THE SCRIPTURES

2009 EDITION

THE
SCRIPTURES

TRANSLATED, PUBLISHED AND DISTRIBUTED BY

INSTITUTE FOR SCRIPTURE RESEARCH

P.O. Box 1830
Northriding
2162
South Africa

Internet Web Page - http://www.messianic.co.za
Email - isr.mail@messianic.co.za

THE SCRIPTURES

We wish to thank all the brothers, sisters and friends,

from across the world,

who worked on this translation, or helped with it.

They did this voluntarily, without asking for remuneration.

Elohim bless them!

We wish to thank our wives and children

for being ever so patient while we worked on this project.

Above all, we thank our Heavenly Father

for sending His Son to earth, and into our lives,

to save us from our sins (Mt. 1:21),

to redeem us from all lawlessness (Titos 2:14),

to destroy the works of the devil (Yn.א 3:8).

INSTITUTE FOR SCRIPTURE RESEARCH, SOUTH AFRICA
P.O. Box 1830
2162 Northriding
Republic of South Africa

Typesetting by Institute for Scripture Research, South Africa
Printed in the United States of America

1st edition - 1993
2nd edition - 1998
Reprinted - 2000, 2002, 2004, 2005, 2006, 2007, 2008
3rd edition - 2009

Soft Cover edition - ISBN 0-9585045-4-7
Hard Cover edition - ISBN 0-9585045-5-5
Leather Cover edition - ISBN 0-9585045-6-3
Hard Cover Large Print edition - ISBN 0-9585045-7-1
Leather Cover Large Print edition - ISBN 0-9585045-9-8
Soft Cover Pocket Edition - ISBN 0-9585045-8-X

BOOKS OF THE SCRIPTURES

TABLE OF CONTENTS

THE PRE-MESSIANIC SCRIPTURES

Torah – Teaching (commonly called *Law*)

Neḇi'im – Prophets

Kethuḇim Aleph – Writings

Bookname (Alternate name) *Abbreviation* *Page*

THE MESSIANIC SCRIPTURES

Kethuḇim Bět – Writings

Table of Conents - Continue next page.

TABLE OF CONTENTS (continue)

ABBREVIATIONS

Gk. .... *Greek*
Heb. .... *Hebrew*
MT.. .... *Massoretic Text*
DSS .... *Dead Sea Scrolls*
LXX .... *Septuagint*

THE SCRIPTURES

Presented by

....

to

....

Family record

Husband.. Born

Father.. Born

Mother... Born

Wife... Born

Father.. Born

Mother... Born

Married.. Date

Place..

Children

Name...Born

Name...Born

Name...Born

Name...Born

Name...Born

Name...Born

Name...Born

Name...Born

Name...Born

Name...Born

Name...Born

Name...Born

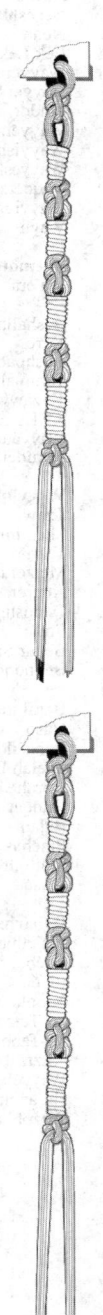

TORAH AND HAFTARAH READINGS

Name	Meaning	Torah	Haftarah *
Berěshith	In (the) beginning	Ber. 1:1-6:8	Yesh. 42:5-43:10
Noaḥ	Noaḥ (Comfort)	Ber. 6:9-11:32	Yesh. 54:1-55:5
Leḵ Leḵa	You go	Ber. 12:1-17:27	Yesh. 40:27-41:16
Wayyěra	And he appeared	Ber. 18:1-22:24	Mel. ב 4:1-37
Ḥayyei Sarah	Life of Sarah	Ber. 23:1-25:18	Mel. א 1:1-31
Toldot	Generatings / births	Ber. 25:19-28:9	Mal. 1:1-2:7
Wayyětze	And he went out	Ber. 28:10-32:2	Hosh. 12:12-14:9
Wayyishlaḥ	And he sent	Ber. 32:3-36:43	Hosh. 11:7-12:11
Wayyěsheḇ	And he dwelt	Ber. 37:1-40:23	Amos 2:6-3:8
Miqqětz	At the end	Ber. 41:1-44:17	Mel. א 3:15-4:1
Wayyiggash	And he came near	Ber. 44:18-47:27	Yeḥez. 37:15-28
Wayḥi	And he lived	Ber. 47:28-50:26	Mel. א 2:1-12
Shemoth	Names	Shem. 1:1-6:1	Yesh. 27:6-28:13; 29:22-23
Wa'ěra	And I appeared	Shem. 6:2-9:35	Yeḥez. 28:25-29:21
Bo	Come in	Shem. 10:1-13:16	Yirm. 46:13-28
Beshallaḥ	When he sent	Shem. 13:17-17:16	Shoph. 4:4-5:31
Yitro	His excellency	Shem. 18:1-20:26	Yesh. 6:1-7:6; 9:6-7
Mishpatim	Right-rulings	Shem. 21:1-24:18	Yirm. 34:8-22; 33:25-26
Terumah	Contribution	Shem. 25:1-27:19	Mel. א 5:12-6:13
Tetzawweh	You shall command	Shem. 27:20-30:10	Yeḥez. 43:10-43:27
Ki Tissa	When you lift up	Shem. 30:11-34:35	Mel. א 18:1-39
Wayyaqhěl	And he assembles	Shem. 35:1-38:20	Mel. א 7:40-50
Pekudei	Accounts	Shem. 38:21-40:38	Mel. א 7:51-8:21
Wayyiqra	And he called	Way. 1:1-6:7	Yesh. 43:21-44:23
Tzaw	Command	Way. 6:8-8:36	Yirm. 7:21-8:3; 9:23-24
Shemini	Eighth	Way. 9:1-11:47	Shem. ב 6:1-7:17
Tazria	She is with seed	Way. 12:1-13:59	Mel. ב 4:42-5:19
Metzora	The one with tzara'at	Way. 14:1-15:33	Mel. ב 7:3-20
Aḥarei Moth	After the death	Way. 16:1-18:30	Yeḥez. 22:1-19
Qedoshim	Set apart ones	Way. 19:1-20:27	Amos 9:7-15
Emor	He say	Way. 21:1-24:23	Yeḥez. 44:15-31
Behar Sinai	In Mount Sinai	Way. 25:1-26:2	Yirm. 32:6-27
Beḥuqqotai	In My laws	Way. 26:3-27:34	Yirm. 16:19-17:14
Bemiḏbar	In (the) wilderness	Bem. 1:1-4:20	Hosh. 1:10-2:20
Naso	Lift up	Bem. 4:21-7:89	Shoph. 13:2-25
Beha'aloteḥa	In your ascent	Bem. 8:1-12:16	Zeḵ. 2:14-4:7
Shelaḥ Leḥa	You send	Bem. 13:1-15:41	Yeh. 2:1-24
Qoraḥ	Qoraḥ (Bald)	Bem. 16:1-18:32	Shem. א 11:14-12:22
Ḥuqqat	Laws	Bem. 19:1-22:1	Shoph. 11:1-33
Balaq	Balaq (Devastator)	Bem. 22:2-25:9	Miḵ. 5:7-6:8
Pineḥas	Pineḥas (Mouth of brass)	Bem. 25:10-29:40	Mel. א 18:46-19:21
Mattoth	Tribes	Bem. 30:1-32:42	Yirm. 1:1-2:3
Masěi	Journeys of	Bem. 33:1-36:13	Yirm. 2:4-28; 3:4
Deḇarim	Words	Deḇ. 1:1-3:22	Yesh. 1:1-27
Wa'ethannan	And I sought favour	Deḇ. 3:23-7:11	Yesh. 40:1-26
Ěqeḇ	Because	Deḇ. 7:12-11:25	Yesh. 49:14-51:3
Re'ěh	Look	Deḇ. 11:26-16:17	Yesh. 54:11-55:5
Shophetim	Right rulers	Deḇ. 16:18-21:9	Yesh. 51:12-52:12
Ki-Tětze	When you go out	Deḇ. 21:10-25:19	Yesh. 54:1-10
Ki-Taḇo	When you come in	Deḇ. 26:1-29:9	Yesh. 60:1-22
Nitztzaḇim	You are standing	Deḇ. 29:10-30:20	Yesh. 61:10-63:9
Wayyělek	And he went	Deḇ. 31:1-31:30	Hosh. 14:1-9; Miḵ.7:18-20; Yo'el 2:15-27
Ha'azinu	Give ear	Deḇ. 32:1-32:52	Shem. ב 22:1-51
Wezot haBeraḥah	And this is the blessing	Deḇ. 33:1-34:12	Yeh. 1:1-18

* Ashkenazi rendering

PREFACE

WHY ANOTHER TRANSLATION?

There have been many fine translations of the Scriptures which, over the years, have been such a wonderful source of blessing to so many. Yet the multitude of choices between available translations is in itself a source of confusion for many. Which translation is truly the Word of the Most High? Don't some translations appear to outrightly contradict the reading of certain other translations? Is it really necessary, one may ask, to add yet another one?

The reality is that the inspired Word of the Almighty is not represented adequately in any translation or version made by human beings (including this one!), for the best translation only represents the sincere and prayerful attempt by human beings to render the Word of the Creator into a receptor language which ultimately has its origins at the Tower of Baḇel, and words in one language do not have a one-to-one correspondence with words in any other language. The Scriptures are, after all, those words which were originally breathed out by the very Creator himself. While we definitely believe in the overriding hand of Providence in the transmission of the Scriptures (Rom. 3:2; 9:4,5), no sincere translator (or board of translators) would ever be so pompous as to assert that his or her translation is the very Word of the Almighty himself!

Approaching the task of Scripture translation from different backgrounds, environments, cultural mindsets, etc. inevitably affects the end result. Those with no access to the original language of Scripture become entirely dependent on whichever translations are in their hands. Apart from taking steps to get to grips with the original languages of the Scriptures (something that we would earnestly encourage every genuine student of the Scriptures to do), the only other recourse they have is to acquire and compare as many translations/versions of the Scriptures as possible. This way something, however small, may be grasped, of the multifaceted depth of the original. Thus there remains a real need for further translations which will help to bring forth yet further elements from the original tongue that are not adequately reflected in other translations.

This is precisely where "The Scriptures - 2009 Edition (ISR)" comes into the picture. This edition of the Scriptures, while attempting to be an accurate translation, seeks at the same time to introduce the reader to something of the Hebraic mindset and culture which are very much a part of the original. Indeed, we see this is as absolutely necessary for the serious student of Scripture. The events of Scripture did not occur in the modern western world, with its Anglo-Hellenist mindset, but within the very different world of the ancient middle-east, and the Semitic mindset of the People of Yisra'ěl. While we have sought to accurately translate rather than to interpret, aiming at producing a literal translation rather than a paraphrase, we have tried to provide the student of Scripture with a tool which in some way helps him or her to "experience" the Scriptures as Semitic rather than Hellenistic. In so doing we have taken much further the work of the 1993 and 1998 editions of the ISR "Scriptures" toward this end.

As in the earlier editions, our aims have included:

"A translation of the Scriptures which:

i. restores the Name of the Almighty to its rightful place in the text (see THE RESTORATION OF THE NAME, below).
ii. is recognisably Messianic in that it affirms the Hebraic roots of the Messianic belief by its appearance, by the use of Hebraic forms of certain words and titles, and by its usage of the same division of the pre-Messianic books of Scripture (the Tanaḵ or "Old Testament") that was current at the time of our Messiah.
iii. restores the meaning to so many words which have become popular to use, but do not accurately reflect the meaning of the original - for example, church, glory, holy, sacrifice, soul, etc.
iv. seeks to be as far as possible a "literal" translation, wherever possible rendering key words uniformly (exceptions being noted in footnotes or the Explanatory Notes)."

To this may be added:

i. the further restoration of the Semitic form of the names of the books of Scripture.
ii The rendering of words such as Hades (a Greek term, loaded with pagan connotations, variously rendered by different translators as "pit", "grave", and "hell") by their Hebrew or Aramaic equivalent instead, such as She'ol.
iii. The deletion of notes, footnotes and explanatory notes of a doctrinal nature, other than those 'doctrinal agendas' expressed in this Preface.
iv. The addition of notes, footnotes, and/or explanatory notes which may be more useful to students of Scripture, in equipping them for their studies, rather than in doing studies for them.
v. Highlighting by means of bold typeface those passages in the Second Writings (also known as Kethuḇim Bĕt, Netzarim Writings, haBrit haḤadasha, New Testament, etc.), which quote allusions from the Tanaḵ (also known as the Old Testament).

THE ORDER AND TITLES OF THE BOOKS

In accordance with our aim to affirm the Hebraic roots of our Belief we have:

i. transliterated the names of the books of the Tanaḵ (Old Testament), and where appropriate have done the same in the Second Writings (Messianic Writings, New Testament). For your convenience the traditional English names of the books may be found facing the Hebraic form at the top of each page. They are also together with the transliterated forms in the Table of Contents.

ii. followed the traditional Hebraic order of the Tanaḵ, (Torah, Neḇi'im, Kethuḇim).

THE TANAḴ *(Torah, Neḇi'im, Kethuḇim)*

First, **The Torah** - *Law*

We have rendered it by the Hebrew word itself, Torah, i.e. the five books of Mosheh (Moses), also known as the Ḥumash, or (The Pentateuch), Law or Teaching. They consist of the following 5 books:

Berĕshith (Genesis)
Shemoth (Exodus)
Wayyiqra (Leviticus)
Bemiḏbar (Numbers)
Deḇarim (Deuteronomy)

Then, **The Neḇi'im** - *Prophets*

These books are known as The Prophets, not because of the element of prediction (a considerable amount of their content is historical rather than predictive!), but because of being written by prophets. They are divided into two categories, the Former Prophets, and the Latter Prophets, referring to their time of writing. The Latter Prophets were further divided into Major Prophets, and Minor Prophets (known as Shnĕm Asar, i.e. The Twelve).

Please note that we have restored the book of Dani'ĕl to its rightful place among the Prophets*, as also did Josephus. We have placed it between Yeḥezqĕl / Ezekiel (the third of the Latter Prophets), and Shnĕm Asar / The Twelve (the fourth of the Latter Prophets), instead of including it among The Kethubim (Writings), as is usually done. They consist of the following 9 books, i.e. 8 books, plus Dani'ĕl:

The Former Prophets (4 books)	*The Latter Prophets (4 books, plus Dani'ĕl)*
Yehoshua (Joshua)	Yeshayahu (Isaiah)
Shophetim (Judges)	Yirmeyahu (Jeremiah)
Shemu'ĕl (Aleph & Bĕt)	Yeḥezqĕl (Ezekiel)
	+Dani'ĕl (Daniel)
Melaḵim (Aleph & Bĕt)	Shnĕm Asar* (The Twelve)

[**Shnĕm Asar* is one book, containing the works of twelve prophets:

Hoshĕa (Hosea)
Yo'ĕl (Joel)
Amos (Amos)
Oḇaḏyah (Obadiah)
Yonah (Jonah)
Miḵah (Micah)
Naḥum (Nahum)
Ḥaḇaqquq (Habakkuk)
Tsephanyah (Zephaniah)
Ḥaggai
Zeḵaryah (Zechariah)
Mal'aḵi (Malachi)]

Then, **The Kethuḇim** - *Writings*
They are the remaining books of the Tanaḵ, (10 books, i.e. 11 less Dani'ěl)
Tehillim (Psalms)
Mishlě (Proverbs)
Iyoḇ (Job)
Shir haShirim (Song of Songs)
Ruth
Ěḵah (Lamentations)
Qoheleth (Ecclesiastes, Convener)
Estěr (Esther)
Ezra - Neḥemyah (Nehemiah)
Diḇre haYamim (Aleph & Bět) (Chronicles, Annals)

Thus, the Torah, Neḇi'im, and Kethuḇim go to make up the TaNaḴ, which is commonly known as the "Old Testament". There are 24 books in all, according to the Hebraic reckoning (as given above), although the same books are reckoned by others to add up to 39, by counting the individual segments (such as Shemu'ěl Aleph, Shemu'ěl Bět, Ezra, Neḥemyah, etc.)

THE SECOND WRITINGS (variously called The Netzarim Writings, The Messianic Writings, The New Covenant, haBrit haḤadasha, The New Testament, etc.)

The 'correct' order of the books has been debated by some. The traditional order since Jerome is a roughly chronological arrangement, and there is much to be said for this approach. In Western Christianity since the time of Jerome the letters of Ya`aqoḇ, Kěpha, Yoḥanan and Yehuḏah have been placed after those of Sha'ul/Paul. An earlier arrangement (still preferred by Eastern Christianity) is to to place these letters before Sha'ul/Paul. Others contend that a more consistent approach is to follow a topical arrangement, as in the traditional Hebraic arrangement of the Tanaḵ.

Each arrangement has its merits, but the reality is that there is no 'original' arrangement for the simple but obvious reason that the Second writings were not written as one book! Instead, they came about over time through the careful collation of those documents which had been preserved by various persons and congregations of individual 'books', letters, etc. written by those whom יהושע Rabbeinu appointed as his 'personal representatives' (shliḥim = 'apostles')

These writings of men inspired by יהוה had been written under different circumstances in different places, at different times, yet were regarded all along as inspired documents because of the anointing on their authors. Each shaliaḥ / 'apostle' was writing as a personal representative of יהושע, and therefore also of יהוה, the anointing was on the very Writings themselves, from the very beginning.

However, they still had to be collected into a single collection, before they became what we today know as the Second Writings (or 'New Testament'), and that took place over time, with many collations of these Writings not having all the books we have today, and as could be expected, differing in their ordering of the books. Let us not forget that the original "Second-Writings-Believers" had no copy of the Second Writings. They wrote it! Naturally then, different ones in different places had only parts of the Second Writings until all those parts which we now have had been collected, and bound together.

Thus, there is no 'correct' order of the books of the Second Writings.

Are the Second Writings then really necessary? Absolutely! That is why יהוה Eloheinu inspired them to be written, and anointed the Shliḥim (personal representatives) of יהושע to the task. These works are unique in their guidance concerning how those who follow יהושע the Messiah are to apply יהוה's Torah to their lives. Truly, we are to live by "every Word of יהוה ", as Torah and יהושע Rabbeinu both exhort us to do (Deḇ. 8:3; Mt. 4:4), and that includes all of the Second Writings (Kěpha ב 3:15, 16; Tim. ב 3:16, 17).

Since there is no 'correct' order of the books, we have decided to stay with the traditional Western order that we have followed in previous editions of The Scriptures until further consideration more strongly motivates our change to a different order of books.

Thus there is a total of 27 books in all, or if reckoned Hebraically (e.g. counting Kěpha א & Kěpha ב as one book consisting of two letters, etc.), a total of 21.

THE RESTORATION OF THE NAME

The restoration of the Name of the Almighty to any translation of the Scriptures should require no justification. After all it was the Almighty himself who originally placed his name in the Scriptures at least 6 823 times! It was human beings who decided, for reasons that made sense to them, to delete His Name and to replace it with something "more appropriate" in their view. This, in spite of the Creator's own statement to and through Mosheh (Moses) that: "This is My Name forever, and this is My remembrance to all generations." (Shemoth / Exodus 3:15, The Scriptures - 2009 Edition (ISR).

The reference in this passage is to the Name which, in Hebrew, consists of four letters Yod, Hey, Waw, Hey, and which is frequently referred to as 'The Tetragrammaton'. These letters are often brought across into English characters by the use of the four letters, YHWH (or as YHVH). This has been variously pronounced as YaHWeH, YaHoWeH, YaHuWeH, YaHVeH, etc. We have chosen not to enter the pronunciation debate, but rather give the Name exactly as it appears in the unpointed Hebrew text, i.e. יהוה.

While there has been some debate over what is the most accurate and precise pronunciation, three things are clear however:

Firstly, the word Jehovah is definitely an erroneous pronunciation. This is so because it derives from a combination of the letters JHVH and Hebrew vowel points belonging to an altogether different word. Incidentally, the J was originally pronounced as a capital I (or Y), and thus the term Jehovah would have been read by early readers of the King James Version as Iehovah (or Yehovah).

Secondly, any one of the various attempts to pronounce the Name is infinitely superior to the actual removal of the Name, and its substitution by an altogether different term! Substitution by a 'good' term does not alter the fact that it is a substitution, a replacement word. Further, some of the terms traditionally substituted for the Name are actually the names of pagan deities! This is true, not only in English, but also in the other languages of the world!

Thirdly, in spite of the above facts, many translations perpetuate a "tradition" of substituting "LORD" or "GOD", all in capital letters, for our heavenly Father's chosen Name, יהוה. Why? Many, and varied are the reasons which have been given, amongst both Christian and Jewish communities, for this serious error. Nevertheless, the fact remains that a translation purporting to be literal, yet resorting to the "device", however well intentioned, of adding and subtracting from our heavenly Father's own choice of Personal Name, would be doing a grave disservice to His cause. At best it would display ignorance, but at worst would show disrespect, or blatant disregard for the plain Word of the Almighty Himself!

This is a matter that the ISR has taken seriously from the very beginning. In the 1993 edition of "The Scriptures" we stated: "The Scriptures differs radically from most other translations in that it does not continue in the tradition of substituting the Name of the Father and of the Son with names ascribed to gentile (pagan) deities. All the names of deities which in the past have been ascribed to the Father, the Son, and even used when engaged in worship, have been avoided". Our position has NOT changed.

But surely He has many Names, one may ask? Not so! Men have called Him by many names, and indeed there are many titles by which He is known in Scripture (mistakenly called 'names' by some), but there is only ONE Name by which He urges us to remember Him to all generations! That is the Name יהוה! You may be surprised to find that the expression "I AM", quoted by so many people from Shemoth /Ex. 3:14 as the special Name of the Almighty is not His special Name at all. It is in fact a declaration made by Himself, as He leads up to His statement in verse 15 that His Name - the one by which He is to be always remembered - is יהוה. The actual term translated in 3:14 as "I am" is only used in the Tanaḵ (Old Testament) 30 times. The remaining 29 times it is NEVER used as a proper name for the Almighty - as the Name יהוה is used. The Name יהוה is used throughout the Tanaḵ, both before and after this passage, a total of 6 823 times in the Masoretic text of the Tanaḵ alone. A rose, by any other name may smell just as sweet, but clearly this is not the case with יהוה! One may not simply substitute His Name with that of a pagan deity, be it God, Gott, Zeus, Theos, Pan, Allah, Lord, Lordo, Lard, Hlafweard, or any other. Nor can we refer to Him by even a generic Lord, referencing Krishna, Vishnu, or any other "Lord" of choice. Doing so is to attribute to another the work, power, esteem and wisdom which belongs only to יהוה Elohim (Yeshayahu /Is. 42:8). By His Name יהוה, He is to be distinguished from all "other deities".

Many misguided individuals are under the false impression that, for instance, the words "Lord, LORD, God, GOD, Adonai or HaShem are "translations" of the Name of the Almighty. Nothing could be further from the truth! Consider once more the passage quoted above (Shemoth / Ex. 3:15) in which the ELOHIM (Heb. = "Mighty One") of Aḇraham, Yitsḥaq and Ya'aqoḇ declares that his Name is יהוה and that this Name is to be His remembrance to all generations. Should this not then be the case in this generation also?

While names, especially in the Scriptures, frequently do have meanings, it is erroneous to think that we should call anyone or refer to anyone by the "translation" of his or her name. And the same holds true in Scripture. Giuseppe in Italian corresponds to Joseph in English; however, Giuseppe Verdi cannot be translated as Joseph Green in English, even if that is what it means in English! The proper name of any individual is not translated; it is always transliterated or transcribed in order to approximate its original pronunciation. We repeat: the proper name of any individual is simply not translated, more especially when we are dealing with the most important Ones: the Most High (יהוה) and His Son (יהושע)!

For all of these reasons, we have returned these Most Set Apart Names to their rightful place in our translation of the Scriptures, and have done so by using the Hebrew characters rather than any English rendering. Such a rendering has solid historical precedent in the earliest copies of the Septuagint (LXX), and has the merit of being true to the text, neither adding nor subtracting by means of substitutions (however well-intended). It has also the additional merit of allowing the individual reader to progress in his own quest for accuracy of pronunciation, as he seeks to obey the scriptural injunctions to call on the Name (Shemoth / Ex. 3:15; Yeshayahu / Is.12:4; Yirmeyahu / Jer. 10:25; Tehillim / Ps. 105:1,3), to make it known (Shemoth / Ex. 9:16; Yeshayahu / Is. 64:1,2; Yeḥezqěl / Ez. 39:7), and to not obliterate or forget it (Deḇarim / Dt. 12:3,4; Yeshayahu / Is. 65:11; Yirmeyahu / Jer. 23:27; Tehillim / Ps. 44:20)!

In the same way the Messiah's Name in Hebrew, יהושע, was chosen in order to avoid controversy. All the available authoritative sources and references are in agreement and clearly admit that our Messiah's Name was יהושע (see for instance Kittel's Theological Dictionary of the New Testament, under Iesous). While the short form "Yeshua" (ישוע) is popular with many (indeed the Shem Toḇ Hebrew text of Mattithyahu renders it as such, as also the Hebrew translation of the "New Testament" by F. Delitzch), Dr. Solomon Zeitlin refutes this form as the Name of our Messiah, favouring instead the form יהושע (see The Jewish Quarterly Review, Jan. 1970, p.195).

At this stage we need to explain the word "Elohim" used in this translation. English translations have traditionally rendered it as "God" or as "god(s)" in most instances. However, the Hebrew word "elohim" is the plural form of "eloah", which has the basic meaning of "mighty one". This word is not only used for deity, but is used in Scripture for judges, angels and idols (Shemoth / Ex. 7:1; 9:28; 12:12; 22:8, 9; Tehillim / Ps. 8:5; 82:1, 6) besides being used frequently for the Almighty. The shorter forms, "el" and "elim" have the same basic meaning and similar usage. (Needless to say, the same would apply to the Aramaic equivalents, such as "elah" and "elahin"). By transliterating these expressions instead of translating them as "Mighty One" something of the richness of the Hebrew is communicated, and we therefore retained them, with the exception of a few instances, such as Bereshith / Gen. 10:8; 31:30,32; 35:2,4; Shemoth / Ex. 12:12; 15:11; 18:11; 20:3,23; 23:13,24, where the translation of "mighty one" or "mighty ones" seemed more appropriate.

THE TEXT OF THE TANAḴ AND SECOND WRITINGS

THE TANAḴ (Pre-Second Writings Scripture, commonly called The Old Testament):

The Tanaḵ in this translation is based on the Masoretic Hebrew and Aramaic text of the Scriptures, printed in the 1937 edition of Rudolph Kittel's Biblia Hebraica. This is based on the ben Asher text of Leningrad, B 19a. Generally speaking, there are few problems with the Masoretic text, because the Masoretes copied the Scriptures in great fear of making mistakes and altering the text. They used the device of the Kethiḇ and Qerě by means of which they indicated in the margins their preferred readings.

However, they did make a few changes in the text itself which have been recorded for us, but unfortunately not all in one manuscript. In 134 places the Sopherim (Scribes) removed the Name יהוה and substituted the term Adonai. In a further 8 places the Name יהוה was substituted by the term Elohim. These have been collected by Dr. C.D. Ginsberg in his Introduction to the Massoretico-Critical Edition of the Hebrew Bible, (Ktav Publishing House Inc. New York).

We have accordingly restored the text to its original readings in these 142 places, and have also restored the text in accordance with the "Eighteen emendations of the Sopherim", which are also recorded for us by Dr. C.D. Ginsberg. A list of these 160 places is provided in the Explanatory Notes for your convenience.

THE SECOND WRITINGS (variously called The Netzarim Writings, The Messianic Writings, The New Covenant, haBrit haḤadasha, The New Testament, etc.):

THE ISSUES:

An issue that presents itself to anyone wanting to get to the "original" words behind those of the various translations available in any language is the matter of Primacy. In other words, in what language were the words of the Second Writings originally inspired? Unfortunately, we do not have the original text. Only very old copies are currently available, until the archaeologists give us something more. The oldest, but not necessarily the 'best' copies currently available are in Greek. Were these (ultimately) copies of Greek or Semitic (i.e. Hebrew / Aramaic) originals?

Positions vary on the matter of Primacy, most scholars opting for the more traditional view of Western Christianity, that they were originally written in Greek. However, there are various scholars who dispute this intensely, maintaining that at least part, if not all of the Second Writings are of Semitic origin. Indeed, this represents the position of Eastern Christianity, where for example, the 'authorized version' of the Church of the East is the Peshitta, in which the Second Writings are entirely in Aramaic. The Peshitta in its current form does not go back beyond the fourth century, but its advocates strongly maintain that it rests firmly upon Aramaic originals.

We are not going to go argue the case here, beyond stating that we believe that there is a very strong case to be made for the view that the originals were inspired in a Semitic language and not in Greek, as is commonly supposed. The Institute for Scripture Research is firmly of the persuasion that the originals were written in a Semitic tongue, and that they are intended by יהוה our Elohim to find their natural place in the Tanaḵ (Torah, Neḇi'im, Kethuḇim) as part of the Kethuḇim (Writings).

This view, that the Scriptures in their entirety, consist of Semitic Writings, originally given to Semitic people, within a Semitic religious and cultural context should not seem so strange, against the background of Sha'ul's/Paul's statement concerning the Yehuḏim (Jews) that "they were entrusted with the Words of Elohim" (Rom.3:2). This is in no way to be seen as contradicting the commission of יהושע Rabbeinu, our Master the Messiah, to make talmidim (taught ones) of all the nations (Mattityahu / Mt. 28:19,20; Luqas / Luke. 24:47; Ma`asei / Acts 1:8), for was it not he who taught that "deliverance/salvation is of the Yehuḏim" (Yoḥanan / Jn. 4:22)?

In addition to the above, there is the matter of substituting the Name of the Father and the Son with other terms, especially in light of the scriptural prohibition against adding to or diminishing from the words of the Most High (Deḇarim / Dt. 4:2;12:32; Mishlě / Pr.30:4-6). And if it be further admitted (see for example, Explanatory Notes, under Jesus) that the Greek text uses terms that come direct from pagan deities for both the Father and the Son, then it becomes abundantly clear from Scripture itself (Shemoth / Ex. 23:13; Yehoshua / Jos. 23:7; etc.) that such texts could not possibly be the inspired originals, but rather they are translations, ultimately descending from the Semitic originals.

This means of course, for the ISR, that we have to attempt to put before the reader an English text that truthfully and accurately reflects the inspired Semitic originals, when in fact the oldest and vast majority of texts we have available are Greek! A daunting task indeed. To the extent that we have succeeded in this, we can only give praise to the Most High. However we are well aware of our shortcomings, and the possibility, even the probability that we have fallen far short of our goal. In this respect, let it be said that we do not view our work as in any way final or definitive. Rather, we hope that it will encourage others to re-examine what they may have always taken for granted, and to research these matters for themselves. (We extend an ongoing invitation to any who can give input that will improve future editions of The Scriptures, especially in regard to the matter of Semitic originals).

WHICH TEXT?

What text then were we to use? Since the originals are no longer extant, there was no alternative but to make use of the existing Greek manuscripts, carefully considering the additional testimony of Semitic texts such as the Peshitta (Aramaic), the Shem Toḇ (Hebrew), etc. Even here, however there are problems, in that for each of the main streams of textual types (e.g. Byzantine / Textus Receptus vs. Alexandrinus, Sinaiticus, and Vaticanus) there are those who contend that a particular type and that one alone represents the true original.

We determined however, not to become embroiled in such controversies, since our position advocates a Semitic original, true to the Tanaḵ / *Old Testament*. Hence whatever readings we have adopted will inevitably offend those contending for any one of the main textual types as the true original. We cannot therefore claim that our text represents a translation of any particular underlying text.

As a modus operandi then, we have started out using the Textus Receptus, modifying our rendering as seemed appropriate in light of those other texts which we consulted, such as the Nestlé-Aland text and the Shem Toḇ text, noting certain differences in the footnotes, where necessary.

In harmony therefore with the above principles, we restored the Names of the Father and of the Son, and the names of all the Hebrew individuals, in accordance with the Hebrew, especially as found in the Tanaḵ / *Old Testament*. We also restored the names of the places in Yisra'ěl, for after all, we are dealing with a Jewish worship; we are dealing with the Elohim of Yisra'ěl; we are dealing with יהושע haMashiach (the Messiah), Rabbeinu (our Rabbi - Mt.23:8), the Sovereign of the Yehuḏim - as He is called in no less than 23 places in the Second Writings (Messianic Writings, New Testament).

TRANSLITERATION

In rendering Hebrew names we tried to be as exact as possible. However, with a few names there was a problem, e.g. the name Dani'ěl is spelt in three different ways, but all three of these spellings result in the same pronunciation. Therefore it was decided to strive for consistency and render such names according to a single spelling, in order to retain the original pronunciation as best we could. We departed from this, however, in two cases, viz. in those names containing part of the Name יהוה, where we felt compelled to add the suffix -yah or - yahu, exactly as it appears in the Hebrew text, and in the case of certain terms such as Ělohim, where we opted to use the form, Elohim, instead.

CONCLUSION

As in previous editions of The Scriptures, we stand in awe and fear before the Most High, knowing that account shall be given for every word rendered in this version, The Scriptures - 2009 Edition (ISR). Much is going to be required from those to whom much has been given (Luqas / Lk. 12:48). As previously stated, we do not offer our labours to the public as the "last word" on these matters, and welcome feedback and useful input from any who have insight or information relevant to the improvement of this translation.

With this new edition of The Scriptures, we continue to reach out a hand of love toward all Scripture-believers of all backgrounds, pleading that we join hands and turn back to יהוה who will then turn back to us (Zeḵaryah / Zec. 1:3 and Hoshěa 6:1-3). Let us do so by turning to his Torah. This will lead to belief in יהושע and his Words (Yoḥanan / Jn. 5:45-47), and for those who come into the (re-)new(-d) covenant, this will result in reconciliation to his Father.

Institute for Scripture Research

PRONUNCIATION TABLE

English letter	Hebrew	Name of Hebrew letter	Pronounced like
Ḇ and ḇ	ב	Bet(h)	*bh*, as *-v* in *view*
Ḏ and ḏ	ד	Dalet(h)	*dh*, as *-th* in *this* and *that*
Ḡ and ḡ	ג	Gimel	*gh*, a soft *g*
Ḥ and ḥ	ח	Ḥet(h)	*ḥ* as *-ch* in the Scottish *loch*
Ḵ and ḵ	כ	Kaf	*kh*, as *-ch* in the Scottish *loch* or *-g* in Afrikaans *gee*
Q and q	ק	Qof	*k* in *kitten*
Ě and ě		the vowel *tsěrě*	*ey* as in *they*
I and i		the vowel *ḥireq*	*i* as *-ee* in *tree*

Please note that the ' within a Hebrew name represents an *aleph*, a smooth breathing, and for practical purposes may be considered a 'silent' letter.

Similarly, the ʽ represents the letter *ayin*, a rough breathing, and it too, may for practical purposes be considered a 'silent' letter. So ʽAmorah (Gomorrah) may be read as Amorah, and in fact we have rendered it as such. Thus *aleph* and *ayin* take on the sound of the vowel that they 'carry'.

Other

Words in italics are not found in the original text but were added for context and/or readability.

Text in bold type face in the Second Writings (Messianic) reference allusions or quotations from the Tanaḵ.

In connection with *The Scriptures* or Appendices thereto, any reference to copyright holders other than the Institute for Scripture Research, is not to be construed as endorsement of any views held by such copyright holders.

THE

TANAḴ

Torah – Teaching

Neḇi'im – Prophets

Kethuḇim – Writings

BERĚSHITH

GENESIS

1 In the beginning Elohim created the
heavens and the earth.
2 And the earth came to be [a] formless and
empty, and darkness was on the face of the
deep. And the Spirit of Elohim was moving on the face of the waters.
3 And Elohim said, "Let light come to
be," and light came to be.
4 And Elohim saw the light, that it was
good. And Elohim separated the light from
the darkness.
5 And Elohim called the light 'day' and
the darkness He called 'night.' And there
came to be evening and there came to be
morning, one day.
6 And Elohim said, "Let an expanse
come to be in the midst of the waters, and
let it separate the waters from the waters."
7 And Elohim made the expanse, and
separated the waters which were under the
expanse from the waters which were above
the expanse. And it came to be so.
8 And Elohim called the expanse 'heavens.' And there came to be evening and
there came to be morning, the second day.
9 And Elohim said, "Let the waters under
the heavens be gathered together into one
place, and let the dry land appear." And it
came to be so.
10 And Elohim called the dry land 'earth,'
and the collection of the waters He called
'seas.' And Elohim saw that it was good.
11 And Elohim said, "Let the earth bring
forth grass, the plant that yields seed, and
the fruit tree that yields fruit according to
its kind, whose seed is in itself, on the
earth." And it came to be so.
12 And the earth brought forth grass, the
plant that yields seed according to its kind,
and the tree that yields fruit, whose seed is
in itself according to its kind. And Elohim
saw that it was good.
13 And there came to be evening and there
came to be morning, the third day.
14 And Elohim said, "Let lights come to
be in the expanse of the heavens to separate the day from the night, and let them be
for signs and appointed times, and for days
and years,
15 and let them be for lights in the expanse
of the heavens to give light on the earth."
And it came to be so.
16 And Elohim made two great lights: the
greater light to rule the day, and the lesser
light to rule the night, and the stars.
17 And Elohim set them in the expanse of
the heavens to give light on the earth,
18 and to rule over the day and over the
night, and to separate the light from the
darkness. And Elohim saw that it was
good.
19 And there came to be evening and there
came to be morning, the fourth day.
20 And Elohim said, "Let the waters teem
with shoals of living being*s*, and let birds
fly above the earth on the face of the
expanse of the heavens."
21 And Elohim created great sea creatures
and every living being that moves, with
which the waters teemed, according to
their kind, and every winged bird according to its kind. And Elohim saw that it was
good.
22 And Elohim blessed them, saying, "Be
fruitful and increase, and fill the waters in
the seas, and let the birds increase on the
earth."
23 And there came to be evening and there
came to be morning, the fifth day.
24 And Elohim said, "Let the earth bring
forth the living being according to its kind:
livestock and creeping *creatures* and
beasts of the earth, according to its kind."
And it came to be so.
25 And Elohim made the beast of the earth
according to its kind, livestock according

1a Or *the earth became.*

to its kind, and all that creep on the earth according to its kind. And Elohim saw that it was good.

26 And Elohim said, "Let Us make man in Our image, according to Our likeness, and let them rule over the fish of the sea, and over the birds of the heavens, and over the livestock, and over all the earth and over all the creeping *creatures* that creep on the ground."

27 And Elohim created the man in His image, in the image of Elohim He created him – male and female He created them.

28 And Elohim blessed them, and Elohim said to them, "Be fruitful and increase, and fill the earth and subdue it, and rule over the fish of the sea, and over the birds of the heavens, and over all creeping *creatures* on the earth."

29 And Elohim said, "See, I have given you every plant that yields seed which is on the face of all the earth, and every tree whose fruit yields seed, to you it is for food.

30 "And to every beast of the earth, and to every bird of the heavens, and to every creeping *creature* on the earth, in which there is a living being, every green plant is for food." And it came to be so.

31 And Elohim saw all that He had made, and see, it was very good. And there came to be evening and there came to be morning, the sixth day.

2 Thus the heavens and the earth were completed, and all their array.

2 And in the seventh day [a] Elohim completed His work which He had done, and He rested on the seventh day from all His work which He had made.

3 And Elohim blessed the seventh day and set it apart, because on it He rested from all His work which Elohim in creating had made.

4 These are the births of the heavens and the earth when they were created, in the day that יהוה Elohim made earth and heavens.

5 Now no shrub of the field was yet on the earth, and no plant of the field had yet sprung up, for יהוה Elohim had not sent rain on the earth, and there was no man to till the ground,

6 but a mist went up from the earth and watered the entire surface of the ground.

7 And יהוה Elohim formed the man out of dust from the ground, and breathed into his nostrils breath of lives. And the man became a living being.

8 And יהוה Elohim planted a garden in Ěḏen, to the east, and there He put the man whom He had formed.

9 And out of the ground יהוה Elohim made every tree grow that is pleasant to the sight and good for food, with the tree of life in the midst of the garden and the tree of the knowledge of good and evil.

10 And a river went out of Ěḏen to water the garden, and from there it divided and became four riverheads.

11 The name of the first is Pishon, it is the one surrounding the entire land of Ḥawilah, where there is gold.

12 And the gold of that land is good. Bdellium is there, and the shoham stone.

13 And the name of the second river is Giḥon, it is the one surrounding the entire land of Kush.

14 And the name of the third river is Ḥiddeqel, it is the one which goes toward the east of Ashshur. And the fourth river is the Euphrates.

15 And יהוה Elohim took the man and put him in the garden of Ěḏen to work it and to guard it.

16 And יהוה Elohim commanded the man, saying, "Eat of every tree of the garden,

17 but do not eat of the tree of the knowledge of good and evil, for in the day that you eat of it you shall certainly die."

18 And יהוה Elohim said, "It is not good for the man to be alone, I am going to make a helper for him, as his counterpart."

19 And from the ground יהוה Elohim formed every beast of the field and every bird of the heavens, and brought them to the man to see what he would call them. And whatever the man called each living

2a In (not 'by' or 'on') the seventh day - Hebrew: Bayyom haShḇi'i.

being, that was its name.
20 So the man gave names to all livestock, and to the birds of the heavens, and to every beast of the field. But for the man there was not found a helper for him, as his counterpart.
21 So יהוה Elohim caused a deep sleep to fall on the man, and he slept. And He took one of his ribs, and closed up the flesh in its place.
22 And the rib which יהוה Elohim had taken from the man He made into a woman, and He brought her to the man.
23 And the man said, "This is now bone of my bones and flesh of my flesh. This one is called 'woman,' because she was taken out of man."
24 For this cause a man shall leave his father and mother, and cleave to his wife, and they shall become one flesh.
25 And they were both naked, the man and his wife, yet they were not ashamed.

3 And the naḥash [a] was more crafty than all the lives of the field which יהוה Elohim had made, and he said to the woman, "Is it true that Elohim has said, 'Do not eat of every tree of the garden'?"
2 And the woman said to the naḥash, "We are to eat of the fruit of the trees of the garden,
3 but of the fruit of the tree which is in the midst of the garden, Elohim has said, 'Do not eat of it, nor touch it, lest you die.' "
4 And the naḥash said to the woman, "You shall certainly not die.
5 "For Elohim knows that in the day you eat of it your eyes shall be opened, and you shall be like Elohim, knowing good and evil."
6 And the woman saw that the tree was good for food, that it was pleasant to the eyes, and a tree desirable to make one wise, and she took of its fruit and ate. And she also gave to her husband with her, and he ate.
7 Then the eyes of both of them were opened, and they knew that they were naked. And they sewed fig leaves together and made loin coverings for themselves.
8 And they heard the voice of יהוה Elohim walking about in the garden in the cool of the day, and Aḏam and his wife hid themselves from the presence of יהוה Elohim among the trees of the garden.
9 And יהוה Elohim called unto Aḏam and said to him, "Where are you?"
10 And he said, "I heard Your voice in the garden, and I was afraid because I was naked, so I hid myself."
11 And He said, "Who made you know that you were naked? Have you eaten of the tree of which I commanded you that you should not eat?"
12 And the man said, "The woman whom You gave to be with me, she gave me of the tree and I ate."
13 And יהוה Elohim said to the woman, "What is this you have done?" And the woman said, "The naḥash deceived me, and I ate."
14 And יהוה Elohim said to the naḥash, "Because you have done this, you are cursed more than all livestock and more than every beast of the field. On your belly you are to go, and eat dust all the days of your life.
15 "And I put enmity between you and the woman, and between your seed and her Seed. [b] He shall crush your head, and you shall crush His heel."
16 To the woman He said, "I greatly increase your sorrow and your conception – bring forth children in pain. And your desire is for your husband, and he does rule over you."
17 And to the man He said, "Because you have listened to the voice of your wife, and have eaten of the tree of which I commanded you, saying, 'Do not eat of it': "Cursed is the ground because of you, in toil you are to eat of it all the days of your life,
18 and *the ground* shall bring forth thorns and thistles for you, and you shall eat the

3a Or Naḥash.Traditionally rendered the "serpent". See Explanatory notes "Serpent" and "Naḥash".
3b First promise of the Messiah.

plants of the field.

19 “By the sweat of your face you are to eat bread until you return to the ground, for out of it you were taken. For dust you are, and to dust you return.”

20 And the man called his wife’s name Ḥawwah, because she became the mother of all living.

21 And יהוה Elohim made coats of skin for the man and his wife and dressed them.

22 And יהוה Elohim said, “See, the man has become like one of Us, to know good and evil. And now, lest he put out his hand and take also of the tree of life, and eat, and live forever...”

23 so יהוה Elohim sent him out of the garden of Ěḏen to till the ground from which he was taken,

24 and He drove the man out. And He placed keruḇim at the east of the garden of Ěḏen, and a flaming sword which turned every way, to guard the way to the tree of life.

4

And Aḏam knew Ḥawwah his wife, and she conceived and bore Qayin, and said, “I have gained a man, יהוה.”

2 And again, she gave birth to his brother Heḇel. And Heḇel became a keeper of sheep, but Qayin became a tiller of the ground.

3 And it came to be, in the course of time, that Qayin brought an offering of the fruit of the ground to יהוה.

4 And Heḇel also brought of the firstborn of his flock and of their fat. And יהוה looked to Heḇel and his offering,

5 but He did not look to Qayin and his offering. And Qayin was very wroth, and his face fell.

6 And יהוה said to Qayin, “Why is he wroth towards you? And why is your face [a] fallen?

7 “*Is it* not if you do good, you are to be accepted? And if you do not do good, towards the door is a sin. [b] He is lying [c] and towards you is his desire, and you must rule over [d] him.”

8 And Qayin told Heḇel his brother. And it came to be when they were in the field, that Qayin rose up against Heḇel his brother and killed him.

9 And יהוה said to Qayin, “Where is Heḇel your brother?” And he said, “I do not know. Am I my brother’s guard?”

10 And He said, “What have you done? The voice of your brother’s blood cries out to Me from the ground.

11 “And now you are cursed from the earth, which has opened its mouth to receive your brother’s blood from your hand.

12 “If you till the ground, it shall no longer yield its strength to you. You shall be a fugitive and a wanderer on the earth.”

13 And Qayin said to יהוה, “My punishment is too great to bear!

14 “See, You have driven me from the face of the ground today, and I am hidden from Your face. I shall be a fugitive and a wanderer on the earth, and it shall be that anyone who finds me kills me.”

15 And יהוה said to him, “Well, if anyone kills Qayin, vengeance is taken on him sevenfold.” And יהוה set up a sign for Qayin, lest anyone finding him strikes him.

16 So Qayin went out from the presence of יהוה and dwelt in the land of Noḏ on the east of Ěḏen.

17 And Qayin knew his wife, and she conceived and bore Ḥanoḵ. And he built a city, and called the name of the city after the name of his son, Ḥanoḵ.

18 And to Ḥanoḵ was born Iraḏ. And Iraḏ brought forth Meḥuya’ěl, and Meḥuya’ěl brought forth Methusa’ěl, and Methusa’ěl brought forth Lemeḵ.

19 And Lemeḵ took for himself two wives, the name of one was Aḏah, and the name of the second was Tsillah.

20 And Aḏah bore Yaḇal. He was the father of those who dwell in tents, with livestock.

21 And his brother’s name was Yuḇal. He was the father of all those who play the lyre and flute.

22 As for Tsillah, she also bore Tuḇal-Qayin, a smith of all kinds of tools in

4a Lit. faces. *4b* Or, sin-offering (feminine). *4c* Or, reposing or crouching (masculine). *4d* Lit. in

bronze and iron. And the sister of Tuḇal-
Qayin was Naʿamah.
23 And Lemeḵ said to his wives, “Aḏah
and Tsillah, hear my voice! Wives of
Lemeḵ, listen to my words! For I have
killed a man for wounding me, even a
young man for hurting me.
24 “For Qayin is avenged sevenfold, and
Lemeḵ seventy-sevenfold.”
25 And Aḏam knew his wife again, and
she bore a son and called his name Shěth,
“For Elohim has appointed me another
seed instead of Heḇel, because Qayin had
killed him.”
26 And to Shěth, to him also a son was
born. And he called his name Enosh. Then
it was begun to call on the Name of יהוה. [e]

5 This is the book of the genealogy of
Aḏam. In the day that Elohim created
man, He made him in the likeness of
Elohim.
2 Male and female He created them, and
He blessed them, and called their name
‘Aḏam’ in the day they were created.
3 And Aḏam lived one hundred and thirty years, and brought forth a son in his own
likeness, after his image, and called his
name Shěth.
4 And after he brought forth Shěth, the
days of Aḏam were eight hundred years.
And he brought forth sons and daughters.
5 So all the days that Aḏam lived were
nine hundred and thirty years, and he died.
6 And Shěth lived one hundred and five
years, and brought forth Enosh.
7 And after he brought forth Enosh,
Shěth lived eight hundred and seven years,
and brought forth sons and daughters.
8 So all the days of Shěth were nine hundred and twelve years, and he died.
9 And Enosh lived ninety years, and
brought forth Qěynan.
10 And after he brought forth Qěynan,
Enosh lived eight hundred and fifteen
years, and brought forth sons and daughters.
11 So all the days of Enosh were nine hundred and five years, and he died.
12 And Qěynan lived seventy years, and
brought forth Mahalal’ěl.
13 After he brought forth Mahalal’ěl, Qěynan lived eight hundred and forty years,
and brought forth sons and daughters.
14 So all the days of Qěynan were nine
hundred and ten years, and he died.
15 And Mahalal’ěl lived sixty-five years,
and brought forth Yereḏ.
16 And after he brought forth Yereḏ,
Mahalal’ěl lived eight hundred and thirty
years, and brought forth sons and daughters.
17 So all the days of Mahalal’ěl were eight
hundred and ninety-five years, and he died.
18 And Yereḏ lived one hundred and
sixty-two years, and brought forth Ḥanoḵ.
19 And after he brought forth Ḥanoḵ,
Yereḏ lived eight hundred years, and
brought forth sons and daughters.
20 So all the days of Yereḏ were nine hundred and sixty-two years, and he died.
21 And Ḥanoḵ lived sixty-five years, and
brought forth Methushelaḥ.
22 And after he brought forth Methushelaḥ, Ḥanoḵ walked with Elohim three
hundred years, and brought forth sons and
daughters.
23 So all the days of Ḥanoḵ were three
hundred and sixty-five years.
24 And Ḥanoḵ walked with Elohim. Then
he was no more, for Elohim took him.
25 And Methushelaḥ lived one hundred
and eighty-seven years, and brought forth
Lemeḵ.
26 And after he brought forth Lemeḵ,
Methushelaḥ lived seven hundred and
eighty-two years, and brought forth sons
and daughters.
27 So all the days of Methushelaḥ were
nine hundred and sixty-nine years, and he
died.
28 And Lemeḵ lived one hundred and
eighty-two years, and brought forth a son,
29 and called his name Noaḥ, saying,
“This one does comfort us concerning our
work and the toil of our hands, because of
the ground which יהוה has cursed.”
30 And after he brought forth Noaḥ,

4e The first record of “calling on the Name of יהוה.”

Lemeḵ lived five hundred and ninety-five years, and brought forth sons and daughters.

31 So all the days of Lemeḵ were seven hundred and seventy-seven years, and he died.

32 And Noaḥ was five hundred years old, and Noaḥ brought forth Shěm, Ḥam, and Yepheth.

6 And it came to be, when men began to increase on the face of the earth, and daughters were born to them,

2 that the sons of Elohim saw the daughters of men, that they were good. And they took wives for themselves of all whom they chose.

3 And יהוה said, "My Spirit shall not strive with man forever in his going astray. He is flesh, and his days shall be one hundred and twenty years."

4 The Nephilim were on the earth in those days, and also afterward, when the sons of Elohim came in to the daughters of men and they bore children to them. Those were the mighty men who were of old, the men of name.

5 And יהוה saw that the wickedness of man was great in the earth, and that every inclination of the thoughts of his heart was only evil continually.

6 And יהוה was sorry that He had made man on the earth, and He was grieved in His heart.

7 And יהוה said, "I am going to wipe off man whom I have created from the face of the ground, both man and beast, creeping *creature* and birds of the heavens, for I am sorry that I have made them."

8 But Noaḥ found favour in the eyes of יהוה.

9 This is the genealogy of Noaḥ. Noaḥ was a righteous man, perfect in his generations. Noaḥ walked with Elohim.

10 And Noaḥ brought forth three sons: Shěm, Ḥam, and Yepheth.

11 And the earth was corrupt before Elohim, and the earth was filled with violence.

12 And Elohim looked upon the earth and saw that it was corrupt – for all flesh had corrupted their way on the earth –

13 and Elohim said to Noaḥ, "The end of all flesh has come before Me, for the earth is filled with violence through them. And see, I am going to destroy them from the earth.

14 "Make yourself an ark of gopherwood. Make rooms in the ark, and cover it inside and outside with a covering.[a]

15 "And this is how you are to make it: The length of the ark is three hundred cubits, its width fifty cubits, and its height thirty cubits.

16 "Make a window for the ark, and complete it to a cubit from above. And set the door of the ark in its side. Make it with lower, second, and third decks.

17 "And see, I Myself am bringing floodwaters on the earth, to destroy all flesh in which is the breath of life from under the heavens – all that is on the earth is to die.

18 "And I shall establish My covenant with you, and you shall come into the ark, you and your sons and your wife and your sons' wives with you.

19 "And of all the living of all flesh, two of each, you are to bring into the ark, to keep them alive with you – a male and a female.

20 "Of the birds after their kind, and of the cattle after their kind, and of all creeping *creatures* of the ground after their kind, two of each are to come to you, to keep them alive.

21 "As for you, take of all food that is eaten and gather it to yourself. And it shall be food for you and for them."

22 And Noaḥ did according to all that Elohim commanded him, so he did.

7 And יהוה said to Noaḥ, "Come into the ark, you and all your household, because I have seen that you are righteous before Me in this generation.

2 "Of all the clean beasts take with you seven pairs, a male and his female; and of the beasts that are unclean two, a male and

6a Pitch, tar or other.

his female;
3 and of birds of the heavens seven pairs,
male and female, to keep offspring alive on
the face of all the earth.
4 "For after seven more days I am sending rain on the earth, forty days and forty
nights, and shall wipe from the face of the
earth all that stand that I created."
5 And Noaḥ did according to all that
יהוה commanded him.
6 Now Noaḥ was six hundred years old
when the flood-waters were on the earth.
7 And Noaḥ and his sons and his wife
and his sons' wives went into the ark
because of the waters of the flood.
8 Of the clean beasts and of the beasts
that are unclean, and of birds, and of all
that creep on the earth,
9 two by two they went into the ark to
Noaḥ, male and female, as Elohim had
commanded Noaḥ.
10 And it came to be after seven days that
the waters of the flood were on the earth.
11 In the six hundredth year of Noaḥ's
life, in the second new *moon*, [a] the seventeenth day of the new *moon*, [a] on that day
all the fountains of the great deep were
broken up, and the windows of the heavens
were opened.
12 And the rain was on the earth forty days
and forty nights.
13 On that same day Noaḥ and Shěm and
Ḥam and Yepheth, the sons of Noaḥ, and
Noaḥ's wife and the three wives of his
sons with them, went into the ark,
14 they and every life *form* after its kind,
and every beast after its kind, and every
creeping *creature* that creeps on the earth
after its kind, and every bird after its kind,
every bird of every sort.
15 And they went into the ark to Noaḥ,
two by two, of all flesh in which is the
breath of life.
16 And those going in, male and female of
all flesh, went in as Elohim had commanded him, and יהוה shut him in.
17 And the flood was on the earth forty
days, and the waters increased and lifted
up the ark, and it rose high above the earth.
18 And the waters were mighty and greatly increased on the earth, and the ark
moved about on the surface of the waters.
19 And the waters were exceedingly
mighty on the earth, and all the high mountains under all the heavens were covered.
20 The waters became mighty, fifteen
cubits upward, and the mountains were
covered.
21 And all flesh died – the creeping *creature* on the earth – birds and cattle and
beasts and every swarming *creature* that
swarms on the earth, and all mankind.
22 All in whose nostrils was the breath of
the spirit of life, all that was on the dry
land, died.
23 So He wiped off all that stand, which
were on the face of the ground – both man
and beast, creeping *creature* and bird of the
heavens. And they were wiped off from the
earth. And only Noaḥ was left, and those
with him in the ark.
24 And the waters were mighty on the
earth, one hundred and fifty days.

8 And Elohim remembered Noaḥ, and
all the beasts and all the cattle that
were with him in the ark. And Elohim
made a wind to pass over the earth, and the
waters subsided.
2 And the fountains of the deep and the
windows of the heavens were stopped, and
the rain from the heavens was withheld.
3 And the waters receded steadily from
the earth, and at the end of the hundred and
fifty days the waters diminished.
4 And in the seventh new *moon*, the seventeenth day of the new *moon*, the ark rested on the mountains of Ararat.
5 And the waters decreased steadily until
the tenth new *moon*. In the tenth *new
moon*, on the first day of the new *moon*, the
tops of the mountains became visible.
6 And it came to be, at the end of forty
days, that Noaḥ opened the window of the
ark which he had made,
7 and he sent out a raven, which kept
going out and turning back until the waters
had dried up from the earth.

7a Month.

8 Then he sent out a dove from him, to see if the waters had receded from the face of the ground.

9 But the dove found no resting place for its feet and returned into the ark to him, for the waters were on the face of all the earth. So he put out his hand and took it, and pulled it into the ark to himself.

10 And he waited yet another seven days, and again he sent the dove out from the ark.

11 And the dove came to him in the evening, and see, a freshly plucked olive leaf was in its mouth. And Noaḥ knew that the waters had receded from the earth.

12 And he waited yet another seven days and sent out the dove, which did not return to him again.

13 And it came to be in the six hundred and first year, in the first *month*, the first day of the new *moon*, that the waters were dried up from the earth. And Noaḥ removed the covering of the ark and looked, and saw the surface of the ground was dry.

14 And in the second new *moon*, on the twenty-seventh day of the new *moon*, the earth was dry.

15 And Elohim spoke to Noaḥ, saying,

16 "Go out of the ark, you and your wife and your sons and your sons' wives with you.

17 "Bring out with you every life *form* of all flesh that is with you: of birds, of cattle and all creeping *creatures* – the creeping *creatures* on the earth. And let them teem on the earth, and bear and increase on the earth."

18 So Noaḥ went out, and his sons and his wife and his sons' wives with him,

19 every beast, every creeping *creature*, and every bird, whatever creeps on the earth, according to their kinds, went out of the ark.

20 And Noaḥ built a slaughter-place to יהוה, and took of every clean beast and of every clean bird, and offered ascending offerings on the slaughter-place.

21 And יהוה smelled a soothing fragrance, and יהוה said in His heart, "Never again shall I curse the ground because of man, although the inclination of man's heart is evil from his youth, and never again strike all living *creatures*, as I have done,

22 as long as the earth remains, seedtime and harvest, and cold and heat, and winter and summer, and day and night shall not cease."

9 And Elohim blessed Noaḥ and his sons, and said to them, "Be fruitful and increase, and fill the earth.

2 "And the fear of you and the dread of you is on every beast of the earth, on every bird of the heavens, on all that creeps on the ground, and on all the fish of the sea – into your hand they have been given.

3 "Every creeping *creature* that lives is food for you. I have given you all, as *I gave* the green plants.

4 "But do not eat flesh with its life, its blood.

5 "But only your blood for your lives I require, from the hand of every beast I require it, and from the hand of man. From the hand of every man's brother I require the life of man.

6 "Whoever sheds man's blood, by man his blood is shed, for in the image of Elohim has He made man.

7 "As for you, be fruitful and increase, bring forth teemingly in the earth and increase in it."

8 And Elohim spoke to Noaḥ and to his sons with him, saying,

9 "And I, see, I establish My covenant with you and with your seed after you,

10 and with every living being that is with you: of the birds, of the cattle, and of every beast of the earth with you, of all that go out of the ark, every beast of the earth.

11 "And I shall establish My covenant with you, and never again is all flesh cut off by the waters of the flood, and never again is there a flood to destroy the earth."

12 And Elohim said, "This is the sign of the covenant which I make between Me and you, and every living being that is with you, for all generations to come:

13 "I shall set My rainbow in the cloud, and it shall be for the sign of the covenant between Me and the earth.

14 "And it shall be, when I bring a cloud
over the earth, that the rainbow shall be
seen in the cloud,
15 and I shall remember My covenant
which is between Me and you and every
living being of all flesh, and never again
let the waters become a flood to destroy all
flesh.
16 "And the rainbow shall be in the cloud,
and I shall see it, to remember the everlasting covenant between Elohim and every
living being of all flesh that is on the
earth."
17 And Elohim said to Noaḥ, "This is the
sign of the covenant which I have established between Me and all flesh that is on
the earth."
18 And the sons of Noaḥ who went out of
the ark were Shěm and Ḥam and Yepheth.
And Ḥam was the father of Kenaʿan.
19 These three were the sons of Noaḥ, and
all the earth was overspread from them.
20 And Noaḥ, a man of the soil, began and
planted a vineyard.
21 And he drank of the wine and was
drunk, and became uncovered in his tent.
22 And Ḥam, the father of Kenaʿan, saw
the nakedness of his father, and told his
two brothers outside.
23 So Shěm and Yepheth took a garment,
laid it on both their shoulders, and went
backward and covered the nakedness of
their father, but their faces were turned
away, and they did not see their father's
nakedness.
24 And Noaḥ awoke from his wine, and he
knew what his younger son had done to
him,
25 and he said, "Cursed is Kenaʿan, let
him become a servant of servants to his
brothers."
26 And he said, "Blessed be יהוה, the
Elohim of Shěm, and let Kenaʿan become
his servant.
27 "Let Elohim enlarge Yepheth, and let
him dwell in the tents of Shěm. And let
Kenaʿan become his servant."
28 And Noaḥ lived after the flood three
hundred and fifty years.
29 So all the days of Noaḥ were nine hundred and fifty years, and he died.

10 And this is the genealogy of the
sons of Noaḥ: Shěm, Ḥam, and
Yepheth. And sons were born to them after
the flood.
2 The sons of Yepheth: Gomer, and
Maḡoḡ, and Maḏai, and Yawan, and Tuḇal,
and Mesheḵ, and Tiras.
3 And the sons of Gomer: Ashkenaz, and
Riphath, and Toḡarmah.
4 And the sons of Yawan: Elishah and
Tarshish, Kittim and Doḏanim.
5 From these the coastland peoples of the
nations were separated into their lands,
everyone according to his language,
according to their clans, into their nations.
6 And the sons of Ḥam: Kush, and
Mitsrayim, and Put, and Kenaʿan.
7 And the sons of Kush: Seḇa, and
Ḥawilah, and Saḇtah, and Raʿmah, and
Saḇteḵa. And the sons of Raʿmah: Sheḇa
and Deḏan.
8 And Kush brought forth Nimroḏ, he
began to be a mighty one on the earth.
9 He was a mighty hunter before יהוה,
therefore it is said, "Like Nimroḏ the
mighty hunter before יהוה."
10 And the beginning of his reign was
Baḇel, and Ereḵ, and Akkaḏ, and Kalněh,
in the land of Shinʿar.
11 From that land he went to Ashshur and
built Nineweh, and Reḥoḇoth Ir, and
Kelaḥ,
12 and Resen between Nineweh and
Kelaḥ, the great city.
13 And Mitsrayim brought forth Luḏim,
and Anamim, and Lehaḇim, and
Naphtuḥim,
14 and Pathrusim, and Kasluḥim, from
whom came the Philistines and Kaphtorim.
15 And Kenaʿan brought forth Tsiḏon his
first-born, and Ḥěth,
16 and the Yeḇusite, and the Amorite, and
the Girgashite,
17 and the Ḥiwwite, and the Arqite, and
the Sinite,
18 and the Arwaḏite, and the Tsemarite,
and the Ḥamathite. And afterward the
clans of the Kenaʿanites were spread
abroad.
19 And the border of the Kenaʿanites was
from Tsiḏon as you go toward Gerar, as far

as Azzah, as you go toward Seḏom, and
Amorah, and Aḏmah, and Tseḇoyim, as far
as Lasha.
20 These were the sons of Ḥam, according
to their clans, according to their languages,
in their lands, in their nations.
21 And also to Shĕm, the father of all the
children of Ěḇer, the brother of Yepheth
the elder, *children* were born.
22 The sons of Shĕm: Ěylam, and Asshur,
and Arpaḵshaḏ, and Luḏ, and Aram.
23 And the sons of Aram: Uts, and Ḥul,
and Gether, and Mash.
24 And Arpaḵshaḏ brought forth Shelaḥ,
and Shelaḥ brought forth Ěḇer.
25 And to Ěḇer were born two sons, the
name of one was Peleḡ, for in his days the
earth was divided, and his brother's name
was Yoqtan.
26 And Yoqtan brought forth Almoḏaḏ,
and Sheleph, and Ḥatsarmaweth, and
Yeraḥ,
27 and Haḏoram, and Uzal, and Diqlah,
28 and Oḇal, and Aḇima'ĕl, and Sheḇa,
29 and Ophir, and Ḥawilah, and Yoḇaḇ.
All these were sons of Yoqtan.
30 And their dwelling place was from
Mĕysha as you go toward Sephar, a mountain of the east.
31 These were the sons of Shĕm, according to their clans, according to their languages, in their lands, according to their
nations.
32 These were the clans of the sons of
Noaḥ, according to their generations, in
their nations. And from these the nations
were divided on the earth after the flood.

11 And all the earth had one
language [a] and one speech.
2 And it came to be, as they set out from
the east, that they found a plain in the land
of Shin'ar, [b] and they dwelt there.
3 And they said to each other, "Come, let
us make bricks and bake them thoroughly."
And they had brick for stone, and they had
asphalt for mortar.
4 And they said, "Come, let us build
ourselves a city, and a tower whose top
is in the heavens, and make a name for
ourselves, lest we be scattered over all the
face of the earth."
5 Then יהוה came down to see the city
and the tower which the sons of men had
built.
6 And יהוה said, "Look, they are one
people and they all have one language, and
this is what they begin to do! And now,
they are not going to be withheld from
doing whatever they plan to do.
7 "Come, let Us go there and confuse
their language, so that they do not understand one another's speech."
8 And יהוה scattered them from there,
over the face of all the earth, and they left
off building the city.
9 That is why its name was called Baḇel, [c]
because there יהוה confused the language
of all the earth, and from there יהוה scattered them over the face of all the earth.
10 This is the genealogy of Shĕm: Shĕm
was a hundred years old and brought forth
Arpaḵshaḏ, two years after the flood.
11 And after he brought forth Arpaḵshaḏ,
Shĕm lived five hundred years, and
brought forth sons and daughters.
12 And Arpaḵshaḏ lived thirty-five years,
and brought forth Shelaḥ.
13 And after he brought forth Shelaḥ,
Arpaḵshaḏ lived four hundred and three
years, and brought forth sons and daughters.
14 And Shelaḥ lived thirty years, and
brought forth Ěḇer.
15 And after he brought forth Ěḇer, Shelaḥ
lived four hundred and three years, and
brought forth sons and daughters.
16 And Ěḇer lived thirty-four years, and
brought forth Peleḡ.
17 And after he brought forth Peleḡ, Ěḇer
lived four hundred and thirty years, and
brought forth sons and daughters.
18 And Peleḡ lived thirty years, and
brought forth Re'u.
19 And after he brought forth Re'u, Peleḡ
lived two hundred and nine years, and
brought forth sons and daughters.
20 And Re'u lived thirty-two years, and

11a Heb. *lip*. *11b* Earlier name for Baḇel. *11c* Baḇel is derived from a verb which means "to confuse."

brought forth Seruḡ.
21 And after he brought forth Seruḡ, Reʽu
lived two hundred and seven years, and
brought forth sons and daughters.
22 And Seruḡ lived thirty years, and
brought forth Naḥor.
23 And after he brought forth Naḥor,
Seruḡ lived two hundred years, and
brought forth sons and daughters.
24 And Naḥor lived twenty-nine years,
and brought forth Teraḥ.
25 And after he brought forth Teraḥ,
Naḥor lived one hundred and nineteen
years, and brought forth sons and
daughters.
26 And Teraḥ lived seventy years, and
brought forth Aḇram, Naḥor, and Haran.
27 And this is the genealogy of Teraḥ:
Teraḥ brought forth Aḇram, Naḥor, and
Haran. And Haran brought forth Lot.
28 And Haran died before his father Teraḥ
in the land of his birth, in Ur-kasdim.
29 And Aḇram and Naḥor took wives: the
name of Aḇram's wife was Sarai, and the
name of Naḥor's wife, Milkah, the daughter of Haran the father of Milkah and the
father of Yiskah.
30 And Sarai was barren, she had no child.
31 And Teraḥ took his son Aḇram and his
grandson Lot, son of Haran, and his daughter-in-law Sarai, his son Aḇram's wife, and
they went out with them from Ur-kasdim
to go to the land of Kenaʽan. And they
came to Ḥaran and dwelt there.
32 And the days of Teraḥ came to be two
hundred and five years, and Teraḥ died in
Ḥaran.

12 And יהוה said to Aḇram, "Go
yourself out of your land, from
your relatives and from your father's
house, to a land which I show you.
2 "And I shall make you a great nation,
and bless you and make your name great,
and you shall be a blessing!
3 "And I shall bless those who bless you,
and curse him who curses you. And in you
all the clans of the earth shall be blessed."
4 So Aḇram left, as יהוה had commanded
him, and Lot went with him. And Aḇram
was seventy-five years old when he set out
from Ḥaran.
5 And Aḇram took Sarai his wife and Lot
his brother's son, and all their possessions
that they had gathered, and the beings
whom they had acquired in Ḥaran, and
they set out for the land of Kenaʽan. And
they came to the land of Kenaʽan.
6 And Aḇram passed through the land to
the place of Sheḵem, as far as the terebinth
tree of Moreh. At that time the Kenaʽanites
were in the land.
7 And יהוה appeared to Aḇram and said,
"To your seed I give this land." And he
built there a slaughter-place to יהוה, who
had appeared to him.
8 And from there he moved to the mountain east of Běyth Ěl, and he pitched his
tent, with Běyth Ěl on the west and Ai on
the east. And he built there a slaughter-
place to יהוה, and called on the Name of
יהוה.
9 And Aḇram set out, continuing toward
the South.
10 And a scarcity of food came to be in the
land, and Aḇram went down to Mitsrayim
to dwell there, for the scarcity of food was
severe in the land.
11 And it came to be, when he was close
to entering Mitsrayim, that he said to Sarai
his wife, "See, I know that you are a
beautiful woman to look at.
12 "And it shall be, when the Mitsrites see
you, that they shall say, 'This is his wife.'
And they shall kill me, but let you live.
13 "Please say you are my sister, so that it
shall be well with me for your sake, and
my life be spared because of you."
14 And it came to be, when Aḇram came
into Mitsrayim, that the Mitsrites saw the
woman, that she was very beautiful.
15 And Pharaoh's officials saw her and
praised her before Pharaoh, and the
woman was taken to Pharaoh's house.
16 And he treated Aḇram well for her
sake, and he had sheep, and cattle, and
male donkeys, and male and female
servants, and female donkeys, and camels.
17 But יהוה plagued Pharaoh and his
house with great plagues because of Sarai,
Aḇram's wife.
18 And Pharaoh called Aḇram and said,

“What is this you have done to me? Why
did you not inform me that she was your
wife?
19 “Why did you say, ‘She is my sister’?
And so I was going to take her for my
wife. Look, here is your wife, take her and
go.”
20 And Pharaoh commanded his men
concerning him, and they sent him away,
with his wife and all that he had.

13 And Aḇram went up from
Mitsrayim into the South, he and
his wife and all that he had, and Lot with
him.
2 And Aḇram was very rich in livestock,
in silver, and in gold.
3 And he went on his journey from the
South as far as Běyth Ěl, to the place where
his tent had been at the beginning, between
Běyth Ěl and Ai,
4 to the place of the slaughter-place
which he had made there at first. And there
Aḇram called on the Name of יהוה.
5 Now Lot, who went with Aḇram, also
had flocks and herds and tents.
6 And the land was not able to bear them,
that they might dwell together, for their
possessions were great, so that they could
not dwell together.
7 And there was strife between the herdsmen of Aḇram’s livestock and the herdsmen of Lot’s livestock. And at that time
the Kenaʿanites and the Perizzites dwelt in
the land.
8 Then Aḇram said to Lot, “Let there be
no strife between you and me, and between
my herdsmen and your herdsmen, for we
are brothers.
9 “Is not all the land before you? Please
separate from me. If you take the left, then
I go to the right; or, if you go to the right,
then I go to the left.”
10 And Lot lifted his eyes and saw all the
plain of the Yarděn, that it was well
watered everywhere – before יהוה
destroyed Seḏom and Amorah – like the
garden of יהוה, like the land of Mitsrayim
as you go toward Tsoʿar.
11 So Lot chose for himself all the plain of
the Yarděn, and Lot moved east. Thus they
separated from each other,
12 Aḇram dwelling in the land of Kenaʿan,
and Lot dwelling in the cities of the plain
and pitched his tent as far as Seḏom.
13 But the men of Seḏom were evil and
sinned before יהוה, exceedingly so.
14 And after Lot had separated from him,
יהוה said to Aḇram, “Now lift up your
eyes and look from the place where you
are, northward and southward and eastward and westward,
15 for all the land which you see I shall
give to you and your seed forever.
16 “And I shall make your seed as the dust
of the earth, so that, if a man could count
the dust of the earth, then your seed also
could be counted.
17 “Arise, walk in the land through its
length and its width, for I give it to you.”
18 So Aḇram moved his tent, and went
and dwelt by the terebinth trees of Mamrě,
which are in Ḥeḇron, and built a slaughter-
place there to יהוה.

14 And it came to be in the days of
Amraphel sovereign of Shinʿar,
Aryoḵ sovereign of Ellasar, Keḏorlaʿomer
sovereign of Ěylam, and Tiḏʿal sovereign
of Goyim,
2 that they fought against Bera sovereign
of Seḏom, Birsha sovereign of Amorah,
Shinaḇ sovereign of Aḏmah, Shem’ěḇer
sovereign of Tseḇoyim, and the sovereign
of Bela, that is Tsoʿar.
3 All these joined together in the Valley
of Siddim, that is the Salt Sea.
4 Twelve years they served Keḏorlaʿomer, and in the thirteenth year they
rebelled.
5 And in the fourteenth year Keḏorlaʿomer and the sovereigns that were with
him came and struck the Repha’im in
Ashteroth Qarnayim, and the Zuzim in
Ḥam, and the Ěmites in Shawěh
Qiryathayim,
6 and the Ḥorites in their mountain of
Sěʿir, as far as Ěl Paran, which is by the
wilderness.
7 And they turned back and came to Ěn
Mishpat, that is Qaḏěsh, and struck all the
country of the Amalěqites, and also the

Amorites who dwelt in Ḥatsetson Tamar.
8 And the sovereign of Seḏom, and the sovereign of Amorah, and the sovereign of Aḏmah, and the sovereign of Tseḇoyim, and the sovereign of Bela, that is Tsoʽar, went out and joined together in battle in the Valley of Siddim,
9 against Keḏorlaʽomer sovereign of Ěylam, and Tiḏʽal sovereign of Goyim, and Amraphel sovereign of Shinʽar, and Aryoḵ sovereign of Ellasar – four sovereigns against five.
10 And the Valley of Siddim had many tar pits. And the sovereigns of Seḏom and Amorah fled and fell there, and the remainder fled to the mountains.
11 And they took all the goods of Seḏom and Amorah, and all their food, and went away.
12 And they took Lot, Aḇram's brother's son who dwelt in Seḏom, and his goods, and left.
13 And one who had escaped came and informed Aḇram the Hebrew, for he dwelt by the terebinth trees of Mamrě the Amorite, brother of Eshkol and brother of Aněr, and they had a covenant with Aḇram.
14 And when Aḇram heard that his brother was taken captive, he armed his three hundred and eighteen trained servants who were born in his own house, and went in pursuit as far as Dan.
15 And he and his servants divided against them by night, and struck them and pursued them as far as Ḥoḇah, which is on the left of Dammeseq.
16 So he brought back all the goods, and also brought back his brother Lot and his goods, as well as the women and the people.
17 And after his return from the striking of Keḏorlaʽomer and the sovereigns who were with him, the sovereign of Seḏom came out to meet him at the Valley of Shawěh, that is, the Sovereign's Valley.
18 And Malkitseḏeq sovereign of Shalěm brought out bread and wine. Now he was the priest of the Most High Ěl.
19 And he blessed him and said, "Blessed be Aḇram of the Most High Ěl, Possessor of the heavens and earth.
20 "And blessed be the Most High Ěl who has delivered your enemies into your hand." And he gave him a tenth of all.
21 And the sovereign of Seḏom said to Aḇram, "Give me the people, and take the goods for yourself."
22 But Aḇram said to the sovereign of Seḏom, "I have lifted my hand to יהוה, the Most High Ěl, the Possessor of the heavens and earth,
23 not to take a thread or a sandal strap or whatever is yours, lest you should say, 'I have made Aḇram rich,'
24 except only what the young men have eaten, and the portion of the men who went with me: Aněr, Eshkol, and Mamrě. Let them take their portion."

15 After these events the word of יהוה came to Aḇram in a vision, saying, "Do not be afraid, Aḇram. I am your shield, your reward is exceedingly great."
2 And Aḇram said, "Master יהוה, what would You give me, seeing I go childless, and the heir of my house is Eliʽezer of Dammeseq?"
3 And Aḇram said, "See, You have given me no seed, and see, one born in my house is my heir!"
4 And see, the word of יהוה came to him, saying, "This one is not your heir, but he who comes from your own body is your heir."
5 And He brought him outside and said, "Look now toward the heavens, and count the stars if you are able to count them." And He said to him, "So are your seed."
6 And he believed in יהוה, and He reckoned it to him for righteousness.
7 And He said to him, "I am יהוה, who brought you out of Ur-kasdim, to give you this land to inherit it."
8 And he said, "Master יהוה, whereby do I know that I possess it?"
9 And He said to him, "Bring Me a three-year-old heifer, and a three-year-old female goat, and a three-year-old ram, and a turtledove, and a young pigeon."
10 And he took all these to Him and cut

them in the middle, and placed each half opposite the other, but he did not cut the birds.

11 And the birds of prey came down on the carcasses, and Aḇram drove them away.

12 And it came to be, when the sun was going down, and a deep sleep fell upon Aḇram, that see, a frightening great darkness fell upon him.

13 And He said to Aḇram, "Know for certain that your seed are to be sojourners in a land that is not theirs, and shall serve them, and they shall afflict them four hundred years.

14 "But the nation whom they serve I am going to judge, and afterward let them come out with great possessions.

15 "Now as for you, you are to go to your fathers in peace, you are to be buried at a good old age.

16 "Then, in the fourth generation they shall return here, for the crookedness of the Amorites is not yet complete."

17 And it came to be, when the sun went down and it was dark, that see, a smoking oven and a burning torch passing between those pieces.

18 On the same day יהוה made a covenant with Aḇram, saying, "I have given this land to your seed, from the river of Mitsrayim to the great river, the River Euphrates,

19 with the Qěynite, and the Qenizzite, and the Qaḏmonite,

20 and the Ḥittite, and the Perizzite, and the Repha'im,

21 and the Amorite, and the Kena'anite, and the Girgashite, and the Yeḇusite."

16 And Sarai, Aḇram's wife, had borne him no child. And she had a Mitsrian female servant whose name was Haḡar.

2 And Sarai said to Aḇram, "See, יהוה has kept me from bearing children. Please, go in to my female servant. It might be that I am built up by her." And Aḇram listened to the voice of Sarai.

3 And Sarai, Aḇram's wife, took Haḡar her female servant, the Mitsrian, and gave her to her husband Aḇram to be his wife, after Aḇram had dwelt ten years in the land of Kena'an.

4 And he went in to Haḡar, and she conceived. And when she saw that she had conceived, her mistress was despised in her eyes.

5 And Sarai said to Aḇram, "My wrong be upon you! I gave my female servant into your bosom. And when she saw that she had conceived, I was despised in her eyes. Let יהוה judge between you and me."

6 And Aḇram said to Sarai, "See, your female servant is in your hand, do to her what is good in your eyes." And Sarai treated her harshly, and she fled from her presence.

7 And the Messenger of יהוה found her by a spring of water in the wilderness, by the spring on the way to Shur,

8 and He said, "Haḡar, Sarai's female servant, where have you come from, and where are you going?" And she said, "I am fleeing from the presence of Sarai, my mistress."

9 And the Messenger of יהוה said to her, "Return to your mistress, and humble yourself under her hand."

10 And the Messenger of יהוה said to her, "I am going to increase your seed greatly, too numerous to be counted."

11 And the Messenger of יהוה said to her, "See, you are conceiving and bearing a son, and shall call his name Yishma'ěl, because יהוה has heard your affliction.

12 "And he is to be a wild man, his hand against every one and every one's hand against him, and dwell over against all his brothers."

13 And she called the Name of יהוה who spoke to her, "You are the Ěl who sees," for she said, "Even here have I seen after Him who sees me?"

14 That is why the well was called Be'ěr Laḥai Ro'i, see, it is between Qaḏěsh and Bereḏ.

15 And Haḡar bore Aḇram a son, and Aḇram called the name of his son, whom Haḡar bore, Yishma'ěl.

16 And Aḇram was eighty-six years old

when Haḡar bore Yishmaʿěl to Aḇram.

17 And it came to be when Aḇram
was ninety-nine years old, that
יהוה appeared to Aḇram and said to him,
"I am Ěl Shaddai – walk before Me and be
perfect.
2 "And I give My covenant between Me
and you, and shall greatly increase you."
3 And Aḇram fell on his face, and
Elohim spoke with him, saying,
4 "As for Me, look, My covenant is with
you, and you shall become a father of
many nations.
5 "And no longer is your name called
Aḇram, but your name shall be Aḇraham,
because I shall make you a father of many
nations.
6 "And I shall make you exceedingly
fruitful, and make nations of you, and sovereigns shall come from you.
7 "And I shall establish My covenant
between Me and you and your seed after
you in their generations, for an everlasting
covenant, to be Elohim to you and your
seed after you.
8 "And I shall give to you and your seed
after you the land of your sojournings,
all the land of Kenaʿan, as an everlasting
possession. And I shall be their Elohim."
9 And Elohim said to Aḇraham, "As for
you, guard My covenant, you and your
seed after you throughout their generations.
10 "This is My covenant which you guard
between Me and you, and your seed after
you: Every male child among you is to be
circumcised.
11 "And you shall circumcise the flesh of
your foreskin, and it shall become a sign of
the covenant between Me and you.
12 "And a son of eight days is circumcised
by you, every male child in your generations, he who is born in your house or
bought with silver from any foreigner who
is not of your seed.
13 "He who is born in your house, and he
who is bought with your silver, has to be
circumcised. So shall My covenant be in
your flesh, for an everlasting covenant.
14 "And an uncircumcised male child,
who is not circumcised in the flesh of his
foreskin, his life shall be cut off from his
people – he has broken My covenant."
15 And Elohim said to Aḇraham, "As for
Sarai your wife, do not call her name Sarai,
for Sarah is her name.
16 "And I shall bless her and also give you
a son by her. And I shall bless her, and she
shall become nations – sovereigns of peoples are to be from her."
17 And Aḇraham fell on his face and
laughed, and said in his heart, "Is a *child*
born to a man who is a hundred years old?
Or is Sarah, who is ninety years old, to
bear a child?"
18 And Aḇraham said to Elohim, "Oh, let
Yishmaʿěl live before You!"
19 And Elohim said, "No, Sarah your wife
is truly bearing a son to you, and you shall
call his name Yitsḥaq. And I shall establish
My covenant with him for an everlasting
covenant, and with his seed after him.
20 "And as for Yishmaʿěl, I have heard
you. See, I shall bless him, and shall make
him fruitful, and greatly increase him. He
is to bring forth twelve princes, and I shall
make him a great nation.
21 "But My covenant I establish with
Yitsḥaq, whom Sarah is to bear to you at
this appointed time next year."
22 And when He had ended speaking with
him, Elohim went up from Aḇraham.
23 And Aḇraham took Yishmaʿěl his son,
and all those born in his house and all
those bought with his silver, every male
among the men of Aḇraham's house, and
circumcised the flesh of their foreskins that
same day, as Elohim told him.
24 And Aḇraham was ninety-nine years
old when he was circumcised in the flesh
of his foreskin.
25 And Yishmaʿěl his son was thirteen
years old when he was circumcised in the
flesh of his foreskin.
26 Aḇraham and his son Yishmaʿěl were
circumcised that same day.
27 And all the men of his house, born in
the house or bought with silver from a foreigner, were circumcised with him.

18 And יהוה appeared to him by the terebinth trees of Mamrě, while he was sitting in the tent door in the heat of the day.

2 So he lifted his eyes and looked, and saw three men standing opposite him. And when he saw them, he ran from the tent door to meet them, and bowed himself to the ground,

3 and said, "יהוה, if I have now found favour in Your eyes, please do not pass Your servant by.

4 "Please let a little water be brought, and wash your feet, and rest yourselves under the tree.

5 "And let me bring a piece of bread and refresh your hearts, and then go on, for this is why you have come to your servant." And they said, "Do as you have said."

6 So Aḇraham ran into the tent to Sarah and said, "Hurry, make ready three measures of fine flour, knead it and make cakes."

7 And Aḇraham ran to the herd, took a tender and good calf, gave it to a young man, and he hurried to prepare it.

8 And he took curds and milk and the calf which he had prepared, and set it before them, and he stood by them under the tree as they ate.

9 And they said to him, "Where is Sarah your wife?" And he said, "See, in the tent."

10 And He said, "I shall certainly return to you according to the time of life, and see, Sarah your wife is to have a son!" And Sarah was listening in the tent door which was behind him.

11 Now Aḇraham and Sarah were old, well advanced in age, and Sarah was past the way of women.

12 And Sarah laughed within herself, saying, "After I have grown old, shall I have pleasure, my master being old too?"

13 And יהוה said to Aḇraham, "Why did Sarah laugh, saying, 'Shall I truly have a child, since I am old?'

14 "Is any matter too hard for יהוה? At the appointed time I am going to return to you, according to the time of life, and Sarah is to have a son."

15 But Sarah denied it, saying, "I did not laugh," for she was afraid. And He said, "No, but you did laugh!"

16 And the men rose up from there and looked toward Seḏom, and Aḇraham went with them to send them away.

17 And יהוה said, "Shall I hide from Aḇraham what I am doing,

18 since Aḇraham is certainly going to become a great and mighty nation, and all the nations of the earth shall be blessed in him?

19 "For I have known him, so that he commands his children and his household after him, to guard the way of יהוה, to do righteousness and right-ruling, so that יהוה brings to Aḇraham what He has spoken to him."

20 And יהוה said, "Because the outcry against Seḏom and Amorah is great, and because their sin is very heavy,

21 "I am going down now to see whether they have done altogether according to the outcry against it that has come to Me, and if not, I know."

22 So the men turned away from there and went toward Seḏom, but יהוה still stood before Aḇraham.

23 And Aḇraham drew near and said, "Would You also destroy the righteous with the wrong?

24 "Suppose there are fifty righteous within the city, would You also destroy the place and not spare it for the fifty righteous that were in it?

25 "Far be it from You to act in this way, to slay the righteous with the wrong, so that the righteous should be as the wrong. Far be it from You! Does the Judge of all the earth not do right?"

26 And יהוה said, "If I find in Seḏom fifty righteous within the city, then I shall spare all the place for their sakes."

27 And Aḇraham answered and said, "Look, please, I who am but dust and ashes have taken it upon myself to speak to יהוה,

28 "Suppose there are five less than the fifty righteous, would You destroy all of the city for lack of five?" And He said, "If I find there forty-five, I do not destroy it."

29 And he spoke to Him yet again and said, "Suppose there are found forty?" And

He said, "I would not do it for the sake of forty."

30 And he said, "Let not יהוה be displeased, and let me speak: Suppose there are found thirty?" And He said, "I would not do it if I find thirty there."

31 And he said, "Look, please, I have taken it upon myself to speak to יהוה: Suppose there are found twenty?" And He said, "I would not destroy it for the sake of twenty."

32 And he said, "Let not יהוה be displeased, and let me speak only this time: Suppose there are found ten?" And He said, "I would not destroy it for the sake of ten."

33 Then יהוה went away as soon as He had ended speaking to Aḇraham. And Aḇraham returned to his place.

19 And the two messengers came to Seḏom in the evening, and Lot was sitting in the gate of Seḏom. And when Lot saw them, he rose up to meet them, and he bowed himself with his face toward the ground,

2 and he said, "Look, please my masters, please turn in to your servant's house and spend the night, and wash your feet, and rise early and go your way." And they said, "No, but let us spend the night in the open square."

3 But he urged them strongly, and they turned in to him and came into his house. And he made them a feast, and baked unleavened bread, and they ate.

4 Before they lay down, the men of the city, the men of Seḏom, both old and young, all the people from every part, surrounded the house.

5 And they called to Lot and said to him, "Where are the men who came to you tonight? Bring them out to us, and let us 'know' them."

6 So Lot went out to them through the doorway, and shut the door behind him,

7 and said, "Please, my brothers, do not do evil!

8 "Look, please, I have two daughters who have not known a man. Please, let me bring them out to you, and do to them as you wish, only do no deed to these men, because they have come under the shadow of my roof."

9 But they said, "Stand back!" And they said, "This one came in to sojourn, and should he always judge? Now we are going to treat you worse than them." So they pressed hard against the man Lot, and came near to break down the door.

10 But the men reached out their hands and pulled Lot into the house with them, and shut the door.

11 Then they struck the men who were at the doorway of the house with blindness, both small and great, and they wearied themselves to find the door.

12 And the men said to Lot, "Have you anyone else here? A son-in-law, and your sons, and your daughters, and whomever you have in the city – bring them out of this place!

13 "For we are going to destroy this place, because the cry against them has grown great before the face of יהוה, and יהוה has sent us to destroy it."

14 And Lot went out and spoke to his sons-in-law, who had married his daughters, and said, "Get up, get out of this place, for יהוה is going to destroy this city!" But to his sons-in-law he seemed to be as one joking.

15 And when morning dawned, the messengers urged Lot to hurry, saying, "Get up, take your wife and your two daughters who are here, lest you be consumed in the punishment of the city."

16 And while he loitered, the men took hold of his hand, and his wife's hand, and the hands of his two daughters, יהוה having compassion on him, and they brought him out and set him outside the city.

17 And it came to be, when they had brought them outside, that he said, "Escape for your life! Do not look behind you nor stay anywhere in the plain. Escape to the mountains, lest you be consumed."

18 And Lot said to them, "Oh no, יהוה!

19 "Look, please, your servant has found favour in your eyes, and you have increased your loving-commitment which you have shown me by saving my life, but

I am unable to escape to the mountains, lest calamity overtake me and I die.
20 "Look, please, this city is near enough to flee to, and it is small. Please let me escape there – is it not a small matter – and let my life be saved?"
21 And He said to him, "Look, I have favoured you concerning this matter also, without overthrowing this city for which you have spoken.
22 "Hurry, escape there. For I am not able to do any deed until you arrive there." So the name of the city was called Tsoʻar.
23 The sun had risen upon the earth when Lot entered Tsoʻar.
24 And יהוה rained sulphur and fire on Seḏom and Amorah, from יהוה out of the heavens.
25 So He overthrew those cities, and all the plain, and all the inhabitants of the cities, and what grew on the ground.
26 But his wife looked back from behind him, and she became a post of salt.
27 And Aḇraham arose early in the morning *and went* to the place where he had stood before יהוה,
28 and he looked toward Seḏom and Amorah, and toward all the land of the plain. And he looked and saw the smoke of the land which went up like the smoke of a furnace.
29 Thus it came to be, when Elohim destroyed the cities of the plain, that Elohim remembered Aḇraham, and sent Lot out of the midst of the overthrow, when He overthrew the cities in which Lot had dwelt.
30 And Lot went up out of Tsoʻar and dwelt in the mountains, and his two daughters were with him, for he was afraid to dwell in Tsoʻar. And he and his two daughters dwelt in a cave.
31 And the first-born said to the younger, "Our father is old, and there is no man on the earth to come in to us, as is the way of all the earth.
32 "Come, let us make our father drink wine and lie with him, so that we preserve the seed of our father."
33 So they made their father drink wine that night. And the first-born went in and lay with her father, and he was not aware of it when she lay down or when she arose.
34 And it came to be on the next day that the first-born said to the younger, "See, I lay with my father last night. Let us make him drink wine tonight as well, and you go in and lie with him, so that we keep the seed of our father."
35 So they made their father drink wine that night as well. And the younger arose and lay with him, and he was not aware of it when she lay down or when she arose.
36 Thus both the daughters of Lot became pregnant by their father.
37 And the first-born bore a son and called his name Mo'aḇ, he is the father of the Mo'aḇites to this day.
38 And the younger, she also bore a son and called his name Ben-Ammi, he is the father of the children of Ammon to this day.

20 And Aḇraham set out from there to the land of the South, and dwelt between Qaḏēsh and Shur, and stayed in Gerar.
2 And Aḇraham said concerning Sarah his wife, "She is my sister." And Aḇimeleḵ sovereign of Gerar sent and took Sarah.
3 But Elohim came to Aḇimeleḵ in a dream by night, and said to him, "See, you are a dead man because of the woman whom you have taken, for she is a man's wife."
4 However, Aḇimeleḵ had not come near her, and he said, "יהוה, would You kill a righteous nation also?
5 "Did he not say to me, 'She is my sister'? And she, even she herself said, 'He is my brother.' In the integrity of my heart and in the innocence of my hands I have done this."
6 And Elohim said to him in a dream, "Yes, I know that you did this in the integrity of your heart, and so I kept you from sinning against Me. For this reason I did not let you touch her.
7 "And now, return the man's wife, for he is a prophet, and let him pray for you and you live. But if you do not return her, know that you shall certainly die, you and

all that are yours.”
8 So Aḇimeleḵ rose early in the morning,
and called all his servants, and spoke all
these words in their hearing. And the men
were greatly frightened.
9 And Aḇimeleḵ called Aḇraham and
said to him, “What have you done to us? In
what have I sinned against you, that you
have brought on me and on my reign a
great sin? You have done matters to me
that should not be done.”
10 And Aḇimeleḵ said to Aḇraham, “What
did you have in view, that you have done
this matter?”
11 And Aḇraham said, “Only because I
said *to myself*, the fear of Elohim is not in
this place, and they shall kill me for the
sake of my wife.
12 “And yet, she is truly my sister. She is
the daughter of my father, but not the
daughter of my mother, and she became
my wife.
13 “And it came to be, when Elohim
caused me to wander from my father’s
house, that I said to her, ‘This is your
loving-commitment that you should do for
me: in every place, wherever we go, say of
me, “He is my brother.” ’ ”
14 Then Aḇimeleḵ took sheep, and cattle,
and male and female servants, and gave
them to Aḇraham. And he returned Sarah
his wife to him.
15 And Aḇimeleḵ said, “See, my land is
before you, dwell wherever it is good in
your eyes.”
16 And to Sarah he said, “See, I have
given your brother a thousand pieces of
silver. See, it is to you a covering of eyes
before all who are with you and before
all others, and you are cleared before
everyone.”
17 And Aḇraham prayed to Elohim, and
Elohim healed Aḇimeleḵ, and his wife, and
his female servants, so they bore children,
18 for יהוה had closed up all the wombs of
the house of Aḇimeleḵ because of Sarah,
Aḇraham’s wife.

21 And יהוה visited Sarah as He had
said, and יהוה did for Sarah as He
had spoken.
2 So Sarah conceived and bore Aḇraham
a son in his old age, at the appointed time
of which Elohim had spoken to him.
3 And Aḇraham called the name of his
son who was born to him, whom Sarah
bore to him, Yitsḥaq.
4 And Aḇraham circumcised his son
Yitsḥaq when he was eight days old, as
Elohim had commanded him.
5 And Aḇraham was one hundred years
old when his son Yitsḥaq was born to him.
6 And Sarah said, “Elohim has made me
laugh, and everyone who hears of it laughs
with me.”
7 And she said, “Who would have said to
Aḇraham that Sarah would nurse children?
For I have borne him a son in his old age.”
8 And the child grew and was weaned,
and Aḇraham made a great feast on the day
that Yitsḥaq was weaned.
9 And Sarah saw the son of Haḡar the
Mitsrian, whom she had borne to
Aḇraham, mocking.
10 So she said to Aḇraham, “Drive out this
female servant and her son, for the son of
this female servant shall not inherit with
my son, with Yitsḥaq.”
11 And the matter was very evil in the
eyes of Aḇraham because of his son.
12 But Elohim said to Aḇraham, “Let it
not be evil in your eyes because of the boy
and because of your female servant.
Whatever Sarah has said to you, listen to
her voice, for in Yitsḥaq your seed is
called.
13 “And of the son of the female servant I
also make a nation, because he is your
seed.”
14 And Aḇraham rose early in the morning, and took bread and a skin of water,
which he gave to Haḡar, putting it on her
shoulder, also the boy, and sent her away.
And she left and wandered in the
Wilderness of Be’ĕrsheḇa.
15 And the water in the skin was used up,
and she placed the boy under one of the
shrubs.
16 And she went and sat down about a
bowshot away, for she said, “Let me not
see the death of the boy.” And she sat
opposite him, and lifted her voice and

wept.
[17]And Elohim heard the voice of the boy, and the messenger of Elohim called to Hağar from the heavens, and said to her, "What is the matter with you, Hağar? Do not fear, for Elohim has heard the voice of the boy where he is.
[18]"Arise, lift up the boy and hold him with your hand, for I make a great nation of him."
[19]And Elohim opened her eyes, and she saw a well of water. And she went and filled the skin with water, and gave the boy a drink.
[20]And Elohim was with the boy, and he grew and dwelt in the wilderness, and became an archer.
[21]And he dwelt in the Wilderness of Paran, and his mother took a wife for him from the land of Mitsrayim.
[22]And it came to be at that time that Aḇimeleḵ and Piḵol, the commander of his army, spoke to Aḇraham, saying, "Elohim is with you in all that you do.
[23]"And now, swear to me by Elohim, not to be untrue to me, to my offspring, or to my descendants. Do to me according to the loving-commitment that I have done to you and to the land in which you have dwelt."
[24]And Aḇraham said, "I swear."
[25]And Aḇraham reproved Aḇimeleḵ because of a well of water which Aḇimeleḵ's servants had seized.
[26]And Aḇimeleḵ said, "I do not know who has done this deed. Neither did you inform me, nor did I hear until today."
[27]So Aḇraham took sheep and cattle and gave them to Aḇimeleḵ, and the two of them made a covenant.
[28]And Aḇraham set seven ewe lambs of the flock by themselves.
[29]And Aḇimeleḵ asked Aḇraham, "What are these seven ewe lambs which you have set by themselves?"
[30]And he said, "Take these seven ewe lambs from my hand, to be my witness that I have dug this well."
[31]So he called that place Be'ĕrsheḇa, because the two of them swore an oath there.
[32]Thus they made a covenant at Be'ĕrsheḇa. And Aḇimeleḵ rose with Piḵol, the commander of his army, and they returned to the land of the Philistines.
[33]And he planted a tamarisk tree in Be'ĕrsheḇa, and there called on the Name of יהוה, the Everlasting Ěl.
[34]And Aḇraham sojourned in the land of the Philistines many days.

22

And it came to be after these events that Elohim tried Aḇraham, and said to him, "Aḇraham!" And he said, "Here I am."
[2]And He said, "Take your son, now, your only son Yitsḥaq, whom you love, and go to the land of Moriyah, and offer him there as an ascending offering on one of the mountains which I command you."
[3]And Aḇraham rose early in the morning and saddled his donkey, and took two of his young men with him, and Yitsḥaq his son. And he split the wood for the ascending offering, and arose and went to the place which Elohim had commanded him.
[4]And on the third day Aḇraham lifted his eyes and saw the place from a distance.
[5]So Aḇraham said to his young men, "Stay here with the donkey while the boy and I go over there and worship, and come back to you."
[6]And Aḇraham took the wood of the ascending offering and laid it on Yitsḥaq his son. And he took the fire in his hand, and a knife, and the two of them went together.
[7]And Yitsḥaq spoke to Aḇraham his father and said, "My father!" And he said, "Here I am, my son." And he said, "See, the fire and the wood! But where is the lamb for an ascending offering?"
[8]And Aḇraham said, "My son, Elohim does provide for Himself the lamb for an ascending offering." And the two of them went together.
[9]And they came to the place which Elohim had commanded him, and Aḇraham built a slaughter-place there and placed the wood in order. And he bound Yitsḥaq his son and laid him on the slaughter-place, upon the wood.

10 And Aḇraham stretched out his hand
and took the knife to slay his son,
11 but the Messenger of יהוה called to
him from the heavens and said, "Aḇraham,
Aḇraham!" And he said, "Here I am."
12 And He said, "Do not lay your hand on
the boy, nor touch him. For now I know
that you fear Elohim, seeing you have not
withheld your son, your only son, from
Me."
13 And Aḇraham lifted his eyes and
looked and saw behind him a ram caught
in a bush by its horns, and Aḇraham went
and took the ram and offered it up for an
ascending offering instead of his son.
14 And Aḇraham called the name of the
place, 'יהוה Yireh,' as it is said to this day,
"On the mountain יהוה provides."
15 And the Messenger of יהוה called to
Aḇraham a second time from the heavens,
16 and said, "By Myself I have sworn,
declares יהוה, because you have done this,
and have not withheld your son, your only
son,
17 that I shall certainly bless you, and I
shall certainly increase your seed as the
stars of the heavens and as the sand which
is on the seashore, and let your seed possess the gate of their enemies.
18 "And in your seed all the nations of the
earth shall be blessed, because you have
obeyed My voice."
19 Then Aḇraham returned to his young
men, and they rose up and went together
to Be'ěrsheḇa. And Aḇraham dwelt at
Be'ěrsheḇa.
20 And it came to be after these events that
it was reported to Aḇraham, saying, "See,
Milkah too has borne children to your
brother Naḥor:
21 "Uts his first-born, and Buz his brother,
and Qemu'ěl the father of Aram,
22 and Keseḏ, and Ḥazo, and Pildash, and
Yiḏlaph, and Bethu'ěl."
23 And Bethu'ěl brought forth Riḇqah.
These eight Milkah bore to Naḥor,
Aḇraham's brother.
24 And his concubine, whose name was
Re'uwmah, also bore Teḇaḥ, and Gaḥam,
and Taḥash, and Maʽaḵah.

23 And Sarah lived one hundred and
twenty-seven years, the years of
the life of Sarah.
2 And Sarah died in Qiryath Arba, that is
Ḥeḇron, in the land of Kenaʽan, and
Aḇraham came to mourn for Sarah and to
weep for her.
3 Then Aḇraham rose up from beside his
dead, and spoke to the sons of Ḥěth,
saying,
4 "I am a foreigner and a sojourner
among you. Give me property for a burial-
site among you, so that I bury my dead
from my presence."
5 And the sons of Ḥěth answered
Aḇraham, saying to him,
6 "Hear us, my master: You are a prince
of Elohim among us. Bury your dead in the
choicest of our burial-sites. None of us
withholds from you his burial-site, from
burying your dead."
7 So Aḇraham rose and bowed himself to
the people of the land, the sons of Ḥěth.
8 And he spoke with them, saying, "If it
is your desire that I bury my dead from my
presence, hear me, and approach Ephron
son of Tsoḥar for me,
9 and let me have the cave of Maḵpělah
which he has, which is at the end of his
field. Let him give it to me for the complete amount of silver, as property for a
burial-site among you."
10 And Ephron dwelt among the sons of
Ḥěth. And Ephron the Ḥittite answered
Aḇraham in the hearing of the sons of
Ḥěth, all who entered at the gate of his city,
saying,
11 "No, my master, listen to me! I shall
give you the field and the cave that is in it.
I shall give it to you in the presence of the
sons of my people. I shall give it to you.
Bury your dead!"
12 And Aḇraham bowed himself down
before the people of the land,
13 and he spoke to Ephron in the hearing
of the people of the land, saying, "If only
you would hear me. I shall give the amount
of silver for the field, take it from me, and
let me bury my dead there."
14 And Ephron answered Aḇraham, saying to him,

15 "My master, listen to me! The land is worth four hundred sheqels of silver. What is that between you and me? So bury your dead."

16 And Aḇraham listened to Ephron, and Aḇraham weighed out the silver for Ephron which he had named in the hearing of the sons of Ḥěth, four hundred sheqels of silver, currency of the merchants.

17 Thus the field of Ephron which was in Maḵpělah, which was before Mamrě, the field and the cave which was in it, and all the trees that were in the field, which were within all the surrounding borders, were deeded

18 to Aḇraham as a possession in the presence of the sons of Ḥěth, before all who went in at the gate of his city.

19 And after this Aḇraham buried Sarah his wife in the cave of the field of Maḵpělah, before Mamrě, that is Ḥeḇron, in the land of Kenaʽan.

20 Thus the field and the cave that is in it were deeded to Aḇraham by the sons of Ḥěth as property for a burial-site.

24 And Aḇraham was old, advanced in years. And יהוה had blessed Aḇraham in every way.

2 And Aḇraham said to the oldest servant of his house, who ruled over all that he had, "Please, put your hand under my thigh,

3 so that I make you swear by יהוה, the Elohim of the heavens and the Elohim of the earth, that you do not take a wife for my son from the daughters of the Kenaʽanites, among whom I dwell,

4 but to go to my land and to my relatives, and take a wife for my son Yitsḥaq."

5 And the servant said to him, "What if the woman refuses to follow me to this land? Do I then take your son back to the land from which you came?"

6 And Aḇraham said to him, "Beware lest you take my son back there!

7 "יהוה, Elohim of the heavens, who took me from my father's house and from the land of my relatives, and who spoke to me and swore to me, saying, 'To your seed I give this land,' He sends His messenger before you, and you shall take a wife for my son from there.

8 "And if the woman refuses to follow you, then you shall be released from this oath; only, do not take my son back there."

9 Then the servant put his hand under the thigh of Aḇraham his master, and swore to him concerning this matter.

10 And the servant took ten of his master's camels and left, for all his master's good *gifts* were in his hand. And he arose and went to Aram Naharayim, to the city of Naḥor.

11 And he made his camels kneel down outside the city by a fountain of water at evening time, the time when women go out to draw water.

12 And he said, "יהוה, Elohim of my master Aḇraham, please cause *her* to meet before me this day, and show loving-commitment to my master Aḇraham.

13 "See, I am standing here by the fountain of water, and the daughters of the men of the city are coming out to draw water.

14 "Now let it be that the young woman to whom I say, 'Please let down your jar to let me drink,' and she says, 'Drink, and let me water your camels too,' let her be the one whom You have appointed for Your servant Yitsḥaq. And let me know by this that You have shown loving-commitment to my master."

15 And it came to be, before he had ended speaking, that see, Riḇqah, who was born to Bethu'ěl, son of Milkah, the wife of Naḥor, Aḇraham's brother, came out with her jar on her shoulder.

16 And the young woman was very good-looking, a maiden, no man having known her. And she went down to the fountain, filled her jar, and came up.

17 And the servant ran to meet her and said, "Please let me drink a little water from your jar."

18 And she said, "Drink, my master." And she hurried and let her jar down to her hand, and gave him a drink.

19 And when she had finished giving him a drink, she said, "Let me draw water for your camels too, until they have finished drinking."

20 And she hurried and emptied her jar into the trough, ran back to the fountain to draw water, and drew for all his camels.
21 And watching her, the man remained silent in order to know whether יהוה had prospered his way or not.
22 And it came to be, when the camels had finished drinking, that the man took a golden nose ring weighing half a sheqel, and two bracelets for her wrists weighing ten sheqels of gold,
23 and said, "Whose daughter are you? Please inform me, is there room in your father's house for us to spend the night?"
24 And she said to him, "I am the daughter of Bethu'ĕl, Milkah's son, whom she bore to Naḥor."
25 And she said to him, "We have both straw and fodder enough, and room to spend the night."
26 And the man bowed down his head and worshipped יהוה.
27 And he said, "Blessed be יהוה Elohim of my master Aḇraham, who has not forsaken His loving-commitment and His truth toward my master. As for me, being on the way, יהוה led me to the house of my master's brothers."
28 Then the young woman ran and informed those of her mother's house these matters.
29 And Riḇqah had a brother whose name was Laḇan, and Laḇan ran out to the man, to the fountain.
30 And it came to be, when he saw the nose ring, and the bracelets on his sister's wrists, and when he heard the words of his sister Riḇqah, saying, "Thus the man spoke to me," that he went to the man and saw him standing by the camels at the fountain.
31 And he said, "Come in, O blessed of יהוה! Why do you stand outside? I myself have prepared the house, and a place for the camels."
32 So the man came into the house, while he unloaded the camels and provided straw and fodder for the camels and water to wash his feet and the feet of the men who were with him,
33 and set food before him to eat. But he said, "Let me not eat until I have spoken my word." And he said, "Speak on."
34 And he said, "I am Aḇraham's servant.
35 "And יהוה has blessed my master exceedingly, and he has become great. And He has given him flocks and herds, and silver and gold, and male and female servants, and camels and donkeys.
36 "And Sarah my master's wife bore a son to my master when she was old. And he has given to him all that he has.
37 "And my master made me swear, saying, 'Do not take a wife for my son from the daughters of the Kenaʽanites, in whose land I dwell,
38 but go to my father's house and to my relatives, and take a wife for my son.'
39 "And I said to my master, 'What if the woman does not follow me?'
40 "But he said to me, 'יהוה, before whom I walk, sends His messenger with you and shall prosper your way. And you shall take a wife for my son from my relatives and from my father's house.
41 'Then, when you go to my relatives, you are to be released from this oath. And if they do not give her to you, then you are released from my oath.'
42 "And this day I came to the fountain and said, 'יהוה, Elohim of my master Aḇraham, please, if You are prospering the way in which I am going,
43 see, I am standing by the fountain of water, and when the young woman [a] comes out to draw water, and I say to her, "Please give me a little water from your jar to drink,"
44 and she says to me, "Drink, and let me draw for your camels too," let her be the woman whom יהוה has appointed for my master's son.'
45 "I had not yet ended speaking in my heart, then see, Riḇqah was coming out with her jar on her shoulder. And she went down to the fountain and drew water. And I said to her, 'Please let me drink.'
46 "And she hurried and let her jar down from her shoulder, and said, 'Drink, and let

24a See Explanatory notes: Maiden

me water your camels too.' So I drank, and
she watered the camels too.
47 "And I asked her, and said, 'Whose
daughter are you?' And she said, 'The
daughter of Bethu'ěl, Naḥor's son, whom
Milkah bore to him.' Then I put the nose
ring on her nose and the bracelets on her
wrists.
48 "And I bowed my head and worshipped
יהוה, and blessed יהוה, Elohim of my
master Aḇraham, who had led me in
the true way to take the daughter of my
master's brother for his son.
49 "And now, if you are going to show
loving-commitment and truth to my master, let me know, and if not, let me know,
so that I turn to the right or to the left."
50 And Laḇan answered – Bethu'ěl too –
and said, "The matter comes from יהוה,
we are not able to speak to you either evil
or good.
51 "See, Riḇqah is before you. Take her
and go, and let her be your master's son's
wife, as יהוה has spoken."
52 And it came to be, when Aḇraham's
servant heard their words, that he bowed
himself towards the earth before יהוה.
53 And the servant brought out ornaments
of silver, and ornaments of gold, and garments, and gave them to Riḇqah. He also
gave costly gifts to her brother and to her
mother.
54 And he and the men who were with him
ate and drank and spent the night. When
they arose in the morning he said, "Let me
go to my master."
55 But her brother and her mother said,
"Let the young woman stay with us a few
days, at least ten, then you go."
56 And he said to them, "Do not delay me,
since יהוה has prospered my way. Let me
go so that I go to my master."
57 And they said, "Let us call the young
woman and ask her."
58 So they called Riḇqah and said to her,
"Are you going with this man?" And she
said, "I shall go."
59 So they let go Riḇqah their sister and
her nurse, and Aḇraham's servant and his
men.
60 And they blessed Riḇqah and said to
her, "Let our sister become the mother of
thousands of ten thousands, and let your
seed possess the gates of those who hate
them."
61 And Riḇqah and her young women
arose, and they rode on the camels and
followed the man. So the servant took
Riḇqah and left.
62 And Yitsḥaq came from the way of
Be'ěr Laḥai Ro'i, for he dwelt in the
South.
63 And Yitsḥaq went out to meditate in the
field in the evening. And he lifted his eyes
and looked and saw the camels coming.
64 And Riḇqah lifted her eyes, and when
she saw Yitsḥaq she dismounted from her
camel,
65 and she had said to the servant, "Who is
this man walking in the field to meet us?"
And the servant said, "It is my master."
So she took a veil and covered herself.
66 And the servant told Yitsḥaq all the
matters he had done.
67 And Yitsḥaq brought her into his
mother Sarah's tent. And he took Riḇqah
and she became his wife, and he loved her.
Thus Yitsḥaq was comforted after his
mother's death.

25 And Aḇraham took another wife,
whose name was Qeturah.
2 And she bore him Zimran, and Yoqshan, and Meḏan, and Miḏyan, and
Yishbaq, and Shuwaḥ.
3 And Yoqshan brought forth Sheḇa and
Deḏan. And the sons of Deḏan were
Asshurim, and Letushim, and Le'ummim.
4 And the sons of Miḏyan were Ěphah,
and Ěpher, and Ḥanoḵ, and Aḇiḏa, and
Elda'ah. All these were the children of
Qeturah.
5 Now Aḇraham gave all that he had to
Yitsḥaq,
6 but to the sons of the concubines whom
Aḇraham had, Aḇraham gave gifts while
he was still living, and sent them away
from his son Yitsḥaq, eastward, to the land
of the east.
7 And these are all the years of
Aḇraham's life which he lived: one hundred and seventy-five years.

8 And Aḇraham breathed his last and
died in a good old age, aged and satisfied,
and was gathered to his people.
9 And his sons Yitsḥaq and Yishmaʽĕl
buried him in the cave of Maḵpĕlah, which
is before Mamrĕ, in the field of Ephron son
of Tsoḥar the Ḥittite,
10 the field which Aḇraham purchased
from the sons of Ḥĕth. There Aḇraham was
buried with Sarah his wife.
11 And it came to be, after the death of
Aḇraham, that Elohim blessed his son
Yitsḥaq. And Yitsḥaq dwelt at Be'ĕr Laḥai
Ro'i.
12 And this is the genealogy of Yishmaʽĕl,
Aḇraham's son, whom Haḡar the Mitsrian,
Sarah's female servant, bore to Aḇraham.
13 And these were the names of the sons
of Yishmaʽĕl, by their names, according to
their generations: The first-born of
Yishmaʽĕl, Neḇayoth; then Qĕḏar, and
Aḏbe'ĕl, and Miḇsam,
14 and Mishma, and Dumah, and Massa,
15 Ḥaḏar, and Tĕma, Yetur, Naphish, and
Qĕḏemah.
16 These were the sons of Yishmaʽĕl and
these were their names, by their towns and
their settlements, twelve chiefs according
to their tribes.
17 And these were the years of the life of
Yishmaʽĕl: one hundred and thirty-seven
years. And he breathed his last and died,
and was gathered to his people.
18 And they dwelt from Ḥawilah as far as
Shur, which is east of Mitsrayim as you go
toward Ashshur. He settled before all his
brothers.
19 And this is the genealogy of Yitsḥaq,
Aḇraham's son. Aḇraham brought forth
Yitsḥaq.
20 And Yitsḥaq was forty years old when
he took Riḇqah as wife, the daughter of
Bethu'ĕl the Aramean of Paddan Aram, the
sister of Laḇan the Aramean.
21 And Yitsḥaq prayed to יהוה for his
wife, because she was barren. And יהוה
answered his prayer, and Riḇqah his wife
conceived.
22 And within her the children struggled
together, and she said, "If all is right, why
am I this way?" So she went to ask יהוה.
23 And יהוה said to her, "Two nations are
in your womb, and two peoples shall be
separated from your body. And one people
shall be stronger than the other, and the
older serve the younger."
24 And when the days were filled for her
to give birth, and see, twins were in her
womb!
25 And the first came out red all over, like
a hairy garment, so they called his name
Ĕsaw.
26 And afterward his brother came out,
with his hand holding on to Ĕsaw's heel,
so his name was called Yaʽaqoḇ. And
Yitsḥaq was sixty years old when she bore
them.
27 And the boys grew up. And Ĕsaw
became a man knowing how to hunt,
a man of the field, while Yaʽaqoḇ was a
complete man, dwelling in tents.
28 And Yitsḥaq loved Ĕsaw because he ate
of his wild game, but Riḇqah loved
Yaʽaqoḇ.
29 And Yaʽaqoḇ cooked a stew, and Ĕsaw
came in from the field, and he was weary.
30 And Ĕsaw said to Yaʽaqoḇ, "Please feed
me with that same red stew, for I am
weary." That is why his name was called
Eḏom.
31 But Yaʽaqoḇ said, "Sell me your birthright today."
32 And Ĕsaw said, "Look, I am going to
die, so why should I have birthright?"
33 Then Yaʽaqoḇ said, "Swear to me
today." And he swore to him, and sold his
birthright to Yaʽaqoḇ.
34 Yaʽaqoḇ then gave Ĕsaw bread and
stew of lentils. And he ate and drank, and
rose up and left. Thus Ĕsaw despised his
birthright.

26 And there was a scarcity of food in
the land, besides the first scarcity
of food which was in the days of Aḇraham.
And Yitsḥaq went to Aḇimeleḵ, sovereign
of the Philistines, in Gerar.
2 And יהוה appeared to him and said,
"Do not go down to Mitsrayim, live in the
land which I command you.
3 "Sojourn in this land. And I shall be
with you and bless you, for I give all these

lands to you and your seed. And I shall establish the oath which I swore to Aḇraham your father.
4 "And I shall increase your seed like the stars of the heavens, and I shall give all these lands to your seed. And in your seed all the nations of the earth shall be blessed,
5 because Aḇraham obeyed My voice and guarded My Charge: My commands, My laws, and My Torot." [a]
6 And Yitsḥaq dwelt in Gerar.
7 And when the men of the place asked about his wife, he said, "She is my sister." For he was afraid to say, "She is my wife," *thinking*, "lest the men of the place should kill me for Riḇqah, because she is good-looking."
8 And it came to be, when he had been there a long time, that Aḇimeleḵ sovereign of the Philistines looked through a window, and he watched and saw Yitsḥaq playing with Riḇqah his wife.
9 So Aḇimeleḵ called Yitsḥaq and said, "See, truly she is your wife! So how could you say, 'She is my sister'?" And Yitsḥaq said to him, "Because I said, 'Lest I die on account of her.' "
10 And Aḇimeleḵ said, "What is this you have done to us? One of the people had almost lain with your wife, and you would have brought guilt on us."
11 And Aḇimeleḵ commanded all his people, saying, "He who touches this man or his wife shall certainly be put to death."
12 And Yitsḥaq sowed in that land, and reaped in the same year a hundredfold, and יהוה blessed him.
13 And the man grew great and went forward until he became very great.
14 And he came to have possessions of flocks and possessions of herds and a great body of servants, and the Philistines envied him.
15 And the Philistines had stopped up all the wells which his father's servants had dug in the days of Aḇraham his father, and filled them with dirt.
16 And Aḇimeleḵ said to Yitsḥaq, "Go away from us, for you are much mightier than we."
17 So Yitsḥaq went from there and pitched his tent in the wadi Gerar, and dwelt there.
18 And Yitsḥaq dug again the wells of water which they had dug in the days of Aḇraham his father, for the Philistines had stopped them up after the death of Aḇraham. And he called them by the names which his father had called them.
19 But when Yitsḥaq's servants dug in the wadi and found a well of running water there,
20 the herdsmen of Gerar strove with Yitsḥaq's herdsmen, saying, "The water is ours." And he called the name of the well Ěseq, because they strove with him.
21 And they dug another well, and they strove over that one too, and he called its name Sitnah.
22 And he moved from there and dug another well, and they did not strive over it. And he called its name Reḥoḇoth, and said, "For now יהוה has made room for us, and we shall be fruitful in the land."
23 And from there he went up to Be'ěrsheḇa.
24 And יהוה appeared to him the same night and said, "I am the Elohim of your father Aḇraham. Do not fear, for I am with you, and shall bless you and increase your seed for My servant Aḇraham's sake."
25 And he built a slaughter-place there, and called on the Name of יהוה, and he pitched his tent there, and the servants of Yitsḥaq dug a well there.
26 And Aḇimeleḵ came to him from Gerar, with Aḥuzzath, one of his friends, and Piḵol the commander of his army.
27 And Yitsḥaq said to them, "Why have you come to me, seeing you have hated me and have sent me away from you?"
28 But they said, "We have clearly seen that יהוה is with you. And we said, 'Please, let there be an oath between us, between you and us. And let us make a covenant with you,
29 that you do no evil to us, as we have not touched you, and as we have done only good toward you, and have sent you away

26a Torot - plural of Torah, teaching

in peace. You are now blessed by יהוה.' "

30 And he made them a feast, and they ate and drank.

31 And they rose early in the morning and swore an oath with one another. And Yitsḥaq let them go, and they departed from him in peace.

32 And on the same day it came to be that the servants of Yitsḥaq came and informed him about the well which they had dug, and said to him, "We have found water."

33 So he called it Shiḇah. Therefore the name of the city is Be'ěrsheḇa to this day.

34 And when Ěsaw was forty years old, he took as wives Yehuḏith the daughter of Be'ěri the Ḥittite, and Basemath the daughter of Ělon the Ḥittite.

35 And they were a bitterness of spirit to Yitsḥaq and Riḇqah.

27 And it came to be, when Yitsḥaq was old and his eyes were too dim to see, that he called Ěsaw his elder son and said to him, "My son." And he answered him, "Here I am."

2 And he said, "See now, I am old, I do not know the day of my death.

3 "Now then, please take your weapons, your quiver and your bow, and go out to the field and hunt wild game for me.

4 "And make me a tasty dish, such as I love, and bring it to me to eat, in order that my being does bless you before I die."

5 And Riḇqah heard when Yitsḥaq spoke to Ěsaw his son. And Ěsaw went to the field to hunt wild game and to bring it.

6 And Riḇqah spoke to Ya'aqoḇ her son, saying, "See, I heard your father speak to Ěsaw your brother, saying,

7 'Bring me wild game and make me a tasty dish to eat, and bless you in the presence of יהוה before my death.'

8 "And now my son, listen to my voice according to what I command you.

9 "Please go to the flock and bring me two choice young goats, and I make a tasty dish from them for your father, such as he loves.

10 "And you shall take it to your father, and he shall eat it, so that he might bless you before his death."

11 And Ya'aqoḇ said to Riḇqah his mother, "See, Ěsaw my brother is a hairy man, and I am a smooth-skinned man.

12 "What if my father touches me? Then I shall be like a deceiver in his eyes, and shall bring a curse on myself and not a blessing."

13 But his mother said to him, "Let your curse be on me, my son. Only obey my voice, and go, get them for me."

14 And he went and fetched them and brought them to his mother, and his mother made a tasty dish, such as his father loved.

15 And Riḇqah took the best garments of her elder son Ěsaw, which were with her in the house, and put them on Ya'aqoḇ her younger son.

16 And she put the skins of the young goats on his hands and on the smooth part of his neck.

17 Then she gave the tasty dish and the bread, which she had prepared, into the hand of her son Ya'aqoḇ.

18 And he went to his father and said, "My father." And he said, "Here I am. Who are you, my son?"

19 And Ya'aqoḇ said to his father, "I am Ěsaw your first-born, I have done as you said to me. Please rise, sit and eat of my wild game, so that your being might bless me."

20 But Yitsḥaq said to his son, "How is it that you have found it so quickly, my son?" And he said, "Because יהוה your Elohim brought it to me."

21 Then Yitsḥaq said to Ya'aqoḇ, "Please come near, so that I feel you, my son, whether you truly are my son Ěsaw or not."

22 And Ya'aqoḇ went near to Yitsḥaq his father, and he felt him and said, "The voice is the voice of Ya'aqoḇ, but the hands are the hands of Ěsaw."

23 And he did not recognise him, for his hands were hairy like his brother Ěsaw's hands, and he blessed him.

24 And he said, "Are you truly my son Ěsaw?" And he said, "I am."

25 And he said, "Bring it near to me, and let me eat of my son's wild game, so that my being might bless you." So he brought

it near to him, and he ate. And he brought him wine, and he drank.

26 And his father Yitsḥaq said to him, "Please come near and kiss me, my son."

27 And he came near and kissed him. And he smelled the smell of his garments, and blessed him and said, "See, the smell of my son is like the smell of a field which יהוה has blessed.

28 And Elohim give you of the dew of the heavens, of the fatness of the earth, and plenty of grain and wine.

29 Let peoples serve you, and nations bow down to you. Be master over your brothers, and let your mother's sons bow down to you. Cursed be those cursing you, and blessed be those blessing you!"

30 And it came to be, as soon as Yitsḥaq had finished blessing Ya'aqoḇ, and Ya'aqoḇ had hardly left the presence of Yitsḥaq his father, that Ěsaw his brother came in from his hunting.

31 And he too had made a tasty dish and brought it to his father, and said to his father, "Let my father rise and eat of his son's wild game, so that your being might bless me."

32 And his father Yitsḥaq said to him, "Who are you?" And he said, "I am your son, your first-born, Ěsaw."

33 Then Yitsḥaq trembled exceedingly, and said, "Who was it then who hunted wild game and brought it to me? And I ate all of it before you came, and I have blessed him. Yes, he is blessed."

34 When Ěsaw heard the words of his father, he cried with an exceedingly great and bitter cry, and said to his father, "Bless me, me too, O my father!"

35 And he said, "Your brother came with deceit and took your blessing."

36 And Ěsaw said, "Was his name, then, called Ya'aqoḇ? For he has caught me by the heel these two times. He took my birthright, and see, now he has taken my blessing!" And he said, "Have you not reserved a blessing for me?"

37 Then Yitsḥaq answered and said to Ěsaw, "See, I have made him your master, and all his brothers I have given to him as servants. And I have sustained him with grain and wine. And what, then, shall I do for you, my son?"

38 And Ěsaw said to his father, "Have you only one blessing, my father? Bless me, me too, O my father!" And Ěsaw lifted up his voice and wept.

39 And Yitsḥaq his father answered and said to him, "See, your dwelling is of the fatness of the earth, and of the dew of the heavens from above.

40 And by your sword you are to live, and serve your brother. And it shall be, when you grow restless, that you shall break his yoke from your neck."

41 And Ěsaw hated Ya'aqoḇ because of the blessing with which his father blessed him, and Ěsaw said in his heart, "The days of mourning for my father draw near, then I am going to kill my brother Ya'aqoḇ."

42 And the words of Ěsaw her older son were reported to Riḇqah, and she sent and called Ya'aqoḇ her younger son, and said to him, "See, your brother Ěsaw comforts himself concerning you, to kill you.

43 "And now, my son, listen to my voice, and rise, flee to my brother Laḇan in Ḥaran.

44 "And stay with him a few days, until your brother's wrath turns away,

45 until your brother's displeasure turns away from you, and he forgets what you have done to him. And I shall send and bring you from there. Why should I be bereaved of you both in one day?"

46 And Riḇqah said to Yitsḥaq, "I am disgusted with my life because of the daughters of Ḥěth. If Ya'aqoḇ takes a wife from the daughters of Ḥěth, like these who are the daughters of the land, what is my life to me?"

28

And Yitsḥaq called Ya'aqoḇ and blessed him, and commanded him, and said to him, "Do not take a wife from the daughters of Kena'an.

2 "Arise, go to Paddan Aram, to the house of Bethu'ěl your mother's father. And take a wife for yourself from there, from the daughters of Laḇan your mother's brother.

3 "And Ěl Shaddai bless you, and make

you fruitful and increase you, and you
shall become an assembly of peoples,
4 and give you the blessing of Aḇraham,
to you and your seed with you, so that you
inherit the land of your sojournings, which
Elohim gave to Aḇraham."
5 So Yitsḥaq sent Yaʿaqoḇ away, and he
went to Paddan Aram, to Laḇan son of
Bethu'ěl the Aramean, the brother of
Riḇqah, the mother of Yaʿaqoḇ and Ěsaw.
6 And Ěsaw saw that Yitsḥaq had blessed
Yaʿaqoḇ and sent him away to Paddan
Aram to take himself a wife from there,
and that as he blessed him he gave him a
command, saying, "Do not take a wife
from the daughters of Kenaʿan,"
7 and that Yaʿaqoḇ had obeyed his father
and his mother and had gone to Paddan
Aram.
8 So Ěsaw saw that the daughters of
Kenaʿan did not please his father Yitsḥaq,
9 and Ěsaw went to Yishmaʿěl and took
Maḥalath the daughter of Yishmaʿěl,
Aḇraham's son, the sister of Neḇayoth, to
be his wife, besides the wives he had.
10 And Yaʿaqoḇ went out from Be'ěrsheḇa
and went toward Ḥaran.
11 And he came upon a place and stopped
over for the night, for the sun had set. And
he took one of the stones of that place and
put it at his head, and he lay down in that
place to sleep.
12 And he dreamed and saw a ladder set
up on the earth, and its top reached to the
heavens, and saw messengers of Elohim
going up and coming down on it.
13 And see, יהוה stood above it and said,
"I am יהוה Elohim of Aḇraham your father
and the Elohim of Yitsḥaq. The land on
which you are lying, I give it to you and
your seed.
14 "And your seed shall be as the dust of
the earth, and you shall break forth to the
west and to the east, to the north and the
south. And all the clans of the earth shall
be blessed in you and in your seed.
15 "And see, I am with you and shall
guard you wherever you go, and shall
bring you back to this land. For I am not
going to leave you until I have done what I
have spoken to you."
16 And Yaʿaqoḇ awoke from his sleep and
said, "Truly, יהוה is in this place, and I did
not know it."
17 And he was afraid and said, "How awesome is this place! This is none other than
the house of Elohim, and this is the gate of
the heavens!"
18 And Yaʿaqoḇ rose early in the morning,
and took the stone that he had put at his
head, set it up as a standing column, and
poured oil on top of it.
19 And he called the name of that place
Běyth Ěl, however, the name of that city
had been Luz previously.
20 And Yaʿaqoḇ made a vow, saying,
"Seeing Elohim is with me, and has kept
me in this way that I am going, and has
given me bread to eat and a garment to put
on –
21 when I have returned to my father's
house in peace, and יהוה has been my
Elohim,
22 then this stone which I have set as a
standing column shall be Elohim's house,
and of all that You give me, I shall certainly give a tenth to You."

29 And Yaʿaqoḇ moved on and came
to the land of the people of the
East.
2 And he looked and saw a well in the
field, and saw three flocks of sheep lying
by it, for out of that well they watered the
flocks, and a large stone was on the well's
mouth.
3 And all the flocks would be gathered
there, then they would roll the stone from
the well's mouth and water the sheep, and
put the stone back in its place on the well's
mouth.
4 So Yaʿaqoḇ said to them, "My brothers,
where are you from?" And they said, "We
are from Ḥaran."
5 And he said to them, "Do you know
Laḇan son of Naḥor?" And they said, "We
know him."
6 So he said to them, "Is he well?" And
they said, "Well. And see, his daughter
Raḥěl is coming with the sheep."
7 And he said, "See, it is still high day,
not the time for the livestock to be gath-

ered together. Water the sheep, and go and
feed them."
8 But they said, "We are not allowed until
all the flocks are gathered together, and
they have rolled the stone from the well's
mouth, then we shall water the sheep."
9 While he was still speaking with them,
Raḥěl came with her father's sheep, for she
was a shepherdess.
10 And it came to be, when Ya'aqoḇ saw
Raḥěl the daughter of Laḇan his mother's
brother, and the sheep of Laḇan his mother's brother, that Ya'aqoḇ went near and
rolled the stone from the well's mouth, and
watered the flock of Laḇan his mother's
brother.
11 And Ya'aqoḇ kissed Raḥěl, and lifted
up his voice and wept.
12 And when Ya'aqoḇ told Raḥěl that he
was her father's relative and that he was
Riḇqah's son, she ran and told her father.
13 And it came to be, when Laḇan heard
the report about Ya'aqoḇ his sister's son,
that he ran to meet him, and embraced
him and kissed him, and brought him to
his house. Then he told Laḇan all these
matters.
14 And Laḇan said to him, "You are
indeed my bone and my flesh." And he
stayed with him for a new *moon*.
15 Then Laḇan said to Ya'aqoḇ, "Because
you are my relative, should you therefore
serve me for naught? Let me know, what
should your wages be?"
16 And Laḇan had two daughters, the
name of the elder was Lě'ah, and the name
of the younger was Raḥěl.
17 And Lě'ah's eyes were weak, but Raḥěl
was beautiful of form and beautiful of
appearance.
18 And Ya'aqoḇ loved Raḥěl, so he said,
"Let me serve you seven years for Raḥěl
your younger daughter."
19 And Laḇan said, "It is better that I give
her to you than that I should give her to
another man. Stay with me."
20 So Ya'aqoḇ served seven years for
Raḥěl, and they seemed to him but a few
days because of the love he had for her.
21 Then Ya'aqoḇ said to Laḇan, "Give me
my wife, for my days are completed, and
let me go in to her."
22 And Laḇan gathered all the men of the
place and made a feast.
23 And it came to be in the evening, that
he took Lě'ah his daughter and brought her
to Ya'aqoḇ. And he went in to her.
24 And Laḇan gave his female servant
Zilpah to his daughter Lě'ah as a female
servant.
25 And in the morning it came to be, that
see, it was Lě'ah. So he said to Laḇan,
"What is this you have done to me? Was it
not for Raḥěl that I served you? Why then
have you deceived me?"
26 And Laḇan said, "It is not done this
way in our place, to give the younger
before the first-born.
27 "Complete the week of this one, then
we give you this one too, for the service
which you shall serve with me still another
seven years."
28 And Ya'aqoḇ did so and completed her
week. Then he gave him his daughter
Raḥěl too, as wife.
29 And Laḇan gave his female servant
Bilhah to his daughter Raḥěl as a female
servant.
30 And he also went in to Raḥěl, and he
also loved Raḥěl more than Lě'ah. And he
served with Laḇan still another seven
years.
31 And יהוה saw that Lě'ah was unloved,
and He opened her womb, but Raḥěl was
barren.
32 And Lě'ah conceived and bore a son,
and she called his name Re'uḇěn, for she
said, "For יהוה has looked on my affliction, because now my husband is going to
love me."
33 And she conceived again and bore a
son, and said, "Because יהוה has heard
that I am unloved, He gave me this son
too." And she called his name Shim'on.
34 And she conceived again and bore a
son, and said, "Now this time my husband
is joined to me, because I have borne him
three sons." So his name was called Lěwi.
35 And she conceived again and bore a
son, and said, "Now I praise יהוה." So she
called his name Yehuḏah. And she ceased
bearing.

30 And when Raḥěl saw that she bore Yaʽaqoḇ no children, Raḥěl envied her sister, and said to Yaʽaqoḇ, "Give me children, or else I am going to die!"

2 And Yaʽaqoḇ's displeasure burned against Raḥěl, and he said, "Am I in the place of Elohim, who has withheld from you the fruit of the womb?"

3 And she said, "See, my female servant Bilhah; go in to her, and let her bear for me, and let me be built up from her as well."

4 So she gave him Bilhah her female servant as wife, and Yaʽaqoḇ went in to her.

5 And Bilhah conceived and bore Yaʽaqoḇ a son.

6 And Raḥěl said, "Elohim has rightly ruled my case, and has also heard my voice and given me a son." So she called his name Dan.

7 And Raḥěl's female servant Bilhah conceived again and bore Yaʽaqoḇ a second son.

8 And Raḥěl said, "With great wrestlings I have wrestled with my sister, and I have overcome." So she called his name Naphtali.

9 And Lě'ah saw that she had ceased bearing, and she took Zilpah her female servant and gave her to Yaʽaqoḇ as wife.

10 And Lě'ah's female servant Zilpah bore Yaʽaqoḇ a son.

11 And Lě'ah said, "With Gaḏ!" So she called his name Gaḏ.

12 And Lě'ah's female servant Zilpah bore Yaʽaqoḇ a second son.

13 And Lě'ah said, "I am blessed, for the daughters shall call me blessed." So she called his name Ashěr.

14 And Re'uḇěn went in the days of wheat harvest and found love-apples in the field, and brought them to his mother Lě'ah. And Raḥěl said to Lě'ah, "Please give me some of your son's love-apples."

15 But she said to her, "Is it a small matter that you have taken away my husband? Would you take away my son's love-apples too?" And Raḥěl said, "Therefore let him lie with you tonight for your son's love-apples."

16 And when Yaʽaqoḇ came out of the field in the evening, Lě'ah went out to meet him and said, "Do come in to me, for indeed, I have hired you with my son's love-apples." And he lay with her that night.

17 And Elohim listened to Lě'ah, and she conceived and bore Yaʽaqoḇ a fifth son.

18 And Lě'ah said, "Elohim has given me my hire, because I have given my female servant to my husband." So she called his name Yissasḵar.

19 And Lě'ah conceived again and bore Yaʽaqoḇ a sixth son.

20 And Lě'ah said, "Elohim has presented me with a good present. Now my husband is going to dwell with me, because I have borne him six sons." So she called his name Zeḇulun.

21 And afterward she bore a daughter, and called her name Dinah.

22 And Elohim remembered Raḥěl, and Elohim listened to her and opened her womb.

23 And she conceived, and bore a son, and said, "Elohim has taken away my reproach."

24 So she called his name Yosěph, and said, "יהוה has added to me another son."

25 And it came to be, when Raḥěl had borne Yosěph, that Yaʽaqoḇ said to Laḇan, "Send me on my way, to go to my own place and to my land.

26 "Give my wives and my children for whom I have served you, and let me go, for you yourself know my service which I have done for you."

27 And Laḇan said to him, "If I have found favour in your eyes, please stay, for I have diligently watched that יהוה has blessed me for your sake."

28 And he said, "Name me your wages, and I give it."

29 So he said to him, "You know how I have served you and how your livestock has been with me.

30 "For the little you had before I came has increased greatly, and יהוה has blessed you since my coming. But now, when am I to provide for my own house too?"

31 And he said, "What do I give you?" And Yaʽaqoḇ said, "Give me naught! If

you do this for me, I shall again feed and guard your flocks:

32 “Let me pass through all your flock today, removing from there all the speckled and spotted sheep, and all the black ones among the lambs, and the spotted and speckled among the goats. And these shall be my wages.

33 “And my righteousness shall answer for me in time to come, when you come concerning my wages: every one that is not speckled and spotted among the goats, and black among the lambs, it is stolen if it is with me.”

34 And Laḇan said, “See, let it be according to your word!”

35 And on that day he set aside the male goats that were speckled and spotted, and all the female goats that were speckled and spotted, every one that had some white in it, and all the black ones among the lambs, and gave them into the hand of his sons.

36 And he put three days’ journey between himself and Yaʿaqoḇ, and Yaʿaqoḇ fed the rest of Laḇan’s flocks.

37 And Yaʿaqoḇ took for himself rods of green poplar and of the almond and chestnut trees, peeled white strips in them, and exposed the white which was in the rods.

38 And he set the rods which he had peeled before the flocks in the gutters, in the watering troughs where the flocks came to drink, and they conceived when they came to drink.

39 So the flocks conceived before the rods, and the flocks brought forth streaked, speckled, and spotted.

40 And Yaʿaqoḇ separated the lambs, and made the flocks face toward the streaked and all the black in the flock of Laḇan, but he put his own flocks by themselves and did not put them with Laḇan’s flock.

41 And it came to be, whenever the strong ones of the flock conceived, that Yaʿaqoḇ placed the rods before the eyes of the flock in the gutters, so they would conceive among the rods.

42 But when the flocks were weak, he did not put them in, so the weak ones were Laḇan’s and the strong ones Yaʿaqoḇ’s.

43 Thus the man increased very much, and had many flocks, and female and male servants, and camels and donkeys.

31 And he heard the words of Laḇan’s sons, saying, “Yaʿaqoḇ has taken away all that was our father’s, and from what belonged to our father he has made all this wealth.”

2 And Yaʿaqoḇ would look at the face of Laḇan and see that it was not toward him as before.

3 And יהוה said to Yaʿaqoḇ, “Return to the land of your fathers and to your relatives. And I am with you.”

4 And Yaʿaqoḇ sent and called Raḥěl and Lě’ah to the field, to his flock,

5 and said to them, “I see your father’s face, that it is not toward me as before, but the Elohim of my father has been with me.

6 “And you know that I have served your father with all my strength.

7 “Yet your father has deceived me and changed my wages ten times, but Elohim did not allow him to do evil to me.

8 “When he said this, ‘The speckled are your wages,’ then all the flocks bore speckled. And when he said this, ‘The streaked are your wages,’ then all the flocks bore streaked.

9 “So Elohim has taken away the livestock of your father and given them to me.

10 “And it came to be, at the time when the flocks conceived, that I lifted my eyes and looked in a dream and saw the rams which leaped upon the flocks were streaked, speckled, and mottled.

11 “And the Messenger of Elohim spoke to me in a dream, saying, ‘Yaʿaqoḇ.’ And I said, ‘Here I am.’

12 “And He said, ‘Lift your eyes now and see, all the rams which leap on the flocks are streaked, speckled, and mottled, for I have seen all that Laḇan is doing to you.

13 ‘I am the Ěl of Běyth Ěl, where you anointed the standing column and where you made a vow to Me. Now rise up, get out of this land, and return to the land of your relatives.’ ”

14 And Raḥěl and Lě’ah answered and said to him, “Do we still have any portion or inheritance in our father’s house?

15 "Are we not reckoned by him as strangers? For he has sold us, and also entirely consumed our silver.

16 "For all the wealth which Elohim has taken from our father are ours and our children's. Now then, do whatever Elohim has told you."

17 So Ya'aqoḇ rose and put his sons and his wives on camels,

18 and he drove off all his livestock and all his possessions which he had acquired, his property of the livestock which he had acquired in Paddan Aram, to go to his father Yitsḥaq in the land of Kena'an.

19 And when Laḇan had gone to shear his sheep, Raḥĕl stole the house idols that were her father's.

20 And Ya'aqoḇ deceived Laḇan the Aramean, because he did not inform him that he was about to flee.

21 And he fled with all that he had. And he rose up and passed over the river, and headed toward the mountains of Gil'aḏ.

22 And on the third day Laḇan was told that Ya'aqoḇ had fled.

23 Then he took his brothers with him and pursued him for seven days' journey, and he overtook him in the mountains of Gil'aḏ.

24 But in a dream by night Elohim came to Laḇan the Aramean, and said to him, "Guard yourself, that you do not speak to Ya'aqoḇ either good or evil."

25 Then Laḇan overtook Ya'aqoḇ. Now Ya'aqoḇ had pitched his tent in the mountains, and Laḇan with his brothers pitched in the mountains of Gil'aḏ.

26 And Laḇan said to Ya'aqoḇ, "What have you done, that you have deceived me, and driven my daughters off like captives taken with the sword?

27 "Why did you flee secretly and deceive me, and not inform me, and I would have sent you away with joy and songs, with tambourine and lyre?

28 "And you did not allow me to kiss my sons and my daughters. Now you have been foolish to do this.

29 "It is in the power of my hand to do evil to you, but the Elohim of your father spoke to me last night, saying, 'Guard yourself, that you do not speak to Ya'aqoḇ either good or evil.'

30 "And now you have gone because you greatly long for your father's house, but why did you steal my mighty ones?"

31 And Ya'aqoḇ answered and said to Laḇan, "Because I was afraid, for I said, 'Lest you tear your daughters away from me.'

32 "With whomever you find your mighty ones, do not let him live. In the presence of our brothers, see for yourself what is with me and take it with you." For Ya'aqoḇ did not know that Raḥĕl had stolen them.

33 And Laḇan went into Ya'aqoḇ's tent, and into Lĕ'ah's tent, and into the tents of the two female servants, but he did not find them. And he came out of Lĕ'ah's tent and entered Raḥĕl's tent.

34 Now Raḥĕl had taken the house idols and put them in the camel's saddle, and sat on them. And Laḇan searched all about the tent but did not find them.

35 And she said to her father, "Let it not displease my master that I am unable to rise before you, for the way of women is with me." And he searched but did not find the house idols.

36 And Ya'aqoḇ was wroth and contended with Laḇan, and Ya'aqoḇ answered and said to Laḇan, "What is my transgression? What is my sin, that you have hotly pursued me?

37 "Now that you have searched all my goods what have you found of all your household goods? Set it here before my brothers and your brothers, and let them decide between the two of us!

38 "These twenty years I have been with you. Your ewes and your female goats have not miscarried their young, and I have not eaten the rams of your sheep.

39 "That which was torn by beasts I did not bring to you, I myself bore the loss of it. You required it from my hand, whether stolen by day or stolen by night.

40 "*Thus* I was! By day the heat consumed me, and the frost by night, and my sleep fled from my eyes.

41 "These twenty years I have been in your house. I served you fourteen years for

your two daughters, and six years for your
flock, and you have changed my wages ten
times.
42 "Unless the Elohim of my father, the
Elohim of Aḇraham and the Fear of
Yitsḥaq, had been with me, you would
now have sent me away empty-handed.
Elohim has seen my affliction and the
labour of my hands, and rendered judgment last night."
43 And Laḇan answered and said to
Ya'aqoḇ, "These daughters are my daughters, and these children are my children,
and this flock is my flock, and all that you
see is mine. But what shall I do today to
these, my daughters or to their children
whom they have borne?
44 "And now, come, let us make a
covenant, you and I, and it shall be a witness between you and me."
45 So Ya'aqoḇ took a stone and set it up as
a standing column.
46 And Ya'aqoḇ said to his brothers,
"Gather stones." And they took stones and
made a heap, and they ate there on the
heap.
47 And Laḇan called it Yeḡar Sahaḏutha,
but Ya'aqoḇ called it Gal'ěḏ.
48 And Laḇan said, "This heap is a witness between you and me today." That is
why its name was called Gal'ěḏ,
49 also Mitspah, because he said, "Let
יהוה watch between you and me when we
are out of each other's sight.
50 "If you afflict my daughters, or if you
take other wives besides my daughters,
although no man is with us; see, Elohim is
witness between you and me!"
51 And Laḇan said to Ya'aqoḇ, "See this
heap and see this standing column, which I
have placed between you and me.
52 "This heap is a witness, and this standing column is a witness, that I do not pass
beyond this heap to you, and you do not
pass beyond this heap and this standing
column to me, for evil.
53 "The Elohim of Aḇraham, the Elohim
of Naḥor, and the Elohim of their father
rightly rule between us!" And Ya'aqoḇ
swore by the Fear of his father Yitsḥaq.
54 And Ya'aqoḇ slaughtered a slaughtering on the mountain, and called his brothers to eat bread. And they ate bread and
spent the night on the mountain.
55 And Laḇan rose up early in the morning, and kissed his sons and daughters and
blessed them. And Laḇan left and returned
to his place.

32 And Ya'aqoḇ went on his way, and
the messengers of Elohim met him.
2 And when Ya'aqoḇ saw them, he said,
"This is the camp of Elohim." And he
called the name of that place Maḥanayim.
3 And Ya'aqoḇ sent messengers before
him to Ěsaw his brother in the land of Sě'ir,
the field of Eḏom
4 and he commanded them, saying, "Say
this to my master Ěsaw, 'Your servant
Ya'aqoḇ said this, "I have sojourned with
Laḇan and stayed there until now.
5 "And I have bulls, and donkeys, flocks,
and male and female servants. And I have
sent to inform my master, to find favour in
your eyes." ' "
6 So the messengers returned to Ya'aqoḇ,
saying, "We came to your brother Ěsaw,
and he also is coming to meet you, and
four hundred men with him."
7 And Ya'aqoḇ was greatly afraid and
distressed. So he divided the people that
were with him, and the flocks and herds
and camels, into two groups,
8 and he said, "If Ěsaw comes to the one
group and strikes it, then the other group
which is left shall escape."
9 And Ya'aqoḇ said, "O Elohim of my
father Aḇraham and Elohim of my father
Yitsḥaq, יהוה who said to me, 'Return to
your land and to your relatives, and I do
good to you,'
10 "I do not deserve the least of all the loving-commitment and all the truth which
You have shown Your servant, for I passed
over this Yarděn with my staff, and now I
have become two groups.
11 "Deliver me, I pray, from the hand of
my brother, from the hand of Ěsaw, for I
fear him, lest he come and shall strike me
and the mother with the children.
12 "For You said, 'I shall certainly do
good to you, and shall make your seed as

the sand of the sea, which are too numerous to count.' "
13 And he spent the night there, and took
what came to his hand as a present for
Ěsaw his brother –
14 two hundred female goats and twenty
male goats, two hundred ewes and twenty
rams,
15 thirty suckling-camels with their colts,
forty cows and ten bulls, twenty female
donkeys and ten foals.
16 And he gave into the hand of his servants, every drove by itself, and said to his
servants, "Pass over before me, and put
some distance between drove and drove."
17 And he commanded the first one,
saying, "When Ěsaw my brother meets
you and asks you, saying, 'To whom do
you belong, and where are you going?
And whose are these in front of you?'
18 then you shall say, 'They are your servant Yaʻaqoḇ's. It is a present sent to my
master Ěsaw. And see, he also is behind
us.' "
19 So he commanded the second, and the
third, and all who followed the droves,
saying, "Speak to Ěsaw this same word
when you find him,
20 and you shall say, 'Also look, your servant Yaʻaqoḇ is behind us.' " For he said,
"Let me appease him with the present that
goes before me, and after that see his face.
He might accept me."
21 And the present passed over before
him, but he himself spent the night in the
camp.
22 And he rose up that night and took his
two wives, and his two female servants,
and his eleven sons, and passed over the
ford of Yabboq.
23 And he took them and sent them over
the stream, and sent over what he had.
24 And Yaʻaqoḇ was left alone. And a Man
wrestled with him until the breaking of
day.
25 And when He saw that He did not overcome him, He touched the socket of his
hip. And the socket of Yaʻaqoḇ's hip was
dislocated as He wrestled with him.
26 And He said, "Let Me go, for the day
breaks." But he said, "I am not letting You
go until You have blessed me!"
27 So He asked him, "What is your
name?" And he said, "Yaʻaqoḇ."
28 And He said, "Your name is no longer
called Yaʻaqoḇ, but Yisra'ĕl, [a] because you
have striven with Elohim and with men,
and have overcome."
29 And Yaʻaqoḇ asked Him, saying,
"Please let me know Your Name." And He
said, "Why do you ask about My Name?"
And He blessed him there.
30 And Yaʻaqoḇ called the name of the
place Peni'ĕl, "For I have seen Elohim face
to face, and my life is preserved."
31 And the sun rose on him as he passed
over Penu'ĕl, and he limped on his hip.
32 That is why the children of Yisra'ĕl to
this day do not eat the sinew of the hip,
which is on the socket of the thigh,
because He touched the socket of the thigh
of Yaʻaqoḇ, in the sinew of the hip.

33 And Yaʻaqoḇ lifted his eyes and
looked and saw Ěsaw coming, and
with him four hundred men. And he divided the children among Lě'ah, and Raḥěl,
and the two female servants.
2 And he put the female servants and
their children in front, and Lě'ah and her
children behind, and Raḥěl and Yosěph
last.
3 And he himself passed over before
them and bowed himself to the ground
seven times, until he came near to his
brother.
4 And Ěsaw ran to meet him, and
embraced him, and fell on his neck and
kissed him, and they wept.
5 And he lifted his eyes and saw the
women and children, and said, "Who are
these with you?" And he said, "The
children with whom Elohim has favoured
your servant."
6 Then the female servants came near,
they and their children, and bowed themselves.
7 And Lě'ah also came near with her

32a Yisra'ĕl means "to strive with Ěl; to overcome with Ěl; to rule with Ěl"

children, and they bowed themselves. And
Yosěph and Raḥěl came near, and they
bowed themselves.
8 Then Ěsaw said, "What do you mean
by all this company which I met?" And he
said, "To find favour in the eyes of my
master."
9 But Ěsaw said, "I have enough, my
brother, let what you have remain yours."
10 And Ya'aqoḇ said, "No, please, if I
have now found favour in your eyes, then
receive my present from my hand, because
I have seen your face like seeing the face
of Elohim, and you were pleased with me.
11 "Please, take my blessing that is
brought to you, because Elohim has
favoured me, and because I have all *I
need.*" And he urged him, and he took it.
12 And he said, "Let us depart and go, and
let me go before you."
13 But he said to him, "My master knows
that the children are weak, and the flocks
and herds which are nursing are with me.
And if the men should drive them hard one
day, all the flocks shall die.
14 "Please let my master go before his servant, and let me lead on slowly according
to the pace of the livestock that go before
me, and according to the pace of the children, until I come to my master in Sě'ir."
15 And Ěsaw said, "Please let me leave
with you some of the people who are with
me." But he said, "Why this? Let me find
favour in the eyes of my master."
16 And Ěsaw returned that day on his way
to Sě'ir.
17 And Ya'aqoḇ set out to Sukkoth, and
built himself a house, and made booths for
his livestock. That is why the name of the
place is called Sukkoth.
18 And Ya'aqoḇ came safely to the city of
Sheḵem, which is in the land of Kena'an,
when he came from Paddan Aram. And he
pitched his tent before the city.
19 And he bought the portion of the field
where he had pitched his tent, from the
children of Ḥamor, Sheḵem's father, for
one hundred qesitah. [a]
20 And he set up a slaughter-place there
and called it Ěl Elohě Yisra'ěl.

34 And Dinah, the daughter of Lě'ah,
whom she had borne to Ya'aqoḇ,
went out to see the daughters of the land.
2 And Sheḵem, son of Ḥamor the
Ḥiwwite, prince of the land, saw her and
took her and lay with her, and humbled her.
3 And his being clung to Dinah the
daughter of Ya'aqoḇ, and he loved the girl
and spoke kindly to the girl.
4 And Sheḵem spoke to his father
Ḥamor, saying, "Take this girl for me for a
wife."
5 And Ya'aqoḇ heard that he had defiled
Dinah his daughter. Now his sons were
with his livestock in the field, so Ya'aqoḇ
kept silent until they came.
6 And Ḥamor, the father of Sheḵem,
went out to Ya'aqoḇ to speak with him.
7 And the sons of Ya'aqoḇ came in from
the field when they heard it. And the men
were grieved and very wroth, because he
had done a senseless deed in Yisra'ěl by
lying with Ya'aqoḇ's daughter, which
should not be done.
8 But Ḥamor spoke with them, saying,
"My son Sheḵem's being longs for your
daughter. Please give her to him for a wife.
9 "And intermarry with us, give us your
daughters and take our daughters for yourselves,
10 and dwell with us, and let the land be
before you. Dwell and move about in it,
and have possessions in it."
11 And Sheḵem said to her father and her
brothers, "Let me find favour in your eyes,
and whatever you say to me I give.
12 "Ask of me a bride price and gift ever
so high, and I give according to what you
say to me, but give me the girl for a wife."
13 But the sons of Ya'aqoḇ answered
Sheḵem and Ḥamor his father, and spoke
with deceit, because he had defiled Dinah
their sister.
14 And they said to them, "We are not able
to do this matter, to give our sister to one
who is uncircumcised, for that would be a
reproach to us.

33a A monetary unit of uncertain value, perhaps in the form of a lamb.

15 "Only on this *condition* would we agree
to you: If you become as we are, to have
every male of you circumcised,
16 then we shall give our daughters to you,
and take your daughters to us. And we
shall dwell with you, and shall become one
people.
17 "But if you do not listen to us and be
circumcised, we shall take our daughter
and go."
18 And their words pleased Ḥamor and
Sheḵem, Ḥamor's son.
19 And the young man did not delay to do
this because he delighted in Yaʿaqoḇ's
daughter. Now he was more respected than
all the household of his father.
20 And Ḥamor and Sheḵem his son came
to the gate of their city, and spoke with the
men of their city, saying,
21 "These men are at peace with us, so let
them dwell in the land and move about in
it. And see, the land is large enough for
them. Let us take their daughters for us for
wives, and let us give them our daughters.
22 "Only on this *condition* would the men
agree to dwell with us, to be one people: if
every male among us is circumcised as
they are circumcised.
23 "Their herds and their possessions, and
all their beasts, should they not be ours?
Only let us agree with them, and let them
dwell with us."
24 And all who went out of the gate of his
city listened to Ḥamor and Sheḵem his
son; every male was circumcised, all who
went out of the gate of his city.
25 And it came to be on the third day,
when they were in pain, that two of the
sons of Yaʿaqoḇ, Shimʿon and Lěwi,
Dinah's brothers, each took his sword and
came boldly upon the city and killed all the
males.
26 And they killed Ḥamor and Sheḵem his
son with the edge of the sword, and took
Dinah from Sheḵem's house, and went
out.
27 The sons of Yaʿaqoḇ came upon the
slain, and plundered the city, because they
had defiled their sister.
28 They took their flocks and their herds,
and their donkeys, and that which was in
the city and that which was in the field,
29 and all their wealth. And all their little
ones and their wives they took captive, and
they plundered all that was in the houses.
30 And Yaʿaqoḇ said to Shimʿon and Lěwi,
"You have troubled me by making me a
stench among the inhabitants of the land,
among the Kenaʿanites and the Perizzites.
And I am few in number, they shall gather
themselves against me and shall strike me,
and I shall be destroyed, my household
and I."
31 But they said, "Should he treat our
sister like a whore?"

35

And Elohim said to Yaʿaqoḇ,
"Arise, go up to Běyth Ěl and
dwell there. And make a slaughter-place
there to Ěl who appeared to you when you
fled from the face of Ěsaw your brother."
2 And Yaʿaqoḇ said to his household and
to all who were with him, "Put away the
foreign mighty ones that are among you,
and cleanse yourselves, and change your
garments.
3 "And let us arise and go up to Běyth Ěl,
and let me make there a slaughter-place to
Ěl, who answered me in the day of my distress, and has been with me in the way
which I have gone."
4 So they gave Yaʿaqoḇ all the foreign
mighty ones which were in their hands,
and all their earrings which were in their
ears. And Yaʿaqoḇ hid them under the terebinth tree which was near Sheḵem.
5 And they departed, and the fear of
Elohim was upon the cities that were all
around them, and they did not pursue the
sons of Yaʿaqoḇ.
6 And Yaʿaqoḇ came to Luz, that is Běyth
Ěl, which is in the land of Kenaʿan, he and
all the people who were with him.
7 And he built there a slaughter-place and
called the place El Běyth Ěl, because there
Elohim appeared to him when he fled from
the face of his brother.
8 And Deḇorah, Riḇqah's nurse, died,
and she was buried below Běyth Ěl under
the terebinth tree. So the name of it was
called Allon Baḵuth.
9 And Elohim appeared to Yaʿaqoḇ again,

when he came from Paddan Aram, and blessed him.

10 And Elohim said to him, "Your name is Ya'aqoḇ, your name is no longer called Ya'aqoḇ, but Yisra'ěl is your name." So He called his name Yisra'ěl.

11 And Elohim said to him, "I am Ěl Shaddai. Be fruitful and increase, a nation and a company of nations shall be from you, and sovereigns come from your body.

12 "And the land which I gave Aḇraham and Yitsḥaq I give to you. And to your seed after you I give this land."

13 And Elohim went up from him in the place where He had spoken with him.

14 And Ya'aqoḇ set up a standing column in the place where He had spoken with him, a monument of stone. And he poured a drink offering on it, and he poured oil on it.

15 And Ya'aqoḇ called the name of the place where Elohim spoke with him, Běyth Ěl.

16 Then they set out from Běyth Ěl. And it came to be, when there was but a little distance to go to Ephrath, that Raḥěl began to give birth, and had great difficulty giving birth.

17 And it came to be, as she was having great difficulty giving birth, that the midwife said to her, "Do not fear, for it is another son for you."

18 And it came to be, as her life was going out – for she died – that she called his name Ben-Oni. But his father called him Binyamin.

19 So Raḥěl died and was buried on the way to Ephrath, that is Běyth Leḥem.

20 And Ya'aqoḇ set a standing column on her burial-place, which is the monument of Raḥěl's burial-place to this day.

21 And Yisra'ěl set out and pitched his tent beyond the tower of Ěḏer.

22 And it came to be, when Yisra'ěl dwelt in that land, that Re'uḇěn went and lay with Bilhah his father's concubine. And Yisra'ěl heard about it. Now the sons of Ya'aqoḇ were twelve:

23 the sons of Lě'ah were Re'uḇěn, Ya'aqoḇ's first-born, and Shim'on, and Lěwi, and Yehuḏah, and Yissasḵar, and Zeḇulun;

24 the sons of Raḥěl were Yosěph and Binyamin;

25 the sons of Bilhah, Raḥěl's female servant, were Dan and Naphtali;

26 and the sons of Zilpah, Lě'ah's female servant, were Gaḏ and Ashěr. These were the sons of Ya'aqoḇ who were born to him in Paddan Aram.

27 And Ya'aqoḇ came to his father Yitsḥaq at Mamrě, or Qiryath Arba, that is Ḥeḇron, where Aḇraham and Yitsḥaq had dwelt.

28 And the days of Yitsḥaq were one hundred and eighty years.

29 So Yitsḥaq breathed his last and died, and was gathered to his people, aged and satisfied of days. And his sons Ěsaw and Ya'aqoḇ buried him.

36 And this is the genealogy of Ěsaw, who is Eḏom.

2 Ěsaw took his wives from the daughters of Kena'an: Aḏah the daughter of Ělon the Ḥittite, and Oholiḇamah the daughter of Anah, the daughter of Tsiḇ'on the Ḥiwwite;

3 and Basemath, Yishma'ěl's daughter, sister of Neḇayoth.

4 And Aḏah bore Eliphaz to Ěsaw, and Basemath bore Re'u'ěl.

5 And Oholiḇamah bore Ye'ush, and Ya'lam, and Qoraḥ. These were the sons of Ěsaw who were born to him in the land of Kena'an.

6 And Ěsaw took his wives, and his sons, and his daughters, and all the beings of his household, and his herds and all his beasts, and all his possessions which he had gained in the land of Kena'an, and went to a land away from the presence of his brother Ya'aqoḇ.

7 For their possessions were too great for them to dwell together, and the land of their sojournings could not support them because of their herds.

8 So Ěsaw dwelt in Mount Sě'ir. Ěsaw is Eḏom.

9 And this is the genealogy of Ěsaw the father of the Eḏomites in Mount Sě'ir.

10 These were the names of Ěsaw's sons: Eliphaz son of Aḏah, wife of Ěsaw, and

Re‘u’ĕl son of Basemath, wife of Ěsaw.
11 And the sons of Eliphaz were Těman,
Omar, Tsepho, and Gatam, and Qenaz.
12 And Timna was the concubine of
Eliphaz, Ěsaw’s son, and she bore Amalěq
to Eliphaz. These were the sons of Aḏah,
Ěsaw’s wife.
13 These were the sons of Re‘u’ĕl: Naḥath
and Zeraḥ, Shammah and Mizzah. These
were the sons of Basemath, Ěsaw’s wife.
14 These were the sons of Oholiḇamah,
Ěsaw’s wife, the daughter of Anah, the
daughter of Tsiḇ‘on. And she bore to Ěsaw:
Ye‘ush, and Ya‘lam, and Qoraḥ.
15 These were the chiefs of the sons of
Ěsaw. The sons of Eliphaz, the first-born
son of Ěsaw, were Chief Těman, Chief
Omar, Chief Tsepho, Chief Qenaz,
16 Chief Qoraḥ, Chief Gatam, Chief
Amalěq. These were the chiefs of Eliphaz
in the land of Eḏom. They were the sons of
Aḏah.
17 And these were the sons of Re‘u’ĕl,
Ěsaw’s son: Chief Naḥath, Chief Zeraḥ,
Chief Shammah, and Chief Mizzah. These
were the chiefs of Re‘u’ĕl in the land of
Eḏom. These were the sons of Basemath,
Ěsaw’s wife.
18 And these were the sons of
Oholiḇamah, Ěsaw’s wife: Chief Ye‘ush,
Chief Ya‘lam, and Chief Qoraḥ. These
were the chiefs *descending* from
Oholiḇamah, Ěsaw’s wife, the daughter of
Anah.
19 These were the sons of Ěsaw, who is
Eḏom, and these were their chiefs.
20 These were the sons of Sě‘ir the Ḥorite
who inhabited the land: Lotan, and Shoḇal,
and Tsiḇ‘on, and Anah,
21 and Dishon, and Ětser, and Dishan.
These were the chiefs of the Ḥorites, the
sons of Sě‘ir, in the land of Eḏom.
22 And the sons of Lotan were Ḥori and
Hěmam. Lotan’s sister was Timna.
23 And these were the sons of Shoḇal:
Alwan, and Manaḥath, and Ěyḇal, Shepho,
and Onam.
24 And these were the sons of Tsiḇ‘on:
both Ayah and Anah. This was the Anah
who found the water in the wilderness as
he fed the donkeys of his father Tsiḇ‘on.
25 And these were the children of Anah:
Dishon and Oholiḇamah the daughter of
Anah.
26 And these were the sons of Dishon:
Ḥemdan, and Eshban, and Yithran, and
Keran.
27 These were the sons of Ětser: Bilhan,
and Za‘awan, and Aqan.
28 These were the sons of Dishan: Uts and
Aran.
29 These were the chiefs of the Ḥorites:
Chief Lotan, Chief Shoḇal, Chief Tsiḇ‘on,
Chief Anah,
30 Chief Dishon, Chief Ětser, and Chief
Dishan. These were the chiefs of the
Ḥorites, according to their chiefs in the
land of Sě‘ir.
31 And these were the sovereigns who
reigned in the land of Eḏom before any
sovereign reigned over the children of
Yisra’ĕl.
32 And Bela the son of Be‘or reigned in
Eḏom, and the name of his city was
Dinhaḇah.
33 And Bela died, and Yoḇaḇ son of Zeraḥ
of Botsrah reigned in his place.
34 And Yoḇaḇ died, and Ḥusham of the
land of the Těmanites reigned in his place.
35 And Ḥusham died, and Haḏaḏ son of
Beḏaḏ, who struck Miḏyan in the field of
Mo’aḇ, reigned in his place. And the name
of his city was Awith.
36 And Haḏaḏ died, and Samlah of
Masrěqah reigned in his place.
37 And Samlah died, and Sha’ul of
Reḥoḇoth by the River reigned in his
place.
38 And Sha’ul died, and Ba‘al-Ḥanan son
of Aḵbor reigned in his place.
39 And Ba‘al-Ḥanan son of Aḵbor died,
and Haḏar reigned in his place. And the
name of his city was Pa‘u. And his wife’s
name was Mehětab’ĕl, the daughter of
Matrěḏ, the daughter of Měyzahaḇ.
40 And these were the names of the chiefs
of Ěsaw, according to their clans and their
places, by their names: Chief Timnah,
Chief Alwah, Chief Yethěth,
41 Chief Oholiḇamah, Chief Ělah, Chief
Pinon,
42 Chief Qenaz, Chief Těman, Chief

Miḇtsar,
43 Chief Maḡdi'ěl, Chief Iram. These
were the chiefs of Eḏom, according to their
dwelling places in the land of their possession. Ěsaw was the father of the Eḏomites.

37 And Ya'aqoḇ dwelt in the land of
his father's sojournings, in the land
of Kena'an.
2 This is the genealogy of Ya'aqoḇ.
Yosěph, being seventeen years old, was
feeding the flock with his brothers. And
the young man was with the sons of Bilhah
and the sons of Zilpah, his father's wives.
And Yosěph brought an evil report of them
to his father.
3 And Yisra'ěl loved Yosěph more than
all his children, because he was the son of
his old age. And he made him a long robe.
4 But when his brothers saw that their
father loved him more than all his brothers,
they hated him and were not able to speak
peaceably to him.
5 And Yosěph dreamed a dream, and told
it to his brothers. So they hated him even
more.
6 And he said to them, "Please listen to
this dream which I have dreamed:
7 "See, we were binding sheaves in the
midst of the field, and see, my sheaf rose
up and also stood up. And see, your
sheaves stood all around and bowed down
to my sheaf."
8 And his brothers said to him, "Shall
you indeed reign over us? Shall you indeed
rule over us?" So they hated him even
more for his dreams and for his words.
9 And he dreamed still another dream
and related it to his brothers, and said,
"See, I have dreamed another dream, and
see, the sun and the moon and the eleven
stars bowed down to me."
10 And he related it to his father and his
brothers. And his father rebuked him and
said to him, "What is this dream that you
have dreamed? Shall we, your mother and
I and your brothers, indeed come to bow
down to the earth before you?"
11 And his brothers envied him, but his
father guarded the word.
12 And his brothers went to feed their
father's flock in Sheḵem.
13 And Yisra'ěl said to Yosěph, "Are not
your brothers feeding *the flock* in Sheḵem?
Come, I send you to them." So he said to
him, "Here I am."
14 And he said to him, "Please go and see
if it is well with your brothers and well
with the sheep, and bring back word to
me." So he sent him out of the Valley of
Ḥeḇron, and he went to Sheḵem.
15 And a certain man found him, and see,
he was wandering in the field. And the
man asked him, saying, "What do you
seek?"
16 And he said, "I am seeking my brothers. Please inform me where they are feeding their sheep."
17 And the man said, "They have left here,
for I heard them say, 'Let us go towards
Dothan.' " So Yosěph went after his brothers and found them in Dothan.
18 And they saw him from a distance, and
before he came near them, they plotted
against him, to kill him.
19 And they said to each other, "See, this
master of dreams is coming!
20 "Now, then, come and let us now kill
him and throw him into some pit, and shall
say, 'Some wild beast has devoured him.'
Let us then see what comes of his dreams!"
21 But Re'uḇěn heard and rescued him
from their hands, and said, "Let us not
strike his being."
22 And Re'uḇěn said to them, "Shed no
blood. Throw him into this pit which is in
the wilderness, and do not lay a hand on
him" – in order to rescue him out of their
hands, and bring him back to his father.
23 So it came to be, when Yosěph had
come to his brothers, that they stripped
Yosěph of his robe, the long robe which
was on him.
24 And they took him and threw him into a
pit. And the pit was empty, there was no
water in it.
25 And they sat down to eat a meal. And
they lifted their eyes and looked and saw a
company of Yishma'ělites, coming from
Gil'aḏ with their camels, bearing spices,
and balm, and myrrh, going to take them
down to Mitsrayim.

[26]And Yehuḏah said to his brothers,
"What would we gain if we kill our brother
and conceal his blood?
[27]"Come and let us sell him to the
Yishmaʿĕlites, and let not our hand be upon
him, for he is our brother, our flesh." And
his brothers listened.
[28]And men, Miḏyanite traders passed by,
so they pulled Yosĕph up and lifted him
out of the pit, and sold him to the
Yishmaʿĕlites for twenty pieces of silver.
And they took Yosĕph to Mitsrayim.
[29]And Re'uḇěn returned to the pit, and
see, Yosĕph was not in the pit. And he tore
his garments.
[30]And he returned to his brothers and
said, "The boy is gone! And I, where am I
to go?"
[31]So they took Yosĕph's robe, slew a
male goat, and dipped the robe in the
blood,
[32]and sent the long robe and brought it to
their father and said, "We have found this.
Please look, is it the robe of your son or
not?"
[33]And he recognised it and said, "It is my
son's robe. An evil beast has devoured
him. Yosĕph is torn, torn to pieces."
[34]And Yaʿaqoḇ tore his garments, and put
sackcloth on his waist, and mourned for
his son many days.
[35]And all his sons and all his daughters
arose to comfort him, but he refused to be
comforted, and he said, "Now let me go
down into She'ol [a] to my son in mourning." So his father wept for him.
[36]And the Miḏanites had sold him in
Mitsrayim to Potiphar, an officer of
Pharaoh and captain of the guard.

38 And at that time it came to be that
Yehuḏah left his brothers, and
turned aside to a man, an Aḏullamite
whose name was Ḥirah.
[2]And Yehuḏah saw there a daughter of a
certain Kenaʿanite whose name was
Shuwa. And he took her and went in to her.
[3]So she conceived and bore a son, and
he called his name Ěr.
[4]And she conceived again and bore a
son, and she called his name Onan.
[5]And she conceived yet again and bore a
son, and called his name Shĕlah. And he
was at Keziḇ when she bore him.
[6]And Yehuḏah took a wife for Ěr his
first-born, and her name was Tamar.
[7]But Ěr, Yehuḏah's first-born, was evil
in the eyes of יהוה, and יהוה took his life.
[8]And Yehuḏah said to Onan, "Go in to
your brother's wife and marry her, and
raise up an heir to your brother."
[9]And Onan knew that the offspring
would not be his. And it came to be, when
he went in to his brother's wife, that he
spilled on the ground, lest he should give
an offspring to his brother.
[10]But what he did displeased יהוה, so He
took his life too.
[11]Then Yehuḏah said to Tamar his daughter-in-law, "Remain a widow in your
father's house until my son Shĕlah is
grown." For he said, "Lest he also die as
his brothers did." And Tamar went and
dwelt in her father's house.
[12]And after a long time the daughter of
Shuwa, Yehuḏah's wife, died. And
Yehuḏah was comforted, and went up to
his sheep-shearers at Timnah, he and his
friend Ḥirah the Aḏullamite.
[13]And it was reported to Tamar, saying,
"See, your father-in-law is going up to
Timnah to shear his sheep."
[14]And she took off her widow's garments, and covered herself with a veil and
wrapped herself, and sat at the entrance to
Ěnayim which was on the way to Timnah.
For she saw that Shĕlah was grown, and
she was not given to him as a wife.
[15]And Yehuḏah saw her, and reckoned
her for a whore, for she had covered her
face.
[16]And he turned aside to her by the way,
and said, "Please let me come in to you,"
for he did not know that she was his
daughter-in-law. And she said, "What do
you give me to come in to me?"
[17]And he said, "Let me send you a young
goat from the flock." And she said, "Do

37a See Explanatory notes - She'ol.

you give me a pledge until you send it?"
18 So he said, "What pledge should I give
you?" And she said, "Your seal and your
cord and your staff that is in your hand."
And he gave them to her, and went in to
her, and she conceived by him.
19 And she arose and went away, and
removed her veil and put on the garments
of her widowhood.
20 And Yehuḏah sent the young goat by
the hand of his friend the Aḏullamite, to
receive his pledge from the woman's hand,
but he did not find her.
21 And he asked the men of that place,
saying, "Where is the cult prostitute who
was beside the way to Ěnayim?" And they
said, "There was no cult prostitute in this
place."
22 And he returned to Yehuḏah and said,
"I have not found her. And the men of the
place also said there was no cult prostitute
in this place."
23 And Yehuḏah said, "Let her take them
for herself, lest we become despised, for I
sent this young goat and you have not
found her."
24 And it came to be, about three new
moons after, that Yehuḏah was informed,
saying, "Tamar your daughter-in-law has
whored, and see, she has conceived by
whoring." And Yehuḏah said, "Bring her
out and let her be burned!"
25 When she was brought out, she sent to
her father-in-law, saying, "By the man to
whom these belong, I am pregnant." And
she said, "Please examine whose these are:
the seal and the cord and the staff."
26 And Yehuḏah examined and said, "She
has been more righteous than I, because I
did not give her to Shělah my son." And he
never knew her again.
27 And it came to be, at the time for giving
birth, that see, twins were in her womb.
28 And it came to be, when she was giving
birth, that the one put out his hand. And the
midwife took a scarlet thread and bound it
on his hand, saying, "This one came out
first."
29 And it came to be, as he drew back his
hand, that see, his brother came out! And
she said, "How did you break through?
This breach be upon you!" So his name
was called Perets.
30 And afterward his brother came out
who had the scarlet thread on his hand. So
his name was called Zeraḥ.

39 And Yosěph had been taken down
to Mitsrayim. And Potiphar, an
officer of Pharaoh, captain of the guard, a
Mitsrian, bought him from the
Yishma'ělites who had taken him down
there.
2 And it came to be that יהוה was with
Yosěph, and he became a prosperous man,
and was in the house of his master the
Mitsrian.
3 And his master saw that יהוה was with
him and that יהוה made all he did to prosper in his hand.
4 So Yosěph found favour in his eyes,
and served him, and he appointed him over
his house, and gave into his hand all that
he had.
5 And it came to be, from the time that he
appointed him over his house and all that
he had, that יהוה blessed the Mitsrian's
house for Yosěph's sake. And the blessing
of יהוה was on all that he had in the house
and in the field.
6 And he left in Yosěph's hand all that he
had, and he did not know what he had
except for the bread which he ate. And
Yosěph was handsome in form and handsome in appearance.
7 And after these events it came to be that
his master's wife lifted up her eyes to
Yosěph and said, "Lie with me."
8 But he refused and said to his master's
wife, "Look, my master does not know
what is with me in the house, and he has
given into my hand all that he has.
9 "No one is greater in this house than I,
and he has not withheld whatever from me
but you, because you are his wife. And
how shall I do this great evil and sin
against Elohim?"
10 And it came to be, as she spoke to
Yosěph day by day, that he did not listen to
her, to lie with her, to be with her.
11 And it came to be on a certain day,
when Yosěph went into the house to do his

work, and none of the men of the house
was inside,
12 that she caught him by his garment,
saying, "Lie with me." But he left his garment in her hand, and fled and ran outside.
13 And it came to be, when she saw that
he had left his garment in her hand and fled
outside,
14 that she called to the men of her house
and spoke to them, saying, "See, he has
brought in to us a Hebrew to mock us. He
came in to me to lie with me, and I cried
out with a loud voice.
15 "And it came to be, when he heard that
I lifted my voice and cried out, that he left
his garment with me, and fled and went
outside."
16 And she kept his garment with her until
his master came home.
17 And she spoke to him these same
words, saying, "The Hebrew servant
whom you brought to us came in to me, to
mock me,
18 so it came to be, as I lifted my voice
and cried out, that he left his garment with
me and fled outside."
19 And it came to be, when his master
heard the words which his wife spoke to
him, saying, "Your servant did to me
according to these words," that his displeasure burned.
20 Then Yosěph's master took him and put
him into the prison, a place where the
sovereign's prisoners were confined. And
he was there in the prison.
21 But יהוה was with Yosěph and extended loving-commitment to him, and He
gave him favour in the eyes of the prison
warden.
22 And the prison warden gave into the
hand of Yosěph all the prisoners who were
in the prison, and whatever was done there
was his doing.
23 The prison warden did not look into
any point that was under Yosěph's hand,
because יהוה was with him. And whatever
he did, יהוה made it prosper.

40 And after these events it came to
be that the cupbearer and the baker
of the sovereign of Mitsrayim sinned
against their master, the sovereign of
Mitsrayim.
2 And Pharaoh was wroth with his two
officers, the chief cupbearer and the chief
baker.
3 So he put them in confinement in the
house of the captain of the guard, in the
prison, the place where Yosěph was a prisoner.
4 And the captain of the guard put
Yosěph in charge of them, and he served
them. So they were in confinement for
some time.
5 Then the cupbearer and the baker of
the sovereign of Mitsrayim, who were
confined in the prison, dreamed a dream,
both of them, each man's dream in one
night and each man's dream with its own
interpretation.
6 And Yosěph came in to them in the
morning and looked at them and saw that
they were sad.
7 And he asked Pharaoh's officers who
were with him in confinement of his master's house, saying, "Why do you look so
sad today?"
8 And they said to him, "We each have
dreamed a dream, and there is no one to
interpret it." And Yosěph said to them, "Do
not interpretations belong to Elohim?
Relate them to me, please."
9 So the chief cupbearer related his
dream to Yosěph, and said to him, "See, in
my dream a vine was before me,
10 and in the vine were three branches,
and it was as though it budded – its
blossoms shot forth, and its clusters
brought forth ripe grapes.
11 "And Pharaoh's cup was in my hand.
So I took the grapes and pressed them into
Pharaoh's cup, and placed the cup in
Pharaoh's hand."
12 And Yosěph said to him, "This is the
interpretation of it: The three branches are
three days.
13 "Yet, within three days Pharaoh is
going to lift up your head and restore you
to your place, and you shall put Pharaoh's
cup in his hand according to the former
ruling, when you were his cupbearer.
14 "But remember me when it is well with

you, and please show loving-commitment to me. And mention me to Pharaoh, and get me out of this house.

15 “For truly I was stolen away from the land of the Hebrews. And also I have done naught that they should put me into the dungeon.”

16 And the chief baker saw that the interpretation was good, and he said to Yosĕph, “I also was in my dream and saw three white baskets were on my head,

17 and in the uppermost basket all kinds of baked goods for Pharaoh, and the birds ate them out of the basket on my head.”

18 And Yosĕph answered and said, “This is the interpretation of it: The three baskets are three days.

19 “Yet, within three days Pharaoh is going to lift off your head from you and hang you on a tree. And the birds shall eat your flesh from you.”

20 And on the third day, Pharaoh’s birthday, it came to be that he made a feast for all his servants. And he lifted up the head of the chief cupbearer and of the chief baker among his servants,

21 and he restored the chief cupbearer to his post of cupbearer again, and he placed the cup in Pharaoh’s hand,

22 but he hanged the chief baker, as Yosĕph had interpreted to them.

23 And the chief cupbearer did not remember Yosĕph, but forgot him.

41 And it came to be, at the end of two years’ time, that Pharaoh had a dream, and saw him standing by the river,

2 and saw seven cows coming up out of the river, beautiful looking and fat, and they fed amongst the reeds,

3 then saw seven other cows coming up after them out of the river, ugly and lean of flesh, and stood by the other cows on the bank of the river.

4 And the ugly and lean of flesh cows ate up the seven beautiful looking and fat cows. Then Pharaoh awoke.

5 And he slept and dreamed a second time and saw seven heads of grain coming up on one stalk, plump and good,

6 and saw seven lean heads, scorched by the east wind, coming up after them.

7 And the seven lean heads swallowed the seven plump and complete heads. Then Pharaoh awoke and saw it was a dream.

8 And it came to be in the morning that his spirit was moved, and he sent and called for all the magicians of Mitsrayim and all its wise men. And Pharaoh related to them his dreams, but there was no one who could interpret them for Pharaoh.

9 Then the chief cupbearer spoke to Pharaoh, saying, “I remember my crimes this day.

10 “When Pharaoh was wroth with his servants, and put me in confinement in the house of the captain of the guard, both me and the chief baker,

11 each one of us dreamed a dream in one night, he and I. Each of us dreamed according to the interpretation of his own dream.

12 “And there was with us a Hebrew youth, a servant of the captain of the guard. And we related to him, and he interpreted our dreams for us. To each man he interpreted according to his own dream.

13 “And it came to be, as he interpreted for us, so it came to be. He restored me to my office, and he hanged him.”

14 Then Pharaoh sent and called Yosĕph, and they hurriedly brought him out of the dungeon. And he shaved and changed his garments, and came to Pharaoh.

15 And Pharaoh said to Yosĕph, “I have dreamed a dream, and there is no one to interpret it. Now I myself have heard it said of you that you understand a dream, to interpret it.”

16 And Yosĕph answered Pharaoh, saying, “It is not in me, let Elohim answer Pharaoh with peace.”

17 And Pharaoh said to Yosĕph, “See, in my dream I stood on the bank of the river

18 and saw seven cows coming up out of the river, beautiful looking and fat, and they fed amongst the reeds,

19 then saw seven other cows coming up after them, poor and very ugly and lean of flesh, such ugliness as I have never seen in all the land of Mitsrayim.

20 “And the lean of flesh and ugly cows

ate up the first seven, the fat cows.
21"Yet when they had eaten them up, no
one would have known that they had eaten
them, for they were as ugly as at the beginning. Then I awoke.
22"Also, I looked in my dream and saw
seven heads coming up on one stalk, complete and good,
23then saw seven heads, withered, lean,
scorched by the east wind, coming up after
them.
24"And the lean heads swallowed the
seven good heads. And I spoke to the
magicians, but there was no one who could
explain it to me."
25And Yosĕph said to Pharaoh, "The
dream of Pharaoh is one. Elohim has
shown Pharaoh what He is about to do:
26"The seven good cows are seven years,
and the seven good heads are seven years –
it is one dream.
27"And the seven lean and ugly cows
which came up after them are seven years,
and the seven empty heads scorched by the
east wind are seven years of scarcity of
food.
28"This is the word which I spoke to
Pharaoh: Elohim has shown Pharaoh what
He is about to do.
29"See, seven years of great plenty are
coming in all the land of Mitsrayim,
30but after them seven years of scarcity of
food shall arise and all the plenty be forgotten in the land of Mitsrayim. And the
scarcity of food shall destroy the land,
31and the plenty shall not be remembered
in the land, because of the scarcity of food
following, for it is very severe.
32"And the dream was repeated to
Pharaoh twice because the word is established by Elohim, and Elohim is hastening
to do it.
33"And now, let Pharaoh look for a discerning and wise man, and set him over the
land of Mitsrayim.
34"Let Pharaoh do this, and let him
appoint overseers over the land, to take up
one-fifth of the land of Mitsrayim in the
seven years of plenty.
35"And let them gather all the food of
those good years that are coming, and store
up grain under the hand of Pharaoh, and let
them keep food in the cities.
36"And the food shall be for a store for
the land for the seven years of scarcity of
food which shall be in the land of
Mitsrayim, and do not let the land be cut
off by the scarcity of food."
37And the word was good in the eyes of
Pharaoh and in the eyes of all his servants.
38And Pharaoh said to his servants,
"Could we find another like him, a man in
whom is the Spirit of Elohim?"
39Then Pharaoh said to Yosĕph, "Since
Elohim has shown you all this, there is no
one as discerning and wise as you.
40"Be over my house, you yourself, and
at your mouth all my people shall kiss –
only in the throne I am greater than you."
41And Pharaoh said to Yosĕph, "See, I
have set you over all the land of Mitsrayim."
42And Pharaoh took his seal-ring off his
hand and put it on Yosĕph's hand. And he
dressed him in garments of fine linen and
put a gold chain around his neck.
43And he had him ride in the second chariot which he had. And they cried out
before him, "Bow the knee!" And he set
him over all the land of Mitsrayim.
44And Pharaoh said to Yosĕph, "I am
Pharaoh, and without *a word* from you let
no man lift his hand or foot in all the land
of Mitsrayim."
45And Pharaoh called Yosĕph's name
Zaphnath-Paʽnĕaḥ. And he gave him as a
wife Asenath, the daughter of Poti-Pherah
priest of On. And Yosĕph went out over all
the land of Mitsrayim.
46Now Yosĕph was thirty years old when
he stood before Pharaoh sovereign of
Mitsrayim. And Yosĕph went out from the
presence of Pharaoh, and went throughout
all the land of Mitsrayim.
47And in the seven years of plenty the
ground brought forth generously.
48And he gathered all the food of the
seven years which were in the land of
Mitsrayim, and laid up the food in the
cities. He laid up in every city the food of
the fields which surrounded them.
49Thus Yosĕph gathered very much grain,

as the sand of the sea, until he ceased
counting, for it was without number.
50 And to Yosěph were born two sons
before the years of scarcity of food came,
whom Asenath, the daughter of Poti-
Pherah priest of On, bore to him.
51 And Yosěph called the name of the
first-born Menashsheh, "For Elohim has
made me forget all my toil and all my
father's house."
52 And the name of the second he called
Ephrayim, "For Elohim has caused me to
be fruitful in the land of my affliction."
53 And the seven years of plenty which
were in the land of Mitsrayim came to an
end,
54 and the seven years of scarcity of food
began to come, as Yosěph had said. And
the scarcity of food was in all lands, but in
all the land of Mitsrayim there was bread.
55 But when all the land of Mitsrayim
hungered, and the people cried to Pharaoh
for bread, Pharaoh said to all the Mitsrites,
"Go to Yosěph, do whatever he says to
you."
56 And the scarcity of food was over all
the face of the earth, and Yosěph opened
all the storehouses and sold to the
Mitsrites. And the scarcity of food was
severe in the land of Mitsrayim.
57 And all the earth came to Yosěph in
Mitsrayim to buy grain, because the scarcity of food was severe in all the earth.

42 And when Yaʿaqoḇ saw that there
was grain in Mitsrayim, Yaʿaqoḇ
said to his sons, "Why do you look at each
other?"
2 And he said, "See, I have heard that
there is grain in Mitsrayim. Go down to
that place and buy for us there, and let us
live and not die."
3 And Yosěph's ten brothers went down
to buy grain in Mitsrayim.
4 But Yaʿaqoḇ did not send Yosěph's
brother Binyamin with his brothers, for he
said, "Lest some harm come to him."
5 And the sons of Yisra'ěl went to buy
grain among those who journeyed, for the
scarcity of food was in the land of
Kenaʿan.
6 And Yosěph was the governor over the
land, he was the one who sold to all the
people of the land. And Yosěph's brothers
came and bowed down before him with
their faces to the earth.
7 And Yosěph saw his brothers and
recognised them, but he acted as a stranger
to them and spoke to them harshly, and
said to them, "Where do you come from?"
And they said, "From the land of Kenaʿan
to buy food."
8 So Yosěph recognised his brothers, but
they did not recognise him.
9 And Yosěph remembered the dreams
which he had dreamed about them, and
said to them, "You are spies! You have
come to see the nakedness of the land!"
10 And they said to him, "No, my master,
but your servants have come to buy food.
11 "We are all one man's sons, we are
trustworthy, your servants are not spies."
12 But he said to them, "No, but you have
come to see the nakedness of the land."
13 And they said, "Your servants are
twelve brothers, the sons of one man in
the land of Kenaʿan. And see, the youngest
is with our father today, and one is no
more."
14 And Yosěph said to them, "It is as I
spoke to you, saying, 'You are spies!'
15 "By this you shall be proven: By the
life of Pharaoh, you do not leave this place
unless your youngest brother comes here.
16 "Send one of you, and let him bring
your brother, while you are kept in prison.
So let your words be proven to see whether
there is any truth in you, or else, by the life
of Pharaoh, you are spies!"
17 And he put them all together in prison
for three days.
18 Now Yosěph said to them the third day,
"Do this and live, for I fear Elohim:
19 "If you are trustworthy, let one of your
brothers be confined to your prison house,
and you, go, bring grain for the scarcity of
food of your houses.
20 "And bring your youngest brother to
me, and let your words be confirmed, and
you do not die." And so they did.
21 And they said to each other, "Truly, we
are guilty concerning our brother, for we

saw the distress of his life when he pleaded with us, yet we did not listen, that is why this distress has come upon us."

22 And Re'uḇěn answered them, saying, "Did I not speak to you, saying, 'Do not sin against the boy,' and you would not listen? And see, his blood is now required of us."

23 And they did not know that Yosěph understood them, for he spoke to them through an interpreter.

24 And he turned himself away from them and wept, but came back to them and spoke to them. And he took Shimʽon from them and bound him before their eyes.

25 And Yosěph commanded and they filled their sacks with grain, also to put back every man's silver to his sack, and to give them food for the journey. And thus it was done for them.

26 So they loaded their donkeys with the grain and went from there.

27 And as one of them opened his sack to give his donkey fodder at the lodging place, he saw his silver, for there it was in the mouth of his sack!

28 And he said to his brothers, "My silver has been returned, and there it is, in my sack!" And their hearts sank and they were afraid, saying to each other, "What is this that Elohim has done to us?"

29 So they came to Yaʽaqoḇ their father in the land of Kenaʽan and reported to him all that befell them, saying,

30 "The man, the master of the land, spoke to us harshly, and took us for spies of the land.

31 "But we said to him, 'We are trustworthy, we are not spies.

32 'We are twelve brothers, sons of our father. One is no more, and the youngest is today with our father in the land of Kenaʽan.'

33 "And the man, the master of the land, said to us, 'By this I know that you are trustworthy: Leave one of your brothers here with me, and take food for the scarcity of food of your households, and go.

34 'And bring your youngest brother to me, then I know that you are not spies, but that you are trustworthy – I give your brother to you, and you move about in the land.' "

35 And it came to be as they emptied their sacks, that look, the bundle of each man's silver was in his sack! And when they and their father saw the bundles of silver, they were afraid.

36 And Yaʽaqoḇ their father said to them, "You have bereaved me – Yosěph is no more, and Shimʽon is no more, and you would take Binyamin! All this is against me."

37 So Re'uḇěn spoke to his father, saying, "Take the lives of my two sons if I do not bring him back to you. Put him in my hands, and I myself bring him back to you."

38 But he said, "My son is not going down with you, for his brother is dead, and he is left alone. If any harm should come to him along the way in which you go, then you would bring down my grey hair with sorrow to She'ol."

43

But the scarcity of food was severe in the land.

2 And it came to be, when they had eaten up the grain which they had brought from Mitsrayim, that their father said to them, "Go back, buy us a little food."

3 But Yehuḏah spoke to him, saying, "The man vehemently warned us, saying, 'You do not see my face unless your brother is with you.' "

4 "If you let our brother go with us, we go down and buy you food.

5 "But if you do not let him go, we do not go down, because the man said to us, 'You do not see my face unless your brother is with you.' "

6 And Yisra'ěl said, "Why did you do evil to me to inform the man that you still had *another* brother?"

7 And they said, "The man kept asking about us and our relatives, saying, 'Is your father still alive? Have you *another* brother?' And we informed him according to these words. How could we know that he would say, 'Bring your brother down'?"

8 And Yehuḏah said to Yisra'ěl his father, "Send the boy with me, and let us arise and

go, and live and not die, both we and you and also our little ones.

9 "I myself shall stand guaranty for him – from my hand you are to require him. If I do not bring him back to you and set him before you, then let me bear the blame forever.

10 "For if we had not delayed, truly by now we could have returned this second time."

11 And their father Yisra'ĕl said to them, "If so, then do this: Take some of the best fruit of the land in your vessels and bring a present down for the man, a little balm and a little honey, spices and myrrh, nuts and almonds.

12 "And take double silver in your hand, and take back in your hand the silver that was returned in the mouth of your sacks. It could have been a mistake.

13 "And take your brother, and arise, go back to the man.

14 "And Ĕl Shaddai give to you compassion before the man, so that he shall release your other brother and Binyamin. And I, if I am bereaved, I am bereaved!"

15 And the men took that present and Binyamin, and they took double the amount of silver in their hand, and arose and went down to Mitsrayim, and stood before Yosĕph.

16 And Yosĕph saw Binyamin with them, and said to the one over his house, "Bring the men home, and make a great slaughter, and prepare, for these men are to eat with me at noon."

17 And the man did as Yosĕph said, and the man brought the men into Yosĕph's house.

18 And the men were afraid because they were brought into Yosĕph's house. And they said, "It is because of the silver, which was put back into our sacks the first time, that we are brought in, to throw himself upon us and fall upon us, to take us as slaves, our donkeys too."

19 So they came near to the man over the house of Yosĕph, and spoke to him at the door of the house,

20 and said, "O my master, we indeed came down the first time to buy food,

21 but it came to be, when we came to the lodging place, that we opened our sacks and saw each man's silver in the mouth of his sack, our silver in its weight. And we have brought it back in our hand.

22 "And we have brought down other silver in our hands to buy food. We do not know who put our silver in our sacks."

23 But he said, "Peace be with you, do not be afraid. Your Elohim and the Elohim of your father has given you treasure in your sacks – your silver had come to me!" And he brought Shim'on out to them.

24 And the man brought the men into Yosĕph's house and gave them water, and they washed their feet. And he gave their donkeys fodder.

25 And they made the present ready for Yosĕph's coming at noon, for they heard that they were to eat there.

26 And when Yosĕph came home, they brought him the present which was in their hand, into the house, and bowed down before him to the earth.

27 And he asked them about their welfare, and said, "Is your father well, the old man of whom you spoke? Is he still alive?"

28 And they said, "Your servant our father is in good health, he is still alive." And they bowed their heads down and did obeisance.

29 And he lifted his eyes and saw his brother Binyamin, his mother's son, and said, "Is this your younger brother of whom you spoke to me?" And he said, "Elohim show favour to you, my son."

30 And Yosĕph hurried, for his emotions were deeply moved towards his brother, and he looked for *a place* to weep, and went into his room and wept there.

31 Then he washed his face and came out, and controlled himself, and said, "Serve the food."

32 And they set him a place by himself, and them by themselves, and the Mitsrites who ate with him by themselves, for the Mitsrites could not eat food with the Hebrews, for that is an abomination to the Mitsrites.

33 And they sat before him, the first-born according to his birthright and the

youngest according to his youth, and the men looked at each other in astonishment.
34 And he took portions to them from before him, but Binyamin's portion was five times as much as any of theirs. And they feasted and they drank with him.

44 And he commanded the one over his house, saying, "Fill the men's sacks with food, as they are able to bear, and put each man's silver in the mouth of his sack.
2 "And put my cup, the silver cup, in the mouth of the sack of the youngest, and the silver for his grain." And he did according to the word of Yosěph which he spoke.
3 As soon as the morning was light, the men were sent away, they and their donkeys.
4 And when they had gone out of the city, not having gone far, Yosěph said to the one over his house, "Rise up, follow the men, and when you overtake them, say to them, 'Why have you repaid evil for good?
5 'Is this not the one from which my master drinks, and with which he indeed divines? You have done evil in what you have done.' "
6 So he overtook them and spoke these words to them.
7 And they said to him, "Why does my master say these words? Far be it from us that your servants should do according to this word.
8 "See, we brought back to you from the land of Kena'an the silver which we found in the mouth of our sacks. How then should we steal silver or gold from your master's house?
9 "With whomever of your servants it is found – he shall die and we shall become my master's slaves as well."
10 And he said, "Now also let it be according to your words: he with whom it is found becomes my slave, and you are innocent."
11 And they hurried, each man let down his sack to the ground, and each opened his sack.
12 And he searched, with the oldest first and with the youngest last, and the cup was found in Binyamin's sack.
13 And they tore their garments, and each man loaded his donkey and went back to the city.
14 And Yehuḏah and his brothers came to Yosěph's house, and he was still there. And they fell before him on the ground.
15 And Yosěph said to them, "What deed is this you have done? Did you not know that a man like me indeed divines?"
16 And Yehuḏah said, "What do we say to my master? What do we speak? Or how do we clear ourselves? Elohim has found out the crookedness of your servants. See, we are my master's slaves, both we and he also with whom the cup was found."
17 But he said, "Far be it from me to do this. The man in whose hand the cup was found, he becomes my slave. And you, go up in peace to your father."
18 And Yehuḏah came near to him and said, "O my master, please let your servant speak a word in my master's hearing, and do not let your displeasure burn against your servant, for you are like Pharaoh.
19 "My master asked his servants, saying, 'Have you a father or a brother?'
20 "And we said to my master, 'We have a father, an old man, and a young child of *his* old age, and his brother is dead, and he alone is left of his mother's children, and his father loves him.'
21 "And you said to your servants, 'Bring him down to me, and let me set my eyes on him.'
22 "And we said to my master, 'The boy is not able to leave his father, for if he leaves his father, his father shall die.'
23 "But you said to your servants, 'Unless your youngest brother comes down with you, you do not see my face again.'
24 "And it came to be, when we went up to your servant my father, that we told him the words of my master.
25 "And our father said, 'Go back and buy us a little food.'
26 "But we said, 'We are not able to go down. If our youngest brother is with us, then we shall go down, for we are not able to see the man's face unless our youngest brother is with us.'

27 “Then your servant my father said to us, ‘You know that my wife bore me two sons,

28 and the one went out from me, and I said, “Truly, he is torn, torn to pieces!” And I have not seen him since.

29 ‘And if you take this one from me too, and harm comes to him, you shall bring down my grey hair with evil to She’ol.’

30 “And now, if I come to your servant my father and the boy is not with us – since his own life is bound up in his life –

31 then it shall be, when he sees that the boy is not with us, that he shall die. So your servants shall bring down the grey hair of your servant our father with evil to She’ol.

32 “For your servant went guaranty for the boy to my father, saying, ‘If I do not bring him back to you, then I shall be a sinner before my father forever.’

33 “And now, please let your servant remain instead of the boy as a slave to my master, and let the boy go up with his brothers.

34 “For how do I go up to my father if the boy is not with me, lest I see the evil that would come upon my father?”

45 And Yosĕph was unable to restrain himself before all those who stood by him, and he called out, “Have everyone go out from me!” So no one stood with him while Yosĕph made himself known to his brothers.

2 And he wept aloud, and the Mitsrites and the house of Pharaoh heard it.

3 And Yosĕph said to his brothers, “I am Yosĕph, is my father still alive?” But his brothers were unable to answer him, for they trembled before him.

4 Then Yosĕph said to his brothers, “Please come near to me.” And when they came near, he said, “I am Yosĕph your brother, whom you sold into Mitsrayim.

5 “And now, do not be grieved nor displeased with yourselves because you sold me here, for Elohim sent me before you to preserve life.

6 “For two years now the scarcity of food has been in the land, and there are still five years in which there is neither ploughing nor harvesting.

7 “And Elohim sent me before you to preserve for you a remnant in the earth, and to give life to you by a great escape.

8 “So then, you did not send me here, but Elohim. And He has set me for a father to Pharaoh, and master of all his house, and a ruler throughout all the land of Mitsrayim.

9 “Hurry and go up to my father, and say to him, ‘Thus says your son Yosĕph, “Elohim has made me master of all Mitsrayim. Come down to me, do not delay.

10 “And you shall dwell in the land of Goshen, and be near to me, you and your children, your children’s children, your flocks and your herds, and all that you have.

11 “And I shall provide for you there, lest you and your household, and all that you have, come to poverty, because five years of scarcity of food are still to come.” ’

12 “And look, your eyes and the eyes of my brother Binyamin see that it is my mouth that speaks to you.

13 “And you shall inform my father of all my esteem in Mitsrayim, and of all that you have seen. And you shall hurry and bring my father down here.”

14 And he fell on his brother Binyamin’s neck and wept, and Binyamin wept on his neck.

15 And he kissed all his brothers and wept over them, and after that his brothers spoke with him.

16 And the report of it was heard by the house of Pharaoh, saying, “The brothers of Yosĕph have come.” And it was good in the eyes of Pharaoh and in the eyes of his servants.

17 And Pharaoh said to Yosĕph, “Say to your brothers, ‘Do this: Load your beasts and go, enter the land of Kenaʿan,

18 and take your father and your households and come to me, and I give you the best of the land of Mitsrayim, and you eat the fat of the land.

19 ‘And you, you have been commanded, do this: Take wagons out of the land of

Mitsrayim for your little ones and your
wives. And you shall bring your father, and
come.
20 'And do not be concerned about your
goods, for the best of all the land of
Mitsrayim is yours.' "
21 And the sons of Yisra'ěl did so. And
Yosěph gave them wagons, according to
the mouth of Pharaoh, and he gave them
food for the journey.
22 He gave to all of them, to each man,
changes of garments, but to Binyamin he
gave three hundred pieces of silver and
five changes of garments.
23 And he sent to his father this: ten
donkeys loaded with the best of
Mitsrayim, and ten female donkeys loaded
with grain, and bread, and food for his
father for the journey.
24 So he sent his brothers away, and they
left. And he said to them, "Do not quarrel
along the way."
25 And they went up out of Mitsrayim,
and came to the land of Kenaʻan to
Yaʻaqoḇ their father.
26 And they told him, saying, "Yosěph is
still alive, and he is governor over all the
land of Mitsrayim." And Yaʻaqoḇ's heart
ceased, for he did not believe them.
27 But when they spoke to him all the
words which Yosěph had spoken to them,
and when he saw the wagons which
Yosěph had sent to transport him, the spirit
of Yaʻaqoḇ their father revived.
28 And Yisra'ěl said, "Enough! My son
Yosěph is still alive. Let me go and see him
before I die."

46 And Yisra'ěl set out with all that he
had, and came to Be'ěrsheḇa, and
slaughtered slaughterings to the Elohim of
his father Yitsḥaq.
2 And Elohim spoke to Yisra'ěl in the
visions of the night, and said, "Yaʻaqoḇ,
Yaʻaqoḇ!" And he said, "Here I am."
3 And He said, "I am the Ěl, Elohim of
your father. Do not be afraid to go down
to Mitsrayim, for I shall make you there
into a great nation.
4 "I Myself am going down with you to
Mitsrayim and I Myself shall certainly
bring you up again. And let Yosěph put his
hand on your eyes."
5 And Yaʻaqoḇ rose up from Be'ěrsheḇa.
And the sons of Yisra'ěl brought their
father Yaʻaqoḇ, and their little ones, and
their wives, in the wagons which Pharaoh
had sent to transport him.
6 And they took their livestock and their
property which they had acquired in the
land of Kenaʻan, and came into Mitsrayim,
Yaʻaqoḇ and all his seed with him.
7 His sons and his sons' sons, his daughters and his sons' daughters, and all his
seed he brought with him to Mitsrayim.
8 And these were the names of the
children of Yisra'ěl, Yaʻaqoḇ and his sons,
who came into Mitsrayim: Re'uḇěn was
Yaʻaqoḇ's first-born.
9 And the sons of Re'uḇěn: Ḥanoḵ, and
Pallu, and Ḥetsron, and Karmi.
10 And the sons of Shimʻon: Yemu'ěl, and
Yamin, and Ohaḏ, and Yaḵin, and Tsoḥar,
and Sha'ul, son of a Kenaʻanite woman.
11 And the sons of Lěwi: Gěrshon,
Qehath, and Merari.
12 And the sons of Yehuḏah: Ěr, and
Onan, and Shělah, and Perets, and Zeraḥ –
but Ěr and Onan died in the land of
Kenaʻan. And the sons of Perets were
Ḥetsron and Ḥamul.
13 And the sons of Yissasḵar: Tola, and
Puwʻah, and Yoḇ, and Shimron.
14 And the sons of Zeḇulun: Sereḏ, and
Ělon, and Yaḥle'ěl.
15 These were the sons of Lě'ah, whom
she bore to Yaʻaqoḇ in Paddan Aram, with
his daughter Dinah. All the beings, his
sons and his daughters, were thirty-three.
16 And the sons of Gaḏ: Tsiphyon and
Ḥaggi, Shuni and Etsbon, Ěri and Aroḏi,
and Arěli.
17 And the sons of Asher: Yimnah, and
Yishwah, and Yishwi, and Beriʻah, and
Seraḥ, their sister. And the sons of Beriʻah:
Ḥeḇer and Malki'ěl.
18 These were the sons of Zilpah, whom
Laḇan gave to Lě'ah his daughter. And
these she bore to Yaʻaqoḇ: sixteen beings.
19 The sons of Raḥěl, Yaʻaqoḇ's wife:
Yosěph and Binyamin.
20 And to Yosěph in the land of Mitsrayim

were born Menashsheh and Ephrayim,
whom Asenath, the daughter of Poti-
Pherah priest of On, bore to him.
21 And the sons of Binyamin: Belah, and
Beḵer, and Ashběl, Gěra and Na'aman,
Ěḥi and Rosh, Muppim and Ḥuppim, and
Ard.
22 These were the sons of Raḥěl who were
born to Ya'aqoḇ: fourteen beings in all.
23 And the son of Dan: Ḥushim.
24 And the sons of Naphtali: Yaḥtse'ěl,
and Guni, and Yětser, and Shillěm.
25 These were the sons of Bilhah, whom
Laḇan gave to Raḥěl his daughter, and she
bore these to Ya'aqoḇ: seven beings in all.
26 All the beings who went with Ya'aqoḇ
to Mitsrayim, who came from his body,
besides Ya'aqoḇ's sons' wives, were sixty-
six beings in all.
27 And the sons of Yosěph who were born
to him in Mitsrayim were two beings. All
the beings of the house of Ya'aqoḇ who
went to Mitsrayim were seventy.
28 And he sent Yehuḏah before him to
Yosěph, to point out before him the way to
Goshen. And they came to the land of
Goshen.
29 And Yosěph made ready his chariot and
went up to Goshen to meet his father
Yisra'ěl. And he appeared to him, and fell
on his neck and wept on his neck a long
time.
30 And Yisra'ěl said to Yosěph, "Now let
me die, since I have seen your face, that
you are still alive."
31 And Yosěph said to his brothers and to
his father's household, "I am going up to
inform Pharaoh, and say to him, 'My
brothers and those of my father's house,
who were in the land of Kena'an, have
come to me.
32 'And the men are shepherds, that they
have been men of livestock, and they have
brought their flocks and their herds, and all
that they have.'
33 "And it shall be, when Pharaoh calls
you and says, 'What is your occupation?'
34 that you shall say, 'Your servants have
been men of livestock from our youth even
till now, both we and also our fathers,' so
that you dwell in the land of Goshen, for
every shepherd is an abomination to the
Mitsrites."

47 Then Yosěph went and spoke to
Pharaoh, and said, "My father and
my brothers, their flocks and their herds
and all that they possess, have come from
the land of Kena'an. And see, they are in
the land of Goshen."
2 And he took five men from among his
brothers and presented them to Pharaoh.
3 And Pharaoh said to his brothers,
"What is your occupation?" And they said
to Pharaoh, "Your servants are shepherds,
both we and also our fathers."
4 And they said to Pharaoh, "We have
come to dwell in the land, because there is
no pasture for your servant's flocks, for the
scarcity of food is severe in the land of
Kena'an. And now, please let your servants
dwell in the land of Goshen."
5 And Pharaoh spoke to Yosěph, saying,
"Your father and your brothers have come
to you.
6 "The land of Mitsrayim is before you.
Settle your father and brothers in the best
of the land, let them dwell in the land of
Goshen. And if you know of capable men
among them, then make them chief herdsmen over my livestock."
7 And Yosěph brought in his father
Ya'aqoḇ and set him before Pharaoh. And
Ya'aqoḇ blessed Pharaoh.
8 And Pharaoh said to Ya'aqoḇ, "How
old are you?"
9 And Ya'aqoḇ said to Pharaoh, "The
days of the years of my sojournings are
one hundred and thirty years. Few and evil
have been the days of the years of my life,
and they have not reached the days of the
years of the life of my fathers in the days
of their sojournings."
10 And Ya'aqoḇ blessed Pharaoh, and
went out from before Pharaoh.
11 So Yosěph settled his father and his
brothers, and gave them a possession in the
land of Mitsrayim, in the best of the land,
in the land of Ra'meses, as Pharaoh had
commanded.
12 And Yosěph provided his father, and
his brothers, and all his father's household

with bread for the mouth of the little ones.
13 Now there was no bread in all the land,
because the scarcity of food was very
severe, and the land of Mitsrayim and all
the land of Kenaʽan became exhausted
from the scarcity of food.
14 And Yosěph gathered up all the silver
that was found in the land of Mitsrayim
and in the land of Kenaʽan, for the grain
which they bought. And Yosěph brought
the silver into Pharaoh's house.
15 And when the silver was all spent in the
land of Mitsrayim and in the land of
Kenaʽan, all the Mitsrites came to Yosěph
and said, "Give us bread, for why should
we die in your presence? For the silver is
gone!"
16 And Yosěph said, "Give your livestock,
and I give you bread for your livestock, if
the silver is gone."
17 So they brought their livestock to
Yosěph, and Yosěph gave them bread in
exchange for the horses, and for the flocks
they owned, and for the herds they owned,
and for the donkeys. Thus he fed them
with bread in exchange for all their livestock that year.
18 And when that year had ended, they
came to him the next year and said to him,
"We do not hide from my master that our
silver is all spent, and my master also has
the livestock we owned. There has not
been left any before my master but our
bodies and our lands.
19 "Why should we die before your eyes,
both we and our land? Buy us and our land
for bread, and let us and our land be servants of Pharaoh. And give us seed, and let
us live and not die, and let the land not lie
waste."
20 And Yosěph bought the entire land of
Mitsrayim for Pharaoh, because every man
of the Mitsrites sold his field, because the
scarcity of food was severe upon them.
And the land came to be Pharaoh's.
21 And as for the people, he moved them
into the cities, from one end of the borders
of Mitsrayim to the other end.
22 Only the ground of the priests he did
not buy, for the priests had from what
Pharaoh gave them *by* law, and they ate
that which Pharaoh gave them by law.
Therefore they did not sell their ground.
23 And Yosěph said to the people, "Look,
I have bought you and your land today for
Pharaoh. Look, here is seed for you, and
you shall sow the land.
24 "And it shall be that in the harvest you
shall give one-fifth to Pharaoh. And four-
fifths is your own, as seed for the field and
for your food, for those of your households
and as food for your little ones."
25 And they said, "You have saved our
lives. Let us find favour in the eyes of my
master, and we shall become Pharaoh's
servants."
26 And Yosěph made it a law over the land
of Mitsrayim to this day, that Pharaoh
should have one-fifth, except for the
ground of the priests only, which did not
become Pharaoh's.
27 And Yisra'ěl dwelt in the land of
Mitsrayim, in the land of Goshen. And
they had possessions there and bore fruit
and increased exceedingly.
28 And Yaʽaqoḇ lived in the land of
Mitsrayim seventeen years. So the length
of Yaʽaqoḇ's life was one hundred and
forty-seven years.
29 And the time for Yisra'ěl to die drew
near, and he called his son Yosěph and said
to him, "Now if I have found favour in
your eyes, please put your hand under my
thigh, and show loving-commitment and
truth to me. Please do not bury me in
Mitsrayim,
30 but I shall lie with my fathers, and you
shall take me up out of Mitsrayim and bury
me in their burial-place." And he said, "I
do as you have said."
31 And he said, "Swear to me." And he
swore to him, and Yisra'ěl bowed himself
on the head of the bed.

48

And after these events it came to
be that it was said to Yosěph, "See,
your father is sick." And he took with him
his two sons, Menashsheh and Ephrayim.
2 And Yaʽaqoḇ was told, "See, your son
Yosěph is coming to you." And Yisra'ěl
strengthened himself and sat up on the bed.
3 And Yaʽaqoḇ said to Yosěph, "Ěl

Shaddai appeared to me at Luz in the land
of Kenaʿan and blessed me,
4 and said to me, ‘See, I am making you
fruitful and shall increase you and make of
you an assembly of peoples, and give this
land to your seed after you as an everlasting possession.’
5 “And now, your two sons, Ephrayim
and Menashsheh, who were born to you in
the land of Mitsrayim before I came to you
in Mitsrayim, are mine – as Re’uḇěn and
Shimʿon, they are mine.
6 “Your offspring whom you shall bring
forth after them are yours, and let them be
called by the name of their brothers in their
inheritance.
7 “And I, when I came from Paddan,
Raḥěl died beside me in the land of
Kenaʿan on the way, when there was but a
little distance to go to Ephrath. And I
buried her there on the way to Ephrath,
that is Běyth Leḥem.”
8 And Yisra’ěl saw Yosěph’s sons, and
said, “Who are these?”
9 And Yosěph said to his father, “They
are my sons, whom Elohim has given me
in this place.” And he said, “Please bring
them to me, and let me bless them.”
10 And the eyes of Yisra’ěl were dim with
age, and he was unable to see. And he
drew them near him, and he kissed them
and embraced them.
11 And Yisra’ěl said to Yosěph, “I had not
thought to see your face. But see, Elohim
has also shown me your seed!”
12 So Yosěph brought them from between
his knees, and he bowed down with his
face to the earth.
13 And Yosěph took them both, Ephrayim
with his right hand toward Yisra’ěl’s left
hand, and Menashsheh with his left hand
toward Yisra’ěl’s right hand, and brought
them near him.
14 And Yisra’ěl stretched out his right
hand and laid it on Ephrayim’s head, who
was the younger, and his left hand on
Menashsheh’s head, consciously directing
his hands, for Menashsheh was the first-
born.
15 And he blessed Yosěph, and said, “The
Elohim before whom my fathers Aḇraham
and Yitsḥaq walked, the Elohim who has
fed me all my life long to this day,
16 the Messenger who has redeemed me
from all evil – bless the youths! And let my
name be called upon them, and the name
of my fathers Aḇraham and Yitsḥaq. And
let them increase to a multitude in the
midst of the earth.”
17 And when Yosěph saw that his father
laid his right hand on the head of
Ephrayim, it was evil in his eyes; and he
took hold of his father’s hand to remove it
from the head of Ephrayim to the head of
Menashsheh.
18 And Yosěph said to his father, “Not so,
my father, for this one is the first-born, put
your right hand on his head.”
19 But his father refused and said, “I
know, my son, I know. He also becomes a
people, and he also is great. And yet, his
younger brother is greater than he, and his
seed is to become the completeness of the
nations.”
20 And he blessed them on that day, saying, “In you Yisra’ěl shall bless, saying,
‘Elohim make you as Ephrayim and as
Menashsheh!’ ” Thus he put Ephrayim
before Menashsheh.
21 And Yisra’ěl said to Yosěph, “See, I am
dying, but Elohim shall be with you and
bring you back to the land of your fathers.
22 “And I, I have given to you one portion
above your brothers, which I took from the
hand of the Amorite with my sword and
with my bow.”

49 And Yaʿaqoḇ called his sons and
said, “Gather together, so that I
declare to you what is to befall you in the
last days:
2 “Gather together and hear, you sons of
Yaʿaqoḇ, and listen to Yisra’ěl your father.
3 “Re’uḇěn, you are my first-born, my
power and the beginning of my strength,
the excellency of exaltation and the excellency of power.
4 “Boiling like water, you do not excel,
because you went up to your father’s bed,
then you defiled it – he went up to my
couch.
5 “Shimʿon and Lěwi are brothers, their

weapons are implements of violence.
6 "Let my being not enter their council,
let my esteem not be united to their assembly; because they killed a man in their displeasure, and they lamed an ox in pleasure.
7 "Cursed be their displeasure for it is
fierce, and their wrath for it is cruel! I
divide them in Ya'aqoḇ and scatter them in
Yisra'ěl.
8 "You, Yehuḏah, your brothers praise
you; your hand is on the neck of your
enemies; your father's children bow down
before you.
9 "Yehuḏah is a lion's cub; from the prey
you have gone up, my son! He bowed
down, he crouched like a lion. And like a
lion, who does rouse him?
10 "The sceptre shall not turn aside from
Yehuḏah, nor an Inscriber from between
his feet, until Shiloh comes, and to Him is
the obedience of peoples.
11 "Binding his donkey to the vine, and
his donkey's colt to the choice vine, he
washed his garments in wine, and his robes
in the blood of grapes.
12 "His eyes are darker than wine, and his
teeth whiter than milk.
13 "Zeḇulun dwells at the seashore, he is
for a haven for ships, and his border is unto
Tsiḏon.
14 "Yissasḵar is a strong donkey lying
down between two burdens,
15 and he saw that a resting place was
good, and that the land was pleasant, and
he inclined his shoulder to bear a burden,
and became a subject to slave labour.
16 "Dan rightly rules his people as one of
the tribes of Yisra'ěl.
17 "Dan is a serpent by the way, an adder
by the path, that bites the horse's heels so
that its rider falls backward.
18 "I have waited for your deliverance, O
יהוה!
19 "Gaḏ, a raiding band raids him, but he
raids its heel.
20 "Bread from Ashěr is rich, and he gives
delicacies of a sovereign.
21 "Naphtali is a deer let loose, he gives
words of elegance.
22 "Yosěph is an offshoot of a fruit-bearing tree, an offshoot of a fruit-bearing tree
by a fountain, his branches run over a wall.
23 "And the archers have bitterly grieved
him, shot at him and hated him.
24 "But his bow remained in strength, and
the arms of his hands were made strong by
the hands of the Mighty One of Ya'aqoḇ –
from there is the Shepherd, the Stone of
Yisra'ěl –
25 from the Ěl of your father who helps
you, and by the Almighty who blesses you
with blessings of the heavens from above,
blessings of the deep that lies beneath,
blessings of the breasts and of the womb.
26 "The blessings of your father have
excelled the blessings of my ancestors, up
to the limit of the everlasting hills. They
are on the head of Yosěph, and on the
crown of the head of him who was separated from his brothers.
27 "Binyamin is a wolf that tears, in the
morning he eats prey, and at night he
divides the spoil."
28 All these are the twelve tribes of
Yisra'ěl, and this is what their father spoke
to them. And he blessed them, he blessed
each one according to his own blessing.
29 And he commanded them, and said to
them, "I am to be gathered to my people,
bury me with my fathers in the cave that is
in the field of Ephron the Ḥittite,
30 in the cave that is in the field of
Maḵpělah, which is before Mamrě in the
land of Kena'an, which Aḇraham bought
with the field of Ephron the Ḥittite as a
possession for a burial-site.
31 There they buried Aḇraham and Sarah
his wife, there they buried Yitsḥaq and
Riḇqah his wife, and there I buried Lě'ah –
32 the field purchased, and the cave which
is in it, from the sons of Ḥěth."
33 And when Ya'aqoḇ ended commanding
his sons, he drew his feet up into the bed
and breathed his last, and was gathered to
his people.

50 And Yosěph fell on his father's
face, and wept over him, and
kissed him.
2 And Yosěph commanded his servants
the physicians to embalm his father. So the
physicians embalmed Yisra'ěl.

3 And forty days were completed for him, for so are completed the days of embalming. And the Mitsrites wept for him seventy days.

4 And when the days of weeping for him were past, Yosěph spoke to the household of Pharaoh, saying, "If, now, I have found favour in your eyes, please speak in the hearing of Pharaoh, saying,

5 'My father made me swear, saying, "See, I am dying, bury me in my burial-site which I dug for myself in the land of Kenaʽan." And now, please let me go up and bury my father, and return.' "

6 And Pharaoh said, "Go up and bury your father, as he made you swear."

7 And Yosěph went up to bury his father. And with him went up all the servants of Pharaoh, the elders of his house, and all the elders of the land of Mitsrayim,

8 and all the house of Yosěph, and his brothers, and his father's house. Only their little ones, and their flocks, and their herds they left in the land of Goshen.

9 And there went up with him both chariots and horsemen, and it was a very great company.

10 And they came to the threshing-floor of Atad̲, which is beyond the Yarděn, and they lamented there with a great and very heavy lamentation. And he performed seven days of mourning for his father.

11 And when the inhabitants of the land, the Kenaʽanites, saw the mourning at the threshing-floor of Atad̲, they said, "This is a grievous mourning for the Mitsrites." That is why its name was called Ab̲ěl Mitsrayim, which is beyond the Yarděn.

12 And his sons did to him as he had commanded them,

13 for his sons brought him to the land of Kenaʽan, and buried him in the cave of the field of Mak̲pělah, before Mamrě, which Ab̲raham bought with the field from Ephron the Ḥittite as property for a burial-site.

14 And after he had buried his father, Yosěph returned to Mitsrayim, he and his brothers and all who went up with him to bury his father.

15 And when Yosěph's brothers saw that their father was dead, they said, "What if Yosěph hates us, and pays us back all the evil which we did to him?"

16 And they sent word to Yosěph, saying, "Before your father died he commanded, saying,

17 'This is what you are to say to Yosěph, "I beg you, please forgive the transgression of your brothers and their sin, for they did evil to you." ' And now, please forgive the transgression of the servants of the Elohim of your father." And Yosěph wept when they spoke to him.

18 And his brothers also went and fell down before his face, and they said, "See, we are your servants."

19 And Yosěph said to them, "Do not fear, for am I in the place of Elohim?

20 "And you, you intended evil against me, but Elohim intended it for good, in order to do it as it is this day, to keep a great many people alive.

21 "And now, do not fear, I provide for you and your little ones." So he comforted them and spoke kindly to them.

22 And Yosěph dwelt in Mitsrayim, he and his father's household. And Yosěph lived one hundred and ten years.

23 And Yosěph saw Ephrayim's children to the third *generation*. The children of Mak̲ir, son of Menashsheh, were also born on Yosěph's knees.

24 And Yosěph said to his brothers, "I am dying, but Elohim shall certainly visit you and bring you out of this land to the land of which He swore to Ab̲raham, to Yitsḥaq, and to Yaʽaqob̲."

25 And Yosěph made the children of Yisra'ěl swear, saying, "Elohim shall certainly visit you, and you shall bring up my bones from here."

26 And Yosěph died, being one hundred and ten years old. And they embalmed him, and he was placed in a coffin in Mitsrayim.

SHEMOTH

EXODUS

1 And these are the names of the children of Yisra’ěl who came to Mitsrayim with Yaʿaqoḇ, each one with his household:

2 Re’uḇěn, Shimʿon, Lěwi, and Yehuḏah;

3 Yissasḵar, Zeḇulun, and Binyamin;

4 Dan and Naphtali, Gaḏ and Ashěr.

5 And all those who were descendants of Yaʿaqoḇ were seventy beings, as Yosěph was already in Mitsrayim.

6 And Yosěph died, and all his brothers, and all that generation.

7 And the children of Yisra’ěl bore fruit and increased very much, multiplied and became very strong, and the land was filled with them.

8 Then a new sovereign arose over Mitsrayim, who did not know Yosěph,

9 and he said to his people, “See, the people of the children of Yisra’ěl are more and stronger than we,

10 come, let us act wisely towards them, lest they increase, and it shall be when fighting befalls us, that they shall join our enemies and fight against us, and shall go up out of the land.”

11 So they set slave-masters over them to afflict them with their burdens, and they built for Pharaoh supply cities, Pithom and Raʿamses.

12 But the more they afflicted them, the more they increased and grew, and they were in dread of the children of Yisra’ěl.

13 And the Mitsrites made the children of Yisra’ěl serve with harshness,

14 and they made their lives bitter with hard bondage, in mortar, and in brick, and in all kinds of work in the field, all their work which they made them do was with harshness.

15 Then the sovereign of Mitsrayim spoke to the Hebrew midwives, of whom the name of one was Shiphrah and the name of the other Puʿah,

16 and he said, “When you deliver the Hebrew women, and see them on the birth-stools, if it is a son, then you shall put him to death, but if it is a daughter, then she shall live.”

17 But the midwives feared Elohim, and did not do as the sovereign of Mitsrayim commanded them, and kept the male children alive.

18 So the sovereign of Mitsrayim called for the midwives and said to them, “Why have you done this, and kept the male children alive?”

19 And the midwives said to Pharaoh, “Because the Hebrew women are not like the Mitsrian women. For they are lively and give birth before the midwives come to them.”

20 So Elohim was good to the midwives, and the people increased and became very numerous.

21 And it came to be, because the midwives feared Elohim, that He provided households for them.

22 And Pharaoh commanded all his people, saying, “Throw every son who is born into the river, and keep alive every daughter.”

2 And a man of the house of Lěwi went and married a daughter of Lěwi.

2 And the woman conceived and bore a son. And she saw that he was a lovely child, and she hid him three months.

3 And when she could hide him no longer, she took an ark of wicker for him, and coated it with tar and pitch, and put the child in it, and laid it in the reeds by the edge of the river.

4 And his sister stood at a distance, to know what would be done to him.

5 And the daughter of Pharaoh came down to wash herself at the river, and her young women were walking by the riverside. And when she saw the ark among the reeds, she sent her female servant to get it,

6 and opened it and saw the child, and see, the baby wept. So she had compassion on him, and said, "This is one of the children of the Hebrews."

7 And his sister said to Pharaoh's daughter, "Shall I go and call a nurse for you from the Hebrew women to nurse the child for you?"

8 And Pharaoh's daughter said to her, "Go." And the young woman [a] went and called the child's mother.

9 And Pharaoh's daughter said to her, "Take this child away and nurse him for me, then I shall pay your wages." So the woman took the child and nursed him.

10 And the child grew, and she brought him to Pharaoh's daughter, and he became her son. And she called his name Mosheh, saying, "Because I have drawn him out of the water."

11 And in those days it came to be, when Mosheh was grown, that he went out to his brothers and looked at their burdens. And he saw a Mitsrian striking a Hebrew, one of his brothers.

12 So he turned this way and that way, and when he saw no one, he struck the Mitsrian and hid him in the sand.

13 And he went out the second day and saw two Hebrew men fighting, and he said to the one who did the wrong, "Why do you strike your neighbour?"

14 And he said, "Who made you a head and a judge over us? Do you intend to kill me as you killed the Mitsrian?" And Mosheh feared and said, "Truly, the matter is known!"

15 And Pharaoh heard of this matter, and he sought to kill Mosheh. But Mosheh fled from the face of Pharaoh and dwelt in the land of Miḏyan. And he sat down by a well.

16 And the priest of Miḏyan had seven daughters. And they came and drew water, and they filled the troughs to water their father's flock,

17 but the shepherds came and drove them away. Then Mosheh stood up and came to their rescue, and watered their flock.

18 And they came to Reʽu'ĕl [b] their father, and he said, "How is it that you have come so soon today?"

19 And they said, "A Mitsrian rescued us from the hand of the shepherds, and he also drew enough water for us and watered the flock."

20 And he said to his daughters, "And where is he? Why did you leave the man? Call him and let him eat bread."

21 And Mosheh agreed to dwell with the man, and he gave Tsipporah his daughter to Mosheh.

22 And she bore him a son, and he called his name Gĕreshom, for he said, "I have become a sojourner in a foreign land."

23 And it came to be after these many days that the sovereign of Mitsrayim died. And the children of Yisra'ĕl groaned because of the slavery, and they cried out. And their cry came up to Elohim because of the slavery.

24 And Elohim heard their groaning, and Elohim remembered His covenant with Aḇraham, with Yitsḥaq, and with Yaʽaqoḇ.

25 And Elohim looked on the children of Yisra'ĕl, and Elohim knew!

3 And Mosheh was shepherding the flock of Yithro his father-in-law, the priest of Miḏyan. And he led the flock to the back of the wilderness, and came to Ḥorĕḇ, the mountain of Elohim.

2 And the Messenger of יהוה appeared to him in a flame of fire from the midst of a bush. And he looked and saw the bush burning with fire, but the bush was not consumed.

3 And Mosheh said, "Let me turn aside now, and see this great sight, why the bush does not burn."

4 And יהוה saw that he turned aside to see, and Elohim called to him from the midst of the bush and said, "Mosheh! Mosheh!" And he said, "Here I am."

5 And He said, "Do not come near here. Take your sandals off your feet, for the place on which you are standing is set-apart ground."

2a See Explanatory notes: Maiden. *2b* His title was Yithro (Excellency).

6 And He said, "I am the Elohim of your
father, the Elohim of Aḇraham, the Elohim
of Yitsḥaq, and the Elohim of Ya'aqoḇ."
And Mosheh hid his face, for he was afraid
to look at Elohim.
7 And יהוה said, "I have indeed seen the
oppression of My people who are in
Mitsrayim, and have heard their cry
because of their slave-drivers, for I know
their sorrows.
8 "And I have come down to deliver
them from the hand of the Mitsrites, and to
bring them up from that land to a good and
spacious land, to a land flowing with milk
and honey, to the place of the Kena'anites
and the Ḥittites and the Amorites and the
Perizzites and the Ḥiwwites and the
Yeḇusites.
9 "And now, see, the cry of the children
of Yisra'ěl has come to Me, and I have also
seen the oppression with which the
Mitsrites oppress them.
10 "And now, come, I am sending you to
Pharaoh, to bring My people, the children
of Yisra'ěl, out of Mitsrayim."
11 And Mosheh said to Elohim, "Who am
I that I should go to Pharaoh, and that I
should bring the children of Yisra'ěl out of
Mitsrayim?"
12 And He said, "Because I am with you.
And this is to you the sign that I have sent
you: When you have brought the people
out of Mitsrayim, you are to serve Elohim
on this mountain."
13 And Mosheh said to Elohim, "See,
when I come to the children of Yisra'ěl and
say to them, 'The Elohim of your fathers
has sent me to you,' and they say to me,
'What is His Name?' what shall I say to
them?"
14 And Elohim said to Mosheh, "I am that
which I am." [a] And He said, "Thus you
shall say to the children of Yisra'ěl, 'I am
has sent me to you.' "
15 And Elohim said further to Mosheh,
"Thus you are to say to the children of
Yisra'ěl, 'יהוה Elohim of your fathers, the
Elohim of Aḇraham, the Elohim of
Yitsḥaq, and the Elohim of Ya'aqoḇ,
has sent me to you. This is My Name
forever, and this is My remembrance to all
generations.'
16 "Go, and you shall gather the elders of
Yisra'ěl together, and say to them, 'יהוה
Elohim of your fathers, the Elohim of
Aḇraham, of Yitsḥaq, and of Ya'aqoḇ,
appeared to me, saying, "I have indeed
visited you and seen what is done to you
in Mitsrayim;
17 and I say: I am bringing you up out of
the affliction of Mitsrayim to the land of
the Kena'anite and the Ḥittite and the
Amorite and the Perizzite and the Ḥiwwite
and the Yeḇusite, to a land flowing with
milk and honey." '
18 "And they shall listen to your voice.
And you shall come, you and the elders of
Yisra'ěl, to the sovereign of Mitsrayim,
and you shall say to him, 'יהוה Elohim of
the Hebrews has met with us. And now,
please, let us go three days' journey into
the wilderness to slaughter to יהוה our
Elohim.'
19 "But I know that the sovereign of Mitsrayim is not going to let you go, not even
by a strong hand.
20 "And I shall stretch out My hand and
strike Mitsrayim with all My wonders
which I shall do in its midst. And after that
he shall let you go.
21 "And I shall give this people favour
in the eyes of the Mitsrites. And it shall
be, that when you go, you shall not go
empty-handed.
22 "But every woman shall ask from her
neighbour and from the stranger in her
house, objects of silver, and objects of
gold, and garments. And you shall put
them on your sons and on your daughters,
and shall plunder the Mitsrites."

4 And Mosheh answered and said, "And
if they do not believe me, nor listen to
my voice, and say, 'יהוה has not appeared
to you?' "
2 And יהוה said to him, "What is that in

3a The Hebrew text reads: *'eheyeh 'asher 'eheyeh*, the word *'eheyeh* being derived from *hayah* which means *to be, to exist*, but the Aramaic text here in v. 14 reads: *ayah ashar ayah*.

your hand?" And he said, "A rod."

3 And He said, "Throw it on the ground." So he threw it on the ground, and it became a serpent. And Mosheh fled from it.

4 And יהוה said to Mosheh, "Reach out your hand and seize it by the tail" – so he reached out his hand and took hold of it, and it became a rod in his hand –

5 so that they believe that יהוה Elohim of their fathers, the Elohim of Aḇraham, the Elohim of Yitsḥaq, and the Elohim of Ya'aqoḇ, has appeared to you."

6 And יהוה said to him again, "Now put your hand in your bosom." And he put his hand in his bosom, and when he took it out, and see, his hand was leprous, like snow.

7 And He said, "Put your hand in your bosom again." So he put his hand in his bosom again, and drew it out of his bosom, and see, it was restored like his other flesh.

8 "And it shall be, if they do not believe you, nor listen to the voice of the first sign, they shall believe the voice of the latter sign.

9 "And it shall be, if they do not believe even these two signs, or listen to your voice, that you shall take water from the river and pour it on the dry land. And the water which you take from the river shall become blood on the dry land."

10 And Mosheh said to יהוה, "O יהוה, I am not a man of words, neither before nor since You have spoken to Your servant, for I am slow of speech and slow of tongue."

11 And יהוה said to him, "Who has made man's mouth? Or who makes dumb, or deaf, or seeing, or blind? Is it not I, יהוה?

12 "And now, go, and I shall be with your mouth and teach you what to say."

13 But he said, "O יהוה, please send by the hand of him whom You would send."

14 And the displeasure of יהוה burned against Mosheh, and He said, "Is not Aharon the Lěwite your brother? I know that he speaks well. And see, he is also coming out to meet you. And when he sees you, he shall be glad in his heart.

15 "And you shall speak to him and put the words in his mouth. And I am with your mouth and with his mouth, and I shall teach you what to do.

16 "And he shall speak for you to the people. And it shall be that he shall be a mouth for you, and you shall be an elohim [a] for him.

17 "And take this rod in your hand, with which you shall do the signs."

18 Then Mosheh went and returned to Yether [b] his father-in-law, and said to him, "Please let me go and return to my brothers who are in Mitsrayim to see whether they are still alive." And Yithro [c] said to Mosheh, "Go in peace."

19 And יהוה said to Mosheh in Miḏyan, "Go, return to Mitsrayim, for all the men are dead who sought your life."

20 So Mosheh took his wife and his sons and set them on a donkey, and he returned to the land of Mitsrayim. And Mosheh took the rod of Elohim in his hand.

21 And יהוה said to Mosheh, "As you go back to Mitsrayim, see that you do all those wonders before Pharaoh which I have put in your hand. But I am going to strengthen his heart, so that he does not let the people go.

22 "And you shall say to Pharaoh, 'Thus said יהוה, "Yisra'ěl is My son, My first-born,

23 so I say to you, let My son go to serve Me. But if you refuse to let him go, see, I am killing your son, your first-born." ' "

24 And it came to be on the way, in the lodging place, that יהוה met him and sought to kill him.

25 And Tsipporah took a sharp stone and cut off the foreskin of her son and threw it at Mosheh's feet, and said, "You are indeed a bridegroom of blood to me!"

26 So He let him go. Then she said, "You are a bridegroom of blood," because of the circumcision.

27 And יהוה said to Aharon, "Go to meet Mosheh in the wilderness." And he went and met him on the mountain of Elohim, and kissed him.

28 Mosheh then told Aharon all the words

4a Or *mighty one*. *4b* A title meaning "Excellency." *4c* A title meaning "his Excellency."

of יהוה who had sent him, and all the signs
which He had commanded him.
29 And Mosheh went with Aharon and
gathered together all the elders of the children of Yisra'ěl.
30 And Aharon spoke all the words which
יהוה had spoken to Mosheh. Then he did
the signs before the eyes of the people.
31 And the people believed. And they
heard that יהוה had visited the children of
Yisra'ěl and that He had looked on their
affliction, and they bowed their heads and
did obeisance.

5 And afterwards Mosheh and Aharon
went in and said to Pharaoh, "Thus
said יהוה Elohim of Yisra'ěl, 'Let My
people go, so that they celebrate a festival
to Me in the wilderness.' "
2 And Pharaoh said, "Who is יהוה, that I
should obey His voice to let Yisra'ěl go? I
do not know יהוה, nor am I going to let
Yisra'ěl go."
3 And they said, "The Elohim of the
Hebrews has met with us. Please, let us go
three days' journey into the wilderness and
slaughter to יהוה our Elohim, lest He fall
upon us with pestilence or with the
sword."
4 But the sovereign of Mitsrayim said to
them, "Mosheh and Aharon, why do you
take the people from their work? Get back
to your burdens."
5 And Pharaoh said, "See, the people of
the land are many now, and you make
them cease from their burdens!"
6 And the same day Pharaoh commanded
the slave-drivers of the people and their
foremen, saying,
7 "You are no longer to give the people
straw to make bricks as before. Let them
go and gather straw for themselves.
8 "And lay on them the required amount
of bricks which they made before, do not
diminish it. For they are idle, that is why
they cry out, saying, 'Let us go and slaughter to our Elohim.'
9 "Let more work be laid on the men, so
that they labour in it, and not pay attention
to words of falsehood."
10 And the slave-drivers of the people and
their foremen went out and spoke to the
people, saying, "Thus said Pharaoh, 'I do
not give you straw.
11 'Go, take straw for yourselves, where
ever you find it, for your work shall not be
diminished.' "
12 And the people were scattered in all the
land of Mitsrayim – to gather stubble for
straw.
13 And the slave-drivers were hurrying
them on, saying, "Fulfill your actions, your
daily matters, as when there was straw."
14 Also the foremen of the children of
Yisra'ěl, whom Pharaoh's slave-drivers
had set over them, were struck and were
asked, "Why have you not fulfilled your
law in making bricks both yesterday and
today, as before?"
15 And the foremen of the children of
Yisra'ěl came and cried out to Pharaoh,
saying, "Why do you treat your servants
this way?
16 "There is no straw given to your servants, and they say to us, 'Make bricks!'
And see, your servants are struck, but your
own people are at fault."
17 But he said, "You are idle! You are idle!
That is why you say, 'Let us go and
slaughter to יהוה.'
18 "So now go, work. And straw is not
given to you, but deliver the amount of
bricks."
19 And the foremen of the children of
Yisra'ěl saw that they were in trouble after
it was said, "You are not to diminish your
daily amount of bricks."
20 And when they came out from Pharaoh,
they met Mosheh and Aharon who stood
there to meet them.
21 And they said to them, "Let יהוה look
on you and judge, because you have made
us loathsome in the eyes of Pharaoh and in
the eyes of his servants, to give a sword in
their hand to kill us."
22 And Mosheh returned to יהוה and said,
"יהוה, why have You done evil to this
people? Why did You send me?
23 "For ever since I came to Pharaoh to
speak in Your Name, he has done evil to
this people. And You have not delivered
Your people at all."

6 And יהוה said to Mosheh, "Now see
what I do to Pharaoh, for with a strong
hand he is going to let them go, and with a
strong hand he is going to drive them out
of his land."
2 And Elohim spoke to Mosheh and said
to him, "I am יהוה.
3 "And I appeared to Aḇraham, to
Yitsḥaq, and to Yaʽaqoḇ, as Ěl Shaddai.
And by My Name, יהוה, was I not known
to them?
4 "And I also established My covenant
with them, to give them the land of
Kenaʽan, the land of their sojournings, in
which they have sojourned.
5 "And I have also heard the groaning of
the children of Yisra'ěl whom the Mitsrites
are enslaving, and I have remembered My
covenant.
6 "Say, therefore, to the children of
Yisra'ěl, 'I am יהוה, and I shall bring you
out from under the burdens of the
Mitsrites, and shall deliver you from their
enslaving, and shall redeem you with an
outstretched arm, and with great judgments,
7 and shall take you as My people, and I
shall be your Elohim. And you shall know
that I am יהוה your Elohim who is bringing you out from under the burdens of the
Mitsrites.
8 'And I shall bring you into the land
which I swore to give to Aḇraham, to
Yitsḥaq, and to Yaʽaqoḇ, to give it to you
as an inheritance. I am יהוה.' "
9 And Mosheh spoke thus to the children
of Yisra'ěl, but they did not listen to
Mosheh, because of shortness of spirit, and
from hard slavery.
10 And יהוה spoke to Mosheh, saying,
11 "Go in, speak to Pharaoh sovereign of
Mitsrayim, to let the children of Yisra'ěl
go out of his land."
12 And Mosheh spoke before יהוה,
saying, "The children of Yisra'ěl have not
listened to me, and why would Pharaoh listen to me, for I am of uncircumcised lips?"
13 And יהוה spoke to Mosheh and to
Aharon, and gave them a command for the
children of Yisra'ěl and for Pharaoh, sovereign of Mitsrayim, to bring the children
of Yisra'ěl out of the land of Mitsrayim.
14 These are the heads of their fathers'
houses: The sons of Re'uḇěn, the first-born
of Yisra'ěl: Ḥanoḵ and Pallu, Ḥetsron and
Karmi. These are the clans of Re'uḇěn.
15 And the sons of Shimʽon: Yemu'ěl, and
Yamin, and Ohaḏ, and Yaḵin, and Tsoḥar,
and Sha'ul the son of a Kenaʽanite woman.
These are the clans of Shimʽon.
16 These are the names of the sons of
Lěwi according to their generations:
Gěrshon, and Qehath, and Merari. And the
years of the life of Lěwi were one hundred
and thirty-seven.
17 The sons of Gěrshon: Liḇni and Shimʽi
according to their clans.
18 And the sons of Qehath: Amram, and
Yitshar, and Ḥeḇron, and Uzzi'ěl. And the
years of the life of Qehath were one hundred and thirty-three.
19 And the sons of Merari: Maḥli and
Mushi. These are the clans of Lěwi according to their generations.
20 And Amram took for himself Yoḵeḇeḏ,
his father's sister, as wife. And she bore
him Aharon and Mosheh. And the years of
the life of Amram were one hundred and
thirty-seven.
21 And the sons of Yitshar: Qoraḥ, and
Nepheḡ, and Ziḵri.
22 And the sons of Uzzi'ěl: Misha'ěl, and
Eltsaphan, and Sithri.
23 Aharon took to himself Elisheḇa,
daughter of Amminaḏaḇ, sister of
Naḥshon, as wife. And she bore him
Naḏaḇ, and Aḇihu, Elʽazar, and Ithamar.
24 And the sons of Qoraḥ: Assir, Elqanah,
and Aḇiyasaph. These are the clans of the
Qorḥites.
25 And Elʽazar, Aharon's son, took for
himself one of the daughters of Puti'ěl as
wife. And she bore him Pineḥas. These are
the heads of the fathers of the Lěwites
according to their clans.
26 This is Aharon, and Mosheh, to whom
יהוה said, "Bring out the children of
Yisra'ěl from the land of Mitsrayim
according to their divisions."
27 They were the ones who spoke to
Pharaoh sovereign of Mitsrayim, to bring
out the children of Yisra'ěl from Mits-

rayim. This is Mosheh, and Aharon.
28 And it came to be, on the day when
יהוה spoke to Mosheh in the land of
Mitsrayim,
29 that יהוה spoke to Mosheh, saying,
"I am יהוה. Speak to Pharaoh sovereign
of Mitsrayim all that I say to you."
30 And Mosheh said before יהוה, "See, I
am of uncircumcised lips, and why would
Pharaoh listen to me?"

7 So יהוה said to Mosheh, "See, I have
made you an elohim [a] to Pharaoh, and
Aharon your brother is your prophet.
2 "You shall speak all that I command
you, and Aharon your brother shall speak
to Pharaoh, to let the children of Yisra'ĕl
go out of his land.
3 "But I am going to harden the heart of
Pharaoh, and shall increase My signs and
My wonders in the land of Mitsrayim.
4 "And Pharaoh is not going to listen to
you, and I shall lay My hand on Mitsrayim,
and bring My divisions and My people, the
children of Yisra'ĕl, out of the land of
Mitsrayim by great judgments.
5 "And the Mitsrites shall know that I am
יהוה, when I stretch out My hand on
Mitsrayim. And I shall bring the children
of Yisra'ĕl out from among them."
6 And Mosheh and Aharon did as יהוה
commanded them, so they did.
7 Now Mosheh was eighty years old and
Aharon eighty-three years old when they
spoke to Pharaoh.
8 And יהוה spoke to Mosheh and to
Aharon, saying,
9 "When Pharaoh speaks to you, saying,
'Show a miracle for yourselves,' then you
shall say to Aharon, 'Take your rod and
throw it before Pharaoh, and let it become
a serpent.' "
10 So Mosheh and Aharon went in to
Pharaoh, and they did so, as יהוה commanded. And Aharon threw his rod before
Pharaoh and before his servants, and it
became a serpent.
11 But Pharaoh also called the wise men
and the practisers of witchcraft. And they,
the magicians of Mitsrayim, also did so
with their magic.
12 And they, each one, threw down his
rod, and they became serpents. But the rod
of Aharon swallowed up their rods.
13 And Pharaoh's heart was strengthened,
and he did not listen to them, as יהוה had
said.
14 And יהוה said to Mosheh, "The heart
of Pharaoh is hard, he refuses to let the
people go.
15 "Go to Pharaoh in the morning, as he
goes out to the water, and you shall stand
by the river's bank to meet him. And take
in your hand the rod which was turned into
a serpent.
16 "And you shall say to him, 'יהוה the
Elohim of the Hebrews has sent me to you,
saying, "Let My people go, so that they
serve Me in the wilderness," but see, until
now you have not listened!
17 'Thus said יהוה, "By this you know
that I am יהוה. See, I am striking the
waters which are in the river with the rod
that is in my hand, and they shall be turned
to blood,
18 and the fish in the river shall die. And
the river shall stink, and the Mitsrites shall
find it impossible to drink the water of the
river." ' "
19 And יהוה spoke to Mosheh, "Say to
Aharon, 'Take your rod and stretch out
your hand over the waters of Mitsrayim,
over their streams, over their rivers, over
their ponds, and over all their pools of
water, that they become blood. And there
shall be blood in all the land of Mitsrayim,
both in wooden and in stone *containers*.' "
20 And Mosheh and Aharon did so, as
יהוה commanded. And he lifted up the rod
and struck the waters that were in the river,
in the eyes of Pharaoh and in the eyes of
his servants. And all the waters that were
in the river were turned to blood.
21 And the fish that were in the river died,
and the river stank, and the Mitsrites were
unable to drink the water of the river. And
the blood was in all the land of Mitsrayim.
22 And the magicians of Mitsrayim did the

7a Or *mighty one* – see footnote at 4:16.

same with their magic. And the heart of
Pharaoh was strengthened, and he did not
listen to them, as יהוה had said.
23 And Pharaoh turned and went into his
house, and his heart was not moved by this
either.
24 And all the Mitsrites dug all around the
river for water to drink, for they were
unable to drink the water of the river.
25 And seven days were completed after
יהוה had struck the river.

8 And יהוה spoke to Mosheh, "Go to
Pharaoh and say to him, 'Thus said
יהוה, "Let My people go, so that they
serve Me.
2 "But if you refuse to let them go, see,
I am smiting all your border with frogs.
3 "And the river shall swarm with frogs,
which shall go up and shall come into your
house, and into your bedroom, and on your
bed, and into the houses of your servants,
and on your people, and into your ovens,
and into your kneading bowls,
4 and the frogs shall come up on you and
on your people and on all your servants." ' "
5 And יהוה said to Mosheh, "Say to
Aharon, 'Stretch out your hand with your
rod over the streams, over the rivers, and
over the ponds, and cause frogs to come up
on the land of Mitsrayim.' "
6 So Aharon stretched out his hand over
the waters of Mitsrayim, and the frogs
came up, and covered the land of Mitsrayim.
7 And the magicians did so with their
magic, and brought up frogs on the land of
Mitsrayim.
8 Pharaoh then called for Mosheh and
Aharon, and said, "Pray to יהוה to take
away the frogs from me and from my
people, and I shall let the people go to
slaughter to יהוה."
9 And Mosheh said to Pharaoh, "Explain
yourself to me: When am I to pray for you,
and for your servants, and for your people,
to destroy the frogs from you and your
houses, and remain only in the river?"
10 So he said, "Tomorrow." And he said,
"Let it be according to your word, so that
you know that there is no one like יהוה our
Elohim.
11 "And the frogs shall turn aside from
you, and from your houses, and from your
servants, and from your people – they shall
remain in the river only."
12 And Mosheh and Aharon went out
from Pharaoh. And Mosheh cried out to
יהוה concerning the frogs which He had
brought against Pharaoh.
13 And יהוה did according to the word of
Mosheh. And the frogs died out of the
houses, out of the courtyards, and out of
the fields.
14 And they gathered them together in
heaps, and the land stank.
15 And when Pharaoh saw that there was
relief, he hardened his heart and did not
listen to them, as יהוה had said.
16 And יהוה said to Mosheh, "Say to
Aharon, 'Stretch out your rod, and strike
the dust of the land, so that it becomes
gnats in all the land of Mitsrayim.' "
17 And they did so, and Aharon stretched
out his hand with his rod and struck the
dust of the earth, and it became gnats on
man and beast. All the dust of the land
became gnats in all the land of Mitsrayim.
18 And the magicians did similarly with
their magic to bring forth gnats, but they
were unable. And there were gnats on man
and beast.
19 The magicians then said to Pharaoh,
"This is the finger of Elohim!" But the
heart of Pharaoh was strengthened, and he
did not listen to them, as יהוה had said.
20 And יהוה said to Mosheh, "Rise early
in the morning and stand before Pharaoh as
he comes out to the water, and say to him,
'Thus said יהוה, "Let My people go, so
that they serve Me.
21 "Or else, if you do not let My people
go, see, I am sending swarms of flies on
you and your servants, and on your people
and into your houses. And the houses of
the Mitsrites shall be filled with swarms of
flies, and also the ground on which they
stand.
22 "And in that day I shall separate the
land of Goshen, in which My people dwell,
that no swarms of flies shall be there, so
that you know that I am יהוה in the midst

of the land.
23 “And I shall put a ransom between My
people and your people. Tomorrow this
sign shall be.” ’ ”
24 And יהוה did so, and thick swarms of
flies came into the house of Pharaoh, and
into his servants’ houses, and into all the
land of Mitsrayim, and the land was ruined
because of the swarms of flies.
25 Pharaoh then called for Mosheh and
Aharon, and said, “Go, slaughter to your
Elohim in the land.”
26 And Mosheh said, “It is not right to do
so, for we would be slaughtering the
abomination of the Mitsrites to יהוה our
Elohim. See, if we slaughter the abomination of the Mitsrites before their eyes,
would they not stone us?
27 “Let us go three days’ journey into the
wilderness, then we shall slaughter to יהוה
our Elohim, as He commands us.”
28 And Pharaoh said, “I am letting you go,
then you shall slaughter to יהוה your
Elohim in the wilderness. Only, do not go
very far away! Pray for me.”
29 And Mosheh said, “See, when I leave
you I shall pray to יהוה, and tomorrow the
swarms of flies shall depart from Pharaoh,
from his servants, and from his people. But
do not let Pharaoh again deceive, not to let
the people go to slaughter to יהוה.”
30 And Mosheh went out from Pharaoh
and prayed to יהוה.
31 And יהוה did according to the word of
Mosheh and removed the swarms of flies
from Pharaoh, from his servants, and from
his people. Not one remained.
32 But Pharaoh hardened his heart at this
time too, and did not let the people go.

9 And יהוה said to Mosheh, “Go in to
Pharaoh and speak to him, ‘Thus said
יהוה Elohim of the Hebrews, “Let My
people go, so that they serve Me.
2 “For if you refuse to let them go, and
are still holding them,
3 see, the hand of יהוה is on your livestock in the field, on the horses, on the
donkeys, on the camels, on the cattle, and
on the sheep – a very grievous pestilence.
4 “And יהוה shall separate between the
livestock of Yisra’ĕl and the livestock of
Mitsrayim, and let no matter die of all that
belongs to the children of Yisra’ĕl.” ’ ”
5 And יהוה set an appointed time, saying, “Tomorrow יהוה is going to do this
word in the land.”
6 And יהוה did this word on the next day,
and all the livestock of Mitsrayim died, but
of the livestock of the children of Yisra’ĕl,
not one died.
7 Then Pharaoh sent, and see, not even
one of the livestock of Yisra’ĕl was dead.
But the heart of Pharaoh was hardened,
and he did not let the people go.
8 And יהוה said to Mosheh and Aharon,
“Fill your hands with ashes from a furnace
and let Mosheh scatter it toward the heavens before the eyes of Pharaoh.
9 “And it shall become fine dust in all the
land of Mitsrayim, and it shall cause boils
that break out in sores on man and beast in
all the land of Mitsrayim.”
10 So they took ashes from the furnace
and stood before Pharaoh, and Mosheh
scattered them toward the heavens. And
they caused boils, breaking out in sores on
man and beast.
11 And the magicians were unable to stand
before Mosheh because of the boils, for the
boils were on the magicians and on all the
Mitsrites.
12 But יהוה strengthened the heart of
Pharaoh, and he did not listen to them, as
יהוה had said to Mosheh.
13 And יהוה said to Mosheh, “Rise early
in the morning and stand before Pharaoh,
and say to him, ‘Thus said יהוה Elohim of
the Hebrews, “Let My people go, so that
they serve Me,
14 for at this time I am sending all My
plagues unto your heart, and on your
servants and on your people, so that you
know that there is no one like Me in all the
earth.
15 “Now if I had stretched out My hand
and struck you and your people with pestilence, then you would have been cut off
from the earth.
16 “And for this reason I have raised you
up, in order to show you My power, and in
order to declare My Name in all the earth.

17 "You still exalt yourself against My
people in that you do not let them go!
18 "See, tomorrow about this time I am
causing very heavy hail to rain down, such
as has not been in Mitsrayim, from the day
of its founding until now.
19 "And now send, bring your livestock
to safety, and all that you have in the field,
for the hail shall come down on every man
and every beast which is found in the field
and is not brought home, and they shall
die." ' "
20 Those among the servants of Pharaoh
who feared the word of יהוה made their
servants and livestock flee to the houses.
21 But those who did not set their heart on
the word of יהוה left their servants and
livestock in the field.
22 Then יהוה said to Mosheh, "Stretch out
your hand toward the heavens, and let
there be hail in all the land of Mitsrayim –
on man, and on beast, and on every plant
of the field, throughout the land of
Mitsrayim."
23 Then Mosheh stretched out his rod
toward the heavens. And יהוה sent thunder
and hail, and fire came down to the earth.
And יהוה rained hail on the land of
Mitsrayim.
24 Thus there came to be hail, and fire
flashing continually in the midst of the
hail, very heavy, such as had not been in all
the land of Mitsrayim since it became a
nation.
25 And the hail struck in all the land of
Mitsrayim all that was in the field, both
man and beast. And the hail struck every
plant of the field and broke every tree of
the field.
26 Only in the land of Goshen, where the
children of Yisra'ěl were, there was no
hail.
27 Pharaoh then sent and called for
Mosheh and for Aharon, and said to them,
"I have sinned this time. יהוה is righteous,
and my people and I are wrong.
28 "Pray to יהוה, for there has been
enough of the thunder and hail of Elohim.
And I am letting you go, so that you stay
no longer."
29 And Mosheh said to him, "As soon as I
go out of the city, let me spread out my
hands to יהוה, let the thunder cease and the
hail be no more, so that you know that the
earth belongs to יהוה.
30 "But as for you and your servants,
I know that you do not yet fear before יהוה
Elohim."
31 And the flax and the barley were
struck, for the barley was in the head and
the flax was in bud.
32 But the wheat and the spelt were not
struck, for they were late crops.
33 And Mosheh went out of the city from
Pharaoh and spread out his hands to יהוה,
and the thunder and the hail ceased, and
the rain was not poured on the earth.
34 And Pharaoh saw that the rain, and the
hail, and the thunder had ceased, yet he
sinned again and he hardened his heart, he
and his servants.
35 And the heart of Pharaoh was strengthened, and he did not let the children of
Yisra'ěl go, as יהוה had said through
Mosheh.

10 And יהוה said to Mosheh, "Go in
to Pharaoh, for I have hardened his
heart and the hearts of his servants, so that
I show these signs of Mine before him,
2 and that you relate in the hearing of
your son and your son's son what I have
done in Mitsrayim, and My signs which I
have done among them. And you shall
know that I am יהוה."
3 And Mosheh and Aharon came in to
Pharaoh and said to him, "Thus said יהוה
Elohim of the Hebrews, 'Till when shall
you refuse to humble yourself before Me?
Let My people go, so that they serve Me.
4 'Or else, if you refuse to let My people
go, see, tomorrow I am bringing locusts
within your borders.
5 'And they shall cover the surface of the
land, so that no one is able to see the land.
And they shall eat the rest of what has
escaped, which remains to you from the
hail, and they shall eat every tree which
grows up for you out of the field.
6 'And they shall fill your houses, and
the houses of all your servants, and the
houses of all the Mitsrites, which neither

your fathers nor your fathers' fathers have seen, since the day that they were on the earth to this day.' " Then he turned and went out from Pharaoh.

7 And Pharaoh's servants said to him, "Till when would this one be a snare to us? Let the men go, so that they serve יהוה their Elohim. Do you not yet know that Mitsrayim is destroyed?"

8 And Mosheh and Aharon were brought back to Pharaoh, and he said to them, "Go, serve יהוה your Elohim. Who are the ones that are going?"

9 And Mosheh said, "We are going with our young and our old, with our sons and our daughters, with our flocks and our herds we are going, for we have a festival to יהוה."

10 And he said to them, "Let יהוה be with you as I let you and your little ones go! Watch, for evil is before your face!

11 "Not so! You men go now, and serve יהוה, for that is what you desired." And they were driven out from the presence of Pharaoh.

12 And יהוה said to Mosheh, "Stretch out your hand over the land of Mitsrayim for the locusts to come upon the land of Mitsrayim, and eat every plant of the land – all that the hail has left."

13 And Mosheh stretched out his rod over the land of Mitsrayim, and יהוה brought an east wind on the land all that day and all that night. Morning came, and the east wind brought the locusts.

14 And the locusts went up over all the land of Mitsrayim and settled within all the borders of Mitsrayim, very grievous. There had never been locusts like them before, nor would there again be like them.

15 And they covered the surface of all the land, so that the land was darkened. And they ate every plant of the land and all the fruit of the trees which the hail had left, and no greenness was left on the trees or on the plants of the field, in all the land of Mitsrayim.

16 Pharaoh then called for Mosheh and Aharon in haste, and said, "I have sinned against יהוה your Elohim and against you.

17 "And now, please forgive my sin only this once, and pray to יהוה your Elohim, that He would only turn away this death from me."

18 And he went out from Pharaoh and prayed to יהוה.

19 And יהוה turned a very strong west wind, which took the locusts away and blew them into the Sea of Reeds. Not one locust was left within all the border of Mitsrayim.

20 However, יהוה strengthened the heart of Pharaoh, and he did not let the children of Yisra'ěl go.

21 And יהוה said to Mosheh, "Stretch out your hand toward the heavens, and let there be darkness over the land of Mitsrayim, even a darkness which is felt."

22 And Mosheh stretched out his hand toward the heavens, and there was thick darkness in all the land of Mitsrayim for three days.

23 They did not see one another, nor did anyone rise from his place for three days, while all the children of Yisra'ěl had light in their dwellings.

24 And Pharaoh called to Mosheh and said, "Go, serve יהוה, only leave your flocks and your herds behind. Let your little ones go with you too."

25 But Mosheh said, "You yourself are to provide us with slaughterings and ascending offerings, to prepare for יהוה our Elohim.

26 "And our livestock are to go with us too, not a hoof is to be left behind, for we have to take some of them to serve יהוה our Elohim, and we ourselves do not know with what we are to serve יהוה until we come there."

27 However, יהוה strengthened the heart of Pharaoh, and he would not let them go.

28 And Pharaoh said to him, "Get away from me! Watch yourself and see my face no more, for in the day you see my face you die!"

29 And Mosheh said, "You have spoken rightly – never again do I see your face!"

11 And יהוה said to Mosheh, "I am bringing yet one more plague on Pharaoh and on Mitsrayim. After that he is

going to let you go from here. When he lets you go, he shall drive you out from here altogether.

2 “Speak now in the hearing of the people, and let every man ask from his neighbour and every woman from her neighbour, objects of silver and objects of gold.”

3 And יהוה gave the people favour in the eyes of the Mitsrites. And the man Mosheh was very great in the land of Mitsrayim, in the eyes of Pharaoh’s servants and in the eyes of the people.

4 And Mosheh said, “Thus said יהוה, ‘About midnight I am going out into the midst of Mitsrayim,

5 and all the first-born in the land of Mitsrayim shall die, from the first-born of Pharaoh who sits on his throne, even to the first-born of the female servant who is behind the handmill, and all the first-born of cattle.

6 ‘And there shall be a great cry throughout all the land of Mitsrayim, such as has never been or ever shall be again.

7 ‘But against any of the children of Yisra’ěl no dog shall move its tongue, against man or against beast, so that you know that יהוה makes distinction between Mitsrayim and Yisra’ěl.’

8 “And all these servants of yours shall come down to me and bow down to me, saying, ‘Get out, you and all the people at your feet!’ And after that I shall go out.” And he went out from Pharaoh in great displeasure.

9 But יהוה said to Mosheh, “Pharaoh is not going to listen to you, in order to multiply My wonders in the land of Mitsrayim.”

10 And Mosheh and Aharon did all these wonders before Pharaoh, however, יהוה strengthened the heart of Pharaoh, and he did not let the children of Yisra’ěl go out of his land.

12 And יהוה spoke to Mosheh and to Aharon in the land of Mitsrayim, saying,

2 “This new *moon* is the beginning of new *moons* for you, it is the first new *moon* of the year for you.

3 “Speak to all the congregation of Yisra’ěl, saying, ‘On the tenth day of this new *moon* each one of them is to take for himself a lamb, according to the house of his father, a lamb for a household.

4 ‘And if the household is too small for the lamb, let him and his neighbour next to his house take it according to the number of the beings, according to each man’s need you make your count for the lamb.

5 ‘Let the lamb be a perfect one, a year old male. Take it from the sheep or from the goats.

6 ‘And you shall keep it until the fourteenth day of the same new *moon*. Then all the assembly of the congregation of Yisra’ěl shall slay it between the evenings.

7 ‘And they shall take some of the blood and put it on the two doorposts and on the lintel of the houses where they eat it.

8 ‘And they shall eat the flesh on that night, roasted in fire – with unleavened bread and with bitter herbs they shall eat it.

9 ‘Do not eat it raw, nor boiled at all with water, but roasted in fire, its head with its legs and its inward parts.

10 ‘And do not leave of it until morning, and what remains of it until morning you are to burn with fire.

11 ‘And this is how you eat it: your loins girded, your sandals on your feet, and your staff in your hand. And you shall eat it in haste. It is the Pěsaḥ [a] of יהוה.

12 ‘And I shall pass through the land of Mitsrayim on that night, and shall strike all the first-born in the land of Mitsrayim, both man and beast. And on all the mighty ones of Mitsrayim I shall execute judgment. I am יהוה.

13 ‘And the blood shall be a sign for you on the houses where you are. And when I see the blood, I shall pass over you, and let the plague not come on you to destroy you when I strike the land of Mitsrayim.

14 ‘And this day shall become to you a remembrance. And you shall celebrate it as a festival to יהוה throughout your

12a - Pěsaḥ - See Explanatory notes - Passover.

generations – celebrate it as a festival, an
everlasting law.
15 'Seven days you shall eat unleavened
bread. Indeed on the first day you cause
leaven to cease from your houses. For
whoever eats leavened bread from the first
day until the seventh day, that being shall
be cut off from Yisra'ěl.
16 'And on the first day is a set-apart gathering, and on the seventh day you have a
set-apart gathering. No work at all is done
on them, only that which is eaten by every
being, that alone is prepared by you.
17 'And you shall guard the *Festival of*
Matzot,[b] for on this same day I brought
your divisions out of the land of
Mitsrayim. And you shall guard this day
throughout your generations, an everlasting law.
18 'In the first *month*, on the fourteenth
day of the new *moon*, in the evening, you
shall eat unleavened bread until the twenty-first day of the new *moon* in the
evening.
19 'For seven days no leaven is to be
found in your houses, for if anyone eats
what is leavened, that same being shall be
cut off from the congregation of Yisra'ěl,
whether sojourner or native of the land.
20 'Do not eat that which is leavened – in
all your dwellings you are to eat unleavened bread.' "
21 And Mosheh called for all the elders of
Yisra'ěl and said to them, "Go out and take
lambs for yourselves according to your
clans, and slay the Pěsaḥ.
22 "And you shall take a bunch of hyssop,
and dip it in the blood that is in the basin,
and strike the lintel and the two doorposts
with the blood that is in the basin, and you,
none of you shall go out of the door of his
house until morning.
23 "And יהוה shall pass on to smite the
Mitsrites, and shall see the blood on the
lintel and on the two doorposts, and יהוה
shall pass over the door and not allow the
destroyer to come into your houses to
smite you.
24 "And you shall guard this word as a law
for you and your sons, forever.
25 "And it shall be, when you come to the
land which יהוה gives you, as He
promised, that you shall guard this service.
26 "And it shall be, when your children
say to you, 'What does this service mean
to you?'
27 then you shall say, 'It is the Pěsaḥ
slaughtering of יהוה, who passed over the
houses of the children of Yisra'ěl in Mitsrayim when He smote the Mitsrites and
delivered our households.' " And the people bowed their heads and did obeisance.
28 And the children of Yisra'ěl went away
and did so – as יהוה had commanded
Mosheh and Aharon, so they did.
29 And it came to be at midnight that יהוה
struck all the first-born in the land of
Mitsrayim, from the first-born of Pharaoh
who sat on his throne to the first-born of
the captive who was in the dungeon, and
all the first-born of livestock.
30 And Pharaoh rose up in the night, he
and all his servants, and all the Mitsrites.
And there was a great cry in Mitsrayim, for
there was not a house where there was not
a dead one.
31 Then he called for Mosheh and Aharon
by night, and said, "Arise, go out from the
midst of my people, both you and the
children of Yisra'ěl. And go, serve יהוה as
you have said.
32 "Take both your flocks and your herds,
as you have said, and go. Then you shall
bless me too."
33 And the Mitsrites were strong on the
people, to hasten to send them away out of
the land. For they said, "We are all dying!"
34 And the people took their dough before
it was leavened, having their kneading
bowls bound up in their garments on their
shoulders.
35 And the children of Yisra'ěl had done
according to the word of Mosheh, and they
had asked from the Mitsrites objects of
silver, and objects of gold, and garments.
36 And יהוה gave the people favour in the
eyes of the Mitsrites, so that they gave
them what they asked, and they plundered

12b - Unleavened Bread

the Mitsrites.
37 And the children of Yisra'ĕl set out
from Ra'meses to Sukkoth, about six
hundred thousand men on foot, besides the
little ones.
38 And a mixed multitude went up with
them too, also flocks and herds, very much
livestock.
39 And they baked unleavened cakes of
the dough which they had brought out of
Mitsrayim, for it was not leavened, since
they were driven out of Mitsrayim, and
had not been able to delay, nor had they
prepared food for themselves.
40 And the sojourn of the children of
Yisra'ĕl who lived in Mitsrayim was four
hundred and thirty years.
41 And it came to be at the end of the four
hundred and thirty years, on that same day
it came to be that all the divisions of יהוה
went out from the land of Mitsrayim.
42 It is a night of watches unto יהוה for
bringing them out of the land of Mitsrayim. This is that night of watches unto
יהוה, for all the children of Yisra'ĕl
throughout their generations.
43 And יהוה said to Mosheh and Aharon,
"This is the law of the Pĕsaḥ: No son of a
stranger is to eat of it,
44 but any servant a man has bought for
silver, when you have circumcised him,
then let him eat of it.
45 "A sojourner and a hired servant does
not eat of it.
46 "It is eaten in one house, you are not to
take any of the flesh outside the house, nor
are you to break any bone of it.
47 "All the congregation of Yisra'ĕl are to
perform it.
48 "And when a stranger sojourns with
you and shall perform the Pĕsaḥ to יהוה,
let all his males be circumcised, and then
let him come near and perform it, and he
shall be as a native of the land. But let no
uncircumcised eat of it.
49 "There is one Torah for the native-born
and for the stranger who sojourns among
you."
50 And all the children of Yisra'ĕl did as
יהוה commanded Mosheh and Aharon, so
they did.
51 And it came to be on that same day that
יהוה brought the children of Yisra'ĕl out of
the land of Mitsrayim according to their
divisions.

13 And יהוה spoke to Mosheh, saying,
2 "Set apart to Me all the first-
born, the one opening the womb among
the children of Yisra'ĕl, among man and
among beast, it is Mine."
3 And Mosheh said to the people,
"Remember this day in which you went
out of Mitsrayim, out of the house of
slavery. For by strength of hand יהוה
brought you out of this place, and whatever is leavened shall not be eaten.
4 "Today you are going out, in the new
moon Aḇiḇ.
5 "And it shall be, when יהוה brings you
into the land of the Kena'anites, and the
Ḥittites, and the Amorites, and the
Ḥiwwites, and the Yeḇusites, which He
swore to your fathers to give you, a land
flowing with milk and honey, that you
shall keep this service in this new *moon*.
6 "Seven days you eat unleavened bread,
and on the seventh day is a festival to יהוה.
7 "Unleavened bread is to be eaten the
seven days, and whatever is leavened is
not to be seen with you, and leaven is not
to be seen with you within all your border.
8 "And you shall inform your son in that
day, saying, 'It is because of what יהוה did
for me when I came up from Mitsrayim.'
9 "And it shall be as a sign to you on
your hand and as a reminder between your
eyes, that the Torah of יהוה is to be in your
mouth, for with a strong hand יהוה has
brought you out of Mitsrayim.
10 "And you shall guard this law at its
appointed time from year to year.
11 "And it shall be, when יהוה brings you
into the land of the Kena'anites, as He
swore to you and your fathers, and gives
it to you,
12 that you shall give over to יהוה every
one opening the womb, and every first-
born that comes from your livestock, the
males belong to יהוה.
13 "But every first-born of a donkey you
are to ransom with a lamb. And if you do

not ransom it, then you shall break its neck. And every first-born of man among your sons you are to ransom.

14 “And it shall be, when your son asks you in time to come, saying, ‘What is this?’ then you shall say to him, ‘By strength of hand יהוה brought us out of Mitsrayim, out of the house of bondage.

15 ‘And it came to be, when Pharaoh was too hardened to let us go, that יהוה killed every first-born in the land of Mitsrayim, both the first-born of man and the first-born of beast. Therefore I am slaughtering to יהוה every male that open the womb, but every first-born of my sons I ransom.’

16 “And it shall be as a sign on your hand and as frontlets between your eyes, for by strength of hand יהוה brought us out of Mitsrayim.”

17 And it came to be, when Pharaoh had let the people go, that Elohim did not lead them by way of the land of the Philistines, though that was nearer, for Elohim said, “Lest the people regret when they see fighting, and return to Mitsrayim.”

18 So Elohim led the people around by way of the wilderness of the Sea of Reeds. And the children of Yisra’ěl went up in fives [a] from the land of Mitsrayim.

19 And Mosheh took the bones of Yosěph with him, for he certainly made the children of Yisra’ěl swear, saying, “Elohim shall certainly visit you, and you shall bring my bones from here with you.”

20 And they departed from Sukkoth and camped in Ětham at the edge of the wilderness.

21 And יהוה went before them by day in a column of cloud to lead the way, and by night in a column of fire to give them light, so as to go by day and night.

22 The column of cloud did not cease by day, nor the column of fire by night, before the people.

14 And יהוה spoke to Mosheh, saying,
2 “Speak to the children of Yisra’ěl, that they turn and camp before Pi Haḥiroth, between Miḡdol and the sea, opposite Ba‘al Tsephon – camp before it by the sea.

3 “For Pharaoh shall say of the children of Yisra’ěl, ‘They are entangled in the land, the wilderness has closed them in.’

4 “And I shall strengthen the heart of Pharaoh, and he shall pursue them. But I am to be esteemed through Pharaoh and over all his army, and the Mitsrites shall know that I am יהוה.” And they did so.

5 And it was reported to the sovereign of Mitsrayim that the people had fled, and the heart of Pharaoh and his servants was turned against the people. And they said, “Why have we done this, that we have let Yisra’ěl go from serving us?”

6 So he made his chariot ready and took his people with him.

7 And he took six hundred choice chariots, and all the chariots of Mitsrayim with officers over all of them.

8 And יהוה strengthened the heart of Pharaoh sovereign of Mitsrayim, and he pursued the children of Yisra’ěl, but the children of Yisra’ěl went out defiantly.

9 And the Mitsrites pursued them, and all the horses and chariots of Pharaoh, and his horsemen and his army, and overtook them camping by the sea beside Pi Haḥiroth, before Ba‘al Tsephon.

10 And when Pharaoh drew near, the children of Yisra’ěl lifted their eyes and saw the Mitsrites coming up after them. And they were greatly afraid, so the children of Yisra’ěl cried out to יהוה.

11 And they said to Mosheh, “Did you take us away to die in the wilderness because there are no burial-sites in Mitsrayim? What is this you have done to us, to bring us up out of Mitsrayim?

12 “Is this not the word that we spoke to you in Mitsrayim, saying, ‘Leave us alone and let us serve the Mitsrites?’ For it would have been better for us to serve the Mitsrites than to die in the wilderness.”

13 And Mosheh said to the people, “Do not be afraid. Stand still, and see the deliverance of יהוה, which He does for you today. For the Mitsrites whom you see

13a Marching formation.

today, you are never, never to see again.
[14]"יהוה does fight for you, and you keep silent."
[15]And יהוה said to Mosheh, "Why do you cry to Me? Speak to the children of Yisra'ěl, and let them go forward.
[16]"And you, lift up your rod, and stretch out your hand over the sea and divide it, and let the children of Yisra'ěl go on dry ground through the midst of the sea.
[17]"And I, see I am strengthening the hearts of the Mitsrites, and they shall follow them. And I am to be esteemed through Pharaoh and over all his army, his chariots, and his horsemen.
[18]"And the Mitsrites shall know that I am יהוה, when I am esteemed through Pharaoh, his chariots, and his horsemen."
[19]And the Messenger of Elohim, who went before the camp of Yisra'ěl, moved and went behind them. And the column of cloud went from before them and stood behind them,
[20]and came between the camp of the Mitsrites and the camp of Yisra'ěl. And it was the cloud and the darkness, and it gave light by night, and the one did not come near the other all the night.
[21]And Mosheh stretched out his hand over the sea. And יהוה caused the sea to go back by a strong east wind all that night, and made the sea into dry land, and the waters were divided.
[22]And the children of Yisra'ěl went into the midst of the sea on dry ground, and the waters were a wall to them on their right and on their left.
[23]And the Mitsrites pursued and went after them into the midst of the sea, all the horses of Pharaoh, his chariots, and his horsemen.
[24]And it came to be, in the morning watch, that יהוה looked down upon the army of the Mitsrites through the column of fire and cloud, and He brought the army of the Mitsrites into confusion.
[25]And He took off their chariot wheels, so that they drove them with difficulty. And the Mitsrites said, "Let us flee from the face of Yisra'ěl, for יהוה fights for them against the Mitsrites."
[26]Then יהוה said to Mosheh, "Stretch out your hand over the sea, and let the waters come back upon the Mitsrites, on their chariots, and on their horsemen."
[27]And Mosheh stretched out his hand over the sea, and the sea returned to its usual flow, at the break of day, with the Mitsrites fleeing into it. Thus יהוה overthrew the Mitsrites in the midst of the sea,
[28]and the waters returned and covered the chariots, and the horsemen, and all the army of Pharaoh that came into the sea after them, and not even one was left of them.
[29]And the children of Yisra'ěl walked on dry ground in the midst of the sea, and the waters were a wall to them on their right and on their left.
[30]Thus יהוה saved Yisra'ěl that day out of the hand of the Mitsrites, and Yisra'ěl saw the Mitsrites dead on the seashore.
[31]And Yisra'ěl saw the great work which יהוה had done in Mitsrayim, and the people feared יהוה, and believed יהוה and His servant Mosheh.

15

Then Mosheh and the children of Yisra'ěl sang this song to יהוה, and spoke, saying, "I sing to יהוה, for He is highly exalted! The horse and its rider He has thrown into the sea!
[2]"Yah is my strength and song, and He has become my deliverance. [a] He is my Ěl, and I praise Him – Elohim of my father, and I exalt Him.
[3]"יהוה is a man of battle, יהוה is His Name.
[4]"He has cast Pharaoh's chariots and his army into the sea, and his chosen officers are drowned in the Sea of Reeds.
[5]"The depths covered them, they went down to the bottom like a stone.
[6]"Your right hand, O יהוה, has become great in power. Your right hand, O יהוה, has crushed the enemy.
[7]"And in the greatness of Your excellence You pulled down those who rose up

15a See Teh. 118:14 and Yesh. 12:2.

against You. You sent forth Your wrath, it
consumed them like stubble.
8 “And with the wind of Your nostrils the
waters were heaped up, the floods stood
like a wall, the depths became stiff in the
heart of the sea.
9 “The enemy said, ‘I pursue, I overtake,
I divide the spoil, my being is satisfied on
them. I draw out my sword, my hand
destroys them.’
10 “You did blow with Your wind, the sea
covered them, they sank like lead in the
mighty waters.
11 “Who is like You, O יהוה, among the
mighty ones? Who is like You, great in set-
apartness, awesome in praises, working
wonders?
12 “You stretched out Your right hand, the
earth swallowed them.
13 “In Your loving-commitment You led
the people whom You have redeemed, in
Your strength You guided them to Your
set-apart dwelling.
14 “Peoples heard, they trembled, anguish
gripped the inhabitants of Philistia.
15 “Then the chiefs of Eḏom were troubled, the mighty men of Mo’aḇ, trembling
grips them, all the inhabitants of Kena‘an
melted.
16 “Fear and dread fell on them, by the
greatness of Your arm they are as silent as
a stone, until Your people pass over, O
יהוה, until the people, whom You have
bought, pass over.
17 “You bring them in and plant them in
the mountain of Your inheritance, in the
place, O יהוה, which You have made for
Your own dwelling, the set-apart place, O
יהוה, which Your hands have prepared.
18 “יהוה reigns forever and ever.”
19 For the horses of Pharaoh went with his
chariots and his horsemen into the sea, and
יהוה brought back the waters of the sea
upon them. And the children of Yisra’ěl
went on dry ground in the midst of the sea.
20 And Miryam the prophetess, the sister
of Aharon, took the timbrel in her hand.
And all the women went out after her with
timbrels and with dances.
21 And Miryam answered them, “Sing to
יהוה, for He is highly exalted! The horse
and its rider He has thrown into the sea!”
22 And Mosheh brought Yisra’ěl from the
Sea of Reeds, and they went out into the
Wilderness of Shur. And they went three
days in the wilderness and found no water.
23 And they came to Marah, and they
were unable to drink the waters of Marah,
for they were bitter. So the name of it was
called Marah.
24 And the people grumbled against
Mosheh, saying, “What are we to drink?”
25 Then he cried out to יהוה, and יהוה
showed him a tree. And when he threw it
into the waters, the waters were made
sweet. There He made a law and a right-
ruling for them, and there He tried them.
26 And He said, “If you diligently obey
the voice of יהוה your Elohim and do what
is right in His eyes, and shall listen to His
commands and shall guard all His laws, I
shall bring on you none of the diseases I
brought on the Mitsrites, for I am יהוה
who heals you.”
27 And they came to Ělim, where there
were twelve fountains of water and seventy palm trees. And they camped there by
the waters.

16 And they set out from Ělim, and all
the congregation of the children of
Yisra’ěl came to the Wilderness of Sin,
which is between Ělim and Sinai, on the
fifteenth day of the second new *moon* after
their going out of the land of Mitsrayim.
2 And all the congregation of the children
of Yisra’ěl grumbled against Mosheh and
Aharon in the wilderness.
3 And the children of Yisra’ěl said to
them, “If only we had died by the hand of
יהוה in the land of Mitsrayim, when we sat
by the pots of meat and when we ate bread
to satisfaction! For you have brought us
out into this wilderness to put all this
assembly to death with hunger.”
4 And יהוה said to Mosheh, “See, I am
raining bread from the heavens for you.
And the people shall go out and gather a
day’s portion every day, in order to try
them, whether they walk in My Torah or
not.
5 “And it shall be on the sixth day that

they shall prepare what they bring in, and
it shall be twice as much as they gather
daily."
6 And Mosheh and Aharon said to all the
children of Yisra'ĕl, "At evening you shall
know that יהוה has brought you out of the
land of Mitsrayim.
7 "And in the morning you shall see the
esteem of יהוה, for He hears your grumblings against יהוה. And what are we, that
you grumble against us?"
8 And Mosheh said, "In that יהוה gives
you meat to eat in the evening, and in the
morning bread to satisfaction, for יהוה
hears your grumblings which you make
against Him. And what are we? Your
grumblings are not against us but against
יהוה."
9 And Mosheh said to Aharon, "Say to
all the congregation of the children of
Yisra'ĕl, 'Come near before יהוה, for He
has heard your grumblings.' "
10 And it came to be, as Aharon spoke to
all the congregation of the children of
Yisra'ĕl, that they looked toward the
wilderness and see, the esteem of יהוה
appeared in the cloud.
11 And יהוה spoke to Mosheh, saying,
12 "I have heard the grumblings of the
children of Yisra'ĕl. Speak to them, saying,
'Between the evenings you are to eat meat,
and in the morning you are to be satisfied
with bread. And you shall know that I am
יהוה your Elohim.' "
13 And it came to be that quails came up at
evening and covered the camp, and in the
morning the dew lay all around the camp.
14 And the layer of dew went up, and see,
on the surface of the wilderness, was a
small round substance, as fine as frost on
the ground.
15 And the children of Yisra'ĕl saw, and
they said to each other, "What is it?" For
they did not know what it was. And
Mosheh said to them, "It is the bread
which יהוה has given you to eat.
16 "This is the word which יהוה has commanded: 'Let every man gather it according to each one's need, an omer for each
being, according to the number of beings.
Let every man take for those who are in his
tent.' "
17 And the children of Yisra'ĕl did so and
gathered, some more, some less.
18 And they measured it by omers, and he
who gathered much did not have too much,
and he who gathered little did not have too
little. Each one gathered according to his
need.
19 And Mosheh said, "Let no one leave
any of it until morning."
20 And they did not listen to Mosheh, so
some of them left part of it until morning,
and it bred worms and stank. And Mosheh
was wroth with them.
21 And they gathered it every morning,
each one according to his need. And when
the sun became hot, it melted.
22 And it came to be, on the sixth day, that
they gathered twice as much bread, two
omers for each one. And all the rulers of
the congregation came and told Mosheh.
23 And he said to them, "This is what יהוה
has said, 'Tomorrow is a rest, a Sabbath
set-apart to יהוה. That which you bake,
bake; and that which you cook, cook. And
lay up for yourselves all that is left over, to
keep it until morning.' "
24 And they laid it up till morning, as
Mosheh commanded. And it did not stink,
and no worm was in it.
25 And Mosheh said, "Eat it today, for
today is a Sabbath to יהוה, today you do
not find it in the field.
26 "Gather it six days, but on the seventh
day, which is the Sabbath, there is none."
27 And it came to be that some of the
people went out on the seventh day to
gather, but they found none.
28 And יהוה said to Mosheh, "How long
shall you refuse to guard My commands
and My Torot [a]?
29 "See, because יהוה has given you the
Sabbath, therefore He is giving you bread
for two days on the sixth day. Let each one
stay in his place, do not let anyone go out
of his place on the seventh day."
30 So the people rested on the seventh

16a Torot - plural of Torah, teaching.

day. [b]

31 And the house of Yisra'ěl called its name Manna. And it was like white coriander seed, and the taste of it was like thin cakes made with honey.

32 And Mosheh said, "This is the word which יהוה has commanded: 'Fill an omer with it, to keep for your generations, so that they see the bread with which I fed you in the wilderness, when I brought you out of the land of Mitsrayim.'"

33 And Mosheh said to Aharon, "Take a pot and put an omer of manna in it, and set it down before יהוה, to keep for your generations."

34 As יהוה commanded Mosheh, so did Aharon set it down before the Witness, to keep.

35 And the children of Yisra'ěl ate manna forty years, until they came to an inhabited land. They ate manna until they came to the border of the land of Kena'an.

36 And an omer is one-tenth of an ěphah.

17 And all the congregation of the children of Yisra'ěl set out on their journey from the Wilderness of Sin, according to the mouth of יהוה, and camped in Rephiḏim. And there was no water for the people to drink.

2 Therefore the people strove with Mosheh, and said, "Give us water to drink." And Mosheh said to them, "Why do you strive with me? Why do you try יהוה?"

3 And the people thirsted there for water, and the people grumbled against Mosheh, and said, "Why did you bring us out of Mitsrayim, to kill us and our children and our livestock with thirst?"

4 Then Mosheh cried out to יהוה, saying, "What am I to do with this people? Yet a little and they shall stone me!"

5 And יהוה said to Mosheh, "Pass over before the people, and take with you some of the elders of Yisra'ěl. And take in your hand your rod with which you struck the river, and go.

6 "See, I am standing before you there on the rock in Ḥorěḇ. And you shall strike the rock, and water shall come out of it, and the people shall drink." And Mosheh did so before the eyes of the elders of Yisra'ěl.

7 And he called the name of the place Massah and Meriḇah, because of the 'strife' of the children of Yisra'ěl, and because they 'tried' יהוה, saying, "Is יהוה in our midst or not?"

8 And Amalěq came and fought with Yisra'ěl in Rephiḏim.

9 And Mosheh said to Yehoshua, "Choose for us men and go out, fight with Amalěq. Tomorrow I am stationing myself on the top of the hill with the rod of Elohim in my hand."

10 And Yehoshua did as Mosheh said to him, to fight with Amalěq. And Mosheh, Aharon, and Ḥur went up to the top of the hill.

11 And it came to be, when Mosheh held up his hand, that Yisra'ěl prevailed. And when he let down his hand, Amalěq prevailed.

12 But Mosheh's hands were heavy, so they took a stone and put it under him, and he sat on it. And Aharon and Ḥur supported his hands, one on one side, and the other on the other side. And his hands were steady until the going down of the sun.

13 And Yehoshua defeated Amalěq and his people with the edge of the sword.

14 And יהוה said to Mosheh, "Write this for a remembrance in the book and recite it in the hearing of Yehoshua, that I shall completely blot out the remembrance of Amalěq from under the heavens."

15 And Mosheh built a slaughter-place and called its name, יהוה Nissi,

16 for he said, "Because a hand is on the throne of Yah, יהוה is to fight against Amalěq, from generation to generation."

18 And Yithro, the priest of Miḏyan, Mosheh's father-in-law, heard of all that Elohim had done for Mosheh and for Yisra'ěl His people, that יהוה had brought Yisra'ěl out of Mitsrayim.

2 And Yithro, Mosheh's father-in-law,

16b See Ber. 2:2 & 3.

took Tsipporah, the wife of Mosheh – after
he had sent her back,
3 and her two sons, of whom the name of
one was Gĕreshom, for he said, "I have
been a sojourner in a foreign land,"
4 and the name of the other was Eli'ezer,
for he said, "The Elohim of my father was
my help, and delivered me from the sword
of Pharaoh."
5 Yithro, Mosheh's father-in-law, came
with his sons and his wife to Mosheh in the
wilderness, where he was encamped at the
mountain of Elohim.
6 And he had said to Mosheh, "I, your
father-in-law Yithro, am coming to you
with your wife and her two sons with her."
7 And Mosheh went out to meet his
father-in-law, and bowed down, and kissed
him. And they asked each other about their
welfare, and they went into the tent.
8 And Mosheh told his father-in-law all
that יהוה had done to Pharaoh and to the
Mitsrites for Yisra'ĕl's sake, all the hardship that had come upon them on the way,
and how יהוה had delivered them.
9 And Yithro rejoiced for all the good
which יהוה had done for Yisra'ĕl, whom
He had delivered out of the hand of the
Mitsrites.
10 And Yithro said, "Blessed be יהוה,
who has delivered you out of the hand of
the Mitsrites and out of the hand of
Pharaoh, and who has delivered the people
from under the hand of the Mitsrites.
11 "Now I know that יהוה is greater than
all the mighty ones, indeed in the matter in
which they acted proudly, above them."
12 Then Yithro, the father-in-law of
Mosheh, brought an ascending offering
and other slaughterings unto Elohim. And
Aharon came with all the elders of Yisra'ĕl
to eat bread with the father-in-law of
Mosheh before Elohim.
13 And it came to be, on the next day, that
Mosheh sat to rightly rule the people. And
the people stood before Mosheh from
morning until evening.
14 And when the father-in-law of Mosheh
saw all that he did for the people, he said,
"What is this that you are doing for the
people? Why do you sit by yourself, and
all the people stand before you from morning until evening?"
15 And Mosheh said to his father-in-law,
"Because the people come to me to seek
Elohim.
16 "When they have a matter, they come
to me, and I rightly rule between one and
another, and make known the laws of
Elohim and His Torot. [a]"
17 And the father-in-law of Mosheh said
to him, "What you are doing is not good.
18 "Both you and these people with you
shall certainly wear yourselves out. For the
matter is too heavy for you. You are not
able to do it by yourself.
19 "Now listen to my voice. Let me counsel you and Elohim be with you: Stand
before Elohim for the people, and you
shall bring the matters to Elohim.
20 "And you shall enlighten them *concerning* the laws and the Torot, and show
them the way in which they should walk
and the work which they do.
21 "But you yourself, seek out from all the
people able men, who fear Elohim, men of
truth, hating unfair gain. And place *these*
over them to be rulers of thousands, rulers
of hundreds, rulers of fifties, and rulers of
tens.
22 "And they shall rightly rule the people
at all times. And it shall be that they bring
every great matter to you, but they themselves rightly rule every small matter. So,
make it lighter for yourself, for they shall
bear with you.
23 "If you do this word, and Elohim shall
command you, then you shall be able to
stand and all this people also go to their
place in peace."
24 And Mosheh listened to the voice of his
father-in-law and did all that he said.
25 And Mosheh chose able men out of all
Yisra'ĕl, and made them heads over the
people: rulers of thousands, rulers of hundreds, rulers of fifties, and rulers of tens.
26 And they rightly ruled the people at all
times – the hard matters they brought to

18a Torot - plural of Torah, teaching.

Mosheh, but they rightly ruled every small matter themselves.

27 And Mosheh sent off his father-in-law, and he went away to his own land.

19

In the third new *moon* after the children of Yisra'ěl had come out of the land of Mitsrayim, on this day they came to the Wilderness of Sinai.

2 For they set out from Rephiḏim, and had come to the Wilderness of Sinai, and camped in the wilderness. So Yisra'ěl camped there before the mountain.

3 And Mosheh went up to Elohim, and יהוה called to him from the mountain, saying, "This is what you are to say to the house of Ya'aqoḇ, and declare to the children of Yisra'ěl:

4 'You have seen what I did to the Mitsrites, and how I bore you on eagles' wings and brought you to Myself.

5 'And now, if you diligently obey My voice, and shall guard My covenant, then you shall be My treasured possession above all the peoples – for all the earth is Mine –

6 'and you shall be to Me a reign of priests and a set-apart nation.' Those are the words which you are to speak to the children of Yisra'ěl."

7 And Mosheh came and called for the elders of the people, and set before them all these words which יהוה commanded him.

8 And all the people answered together and said, "All that יהוה has spoken we shall do." So Mosheh brought back the words of the people to יהוה.

9 And יהוה said to Mosheh, "See, I am coming to you in the thick cloud, so that the people hear when I speak with you, and believe you forever." And Mosheh reported the words of the people to יהוה.

10 And יהוה said to Mosheh, "Go to the people and set them apart today and tomorrow. And they shall wash their garments,

11 and shall be prepared by the third day. For on the third day יהוה shall come down upon Mount Sinai before the eyes of all the people.

12 "And you shall make a border for the people all around, saying, 'Take heed to yourselves that you do not go up to the mountain or touch the border of it. Whoever touches the mountain shall certainly be put to death.

13 'Not a hand is to touch it, but he shall certainly be stoned or shot with an arrow, whether man or beast, he shall not live.' When the Yoḇel [a] sounds long, let them come near the mountain."

14 And Mosheh came down from the mountain to the people and set the people apart, and they washed their garments.

15 And he said to the people, "Be prepared by the third day. Do not come near a wife."

16 And it came to be, on the third day in the morning, that there were thunders and lightnings, and a thick cloud on the mountain. And a voice of a shophar [b] was very strong, and all the people who were in the camp trembled.

17 And Mosheh brought the people out of the camp to meet with Elohim, and they stood at the foot of the mountain.

18 And Mount Sinai was in smoke, all of it, because יהוה descended upon it in fire. And its smoke went up like the smoke of a furnace, and all the mountain trembled exceedingly.

19 And when a voice of the shophar [b] sounded long and became very strong, Mosheh spoke, and Elohim answered him by voice.

20 And יהוה came down upon Mount Sinai, on the top of the mountain. And יהוה called Mosheh to the top of the mountain, and Mosheh went up.

21 And יהוה said to Mosheh, "Go down, *and* warn the people, lest they break through unto יהוה to see, and many of them fall.

22 "And let the priests who come near יהוה set themselves apart too, lest יהוה break out against them."

23 And Mosheh said to יהוה, "The people are not able to come up to Mount Sinai, for You warned us, saying, 'Make a border

19a See Explanatory notes: Yoḇel. *19b* Animal horn - traditionally a ram's horn.

around the mountain and set it apart.' "
24 And יהוה said to him, "Come, go down
and then come up, you and Aharon with
you. But do not let the priests and the
people break through to come up to יהוה,
lest He break out against them."
25 And Mosheh went down to the people
and spoke to them.

20 And Elohim spoke all these Words,
saying,
2 "I am יהוה your Elohim, who brought
you out of the land of Mitsrayim, out of the
house of slavery.
3 "You have no other mighty ones against
My face.
4 "You do not make for yourself a carved
image, or any likeness of that which is in
the heavens above, or which is in the earth
beneath, or which is in the waters under
the earth,
5 you do not bow down to them nor serve
them. For I, יהוה your Elohim am a jealous
Ěl, visiting the crookedness of the fathers
on the children to the third and fourth
generations of those who hate Me,
6 but showing loving-commitment to
thousands, to those who love Me and
guard My commands.
7 "You do not bring [a] the Name of יהוה
your Elohim to naught, for יהוה does not
leave the one unpunished who brings His
Name to naught.
8 "Remember the Sabbath day, to set it
apart.
9 "Six days you labour, and shall do all
your work,
10 but the seventh day is a Sabbath [b] of
יהוה your Elohim. You do not do any work
– you, nor your son, nor your daughter, nor
your male servant, nor your female servant, nor your cattle, nor your stranger
who is within your gates.
11 "For in six days יהוה made the heavens
and the earth, the sea, and all that is in
them, and rested the seventh day.
Therefore יהוה blessed the Sabbath day
and set it apart.
12 "Respect your father and your mother,
so that your days are prolonged upon the
soil which יהוה your Elohim is giving you.
13 "You do not murder.
14 "You do not commit adultery.
15 "You do not steal.
16 "You do not bear false witness against
your neighbour.
17 "You do not covet your neighbour's
house, you do not covet your neighbour's
wife, nor his male servant, nor his female
servant, nor his ox, nor his donkey, or
whatever belongs to your neighbour."
18 And all the people saw the thunders,
the lightning flashes, the voice of the
shophar, and the mountain smoking. And
the people saw it, and they trembled and
stood at a distance,
19 and said to Mosheh, "You speak with
us and we hear, but let not Elohim speak
with us, lest we die."
20 And Mosheh said to the people, "Do
not fear, for Elohim has come to prove
you, and in order that His fear be before
you, so that you do not sin."
21 So the people stood at a distance, but
Mosheh drew near the thick darkness
where Elohim was.
22 And יהוה said to Mosheh, "Say this to
the children of Yisra'ěl: 'You yourselves
have seen that I have spoken to you from
the heavens.
23 'You do not make besides Me mighty
ones of silver, and you do not make mighty
ones of gold for yourselves.
24 'Make a slaughter-place of earth for
Me, and you shall slaughter on it your
ascending offerings and your peace offerings, your sheep and your cattle. In every
place where I cause My Name to be
remembered I shall come to you and bless
you.
25 'And if you make Me a slaughter-place
of stone, do not build it of cut stone, for if
you use your chisel on it, you have profaned it.
26 'Nor do you go up by steps to My
slaughter-place, lest your nakedness be
exposed on it.'

20a Or *lift up*, or *take*. *20b* There are other Sabbaths, but this is the weekly Sabbath.

21 “These are the right-rulings which you are to set before them:

2 “When you buy a Hebrew servant, he serves six years, and in the seventh he goes out free, for naught.

3 “If he comes in by himself, he goes out by himself; if he comes in married, then his wife shall go out with him.

4 “If his master has given him a wife, and she has borne him sons or daughters, the wife and her children are her master’s, and he goes out by himself.

5 “And if the servant truly says, ‘I love my master, my wife, and my children, let me not go out free,’

6 then his master shall bring him before Elohim, and shall bring him to the door, or to the doorpost, and his master shall pierce his ear with an awl. And he shall serve him forever.

7 “And when a man sells his daughter to be a female servant, she does not go out as the male servants do.

8 “If she is displeasing in the eyes of her master who has engaged her to himself, then he shall let her be ransomed. He shall have no authority to sell her to a foreign people, because of him deceiving her.

9 “And if he has engaged her to his son, he is to do to her as is the right of daughters.

10 “If he takes another *wife*, her food, her covering, and her marriage rights are not to be diminished.

11 “And if he does not do these three for her, then she shall go out for naught, without silver.

12 “He who strikes a man so that he dies shall certainly be put to death.

13 “But if he did not lie in wait, but Elohim delivered him into his hand, then I shall appoint for you a place where he is to flee.

14 “But when a man acts presumptuously against his neighbour, to kill him by treachery, you are to take him *even* from My slaughter-place to die.

15 “And he who strikes his father or his mother shall certainly be put to death.

16 “And he who kidnaps a man and sells him, or if he is found in his hand, shall certainly be put to death.

17 “And he who curses his father or his mother shall certainly be put to death.

18 “And when men strive together, and one strikes the other with a stone or with his fist, and he does not die but is confined to his bed,

19 if he rises again and walks about outside with his staff, then he who struck him shall be innocent. He only pays for lost time and sees to it that he is completely healed.

20 “And when a man strikes his male or female servant with a rod, so that he dies under his hand, he shall certainly be punished.

21 “But if he remains alive a day or two, he is not punished; for he is his property.

22 “And when men strive and they shall smite a pregnant woman, and her children come out, yet there is no injury, he shall certainly be punished accordingly as the woman’s husband lays upon him. And he shall give through the judges.

23 “But if there is injury, then you shall give life for life,

24 eye for eye, tooth for tooth, hand for hand, foot for foot,

25 burn for burn, wound for wound, lash for lash.

26 “And when a man strikes the eye of his male or female servant, and destroys it, he is to let him go free for the sake of his eye.

27 “And if he knocks out the tooth of his male or female servant, he is to let him go free for the sake of his tooth.

28 “And when an ox gores a man or a woman to death, then the ox shall certainly be stoned, and its flesh is not eaten, and the owner of the ox is innocent.

29 “However, if the ox was previously in the habit of goring, and its owner has been warned, and he has not kept it confined, so that it has killed a man or a woman, the ox is stoned and its owner also is put to death.

30 “If a *sin*-covering is laid upon him, then he shall give the ransom of his life, whatever is laid on him.

31 “Whether it has gored a son or gored a daughter, according to this right-ruling it is done to him.

32 "If the ox gores a male or female servant, he is to give to their master thirty sheqels of silver, and the ox is stoned.

33 "And when a man opens a pit, or if a man digs a pit and does not cover it, and an ox or a donkey falls in it,

34 the owner of the pit is to repay, he is to give silver to their owner, and the dead *beast* is his.

35 "And when the ox of a man smites the ox of his neighbour and it dies, then they shall sell the live ox and divide the silver from it, and also divide the dead ox.

36 "Or if it was known that the ox was previously in the habit of goring, and its owner has not kept it confined, he shall certainly repay ox for ox, while the dead *beast* is his.

22 "When a man steals an ox or a sheep, and shall slaughter it or sell it, he repays five cattle for an ox and four sheep for a sheep.

2 "If the thief is found breaking in, and he is struck so that he dies, there is no guilt for his bloodshed.

3 "If the sun has risen on him, there is guilt for his bloodshed, he shall certainly repay. If he has not the means, then he shall be sold for his theft.

4 "If the theft is indeed found alive in his hand, whether it is an ox or donkey or sheep, he repays double.

5 "When a man lets a field or vineyard be grazed *bare*, and lets loose his livestock, and it feeds in another man's field, he repays from the best of his own field and the best of his own vineyard.

6 "When fire breaks out and spreads to thorn bushes, so that stacked grain, or standing grain, or the field is consumed, he who kindled the fire shall certainly repay.

7 "When a man gives silver or goods to his neighbour to guard, and it is stolen out of the man's house, if the thief is found, he repays double.

8 "If the thief is not found, then the master of the house shall be brought before Elohim to see whether he has put his hand into his neighbour's goods.

9 "For every matter of transgression, for ox, for donkey, for sheep, for garment, or for whatever is lost which another claims to be his, let the matter of them both come before Elohim. And whomever Elohim declares wrong repays double to his neighbour.

10 "When a man gives to his neighbour a donkey, or ox, or sheep, or any beast to watch over, and it dies, or is injured, or is driven away while no one is looking,

11 let an oath of יהוה be between them both, that he has not put his hand into his neighbour's goods. And the owner of it shall accept that, and he does not repay.

12 "But if it is indeed stolen from him, he repays to its owner.

13 "If it is torn to pieces, then let him bring it for evidence, he does not repay what was torn.

14 "And when a man borrows from his neighbour, and it is injured or dies while the owner of it is not present, he shall certainly repay.

15 "But if its owner was with it, he does not repay. If it was hired, he is entitled to the hire.

16 "And when a man entices a maiden who is not engaged, and lies with her, he shall certainly pay the bride-price for her to be his wife.

17 "If her father absolutely refuses to give her to him, he pays according to the bride-price of maidens.

18 "Do not allow a practiser of witchcraft to live.

19 "Anyone lying with a beast shall certainly be put to death.

20 "He who slaughters to an elohim, except to יהוה only, is put under the ban.

21 "Do not tread down a sojourner or oppress him, for you were sojourners in the land of Mitsrayim.

22 "Do not afflict any widow or fatherless child.

23 "If you do afflict them at all – if they cry out to Me at all, I shall certainly hear their cry,

24 and My wrath shall burn and I shall kill you with the sword, your wives shall be widows and your children fatherless.

25 "If you do lend silver to any of My peo-

ple, the poor among you, you are not to be like one that lends on interest to him. Do not lay interest on him.

26 "If you take your neighbour's garment as a pledge at all, you are to return it to him before the sun goes down.

27 "For that is his only covering, it is his garment for his skin. What does he sleep in? And it shall be that when he cries to Me, I shall hear, for I show favour.

28 "Do not revile an elohim, nor curse a ruler of your people.

29 "Do not delay *giving* your harvest and your vintage. Give Me the first-born of your sons.

30 "Likewise you are to do with your oxen, with your sheep. It is to be with its mother seven days. On the eighth day you give it to Me.

31 "And you are set-apart men to Me, and you do not eat any meat which is torn to pieces in the field, you throw it to the dogs.

23 "Do not bring a false report. Do not put your hand with the wrong to be a malicious witness.

2 "Do not follow a crowd to do evil, nor bear witness in a strife so as to turn aside after many, to turn aside *what is right*.

3 "And do not favour a poor man in his strife.

4 "When you meet your enemy's ox or his donkey going astray, you shall certainly return it to him.

5 "When you see the donkey of him who hates you lying under its burden, you shall refrain from leaving it to him, you shall certainly help him.

6 "Do not turn aside the right-ruling of your poor in his strife.

7 "Keep yourself far from a false matter, and do not kill the innocent and the righteous, for I do not declare the wrong right.

8 "And do not take a bribe, for a bribe blinds the seeing one and twists the words of the righteous.

9 "And do not oppress a sojourner, as you yourselves know the heart of a sojourner, because you were sojourners in the land of Mitsrayim.

10 "And for six years you are to sow your land, and shall gather its increase,

11 but the seventh year you are to let it rest, and shall leave it, and the poor of your people shall eat. And what they leave, the beasts of the field eat. Do the same with your vineyard and your oliveyard.

12 "Six days you are to do your work, and on the seventh day you rest, in order that your ox and your donkey might rest, and the son of your female servant and the sojourner be refreshed.

13 "And in all that I have said to you take heed. And make no mention of the name of other mighty ones, let it not be heard from your mouth.

14 "Three [a] times in the year you are to celebrate a festival to Me:

15 "Guard the Festival of Matzot. [b] Seven days you eat unleavened bread, as I commanded you, at the time appointed in the new *moon* of Aḇiḇ – for in it you came out of Mitsrayim – and do not appear before Me empty-handed;

16 and the Festival of the Harvest, [c] the first-fruits of your labours which you have sown in the field; and the Festival of the Ingathering [d] at the outgoing of the year, when you have gathered in the fruit of your labours from the field.

17 "Three times in the year all your males are to appear before the Master יהוה.

18 "Do not slaughter the blood of My slaughtering with leavened bread, and the fat of My festival shall not remain until morning.

19 "Bring the first of the first-fruits of your land into the House of יהוה your Elohim. Do not cook a young goat in its mother's milk.

20 "See, I am sending a Messenger before you to guard you in the way and to bring you into the place which I have prepared.

21 "Be on guard before Him and obey His voice. Do not rebel against Him, for He is not going to pardon your transgression, for

23a The Festivals of יהוה are grouped in three, for three different times of the year.
23b Unleavened Bread. *23c* - Shaḇu'ot (Festival of Weeks). *23d* - Sukkot (Festival of Booths).

My Name is in Him.
22"But if you diligently obey His voice and shall do all that I speak, then I shall be an enemy to your enemies and a distresser to those who distress you.
23"For My Messenger shall go before you and shall bring you in to the Amorites and the Ḥittites and the Perizzites and the Kenaʽanites and the Ḥiwwites and the Yeḇusites, and I shall cut them off.
24"Do not bow down to their mighty ones, nor serve them, nor do according to their works, but without fail overthrow them and without fail break down their pillars.
25"And you shall serve יהוה your Elohim, and He shall bless your bread and your water. And I shall remove sickness from your midst.
26"None shall miscarry or be barren in your land. I shall fill the number of your days.
27"I shall send My fear before you, and cause confusion among all the people to whom you come, and make all your enemies turn their backs to you.
28"And I shall send hornets before you, which shall drive out the Ḥiwwite, the Kenaʽanite, and the Ḥittite from before you.
29"I shall not drive them out from before you in one year, lest the land become a waste and the beast of the field become too numerous for you.
30"Little by little I shall drive them out from before you, until you have increased, and you inherit the land.
31"And I shall set your border from the Sea of Reeds to the Sea of the Philistines, and from the wilderness to the River, for I shall give the inhabitants of the land into your hand, and you shall drive them out before you.
32"Do not make a covenant with them nor with their mighty ones.
33"Let them not dwell in your land, lest they make you sin against Me when you serve their mighty ones, when it becomes a snare to you."

24 And to Mosheh He said, "Come up
to יהוה, you and Aharon, Naḏaḇ
and Aḇihu, and seventy of the elders of Yisra'ěl, and you shall bow yourselves from a distance.
2"But Mosheh shall draw near to יהוה
by himself, and let them not draw near, nor let the people go up with him."
3And Mosheh came and related to the
people all the Words of יהוה and all the right-rulings. And all the people answered with one voice and said, "All the Words which יהוה has spoken we shall do."
4And Mosheh wrote down all the Words
of יהוה, and rose up early in the morning, and built a slaughter-place at the foot of the mountain, and twelve standing columns for the twelve tribes of Yisra'ěl.
5And he sent young men of the children
of Yisra'ěl, and they offered ascending offerings and slaughtered slaughterings of peace *offerings* to יהוה of bulls.
6And Mosheh took half the blood and
put it in basins, and half the blood he sprinkled on the slaughter-place.
7And he took the Book of the Covenant
and read in the hearing of the people. And they said, "All that יהוה has spoken we shall do, and obey."
8And Mosheh took the blood and sprin-
kled it on the people, and said, "See, the blood of the covenant which יהוה has made with you concerning all these Words."
9And Mosheh went up, also Aharon,
Naḏaḇ, and Aḇihu, and seventy of the elders of Yisra'ěl,
10and they saw the Elohim of Yisra'ěl,
and under His feet like a paved work of sapphire stone, and like the heavens for brightness.
11Yet He did not stretch out His hand
against the chiefs of the children of Yisra'ěl! And they saw Elohim, and they ate and drank.
12And יהוה said to Mosheh, "Come up to
Me on the mountain and be there, while I give you tablets of stone, and the Torah and the command which I have written, to teach them."
13And Mosheh arose with his assistant

Yehoshua, and Mosheh went up to the
mountain of Elohim.
14 And he said to the elders, "Wait here
for us until we come back to you. And see,
Aharon and Ḥur are with you. Whoever
has matters, let him go to them."
15 And Mosheh went up into the mountain, and a cloud covered the mountain.
16 And the esteem of יהוה dwelt on
Mount Sinai, and the cloud covered it for
six days. And on the seventh day He called
to Mosheh out of the midst of the cloud.
17 And the appearance of the esteem of
יהוה was like a consuming fire on the top
of the mountain, before the eyes of the
children of Yisra'ěl.
18 And Mosheh went into the midst of the
cloud and went up into the mountain. And
it came to be that Mosheh was on the
mountain forty days and forty nights.

25 And יהוה spoke to Mosheh, saying,
2 "Speak to the children of Yisra'ěl,
that they take up a contribution for Me.
From everyone whose heart moves him
you shall take up My contribution.
3 "And this is the contribution which you
take up from them: gold, and silver, and
bronze,
4 and blue and purple and scarlet *material*, and fine linen, and goats' *hair*,
5 and rams' skins dyed red, and fine
leather, and acacia wood,
6 oil for the light, spices for the anointing
oil and for the sweet incense,
7 shoham stones, and stones to be set in
the shoulder garment and in the breastplate.
8 "And they shall make Me a Set-apart
Place, and I shall dwell in their midst.
9 "According to all that I show you – the
pattern of the Dwelling Place and the pattern of all its furnishings – make it exactly
so.
10 "And they shall make an ark of acacia
wood two and a half cubits long, a cubit
and a half wide, and a cubit and a half
high.
11 "And you shall overlay it with clean
gold, inside and outside you shall overlay
it. And you shall make on it a moulding of
gold all around.
12 "And you shall cast four rings of gold
for it, and put them in its four corners, two
rings on one side, and two rings on the
other side.
13 "And you shall make poles of acacia
wood, and overlay them with gold,
14 and shall put the poles into the rings on
the sides of the ark, to lift up the ark by
them.
15 "The poles are in the rings of the ark,
they are not taken from it.
16 "And into the ark you shall put the
Witness which I give you.
17 "And you shall make a lid of atonement
of clean gold, two and a half cubits long
and a cubit and a half wide.
18 "And you shall make two kerubim of
gold, make them of beaten work, at the two
ends of the lid of atonement.
19 "And make one kerub at one end, and
the other kerub at the other end. Make the
kerubim from the lid of atonement, at its
two ends.
20 "And the kerubim shall be spreading
out their wings above, covering the lid of
atonement with their wings, with their
faces toward each other, the faces of the
kerubim *turned* toward the lid of atonement.
21 "And you shall put the lid of atonement
on top of the ark, and put into the ark the
Witness which I give you.
22 "And I shall meet with you there, and
from above the lid of atonement, from
between the two kerubim which are on the
ark of the Witness, I shall speak to you all
that which I command you concerning the
children of Yisra'ěl.
23 "And you shall make a table of acacia
wood two cubits long, a cubit wide, and a
cubit and a half high.
24 "And you shall overlay it with clean
gold, and shall make a moulding of gold
all around,
25 and shall make for it a rim of a handbreadth all around, and shall make a gold
moulding for the rim all around.
26 "And you shall make for it four rings of
gold, and put the rings on the four corners
that are at its four legs.

27 “The rings are close to the rim, as holders for the poles to lift the table.
28 “And you shall make the poles of acacia wood, and overlay them with gold, and the table shall be lifted with them.
29 “And you shall make its dishes, and its ladles, and its jars, and its bowls for pouring. Make them of clean gold.
30 “And you shall put the showbread on the table before Me, continually.
31 “And you shall make a lampstand of clean gold – the lampstand is made of beaten work. Its base and its shaft, its cups, its ornamental knobs and blossoms are from it,
32 and six branches shall come out of its sides: three branches of the lampstand out of one side, and three branches of the lampstand out of the other side;
33 three cups made like almond flowers on one branch, with ornamental knob and blossom, and three cups made like almond flowers on the other branch, with ornamental knob and blossom – so for the six branches coming out of the lampstand.
34 “And on the lampstand itself are four cups made like almond flowers, with ornamental knob and blossom,
35 and a knob under the first two branches of the same, and a knob under the second two branches of the same, and a knob under the third two branches of the same, according to the six branches coming out of the lampstand.
36 “Their knobs and their branches are of the same – all of it one beaten work of clean gold.
37 “And you shall make seven lamps for it, and they shall mount its lamps so that they give light in front of it.
38 “And its snuffers and their trays are of clean gold.
39 “It is made of a talent of clean gold, with all these utensils.
40 “So see, and do according to the pattern which was shown to you on the mountain.

26 “And make the Dwelling Place with ten curtains of fine woven linen and blue and purple and scarlet *material*. Make them, with keruḇim, the work of a skilled workman.
2 “The length of each curtain is twenty-eight cubits, and the width of each curtain four cubits, all the curtains having one measure.
3 “Five curtains are joined to each other, and five curtains are joined to each other.
4 “And you shall make loops of blue on the edge of the end curtain on one set, and do the same on the edge of the end curtain of the second set.
5 “Make fifty loops in the one curtain and make fifty loops on the edge of the end curtain of the second set, the loops being opposite to each other.
6 “And you shall make fifty hooks of gold, and shall join the curtains together with the hooks, and the Dwelling Place shall be one.
7 “And you shall make curtains of goats’ *hair*, for a tent over the Dwelling Place, make eleven curtains.
8 “The length of each curtain is thirty cubits, and the width of each curtain four cubits, one measure to the eleven curtains.
9 “And you shall join the five curtains by themselves, and the six curtains by themselves, and you shall double over the six curtains at the front of the Tent.
10 “And you shall make fifty loops on the edge of the curtain that is outermost in one set, and fifty loops on the edge of the curtain of the second set.
11 “And you shall make fifty bronze hooks, and put the hooks into the loops, and join the tent together, and it shall be one.
12 “And the overlapping part of the rest of the curtains of the Tent, the half curtain that remains, shall hang over the back of the Dwelling Place.
13 “And a cubit on one side and a cubit on the other side, of what remains of the length of the curtains of the Tent, is to hang over the sides of the Dwelling Place, on this side and on that side, to cover it.
14 “And you shall make a covering of ram skins dyed red for the Tent, and a covering of fine leather above that.
15 “And for the Dwelling Place you shall make the boards of acacia wood, standing

up.
16 “Ten cubits is the length of a board, and
a cubit and a half the width of each board,
17 two tenons in each board for binding
one to another. Do the same for all the
boards of the Dwelling Place.
18 “And you shall make the boards for the
Dwelling Place, twenty boards for the
south side,
19 and make forty sockets of silver under
the twenty boards, two sockets under each
of the boards for its two tenons.
20 “And for the second side of the
Dwelling Place, on the north side, twenty
boards,
21 and their forty sockets of silver, two
sockets under each of the boards.
22 “And for the extreme parts of the
Dwelling Place, westward, make six
boards,
23 and make two boards for the two back
corners of the Dwelling Place.
24 “And they are double beneath and similarly they are complete to the top, to the
one ring. So it is for both of them, they are
for the two corners.
25 “And they shall be eight boards, and
their sockets of silver, sixteen sockets –
two sockets under the one board, and two
sockets under the other board.
26 “And you shall make bars of acacia
wood, five for the boards on one side of
the Dwelling Place,
27 and five bars for the boards on the other
side of the Dwelling Place, and five bars
for the boards of the side of the Dwelling
Place, for the extreme parts westward,
28 with the middle bar in the midst of the
boards, going through from end to end.
29 “And overlay the boards with gold, and
make their rings of gold as holders for the
bars, and overlay the bars with gold.
30 “And you shall raise up the Dwelling
Place according to its pattern which you
were shown on the mountain.
31 “And you shall make a veil of blue and
purple and scarlet *material*, and fine
woven linen, the work of a skilled workman, made with keruḇim.
32 “And you shall put it on the four
columns of acacia wood overlaid with
gold, their hooks of gold, upon four sockets of silver.
33 “And you shall hang the veil from the
hooks, and shall bring the ark of the
Witness there, behind the veil. And the veil
shall make a separation for you between
the Set-apart and the Most Set-apart Place.
34 “And you shall put the lid of atonement
upon the ark of the Witness in the Most
Set-apart Place.
35 “And you shall set the table outside the
veil, and the lampstand opposite the table
on the side of the Dwelling Place toward
the south, and put the table on the north
side.
36 “And you shall make a covering for
the door of the Tent, of blue and purple and
scarlet *material*, and fine woven linen,
made by a weaver.
37 “And you shall make for the covering
five columns of acacia wood, and overlay
them with gold, their hooks of gold, and
you shall cast five sockets of bronze for
them.

27 “And you shall make a slaughter-
place of acacia wood, five cubits
long and five cubits wide – the slaughter-
place is square – and its height three
cubits.
2 “And you shall make its horns on its
four corners, its horns are of the same. And
you shall overlay it with bronze.
3 “And you shall make its pots to receive
its ashes, and its shovels and its basins and
its forks and its fire holders. Make all its
utensils of bronze.
4 “And you shall make a grating for it, a
bronze network, and shall make on the network four bronze rings at its four corners,
5 and shall put it under the rim of the
slaughter-place beneath, so that the network is halfway up the slaughter-place.
6 “And you shall make poles for the
slaughter-place, poles of acacia wood, and
shall overlay them with bronze.
7 “And the poles shall be put in the rings,
and the poles shall be on the two sides of
the slaughter-place for lifting it.
8 “Make it hollow with boards. As it was
shown to you on the mountain, so they are

to make it.
9 "And you shall make the courtyard of the Dwelling Place: for the south side screens for the courtyard made of fine woven linen, one hundred cubits long for one side,
10 and its twenty columns and their twenty sockets of bronze, the hooks of the columns and their bands of silver,
11 and so for the north side in length, screens one hundred *cubits* long, with its twenty columns and their twenty sockets of bronze, and the hooks of the columns and their bands of silver.
12 "And the width of the courtyard on the west side screens of fifty cubits, with their ten columns and their ten sockets.
13 "And the width of the courtyard on the east side fifty cubits.
14 "And the screens on one side of the gate fifteen cubits, with their three columns and their three sockets.
15 "And on the other side screens of fifteen *cubits*, with their three columns and their three sockets.
16 "And for the gate of the courtyard a covering twenty cubits long, of blue and purple and scarlet *material*, and fine woven linen, made by a weaver – four columns and four sockets.
17 "All the columns around the courtyard have bands of silver, their hooks silver and their sockets bronze.
18 "The length of the courtyard is one hundred cubits, and the width fifty by fifty, and the height five cubits, woven of fine linen thread, and its sockets of bronze.
19 "All the utensils of the Dwelling Place for all its service, all its pegs, and all the pegs of the courtyard, are bronze.
20 "And you, you are to command the children of Yisra'ěl to bring you clear oil of pressed olives for the light, to cause the lamp to burn continually.
21 "In the Tent of Appointment, outside the veil which is before the Witness, Aharon and his sons are to tend it from evening until morning before יהוה – a law forever to their generations, from the children of Yisra'ěl.

28 "And you, bring near Aharon your brother and his sons with him, from among the children of Yisra'ěl, for serving as priest to Me: Aharon, Naḏaḇ and Aḇihu, El'azar and Ithamar, the sons of Aharon.
2 "And you shall make set-apart garments for Aharon your brother, for esteem and for comeliness.
3 "And you, speak to all the wise of heart, whom I have filled with a spirit of wisdom, and they shall make the garments of Aharon, to set him apart, for him to serve as priest to Me.
4 "And these are the garments which they make: a breastplate, a shoulder garment, a robe, an embroidered long shirt, a turban, and a girdle. And they shall make set-apart garments for Aharon your brother and his sons, for him to serve as priest to Me.
5 "And they shall take the gold, and the blue and the purple and the scarlet *material*, and the fine linen,
6 and shall make the shoulder garment of gold, of blue and purple and scarlet *material*, and fine woven linen, the work of a skilled workman.
7 "It is to have two shoulder pieces joined at its two edges, and so it is joined together.
8 "And the embroidered band of the shoulder garment, which is on it, is of the same workmanship, made of gold, of blue and purple and scarlet *material*, and fine woven linen.
9 "And you shall take two shoham stones and engrave on them the names of the sons of Yisra'ěl,
10 six of their names on one stone, and the remaining six names on the other stone, according to their birth.
11 "With the work of an engraver in stone, like the engravings of a signet, engrave the two stones with the names of the sons of Yisra'ěl. Set them in settings of gold.
12 "And you shall put the two stones on the shoulder pieces of the shoulder garment as stones of remembrance for the sons of Yisra'ěl. And Aharon shall bear their names before יהוה on his two shoulders, for a remembrance.

13"And you shall make settings of gold,
14and two chains of clean gold like braided cords, and fasten the braided chains to
the settings.
15"And you shall make a breastplate of
right-ruling, a work of a skilled workman,
like the work of the shoulder garment.
Make it of gold, of blue and purple and
scarlet *material*, and fine woven linen.
16"It is square, doubled, a span its length,
and a span its width.
17"And you shall put settings of stones in
it, four rows of stones: The first row is a
ruby, a topaz, and an emerald;
18and the second row is a turquoise, a
sapphire, and a diamond;
19and the third row is a jacinth, an agate,
and an amethyst;
20and the fourth row is a beryl, and a
shoham, and a jasper. They are set in gold
settings.
21"And the stones are according to the
names of the sons of Yisra'ĕl, twelve
according to their names, like the engravings of a signet, each one with its own
name, for the twelve tribes.
22"And you shall make braided chains of
corded work for the breastplate at the end,
of clean gold.
23"And you shall make two rings of gold
for the breastplate, and shall put the two
rings on the two ends of the breastplate.
24"And you shall put the two cords of
gold in the two rings which are on the ends
of the breastplate,
25and the other two ends of the two cords
you fasten to the two settings, and put
them on the shoulder pieces of the shoulder garment in the front.
26"And you shall make two rings of gold,
and shall put them on the two ends of the
breastplate, on the edge of it, which is on
the inner side of the shoulder garment.
27"And you shall make two rings of gold,
and put them on the two shoulder pieces,
underneath the shoulder garment, on the
front of it, close to the seam above the
embroidered band of the shoulder garment,
28and they bind the breastplate by means
of its rings to the rings of the shoulder
garment, using a blue cord, so that it is
above the embroidered band of the shoulder garment, so that the breastplate does
not come loose from the shoulder garment.
29"And Aharon shall bear the names of
the sons of Yisra'ĕl on the breastplate of
right-ruling over his heart, when he goes
into the set-apart place, for a remembrance
before יהוה, continually.
30"And into the breastplate of right-ruling
you shall put the Urim and the Tummim,
and they shall be on the heart of Aharon
when he goes in before יהוה. And Aharon
shall bear the right-ruling of the children
of Yisra'ĕl on his heart before יהוה, continually.
31"And you shall make the robe of the
shoulder garment all of blue.
32"And the opening for his head shall be
in the middle of it, a woven binding all
around its opening, like the opening in a
scaled armour, so that it does not tear.
33"And on its hem you shall make pomegranates of blue and purple and scarlet
material, all around its hem, and bells of
gold between them all around:
34a golden bell and a pomegranate, a
golden bell and a pomegranate, on the hem
of the robe all around.
35"And it shall be upon Aharon to attend
in, and its sound shall be heard when he
goes into the set-apart place before יהוה
and when he comes out, so that he does not
die.
36"And you shall make a plate of clean
gold and engrave on it, like the engraving
of a signet: SET-APARTNESS TO יהוה.
37"And you shall put it on a blue cord,
and it shall be on the turban – it is to be on
the front of the turban.
38"And it shall be on the forehead of
Aharon, and Aharon shall bear the guilt of
the set-apart gifts which the children of
Yisra'ĕl set apart in all their set-apart gifts.
And it shall always be on his forehead, for
acceptance for them before יהוה.
39"And you shall weave the long shirt of
fine linen, and shall make the turban of
fine linen, and you shall make the girdle of
woven work.
40"And make long shirts for Aharon's
sons. And you shall make girdles for them,

and you shall make turbans for them, for esteem and comeliness.

41 "And you shall put them on Aharon your brother and on his sons with him, and shall anoint them, and shall ordain them, and shall set them apart, and they shall serve as priests to Me.

42 "And make linen trousers for them, to cover their nakedness, reaching from the waist to the thighs.

43 "And they shall be on Aharon and on his sons when they come into the Tent of Appointment, or when they come near the slaughter-place to attend in the Set-apart Place, so that they do not bear crookedness and die – a law forever to him, and to his seed after him.

29 "And this is the task you shall do to them to set them apart to serve Me as priests: Take one young bull and two rams, perfect ones,

2 and unleavened bread, and unleavened cakes mixed with oil, and unleavened wafers anointed with oil – make these of wheat flour.

3 "And you shall put them in one basket and bring them in the basket, along with the bull and the two rams.

4 "Then you shall bring Aharon and his sons to the door of the Tent of Appointment, and wash them with water.

5 "And you shall take the garments, and shall put on Aharon the long shirt, and the robe of the shoulder garment, and the shoulder garment, and the breastplate, and shall gird him with the embroidered band of the shoulder garment,

6 and shall put the turban on his head, and shall put the set-apart sign of dedication on the turban,

7 and shall take the anointing oil, and pour it on his head and anoint him.

8 "Then you shall bring his sons and put long shirts on them,

9 and shall gird them with girdles – Aharon and his sons – and put the turbans on them. And the priesthood shall be theirs for an everlasting law. So you shall ordain Aharon and his sons.

10 "And you shall bring near the bull before the Tent of Appointment, and Aharon and his sons shall lay their hands on the head of the bull.

11 "And you shall slay the bull before יהוה, by the door of the Tent of Appointment,

12 and take some of the blood of the bull and put it on the horns of the slaughter-place with your finger, and pour all the blood beside the base of the slaughter-place.

13 "And you shall take all the fat that covers the entrails, and the appendage on the liver, and the two kidneys and the fat that is on them, and burn them on the slaughter-place.

14 "But the flesh of the bull, and its skin and its dung, you shall burn with fire outside the camp. It is a sin offering.

15 "And take one ram, and Aharon and his sons shall lay their hands on the head of the ram,

16 and you shall slay the ram, and you shall take its blood and sprinkle it all around on the slaughter-place.

17 "And cut the ram in pieces, and wash its entrails and its legs, and place them upon its pieces and on its head.

18 "And you shall burn the entire ram on the slaughter-place. It is an ascending offering to יהוה, it is a sweet fragrance, an offering made by fire to יהוה.

19 "And you shall take the second ram, and Aharon and his sons shall lay their hands on the head of the ram,

20 and you shall slay the ram, and take some of its blood and put it on the tip of the right ear of Aharon and on the tip of the right ear of his sons, on the thumb of their right hand and on the big toe of their right foot, and sprinkle the blood all around on the slaughter-place.

21 "And you shall take some of the blood that is on the slaughter-place, and some of the anointing oil, and sprinkle it on Aharon and on his garments, on his sons and on the garments of his sons with him. And he and his garments shall be set-apart, and his sons and the garments of his sons with him.

22 "And you shall take the fat of the ram,

and the fat tail, and the fat that covers the entrails, and the appendage on the liver, and the two kidneys and the fat on them, and the right thigh – it is for a ram of ordination –

23 and one loaf of bread, and one cake made with oil, and one thin cake from the basket of the unleavened bread that is before יהוה.

24 "And you shall put all these in the hands of Aharon and in the hands of his sons, and you shall wave them – a wave offering before יהוה.

25 "Then you shall take them from their hands and burn them on the slaughter-place as an ascending offering, as a sweet fragrance before יהוה. It is an offering made by fire to יהוה.

26 "And you shall take the breast of the ram of Aharon's ordination and wave it – a wave offering before יהוה, and it shall be your portion.

27 "And from the ram of ordination you shall set apart the breast of the wave offering which is waved, and the thigh of the contribution which is raised, of that which is for Aharon and of that which is for his sons.

28 "And it shall be from the children of Yisra'ěl for Aharon and his sons by a law forever, for it is a contribution. And it is a contribution from the children of Yisra'ěl from the slaughters of their peace offerings – their contribution to יהוה.

29 "And the set-apart garments of Aharon are for his sons after him, to be anointed in them and to be ordained in them.

30 "The priest from his sons in his place, puts them on for seven days, when he enters the Tent of Appointment to attend in the set-apart place.

31 "And take the ram of ordination and cook its flesh in a set-apart place.

32 "And Aharon and his sons shall eat the flesh of the ram, and the bread that is in the basket, by the door of the Tent of Appointment,

33 and they shall eat those *offerings* with which the atonement was made, to ordain them, to set them apart. But let a stranger not eat them, because they are set-apart.

34 "And if any of the flesh of the ordination offerings, or of the bread, be left over until the morning, then you shall burn up what is left over. It is not eaten, because it is set-apart.

35 "And so you shall do to Aharon and his sons, according to all I have commanded you. Seven days you shall ordain them,

36 and prepare a bull each day as a sin offering for atonement. And you shall cleanse the slaughter-place when you make atonement for it, and you shall anoint it to set it apart.

37 "For seven days you shall make atonement for the slaughter-place, and set it apart. And the slaughter-place shall be most set-apart – whatever touches the slaughter-place is to be set-apart.

38 "And this is what you prepare on the slaughter-place: two lambs, a year old, daily, continually.

39 "Prepare the one lamb in the morning, and the other lamb you prepare between the evenings,

40 and one-tenth of an ěphah of flour mixed with one-fourth of a hin of pressed oil, and one-fourth of a hin of wine as a drink offering, with the one lamb.

41 "And prepare the other lamb between the evenings. And with it prepare the grain offering and the drink offering, as in the morning, for a sweet fragrance, an offering made by fire to יהוה –

42 a continual ascending offering for your generations at the door of the Tent of Appointment before יהוה, where I shall meet with you to speak with you.

43 "And there I shall meet with the children of Yisra'ěl, and it shall be set apart by My esteem.

44 "And I shall set apart the Tent of Appointment and the slaughter-place. And Aharon and his sons I set apart to serve as priests to Me.

45 "And I shall dwell in the midst of the children of Yisra'ěl and shall be their Elohim.

46 "And they shall know that I am יהוה their Elohim, who brought them up out of the land of Mitsrayim, to dwell in their midst. I am יהוה their Elohim.

30 "And you shall make a slaughter-place to burn incense on, make it of acacia wood,

2 a cubit long and a cubit wide – it is a square – and two cubits high, its horns of the same.

3 "And you shall overlay its top, and its sides all around, and its horns with clean gold. And you shall make for it a moulding of gold all around.

4 "And make two gold rings for it, under the moulding on both its sides. Make them on its two sides, and they shall be holders for the poles to lift it with.

5 "And you shall make the poles of acacia wood, and overlay them with gold.

6 "And you shall put it before the veil that is before the ark of the Witness, before the lid of atonement that is over the Witness, where I am to meet with you.

7 "And Aharon shall burn on it sweet incense, morning by morning. As he tends the lamps, he shall burn incense on it.

8 "And when Aharon lights the lamps between the evenings, he shall burn incense on it – a continual incense before יהוה throughout your generations.

9 "Do not offer strange incense on it, or an ascending offering, or a grain offering, and do not pour a drink offering on it.

10 "And Aharon shall make atonement upon its horns once a year with the blood of the sin offering of atonement – once a year he makes atonement upon it throughout your generations. It is most set-apart to יהוה."

11 And יהוה spoke to Mosheh, saying,

12 "When you take the census of the children of Yisra'ĕl, to register them, then each one shall give an atonement for his life to יהוה, when you register them, so that there is no plague among them when you register them.

13 "Everyone among those who are registered is to give this: half a sheqel according to the sheqel of the set-apart place, twenty gĕrahs being a sheqel. The half-sheqel is the contribution to יהוה.

14 "Everyone passing over to be registered, from twenty years old and above, gives a contribution to יהוה.

15 "The rich does not give more and the poor does not give less than half a sheqel, when you give a contribution to יהוה, to make atonement for yourselves.

16 "And you shall take the silver for the atonement from the children of Yisra'ĕl, and give it for the service of the Tent of Appointment. And it shall be to the children of Yisra'ĕl for a remembrance before יהוה, to make atonement for yourselves."

17 And יהוה spoke to Mosheh, saying,

18 "And you shall make a basin of bronze, with its stand also of bronze, for washing. And you shall put it between the Tent of Appointment and the slaughter-place, and shall put water in it.

19 "And Aharon and his sons shall wash from it their hands and their feet.

20 "When they go into the Tent of Appointment, or when they come near the slaughter-place to attend, to burn an offering made by fire to יהוה, they wash with water, lest they die.

21 "And they shall wash their hands and their feet, lest they die. And it shall be a law forever to them, to him and his seed throughout their generations."

22 And יהוה spoke to Mosheh, saying,

23 "And take for yourself choice spices, five hundred *sheqels* of liquid myrrh, and half as much – two hundred and fifty – of sweet-smelling cinnamon, and two hundred and fifty of sweet-smelling cane,

24 and five hundred of cassia, according to the sheqel of the set-apart place, and a hin of olive oil.

25 "And you shall make from these a set-apart anointing oil, a compound, blended, the work of a perfumer. It is a set-apart anointing oil.

26 "And with it you shall anoint the Tent of Appointment and the ark of the Witness,

27 and the table and all its utensils, and the lampstand and its utensils, and the slaughter-place of incense,

28 and the slaughter-place of ascending offering with all its utensils, and the basin and its stand.

29 "And you shall set them apart, and they shall be most set-apart. Whatever touches them is to be set-apart.

30 "And you shall anoint Aharon and his
sons, and set them apart, to serve as priests
to Me.
31 "And speak to the children of Yisra'ĕl,
saying, 'This is a set-apart anointing oil to
Me throughout your generations.
32 'It shall not be poured on the flesh of a
man, and make no other like it, according
to its composition. It is set-apart, it is set-
apart to you.
33 'Whoever compounds *any* like it, or
whoever puts any of it on a stranger, shall
be cut off from his people.' "
34 And יהוה said to Mosheh, "Take sweet
spices, fragrant gum and cinnamon and
galbanam, and clear frankincense with
these sweet spices, all in equal amounts.
35 "Then you shall make of these an
incense, a compound, work of a perfumer,
salted, clean, set-apart.
36 "And you shall beat some of it very
fine, and put some of it before the Witness
in the Tent of Appointment where I meet
with you, it is most set-apart to you.
37 "And the incense which you make, do
not make any for yourselves, according to
its composition, it is set-apart to you for
יהוה.
38 "Whoever makes *any* like it, to smell it,
he shall be cut off from his people."

31 And יהוה spoke to Mosheh, saying,
2 "See, I have called by name
Betsal'ĕl son of Uri, son of Ḥur, of the
tribe of Yehuḏah,
3 and I have filled him with the Spirit of
Elohim in wisdom, and in understanding,
and in knowledge, and in all work,
4 to make designs for work in gold, and
in silver, and in bronze,
5 and in cutting stones for setting, and in
carving wood, and to work in all work.
6 "And I, look I have appointed with him
Oholiaḇ son of Aḥisamaḵ, of the tribe of
Dan. And I have put wisdom in the hearts
of everyone who is wise-hearted, and they
shall make all that I have commanded you:
7 the Tent of Appointment, and the ark of
the Witness and the lid of atonement that is
on it, and all the utensils of the Tent,
8 and the table and its utensils, and the
clean gold lampstand with all its utensils,
and the slaughter-place of incense,
9 and the slaughter-place of ascending
offering with all its utensils, and the basin
and its stand,
10 and the woven garments, and the set-
apart garments for Aharon the priest and
the garments of his sons, for serving as
priests,
11 and the anointing oil and sweet incense
for the Set-apart Place. According to all
that I have commanded you, they are to
do."
12 And יהוה spoke to Mosheh, saying,
13 "And you, speak to the children of
Yisra'ĕl, saying, 'My Sabbaths you are to
guard, by all means, for it is a sign [a]
between Me and you throughout your
generations, to know that I, יהוה, am
setting you apart.
14 'And you shall guard the Sabbath, for it
is set-apart to you. Everyone who profanes
it shall certainly be put to death, for anyone who does work on it, that being shall
be cut off from among his people.
15 'Six days work is done, and on the
seventh is a Sabbath of rest, set-apart to
יהוה. Everyone doing work on the Sabbath
day shall certainly be put to death.
16 'And the children of Yisra'ĕl shall
guard the Sabbath, to perform the Sabbath
throughout their generations as an everlasting covenant.
17 'Between Me and the children of Yisra'ĕl it is a sign forever. For in six days
יהוה made the heavens and the earth, and
on the seventh day He rested and was
refreshed.' "
18 And when He had ended speaking with
him on Mount Sinai, He gave Mosheh two
tablets of the Witness, tablets of stone,
written with the finger of Elohim.

32 And when the people saw that
Mosheh was so long in coming
down from the mountain, the people gathered together to Aharon, and said to him,

31a Also see Yeḥ. 20:12 & 20.

"Arise, make us mighty ones who go before us. For this Mosheh, the man who brought us up out of the land of Mitsrayim, we do not know what has become of him."

2 And Aharon said to them, "Take off the golden earrings which are in the ears of your wives, your sons, and your daughters, and bring them to me."

3 "And all the people took off the golden earrings which were in their ears, and brought them to Aharon.

4 And he took *this* from their hand, and he formed it with an engraving tool, and made a moulded calf. And they said, "This is your mighty one, O Yisra'ĕl, that brought you out of the land of Mitsrayim!"

5 And Aharon saw and built a slaughter-place before it. And Aharon called out and said, "Tomorrow is a festival to יהוה."

6 And they rose early on the next day, and offered ascending offerings, and brought peace offerings. And the people sat down to eat and drink, and rose up to play.

7 And יהוה said to Mosheh, "Go, get down! For your people whom you brought out of the land of Mitsrayim have corrupted themselves.

8 "They have turned aside quickly out of the way which I commanded them. They have made themselves a moulded calf, and have bowed themselves to it and slaughtered to it, and said, 'This is your mighty one, O Yisra'ĕl, who brought you out of the land of Mitsrayim!' "

9 And יהוה said to Mosheh, "I have seen this people, and see, it is a stiff-necked people!

10 "And now, let Me alone, that My wrath might burn against them and I consume them and I make of you a great nation."

11 But Mosheh pleaded with יהוה his Elohim, and said, "יהוה, why does Your wrath burn against Your people whom You have brought out of the land of Mitsrayim with great power and with a strong hand?

12 "Why should the Mitsrites speak, and say, 'For evil He brought them out to kill them in the mountains, and to consume them from the face of the earth'? Turn from the heat of Your wrath, and relent from this evil to Your people.

13 "Remember Aḇraham, Yitsḥaq, and Yisra'ĕl, Your servants, to whom You swore by Yourself, and said to them, 'I increase your seed like the stars of the heavens. And all this land that I have spoken of I give to your seed, and they shall inherit it forever.' "

14 And יהוה relented from the evil which He said He would do to His people.

15 And Mosheh turned and went down from the mountain, and in his hand were the two tablets of the Witness, tablets written on both their sides, written on the one and on the other.

16 And the tablets were the work of Elohim, and the writing was the writing of Elohim engraved on the tablets.

17 And Yehoshua heard the noise of the people as they shouted and he said to Mosheh, "A noise of battle in the camp!"

18 But he said, "It is not the sound of those who shout of might, nor is it the sound of those who cry out in weakness, but the sound of singing that I hear."

19 And it came to be, as soon as he came near the camp, that he saw the calf and the dancing. And Mosheh's displeasure burned, and he threw the tablets out of his hands and broke them at the foot of the mountain.

20 And he took the calf which they had made, and burned it in the fire, and ground it into powder, and scattered it on the face of the water and made the children of Yisra'ĕl drink it.

21 And Mosheh said to Aharon, "What did this people do to you that you have brought so great a sin upon them?"

22 And Aharon said, "Do not let the displeasure of my master burn. You know the people, that it is in evil.

23 "And they said to me, 'Make us mighty ones who go before us. For this Mosheh, the man who brought us out of the land of Mitsrayim, we do not know what has become of him.'

24 "And I said to them, 'Whoever has gold, let them take it off.' And they gave it to me, and I threw it into the fire, and this calf came out."

25 And Mosheh saw that the people were
let loose, for Aharon had let them loose, to
their shame among their enemies.
26 And Mosheh stood in the entrance of
the camp, and said, "Who is for יהוה?
Come to me." And all the sons of Lěwi
gathered themselves to him.
27 And he said to them, "Thus said יהוה
Elohim of Yisra'ěl: 'Each one put his
sword on his side, pass over to and fro
from gate to gate in the camp, and each
one kill his brother, and each one his
friend, and each one his relative.' "
28 And the sons of Lěwi did according to
the word of Mosheh. And about three
thousand men of the people fell that day.
29 And Mosheh said, "You are ordained
for יהוה today – since each one has been
against his son and his brother – so as to
bring upon you a blessing today."
30 And it came to be on the next day that
Mosheh said to the people, "You, you have
sinned a great sin. And now I am going up
to יהוה – if I might atone for your sin."
31 And Mosheh returned to יהוה and said,
"Oh, these people have sinned a great sin,
and have made for themselves a mighty
one of gold!
32 "And now, if You would forgive their
sin, but if not, please blot me out of Your
book which You have written."
33 And יהוה said to Mosheh, "Whoever
has sinned against Me, I blot him out of
My book.
34 "And now, go, lead the people to the
place of which I have spoken to you. See,
My Messenger goes before you. And in the
day of My visitation I shall visit their sin
upon them."
35 And יהוה plagued the people because
they made the calf, which Aharon made.

33 And יהוה said to Mosheh, "Come,
go up from here, you and the people whom you have brought out of the land
of Mitsrayim, to the land of which I swore
to Aḇraham, to Yitsḥaq, and to Ya'aqoḇ,
saying, 'To your seed I give it.'
2 "And I shall send My Messenger before
you, and I shall drive out the Kena'anite
and the Amorite and the Ḥittite and the
Perizzite and the Ḥiwwite and the
Yeḇusite,
3 to a land flowing with milk and honey.
For I do not go up in your midst because
you are a stiff-necked people, lest I consume you on the way."
4 And when the people heard this evil
word, they mourned, and no one put on his
ornaments.
5 And יהוה said to Mosheh, "Say to the
children of Yisra'ěl, 'You are a stiff-
necked people. Should I go up in your
midst for one moment I shall consume
you. And now, take off your ornaments,
and I shall know what to do to you.' "
6 So the children of Yisra'ěl took off
their ornaments at Mount Ḥorěḇ.
7 And Mosheh took his tent and pitched
it outside the camp, far from the camp, and
called it the Tent of Appointment. And it
came to be that everyone who sought יהוה
went out to the Tent of Appointment which
was outside the camp.
8 And it came to be, whenever Mosheh
went out to the Tent, that all the people
rose, and each man stood at his tent door
and watched Mosheh until he entered the
Tent.
9 And it came to be, when Mosheh
entered the Tent, that the column of cloud
descended and stood at the door of the
Tent, and He spoke with Mosheh.
10 And all the people saw the column of
cloud standing at the Tent door, and all the
people rose and bowed themselves, each
one at the door of his tent.
11 Thus יהוה spoke to Mosheh face to
face, as a man speaks to his friend. And he
would return to the camp, but his servant
Yehoshua son of Nun, a young man, did
not leave the Tent.
12 And Mosheh said to יהוה, "See, You
are saying to me, 'Bring up this people.'
But You have not made known to me
whom You would send with me, though
You have said, 'I know you by name, and
you have also found favour in My eyes.'
13 "And now, please, if I have found
favour in Your eyes, please show me Your
way, and let me know You, so that I find
favour in Your eyes. And consider that this

nation is Your people."
14 And He said, "My Presence does go, and I shall give you rest."
15 And he said to Him, "If Your Presence is not going, do not lead us up from here.
16 "For how then shall it be known that I have found favour in Your eyes, I and Your people, except You go with us? Then we shall be distinguished, I and Your people, from all the people who are upon the face of the earth."
17 And יהוה said to Mosheh, "Even this word you have spoken I shall do, for you have found favour in My eyes, and I know you by name."
18 Then he said, "Please, show me Your esteem."
19 And He said, "I shall cause all My goodness to pass before you, and I shall proclaim the Name of יהוה before you. And I shall favour him whom I favour, and shall have compassion on him whom I have compassion."
20 But He said, "You are unable to see My face, for no man does see Me and live."
21 And יהוה said, "See, there is a place with Me! And you shall stand on the rock.
22 "And it shall be, while My esteem passes by, that I shall put you in the cleft of the rock and cover you with My hand while I pass by.
23 "Then I shall take away My hand and you shall see My back, but My face shall not be seen."

34 And יהוה said to Mosheh, "Cut two tablets of stone like the first ones, and I shall write on these tablets the Words that were on the first tablets which you broke.
2 "And be ready in the morning. Then you shall come up in the morning to Mount Sinai, and present yourself to Me there on the top of the mountain.
3 "And let no man come up with you, and let no man be seen in all the mountain, and let not even the flock or the herd feed in front of that mountain."
4 And he cut two tablets of stone like the first ones. Then Mosheh rose early in the morning and went up Mount Sinai, as יהוה had commanded him, and he took two tablets of stone in his hand.
5 And יהוה came down in the cloud and stood with him there, and proclaimed the Name, יהוה.
6 And יהוה passed before him and proclaimed, "יהוה, יהוה, an Ěl compassionate and showing favour, patient, and great in loving-commitment and truth,
7 watching over loving-commitment for thousands, forgiving crookedness and transgression and sin, but by no means leaving unpunished, [a] visiting the crookedness of the fathers upon the children and the children's children to the third and the fourth *generation*."
8 And Mosheh hurried and bowed himself toward the earth, and did obeisance,
9 and said, "If, now, I have found favour in Your eyes, O יהוה, I pray, let יהוה go on in our midst, even though we are a stiff-necked people. And forgive our crookedness and our sin, and take us as Your inheritance."
10 And He said, "See, I am making a covenant. Before all your people I am going to do wonders such as have not been done in all the earth, nor in any nation. And all the people among whom you are shall see the work of יהוה. For what I am doing with you is awesome.
11 "Guard what I command you today. See, I am driving out from before you the Amorite and the Kena'anite and the Ḥittite and the Perizzite and the Ḥiwwite and the Yeḇusite.
12 "Guard yourself, lest you make a covenant with the inhabitants of the land where you are going, lest it be a snare in your midst.
13 "But break down their slaughter-places, and smash their pillars, and cut down their Ashĕrim –
14 for you do not bow yourselves to another mighty one, for יהוה, whose Name is jealous, is a jealous Ěl –
15 lest you make a covenant with the

34a Also see Bem. 14:18 and Yirm. 30:11.

inhabitants of the land, and they whore after their mighty ones, and slaughter to their mighty ones, and one of them invites you and you eat of his slaughterings,

16 and you take of his daughters for your sons, and his daughters whore after their mighty ones, and make your sons whore after their mighty ones.

17 "Do not make a moulded mighty one for yourselves.

18 "Guard the Festival of Matzot.[b] For seven days you eat unleavened bread, as I commanded you, in the appointed time of the new *moon* of Aḇiḇ, because in the new *moon* of Aḇiḇ you came out from Mitsrayim.

19 "Everyone opening the womb is Mine, and every male first-born among your livestock, whether bull or sheep.

20 "But the first-born of a donkey you ransom with a lamb. And if you do not ransom, then you shall break his neck. Every first-born of your sons you shall ransom. And they shall not appear before Me empty-handed.

21 "Six days you work, but on the seventh day you rest – in ploughing time and in harvest you rest.

22 "And perform the Festival of Shaḇu'ot[c] for yourself, of the first-fruits of wheat harvest, and the Festival of Ingathering[d] at the turn of the year.

23 "Three times in the year all your men are to appear before the Master, יהוה, the Elohim of Yisra'ěl,

24 for I dispossess nations before you, and shall enlarge your borders, and let no one covet your land when you go up to appear before יהוה your Elohim three times in the year.

25 "Do not slay the blood of My slaughtering with leaven, and do not let the slaughtering of the Festival of the Pěsaḥ[e] remain until morning.

26 "Bring the first of the first-fruits of your land to the House of יהוה your Elohim. Do not cook a young goat in its mother's milk."

27 And יהוה said to Mosheh, "Write these Words, for according to the mouth of these Words I have made a covenant with you and with Yisra'ěl."

28 And he was there with יהוה forty days and forty nights. He did not eat bread and he did not drink water. And He wrote on the tablets the Words of the covenant, the Ten Words.

29 And it came to be, when Mosheh came down from Mount Sinai, while the two tablets of the Witness were in Mosheh's hand when he came down from the mountain, that Mosheh did not know that the skin of his face shone since he had spoken with Him.

30 And Aharon and all the children of Yisra'ěl looked at Mosheh and saw the skin of his face shone, and they were afraid to come near him.

31 But Mosheh called out to them, and Aharon and all the rulers of the congregation returned to him, and Mosheh spoke to them.

32 And afterward all the children of Yisra'ěl came near, and he commanded them all that יהוה had spoken with him on Mount Sinai.

33 And when Mosheh ended speaking with them, he put a veil on his face.

34 But whenever Mosheh went in before יהוה to speak with Him, he would remove the veil until he came out. And when he came out he spoke to the children of Yisra'ěl what he had been commanded,

35 and the children of Yisra'ěl would see the face of Mosheh, that the skin of Mosheh's face shone, and Mosheh would put the veil on his face again, until he went in to speak with Him.

35

And Mosheh assembled all the congregation of the children of Yisra'ěl, and said to them, "These are the Words which יהוה has commanded you to do:

2 "Work is done for six days, but on the seventh day it shall be set-apart to you, a Sabbath of rest to יהוה. Anyone doing work on it is put to death.

34b - Unleavened Bread. *34c* - Weeks. *34d* - Festival of Sukkot (Booths). *34e* - Passover.

3 "Do not kindle a fire in any of your
dwellings on the Sabbath day."
4 And Mosheh spoke to all the congregation of the children of Yisra'ěl, saying, "This is the word which יהוה commanded, saying,
5 'Take from among you a contribution to יהוה. Everyone whose heart so moves him, let him bring it as a contribution to יהוה: gold, and silver, and bronze,
6 and blue, and purple, and scarlet *material*, and fine linen, and goats' *hair*,
7 and ram skins dyed red, and fine leather, and acacia wood,
8 and oil for the light, and spices for the anointing oil and for the sweet incense,
9 and shoham stones, and stones to be set in the shoulder garment and in the breastplate.
10 'And let all the wise-hearted among you come and make all that יהוה has commanded:
11 the Dwelling Place, its tent and its covering, its hooks and its boards, its bars, its columns, and its sockets,
12 the ark and its poles, the lid of atonement and the veil of the covering,
13 the table and its poles, and all its utensils, and the showbread,
14 and the lampstand for the light, and its utensils, and its lamps, and the oil for the light,
15 and the incense slaughter-place, and its poles, and the anointing oil, and the sweet incense, and the covering for the door at the entrance of the Dwelling Place,
16 the slaughter-place of ascending offering with its bronze grating, its poles, and all its utensils, the basin and its stand,
17 the screens of the courtyard, its columns, and their sockets, and the covering for the gate of the courtyard,
18 the pegs of the Dwelling Place, and the pegs of the courtyard, and their cords,
19 the woven garments to do service in the set-apart place, the set-apart garments for Aharon the priest and the garments of his sons to serve as priests.' "
20 And all the congregation of the children of Yisra'ěl withdrew from the presence of Mosheh.
21 And everyone whose heart lifted him up and everyone whose spirit moved him came, and they brought the contribution to יהוה for the work of the Tent of Appointment, and for all its service, and for the set-apart garments.
22 And they came, both men and women, all whose hearts moved them, and brought earrings and nose rings, and rings and necklaces, all golden goods, even every one who made a wave offering of gold to יהוה.
23 And every man, with whom was found blue and purple and scarlet *material*, and fine linen, and goats' *hair*, and rams' skins dyed red, and fine leather, brought them.
24 Everyone who would make a contribution to יהוה of silver or bronze, brought it. And everyone with whom was found acacia wood for any work of the service, brought it.
25 And all the wise-hearted women spun yarn with their hands, and brought what they had spun, the blue and the purple, the scarlet *material,* and the fine linen.
26 And all the women whose hearts lifted them up in wisdom spun the goats' *hair*.
27 And the rulers brought shoham stones, and the stones to be set in the shoulder garment and in the breastplate,
28 and the spices and the oil for the light, and for the anointing oil, and for the sweet incense.
29 The children of Yisra'ěl brought a voluntary offering to יהוה, all the men and women whose hearts moved them to bring all kinds of work which יהוה, by the hand of Mosheh, had commanded to be done.
30 And Mosheh said to the children of Yisra'ěl, "See, יהוה has called by name Betsal'ěl son of Uri, son of Ḥur, of the tribe of Yehuḏah,
31 and He has filled him with the Spirit of Elohim, in wisdom, in understanding, and in knowledge, and in all work,
32 to make designs, to work in gold and in silver and in bronze,
33 and in cutting of stones for setting, and in carving wood, and to work in all workmanship of design.
34 "And He has put in his heart the ability

to teach, in him and Oholiaḇ son of Aḥisamaḵ, of the tribe of Dan.

35 “He has filled them with skill to do all work of the engraver and the designer and embroiderer, in blue and in purple, in scarlet *material,* and in fine linen, and a weaver, doing any work, and makers of designs.

36 “And Betsal’ĕl and Oholiaḇ, and every wise-hearted man in whom יהוה has given wisdom and understanding, to know how to do all work for the service of the set-apart place, shall do according to all that יהוה has commanded.”

2 And Mosheh called Betsal’ĕl and Oholiaḇ, and every wise-hearted man in whose heart יהוה had given wisdom, everyone whose heart lifted him up, to come and do the work.

3 And they received from Mosheh all the contribution which the children of Yisra’ĕl had brought for the work of the service of making the set-apart place. But they still brought to him voluntary offerings every morning,

4 so all the craftsmen who were doing all the work of the set-apart place came, each from the work he was doing,

5 and they spoke to Mosheh, saying, “The people bring much more than enough for the service of the work which יהוה commanded us to do.”

6 Then Mosheh commanded and they sent this word throughout the camp, saying, “Let neither man nor woman do any more work for the contribution of the set-apart place.” And the people were withheld from bringing,

7 for what they had was enough for all the work to be done, more than enough.

8 Then all the wise-hearted ones among them who worked on the Dwelling Place made ten curtains woven of fine linen and blue and purple and scarlet *material*. They made them with keruḇim, the work of a skilled workman.

9 The length of each curtain was twenty-eight cubits, and the width of each curtain four cubits, all the curtains having one measure.

10 And he joined five curtains, one to another; and the other five curtains he joined, one to another.

11 And he made loops of blue on the edge of the end curtain of one set, the same he did on the edge of the end curtain of the other set.

12 Fifty loops he made on one curtain, and fifty loops he made on the edge of the end curtain of the second set; the loops held one curtain to another.

13 And he made fifty hooks of gold, and joined the curtains to each other with the hooks, and the Dwelling Place became one.

14 And he made curtains of goats’ *hair* for the tent over the Dwelling Place, he made eleven curtains.

15 The length of each curtain was thirty cubits, and the width of each curtain four cubits, the eleven curtains having one measure.

16 And he joined five curtains by themselves and six curtains by themselves.

17 And he made fifty loops on the edge of the end curtain in one set, and fifty loops he made on the edge of the curtain of the second set.

18 And he made fifty bronze hooks to join the tent, to be one.

19 And he made a covering for the tent of rams’ skins, dyed red, and a covering of fine leather above that.

20 And for the Dwelling Place he made boards of acacia wood, standing up.

21 The length of each board was ten cubits, and the width of each board a cubit and a half.

22 Each board had two tenons for binding one to another. So he did to all the boards of the Dwelling Place.

23 And he made boards for the Dwelling Place, twenty boards for the south side.

24 And he made forty sockets of silver to go under the twenty boards, and two sockets under each of the boards for its two tenons.

25 And for the other side of the Dwelling Place, for the north side, he made twenty boards,

26 and their forty sockets of silver, two

sockets under the one board, and two
sockets under the other board.
27 And he made six boards for the west
side of the Dwelling Place.
28 And he made two boards for the two
back corners of the Dwelling Place.
29 And they were double beneath, and
similarly they were complete to the top by
one ring. So he did to both of them for the
two corners.
30 And there were eight boards, and their
silver sockets, sixteen sockets, two sockets
under each of the boards.
31 And he made bars of acacia wood, five
for the boards on one side of the Dwelling
Place,
32 and five bars for the boards on the other
side of the Dwelling Place, and five bars
for the boards of the Dwelling Place at the
rear, westward.
33 And he made the middle bar to pass
through the boards from one end to the
other.
34 And he overlaid the boards with gold,
and their rings he made of gold to be holders for the bars, and overlaid the bars with
gold.
35 And he made a veil of blue and purple
and scarlet *material*, and fine worked
linen. It was made with keruḇim, the work
of a skilled workman.
36 And he made four columns of acacia
wood for it, and overlaid them with gold,
with their hooks of gold. And he cast four
sockets of silver for them.
37 And he made a covering for the Tent
door of blue and purple and scarlet *material* and fine woven linen, made by a weaver,
38 and its five columns with their hooks.
And he overlaid their tops and their rings
with gold, but their five sockets were of
bronze.

37 And Betsal'ěl made the ark of
acacia wood, two and a half cubits
long, and a cubit and a half wide, and a
cubit and a half high.
2 And he overlaid it with clean gold
inside and outside, and made a moulding
of gold all around it.
3 And he cast four rings of gold for it, for
its four feet, two rings on its one side, and
two rings on its other side.
4 And he made poles of acacia wood, and
overlaid them with gold.
5 And he put the poles into the rings at
the sides of the ark, to lift the ark.
6 And he made a lid of atonement of
clean gold, two and a half cubits long and a
cubit and a half wide.
7 And he made two keruḇim of beaten
gold. He made them from the two ends of
the lid of atonement,
8 one keruḇ at one end on this side, and
the other keruḇ at the other end on that
side. He made the keruḇim from the lid of
atonement, from the two ends.
9 And the keruḇim spread out their wings
above, and covered the lid of atonement
with their wings, with their faces toward
each other, the faces of the keruḇim were
turned toward the lid of atonement.
10 And he made the table of acacia wood,
two cubits long, and a cubit wide, and a
cubit and a half high.
11 And he overlaid it with clean gold, and
made a moulding of gold all around it.
12 And he made a rim of a handbreadth all
around it, and made a moulding of gold for
the rim all around it.
13 And he cast four rings of gold for it,
and put the rings on the four corners that
were at its four legs.
14 The rings were next to the rim, as holders for the poles to lift the table.
15 And he made the poles of acacia wood
to lift the table, and overlaid them with
gold.
16 And he made the utensils which were
on the table, its dishes, and its cups, and its
bowls, and its jars for pouring, of clean
gold.
17 And he made the lampstand of clean
gold. He made the lampstand of beaten
work, its base, and its shaft, its cups, its
ornamental knobs, and its blossoms were
from it.
18 And six branches came out of its sides:
three branches of the lampstand out of one
side, and three branches of the lampstand
out of the other side.
19 There were three cups like almond

flowers on one branch, with ornamental
knob and blossom, and three cups like
almond flowers on the other branch, a
knob and a blossom – so for the six
branches coming out of the lampstand.
20 And on the lampstand were four
cups like almond flowers, its knobs and
blossoms,
21 and a knob under the first two branches
of the same, and a knob under the second
two branches of the same, and a knob
under the third two branches of the same,
for the six branches coming out of it.
22 Their knobs and their branches were of
it, all of it was one beaten work of clean
gold.
23 And he made its seven lamps, and its
snuffers, and its trays, of clean gold.
24 He made it of a talent of clean gold, and
all its utensils.
25 And he made the incense slaughter-
place of acacia wood, a cubit long and a
cubit wide, square, and two cubits high. Its
horns were of it.
26 And he overlaid it with clean gold, its
top and its sides all around, and its horns.
And he made a moulding for it of gold all
around it.
27 And he made two rings of gold for it
under its moulding, at its two corners on
both sides, as holders for the poles with
which to lift it.
28 And he made the poles of acacia wood,
and overlaid them with gold.
29 And he made the set-apart anointing oil
and the clean incense of sweet spices,
according to the work of the perfumer.

38 And he made the slaughter-place
of ascending offering of acacia
wood, five cubits long and five cubits
wide, square, and three cubits high.
2 And he made its horns on its four
corners, the horns were of it. And he overlaid it with bronze.
3 And he made all the utensils for the
slaughter-place: the pots, and the shovels,
and the basins, and the forks, and the fire
holders. He made all its utensils of bronze.
4 And he made a grating for the slaughter-place, a bronze network, under its rim,
midway from the bottom.
5 And he cast four rings for the four
corners of the bronze grating, as holders
for the poles.
6 And he made the poles of acacia wood,
and overlaid them with bronze.
7 And he put the poles into the rings on
the sides of the slaughter-place, with which
to lift it. He made the slaughter-place hollow with boards.
8 And he made the basin of bronze and
its stand of bronze, from the bronze
mirrors of the serving women who did
service at the door of the Tent of
Appointment.
9 And he made the courtyard: for the
south side the screens of the courtyard
were of fine woven linen, one hundred
cubits long,
10 their twenty columns and their twenty
sockets, of bronze. The hooks of the
columns and their bands were of silver.
11 And for the north side the screens were
one hundred cubits long, their twenty
columns and their twenty sockets, of
bronze. The hooks of the columns and
their bands were of silver.
12 And for the west side there were
screens of fifty cubits, their ten columns
and their ten sockets. The hooks of the
columns and their bands were of silver.
13 And for the east side eastward, fifty
cubits:
14 fifteen cubits of screens on the one
side, with their three columns and their
three sockets,
15 and fifteen cubits of screens the other
side of the courtyard gate, on this side and
that side, with their three columns and
their three sockets.
16 All the screens of the courtyard all
around were of fine woven linen.
17 And the sockets for the columns were
of bronze, the hooks of the columns and
their bands were of silver, and the overlay
of their tops was of silver. And all the
columns of the courtyard had bands of
silver.
18 And the covering for the gate of the
courtyard was the work of an embroiderer,
of blue and purple and scarlet *material*,

and of fine woven linen, and twenty cubits long, and the height along its width was five cubits, corresponding to the screens of the courtyard.
19 And the columns were four, and their sockets of bronze four, their hooks were of silver, and the overlay of their tops and their bands was of silver.
20 And all the pegs of the Dwelling Place, and of the courtyard all around, were of bronze.
21 These were the appointments of the Dwelling Place, the Dwelling Place of the Witness, which was appointed by the mouth of Mosheh, for the service of the Lĕwites, by the hand of Ithamar, son of Aharon the priest.
22 And Betsal'ĕl son of Uri, son of Ḥur, of the tribe of Yehuḏah, made all that יהוה had commanded Mosheh.
23 And with him: Oholiaḇ son of Aḥisamaḵ, of the tribe of Dan, an engraver and designer, an embroiderer in blue and purple and scarlet *material,* and in fine linen.
24 All the gold prepared for the work, in all the work of the set-apart place – and it was the gold of the wave offering – came to be twenty-nine talents and seven hundred and thirty sheqels, according to the sheqel of the set-apart place.
25 And the silver from the ones counted of the congregation was one hundred talents and one thousand seven hundred and seventy-five sheqels, according to the sheqel of the set-apart place:
26 a beqa, half a sheqel for a head, according to the sheqel of the set-apart place, for everyone passing over to those counted, from twenty years old and above, for six hundred and three thousand, five hundred and fifty *men*.
27 And the hundred talents of silver were for casting the sockets of the set-apart place and the bases of the veil: one hundred sockets from the hundred talents, a talent for each socket.
28 And of the one thousand seven hundred and seventy-five *sheqels* he made hooks for the columns, and overlaid their tops, and made bands for them.
29 And the bronze of the wave offering was seventy talents and two thousand four hundred sheqels.
30 And with it he made the sockets for the door of the Tent of Appointment, and the bronze slaughter-place, and the bronze grating for it, and all the utensils for the slaughter-place,
31 and the sockets for the courtyard all around, and the bases for the courtyard gate, and all the pegs for the Dwelling Place, and all the pegs for the courtyard all around.

39 And of the blue and purple and scarlet *material* they made woven garments, to do service in the set-apart place. And they made the set-apart garments which were for Aharon, as יהוה had commanded Mosheh.
2 And he made the shoulder garment of gold, of blue and purple and scarlet *material*, and of fine woven linen.
3 And they beat out sheets of gold and cut it into threads, to work it in with the blue and purple and scarlet *material,* and the fine linen, the work of a skilled workman.
4 They made shoulder pieces for it to join it, it was joined at its two edges.
5 And the embroidered band of his shoulder garment that was on it was of the same work of gold, and blue and purple and scarlet *material*, and of fine woven linen, as יהוה had commanded Mosheh.
6 And they made the shoham stones, set in plated work of gold, engraved as signets are engraved, according to the names of the sons of Yisra'ĕl.
7 And he put them on the shoulders of the shoulder garment, stones of remembrance for the sons of Yisra'ĕl, as יהוה had commanded Mosheh.
8 And he made the breastplate, a work of a skilled workman, like the work of the shoulder garment, of gold, of blue and purple and scarlet *material*, and of fine woven linen.
9 It was square, they made the breastplate double, its length a span, its width a span, doubled.
10 And they filled it with four rows of

stones: a row of ruby, a topaz, and an
emerald was the first row;
11 and the second row a turquoise, a sapphire, and a diamond;
12 and the third row a jacinth, an agate,
and an amethyst;
13 and the fourth row a beryl, a shoham,
and a jasper – set in plated work of gold in
their settings.
14 And the stones were according to the
names of the sons of Yisra'ěl, twelve
according to their names, engraved like a
signet, each one with its own name according to the twelve tribes.
15 And they made braided chains of corded work for the breastplate at the ends, of
clean gold.
16 And they made two settings of gold and
two gold rings, and put the two rings on
the two ends of the breastplate.
17 And they put the two cords of gold in
the two rings on the ends of the breastplate.
18 And the two ends of the two cords they
fastened in the two settings, and put them
on the shoulder pieces of the shoulder
garment in the front.
19 And they made two rings of gold and
put them on the two ends of the breastplate, on the edge of it, which was on the
inward side of the shoulder garment.
20 And they made two gold rings and put
them on the two shoulder pieces, underneath the shoulder garment, on the front of
it, close to its seam above the embroidered
band of the shoulder garment.
21 And they bound the breastplate by
means of its rings to the rings of the shoulder garment with a blue cord, so that it
would be above the embroidered band of
the shoulder garment, and that the breastplate would not come loose from the
shoulder garment, as יהוה had commanded
Mosheh.
22 And he made the robe of the shoulder
garment of woven work, all of blue.
23 And the opening of the robe was in the
middle, like the opening in a scaled
armour, with a woven binding all around
the opening, so that it would not tear.
24 And they made on the hem of the robe
pomegranates of blue and purple and scarlet *material*, twined.
25 And they made bells of clean gold, and
put the bells between the pomegranates on
the hem of the robe all around between the
pomegranates:
26 a bell and a pomegranate, a bell and
a pomegranate, all around the hem of
the robe, for the service, as יהוה had
commanded Mosheh.
27 And they made the long shirt of fine
linen, the work of a weaver, for Aharon
and his sons,
28 and a turban of fine linen, and the
turban ornaments of fine linen, and short
trousers of fine woven linen,
29 and a girdle of fine woven linen with
blue and purple and scarlet *material*, the
work of an embroiderer, as יהוה had commanded Mosheh.
30 And they made the plate of the set-apart
sign of dedication of clean gold, and wrote
on it an inscription like the engraving of a
signet: SET-APARTNESS TO יהוה.
31 And they put on it a blue cord, to fasten
it above on the turban, as יהוה had commanded Mosheh.
32 And all the work of the Dwelling Place
of the Tent of Appointment was completed. And the children of Yisra'ěl did
according to all that יהוה had commanded
Mosheh, so they did.
33 And they brought the Dwelling Place to
Mosheh, the tent and all its furnishings, its
hooks, its boards, its bars, and its columns,
and its sockets,
34 and the covering of rams' skins dyed
red, and the covering of fine leather, and
the veil of the covering,
35 the ark of the Witness with its poles,
and the lid of atonement,
36 the table, and all its utensils, and the
showbread,
37 the clean lampstand with its lamps, the
lamps to be put in order, and all its utensils, and the oil for light,
38 and the slaughter-place of gold, and the
anointing oil, and the sweet incense, and
the covering for the Tent door,
39 the bronze slaughter-place and its
bronze grating, its poles, and all its uten-

sils, the basin with its stand,
40 the screens of the courtyard, its
columns and its sockets, the covering for
the courtyard gate, its cords, and its pegs,
and all the utensils for the service of the
Dwelling Place, for the Tent of
Appointment,
41 the woven garments, to do service in
the set-apart place: the set-apart garments
for Aharon the priest, and his sons'
garments, to serve as priests.
42 According to all that יהוה had commanded Mosheh, so the children of
Yisra'ĕl did all the work.
43 And Mosheh looked over all the work
and saw they did it as יהוה had commanded, so they had done. And Mosheh
blessed them.

40 And יהוה spoke to Mosheh, saying,
2 "On the first day of the first new
moon, you are to raise up the Dwelling
Place of the Tent of Appointment,
3 and shall put in it the ark of the
Witness, and screen the ark with the veil.
4 "And you shall bring in the table and
arrange what belongs on it, and bring in
the lampstand and light its lamps.
5 "And you shall set the slaughter-place
of gold for the incense before the ark of the
Witness, and put up the covering of the
door to the Dwelling Place.
6 "And you shall set the slaughter-place
of the ascending offering before the door
of the Dwelling Place of the Tent of
Appointment,
7 and shall set the basin between the Tent
of Appointment and the slaughter-place,
and shall put water therein.
8 "And you shall set up the courtyard all
around, and shall place the covering of the
courtyard gate,
9 and shall take the anointing oil, and
anoint the Dwelling Place and all that is in
it, and shall set it and all its utensils apart,
and it shall be set-apart.
10 "And you shall anoint the slaughter-
place of the ascending offering and all its
utensils, and set the slaughter-place apart,
and the slaughter-place shall be most set-
apart.
11 "And you shall anoint the basin and its
stand, and set it apart.
12 "And you shall bring Aharon and his
sons to the door of the Tent of
Appointment and wash them with water.
13 "And you shall put the set-apart garments on Aharon, and anoint him and set
him apart to serve as priest to Me.
14 "And you shall bring his sons and put
long shirts on them,
15 and shall anoint them, as you anointed
their father, and they shall serve as priests
to Me. And their anointing shall be for
them an everlasting priesthood throughout
their generations."
16 And Mosheh did according to all that
יהוה had commanded him, so he did.
17 And it came to be in the first new *moon*
of the second year, on the first day of the
new *moon*, that the Dwelling Place was
raised up.
18 And Mosheh raised up the Dwelling
Place and placed its sockets, and set up its
boards, and put in its bars, and raised up its
columns,
19 and spread the tent over the Dwelling
Place and put the covering of the tent on
top of it, as יהוה had commanded Mosheh.
20 And he took the Witness and put it into
the ark, and he put the poles through the
rings of the ark, and put the lid of atonement on top of the ark,
21 and brought the ark into the Dwelling
Place, and placed the veil of the covering
to screen off the ark of the Witness, as
יהוה had commanded Mosheh.
22 And he put the table in the Tent of
Appointment, on the north side of the
Dwelling Place, outside the veil,
23 and set the bread in order upon it before
יהוה, as יהוה had commanded Mosheh.
24 And he put the lampstand in the Tent of
Appointment, opposite the table, on the
south side of the Dwelling Place,
25 and lit the lamps before יהוה, as יהוה
had commanded Mosheh.
26 And he put the gold slaughter-place in
the Tent of Appointment in front of the
veil,
27 and burned sweet incense on it, as יהוה
had commanded Mosheh.

28 And he set up the covering to the door of the Dwelling Place.

29 And he put the slaughter-place of ascending offering before the door of the Dwelling Place of the Tent of Appointment, and offered upon it the ascending offering and the grain offering, as יהוה had commanded Mosheh.

30 And he put the basin between the Tent of Appointment and the slaughter-place, and put water therein for washing.

31 And Mosheh, and Aharon, and his sons washed their hands and their feet with water from it,

32 as they went into the Tent of Appointment, and as they came near the slaughter-place. They would wash, as יהוה had commanded Mosheh.

33 And he raised up the courtyard all around the Dwelling Place and the slaughter-place, and placed the covering of the courtyard gate. And Mosheh completed the work.

34 And the cloud covered the Tent of Appointment, and the esteem of יהוה filled the Dwelling Place.

35 And Mosheh was not able to come into the Tent of Appointment, because the cloud dwelt on it, and the esteem of יהוה filled the Dwelling Place.

36 And when the cloud was taken up from above the Dwelling Place, the children of Yisra'ěl went onward in all their journeys.

37 But if the cloud was not taken up, then they did not set out till the day that it was taken up.

38 For the cloud of יהוה was on the Dwelling Place by day, and fire was on it by night, before the eyes of all the house of Yisra'ěl, in all their journeys.

WAYYIQRA

LEVITICUS

1 And יהוה called to Mosheh, and spoke to him from the Tent of Appointment, saying,

2 "Speak to the children of Yisra'ěl, and say to them, 'When anyone of you brings an offering to יהוה, you bring your offering of the livestock, of the herd or of the flock.

3 'If his offering is an ascending offering of the herd, let him bring a male, a perfect one. Let him bring it at the door of the Tent of Appointment, for his acceptance before יהוה.

4 'And he shall lay his hand on the head of the ascending offering, and it shall be accepted on his behalf to make atonement for him.

5 'And he shall slay the bull before יהוה. And the sons of Aharon, the priests, shall bring the blood and sprinkle the blood all around on the slaughter-place which is at the door of the Tent of Appointment.

6 'And he shall skin the ascending offering and cut it into its pieces.

7 'And the sons of Aharon the priest shall put fire on the slaughter-place, and lay the wood in order on the fire.

8 'And the sons of Aharon, the priests, shall arrange the pieces, with the head and the fat on the wood which is on the fire on the slaughter-place.

9 'But its entrails and its legs he washes with water. And the priest shall burn all of it on the slaughter-place as an ascending offering, an offering made by fire, a sweet fragrance to יהוה.

10 'And if his offering is from the flock, from the sheep or from the goats as an ascending offering, let him bring a male, a perfect one.

11 'And he shall slay it on the north side of the slaughter-place before יהוה. And the sons of Aharon, the priests, shall sprinkle its blood on the slaughter-place all around.

12 'And he shall cut it into its pieces, with its head and its fat, and the priest shall arrange them on the wood which is on the fire on the slaughter-place.

13 'But the entrails and the legs he washes with water. And the priest shall bring it all and burn it on the slaughter-place. It is an ascending offering, an offering made by fire, a sweet fragrance to יהוה.

14 'And if the ascending offering of his offering to יהוה is of birds, then he shall bring his offering of turtledoves or young pigeons.

15 'And the priest shall bring it to the slaughter-place, and shall wring off its head, and burn it on the slaughter-place, and its blood shall be drained out at the side of the slaughter-place.

16 'And he shall remove its crop with its feathers and throw it beside the slaughter-place on the east side, into the place for ashes.

17 'And he shall split it at its wings, but not sever it. And the priest shall burn it on the slaughter-place, on the wood that is on the fire. It is an ascending offering, an offering made by fire, a sweet fragrance to יהוה.

2 'And when anyone brings a grain offering to יהוה, his offering is to be of fine flour. And he shall pour oil on it, and put frankincense on it,

2 and he shall bring it to the sons of Aharon, the priests, and he shall take from it his hand filled with fine flour and oil with all the frankincense. And the priest shall burn it as a remembrance portion on the slaughter-place, an offering made by fire, a sweet fragrance to יהוה.

3 'And the rest of the grain offering is for Aharon and his sons, most set-apart of the offerings to יהוה by fire.

4 'And when you bring as an offering a grain offering baked in the oven, *it is of* unleavened cakes of fine flour mixed with

oil, or unleavened thin cakes anointed with oil.

5 'But if your offering is a grain offering on the griddle, it is of fine flour, unleavened, mixed with oil.

6 'Divide it into bits and pour oil on it, it is a grain offering.

7 'And if your offering is a grain offering, in a stewing-pot, it is made of fine flour with oil.

8 'And you shall bring to יהוה the grain offering that is made of these, and shall present it to the priest, and he shall bring it to the slaughter-place.

9 'And the priest shall take from the grain offering a remembrance portion, and burn it on the slaughter-place, an offering made by fire, a sweet fragrance to יהוה.

10 'And the rest of the grain offering is for Aharon and his sons, most set-apart of the offerings to יהוה made by fire.

11 'No grain offering which you bring to יהוה is made with leaven, for you do not burn any leaven or any honey in an offering to יהוה made by fire.

12 'Bring them to יהוה as an offering of the first-fruits, but they are not burned on the slaughter-place for a sweet fragrance.

13 'And season with salt every offering of your grain offering, and do not allow the salt of the covenant of your Elohim to be lacking from your grain offering. With all your offerings you bring salt.

14 'And if you bring a grain offering of your first-fruits to יהוה, bring for the grain offering of your first-fruits green heads of grain roasted on the fire, crushed heads of new grain.

15 'And you shall put oil on it, and lay frankincense on it. It is a grain offering.

16 'And the priest shall burn the remembrance portion, from its crushed grain and from its oil, with all the frankincense, an offering made by fire to יהוה.

3 'And if that which he presents is a slaughtering of peace *offerings*, if he is bringing it of the herd, whether male or female, he brings a perfect one before יהוה.

2 'And he shall lay his hand on the head of his offering, and slay it at the door of the Tent of Appointment. And the sons of Aharon, the priests, shall sprinkle the blood on the slaughter-place all around.

3 'And from the slaughtering of peace *offerings* he shall bring a fire *offering* to יהוה, the fat that covers the entrails and all the fat that is on the entrails,

4 and the two kidneys, and the fat that is on them by the loins, and the appendage on the liver which he removes with the kidneys.

5 'And the sons of Aharon shall burn it on the slaughter-place upon the ascending offering, which is on the wood, which is on the fire, as an offering made by fire, a sweet fragrance to יהוה.

6 'And if that which he presents is from the flock, for a slaughtering of peace *offerings* to יהוה, male or female, he brings a perfect one.

7 'If he is bringing a lamb as his offering, then he shall bring it before יהוה,

8 and shall lay his hand on the head of his offering, and slay it in front of the Tent of Appointment, and the sons of Aharon shall sprinkle its blood on the slaughter-place round about.

9 'And from the slaughtering of peace *offerings* he shall bring near – as a fire *offering* to יהוה – its fat, all the fat tail which he removes close to the backbone, and the fat that covers the entrails and all the fat that is on the entrails,

10 and the two kidneys and the fat that is on them by the loins, and the appendage on the liver, which he removes with the kidneys.

11 'And the priest shall burn them on the slaughter-place as food, an offering made by fire to יהוה.

12 'And if his offering is a goat, then he shall bring it before יהוה,

13 and shall lay his hand on its head and slay it before the Tent of Appointment. And the sons of Aharon shall sprinkle its blood on the slaughter-place all around.

14 'And from it he shall bring his offering, as an offering made by fire to יהוה, the fat that covers the entrails and all the fat that is on the entrails,

15 and the two kidneys and the fat that is on them by the loins, and the appendage on the liver, which he removes with the kidneys.

16 'And the priest shall burn them on the slaughter-place as food, an offering made by fire for a sweet fragrance. All the fat belongs to יהוה.

17 'An everlasting law throughout your generations in all your dwellings: you do not eat any fat or any blood.' "

4 And יהוה spoke to Mosheh, saying,

2 "Speak to the children of Yisra'ěl, saying, 'When a being sins by mistake against any of the commands of יהוה, which are not to be done, and shall do any of them:

3 'If the anointed priest sins, bringing guilt on the people, then he shall bring to יהוה for his sin which he has sinned a young bull, a perfect one, as a sin offering,

4 and he shall bring the bull to the door of the Tent of Appointment before יהוה, and shall lay his hand on the bull's head, and slay the bull before יהוה.

5 'And the anointed priest shall take some of the bull's blood and bring it to the Tent of Appointment,

6 and the priest shall dip his finger in the blood and sprinkle some of the blood seven times before יהוה, in front of the veil of the set-apart place.

7 'And the priest shall put some of the blood on the horns of the slaughter-place of sweet incense before יהוה, which is in the Tent of Appointment, and pour all the blood of the bull at the base of the slaughter-place of the ascending offering, which is at the door of the Tent of Appointment.

8 'Then he takes all the fat of the bull as the sin offering, the fat that covers the entrails and all the fat which is on the entrails,

9 and the two kidneys and the fat that is on them by the loins, and the appendage on the liver, which he removes with the kidneys,

10 as it was taken from the bull of the slaughtering of peace *offerings*. And the priest shall burn them on the slaughter-place of the ascending offering.

11 'But the skin of the bull, and all its flesh, with its head and legs, its entrails and dung –

12 all of the bull – he shall bring outside the camp to a clean place, where the ashes are poured out, and burn it on wood with fire. Where the ashes are poured out it is burned.

13 'And if the entire congregation of Yisra'ěl strays by mistake, and the matter has been hidden from the eyes of the assembly, and they have done *against* any of the commands of יהוה, which are not to be done, and shall be guilty,

14 when the sin which they have sinned becomes known, then the assembly shall bring a young bull for the sin, and bring it before the Tent of Appointment.

15 'And the elders of the congregation shall lay their hands on the head of the bull before יהוה, and the bull shall be slain before יהוה.

16 'And the anointed priest shall bring some of the bull's blood to the Tent of Appointment,

17 and the priest shall dip his finger in the blood and sprinkle it seven times before יהוה, in front of the veil,

18 and put some of the blood on the horns of the slaughter-place which is before יהוה, which is in the Tent of Appointment, and pour all the blood at the base of the slaughter-place of ascending offering, which is at the door of the Tent of Appointment.

19 'Then he takes all the fat from it and shall burn it on the slaughter-place.

20 'And he shall do with the bull as he did with the bull as a sin offering – so shall he do it. And the priest shall make atonement for them, and it shall be forgiven them.

21 'And he shall bring the bull outside the camp, and burn it as he burned the first bull. It is a sin offering for the assembly.

22 'When a ruler sins, and by mistake has done *against* any of the commands of יהוה his Elohim which are not to be done, and shall be guilty,

23 or if his sin which he has sinned is made known to him, then he shall bring as his offering a buck of the goats, a male,

a perfect one.
24 'And he shall lay his hand on the head of the goat, and slay it at the place where they slay the ascending offering before יהוה. It is a sin offering.
25 'And the priest shall take some of the blood of the sin offering with his finger, and shall put it on the horns of the slaughter-place of ascending offering, and pour its blood at the base of the slaughter-place of ascending offering,
26 and burn all its fat on the slaughter-place, like the fat of the slaughtering of the peace *offerings*. And the priest shall make atonement for him for his sin, and it shall be forgiven him.
27 'And if any being of the people of the land sins by mistake by doing *against* any of the commands of יהוה which are not to be done, and shall be guilty,
28 or if his sin which he has sinned shall be made known to him, then he shall bring as his offering a female goat, a perfect one, for his sin which he has sinned.
29 'And he shall lay his hand on the head of the sin offering, and slay the sin offering at the place of the ascending offering.
30 'And the priest shall take some of its blood with his finger, and shall put it on the horns of the slaughter-place of ascending offering, and pour all the blood at the base of the slaughter-place,
31 then remove all its fat, as fat is removed from the slaughtering of the peace *offerings*. And the priest shall burn it on the slaughter-place for a sweet fragrance to יהוה. And the priest shall make atonement for him, and it shall be forgiven him.
32 'And if he brings a lamb as his sin offering, he brings a female, a perfect one.
33 'And he shall lay his hand on the head of the sin offering, and slay it as a sin offering at the place where they slay the ascending offering.
34 'And the priest shall take some of the blood of the sin offering with his finger, and shall put it on the horns of the slaughter-place of ascending offering, and pour all the blood at the base of the slaughter-place.
35 'Then he removes all its fat, as the fat of the lamb is removed from the slaughtering of the peace *offerings*. And the priest shall burn it on the slaughter-place, according to the fire *offerings* to יהוה. So the priest shall make atonement for his sin that he has sinned, and it shall be forgiven him.

5 'And when a being sins in that he has heard the voice of swearing, and is a witness, or has seen, or has known, but does not reveal it, he shall bear his crookedness.
2 'Or when a being touches any unclean matter, or the carcass of an unclean beast, or the carcass of unclean livestock, or the carcass of unclean creeping creatures, and it has been hidden from him, he is unclean and guilty.
3 'Or when he touches uncleanness of man, any of his uncleanness by which he is unclean, and it has been hidden from him, when he shall know it, then he shall be guilty.
4 'Or when a being swears, speaking rashly with his lips to do evil or to do good, whatever it is that a man swears rashly with an oath, and it has been hidden from him, when he shall know it, then he shall be guilty of one of these.
5 'And it shall be, when he is guilty of one of these, that he shall confess that in which he has sinned,
6 and shall bring his guilt offering to יהוה for his sin which he has sinned, a female from the flock, a lamb or a female goat as a sin offering. And the priest shall make atonement for him, for his sin.
7 'And if he is unable to bring a lamb, then he shall bring to יהוה, he who has sinned, two turtledoves or two young pigeons, one for a sin offering and the other for an ascending offering.
8 'And he shall bring them to the priest, who shall bring near that which is for the sin offering first, and nib off its head from its neck, but not sever it.
9 'And he shall sprinkle some of the blood of the sin offering on the side of the slaughter-place, and the rest of the blood shall be drained out at the base of the slaughter-place. It is a sin offering.

10 'And he shall prepare the second as an ascending offering according to the right-ruling, and the priest shall make atonement for him, for his sin which he has sinned, and it shall be forgiven him.

11 'But if he is unable to bring two turtle-doves or two young pigeons, then he who sinned shall bring for his offering one-tenth of an ĕphah of fine flour as a sin offering. He puts no oil on it, nor does he put any frankincense on it, for it is a sin offering.

12 'And he shall bring it to the priest, and the priest shall take his hand filled with it as a remembrance portion, and burn it on the slaughter-place according to the offerings made by fire to יהוה. It is a sin offering.

13 'And the priest shall make atonement for him, for his sin that he has sinned in any of these, and it shall be forgiven him. And it shall be the priest's, like a grain offering.' "

14 And יהוה spoke to Mosheh, saying,

15 "When a being commits a trespass, and has sinned by mistake against the set-apart matters of יהוה, then he shall bring to יהוה as his guilt offering a ram, a perfect one, from the flock, with your valuation in sheqels of silver according to the sheqel of the set-apart place, as a guilt offering.

16 "And he shall make good for the sin that he has done against that which is set-apart, and shall add one-fifth to it and give it to the priest. And the priest shall make atonement for him with the ram of the guilt offering, and it shall be forgiven him.

17 "And when any being sins, and has done what is not to be done, *against* any of the commands of יהוה, though he knew it not, yet he shall be guilty and shall bear his crookedness.

18 "Then he shall bring to the priest a ram, a perfect one, from the flock, with your valuation, as a guilt offering. And the priest shall make atonement for his mistake he committed unintentionally, though he did not know it, and it shall be forgiven him –

19 it is a guilt offering, he was truly guilty before יהוה."

6 And יהוה spoke to Mosheh, saying,

2 "When any being sins, and committed a trespass against יהוה, and has lied to his neighbour about a deposit, or about a pledge, or about a robbery, or shall extort from his neighbour,

3 or has found what was lost and has lied concerning it, or did swear falsely, so that he sins in regard to any one of all these that a man does,

4 then it shall be, when he sins, and shall be guilty, that he shall return what he took by robbery, or what he has extorted, or the deposit which was deposited with him, or the lost item which he found,

5 or all that about which he swore falsely. He shall repay its total value, add one-fifth more to it, and give it to whom it belongs, on the day of his guilt offering.

6 "Then he brings his guilt offering to יהוה, a ram, a perfect one, from the flock, with your valuation, as a guilt offering, to the priest.

7 "And the priest shall make atonement for him before יהוה, and he shall be forgiven for whatever he did that made him guilty."

8 And יהוה spoke to Mosheh, saying,

9 "Command Aharon and his sons, saying, 'This is the Torah of the ascending offering: This is the ascending offering, because it is burned on the slaughter-place all night until morning, and the fire of the slaughter-place is kept burning on it.

10 'And the priest shall put on his linen garment, and put his linen trousers on his body, and shall take up the ashes of the ascending offering which the fire has consumed on the slaughter-place, and shall put them beside the slaughter-place.

11 'And he shall take off his garments, and put on other garments, and shall bring the ashes outside the camp to a clean place.

12 'And the fire on the slaughter-place is kept burning on it, it is not put out. And the priest shall burn wood on it every morning, and arrange the ascending offering on it, and shall burn on it the fat of the peace offerings –

13 fire is continually kept burning on the slaughter-place, it is not put out.

14 'And this is the Torah of the grain offering: The sons of Aharon shall bring it near
before יהוה, in front of the slaughter-place,
15 and shall take from it with his hand
from the fine flour of the grain offering,
and from its oil, and all the frankincense
which is on the grain offering, and shall
burn it on the slaughter-place for a sweet
fragrance, as its remembrance portion to
יהוה.
16 'Then Aharon and his sons eat the rest
of it. It is eaten with unleavened bread, in
the set-apart place. They eat it in the courtyard of the Tent of Appointment.
17 'It is not baked with leaven. I have
given it to them as their portion of My
offerings made by fire, it is most set-apart,
like the sin offering and the guilt offering.
18 'All the males among the children of
Aharon eat it – a law forever in your generations concerning the offerings made by
fire to יהוה. All that touches them is to be
set-apart.' "
19 And יהוה spoke to Mosheh, saying,
20 "This is the offering of Aharon and
his sons, which they bring near to יהוה,
beginning on the day when he is anointed:
one-tenth of an ĕphah of fine flour as a
daily grain offering, half of it in the morning and half of it at night.
21 "It is made on a griddle with oil. Bring
it in mixed, bring the baked portions of the
grain offering near, a sweet fragrance to
יהוה.
22 "And the anointed priest from among
his sons, who is in his place, prepares it –
a law forever to יהוה. All of it has to be
burned,
23 and every grain offering for the priest is
completely burned, it is not eaten."
24 And יהוה spoke to Mosheh, saying,
25 "Speak to Aharon and to his sons, saying, 'This is the Torah of the sin offering:
In the place where the ascending offering is
slain, the sin offering is slain before יהוה,
it is most set-apart.
26 'The priest who is making atonement
eats it, in the set-apart place it is eaten, in
the courtyard of the Tent of Appointment.
27 'All that touches its flesh is to be set-
apart. And when its blood is sprinkled on
any garment, you wash that on which it
was sprinkled, in a set-apart place.
28 'But the earthen vessel in which it is
cooked is to be broken. And if it is cooked
in a bronze pot, then it is scoured and
rinsed in water.
29 'Every male among the priests eats it, it
is most set-apart.
30 'And no sin offering from which any of
the blood is brought into the Tent of
Appointment, to make atonement in the
set-apart place, is eaten, it is burned with
fire.

7 'And this is the Torah of the guilt
offering – it is most set-apart.
2 'The guilt offering is slain in the place
where they slay the ascending offering, and
its blood is sprinkled on the slaughter-place
all around.
3 'Then he brings from it all its fat: the fat
tail and the fat that covers the entrails,
4 and the two kidneys and the fat that
is on them by the loins, and the appendage
on the liver, which he removes with the
kidneys.
5 'And the priest shall burn them on the
slaughter-place as an offering made by fire
to יהוה. It is a guilt offering.
6 'Every male among the priests eats it. It
is eaten in the set-apart place, it is most set-
apart.
7 'The guilt offering is like the sin offering, there is one Torah for them both: the
priest who makes atonement with it, it is
his.
8 'And the priest who brings anyone's
ascending offering, the skin of the ascending offering which he has brought is the
priest's, it is his.
9 'And every grain offering that is baked
in the oven and all that is prepared in the
stewing-pot, or on a griddle, is the priest's
who brings it, it is his.
10 'And every grain offering mixed with
oil, or dry, is for all the sons of Aharon, for
all alike.
11 'And this is the Torah of the slaughtering of peace *offerings* which is brought to
יהוה:
12 'If he brings it for a thanksgiving, then

he shall bring with the slaughtering of thanksgiving unleavened cakes mixed with oil, and unleavened thin cakes anointed with oil, or cakes of finely blended flour mixed with oil.

13 ‘Besides the cakes, he brings as his offering leavened bread together with the slaughtering of thanksgiving of his peace *offerings*.

14 ‘And from it he shall bring one cake from each offering as a contribution to יהוה: to the priest who sprinkles the blood of the peace *offerings*, it is his.

15 ‘As for the flesh of the slaughtering of his peace *offerings* for thanksgiving, it is eaten the same day it is offered, he does not leave any of it until morning.

16 ‘And if the slaughtering he brings is a vow or a voluntary offering, it is eaten the same day that he brings his slaughtering, and what is left of it is eaten the next day,

17 but whatever is left of the flesh of the slaughtering on the third day is burned with fire.

18 ‘However, if any of the flesh of the slaughtering of his peace *offerings* is eaten at all on the third day, it is not accepted. It is not reckoned to him who brings it, it is unclean to him, and the being who eats of it bears his crookedness.

19 ‘And the flesh that touches that which is unclean is not eaten, it is burned with fire. And as for the clean flesh, all who are clean eat of it.

20 ‘But the being who eats the flesh of the slaughtering of peace *offerings* that belongs to יהוה, while he is unclean, that being shall be cut off from his people.

21 ‘And when a being who touches that which is unclean, of the uncleanness of man, or of the uncleanness of beast, or of any unclean abomination, and shall eat the flesh of the slaughtering of peace *offerings* that belongs to יהוה, that being shall be cut off from his people.’ ”

22 And יהוה spoke to Mosheh, saying,

23 “Speak to the children of Yisra’ĕl, saying, ‘Do not eat any fat, of bull or sheep or goat.

24 ‘And the fat of a dead body, and the fat of what is torn, is used for any purpose, but you do not eat it at all.

25 ‘For whoever eats the fat of the beast of which men bring as an offering made by fire to יהוה, even the being who eats it shall be cut off from his people.

26 ‘And do not eat any blood in any of your dwellings, of bird or of beast.

27 ‘Any being who eats any blood, even that being shall be cut off from his people.’ ”

28 And יהוה spoke to Mosheh, saying,

29 “Speak to the children of Yisra’ĕl, saying, ‘He who brings his slaughtering of peace *offerings* to יהוה brings his offering to יהוה from the slaughtering of his peace *offerings*.

30 ‘With his own hands he bring the offerings made by fire to יהוה. He brings the fat with the breast, to be waved as a wave offering before יהוה.

31 ‘And the priest shall burn the fat on the slaughter-place, but the breast shall be Aharon’s and his sons.’

32 ‘And the right thigh you give to the priest as a contribution from the slaughtering of your peace *offerings*.

33 ‘He among the sons of Aharon, who brings the blood of the peace *offerings*, and the fat, the right thigh is his for a portion.

34 ‘For the breast of the wave offering and the thigh of the contribution I have taken from the children of Yisra’ĕl, from the slaughterings of their peace *offerings*, and I give them to Aharon the priest and to his sons, as a law forever, from the children of Yisra’ĕl.’ ”

35 This is the anointed portion for Aharon and the anointed portion for his sons, from the offerings made by fire to יהוה, on the day when Mosheh presented them to serve as priests to יהוה,

36 which יהוה commanded to be given to them by the children of Yisra’ĕl, on the day that He anointed them, a law forever throughout their generations.

37 This is the Torah of the ascending offering, of the grain offering, and of the sin offering, and of the guilt offering, and of the ordinations, and of the slaughtering of peace *offerings*,

38 which יהוה commanded Mosheh on

Mount Sinai, on the day when He commanded the children of Yisra'ěl to bring
their offerings to יהוה, in the Wilderness of
Sinai.

8 And יהוה spoke to Mosheh, saying,
2 "Take Aharon and his sons with him,
and the garments, and the anointing oil,
and the bull of the sin offering, and the two
rams, and the basket of unleavened bread,
3 and assemble all the congregation at the
door of the Tent of Appointment."
4 And Mosheh did as יהוה commanded
him, and the congregation was assembled
at the door of the Tent of Appointment.
5 And Mosheh said to the congregation,
"This is the word יהוה commanded to
be done."
6 So Mosheh brought Aharon and his
sons and washed them with water,
7 and put the long shirt on him, and girded him with the girdle, and dressed him in
the robe, and put the shoulder garment on
him, and girded him with the embroidered
band of the shoulder garment, and with it
tied the shoulder garment on him,
8 and put the breastplate on him, and put
the Urim and the Tummim in the breastplate,
9 and put the turban on his head. And on
the turban, on its front, he put the golden
plate, the set-apart sign of dedication, as
יהוה had commanded Mosheh.
10 And Mosheh took the anointing oil and
anointed the Dwelling Place and all that
was in it, and set them apart.
11 And he sprinkled some of it on the
slaughter-place seven times, and anointed
the slaughter-place and all its utensils, and
the basin and its base, to set them apart.
12 And he poured some of the anointing
oil on Aharon's head and anointed him, to
set him apart.
13 And Mosheh brought the sons of
Aharon and put long shirts on them, and
girded them with girdles, and put turbans
on them, as יהוה had commanded Mosheh.
14 And he brought the bull for the sin
offering, and Aharon and his sons laid their
hands on the head of the bull for the sin
offering,
15 and it was slain. And Mosheh took the
blood, and put some on the horns of the
slaughter-place all around with his finger,
and cleansed the slaughter-place. And he
poured the blood at the base of the slaughter-place, and set it apart, to make atonement for it.
16 And he took all the fat that was on the
entrails, and the appendage on the liver,
and the two kidneys with their fat, and
Mosheh burned them on the slaughter-
place.
17 And the bull, and its skin, and its flesh,
and its dung, he burned with fire outside
the camp, as יהוה had commanded
Mosheh.
18 And he brought the ram of the ascending offering, and Aharon and his sons laid
their hands on the head of the ram,
19 and it was slain. And Mosheh sprinkled
the blood on the slaughter-place all around,
20 and he cut the ram into pieces. And
Mosheh burned the head, and the pieces,
and the fat,
21 and he washed the entrails and the legs
in water. And Mosheh burned the entire
ram on the slaughter-place. It was an
ascending offering for a sweet fragrance,
and an offering made by fire to יהוה, as
יהוה had commanded Mosheh.
22 And he brought the second ram, the ram
of ordination, and Aharon and his sons laid
their hands on the head of the ram,
23 and it was slain. And Mosheh took
some of its blood and put it on the tip of
Aharon's right ear, and on the thumb of his
right hand, and on the big toe of his right
foot.
24 And he brought near the sons of
Aharon, and Mosheh put some of the blood
on the tips of their right ears, and on the
thumbs of their right hands, and on the big
toes of their right feet. And Mosheh sprinkled the blood on the slaughter-place all
around,
25 and took the fat and the fat tail, and
all the fat that was on the entrails, and
the appendage on the liver, and the two
kidneys and their fat, and the right thigh,
26 and from the basket of unleavened
bread that was before יהוה he took one

unleavened cake, and a cake of bread anointed with oil, and one thin cake, and put them on the fat and on the right thigh,

27 and placed all these in the hands of Aharon and in the hands of his sons, and waved them as a wave offering before יהוה.

28 Mosheh then took them from their hands and burned them on the slaughter-place, on the ascending offering. They were ordinations for a sweet fragrance. It was an offering by fire to יהוה.

29 And Mosheh took the breast and waved it, a wave offering before יהוה. It was Mosheh's portion of the ram of ordination, as יהוה had commanded Mosheh.

30 And Mosheh took some of the anointing oil and some of the blood which was on the slaughter-place, and sprinkled it on Aharon, on his garments, and on his sons, and on the garments of his sons with him. And he set apart Aharon, his garments, and his sons, and the garments of his sons with him.

31 And Mosheh said to Aharon and his sons, "Cook the flesh at the door of the Tent of Appointment, and eat it there with the bread that is in the basket of the ordinations, as I have commanded, saying, 'Aharon and his sons are to eat it.'

32 "Then burn the rest of the flesh and the bread with fire.

33 "And do not go outside the door of the Tent of Appointment for seven days, until the days of your ordination are completed – for he fills your hands for seven days.

34 "יהוה has commanded to do, as he has done this day, to make atonement for you.

35 "And stay at the door of the Tent of Appointment day and night for seven days. And you shall guard the duty of יהוה, and not die, for so I have been commanded."

36 And Aharon and his sons did all the words that יהוה had commanded by the hand of Mosheh.

9 And on the eighth day it came to be that Mosheh called Aharon and his sons and the elders of Yisra'ěl.

2 And he said to Aharon, "Take for yourself a young bull as a sin offering and a ram as an ascending offering, a perfect one, and bring them before יהוה.

3 "And speak to the children of Yisra'ěl, saying, 'Take a male goat as a sin offering, and a calf and a lamb, both a year old, perfect ones, as an ascending offering,

4 and a bull and a ram as peace offerings, to slaughter before יהוה, and a grain offering mixed with oil. For today יהוה shall appear to you.' "

5 And they took what Mosheh commanded before the Tent of Appointment, and all the congregation drew near and stood before יהוה.

6 And Mosheh said, "This is the word which יהוה commanded you to do, so that the esteem of יהוה appears to you."

7 And Mosheh said to Aharon, "Go to the slaughter-place, and prepare your sin offering and your ascending offering, and make atonement for yourself and for the people. And make the offering of the people, and make atonement for them, as יהוה has commanded."

8 So Aharon came near to the slaughter-place and slew the calf of the sin offering, which was for himself.

9 And the sons of Aharon brought the blood to him, and he dipped his finger in the blood, and put it on the horns of the slaughter-place, and poured the blood at the base of the slaughter-place.

10 And the fat, and the kidneys, and the appendage on the liver of the sin offering he burned on the slaughter-place, as יהוה had commanded Mosheh.

11 And the flesh and the skin he burned with fire outside the camp.

12 And he slew the ascending offering, and the sons of Aharon presented to him the blood, which he sprinkled on the slaughter-place all around.

13 And they presented the ascending offering to him, with its pieces and head, and he burned them on the slaughter-place.

14 And he washed the entrails and the legs, and burned them with the ascending offering on the slaughter-place.

15 And he brought the people's offering, and took the goat, which was the sin offering for the people, and slew it and made it a

sin offering, like the first one.
16 And he brought the ascending offering
and made it, according to the right-ruling.
17 He also brought the grain offering, and
filled his hand with it, and burned it on the
slaughter-place, besides the ascending
offering of the morning.
18 And he slew the bull and the ram as a
slaughtering of peace *offerings*, which
were for the people. And Aharon's sons
presented to him the blood, which he sprinkled on the slaughter-place all around,
19 and the fat from the bull and the ram,
the fat tail, and the covering, and the
kidneys, and the appendage on the liver,
20 and they placed the fat on the breasts,
and he burned the fat on the slaughter-
place.
21 But the breasts and the right thigh
Aharon waved as a wave offering before
יהוה, as Mosheh had commanded.
22 Aharon then lifted up his hand toward
the people and blessed them, and came
down from making the sin offering, and the
ascending offering, and the peace offerings.
23 And Mosheh and Aharon went into the
Tent of Appointment, and came out and
blessed the people. And the esteem of יהוה
appeared to all the people,
24 and fire came out from before יהוה and
consumed the ascending offering and the
fat on the slaughter-place. And all the people saw and cried aloud and fell on their
faces.

10 And Naḏaḇ and Aḇihu, the sons of
Aharon, each took his fire holder
and put fire in it, and put incense on it, and
brought strange fire before יהוה, which He
had not commanded them.
2 And fire came out from יהוה and consumed them, and they died before יהוה.
3 Then Mosheh said to Aharon, "This is
what יהוה spoke, saying, 'By those who
come near Me let Me be set-apart! And
before all the people let Me be
esteemed!' " And Aharon was silent.
4 And Mosheh called to Misha'ěl and to
Eltsaphan, the sons of Uzzi'ěl the uncle of
Aharon, and said to them, "Come near,
take your brothers from before the set-apart
place out of the camp."
5 So they came near and took them by
their long shirts out of the camp, as
Mosheh had said.
6 And Mosheh said to Aharon, and to
El'azar and to Ithamar, his sons, "Do not
unbind your heads nor tear your garments,
lest you die, and wrath come upon all the
people. But let your brothers, all the house
of Yisra'ěl, bewail the burning which יהוה
has kindled.
7 "And do not go out from the door of the
Tent of Appointment, lest you die, for the
anointing oil of יהוה is upon you." And
they did according to the word of Mosheh.
8 And יהוה spoke to Aharon, saying,
9 "Do not drink wine or strong drink,
you, nor your sons with you, when you go
into the Tent of Appointment, lest you die
– a law forever throughout your generations,
10 so as to make a distinction between the
set-apart and the profane, and between the
unclean and the clean,
11 and to teach the children of Yisra'ěl all
the laws which יהוה has spoken to them by
the hand of Mosheh."
12 And Mosheh spoke to Aharon, and to
El'azar and Ithamar, his sons who were
left, "Take the grain offering that is left
over from the offerings made by fire to
יהוה, and eat it without leaven beside the
slaughter-place, for it is most set-apart.
13 "And you shall eat it in a set-apart
place, because it is yours by law and your
sons' by law, of the offerings made by fire
to יהוה, for so I have been commanded.
14 "And the breast of the wave offering
and the thigh of the contribution you eat in
a clean place, you, and your sons, and your
daughters with you. For they are yours by
law and your sons' by law, which are given
from the slaughterings of peace *offerings*
of the children of Yisra'ěl.
15 "The thigh of the contribution and the
breast of the wave offering they bring with
the offerings of fat made by fire, to bring as
a wave offering before יהוה. And it shall
be yours and your sons' with you, by a law
forever, as יהוה has commanded."

16 And Mosheh diligently looked for the
goat of the sin offering and saw it was
burned up. And he was wroth with El'azar
and Ithamar, the sons of Aharon who were
left, saying,
17 "Why have you not eaten the sin offering in a set-apart place, since it is most set-
apart, and Elohim has given it to you to
bear the crookedness of the congregation,
to make atonement for them before יהוה?
18 "See, its blood was not brought inside
the set-apart place. You should have eaten
it without fail in a set-apart place, as I have
commanded."
19 And Aharon said to Mosheh, "See,
today they have brought their sin offering
and their ascending offering before יהוה,
and *matters* like these have come to me! If
I had eaten the sin offering today, would it
have been right in the eyes of יהוה?"
20 And when Mosheh heard that, it was
good in his eyes.

11 And יהוה spoke to Mosheh and to
Aharon, saying to them,
2 "Speak to the children of Yisra'ĕl,
saying, 'These are the living creatures
which you do eat among all the beasts that
are on the earth:
3 'Whatever has a split hoof completely
divided, chewing the cud, among the
beasts, that you do eat.
4 'Only, these you do not eat among those
that chew the cud or those that have a split
hoof: the camel, because it chews the cud
but does not have a split hoof, it is unclean
to you;
5 and the rabbit, because it chews the cud
but does not have a split hoof, it is unclean
to you;
6 and the hare, because it chews the cud
but does not have a split hoof, it is unclean
to you;
7 and the pig, though it has a split hoof,
completely divided, yet does not chew the
cud, it is unclean to you.
8 'Their flesh you do not eat, and their
carcasses you do not touch. They are
unclean to you.
9 'These you do eat of all that are in the
waters: any one that has fins and scales in
the waters, in the seas or in the rivers, that
you do eat.
10 'But all that have not fins and scales in
the seas and in the rivers, all that move in
the waters or any living being which is in
the waters, they are an abomination to you.
11 'They are an abomination to you – of
their flesh you do not eat, and their carcasses you abominate.
12 'All that have not fins or scales in the
waters are an abomination to you.
13 'And these you do abominate among
the birds, they are not eaten, they are an
abomination: the eagle, and the vulture,
and the black vulture,
14 and the hawk, and the falcon after its
kind,
15 every raven after its kind,
16 and the ostrich, and the nighthawk, and
the seagull, and the hawk after its kind,
17 and the little owl, and the fisher owl,
and the great owl,
18 and the white owl, and the pelican, and
the carrion vulture,
19 and the stork, the heron after its kind,
and the hoopoe, and the bat.
20 'All flying insects that creep on all
fours is an abomination to you.
21 'Only, these you do eat of every flying
insect that creeps on all fours: those which
have jointed legs above their feet with
which to leap on the earth.
22 'These of them you do eat: the arbeh-
locust after its kind, and the solam-*locust*
after its kind, and the ḥargol-*locust* after its
kind, and the ḥagaḇ-*locust* after its kind.
23 'But all other flying insects which have
four feet are an abomination to you.
24 'And by these you are made unclean,
anyone touching the carcass of any of them
is unclean until evening,
25 and anyone picking up part of the carcass of any of them has to wash his garments, and shall be unclean until evening.
26 'Every beast that has a split hoof not
completely divided, or does not chew the
cud, is unclean to you. Anyone who touches their carcass is unclean.
27 'And whatever goes on its paws, among
all the creatures that go on all fours, those
are unclean to you. Anyone who touches

their carcass is unclean until evening,
28 and he who picks up their carcass has to wash his garments, and shall be unclean until evening. They are unclean to you.
29 'And these are unclean to you among the creeping creatures that creep on the earth: the mole, and the mouse, and the tortoise after its kind,
30 and the gecko, and the land crocodile, and the sand reptile, and the sand lizard, and the chameleon.
31 'These are unclean to you among all that creep. Anyone who touches them when they are dead becomes unclean until evening.
32 'And whatever any of them in its dead state falls upon, becomes unclean, whether it is any wooden object or garment or skin or sack, any object in which work is done, it is put in water. And it shall be unclean until evening, then it shall be clean.
33 'Any earthen vessel into which any of them falls, whatever is in it becomes unclean, and you break it.
34 'Any of the food which might be eaten, on which water comes, becomes unclean, and any drink which might be drunk from it becomes unclean.
35 'And on whatever *any* of their carcass falls becomes unclean – an oven or cooking range – it is broken down. They are unclean, and are unclean to you.
36 'But a fountain or a well, a collection of water, is clean, but whatever touches their carcass is unclean.
37 'And when *any* of their carcass falls on any planting seed which is to be sown, it is clean.
38 'But when any water is put on the seed and any part of any such carcass falls on it, it is unclean to you.
39 'And when any of the beasts which are yours for food dies, he who touches its carcass becomes unclean until evening.
40 'And he who eats of its carcass has to wash his garments, and shall be unclean until evening. And he who picks up its carcass has to wash his garments, and shall be unclean until evening.
41 'And every swarming *creature* – the one that swarms on the earth is an abomination, it is not eaten.
42 'Whatever crawls on its stomach, and whatever goes on *all* fours, and whatever has many feet among all swarming *creatures* – the ones swarming on the earth, these you do not eat, for they are an abomination.
43 'Do not make yourselves abominable with any swarming *creature* – the one swarming, and do not make yourselves unclean with them, lest you be defiled by them.
44 'For I am יהוה your Elohim, and you shall set yourselves apart. And you shall be set-apart, for I am set-apart. And do not defile yourselves with any swarming *creature* – the one creeping on the earth.
45 'For I am יהוה who is bringing you up out of the land of Mitsrayim, to be your Elohim. And you shall be set-apart, for I am set-apart.
46 'This is the Torah of the beasts and the birds and every living being – the creeping creature in the waters, and of every being that swarms on the earth,
47 to make a distinction between the unclean and the clean, and between the living *creature* that is eaten and the living *creature* that is not eaten.' "

12 And יהוה spoke to Mosheh, saying,
2 "Speak to the children of Yisra'ěl, saying, 'When a woman has conceived, and has given birth to a male child, then she shall be unclean seven days, as in the days of her monthly separation she is unclean.
3 'And on the eighth day the flesh of his foreskin is circumcised.
4 'And she remains in the blood of her cleansing thirty-three days. She does not touch whatever is set-apart, and she does not come into the set-apart place until the days of her cleansing are completed.
5 'But if she gives birth to a female child, then she shall be unclean for two weeks, as in her monthly separation, and she remains in the blood of her cleansing for sixty-six days.
6 'And when the days of her cleansing are completed, for a son or for a daughter,

she brings to the priest a lamb a year old, as an ascending offering, and a young pigeon or a turtledove as a sin offering, to the door of the Tent of Appointment.

7 'And he shall bring it before יהוה, and make atonement for her, and she shall be cleansed from the flow of her blood. This is the Torah for her who has given birth to a male or a female.

8 'And if she is not able to bring a lamb, then she shall bring two turtledoves or two young pigeons, one as an ascending offering and the other as a sin offering. And the priest shall make atonement for her, and she shall be clean.' "

13 And יהוה spoke to Mosheh and to Aharon, saying,

2 "When a man has on the skin of his body a swelling, a scab, or a bright spot, and it shall become on the skin of his body like a leprous infection, then he shall be brought to Aharon the priest or to one of his sons the priests.

3 "And the priest shall look at the infection on the skin of the body. And if the hair on the infection has turned white, and the infection appears to be deeper than the skin of his body, it is a leprous infection. And the priest shall look at him, and pronounce him unclean.

4 "But if the bright spot is white on the skin of his body, and does not appear to be deeper than the skin, and its hair has not turned white, then the priest shall shut up the infected one seven days.

5 "And the priest shall look at him on the seventh day and see, if the infection appears to be as it was, and the infection has not spread on the skin, then the priest shall shut him up another seven days.

6 "And the priest shall look at him again on the seventh day and see, if the infection has darkened, and the infection has not spread on the skin, then the priest shall pronounce him clean. It is a scab, and he shall wash his garments and be clean.

7 "But if the scab spreads further over the skin, after he has been seen by the priest for his cleansing, he shall be seen by the priest again.

8 "And the priest shall look and see, if the scab has spread on the skin, then the priest shall pronounce him unclean, it is leprosy.

9 "When the infection of leprosy is on a man, then he shall be brought to the priest.

10 "And the priest shall look and see, if the swelling on the skin is white, and it has turned the hair white, and there is a spot of raw flesh in the swelling,

11 it is an old leprosy on the skin of his body, and the priest shall pronounce him unclean. He does not shut him up, for he is unclean.

12 "And if leprosy breaks out all over the skin, and the leprosy shall cover all the skin of the infected one, from his head to his foot, wherever the priest looks,

13 then the priest shall look and see, if the leprosy has covered all his body, he shall pronounce the infected one clean. It has all turned white, he is clean.

14 "But the day raw flesh appears on him, he is unclean.

15 "And the priest shall look at the raw flesh and pronounce him to be unclean – the raw flesh is unclean, it is leprosy.

16 "Or when the raw flesh changes and turns white again, he shall come to the priest.

17 "And the priest shall look at him and see, if the infection has turned white, then the priest shall pronounce the infected one clean, he is clean.

18 "And when the body has a boil in the skin, and it is healed,

19 and in the place of the boil there comes a white swelling or a bright spot, reddish-white, then it shall be seen by the priest.

20 "And the priest shall look and see, if it appears deeper than the skin, and its hair has turned white, the priest shall pronounce him unclean, it is a leprous infection which has broken out of the boil.

21 "But if the priest looks at it and sees no white hairs in it, and it is not deeper than the skin, but has faded, then the priest shall shut him up seven days;

22 and if it has spread further over the skin, then the priest shall pronounce him unclean, it is a leprous infection.

23 "But if the bright spot stays in its place,

it has not spread, it is the scar of the boil,
and the priest shall pronounce him clean.
24 "Or when the body receives a burn on
its skin by fire, and the raw flesh of the
burn shall become a bright spot, reddish-
white or white,
25 then the priest shall look at it and see, if
the hair of the bright spot has turned white,
and it appears deeper than the skin, it is
leprosy broken out in the burn. And the
priest shall pronounce him unclean, it is a
leprous infection.
26 "But if the priest looks at it and sees
there are no white hairs in the bright spot,
and it is not deeper than the skin, but has
faded, then the priest shall shut him up
seven days.
27 "And the priest shall look at him on the
seventh day. If it spreads further over the
skin, then the priest shall pronounce him
unclean, it is a leprous infection.
28 "But if the bright spot stays in its place,
and has not spread on the skin, but has
faded, it is a swelling from the burn. And
the priest shall pronounce him clean, for it
is the scar from the burn.
29 "And when a man, or a woman, has an
infection on the head or in the beard,
30 then the priest shall look at the infection
and see, if it appears deeper than the skin,
and there is thin yellow hair in it, then the
priest shall pronounce him unclean, it is an
eruption, a leprosy of the head or beard.
31 "But when the priest looks at the infection of the eruption and sees that it does not
appear deeper than the skin, and there is no
black hair in it, then the priest shall shut up
the one with the infection of the eruption
seven days.
32 "And on the seventh day the priest shall
look at the infection and see, if the eruption
has not spread, and there is no yellow hair
in it, and the eruption does not appear
deeper than the skin,
33 then he shall shave himself, but the
eruption he does not shave. And the priest
shall shut up *the one with* the eruption
another seven days.
34 "And on the seventh day the priest shall
look at the eruption and see, if the eruption
has not spread over the skin, and does not
appear deeper than the skin, then the priest
shall pronounce him clean. And he shall
wash his garments, and he shall be clean.
35 "But if the eruption spreads further over
the skin after his cleansing,
36 then the priest shall look at him and see,
if the eruption has spread over the skin, the
priest need not seek for yellow hair, he is
unclean.
37 "But if the eruption appears to have
stayed, and there is black hair grown up in
it, the eruption has healed. He is clean, and
the priest shall pronounce him clean.
38 "And when a man or a woman has
bright spots on the skin of the body, white
bright spots,
39 then the priest shall look and see, if the
bright spots on the skin of the body are dull
white, it is a white spot that grows on the
skin, he is clean.
40 "And when a man loses the hair of his
head, he is bald, he is clean.
41 "And if the hair has fallen from his
forehead, he is bald on the forehead, he is
clean.
42 "And when there is on the bald head or
bald forehead a reddish-white infection, it
is leprosy breaking out on his bald head or
his bald forehead.
43 "And the priest shall look at it and see,
if the swelling of the infection is reddish-
white on his bald head or on his bald forehead, as the appearance of leprosy on the
skin of the body,
44 he is a leprous man, he is unclean. The
priest shall pronounce him unclean, without fail, his infection is on his head.
45 "As for the leper who has the infection,
his garments are torn, and his head is
uncovered, and he has to cover his upper
lip and cry, 'Unclean! Unclean!'
46 "He is unclean – all the days he has the
infection he is unclean. He is unclean,
and he dwells alone, his dwelling place is
outside the camp.
47 "And when a garment has an infection
of leprosy in it, in a woollen garment or in
a linen garment,
48 or in the warp or in the weft of linen or
wool, or in leather or in any leather-work,
49 and the infection shall be greenish or

reddish in the garment or in the leather, or in the warp or in the weft, or in any leather object, it is an infection of leprosy and shall be shown to the priest.

50 “And the priest shall look at the infection and shut up the infected one seven days.

51 “And he shall look at the infection on the seventh day. And when the infection has spread in the garment, or in the warp or in the weft, or in the leather or any leatherwork, the infection is an active leprosy, it is unclean.

52 “And he shall burn that garment, or the warp or the weft, in wool or in linen, or any leather object in which the infection is, for it is an active leprosy. It is burned with fire.

53 “But if the priest looks and sees that the infection has not spread in the garment, or in the warp or in the weft, or in any leather object,

54 then the priest shall give command, and they shall wash that in which the infection is. And he shall shut it up another seven days.

55 “And the priest shall look at the infection after it has been washed and see, if the infection has not changed its appearance, though the infection has not spread, it is unclean, and burn it in the fire – it is eaten away, in its inside or outside.

56 “And if the priest shall look and see that the infection has faded after washing it, then he shall tear it out of the garment, or out of the warp, or out of the weft, or out of the leather.

57 “And if it is still seen in the garment, or in the warp or in the weft, or in any leather object, it is a spreading infection. Burn it with fire, that in which the infection is.

58 “And if you wash the garment, or the warp or the weft, or any leather object, if the infection has disappeared from it, then it shall be washed a second time, and shall be clean.

59 “This is the Torah of the infection of leprosy in a garment of wool or linen, or in the warp or in the weft, or in any leather object, to pronounce it clean or to pronounce it unclean.”

14 And יהוה spoke to Mosheh, saying,

2 “This shall be the Torah of the leper for the day of his cleansing: He shall be brought to the priest,

3 and the priest shall go out of the camp, and the priest shall look and see, if the leprosy is healed in the leper,

4 then the priest shall command, and he shall take for him who is to be cleansed two live and clean birds, and cedar wood, and scarlet, and hyssop.

5 “And the priest shall command, and he shall slay one of the birds in an earthen vessel over running water.

6 “Let him take the live bird and the cedar wood and the scarlet and the hyssop, and dip them and the live bird in the blood of the bird that was slain over the running water.

7 “And he shall sprinkle it seven times on him who is to be cleansed from the leprosy, and shall pronounce him clean, and shall let the live bird loose in the open field.

8 “And he who is to be cleansed shall wash his garments, and shall shave off all his hair and wash himself in water, and shall be clean. Then after that he comes into the camp, but shall stay outside his tent seven days.

9 “And on the seventh day it shall be that he shaves all the hair off his head and his beard and his eyebrows, even all his hair he shaves off. And he shall wash his garments and wash his body in water, and shall be clean.

10 “And on the eighth day he takes two male lambs, perfect ones, and one ewe lamb a year old, a perfect one, and three-tenths *of an ĕphah* of fine flour mixed with oil as a grain offering, and one log of oil.

11 “And the priest who is cleansing shall present the man who is to be cleansed, with these *offerings*, before יהוה, at the door of the Tent of Appointment.

12 “And the priest shall take one male lamb and bring it as a guilt offering, and the log of oil, and wave them as a wave offering before יהוה.

13 “And he shall slay the lamb in the place where he slays the sin offering and the ascending offering, in a set-apart place. For

the guilt offering, like the sin offering, belongs to the priest. It is most set-apart.
14 "And the priest shall take some of the blood of the guilt offering, and the priest shall put it on the tip of the right ear of him who is to be cleansed, and on the thumb of his right hand, and on the big toe of his right foot.
15 "And the priest shall take some of the log of oil, and pour it into the palm of his own left hand.
16 "And the priest shall dip his right finger in the oil that is in his left hand, and shall sprinkle some of the oil with his finger seven times before יהוה.
17 "And of the rest of the oil in his hand, the priest puts some on the tip of the right ear of him who is to be cleansed, and on the thumb of his right hand, and on the big toe of his right foot, on the blood of the guilt offering.
18 "And the rest of the oil that is in the priest's hand he puts on the head of him who is to be cleansed. And the priest shall make atonement for him before יהוה.
19 "And the priest shall make the sin offering, and make atonement for him who is to be cleansed from his uncleanness. Then afterwards he slays the ascending offering.
20 "And the priest shall offer the ascending offering and the grain offering on the slaughter-place. And the priest shall make atonement for him, and he shall be clean.
21 "But if he is poor and is unable to afford it, then he shall take one male lamb as a guilt offering to be waved, to make atonement for him, and one-tenth *of an ĕphah* of fine flour mixed with oil as a grain offering, and a log of oil,
22 and two turtledoves or two young pigeons, such as he is able to afford, and one shall be a sin offering and the other an ascending offering.
23 "And he shall bring them to the priest on the eighth day for his cleansing, to the door of the Tent of Appointment, before יהוה.
24 "And the priest shall take the lamb of the guilt offering and the log of oil, and the priest shall wave them as a wave offering before יהוה.
25 "And he shall slay the lamb of the guilt offering, and the priest shall take some of the blood of the guilt offering and put it on the tip of the right ear of him who is to be cleansed, and on the thumb of his right hand, and on the big toe of his right foot.
26 "Then the priest pours some of the oil into the palm of his own left hand.
27 "And the priest shall sprinkle with his right finger some of the oil that is in his left hand seven times before יהוה.
28 "And the priest shall put some of the oil that is in his hand on the tip of the right ear of him who is to be cleansed, and on the thumb of the right hand, and on the big toe of his right foot, on the place of the blood of the guilt offering.
29 "And the rest of the oil that is in the priest's hand he puts on the head of him who is to be cleansed, to make atonement for him before יהוה.
30 "And he shall prepare one of the turtledoves or young pigeons, such as he is able to afford,
31 that which he is able to afford, the one as a sin offering and the other as an ascending offering, with the grain offering. And the priest shall make atonement for him who is to be cleansed before יהוה.
32 "This is the Torah for one who had an infection of leprosy, who is unable to afford for his cleansing."
33 And יהוה spoke to Mosheh and to Aharon, saying,
34 "When you come into the land of Kenaʽan, which I am giving you as a possession, and I put a plague of leprosy in a house in the land of your possession,
35 then shall the one who owns the house come and inform the priest, saying, 'It seems to me that there is some plague in the house.'
36 "And the priest shall command, and they shall empty the house, before the priest goes in to look at the plague, so that all that is in the house is not made unclean. And after that the priest goes in to look at the house.
37 "And he shall look at the plague and see, if the plague is on the walls of the house with sunken places, greenish or red-

dish, which appear to be deep in the wall,
38 then the priest shall go out of the house,
to the door of the house, and shut up the
house seven days.
39 "And the priest shall come again on the
seventh day and look and see, if the plague
has spread on the walls of the house,
40 then the priest shall command, and they
shall remove the stones with the plague in
them, and they shall throw them outside
the city, into an unclean place,
41 while he lets the house be scraped
inside, all around, and the dust that they
scrape off they shall pour out in an unclean
place outside the city.
42 "And they shall take other stones and
put them in the place of those stones, and
take other mortar and plaster the house.
43 "And if the plague comes back and
breaks out in the house, after he has
removed the stones, after he has scraped
the house, and after it is plastered,
44 then the priest shall come and look and
see, if the plague has spread in the house, it
is an active leprosy in the house, it is
unclean.
45 "And he shall break down the house, its
stones, and its timber, and all the plaster of
the house, and he shall bring them outside
the city to an unclean place.
46 "And he who goes into the house, all
the days while it is shut up, becomes unclean until evening.
47 "And he who lies down in the house has
to wash his garments, and he who eats in
the house has to wash his garments.
48 "However, if the priest indeed comes in
and looks at it and sees that the plague has
not spread in the house after the house was
plastered, then the priest shall pronounce
the house clean, because the plague is
healed.
49 "And to cleanse the house, he shall take
two birds, and cedar wood, and scarlet, and
hyssop.
50 "And he shall slay one of the birds in an
earthen vessel over running water,
51 and he shall take the cedar wood, and
the hyssop, and the scarlet, and the live
bird, and dip them in the blood of the slain
bird and in the running water, and shall
sprinkle the house seven times.
52 "He shall thus cleanse the house with
the blood of the bird and the running water
and the live bird, and with the cedar wood,
and with the hyssop, and with the scarlet,
53 and he shall let the live bird loose
outside the city in the open field, and
shall make atonement for the house, and
it shall be clean.
54 "This is the Torah for any infection of
leprosy, and eruption,
55 and for leprosy of a garment, and of a
house,
56 and for a swelling, and for a scab, and
for a bright spot,
57 to teach when it is unclean and when it
is clean. This is the Torah of leprosy."

15 And יהוה spoke to Mosheh and to
Aharon, saying,
2 "Speak to the children of Yisra'ěl, and
say to them, 'When any man has a
discharge from his flesh, his discharge is
unclean.
3 'And this is his uncleanness in regard to
his discharge; whether his flesh runs with
his discharge, or his flesh is stopped up by
his discharge, it is his uncleanness.
4 'Any bed becomes unclean on which he
who has the discharge lies, and any object
on which he sits becomes unclean.
5 'And anyone who touches his bed has
to wash his garments, and shall bathe in
water, and be unclean until evening.
6 'And he who sits on any object on
which he who has the discharge sat, has to
wash his garments, and shall bathe in
water, and be unclean until evening.
7 'And he who touches the flesh of him
who has the discharge has to wash his
garments, and shall bathe in water, and
shall be unclean until evening.
8 'And when he who has the discharge
spits on him who is clean, then he shall
wash his garments, and shall bathe in
water, and be unclean until evening.
9 'Any saddle on which he who has the
discharge rides becomes unclean.
10 'And whoever touches any of that
which was under him is unclean until
evening. And he who is carrying them up

has to wash his garments, and shall bathe
in water, and be unclean until evening.
11 'And anyone whom he who has the discharge touches without rinsing his hands in
water, shall wash his garments and bathe in
water, and be unclean until evening.
12 'And the earthen vessel which he who
has the discharge touches has to be broken,
and every wooden vessel has to be rinsed
in water.
13 'And when he who has a discharge is
cleansed of his discharge, then he shall
count for himself seven days for his cleansing, and shall wash his garments, and shall
bathe his flesh in running water, and be
clean.
14 'And on the eighth day he takes for
himself two turtledoves or two young
pigeons, and shall come before יהוה, to the
door of the Tent of Appointment, and shall
give them to the priest.
15 'And the priest shall prepare them, the
one as a sin offering and the other as an
ascending offering. And the priest shall
make atonement for him before יהוה
because of his discharge.
16 'And when a man has an emission of
semen, then he shall wash all his flesh in
water, and be unclean until evening.
17 'And any garment and any leather on
which there is semen, shall also be washed
with water, and be unclean until evening.
18 'And when a woman lies with a man,
and there is an emission of semen, they
both shall bathe in water, and be unclean
until evening.
19 'And when a woman has a discharge,
and the discharge from her flesh is blood,
she has to be in her separation for seven
days. And whoever touches her is unclean
until evening.
20 'And whatever she lies on during her
separation is unclean. And whatever she
sits on is unclean.
21 'And anyone who touches her bed has
to wash his garments, and shall bathe in
water, and be unclean until evening.
22 'And whoever touches any object that
she sat on has to wash his garments, and
shall bathe in water, and be unclean until
evening.
23 'And if it is on the bed or on any object
on which she sits, when he touches it, he is
unclean until evening.
24 'And if a man lies with her at all, and
her monthly flow is on him, he shall be
unclean seven days. And any bed he lies on
is unclean.
25 'And when a woman has a discharge of
blood for many days, other than at the time
of her monthly separation, or when she dis-
charges beyond her usual time of monthly
separation, all the days of her unclean discharge shall be as the days of her monthly
separation. She is unclean.
26 'Any bed on which she lies all the days
of her discharge is to her as the bed of her
monthly separation. And whatever she sits
on is unclean, as the uncleanness of her
monthly separation.
27 'And anyone who touches them is
unclean, and shall wash his garments, and
shall bathe in water, and be unclean until
evening.
28 'But if she is cleansed of her discharge,
then she shall count for herself seven days,
and after that she is clean.
29 'And on the eighth day she takes for
herself two turtledoves or two young
pigeons, and shall bring them to the priest,
to the door of the Tent of Appointment.
30 'And the priest shall prepare the one as
a sin offering and the other as an ascending
offering, and the priest shall make atonement for her before יהוה for the discharge
of her uncleanness.
31 'Thus you shall separate the children of
Yisra'ěl from their uncleanness, lest they
die in their uncleanness when they defile
My Dwelling Place which is in their midst.
32 'This is the Torah for one who has a discharge, and for him who emits semen and
is unclean thereby,
33 and for her who is sick in her monthly
separation, and for one who has a discharge, either man or woman, and for him
who lies with an unclean woman.' "

16 And יהוה spoke to Mosheh after
the death of the two sons of
Aharon, as they drew near before יהוה, and
died.

2And יהוה said to Mosheh, "Speak to Aharon your brother not to come in at all times to the Set-apart Place inside the veil, before the lid of atonement which is on the ark, lest he die, because I appear in the cloud above the lid of atonement.

3"With this Aharon should come into the Set-apart Place: with the blood of a young bull as a sin offering, and of a ram as an ascending offering.

4"He should put on the set-apart linen long shirt, with linen trousers on his flesh, and gird himself with a linen girdle, and be dressed with the linen turban – they are set-apart garments. And he shall bathe his body in water, and shall put them on.

5"And from the congregation of the children of Yisra'ěl he takes two male goats as a sin offering, and one ram as an ascending offering.

6"And Aharon shall bring the bull as a sin offering, which is for himself, and make atonement for himself and for his house.

7"And he shall take the two goats and let them stand before יהוה at the door of the Tent of Appointment.

8"And Aharon shall cast lots for the two goats, one lot for יהוה and the other lot for Azazel.

9"And Aharon shall bring the goat on which the lot for יהוה fell, and shall prepare it as a sin offering.

10"But the goat on which the lot for Azazel fell is caused to stand alive before יהוה, to make atonement upon it, to send it into the wilderness to Azazel.

11"And Aharon shall bring the bull of the sin offering, which is for himself, and make atonement for himself and for his house, and shall slay the bull as the sin offering which is for himself,

12and shall take a fire holder filled with burning coals of fire from the slaughter-place before יהוה, with his hands filled with sweet incense beaten fine, and shall bring it inside the veil.

13"And he shall put the incense on the fire before יהוה, and the cloud of incense shall cover the lid of atonement which is on the Witness, lest he die.

14"And he shall take some of the blood of the bull and sprinkle it with his finger on the lid of atonement on the east side, also in front of the lid of atonement he sprinkles some of the blood with his finger seven times.

15"And he shall slay the goat of the sin offering, which is for the people, and shall bring its blood inside the veil, and shall do with that blood as he did with the blood of the bull, and sprinkle it on the lid of atonement and in front of the lid of atonement.

16"And he shall make atonement for the Set-apart Place, because of the uncleanness of the children of Yisra'ěl, and because of their transgressions in all their sins. And so he does for the Tent of Appointment which is dwelling with them in the midst of their uncleanness.

17"And no man should be in the Tent of Appointment when he goes in to make atonement in the Set-apart Place, until he comes out. And he shall make atonement for himself, and for his household, and for all the assembly of Yisra'ěl.

18"And he shall go out to the slaughter-place that is before יהוה, and make atonement for it. And he shall take some of the blood of the bull and some of the blood of the goat, and put it on the horns of the slaughter-place all around.

19"And he shall sprinkle some of the blood on it with his finger seven times, and cleanse it, and set it apart from the uncleanness of the children of Yisra'ěl.

20"And when he has finished atoning for the Set-apart Place, and the Tent of Appointment, and the slaughter-place, he shall bring the live goat.

21"Then Aharon shall lay both his hands on the head of the live goat, and shall confess over it all the crookednesses of the children of Yisra'ěl, and all their transgressions in all their sins, and shall put them on the head of the goat, and shall send it away into the wilderness by the hand of a fit man.

22"And the goat shall bear on itself all their crookednesses, to a land cut off. Thus he shall send the goat away into the wilderness.

23 "Aharon shall then come into the Tent of Appointment, and shall take off the linen garments which he put on when he went into the Set-apart Place, and shall leave them there.

24 "And he shall bathe his body in water in the set-apart place, and shall put on his garments, and shall come out and prepare his ascending offering and the ascending offering of the people, and make atonement for himself and for the people,

25 and burn the fat of the sin offering on the slaughter-place.

26 "And he who sent away the goat to Azazel washes his garments, and shall bathe his body in water, and afterward he comes into the camp.

27 "And the bull for the sin offering and the goat for the sin offering, whose blood was brought in to make atonement in the Set-apart Place, is brought outside the camp. And they shall burn their skins, and their flesh, and their dung with fire.

28 "And he who burns them washes his garments, and shall bathe his body in water, and afterward he comes into the camp.

29 "And this shall be for you a law forever: In the seventh new *moon*, on the tenth day of the new *moon*, you afflict your beings, and do no work, the native or the stranger who sojourns among you.

30 "For on that day he makes atonement for you, to cleanse you, to be clean from all your sins before יהוה.

31 "It is a Sabbath of rest for you, and you shall afflict your beings – a law forever.

32 "And the priest, who is anointed and ordained to serve as priest in his father's place, shall make atonement, and shall put on the linen garments, the set-apart garments,

33 and he shall make atonement for the Most Set-apart Place, and make atonement for the Tent of Appointment and for the slaughter-place, and make atonement for the priests and for all the people of the assembly.

34 "And this shall be for you a law forever, to make atonement for the children of Yisra'ěl, for all their sins, once a year." And he did as יהוה commanded Mosheh.

17

And יהוה spoke to Mosheh, saying,

2 "Speak to Aharon, to his sons, and to all the children of Yisra'ěl, and say to them, 'This is the word which יהוה has commanded, saying,

3 "Any man from the house of Yisra'ěl who slays a bull or a lamb or a goat in the camp, or who slays it outside the camp,

4 and does not bring it to the door of the Tent of Appointment, to bring an offering to יהוה before the Dwelling Place of יהוה, blood-guilt is reckoned to that man. He has shed blood, and that man shall be cut off from among his people,

5 in order that the children of Yisra'ěl bring their slaughterings which they slaughter in the open field. And they shall bring them to יהוה at the door of the Tent of Appointment, to the priest, and slaughter them as slaughterings of peace *offerings* to יהוה.

6 "And the priest shall sprinkle the blood on the slaughter-place of יהוה at the door of the Tent of Appointment, and shall burn the fat for a sweet fragrance to יהוה.

7 "And let them no longer slaughter their slaughterings to demons, after whom they whored. This is a law forever for them throughout their generations." '

8 "And say to them, 'Any man of the house of Yisra'ěl, or of the strangers who sojourn among you, who offers an ascending offering or slaughtering,

9 and does not bring it to the door of the Tent of Appointment, to do it to יהוה, that man shall be cut off from among his people.

10 'And any man of the house of Yisra'ěl, or of the strangers who sojourn among you, who eats any blood, I shall set My face against that being who eats blood, and shall cut him off from among his people.

11 'For the life of the flesh is in the blood, and I have given it to you upon the slaughter-place to make atonement for your lives, for it is the blood that makes atonement for the life.'

12 "Therefore I said to the children of Yisra'ěl, 'No being among you eats blood,

nor does any stranger who sojourns among you eat blood.'

13 "And any man from the children of Yisra'ěl, or from the strangers who sojourn among you, who hunts and catches any beast or bird, which is eaten, shall pour out its blood and cover it with dust,

14 for it is the life of all flesh. Its blood is for its life. And I said to the children of Yisra'ěl, 'Do not eat the blood of any flesh, for the life of all flesh is its blood. Anyone eating it is cut off.'

15 "And any being who eats a carcass or what was torn *by a beast*, be he a native or a stranger, he shall wash his garments and bathe in water, and shall be unclean until evening. Then he shall be clean.

16 "And if he does not wash or bathe his body, then he shall bear his crookedness."

18 And יהוה spoke to Mosheh, saying,

2 "Speak to the children of Yisra'ěl, and say to them, 'I am יהוה your Elohim.

3 'Do not do as they do in the land of Mitsrayim, where you dwelt. And do not do as they do in the land of Kena'an, where I am bringing you, and do not walk in their laws.

4 'Do My right-rulings and guard My laws, to walk in them. I am יהוה your Elohim.

5 'And you shall guard My laws and My right-rulings, which a man does and lives by them. I am יהוה.

6 'No one is to approach anyone of his own flesh to uncover his nakedness. I am יהוה.

7 'The nakedness of your father or the nakedness of your mother you do not uncover. She is your mother, you do not uncover her nakedness.

8 'The nakedness of your father's wife you do not uncover, it is your father's nakedness.

9 'The nakedness of your sister, the daughter of your father, or the daughter of your mother, whether born at home or elsewhere, their nakedness you do not uncover.

10 'The nakedness of your son's daughter or your daughter's daughter, their nakedness you do not uncover, for theirs is your own nakedness.

11 'The nakedness of your father's wife's daughter, brought forth by your father, she is your sister, you do not uncover her nakedness.

12 'The nakedness of your father's sister you do not uncover, she is your father's flesh.

13 'The nakedness of your mother's sister you do not uncover, for she is your mother's flesh.

14 'The nakedness of your father's brother you do not uncover, you do not approach his wife, she is your aunt.

15 'The nakedness of your daughter-in-law you do not uncover, she is your son's wife, you do not uncover her nakedness.

16 'The nakedness of your brother's wife you do not uncover, it is your brother's nakedness.

17 'The nakedness of a woman and her daughter you do not uncover, nor do you take her son's daughter or her daughter's daughter, to uncover her nakedness. They are her relatives – it is wickedness.

18 'And do not take a woman as a rival to her sister, to uncover her nakedness while the other is alive.

19 'And do not approach a woman to uncover her nakedness in her monthly separation of uncleanness.

20 'And do not have intercourse with the wife of your neighbour, to defile yourself with her.

21 'And do not give any of your offspring to pass through to Moleḵ. And do not profane the Name of your Elohim. I am יהוה.

22 'And do not lie with a male as with a woman, it is an abomination.

23 'And do not have intercourse with any beast, to defile yourself with it. And a woman does not stand before a beast to mate with it, it is a perversion.

24 'Do not defile yourselves with all these, for by all these the nations are defiled, which I am driving out before you.

25 'Thus the land became defiled, therefore I punished it for its crookedness, and the land vomited out its inhabitants.

26 'But you, you shall guard My laws and My right-rulings, and not do any of these

abominations, the native nor stranger who sojourns among you,

27 because the men of the land who were before you have done all these abominations, and thus the land became defiled,

28 'So let not the land vomit you out for defiling it, as it vomited out the nations that were before you.

29 'For whoever does any of these abominations, those beings who do them shall be cut off from among their people.

30 'And you shall guard My Charge, so as not to do any of these abominable laws which were done before you, so as not to defile yourselves by them. I am יהוה your Elohim.' "

19 And יהוה spoke to Mosheh, saying,

2 "Speak to all the congregation of the children of Yisra'ěl, and say to them, 'Be set-apart, for I יהוה your Elohim am set-apart.

3 'Each one of you should fear his mother and his father, and guard My Sabbaths. I am יהוה your Elohim.

4 'Do not turn to idols, and do not make for yourselves moulded mighty ones. I am יהוה your Elohim.

5 'And when you slaughter a slaughtering of peace *offerings* to יהוה, slaughter it for your acceptance.

6 'It is eaten the same day you slaughter it, and on the next day. And that which is left on the third day is burned with fire.

7 'So if it is eaten at all on the third day, it is abominable, it is not accepted,

8 and he who eats it bears his crookedness, because he has profaned the set-apart *offering* of יהוה, and that being shall be cut off from his people.

9 'And when you reap the harvest of your land, do not completely reap the corners of your field or gather the gleanings of your harvest.

10 'And do not glean your vineyard or gather every grape of your vineyard, leave them for the poor and the stranger. I am יהוה your Elohim.

11 'Do not steal, do not lie, do not deceive one another.

12 'And do not swear falsely by My Name and so profane the Name of your Elohim. I am יהוה.

13 'Do not oppress your neighbour or rob *him*. The wages of him who is hired is not to remain with you all night until morning.

14 'Do not curse the deaf or put a stumbling-block before the blind, but fear your Elohim. I am יהוה.

15 'Do no unrighteousness in right-ruling. Do not be partial to the poor or favour the face of the great, but rightly rule your neighbour in righteousness.

16 'Do not go slandering among your people. Do not stand against the blood of your neighbour. I am יהוה.

17 'Do not hate your brother in your heart. Reprove your neighbour, for certain, and bear no sin because of him.

18 'Do not take vengeance or bear a grudge against the children of your people. And you shall love your neighbour as yourself. I am יהוה.

19 'Guard My laws. Do not let your livestock mate with another kind. Do not sow your field with mixed seed. And do not put a garment woven of two sorts of thread upon you.

20 'And when a man has intercourse with a woman who is a female servant, engaged to a man, and to be ransomed, *but* she has not been ransomed nor set free, there should be an inquiry. But they are not put to death, because she was not free.

21 'And he shall bring his guilt offering to יהוה, to the door of the Tent of Appointment, a ram as a guilt offering.

22 'And the priest shall make atonement for him with the ram of the guilt offering before יהוה for his sin which he has done. And the sin which he has sinned shall be forgiven him.

23 'And when you come into the land, and have planted all kinds of trees for food, then you shall reckon their fruit as uncircumcised. For three years it is as uncircumcised to you, it is not eaten.

24 'And in the fourth year all its fruit is set-apart – praises to יהוה.

25 'And in the fifth year you eat its fruit, so that it increases its yield to you. I am יהוה your Elohim.

26 'Do not eat *meat* with the blood. Do not practise divination or magic.
27 'Do not round the corner of your head, nor destroy the corner of your beard.
28 'And do not make any cuttings in your flesh for the dead, nor put tattoo marks on you. I am יהוה.
29 'Do not profane your daughter by making her a whore, so that the land does not whore, and the land becomes filled with wickedness.
30 'Guard My Sabbaths and reverence My set-apart place. I am יהוה.
31 'Do not turn to mediums, and do not seek after spiritists to be defiled by them. I am יהוה your Elohim.
32 'Rise up before the grey-headed. And you shall favour the face of an old man, and shall fear your Elohim. I am יהוה.
33 'And when a stranger sojourns with you in your land, do not oppress him.
34 'Let the stranger who dwells among you be to you as the native among you, and you shall love him as yourself. For you were strangers in the land of Mitsrayim. I am יהוה your Elohim.
35 'Do no unrighteousness in right-ruling, in measurement of length, in weight, or in measuring liquids.
36 'Have right scales, right weights, a right ĕphah, and a right hin. I am יהוה your Elohim, who brought you out of the land of Mitsrayim.
37 'And you shall guard all My laws and all My right-rulings, and do them. I am יהוה.' "

20 And יהוה spoke to Mosheh, saying,
2 "Say to the children of Yisra'ĕl, 'Any man of the children of Yisra'ĕl, or of the strangers who sojourn in Yisra'ĕl, who gives any of his offspring to Molek̲, shall certainly be put to death. The people of the land shall stone him with stones.
3 'And I, I shall set My face against that man, and shall cut him off from the midst of his people, because he has given of his offspring to Molek̲, so as to defile My set-apart place and to profane My set-apart Name.
4 'And if the people of the land at all hide their eyes from the man, as he gives any of his offspring to Molek̲, and they do not kill him,
5 then I shall set My face against that man and against his clan, and shall cut him off – and all who go whoring after him, even go whoring after Molek̲ – from the midst of their people.
6 'And the being who turns to mediums, and to spiritists, to go whoring after them, I shall set My face against that being and cut him off from the midst of his people.
7 'And you shall set yourselves apart, and shall be set-apart, for I am יהוה your Elohim,
8 and you shall guard My laws and do them. I am יהוה, who sets you apart.
9 'For everyone who curses his father or his mother shall certainly be put to death – he has cursed his father or his mother, his blood is on him.
10 'And a man who commits adultery with the wife of another man, who commits adultery with the wife of his neighbour: the adulterer and the adulteress shall certainly be put to death.
11 'And a man who lies with the wife of his father has uncovered the nakedness of his father, both of them shall certainly be put to death, their blood is upon them.
12 'And a man who lies with his daughter-in-law: both of them shall certainly be put to death, they have made confusion, their blood is upon them.
13 'And a man who lies with a male as he lies with a woman: both of them have done an abomination, they shall certainly be put to death, their blood is upon them.
14 'And a man who marries a woman and her mother: it is wickedness, they are burned with fire, both he and they, that there be no wickedness in your midst.
15 'And a man who has intercourse with a beast: he shall certainly be put to death, and the beast you kill.
16 'And a woman who approaches any beast and mates with it: you shall kill the woman and the beast, they shall certainly be put to death, their blood is upon them.
17 'And a man who takes his sister, his father's daughter or his mother's daughter,

and sees her nakedness and she sees his
nakedness: is it loving-commitment? And
they shall be cut off before the eyes of their
people. He has uncovered his sister's
nakedness, he bears his crookedness.
18 'And a man who lies with a woman
during her sickness and uncovers her
nakedness: he has laid bare her flow, and
she has uncovered the flow of her blood,
both of them shall be cut off from the midst
of their people.
19 'And do not uncover the nakedness of
your mother's sister nor of your father's
sister, for that is laying bare one's own
flesh, they bear their crookedness.
20 'And a man who lies with his uncle's
wife: he has uncovered his uncle's nakedness, they bear their sin, they die childless.
21 'And a man who takes his brother's
wife: it is uncleanness, he has uncovered
his brother's nakedness, they are childless.
22 'And you shall guard all My laws and
all My right-rulings, and do them, so that
the land where I am bringing you to dwell
does not vomit you out.
23 'And do not walk in the laws of the
nation which I am driving out before you,
for they do all these, and therefore I
loathed them.
24 'But I say to you, "You are going to
possess their land, and I Myself give it to
you to possess it, a land flowing with milk
and honey." I am יהוה your Elohim, who
has separated you from the peoples.
25 'And you shall make a distinction
between clean beasts and unclean, and
between unclean birds and clean. And do
not make yourselves abominable by beast
or by bird, or whatever creeps on the
ground, which I have separated from you
as unclean.
26 'And you shall be set-apart to Me, for I
יהוה am set-apart, and have separated you
from the peoples to be Mine.
27 'And a man or a woman in whom there
is a medium, or who are spiritists, shall certainly be put to death, they are to stone
them with stones. Their blood is upon
them.' "

21 And יהוה said to Mosheh, "Speak
to the priests, the sons of Aharon,
and say to them: 'No one is to be defiled
for the dead among his people,
2 except for his relatives who are nearest
to him: for his mother, and for his father,
and for his son, and for his daughter, and
for his brother;
3 and for his maiden sister who is near to
him, who has had no husband – for her he
is defiled.
4 'A leader does not defile himself
among his people, to profane himself;
5 they do not make any bald place on
their heads, and they do not shave the corner of their beard, and they do not make a
cutting in their flesh.
6 'They are set-apart to their Elohim and
do not profane the Name of their Elohim,
for they bring the fire *offerings* of יהוה,
and the bread of their Elohim, and shall be
set-apart.
7 'They do not take a woman who is a
whore or a defiled woman, and they do not
take a woman put away from her husband,
for he is set-apart to his Elohim.
8 'And you shall set him apart, for he
brings the bread of your Elohim, he is set-
apart to you. For I, יהוה, setting you apart,
am set-apart.
9 'And when the daughter of any priest
profanes herself by whoring, she profanes
her father. She is burned with fire.
10 'And the high priest among his brothers, on whose head the anointing oil was
poured and who is ordained to wear the
garments, does not unbind his head nor tear
his garments,
11 nor come near any dead body, nor defile
himself for his father or his mother,
12 nor go out of the set-apart place, nor
profane the set-apart place of his Elohim,
for the sign of dedication of the anointing
oil of his Elohim is upon him. I am יהוה.
13 'And let him take a wife in her maidenhood.
14 'A widow or one put away or a defiled
woman or a whore – these he does not take.
But a maiden of his own people he does
take as a wife.
15 'And he does not profane his offspring

among his people, for I am יהוה, who sets
him apart.' "
16 And יהוה spoke to Mosheh, saying,
17 "Speak to Aharon, saying, 'No man of
your offspring throughout their generations, who has any defect, is to draw near
to bring the bread of his Elohim.
18 'For any man who has a defect is not to
draw near: a man blind or one lame or dis-
figured or deformed,
19 a man who has a broken foot or broken
hand,
20 or is a hunchback or a dwarf, or a man
who has a defect in his eye, or eczema or
scab, or is a eunuch.
21 'No man among the offspring of
Aharon the priest, who has a defect, is to
come near to bring the offerings made by
fire to יהוה – he has a defect, he does not
come near to bring the bread of his Elohim.
22 'He does eat the bread of his Elohim,
both the most set-apart and the set-apart,
23 only, he does not go near the veil or
approach the slaughter-place, because he
has a defect, lest he profanes My set-apart
places. For I am יהוה, who sets them
apart.' "
24 Thus Mosheh spoke to Aharon and his
sons, and to all the children of Yisra'ĕl.

22

And יהוה spoke to Mosheh, saying,
2 "Speak to Aharon and his sons,
that they separate themselves from the set-
apart *offerings* of the children of Yisra'ĕl,
and that they do not profane My set-apart
Name in what they set apart to Me. I am
יהוה.
3 "Say to them, 'Any man of all your offspring throughout your generations who
draws near the set-apart *offerings* which
the children of Yisra'ĕl set apart to יהוה,
while he has uncleanness upon him, that
being shall be cut off from before Me. I am
יהוה.
4 'Any man of the offspring of Aharon,
who is a leper or has a discharge, does not
eat the set-apart *offerings* until he is clean.
And whoever touches what is rendered
unclean by a being, or a man who has had
an emission of semen,
5 or a man who touches any swarming
creature by which he would be made
unclean, or any being by whom he would
become unclean, even any of his uncleanness;
6 the being who has touched it shall be
unclean until evening, and does not eat the
set-apart *offerings*, but shall bathe his body
in water.
7 'And when the sun goes down he shall
be clean, and afterward eat the set-apart
offerings, because it is his food.
8 'He does not eat that which dies or is
torn *by beasts,* becoming unclean by it.
I am יהוה.
9 'And they shall guard My Charge, lest
they bear sin for it and die thereby, when
they profane it. I יהוה set them apart.
10 'And no stranger eats the set-apart
offering. A sojourner with the priest, or a
hired servant, does not eat the set-apart
offering.
11 'But when the priest buys a being with
his silver, he does eat of it. And one who is
born in his house does eat his food.
12 'And when a priest's daughter is
married to a stranger, she does not eat of
the set-apart *offerings.*
13 'But when a priest's daughter is a
widow or put away, and has no child, and
has returned to her father's house as in her
youth, she does eat her father's food, but
no stranger eats of it.
14 'And when a man eats the set-apart
offering by mistake, then he shall give a
set-apart offering to the priest, and add
one-fifth to it.
15 'And let *the priests* not profane the set-
apart offerings of the children of Yisra'ĕl,
which they lift up to יהוה,
16 or allow them to bear the crookedness
of trespass when they eat their set-apart
offerings. For I am יהוה, who sets them
apart.' "
17 And יהוה spoke to Mosheh, saying,
18 "Speak to Aharon and his sons, and to
all the children of Yisra'ĕl, and say to
them, 'Any man of the house of Yisra'ĕl, or
of the strangers in Yisra'ĕl, who brings his
offering for any of his vows or for any of
his voluntary offerings, which they bring to
יהוה as an ascending offering,

19 for your acceptance, is a male, a perfect one from the cattle, from the sheep, or from the goats.

20 'Whatever has a defect, you do not bring, for it is not acceptable for you.

21 'And when a man brings a slaughtering of peace *offerings* to יהוה, to complete a vow, or a voluntary offering from the cattle or the sheep, it is to be perfect to be accepted, let there be no defect in it.

22 '*Those* blind or broken or cut, or having an ulcer or eczema or scabs, you do not bring to יהוה, nor make an offering by fire of them on the slaughter-place to יהוה.

23 'As for a bull or a lamb that has any limb deformed or dwarfed you do prepare as a voluntary offering, but for a vow it is not accepted.

24 'Do not bring to יהוה what is bruised or crushed, or torn or cut, nor do it in your land.

25 'And from a son of a stranger's hand you do not bring any of these as the bread of your Elohim, for their corruption is in them, and defects are in them, they are not acceptable for you.' "

26 And יהוה spoke to Mosheh, saying,

27 "When a bull or a sheep or a goat is born, it shall be seven days with its mother. And from the eighth day and thereafter it is acceptable as an offering made by fire to יהוה.

28 "But do not slay a cow or a sheep and its young on the same day.

29 "And when you slaughter a slaughtering of thanksgiving to יהוה, slaughter it for your acceptance.

30 "It is eaten that same day, leave none of it till morning. I am יהוה.

31 "And you shall guard My commands and do them. I am יהוה.

32 "And do not profane My set-apart Name, and I shall be set-apart among the children of Yisra'ĕl. I am יהוה, who sets you apart,

33 who brought you out of the land of Mitsrayim, to be your Elohim. I am יהוה."

23

And יהוה spoke to Mosheh, saying,

2 "Speak to the children of Yisra'ĕl, and say to them, 'The appointed times of יהוה, which you are to proclaim as set-apart gatherings, My appointed times, are these:

3 'Six days work is done, but the seventh day is a Sabbath of rest, a set-apart gathering. You do no work, it is a Sabbath to יהוה in all your dwellings.

4 'These are the appointed times of יהוה, set-apart gatherings which you are to proclaim at their appointed times.

5 'In the first new *moon*, on the fourteenth day of the new *moon*, between the evenings, is the Pĕsaḥ [a] to יהוה.

6 'And on the fifteenth day of this new *moon* is the Festival of Matzot [b] to יהוה – seven days you eat unleavened bread.

7 'On the first day you have a set-apart gathering, you do no servile work.

8 'And you shall bring an offering made by fire to יהוה for seven days. On the seventh day is a set-apart gathering, you do no servile work.' "

9 And יהוה spoke to Mosheh, saying,

10 "Speak to the children of Yisra'ĕl, and you shall say to them, 'When you come into the land which I give you, and shall reap its harvest, then you shall bring a sheaf of the first-fruits of your harvest to the priest.

11 'And he shall wave the sheaf before יהוה, for your acceptance. On the morrow after the Sabbath the priest waves it.

12 'And on that day when you wave the sheaf, you shall prepare a male lamb a year old, a perfect one, as an ascending offering to יהוה,

13 and its grain offering: two-tenths of an ĕphah of fine flour mixed with oil, an offering made by fire to יהוה, a sweet fragrance, and its drink offering: one-fourth of a hin of wine.

14 'And you do not eat bread or roasted grain or fresh grain until the same day that you have brought an offering to your Elohim – a law forever throughout your generations in all your dwellings.

23a - Passover. *23b* - Unleavened Bread.

15 'And from the morrow after the Sabbath, from the day that you brought the sheaf of the wave offering, you shall count for yourselves: seven completed Sabbaths.

16 'Until the morrow after the seventh Sabbath you count fifty days, then you shall bring a new grain offering to יהוה.

17 'Bring from your dwellings for a wave offering two *loaves of* bread, of two-tenths of an ĕphah of fine flour they are, baked with leaven, first-fruits to יהוה.

18 'And besides the bread, you shall bring seven lambs a year old, perfect ones, and one young bull and two rams. They are an ascending offering to יהוה, with their grain offering and their drink offerings, an offering made by fire for a sweet fragrance to יהוה.

19 'And you shall offer one male goat as a sin offering, and two male lambs a year old, as a slaughter of peace *offerings*.

20 'And the priest shall wave them, besides the bread of the first-fruits, as a wave offering before יהוה, besides the two lambs. They are set-apart to יהוה for the priest.

21 'And on this same day you shall proclaim a set-apart gathering for yourselves, you do no servile work on it – a law forever in all your dwellings throughout your generations.

22 'And when you reap the harvest of your land do not completely reap the corners of your field when you reap, and do not gather any gleaning from your harvest. Leave them for the poor and for the stranger. I am יהוה your Elohim.' "

23 And יהוה spoke to Mosheh, saying,

24 "Speak to the children of Yisra'ĕl, saying, 'In the seventh new *moon*, on the first day of the new *moon*, you have a rest, a remembrance of Teruʻah,[c] a set-apart gathering.

25 'You do no servile work, and you shall bring an offering made by fire to יהוה.' "

26 And יהוה spoke to Mosheh, saying,

27 "On the tenth day of this seventh new *moon* is Yom haKippurim.[d] It shall be a set-apart gathering for you. And you shall afflict your beings, and shall bring an offering made by fire to יהוה.

28 "And you do no work on that same day, for it is Yom Kippurim, to make atonement for you before יהוה your Elohim.

29 "For any being who is not afflicted on that same day, he shall be cut off from his people.

30 "And any being who does any work on that same day, that being I shall destroy from the midst of his people.

31 "You do no work – a law forever throughout your generations in all your dwellings.

32 'It is a Sabbath of rest to you, and you shall afflict your beings. On the ninth day of the new *moon* at evening, from evening to evening, you observe your Sabbath."

33 And יהוה spoke to Mosheh, saying,

34 "Speak to the children of Yisra'ĕl, saying, 'On the fifteenth day of this seventh new *moon* is the Festival of Sukkot[e] for seven days to יהוה.

35 'On the first day is a set-apart gathering, you do no servile work.

36 'For seven days you bring an offering made by fire to יהוה. On the eighth day there shall be a set-apart gathering for you, and you shall bring an offering made by fire to יהוה. It is a closing festival, you do no servile work.

37 'These are the appointed times of יהוה which you proclaim as set-apart gatherings, to bring an offering made by fire to יהוה, an ascending offering and a grain offering, a slaughtering and drink offerings, as commanded for every day –

38 besides the Sabbaths of יהוה, and besides your gifts, and besides all your vows, and besides all your voluntary offerings which you give to יהוה.

39 'On the fifteenth day of the seventh new *moon*, when you gather in the fruit of the land, celebrate the festival of יהוה for seven days. On the first day is a rest, and on the eighth day a rest.

40 'And you shall take for yourselves on the first day the fruit of good trees, branches of palm trees, twigs of leafy trees, and

23c Lit. Soundings, by instrument or human voice. *23d* Day of Atonement or Day of the Coverings. *23e* Booths.

willows of the stream, and shall rejoice
before יהוה your Elohim for seven days.
41 'And you shall celebrate it as a festival
to יהוה for seven days in the year – a law
forever in your generations. Celebrate it in
the seventh new *moon*.
42 'Dwell in booths for seven days; all
who are native born in Yisra'ĕl dwell in
booths,
43 so that your generations know that
I made the children of Yisra'ĕl dwell in
booths when I brought them out of the land
of Mitsrayim. I am יהוה your Elohim.' "
44 Thus did Mosheh speak of the appointed times of יהוה to the children of Yisra'ĕl.

24 And יהוה spoke to Mosheh, saying,
2 "Command the children of Yis-
ra'ĕl that they bring to you clear oil of
pressed olives for the light, to make the
lamps burn continually.
3 "Outside the veil of the Witness, in the
Tent of Appointment, Aharon is to arrange
it from evening until morning before יהוה
continually – a law forever throughout
your generations.
4 "He is to arrange the lamps on the clean
gold lampstand before יהוה continually.
5 "And you shall take fine flour and bake
twelve cakes with it, two-tenths *of an
ĕphah* in each cake.
6 "And you shall set them in two rows,
six in a row, on the clean table before יהוה.
7 "And you shall put clear frankincense
on each row, and it shall be on the bread as
a remembrance portion, an offering made
by fire to יהוה.
8 "On every Sabbath he is to arrange it
before יהוה continually, from the children
of Yisra'ĕl – an everlasting covenant.
9 "And it shall be for Aharon and his
sons, and they shall eat it in the set-apart
place, because it is most set-apart to him
from the offerings of יהוה made by fire –
an everlasting law."
10 And the son of an Yisra'ĕli woman,
whose father was a Mitsrian man, went out
among the children of Yisra'ĕl. And the
Yisra'ĕli woman's son and a man of
Yisra'ĕl strove in the camp.
11 And the Yisra'ĕli woman's son blasphemed the Name, and cursed. So they
brought him to Mosheh. Now his mother's
name was Shelomith the daughter of Diḇri,
of the tribe of Dan.
12 And they put him under guard, that
it might be declared to them at the mouth
of יהוה.
13 And יהוה spoke to Mosheh, saying,
14 "Bring the one who has cursed outside
the camp, and all those who heard him
shall lay their hands on his head, and all the
congregation shall stone him.
15 "And speak to the children of Yisra'ĕl,
saying, 'Anyone who curses his Elohim
shall bear his sin.
16 'And he who blasphemes the Name of
יהוה shall certainly be put to death, and all
the congregation certainly stone him, the
stranger as well as the native. When he
blasphemes the Name, he is put to death.
17 'And a man who strikes the being of
any man shall certainly be put to death.
18 'And he who strikes a beast repays it,
body for body.
19 'And when a man inflicts a blemish
upon his neighbour, as he has done so it is
done to him:
20 'Fracture for fracture, eye for eye, tooth
for tooth; as he inflicts a blemish upon him,
so it is done to him.
21 'And he who strikes a beast repays it,
and he who strikes a man *to death* is put to
death.
22 'You are to have one right-ruling, for
the stranger and for the native, for I am
יהוה your Elohim.' "
23 And Mosheh spoke to the children of
Yisra'ĕl, and they brought the one who
cursed outside the camp, and stoned him
with stones. And the children of Yisra'ĕl
did as יהוה commanded Mosheh.

25 And יהוה spoke to Mosheh on
Mount Sinai, saying,
2 "Speak to the children of Yisra'ĕl, and
say to them, 'When you come into the land
which I give you, then the land shall
observe a Sabbath to יהוה.
3 'Six years you sow your field, and six
years you prune your vineyard, and gather
in its fruit,

4 but in the seventh year the land is to
have a Sabbath of rest, a Sabbath to יהוה.
Do not sow your field and do not prune
your vineyard.
5 'Do not reap what grows of its own of
your harvest, and do not gather the grapes
of your unpruned vine, for it is a year of
rest for the land.
6 'And the Sabbath of the land shall be
to you for food, for you and your servant,
and for your female servant and your hired
servant, and for the stranger who sojourns
with you,
7 and for your livestock and the beasts
that are in your land. All its crops are for
food.
8 'And you shall count seven Sabbaths of
years for yourself, seven times seven years.
And the time of the seven Sabbaths of
years shall be to you forty-nine years.
9 'You shall then sound a shophar-sound
on the tenth day of the seventh new *moon*,
on Yom haKippurim [a] cause a shophar [b] to
sound through all your land.
10 'And you shall set the fiftieth year
apart, and proclaim release throughout all
the land to all its inhabitants, it is a Yoḇel [c]
for you. And each of you shall return to his
possession, and each of you return to his
clan.
11 'The fiftieth year is a Yoḇel [c] to you. Do
not sow, nor reap what grows of its own,
nor gather from its unpruned vine.
12 'It is a Yoḇel, it is set-apart to you. Eat
from the field its crops.
13 'In the Year of this Yoḇel let each one
of you return to his possession.
14 'And when you sell whatever to your
neighbour or buy from the hand of your
neighbour, do not exploit one another.
15 'According to the number of years after
the Yoḇel you buy from your neighbour,
and according to the number of years of
crops he sells to you.
16 'According to the greater number of
years you increase its price, and according
to the fewer number of years you diminish
its price, because he sells to you according
to the number of the years of the crops.
17 'And do not oppress one another, but
you shall fear your Elohim. For I am יהוה
your Elohim.
18 'And you shall do My laws and guard
My right-rulings, and shall do them. And
you shall dwell in the land in safety,
19 'and the land shall yield its fruit, and
you shall eat to satisfaction, and shall dwell
there in safety.
20 'And since you might say, "What do we
eat in the seventh year, since we do not sow
nor gather in our crops?"
21 'Therefore I have commanded My
blessing on you in the sixth year, and it
shall bring forth the crop for three years.
22 'And you shall sow in the eighth year,
and eat of the old crop until the ninth year.
Eat of the old until its crop comes in.
23 'And the land is not to be sold beyond
reclaim, for the land is Mine, for you are
sojourners and settlers with Me.
24 'And provide for a redemption for the
land, in all the land of your possession.
25 'When your brother becomes poor, and
has sold some of his possession, and his
redeemer, a close relative comes to redeem
it, then he shall redeem what his brother
sold.
26 'And when the man has no one to
redeem it, but he himself becomes able to
redeem it,
27 then let him count the years since its
sale, and return the remainder to the man to
whom he sold it, that he shall return to his
possession.
28 'And if his hand has not found enough
to give back to him, then what was sold
shall remain in the hand of him who bought
it until the Year of Yoḇel. And it shall be
released in the Yoḇel, and he shall return to
his possession.
29 'And when a man sells a house in a
walled city, then his right of redemption
shall be at the end of the year after it is
sold. His right of redemption lasts a year.
30 'But if it is not redeemed within a complete year, then the house in the walled city

25a Day of the Coverings or Day of Atonement. *25b* Animal horn - traditionally a ram's horn.
25c See Explanatory notes: Yoḇel.

shall be established beyond reclaim to the buyer of it, throughout his generations. It is not released in the Yoḇel.
31 'The houses of villages, however, which have no wall around them are reckoned as the field of the country. A right of redemption belongs to it, and they are released in the Yoḇel.
32 'As for the cities of the Lěwites, and the houses in the cities of their possession, the Lěwites have a right of redemption forever.
33 'And that which is redeemed from the Lěwites, both the sale of a house and the city of his possession shall be released in the Year of Yoḇel, because the houses in the cities of the Lěwites are their possession in the midst of the children of Yisra'ěl.
34 'But the field of the open land of their cities is not sold, for it is their everlasting possession.
35 'And when your brother becomes poor, and his hand has failed with you, then you shall strengthen him, and he shall live with you, like a stranger or a sojourner.
36 'Take no interest from him, or profit, but you shall fear your Elohim, and your brother shall live with you.
37 'Do not lend him your silver on interest, and do not lend him your food for profit.
38 'I am יהוה your Elohim, who brought you out of the land of Mitsrayim, to give you the land of Kena'an, to be your Elohim.
39 'And when your brother who dwells by you becomes poor, and sells himself to you, do not make him serve as a slave.
40 'But as a hired servant, as a settler he is with you, and serves you until the Year of Yoḇel.
41 'And then he shall leave you, he and his children with him, and shall return to his own clan, even return to the possession of his fathers.
42 'For they are My servants, whom I brought out of the land of Mitsrayim, they are not sold as slaves.
43 'Do not rule over him with harshness, but you shall fear your Elohim.
44 'And your male and female slaves whom you have from the nations that are around you, from them you buy male and female slaves,
45 and also from the sons of the strangers sojourning among you, from them you buy, and from their clans who are with you, which they shall bring forth in your land, and they shall be your property.
46 'And you shall take them as an inheritance for your children after you, to inherit them as a possession, they are your slaves for all time. But over your brothers, the children of Yisra'ěl, you do not rule with harshness, one over another.
47 'Now when a sojourner or a settler with you becomes rich, and your brother with him becomes poor, and sells himself to the settler or sojourner with you, or to a member of the sojourner's clan,
48 after he has been sold, there is a right of redemption to him – one of his brothers does redeem him,
49 or his uncle or his uncle's son does redeem him, or anyone who is a close relative to him in his clan does redeem him, or if he is able, then he shall redeem himself.
50 'And he shall reckon with him who bought him: The price of his release shall be according to the number of years, from the year that he was sold to him until the Year of Yoḇel; as the days of a hired servant it is with him.
51 'If there are yet many years, according to them he repays the price of his redemption, from the silver of his purchase.
52 'And if few years are left until the Year of Yoḇel, then he shall reckon with him, and according to his years he repays him the price of his redemption.
53 'He is with him as a yearly hired servant, and he does not rule with harshness over him before your eyes.
54 'And if he is not redeemed in these years, then he shall be released in the Year of Yoḇel, he and his children with him.
55 'Because the children of Yisra'ěl are servants to Me, they are My servants whom I brought out of the land of Mitsrayim. I am יהוה your Elohim.

26 'Do not make idols for yourselves, and do not set up a carved image or a pillar for yourselves, and do not place a

stone image in your land, to bow down to it. For I am יהוה your Elohim.

2 'Guard My Sabbaths and reverence My set-apart place. I am יהוה.

3 'If you walk in My laws and guard My commands, and shall do them,

4 then I shall give you rain in its season, and the land shall yield its crops, and the trees of the field yield their fruit.

5 'And your threshing shall last till the time of the grape harvest, and the grape harvest shall last till the time of sowing. And you shall eat your bread until you have enough, and shall dwell in your land safely.

6 'And I shall give peace in the land, and you shall lie down and no one make you afraid. And I shall clear the land of evil beasts, and not let the sword go through your land.

7 'And you shall pursue your enemies, and they shall fall by the sword before you.

8 'And five of you shall pursue a hundred, and a hundred of you pursue ten thousand. And your enemies shall fall by the sword before you.

9 'And I shall turn to you and make you fruitful, and shall increase you, and shall establish My covenant with you.

10 'And you shall eat the old supply, and clear out the old because of the new.

11 'And I shall set My Dwelling Place in your midst, and My being shall not reject you.

12 'And I shall walk in your midst, and shall be your Elohim, and you shall be My people.

13 'I am יהוה your Elohim, who brought you out of the land of Mitsrayim, from being their slaves. And I have broken the bars of your yoke and made you walk upright.

14 'But if you do not obey Me, and do not do all these commands,

15 and if you reject My laws, or if your being loathes My right-rulings, so that you do not do all My commands, but break My covenant,

16 I also do this to you: And I shall appoint sudden alarm over you, wasting disease and inflammation, destroying the eyes, and consuming the life. And you shall sow your seed in vain, for your enemies shall eat it.

17 'And I shall set My face against you, and you shall be smitten before your enemies. And those who hate you shall rule over you, and you shall flee when no one pursues you.

18 'And after all this, if you do not obey Me, then I shall punish you seven times more for your sins.

19 'And I shall break the pride of your power, and shall make your heavens like iron and your earth like bronze.

20 'And your strength shall be spent in vain and your land not yield its crops, nor the trees of the land yield their fruit.

21 'And if you walk contrary to Me, and refuse to obey Me, I shall bring on you seven times more plagues, according to your sins,

22 and send wild beasts among you, which shall bereave you of your children. And I shall cut off your livestock, and make you few in number, and your highways shall be deserted.

23 'And if you are not instructed by Me by these, but walk contrary to Me,

24 then I also shall walk contrary to you, and I Myself shall strike you seven times for your sins.

25 'And I shall bring against you a sword executing the vengeance of My covenant, and you shall gather together in your cities, and I shall send pestilence among you, and you shall be given into the hand of the enemy.

26 'When I have cut off your supply of bread, ten women shall bake your bread in one oven, and they shall bring back to you your bread by weight, and you shall eat and not be satisfied.

27 'And if in spite of this, you do not obey Me, but walk contrary to Me,

28 then I shall walk contrary to you in wrath. And I Myself shall punish you seven times for your sins.

29 'And you shall eat the flesh of your sons, and eat the flesh of your daughters.

30 'And I shall destroy your high places, and cut down your sun-pillars, and put

your carcasses on the carcasses of your
idols. And My being shall loathe you.
31 'And I shall turn your cities into ruins
and lay your set-apart places waste, and not
smell your sweet fragrances.
32 'And I shall lay the land waste, and
your enemies who dwell in it shall be
astonished at it.
33 'And I shall scatter you among the
nations and draw out a sword after you.
And your land shall be desert and your
cities ruins,
34 and the land enjoy its Sabbaths as long
as it lies waste and you are in your
enemies' land. Then the land would rest
and enjoy its Sabbaths.
35 'As long as it lies waste it rests, for the
time it did not rest on your Sabbaths when
you dwelt in it.
36 'And as for those of you who are left, I
shall send faintness into their hearts in the
lands of their enemies, and the sound of a
shaken leaf shall cause them to flee. And
they shall flee as though retreating from
a sword, and they shall fall when no one
pursues.
37 'And they shall stumble over one
another, as from before a sword, when no
one pursues. And you shall be unable to
stand before your enemies.
38 'And you shall perish among the
nations, and the land of your enemies shall
eat you up,
39 and those of you who are left rot away
in their crookedness in your enemies'
lands, and also in their fathers' crookednesses rot away with them.
40 'But if they confess their crookedness
and the crookedness of their fathers, with
their trespass in which they trespassed
against Me, and that they also have walked
contrary to Me,
41 and that I also have walked contrary to
them and have brought them into the land
of their enemies – if their uncircumcised
heart is then humbled, and they accept the
punishment of their crookedness,
42 then I shall remember My covenant
with Ya'aqoḇ, and also My covenant with
Yitsḥaq, and also remember My covenant
with Aḇraham, and remember the land.
43 'For the land was abandoned by them,
and enjoying its Sabbaths while lying
waste without them, and they were paying
for their crookedness, because they rejected My right-rulings and because their
being loathed My laws.
44 'And yet for all this, when they are in
the land of their enemies, I shall not reject
them, nor shall I loathe them so as to
destroy them and break My covenant with
them. For I am יהוה their Elohim.
45 'Then I shall remember for their sake
the covenant of the ancestors whom I
brought out of the land of Mitsrayim before
the eyes of the nations to be their Elohim. I
am יהוה.' "
46 These are the laws and the right-rulings
and the Torot [a] which יהוה made between
Himself and the children of Yisra'ěl on
Mount Sinai by the hand of Mosheh.

27
And יהוה spoke to Mosheh, saying,
2 "Speak to the children of Yisra'ěl,
and say to them, 'When a man separates a
vow, by your evaluation of lives unto יהוה,
3 when your evaluation is of a male from
twenty years old up to sixty years old, then
your evaluation shall be fifty sheqels of silver, according to the sheqel of the set-apart
place.
4 'And if it is a female, then your evaluation shall be thirty sheqels;
5 and if from five years old up to twenty
years old, then your evaluation for a male
shall be twenty sheqels, and for a female
ten sheqels;
6 and if from a new *moon* [a] old up to five
years old, then your evaluation for a male
shall be five sheqels of silver, and for a
female your evaluation shall be three sheqels of silver;
7 and if from sixty years old and above,
if it is a male, then your evaluation shall
be fifteen sheqels, and for a female ten sheqels.
8 'But if he is too poor to pay your evaluation, then he shall present himself before

26a Torot - plural of Torah - teaching. *27a* Or a month.

the priest, and the priest shall set a value for him. According to the ability of him who vowed, the priest shall value him.
9 'And if it is a beast of which they bring an offering to יהוה, all such given to יהוה is set-apart.
10 'He is not to replace it or exchange it, good for spoilt or spoilt for good. And if he at all exchanges beast for beast, then both it and the one exchanged for it is set-apart.
11 'And if it is any unclean beast of which they do not bring an offering to יהוה, then he shall present the beast before the priest;
12 and the priest shall value it, whether it is good or spoilt. According to your evaluation, O priest, so it shall be.
13 'But if he indeed redeems it, then he shall add one-fifth to your evaluation.
14 'And when a man sets his house apart, to be set-apart to יהוה, then the priest shall value it, whether it is good or spoilt. As the priest values it, so it stands.
15 'And if he who sets it apart does redeem his house, then he shall add one-fifth of the silver of your evaluation to it, and it shall be his.
16 'And if a man sets apart to יהוה a field he owns, then your evaluation shall be according to the seed for it – a ḥomer of barley seed at fifty sheqels of silver.
17 'If he sets his field apart from the Year of Yoḇel, according to your evaluation it stands.
18 'But if he sets his field apart after the Yoḇel, then the priest shall reckon to him the silver due according to the years that remain till the Year of Yoḇel, and it shall be deducted from your evaluation.
19 'And if he who sets the field apart ever wishes to redeem it, then he shall add one-fifth of the silver of your evaluation to it, and it shall be his.
20 'And if he does not redeem the field, or if he has sold the field to another man, it is no longer redeemed,
21 but the field, when it is released in the Yoḇel, is set-apart to יהוה as a dedicated field, to be the possession of the priest.
22 'And if a man sets apart to יהוה a field which he has bought, which is not the field of his possession,
23 then the priest shall reckon to him the amount of your evaluation, up to the Year of Yoḇel, and he shall give your evaluation on that day, set-apart to יהוה.
24 'In the Year of Yoḇel the field returns to him from whom he bought it, to him whose is the possession of the land.
25 'And all your evaluations are to be according to the sheqel of the set-apart place: twenty gĕrahs to the sheqel.
26 'However, a first-born of the beasts, which is first-born to יהוה, no man sets it apart – whether bull or sheep, it belongs to יהוה.
27 'And if among the unclean beasts, then he shall ransom it according to your evaluation, and shall add one-fifth to it. And if it is not redeemed, then it shall be sold according to your evaluation.
28 'However, whatever a man lays under ban for יהוה of all that he has, man and beast, or the field of his possession, is not sold or redeemed. Whatever is laid under ban is most set-apart to יהוה.
29 'No one under the ban, under the ban among men, is ransomed, but shall certainly be put to death.
30 'And all the tithe of the land – of the seed of the land or of the fruit of the tree – belongs to יהוה. It is set-apart to יהוה.
31 'If a man indeed redeems any of his tithes, he adds one-fifth to it.
32 'And the entire tithe of the herd and of the flock, all that passes under the rod, the tenth one is set-apart to יהוה.
33 'He does not inquire whether it is good or spoilt, nor does he exchange it. And if he exchanges it at all, then both it and the one exchanged for it are set-apart, it is not redeemed.' "
34 These are the commands which יהוה commanded Mosheh for the children of Yisra'ĕl on Mount Sinai.

BEMIḎBAR

NUMBERS

1 And יהוה spoke to Mosheh in the Wilderness of Sinai, in the Tent of Appointment, on the first day to the second new *moon*, in the second year after they had come out of the land of Mitsrayim, saying,

2 “Take a census of all the congregation of the children of Yisra’ěl, by their clans, by their fathers’ houses, according to the number of names, every male, head by head,

3 from twenty years old and above, everyone going out to the army in Yisra’ěl. Number them by their divisions, you and Aharon.

4 “And a man from every tribe should be with you, each one the head of his father’s house.

5 “And these are the names of the men who stand with you. From Re’uḇěn: Elitsur, son of Sheḏěy’ur.

6 “From Shimʽon: Shelumi’ěl, son of Tsurishaddai.

7 “From Yehuḏah: Naḥshon, son of Amminaḏaḇ.

8 “From Yissasḵar: Nethaně’l, son of Tsuʽar.

9 “From Zeḇulun: Eliyaḇ, son of Ḥělon.

10 “From the sons of Yosěph: From Ephrayim: Elishama, son of Ammihuḏ. From Menashsheh: Gamli’ěl, son of Peḏahtsur.

11 “From Binyamin: Aḇiḏan, son of Giḏʽoni.

12 “From Dan: Aḥiʽezer, son of Ammishaddai.

13 “From Ashěr: Paḡʽi’ěl, son of Oḵran.

14 “From Gaḏ: Elyasaph, son of Deʽu’ěl.

15 “From Naphtali: Aḥira, son of Ěnan.”

16 These are the ones called from the congregation, leaders of their fathers’ tribes, heads of the thousands of Yisra’ěl.

17 And Mosheh and Aharon took these men who were called by name,

18 and they assembled all the congregation together on the first day of the second new *moon*. And they declared their ancestry by clans, by their fathers’ houses, according to the number of names, from twenty years old and above, each one head by head.

19 As יהוה commanded Mosheh, so he registered them in the Wilderness of Sinai.

20 And the children of Re’uḇěn, Yisra’ěl’s first-born, their genealogies by their clans, by their fathers’ house, according to the number of names, every male head by head, from twenty years old and above, everyone going out to the army,

21 those who were registered of the tribe of Re’uḇěn were forty-six thousand five hundred.

22 From the children of Shimʽon, their genealogies by their clans, by their fathers’ house, of those who were registered, according to the number of names, every male head by head, from twenty years old and above, everyone going out to the army,

23 those who were registered of the tribe of Shimʽon were fifty-nine thousand three hundred.

24 From the children of Gaḏ, their genealogies by their clans, by their fathers’ house, according to the number of names, from twenty years old and above, everyone going out to the army,

25 those who were registered of the tribe of Gaḏ were forty-five thousand six hundred and fifty.

26 From the children of Yehuḏah, their genealogies by their clans, by their fathers’ house, according to the number of names, from twenty years old and above, everyone going out to the army,

27 those who were registered of the tribe of Yehuḏah were seventy-four thousand six hundred.

28 From the children of Yissasḵar, their genealogies by their clans, by their fathers’

house, according to the number of names,
from twenty years old and above, everyone
going out to the army,
29 those who were registered of the tribe
of Yissasḵar were fifty-four thousand four
hundred.
30 From the children of Zeḇulun, their
genealogies by their clans, by their fathers'
house, according to the number of names,
from twenty years old and above, everyone
going out to the army,
31 those who were registered of the tribe
of Zeḇulun were fifty-seven thousand four
hundred.
32 From the sons of Yosěph, the children
of Ephrayim, their genealogies by their
clans, by their fathers' house, according to
the number of names, from twenty years
old and above, everyone going out to the
army,
33 those who were registered of the tribe
of Ephrayim were forty thousand five
hundred.
34 From the children of Menashsheh, their
genealogies by their clans, by their fathers'
house, according to the number of names,
from twenty years old and above, everyone
going out to the army,
35 those who were registered of the tribe
of Menashsheh were thirty-two thousand
two hundred.
36 From the children of Binyamin, their
genealogies by their clans, by their fathers'
house, according to the number of names,
from twenty years old and above, everyone
going out to the army,
37 those who were registered of the tribe
of Binyamin were thirty-five thousand four
hundred.
38 From the children of Dan, their
genealogies by their clans, by their fathers'
house, according to the number of names,
from twenty years old and above, everyone
going out to the army,
39 those who were registered of the tribe
of Dan were sixty-two thousand seven
hundred.
40 From the children of Ashěr, their
genealogies by their clans, by their fathers'
house, according to the number of names,
from twenty years old and above, everyone
going out to the army,
41 those who were registered of the tribe
of Ashěr were forty-one thousand five
hundred.
42 From the children of Naphtali, their
genealogies by their clans, by their fathers'
house, according to the number of names,
from twenty years old and above, everyone
going out to the army,
43 those who were registered of the tribe
of Naphtali were fifty-three thousand four
hundred.
44 These were those registered, whom
Mosheh and Aharon registered, with the
leaders of Yisra'ěl, twelve men, each one
for his father's house.
45 And all those that were registered of the
children of Yisra'ěl, by their fathers' houses, from twenty years old and above,
everyone going out to the army in Yisra'ěl,
46 all those that were registered were six
hundred and three thousand five hundred
and fifty.
47 But the Lěwites were not registered
among them by their fathers' tribe,
48 because יהוה had spoken to Mosheh,
saying,
49 "Only the tribe of Lěwi you do not
register, nor take a census of them among
the children of Yisra'ěl.
50 "Instead, appoint the Lěwites over the
Dwelling Place of the Witness, over all its
furnishings, and over all that belongs to it.
They bear the Dwelling Place and all its
furnishings, and they attend to it, and camp
around the Dwelling Place.
51 "And when the Dwelling Place is to go
forward, the Lěwites take it down. And
when the Dwelling Place is to be set up,
the Lěwites set it up. And the stranger who
comes near is put to death.
52 "And the children of Yisra'ěl shall
pitch their tents, everyone by his own
camp, everyone by his own banner,
according to their divisions,
53 but let the Lěwites camp around the
Dwelling Place of the Witness, so that
there be no wrath on the congregation of
the children of Yisra'ěl. And the Lěwites
shall guard the duty of the Dwelling Place
of the Witness."

54 And the children of Yisra'ĕl did according to all that יהוה commanded Mosheh,
so they did.

2 And יהוה spoke to Mosheh and to
Aharon, saying,
2 "The children of Yisra'ĕl are to camp,
each one by his own banner, beside the
sign of his father's house. Let them camp
around the Tent of Appointment at a distance."
3 And on the east side, towards sunrise:
those of the banner of the camp of
Yehuḏah camp according to their divisions. And the leader of the children of
Yehuḏah: Naḥshon, son of Amminaḏaḇ.
4 And his army with their registered
ones: seventy-four thousand six hundred.
5 And those camping next to him is the
tribe of Yissasḵar, and the leader of the
children of Yissasḵar: Nethanĕ'l, son of
Tsuʽar.
6 And his army with its registered ones:
fifty-four thousand four hundred.
7 Then the tribe of Zeḇulun, and the
leader of the children of Zeḇulun: Eliyaḇ,
son of Ḥĕlon.
8 And his army with its registered ones:
fifty-seven thousand four hundred.
9 All the registered ones of the camp of
Yehuḏah, according to their divisions: one
hundred and eighty-six thousand four
hundred. These depart first.
10 On the south side: the banner of
the camp of Re'uḇĕn according to their
divisions, and the leader of the children of
Re'uḇĕn: Elitsur, son of Sheḏĕy'ur.
11 And his army with its registered ones:
forty-six thousand five hundred.
12 And those who camp next to him: the
tribe of Shimʽon, and the leader of the
children of Shimʽon: Shelumi'ĕl, son of
Tsurishaddai.
13 And his army with their registered
ones: fifty-nine thousand three hundred.
14 Then the tribe of Gaḏ, and the leader
of the children of Gaḏ: Elyasaph, son of
Reʽu'ĕl. [a]
15 And his army with their registered
ones: forty-five thousand six hundred and
fifty.
16 All the registered ones of the camp of
Re'uḇĕn, according to their divisions: one
hundred and fifty-one thousand four hundred and fifty. And they are the second to
depart.
17 And the Tent of Appointment, the camp
of the Lĕwites, shall move out in the middle of the camps. As they camp, so they
move out, everyone in his place, by their
banners.
18 On the west side: the banner of the
camp of Ephrayim according to their divisions, and the leader of the children of
Ephrayim: Elishama, son of Ammihuḏ.
19 And his army with their registered
ones: forty thousand five hundred.
20 And next to him the tribe of
Menashsheh, and the leader of the children
of Menashsheh: Gamli'ĕl, son of
Peḏahtsur.
21 And his army with their registered
ones: thirty-two thousand two hundred.
22 Then the tribe of Binyamin, and the
leader of the children of Binyamin:
Aḇiḏan, son of Giḏʽoni.
23 And his army with their registered
ones: thirty-five thousand four hundred.
24 All the registered ones of the camp of
Ephrayim, according to their divisions:
one hundred and eight thousand one hundred. And they are the third to depart.
25 On the north side: the banner of the
camp of Dan, according to their divisions,
and the leader of the children of Dan:
Aḥiʽezer, son of Ammishaddai.
26 And his army with their registered
ones: sixty-two thousand seven hundred.
27 And those who camp next to him: the
tribe of Ashĕr, and the leader of the children of Ashĕr: Paḡʽi'ĕl, son of Oḵran.
28 And his army with their registered
ones: forty-one thousand five hundred.
29 Then the tribe of Naphtali, and the
leader of the children of Naphtali: Aḥira,
son of Ĕnan.
30 And his army with their registered
ones: fifty-three thousand four hundred.

2a See Explanatory notes: Deʽu'ĕl.

31 All the registered ones of the camp of
Dan: one hundred and fifty-seven thousand
six hundred. They depart last, with their
banners.
32 These were registered ones of the children of Yisra'ěl by their fathers' houses.
All who were registered according to their
divisions of the camps: six hundred and
three thousand five hundred and fifty.
33 But the Lěwites were not registered
among the children of Yisra'ěl, as יהוה
commanded Mosheh.
34 And the children of Yisra'ěl did according to all that יהוה commanded Mosheh.
So they camped by their banners and so
they departed, each one by his clan,
according to their fathers' houses.

3

And these are the generations of
Aharon and Mosheh when יהוה spoke
with Mosheh on Mount Sinai.
2 And these are the names of the sons of
Aharon: Naḏaḇ, the first-born, and Aḇihu,
El'azar, and Ithamar.
3 These are the names of the sons of
Aharon, the anointed priests, whom he
ordained to act as priests.
4 And Naḏaḇ and Aḇihu had died before
יהוה when they brought strange fire before
יהוה in the Wilderness of Sinai. And they
had no children. So El'azar and Ithamar
acted as priests in the presence of Aharon
their father.
5 And יהוה spoke to Mosheh, saying,
6 "Bring the tribe of Lěwi near, and set
them before Aharon the priest, and they
shall serve him,
7 and shall guard his duty and the duty of
all the congregation before the Tent of
Appointment, to do the service of the
Dwelling Place.
8 "And they shall guard all the furnishings of the Tent of Appointment, and the
duty of the children of Yisra'ěl, to do the
service of the Dwelling Place.
9 "And you shall give the Lěwites to
Aharon and his sons. They are the given
ones, given to him from among the children of Yisra'ěl.
10 "And appoint Aharon and his sons, and
they shall guard their priesthood. And the
stranger who comes near shall be put to
death."
11 And יהוה spoke to Mosheh, saying,
12 "Now look, I Myself have taken the
Lěwites from among the children of
Yisra'ěl instead of every first-born who
opens the womb among the children of
Yisra'ěl. And the Lěwites shall be Mine,
13 because all the first-born are Mine. On
the day that I struck all the first-born in the
land of Mitsrayim, I set apart to Myself all
the first-born in Yisra'ěl, both man and
beast. They are Mine, I am יהוה."
14 And יהוה spoke to Mosheh in the
Wilderness of Sinai, saying,
15 "Register the children of Lěwi by their
fathers' houses, by their clans. Register
every male from a new *moon* [a] old and
above."
16 So Mosheh registered them according
to the word of יהוה, as he had been commanded.
17 And these were the sons of Lěwi by
their names: Gěrshon, and Qehath, and
Merari.
18 And these are the names of the sons of
Gěrshon by their clans: Liḇni and Shim'i.
19 And the sons of Qehath by their clans:
Amram and Yitshar, Ḥeḇron and Uzzi'ěl.
20 And the sons of Merari by their clans:
Maḥli and Mushi. These are the clans of
the Lěwites by their fathers' houses.
21 From Gěrshon came the clan of the
Liḇnites and the clan of the Shim'ites.
These were the clans of the Gěrshonites.
22 Their registered ones, according to the
number of all the males from a new *moon* [a]
old and above, their registered ones were
seven thousand five hundred.
23 The clans of the Gěrshonites were
to camp westward, behind the Dwelling
Place,
24 and the leader of the fathers' house of
the Gěrshonites: Elyasaph, son of La'ěl.
25 And the duty of the children of Gěrshon
in the Tent of Appointment was the
Dwelling Place, and the tent with its cover-

3a Or a month.

ing, and the covering of the door of the Tent of Appointment,

26 and the screens of the courtyard and the covering of the door of the courtyard, which is around the Dwelling Place and the slaughter-place, and their cords, according to all its service.

27 And from Qehath came the clan of the Amramites, and the clan of the Yitsharites, and the clan of the Ḥeḇronites, and the clan of the Uzzi'ĕlites. These were the clans of the Qehathites.

28 In number, all the males, from a new *moon* [a] old and above, were eight thousand six hundred, guarding the duty of the set-apart place.

29 The clans of the children of Qehath were to camp on the south side of the Dwelling Place.

30 And the leader of the fathers' house of the clans of the Qehathites was Elitsaphan, son of Uzzi'ĕl.

31 And their duty was the ark, and the table, and the lampstand, and the slaughter-places, and the utensils of the set-apart place used in the service, and the covering, and all its service.

32 And El'azar, son of Aharon the priest, was to be chief over the leaders of the Lĕwites, with oversight of those who guard the duty of the set-apart place.

33 From Merari came the clan of the Maḥlites and the clan of the Mushites. These were the clans of Merari.

34 And the number of their registered ones, all the males from a new *moon* [a] old and above, were six thousand two hundred.

35 And the leader of the fathers' house of the clans of Merari was Tsuri'ĕl, son of Aḇiḥayil. These were to camp on the north side of the Dwelling Place.

36 And the appointed duty of the children of Merari was the boards of the Dwelling Place, and its bars, and its columns, and its sockets, and its utensils, and all its service,

37 and the columns of the courtyard all around, with their sockets, and their pegs, and their cords.

38 And those who were to camp before the Dwelling Place on the east, before the Tent of Appointment, were Mosheh and Aharon, and his sons, guarding the duty of the set-apart place, and the duty of the children of Yisra'ĕl. But the stranger who came near was to be put to death.

39 All the registered ones of the Lĕwites, whom Mosheh and Aharon registered at the mouth of יהוה, by their clans, all the males from a new *moon* [a] old and above, were twenty-two thousand.

40 And יהוה said to Mosheh, "Register all the first-born males of the children of Yisra'ĕl from a new *moon* [a] old and above, and take the number of their names.

41 "And you shall take the Lĕwites for Me – I am יהוה – instead of all the first-born among the children of Yisra'ĕl, and the livestock of the Lĕwites instead of all the first-born among the livestock of the children of Yisra'ĕl."

42 And Mosheh registered all the first-born among the children of Yisra'ĕl as יהוה had commanded him.

43 And all the first-born males, by the number of names, from one new *moon* [a] old and above of their registered ones, were twenty-two thousand two hundred and seventy-three.

44 And יהוה spoke to Mosheh, saying,

45 "Take the Lĕwites instead of all the first-born among the children of Yisra'ĕl, and the livestock of the Lĕwites instead of their livestock. And the Lĕwites shall be Mine, I am יהוה.

46 "And for the ransom of the two hundred and seventy-three of the first-born of the children of Yisra'ĕl, who are more than the number of the Lĕwites,

47 you shall take five sheqels for each one, head by head – take it by the sheqel of the set-apart place, the sheqel of twenty gĕrahs.

48 "And you shall give the silver, the ransom of those who are in excess among them, to Aharon and his sons."

49 And Mosheh took the ransom silver from those who were over and above those who were ransomed by the Lĕwites.

3a Or a month.

50 From the first-born of the children of
Yisra'ěl he took the silver, one thousand
three hundred and sixty-five pieces,
according to the sheqel of the set-apart
place.
51 And Mosheh gave their ransom silver
to Aharon, and to his sons, according to
the word of יהוה, as יהוה had commanded
Mosheh.

4 And יהוה spoke to Mosheh, and to
Aharon, saying,
2 "Take a census of the sons of Qehath
from among the children of Lěwi, by their
clans, by their fathers' house,
3 from thirty years old and above, even to
fifty years old, all who enter the service to
do the work in the Tent of Appointment.
4 "This is the service of the sons of
Qehath in the Tent of Appointment, the
most set-apart matters:
5 "At the breaking of camp, Aharon and
his sons shall come, and they shall take
down the covering veil and cover the ark
of the Witness with it,
6 and shall put on it a covering of fine
leather, and spread over that an all-blue
wrapper, and shall insert its poles.
7 "And on the table of showbread they
shall spread a blue wrapper, and shall put
on it the dishes, and the ladles, and the
bowls, and the jars for pouring, and the
showbread on it.
8 "And they shall spread over them a
scarlet wrapper, and cover the same with a
covering of fine leather, and shall insert its
poles,
9 and shall take a blue wrapper and cover
the lampstand of the light, with its lamps,
and its snuffers, and its trays, and all its oil
vessels, by which they serve it.
10 "And they shall put it with all its utensils in a covering of fine leather, and put it
on a bar.
11 "And over the golden slaughter-place
they shall spread a blue wrapper, and cover
it with a covering of fine leather, and shall
insert its poles,
12 and shall take all the utensils of service
with which they serve in the set-apart
place, and shall put them in a blue wrapper,
cover them with a covering of fine leather,
and put them on a bar,
13 and shall remove the ashes from the
slaughter-place, and spread a purple wrapper over it,
14 and shall put on it all its utensils by
which they serve there: the fire holders, the
forks, and the shovels, and the basins, and
all the utensils of the slaughter-place, and
shall spread on it a covering of fine leather,
and insert its poles.
15 "And when Aharon and his sons have
finished covering the set-apart *objects* and
all the furnishings of the Set-apart Place at
the breaking of camp, then the sons of
Qehath shall come to lift them, but let
them not touch that which is set-apart, lest
they die. These *matters* are the burden of
the sons of Qehath in the Tent of
Appointment.
16 "And the oversight of El'azar, son of
Aharon the priest, is the oil for the light,
and the sweet incense, and the daily grain
offering, and the anointing oil, and the
oversight of all the Dwelling Place and all
that is in it, with the set-apart place and its
furnishings."
17 And יהוה spoke to Mosheh, and to
Aharon, saying,
18 "Do not cut off the tribe of the clans of
the Qehathites from among the Lěwites,
19 but do this to them, and they shall live
and not die when they approach the most
set-apart *objects*: Aharon and his sons shall
go in and appoint each of them to his
service and his burden.
20 "They are not, however, to go in to
watch while the set-apart *objects* are being
covered, lest they die."
21 And יהוה spoke to Mosheh, saying,
22 "Take a census also of the sons of
Gěrshon, by their fathers' house, by their
clans.
23 "Register them, from thirty years old
and above, even to fifty years old, all who
enter to perform the service, to do the
service in the Tent of Appointment.
24 "This is the service of the clans of the
Gěrshonites, in serving and in bearing burdens:
25 "And they shall bear the curtains of the

Dwelling Place and the Tent of
Appointment with its covering, the covering of fine leather that is on it, the covering
for the door of the Tent of Appointment,
26 and the screens of the courtyard and the
covering for the door of the gate of
the courtyard, which is around the
Dwelling Place and slaughter-place, and
their cords, all the equipment for their service and all that is made for them – so shall
they serve.
27 "At the mouth of Aharon and his sons
is all the service of the sons of the
Gĕrshonites, all their burden and all their
service. And you shall appoint to them all
the duty of all their burden.
28 "This is the service of the clans of the
sons of Gĕrshon in the Tent of
Appointment. And let their duties be under
the hand of Ithamar, son of Aharon the
priest.
29 "As for the sons of Merari, register
them by their clans and by their fathers'
house.
30 "Register them, from thirty years old
and above, even to fifty years old, all who
enter the service to do the work of the Tent
of Appointment.
31 "And this is the duty of their burden,
according to all their service for the Tent
of Meeting: the boards of the Dwelling
Place, and its bars, and its columns, and its
sockets,
32 and the columns around the courtyard
with their sockets, and their pegs, and their
cords, with all their equipment and all their
service. And assign *to each* by name the
equipment of the duty of their burden.
33 "This is the service of the clans of the
sons of Merari, as all their service for the
Tent of Appointment, under the hand of
Ithamar, son of Aharon the priest."
34 So Mosheh and Aharon and the leaders
of the congregation registered the sons of
the Qehathites by their clans and by their
fathers' house,
35 from thirty years old and above, even to
fifty years old, all who entered the service
for work in the Tent of Appointment.
36 And their registered ones, by their
clans, were two thousand seven hundred
and fifty.
37 These were the registered ones of the
clans of the Qehathites, all those serving in
the Tent of Appointment, whom Mosheh
and Aharon registered according to the
mouth of יהוה by the hand of Mosheh.
38 And those registered ones of the sons of
Gĕrshon, by their clans and by their
fathers' house,
39 from thirty years old and above, even to
fifty years old, all who entered the service
for work in the Tent of Appointment,
40 the registered ones, by their clans, by
their fathers' house, were two thousand six
hundred and thirty.
41 These were the registered ones of the
clans of the sons of Gĕrshon, of all who
serve in the Tent of Appointment, whom
Mosheh and Aharon registered according
to the mouth of יהוה.
42 And those of the clans of the sons of
Merari who were registered, by their clans,
by their fathers' house,
43 from thirty years old and above, even to
fifty years old, all who entered the service
for work in the Tent of Appointment,
44 the registered ones, by their clans were
three thousand two hundred.
45 These were the registered ones of the
clans of the sons of Merari, whom Mosheh
and Aharon registered according to the
mouth of יהוה by the hand of Mosheh.
46 All the registered ones of the Lĕwites,
whom Mosheh and Aharon and the leaders
of Yisra'ĕl registered, by their clans and by
their fathers' houses,
47 from thirty years old and above, even to
fifty years old, all who came to do the
work of service and the work of bearing
burdens in the Tent of Appointment,
48 their registered ones were eight thousand five hundred and eighty.
49 According to the mouth of יהוה they
were registered by the hand of Mosheh,
each according to his service and according to his burden, thus were they registered
by him, as יהוה commanded Mosheh.

5 And יהוה spoke to Mosheh, saying,
2 "Command the children of Yisra'ĕl
to send out of the camp every leper,

and everyone who has a discharge, and whoever becomes defiled for a being.

3 "Send out both male and female, send them outside the camp, so that they do not defile their camps in the midst of which I dwell."

4 And the children of Yisra'ĕl did so, to send them outside the camp. As יהוה had spoken to Mosheh, so the children of Yisra'ĕl did.

5 And יהוה spoke to Mosheh, saying,

6 "Speak to the children of Yisra'ĕl, 'When a man or woman commits any sin that men commit in trespass against יהוה, and that being is guilty,

7 then they shall confess their sin which they have done. And he shall restore his guilt in its principal, plus one-fifth of it, and give it to whom he has been guilty.

8 'But if the man has no relative to restore the guilt to, the guilt which is restored goes to יהוה, for the priest, in addition to the ram of the atonement with which atonement is made for him.

9 'And every contribution of all the set-apart *gifts* of the children of Yisra'ĕl, which they bring to the priest, becomes his.

10 'And every man's set-apart *gifts* becomes his, whatever any man gives the priest becomes his.' "

11 And יהוה spoke to Mosheh, saying,

12 "Speak to the children of Yisra'ĕl, and say to them, 'When any man's wife turns aside and has committed a trespass against him,

13 and a man has intercourse with her, and it is hidden from the eyes of her husband, and it is concealed that she has defiled herself, and there was no witness against her, nor was she caught,

14 and a spirit of jealousy comes upon him and he becomes jealous of his wife who has defiled herself, or a spirit of jealousy comes upon him and he becomes jealous of his wife although she has not defiled herself,

15 then the man shall bring his wife to the priest. And he shall bring the offering for her, one-tenth of an ĕphah of barley flour. He is not to pour oil on it or put frankincense on it, because it is a grain offering of jealousy, an offering for remembering, for bringing crookedness to remembrance.

16 'And the priest shall bring her near, and shall make her stand before יהוה.

17 'And the priest shall take set-apart water in an earthen vessel, and take some of the dust that is on the floor of the Dwelling Place and put it into the water.

18 'And the priest shall make the woman stand before יהוה, and shall uncover the woman's head, and put the offering for remembering in her hands, which is the grain offering of jealousy, while the priest holds in his hand the bitter water that brings a curse.

19 'And the priest shall make her swear, and say to the woman, "If no man has lain with you, and if you have not turned aside to uncleanness under your husband's *authority*, be free from this bitter water that brings a curse.

20 "But if you have turned aside under your husband's *authority*, and if you have defiled yourself and some man other than your husband has lain with you" –

21 then the priest shall make the woman swear with the oath of the curse, and he shall say to the woman – "יהוה make you a curse and an oath among your people, when יהוה makes your thigh waste away and your belly swell,

22 and this water that causes the curse shall go into your inward parts, and make your belly swell and your thigh waste away." And the woman shall say, "Amĕn, amĕn."

23 'And the priest shall write these curses in a book, and shall wipe them off into the bitter water,

24 and shall make the woman drink the bitter water that brings the curse, and the water that brings the curse shall enter her to become bitter.

25 'And the priest shall take the grain offering of jealousy from the woman's hand, and shall wave the offering before יהוה, and bring it to the slaughter-place.

26 'And the priest shall take a hand filled with the offering, as its remembrance offering, and burn it on the slaughter-place,

and afterward make the woman drink the
water.
27 'And when he has made her drink the
water, then it shall be, if she has defiled
herself and has committed a trespass
against her husband, that the water that
brings the curse shall enter her and become
bitter, and her belly shall swell, and her
thigh shall waste away, and the woman
shall become a curse among her people.
28 'But if the woman has not defiled herself, and is clean, then she shall be clear
and shall conceive children.
29 'This is the Torah of jealousy, when a
wife turns aside under her husband's
authority and defiles herself,
30 or when a spirit of jealousy comes upon
a man, and he becomes jealous of his wife.
Then he shall make the woman stand
before יהוה, and the priest shall do to her
all this Torah.
31 'And the man shall be clear from
crookedness, but the woman bear her
crookedness.' "

6 And יהוה spoke to Mosheh, saying,
2 "Speak to the children of Yisra'ěl,
and say to them, 'When a man or woman
does separate, by making a vow of a
Nazirite, to be separate to יהוה,
3 he separates *himself* from wine and
strong drink – he drinks neither vinegar of
wine nor vinegar of strong drink, neither
does he drink any grape juice, nor eat
grapes or raisins.
4 'All the days of his separation he does
not eat whatever is made of the grapevine,
from seed to skin.
5 'All the days of the vow of his separation a razor does not come upon his head.
Until the days are completed for which he
does separate himself to יהוה, he is set-
apart. He shall let the locks of the hair of
his head grow long.
6 'All the days of his separation to יהוה
he does not go near a dead body.
7 'He does not make himself unclean for
his father, or for his mother, for his brother
or his sister, when they die, because his
separation to Elohim is on his head.
8 'All the days of his separation he is set-
apart to יהוה.
9 'And when anyone dies beside him in
an instant, suddenly, and he has defiled the
head of his separation, then he shall shave
his head on the day of his cleansing – on
the seventh day he shaves it.
10 'And on the eighth day he brings two
turtledoves or two young pigeons to the
priest, to the door of the Tent of
Appointment,
11 and the priest shall prepare one as a sin
offering and the other as an ascending
offering, and shall make atonement for
him, because he sinned by reason of the
dead body. And he shall set apart his head
on that day,
12 and shall separate to יהוה the days of
his separation, and shall bring a male lamb
a year old, as a guilt offering. But the
former days are not counted, because his
separation was defiled.
13 'And this is the Torah of the Nazirite:
When the days of his separation are completed, he is brought to the door of the Tent
of Appointment,
14 and he shall bring his offering to יהוה:
one male lamb a year old, a perfect one, as
an ascending offering, and one ewe lamb a
year old, a perfect one, as a sin offering,
and one ram, a perfect one, as a peace
offering,
15 and a basket of unleavened bread,
cakes of fine flour mixed with oil, and
unleavened thin cakes anointed with oil,
and their grain offering with their drink
offerings.
16 'And the priest shall bring them before
יהוה and prepare his sin offering and his
ascending offering.
17 'And he shall prepare the ram as a
slaughtering of peace *offerings* to יהוה,
together with the basket of unleavened
bread. And the priest shall prepare its grain
offering and its drink offering.
18 'And the Nazirite shall shave the head
of his separation at the door of the Tent of
Appointment, and shall take the hair from
the head of his separation and shall put it
on the fire which is under the slaughtering
of the peace *offerings*.
19 'And the priest shall take the boiled

shoulder of the ram, and one unleavened cake from the basket, and one unleavened thin cake, and put them upon the hands of the Nazirite after he has shaved his *hair of* separation.

20 'Then the priest shall wave them, a wave offering before יהוה. It is set-apart for the priest, besides the breast of the wave offering and besides the thigh of the contribution. And afterwards the Nazirite shall drink wine.'

21 "This is the Torah of the Nazirite who vows to יהוה the offering for his separation, and besides that, whatever else his hand is able to provide. According to the vow which he takes, so he shall do according to the Torah of his separation."

22 And יהוה spoke to Mosheh, saying,

23 "Speak to Aharon and his sons, saying, 'This is how you bless the children of Yisra'ěl. Say to them:

24 "יהוה bless you and guard you;

25 יהוה make His face shine upon you, and show favour to you;

26 יהוה lift up His face upon you, and give you peace." '

27 "Thus they shall put My Name on the children of Yisra'ěl, and I Myself shall bless them."

7

And it came to be, when Mosheh finished setting up the Dwelling Place, that he anointed it and set it apart and all its furnishings, as well as the slaughter-place and all its utensils. Thus he anointed them and set them apart.

2 And the leaders of Yisra'ěl, heads of their fathers' houses who were the leaders of the tribes and over the ones registered, drew near,

3 and they brought their offering before יהוה: six covered wagons and twelve cattle, a wagon for every two of the leaders, and for each one a bull. And they brought them near before the Dwelling Place.

4 And יהוה spoke to Mosheh, saying,

5 "Accept *these* from them, and they shall be used in doing the service of the Tent of Appointment. And you shall give them to the Lěwites, each one according to his service."

6 And Mosheh took the wagons and the cattle, and gave them to the Lěwites.

7 He gave two wagons and four cattle to the sons of Gěrshon, according to their service.

8 And he gave four wagons and eight cattle to the sons of Merari, according to their service, under the hand of Ithamar, son of Aharon the priest.

9 But to the sons of Qehath he gave none, because theirs was the service of the set-apart *objects*, which they bore on their shoulders.

10 And the leaders brought the dedication *offering* of the slaughter-place in the day it was anointed. So the leaders brought their offering before the slaughter-place.

11 And יהוה said to Mosheh, "Let them bring their offering, one leader each day, for the dedication of the slaughter-place."

12 And the one who brought his offering on the first day was Naḥshon, son of Amminaḏaḇ, from the tribe of Yehuḏah.

13 And his offering was one silver dish, the weight of which was one hundred and thirty *sheqels*, one silver bowl of seventy sheqels, according to the sheqel of the set-apart place, both of them filled with fine flour mixed with oil as a grain offering;

14 one gold ladle of ten *sheqels*, filled with incense;

15 one young bull, one ram, one male lamb a year old, as an ascending offering;

16 one male goat as a sin offering;

17 and as a slaughtering of peace *offerings*: two cattle, five rams, five male goats, five male lambs a year old. This was the offering of Naḥshon, son of Amminaḏaḇ.

18 On the second day Nethaně'l, son of Tsu'ar, leader of Yissasḵar, brought near.

19 He brought his offering, one silver dish, the weight of which was one hundred and thirty *sheqels*, one silver bowl of seventy sheqels, according to the sheqel of the set-apart place, both of them filled with fine flour mixed with oil as a grain offering;

20 one gold ladle of ten *sheqels*, filled with incense;

21 one young bull, one ram, one male lamb a year old, as an ascending offering;

22 one male goat as a sin offering;
23 and as a slaughtering of peace *offerings*: two cattle, five rams, five male goats, five male lambs a year old. This was the offering of Nethanĕ'l, son of Tsuʽar.
24 On the third day Eliyaḇ, son of Ḥĕlon, leader of the children of Zeḇulun:
25 his offering was one silver dish, the weight of which was one hundred and thirty *sheqels*, one silver bowl of seventy sheqels, according to the sheqel of the set-apart place, both of them filled with fine flour mixed with oil as a grain offering;
26 one gold ladle of ten *sheqels*, filled with incense;
27 one young bull, one ram, one male lamb a year old, as an ascending offering;
28 one male goat as a sin offering;
29 and as a slaughtering of peace *offerings*: two cattle, five rams, five male goats, five male lambs a year old. This was the offering of Eliyaḇ, son of Ḥĕlon.
30 On the fourth day Elitsur, son of Sheḏĕy'ur, leader of the children of Re'uḇĕn:
31 his offering was one silver dish, the weight of which was one hundred and thirty *sheqels*, one silver bowl of seventy sheqels, according to the sheqel of the set-apart place, both of them filled with fine flour mixed with oil as a grain offering;
32 one gold ladle of ten *sheqels*, filled with incense;
33 one young bull, one ram, one male lamb a year old, as an ascending offering;
34 one male goat as a sin offering;
35 and as a slaughtering of peace *offerings*: two cattle, five rams, five male goats, five male lambs a year old. This was the offering of Elitsur, son of Sheḏĕy'ur.
36 On the fifth day Shelumi'ĕl, son of Tsurishaddai, leader of the children of Shimʽon:
37 his offering was one silver dish, the weight of which was one hundred and thirty *sheqels*, one silver bowl of seventy sheqels, according to the sheqel of the set-apart place, both of them filled with fine flour mixed with oil as a grain offering;
38 one gold ladle of ten *sheqels*, filled with incense;
39 one young bull, one ram, one male lamb a year old, as an ascending offering;
40 one male goat as a sin offering;
41 and as a slaughtering of peace *offerings*: two cattle, five rams, five male goats, five male lambs a year old. This was the offering of Shelumi'ĕl, son of Tsurishaddai.
42 On the sixth day Elyasaph, son of Deʽu'ĕl,[a] leader of the children of Gaḏ:
43 his offering was one silver dish, the weight of which was one hundred and thirty *sheqels*, one silver bowl of seventy sheqels, according to the sheqel of the set-apart place, both of them filled with fine flour mixed with oil as a grain offering;
44 one gold ladle of ten *sheqels*, filled with incense;
45 one young bull, one ram, one male lamb a year old, as an ascending offering;
46 one male goat as a sin offering;
47 and as a slaughtering of peace *offerings*: two cattle, five rams, five male goats, five male lambs a year old. This was the offering of Elyasaph, son of Deʽu'ĕl. [a]
48 On the seventh day Elishama, son of Ammihuḏ, leader of the children of Ephrayim:
49 his offering was one silver dish, the weight of which was one hundred and thirty *sheqels*, one silver bowl of seventy sheqels, according to the sheqel of the set-apart place, both of them filled with fine flour mixed with oil as a grain offering;
50 one gold ladle of ten *sheqels*, filled with incense;
51 one young bull, one ram, one male lamb a year old, as an ascending offering;
52 one male goat as a sin offering;
53 and as a slaughtering of peace *offerings*: two cattle, five rams, five male goats, five male lambs a year old. This was the offering of Elishama, son of Ammihuḏ.
54 On the eighth day Gamli'ĕl, son of Peḏahtsur, leader of the children of Menashsheh:
55 his offering was one silver dish, the

7a See Explanatory notes: Deʽu'ĕl.

weight of which was one hundred and thirty *sheqels*, one silver bowl of seventy sheqels, according to the sheqel of the set-apart place, both of them filled with fine flour mixed with oil as a grain offering;
56 one gold ladle of ten *sheqels*, filled with incense;
57 one young bull, one ram, one male lamb a year old, as an ascending offering;
58 one male goat as a sin offering;
59 and as a slaughtering of peace *offerings*: two cattle, five rams, five male goats, five male lambs a year old. This was the offering of Gamli'ěl, son of Peḏahtsur.
60 On the ninth day Aḇiḏan, son of Giḏʽoni, leader of the children of Binyamin:
61 his offering was one silver dish, the weight of which was one hundred and thirty *sheqels*, one silver bowl of seventy sheqels, according to the sheqel of the set-apart place, both of them filled with fine flour mixed with oil as a grain offering;
62 one gold ladle of ten *sheqels*, filled with incense;
63 one young bull, one ram, one male lamb a year old, as an ascending offering;
64 one male goat as a sin offering;
65 and as a slaughtering of peace *offerings*: two cattle, five rams, five male goats, five male lambs a year old. This was the offering of Aḇiḏan, son of Giḏʽoni.
66 On the tenth day Aḥiʽezer, son of Ammishaddai, leader of the children of Dan:
67 his offering was one silver dish, the weight of which was one hundred and thirty *sheqels*, one silver bowl of seventy sheqels, according to the sheqel of the set-apart place, both of them filled with fine flour mixed with oil as a grain offering;
68 one gold ladle of ten *sheqels*, filled with incense;
69 one young bull, one ram, one male lamb a year old, as an ascending offering;
70 one male goat as a sin offering;
71 and as a slaughtering of peace *offerings*: two cattle, five rams, five male goats, five male lambs a year old. This was the offering of Aḥiʽezer, son of Ammishaddai.
72 On the eleventh day Paḡʽi'ěl, son of Oḵran, leader of the children of Ashěr:
73 his offering was one silver dish, the weight of which was one hundred and thirty *sheqels*, one silver bowl of seventy sheqels, according to the sheqel of the set-apart place, both of them filled with fine flour mixed with oil as a grain offering;
74 one gold ladle of ten *sheqels*, filled with incense;
75 one young bull, one ram, one male lamb a year old, as an ascending offering;
76 one male goat as a sin offering;
77 and as a slaughtering of peace *offerings*: two cattle, five rams, five male goats, five male lambs a year old. This was the offering of Paḡʽi'ěl, son of Oḵran.
78 On the twelfth day Aḥira, son of Ěnan, leader of the children of Naphtali:
79 his offering was one silver dish, the weight of which was one hundred and thirty *sheqels*, one silver bowl of seventy sheqels, according to the sheqel of the set-apart place, both of them filled with fine flour mixed with oil as a grain offering;
80 one gold ladle of ten *sheqels*, filled with incense;
81 one young bull, one ram, one male lamb a year old, as an ascending offering;
82 one male goat as a sin offering;
83 and as a slaughtering of peace *offerings*: two cattle, five rams, five male goats, five male lambs a year old. This was the offering of Aḥira, son of Ěnan.
84 This was the dedication of the slaughter-place from the leaders of Yisra'ěl, when it was anointed: twelve silver dishes, twelve silver bowls, twelve gold ladles.
85 Each silver dish was one hundred and thirty *sheqels* and each bowl seventy *sheqels*. All the silver of the vessels was two thousand four hundred *sheqels*, according to the sheqel of the set-apart place.
86 The twelve gold ladles filled with incense was ten *sheqels* each, according to the sheqel of the set-apart place. All the gold of the ladles was one hundred and twenty *sheqels*.
87 All the cattle for the ascending offering were twelve young bulls, the rams twelve, the male lambs a year old twelve, with

their grain offering, and the male goats as a
sin offering twelve.
88 And all the cattle for the slaughtering of
peace *offerings* were twenty-four bulls, the
rams sixty, the male goats sixty, the lambs
a year old sixty. This was the dedication of
the slaughter-place after it was anointed.
89 And when Mosheh went into the Tent
of Appointment to speak with Him, he
heard the voice of One speaking to him
from above the lid of atonement that was
on the ark of the Witness, from between
the two kerubim. Thus He spoke to him.

8 And יהוה spoke to Mosheh, saying,
2 "Speak to Aharon, and say to him,
'When you ascend to trim the lamps, let
the seven lamps give light in front of the
lampstand.' "
3 And Aharon did so. He set up the lamps
to face toward the front of the lampstand,
as יהוה commanded Mosheh.
4 And this is the work of the lampstand:
beaten work of gold, from its base to its
blossoms it is beaten work. According to
the pattern which יהוה had shown
Mosheh, so he made the lampstand.
5 And יהוה spoke to Mosheh, saying,
6 "Take the Lĕwites from among the
children of Yisra'ĕl, and you shall cleanse
them,
7 and do this to them to cleanse them:
Sprinkle water of sin *offering* on them,
and they shall shave all their body, and
shall wash their garments, and cleanse
themselves,
8 and shall take a young bull with its
grain offering of fine flour mixed with oil,
while you take another young bull as a sin
offering.
9 "And you shall bring the Lĕwites
before the Tent of Appointment, and you
shall assemble all the congregation of the
children of Yisra'ĕl.
10 "And you shall bring the Lĕwites
before יהוה, and the children of Yisra'ĕl
shall lay their hands on the Lĕwites,
11 and Aharon shall wave the Lĕwites
before יהוה, a wave offering from the
children of Yisra'ĕl – so shall they be for
doing the service of יהוה.
12 "And the Lĕwites shall lay their hands
on the heads of the young bulls. And one
shall be prepared as a sin offering and the
other as an ascending offering to יהוה, to
make atonement for the Lĕwites.
13 "And you shall have the Lĕwites stand
before Aharon and his sons, and then wave
them, a wave offering to יהוה.
14 "Thus you shall separate the Lĕwites
from among the children of Yisra'ĕl, and
the Lĕwites shall be Mine.
15 "Then after that the Lĕwites shall go in
to do service in the Tent of Appointment,
when you have cleansed them and waved
them as a wave offering.
16 "For they are given ones, given to Me
from among the children of Yisra'ĕl. I have
taken them for Myself instead of all who
open the womb, the first-born of all the
children of Yisra'ĕl.
17 "For all the first-born among the
children of Yisra'ĕl are Mine, both man
and beast. On the day that I struck all the
first-born in the land of Mitsrayim I set
them apart unto Myself.
18 "And I have taken the Lĕwites instead
of all the first-born of the children of
Yisra'ĕl.
19 "And I have given the Lĕwites as a gift
to Aharon and his sons from among the
children of Yisra'ĕl, to do the service of the
children of Yisra'ĕl in the Tent of
Appointment, and to make atonement for
the children of Yisra'ĕl, that there be no
plague among the children of Yisra'ĕl
when the children of Yisra'ĕl come near
the set-apart place."
20 Thus Mosheh and Aharon and all the
congregation of the children of Yisra'ĕl did
to the Lĕwites according to all that יהוה
commanded Mosheh concerning the
Lĕwites, so the children of Yisra'ĕl did to
them.
21 And the Lĕwites cleansed themselves
and washed their garments, and Aharon
waved them, a wave offering before יהוה,
and Aharon made atonement for them to
cleanse them.
22 Then after that the Lĕwites went in to
do their service in the Tent of Appointment
before Aharon and his sons as יהוה com-

manded Mosheh concerning the Lĕwites, so they did to them.

[23] And יהוה spoke to Mosheh, saying,

[24] "This applies to the Lĕwites: From twenty-five years old and above let him come into active service in the service of the Tent of Appointment,

[25] and at the age of fifty years they retire from active service of the service, and serve no more,

[26] but they shall attend with their brothers in the Tent of Appointment, to guard the duty, but shall do no service. Thus you shall do to the Lĕwites regarding their duties."

9 And יהוה spoke to Mosheh in the Wilderness of Sinai, in the first new *moon* [a] of the second year after they had come out of the land of Mitsrayim, saying,

[2] "Now, let the children of Yisra'ĕl perform the Pĕsaḥ at its appointed time.

[3] "On the fourteenth day of this new *moon*, between the evenings, perform it at its appointed time. According to all its laws and right-rulings you perform it."

[4] And Mosheh spoke to the children of Yisra'ĕl to perform the Pĕsaḥ.

[5] So they performed the Pĕsaḥ on the fourteenth day of the first new *moon*, between the evenings, in the Wilderness of Sinai. According to all that יהוה commanded Mosheh, so the children of Yisra'ĕl did.

[6] But there were men who were defiled for a being of a man, so that they were not able to perform the Pĕsaḥ on that day. So they came before Mosheh and Aharon that day,

[7] and those men said to him, "We are defiled for the being of a man. Why are we withheld from bringing near the offering of יהוה at its appointed time among the children of Yisra'ĕl?"

[8] And Mosheh said to them, "Wait, let me hear what יהוה commands concerning you."

[9] And יהוה spoke to Mosheh, saying,

[10] "Speak to the children of Yisra'ĕl, saying, 'When any male of you or your generations is unclean for a being, or is far away on a journey, he shall still perform the Pĕsaḥ of יהוה.

[11] 'On the fourteenth day of the second new *moon*, between the evenings, they perform it – with unleavened bread and bitter herbs they eat it.

[12] 'They do not leave of it until morning, and they do not break a bone of it. According to all the laws of the Pĕsaḥ they perform it.

[13] 'But the man who is clean and is not on a journey, and has failed to perform the Pĕsaḥ, that same being shall be cut off from among his people, because he did not bring the offering of יהוה at its appointed time – that man bears his sin.

[14] 'And when a stranger sojourns among you, then he shall perform the Pĕsaḥ of יהוה. He shall do so according to the law of the Pĕsaḥ and according to its right-ruling. You have one law, both for the stranger and the native of the land.' "

[15] And on the day that the Dwelling Place was raised up, the cloud covered the Dwelling Place, the Tent of the Witness. From evening until morning it was above the Dwelling Place like the appearance of fire.

[16] Thus it was continually: the cloud covered it by day, and the appearance of fire by night.

[17] And whenever the cloud was taken up from above the Tent, after that the children of Yisra'ĕl would depart. And in the place where the cloud dwelt, there the children of Yisra'ĕl would camp.

[18] At the mouth of יהוה the children of Yisra'ĕl departed, and at the command of יהוה they camped. They remained camped as long as the cloud dwelt above the Dwelling Place.

[19] Even when the cloud lingered many days above the Dwelling Place, the children of Yisra'ĕl guarded the Charge of יהוה, and did not depart.

[20] And so it was, when the cloud was above the Dwelling Place a few days:

9a Or a month.

according to the mouth of יהוה they
camped, and according to the mouth of
יהוה they would depart.
21 And so it was, when the cloud dwelt
only from evening until morning: when the
cloud was taken up in the morning, then
they departed. Whether by day or by night,
whenever the cloud was taken up, they
departed.
22 Whether two days, or a new *moon*, [a] or
a year that the cloud lingered above the
Dwelling Place to dwell upon it, the children of Yisra'ěl camped, and did not
depart. But when it was taken up, they
departed.
23 At the mouth of יהוה they camped, and
at the mouth of יהוה they departed. They
guarded the Charge of יהוה, at the mouth
of יהוה by the hand of Mosheh.

10 And יהוה spoke to Mosheh, saying,
2 "Make two silver trumpets for
yourself, make them of beaten work. And
you shall use them for the gathering of the
congregation and for breaking camp.
3 "And when they blow both of them, all
the congregation shall meet before you at
the door of the Tent of Appointment.
4 "And if they blow one, then the leaders,
the heads of the thousands of Yisra'ěl,
shall gather to you.
5 "And when you blow a shout, the
camps that lie on the east side shall depart.
6 "And when you blow a shout the
second time, then the camps that lie on the
south side shall depart – they blow a shout
for them to depart.
7 "And when the assembly is to be
assembled, you blow, but do not shout.
8 "And the sons of Aharon, the priests,
blow with the trumpets. And it shall be
to you for a law forever throughout your
generations.
9 "And when you go into battle in your
land against the enemy that distresses you,
then you shall shout with the trumpets, and
you shall be remembered before יהוה your
Elohim, and you shall be saved from your
enemies.
10 "And in the day of your gladness, and
in your appointed times, and at the beginning of your new *moons*, you shall blow
the trumpets over your ascending offerings
and over your slaughterings of peace *offerings*. And they shall be a remembrance for
you before your Elohim. I am יהוה your
Elohim."
11 And it came to be on the twentieth day
of the second new *moon*, in the second
year, that the cloud was taken up from
above the Dwelling Place of the Witness.
12 And the children of Yisra'ěl departed,
setting out from the Wilderness of Sinai.
And the cloud dwelt *on it* in the Wilderness
of Paran.
13 Thus they departed the first time,
according to the mouth of יהוה by the hand
of Mosheh.
14 And the banner of the camp of the children of Yehuḏah departed first according
to their divisions. And over their army was
Naḥshon, son of Amminaḏaḇ.
15 And over the army of the tribe of the
children of Yissasḵar was Nethaněʼl, son
of Tsuʻar.
16 And over the army of the tribe of the
children of Zeḇulun was Eliyaḇ, son of
Ḥělon.
17 And the Dwelling Place was taken
down. And the sons of Gěrshon and the
sons of Merari departed, bearing the
Dwelling Place.
18 And the banner of the camp of Re'uḇěn
departed according to their divisions. And
over their army was Elitsur, son of
Sheḏěy'ur.
19 And over the army of the tribe of the
children of Shimʻon was Shelumi'ěl, son
of Tsurishaddai.
20 And over the army of the tribe of the
children of Gaḏ was Elyasaph, the son of
Deʻu'ěl.
21 And the Qehathites departed, bearing
the set-apart *objects*, while the Dwelling
Place was set up before they came.
22 And the banner of the camp of the
children of Ephrayim departed according
to their divisions. And over their army was
Elishama, son of Ammihuḏ.
23 And over the army of the tribe of the
children of Menashsheh was Gamli'ěl, son
of Peḏahtsur.

24 And over the army of the tribe of the children of Binyamin was Aḇiḏan, son of Giḏʿoni.
25 Then the banner of the camp of the children of Dan, which formed the rear guard of all the camps, departed according to their divisions. And over their army was Aḥiʿezer, son of Ammishaddai.
26 And over the army of the tribe of the children of Ashěr was Paḡʿi'ěl, the son of Oḵran.
27 And over the army of the tribe of the children of Naphtali was Aḥira, the son of Ěnan.
28 Such was the order of setting out of the children of Yisra'ěl, according to their divisions, when they departed.
29 And Mosheh said to Ḥoḇaḇ, the son of Reʿuw'ěl the Miḏyanite, Mosheh's father-in-law, "We are setting out for the place of which יהוה said, 'I give it to you.' Come with us, and we shall do good to you, for יהוה has spoken good concerning Yisra'ěl."
30 And he replied to him, "I am not going, but I am going to my own land and to my relatives."
31 Then he said, "Please do not leave us, because you know how we are to camp in the wilderness, and you shall be our eyes.
32 "And it shall be, when you go with us, then it shall be that whatever good יהוה does to us, the same we shall do to you."
33 So they set out from the mountain of יהוה on a journey of three days. And the ark of the covenant of יהוה went before them for the three days' journey, to seek out a resting place for them.
34 And the cloud of יהוה was above them by day when they went out from the camp.
35 And it came to be, whenever the ark set out, that Mosheh said, "Rise up, O יהוה! And let Your enemies be scattered, and let those who hate You flee before You."
36 And when it rested, he said, "Return, O יהוה, to the countless thousands of Yisra'ěl."

11 And it came to be, when the people were as complainers, it was evil in the ears of יהוה. And יהוה heard it, and His displeasure burned. And the fire of יהוה burned among them, and consumed those in the outskirts of the camp.
2 And the people cried out to Mosheh, and Mosheh prayed to יהוה, and the fire died down.
3 Then he called the name of the place Taḇʿěrah, because the fire of יהוה had burned among them.
4 And the mixed multitude who were in their midst lusted greatly, so the children of Yisra'ěl also wept again and said, "Who is giving us meat to eat?
5 "We remember the fish which we ate without cost in Mitsrayim, the cucumbers, and the melons, and the leeks, and the onions, and the garlic,
6 but now our being is dried up. There is naught to look at but this manna!"
7 Now the manna was like coriander seed, and its appearance like the appearance of bdellium.
8 The people went about and gathered it, ground it on millstones or beat it in the mortar, and cooked it in a pot, and made cakes of it. And its taste was as the taste of cakes baked with oil.
9 And when the dew fell on the camp at night, the manna fell on it.
10 And Mosheh heard the people weeping throughout their clans, each man at the door of his tent. And the displeasure of יהוה burned exceedingly. And in the eyes of Mosheh it was evil,
11 so Mosheh said to יהוה, "Why have You done evil to Your servant? And why have I not found favour in Your eyes, to put the burden of all these people on me?
12 "Was it I who conceived all these people? Was it I who brought them forth, that You should say to me, 'Carry them in your bosom, as the foster father carries a nursing child,' to the land which You swore to their fathers?
13 "Where am I to get meat to give to all these people? For they weep before me, saying, 'Give us meat to eat.'
14 "I am unable to bear all these people alone, because the burden is too heavy for me.
15 "And if You are doing *this* to me, kill

me – please kill me, if I have found favour
in Your eyes, and let me not see my evil!"
16 Then יהוה said to Mosheh, "Gather to
Me seventy men of the elders of Yisra'ěl,
whom you know to be the elders of the
people and officers over them. And bring
them to the Tent of Appointment, and let
them stand there with you.
17 "And I shall come down and speak with
you there, and shall take of the Spirit that
is on you, and put on them. And they shall
bear the burden of the people with you, so
that you do not bear it yourself alone.
18 "And say to the people, 'Set yourselves
apart for tomorrow, and you shall eat meat,
because you have wept in the hearing of
יהוה, saying, "Who is giving us meat to
eat? For it was well with us in Mitsrayim."
And יהוה shall give you meat, and you
shall eat.
19 'You are going to eat, not one day, nor
two days, nor five days, nor ten days, nor
twenty days,
20 but for a new *moon* [a] of days, until it
comes out of your nostrils and becomes an
abomination to you, because you have
rejected יהוה who is among you, and have
wept before Him, saying, "Why did we
come up out of Mitsrayim?" ' "
21 And Mosheh said, "The people in
whose midst I am are six hundred thousand
men on foot, and You, You have said, 'I
give them meat to eat for a new *moon* [a] of
days.'
22 "Could flocks and herds be slain for
them, to be sufficient for them? Or could
all the fish of the sea be gathered together
for them, to be sufficient for them?"
23 And יהוה said to Mosheh, "Is the arm
of יהוה too short? Now see whether My
word meets you or not!"
24 And Mosheh went out and spoke to the
people the words of יהוה, and he gathered
the seventy men of the elders of the people
and placed them around the Tent.
25 And יהוה came down in the cloud, and
spoke to him, and took of the Spirit that
was upon him, and placed the same upon
the seventy elders. And it came to be,
when the Spirit rested upon them, that they
prophesied, but did not continue.
26 However, two men had remained in the
camp. The name of one was Eldaḏ, and the
name of the other Měyḏaḏ. And the Spirit
rested upon them. Now they were among
those listed, but did not go out to the Tent.
And they prophesied in the camp.
27 And a young man ran and informed
Mosheh, and said, "Eldaḏ and Měyḏaḏ are
prophesying in the camp."
28 And Yehoshua son of Nun, Mosheh's
assistant from his youth, answered and
said, "Mosheh my master, forbid them!"
29 Then Mosheh said to him, "Are you
jealous for my sake? Oh, that all the people
of יהוה were prophets, that יהוה would put
His Spirit upon them!"
30 And Mosheh returned to the camp, both
he and the elders of Yisra'ěl.
31 And a wind went forth from יהוה, and
it brought quail from the sea and let them
fall beside the camp, about a day's journey
on this side and about a day's journey on
the other side, all around the camp, and
about two cubits above the surface of the
ground.
32 And the people were up all that day,
and all that night, and all the next day, and
gathered the quail. He who has least gathered ten ḥomers. And they spread them out
for themselves all around the camp.
33 The meat was still between their teeth,
before it was chewed, and the wrath of
יהוה burned against the people, and יהוה
struck the people with an exceeding great
plague.
34 Then he called the name of that place
Qiḇroth Hatta'awah, because there they
buried the people who had lusted.
35 From Qiḇroth Hatta'awah the people
set out for Ḥatsěroth – and they were at
Ḥatsěroth.

12 Now Miryam and Aharon spoke
against Mosheh because of the
Kushite woman whom he had taken, for he
had taken a Kushite woman.
2 And they said, "Has יהוה spoken only

11a Or a month.

through Mosheh? Has He not also spoken
through us?" And יהוה heard it.
[3] And the man Mosheh was very humble,
more than all men who were on the face of
the earth.
[4] And suddenly יהוה said to Mosheh,
and Aharon, and Miryam, "You three,
come out to the Tent of Appointment!" So
the three came out.
[5] And יהוה came down in the column of
cloud and stood in the door of the Tent,
and called Aharon and Miryam. And they
both went forward.
[6] And He said, "Hear now My words: If
your prophet is of יהוה, I make Myself
known to him in a vision, and I speak to
him in a dream.
[7] "Not so with My servant Mosheh, he is
trustworthy in all My house.
[8] "I speak with him mouth to mouth, and
plainly, and not in riddles. And he sees the
form of יהוה. So why were you not afraid
to speak against My servant Mosheh?"
[9] And the displeasure of יהוה burned
against them, and He left.
[10] And the cloud turned away from above
the Tent, and look: Miryam was leprous, as
white as snow! And Aharon turned toward
Miryam, and look: a leper!
[11] And Aharon said to Mosheh, "Oh, my
master! Please do not hold against us the
sin in which we have done foolishly and in
which we have sinned.
[12] "Please do not let her be as one dead
when coming out of its mother's womb,
with our flesh half consumed!"
[13] And Mosheh cried out to יהוה, saying,
"O Ěl, please heal her, please!"
[14] And יהוה said to Mosheh, "If her father
had but spit in her face, would she not be
ashamed seven days? Let her be shut out of
the camp seven days, and after that let her
be readmitted."
[15] And Miryam was shut out of the camp
seven days, and the people did not set out
until Miryam was readmitted.
[16] And afterward the people departed
from Ḥatsěroth, and they camped in the
Wilderness of Paran.

13 And יהוה spoke to Mosheh, saying,
[2] "Send men to spy out the land of
Kena'an, which I am giving to the children
of Yisra'ěl. Send one man from each tribe
of their fathers, every one a leader among
them."
[3] And by the mouth of יהוה Mosheh sent
them from the Wilderness of Paran,
all of them men who were heads of the
children of Yisra'ěl.
[4] And these were their names. From the
tribe of Re'uḇěn: Shammua, son of
Zakkur.
[5] From the tribe of Shim'on: Shaphat,
son of Ḥori.
[6] From the tribe of Yehuḏah: Kalěḇ, son
of Yephunneh.
[7] From the tribe of Yissasḵar: Yiḡ'al, son
of Yosěph.
[8] From the tribe of Ephrayim: Hoshěa,
son of Nun.
[9] From the tribe of Binyamin: Palti, son
of Raphu.
[10] From the tribe of Zeḇulun: Gaddi'ěl,
son of Soḏi.
[11] From the tribe of Yosěph, from the tribe
of Menashsheh: Gaddi, son of Susi.
[12] From the tribe of Dan: Ammi'ěl, son of
Gemalli.
[13] From the tribe of Ashěr: Shěthur, son of
Miḵa'ěl.
[14] From the tribe of Naphtali: Naḥbi, son
of Wophsi.
[15] From the tribe of Gaḏ: Geu'ěl, son of
Maḵi.
[16] These are the names of the men whom
Mosheh sent to spy out the land. And
Mosheh called Hoshěa the son of Nun,
Yehoshua.
[17] And Mosheh sent them to spy out the
land of Kena'an, and said to them, "Go
up here into the South, and go up to the
mountains,
[18] and see what the land is like, and the
people who dwell in it, whether strong or
weak, whether few or many,
[19] and whether the land they dwell in is
good or evil, whether the cities they inhabit are in camps or strongholds,
[20] and whether the land is rich or poor,
and whether there are forests there or not.

And you shall be strong, and bring some of
the fruit of the land." Now the time was the
season of the first-fruits of grapes.
21 So they went up and spied out the land
from the Wilderness of Tsin as far as
Reḥoḇ, near the entrance of Ḥamath.
22 And they went up through the South
and came to Ḥeḇron. And Aḥiman,
Shěshai, and Talmai, the descendants of
Anaq, were there. Now Ḥeḇron had been
built seven years before Tsoʽan in Mitsrayim.
23 And they came to the wadi Eshkol, and
cut down from there a branch with one
cluster of grapes. And they bore it between
two of them on a pole, also of the pomegranates and of the figs.
24 That place was called the wadi Eshkol,
because of the cluster which the men of
Yisra'ěl cut down from there.
25 And they returned from spying out the
land after forty days.
26 And they went and came to Mosheh
and Aharon and all the congregation of the
children of Yisra'ěl in the Wilderness of
Paran, at Qaḏěsh. And they brought back
word to them and to all the congregation,
and showed them the fruit of the land.
27 And they reported to him, and said,
"We went to the land where you sent us.
And truly, it flows with milk and honey,
and this is its fruit.
28 "But the people who dwell in the land
are strong, and the cities are walled, very
great. And we saw the descendants of
Anaq there too.
29 "The Amalěqites dwell in the land of
the South, while the Ḥittites and the
Yeḇusites and the Amorites dwell in the
mountains. And the Kenaʽanites dwell by
the sea and along the banks of the Yarděn."
30 And Kalěḇ silenced the people before
Mosheh, and said, "Let us go up at once
and take possession, for we are certainly
able to overcome it."
31 But the men who had gone up with him
said, "We are not able to go up against the
people, for they are stronger than we."
32 And they gave the children of Yisra'ěl
an evil report of the land which they had
spied out, saying, "The land through which
we have gone as spies is a land eating up
its inhabitants, and all the people whom we
saw in it are men of great size.
33 "And we saw there the Nephilim, sons
of Anaq, of the Nephilim. And we were
like grasshoppers in our own eyes, and so
we were in their eyes."

14 Then all the congregation lifted up
their voices and cried, and the people wept that night.
2 And all the children of Yisra'ěl grumbled against Mosheh and against Aharon,
and all the congregation said to them, "If
only we had died in the land of Mitsrayim!
Or if only we had died in this wilderness!
3 "And why is יהוה bringing us to this
land to fall by the sword, that our wives
and children should become a prey? Would
it not be better for us to turn back to
Mitsrayim?"
4 And they said to each other, "Let us
appoint a leader, and let us turn back to
Mitsrayim."
5 Then Mosheh and Aharon fell on their
faces before all the assembly of the
congregation of the children of Yisra'ěl.
6 And Yehoshua son of Nun, and Kalěḇ
son of Yephunneh, who were among those
who had spied out the land, tore their
garments,
7 and they spoke to all the congregation
of the children of Yisra'ěl, saying, "The
land we passed through to spy out is an
exceedingly good land.
8 "If יהוה has delighted in us, then He
shall bring us into this land and give it to
us, 'a land which is flowing with milk and
honey.'
9 "Only, do not rebel against יהוה, nor
fear the people of the land, for they are our
bread. Their defence has turned away from
them, and יהוה is with us. Do not fear
them."
10 But all the congregation said to stone
them with stones. Then the esteem of יהוה
appeared in the Tent of Appointment
before all the children of Yisra'ěl.
11 And יהוה said to Mosheh, "How long
shall I be scorned by these people? And
how long shall I not be trusted by them,

with all the signs which I have done in
their midst?
[12] "Let Me strike them with the pestilence
and disinherit them, and make of you a
nation greater and mightier than they."
[13] And Mosheh said to יהוה, "Then the
Mitsrites shall hear it, for by Your power
You brought these people up from their
midst,
[14] and they shall say to the inhabitants of
this land they have heard that You, יהוה,
are in the midst of these people, that You,
יהוה, are seen eye to eye and that Your
cloud stands above them, and You go
before them in a column of cloud by day
and in a column of fire by night.
[15] "Now if You shall kill these people as
one man, then the nations which have
heard of Your report shall speak, saying,
[16] 'Because יהוה was not able to bring
this people to the land which He swore to
give them, therefore He slew them in the
wilderness.'
[17] "And now, I pray, let the power of יהוה
be great, as You have spoken, saying,
[18] 'יהוה is patient and of great loving-
commitment, forgiving crookedness and
transgression, but by no means leaving
unpunished; [a] visiting the crookedness of
the fathers on the children to the third and
fourth *generation*.'
[19] "Please forgive the crookedness of this
people, according to the greatness of Your
loving-commitment, as You have forgiven
this people, from Mitsrayim even until
now."
[20] And יהוה said, "I shall forgive, according to your word,
[21] but truly, as I live and all the earth is
filled with the esteem of יהוה,
[22] for none of these men who have seen
My esteem and the signs which I did in
Mitsrayim and in the wilderness, and have
tried Me now these ten times, and have
disobeyed My voice,
[23] shall see the land of which I swore to
their fathers, nor any of those who scorned
Me see it.
[24] "But My servant Kalĕḇ, because he has
a different spirit in him and has followed
Me completely, I shall bring into the land
where he went, and his seed shall inherit it.
[25] "Since the Amalĕqites and the
Kenaʽanites are dwelling in the valley, turn
back tomorrow and set out into the wilderness by the Way of the Sea of Reeds."
[26] And יהוה spoke to Mosheh, and to
Aharon, saying,
[27] "How long shall this evil congregation
have this grumbling against Me? I have
heard the grumblings which the children of
Yisra'ĕl are grumbling against Me.
[28] "Say to them, 'As I live,' declares יהוה,
'as you have spoken in My hearing, so I do
to you:
[29] 'The carcasses of you who have grumbled against Me are going to fall in this
wilderness, all of you who were registered,
according to your entire number, from
twenty years old and above.
[30] 'None of you except Kalĕḇ son of
Yephunneh, and Yehoshua son of Nun,
shall enter the land which I swore I would
make you dwell in.
[31] 'But your little ones, whom you said
would become a prey, I shall bring in, and
they shall know the land which you have
rejected.
[32] 'But as for you, your carcasses are
going to fall in this wilderness.
[33] 'And your sons shall be wanderers in
the wilderness forty years, and shall bear
your whorings, until your carcasses are
consumed in the wilderness.
[34] 'According to the number of the days in
which you spied out the land, forty days –
a day for a year, a day for a year – you are
to bear your crookednesses forty years,
and you shall know My breaking off.
[35] 'I am יהוה, I have spoken, I shall do
this to all this evil congregation who are
meeting against Me: In this wilderness
they are consumed, and there they die.' "
[36] And the men whom Mosheh sent to spy
out the land, who returned and made all the
congregation grumble against him by
bringing an evil report of the land,
[37] even those men who brought the evil

14a This is confirmed in Shem. 34:7 and in Yirm. 30:11.

report about the land, died by the plague
before יהוה.
38Of those men who went to spy out the
land, only Yehoshua son of Nun, and
Kalěḇ son of Yephunneh remained alive.
39And when Mosheh spoke these words
to all the children of Yisra'ěl, the people
mourned greatly.
40And they rose up early in the morning
and went up to the top of the mountain,
saying, "See, we have indeed sinned, but
we shall go up to the place which יהוה had
spoken of!"
41But Mosheh said, "Why do you now
transgress the mouth of יהוה, since it does
not prosper?
42"Do not go up, lest you be smitten by
your enemies, for יהוה is not in your
midst.
43"Because the Amalěqites and the
Kenaʽanites are there before you, and you
shall fall by the sword. Because you have
turned away from יהוה, יהוה is not with
you."
44But they presumed to go up to the
mountaintop, but neither the ark of the
covenant of יהוה nor Mosheh left the
camp.
45So the Amalěqites and the Kenaʽanites
who dwelt in that mountain came down
and struck them, and beat them down, even
to Ḥormah.

15 And יהוה spoke to Mosheh, saying,
2"Speak to the children of Yisra'ěl,
and say to them, 'When you have come
into the land of your dwellings, which I am
giving you,
3and you make an offering by fire to
יהוה, an ascending offering or a slaughtering, to accomplish a vow or as a voluntary
offering or in your appointed times, to
make a sweet fragrance to יהוה, from the
herd or the flock,
4then he who brings near his offering to
יהוה shall bring near a grain offering of
one-tenth *of an ěphah* of fine flour mixed
with one-fourth of a hin of oil,
5and one-fourth of a hin of wine as a
drink offering you prepare with the
ascending offering or the slaughtering, for
each lamb.
6'Or for a ram you prepare as a grain
offering two-tenths *of an ěphah* of fine
flour mixed with one-third of a hin of oil,
7and as a drink offering you bring one-
third of a hin of wine as a sweet fragrance
to יהוה.
8'And when you prepare a young bull as
an ascending offering, or as a slaughtering
to accomplish a vow, or as a peace offering
to יהוה,
9then shall be brought with the young
bull a grain offering of three-tenths *of an
ěphah* of fine flour mixed with half a hin
of oil,
10and bring as the drink offering half a
hin of wine as an offering made by fire, a
sweet fragrance to יהוה.
11'This is what is done for each young
bull, for each ram, or for each lamb or
young goat.
12'According to the number that you
prepare, so you do for each one according
to their number.
13'Let all who are native do so with them,
in bringing near an offering made by fire,
a sweet fragrance to יהוה.
14'And when a stranger sojourns with
you, or whoever is among you throughout
your generations, and would make an
offering made by fire, a sweet fragrance to
יהוה, as you do, so he does.
15'One law is for you of the assembly and
for the stranger who sojourns with you – a
law forever throughout your generations.
As you are, so is the stranger before יהוה.
16'One Torah and one right-ruling is for
you and for the stranger who sojourns with
you.' "
17And יהוה spoke to Mosheh, saying,
18"Speak to the children of Yisra'ěl, and
say to them, 'When you come into the land
to which I bring you,
19then it shall be, when you eat of
the bread of the land, that you present a
contribution to יהוה.
20'Present a cake of the first of your
dough as a contribution – as a contribution
of the threshing-floor you present it.
21'Of the first of your dough you are to
give to יהוה a contribution throughout

your generations.

22 'And when you sin by mistake,[a] and do not do all these commands which יהוה has spoken to Mosheh,

23 all that יהוה has commanded you by the hand of Mosheh, from the day יהוה gave command and onward throughout your generations,

24 then it shall be, if it is done by mistake, without the knowledge of the congregation, that all the congregation shall prepare one young bull as an ascending offering, as a sweet fragrance to יהוה, with its grain offering and its drink offering, according to the right-ruling, and one male goat as a sin offering.

25 'Then the priest shall make atonement for all the congregation of the children of Yisra'ěl, and it shall be forgiven them, for it was by mistake. And they shall bring their offering, an offering made by fire to יהוה, and their sin offering before יהוה, for their mistake.

26 'And it shall be forgiven all the congregation of the children of Yisra'ěl and the stranger who sojourns in their midst, because all the people did it by mistake.

27 'And if a being sins by mistake, then he shall bring a female goat a year old as a sin offering.

28 'And the priest shall make atonement for the being who strays by mistake, when he sins by mistake before יהוה, to make atonement for him, and it shall be forgiven him.

29 'For him who does *whatever* by mistake there is one Torah, both for him who is native among the children of Yisra'ěl and for the stranger who sojourns in their midst.

30 'But the being who does *whatever* defiantly, whether he is native or a stranger, he reviles יהוה, and that being shall be cut off from among his people.

31 'Because he has despised the word of יהוה, and has broken His command, that being shall certainly be cut off, his crookedness is upon him.' "

32 And while the children of Yisra'ěl were in the wilderness, they found a man gathering sticks on the Sabbath day.

33 And those who found him gathering sticks brought him to Mosheh and to Aharon, and to all the congregation.

34 And they put him in under guard, because it had not been declared what should be done to him.

35 And יהוה said to Mosheh, "The man shall certainly be put to death, all the congregation stoning him with stones outside the camp."

36 And all the congregation brought him outside the camp and stoned him with stones, as יהוה commanded Mosheh, and he died.

37 And יהוה spoke to Mosheh, saying,

38 "Speak to the children of Yisra'ěl, and you shall say to them to make tzitzit [b] on the corners of their garments throughout their generations, and to put a blue cord in the tzitzit [b] of the corners.

39 "And it shall be to you for a tzitzit [b], and you shall see it, and shall remember all the commands of יהוה and shall do them, and not search after your own heart and your own eyes after which you went whoring,

40 so that you remember, and shall do all My commands, and be set-apart unto your Elohim.[c]

41 "I am יהוה your Elohim, who brought you out of the land of Mitsrayim, to be your Elohim. I am יהוה your Elohim."

16 And Qoraḥ, son of Yitshar, son of Qehath, son of Lěwi, took both Dathan and Aḇiram the sons of Eliyaḇ, and On, son of Peleth, sons of Re'uḇěn,

2 and they rose up before Mosheh with some of the children of Yisra'ěl, two hundred and fifty leaders of the congregation, called ones of the meeting, men of name.

15a Verse 22 - 31 shows the difference between sinning by mistake (unintentional sin) on the one hand, and sinning defiantly (intentional sin) on the other hand. Sinning by mistake is also dealt with in Wayyiqra chapter 4.
15b See Explanatory notes - "Tzitzit". *15c* Also see Shemoth 20:6, Deḇ. 7:9, Deḇ. 11:1, Deḇ. 30:16, Neḥ. 1:5, Dan. 9:4, Yn. א 5:2-3, Yn. ב v. 6.

[3] And they assembled against Mosheh and against Aharon, and said to them, "Enough of you! For all the congregation is set-apart, all of them, and יהוה is in their midst. Why then do you lift up yourselves above the assembly of יהוה?"

[4] And when Mosheh heard, he fell on his face,

[5] and spoke to Qoraḥ and all his company, saying, "Tomorrow morning יהוה shall make known who is His and who is set-apart, and bring *him* near to Him. And let Him bring near to Him the one whom He chooses.

[6] "Do this: Take fire holders, Qoraḥ and all your company,

[7] and put fire in them and put incense in them before יהוה tomorrow. And it shall be that the one whom יהוה chooses is the set-apart one. Enough of you, sons of Lěwi!"

[8] And Mosheh said to Qoraḥ, "Hear now, you sons of Lěwi:

[9] "Is it little to you that the Elohim of Yisra'ěl has separated you from the congregation of Yisra'ěl, to bring you near to Himself, to perform the service of the Dwelling Place of יהוה, and to stand before the congregation to serve them,

[10] and that He has brought you near to Himself, you and all your brothers, the sons of Lěwi, with you? Yet you seek the priesthood as well?

[11] "Therefore you and all your company are set against יהוה. And Aharon, what is he that you grumble against him?"

[12] And Mosheh sent to call Dathan and Aḇiram the sons of Eliyaḇ, but they said, "We are not coming up!

[13] "Is it little that you have brought us up out of a land flowing with milk and honey, to kill us in the wilderness, that you would also seize total rule over us?

[14] "Also, you have not brought us into a land flowing with milk and honey, nor given us inheritance of fields and vineyards. Would you bore out the eyes of these men? We are not coming up!"

[15] And Mosheh became very displeased, and said to יהוה, "Do not respect their offering. I have not taken one donkey from them, nor have I done harm to any of them."

[16] Then Mosheh said to Qoraḥ, "Tomorrow, you and all your company shall be there before יהוה, you and they and Aharon.

[17] "And take each one his fire holder, and you shall put incense in it. And let each one bring his fire holder before יהוה, two hundred and fifty fire holders, and you and Aharon, each one with his fire holder."

[18] So each one took his fire holder, and put fire in it, and laid incense on it, and stood at the door of the Tent of Appointment with Mosheh and Aharon.

[19] And Qoraḥ assembled all the congregation against them at the door of the Tent of Appointment. Then the esteem of יהוה appeared to all the congregation.

[20] And יהוה spoke to Mosheh, and to Aharon, saying,

[21] "Separate yourselves from the midst of this congregation, and let Me consume them in a moment."

[22] But they fell on their faces, and said, "O Ěl, Elohim of the spirits of all flesh! When one man sins, are You wroth with all the congregation?"

[23] And יהוה spoke to Mosheh, saying,

[24] "Speak to the congregation, saying, 'Move away from around the tents of Qoraḥ, Dathan, and Aḇiram.' "

[25] So Mosheh rose up and went to Dathan and Aḇiram, and the elders of Yisra'ěl followed him.

[26] And he spoke to the congregation, saying, "Please turn away from the tents of these wrong men! Do not touch whatever belongs to them, lest you be consumed in all their sins."

[27] Then they moved away from around the tents of Qoraḥ, Dathan, and Aḇiram. And Dathan and Aḇiram came out and stood at the door of their tents, with their wives, and their sons, and their little children.

[28] And Mosheh said, "By this you know that יהוה has sent me to do all these works, that *they are* not from my own heart.

[29] "If these die as all men do, or if they are visited as all men are visited, then יהוה has

not sent me.

30 “But if יהוה creates what is unheard of, and the earth opens its mouth and swallows them up with all that belongs to them, and they go down alive into She’ol, [a] then you shall know that these men have scorned יהוה.”

31 And it came to be, as he ended speaking all these words, that the ground under them split apart,

32 and the earth opened its mouth and swallowed them up, with their households and all the men with Qoraḥ, with all their goods.

33 So they and all those with them went down alive into She’ol, and the earth closed over them, and they perished from the midst of the assembly.

34 And all Yisra’ĕl who were round about them fled at their cry, for they said, “Lest the earth swallow us up!”

35 And a fire came out from יהוה and consumed the two hundred and fifty men who were offering incense.

36 And יהוה spoke to Mosheh, saying,

37 “Say to El‘azar, son of Aharon the priest, to pick up the fire holders out of the blaze, for they are set-apart, and scatter the fire some distance away.

38 “The fire holders of these men who sinned against their own lives, let them be made into beaten plates as a covering for the slaughter-place. Because they brought them before יהוה, therefore they are set-apart. And let them become a sign to the children of Yisra’ĕl.”

39 And El‘azar the priest took the bronze fire holders, which those who were burned up had brought, and they were beaten out as a covering on the slaughter-place –

40 a remembrance to the children of Yisra’ĕl that no stranger who is not of the seed of Aharon, should come near to offer incense before יהוה, and not be like Qoraḥ and his company – as יהוה had said to him through Mosheh.

41 But all the congregation of the children of Yisra’ĕl grumbled against Mosheh and against Aharon on the next day, saying, “You, you have killed the people of יהוה.”

42 And it came to be, when the congregation assembled against Mosheh and against Aharon, that they turned toward the Tent of Appointment. And see, the cloud covered it, and the esteem of יהוה appeared.

43 And Mosheh and Aharon came before the Tent of Appointment.

44 And יהוה spoke to Mosheh, saying,

45 “Arise from amidst this congregation, and let Me consume them in a moment.” And they fell on their faces.

46 So Mosheh said to Aharon, “Take the fire holder and put fire in it from the slaughter-place, and lay incense on, and go, hurry to the congregation and make atonement for them, for wrath has gone out from יהוה, the plague has begun.”

47 And Aharon took it as Mosheh commanded, and ran into the midst of the assembly, and saw that the plague had begun among the people. And he laid on the incense and made atonement for the people,

48 and stood between the dead and the living. And the plague was stopped.

49 And those who died in the plague were fourteen thousand seven hundred, besides those who died on account of Qoraḥ.

50 Then Aharon returned to Mosheh at the door of the Tent of Appointment, for the plague had stopped.

17

And יהוה spoke to Mosheh, saying,
2 “Speak to the children of Yisra’ĕl, and take from them a rod from each father’s house, all their leaders according to their fathers’ houses, twelve rods. Write each one’s name on his rod,

3 and write Aharon’s name on the rod of Lĕwi, for there is one rod for the head of each father’s house.

4 “You shall then place them in the Tent of Appointment before the Witness, where I meet with you.

5 “And it shall be that the rod of the man whom I choose buds, and I shall rid Myself of the grumblings of the children of Yisra’ĕl, which they grumble against you.”

16a See Explanatory notes - She’ol.

6 And Mosheh spoke to the children of
Yisra'ěl, and all their leaders gave him a
rod each, for each leader according to their
fathers' houses, twelve rods. And the rod
of Aharon was among their rods.
7 So Mosheh placed the rods before יהוה
in the Tent of the Witness.
8 And it came to be on the next day that
Mosheh went into the Tent of the Witness
and saw that the rod of Aharon, of the
house of Lěwi, had budded, and brought
forth buds, and blossomed and bore ripe
almonds.
9 And Mosheh brought out all the rods
from before יהוה to all the children of
Yisra'ěl. And they looked, and each man
took his rod.
10 And יהוה said to Mosheh, "Bring
Aharon's rod back before the Witness, to
be kept as a sign against the rebels, so that
you put an end to their grumblings against
Me, lest they die."
11 And Mosheh did as יהוה had commanded him, so he did.
12 And the children of Yisra'ěl spoke to
Mosheh, saying, "See, we shall die, we
shall perish, we shall all perish!
13 "Anyone who comes near the Dwelling
Place of יהוה dies. Shall we be consumed
– to die?"

18 And יהוה said to Aharon, "You
and your sons and your father's
house with you are to bear the crookedness
against the set-apart place, and you and
your sons with you are to bear the crookedness against your priesthood.
2 "But bring with you your brothers of
the tribe of Lěwi too, the tribe of your
father to join you and serve you while you
and your sons are with you before the Tent
of the Witness.
3 "And they shall guard your charge, and
the duty of all the Tent, but they do not
come near the furnishings of the set-apart
place and the slaughter-place, lest they die,
both they and you.
4 "And they shall be joined with you and
guard the duty to the Tent of Appointment,
for all the service of the Tent, but a
stranger does not come near you.
5 "And you shall guard the duty of the
set-apart place and the duty of the slaughter-place, so that there be no more wrath on
the children of Yisra'ěl.
6 "And see, I Myself have taken your
brothers the Lěwites from the midst of the
children of Yisra'ěl – a gift to you, given
by יהוה, to do the service of the Tent of
Appointment.
7 "But you and your sons with you are to
guard your priesthood for all matters at the
slaughter-place and behind the veil, and
you shall serve. I have given you the
priesthood as a gift for service, but the
stranger who comes near is put to death."
8 And יהוה spoke to Aharon, "And see, I
Myself have also given you the charge of
My contributions, all the set-apart gifts of
the children of Yisra'ěl. I have given them
to you for the anointing, and to your sons,
as a law forever.
9 "This is yours of the most set-apart
gifts, from the fire: all their offerings, all
their grain offerings and all their sin offerings and all their guilt offerings which they
render to Me, are most set-apart for you
and your sons.
10 "Eat it in the most set-apart place –
every male eats it. It is set-apart to you.
11 "This also is yours: the contribution of
their gift, with all the wave offerings of the
children of Yisra'ěl. I have given them to
you, and your sons and daughters with
you, as a law forever. Everyone who is
clean in your house eats it.
12 "All the best of the oil, and all the best
of the new wine and the grain – their first-
fruits which they give to יהוה – I have
given them to you.
13 "The first-fruits of all that is in their
land, which they bring to יהוה, are yours.
Everyone who is clean in your house
eats it.
14 "All that is dedicated in Yisra'ěl is
yours.
15 "Everyone opening a womb of all flesh,
which they bring to יהוה, whether man or
beast, is yours. But to ransom: you shall
ransom the first-born of man, and the first-
born of the unclean beast you ransom.
16 "And ransom their ransomed ones

when one new *moon* [a] old, according to
your valuation, five sheqels of silver,
according to the sheqel of the set-apart
place, which is twenty gĕrahs.
17 “But the first-born of a cow, or the first-
born of a sheep, or the first-born of a goat
you do not ransom, they are set-apart.
Sprinkle their blood on the slaughter-place,
and burn their fat as an offering made by
fire for a sweet fragrance to יהוה.
18 “And their flesh is yours, as the wave
breast and as the right thigh, it is yours.
19 “All the contributions of the set-apart
gifts, which the children of Yisra’ĕl present
to יהוה, I have given to you and your sons
and daughters with you as a law forever. It
is a covenant of salt forever before יהוה
with you and your seed with you.”
20 And יהוה said to Aharon, “You are not
to have an inheritance in their land, nor
have any portion in their midst. I am your
portion and your inheritance among the
children of Yisra’ĕl.
21 “And see, I have given the children of
Lĕwi all the tithes in Yisra’ĕl as an inheritance in return for the service which they
are serving, the service of the Tent of
Appointment.
22 “And let the children of Yisra’ĕl no
more come near the Tent of Appointment,
lest they bear sin and die,
23 because the Lĕwites shall do the service
of the Tent of Appointment, so they themselves bear their crookedness. A law forever, throughout your generations: that
among the children of Yisra’ĕl they are to
have no inheritance,
24 but the tithes of the children of Yisra’ĕl,
which they present as a contribution to
יהוה, I have given to the Lĕwites as an
inheritance. That is why I have said to
them, ‘Among the children of Yisra’ĕl they
have no inheritance.’ ”
25 And יהוה spoke to Mosheh, saying,
26 “Speak to the Lĕwites and say to them,
‘When you take from the children of
Yisra’ĕl the tithes which I have given you
from them as your inheritance, then you
shall present a contribution of it to יהוה,
a tenth of the tithe.
27 ‘And your contribution shall be reckoned to you as grain from the threshing-
floor and as filling from the winepress.
28 ‘Thus you also present a contribution
unto יהוה from all your tithes which you
receive from the children of Yisra’ĕl. And
you shall give from it the contribution to
יהוה to Aharon the priest.
29 ‘From all your gifts you present every
contribution due to יהוה, from all the best
of them, the set-apart part of them.’
30 “And you shall say to them, ‘When you
have presented the best of it, then the rest
shall be reckoned to the Lĕwites as the
yield of the threshing-floor and as the yield
of the winepress.
31 ‘And you shall eat it in any place, you
and your households, for it is your reward
for your service in the Tent of
Appointment,
32 and bear no sin because of it, when you
have presented the best of it, and do not
profane the set-apart gifts of the children
of Yisra’ĕl, lest you die.’ ”

19 And יהוה spoke to Mosheh and to
Aharon, saying,
2 “This is a law of the Torah which יהוה
has commanded, saying, ‘Speak to the
children of Yisra’ĕl, that they bring you a
red heifer, a perfect one, in which there is
no blemish and on which a yoke has never
come.
3 ‘And you shall give it to El‘azar the
priest, and he shall bring it outside the
camp, and shall slay it before him.
4 ‘And El‘azar the priest shall take some
of its blood with his finger, and sprinkle
some of its blood seven times toward the
front of the Tent of Appointment.
5 ‘And the heifer shall be burned before
his eyes – he burns its hide, and its flesh,
and its blood, and its dung.
6 ‘And the priest shall take cedar wood
and hyssop and scarlet, and throw them
into the midst of the fire burning the heifer.
7 ‘The priest shall then wash his garments, and shall bathe his body in water,

18a Or a month.

and afterward come into the camp, but the priest is unclean until evening.

8 'And he who is burning it washes his garments in water, and shall bathe his body in water, and is unclean until evening.

9 'And a clean man shall gather up the ashes of the heifer, and shall place them outside the camp in a clean place. And they shall be kept for the congregation of the children of Yisra'ěl for the water for uncleanness, it is for cleansing from sin.

10 'And he who gathers the ashes of the heifer shall wash his garments, and is unclean until evening. And it shall be a law forever to the children of Yisra'ěl and to the stranger who sojourns in their midst.

11 'He who touches the dead of any human being is unclean for seven days.

12 'He is to cleanse himself with the water on the third day, and on the seventh day he is clean. But if he does not cleanse himself on the third day, then on the seventh day he is not clean.

13 'Anyone who touches the dead of a human being, and does not cleanse himself, defiles the Dwelling Place of יהוה. And that being shall be cut off from Yisra'ěl. He is unclean, for the water for uncleanness was not sprinkled on him, his uncleanness is still upon him.

14 'This is the Torah when a man dies in a tent: All who come into the tent and all who are in the tent are unclean for seven days,

15 and every open vessel which has no cover fastened on it, is unclean.

16 'Anyone in the open field who touches someone slain by a sword or who has died, or a bone of a man, or a burial-site, is unclean for seven days.

17 'And for the unclean being they shall take some of the ashes of the heifer burnt for cleansing from sin, and running water shall be put on them in a vessel.

18 'And a clean man shall take hyssop and dip it in the water, and shall sprinkle it on the tent, and on all the vessels, and on the beings who were there, or on the one who touched a bone, or the slain, or the dead, or a burial-site.

19 'And the clean one shall sprinkle the unclean on the third day and on the seventh day. And on the seventh day he shall cleanse himself, and shall wash his garments and bathe in water, and shall be clean in the evening.

20 'But the man who is unclean and does not cleanse himself, that being shall be cut off from among the assembly, because he has defiled the set-apart place of יהוה – water for uncleanness has not been sprinkled on him, he is unclean.

21 'And it shall be a law for them forever. And the one who sprinkles the water for uncleanness washes his garments. And the one who touches the water for uncleanness is unclean until evening.

22 'And whatever the unclean being touches is unclean. And the being who touches it is unclean until evening.' "

20 And the children of Yisra'ěl, all the congregation, came into the Wilderness of Tsin in the first new *moon*, and the people stayed in Qaḏěsh. And Miryam died there and was buried there.

2 Now there was no water for the congregation and they assembled against Mosheh and against Aharon.

3 And the people contended with Mosheh and spoke, saying, "If only we had died when our brothers died before יהוה!

4 "Why have you brought up the assembly of יהוה into this wilderness, that we and our livestock should die here?

5 "And why have you brought us up out of Mitsrayim, to bring us to this evil place? – not a place of grain or figs or vines or pomegranates, and there is no water to drink."

6 Then Mosheh and Aharon went from the presence of the assembly to the door of the Tent of Appointment, and they fell on their faces. And the esteem of יהוה appeared to them.

7 And יהוה spoke to Mosheh, saying,

8 "Take the rod and assemble the congregation, you and your brother Aharon. And you shall speak to the rock before their eyes, and it shall give its water. And you shall bring water for them out of the rock and give drink to the congregation and

their livestock."
9 And Mosheh took the rod from before
יהוה as He commanded him.
10 And Mosheh and Aharon assembled
the assembly before the rock. And he said
to them, "Hear now, you rebels, shall we
bring water for you out of this rock?"
11 Then Mosheh lifted his hand and struck
the rock twice with his rod. And much
water came out, and the congregation and
their livestock drank.
12 But יהוה spoke to Mosheh and to
Aharon, "Because you did not believe Me,
to set Me apart in the eyes of the children
of Yisra'ěl, therefore you do not bring this
assembly into the land which I have given
them."
13 These were the waters of Meriḇah,
because the children of Yisra'ěl contended
with יהוה, and He was set apart among
them.
14 And Mosheh sent messengers from
Qaḏěsh to the sovereign of Eḏom. "This is
what your brother Yisra'ěl said, 'You know
all the hardship that has befallen us,
15 that our fathers went down to Mitsrayim, and we dwelt in Mitsrayim a long
time, and the Mitsrites did evil to us and
our fathers.
16 'And we cried out to יהוה, and He
heard our voice and sent the Messenger
and brought us up out of Mitsrayim. And
see, we are in Qaḏěsh, a city on the edge of
your border.
17 'Please let us pass over, through your
land. We shall not pass over through fields
or vineyards, nor drink water from wells,
we shall go along the sovereign's highway.
We shall not turn aside, right or left, until
we have passed over your border.' "
18 But Eḏom said to him, "You do not
pass over through me, lest I come out
against you with the sword."
19 And the children of Yisra'ěl said to
him, "We shall go by the highway, and if I
or my livestock drink any of your water,
then I shall pay for it. Let me only pass
over on foot, without a word."
20 But he said, "You do not pass over."
And Eḏom came out against them with
many men and with a strong hand.
21 So when Eḏom refused to let Yisra'ěl
pass over through his border, Yisra'ěl
turned away from him.
22 And the children of Yisra'ěl, all the
company, departed from Qaḏěsh and came
to Mount Hor.
23 And יהוה spoke to Mosheh and to
Aharon in Mount Hor near the border of
the land of Eḏom, saying,
24 "Aharon is to be gathered to his people,
for he is not to enter the land which I have
given to the children of Yisra'ěl, because
you rebelled against My mouth at the
water of Meriḇah.
25 "Take Aharon and El'azar his son, and
bring them up to Mount Hor,
26 and strip Aharon of his garments and
put them on El'azar his son, for Aharon is
to be gathered to his people and die there."
27 And Mosheh did as יהוה commanded,
and they went up to Mount Hor before the
eyes of all the congregation.
28 And Mosheh stripped Aharon of his
garments and put them on El'azar his son.
And Aharon died there on the top of the
mountain. And Mosheh and El'azar came
down from the mountain.
29 And when all the congregation saw that
Aharon was dead, all the house of Yisra'ěl
wept for Aharon, thirty days.

21 And the sovereign of Araḏ, the
Kena'anite, who dwelt in the
South, heard that Yisra'ěl was coming on
the way to Atharim, and he fought against
Yisra'ěl and took some of them captive.
2 Then Yisra'ěl made a vow to יהוה, and
said, "If You deliver this people into my
hand indeed, then I shall put their cities
under the ban."
3 And יהוה listened to the voice of
Yisra'ěl and gave up the Kena'anites, and
they put them and their cities under the
ban. So the name of that place was called
Ḥormah.
4 And they departed from Mount Hor by
the Way of the Sea of Reeds, to go around
the land of Eḏom. But the being of the
people grew impatient because of the way.
5 And the people spoke against Elohim
and against Mosheh, "Why have you

brought us up out of Mitsrayim to die in
the wilderness? For there is no food and no
water, and our being loathes this light
bread."
6 And יהוה sent fiery serpents among the
people, and they bit the people. And many
of the people of Yisra'ĕl died.
7 Then the people came to Mosheh, and
said, "We have sinned, for we have spoken
against יהוה and against you. Pray to יהוה
to take away the serpents from us." So
Mosheh prayed on behalf of the people.
8 And יהוה said to Mosheh, "Make a
fiery serpent, and set it on a pole. And it
shall be that everyone who is bitten, when
he looks at it, shall live."
9 So Mosheh made a bronze serpent, and
put it on a pole. And it came to be, if a
serpent had bitten anyone, when he looked
at the bronze serpent, he lived.
10 And the children of Yisra'ĕl set out and
camped in Oḇoth.
11 And they departed from Oḇoth and
camped at Iyĕ Ha-Aḇarim, in the wilderness which is east of Mo'aḇ, toward sunrise.
12 From there they set out and camped at
the wadi Zereḏ.
13 From there they set out and camped on
the other side of the Arnon, which is in the
wilderness that extends from the border of
the Amorites, for the Arnon is the border
of Mo'aḇ, between Mo'aḇ and the
Amorites.
14 Therefore it is said in the Book of the
Battles of יהוה, "Wahĕḇ in Suphah, the
wadi Arnon,
15 and the slope of the wadi that turns
aside to the dwelling of Ar, and lies on the
border of Mo'aḇ."
16 And from there on to Be'ĕr, which is
the well where יהוה said to Mosheh,
"Gather the people, and let Me give them
water."
17 Yisra'ĕl then sang this song: "Spring
up, O well! Sing to it,
18 a well the leaders sank, which the
nobles of the people dug with their staves,
by *the word of* the Inscriber." Then from
the wilderness on to Mattanah,
19 from Mattanah to Naḥali'ĕl, from
Naḥali'ĕl to Bamoth,
20 and from Bamoth, in the valley that is
in the country of Mo'aḇ, to the top of
Pisgah which looks down on the wasteland.
21 And Yisra'ĕl sent messengers to Siḥon
sovereign of the Amorites, saying,
22 "Let me pass through your land. We
shall not turn off into fields or vineyards,
we shall not drink water from wells, but go
by the sovereign's highway until we have
passed over your border."
23 But Siḥon would not allow Yisra'ĕl to
pass through his border. So Siḥon gathered
all his people together and went out against
Yisra'ĕl in the wilderness, and he came to
Yahats and fought against Yisra'ĕl.
24 And Yisra'ĕl struck him with the edge
of the sword, and took possession of his
land from the Arnon to the Yabboq, as far
as the children of Ammon, for the border
of the children of Ammon was strong.
25 And Yisra'ĕl took all these cities, and
Yisra'ĕl dwelt in all the cities of the
Amorites – in Ḥeshbon and in all its
villages,
26 for Ḥeshbon was the city of Siḥon the
sovereign of the Amorites, who had fought
against the former sovereign of Mo'aḇ, and
had taken all his land from his hand as far
as the Arnon.
27 That is why those who speak in
proverbs say, "Come to Ḥeshbon, let the
city of Siḥon be built and established.
28 "For fire went out from Ḥeshbon, a
flame from the city of Siḥon. It consumed
Ar of Mo'aḇ, the masters of the heights of
the Arnon.
29 "Woe to you, Mo'aḇ! You have perished, O people of Kemosh! He has given
his sons as fugitives, and his daughters into
captivity, to Siḥon the sovereign of the
Amorites.
30 "Then we shot them – Ḥeshbon has
perished as far as Diḇon. And we laid
waste as far as Nophaḥ, which reaches to
Mĕyḏeḇa."
31 So Yisra'ĕl dwelt in the land of the
Amorites.
32 And Mosheh sent to spy out Ya'zĕr.
And they took its villages and drove out

the Amorites who were there,
33 and turned and went up by the way to
Bashan. And Oḡ sovereign of Bashan went
out against them, he and all his people, to
battle at Eḏreʽi.
34 And יהוה said to Mosheh, "Do not fear
him, for I have given him into your hand,
with all his people and his land. And you
shall do to him as you did to Siḥon sovereign of the Amorites, who dwelt at Ḥeshbon."
35 And they struck him, and his sons, and
all his people, until no remnant was left to
him. And they took possession of his land.

22 And the children of Yisra'ĕl set out
and camped in the desert plains of
Mo'aḇ beyond the Yardĕn of Yeriḥo.
2 And Balaq son of Tsippor saw all that
Yisra'ĕl had done to the Amorites.
3 And Mo'aḇ was exceedingly afraid of
the people because they were many, and
Mo'aḇ was in dread because of the
children of Yisra'ĕl.
4 And Mo'aḇ said to the elders of
Miḏyan, "Now this company is licking up
all that is around us, as an ox licks up the
grass of the field." Now Balaq son of
Tsippor was sovereign of the Mo'aḇites at
that time,
5 and he sent messengers to Bilʽam son
of Beʽor at Pethor, which is near the River
in the land of the sons of his people, to
call him, saying, "See, a people has come
from Mitsrayim. See, they have covered
the surface of the land, and are settling
next to me!
6 "And now, please come at once, curse
this people for me, for they are too strong
for me. It might be that I strike them and
drive them out of the land, for I know that
he whom you bless is blessed, and he
whom you curse is cursed."
7 And the elders of Mo'aḇ and the elders
of Miḏyan left with *the fees for* divination
in their hand, and they came to Bilʽam and
spoke the words of Balaq to him.
8 And he said to them, "Spend the night
here, and I shall bring back word to you, as
יהוה speaks to me." So the heads of Mo'aḇ
stayed with Bilʽam.
9 And Elohim came to Bilʽam and said,
"Who are these men with you?"
10 And Bilʽam said to Elohim, "Balaq, son
of Tsippor, sovereign of Mo'aḇ, has sent to
me, saying,
11 'See, a people has come out of Mitsrayim and cover the surface of the land.
Come now, curse them for me. It might be
that I am able to fight against them and
drive them out.' "
12 And Elohim said to Bilʽam, "Do not go
with them. You do not curse the people, for
they are blessed."
13 And Bilʽam rose in the morning and
said to the heads of Balaq, "Go back to
your land, for יהוה has refused to allow me
to go with you."
14 And the heads of Mo'aḇ arose and went
to Balaq, and said, "Bilʽam refuses to come
with us."
15 Then Balaq again sent heads, more
numerous and more esteemed than they.
16 And they came to Bilʽam and said to
him, "This is what Balaq son of Tsippor
said: 'Do not be withheld from coming to
me, please,
17 for I esteem you very greatly, and whatever you say to me, I do. Therefore please
come, curse this people for me.' "
18 And Bilʽam answered and said to the
servants of Balaq, "Though Balaq were to
give me his house filled with silver and
gold, I am unable to go beyond the word of
יהוה my Elohim, to do less or more.
19 "And now, please, you also stay here
tonight, and let me find out what more
יהוה says to me."
20 And Elohim came to Bilʽam at night
and said to him, "If the men come to call
you, rise and go with them, but only the
word which I speak to you that you do."
21 And Bilʽam rose in the morning and
saddled his donkey, and went with the
heads of Mo'aḇ.
22 But the displeasure of Elohim burned
because he went, and the Messenger of
יהוה stationed Himself in the way as an
adversary against him. And he was riding
on his donkey, and his two servants were
with him.
23 And the donkey saw the Messenger of

יהוה standing in the way with His drawn
sword in His hand, and the donkey turned
aside out of the way and went into the
field. So Bilʽam struck the donkey to turn
her back onto the way.
24 Then the Messenger of יהוה stood in a
narrow passage between the vineyards,
with a wall on this side and a wall on that
side.
25 And when the donkey saw the
Messenger of יהוה, she pushed herself
against the wall and crushed Bilʽam's foot
against the wall, so he struck her again.
26 And the Messenger of יהוה went
further, and stood in a narrow place where
there was no way to turn aside, right or
left.
27 And when the donkey saw the
Messenger of יהוה, she lay down under
Bilʽam. So Bilʽam's displeasure burned,
and he struck the donkey with his staff.
28 Then יהוה opened the mouth of the
donkey, and she said to Bilʽam, "What
have I done to you, that you have stricken
me these three times?"
29 And Bilʽam said to the donkey,
"Because you have mocked me. I wish
there were a sword in my hand, for I would
have killed you by now!"
30 And the donkey said to Bilʽam, "Am
I not your donkey on which you have
ridden, ever since I became yours, to this
day? Was I ever known to do so to you?"
And he said, "No."
31 Then יהוה opened Bilʽam's eyes, and
he saw the Messenger of יהוה standing in
the way with His drawn sword in His hand.
And he bowed his head and fell on his
face.
32 And the Messenger of יהוה said to him,
"Why have you struck your donkey these
three times? See, I have come out to stand
against you, because your way is reckless
before Me.
33 "And the donkey saw Me and turned
aside from Me these three times. If she had
not turned aside from Me, I certainly
would have killed you by now, and let her
live."
34 And Bilʽam said to the Messenger of
יהוה, "I have sinned, for I did not know
You stood in the way against me. And now,
if evil is in Your eyes, let me turn back."
35 And the Messenger of יהוה said to
Bilʽam, "Go with the men, but only the
word that I speak to you, that you speak."
Bilʽam then went with the heads of Balaq.
36 And when Balaq heard that Bilʽam was
coming, he went out to meet him at the city
of Mo'aḇ, which is on the border at the
Arnon, which was in the extremity of the
border.
37 And Balaq said to Bilʽam, "Did I not
urgently send to you, calling for you? Why
did you not come to me? Am I not able to
esteem you?"
38 And Bilʽam said to Balaq, "See, I have
come to you! Now, am I at all able to say
somewhat? The word that Elohim puts in
my mouth, that I speak."
39 And Bilʽam went with Balaq, and they
came to Qiryath Ḥutsoth.
40 And Balaq slaughtered cattle and
sheep, and he sent some to Bilʽam and to
the heads who were with him.
41 And it came to be in the morning, that
Balaq took Bilʽam and brought him up to
the high places of Baʽal, and from there he
saw the extremity of the camp.

23

And Bilʽam said to Balaq, "Build
seven slaughter-places for me here,
and prepare seven bulls and seven rams for
me here."
2 And Balaq did as Bilʽam had spoken,
and Balaq and Bilʽam offered a bull and a
ram on each slaughter-place.
3 Bilʽam then said to Balaq, "Stand by
your ascending offering, and let me go on.
It might be that יהוה does come to meet
me, and whatever He shows me I shall
declare to you." And he went to a bare
height.
4 And Elohim came to Bilʽam, and he
said to Him, "I have prepared the seven
slaughter-places, and I have offered on
each slaughter-place a bull and a ram."
5 And יהוה put a word in the mouth of
Bilʽam, and said, "Return to Balaq, and
this is what you say."
6 And he returned to him and saw him
standing by his ascending offering, he and

all the heads of Mo'aḇ.
7 And he took up his proverb and said,
"Balaq the sovereign of Mo'aḇ has brought
me from Aram, from the mountains of the
east. 'Come, curse Ya'aqoḇ for me, and
come, rage at Yisra'ěl!'
8 "How do I curse whom Ěl has not
cursed? And how do I rage at whom יהוה
has not raged?
9 "For from the top of the rocks I see
him, and from the hills I observe him.
Look, a people dwelling alone, not reckoning itself among the nations.
10 "Who shall count the dust of Ya'aqoḇ,
and the number of one-fourth of Yisra'ěl?
Let me die the death of the upright, and let
my end be like his!"
11 And Balaq said to Bil'am, "What have
you done to me? I took you to curse
my enemies, and look, you have kept on
blessing!"
12 And he answered and said, "Should I
not take heed to speak what יהוה has put in
my mouth?"
13 And Balaq said to him, "Please come
with me to another place from where you
see them. You only see the extremity but
not all of them. Curse them for me from
there."
14 And he took him to the field of
Tsophim, to the top of Pisgah, and built
seven slaughter-places, and offered a bull
and a ram on each slaughter-place.
15 And he said to Balaq, "Stand here by
your ascending offering while I meet over
there."
16 And יהוה came to Bil'am, and put a
word in his mouth, and said, "Go back to
Balaq, and say this."
17 So he went to him and saw him standing by his ascending offering, and the
heads of Mo'aḇ with him. And Balaq
asked him, "What did יהוה say?"
18 And he took up his proverb and said,
"Rise up, Balaq, and hear! Listen to me,
son of Tsippor!
19 "Ěl is not a man, to lie; nor a son of
man, to repent! Has He said, and would He
not do it; or spoken, and would not confirm it?
20 "See, I have received, to bless. And He
has blessed, and I do not reverse it.
21 "He has not looked upon wickedness in
Ya'aqoḇ, nor has He seen trouble in
Yisra'ěl. יהוה his Elohim is with him, and
the shout of a Sovereign is in him.
22 "Ěl who brought them out of Mitsrayim, is for them like the horns of a wild ox.
23 "For there is no sorcery against
Ya'aqoḇ, nor is there any divination against
Yisra'ěl. Now it is said to Ya'aqoḇ and to
Yisra'ěl, 'What has Ěl done!'
24 "Look, a people rises like a lioness, and
lifts itself up like a lion; it lies not down
until it devours the prey, and drinks the
blood of the slain."
25 And Balaq said to Bil'am, "Do not
curse them at all, nor bless them at all!"
26 And Bil'am answered and said to
Balaq, "Have I not spoken to you, saying,
'All that יהוה speaks, that I do'?"
27 And Balaq said to Bil'am, "Please
come, let me take you to another place. It
might be right in the eyes of Elohim that
you curse them for me from there."
28 And Balaq took Bil'am to the top of
Pe'or, that overlooks the wasteland.
29 And Bil'am said to Balaq, "Build seven
slaughter-places for me here, and prepare
seven bulls and seven rams for me here."
30 And Balaq did as Bil'am had said, and
offered a bull and a ram on each slaughter-
place.

24 And when Bil'am saw that it
pleased יהוה to bless Yisra'ěl, he
did not go as at other times, to seek to use
sorcery, but he set his face toward the
wilderness.
2 And Bil'am lifted up his eyes and saw
Yisra'ěl encamped according to their
tribes. And the Spirit of Elohim came upon
him.
3 And he took up his proverb and said,
"The saying of Bil'am, son of Be'or, and
the saying of the man whose eyes are
opened,
4 the saying of him who hears the words
of Ěl, who sees the vision of the Almighty,
who falls down, with eyes opened wide:
5 "How good are your tents, O Ya'aqoḇ,
your dwellings, O Yisra'ěl!

6 “Like wadis that stretch out, like gardens by a river, like aloes planted by יהוה, like cedars beside waters.

7 “He makes water flow from his buckets, and his seed is in many waters. His sovereign is higher than Aḡaḡ, and his reign is exalted.

8 “Ěl who brought him out of Mitsrayim is for them like the horns of a wild ox; he devours nations, his enemies; and he breaks their bones, and with his arrows he smites.

9 “He bowed down, he lay down like a lion. And, like a lion, who would rouse him? Blessed is he who blesses you, and cursed is he who curses you.”

10 Then the displeasure of Balaq burned against Bilʿam, and he struck his hands together. Balaq then said to Bilʿam, “I summoned you to curse my enemies, and see, you have kept on blessing, these three times!

11 “And now flee to your place. I said I would greatly esteem you, and see, יהוה has kept you back from esteem.”

12 And Bilʿam said to Balaq, “Did I not also speak to your messengers whom you sent to me, saying,

13 ‘If Balaq should give me his house filled with silver and gold, I am unable to go beyond the word of יהוה, to do either good or evil of my own heart. What יהוה speaks, that I speak’?

14 “And now, see, I am going to my people. Come, let me advise you what this people is going to do to your people in the latter days.”

15 And he took up his proverb and said, “The saying of Bilʿam, son of Beʿor, and the saying of the man whose eyes are opened,

16 the saying of him who hears the words of Ěl, and knows the knowledge of the Most High, who sees the vision of the Almighty, who falls down, with eyes opened wide:

17 “I see Him, [a] but not now; I observe Him, but not near. A Star shall come out of Yaʿaqoḇ, and a Sceptre shall rise out of Yisra’ěl, and shall smite the corners of Mo’aḇ, and shall destroy all the sons of Shěth.

18 “And Eḏom shall be a possession; and Sěʿir shall be a possession – enemies – and Yisra’ěl is doing mightily.

19 “And out of Yaʿaqoḇ *One* shall rule and destroy the remnant from Ar.”

20 He then looked on Amalěq, and he took up his proverb and said, “Amalěq was first among the nations, but his latter end is to perish forever.”

21 He then looked on the Qěynites, and he took up his proverb and said, “Firm is your dwelling place, and your nest is set in the rock,

22 but Qayin is to be burned. Till when does Asshur keep you captive?”

23 And he took up his proverb and said, “Oh, who does live when Ěl does this?

24 And ships shall come from the coast of Kittim, and they shall afflict Asshur and afflict Ěḇer, and so shall Amalěq, and he also perishes.”

25 And Bilʿam arose and left, and returned to his place. And Balaq also went his way.

25 And Yisra’ěl dwelt in Shittim, and the people began to whore with the daughters of Mo’aḇ,

2 and they invited the people to the slaughterings of their mighty ones, and the people ate and bowed down to their mighty ones.

3 Thus Yisra’ěl was joined to Baʿal Peʿor, and the displeasure of יהוה burned against Yisra’ěl.

4 And יהוה said to Mosheh, “Take all the leaders of the people and hang them up before יהוה, before the sun, so that the burning displeasure of יהוה turns away from Yisra’ěl.”

5 And Mosheh said to the judges of Yisra’ěl, “Each one of you kill his men who were joined to Baʿal Peʿor.”

6 And see, one of the children of Yisra’ěl came and brought to his brothers a

24a Also see 31:16 and 25:3, also Kěpha ב 2:15.

Miḏyanite woman before the eyes of
Mosheh and before the eyes of all the congregation of the children of Yisra'ěl, who
were weeping at the door of the Tent of
Appointment.
7 And when Pineḥas, son of El'azar, son
of Aharon the priest, saw it, he rose up
from among the congregation and took a
spear in his hand,
8 and he went after the man of Yisra'ěl
into the tent and thrust both of them
through, the man of Yisra'ěl, and the
woman through her belly. Thus the plague
among the children of Yisra'ěl came to a
stop.
9 And those who died in the plague were
twenty-four thousand.
10 And יהוה spoke to Mosheh, saying,
11 "Pineḥas, son of El'azar, son of Aharon
the priest, has turned back My wrath from
the children of Yisra'ěl, because he was
ardent with My ardour in their midst, so
that I did not consume the children of
Yisra'ěl in My ardour.
12 "Therefore say, 'See, I am giving him
My covenant of peace,
13 and it shall be to him and to his seed
after him a covenant of an everlasting
priesthood, because he was ardent for his
Elohim, and made atonement for the children of Yisra'ěl.' "
14 And the name of the man of Yisra'ěl
who was struck, who was struck with the
Miḏyanite woman, was Zimri, son of Salu,
a leader of a father's house among the
Shim'onites.
15 And the name of the Miḏyanite woman
who was struck was Kozbi the daughter of
Tsur. He was head of the people of a
father's house in Miḏyan.
16 And יהוה spoke to Mosheh, saying,
17 "Distress the Miḏyanites! And you
shall strike them,
18 for they distressed you with their tricks
with which they deceived you in the matter
of Pe'or and in the matter of Kozbi, the
daughter of a leader of Miḏyan, their sister,
who was struck in the day of the plague
because of Pe'or."

26
And it came to be, after the plague,
that יהוה spoke to Mosheh and
El'azar, son of Aharon the priest, saying,
2 "Take a census of all the congregation
of the children of Yisra'ěl from twenty
years old and above, by their fathers' houses, everyone going out to the army in
Yisra'ěl."
3 So Mosheh and El'azar the priest spoke
with them in the desert plains of Mo'aḇ by
the Yarděn of Yeriḥo, saying,
4 "*Take a census of the people* from twenty years old and above, as יהוה commanded Mosheh and the children of Yisra'ěl
who came out of the land of Mitsrayim."
5 Re'uḇěn, first-born of Yisra'ěl, sons of
Re'uḇěn: *of* Ḥanoḵ, the clan of the
Ḥanoḵites; of Pallu, the clan of the
Palluites;
6 of Ḥetsron, the clan of the Ḥetsronites;
of Karmi, the clan of the Karmites.
7 These are the clans of the Re'uḇěnites,
and their registered ones were forty-three
thousand seven hundred and thirty.
8 And the son of Pallu: Eliyaḇ.
9 And the sons of Eliyaḇ: Nemu'ěl, and
Dathan, and Aḇiram. This Dathan and
Aḇiram, were the called ones of the congregation, who contended against Mosheh
and against Aharon in the company of
Qoraḥ, when they contended against יהוה,
10 and the earth opened its mouth and
swallowed them up together with Qoraḥ
when that company died, when the fire
consumed two hundred and fifty men. And
they became a sign,
11 but the sons of Qoraḥ did not die.
12 Sons of Shim'on according to their
clans: of Nemu'ěl, the clan of the
Nemu'ělites; of Yamin, the clan of the
Yaminites; of Yaḵin, the clan of the
Yaḵinites;
13 of Zeraḥ, the clan of the Zarḥites; of
Sha'ul, the clan of the Sha'ulites.
14 These are the clans of the Shim'onites:
twenty-two thousand two hundred.
15 Sons of Gaḏ according to their clans: of
Tsephon, the clan of the Tsephonites; of
Ḥaggi, the clan of the Ḥaggites; of Shuni,
the clan of the Shunites;
16 of Ozni, the clan of the Oznites; of Ěri,

the clan of the Ěrites;
17 of Aroḏ, the clan of the Aroḏites; of
Arěli, the clan of the Arělites.
18 These are the clans of the sons of Gaḏ
according to their registered ones: forty
thousand five hundred.
19 Sons of Yehuḏah: Ěr and Onan. And Ěr
and Onan died in the land of Kenaʽan.
20 And sons of Yehuḏah according to their
clans: of Shělah, the clan of the Shělanites;
of Perets, the clan of the Partsites; of
Zeraḥ, the clan of the Zarḥites.
21 And sons of Perets: of Ḥetsron, the clan
of the Ḥetsronites; of Ḥamul, the clan of
the Ḥamulites.
22 These are the clans of Yehuḏah according to their registered ones: seventy-six
thousand five hundred.
23 Sons of Yissasḵar according to their
clans: of Tola, the clan of the Tolaites; of
Puwwah, the clan of the Punites;
24 of Yashuḇ, the clan of the Yashuḇites;
of Shimron, the clan of the Shimronites.
25 These are the clans of Yissasḵar
according to their registered ones: sixty-
four thousand three hundred.
26 Sons of Zeḇulun according to their
clans: of Sereḏ, the clan of the Sardites; of
Ělon, the clan of the Ělonites; of Yaḥle'ěl,
the clan of the Yaḥle'ělites.
27 These are the clans of the Zeḇulunites
according to their registered ones: sixty
thousand five hundred.
28 Sons of Yosěph according to their
clans, by Menashsheh and Ephrayim:
29 Sons of Menashsheh: of Maḵir, the clan
of the Maḵirites. And Maḵir brought forth
Gilʽaḏ; of Gilʽaḏ, the clan of the Gilʽaḏites.
30 These are sons of Gilʽaḏ: of Iyezer, the
clan of the Iyezerites; of Ḥěleq, the clan of
the Ḥěleqites;
31 of Asri'ěl, the clan of the Asri'ělites; of
Sheḵem, the clan of the Sheḵemites;
32 of Shemiḏa, the clan of the
Shemiḏaites; of Ḥěpher, the clan of the
Ḥěpherites.
33 And Tselophḥaḏ son of Ḥěpher had no
sons, but daughters. And the names of the
daughters of Tselophḥaḏ: Maḥlah, and
Noʽah, Ḥoḡlah, Milkah, and Tirtsah.
34 These are the clans of Menashsheh, and
their registered ones: fifty-two thousand
seven hundred.
35 These are the sons of Ephrayim according to their clans: of Shuthelaḥ, the clan of
the Shuthalḥites; of Beḵer, the clan of the
Baḵrites; of Taḥan, the clan of the
Taḥanites.
36 And these are sons of Shuthelaḥ: of
Ěran, the clan of the Ěranites.
37 These are the clans of the sons of
Ephrayim according to their registered
ones: thirty-two thousand five hundred.
These are the sons of Yosěph according to
their clans.
38 Sons of Binyamin according to their
clans: of Bela, the clan of the Belaites; of
Ashběl, the clan of the Ashbělites; of
Aḥiram, the clan of the Aḥiramites;
39 of Shephupham, the clan of the
Shephuphamites; of Ḥupham, the clan of
the Ḥuphamites.
40 And sons of Bela were Ard and
Naʽaman: of Ard, the clan of the Ardites;
of Naʽaman, the clan of the Naʽamites.
41 These are sons of Binyamin according
to their clans, and their registered ones:
forty-five thousand six hundred.
42 These are sons of Dan according to
their clans: of Shuḥam, the clan of the
Shuḥamites. These are the clans of Dan
according to their clans.
43 All the clans of the Shuḥamites,
according to their registered ones: sixty-
four thousand four hundred.
44 Sons of Asher according to their clans:
of Yimna, the clan of the Yimnahites; of
Yishwi, the clan of the Yishwites; of
Beriʽah, the clan of the Beriʽites.
45 Of the sons of Beriʽah: of Ḥeḇer, the
clan of the Ḥeḇerites; of Malki'ěl, the clan
of the Malki'ělites.
46 And the name of the daughter of Asher
was Seraḥ.
47 These are the clans of the sons of Asher
according to their registered ones: fifty-
three thousand four hundred.
48 Sons of Naphtali according to their
clans: of Yaḥtse'ěl, the clan of the
Yaḥtse'ělites; of Guni, the clan of the
Gunites;
49 of Yětser, the clan of the Yětserites; of

Shillēm, the clan of the Shillēmites.
50 These are the clans of Naphtali according to their clans, and their registered ones:
forty-five thousand four hundred.
51 These are the registered ones of the
children of Yisra'ēl: six hundred and one
thousand seven hundred and thirty.
52 And יהוה spoke to Mosheh, saying,
53 "The land is to be divided to these as an
inheritance, according to the number of
names.
54 "To the large one you give a larger
inheritance, and to the small one you give
a smaller inheritance. Each shall be given
its inheritance according to their registered
ones.
55 "But the land is divided by lot, they
inherit according to the names of the tribes
of their fathers.
56 "According to the lot their inheritance
is divided between the larger and the
smaller."
57 And these are the registered ones of the
Lēwites according to their clans: of
Gērshon, the clan of the Gērshonites; of
Qehath, the clan of the Qehathites; of
Merari, the clan of the Merarites.
58 These are the clans of the Lēwites: the
clan of the Libnites, the clan of the
Ḥebronites, the clan of the Maḥlites, the
clan of the Mushites, and the clan of the
Qorḥites. And Qehath brought forth Amram.
59 And the name of Amram's wife was
Yokebed the daughter of Lēwi, who was
born to Lēwi in Mitsrayim. And to Amram
she bore Aharon and Mosheh and their
sister Miryam.
60 And to Aharon were born Nadab and
Abihu, El'azar and Ithamar.
61 And Nadab and Abihu died when they
brought strange fire before יהוה.
62 And their registered ones were twenty-
three thousand, every male from a new
moon [a] old and above. For they were not
registered among the other children of
Yisra'ēl, because there was no inheritance
given to them among the children of
Yisra'ēl.
63 These are the ones registered by
Mosheh and El'azar the priest, who registered the sons of Yisra'ēl in the desert
plains of Mo'ab by the Yardēn of Yeriḥo.
64 But among these there was not a man of
those registered by Mosheh and Aharon
the priest when they registered the sons of
Yisra'ēl in the Wilderness of Sinai.
65 For יהוה had said of them, "They shall
certainly die in the wilderness." And not a
man was left of them, except Kalēb son of
Yephunneh, and Yehoshua son of Nun.

27 Then came the daughters of
Tselophḥad, son of Ḥēpher, son of
Gil'ad, son of Makir, son of Menashsheh,
from the clans of Menashsheh, son of
Yosēph. And these were the names of his
daughters: Maḥlah, No'ah, and Ḥoglah,
and Milkah, and Tirtsah.
2 And they stood before Mosheh, and
before El'azar the priest, and before the
leaders and all the congregation, by the
doorway of the Tent of Appointment, saying,
3 "Our father died in the wilderness, yet
he was not in the company of those who
were met together against יהוה, in company with Qoraḥ, but he died in his own sin.
And he had no sons.
4 "Why should the name of our father be
removed from among his clan because he
had no son? Give us a possession among
the brothers of our father."
5 Mosheh then brought their case before
יהוה.
6 And יהוה spoke to Mosheh, saying,
7 "The daughters of Tselophḥad speak
what is right. You should certainly give
them a possession of inheritance among
their father's brothers, and cause the inheritance of their father to pass to them.
8 "And speak to the children of Yisra'ēl,
saying, 'When a man dies and has no son,
then you shall cause his inheritance to pass
to his daughter.
9 'And if he has no daughter, then you
shall give his inheritance to his brothers.
10 'And if he has no brothers, then you

26a Or a month.

shall give his inheritance to his father's brothers.
11 'And if his father has no brothers, then you shall give his inheritance to the nearest relative in his clan, and he shall possess it.' " And it shall be to the children of Yisra'ěl a law of right-ruling, as יהוה commanded Mosheh.
12 And יהוה said to Mosheh, "Go up into this Mount Aḇarim, and see the land which I have given to the children of Yisra'ěl.
13 "And when you have seen it, you also shall be gathered to your people as Aharon your brother was gathered,
14 because you rebelled against My mouth in the Wilderness of Tsin, in the strife of the congregation, to set Me apart at the waters before their eyes." These were the waters of Meriḇah, at Qaḏěsh in the Wilderness of Tsin.
15 And Mosheh spoke to יהוה, saying,
16 "Let יהוה, the Elohim of the spirits of all flesh, appoint a man over the congregation,
17 who goes out before them and comes in before them, who leads them out and brings them in, so that the congregation of יהוה be not like sheep without a shepherd."
18 And יהוה said to Mosheh, "Take Yehoshua son of Nun with you, a man in whom is the Spirit. And you shall lay your hand on him,
19 and shall set him before El'azar the priest and before all the congregation, and give him command before their eyes,
20 and shall put some of your esteem upon him, so that all the congregation of the children of Yisra'ěl obey *him*.
21 "And he is to stand before El'azar the priest, who shall inquire before יהוה for him by the right-ruling of the Urim. At his word they go out, and at his word they come in, both he and all the children of Yisra'ěl with him, all the congregation."
22 And Mosheh did as יהוה commanded him, and took Yehoshua and set him before El'azar the priest and before all the congregation,
23 and laid his hands on him and commissioned him, as יהוה commanded by the hand of Mosheh.

28 And יהוה spoke to Mosheh, saying,
2 "Command the children of Yisra'ěl, and you shall say to them, 'Take heed to bring My offering, My food for My offerings made by fire as a sweet fragrance to Me, at their appointed time.'
3 "And you shall say to them, 'This is the offering made by fire which you bring to יהוה: two male lambs a year old, perfect ones, daily, a continual ascending offering.
4 'The one lamb you prepare in the morning, and the other lamb you prepare between the evenings,
5 with one-tenth of an ěphah of fine flour as a grain offering mixed with one-fourth of a hin of pressed oil,
6 a continual ascending offering which was offered at Mount Sinai for a sweet fragrance, an offering made by fire to יהוה,
7 and its drink offering, one-fourth of a hin for each lamb. Pour out the drink to יהוה as an offering in the set-apart place.
8 'And the other lamb you prepare between the evenings. As the morning grain offering and its drink offering, you prepare it as an offering made by fire, a sweet fragrance to יהוה.
9 'And on the Sabbath day two lambs a year old, perfect ones, and two-tenths *of an ěphah* of fine flour as a grain offering, mixed with oil, with its drink offering,
10 the ascending offering for every Sabbath, besides the continual ascending offering with its drink offering.
11 'And on the beginnings of your new *moons* you bring near an ascending offering to יהוה: two young bulls and one ram, and seven lambs a year old, perfect ones;
12 three-tenths *of an ěphah* of fine flour as a grain offering, mixed with oil, for each bull; two-tenths *of an ěphah* of fine flour as a grain offering, mixed with oil, for the one ram;
13 and one-tenth *of an ěphah* of fine flour, mixed with oil, as a grain offering for each lamb, as an ascending offering of sweet fragrance, an offering made by fire to יהוה.
14 'And their drink offering is half a hin of

wine for a bull, and one-third of a hin for a
ram, and one-fourth of a hin for a lamb.
This is the ascending offering for each new
moon throughout the new *moons* of the
year,
15 and one male goat as a sin offering to
יהוה is prepared, besides the continual
ascending offering and its drink offering.
16 'And in the first new *moon*, on the fourteenth day, is the Pěsaḥ [a] of יהוה,
17 and on the fifteenth day of this new
moon is a festival. For seven days unleavened bread is eaten.
18 'On the first day is a set-apart gathering, you do no servile work.
19 'And you shall bring near an offering
made by fire as an ascending offering to
יהוה: two young bulls and one ram, and
seven lambs a year old, perfect ones they
are for you,
20 and their grain offering, fine flour
mixed with oil. Prepare three-tenths *of an*
ěphah for a bull, and two-tenths for a ram.
21 'Prepare one-tenth *of an ěphah* for each
of the seven lambs,
22 and one goat as a sin offering, to make
atonement for you.
23 'Prepare these besides the ascending
offering of the morning, which is for a continual ascending offering.
24 'According to these you are to prepare
the food of the offering made by fire daily
for seven days, as a sweet fragrance to
יהוה. It is prepared besides the continual
ascending offering and its drink offering.
25 'And on the seventh day you have a set-
apart gathering, you do no servile work.
26 'And on the day of the first-fruits, when
you bring a new grain offering to יהוה at
your Festival of Shaḇu'ot, [b] you have a set-
apart gathering, you do no servile work.
27 'And you shall bring near an ascending
offering as a sweet fragrance to יהוה: two
young bulls, one ram, and seven lambs a
year old,
28 with their grain offering of fine flour
mixed with oil: three-tenths *of an ěphah*
for each bull, two-tenths for the one ram,
29 one-tenth for each of the seven lambs,
30 one male goat to make atonement for
you,
31 perfect ones they are for you. Prepare
them with their drink offerings, besides the
continual ascending offering with its grain
offering.

29

'And in the seventh new *moon*, on
the first *day* of the new *moon*, you
have a set-apart gathering, you do no
servile work, it is Yom Teruʿah [a] for you.
2 'And you shall prepare an ascending
offering as a sweet fragrance to יהוה: one
young bull, one ram, seven lambs a year
old, perfect ones,
3 and their grain offering: fine flour
mixed with oil, three-tenths *of an ěphah*
for the bull, two-tenths for the ram,
4 and one-tenth for each of the seven
lambs,
5 and one male goat as a sin offering, to
make atonement for you,
6 besides the ascending offering with its
grain offering for the New Moon, the continual ascending offering with its grain
offering, and their drink offerings, according to their right-ruling, as a sweet fragrance, an offering made by fire to יהוה.
7 'And on the tenth *day* of this seventh
new *moon* you have a set-apart gathering,
and you shall afflict your beings, you do no
work.
8 'And you shall bring near an ascending
offering to יהוה, a sweet fragrance: one
young bull, one ram, seven lambs a year
old, perfect ones they are for you,
9 and their grain offering: fine flour
mixed with oil, three-tenths *of an ěphah*
for the bull, two-tenths for the one ram,
10 one-tenth for each of the seven lambs,
11 one male goat as a sin offering, besides
the sin offering for atonement, the continual ascending offering with its grain offering, and their drink offerings.
12 'And on the fifteenth day of the seventh
new *moon* you have a set-apart gathering,
you do no servile work. And you shall celebrate a festival to יהוה seven days,
13 and you shall bring near an ascending

28a - Passover. *28b* - Weeks. *29a* Day of Soundings or Noisings.

offering, an offering made by fire, a sweet fragrance to יהוה: thirteen young bulls, two rams, fourteen lambs a year old, perfect ones they are,
14 and their grain offering: fine flour mixed with oil, three-tenths *of an ĕphah* for each of the thirteen bulls, two-tenths for each of the two rams,
15 and one-tenth for each of the fourteen lambs,
16 and one male goat as a sin offering, besides the continual ascending offering, its grain offering, and its drink offering.
17 'Then on the second day: twelve young bulls, two rams, fourteen lambs a year old, perfect ones,
18 and their grain offering and their drink offerings for the bulls, for the rams, and for the lambs, by their number, according to the right-ruling,
19 and one male goat as a sin offering, besides the continual ascending offering with its grain offering, and their drink offerings.
20 'And on the third day eleven bulls, two rams, fourteen lambs a year old, perfect ones,
21 and their grain offering and their drink offerings for the bulls, for the rams, and for the lambs, by their number, according to the right-ruling,
22 and one goat as a sin offering, besides the continual ascending offering, its grain offering, and its drink offering.
23 'Then on the fourth day: ten bulls, two rams, fourteen lambs a year old, perfect ones,
24 and their grain offering and their drink offerings for the bulls, for the rams, and for the lambs, by their number, according to the right-ruling,
25 and one male goat as a sin offering, besides the continual ascending offering, its grain offering, and its drink offering.
26 'Then on the fifth day: nine bulls, two rams, fourteen lambs a year old, perfect ones,
27 and their grain offering and their drink offerings for the bulls, for the rams, and for the lambs, by their number, according to the right-ruling,
28 and one goat as a sin offering, besides the continual ascending offering, its grain offering, and its drink offering.
29 'Then on the sixth day: eight bulls, two rams, fourteen lambs a year old, perfect ones,
30 and their grain offering and their drink offerings for the bulls, for the rams, and for the lambs, by their number, according to the right-ruling,
31 and one goat as a sin offering, besides the continual ascending offering, its grain offering, and its drink offering.
32 'Then on the seventh day: seven bulls, two rams, fourteen lambs a year old, perfect ones,
33 and their grain offering and their drink offerings for the bulls, for the rams, and for the lambs, by their number, according to the right-ruling,
34 and one goat as a sin offering, besides the continual ascending offering, its grain offering, and its drink offering.
35 'On the eighth day you have an assembly, you do no servile work,
36 and you shall bring near an ascending offering, an offering made by fire, a sweet fragrance to יהוה: one bull, one ram, seven lambs a year old, perfect ones,
37 their grain offering and their drink offerings for the bull, for the ram, and for the lambs, by their number, according to the right-ruling,
38 and one goat as a sin offering, besides the continual ascending offering, its grain offering, and its drink offering.
39 'These you prepare to יהוה at your appointed times, besides your vowed offerings and your voluntary offerings, as your ascending offerings and your grain offerings, as your drink offerings and your peace offerings.' "
40 And Mosheh spoke to the children of Yisra'ĕl according to all יהוה had commanded Mosheh.

30 And Mosheh spoke to the heads of the tribes concerning the children of Yisra'ĕl, saying, "This is the word which יהוה has commanded:
2 "When a man vows a vow to יהוה, or

swears an oath to bind himself by some agreement, he does not break his word, he does according to all that comes out of his mouth.

3 “Or if a woman vows a vow to יהוה, and binds herself by some agreement while in her father’s house in her youth,

4 and her father hears her vow and the agreement by which she has bound herself, and her father has kept silent towards her, then all her vows shall stand, and every agreement with which she has bound herself stands.

5 “But if her father forbids her on the day that he hears, then none of her vows nor her agreements by which she has bound herself stand. And יהוה pardons her, because her father has forbidden her.

6 “But if she at all belongs to a husband, while bound by her vows or by a rash utterance from her lips by which she bound herself,

7 and her husband hears it, and he has kept silent towards her on the day that he hears, then her vows shall stand, and her agreements by which she bound herself do stand.

8 “But if her husband forbids her on the day that he hears it, then he has nullified her vow which she vowed, and the rash utterance of her lips by which she bound herself, and יהוה pardons her.

9 “But any vow of a widow or a divorced woman, by which she has bound herself, stands against her.

10 “And if she vowed in her husband’s house, or bound herself by an agreement with an oath,

11 and her husband heard it, and has kept silent towards her and did not forbid her, then all her vows shall stand, and every agreement by which she bound herself stands.

12 “But if her husband clearly nullified them on the day he heard them, then whatever came from her lips concerning her vows or concerning the agreement binding her, it does not stand – her husband has nullified them, and יהוה pardons her.

13 “Every vow and every binding oath to afflict her being, let her husband confirm it, or let her husband nullify it.

14 “But if her husband is altogether silent at her from day to day, then he confirms all her vows or all the agreements that bind her – he confirms them, because he kept silent towards her on the day that he heard.

15 “But if he nullifies them after he has heard, then he shall bear her crookedness.”

16 These are the laws which יהוה commanded Mosheh, between a man and his wife, and between a father and his daughter in her youth in her father’s house.

31

And יהוה spoke to Mosheh, saying,

2 “Take vengeance for the children of Yisra’ěl on the Miḏyanites. After that you are to be gathered to your people.”

3 And Mosheh spoke to the people, saying, “Arm some of yourselves for the campaign, and let them go against the Miḏyanites to take vengeance for יהוה on Miḏyan.

4 “Send a thousand from each tribe of all the tribes of Yisra’ěl for the campaign.”

5 So there were supplied from the tribes of Yisra’ěl one thousand from each tribe, twelve thousand armed ones for the campaign.

6 And Mosheh sent them on the campaign, one thousand from each tribe, them and Pineḥas son of El‘azar the priest on the campaign, with the set-apart utensils and the trumpets for sounding in his hand.

7 And they fought against the Miḏyanites, as יהוה commanded Mosheh, and killed all the males.

8 And they killed the sovereigns of Miḏyan with the rest of those who were pierced: Ewi, and Reqem, and Tsur, and Ḥur, and Reḇa, the five sovereigns of Miḏyan. And they killed Bil‘am son of Be‘or with the sword.

9 And the sons of Yisra’ěl took all the women of Miḏyan captive, with their little ones, and took as spoil all their livestock, and all their possessions.

10 And they burned with fire all the cities where they dwelt, and all their settlements.

11 And they took all the spoil and all the booty, both of man and beast.

12 And they brought the captives, and the

booty, and the spoil to Mosheh, and to El'azar the priest, and to the congregation of the children of Yisra'ěl, to the camp in the desert plains of Mo'aḇ by the Yarděn of Yeriḥo.
13 And Mosheh, and El'azar the priest, and all the leaders of the congregation, went to meet them outside the camp.
14 But Mosheh was wroth with the officers of the army, with the commanders of thousands and commanders of hundreds, who had come from the campaign.
15 And Mosheh said to them, "Have you kept all the women alive?
16 "Look, they are the ones who caused the children of Yisra'ěl, through the word of Bil'am, to trespass against יהוה in the matter of Pe'or, and there was a plague among the congregation of יהוה.
17 "And now, kill every male among the little ones. And every woman who has known a man by lying with a man you shall kill.
18 "But keep alive for yourselves all the female children who have not known a man by lying with a man.
19 "And you, camp outside the camp seven days. Whoever has killed any being, and whoever has touched any slain, cleanse yourselves and your captives on the third day and on the seventh day.
20 "And cleanse every garment, and every object of leather and all the work of goats' *hair*, and every object of wood."
21 And El'azar the priest said to the men of the campaign who went to the battle, "This is the law of the Torah which יהוה commanded Mosheh:
22 "Only the gold, and the silver, the bronze, the iron, the tin, and the lead,
23 every object that passes through fire, you put through the fire, and it shall be clean; only, let it be cleansed with the water for uncleanness. And whatever does not pass through fire you pass through water.
24 "And you shall wash your garments on the seventh day and be clean, and afterwards come into the camp."
25 And יהוה spoke to Mosheh, saying,
26 "Count up the plunder that was taken, of man and of beast, you and El'azar the priest and the heads of the fathers of the congregation.
27 "And you shall divide the plunder into two parts, between those who took part in the battle, who went out on the campaign, and all the congregation.
28 "And set aside a levy for יהוה on the men of battle who went out on the campaign: one out of every five hundred, of man, and of the cattle, and of the donkeys, and of the sheep.
29 "Take it from their half, and give it to El'azar the priest as a contribution to יהוה.
30 "And from the children of Yisra'ěl's half you shall take one of every fifty, of man, of the cattle, of the donkeys, and of the sheep, of all the livestock, and give them to the Lěwites guarding the duty of the Dwelling Place of יהוה."
31 And Mosheh and El'azar the priest did as יהוה commanded Mosheh.
32 And the booty remaining from the plunder, which the people of the campaign had taken, was six hundred and seventy-five thousand sheep,
33 and seventy-two thousand cattle,
34 and sixty-one thousand donkeys,
35 and thirty-two thousand human beings in all, of women who had not known a man by lying with a man.
36 And the half, the portion for those who went out on the campaign, was in number three hundred and thirty-seven thousand five hundred sheep,
37 and the levy unto יהוה of the sheep was six hundred and seventy-five.
38 And the cattle were thirty-six thousand, of which the levy unto יהוה was seventy-two.
39 And the donkeys were thirty thousand five hundred, of which the levy unto יהוה was sixty-one.
40 And the human beings were sixteen thousand, of which the levy unto יהוה was thirty-two beings.
41 So Mosheh gave the levy which was the contribution unto יהוה to El'azar the priest, as יהוה commanded Mosheh.
42 And from the children of Yisra'ěl's half, which Mosheh divided from the men

who campaigned:
43 now the half belonging to the congregation was three hundred and thirty-seven thousand five hundred sheep,
44 and thirty-six thousand cattle,
45 and thirty thousand five hundred donkeys,
46 and sixteen thousand human beings.
47 Then Mosheh took from the children of Yisra'ěl's half: one out of every fifty, drawn from man and beast, and gave them to the Lěwites, who guarded the duty of the Dwelling Place of יהוה, as יהוה commanded Mosheh.
48 And the officers who were over thousands of the campaign, the commanders of thousands and commanders of hundreds, came near to Mosheh,
49 and they said to Mosheh, "Your servants have taken a count of the fighting men under our command, and not a man of us is missing.
50 "So we have brought an offering for יהוה, what every man found of ornaments of gold: armlets and bracelets and signet rings and earrings and necklaces, to make atonement for ourselves before יהוה."
51 And Mosheh and El'azar the priest received the gold from them, all the fashioned ornaments.
52 And all the gold of the offering that they presented to יהוה, from the commanders of thousands and commanders of hundreds, was sixteen thousand seven hundred and fifty sheqels.
53 The men of the campaign had taken spoil, every man for himself.
54 And Mosheh and El'azar the priest received the gold from the commanders of thousands and of hundreds, and brought it into the Tent of Appointment as a remembrance for the children of Yisra'ěl before יהוה.

32 And the children of Re'uḇěn and the children of Gaḏ had much livestock, a large number. And they saw the land of Ya'zěr and the land of Gil'aḏ and saw that the place was a place for livestock.
2 So the children of Gaḏ and the children of Re'uḇěn came and spoke to Mosheh, and to El'azar the priest, and to the leaders of the congregation, saying,
3 "Ataroth, and Diḇon, and Ya'zěr, and Nimrah, and Ḥeshbon, and El'alěh, and Seḇam, and Neḇo, and Be'on,
4 the land which יהוה had stricken before the congregation of Yisra'ěl, is a land for livestock, and your servants have livestock."
5 And they said, "If we have found favour in your eyes, let this land be given to your servants as a possession, and do not let us pass over the Yarděn."
6 And Mosheh said to the children of Gaḏ and to the children of Re'uḇěn, "Are your brothers to go into the battle while you yourselves sit here?
7 "Now why do you discourage the heart of the children of Yisra'ěl from passing over into the land which יהוה has given them?
8 "Thus your fathers did when I sent them away from Qaḏěsh Barněa to see the land.
9 "For when they went up to the wadi Eshkol and saw the land, they discouraged the heart of the children of Yisra'ěl, so that they did not go into the land which יהוה had given them.
10 "Then the displeasure of יהוה burned on that day, and He swore an oath, saying,
11 'Not one of the men who came up from Mitsrayim, from twenty years old and above, is to see the land of which I swore to Aḇraham, Yitsḥaq, and Ya'aqoḇ, because they did not follow Me completely,
12 except Kalěḇ son of Yephunneh, the Qenizzite, and Yehoshua son of Nun, for they have followed יהוה completely.'
13 "So the displeasure of יהוה burned against Yisra'ěl, and He made them wander in the wilderness forty years, until all the generation that had done evil in the eyes of יהוה was destroyed.
14 "And see, you have risen in your father's place, an increase of men, sinners, to add still more the burning displeasure of יהוה against Yisra'ěl.
15 "For if you turn away from following

Him, He shall once again leave them in the wilderness, and you shall destroy all these people."

16 Then they came near to him and said, "Let us build sheep-enclosures here for our livestock, and cities for our little ones,

17 but let us ourselves be armed, hastening before the children of Yisra'ěl until we have brought them to their place. And our little ones shall dwell in the walled cities because of the inhabitants of the land.

18 "We shall not return to our homes until every one of the children of Yisra'ěl has received his inheritance.

19 "For we shall not inherit with them on the other side of the Yarděn and beyond, because our inheritance has fallen to us on this eastern side of the Yarděn."

20 And Mosheh said to them, "If you make this promise: if you arm yourselves before יהוה for battle,

21 and all your armed ones pass over the Yarděn before יהוה until He has driven out His enemies from before Him,

22 and the land has been subdued before יהוה, then afterward you shall return, and be guiltless before יהוה and before Yisra'ěl. And this land shall be your possession before יהוה.

23 "But if you do not do so, then see, you shall sin against יהוה, and know: your sin is going to find you out.

24 "Build cities for your little ones and enclosures for your sheep, and do what you have promised."

25 And the children of Gaḏ and the children of Re'uḇěn spoke to Mosheh, saying, "Your servants are going to do as my master commands.

26 "Our little ones, our wives, our flocks, and all our livestock are going to be there in the cities of Gilʿaḏ,

27 but your servants are passing over, every armed one of the army, before יהוה, to battle, as my master says."

28 And Mosheh gave command concerning them to Elʿazar the priest, to Yehoshua son of Nun, and to the heads of the fathers of the tribes of the children of Yisra'ěl.

29 And Mosheh said to them, "If the children of Gaḏ and the children of Re'uḇěn pass over the Yarděn with you, every man armed for battle before יהוה, and the land has been subdued before you, then you shall give them the land of Gilʿaḏ as a possession.

30 "But if they do not pass over armed with you, they shall have possessions among you in the land of Kenaʿan."

31 Then the children of Gaḏ and the children of Re'uḇěn answered, saying, "As יהוה has said to your servants, so we do.

32 "We ourselves are passing over armed before יהוה into the land of Kenaʿan, but the possession of our inheritance remains with us beyond the Yarděn."

33 So Mosheh gave to the children of Gaḏ, to the children of Re'uḇěn, and to half the tribe of Menashsheh, son of Yosěph, the reign of Siḥon sovereign of the Amorites and the reign of Oḡ sovereign of Bashan, the land with its cities within the borders, the cities of the land round about.

34 And the children of Gaḏ built Diḇon and Ataroth and Aroʿěr,

35 and Atroth, Shophan and Yaʿzěr and Yoḡbehah,

36 and Běyth Nimrah and Běyth Haran, walled cities, and enclosures for sheep.

37 And the children of Re'uḇěn built Ḥeshbon and Elʿalěh and Qiryathayim,

38 Neḇo and Baʿal Meʿon – the names being changed – and Shiḇmah. And they gave other names to the cities which they built.

39 And the sons of Maḵir son of Menashsheh went to Gilʿaḏ and took it, and dispossessed the Amorites who were in it.

40 So Mosheh gave Gilʿaḏ to Maḵir, son of Menashsheh, and he dwelt in it.

41 And Ya'ir son of Menashsheh went and took its small towns, and called them Ḥawoth Ya'ir.

42 And Noḇaḥ went and took Qenath and its villages, and he called it Noḇaḥ, after his own name.

33 These are the departures of the children of Yisra'ěl, who went out of the land of Mitsrayim by their divisions under the hand of Mosheh and Aharon.

2 And Mosheh wrote down the starting points of their departures at the mouth of יהוה, and these are their departures according to their starting points:
3 So they departed from Ra'meses in the first new *moon*, on the fifteenth day of the first new *moon*, on the morrow of the Pěsaḥ the children of Yisra'ěl went out with boldness before the eyes of all the Mitsrites,
4 and the Mitsrites were burying all their first-born, whom יהוה had stricken among them. Also on their mighty ones יהוה had executed judgments.
5 Then the children of Yisra'ěl departed from Ra'meses and camped at Sukkoth.
6 And they departed from Sukkoth and camped at Ětham, which is on the edge of the wilderness.
7 And they departed from Ětham and turned back to Pi Haḥiroth, which is east of Ba'al Tsephon. And they camped near Miḡdol.
8 And they departed from before Haḥiroth and passed over through the midst of the sea into the wilderness, went three days' journey in the Wilderness of Ětham, and camped at Marah.
9 And they departed from Marah and came to Ělim. And at Ělim were twelve springs of water and seventy palm trees, so they camped there.
10 And they departed from Ělim and camped by the Sea of Reeds.
11 And they departed from the Sea of Reeds and camped in the Wilderness of Sin.
12 And they departed from the Wilderness of Sin and camped at Dophqah.
13 And they departed from Dophqah and camped at Alush.
14 And they departed from Alush and camped at Rephiḏim, and there was no water for the people to drink.
15 And they departed from Rephiḏim and camped in the Wilderness of Sinai.
16 And they departed from the Wilderness of Sinai and camped at Qiḇroth Hatta'awah.
17 And they departed from Qiḇroth Hatta'awah and camped at Ḥatsěroth.
18 And they departed from Ḥatsěroth and camped at Rithmah.
19 And they departed from Rithmah and camped at Rimmon Perets.
20 And they departed from Rimmon Perets and camped at Liḇnah.
21 And they departed from Liḇnah and camped at Rissah.
22 And they departed from Rissah and camped at Qehělathah.
23 And they departed from Qehělathah and camped at Mount Shapher.
24 And they departed from Mount Shapher and camped at Ḥaraḏah.
25 And they departed from Ḥaraḏah and camped at Maqhěloth.
26 And they departed from Maqhěloth and camped at Taḥath.
27 And they departed from Taḥath and camped at Teraḥ.
28 And they departed from Teraḥ and camped at Mithqah.
29 And they departed from Mithqah and camped at Ḥashmonah.
30 And they departed from Ḥashmonah and camped at Mosěroth.
31 And they departed from Mosěroth and camped at Beněi Ya'aqan.
32 And they departed from Beněi Ya'aqan and camped at Ḥor Haggiḏgaḏ.
33 And they departed from Ḥor Haggiḏgaḏ and camped at Yotḇathah.
34 And they departed from Yotḇathah and camped at Aḇronah.
35 And they departed from Aḇronah and camped at Etsyon Geḇer.
36 And they departed from Etsyon Geḇer and camped in the Wilderness of Tsin, which is Qaḏěsh.
37 And they departed from Qaḏěsh and camped at Mount Hor, on the boundary of the land of Eḏom.
38 Then Aharon the priest went up to Mount Hor at the mouth of יהוה, and died there in the fortieth year after the children of Yisra'ěl had come out of the land of Mitsrayim, on the first *day* of the fifth new *moon*.
39 Now Aharon was one hundred and twenty-three years old when he died on Mount Hor.

[40]And the sovereign of Araḏ, the Kenaʽanite, who dwelt in the South in the land of Kenaʽan, heard of the coming of the children of Yisra'ĕl.
[41]So they departed from Mount Hor and camped at Tsalmonah.
[42]And they departed from Tsalmonah and camped at Punon.
[43]And they departed from Punon and camped at Oḇoth.
[44]And they departed from Oḇoth and camped at Iyĕ Ha-Aḇarim, at the border of Mo'aḇ.
[45]And they departed from Iyim and camped at Diḇon Gaḏ.
[46]And they departed from Diḇon Gaḏ and camped at Almon Diḇlathayemah.
[47]And they departed from Almon Diḇlathayemah and camped in the mountains of Aḇarim, before Neḇo.
[48]And they departed from the mountains of Aḇarim and camped in the desert plains of Mo'aḇ by the Yardĕn of Yeriḥo.
[49]And they camped by the Yardĕn, from Bĕyth Yeshimoth as far as the Aḇĕl Shittim in the desert plains of Mo'aḇ.
[50]And יהוה spoke to Mosheh in the desert plains of Mo'aḇ by the Yardĕn of Yeriḥo, saying,
[51]"Speak to the children of Yisra'ĕl, and say to them, 'When you have passed over the Yardĕn into the land of Kenaʽan,
[52]then you shall drive out all the inhabitants of the land from before you, and shall destroy all their engraved stones, and shall destroy all their moulded images, and lay waste all their high places,
[53]and you shall possess the land and dwell in it, for I have given you the land to possess.
[54]'And you shall divide the land by lot as an inheritance among your clans. To the larger you give a larger inheritance, and to the smaller you give a smaller inheritance. Wherever the lot falls to anyone, that is his. You inherit according to the tribes of your fathers.
[55]'And if you do not drive out the inhabitants of the land from before you, then it shall be that those whom you let remain shall be pricks in your eyes and thorns in your sides, and they shall trouble you in the land where you dwell.
[56]'And it shall be that I do to you as I thought to do to them.' "

34 And יהוה spoke to Mosheh, saying,
[2]"Command the children of Yisra'ĕl, and say to them, 'When you come into the land of Kenaʽan, this is the land which falls to you as an inheritance, the land of Kenaʽan to its boundaries:
[3]'Then your southern border shall be from the Wilderness of Tsin along the border of Eḏom, and your southern border shall be eastward from the end of the Salt Sea.
[4]'Then your border shall turn from the southern side of the Ascent of Aqrabbim, continue to Tsin, and be on the south of Qaḏĕsh Barnĕa, and it shall go on to Ḥatsar Addar, and continue to Atsmon.
[5]'And the border shall turn from Atsmon to the wadi of Mitsrayim, and it shall end at the Sea.
[6]'As for the western border, you shall have the Great Sea for a border, this is your western border.
[7]'And this is your northern border: From the Great Sea you mark out your borderline to Mount Hor,
[8]from Mount Hor you mark out your border to the entrance of Ḥamath, and the edge of the border shall be toward Tseḏaḏ,
[9]and the border shall proceed to Ziphron, and it shall end at Ḥatsar Ĕnan. This is your northern border.
[10]'And you shall mark out your eastern border from Ḥatsar Ĕnan to Shepham,
[11]and the border shall go down from Shepham to Riḇlah on the east side of Ayin, and the border shall go down and reach to the eastern side of the Sea of Kinnereth.
[12]'And the border shall go down along the Yardĕn, and it shall end at the Salt Sea. This is your land with its surrounding boundaries.' "
[13]And Mosheh commanded the children of Yisra'ĕl, saying, "This is the land which you inherit by lot, which יהוה has commanded to give to the nine tribes and to the

half-tribe.
14 "For the tribe of the children of Re'uḇěn according to the house of their fathers, and the tribe of the children of Gaḏ according to the house of their fathers, have received their inheritance. And the half-tribe of Menashsheh has received its inheritance.
15 "The two tribes and the half-tribe have received their inheritance beyond the Yarděn of Yeriḥo eastward, toward the sunrise."
16 And יהוה spoke to Mosheh, saying,
17 "These are the names of the men who divide the land among you as an inheritance: El'azar the priest, and Yehoshua son of Nun.
18 "And take one leader of every tribe to divide the land for the inheritance.
19 "And these are the names of the men. From the tribe of Yehuḏah: Kalěḇ son of Yephunneh.
20 "And from the tribe of the children of Shim'on: Shemu'ěl son of Ammihuḏ.
21 "From the tribe of Binyamin: Eliḏaḏ son of Kislon.
22 "And a leader from the tribe of the children of Dan: Buqqi son of Yoḡli.
23 "From the sons of Yosěph: a leader from the tribe of the children of Menashsheh, Ḥanni'ěl son of Ěphoḏ.
24 "And a leader from the tribe of the children of Ephrayim: Qemu'ěl son of Shiphtan.
25 "And a leader from the tribe of the children of Zeḇulun: Elitsaphan son of Parnaḵ.
26 "And a leader from the tribe of the children of Yissasḵar: Palti'ěl son of Azzan.
27 "And a leader from the tribe of the children of Ashěr: Aḥihuḏ son of Shelomi.
28 "And a leader from the tribe of the children of Naphtali: Peḏah'ěl son of Ammihuḏ."
29 These are the ones יהוה commanded to divide the inheritance among the children of Yisra'ěl in the land of Kena'an.

35 And יהוה spoke to Mosheh in the desert plains of Mo'aḇ by the Yarděn of Yeriḥo, saying,
2 "Command the children of Yisra'ěl that they shall give the Lěwites cities to dwell in from the inheritance of their possession. Also give the Lěwites open land around the cities.
3 "And they shall have the cities to dwell in, and their open land for their cattle, and for their herds, and for all their livestock.
4 "And the open land of the cities which you give the Lěwites are from the wall of the city outward a thousand cubits all around.
5 "And you shall measure outside the city on the east side two thousand cubits, and on the south side two thousand cubits, and on the west side two thousand cubits, and on the north side two thousand cubits. And the city is in the middle. This is to them the open land for the cities.
6 "And the cities which you give to the Lěwites are the six cities of refuge, which you give to the man-slayer to flee to, and to these you add forty-two cities.
7 "All the cities which you give to the Lěwites are forty-eight, these with their open land.
8 "And the cities which you give are from the possession of the children of Yisra'ěl. From the larger *tribe* you give many, from the smaller you give few, each one gives some of its cities to the Lěwites, in proportion to the inheritance that each inherits."
9 And יהוה spoke to Mosheh, saying,
10 "Speak to the children of Yisra'ěl, and say to them, 'When you pass over the Yarděn into the land of Kena'an,
11 then you shall choose cities to be cities of refuge for you, that the man-slayer who struck someone mistakenly shall flee there.
12 'And they shall be cities of refuge for you from the revenger, and the man-slayer is not to die until he stands before the congregation for right-ruling.
13 'And of the cities which you give, six are to be cities of refuge.
14 'Give three cities beyond the Yarděn, and give three cities in the land of Kena'an, as cities of refuge.
15 'These six cities are for refuge for the children of Yisra'ěl, and for the sojourner, and for the settler in their midst, for any-

one who mistakenly strikes someone to flee there.

16 'But if he has stricken him with an instrument of iron, so that he dies, he is a murderer. The murderer shall certainly be put to death.

17 'And if he has stricken him with a stone in the hand, by which one could die, and he does die, he is a murderer. The murderer shall certainly be put to death.

18 'Or if he has stricken him with a wooden instrument that could kill, and he does die, he is a murderer. The murderer shall certainly be put to death.

19 'The revenger of blood himself puts the murderer to death. When he meets him, he puts him to death.

20 'And if he thrusts him through in hatred, or throws *an object* at him while lying in wait, so that he dies,

21 or in enmity he strikes him with his hand so that he dies, the one who struck him shall certainly be put to death, for he is a murderer. The revenger of blood puts the murderer to death when he meets him.

22 'But if he pushes him suddenly without enmity, or throws *an object* at him without lying in wait,

23 or uses a stone, by which a man could die, throwing it at him without seeing him, so that he dies, while he was not his enemy or seeking his harm,

24 then the congregation shall judge between him who struck someone and the revenger of blood, according to these right-rulings.

25 'And the congregation shall rescue the man-slayer from the hand of the revenger of blood, and the congregation shall return him to the city of refuge where he had fled, and he shall remain there until the death of the high priest who was anointed with the set-apart oil.

26 'But if the man-slayer at any time goes outside the limits of the city of refuge where he fled,

27 and the revenger of blood finds him outside the limits of his city of refuge, and the revenger of blood executes the man-slayer, he is not guilty of blood,

28 because he should have remained in his city of refuge until the death of the high priest. But after the death of the high priest the man-slayer is to return to the land of his possession.

29 'And these shall be for a law of right-ruling to you throughout your generations in all your dwellings.

30 'Whoever strikes a being, the murderer shall be executed by the mouth of witnesses, but one witness does not bear witness against someone to die.

31 'And take no ransom for the life of a murderer who is guilty of death, but he shall certainly be put to death.

32 'And take no ransom for him who has fled to his city of refuge to return to dwell in the land before the death of the priest.

33 'And do not profane the land where you are, for blood profanes the land, and the land is not pardoned for the blood that is shed on it, except by the blood of him who shed it.

34 'And do not defile the land which you inhabit, in the midst of which I dwell, for I, יהוה, am dwelling in the midst of the children of Yisra'ěl.' "

36 And the heads of the fathers of the clans of the children of Gil'aḏ, son of Maḵir, son of Menashsheh, of the clans of the sons of Yosěph, came near and spoke before Mosheh and before the leaders, the heads of the fathers of the children of Yisra'ěl,

2 and said, "יהוה commanded my master to give the land as an inheritance by lot to the children of Yisra'ěl, and my master was commanded by יהוה to give the inheritance of our brother Tselophḥaḏ to his daughters.

3 "Now if they are married to any of the sons of the other tribes of the children of Yisra'ěl, then their inheritance shall be taken from the inheritance of our fathers, and shall be added to the inheritance of the tribe into which they marry, and taken from the lot of our inheritance.

[4]"And if the Yoḇel [a] of the children of Yisra'ěl takes place, then their inheritance shall be added to the inheritance of the tribe into which they marry, and their inheritance taken away from the inheritance of the tribe of our fathers."

[5]And Mosheh commanded the children of Yisra'ěl according to the word of יהוה, saying, "What the tribe of the sons of Yosěph speaks is right.

[6]"This is the word which יהוה has commanded, for the daughters of Tselophḥaḏ, saying, 'Let them marry who is good in their eyes, but let them marry only within the clan of their father's tribe.'

[7]"And the inheritance of the children of Yisra'ěl is not to change hands from tribe to tribe, for every one of the children of Yisra'ěl is to cling to the inheritance of the tribe of his fathers.

[8]"And every daughter possessing an inheritance in any tribe of the children of Yisra'ěl is to be the wife of one of the clan of her father's tribe, so that the children of Yisra'ěl possess each the inheritance of his fathers.

[9]"Thus the inheritance is not to change hands from one tribe to another, but every tribe of the children of Yisra'ěl is to cling to its own inheritance."

[10]As יהוה commanded Mosheh, so did the daughters of Tselophḥaḏ.

[11]For Maḥlah, Tirtsah, and Ḥoḡlah, and Milkah, and No'ah, the daughters of Tselophḥaḏ, were married to the sons of their father's brothers.

[12]And they were married into the clans of the children of Menashsheh, the son of Yosěph, and their inheritance remained in the tribe of their father's clan.

[13]These are the commands and the right-rulings which יהוה commanded the children of Yisra'ěl by the hand of Mosheh in the desert plains of Mo'aḇ by the Yarděn of Yeriḥo.

36a See Explanatory notes: Yoḇel

DEḆARIM

DEUTERONOMY

1 These are the words which Mosheh
spoke to all Yisra'ěl beyond the
Yarděn in the wilderness, in the desert
plain opposite Suph, between Paran and
Tophel, and Laḇan, and Ḥatsěroth, and Di
Zahaḇ,
2 eleven days' *journey* from Ḥorěḇ by
way of Mount Sě'ir to Qaḏěsh Barněa.
3 And it came to be in the fortieth year, in
the eleventh new *moon*, on the first *day* of
the new *moon*, that Mosheh spoke to the
children of Yisra'ěl according to all that
יהוה had commanded him concerning
them,
4 after he had stricken Siḥon sovereign of
the Amorites, who dwelt in Ḥeshbon, and
Oḡ sovereign of Bashan, who dwelt at
Ashtaroth in Eḏre'i.
5 Beyond the Yarděn, in the land of
Mo'aḇ, Mosheh undertook to declare this
Torah, saying,
6 "יהוה our Elohim spoke to us in Ḥorěḇ,
saying, 'You have dwelt long enough at
this mountain.
7 'Turn and set out on your way, and go
into the mountains of the Amorites, and to
all the neighbouring places in the desert
plain, in the mountains and in the low
country, and in the Negeḇ and on the seacoast, to the land of the Kena'anites and to
Leḇanon, as far as the great river, the River
Euphrates.
8 'See, I have set the land before you. Go
in and possess the land which יהוה swore
to your fathers, to Aḇraham, to Yitsḥaq,
and to Ya'aqoḇ, to give to them and their
seed after them.'
9 "And I spoke to you at that time,
saying, 'I am unable to bear you by myself.
10 'יהוה your Elohim has increased you,
and see, you are today as numerous as the
stars of the heavens.
11 'יהוה Elohim of your fathers is going to
add to you a thousand times more than you
are, and bless you as He has spoken to you!
12 'How do I bear your pressure and your
burden and your strife, by myself?
13 'Choose men, wise and understanding,
and known to your tribes, and let me
appoint them as your heads.'
14 "And you answered me and said, 'The
word which you have spoken to us to do is
good.'
15 "And I took the heads of your tribes,
wise men and known, and made them
heads over you, leaders of thousands, and
leaders of hundreds, and leaders of fifties,
and leaders of tens, and officers for your
tribes.
16 "And I commanded your judges at that
time, saying, 'When hearing between your
brothers, judge righteously between a man
and his brother or the stranger who is with
him.
17 'Do not show partiality in right-ruling,
hear the small as well as the great. Do not
be afraid of anyone's face, for the right-
ruling belongs to Elohim. And the case
which is too hard for you, bring it to me,
and I shall hear it.'
18 "And I commanded you at that time all
the words which you should do.
19 "Then we set out from Ḥorěḇ, and went
through all that great and awesome wilderness which you saw on the way to the
mountains of the Amorites, as יהוה our
Elohim had commanded us. And we came
to Qaḏěsh Barněa.
20 "And I said to you, 'You have come to
the mountains of the Amorites, which יהוה
our Elohim is giving us.
21 'See, יהוה your Elohim has set the land
before you. Go up and possess it, as יהוה
Elohim of your fathers has spoken to you.
Do not fear, nor be discouraged.'
22 "And all of you came near to me and
said, 'Let us send men before us, and let
them search out the land for us, and bring
back word to us of the way by which we
should go up, and of the cities into which

we would come.’

23 “And the matter was good in my eyes, so I took twelve of your men, one man from each tribe.

24 “And they turned and went up into the mountains, and came to the wadi Eshkol, and spied it out.

25 “And they took some of the fruit of the land in their hands and brought it down to us. And they brought back word to us, saying, ‘The land which יהוה our Elohim is giving us is good.’

26 “But you would not go up and rebelled against the mouth of יהוה your Elohim,

27 and grumbled in your tents, and said, ‘Because יהוה was hating us, He has brought us out of the land of Mitsrayim to give us into the hand of the Amorites, to destroy us.

28 ‘Where are we going to? Our brothers have made our hearts melt, saying, “The people are greater and taller than we, the cities are great and walled up to the heavens, and we saw the sons of the Anaqim there too.” ’

29 “Then I said to you, ‘Have no dread or fear of them.

30 ‘יהוה your Elohim, who is going before you, He does fight for you, according to all He did for you in Mitsrayim before your eyes,

31 and in the wilderness, where you saw how יהוה your Elohim has borne you, as a man bears his son, in all the way that you went until you came to this place.’

32 “Yet in this matter you are putting no trust in יהוה your Elohim,

33 who is going before you in the way to seek out a place for you to pitch your tents, to show you the way you should go, in fire by night and in a cloud by day.

34 “And יהוה heard the voice of your words, and was wroth, and took an oath, saying,

35 ‘Not one of these men of this evil generation shall see that good land of which I swore to give to your fathers,

36 except Kalĕḇ son of Yephunneh. He shall see it, and to him and his children I give the land on which he walked, because he followed יהוה completely.’

37 “And יהוה was enraged with me for your sakes, saying, ‘You do not go in there, either.

38 ‘Yehoshua the son of Nun, who stands before you, he shall go in there. Strengthen him, for he shall cause Yisra’ĕl to inherit.

39 ‘And your little ones and your children, who you say are for a prey, who today have no knowledge of good and evil, they are going in there. And to them I give it, and they are to possess it.

40 ‘But you, turn and take your journey into the wilderness by the Way of the Sea of Reeds.’

41 “Then you answered and said to me, ‘We have sinned against יהוה. We ourselves are going up, and we shall fight, as יהוה our Elohim commanded us.’ And when each one of you had girded on his battle gear, you were ready to go up into the mountain.

42 “And יהוה said to me, ‘Say to them, “Do not go up nor fight, for I am not in your midst, lest you be smitten before your enemies.” ’

43 “So I spoke to you, but you would not listen and rebelled against the mouth of יהוה, and acted proudly, and went up into the mountain.

44 “Then the Amorites who dwelt in that mountain came out against you and chased you as bees do, and drove you back from Sĕ‘ir to Ḥormah.

45 “And you returned and wept before יהוה, but יהוה would not listen to your voice nor give ear to you.

46 “So you dwelt in Qaḏĕsh many days, according to the days that you dwelt.

2 “Then we turned and set out into the wilderness, the way of the Sea of Reeds, as יהוה spoke to me, and we went round Mount Sĕ‘ir, many days.

2 “And יהוה spoke to me, saying,

3 ‘You have gone around this mountain long enough, turn northward.

4 ‘And command the people, saying, “You are about to pass over into the border of your brothers, the descendants of Ĕsaw, who live in Sĕ‘ir, and they are afraid of you. So be on your guard.

5 "Do not strive with them, for I do not
give you any of their land, no, not so much
as one footstep, because I have given
Mount Sĕ'ir to Ěsaw as a possession.
6 "What food you buy from them with
silver you shall eat. And also, what water
you buy from them with silver you shall
drink.
7 "For יהוה your Elohim has blessed you
in all the work of your hand. He has known
your wandering through this great wilderness. These forty years יהוה your Elohim
has been with you, you have not lacked
any matter." '
8 "And when we passed beyond our
brothers, the descendants of Ěsaw who
dwell in Sĕ'ir, away from the way of the
desert plain, away from Ěylath and Etsyon
Geḇer, we turned and passed over by way
of the Wilderness of Mo'aḇ.
9 "And יהוה said to me, 'Do not distress
Mo'aḇ, nor stir yourself up against them
in battle, for I do not give you any of their
land as a possession, because I have given
Ar to the descendants of Lot as a possession.' "
10 (The Ěmites had dwelt there formerly, a
people as great and numerous and tall as
the Anaqim.
11 They were also reckoned as Repha'ites,
like the Anaqim, but the Mo'aḇites call
them Ěmites.
12 And the Ḥorites formerly dwelt in Sĕ'ir,
but the descendants of Ěsaw dispossessed
them and destroyed them from before
them, and dwelt in their place, as Yisra'ĕl
did to the land of their possession which
יהוה gave them).
13 " 'Now rise up, and pass over the wadi
Zereḏ.' So we passed over the wadi Zereḏ.
14 "And the time we took to come from
Qaḏĕsh Barněa until we passed over the
wadi Zereḏ was thirty-eight years, until all
the generation of the men of battle was
consumed from the midst of the camp, as
יהוה had sworn to them.
15 "And also, the hand of יהוה was against
them, to destroy them from the midst of the
camp until they were consumed.
16 "And it came to be, when all the men of
battle had finally perished from among the
people,
17 that יהוה spoke to me, saying,
18 'This day you are to pass over at Ar, the
boundary of Mo'aḇ.
19 'And when you come near the children
of Ammon, do not distress them nor stir
yourself up against them, for I do not give
you any of the land of the children of
Ammon as a possession, because I have
given it to the descendants of Lot as a
possession.'
20 (That was also reckoned as a land of
Repha'ites. Repha'ites formerly dwelt
there. But the Ammonites call them
Zamzummim,
21 a people as great and numerous and tall
as the Anaqim. But יהוה destroyed them
before them, and they dispossessed them
and dwelt in their place,
22 as He had done for the descendants of
Ěsaw, who dwelt in Sĕ'ir, when He
destroyed the Ḥorites from before them.
They dispossessed them and dwelt in their
place, even to this day.
23 And the Awwim who dwelt in villages
as far as Azzah, the Kaphtorim who came
from Kaphtor, destroyed them and dwelt in
their place).
24 'Arise, set out and pass over the wadi
Arnon. See, I have given into your hand
Siḥon the Amorite, sovereign of Ḥeshbon,
and his land. Begin to possess it, and stir
up yourself against him in battle.
25 'This day I begin to put the dread and
fear of you upon the peoples under all the
heavens, who, when they hear the report of
you, shall tremble and shake because of
you.'
26 "Then I sent messengers from the
Wilderness of Qeḏĕmoth to Siḥon sovereign of Ḥeshbon, with words of peace,
saying,
27 'Let me pass over through your land on
the highway. I shall go on the highway and
turn neither to the right nor to the left.
28 'What food you sell me for silver I shall
eat, and what water you give me for silver I
shall drink. Only let me pass over on foot,
29 as the descendants of Ěsaw who dwell
in Sĕ'ir and the Mo'aḇites who dwell in Ar
did for me – until I pass over the Yarděn to

the land יהוה our Elohim is giving us.’

30 “But Siḥon sovereign of Ḥeshbon would not let us pass over, for יהוה your Elohim hardened his spirit and strengthened his heart, to give him into your hand, as it is this day.

31 “And יהוה said to me, ‘See, I have begun to give Siḥon and his land over to you. Begin to possess – in order to possess his land.’

32 “And Siḥon and all his people came out against us to fight at Yahats,

33 and יהוה our Elohim gave him over to us, so we struck him, and his sons, and all his people.

34 “And we took all his cities at that time, and we put the men, women, and little ones of every city under the ban, we left none remaining.

35 “Only the livestock we took as plunder for ourselves, and the spoil of the cities which we captured.

36 “From Aro‛ĕr, which is on the edge of the wadi Arnon, and the city that is by the wadi, as far as Gil‛aḏ, there was not one city too high for us. יהוה our Elohim gave all to us.

37 “Only you did not go near the land of the children of Ammon – anywhere along the wadi Yabboq, or to the cities of the mountains, or anywhere as יהוה our Elohim commanded us.

3 “Then we turned and went up the way to Bashan. And Oḡ sovereign of Bashan came out against us, he and all his people, to battle at Eḏre‛i.

2 “And יהוה said to me, ‘Do not fear him, for I have given him and all his people and his land into your hand. And you shall do to him as you did to Siḥon sovereign of the Amorites, who dwelt at Ḥeshbon.’

3 “So יהוה our Elohim also gave into our hands Oḡ sovereign of Bashan, with all his people, and we struck him until he had no survivors remaining.

4 “And we captured all his cities at that time. There was not a city which we did not take from them: sixty cities, all the district of Argoḇ, the reign of Oḡ in Bashan.

5 “All these cities were fenced with high walls, gates and bars, besides a great many unwalled towns.

6 “And we put them under the ban, as we did to Siḥon sovereign of Ḥeshbon, putting the men, the women, and the children of every city under the ban.

7 “But all the livestock and the spoil of the cities we took as booty for ourselves.

8 “And at that time we took the land, from the hand of the two sovereigns of the Amorites, that was beyond the Yardĕn, from the wadi Arnon to Mount Ḥermon

9 “(Tsiḏonians call Ḥermon, Siryon – and the Amorites call it Senir),

10 all the cities of the plain, all Gil‛aḏ, and all Bashan, as far as Salḵah and Eḏre‛i, cities of the reign of Oḡ in Bashan.

11 “For only Oḡ sovereign of Bashan was left of the remnant of the Repha’ites. See, his bedstead was an iron bedstead. Is it not in Rabbah of the children of Ammon? Nine cubits is its length and four cubits its width, according to the cubit of a man.

12 “And this land, which we possessed at that time, from Aro‛ĕr, which is by the wadi Arnon, and half the mountains of Gil‛aḏ and its cities, I gave to the Re’uḇĕnites and the Gaḏites.

13 “And the rest of Gil‛aḏ, and all Bashan, the reign of Oḡ, I gave to half the tribe of Menashsheh – all the district of Argoḇ, with all Bashan, called the land of the Repha’ites.

14 “Ya‛ir son of Menashsheh had taken all the district of Argoḇ, as far as the border of the Geshurites and the Ma‛aḵathites, and called them after his own name: the Bashan of Hawoth Ya‛ir, to this day.

15 “And to Maḵir I gave Gil‛aḏ.

16 “And to the Re’uḇĕnites and the Gaḏites I gave from Gil‛aḏ as far as the wadi Arnon, the middle of the wadi as the border, as far as the wadi Yabboq, the border of the children of Ammon,

17 and the desert plain, with the Yardĕn as the border, from Kinnereth as far as the Sea of the Araḇah, the Salt Sea, below the slopes of Pisgah on the east.

18 “And I commanded you at that time, saying, ‘יהוה your Elohim has given you

this land to possess. All you sons of might, pass over armed before your brothers, the children of Yisra'ěl.

19 'But let your wives and your little ones, and your livestock – I know that you have much livestock – stay in your cities which I have given you,

20 until יהוה has given rest to your brothers as to you, and they also possess the land which יהוה your Elohim is giving them beyond the Yarděn. Then you shall return, each man to his possession which I have given you.'

21 "And I commanded Yehoshua at that time, saying, 'Your eyes have seen all that יהוה your Elohim has done to these two sovereigns. יהוה does the same to all the reigns which you are passing over.

22 'Do not fear them, for יהוה your Elohim Himself fights for you.'

23 "And I pleaded with יהוה at that time, saying,

24 'O Master יהוה, You have begun to show Your servant Your greatness and Your strong hand, for who is a mighty one in the heavens or on earth who does according to Your works and according to Your might?

25 'I pray, let me pass over and see the good land beyond the Yarděn, this good hill country, and Leḇanon.'

26 "But יהוה was enraged with me, for your sake, and would not listen to me, and יהוה said to me, 'Enough of that! Speak no more to Me about this matter.

27 'Go up to the top of Pisgah, and lift up your eyes westward, and northward, and southward, and eastward, and look with your eyes, for you do not pass over this Yarděn.

28 'But command Yehoshua, and strengthen him and make him brave, for he shall pass over before this people and cause them to inherit the land which you see.'

29 "And we dwelt in the valley opposite Běyth Pe'or.

4 "And now, O Yisra'ěl, listen to the laws and the right-rulings which I am teaching you to do, so that you live, and shall go in and possess the land which יהוה Elohim of your fathers is giving you.

2 "Do not add to the Word which I command you, and do not take away from it,[a] so as to guard the commands of יהוה your Elohim which I am commanding you.

3 "Your eyes have seen what יהוה did at Ba'al Pe'or, for יהוה your Elohim has destroyed from your midst all the men who followed Ba'al Pe'or.

4 "But you who are clinging to יהוה your Elohim are alive today, every one of you.

5 "See, I have taught you laws and right-rulings, as יהוה my Elohim commanded me, to do thus in the land which you go to possess.

6 "And you shall guard and do them, for this is your wisdom and your understanding before the eyes of the peoples who hear all these laws, and they shall say, 'Only a wise and understanding people is this great nation!'

7 "For what great nation is there which has Elohim so near to it, as יהוה our Elohim is to us, whenever we call on Him?

8 "And what great nation is there that has such laws and righteous right-rulings like all this Torah which I set before you this day?

9 "Only, guard yourself, and guard your life diligently, lest you forget the Words your eyes have seen, and lest they turn aside from your heart all the days of your life. And you shall make them known to your children and your grandchildren.

10 "The day when you stood before יהוה your Elohim in Ḥorěḇ, יהוה said to me, 'Assemble the people to Me and I make them hear My Words, so that they learn to fear Me all the days they live on the earth and teach *them to* their children.'

11 "And you came near and stood at the foot of the mountain, and the mountain burned with fire to the heart of the heavens – darkness, cloud, and thick darkness.

12 "And יהוה spoke to you out of the

4a See also 12:32, Mish. 30:6, Ḥazon 22:18-19.

midst of the fire. You heard a voice of words, but saw no form, you only heard a voice.

13 "And He made known to you His covenant which He commanded you to do, the Ten Words, and He wrote them on two tablets of stone.

14 "And יהוה commanded me at that time to teach you laws and right-rulings, for you to do them in the land which you pass over to possess.

15 "Therefore, diligently guard yourselves, for you saw no form when יהוה spoke to you at Ḥorěḇ out of the midst of the fire,

16 lest you should do corruptly and shall make for yourselves a carved image in the form of any figure – the likeness of male or female,

17 the likeness of any beast that is on the earth or the likeness of any winged bird that flies in the heavens,

18 the likeness of any *creature* that creeps on the ground or the likeness of any fish that is in the water under the earth;

19 and lest you lift up your eyes to the heavens, and shall see the sun, and the moon, and the stars – all the host of the heavens – and you be drawn away into bowing down to them and serving them, which יהוה your Elohim has allotted to all the peoples under all the heavens.

20 "But יהוה has taken you and brought you out of the iron furnace, out of Mitsrayim, to be His people, an inheritance, as it is today.

21 "And יהוה was enraged with me because of your words, and swore that I would not pass over the Yarděn, and that I would not enter the good land which יהוה your Elohim is giving you as an inheritance.

22 "For I am to die in this land, I am not passing over the Yarděn, but you are passing over, and shall possess that good land.

23 "Guard yourselves, lest you forget the covenant of יהוה your Elohim which He made with you, and shall make for yourselves a carved image in any form, as יהוה your Elohim has commanded you.

24 "For יהוה your Elohim is a consuming fire, a jealous Ěl.

25 "When you bring forth children and grandchildren, and shall grow old in the land, and shall do corruptly and make a carved image in the form of whatever, and shall do what is evil in the eyes of יהוה your Elohim to provoke Him,

26 "I shall call the heavens and earth to witness against you on that day, that you soon completely perish from the land which you pass over the Yarděn to possess – you do not prolong your days in it but are completely destroyed.

27 "And יהוה shall scatter you among the peoples, and you shall be left few in number among the nations where יהוה drives you.

28 "And there you shall serve mighty ones, the work of men's hands, wood and stone, which neither see nor hear nor eat nor smell.

29 "But from there you shall seek יהוה your Elohim, and shall find, when you search for Him with all your heart [b] and with all your being.

30 "In your distress, when all these words shall come upon you in the latter days, then you shall return to יהוה your Elohim and shall obey His voice.

31 "For יהוה your Elohim is a compassionate Ěl, He does not forsake you, nor destroy you, nor forget the covenant of your fathers which He swore to them.

32 "For ask now of the days that are past, which were before you, since the day that Elohim created man on the earth, and ask from one end of the heavens to the other end of the heavens, whether there has been a Word as great as this, or has been heard like it.

33 "Has a people heard the voice of Elohim speaking out of the midst of the fire, as you have heard, and live?

34 "Or has Elohim tried to go and take for Himself a nation from the midst of a nation by trials, and by signs, and by wonders, and by battle, and by a strong hand and an

4b Yirm. 29:13.

outstretched arm, and by great fearsome
deeds, according to all that יהוה your
Elohim did for you in Mitsrayim before
your eyes?
35 "You have been shown it, to know that
יהוה Himself is Elohim; there is no one
beside Him.
36 "From the heavens He let you hear His
voice, to instruct you, and on earth He
showed you His great fire, and you heard
His words out of the midst of the fire.
37 "And because He loved your fathers,
therefore He chose their seed after them,
and brought you out of Mitsrayim with His
Presence, with His great power,
38 to drive out from before you nations
greater and stronger than you, to bring you
in, to give you their land as an inheritance,
as it is today.
39 "And you shall know today, and shall
recall to your heart that יהוה Himself is
Elohim in the heavens above and on the
earth beneath; there is none else.
40 "And you shall guard His laws and His
commands which I command you today,
so that it is well with you and with your
children after you, and so that you prolong
your days on the soil which יהוה your
Elohim is giving you for all time."
41 Then Mosheh separated three cities
beyond the Yardĕn, toward the rising of the
sun,
42 for a man-slayer to flee there, he who
unknowingly murdered his neighbour,
without having hated him in time past, and
might flee to one of these cities and live:
43 Betser in the wilderness in the level
land for the Re'uḇĕnites, and Ramoth in
Gil'aḏ for the Gaḏites, and Golan in
Bashan for the Menashshites.
44 And this is the Torah which Mosheh set
before the children of Yisra'ĕl.
45 These are the witnesses, and the laws,
and the right-rulings which Mosheh spoke
to the children of Yisra'ĕl after they came
out of Mitsrayim,
46 beyond the Yardĕn, in the valley opposite Bĕyth Pe'or, in the land of Siḥon
sovereign of the Amorites, who dwelt at
Ḥeshbon, whom Mosheh and the children
of Yisra'ĕl had stricken after they came out
of Mitsrayim.
47 And they took possession of his land
and the land of Oḡ sovereign of Bashan,
two sovereigns of the Amorites, who were
beyond the Yardĕn, toward the rising of the
sun,
48 from Aro'ĕr, which is on the bank of the
wadi Arnon, even to Mount Siyon, which
is Ḥermon,
49 and all the desert plain beyond the
Yardĕn as far as the Sea of the Araḇah,
below the slopes of Pisgah.

5 And Mosheh called all Yisra'ĕl, and
said to them, "Hear, O Yisra'ĕl, the
laws and right-rulings which I speak in
your hearing today. And you shall learn
them, and guard to do them.
2 "יהוה our Elohim made a covenant
with us in Ḥorĕḇ.
3 "יהוה did not make this covenant with
our fathers, but with us, those who are here
today, all of us who are alive.
4 "יהוה spoke with you face to face on
the mountain from the midst of the fire.
5 "I stood between יהוה and you at that
time, to declare to you the Word of יהוה –
for you were afraid because of the fire, and
you did not go up the mountain – saying:
6 'I am יהוה your Elohim who brought
you out of the land of Mitsrayim, out of the
house of bondage.
7 'You have no other mighty ones against
My face.
8 'You do not make for yourself a carved
image, any likeness of which is in the
heavens above, or which is in the earth
beneath, or which is in the waters under the
earth,
9 you do not bow down to them nor serve
them. For I, יהוה your Elohim, am a jealous Ĕl, visiting the crookedness of the
fathers upon the children to the third and
fourth *generations* of those who hate Me,
10 but showing loving-commitment to
thousands, to those who love Me and guard
My commands.

[11]'You do not bring [a] the Name of יהוה your Elohim to naught, for יהוה does not leave him unpunished who brings His Name to naught.

[12]'Guard the Sabbath day, to set it apart, as יהוה your Elohim commanded you.

[13]'Six days you labour, and shall do all your work,

[14]but the seventh day is a Sabbath [b] of יהוה your Elohim. You do not do any work – you, nor your son, nor your daughter, nor your male servant, nor your female servant, nor your ox, nor your donkey, nor any of your cattle, nor your stranger who is within your gates, so that your male servant and your female servant rest as you do.

[15]'And you shall remember that you were a slave in the land of Mitsrayim, and that יהוה your Elohim brought you out from there by a strong hand and by an outstretched arm. Therefore יהוה your Elohim commanded you to perform the Sabbath day.

[16]'Respect your father and your mother, as יהוה your Elohim has commanded you, so that your days are prolonged, and so that it is well with you on the soil which יהוה your Elohim is giving you.

[17]'You do not murder.

[18]'You do not commit adultery.

[19]'You do not steal.

[20]'You do not bear false witness against your neighbour.

[21]'You do not covet your neighbour's wife, nor do you desire your neighbour's house, his field, nor his male servant, nor his female servant, his ox, nor his donkey, or whatever belongs to your neighbour.'

[22]"These Words [c] יהוה spoke to all your assembly, in the mountain from the midst of the fire, of the cloud, and of the thick darkness, with a loud voice, and He added no more. And He wrote them on two tablets of stone and gave them to me.

[23]"And it came to be, when you heard the voice from the midst of the darkness, while the mountain was burning with fire, that you came near to me, all the heads of your tribes and your elders,

[24]and said, 'See, יהוה our Elohim has shown us His esteem and His greatness, and we have heard His voice from the midst of the fire. Today we have seen that Elohim speaks with man – and he lives!

[25]'And now why should we die? For this great fire is consuming us. If we hear the voice of יהוה our Elohim any more, then we shall die.

[26]'For who is there of all flesh who has heard the voice of the living Elohim speaking from the midst of the fire, as we have, and does live?

[27]'You go near and hear all that יהוה our Elohim says, and speak to us all that יהוה our Elohim says to you, and we shall hear and do it.'

[28]"And יהוה heard the voice of your words when you spoke to me, and יהוה said to me, 'I have heard the voice of the words of this people which they have spoken to you. They have done well in all that they have spoken.

[29]'Oh, that they had such a heart in them, to fear Me and to guard all My commands always, so that it might be well with them and with their children forever!

[30]'Go, say to them, "Return to your tents."

[31]'But you, stand here by Me, and let Me speak to you all the commands, and the laws, and the right-rulings which you are to teach them. And they shall do them in the land which I am giving them to possess.'

[32]"And you shall guard to do as יהוה your Elohim has commanded you – do not turn aside, to the right or to the left.

[33]"Walk in all the ways which יהוה your Elohim has commanded you, so that you live and it be well with you. And you shall prolong your days in the land which you possess.

6 "And this is the command, the laws and right-rulings which יהוה your

5a Or *lift up*, or *take*. 5b See footnote at Shem. 20:10.
5c "Word(s)" is very often used as a synonym for "command(s)," in the Messianic Writings too.

Elohim has commanded, to teach you to do in the land which you are passing over to possess,

2so that you fear יהוה your Elohim, to guard all His laws and His commands which I command you, you and your son and your grandson, all the days of your life, and that your days be prolonged.

3"And you shall hear, O Yisra'ěl, and shall guard to do, that it might be well with you, and that you increase greatly as יהוה Elohim of your fathers has spoken to you, *in* a land flowing with milk and honey.

4"Hear, O Yisra'ěl: יהוה our Elohim, יהוה is one!

5"And you shall love יהוה your Elohim with all your heart, and with all your being, and with all your might.

6"And these Words[a] which I am commanding you today shall be in your heart,

7and you shall impress them upon your children, and shall speak of them when you sit in your house, and when you walk by the way, and when you lie down, and when you rise up,

8and shall bind them as a sign on your hand, and they shall be as frontlets between your eyes.

9"And you shall write them on the doorposts of your house and on your gates.

10"And it shall be, when יהוה your Elohim brings you into the land of which He swore to your fathers, to Aḇraham, to Yitsḥaq, and to Ya'aqoḇ, to give you great and good cities which you did not build,

11and houses filled with all kinds of goods, which you did not fill, and wells dug which you did not dig, vineyards and olive trees which you did not plant, and you shall eat and be satisfied –

12be on guard, lest you forget יהוה who brought you out of the land of Mitsrayim, from the house of bondage.

13"Fear יהוה your Elohim and serve Him, and swear by His Name.

14"Do not go after other mighty ones, the mighty ones of the peoples who are all around you,

15for יהוה your Elohim is a jealous Ěl in your midst, lest the displeasure of יהוה your Elohim burn against you, then He shall destroy you from the face of the earth.

16"Do not try יהוה your Elohim as you tried Him in Massah.

17"Diligently guard the commands of יהוה your Elohim, and His witnesses, and His laws which He has commanded you.

18"And you shall do what is right and good in the eyes of יהוה, that it might be well with you, and you shall go in and possess the good land of which יהוה swore to your fathers,

19to drive out all your enemies from before you, as יהוה has spoken.

20"When your son asks you in time to come, saying, 'What is the meaning of the witnesses, and the laws, and the right-rulings which יהוה our Elohim has commanded you?'

21then you shall say to your son, 'We were slaves of Pharaoh in Mitsrayim, and יהוה brought us out of Mitsrayim with a strong hand,

22and יהוה sent signs and wonders, great and grievous, upon Mitsrayim, upon Pharaoh, and upon all his household, before our eyes.

23'And He brought us out from there, to bring us in, to give us the land of which He swore to our fathers.

24'And יהוה commanded us to do all these laws, to fear יהוה our Elohim, for our good always, to keep us alive, as it is today.

25'And it is righteousness for us when we guard to do all this command[b] before יהוה our Elohim, as He has commanded us.'

7

"When יהוה your Elohim brings you into the land which you go to possess, He shall also clear away many nations before you: the Ḥittites and the Girgashites and the Amorites and the Kena'anites and the Perizzites and the Ḥiwwites and the Yeḇusites, seven nations greater and

6a See footnote at 5:22. *6b* "Command," singular, very often has the meaning of "commands," plural. See also Teh. 119:172 and in Yesh. 51:7.

mightier than you.
[2]"And when יהוה your Elohim gives
them over to you, you shall strike them and
put them under the ban, completely. Make
no covenant with them, and show them no
favour.
[3]"And do not intermarry with them –
you do not give your daughter to his son,
and you do not take his daughter for your
son,
[4]for he turns your sons away from following Me, to serve other mighty ones.
Then the displeasure of יהוה shall burn
against you and promptly destroy you.
[5]"But this is what you do to them: Break
down their slaughter-places, and smash
their pillars, and cut down their Ashĕrim,
and burn their carved images with fire.
[6]"For you are a set-apart people to יהוה
your Elohim. יהוה your Elohim has chosen
you to be a people for Himself, a treasured
possession above all the peoples on the
face of the earth.
[7]"יהוה did not set His love on you nor
choose you because you were more numerous than any other people, for you were the
least of all peoples,
[8]but because of יהוה loving you, and
because of Him guarding the oath which
He swore to your fathers, יהוה has brought
you out with a strong hand, and ransomed
you from the house of bondage, from the
hand of Pharaoh sovereign of Mitsrayim.
[9]"And you shall know that יהוה your
Elohim, He is Elohim, the trustworthy Ěl
guarding covenant and loving-commitment
for a thousand generations with those who
love Him, and those who guard His commands,
[10]but repaying those who hate Him to
their face, to destroy them. He does not
delay *to do so* with him who hates Him, He
repays him to his face.
[11]"And you shall guard the command,
and the laws, and the right-rulings which I
command you today, to do them.
[12]"And it shall be, because you hear these
right-rulings, and shall guard and do them,
that יהוה your Elohim shall guard with you
the covenant and the loving-commitment
which He swore to your fathers,
[13]and shall love you and bless you and
increase you, and shall bless the fruit of
your womb and the fruit of your land, your
grain and your new wine and your oil, the
increase of your cattle and the offspring of
your flock, in the land of which He swore
to your fathers to give you.
[14]"Blessed are you above all peoples –
there is not going to be a barren man or a
barren woman among you or among your
livestock.
[15]"And יהוה shall turn away from you all
sickness and put on you none of the evil
diseases of Mitsrayim which you have
known, but He shall put them on all those
who hate you.
[16]"And you shall consume all the peoples
whom יהוה your Elohim is delivering over
to you – your eye shall not pardon them.
And do not serve their mighty ones, for
that is a snare to you.
[17]"When you say in your heart, 'These
nations are greater than I, I am unable to
drive them out,'
[18]do not be afraid of them. Remember
well what יהוה your Elohim did to Pharaoh
and to all Mitsrayim,
[19]the great trials which your eyes saw,
and the signs and the wonders, the strong
hand and the outstretched arm, by which
יהוה your Elohim brought you out. יהוה
your Elohim does so to all the peoples of
whom you are afraid.
[20]"And יהוה your Elohim also sends the
hornet among them until those who are
left, who hide themselves from you, are
destroyed.
[21]"Do not be afraid of them, for יהוה
your Elohim, the great and awesome Ěl, is
in your midst.
[22]"And יהוה your Elohim shall drive out
those nations before you, little by little.
You are not allowed to destroy them at
once, lest the beasts of the field become
too numerous for you.
[23]"But יהוה your Elohim shall deliver
them over to you and destroy them with a
great destruction until they are consumed.
[24]"And He shall give their sovereigns
into your hand, and you shall destroy their
name from under the heavens. No one is

going to be able to stand against you until
you have destroyed them.
25 "The carved images of their mighty
ones you are to burn with fire. Do not
covet the silver or gold that is on them, nor
take it for yourselves, lest you be snared by
it, for it is an abomination to יהוה your
Elohim.
26 "And do not bring an abomination into
your house, lest you be accursed like it.
Utterly loathe it and utterly hate it, for it is
accursed.

8 "Guard to do every command which I
command you today, that you might
live, and shall increase, and go in, and shall
possess the land of which יהוה swore to
your fathers.
2 "And you shall remember that יהוה
your Elohim led you all the way these forty
years in the wilderness, to humble you,
prove you, to know what is in your heart,
whether you guard His commands or not.
3 "And He humbled you, and let you suffer hunger, and fed you with manna which
you did not know nor did your fathers
know, to make you know that man does
not live by bread alone, but by every *Word*
that comes from the mouth of יהוה. [a]
4 "Your garments did not wear out on
you, nor did your foot swell these forty
years.
5 "Thus you shall know in your heart that
as a man disciplines his son, so יהוה your
Elohim disciplines you,
6 therefore you shall guard the commands of יהוה your Elohim, to walk in His
ways and to fear Him.
7 "For יהוה your Elohim is bringing you
into a good land, a land of streams of
water, of fountains and springs, that flow
out of valleys and hills,
8 a land of wheat and barley, of vines and
fig trees and pomegranates, a land of olive
oil and honey,
9 a land in which you eat bread without
scarcity, in which you do not lack at all, a
land whose stones are iron and out of
whose hills you dig copper.
10 "And you shall eat and be satisfied, and
shall bless יהוה your Elohim for the good
land which He has given you.
11 "Be on guard, lest you forget יהוה your
Elohim by not guarding His commands,
and His right-rulings, and His laws which I
command you today,
12 lest you eat and shall be satisfied, and
build lovely houses and shall dwell in
them,
13 and your herds and your flocks
increase, and your silver and your gold are
increased, and all that you have is
increased,
14 that your heart then becomes lifted up,
and you forget יהוה your Elohim who
brought you out of the land of Mitsrayim,
from the house of bondage,
15 who led you through that great and
awesome wilderness – fiery serpents and
scorpions and thirst – where there was no
water, who brought water for you out of
the flinty rock,
16 who fed you in the wilderness with
manna, which your fathers did not know,
in order to humble you and to try you, to
do you good in the end,
17 you then shall say in your heart, 'My
power and the strength of my hand have
made for me this wealth!'
18 "But you shall remember יהוה your
Elohim, for it is He who gives you power
to get wealth, in order to establish His
covenant which He swore to your fathers,
as it is today.
19 "And it shall be, if you by any means
forget יהוה your Elohim, and follow other
mighty ones, and serve them and bow
yourself to them, I have warned you this
day that you shall certainly perish.
20 "Like the nations which יהוה is
destroying before you, so you are to perish,
because you did not obey the voice of יהוה
your Elohim.

9 "Hear, O Yisra'ěl: You are passing
over the Yarděn today, to go in to
dispossess nations greater and stronger
than yourself, cities great and walled up to

8a See also Mt. 4:4 and in Lq. 4:4.

the heavens,
2 a people great and tall, the descendants
of the Anaqim, whom you know, and of
whom you heard it said, ‘Who does stand
before the descendants of Anaq?’
3 “And you shall know today that יהוה
your Elohim is He who is passing over
before you as a consuming fire – He does
destroy them and subdue them before you.
So you shall dispossess them and destroy
them quickly, as יהוה has said to you.
4 “Do not think in your heart, after יהוה
your Elohim has driven them out before
you, saying, ‘Because of my righteousness
יהוה has brought me in to possess this
land.’ But it is because of the wrong of
these nations that יהוה is driving them out
from before you.
5 “It is not because of your righteousness
or the uprightness of your heart that you go
in to possess their land, but because of the
wrong of these nations that יהוה your
Elohim drives them out from before you,
in order to establish the word which יהוה
swore to your fathers, to Aḇraham, to
Yitsḥaq, and to Ya‘aqoḇ.
6 “And you shall know that יהוה your
Elohim is not giving you this good land to
possess because of your righteousness, for
you are a stiff-necked people.
7 “Remember, do not forget how you
provoked to wrath יהוה your Elohim in the
wilderness. From the day that you came
out of the land of Mitsrayim until you
came to this place, you have been rebellious against יהוה.
8 “Even in Ḥorěḇ you made יהוה wroth,
so that יהוה was enraged with you, to
destroy you.
9 “When I went up into the mountain to
receive the tablets of stone, the tablets of
the covenant which יהוה made with you,
then I stayed on the mountain forty days
and forty nights. I did not eat bread nor did
I drink water.
10 “Then יהוה gave me the two tablets of
stone written with the finger of Elohim,
and on them were all the Words which
יהוה had spoken to you on the mountain
from the midst of the fire in the day of the
assembly.
11 “And it came to be, at the end of forty
days and forty nights, that יהוה gave me
the two tablets of stone, the tablets of the
covenant.
12 “Then יהוה said to me, ‘Arise, go down
quickly from here, for your people whom
you brought out of Mitsrayim have acted
corruptly. They have quickly turned aside
from the way which I commanded them,
they have made themselves a moulded
image.’
13 “And יהוה spoke to me, saying, ‘I have
seen this people, and look, they are a stiff-
necked people.
14 ‘Leave Me alone, so that I destroy them
and blot out their name from under the
heavens, and make of you a nation stronger
and greater than they.’
15 “So I turned and came down from the
mountain, and the mountain burned with
fire. And the two tablets of the covenant
were in my two hands.
16 “And I looked and saw that you had
sinned against יהוה your Elohim, and had
made for yourselves a moulded calf! You
had quickly turned aside from the way
which יהוה had commanded you.
17 “And I took the two tablets and threw
them out of my two hands and broke them
before your eyes,
18 “and I fell down before יהוה, as at the
first, forty days and forty nights. I did not
eat bread and I did not drink water,
because of all your sins which you committed in doing evil in the eyes of יהוה, to
provoke Him.
19 “For I was afraid of the displeasure and
rage with which יהוה was wroth with you,
to destroy you. But יהוה listened to me that
time once more.
20 “And יהוה was very enraged with
Aharon, to destroy him, so I prayed for
Aharon at that time also.
21 “And I took your sin, the calf which
you had made, and burned it with fire and
crushed it and ground it very small, until it
was as fine as dust. And I threw its dust
into the stream that came down from the
mountain.
22 “And at Taḇ‘ěrah and at Massah and at
Qiḇroth Hatta’awah you made יהוה wroth.

23 "And when יהוה sent you from Qaḏěsh
Barněa, saying, 'Go up and possess the
land which I have given you,' then you
rebelled against the mouth of יהוה your
Elohim, and you neither trusted Him nor
listened to His voice.
24 "You have been rebellious against יהוה
from the day that I knew you.
25 "So I fell down before יהוה the forty
days and forty nights, for I fell down
because יהוה had said He would destroy
you.
26 "And I prayed to יהוה, and said, 'O
Master יהוה, do not destroy Your people
and Your inheritance whom You have ransomed in Your greatness, whom You have
brought out of Mitsrayim with a strong
hand.
27 'Remember Your servants, Aḇraham,
Yitsḥaq, and Ya'aqoḇ. Do not look on the
stubbornness of this people, or on their
wrong or on their sin,
28 lest the land from which You brought
us should say, "Because יהוה was not able
to bring them to the land which He
promised them, and because He hated
them, He has brought them out to kill them
in the wilderness."
29 'And they are Your people and Your
inheritance, whom You brought out by
Your great power and by Your outstretched arm.'

10

"At that time יהוה said to me,
'Hew for yourself two tablets of
stone like the first, and come up to Me on
the mountain. And you shall make yourself
an ark of wood,
2 then I write on the tablets the Words
that were on the first tablets, which you
broke. And you shall put them in the ark.'
3 "So I made an ark of acacia wood,
hewed two tablets of stone like the first,
and went up the mountain, with the two
tablets in my hand.
4 "And He wrote on the tablets according
to the first writing, the Ten Words, which
יהוה had spoken to you in the mountain
from the midst of the fire in the day of the
assembly. Then יהוה gave them to me,
5 and I turned and came down from the
mountain, and put the tablets in the ark
which I had made. And they are there, as
יהוה commanded me."
6 Now the children of Yisra'ěl set out
from the wells of Beněi Ya'aqan to
Mosěrah. Aharon died there, and he was
buried there. And El'azar his son became
priest in his place.
7 From there they set out to Guḏgoḏah,
and from Guḏgoḏah to Yotḇathah, a land
of rivers of water.
8 At that time יהוה separated the tribe of
Lěwi to bear the ark of the covenant of
יהוה, to stand before יהוה, to serve Him,
and to bless in His Name, to this day.
9 Therefore Lěwi has no portion nor
inheritance with his brothers. יהוה is his
inheritance, as יהוה your Elohim promised
him.
10 "And I stayed in the mountain for forty
days and forty nights. And יהוה heard me
at that time also, and יהוה chose not to
destroy you.
11 "And יהוה said to me, 'Arise, go before
the people, to set out, and let them go in
and possess the land which I swore to their
fathers to give them.'
12 "And now, Yisra'ěl, what is יהוה your
Elohim asking of you, but to fear יהוה
your Elohim, to walk in all His ways and to
love Him, and to serve יהוה your Elohim
with all your heart and with all your being,
13 to guard the commands of יהוה and His
laws which I command you today for your
good?
14 "See, the heavens and the heaven of
heavens belong to יהוה your Elohim, also
the earth with all that is in it.
15 "יהוה delighted only in your fathers, to
love them. And He chose their seed after
them, you above all peoples,[a] as it is today.
16 "And you shall circumcise the foreskin
of your heart,[b] and harden your neck no
more.
17 "For יהוה your Elohim is Elohim of

10a See also 7:6, 14:2, 26:18, Teh. 135:4 and Amos. *10b* See also 30:6-8, Rom. 2:26-29, and Qor. א 7:19.

mighty ones and Master of masters, the great Ěl, mighty and awesome, who shows no partiality nor takes a bribe.

18 "He executes right-ruling for the fatherless and the widow, and loves the stranger, giving him food and a garment.

19 "And you shall love the stranger, for you were strangers in the land of Mitsrayim.

20 "Fear יהוה your Elohim. Serve Him, and cling to Him, and swear by His Name.

21 "He is your praise, and He is your Elohim, who has done for you these great and awesome deeds which your eyes have seen.

22 "Your fathers went down to Mitsrayim with seventy beings, and now יהוה your Elohim has made you as numerous as the stars of the heavens.

11 "And you shall love יהוה your Elohim and guard His charge:[a] even His laws, and His right-rulings, and His commands, always.

2 "And you shall know today – for it is not your children who have not known and who have not seen the discipline of יהוה your Elohim, His greatness, His strong hand and His outstretched arm,

3 and His signs, and His works which He had done in the midst of Mitsrayim, to Pharaoh sovereign of Mitsrayim, and to all his land;

4 and that which He had done to the army of Mitsrayim, to their horses and their chariots, when He made the waters of the Sea of Reeds overflow them as they pursued you, and how יהוה has destroyed them to this day;

5 and what He had done for you in the wilderness till you came to this place;

6 and what He had done to Dathan and Aḇiram the sons of Eliyaḇ, son of Re'uḇěn, when the earth opened its mouth and swallowed them up, and their households, and their tents, and all the living creatures that were in their possession, in the midst of all Yisra'ěl.

7 "For yours are the eyes that saw all the great work of יהוה, which He did.

8 "And you shall guard every command which I command you today, so that you are strong, and shall go in, and shall possess the land which you are passing over to possess,

9 and to prolong your days in the land which יהוה swore to give your fathers, to them and their descendants, a land flowing with milk and honey.

10 "For the land which you are going in to possess is not like the land of Mitsrayim from which you have come, where you sowed your seed and watered it by foot, as a vegetable garden,

11 but the land which you are passing over to possess is a land of hills and valleys, which drinks water from the rain of the heavens,

12 a land which יהוה your Elohim looks after. The eyes of יהוה your Elohim are always on it, from the beginning of the year to the latter end of the year.

13 'And it shall be that if you diligently obey My commands which I command you today, to love יהוה your Elohim and to serve Him with all your heart and with all your being,

14 then I shall give you the rain for your land in its season, the early rain and the latter rain, and you shall gather in your grain, and your new wine, and your oil.

15 'And I shall give grass in your fields for your livestock, and you shall eat and be satisfied.

16 'Guard yourselves, lest your heart be deceived, and you turn aside and serve other mighty ones and bow down to them.

17 'Then the displeasure of יהוה shall burn against you, and He shall shut up the heavens, and there be no rain, and the land not give its increase. And you shall perish quickly from the good land which יהוה is giving you.

18 'And you shall lay up these Words[b] of Mine in your heart and in your being, and shall bind them as a sign on your hand, and they shall be as frontlets between your eyes.

11a See Ber. 26:5. *11b* See footnote at 5:22.

19 'And you shall teach them to your children, speaking of them when you sit in your house, and when you walk by the way, and when you lie down, and when you rise up,
20 and shall write them on the doorposts of your house and on your gates,
21 so that your days and the days of your children are increased on the soil of which יהוה swore to your fathers to give them, as the days of the heavens on the earth.
22 'For if you diligently guard all these commands which I command you, to do it, to love יהוה your Elohim, to walk in all His ways, and to cling to Him,
23 then יהוה shall drive out all these nations before you, and you shall dispossess greater and stronger nations than you.
24 'Every place on which the sole of your foot treads is yours: from the wilderness, and Leḇanon, from the river, the River Euphrates, even to the Western Sea is your border.
25 'No man shall stand against you. יהוה your Elohim shall put the dread of you and the fear of you upon all the land where you tread, as He has spoken to you.
26 'See, I am setting before you today a blessing and a curse:
27 the blessing, when you obey the commands of יהוה your Elohim which I command you today;
28 and the curse, if you do not obey the commands of יהוה your Elohim, but turn aside from the way which I command you today, to go after other mighty ones which you have not known.
29 'And it shall be, when יהוה your Elohim has brought you into the land which you go to possess, that you shall put the blessing on Mount Gerizim and the curse on Mount Ěyḇal.
30 'Are they not beyond the Yarděn, toward the setting sun, in the land of the Kena'anites who dwell in the desert plain opposite Gilgal, beside the terebinth trees of Moreh?
31 'For you are passing over the Yarděn to go in to possess the land which יהוה your Elohim is giving you, and you shall possess it and dwell in it,
32 and shall guard to do all the laws and right-rulings which I am setting before you today.'

12 "These are the laws and right-rulings which you guard to do in the land which יהוה Elohim of your fathers is giving you to possess, all the days that you live on the soil.
2 "Completely destroy all the places where the nations which you are dispossessing served their mighty ones, on the high mountains and on the hills and under every green tree.
3 "And you shall break down their slaughter-places, and smash their pillars, and burn their Ashěrim with fire. And you shall cut down the carved images of their mighty ones and shall destroy their name [a] out of that place.
4 "Do not do so to יהוה your Elohim,
5 but seek the place which יהוה your Elohim chooses, out of all your tribes, to put His Name there, for His Dwelling Place, and there you shall enter.
6 "And there you shall take your ascending offerings, and your slaughters, and your tithes, and the contributions of your hand, and your vowed offerings, and your voluntary offerings, and the firstlings of your herd and of your flock.
7 "And there you shall eat before יהוה your Elohim, and shall rejoice in all that you put your hand to, you and your households, in which יהוה your Elohim has blessed you.
8 "Do not do as we are doing here today – each one *doing* whatever is right in his own eyes. [b]
9 "Because you have not yet entered the rest and the inheritance which יהוה your Elohim is giving you.
10 "But you shall pass over the Yarděn, and shall dwell in the land which יהוה your Elohim is giving you to inherit, and He shall give you rest from all your enemies round about, and you shall dwell in safety.

12a The names of the gentile deities (mighty ones). *12b* See Shoph. 17:6 & 21:25.

11 "And it shall be, that unto the place which יהוה your Elohim chooses to make His Name dwell there, there you are to bring all that I command you: your ascending offerings, and your slaughters, and your tithes, and the contributions of your hand, and all your choice offerings which you vow to יהוה.

12 "And you shall rejoice before יהוה your Elohim, you and your sons and your daughters, and your male servants and your female servants, and the Lěwite who is within your gates, since he has no portion nor inheritance with you.

13 "Guard yourself that you do not offer your ascending offerings in every place that you see,

14 except in the place which יהוה chooses, in one of your tribes, there you are to offer your ascending offerings, and there you are to do all that I command you.

15 "Only, whatever your being desires you shall slaughter and eat, according to the blessing of יהוה your Elohim which He has given you, within all your gates. The unclean and the clean do eat of it, of the gazelle and the deer alike.

16 "Only, the blood you do not eat, pour it on the earth like water.

17 "You are not allowed to eat within your gates the tithe of your grain, or of your new wine, or of your oil, or of the firstlings of your herd or your flock, or of any of your offerings which you vow, or of your voluntary offerings, or of the contribution of your hand.

18 "But eat them before יהוה your Elohim, in the place which יהוה your Elohim chooses, you and your son and your daughter, and your male servant and your female servant, and the Lěwite who is within your gates. And you shall rejoice before יהוה your Elohim in all that you put your hands to.

19 "Guard yourself that you do not forsake the Lěwite as long as you live in your land.

20 "When יהוה your Elohim enlarges your border as He has promised you, and you say, 'Let me eat meat,' because you long to eat meat, you eat as much meat as your being desires.

21 "When the place where יהוה your Elohim chooses to put His Name is too far from you, then you shall slaughter from your herd and from your flock which יהוה has given you, as I have commanded you, and you shall eat within your gates as much as your being desires.

22 "Only, as the gazelle and the deer are eaten, so you are to eat of it. The unclean and the clean alike eat of it.

23 "Only, be strong not to eat the blood, for the blood is the life, do not eat the life with the meat.

24 "Do not eat it, you pour it on the earth like water.

25 "Do not eat it, that it might be well with you and your children after you, when you do what is right in the eyes of יהוה.

26 "Only, the set-apart *gifts* which you have, and your vowed offerings, you are to take up and go to the place which יהוה chooses.

27 "And you shall make your ascending offerings, the meat and the blood, on the slaughter-place of יהוה your Elohim. And the blood of your slaughterings is poured out on the slaughter-place of יהוה your Elohim, and you eat the meat.

28 "Guard, and obey all these words which I command you, that it might be well with you and your children after you forever, when you do what is good and right in the eyes of יהוה your Elohim.

29 "When יהוה your Elohim does cut off from before you the nations which you go to dispossess, and you dispossess them and dwell in their land,

30 guard yourself that you are not ensnared to follow them, after they are destroyed from before you, and that you do not inquire about their mighty ones, saying, 'How did these nations serve their mighty ones? And let me do so too.' [c]

31 "Do not do so to יהוה your Elohim, for every abomination which יהוה hates they

12c See also 18:9, Way. 18:3, Yirm.10:2, Yeḥez. 11:12 & 20:32, Eph. 4:17, and Kěpha א 4:3.

have done to their mighty ones, for they
even burn their sons and daughters in the
fire to their mighty ones.
32 “All the words I am commanding you,
guard to do it – do not add to it nor take
away from it. [d]

13 “When there arises among you a
prophet or a dreamer of dreams,
and he shall give you a sign or a wonder,
2 and the sign or the wonder shall come
true, of which he has spoken to you, saying, ‘Let us go after other mighty ones –
which you have not known – and serve
them,’
3 do not listen to the words of that
prophet or that dreamer of dreams, for
יהוה your Elohim is trying you to know
whether you love יהוה your Elohim with
all your heart and with all your being.
4 “Walk after יהוה your Elohim and fear
Him, and guard His commands and obey
His voice, and serve Him and cling to Him.
5 “And that prophet or that dreamer of
dreams is put to death, because he has spoken apostasy against יהוה your Elohim –
who brought you out of the land of
Mitsrayim and ransomed you from the
house of bondage – to make you stray from
the way in which יהוה your Elohim commanded you to walk. Thus you shall purge
the evil from your midst.
6 “When your brother, the son of your
mother, or your son or your daughter, or
the wife of your bosom, or your friend who
is as your own being, entices you secretly,
saying, ‘Let us go and serve other mighty
ones’– which you have not known, neither
you nor your fathers,
7 of the mighty ones of the people which
are all around you, near to you or far off
from you, from one end of the earth to the
other end of the earth –
8 do not agree with him or listen to him,
nor shall your eye pardon him, nor spare
him or conceal him,
9 but you shall certainly kill him. Your
hand is first against him to put him to
death, and afterward the hand of all the
people,
10 and you shall stone him with stones
until he dies, because he sought to entice
you away from יהוה your Elohim, who
brought you out of the land of Mitsrayim,
from the house of bondage.
11 “And let all Yisra’ĕl hear and fear, and
not again do any such evil matter as this in
your midst.
12 “When you hear someone in one of
your cities, which יהוה your Elohim gives
you to dwell in, saying,
13 ‘Some men, sons of Beliyaʽal, have
gone out of your midst and led the inhabitants of their city astray, saying, “Let us go
and serve other mighty ones” ’ – mighty
ones whom you have not known –
14 then you shall inquire, search out, and
ask diligently. And see if the matter is true
and established that this abomination was
done in your midst,
15 you shall certainly strike the inhabitants
of that city with the edge of the sword,
putting it under the ban, and all that is in it
and its livestock, with the edge of the
sword.
16 “And gather all its plunder into the middle of the street, and completely burn with
fire the city and all its plunder, before יהוה
your Elohim. And it shall be a heap forever, never to be built again.
17 “And none of that which is put under
the ban is to cling to your hand, so that
יהוה turns from the fierceness of His displeasure and shall show you compassion,
love you and increase you, as He swore to
your fathers,
18 when you obey the voice of יהוה your
Elohim, to guard all His commands which
I command you today, to do what is right
in the eyes of יהוה your Elohim.

14 “You are the children of יהוה your
Elohim. Do not cut yourselves nor
shave the front of your head for the dead,
2 for you are a set-apart people to יהוה
your Elohim, and יהוה has chosen you to
be a people for Himself, a treasured possession above all the peoples who are on

12d See also 4:2, Mish. 30:6, Ḥazon 22:18-19.

the face of the earth.
3 "Do not eat whatever is abominable.
4 "These are the living creatures which you do eat: ox, sheep, and goat,
5 deer, and gazelle, and roebuck, and wild goat, and mountain goat, and antelope, and mountain sheep.
6 "And every beast that has a split hoof divided in two, chewing the cud, among the beasts, you do eat.
7 "But of those chewing the cud or those having a split hoof completely divided, you do not eat, such as these: the camel, and the hare, and the rabbit, for they chew the cud but do not have a split hoof, they are unclean for you.
8 "And the pig is unclean for you, because it has a split hoof, but does not chew the cud. You do not eat their flesh or touch their dead carcasses.
9 "These you do eat of all that are in the waters: all that have fins and scales you do eat.
10 "And whatever does not have fins and scales you do not eat, it is unclean for you.
11 "Any clean bird you do eat,
12 but these you do not eat: the eagle, and the vulture, and the black vulture,
13 and the red kite, and the falcon, and the buzzard after their kinds,
14 and every raven after its kind,
15 and the ostrich, and the nighthawk, and the seagull, and the hawk after their kinds,
16 the little owl, and the great owl, and the white owl,
17 and the pelican, and the carrion vulture, and the fisher owl,
18 and the stork, and the heron after its kind, and the hoopoe and the bat.
19 "And every creeping *insect* that flies is unclean for you, they are not eaten.
20 "Any clean bird you do eat.
21 "Do not eat whatever dies of itself. Give it to the stranger who is within your gates, to eat it, or sell it to a foreigner. For you are a set-apart people to יהוה your Elohim. Do not cook a young goat in its mother's milk.
22 "You shall tithe without fail all the yield of your grain that the field brings forth year by year.
23 "And you shall eat before יהוה your Elohim, in the place where He chooses to make His Name dwell, the tithe of your grain and your new wine and your oil, and of the firstlings of your herds and your sheep, so that you learn to fear יהוה your Elohim always.
24 "But when the way is too long for you, so that you are not able to bring the tithe, or when the place where יהוה your Elohim chooses to put His Name is too far from you, when יהוה your Elohim is blessing you,
25 then you shall give it in silver, and shall take the silver in your hand and go to the place which יהוה your Elohim chooses.
26 "And you shall use the silver for whatever your being desires: for cattle or sheep, for wine or strong drink, for whatever your being desires. And you shall eat there before יהוה your Elohim, and you shall rejoice, you and your household.
27 "And do not forsake the Lĕwite who is within your gates, for he has no part nor inheritance with you.
28 "At the end of every third year you bring out all the tithe of your increase of that year and store it up within your gates.
29 "And the Lĕwite, because he has no portion nor inheritance with you, and the sojourner and the fatherless and the widow who are within your gates, shall come and eat and be satisfied, so that יהוה your Elohim does bless you in all the work of your hand which you do.

15 "At the end of every seven years you make a release *of debts*.
2 "And this is the word of the release: Every creditor is to release what he has loaned to his neighbour, he does not require it of his neighbour or his brother, because it is called the release of יהוה.
3 "Of a foreigner you could require it, but your hand is to release whatever is owed by your brother.
4 "Only, there should be no poor among you. For יהוה does greatly bless you in the land which יהוה your Elohim is giving you to possess as an inheritance,

5 only if you diligently obey the voice of יהוה your Elohim, to guard to do all these commands which I am commanding you today.

6 “For יהוה your Elohim shall bless you as He promised you. And you shall lend to many nations, but you shall not borrow. And you shall rule over many nations, but they do not rule over you.

7 “When there is a poor man with you, one of your brothers, within any of the gates in your land which יהוה your Elohim is giving you, do not harden your heart nor shut your hand from your poor brother,

8 for you shall certainly open your hand to him and certainly lend him enough for his need, whatever he needs.

9 “Be on guard lest there be a thought of Beliya‘al in your heart, saying, ‘The seventh year, the year of release, is near,’ and your eye is evil against your poor brother and you give him naught. And he shall cry out to יהוה against you, and it shall be a sin in you.

10 “You shall certainly give to him, and your heart should not be grieved when you give to him, because for this reason יהוה your Elohim does bless you in all your works and in all to which you put your hand.

11 “Because the poor one does not cease from the land. Therefore I am commanding you, saying, ‘You shall certainly open your hand to your brother, to your poor and to your needy one, in your land.’

12 “When your brother is sold to you, a Hebrew man or a Hebrew woman, and shall serve you six years, then let him go free from you in the seventh year.

13 “And when you send him away free from you, let him not go away empty-handed.

14 “You shall richly supply him from your flock, and from your threshing-floor, and from your winepress. With that which יהוה has blessed you with, give to him.

15 “And you shall remember that you were a slave in the land of Mitsrayim, and יהוה your Elohim ransomed you. Therefore I am commanding you this word today.

16 “And it shall be, when he says to you, ‘I do not go away from you,’ because he loves you and your house, because it is good for him with you,

17 then you shall take an awl and thrust it through his ear to the door, and he shall be your servant forever. Do the same to your female servant.

18 “Let it not be hard in your eyes when you send him away free from you, for he has been worth a double hired servant in serving you six years. And יהוה your Elohim shall bless you in all that you do.

19 “Set apart to יהוה your Elohim all the first-born males that come from your herd and your flock. Do no work with the first-born of your herd, nor shear the first-born of your flock.

20 “You and your household are to eat it before יהוה your Elohim year by year in the place which יהוה chooses.

21 “But when there is any defect in it, lame or blind, or has any evil defect, do not slaughter it to יהוה your Elohim.

22 “Eat it within your gates – the unclean and the clean alike – as the gazelle, and as the deer.

23 “Only, do not eat its blood, pour it on the ground like water.

16 “Guard the new *moon* of Aḇiḇ, and perform the Pěsaḥ [a] to יהוה your Elohim, for in the new *moon* [b] of Aḇiḇ יהוה your Elohim brought you out of Mitsrayim by night.

2 “And you shall slaughter the Pěsaḥ to יהוה your Elohim, from the flock and the herd, in the place where יהוה chooses to put His Name.

3 “Eat no leavened bread with it. For seven days you eat unleavened bread with it, bread of affliction, because you came out of the land of Mitsrayim in haste – so that you remember the day in which you came out of the land of Mitsrayim, all the days of your life.

4 “And no leaven should be seen with you in all your border for seven days,

16a - Pěsaḥ - See Explanatory notes - Passover. *16b* Or month.

neither should *any* of the meat which you slaughter in the evening on the first day stay all night until morning.
5 "You are not allowed to slaughter the Pěsaḥ within any of your gates which יהוה your Elohim gives you,
6 but at the place where יהוה your Elohim chooses to make His Name dwell, there you slaughter the Pěsaḥ in the evening, at the going down of the sun, at the appointed time you came out of Mitsrayim.
7 "And you shall roast and eat it in the place which יהוה your Elohim chooses, and in the morning you shall turn and go to your tents.
8 "Six days you eat unleavened bread, and on the seventh day there is a closing festival to יהוה your Elohim – you do no work.
9 "Count seven weeks for yourself. Begin to count seven weeks from the time you begin to put the sickle to the grain.
10 "And you shall perform the Festival of Shaḇu'ot [c] to יהוה your Elohim, according to the voluntary offering from your hand, which you give as יהוה your Elohim blesses you.
11 "And you shall rejoice before יהוה your Elohim, you and your son and your daughter, and your male servant and your female servant, and the Lěwite who is within your gates, and the stranger and the fatherless and the widow who are in your midst, at the place where יהוה your Elohim chooses to make His Name dwell.
12 "And you shall remember that you were a slave in Mitsrayim, and you shall guard and do these laws.
13 "Perform the Festival of Sukkot [d] for seven days after the ingathering from your threshing-floor and from your winepress,
14 and you shall rejoice in your festival, you and your son and your daughter, and your male servant and your female servant, and the Lěwite, and the stranger and the fatherless and the widow who are within your gates.
15 "For seven days you shall celebrate to יהוה your Elohim in the place which יהוה chooses, because יהוה your Elohim does bless you in all your increase and in all the work of your hands, and you shall be only rejoicing!
16 "Three times a year all your males appear before יהוה your Elohim in the place which He chooses: at the Festival of Matzot, [e] and at the Festival of Shaḇu'ot, [c] and at the Festival of Sukkot [d]. And none should appear before יהוה empty-handed,
17 *but* each one with the gift of his hand, according to the blessing of יהוה your Elohim which He has given you.
18 "Appoint judges and officers within all your gates, which יהוה your Elohim is giving you, according to your tribes. And they shall judge the people with righteous right-ruling.
19 "Do not distort right-ruling. Do not show partiality, nor take a bribe, for a bribe blinds the eyes of the wise and twists the words of the righteous.
20 "Follow righteousness, righteousness *alone*, so that you live and inherit the land which יהוה your Elohim is giving you.
21 "Do not plant for yourself any tree as an Ashěrah near the slaughter-place of יהוה your Elohim that you make for yourself.
22 "And do not set up a pillar, which יהוה your Elohim hates.

17 "Do not slaughter to יהוה your Elohim a bull or sheep which has any blemish, any evil matter, for that is an abomination to יהוה your Elohim.
2 "When there is found in your midst, in any of your cities which יהוה your Elohim is giving you, a man or a woman who does what is evil in the eyes of יהוה your Elohim, in transgressing His covenant,
3 and has gone and served other mighty ones and bowed down to them, or to the sun or to the moon or to any of the host of the heavens, which I have not commanded,
4 and it has been made known to you and you have heard, and have searched diligently. Then see, if true: the matter is

16c - Weeks. *16d* - Booths. *16e* - Unleavened Bread.

confirmed that such an abomination has
been done in Yisra'ěl,
5 then you shall bring out to your gates
that man or woman who has done this evil
matter, and you shall stone to death that
man or woman with stones.
6 "At the mouth of two or three witnesses
shall he that is to die be put to death. He
is not put to death by the mouth of one
witness.
7 "The hand of the witnesses shall be first
against him to put him to death, and the
hand of all the people last. So you shall
purge the evil from your midst.
8 "When any matter arises which is too
hard for you to judge, between blood and
blood, between plea and plea, or between
stroke and stroke – matters of strife within
your gates – then you shall rise and go up
to the place which יהוה your Elohim
chooses,
9 and shall come to the priests, the
Lěwites, and to the judge who is in those
days, and shall inquire. And they shall
declare to you the word of right-ruling,
10 and you shall do according to the word
which they declare to you from that place
which יהוה chooses. And you shall guard
to do according to all that they instruct
you.
11 "Do according to the Torah in which
they teach you, according to the right-
ruling which they say to you. You do not
turn to the right or to the left from the word
which they declare to you.
12 "And the man who acts arrogantly, so
as not to listen to the priest who stands to
serve there before יהוה your Elohim, or to
the judge, that man shall die. So you shall
purge the evil from Yisra'ěl.
13 "And let all the people hear and fear,
and no longer do arrogantly.
14 "When you come to the land which
יהוה your Elohim is giving you, and shall
possess it and shall dwell in it, and you
shall say, 'Let me set a sovereign over me
like all the nations that are around me,'
15 you shall certainly set a sovereign over
you whom יהוה your Elohim shall choose.
Set a sovereign over you from among your
brothers, you are not allowed to
set a foreigner over you, who is not your
brother.
16 "Only, he is not to increase horses for
himself, nor cause the people to return to
Mitsrayim to increase horses, for יהוה has
said to you, 'Do not return that way again.'
17 "And he is not to increase wives for
himself, lest his heart turn away, nor is
he to greatly increase silver and gold for
himself.
18 "And it shall be, when he sits on the
throne of his reign, that he shall write for
himself a copy of this Torah in a book,
from the one before the priests, the
Lěwites.
19 "And it shall be with him, and he shall
read it all the days of his life, so that he
learns to fear יהוה his Elohim and guard all
the Words of this Torah and these laws, to
do them,
20 so that his heart is not lifted up above
his brothers, and so as not to turn aside
from the command, right or left, so that he
prolongs his days in his reign, he and his
children, in the midst of Yisra'ěl.

18 "The priests, the Lěwites, all the
tribe of Lěwi, have no part nor
inheritance with Yisra'ěl. They are to eat
the offerings of יהוה made by fire, and His
inheritance.
2 "But among his brothers *Lěwi* has no
inheritance. יהוה is his inheritance, as He
has spoken to him.
3 "And this is the priest's right from the
people, from those who slaughter a slaughtering, whether it is bull or sheep: they
shall give to the priest the shoulder, and the
two cheeks, and the stomach;
4 the first-fruits of your grain and your
new wine and your oil, and the first of the
fleece of your sheep, you give to him.
5 "For יהוה your Elohim has chosen him
out of all your tribes to stand to serve in the
Name of יהוה, him and his sons forever.
6 "And when the Lěwite comes from one
of your gates, from where he has sojourned
among all Yisra'ěl, and shall come with all
the desire of his being to the place which
יהוה chooses,
7 then he shall serve in the Name of יהוה

his Elohim, like all his brothers the
Lěwites, who are standing there before
יהוה.
8 "They are to have portion for portion to
eat, besides what comes from the sale of
his inheritance.
9 "When you come into the land which
יהוה your Elohim is giving you, do not
learn to do according to the abominations
of those nations. [a]
10 "Let no one be found among you who
makes his son or his daughter pass through
the fire, or one who practises divination, or
a user of magic, or one who interprets
omens or a sorcerer,
11 or one who conjures spells, or a medium, or a spiritist, or one who calls up the
dead.
12 "For whoever does these are an abomination to יהוה, and because of these abominations יהוה your Elohim drives them out
from before you.
13 "Be perfect before יהוה your Elohim,
14 for these nations whom you are possessing do listen to those using magic and
to diviners. But as for you, יהוה your
Elohim has not appointed such for you.
15 "יהוה your Elohim shall raise up for
you a Prophet [b] like me from your midst,
from your brothers. Listen to Him,
16 according to all you asked of יהוה your
Elohim in Ḥorěḇ in the day of the assembly, saying, 'Let me not hear again the
voice of יהוה my Elohim, nor let me see
this great fire any more, lest I die.'
17 "And יהוה said to me, 'What they have
spoken is good.
18 'I shall raise up for them a Prophet [c]
like you out of the midst of their brothers.
And I shall put My Words in His mouth,
and He shall speak to them all that I command Him.
19 'And it shall be, the man who does not
listen to My Words which He speaks in My
Name, I require it of him.
20 'But the prophet who presumes to
speak a word in My Name, which I have
not commanded him to speak, or who
speaks in the name of other mighty ones,
even that prophet shall die.'
21 "And when you say in your heart, 'How
do we know the word which יהוה has not
spoken?' –
22 when the prophet speaks in the Name of
יהוה and the word is not, or comes
not, that is the word which יהוה has not
spoken. The prophet has spoken it presumptuously. Do not be afraid of him.

19 "When יהוה your Elohim cuts off
the nations whose land יהוה your
Elohim is giving you, and you dispossess
them and dwell in their cities and in their
houses,
2 separate three cities for yourself in the
midst of your land which יהוה your
Elohim is giving you to possess.
3 "Prepare a way for yourself, and divide
into three parts the border of your land
which יהוה your Elohim is giving you to
inherit, that any man-slayer shall flee there.
4 "And this matter of the man-slayer who
flees there and lives: he who strikes his
neighbour unknowingly, not having hated
him in time past,
5 even he who goes to the forest with his
neighbour to cut timber, and his hand
swings a stroke with the axe to cut down
the tree, and the head slips from the handle
and strikes his neighbour so that he dies –
let him flee to one of these cities and live,
6 lest the revenger of blood, while his
displeasure is hot, pursue the man-slayer
and overtake him, because the way is long,
and shall strike his being, though he was
not worthy of death, since he had not hated
him before.
7 "Therefore I am commanding you, saying, 'Separate three cities for yourself.'
8 "And if יהוה your Elohim enlarges
your border, as He swore to your fathers,
and has given you the land which He
promised to give to your fathers –
9 when you guard all this command to do
it, which I am commanding you today, to
love יהוה your Elohim and to walk in His
ways all the days – then you shall add three
more cities for yourself besides these three,

18a See footnote at 12:30. *18b* See footnote at v. 18. *18c* See also Ma. 3:22-26, and Ma. 7:37.

10 so that innocent blood is not shed in the
midst of your land which יהוה your
Elohim is giving you as an inheritance, or
blood-guilt shall be upon you.
11 "But when anyone hates his neighbour,
and shall lie in wait for him and rise
against him and strike his being so that he
dies, then he shall flee to one of these
cities,
12 and the elders of his city shall send and
bring him from there, and give him into the
hand of the revenger of blood, and he shall
die.
13 "Your eye shall not pardon him, but
you shall purge the blood of innocent
blood from Yisra'ěl, so that it might be
well with you.
14 "Do not remove your neighbour's
boundary, which those in the past have set,
in your inheritance which you inherit in the
land that יהוה your Elohim is giving you to
possess.
15 "One witness does not rise up against a
man concerning any crookedness or any
sin that he commits. At the mouth of two
witnesses or at the mouth of three witnesses a matter is established.
16 "When a malicious witness rises up
against any man to accuse him of turning
aside,
17 then both men who have the dispute
shall stand before יהוה, before the priests
and the judges who serve in those days.
18 "And the judges shall diligently search
and see if the witness is a false witness,
who has falsely accused his brother,
19 then you shall do to him as he thought
to have done to his brother. Thus you shall
purge the evil from your midst.
20 "And let the rest hear and fear, and
never again do this evil matter in your
midst.
21 "And let your eye not pardon, life for
life, eye for eye, tooth for tooth, hand for
hand, foot for foot.

20 "When you go out to battle against
your enemies, and shall see horses
and chariots and people more numerous
than you, do not be afraid of them, for יהוה
your Elohim, who brought you up from the
land of Mitsrayim, is with you.
2 "And it shall be, when you draw near to
the battle, that the priest shall come and
speak to the people,
3 and shall say to them, 'Hear, O Yisra'ěl: You are drawing near today to battle
with your enemies. Do not let your heart
faint, do not fear, or tremble, or be afraid
before them,
4 for יהוה your Elohim is He who goes
with you, to fight for you against your
enemies, to save you.'
5 "And the officers shall speak to the
people, saying, 'Who is the man who has
built a new house and has not dedicated it?
Let him go and return to his house, lest he
die in the battle and another man dedicate
it.
6 'And who is the man who has planted a
vineyard and has not begun to use it? Let
him also go and return to his house, lest he
die in the battle and another man should
begin to use it.
7 'And who is the man who is engaged to
a woman and has not taken her? Let him go
and return to his house, lest he die in the
battle and another man take her.'
8 "And the officers shall speak further to
the people, and say, 'Who is the man who
is afraid and tender of heart? Let him go
and return to his house, lest the heart of his
brothers faint like his heart.'
9 "And it shall be, when the officers have
finished speaking to the people, that they
shall appoint commanders of the divisions
to lead the people.
10 "When you draw near to a city to fight
against it, then you shall make a call for
peace to it.
11 "And it shall be that if it accepts your
call for peace, and shall open to you, then
all the people found in it are to be your
compulsory labour, and serve you.
12 "But if it does not make peace with
you, and shall fight against you, then you
shall besiege it,
13 and יהוה your Elohim shall give it into
your hands, and you shall strike every male
in it with the edge of the sword.
14 "Only the women, and the little ones,
and the livestock, and all that is in the city,

all its spoil, you take as plunder for yourself. And you shall eat the enemies' plunder which יהוה your Elohim gives you.

15 "Do so to all the cities which are very far from you, which are not of the cities of these nations.

16 "Only, of the cities of these peoples which יהוה your Elohim gives you as an inheritance, you do not keep alive any that breathe,

17 but you shall certainly put them under the ban: the Ḥittite and the Amorite and the Kenaʽanite and the Perizzite and the Ḥiwwite and the Yeḇusite, as יהוה your Elohim has commanded you,

18 lest they teach you to do according to all their abominations which they have done for their mighty ones, and you sin against יהוה your Elohim.

19 "When you besiege a city for a long time by fighting against it to take it, you do not destroy its trees by wielding an axe against them. If you do eat of them, do not cut them down. For is the tree of the field a man to be besieged by you?

20 "Only the trees which you know are not trees for food you do destroy and cut down, to build siege-works against the city that is fighting against you, until it falls.

21

"When anyone is found slain, lying in the field in the land which יהוה your Elohim is giving you to possess, and it is not known who struck him,

2 then your elders and your judges shall go out, and they shall measure the distance from the slain man to the cities round about.

3 "And it shall be that the elders of the city nearest to the slain man shall take a heifer which has not been worked and which has not pulled with a yoke,

4 and the elders of that city shall bring the heifer down to a wadi with flowing water, which is neither ploughed nor sown, and they shall break the heifer's neck there in the wadi.

5 "And the priests, the sons of Lěwi, shall come near, for יהוה your Elohim has chosen them to serve Him and to bless in the Name of יהוה, and by their mouth every strife and every stroke is *tried.*

6 "And let all the elders of that city nearest to the slain man wash their hands over the heifer whose neck was broken in the wadi.

7 "And they shall answer and say, 'Our hands have not shed this blood, nor have our eyes seen it.

8 'O יהוה, forgive Your people Yisra'ěl, whom You have ransomed, and do not allow innocent blood in the midst of Your people Yisra'ěl.' And the blood-guilt shall be pardoned to them.

9 "Thus you purge the guilt of innocent blood from your midst when you do what is right in the eyes of יהוה.

10 "When you go out to fight against your enemies, and יהוה your Elohim shall give them into your hand, and you shall take them captive,

11 and shall see among the captives a woman fair of form, and shall delight in her and take her for your wife,

12 then you shall bring her home to your house, and she shall shave her head and trim her nails,

13 and put aside the mantle of her captivity, and shall dwell in your house, and mourn her father and her mother a month of days. And after that you shall go in to her and be her husband, and she shall be your wife.

14 "And it shall be, if you are not pleased with her, then you shall let her go at her desire, but you do not sell her at all for silver. Do not treat her harshly, since you have humbled her.

15 "When a man has two wives, one loved and the other unloved, and they have borne him children, both the loved and the unloved, and the first-born son is of her who is unloved,

16 then it shall be, on the day he makes his sons to inherit his possessions, he is not allowed to treat the son of the beloved wife as first-born in the face of the son of the unloved, who is *truly* the first-born.

17 "But he is to acknowledge the son of the unloved wife as the first-born by giving him a double portion of all that he has, for he is the beginning of his strength – the

right of the first-born is his.
18 “When a man has a wayward and rebellious son who is not listening to the voice
of his father or the voice of his mother, and
who, when they have disciplined him, does
not listen to them,
19 then his father and his mother shall take
hold of him and bring him out to the elders
of his city, to the gate of his city,
20 and shall say to the elders of his city,
‘This son of ours is wayward and rebellious. He is not listening to our voice, he is
a glutton and a drunkard.’
21 “Then all the men of his city shall stone
him to death with stones. Thus you shall
purge the evil from your midst. And let all
Yisra’ĕl hear, and fear.
22 “And when a man has committed a sin
worthy of death, then he shall be put to
death and you shall hang him on a tree.
23 “Let his body not remain overnight on
the tree, for you shall certainly bury him
the same day – for he who is hanged is
accursed of Elohim – so that you do not
defile the land which יהוה your Elohim is
giving you as an inheritance.

22 “When you see your brother’s ox
or his sheep straying away, you
shall not hide yourself from them. Return
them to your brother without fail.
2 “And if your brother is not near you, or
if you do not know him, then you shall
bring it to your own house, and it shall be
with you until your brother seeks it, then
you shall return it to him.
3 “And so you do with his donkey, and so
you do with his garment, and so you do
with whatever your brother loses, which he
has lost and you have found. You are not
allowed to hide yourself.
4 “When you see your brother’s donkey
or his ox fall down on the way, you shall
not hide yourself from them. Help him
raise them without fail.
5 “A woman does not wear that which
pertains to a man, nor does a man put on a
woman’s garment, for whoever does this
is an abomination to יהוה your Elohim.
6 “When you come upon a bird’s nest
along the way, in any tree or on the ground,
with young ones or eggs, with the mother
sitting on the young or on the eggs, do not
take the mother with the young –
7 let the mother go without fail, and take
the young for yourself, so that it might be
well with you, and that you shall prolong
your days.
8 “When you build a new house, then you
shall make a parapet for your roof, so that
you do not bring blood-guilt on your house
when one falls from it.
9 “Do not sow your vineyard with different kinds of seed, lest the yield of the seed
which you have sown and the fruit of your
vineyard be defiled.
10 “Do not plough with an ox and a
donkey together.
11 “Do not put on a garment of different
kinds, of wool and linen together.
12 “Make tassels on the four corners of the
garment with which you cover yourself.
13 “When any man takes a wife, and shall
go in to her, and shall hate her,
14 and shall make abusive charges against
her and bring an evil name on her and say,
‘I took this woman, and when I came to her
I did not find her a maiden,’
15 then the father and mother of the young
woman shall take and bring out the *proof*
of the girl’s maidenhood to the elders of
the city at the gate.
16 “And the girl’s father shall say to the
elders, ‘I gave my daughter to this man as
wife, and he hates her.
17 ‘And see, he has made abusive charges
against her, saying, “I did not find your
daughter a maiden,” and yet these are the
proofs of my daughter’s maidenhood.’
And they shall spread the garment before
the elders of the city.
18 “And the elders of that city shall take
that man and punish him,
19 and fine him one hundred pieces of silver and give them to the father of the
young woman, because he has brought an
evil name on a maiden of Yisra’ĕl. And she
is to be his wife, he is not allowed to put
her away all his days.
20 “But if the matter is true, that the girl
was not found a maiden,
21 then they shall bring out the girl to the

door of her father's house, and the men of her city shall stone her to death with stones, because she has done wickedness in Yisra'ěl, to whore in her father's house. Thus you shall purge the evil from your midst.

22 "When a man is found lying with a woman married to a husband, then both of them shall die, both the man that lay with the woman, and the woman. Thus you shall purge the evil from Yisra'ěl.

23 "When a girl who is a maiden is engaged to a husband, and a man finds her in the city and lies with her,

24 then you shall bring them both out to the gate of that city, and shall stone them to death with stones, the girl because she did not cry out in the city, and the man because he has humbled his neighbour's wife. Thus you shall purge the evil from your midst.

25 "But if a man finds the girl who is engaged in the field, and the man takes hold of her and lies with her, then only the man who lay with her shall die.

26 "But you shall do no matter to the girl. The girl has no sin worthy of death – for the matter is like a man who rises against his neighbour and murders him – a being –

27 for he found her in the field, and she cried out, the engaged girl, but without anyone to save her.

28 "When a man finds a girl who is a maiden, who is not engaged, and he seizes her and lies with her, and they are found out,

29 then the man who lay with her shall give to the girl's father fifty pieces of silver, and she is to be his wife because he has humbled her. He is not allowed to put her away all his days.

30 "A man does not take his father's wife, nor uncover his father's skirt [a].

23 "He who is wounded by crushing of testicles or whose penis is cut off, shall not enter into the community of יהוה.

2 "A mamzer [a] shall not enter the community of יהוה, even a tenth generation of his shall not enter the community of יהוה.

3 "An Ammonite or Mo'aḇite shall not enter the assembly of יהוה, even a tenth generation of them shall not ever enter the assembly of יהוה,

4 because they did not meet you with bread and water on the way when you came out of Mitsrayim, and because they hired against you Bil'am son of Be'or from Pethor of Aram Naharayim, to curse you.

5 "But יהוה your Elohim refused to listen to Bil'am, and יהוה your Elohim turned the curse into a blessing for you, because יהוה your Elohim loves you.

6 "Do not seek their peace nor their good, all your days, forever.

7 "Do not loathe an Eḏomite, for he is your brother. Do not loathe a Mitsrian, because you were a stranger in his land.

8 "The children of the third generation born to them do enter the assembly of יהוה.

9 "When the camp goes out against your enemies, then you shall guard yourself from every evil matter.

10 "When there is any man among you who is not clean because of an emission in the night, then he shall go outside the camp. Let him not come into the midst of the camp.

11 "And it shall be, at the approach [b] of evening, that he bathes with water. And when the sun sets let him come into the midst of the camp.

12 "And you shall have a place outside the camp, where you shall go out,

13 and you shall have a sharp implement among your equipment, and when you sit down outside, you shall dig with it and turn and cover your excrement.

14 "For יהוה your Elohim walks in the midst of your camp, to deliver you and give your enemies over to you. Therefore your camp shall be set-apart, so that He does not see unclean matter among you,

22a Hebrew - kanaph: wing, extremity, border or robe. *23a* Mamzer (Hebrew) - Born from prohibited union - See Explanatory notes - Mamzer. *23b* Lit. To the face of evening.

and shall turn away from you.

15 "You do not hand over to his master the slave who has escaped from his master to you.

16 "Let him dwell with you in your midst, in the place which he chooses within one of your gates, where it is pleasing to him. Do not oppress him.

17 "None of the daughters of Yisra'ĕl is to be a cult prostitute, nor any of the sons of Yisra'ĕl be a cult prostitute.

18 "Do not bring the harlot-fee of a whore or the pay of a dog[c] to the House of יהוה your Elohim for any vowed offering, for both of these are an abomination to יהוה your Elohim.

19 "Do not lend at interest to your brother, interest of silver, interest of food, or interest of whatever is lent at interest.

20 "To a foreigner you lend at interest, but to your brother you do not lend at interest, so that יהוה your Elohim might bless you in all that you put your hand to in the land which you are entering to possess.

21 "When you make a vow to יהוה your Elohim, do not delay to pay it, for יהוה your Elohim is certainly requiring it of you, and it shall be sin in you.

22 "But when you abstain from vowing, it is not sin in you.

23 "That which has gone from your lips you shall guard and do, for you voluntarily vowed to יהוה your Elohim what you have promised with your mouth.

24 "When you come into your neighbour's vineyard, you shall eat to the satisfaction of your desire, but do not put any in a receptacle of yours.

25 "When you come into your neighbour's standing grain, you shall pluck the heads with your hand, but do not use a sickle on your neighbour's standing grain.

24

"When a man takes a wife and shall marry her, then it shall be, if she finds no favour in his eyes because he has found a matter of uncoveredness[a] in her, and he shall write her a certificate of divorce, and put it in her hand, and send her out of his house,

2 and if she left his house and went and became another man's wife,

3 and the latter husband shall hate her and write her a certificate of divorce, and put it in her hand, and send her out of his house, or when the latter husband dies who took her to be his wife,

4 then her former husband who sent her away is not allowed to take her back to be his wife after she has been defiled, for that would be an abomination before יהוה. And do not bring sin on the land which יהוה your Elohim is giving you as an inheritance.

5 "When a man has taken a new wife, let him not go out into the army nor let any matter be imposed upon him. He shall be exempt one year for the sake of his home, to rejoice with his wife whom he has taken.

6 "No one takes in pledge the lower or the upper millstone, for he would be taking a life in pledge.

7 "When a man is found kidnapping any of his brothers of the children of Yisra'ĕl, and treats him harshly or sells him, then that kidnapper shall die. Thus you shall purge the evil from your midst.

8 "Take heed, in an outbreak of leprosy, to diligently guard and do according to all that the priests, the Lĕwites, teach you. As I have commanded them, so you shall guard to do.

9 "Remember what יהוה your Elohim did to Miryam on the way when you came out of Mitsrayim.

10 "When you lend your brother a loan, do not go into his house to get his pledge.

11 "Stand outside, and let the man to whom you lend bring the pledge out to you.

12 "And if the man is poor, do not sleep with his pledge.

13 "By all means return the pledge to him at sundown, and he shall sleep in his own garment, and shall bless you. And it shall be righteousness to you before יהוה your

23c Male prostitute. *24a* Proof that she is not a maiden, indicating that she had previously been fornicating. See also Mt. 5:32 and Mt. 19:9.

Elohim.

14 “Do not oppress a hired servant who is poor and needy, of your brothers or of your strangers who are in your land within your gates.

15 “Give him his wages on the same day, and do not let the sun go down on it, for he is poor and lifts up his being to it, so that he does not cry out against you to יהוה, and it shall be sin in you.

16 “Fathers are not put to death for their children, and children are not put to death for their fathers, each is to die for his own sin.

17 “Do not twist the right-ruling of a stranger or the fatherless, nor take the garment of a widow.

18 “But you shall remember that you were a slave in Mitsrayim, and that יהוה your Elohim ransomed you from there. Therefore I am commanding you to do this word.

19 “When you reap your harvest in your field, and have forgotten a sheaf in the field, do not go back to get it. Let it be for the stranger, for the fatherless, and for the widow, so that יהוה your Elohim might bless you in all the work of your hands.

20 “When you beat your olive trees, do not examine the branch behind you. Let it be for the stranger, for the fatherless, and for the widow.

21 “When you gather the grapes of your vineyard, do not glean behind you. Let it be for the stranger, for the fatherless, and for the widow.

22 “And you shall remember that you were a slave in the land of Mitsrayim. Therefore I am commanding you to do this word.

25 “When there is a dispute between men, then they shall come unto judgment, and they shall be judged, and the righteous declared righteous and the wrongdoer declared wrong.

2 “And it shall be, if the wrongdoer is to be struck, that the judge shall cause him to lie down and be struck in his presence with the number of blows according to his wrong.

3 “Forty strikes he gives him but no more, lest he strike him with many more blows than these, and your brother be degraded before your eyes.

4 “Do not muzzle an ox while it is threshing.

5 “When brothers dwell together, and one of them has died, and has no son, the widow of the dead man shall not become a stranger's outside. Her husband's brother does go in to her, and shall take her as his wife, and perform the duty of a husband's brother to her.

6 “And it shall be that the first-born son which she bears does rise up for the name of his dead brother, so that his name is not blotted out of Yisra'ěl.

7 “But if the man does not desire to take his brother's wife, then let his brother's wife go up to the gate to the elders, and say, ‘My husband's brother refuses to raise up a name to his brother in Yisra'ěl, he does not agree to perform the duty of my husband's brother.’

8 “The elders of his city shall then call him and speak to him, and he shall stand and say, ‘I have no desire to take her,’

9 then his brother's wife shall come to him in the presence of the elders, and remove his sandal from his foot, and shall spit in his face, and answer and say, ‘Thus it is done to the man who does not build up his brother's house.’

10 “And in Yisra'ěl his name shall be called, ‘The house of him who had his sandal removed.’

11 “When men fight with one another, a man and his brother, and the wife of one shall draw near to rescue her husband from the hand of the one striking him, and shall put out her hand and take hold of him by the genitals,

12 then you shall cut off her hand – your eye does not pardon.

13 “You shall not have in your bag differing weights, a heavy and a light.

14 “You shall not have in your house differing measures, a large and a small.

15 “You shall have a perfect and right weight, a perfect and right measure, so that they prolong your days on the soil which יהוה your Elohim is giving you.

16 “For all who do these, and all who do unrighteously, are an abomination to יהוה your Elohim.

17 “Remember what Amalěq did to you on the way as you were coming out of Mitsrayim,

18 how he met you on the way and attacked your back, all the feeble ones in your rear, when you were tired and weary. And he did not fear Elohim.

19 “Therefore it shall be, when יהוה your Elohim has given you rest from your enemies all around, in the land which יהוה your Elohim is giving you to possess as an inheritance, that you blot out the remembrance of Amalěq from under the heavens. Do not forget!

26 “And it shall be, when you come into the land which יהוה your Elohim is giving you as an inheritance, and you possess it and dwell in it,

2 that you shall take some of the first of all the fruits of the soil which you bring from your land that יהוה your Elohim is giving you, and shall put it in a basket and go to the place where יהוה your Elohim chooses to make His Name dwell there.

3 “And you shall come to the one who is priest in those days, and say to him, ‘I shall declare today to יהוה your Elohim that I have come to the land which יהוה swore to our fathers to give us.’

4 “And the priest shall take the basket from your hand and place it before the slaughter-place of יהוה your Elohim.

5 “And you shall answer and say before יהוה your Elohim, ‘My father was a perishing Aramean, and he went down to Mitsrayim and sojourned there with few men. And there he became a nation, great, mighty, and numerous.

6 ‘But the Mitsrites did evil to us, and afflicted us, and imposed hard labour on us.

7 ‘Then we cried out to יהוה Elohim of our fathers, and יהוה heard our voice and saw our affliction and our toil and our oppression.

8 ‘And יהוה brought us out of Mitsrayim with a strong hand and with an outstretched arm, with great fear and with signs and wonders.

9 ‘And He brought us to this place and has given us this land, “a land flowing with milk and honey.”

10 ‘And now, see, I have brought the first-fruits of the land which You, O יהוה, have given me.’ Then you shall place it before יהוה your Elohim, and bow down before יהוה your Elohim,

11 and shall rejoice in all the good which יהוה your Elohim has given to you and your house, you and the Lěwite and the stranger who is among you.

12 “When you have completed tithing all the tithe of your increase in the third year, which is the year of tithing, and have given it to the Lěwite, to the stranger, to the fatherless, and to the widow, and they have eaten within your gates and have been satisfied,

13 then you shall say before יהוה your Elohim, ‘I have put away the set-apart *portion* from my house, and also have given it to the Lěwite, and to the stranger, and to the fatherless, and to the widow, according to all Your command which You have commanded me. I have not transgressed Your commands, nor have I forgotten.

14 ‘I have not eaten any of it when in mourning, nor have I removed any of it for any unclean use, nor given any of it for the dead. I have obeyed the voice of יהוה my Elohim, I have done according to all that You have commanded me.

15 ‘Look from Your set-apart dwelling place, from the heavens, and bless Your people Yisra’ěl and the land which You have given us, as You swore to our fathers, “a land flowing with milk and honey.” ’

16 “Today יהוה your Elohim is commanding you to do these laws and right-rulings. And you shall guard and do them with all your heart and with all your being.

17 “You have today caused יהוה to proclaim to be your Elohim, and to walk in His ways and guard His laws, and His commands, and His right-rulings, and to obey His voice.

18 “And יהוה has caused you to proclaim today to be His people, a treasured posses-

sion, as He has spoken to you, and to guard
all His commands,
19 so as to set you high above all nations
which He has made, for a praise, and for a
name, and for esteem, and for you to be a
set-apart people to יהוה your Elohim, as
He has spoken."

27 And Mosheh, with the elders of
Yisra'ěl, commanded the people,
saying, "Guard all the commands which I
am commanding you today.
2 "And it shall be, on the day when you
pass over the Yarděn to the land which
יהוה your Elohim is giving you, that you
shall set up for yourselves large stones, and
plaster them with plaster,
3 and write on them all the Words of this
Torah, when you have passed over, so that
you go into the land which יהוה your
Elohim is giving you, 'a land flowing with
milk and honey,' as יהוה Elohim of your
fathers has spoken to you.
4 "And it shall be, when you have passed
over the Yarděn, that on Mount Ěyḇal you
set up these stones, which I command you
today, and you shall plaster them with
plaster,
5 and build an slaughter-place to יהוה
your Elohim there, a slaughter-place of
stones – do not use an iron *tool* on them.
6 "Build the slaughter-place of יהוה your
Elohim with complete stones, and you
shall offer ascending offerings on it to יהוה
your Elohim,
7 and shall slaughter peace *offerings*, and
eat there, and rejoice before יהוה your
Elohim.
8 "And you shall write all the Words of
this Torah on the stones – plainly and
well."
9 And Mosheh and the priests, the
Lěwites, spoke to all Yisra'ěl, saying, "Be
silent and hear, O Yisra'ěl: This day you
have become the people of יהוה your
Elohim,
10 and you shall obey the voice of יהוה
your Elohim, and do His commands and
His laws which I command you today."
11 And Mosheh commanded the people on
that day, saying,
12 "These are to stand on Mount Gerizim
to bless the people, when you have passed
over the Yarděn: Shimʿon, and Lěwi, and
Yehuḏah, and Yissasḵar, and Yosěph, and
Binyamin.
13 "And these are to stand on Mount Ěyḇal
to curse: Re'uḇěn, Gaḏ, and Ashěr, and
Zeḇulun, Dan, and Naphtali.
14 "And the Lěwites shall speak with a
loud voice and say to all the men of
Yisra'ěl:
15 'Cursed is the man who makes a carved
or moulded image, an abomination to יהוה,
the work of the hands of the craftsman, and
sets it up in secret.' And all the people
shall answer and say, 'Aměn!'
16 'Cursed is he who makes light of his
father or his mother.' And all the people
shall say, 'Aměn!'
17 'Cursed is he who moves his neighbour's boundary.' And all the people shall
say, 'Aměn!'
18 'Cursed is he who misleads the blind in
the way.' And all the people shall say,
'Aměn!'
19 'Cursed is he who twists the right-
ruling of the stranger, the fatherless, and
widow.' And all the people shall say,
'Aměn!'
20 'Cursed is he who lies with his father's
wife, because he has uncovered his father's
bed.' And all the people shall say, 'Aměn!'
21 'Cursed is he who lies with any beast.'
And all the people shall say, 'Aměn!'
22 'Cursed is he who lies with his sister,
the daughter of his father or the daughter of
his mother.' And all the people shall say,
'Aměn!'
23 'Cursed is he who lies with his mother-
in-law.' And all the people shall say,
'Aměn!'
24 'Cursed is he who strikes his neighbour
secretly.' And all the people shall say,
'Aměn!'
25 'Cursed is he who takes a bribe to strike
an innocent being.' And all the people
shall say, 'Aměn!'
26 'Cursed is he who does not establish the
Words of this Torah.' And all the people
shall say, 'Aměn!'

28 "And it shall be, if you diligently obey the voice of יהוה your Elohim, to guard to do all His commands which I command you today, that יהוה your Elohim shall set you high above all nations of the earth.
2 "And all these blessings shall come upon you and overtake you, if you obey the voice of יהוה your Elohim:
3 "Blessed are you in the city, and blessed are you in the field.
4 "Blessed is the fruit of your body, and the fruit of your ground and the fruit of your livestock – the increase of your cattle and the offspring of your flocks.
5 "Blessed is your basket and your kneading bowl.
6 "Blessed are you when you come in, and blessed are you when you go out.
7 "יהוה causes your enemies who rise against you to be smitten before your face – they come out against you one way and flee before you seven ways.
8 "יהוה commands the blessing on you in your storehouses and in all to which you set your hand, and shall bless you in the land which יהוה your Elohim is giving you.
9 "יהוה does establish you as a set-apart people to Himself, as He has sworn to you, if you guard the commands of יהוה your Elohim and walk in His ways.
10 "And all peoples of the earth shall see that the Name of יהוה is called upon you, and they shall be afraid of you.
11 "And יהוה shall make you to have plenty of what is good, in the fruit of your body, in the fruit of your livestock, and in the fruit of your ground, in the land of which יהוה swore to your fathers to give you.
12 "יהוה opens to you His good treasure, the heavens, to give the rain to your land in its season, and to bless all the work of your hand. And you shall lend to many nations, but you do not borrow.
13 "And יהוה shall make you the head and not the tail. And you shall be only on top, and not be beneath, if you obey the commands of יהוה your Elohim, which I command you today, to guard and do.
14 "And do not turn aside from any of the Words which I am commanding you today, right or left, to go after other mighty ones to serve them.
15 "And it shall be, if you do not obey the voice of יהוה your Elohim, to guard to do all His commands and His laws which I command you today, that all these curses shall come upon you and overtake you:
16 "Cursed are you in the city, and cursed are you in the field.
17 "Cursed is your basket and your kneading bowl.
18 "Cursed is the fruit of your body and the fruit of your land, the increase of your cattle and the offspring of your flocks.
19 "Cursed are you when you come in, and cursed are you when you go out.
20 "יהוה sends on you the curse, the confusion, and the rebuke in all that you set your hand to do, until you are destroyed and until you perish quickly, because of the evil of your doings by which you have forsaken Me.
21 "יהוה makes the plague cling to you until He has consumed you from the land which you are going to possess.
22 "יהוה strikes you with wasting disease, and with inflammation, and with burning, and with extreme heat, and with the sword, and with blight, and with mildew. And they shall pursue you until you perish.
23 "And your heavens which are over your head shall be bronze, and the earth which is under you iron.
24 "יהוה makes the rain of your land powder and dust; from the heavens it comes down on you until you are destroyed.
25 "יהוה causes you to be defeated before your enemies – you go out one way against them and flee seven ways before them. And you shall become a horror to all the reigns of the earth.
26 "And your carcasses shall be food for all the birds of the heavens and the beasts of the earth, with no one to frighten them away.
27 "יהוה shall strike you with the boils of Mitsrayim, with tumours, with the scab, and with the itch, from which you are unable to be healed.

[28]"יהוה shall strike you with madness and blindness and bewilderment of heart.
[29]"And you shall be groping at noon, as a blind man gropes in darkness, and not prosper in your ways. And you shall be only oppressed and plundered all the days, with no one to save you.
[30]"You become engaged to a wife, but another man does lie with her. You build a house, but do not dwell in it. You plant a vineyard, but do not use its fruit.
[31]"Your ox is slaughtered before your eyes, but you do not eat of it. Your donkey is violently taken from before you, and it is not given back to you. Your sheep are given to your enemies, with no one to save them.
[32]"Your sons and your daughters are given to another people, and your eyes look and fail for them all day long, and your hand powerless.
[33]"A people whom you have not known eat the fruit of your land and all your labours. And you shall be only oppressed and crushed all the days.
[34]"And you shall be maddened because of the sight which your eyes see.
[35]"יהוה strikes you in the knees and on the legs with evil boils of which you are unable to be healed, and from the sole of your foot to the top of your head.
[36]"יהוה brings you and the sovereign whom you set over you to a nation which neither you nor your fathers have known, and there you shall serve other mighty ones, wood and stone.
[37]"Thus you shall become an astonishment, a proverb, and a mockery among all the peoples to which יהוה drives you.
[38]"You take much seed out into the field but gather little in, for the locust consumes it.
[39]"You plant vineyards, and shall labour, but you neither drink of the wine nor gather, for the worm eats it.
[40]"You have olive trees in all your border, but do not anoint with oil, for your olives drop off.
[41]"You bring forth sons and daughters, but they are not with you, for they go into captivity.
[42]"Locusts possess all your trees and the fruit of your ground.
[43]"The sojourner who is among you rises higher and higher above you, but you come down lower and lower.
[44]"He lends to you, but you do not lend to him. He is the head, and you are the tail.
[45]"And all these curses shall come upon you, and they shall pursue and overtake you, until you are destroyed, because you did not obey the voice of יהוה your Elohim, to guard His commands and His laws which He commanded you.
[46]"And they shall be upon you for a sign and for a wonder, and on your seed, forever.
[47]"Because you did not serve יהוה your Elohim with joy and gladness of heart for all the plenty,
[48]you shall serve your enemies whom יהוה sends against you, in hunger, and in thirst, and in nakedness, and in need of all. And he shall put a yoke of iron on your neck until he has destroyed you.
[49]"יהוה shall bring a nation against you from afar, from the end of the earth, as swift as the eagle flies, a nation whose language you shall not understand,
[50]a fierce-looking nation, which shall show no regard for the elderly nor show favour to the young,
[51]and they shall eat the fruit of your livestock and the fruit of your land, until you are destroyed. They leave you no grain, nor new wine, nor oil, nor the increase of your cattle or the offspring of your flocks, until they have destroyed you.
[52]"And they shall besiege you at all your gates till your high and fenced walls, in which you are trusting, come down in all your land. And they shall besiege you at all your gates in all your land which יהוה your Elohim has given you.
[53]"And you shall eat the fruit of your own body, the flesh of your sons and your daughters whom יהוה your Elohim has given you, in the siege and distress in which your enemies distress you.
[54]"The man among you who is tender, and who is very delicate, his eye is evil against his brother, against the wife of his

bosom, and against the rest of his children
whom he leaves behind,
55 against giving any of them the flesh of
his children that he eats, because it is all
that has been left to him in the siege and
distress with which your enemy distresses
you in all your gates.
56 "The tender and the delicate woman
among you, who has not tried to set the
sole of her foot on the ground because of
her delicateness and tenderness, her eye is
evil against the husband of her bosom, and
against her son, and against her daughter,
57 and against her seed which comes out
from between her feet, and her children
whom she bears, for she eats them in secret
for lack of all, in the siege and distress with
which your enemy distresses you in all
your gates.
58 "If you do not guard to do all the Words
of this Torah that are written in this book,
to fear this esteemed and awesome Name,
יהוה your Elohim,
59 then יהוה shall bring upon you and
your descendants extraordinary plagues,
great and lasting plagues, and grievous and
lasting sicknesses.
60 "And He shall bring back on you all the
diseases of Mitsrayim, of which you were
afraid, and they shall cling to you,
61 also every sickness and every plague,
which is not written in the book of this
Torah, יהוה does bring upon you until you
are destroyed.
62 "And you shall be left with few men,
although you had become as numerous as
the stars of the heavens, because you did
not obey the voice of יהוה your Elohim.
63 "And it shall be, that as יהוה rejoiced
over you to do you good and increase you,
so יהוה does rejoice over you to destroy
you and lay you waste. And you shall be
plucked from off the land which you go to
possess.
64 "And יהוה shall scatter you among all
peoples, from one end of the earth to the
other, and there you shall serve other
mighty ones, which neither you nor your
fathers have known, wood and stone.
65 "And among those nations you are to
find no rest, nor have a resting place for the
sole of your foot. But there יהוה shall give
you a trembling heart, and failing eyes, and
sorrow of being.
66 "And your life shall be hanging in suspense before you, and you shall fear night
and day, and not be certain of your life.
67 "In the morning you say, 'Oh, that it
were evening!' And at evening you say,
'Oh, that it were morning!' because of the
fear of your heart, with which you fear, and
because of the sight which your eyes see.
68 "And יהוה shall bring you back to
Mitsrayim in ships, by a way of which I
said to you, 'You are never to see it again.'
And there you shall be sold to your
enemies as male and female slaves, but no
one to buy."

29

These are the words of the
covenant which יהוה commanded
Mosheh to make with the children of
Yisra'ěl in the land of Mo'aḇ, besides the
covenant which He made with them in
Ḥorěḇ.
2 And Mosheh called all Yisra'ěl and
said to them, "You yourselves saw all that
יהוה did before your eyes in the land
of Mitsrayim, to Pharaoh and to all his
servants and to all his land.
3 "Your eyes saw the great trials, the
signs, and those great wonders.
4 "But יהוה has not given you a heart to
know and eyes to see and ears to hear, till
this day.
5 "And I have led you forty years in the
wilderness. Your garments have not worn
out on you, and your sandals have not
worn out on your feet.
6 "You ate no bread and drank no wine
nor strong drink, so that you might know
that I am יהוה your Elohim.
7 "And when you came to this place,
Siḥon sovereign of Ḥeshbon and Oḡ
sovereign of Bashan came out against us to
battle, and we struck them,
8 and took their land and gave it as an
inheritance to the Re'uḇěnites, and to the
Gaḏites, and to half the tribe of Menashsheh.
9 "Therefore you shall guard the words of
this covenant, and do them, so that you

prosper in all that you do.

10 "All of you are standing today before יהוה your Elohim: your leaders, your tribes, your elders and your officers, all the men of Yisra'ěl,

11 your little ones, your wives, and your sojourner who is in the midst of your camp, from the one who cuts your wood to the one who draws your water,

12 so that you should enter into covenant with יהוה your Elohim, and into His oath, which יהוה your Elohim makes with you today,

13 in order to establish you today as a people for Himself, and He Himself be your Elohim, as He has spoken to you, and as He has sworn to your fathers, to Aḇraham, to Yitsḥaq, and to Ya'aqoḇ.

14 "And not with you alone I am making this covenant and this oath,

15 but with him who stands here with us today before יהוה our Elohim, as well as with him who is not here with us today.

16 "For you know how we dwelt in the land of Mitsrayim and how we passed through the nations which you passed through,

17 and you saw their abominations and their idols, wood and stone, silver and gold, which were with them,

18 lest there should be among you a man or woman or clan or tribe, whose heart turns away today from יהוה our Elohim, to go and serve the mighty ones of these nations, lest there should be among you a root bearing bitterness or wormwood.

19 "And it shall be, when he hears the words of this curse, that he should bless himself in his heart, saying, 'I have peace though I walk in the stubbornness of my heart,' in order to add drunkenness to thirst.

20 "יהוה would not forgive him, but rather, the displeasure of יהוה and His jealousy shall burn against that man, and every curse that is written in this book shall settle on him, and יהוה shall blot out his name from under the heavens.

21 "And יהוה shall separate him for evil, out of all the tribes of Yisra'ěl, according to all the curses of the covenant that are written in this Book of the Torah.

22 "And the generation to come of your children who rise up after you, and the foreigner who comes from a far land, shall say when they see the plagues of that land and the sicknesses which יהוה has sent into it:

23 'All its land is sulphur, salt, and burning; it is not sown, nor does it bear, nor does any grass grow there, like the overthrow of Seḏom and Amorah, Aḏmah and Tseḇoyim, which יהוה overthrew in His displeasure and His wrath.'

24 "And all nations shall say, 'Why has יהוה done so to this land? What does the heat of this great displeasure mean?'

25 "And it shall be said, 'Because they have forsaken the covenant of יהוה Elohim of their fathers, which He made with them when He brought them out of the land of Mitsrayim.

26 'And they went and served other mighty ones and bowed themselves to them, mighty ones that they did not know and that He had not given to them,

27 therefore the displeasure of יהוה burned against this land, to bring on it every curse that is written in this book.

28 'And יהוה uprooted them from their land in displeasure, and in wrath, and in great rage, and cast them into another land, as it is today.'

29 "The secret *matters* belong to יהוה our Elohim, but what is revealed belongs to us and to our children forever, to do all the Words of this Torah.

30

"And it shall be, when all these words come upon you, the blessing and the curse which I have set before you, and you shall bring them back to your heart among all the nations where יהוה your Elohim drives you,

2 and shall turn back to יהוה your Elohim and obey His voice, according to all that I command you today, with all your heart and with all your being, you and your children,

3 then יהוה your Elohim shall turn back your captivity, and shall have compassion on you, and He shall turn back and gather

you from all the peoples where יהוה your Elohim has scattered you.

4 "If any of you are driven out to the farthest parts under the heavens, from there יהוה your Elohim does gather you, and from there He does take you.

5 "And יהוה your Elohim shall bring you to the land which your fathers possessed, and you shall possess it. And He shall do good to you, and increase you more than your fathers.

6 "And יהוה your Elohim shall circumcise your heart and the heart of your seed, to love יהוה your Elohim with all your heart and with all your being, so that you might live,

7 and יהוה your Elohim shall put all these curses on your enemies and on those who hate you, who persecuted you.

8 "And you shall turn back and obey the voice of יהוה and do all His commands which I command you today.

9 "And יהוה your Elohim shall make you have excess in all the work of your hand, in the fruit of your body, and in the fruit of your livestock, and in the fruit of your ground for good. For יהוה turns back to rejoice over you for good as He rejoiced over your fathers,

10 if you obey the voice of יהוה your Elohim, to guard His commands and His laws which are written in this Book of the Torah, if you turn back to יהוה your Elohim with all your heart and with all your being.

11 "For this command which I am commanding you today, it is not too hard for you, nor is it far off.

12 "It is not in the heavens, to say, 'Who shall ascend into the heavens for us, and bring it to us, and cause us to hear it, so that we do it?'

13 "Nor is it beyond the sea, to say, 'Who shall go over the sea for us, and bring it to us, and cause us to hear it, so that we do it?'

14 "For the Word is very near you, in your mouth and in your heart – to do it.

15 "See, I have set before you today life and good, and death and evil,

16 in that I am commanding you today to love יהוה your Elohim, to walk in His ways, and to guard His commands, and His laws, and His right-rulings. And you shall live and increase, and יהוה your Elohim shall bless you in the land which you go to possess.

17 "But if your heart turns away, and you do not obey, and shall be drawn away, and shall bow down to other mighty ones and serve them,

18 "I have declared to you today that you shall certainly perish, you shall not prolong your days in the land which you are passing over the Yardĕn to enter and possess.

19 "I have called the heavens and the earth as witnesses today against you: I have set before you life and death, the blessing and the curse. Therefore you shall choose life, so that you live, both you and your seed,

20 to love יהוה your Elohim, to obey His voice, and to cling to Him – for He is your life and the length of your days – to dwell in the land which יהוה swore to your fathers, to Aḇraham, to Yitsḥaq, and to Ya'aqoḇ, to give them."

31 And Mosheh went and spoke these words to all Yisra'ĕl,

2 and he said to them, "I am one hundred and twenty years old today. I am no longer able to go out and come in. And יהוה has said to me, 'You do not pass over this Yardĕn.'

3 "יהוה your Elohim Himself is passing over before you. He shall destroy these nations from before you and you possess them. Yehoshua himself is passing over before you, as יהוה has spoken.

4 "And יהוה shall do to them as He did to Siḥon and to Oḡ, the sovereigns of the Amorites and their land, when He destroyed them.

5 "And יהוה shall give them over to you, and you shall do to them according to all the command which I have commanded you.

6 "Be strong and courageous, do not fear nor be afraid of them. For it is יהוה your Elohim who is going with you. He does not fail you nor forsake you."

7 And Mosheh called Yehoshua and said

to him before the eyes of all Yisra'ěl, "Be
strong and courageous, for you are going
with this people to the land which יהוה
has sworn to their fathers to give them, and
you are to let them inherit it.
8 "And it is יהוה who is going before
you, He Himself is with you. He does not
fail you nor forsake you. Do not fear nor be
discouraged."
9 And Mosheh wrote this Torah and gave
it to the priests, the sons of Lěwi, who bore
the ark of the covenant of יהוה, and to all
the elders of Yisra'ěl.
10 And Mosheh commanded them, saying,
"At the end of seven years, at the appointed time, the year of release, at the Festival
of Sukkot [a],
11 when all Yisra'ěl comes to appear
before יהוה your Elohim in the place
which He chooses, read this Torah before
all Yisra'ěl in their hearing.
12 "Assemble the people, the men and the
women and the little ones, and your
sojourner who is within your gates, so that
they hear, and so that they learn to fear
יהוה your Elohim and guard to do all the
Words of this Torah.
13 "And their children, who have not
known it, should hear and learn to fear
יהוה your Elohim as long as you live in the
land you are passing over the Yarděn to
possess."
14 And יהוה said to Mosheh, "See, the
days have drawn near for you to die. Call
Yehoshua, and present yourselves in the
Tent of Appointment, so that I command
him." And Mosheh and Yehoshua went
and presented themselves in the Tent of
Appointment.
15 And יהוה appeared at the Tent in a
column of a cloud, and the column of a
cloud stood above the door of the Tent.
16 And יהוה said to Mosheh, "See, you
are about to sleep with your fathers. And
this people shall rise and whore after the
mighty ones of the strangers of the land
into the midst of which they shall enter,
and forsake Me and break My covenant
which I have made with them.
17 "Then My displeasure shall burn
against them in that day, and I shall forsake
them and hide My face from them, and
they shall be consumed. And many evils
and distresses shall come upon them, and it
shall be said in that day, 'Is it not because
our Elohim is not in our midst that these
evils have come upon us?'
18 "And I shall certainly hide My face in
that day, because of all the evil which they
have done, for they shall turn to other
mighty ones.
19 "And now write down this song for
yourselves, and teach it to the children of
Yisra'ěl. Put it in their mouths, so that
this song is to Me for a witness against the
children of Yisra'ěl.
20 "And I shall bring them to the land
flowing with milk and honey, of which I
swore to their fathers, and they shall eat
and be satisfied and be fat, then they shall
turn to other mighty ones, and they shall
serve them, and scorn Me and break My
covenant.
21 "And it shall be, when many evils and
distresses come upon them, that this song
shall answer before them as a witness. For
it is not to be forgotten in the mouths of
their seed, for I know their thoughts which
they are forming today, even before I bring
them to the land of which I swore to give
them."
22 And Mosheh wrote this song the same
day, and taught it to the children of
Yisra'ěl.
23 And He commanded Yehoshua son of
Nun, and said, "Be strong and courageous,
for you are to bring the children of Yisra'ěl
into the land of which I swore to them, and
I Myself am with you."
24 And it came to be, when Mosheh had
completed writing the Words of this Torah
in a book, until their completion,
25 that Mosheh commanded the Lěwites,
who bore the ark of the covenant of יהוה,
saying,
26 "Take this Book of the Torah, and you
shall place it beside the ark of the covenant
of יהוה your Elohim, and it shall be there

31a - Booths.

as a witness against you,
27 for I myself know your rebellion and
your stiff neck. See, while I am still alive
with you today, you have been rebellious
against יהוה, then how much more after
my death?
28 "Assemble unto me all the elders of
your tribes, and your officers, so that I
speak these words in their hearing and call
the heavens and the earth to witness
against them.
29 "For I know that after my death you
shall do very corruptly and turn aside from
the way which I have commanded you.
And evil shall come to you in the latter
days, because you do what is evil in the
eyes of יהוה, to provoke Him through the
work of your hands."
30 So Mosheh spoke in the hearing of all
the assembly of Yisra'ěl the words of this
song till their completion:

32 "Give ear, O heavens, and let me speak;
And hear, O earth,
The words of my mouth.
2 "Let my instruction fall as rain,
My speech drop down as dew,
As fine rain on the tender plants,
And as showers on the grass.
3 "For I proclaim the Name of יהוה,
Ascribe greatness to our Elohim.
4 "The Rock! His work is perfect,
For all His ways are right-ruling,
An Ěl of truth and without unrighteousness,
Righteous and straight is He.
5 "A twisted and crooked generation has corrupted itself,
Their blemish, *they are* not His children.
6 "Do you do this to יהוה,
O foolish and unwise people?
Is He not your Father, who bought you,
Who created you and established you?
7 "Remember the days of old,
Consider the years of many generations.
Ask your father and let him show you,
Your elders, and let them say to you:
8 "When the Most High gave the nations their inheritance
When He separated the sons of Aḏam,
He set the boundaries of the peoples
According to the number of the children of Yisra'ěl.
9 "For the portion of יהוה is His people,
Ya'aqoḇ His allotted inheritance.
10 "He found him in a wilderness,
And in a wasted, howling desert.
He encompassed him,
He made him understand,
He watched over him as the apple of His eye. [a]
11 "As an eagle stirs up its nest,
Flutters over its young,
Spreading out its wings, taking them up,
Bearing them on its wings.
12 "יהוה alone led him,
And there was no strange mighty one with him.
13 "He made him ride in the heights of the earth,
And he ate the fruit of the fields,
And He made him to draw honey from the rock,
And oil from the flinty rock,
14 "Curds from the cattle,
And milk of the flock,
With fat of lambs,
And rams of the breed of Bashan,
And goats, with the choicest wheat;
And you drank wine, the blood of the grapes.
15 "But Yeshurun grew fat and kicked;
You grew fat, you grew thick,
You are covered with fat;
So he forsook Eloah who made him,
And scorned the Rock of his deliverance.
16 "They moved Him to jealousy with foreign *matters*,
With abominations they provoked Him.
17 "They slaughtered to demons – not Eloah –
Mighty ones they did not know,

32a See Zeḵ. 2:8.

New ones who came lately,
Which your fathers did not fear.
18 "You neglected the Rock who brought you forth,
And forgot the Ěl who fathered you.
19 "And יהוה saw, and despised,
Because of the provocation of His sons and His daughters.
20 "And He said, 'Let Me hide My face from them,
Let Me see what their end is,
For they are a perverse generation,
Children in whom there is no trusting.
21 "They made Me jealous by what is not Ěl,
They provoked Me with their worthless *matters*.
But I make them jealous by those who are no people,
I provoke them with a foolish nation.
22 "For a fire was kindled in My wrath
And burns to the bottom of She'ol, [b]
And consumes the earth and its increase,
And sets on fire the foundations of mountains.
23 "I gather evils upon them,
I use up My arrows upon them –
24 "Wasted by scarcity of food,
And consumed by heat and bitter destruction,
And the teeth of beasts I send upon them,
With the poison of serpents of the dust.
25 "The sword bereaves from the outside,
And fear from within,
Both young man and maiden,
Nursing child with the man of grey hairs.
26 "I said, 'I should blow them away,
I should make the remembrance of them
To cease from among men,
27 'If I did not fear the enemy's taunt,
Lest their adversaries misunderstand,
Lest they say, "Our hand is high,
And יהוה has not done all this." '
28 "For they are a nation lost to counsel,
And there is no understanding in them.
29 "If they were wise,
They would understand this,
They would consider their latter end!
30 "How would one chase a thousand,
And two put ten thousand to flight,
Unless their Rock had sold them,
And יהוה had given them up?
31 "For their rock is not like our Rock –
Even our enemies are judges.
32 "Their vine is of the vine of Seḏom
And of the fields of Amorah;
Their grapes are grapes of gall,
Their clusters are bitter.
33 "Their wine is the poison of serpents,
And the fierce venom of cobras.
34 'Is it not stored up with Me,
Sealed up among My treasures?
35 'Vengeance is Mine, and repayment,
At the time their foot slips;
For near is the day of their calamity,
And the *matters* prepared are hastening to them.'
36 "For יהוה rightly rules His people
And has compassion on His servants,
When He sees that their power is gone,
And there is no one remaining,
Shut up or at large.
37 "And He shall say,
'Where are their mighty ones,
The rock in whom they sought refuge?
38 'Who ate the fat of their slaughterings,
And drank the wine of their drink offering?
Let them arise and help you,
Let it be a hiding-place for you!
39 'See now that I, I am He,
And there is no Elohim besides Me.
I put to death and I make alive.
I have wounded, and I heal.
And from My hand no one delivers!
40 'For I lift My hand to the heavens,
And shall say: As I live forever,
41 'If I have sharpened My flashing sword,
And My hand takes hold on judgment,
I shall return vengeance to My enemies,
And repay those who hate Me.
42 'I make My arrows drunk with blood,

32b See Explanatory notes - She'ol.

And My sword devours flesh,
With the blood of the slain and the captives,
From the long-haired enemy chiefs.’
43 “O nations, acclaim His people!
For He avenges the blood of His servants,
And returns vengeance to His adversaries,
And shall pardon His land, His people.”
44 Then Mosheh came, with Hoshěa son
of Nun, and spoke all the words of this
song in the hearing of the people.
45 And when Mosheh ended speaking all
these words to all Yisra’ěl,
46 he said to them, “Set your heart on all
the words with which I warn you today, so
that you command your children to guard
to do all the Words of this Torah.
47 “For it is not a worthless Word for you,
because it is your life, and by this Word
you prolong your days on the soil which
you pass over the Yarděn to possess.”
48 And יהוה spoke to Mosheh that same
day, saying,
49 “Go up this mountain of the Aḇarim,
Mount Neḇo, which is in the land of
Mo’aḇ, which is opposite Yeriḥo, and look
at the land of Kenaʽan, which I give to the
children of Yisra’ěl as a possession,
50 and die on the mountain which you
ascend, and be gathered to your people, as
Aharon your brother died on Mount Hor
and was gathered to his people,
51 because you trespassed against Me in
the midst of the children of Yisra’ěl at the
waters of Meriḇah Qaḏěsh, in the Wilderness of Tsin, because you did not set Me
apart in the midst of the children of Yisra’ěl.
52 “For you are to look at the land before
you, but not enter there, into the land
which I am giving to the children of
Yisra’ěl.”

33 And this is the blessing with which
Mosheh the man of Elohim blessed
the children of Yisra’ěl before his death.
2 And he said, “יהוה came from Sinai,
and rose from Sěʽir for them. He shone
forth from Mount Paran, and came with ten
thousands of set-apart ones – at His right
hand a law of fire for them.
3 Indeed, He loves the peoples, all His
set-apart ones are in Your hand. And they,
they sat down at Your feet, receiving Your
Words.
4 Mosheh commanded us a Torah, an
inheritance of the assembly of Yaʽaqoḇ.
5 And He was Sovereign in Yeshurun,
when the heads of the people were gathered, the tribes of Yisra’ěl.
6 “Let Re’uḇěn live, and not die, and let
his men be numbered.”
7 And this of Yehuḏah, and he said,
“Hear, יהוה, the voice of Yehuḏah, and
bring him to his people. His hands shall
fight for him, and You be a help against his
enemies.”
8 And of Lěwi he said, “Your Tummim
and Your Urim belong to Your lovingly-
commited one, whom You tried at Massah,
with whom You contended at the waters of
Meriḇah,
9 who said of his father and mother, ‘I
have not seen them.’ And he did not
acknowledge his brothers, or know his
own children, for they have guarded Your
Word and watched over Your covenant.
10 “They teach Your right-rulings to
Yaʽaqoḇ, and Your Torah to Yisra’ěl. They
put incense before You, and a complete
ascending offering on Your slaughter-
place.
11 “O יהוה, bless his strength, and accept
the work of his hands. Smite the loins of
those who rise against him, and of those
who hate him, that they rise no more.”
12 Of Binyamin he said, “Let the beloved
of יהוה dwell in safety by Him, shielding
him all the day, as he dwells between His
shoulders.”
13 And of Yosěph he said, “Blessed of
יהוה is his land, with the choicest from the
heavens, with the dew, and the deep lying
beneath,
14 with the choice fruits of the sun, with
the choice yield of the months,
15 with the finest of the ancient mountains, with the choicest of the everlasting
hills,

[16]with the choicest of the earth and all that fills it, and the good pleasure of Him who dwelt in the bush. Let it come on the head of Yosěph, and on the crown of the head of him who was separate from his brothers.
[17]"His splendour is like a first-born bull, and his horns are like the horns of the wild ox. With them he pushes the peoples to the ends of the earth. And they are the ten thousands of Ephrayim, and they are the thousands of Menashsheh."
[18]And of Zeḇulun he said, "Rejoice, O Zeḇulun, in your going out, and Yissasḵar in your tents!
[19]"They call peoples to the mountain, there they slaughter slaughterings of righteousness, for they draw from the riches of the seas, and treasures hidden in the sand."
[20]And of Gaḏ he said, "Blessed is he who enlarges Gaḏ. He dwells as a lion, and shall tear off the arm, also the crown.
[21]"And he chose the best for himself, for there the portion of the inscriber was hidden. And he came with the heads of the people. The righteousness of יהוה he did, and His right-rulings with Yisra'ěl."
[22]And of Dan he said, "Dan is a lion's cub, that leaps from Bashan."
[23]And of Naphtali he said, "O Naphtali, satisfied with pleasure, and filled with the blessing of יהוה, possess the west and the south."
[24]And of Ashěr he said, "Ashěr is most blessed of sons. Let him be accepted by his brothers, and dip his foot in oil.
[25]"Your sandals are iron and bronze, and your strength as your days.
[26]"O Yeshurun, there is no one like Ěl, riding the heavens to help you, and on the clouds, in His excellency.
[27]"The Elohim of old is a refuge, and beneath are everlasting arms. And He drives out the enemy from before you and says, 'Destroy!'
[28]"Thus Yisra'ěl dwells in safety, the fountain of Ya'aqoḇ alone, in a land of grain and new wine. His heavens also drop down dew.
[29]"Blessed are you, O Yisra'ěl! Who is like you, a people saved by יהוה, the shield of your help, and He who is the sword of your excellency! And your enemies are subdued for you, and you tread down their high places."

34 And Mosheh went up from the desert plains of Mo'aḇ to Mount Neḇo, to the top of Pisgah, which is opposite Yeriḥo. And יהוה showed him all the land of Gil'aḏ as far as Dan,
[2]and all Naphtali and the land of Ephrayim and Menashsheh, all the land of Yehuḏah as far as the Western Sea,
[3]and the Negeḇ, and the plain of the Valley of Yeriḥo, the city of palm trees, as far as Tso'ar.
[4]And יהוה said to him, "This is the land of which I swore to Aḇraham, to Yitsḥaq, and to Ya'aqoḇ, saying, 'To your seed I give it.' I have let you look at it with your eyes, but you do not pass over there."
[5]And Mosheh the servant of יהוה died there in the land of Mo'aḇ, according to the mouth of יהוה.
[6]And He buried him in a valley in the land of Mo'aḇ, opposite Běyth Pe'or, and no one knows his burial-place to this day.
[7]And Mosheh was one hundred and twenty years old when he died. His eyes were not dim nor his freshness gone.
[8]And the children of Yisra'ěl wept for Mosheh in the desert plains of Mo'aḇ thirty days. And the days of weeping and mourning for Mosheh were completed.
[9]And Yehoshua son of Nun was filled with the spirit of wisdom, for Mosheh had laid his hands on him. And the children of Yisra'ěl listened to him, and did as יהוה had commanded Mosheh.
[10]And since then no prophet has arisen in Yisra'ěl like Mosheh, whom יהוה knew face to face,
[11]for all the signs and wonders which יהוה sent him to do in the land of Mitsrayim, before Pharaoh, and before all his servants, and in all his land,
[12]and for all that strong hand and all the great fearsome deeds which Mosheh did before the eyes of all Yisra'ěl.

YEHOSHUA

JOSHUA

1 And it came to be, after the death of
Mosheh the servant of יהוה, that יהוה
spoke to Yehoshua son of Nun, the assistant of Mosheh, saying,
2 “Mosheh My servant is dead, so now,
arise, pass over this Yarděn, you and all
this people, to the land which I am giving
to them, to the children of Yisra’ěl.
3 “Every place on which the sole of your
foot treads I have given you, as I spoke to
Mosheh.
4 “From the wilderness and this Leḇanon
even as far as the great river, the River
Euphrates, all the land of the Ḥittites, and
to the Great Sea toward the going down of
the sun, is your border.
5 “No man is going to stand before you
all the days of your life. As I was with
Mosheh, so I am with you. I do not fail you
nor forsake you.
6 “Be strong and courageous, for you are
to let this people inherit the land which I
swore to their fathers to give them.
7 “Only be strong and very courageous,
to guard to do according to all the Torah
which Mosheh My servant commanded
you. Do not turn from it right or left, so
that you act wisely wherever you go.
8 “Do not let this Book of the Torah
depart from your mouth, but you shall
meditate on it day and night, so that you
guard to do according to all that is written
in it. For then you shall make your way
prosperous, and act wisely.
9 “Have I not commanded you? Be
strong and courageous. Do not be afraid,
nor be discouraged, for יהוה your Elohim
is with you wherever you go.”
10 And Yehoshua commanded the officers
of the people, saying,
11 “Pass through the midst of the camp
and command the people, saying, ‘Prepare
food for yourselves, for within three days
you are passing over this Yarděn, to go in
to possess the land which יהוה your
Elohim is giving you to possess.’ ”
12 And Yehoshua spoke to the Re’uḇěnites
and to the Gaḏites and to half the tribe of
Menashsheh, saying,
13 “Remember the word which Mosheh,
servant of יהוה, commanded you, saying,
‘יהוה your Elohim is giving you rest, and
He shall give you this land.’
14 “Let your wives, your little ones, and
your livestock stay in the land which
Mosheh gave you beyond the Yarděn. But
you shall pass before your brothers in
fives, all your brave fighters, and shall help
them,
15 until יהוה has given your brothers rest,
as unto you. So shall they also take possession of the land which יהוה your Elohim is
giving them. Then you shall return to the
land of your possession, and shall possess
that which Mosheh the servant of יהוה
gave you beyond the Yarděn toward the
rising of the sun.”
16 And they answered Yehoshua, saying,
“All that you have commanded us we do,
and wherever you send us we go.
17 “According to all that we obeyed
Mosheh, so we obey you. Only, let יהוה
your Elohim be with you, as He was with
Mosheh.
18 “Whoever rebels against your mouth
and does not obey your words, in all that
you command him, is put to death. Only be
strong and courageous.”

2 And Yehoshua son of Nun secretly
sent out two men from Shittim to spy,
saying, “Go, see the land, and Yeriḥo.”
And they went, and came to the house of
a woman, a whore, and her name was
Raḥaḇ, and they lay down there.
2 But it was reported to the sovereign of
Yeriḥo, saying, “See, men from the children of Yisra’ěl have come here tonight to
search out the land.”
3 And the sovereign of Yeriḥo sent to

Raḥaḇ, saying, "Bring out the men who have come to you, who have entered your house, for they have come to search out all the land."

4 But the woman had taken the two men and hid them. So she said, "The men came to me, but I did not know where they were from.

5 "Then it came to be as the gate was being shut, when it was dark, that the men went out. I do not know where the men went. Pursue them quickly, so that you overtake them."

6 But she had brought them up to the roof and hidden them with the stalks of flax, which she had laid out on the roof.

7 And the men pursued them by the way to the Yardĕn, to the fords. And they shut the gate afterwards as soon as the pursuers had gone out.

8 And before they lay down, she came up to them on the roof,

9 and she said to the men, "I know that יהוה has given you the land, and that the fear of you has fallen on us, and that all the inhabitants of the land melt away because of you.

10 "For we have heard how יהוה dried up the water of the Sea of Reeds for you when you came out of Mitsrayim, and what you did to the two sovereigns of the Amorites who were beyond the Yardĕn, Siḥon and Oḡ, whom you put under the ban.

11 "And when we heard, our hearts melted, and there was no spirit left in anyone because of you, for יהוה your Elohim, He is Elohim in the heavens above and on earth beneath.

12 "And now, please swear to me by יהוה, since I have shown you loving-commitment, that you also show loving-commitment to my father's house, and shall give me a true token,

13 and shall spare my father, and my mother, and my brothers, and my sisters, and all that they have, and shall deliver our lives from death."

14 And the men said to her, "Our lives for yours, if you do not expose this matter of ours, then it shall be, when יהוה has given us the land, that we shall treat you in loving-commitment and truth."

15 So she let them down by a rope through the window, for her house was on the city wall and she dwelt on the wall.

16 And she said to them, "Go to the mountain, lest the pursuers come upon you. And you shall hide there three days, until the pursuers have returned, and afterwards go on your way."

17 And the men said to her, "We are released from this oath of yours which you have made us swear,

18 unless, when we come into the land, you bind this line of scarlet cord in the window through which you let us down, and unless you bring your father, and your mother, and your brothers, and all your father's household to your own home.

19 "And it shall be that anyone who goes outside the doors of your house into the street, his blood is on his own head, and we are innocent. And anyone who is with you in the house, his blood is on our head if a hand is laid on him.

20 "And if you expose this matter of ours, then we shall be released from your oath which you made us swear."

21 And she said, "Let it be according to your words." And she sent them away, and they went. And she bound the scarlet cord in the window.

22 So they left and came to the mountain, and stayed there three days until the pursuers returned. And the pursuers sought them in all the way, but did not find them.

23 Then the two men returned and came down from the mountain, and passed over. And they came to Yehoshua son of Nun, and related to him all that had befallen them.

24 And they said to Yehoshua, "Truly יהוה has given all the land into our hands, and also, all the inhabitants of the land have melted away because of us."

3 And Yehoshua rose early in the morning, and they set out from Shittim and came to the Yardĕn, he and all the children of Yisra'ĕl, and stayed there before they passed over.

2 And it came to be, after three days, that

the officers went into the midst of the camp,

3 and they commanded the people, saying, "When you see the ark of the covenant of יהוה your Elohim, and the priests, the Lĕwites, bearing it, then you shall set out from your place and follow it.

4 "Only, keep a distance between you and it, about two thousand cubits by measure. Do not come near it, so that you know which way to go, for you have not passed over this way before."

5 And Yehoshua said to the people, "Set yourselves apart, for tomorrow יהוה is doing wonders in your midst."

6 And Yehoshua spoke to the priests, saying, "Take up the ark of the covenant and pass over before the people." So they took up the ark of the covenant and went before the people.

7 And יהוה said to Yehoshua, "This day I begin to make you great before the eyes of all Yisra'ĕl, so that they know that I am with you as I was with Mosheh.

8 "And you, command the priests who bear the ark of the covenant, saying, 'When you come to the edge of the water of the Yardĕn, stand in the Yardĕn.' "

9 And Yehoshua said to the children of Yisra'ĕl, "Come near, and hear the words of יהוה your Elohim."

10 And Yehoshua said, "By this you shall know that the living Ĕl is in your midst, and that He is certainly driving out from before you the Kena'anites and the Ḥittites and the Ḥiwwites and the Perizzites and the Girgashites and the Amorites and the Yeḇusites:

11 "See, the ark of the covenant of the Master of all the earth is passing over before you into the Yardĕn.

12 "And now, take for yourselves twelve men from the tribes of Yisra'ĕl, one man from every tribe.

13 "And it shall be, as soon as the soles of the feet of the priests who bear the ark of יהוה, the Master of all the earth, come to rest in the waters of the Yardĕn, that the waters of the Yardĕn are cut off, the waters that come down from upstream, and stand as a heap."

14 And it came to be, when the people set out from their tents to pass over the Yardĕn, with the priests bearing the ark of the covenant before the people,

15 and as those bearing the ark came to the Yardĕn, and the feet of the priests bearing the ark dipped in the edge of the water – now the Yardĕn overflows all its banks during all the time of harvest –

16 that the waters which came down from upstream stood still, and rose in a heap very far away at Aḏam, the city that is beside Tsarethan. And the waters going down into the Sea of the Araḇah, the Salt Sea, were completely cut off. And the people passed over opposite Yeriḥo.

17 And the priests bearing the ark of the covenant of יהוה stood firm on dry ground in the midst of the Yardĕn. And all Yisra'ĕl passed over on dry ground, until all the nation had completely passed over the Yardĕn.

4

And it came to be, when the entire nation had completely passed over the Yardĕn, that יהוה spoke to Yehoshua, saying,

2 "Take for yourselves twelve men from the people, one man from every tribe,

3 and command them, saying, 'Take for yourselves twelve stones from here, out of the midst of the Yardĕn, from the place where the priests' feet stood firm. And you shall bring them with you and leave them in the camp in which you spend the night.' "

4 And Yehoshua called the twelve men whom he had appointed from the children of Yisra'ĕl, one man from every tribe,

5 and Yehoshua said to them, "Pass over before the ark of יהוה your Elohim into the midst of the Yardĕn, and each one of you take up a stone on his shoulder, according to the number of the tribes of the children of Yisra'ĕl,

6 so that this shall be a sign in your midst when your children ask in time to come, saying, 'What do these stones mean to you?'

7 "Then you shall answer them that the waters of the Yardĕn were cut off before

the ark of the covenant of יהוה. When it
passed over the Yarděn, the waters of the
Yarděn were cut off. And these stones shall
be for a remembrance to the children of
Yisra'ěl forever."

8 And the children of Yisra'ěl did so, as
Yehoshua commanded, and took up twelve
stones from the midst of the Yarděn, as
יהוה had spoken to Yehoshua, according to
the number of the tribes of the children of
Yisra'ěl, and took them over with them to
their camp, and laid them down there.

9 Yehoshua also set up twelve stones in
the midst of the Yarděn, in the place where
the feet of the priests who bore the ark of
the covenant stood. And they are there to
this day.

10 And the priests who bore the ark stood
in the midst of the Yarděn until every matter was finished that יהוה had commanded
Yehoshua to speak to the people, according
to all that Mosheh had commanded Yehoshua. And the people hastened and passed
over.

11 And it came to be, when all the people
had completely passed over, that the ark of
יהוה and the priests passed over in the
presence of the people.

12 And the sons of Re'uḇěn, and the sons
of Gaḏ, and half the tribe of Menashsheh
passed over in fives before the children of
Yisra'ěl, as Mosheh had spoken to them.

13 About forty thousand armed ones of the
army passed over before יהוה for battle, to
the desert plains of Yeriḥo.

14 On that day יהוה made Yehoshua great
before the eyes of all Yisra'ěl. And they
feared him, as they had feared Mosheh, all
the days of his life.

15 And יהוה spoke to Yehoshua, saying,

16 "Command the priests who bear the ark
of the Witness, and let them come up from
the Yarděn."

17 And Yehoshua commanded the priests,
saying, "Come up from the Yarděn."

18 And it came to be, when the priests
who bore the ark of the covenant of יהוה
had come from the midst of the Yarděn,
and the soles of the priests' feet touched
the dry land, that the waters of the Yarděn
returned to their place and flowed over all
its banks as before.

19 And the people came up from the
Yarděn on the tenth day of the first new
moon, and they camped in Gilgal on the
east border of Yeriḥo.

20 And those twelve stones which they
took out of the Yarděn, Yehoshua set up in
Gilgal.

21 And he said to the children of Yisra'ěl,
saying, "When your children ask their
fathers in time to come, saying, 'What are
these stones?'

22 then you shall let your children know,
saying, 'Yisra'ěl passed over this Yarděn
on dry land,'

23 for יהוה your Elohim dried up the
waters of the Yarděn before you until you
had passed over, as יהוה your Elohim did
to the Sea of Reeds, which He dried up
before us until we had passed over,

24 so that all the peoples of the earth shall
know the hand of יהוה, that it is strong, so
that you shall fear יהוה your Elohim
forever."

5 And it came to be, when all the
sovereigns of the Amorites who were
beyond the Yarděn westward, and all the
sovereigns of the Kena'anites who were by
the sea, heard that יהוה had dried up the
waters of the Yarděn from before the
children of Yisra'ěl until we had passed
over, that their heart melted. And there was
no spirit in them any longer, because of the
children of Yisra'ěl.

2 At that time יהוה said to Yehoshua,
"Make knives of flint for yourself, and
circumcise the sons of Yisra'ěl again the
second time."

3 So Yehoshua made knives of flint for
himself, and circumcised the sons of
Yisra'ěl at the Hill of Foreskins.

4 And this is why Yehoshua circumcised
them: All the people who came out of
Mitsrayim who were males, all the men of
battle, had died in the wilderness on the
way, after they had come out of Mitsrayim.

5 For all the people who came out had
been circumcised, but all the people who
were born in the wilderness on the way as
they came out of Mitsrayim had not been

circumcised.
[6]For the children of Yisra'ěl walked forty years in the wilderness, till all the nation – the men of battle who came out of Mitsrayim – were consumed, because they did not obey the voice of יהוה, to whom יהוה swore not to show them the land which יהוה had sworn to their fathers that He would give us, "a land flowing with milk and honey."
[7]And Yehoshua circumcised their sons whom He raised up in their place; for they were uncircumcised, because they had not been circumcised on the way.
[8]And it came to be, when they had completed circumcising all the nation, that they stayed in their places in the camp till they were healed.
[9]And יהוה said to Yehoshua, "Today I have rolled away the reproach of Mitsrayim from you." So the name of the place is called Gilgal to this day.
[10]And the children of Yisra'ěl camped in Gilgal, and performed the Pěsaḥ on the fourteenth day of the new *moon* at evening on the desert plains of Yeriḥo.
[11]And they ate of the stored grain of the land on the morrow after the Pěsaḥ, unleavened bread and roasted grain on this same day.
[12]And the manna ceased on the day after they had eaten the stored grain of the land. And the children of Yisra'ěl no longer had manna, but they ate the food of the land of Kenaʽan that year.
[13]And it came to be, when Yehoshua was by Yeriḥo, that he lifted his eyes and looked and saw a Man standing opposite him with His sword drawn in His hand. And Yehoshua went to Him and said to Him, "Are You for us or for our adversaries?"
[14]And He said, "No, for I have now come as Captain of the host of יהוה." And Yehoshua fell on his face to the earth and did obeisance, and said to Him, "What is my Master saying to His servant?"
[15]And the Captain of the host of יהוה said to Yehoshua, "Take your sandal off your foot, for the place where you stand is set-apart." And Yehoshua did so.

6 And Yeriḥo was shut up tight because of the presence of the sons of Yisra'ěl – none going out, and none coming in.
[2]And יהוה said to Yehoshua, "See! I have given Yeriḥo and its sovereign, mighty brave men, into your hand.
[3]"And you shall go around the city, all the men of battle going around the city once. Do this for six days.
[4]"And let seven priests bear seven shopharot [a] of the yoḇelim [b] before the ark, and on the seventh day go around the city seven times while the priests blow with the shopharot.
[5]"And it shall be, when they make a long blast with the horn of a yoḇel, and when you hear the voice of the shophar, [c] that all the people shout with a great sound. And the wall of the city shall fall down flat, and the people shall go up every man straight before him."
[6]And Yehoshua son of Nun called the priests and said to them, "Take up the ark of the covenant, and let seven priests bear seven shopharot of yoḇelim before the ark of יהוה."
[7]And he said to the people, "Pass over, and go around the city, and let him who is armed pass over before the ark of יהוה."
[8]And it came to be, when Yehoshua had spoken to the people, that the seven priests bearing the seven shopharot of the yoḇelim before יהוה passed over and blew with the shopharot, and the ark of the covenant of יהוה went after them.
[9]And the armed men went before the priests who blew the shopharot, and the rear guard came after the ark, going on and blowing with the shopharot.
[10]But Yehoshua had commanded the people, saying, "Do not *make* a sound or cause your voice to be heard, nor let any word come out of your mouth, until the day I say to you, 'Shout!' Then you shall shout."
[11]And the ark of יהוה went around the city, going around once. And they came

6a Plural of Shophar. *6b* Plural of Yoḇel. See Explanatory notes: Yoḇel. *6c* Animal horn, traditionally ram's horn.

into the camp and stayed in the camp.
12 And Yehoshua rose early in the morning, and the priests took up the ark of יהוה.
13 And seven priests bearing seven
shopharot of the yoḇelim before the ark of
יהוה were walking, going on, and they
blew with the shopharot, and the armed
men went before them. But the rear guard
came after the ark of יהוה, going on, and
blowing with the shopharot.
14 And the second day they went around
the city once and returned to the camp.
Thus they did six days.
15 And it came to be on the seventh day
that they rose early, about the dawning of
the day, and went around the city seven
times in this way. Only on that day they
went around the city seven times.
16 And it came to be at the seventh time,
when the priests blew with the shopharot,
that Yehoshua said to the people, "Shout,
for יהוה has given you the city!
17 "And the city shall be put under the
ban, it and all that is in it belongs to יהוה.
Only Raḥaḇ the whore is to live, she and
all who are with her in the house, because
she hid the messengers that we sent.
18 "And you, by all means guard yourselves from that which is under the ban,
lest you come under the ban when you take
of that which is under the ban, and make
the camp of Yisra'ěl a curse, and shall
trouble it.
19 "But all the silver and gold, and vessels
of bronze and iron, are set-apart to יהוה,
they go into the treasury of יהוה."
20 And the people shouted when the
priests blew the shopharot. And it came to
be when the people heard the voice of the
shophar, and the people shouted with a
great shout, that the wall fell down flat.
And the people went up into the city, every
man straight before him, and they captured
the city.
21 And they put under the ban all that was
in the city, both man and woman, young
and old, and ox and sheep and donkey,
with the edge of the sword.
22 And to the two men who had spied out
the land Yehoshua said, "Go into the house
of the woman, the whore, and from there
bring out the woman and all that she has,
as you swore to her."
23 And the young men, the spies, went in
and brought out Raḥaḇ, and her father, and
her mother, and her brothers, and all that
she had. So they brought out all her relatives and set them outside the camp of
Yisra'ěl.
24 And they burned the city and all that
was in it with fire. Only the silver and
gold, and the vessels of bronze and of iron,
they put into the treasury of the House of
יהוה.
25 However, Yehoshua kept alive Raḥaḇ
the whore, and her father's household, and
all that she had. And she dwelt in the midst
of Yisra'ěl to this day, because she hid the
messengers whom Yehoshua sent to spy
out Yeriḥo.
26 And Yehoshua warned them at that
time, saying, "Cursed is the man before
יהוה who rises up and builds this city
Yeriḥo – he lays its foundation with his
first-born, and with his youngest he sets up
its gates."
27 And יהוה was with Yehoshua, and a
report about him was in all the land.

7 But the children of Yisra'ěl committed a trespass regarding that which is
under the ban, for Aḵan son of Karmi, son
of Zaḇdi, son of Zeraḥ, of the tribe of
Yehuḏah, took of that which is under the
ban. And the displeasure of יהוה burned
against the children of Yisra'ěl.
2 Now Yehoshua sent men from Yeriḥo
to Ai, which is beside Běyth Awen, on the
east side of Běyth Ěl, and spoke to them,
saying, "Go up and spy out the land." And
the men went up and spied out Ai.
3 And they returned to Yehoshua and said
to him, "Let not all the people go up, but
let about two or three thousand men go up
and strike Ai. Do not make all the people
toil up there, for the people of Ai are few."
4 And about three thousand men went up
there from the people, but they fled before
the men of Ai.
5 And the men of Ai struck about thirty-
six men, for they pursued them from
before the gate as far as Sheḇarim, and

smote them on the descent. So the hearts of
the people melted and became like water.
6 And Yehoshua tore his garments, and
fell to the earth on his face before the ark
of יהוה until evening, both he and the
elders of Yisra'ěl, and they put dust on
their heads.
7 And Yehoshua said, "Oh Master יהוה,
why have You brought this people over the
Yarděn at all, to give us into the hand of
the Amorites, to destroy us? If only we had
been content to stay beyond the Yarděn!
8 "O יהוה, what do I say when Yisra'ěl
turns its back before its enemies,
9 and the Kena'anites and all the inhabitants of the land hear, and shall surround
us, and cut off our name from the earth.
What then do You do for Your great
Name?"
10 And יהוה said to Yehoshua, "Rise up!
Why are you lying on your face?
11 "Yisra'ěl has sinned, and they have also
transgressed My covenant which I commanded them. And they have even taken
some of that which is under the ban, and
have both stolen and deceived, and also
put it among their own goods.
12 "And the sons of Yisra'ěl shall not be
able to stand before their enemies. They
are going to turn their backs before their
enemies, for they have become accursed. I
am not with you any more, unless you
destroy that which is under the ban from
your midst.
13 "Rise up, set the people apart, and you
shall say, 'Set yourselves apart for tomorrow, because thus said יהוה Elohim of
Yisra'ěl, "That which is under the ban is in
your midst, O Yisra'ěl. You are not able to
stand before your enemies until you put
away that which is under the ban out of
your midst."
14 'And you shall be brought near in the
morning, according to your tribes. And it
shall be, the tribe which יהוה takes comes
according to clans. And the clan which
יהוה takes comes by households. And the
household which יהוה takes comes by
men.
15 'And it shall be that he who is taken
with that which is under the ban is burned
with fire, he and all that he has, because he
has transgressed the covenant of יהוה, and
because he has committed wickedness in
Yisra'ěl.' "
16 So Yehoshua arose early in the morning
and brought Yisra'ěl by their tribes, and
the tribe of Yehuḏah was taken,
17 and he brought the clan of Yehuḏah,
and he took the clan of the Zarḥites. And
he brought the clan of the Zarḥites by men,
and Zaḇdi was taken.
18 And he brought his household by men,
and Aḵan son of Karmi, son of Zaḇdi, son
of Zeraḥ, of the tribe of Yehuḏah, was
taken.
19 Then Yehoshua said to Aḵan, "My son,
now give esteem to יהוה Elohim of Yisra'ěl, and make confession to Him. And
please declare to me what you have done,
do not hide it from me."
20 So Aḵan answered Yehoshua and said,
"Truly, I have sinned against יהוה Elohim
of Yisra'ěl, and this is what I did:
21 "When I saw among the spoil a lovely
garment from Shin'ar, and two hundred
sheqels of silver, and a wedge of gold
weighing fifty sheqels, I coveted them and
took them. And see, they are hidden in the
ground in the midst of my tent, with the
silver under it."
22 And Yehoshua sent messengers, and
they ran to the tent. And see, it was hidden
in his tent, with the silver under it.
23 And they took them from the midst of
the tent, brought them to Yehoshua and to
all the children of Yisra'ěl, and laid them
out before יהוה.
24 Then Yehoshua, and all Yisra'ěl with
him, took Aḵan son of Zeraḥ, and the
silver, and the garment, and the wedge of
gold, and his sons, and his daughters, and
his oxen, and his donkeys, and his sheep,
and his tent, and all that he had, and they
brought them to the Valley of Aḵor.
25 And Yehoshua said, "Why have you
troubled us? יהוה does trouble you today!"
Then all Yisra'ěl stoned him with stones.
And they burned them with fire after they
had stoned them with stones.
26 And they raised over him a great heap
of stones, which remains to this day. Then

יהוה turned from the fierceness of His displeasure. Therefore the name of that place has been called the Valley of Aḵor to this day.

8 And יהוה said to Yehoshua, "Do not be afraid, nor be discouraged. Take all the soldiers with you, and arise, go up to Ai. See, I have given into your hand the sovereign of Ai, and his people, and his city, and his land.

2 "So you shall do to Ai and its sovereign as you did to Yeriḥo and its sovereign. Only its spoil and its livestock you take as plunder for yourselves. Set for yourselves an ambush for the city, behind it."

3 And Yehoshua and all the soldiers rose up, to go up to Ai. And Yehoshua chose thirty thousand mighty brave men and sent them away by night,

4 and commanded them, saying, "See, you are going to lie in ambush against the city, behind the city. Do not go very far from the city, but all of you shall be prepared,

5 while I and all the people who are with me approach the city. And it shall be, when they come out against us, as formerly, that we shall flee before them,

6 and they shall come out after us till we have drawn them from the city, as though saying, 'They are fleeing before us as formerly.' And we shall flee before them,

7 then you shall rise from the ambush and seize the city. And יהוה your Elohim shall give it into your hand.

8 "And it shall be, when you capture the city, that you burn the city with fire. Do according to the word of יהוה. See, I have commanded you."

9 And Yehoshua sent them out. And they went to lie in ambush, and stayed between Běyth Ěl and Ai, on the west side of Ai. But Yehoshua stayed that night in the midst of the people.

10 And Yehoshua rose up early in the morning and inspected the people, and went up, he and the elders of Yisra'ěl, before the people to Ai.

11 And all the soldiers who were with him went up and drew near, and came before the city and camped on the north side of Ai, with the valley between them and Ai.

12 And he took about five thousand men and set them in ambush between Běyth Ěl and Ai, on the west side of the city.

13 So they stationed the people, all the army that was on the north of the city, and its rear guard on the west of the city, and Yehoshua went that night into the midst of the valley.

14 And it came to be, when the sovereign of Ai saw it, that the men of the city hastened and rose up early and went out against Yisra'ěl to battle, he and all his people, at an appointed place before the desert plain. But he did not know that there was an ambush against him behind the city.

15 And Yehoshua and all Yisra'ěl let themselves be beaten before them, and fled by the way of the wilderness.

16 And all the people who were in Ai were called together to pursue them. And they pursued Yehoshua and were drawn away from the city.

17 So there was not a man left in Ai or Běyth Ěl who did not go out after Yisra'ěl, and they left the city open and pursued Yisra'ěl.

18 And יהוה said to Yehoshua, "Stretch out the spear that is in your hand toward Ai, for I give it into your hand." And Yehoshua stretched out the spear that he had in his hand toward the city,

19 and the ambush rose up quickly from their place, and they ran at the stretching out of his hand, and entered the city and took it, and hastened to burn the city with fire.

20 And the men of Ai looked behind them and saw the smoke of the city rising to the heavens. And there was no power in them to flee this way or that way, for the people who had fled to the wilderness turned back on the pursuers.

21 For when Yehoshua and all Yisra'ěl saw that the ambush had captured the city and that the smoke of the city went up, they turned back and struck the men of Ai.

22 The others also came out of the city against them, so they were in the midst of

Yisra'ěl, some on this side and some on
that side. And they struck them until none
were left, and none had escaped.
23 But the sovereign of Ai they caught
alive, and brought him to Yehoshua.
24 And it came to be, when Yisra'ěl ended
killing all the inhabitants of Ai in the field,
in the wilderness where they pursued
them, and when they all had fallen by the
edge of the sword until they were consumed, that all Yisra'ěl returned to Ai and
struck it with the edge of the sword.
25 And it came to be that all who fell that
day, both men and women, were twelve
thousand – all men of Ai.
26 And Yehoshua did not draw back his
hand, with which he stretched out the
spear, until he had put all the inhabitants of
Ai under the ban.
27 Only the livestock and the spoil of that
city Yisra'ěl took as booty for themselves,
according to the word of יהוה which He
had commanded Yehoshua.
28 And Yehoshua burned Ai and made it a
heap forever, a ruin to this day.
29 And he hanged the sovereign of Ai on a
tree until evening. And at sunset Yehoshua
commanded that they should take his
corpse down from the tree, and throw it at
the entrance of the gate of the city, and
raise over it a great heap of stones, to this
day.
30 And Yehoshua built a slaughter-place
to יהוה Elohim of Yisra'ěl in Mount
Ěyḇal,
31 as Mosheh the servant of יהוה had
commanded the children of Yisra'ěl, as it
is written in the Book of the Torah of
Mosheh, "a slaughter-place of unhewn
stones over which no man has wielded
iron." And they offered on it ascending
offerings to יהוה, and slaughtered peace
offerings.
32 And there, in the presence of the
children of Yisra'ěl, he wrote on the stones
a copy of the Torah of Mosheh, which he
had written.
33 And all Yisra'ěl – the sojourner as well
as the native – with their elders and officers and judges, stood on either side of the
ark before the priests, the Lěwites, who
bore the ark of the covenant of יהוה. Half
of them were in front of Mount Gerizim
and half of them in front of Mount Ěyḇal,
as Mosheh the servant of יהוה had commanded before, that they should bless the
people of Yisra'ěl.
34 And afterward he read all the words of
the Torah, the blessings and the cursings,
according to all that is written in the Book
of the Torah.
35 There was not a word of all that
Mosheh had commanded which Yehoshua
did not read before all the assembly of
Yisra'ěl, with the women, and the little
ones, and the sojourners who accompanied
them.

9 And it came to be, when all the
sovereigns who were beyond the
Yarděn, in the hills and in the low country
and in all the coasts of the Great Sea
toward Leḇanon – the Ḥittite and the
Amorite, the Kena'anite and the Perizzite,
the Ḥiwwite and the Yeḇusite – heard,
2 they gathered together to fight with
Yehoshua and Yisra'ěl with one accord.
3 And the inhabitants of Giḇ'on heard
what Yehoshua had done to Yeriḥo and Ai,
4 and they acted slyly and went and pretended to be envoys. And they took old
sacks on their donkeys, old wineskins torn
and mended,
5 and old and patched sandals on their
feet, and old garments on themselves. And
all the bread of their provision was dry, it
was crumbs.
6 And they went to Yehoshua, to the
camp at Gilgal, and said to him and to the
men of Yisra'ěl, "We have come from a far
land, and now, make a covenant with us."
7 But the men of Yisra'ěl said to the
Ḥiwwites, "It could be that you dwell in
our midst, so how would we make a
covenant with you?"
8 And they said to Yehoshua, "We are
your servants." And Yehoshua said to
them, "Who are you, and where do you
come from?"
9 So they said to him, "From a land very
far off your servants have come, because
of the Name of יהוה your Elohim. For we

have heard the report of Him, and all that
He did in Mitsrayim,
10 and all that He had done to the two
sovereigns of the Amorites who were
beyond the Yarděn, to Siḥon sovereign of
Ḥeshbon, and Og̃ sovereign of Bashan,
who was at Ashtaroth.
11 "So our elders and all the inhabitants of
our land spoke to us, saying, 'Take food
with you for the journey, and go to meet
them, and say to them, "We are your
servants, and now, make a covenant with
us." '
12 "This bread of ours we took hot for our
provision from our houses on the day that
we left to come to you. But now, see, it is
dry and it is crumby.
13 "And these wineskins which we filled
were new, and see, they are torn. And these
our garments and our sandals have become
old because of the very long journey."
14 And the men of Yisra'ěl took some of
their food, but they did not ask the mouth
of יהוה.
15 And Yehoshua made peace with them,
and made a covenant with them to let them
live, and the rulers of the congregation
swore to them.
16 And it came to be at the end of three
days, after they had made a covenant with
them, that they heard that they were their
neighbours who dwelt near them.
17 And the children of Yisra'ěl set out and
came to their cities on the third day. Now
their cities were Giḇʿon, and Kephirah, and
Be'ěroth, and Qiryath Yeʿarim.
18 But the children of Yisra'ěl did not
strike them, because the rulers of the
congregation had sworn to them by יהוה
Elohim of Yisra'ěl. And all the congregation grumbled against the rulers.
19 But all the rulers said to all the congregation, "We have sworn to them by
יהוה Elohim of Yisra'ěl, and we are unable
to touch them now.
20 "Let us do this to them: We shall keep
them alive, lest wrath be upon us because
of the oath which we swore to them."
21 And the rulers said to them, "Let them
live, but let them be woodcutters and
drawers of water for all the congregation,
as the rulers had promised them."
22 Then Yehoshua called for them, and he
spoke to them, saying, "Why have you
deceived us, saying, 'We are very far from
you,' yet you are dwelling in our midst?
23 "And now you are cursed, and you
shall not cease from being slaves, and
woodcutters and drawers of water for the
House of my Elohim."
24 And they answered Yehoshua and said,
"Your servants were clearly told that יהוה
your Elohim commanded His servant
Mosheh to give you all the land, and to
destroy all the inhabitants of the land from
before you. So we were very much afraid
for our lives because of you, and have
done this deed.
25 "And now, see, we are in your hands.
Do with us as it seems good and right to
do to us."
26 And he did so to them, and delivered
them out of the hand of the children of
Yisra'ěl, and they did not kill them.
27 And that day Yehoshua made them
woodcutters and drawers of water for the
congregation and for the slaughter-place of
יהוה, even to this day, at the place that He
should choose.

10 And it came to be when Aḏoni-
Tseḏeq sovereign of Yerushalayim
heard that Yehoshua had captured Ai and
had put it under the ban, that he had done
to Ai and its sovereign as he had done to
Yeriḥo and its sovereign, and that the
inhabitants of Giḇʿon had made peace with
Yisra'ěl and were in their midst,
2 that they feared greatly, because Giḇʿon
was a great city, as one of the royal cities,
and because it was greater than Ai, and all
its men were mighty.
3 And Aḏoni-Tseḏeq sovereign of
Yerushalayim sent to Hoham sovereign of
Ḥeḇron, and to Piram sovereign of
Yarmuth, and to Yaphiya sovereign of
Laḵish, and to Deḇir sovereign of Eg̃lon,
saying,
4 "Come up to me and help me, and let us
strike Giḇʿon, for it has made peace with
Yehoshua and with the children of
Yisra'ěl."

5 So the five sovereigns of the Amorites – the sovereign of Yerushalayim, the sovereign of Ḥeḇron, the sovereign of Yarmuth, the sovereign of Laḵish, the sovereign of Eḡlon – gathered together and went up, they and all their armies, and camped before Giḇʽon and fought against it.

6 And the men of Giḇʽon sent to Yehoshua at the camp at Gilgal, saying, "Do not withdraw your hand from your servants. Come up to us quickly, and save us and help us, for all the sovereigns of the Amorites who dwell in the mountains have assembled against us."

7 And Yehoshua went up from Gilgal, he and all the soldiers with him, and all the mighty brave men.

8 And יהוה said to Yehoshua, "Do not fear them, for I have given them into your hand. Not one of them does stand before you."

9 So then Yehoshua came upon them suddenly, having gone up all night from Gilgal.

10 And יהוה threw them into confusion before Yisra'ěl, and they struck them with a great slaughter at Giḇʽon, and pursued them along the way that goes to Běyth Ḥoron, and struck them as far as Azěqah and Maqqěḏah.

11 And it came to be, as they fled before Yisra'ěl and were on the descent of Běyth Ḥoron, that יהוה threw down large hailstones from the heavens on them as far as Azěqah, and they died. There were more who died from the hailstones than those whom the sons of Yisra'ěl had killed with the sword.

12 Then Yehoshua spoke to יהוה in the day when יהוה gave the Amorites over to the children of Yisra'ěl, and he said before the eyes of Yisra'ěl, "Sun, stand still over Giḇʽon; and moon, in the Valley of Ayalon."

13 So the sun stood still, and the moon stopped, till the nation avenged itself upon their enemies. Is this not written in the Book of Yashar? Thus the sun stopped in the midst of the heavens, and did not hasten to go down for an entire day.

14 And there has been no day like that, before it or after it, that יהוה listened to the voice of a man, because יהוה fought for Yisra'ěl.

15 So Yehoshua returned, and all Yisra'ěl with him, to the camp at Gilgal.

16 Now these five sovereigns had fled and hidden themselves in a cave at Maqqěḏah.

17 And it was reported to Yehoshua, saying, "The five sovereigns have been found hidden in the cave at Maqqěḏah."

18 And Yehoshua said, "Roll large stones against the mouth of the cave, and set men by it to guard them.

19 "And you, do not stand still, but pursue your enemies. And you shall smite them in the rear. Do not allow them to enter their cities, for יהוה your Elohim has given them into your hand."

20 And it came to be, when Yehoshua and the children of Yisra'ěl had ended striking them with a very great slaughter, till they had finished – but those who escaped went into walled cities –

21 that all the people returned to the camp, to Yehoshua at Maqqěḏah, in peace. No one moved his tongue against any of the sons of Yisra'ěl.

22 Then Yehoshua said, "Open the mouth of the cave, and bring out those five sovereigns to me from the cave."

23 And they did so, and brought those five sovereigns to him from the cave: the sovereign of Yerushalayim, the sovereign of Ḥeḇron, the sovereign of Yarmuth, the sovereign of Laḵish, the sovereign of Eḡlon.

24 And it came to be, when they brought out those sovereigns to Yehoshua, that Yehoshua called for all the men of Yisra'ěl, and said to the chiefs of the men of battle who went with him, "Come near, put your feet on the necks of these sovereigns." And they drew near and put their feet on their necks.

25 Then Yehoshua said to them, "Do not be afraid nor be discouraged, be strong and courageous, for this is what יהוה is going to do to all your enemies whom you are fighting."

26 And afterward Yehoshua struck them and killed them, and hanged them on five

trees. And they were hanging on the trees
until evening.
27 And it came to be, at the time of the
going down of the sun, that Yehoshua
commanded, and they took them down
from the trees, and threw them into the
cave where they had been hidden, and laid
large stones against the cave's mouth, to
this day.
28 And on that day Yehoshua captured
Maqqěḏah, and he struck it with the edge
of the sword, and he put its sovereign
under the ban – them and all the people
who were in it, he left no survivor. And he
did to the sovereign of Maqqěḏah as he
had done to the sovereign of Yeriḥo.
29 Then Yehoshua passed over, and all
Yisra'ěl with him, from Maqqěḏah to
Liḇnah. And they fought against Liḇnah.
30 And יהוה also gave it and its sovereign
into the hand of Yisra'ěl. And he struck it
and all the people who were in it with the
edge of the sword, he left no survivor in it.
And he did to its sovereign as he had done
to the sovereign of Yeriḥo.
31 Then Yehoshua passed over, and all
Yisra'ěl with him, from Liḇnah to Laḵish,
and encamped against it and fought against
it.
32 And יהוה gave Laḵish into the hand of
Yisra'ěl, who captured it on the second
day, and struck it and all the people who
were in it with the edge of the sword,
according to all that he had done to
Liḇnah.
33 Then Horam sovereign of Gezer came
up to help Laḵish. And Yehoshua struck
him and his people, until he left him no
survivor.
34 Then Yehoshua passed over, and all
Yisra'ěl with him, from Laḵish to Eḡlon.
And they encamped against it and fought
against it,
35 and captured it on that day and struck it
with the edge of the sword. And all the
beings who were in it he put under the ban
that day, according to all that he had done
to Laḵish.
36 Then Yehoshua went up, and all
Yisra'ěl with him, from Eḡlon to Ḥeḇron,
and they fought against it,
37 and captured it and struck it with the
edge of the sword, and its sovereign, and
all its cities, and all the people who were in
it. He left no survivor, according to all
that he had done to Eḡlon, but put it and all
the people who were in it under the ban.
38 Then Yehoshua returned, and all
Yisra'ěl with him, to Deḇir, and fought
against it,
39 and captured it and its sovereign and all
its cities. And they struck them with the
edge of the sword and put all the people
who were in it under the ban, he left no
survivor. As he had done to Ḥeḇron, so he
did to Deḇir and its sovereign, as he had
done also to Liḇnah and its sovereign.
40 Thus Yehoshua struck all the land: the
mountain country and the South and the
low country and the wilderness slopes, and
all their sovereigns. He left no survivor,
but put all that breathed under the ban, as
יהוה Elohim of Yisra'ěl had commanded.
41 And Yehoshua struck them from
Qaḏěsh Barněa as far as Azzah, and all the
land of Goshen, even as far as Giḇ'on.
42 And Yehoshua captured all these sovereigns and their land at one time, because
יהוה Elohim of Yisra'ěl fought for Yisra'ěl.
43 And Yehoshua returned, and all Yisra'ěl with him, to the camp at Gilgal.

11 And it came to be, when Yaḇin
sovereign of Ḥatsor heard, that he
sent to Yoḇaḇ sovereign of Maḏon, and to
the sovereign of Shimron, and to the
sovereign of Aḵshaph,
2 and to the sovereigns who were from
the north, in the mountains, and in the
desert plain south of Kinneroth, and in the
low country, and in the heights of Dor on
the west –
3 the Kena'anites in the east and in the
west, and the Amorite, and the Ḥittite, and
the Perizzite, and the Yeḇusite in the
mountains, and the Ḥiwwite below
Ḥermon in the land of Mitspah.
4 And they went out, they and all their
armies with them, as many people as
numerous as the sand on the seashore, with
very many horses and chariots.

5 And all these sovereigns met together, and they came and camped together at the waters of Měrom to fight against Yisra'ěl.

6 And יהוה said to Yehoshua, "Do not be afraid of their presence, for tomorrow about this time I am giving all of them over to Yisra'ěl, slain. Hamstring their horses and burn their chariots with fire."

7 And Yehoshua, and all the soldiers with him, came against them suddenly by the waters of Měrom, and they fell on them.

8 And יהוה gave them into the hand of Yisra'ěl, and they struck them and pursued them to Great Tsiḏon, and to Misrephoth Mayim, and to the Valley of Mitspeh eastward. And they struck them until no survivor was left to them.

9 And Yehoshua did to them as יהוה said to him: he hamstrung their horses and burned their chariots with fire.

10 And Yehoshua turned back at that time and captured Ḥatsor, and struck its sovereign with the sword, for Ḥatsor was formerly the head of all those reigns.

11 And they struck all the beings who were in it with the edge of the sword, putting them under the ban. He did not leave anyone breathing. Then he burned Ḥatsor with fire.

12 And Yehoshua captured all the cities of those sovereigns, and all their sovereigns, and he struck them with the edge of the sword. He put them under the ban, as Mosheh the servant of יהוה commanded.

13 However, Yisra'ěl did not burn any cities that stood on their mounds, but Yehoshua burned only Ḥatsor.

14 And all the spoil of these cities and the livestock, the children of Yisra'ěl took as booty for themselves. But they struck every man with the edge of the sword until they had destroyed them, and they did not leave anyone breathing.

15 As יהוה had commanded Mosheh his servant, so Mosheh commanded Yehoshua, and so Yehoshua did. He did not turn aside a word of all that יהוה had commanded Mosheh.

16 Thus Yehoshua took all this land: the mountain country, and all the South, and all the land of Goshen, and the low country, and the desert plain, and the mountains of Yisra'ěl and its low lands,

17 from Mount Ḥalaq that goes up to Sě'ir, and as far as Ba'al Gaḏ in the Valley of Leḇanon below Mount Ḥermon. And he captured all their sovereigns, and struck them and killed them.

18 Yehoshua fought with all those sovereigns for a long time.

19 There was not a city that made peace with the children of Yisra'ěl, except the Ḥiwwites, the inhabitants of Giḇ'on. All the others they took in battle.

20 For it was of יהוה to strengthen their hearts, that they should come against Yisra'ěl in battle, in order to put them under the ban, so that they might have no favour, but that He might annihilate them, as יהוה had commanded Mosheh.

21 And at that time Yehoshua came and cut off the Anaqim from the mountains, from Ḥeḇron, from Deḇir, from Anaḇ, and from all the mountains of Yehuḏah, and from all the mountains of Yisra'ěl. Yehoshua put them with their cities under the ban.

22 There were none of the Anaqim left in the land of the children of Yisra'ěl; only in Azzah, in Gath, and in Ashdoḏ some remained.

23 Thus Yehoshua took the entire land, according to all that יהוה had said to Mosheh. And Yehoshua gave it as an inheritance to Yisra'ěl according to their divisions by their tribes. And the land rested from fighting.

12 And these are the sovereigns of the land whom the children of Yisra'ěl struck, and whose land they possessed beyond the Yarděn towards the sun-rising, from the wadi Arnon to Mount Ḥermon, and all the desert plain eastward:

2 Siḥon sovereign of the Amorites, who dwelt in Ḥeshbon, ruling from Aro'ěr, which is on the bank of the wadi Arnon, from the middle of that wadi, and half Gil'aḏ, even as far as the wadi Yabboq, the border of the children of Ammon,

3 and the desert plain from the Sea of Kinneroth eastward as far as the Sea of the

Araḇah, the Salt Sea, the way to Běyth
Yeshimoth, and southward below the
slopes of Pisgah,
4 and the border of Oḡ, sovereign of
Bashan, who was of the remnant of the
Repha'ites, who dwelt at Ashtaroth and at
Eḏre'i,
5 and ruled in Mount Ḥermon, and in
Salḵah, and in all Bashan, as far as the border of the Geshurites and the Ma'aḵathites,
and the half of Gil'aḏ as far as the border
of Siḥon sovereign of Ḥeshbon.
6 Mosheh the servant of יהוה and the
children of Yisra'ěl had stricken them. And
Mosheh the servant of יהוה had given it as
a possession to the Re'uḇěnites, and to the
Gaḏites, and to half the tribe of Menashsheh.
7 And these are the sovereigns of the land
which Yehoshua and the children of
Yisra'ěl struck beyond the Yarděn, on the
west, from Ba'al Gaḏ in the Valley of
Leḇanon as far as Mount Ḥalaq that goes
up to Sě'ir, which Yehoshua gave to the
tribes of Yisra'ěl as a possession according
to their divisions,
8 in the mountain country, and in the low
country, and in the desert plain, and in the
slopes, and in the wilderness, and in the
South, the Ḥittites, the Amorites and the
Kena'anites, the Perizzites, the Ḥiwwites,
and the Yeḇusites:
9 the sovereign of Yeriḥo, one; the sovereign of Ai, which is beside Běyth Ěl, one;
10 the sovereign of Yerushalayim, one; the
sovereign of Ḥeḇron, one;
11 the sovereign of Yarmuth, one; the
sovereign of Laḵish, one;
12 the sovereign of Eḡlon, one; the
sovereign of Gezer, one;
13 the sovereign of Deḇir, one; the
sovereign of Geḏer, one;
14 the sovereign of Ḥormah, one; the
sovereign of Araḏ, one;
15 the sovereign of Liḇnah, one; the
sovereign of Aḏullam, one;
16 the sovereign of Maqqěḏah, one; the
sovereign of Běyth Ěl, one;
17 the sovereign of Tappuwaḥ, one; the
sovereign of Ḥěpher, one;
18 the sovereign of Aphěq, one; the
sovereign of Sharon, one;
19 the sovereign of Maḏon, one; the
sovereign of Ḥatsor, one;
20 the sovereign of Shimron Měron, one;
the sovereign of Aḵshaph, one;
21 the sovereign of Ta'anaḵ, one; the
sovereign of Meḡiddo, one;
22 the sovereign of Qeḏesh, one; the
sovereign of Yoqne'am in Karmel, one;
23 the sovereign of Dor in the heights of
Dor, one; the sovereign of the nations of
Gilgal, one;
24 the sovereign of Tirtsah, one – thirty-
one sovereigns in all.

13 And Yehoshua was old, advanced
in years. And יהוה said to him,
"You are old, advanced in years, and still
much of the land remains to be possessed.
2 "This is the land that remains: all the
districts of the Philistines and all the
Geshurites,
3 from Shiḥor which is in front of
Mitsrayim, and up to the border of Eqron
northward, are considered as Kena'anite
– the five princes of the Philistines,
the Azzathites, and the Ashdoḏites, the
Eshqelonites, the Gittites, and the Eqronites; also the Awwites
4 on the south; all the land of the
Kena'anites, and Me'arah that belongs to
the Tsiḏonians as far as Aphěq, to the
border of the Amorites;
5 and the land of the Geḇalites, and all
Leḇanon, toward the sunrise, from Ba'al
Gaḏ below Mount Ḥermon as far as the
entrance to Ḥamath;
6 all the inhabitants of the mountains
from Leḇanon as far as Misrephoth
Mayim, and all the Tsiḏonians. I Myself
drive them out from before the children of
Yisra'ěl. Only, divide it by lot to Yisra'ěl
as an inheritance, as I have commanded
you.
7 "And now, divide this land as an
inheritance to the nine tribes and half the
tribe of Menashsheh."
8 With them the other half tribe the
Re'uḇěnites and the Gaḏites received their
inheritance, which Mosheh had given
them, beyond the Yarděn eastward, as

Mosheh the servant of יהוה had given
them:
9 from Aro'ěr which is on the bank of
the wadi Arnon, and the city that is in the
middle of the wadi, and all the plain of
Měyḏeḇa as far as Diḇon;
10 and all the cities of Siḥon sovereign of
the Amorites, who reigned in Ḥeshbon, as
far as the border of the children of
Ammon;
11 and Gil'aḏ, and the border of the
Geshurites, and of the Ma'aḵathites, and
all Mount Ḥermon, and all Bashan as far as
Salḵah;
12 all the reign of Oḡ in Bashan, who
reigned in Ashtaroth and Eḏre'i, who
remained of the remnant of the Repha'ites,
for Mosheh had stricken and dispossessed
them.
13 However, the children of Yisra'ěl did
not drive out the Geshurites nor the
Ma'aḵathites, so the Geshurites and the
Ma'aḵathites dwell in the midst of Yisra'ěl
to this day.
14 Only to the tribe of Lěwi he had given
no inheritance – the offerings made by fire
to יהוה Elohim of Yisra'ěl were their
inheritance, as He said to them.
15 And Mosheh gave to the tribe of the
children of Re'uḇěn, for their clans:
16 and their border was from Aro'ěr,
which is on the bank of the wadi Arnon,
and the city that is in the middle of the
wadi, and all the plain by Měyḏeḇa,
17 Ḥeshbon and all its cities that are in the
plain: Diḇon, and Bamoth Ba'al, and Běyth
Ba'al Me'on,
18 and Yahtsah, and Qeḏěmoth, and
Měpha'ath,
19 and Qiryathayim, and Siḇmah, and
Tsereth Shaḥar on the mountain of the
valley,
20 and Běyth Pe'or, and the slopes of
Pisgah, and Běyth Yeshimoth;
21 and all the cities of the plain, and all the
reign of Siḥon sovereign of the Amorites,
who reigned in Ḥeshbon, whom Mosheh
had stricken with the princes of Miḏyan:
Ewi, and Reqem, and Tsur, and Ḥur, and
Reḇa, princes of Siḥon dwelling in the
land.
22 And the sons of Yisra'ěl killed with the
sword Bil'am son of Be'or, the diviner,
among those who were killed by them.
23 And the border of the children of
Re'uḇěn was the bank of the Yarděn. This
was the inheritance of the children of
Re'uḇěn for their clans, the cities and their
villages.
24 And Mosheh gave to the tribe of Gaḏ,
to the children of Gaḏ for their clans:
25 and their border was Ya'zěr, and all the
cities of Gil'aḏ, and half the land of the
children of Ammon as far as Aro'ěr, which
is before Rabbah,
26 and from Ḥeshbon to Ramath Mitspeh
and Betonim, and from Maḥanayim to the
border of Deḇir,
27 and in the valley Běyth Haram, and
Běyth Nimrah, and Sukkoth, and Tsaphon,
the rest of the reign of Siḥon sovereign of
Ḥeshbon, the Yarděn being its border, as
far as the edge of the Sea of Kinnereth,
beyond the Yarděn eastward.
28 This is the inheritance of the children of
Gaḏ for their clans, the cities and their
villages.
29 And Mosheh gave to half the tribe of
Menashsheh, and it was for half the tribe
of the children of Menashsheh for their
clans:
30 and their border was from Maḥanayim,
all Bashan, all the reign of Oḡ sovereign of
Bashan, and all the small towns of Ya'ir
which are in Bashan, sixty cities;
31 and the half of Gil'aḏ, and Ashtaroth
and Eḏre'i, cities of the reign of Oḡ in
Bashan, were for the children of Maḵir son
of Menashsheh, to the half of the children
of Maḵir for their clans.
32 These Mosheh gave as an inheritance in
the desert plains of Mo'aḇ beyond the
Yarděn, by Yeriḥo eastward.
33 But to the tribe of Lěwi Mosheh gave
no inheritance. יהוה, Elohim of Yisra'ěl,
He was their inheritance, as He had said to
them.

14 Now these the children of Yisra'ěl
inherited in the land of Kena'an,
which El'azar the priest, and Yehoshua son
of Nun, and the heads of the fathers of the

tribes of the children of Yisra'ěl caused them to inherit.

2 Their inheritance was by lot, as יהוה had commanded by the hand of Mosheh, for the nine tribes and the half-tribe.

3 For Mosheh had given the inheritance of the two tribes and the half-tribe beyond the Yarděn, but to the Lěwites he gave no inheritance in their midst.

4 For the children of Yosěph had become two tribes: Menashsheh and Ephrayim. And they gave no part to the Lěwites in the land, except cities to dwell in, with their open land for their livestock and their possessions.

5 As יהוה had commanded Mosheh, so the children of Yisra'ěl did, and they divided the land.

6 And the children of Yehuḏah came to Yehoshua in Gilgal, and Kalěḇ son of Yephunneh the Kenizzite said to him, "You know the word which יהוה said to Mosheh the man of Elohim concerning you and me in Qaḏěsh Barněa.

7 "I was forty years old when Mosheh the servant of יהוה sent me from Qaḏěsh Barněa to spy out the land, and I brought back word to him as it was in my heart.

8 "But my brothers who went up with me made the heart of the people melt, but I followed יהוה my Elohim completely.

9 "So Mosheh swore on that day, saying, 'The land on which your foot has trodden is your inheritance and your children's forever, because you have followed יהוה my Elohim completely.'

10 "And now, see, יהוה has kept me alive, as He said, these forty-five years since יהוה spoke this word to Mosheh while Yisra'ěl walked in the wilderness. And now, see, I am eighty-five years old today.

11 "Yet I am still as strong today as I was on the day that Mosheh sent me. As my strength was then, so my strength is now, for battle, and for going out and for coming in.

12 "And now, give me this mountain of which יהוה spoke in that day, for you heard in that day how the Anaqim were there, and that the cities were great and walled. If יהוה is with me, then I shall dispossess them, as יהוה said."

13 Yehoshua then blessed him, and gave Ḥeḇron to Kalěḇ son of Yephunneh as an inheritance.

14 So Ḥeḇron became the inheritance of Kalěḇ son of Yephunneh the Qenizzite to this day, because he followed יהוה Elohim of Yisra'ěl completely.

15 Now the name of Ḥeḇron was formerly Qiryath Arba (*Arba was* the greatest man among the Anaqim). And the land had rest from fighting.

15

And the lot of the tribe of the children of Yehuḏah for their clans was to the border of Eḏom, the Wilderness of Tsin southward in the extreme south.

2 And their southern border began at the edge of the Salt Sea, from the bay that faces southward.

3 And it went out to the southern side of the Ascent of Aqrabbim, passed over to Tsin, and went up on the south side of Qaḏěsh Barněa, and passed over to Ḥetsron, went up to Aḏar, and went around to Qarqa,

4 and passed over to Atsmon, and went out to the wadi of Mitsrayim, and the border ended at the sea. This is your southern border.

5 And the east border was the Salt Sea as far as the end of the Yarděn. And the border on the northern quarter began at the bay of the sea at the end of the Yarděn.

6 And the border went up to Běyth Ḥoḡlah and passed over north of Běyth Araḇah. And the border went up to the stone of Bohan son of Re'uḇěn.

7 And the border went up toward Deḇir from the Valley of Aḵor, and it turned northward toward Gilgal, which is before the Ascent of Aḏummim, which is south of the wadi. And the border passed over to the waters of Ěn Shemesh and ended at Ěn Roḡěl.

8 And the border went up by the Valley of the Son of Hinnom to the southern slope of the Yeḇusite city, that is Yerushalayim. And the border went up to the top of the mountain that lies before the Valley of Hinnom westward, which is at the end of

the Valley of Repha'im northward.
9 And the border went around from the
top of the hill to the fountain of the water
of Nephtowaḥ, and went up to the cities of
Mount Ephron. And the border went
around to Baʿalah, that is Qiryath Yeʿarim.
10 And the border turned around from
Baʿalah westward to Mount Sĕʿir, and
passed over to the side of Mount Yeʿarim
on the north, that is Kesalon, and went
down to Bĕyth Shemesh, and passed over
to Timnah.
11 And the border went out to the side of
Eqron northward. And the border went
around to Shikkeron, and passed over to
Mount Baʿalah, and went out to Yaḇne'ĕl.
And the border ended at the sea.
12 And the west border was the coastline
of the Great Sea. This is the boundary of
the children of Yehuḏah all around for
their clans.
13 And to Kalĕḇ son of Yephunneh he
gave a portion in the midst of the children
of Yehuḏah, according to the mouth of
יהוה to Yehoshua: Qiryath Arba, that is
Ḥeḇron – *Arba was* the father of Anaq.
14 And Kalĕḇ drove out the three sons of
Anaq from there: Shĕshai, and Aḥiman,
and Talmai, the children of Anaq.
15 And he went up from there to the
inhabitants of Deḇir, and the name of
Deḇir formerly was Qiryath Sĕpher.
16 And Kalĕḇ said, "He who strikes
Qiryath Sĕpher and shall capture it, to him
I shall give Aḵsah my daughter as wife."
17 And Othni'ĕl son of Qenaz, the brother
of Kalĕḇ, did capture it, so he gave him
Aḵsah his daughter as wife.
18 And it came to be, when she came to
him, that she persuaded him to ask her
father for a field. And when she got off
from the donkey, Kalĕḇ said to her, "What
is the matter?"
19 And she said, "Give me a blessing.
Since you have given me land in the South,
give me also fountains of water." And he
gave her the upper fountains and the lower
fountains.
20 This was the inheritance of the tribe of
the children of Yehuḏah for their clans:
21 And the cities at the furthest border of
the tribe of the children of Yehuḏah,
toward the border of Eḏom in the South,
were Qaḇtse'ĕl, and Ĕḏer, and Yaḡur,
22 and Qinah, and Dimonah, and Aḏaḏah,
23 and Qeḏesh, and Ḥatsor, and Yithnan,
24 Ziph, and Telem, and Beʿaloth,
25 and Ḥatsor, Ḥaḏattah, and Qeriyoth,
Ḥetsron, that is Ḥatsor,
26 Amam, and Shema, and Molaḏah,
27 and Ḥatsar Gaddah, and Ḥeshmon, and
Bĕyth Pelet,
28 and Ḥatsar Shuʿal, and Be'ĕrsheḇa, and
Bizyothyah,
29 Baʿalah, and Iyim, and Etsem,
30 and Eltolaḏ, and Kesil, and Ḥormah,
31 and Tsiqlaḡ, and Maḏmannah, and
Sansannah,
32 and Leḇa'oth, and Shilḥim, and Ayin,
and Rimmon. All the cities were twenty-
nine, with their villages.
33 In the low country: Eshta'ol, and
Tsorʿah, and Ashnah,
34 and Zanowaḥ, and Ĕn Gannim,
Tappuwaḥ and Ĕnam,
35 Yarmuth and Aḏullam, Soḵoh and
Azĕqah,
36 and Shaʿarayim, and Aḏithayim, and
Geḏĕrah, and Geḏĕrothayim – fourteen
cities with their villages.
37 Tsenan, and Ḥaḏashah, and Miḡdal
Gaḏ,
38 and Dilʿan, and Mitspeh, and Yoqthe'ĕl,
39 Laḵish, and Botsqath, and Eḡlon,
40 and Kabbon, and Laḥmam, and Kith-
lish,
41 and Geḏĕroth, Bĕyth Daḡon, and
Naʿamah, and Maqqĕḏah – sixteen cities
with their villages.
42 Liḇnah, and Ether, and Ashan,
43 and Yiphtaḥ, and Ashnah, and Netsiḇ,
44 and Qeʿilah, and Aḵziḇ, and Marĕshah
– nine cities with their villages.
45 Eqron with its towns and its villages,
46 from Eqron to the sea, all that were by
the side of Ashdoḏ, with their villages.
47 Ashdoḏ, its towns and its villages;
Azzah, its towns and its villages; as far as
the wadi of Mitsrayim and the Great Sea
with its coastline.
48 And in the mountain country: Shamur,
and Yattir, and Soḵoh,

49 and Dannah, and Qiryath Sannah, that
is Deḇir,
50 and Anaḇ, and Eshtemoh, and Anim,
51 and Goshen, and Ḥolon, and Giloh –
eleven cities with their villages.
52 Araḇ, and Dumah, and Eshʽan,
53 and Yanim, and Běyth Tappuwaḥ, and
Aphěqah,
54 and Ḥumtah, and Qiryath Arba, that is
Ḥeḇron, and Tsiʽor – nine cities with their
villages.
55 Maʽon, Karmel, and Ziph, and Yutah,
56 and Yizreʽěl, and Yoqdeʽam, and
Zanowaḥ,
57 Qayin, Giḇʽah, and Timnah – ten cities
with their villages.
58 Ḥalḥul, Běyth Tsur, and Geḏor,
59 and Maʽarath, and Běyth Anoth, and
Elteqon – six cities with their villages.
60 Qiryath Baʽal, that is Qiryath Yeʽarim,
and Rabbah – two cities with their villages.
61 In the wilderness: Běyth Araḇah,
Middin, and Seḵaḵah,
62 and Niḇshan, and the City of Salt, and
Ěn Geḏi – six cities with their villages.
63 As for the Yeḇusites, the inhabitants of
Yerushalayim, the children of Yehuḏah
were unable to drive them out, so the
Yeḇusites have dwelt with the children
of Yehuḏah at Yerushalayim to this day.

16 And the lot for the children of
Yosěph went out from the Yarděn,
by Yeriḥo, to the waters of Yeriḥo on the
east, to the wilderness going up from
Yeriḥo through the mountains to Běyth Ěl,
2 and went out from Běyth Ěl to Luz, and
passed over to the border of the Arkites at
Ataroth,
3 and went down westward to the
boundary of the Yaphlětites, as far as the
boundary of Lower Běyth Ḥoron to Gezer,
and it ended at the sea.
4 Thus the children of Yosěph, Menashsheh and Ephrayim, inherited.
5 And the border of the children of
Ephrayim, according to their clans, was:
The border of their inheritance on the east
side was Ataroth Addar as far as Upper
Běyth Ḥoron.
6 And the border went out toward the
sea, to Miḵmethath on the north, then
the border went around eastward to
Ta'anath Shiloh, and passed over it on the
east of Yanoḥah,
7 and went down from Yanoḥah to
Ataroth and Naʽarah, reached to Yeriḥo,
and came out at the Yarděn.
8 From Tappuwaḥ the border went westward to the wadi Qanah, and it ended at the
sea. This was the inheritance of the tribe of
the children of Ephrayim for their clans.
9 And the separate cities for the children
of Ephrayim were in the midst of the
inheritance of the children of Menashsheh,
all the cities with their villages.
10 And they did not drive out the
Kenaʽanites who dwelt in Gezer, so the
Kenaʽanites dwell among the Ephrayimites
to this day and have become compulsory
labour.

17 And the lot for the tribe of
Menashsheh, for he was the first-
born of Yosěph, was: for Maḵir the
first-born of Menashsheh, father of Gilʽaḏ,
because he was a man of battle, therefore
he had Gilʽaḏ and Bashan.
2 And for the rest of the children of
Menashsheh for their clans there was: for
the children of Aḇiʽezer, and for the
children of Ḥěleq, and for the children of
Asri'ěl, and for the children of Sheḵem,
and for the children of Ḥěpher, and for the
children of Shemiḏa. These were the male
children of Menashsheh son of Yosěph
according to their clans.
3 But Tselophḥaḏ son of Ḥěpher, son of
Gilʽaḏ, son of Maḵir, son of Menashsheh,
had no sons, but only daughters. And these
were the names of his daughters: Maḥlah
and Noʽah, Ḥoḡlah, Milkah and Tirtsah.
4 And they came near before Elʽazar the
priest, before Yehoshua son of Nun, and
before the rulers, saying, "יהוה commanded Mosheh to give us an inheritance
among our brothers." So he gave them an
inheritance among their father's brothers,
according to the mouth of יהוה.
5 And ten portions fell to Menashsheh,
besides the land of Gilʽaḏ and Bashan,
which were beyond the Yarděn,

6 because the daughters of Menashsheh received an inheritance among his sons. And the rest of Menashsheh's sons had the land of Gilʽaḏ.

7 And the border of Menashsheh was from Ashěr to Miḵmethath, which faces Sheḵem. And the border went up to the right to the inhabitants of Ěn Tappuwaḥ.

8 The land of Tappuwaḥ belonged to Menashsheh, but Tappuwaḥ on the border of Menashsheh belonged to the children of Ephrayim.

9 And the border went down to the wadi Qanah, southward to the wadi. These cities of Ephrayim were in the midst of the cities of Menashsheh, but the border of Menashsheh was north of the wadi, and it ended at the sea.

10 Southward it was Ephrayim's, and northward it was Menashsheh's, and the sea was its border, and they reached to Ashěr on the north and to Yissasḵar on the east.

11 And in Yissasḵar and in Ashěr, Menashsheh had Běyth She'an and its towns, and Yiḇleʽam and its towns, and the inhabitants of Dor and its towns, and the inhabitants of Ěn Dor and its towns, and the inhabitants of Taʽanaḵ and its towns, and the inhabitants of Meḡiddo and its towns – three of the heights.

12 But the children of Menashsheh were unable to drive out the inhabitants of those cities, for the Kenaʽanites desired to dwell in that land.

13 And it came to be, when the children of Yisra'ěl grew strong, that they put the Kenaʽanites to compulsory labour, but did not utterly drive them out.

14 And the children of Yosěph spoke to Yehoshua, saying, "Why have you given us but one lot and one portion to inherit, seeing we are a great people whom יהוה has blessed until now?"

15 And Yehoshua said to them, "If you are a great people, go up to the forest and clear a place for yourself there in the land of the Perizzites and the Repha'ites, since the hill country of Ephrayim is too narrow for you."

16 Then the children of Yosěph said, "The hill country is not enough for us, and all the Kenaʽanites who dwell in the land of the valley have chariots of iron, both those who are of Běyth She'an and its towns and those who are of the Valley of Yizreʽěl."

17 And Yehoshua spoke to the house of Yosěph, to Ephrayim and to Menashsheh, saying, "You are a great people and have great power, you are not to have one lot,

18 for the hill country shall be yours. For though it is a forest, you shall cut it down, and its farthest limits shall be yours. For you are to drive out the Kenaʽanites, though they have iron chariots and are strong."

18 And all the congregation of the children of Yisra'ěl assembled at Shiloh, and they let the Tent of Appointment dwell there. And the land was subdued before them.

2 And seven tribes were left among the children of Yisra'ěl who had not yet shared their inheritance.

3 So Yehoshua said to the children of Yisra'ěl, "Till when are you going to fail to go in and possess the land which יהוה Elohim of your fathers has given you?

4 "Appoint three men from each tribe, and let me send them out to go through the land and describe it according to their inheritance, and come back to me.

5 "And they shall divide it into seven portions – Yehuḏah stays within their border on the south, and the house of Yosěph stays within their border on the north –

6 and you shall describe the land in seven portions, and shall bring it to me. Then I shall cast lots for you here before יהוה our Elohim.

7 "But the Lěwites have no portion among you, for the priesthood of יהוה is their inheritance. And Gaḏ, and Re'uḇěn, and half the tribe of Menashsheh have received their inheritance beyond the Yarděn on the east, which Mosheh the servant of יהוה gave them."

8 So the men rose up and went. And Yehoshua commanded those who went to describe the land, saying, "Go, walk through the land, and describe it, and come

back to me, and let me cast lots for you
here before יהוה in Shiloh."
9 So the men went, and passed through
the land, and described it in a book in
seven portions by cities. And they came to
Yehoshua at the camp in Shiloh.
10 And Yehoshua cast lots for them in
Shiloh before יהוה, and there Yehoshua
divided the land to the children of Yisra'ěl
according to their portions.
11 And the lot of the tribe of the children
of Binyamin came up for their clans, and
the border of their lot came out between
the children of Yehuḏah and the children
of Yosěph.
12 And their border was on the north side
from the Yarděn, and the border went up to
the side of Yeriḥo on the north, and went
up through the mountains westward, and
ended at the Wilderness of Běyth Awen.
13 And the border went over from there
toward Luz, to the side of Luz, that is
Běyth Ěl, southward. And the border went
down to Ataroth Aḏar, by the hill that lies
on the south side of Lower Běyth Ḥoron.
14 And the border was drawn and went
around the west side to the south, from the
hill that faces Běyth Ḥoron southward, and
it ended at Qiryath Ba'al, that is Qiryath
Ye'arim, a city of the children of Yehuḏah.
This was the west side.
15 And the south side was from the end of
Qiryath Ye'arim, and the border went out
westward, and went out to the fountain of
the waters of Nephtowaḥ.
16 And the border came down to the end
of the mountain that faces the Valley of the
Son of Hinnom, which is in the Valley of
the Repha'im on the north, and went down
to the Valley of Hinnom, to the side of the
Yeḇusite city on the south, and went down
to Ěn Roḡěl.
17 And it was drawn from the north, went
out to Ěn Shemesh, and went out toward
Geliloth, which is opposite the Ascent of
Aḏummim, and went down to the stone of
Bohan son of Re'uḇěn,
18 and passed over to the side opposite
Araḇah northward, and went down to
Araḇah.
19 And the border passed over to the side
of Běyth Ḥoḡlah northward, and the border
ended at the north bay at the Salt Sea, at
the south end of the Yarděn. This was the
southern boundary,
20 and the Yarděn borders it on the east
side. This was the inheritance of the
children of Binyamin, according to its
boundaries all around, for their clans.
21 And the cities for the tribe of the children of Binyamin, for their clans, were
Yeriḥo, and Běyth Ḥoḡlah, and Ěmeq
Qetsits,
22 and Běyth Araḇah, and Tsemarayim,
and Běyth Ěl,
23 and Awwim, and Parah, and Ophrah,
24 and Kephar Ha'ammoni, and Ophni,
and Gaḇa – twelve cities with their
villages.
25 Giḇ'on, and Ramah, and Be'ěroth,
26 and Mitspeh, and Kephirah, and
Motsah,
27 and Reqem, and Yirpe'ěl, and Taralah,
28 and Tsela, Eleph, and the Yeḇusite, that
is Yerushalayim, Giḇ'ath, and Qiryath –
fourteen cities with their villages. This was
the inheritance of the children of Binyamin
for their clans.

19 And the second lot came out for
Shim'on, for the tribe of the children of Shim'on for their clans. And their
inheritance was within the inheritance of
the children of Yehuḏah.
2 And they had in their inheritance
Be'ěrsheḇa, or Sheḇa, and Molaḏah,
3 and Ḥatsar Shu'al, and Balah, and
Etsem,
4 and Eltolaḏ, and Bethul, and Ḥormah,
5 and Tsiqlaḡ, and Běyth Markaḇoth, and
Ḥatsar Susah,
6 and Běyth Leḇa'oth, and Sharuḥen –
thirteen cities and their villages.
7 Ayin, Rimmon, and Ether, and Ashan –
four cities and their villages;
8 and all the villages that were all around
these cities as far as Ba'alath Be'ěr,
Ramath Neḡeḇ. This was the inheritance of
the tribe of the children of Shim'on for
their clans.
9 The inheritance of the children of
Shim'on was out of the portion of the

children of Yehuḏah, for the portion of the children of Yehuḏah was too much for them. So the children of Shimʿon had their inheritance within their inheritance.
10 And the third lot came up for the children of Zeḇulun for their clans, and the border of their inheritance was as far as Sariḏ.
11 And their border went toward the sea, and Maralah, and reached to Dabbesheth, and reached to the wadi that faced Yoqneʿam,
12 and turned back from Sariḏ eastward toward the sunrise, to the border of Kisloth Taḇor, and went out toward Daḇerath, and went up to Yaphiya.
13 And from there it passed over eastward, to the east of Gath Ḥěpher, toward Eth Qatsin, and went out to Rimmon, which borders on Něʿah.
14 And the border went around it on the north side of Ḥannathon, and it ended in the Valley of Yiphthaḥ Ěl;
15 also Qattath, and Nahalal, and Shimron, and Yiḏalah, and Běyth Leḥem – twelve cities with their villages.
16 This was the inheritance of the children of Zeḇulun for their clans, these cities with their villages.
17 The fourth lot came out to Yissasḵar, for the children of Yissasḵar, for their clans.
18 And their border was toward Yizreʿěl, and Kesulloth, and Shuněm,
19 and Ḥapharayim, and Shiyon, and Anaḥarath,
20 and Rabbith, and Qishyon, and Eḇets,
21 and Remeth, and Ěn Gannim, and Ěn Ḥaddah, and Běyth Patstsěts.
22 And the border reached to Taḇor, and Shaḥatsimah, and Běyth Shemesh, and their border ended at the Yarděn – sixteen cities with their villages.
23 This was the inheritance of the tribe of the children of Yissasḵar for their clans, the cities and their villages.
24 And the fifth lot came out for the tribe of the children of Ashěr for their clans.
25 And their border was Ḥelqath, and Ḥali, and Beten, and Aḵshaph,
26 and Allammeleḵ, and Amaḏ, and Mish'al. And it reached to Mount Karmel westward, and to Brook Shiḥor Liḇnath,
27 and turned toward the sunrise, to Běyth Daḡon, and reached to Zeḇulun and to the Valley of Yiphthaḥ Ěl, then northward beyond Běyth Ěmeq and Neʿi'ěl, and went out to Kaḇul which was on the left,
28 and Ḥeḇron, and Reḥoḇ, and Ḥammon, and Qanah, as far as Great Tsiḏon.
29 And the border turned to Ramah and to the strong city Tsor, and the border turned to Ḥosah, and ended at the sea, from the coast to Aḵziḇ.
30 And Ummah, and Aphěq, and Reḥoḇ were included – twenty-two cities with their villages.
31 This was the inheritance of the tribe of the children of Ashěr for their clans, these cities with their villages.
32 The sixth lot came out to the children of Naphtali, for the children of Naphtali for their clans.
33 And their border was from Ḥeleph, from the terebinth tree in Tsa'anannim, and Aḏami Neqeḇ, and Yaḇne'ěl, as far as Laqqum, and it ended at the Yarděn.
34 And the border turned westward to Aznoth Taḇor, and went out from there toward Ḥuqqoq, and reached to Zeḇulun on the south side and Ashěr on the west side, and ended at Yehuḏah by the Yarděn toward the sunrise.
35 And the cities of defence were Tsiddim, Tsěr, and Ḥammath, Raqqath, and Kinnereth,
36 and Aḏamah, and Ramah, and Ḥatsor,
37 and Qeḏesh, and Eḏreʿi, and Ěn Ḥatsor,
38 and Yiron, and Miḡdal Ěl, Ḥorěm, and Běyth Anath, and Běyth Shemesh – nineteen cities with their villages.
39 This was the inheritance of the tribe of the children of Naphtali for their clans, the cities with their villages.
40 The seventh lot came out for the tribe of the children of Dan for their clans.
41 And the border of their inheritance was Tsorʿah, and Eshta'ol, and Ir Shemesh,
42 and Shaʿalabbin, and Ayalon, and Yithlah,
43 and Ělon, and Timnathah, and Eqron,
44 and Elteqěh, and Gibbethon, and

Baʿalath,
45 and Yehuḏ, and Beněi Beraq, and Gath
Rimmon,
46 and Měy Yarqon, and Raqqon, with the
border before Yapho.
47 And the border of the children of Dan
went out from them. And the children of
Dan went up to fight against Leshem and
captured it. And they struck it with the
edge of the sword, and possessed it, and
dwelt in it, and called it Leshem, Dan, after
the name of Dan their father.
48 This is the inheritance of the tribe of the
children of Dan for their clans, these cities
with their villages.
49 And when they had ended dividing the
land as an inheritance according to their
borders, the children of Yisra'ěl gave an
inheritance to Yehoshua son of Nun in
their midst.
50 According to the mouth of יהוה they
gave him the city which he asked for,
Timnath Seraḥ in the mountains of
Ephrayim. And he built the city and dwelt
in it.
51 These were the inheritances which
Elʿazar the priest, and Yehoshua son of
Nun, and the heads of the fathers of the
tribes of the children of Yisra'ěl divided as
an inheritance by lot in Shiloh before יהוה,
at the door of the Tent of Appointment.
And they ended dividing the country.

20 And יהוה spoke to Yehoshua,
saying,
2 "Speak to the children of Yisra'ěl,
saying, 'Appoint for yourselves cities of
refuge, of which I spoke to you through
Mosheh,
3 for the man-slayer who strikes any
being mistakenly, unknowingly, to flee
there. And they shall be your refuge from
the revenger of blood.
4 'And he shall flee to one of those cities,
and stand at the entrance of the gate of the
city, and declare his case in the hearing of
the elders of that city. And they shall take
him into the city as one of them, and give
him a place, and he shall dwell among
them.
5 'And when the revenger of blood
pursues him, they do not give the man-
slayer into his hand, because he struck his
neighbour unknowingly, and did not hate
him beforehand.
6 'And he shall dwell in that city until he
stands before the congregation for right-
ruling, and until the death of the one who
is high priest in those days. Then let the
man-slayer return and come to his own city
and his own house, to the city from which
he fled.'"
7 So they set apart Qeḏesh in Galil, in the
mountains of Naphtali, and Sheḵem in the
mountains of Ephrayim, and Qiryath Arba,
that is Ḥeḇron, in the mountains of
Yehuḏah.
8 And beyond the Yarděn, by Yeriḥo
eastward, they appointed Betser in the
wilderness on the plain, from the tribe of
Re'uḇěn, and Ramoth in Gilʿaḏ, from the
tribe of Gaḏ, and Golan in Bashan, from
the tribe of Menashsheh.
9 These were the cities appointed for all
the children of Yisra'ěl and for the stranger
who sojourned in their midst, for anyone
striking any being unknowingly, to flee
there, and not die by the hand of the
revenger of blood until he stood before the
congregation.

21 And the heads of the fathers of the
Lěwites came near to Elʿazar the
priest, to Yehoshua son of Nun, and to the
heads of the fathers of the tribes of the
children of Yisra'ěl.
2 And they spoke to them at Shiloh in the
land of Kenaʿan, saying, "יהוה commanded through Mosheh to give us cities to
dwell in, with their open land for our
livestock."
3 So the children of Yisra'ěl gave to the
Lěwites from their inheritance, at the
mouth of יהוה, these cities and their open
land:
4 And the lot came out for the clans of
the Qehathites. And the children of Aharon
the priest, who were of the Lěwites, had
thirteen cities by lot from the tribe of
Yehuḏah, from the tribe of Shimʿon, and
from the tribe of Binyamin.
5 And the rest of the children of Qehath

had ten cities by lot from the clans of the
tribe of Ephrayim, from the tribe of Dan,
and from the half-tribe of Menashsheh.
6 And the children of Gĕrshon had
thirteen cities by lot from the clans of the
tribe of Yissasḵar, from the tribe of Ashĕr,
from the tribe of Naphtali, and from the
half-tribe of Menashsheh in Bashan.
7 The children of Merari for their clans
had twelve cities from the tribe of
Re'uḇĕn, and from the tribe of Gaḏ, and
from the tribe of Zeḇulun.
8 Thus the children of Yisra'ĕl gave these
cities with their open land by lot to the
Lĕwites, as יהוה had commanded by the
hand of Mosheh.
9 So from the tribe of the children of
Yehuḏah and from the tribe of the children
of Shimʽon they gave these cities which
are mentioned by name,
10 and they were for the children of
Aharon, one of the clans of the Qehathites,
who were of the children of Lĕwi, for the
lot was theirs first.
11 And they gave them Qiryath Arba, that
is Ḥeḇron – *Arba was* the father of Anaq –
in the mountains of Yehuḏah, with the
open land surrounding it.
12 And the fields of the city and its
villages they gave to Kalĕḇ son of
Yephunneh as his possession.
13 But to the children of Aharon the priest
they gave Ḥeḇron with its open land – a
city of refuge for the man-slayer – and
Liḇnah with its open land,
14 and Yattir with its open land, and
Eshtemoa with its open land,
15 and Ḥolon with its open land, and
Deḇir with its open land,
16 and Ayin with its open land, and Yuttah
with its open land, and Bĕyth Shemesh
with its open land – nine cities from those
two tribes.
17 And from the tribe of Binyamin, Giḇʽon
with its open land, Geḇa with its open land,
18 Anathoth with its open land, and
Almon with its open land – four cities.
19 All the cities of the children of Aharon,
the priests, were thirteen cities with their
open lands.
20 And the clans of the children of
Qehath, the Lĕwites, the rest of the
children of Qehath, even they had the
cities of their lot from the tribe of
Ephrayim.
21 And they gave them Sheḵem with its
open land in the mountains of Ephrayim as
a city of refuge for the man-slayer, and
Gezer with its open land,
22 and Qiḇtsayim with its open land, and
Bĕyth Ḥoron with its open land – four
cities.
23 And from the tribe of Dan, Elteqĕh
with its open land, Gibbethon with its open
land,
24 Ayalon with its open land, and Gath
Rimmon with its open land – four cities.
25 And from the half-tribe of Menashsheh,
Taʽnaḵ with its open land, and Gath
Rimmon with its open land – two cities.
26 All the ten cities with their open lands
were for the rest of the clans of the
children of Qehath.
27 And to the children of Gĕrshon, of the
clans of the Lĕwites, from the other half-
tribe of Menashsheh, they gave Golan in
Bashan with its open land as a city of
refuge for the man-slayer, and Beʽeshterah
with its open land – two cities.
28 And from the tribe of Yissasḵar,
Qishyon with its open land, Daḇerath with
its open land,
29 Yarmuth with its open land, and Ĕn
Gannim with its open land – four cities.
30 And from the tribe of Ashĕr, Mish'al
with its open land, Aḇdon with its open
land,
31 Ḥelqath with its open land, and Reḥoḇ
with its open land – four cities.
32 And from the tribe of Naphtali, Qeḏesh
in Galil with its open land as a city of
refuge for the man-slayer, and Ḥammoth
Dor with its open land, and Qartan with its
open land – three cities.
33 All the cities of the Gĕrshonites for
their clans were thirteen cities with their
open land.
34 And to the clans of the children of
Merari, the rest of the Lĕwites, from the
tribe of Zeḇulun, Yoqneʽam with its open
land, Qartah with its open land,
35 Dimnah with its open land, Nahalal

with its open land – four cities.
[36]And from the tribe of Re'uḇěn, Betser
with its open land, Yahtsah with its open
land,
[37]Qeḏěmoth with its open land, and
Měpha'ath with its open land – four cities.
[38]And from the tribe of Gaḏ, Ramoth in
Gil'aḏ with its open land as a city of refuge
for the man-slayer, and Maḥanayim with
its open land,
[39]Ḥeshbon with its open land, Ya'zěr with
its open land – four cities in all.
[40]All the cities for the children of Merari
for their clans, the rest of the clans of the
Lěwites, were by their lot twelve cities.
[41]All the cities of the Lěwites within the
possession of the children of Yisra'ěl were
forty-eight cities with their open lands.
[42]Each of these cities had its open land
surrounding it. So it was with all these
cities.
[43]Thus יהוה gave to Yisra'ěl all the land
of which He had sworn to give to their
fathers, and they took possession of it, and
dwelt in it.
[44]And יהוה gave them rest all around,
according to all that He had sworn to their
fathers. And not a man of all their enemies
stood against them, יהוה gave all their
enemies into their hand.
[45]Not a word failed of any good word
which יהוה had spoken to the house of
Yisra'ěl – all came in.

22 Then Yehoshua called for the
Re'uḇěnites, and the Gaḏites, and
half the tribe of Menashsheh,
[2]and said to them, "You, you have
guarded all that Mosheh the servant of
יהוה commanded you, and have obeyed
my voice in all that I commanded you.
[3]"You have not left your brothers these
many days, up to this day, but have
guarded the Charge, the command of יהוה
your Elohim.
[4]"And now יהוה your Elohim has given
rest to your brothers, as He promised them.
So now, return and go to your tents and to
the land of your possession, which Mosheh
the servant of יהוה gave you beyond the
Yarděn.
[5]"Only, diligently guard to do the
command and the Torah which Mosheh the
servant of יהוה commanded you, to love
יהוה your Elohim, and to walk in all His
ways, and to guard His commands, and to
cling to Him, and to serve Him with all
your heart and with all your being."
[6]And Yehoshua blessed them and sent
them away, and they went to their tents.
[7]And to half the tribe of Menashsheh
Mosheh had given a possession in Bashan,
but to the *other* half of it Yehoshua gave
land among their brothers beyond the
Yarděn, westward. So when Yehoshua sent
them away to their tents, he also blessed
them,
[8]and spoke to them, saying, "Return to
your tents with great riches, and with very
much livestock, and with silver, and with
gold, and with bronze, and with iron, and
with countless garments. Divide the spoil
of your enemies with your brothers."
[9]And the children of Re'uḇěn, and the
children of Gaḏ, and half the tribe of
Menashsheh returned, and left the children
of Yisra'ěl at Shiloh, which is in the land
of Kena'an, to go to the land of Gil'aḏ, to
the land of their possession, which they
possessed according to the mouth of יהוה
by the hand of Mosheh.
[10]And they came to the districts of the
Yarděn which is in the land of Kena'an,
and the children of Re'uḇěn, and the
children of Gaḏ, and half the tribe of
Menashsheh built a slaughter-place there
by the Yarděn, a great conspicuous slaughter-place.
[11]And the children of Yisra'ěl heard it
said, "See, the children of Re'uḇěn, and the
children of Gaḏ, and half the tribe of
Menashsheh have built a slaughter-place
opposite the land of Kena'an, in the districts of the Yarděn, at the border of the
children of Yisra'ěl."
[12]And when the children of Yisra'ěl
heard, all the congregation of the children
of Yisra'ěl assembled at Shiloh to go to
fight against them.
[13]So the children of Yisra'ěl sent Pineḥas
son of El'azar the priest to the children of
Re'uḇěn, and to the children of Gaḏ, and to

half the tribe of Menashsheh, into the land of Gil'aḏ,

14 and ten rulers with him, one ruler each from the chief house of every tribe of Yisra'ěl. And each one was the head of the house of his father among the divisions of Yisra'ěl.

15 And they came to the children of Re'uḇěn and to the children of Gaḏ, and to half the tribe of Menashsheh, to the land of Gil'aḏ, and spoke with them, saying,

16 "Thus says all the congregation of יהוה, 'What is this trespass you have committed against the Elohim of Yisra'ěl, to turn away this day from following יהוה, in that you have built for yourselves a slaughter-place, to rebel against יהוה this day?

17 'Is the crookedness of Pe'or not enough for us, from which we have not been cleansed till this day, although there was a plague in the congregation of יהוה,

18 that you turn away today from following יהוה? And it shall be, if you rebel today against יהוה, that tomorrow He is wroth with all the congregation of Yisra'ěl.

19 'And indeed, if the land of your possession is unclean, then pass over to the land of the possession of יהוה, where the Dwelling Place of יהוה dwells, and take possession among us. But do not rebel against יהוה, nor rebel against us, by building yourselves a slaughter-place besides the slaughter-place of יהוה our Elohim.

20 'Did not Aḵan son of Zeraḥ commit a trespass in that which is under the ban, and wrath fell on all the congregation of Yisra'ěl? And he was not the only one to die in his crookedness.' "

21 Then the children of Re'uḇěn, and the children of Gaḏ, and half the tribe of Menashsheh answered and said to the heads of the divisions of Yisra'ěl,

22 "Ěl Elohim יהוה, Ěl Elohim יהוה, He knows, and let Yisra'ěl itself know. If this has been in rebellion, or if in trespass against יהוה, do not save us this day.

23 "If we have built ourselves a slaughter-place to turn from following יהוה, or if to offer ascending offerings or grain offerings on it, or if to make slaughterings of peace *offerings* on it, let יהוה Himself require it.

24 "But truly, from fear, for a reason we did this, saying, 'In time to come your sons might speak to our sons, saying, "What have you to do with יהוה Elohim of Yisra'ěl?

25 "For יהוה has made the Yarděn a border between you and us, you children of Re'uḇěn and children of Gaḏ. You have no portion with יהוה." So your sons would make our sons stop fearing יהוה.'

26 "So we said, 'Let us now prepare to build ourselves a slaughter-place, not for ascending offering nor for slaughtering,

27 but to be a witness between you and us and our generations after us, to do the service of יהוה before Him with our ascending offerings, with our slaughterings, and with our peace *offerings*, that your sons should not say to our sons in time to come, "You have no portion with יהוה." '

28 "So we said that it shall be, when they say this to us or to our generations in time to come, that we shall say, 'See the pattern of the slaughter-place of יהוה which our fathers made, though not for ascending offerings nor for slaughterings, but it is a witness between you and us.'

29 "Far be it from us to rebel against יהוה, and to turn from following יהוה this day, to build a slaughter-place for ascending offerings, for grain offerings, or for slaughterings, besides the slaughter-place of יהוה our Elohim which is before His Dwelling Place."

30 And Pineḥas the priest and the rulers of the congregation, and the heads of the thousands of Yisra'ěl who were with him, heard the words that the children of Re'uḇěn, and the children of Gaḏ, and the children of Menashsheh spoke, and it was good in their eyes.

31 And Pineḥas son of El'azar the priest said to the children of Re'uḇěn, and to the children of Gaḏ, and to the children of Menashsheh, "Today we know that יהוה is in our midst, because you have not committed against יהוה this trespass. Now you have delivered the children of Yisra'ěl

out of the hand of יהוה."
32 And Pineḥas son of El'azar the priest, and the rulers, returned from the children of Re'uḇěn and the children of Gaḏ, from the land of Gil'aḏ to the land of Kena'an, to the children of Yisra'ěl, and brought back word to them.
33 So the matter was good in the eyes of the children of Yisra'ěl, and the children of Yisra'ěl blessed Elohim. And they spoke no more of going against to fight, to destroy the land where the children of Re'uḇěn and Gaḏ dwelt.
34 And the children of Re'uḇěn and the children of Gaḏ called the slaughter-place, "A witness between us that יהוה is Elohim."

23 And it came to be, a long time after יהוה had given rest to Yisra'ěl from all their enemies round about, that Yehoshua was old, advanced in years.
2 And Yehoshua called for all Yisra'ěl, and for their elders, and for their heads, and for their judges, and for their officers, and said to them, "I am old, advanced in years.
3 "And you, you have seen all that יהוה your Elohim has done to all these nations because of you, for יהוה your Elohim is He who was fighting for you.
4 "See, I have divided to you by lot these nations that remain, to be an inheritance for your tribes, from the Yarděn, with all the nations that I have cut off, as far as the Great Sea toward the setting of the sun.
5 "And יהוה your Elohim thrust them out from before you, and shall drive them out from before you, and you shall possess their land, as יהוה your Elohim has promised you.
6 "And you shall be very strong to guard and to do all that is written in the Book of the Torah of Mosheh, so as not to turn aside from it right or left,
7 so as not to go in among these nations, these who remain among you. And make no mention of the name of their mighty ones,[a] nor swear *by them*, nor serve them nor bow down to them.
8 "But cling to יהוה your Elohim, as you have done to this day.
9 "For יהוה has driven out from before you great and strong nations. As for you, no one has stood against you to this day.
10 "One man of you put a thousand to flight, for יהוה your Elohim is He who is fighting for you, as He has promised you.
11 "And you shall diligently guard yourselves, to love יהוה your Elohim.
12 "But if you do turn back at all, and cling to the remnant of these nations, these that remain among you, and intermarry with them, and go in to them and they to you,
13 know for certain that יהוה your Elohim shall no longer drive these nations out from before you. And they shall be snares and traps to you, and a whip on your sides and thorns in your eyes, until you perish from this good land which יהוה your Elohim has given you.
14 "And see, this day I am going the way of all the earth. And you know in all your hearts and in all your beings that not one word has failed of all the good words which יהוה your Elohim spoke concerning you. All of it has come to you, and not one word of them has failed.
15 "And it shall be, that as every good word has come upon you which יהוה your Elohim promised you, so יהוה does bring upon you every evil word, until He has destroyed you from this good land which יהוה your Elohim has given you,
16 when you transgress the covenant of יהוה your Elohim, which He commanded you, and shall go and serve other mighty ones, and bow down to them. And the displeasure of יהוה shall burn against you, and you shall perish quickly from the good land which He has given you."

24 And Yehoshua gathered all the tribes of Yisra'ěl to Sheḵem and called for the elders of Yisra'ěl, and for their heads, and for their judges, and for their officers. And they presented them-

23a See Shem. 23:13.

selves before Elohim.
2 And Yehoshua said to all the people,
"Thus said יהוה Elohim of Yisra'ěl, 'Long
ago your fathers dwelt beyond the River –
Teraḥ, the father of Aḇraham and the
father of Naḥor. And they served other
mighty ones.
3 'So I took your father Aḇraham from
beyond the River, and caused him to go
through all the land of Kenaʽan, and multiplied his offspring and gave him Yitsḥaq.
4 'And to Yitsḥaq I gave Yaʽaqoḇ and
Ěsaw. And to Ěsaw I gave the mountains
of Sěʽir to possess, but Yaʽaqoḇ and his
children went down to Mitsrayim.
5 'Then I sent Mosheh and Aharon, and
plagued Mitsrayim, as I did in their midst.
And afterward I brought you out.
6 'And I brought your fathers out of
Mitsrayim, and you came to the sea. And
the Mitsrians pursued your fathers with
chariots and horsemen to the Sea of Reeds.
7 'And they cried out to יהוה, and He put
thick darkness between you and the
Mitsrians, and brought the sea upon them,
and covered them. And your eyes saw
what I did in Mitsrayim. And you dwelt in
the wilderness a long time.
8 'And I brought you into the land of the
Amorites, who dwelt beyond the Yarděn,
and they fought with you. But I gave them
into your hand, and you possessed their
land, and I destroyed them from before
you.
9 'And Balaq son of Tsippor, sovereign
of Mo'aḇ, rose up and fought against
Yisra'ěl, and sent and called for Bilʽam son
of Beʽor to curse you.
10 'But I refused to listen to Bilʽam, so he
continued to bless you, and I delivered you
out of his hand.
11 'And you passed over the Yarděn and
came to Yeriḥo. And the masters of Yeriḥo,
the Amorite, and the Perizzite, and the
Kenaʽanite, and the Ḥittite, and the
Girgashite, and the Ḥiwwite, and the
Yeḇusite fought against you. But I gave
them into your hand.
12 'And I sent the hornet before you which
drove them out from before you, also the
two sovereigns of the Amorites, but not
with your sword or with your bow.
13 'And I gave you a land for which you
did not labour, and cities which you did not
build. And you dwell in them, you eat of
the vineyards and olive-trees which you
did not plant.'
14 "And now, fear יהוה, serve Him in
perfection and in truth, and put away the
mighty ones which your fathers served
beyond the River and in Mitsrayim, and
serve יהוה!
15 "And if it seems evil in your eyes to
serve יהוה, choose for yourselves this day
whom you are going to serve, whether the
mighty ones which your fathers served that
were beyond the River, or the mighty ones
of the Amorites, in whose land you dwell.
But I and my house, we serve יהוה."
16 And the people answered and said, "Far
be it from us to forsake יהוה, to serve other
mighty ones,
17 for יהוה our Elohim is He who has
brought us and our fathers up out of the
land of Mitsrayim, from the house of
bondage, who did those great signs before
our eyes, and has guarded us in all the way
that we went and among all the people
through whom we passed.
18 "And יהוה drove out from before us all
the people, even the Amorites who dwelt
in the land. We too serve יהוה, for He is
our Elohim."
19 Then Yehoshua said to the people,
"You are not able to serve יהוה, for He is
a set-apart Elohim, a jealous Ěl is He. He
does not bear with your transgression and
with your sins,
20 if you forsake יהוה and shall serve
mighty ones of a stranger. Then He shall
turn back and do you evil and consume
you, after He has been good to you."
21 And the people said to Yehoshua, "No,
but we do serve יהוה!"
22 Then Yehoshua said to the people,
"You are witnesses against yourselves that
you have chosen יהוה for yourselves, to
serve Him." And they said, "Witnesses!"
23 "And now, put away the mighty ones of
the stranger which are in your midst, and
incline your heart to יהוה Elohim of
Yisra'ěl."

24 And the people said to Yehoshua, "יהוה our Elohim we serve, and His voice we obey."

25 And Yehoshua made a covenant with the people that day, and laid on them a law and a right-ruling in Sheḵem.

26 Then Yehoshua wrote these words in the Book of the Torah of Elohim. And he took a large stone, and set it up there under the oak that was by the set-apart place of יהוה.

27 And Yehoshua said to all the people, "See, this stone is a witness to us, for it has heard all the words of יהוה which He spoke to us. And it shall be a witness against you, lest you lie against your Elohim."

28 Then Yehoshua sent the people away, each to his own inheritance.

29 And after these events it came to be that Yehoshua son of Nun, the servant of יהוה, died, one hundred and ten years old.

30 And they buried him within the border of his inheritance at Timnath Seraḥ, which is in the mountains of Ephrayim, on the north side of Mount Gaʽash.

31 And Yisra'ěl served יהוה all the days of Yehoshua, and all the days of the elders who outlived Yehoshua, who had known all the works of יהוה which He had done for Yisra'ěl.

32 And the bones of Yosěph, which the children of Yisra'ěl had brought up out of Mitsrayim, they buried at Sheḵem, in the plot of ground which Yaʽaqoḇ had bought from the sons of Ḥamor the father of Sheḵem for one hundred qesitah,[a] and which had become an inheritance of the children of Yosěph.

33 And Elʽazar son of Aharon died, and they buried him in a hill that belonged to Pineḥas his son, which was given to him in the hill country of Ephrayim.

24a A monetary unit of uncertain value, perhaps in the form of a lamb.

SHOPHETIM

JUDGES — RULERS

1 And it came to be, after the death of
Yehoshua, that the children of Yisra'ěl
asked יהוה, saying, "Who of us should go
up first against the Kena'anites to fight
against them?"
2 And יהוה said, "Yehuḏah does go up.
See, I have given the land into his hand."
3 And Yehuḏah said to Shim'on his brother, "Come up with me into my allotment,
and let us fight against the Kena'anites.
And I myself shall also go with you into
your allotment." So Shim'on went with
him.
4 And Yehuḏah went up, and יהוה gave
the Kena'anites and the Perizzites into their
hand. And they struck ten thousand men at
Bezeq.
5 And they found Aḏoni-Ḇezeq in Bezeq,
and fought against him, and struck the
Kena'anites and the Perizzites.
6 But Aḏoni-Ḇezeq fled, and they pursued him and caught him and cut off his
thumbs and big toes.
7 And Aḏoni-Ḇezeq said, "Seventy sovereigns with their thumbs and big toes cut
off used to gather *food* under my table. As I
have done, so Elohim has repaid me." And
they brought him to Yerushalayim, and he
died there.
8 And the children of Yehuḏah fought
against Yerushalayim and captured it, and
struck it with the edge of the sword and set
the city on fire.
9 And afterward the children of Yehuḏah
went down to fight against the Kena'anites
who dwelt in the mountains, in the South,
and in the low country.
10 And Yehuḏah went against the Ken-
a'anites who dwelt in Ḥeḇron – now the
name of Ḥeḇron was formerly Qiryath
Arba – and they struck Shěshai, and
Aḥiman, and Talmai.
11 And from there they went against the
inhabitants of Deḇir – now the name of
Deḇir was formerly Qiryath Sěpher.
12 And Kalěḇ said, "He who smites
Qiryath Sěpher, and shall capture it, to him
I shall give my daughter Aḵsah as wife."
13 And Othni'ěl son of Qenaz, Kalěḇ's
younger brother, captured it. And he gave
him his daughter Aḵsah as wife.
14 And it came to be, when she came in,
that she urged him to ask her father for a
field. And when she got off from her
donkey, Kalěḇ said to her, "What is the
matter?"
15 And she said to him, "Give me a blessing. Since you have given me land in the
South, give me also springs of water." So
Kalěḇ gave her the upper springs and the
lower springs.
16 And the children of the Qěynite, father-
in-law of Mosheh, went up from the city of
palms with the children of Yehuḏah into
the Wilderness of Yehuḏah, which is in the
Neḡeḇ of Araḏ. And they went and dwelt
among the people.
17 And Yehuḏah went with Shim'on his
brother, and they struck the Kena'anites
who inhabited Tsephath, and put it under
the ban. So the name of the city was called
Ḥormah.
18 And Yehuḏah captured Azzah and its
border, and Ashqelon and its border, and
Eqron and its border.
19 And יהוה was with Yehuḏah, so they
took possession of the mountains, but they
were unable to drive out the inhabitants of
the plain, because they had chariots of iron.
20 And they gave Ḥeḇron to Kalěḇ, as
Mosheh had said, and he drove out from
there the three sons of Anaq.
21 However, the children of Binyamin did
not drive out the Yeḇusites who inhabited
Yerushalayim, so the Yeḇusites have dwelt
with the children of Binyamin in Yerushalayim to this day.
22 And the house of Yosěph also went up
against Běyth Ěl, and יהוה was with them.
23 And the house of Yosěph sent men to

spy out Běyth Ěl – now the name of the city was formerly Luz.

24 And the watchmen saw a man coming out of the city, and they said to him, "Please show us the entrance to the city, and we shall show you loving-commitment."

25 So he showed them the entrance to the city, and they struck the city with the edge of the sword. But the man and all his clan they let go,

26 and the man went to the land of the Ḥittites and built a city, and called its name Luz, which is its name to this day.

27 And Menashsheh did not dispossess Běyth She'an and its villages, nor Ta'anaḵ and its villages, nor the inhabitants of Dor and its villages, nor the inhabitants of Yiḇle'am and its villages, nor the inhabitants of Meḡiddo and its villages, for the Kena'anites desired to dwell in that land.

28 And it came to be, when Yisra'ěl was strong, that they put the Kena'anites into compulsory labour, but did not completely drive them out.

29 Neither did Ephrayim drive out the Kena'anites who dwelt in Gezer, so the Kena'anites dwelt in their midst, in Gezer.

30 Neither did Zeḇulun drive out the inhabitants of Qitron or the inhabitants of Nahalol, so the Kena'anites dwelt in their midst, and became compulsory labour.

31 Neither did Ashěr drive out the inhabitants of Akko nor the inhabitants of Tsiḏon, nor of Aḥlaḇ, nor of Aḵziḇ, nor of Ḥelbah, nor of Aphiq, nor of Reḥoḇ.

32 So the Ashěrites dwelt in the midst of the Kena'anites, the inhabitants of the land, because they did not drive them out.

33 Neither did Naphtali drive out the inhabitants of Běyth Shemesh nor the inhabitants of Běyth Anath, but they dwelt among the Kena'anites, the inhabitants of the land. And the inhabitants of Běyth Shemesh and of Běyth Anath became compulsory labour for them.

34 And the Amorites pressed the children of Dan into the mountains, for they would not allow them to come down to the valley,

35 and the Amorites desired to dwell in Mount Ḥeres, in Ayalon, and in Sha'alḇim. But when the hand of the house of Yosěph became stronger, they became compulsory labour.

36 And the border of the Amorites was from the Ascent of Aqrabbim, from Sela, and upward.

2 And the Messenger of יהוה came up from Gilgal to Boḵim, and said, "I led you up from Mitsrayim and brought you to the land of which I swore to your fathers, and I said, 'I do not break My covenant with you,

2 and as for you, do not make a covenant with the inhabitants of this land – break down their slaughter-places.' But you have not obeyed My voice. What is this you have done?

3 "Therefore I also said, 'I am not driving them out before you, and they shall be adversaries to you, and their mighty ones shall be a snare to you.' "

4 And it came to be, when the Messenger of יהוה spoke these words to all the children of Yisra'ěl, that the people lifted up their voice and wept.

5 So they called the name of that place Boḵim, and slaughtered there to יהוה.

6 Then Yehoshua dismissed the people, and the children of Yisra'ěl went each to his own inheritance to possess the land.

7 And the people served יהוה all the days of Yehoshua, and all the days of the elders who outlived Yehoshua, who had seen all the great works of יהוה which He had done for Yisra'ěl.

8 And Yehoshua son of Nun, the servant of יהוה, died, one hundred and ten years old.

9 And they buried him within the border of his inheritance at Timnath Ḥeres, in the mountains of Ephrayim, on the north side of Mount Ga'ash.

10 And all that generation were likewise gathered to their fathers, and another generation arose after them who did not know יהוה nor the work which He had done for Yisra'ěl.

11 Then the children of Yisra'ěl did evil in the eyes of יהוה, and served the Ba'als,

12 and forsook יהוה Elohim of their

fathers, who had brought them out of the
land of Mitsrayim, and went after other
mighty ones, of the mighty ones of the people who were all around them, and they
bowed down to them, and provoked יהוה.
13 So they forsook יהוה and served Ba'al
and the Ashtoreths.
14 And the displeasure of יהוה burned
against Yisra'ěl. Therefore He gave them
into the hands of plunderers who despoiled
them. And He sold them into the hands of
their enemies all around, and they were
unable to stand before their enemies any
longer.
15 Wherever they went out, the hand of
יהוה was against them for evil, as יהוה had
spoken, and as יהוה had sworn to them.
And they were distressed – greatly.
16 Then יהוה raised up rulers who saved
them from the hand of those who plundered
them.
17 However, they did not listen to their
rulers either, but went whoring after other
mighty ones, and bowed down to them.
They soon turned aside from the way in
which their fathers walked, in obeying the
commands of יהוה – they did not do so.
18 And when יהוה raised up rulers for
them, יהוה was with the ruler and saved
them from the hand of their enemies all the
days of the ruler, for יהוה had compassion
on their groaning because of those who
oppressed them and crushed them.
19 And it came to be, when the ruler was
dead, that they would turn back and do
more corruptly than their fathers, to go
after other mighty ones, to serve them and
bow down to them. They did not refrain
from their practices and from their stubborn way.
20 And the displeasure of יהוה burned
against Yisra'ěl, and He said, "Because this
nation has transgressed My covenant that I
commanded their fathers, and has not
obeyed My voice,
21 I also shall no longer drive out before
them any of the nations which Yehoshua
left when he died,
22 in order to try [a] Yisra'ěl by them,
whether they would guard the way of יהוה,
to walk in them as their fathers guarded
them, or not."
23 So יהוה left those nations, without
driving them out at once, and did not give
them into the hand of Yehoshua.

3 And these are the nations which יהוה
left, to try Yisra'ěl by them, all those
who had not known all the battles in
Kena'an,
2 only that the generations of the children
of Yisra'ěl might know, to teach them
battle, only those who before did not know
them:
3 five princes of the Philistines, and all
the Kena'anites, and the Tsiḏonians, and
the Ḥiwwites who dwelt in Mount
Leḇanon, from Mount Ba'al Ḥermon to the
entrance of Ḥamath.
4 And they were to try Yisra'ěl by them,
to know whether they would obey the commands of יהוה, which He had commanded
their fathers by the hand of Mosheh.
5 Thus the children of Yisra'ěl dwelt in
the midst of the Kena'anites, the Ḥittites,
and the Amorites, and the Perizzites, and
the Ḥiwwites, and the Yeḇusites,
6 and took their daughters to be their
wives, and gave their daughters to their
sons, and they served their mighty ones.
7 Thus the children of Yisra'ěl did evil in
the eyes of יהוה, and forgot יהוה their
Elohim, and served the Ba'als and the
Ashěrahs.
8 And the displeasure of יהוה burned
against Yisra'ěl, and He sold them into the
hand of Kushan-Rish'athayim sovereign of
Aram Naharayim. And the children of
Yisra'ěl served Kushan-Rish'athayim eight
years.
9 And when the children of Yisra'ěl cried
out to יהוה, יהוה raised up a saviour for the
children of Yisra'ěl, who saved them:
Othni'ěl son of Qenaz, Kalěḇ's younger
brother.
10 And the Spirit of יהוה came upon him,
and he ruled Yisra'ěl, and went out to
battle, and יהוה gave into his hand Kushan-

2a See footnote at Deḇ. 8:2.

Rish'athayim sovereign of Aram Naharayim. And his hand prevailed over Kushan-Rish'athayim,

11 and the land had rest for forty years. Then Othni'ěl son of Qenaz died,

12 and the children of Yisra'ěl again did evil in the eyes of יהוה. And יהוה made Eḡlon sovereign of Mo'aḇ strong against Yisra'ěl, because they had done evil in the eyes of יהוה.

13 And he gathered to himself the children of Ammon and Amalěq, and went and struck Yisra'ěl, and they took possession of the city of palms.

14 And the children of Yisra'ěl served Eḡlon sovereign of Mo'aḇ eighteen years.

15 And when the children of Yisra'ěl cried out to יהוה, יהוה raised up a saviour for them: Ěhuḏ son of Gěra, a Binyamite, a man impeded in his right hand. And by him the children of Yisra'ěl sent a present to Eḡlon sovereign of Mo'aḇ.

16 And Ěhuḏ made himself a sword, it was double-edged and a cubit in length, and he girded it under his long robe on his right thigh.

17 And he brought the present to Eḡlon sovereign of Mo'aḇ. Now Eḡlon was a very fat man.

18 And it came to be that when he had finished bringing near the present, he sent away the people bearing the present.

19 But he himself turned back from the stone images that were at Gilgal, and said, "I have a secret message for you, O sovereign." And he said, "Be silent!" And all those standing beside him went out from him.

20 And Ěhuḏ came to him while he was sitting in his cool roof room. And Ěhuḏ said, "I have a message from Elohim for you." So he arose from his seat.

21 And Ěhuḏ reached with his left hand, and took the sword from his right thigh, and thrust it into his stomach.

22 And the handle went in after the blade, and the fat closed over the blade, for he did not draw the sword out of his stomach, and it came out behind.

23 Then Ěhuḏ went out to the porch and shut the doors of the upper room behind him and locked them.

24 And when he had gone out, his servants came to look and saw the doors of the roof room were locked. So they said, "He is only covering his feet in the cool roof room."

25 And they waited until they were ashamed, but saw he was not opening the doors of the upper room. So they took the key and opened them and saw their master, fallen to the ground, dead.

26 But while they were delaying Ěhuḏ escaped and had passed beyond the stone images, and escaped to Se'irah.

27 And it came to be, when he arrived, that he blew the shophar [a] in the mountains of Ephrayim, and the children of Yisra'ěl went down with him from the mountains, with him leading them.

28 And he said to them, "Follow me, for יהוה has given your enemies the Mo'aḇites into your hand." And they went down after him, and took the fords of Yarděn leading to Mo'aḇ, and did not allow anyone to pass over.

29 And they struck about ten thousand men of Mo'aḇ at that time, all robust and brave men, and not a man escaped.

30 And on that day Mo'aḇ was humbled under the hand of Yisra'ěl. And the land had rest for eighty years.

31 And after him was Shamgar son of Anath, and he struck six hundred men of the Philistines with an ox goad. And he too saved Yisra'ěl.

4 And when Ěhuḏ was dead, the children of Yisra'ěl again did evil in the eyes of יהוה.

2 Therefore יהוה sold them into the hand of Yaḇin the sovereign of Kena'an, who reigned in Ḥatsor. And the commander of his army was Sisera, who was dwelling in Ḥarosheth Haggoyim.

3 And the children of Yisra'ěl cried out to יהוה, because he had nine hundred chariots of iron, and for twenty years he harshly

3a Animal horn, traditionally a ram's horn.

oppressed the children of Yisra'ěl.
[4] And Deḇorah, a prophetess, the wife of
Lappiḏoth, was ruling Yisra'ěl at that time.
[5] And she was dwelling under the palm
tree of Deḇorah between Ramah and Běyth
Ěl in the mountains of Ephrayim. And the
children of Yisra'ěl came up to her for
right-ruling.
[6] And she sent and called for Baraq son
of Aḇino'am from Qeḏesh in Naphtali, and
said to him, "Has not יהוה Elohim of
Yisra'ěl commanded, 'Go, and you shall
draw towards Mount Taḇor, and shall take
with you ten thousand men of the sons of
Naphtali and of the sons of Zeḇulun,
[7] and I shall draw unto you Sisera, the
commander of Yaḇin's army, with his chariots and his company at the wadi Qishon,
and shall give him into your hand'?"
[8] And Baraq said to her, "If you go with
me, then I shall go; but if you do not go
with me, I do not go."
[9] And she said, "I shall certainly go with
you. Only, there shall be no esteem for you
in the journey you are taking, for יהוה is
going to sell Sisera into the hand of a
woman." So Deḇorah arose and went with
Baraq to Qeḏesh.
[10] And Baraq called Zeḇulun and Naphtali
to Qeḏesh. And he went up – ten thousand
men under his command – and Deḇorah
went up with him.
[11] And Ḥeḇer the Qěynite, of the children
of Ḥoḇaḇ the father-in-law of Mosheh, had
separated himself from the Qěynites and
pitched his tent near the terebinth tree at
Tsa'anayim, which is beside Qeḏesh.
[12] And they reported to Sisera that Baraq
son of Aḇino'am had gone up to Mount
Taḇor.
[13] So Sisera called all his chariots, nine
hundred chariots of iron, and all the people
who were with him, from Ḥarosheth
Haggoyim to the wadi Qishon.
[14] And Deḇorah said to Baraq, "Rise up!
For this is the day in which יהוה has given
Sisera into your hand. Has not יהוה gone
out before you?" And Baraq went down
from Mount Taḇor with ten thousand men
after him.
[15] And יהוה destroyed Sisera and all his
chariots and all his army with the edge of
the sword before Baraq. And Sisera leaped
from his chariot and fled away on foot.
[16] But Baraq pursued the chariots and the
army as far as Ḥarosheth Haggoyim, and
all the army of Sisera fell by the edge of the
sword, not one was left.
[17] Sisera, meanwhile, had fled on foot to
the tent of Ya'ěl, the wife of Ḥeḇer the
Qěynite, for there was peace between
Yaḇin sovereign of Ḥatsor and the house of
Ḥeḇer the Qěynite.
[18] And Ya'ěl went out to meet Sisera, and
said to him, "Turn aside, my master, turn
aside to me, do not fear." So he turned
aside with her into the tent, and she
covered him with a blanket.
[19] And he said to her, "Please give me a
little water to drink, for I am thirsty." So
she opened a bottle of milk, and gave him a
drink, and covered him.
[20] And he said to her, "Stand at the door of
the tent, and it shall be if anyone comes and
asks you, and says, 'Is there a man here?'
you shall say, 'No.' "
[21] But Ya'ěl, Ḥeḇer's wife, took a tent
peg and took a hammer in her hand, and
went softly to him and drove the peg into
the side of his head, and it went down into
the ground – for he was fast asleep and
exhausted – and he died.
[22] And see, as Baraq pursued Sisera, Ya'ěl
came out to meet him, and said to him,
"Come, let me show you the man whom
you are seeking." And when he went into
her tent, there lay Sisera, dead with the peg
in the side of his head.
[23] And on that day Elohim humbled Yaḇin
sovereign of Kena'an in the presence of the
children of Yisra'ěl.
[24] And the hand of the children of Yisra'ěl
grew stronger and stronger against Yaḇin
sovereign of Kena'an, until they had cut off
Yaḇin sovereign of Kena'an.

5

And on that day Deḇorah and Baraq
son of Aḇino'am sang, saying,
[2] "For leaders leading in Yisra'ěl, for the
people volunteering, bless יהוה!
[3] "Hear, O sovereigns! Give ear, O
princes! I, I do sing to יהוה; I sing praise to

יהוה Elohim of Yisra’ěl.
4“יהוה, when You went out from Sě‘ir,
when You stepped from the field of Eḏom,
the earth shook and the heavens poured, the
clouds also poured water.
5“The mountains flowed at the presence
of יהוה, this Sinai, at the presence of יהוה
Elohim of Yisra’ěl.
6“In the days of Shamgar, the son of
Anath, in the days of Ya‘ěl, the highways
were deserted, and the travellers went in
crooked ways.
7“Leadership ceased, it ceased in Yisra’ěl, until I, Deḇorah, arose – a mother in
Yisra’ěl arose.
8“They chose new mighty ones, then
fighting was in the gates! Neither a shield
nor spear was seen among forty thousand
in Yisra’ěl.
9“My heart is towards the inscribers of
Yisra’ěl, the volunteers among the people.
Bless יהוה!
10“You who ride on white donkeys, you
who sit on rich carpets, and you who walk
along the way, declare it!
11“By the voice of shouters, between the
places of drawing water, there they recount
the righteous acts of יהוה, the righteous
acts of His leadership in Yisra’ěl; then the
people of יהוה shall go down to the gates.
12“Wake up, wake up, Deḇorah! Wake up,
wake up, sing a song! Arise, Baraq, and
lead your captives away, O son of
Aḇino‘am!
13“Then He set the remnant to rule the
nobles; יהוה came down for me against the
mighty ones.
14“Out of Ephrayim their root is against
Amalěq. After you, Binyamin, with your
peoples, out of Maḵir inscribers came
down, and out of Zeḇulun those who handle the scribe’s reed.
15“And the heads of Yissasḵar were with
Deḇorah. And as Yissasḵar, so was Baraq
sent into the valley under his command.
Among the divisions of Re’uḇěn there were
great searchings of heart.
16“Why did you remain among the sheepfolds, to hear the bleatings of the flocks?
The divisions of Re’uḇěn have great
searchings of heart.
17“Gil‘aḏ remained beyond the Yarděn,
and why did Dan remain on ships? Ashěr
continued at the seashore, and remained by
its landing places.
18“Zeḇulun is a people who risked their
lives to the point of death, Naphtali also, on
the heights of the field.
19“Sovereigns came, they fought, then the
sovereigns of Kena‘an fought in Ta‘anaḵ,
by the waters of Meḡiddo; they took no
spoils of silver.
20“From the heavens they fought; the
stars from their courses fought against
Sisera.
21“The wadi of Qishon swept them away,
that age-old wadi, the wadi of Qishon. O
my being, you have trampled in strength!
22“Then stamped hoofs of horses, with
the galloping, galloping of his steeds.
23‘Curse Měroz,’ said a messenger of
יהוה, ‘curse, curse its inhabitants, because
they did not come to the help of יהוה, to
the help of יהוה among the mighty.’
24“Blessed above women is Ya‘ěl, the
wife of Ḥeḇer the Qěynite – above women
in tents she is blessed.
25“He asked for water, she gave milk; she
brought out curdled milk in a bowl for
nobles.
26“She stretched her hand to the tent peg,
and her right hand to the workmen’s hammer. Then she pounded Sisera, she
smashed his head, she pierced and struck
through the side of his head.
27“Between her feet he bowed, he fell, he
lay still; between her feet he bowed, he fell;
where he bowed, there he fell – destroyed.
28“Through the window the mother of
Sisera looked, and cried out through the lattice, ‘Why does his chariot delay to come?
Why have the steps of his chariots tarried?’
29“The wise ones of her princesses
answered her, indeed, she answered herself,
30‘Do they not find and divide the spoil: a
girl or two for each man; a spoil of dyed
work for Sisera, a spoil of dyed work
embroidered, dyed work richly embroidered for the necks of the looter?’
31“So do all Your enemies perish, O יהוה!
But let those who love Him be like the sun

rising in its might!"

And the land had rest forty years.

6 And the children of Yisra'ĕl did evil in the eyes of יהוה, and יהוה gave them into the hand of Miḏyan for seven years,

2 and the hand of Miḏyan was strong against Yisra'ĕl. And before the faces of the Miḏyanites the children of Yisra'ĕl made for themselves the refuges which are in the mountains, and the caves, and the strongholds.

3 And it came to be, whenever Yisra'ĕl had sown, that Miḏyan would come up, and Amalĕq and the people of the East would come up against them,

4 and encamp against them and destroy the increase of the soil as far as Azzah, and leave no food in Yisra'ĕl, neither sheep nor ox nor donkey.

5 For they came up with their livestock and their tents, coming in as numerous as locusts. And they and their camels were without number. And they came into the land to destroy it.

6 Thus Yisra'ĕl was brought very low because of Miḏyan, and the children of Yisra'ĕl cried out to יהוה.

7 And it came to be, when the children of Yisra'ĕl cried out to יהוה because of Miḏyan,

8 that יהוה sent a prophet to the children of Yisra'ĕl, who said to them, "Thus said יהוה Elohim of Yisra'ĕl, 'I have brought you up from Mitsrayim and I brought you out of the house of bondage,

9 and I delivered you out of the hand of the Mitsrites and out of the hand of all your oppressors, and drove them out before you and gave you their land.

10 'And I said to you, "I am יהוה your Elohim, do not fear the mighty ones of the Amorites, in whose land you dwell. And you have not obeyed My voice." ' "

11 And the Messenger of יהוה came and sat under the terebinth tree which was in Ophrah, which belonged to Yo'ash the Aḇi'ezerite, while his son Giḏ'on threshed wheat in the winepress, to hide it from the eyes of the Miḏyanites.

12 And the Messenger of יהוה appeared to him, and said to him, "יהוה is with you, you mighty brave one!"

13 And Giḏ'on said to Him, "O my master, if יהוה is with us, why has all this come upon us? And where are all His wonders which our fathers related to us, saying, 'Did not יהוה bring us up from Mitsrayim?' But now יהוה has left us and given us into the hands of Miḏyan."

14 And יהוה turned to him and said, "Go in this strength of yours, and you shall save Yisra'ĕl from the hand of the Miḏyanites. Have I not sent you?"

15 And he said to Him, "O יהוה, with what do I save Yisra'ĕl? See, my clan is the weakest in Menashsheh, and I am the least in my father's house."

16 And יהוה said to him, "Because I am with you, you shall strike the Miḏyanites as one man."

17 And he said to Him, "Please, if I have found favour in Your eyes, then show me a sign that it is You who are speaking with me.

18 "Please do not move away from here, until I come to You and bring out my offering and set it before You." And He said, "I shall stay until you return."

19 And Giḏ'on went in, and prepared a young goat, and unleavened bread from an ĕphah of flour. The meat he put in a basket, and he put the broth in a pot. And he brought them out to Him, under the terebinth tree, and presented it.

20 And the Messenger of Elohim said to him, "Take the meat and the unleavened bread and lay them on this rock, and pour out the broth." And he did so.

21 And the Messenger of יהוה put forth the end of the staff that was in His hand, and touched the meat and the unleavened bread. And fire went up out of the rock and consumed the meat and the unleavened bread. And the Messenger of יהוה went from his sight.

22 And when Giḏ'on saw that He was a Messenger of יהוה, Giḏ'on said, "Oh Master יהוה! For I have seen a Messenger of יהוה face to face."

23 And יהוה said to him, "Peace be with you! Do not fear, you do not die."

24 And Giḏʿon built a slaughter-place there to יהוה, and called it: יהוה Shalom. To this day it is still in Ophrah of the Aḇiʿezerites.

25 And the same night it came to be that יהוה said to him, "Take the young bull of your father, and the second bull of seven years old, and you shall throw down the slaughter-place of Baʿal that your father has, and cut down the Ashĕrah that is beside it.

26 "And you shall build a slaughter-place to יהוה your Elohim on top of this rock in an orderly way, and shall take the second bull and offer an ascending offering with the wood of the image which you cut down."

27 And Giḏʿon took ten men from among his servants and did as יהוה had said to him. And it came to be, because he feared his father's household and the men of the city too much to do it by day, that he did it by night.

28 And the men of the city arose early in the morning and saw the slaughter-place of Baʿal was broken down, and the Ashĕrah that was beside it had been cut down, and the second bull was being offered on the slaughter-place which was built.

29 And they said to each other, "Who has done this deed?" And when they had inquired and asked, they said, "Giḏʿon son of Yo'ash has done this deed."

30 And the men of the city said to Yo'ash, "Bring out your son, so that he dies, for he has broken down the slaughter-place of Baʿal, and because he has cut down the Ashĕrah that was beside it."

31 And Yo'ash said to all who stood against him, "You, would you plead for Baʿal? You, would you save him? Let the one who would plead for him be put to death by morning! If he is a mighty one, let him plead for himself, because his slaughter-place has been broken down!"

32 So that day he called him Yerubbaʿal, saying, "Let Baʿal plead against him, because he has broken down his slaughter-place."

33 Now all Miḏyan and Amalĕq and the people of the East, were gathered together. And they passed over and encamped in the Valley of Yizreʿĕl.

34 Then the Spirit of יהוה came upon Giḏʿon, and he blew the shophar, and the Aḇiʿezerites gathered behind him.

35 And he sent messengers throughout all Menashsheh, who also gathered behind him. And he sent messengers to Ashĕr, and to Zeḇulun, and to Naphtali. And they came up to meet them.

36 And Giḏʿon said to Elohim, "If You are saving Yisra'ĕl by my hand as You have said,

37 see, I am placing a fleece of wool on the threshing-floor. If there is dew only on the fleece, and it is dry on all the ground, then I shall know that You are saving Yisra'ĕl by my hand, as You have said."

38 And it was so, and he rose early the next morning and pressed the fleece, and wrung dew out of the fleece, to fill a bowl with water.

39 And Giḏʿon said to Elohim, "Do not be displeased with me, and let me speak only this time: Please let me try only this time with the fleece, please let it be dry only on the fleece, and let there be dew on all the ground."

40 And Elohim did so that night, and it was dry on the fleece only, but there was dew on all the ground.

7 And Yerubbaʿal, that is Giḏʿon, and all the people who were with him rose up early and encamped by the fountain of Ḥaroḏ, so that the camp of Miḏyan was on the north side of them by the hill of Moreh in the valley.

2 And יהוה said to Giḏʿon, "The people who are with you are too many for Me to give Miḏyan into their hands, lest Yisra'ĕl boast against Me, saying, 'My own hand has saved me.'

3 "And now, proclaim in the hearing of the people, saying, 'Whoever is afraid and trembling, let him turn back, and leave Mount Gilʿaḏ.' " And twenty-two thousand of the people turned back, while ten thousand remained.

4 And יהוה said to Giḏʿon, "The people are still too many. Bring them down to the water, and let Me prove them for you there.

And it shall be, that of whom I say to you, 'This one goes with you,' let him go with you. And of whomever I say to you, 'This one does not go with you,' let him not go."
5 So he brought the people down to the water. And יהוה said to Giḏ'on, "Everyone who laps the water with his tongue, as a dog laps, separate him from everyone who bows down on his knees to drink."
6 And the number of those who lapped, putting their hand to their mouth, was three hundred men, and all the rest of the people bowed down on their knees to drink water.
7 And יהוה said to Giḏ'on, "By the three hundred men who lapped I save you, and shall give Miḏyan into your hand. Let all the other people go, each to his place."
8 And the people took food and their shopharot[a] in their hands. And he sent away all *the rest* of Yisra'ěl, each to his tent, but held onto those three hundred men. Now the camp of Miḏyan was below him in the valley.
9 And it came to be, on that night, that יהוה said to him, "Arise, go down against the camp, for I have given it into your hand.
10 "But if you are afraid to go down, go down, you and Purah your servant, to the camp.
11 "And you shall hear what they say, and after that let your hands be strengthened. And you shall go down against the camp." So he went down with Purah his servant to the edge of the *formation of* fives who were in the camp.
12 And Miḏyan and Amalěq, and all the people of the East, were lying in the valley as many as locusts. And their camels were as numerous as the sand by the seashore.
13 And Giḏ'on came, and see, a man was relating a dream to his companion, and said, "See I had a dream, and see, a loaf of barley bread tumbled into the camp of Miḏyan, and it came to a tent and struck it so that it fell and overturned, and the tent fell down."
14 And his companion answered and said, "This is nil else than the sword of Giḏ'on son of Yo'ash, a man of Yisra'ěl. Elohim has given Miḏyan and all the camp into his hand."
15 And it came to be, when Giḏ'on heard this dream related, and its interpretation, that he bowed himself down. And he returned to the camp of Yisra'ěl, and said, "Arise, for יהוה has given the camp of Miḏyan into your hand."
16 And he divided the three hundred men into three companies, and he put shopharot into the hands of all of them, with empty jars, and torches inside the jars.
17 And he said to them, "Watch me and do likewise. And see, when I come to the edge of the camp do as I do.
18 "And I shall blow with the shophar, I and all those with me, then you shall also blow with the shopharot round about all the camp, and say, 'For יהוה and for Giḏ'on!' "
19 And Giḏ'on and the hundred men who were with him came to the edge of the camp at the beginning of the middle watch, as they had but newly posted the watch. And they blew with the shopharot and broke the jars that were in their hands.
20 And the three companies blew with the shopharot and broke the jars, and held the torches in their left hands and the shopharot in their right hands for blowing. And they cried, "For יהוה and for Giḏ'on!"
21 And each stood in his place, round about the camp. And all the army ran and cried out and fled,
22 and the three hundred blew the shopharot, and יהוה set the sword of each one against the other throughout all the camp. And the army fled to Běyth Shittah, toward Tserěrah, as far as the border of Aḇěl Meḥolah, by Tabbath.
23 And the men of Yisra'ěl were called from Naphtali, and from Ashěr, and from all Menashsheh, and pursued Miḏyan.
24 Then Giḏ'on sent messengers throughout all the mountains of Ephrayim, saying, "Come down to meet Miḏyan, and capture from them the watering places as far as Běyth Barah and the Yarděn." So all the men of Ephrayim were called and captured

7a Plural of shophar, an animal horn; traditionally a ram's horn.

the watering places as far as Běyth Barah and the Yarděn.

25 And they captured two princes of Miḏyan, Orěḇ and Ze'ěḇ, and killed Orěḇ at the rock of Orěḇ, and Ze'ěḇ they killed at the winepress of Ze'ěḇ while they pursued Miḏyan. And they brought the heads of Orěḇ and Ze'ěḇ to Giḏʿon beyond the Yarděn.

8 And the men of Ephrayim said to him, "What is this you have done to us by not calling us when you went to fight with Miḏyan?" And they contended with him sharply,

2 and he said to them, "What have I done as compared with you? Are the gleanings of Ephrayim not better than the grape harvest of Aḇiʿezer?

3 "Elohim has given into your hands the princes of Miḏyan, Orěḇ and Ze'ěḇ. And what was I able to do as compared with you?" And when he had said that their rage toward him subsided.

4 And Giḏʿon and the three hundred men who were with him came to the Yarděn, passing over, weary yet pursuing.

5 And he said to the men of Sukkoth, "Please give loaves of bread to the people who follow me, for they are weary, and I am pursuing Zeḇaḥ and Tsalmunna, sovereigns of Miḏyan."

6 But the leaders of Sukkoth said, "Are the hands of Zeḇaḥ and Tsalmunna now in your hand, that we should give bread to your army?"

7 And Giḏʿon said, "Because of this, when יהוה has given Zeḇaḥ and Tsalmunna into my hand, I shall tear your flesh with the thorns of the wilderness and with briers!"

8 And he went up from there to Penu'ěl and spoke to them in the same way. And the men of Penu'ěl answered him as the men of Sukkoth had answered him.

9 So he spoke also to the men of Penu'ěl, saying, "When I come back in peace I shall break down this tower!"

10 And Zeḇaḥ and Tsalmunna were at Qarqor, and their armies with them, about fifteen thousand men, all who were left of all the army of the people of the East. Now those who had *already* fallen were one hundred and twenty thousand men who drew the sword.

11 And Giḏʿon went up by the way of those who dwell in tents on the east of Noḇaḥ and Yoḡbehah. And he struck the camp while the camp was at ease.

12 And Zeḇaḥ and Tsalmunna fled, and he pursued them, and captured the two sovereigns of Miḏyan, Zeḇaḥ and Tsalmunna, and shuddered the entire army.

13 And Giḏʿon son of Yo'ash returned from battle, from the Ascent of Ḥeres,

14 and captured a youth of the men of Sukkoth and questioned him. So *the youth* wrote down for him the leaders of Sukkoth and its elders, seventy-seven men.

15 And he came to the men of Sukkoth and said, "See: Zeḇaḥ and Tsalmunna, about whom you taunted me, saying, 'Are the hands of Zeḇaḥ and Tsalmunna now in your hand, that we should give bread to your men who are weary?' "

16 And he took the elders of the city, and thorns of the wilderness and briers, and with them he taught the men of Sukkoth *a lesson.*

17 And he broke down the tower of Penu'ěl and killed the men of the city.

18 And he said to Zeḇaḥ and Tsalmunna, "How were the men whom you killed at Taḇor?" So they answered, "They were like you, each one looked like the son of a sovereign ."

19 And he said, "They were my brothers, the sons of my mother. As יהוה lives, if you had let them live, I would not kill you."

20 And he said to Yether his first-born, "Rise, kill them!" But the youth would not draw his sword, for he was afraid, because he was still a youth.

21 Then Zeḇaḥ and Tsalmunna said, "Rise yourself, and fall on us. For as a man is, so is his might." So Giḏʿon arose and killed Zeḇaḥ and Tsalmunna, and took the crescent ornaments which were on their camels' necks.

22 So the men of Yisra'ěl said to Giḏʿon, "Rule over us, both you and your son, also your son's son, for you have saved us from

the hand of Miḏyan."
23 But Giḏʽon said to them, "I do not rule
over you, nor does my son rule over you.
יהוה does rule over you."
24 And Giḏʽon said to them, "I have a
request to make of you, that each of you
give me the ring from his spoil." For they
had rings of gold, because they were
Yishmaʽĕlites.
25 And they said, "We shall certainly give
them." And they spread out a garment, and
each man threw into it the ring from his
spoil.
26 And the weight of the gold rings that he
requested was one thousand seven hundred
pieces of gold – besides the crescent
ornaments, and the pendants, and purple
robes which were on the sovereigns of
Miḏyan, and besides the chains that were
around their camels' necks.
27 And Giḏʽon made it into a shoulder
garment and set it up in his city, Ophrah.
And all Yisra'ĕl went whoring after it there.
And it became a snare to Giḏʽon and to his
house.
28 Thus Miḏyan was humbled before the
children of Yisra'ĕl, and they lifted their
heads no more. And the land had rest for
forty years in the days of Giḏʽon.
29 And Yerubbaʽal son of Yo'ash went and
dwelt in his own house.
30 And Giḏʽon had seventy sons who were
his own offspring, for he had many wives.
31 And his concubine who was in Sheḵem
also bore him a son, and he gave him the
name Aḇimeleḵ.
32 And Giḏʽon son of Yo'ash died at a
good old age, and was buried in the burial-
site of Yo'ash his father, in Ophrah of the
Aḇiʽezerites.
33 And it came to be, when Giḏʽon was
dead, that the children of Yisra'ĕl again
went whoring after the Baʽals, and made
Baʽal-Berith their mighty one.
34 Thus the children of Yisra'ĕl did not
remember יהוה their Elohim, who had
delivered them from the hands of all their
enemies round about,
35 nor did they show loving-commitment
to the house of Yerubbaʽal, Giḏʽon, according to all the good which he did for
Yisra'ĕl.

9 And Aḇimeleḵ son of Yerubbaʽal went
to Sheḵem, to his mother's brothers,
and spoke with them and with all the clan
of the house of his mother's father, saying,
2 "Please speak in the hearing of all the
masters of Sheḵem, 'Which is better for
you, that seventy men, all the sons of
Yerubbaʽal rule over you, or that one man
rule over you?' And you shall remember
that I am your own flesh and bone."
3 And his mother's brothers spoke all
these words concerning him in the hearing
of all the masters of Sheḵem. And their
heart inclined toward Aḇimeleḵ, for they
said, "He is our brother."
4 And they gave him seventy pieces of
silver from the house of Baʽal-Berith, with
which Aḇimeleḵ hired worthless and
reckless men. And they followed him.
5 And he went to his father's house at
Ophrah and killed his brothers, the seventy
sons of Yerubbaʽal, on one stone. But
Yotham the youngest son of Yerubbaʽal
was left, because he hid himself.
6 And all the masters of Sheḵem gathered
together, and all of Bĕyth Millo, and they
went and made Aḇimeleḵ sovereign beside
the terebinth tree at the post that was in
Sheḵem.
7 And they informed Yotham, and he
went and stood on top of Mount Gerizim,
and lifted his voice and cried out, and said
to them, "Hear me, you masters of Sheḵem,
and let Elohim hear you!
8 "The trees went forth to anoint a sovereign over them. And they said to the olive
tree, 'reign over us!'
9 "And the olive tree said to them, 'Shall
I leave my oil, with which they esteem
mighty ones and men, and go to sway over
trees?'
10 "Then the trees said to the fig tree,
'Come, reign over us!'
11 "And the fig tree said to them, 'Shall I
leave my sweetness and my good fruit, and
go to sway over trees?'
12 "Then the trees said to the vine, 'Come,
reign over us!'
13 "And the vine said to them, 'Shall I

leave my new wine, which rejoices mighty
ones and men, and go to sway over trees?'
14 "Then all the trees said to the bramble,
'Come, reign over us!'
15 "And the bramble said to the trees, 'If in
truth you anoint me as sovereign over you,
come, take shelter in my shade. But if not,
let fire come out of the bramble and devour
the cedars of Leḇanon!'
16 "And now, if you have acted in truth
and integrity in setting up Aḇimeleḵ to
reign, and if you have acted well with
Yerubbaʽal and his house, and have done to
him as his hands did to you –
17 for my father fought for you and risked
his life, and delivered you out of the hand
of Miḏyan,
18 but you have risen up against my
father's house today, and killed his seventy
sons on one stone, and set up Aḇimeleḵ,
the son of his female servant, to reign over
the masters of Sheḵem, because he is your
brother –
19 if then you have acted in truth and
integrity with Yerubbaʽal and with his
house this day, then rejoice in Aḇimeleḵ,
and let him also rejoice in you.
20 "But if not, let fire come out from
Aḇimeleḵ and devour the masters of
Sheḵem and Bĕyth Millo, and let fire come
out from the masters of Sheḵem and from
Bĕyth Millo and devour Aḇimeleḵ!"
21 Then Yotham ran away and fled, and he
went to Be'ĕr and dwelt there, for fear of
Aḇimeleḵ his brother.
22 And Aḇimeleḵ governed Yisra'ĕl three
years,
23 and Elohim sent an evil spirit between
Aḇimeleḵ and the masters of Sheḵem. And
the masters of Sheḵem acted treacherously
against Aḇimeleḵ,
24 in order that the violence done to the
seventy sons of Yerubbaʽal might come,
and their blood be laid on Aḇimeleḵ their
brother, who killed them, and on the masters of Sheḵem, who strengthened his
hands to kill his brothers.
25 And the masters of Sheḵem set men in
ambush against him on the tops of the
mountains, and they robbed all who passed
over by them along that way. And it was
reported to Aḇimeleḵ.
26 And Gaʽal son of Eḇeḏ came with his
brothers and passed over to Sheḵem. And
the masters of Sheḵem put their trust in
him,
27 and went out into the fields, and
gathered their vineyards and trod out, and
held a feast. And they went into the house
of their mighty one, and ate and drank, and
cursed Aḇimeleḵ.
28 And Gaʽal son of Eḇeḏ said, "Who is
Aḇimeleḵ, and who is Sheḵem, that we
should serve him? Is he not the son of
Yerubbaʽal, and is not Zeḇul his officer?
Serve the men of Ḥamor the father of
Sheḵem! But why should we serve him?
29 "If only this people were under my
hand! Then I would remove Aḇimeleḵ."
And he said to Aḇimeleḵ, "Increase your
army and come out!"
30 And when Zeḇul, the governor of the
city, heard the words of Gaʽal son of Eḇeḏ,
his displeasure burned.
31 And he sent messengers to Aḇimeleḵ by
deceit, saying, "See, Gaʽal son of Eḇeḏ and
his brothers have come to Sheḵem. And
see, they are besieging the city against you.
32 "And now, get up by night, you and the
people who are with you, and lie in wait in
the field.
33 "And it shall be, as soon as the sun is up
in the morning, then rise early and rush
upon the city. And see, when he and the
people who are with him come out against
you, you shall do to them as your hand
finds to do."
34 And Aḇimeleḵ and all the people who
were with him rose up by night, and laid in
wait against Sheḵem in four companies.
35 Now Gaʽal son of Eḇeḏ went out and
stood in the entrance to the city gate, and
Aḇimeleḵ and the people who were with
him rose from lying in wait.
36 And when Gaʽal saw the people, he said
to Zeḇul, "See, people are coming down
from the tops of the mountains!" But Zeḇul
said to him, "You are seeing the shadows of
the mountains like men."
37 And Gaʽal spoke again and said, "See,
people are coming down from the high part
of the land, and another company is com-

ing from the Diviners' Terebinth Tree."
38 And Zeḇul said to him, "Now where is
your mouth with which you said, 'Who is
Aḇimeleḵ, that we should serve him?' Are
not these the people whom you despised?
I beg you, go out and fight them now."
39 So Gaʽal went out, leading the masters
of Sheḵem, and fought Aḇimeleḵ.
40 And Aḇimeleḵ pursued him, and he fled
from him. And many fell wounded, up to
the entrance of the gate.
41 And Aḇimeleḵ stayed at Arumah, and
Zeḇul drove out Gaʽal and his brothers, so
that they would not dwell in Sheḵem.
42 And it came to be the next day that the
people went out into the field, and they
informed Aḇimeleḵ.
43 And he took his people, and divided
them into three companies, and laid in wait
in the field, and looked and saw the people
coming out of the city. And he rose against
them and struck them.
44 And Aḇimeleḵ and the company that
was with him rushed forward and stood at
the entrance of the gate of the city. And the
other two companies rushed upon all who
were in the fields and struck them.
45 And Aḇimeleḵ fought against the city
all that day, and captured the city and killed
the people who were in it. And he broke
down the city and sowed it with salt.
46 And all the masters of the tower of
Sheḵem had heard that, and entered the
stronghold of the house of Ěl Berith.
47 And it was reported to Aḇimeleḵ that all
the masters of the tower of Sheḵem were
gathered together.
48 So Aḇimeleḵ went up to Mount Tsalmon, he and all the people who were with
him. And Aḇimeleḵ took an axe in his hand
and cut down a branch from the trees, and
took it and laid it on his shoulder. Then he
said to the people who were with him,
"What you have seen me do, hurry, do as I
have done."
49 And all the people likewise cut down
each one his own branch and followed
Aḇimeleḵ, and put them against the stronghold, and set the stronghold on fire above
them, so that all the men of the tower of
Sheḵem died, about a thousand men and
women.
50 Aḇimeleḵ then went to Thěḇěts, and he
encamped against Thěḇěts and captured it.
51 However, there was a strong tower in
the city, and all the men and women and all
the masters of the city fled there and shut
themselves in, and went up to the top of the
tower.
52 And Aḇimeleḵ came to the tower and
fought against it, and approached the door
of the tower to burn it with fire.
53 But a certain woman dropped an upper
millstone on the head of Aḇimeleḵ, and
crushed his skull.
54 He then immediately called the young
man, his armour-bearer, and said to him,
"Draw your sword and kill me, lest men
say of me, 'A woman killed him.' " And
his young man thrust him through, and he
died.
55 And when the men of Yisra'ěl saw that
Aḇimeleḵ was dead, each one went to his
own place.
56 Thus did Elohim repay the evil of Aḇimeleḵ, which he had done to his father to
kill his seventy brothers.
57 And all the evil of the men of Sheḵem
Elohim turned back on their own heads,
and the curse of Yotham son of Yerubbaʽal
came on them.

10 And after Aḇimeleḵ there arose
Tola son of Pu'ah, son of Dodo, a
man of Yissasḵar, to save Yisra'ěl. And he
dwelt in Shamur in the mountains of
Ephrayim.
2 And he ruled Yisra'ěl twenty-three
years. Then he died and was buried in
Shamur.
3 And after him arose Ya'ir, a Gilʽaḏite,
and he ruled Yisra'ěl twenty-two years.
4 And he had thirty sons who rode on
thirty donkeys. And they had thirty towns,
which are called Hawoth Yair to this day,
which are in the land of Gilʽaḏ.
5 And Ya'ir died, and was buried in
Qamon.
6 And the children of Yisra'ěl again did
evil in the eyes of יהוה, and served the
Baʽals and the Ashtoreths, and the mighty
ones of Aram, and the mighty ones of

Tsiḏon, and the mighty ones of Mo'aḇ, and
the mighty ones of the children of Ammon,
and the mighty ones of the Philistines – and
forsook יהוה and did not serve Him.
7 Therefore the displeasure of יהוה
burned against Yisra'ěl. And He sold them
into the hands of the Philistines and into the
hands of the children of Ammon.
8 And they crushed and oppressed the
children of Yisra'ěl that year – for eighteen
years – all the children of Yisra'ěl who
were beyond the Yarděn in the land of the
Amorites, in Gilʽaḏ.
9 And the children of Ammon passed
over the Yarděn to fight against Yehuḏah,
and against Binyamin, and against the
house of Ephrayim, so that Yisra'ěl had
great distress.
10 And the children of Yisra'ěl cried out to
יהוה, saying, "We have sinned against You,
because we have both forsaken our Elohim
and served the Baʽals!"
11 So יהוה said to the children of Yisra'ěl,
"Was it not from the Mitsrites and from the
Amorites and from the children of Ammon
and from the Philistines *that I saved you*?
12 "And the Tsiḏonians and Amalěq and
Maʽon oppressed you. And you cried out to
Me, and I saved you from their hand.
13 "But you, you have forsaken Me and
served other mighty ones. Therefore I do
not save you again.
14 "Go and cry out to the mighty ones
which you have chosen, let them save you
in your time of distress."
15 And the children of Yisra'ěl said to
יהוה, "We have sinned! Do to us whatever
is good in Your eyes, only deliver us today,
please."
16 So they put away the foreign mighty
ones from their midst and served יהוה. And
His being was grieved with the trouble of
Yisra'ěl.
17 Then the children of Ammon were
called together and encamped in Gilʽaḏ.
And the children of Yisra'ěl gathered
together and encamped in Mitspah.
18 And the people, the heads of Gilʽaḏ,
said to each other, "Let the man who is the
first to fight against the children of Ammon
be head over all the inhabitants of Gilʽaḏ."

11 And Yiphtaḥ the Gilʽaḏite was a
mighty brave one, but he was the
son of a whore. And Gilʽaḏ brought forth
Yiphtaḥ.
2 And the wife of Gilʽaḏ bore sons. And
when his wife's sons grew up, they drove
Yiphtaḥ out, and said to him, "You shall
not have an inheritance in the house of our
father, for you are the son of another
woman."
3 And Yiphtaḥ fled from his brothers and
dwelt in the land of Toḇ. And worthless
men banded together with Yiphtaḥ and
went out with him.
4 And it came to be, some time later, that
the children of Ammon fought against Yisra'ěl.
5 And it came to be, when the children of
Ammon fought against Yisra'ěl, that the
elders of Gilʽaḏ went to bring Yiphtaḥ out
of the land of Toḇ.
6 And they said to Yiphtaḥ, "Come, and
you shall be our commander, and let us
fight against the children of Ammon."
7 But Yiphtaḥ said to the elders of Gilʽaḏ,
"Did you not hate me, and drive me from
my father's house? Why have you come to
me now when you are in trouble?"
8 And the elders of Gilʽaḏ said to
Yiphtaḥ, "That is the reason we have
turned to you, that you shall go with us and
fight against the children of Ammon, and
be our head over all the inhabitants of
Gilʽaḏ."
9 And Yiphtaḥ said to the elders of
Gilʽaḏ, "If you take me back home to fight
against the children of Ammon, and יהוה
gives them to me, am I to be your head?"
10 And the elders of Gilʽaḏ said to
Yiphtaḥ, "יהוה is witness between us, if we
do not do according to your words."
11 Then Yiphtaḥ went with the elders of
Gilʽaḏ, and the people set him over them,
as head and commander. And Yiphtaḥ
spoke all his words before יהוה in Mitspah.
12 And Yiphtaḥ sent messengers to the
sovereign of the children of Ammon,
saying, "What is between you and me,
that you have come to fight against me in
my land?"
13 And the sovereign of the children of

Ammon said to the messengers of Yiphtaḥ,
"Because Yisra'ĕl took my land when they
came up out of Mitsrayim, from the Arnon
as far as the Yabboq, and to the Yardĕn.
And now, give back those lands in peace."
14 But Yiphtaḥ again sent messengers to
the sovereign of the children of Ammon,
15 and said to him, "This is what Yiphtaḥ
said, 'Yisra'ĕl did not take the land of
Mo'aḇ, nor the land of the children of
Ammon.
16 'For when they came up from Mitsrayim, and Yisra'ĕl walked through the
wilderness as far as the Sea of Reeds and
came to Qaḏĕsh,
17 then Yisra'ĕl sent messengers to the
sovereign of Eḏom, saying, "Please let me
pass over, through your land." But the sovereign of Eḏom would not listen. And they
also sent to the sovereign of Mo'aḇ, but he
refused, so Yisra'ĕl stayed at Qaḏĕsh.
18 'Then they went through the wilderness
and around the land of Eḏom and the land
of Mo'aḇ, and came to the east side of the
land of Mo'aḇ, and encamped beyond
Arnon. But they did not enter the border of
Mo'aḇ, for Arnon was the border of Mo'aḇ.
19 'And Yisra'ĕl sent messengers to Siḥon
sovereign of the Amorites, sovereign of
Ḥeshbon, and Yisra'ĕl said to him, "Please
let us pass over, through your land into our
place."
20 'But Siḥon did not trust Yisra'ĕl to pass
over through his border, and Siḥon
gathered all his people together, and they
encamped in Yahats, and fought against
Yisra'ĕl.
21 'And יהוה Elohim of Yisra'ĕl gave
Siḥon and all his people into the hand of
Yisra'ĕl, and they struck them. So Yisra'ĕl
took possession of all the land of the
Amorites, the inhabitants of that land.
22 'Thus they took possession of all the
border of the Amorites, from Arnon to the
Yabboq and from the wilderness to the
Yardĕn.
23 'And now, יהוה Elohim of Yisra'ĕl has
driven out the Amorites from before His
people Yisra'ĕl, should you then possess it?
24 'Whatever Kemosh your mighty one
gives you to possess, do you not possess it?
And all that which יהוה our Elohim takes
possession of before us, we possess.
25 'And now are you any better than Balaq
son of Tsippor, sovereign of Mo'aḇ? Did he
ever strive against Yisra'ĕl? Did he ever
fight against them?
26 'While Yisra'ĕl dwelt in Ḥeshbon and
its villages, and in Aro'ĕr and its villages,
and in all the cities along the banks of
Arnon, for three hundred years, why did
you not recover them within that time?
27 'So I have not sinned against you, but
you are doing me evil by fighting against
me. Let יהוה the Judge, judge today
between the children of Yisra'ĕl and the
children of Ammon.'"
28 But the sovereign of the children of
Ammon did not listen to the words which
Yiphtaḥ sent him.
29 And the Spirit of יהוה came upon
Yiphtaḥ, and he passed through Gil'aḏ and
Menashsheh, and passed through Mitspeh
of Gil'aḏ. And from Mitspeh of Gil'aḏ he
passed on toward the children of Ammon.
30 And Yiphtaḥ made a vow to יהוה, and
said, "If You give the children of Ammon
into my hands,
31 then it shall be that whatever comes out
of the doors of my house to meet me, when
I return in peace from the children of
Ammon, shall belong to יהוה, and I shall
offer it up as an ascending offering."
32 Yiphtaḥ then passed on toward the
children of Ammon to fight against them,
and יהוה gave them into his hands.
33 And he struck them from Aro'ĕr as far
as Minnith, twenty cities, and to Aḇĕl
Keramim, with a very great slaughter. Thus
the children of Ammon were humbled
before the children of Yisra'ĕl.
34 And Yiphtaḥ came to his house at
Mitspah, and saw his daughter coming out
to meet him with timbrels and dancing.
Now except for her he had neither son nor
daughter.
35 And it came to be, when he saw her,
that he tore his garments, and said, "Oh my
daughter! You have brought me very low,
and you are among those who trouble me!
And I, I have given my word to יהוה, and I
am unable to turn back."

36 And she said to him, "My father, if you
have given your word to יהוה, do to me
according to what has gone out of your
mouth, because יהוה has taken vengeance
for you upon your enemies, the children of
Ammon."
37 And she said to her father, "Let this be
done for me: let me alone for two new
moons, and let me go and wander on the
mountains and bewail my maidenhood, my
friends and I."
38 Then he said, "Go." And he sent her
away for two new *moons*. And she went
with her friends, and bewailed her maidenhood on the mountains.
39 And it came to be at the end of two new
moons that she returned to her father, and
he did to her as he had vowed, and she
knew no man. And it became a statute in
Yisra'ĕl
40 that the daughters of Yisra'ĕl went
every year for four days to lament the
daughter of Yiphtaḥ the Gil'aḏite.

12 And the men of Ephrayim gathered
together, and passed over toward
Tsaphon, and said to Yiphtaḥ, "Why did
you pass over to fight against the children
of Ammon, and did not call us to go with
you? We are going to burn your house over
you with fire!"
2 And Yiphtaḥ said to them, "My people
and I were in a great struggle with the children of Ammon. And when I called you,
you did not save me out of their hands.
3 "And I saw that you would not save me,
then I took my life in my hands and went
over against the children of Ammon. And
יהוה gave them into my hand. And why
have you come up to me today to fight
against me?"
4 Yiphtaḥ then gathered together all
the men of Gil'aḏ and fought against
Ephrayim. And the men of Gil'aḏ struck
Ephrayim, because they had said, "You
Gil'aḏites are fugitives of Ephrayim in the
midst of Ephrayim, in the midst of
Menashsheh."
5 And Gil'aḏ captured the fords of the
Yardĕn that faced Ephrayim. And it came
to be, when the fugitives from Ephrayim
said, "Let me pass over," the men of Gil'aḏ
said to him, "You are an Ephrayimite!" If
he said, "No,"
6 then they would say to him, "Please say,
'Shibboleth'!" And he would say,
"Sibboleth," for he was unable to pronounce it right. Then they seized him and
slew him at the fords of the Yardĕn. And at
that time there fell forty-two thousand
Ephrayimites.
7 And Yiphtaḥ ruled Yisra'ĕl six years.
And Yiphtaḥ the Gil'aḏite died and was
buried in one of the cities of Gil'aḏ.
8 And after him, Iḇtsan of Bĕyth Leḥem
ruled Yisra'ĕl.
9 And he came to have thirty sons and
thirty daughters – he sent abroad and
brought in thirty daughters for his sons.
And he ruled Yisra'ĕl seven years.
10 And Iḇtsan died and was buried at
Bĕyth Leḥem.
11 And after him Ĕlon the Zeḇulunite ruled
Yisra'ĕl. And he ruled Yisra'ĕl ten years.
12 And Ĕlon the Zeḇulunite died and was
buried at Ayalon in the land of Zeḇulun.
13 And after him, Aḇdon son of Hillĕl the
Pirathonite ruled Yisra'ĕl,
14 and he had forty sons and thirty grandsons, who rode on seventy young donkeys.
And he ruled Yisra'ĕl eight years.
15 And Aḇdon son of Hillĕl the Pirathonite
died and was buried in Pirathon in the land
of Ephrayim, in the mountains of the
Amalĕqites.

13 And again the children of Yisra'ĕl
did evil in the eyes of יהוה, so יהוה
gave them into the hand of the Philistines
for forty years.
2 And there was a certain man from
Tsor'ah, of the clan of the Danites, whose
name was Manowaḥ. And his wife was
barren and had not borne.
3 And a Messenger of יהוה appeared to
the woman and said to her, "See now, you
are barren and have not borne, but you
shall conceive, and you shall bear a son.
4 "And now, please guard, and do not
drink wine or strong drink, and do not eat
any unclean *food*.
5 "For look, you are conceiving and

bearing a son. And let no razor come upon
his head, for the youth is a Nazirite to
Elohim from the womb on. And he shall
begin to save Yisra'ěl out of the hand of the
Philistines."
6 And the woman came and spoke to her
husband, saying, "A Man of Elohim came
to me, and His appearance was like the
appearance of a Messenger of Elohim, very
awesome. But I did not ask Him where He
was from, and He did not declare to me His
name.
7 "And He said to me, 'See, you are
conceiving and bearing a son. And now,
drink no wine or strong drink, nor eat any
unclean *food*, for the youth is a Nazirite to
Elohim from the womb to the day of his
death.' "
8 And Manowaḥ prayed to יהוה, and
said, "O יהוה, please let the Man of Elohim
whom You sent come to us again and teach
us what to do for the youth who is to be
born."
9 And Elohim listened to the voice of
Manowaḥ, and the Messenger of Elohim
came to the woman again as she was sitting
in the field, but Manowaḥ her husband was
not with her.
10 And the woman ran hurriedly and
informed her husband, and said to him,
"See, He has appeared to me, the Man who
came to me the other day!"
11 And Manowaḥ arose and went after his
wife, and came to the Man, and he said to
Him, "Are You the Man who spoke to this
woman?" And He said, "I am."
12 And Manowaḥ said, "Now let Your
words come true! What is to be the rule for
the youth's life and his work?"
13 And the Messenger of יהוה said to
Manowaḥ, "Let the woman guard all that I
said to her.
14 "Let her not eat any *food* that comes
from the vine, neither let her drink wine or
strong drink, or eat any unclean *food*. Let
her guard all that which I have commanded
her."
15 And Manowaḥ said to the Messenger of
יהוה, "Please let us detain You, and prepare
a young goat for You."
16 And the Messenger of יהוה said to
Manowaḥ, "Though you detain Me, I do
not eat your food. But if you offer an
ascending offering, offer it to יהוה." For
Manowaḥ did not know He was a
Messenger of יהוה.
17 Then Manowaḥ said to the Messenger
of יהוה, "What is Your name? When Your
words come true, then we shall esteem
You."
18 And the Messenger of יהוה said to him,
"Why do you ask My name, since it is
wondrous?"
19 And Manowaḥ took the young goat
with the grain offering, and offered it upon
the rock to יהוה. And He did wondrously
while Manowaḥ and his wife looked on.
20 And it came to be, as the flame went up
toward the heavens from the slaughter-
place, that the Messenger of יהוה went up
in the flame of the slaughter-place. And
Manowaḥ and his wife were watching, and
they fell on their faces to the ground.
21 And the Messenger of יהוה did not
appear any more to Manowaḥ and his wife.
Then Manowaḥ knew that He was a
Messenger of יהוה.
22 And Manowaḥ said to his wife, "We
shall certainly die, because we have seen
Elohim!"
23 But his wife said to him, "If יהוה had
been pleased to put us to death, He would
not have accepted an ascending offering
and a grain offering from our hands, nor
would He have shown us all this, nor
would He have let us hear the like of this!"
24 So the woman bore a son and called his
name Shimshon. And the child grew, and
יהוה blessed him.
25 And the Spirit of יהוה began to move
him at Maḥaněh Dan, between Tsorʽah and
Eshta'ol.

14

And Shimshon went down to
Timnah, and saw a woman in
Timnah of the daughters of the Philistines.
2 And he went up and informed his father
and mother, saying, "I have seen a woman
in Timnah of the daughters of the
Philistines. And now, take her for me for a
wife."
3 But his father and mother said to him,

"Is there no woman among the daughters of your brothers, or among all my people, that you should take a wife from the uncircumcised Philistines?" And Shimshon said to his father, "Take her for me, for she is pleasing in my eyes."

4 However, his father and mother did not know that it was of יהוה, that He was seeking an occasion to move against the Philistines. For at that time the Philistines were ruling over Yisra'ĕl.

5 Then Shimshon went down to Timnah with his father and mother, and came to the vineyards of Timnah, and saw a young lion roaring as it met him.

6 And the Spirit of יהוה came mightily upon him, and he tore it apart as the tearing apart of a young goat, with naught in his hand. But he did not make known to his father or his mother what he had done.

7 And he went down and spoke to the woman, and she pleased Shimshon well.

8 And when he returned later to take her, he turned aside to look at the carcass of the lion, and saw a swarm of bees and honey in the carcass of the lion.

9 And he took some of it in his hands and went along, eating. And he came to his father and mother, and gave them, and they ate. But he did not make known to them that he took the honey out of the carcass of the lion.

10 So his father went down to the woman. And Shimshon gave a feast there, for young men used to do so.

11 And it came to be, when they saw him, that they brought thirty companions to be with him.

12 And Shimshon said to them, "Please let me put forth a riddle to you. If you clearly solve and explain it to me within the seven days of the feast, then I shall give you thirty linen garments and thirty changes of garments.

13 "But if you are unable to explain it to me, then you shall give me thirty linen shirts and thirty changes of garments." And they said to him, "Put forth your riddle and let us hear it."

14 And he said to them, "Out of the eater came forth food, and out of the strong came forth sweetness." And for three days they were unable to explain the riddle.

15 And it came to be on the seventh day that they said to Shimshon's wife, "Entice your husband to explain the riddle to us, or else we burn you and your father's house with fire. Have you invited us in order to take what is ours? Is it not?"

16 And Shimshon's wife wept before him, and said, "You only hate me, and do not love me! You have put forth a riddle to the sons of my people, but you have not explained it to me." And he said to her, "Look, I have not explained it to my father or my mother, and should I explain it to you?"

17 And she had wept before him the seven days while their feast lasted. And it came to be on the seventh day that he informed her, because she pressed him so much. She then explained the riddle to the sons of her people.

18 And the men of the city said to him on the seventh day before the sun went down, "What is sweeter than honey? And what is stronger than a lion?" And he said to them, "If you had not ploughed with my heifer, you would not have solved my riddle!"

19 Then the Spirit of יהוה came upon him mightily, and he went down to Ashqelon and struck thirty of their men, stripped them, and gave the changes *of garments* to those who had explained the riddle. And his displeasure burned, and he went back up to his father's house.

20 And Shimshon's wife was given to his companion, who had been his friend.

15

And it came to be, after some time, in the days of wheat harvest, that Shimshon visited his wife with a young goat. And he said, "Let me go in to my wife, into her room." But her father would not permit him to go in.

2 And her father said, "Indeed, I thought that you hated her intensely; so I gave her to your companion. Is not her younger sister better than she? Please, take her instead."

3 And Shimshon said to them, "This time I am blameless regarding the Philistines

if I do evil to them!"
4 And Shimshon went and caught three
hundred foxes, and took torches, and
turned them tail to tail, and put a torch
between each pair of tails,
5 and set the torches on fire, and sent
them out into the standing grain of the
Philistines, and burned up both the shocks
and the standing grain, even the vineyards
and olive-trees.
6 And the Philistines said, "Who did
this?" And they answered, "Shimshon, the
son-in-law of the Timnite, because he took
away his wife and gave her to his companion." Then the Philistines went up and
burned her and her father with fire.
7 And Shimshon said to them, "Though
you do this, yet I shall take revenge on you,
and after that I cease."
8 And he struck them hip and thigh, a
great slaughter, and went down and dwelt
in the cleft of the rock of Ěytam.
9 The Philistines then went up and
encamped in Yehuḏah, and spread out
against Leḥi.
10 And the men of Yehuḏah said, "Why
have you come up against us?" And they
answered, "We have come up to bind
Shimshon, to do to him as he has done to
us."
11 Then three thousand men of Yehuḏah
went down to the cleft of the rock of Ěytam
and said to Shimshon, "Do you not know
that the Philistines are rulers over us? Why
have you done this to us?" And he said to
them, "As they did to me, so I did to them."
12 And they said to him, "We have come
down to bind you, to give you into the hand
of the Philistines." And Shimshon said to
them, "Swear to me not to fall on me yourselves."
13 And they spoke to him, saying, "No, but
we are certainly going to bind you, and
shall give you into their hand but certainly
not kill you." So they bound him with two
new ropes and brought him up from the
rock.
14 When he came to Leḥi, the Philistines
came shouting to meet him. And the Spirit
of יהוה came mightily upon him. And the
ropes that were on his arms became like
flax that is burned with fire, and his bonds
broke loose from his hands.
15 And he found a fresh jawbone of a
donkey, and put out his hand and took it,
and struck a thousand men with it.
16 And Shimshon said, "With the jawbone
of a donkey, one heap, two heaps, with the
jawbone of a donkey I have stricken a thousand men!"
17 And it came to be, when he had ended
speaking, that he threw the jawbone from
his hand, and called that place Ramath
Leḥi.
18 And he became very thirsty, and cried
out to יהוה and said, "You have given this
great deliverance by the hand of Your servant. And now, am I to die of thirst and fall
into the hand of the uncircumcised?"
19 And Elohim split the hollow place that
is in Leḥi, and water came out, and he
drank. And his spirit came back, and he
revived. So he called its name Ěn Haqqore,
which is in Leḥi to this day.
20 And he ruled Yisra'ěl twenty years in
the days of the Philistines.

16 And Shimshon went to Azzah and
saw a woman there, a whore, and
went in to her –
2 the Azzathites saying, "Shimshon has
come here!" So they went round and lay in
wait for him all night at the gate of the city,
and kept silent all night, saying, "In the
morning, when it is daylight, then we shall
kill him."
3 Now Shimshon lay until midnight, and
rose at midnight, and took hold of the doors
of the gate of the city and the two
gateposts, and pulled them up with the bar,
put them on his shoulders, and took them to
the top of the hill that faces Ḥeḇron.
4 And it came to be afterward that he
loved a woman in the wadi Soréq, whose
name was Delilah.
5 And the princes of the Philistines came
up to her and said to her, "Entice him, and
find out where his great strength lies, and
see by what we might overpower him, then
we shall bind him to humble him. And let
us give you, each one of us, eleven hundred
pieces of silver."

6 And Delilah said to Shimshon, "Please reveal to me where your great strength lies, and by what you might be bound, to humble you."

7 And Shimshon said to her, "If they bind me with seven fresh cords, not yet dried, then I shall be weak, and be like any other man."

8 The princes of the Philistines then brought her seven fresh cords, not yet dried, and she bound him with them,

9 while those lying in wait stayed with her in the room. And she said to him, "The Philistines are upon you, Shimshon!" But he broke the cords as a strand of yarn breaks when it touches fire. So the secret of his strength remained unknown.

10 And Delilah said to Shimshon, "Look, you have mocked me and spoken lies to me. Now, please reveal to me by what you might be bound."

11 And he said to her, "If they bind me tightly with new ropes that have never been used, then I shall be weak, and be like any other man."

12 And Delilah took new ropes and bound him with them, and said to him, "The Philistines are upon you, Shimshon!" And those lying in wait were sitting in the inner room. But he broke them off his arms like a thread.

13 So Delilah said to Shimshon, "Until now you have mocked me and spoken lies to me, reveal to me how you might be bound." And he said to her, "If you weave the seven locks of my head with the web."

14 Then she fastened it with a pin, and said to him, "The Philistines are upon you, Shimshon!" But he awoke from his sleep, and pulled out the pin of the loom and the web.

15 Then she said to him, "How do you say, 'I love you,' when your heart is not with me? You have mocked me these three times, and have not made known to me where your great strength lies."

16 And it came to be, when she pressed him daily with her words and urged him, so that his being was wearied to death,

17 that he made known to her all his heart, and said to her, "No razor has ever come upon my head, for I have been a Nazirite to Elohim from my mother's womb. If I were shaven, then my strength would leave me, and I would become as weak as any other man."

18 And Delilah saw that he had made known to her all his heart, and she sent and called for the princes of the Philistines, saying, "Come up once more, for he has made known to me all his heart." So the princes of the Philistines came up to her and brought the silver in their hand.

19 And she made him sleep on her knees, and called for a man and shaved off the seven locks of his head. Thus she began to humble him, and his strength left him.

20 And she said, "The Philistines are upon you, Shimshon!" And he awoke from his sleep, and said, "Let me go out as before, at other times, and shake myself loose!" But he did not know that יהוה had turned aside from him.

21 So the Philistines took him and put out his eyes, and brought him down to Azzah, and bound him with bronze shackles. And he became a grinder in the prison.

22 But the hair of his head began to grow again after it had been shaven.

23 And the princes of the Philistines gathered to slaughter a great slaughtering to Dağon their mighty one, and to rejoice. And they said, "Our mighty one has given Shimshon our enemy into our hands!"

24 And the people saw him, and praised their mighty one, for they said, "Our mighty one has given into our hands our enemy, the destroyer of our land, who slew many of us."

25 And it came to be, when their hearts were glad, that they said, "Call for Shimshon, and let him entertain us." So they called for Shimshon from the prison, and he entertained them. And they made him stand between the columns.

26 And Shimshon said to the young man who who was holding his hand, "Let me alone and let me feel the columns which support the house, so that I lean on them."

27 And the house was filled with men and women. And all the princes of the

Philistines were there. And about three
thousand men and women were on the roof
who watched Shimshon entertaining.
28 And Shimshon called to יהוה, saying,
"O Master יהוה, remember me, I pray!
Strengthen me, I pray, only this time, O
Elohim, and let me avenge myself on the
Philistines with vengeance for my two
eyes!"
29 And Shimshon took hold of the two
middle columns which supported the
house, and he braced himself against them,
one on his right and the other on his left.
30 And Shimshon said, "Let me die with
the Philistines!" And he bowed himself
mightily, and the house fell on the princes
and all the people in it. And the dead that
he killed at his death were more than he
had killed in his life.
31 And his brothers and all his father's
household came down and took him, and
brought him up and buried him between
Tsorʻah and Eshta'ol in the burial-site of his
father Manowaḥ. And he had ruled Yisra'ĕl
twenty years.

17 And there was a man from the hill
country of Ephrayim, whose name
was Miḵahu.
2 And he said to his mother, "The eleven
hundred pieces of silver that were taken
from you, and on which you put a curse,
even saying it in my ears. Look, the silver
is with me, I took it." And his mother said,
"Blessed of יהוה be my son!"
3 And he gave back the eleven hundred
pieces of silver to his mother, and his mother said, "I had truly set apart the silver from
my hand to יהוה for my son, to make a
carved image and a moulded image, and
now, I give it back to you."
4 And he gave the silver back to his
mother, and his mother took two hundred
pieces of silver and gave them to the silversmith, and he made it into a carved image
and a moulded image. And they were in the
house of Miḵahu.
5 Now the man Miḵah had a house of
mighty ones, and made a shoulder garment
and house idols. And he ordained one of
his sons, who became his priest.
6 In those days there was no sovereign in
Yisra'ĕl – everyone did what was right in
his own eyes.[a]
7 And there was a young man from Bĕyth
Leḥem in Yehuḏah, of the clan of Yehuḏah.
And he was a Lĕwite, and he was sojourning there.
8 And the man went out of the city of
Bĕyth Leḥem in Yehuḏah to sojourn wherever he could find a place. And he came to
the mountains of Ephrayim, to the house of
Miḵah, as he journeyed.
9 And Miḵah said to him, "Where do you
come from?" And he said to him, "I am a
Lĕwite from Bĕyth Leḥem in Yehuḏah, and
I am on my way to find a place to sojourn."
10 And Miḵah said to him, "Dwell with
me, and be a father and a priest to me, and I
give you ten pieces of silver per year, and a
suit of garments, and your food." And the
Lĕwite went in.
11 So the Lĕwite agreed to dwell with the
man. And the young man became like one
of his sons to him.
12 Then Miḵah ordained the Lĕwite, and
the young man became his priest, and he
was in the house of Miḵah.
13 And Miḵah said, "Now I know that
יהוה does good to me, since I have a
Lĕwite as priest!"

18 In those days there was no sovereign in Yisra'ĕl. And in those days
the tribe of the Danites was seeking an
inheritance for itself to dwell in, for until
that day all their inheritance among the
tribes of Yisra'ĕl had not yet fallen to them.
2 And the children of Dan sent five men
of their clan, brave men from Tsorʻah and
Eshta'ol, to spy out the land and search it.
And they said to them, "Go, search the
land," so they went to the mountains of
Ephrayim, to the house of Miḵah, and
spent the night there.
3 When they were near the house of
Miḵah, they recognised the voice of the
young Lĕwite, and turned aside and said to

17a See also 21:25, and Deḇ. 12:8.

him, "Who brought you here? What are you doing in this place, and what do you have here?"
4 And he said to them, "Miḵah did such and such for me. And he hired me, and I have become his priest."
5 And they said to him, "Please inquire of Elohim, and we shall know whether the journey on which we are going is prosperous."
6 And the priest said to them, "Go in peace. Your journey on which you go is before יהוה."
7 Then the five men left and came to Layish, and saw the people who were in their midst, how they dwelt safely, according to the ruling of the Tsiḏonians, at rest and unsuspecting. And no one possessing authority in the land was reproaching for any matter. And they were far from the Tsiḏonians, and they had no word with anyone.
8 And the spies came back to their brothers at Tsorʽah and Eshta'ol, and their brothers said to them, "What do you *say*?"
9 And they said, "Arise, and let us go up against them. For we have seen the land, and look, it is very good. And you sit still! Do not hesitate to go to enter in to possess the land.
10 "When you go, you are to come to an unsuspecting people, and the land is spacious. For Elohim has given it into your hands, a place in which there is no lack of any matter which is on the earth."
11 And six hundred men of the clan of the Danites went from there, from Tsorʽah and Eshta'ol, armed for battle.
12 And they went up and encamped in Qiryath Yeʽarim in Yehuḏah. Therefore they call that place Maḥanĕh Ḏan to this day. See, it is west of Qiryath Yeʽarim.
13 And they passed over from there to the mountains of Ephrayim, and came to the house of Miḵah.
14 And the five men who had gone to spy out the land of Layish answered and said to their brothers, "Do you know that there are in these houses a shoulder garment, and house idols, and a carved image, and a moulded image? And now, you know what to do."
15 And they turned aside there, and came to the house of the young Lĕwite man, the house of Miḵah, and greeted him.
16 And the six hundred men, armed for battle, who were of the children of Dan, stood by the entrance of the gate.
17 And the five men who had gone to spy out the land went up, and entering there, they took the carved image, and the shoulder garment, and the house idols, and the moulded image, while the priest stood at the entrance of the gate with the six hundred men who were armed for battle.
18 And these went into Miḵah's house and took the idol, and the shoulder garment, and the house idols, and the moulded image. Then the priest said to them, "What are you doing?"
19 And they said to him, "Be silent, put your hand over your mouth, and come with us, and be a father and a priest to us. Is it better for you to be a priest to the household of one man, or that you be a priest to a tribe and a clan in Yisra'ĕl?"
20 And the heart of the priest was glad. And he took the shoulder garment, and the house idols, and the carved image, and took his place among the people.
21 And they turned and went, and put the little ones, and the livestock, and the valuables in front of them.
22 They had gone some distance from the house of Miḵah, when the men who were in the houses near Miḵah's house gathered together and overtook the children of Dan,
23 and called out to the children of Dan. So they turned around and said to Miḵah, "What is the matter, that you have gathered such a company?"
24 And he said, "You have taken away my mighty ones which I made, and the priest, and you are leaving. Now what more do I have? What is this you say to me, 'What is the matter?' "
25 And the children of Dan said to him, "Do not let your voice be heard among us, lest men, bitter of being, fall upon you, and you lose your life, with the lives of your household!"
26 And the children of Dan went their way.

And when Miḵah saw that they were too
strong for him, he turned and went back to
his house.
27 Then they took what Miḵah had made,
and the priest who had belonged to him,
and went to Layish, to a people who were
at rest and unsuspecting, and struck them
with the edge of the sword and burned the
city with fire.
28 And there was no deliverer, because it
was far from Tsiḏon, and they had no word
with anyone. And it was in the valley that
belongs to Bĕyth Reḥoḇ. And they rebuilt
the city and dwelt there.
29 And they called the name of the city
Dan, after the name of Dan their father,
who was born to Yisra'ĕl. But previously
the name of the city was Layish.
30 And the children of Dan set up for
themselves the carved image. And Yehonathan son of Gĕreshom, son of Menashsheh, and his sons were priests to the tribe
of Dan until the day the land was taken into
exile.
31 And they set up for themselves the
carved image of Miḵah, which he had
made, all the days that the house of Elohim
was in Shiloh.

19 And it came to be in those days,
when there was no sovereign in
Yisra'ĕl, that there was a certain Lĕwite
sojourning on the further side of the
mountains of Ephrayim. And he took for
himself a concubine from Bĕyth Leḥem in
Yehuḏah.
2 And his concubine committed whoring
against him, and went away from him to
her father's house at Bĕyth Leḥem in
Yehuḏah, and was there four new *moons* of
days. [a]
3 And her husband arose and went after
her, to speak to her heart and bring her
back, having his servant and a couple of
donkeys with him. And she brought him
into her father's house. And the father of
the young woman saw him, and he was
glad to meet him.
4 And his father-in-law, the young woman's father, took hold of him, and he dwelt
with him three days. And they ate and
drank and spent the nights there.
5 And it came to be on the fourth day that
they arose early in the morning. And he
prepared to leave, but the young woman's
father said to his son-in-law, "Refresh your
heart with a piece of bread, and afterward
go your way."
6 So they sat down, and the two of them
ate and drank together. And the young
woman's father said to the man, "Please
agree to stay all night, and let your heart be
glad."
7 And when the man arose to go, his
father-in-law urged him. So he spent the
night there again.
8 And he arose early in the morning on
the fifth day to go. But the young woman's
father said, "Please refresh your heart." So
they delayed until afternoon, and both of
them ate.
9 And the man arose to go, he and his
concubine and his servant. But his father-
in-law, the young woman's father, said to
him, "See, the day is now drawing toward
evening. Please spend the night. See, the
day is coming to an end. Stay here, and let
your heart be glad. And you shall rise early
tomorrow for your journey, and you shall
go to your tent."
10 But the man would not stay that night.
And he arose and left, and came to a place
opposite Yeḇus, that is Yerushalayim. And
with him were the two saddled donkeys,
and his concubine with him.
11 They were near Yeḇus, and the day was
far spent. And the servant said to his
master, "Come, please, and let us turn aside
into this city of the Yeḇusites and spend the
night in it."
12 And his master said to him, "Let us not
turn aside here into a city of foreigners,
who are not of the children of Yisra'ĕl. But
we shall pass over to Giḇ'ah."
13 And he said to his servant, "Come, let
us draw near to one of these places, and
spend the night in Giḇ'ah or in Ramah."
14 And they passed over and went their

19a Four whole months.

way. And the sun went down on them near
Giḇʿah, which belongs to Binyamin,
15 and they turned off there to go in to
spend the night in Giḇʿah. So he went in,
and he sat down in the open square of the
city, for no one would take them into his
house to spend the night.
16 But see, an old man came in from his
work in the field at evening, who also was
from the mountains of Ephrayim. And he
was sojourning in Giḇʿah, whereas the men
of the place were Binyamites.
17 And when he lifted up his eyes, he saw
the traveller in the open square of the city.
And the old man said, "Where are you
going, and where do you come from?"
18 And he said to him, "We are passing
over from Běyth Leḥem in Yehuḏah to the
other side of the mountains of Ephrayim. I
am from there, and I went to Běyth Leḥem
in Yehuḏah, and I am going to the House of
יהוה. But there is no one taking me into his
house,
19 yet there is both straw and fodder for
our donkeys, and bread and wine for
myself, and for your female servant, and
for the young man who is with your servant; there is no lack of any matter."
20 And the old man said, "Peace be with
you! However, let all your needs be on me,
only do not spend the night in the open
square."
21 And he brought him into his house, and
gave fodder to the donkeys. And they
washed their feet, and ate and drank.
22 They were making their hearts glad, and
see, men of the city, sons of Beliyaʿal, surrounded the house, beating on the door.
And they spoke to the master of the house,
the old man, saying, "Bring out the man
who came to your house, so that we know
him!"
23 But the man, the master of the house,
went out to them and said to them, "No, my
brothers! I beg you, do no evil! Since this
man has come into my house, do not do
this folly.
24 "Look, here is my maiden daughter and
the man's concubine. Let me bring them
out now, and humble them, and do with
them what is good in your eyes, but do not
do such a foolish matter to this man!"
25 But the men would not listen to him. So
the man took hold of his concubine and
brought her out to them. And they knew
her and rolled themselves on her all night
until morning, and let her go when the day
began to break.
26 And as morning appeared the woman
came back and fell down at the door of the
man's house where her master was, till it
was light.
27 And her master rose up in the morning,
and opened the doors of the house and went
out to go his way, and saw his concubine,
fallen at the door of the house with her
hands on the threshold.
28 And he said to her, "Rise up and let us
go." But there was no answer. Then he took
her on the donkey, and the man rose and
went to his place,
29 and came into his house and took a
knife, then took hold of his concubine, and
cut her up limb by limb into twelve pieces,
and sent her throughout all the borders of
Yisra'ěl.
30 And it came to be that all who saw it
said, "There has never been, and there has
not been seen the like of this, from the day
that the children of Yisra'ěl came up from
the land of Mitsrayim until this day. Set
your *heart* on it, take counsel, and speak
up!"

20 And all the children of Yisra'ěl
came out, from Dan to Be'ěrsheḇa,
and from the land of Gilʿaḏ, and the congregation assembled as one man before
יהוה at Mitspah.
2 And the leaders of all the people, all the
tribes of Yisra'ěl, presented themselves in
the assembly of the people of Elohim, four
hundred thousand foot soldiers who drew
the sword.
3 And the children of Binyamin heard
that the children of Yisra'ěl had gone up to
Mitspah. And the children of Yisra'ěl said,
"Speak up, how did this evil come about?"
4 And the man, the Lěwite, husband of
the woman who was murdered, answered
and said, "My concubine and I went into
Giḇʿah, which belongs to Binyamin, to

spend the night.
5 "And the masters of Giḇʿah rose against
me, and surrounded the house at night
because of me. They thought to kill me, but
instead they humbled my concubine, and
she died.
6 "Then I took my concubine, and cut her
in pieces, and sent her throughout all the
land of the inheritance of Yisra'ěl, because
they committed wickedness and folly in
Yisra'ěl.
7 "Look, you are all children of Yisra'ěl,
speak and give your counsel here!"
8 And all the people rose as one man, saying, "Let not one of us go to his tent, nor
any of us turn back to his house.
9 "And now, this is what we do to Giḇʿah:
go against it by lot.
10 "And we shall take ten men out of every
hundred throughout all the tribes of
Yisra'ěl, and a hundred out of every
thousand, and a thousand out of every ten
thousand, to make food for the people,
to prepare for their going to Giḇʿah in
Binyamin, for all the folly they did in
Yisra'ěl."
11 And all the men of Yisra'ěl were
gathered against the city, knit together as
one man.
12 And the tribes of Yisra'ěl sent men
through all the tribe of Binyamin, saying,
"What is this evil that has come about
among you?
13 "And now, give us the men, the sons of
Beliyaʿal who are in Giḇʿah, so that we put
them to death and put away evil from
Yisra'ěl!" But the children of Binyamin
would not listen to the voice of their
brothers, the children of Yisra'ěl.
14 So the children of Binyamin gathered
together from their cities to Giḇʿah, to go to
battle against the children of Yisra'ěl.
15 And from their cities at that time the
children of Binyamin registered twenty-six
thousand men who drew the sword, besides
the inhabitants of Giḇʿah, who registered
seven hundred chosen men.
16 Among all this people there were seven
hundred chosen men who were left-handed, each one could sling a stone at a hair's
breadth and not miss.
17 And besides Binyamin, the men of
Yisra'ěl registered four hundred thousand
men who drew the sword, all of these were
men of battle.
18 And the children of Yisra'ěl rose and
went up to Běyth Ěl to ask of Elohim, and
they said, "Who of us go up first to battle
against the children of Binyamin?" And
יהוה said, "Yehuḏah first."
19 And the children of Yisra'ěl rose in the
morning and encamped against Giḇʿah.
20 And the men of Yisra'ěl went out to battle against Binyamin, and the men of
Yisra'ěl put themselves in battle array to
fight against them at Giḇʿah.
21 And the children of Binyamin came out
of Giḇʿah, and on that day cut down to the
ground twenty-two thousand men of
Yisra'ěl.
22 But the people, the men of Yisra'ěl,
strengthened themselves and again formed
the battle line at the place where they had
put themselves in array on the first day.
23 And the children of Yisra'ěl went up
and wept before יהוה until evening, and
asked of יהוה, saying, "Should I again
draw near for battle against the children of
my brother Binyamin?" And יהוה said,
"Go up against him."
24 And the children of Yisra'ěl drew near
to the children of Binyamin on the second
day.
25 And Binyamin went out against them
from Giḇʿah on the second day, and cut
down to the ground eighteen thousand
more of the children of Yisra'ěl – all these
drew the sword.
26 And all the children of Yisra'ěl, even all
the people, went up and came to Běyth Ěl
and wept, and sat there before יהוה and
fasted that day until evening. And they
offered ascending offerings and peace
offerings before יהוה.
27 And the children of Yisra'ěl asked of
יהוה – the ark of the covenant of Elohim
was there in those days,
28 and Pineḥas son of Elʿazar, son of
Aharon, stood before it in those days – saying, "Should I yet again go out to battle
against the children of my brother
Binyamin, or should I cease?" And יהוה

said, "Go up, for tomorrow I give them into
your hand."
29 And Yisra'ĕl set ambushers all around
Giḇʿah.
30 And the children of Yisra'ĕl went up
against the children of Binyamin on the
third day, and put themselves in battle array
against Giḇʿah as at the other times.
31 And the children of Binyamin came out
to meet the people – drawn away from the
city. And they began to strike some of the
people, slaying, as at the other times, in the
highways, of which one went up to Bĕyth
Ĕl and the other to Giḇʿah in the field,
about thirty men of Yisra'ĕl.
32 And the children of Binyamin said,
"They are going to be smitten before us, as
previously." But the children of Yisra'ĕl
said, "Let us flee and draw them away from
the city to the highways."
33 And all the men of Yisra'ĕl rose from
their place and put themselves in battle
array at Baʿal Tamar. And the ambush of
Yisra'ĕl broke forth from their position at
Maʿareh Ḡeḇa.
34 And ten thousand chosen men from all
Yisra'ĕl came against Giḇʿah, and the battle
was fierce. But they did not know that
calamity was close to them.
35 And יהוה smote Binyamin before
Yisra'ĕl. And the children of Yisra'ĕl
destroyed twenty-five thousand one hundred men on that day in Binyamin – all
these drew the sword.
36 And the children of Binyamin saw that
they were smitten. And the men of Yisra'ĕl
had given ground to the Binyamites,
because they trusted in the ambush that
they had set against Giḇʿah,
37 and the ambush hurried and came
against Giḇʿah, and the ambush spread out
and struck the entire city with the edge of
the sword.
38 And the appointed signal between the
men of Yisra'ĕl and the ambush was that
they would make a great cloud of smoke
rise up from the city,
39 then the men of Yisra'ĕl would turn in
battle, and Binyamin began to strike dead
about thirty of the men of Yisra'ĕl. For they
said, "They are indeed smitten before us, as
at the first battle."
40 Then the cloud began to rise from the
city in a column of smoke, and the
Binyamites looked behind them, and saw
the entire city going up in smoke to the
heavens.
41 And when the men of Yisra'ĕl turned
back, the men of Binyamin were troubled,
for they saw that calamity was close to
them.
42 And they turned their backs before the
men of Yisra'ĕl toward the way of the
wilderness, but the battle overtook them,
while those who had come out of the cities
were destroying them in their midst.
43 They surrounded the Binyamites and
pursued them, and with ease trampled them
down as far as the front of Giḇʿah toward
the east.
44 And there fell of Binyamin eighteen
thousand men – all of these were mighty
men.
45 And they turned and fled toward the
wilderness to the rock of Rimmon. And
they cut down five thousand of them on the
highways, and followed after them up to
Giḏom, and struck two thousand of them.
46 And all who fell of Binyamin that day
were twenty-five thousand men who drew
the sword, all of these were mighty men.
47 But six hundred men turned and fled
toward the wilderness to the rock of
Rimmon, and they dwelt at the rock of
Rimmon for four new *moons*.
48 And the men of Yisra'ĕl turned back
against the children of Binyamin, and
struck them with the edge of the sword
from every city, men and beasts, all who
were found. And they set fire to all the
cities they came to.

21 And the men of Yisra'ĕl had sworn
an oath at Mitspah, saying, "Not
one of us shall give his daughter to
Binyamin as a wife."
2 So the people came to Bĕyth Ĕl, and sat
there until evening before Elohim, and
lifted up their voices and wept bitterly,
3 and said, "O יהוה Elohim of Yisra'ĕl,
why has this come about in Yisra'ĕl, that
today there should be one tribe missing in

Yisra'ĕl?"
4 And it came to be on the morrow, that
the people rose early and built a slaughter-
place there, and brought ascending offerings and peace offerings.
5 And the children of Yisra'ĕl said, "Who
is there among all the tribes of Yisra'ĕl who
did not come up with the assembly to
יהוה?" For they had made a great oath concerning anyone who had not come up to
יהוה at Mitspah, saying, "He shall certainly
be put to death."
6 And the children of Yisra'ĕl were sorry
for Binyamin their brother, and said, "One
tribe is cut off from Yisra'ĕl today.
7 "What do we do for wives for those
who remain, seeing we have sworn by יהוה
not to give them our daughters as wives?"
8 And they said, "Which one of the tribes
of Yisra'ĕl did not come up to Mitspah to
יהוה?" And see, no one had come to the
camp from Yaḇĕsh Gil'aḏ to the assembly.
9 For when the people called a roll, see,
not one of the inhabitants of Yaḇĕsh Gil'aḏ
was there.
10 And the congregation sent out there
twelve thousand of their bravest men, and
commanded them, saying, "Go, and you
shall strike the inhabitants of Yaḇĕsh Gil'aḏ
with the edge of the sword, even the
women and children.
11 "And this is what you do: Put under the
ban every male, and every woman who has
known a man by lying with him."
12 And they found among the inhabitants
of Yaḇĕsh Gil'aḏ four hundred young
maidens who had not known a man. And
they brought them to the camp at Shiloh,
which is in the land of Kena'an.
13 Then all the congregation sent, and
spoke to the children of Binyamin who
were at the rock of Rimmon, and proclaimed peace to them.
14 And Binyamin turned back at that time,
and they gave them the women whom they
had saved alive of the women of Yaḇĕsh
Gil'aḏ. But even so there were not enough
for them.
15 And the people were sorry for Binyamin, because יהוה had made a breach in
the tribes of Yisra'ĕl.
16 And the elders of the congregation said,
"What do we do for wives for those who
remain, since the women have been
destroyed out of Binyamin?"
17 And they said, "There is an inheritance
for the survivors of Binyamin, and no tribe
is to be destroyed from Yisra'ĕl.
18 "But we are unable to give them wives
from our daughters, for the children of
Yisra'ĕl have sworn an oath, saying,
'Cursed be the one who gives a wife to
Binyamin.' "
19 So they said, "See, there is a yearly festival of יהוה in Shiloh, which is north of
Bĕyth Ĕl, on the east side of the highway
that goes up from Bĕyth Ĕl to Sheḵem, and
south of Leḇonah."
20 And they commanded the children of
Binyamin, saying, "Go, lie in wait in the
vineyards,
21 "and watch. And see, when the daughters of Shiloh come out to perform their
dances, then you shall come out from the
vineyards, and every man catch a wife for
himself from the daughters of Shiloh, and
go to the land of Binyamin.
22 "And it shall be, when their fathers or
their brothers come to us to complain, that
we shall say to them, 'Favour us with them,
because we did not take a wife for any of
them in battle, neither have you given them
to them, making yourselves guilty of your
oath.' "
23 And the children of Binyamin did so,
and took enough wives for their number
from those who danced, whom they caught.
Then they went and returned to their inheritance, and they rebuilt the cities and dwelt
in them.
24 And the children of Yisra'ĕl went from
there at that time, each one to his tribe and
clan. And they went from there, each one to
his inheritance.
25 In those days there was no sovereign in
Yisra'ĕl – everyone did what was right in
his own eyes.[a]

21a - See 17:6 and Deḇ. 12:8.

SHEMU'ĚL ALEPH

1 SAMUEL

1 And there was a certain man of
Ramathayim Tsophim, of the mountains of Ephrayim, and his name was
Elqanah son of Yeroḥam, son of Elihu, son
of Tohu, son of Tsuph, an Ephrayimite.
2 And he had two wives, the name of one
was Ḥannah, and the name of the other
Peninnah. And Peninnah had children, but
Ḥannah had no children.
3 Now this man went up from his city
year by year to worship and to slaughter to
יהוה of hosts in Shiloh. And the two sons
of Ěli, Ḥophni and Pineḥas, the priests of
יהוה, were there.
4 And when the day came for Elqanah to
make a slaughtering, he gave portions to
Peninnah his wife and to all her sons and
daughters,
5 but, although he loved Ḥannah, he gave
only one portion to Ḥannah, because יהוה
had shut up her womb.
6 Moreover, her rival also provoked her
greatly, to make her irritable, because יהוה
had shut up her womb.
7 And so he did, year by year. Whenever
she went up to the House of יהוה, she was
provoked, so that she wept and did not eat.
8 And her husband Elqanah said to her,
"Ḥannah, why do you weep? Why do you
not eat? And why is your heart sad? Am I
not better to you than ten sons?"
9 And Ḥannah rose up after eating and
drinking in Shiloh, while Ěli the priest was
sitting on the seat by the doorpost of the
Hěḵal of יהוה.
10 And she was bitter in life, and prayed to
יהוה and wept greatly.
11 And she made a vow and said, "O יהוה
of hosts, if You would indeed look on the
affliction of your female servant and
remember me, and not forget your female
servant, but shall give your female servant
a male child, then I shall give him to יהוה
all the days of his life, and let no razor
come upon his head."
12 And it came to be, as she kept on
praying before יהוה, that Ěli was watching
her mouth.
13 And Ḥannah spoke in her heart, only
her lips moved, but her voice was not
heard. So Ěli thought she was drunk.
14 Then Ěli said to her, "How long are you
going to be drunk? Put your wine away
from you!"
15 And Ḥannah answered and said, "No,
my master, I am a woman pained in spirit.
And I have drunk neither wine nor strong
drink, but have poured out my being
before יהוה.
16 "Do not take your female servant for a
daughter of Beliya'al, for it is out of my
great concern and provocation that I have
spoken until now."
17 And Ěli answered and said, "Go in
peace, and the Elohim of Yisra'ěl give you
your petition which you have asked of
Him."
18 And she said, "Let your female servant
find favour in your eyes." And the woman
went her way and ate, and her face was no
more *sad*.
19 And they rose up early in the morning
and worshipped before יהוה, and returned
and came to their house at Ramah. And
Elqanah knew Ḥannah his wife, and יהוה
remembered her.
20 And it came to be at the turn of days,
that Ḥannah conceived and bore a son, and
called his name Shemu'ěl, "Because I have
asked יהוה for him."
21 And the man Elqanah and all his house
went up to slaughter to יהוה the yearly
slaughtering and his vow.
22 But Ḥannah did not go up, for she said
to her husband, "When the child is
weaned, then I shall take him. And he shall
appear before יהוה and remain forever
there."
23 And her husband Elqanah said to her,
"Do what is good in your eyes. Remain

until you have weaned him. Only let יהוה
establish His word." And the woman
remained and nursed her son until she had
weaned him.
24 And when she had weaned him, she
took him up with her, with three bulls, [a]
and one ĕphah of flour, and a skin of wine,
and brought him to the House of יהוה in
Shiloh. And the child was young.
25 And they slew a bull, and brought the
child to Ěli.
26 And she said, "O my master! As your
being lives, my master, I am the woman
who stood by you here, praying to יהוה.
27 "I prayed for this youth, and יהוה has
granted me what I asked of Him.
28 "So I have also loaned him to יהוה. All
the days that he lives he shall be loaned to
יהוה." And he worshipped there before
יהוה.

2 And Ḥannah prayed and said, "My
heart rejoices in יהוה, my horn has
been high in יהוה. My mouth is opened
wide over my enemies, for I have rejoiced
in Your deliverance.
2 "There is no one set-apart like יהוה, for
there is no one besides You, and there is no
rock like our Elohim.
3 "Do not multiply words so proudly,
proudly; let no arrogance come from your
mouth, for יהוה is an Ěl of knowledge, and
by Him deeds are weighed.
4 "Bows of the mighty are broken, and
those who stumble shall be girded with
strength.
5 "The satisfied have hired themselves
out for bread, and the hungry have ceased.
Even the barren has borne seven, and she
who has many children pines away.
6 "יהוה puts to death and makes alive,
He brings down to She'ol and raises up.
7 "יהוה makes poor and makes rich, He
brings low and lifts up.
8 "He raises the poor from the dust, He
lifts the needy from the dunghill, to sit
with princes, and make them inherit a
throne of esteem. For the supports of the
earth belong to יהוה, and He has set the
world upon them.
9 "He guards the feet of His lovingly-
commited ones, but the wrong are silent in
darkness, for man does not become mighty
by power.
10 "Those who oppose יהוה are shattered,
from the heavens He thunders against
them. יהוה judges the ends of the earth,
and gives strength to His sovereign, and
exalts the horn of His anointed."
11 And Elqanah went to his house at
Ramah. But the youth served יהוה before
Ěli the priest.
12 And the sons of Ěli were sons of
Beliyaʽal – they did not know יהוה.
13 And the ruling of the priests with the
people was that when any man slaughtered
a slaughtering, the priest's servant shall
come with a three-pronged flesh-hook in
his hand while the meat was cooking,
14 and shall strike it into the basin, or
kettle, or cauldron, or pot. And the priest
would take for himself all that the flesh-
hook brought up. Thus they did in Shiloh
to all Yisra'ěl who came there.
15 Also, before they burned the fat, the
priest's servant would come and say to the
man who slaughtered, "Give meat for
roasting to the priest, for he does not
accept cooked meat from you, but raw."
16 And if the man said to him, "Let the fat
be burned up first, then take as much as
your being desires," he would then answer
him, "No, but give it to me now. And if
not, I shall take it by strength."
17 And the sin of the young men was very
great before יהוה, for the men despised the
offering of יהוה.
18 But Shemu'ěl was attending before
יהוה – a youth, wearing a linen shoulder
garment.
19 And his mother would make him a little
robe, and bring it to him year by year when
she came up with her husband to slaughter
the yearly slaughtering.
20 And Ěli blessed Elqanah and his wife,
and said, "יהוה give you offspring from
this woman for the one she prayed for and
gave to יהוה." Then they would go to their

1a - DSS read a 'one three year old bull'. Also see Ber. 15:9.

own home.

21 And יהוה visited Ḥannah, so that she conceived and bore three sons and two daughters, while the young Shemu'ěl grew before יהוה.

22 And Ěli was very old, and had heard all that his sons were doing to all Yisra'ěl, and how they lay with the women who were assembling at the door of the Tent of Appointment.

23 And he said to them, "Why do you do deeds like these? For I hear of your evil deeds from all the people.

24 "No, my sons! For it is not a good report that I hear: making the people of יהוה transgress.

25 "If one man sins against another, Elohim shall judge him. But if a man sins against יהוה, who shall pray for him?" But they did not listen to the voice of their father, though יהוה was pleased to put them to death.

26 And the young Shemu'ěl was growing in stature, and was in favour with יהוה and also with men.

27 And a man of Elohim came to Ěli and said to him, "Thus said יהוה, 'Did I not clearly reveal Myself to the house of your father when they were in Mitsrayim in Pharaoh's house,

28 even to choose him out of all the tribes of Yisra'ěl to be My priest, to offer upon My slaughter-place, to burn incense, and to wear a shoulder garment before Me? And did I not give to the house of your father all the offerings of the children of Yisra'ěl made by fire?

29 'Why do you kick at My slaughtering and My offering which I have commanded in My Dwelling Place, and esteem your sons above Me, to make yourselves fat with the best of all the offerings of Yisra'ěl My people?'

30 "Therefore יהוה Elohim of Yisra'ěl declares, 'I said indeed that your house and the house of your father would walk before Me forever.' But now יהוה declares, 'Far be it from Me, for those who *highly* esteem Me I *highly* esteem, and those who despise Me are lightly esteemed.

31 'See, the days are coming that I shall cut off your arm and the arm of your father's house, so that an old man shall not be *found* in your house.

32 'And you shall see an enemy in My Dwelling Place, despite all the good which Elohim does for Yisra'ěl, and there shall not be an old man in your house forever.

33 'But any of your men whom I do not cut off from My slaughter-place is to consume your eyes and grieve your life, and all the increase of your house die as men.

34 'And this is the sign to you that comes upon your two sons, upon Ḥophni and Pineḥas: in one day they are going to die, both of them.

35 'And I shall raise up for Myself a trustworthy priest who does according to what is in My heart and in My being. And I shall build him a steadfast house, and he shall walk before My anointed forever.

36 'And it shall be that everyone who is left in your house shall come and bow down to him for a piece of silver and a cake of bread, and say, "Please, put me in one of the priestly positions to eat a piece of bread." ' "

3

And the young Shemu'ěl was serving יהוה before Ěli. And the word of יהוה was rare in those days – no vision breaking forth.

2 And it came to be in that day, that Ěli was lying down in his place. And his eyes had begun to grow so dim that he was unable to see,

3 And the lamp of Elohim had not gone out in the Hěḵal of יהוה where the ark of Elohim was, and Shemu'ěl was lying down to sleep.

4 And יהוה called Shemu'ěl, and he answered, "Here I am!"

5 He then ran to Ěli and said, "Here I am, for you called me." But he said, "I did not call – lie down again." So he went and lay down.

6 And יהוה again called, "Shemu'ěl!" And Shemu'ěl arose and went to Ěli, and said, "Here I am, for you called me." But he answered, "My son, I did not call – lie down again."

7 Now Shemu'ěl did not yet know יהוה,

and the word of יהוה was not yet revealed
to him.
8 And יהוה called Shemu'ĕl again the
third time, and he arose and went to Ĕli,
and said, "Here I am, for you did call me."
Then Ĕli understood that יהוה had called
the youth.
9 So Ĕli said to Shemu'ĕl, "Go, lie down.
And it shall be, if He calls you, say,
'Speak, יהוה, for Your servant hears.' "
And Shemu'ĕl went and lay down in his
place.
10 And יהוה came and stood and called as
at other times, "Shemu'ĕl! Shemu'ĕl!"
And Shemu'ĕl answered, "Speak, for Your
servant hears."
11 And יהוה said to Shemu'ĕl, "See, I am
doing a matter in Yisra'ĕl at which both
ears of everyone who hears it shall tingle.
12 "In that day I shall confirm against Ĕli
all that I have spoken concerning his
house, from beginning to end.
13 "For I have declared to him that I am
judging his house forever for the crookedness which he knows, because his sons
cursed Elohim, and he did not rebuke
them.
14 "And therefore I have sworn to the
house of Ĕli that the crookedness of the
house of Ĕli shall never be atoned for, by
slaughtering or grain offering."
15 And Shemu'ĕl lay down until morning,
and opened the doors of the House of יהוה.
And Shemu'ĕl was afraid to report the
vision to Ĕli.
16 Then Ĕli called Shemu'ĕl and said,
"Shemu'ĕl, my son!" And he answered,
"Here I am."
17 And he said, "What is the word that He
spoke to you? Please do not hide it from
me. Elohim do so to you, and more also,
if you hide a word from me of all the
words that He spoke to you."
18 And Shemu'ĕl reported to him all the
words, and hid none from him. And he
said, "It is יהוה. Let Him do what is good
in His eyes."
19 And Shemu'ĕl grew up, and יהוה was
with him and did not let any of his words
fall to the ground.
20 And all Yisra'ĕl from Dan to
Be'ĕrsheḇa knew that Shemu'ĕl had been
established as a prophet of יהוה.
21 And יהוה continued to appear in
Shiloh, because יהוה revealed Himself to
Shemu'ĕl in Shiloh by the word of יהוה.

4 Thus the word of Shemu'ĕl was to all
Yisra'ĕl. And Yisra'ĕl went out to battle against the Philistines, and encamped
beside Eḇen Haʽĕzer, while the Philistines
encamped in Aphĕq.
2 And the Philistines put themselves in
battle array against Yisra'ĕl. And when the
battle spread, Yisra'ĕl was stricken by the
Philistines, who killed about four thousand
men of the army in the field.
3 And when the people came into the
camp, the elders of Yisra'ĕl said, "Why has
יהוה smitten us today before the
Philistines? Let us bring the ark of the
covenant of יהוה from Shiloh to us, so that
He comes into our midst and save us from
the hand of our enemies."
4 And the people sent to Shiloh, and they
brought from there the ark of the covenant
of יהוה of hosts, dwelling between the
keruḇim. And the two sons of Ĕli, Ḥophni
and Pineḥas, were there with the ark of the
covenant of Elohim.
5 And when the ark of the covenant of
יהוה came into the camp, all Yisra'ĕl
shouted so loudly that the earth shook.
6 And when the Philistines heard the
noise of the shout, they said, "What is the
noise of this great shout in the camp of the
Hebrews?" And when they knew that the
ark of יהוה had come into the camp,
7 the Philistines were afraid, for they
said, "Elohim has come into the camp!"
And they said, "Woe to us! For it has never
been like this before.
8 "Woe to us! Who shall deliver us from
the hand of these mighty Elohim? These
are the Elohim who struck the Mitsrites
with all the plagues in the wilderness.
9 "Be strong and be men, you Philistines,
that you do not become servants of the
Hebrews, as they have been to you. Be
men, and fight!"
10 And the Philistines fought, and Yisra'ĕl
was smitten, and every man fled to his tent.

And the slaughter was very great, and
there fell of Yisra'ěl thirty thousand foot
soldiers.
11 And the ark of Elohim was captured,
and the two sons of Ěli died, Ḥophni and
Pineḥas.
12 And a man of Binyamin ran from the
battle line the same day, and came to
Shiloh with his garments torn and dirt on
his head.
13 And he came in and saw Ěli, sitting on
a seat by the wayside watching, for his
heart trembled for the ark of Elohim. And
the man came into the city and reported it,
and all the city cried out.
14 And Ěli heard the noise of the outcry
and said, "What is the noise of this
uproar?" And the man came hastily and
informed Ěli.
15 Now Ěli was ninety-eight years old and
his eyes were so dim that he was unable to
see.
16 And the man said to Ěli, "I am he who
came from the battle. And I fled today
from the battle line." And he said, "What
was the matter, my son?"
17 And the messenger answered and said,
"Yisra'ěl has fled before the Philistines,
and there has been a great slaughter among
the people. And your two sons have died,
Ḥophni and Pineḥas, and the ark of Elohim
has been captured."
18 And it came to be, when he made
mention of the ark of Elohim, that Ěli fell
off the seat backward by the side of the
gate. And his neck was broken and he died,
for the man was old and heavy. And he
ruled Yisra'ěl forty years.
19 And his daughter-in-law, Pineḥas' wife,
was pregnant, about to bear. And when she
heard the news that the ark of Elohim was
captured, and that her father-in-law and her
husband were dead, she bowed herself and
gave birth, because her pains came upon
her.
20 And about the time of her death the
women who stood by her said to her, "Do
not fear, for you have borne a son." But
she did not answer, nor did she set her
heart to it.
21 And she called the child Iḵaḇoḏ, saying, "The esteem has departed from
Yisra'ěl!" because the ark of Elohim was
taken and because of her father-in-law and
her husband.
22 And she said, "The esteem has departed
from Yisra'ěl, for the ark of Elohim was
taken."

5 And the Philistines took the ark of
Elohim and brought it from Eḇen
Ha'ězer to Ashdoḏ,
2 and the Philistines took the ark of
Elohim and brought it into the house of
Dag̅on and set it by Dag̅on.
3 And the Ashdoḏites rose early in the
morning and saw Dag̅on fallen on its face
to the ground before the ark of יהוה.
So they took Dag̅on and put it in its place
again.
4 And they arose early the next morning
and saw Dag̅on fallen on its face to the
ground before the ark of יהוה, and the
head of Dag̅on and both the palms of its
hands cut off, on the threshold, only Dag̅on
itself was left of it.
5 That is why, to this day, the priests of
Dag̅on and all who come into Dag̅on's
house do not tread on the threshold of
Dag̅on in Ashdoḏ.
6 But the hand of יהוה was heavy on the
Ashdoḏites, and He wasted them and
struck them with tumours – Ashdoḏ and
its borders.
7 And when the men of Ashdoḏ saw this,
they said, "Let not the ark of the Elohim of
Yisra'ěl remain with us, for His hand has
been hard on us, and on Dag̅on our mighty
one."
8 Then they sent and gathered to them all
the princes of the Philistines, and said,
"What do we do with the ark of the Elohim
of Yisra'ěl?" And they answered, "Let the
ark of the Elohim of Yisra'ěl be removed
to Gath." And they removed the ark of the
Elohim of Yisra'ěl.
9 And it came to be, after they removed
it, that the hand of יהוה was against the
city with a very great destruction. And He
struck the men of the city, from the least to
the greatest, and tumours broke out
on them.

10 They then sent the ark of Elohim to Eqron. And it came to be, as the ark of Elohim came to Eqron, that the Eqronites cried out, saying, "They have removed the ark of the Elohim of Yisra'ěl to us, to kill us and our people!"

11 And they sent and gathered together all the princes of the Philistines, and said, "Send away the ark of the Elohim of Yisra'ěl, and let it return to its own place, so that it does not kill us and our people." For there had come a deadly destruction throughout all the city – the hand of Elohim was very heavy there.

12 And the men who did not die were stricken with tumours, and the cry of the city went up to the heavens.

6 And the ark of יהוה was in the field of the Philistines for seven new *moons*.

2 And the Philistines called for the priests and the diviners, saying, "What do we do with the ark of יהוה? Let us know with what we should send it to its place."

3 And they said, "If you send away the ark of the Elohim of Yisra'ěl, do not send it empty, but you shall certainly return it to Him with a guilt offering. Then you are going to be healed, and it shall be known to you why His hand does not turn aside from you."

4 And they said, "What is the guilt offering which we return to Him?" And they answered, "The number of the princes of the Philistines: five golden tumours and five golden rats. For the same plague was on all of you and on your princes.

5 "And you shall make images of your tumours and images of your rats that ruin the land, and you shall give esteem to the Elohim of Yisra'ěl. It could be that He does lift His hand from you, from your mighty ones, and from your land.

6 "And why do you harden your hearts as the Mitsrites and Pharaoh hardened their hearts? When He had severely dealt with them, did they not send them away, and they went?

7 "And now, take and make a new wagon, and two milk cows which have never been yoked, and hitch the cows to the wagon. And take their calves home, away from them.

8 "And take the ark of יהוה and put it on the wagon. And put the objects of gold which you are returning to Him as a guilt offering in a chest by its side, and send it away, and it shall go.

9 "And you shall see, if it goes up the way to its own border, to Běyth Shemesh, then He has done us this great evil. But if not, then we shall know that His hand has not come against us – an accident it was to us."

10 And the men did so and took two milk cows and hitched them to the wagon, and shut up their calves at home.

11 And they put the ark of יהוה on the wagon, and the chest with the gold rats and the images of their tumours.

12 And the cows went straight for the way to Běyth Shemesh, and went along the highway, bellowing as they went, and did not turn aside, right or left. And the princes of the Philistines went after them to the border of Běyth Shemesh.

13 And *they of* Běyth Shemesh were reaping their wheat harvest in the valley. And they lifted their eyes and saw the ark, and rejoiced to see it.

14 And the wagon came into the field of Yehoshua of Běyth Shemesh and stood there, and there was a great stone. So they split the wood of the wagon and offered the cows as a ascending offering to יהוה.

15 And the Lěwites took down the ark of יהוה and the chest that was with it, in which were the objects of gold, and put them on the great stone. And the men of Běyth Shemesh offered ascending offerings and slaughtered slaughterings the same day to יהוה.

16 And when the five princes of the Philistines saw it, they returned to Eqron the same day.

17 And these are the gold tumours which the Philistines returned as a guilt offering to יהוה: one for Ashdoḏ, one for Azzah, one for Ashqelon, one for Gath, one for Eqron,

18 and the gold rats, by the number of all the cities of the Philistines belonging to the

five princes, both walled cities and country villages, even as far as the great meadow on which they placed the ark of יהוה, *remain* to this day in the field of Yehoshua of Bĕyth Shemesh.

19 And He struck among the men of Bĕyth Shemesh, for they had looked into the ark of יהוה. He struck among the people seventy men, and the people mourned because יהוה struck among the people, a great smiting.

20 And the men of Bĕyth Shemesh said, "Who is able to stand before this set-apart יהוה Elohim? And to whom shall He go from us?"

21 And they sent messengers to the inhabitants of Qiryath Ye'arim, saying, "The Philistines have brought back the ark of יהוה. Come down, take it up to you."

7 And the men of Qiryath Ye'arim came and took the ark of יהוה, and brought it into the house of Aḇinaḏaḇ on the hill, and set apart El'azar his son to guard the ark of יהוה.

2 And it came to be, from the day that the ark remained in Qiryath Ye'arim, that the time increased, it came to be twenty years. And all the house of Yisra'ĕl lamented after יהוה.

3 And Shemu'ĕl spoke to all the house of Yisra'ĕl, saying, "If you return to יהוה with all your hearts, then put away the foreign mighty ones and Ashtaroth from among you, and prepare your hearts for יהוה, and serve Him only, so that He delivers you from the hand of the Philistines."

4 And the children of Yisra'ĕl put away the Ba'als and Ashtaroth, and served יהוה only.

5 And Shemu'ĕl said, "Gather all Yisra'ĕl to Mitspah and let me pray to יהוה for you."

6 And they gathered to Mitspah and drew water, and poured it out before יהוה. And they fasted that day, and said there, "We have sinned against יהוה." And Shemu'ĕl rightly ruled the children of Yisra'ĕl at Mitspah.

7 And when the Philistines heard that the children of Yisra'ĕl had gathered together at Mitspah, the princes of the Philistines went up against Yisra'ĕl. And the children of Yisra'ĕl heard of it, and were afraid of the Philistines.

8 And the children of Yisra'ĕl said to Shemu'ĕl, "Do not cease to cry out to יהוה our Elohim for us, that He would save us from the hand of the Philistines."

9 And Shemu'ĕl took a suckling lamb and offered it as a ascending offering, completely, to יהוה. And Shemu'ĕl cried out to יהוה for Yisra'ĕl, and יהוה answered him.

10 And it came to be, as Shemu'ĕl offered up the ascending offering, the Philistines drew near to battle against Yisra'ĕl. But יהוה thundered with a great noise on that day on the Philistines, and troubled them, and they were smitten before Yisra'ĕl.

11 And the men of Yisra'ĕl went out from Mitspah and pursued the Philistines, and struck them as far as below Bĕyth Kar.

12 And Shemu'ĕl took a stone and set it up between Mitspah and Shĕn, and called its name Eḇen Ha'ĕzer, saying, "Thus far יהוה has helped us."

13 Thus the Philistines were humbled, and no longer came into the border of Yisra'ĕl. And the hand of יהוה was against the Philistines all the days of Shemu'ĕl.

14 And the cities which the Philistines had taken from Yisra'ĕl were returned to Yisra'ĕl, from Eqron to Gath. And Yisra'ĕl recovered its border from the hands of the Philistines. And there was peace between Yisra'ĕl and the Amorites.

15 And Shemu'ĕl rightly ruled Yisra'ĕl all the days of his life,

16 and each year he made the rounds of Bĕyth Ĕl, and Gilgal, and Mitspah, and rightly ruled Yisra'ĕl in all those places.

17 Then he returned to Ramah, for his home was there. And there he rightly ruled Yisra'ĕl, and there he built a slaughter-place to יהוה.

8 And it came to be, when Shemu'ĕl was old, that he made his sons rulers over Yisra'ĕl.

2 And the name of his first-born was Yo'ĕl, and the name of his second, Aḇiyah,

rulers in Be’ĕrsheḇa.
3 But his sons did not walk in his ways,
and turned aside after own gain, and took
bribes, and twisted right-ruling.
4 And all the elders of Yisra’ĕl gathered
together and came to Shemu’ĕl at Ramah,
5 and said to him, “Look, you are old,
and your sons do not walk in your ways.
Now appoint for us a sovereign to rule us
like all the nations.”
6 But the word was evil in the eyes of
Shemu’ĕl when they said, “Give us a
sovereign to rule us.” So Shemu’ĕl prayed
to יהוה.
7 And יהוה said to Shemu’ĕl, “Listen to
the voice of the people in all that they say
to you, for they have not rejected you, but
they have rejected Me from reigning over
them.
8 “According to all the works which they
have done since the day that I brought
them up out of Mitsrayim, even to this day
– forsaking Me and serving other mighty
ones – so they are doing to you too.
9 “And now, listen to their voice, but you
shall certainly warn them, and shall make
known to them the ruling of the sovereign
who does reign over them.”
10 And Shemu’ĕl spoke all the words of
יהוה to the people who asked him for a
sovereign,
11 and said, “This is the ruling of the
sovereign who does reign over you: He
shall take your sons and appoint them for
his own chariots and to be his horsemen,
and they shall run before his chariots,
12 and appoint commanders over his thousands and commanders over his fifties, or
to plough his ground and reap his harvest,
or to make his weapons, and equipment for
his chariots.
13 “And your daughters he is going to take
to be perfumers, and cooks, and bakers.
14 “And the best of your fields, and your
vineyards, and your olive-trees he is going
to take and give them to his servants.
15 “And a tenth of your grain and your
vintage he is going to take and give it to
his officers and servants.
16 “And your male servants and your
female servants and your best young men
and your donkeys he is going to take and
use for his own work.
17 “A tenth of your sheep he is going to
take, and you are to be his servants.
18 “And you shall cry out in that day
because of your sovereign whom you have
chosen for yourselves, but יהוה is not
going to answer you in that day.”
19 However, the people refused to listen to
the voice of Shemu’ĕl, and said, “No, but
let a sovereign be over us.
20 Then we shall be, we also, like all the
nations, and our sovereign shall rule us and
go out before us and fight our battles.”
21 And Shemu’ĕl heard all the words of
the people, and he repeated them in the
hearing of יהוה.
22 And יהוה said to Shemu’ĕl, “Listen to
their voice, and make them a sovereign.”
And Shemu’ĕl said to the men of Yisra’ĕl,
“Each of you go to his city.”

9 And there was a man of Binyamin
whose name was Qish, son of Aḇi’ĕl,
son of Tseror, son of Beḵorath, son of
Aphiyaḥ, a Binyamite, a mighty man of
power.
2 And he had a son whose name was
Sha’ul, young and handsome. And there
was not a more handsome man than he
among the children of Yisra’ĕl, taller than
any of the people by the shoulders and
upwards.
3 And the donkeys of Qish, father of
Sha’ul, were lost. And Qish said to his son
Sha’ul, “Please take one of the servants
with you, and arise, go seek the donkeys.”
4 And he passed through the mountains
of Ephrayim and through the land of
Shalishah, but they did not find them. Then
they passed through the land of Sha‘alim,
but they were not. Then he passed through
the land of the Binyamites, but they did not
find them.
5 They came to the land of Tsuph, and
Sha’ul said to his servant who was with
him, “Come, let us turn back, lest my
father stops *thinking* about the donkeys
and become worried about us.”
6 And he said to him, “See, there is in
this city a man of Elohim, and the man is

esteemed. All that he says comes true,
without fail. Now, let us go there. It could
be that he shows us the way to go."
7 And Sha'ul said to his servant, "But
look, if we go, what do we bring the man?
For the bread in our bags is all gone, and
there is no present to bring to the man of
Elohim. What do we have?"
8 And the servant answered Sha'ul again
and said, "Look, I have here at hand one
fourth of a sheqel of silver. And I shall
give that to the man of Elohim, and he
shall make known to us our way."
9 Formerly, in Yisra'ĕl, when a man went
to inquire of Elohim, he spoke thus,
"Come, let us go to the seer," for the
prophet of today was formerly called a
seer.
10 And Sha'ul said to his servant, "Your
word is good. Come, let us go." And they
went to the city where the man of Elohim
was.
11 As they went up the hill to the city, they
met some young women going out to draw
water, and said to them, "Is the seer here?"
12 And they answered them and said, "He
is. Look, ahead of you. Hurry now, for he
came to this city today, for the people have
a slaughtering on the high place today.
13 "As you come into the city, you are
going to find him before he goes up to the
high place to eat. For the people do not eat
until he comes, for he blesses the slaughtering, afterward they who are invited eat.
And now, go up, for you should find him
about this time."
14 And they went up to the city. They
were coming into the midst of the city, and
saw Shemu'ĕl coming out toward them to
go up to the high place.
15 And יהוה had revealed to Shemu'ĕl in
his ear the day before Sha'ul came, saying,
16 "At this time tomorrow I shall send you
a man from the land of Binyamin, and you
shall anoint him leader over My people
Yisra'ĕl, and he shall save My people
from the hand of the Philistines. For I have
seen My people, because their cry has
come to me."
17 And when Shemu'ĕl saw Sha'ul, יהוה
said to him, "See, the man of whom I
spoke to you. Let this one govern My
people."
18 And Sha'ul drew near to Shemu'ĕl in
the gate, and said, "Please inform me,
where is the house of the seer?"
19 And Shemu'ĕl answered Sha'ul and
said, "I am the seer. Go up before me to the
high place, for you shall eat with me today.
And tomorrow I shall let you go and make
known to you all that is in your heart.
20 "As for your donkeys that were lost
three days ago, do not set your heart on
them, for they have been found. And on
whom is all the desire of Yisra'ĕl? Is it not
on you and on all your father's house?"
21 And Sha'ul answered and said, "Am I
not a Binyamite – of the smallest of the
tribes of Yisra'ĕl, and my clan the least of
all the clans of the tribe of Binyamin? Why
then do you speak like this to me?"
22 And Shemu'ĕl took Sha'ul and his
servant and brought them into the hall, and
gave to them a place at the head of those
who were invited, and there were about
thirty men.
23 And Shemu'ĕl said to the cook, "Bring
the portion which I gave you, of which I
told you to set it aside."
24 And the cook brought out the thigh
with its upper part and set it before Sha'ul.
And Shemu'ĕl said, "See what was kept
back. It was set aside for you. Eat, for it
has been kept for you for this appointed
time, saying, I have invited the people."
And Sha'ul ate with Shemu'ĕl on that day.
25 And they came down from the high
place into the city, and Shemu'ĕl spoke
with Sha'ul on the roof.
26 And they rose early. And it came to be
about the dawning of the day that
Shemu'ĕl called to Sha'ul on the roof,
saying, "Rise, so that I send you on your
way." And Sha'ul rose, and both of them
went outside, he and Shemu'ĕl.
27 As they were walking toward the edge
of the city, Shemu'ĕl said to Sha'ul, "Say
to the servant to go on ahead of us." And
he went on. "But you stand here a moment,
so that I let you hear the word of Elohim."

10 And Shemu’ĕl took a flask of oil and poured it on his head, and kissed him and said, “Is it not because יהוה has anointed you leader over His inheritance?

2 “When you leave me today, you shall find two men by Raḥĕl’s burial-place in the border of Binyamin at Tseltsaḥ, and they shall say to you, ‘The donkeys which you went to look for have been found. And see, your father has left the matters of the donkeys and is worrying about you, saying, “What shall I do for my son?” ’

3 “And you shall pass on from there, and beyond, and shall come to the terebinth tree of Taḇor. And three men going up to Elohim at Bĕyth Ĕl shall find you there, one bearing three young goats, another bearing three loaves of bread, and another bearing a skin of wine.

4 “And they shall greet you and give you two loaves of bread, which you shall accept from their hand.

5 “After that go to the hill of Elohim where the Philistine watch-post is. And it shall be, when you have come there to the city, that you shall meet a group of prophets coming down from the high place with a stringed instrument, and a tambourine, and a flute, and a lyre before them, and they are prophesying.

6 “And the Spirit of יהוה shall come upon you, and you shall prophesy with them and be turned into another man.

7 “And it shall be, when these signs come to you, do for yourself as your hand finds to do, for Elohim is with you.

8 “And you shall go down before me to Gilgal. And see, I am coming down to you to offer ascending offerings and slaughter slaughterings of peace *offerings*. Wait seven days, till I come to you, then I shall make known to you what you should do.”

9 And it came to be, when he had turned his back to go from Shemu’ĕl, that Elohim gave him another heart. And all those signs came on that day.

10 And they came there to the hill and saw a group of prophets, to meet him. And the Spirit of Elohim came upon him, and he prophesied in their midst.

11 And it came to be, all who knew him formerly looked and saw that he prophesied among the prophets. So the people said to each other, “What is this that has come upon the son of Qish? Is Sha’ul also among the prophets?”

12 And a man there answered and said, “And who is their father?” That is why it became a proverb, “Is Sha’ul also among the prophets?”

13 And when he stopped prophesying, he went to the high place.

14 And the uncle of Sha’ul asked him and his servant, “Where did you go?” And he said, “To look for the donkeys. And when we saw that they were nowhere to be found, we went to Shemu’ĕl.”

15 And the uncle of Sha’ul said, “Please inform me what Shemu’ĕl said to you.”

16 And Sha’ul said to his uncle, “He informed us plainly that the donkeys had been found.” But he did not disclose to him about the matter of the reign, what Shemu’ĕl had said.

17 And Shemu’ĕl called the people together to יהוה at Mitspah,

18 and said to the children of Yisra’ĕl, “Thus said יהוה, the Elohim of Yisra’ĕl, ‘I have brought Yisra’ĕl up out of Mitsrayim, and delivered you from the hand of the Mitsrites and from the hand of all reigns and from those who oppressed you.’

19 “And today you have rejected your Elohim, who Himself saved you out of all your evils and your distresses. And you have said to Him, ‘No, but set a sovereign over us!’ And now, present yourselves before יהוה by your tribes and by your clans.”

20 And Shemu’ĕl brought near all the tribes of Yisra’ĕl, and the tribe of Binyamin was taken.

21 Then he brought near the tribe of Binyamin, by their clans, and the clan of Matri was taken, and Sha’ul son of Qish was taken. And when they sought him, he could not be found.

22 And they asked again of יהוה, “Has the man come here yet?” And יהוה answered, “See, he has hidden by the baggage.”

23 And they ran and brought him from there. And he stood in the midst of the people, and he was taller than any of the people, from his shoulders and upwards.

24 And Shemu'ĕl said to all the people, "Do you see him whom יהוה has chosen, that there is no one like him among all the people?" And all the people shouted and said, "Let the sovereign live!"

25 And Shemu'ĕl declared to the people the rulings of the reign, and wrote it in a book and placed it before יהוה. And Shemu'ĕl sent all the people away, each to his house.

26 And Sha'ul went to his house too, to Giḇ'ah. And with him went brave men whose hearts Elohim had touched.

27 But the sons of Beliya'al said, "What! Does this one save us?" And they despised him, and brought him no presents. But he kept silent.

11 And Naḥash the Ammonite came up and camped against Yaḇĕsh Gil'aḏ. And all the men of Yaḇĕsh said to Naḥash, "Make a covenant with us, and we shall serve you."

2 Then Naḥash the Ammonite answered them, "For this I make a covenant with you, that I dig out all your right eyes, and I shall bring reproach on all Yisra'ĕl."

3 And the elders of Yaḇĕsh said to him, "Leave us alone for seven days, so that we send messengers to all the borders of Yisra'ĕl. And then, if there is no one to save us, we shall come out to you."

4 And the messengers came to Giḇ'ah of Sha'ul and spoke the words in the hearing of the people. And all the people lifted up their voices and wept.

5 And look, Sha'ul was coming behind the herd from the field. And Sha'ul said, "Why are the people weeping?" And they related to him the words of the men of Yaḇĕsh.

6 And the Spirit of Elohim came upon Sha'ul mightily as he heard these words, and his displeasure burned greatly.

7 And he took a yoke of cattle and cut them in pieces, and sent them throughout all the border of Yisra'ĕl by the hands of messengers, saying, "Whoever does not go out with Sha'ul and Shemu'ĕl to battle, let this be done to his cattle." And the fear of יהוה fell on the people, and they came out as one man.

8 And he mustered them in Bezeq, and the children of Yisra'ĕl were three hundred thousand, and the men of Yehuḏah thirty thousand.

9 And they said to the messengers who came, "Say this to the men of Yaḇĕsh Gil'aḏ, 'Tomorrow, by the time the sun is hot, you shall have help.' " Then the messengers came and informed the men of Yaḇĕsh, and they rejoiced.

10 So the men of Yaḇĕsh said, "Tomorrow we come out to you, and you shall do to us whatever seems good to you."

11 And it came to be, on the next day, that Sha'ul put the people in three companies. And they came into the midst of the camp in the morning watch and struck Ammon until the heat of the day. And it came to be that those left were scattered, so that no two of them were left together.

12 And the people said to Shemu'ĕl, "Who said, 'Shall Sha'ul reign over us?' Bring the men, so that we put them to death."

13 But Sha'ul said, "No man is put to death this day, for today יהוה has wrought deliverance in Yisra'ĕl."

14 And Shemu'ĕl said to the people, "Come, and let us go to Gilgal and renew the reign there."

15 And all the people went to Gilgal, and there they set up Sha'ul to reign before יהוה in Gilgal, and there they slaughtered slaughterings of peace *offerings* before יהוה. And there Sha'ul rejoiced, and all the men of Yisra'ĕl, very greatly.

12 And Shemu'ĕl said to all Yisra'ĕl, "Look, I have listened to your voice in all that you said to me, and have set a sovereign over you.

2 "And now, look, the sovereign is walking before you. And I am old and grey, and look, my sons are with you. And I have walked before you from my youth to this day.

3 "Look, here I am. Witness against me

before יהוה and before His anointed:
Whose ox have I taken, or whose donkey
have I taken, or whom have I oppressed?
Whom have I abused, or from whose hand
have I received any bribe with which to
blind my eyes? – then I restore it to you."
4 And they said, "You have not
oppressed us or abused us, nor have you
taken any *bribe* from anyone's hand."
5 So he said to them, "יהוה is witness
against you, and His anointed is witness
today, that you have found naught in my
hand." And they answered, "He is witness."
6 And Shemu'ěl said to the people, "It is
יהוה who appointed Mosheh and Aharon,
and who brought your fathers up from the
land of Mitsrayim.
7 "And now, stand still, so that I judge
you before יהוה concerning all the
righteous acts of יהוה which He did to you
and your fathers:
8 "When Ya'aqoḇ had come to Mitsrayim, and your fathers cried out to יהוה,
then יהוה sent Mosheh and Aharon, who
brought your fathers out of Mitsrayim and
made them dwell in this place.
9 "But they forgot יהוה their Elohim, so
He sold them into the hand of Sisera,
commander of the army of Ḥatsor, and into
the hand of the Philistines, and into the
hand of the sovereign of Mo'aḇ. And they
fought against them.
10 "And they cried out to יהוה, and said,
'We have sinned, because we have forsak-
en יהוה and served the Ba'als and the
Ashtaroth. And now, deliver us from the
hand of our enemies, and we serve You.'
11 "And יהוה sent Yerubba'al, and Bedan,
and Yiphtaḥ, and Shemu'ěl, and delivered
you out of the hand of your enemies round
about, and you dwelt in safety.
12 "And when you saw that Naḥash
sovereign of the children of Ammon came
against you, you said to me, 'No, but let
a sovereign reign over us,' when יהוה your
Elohim was your sovereign.
13 "And now, here is the sovereign whom
you have chosen and whom you have
asked. And see, יהוה has set a sovereign
over you.
14 "If you fear יהוה, and shall serve Him
and obey His voice, and not rebel against
the command of יהוה, then both you and
the sovereign who reigns over you shall
follow יהוה your Elohim.
15 "But if you do not obey the voice of
יהוה, and shall rebel against the mouth of
יהוה, then the hand of יהוה shall be
against you, as it was against your fathers.
16 "And now, stand and see this great
matter which יהוה does before your eyes:
17 "Is today not the wheat harvest? Let me
call to יהוה, so that He sends thunder and
rain – know then and see that your evil is
great, which you have done in the eyes of
יהוה, in asking for yourselves a sovereign."
18 And Shemu'ěl called to יהוה, and יהוה
sent thunder and rain that day. And all the
people greatly feared יהוה and Shemu'ěl.
19 And all the people said to Shemu'ěl,
"Pray for your servants to יהוה your
Elohim, that we do not die, for we have
added to all our sins *this* evil of asking for
ourselves a sovereign."
20 And Shemu'ěl said to the people, "Do
not fear. You have done all this evil. Only,
do not turn aside from following יהוה.
And you shall serve יהוה with all your
heart,
21 and do not turn aside after worthless
matters which do not profit or deliver, for
they are worthless.
22 "For יהוה would not cast away His
people, for His great Name's sake, seeing
it has pleased יהוה to make you His people.
23 "Also, as for me, far be it from me that
I should sin against יהוה in ceasing to pray
for you, but I shall teach you the good and
straight way.
24 "Only fear יהוה, and you shall serve
Him in truth with all your heart, for consider what marvels He has done for you.
25 "But if you persist in doing evil, both
you and your sovereign are consumed."

13

Sha'ul was ... years old when he
began to reign. And when he had
reigned two years over Yisra'ěl,
2 Sha'ul chose for himself three thousand

men of Yisra'ěl. And two thousand were with Sha'ul in Miḵmash and in the mountains of Běyth Ěl, and a thousand were with Yonathan in Giḇ'ah of Binyamin. And the rest of the people he sent away, each to his tent.

3 And Yonathan struck the watch-post of the Philistines that was in Geḇa, and the Philistines heard of it. And Sha'ul blew with the shophar[a] throughout all the land, saying, "Let the Hebrews hear!"

4 And all Yisra'ěl heard the news that Sha'ul had stricken a watch-post of the Philistines, and also that Yisra'ěl had become a stench to the Philistines. And the people were summoned to Sha'ul at Gilgal.

5 And the Philistines gathered to fight Yisra'ěl, thirty thousand chariots and six thousand horsemen, and people as numerous as the sand on the seashore. And they came up and encamped in Miḵmash, east of Běyth Awen.

6 And the men of Yisra'ěl saw that they were in trouble, for the people were distressed, and the people hid in caves, and in thorny bushes, and in rocks, and in holes, and in pits.

7 And *some* Hebrews passed over the Yarděn to the land of Gaḏ and Gil'aḏ. But Sha'ul was still in Gilgal, and all the people followed him, trembling.

8 And he waited for seven days, according to the appointment with Shemu'ěl. But Shemu'ěl did not come to Gilgal, and the people were scattered from him.

9 And Sha'ul said, "Bring a ascending offering and peace offerings here to me." And he offered the ascending offering.

10 And it came to be, as he had finished offering the ascending offering, look, Shemu'ěl came. And Sha'ul went out to meet him, to bless him.

11 Then Shemu'ěl said, "What have you done?" And Sha'ul said, "Because I saw that the people were scattered from me, and that you did not come within the days appointed, and that the Philistines gathered at Miḵmash,

12 so I said, 'The Philistines are going to come down on me at Gilgal, and I have not appeased the face of יהוה.' So I felt compelled, and offered a ascending offering."

13 And Shemu'ěl said to Sha'ul, "You have been foolish. You have not guarded the command of יהוה your Elohim, which He commanded you. For now יהוה would have established your reign over Yisra'ěl forever.

14 "But now, your reign is not going to stand. יהוה shall seek for Himself a man after His own heart,[b] and יהוה shall command him to be leader over His people, because you have not guarded what יהוה commanded you."

15 And Shemu'ěl arose and went up from Gilgal to Giḇ'ah of Binyamin. And Sha'ul mustered the people who were present with him, about six hundred men.

16 And Sha'ul, and Yonathan his son, and the people who were present with them remained in Giḇ'ah of Binyamin, while the Philistines camped at Miḵmash.

17 And from the camp of the Philistines raiders went out in three companies. The one company turned to the way that leads to Ophrah, to the land of Shu'al,

18 and another company turned toward the way of Běyth Ḥoron, and another company turned toward the way of the border that overlooks the Valley of Tseḇo'im toward the wilderness.

19 Now no blacksmith could be found in all the land of Yisra'ěl, for the Philistines said, "Lest the Hebrews make swords or spears."

20 And all Yisra'ěl went down to the Philistines, each one to sharpen his ploughshare, and his mattock, and his axe, and his sickle.

21 And the charge was a pim for the ploughshares, and the mattocks, and the forks, and the axes, and to set the points of the goads.

22 And it came to be, on the day of battle, that there was neither sword nor spear found in the hand of any of the people who

13a An animal horn. Traditionally a ram's horn. *13b* Ma. 13:22.

were with Sha'ul and Yonathan. But they were found with Sha'ul and Yonathan his son.

23 And the outpost of the Philistines went out to the pass of Miḵmash.

14 And it came to be one day that Yonathan son of Sha'ul said to the young man who bore his armour, "Come, and let us go over to the outpost of the Philistines which is on the other side." But he did not inform his father.

2 And Sha'ul remained at the outskirts of Giḇʿah under a pomegranate tree at Miḡron, and the people who were with him were about six hundred men.

3 And Aḥiyah son of Aḥituḇ, Iḵaḇoḏ's brother, son of Pineḥas, son of Ěli, the priest of יהוה in Shiloh, was wearing a shoulder garment. And the people did not know that Yonathan had gone.

4 And between the passes, by which Yonathan sought to go over to the outpost of the Philistines, there was an edge of a rock on one side and an edge of a rock on the other side. And the name of one was Botsěts, and the name of the other Seneh.

5 The one edge was on the north opposite Miḵmash, and the other on the south opposite Giḇʿah.

6 And Yehonathan said to the young man who bore his armour, "Come, and let us go over to the outpost of these uncircumcised. If so be, יהוה does work for us. For there is no hindrance for יהוה to save by many or by few."

7 And his armour-bearer said to him, "Do all that is in your heart, incline yourself. See, I am with you, according to your heart."

8 And Yehonathan said, "See, we are passing over to the men – and show ourselves to them.

9 "If they say this to us, 'Wait until we come to you,' then we shall stand still in our place and not go up to them.

10 "But if they say this, 'Come up to us,' then we shall go up. For יהוה has given them into our hand, and this is the sign to us."

11 And both of them disclosed themselves to the outpost of the Philistines, and the Philistines said, "See, the Hebrews are coming out of the holes where they have hidden."

12 And the men of the outpost called to Yonathan and his armour-bearer, and said, "Come up to us, and let us teach you a lesson." Then Yonathan said to his armour-bearer, "Come up after me, for יהוה has given them into the hand of Yisra'ěl."

13 And Yonathan climbed up on his hands and knees with his armour-bearer after him. And they fell before Yonathan, and his armour-bearer was putting them to death behind him.

14 And that first smiting which Yonathan and his armour-bearer struck was about twenty men, in about half an acre of land.

15 And there was trembling in the camp, in the field, and among all the people. The outpost and the raiders also trembled, and the ground shook. And it became a trembling of Elohim.

16 And the watchmen of Sha'ul in Giḇʿah of Binyamin looked and saw the crowd melting away, and they went here and there.

17 And Sha'ul said to the people who were with him, "Please inspect and see who has gone from us." So they inspected and saw that Yonathan and his armour-bearer were missing.

18 And Sha'ul said to Aḥiyah, "Bring the ark of Elohim here." For the ark of Elohim was with the children of Yisra'ěl on that day.

19 And it came to be, while Sha'ul talked to the priest, that the noise which was in the camp of the Philistines went on, and became great, so Sha'ul said to the priest, "Withdraw your hand."

20 And Sha'ul was called, and all the people who were with him , and they went to the battle. And see, every man's sword was against his neighbour – a very great confusion.

21 And the Hebrews who were with the Philistines before that time, who went up with them into the camp, turned round, they too, to be with Yisra'ěl, who were with Sha'ul and Yonathan.

22 And all the men of Yisra'ĕl who had hidden in the mountains of Ephrayim, heard that the Philistines fled, and they also pursued them in the battle.

23 Thus יהוה saved Yisra'ĕl that day, and the battle passed over to Bĕyth Awen.

24 And the men of Yisra'ĕl were distressed that day, for Sha'ul had placed the people under oath, saying, "Cursed be the man who eats food until evening, and I have taken revenge on my enemies." Therefore none of the people tasted food.

25 And all *they of* the land came into the woods, and there was honey on the ground.

26 And the people came into the woods and saw the honey, dripping. But no one put his hand to his mouth, for the people feared the oath.

27 But Yonathan had not heard that his father had taken an oath of the people, and he stretched out the end of the rod that was in his hand and dipped it in a honeycomb, and put his hand to his mouth. And his eyes lit up.

28 Then one of the people said, "Your father strictly took an oath of the people, saying, 'Cursed be the man who eats food today.' " And the people were weary.

29 And Yonathan said, "My father has troubled the land. Now see how my eyes lit up when I tasted a little of this honey.

30 "How much better if the people had well eaten today of the spoil of their enemies which they found! For then, would not the slaughter among the Philistines have been greater?"

31 And they struck the Philistines that day from Miḵmash to Ayalon. So the people were very weary,

32 and the people pounced on the spoil, and took sheep, and cattle, and calves, and slew them on the ground. And the people ate with the blood.

33 And they told Sha'ul, saying, "Look, the people are sinning against יהוה by eating with the blood!" And he said, "You have acted treacherously. Roll a large stone to me today."

34 And Sha'ul said, "Scatter among the people, and say to them, 'Each one bring his ox near to me, and each one his sheep, and you shall slay them here, and eat. And do not sin against יהוה by eating with the blood.' " So every one of the people brought his ox with him that night, and slew it there.

35 And Sha'ul built a slaughter-place to יהוה. It was the first slaughter-place he built to יהוה.

36 And Sha'ul said, "Let us go down after the Philistines by night, and plunder them until the morning light, and not leave a man of them." And they said, "Do whatever seems good to you." But the priest said, "Let us draw near to Elohim here."

37 And Sha'ul asked of Elohim, "Should I go down after the Philistines? Do You give them into the hand of Yisra'ĕl?" But He did not answer him that day.

38 And Sha'ul said, "Come over here, all you chiefs of the people, and know and see what this sin was today.

39 "For as יהוה lives, who saves Yisra'ĕl, though it be in Yonathan my son, he shall certainly die." But not one among all the people answered him.

40 And he said to all Yisra'ĕl, "You be on one side, and my son Yonathan and I be on the other side." And the people said to Sha'ul, "Do what seems good to you."

41 Then Sha'ul said to יהוה Elohim of Yisra'ĕl, "Give a perfect *lot*." And Sha'ul and Yonathan were taken, but the people escaped.

42 And Sha'ul said, "Cast *lots* between my son Yonathan and me." And Yonathan was taken.

43 Sha'ul then said to Yonathan, "Explain to me what you have done." And Yonathan explained to him, and said, "I only tasted a little honey with the end of the rod that was in my hand. See, let me die!"

44 And Sha'ul answered, "Elohim do so and more also, for you shall certainly die, Yonathan."

45 But the people said to Sha'ul, "Should Yonathan die, who has wrought this great salvation in Yisra'ĕl? Far be it! As יהוה lives, let not one hair of his head fall to the ground, for he has wrought with Elohim this day." Thus the people ransomed Yonathan, and he did not die.

46 And Sha'ul returned from pursuing the
Philistines, and the Philistines went to their
own place.
47 And Sha'ul took the reign over Yisra'ĕl, and fought against all his enemies
round about, against Mo'aḇ, and against
the children of Ammon, and against Eḏom,
and against the sovereigns of Tsoḇah, and
against the Philistines. And wherever he
turned, he inflicted punishment.
48 And he gathered an army and struck the
Amalĕqites, and delivered Yisra'ĕl from
the hands of those who plundered them.
49 And the sons of Sha'ul were Yonathan
and Yishwi and Malkishua. And the names
of his two daughters were these: the name
of the first-born Mĕraḇ, and the name of
the younger Miḵal.
50 And the name of Sha'ul's wife was
Aḥino'am the daughter of Aḥima'ats. And
the name of the commander of his army
was Aḇnĕr son of Nĕr, uncle of Sha'ul.'
51 And Qish was the father of Sha'ul, and
Nĕr the father of Aḇnĕr was the son of
Aḇi'ĕl.
52 And there was tough [a] fighting against
the Philistines all the days of Sha'ul. And
when Sha'ul saw any mighty man or any
brave man, he took him for himself.

15 And Shemu'ĕl said to Sha'ul,
"יהוה sent me to anoint you sovereign over His people, over Yisra'ĕl. And
now, listen to the voice of the words of
יהוה.
2 "Thus said יהוה of hosts, 'I shall punish Amalĕq for what he did to Yisra'ĕl,
how he set himself against him on the way
when he came up from Mitsrayim.
3 'Now go, and you shall strike Amalĕq
and put under the ban all that he has, and
you shall not spare them, and put to death
from man to woman, from infant to
nursing child, from ox to sheep, from
camel to donkey.' "
4 Then Sha'ul summoned the people and
mustered them in Tela'im, two hundred
thousand foot soldiers and ten thousand
men of Yehuḏah.
5 And Sha'ul came to a city of Amalĕq,
and lay in wait in the wadi.
6 And Sha'ul said to the Qĕynites, "Go,
turn aside, come down from among the
Amalĕqites, lest I destroy you with them.
For you did show loving-commitment to
all the children of Yisra'ĕl when they came
up out of Mitsrayim." So the Qĕynites
turned aside from the midst of the
Amalĕqites.
7 And Sha'ul struck the Amalĕqites, from
Ḥawilah all the way to Shur, which is
before Mitsrayim.
8 And he caught Aḡaḡ sovereign of the
Amalĕqites alive, and put under the ban all
the people with the edge of the sword.
9 But Sha'ul and the people spared Aḡaḡ
and the best of the sheep, and the cattle,
and the fatlings, and the lambs, and all that
was good, and would not put them under
the ban. But all goods despised and worthless, that they put under the ban.
10 And the word of יהוה came to
Shemu'ĕl, saying,
11 "I am grieved that I have set up Sha'ul
as sovereign, for he has turned back from
following Me, and has not performed My
words." And it displeased Shemu'ĕl, and
he cried to יהוה all night.
12 And Shemu'ĕl rose early in the morning to meet Sha'ul, and it was told to
Shemu'ĕl, saying, "Sha'ul went to Karmel,
and see, he set up a monument for himself,
then turned and passed over, and went
down to Gilgal."
13 And Shemu'ĕl came to Sha'ul, and
Sha'ul said to him, "Blessed are you of
יהוה! I have performed the word of יהוה."
14 But Shemu'ĕl said, "What then is this
bleating of the sheep in my ears, and the
lowing of the cattle which I hear?"
15 And Sha'ul said, "They have brought
them from Amalĕq, because the people
spared the best of the sheep and the cattle,
to slaughter to יהוה your Elohim. And the
rest we have put under the ban."
16 And Shemu'ĕl said to Sha'ul, "Wait,
and let me declare to you what יהוה said
to me last night." And he said to him,

14a Lit. strong.

"Speak."
17 And Shemu'ĕl said, "Though you were
little in your own eyes, were you not head
of the tribes of Yisra'ĕl? And did not יהוה
anoint you sovereign over Yisra'ĕl?
18 "And יהוה sent you on the way, and
said, 'Go, and you shall put under the ban
the sinners, the Amalĕqites, and fight
against them until they are consumed.'
19 "And why did you not obey the voice
of יהוה, but swooped down on the spoil,
and did evil in the eyes of יהוה?"
20 And Sha'ul said to Shemu'ĕl, "I did
obey the voice of יהוה, and I went on the
way on which יהוה sent me, and brought
back Ağağ sovereign of Amalĕq, and I put
Amalĕq under the ban.
21 "But the people took of the spoil, of the
sheep and cattle, the best of that which
should have been put under the ban, to
slaughter to יהוה your Elohim in Gilgal."
22 Then Shemu'ĕl said, "Does יהוה
delight in ascending offerings and slaughterings, as in obeying the voice of יהוה?
Look, to obey is better than a slaughtering,
to heed *is better* than the fat of rams.
23 "For rebellion is as the sin of divination, and stubbornness is as wickedness
and idolatry. Because you have rejected the
word of יהוה, He also does reject you as
sovereign."
24 And Sha'ul said to Shemu'ĕl, "I have
sinned, for I have transgressed the mouth
of יהוה and your words, because I feared
the people and listened to their voice.
25 "And now, please pardon my sin, and
return with me, and let me bow myself to
יהוה."
26 But Shemu'ĕl said to Sha'ul, "I do not
return with you, for you have rejected the
word of יהוה, and יהוה does reject you
from being sovereign over Yisra'ĕl."
27 And as Shemu'ĕl turned around to go
away, *Sha'ul* took hold of the edge of his
robe, and it tore.
28 And Shemu'ĕl said to him, "יהוה has
torn the reign of Yisra'ĕl from you today,
and has given it to a neighbour of yours,
better than you.
29 "Moreover, the Eminence of Yisra'ĕl
does not lie nor relent. For He is not a man,
that He should relent."
30 Then he said, "I have sinned. But
esteem me now, please, before the elders
of my people and before Yisra'ĕl, and
return with me, and I shall bow myself
to יהוה your Elohim."
31 And Shemu'ĕl turned back after Sha'ul,
and Sha'ul bowed himself to יהוה.
32 And Shemu'ĕl said, "Bring Ağağ sovereign of the Amalĕqites here to me." So
Ağağ came to him delightedly, and Ağağ
said, "Truly, the bitterness of death has
turned aside."
33 And Shemu'ĕl said, "As your sword
bereaved women, let your mother be
bereaved among women too." Shemu'ĕl
then hewed Ağağ to pieces before יהוה in
Gilgal.
34 And Shemu'ĕl went to Ramah, while
Sha'ul went up to his house at Giḇʿah of
Sha'ul.
35 And Shemu'ĕl did not see Sha'ul again
until the day of his death, for Shemu'ĕl
mourned for Sha'ul. And יהוה was grieved
that He had made Sha'ul to reign over
Yisra'ĕl.

16 And יהוה said to Shemu'ĕl, "How
long are you going to mourn for
Sha'ul, seeing I have rejected him from
reigning over Yisra'ĕl? Fill your horn with
oil, and go, I am sending you to Yishai the
Bĕyth Leḥemite. For I have seen among
his sons a sovereign for Myself."
2 And Shemu'ĕl said, "How would I go?
When Sha'ul hears it, he shall kill me."
And יהוה said, "Take a heifer with you,
and say, 'I have come to slaughter to יהוה.'
3 "And you shall invite Yishai to the
slaughtering, then let Me show you what to
do. And you shall anoint for Me the one I
say to you."
4 And Shemu'ĕl did what יהוה said, and
went to Bĕyth Leḥem. And the elders of
the town trembled at his coming, and said,
"Do you come in peace?"
5 And he said, "In peace. I have come to
slaughter to יהוה. Set yourselves apart, and
you shall come with me to the slaughtering." And he set Yishai and his sons apart,
and invited them to the slaughtering.

6 And it came to be, when they came,
that he saw Eliyaḇ and thought, "The
anointed of יהוה is indeed before Him."
7 But יהוה said to Shemu'ěl, "Do not
look at his appearance or at the height of
his stature, because I have refused him, for
not as man sees, for man looks at the eyes,
but יהוה looks at the heart."
8 Then Yishai called Aḇinaḏaḇ, and
made him pass before Shemu'ěl. And he
said, "Neither has יהוה chosen this one."
9 Next Yishai made Shammah pass by.
And he said, "Neither has יהוה chosen this
one."
10 And Yishai made seven of his sons pass
before Shemu'ěl. And Shemu'ěl said to
Yishai, "יהוה has not chosen these."
11 And Shemu'ěl said to Yishai, "Are
these all the young men?" And he said,
"There remains yet the youngest, and see,
he is tending the sheep." And Shemu'ěl
said to Yishai, "Send and bring him, for we
do not turn round till he comes here."
12 And he sent and brought him in. And
he was ruddy, with bright eyes, and handsome. And יהוה said, "Arise, anoint him,
for this is the one!"
13 And Shemu'ěl took the horn of oil and
anointed him in the midst of his brothers.
And the Spirit of יהוה came upon Dawiḏ
from that day and onwards. And Shemu'ěl
arose and went to Ramah.
14 And the Spirit of יהוה turned aside
from Sha'ul, and an evil spirit from יהוה
troubled him.
15 And the servants of Sha'ul said to him,
"Look, now, an evil spirit from Elohim is
troubling you.
16 "Please, let our master command your
servants who are before you, to seek out a
man who is a skilled player on the lyre.
And it shall be that when the evil spirit
from Elohim is upon you, that he shall
play with his hand, and you be well."
17 And Sha'ul said to his servants, "Please
get me a man that plays well, and bring
him to me."
18 And one of the servants answered and
said, "Look, I have seen a son of Yishai the
Běyth Leḥemite, who knows how to play, a
brave one, and a man of battle, and skilled
in words, and a handsome man. And יהוה
is with him."
19 So Sha'ul sent messengers to Yishai,
and said, "Send me your son Dawiḏ, who
is with the sheep."
20 And Yishai took a donkey loaded with
bread, and a skin of wine, and a young
goat, and sent them by his son Dawiḏ to
Sha'ul.
21 And Dawiḏ came to Sha'ul and stood
before him. And he loved him greatly, and
he became his armour-bearer.
22 Sha'ul therefore sent to Yishai, saying,
"Please let Dawiḏ stand before me, for he
has found favour in my eyes."
23 And it came to be, whenever the *evil*
spirit from Elohim was upon Sha'ul, that
Dawiḏ would take a lyre and play it with
his hand. Then Sha'ul would become
refreshed and well, and the evil spirit
would leave him.

17 And the Philistines had gathered
their armies for battle, and came
together at Soḵoh, which belongs to Yehuḏah, and encamped between Soḵoh and
Azěqah, in Ephes Dammim.
2 And Sha'ul and the men of Yisra'ěl
were gathered and encamped in the Valley
of Ělah, and drew up in battle array to meet
the Philistines.
3 And the Philistines stood on a mountain
on one side, and Yisra'ěl stood on a mountain on the other side, with the valley
between them.
4 Then a champion came out from the
camp of the Philistines, named Golyath,
from Gath, whose height was six cubits
and a span.
5 And a bronze helmet was on his head,
and he was armed with a scaled armour,
and the weight of the coat was five thousand sheqels of bronze,
6 and bronze shin guards on his legs and
a bronze spear between his shoulders.
7 And the wood of his spear was like a
weaver's beam, and his iron spearhead
weighed six hundred sheqels, and a shield-
bearer went before him.
8 And he stood and shouted to the armies
of Yisra'ěl, and said to them, "Why have

you come out to line up for battle? Am I
not a Philistine, and you the servants of
Sha'ul? Choose a man for yourselves, and
let him come down to me.
9 "If he is able to fight with me, and shall
strike me, then we shall be your servants.
But if I overcome him and shall strike him,
then you shall be our servants and serve
us."
10 Then the Philistine said, "This day I
shall reproach the armies of Yisra'ěl. Give
me a man, and let us fight together."
11 And Sha'ul and all Yisra'ěl heard these
words of the Philistine, and they were
broken down and in great fear.
12 Now Dawiḏ was the son of that
Ephrathite of Běyth Leḥem in Yehuḏah,
whose name was Yishai, and he had eight
sons, and in the days of Sha'ul the man
was old among men.
13 And the three oldest sons of Yishai
went, they had gone to follow Sha'ul to the
battle, and the names of his three sons who
went to the battle were Eliyaḇ the first-
born, and his second Aḇinaḏaḇ, and the
third Shammah.
14 And Dawiḏ was the youngest. And the
three oldest followed Sha'ul,
15 but Dawiḏ went and returned from
Sha'ul to feed his father's sheep at Běyth
Leḥem.
16 And for forty days the Philistine drew
near, morning and evening, and took his
stand.
17 Then Yishai said to his son Dawiḏ,
"Please take to your brothers an ěphah of
this dried grain and these ten loaves, and
run to your brothers at the camp.
18 "And take these ten cheeses to the
commander of the thousand, and see how
your brothers are, and bring back news of
them."
19 For Sha'ul and they and all the men of
Yisra'ěl were in the Valley of Ělah, fighting with the Philistines.
20 And Dawiḏ rose up early in the morning, and left the sheep with a herdsman,
and took and went as Yishai had commanded him. And he came to the camp as
the army was going out to the fight, and
they shouted for the battle.
21 And Yisra'ěl and the Philistines drew
up in battle array, army against army.
22 And Dawiḏ left his supplies in the hand
of the keeper of the supplies, and ran to the
army, and came and greeted his brothers.
23 And he was speaking with them and
saw the champion, the Philistine of Gath,
Golyath by name, coming up from the
armies of the Philistines. And he spoke
according to the same words, and Dawiḏ
heard.
24 And all the men of Yisra'ěl, when they
saw the man, ran from him and were in
great fear.
25 And the men of Yisra'ěl said, "Have
you seen this man who has come up? For
he has come up to reproach Yisra'ěl. And it
shall be that the man who strikes him, the
sovereign is going to enrich him with great
riches, and give him his daughter, and give
his father's house exemption in Yisra'ěl."
26 And Dawiḏ spoke to the men who
stood by him, saying, "What shall be done
for the man who strikes this Philistine and
shall take away reproach from Yisra'ěl?
For who is this uncircumcised Philistine,
that he should reproach the armies of the
living Elohim?"
27 And the people answered him according to this word, saying, "This is what is
done for the man who strikes him."
28 And Eliyaḇ his oldest brother heard
when he spoke to the men. And Eliyaḇ's
displeasure burned against Dawiḏ, and he
said, "Why did you come down here? And
with whom have you left those few sheep
in the wilderness? I know your pride and
the evil of your heart, for you have come
down to see the battle."
29 And Dawiḏ said, "Now what have I
done? Was it not but a word?"
30 And he turned around from him toward
another and said the same word. And these
people answered him a word like the first
word.
31 And when the words which Dawiḏ
spoke were heard, they reported them to
Sha'ul, and he sent for him.
32 And Dawiḏ said to Sha'ul, "Let no
man's heart fail because of him, your servant is going, and shall fight with this

Philistine."
33 And Sha'ul said to Dawiḏ, "You are not
able to go against this Philistine to fight
with him, for you are but a youth, and he a
man of battle from his youth."
34 Then Dawiḏ said to Sha'ul, "Your
servant has been tending sheep for his
father, and when a lion or a bear came and
took a lamb out of the flock,
35 I went out after it and struck it, and
rescued *it* from its mouth. And when it
rose against me, I took hold of *it* by its
beard, and struck it and killed it.
36 "Your servant has stricken both lion
and bear. And this uncircumcised
Philistine shall be like one of them, seeing
he has reproached the armies of the living
Elohim."
37 And Dawiḏ said, "יהוה, who delivered
me from the paw of the lion and from the
paw of the bear, He does deliver me from
the hand of this Philistine." And Sha'ul
said to Dawiḏ, "Go, and יהוה be with
you!"
38 And Sha'ul dressed Dawiḏ with his
garments, and he put a bronze helmet on
his head, and put a coat of armour on him.
39 And Dawiḏ girded his sword over his
garments, and began to go, but he had not
tried them. Then Dawiḏ said to Sha'ul, "I
am not able to go with these, for I have not
tried them." So Dawiḏ took them off.
40 And he took his staff in his hand, and
chose for himself five smooth stones from
the wadi, and put them in a shepherd's bag,
in a pouch which he had, and his sling was
in his hand. And he drew near to the
Philistine.
41 And the Philistine came, and began
drawing near to Dawiḏ, and the man who
bore the shield went before him.
42 And when the Philistine looked about
and saw Dawiḏ, he despised him, for he
was a youth, and ruddy and of handsome
appearance.
43 And the Philistine said to Dawiḏ, "Am
I a dog, that you come to me with sticks?"
And the Philistine cursed Dawiḏ by his
mighty ones.
44 And the Philistine said to Dawiḏ,
"Come to me, and I give your flesh to the
birds of the heavens and the beasts of
the field!"
45 But Dawiḏ said to the Philistine, "You
come to me with a sword, and with a spear,
and with a javelin. But I come to you in the
Name of יהוה of hosts, the Elohim of the
armies of Yisra'ěl, whom you have
reproached.
46 "This day יהוה shall deliver you into
my hand, and I shall strike you and take
your head from you, and give the carcasses
of the camp of the Philistines today to the
birds of the heavens and the wild beasts of
the earth, so that all the earth know that
Elohim is for Yisra'ěl,
47 and all this assembly know that יהוה
does not save with sword and spear, for the
battle belongs to יהוה, and He shall give
you into our hands."
48 And it came to be, when the Philistine
arose and came and drew near to meet
Dawiḏ, that Dawiḏ hurried and ran toward
the army to meet the Philistine.
49 And Dawiḏ put his hand in his bag and
took out a stone, and slung it and struck the
Philistine on his forehead, so that the stone
sank into his forehead, and he fell on his
face to the ground.
50 Thus Dawiḏ was stronger than the
Philistine with a sling and a stone, and
struck the Philistine and killed him, and
there was no sword in the hand of Dawiḏ.
51 Then Dawiḏ ran and stood over the
Philistine, and took his sword and drew it
out of its sheath and killed him, and cut off
his head with it. And when the Philistines
saw that their champion was dead, they
fled.
52 And the men of Yisra'ěl and Yehuḏah
arose and shouted, and pursued the
Philistines as far as the entrance of the
valley and to the gates of Eqron. And the
wounded of the Philistines fell along the
way to Sha'arayim, even as far as Gath
and Eqron.
53 Then the children of Yisra'ěl turned
back from chasing the Philistines, and they
plundered their camps.
54 And Dawiḏ took the head of the
Philistine and brought it to Yerushalayim,
but he put his weapons in his tent.

55 And when Sha'ul saw Dawiḏ going out against the Philistine, he said to Aḇněr, the commander of the army, "Aḇněr, whose son is this youth?" And Aḇněr said, "As your being lives, O sovereign, I do not know."

56 And the sovereign said, "Ask whose son this young man is."

57 And when Dawiḏ returned from the striking of the Philistine, Aḇněr took him and brought him before Sha'ul with the head of the Philistine in his hand.

58 And Sha'ul said to him, "Whose son are you, young man?" And Dawiḏ said, "The son of your servant Yishai the Běyth Leḥemite."

18 And it came to be, when he had ended speaking to Sha'ul, that the being of Yehonathan was knit to the being of Dawiḏ, and Yehonathan loved him as his own being.

2 And Sha'ul took him that day, and would not let him return to his father's house any more.

3 And Yehonathan and Dawiḏ made a covenant, because he loved him as his own being.

4 And Yehonathan took off the robe that was on him and gave it to Dawiḏ, and his garments, even to his sword and his bow and his girdle.

5 And Dawiḏ went out wherever Sha'ul sent him. He acted wisely, and Sha'ul set him over the men of battle, and it was right in the eyes of all the people and also in the eyes of Sha'ul's servants.

6 And it came to be, as they came in, as Dawiḏ was returning from striking the Philistine, that the women came out from all the cities of Yisra'ěl, singing and dancing, to meet Sha'ul the sovereign with tambourines, with joy, and with musical instruments.

7 And the women sang as they danced, and said, "Sha'ul struck his thousands, and Dawiḏ his ten thousands."

8 And Sha'ul was very wroth, and this matter was evil in his eyes, and he said, "To Dawiḏ they have given ten thousands, and to me they have given thousands. So what more for him, except the reign?"

9 And from that day on Sha'ul eyed Dawiḏ.

10 And it came to be on the next day that an evil spirit from Elohim came upon Sha'ul, and he prophesied inside the house, while Dawiḏ was playing *the lyre* with his hand, as usual. And the spear was in the hand of Sha'ul.

11 Then Sha'ul hurled the spear, for he said, "Let me strike Dawiḏ, even to the wall." But twice Dawiḏ withdrew from his presence.

12 And Sha'ul was afraid of Dawiḏ, because יהוה was with him, but from Sha'ul He had turned away.

13 Sha'ul therefore removed him from his presence, and made him his commander over a thousand. And he went out and came in before the people.

14 And Dawiḏ was acting wisely in all his ways, and יהוה was with him.

15 And Sha'ul saw that he was acting very wisely, and was afraid of him.

16 But all Yisra'ěl and Yehuḏah loved Dawiḏ, as he went out and came in before them.

17 And Sha'ul said to Dawiḏ, "See my older daughter Měraḇ! I give her to you as a wife. Only be brave for me, and fight the battles of יהוה." For Sha'ul thought, "Let not my hand be against him, but let the hand of the Philistines be against him."

18 And Dawiḏ said to Sha'ul, "Who am I, and what is my life or my father's clan in Yisra'ěl, that I should be son-in-law to the sovereign?"

19 And it came to be at the time when Měraḇ, Sha'ul's daughter, should have been given to Dawiḏ, that she was given to Aḏri'ěl the Meḥolathite as a wife.

20 And Miḵal, Sha'ul's daughter, loved Dawiḏ. And they told Sha'ul, and the matter was right in his eyes.

21 And Sha'ul said, "Let me give her to him and let her be a snare to him, and the hand of the Philistines be against him." So Sha'ul said to Dawiḏ a second time, "Become my son-in-law today."

22 And Sha'ul commanded his servants, "Speak to Dawiḏ gently, and say, 'See, the

sovereign has delighted in you, and all his servants have loved you. And now, be the sovereign's son-in-law!' "

23 And the servants of Sha'ul spoke those words in the hearing of Dawiḏ. And Dawiḏ said, "Does it seem to you a small matter to be a sovereign's son-in-law, seeing I am a poor man, and lightly esteemed?"

24 And the servants of Sha'ul told him, saying, "Dawiḏ has spoken according to these words."

25 And Sha'ul said, "Say to Dawiḏ, 'The sovereign has no delight in any payment for the bride but one hundred foreskins of the Philistines, to take vengeance on the sovereign's enemies.' " But Sha'ul intended to have Dawiḏ fall by the hand of the Philistines.

26 And his servants declared these words to Dawiḏ, and it pleased Dawiḏ well to become the sovereign's son-in-law. And the days had not expired,

27 and Dawiḏ arose and went, he and his men, and struck two hundred men of the Philistines. And Dawiḏ brought their foreskins, and they set them before the sovereign, to become the sovereign's son-in-law. And Sha'ul gave him Miḵal his daughter as a wife.

28 And Sha'ul saw and knew that יהוה was with Dawiḏ, and Miḵal daughter of Sha'ul did love him.

29 So then Sha'ul was still more afraid of Dawiḏ. And Sha'ul came to be an enemy of Dawiḏ all the days.

30 And the princes of the Philistines went out *to fight*. And it came to be, whenever they went out, that Dawiḏ acted more wisely than all the servants of Sha'ul, so that his name came to be very precious.

19 And Sha'ul spoke to Yonathan his son and to all his servants, to put Dawiḏ to death. But Yehonathan, Sha'ul's son, delighted much in Dawiḏ,

2 and Yehonathan declared to Dawiḏ, saying, "My father Sha'ul seeks to put you to death. And now, please be on your guard until morning, and dwell in secrecy, and hide.

3 "And I myself shall go out and stand beside my father in the field where you are, and speak with my father about you, and shall see, and shall let you know."

4 And Yehonathan spoke well of Dawiḏ to Sha'ul his father, and said to him, "Let not the sovereign sin against his servant, against Dawiḏ, because he has not sinned against you, and because his works have been very good toward you.

5 "For he took his life in his hands and struck the Philistine, and יהוה wrought a great deliverance for all Yisra'ĕl. You saw it and rejoiced. Why then do you sin against innocent blood, to put Dawiḏ to death without cause?"

6 And Sha'ul listened to the voice of Yehonathan, and Sha'ul swore, "As יהוה lives, he does not die."

7 Yehonathan then called Dawiḏ, and Yehonathan told him all these words. So Yehonathan brought Dawiḏ to Sha'ul, and he was in his presence as before.

8 And there was fighting again, and Dawiḏ went out and fought with the Philistines, and struck them, a great smiting, and they fled before him.

9 And an evil spirit from יהוה came upon Sha'ul as he sat in his house with his spear in his hand. And Dawiḏ was playing *the lyre* with his hand,

10 and Sha'ul sought to strike the spear through Dawiḏ, and into the wall, but he slipped away from the presence of Sha'ul, so he struck the spear into the wall. And Dawiḏ fled and escaped that night.

11 And Sha'ul sent messengers to Dawiḏ's house to watch him and to put him to death in the morning. And Miḵal, Dawiḏ's wife, informed him, saying, "If you do not save your life tonight, tomorrow you are put to death."

12 So Miḵal let Dawiḏ down through a window, and he went and fled and escaped.

13 And Miḵal took the household idol and laid it in the bed, and put a cover of goats' *hair* for his head, and covered it with a garment.

14 And when Sha'ul sent messengers to take Dawiḏ, she said, "He is sick."

15 And Sha'ul sent the messengers back to see Dawiḏ, saying, "Bring him up to me in

the bed to put him to death."
16 And the messengers came in and saw
the household idol in the bed, with a cover
of goats' *hair* for his head.
17 Sha'ul then said to Miḵal, "Why have
you deceived me like this, and sent my
enemy away, so that he escaped?" And
Miḵal answered Sha'ul, "He said to me,
'Let me go, why should I put you to
death?' "
18 Now Dawiḏ fled and escaped, and went
to Shemu'ěl at Ramah, and told him all
that Sha'ul had done to him. And he and
Shemu'ěl went and dwelt in Nawith.
19 And it was reported to Sha'ul, saying,
"See, Dawiḏ is in Nawith in Ramah!"
20 And Sha'ul sent messengers to take
Dawiḏ. And they saw the assembly of the
prophets prophesying, and Shemu'ěl
standing as leader over them, and the Spirit
of Elohim came upon the messengers of
Sha'ul, and they also prophesied.
21 And when Sha'ul was told, he sent
other messengers, and they prophesied
likewise. So Sha'ul sent messengers again,
the third time, and they prophesied also.
22 Then he himself went to Ramah, and
came to the great well that is at Seḵu. And
he asked, and said, "Where are Shemu'ěl
and Dawiḏ?" And one said, "There in
Nawith in Ramah."
23 So he went there to Nawith in Ramah.
And the Spirit of Elohim was upon him
too, and he went on and prophesied until
he came to Nawith in Ramah.
24 And he also stripped off his garments
and prophesied before Shemu'ěl, and lay
down naked all that day and all that night.
Therefore they say, "Is Sha'ul also among
the prophets?"

20 And Dawiḏ fled from Nawith in
Ramah, and went and said to
Yehonathan, "What have I done? What is
my crookedness, and what is my sin before
your father, that he seeks my life?"
2 And Yehonathan said to him, "Far be it!
You are not going to die! See, my father
does no big matter nor small matter
without disclosing it to me. And why
should my father hide this matter from me?
It is not so!"
3 But Dawiḏ swore again, and said,
"Your father knows well that I have found
favour in your eyes, and he says, 'Do not
let Yehonathan know this, lest he be
grieved.' But truly, as יהוה lives and as
your being lives, there is but a step
between me and death."
4 And Yehonathan said to Dawiḏ,
"Whatever your desire is, I do it for you."
5 And Dawiḏ said to Yehonathan, "See,
tomorrow is the new *moon*, and I ought to
sit with the sovereign to eat. But let me go,
and I shall hide in the field until the third
day at evening.
6 "If your father misses me at all, then
you shall say, 'Dawiḏ earnestly asked my
permission to run over to Běyth Leḥem,
his city, for a yearly slaughtering is made
there for all the clan.'
7 "If he says thus, 'It is well,' your servant is safe. But if he is very displeased,
then know that he has resolved to do evil.
8 "And you shall show loving-commitment to your servant, for you have brought
your servant into a covenant of יהוה with
you. And if there is crookedness in me, put
me to death yourself, for why should you
bring me to your father?"
9 And Yehonathan said, "Far be it from
you! For if I knew with certainty that my
father has resolved that evil is to come
upon you, then would I not make it known
to you?"
10 And Dawiḏ said to Yehonathan, "Who
would make it known to me, or what if
your father answers you sharply?"
11 And Yehonathan said to Dawiḏ,
"Come, and let us go out into the field."
And they both went out into the field.
12 And Yehonathan said to Dawiḏ, "יהוה
Elohim of Yisra'ěl *be witness*! When I
search out my father sometime tomorrow,
or the third day, and see if there is good
toward Dawiḏ, and I do not send to you
or disclose it to you,
13 so let יהוה do so and much more to
Yehonathan. And if it pleases my father to
do you evil, then I shall disclose it to you
and send you away, and you shall go in
peace. And יהוה be with you as He has

been with my father.
14 “But show me the loving-commitment
of יהוה, not only while I still live, so that I
do not die,
15 and do not cut off your loving-commitment from my house forever, no, not when
יהוה has cut off every one of the enemies
of Dawiḏ from the face of the earth.”
16 And Yehonathan made a covenant with
the house of Dawiḏ, *saying*, “יהוה shall
require it at the hand of the enemies of
Dawiḏ.”
17 And Yehonathan again made Dawiḏ
swear, because he loved him, for he loved
him as he loved his own being.
18 So Yehonathan said to him, “Tomorrow
is the new *moon*, and you shall be missed,
because your seat shall be empty.
19 “And on the third day, go down quickly
and you shall come to the place where you
hid on the day of the deed, and shall
remain by the stone Ĕtsel.
20 “And let me shoot three arrows to the
side of it as though shooting at a target,
21 and see, I shall send the youth, saying,
‘Go, find the arrows.’ If I expressly say to
the youth, ‘Look, the arrows are on this
side of you, get them and come,’ then, as
יהוה lives, there is safety for you and no
concern.
22 “But if I say thus to the youth, ‘Look,
the arrows are beyond you,’ go your way,
for יהוה has sent you away.
23 “And as for the word which you and I
have spoken of, see, יהוה is between you
and me forever.”
24 And Dawiḏ hid in the field. And when
the new *moon* came, the sovereign sat
down by the food to eat.
25 And the sovereign sat on his seat, as at
other times, on a seat by the wall, with
Yehonathan standing, and Aḇnĕr sitting by
Sha’ul’s side, but the place of Dawiḏ was
empty.
26 But Sha’ul spoke not *a word* that day,
for he thought, “It is an accident; he is not
clean, for he has not been cleansed.”
27 And it came to be the next day, the second *day* of the new *moon*, that Dawiḏ’s
place was empty. And Sha’ul said to
Yehonathan his son, “Why has the son of
Yishai not come to eat, either yesterday or
today?”
28 And Yehonathan answered Sha’ul,
“Dawiḏ earnestly asked my permission *to
go* to Bĕyth Leḥem.
29 “And he said, ‘Please let me go, for our
clan has a slaughtering in the city, and my
brother has commanded me to be there.
And now, if I have found favour in your
eyes, please let me get away and see my
brothers.’ That is why he has not come to
the sovereign’s table.”
30 Then the displeasure of Sha’ul burned
against Yehonathan, and he said to him,
“You son of a perverse, rebellious woman!
Do I not know that you have chosen the
son of Yishai to your own shame and to the
shame of your mother’s nakedness?
31 “For as long as the son of Yishai lives
on the earth, you shall not be established,
you and your reign. And now, send and
bring him to me, for he is a son of death.”
32 And Yehonathan answered Sha’ul his
father, and said to him, “Why should he
be put to death? What has he done?”
33 At that, Sha’ul hurled a spear at him to
smite him. Then Yehonathan knew that his
father had resolved to put Dawiḏ to death.
34 And Yehonathan rose up from the table
in the heat of displeasure, and ate no food
the second day of the new *moon*, for he
was grieved for Dawiḏ, because his father
put him to shame.
35 And it came to be, in the morning, that
Yehonathan went out into the field at the
time appointed with Dawiḏ, and a small
youth was with him.
36 And he said to the youth, “Now run,
find the arrows which I shoot.” As the
youth ran, he shot an arrow beyond him.
37 And when the youth came to the place
where the arrow was which Yehonathan
had shot, Yehonathan called out after the
youth and said, “Is not the arrow beyond
you?”
38 And Yehonathan shouted after the
youth, “Make haste, hurry, do not stand
still!” And Yehonathan’s youth picked up
the arrows and came to his master.
39 But the youth knew not a speck. Only
Yehonathan and Dawiḏ knew of the matter.

40 Then Yehonathan gave his weapons to the youth and said to him, “Go, take them to the city.”

41 And as soon as the youth had gone, Dawiḏ rose up from the south side, and fell on his face to the ground, and bowed down three times. And they kissed one another. And they wept together, but Dawiḏ more so.

42 And Yehonathan said to Dawiḏ, “Go in peace, since we have both sworn in the Name of יהוה, saying, ‘יהוה is between you and me, and between your seed and my seed, forever.’ ” Then he arose and left, and Yehonathan went into the city.

21 And Dawiḏ came to Noḇ, to Aḥimeleḵ the priest. And Aḥimeleḵ trembled when he met Dawiḏ, and asked him, “Why are you alone, and no one is with you?”

2 And Dawiḏ said to Aḥimeleḵ the priest, “The sovereign has commanded me a word, and said to me, ‘Let no one know whatever of the word about which I send you, and which I have commanded you.’ And I have directed my young men to such and such a place.

3 “And now, what do you have on hand? Give five loaves into my hand, or whatever is found.”

4 And the priest answered Dawiḏ and said, “There is no ordinary bread on hand, but there is set-apart bread – provided the young men have kept themselves from women.”

5 And Dawiḏ answered the priest, and said to him, “Truly, women have been kept from us about three days since I came out. And the vessels of the young men are set-apart, and it is an ordinary mission, and also, it was set-apart in the vessel today.”

6 Then the priest gave him set-apart *bread*, for there was no bread there except the showbread which had been taken from before יהוה, in order to put hot bread in on the day it is taken away.

7 Now one of the servants of Sha’ul was there that day, detained before יהוה. And his name was Do’ěḡ, an Eḏomite, the chief of the herdsmen who belonged to Sha’ul.

8 And Dawiḏ said to Aḥimeleḵ, “Is there not here on hand a spear or a sword? For I have brought neither my sword nor my weapons with me, because the matter of the sovereign was urgent.”

9 And the priest said, “The sword of Golyath the Philistine, whom you struck in the Valley of Ělah. See, it is wrapped in a garment behind the shoulder garment. If you would take it, take it. For there is none other except this one here.” And Dawiḏ said, “There is none like it, give it to me.”

10 And Dawiḏ rose and fled that day from before Sha’ul, and went to Aḵish the sovereign of Gath.

11 But the servants of Aḵish said to him, “Is this not Dawiḏ the sovereign of the land? Did they not sing of him to each other in dances, saying, ‘Sha’ul struck his thousands, and Dawiḏ his ten thousands’?”

12 And Dawiḏ took these words to heart, and was very much afraid of Aḵish the sovereign of Gath,

13 and changed his behaviour before them, and feigned madness in their hands, and scratched on the doors of the gate, and let his saliva run down on his beard.

14 Then Aḵish said to his servants, “Look, you see the man is acting like a madman. Why do you bring him to me?

15 “Am I short of madmen, that you have brought this one to act as a madman near me? Should this one come into my house?”

22 And Dawiḏ went from there and escaped to the cave of Aḏullam. And his brothers and all his father’s house heard it, and went down to him there.

2 And everyone who was in distress, everyone who was in debt, and everyone bitter in being gathered to him. So he became head over them, and there were about four hundred men with him.

3 And Dawiḏ went from there to Mitspeh of Mo’aḇ and said to the sovereign of Mo’aḇ, “Please let my father and mother come here with you, till I know what Elohim does for me.”

4 And he left them with the sovereign of Mo’aḇ, and they dwelt with him all the time that Dawiḏ was in the stronghold.

5 And the prophet Gaḏ said to Dawiḏ,
"Do not remain in the stronghold. Leave,
and go to the land of Yehuḏah." So Dawiḏ
left and went into the Ḥereth woods.
6 And Sha'ul heard that Dawiḏ and the
men who were with him had been discovered, while Sha'ul was in Giḇ'ah, sitting
under a tamarisk tree in Ramah, with his
spear in his hand, and all his servants
standing about him.
7 And Sha'ul said to his servants who
were standing around him, "Hear now, you
Binyamites! Does the son of Yishai give
every one of you fields and vineyards, and
make you all commanders of thousands
and commanders of hundreds?
8 "For all of you have conspired against
me, and there is no one who reveals to me
that my son has made a covenant with the
son of Yishai. And there is not one of you
who is grieved for me or reveals to me that
my son has stirred up my servant against
me, to lie in wait, as it is this day."
9 And Do'ēḡ the Eḏomite, who was set
over the servants of Sha'ul, answered and
said, "I saw the son of Yishai going to
Noḇ, to Aḥimeleḵ son of Aḥituḇ.
10 "And he inquired of יהוה for him, gave
him food, and gave him the sword of
Golyath the Philistine."
11 And the sovereign sent someone to call
Aḥimeleḵ the priest, son of Aḥituḇ, and all
his father's house, the priests who were in
Noḇ. And they all came to the sovereign,
12 and Sha'ul said, "Hear now, son of
Aḥituḇ!" And he answered, "Here I am,
my master."
13 And Sha'ul said to him, "Why have
you conspired against me, you and the son
of Yishai, by giving him bread and a
sword, and have inquired of Elohim for
him, to rise against me, to lie in wait, as it
is this day?"
14 And Aḥimeleḵ answered the sovereign
and said, "And who among all your servants is so trustworthy as Dawiḏ, who is
the sovereign's son-in-law, and has turned
aside to your counsel, and is esteemed in
your house?
15 "Have I today begun to inquire of
Elohim for him? Far be it from me! Let not
the sovereign lay a case against his
servant, or against any in the house of my
father. For your servant knew not of all
this, little or much."
16 And the sovereign said, "You shall
certainly die, Aḥimeleḵ, you and all your
father's house!"
17 The sovereign then said to the guards
who stood about him, "Turn and put the
priests of יהוה to death, because their hand
also is with Dawiḏ, and because they knew
when he fled and did not reveal it to me."
But the servants of the sovereign would
not lift their hands to come against the
priests of יהוה.
18 And the sovereign said to Do'ēḡ, "You
turn and come against the priests!" So
Do'ēḡ the Eḏomite turned and came
against the priests, and put to death on that
day eighty-five men who wore a linen
shoulder garment.
19 And he struck Noḇ, the city of the
priests, with the edge of the sword, from
men even to women, from children even to
nursing infants, and oxen and donkeys
and sheep, with the edge of the sword.
20 And one of the sons of Aḥimeleḵ son of
Aḥituḇ, named Eḇyathar, escaped and fled
after Dawiḏ.
21 And Eḇyathar reported to Dawiḏ that
Sha'ul had killed the priests of יהוה.
22 And Dawiḏ said to Eḇyathar, "I knew
that day, when Do'ēḡ the Eḏomite was
there, that he would certainly inform
Sha'ul. I am accountable for all the lives of
your father's house.
23 "Remain with me, do not fear. For he
who seeks my life seeks your life, but with
me you are safe."

23 And they informed Dawiḏ, saying,
"See, the Philistines are fighting
against Qe'ilah, and they are plundering
the threshing-floors."
2 So Dawiḏ inquired of יהוה, saying,
"Shall I go and strike these Philistines?"
And יהוה said to Dawiḏ, "Go and smite
the Philistines, and save Qe'ilah."
3 And Dawiḏ's men said to him, "See,
we here in Yehuḏah are afraid. How much
more, then, if we go to Qe'ilah against the

armies of the Philistines?"
4 And Dawiḏ inquired of יהוה once
again. And יהוה answered him and said,
"Arise, go down to Qe'ilah, for I am giving
the Philistines into your hand."
5 So Dawiḏ and his men went to Qe'ilah
and fought with the Philistines, and he led
away their livestock and struck them,
a great smiting. Thus Dawiḏ saved the
inhabitants of Qe'ilah.
6 And it came to be, when Eḇyathar son
of Aḥimeleḵ fled to Dawiḏ at Qe'ilah, that
he went down with a shoulder garment in
his hand.
7 And Sha'ul was informed that Dawiḏ
had gone to Qe'ilah. Then Sha'ul said,
"Elohim has estranged him into my hand,
for he has shut himself in by entering a
town that has gates and bars."
8 And Sha'ul summoned all the people to
battle, to go down to Qe'ilah to besiege
Dawiḏ and his men.
9 And Dawiḏ knew that Sha'ul was
plotting evil against him, and said to
Eḇyathar the priest, "Bring the shoulder
garment here."
10 And Dawiḏ said, "O יהוה Elohim of
Yisra'ěl, Your servant has heard for certain
that Sha'ul seeks to come to Qe'ilah to
destroy the city for my sake.
11 "Are the landowners of Qe'ilah going
to surrender me into his hand? Is Sha'ul
coming down, as Your servant has heard?
O יהוה Elohim of Yisra'ěl, I pray, let Your
servant know." And יהוה said, "He is
coming down."
12 And Dawiḏ said, "Are the landowners
of Qe'ilah going to surrender me and my
men into the hand of Sha'ul?" And יהוה
said, "They are going to surrender you."
13 Then Dawiḏ and his men, about six
hundred, arose and left Qe'ilah and went
wherever they could go. And Sha'ul was
informed that Dawiḏ had escaped from
Qe'ilah, and he ceased to go out.
14 And Dawiḏ remained in the wilderness,
in strongholds, and remained in the hill
country in the Wilderness of Ziph. And
Sha'ul sought him every day, but Elohim
did not give him into his hand.
15 And Dawiḏ saw that Sha'ul had come
out to seek his life while Dawiḏ was in the
Wilderness of Ziph at Ḥoresh.
16 And Yehonathan, Sha'ul's son, arose
and went to Dawiḏ at Ḥoresh and strengthened his hand in Elohim,
17 and said to him, "Do not fear, for the
hand of Sha'ul my father is not going
to find you, and you are to reign over
Yisra'ěl, and I am to be next to you. Even
my father Sha'ul knows that."
18 And they made a covenant before יהוה.
And Dawiḏ remained at Ḥoresh while
Yehonathan went to his own house.
19 And the Ziphites came up to Sha'ul at
Giḇ'ah, saying, "Is Dawiḏ not hiding with
us in strongholds Ḥoresh, in the hill of
Ḥaḵilah, which is on the south of the
wasteland?
20 "And now, O sovereign, by all the
desire of your being, come down, come
down, and our part is to surrender him into
the sovereign's hand."
21 And Sha'ul said, "Blessed are you of
יהוה, for you have sympathy with me.
22 "Please go, prepare yet further and find
out and see the place where his hide-out is,
who has seen him there. For I am told that
he is very cunning.
23 "So look, and learn all about the hiding
places where he hides. And you shall come
back to me with certainty, then I shall go
with you. And it shall be, if he is in the
land, that I shall search for him throughout
all the clans of Yehuḏah."
24 And they rose up and went to Ziph
before Sha'ul, while Dawiḏ and his men
were in the Wilderness of Ma'on, in the
desert plain on the south of the wasteland.
25 And Sha'ul and his men went to seek
him, and they informed Dawiḏ, so he went
down to the rock, and remained in the
Wilderness of Ma'on. And when Sha'ul
heard this, he pursued Dawiḏ in the
Wilderness of Ma'on.
26 And Sha'ul went on one side of the
mountain, and Dawiḏ and his men on the
other side of the mountain. And Dawiḏ
was hurrying to get away from Sha'ul, for
Sha'ul and his men were surrounding
Dawiḏ and his men to take them.
27 Then a messenger came to Sha'ul, say-

ing, "Hurry and come, for the Philistines have invaded the land!"
28 So Sha'ul turned back from pursuing Dawiḏ, and went against the Philistines. Therefore they called that place Sela Hammaḥleqoth.
29 And Dawiḏ went up from there and remained in strongholds at Ěn Geḏi.

24 And it came to be, when Sha'ul had returned from pursuing the Philistines, that it was reported to him, saying, "See, Dawiḏ is in the Wilderness of Ěn Geḏi."
2 So Sha'ul took three thousand chosen men from all Yisra'ěl, and went to seek Dawiḏ and his men on the Rocks of the Wild Goats.
3 And he came to the sheepfolds, on the way, and there was a cave. And Sha'ul went in to relieve himself. Now Dawiḏ and his men were sitting in the sides of the cave.
4 And the men of Dawiḏ said to him, "See, the day of which יהוה said to you, 'See, I am giving your enemy into your hand, and you shall do to him as it seems good to you!' " And Dawiḏ arose and gently cut off a corner of Sha'ul's robe.
5 And it came to be afterward that the heart of Dawiḏ struck him because he had cut the robe of Sha'ul.
6 So he said to his men, "Far be it from me, by יהוה, that I should do this matter to my master, anointed of יהוה, to stretch out my hand against him, for he is the anointed of יהוה."
7 And Dawiḏ dispersed his servants with words, and did not allow them to rise against Sha'ul. And Sha'ul rose up from the cave and went on his way.
8 And afterward Dawiḏ arose and went out of the cave, and called out to Sha'ul, saying, "My master the sovereign!" And when Sha'ul looked behind him, Dawiḏ bowed with his face to the earth, and did obeisance.
9 And Dawiḏ said to Sha'ul, "Why do you listen to the words of men who say, 'See, Dawiḏ seeks to do you evil'?
10 "See, this day your eyes have seen that יהוה gave you today into my hand in the cave, and *one* said to kill you. But my eye pardoned you, and I said, 'I do not stretch out my hand against my master, for he is the anointed of יהוה.'
11 "And my father, see! Yes, see the corner of your robe in my hand! For in that I cut off the corner of your robe, and did not kill you, know and see that there is neither evil nor rebellion in my hand, and I have not sinned against you, while you are hunting my life to take it.
12 "Let יהוה judge between you and me, and let יהוה revenge me on you, but my hand is not against you.
13 "As the proverb of the ancients says, 'Wrong comes from the wrongdoer.' But my hand is not against you.
14 "After whom has the sovereign of Yisra'ěl come out? Whom do you pursue? A dead dog? A flea?
15 "And יהוה shall be judge, and rightly rule between you and me, and see and plead my case, and rightly rule me out of your hand."
16 And it came to be, when Dawiḏ had ended speaking these words to Sha'ul, that Sha'ul said, "Is this your voice, my son Dawiḏ?" So Sha'ul lifted up his voice and wept.
17 And he said to Dawiḏ, "You are more righteous than I, for you have rewarded me with good, whereas I have rewarded you with evil.
18 "And you have shown today how you have done good to me, for when יהוה surrendered me into your hand you did not kill me.
19 "For if a man finds his enemy, shall he let him get away safely? And let יהוה reward you with good for what you have done to me today.
20 "And now look, I know that you shall certainly reign, and that the reign of Yisra'ěl shall be established in your hand.
21 "And now, swear to me by יהוה that you do not cut off my seed after me, nor destroy my name from my father's house."
22 And Dawiḏ swore to Sha'ul. Then Sha'ul went home, and Dawiḏ and his men went up to the stronghold.

25 And Shemu'ěl died, and all
Yisra'ěl gathered and mourned for
him, and buried him at his home in Ramah.
And Dawiḏ arose and went down into the
Wilderness of Paran.
2 Now there was a man in Maʽon and his
work was in Karmel, and the man was very
great. And he had three thousand sheep
and a thousand goats. And he came to be
shearing his sheep in Karmel.
3 And the name of the man was Naḇal,
and the name of his wife Aḇiḡayil. And
she was a woman of good understanding
and beautiful. But the man was hard and
evil in his doings. And he was of Kalěḇ.
4 And Dawiḏ heard in the wilderness that
Naḇal was shearing his sheep.
5 And Dawiḏ sent ten young men, and
Dawiḏ said to the young men, "Go up to
Karmel, and you shall come to Naḇal,
and greet him in my name,
6 and say this, 'Long life and peace to
you! And peace to your house, and peace
to all that you have!
7 'And now, I have heard that you have
shearers. Now your shepherds have been
with us. We did not put them to shame, and
not a speck of theirs was missing all the
days they were in Karmel.
8 'Ask your young men, and let them
inform you. So let *my* young men find
favour in your eyes, for we come on a
good day. Please give whatever comes to
your hand to your servants and to your
son Dawiḏ.' "
9 And the young men of Dawiḏ came and
spoke to Naḇal according to all these
words in the name of Dawiḏ, and waited.
10 But Naḇal answered the servants of
Dawiḏ and said, "Who is Dawiḏ, and who
is the son of Yishai? The servants who are
running away from their masters, have
become many nowadays.
11 "And shall I take my bread and my
water and my meat that I have slaughtered
for my shearers, and give it to men coming
from who knows where?"
12 And the young men of Dawiḏ turned
around on their way and went back, and
came and reported to him all these words.
13 And Dawiḏ said to his men, "Each one
gird on his sword." So they each girded on
his sword, and Dawiḏ also girded on his
sword. And about four hundred men went
with Dawiḏ, and two hundred remained
with the baggage.
14 And one of the young men informed
Aḇiḡayil, the wife of Naḇal, saying, "See,
Dawiḏ has sent messengers from the
wilderness to greet our master, but he
scoffed at them.
15 "But the men were very good to us, and
did not put us to shame, nor did we miss
any *item* all the days we accompanied
them, when we were in the fields.
16 "They were a wall to us both by night
and day, all the days we were with them
tending the sheep.
17 "And now, know and see what you
should do, for evil has been resolved
against our master, and against all his
household, and he is too much of a son of
Beliyaʽal to speak to."
18 Then Aḇiḡayil made haste and took two
hundred loaves, and two skins of wine, and
five sheep made ready, five measures of
roasted grain, and one hundred clusters of
raisins, and two hundred cakes of figs, and
loaded them on donkeys.
19 And she said to her servants, "Pass over
before me. See, I am coming after you."
But she did not inform her husband Naḇal.
20 And it came to be, as she rode on the
donkey, that she went down under cover of
the hill, and there were Dawiḏ and his
men, coming down toward her, and she
met them.
21 And Dawiḏ had said, "Only in vain
have I protected all that this one has in the
wilderness, so that not a speck was missing
of all that belongs to him. And he has
repaid me evil for good.
22 "Let Elohim do so, and more also, to
the enemies of Dawiḏ, if I leave one male
of all who belong to him by morning
light."
23 And Aḇiḡayil saw Dawiḏ, and she
hastened to come down from the donkey,
and fell on her face before Dawiḏ, and
bowed down to the ground,
24 and fell at his feet and said, "On me,
my master, let this crookedness be on me!

And please let your female servant speak in your ears, and hear the words of your female servant.

25 "Please, let not my master regard this man of Beliya'al, Naḇal. For as his name is, so is he: Naḇal is his name, and folly is with him. But I, your female servant, did not see the young men of my master whom you sent.

26 "And now my master, as יהוה lives and as your being lives, since יהוה has withheld you from coming to bloodshed and from avenging yourself with your own hand, now then, let your enemies be as Naḇal, even those seeking evil against my master.

27 "And now this present which your female servant has brought to my master, let it be given to the young men who follow my master.

28 "Please forgive the transgression of your female servant. For יהוה is certainly making a steadfast house for my master, because my master fights the battles of יהוה, and evil is not found in you in *all* your days.

29 "And if a man rises to pursue you and seek your life, and the life of my master has been bound in the bundle of the living with יהוה your Elohim, then the lives of your enemies He shall sling out, as from the pocket of a sling.

30 "And it shall be, when יהוה has done for my master according to all the good that He has spoken concerning you, and has commanded you to be ruler over Yisra'ěl,

31 do not let this be a staggering and stumbling of heart to my master, that you have shed blood without cause, or that my master has saved himself. And when יהוה has done good to my master, then remember your female servant."

32 And Dawiḏ said to Aḇiḡayil, "Blessed be יהוה Elohim of Yisra'ěl, who sent you to meet me today!

33 "And blessed is your good taste, and blessed are you, because you have kept me this day from coming to bloodshed and from avenging myself with my own hand.

34 "Nevertheless, as יהוה Elohim of Yisra'ěl lives, who has kept me back from doing evil to you, if you had not hurried and come to meet me, not a male would have been left to Naḇal by break of day, for certain."

35 And Dawiḏ received from her hand what she had brought him, and said to her, "Go up in peace to your house. See, I have listened to your voice and have accepted your face."

36 And Aḇiḡayil went to Naḇal, and see, he was at a feast in his house, like the feast of a sovereign. And Naḇal's heart was glad within him, and he was exceedingly drunk. So she told him not a word, little or much, until morning light.

37 And it came to be, in the morning, when the wine had gone from Naḇal, and his wife had told him these matters, that his heart died within him, and he became like a stone.

38 And it came to be in about ten days, that יהוה smote Naḇal, and he died.

39 And Dawiḏ heard that Naḇal was dead, and he said, "Blessed be יהוה, who has pleaded the cause of my reproach from the hand of Naḇal, and has kept His servant from evil! For יהוה has returned the evil of Naḇal on his own head." And Dawiḏ sent and spoke to Aḇiḡayil, to take her as his wife.

40 And when the servants of Dawiḏ had come to Aḇiḡayil at Karmel, they spoke to her saying, "Dawiḏ sent us to you, to ask you to become his wife."

41 And she arose, bowed her face to the earth, and said, "Here is your female servant, a servant to wash the feet of the servants of my master."

42 And Aḇiḡayil hurried and rose, and rode on a donkey, with five of her female attendants. And she followed the messengers of Dawiḏ, and became his wife.

43 Dawiḏ had also taken Aḥino'am of Yizre'ěl, and so both of them were his wives.

44 But Sha'ul had given Miḵal his daughter, Dawiḏ's wife, to Palti son of Layish, who was from Galliym.

26 And the Ziphites came to Sha'ul at Giḇ'ah, saying, "Is not Dawiḏ hiding himself in the hill of Ḥaḵilah, overlooking the wasteland?"

2 And Sha'ul rose up and went down to the Wilderness of Ziph, and with him three thousand chosen men of Yisra'ěl, to seek Dawiḏ in the Wilderness of Ziph.

3 And Sha'ul encamped in the hill of Ḥaḵilah, overlooking the wasteland, by the way, while Dawiḏ was dwelling in the wilderness, and he saw that Sha'ul came after him into the wilderness.

4 And Dawiḏ sent out spies, and learned that Sha'ul had indeed come.

5 And Dawiḏ rose up and came to the place where Sha'ul had encamped. And Dawiḏ saw the place where Sha'ul lay, and Aḇněr son of Něr, the commander of his army. And Sha'ul was lying within the enclosure, with the people encamped all around him.

6 And Dawiḏ spoke up and said to Aḥimeleḵ the Ḥittite and to Aḇishai son of Tseruyah, brother of Yo'aḇ, saying, "Who does go down with me to Sha'ul in the camp?" And Aḇishai said, "I, I go down with you."

7 And Dawiḏ and Aḇishai came to the people by night and saw Sha'ul lying asleep within the camp, with his spear stuck in the ground by his head, and Aḇněr and the people lay all around him.

8 And Aḇishai said to Dawiḏ, "Elohim has surrendered your enemy into your hand this day. And now, please, let me strike him at once with the spear, right into the earth, and not a second time!"

9 But Dawiḏ said to Aḇishai, "Do not destroy him, for who shall stretch out his hand against the anointed of יהוה, and be guiltless?"

10 Dawiḏ also said, "As יהוה lives, except יהוה does smite him, or his day come that he shall die, or he shall go out to battle and perish,

11 far be it from me, by יהוה, that I stretch out my hand against the anointed of יהוה. And now, please take the spear and the jug of water that are by his head, and let us go."

12 So Dawiḏ took the spear and the jug of water by Sha'ul's head, and they went away. And no man saw it or knew it or awoke, for they were all asleep, because a deep sleep from יהוה had fallen on them.

13 And Dawiḏ passed over to the other side, and stood on the top of a hill far away, a great distance being between them.

14 And Dawiḏ called out to the people and to Aḇněr son of Něr, saying, "Do you not answer, Aḇněr?" And Aḇněr answered and said, "Who are you, calling out to the sovereign?"

15 And Dawiḏ said to Aḇněr, "Are you not a man? And who is like you in Yisra'ěl? Why then have you not guarded your master the sovereign? For one of the people came in to destroy your master the sovereign.

16 "What you have done is not good. As יהוה lives, you are worthy to die, because you have not guarded your master, the anointed of יהוה. And now see where the sovereign's spear is, and the jug of water that was by his head."

17 And Sha'ul recognised Dawiḏ's voice, and said, "Is that your voice, my son Dawiḏ?" And Dawiḏ said, "It is my voice, my master, O sovereign."

18 And he said, "Why is this that my master is pursuing his servant? For what have I done, or what evil is in my hand?

19 "And now, please, let my master the sovereign hear the words of his servant: If יהוה has moved you against me, let Him accept an offering. But if it is the children of men, then they are cursed before יהוה, for they have driven me out today that I should not join myself to the inheritance of יהוה, saying, 'Go, serve other mighty ones.'

20 "And now, do not let my blood fall to the earth before the face of יהוה. For the sovereign of Yisra'ěl has come out to seek a flea, as when one hunts a partridge in the mountains."

21 And Sha'ul said, "I have sinned. Come back, my son Dawiḏ. For no more am I going to do evil to you, because my life was precious in your eyes today. See, I have acted foolishly, and have greatly

strayed."
22 And Dawiḏ answered and said, "See,
the sovereign's spear! And let one of the
young men come over and get it.
23 "And let יהוה reward every man for his
righteousness and his trustworthiness, for
this day יהוה gave you into my hand, but I
would not stretch out my hand against
the anointed of יהוה.
24 "And see, as your life has been valued
in my eyes today, so let my life be valued
in the eyes of יהוה, and let Him deliver me
out of all distress."
25 And Sha'ul said to Dawiḏ, "Blessed are
you, my son Dawiḏ, achieving much, and
indeed prevailing!" Then Dawiḏ went on
his way, and Sha'ul returned to his place.

27 And Dawiḏ said in his heart, "Now
I shall perish by the hand of
Sha'ul, some day. There is naught better
for me than to escape to the land of the
Philistines. Then Sha'ul shall give up
searching for me any longer in any part of
Yisra'ĕl, and I shall escape out of his
hand."
2 So Dawiḏ rose up and passed over with
the six hundred men who were with him to
Aḵish son of Maʿoḵ, sovereign of Gath.
3 And Dawiḏ dwelt with Aḵish at Gath,
he and his men, each man with his household – Dawiḏ with his two wives,
Aḥinoʿam the Yizreʿĕlitess, and Aḇiḡayil
the Karmelitess, Naḇal's widow.
4 And it was reported to Sha'ul that
Dawiḏ had fled to Gath, so he sought him
no more.
5 And Dawiḏ said to Aḵish, "If I have
now found favour in your eyes, let them
give me a place in some town in the country, to dwell there. For why should your
servant dwell in the royal city with you?"
6 And Aḵish gave him Tsiqlaḡ that day.
That is why Tsiqlaḡ has belonged to the
sovereigns of Yehuḏah to this day.
7 And the time that Dawiḏ dwelt in the
country of the Philistines came to be a year
and four new *moons*.
8 And Dawiḏ and his men went up and
raided the Geshurites, and the Girzites, and
the Amalĕqites. For those nations were the
inhabitants of the land from of old, as you
go to Shur, even as far as the land of
Mitsrayim.
9 And when Dawiḏ had stricken the land,
he left neither man nor woman alive, but
took away sheep, and cattle, and donkeys,
and camels, and garments, and returned
and came to Aḵish.
10 And Aḵish would say, "Where have
you made a raid today?" And Dawiḏ
would say, "Against the South of Yehuḏah,
or against the South of the Yeraḥme'ĕlites,
or against the South of the Qĕynites."
11 Dawiḏ did not keep alive man nor
woman, to bring news to Gath, saying,
"Lest they inform against us, saying, 'Thus
Dawiḏ did.' " And this was his practice all
the days that he dwelt in the country of
the Philistines.
12 And Aḵish trusted Dawiḏ, saying *to
himself*, "He has indeed made himself a
stench to his people in Yisra'ĕl, and has
become my servant forever."

28 And it came to be in those days
that the Philistines gathered their
armies for battle, to fight with Yisra'ĕl.
And Aḵish said to Dawiḏ, "You know, of
course, that you are to go out with me in
the army, you and your men."
2 And Dawiḏ said to Aḵish, "Very well,
you shall know what your servant should
do." And Aḵish said to Dawiḏ, "Very well,
I make you one of my chief guardians forever."
3 And Shemu'ĕl had died, and all Yisra'ĕl had mourned for him and buried him
in Ramah, in his own city. And Sha'ul had
put away the mediums and the spiritists
from the land.
4 And the Philistines were gathered, and
came and encamped at Shunĕm. And
Sha'ul gathered all Yisra'ĕl, and they
encamped at Gilboa.
5 And when Sha'ul saw the army of the
Philistines, he was afraid, and his heart
trembled greatly.
6 And Sha'ul inquired of יהוה, but יהוה
did not answer him, either by dreams or by
Urim or by the prophets.
7 Sha'ul then said to his servants, "Find

me a woman who is a medium, to go to her
and inquire of her." And his servants said
to him, "Look, there is a woman who is
a medium at Ěn Dor."
8 And Sha'ul disguised himself and put
on other garments, and went, he and two
men with him. And they came to the
woman by night. And he said, "Please
divine for me, and bring up for me the one
I shall name."
9 But the woman said to him, "Look, you
know what Sha'ul has done, how he has
cut off the mediums and the spiritists from
the land. Why then do you lay a snare for
my life, to put me to death?"
10 And Sha'ul swore to her by יהוה,
saying, "As יהוה lives, no punishment
comes upon you for this matter."
11 And the woman said, "Whom do I
bring up for you?" So he said, "Bring up
Shemu'ěl for me."
12 And when the woman saw Shemu'ěl,
she cried out with a loud voice. And the
woman spoke to Sha'ul, saying, "Why
have you deceived me? You yourself are
Sha'ul!"
13 And the sovereign said to her, "Do not
be afraid. What did you see?" And the
woman said to Sha'ul, "I saw a spirit
coming up out of the earth."
14 And he said to her, "What is his form?"
And she said, "An old man is coming up,
and he is covered with a mantle." And
Sha'ul knew that it was Shemu'ěl, and he
bowed with his face to the ground and
did obeisance.
15 And Shemu'ěl said to Sha'ul, "Why
have you disturbed me by bringing me
up?" And Sha'ul answered, "I am deeply
distressed, for the Philistines are fighting
against me, and Elohim has turned aside
from me and does not answer me any
more, neither by prophets nor by dreams.
So I have called you, to reveal to me what
I should do."
16 Then Shemu'ěl said, "And why do you
ask me, seeing יהוה has turned aside from
you and has become your enemy?
17 "And יהוה has done for Himself as He
spoke by me. For יהוה has torn the reign
out of your hand and given it to your
neighbour, to Dawiḏ.
18 "Because you did not obey the voice of
יהוה nor execute His burning wrath upon
Amalěq, therefore יהוה has done this
matter to you today.
19 "Further, יהוה also gives Yisra'ěl with
you into the hand of the Philistines. And
tomorrow you and your sons are with me.
יהוה also gives the army of Yisra'ěl into
the hand of the Philistines."
20 And immediately Sha'ul fell on the
ground, his complete length, and greatly
feared because of the words of Shemu'ěl.
And there was no strength in him, for he
had eaten no food all day or all night.
21 And the woman came to Sha'ul and
saw that he had been greatly disturbed, and
said to him, "See, your female servant has
obeyed your voice, and I have put my life
in my hands and have listened to the words
which you spoke to me.
22 "And now, please listen to the voice of
your female servant too, and let me set a
piece of bread before you. And eat, so that
you have strength when you go on your
way."
23 But he refused and said, "I am not
going to eat." But his servants, together
with the woman, urged him. And he
listened to their voice. So he rose from the
ground and sat on the bed.
24 And the woman had a fatted calf in the
house, and she quickly slaughtered it. And
she took flour and kneaded it, and baked
unleavened bread from it.
25 And she brought it before Sha'ul and
his servants. And they ate, and rose up and
went away that night.

29
And the Philistines gathered all
their armies at Aphěq, while Yisra'ěl encamped by a fountain which is in
Yizre'ěl.
2 And the princes of the Philistines were
passing on by hundreds and by thousands,
and Dawiḏ and his men were passing on in
the rear with Aḵish.
3 And the princes of the Philistines said,
"Who are these Hebrews?" And Aḵish
said to the princes of the Philistines, "Is
this not Dawiḏ, the servant of Sha'ul

sovereign of Yisra'ĕl, who has been with me these days, or these years? And to this day I have found no *evil* in him since he came over."

4 But the princes of the Philistines were wroth with him, and the princes of the Philistines said to him, "Send the man back, let him return to the place which you have appointed for him, and do not let him go down with us to battle, lest in the battle he become our adversary. For with what could he appease his master, if not with the heads of these men?

5 "Is this not Dawiḏ, of whom they sang to each other in dances, saying, 'Sha'ul struck his thousands, and Dawiḏ his ten thousands'?"

6 And Aḵish called Dawiḏ and said to him, "As יהוה lives, you have been straight, and your going out and your coming in with me in the army is good in my eyes. For to this day I have not found evil in you since the day of your coming to me. But in the eyes of the princes you are not good.

7 "And now, return, and go in peace, and do no evil in the eyes of the princes of the Philistines."

8 And Dawiḏ said to Aḵish, "But what have I done? And to this day what have you found in your servant as long as I have been with you, that I should not go and fight against the enemies of my master the sovereign?"

9 But Aḵish answered and said to Dawiḏ, "I know that you are as good in my eyes as a messenger of Elohim, but the princes of the Philistines have said, 'Let him not go up with us to the battle.'

10 "And now, rise early in the morning with your master's servants who have come with you. And as soon as you are up early in the morning and have light, then go."

11 And Dawiḏ and his men rose up early to go in the morning, to return to the land of the Philistines, and the Philistines went up to Yizre'ĕl.

30 And it came to be, when Dawiḏ and his men came to Tsiqlaḡ, on the third day, that the Amalĕqites had invaded the South and Tsiqlaḡ, and struck Tsiqlaḡ and burned it with fire.

2 And they took captive the women and those who were there, from small to great. They did not kill anyone, but they led them away and went their way.

3 And Dawiḏ and his men came to the city and saw it burned with fire, and their wives and their sons and their daughters had been taken captive.

4 And Dawiḏ and the people who were with him lifted up their voices and wept, until they had no more power to weep.

5 And Dawiḏ's two wives, Aḥino'am the Yizre'ĕlitess, and Aḇiḡayil the widow of Naḇal the Karmelite, had been taken captive.

6 And Dawiḏ was greatly distressed, for the people spoke of stoning him, because the being of all the people was grieved, each for his sons and his daughters. But Dawiḏ strengthened himself in יהוה his Elohim.

7 And Dawiḏ said to Eḇyathar the priest, son of Aḥimeleḵ, "Please bring the shoulder garment here to me." So Eḇyathar brought the shoulder garment to Dawiḏ.

8 And Dawiḏ inquired of יהוה, saying, "Do I pursue this band? Do I overtake them?" And He answered him, "Pursue, for you shall certainly overtake them, and certainly rescue."

9 So Dawiḏ went, he and the six hundred men who were with him, and came to the wadi Besor, where a halt was made by those who were left behind,

10 while Dawiḏ pursued, he and four hundred men – for two hundred halted, who were too faint to pass over the wadi Besor.

11 And they found a man in the field, a Mitsrian, and took him to Dawiḏ. And they gave him bread and he ate, and they let him drink water,

12 and gave him a piece of a cake of figs and two clusters of raisins. And when he had eaten, his strength came back to him, for he had not eaten bread nor drunk water for three days and three nights.

13 And Dawiḏ said to him, "To whom do you belong, and where are you from?"

And he said, "I am a young man from
Mitsrayim, servant of an Amalěqite. And
my master left me behind, for I had been
sick three days.
14 "We attacked the south of the
Kerěthites and against that which belongs
to Yehuḏah, and upon the south of Kalěḇ,
and we burned Tsiqlaḡ with fire."
15 And Dawiḏ said to him, "Could you
bring me down to this marauding band?"
And he said, "Swear to me by Elohim that
you neither kill me nor surrender me into
the hands of my master, then I bring you
down to this marauding band."
16 And he brought him down and saw they
were spread out over all the land, eating
and drinking and celebrating, because of
all the great spoil which they had taken
from the land of the Philistines and from
the land of Yehuḏah.
17 And Dawiḏ struck them from twilight
until the evening of the next day. And none
of them escaped, except four hundred
young men who rode on camels and fled.
18 And Dawiḏ rescued all that the
Amalěqites had taken. Dawiḏ also rescued
his two wives.
19 And there was none missing to them,
whether small or great, whether sons or
daughters, or spoil or whatever they had
taken from them. Dawiḏ recovered all.
20 Besides, Dawiḏ captured all the flocks
and herds they had driven before those
livestock, and they said, "This is Dawiḏ's
spoil."
21 And Dawiḏ came to the two hundred
men who were too faint to follow Dawiḏ,
who had also been left at the wadi Besor.
And they went out to meet Dawiḏ and to
meet the people who were with him. And
when Dawiḏ came near the people, he
greeted them.
22 And all the evil and worthless men of
those who went with Dawiḏ answered and
said, "Because they did not go with us, we
do not give them any of the spoil that we
have rescued, except for every man's wife
and children, and let them take them and
go."
23 But Dawiḏ said, "My brothers, do not
do so with what יהוה has given us, who
has protected us and gave into our hand the
band that came against us.
24 "And who would listen to you in this
matter? For as his portion is who goes
down to the battle, so is his portion who
remains with the baggage, they share
alike."
25 And it came to be, from that day
forward, he appointed it for a law and a
right-ruling for Yisra'ěl to this day.
26 And when Dawiḏ came to Tsiqlaḡ, he
sent some of the spoil to the elders of
Yehuḏah, to his friends, saying, "Here is a
present for you from the spoil of the
enemies of יהוה,"
27 to those in Běyth Ěl, and to those in
Ramoth of the South, and to those in Yattir,
28 and to those in Aroʽěr, and to those in
Siphmoth, and to those in Eshtemoa,
29 and to those in Raḵal, and to those in
the cities of the Yeraḥme'ělites, and to
those in the cities of the Qěynites,
30 and to those in Ḥormah, and to those in
Korashan, and to those in Athaḵ,
31 and to those in Ḥeḇron, and to all the
places where Dawiḏ had gone up and
down, he and his men.

31 And the Philistines were fighting
against Yisra'ěl, and the men of
Yisra'ěl fled from before the Philistines,
and fell slain on Mount Gilboa.
2 And the Philistines followed hard after
Sha'ul and his sons. And the Philistines
struck Yehonathan, and Aḇinaḏaḇ, and
Malkishua, sons of Sha'ul.
3 And the battle went hard against
Sha'ul, and the archers hit him, so that
he was severely wounded by the archers.
4 And Sha'ul said to his armour-bearer,
"Draw your sword, and thrust me through
with it, lest these uncircumcised men come
and thrust me through and roll themselves
on me." But his armour-bearer would not,
for he was greatly afraid. So Sha'ul took
the sword and fell on it.
5 And when his armour-bearer saw that
Sha'ul was dead, he also fell on his sword,
and died with him.
6 Thus Sha'ul died, and three of his sons,
and his armour-bearer, also all his men,

together on that day.
7 And they saw – the men of Yisra'ĕl
who were beyond the valley, and those
who were beyond the Yardĕn – that the
men of Yisra'ĕl had fled and that Sha'ul
and his sons were dead. So they forsook
the cities and fled, and the Philistines came
and dwelt in them.
8 And the next day it came to be, when
the Philistines came to strip the slain, that
they found Sha'ul and his three sons fallen
on Mount Gilboa.
9 And they cut off his head and stripped
off his armour, and sent word throughout
the land of the Philistines, to announce it in
the house of their idols and to the people.
10 And they placed his armour in the
house of the Ashtaroth, and they fastened
his body to the wall of Bĕyth Shan.
11 And the inhabitants of Yaḇĕsh Gilʽaḏ
heard what the Philistines had done to
Sha'ul,
12 and all the brave men arose and went
all night, and took the body of Sha'ul and
the bodies of his sons from the wall of
Bĕyth Shan. And they came to Yaḇĕsh and
burned them there.
13 And they took their bones and buried
them under the tamarisk tree at Yaḇĕsh,
and fasted for seven days.

SHEMU'ĔL BĔT

2 SAMUEL

1 And it came to be after the death of
Sha'ul, when Dawiḏ had returned
from striking the Amalĕqites, that Dawiḏ
remained two days in Tsiqlaḡ.
2 And it came to be on the third day, that
see, a man came out of the camp from
Sha'ul with his garments torn and dust on
his head. And it came to be, when he came
to Dawiḏ, that he fell to the ground and did
obeisance.
3 And Dawiḏ said to him, "From where
do you come?" And he said to him, "I have
escaped from the camp of Yisra'ĕl."
4 And Dawiḏ said to him, "What was the
matter? Please inform me." And he said,
"The people have fled from the battle, and
also many of the people have fallen and are
dead, and Sha'ul and Yehonathan his son
are dead too."
5 And Dawiḏ said to the young man who
informed him, "How do you know that
Sha'ul and Yehonathan his son are dead?"
6 And the young man who informed him
said, "By chance I was on Mount Gilboa
and saw Sha'ul leaning on his spear. And
see, the chariots and horsemen followed
hard after him.
7 "And when he looked behind him, he
saw me and called to me, and I answered,
'Here I am.'
8 "And he said to me, 'Who are you?' So
I answered him, 'I am an Amalĕqite.'
9 "And he said to me, 'Please stand over
me and put me to death, for agony has
seized me, but my life is still in me.'
10 "So I stood beside him and put him to
death, for I knew he would not live after he
had fallen. And I took the diadem that was
on his head and the bracelet that was on his
arm, and have brought them here to my
master."
11 And Dawiḏ took hold of his garments
and tore them, and also all the men who
were with him.
12 And they mourned and wept and fasted
until evening for Sha'ul and for Yehonathan his son, and for the people of יהוה
and for the house of Yisra'ĕl, because they
had fallen by the sword.
13 Then Dawiḏ asked the young man who
informed him, "Where are you from?" And
he answered, "I am the son of a sojourner,
an Amalĕqite."
14 And Dawiḏ said to him, "How was it
you were not afraid to stretch out your
hand to destroy the anointed of יהוה?"
15 And Dawiḏ called one of the young
men and said, "Draw near and fall on
him!" And he struck him so that he died.
16 And Dawiḏ said to him, "Your blood is
on your own head, for your own mouth has
witnessed against you, saying, 'I myself
have put to death the anointed of יהוה.' "
17 Then Dawiḏ lamented with this lamentation over Sha'ul and over Yehonathan his
son,
18 and he ordered "The Bow" to be taught
to the children of Yehuḏah. See, it is written in the Book of Yashar:
19 "The splendour of Yisra'ĕl
Is slain on your high places!
How the mighty have fallen!
20 "Declare it not in Gath,
Proclaim it not in the streets of Ashqelon,
Lest the daughters of the Philistines rejoice,
Lest the daughters of the uncircumcised exult.
21 "Mountains of Gilboa!
No dew or rain be upon you,
Nor fields of offerings.
For there the shield of the mighty lay rejected,
The shield of Sha'ul, not anointed with oil.
22 "From the blood of the slain,
From the fat of the mighty,
The bow of Yehonathan did not turn back,

And the sword of Sha'ul did not return
empty.
23 "Sha'ul and Yehonathan were beloved
And pleasant in their lives,
And in their death they were not parted.
They were swifter than eagles,
They were stronger than lions.
24 "Daughters of Yisra'ěl – weep over
Sha'ul,
Who wrapped you in scarlet, with
finery;
Who decked your robes with ornaments
of gold.
25 "How the mighty have fallen
In the midst of the battle!
Yehonathan was slain in your high
places.
26 "I am distressed for you, my brother
Yehonathan.
You have been very pleasant to me.
Your love to me was wondrous,
Surpassing the love of women.
27 "How the mighty have fallen,
And the weapons of battle perish!"

2 And it came to be afterwards that
Dawiḏ inquired of יהוה, saying, "Do I
go up to any of the cities of Yehuḏah?"
And יהוה said to him, "Go up." And
Dawiḏ said, "Where should I go up?" And
He said, "To Ḥeḇron."
2 And Dawiḏ went up there, as well as
his two wives, Aḥino'am the Yizre'ělitess,
and Aḇiḡayil the widow of Naḇal the Karmelite.
3 And Dawiḏ brought up the men who
were with him, each man with his household, and they dwelt in the cities of
Ḥeḇron.
4 And the men of Yehuḏah came, and
anointed Dawiḏ sovereign over the house
of Yehuḏah there. They also reported to
Dawiḏ, saying, "The men of Yaḇěsh Gil'aḏ
are they who buried Sha'ul."
5 Dawiḏ then sent messengers to the men
of Yaḇěsh Gil'aḏ, and said to them, "You
are blessed of יהוה, for you have shown
this loving-commitment to your master, to
Sha'ul, that you buried him.
6 "And now, יהוה show loving-commitment and truth to you, and I am also going
to do you good, because you have done this
deed.
7 "And now, let your hands be strengthened and be brave, for your master Sha'ul
is dead, and also the house of Yehuḏah
has anointed me sovereign over them."
8 But Aḇněr son of Něr, commander
of the army of Sha'ul, took Ishbosheth the
son of Sha'ul, and brought him over to
Maḥanayim,
9 and set him up to reign over Gil'aḏ, and
over the Ashěrites, and over Yizre'ěl, and
over Ephrayim, and over Binyamin, and
over all Yisra'ěl.
10 Ishbosheth, son of Sha'ul, was forty
years old when he began to reign over
Yisra'ěl, and he reigned two years. Only
the house of Yehuḏah followed Dawiḏ.
11 And the time that Dawiḏ was sovereign
in Ḥeḇron over the house of Yehuḏah was
seven years and six new *moons*.
12 And Aḇněr son of Něr, and the servants
of Ishbosheth son of Sha'ul, went out from
Maḥanayim to Giḇ'on.
13 And Yo'aḇ son of Tseruyah, and the
servants of Dawiḏ, went out and met them
by the pool of Giḇ'on. And they sat down,
one on one side of the pool and the other
on the other side of the pool.
14 And Aḇněr said to Yo'aḇ, "Let the
young men now rise and compete before
us." And Yo'aḇ said, "Let them rise."
15 And they rose and went over by
number, twelve from Binyamin, followers
of Ishbosheth son of Sha'ul, and twelve
from the servants of Dawiḏ.
16 And each man took hold of his opponent by the head and *thrust* his sword in his
opponent's side, and they fell down together. So that place was called the Field of
Sharp Swords, which is in Giḇ'on.
17 And the battle was fierce that day, and
Aḇněr and the men of Yisra'ěl were smitten before the servants of Dawiḏ.
18 And there were three sons of Tseruyah
there, Yo'aḇ and Aḇishai and Asah'ěl. And
Asah'ěl was light on his feet, as one of the
gazelles in the field.
19 And Asah'ěl pursued Aḇněr, and in
going he did not turn aside to the right or
to the left from following Aḇněr.

20 And Aḇnĕr looked behind him and said, "Are you Asah'ĕl?" And he answered, "I am."

21 And Aḇnĕr said to him, "Turn aside to your right hand or to your left, and lay hold on one of the young men and take his armour for yourself." But Asah'ĕl would not turn aside from following him.

22 And Aḇnĕr again said to Asah'ĕl, "Turn aside from following me. Why should I strike you to the ground? How then could I face your brother Yo'aḇ?"

23 But he refused to turn aside, and Aḇnĕr struck him with the blunt end of the spear in the stomach, so that the spear came out of his back. And he fell down there and died on the spot. And it came to be that as many as came to the place where Asah'ĕl fell down and died, stood still.

24 And Yo'aḇ and Aḇishai pursued Aḇnĕr. And the sun was going down and they came to the hill of Ammah, which overlooks Giyaḥ by the way to the Wilderness of Giḇʽon.

25 And the children of Binyamin gathered together behind Aḇnĕr and became a single company, and took their stand on top of a hill.

26 And Aḇnĕr called to Yo'aḇ and said, "Should the sword devour forever? Do you not know that it is bitter in the latter end? And when are you going to say to the people to turn back from pursuing their brothers?"

27 And Yo'aḇ said, "As Elohim lives, if you had not spoken, then all the people would have given up pursuing their brothers only the next morning."

28 Yo'aḇ then blew with a shophar, and all the people halted and pursued Yisra'ĕl no further, nor did they fight any more.

29 And Aḇnĕr and his men went on all that night through the desert plain, and passed over the Yardĕn, and went through all Bithron. And they came to Maḥanayim.

30 And Yo'aḇ turned back from pursuing Aḇnĕr. And when he had gathered all the people together, there were missing of Dawiḏ's servants nineteen men and Asah'ĕl.

31 But the servants of Dawiḏ had stricken, of Binyamin and Aḇnĕr's men, three hundred and sixty men who died.

32 And they brought Asah'ĕl and buried him in his father's burial-site, which was in Bĕyth Leḥem. And Yo'aḇ and his men went all night, and they came to Ḥeḇron at daybreak.

3 And the fighting between the house of Sha'ul and the house of Dawiḏ was long drawn out. But Dawiḏ was going on and was strong, and the house of Sha'ul was going on and was weak.

2 And sons were born to Dawiḏ in Ḥeḇron. And his first-born was Amnon by Aḥinoʽam the Yizreʽĕlitess;

3 and his second, Kil'aḇ, by Aḇiḡayil the widow of Naḇal the Karmelite; and the third, Aḇshalom son of Maʽaḵah, the daughter of Talmai, sovereign of Geshur;

4 and the fourth, Aḏoniyah son of Ḥaggith; and the fifth, Shephatyah son of Aḇital;

5 and the sixth, Yithreʽam, by Dawiḏ's wife Eḡlah. These were born to Dawiḏ in Ḥeḇron.

6 And it came to be, while there was fighting between the house of Sha'ul and the house of Dawiḏ, that Aḇnĕr was strengthening himself in the house of Sha'ul.

7 And Sha'ul had a concubine, whose name was Ritspah, daughter of Ayah. And *Ishbosheth* said to Aḇnĕr, "Why have you gone in to my father's concubine?"

8 And Aḇnĕr was very displeased at the words of Ishbosheth, and said, "Am I a dog's head that belongs to Yehuḏah, that I show loving-commitment to the house of Sha'ul your father, to his brothers, and to his friends today, and have not let you fall into the hand of Dawiḏ, that you charge me today with a sin concerning this woman?

9 "Elohim does so to Aḇnĕr, and more also, if I do not do for Dawiḏ as יהוה has sworn to him:

10 to cause the reign to pass over from the house of Sha'ul, and to raise up the throne of Dawiḏ over Yisra'ĕl and over Yehuḏah, from Dan to Be'ĕrsheḇa."

11 And he was unable to answer Aḇnĕr

another word, because he feared him.

12 And Aḇnĕr sent messengers on his behalf to Dawiḏ, saying, "Whose is the land?" saying also, "Make your covenant with me, and see, my hand is with you to bring all Yisra'ĕl to you."

13 And Dawiḏ said, "Good, I make a covenant with you. Only one matter I am asking of you: you do not see my face unless you first bring Miḵal, daughter of Sha'ul, when you come to see my face."

14 Dawiḏ then sent messengers to Ishbosheth son of Sha'ul, saying, "Give me my wife Miḵal, to whom I became engaged for a hundred foreskins of the Philistines."

15 And Ishbosheth sent and took her from her husband, from Palti'ĕl son of Layish.

16 But her husband went with her to Baḥurim, going on and weeping behind her. And Aḇnĕr said to him, "Go, turn back!" And he turned back.

17 And Aḇnĕr had a word with the elders of Yisra'ĕl, saying, "In time past you were seeking for Dawiḏ to be sovereign over you.

18 "And now, do it! For יהוה has spoken of Dawiḏ, saying, 'By the hand of My servant Dawiḏ, I save My people Yisra'ĕl from the hand of the Philistines and the hand of all their enemies.' "

19 And Aḇnĕr also spoke in the hearing of Binyamin. And Aḇnĕr also went to speak in the hearing of Dawiḏ in Ḥeḇron all that seemed good to Yisra'ĕl and all the house of Binyamin.

20 And Aḇnĕr and twenty men with him came to Dawiḏ at Ḥeḇron. And Dawiḏ made a feast for Aḇnĕr and the men who were with him.

21 And Aḇnĕr said to Dawiḏ, "Let me arise and go, and gather all Yisra'ĕl to my master the sovereign, and let them make a covenant with you, and you shall reign over all that your being desires." And Dawiḏ sent Aḇnĕr away, and he went in peace.

22 And see, the servants of Dawiḏ and Yo'aḇ came from a raid and brought much spoil with them. But Aḇnĕr was not with Dawiḏ in Ḥeḇron, for he had sent him away, and he had gone in peace.

23 And Yo'aḇ and all the army that was with him came, and they reported to Yo'aḇ, saying, "Aḇnĕr son of Nĕr came to the sovereign, and he sent him away, and he has gone in peace."

24 And Yo'aḇ went to the sovereign and said, "What have you done? See, Aḇnĕr has come to you! Why is it that you sent him away, and he has already gone?

25 "You know that Aḇnĕr son of Nĕr came to deceive you, to know your going out and your coming in, and to know all that you are doing."

26 Yo'aḇ then left Dawiḏ, and he sent messengers after Aḇnĕr, who brought him back from the well of Sirah. But Dawiḏ did not know it.

27 Thus Aḇnĕr returned to Ḥeḇron, and Yo'aḇ took him aside in the gate to speak with him privately, and there struck him in the stomach, so that he died for the blood of Asah'ĕl his brother.

28 And when Dawiḏ heard it afterwards, he said, "My reign and I are guiltless before יהוה forever of the blood of Aḇnĕr son of Nĕr.

29 "Let it rest on the head of Yo'aḇ and on all his father's house. And let there never fail to be in the house of Yo'aḇ one who has a discharge or is a leper, or who is taking hold of a staff or falls by the sword, or who lacks bread."

30 So Yo'aḇ and Aḇishai his brother killed Aḇnĕr, because he had killed their brother Asah'ĕl at Giḇ'on in the battle.

31 And Dawiḏ said to Yo'aḇ and to all the people who were with him, "Tear your garments, gird yourselves with sackcloth, and mourn for Aḇnĕr." And Sovereign Dawiḏ followed the coffin.

32 And they buried Aḇnĕr in Ḥeḇron. And the sovereign lifted up his voice and wept at the burial-site of Aḇnĕr, and all the people wept.

33 And the sovereign sang a lament over Aḇnĕr and said, "Should Aḇnĕr die as a fool dies?

34 "Your hands were not bound nor your feet put into shackles. As one falls before sons of evil, so you fell." And all the peo-

ple wept over him again.
35 And all the people came to cause
Dawiḏ to eat food while it was still day, but
Dawiḏ swore, saying, "Elohim do so to
me, and more also, if I taste bread or
whatever else till the sun goes down!"
36 And all the people took note of it, and
it was good in their eyes, since whatever
the sovereign did was good in the eyes of
all the people.
37 And all the people and all Yisra'ěl
knew that day that it had not been the
sovereign's intent to kill Aḇněr son of Něr.
38 The sovereign also said to his servants,
"Do you not know that a prince and a great
one has fallen in Yisra'ěl today?
39 "And I am weak today, though anointed
sovereign. And these men, the sons of
Tseruyah, are too harsh for me. Let יהוה
repay the evil-doer according to his evil."

4 And the son of Sha'ul heard that
Aḇněr had died in Ḥeḇron, and he lost
heart, and all Yisra'ěl was troubled.
2 And the son of Sha'ul had two men,
commanders of bands, and the name of one
was Ba'anah and the name of the other
Rěḵaḇ, sons of Rimmon the Be'ěrothite, of
the children of Binyamin. For Be'ěroth
was also reckoned to Binyamin,
3 because the Be'ěrothites fled to Gittayim and have been sojourners there until
this day.
4 Now Yehonathan, son of Sha'ul, had a
son who was lame in his feet. He was five
years old when the news about Sha'ul and
Yehonathan came from Yizre'ěl, and his
nurse took him up and fled. And it came to
be, as she hurried to flee, that he fell and
became lame. And his name was Mephiḇosheth.
5 So the sons of Rimmon the Be'ěrothite,
Rěḵaḇ and Ba'anah, went and came at
about the heat of the day to the house of
Ishbosheth, who was lying on his bed at
noon.
6 And they came into the midst of the
house, to fetch wheat, and they struck him
in the stomach, and Rěḵaḇ and Ba'anah his
brother escaped.
7 Thus they came into the house when he
was lying on his bed in his bedroom, and
they struck him, and slew him, and beheaded him. And they took his head, and went
the way of the desert plain all night,
8 and brought the head of Ishbosheth to
Dawiḏ at Ḥeḇron, and said to the sovereign, "See, the head of Ishbosheth, the son
of Sha'ul your enemy, who sought your
life. So יהוה has given my master the sovereign vengeance on Sha'ul and his seed
this day."
9 And Dawiḏ answered Rěḵaḇ and
Ba'anah his brother, sons of Rimmon the
Be'ěrothite, and said to them, "As יהוה
lives, who has ransomed my life out of all
distress,
10 when someone reported to me, saying,
'See, Sha'ul is dead,' and he was a bearer
of good news in his own eyes, I then took
hold of him and killed him in Tsiqlaḡ,
which was the reward I gave him for his
news.
11 "How much more, when wrong men
have killed a righteous man in his own
house on his bed, should I not now require
his blood at your hand and remove you
from the earth?"
12 And Dawiḏ commanded his young
men, and they killed them, and cut off their
hands and feet, and hanged them by the
pool in Ḥeḇron. And they took the head of
Ishbosheth and buried it in the burial-site
of Aḇněr in Ḥeḇron.

5 And all the tribes of Yisra'ěl came to
Dawiḏ at Ḥeḇron and spoke, saying,
"Look, we are your bone and your flesh.
2 "Formerly, when Sha'ul was sovereign
over us, you were the one who led Yisra'ěl
out and brought them in. And יהוה said to
you, 'Shepherd My people Yisra'ěl, and be
ruler over Yisra'ěl.' "
3 And all the elders of Yisra'ěl came to
the sovereign at Ḥeḇron, and Sovereign
Dawiḏ made a covenant with them at
Ḥeḇron before יהוה. And they anointed
Dawiḏ sovereign over Yisra'ěl.
4 Dawiḏ was thirty years old when he
began to reign, and he reigned forty years.
5 In Ḥeḇron he reigned over Yehuḏah
seven years and six new *moons*, and in

Yerushalayim he reigned thirty-three years
over all Yisra'ěl and Yehuḏah.
6 And the sovereign and his men went to
Yerushalayim against the Yeḇusites, the
inhabitants of the land. And they spoke to
Dawiḏ, saying, "Except you take away the
blind and the lame, you are not going to
come in here," thinking, "Dawiḏ is not
going to come in here."
7 But Dawiḏ captured the stronghold of
Tsiyon, the City of Dawiḏ.
8 And Dawiḏ said on that day, "Anyone
who strikes the Yeḇusites, let him go by the
water-shaft and *take* the lame and the
blind, who are hated by Dawiḏ's being."
That is why they say, "The blind and the
lame do not come into the house."
9 And Dawiḏ dwelt in the stronghold,
and called it the City of Dawiḏ. And
Dawiḏ built all around from the Millo and
inward.
10 And Dawiḏ went on and became great,
and יהוה Elohim of hosts was with him.
11 Now Ḥiram sovereign of Tsor sent messengers to Dawiḏ, and cedar trees, and carpenters and masons. And they built a house
for Dawiḏ.
12 And Dawiḏ knew that יהוה had established him as sovereign over Yisra'ěl, and
that He had exalted His reign, because of
His people Yisra'ěl.
13 And Dawiḏ took more concubines and
wives from Yerushalayim, after he had
come from Ḥeḇron, and more sons and
daughters were born to Dawiḏ.
14 And these were the names of those born
to him in Yerushalayim: Shammua, and
Shoḇaḇ, and Nathan, and Shelomoh,
15 and Yiḇḥar, and Elishua, and Nepheḡ,
and Yaphiya,
16 and Elishama, and Elyaḏa, and
Eliphelet.
17 And the Philistines heard that they had
anointed Dawiḏ sovereign over Yisra'ěl,
and all the Philistines went up to search for
Dawiḏ, but Dawiḏ heard and went down to
the stronghold.
18 And the Philistines came and spread
themselves out in the Valley of Repha'im.
19 And Dawiḏ inquired of יהוה, saying,
"Do I go up against the Philistines? Do
You give them into my hand?" And יהוה
said to Dawiḏ, "Go up, for I shall certainly
give the Philistines into your hand."
20 And Dawiḏ came to Ba'al Peratsim, and
Dawiḏ struck them there. And he said,
"יהוה has broken through my enemies
before me, like a breakthrough of water."
So he called the name of that place Ba'al
Peratsim.
21 And they left their images there, and
Dawiḏ and his men took them away.
22 And the Philistines again came up and
were spread out in the Valley of Repha'im.
23 And when Dawiḏ inquired of יהוה, He
said, "Do not go up, turn around behind
them, and you shall come upon them in
front of the mulberry trees.
24 "And it shall be, when you hear the
sound of stepping in the tops of the mulberry trees, then act promptly, for then
יהוה shall go out before you to strike the
camp of the Philistines."
25 And Dawiḏ did so, as יהוה commanded
him, and smote the Philistines from Geḇa
as far as Gezer.

6 Now Dawiḏ again gathered all the
chosen men of Yisra'ěl, thirty thousand.
2 And Dawiḏ rose up and went with all
the people who were with him from Ba'alě
Yehuḏah, to bring up from there the ark of
Elohim, that is called by the Name, the
Name יהוה of Hosts, who dwells between
the keruḇim.
3 And they placed the ark of Elohim on a
new wagon, and brought it from the house
of Aḇinaḏaḇ, which was on the hill. And
Uzzah and Aḥyo, sons of Aḇinaḏaḇ, were
leading the new wagon.
4 And they brought it from the house of
Aḇinaḏaḇ, which was on the hill, with the
ark of Elohim. And Aḥyo was walking
before the ark.
5 And Dawiḏ and all the house of
Yisra'ěl were dancing before יהוה, with all
instruments of fir wood, and with lyres,
and with harps, and with tambourines, and
with sistrums, and with cymbals.
6 And when they came to the threshing-
floor of Naḵon, Uzzah reached out toward

the ark of Elohim and took hold of it,
for the oxen stumbled.
7 And the wrath of יהוה burned against
Uzzah, and Elohim struck him there for the
fault. And he died there by the ark of
Elohim.
8 And Dawiḏ was displeased because
יהוה had broken out against Uzzah. And he
called the name of the place Perets Uzzah,
until this day.
9 And Dawiḏ was afraid of יהוה on that
day, and said, "How shall the ark of יהוה
come to me?"
10 And Dawiḏ would not move the ark of
יהוה with him into the City of Dawiḏ, but
Dawiḏ turned it aside to the house of
Oḇěḏ-Eḏom the Gittite.
11 And the ark of יהוה remained in the
house of Oḇěḏ-Eḏom the Gittite three new
moons, and יהוה blessed Oḇěḏ-Eḏom and
all his house.
12 And it was reported to Sovereign
Dawiḏ, saying, "יהוה has blessed the
house of Oḇěḏ-Eḏom and all that he has,
because of the ark of Elohim." Dawiḏ then
went and brought up the ark of Elohim
from the house of Oḇěḏ-Eḏom to the City
of Dawiḏ with rejoicing.
13 And it came to be, when those bearing
the ark of יהוה had gone six steps, that he
slaughtered bulls and fatted sheep.
14 And Dawiḏ danced before יהוה with all
his might. And Dawiḏ was wearing a linen
shoulder garment.
15 Thus Dawiḏ and all the house of
Yisra'ěl brought up the ark of יהוה with
shouting and with a voice of a shophar.
16 And it came to be, when the ark of יהוה
came into the City of Dawiḏ, that Miḵal,
daughter of Sha'ul, looked through a window and saw Sovereign Dawiḏ leaping and
dancing before יהוה, and she despised him
in her heart.
17 So they brought the ark of יהוה in, and
set it in its place in the midst of the Tent
that Dawiḏ had pitched for it. And Dawiḏ
brought ascending offerings before יהוה,
and peace offerings.
18 And when Dawiḏ had finished bringing
ascending offerings and peace offerings, he
blessed the people in the Name of יהוה
of hosts.
19 And he apportioned to all the people, to
all the crowd of Yisra'ěl, from man even to
women, to each one a loaf of bread, and a
measure, and a cake of raisins. And all the
people left, each one to his house.
20 And Dawiḏ returned to bless his household, and Miḵal the daughter of Sha'ul
came out to meet Dawiḏ, and said, "How
esteemed was the sovereign of Yisra'ěl
today, uncovering himself today in the eyes
of the female servants of his servants, as
one of the foolish ones shamelessly uncovers himself!"
21 So Dawiḏ said to Miḵal, "Before יהוה,
who chose me instead of your father and
all his house, commanded me to be ruler
over the people of יהוה, over Yisra'ěl, so I
danced before יהוה.
22 "And I shall be even more slight than
this, and shall be humble in my own eyes.
But as for the female servants of whom
you have spoken, by them I am esteemed."
23 And Miḵal the daughter of Sha'ul had
no children to the day of her death.

7 And it came to be when the sovereign
was dwelling in his house, and יהוה
had given him rest from all his enemies all
around,
2 that the sovereign said to Nathan the
prophet, "See now, I am dwelling in a
house of cedar, but the ark of Elohim
dwells within curtains."
3 And Nathan said to the sovereign, "Go,
do all that is in your heart, for יהוה is with
you."
4 And it came to be that night that the
word of יהוה came to Nathan, saying,
5 "Go and say to My servant Dawiḏ,
'Thus said יהוה, "Would you build a house
for Me to dwell in?
6 "For I have not dwelt in a house since
the time that I brought the children of
Yisra'ěl up from Mitsrayim, even to this
day, but have moved about in a Tent and in
a Dwelling Place.
7 "Wherever I have walked with all the
children of Yisra'ěl, have I ever spoken a
word to anyone from the tribes of Yisra'ěl,
whom I commanded to shepherd My

people Yisra’ĕl, saying, ‘Why have you not built Me a house of cedar?’ ” ’

8 “And now, say to My servant Dawiḏ, ‘Thus said יהוה of hosts, “I took you from the pasture, from following the flock, to be ruler over My people, over Yisra’ĕl.

9 “And I have been with you wherever you have gone, and have cut off all your enemies from before you, and have made you a great name, like the name of the great ones who are on the earth.

10 “And I shall appoint a place for My people Yisra’ĕl, and shall plant them, and they shall dwell in a place of their own and no longer be afraid, neither shall the children of wickedness oppress them again, as at the first,

11 even from the day I commanded rulers over My people Yisra’ĕl, and have caused you to rest from all your enemies. And יהוה has declared to you that He would make you a house.

12 “When your days are filled and you rest with your fathers, I shall raise up your seed after you, who comes from your inward parts, and shall establish his reign.

13 “He does build a house for My Name, and I shall establish the throne of his reign forever.

14 “I am to be his Father, and he is My son. If he does perversely, I shall reprove him with the rod of men and with the blows of the sons of men.

15 “But My loving-commitment does not turn aside from him, as I turned it aside from Sha’ul, whom I removed from before you.

16 “And your house and your reign are to be steadfast forever before you – your throne is established forever.” ’ ”

17 According to all these words and according to all this vision, so Nathan spoke to Dawiḏ.

18 And Sovereign Dawiḏ went in and sat before יהוה and he said, “Who am I, O Master יהוה? And what is my house, that You have brought me this far?

19 “And yet this was a small matter in Your eyes, O Master יהוה. And You have also spoken of Your servant’s house for a great while to come. And is this the teaching of man, O Master יהוה?

20 “And what more does Dawiḏ say to You? For You, Master יהוה, know Your servant.

21 “Because of Your word, and according to Your own heart, You have done all this greatness, to make it known to Your servant.

22 “You are great indeed, O Master יהוה. For there is none like You, and there is no Elohim but You, according to all that we have heard with our ears.

23 “And who is like Your people, like Yisra’ĕl, the one nation on the earth whom Elohim went to ransom for Himself as a people, to make for Himself a Name, and to do for You greatness, and awesome deeds for Your land before Your people, whom You ransomed for Yourself from Mitsrayim, from the nations and their mighty ones?

24 “And You have established for Yourself Your people Yisra’ĕl as Your own people forever, and You, יהוה, have become their Elohim.

25 “And now, O יהוה Elohim, the word which You have spoken concerning Your servant and concerning his house, establish it forever and do as You have said.

26 “And let Your Name be made great forever, saying, ‘יהוה of hosts is the Elohim over Yisra’ĕl.’ And let the house of Your servant Dawiḏ be established before You.

27 “For You, O יהוה of hosts, the Elohim of Yisra’ĕl, have revealed this to Your servant, saying, ‘I build you a house.’ Therefore Your servant has taken heart to pray this prayer to You.

28 “And now, O Master יהוה, You are Elohim, and Your words are true, and You have spoken this goodness to Your servant.

29 “And now, be pleased to bless the house of Your servant, to be before You, forever. For You, O Master יהוה, have spoken it, and with Your blessing let the house of Your servant be blessed forever.”

8 And after this it came to be that Dawiḏ struck the Philistines and humbled them. And Dawiḏ took the bridle of the

mother city out of the hand of the Philistines.

2 He also struck Mo’aḇ, and measured them off with a line, causing them to lie down on the earth. With two lines he measured off those to be put to death, and with one complete line those to be kept alive. And the Mo’aḇites became Dawiḏ’s servants, and brought presents.

3 Dawiḏ also struck Haḏaḏezer son of Reḥoḇ, sovereign of Tsoḇah, as he went to restore his rule at the River Euphrates.

4 And Dawiḏ captured from him one thousand and seven hundred horsemen, and twenty thousand foot soldiers. And Dawiḏ destroyed all the chariots, but he left of them a hundred chariots.

5 And the Arameans of Dammeseq came to help Haḏaḏezer sovereign of Tsoḇah, and Dawiḏ struck twenty-two thousand of the Arameans.

6 Then Dawiḏ put watch-posts in Aram of Dammeseq. And the Arameans became Dawiḏ’s servants, and brought presents. And יהוה saved Dawiḏ wherever he went.

7 And Dawiḏ took the shields of gold which were on the servants of Haḏaḏezer, and brought them to Yerushalayim.

8 And from Betaḥ and from Bĕrothai, cities of Haḏaḏezer, Sovereign Dawiḏ took very much bronze.

9 And To‘i sovereign of Ḥamath heard that Dawiḏ had stricken all the army of Haḏaḏezer,

10 so To‘i sent Yoram his son to Sovereign Dawiḏ, to ask peace of him and bless him, because he had fought against Haḏaḏezer and struck him, for Haḏaḏezer had battles with To‘i. And *Yoram* brought with him objects of silver, and objects of gold, and objects of bronze.

11 Sovereign Dawiḏ also set these apart to יהוה, along with the silver and gold that he had set apart from all the nations which he had humbled:

12 from Aram, and from Mo’aḇ, and from the children of Ammon, and from the Philistines, and from Amalĕq, and from the spoil of Haḏaḏezer son of Reḥoḇ, sovereign of Tsoḇah.

13 And Dawiḏ made a name *for himself* when he returned from striking eighteen thousand Arameans in the Valley of Salt.

14 And he put watch-posts in Eḏom. Throughout all Eḏom he put watch-posts, and all the Eḏomites became Dawiḏ’s servants. And יהוה saved Dawiḏ wherever he went.

15 And Dawiḏ reigned over all Yisra’ĕl, and Dawiḏ was doing right-ruling and righteousness to all his people.

16 And Yo’aḇ son of Tseruyah was over the army, and Yehoshaphat son of Aḥiluḏ was recorder,

17 and Tsaḏoq son of Aḥituḇ and Aḥimeleḵ son of Eḇyathar were the priests, and Serayah was the scribe,

18 and Benayahu son of Yehoyaḏa was over both the Kerĕthites and the Pelĕthites, and Dawiḏ’s sons were priests.

9 And Dawiḏ said, “Is there still anyone who is left of the house of Sha’ul, that I might show him loving-commitment, because of Yehonathan?”

2 And the house of Sha’ul had a servant whose name was Tsiḇa. And they had called him to Dawiḏ, and the sovereign said to him, “Are you Tsiḇa?” And he said, “Your servant!”

3 And the sovereign said, “Is there not still someone of the house of Sha’ul, so that I show him the loving-commitment of Elohim?” And Tsiḇa said to the sovereign, “There is still a son of Yehonathan, lame in his feet.”

4 So the sovereign said to him, “Where is he?” And Tsiḇa said to the sovereign, “See, he is in the house of Maḵir son of Ammi’ĕl, in Lo Ḏeḇar.”

5 And Sovereign Dawiḏ sent and brought him out of the house of Maḵir son of Ammi’ĕl, from Lo Ḏeḇar.

6 And Mephiḇosheth son of Yehonathan, son of Sha’ul, came to Dawiḏ, and fell on his face and did obeisance. And Dawiḏ said, “Mephiḇosheth!” And he answered, “Here is your servant!”

7 Dawiḏ then said to him, “Do not fear, for I shall certainly show you loving-commitment because of Yehonathan your father, and shall return to you all the land

of Sha'ul your grandfather, and let you eat
bread at my table continually."
8 And he bowed himself and said, "What
is your servant, that you should turn to
such a dead dog as I?"
9 And the sovereign called Tsiḇa servant
of Sha'ul, and said to him, "I have given to
your master's son all that belonged to
Sha'ul and to all his house.
10 "And you and your sons and your
servants, shall work the land for him, and
you shall bring in *its yield*, and your master's son shall have food to eat. But let
Mephiḇosheth your master's son eat bread
at my table always." And Tsiḇa had fifteen
sons and twenty servants.
11 And Tsiḇa said to the sovereign,
"According to all that my master the sovereign has commanded his servant, so your
servant does." "As for Mephiḇosheth,"
said the sovereign, "he shall eat at my table
as one of the sons of the sovereign."
12 And Mephiḇosheth had a young son
whose name was Miḵa. And all who dwelt
in the house of Tsiḇa were servants of
Mephiḇosheth.
13 And Mephiḇosheth was dwelling in
Yerushalayim, for he ate continually at the
sovereign's table. And he was lame in
both his feet.

10

And after this it came to be that the
sovereign of the children of
Ammon died, and Ḥanun his son reigned
in his place.
2 And Dawiḏ said, "Let me show loving-
commitment to Ḥanun son of Naḥash, as
his father showed loving-commitment to
me." So Dawiḏ sent by the hand of his servants to comfort him concerning his father.
And when Dawiḏ's servants came into the
land of the children of Ammon,
3 the chiefs of the children of Ammon
said to Ḥanun their master, "Is Dawiḏ
esteeming your father in your eyes in that
he has sent comforters to you? Has Dawiḏ
not rather sent his servants to you to search
the city, and to spy it out, and to overthrow
it?"
4 So Ḥanun took Dawiḏ's servants and
shaved off half of their beards, and cut off
their garments in the middle, as far as their
buttocks, and sent them away.
5 And they informed Dawiḏ, and he sent
to meet them, because the men were greatly ashamed. And the sovereign said, "Wait
at Yeriḥo until your beards have grown,
and then return."
6 And when the children of Ammon saw
that they had become a stench to Dawiḏ,
the children of Ammon sent and hired
Arameans of Běyth Reḥoḇ and Arameans
of Tsoḇa, twenty thousand foot soldiers,
and the sovereign of Ma'aḵah, one thousand men, and men of Toḇ, twelve thousand men.
7 And Dawiḏ heard, and sent Yo'aḇ and
the entire army, the mighty men.
8 And the children of Ammon came out
and put themselves in battle array at the
entrance of the gate. And the Arameans of
Tsoḇa, and Reḥoḇ, and men of Toḇ, and
Ma'aḵah were by themselves in the field.
9 And Yo'aḇ saw that the battle line was
against him before and behind, and he
chose out of all the chosen men of Yisra'ěl
and put them in battle array against the
Arameans.
10 And the rest of the people he gave
under the hand of Aḇishai his brother, and
he put them in battle array against the
children of Ammon.
11 And he said, "If the Arameans are too
strong for me, then you shall help me. But
if the children of Ammon are too strong for
you, then I shall come and help you.
12 "Be strong, and let us show strength for
our people and for the cities of our Elohim,
and let יהוה do what is good in His eyes."
13 And Yo'aḇ drew near, and the people
with him, to battle against Aram, and they
fled before him.
14 And when the children of Ammon saw
that the Arameans were fleeing, they also
fled before Aḇishai, and went into the city.
And Yo'aḇ returned from the children of
Ammon and came to Yerushalayim.
15 And Aram saw that they were smitten
before Yisra'ěl, and they gathered together,
16 and Haḏaḏezer sent and brought out
the Arameans who were beyond the River,
and they came to Ḥělam. And Shoḇaḵ the

commander of the army of Haḏaḏezer went before them.

17 And it was reported to Dawiḏ, and he gathered all Yisra'ěl, and passed over the Yarděn, and came to Ḥělam. And Aram set themselves in battle array against Dawiḏ and they fought with him.

18 And Aram fled before Yisra'ěl, and Dawiḏ killed seven hundred charioteers and forty thousand horsemen of Aram, and he struck Shoḇaḵ, commander of their army, who died there.

19 And all the sovereigns, the servants of Haḏaḏezer, saw that they were smitten by Yisra'ěl, and made peace with Yisra'ěl, and served them. And the Arameans were afraid to help the children of Ammon any more.

11 And it came to be at the turn of the year, at the time sovereigns go out *to battle*, that Dawiḏ sent Yo'aḇ and his servants with him, and all Yisra'ěl, and they destroyed the children of Ammon and besieged Rabbah. But Dawiḏ remained at Yerushalayim.

2 And it came to be, at evening time, that Dawiḏ rose up from his bed and walked about on the roof of the sovereign's house. And from the roof he saw a woman bathing, and the woman was very good to look at.

3 And Dawiḏ sent and asked about the woman, and one said, "Is this not Bathsheḇa, the daughter of Eliyam, the wife of Uriyah the Ḥittite?"

4 And Dawiḏ sent messengers, to fetch her. And she came to him, and he lay with her – for she was cleansing herself from her uncleanness – and she returned to her house.

5 And the woman conceived, and sent and informed Dawiḏ, and said, "I am pregnant."

6 Then Dawiḏ sent to Yo'aḇ, "Send Uriyah the Ḥittite to me." And Yo'aḇ sent Uriyah to Dawiḏ.

7 And Uriyah came to him, and Dawiḏ asked how Yo'aḇ was doing, and how the people were doing, and how the fighting was going.

8 And Dawiḏ said to Uriyah, "Go down to your house and wash your feet." And Uriyah went out from the sovereign's house, and a gift from the sovereign followed him.

9 But Uriyah lay down at the door of the sovereign's house with all the servants of his master, and did not go down to his house.

10 And they informed Dawiḏ, saying, "Uriyah did not go down to his house," So Dawiḏ said to Uriyah, "Did you not come from a journey? Why did you not go down to your house?"

11 And Uriyah said to Dawiḏ, "The ark and Yisra'ěl and Yehuḏah are dwelling in booths, and my master Yo'aḇ and the servants of my master are encamped in the open fields. And I, should I go to my house to eat and to drink, and to lie with my wife? As you live, and as your being lives, let me not do this."

12 And Dawiḏ said to Uriyah, "Remain here today also, and tomorrow I let you go." So Uriyah remained in Yerushalayim, that day and the next.

13 And Dawiḏ called him, and he ate and drank before him, and he made him drunk. And at evening he went out to lie on his bed with the servants of his master, but he did not go down to his house.

14 And it came to be in the morning that Dawiḏ wrote a letter to Yo'aḇ and sent it by the hand of Uriyah.

15 And he wrote in the letter, saying, "Set Uriyah in the front of the toughest[a] battle, and you shall turn away from him, and he shall be stricken and shall die."

16 And it came to be, as Yo'aḇ watched the city, that he appointed Uriyah to the place where he knew there were brave men.

17 And the men of the city came out and fought with Yo'aḇ. And some of the people of the servants of Dawiḏ fell. And Uriyah the Ḥittite also died.

18 And Yo'aḇ sent and reported to Dawiḏ

11a Lit. strong.

all the events of the battle,

19 and commanded the messenger, saying, "When you have finished reporting all the events of the battle to the sovereign,

20 then it shall be, if the sovereign's wrath rises and he says to you, 'Why did you go so near to the city when you fought? Did you not know that they would shoot from the wall?

21 'Who struck Aḇimeleḵ the son of Yerubbesheth? Was it not a woman who threw an upper millstone on him from the wall, so that he died in Thĕḇĕts? Why did you go near the wall?' Then you shall say, 'Your servant Uriyah the Ḥittite is also dead.' "

22 And the messenger went, and came and reported to Dawiḏ all with which Yo'aḇ had sent him.

23 And the messenger said to Dawiḏ, "The men have been mighty against us and came out to us in the field, but we drove them back as far as the entrance of the gate.

24 "And the archers shot from the wall at your servants. And some of the sovereign's servants are dead, and your servant Uriyah the Ḥittite is also dead."

25 And Dawiḏ said to the messenger, "Say to Yo'aḇ, 'Do not let this matter be evil in your eyes, for the sword devours one as well as another. Strengthen your attack against the city, and overthrow it.' And strengthen him."

26 And the wife of Uriyah heard that Uriyah her husband was dead, and she lamented for her husband.

27 And when her mourning was over, Dawiḏ sent and brought her to his house, and she became his wife and bore him a son. But the deed that Dawiḏ had done was evil in the eyes of יהוה.

12 Then יהוה sent Nathan to Dawiḏ. And he came to him, and said to him, "There were two men in one city, one rich and the other poor.

2 "The rich one had flocks and herds, very many.

3 "But the poor one had only one little ewe lamb which he had bought and kept alive. And it grew up with him and with his children together. It ate of his own food and drank from his own cup and lay in his bosom. And it was like a daughter to him.

4 "And a traveller came to the rich man, who refused to take from his own flock and from his own herd to prepare one for the wayfaring man who had come to him, but he took the poor man's lamb and prepared it for the man who had come to him."

5 And the wrath of Dawiḏ burned greatly against the man, and he said to Nathan, "As יהוה lives, the man who has done this is a son of death!

6 "Also, he has to repay fourfold for the lamb, because he did this deed and because he had no compassion."

7 Then Nathan said to Dawiḏ, "You are the man! Thus said יהוה Elohim of Yisra'ĕl, 'I anointed you sovereign over Yisra'ĕl, and I delivered you from the hand of Sha'ul.

8 'And I gave you your master's house and your master's wives into your bosom, and gave you the house of Yisra'ĕl and Yehuḏah. And if that were not enough, I also would have given you much more!

9 'Why have you despised the Word of יהוה to do evil in His eyes? You have struck Uriyah the Ḥittite with the sword, and his wife you took to be your wife, and you have killed him with the sword of the children of Ammon.

10 'And now, the sword does not turn aside from your house, because you have despised Me, and have taken the wife of Uriyah the Ḥittite to be your wife.'

11 "Thus said יהוה, 'See, I am raising up evil against you, from your own house, and shall take your wives before your eyes and give them to your neighbour, and he shall lie with your wives in the sight of this sun.

12 'For you did it in secret, but I shall do this deed before all Yisra'ĕl, and before the sun.' "

13 And Dawiḏ said to Nathan, "I have sinned against יהוה." And Nathan said to Dawiḏ, "Also, יהוה has put away your sin, you shall not die.

14 "However, because by this deed you have greatly scorned יהוה, the child also

who is born to you shall certainly die."
15 And Nathan went to his house, and יהוה smote the child that Uriyah's wife had born to Dawiḏ, and he was sick.
16 And Dawiḏ sought Elohim for the child, and Dawiḏ fasted and went in and spent all night lying on the ground.
17 So the elders of his house stood up over him, to raise him up from the earth. But he would not, nor did he eat food with them.
18 And on the seventh day it came to be that the child died. And the servants of Dawiḏ were afraid to inform him that the child was dead, for they said, "Look, while the child was still alive, we spoke to him, and he would not listen to our voice. And how do we say to him that the child is dead? Then he shall do evil!"
19 And Dawiḏ saw that his servants were whispering, and Dawiḏ perceived that the child was dead. Then Dawiḏ said to his servants, "Is the child dead?" And they said, "He is dead."
20 Dawiḏ then rose up from the ground, and washed and anointed himself, and changed his garments. And he went into the House of יהוה and bowed himself, then came to his own house, and asked, and they set food before him, so he ate.
21 And his servants said to him, "What is this that you have done? You fasted and wept because of the living child, but when the child died, you rose up and ate food."
22 And he said, "While the child was alive I fasted and wept, for I said, 'Who knows whether יהוה shows favour unto me, and the child shall live?'
23 "But now he is dead, why should I fast? Am I able to bring him back again? I am going to him, but he does not return to me."
24 And Dawiḏ comforted Bathsheḇa his wife, and went in to her and lay with her. So she bore a son, and he called his name Shelomoh. And יהוה loved him,
25 and sent by the hand of Nathan the prophet, and called his name Yeḏiḏeyah, because of יהוה.
26 And Yo'aḇ fought against Rabbah of the children of Ammon, and captured the royal city.
27 And Yo'aḇ sent messengers to Dawiḏ, and said, "I have fought against Rabbah, and I have captured the city's water supply.
28 "And now, gather the rest of the people together and encamp against the city and capture it, lest I capture the city and it be called after my name."
29 And Dawiḏ gathered all the people and went to Rabbah, and fought against it, and captured it.
30 And he took their sovereign's crown from his head. And its weight was a talent of gold, with precious stones, and it was on Dawiḏ's head. And he brought out the spoil of the city, a very great amount.
31 And he brought out the people who were in it, and set them to the saw and to sharp instruments of iron and to axes of iron, and made them pass over to the brick works. And so he did with all the cities of the children of Ammon. And Dawiḏ and all the people returned to Yerushalayim.

13 And after this it came to be that Aḇshalom son of Dawiḏ had a beautiful sister, whose name was Tamar, and Amnon son of Dawiḏ loved her.
2 And Amnon was distressed, even to become sick, because of his sister Tamar – for she was a maiden – and it was hard in the eyes of Amnon to do whatever to her.
3 And Amnon had a friend whose name was Yonaḏaḇ son of Shim'ah, Dawiḏ's brother. Now Yonaḏaḇ was a very wise man.
4 And he said to him, "Why are you, the sovereign's son, becoming thinner day after day? Explain it to me." And Amnon said to him, "I love Tamar, my brother Aḇshalom's sister."
5 And Yonaḏaḇ said to him, "Lie down on your bed and pretend to be sick. And when your father comes to see you, say to him, 'Please let my sister Tamar come and give me food, and make the food before my eyes so that I see it, and eat it from her hand.' "
6 So Amnon lay down and pretended to be sick. And when the sovereign came to see him, Amnon said to the sovereign, "Please let Tamar my sister come and make

a couple of cakes for me before my eyes,
so that I eat from her hand."
7 And Dawiḏ sent to Tamar, to the house,
saying, "Please go to the house of your
brother Amnon, and make food for him."
8 So Tamar went to her brother Amnon's
house, while he was lying down. And she
took dough and kneaded it, and made cakes
before his eyes, and baked the cakes.
9 And she took the pan and turned them
out before him, but he refused to eat. And
Amnon said, "Make everyone go away
from me." And they all went out from him.
10 And Amnon said to Tamar, "Bring the
food into the bedroom, that I eat from your
hand." And Tamar took the cakes which
she had made, and brought them to Amnon
her brother in the bedroom.
11 And she brought them to him to eat,
and he took hold of her and said to her,
"Come, lie with me, my sister."
12 And she answered him, "No, my brother, do not humble me, for it is not done so
in Yisra'ěl. Do not do this wickedness!
13 "And I, where could I take my shame?
And you – you would be like one of the
fools in Yisra'ěl. And now, please speak to
the sovereign, for he would not withhold
me from you."
14 But he would not listen to her voice,
and being stronger than she, he humbled
her and lay with her.
15 Amnon then hated her exceedingly, so
that the hatred with which he hated her was
greater than the love with which he had
loved her. And Amnon said to her, "Arise,
go!"
16 And she said to him, "No, for this evil
of sending me away is worse than the other
you have done to me." But he would not
listen to her.
17 And he called his young man serving
him, and said, "Now put this one out, away
from me, and bolt the door behind her."
18 And she had on a long coat, for the
sovereign's maiden daughters wore such
garments. And his servant put her out and
bolted the door behind her.
19 And Tamar put ashes on her head, and
tore her long coat that was on her, and put
her hand on her head and went away crying
bitterly.
20 And Aḇshalom her brother said to her,
"Has Amnon your brother been with you?
But now, keep silent, my sister. He is your
brother, do not take this matter to heart."
So Tamar remained in the house of her
brother Aḇshalom, but was ruined.
21 And Sovereign Dawiḏ heard all these
reports, and he was very wroth.
22 And Aḇshalom spoke to his brother
Amnon neither good nor evil. For
Aḇshalom hated Amnon, because he had
humbled his sister Tamar.
23 And it came to be, after two years, that
Aḇshalom had sheep-shearers in Baʿal
Hatsor, which is beside Ephrayim, and
Aḇshalom invited all the sons of the sovereign.
24 And Aḇshalom came to the sovereign
and said, "See, your servant has sheep-
shearers. Please, let the sovereign and his
servants go with your servant."
25 But the sovereign said to Aḇshalom,
"No, my son, let us not all go now, lest we
be too heavy on you." And he urged him,
but he would not go. And he blessed him.
26 And Aḇshalom said, "If not, please let
my brother Amnon go with us." And the
sovereign said to him, "Why should he go
with you?"
27 And Aḇshalom urged him, so he let
Amnon and all the sons of the sovereign go
with him.
28 And Aḇshalom had commanded his
servants, saying, "Watch, and when the
heart of Amnon is glad with wine, and I
shall say to you, 'Strike Amnon!' then kill
him. Do not be afraid. Have I not commanded you? Be strong and brave."
29 Then the servants of Aḇshalom did to
Amnon as Aḇshalom had commanded.
Then all the sons of the sovereign rose up,
and each one mounted his mule and fled.
30 And it came to be, while they were on
the way, that news came to Dawiḏ, saying,
"Aḇshalom has stricken all the sons of the
sovereign, and not one of them is left!"
31 And the sovereign rose up and tore his
garments and lay on the ground, and all his
servants stood by with their garments torn.
32 And Yonaḏaḇ son of Shimʿah, Dawiḏ's

brother, answered and said, "Do not let my master say they have killed all the young men, the sons of the sovereign, for only Amnon is dead. For by the mouth of Aḇshalom this has been appointed from the day that he humbled his sister Tamar.

33 "And now, let not my master the sovereign take the matter to his heart, to think that all the sons of the sovereign are dead. For only Amnon is dead."

34 And Aḇshalom fled, and the young man who was watching lifted up his eyes and looked and saw many people were coming from the way behind him, on the side of the hill.

35 Then Yonaḏaḇ said to the sovereign, "Look, the sons of the sovereign are coming; as your servant said, so it is."

36 And it came to be, as soon as he had finished speaking, that look, the sons of the sovereign came, and they lifted up their voice and wept. And the sovereign too, and all his servants wept very bitterly.

37 But Aḇshalom fled and went to Talmai son of Ammihuḏ, sovereign of Geshur. And *Dawiḏ* mourned for his son all the days.

38 So Aḇshalom fled and went to Geshur, and was there three years.

39 Sovereign Dawiḏ then longed to go to Aḇshalom, for he had been comforted concerning Amnon, because he was dead.

14 And Yo'aḇ son of Tseruyah knew that the heart of the sovereign was towards Aḇshalom.

2 And Yo'aḇ sent to Teqowa and brought from there a wise woman, and said to her, "Please pretend to be a mourner, and put on mourning garments, and do not anoint yourself with oil, but act like a woman who has been mourning a long time for the dead.

3 "Then you shall go to the sovereign and speak to him according to this word." And Yo'aḇ put the words in her mouth.

4 And when the woman of Teqowa spoke to the sovereign, she fell on her face to the ground and did obeisance, and said, "Save, O sovereign!"

5 And the sovereign said to her, "What is your trouble?" And she answered, "Truly I am a widow, my husband is dead.

6 "And your female servant had two sons. And the two fought with each other in the field, and there was no one to part them, but the one struck the other and killed him.

7 "And see, the entire clan has risen up against your female servant and said, 'Give him who struck his brother, so that we put him to death for the life of his brother whom he killed, and destroy the heir also.' Thus they would extinguish my burning coal that is left, and leave to my husband neither name nor remnant on the earth."

8 And the sovereign said to the woman, "Go to your house, and let me give commands concerning you."

9 And the woman of Teqowa said to the sovereign, "My master, O sovereign, let the crookedness be on me and on my father's house, and the sovereign and his throne be guiltless."

10 And the sovereign said, "Whoever speaks to you, bring him to me, and let him no longer touch you."

11 And she said, "Please let the sovereign remember יהוה your Elohim, and the redeemer of blood not destroy any more, lest they destroy my son." And he said, "As יהוה lives, not one hair of your son shall fall to the ground."

12 And the woman said, "Please, let your female servant speak a word to my master the sovereign." And he said, "Speak."

13 And the woman said, "And why have you reasoned like this against the people of Elohim? For in speaking this word the sovereign is as one who is guilty, in that the sovereign does not bring his outcast one home again.

14 "For we shall certainly die and become like water spilled on the ground, which is not gathered up again. Yet Elohim does not take away a life, but shall devise ways, so that His outcast ones are not cast out from Him.

15 "And now I have come to speak this word to my master the sovereign because the people have made me afraid. And your female servant said, 'Please let me speak to the sovereign, it could be that the sovereign

does what his female servant asks,
[16]for the sovereign has listened to deliver his female servant from the hand of the man *seeking* to destroy me and my son together from the inheritance of Elohim.'
[17]"Then your female servant said, 'Please let the word of my master the sovereign be comforting, for my master the sovereign is as the messenger of Elohim, in discerning the good and the evil. And יהוה your Elohim is with you.' "
[18]And the sovereign answered and said to the woman, "Please do not hide from me the matter that I am asking you." And the woman said, "Please, let my master the sovereign speak."
[19]And the sovereign said, "Is the hand of Yo'aḇ with you in all this?" And the woman answered and said, "As your being lives, my master the sovereign, no one *turns* to the right or to the left from all that my master the sovereign has spoken. For your servant Yo'aḇ commanded me, and he put all these words in the mouth of your female servant.
[20]"Your servant Yo'aḇ has done this to change the appearance of the matter. But my master is wise, according to the wisdom of a messenger of Elohim, to know all that is in the earth."
[21]And the sovereign said to Yo'aḇ, "See now, you shall do this matter. And go, bring back the young man Aḇshalom."
[22]And Yo'aḇ fell to the ground on his face and did obeisance, and blessed the sovereign. And Yo'aḇ said, "Today your servant knows that I have found favour in your eyes, my master, O sovereign, in that the sovereign has done the word of his servant."
[23]And Yo'aḇ rose up and went to Geshur, and brought Aḇshalom to Yerushalayim.
[24]And the sovereign said, "Let him return to his own house, but do not let him see my face." And Aḇshalom went to his own house, and did not see the sovereign's face.
[25]And in all Yisra'ĕl there was no one who was praised as much as Aḇshalom for his handsomeness. From the sole of his foot to the crown of his head there was no blemish in him.
[26]And when he cut the hair of his head – for it was at every year's end that he cut it because it was heavy on him – when he cut it, he weighed the hair of his head at two hundred sheqels by the sovereign's weight.
[27]And to Aḇshalom were born three sons, and one daughter whose name was Tamar. She was a woman of beautiful appearance.
[28]And Aḇshalom dwelt in Yerushalayim, two years, and he had not seen the sovereign's face.
[29]Then Aḇshalom sent for Yo'aḇ, to send him to the sovereign, but he would not come to him. And he sent again the second time, but he would not come.
[30]And he said to his servants, "See, Yo'aḇ's field is near mine, and he has barley there. Go and set it on fire." And Aḇshalom's servants set the field on fire.
[31]Then Yo'aḇ rose up and came to the house of Aḇshalom, and said to him, "Why have your servants set my field on fire?"
[32]And Aḇshalom said to Yo'aḇ, "Look, I sent to you, saying, 'Come here, so that I send you to the sovereign, to say, "Why have I come from Geshur? It was good for me while I was there." ' And now, let me see the sovereign's face. And if there is any crookedness in me, then you shall put me to death."
[33]Yo'aḇ then went to the sovereign and informed him. And he called for Aḇshalom, and he came to the sovereign and bowed himself on his face to the ground before the sovereign. Then the sovereign kissed Aḇshalom.

15 And it came to be after this that Aḇshalom prepared a chariot and horses for himself, and fifty men to run before him.
[2]And Aḇshalom used to rise early and stand beside the way to the gate. And it came to be, whenever anyone who had a complaint came to the sovereign for a right-ruling, that Aḇshalom would call to him and say, "What city are you from?" And when he said, "Your servant is from such and such a tribe of Yisra'ĕl,"
[3]Aḇshalom would say to him, "Look, your matters are good and right, but you

have nobody from the sovereign to hear
you."
4 And Aḇshalom would say, "Oh, that I
were made judge in the land, and everyone
who has any complaint or case would
come to me, and I shall let right be done to
him."
5 And it came to be, whenever anyone
came near him to bow down to him, that he
would put out his hand and take hold of
him and kiss him.
6 And Aḇshalom did this to all Yisra'ěl
who came to the sovereign for right-ruling.
And Aḇshalom stole the hearts of the men
of Yisra'ěl.
7 And it came to be at the end of forty
years that Aḇshalom said to the sovereign,
"Please, let me go to Ḥeḇron and pay the
vow which I vowed to יהוה.
8 "For your servant vowed a vow while I
dwelt at Geshur in Aram, saying, 'If יהוה
indeed brings me back to Yerushalayim,
then I shall serve יהוה.' "
9 And the sovereign said to him, "Go in
peace." And he rose up and went to
Ḥeḇron.
10 But Aḇshalom sent spies throughout all
the tribes of Yisra'ěl, saying, "As soon as
you hear the voice of the shophar, then you
shall say, 'Aḇshalom is sovereign in
Ḥeḇron!' "
11 And with Aḇshalom went two hundred
men from Yerushalayim who were invited,
and they went along unsuspectingly, and
did not know the matter at all.
12 Aḇshalom also sent for Aḥithophel the
Gilonite, counsellor of Dawiḏ, from his
city, from Giloh, while he slaughtered
slaughterings. And it came to be that the
conspiracy became potent, for the people
with Aḇshalom kept increasing.
13 Then a messenger came to Dawiḏ,
saying, "The hearts of the men of Yisra'ěl
are with Aḇshalom."
14 And Dawiḏ said to all his servants who
were with him at Yerushalayim, "Rise up,
and let us flee, for none of us shall escape
from Aḇshalom. Go in haste, lest he overtake us quickly and bring evil upon us, and
strike the city with the edge of the sword."
15 And the sovereign's servants said to the
sovereign, "Look, your servants *shall do*
according to all my master the sovereign
chooses."
16 And the sovereign went out, and all
his household at his feet. But the sovereign
left ten women, concubines, to look after
the house.
17 So the sovereign went out, and all the
people at his feet, and they stood still at the
last house.
18 And all his servants were passing on at
his side. And all the Kerěthites, and all the
Pelěthites, and all the Gittites, six hundred
men who had followed him from Gath,
were passing on before the sovereign.
19 And the sovereign said to Ittai the
Gittite, "Why do you go, you also, with us?
Turn back and remain with the sovereign,
for you are a foreigner, and also an exile
from your own place.
20 "You came yesterday, and should I
today make you wander up and down with
us, when I am going wherever I am going?
Return, and take your brothers back.
Loving-commitment and truth be with
you."
21 And Ittai answered the sovereign and
said, "As יהוה lives, and as my master
the sovereign lives, in whatever place my
master the sovereign is, whether in death or
life, let your servant also be there."
22 Therefore Dawiḏ said to Ittai, "Go, and
pass over." And Ittai the Gittite and all his
men and all the little ones who were with
him passed over.
23 And all the land was weeping with a
loud voice, and all the people were passing
over. And the sovereign himself was
passing over the wadi Qiḏron, and all
the people were passing over toward
the way of the wilderness.
24 And see, Tsaḏoq also *came*, and all the
Lěwites with him, bearing the ark of the
covenant of Elohim. And they set down the
ark of Elohim, and Eḇyathar went up until
all the people completed passing over from
the city.
25 And the sovereign said to Tsaḏoq,
"Take the ark of Elohim back to the city. If
I find favour in the eyes of יהוה, then He
shall bring me back and show me both

it and His dwelling.
26 "But if He says thus, 'I have not
delighted in you,' here I am, let Him do
to me as *seems* good in His eyes."
27 And the sovereign said to Tsaḏoq the
priest, "Are you not a seer? Return to the
city in peace, and your two sons with you,
Aḥima'ats your son, and Yehonathan son
of Eḇyathar.
28 "See, I am waiting in the desert plains
of the wilderness until word comes from
you to inform me."
29 And Tsaḏoq and Eḇyathar took the ark
of Elohim back to Yerushalayim, and they
remained there.
30 And Dawiḏ went up by the ascent of the
Mount of Olives, and wept as he went up.
And he had his head covered and went
barefoot. And all the people who were with
him covered their heads and went up,
weeping as they went up.
31 And Dawiḏ was informed, saying,
"Aḥithophel is among the conspirators
with Aḇshalom." And Dawiḏ said, "O
יהוה, I pray You, make the counsel of
Aḥithophel foolish!"
32 And it came to be that Dawiḏ came to
the summit, where he bowed himself
before Elohim, and saw Ḥushai the Arkite,
coming to meet him with his robe torn and
dust on his head.
33 And Dawiḏ said to him, "If you pass on
with me, then you shall become a burden to
me,
34 but if you return to the city, and say to
Aḇshalom, 'I am your servant, O sovereign
– once servant of your father, but now I am
your servant,' then you shall nullify the
counsel of Aḥithophel for me.
35 "And are not Tsaḏoq and Eḇyathar the
priests with you there? And it shall be that
every matter you hear from the sovereign's
house, you should report to Tsaḏoq and
Eḇyathar the priests.
36 "See, there with them are their two
sons, Aḥima'ats, Tsaḏoq's son, and Yehonathan, Eḇyathar's son. And by them you
shall send me every matter you hear."
37 And Ḥushai, Dawiḏ's friend, went into
the city. And Aḇshalom came into Yerushalayim.

16 And Dawiḏ had passed on a little
from the summit, and saw Tsiḇa the
servant of Mephiḇosheth, who met him
with a couple of saddled donkeys, and on
them two hundred loaves, and one hundred
cakes of raisins, and one hundred summer
fruit, and a skin of wine.
2 And the sovereign said to Tsiḇa, "Why
do you have these?" And Tsiḇa said, "The
donkeys are for the sovereign's household
to ride on, and the bread and summer fruit
for the young men to eat, and the wine for
the wearied to drink in the wilderness."
3 And the sovereign said, "And where is
the son of your master?" And Tsiḇa said to
the sovereign, "See, he remains in Yerushalayim, for he said, 'Today the house of
Yisra'ĕl is going to return the reign of my
father to me.' "
4 And the sovereign said to Tsiḇa, "See,
all that belongs to Mephiḇosheth is yours."
And Tsiḇa said, "I have bowed myself,
let me find favour in your eyes, my master,
O sovereign!"
5 And when Sovereign Dawiḏ came to
Baḥurim he saw a man from the clan of the
house of Sha'ul, whose name was Shim'i
son of Gĕra, coming from there. He came
out, cursing as he came.
6 And he threw Dawiḏ with stones, and
all the servants of Sovereign Dawiḏ. And
all the people and all the mighty men were
on his right and on his left.
7 And this is what Shim'i said as he
cursed, "Get out! Get out! O man of blood,
and man of Beliya'al!
8 "יהוה has brought upon you all the
blood of the house of Sha'ul, in whose
place you have reigned. And יהוה has
given the reign into the hand of Aḇshalom
your son. And see, you are in your own
evil, for you are a man of blood!"
9 And Aḇishai son of Tseruyah said to the
sovereign, "Why should this dead dog
curse my master the sovereign? Please, let
me pass over and take off his head!"
10 And the sovereign said, "What have I to
do with you, you sons of Tseruyah? For let
him curse, even because יהוה has said to
him, 'Curse Dawiḏ.' And who should say,
'Why did you do that?' "

11 And Dawiḏ said to Aḇishai and all his
servants, "See how my son who came from
my own body seeks my life, and how much
more now this Binyamite? Leave him
alone, and let him curse, for יהוה has spoken to him.
12 "If so be, יהוה does look on my affliction, and יהוה shall return good to me for
his cursing today."
13 And as Dawiḏ and his men went in the
way, Shim'i walked alongside him on the
hillside, and cursed as he went, and threw
stones at him and kicked up dust.
14 And the sovereign and all the people
who were with him became weary, and
they refreshed themselves there.
15 And Aḇshalom and all the people, the
men of Yisra'ěl, came to Yerushalayim,
and Aḥithophel was with him.
16 And it came to be, when Ḥushai the
Arkite, the friend of Dawiḏ, had come to
Aḇshalom, that Ḥushai said to Aḇshalom,
"Let the sovereign live! Let the sovereign
live!"
17 And Aḇshalom said to Ḥushai, "Is this
your loving-commitment to your friend?
Why did you not go with your friend?"
18 And Ḥushai said to Aḇshalom, "No, I
am for the one whom יהוה and this people
and all the men of Yisra'ěl have chosen,
and with him I remain.
19 "And besides, whom should I serve?
Should it not be before his son? As I have
served before your father, so I am before
you."
20 And Aḇshalom said to Aḥithophel,
"Give your advice. What should we do?"
21 And Aḥithophel said to Aḇshalom, "Go
in to your father's concubines, whom he
has left to look after the house. And all
Yisra'ěl shall hear that you have made
yourself a stench to your father. And the
hands of all who are with you shall be
strong."
22 So they pitched a tent for Aḇshalom on
the top of the house, and Aḇshalom went in
to his father's concubines before the eyes
of all Yisra'ěl.
23 Now the advice Aḥithophel gave in
those days was as if one had inquired at the
word of Elohim. So was all the advice of
Aḥithophel both to Dawiḏ and to
Aḇshalom.

17 And Aḥithophel said to Aḇshalom,
"Please let me choose twelve thousand men, and let me arise and pursue
Dawiḏ tonight,
2 and come upon him while he is weary
and weak. And I shall make him afraid and
all the people who are with him shall flee.
And I shall strike the sovereign alone,
3 and bring back all the people to you.
When all return except the man whom you
seek, all the people should be at peace."
4 And the saying pleased Aḇshalom and
all the elders of Yisra'ěl.
5 But Aḇshalom said, "Now call Ḥushai
the Arkite also, and let us hear what he
says too."
6 And Ḥushai came to Aḇshalom, and
Aḇshalom spoke to him, saying, "Aḥithophel has spoken according to this word.
Should we do as he says? If not, speak up."
7 And Ḥushai said to Aḇshalom, "The
advice that Aḥithophel has given is not
good at this time."
8 And Ḥushai said, "You know your
father and his men, that they are mighty
men, and they are as bitter in being as a
bear robbed of her cubs in the field. And
your father is a man of battle, and would
not spend the night with the people.
9 "See, by now he is hidden in some pit,
or in some place. And it shall be, when
some of them fall at the first, that whoever
hears it shall say, 'There has been a slaughter among the people who are following
Aḇshalom.'
10 "And even he who is brave, whose
heart is like the heart of a lion, would
utterly melt. For all Yisra'ěl knows that
your father is a mighty man, and those who
are with him are brave men.
11 "But I advise: Let all Yisra'ěl without
fail be gathered to you, from Dan to
Be'ěrsheḇa, as numerous as the sand by the
sea, and that you yourself go to battle.
12 "And we shall come upon him in some
place where he is found, and fall on him as
the dew falls on the ground. And there
shall be left of him and of all the men with

him not even one.
13"And if he withdraws into a city, then
all Yisra'ěl shall bring ropes to that city.
And we shall pull it into the wadi, until
there is not one small stone found there."
14Aḇshalom and all the men of Yisra'ěl
then said, "The advice of Ḥushai the Arkite
is better than the advice of Aḥithophel."
For יהוה had ordained to nullify the good
advice of Aḥithophel, for the sake of יהוה
bringing evil upon Aḇshalom.
15Ḥushai then said to Tsaḏoq and to
Eḇyathar the priests, "Aḥithophel has
advised Aḇshalom and the elders of
Yisra'ěl such and such, but I have advised
so and so.
16"And now, send hastily and inform
Dawiḏ, saying, 'Do not spend this night in
the desert plains of the wilderness, but pass
over without fail, lest the sovereign and all
the people with him be swallowed up.' "
17And Yehonathan and Aḥimaʽats were
stationed at Ěn Roḡěl, and a female servant
would come and inform them, and they
would go and inform Sovereign Dawiḏ, for
they could not be seen entering the city.
18But a youth saw them, and informed
Aḇshalom. So the two of them went away
at once and came to a man's house in
Baḥurim, who had a well in his courtyard,
and they went down into it.
19And the woman took and spread a
covering over the well's mouth, and spread
ground grain on it, so the matter was not
known.
20And the servants of Aḇshalom came to
the woman at the house and said, "Where
are Aḥimaʽats and Yehonathan?" And the
woman said to them, "They have passed
over the stream of water." And they looked
and did not find them, and returned to
Yerushalayim.
21And it came to be, after they had left,
that they came up out of the well and went
and informed Sovereign Dawiḏ, and said to
Dawiḏ, "Arise and pass over the water
quickly. For thus Aḥithophel has advised
against you."
22And Dawiḏ and all the people who
were with him rose up and passed over the
Yarděn. And by morning light not even one
remained who had not gone over the
Yarděn.
23And Aḥithophel saw that his advice
was not followed, so he saddled his donkey, and rose up and went home to his
house, to his city. Then he gave command
to his house, and hanged himself, and died.
And he was buried in his father's burial-
site.
24And Dawiḏ came to Maḥanayim. And
Aḇshalom passed over the Yarděn, he and
all the men of Yisra'ěl with him.
25And Aḇshalom appointed Amasa over
the army instead of Yo'aḇ. Now Amasa
was the son of a man whose name was
Yithra, a Yisra'ěli, who had gone in to
Aḇiḡayil the daughter of Naḥash, sister
of Tseruyah, Yo'aḇ's mother.
26And Yisra'ěl and Aḇshalom encamped
in the land of Gilʽaḏ.
27And it came to be, when Dawiḏ had
come to Maḥanayim, that Shoḇi son of
Naḥash from Rabbah of the children of
Ammon, and Maḵir son of Ammi'ěl from
Lo Ḏeḇar, and Barzillai the Gilʽaḏite from
Roḡelim,
28brought beds and basins, and earthen
vessels and wheat, and barley and flour,
and roasted *grain* and beans, and lentils,
and parched *vegetables*,
29and honey and curds, and sheep and
cheese of the herd, for Dawiḏ and the
people who were with him to eat. For they
said, "The people are hungry and weary
and thirsty in the wilderness."

18 And Dawiḏ mustered the people
who were with him, and set commanders of thousands and commanders of
hundreds over them.
2And Dawiḏ sent out one third of the
people under the hand of Yo'aḇ, and one
third under the hand of Aḇishai son of
Tseruyah, Yo'aḇ's brother, and one third
under the hand of Ittai the Gittite. And the
sovereign said to the people, "I shall certainly go out with you too."
3But the people answered, "Do not go
out, for if we flee away, they would not set
heart upon us. Even if half of us die, they
would not set heart upon us. For now, ten

thousand are like us. Therefore, it is better for you to support us from the city."

4 And the sovereign said to them, "That which is good in your eyes I do." And the sovereign stood beside the gate, and all the people went out by hundreds and by thousands.

5 And the sovereign ordered Yo'aḇ, and Aḇishai and Ittai, saying, "Be gentle with the young man Aḇshalom for my sake." And all the people heard when the sovereign gave all the commanders orders concerning Aḇshalom.

6 So the people went out into the field to meet Yisra'ěl. And the battle was in the forest of Ephrayim,

7 and the people of Yisra'ěl were smitten there before the servants of Dawiḏ. And the slaughter there that day was great – twenty thousand.

8 And the battle there was scattered over the face of all the land, and the forest devoured more people that day than the sword devoured.

9 And when Aḇshalom met the servants of Dawiḏ, Aḇshalom was riding on a mule, and the mule went under the thick branches of a great terebinth tree, and his head caught hold in the terebinth. And he was suspended between the heavens and earth while the mule which was under him passed on.

10 And a certain man saw it and informed Yo'aḇ, and said, "Look, I saw Aḇshalom hanging in a terebinth tree!"

11 And Yo'aḇ said to the man who informed him, "Now look, you saw, and why did you not strike him to the earth there? Then I would have given you ten pieces of silver and a belt."

12 But the man answered Yo'aḇ, "Though I were to receive a thousand pieces of silver in my hand, I would not raise my hand against the son of the sovereign. Because in our hearing the sovereign commanded you and Aḇishai and Ittai, saying, 'Take heed, you who go against the youth, against Aḇshalom!'

13 "Otherwise I would have been untrue to my own life. For no matter is hidden from the sovereign, and you yourself would have set yourself against me."

14 And Yo'aḇ said, "Let me not waste time here with you." And he took three spears in his hand and thrust them through Aḇshalom's heart, while he was still alive in the midst of the terebinth tree.

15 And ten young men who bore Yo'aḇ's armour went around, and struck Aḇshalom and put him to death.

16 And Yo'aḇ blew with the shophar, and the people returned from pursuing Yisra'ěl, for Yo'aḇ had held the people back.

17 And they took Aḇshalom and threw him into a large pit in the forest, and heaped a very large pile of stones over him. And all Yisra'ěl fled, each one to his tent.

18 And Aḇshalom in his lifetime had taken and set up a monument for himself, which is in the Sovereign's Valley. For he said, "I have no son to keep my name in remembrance." And he called the monument after his own name. And to this day it is called Aḇshalom's Monument.

19 And Aḥima'ats son of Tsaḏoq said, "Please let me run and take the news to the sovereign, for יהוה has avenged him of his enemies."

20 But Yo'aḇ said to him, "You are not the man to take the news today, but you shall take the news another day. But today you do not take news, because the sovereign's son is dead."

21 And Yo'aḇ said to the Kushite, "Go, inform the sovereign what you have seen." And the Kushite bowed himself to Yo'aḇ and ran.

22 And Aḥima'ats son of Tsaḏoq said again to Yo'aḇ, "And whatever might be, please let me also run after the Kushite." And Yo'aḇ said, "Why would you run, my son, there is no news to bring you reward."

23 "And whatever might be," *he said*, "let me run." So he said to him, "Run." And Aḥima'ats ran by the way of the plain, and passed the Kushite.

24 Now Dawiḏ was sitting between the two gates. And the watchman went up to the roof over the gate, to the wall, and lifted his eyes and looked and saw a man, running alone.

25 So the watchman called out and told the

sovereign. And the sovereign said, "If he
is alone, there is news in his mouth." And
he came nearer and nearer.
26 And the watchman saw another man
running, and the watchman called out to
the gatekeeper and said, "See, a man, running by himself!" And the sovereign said,
"This one is also bringing news."
27 And the watchman said, "I see the
running of the first is like the running of
Aḥima'ats son of Tsaḏoq." And the sovereign said, "This is a good man, and he
comes with good news."
28 And Aḥima'ats called out and said to
the sovereign, "Peace!" Then he bowed
down with his face to the earth before the
sovereign, and said, "Blessed be יהוה your
Elohim, who has surrendered the men who
raised their hand against my master the
sovereign!"
29 And the sovereign said, "Peace to the
young man, to Aḇshalom?" And Aḥima'ats
answered, "When Yo'aḇ sent the sovereign's servant and me your servant, I saw a
great crowd, but I did not know why."
30 And the sovereign said, "Turn aside and
stand here." And he turned aside and stood
still.
31 And see, the Kushite came, and the
Kushite said, "Receive news, my master
the sovereign! For יהוה has avenged you
this day of all those who rose against you."
32 And the sovereign said to the Kushite,
"Peace to the young man, to Aḇshalom?"
And the Kushite answered, "Let the
enemies of my master the sovereign, and
all who rise against you for evil, be as that
young man is!"
33 And the sovereign was shaken, and
went up to the room over the gate, and
wept. And as he went, he said this, "O my
son Aḇshalom! My son, my son Aḇshalom,
if only I had died instead of you! O
Aḇshalom my son, my son!"

19

And it was reported to Yo'aḇ, "See,
the sovereign is weeping and
mourning for Aḇshalom."
2 So the deliverance that day was turned
into mourning for all the people. For the
people heard on that day, saying, "The sovereign has been grieved for his son."
3 And the people stole back into the city
that day, as people who are ashamed steal
away when they flee in battle.
4 And the sovereign covered his face, and
the sovereign cried out with a loud voice,
"O my son Aḇshalom! O Aḇshalom, my
son, my son!"
5 And Yo'aḇ came into the house to the
sovereign, and said, "Today you have put
to shame all your servants who today have
saved your life, and the lives of your sons
and daughters, and the lives of your wives
and the lives of your concubines,
6 by loving those who hate you, and by
hating those who love you. For you have
made it clear today that you have neither
commanders nor servants, for today I know
that if Aḇshalom had lived and all of us
had died today, then it would be right in
your eyes.
7 "And now, arise, go out and speak to
the heart of your servants. For I swear by
יהוה, if you do not go out, not one passes
the night with you. And that is worse for
you than all the evil that has come upon
you from your youth until now."
8 So the sovereign rose up and sat in the
gate. And they told all the people, saying,
"Look, the sovereign is sitting in the gate."
And all the people came before the
sovereign. As for Yisra'ěl, they had fled,
each one to his tent.
9 And it came to be, that all the people
were contending throughout all the tribes
of Yisra'ěl, saying, "The sovereign delivered us from the hand of the enemies, he
rescued us from the hand of the Philistines,
and now he has fled from the land because
of Aḇshalom,
10 and Aḇshalom, whom we anointed over
us, has died in battle. And now, why are
you silent about bringing back the sovereign?"
11 And Sovereign Dawiḏ sent to Tsaḏoq
and Eḇyathar the priests, saying, "Speak to
the elders of Yehuḏah, saying, 'Why are
you the last to bring the sovereign back to
his house, since the words of all Yisra'ěl
have come to the sovereign, to his house?
12 'You are my brothers, you are my bone

and my flesh. Why then are you the last to
bring back the sovereign?'
13 "And say to Amasa, 'Are you not my
bone and my flesh? Elohim do so to me,
and more also, if you are not commander
of the army before me all the days in place
of Yo'aḇ.' "
14 Thus he swayed the hearts of all the
men of Yehuḏah as one man, so that they
sent to the sovereign, *saying* "Return, you
and all your servants!"
15 So the sovereign returned and came to
the Yardĕn. And Yehuḏah came to Gilgal,
to go to meet the sovereign, to bring the
sovereign over the Yardĕn.
16 And Shim'i son of Gĕra, a Binyamite,
who was from Baḥurim, hastened and
came down with the men of Yehuḏah to
meet Sovereign Dawiḏ.
17 And with him were a thousand men of
Binyamin, and Tsiḇa the servant of the
house of Sha'ul, and his fifteen sons,
and his twenty servants with him. And they
rushed over the Yardĕn before the sovereign.
18 And they passed over the ford to bring
over the sovereign's household, and to do
what was good in his eyes. And Shim'i son
of Gĕra fell down before the sovereign
when he had passed over the Yardĕn,
19 and said to the sovereign, "Do not let
my master reckon crookedness to me,
neither remember what wrong your servant
did on the day that my master the sovereign left Yerushalayim, that the sovereign
should take it to heart.
20 "For I, your servant, know that I have
sinned. And see, I have come today, first of
all the house of Yosĕph, to go down to
meet my master the sovereign."
21 But Aḇishai son of Tseruyah answered
and said, "Should Shim'i not be put to
death for this, because he cursed the
anointed of יהוה?"
22 And Dawiḏ said, "What have I to do
with you, you sons of Tseruyah, that you
are to be adversaries to me today? Should
any man be put to death in Yisra'ĕl today?
For do I not know that I am sovereign over
Yisra'ĕl today?"
23 So the sovereign said to Shim'i, "You
do not die." And the sovereign swore to
him.
24 And Mephiḇosheth son of Sha'ul came
down to meet the sovereign. And he had
not attended to his feet, nor trimmed his
moustache, nor washed his garments, from
the day the sovereign went away until the
day he came back in peace.
25 And it came to be, when he had come to
Yerushalayim to meet the sovereign, that
the sovereign said to him, "Why did you
not go with me, Mephiḇosheth?"
26 And he answered, "My master, O
sovereign, my servant deceived me. For
your servant said, 'I am saddling a donkey
for myself to ride on it and go to the
sovereign,' because your servant is lame.
27 "And he spoke slander against your
servant to my master the sovereign, but my
master the sovereign is as a messenger of
Elohim. Therefore do what is good in your
eyes.
28 "For all of my father's house were but
dead men before my master the sovereign.
Yet you set your servant among those who
eat at your own table. Therefore what right
have I still to cry out any more to the
sovereign?"
29 Then the sovereign said to him, "Why
do you speak any more of your matters? I
have said, 'You and Tsiḇa share the land.' "
30 And Mephiḇosheth said to the sovereign, "Rather, let him take it all, since my
master the sovereign has come back in
peace to his own house."
31 And Barzillai the Gil'aḏite came down
from Roḡelim and passed over the Yardĕn
with the sovereign, to send him on his way
over the Yardĕn.
32 And Barzillai was a very aged man,
eighty years old. And he had sustained the
sovereign while he was dwelling at
Maḥanayim, for he was a very rich man.
33 And the sovereign said to Barzillai,
"Pass over with me, and I shall provide for
you with me in Yerushalayim."
34 But Barzillai said to the sovereign,
"How many are the days of my life, that
I should go up with the sovereign to Yerushalayim?
35 "I am now eighty years old. Do I dis-

cern between the good and evil? Does your
servant taste what I eat or what I drink? Do
I still hear the voice of singing men and
singing women? Why then should your
servant be a further burden to my master
the sovereign?
36 “Your servant would only pass over the
Yarděn with the sovereign for a short distance. And why should the sovereign repay
me with such a reward?
37 “Please let your servant turn back again
to die in my own city, near the burial-site
of my father and mother. But here is your
servant Kimham, let him pass over with
my master the sovereign, and do for him
what is good in your eyes.”
38 And the sovereign answered, “Kimham
is passing over with me, and let me do
for him what is good in your eyes. Now
whatever you choose of me, I do for you.”
39 Then all the people went over the
Yarděn. And when the sovereign had
passed over, the sovereign kissed Barzillai
and blessed him, and he returned to his
own place.
40 And the sovereign passed over to
Gilgal, and Kimham passed over with him.
And all the people of Yehuḏah brought the
sovereign over, and also half the people
of Yisra’ěl.
41 And see, all the men of Yisra’ěl were
coming to the sovereign! And they said to
the sovereign, “Why have our brothers, the
men of Yehuḏah, stolen you away and
brought the sovereign, and his household,
and all Dawiḏ’s men with him over the
Yarděn?”
42 And all the men of Yehuḏah answered
the men of Yisra’ěl, “Because the sovereign is our relative. And why are you displeased over this matter? Have we at all
eaten at the sovereign’s cost? Or has he
given us any gift?”
43 And the men of Yisra’ěl answered the
men of Yehuḏah, and said, “We have ten
parts in the sovereign, and in Dawiḏ too,
we have more than you. Why then did you
despise us? Was it not our advice first to
bring back our sovereign?” But the words
of the men of Yehuḏah were harsher than
the words of the men of Yisra’ěl.

20 And there came to be a man of
Beliya‘al, whose name was Sheḇa
son of Biḵri, a Binyamite. And he blew
with the shophar, and said, “We have no
part in Dawiḏ, nor do we have inheritance
in the son of Yishai – each one to his tents,
O Yisra’ěl!”
2 Then all the men of Yisra’ěl deserted
Dawiḏ, to follow Sheḇa the son of Biḵri.
But the men of Yehuḏah, from the Yarděn
as far as Yerushalayim, clung to their sovereign.
3 And Dawiḏ came to his house at
Yerushalayim. And the sovereign took the
ten women, his concubines whom he had
left to look after the house, and put them in
a protected house and supported them, but
did not go in to them. So they were shut up
to the day of their death, living in widowhood.
4 And the sovereign said to Amasa, “Call
the men of Yehuḏah for me within three
days, and be present here yourself.”
5 And Amasa went to call the men of
Yehuḏah. But he delayed longer than the
appointed time which Dawiḏ had appointed him.
6 And Dawiḏ said to Aḇishai, “Now
Sheḇa son of Biḵri is going to do us more
evil than Aḇshalom. Take the servants of
your master, and pursue him, lest he find
for himself walled cities, and escape us.”
7 Then the men of Yo’aḇ went out after
him, with the Kerěthites and the Pelěthites,
and all the mighty men. And they went out
of Yerushalayim to pursue Sheḇa son of
Biḵri.
8 When they were near the large stone
which is in Giḇ‘on, Amasa came before
them. And Yo’aḇ was dressed in battle
armour, and on it was a girdle with a sword
fastened in its sheath at his hips. And as he
went forward, it fell out.
9 And Yo’aḇ said to Amasa, “Peace, my
brother?” And Yo’aḇ took Amasa by the
beard with his right hand to kiss him.
10 But Amasa was not on guard against
the sword in Yo’aḇ’s hand. And he struck
him with it in the stomach, and his inward
parts poured out on the ground, and he did
not *strike* him again, and he died. Then

Yo'aḇ and Aḇishai his brother pursued Sheḇa son of Biḵri.

11 And a man, one of Yo'aḇ's men, stood beside him, and said, "Whoever is well pleased with Yo'aḇ and whoever is for Dawiḏ, let him follow Yo'aḇ!"

12 And Amasa was rolling in his blood in the middle of the highway. And the man saw that all the people stood still, so he moved Amasa from the highway to the field and threw a garment over him, when he saw that everyone who came upon him halted.

13 When he was removed from the highway, all the men passed on after Yo'aḇ to pursue Sheḇa son of Biḵri.

14 And he passed over through all the tribes of Yisra'ěl to Aḇěl, and to Běyth Ma'aḵah, and to all the Běrites. And they were assembled and went after him too.

15 And they went and besieged him in Aḇěl of Běyth Ma'aḵah, and they cast up a siege mound against the city. And it stood in a rampart, and all the people who were with Yo'aḇ battered the wall to throw it down.

16 Then a wise woman called out from the city, "Listen, listen! Please say to Yo'aḇ, 'Come nearby, so that I speak to you.' "

17 And he came near to her, and the woman said, "Are you Yo'aḇ?" And he answered, "I am." Then she said to him, "Listen to the words of your female servant." And he answered, "I am listening."

18 Then she spoke, saying, "In former times they often spoke, saying, 'Let them inquire of Aḇěl,' and so they ended *the matter*.

19 "I am of the peaceable and trustworthy ones in Yisra'ěl. You seek to destroy a city and a mother in Yisra'ěl. Why do you swallow up the inheritance of יהוה?"

20 And Yo'aḇ answered and said, "Far be it, far be it from me to swallow up or to destroy!

21 "That is not the case. But a man from the mountains of Ephrayim, Sheḇa son of Biḵri by name, has raised his hand against the sovereign, against Dawiḏ. Hand him over, him alone, and I withdraw from the city." And the woman said to Yo'aḇ, "Look, his head is going to be thrown to you over the wall."

22 So the woman in her wisdom went to all the people. And they cut off the head of Sheḇa son of Biḵri, and threw it out to Yo'aḇ. Then he blew with the shophar, and they dispersed from the city, each one to his tent. And Yo'aḇ returned to the sovereign at Yerushalayim.

23 Now Yo'aḇ was over all the army of Yisra'ěl, and Benayah son of Yehoyaḏa was over the Kerěthites and the Pelěthites,

24 and Aḏoram was over the compulsory labour, and Yehoshaphat son of Aḥiluḏ was recorder,

25 and Shewa was scribe, and Tsaḏoq and Eḇyathar were the priests,

26 and Ira the Ya'irite was priest to Dawiḏ.

21

And there was a scarcity of food in the days of Dawiḏ for three years, year after year. And Dawiḏ sought the face of יהוה, and יהוה answered, "Because of Sha'ul and his bloodthirsty house, because he killed the Giḇ'onites."

2 The sovereign therefore called the Giḇ'onites and spoke to them. Now the Giḇ'onites were not of the children of Yisra'ěl, but of the remnant of the Amorites. And the children of Yisra'ěl had sworn protection to them, but Sha'ul had sought to strike them in his ardour for the children of Yisra'ěl and Yehuḏah.

3 So Dawiḏ said to the Giḇ'onites, "What should I do for you? And with what do I make atonement, so that you bless the inheritance of יהוה?"

4 And the Giḇ'onites said to him, "It is no matter of silver or gold between us and Sha'ul, or his house, neither is it for us to put to death any man in Yisra'ěl." And he said, "Whatever you say I do for you."

5 And they said to the sovereign, "The man who consumed us and plotted against us, that we should be destroyed from remaining in all the border of Yisra'ěl,

6 let seven men of his sons be given to us, and we shall hang them before יהוה in Giḇ'ah of Sha'ul, whom יהוה chose." And the sovereign said, "I give them."

7 But the sovereign spared Mephiḇosheth

son of Yehonathan, son of Sha'ul, because of the oath of יהוה that was between them, between Dawiḏ and Yehonathan son of Sha'ul.

8 And the sovereign took the two sons of Ritspah the daughter of Ayah, whom she bore to Sha'ul: Armoni and *the other* Mephiḇosheth, and the five sons of Miḵal the daughter of Sha'ul, whom she brought up for Aḏri'ěl the son of Barzillai, the Meḥolathite,

9 and gave them into the hands of the Giḇ'onites, and they hanged them on the hill before יהוה. So the seven fell together, and were put to death in the days of harvest, in the first days, in the beginning of barley harvest.

10 And Ritspah the daughter of Ayah took sackcloth and spread it for herself on the rock, from the beginning of harvest until the late rains poured on them from the heavens. And she did not allow the birds of the heavens to rest on them by day nor the beasts of the field by night.

11 And Dawiḏ was informed what Ritspah the daughter of Ayah, the concubine of Sha'ul, had done.

12 And Dawiḏ went and took the bones of Sha'ul, and the bones of Yehonathan his son, from the men of Yaḇěsh Gil'aḏ who had stolen them from the street of Běyth Shan, where the Philistines had hung them up, after the Philistines had struck down Sha'ul in Gilboa.

13 And he brought up the bones of Sha'ul and the bones of Yehonathan his son from there, and they gathered the bones of those who had been hanged,

14 and buried the bones of Sha'ul and Yehonathan his son in the land of Binyamin in Tsela, in the burial-site of Qish his father, and did all that the sovereign commanded. And after that Elohim heard prayer for the land.

15 And the Philistines were again fighting against Yisra'ěl, so Dawiḏ and his servants with him went down and fought against the Philistines. And Dawiḏ was weary,

16 and Yishbo-Benoḇ – who was one of the sons of the giant, the weight of whose bronze spear was three hundred pieces, who was bearing a new sword – spoke of striking Dawiḏ.

17 But Aḇishai son of Tseruyah came to help him, and struck the Philistine and killed him. Then Dawiḏ's men swore to him, saying, "Do not go out with us to battle any more, lest you put out the lamp of Yisra'ěl."

18 And it came to be afterward, that there was a battle again with the Philistines at Goḇ. Then Sibbeḵai the Ḥushathite struck Saph, who was one of the sons of the giant.

19 And there was a battle with the Philistines again at Goḇ, where Elḥanan son of Ya'arěy-Oreğim the Běyth Leḥemite struck Golyath the Gittite, the shaft of whose spear was like a weaver's beam.

20 And there was a battle in Gath again, where there was a man of great height, who had six fingers on each hand and six toes on each foot, twenty-four in number. And he also was descended from the giants.

21 And he reproached Yisra'ěl, and Yehonathan son of Shim'i, the brother of Dawiḏ, struck him.

22 These four were born to the giant in Gath, and they fell by the hand of Dawiḏ and by the hand of his servants.

22 Then Dawiḏ spoke to יהוה the words of this song, on the day when יהוה had delivered him from the hand of all his enemies, and from the hand of Sha'ul.

2 And he said, "יהוה is my rock and my stronghold and my deliverer.
3 "My Elohim is my rock, I take refuge in Him,
My shield and the horn of my deliverance,
My high tower and my refuge.
My Saviour, You save me from violence.
4 "I call on יהוה, the One to be praised,
And I am saved from my enemies.
5 "For the waves of death surrounded me,
Floods of Beliya'al made me afraid,
6 "The cords of She'ol were all around me;
The snares of death were before me.
7 "In my distress I called upon יהוה,

And to my Elohim I cried.
And from His Hěḵal He heard my voice,
And my cry was in His ears.
8 "And the earth shook and trembled,
The foundations of the heavens were troubled,
Because He was wroth.
9 "Smoke went up from His nostrils,
And devouring fire from His mouth;
Coals were kindled by it.
10 "And He bowed the heavens and came down,
And thick darkness was under His feet.
11 "And He rode upon a keruḇ, and flew,
And was seen upon the wings of the wind.
12 "And He put darkness around Him as booths,
Darkness of waters, thick clouds.
13 "From the brightness before Him
Coals of fire were kindled.
14 "יהוה thundered from the heavens,
And the Most High sent forth His voice.
15 "And He sent out arrows and scattered them,
Lightning, and confused them.
16 "And the channels of the sea were seen,
The foundations of the world were uncovered
At the rebuke of יהוה,
At the blast of the breath of His nostrils.
17 "He sent from above, He took me,
He drew me out of many waters.
18 "He delivered me from my strong enemy,
From those hating me,
For they were stronger than I.
19 "They confronted me in the day of my calamity,
But יהוה was my support.
20 "And He brought me out into a large place,
He delivered me for He delighted in me.
21 "יהוה rewarded me according to my righteousness;
According to the cleanness of my hands He repaid me.
22 "For I have guarded the ways of יהוה,
And have not acted wrongly against my Elohim.
23 "For all His right-rulings are before me;
As for His laws, I do not turn from them.
24 "And I am perfect before Him,
And I guard myself from my crookedness.
25 "And יהוה repays me according to my righteousness,
According to my cleanness before His eyes.
26 "With the lovingly-commited *ones* You show Yourself lovingly-commited,
With the perfect one You show Yourself perfect,
27 "With the clean You show Yourself clean,
And with the crooked You show Yourself twisted.
28 "For You save the humble people,
But Your eyes are on the haughty to bring them low.
29 "For You are my lamp, O יהוה,
And יהוה makes my darkness light.
30 "For with You I run against a band,
With my Elohim I leap over a wall.
31 "The Ěl – His way is perfect;
The Word of יהוה is proven;
He is a shield to all who take refuge in Him.
32 "For who is Ěl, besides יהוה?
And who is a rock, besides our Elohim?
33 "Ěl is my mighty stronghold,
And He makes my way perfect,
34 "Making my feet like the feet of deer,
And sets me on my high places,
35 "Teaching my hands for battle,
So that my arms bend a bow of bronze.
36 "And You give me the shield of Your deliverance,
And Your lowliness makes me great.
37 "You enlarge my step under me,
So that my feet shall not slip.
38 "I pursue my enemies and destroy them,
And I do not turn back till they are destroyed.
39 "And I destroy them and crush them,
So that they do not rise,
And fall under my feet.

40"And You gird me with strength for battle,
You cause my adversaries to bow under me.
41"And You make my enemies turn their backs,
Those hating me, and I cut them off.
42"They look but there is no saviour,
Unto יהוה, but He shall not answer them.
43"And I beat them as dust of the earth,
I beat them small as dirt in the streets –
I spread them out.
44"And You deliver me from the strivings of my people,
You safeguard me as the head of the nations;
A people I have not known serve me.
45"Sons of the foreigner submit to me,
As soon as they hear they obey me.
46"Sons of the foreigner fade away,
And gird themselves from their strongholds.
47"יהוה lives! And blessed is my Rock!
And exalted is my Elohim,
The Rock of my deliverance,
48"Ěl who avenges me,
And bringing peoples down under me,
49"And bringing me out from my enemies;
You raise me up above those rising up against me;
You deliver me from a man of violence.
50"Therefore I give thanks to You, O יהוה, among nations,
And I sing praise to Your Name.
51"A tower of deliverance is He to His sovereign,
And showing loving-commitment to His anointed,
To Dawiḏ and his seed, forever."

23 And these are the last words of
Dawiḏ, the saying of Dawiḏ son of
Yishai, the saying of the man raised above,
the anointed of the Elohim of Ya'aqoḇ, and
the sweet singer of Yisra'ěl:
2"The Spirit of יהוה has spoken through me,
And His word is on my tongue.
3"The Elohim of Yisra'ěl said,
The Rock of Yisra'ěl spoke to me,
'One who rules over man righteously,
4"Who rules in the fear of Elohim,
Is like the light of the morning when the sun rises,
A morning without clouds,
Tender grass from the earth
From sunshine, from rain.'
5"For is not my house so with Ěl?
For He has made an everlasting covenant with me,
Ordered in all *matters*, and guarded.
For all my deliverance and all desire,
Shall He not make it send forth a Branch?
6"But the worthless are all as thorns thrust away,
For they are not taken with hands,
7"But the man who touches them
Uses iron or the shaft of a spear,
And with fire they are burned up in *their* place."
8These are the names of the mighty men
whom Dawiḏ had: Yoshěḇ-Bassheḇeth the
Taḥkemonite, chief among the officers, he
was Aḏino the Etsnite, for eight hundred
slain at one time.
9And after him was El'azar son of Doḏo,
the Aḥoḥite, one of the three mighty men
with Dawiḏ when they taunted the
Philistines who were gathered there for
battle, and the men of Yisra'ěl had gone up.
10He arose and struck the Philistines until
his hand was weary, but his hand clung to
the sword, so יהוה brought about a great
deliverance that day. And the people
returned after him only to plunder.
11And after him was Shammah son of
Aḡě the Hararite. And the Philistines had
gathered into a company where there was a
plot of ground covered with lentils, and the
people fled from the Philistines.
12But he took his stand in the middle of
the field, and delivered it, and struck the
Philistines, and יהוה wrought a great deliverance.
13And three of the thirty chief men went
down at harvest time and came to Dawiḏ at
the cave of Aḏullam, while the army of
Philistines encamped in the Valley of
Repha'im.

[14]And Dawiḏ was then in the stronghold,
while a watch-post of the Philistines was
then in Bĕyth Leḥem.
[15]And Dawiḏ longed and said, "Oh that
someone would give me a drink of the
water from the well of Bĕyth Leḥem,
which is by the gate!"
[16]And the three mighty men broke
through the camp of the Philistines, and
drew water from the well of Bĕyth Leḥem
that was by the gate, and took it and
brought it to Dawiḏ. But he would not
drink it, but poured it out to יהוה.
[17]And he said, "Far be it from me, O
יהוה, to do this – the blood of the men who
went at the risk of their lives!" So he would
not drink it. This is what the three mighty
men did.
[18]And Aḇishai the brother of Yo'aḇ, son
of Tseruyah, was chief of another three.
And he lifted his spear against three hundred men whom he slew, and had a name
among these three.
[19]Was he not the most esteemed of three?
And he became their commander, but he
did not come to the first three.
[20]And Benayahu was the son of Yehoyaḏa, son of a brave man from Qaḇtse'ĕl,
great in deeds. He struck two lion-like men
of Mo'aḇ. And he went down and struck a
lion in the midst of a pit on a snowy day.
[21]And he struck a Mitsrian, an impressive
man. And the Mitsrian had a spear in his
hand, so he went down to him with a staff,
wrested the spear out of the Mitsrian's
hand, and killed him with his own spear.
[22]This is what Benayahu son of Yehoyaḏa
did, and had a name among three mighty
men.
[23]He was more esteemed than the thirty,
but he did not come to the first three. And
Dawiḏ set him over his guard.
[24]Asah'ĕl the brother of Yo'aḇ was one of
the thirty; Elḥanan son of Doḏo of Bĕyth
Leḥem,
[25]Shammah the Ḥaroḏite, Eliqa the
Ḥaroḏite,
[26]Ḥelets the Paltite, Ira son of Iqqĕsh the
Teqowite,
[27]Aḇi'ezer the Anethothite, Meḇunnai the
Ḥushathite,
[28]Tsalmon the Aḥoḥite, Maharai the
Netophathite,
[29]Ḥĕleḇ son of Ba'anah the Netophathite,
Ittai son of Riḇai from Giḇ'ah of the
children of Binyamin,
[30]Benayahu the Pirathonite, Hiddai from
the wadis of Ga'ash,
[31]Aḇi-Alḇon the Arbathite, Azmaweth
the Barḥumite,
[32]Elyaḥba the Sha'albonite of the sons of
Yashĕn, Yehonathan,
[33]Shammah the Hararite, Aḥyam son of
Sharar the Hararite,
[34]Eliphelet son of Aḥasbai, son of the
Ma'aḵathite, Eliyam son of Aḥithophel the
Gilonite,
[35]Ḥetsrai the Karmelite, Pa'arai the
Arbite,
[36]Yiḡ'al son of Nathan of Tsoḇah, Bani
the Gaḏite,
[37]Tseleq the Ammonite, Naḥarai the
Be'ĕrothite, armour-bearer of Yo'aḇ son of
Tseruyah,
[38]Ira the Yithrite, Garĕḇ the Yithrite,
[39]and Uriyah the Ḥittite – thirty-seven in
all.

24 And again the displeasure of יהוה
burned against Yisra'ĕl, and moved
Dawiḏ against them to say, "Go, number
Yisra'ĕl and Yehuḏah."
[2]And the sovereign said to Yo'aḇ the
commander of the army who was with him,
"Go please, throughout all the tribes of
Yisra'ĕl, from Dan to Be'ĕrsheḇa, and register the people, so that I know the number
of the people."
[3]And Yo'aḇ said to the sovereign, "Even
if יהוה your Elohim does add to the people
a hundredfold more than there are, and the
eyes of my master the sovereign see it, but
why does my master the sovereign delight
in this matter?"
[4]However, the sovereign's word was
strong towards Yo'aḇ and against the commanders of the army. And Yo'aḇ and the
commanders of the army went out from the
presence of the sovereign to register the
people of Yisra'ĕl.
[5]And they passed over the Yardĕn and
camped in Aro'ĕr, on the right side of the

town which is in the midst of the wadi of
Gaḏ, and toward Yaʽzěr.
6 Then they came to Gilʽaḏ and to the
land of Taḥtim Ḥoḏshi, and they came to
Dan Yaʽan and around to Tsiḏon.
7 And they came to the stronghold of
Tsor and to all the cities of the Ḥiwwites
and the Kenaʽanites, and went out to South
Yehuḏah as far as Be'ěrsheḇa.
8 And when they had gone through all the
land, they came to Yerushalayim at the end
of nine new *moons* and twenty days.
9 And Yo'aḇ gave the number of the
registration of the people to the sovereign,
and there were in Yisra'ěl eight hundred
thousand brave men who drew the sword,
and the men of Yehuḏah were five hundred
thousand men.
10 And the heart of Dawiḏ struck him after
he had numbered the people. And Dawiḏ
said to יהוה, "I have sinned greatly in what
I have done. But now, I pray, O יהוה, take
away the crookedness of Your servant, for I
have done very foolishly."
11 And Dawiḏ rose up in the morning, and
the word of יהוה came to the prophet Gaḏ,
Dawiḏ's seer, saying,
12 "Go, and you shall speak to Dawiḏ,
'Thus said יהוה, "I hold three *options*
before you. Choose one of them, and I do
it to you." ' "
13 Gaḏ then came to Dawiḏ and informed
him. And he said to him, "Should seven
years of scarcity of food come to you in
your land? Or would you flee three new
moons before your enemies, while they
pursue you? Or should there be three days'
plague in your land? Now know and see
what answer I take back to Him who sent
me."
14 And Dawiḏ said to Gaḏ, "I am in great
trouble. Please let us fall into the hand of
יהוה, for His compassion is great, but do
not let me fall into the hand of man."
15 And יהוה sent a plague upon Yisra'ěl
from the morning till the appointed time,
and from Dan to Be'ěrsheḇa seventy thousand men of the people died.
16 And the messenger stretched out His
hand over Yerushalayim to destroy it, and
יהוה relented concerning the evil, and said
to the messenger who was destroying the
people, "It is enough, now stop Your
hand." And the messenger of יהוה was by
the threshing-floor of Arawnah the
Yeḇusite.
17 And Dawiḏ spoke to יהוה when he saw
the messenger who was striking the people,
and said, "See, I have sinned, and I have
done perversely. But these sheep, what
have they done? Let Your hand, I pray, be
against me and against my father's house."
18 And Gaḏ came that day to Dawiḏ and
said to him, "Go up, raise a slaughter-place
to יהוה on the threshing-floor of Arawnah
the Yeḇusite."
19 And Dawiḏ, according to the word of
Gaḏ, went up as יהוה commanded.
20 And Arawnah looked and saw the
sovereign and his servants coming toward
him. And Arawnah went out and bowed
before the sovereign with his face to the
ground.
21 And Arawnah said, "Why has my master the sovereign come to his servant?"
And Dawiḏ said, "To buy the threshing-
floor from you, to build a slaughter-place
to יהוה, so that the plague be withdrawn
from the people."
22 And Arawnah said to Dawiḏ, "Let my
master the sovereign take and offer that
which seems good to him. Here are cattle
for ascending offering, and threshing
implements and the yokes of the cattle for
wood.
23 "All these, O sovereign, Arawnah has
given to the sovereign." And Arawnah said
to the sovereign, "יהוה your Elohim accept
you!"
24 And the sovereign said to Arawnah,
"No, let me buy it from you for a price, for
certain. I am not offering ascending offerings to יהוה my Elohim without cost." So
Dawiḏ bought the threshing-floor and the
cattle for fifty sheqels of silver.
25 And Dawiḏ built a slaughter-place to
יהוה there, and offered ascending offerings
and peace offerings. And יהוה answered
the prayers for the land, and the plague was
withdrawn from Yisra'ěl.

MELAḴIM ALEPH

1 KINGS

1 And Sovereign Dawiḏ was old,
advanced in years. And they covered
him with garments, but he could not get
warm.
2 So his servants said to him, "Let them
seek for our master the sovereign a young
woman, a maiden, and she shall stand
before the sovereign and be his companion, and shall lie in your bosom, so that our
master the sovereign gets warm."
3 And they sought for a beautiful young
woman in all the border of Yisra'ěl, and
found Aḇishaḡ the Shunammite, and
brought her to the sovereign.
4 And the young woman was very beautiful. And she was a companion for the sovereign, and served him, but the sovereign
did not know her.
5 And Aḏoniyah son of Ḥaggith exalted
himself, saying, "I reign." And he prepared
for himself a chariot and horsemen, and
fifty men to run before him.
6 Now his father had not worried him at
any time by saying, "Why have you done
so?" He was also very good-looking. And
he was born after Aḇshalom.
7 And he talked with Yo'aḇ son of
Tseruyah and with Eḇyathar the priest, and
they supported Aḏoniyah.
8 But Tsaḏoq the priest, and Benayahu
son of Yehoyaḏa, and Nathan the prophet,
and Shim'i, and Rě'i, and the mighty men
who belonged to Dawiḏ were not with
Aḏoniyahu.
9 And Aḏoniyahu slaughtered sheep and
cattle and fatlings by the stone of Zoḥeleth,
which is by Ěn Roḡěl. He also invited all
his brothers, the sovereign's sons, and all
the men of Yehuḏah, servants of the
sovereign.
10 But he did not invite Nathan the
prophet, or Benayahu, or the mighty men,
or Shelomoh his brother.
11 Nathan then spoke to Bathsheḇa the
mother of Shelomoh, saying, "Have you
not heard that Aḏoniyahu son of Ḥaggith
has become sovereign, and Dawiḏ our
master does not know it?
12 "And now, come let me give you
advice, and deliver your own life and the
life of your son Shelomoh.
13 "Go immediately to Sovereign Dawiḏ
and say to him, 'Did you not, my master, O
sovereign, swear to your female servant,
saying, "Certainly, your son Shelomoh
shall reign after me, and he shall sit on my
throne"? Why then has Aḏoniyahu become
sovereign?'
14 "Look, while you are still speaking
there with the sovereign let me come in
after you and confirm your words."
15 And Bathsheḇa went into the room to
the sovereign. Now the sovereign was very
old, and Aḇishaḡ the Shunammite was
serving the sovereign.
16 And Bathsheḇa bowed and did obeisance to the sovereign. And the sovereign
said, "What do you wish?"
17 And she said to him, "My master, you
swore by יהוה your Elohim to your female
servant, saying, 'Certainly, Shelomoh your
son shall reign after me, and he shall sit on
my throne.'
18 "And now, look! Aḏoniyah has become
sovereign. And now, my master the sovereign, you do not know about it.
19 "And he has slaughtered great numbers
of bulls and fatlings and sheep, and has
invited all the sons of the sovereign, and
Eḇyathar the priest, and Yo'aḇ the commander of the army, but he did not invite
Shelomoh your servant.
20 "And you my master, O sovereign, the
eyes of all Yisra'ěl are on you, to declare to
them who is going to sit on the throne of
my master the sovereign after him.
21 "Otherwise it shall be, when my master
the sovereign rests with his fathers, that I
and my son Shelomoh shall be considered
sinners."

22 And see, while she was still speaking
with the sovereign, Nathan the prophet
also came in.
23 So they informed the sovereign, saying,
"Here is Nathan the prophet." And when
he came in before the sovereign, he bowed
down before the sovereign with his face to
the ground.
24 And Nathan said, "My master, O sovereign, have you said, 'Aḏoniyahu shall
reign after me, and he shall sit on my
throne'?
25 "For he has gone down today, and has
slaughtered great numbers of bulls and
fatlings and sheep, and has invited all the
sovereign's sons, and the commanders of
the army, and Eḇyathar the priest. And
look! They are eating and drinking before
him. And they say, 'Let Sovereign
Aḏoniyahu live!'
26 "But he has not invited me, me your
servant, nor Tsaḏoq the priest, nor Benayahu son of Yehoyaḏa, nor your servant
Shelomoh.
27 "If this matter is from my master the
sovereign, then you did not let your
servant know who should sit on the throne
of my master the sovereign after him."
28 And Sovereign Dawiḏ answered and
said, "Call Bathsheḇa to me." So she came
into the sovereign's presence and stood
before the sovereign.
29 And the sovereign took an oath and
said, "As יהוה lives, who has ransomed
my life out of all distress,
30 even as I swore to you by יהוה Elohim
of Yisra'ěl, saying, 'Certainly, Shelomoh
your son shall reign after me, and he shall
sit on my throne in my place,' even so I do
this day."
31 And Bathsheḇa bowed with her face to
the earth, and did obeisance to the sovereign, and said, "Let my master Sovereign
Dawiḏ live forever!"
32 And Sovereign Dawiḏ said, "Call me
Tsaḏoq the priest, and Nathan the prophet,
and Benayahu son of Yehoyaḏa." And they
came before the sovereign.
33 And the sovereign said to them, "Take
with you the servants of your master, and
you shall have Shelomoh my son ride on
my own mule, and take him down to
Giḥon.
34 "And there Tsaḏoq the priest and
Nathan the prophet shall anoint him sovereign over Yisra'ěl. And blow the shophar,
and say, 'Let Sovereign Shelomoh live!'
35 "And you shall come up after him, and
he shall come and sit on my throne, and
he shall reign in my place. For I have commanded him to be ruler over Yisra'ěl and
over Yehuḏah."
36 And Benayahu son of Yehoyaḏa
answered the sovereign and said, "Aměn!
So says יהוה Elohim of my master the
sovereign.
37 "As יהוה has been with my master the
sovereign, so let Him be with Shelomoh
and make his throne greater than the throne
of my master Sovereign Dawiḏ."
38 Then Tsaḏoq the priest, and Nathan the
prophet, and Benayahu son of Yehoyaḏa,
and the Kerěthites, and the Pelěthites went
down and had Shelomoh ride on Sovereign
Dawiḏ's mule, and took him to Giḥon.
39 And Tsaḏoq the priest took a horn of oil
from the Tent and anointed Shelomoh. And
they blew with the shophar, and all the
people said, "Let Sovereign Shelomoh
live!"
40 And all the people came up after him.
And the people played the flutes and
rejoiced with great joy, so that the earth
was split by their noise!
41 And Aḏoniyahu and all the guests who
were with him heard it as they had finished
eating. And Yo'aḇ heard the voice of the
shophar, and said, "Why is the city in such
a noisy uproar?"
42 And he was still speaking, then see,
Yonathan came, son of Eḇyathar the priest.
And Aḏoniyahu said to him, "Come in, for
you are a brave man, and you bring good
news."
43 But Yonathan answered and said to
Aḏoniyahu, "No! Our master Sovereign
Dawiḏ has made Shelomoh sovereign,
44 and the sovereign has sent with him
Tsaḏoq the priest, and Nathan the prophet,
and Benayahu son of Yehoyaḏa, and the
Kerěthites, and the Pelěthites. And they
had him ride on the sovereign's mule.

45"And Tsaḏoq the priest and Nathan the
prophet have anointed him sovereign at
Giḥon. And they have gone up from there
rejoicing, and the city is moved. This is the
noise you heard.
46"And further, Shelomoh sits on the
throne of the reign.
47"And further, the servants of the sovereign have gone to bless our master
Sovereign Dawiḏ, saying, 'Let your
Elohim make the name of Shelomoh better
than your name, and his throne greater
than your throne.' And the sovereign
bowed himself on the bed.
48"And the sovereign also said thus,
'Blessed be יהוה Elohim of Yisra'ěl, who
has given one to sit on my throne this day,
while my eyes see it!' "
49And all the guests who were invited by
Aḏoniyahu were afraid, and rose, and each
one went his way.
50And Aḏoniyahu was afraid of Shelomoh, and rose, and went and took hold of
the horns of the slaughter-place.
51And it was reported to Shelomoh,
saying, "Look, Aḏoniyahu is afraid of
Sovereign Shelomoh. And look, he has
taken hold of the horns of the slaughter-
place, saying, 'Let Sovereign Shelomoh
swear to me today that he does not put his
servant to death with the sword.' "
52And Shelomoh said, "If he proves himself a worthy man, not one hair of him is
going to fall to the earth, but if evil is
found in him, then he shall die."
53And Sovereign Shelomoh sent, and
they brought him down from the slaughter-
place. And he came and fell down before
Sovereign Shelomoh. And Shelomoh said
to him, "Go to your house."

2 And the days of Dawiḏ drew near to
die, and he commanded Shelomoh
his son, saying,
2"I am going the way of all the earth.
And you shall be strong, and be a man.
3"And guard the Charge of יהוה your
Elohim: to walk in His ways, to guard His
laws, His commands, His right-rulings,
and His witnesses, as it is written in the
Torah of Mosheh, so that you do wisely all
that you do and wherever you turn;
4so that יהוה does establish His word
which He spoke concerning me, saying, 'If
your sons guard their way, to walk before
Me in truth with all their heart and with all
their being,' saying, 'there is not to cease a
man of yours on the throne of Yisra'ěl.'
5"And also, you know what Yo'aḇ son
of Tseruyah did to me, and what he did
to the two commanders of the armies of
Yisra'ěl, to Aḇněr son of Něr and Amasa
son of Yether, that he killed them, and shed
the blood of battle in peace, and put the
blood of battle on his belt that was around
his waist, and on his sandals that were on
his feet.
6"So act according to your wisdom, and
do not let his grey hair go down to She'ol
in peace.
7"But show loving-commitment to the
sons of Barzillai the Gilʽaḏite, and let them
be among those who eat at your table, for
so they came to me when I fled from
Aḇshalom your brother.
8"And see, with you is Shimʽi son of
Gěra, the Binyamite from Baḥurim, who
cursed me with a grievous cursing in the
day when I went to Maḥanayim. But he
came down to meet me at the Yarděn, and I
swore to him by יהוה, saying, 'I shall not
put you to death with the sword.'
9"And now, do not leave him unpunished, for you are a wise man and know
what you should do to him, and shall bring
his grey hair down to She'ol with blood."
10And Dawiḏ slept with his fathers, and
was buried in the City of Dawiḏ.
11And the days that Dawiḏ reigned over
Yisra'ěl was forty years. He reigned seven
years in Ḥeḇron, and in Yerushalayim he
reigned thirty-three years.
12And Shelomoh sat on the throne of his
father Dawiḏ. And his reign was firmly
established.
13And Aḏoniyahu son of Ḥaggith came
to Bathsheḇa the mother of Shelomoh, and
she said, "Do you come in peace?" And he
said, "Peace."
14And he said, "I have a word for you,"
and she said, "Speak."
15And he said, "You know that the reign

was mine, and all Yisra'ěl had set their faces toward me, that I should reign. But the reign has been turned around, and has become my brother's, for it was his from יהוה.

16 "And now, I am making one request of you, do not refuse me." And she said to him, "Say it."

17 And he said, "Please speak to Sovereign Shelomoh – for he would not refuse you – to give me Aḇishaḡ the Shunammite as wife."

18 And Bathsheḇa said, "Good, let me speak for you to the sovereign."

19 And Bathsheḇa came to Sovereign Shelomoh, to speak to him for Aḏoniyahu. And the sovereign rose up to meet her and bowed down to her, and sat down on his throne and had a throne set for the sovereign's mother. So she sat at his right hand.

20 And she said, "I am making one small request of you, do not refuse me." And the sovereign said to her, "Ask it, my mother, for I do not refuse you."

21 Then she said, "Let Aḇishaḡ the Shunammite be given to Aḏoniyahu your brother as wife."

22 And Sovereign Shelomoh answered and said to his mother, "Now why do you ask Aḇishaḡ the Shunammite for Aḏoniyahu? Ask for him the reign also – for he is my older brother – for him, and for Eḇyathar the priest, and for Yo'aḇ son of Tseruyah."

23 And Sovereign Shelomoh swore by יהוה, saying, "Elohim does so to me, and more also, if Aḏoniyahu has not spoken this word against his own life!

24 "And now, as יהוה lives, who established me and set me on the throne of Dawiḏ my father, and who has made me a house, as He promised, Aḏoniyahu shall be put to death today!"

25 And Sovereign Shelomoh sent by the hand of Benayahu son of Yehoyaḏa, and he fell upon him, and he died.

26 Then the sovereign said to Eḇyathar the priest, "Go to Anathoth, to your own fields, for you deserve death. But I do not put you to death at this time, because you did bear the ark of the Master יהוה before my father Dawiḏ, and because you were afflicted in all my father was afflicted in."

27 So Shelomoh dismissed Eḇyathar from being priest to יהוה, to fill the word of יהוה which He spoke concerning the house of Ěli at Shiloh.

28 And news came to Yo'aḇ, for Yo'aḇ had turned aside after Aḏoniyah, though he did not turn aside after Aḇshalom. And Yo'aḇ fled to the Tent of יהוה, and took hold of the horns of the slaughter-place.

29 And the report came to Sovereign Shelomoh that Yo'aḇ had fled to the Tent of יהוה, and see, he is by the slaughter-place. Then Shelomoh sent Benayahu son of Yehoyaḏa, saying, "Go, fall on him."

30 So Benayahu came to the Tent of יהוה and said to him, "Thus said the sovereign, 'Come out!' " And he said, "No, for here I die." And Benayahu brought back word to the sovereign, saying, "Thus said Yo'aḇ, and thus he answered me."

31 And the sovereign said to him, "Do as he has said, and fall upon him. And you shall bury him, so that you take away from me and from the house of my father the blood which Yo'aḇ shed without cause.

32 "Thus יהוה shall return his blood on his head, because he had fallen on two men more righteous and better than he, and killed them with the sword, while my father Dawiḏ did not know it: Aḇněr son of Něr, commander of the army of Yisra'ěl, and Amasa son of Yether, commander of the army of Yehuḏah.

33 "So shall their blood return upon the head of Yo'aḇ and upon the head of his seed forever. But upon Dawiḏ and his seed, upon his house and his throne, there is to be peace forever from יהוה."

34 Then Benayahu son of Yehoyaḏa went up and fell upon him and put him to death. And he was buried in his own house in the wilderness.

35 And the sovereign put Benayahu son of Yehoyaḏa in his place over the army, and the sovereign put Tsaḏoq the priest in the place of Eḇyathar.

36 And the sovereign sent and called for Shim'i, and said to him, "Build yourself a house in Yerushalayim and dwell there,

and do not go out from there anywhere.
37 “And it shall be, on the day you go out
and pass over the wadi Qiḏron, know for
certain that you shall die – your blood is on
your own head.”
38 And Shim‘i said to the sovereign, “The
word is good. As my master the sovereign
has said, so your servant does.” So Shim‘i
dwelt in Yerushalayim many days.
39 And it came to be at the end of three
years, that two slaves of Shim‘i fled to
Aḵish son of Ma‘aḵah, sovereign of Gath.
And they informed Shim‘i, saying, “See,
your slaves are in Gath!”
40 And Shim‘i rose up, and saddled his
donkey, and went to Aḵish at Gath to look
for his slaves. And Shim‘i went and
brought his slaves from Gath.
41 And Shelomoh was told that Shim‘i had
gone from Yerushalayim to Gath and had
come back.
42 So the sovereign sent and called for
Shim‘i, and said to him, “Did I not make
you swear by יהוה, and warn you, saying,
‘Know for certain that on the day you
leave to go anywhere, you shall certainly
die’? And you said to me, ‘The word I
have heard is good.’
43 “And why have you not guarded the
oath of יהוה and the command that I gave
you?”
44 The sovereign also said to Shim‘i, “You
shall know all the evil that your heart has
known, that you did to my father Dawiḏ.
And יהוה shall return your evil on your
own head.
45 “But Sovereign Shelomoh is blessed,
and the throne of Dawiḏ is established
before יהוה forever.”
46 So the sovereign commanded
Benayahu son of Yehoyaḏa, and he went
out and fell on him, and he died. And the
reign was established in the hand of
Shelomoh.

3 And Shelomoh joined in marriage
with Pharaoh sovereign of Mitsrayim,
and took the daughter of Pharaoh, and
brought her to the City of Dawiḏ until he
had completed building his own house,
and the House of יהוה, and the wall all
around Yerushalayim.
2 Only, the people slaughtered at the high
places, for a house for the Name of יהוה
had not been built until those days.
3 And Shelomoh loved יהוה, walking
in the laws of his father Dawiḏ, except that
he slaughtered and burned incense at the
high places.
4 And the sovereign went to Giḇ‘on to
slaughter there, for that was the great high
place. Shelomoh offered a thousand
ascending offerings on that slaughter-
place.
5 At Giḇ‘on יהוה appeared to Shelomoh
in a dream by night, and Elohim said, “Ask
what I should give you.”
6 And Shelomoh said, “You have shown
great loving-commitment to your servant
Dawiḏ my father, as he walked before You
in truth, and in righteousness, and in
uprightness of heart with You. And You
have guarded for him this great loving-
commitment, and did give him a son to sit
on his throne, as it is this day.
7 “And now, O יהוה my Elohim, You
have set up Your servant to reign instead of
my father Dawiḏ. But I am a little child, I
do not know how to go out or to come in.
8 “And Your servant is in the midst of
Your people whom You have chosen, a
great people, too numerous to be numbered or counted.
9 “Shall You then give to Your servant an
understanding heart to rule Your people, to
discern between good and evil? For who is
able to rule this great people of Yours?”
10 And the word was good in the eyes of
יהוה, that Shelomoh had asked this.
11 So Elohim said to him, “Because you
have asked this, and have not asked long
life for yourself, nor have asked riches for
yourself, nor have asked the life of your
enemies, but have asked for yourself
discernment to understand right-ruling,
12 see, I shall do according to your words.
See, I shall give you a wise and understanding heart, so that there was none like
you before you, and none like you shall
arise after you.
13 “And I shall also give you what you
have not asked: both riches and esteem, so

that there shall not be anyone like you
among the sovereigns all your days.
14 "And if you walk in My ways, to guard
My laws and My commands, as your
father Dawiḏ walked, then I shall prolong
your days."
15 And Shelomoh awoke, and see, it was a
dream! And he came into Yerushalayim
and stood before the ark of the covenant of
יהוה, and offered up ascending offerings
and made peace offerings. And he made a
feast for all his servants.
16 Then two women, whores, came to the
sovereign, and stood before him.
17 And one woman said, "O my master,
this woman and I dwell in the same house.
And I gave birth while she was in the
house.
18 "And it came to be, the third day after I
had given birth, that this woman also gave
birth. And we were together. There was no
one else with us in the house, only the two
of us in the house.
19 "Then this woman's son died in the
night, because she lay on him.
20 "And she rose up in the middle of the
night and took my son from my side, while
your female servant slept, and laid him in
her bosom, and laid her dead child in my
bosom.
21 "And I rose up in the morning to nurse
my son and saw he was dead. But I looked
at him closely in the morning, and saw he
was not my son whom I had borne."
22 And the other woman said, "No! But
the living one is my son, and the dead one
is your son." And the first woman said,
"No! For the dead one is your son, and the
living one is my son." And they spoke
before the sovereign.
23 And the sovereign said, "The one says,
'This is my son, who lives, and your son is
the dead one,' while the other says, 'No!
For your son is the dead one, and my son is
the living one.' "
24 And the sovereign said, "Bring me a
sword." So they brought a sword before
the sovereign.
25 And the sovereign said, "Divide the
living child in two, and give half to one,
and half to the other."
26 And the woman whose son was living
spoke to the sovereign, for she was overcome with compassion for her son. And
she said, "O my master, give her the living
child, and by no means kill him!" But the
other said, "Let him be neither mine nor
yours, but divide him."
27 And the sovereign answered and said,
"Give the first woman the living child, and
by no means kill him – she is his mother."
28 And all Yisra'ěl heard of the right-
ruling which the sovereign had rendered.
And they feared the sovereign, for they
saw that the wisdom of Elohim was in him
to do right-ruling.

4 And it came to be that Sovereign
Shelomoh was sovereign over all
Yisra'ěl.
2 And these were his chief officials:
Azaryahu son of Tsaḏoq, the priest;
3 Eliḥoreph and Aḥiyah, sons of Shisha,
scribes; Yehoshaphat son of Aḥiluḏ, the
recorder;
4 and Benayahu son of Yehoyaḏa, over
the army; and Tsaḏoq and Eḇyathar, the
priests;
5 and Azaryahu son of Nathan, over the
officers; Zaḇuḏ son of Nathan, a priest,
friend of the sovereign;
6 and Aḥishar, over the household; and
Aḏoniram son of Aḇda, over the compulsory labour.
7 And Shelomoh had twelve governors
over all Yisra'ěl, who provided food for
the sovereign and his household – each one
made provision for one new *moon* of the
year –
8 and these were their names: Ben-Ḥur,
in the mountains of Ephrayim;
9 Ben-Deqer, in Maqats and Sha'alḇim
and Běyth Shemesh and Ělon Běyth
Ḥanan;
10 Ben-Ḥeseḏ in Arubboth, Soḵoh and all
the land of Ḥěpher were his;
11 Ben-Aḇinaḏaḇ, all the height of Dor,
Taphath the daughter of Shelomoh became
his wife;
12 Ba'ana son of Aḥiluḏ, in Ta'anaḵ and
Meḡiddo, and all Běyth She'an, which is
beside Tsarethan below Yizre'ěl, from

Bĕyth She'an to Aḇĕl Meḥolah, as far as
the other side of Yoqne'am;
13 Ben-Geḇer, in Ramoth Gil'aḏ, the
towns of Ya'ir son of Menashsheh in
Gil'aḏ were his; the portion of Argoḇ in
Bashan, sixty large cities with walls and
bronze gate-bars, were his;
14 Aḥinaḏaḇ son of Iddo, in Maḥanayim;
15 Aḥima'ats in Naphtali; he also took
Basemath the daughter of Shelomoh as
wife;
16 Ba'anah son of Ḥushai, in Ashĕr and in
Aloth;
17 Yehoshaphat son of Paruwaḥ, in Yissasḵar;
18 Shim'i son of Ĕlah, in Binyamin;
19 Geḇer son of Uri, in the land of Gil'aḏ,
in the land of Siḥon sovereign of the
Amorites and of Oḡ sovereign of Bashan,
and one governor was in the land.
20 Yehuḏah and Yisra'ĕl were as numerous as the sand by the sea, eating and
drinking and rejoicing.
21 And Shelomoh was ruling over all
reigns from the River to the land of the
Philistines, as far as the border of Mitsrayim. They did taskwork and served
Shelomoh all the days of his life.
22 And Shelomoh's food supply for one
day was thirty kors of fine flour, and sixty
kors of meal,
23 ten fatted cattle and twenty cattle from
the pastures, and one hundred sheep,
besides deer, and gazelles, and roebucks,
and fatted fowl.
24 For he was ruling over all on this side
of the River from Tiphsaḥ even to Azzah,
over all the sovereigns on this side of the
River. And he had peace on all sides round
about him.
25 And Yehuḏah and Yisra'ĕl dwelt safely,
each man under his vine and his fig tree,
from Dan as far as Be'ĕrsheḇa, all the days
of Shelomoh.
26 And Shelomoh had forty thousand
stalls of horses for his chariots, and twelve
thousand horsemen.
27 And these governors, each one in his
new *moon*, provided food for Sovereign
Shelomoh and for all who came to the
table of Sovereign Shelomoh. There was
no lack in their supply.
28 They also brought barley and straw to
the appointed place, for the horses and
steeds, each one according to his right-
ruling.
29 And Elohim gave Shelomoh exceeding
great wisdom and understanding, and
largeness of heart like the sand on the
seashore.
30 And Shelomoh's wisdom excelled the
wisdom of all the men of the East and all
the wisdom of Mitsrayim.
31 For he was wiser than all men, than
Ĕythan the Ezrahite, and Hĕman, and
Kalkol, and Darda, the sons of Maḥol. And
his name was in all the nations round
about.
32 And he spoke three thousand proverbs,
and his songs were one thousand and five.
33 And he spoke of trees, from the cedar
tree of Leḇanon even to the hyssop that
springs out of the wall. And he spoke
of beasts, and of birds, and of creeping
creatures, and of fish.
34 And there came from all peoples, from
all the sovereigns of the earth who had
heard of his wisdom, to hear the wisdom of
Shelomoh.

5 And Ḥiram sovereign of Tsor sent his
servants to Shelomoh, because he
heard that they had anointed him sovereign
in place of his father, for Ḥiram had always
loved Dawiḏ.
2 And Shelomoh sent to Ḥiram, saying,
3 "You know my father Dawiḏ was
unable to build a house for the Name of
יהוה his Elohim because of the battles
which were all around him, until יהוה put
them under the soles of his feet.
4 "But now יהוה my Elohim has given
me rest all around, there is neither
adversary nor evil incident.
5 "And see, I intend to build a house for
the Name of יהוה my Elohim, as יהוה
spoke to my father Dawiḏ, saying, 'Your
son, whom I set on your throne in your
place, he does build the house for My
Name.'
6 "And now, command that they cut
down cedars for me from Leḇanon. And let

my servants be with your servants, and let me pay you wages for your servants according to whatever you say. For you know there is none among us who knows to cut timber like the Tsiḏonians.”

7 And it came to be, when Ḥiram heard the words of Shelomoh, that he rejoiced greatly and said, “Blessed be יהוה this day, for He has given Dawiḏ a wise son over this great people!”

8 And Ḥiram sent to Shelomoh, saying, “I have heard that which you sent me. Let me do all you desire concerning the cedar and cypress logs.

9 “Let my servants bring them down from Leḇanon to the sea, then I put them in rafts by sea to the place you direct me. And I shall spread them out there, then you take them up, while you do my desire by giving food for my household.”

10 And Ḥiram gave Shelomoh cedar and cypress logs – all his desire.

11 And Shelomoh gave Ḥiram twenty thousand kors of wheat as food for his household, and twenty kors of pressed oil. Thus Shelomoh gave to Ḥiram year by year.

12 And יהוה gave Shelomoh wisdom, as He promised him. And there was peace between Ḥiram and Shelomoh, and the two of them made a covenant.

13 And Sovereign Shelomoh raised up compulsory labour out of all Yisra’ěl. And the compulsory labour was thirty thousand men.

14 And he sent them to Leḇanon, ten thousand *per* new *moon* by courses – they were one new *moon* in Leḇanon, two new *moons* at home. And Aḏoniram was over the compulsory labour.

15 And Shelomoh had seventy thousand bearing burdens, and eighty thousand hewing *stone* in the mountains,

16 besides three thousand three hundred from the chiefs of Shelomoh’s deputies who were over the work, those ruling over the people who laboured in the work.

17 And the sovereign commanded, and they brought large stones, precious stones, to lay the foundation of the House with hewn stones.

18 And Shelomoh’s builders, and Ḥiram’s builders, and the men of Geḇal did hew, and prepared timber and stones to build the House.

6 And it came to be, in the four hundred and eightieth year after the children of Yisra’ěl had come out of the land of Mitsrayim, in the fourth year of the reign of Shelomoh over Yisra’ěl, in the new *moon* of Ziw, which is the second new *moon*, that he began to build the House of יהוה.

2 And the house which Sovereign Shelomoh built for יהוה was sixty cubits long, and twenty wide, and thirty cubits high.

3 And the porch at the front of the Hěḵal of the House was twenty cubits long, according to the breadth of the House, and its width ten cubits, from the front of the House.

4 And he made for the House windows with narrowed frames.

5 And against the wall of the House he built rooms all around, *against* the walls of the House, all around the Hěḵal and the Speaking Place. Thus he made side rooms all around.

6 The lowest side room was five cubits wide, and the middle one was six cubits wide, and the third one was seven cubits wide; for he made narrow ledges around the outside of the House, so as not to lay hold on the walls of the House.

7 And the House, when it was being built, was built with finished stone made ready beforehand, so that no hammer or chisel or any iron tool was heard in the House while it was being built.

8 The doorway for the middle side room was on the right side of the House. And they went up by stairs to the middle side rooms, and from the middle to the third.

9 So he built the House and completed it, and he panelled the House with beams and boards of cedar.

10 And he built the side rooms of the structure against all the House, each five cubits high, and they were fastened to the House with cedar beams.

11 And the word of יהוה came to
Shelomoh, saying,
12 "This House which you are building –
if you walk in My laws, and do My right-rulings, and shall guard all My commands
and walk in them, then I shall confirm My
word with you, which I spoke to your
father Dawiḏ,
13 and shall dwell in the midst of the children of Yisra'ěl, and not forsake My people Yisra'ěl."
14 So Shelomoh built the House and completed it.
15 And he built the walls of the House
inside with cedar boards, from the floor of
the House to the ceiling he panelled them
on the inside with wood, and covered the
floor of the House with planks of cypress.
16 And he built twenty cubits at the rear of
the House, from floor to the walls, with
cedar boards. And he built it inside as the
Speaking Place, as the Most Set-apart
Place.
17 And the House was forty cubits, it is
the Hěḵal before it.
18 And the cedar for the House inside was
carved with ornaments and open flowers;
all was cedar, not a stone was seen.
19 And he prepared the Speaking Place in
the midst of the House, to place the ark of
the covenant of יהוה there.
20 And the front of the Speaking Place
was twenty cubits long, and twenty cubits
wide, and twenty cubits high. And he
overlaid it with refined gold, and overlaid
the slaughter-place of cedar.
21 And Shelomoh overlaid the inside of
the House with refined gold, and made
gold chains pass over the front of the
Speaking Place, and overlaid it with gold.
22 Thus he overlaid the entire House with
gold, until the entire House was completed. And the entire slaughter-place that was
by the Speaking Place he overlaid with
gold.
23 And inside the Speaking Place he made
two keruḇim of olive wood, ten cubits
high.
24 And one wing of the keruḇ was five
cubits, and the other wing of the keruḇ five
cubits – ten cubits from the tip of one wing
to the tip of the other.
25 And the other keruḇ was ten cubits.
Both keruḇim were of the same size and
shape.
26 The height of one keruḇ was ten cubits,
and so was the other keruḇ.
27 And he placed the keruḇim in the midst
of the inner house. And they stretched out
the wings of the keruḇim so that the wing
of the one touched one wall, and the wing
of the other keruḇ touched the other wall.
And their wings touched each other in the
middle of the room.
28 And he overlaid the keruḇim with gold.
29 And he carved all the walls of the
House all around, both inside and outside,
with carved figures of keruḇim, and palm
trees, and open flowers.
30 And he overlaid the floor of the House
with gold, inside and outside.
31 And for the entrance of the Speaking
Place he made doors of olive wood: the
lintel, doorposts, a fifth.
32 And the two doors were of olive wood.
And he carved on them figures of keruḇim,
and palm trees, and open flowers, and
overlaid them with gold. And he spread the
gold on the keruḇim and on the palm trees.
33 And so he made doorposts for the door
of the Hěḵal of olive wood – a fourth part.
34 And the two doors were of cypress
wood, the two leaves of the one folded,
and two leaves of the other door folded.
35 And he carved keruḇim, and palm trees,
and open flowers, and overlaid them with
gold laid smoothly on the carved work.
36 And he built the inner courtyard with
three rows of hewn stone and a row of
cedar beams.
37 In the fourth year the foundation of the
House of יהוה was laid, in the month Ziw.
38 And in the eleventh year, in the month
Bul, the eighth new *moon*, the house was
completed in all its matters and according
to all its plans. Thus he built it for seven
years.

7 And Shelomoh built his own house
for thirteen years, and he completed
his entire house.
2 And he built the house of the forest of

Leḇanon. It was one hundred cubits long, and fifty cubits wide, and thirty cubits high, with four rows of cedar columns, and cedar beams on the columns.
3 And it was panelled with cedar above the beams that were on forty-five columns, fifteen to a row.
4 And there were windows with narrowed frames in three rows, and window was opposite window, three times.
5 And all the doorways and doorposts had square frames. And window was opposite window, three times.
6 And he made the porch of the columns, fifty cubits long and thirty cubits wide. And the porch was in front of them, and the columns and the roof was in front of them.
7 And he made a hall for the throne, the Hall of Right-ruling, where he ruled. And it was panelled with cedar from floor to floor.
8 And the house where he was to dwell, *in* the other courtyard, within the hall was of like workmanship. And Shelomoh made a house like this hall for Pharaoh's daughter, whom he had taken.
9 All these were of precious stone hewn to size, sawed with a saw, inside and out, from the foundation to the coping, and also on the outside to the great courtyard.
10 And the foundation was of precious stone, large stones, stones of ten cubits and stones of eight cubits.
11 And above were precious stones, hewn to size, and cedar wood.
12 So the great courtyard all around had three rows of hewn stones and a row of cedar beams, as was the inner courtyard of the House of יהוה and the porch of the House.
13 And Sovereign Shelomoh sent and brought Ḥiram from Tsor.
14 He was the son of a widow from the tribe of Naphtali, and his father was a man of Tsor, a bronze worker. And he was filled with wisdom and understanding and skill in working with all kinds of bronze work. So he came to Sovereign Shelomoh and did all his work.
15 And he cast two columns of bronze, each one eighteen cubits high, and a line of twelve cubits measured the circumference of each.
16 And he made two capitals of cast bronze, to put on the tops of the columns – the height of one capital was five cubits, and the height of the other capital was five cubits –
17 a lattice network, with wreaths of chainwork, for the capitals which were on top of the columns, seven chains for one capital and seven for the other capital.
18 And he made the columns, and two rows of pomegranates above the network all around to cover the capitals that were on top, and so he did for the other capital.
19 And the capitals that were on top of the columns in the hall were in the shape of lilies, four cubits.
20 And there were capitals above also on the two columns, by the bulge which was next to the network. And the pomegranates were two hundred, in rows on each of the capitals all around.
21 And he set up the columns by the porch of the Hěḵal. And he set up the column on the right and called its name Yaḵin, and he set up the column on the left and called its name Boʽaz.
22 And on the top of the columns was lily work. Thus the work of the columns was completed.
23 And he made the Sea of cast *metal*, ten cubits from one rim to the other, round all about, and five cubits high, and a line of thirty cubits measured around it.
24 And below its rim were ornaments all around, ten to a cubit, all the way around the Sea. The ornaments were cast in two rows when it was cast.
25 It stood on twelve oxen, three facing north, and three facing west, and three facing south, and three facing east. And the Sea was set upon them, and all their back parts were inward.
26 And it was a handbreadth thick, and its rim was shaped like the rim of a cup, like a lily blossom. It held two thousand baths.
27 And he made ten stands of bronze, each stand was four cubits long, and four cubits wide, and three cubits high.

[28]And this is how the stands were made:
They had side panels, and the side panels
were between frames,
[29]and on the side panels that were
between the frames were lions, oxen, and
keruḇim, and a pedestal above on the
frame. Below the lions and oxen were
wreaths of beaten work.
[30]And each stand had four bronze wheels
and axles of bronze, and its four feet had
supports. Under the basin were cast supports beside each wreath.
[31]And its opening inside the crown at the
top was one cubit. And the opening was
round, like the work of the pedestal, one
and a half cubits. And also on the opening
were engravings, but the side panels were
square, not round.
[32]And the four wheels were under the
side panels, and the axles of the wheels
were joined to the stand, and the height of
a wheel was one and a half cubits.
[33]And the wheels were made like chariot
wheels. Their axle pins, and their rims, and
their spokes, and their hubs were all cast.
[34]And there were four supports at the
four corners of each stand, its supports
were of the stand itself.
[35]And on the top of the stand, half a cubit
in height – round all around. And on the
top of the stand, its flanges and its side
panels were of the same.
[36]And on the plates of its flanges and on
its side panels he engraved keruḇim, lions,
and palm trees, according to the clear
space on each, with wreaths all around.
[37]He made the ten stands like this: all of
them were of one mould, one measure, and
one shape.
[38]And he made ten basins of bronze; each
basin contained forty baths, and each basin
was four cubits, one basin on each of the
ten stands.
[39]And he put five stands on the right side
of the house, and five on the left side of the
house, and he put the Sea on the right side
of the house to the east, facing the south.
[40]And Ḥiram made the pots and the shovels and the bowls. And Ḥiram completed
doing all the work that he was to do for
Sovereign Shelomoh on the House of
יהוה:
[41]the two columns, and the bowl-shaped
capitals that were on top of the columns,
and the two networks covering the two
bowl-shaped capitals which were on top of
the columns;
[42]and the four hundred pomegranates for
the two networks, two rows of pomegranates for each network to cover the two
bowl-shaped capitals that were on top of
the columns;
[43]and the ten stands, and the ten basins on
the stands;
[44]and the one Sea, and twelve oxen under
the Sea;
[45]and the pots, and the shovels, and the
bowls. And all these utensils which Ḥiram
made for Sovereign Shelomoh for the
House of יהוה were of polished bronze.
[46]The sovereign had them cast in clay in
the district of Yardĕn between Sukkoth and
Tsarethan.
[47]And Shelomoh left all the utensils
unweighed, because they were many, nor
was the weight of the bronze searched out.
[48]So Shelomoh made all the utensils for
the House of יהוה: the slaughter-place of
gold, and the table of gold on which was
the showbread;
[49]and the lampstands of refined gold, five
on the right side and five on the left in
front of the Speaking Place, with the flowers and the lamps and the snuffers of gold;
[50]and the basins, and the snuffers, and the
bowls, and the ladles, and the fire holders
of refined gold, and the hinges of gold,
both for the doors of the inner house, the
Most Set-apart Place, and for the doors of
the house of the Hĕḵal.
[51]Thus all the work which Sovereign
Shelomoh had done for the House of יהוה
was completed. And Shelomoh brought in
the set-apart items of his father Dawiḏ: the
silver and the gold and the utensils, and
he put them in the treasuries of the House
of יהוה.

8 Then Shelomoh assembled the elders
of Yisra'ĕl and all the heads of the
tribes, the chief fathers of the children of
Yisra'ĕl, to Sovereign Shelomoh in Yeru-

shalayim, to bring up the ark of the
covenant of יהוה from the City of Dawiḏ,
which is Tsiyon.
2 And all the men of Yisra'ĕl assembled
to Sovereign Shelomoh at the festival in
the month of Ěythanim, which is the
seventh new *moon*.
3 And all the elders of Yisra'ĕl came, and
the priests took up the ark,
4 and brought up the ark of יהוה, and the
Tent of Appointment, and all the set-apart
utensils that were in the Tent. And the
priests and the Lĕwites brought them up,
5 and Sovereign Shelomoh, and all the
congregation of Yisra'ĕl who had assembled with him, were with him before the
ark, slaughtering so many sheep and cattle,
that they could not be counted or numbered.
6 And the priests brought in the ark of the
covenant of יהוה to its place, into the
Speaking Place of the House, to the Most
Set-apart Place, under the wings of the
keruḇim,
7 for the keruḇim spread two wings over
the place of the ark, and the keruḇim covered over the ark and its poles.
8 And the poles extended so that the ends
of the poles were seen from the set-apart
place, in front of the Speaking Place, but
they were not seen from outside. And they
are there to this day.
9 There was naught in the ark, only the
two tablets of stone which Mosheh put
there at Ḥorĕḇ, where יהוה made a
covenant with the children of Yisra'ĕl,
when they came out of the land of Mitsrayim.
10 And it came to be, when the priests
came out of the Set-apart Place, that the
cloud filled the House of יהוה,
11 so that the priests were unable to stand
and perform the service because of the
cloud, for the esteem of יהוה filled the
House of יהוה.
12 And Shelomoh said, "יהוה has said He
would dwell in the dark cloud.
13 I have indeed built You an exalted
house, an established place for You to
dwell in forever."
14 And the sovereign turned around and
blessed all the assembly of Yisra'ĕl, while
all the assembly of Yisra'ĕl was standing.
15 And he said, "Blessed be יהוה Elohim
of Yisra'ĕl, who spoke with His mouth to
my father Dawiḏ, and with His hand has
filled it, saying,
16 'Since the day I brought My people
Yisra'ĕl out of Mitsrayim, I have chosen
no city from any tribe of Yisra'ĕl in which
to build a house for My Name to be there,
but I chose Dawiḏ to be over My people
Yisra'ĕl.'
17 "And it was in the heart of my father
Dawiḏ to build a house for the Name of
יהוה Elohim of Yisra'ĕl.
18 "But יהוה said to my father Dawiḏ,
'Because it has been in your heart to build
a house for My Name, you did well that it
was in your heart.
19 'Only, you do not build the house, but
your son, who is coming from your loins,
he does build the house for My Name.'
20 "Now יהוה has established His word
which He spoke, and I have been raised up
instead of my father Dawiḏ, and sit on the
throne of Yisra'ĕl, as יהוה promised, and
built a house for the Name of יהוה Elohim
of Yisra'ĕl,
21 and have appointed there a place for the
ark, wherein is the covenant of יהוה which
He made with our fathers, when He
brought them out of the land of Mitsrayim."
22 And Shelomoh stood before the slaughter-place of יהוה in front of all the assembly of Yisra'ĕl, and spread out his hands
toward the heavens,
23 and said, "יהוה Elohim of Yisra'ĕl,
there is no Elohim in the heavens above or
on earth below like You, guarding Your
covenant and loving-commitment with
Your servants who walk before You with
all their heart,
24 who has guarded that which You did
promise Your servant Dawiḏ my father.
Indeed, You have both spoken with Your
mouth and have filled it with Your hand, as
it is this day.
25 "And now, יהוה Elohim of Yisra'ĕl,
guard what You promised Your servant
Dawiḏ my father, saying, 'There is not to

cease a man of yours before Me, sitting on
the throne of Yisra'ĕl – only, if your sons
guard their way, to walk before Me as you
have walked before Me.'
26 "And now, O Elohim of Yisra'ĕl, please
let Your word come true which You have
spoken to Your servant Dawiḏ my father.
27 "For is it true: Elohim dwells on the
earth? See, the heavens and the heavens of
the heavens are unable to contain You,
how much less this House which I have
built!
28 "Yet, shall You turn to the prayer of
Your servant and his supplication, O יהוה
my Elohim, and listen to the cry and the
prayer which Your servant is praying
before You today?
29 "For Your eyes to be open toward this
House night and day, toward the place of
which You said, 'My Name is there,' to listen to the prayer which Your servant makes
toward this place.
30 "Then, shall You hear the supplication
of Your servant and of Your people
Yisra'ĕl when they pray toward this place,
when You hear in Your dwelling place, in
the heavens? And shall You hear, and
forgive?
31 "If anyone sins against his neighbour,
and he has lifted up an oath on him, to
cause him to swear, and comes and swears
before Your slaughter-place in this House,
32 then hear in the heavens, and act and
rightly rule Your servants, declaring the
wrongdoer wrong, bringing his way on his
head, and declaring the righteous right by
giving him according to his righteousness.
33 "When Your people Yisra'ĕl are
smitten before an enemy, because they
have sinned against You, and they shall
turn back to You and confess Your Name,
and pray and make supplication to You
in this House,
34 then hear in the heavens, and forgive
the sin of Your people Yisra'ĕl, and bring
them back to the land which You gave to
their fathers.
35 "When the heavens are shut up and
there is no rain because they sin against
You, when they pray toward this place and
confess Your Name, and turn from their sin
because You afflict them,
36 then hear in the heavens, and forgive
the sin of Your servants, Your people
Yisra'ĕl – for You teach them the good
way in which they should walk – and shall
give rain on Your land which You have
given to Your people as an inheritance.
37 "When there is scarcity of food in the
land; when there is pestilence, blight,
mildew, locusts, grasshoppers; when their
enemy distresses them in the land of their
cities; any plague, any sickness,
38 whatever prayer, whatever supplication
made by anyone of all Your people
Yisra'ĕl, each knowing the plague of his
own heart, and shall spread out his hands
toward this House,
39 then hear in the heavens, Your dwelling
place, and forgive, and act, and render unto
everyone according to all his ways, whose
heart You know. Because You – You alone
– know the hearts of all the sons of men,
40 so that they fear You all the days that
they live in the land which You gave to our
fathers.
41 "Also, concerning a foreigner, who is
not of Your people Yisra'ĕl, but has come
from a far land for Your Name's sake –
42 since they hear of Your great Name and
Your strong hand and Your outstretched
arm – and he shall come and pray toward
this House,
43 hear in the heavens Your dwelling
place, and do according to all for which the
foreigner calls to You, so that all peoples
of the earth know Your Name and fear
You, as do Your people Yisra'ĕl, and know
that this House which I have built is called
by Your Name.
44 "When Your people go out to battle
against their enemy, in the way that You
send them, and they shall pray to יהוה
toward the city which You have chosen
and toward the House which I have built
for Your Name,
45 then shall You hear in the heavens their
prayer and their supplication, and maintain
their cause?
46 "When they sin against You – for there
is no one who does not sin – and You
become enraged with them and give them

to the enemy, and they take them captive to the land of the enemy, far or near;

47 and they shall turn back unto their heart in the land where they have been taken captive, and shall turn, and make supplication to You in the land of those who took them captive, saying, 'We have sinned and acted crookedly, we have committed wrong,'

48 and they shall turn back to You with all their heart and with all their being in the land of their enemies who led them away captive, and shall pray to You toward their land which You gave to their fathers, the city which You have chosen and the House which I have built for Your Name,

49 then shall You hear in the heavens Your dwelling place their prayer and their supplication, and maintain their cause,

50 and forgive Your people who have sinned against You, and all their transgressions which they have transgressed against You? And give them compassion before those who took them captive, and they shall have compassion on them.

51 'For they are Your people and Your inheritance, whom You brought out of Mitsrayim, out of the iron furnace.

52 "Let Your eyes be open to the supplication of Your servant and the supplication of Your people Yisra'ĕl, to listen to them whenever they call to You.

53 "For You have separated them unto Yourself for an inheritance, out of all the peoples of the earth, as You spoke by the hand of Your servant Mosheh, when You brought our fathers out of Mitsrayim, O Master יהוה."

54 And it came to be, when Shelomoh had ended praying all this prayer and supplication to יהוה, that he rose up from before the slaughter-place of יהוה, from kneeling on his knees with his hands spread up to the heavens.

55 And he stood and blessed all the assembly of Yisra'ĕl with a loud voice, saying,

56 "Blessed be יהוה, who has given rest to His people Yisra'ĕl, according to all that He promised. There has not failed one word of all His good word, which He promised through His servant Mosheh.

57 "יהוה our Elohim is with us as He was with our fathers – He does not leave us nor forsake us –

58 to incline our hearts to Himself, to walk in all His ways, and to guard His commands and His laws and His right-rulings, which He commanded our fathers.

59 "And let these words of mine, with which I have made supplication before יהוה, be near יהוה our Elohim day and night, to maintain the cause of His servant and the cause of His people Yisra'ĕl, the matter of each day in its day,

60 so that all the peoples of the earth might know that יהוה is Elohim, there is no one else.

61 "Let your heart therefore be perfect to יהוה our Elohim, to walk in His laws and guard His commands, as at this day."

62 And the sovereign and all Yisra'ĕl with him slaughtered slaughterings before יהוה.

63 And Shelomoh slaughtered slaughterings of peace *offerings*, which he slaughtered to יהוה, twenty-two thousand bulls and one hundred and twenty thousand sheep. Thus the sovereign and all the children of Yisra'ĕl dedicated the House of יהוה.

64 On that day the sovereign set apart the middle of the courtyard that was in front of the House of יהוה, for there he made ascending offerings, and the grain offerings, and the fat of the peace offerings, because the bronze slaughter-place that was before יהוה was too small to contain the ascending offerings, and the grain offerings, and the fat of the peace offerings.

65 And Shelomoh at that time performed the Festival, and all Yisra'ĕl with him, a great assembly from the entrance of Ḥamath to the wadi of Mitsrayim, before יהוה our Elohim, seven days and seven days – fourteen days.[a]

66 On the eighth day he sent the people

8a It seems that the first seven were the Festival of Ḥanukkah (Dedication), and the last seven the Festival of Sukkot (Booths).

away. And they blessed the sovereign, and
went to their tents rejoicing and glad of
heart for all the goodness that יהוה had
done for His servant Dawiḏ, and for
Yisra'ěl His people.

9

And it came to be, when Shelomoh
had finished building the House of
יהוה and the house of the sovereign, and
all the desire of Shelomoh which he was
pleased to do,
2 that יהוה appeared to Shelomoh the
second time, as He had appeared to him
at Gib'on.
3 And יהוה said to him, "I have heard
your prayer and your supplication that you
have made before Me. I have set this house
apart which you have built to put My
Name there forever, and My eyes and My
heart shall always be there.
4 "And you, if you walk before Me as
your father Dawiḏ walked, in integrity of
heart and in uprightness, to do according to
all that I have commanded you, if you
guard My laws and My right-rulings,
5 then I shall establish the throne of your
reign over Yisra'ěl forever, as I promised
Dawiḏ your father, saying, 'There is not to
cease a man of yours on the throne of
Yisra'ěl.'
6 "If you at all turn back, you or your
sons, from following Me, and do not guard
My commands, My laws, which I have set
before you, but shall go and serve other
mighty ones and bow yourselves to them,
7 then I shall cut off Yisra'ěl from the
face of the soil which I have given them,
and send away from My presence this
house which I have set apart for My Name.
And Yisra'ěl shall be a proverb and a
mockery among all the peoples.
8 "And this house, which has been exalted, everyone who passes by it shall be
astonished, and hiss, and say, 'Why has
יהוה done thus to this land and to this
house?'
9 "Then they shall say, 'Because they
have forsaken יהוה their Elohim, who
brought their fathers out of the land of
Mitsrayim, and they took hold of other
mighty ones, and bowed themselves to
them and served them. That is why יהוה
has brought all this evil on them.' "
10 And it came to be, at the end of twenty
years, that Shelomoh had built the two
houses, the House of יהוה and the house of
the sovereign.
11 Ḥiram the sovereign of Tsor had supplied Shelomoh with cedar and cypress
and gold, as much as he desired. Then
Sovereign Shelomoh gave Ḥiram twenty
cities in the land of Galil.
12 And Ḥiram came from Tsor to see the
cities which Shelomoh had given him, but
they were not right in his eyes,
13 and he said, "What are these cities you
have given me, my brother?" And he
called them the land of Kaḇul, as they are
to this day.
14 And Ḥiram sent the sovereign one hundred and twenty talents of gold.
15 And this is the purpose of the compulsory labour which Sovereign Shelomoh
raised, to build the House of יהוה, and his
own house, and Millo, and the wall of
Yerushalayim, and Ḥatsor, and Meḡiddo,
and Gezer –
16 Pharaoh sovereign of Mitsrayim had
gone up and taken Gezer and burned it
with fire, and had killed the Kena'anites
who dwelt in the city, and had given it as a
payment for the bride to his daughter,
Shelomoh's wife –
17 and Shelomoh built Gezer, and Lower
Běyth Ḥoron,
18 and Ba'alath, and Tamar in the wilderness, in the land of Yehuḏah,
19 and all the storage cities that Shelomoh
had, and cities for his chariots and cities
for his cavalry, and whatever Shelomoh
desired to build in Yerushalayim, and in
Leḇanon, and in all the land of his rule.
20 All the people who were left of the
Amorites, the Ḥittites, the Perizzites, the
Ḥiwwites, and the Yeḇusites, who were not
of the children of Yisra'ěl –
21 their descendants who were left in
the land after them, whom the children of
Yisra'ěl had not been able to destroy completely – from these Shelomoh raised compulsory labour, as it is to this day.
22 But Shelomoh did not make slaves of

the children of Yisra'ěl, because they were men of battle, and his servants, and his rulers, and his officers, and commanders of his chariots, and his cavalry.

23 These were the chiefs of the officials who were over the work of Shelomoh: five hundred and fifty, who ruled over the people who did the work.

24 But the daughter of Pharaoh came up from the City of Dawiḏ to her house that he built for her. Then he built Millo.

25 And three times a year Shelomoh brought ascending offerings and peace offerings on the slaughter-place which he had built for יהוה, and he burned incense with that which was before יהוה – thus gave completeness to the House.

26 And Sovereign Shelomoh built a fleet of ships at Etsyon Geḇer, which is near Ěyloth on the shore of the Sea of Reeds, in the land of Eḏom.

27 And Ḥiram sent his servants with the fleet, seamen who knew the sea, to work with the servants of Shelomoh.

28 And they went to Ophir, and took four hundred and twenty talents of gold from there, and brought it to Sovereign Shelomoh.

10 And the sovereigness of Sheḇa heard of the report of Shelomoh concerning the Name of יהוה, and came to try him with hard questions.

2 And she came to Yerushalayim with a very great company, with camels that bore spices, very much gold, and precious stones. And she came to Shelomoh, and she spoke with him about all that was in her heart.

3 And Shelomoh answered all her questions. There was no matter hidden for the sovereign that he did not make known to her.

4 And the sovereigness of Sheḇa saw all the wisdom of Shelomoh, and the house that he had built,

5 and the food on his table, and the seating of his servants, and the service of his waiters and their attire, and his cupbearers, and his ascending offerings which he offered in the House of יהוה, and there was no more spirit in her.

6 Then she said to the sovereign, "The word I heard in my own land about your words and your wisdom was true.

7 "But I did not believe the words until I came and saw with my own eyes. And see, I have not been told the half! Your wisdom and prosperity exceed the report which I heard.

8 "Blessed are your men and blessed are these your servants, who stand continually before you, who are hearing your wisdom!

9 "Blessed be יהוה your Elohim, who delighted in you, to put you on the throne of Yisra'ěl! Because יהוה has loved Yisra'ěl forever, therefore He made you sovereign, to do right-ruling and righteousness."

10 And she gave the sovereign one hundred and twenty talents of gold, and very many spices, and precious stones. Never again did so many spices come as the sovereigness of Sheḇa gave to Sovereign Shelomoh.

11 And also, the ships of Ḥiram, which brought gold from Ophir, brought almug wood, a great many, and precious stones from Ophir.

12 And the sovereign made steps of the almug wood for the House of יהוה and for the sovereign's house, also lyres and harps for singers. No such almug wood has come or been seen to this day.

13 And Sovereign Shelomoh gave the sovereigness of Sheḇa all she desired, whatever she asked, besides what he gave her according to the hand of Sovereign Shelomoh. And she turned and went to her land, she and her servants.

14 And the weight of gold that came to Shelomoh yearly was six hundred and sixty-six talents of gold,

15 besides that from men of travel, and the profit from traders, and from all the sovereigns of Araḇia, and from the governors of the land.

16 And Sovereign Shelomoh made two hundred large shields of beaten gold – six hundred pieces of gold went into each shield;

17 and three hundred shields of beaten

gold – three minas of gold went into each
shield. And the sovereign put them in the
House of the Forest of Leḇanon.
18 And the sovereign made a great throne
of ivory, and overlaid it with refined gold.
19 The throne had six steps, and the top of
the throne was round at the back, and there
were armrests on either side of the place of
the seat, and two lions stood beside the
armrests.
20 And twelve lions were standing there,
one on each side of the six steps. The like
of it was never made in any reign.
21 And all the drinking vessels of
Sovereign Shelomoh were of gold, and all
the vessels of the House of the Forest of
Leḇanon were of refined gold – not of
silver, for this was reckoned of little value
in the days of Shelomoh.
22 For the sovereign had ships of Tarshish
at sea with the fleet of Ḥiram. Once every
three years the ships of Tarshish came
bringing gold, and silver, ivory, and apes,
and baboons.
23 And Sovereign Shelomoh was greater
than any of the sovereigns of the earth in
riches and wisdom.
24 And all the earth sought the presence
of Shelomoh to hear his wisdom, which
Elohim had put in his heart.
25 And they were each bringing his
present: objects of silver and objects of
gold, and garments, and armour, and
spices, horses, and mules, the matter of a
year by year.
26 And Shelomoh gathered chariots and
horsemen, and he had one thousand four
hundred chariots and twelve thousand
horsemen, whom he stationed in the
chariot cities and with the sovereign in
Yerushalayim.
27 And the sovereign made silver as common in Yerushalayim as stones, and he
made cedars as plenty as the sycamores
which are in the low country.
28 And Shelomoh had horses brought out
from Mitsrayim and Quěh; the sovereign's
merchants bought them in Quěh at a price.
29 And a chariot came up and went out
from Mitsrayim for six hundred pieces of
silver, and a horse one hundred and fifty.
And so, by their hand, they brought them
out to all the sovereigns of the Ḥittites and
the sovereigns of Aram.

11 And Sovereign Shelomoh loved
many foreign women in addition to
the daughter of Pharaoh: Mo'aḇite,
Ammonite, Eḏomite, Tsiḏonian, and Ḥittite women;
2 from the nations of whom יהוה had
said to the children of Yisra'ěl, "You do
not go into them, and they do not go into
you, for they shall certainly turn away your
hearts after their mighty ones." Shelomoh
clung to these in love.
3 And he had seven hundred wives,
princesses, and three hundred concubines.
And his wives turned away his heart.
4 And it came to be, when Shelomoh was
old, that his wives turned away his heart
after other mighty ones. And his heart was
not perfect with יהוה his Elohim, as was
the heart of his father Dawiḏ.
5 And Shelomoh went after Ashtoreth
the mighty one of the Tsiḏonians, and
after Milkom the abomination of the
Ammonites.
6 Thus Shelomoh did evil in the eyes of
יהוה, and did not follow יהוה completely,
like his father Dawiḏ.
7 Then Shelomoh built a high place for
Kemosh the abomination of Mo'aḇ, on the
hill that is east of Yerushalayim, and for
Moleḵ the abomination of the children of
Ammon.
8 And so he did for all his foreign wives,
who burned incense and slaughtered to
their mighty ones.
9 Therefore יהוה was enraged with
Shelomoh, because his heart had turned
away from יהוה Elohim of Yisra'ěl, who
had appeared to him twice,
10 and had commanded him concerning
this word, not to go after other mighty
ones. But he did not guard what יהוה
had commanded.
11 And יהוה said to Shelomoh, "Because
you have done this, and have not guarded
My covenant and My laws, which I have
commanded you, I shall certainly tear the
reign away from you and give it to your

servant.
12 "Only, I do not do it in your days, for
the sake of your father Dawiḏ. Out of the
hand of your son I shall tear it.
13 "Only, I shall not tear away all the reign
but give one tribe to your son for the sake
of my servant Dawiḏ, and for the sake of
Yerushalayim which I have chosen."
14 And יהוה raised up an adversary
against Shelomoh, Haḏaḏ the Eḏomite. He
was of the seed of the sovereign in Eḏom.
15 And it came to be, when Dawiḏ was in
Eḏom, and Yo'aḇ the commander of the
army had gone up to bury the slain, after
he had struck every male in Eḏom –
16 Yo'aḇ remained there with all Yisra'ěl
for six new *moons*, until every male in
Eḏom was cut off –
17 that Haḏaḏ fled to go to Mitsrayim, he
and certain Eḏomites of his father's servants with him, while Haḏaḏ was still a
little child.
18 And they arose from Miḏyan and came
to Paran, and took men with them from
Paran and came to Mitsrayim, to Pharaoh
sovereign of Mitsrayim, who gave him a
house, and ordered food for him, and gave
him land.
19 And Haḏaḏ found much favour in the
eyes of Pharaoh, so that he gave him as
wife the sister of his own wife, the sister
of Sovereigness Taḥpeněs.
20 And the sister of Taḥpeněs bore him
Genuḇath his son, whom Taḥpeněs weaned
in Pharaoh's house. And Genuḇath was in
the house of Pharaoh among the sons of
Pharaoh.
21 And Haḏaḏ heard in Mitsrayim that
Dawiḏ slept with his fathers, and that
Yo'aḇ the commander of the army was
dead, and Haḏaḏ said to Pharaoh, "Let me
go to my land."
22 And Pharaoh said to him, "But what
have you lacked with me, that you are now
seeking to go to your own land?" And he
answered, "No, but please let me go."
23 And Elohim raised up another adversary against him, Rezon son of Elyaḏa who
had fled from his master, Haḏaḏezer sovereign of Tsoḇah,
24 and gathered men to him and became
commander over a raiding band, when
Dawiḏ killed those *of Tsoḇah*. And they
went to Dammeseq and dwelt there, and
reigned in Dammeseq.
25 And he was an adversary of Yisra'ěl all
the days of Shelomoh – besides the trouble
that Haḏaḏ caused – and he was hostile to
Yisra'ěl and reigned over Aram.
26 And a servant of Shelomoh, Yaroḇ'am
son of Neḇat, an Ephrayimite from
Tserěḏah, whose mother's name was
Tseru'ah, a widow, also lifted up a hand
against the sovereign.
27 And this is what caused him to lift up a
hand against the sovereign: Shelomoh had
built Millo, repairing the breaks in the City
of Dawiḏ his father.
28 And the man Yaroḇ'am was a brave
man. And Shelomoh, seeing that the young
man was doing his work well, made him
the officer over all the compulsory labour
of the house of Yosěph.
29 And it came to be at that time, when
Yaroḇ'am went out of Yerushalayim, that
the prophet Aḥiyah the Shilonite met him
on the way. And he was wearing a new
garment, and the two were alone in the
field.
30 And Aḥiyah took hold of the new
garment that was on him, and tore it into
twelve pieces,
31 and said to Yaroḇ'am, "Take for yourself ten pieces, for thus said יהוה, the
Elohim of Yisra'ěl, 'See, I am tearing the
reign out of the hand of Shelomoh and
shall give ten tribes to you,
32 but he shall have one tribe for the sake
of My servant Dawiḏ, and for the sake of
Yerushalayim, the city which I have
chosen out of all the tribes of Yisra'ěl.
33 'Because they have forsaken Me, and
bow themselves to Ashtoreth the mighty
one of the Tsiḏonians, to Kemosh the
mighty one of the Mo'aḇites, and to
Milkom the mighty one of the children of
Ammon, and have not walked in My ways
– to do what is right in My eyes, and My
laws and My right-rulings, as did his father
Dawiḏ.
34 'But I do not take all the reign out of his
hand, because I have made him ruler all

the days of his life for the sake of My
servant Dawiḏ, whom I chose because he
guarded My commands and My laws.
35 'And I shall take the reign out of his
son's hand and give it to you, the ten
tribes.
36 'And to his son I give one tribe, so that
My servant Dawiḏ shall always have a
lamp before Me in Yerushalayim, the city
which I have chosen for Myself, to put My
Name there.
37 'So I take you, and you shall reign over
all that your being desires, and you shall be
sovereign over Yisra'ěl.
38 'And it shall be, if you obey all that I
command you, and shall walk in My ways,
and do what is right in My eyes, to guard
My laws and My commands, as My
servant Dawiḏ did, then I shall be with
you and build for you a steadfast house,
as I built for Dawiḏ, and shall give Yisra'ěl
to you.
39 'And because of this I humble the seed
of Dawiḏ, but not forever.' "
40 And Shelomoh sought to kill Yaroḇʽam,
but Yaroḇʽam rose up and fled to Mitsrayim, to Shishaq sovereign of Mitsrayim,
and was in Mitsrayim until the death of
Shelomoh.
41 And the rest of the acts of Shelomoh,
all that he did, and his wisdom, are they
not written in the book of the acts of
Shelomoh?
42 And the days that Shelomoh reigned in
Yerushalayim over all Yisra'ěl was forty
years.
43 So Shelomoh slept with his fathers, and
was buried in the City of Dawiḏ his father,
and Reḥaḇʽam his son reigned in his place.

12 And Reḥaḇʽam went to Sheḵem,
for all Yisra'ěl had gone to
Sheḵem to set him up to reign.
2 And it came to be, when Yaroḇʽam son
of Neḇat heard this – he was still in
Mitsrayim, for he had fled from the
presence of Sovereign Shelomoh and had
been dwelling in Mitsrayim –
3 that they sent and called him. And
Yaroḇʽam and all the assembly of Yisra'ěl
came and spoke to Reḥaḇʽam, saying,
4 "Your father made our yoke hard, and
now, lighten the hard service of your
father, and his heavy yoke which he put on
us, then we serve you."
5 And he said to them, "Go away for
three days, then come back to me." And
the people went.
6 Then Sovereign Reḥaḇʽam consulted
the elders who stood before his father
Shelomoh while he still lived, and he said,
"What do you advise me to answer these
people?"
7 And they spoke to him, saying, "If you
are a servant to these people today, and
shall serve them, and shall answer them
and speak good words to them, then they
shall be your servants all the days."
8 But he ignored the advice the elders
gave him, and consulted the young men
who had grown up with him, who stood
before him.
9 And he said to them, "What advice do
you give? How should we answer this
people who have spoken to me, saying,
'Lighten the yoke which your father put
on us'?"
10 And the young men who had grown up
with him spoke to him, saying, "Say this to
this people who have spoken to you, saying, 'Your father made our yoke heavy, but
you make it lighter on us.' Say this to
them, 'My little finger is thicker than my
father's waist!
11 'And now, my father laid a heavy yoke
on you, but I add to your yoke; my father
flogged you with whips, but I, I flog you
with scourges!' "
12 So Yaroḇʽam and all the people came to
Reḥaḇʽam the third day, as the sovereign
had spoken, saying, "Come back to me the
third day."
13 But the sovereign answered the people
harshly, and ignored the advice which the
elders had given him,
14 and he spoke to them according to the
advice of the young men, saying, "My
father made your yoke heavy, but I add to
your yoke; my father flogged you with
whips, but I, I flog you with scourges!"
15 So the sovereign did not listen to the
people, for the turn *of events* was from

יהוה, in order to establish His word, which
יהוה had spoken by Aḥiyah the Shilonite
to Yaroḇʽam son of Neḇat.
16 And all Yisra'ěl saw that the sovereign
did not listen to them. Then the people
answered the sovereign, saying, "What
portion do we have in Dawiḏ? And there is
no inheritance in the son of Yishai. To your
mighty ones, [a] O Yisra'ěl! Now, see to your
own house, O Dawiḏ!" So Yisra'ěl went to
their tents.
17 But as for the children of Yisra'ěl who
dwelt in the cities of Yehuḏah, Reḥaḇʽam
reigned over them.
18 And when Sovereign Reḥaḇʽam sent
Aḏoram, who was over the compulsory
labour, all Yisra'ěl stoned him with stones,
and he died. And Sovereign Reḥaḇʽam
hastily mounted his chariot to flee to
Yerushalayim.
19 Thus Yisra'ěl revolted against the
house of Dawiḏ to this day.
20 And it came to be when all Yisra'ěl
heard that Yaroḇʽam had come back, they
sent for him and called him to the congregation, and set him up to reign over all
Yisra'ěl. There was none who followed
the house of Dawiḏ, except the tribe of
Yehuḏah only.
21 And Reḥaḇʽam came to Yerushalayim,
and he assembled all the house of Yehuḏah
with the tribe of Binyamin, one hundred
and eighty thousand chosen brave men, to
fight against the house of Yisra'ěl, to bring
back the reign to Reḥaḇʽam son of
Shelomoh.
22 But the word of Elohim came to
Shemayah the man of Elohim, saying,
23 "Speak to Reḥaḇʽam son of Shelomoh,
sovereign of Yehuḏah, and to all the house
of Yehuḏah and Binyamin, and to the rest
of the people, saying,
24 'Thus said יהוה, "Do not go up or fight
against your brothers the children of
Yisra'ěl. Let every man return to his house,
for this matter is from Me." ' " So they
obeyed the word of יהוה, and turned back,
according to the word of יהוה.
25 And Yaroḇʽam built Sheḵem in the
mountains of Ephrayim, and dwelt there.
And he went out from there and built
Penu'ěl.
26 And Yaroḇʽam said in his heart, "Now
the reign shall return to the house of
Dawiḏ.
27 "If these people go up to do slaughterings in the House of יהוה at Yerushalayim,
then the heart of this people shall turn back
to their master, Reḥaḇʽam sovereign of
Yehuḏah, and they shall kill me and go
back to Reḥaḇʽam sovereign of Yehuḏah."
28 So the sovereign took counsel and
made two calves of gold, and said to the
people, "It is too much for you to go up to
Yerushalayim. See, your mighty ones,
O Yisra'ěl, which brought you up from
the land of Mitsrayim!"
29 And he set up one in Běyth Ěl, and the
other he put in Dan.
30 And this matter became a sin, for the
people went before the one as far as Dan.
31 And he made the house of high places,
and made priests from all sorts of people,
who were not of the sons of Lěwi.
32 And Yaroḇʽam performed a festival on
the fifteenth day of the eighth new *moon*,
like the festival that was in Yehuḏah, and
he offered on the slaughter-place. So he
did at Běyth Ěl, slaughtering to the calves
that he had made. And at Běyth Ěl he
appointed the priests of the high places
which he had made.
33 And he made offerings on the slaughter-place which he had made at Běyth Ěl
on the fifteenth day of the eighth new
moon, in the new *moon* which he had
devised in his own heart. And he performed a festival for the children of
Yisra'ěl, and offered on the slaughter-place
and burned incense.

13

And see, a man of Elohim went
from Yehuḏah to Běyth Ěl by the
word of יהוה, while Yaroḇʽam was standing by the slaughter-place to burn incense.
2 And he cried out against the slaughter-
place by the word of יהוה, and said, "O
slaughter-place, slaughter-place! Thus said

12a - Heb. *elohim*, which the Scribes (*Sopherim*) later on emended to read "tents."

יהוה, 'See, a son is to be born to the house
of Dawiḏ, Yoshiyahu is his name. And on
you he shall slaughter the priests of the
high places who burn incense on you, and
men's bones be burned on you.' "
3 And he gave a sign the same day,
saying, "This is the sign which יהוה has
spoken: See, the slaughter-place is split
apart, and the ashes on it is poured out."
4 And it came to be when Sovereign
Yaroḇʽam heard the saying of the man of
Elohim, who cried out against the slaughter-place in Bĕyth Ěl, that he stretched out
his hand from the slaughter-place, saying,
"Seize him!" Then his hand, which he
stretched out toward him, dried up, so that
he was unable to bring it back to him.
5 And the slaughter-place was split apart,
and the ashes poured out from the slaughter-place, according to the sign which the
man of Elohim had given by the word of
יהוה.
6 And the sovereign answered and said to
the man of Elohim, "Please appease the
face of יהוה your Elohim, and pray for me,
that my hand might be restored to me."
And the man of Elohim appeased the face
of יהוה, and the sovereign's hand was
restored to him, and became as it was
before.
7 The sovereign then said to the man of
Elohim, "Come home with me and refresh
yourself, and I give you a gift."
8 But the man of Elohim said to the
sovereign, "If you were to give me half
your house, I do not go in with you, nor do
I eat bread nor drink water in this place.
9 "For so He commanded me by the word
of יהוה, saying, 'Do not eat bread, nor
drink water, nor return by the same way
you came.' "
10 So he went another way and did not
return by the way he came to Bĕyth Ěl.
11 And a certain old prophet was dwelling
in Bĕyth Ěl, and his sons came and told
him all the works that the man of Elohim
had done that day in Bĕyth Ěl, the words
which he had spoken to the sovereign.
12 And their father said to them, "Which
way did he go?" And his sons had seen
which way the man of Elohim went who
came from Yehuḏah.
13 And he said to his sons, "Saddle the
donkey for me." And they saddled the
donkey for him, and he rode on it,
14 and went after the man of Elohim, and
found him sitting under a terebinth. And he
said to him, "Are you the man of Elohim
who came from Yehuḏah?" And he said,
"I am."
15 And he said to him, "Come home with
me and eat bread."
16 And he said, "I am not able to return
with you or to go in with you, nor am I to
eat bread or drink water with you in this
place.
17 "For word came to me by the word of
יהוה, 'Do not eat bread nor drink water
there, nor return by going the way you
came.' "
18 And he said to him, "I too am a prophet
like you, and a messenger spoke to me by
the word of יהוה, saying, 'Bring him back
with you to your house, and let him eat
bread and drink water.' " But he lied to
him.
19 So he turned back with him, and ate
bread in his house, and drank water.
20 And it came to be, as they sat at the
table, that the word of יהוה came to the
prophet who had brought him back,
21 and he cried out to the man of Elohim
who came from Yehuḏah, saying, "Thus
said יהוה, 'Because you have rebelled
against the mouth of יהוה, and have not
guarded the command which יהוה your
Elohim commanded you,
22 and turned back, and ate bread, and
drank water in the place of which He said
to you, "Do not eat bread nor drink water,"
your body shall not enter the burial-site of
your fathers.' "
23 And it came to be, after he had eaten
bread and after he had drunk, that he
saddled the donkey for him, for the
prophet whom he had brought back.
24 And he went, and a lion met him on the
way and killed him. And his body was
thrown on the way. And the donkey was
standing by it, and the lion was standing by
the body.
25 And see, men were passing by and saw

the body thrown on the way, while the lion was standing by the body. And they went and reported it in the city where the old prophet dwelt.

26 And the prophet who had brought him back from the way heard it, and said, "It is the man of Elohim who rebelled against the mouth of יהוה, and יהוה gave him to the lion, and it tore him apart and killed him, according to the word of יהוה which He spoke to him."

27 And he spoke to his sons, saying, "Saddle the donkey for me." And they saddled it.

28 So he went and found his body thrown on the way, and the donkey and the lion standing by the body. The lion had not eaten the body nor mauled the donkey.

29 And the prophet lifted up the body of the man of Elohim, and placed it on the donkey, and brought it back. And the old prophet came to the city to mourn, and to bury him,

30 and he placed his body in his own burial-site. And they lamented over him, saying, "Oh, my brother!"

31 And it came to be, after he had buried him, that he spoke to his sons, saying, "When I am dead, then you shall bury me in the burial-site where the man of Elohim is buried. Lay my bones beside his bones.

32 "For the word which he cried out, by the word of יהוה, against the slaughter-place in Bĕyth Ěl, and against all the houses of the high places which are in the cities of Shomeron, shall certainly come to be."

33 After this event Yaroḇʽam did not turn from his evil way, but again he made priests from all sorts of people for the high places. Whoever wished, he ordained, to become one of the priests of the high places.

34 And this matter was the sin of the house of Yaroḇʽam, even to cut it off and destroy it from the face of the earth.

14

At that time Aḇiyah the son of Yaroḇʽam became sick.

2 And Yaroḇʽam said to his wife, "Please arise, and disguise yourself, so they do not know that you are the wife of Yaroḇʽam, and go to Shiloh. See, Aḥiyah the prophet is there, who spoke to me of *becoming* sovereign over this people.

3 "And you shall take with you ten loaves, and cakes, and a jar of honey, and go to him. Let him declare to you what becomes of the child."

4 And Yaroḇʽam's wife did so, and rose up and went to Shiloh, and came to the house of Aḥiyah. But Aḥiyahu was unable to see, for his eyes had set because of his age.

5 And יהוה had said to Aḥiyahu, "See, the wife of Yaroḇʽam is coming to ask you a word about her son, for he is sick. Speak to her thus and thus. For it shall be, when she comes in, that she makes herself strange."

6 And it came to be, when Aḥiyahu heard the sound of her footsteps as she came through the door, he said, "Come in, wife of Yaroḇʽam. Why are you making yourself strange? And I have been sent to you with a hard *word*.

7 Go, say to Yaroḇʽam, 'Thus said יהוה Elohim of Yisra'ěl, "Because I exalted you from among the people, and made you ruler over My people Yisra'ěl,

8 and tore the reign away from the house of Dawiḏ, and gave it to you – and you have not been as My servant Dawiḏ, who guarded My commands and who followed Me with all his heart, to do only what was right in My eyes,

9 but you have done more evil than all who were before you, for you have gone and made for yourself other mighty ones and moulded images to provoke Me, and have cast Me behind your back –

10 therefore, see, I am bringing evil to the house of Yaroḇʽam, and shall cut off from Yaroḇʽam every male in Yisra'ěl, whether shut up or left at large, and sweep away the remnant of the house of Yaroḇʽam, as one sweeps away dung until it is all gone.

11 Those of Yaroḇʽam who die in the city the dogs do eat, and those who die in the field the birds of the heavens do eat, for יהוה has spoken it!" '

12 "And you, arise, go to your house. When your feet enter the city, the child

shall die.
13“And all Yisra’ěl shall mourn for him
and bury him, for he is the only one of
Yaroḇ‘am who shall come to the burial-
site, because in him there is found a good
report toward יהוה Elohim of Yisra’ěl, in
the house of Yaroḇ‘am.
14“And יהוה shall raise up for Himself
a sovereign over Yisra’ěl who cuts off
the house of Yaroḇ‘am, this day, and even
now!
15“And יהוה shall strike Yisra’ěl, as a
reed is shaken in the water, and shall pluck
Yisra’ěl from this good soil which He gave
to their fathers, and shall scatter them
beyond the River, because they made their
Ashěrim, provoking יהוה,
16and He shall give Yisra’ěl up, because
of the sins of Yaroḇ‘am, who sinned and
who made Yisra’ěl sin.”
17And the wife of Yaroḇ‘am rose up and
went, and came to Tirtsah. When she came
to the threshold of the house, the child
died.
18And they buried him, and all Yisra’ěl
lamented for him, according to the word of
יהוה which He spoke through His servant
Aḥiyahu the prophet.
19And the rest of the acts of Yaroḇ‘am,
how he fought and how he reigned, see,
they are written in the book of the annals
of the sovereigns of Yisra’ěl.
20And the days that Yaroḇ‘am reigned
was twenty-two years. So he slept with his
fathers, and Naḏaḇ his son reigned in his
place.
21Meanwhile Reḥaḇ‘am son of Shelomoh
reigned in Yehuḏah. Reḥaḇ‘am was forty-
one years old when he became sovereign,
and he reigned seventeen years in Yerushalayim, the city which יהוה had chosen
out of all the tribes of Yisra’ěl, to put His
Name there. And his mother’s name was
Na‘amah the Ammonitess.
22And Yehuḏah did evil in the eyes of
יהוה, and they provoked Him to jealousy
with their sins which they committed,
more than all that their fathers had done.
23For they also built for themselves high
places, and pillars, and Ashěrim on every
high hill and under every green tree.
24And there were also cult prostitutes in
the land. They did according to all the
abominations of the nations which יהוה
dispossessed before the children of
Yisra’ěl.
25And it came to be, in the fifth year of
Sovereign Reḥaḇ‘am, that Shishaq sovereign of Mitsrayim came up against Yerushalayim.
26And he took away the treasures of the
House of יהוה and the treasures of the
sovereign’s house, he even took away all.
And he took away all the shields of gold
which Shelomoh had made.
27And Sovereign Reḥaḇ‘am made shields
of bronze to replace them, and entrusted
them into the hands of the chiefs of the
guard, who guarded the entrance of the
sovereign’s house.
28And it came to be, whenever the sovereign went into the House of יהוה, the
guards would bring them, then take them
back into the guardroom.
29And the rest of the acts of Reḥaḇ‘am,
and all that he did, are they not written in
the book of the annals of the sovereigns of
Yehuḏah?
30And there was fighting between
Reḥaḇ‘am and Yaroḇ‘am all the days.
31So Reḥaḇ‘am slept with his fathers, and
was buried with his fathers in the City of
Dawiḏ. And the name of his mother was
Na‘amah the Ammonitess. And Aḇiyam
his son reigned in his place.

15 And in the eighteenth year of
Sovereign Yaroḇ‘am son of Neḇat,
Aḇiyam became sovereign over Yehuḏah.
2He reigned three years in Yerushalayim, and his mother’s name was
Ma‘aḵah the granddaughter of Aḇishalom.
3And he walked in all the sins of his
father, which he had done before him, and
his heart was not perfect to יהוה his
Elohim, as was the heart of his father
Dawiḏ.
4But for Dawiḏ’s sake יהוה his Elohim
gave him a lamp in Yerushalayim, to raise
up his son after him and by establishing
Yerushalayim,
5for Dawiḏ did what was right in the

eyes of יהוה, and did not turn aside from
all that He commanded him all the days of
his life, except in the matter of Uriyah the
Ḥittite.
6 And there was fighting between
Reḥaḇʽam and Yaroḇʽam all the days of his
life.
7 And the rest of the acts of Aḇiyam, and
all that he did, are they not written in the
book of the annals of the sovereigns of
Yehuḏah? And there was fighting between
Aḇiyam and Yaroḇʽam.
8 So Aḇiyam slept with his fathers, and
they buried him in the City of Dawiḏ. And
Asa his son reigned in his place.
9 And in the twentieth year of Yaroḇʽam
sovereign of Yisra'ěl, Asa became sovereign over Yehuḏah.
10 And he reigned forty-one years in
Yerushalayim, and his grandmother's
name was Maʽaḵah the granddaughter of
Aḇishalom.
11 And Asa did what was right in the eyes
of יהוה, as his father Dawiḏ had done,
12 and put away the cult prostitutes from
the land, and removed all the idols that his
fathers had made.
13 And he also removed Maʽaḵah his
grandmother from being sovereigness
mother, because she had made an abominable image for Ashěrah. And Asa cut
down her abominable image and burned it
by the wadi Qiḏron.
14 But the high places were not removed.
However, Asa's heart was perfect with
יהוה all his days.
15 And he brought into the House of יהוה
the set-apart items of his father, and his
own set-apart items: silver and gold and
utensils.
16 And there was fighting between Asa
and Baʽasha sovereign of Yisra'ěl all their
days.
17 And Baʽasha sovereign of Yisra'ěl
came up against Yehuḏah, and built
Ramah, to keep anyone from going out or
coming in to Asa sovereign of Yehuḏah.
18 And Asa took all the silver and gold
that was left in the treasuries of the House
of יהוה and the treasuries of the sovereign's house, and gave them into the hand
of his servants. And Sovereign Asa sent
them to Ben-Haḏaḏ son of Taḇrimmon,
son of Ḥezyon, sovereign of Aram, who
dwelt in Dammeseq, saying,
19 "Let there be a covenant between you
and me, as there was between my father
and your father. Look, I have sent you a
present of silver and gold. Come, break
your covenant with Baʽasha sovereign of
Yisra'ěl, so that he withdraws from me."
20 And Ben-Haḏaḏ listened to Sovereign
Asa, and sent the commanders of his
armies against the cities of Yisra'ěl, and
struck Iyon, and Dan, and Aḇěl Běyth
Maʽaḵah, and all Kinneroth, with all the
land of Naphtali.
21 And it came to be, when Baʽasha heard
it, that he stopped building Ramah, and
remained in Tirtsah.
22 Then Sovereign Asa summoned all
Yehuḏah – none was exempted – and they
took away the stones and timber of Ramah,
which Baʽasha had used for building. And
with them Sovereign Asa built Geḇa of
Binyamin, and Mitspah.
23 And the rest of all the acts of Asa, and
all his might, and all that he did, and the
cities which he built, are they not written
in the book of the annals of the sovereigns
of Yehuḏah? But in the time of his old age
he was diseased in his feet.
24 So Asa slept with his fathers, and was
buried with his fathers in the City of
Dawiḏ his father. And Yehoshaphat his son
reigned in his place.
25 And Naḏaḇ son of Yaroḇʽam became
sovereign over Yisra'ěl in the second year
of Asa sovereign of Yehuḏah, and he
reigned over Yisra'ěl two years.
26 And he did evil in the eyes of יהוה, and
walked in the way of his father, and in his
sin by which he had made Yisra'ěl sin.
27 Then Baʽasha son of Aḥiyah, of the
house of Yissasḵar, conspired against him.
And Baʽasha struck him at Gibbethon,
which belonged to the Philistines, for
Naḏaḇ and all Yisra'ěl had laid siege to
Gibbethon.
28 And Baʽasha killed him in the third
year of Asa sovereign of Yehuḏah, and
reigned in his place.

29 And it came to be, when he became sovereign, that he struck all the house of Yaroḇʽam. He did not leave to Yaroḇʽam anyone breathing, until he had destroyed him, according to the word of יהוה which He had spoken by His servant Aḥiyah the Shilonite,

30 because of the sins of Yaroḇʽam, which he had sinned and by which he had made Yisra'ěl sin, because of his provocation with which he had provoked יהוה Elohim of Yisra'ěl.

31 And the rest of the acts of Naḏaḇ, and all that he did, are they not written in the book of the annals of the sovereigns of Yisra'ěl?

32 And there was fighting between Asa and Baʽasha sovereign of Yisra'ěl all their days.

33 In the third year of Asa sovereign of Yehuḏah, Baʽasha son of Aḥiyah became sovereign over all Yisra'ěl in Tirtsah, and reigned twenty-four years.

34 And he did evil in the eyes of יהוה, and walked in the way of Yaroḇʽam, and in his sin by which he had made Yisra'ěl sin.

16 Then the word of יהוה came to Yěhu son of Ḥanani, against Baʽasha, saying,

2 "Because I raised you up out of the dust and made you ruler over My people Yisra'ěl, but you walked in the way of Yaroḇʽam, and made My people Yisra'ěl sin, to provoke Me with their sins,

3 see, I am going to sweep away Baʽasha and his house, and shall make your house like the house of Yaroḇʽam the son of Neḇat.

4 "Anyone belonging to Baʽasha who dies in a city the dogs eat, and anyone belonging to him who dies in a field the birds of the heavens eat."

5 And the rest of the acts of Baʽasha, what he did, and his might, are they not written in the book of the annals of the sovereigns of Yisra'ěl?

6 So Baʽasha slept with his fathers and was buried in Tirtsah. And his son Ělah reigned in his place.

7 Moreover, the word of יהוה came by the prophet Yěhu son of Ḥanani against Baʽasha and his house, because of all the evil that he did in the eyes of יהוה in provoking Him with the work of his hands, in being like the house of Yaroḇʽam, and because he struck them.

8 In the twenty-sixth year of Asa sovereign of Yehuḏah, Ělah son of Baʽasha began to reign over Yisra'ěl in Tirtsah, two years.

9 And his servant Zimri, commander of half his chariots, conspired against him as he was in Tirtsah drinking himself drunk in the house of Artsa, who was over his house in Tirtsah.

10 Then Zimri came in and struck him and killed him in the twenty-seventh year of Asa sovereign of Yehuḏah, and reigned in his place.

11 And it came to be, when he began to reign, as soon as he was seated on his throne, that he struck all the household of Baʽasha. He did not leave him one male, neither of his relatives nor of his friends.

12 So Zimri destroyed the entire house of Baʽasha, according to the word of יהוה, which He spoke against Baʽasha by Yěhu the prophet,

13 for all the sins of Baʽasha and the sins of Ělah his son, by which they had sinned and by which they had made Yisra'ěl sin, in provoking יהוה Elohim of Yisra'ěl with their worthlessnesses.

14 And the rest of the acts of Ělah, and all that he did, are they not written in the book of the annals of the sovereigns of Yisra'ěl?

15 In the twenty-seventh year of Asa sovereign of Yehuḏah, Zimri reigned seven days in Tirtsah. And the people were encamped against Gibbethon, which belonged to the Philistines.

16 And the people who were encamped heard it said, "Zimri has conspired and also struck the sovereign." So all Yisra'ěl set up Omri, the commander of the army, to reign over Yisra'ěl that day in the camp.

17 And Omri went up, and all Yisra'ěl with him, from Gibbethon, and they besieged Tirtsah.

18 And it came to be, when Zimri saw that the city was captured, that he went into a

high place of the sovereign's house and burned the sovereign's house down upon himself with fire, and died,

19 because of the sins which he had sinned in doing evil in the eyes of יהוה, in walking in the way of Yaroḇʽam, and in his sin which he had committed to make Yisra'ěl sin.

20 And the rest of the acts of Zimri, and the conspiracy he made, are they not written in the book of the annals of the sovereigns of Yisra'ěl?

21 Then the people of Yisra'ěl were divided into two parts: half of the people followed Tiḇni son of Ginath, to make him reign, and half followed Omri.

22 But the people who followed Omri were stronger than the people who followed Tiḇni son of Ginath. And Tiḇni died and Omri reigned.

23 In the thirty-first year of Asa sovereign of Yehuḏah, Omri became sovereign over Yisra'ěl, and reigned twelve years. He reigned six years in Tirtsah.

24 And he bought the hill of Shomeron from Shemer for two talents of silver, and built on the hill, and called the name of the city which he built, Shomeron, after the name of Shemer, owner of the hill.

25 And Omri did evil in the eyes of יהוה, and did evil more than all those before him,

26 and walked in all the ways of Yaroḇʽam son of Neḇat, and in his sin by which he had made Yisra'ěl sin, provoking יהוה Elohim of Yisra'ěl with their worthlessnesses.

27 And the rest of the acts of Omri which he did, and the might that he attained, are they not written in the book of the annals of the sovereigns of Yisra'ěl?

28 So Omri slept with his fathers and was buried in Shomeron. And Aḥaḇ his son reigned in his place.

29 In the thirty-eighth year of Asa sovereign of Yehuḏah, Aḥaḇ son of Omri became sovereign over Yisra'ěl. And Aḥaḇ son of Omri reigned over Yisra'ěl in Shomeron twenty-two years.

30 And Aḥaḇ son of Omri did evil in the eyes of יהוה, more than all those before him.

31 And it came to be, as though it had been a light matter for him to walk in the sins of Yaroḇʽam son of Neḇat, that he took as wife Izeḇel the daughter of Ethbaʽal, sovereign of the Tsiḏonians. And he went and served Baʽal and bowed himself to it,

32 and raised up a slaughter-place for Baʽal in the house of Baʽal, which he had built in Shomeron.

33 And Aḥaḇ made an Ashěrah. And Aḥaḇ did more to provoke יהוה Elohim of Yisra'ěl than all the sovereigns of Yisra'ěl before him.

34 In his days Ḥi'ěl of Běyth Ěl built Yeriḥo. He laid its foundation at the cost of Aḇiram his first-born, and at the cost of his youngest son Seḡuḇ he set up its gates, according to the word of יהוה, which He had spoken through Yehoshua son of Nun.

17 And Ěliyahu the Tishbite, of the inhabitants of Gilʽaḏ, said to Aḥaḇ, "As יהוה Elohim of Yisra'ěl lives, before whom I stand, there shall be no dew or rain these years, except at my word."

2 And the word of יהוה came to him, saying,

3 "Go away from here and turn eastward, and hide by the wadi Kerith, which flows into the Yarděn.

4 "And it shall be that you drink from the stream, and I shall command the ravens to feed you there."

5 And he went and did according to the word of יהוה, for he went and dwelt by the wadi Kerith, which flows into the Yarděn.

6 And the ravens brought him bread and meat in the morning, and bread and meat in the evening, and he drank from the stream.

7 And it came to be after a while that the stream dried up, because there had been no rain in the land.

8 Then the word of יהוה came to him, saying,

9 "Rise up, go to Tsarephath, which belongs to Tsiḏon, and dwell there. See, I have commanded a widow there to sustain you."

10 And he rose up and went to Tsarephath,

and came to the gate of the city and saw a
widow there gathering sticks. And he
called and said to her, "Please bring me a
little water in a vessel to drink."
11 And as she was going to get it, he
called and said to her, "Please bring me a
piece of bread in your hand."
12 And she said, "As יהוה your Elohim
lives, I do not have bread, only a handful
of flour in a bin, and a little oil in a jar. And
see, I am gathering a couple of sticks and
shall go in and prepare it for myself and
my son, and we shall eat it, and die."
13 And Ěliyah said to her, "Do not fear, go
and do as you have said, but make me a
small cake from it first, and bring it to me.
And afterward make some for yourself and
your son.
14 "For thus said יהוה Elohim of Yisra'ěl,
'The bin of flour shall not be used up, nor
the jar of oil run dry, until the day יהוה
sends rain on the earth.' "
15 So she went and did according to the
word of Ěliyahu, and she and he and her
household ate for many days.
16 The bin of flour was not used up, nor
did the jar of oil run dry, according to the
word of יהוה which He spoke by Ěliyahu.
17 And after these events it came to be that
the son of the woman who owned the
house became sick. And his sickness was
very severe[a] until there was no breath left
in him.
18 And she said to Ěliyahu, "What have I
to do with you, O man of Elohim? Have
you come to me to bring my crookedness
to be remembered, and to kill my son?"
19 And he said to her, "Give me your
son." So he took him from her arms and
took him to the upper room where he was
dwelling, and laid him on his own bed,
20 and cried out to יהוה and said, "O יהוה
my Elohim, have You also brought evil on
the widow with whom I am sojourning, to
kill her son?"
21 And he stretched himself out on the
child three times, and cried out to יהוה and
said, "O יהוה my Elohim, I pray, let the
life of this child come back to him."
22 And יהוה heard the voice of Ěliyahu,
and the life of the child came back to him,
and he lived.
23 And Ěliyahu took the child and brought
him down from the upper room into the
house, and gave him to his mother. And
Ěliyahu said, "See, your son lives!"
24 And the woman said to Ěliyahu, "Now
by this I know that you are a man of
Elohim, and that the word of יהוה in your
mouth is truth."

18

And after many days it came to be
that the word of יהוה came to
Ěliyahu, in the third year, saying, "Go,
present yourself to Aḥab̲, and I give rain
on the earth."
2 Thereupon Ěliyahu went to present
himself to Aḥab̲. And the scarcity of food
in Shomeron was severe.[a]
3 And Aḥab̲ had called Ob̲ad̲yahu, who
was over his house. Now Ob̲ad̲yahu feared
יהוה exceedingly.
4 And it came to be, while Izeb̲el cut
down the prophets of יהוה, that Ob̲ad̲yahu
had taken one hundred prophets and
hidden them, fifty to a cave, and had fed
them with bread and water.
5 And Aḥab̲ had said to Ob̲ad̲yahu, "Go
into the land to all the springs of water and
to all the wadis, it could be that we find
grass to keep the horses and mules alive,
and not have any livestock cut off.
6 And they divided the land between
them to pass over it, Aḥab̲ went one way
by himself, and Ob̲ad̲yahu went another
way by himself.
7 And as Ob̲ad̲yahu was on his way, then
see, Ěliyahu met him. And he recognised
him, and fell on his face, and said, "Is that
you, my master Ěliyahu?"
8 And he answered him, "It is I. Go, say
to your master, 'Ěliyahu is here.' "
9 And he said, "What have I sinned, that
you are giving your servant into the hand
of Aḥab̲, to kill me?
10 "As יהוה your Elohim lives, there is no
nation or reign where my master has not
sent to look for you. And when they said,

17a,18a Lit. strong

'He is not here,' he made the reign or nation swear that they could not find you.

11 "And now you say, 'Go, say to your master, "Ěliyahu is here" '!

12 "And it shall be, as soon as I am gone from you, that the Spirit of יהוה takes you away to a place I do not know. And I shall come to report to Aḥaḇ, and when he does not find you, he shall kill me. But I your servant have feared יהוה from my youth.

13 "Was it not reported to my master what I did when Izeḇel killed the prophets of יהוה, how I hid one hundred men of the prophets of יהוה, fifty to a cave, and fed them with bread and water?

14 "And now you say, 'Go, say to your master, "Ěliyahu is here!" ' Then he shall kill me."

15 And Ěliyahu said, "As יהוה of hosts lives, before whom I stand, I shall indeed show myself to him today."

16 Oḇaḏyahu then went to meet Aḥaḇ and informed him, and Aḥaḇ went to meet Ěliyahu.

17 And it came to be, when Aḥaḇ saw Ěliyahu, that Aḥaḇ said to him, "Is that you, O disturber of Yisra'ěl?"

18 And he answered, "I have not disturbed Yisra'ěl, but you and your father's house, in that you have forsaken the commands of יהוה, and you have followed the Ba'als.

19 "And now, send and gather all Yisra'ěl to me on Mount Karmel, the four hundred and fifty prophets of Ba'al, and the four hundred prophets of Ashěrah, who eat at Izeḇel's table."

20 Aḥaḇ then sent for all the children of Yisra'ěl, and gathered the prophets on Mount Karmel.

21 And Ěliyahu came to all the people, and said, "How long would you keep hopping between two opinions? If יהוה is Elohim, follow Him; and if Ba'al, follow him." But the people answered him not a word.

22 And Ěliyahu said to the people, "I alone am left a prophet of יהוה, but the prophets of Ba'al are four hundred and fifty men.

23 "Now let them give us two bulls. And let them choose one bull for themselves, and cut it in pieces, and lay it on the wood, but set no fire. And I, I prepare the other bull, and shall lay it on the wood, but set no fire.

24 "And you shall call on the name of your mighty one, and I, I call on the Name of יהוה. And the Elohim who answers by fire, He is Elohim." So all the people answered and said, "The word is good."

25 And Ěliyahu said to the prophets of Ba'al, "Choose one bull for yourselves and prepare it first, for you are many. And call on the name of your mighty one, but set no fire."

26 So they took the bull which was given them, and prepared it, and called on the name of Ba'al from morning even until noon, saying, "O Ba'al, answer us!" But there was no voice and no one answered. And they leaped about the slaughter-place which they had made.

27 And it came to be at noon, that Ěliyahu taunted them and said, "Cry aloud, for he is a mighty one; he is meditating, or he is busy, or he is on a journey, or it could be that he is asleep and has to be awakened!"

28 And they cried aloud, and cut themselves, according to their ruling, with knives and spears, until the blood gushed out on them.

29 And it came to be when midday was past, that they prophesied until the time of bringing the *evening* offering. But there was no voice and no one answered, and no one paying attention.

30 Then Ěliyahu said to all the people, "Come closer to me." And all the people came closer to him. And he repaired the slaughter-place of יהוה that was broken down.

31 And Ěliyahu took twelve stones, according to the number of the tribes of the sons of Ya'aqoḇ, to whom the word of יהוה had come, saying, "Yisra'ěl is your name."

32 And with the stones he built a slaughter-place in the Name of יהוה. And he made a trench around the slaughter-place large enough to hold two seahs of seed.

33 And he arranged the wood, and cut the bull in pieces, and laid it on the wood, and said, "Fill four jars with water, and pour it

on the ascending offering and on the
wood."
34 Then he said, "Do it a second time,"
and they did it a second time. And he said,
"Do it a third time," and they did it a third
time.
35 And the water flowed around the
slaughter-place, and he filled the trench
with water too.
36 And it came to be, at the time of bringing the *evening* offering, that Ěliyahu the
prophet came near and said, "יהוה Elohim
of Aḇraham, Yitsḥaq, and Yisra'ěl, let it be
known today: You are Elohim in Yisra'ěl,
and I Your servant, have done all these
matters by Your word.
37 "Answer me, O יהוה, answer me, and
let this people know that You are יהוה
Elohim, and You shall turn their hearts
back to You again."
38 Then the fire of יהוה fell and consumed
the ascending offering, and the wood and
the stones and the dust, and it licked up the
water that was in the trench.
39 And all the people saw, and fell on their
faces, and said, "יהוה, He is the Elohim!
יהוה, He is the Elohim!"
40 And Ěliyahu said to them, "Seize the
prophets of Ba'al! Do not let one of them
escape!" So they seized them, and Ěliyahu
brought them down to the wadi Qishon and
slew them there.
41 And Ěliyahu said to Aḥaḇ, "Go up, eat
and drink, because of the sound of the
noise of rain."
42 And Aḥaḇ went up to eat and to drink.
And Ěliyahu went up to the top of Karmel,
and he bowed down on the ground, and put
his face between his knees,
43 and said to his servant, "Go up, please,
look closely toward the sea." So he went
up and looked closely, and said, "Not
a speck." And seven times he said, "Go
again."
44 And it came to be the seventh time, that
he said, "See, a little cloud as small as a
man's hand is coming out of the sea!" And
he said, "Go up, say to Aḥaḇ, 'Hitch up,
and go down before the rain stops you.' "
45 And in the meantime, it came to be that
the heavens became black with clouds and
wind, and there was a heavy rain, while
Aḥaḇ rode and went to Yizre'ěl.
46 And the hand of יהוה was on Ěliyahu.
And he girded up his loins and ran ahead
of Aḥaḇ to the entrance of Yizre'ěl.

19 And when Aḥaḇ reported to Izeḇel
all that Ěliyahu had done, also how
he slew all the prophets with the sword,
2 Izeḇel sent a messenger to Ěliyahu,
saying, "So let the mighty ones do to me,
and more also, if I do not make your life as
the life of one of them by tomorrow about
this time."
3 And he feared, and rose up and ran for
his life, and went to Be'ěrsheḇa, which
belongs to Yehuḏah, and left his servant
there.
4 But he himself went a day's journey
into the wilderness, and came and sat
down under a broom tree, and prayed that
he might die, and said, "It is enough! Now,
יהוה, take my life, for I am no better than
my fathers!"
5 And he lay and slept under a broom
tree, and see, a messenger touched him,
and said to him, "Rise, eat."
6 And he looked and saw by his head a
cake baked on coals, and a jar of water. So
he ate and drank, and turned and lay down.
7 And the messenger of יהוה came back
the second time, and touched him, and
said, "Rise, eat, for the journey is too much
for you."
8 And he rose up and ate and drank, and
went in the strength of that food forty days
and forty nights as far as Ḥorěḇ, the mountain of Elohim.
9 And there he went into a cave and spent
the night there. And see, the word of יהוה
came to him, and said to him, "What are
you doing here, Ěliyahu?"
10 And he said, "I have been very jealous
for יהוה Elohim of hosts, for the children
of Yisra'ěl have forsaken Your covenant.
They have thrown down Your slaughter-
places, and they have killed Your prophets
with the sword, and I am left, I alone, and
they seek my life, to take it."
11 And He said, "Go out, and stand on the
mountain before יהוה." And see, יהוה

passed by, and a great and strong wind
tearing the mountains and breaking the
rocks in pieces before יהוה – יהוה was not
in the wind. And after the wind an earthquake – יהוה was not in the earthquake,
12 and after the earthquake a fire – יהוה
was not in the fire, and after the fire a still
small voice.
13 And it came to be, when Ěliyahu heard
it, that he wrapped his face in his robe and
went out and stood at the cave opening.
And see, a voice came to him, and said,
"What are you doing here, Ěliyahu?"
14 And he said, "I have been very jealous
for יהוה Elohim of hosts, for the children
of Yisra'ěl have forsaken Your covenant.
They have thrown down Your slaughter-
places, and they have killed Your prophets
with the sword, and I am left, I alone, and
they seek my life, to take it."
15 And יהוה said to him, "Go, return on
your way to the Wilderness of Dammeseq.
And you shall go in and anoint Ḥaza'ěl as
sovereign over Aram.
16 "And anoint Yěhu son of Nimshi as
sovereign over Yisra'ěl. And anoint Elisha
son of Shaphat of Aḇěl Meḥolah as
prophet in your place.
17 "And it shall be that whoever escapes
the sword of Ḥaza'ěl, Yěhu does kill. And
whoever escapes from the sword of Yěhu,
Elisha does kill.
18 "And I shall leave seven thousand in
Yisra'ěl, all whose knees have not bowed
to Ba'al, and every mouth that has not
kissed him."
19 And he went from there, and found
Elisha son of Shaphat, who was ploughing
with twelve yoke *of oxen* before him, and
he was with the twelfth. And Ěliyahu
passed by him and threw his robe on him.
20 And he left the oxen and ran after
Ěliyahu, and said, "Please let me kiss my
father and my mother, and then I follow
you." And he said to him, "Go, turn back,
for what have I done to you?"
21 And he turned back from him, and took
a yoke of oxen and slaughtered them and
cooked their flesh, using the implements of
the oxen, and gave it to the people, and
they ate. Then he rose up and followed
Ěliyahu, and became his servant.

20 And Ben-Haḏaḏ the sovereign of
Aram gathered all his army, and
there were thirty-two sovereigns with him,
with horses and chariots. And he went up
and besieged Shomeron, and fought
against it.
2 And he sent messengers into the city to
Aḥaḇ sovereign of Yisra'ěl, and said to
him, "Thus said Ben-Haḏaḏ,
3 'Your silver and your gold are mine,
and your wives and children, the best, are
mine.' "
4 And the sovereign of Yisra'ěl answered
and said, "As you say, my master, O sovereign, I am yours, and all that I have."
5 And the messengers came back and
said, "Thus speaks Ben-Haḏaḏ, saying,
'Indeed I have sent to you, saying, "Give
me your silver and your gold, your wives
and your children,"
6 but about this time tomorrow I shall
send my servants to you, and they shall
search your house and the houses of your
servants. And it shall be, that whatever is
pleasing in your eyes they shall lay hold of
and take it.' "
7 And the sovereign of Yisra'ěl called all
the elders of the land, and said, "Please
know and see the evil this one is seeking,
for he sent to me for my wives, and for my
children, and for my silver, and for my
gold, and I did not refuse him."
8 And all the elders and all the people
said to him, "Do not listen nor agree."
9 So he said to the messengers of Ben-
Haḏaḏ, "Say to my master the sovereign,
'All that you sent for to your servant the
first time I shall do, but this I am unable to
do.' " And the messengers went and
brought back word to him.
10 And Ben-Haḏaḏ sent to him and said,
"The mighty ones do so to me, and more
also, if enough dust is left of Shomeron
for a handful for each of the people who
follow me."
11 And the sovereign of Yisra'ěl answered
and said, "Speak, 'Him who girds on *his
armour* should not boast like him who lays
it down.' "

12 And it came to be when this word was
heard, as he and the sovereigns were drinking in the booths, that he said to his servants, "Set yourselves." So they set themselves against the city.
13 And see, a prophet came near to Aḥaḇ
sovereign of Yisra'ĕl, saying, "Thus said
יהוה, 'Have you seen all this great company? See, I am giving it into your hand
today, and you shall know that I am
יהוה.' "
14 And Aḥaḇ said, "By whom?" And he
said, "Thus said יהוה, 'By the young rulers
of the provinces.' " And he said, "Who
opens the attack?" Then he answered,
"You."
15 And he mustered the young rulers of
the provinces, and there were two hundred
and thirty-two. And after them he mustered all the people, all the children of
Yisra'ĕl, seven thousand.
16 And they went out at noon, while Ben-
Hadad and the thirty-two sovereigns
helping him were getting drunk in the
booths.
17 And the young rulers of the provinces
went out first. And Ben-Hadad sent out,
and they reported to him, saying, "Men
have come out of Shomeron!"
18 Then he said, "If they have come out
for peace, seize them alive. And if they
have come out for battle, seize them alive."
19 So these young rulers of the provinces
went out of the city with the army which
followed them.
20 And each struck his man, so the
Arameans fled, and Yisra'ĕl pursued them.
And Ben-Hadad the sovereign of Aram
escaped on a horse with the horsemen.
21 And the sovereign of Yisra'ĕl went out
and struck the horses and chariots, and
struck the Arameans, a great smiting.
22 And the prophet came to the sovereign
of Yisra'ĕl and said to him, "Go, strength-
en yourself. And know and see what you
should do, for at the turn of the year the
sovereign of Aram is coming up against
you."
23 And the servants of the sovereign of
Aram said to him, "Their mighty ones are
mighty ones of the hills. That is why they
were stronger than we. But let us fight
against them in the plain – are we not
stronger than they?
24 "Now do this: Take away the sovereigns, each from his position, and put
officers in their places,
25 and number an army like the army that
you have lost, horse for horse and chariot
for chariot, and let us fight against them in
the plain – are we not stronger than they?"
And he listened to their voice and did so.
26 And it came to be, at the turn of the
year, that Ben-Hadad mustered the
Arameans and went up to Aphĕq to fight
against Yisra'ĕl.
27 And the children of Yisra'ĕl were
mustered and were fed, and they went
against them. And the children of Yisra'ĕl
encamped before them like two little
flocks of goats, while the Arameans filled
the land.
28 And there came near a man of Elohim
and spoke to the sovereign of Yisra'ĕl, and
said, "Thus said יהוה, 'Because the
Arameans have said, "יהוה is Elohim of
the hills, but He is not Elohim of the
valleys," therefore I shall give all this great
company into your hand, and you shall
know that I am יהוה.' "
29 And they encamped opposite each
other for seven days. And it came to be
that on the seventh day the battle was
joined. And the children of Yisra'ĕl struck
one hundred thousand foot soldiers of the
Arameans in one day.
30 And those that were left fled to Aphĕq,
into the city, and a wall fell on twenty-
seven thousand of the men who were left.
And Ben-Hadad fled and went into the
city, into an inner room.
31 And his servants said to him, "See now,
we have heard that the sovereigns of the
house of Yisra'ĕl are lovingly-commited
sovereigns. Please, let us put sackcloth
around our waists and ropes around our
heads, and go out to the sovereign of
Yisra'ĕl. It could be that he spares your
life."
32 So they girded sackcloth on their loins
and put ropes around their heads, and came
to the sovereign of Yisra'ĕl and said, "Your

servant Ben-Haḏaḏ said, 'Please let me
live.'" And he said, "Is he still alive? He is
my brother."
33 And the men divined and they quickly
grasped it and said, "Your brother Ben-
Haḏaḏ." And he said, "Go, bring him." So
Ben-Haḏaḏ came out to him, and he let
him come up on the chariot.
34 And Ben-Haḏaḏ said to him, "The
cities which my father took from your
father I return. And set up market-places
for yourself in Dammeseq, as my father
did in Shomeron." And Aḥaḇ said, "I send
you away with this covenant." And he
made a covenant with him and sent him
away.
35 And a certain man of the sons of the
prophets said to his neighbour by the word
of יהוה, "Strike me, please." But the man
refused to strike him.
36 Then he said to him, "Because you
have not obeyed the voice of יהוה, see, as
soon as you leave me a lion shall strike
you." And when he left him, a lion found
him and struck him.
37 And he found another man, and said,
"Strike me, please." So the man struck
him, striking and wounding.
38 Then the prophet went and waited for
the sovereign by the way, and disguised
himself with ashes on his eyes.
39 And as the sovereign passed by, he
cried out to the sovereign and said, "Your
servant went out into the midst of the
battle. And see, a man came over and
brought a man to me, and said, 'Guard this
man. If he should in any way be missing,
your life shall be for his life, or else you
shall pay a talent of silver.'
40 "And it came to be, while your servant
was busy here and there, he was gone."
And the sovereign of Yisra'ěl said to him,
"Your judgment is right, you yourself have
decided it."
41 Then he quickly removed the ashes
from his eyes. And the sovereign of
Yisra'ěl recognised him as one of the
prophets.
42 And he said to him, "Thus said יהוה,
'Because you have let slip out of your hand
a man whom I put under the ban, therefore
your life shall go for his life, and your
people for his people.'"
43 And the sovereign of Yisra'ěl went to
his house embittered and displeased, and
came to Shomeron.

21 And it came to be, after these
events, that Naḇoth the Yizre'ělite
had a vineyard which was in Yizre'ěl, near
the palace of Aḥaḇ the sovereign of
Shomeron.
2 And Aḥaḇ spoke to Naḇoth, saying,
"Give me your vineyard, and it shall be a
vegetable garden for me, since it adjoins
my house. And let me give you a better
vineyard for it. If it is good in your eyes,
let me give you its worth in silver."
3 And Naḇoth said to Aḥaḇ, "Far be it
from me, by יהוה, that I should give the
inheritance of my fathers to you!"
4 And Aḥaḇ went into his house embittered and displeased because of the word
which Naḇoth the Yizre'ělite had spoken to
him when he said, "I do not give you the
inheritance of my fathers." And he lay
down on his bed, and turned away his face,
and did not eat food.
5 And Izeḇel his wife came to him, and
said to him, "Why is your spirit so embittered that you are not eating food?"
6 And he said to her, "Because I spoke to
Naḇoth the Yizre'ělite, and said to him,
'Give me your vineyard for silver, or if you
prefer, I give you another vineyard for it.'
But he answered, 'I do not give you my
vineyard.'"
7 So Izeḇel his wife said to him, "Do you
now rule over Yisra'ěl? Rise up, eat food,
and let your heart be glad. Let me give you
the vineyard of Naḇoth the Yizre'ělite!"
8 Then she wrote letters in Aḥaḇ's name,
and sealed them with his seal, and sent the
letters to the elders and the nobles who
were dwelling in the city with Naḇoth.
9 And she wrote in the letters, saying,
"Proclaim a fast, and seat Naḇoth at the
head of the people,
10 and seat two men, sons of Beliya'al
before him to bear witness against him,
saying, 'You have blasphemed Elohim and
the sovereign.' Then you shall take him

out, and stone him to death."
11 And the men of his city, the elders and nobles who were inhabitants of his city, did as Izeḇel had sent to them, as it was written in the letters which she had sent to them.
12 They proclaimed a fast, and seated Naḇoth at the head of the people.
13 And the men, sons of Beliya'al, came in and sat before him. And the men of Beliya'al witnessed against him, against Naḇoth, in the presence of the people, saying, "Naḇoth has blasphemed Elohim and the sovereign!" So they took him outside the city and stoned him with stones, and he died.
14 And they sent to Izeḇel, saying, "Naḇoth has been stoned and is dead."
15 And it came to be, when Izeḇel heard that Naḇoth had been stoned and was dead, that Izeḇel said to Aḥaḇ, "Arise, take possession of the vineyard of Naḇoth the Yizre'ělite, which he refused to give you for silver, for Naḇoth is not alive but dead."
16 And it came to be, when Aḥaḇ heard that Naḇoth was dead, that Aḥaḇ rose to go down to take possession of the vineyard of Naḇoth the Yizre'ělite.
17 And the word of יהוה came to Ěliyahu the Tishbite, saying,
18 "Rise up, go down to meet Aḥaḇ sovereign of Yisra'ěl, who lives in Shomeron. See, he is in the vineyard of Naḇoth, where he has gone down to take possession of it.
19 "And you shall speak to him, saying, 'Thus said יהוה, "Have you murdered and also taken possession?" ' And you shall speak to him, saying, 'Thus said יהוה, "In the place where dogs licked the blood of Naḇoth, the dogs are going to lick your blood, even yours." ' "
20 And Aḥaḇ said to Ěliyahu, "Have you found me, O my enemy?" And he answered, "I have found you, because you have sold yourself to do evil in the eyes of יהוה:
21 'See, I am bringing evil on you, and shall consume your descendants, and cut off from Aḥaḇ every male in Yisra'ěl, both those shut up and those left at large,
22 and make your house like the house of Yaroḇ'am son of Neḇat, and like the house of Ba'asha son of Aḥiyah, because of the provocation with which you have provoked Me, and made Yisra'ěl sin.'
23 "And also of Izeḇel יהוה has spoken, saying, 'The dogs are going to eat Izeḇel by the wall of Yizre'ěl.'
24 "The dogs are going to eat whoever belongs to Aḥaḇ and dies in the city, and the birds of the heavens are going to eat whoever dies in the field."
25 Indeed, there never was anyone like Aḥaḇ who sold himself to do evil in the eyes of יהוה, because Izeḇel his wife stirred him up.
26 And he acted very abominably in following idols, according to all that the Amorites had done, whom יהוה dispossessed from before the children of Yisra'ěl.
27 And it came to be, when Aḥaḇ heard those words, that he tore his garments and put sackcloth on his body, and fasted and lay in sackcloth, and went softly.
28 And the word of יהוה came to Ěliyahu the Tishbite, saying,
29 "See how Aḥaḇ has humbled himself before Me? Because he has humbled himself before Me, I do not bring the evil in his days, but in the days of his son I bring the evil on his house."

22 And they continued three years without fighting between Aram and Yisra'ěl.
2 And it came to be, in the third year, that Yehoshaphat sovereign of Yehuḏah came down to the sovereign of Yisra'ěl.
3 And the sovereign of Yisra'ěl said to his servants, "Do you know that Ramoth in Gil'aḏ is ours, and we are keeping silent from taking it out of the hand of the sovereign of Aram!"
4 And he said to Yehoshaphat, "Do you go with me to battle at Ramoth Gil'aḏ?" And Yehoshaphat said to the sovereign of Yisra'ěl, "I am as you are, my people as your people, my horses as your horses."
5 And Yehoshaphat said to the sovereign of Yisra'ěl, "Please, first inquire for the word of יהוה."

6 And the sovereign of Yisra'ěl gathered the prophets, about four hundred men, and said to them, "Do I go against Ramoth Gil'aḏ to battle, or do I refrain?" And they said, "Go up, for יהוה does give it into the hand of the sovereign."

7 And Yehoshaphat said, "Is there not here a prophet of יהוה besides, that we might inquire of him?"

8 And the sovereign of Yisra'ěl said to Yehoshaphat, "There is still one man, Miḵayehu son of Yimlah, to inquire of יהוה by him. But I hate him, because he does not prophesy good concerning me, but evil." And Yehoshaphat said, "Let not the sovereign say so!"

9 So the sovereign of Yisra'ěl called an officer and said, "Bring Miḵayehu son of Yimlah at once!"

10 And the sovereign of Yisra'ěl and Yehoshaphat sovereign of Yehuḏah were sitting, each on his throne, dressed in their robes, at a threshing-floor at the entrance of the gate of Shomeron. And all the prophets were prophesying before them.

11 And Tsiḏqiyah son of Kena'anah had made horns of iron for himself, and said, "Thus said יהוה, 'With these you push the Arameans until they are destroyed.' "

12 And all the prophets were prophesying so, saying, "Go up to Ramoth Gil'aḏ and prosper, for יהוה shall give it into the hand of the sovereign."

13 And the messenger who had gone to call Miḵayehu spoke to him, saying, "See now, the words of the prophets with one mouth are good towards the sovereign. Please, let your word be like the word of one of them, and you shall speak good."

14 And Miḵayehu said, "As יהוה lives, whatever יהוה says to me, that I speak."

15 And he came to the sovereign, and the sovereign said to him, "Miḵayehu, do we go against Ramoth Gil'aḏ to battle, or do we refrain?" And he answered him, "Go and prosper, for יהוה shall give it into the hand of the sovereign!"

16 And the sovereign said to him, "How many times have I made you swear that you do not speak to me, except the truth, in the Name of יהוה?"

17 So he said, "I saw all Yisra'ěl scattered on the mountains, as sheep that have no shepherd. And יהוה said, 'These have no master. Let everyone return to his house in peace.' "

18 And the sovereign of Yisra'ěl said to Yehoshaphat, "Have I not said to you that he would not prophesy good concerning me, but evil?"

19 Then he said, "Therefore hear the word of יהוה: I saw יהוה sitting on His throne, and all the host of the heavens standing by Him, on His right and on His left.

20 "And יהוה said, 'Who shall entice Aḥaḇ to go up and fall at Ramoth Gil'aḏ?' And this one said this, and another said that.

21 "And a spirit came forward and stood before יהוה, and said, 'Let me entice him.'

22 "And יהוה said to him, 'In what way?' And he said, 'I shall go out and be a spirit of falsehood in the mouth of all his prophets.' And He said, 'Entice him, and also prevail. Go out and do so.'

23 "And now, see, יהוה has put a spirit of falsehood in the mouth of all these prophets of yours, and יהוה has spoken evil concerning you."

24 And Tsiḏqiyahu son of Kena'anah came near and struck Miḵayehu on the cheek, and said, "Where did the spirit of יהוה pass over from me to speak to you?"

25 And Miḵayehu said, "Look, you shall see on that day when you go into an inner room to hide!"

26 And the sovereign of Yisra'ěl said, "Take Miḵayehu, and return him to Amon the governor of the city, and to Yo'ash son of the sovereign,

27 and say, 'Thus said the sovereign, "Put this one in prison, and feed him with bread of affliction and water of affliction until I come in peace." ' "

28 And Miḵayehu said, "If you ever return in peace, יהוה has not spoken by me." And he said, "Hear, all you people!"

29 And the sovereign of Yisra'ěl and Yehoshaphat the sovereign of Yehuḏah went up to Ramoth Gil'aḏ.

30 And the sovereign of Yisra'ěl said to Yehoshaphat, "Let me disguise myself and

go into battle, but you put on your robes."
So the sovereign of Yisra'ěl disguised himself and went into battle.
31 And the sovereign of Aram had
commanded the thirty-two commanders of
his chariots, saying, "Fight with no one
small or great, but only with the sovereign
of Yisra'ěl."
32 And it came to be, when the commanders of the chariots saw Yehoshaphat, that
they said, "Indeed, it is the sovereign of
Yisra'ěl!" So they turned aside to fight
against him, and Yehoshaphat cried out.
33 And it came to be, when the commanders of the chariots saw that it was not the
sovereign of Yisra'ěl, that they turned back
from pursuing him.
34 And a man drew a bow in his simplicity, and struck the sovereign of Yisra'ěl
between the joints of his armour. And he
said to the driver of his chariot, "Turn
around and take me out of the battle, for I
am wounded."
35 And the battle increased that day. And
the sovereign was propped up in his
chariot, facing the Arameans, and died at
evening, and the blood ran out from the
wound onto the floor of the chariot.
36 And as the sun was going down, a
shout passed through the camp, saying,
"Each to his city, and each to his land!"
37 So the sovereign died and was brought
to Shomeron, and they buried the sovereign in Shomeron.
38 And when the chariot was washed at a
pool in Shomeron, the dogs licked up his
blood, where the whores bathed, according
to the word of יהוה which He had spoken.
39 And the rest of the acts of Aḥaḇ and all
that he did, and the ivory house which he
built and all the cities that he built, are they
not written in the book of the annals of the
sovereigns of Yisra'ěl?
40 So Aḥaḇ slept with his fathers, and
Aḥazyahu his son reigned in his place.
41 And Yehoshaphat son of Asa began to
reign over Yehuḏah in the fourth year of
Aḥaḇ sovereign of Yisra'ěl.
42 Yehoshaphat was thirty-five years old
when he became sovereign, and he reigned
twenty-five years in Yerushalayim. And
his mother's name was Azuḇah the
daughter of Shilḥi.
43 And he walked in all the ways of his
father Asa. He did not turn aside from
them, doing what was right in the eyes of
יהוה. Only, the high places were not taken
away, for the people slaughtered and
burned incense on the high places.
44 And Yehoshaphat made peace with the
sovereign of Yisra'ěl.
45 And the rest of the acts of Yehoshaphat,
and the might that he showed, and how he
fought, are they not written in the book of
the annals of the sovereigns of Yehuḏah?
46 And the rest of the cult prostitutes, who
remained in the days of his father Asa, he
cleared out from the land.
47 And there was then no sovereign in
Eḏom, a deputy was sovereign.
48 Yehoshaphat made Tarshish ships to go
to Ophir for gold. However, they did not
go, for the ships were wrecked at Etsyon
Geḇer.
49 Then Aḥazyahu son of Aḥaḇ said to
Yehoshaphat, "Let my servants go with
your servants in the ships." But Yehoshaphat would not.
50 So Yehoshaphat slept with his fathers,
and was buried with his fathers in the City
of Dawiḏ his father. And Yehoram his son
reigned in his place.
51 Aḥazyahu son of Aḥaḇ began to reign
over Yisra'ěl in Shomeron in the seventeenth year of Yehoshaphat sovereign of
Yehuḏah, and reigned two years over
Yisra'ěl,
52 and did evil in the eyes of יהוה, and
walked in the way of his father and in the
way of his mother and in the way of
Yaroḇ'am son of Neḇat, who had made
Yisra'ěl sin,
53 and served Ba'al and bowed himself to
it, and provoked יהוה Elohim of Yisra'ěl,
according to all that his father had done.

MELAḴIM BĚT

2 KINGS

1 And Mo'aḇ revolted against Yisra'ěl
after the death of Aḥaḇ.
2 And Aḥazyah fell through the lattice of
his upper room in Shomeron, and was
injured, and sent messengers and said to
them, "Go, inquire of Baʿal-Zeḇuḇ, the
mighty one of Eqron, if I shall recover
from this injury."
3 But a messenger of יהוה spoke to
Ěliyah the Tishbite, "Rise up, go up to
meet the messengers of the sovereign of
Shomeron, and say to them, 'Is it because
there is no Elohim in Yisra'ěl that you are
going to inquire of Baʿal-Zeḇuḇ, the
mighty one of Eqron?'
4 "So therefore, thus said יהוה, 'You are
not going to get out of the bed to which
you have gone up, for you shall certainly
die.' " And Ěliyah went.
5 And the messengers returned to him,
and he said to them, "Why have you come
back?"
6 And they said to him, "A man came up
to meet us, and said to us, 'Go, return to
the sovereign who sent you, and say to
him, "Thus said יהוה, 'Is it because there
is no Elohim in Yisra'ěl that you are sending to inquire of Baʿal-Zeḇuḇ, the mighty
one of Eqron? Therefore you are not going
to get out of the bed to which you have
gone up, for you shall certainly die.' " ' "
7 And he said to them, "What was the
man like who came up to meet you and
spoke to you these words?"
8 And they answered him, "He was a
hairy man, and wore a leather girdle
around his waist." And he said, "It is
Ěliyah the Tishbite."
9 He then sent to him a captain of fifty
with his fifty men. And he went up to him,
and see, he was sitting on the top of a hill.
And he spoke to him, "Man of Elohim, the
sovereign has said, 'Come down!' "
10 And Ěliyahu answered and said to the
captain of fifty, "And if I am a man of
Elohim, let fire come down from the heavens and consume you and your fifty men."
And fire came down from the heavens and
consumed him and his fifty.
11 He then sent another captain of fifty
with his fifty men to him. And he answered
and said to him, "Man of Elohim, this is
what the sovereign said, 'Come down at
once!' "
12 And Ěliyah answered and said to them,
"If I am a man of Elohim, let fire come
down from the heavens and consume you
and your fifty men." And a fire of Elohim
came down from the heavens and consumed him and his fifty.
13 And again he sent a third captain of
fifty with his fifty men. And the third captain of fifty went up, and came and fell on
his knees before Ěliyahu, and pleaded with
him, and said to him, "Man of Elohim,
please let my life and the life of these fifty
servants of yours be precious in your eyes.
14 "See, fire has come down from the
heavens and burned up the first two captains of fifties with their fifties. But let my
life be precious in your eyes."
15 And the Messenger of יהוה said to
Ěliyahu, "Go down with him; do not be
afraid of him." So he rose up and went
down with him to the sovereign,
16 and spoke to him, "Thus said יהוה,
'Because you have sent messengers to
inquire of Baʿal-Zeḇuḇ, the mighty one of
Eqron, is it because there is no Elohim in
Yisra'ěl to inquire of His word? Therefore
you are not going to get out of the bed to
which you have gone up, for you shall
certainly die.' "
17 And he died, according to the word of
יהוה which Ěliyahu had spoken. And
Yehoram reigned in his place, in the second year of Yehoram son of Yehoshaphat
sovereign of Yehuḏah, for he had no son.
18 And the rest of the acts of Aḥazyahu
which he did, are they not written in the

book of the annals of the sovereigns of
Yisra'ěl?

2 And it came to be, when יהוה was to
take up Ěliyahu to the heavens by a
whirlwind, that Ěliyahu went with Elisha
from Gilgal.
2 And Ěliyahu said to Elisha, "Please
remain here, for יהוה has sent me on to
Běyth Ěl." And Elisha said, "As יהוה lives,
and as your being lives, I do not leave
you!" And they went down to Běyth Ěl.
3 And the sons of the prophets who were
at Běyth Ěl came out to Elisha, and said to
him, "Do you know that יהוה is taking
away your master from your head?" And
he said, "I also know, be silent!"
4 And Ěliyahu said to him, "Elisha,
please remain here, for יהוה has sent me
on to Yeriḥo." And he said, "As יהוה lives,
and as your being lives, I do not leave
you!" And they came into Yeriḥo.
5 And the sons of the prophets who were
at Yeriḥo came to Elisha and said to him,
"Do you know that יהוה is taking away
your master from over you today?" And he
said, "I also know, be silent!"
6 And Ěliyahu said to him, "Please
remain here, for יהוה has sent me on to the
Yarděn." And he said, "As יהוה lives, and
as your being lives, I do not leave you!"
And the two of them went on.
7 And fifty men of the sons of the
prophets went and stood facing them at a
distance, while the two of them stood by
the Yarděn.
8 And Ěliyahu took his mantle, and rolled
it up, and struck the water. And it was
divided this way and that, so that the two
of them passed over on dry ground.
9 And it came to be, when they had
passed over, that Ěliyahu said to Elisha,
"Ask what I am to do for you, before I am
taken away from you!" And Elisha said,
"Please let a double portion of your spirit
be upon me."
10 And he said, "You have made it hard to
ask, yet if you see me when I am taken
from you, it is yours; but if not, it is not."
11 And it came to be, as they continued on
and spoke, that see, a chariot of fire with
horses of fire which separated the two of
them. And Ěliyahu went up by a whirlwind
into the heavens.
12 And Elisha saw it, and he cried out,
"My father, my father, the chariot of
Yisra'ěl and its horsemen!" And he saw
him no more. Then he took hold of his
garments and tore them into two pieces.
13 And he took up the mantle of Ěliyahu
that had fallen from him, and went back
and stood by the bank of the Yarděn.
14 And he took the mantle of Ěliyahu that
had fallen from him, and struck the water,
and said, "Where is יהוה Elohim of
Ěliyahu?" And he struck the water, and it
was divided this way and that, and Elisha
passed over.
15 And when the sons of the prophets who
were from Yeriḥo saw him, they said, "The
spirit of Ěliyahu rests on Elisha." And they
came to meet him, and bowed to the
ground before him.
16 And they said to him, "Look, there are
fifty strong men with your servants. Please
let them go and search for your master, lest
the Spirit of יהוה has taken him up and
cast him upon some mountain or into some
valley." And he said, "Send no one."
17 But they pressed upon him till he was
ashamed, and he said, "Send." So they sent
fifty men, and they searched for three days
but did not find him.
18 And they returned to him, for he
remained in Yeriḥo, and he said to them,
"Did I not say to you, 'Do not go'?"
19 And the men of the city said to Elisha,
"Look, the site of this city is good, as my
master sees, but the waters are spoilt, and
the soil barren."
20 And he said, "Bring me a new bowl,
and put salt in it." And they brought it to
him.
21 And he went out to the source of the
water, and threw salt in there, and said,
"Thus said יהוה, 'I have healed this water
– no longer shall death or barrenness come
from it.' "
22 And the waters were healed, to this day,
according to the word of Elisha which he
spoke.
23 And he went up from there to Běyth Ěl.

And as he was going up the way, some youths came from the city and mocked him, and said to him, "Go up, baldhead! Go up, baldhead!"

24 And he turned around and looked at them, and pronounced a curse on them in the Name of יהוה. And two female bears came out of the forest and tore to pieces forty-two of the youths.

25 And from there he went to Mount Karmel, and from there he returned to Shomeron.

3 And Yehoram son of Aḥaḇ began to reign over Yisra'ěl at Shomeron in the eighteenth year of Yehoshaphat sovereign of Yehuḏah, and reigned twelve years.

2 And he did evil in the eyes of יהוה, but not like his father and mother; for he removed the statue of Ba'al which his father had made.

3 But he clung to the sins of Yaroḇ'am son of Neḇat, who had made Yisra'ěl sin. He did not turn away from them.

4 And Měysha sovereign of Mo'aḇ was a sheep-breeder, and he paid the sovereign of Yisra'ěl one hundred thousand lambs and the wool of one hundred thousand rams.

5 And it came to be, when Aḥaḇ died, that the sovereign of Mo'aḇ revolted against the sovereign of Yisra'ěl.

6 And Sovereign Yehoram went out of Shomeron at that time and mustered all Yisra'ěl.

7 And he went and sent to Yehoshaphat sovereign of Yehuḏah, saying, "The sovereign of Mo'aḇ has revolted against me. Do you go with me to fight against Mo'aḇ?" And he said, "I go up. I am as you are, my people as your people, my horses as your horses."

8 And he said, "Which way do we go up?" And he said, "By way of the Wilderness of Eḏom."

9 And the sovereign of Yisra'ěl went, and the sovereign of Yehuḏah and the sovereign of Eḏom, and went round a journey of seven days. And there was no water for the army, nor for the cattle that followed them.

10 And the sovereign of Yisra'ěl said, "What? Has יהוה called these three sovereigns to give them into the hand of Mo'aḇ."

11 And Yehoshaphat said, "Is there no prophet of יהוה here? Then let us inquire of יהוה through him." One of the servants of the sovereign of Yisra'ěl then answered and said, "Elisha son of Shaphat is here, who poured water out on the hands of Ěliyahu."

12 And Yehoshaphat said, "The word of יהוה is with him." And the sovereign of Yisra'ěl and Yehoshaphat and the sovereign of Eḏom went down to him.

13 And Elisha said to the sovereign of Yisra'ěl, "What have I to do with you? Go to the prophets of your father and the prophets of your mother." And the sovereign of Yisra'ěl said to him, "No, for יהוה has called these three sovereigns to give them into the hand of Mo'aḇ."

14 And Elisha said, "As יהוה of hosts lives, before whom I stand, if it were not that I regard the presence of Yehoshaphat sovereign of Yehuḏah, I would not look at you nor see you.

15 "And now, bring me a harpist." And it came to be, when the harpist played, that the hand of יהוה came upon him.

16 And he said, "Thus said יהוה, 'Make this wadi ditches – ditches.'

17 "For thus said יהוה, 'You are not going to see wind, nor rain. Yet that wadi is to be filled with water, so that you, your cattle, and your beasts shall drink.'

18 "And this shall be but a light matter in the eyes of יהוה. And He shall give Mo'aḇ into your hand.

19 "And you shall strike every walled city and every choice city, and shall cut down every good tree, and stop up every fountain of water, and ruin every good piece of land with stones."

20 And it came to be in the morning, when the grain offering was offered, that see, water came by way of Eḏom, and the land was filled with water.

21 And when all Mo'aḇ heard that the sovereigns had come up to fight against them, all who were able to bear arms and older were gathered, and they stood at the border.

22 And they rose up early in the morning,
and the sun was shining on the water. And
the Mo'aḇites saw the water on the other
side as red as blood.
23 And they said, "This is blood. The sovereigns have indeed struck swords and
have killed one another. And now, Mo'aḇ,
to the spoil!"
24 And they came to the camp of Yisra'ěl,
and Yisra'ěl rose up and struck the
Mo'aḇites, so that they fled before them.
And striking they struck the Mo'aḇites.
25 And they broke down the cities, and
each man threw a stone on every good
piece of land and filled it. And they
stopped up all the fountains of water and
cut down all the good trees, until *only* the
stones of Qir Ḥaraseth was left. And the
slingers went round and struck it.
26 And when the sovereign of Mo'aḇ saw
that the battle was too strong for him,
he took with him seven hundred men
who drew swords, to break through to the
sovereign of Eḏom, but they could not,
27 then took his eldest son who would
have reigned in his place, and offered him
as an ascending offering upon the wall.
And there was great wrath against Yisra'ěl.
And they left him and returned to the land.

4 And a certain woman of the wives of
the sons of the prophets cried out to
Elisha, saying, "Your servant my husband
is dead, and you know that your servant
feared יהוה. And the lender has come to
take my two sons to be his slaves."
2 And Elisha said to her, "What should I
do for you? Inform me, what do you have
in the house?" And she said, "Your female
servant has none at all in the house except
a pot of oil."
3 And he said, "Go, borrow vessels from
everywhere, from all your neighbours,
empty vessels, do not get a few.
4 "And when you have come in, you shall
shut the door behind you and your sons.
Then pour it into all those vessels, and set
aside the filled ones."
5 So she went from him and shut the door
behind her and her sons, who brought *the
vessels* to her, and she poured it out.
6 And it came to be, when the vessels
were filled, that she said to her son, "Bring
me another vessel." But he said to her,
"There is not another vessel." And the oil
ceased.
7 So she went and informed the man of
Elohim, and he said, "Go, sell the oil and
pay your debt. And you *and* your sons live
on the rest."
8 And it came to be on a day that Elisha
went to Shuněm, where there was a prominent woman, and she took hold of him to
eat some food. And it came to be, as often
as he passed by, that he turned in there to
eat some food.
9 And she said to her husband, "Look, I
know that this is a set-apart man of
Elohim, who passes by us continually.
10 "Please, let us make a small upper room
on the wall, and let us put a bed for him
there, and a table and a chair and a lampstand. And it shall be, whenever he comes
to us, let him turn in there."
11 And it came to be on a day that he came
there, and he turned in to the upper room
and lay down there.
12 And he said to Gěḥazi his servant, "Call
this Shunammite woman." So he called
her, and she stood before him.
13 And he said to him, "Please say to her,
'Look, you have gone to all this trouble for
us. What is there to be done for you?
Should I speak on your behalf to the sovereign or to the commander of the army?' "
And she answered, "I am dwelling among
my own people."
14 And he said, "What then is to be done
for her?" And Gěḥazi answered, "Well, she
has no son, and her husband is old."
15 And he said, "Call her." So he called
her, and she stood in the doorway.
16 And he said, "About this appointed
time next year you shall embrace a son."
And she said, "No, my master, man of
Elohim, do not lie to your female servant!"
17 And the woman conceived, and bore a
son when the appointed time had come, of
which Elisha had spoken to her.
18 And the child grew. And it came to be
on a day that he went out to his father, to
the reapers,

19 and he said to his father, "My head, my
head!" And he said to a servant, "Take him
to his mother."
20 So he took him and brought him to his
mother, and he sat on her knees till noon,
and died.
21 And she went up and laid him on the
bed of the man of Elohim, and shut *the
door* on him, and went out.
22 And she called to her husband, and
said, "Please send me one of the young
men and one of the donkeys, so that I hurry
to the man of Elohim and return."
23 And he said, "Why are you going to
him today? It is neither the new *moon* nor
the sabbath." And she said, "It is well!"
24 And she saddled the donkey and said to
her servant, "Drive and go, do not slow
down, except I speak to you."
25 And she went, and came to the man of
Elohim at Mount Karmel. And it came to
be, when the man of Elohim saw her at a
distance, that he said to his servant Gěḥazi,
"See, the Shunammite woman.
26 "Please run now to meet her, and say to
her, 'Is it well with you? Is it well with
your husband? Is it well with the child?' "
And she answered, "It is well."
27 And she came to the man of Elohim at
the hill, and she took hold of him by the
feet, but Gěḥazi came near to push her
away. But the man of Elohim said, "Leave
her alone, for her being is bitter in her, and
יהוה has hidden it from me, and has not
revealed it to me."
28 And she said, "Did I ask a son of my
master? Did I not say, 'Do not deceive
me'?"
29 And he said to Gěḥazi, "Gird up your
loins, and take my staff in your hand, and
go. When you meet anyone, do not greet
him, and when anyone greets you, do not
answer him. And you shall lay my staff on
the face of the child."
30 And the mother of the child said, "As
יהוה lives, and as your being lives, I do not
leave you." And he rose and followed her.
31 And Gěḥazi went on ahead of them,
and laid the staff on the face of the child.
But there was no voice and there was no
hearing, so he went back to meet him, and
reported to him, saying, "The child has not
awakened."
32 And Elisha came into the house and
saw the child was dead, lying on his bed,
33 and he went in, and shut the door
behind the two of them, and prayed to
יהוה.
34 And he went up and lay on the child,
and put his mouth on his mouth, and his
eyes on his eyes, and his hands on his
hands, and stretched himself out on the
child, and the flesh of the child became
warm.
35 And he returned and walked back and
forth in the house, then went up and
stretched himself out on him. And the child
sneezed seven times, and the child opened
his eyes.
36 And he called Gěḥazi and said, "Call
this Shunammite." So he called her. And
she came in to him, and he said, "Pick up
your son."
37 Then she went in and fell at his feet,
and bowed herself to the ground, and
picked up her son and went out.
38 And Elisha returned to Gilgal. And the
scarcity of food was in the land, and the
sons of the prophets were sitting before
him. And he said to his servant, "Put on the
large pot, and cook stew for the sons of the
prophets."
39 And one went out to the field to gather
plants, and found a wild vine, and gathered
wild cucumbers from it, filling the skirt of
his garment, and came and sliced them into
the pot of stew, though they did not know
what they were.
40 They then served it to the men to eat.
And it came to be, as they were eating the
stew, that they cried out and said, "O man
of Elohim, there is death in the pot!" And
they were unable to eat it.
41 And he said, "Then bring some flour."
And he put it into the pot, and said, "Serve
it to the people to eat." And there was no
evil matter in the pot.
42 Now a man came from Baʿal Shalishah,
and brought the man of Elohim bread of
the first-fruits, twenty loaves of barley
bread, and newly ripened grain in his knap-
sack. And he said, "Give it to the people to

eat."
43 And his servant said, "What? Do I set
this before one hundred men?" And he
said, "Give it to the people to eat. For thus
said יהוה, 'Eat and have some left over.' "
44 And he set it before them, and they ate
and had some left over, according to the
word of יהוה.

5

And Na'aman, commander of the
army of the sovereign of Aram, was a
great man in the eyes of his master, and
highly respected, because by him יהוה had
given deliverance to Aram. And he was a
brave man, *but* leprous.
2 And the Arameans had gone out on
raids, and had brought back captive a
young girl from the land of Yisra'ěl, and
she served the wife of Na'aman.
3 And she said to her mistress, "If only
my master were with the prophet who is in
Shomeron! Then he would recover him of
his leprosy."
4 And Na'aman went in and reported to
his master, saying, "Thus and thus spoke
the girl who is from the land of Yisra'ěl."
5 And the sovereign of Aram said, "Go,
enter, and let me send a letter to the sovereign of Yisra'ěl." And he went and took
with him ten talents of silver, and six thousand *pieces* of gold, and ten changes of
garments.
6 And he brought the letter to the sovereign of Yisra'ěl, which said, "And now,
when this letter comes to you, see I have
sent Na'aman my servant to you, so that
you shall recover him of his leprosy."
7 And it came to be, when the sovereign
of Yisra'ěl read the letter, that he tore his
garments and said, "Am I Elohim, to kill
and keep alive, that this man sends a man
to me to recover him of his leprosy? For
consider now, and see how he is seeking an
occasion with me!"
8 And it came to be, when Elisha the man
of Elohim heard that the sovereign of
Yisra'ěl had torn his garments, that he sent
to the sovereign, saying, "Why have you
torn your garments? Please let him come to
me, so that he knows that there is a prophet
in Yisra'ěl."
9 So Na'aman came with his horses and
chariot, and he stood at the entrance of the
house of Elisha.
10 And Elisha sent a messenger to him,
saying, "Go, and you shall wash seven
times in the Yarděn, that your flesh might
be restored to you, and be clean."
11 But Na'aman became wroth, and went
away and said, "See, I said to myself, 'He
would certainly come out to me, and stand
and call on the Name of יהוה his Elohim,
and wave his hand over the place, and
recover the leprosy.'
12 "Are not the Aḇanah and the Pharpar,
the rivers of Dammeseq, better than all the
waters of Yisra'ěl? Could I not wash in
them and be clean?" And he turned and
went away in a rage.
13 And his servants came near and spoke
to him, and said, "My father, if the prophet
had spoken to you a great matter, would
you not have done it? How much more
then, when he says to you, 'Wash, and be
clean'?"
14 Then he went down and dipped seven
times in the Yarděn, according to the word
of the man of Elohim. And his flesh was
restored like the flesh of a little child, and
he was clean.
15 And he returned to the man of Elohim,
he and all his company, and came and
stood before him and said, "See, now I
know that there is no Elohim in all the
earth, except in Yisra'ěl. And now, please
take a gift from your servant."
16 But he said, "As יהוה lives, before
whom I stand, I do not accept it." And he
pressed on him to accept it, but he refused.
17 Then Na'aman said, "If not, please let
your servant be given two mule-loads of
earth, for no longer is your servant going to
make an ascending offering and slaughtering to other mighty ones, but to יהוה.
18 "יהוה grant forgiveness to your servant
in this matter: when my master goes into
the house of Rimmon to worship there, and
he leans on my hand, and I bow down in
the house of Rimmon; when I bow down in
the house of Rimmon, יהוה, please grant
forgiveness to your servant in this matter."
19 Then he said to him, "Go in peace."

And when he had gone from him some distance,
20 But Gěḥazi, the servant of Elisha the man of Elohim, said *to himself*, "Look, my master has spared Naʽaman this Aramean, while not receiving from his hands what he brought. But as יהוה lives, I shall run after him and take whatever from him."
21 And Gěḥazi pursued Naʽaman. And when Naʽaman saw him running after him, he came down from the chariot to meet him, and said, "Is there peace?"
22 And he said, "Peace. My master has sent me, saying, 'Look, even now two young men of the sons of the prophets have come to me from the mountains of Ephrayim. Please give them a talent of silver and two changes of garments.' "
23 And Naʽaman said, "Please accept two talents." And he urged him, and bound two talents of silver in two bags, with two changes of garments, and handed them to two of his servants. And they bare them ahead of him.
24 And when he came to the high place, he took them from their hand, and stored them away in the house, and let the men go, and they went.
25 And he went in and stood before his master, and Elisha said to him, "Where did you go, Gěḥazi?" And he said, "Your servant did not go anywhere."
26 But he said to him, "Did not my heart go with you when the man turned back from his chariot to meet you? Is it time to accept silver and to accept garments, and olive-trees and vineyards, and sheep and cattle, and male and female servants?
27 "So let the leprosy of Naʽaman cling to you and your descendants forever." And he went out from him as leprous as snow.

6 And the sons of the prophets said to Elisha, "See, the place where we dwell with you is too small for us.
2 "Please, let us go to the Yarděn, and let every man take a log from there, and let us make there a place to dwell." And he answered, "Go."
3 Then the one said, "Please undertake to go with your servants." And he answered, "I shall go."
4 And he went with them, and they came to the Yarděn, and they cut down trees.
5 And it came to be, as one was cutting down a tree, that the iron axe head fell into the water. And he cried out and said, "Oh my master, for it was borrowed!"
6 And the man of Elohim said, "Where did it fall?" And he showed him the place. And he cut off a stick, and threw it in there, and made the iron float.
7 And he said, "Pick it up." And he reached out his hand and took it.
8 And the sovereign of Aram was fighting against Yisra'ěl, and took counsel with his servants, saying, "My camp is in such and such a place."
9 And the man of Elohim sent to the sovereign of Yisra'ěl, saying, "Be on guard, do not pass this place, for the Arameans are coming down there."
10 The sovereign of Yisra'ěl then sent to the place of which the man of Elohim had spoken to him, and warned him, so that he was on his guard there, not once, and not twice.
11 And this greatly troubled the heart of the sovereign of Aram. And he called his servants and said to them, "Declare to me! Who of us is for the sovereign of Yisra'ěl?"
12 And one of his servants said, "None, my master, O sovereign, for Elisha, the prophet who is in Yisra'ěl, declares to the sovereign of Yisra'ěl the words that you speak in your bedroom."
13 And he said, "Go and see where he is, so that I send and get him." And it was reported to him, saying, "See, he is in Dothan."
14 And he sent horses and chariots and a great army there, and they came by night and surrounded the city.
15 And the servant of the man of Elohim rose early and went out, and saw an army, surrounding the city with horses and chariots. And his servant said to him, "Oh, my master! What do we do?"
16 And he answered, "Do not fear, for those who are with us are more than those who are with them."

17 And Elisha prayed, and said, "יהוה, I pray, open his eyes and let him see." And יהוה opened the eyes of the young man, and he looked and saw the mountain covered with horses and chariots of fire all around Elisha.

18 And when they came down to him, Elisha prayed to יהוה, and said, "Strike this nation with blindness, I pray." And He struck them with blindness according to the word of Elisha.

19 And Elisha said to them, "This is not the way, nor is this the city. Follow me, and let me bring you to the man whom you seek." But he led them to Shomeron.

20 And it came to be, when they had come to Shomeron, that Elisha said, "יהוה, open the eyes of these men so that they see." And יהוה opened their eyes, and they looked and saw they were in the midst of Shomeron!

21 And when the sovereign of Yisra'ěl saw them, he said to Elisha, "My father, should I strike? Should I strike?"

22 But he said, "Do not strike. Do you strike those whom you have taken captive with your sword and your bow? Set food and water before them and let them eat and drink and go to their master."

23 And he made a great feast for them. And after they ate and drank, he let them go, and they went to their master. And the bands of Aramean raiders came no more into the land of Yisra'ěl.

24 And after this it came to be that Ben-Haḏaḏ the sovereign of Aram mustered all his army, and went up and besieged Shomeron.

25 And there was a great scarcity of food in Shomeron. And see, they besieged it until a donkey's head went at eighty pieces of silver, and one-fourth of a kab of dove droppings for five pieces of silver.

26 And it came to be, as the sovereign of Yisra'ěl was passing by on the wall, a woman cried out to him, saying, "Help, my master, O sovereign!"

27 And he said, "If יהוה does not help you, where do I find help for you? From the threshing floor or from the winepress?"

28 And the sovereign said to her, "What is troubling you?" And she answered, "This woman said to me, 'Give your son and let us eat him today, and tomorrow we eat my son.'

29 "So we cooked my son, and ate him. And I said to her on the next day, 'Give your son and let us eat him.' But she has hidden her son."

30 And it came to be, when the sovereign heard the words of the woman, that he tore his garments. And as he passed by on the wall, the people looked and saw the sack-cloth on his body, underneath.

31 And he said, "Elohim do so to me and more also, if the head of Elisha son of Shaphat remains on him today."

32 And Elisha was sitting in his house, and the elders were sitting with him. And *the sovereign* sent a man ahead of him, but before the messenger came to him, he said to the elders, "Do you see how this son of a murderer has sent someone to take away my head? Look, when the messenger comes, shut the door, and hold him fast at the door. Is not the sound of his master's feet behind him?"

33 While he was still speaking with them, then see, the messenger came down to him, and he said, "Look, this evil is from יהוה, why should I wait for יהוה any longer?"

7 And Elisha said, "Hear the word of יהוה. Thus said יהוה, 'About this time tomorrow a seah of fine flour for a sheqel, and two seahs of barley for a sheqel, at the gate of Shomeron.' "

2 And an officer on whose hand the sovereign leaned answered the man of Elohim and said, "Look, if יהוה is making windows in the heavens, shall this word come true?" And he said, "Look, you are about to see it with your eyes, but not eat of it."

3 And there were four leprous men at the entrance of the gate. And they said to each other, "Why are we sitting here until we are dead?

4 "If we shall say, 'Let us go into the city,' the scarcity of food is in the city, and we shall die there. And if we sit here, we shall die. And now, come, let us surrender to the army of the Arameans. If they keep

us alive, we live. And if they kill us, we
shall die."
5 So at twilight they rose up to go to the
camp of the Arameans. And when they had
come to the outskirts of the Aramean
camp, look, no one was there.
6 For יהוה had caused the army of the
Arameans to hear the noise of chariots and
the noise of horses, the noise of a great
army, and they said to each other, "Look,
the sovereign of Yisra'ěl has hired against
us the sovereigns of the Ḥittites and the
sovereigns of the Mitsrians to come against
us!"
7 So they rose up and fled at twilight, and
left the camp as it is – their tents, and their
horses, and their donkeys – and they fled
for their lives.
8 And when these lepers came to the outskirts of the camp, they went into one tent
and ate and drank, and took from there
silver and gold and garments, and went and
hid them. And they came back and went
into another tent, and took from there and
went and hid it.
9 Then they said to each other, "We are
not doing right. This day is a day of good
news, and we are keeping silent. And if we
wait until morning light, then evil shall
come upon us. And now, come, let us go
and inform the house of the sovereign."
10 And they came and called to the gatekeepers of the city, and informed them,
saying, "We went to the camp of Aram,
and look, there is not a man or a voice of
man, only horses tied and donkeys tied,
and the tents as they were."
11 And the gatekeepers called, and they
informed the house of the sovereign inside.
12 So the sovereign rose up in the night
and said to his servants, "Let me now
inform you what the Arameans have done
to us. They know that we are starving, so
they have gone out of the camp to hide
themselves in the field, saying, 'When they
come out of the city, we shall catch them
alive, and enter into the city.' "
13 And one of his servants answered and
said, "Please, let some take five of the
horses that are left in the city. Look, they
are like the entire crowd of Yisra'ěl that are
left in it, look, they are like the entire
crowd of Yisra'ěl left from those who are
consumed. So let us send and see."
14 They then took two chariots with horses. And the sovereign sent them in the
direction of the camp of Aram, saying, "Go
and see."
15 And they went after them to the Yarděn.
And look, all the way was littered with garments and weapons which the Arameans
had thrown away in their haste. And the
messengers returned and reported to the
sovereign.
16 Then the people went out and plundered the camp of Aram. So a seah of fine
flour was for a sheqel, and two seahs of
barley for a sheqel, according to the word
of יהוה.
17 And the sovereign had appointed the
officer on whose hand he leaned to be in
charge of the gate. But the people trampled
him in the gate, and he died, as the man of
Elohim had said, who spoke when the
sovereign came down to him.
18 And it came to be, as the man of
Elohim had spoken to the sovereign, saying, "Two seahs of barley for a sheqel, and
a seah of fine flour for a sheqel, at this time
tomorrow in the gate of Shomeron,"
19 that officer answered the man of
Elohim, and said, "Now look, if יהוה is
making windows in the heavens, is it
according to this word?" And he had said,
"Look, you are about to see it with your
eyes, but not eat of it."
20 And so it came to be for him, for the
people trampled him in the gate, and he
died.

8 And Elisha spoke to the woman
whose son he had restored to life, saying, "Rise up and go, you and your household, and sojourn wherever you do
sojourn, for יהוה has called for a scarcity
of food, and also, it is coming upon the
land for seven years."
2 And the woman rose up and did according to the word of the man of Elohim, and
she went with her household and sojourned
in the land of the Philistines, seven years.
3 And it came to be, at the end of seven

years, that the woman returned from the
land of the Philistines. And she went to cry
out to the sovereign for her house and for
her land.
4 And the sovereign was speaking to
Gěḥazi, the servant of the man of Elohim,
saying, "Please relate to me all the great
matters Elisha has done."
5 And it came to be, as he was relating to
the sovereign how he had restored the dead
to life, that see, the woman whose son he
had restored to life, was crying out to the
sovereign for her house and for her land.
And Gěḥazi said, "My master, O sovereign, this is the woman, and this is her son
whom Elisha restored to life."
6 So the sovereign asked the woman, and
she related to him. And the sovereign
appointed a certain eunuch for her, saying,
"Return all that was hers, and all the
increase of the field from the day that she
left the land until now."
7 And Elisha came to Dammeseq, and
Ben-Haḏaḏ sovereign of Aram was sick.
And it was reported to him, saying, "The
man of Elohim has come here."
8 And the sovereign said to Ḥaza'ěl,
"Take a present in your hand, and go to
meet the man of Elohim, and inquire of
יהוה by him, saying, 'Do I recover from
this sickness?' "
9 And Ḥaza'ěl went to meet him and took
a present with him, of all the good *wares* of
Dammeseq, forty camel-loads. And he
came and stood before him, and said,
"Your son Ben-Haḏaḏ sovereign of Aram
has sent me to you, saying, 'Do I recover
from this sickness?' "
10 And Elisha said to him, "Go, say to
him, 'You shall certainly recover.' But
יהוה has shown me that he shall certainly
die."
11 And he looked *at him* steadily until he
was ashamed. Then the man of Elohim
wept.
12 And Ḥaza'ěl said, "Why is my master
weeping?" And he answered, "Because I
know the evil that you are going to do to
the children of Yisra'ěl: Setting their
strongholds on fire, and killing their young
men with the sword, and dashing their children, and ripping open their women with
child."
13 And Ḥaza'ěl said, "But what is your
servant – a dog, that he should perform
this great matter?" And Elisha answered,
"יהוה has shown that you are to be sovereign over Aram!"
14 And he left Elisha, and came to his
master, who said to him, "What did Elisha
say to you?" And he answered, "He said to
me that you shall certainly recover."
15 And on the next day it came to be that
he took a thick cloth and dipped it in water,
and spread it over his face so that he died.
And Ḥaza'ěl reigned in his place.
16 And in the fifth year of Yehoram son of
Aḥaḇ sovereign of Yisra'ěl – Yehoshaphat
was sovereign of Yehuḏah – Yehoram son
of Yehoshaphat began to reign as sovereign of Yehuḏah.
17 He was thirty-two years old when he
began to reign, and he reigned eight years
in Yerushalayim.
18 And he walked in the way of the sovereigns of Yisra'ěl, as the house of Aḥaḇ had
done, for the daughter of Aḥaḇ was his
wife. And he did evil in the eyes of יהוה.
19 However, יהוה would not destroy
Yehuḏah, for the sake of Dawiḏ His servant, as He promised him to give a lamp to
him and his sons forever.
20 In his days Eḏom revolted from under
the hand of Yehuḏah, and made a sovereign over themselves.
21 And Yoram passed over to Tsa'ir, and
all his chariots with him. And he rose by
night and struck the Eḏomites who had
surrounded him and the commanders of the
chariots, but his people fled to their tents.
22 Yet Eḏom has been in revolt from under
the hand of Yehuḏah to this day. Then
Liḇnah revolted at the same time.
23 And the rest of the acts of Yoram, and
all that he did, are they not written in the
book of the annals of the sovereigns of
Yehuḏah?
24 So Yoram slept with his fathers, and
was buried with his fathers in the City of
Dawiḏ. And Aḥazyahu his son reigned in
his place.
25 In the twelfth year of Yoram son of

Aḥaḇ sovereign of Yisra'ĕl, Aḥazyahu son of Yehoram sovereign of Yehuḏah began to reign.

26 Aḥazyahu was twenty-two years old when he began to reign, and he reigned one year in Yerushalayim. And the name of his mother was Athalyahu, the granddaughter of Omri, sovereign of Yisra'ĕl.

27 And he walked in the way of the house of Aḥaḇ, and did evil in the eyes of יהוה, as the house of Aḥaḇ had done, for he was the son-in-law of the house of Aḥaḇ.

28 And he went with Yoram son of Aḥaḇ to battle against Ḥaza'ĕl sovereign of Aram at Ramoth Gilʽaḏ, and the Arameans struck Yoram.

29 And Sovereign Yoram went back to Yizreʽĕl to recover from the wounds with which the Arameans had stricken him at Ramah, when he fought against Ḥaza'ĕl sovereign of Aram. Then Aḥazyahu son of Yehoram, the sovereign of Yehuḏah, went down to see Yoram son of Aḥaḇ in Yizreʽĕl, for he was sick.

9 And Elisha the prophet called one of the sons of the prophets, and said to him, "Gird your loins and take this flask of oil in your hand, and go to Ramoth Gilʽaḏ.

2 "And you shall go there and look there for Yĕhu son of Yehoshaphat, son of Nimshi, and go in and make him rise up from among his brothers, and take him to an inner room,

3 "and take the flask of oil, and pour it on his head, and say, 'Thus said יהוה, "I have anointed you sovereign over Yisra'ĕl." ' Then you shall open the door and flee, and do not wait."

4 So the young man – the young man the prophet – went to Ramoth Gilʽaḏ,

5 and came in and saw the commanders of the army sitting. And he said, "I have a message for you, O commander." And Yĕhu said, "For which one of us?" And he said, "For you, commander."

6 And he rose up and went into the house. And he poured the oil on his head, and said to him, "Thus said יהוה Elohim of Yisra'ĕl, 'I have anointed you sovereign over the people of יהוה, over Yisra'ĕl.

7 'And you shall strike the house of Aḥaḇ your master, and I shall avenge the blood of My servants the prophets, and the blood of all the servants of יהוה, at the hand of Izeḇel.

8 'And all the house of Aḥaḇ shall perish. And I shall cut off from Aḥaḇ all the males in Yisra'ĕl, both those shut up and those left at large.

9 'And I shall give up the house of Aḥaḇ like the house of Yaroḇʽam son of Neḇat, and like the house of Baʽasha son of Aḥiyah.

10 'And the dogs are going to eat Izeḇel in the portion of Yizreʽĕl, with none to bury her.' " Then he opened the door and fled.

11 And Yĕhu came out to the servants of his master, and one said to him, "Is there peace? Why did this madman come to you?" And he said to them, "You know the man and his talk."

12 And they said, "A lie! Reveal it to us now." So he said, "Thus and thus he spoke to me, saying, 'Thus said יהוה, "I have anointed you sovereign over Yisra'ĕl." ' "

13 And they hurried, and each one took his garment and put it under him on the top of the steps. And they blew with the shophar, saying, "Yĕhu reigns!"

14 Thus Yĕhu son of Yehoshaphat, son of Nimshi, conspired against Yoram – now Yoram had been guarding Ramoth Gilʽaḏ, he and all Yisra'ĕl, against Ḥaza'ĕl sovereign of Aram.

15 But Sovereign Yehoram had returned to Yizreʽĕl to recover from the wounds with which the Arameans had stricken him when he fought with Ḥaza'ĕl sovereign of Aram – Yĕhu now said, "If this is your desire, let no one leave or escape from the city to go and make it known in Yizreʽĕl!"

16 And Yĕhu rode in a chariot and went to Yizreʽĕl, for Yoram was laid up there. And Aḥazyah sovereign of Yehuḏah had come down to see Yoram.

17 And a watchman stood on the tower in Yizreʽĕl, and he saw the company of Yĕhu as he came, and said, "I see a company of men." And Yehoram said, "Get a horseman and send him to meet them, and let him say, 'Is there peace?' "

18 And the horseman went to meet him,
and said, “Thus said the sovereign, ‘Is
there peace?’ ” And Yěhu said, “What
have you to do with peace? Turn around
and follow me.” And the watchman spoke,
saying, “The messenger went to them, but
is not coming back.”
19 Then he sent out a second horseman
who came to them, and said, “Thus said the
sovereign, ‘Is there peace?’ ” And Yěhu
answered, “What have you to do with
peace? Turn around and follow me.”
20 And the watchman spoke, saying, “He
went up to them and is not coming back.
And the driving is like the driving of Yěhu
son of Nimshi, for he drives madly!”
21 Then Yehoram said, “Hitch up.” And
his chariot was hitched up. And Yehoram
sovereign of Yisra’ěl and Aḥazyahu sovereign
of Yehuḏah went out, each in his chariot.
And they went out to meet Yěhu, and
met him on the portion of Naḇoth the
Yizreʽělite.
22 And it came to be, when Yehoram saw
Yěhu, that he said, “Is there peace, Yěhu?”
But he answered, “What peace, as long as
the whorings of your mother Izeḇel and her
witchcraft are so many?”
23 Thereupon Yehoram turned his hands
around and fled, and said to Aḥazyahu,
“Treachery, O Aḥazyah!”
24 And Yěhu drew his bow and struck
Yehoram between his arms. And the arrow
came out at his heart, and he sank down in
his chariot.
25 And *Yěhu* said to Biḏqar his officer,
“Take him up, and throw him into the
portion of the field of Naḇoth the
Yizreʽělite. Remember how you and I were
riding together behind Aḥaḇ his father, and
יהוה lifted up this pronouncement against
him:
26 ‘Have I not seen the blood of Naḇoth
and the blood of his sons last night?’
declares יהוה. ‘And I shall repay you in
this portion,’ declares יהוה. And now, take
up, throw him on the portion, according
to the word of יהוה.”
27 And Aḥazyah sovereign of Yehuḏah
saw this and fled up the way to Běyth
Haggan. And Yěhu pursued him, and said,
“Strike him, him too, in the chariot,” at the
ascent to Gur, which is by Yiḇleʽam. And
he fled to Meḡiddo, and died there.
28 Then his servants conveyed him in the
chariot to Yerushalayim, and buried him in
his burial-place with his fathers in the City
of Dawiḏ.
29 And in the eleventh year of Yoram son
of Aḥaḇ, Aḥazyah began to reign over
Yehuḏah.
30 And Yěhu came to Yizreʽěl, and Izeḇel
heard of it. And she put paint on her eyes
and adorned her head, and looked through
a window.
31 And as Yěhu came to the gate, she said,
“Is it peace, Zimri, killer of your master?”
32 And he lifted up his face to the window
and said, “Who is with me? Who?” And
two, three eunuchs looked down to him.
33 And he said, “Throw her down.” And
they threw her down, and some of her
blood spattered on the wall and on the
horses, and he trampled her under foot.
34 And he went in, and he ate and drank,
and said, “Go now, see to this cursed one,
and bury her, for she was a sovereign’s
daughter.”
35 So they went to bury her, but all they
found of her was the skull and the feet and
the palms of the hands.
36 And they came back and informed him.
And he said, “This is the word of יהוה,
which He spoke by His servant Ěliyahu the
Tishbite, saying, ‘In the portion of Yizreʽěl
dogs are going to eat the flesh of Izeḇel,
37 and the corpse of Izeḇel shall be as
dung on the surface of the field, in the
portion of Yizreʽěl, so that they do not say,
“This is Izeḇel.” ’ ”

10 And Aḥaḇ had seventy sons in
Shomeron. And Yěhu wrote letters
and sent to Shomeron, to the rulers of
Yizreʽěl, to the elders, and to the guardians
of Aḥaḇ, saying,
2 And now, when this letter comes to
you, since your master’s sons are with you,
and you have chariots and horses, and a
walled city, and weapons,
3 choose the best and most upright of
your master’s sons, and set him on his

father's throne, and fight for your master's
house.
4 And they were greatly afraid, and said,
"Look, two sovereigns have not stood
before him, how do we stand, we?"
5 And he who was over the house, and he
who was over the city, the elders also, and
the guardians, sent to Yěhu, saying, "We
are your servants, and all that you say to us
we do. We do not set up anyone to reign.
Do what is good in your eyes."
6 And he wrote a second letter to them,
saying, If you are for me, and if you obey
my voice, take the heads of the men, your
master's sons, and come to me at Yizreʽěl
by this time tomorrow. Now the sovereign's sons, seventy beings, were with the
great men of the city, who brought them
up.
7 And it came to be, when the letter came
to them, that they took the sovereign's sons
and slew them, seventy men, and put their
heads in baskets and sent them to him at
Yizreʽěl.
8 Then a messenger came and informed
him, saying, "They have brought the heads
of the sovereign's sons." And he said,
"Make them two heaps at the entrance of
the gate until morning."
9 And it came to be, in the morning, that
he went out and stood, and said to all the
people, "You are righteous. Look, I conspired against my master and killed him,
but who struck all these?
10 "Know now that not one word of יהוה
which יהוה spoke concerning the house of
Aḥaḇ does fall to the ground, for יהוה has
done what He spoke by His servant
Ěliyahu."
11 And Yěhu struck all those left of the
house of Aḥaḇ in Yizreʽěl, and all his great
men and his friends and his priests, until he
left him without a survivor.
12 And he rose up to go, and went to
Shomeron. On the way, at Běyth Ěqeḏ of
the Shepherds,
13 Yěhu met the brothers of Aḥazyahu
sovereign of Yehuḏah, and said, "Who are
you?" And they answered, "We are brothers of Aḥazyahu, and we have come down
to greet the sons of the sovereign and the
sons of the sovereigness mother."
14 And he said, "Take them alive!" So
they took them alive, and slew them at the
well of Běyth Ěqeḏ, forty-two men, and he
left none of them.
15 And he left there and met Yehonaḏaḇ
son of Rěḵaḇ, coming to meet him, and
blessed him and said to him, "Is your heart
right, as my heart is toward your heart?"
And Yehonaḏaḇ answered, "It is." *Yěhu
said*, "If it is, give me your hand." And he
gave him his hand, and he took him up to
him into the chariot.
16 And he said, "Come with me, and see
my ardour for יהוה." And they made him
ride in his chariot.
17 And he came to Shomeron, and struck
all those left of Aḥaḇ in Shomeron, till he
had destroyed them, according to the word
of יהוה which He spoke to Ěliyahu.
18 And Yěhu gathered all the people and
said to them, "Aḥaḇ served Baʽal a little;
Yěhu serves him much.
19 "And now, call to me all the prophets of
Baʽal, all his servants, and all his priests.
Let no one be missing, for I have a great
slaughtering to make to Baʽal. Anyone who
is lacking shall not live!" But Yěhu did this
deceptively, in order to destroy the servants of Baʽal.
20 And Yěhu said, "Set apart an assembly
for Baʽal." So they proclaimed it.
21 And Yěhu sent throughout all Yisra'ěl,
and all the servants of Baʽal came, so that
there was not a man left who did not come.
And they came into the house of Baʽal, and
the house of Baʽal was filled from end
to end.
22 And he said to him who was over the
wardrobe, "Bring out garments for all the
servants of Baʽal." And he brought out garments for them.
23 And Yěhu and Yehonaḏaḇ son of
Rěḵaḇ went into the house of Baʽal, and
said to the servants of Baʽal, "Search and
see that no servants of יהוה are here with
you, but only the servants of Baʽal."
24 So they went in to make slaughterings
and ascending offerings. Now Yěhu had
appointed for himself eighty men on the
outside, and had said, "The man who lets

escape *any* of the men whom I have
brought into your hands – his life for his
life!"
25 And it came to be, when he had finished making the ascending offering, Yěhu
said to the guard and to the officers, "Go
in, strike them, let no one come out!" And
they struck them with the edge of the
sword, and the guards and the officers
threw them out, and went into the inner
room of the house of Ba'al,
26 and brought out the pillars of the house
of Ba'al and burned them,
27 and broke down the statue of Ba'al, and
broke down the house of Ba'al and made it
a latrine to this day.
28 Thus Yěhu destroyed Ba'al out of Yisra'ěl.
29 However, Yěhu did not turn away from
the sins of Yaroḇ'am son of Neḇat, who
had made Yisra'ěl sin, from the golden
calves that were at Běyth Ěl and Dan.
30 And יהוה said to Yěhu, "Because you
have done well by doing what is right in
My eyes, and have done to the house of
Aḥaḇ all that was in My heart, your sons
are going to sit on the throne of Yisra'ěl to
the fourth *generation*."
31 But Yěhu did not guard to walk in the
Torah of יהוה Elohim of Yisra'ěl with all
his heart. For he did not turn away from the
sins of Yaroḇ'am, who had made Yisra'ěl
sin.
32 In those days יהוה began to cut off
some in Yisra'ěl. And Ḥaza'ěl struck them
throughout all the border of Yisra'ěl,
33 from the Yarděn to the sun-rising: all
the land of Gil'aḏ – the Gaḏites, and the
Re'uḇěnites, and the Menashshehites –
from Aro'ěr, which is by the wadi Arnon,
including Gil'aḏ and Bashan.
34 And the rest of the acts of Yěhu, and all
that he did, and all his might, are they not
written in the book of the annals of the sovereigns of Yisra'ěl?
35 So Yěhu slept with his fathers, and they
buried him in Shomeron. And Yeho'aḥaz
his son reigned in his place.
36 And the days that Yěhu reigned over
Yisra'ěl in Shomeron were twenty-eight
years.

11 And Athalyah was the mother of
Aḥazyahu. And when she saw that
her son was dead, she arose and destroyed
all the offspring of the reign.
2 But Yehosheḇa, the daughter of
Sovereign Yoram, sister of Aḥazyahu, took
Yo'ash son of Aḥazyah, and stole him
away from among the sons of the sovereign's sons who were put to death. So they
hid him and his nurse in the bedroom, from
Athalyahu, and he was not put to death.
3 And he remained with her in hiding in
the House of יהוה for six years, while
Athalyah was reigning over the land.
4 And in the seventh year Yehoyaḏa sent
and brought the commanders of hundreds,
with the Karites and the runners, and
brought them into the House of יהוה to
him. And he made a covenant with them
and took an oath from them in the House
of יהוה, and showed them the son of the
sovereign.
5 And he commanded them, saying,
"This is what you are to do: One-third of
you who come in on the Sabbath to be on
guard in the sovereign's house,
6 and one-third at the gate of Sur, and
one-third at the gate behind the runners.
And you shall be on guard in the house,
lest it be broken down.
7 "And the two detachments of you
who are going out on the Sabbath shall
be on guard in the House of יהוה for the
sovereign.
8 "And you shall surround the sovereign
on all sides, every man with his weapons in
his hand. And whoever comes within the
ranks, let him be put to death. And be with
the sovereign as he goes out and as he
comes in."
9 So the commanders of the hundreds did
according to all that Yehoyaḏa the priest
commanded. And each of them took his
men who were going in on the Sabbath,
with those who were going out on the
Sabbath, and came to Yehoyaḏa the priest.
10 And the priest gave the commanders of
hundreds the spears and shields which had
belonged to Sovereign Dawiḏ, that were
in the House of יהוה.
11 And the runners stood, every man with

his weapons in his hand, all around the
sovereign, from the right side of the House
to the left side of the House, by the slaughter-place and the House.
12 And he brought out the son of the sovereign and put on him the diadem and the
Witness. And they set him up to reign and
anointed him, and they clapped[a] their
hands and said, "Let the sovereign live!"
13 And Athalyah heard the noise of the
runners, the people, and she came to the
people, into the House of יהוה,
14 and looked and saw the sovereign
standing by a column, according to the
ruling, and the chiefs and the trumpeters
were beside the sovereign, and all the
people of the land rejoicing and blowing
trumpets. And Athalyah tore her garments
and cried out, "Treason! Treason!"
15 And Yehoyaḏa the priest commanded
the commanders of the hundreds, the officers of the army, and said to them, "Take
her outside the ranks, and slay with the
sword whoever follows her." For the priest
had said, "Do not let her be killed in the
House of יהוה."
16 So they took hold of her, and she went
by way of the horses' entrance to the sovereign's house, and was put to death there.
17 And Yehoyaḏa made a covenant
between יהוה and the sovereign and the
people, to be the people of יהוה – also
between the sovereign and the people.
18 And all the people of the land went to
the house of Baʽal, and broke it down.
They completely broke up its slaughter-
places and images, and killed Mattan the
priest of Baʽal before the slaughter-places.
And the priest appointed inspectors over
the House of יהוה,
19 and took the commanders of hundreds,
and the Karites, and the runners, and all the
people of the land. And they brought the
sovereign down from the House of יהוה,
and went by way of the gate of the runners
to the sovereign's house. And he sat on the
throne of the sovereigns.
20 And all the people of the land rejoiced.
And the city had rest, for they had slain
Athalyahu with the sword in the sovereign's house.
21 Yeho'ash was seven years old when he
began to reign.

12

Yeho'ash began to reign in the seventh year of Yěhu, and he reigned
forty years in Yerushalayim. And his mother's name was Tsiḇyah of Be'ěrsheḇa.
2 And Yeho'ash did what was right in the
eyes of יהוה all the days in which Yehoyaḏa the priest instructed him.
3 However, the high places were not
taken away; the people still slaughtered
and burned incense on the high places.
4 And Yeho'ash said to the priests, "All
the silver of the set-apart gifts that are
brought into the House of יהוה, the silver
coming over, each man's assessment
silver, all the silver that a man purposes in
his heart to bring into the House of יהוה,
5 let the priests take for themselves, each
from his friend. And let them strengthen
the breaches of the House, wherever there
is a breach."
6 And it came to be, by the twenty-third
year of Sovereign Yeho'ash, that the
priests had not strengthened the breaches
of the House,
7 and Sovereign Yeho'ash called Yehoyaḏa the priest and the other priests, and
said to them, "Why have you not strengthened the breaches of the House? And now,
do not take any more silver from your
friends, but give it for the breaches of the
House."
8 And the priests agreed that they would
neither receive any more silver from the
people, nor strengthen the breaches of the
House.
9 And Yehoyaḏa the priest took a chest,
and bored a hole in its lid, and set it beside
the slaughter-place, on the right side as one
comes into the House of יהוה. And the
priests who guarded the door put there all
the silver that was brought into the House
of יהוה.
10 And it came to be, whenever they saw
that there was much silver in the chest, that

11a - Lit. struck

the sovereign's scribe and the high priest
came up and put it in bags, and counted the
silver that was found in the House of יהוה,
11 and gave the silver, weighed out, into
the hands of those who did the work, who
had the oversight of the House of יהוה.
And they paid it out to the carpenters and
builders who worked on the House of
יהוה,
12 and to stonemasons and stonecutters,
and for buying timber and hewn stone to
strengthen the breach of the House of יהוה,
and for all that was paid out to strengthen
the House.
13 However there were not made for the
House of יהוה basins of silver, snuffers,
sprinkling-bowls, trumpets, any objects of
gold, or objects of silver, from the silver
that was brought into the House of יהוה,
14 for they gave that to the workmen, and
they strengthened the House of יהוה with
it.
15 And they did not reckon with the men
into whose hand they gave the silver to be
paid to workmen, for they acted trustworthily.
16 The silver from the trespass offerings
and the silver from the sin offerings was
not brought into the House of יהוה.
It belonged to the priests.
17 And Ḥaza'ĕl sovereign of Aram went
up and fought against Gath, and captured
it. And Ḥaza'ĕl set his face to go up to
Yerushalayim.
18 And Yeho'ash sovereign of Yehuḏah
took all the set-apart gifts that his fathers,
Yehoshaphat and Yehoram and Aḥazyahu,
sovereigns of Yehuḏah, had set apart, and
his own set-apart gifts, and all the gold
found in the treasuries of the House of
יהוה and in the sovereign's house, and sent
them to Ḥaza'ĕl sovereign of Aram. Then
he went away from Yerushalayim.
19 And the rest of the acts of Yo'ash, and
all that he did, are they not written in the
book of the annals of the sovereigns of
Yehuḏah?
20 And his servants rose up and made a
conspiracy, and smote Yo'ash in the house
of Millo, which goes down to Silla.
21 For Yozaḵar son of Shimʽath and
Yehozaḇaḏ son of Shomĕr, his servants,
struck him. So he died, and they buried
him with his fathers in the City of Dawiḏ.
And Amatsyah his son reigned in his place.

13 In the twenty-third year of Yo'ash
son of Aḥazyahu, sovereign of
Yehuḏah, Yeho'aḥaz son of Yĕhu began to
reign over Yisra'ĕl in Shomeron, and
reigned seventeen years.
2 And he did evil in the eyes of יהוה, and
followed the sins of Yaroḇʽam son of
Neḇat, who had made Yisra'ĕl sin. He did
not turn away from them.
3 And the displeasure of יהוה burned
against Yisra'ĕl, and He gave them into
the hand of Ḥaza'ĕl sovereign of Aram,
and into the hand of Ben-Haḏaḏ son of
Ḥaza'ĕl, all the days.
4 Then Yeho'aḥaz sought the face of
יהוה. And יהוה listened to him, for He saw
the oppression of Yisra'ĕl, because the
sovereign of Aram oppressed them.
5 And יהוה gave Yisra'ĕl a saviour, so
that they came out from under the hand of
Aram. And the children of Yisra'ĕl dwelt
in their tents as before.
6 However, they did not turn away from
the sins of the house of Yaroḇʽam, who had
made Yisra'ĕl sin, but walked in them.
Moreover, the Ashĕrah also remained in
Shomeron.
7 For He left of the army of Yeho'aḥaz
only fifty horsemen, and ten chariots, and
ten thousand footmen, for the sovereign of
Aram had destroyed them and made them
like the dust at threshing.
8 And the rest of the acts of Yeho'aḥaz,
and all that he did, and his might, are they
not written in the book of the annals of the
sovereigns of Yisra'ĕl?
9 So Yeho'aḥaz slept with his fathers,
and they buried him in Shomeron. And
Yo'ash his son reigned in his place.
10 In the thirty-seventh year of Yo'ash
sovereign of Yehuḏah, Yeho'ash son of
Yeho'aḥaz began to reign over Yisra'ĕl in
Shomeron, sixteen years.
11 And he did evil in the eyes of יהוה. He
did not turn away from all the sins of
Yaroḇʽam son of Neḇat, who had made

Yisra'ěl sin – he walked in it.
12 And the rest of the acts of Yo'ash, and all that he did, and his might with which he fought against Amatsyah sovereign of Yehuḏah, are they not written in the book of the annals of the sovereigns of Yisra'ěl?
13 So Yo'ash slept with his fathers. And Yaroḇʽam sat on his throne. And Yo'ash was buried in Shomeron with the sovereigns of Yisra'ěl.
14 And Elisha had become sick with the sickness in which he died. And Yo'ash the sovereign of Yisra'ěl came down to him, and wept over his face, and said, "O my father, my father, the chariots of Yisra'ěl and their horsemen!"
15 And Elisha said to him, "Take a bow and some arrows." And he took a bow and some arrows.
16 And he said to the sovereign of Yisra'ěl, "Place your hand on the bow." So he placed his hand, and Elisha placed his hands on the hands of the sovereign,
17 and said, "Open the east window." And he had opened it and Elisha said, "Shoot." And he shot. Then he said, "The arrow of deliverance of יהוה and the arrow of deliverance from Aram, for you shall strike Aram at Aphěq until it is finished."
18 Then he said, "Take the arrows," and he took them. And he said to the sovereign of Yisra'ěl, "Strike the ground," and he struck three times, and stopped.
19 And the man of Elohim was wroth with him and said, "You should have struck five or six times, then you would have stricken Aram till its utter destruction. But now you shall strike Aram only three times."
20 And Elisha died, and they buried him. And the raiding bands from Mo'aḇ came into the land in the spring of the year.
21 And it came to be, they were burying a man, and there they saw a raiding band, and cast the man in the burial-site of Elisha. And the man fell and touched the bones of Elisha, and came to life and stood on his feet.
22 And Ḥaza'ěl sovereign of Aram oppressed Yisra'ěl all the days of Yeho'aḥaz.
23 But יהוה showed favour to them, and had compassion on them, and turned toward them, for the sake of His covenant with Aḇraham, Yitsḥaq, and Yaʽaqoḇ, and would not destroy them or cast them from His presence as yet.
24 And Ḥaza'ěl sovereign of Aram died. And Ben-Haḏaḏ his son reigned in his place.
25 And Yeho'ash son of Yeho'aḥaz recovered from the hand of Ben-Haḏaḏ, son of Ḥaza'ěl, the cities which he had taken out of the hand of Yeho'aḥaz his father in battle. Yo'ash struck him three times, and he recovered the cities of Yisra'ěl.

14 In the second year of Yo'ash son of Yo'aḥaz, sovereign of Yisra'ěl, Amatsyahu son of Yo'ash, sovereign of Yehuḏah, began to reign.
2 He was twenty-five years old when he began to reign, and he reigned twenty-nine years in Yerushalayim. And his mother's name was Yehoʽaddin of Yerushalayim.
3 And he did what was right in the eyes of יהוה, but not like his father Dawiḏ. He did according to all his father Yo'ash did.
4 However, the high places were not taken away. The people still slaughtered and burned incense on the high places.
5 And it came to be, as soon as the reign was strengthened in his hand, that he struck his servants who had stricken his father the sovereign.
6 But he did not put to death the children of the strikers, according to what is written in the Book of the Torah of Mosheh, in which יהוה commanded, saying, "Fathers are not put to death for the children, and children are not put to death for the fathers, but each one is put to death for his own sin."
7 He struck Eḏom in the Valley of Salt, ten thousand, and took Sela in battle, and called its name Yoqthe'ěl to this day.
8 Amatsyah then sent messengers to Yeho'ash son of Yeho'aḥaz, son of Yěhu, sovereign of Yisra'ěl, saying, "Come, let us look each other in the face!"
9 And Yeho'ash sovereign of Yisra'ěl sent to Amatsyahu sovereign of Yehuḏah, saying, "The thistle that was in Leḇanon

sent to the cedar that was in Leḇanon,
saying, ‘Give your daughter to my son as
wife.’ And a wild beast that was in
Leḇanon passed by and trampled the
thistle.
10 “You have certainly stricken Eḏom, and
your heart has lifted you up. Be esteemed
and stay in your house. But why do you stir
up yourself to evil, that you should
fall – you and Yehuḏah with you?”
11 But Amatsyahu did not listen, so
Yeho’ash sovereign of Yisra’ěl went up,
and he and Amatsyahu sovereign of Yehuḏah faced one another at Běyth Shemesh,
which belongs to Yehuḏah.
12 And Yehuḏah was smitten before Yisra’ěl, and they each fled to his tent.
13 And Yeho’ash sovereign of Yisra’ěl
caught Amatsyahu sovereign of Yehuḏah,
son of Yeho’ash, son of Aḥazyahu, at
Běyth Shemesh. And they came to
Yerushalayim and he broke through the
wall of Yerushalayim from the Gate of
Ephrayim to the Corner Gate, four hundred
cubits,
14 and took all the gold and silver, and all
the objects that were found in the House of
יהוה and in the treasuries of the sovereign’s house, and hostages, and returned to
Shomeron.
15 And the rest of the acts of Yeho’ash
which he did, and his might, and how he
fought with Amatsyahu sovereign of
Yehuḏah, are they not written in the book
of the annals of the sovereigns of Yisra’ěl?
16 So Yeho’ash slept with his fathers, and
was buried in Shomeron with the sovereigns of Yisra’ěl. And Yaroḇ‘am his son
reigned in his place.
17 And Amatsyahu son of Yo’ash, sovereign of Yehuḏah, lived fifteen years after
the death of Yeho’ash son of Yeho’aḥaz,
sovereign of Yisra’ěl.
18 And the rest of the acts of Amatsyahu,
are they not written in the book of the
annals of the sovereigns of Yehuḏah?
19 And they made a conspiracy against
him in Yerushalayim, and he fled to
Laḵish. And they sent after him to Laḵish
and killed him there,
20 and brought him on horses, and he was
buried at Yerushalayim with his fathers in
the City of Dawiḏ.
21 And all the people of Yehuḏah took
Azaryah, who was sixteen years old, and
set him up to reign instead of his father
Amatsyahu.
22 He built Ěylath and restored it to
Yehuḏah, after the sovereign slept with his
fathers.
23 In the fifteenth year of Amatsyahu son
of Yo’ash, the sovereign of Yehuḏah,
Yaroḇ‘am son of Yo’ash, the sovereign of
Yisra’ěl, began to reign in Shomeron, and
reigned forty-one years.
24 And he did evil in the eyes of יהוה. He
did not turn away from all the sins of
Yaroḇ‘am son of Neḇat, who had made
Yisra’ěl sin.
25 He restored the border of Yisra’ěl from
the entrance of Ḥamath to the Sea of the
Araḇah, according to the word of יהוה
Elohim of Yisra’ěl, which He had spoken
through His servant Yonah son of Amittai,
the prophet who was from Gath Ḥěpher.
26 For יהוה saw that the affliction of
Yisra’ěl was very bitter. And there was no
one, neither shut up nor left at large, to
help Yisra’ěl.
27 And יהוה had not said that He would
blot out the name of Yisra’ěl from under
the heavens, but saved them by the hand of
Yaroḇ‘am son of Yo’ash.
28 And the rest of the acts of Yaroḇ‘am,
and all that he did, and his might, how he
fought, and how he recovered Dammeseq
and Ḥamath for Yehuḏah in Yisra’ěl, are
they not written in the book of the annals
of the sovereigns of Yisra’ěl?
29 So Yaroḇ‘am slept with his fathers, the
sovereigns of Yisra’ěl. And Zeḵaryah his
son reigned in his place.

15 In the twenty-seventh year of
Yaroḇ‘am sovereign of Yisra’ěl,
Azaryah son of Amatsyah, sovereign of
Yehuḏah, began to reign.
2 He was sixteen years old when he
began to reign, and he reigned fifty-two
years in Yerushalayim. And his mother’s
name was Yeḵolyahu of Yerushalayim.
3 And he did what was right in the eyes

of יהוה, according to all that his father
Amatsyahu did,
4 however, the high places were not taken
away. The people still slaughtered and
burned incense on the high places.
5 And יהוה smote the sovereign, so that
he was a leper until the day of his death,
and he dwelt in a separate house. And
Yotham son of the sovereign was over the
house, ruling the people of the land.
6 And the rest of the acts of Azaryahu,
and all that he did, are they not written in
the book of the annals of the sovereigns of
Yehuḏah?
7 So Azaryah slept with his fathers, and
they buried him with his fathers in the City
of Dawiḏ. And Yotham his son reigned in
his place.
8 In the thirty-eighth year of Azaryahu
sovereign of Yehuḏah, Zeḵaryahu son
of Yaroḇʽam began to reign over Yisra'ěl in
Shomeron, for six new *moons*.
9 And he did evil in the eyes of יהוה, as
his fathers had done. He did not turn away
from the sins of Yaroḇʽam son of Neḇat,
who had made Yisra'ěl sin.
10 And Shallum son of Yaḇěsh conspired
against him, and struck him in front of the
people, and killed him, and reigned in his
place.
11 And the rest of the acts of Zeḵaryah,
see, they are written in the book of the
annals of the sovereigns of Yisra'ěl.
12 This was the word of יהוה which He
spoke to Yěhu, saying, "Your sons to the
fourth *generation* are going to sit on the
throne of Yisra'ěl." And it came to be so.
13 Shallum son of Yaḇěsh began to reign
in the thirty-ninth year of Uzziyah, the sovereign of Yehuḏah. And he reigned a
month of days in Shomeron.
14 And Menaḥěm son of Gaḏi went up
from Tirtsah, and came to Shomeron, and
struck Shallum son of Yaḇěsh in Shomeron
and killed him, and reigned in his place.
15 And the rest of the acts of Shallum, and
the conspiracy which he led, see, they are
written in the book of the annals of the sovereigns of Yisra'ěl.
16 And Menaḥěm struck Tiphsaḥ, and all
who were there, and its borders, from
Tirtsah. Because they did not open it to
him, therefore he struck it. And he ripped
open all the pregnant women.
17 In the thirty-ninth year of Azaryah sovereign of Yehuḏah, Menaḥěm son of Gaḏi
began to reign over Yisra'ěl, ten years in
Shomeron.
18 And he did evil in the eyes of יהוה. He
did not turn away from the sins of
Yaroḇʽam son of Neḇat, who had made
Yisra'ěl sin, all his days.
19 Pul the sovereign of Ashshur came
against the land. And Menaḥěm gave Pul a
thousand talents of silver, for his hand to
be with him to strengthen the reign in his
hand.
20 And Menaḥěm exacted the silver of
Yisra'ěl, of all the mighty men of wealth,
of each man fifty sheqels of silver, to give
to the sovereign of Ashshur. And the sovereign of Ashshur turned back, and did not
stay there in the land.
21 And the rest of the acts of Menaḥěm,
and all that he did, are they not written in
the book of the annals of the sovereigns of
Yisra'ěl?
22 So Menaḥěm slept with his fathers.
And Peqaḥyah his son reigned in his place.
23 In the fiftieth year of Azaryah the sovereign of Yehuḏah, Peqaḥyah the son of
Menaḥěm began to reign over Yisra'ěl in
Shomeron, for two years.
24 And he did evil in the eyes of יהוה.
He did not turn away from the sins of
Yaroḇʽam son of Neḇat, who had made
Yisra'ěl sin.
25 And Peqaḥ son of Remalyahu, a chief
officer of his, conspired against him and
struck him in Shomeron, in the high place
of the sovereign's house, along with Argoḇ
and Aryěh, and with him were fifty men of
Gilʽaḏ. So he killed him and reigned in his
place.
26 And the rest of the acts of Peqaḥyah,
and all that he did, see, they are written in
the book of the annals of the sovereigns of
Yisra'ěl.
27 In the fifty-second year of Azaryah
sovereign of Yehuḏah, Peqaḥ son of
Remalyahu began to reign over Yisra'ěl in
Shomeron, for twenty years.

28 And he did evil in the eyes of יהוה. He
did not turn away from the sins of
Yaroḇʽam son of Neḇat, who had made
Yisra'ěl sin.
29 In the days of Peqaḥ sovereign of
Yisra'ěl, Tiḡlath-Pileser sovereign of
Ashshur came and took Iyon, and Aḇěl
Běyth Maʽaḵah, and Yanowaḥ, and
Qeḏesh, and Ḥatsor, and Gilʽaḏ, and Galil,
all the land of Naphtali, and took them into
exile to Ashshur.
30 And Hoshěa son of Ělah led a conspiracy against Peqaḥ son of Remalyahu, and
struck him, and killed him, and reigned in
his place in the twentieth year of Yotham
son of Uzziyah.
31 And the rest of the acts of Peqaḥ, and
all that he did, see, they are written in the
book of the annals of the sovereigns of
Yisra'ěl.
32 In the second year of Peqaḥ son of
Remalyahu, sovereign of Yisra'ěl, Yotham
son of Uzziyahu, sovereign of Yehuḏah,
began to reign.
33 He was twenty-five years old when he
began to reign, and he reigned sixteen
years in Yerushalayim. And his mother's
name was Yerusha the daughter of Tsaḏoq.
34 And he did what was right in the eyes
of יהוה. He did according to all that his
father Uzziyahu did.
35 However, the high places were not
taken away. The people still slaughtered
and burned incense on the high places. He
built the Upper Gate of the House of יהוה.
36 And the rest of the acts of Yotham, and
all that he did, are they not written in the
book of the annals of the sovereigns of
Yehuḏah?
37 In those days יהוה began to send Retsin
sovereign of Aram and Peqaḥ son of
Remalyahu against Yehuḏah.
38 So Yotham slept with his fathers, and
was buried with his fathers in the City of
Dawiḏ his father. And Aḥaz his son
reigned in his place.

16 In the seventeenth year of Peqaḥ
son of Remalyahu, Aḥaz son of
Yotham, sovereign of Yehuḏah, began
to reign.
2 Aḥaz was twenty years old when he
began to reign, and he reigned sixteen
years in Yerushalayim. And he did not do
what was right in the eyes of יהוה his
Elohim, as his father Dawiḏ had done.
3 But he walked in the way of the sovereigns of Yisra'ěl, and he also made his son
pass through the fire, according to the
abominations of the nations whom יהוה
had dispossessed from before the children
of Yisra'ěl.
4 And he slaughtered and burned incense
on the high places, and on the hills, and
under every green tree.
5 Then Retsin sovereign of Aram and
Peqaḥ son of Remalyahu, sovereign of Yisra'ěl, came up to Yerushalayim, to battle.
And they besieged Aḥaz but were unable
to overcome him.
6 At that time Retsin sovereign of Aram
recovered Ěylath for Aram, and drove the
men of Yehuḏah from Ěylath. And the
Eḏomites went to Ěylath, and have dwelt
there to this day.
7 And Aḥaz sent messengers to Tiḡlath-
Pileser sovereign of Ashshur, saying,
"I am your servant and your son. Come
up and save me from the hand of the
sovereign of Aram and from the hand of
the sovereign of Yisra'ěl, who are rising
up against me."
8 And Aḥaz took the silver and gold that
was found in the House of יהוה, and in the
treasuries of the house of the sovereign,
and sent it as a present to the sovereign of
Ashshur.
9 And the sovereign of Ashshur listened
to him. And the sovereign of Ashshur went
up against Dammeseq and captured it, and
exiled it to Qir, and he killed Retsin.
10 And Sovereign Aḥaz went to meet
Tiḡlath-Pileser sovereign of Ashshur at
Dummeseq, and saw a slaughter-place that
was at Dammaseq. And Sovereign Aḥaz
sent to Uriyah the priest a sketch of the
slaughter-place and its pattern, according
to all its workmanship.
11 And Uriyah the priest built a slaughter-
place according to all that Sovereign Aḥaz
had sent from Dammeseq. And Uriyah the
priest made it before Sovereign Aḥaz came

from Dammeseq.
12 And when the sovereign came from
Dammeseq, the sovereign saw the slaughter-place, and the sovereign approached the
slaughter-place and made offerings on it.
13 And he burned his ascending offering
and his grain offering. And he poured his
drink offering and sprinkled the blood of
his peace offerings on the slaughter-place.
14 And the bronze slaughter-place which
was before יהוה he brought from the front
of the House, from between the new
slaughter-place and the House of יהוה, and
put it on the north side of *his* slaughter-
place.
15 And Sovereign Aḥaz commanded
Uriyah the priest, saying, “On the great
slaughter-place burn the morning ascending offering, and the evening grain offering, and the sovereign’s ascending offering, and his grain offering, with the
ascending offering of all the people of the
land, and their grain offering, and their
drink offerings. And sprinkle on it all the
blood of the ascending offering and all the
blood of the slaughtering. And the bronze
slaughter-place is for me to inquire by.”
16 And Uriyah the priest did according to
all that Sovereign Aḥaz commanded.
17 And Sovereign Aḥaz cut off the side
panels of the stands, and removed the
basins from them. And he took down the
Sea from the bronze oxen that were under
it, and put it on a pavement of stones.
18 And the covered way which they had
built in the House for the Sabbath, and the
sovereign’s outer entrance, he took from
the House of יהוה, because of the sovereign of Ashshur.
19 And the rest of the acts of Aḥaz which
he did, are they not written in the book of
the annals of the sovereigns of Yehuḏah?
20 So Aḥaz slept with his fathers, and was
buried with his fathers in the City of
Dawiḏ. And Ḥizqiyahu his son reigned in
his place.

17 In the twelfth year of Aḥaz sovereign of Yehuḏah, Hoshěa son of
Ělah began to reign over Yisra’ěl in
Shomeron, for nine years.
2 And he did evil in the eyes of יהוה, but
not as the sovereigns of Yisra’ěl who were
before him.
3 Shalmaneser sovereign of Ashshur
came up against him. And Hoshěa became
his servant, and rendered him a present.
4 But the sovereign of Ashshur found a
conspiracy in Hoshěa, for he had sent messengers to So, sovereign of Mitsrayim, and
had not brought a present to the sovereign
of Ashshur, as year by year. And the sovereign of Ashshur shut him up, and bound
him in prison.
5 And the sovereign of Ashshur went
through all the land, and went up to
Shomeron and besieged it for three years.
6 In the ninth year of Hoshěa, the sovereign of Ashshur captured Shomeron and
exiled Yisra’ěl to Ashshur, and settled
them in Ḥalaḥ and Ḥaḇor, the River of
Gozan, and in the cities of the Medes.
7 Now this came to be because the children of Yisra’ěl had sinned against יהוה
their Elohim – who had brought them up
out of the land of Mitsrayim, from under
the hand of Pharaoh sovereign of
Mitsrayim – and feared other mighty ones,
8 and walked in the laws of the nations
whom יהוה had dispossessed from before
the children of Yisra’ěl, and of the sovereigns of Yisra’ěl that they had made.
9 And the children of Yisra’ěl secretly
did against יהוה their Elohim matters that
were not right, and they built for themselves high places in all their cities, from
watchtower unto the walled city,
10 and set up for themselves pillars and
Ashěrim on every high hill and under
every green tree,
11 and burned incense there on all the high
places, like the nations whom יהוה had
removed from their presence. And they did
evil matters to provoke יהוה,
12 and served the idols, of which יהוה had
said to them, “Do not do this.”
13 And יהוה warned Yisra’ěl and
Yehuḏah, through all of His prophets, and
every seer, saying, “Turn back from your
evil ways, and guard My commands and
My laws, according to all the Torah which
I commanded your fathers, and which I

sent to you by My servants the prophets."
14 But they did not listen and hardened
their necks, like the necks of their fathers,
who did not put their trust in יהוה their
Elohim,
15 and rejected His laws and His covenant
that He had made with their fathers, and
His witnesses which He had witnessed
against them, and went after worthlessness,
and became worthless, and after the
nations who were all around them, of
whom יהוה had commanded them not to
do like them.
16 And they left all the commands of יהוה
their Elohim, and made for themselves a
moulded image, two calves, and made an
Ashěrah and bowed themselves to all the
host of the heavens, and served Ba'al,
17 and caused their sons and daughters to
pass through the fire, and practised divination and sorcery, and sold themselves to do
evil in the eyes of יהוה, to provoke Him.
18 So יהוה was very enraged with Yisra'ěl, and removed them from His presence
– none was left but the tribe of Yehuḏah
alone.
19 Yehuḏah, also, did not guard the commands of יהוה their Elohim, but walked in
the laws [a] of Yisra'ěl which they made.
20 And יהוה rejected all the seed of
Yisra'ěl, and afflicted them, and gave them
into the hand of plunderers, until He had
cast them out from His presence.
21 For He tore Yisra'ěl from the house of
Dawiḏ, and they made Yaroḇ'am son of
Neḇat sovereign. And Yaroḇ'am drove
Yisra'ěl from following יהוה, and made
them commit a great sin.
22 And the children of Yisra'ěl walked in
all the sins of Yaroḇ'am which he did. They
did not turn away from them,
23 until יהוה removed Yisra'ěl from His
presence, as He spoke by all His servants
the prophets. So Yisra'ěl was exiled from
their land to Ashshur, as it is to this day.
24 And the sovereign of Ashshur brought
people from Baḇel, and from Kuthah, and
from Awwa, and from Ḥamath, and
Sepharwayim, and placed *them* in the cities
of Shomeron instead of the children of
Yisra'ěl. And they took possession of
Shomeron and dwelt in its cities.
25 And it came to be, at the beginning of
their dwelling there, that they did not fear
יהוה, and יהוה sent lions among them,
which were killing among them.
26 And they spoke to the sovereign of
Ashshur, saying, "The nations whom you
have removed and placed in the cities of
Shomeron do not know the right-ruling of
the Elohim of the land. And He has sent
lions among them, and see, they are slaying among them because they do not know
the right-ruling of the Elohim of the land."
27 And the sovereign of Ashshur commanded, saying, "Send one of the priests
whom you exiled from there, to go there.
Let him go and dwell there, and let him
teach them the right-ruling of the Elohim
of the land."
28 And one of the priests whom they had
exiled from Shomeron came and dwelt
in Běyth Ěl, and taught them how to fear
יהוה.
29 But every nation was making mighty
ones of its own, and put them in the houses
of the high places which the Shomeronim
had made, every nation in the cities where
they dwelt.
30 And the men of Baḇel made Sukkoth
Benoth, and the men of Kuth made Něrḡal,
and the men of Ḥamath made Ashima,
31 and the Awwites made Niḇḥaz and
Tartaq. And the Sepharwites burned their
children in fire to Aḏrammeleḵ and
Anammeleḵ, the mighty ones of Sepharim.
32 They also feared יהוה, and from every
class they made for themselves priests of
the high places, who offered for them in
the house of the high places.
33 They were fearing יהוה, and they were
serving their own mighty ones, [b] according
to the ruling of the nations from among
whom they had been exiled.
34 To this day they are doing according to
the former rulings: they are not fearing
יהוה, nor do they follow their laws or their
right-rulings, or the Torah and command

17a Man-made laws. *17b* Mixed worship, mixing the true with the false – compromise.

which יהוה had commanded the children
of Ya'aqoḇ, whose name He made Yisra'ĕl,
35 with whom יהוה had made a covenant
and commanded them, saying, "Do not
fear other mighty ones, nor bow down to
them nor serve them nor slaughter to them;
36 but יהוה, who brought you up from the
land of Mitsrayim with great power and
with an outstretched arm, Him you shall
fear, and to Him you shall bow yourselves,
and to Him you shall slaughter.
37 "And guard to do forever the laws, and
the right-rulings, and the Torah, and the
command which He wrote for you. And do
not fear other mighty ones.
38 "And do not forget the covenant that I
have made with you, and do not fear other
mighty ones.
39 "But fear יהוה your Elohim, so that
He delivers you from the hand of all your
enemies."
40 And they did not obey, but did according to their former ruling.
41 So these nations were fearing יהוה, and
served their carved images,[c] both their
children and their children's children. As
their fathers did, they are doing to this day.

18 And it came to be in the third year
of Hoshĕa son of Ĕlah, sovereign
of Yisra'ĕl, that Ḥizqiyah son of Aḥaz,
sovereign of Yehuḏah, began to reign.
2 He was twenty-five years old when he
began to reign, and he reigned twenty-nine
years in Yerushalayim. And his mother's
name was Aḇi, daughter of Zeḵaryah.
3 And he did what was right in the eyes
of יהוה, according to all that his father
Dawiḏ did.
4 He took away the high places and broke
the pillars, and cut down the Ashĕrah, and
broke in pieces the bronze serpent which
Mosheh had made, for until those days the
children of Yisra'ĕl burned incense to it,
and called it Neḥushtan.
5 He put his trust in יהוה Elohim of
Yisra'ĕl, and after him was none like him
among all the sovereigns of Yehuḏah, nor
who were before him,
6 and he clung to יהוה. He did not turn
away from following Him, but guarded His
commands, which יהוה had commanded
Mosheh.
7 And יהוה was with him – wherever he
went he acted wisely. And he rebelled
against the sovereign of Ashshur and did
not serve him.
8 He struck the Philistines, as far as
Azzah and its borders – from watchtower
unto the walled city.
9 And it came to be in the fourth year of
Sovereign Ḥizqiyahu, which was the seventh year of Hoshĕa son of Ĕlah, sovereign
of Yisra'ĕl, that Shalmaneser sovereign of
Ashshur came up against Shomeron and
besieged it,
10 and they captured it at the end of three
years. In the sixth year of Ḥizqiyah, that is
the ninth year of Hoshĕa sovereign of
Yisra'ĕl, Shomeron was captured.
11 And the sovereign of Ashshur exiled
Yisra'ĕl to Ashshur, and placed them in
Ḥalaḥ and Ḥaḇor, the River of Gozan, and
in the cities of the Medes,
12 because they did not obey the voice of
יהוה their Elohim, but transgressed His
covenant – all that Mosheh the servant of
יהוה had commanded. And they did not
obey nor do them.
13 And in the fourteenth year of Sovereign
Ḥizqiyahu, Sanḥĕriḇ sovereign of Ashshur
came up against all the walled cities of
Yehuḏah and captured them.
14 And Ḥizqiyah sovereign of Yehuḏah
sent to the sovereign of Ashshur at Laḵish,
saying, "I have done wrong, turn away
from me. I shall bear whatever you impose
on me." And the sovereign of Ashshur
imposed upon Ḥizqiyah, the sovereign of
Yehuḏah, three hundred talents of silver
and thirty talents of gold.
15 And Ḥizqiyah gave him all the silver
that was found in the House of יהוה and in
the treasuries of the sovereign's house.
16 At that time Ḥizqiyah cut off the doors
of the Hĕḵal of יהוה, and the doorposts
which Ḥizqiyah sovereign of Yehuḏah had
overlaid, and gave it to the sovereign of

17c Mixed worship, mixing the true with the false – compromise.

Ashshur.
17 And the sovereign of Ashshur sent the
Tartan, and the Rab̲saris, and the
Rab̲shaqĕh from Lak̲ish, with a great army
against Yerushalayim, to Sovereign Ḥizqiyahu. And they went up and came to
Yerushalayim. And when they had come
up, they came and stood by the channel of
the upper pool, which was on the highway
to the Launderer's Field.
18 And they called to the sovereign. And
Elyaqim son of Ḥilqiyahu, who was over
the household, and Sheb̲nah the scribe, and
Yo'aḥ son of Asaph, the recorder, came out
to them.
19 And the Rab̲shaqĕh said to them,
"Please say to Ḥizqiyahu, 'Thus said the
great sovereign, the sovereign of Ashshur,
"What is this trust in which you have
trusted?
20 "You have spoken of having counsel
and strength for battle, but they are only
words of the lips! And in whom do you
trust, that you rebel against me?
21 "Now look! You have put your trust in
the staff of this crushed reed, Mitsrayim,
on which if a man leans, it shall go into his
hand and pierce it. So is Pharaoh sovereign
of Mitsrayim to all who trust in him.
22 "But when you say to me, 'We trust in
יהוה our Elohim,' is it not He whose high
places and whose slaughter-places
Ḥizqiyahu has taken away, and said to
Yehud̲ah and Yerushalayim, 'Bow yourselves before this slaughter-place in
Yerushalayim'?" '
23 "And now, I urge you, give a pledge to
my master the sovereign of Ashshur, then
I give you two thousand horses, if you are
able to put riders on them!
24 "And how do you turn back the face of
one commander of the least of my master's
servants, and trust in Mitsrayim for chariots and horsemen?
25 "Have I now come up without יהוה
against this place to destroy it? יהוה said to
me, 'Go up against this land, and you shall
destroy it.' "
26 Then said Elyaqim son of Ḥilqiyahu,
and Sheb̲nah, and Yo'aḥ to the Rab̲shaqĕh,
"Please speak to your servants in Aramaic,
for we understand it. And do not speak to
us in the language of Yehud̲ah, in the ears
of the people on the wall."
27 And the Rab̲shaqĕh said to them, "Has
my master sent me to your master and to
you to speak these words, and not to the
men sitting on the wall to eat their own
dung and drink their own urine, with you?"
28 And the Rab̲shaqĕh stood and called
out with a loud voice in the language of
Yehud̲ah, and spoke and said, "Hear the
word of the great sovereign, the sovereign
of Ashshur!
29 "Thus said the sovereign, 'Do not let
Ḥizqiyahu deceive you, for he is unable to
deliver you out of his hand,
30 and do not let Ḥizqiyahu make you
trust in יהוה, saying, "יהוה shall certainly
deliver us, and this city is not given into
the hand of the sovereign of Ashshur." '
31 "Do not listen to Ḥizqiyahu, for thus
said the sovereign of Ashshur, 'Make
peace with me by a present and come out
to me, and let each of you eat from his own
vine and each from his own fig tree, and
each of you drink the waters of his own
cistern,
32 until I come. Then I shall take you
away to a land like your own land, a land
of grain and new wine, a land of bread and
vineyards, a land of olive-trees and honey,
and live, and not die. But do not listen to
Ḥizqiyahu, when he misleads you, saying,
"יהוה shall deliver us."
33 'Has any of the mighty ones of the
nations at all delivered its land from the
hand of the sovereign of Ashshur?
34 'Where are the mighty ones of Ḥamath
and Arpad̲? Where are the mighty ones of
Sepharwayim and Hĕna and Iwwah? Did
they deliver Shomeron from my hand?
35 'Who among all the mighty ones of
the lands have delivered their land out of
my hand, that יהוה should deliver Yerushalayim from my hand?' "
36 But the people were silent and did not
answer him a word, for the command of
the sovereign was, "Do not answer him."
37 And Elyaqim son of Ḥilqiyah, who was
over the household, and Sheb̲nah the
scribe, and Yo'aḥ son of Asaph, the

recorder, came to Ḥizqiyahu with their garments torn, and they reported to him the
words of the Raḇshaqěh.

19 And it came to be, when Sovereign
Ḥizqiyahu heard it, that he tore his
garments, and covered himself with sackcloth, and went into the House of יהוה,
2 and sent Elyaqim, who was over the
household, and Sheḇnah the scribe, and the
elders of the priests, covering themselves
with sackcloth, to Yeshayahu the prophet,
son of Amots.
3 And they said to him, "Thus said
Ḥizqiyahu, 'This day is a day of distress
and rebuke and scorn, for the children have
come to birth but there is no power to bring
forth.
4 'It could be that יהוה your Elohim does
hear all the words of the Raḇshaqěh, whom
his master the sovereign of Ashshur has
sent to reproach the living Elohim, and
shall rebuke the words which יהוה your
Elohim has heard. Therefore lift up your
prayer for the remnant that is left.' "
5 And the servants of Sovereign Ḥizqiyahu came to Yeshayahu,
6 and Yeshayahu said to them, "Say this
to your master, 'Thus said יהוה, "Do
not be afraid of the words which you have
heard, with which the servants of the
sovereign of Ashshur have reviled Me.
7 "See, I am putting a spirit upon him,
and he shall hear a report and return to his
own land. And I shall cause him to fall by
the sword in his land." ' "
8 And the Raḇshaqěh returned and found
the sovereign of Ashshur fighting against
Liḇnah, for he had heard that he had left
Laḵish.
9 And when the sovereign heard concerning Tirhaqah sovereign of Kush, "See,
he has come out to fight against you,"
he again sent messengers to Ḥizqiyahu,
saying,
10 "Speak to Ḥizqiyahu sovereign of
Yehuḏah, saying, 'Do not let your Elohim
in whom you trust deceive you, saying,
"Yerushalayim is not given into the hand
of the sovereign of Ashshur."
11 'See, you have heard what the sovereigns of Ashshur have done to all lands by
putting them under the ban. And are you
going to be delivered?
12 'Have the mighty ones of the nations
delivered those whom my fathers have
destroyed: Gozan and Ḥaran and Retseph,
and the sons of Ěḏen who were in
Telassar?
13 'Where is the sovereign of Ḥamath, and
the sovereign of Arpaḏ, and the sovereign
of the city of Sepharwayim, Hěna, and
Iwwah?' "
14 And Ḥizqiyahu received the letters
from the hand of the messengers, and read
them, and went up to the House of יהוה.
And Ḥizqiyahu spread it before יהוה.
15 And Ḥizqiyahu prayed before יהוה,
and said, "O יהוה Elohim of Yisra'ěl, the
One who dwells between the keruḇim, You
are Elohim, You alone, of all the reigns of
the earth. You have made the heavens and
earth.
16 "Incline Your ear, O יהוה, and hear.
Open Your eyes, O יהוה, and see. And hear
the words of Sanḥěriḇ, which he has sent to
reproach the living Elohim.
17 "Truly, יהוה, the sovereigns of Ashshur
have laid waste the nations and their lands,
18 and have put their mighty ones into the
fire, for they were not mighty ones, but the
work of men's hands, wood and stone, and
destroyed them.
19 "And now, O יהוה our Elohim, I pray,
save us from his hand, so that all the reigns
of the earth know that You are יהוה
Elohim, You alone."
20 Then Yeshayahu son of Amots sent to
Ḥizqiyahu, saying, "Thus said יהוה
Elohim of Yisra'ěl, 'I have heard that
which you have prayed to Me against
Sanḥěriḇ sovereign of Ashshur.'
21 "This is the word which יהוה has
spoken concerning him, 'The maiden, the
daughter of Tsiyon, has despised you,
mocked you; the daughter of Yerushalayim
has shaken her head behind you!
22 'Whom have you reproached and
reviled? Against whom have you raised a
voice, and lifted up your eyes on high?
Against the Set-apart One of Yisra'ěl!
23 'By the hand of your messengers you

have reproached יהוה, and said, "With my
many chariots I have come up to the height
of the mountains, to the sides of Leḇanon.
And I cut down its tall cedars, its choice
cypress trees. And I enter its remotest
parts, its thickest forest.
24 'I have dug and drunk strange water,
and with the soles of my feet I dry up all
the streams of defence."
25 'Have you not heard long ago, I made
it; from days of old I formed it? Now I
have brought it to be, that you should make
walled cities ruinous heaps.
26 'And their inhabitants were powerless,
they were overthrown and put to shame,
they were as the grass of the field and the
green plants, as the grass on the house-tops
and withered before it came up.
27 'But I know your sitting down, and
your going out and your coming in, and
your rage against Me.
28 'Because your rage against Me and
your pride have come up to My ears, I shall
put My hook in your nose and My bridle in
your lips, and I shall turn you back by the
way which you came.
29 'And this is the sign for you: This year
you eat what grows of itself, and in the second year what springs from that, and in the
third year sow and reap and plant vineyards and eat their fruit.
30 'And the remnant who have escaped of
the house of Yehuḏah shall again take root
downward, and be fruitful.
31 'For out of Yerushalayim comes forth a
remnant, and those who escape from
Mount Tsiyon – the ardour of יהוה does
this.'
32 "Therefore thus said יהוה concerning
the sovereign of Ashshur, 'He does not
come into this city, nor does he shoot an
arrow there, nor does he come before it
with shield, nor does he build a siege
mound against it.
33 'By the way that he came, by the same
he turns back. And he does not come into
this city,' declares יהוה.
34 'And I shall defend this city, to save it
for My own sake and for the sake of Dawiḏ
My servant.' "
35 And it came to be in that night that the
messenger of יהוה went out, and struck in
the camp of Ashshur one hundred and
eighty-five thousand. And they rose up
early in the morning and saw all of them
dead bodies.
36 And Sanḥěriḇ sovereign of Ashshur
broke camp and went away, and turned
back, and remained in Nineweh.
37 And it came to be, as he was bowing
himself in the house of Nisroḵ his mighty
one, that his sons Aḏrammeleḵ and
Shar'etser struck him with the sword, and
they escaped into the land of Ararat. And
his son Ěsarḥaddon reigned in his place.

20 In those days Ḥizqiyahu was sick
unto death. And Yeshayahu the
prophet, son of Amots, went to him and
said to him, "Thus said יהוה, 'Command
your house, for you are going to die, and
not live.' "
2 And he turned his face toward the wall,
and prayed to יהוה, saying,
3 "I pray to You, O יהוה, remember how
I have walked before You in truth and with
a perfect heart, and have done what was
good in Your eyes." And Ḥizqiyahu wept
bitterly.
4 And it came to be, before Yeshayahu
had gone out into the middle court, that the
word of יהוה came to him, saying,
5 "Return and say to Ḥizqiyahu the
leader of My people, 'Thus said יהוה, the
Elohim of Dawiḏ your father, "I have
heard your prayer, I have seen your tears.
See, I am going to heal you. On the third
day go up to the House of יהוה.
6 "And I shall add to your days fifteen
years, and deliver you and this city from
the hand of the sovereign of Ashshur, and
shall defend this city for My own sake, and
for the sake of Dawiḏ My servant." ' "
7 And Yeshayahu said, "Take a cake of
figs." And they took and laid it on the boil,
and he recovered.
8 And Ḥizqiyahu said to Yeshayahu,
"What is the sign that יהוה does heal me,
and that I shall go up to the House of יהוה
the third day?"
9 And Yeshayahu said, "This is the sign
for you from יהוה, that יהוה does the word

which He has spoken: shall the shadow go
forward ten degrees or go backward ten
degrees?"
10 And Ḥizqiyahu said, "It would be easy
for the shadow to go down ten degrees; no,
but let the shadow go backward ten
degrees."
11 And Yeshayahu the prophet cried out to
יהוה, and He brought the shadow ten
degrees backward, by which it had gone
down on the sundial of Aḥaz.
12 At that time Berodaḵ-Baladan son of
Baladan, sovereign of Baḇel, sent letters
and a present to Ḥizqiyahu, for he heard
that Ḥizqiyahu had been sick.
13 And Ḥizqiyahu listened to them, and
showed them all his treasure house, the
silver and the gold, and the spices and the
precious ointment, and all his armoury, and
all that was found among his treasures.
There was not an object in his house or
in all his rule that Ḥizqiyahu did not show
them.
14 And Yeshayahu the prophet came to
Sovereign Ḥizqiyahu, and said to him,
"What did these men say, and from where
did they come to you?" And Ḥizqiyahu
said, "They came from a distant land, from
Baḇel."
15 And he said, "What have they seen in
your house?" And Ḥizqiyahu answered,
"They saw all that is in my house; there is
not an object among my treasures that I did
not show them."
16 And Yeshayahu said to Ḥizqiyahu,
"Hear the word of יהוה:
17 'See, the days are coming when all that
is in your house, and what your fathers
have treasured up until this day, shall be
brought to Baḇel – no object is to be left,'
said יהוה.
18 'And they are going to take away some
of your sons who are to be born to you,
whom you bring forth, and they shall be
eunuchs in the palace of the sovereign of
Baḇel.' "
19 And Ḥizqiyahu said to Yeshayahu,
"The word of יהוה which you have spoken
is good!" And he said, "Is it not so, if peace
and truth are to be in my days?"
20 And the rest of the acts of Ḥizqiyahu,
and all his might and how he made a pool
and a channel and brought water into the
city, are they not written in the book of the
annals of the sovereigns of Yehuḏah?
21 So Ḥizqiyahu slept with his fathers.
And Menashsheh his son reigned in his
place.

21 Menashsheh was twelve years old
when he began to reign, and he
reigned fifty-five years in Yerushalayim.
And his mother's name was Ḥephtsiḇah.
2 And he did evil in the eyes of יהוה,
according to the abominations of the
nations whom יהוה dispossessed before
the children of Yisra'ěl.
3 For he turned and built the high places
which Ḥizqiyahu his father had destroyed,
and raised up slaughter-places for Ba'al,
and made an Ashěrah, as Aḥaḇ sovereign
of Yisra'ěl had done, and he bowed himself to all the host of the heavens and
served them.
4 And he built slaughter-places in the
House of יהוה, of which יהוה had said, "In
Yerushalayim I put My Name."
5 And he built slaughter-places for all the
host of the heavens in the two courtyards
of the House of יהוה.
6 And he made his son pass through the
fire, and practised magic, and used divination, and consulted spiritists and mediums.
He did much evil in the eyes of יהוה,
to provoke *Him*.
7 And he placed a carved image of
Ashěrah that he had made in the House of
which יהוה had said to Dawiḏ and to
Shelomoh his son, "In this house and in
Yerushalayim, which I have chosen out of
all the tribes of Yisra'ěl, I put My Name
forever,
8 and no more shall I cause the feet of
Yisra'ěl to move from the soil which I gave
their fathers – only if they guard to do
according to all that I have commanded
them, and according to all the Torah that
My servant Mosheh commanded them."
9 But they did not obey, and Menashsheh
led them astray to do more evil than the
nations whom יהוה had destroyed before
the children of Yisra'ěl.

10 And יהוה spoke by His servants the prophets, saying,

11 "Because Menashsheh sovereign of Yehuḏah has done these abominations, having done more evil than all the Amorites who were before him, and also made Yehuḏah sin with his idols,

12 therefore thus said יהוה Elohim of Yisra'ěl, 'See, I am bringing such evil upon Yerushalayim and Yehuḏah that both ears of those who hear of it shall tingle.

13 'And I shall stretch over Yerushalayim the measuring line of Shomeron and the plummet of the house of Aḥaḇ, and shall wipe Yerushalayim as one wipes a dish, wiping it and turning it upside down.

14 'And I shall forsake the remnant of My inheritance and give them into the hand of their enemies. And they shall be for a prey and for a plunder to all their enemies,

15 because they have done evil in My eyes, and have provoked Me since the day their fathers came out of Mitsrayim, even to this day.' "

16 And also, Menashsheh shed very much innocent blood, until he had filled Yerushalayim from one end to another, besides his sin with which he made Yehuḏah sin, in doing evil in the eyes of יהוה.

17 And the rest of the acts of Menashsheh, and all that he did, and the sin that he committed, are they not written in the book of the annals of the sovereigns of Yehuḏah?

18 So Menashsheh slept with his fathers, and was buried in the garden of his own house, in the garden of Uzza. And his son Amon reigned in his place.

19 Amon was twenty-two years old when he began to reign, and he reigned two years in Yerushalayim. And the name of his mother was Meshullemeth the daughter of Ḥaruts of Yoteḇah.

20 And he did evil in the eyes of יהוה, as his father Menashsheh had done,

21 and walked in all the ways that his father had walked, and served the idols that his father had served, and bowed himself to them,

22 and forsook יהוה Elohim of his fathers, and did not walk in the way of יהוה.

23 And the servants of Amon conspired against him, and killed the sovereign in his own house.

24 But the people of the land struck all those who had conspired against Sovereign Amon, and the people of the land set up his son Yoshiyahu to reign in his place.

25 And the rest of the acts of Amon which he did, are they not written in the book of the annals of the sovereigns of Yehuḏah?

26 And he was buried in his burial-place in the garden of Uzza. And his son Yoshiyahu reigned in his place.

22

Yoshiyahu was eight years old when he began to reign, and he reigned thirty-one years in Yerushalayim. And his mother's name was Yeḏiḏah the daughter of Aḏayah of Botsqath.

2 And he did what was right in the eyes of יהוה, and walked in all the ways of his father Dawiḏ, and did not turn aside, right or left.

3 And it came to be, in the eighteenth year of Sovereign Yoshiyahu, that the sovereign sent Shaphan the scribe, son of Atsalyahu, son of Meshullam, to the House of יהוה, saying,

4 "Go up to Ḥilqiyahu the high priest, and let him weigh the silver which has been brought into the House of יהוה, which the doorkeepers have gathered from the people.

5 "And let them give it into the hand of those doing the work, who are the overseers in the House of יהוה. And let them give it to those who are in the House of יהוה doing the work, to strengthen the breach of the house,

6 to carpenters and to builders and to stonemasons, and to buy timber and hewn stone to strengthen the house.

7 "However, let not the silver given into their hand be reckoned with them, for they are acting trustworthily."

8 And Ḥilqiyahu the high priest said to Shaphan the scribe, "I have found the Book of the Torah in the House of יהוה." And Ḥilqiyah gave the book to Shaphan, and he read it.

9 And Shaphan the scribe came to the

sovereign, and brought word to the sovereign again, saying, "Your servants have gathered the silver that was found in the house, and have given it into the hand of those who do the work, who oversee the House of יהוה."

10 And Shaphan the scribe informed the sovereign, saying, "Ḥilqiyah the priest has given me a book." And Shaphan read it before the sovereign.

11 And it came to be, when the sovereign heard the words of the Book of the Torah, that he tore his garments,

12 and the sovereign commanded Ḥilqiyah the priest, and Aḥiqam son of Shaphan, and Aḵbor son of Miḵayah, and Shaphan the scribe, and Asayah a servant of the sovereign, saying,

13 "Go, inquire of יהוה for me, for the people and for all Yehuḏah, concerning the words of this book that has been found. For great is the wrath of יהוה that is kindled against us, because our fathers have not obeyed the words of this book, to do according to all that is written concerning us."

14 Then Ḥilqiyahu the priest, and Aḥiqam, and Aḵbor, and Shaphan, and Asayah went to Ḥuldah the prophetess, the wife of Shallum son of Tiqwah, son of Ḥarḥas, keeper of the wardrobe. Now she was dwelling in Yerushalayim in the Second Quarter. And they spoke with her.

15 And she said to them, "Thus said יהוה Elohim of Yisra'ĕl, 'Say to the man who sent you to Me,

16 "Thus said יהוה, 'See, I am bringing evil on this place and on its inhabitants, all the words of the book which the sovereign of Yehuḏah has read,

17 because they have forsaken Me and burned incense to other mighty ones to provoke Me with all the works of their hands. And so My wrath shall be kindled against this place and not be quenched.' " '

18 "And to the sovereign of Yehuḏah, who sent you to inquire of יהוה, say this to him, 'Thus said יהוה Elohim of Yisra'ĕl, "As for the words which you have heard,

19 because your heart was tender, and you humbled yourself before יהוה when you heard what I spoke against this place and against its inhabitants, that they would become a ruin and a curse, and did tore your garments and wept before Me, I also have heard," declares יהוה.

20 "Therefore, see, I am gathering you to your fathers, and you shall be gathered to your burial-site in peace, so that your eyes do not see all the evil I am bringing on this place." ' " And they brought word to the sovereign.

23 And the sovereign sent, and they gathered all the elders of Yehuḏah and Yerushalayim to him.

2 And the sovereign went up to the House of יהוה with all the men of Yehuḏah, and all the inhabitants of Yerushalayim with him, and the priests and the prophets and all the people, both small and great. And he read in their hearing all the words of the Book of the Covenant which had been found in the House of יהוה.

3 And the sovereign stood by the column and made a covenant before יהוה, to follow יהוה and to guard His commands and His witnesses and His laws, with all his heart and all his being, to establish the words of this covenant that were written in this book. And all the people stood to the covenant.

4 Then the sovereign commanded Ḥilqiyahu the high priest, and the priests of the second order, and the doorkeepers, to bring out of the Hĕḵal of יהוה all the objects that were made for Baʿal, and for Ashĕrah, and for all the host of the heavens. And he burned them outside Yerushalayim in the fields of Qiḏron, and took their ashes to Bĕyth Ĕl.

5 And he put down the black-robed priests [a] whom the sovereigns of Yehuḏah had appointed to burn incense on the high places in the cities of Yehuḏah and in the places all around Yerushalayim, and those who burned incense to Baʿal, to the sun,

23a Heb. kemarim.

and to the moon, and to the constellations, and to all the host of the heavens.

6 And he brought out the Ashěrah from the House of יהוה, to the wadi Qiḏron outside Yerushalayim, and burned it at the wadi Qiḏron and ground it to ashes, and threw its ashes on the burial-sites of the sons of the people.

7 And he broke down the houses of the male cult prostitutes that were in the House of יהוה, where the women wove tapestries for the Ashěrah.

8 And he brought all the priests from the cities of Yehuḏah, and defiled the high places where the priests had burned incense, from Geḇa to Be'ěrsheḇa, and broke down the high places at the gates which were at the entrance of the Gate of Yehoshua the governor of the city, which were to the left of the city gate.

9 However, the priests of the high places did not come up to the slaughter-place of יהוה in Yerushalayim, but they ate unleavened bread among their brothers.

10 And he defiled Topheth, which is in the Valley of the Son of Hinnom, so that no man could make his son or his daughter pass through the fire to Moleḵ.

11 And he did away with the horses that the sovereigns of Yehuḏah had given to the sun, at the entrance to the House of יהוה, by the room of Nathan-Meleḵ the eunuch, that were in the court. And he burned the chariots of the sun with fire.

12 And the slaughter-places that were on the roof of the upper room of Aḥaz, which the sovereigns of Yehuḏah had made, and the slaughter-places which Menashsheh had made in the two courtyards of the House of יהוה, the sovereign broke down, and rushed from there, and threw their dust into the wadi Qiḏron.

13 And the sovereign defiled the high places that were before Yerushalayim, which were on the right hand of the Mountain of Destruction, which Shelomoh sovereign of Yisra'ěl built for Ashtoreth the abomination of the Tsiḏonians, and for Kemosh the abomination of the Mo'aḇites, and for Milkom the abomination of the children of Ammon.

14 And he broke in pieces the pillars and cut down the Ashěrim, and filled their places with the bones of men.

15 And also the slaughter-place that was at Běyth Ěl, and the high place which Yaroḇ'am son of Neḇat made, by which he made Yisra'ěl sin, both that slaughter-place and the high place he broke down. And he burned the high place and ground it to dust, and burned the Ashěrah.

16 Then Yoshiyahu turned, and saw the burial-sites that were there on the mountain. And he sent and took the bones out of the burial-sites and burned them on the slaughter-place, and defiled it according to the word of יהוה which the man of Elohim proclaimed, who proclaimed these words.

17 And he said, "What tombstone is this that I see?" And the men of the city said to him, "It is the burial-site of the man of Elohim who came from Yehuḏah and proclaimed these matters which you have done against the slaughter-place of Běyth Ěl."

18 And he said, "Let him alone, let no one move his bones." So they left his bones alone, with the bones of the prophet who came from Shomeron.

19 And Yoshiyahu also took away all the houses of the high places that were in the cities of Shomeron, which the sovereigns of Yisra'ěl had made to provoke. And he did to them according to all the deeds he did in Běyth Ěl.

20 And he slaughtered all the priests of the high places who were there, on the slaughter-places, and burned men's bones on them, and went back to Yerushalayim.

21 And the sovereign commanded all the people, saying, "Prepare the Pěsaḥ to יהוה your Elohim, as it is written in this Book of the Covenant."

22 For such a Pěsaḥ had not been prepared since the days of the rulers who ruled Yisra'ěl, nor in all the days of the sovereigns of Yisra'ěl and the sovereigns of Yehuḏah,

23 but in the eighteenth year of Sovereign Yoshiyahu this Pěsaḥ was prepared before יהוה in Yerushalayim.

24 And also, Yoshiyahu put away those

who consulted mediums and spiritists, and
the household mighty ones and idols, and
all the abominations that were seen in the
land of Yehuḏah and in Yerushalayim,
in order to establish the words of the Torah
which were written in the book that
Ḥilqiyahu the priest found in the House
of יהוה.
25 And before him there was no sovereign
like him, who turned back to יהוה with all
his heart, and with all his being, and with
all his might, according to all the Torah of
Mosheh; and after him none rose up like
him.
26 However, יהוה did not turn from the
fierceness of His great wrath, with which
His wrath burned against Yehuḏah,
because of all the provocations with which
Menashsheh had provoked Him.
27 And יהוה said, "Even Yehuḏah I shall
remove from My presence, as I have
removed Yisra'ěl, and I shall reject this
city Yerushalayim which I have chosen,
and the House of which I said, 'My Name
is there.' "
28 And the rest of the acts of Yoshiyahu,
and all that he did, are they not written in
the book of the annals of the sovereigns of
Yehuḏah?
29 In his days Pharaoh Neḵo sovereign of
Mitsrayim went up against the sovereign of
Ashshur, to the River Euphrates. And
Sovereign Yoshiyahu went out to him, and
he killed him at Meḡiddo when he saw
him.
30 And his servants conveyed his body in
a chariot from Meḡiddo, and brought him
to Yerushalayim, and buried him in his
own burial-place. And the people of the
land took Yeho'aḥaz son of Yoshiyahu,
and anointed him, and set him up to reign
in his father's place.
31 Yeho'aḥaz was twenty-three years old
when he began to reign, and he reigned
three new *moons* in Yerushalayim. And his
mother's name was Ḥamutal the daughter
of Yirmeyahu of Liḇnah.
32 And he did evil in the eyes of יהוה,
according to all that his fathers did.
33 And Pharaoh Neḵo imprisoned him at
Riblah in the land of Ḥamath, to keep him
from reigning in Yerushalayim. And he
imposed on the land a fine of one hundred
talents of silver and a talent of gold.
34 And Pharaoh Neḵo set up Elyaqim son
of Yoshiyahu to reign in place of his father
Yoshiyahu, and changed his name to
Yehoyaqim. And Pharaoh took Yeho'aḥaz
and went to Mitsrayim, and he died there.
35 And Yehoyaqim gave the silver and
gold to Pharaoh. Only, he taxed the land to
give silver according to the mouth of
Pharaoh. He exacted the silver and gold
from the people of the land, from every
one according to his assessment, to give it
to Pharaoh Neḵo.
36 Yehoyaqim was twenty-five years old
when he began to reign, and he reigned
eleven years in Yerushalayim. And his
mother's name was Zeḇiḏah the daughter
of Peḏayah of Rumah.
37 And he did evil in the eyes of יהוה,
according to all that his fathers did.

24 In his days Neḇuḵaḏnetstsar sovereign of Baḇel came up, and Yehoyaqim became his servant for three years.
And he turned and rebelled against him.
2 And יהוה sent against him raiding
bands of Kasdim, and raiding bands of
Aram, and raiding bands of Mo'aḇ, and
raiding bands of the children of Ammon.
And He sent them against Yehuḏah to
destroy it, according to the word of יהוה
which He had spoken by His servants the
prophets.
3 Only at the mouth of יהוה this came
upon Yehuḏah, to remove *them* from His
presence, because of the sins of
Menashsheh, according to all that he did,
4 and also because of the innocent blood
that he shed. For he filled Yerushalayim
with innocent blood, which יהוה would not
forgive.
5 And the rest of the acts of Yehoyaqim,
and all that he did, are they not written
in the book of the annals of the sovereigns
of Yehuḏah?
6 So Yehoyaqim slept with his fathers.
And Yehoyaḵin his son reigned in his
place.
7 And the sovereign of Mitsrayim did not

come out of his land again, for the sovereign of Baḇel had taken all that belonged to
the sovereign of Mitsrayim from the wadi
of Mitsrayim to the River Euphrates.
8 Yehoyaḵin was eighteen years old
when he began to reign, and he reigned in
Yerushalayim three new *moons*. And his
mother's name was Neḥushta the daughter
of Elnathan of Yerushalayim.
9 And he did evil in the eyes of יהוה,
according to all that his father did.
10 At that time the servants of Neḇuḵaḏnetstsar sovereign of Baḇel came up
against Yerushalayim, and the city was
besieged.
11 And Neḇuḵaḏnetstsar sovereign of
Baḇel came against the city, as his servants
were besieging it.
12 And Yehoyaḵin sovereign of Yehuḏah,
and his mother, and his servants, and his
heads, and his eunuchs went out to the sovereign of Baḇel. And the sovereign of
Baḇel, in the eighth year of his reign, took
him prisoner.
13 And he took from there all the treasures
of the House of יהוה and the treasures of
the sovereign's house, and he cut in pieces
all the objects of gold which Shelomoh
sovereign of Yisra'ěl had made in the
Hěḵal of יהוה, as יהוה had said.
14 And he exiled all Yerushalayim, and all
the officers and all the mighty brave men –
ten thousand exiles – and all the craftsmen
and smiths. None remained except the
poorest people of the land.
15 And he exiled Yehoyaḵin to Baḇel. And
the sovereign's mother, and the sovereign's wives, and his eunuchs, and the
leading men of the land he exiled from
Yerushalayim to Baḇel.
16 And all the mighty brave men, seven
thousand, and craftsmen and smiths, one
thousand, all who were strong and fit for
battle, these the sovereign of Baḇel
brought to Baḇel into exile.
17 And the sovereign of Baḇel set up
Mattanyah, Yehoyaḵin's uncle, to reign in
his place, and changed his name to
Tsiḏqiyahu.
18 Tsiḏqiyahu was twenty-one years old
when he began to reign, and he reigned
eleven years in Yerushalayim. And his
mother's name was Ḥamutal the daughter
of Yirmeyahu of Liḇnah.
19 And he did evil in the eyes of יהוה,
according to all that Yehoyaqim did.
20 For this took place in Yerushalayim and
Yehuḏah because of the displeasure of
יהוה, until He had cast them out from His
presence. And Tsiḏqiyahu rebelled against
the sovereign of Baḇel.

25 And it came to be in the ninth year
of his reign, in the tenth new *moon*,
on the tenth of the new *moon*, that
Neḇuḵaḏnetstsar sovereign of Baḇel and
all his army came against Yerushalayim
and encamped against it, and they built a
siege wall against it all around.
2 And the city was besieged until the
eleventh year of Sovereign Tsiḏqiyahu.
3 By the ninth of the new *moon* the
scarcity of food had become so severe in
the city that there was no food for the people of the land.
4 Then the city wall was breached, and
all the men of battle *fled* at night by way of
the gate between two walls, which was by
the sovereign's garden, even though the
Kasdim were still encamped all around
against the city. And *the sovereign* went
by way of the desert plain.
5 And the army of the Kasdim pursued
the sovereign, and overtook him in the
desert plains of Yeriḥo, and all his army
was scattered from him.
6 And they seized the sovereign and
brought him up to the sovereign of Baḇel at
Riblah, and they pronounced sentence on
him.
7 And they slew the sons of Tsiḏqiyahu
before his eyes, and put out the eyes of
Tsiḏqiyahu, and bound him with bronze
shackles, and took him to Baḇel.
8 And in the fifth new *moon*, on the seventh of the new *moon*, which was the nineteenth year of Sovereign Neḇuḵaḏnetstsar
sovereign of Baḇel, Neḇuzaraḏan the chief
of the guard, a servant of the sovereign of
Baḇel, came to Yerushalayim.
9 And he burned the House of יהוה and
the house of the sovereign, and all the

houses of Yerushalayim – even every great house he burned with fire.

10 And all the army of the Kasdim who were with the chief of the guard broke down the walls of Yerushalayim all around.

11 And Neḇuzaraḏan the chief of the guard took into exile the rest of the people who were left in the city and the deserters who deserted to the sovereign of Baḇel, with the rest of the multitude.

12 But the chief of the guard left some of the poor of the land as vinedressers and farmers.

13 And the bronze columns that were in the House of יהוה, and the stands and the bronze Sea that were in the House of יהוה, the Kasdim broke in pieces, and took their bronze away to Baḇel.

14 And they took the pots, and the shovels, and the snuffers, and the ladles, and all the bronze utensils the priests used in the service.

15 And the chief of the guard took the fire holders and the basins which were of solid gold and solid silver.

16 The bronze of all these utensils was beyond measure – the two columns, the one Sea, and the stands, which Shelomoh had made for the House of יהוה.

17 The height of one column was eighteen cubits, and the capital on it was of bronze. And the height of the capital was three cubits, and the network and pomegranates all around the capital were all of bronze. And the second column was the same, with a network.

18 And the chief of the guard took Serayah the chief priest, and Tsephanyahu the second priest, and the three doorkeepers.

19 And out of the city he took a certain eunuch who was appointed over the men of battle, and five men of those who saw the sovereign's face, who were found in the city, and the chief scribe of the army who mustered the people of the land, and sixty men of the people of the land who were found in the city.

20 And Neḇuzaraḏan, chief of the guard, took them and made them go to the sovereign of Baḇel at Riblah.

21 And the sovereign of Baḇel struck them and put them to death at Riblah in the land of Ḥamath. So he exiled Yehuḏah from its own land.

22 And he appointed Geḏalyahu son of Aḥiqam, son of Shaphan, over the people who were left in the land of Yehuḏah, whom Neḇuḵaḏnetstsar sovereign of Baḇel had left.

23 And all the commanders of the armies, they and their men, heard that the sovereign of Baḇel had appointed Geḏalyahu. And they came to Geḏalyahu at Mitspah, even Yishmaʽěl son of Nethanyah, and Yoḥanan son of Qarěaḥ, and Serayah son of Tanḥumeth the Netophathite, and Yaʽazanyahu the son of a Maʽaḵathite, they and their men.

24 And Geḏalyahu swore to them and their men, and said to them, "Do not be afraid of the servants of the Kasdim. Dwell in the land and serve the sovereign of Baḇel, and let it be well with you."

25 And in the seventh new *moon* it came to be that Yishmaʽěl son of Nethanyah, son of Elishama, of the seed of the reign, came with ten men and struck Geḏalyahu that he died, and the Yehuḏim, and the Kasdim who were with him at Mitspah.

26 And all the people rose up, small and great, and the commanders of the armies, and went to Mitsrayim, for they were afraid of the Kasdim.

27 And it came to be in the thirty-seventh year of the exile of Yehoyaḵin sovereign of Yehuḏah, in the twelfth new *moon*, on the twenty-seventh of the new *moon*, that Ewil-Meroḏaḵ sovereign of Baḇel, in the year that he began to reign, released Yehoyaḵin sovereign of Yehuḏah from prison,

28 and spoke kindly to him, and set his throne above the throne of the sovereigns who were with him in Baḇel,

29 and changed his prison garments. And he ate bread continually before the sovereign all the days of his life.

30 And as his allowance, a continual allowance was given to him from the sovereign, a quota for each day, all the days of his life.

YESHAYAHU

ISAIAH

1 The vision of Yeshayahu son of
Amots, which he saw concerning
Yehuḏah and Yerushalayim in the days of
Uzziyahu, Yotham, Aḥaz, Ḥizqiyahu –
sovereigns of Yehuḏah.
2 Hear, O heavens, and listen, O earth!
For יהוה has spoken, "I have reared and
brought up children, but they have transgressed against Me.
3 An ox knows its owner and a donkey its
master's crib – Yisra'ěl does not know, My
people have not understood."
4 Alas, sinning nation, a people loaded
with crookedness, a seed of evil-doers,
sons acting corruptly! They have forsaken
יהוה, they have provoked the Set-apart
One of Yisra'ěl, they went backward.
5 Why should you be stricken any more?
You continue in apostasy! All the head is
sick, and all the heart faints.
6 From the sole of the foot, to the head,
there is no soundness in it – wounds and
bruises and open sores; they have not been
closed or bound up, or soothed with ointment.
7 Your land is laid waste, your cities are
burned with fire, strangers devour your
land in your presence. And it is laid waste,
as overthrown by strangers.
8 And the daughter of Tsiyon is left as a
booth in a vineyard, as a hut in a garden of
cucumbers, as a besieged city.
9 Unless יהוה of hosts had left to us a
small remnant, we would have become
like Seḏom, we would have been made
like Amorah.
10 Hear the word [a] of יהוה, you rulers of
Seḏom; give ear to the Torah [a] of our
Elohim, you people of Amorah!
11 "Of what use to Me are your many
slaughterings?" declares יהוה. "I have had
enough of ascending offerings of rams and
the fat of fed beasts. I do not delight in the
blood of bulls, or of lambs or goats.
12 "When you come to appear before Me,
who has required this from your hand, to
trample My courtyards?
13 "Stop bringing futile offerings, incense,
it is an abomination to Me. New Moons,
Sabbaths, the calling of gatherings – I am
unable to bear unrighteousness and assembly.
14 "My being hates your New Moons and
your appointed times, they are a trouble to
Me, I am weary of bearing them.
15 "And when you spread out your hands,
I hide My eyes from you; even though you
make many prayers, I do not hear. Your
hands have become filled with blood.
16 "Wash yourselves, make yourselves
clean; put away the evil of your doings
from before My eyes. Stop doing evil!
17 "Learn to do good! Seek right-ruling,
reprove the oppressor, defend the fatherless, plead for the widow.
18 "Come now, and let us reason together," says יהוה. "Though your sins are like
scarlet, they shall be as white as snow;
though they are red like crimson, they shall
be as wool.
19 "If you submit and obey, you shall eat
the good of the land;
20 but if you refuse and rebel, you shall be
devoured by the sword," for the mouth
of יהוה has spoken.
21 How the steadfast city has become a
whore! I have filled it with right-ruling;
righteousness lodged in it, but now murderers.
22 Your silver has become dross, your
wine is mixed with water.
23 Your rulers are stubborn, and companions of thieves. Everyone loves bribes, and
runs after rewards. They do not defend the

1a "Word" and "Torah" (teaching) are used as synonyms.

fatherless, nor does the cause of the widow
reach them.
24 Therefore the Master declares, יהוה of
hosts, the Mighty *One* of Yisra'ěl, "Ah, I
shall be eased of My adversaries, and I
shall be avenged of My enemies.
25 "And I shall turn My hand against you,
and shall refine your dross as with lye, and
shall remove all your alloy.
26 "And I shall give back your judges as at
the first, and your counsellors as at the
beginning. After this you shall be called
the city of righteousness, a steadfast city."
27 Tsiyon shall be ransomed with right-
ruling, and her returning ones with righteousness.
28 And the destruction of transgressors
and of sinners is together, and those who
forsake יהוה shall be consumed.
29 For they shall be ashamed of the terebinth trees which you have desired. And
you shall be embarrassed because of the
gardens which you have chosen.
30 For you shall be as a terebinth whose
leaf fades, and as a garden that has no
water.
31 The strong shall be for tow, and his
work for a spark. And both shall burn
together, with no one to extinguish.

2 The word that Yeshayahu the son of
Amots saw concerning Yehuḏah and
Yerushalayim:
2 And it shall be in the latter days that the
mountain of the House of יהוה is established on the top of the mountains, and
shall be exalted above the hills. And all
nations shall flow to it.
3 And many peoples shall come and say,
"Come, and let us go up to the mountain of
יהוה, to the House of the Elohim of
Ya'aqoḇ, and let Him teach us His ways,
and let us walk in His paths, for out of
Tsiyon comes forth the Torah, and the
Word of יהוה from Yerushalayim."
4 And He shall judge between the
nations, and shall reprove many peoples.
And they shall beat their swords into
ploughshares, and their spears into pruning
hooks. Nation shall not lift up sword
against nation, neither teach battle any
more.
5 O house of Ya'aqoḇ, come and let us
walk in the light of יהוה.
6 For You have forsaken Your people, the
house of Ya'aqoḇ, because they have been
filled from the East, and practise magic
like the Philistines, and they are pleased
with the children of foreigners.
7 And their land is filled with silver and
gold, and there is no end to their treasures.
And their land is filled with horses, and
there is no end to their chariots.
8 And their land is filled with idols; they
bow themselves to the work of their own
hands, to what their own fingers have
made.
9 And the lowly bows down, and the high
is humbled; therefore You do not forgive
them.
10 Enter into the rock, and hide in the dust,
because of the fear of יהוה and the splendour of His excellency.
11 The lofty looks of man shall be humbled, the pride of men shall be bowed
down, and יהוה alone shall be exalted in
that day.
12 For יהוה of hosts has a day against all
that is proud and lofty, against all that is
lifted up, so that it is brought low;
13 and against all the cedars of Leḇanon
that are high and lifted up, and against all
the oaks of Bashan;
14 and against all the high mountains, and
against all the hills that are lifted up;
15 and against every lofty tower, and
against every strong wall;
16 and against all the ships of Tarshish,
and against all the desirable craft.
17 And the loftiness of man shall be
bowed down, and the pride of men shall be
brought low. And יהוה alone shall be
exalted in that day,
18 and the idols completely pass away.
19 And they shall go into the holes of the
rocks, and into the caves of the earth, from
dread of יהוה and the splendour of His
excellency, when He arises to shake the
earth mightily.
20 In that day man shall throw away his
idols of silver and his idols of gold, which
they made, each for himself to worship, to

the moles and bats,
21 to go into the clefts of the rocks, and
into the crags of the rugged rocks, because
of the fear of יהוה and the splendour of His
excellency, when He arises to shake the
earth mightily.
22 Cease from man, whose breath is in his
nostrils, for in what is he to be reckoned
upon?

3 For look, the Master, יהוה of hosts, is
turning aside from Yerushalayim and
from Yehuḏah the stock and the store, all
the supply of bread and all the supply of
water;
2 the mighty man and the man of battle,
the judge and the prophet, and the diviner
and the elder;
3 the commander of fifty and the highly
respected man, and the counsellor and the
skilled craftsman, and the clever enchanter.
4 "And I shall make youths their heads,
and children shall rule over them.
5 And the people shall exert pressure,
man on man, man on his neighbour; the
young rise up against the older, and the
lightly esteemed against the highly
esteemed."
6 When a man takes hold of his brother in
the house of his father, by the garment, *and
say*, "Come, be a chief over us, and let this
ruin be under your hand,"
7 he shall swear in that day, saying, "I am
not a healer, for in my house is neither
bread nor garment; do not make me a chief
of the people."
8 For Yerushalayim has stumbled, and
Yehuḏah has fallen, because their tongue
and their doings are against יהוה, to
provoke the eyes of His esteem.
9 The look on their faces witnesses
against them, and they declare their sin as
Seḏom; they do not hide it. Woe to their
being! For they have brought evil upon
themselves.
10 "Say to the righteous it is well, for they
eat the fruit of their doings.
11 "Woe to the wrong – evil! For the
reward of his hand is done to him.
12 "My people! Youths exert pressure on
them, and women rule over them. O My
people! Your leaders lead *you* astray, [a] and
swallow the way of your paths."
13 יהוה shall stand up to plead, and is
standing to judge the peoples.
14 יהוה enters into judgment with the
elders of His people and its heads, "It is
you who have eaten up the vineyard, the
plunder of the poor is in your houses.
15 "What do you mean by crushing My
people and grinding the faces of the poor?"
declares the Master, יהוה of hosts.
16 And יהוה says, "Because the daughters
of Tsiyon are haughty, and walk with outstretched necks and seductive eyes, walking and mincing as they go, making a
jingling with their feet,
17 therefore יהוה shall smite with a scab
the crown of the head of the daughters of
Tsiyon, and יהוה expose their nakedness."
18 In that day יהוה takes away the finery
of the anklets, and the headbands, and the
crescents,
19 the pendants, the bracelets and the
veils,
20 the headdresses, and the leg ornaments,
and the sashes, and the perfume bottles,
and the amulets,
21 the rings, and the nose jewels,
22 the costly robes, and the cloaks, and the
shawls, and the purses,
23 the mirrors, and the fine linen, and the
turbans, and the large veils.
24 And it shall be: Instead of a sweet fragrance, a smell of decay; and instead of a
belt, a rope; and instead of well-set hair,
baldness; and instead of a festal robe, a
girding of sackcloth; and branding instead
of loveliness.
25 Your men shall fall by the sword, and
your strength in battle.
26 And her gates shall lament and mourn,
and she, deserted, shall sit on the ground.

4 And in that day seven women shall
take hold of one man, saying, "We
shall eat our own food and wear our own
clothes; only let us be called by your name,

3a 9:16.

to take away our reproach.”
2 In that day the Branch of יהוה shall be
splendid and esteemed. And the fruit of the
earth shall be excellent and comely for the
escaped ones [a] of Yisra’ěl.
3 And it shall be that he who is left in
Tsiyon and he who remains in Yerushalayim is called set-apart, everyone who is
written among the living in Yerushalayim.
4 When יהוה has washed away the filth
of the daughters of Tsiyon, and rinsed
away the blood of Yerushalayim from her
midst, by the spirit of judgment and by the
spirit of burning,
5 then יהוה shall create above every
dwelling place of Mount Tsiyon, and
above her gatherings, a cloud and smoke
by day and the shining of a flaming fire by
night, for over all the esteem shall be a
covering,
6 and a booth for shade in the daytime
from the heat, for a place of refuge, and for
a shelter from storm and rain.

5 Please let me sing to the One I love, a
song for my loved One regarding His
vineyard: my loved One has a vineyard on
a fertile hill.
2 And He dug it up and cleared it of
stones, and planted it with the choicest
vine, and built a watchtower in its midst,
and also made a winepress in it. And He
waited for the yielding of grapes, but it
yielded rotten ones.
3 “And now, O inhabitant of Yerushalayim and man of Yehuḏah, please judge
between Me and My vineyard.
4 “What more could have been done to
My vineyard that I have not done in it?
Why, when I waited for the yielding of
grapes, did it yield rotten ones?
5 “And now, please let Me inform you
what I am doing to My vineyard: To take
away its hedge and it shall be burned; to
break down its wall and it shall be trampled down;
6 and I lay it waste; it is not pruned or
dug and thornbushes and weeds shall come
up; and I command the clouds not to rain
on it.”
7 For the vineyard of יהוה of hosts is the
house of Yisra’ěl, and the man of Yehuḏah
is His pleasant plant. He looked for right-
ruling, but see, oppression; for righteousness, but see, weeping.
8 Woe to those who join house to house,
who add field to field, until there is no
room, and you are made to dwell alone in
the midst of the land!
9 In my hearing יהוה of hosts *said*,
“Truly, many houses shall be a waste – big
and fine ones, without inhabitant.
10 “For ten acres of vineyard yield one
bath, and a ḥomer of seed yields one
ěphah.”
11 Woe to those who rise early in the
morning pursuing strong drink, who stay
up late at night – wine inflames them!
12 And the lyre and the harp, the tambourine and flute, and wine are in their
feasts; but they do not regard the deeds of
יהוה, nor see the work of His hands.
13 Therefore my people have gone into
exile, because they have no knowledge.
And their esteemed men are starved, and
their crowd dried up with thirst.
14 Therefore She’ol has made itself wide
and opened its mouth without law. Their
splendour and their crowd and their uproar,
and he who is exulting within her, shall go
down into it.
15 And man is bowed down, and mortal
man humbled, and the eyes of the proud
are humbled.
16 But יהוה of hosts is exalted in judgment, and the set-apart Ěl is set-apart in
righteousness.
17 And the lambs shall feed in their
pasture, and strangers shall eat in the waste
places of the fat ones.
18 Woe to those who draw crookedness
with cords of falsehood, and sin as with
wagon ropes,
19 who are saying, “Let Him hurry! Let
Him hasten His work, so that we see it!
And let the counsel of the Set-apart One of
Yisra’ěl draw near and come, so that we
know.”

4a Yo’ěl 2:32, Oḇaḏ. v. 17.

20 Woe to those who call evil good, and good evil; who put darkness for light, and light for darkness; who put bitter for sweet, and sweet for bitter!

21 Woe to those who are wise in their own eyes, [a] and clever in their own sight!

22 Woe to the mighty to drink wine, and brave men to mix strong drink,

23 who declare right the wrong for a bribe, and the righteousness of the righteous they turn aside from him!

24 Therefore, as a tongue of fire devours the stubble, and the flame consumes the chaff, their root is as rottenness, and their blossom goes up like dust – because they have rejected the Torah of יהוה of hosts, and despised the Word of the Set-apart One of Yisra'ěl.

25 Therefore the displeasure of יהוה has burned against His people, and He stretches out His hand against them and strikes them, and the mountains tremble. And their carcass is as filth in the middle of the streets. With all this His displeasure has not turned back, and His hand is still stretched out!

26 And He shall lift up a banner to the nations from afar, and shall whistle to them from the end of the earth. And see, they come with speed, swiftly!

27 Not one of them is weary or stumbling, not one slumbers or sleeps. Not a belt shall be loosened on their loins, nor the thong of their sandals be broken.

28 Their arrows are sharp, and all their bows bent; their horses' hooves shall seem like flint, and their wheels like a whirl-wind.

29 Their roar is like that of a lion, they roar like young lions. And they growl and seize prey, and slip away, with no one to rescue.

30 And in that day they shall growl over it as with the growling of the sea. And one shall look at the earth, and see, darkness and distress! And light shall be darkened by the clouds.

6 In the year that Sovereign Uzziyahu died, I saw יהוה sitting on a throne, high and lifted up, and the train of His robe filled the Hěḵal.

2 Above it stood seraphim. Each one had six wings: with two he covered his face, with two he covered his feet, and with two he flew.

3 And one cried to another and said, "Set-apart, set-apart, set-apart is יהוה of hosts; all the earth is filled with His esteem!"

4 And the posts of the door were shaken by the voice of him who cried out, and the house was filled with smoke.

5 And I said, "Woe to me, for I am undone! Because I am a man of unclean lips, and I dwell in the midst of a people of unclean lips – for my eyes have seen the Sovereign, יהוה of hosts."

6 And one of the seraphim flew to me, having in his hand a live coal which he had taken with the tongs from the slaughter-place.

7 And he touched my mouth with it, and said, "See, this has touched your lips; your crookedness is taken away, and your sin is covered."

8 And I heard the voice of יהוה, saying, "Whom do I send, and who would go for Us?" And I said, "Here am I! Send me."

9 And He said, "Go, and you shall say to this people, 'Hearing, you hear, but do not understand; and seeing, you see, but do not know.'

10 "Make the heart of this people fat, and their ears heavy, and shut their eyes; lest they see with their eyes, and hear with their ears, and understand with their heart, and shall turn and be healed."

11 Then I said, "יהוה, until when?" And He answered, "Until the cities are laid waste and without inhabitant, and the houses are without a man, and the land is laid waste, a ruin,

12 and יהוה has removed men far away, and the forsaken places be many in the midst of the land.

13 "But still, there is a tenth part in it, and

5a Mish. 3:7.

it shall again be for a burning, like a terebinth tree and like an oak, whose stump
remains when it is cut down. The set-apart
seed is its stump!"

7

And it came to be in the days of Aḥaz
son of Yotham, son of Uzziyahu, sovereign of Yehuḏah, that Retsin sovereign
of Aram and Peqaḥ son of Remalyahu,
sovereign of Yisra'ěl, went up to Yerushalayim to fight against it, but could not
prevail against it.
2 And it was reported to the house of
Dawiḏ, saying, "Aram has set up camp in
Ephrayim." And his heart and the heart of
his people were moved as the trees of the
forest are moved with the wind.
3 And יהוה said to Yeshayahu, "Go out
now to meet Aḥaz, you and She'ar-Yashuḇ
your son, at the end of the channel of the
upper pool, on the highway of the
Launderer's Field,
4 and say to him, 'Take heed, and be
calm; do not fear or be faint-hearted for
these two stubs of smoking firebrands, for
the fierce displeasure of Retsin and Aram,
and the son of Remalyahu.
5 'Because Aram, Ephrayim, and the son
of Remalyahu have plotted evil against
you, saying,
6 "Let us go up against Yehuḏah and tear
it apart, and break it open for ourselves,
and set a sovereign over them, the son of
Taḇe'ěl."
7 'Thus said the Master יהוה, "It is not
going to stand, nor shall it take place.
8 "For the head of Aram is Dammeseq,
and the head of Dammeseq is Retsin. And
within sixty-five years Ephrayim is to be
broken as a people.
9 "And the head of Ephrayim is Shomeron, and the head of Shomeron is the son of
Remalyahu. If you do not believe, you are
not steadfast." ' "
10 And יהוה spoke again to Aḥaz, saying,
11 "Ask a sign for yourself from יהוה
your Elohim; make deep the request or
make it high."
12 But Aḥaz said, "I do not ask nor try
יהוה!"
13 And he said, "Hear now, O house of
Dawiḏ! Is it not enough that you weary
men, that you weary my Elohim also?
14 "Therefore יהוה Himself gives you a
sign: Look, the 'almah' [a] conceives and
gives birth to a son, and shall call His
Name Immanu'ěl. [b]
15 "He eats curds and honey when He
knows to refuse evil and choose the good.
16 "For before the child knows to refuse
evil and choose the good, the land that
you dread is to be forsaken by both her
sovereigns.
17 "יהוה brings on you and your people
and your father's house days that have not
come since the day that Ephrayim turned
away from Yehuḏah – the sovereign of
Ashshur."
18 And it shall be in that day that יהוה
whistles for the fly that is in the farthest
part of the rivers of Mitsrayim, and for the
bee that is in the land of Ashshur.
19 And they shall come, and all of them
shall rest in the steep ravines and in the
clefts of the rocks, and on all weeds and in
all pastures.
20 In that day יהוה shall shave with a
razor hired beyond the River – with the
sovereign of Ashshur – the head and the
hair of the legs, and also remove the beard.
21 And it shall be in that day that a man
keeps alive a young cow and two sheep.
22 And it shall be, that he shall eat curds
because of the plenty milk he gets, for
everyone left in the land shall eat curds.
23 And it shall be in that day, every place
where there were a thousand vines worth a
thousand sheqels of silver, let it be for
thornbushes and weeds.
24 With arrows and bows one shall go
there, because all the land shall be thornbushes and weeds.
25 And to all the hills which were tilled
with the hoe, you do not go for fear of
thornbushes and weeds; but it shall be for
sending oxen to, and a place for sheep to
roam.

7a Virgin/young woman. See also Explanatory Note: "Maiden". 7b Ěl with us.

8 And יהוה said to me, "Take a large
tablet, and write on it with a man's
pen concerning Mahĕr-Shalal-Ḥash-Baz.
2 "And let Me take reliable witnesses to
record, Uriyah the priest and Zeḵaryahu
son of Yeḇereḵyahu."
3 And I went to the prophetess, and she
conceived and bore a son. And יהוה said to
me, "Call his name Mahĕr-Shalal-Ḥash-
Baz;
4 for before the child knows to cry 'My
father' and 'My mother,' the riches of
Dammeseq and the spoil of Shomeron is
taken away before the sovereign of
Ashshur."
5 And יהוה spoke to me again, saying,
6 "Inasmuch as these people refused the
waters of Shiloaḥ that flow softly, and
rejoice in Retsin and in Remalyahu's son;
7 now therefore, see, יהוה brings up over
them the waters of the River, strong and
mighty – the sovereign of Ashshur and all
his esteem. And he shall come up over all
his channels and go over all his banks.
8 "And he shall pass through Yehuḏah,
he shall overflow and pass over, reaching
up to the neck. And the stretching out of
his wings shall fill the breadth of Your
land, O Immanu'ĕl.
9 "Be shattered, O you peoples, and be
broken in pieces! Give ear, all you from
the far places of the earth. Gird yourselves,
but be broken in pieces; gird yourselves,
but be broken in pieces.
10 "Take counsel, and it comes to naught;
speak a word, and it does not stand, for Ĕl
is with us."
11 For יהוה spoke thus to me with a strong
hand, and instructed me that I should not
walk in the way of this people, saying,
12 "Do not say, 'A conspiracy,' concerning all that this people call a conspiracy,
nor be afraid of their threats, nor be
troubled.
13 "יהוה of hosts, Him you shall set apart.
Let Him be your fear, and let Him be your
dread.
14 "And He shall be for a set-apart place,
but a stone of stumbling and a rock that
makes for falling to both the houses of
Yisra'ĕl, as a trap and a snare to the inhabitants of Yerushalayim.
15 "And many among them shall stumble
and fall, and be broken and snared and
taken."
16 Bind up the witness, seal the Torah
among my taught ones.
17 And I shall wait on יהוה, who hides His
face from the house of Ya'aqoḇ. And I
shall look for Him.
18 Look, I and the children whom יהוה
has given me – for signs and wonders in
Yisra'ĕl from יהוה of hosts, who dwells in
Mount Tsiyon.
19 And when they say to you, "Seek those
who are mediums and wizards, who whisper and mutter," should not a people seek
their Elohim? Should they seek the dead
on behalf of the living?
20 To the Torah and to the witness! If they
do not speak according to this Word, it is
because they have no daybreak. [a]
21 And they shall pass through it hard
pressed and hungry. And it shall be, when
they are hungry, that they shall be wroth
and curse their sovereign and their Elohim,
looking upward.
22 And they shall look to the earth and see
distress and darkness, gloom of hard times,
and be driven into thick darkness.

9 But there is no gloom upon her who is
distressed, as when at first He humbled the land of Zeḇulun and the land of
Naphtali, and afterward more heavily
oppressed her, by the way of the sea,
beyond the Yardĕn, in Galil of the nations.
2 The people who were walking in darkness have seen a great light; upon those
who dwelt in the land of the shadow of
death a light has shone.
3 You shall increase the nation; You shall
make its joy great. They shall rejoice
before You, as in the joy of harvest, as men
rejoice when they divide the spoil.
4 For You shall break the yoke of his burden and the staff of his shoulder, the rod of
his oppressor, as in the day of Miḏyan.

8a Or *light*.

5 For every boot of one trampling in
tumult, and coat rolled in blood, shall be
used for burning and fuel of fire.
6 For a Child is born unto us, a Son is
given unto us, and the rule is on His shoulder. And His Name is called Wonder,
Counsellor, Strong Ěl, Father of
Continuity, Prince of Peace.
7 Of the increase of His rule and peace
there is no end, upon the throne of Dawiḏ
and over His reign, [a] to establish it and sustain it with right-ruling and with righteousness from now on, even forever. The
ardour of יהוה of hosts does this.
8 יהוה sent a word against Ya'aqoḇ, and
it has fallen on Yisra'ěl.
9 And the people shall know, all of them,
Ephrayim and the inhabitant of Shomeron,
who say in pride and greatness of heart:
10 "The bricks have fallen down, but we
rebuild with hewn stones; the sycamores
are cut down, but we replace them with
cedars."
11 And יהוה set up the adversaries of
Retsin against him, and stirred up his enemies,
12 the Arameans before and the Philistines
behind. And they devour Yisra'ěl with an
open mouth. With all this His displeasure
has not turned back, and His hand is still
stretched out.
13 And the people have not turned back to
Him who strikes them, nor have they
sought יהוה of hosts.
14 And יהוה cuts off head and tail from
Yisra'ěl, palm branch and reed in one day.
15 Elder and highly respected, he is the
head; the prophet who teaches falsehood,
he is the tail.
16 For the leaders of this people lead *them*
astray, [b] and those who are guided by them
are swallowed up.
17 Therefore יהוה does not rejoice over
their young men, and has no compassion
on their fatherless and widows; for everyone is defiled and evil, and every mouth
speaks foolishness. With all this His displeasure has not turned back, and His hand
is still stretched out.
18 For wrongness burns as the fire; it consumes thornbushes and weeds, and sets the
bushes of the forest ablaze, and they roll
up like rising smoke.
19 The land shall be burned up by the
wrath of יהוה of hosts, and the people be
as fuel for the fire. A man shall not spare
his brother,
20 and cut down on the right hand, but
shall be hungry; and he devours on the left
hand, but shall not be satisfied; each one
devouring the flesh of his own arm:
21 Menashsheh Ephrayim, and Ephrayim
Menashsheh; together they are against
Yehuḏah. With all this His displeasure has
not turned back, and His hand is still
stretched out.

10

"Woe to those making unrighteous
inscriptions, and writers who have
prescribed toil,
2 to keep the needy back from right-
ruling, and to take what is right from the
poor of My people, that widows become
their prey, and orphans their plunder.
3 "What shall you do in the day of visitation, and in the ruin which comes from
afar? To whom would you run for help?
And where would you leave your wealth?
4 "Without Me they shall bow down
among the prisoners, and fall among the
killed." With all this His displeasure has
not turned back, and His hand is still
stretched out.
5 "Woe to Ashshur, the rod of My displeasure and the staff in whose hand is My
displeasure.
6 "Against a defiled nation I send him,
and against the people of My wrath I command him to seize the spoil, to take the
prey, and to tread them down like the mud
of the streets.
7 "But he does not intend so, nor does his
heart think so, for it is in his heart to
destroy, and cut off not a few nations.
8 "For he says, 'Are not my princes
sovereigns?
9 'Is not Kalno like Karkemish? Is not
Ḥamath like Arpaḏ? Is not Shomeron like

9a See 16:5, Teh. 2, Teh. 45:6, Miḵ. 5:2, Lq. 1:32-33. *9b* 3:12.

Dammeseq?

10 ‘As my hand has found the reigns of the idols, whose carved images excelled those of Yerushalayim and Shomeron,

11 as I have done to Shomeron and her idols, do I not do also to Yerushalayim and her idols?’

12 “And it shall be, when יהוה has performed all His work on Mount Tsiyon and on Yerushalayim, that I shall punish the fruit of the greatness of the heart of the sovereign of Ashshur, and the boasting of his haughty looks.

13 “For he has said, ‘By the power of my hand I have done it, and by my wisdom, for I have been clever. And I remove the boundaries of the people, and have robbed their treasuries. And I put down the inhabitants like a strong one.

14 ‘And my hand finds the riches of the people like a nest. And I have gathered all the earth like forsaken eggs are gathered. And there was no one who moved his wing, nor opened his mouth with even a peep.’ ”

15 Would the axe boast itself over him who chops with it, or the saw exalt itself over him who saws with it? As a rod waving those who lift it up! As a staff lifting up that which is not wood!

16 Therefore the Master, יהוה of hosts, sends leanness among his fat ones. And under his esteem he kindles a burning like the burning of a fire.

17 And the Light of Yisra’ěl shall be for a fire, and his Set-apart One for a flame. And it shall burn and devour his weeds and his thornbushes in one day,

18 and consume the esteem of his forest and of his fertile field, both life and flesh. And they shall be as when a sick man wastes away,

19 and the remaining trees of his forest shall be so few in number that a child records them.

20 And in that day it shall be that the remnant of Yisra’ěl, and those who have escaped of the house of Ya‘aqoḇ, never again lean upon him who struck them, but shall lean upon יהוה, the Set-apart One of Yisra’ěl, in truth.

21 A remnant shall return, the remnant of Ya‘aqoḇ, to the Mighty Ěl.

22 For though your people, O Yisra’ěl, be as the sand of the sea, yet a remnant of them shall return – a decisive end, overflowing with righteousness.

23 For the Master יהוה of hosts is making a complete end, as decided, in the midst of all the earth.

24 Therefore thus said the Master יהוה of hosts, “My people, who dwell in Tsiyon, be not afraid of Ashshur, who struck you with a rod and lifts up his staff against you, in the way of Mitsrayim.

25 “For yet a little while and the displeasure shall be completed, and My displeasure be to their destruction.”

26 And יהוה of hosts stirs up a lash for him as the smiting of Miḏyan at the rock of Orěḇ. And as His rod was on the sea, so shall He lift it up in the way of Mitsrayim.

27 And in that day it shall be that his burden is removed from your shoulder, and his yoke from your neck, and the yoke shall be destroyed because of the anointing oil.

28 He has come upon Ayath, he has passed Miḡron. At Miḵmash he stored his supplies.

29 They have gone through the pass, they have taken up lodging at Geḇa. Ramah is afraid, Giḇ‘ah of Sha’ul has fled.

30 Lift up your voice, O daughter of Galliym! Listen, Layishah – O poor Anathoth!

31 Maḏměnah has fled, the inhabitants of Gěḇim sought refuge.

32 Yet he remains at Noḇ that day; he shakes his fist at the mountain of the daughter of Tsiyon, the hill of Yerushalayim.

33 Look, the Master, יהוה of hosts, is lopping off a branch with an awesome crash, and the tall ones are cut down, and the lofty ones are laid low.

34 And He shall cut down the thickets of the forest with iron, and Leḇanon shall fall as a mighty one!

11

And a Rod shall come forth from the stump of Yishai, and a Sprout

from his roots shall be fruitful.
2 The Spirit of יהוה shall rest upon Him
– the Spirit of wisdom and understanding,
the Spirit of counsel and might, the Spirit
of knowledge and of the fear of יהוה,
3 and shall make Him breathe in the fear
of יהוה. And He shall not judge by the
sight of His eyes, nor decide by the hearing
of His ears.
4 But with righteousness He shall judge
the poor, and shall decide with straightness
for the meek ones of the earth, and shall
strike the earth with the rod of His mouth,
and slay the wrong with the breath of His
lips.
5 And righteousness shall be the girdle of
His loins, and trustworthiness the girdle of
His waist.
6 And a wolf shall dwell with the lamb,
and a leopard lie down with the young
goat, and the calf and the young lion and
the fatling together, and a little child leads
them.
7 And cow and bear shall feed, their
young ones lie down together, and a lion
eat straw like an ox.
8 And the nursing child shall play by the
cobra's hole, and the weaned child shall
put his hand in the adder's den.
9 They do no evil nor destroy in all My
set-apart mountain, for the earth shall be
filled with the knowledge of יהוה as the
waters cover the sea.[a]
10 And in that day there shall be a Root of
Yishai, standing as a banner to the people.
Unto Him the nations[b] shall seek, and His
rest shall be esteem.
11 And it shall be in that day that יהוה sets
His hand again a second time to recover
the remnant of His people who are left,
from Ashshur and from Mitsrayim, from
Pathros and from Kush, from Ěylam and
from Shin'ar, from Ḥamath and from the
islands of the sea.
12 And He shall raise a banner for the
nations, and gather the outcasts of Yisra'ěl,
and assemble the dispersed of Yehuḏah
from the four corners of the earth.
13 And the envy of Ephrayim shall turn
aside, and the adversaries of Yehuḏah be
cut off. Ephrayim shall not envy Yehuḏah,
and Yehuḏah not trouble Ephrayim.
14 But they shall fly down upon the shoulder of the Philistines toward the west;
together they plunder the people of the
east, their hand stretching forth on Eḏom
and Mo'aḇ, and the children of Ammon
shall be subject to them.
15 And יהוה shall put under the ban the
tongue of the Sea of Mitsrayim, and He
shall wave His hand over the River with
the might of His Spirit, and shall strike it in
the seven streams, and shall cause *men* to
tread it in sandals.
16 And there shall be a highway for the
remnant of His people, those left from
Ashshur, as it was for Yisra'ěl in the day
when he came up from the land of
Mitsrayim.

12 And in that day you shall say, "I
thank You יהוה, though You were
enraged with me, Your displeasure has
turned back, and You have comforted me.
2 "See, Ěl is my deliverance, I trust and
am not afraid. For Yah, יהוה, is my
strength and my song; and He has become
my deliverance."[a]
3 And you shall draw water with joy
from the fountains of deliverance.
4 And in that day you shall say, "Praise
יהוה, call upon His Name; make known
His deeds among the peoples, make mention that His Name is exalted.
5 "Sing to יהוה, For He has done excel-
lently; this is known in all the earth.
6 "Cry aloud and shout, O inhabitant of
Tsiyon, for great is the Set-apart One of
Yisra'ěl in your midst!"

13 The message concerning Baḇel
which Yeshayahu son of Amots
saw.
2 "Lift up a banner on the high mountain,
raise your voice to them; wave your hand,
let them enter the gates of the nobles.
3 "I have commanded My set-apart ones;
I have also called My mighty men for My

11a Ḥaḇ. 2:14. *11b* Or *nations*. *12a* See Shem. 15:2, Teh. 118:14.

displeasure, My proudly exulting ones."

4 The noise of an uproar in the mountains, like that of many people! A noise of uproar of the reigns of nations gathered together! יהוה of hosts is gathering an army for battle.

5 They are coming from a distant land, from the end of the heavens, even יהוה and His weapons of displeasure, to destroy all the earth.[a]

6 Howl, for the day of יהוה is near! It comes as a destruction from the Almighty.

7 Therefore all hands go limp, every man's heart melts,

8 and they shall be afraid. Pangs and sorrows take hold of them, they are in pain as a woman in labour; they are amazed at one another, their faces aflame!

9 See, the day of יהוה is coming, fierce, with wrath and heat of displeasure, to lay the earth waste, and destroy its sinners from it.

10 For the stars of the heavens and their constellations do not give off their light. The sun shall be dark at its rising, and the moon not send out its light.

11 "And I shall punish the world for its evil, and the wrong for their crookedness, and shall put an end to the arrogance of the proud, and lay low the pride of the ruthless.

12 "I shall make mortal man scarcer than fine gold, and mankind *scarcer* than the gold of Ophir.

13 "So I shall make the heavens tremble, and the earth shall shake from her place, in the wrath of יהוה of hosts and in the day of the heat of His displeasure.

14 "And it shall be as the hunted gazelle, and as a sheep that no man takes up – every man turns to his own people, and everyone flees to his own land.

15 "Whoever is found is thrust through, and everyone taken falls by the sword.

16 "And their children are dashed to pieces before their eyes, their houses plundered and their wives ravished.

17 "See, I am stirring up the Medes against them, who do not regard silver, and as for gold, they do not delight in it.

18 "And bows dash the young to pieces, and they have no compassion on the fruit of the womb, their eye spare no children.

19 "And Baḇel, the splendour of reigns, the comeliness of the pride of the Kasdim, shall be as when Elohim overthrew Sedom and Amorah.

20 "She shall never be inhabited, nor be settled from generation to generation; nor shall the Araḇian pitch tents there, nor shepherds rest their flocks there.

21 "But wild beasts of the desert shall lie there, and their houses shall be filled with owls. And ostriches shall dwell there, and wild goats frolic there.

22 "And hyenas shall cry in their citadels, and jackals in their pleasant palaces. And her time is near to come, and her days are not drawn out."

14

Because יהוה has compassion on Ya'aqoḇ, and shall again choose Yisra'ěl,[a] and give them rest in their own land. And the strangers shall join them, and they shall cling to the house of Ya'aqoḇ.[b]

2 And peoples shall take them and bring them to their own place. And the house of Yisra'ěl shall possess them for servants and female servants in the land of יהוה. And they shall make captives of their captors, and rule over their oppressors.

3 And it shall be, in the day יהוה gives you rest from your sorrow, and from your trouble and the hard service in which you were made to serve,

4 that you shall take up this proverb against the sovereign of Baḇel, and say, "How the oppressor has ceased, the gold-gatherer ceased!

5 "יהוה has broken the staff of the wrong, the sceptre of the rulers,

6 he who struck the people in wrath with ceaseless blows, he who ruled the nations

13a Also see Yeshayahu chs. 24, 34, 63 & 66.

14a See 45:17, Yirm. 30:11, Yirm. 46:28, Dan. 2:44, Amos 9:8, Zeḵ. 1:16-17, Zeḵ. 2:10-12, Yo'ěl 3:16.

14b See 56:6-8 & 60:3, Amos 9:12, Zeḵ. 2:11, Zeḵ. 8:23, Rom. 11:17-24, Ḥazon 21:24.

in displeasure, is persecuted and no one restrains.

7 "All the earth is at rest and at peace, they shall break forth into singing.

8 "Even the cypress trees rejoice over you, and the cedars of Leḇanon, saying, 'Since you were cut down, no woodcutter has come up against us.'

9 "She'ol from beneath is excited about you, to meet you at your coming; it stirs up the dead for you, all the chief ones of the earth; it has raised up from their thrones all the sovereigns of the nations.

10 "All of them respond and say to you, 'Have you also become as weak as we? Have you become like us?

11 'Your arrogance has been brought down to She'ol, and the sound of your stringed instruments; the maggot is spread under you, and worms cover you.'

12 "How you have fallen from the heavens, O Hělěl,[c] son of the morning! You have been cut down to the ground, you who laid low the nations!

13 "For you have said in your heart, 'Let me go up to the heavens, let me raise my throne above the stars of Ěl, and let me sit in the mount of appointment on the sides of the north;

14 let me go up above the heights of the clouds, let me be like the Most High.'

15 "But you are brought down to She'ol, to the sides of the pit.

16 "Those who see you stare at you, and ponder over you, saying, 'Is this the man who made the earth tremble, who shook reigns,

17 who made the world as a wilderness and destroyed its cities, who would not open the house of his prisoners?'

18 "All the sovereigns of the nations, all of them, were laid in esteem, everyone in his own house;

19 but you have been thrown from your burial-site like an abominable branch, like the garment of those who are killed, thrust through with a sword, who go down to the stones of the pit, like a trampled corpse.

20 "You are not joined with them in the burial-place, for you have destroyed your land and killed your people. Let the seed of evil-doers never be mentioned.

21 "Prepare his children for slaughter, because of the crookedness of their fathers, lest they rise up and possess the land, and fill the face of the world with cities."

22 "And I shall rise up against them," declares יהוה of hosts, "and shall cut off from Baḇel the name and remnant, and offspring and descendant," declares יהוה.

23 "And I shall make it a possession for the porcupine, and marshes of muddy water; and shall sweep it with the broom of destruction," declares יהוה of hosts.

24 יהוה of hosts has sworn, saying, "Truly, as I have planned, so shall it be; and as I have purposed, so it stands:

25 "To break Ashshur in My land, and tread him down on My mountains. And his yoke shall be removed from them, and his burden removed from their shoulders.

26 "This is the counsel that is counselled for all the earth, and this is the hand that is stretched out over all the nations.

27 "For יהוה of hosts has counselled, and who annuls it? And His hand that is stretched out, who turns it back?"

28 This is the message which came in the year that Sovereign Aḥaz died:

29 "Do not rejoice, all you of Philistia, that the rod that struck you is broken; for out of the serpent's roots comes forth an adder, and its offspring is a fiery flying serpent.

30 "And the first-born of the poor shall feed, and the needy lie down in safety. And I shall kill your roots with scarcity of food, and it shall kill your remnant.

31 "Howl, O gate! Cry, O city! Melt away, all you of Philistia! For smoke shall come from the north, and there is no stranger in his ranks."

32 And what does one answer the messengers of a nation? "That יהוה has founded Tsiyon, and the poor of His people take refuge in it."

15

The message concerning Mo'aḇ. Because in the night Ar of Mo'aḇ

14c The Shining One.

was laid waste, was silenced! Because in
the night Qir of Mo'aḇ was laid waste, was
silenced!
2 He has gone up to the house and Diḇon,
to the high places to weep. Mo'aḇ is wailing over Neḇo and over Mĕyḏeḇa; on all
their heads is baldness, and every beard is
cut off.
3 In their streets they shall put on sackcloth; on the tops of their houses and
in their streets everyone wails, weeping
bitterly.
4 And Ḥeshbon and El'alěh cry out, their
voice shall be heard as far as Yahats.
Therefore the armed ones of Mo'aḇ shout;
his being shall tremble within him.
5 My own heart is toward Mo'aḇ; her
fugitives cry unto Tso'ar, like a three-year-
old heifer. For by the ascent of Luḥith they
go up with weeping; for in the way of
Ḥoronayim they raise a cry of destruction.
6 For the waters of Nimrim are wastes,
for the green grass has withered away; the
grass fails, there is no greenness.
7 Therefore the wealth, acquired and
stored up, they take away to the wadi of
the Willows.
8 For the cry has gone all around the
borders of Mo'aḇ, its wailing to Eḡlayim
and its wailing to Be'ĕr Ělim.
9 "For the waters of Dimon shall be filled
with blood; for I shall bring more upon
Dimon, lions upon him who escapes from
Mo'aḇ, and on the remnant of the land."

16 Send a lamb to the ruler of the
land, from Sela to the wilderness,
to the mountain of the daughter of Tsiyon.
2 And it shall be, like a wandering bird, a
nest thrown out, so are the daughters of
Mo'aḇ at the fords of Arnon.
3 "Bring counsel, execute judgment;
make your shadow like the night in the
middle of the day; hide the outcasts, do not
betray him who escapes.
4 "Let My outcasts dwell with you, O
Mo'aḇ; be a shelter to them from the face
of the ravager. For the oppressor has met
his end, destruction has ceased, those trampling down have perished from the land.
5 "And in loving-commitment the throne
shall be established. And One shall sit on it
in truth, in the Tent of Dawiḏ, judging and
seeking right-ruling, and speeding righteousness."
6 We have heard of the pride of Mo'aḇ –
very proud – of his pride, his arrogance
and his rage. His boastings are not true.
7 So Mo'aḇ wails for Mo'aḇ, everyone
wails. For the raisin-cakes of Qir Ḥareseth
they moan. They are utterly smitten.
8 For the fields of Ḥeshbon languish –
the vine of Siḇmah. The masters of the
nations have broken down its choice
plants, which have reached to Ya'zĕr and
wandered through the wilderness. Her
branches are stretched out, they are gone
over the sea.
9 Therefore I bewail the vine of Siḇmah,
with the weeping of Ya'zĕr. I water you
with my tears, O Ḥeshbon and El'alěh, for
acclamation have fallen over your summer
fruit and your harvest.
10 Gladness is taken away, and joy from
the orchard; in the vineyards there is no
singing, nor shouting; No treaders tread
out wine in their presses; I have made their
acclamation cease.
11 Therefore my inward parts sound like a
lyre for Mo'aḇ, and my inner being for Qir
Ḥeres.
12 And it shall be, when it is seen that
Mo'aḇ has wearied herself on the high
place, that she shall come to her set-apart
place to pray, but not be able.
13 This is the word which יהוה has spoken
concerning Mo'aḇ since that time.
14 But now יהוה has spoken, saying,
"Within three years, as the years of a hired
man, the esteem of Mo'aḇ is to be despised
with all its great throng, and the remnant
be few, small and weak."

17 The message concerning
Dammeseq. "See, Dammeseq
ceases to be a city, and shall become a
heap of ruins.
2 "The cities of Aro'ĕr are forsaken, they
are for flocks which shall lie down, with
no one to frighten.
3 "And the stronghold shall cease from
Ephrayim, and the reign from Dammeseq,

and the remnant of Aram be as the esteem
of the sons of Yisra'ěl," declares יהוה of
hosts.
4 "And in that day it shall be that the
esteem of Ya'aqoḇ wanes, and the fatness
of his flesh grows lean.
5 "And it shall be as when the harvester
gathers the grain, and reaps the heads with
his arm. And it shall be as he who gathers
heads of grain in the Valley of Repha'im.
6 "And gleaning grapes shall be left in it,
like the shaking of an olive tree, two or
three olives at the top of the uppermost
branch, four or five in its most fruit-bearing branches," declares יהוה Elohim of
Yisra'ěl.
7 In that day man shall look to his Maker,
and his eyes turn to the Set-apart One of
Yisra'ěl.
8 And he shall not look to the slaughter-
places, the work of his hands; and he shall
not see that which his own fingers made,
nor the Ashěrim nor the sun-pillars.
9 In that day his strong cities become like
a forsaken forest and an uppermost branch,
which they left because of the children of
Yisra'ěl. And it shall become a ruin.
10 Because you have forgotten the Elohim
of your deliverance, and have not remembered the Rock of your stronghold, therefore you shall plant pleasant plants and set
out foreign seedlings,
11 by day make your plant to grow, and in
the morning make your seed to flourish –
but the harvest is a heap in the day of grief
and incurable pain.
12 Woe to the uproar of many people who
make a noise like the roar of the seas, and
to the rushing of nations that make a rushing like the rushing of mighty waters –
13 nations rushing like the rushing of
many waters. But He shall rebuke them
and they shall flee far away, and be chased
like the chaff of the mountains before the
wind, like whirling dust before the whirlwind.
14 At eventide, look! Alarm! Before
morning, it is no more. This is the portion
of those who plunder us, and the lot of
those who rob us.

18

Woe to the land shadowed with
whirring wings, which is beyond
the rivers of Kush,
2 which sends envoys by sea, even in
vessels of reed on the waters, saying, "Go,
swift messengers, to a nation tall and
smooth-skinned, to a people dreaded from
their beginning onward, a nation mighty
and trampling, whose land the rivers
divide."
3 All inhabitants of the world, and you
that dwell on the earth: When a banner is
lifted up on the mountains, look! And
when a shophar is blown, hear!
4 For thus יהוה said to me, "I am still,
and I watch in My dwelling place like
dazzling heat in sunshine, like a cloud of
dew in the heat of harvest."
5 For before harvest, when the bud is
perfect and the sour grape is ripening in the
flower, then He shall cut off the twigs with
pruning hooks, and shall cut down and
take away the spreading branches.
6 They are left together for the mountain
birds of prey and for the beasts of the
earth. And the birds of prey shall summer
on them, and all the beasts of the earth
winter on them.
7 In that time a present shall be brought
to יהוה of hosts from a people tall and
smooth-skinned, and from a people awesome from their beginning onward – a
nation mighty and trampling, whose land
the rivers have divided – to the place of the
Name of יהוה of hosts, to Mount Tsiyon.

19

The message concerning Mitsrayim. See, יהוה is riding on a
swift cloud, and He shall come into
Mitsrayim. And the idols of Mitsrayim
shall tremble at His presence, and the heart
of Mitsrayim melt in its midst.
2 "And I shall stir up Mitsrites against
Mitsrites, and they shall fight, each one
against his brother, and each one against
his neighbour, city against city, reign
against reign.
3 "And the spirit of Mitsrayim shall vanish within them, and I destroy their counsel. And they shall seek the idols and the
mutterers, the mediums and the sorcerers.

4 “And I shall deliver the Mitsrites into the hand of a cruel master, and a fierce sovereign to rule over them,” declares the Master, יהוה of hosts.

5 And waters shall fail from the sea, and the river wasted and dried up.

6 And the rivers shall stink, and the streams shall be weak and dried up. Reeds and rushes shall wither.

7 Bare places by the River, by the mouth of the River, and every sown field by the River shall wither. It shall be driven away, and be no more.

8 And the fishermen shall lament, and all those who cast hooks into the River shall mourn, and they who spread nets on the waters shall pine away.

9 And those who work in fine flax, and those who weave fine fabric shall become ashamed.

10 And its foundations shall be crushed, all the wage workers grieved in being.

11 The princes of Tsoʽan are only fools; the counsel of Pharaoh’s wise ones have become senseless. How do you say to Pharaoh, “I am the son of the wise, the son of ancient sovereigns?”

12 Where are they? Where are your wise men? Let them show you, and let them know what יהוה of hosts has counselled against Mitsrayim.

13 The princes of Tsoʽan have become fools, the princes of Noph are deceived. They, the corner-stone of her tribes, have led Mitsrayim astray.

14 יהוה has mixed a perverse spirit in her midst. And they have led Mitsrayim astray in all her work, as a drunkard strays in his vomit.

15 And there is no work for Mitsrayim, by either head or tail, palm branch or bulrush.

16 In that day Mitsrayim shall become like women, and tremble and fear because of the waving of the hand of יהוה of hosts, which He waves over it.

17 And the land of Yehuḏah shall be a fear to Mitsrayim, everyone who mentions it fears for himself, because of the counsel of יהוה of hosts which He has counselled against it.

18 In that day five cities in the land of Mitsrayim shall speak the language of Kenaʽan and swear by יהוה of hosts, one is called the City of Destruction.

19 In that day a slaughter-place to יהוה shall be in the midst of the land of Mitsrayim, and a standing column to יהוה at its border.

20 And it shall be for a sign and for a witness to יהוה of hosts in the land of Mitsrayim. When they cry to יהוה because of the oppressors, He sends them a Saviour and an Elohim, and shall deliver them.

21 And יהוה shall be known to Mitsrayim, and the Mitsrites shall know יהוה in that day, and make slaughtering and meal offering, and shall make a vow to יהוה and pay it.

22 And יהוה shall smite Mitsrayim, smite it and heal it. And they shall turn to יהוה, and He shall hear them and heal them.

23 In that day there shall be a highway from Mitsrayim to Ashshur, and Ashshur shall come into Mitsrayim and Mitsrayim into Ashshur, and Mitsrayim shall serve with Ashshur.

24 In that day Yisra’ěl shall be one of three with Mitsrayim and Ashshur, even a blessing in the midst of the earth,

25 whom יהוה of hosts shall bless, saying, “Blessed is Mitsrayim My people, and Ashshur the work of My hands, and Yisra’ěl My inheritance.”

20

In the year that Tartan came to Ashdoḏ, when Sargon the sovereign of Ashshur sent him, and he fought against Ashdoḏ and took it,

2 at that same time יהוה spoke by means of Yeshayahu son of Amots, saying, “Go, and remove the sackcloth from your body, and take your sandals off your feet.” And he did so, walking naked and barefoot.

3 And יהוה said, “As My servant Yeshayahu has walked naked and barefoot three years for a sign and a wonder against Mitsrayim and Kush,

4 so does the sovereign of Ashshur lead away the captives of Mitsrayim and the exiles of Kush, young and old, naked and barefoot, with their buttocks uncovered – the shame of Mitsrayim.

5 “And they shall be afraid and ashamed
of Kush, their expectation, and of
Mitsrayim, their boast.
6 “And the inhabitant of this coastland
shall say in that day, ‘See, such is our
expectation, wherever we flee for help to
be delivered from the sovereign of
Ashshur. And how do we escape?’ ”

21 The message concerning the
Wilderness of the Sea. As whirlwinds in the South sweep on, so it comes
from the wilderness, from an awesome
land.
2 A distressing vision is revealed to me:
the treacherous betrays, and the ravager
ravages. Go up, O Ěylam! Besiege, O
Media! All the groaning I bring to an end.
3 Therefore my loins are filled with
anguish; pangs have seized me, like the
pangs of a woman in labour. I was distressed when I heard it; I was troubled
when I saw it.
4 My heart reeled, horror overwhelmed
me; the night for which I longed He turned
into fear for me.
5 Prepare the table, spread the mat, eat
and drink. Arise, you princes, anoint the
shield!
6 For יהוה has said this to me, “Go, set a
watchman, let him declare what he sees.”
7 And he saw a chariot with a pair of
horsemen, a chariot of donkeys, and a
chariot of camels, and he listened attentively, very attentively.
8 Then he cried, “A lion, O יהוה! I stand
continually on the watchtower in the daytime, and I have sat at my post every night.
9 “And see this, a chariot of men coming
with a pair of horsemen!” And he spoke up
and said, “Baḇel is fallen, is fallen! And all
the carved images of her mighty ones He
has broken to the ground.”
10 Oh, my threshing and the grain of my
floor! That which I have heard from יהוה
of hosts, the Elohim of Yisra’ěl, I have
declared to you.
11 The message concerning Dumah. He
calls to me out of Sě‘ir, “Watchman, how
much of the night is passed? Watchman,
how much of the night has passed?”
12 The watchman said, “Morning came,
and also the night. If you inquire, inquire.
Come again!”
13 The message concerning Araḇia. In the
forest in Araḇia you stay, O you travelling
companies of Deḏanites.
14 You who dwell in the land of Těma,
bring water to him who is thirsty, meet the
fugitive with bread.
15 For they fled from the swords, from the
drawn sword, from the bent bow, and from
the stress of battle.
16 For thus יהוה has said to me, “Within a
year, according to the year of a hired man,
all the esteem of Qěḏar shall come to an
end,
17 and the rest of the number of archers,
the mighty men of the people of Qěḏar,
shall be few. For יהוה Elohim of Yisra’ěl
has spoken.”

22 The message concerning the Valley
of Vision. What troubles you now,
that you have all gone up to the house-
tops,
2 you who are filled with turmoils, a
noisy city, a city of revelry? Your slain are
not slain with the sword, nor the dead in
battle.
3 All your rulers have fled together; without a bow they were taken captive. All
who are found in you are bound together,
who have fled from afar.
4 Therefore I said, “Look away from me,
let me weep bitterly. Do not try to comfort
me because of the ravaging of the daughter
of my people.”
5 For it is a day of uproar and treading
down and perplexity by the Master יהוה of
hosts in the Valley of Vision – breaking
down of a wall and of crying to the mountain.
6 And Ěylam bore the quiver with chariots of men and horsemen, and Qir bared
the shield.
7 And it shall be that your choicest
valleys shall be filled with chariots, and
the horsemen shall take up positions at the
gate.
8 Then He removed the covering of
Yehuḏah. And you looked in that day to

the weapons of the House of the Forest.
9 And you saw the breaches of the city of
Dawiḏ, that it was great. And you gathered
together the waters of the lower pool.
10 And you counted the houses of Yerushalayim, and the houses you broke down
to strengthen the wall.
11 And you dug a ditch between the two
walls for the water of the old pool. But you
have not looked to its Maker, nor have you
seen Him who fashioned it long ago.
12 And in that day the Master יהוה of
hosts called for weeping and for mourning,
for baldness and for girding with sackcloth.
13 Then see! Joy and gladness, killing
oxen and slaying sheep, eating meat and
drinking wine, "Let us eat and drink, for
tomorrow we die!"
14 And it was revealed in my hearing by
יהוה of hosts, "For this crookedness shall
certainly not be pardoned until you die,"
said the Master יהוה of hosts.
15 Thus said the Master יהוה of hosts,
"Go, come to this steward, to Sheḇnah,
who is over the house, and say,
16 'What have you here, and whom have
you here, that you have hewn a burial-site
here, as he who hews himself a burial-site
on high, inscribing[a] a resting place for
himself in a rock?
17 'See, יהוה is hurling you away, O man,
and is firmly grasping you,
18 rolling you up tightly like a ball, into a
wide land. There you are to die, and there
your esteemed chariots are to be the shame
of your master's house.
19 'And I shall drive you from your office,
and you shall be ousted from your position.
20 'And it shall be in that day, that I shall
call My servant Elyaqim son of Ḥilqiyahu.
21 'And I shall put your robe on him, and
strengthen him with your girdle, and give
your authority into his hand. And he shall
be a father to the inhabitants of Yerushalayim and to the house of Yehuḏah.
22 'And I shall place the key of the house
of Dawiḏ on his shoulder. And he shall
open, and no one shuts; and shall shut, and
no one opens.
23 'And I shall fasten him like a peg in a
steadfast place, and he shall become a
throne of esteem to his father's house.
24 'And they shall hang on him all the
weight of his father's house, the offspring
and the offshoots, all vessels of small
quantity, from the cups to all the jars.
25 'In that day,' declares יהוה of hosts,
'the peg that is fastened in the steadfast
place shall be removed and be cut down
and fall, and the burden that was on it shall
be cut off. For יהוה has spoken.' "

23 The message concerning Tsor.
Howl, you ships of Tarshish! For it
has been destroyed, without house, without
harbour. From the land of Kittim it has
been revealed to them.
2 Be silent, you inhabitants of the coastland, you merchants of Tsiḏon, who passed
over the sea, they filled you.
3 And on great waters the grain of
Shiḥor, the harvest of the River, was her
increase. And she was a market-place for
the nations.
4 Be ashamed, O Tsiḏon, for the sea has
spoken, the stronghold of the sea, saying,
"I have not laboured, nor brought forth
children; neither have I reared young men,
brought up maidens."
5 Like the report of Mitsrayim, they too
are grieved at the report of Tsor.
6 Pass over to Tarshish; wail, you inhabitants of the coastland!
7 Is this your city of revelry, whose antiq-
uity is from days of old, whose feet carried
her far off to sojourn?
8 Who has counselled this against Tsor,
the crowning city, whose merchants are
chiefs, whose traders are the esteemed of
the earth?
9 יהוה of hosts has counselled it, to defile
the pride of all splendour, and to shame all
the esteemed of the earth.
10 Overflow through your land like the
River, O daughter of Tarshish; there is no
more strength.

22a Engraving.

11 He has stretched out His hand over the
sea, He shook the reigns; יהוה has given a
command against Kenaʽan to destroy its
strongholds.
12 And He said, "Never again shall you
exult, O you oppressed maiden daughter of
Tsiḏon. Arise, pass over to Kittim, even
there you shall find no rest."
13 See the land of the Kasdim – this people did not exist. Ashshur founded it for
wild beasts of the desert. They set up their
siege-towers, they demolished her palaces,
and made her a ruin.
14 Howl, you ships of Tarshish, for your
stronghold is laid waste!
15 And in that day it shall be that Tsor is
forgotten seventy years, according to the
days of one sovereign. At the end of seventy years it shall be to Tsor as in the song of
the whore:
16 "Take a lyre, go about the city, you forgotten whore; make sweet playing, sing
many songs, so that you might be remembered."
17 And at the end of seventy years it shall
be that יהוה visits Tsor. And she shall
return to her harlot-fee and commit whoring with all the reigns of the earth on the
face of the soil.
18 And her goods and her harlot-fee shall
be set apart for יהוה, not treasured nor laid
up, for her gain is for those who dwell
before יהוה, to eat sufficiently, and for a
choice covering.

24 See, יהוה is making the earth
empty and making it waste, and
shall overturn its surface, and shall scatter
abroad its inhabitants.
2 And it shall be – as with the people so
with the priest, as with the servant so with
his master, as with the female servant so
with her mistress, as with the buyer so with
the seller, as with the lender so with the
borrower, as with the creditor so with the
debtor;
3 the earth is completely emptied and
utterly plundered, for יהוה has spoken this
word.
4 The earth shall mourn and wither, the
world shall languish and wither, the
haughty people of the earth shall languish.
5 For the earth has been defiled under its
inhabitants, because they have transgressed the Torot, [a] changed [b] the law, broken the everlasting covenant. [c]
6 Therefore a curse shall consume the
earth, and those who dwell in it be
punished. Therefore the inhabitants of the
earth shall be burned, and few men shall
be left.
7 The new wine shall fail, the vine shall
languish, all those glad at heart shall sigh.
8 The joy of the tambourine shall cease,
the noise of those who rejoice shall end,
the joy of the lyre shall cease.
9 No more do they drink wine with a
song, strong drink is bitter to those who
drink it.
10 The deserted city shall be broken down,
every house shall be shut, no one enters.
11 There is a crying for wine in the streets;
all joy shall be darkened, the gladness of
the earth shall be gone.
12 The city is left in ruins, and the gate is
stricken with destruction.
13 For thus it is to be in the midst of the
earth among the peoples, like the shaking
of an olive tree, like the gleaning of grapes
when the grape harvest is done.
14 They lift up their voice, they sing of the
excellency of יהוה, they shall cry aloud
from the sea.
15 Therefore praise יהוה in the east, the
Name of יהוה Elohim of Yisra'ěl in the
coastlands of the sea.
16 From the ends of the earth we shall hear
songs, "Splendour to the Righteous One!"
But I say, "I waste away, I waste away!
Woe to me! The treacherous betray, with
treachery the treacherous betray."
17 Fear and the pit and the snare are upon
you, O inhabitant of the earth.
18 And it shall be that he who flees from
the noise of the fear falls into the pit, and
he who comes up from the midst of the pit

24a Torot - plural of Torah - teaching. *24b* Yirm. 23:36.
24c See also 13:9, 13:11, 26:21, 66:24, Miḵ. 5:15, Tseph. 1:2-18.

is caught in the snare. For the windows
from on high shall be opened, and the
foundations of the earth be shaken.
19 The earth shall be utterly broken, the
earth shall be completely shattered, the
earth shall be fiercely shaken.
20 The earth shall stagger like a drunkard.
And it shall totter like a hut, and its transgression shall be heavy upon it, and it shall
fall, and not rise again.
21 And in that day it shall be that יהוה
punishes on high the host of exalted ones,
and on the earth the sovereigns of the
earth.
22 And they shall be gathered together, as
prisoners are gathered in the pit, and shall
be shut up in the prison, and be punished
after many days.
23 And the moon shall blush, and the sun
shall be ashamed, for יהוה of hosts shall
reign on Mount Tsiyon, and in Yerushalayim, [d] and before His elders, in
esteem!

25 O יהוה, You are my Elohim. I exalt
You, I praise Your Name, for You
shall do a wonder – counsels of long ago,
trustworthiness, truth.
2 For You shall make a city a heap, a
walled city a ruin, a palace of foreigners to
be a city no more – never to be rebuilt.
3 Therefore a strong people praise You,
the city of the ruthless nations fear You.
4 For You shall be a refuge to the poor, a
refuge to the needy in his distress, a shelter
from the storm, a shade from the heat. For
the spirit of the ruthless is like a storm
against a wall.
5 You subdue the noise of foreigners, as
heat in a dry place; as heat in the shadow
of a cloud, the singing of the ruthless is
subdued.
6 And in this mountain יהוה of hosts
shall make for all people a feast of choice
pieces, a feast of old wines, of choice
pieces with marrow, of old wines, well-
refined.
7 And He shall swallow up on this mountain the surface of the covering which
covers all people, and the veil which is
spread over all nations.
8 He shall swallow up death forever, and
the Master יהוה shall wipe away tears
from all faces, and take away the reproach
of His people from all the earth. For יהוה
has spoken.
9 And it shall be said in that day, "See,
this is our Elohim. We have waited for
Him, and He saves us. This is יהוה, we
have waited for Him, let us be glad and
rejoice in His deliverance."
10 For the hand of יהוה rests on this
mountain, and Mo'aḇ is trodden down
under Him, as straw is trodden down in the
water of a dunghill.
11 And He shall spread out His hands in
their midst as he who swims spreads out
his hands to swim, and He shall bring
down their pride together, with the skill of
His hands.
12 And the high stronghold of your walls
He shall bring down, lay it low, levelled
to the ground, down to the dust.

26 In that day this song is sung in the
land of Yehuḏah, "We have a
strong city – He sets up deliverance, walls
and ramparts.
2 "Open the gates, let the righteous
nation which guards the truth enter in.
3 "The one steadfast of mind You guard
in perfect peace, for he trusts in You.
4 "Trust in יהוה forever, for in Yah, יהוה,
is a rock of ages.
5 "For He shall bring down those who
dwell on high. He lays the exalted city low,
He lays it low to the earth, He brings it
down to the dust.
6 "A foot tramples it down – feet of the
poor, footsteps of the needy."
7 The path of the righteous is uprightness; O upright One, You weigh the course
of the righteous.
8 Also, in the path of Your right-rulings,
O יהוה, we have waited for You; the longing of *our* being is for Your Name and for

24d 12:6, 16:5, 46:13, 52:8, 59:20, Teh.102:16, Yeḥez. 43:7-9, Yo'ěl 3:17 & 21, Miḵ. 4:7-8, Tseph. 3:14-17, Zeḵ. 1:16-17, Zeḵ. 2:10, Zeḵ. 8:3-8, Zeḵ. 14:1-11, Ma. 1:6-7, Ḥazon 21.

the remembrance of You.
[9]My being longs for You in the night,
also, my spirit within me seeks You
earnestly. For when Your right-rulings are
in the earth, the inhabitants of the world
shall learn righteousness.
[10]The wrong finds favour, *yet* he shall not
learn righteousness; in the land of straight-
forwardness he acts perversely, and does
not see the excellency of יהוה.
[11]O יהוה, Your hand is high, they do not
see. They see the ardour of the people and
are ashamed; also, let the fire for Your
adversaries consume them.
[12]O יהוה, You establish peace for us, for
You have also done all our works in us.
[13]O יהוה our Elohim, other masters
besides You have had rule over us; only in
You do we make mention of Your Name.
[14]The dead do not live; the departed
spirits [a] do not rise. Therefore You have
visited and destroyed them, and made all
their remembrance to perish.
[15]You shall increase the nation, O יהוה,
You shall increase the nation; You are
esteemed; You shall expand all the borders
of the land.
[16]O יהוה, in distress they shall visit You,
they shall pour out a prayer when Your disciplining is upon them.
[17]As a woman with child and about to
give birth writhes and cries out in her pain,
so shall we be before Your face, O יהוה.
[18]We have conceived, we writhed in pain;
we have given birth to wind. We have not
accomplished deliverance in the earth, nor
have the inhabitants of the world fallen.
[19]Let Your dead live, *together with* my
dead body, let them arise. Awake and sing,
you who dwell in dust; for Your dew is a
dew of light, and let the earth give birth to
the departed spirits.[a]
[20]Go, my people, enter your rooms, and
shut your doors behind you; hide yourself,
as it were, for a little while, until the displeasure is past.
[21]For look, יהוה is coming out of His
place to punish the inhabitants of the earth
for their crookedness. And the earth shall
disclose her blood, and no longer cover her
killed *ones*.

27

In that day יהוה with His severe
sword, great and strong, punishes
Liwiathan the fleeing serpent, Liwiathan
that twisted serpent. And He shall kill the
monster that is in the sea.
[2]In that day sing to her, "A vineyard of
red wine!
[3]"I, יהוה, do guard it, I water it every
moment; lest any hurt it, I guard it night
and day.
[4]"Wrath is not in Me. Who would set
thornbushes and weeds against Me in
battle? I would go through them, I would
burn them together.
[5]"Or let him take hold of My strength
and make peace with Me. Let him make
peace with Me!"
[6]Those who come He causes to take root
in Yaʿaqoḇ, Yisra'ěl shall blossom and bud.
And they shall fill the face of the world
with fruit.
[7]Has He smitten him as he struck the
ones who were striking him? Or as a killer
– was he killed *as* he was killing?
[8]In measure, by sending her away, You
contended with her. He shall take away by
His rough wind in the day of the east wind.
[9]Therefore by this the crookedness of
Yaʿaqoḇ is covered. And this is all the fruit
of taking away his sin: when he makes all
the stones of the slaughter-place like
chalkstones that are beaten to dust –
Ashěrim and sun-pillars rise no more.
[10]For the city of defence is lonely, a
home forsaken and left like a wilderness –
there the calf feeds, and there it lies down,
and shall consume its branches.
[11]When its twigs are dry, they are broken
off, women come and set them on fire. For
it is a people of no understanding, therefore He who made them has no compassion on them, and He who formed them
shows them no favour.
[12]And in that day it shall be that יהוה
threshes, from the channel of the River to
the wadi of Mitsrayim. And you shall be

26a Departed spirits - the *Repha'im.*

gathered one by one, [a] O children of Yisra'ěl.
13 And in that day it shall be that a great
shophar is blown, and those who were perishing in the land of Ashshur and the outcasts in the land of Mitsrayim shall come,
and shall worship יהוה on the set-apart
mountain, in Yerushalayim.

28

Woe to the proud crown of the
drunkards of Ephrayim, and to the
fading flower of its splendid comeliness
that is on the head of the fertile valley, to
those who are overcome with wine!
2 See, יהוה has one who is strong and
potent, like a downpour of hail and a
destroying storm, like a flood of mighty
waters overflowing, who casts down to the
earth with the hand.
3 The proud crown of the drunkards of
Ephrayim, is trampled under foot;
4 and the fading flower of its splendid
comeliness that is on the head of the fertile
valley, like the first fruit before the summer, which, when one sees it, he eats it up
while it is still in his hand.
5 In that day יהוה of hosts is for a crown
of splendour and a head-dress of comeliness to the remnant of His people,
6 and a spirit of right-ruling to him who
sits in right-ruling, and strength to those
who turn back the battle at the gate.
7 And these too have gone astray through
wine, and through strong drink wandered
about. Priest and prophet have gone astray
through strong drink, they are swallowed
up by wine, they wander about through
strong drink, they go astray in vision, they
stumble in right-ruling.
8 For all tables shall be covered with
vomit, no place without filth.
9 Whom would He teach knowledge?
And whom would He make to understand
the message? Those weaned from milk,
those taken from the breasts!
10 For it is: command upon command,
command upon command, line upon line,
line upon line, here a little, there a little.
11 For with a jabbering lip and a foreign
tongue He speaks to this people,
12 to whom He said, "This is the rest, give
rest to the weary," and, "This is the
refreshing." But they would not hear.
13 But the Word of יהוה was to them,
"Command upon command, command
upon command, line upon line, line upon
line, here a little, there a little," so that they
go and shall stumble backward, and be
broken and snared and taken captive.
14 Therefore hear the Word of יהוה, you
men of scorn, who rule this people who are
in Yerushalayim,
15 because you have said, "We have made
a covenant with death, and with She'ol we
have effected a vision. When the overflowing scourge passes through, it does not
come to us, for we have made lying our
refuge, and under falsehood we have
hidden ourselves."
16 Therefore thus said the Master יהוה,
"See, I am laying in Tsiyon a stone for
a foundation, a tried stone, a precious
corner-stone, a settled foundation. He who
trusts shall not hasten away.
17 And I shall make right-ruling the measuring line, and righteousness the plummet. And the hail shall sweep away the
refuge of lying, and the waters overflow
the hiding place.
18 And your covenant with death shall be
annulled, and your vision with She'ol not
stand. When an overflowing scourge passes through, then you shall be trampled
down by it.
19 As often as it passes through it shall
take you, for it shall pass through every
morning, and by day and by night. And it
shall be only trembling to understand the
message."
20 For the bed shall be too short for a man
to stretch out on, and the covering shall be
too narrow to wrap himself in it.
21 For יהוה rises up as at Mount Peratsim,
and He is wroth as at the Valley of Giḇʽon,
to do His work, His strange work, and to
do His deed, His strange deed.
22 And now, do not be scoffers, lest your
bonds be made strong. For I have heard

27a - Yirm. 3:14-15.

from the Master יהוה of hosts, a destruction decreed upon all the earth.
23 Give ear and hear my voice, listen and
hear my Word.
24 Does the ploughman keep ploughing all
day to sow? Does he keep turning his soil
and breaking the clods?
25 When he has levelled its surface, does
he not sow the caraway and scatter the
cummin, plant the wheat in rows, the
barley in the appointed place, and the spelt
in its place?
26 For He instructs him for right-ruling,
his Elohim teaches him.
27 For caraway is not threshed with a
threshing sledge, nor is a wagon wheel
rolled over cummin, but caraway is beaten
out with a stick, and cummin with a rod.
28 Grain is crushed, so one does not go on
threshing it forever, nor break it with his
wagon wheel, nor crush it with his horsemen.
29 Even this has come from יהוה of hosts,
who did wonders in counsel, who made
wisdom great.

29

Woe to Ari'ěl, to Ari'ěl, the city
where Dawiḏ dwelt! Add year to
year, let festivals come around.
2 "And I shall distress Ari'ěl, and there
shall be mourning and sorrow, and it shall
be to Me as Ari'ěl.
3 "And I shall encamp against you all
around, I shall lay siege against you with a
mound, and I shall raise siege-works
against you.
4 "And you shall be brought low and
speak out of the ground, and your speech
shall be low, out of the dust. And your
voice shall be like a medium's, out of the
ground, and your speech whisper out of the
dust.
5 "But the crowd of those strange to you
shall be like fine dust, and the crowd of the
ruthless ones as chaff blowing away. And
it shall be in an instant, suddenly!"
6 You shall be visited by יהוה of hosts
with thunder and earthquake and great
noise, with whirlwind and storm, and
flame of devouring fire.
7 Then the crowd of all the nations who
fight against Ari'ěl, even all who fight
against her and her stronghold, and distress
her, shall be as a dream of a night vision.
8 And it shall be as when a hungry man
dreams, and see, he eats; but he awakes,
and his being is empty; or as when a thirsty
man dreams, and see, he drinks; but he
awakes, and see, he is faint, and his being
is longing. Thus shall the crowd of all the
nations be who fight against Mount
Tsiyon.
9 Pause and wonder! Blind yourselves
and be blind! They are drunk, but not with
wine; they stagger, but not with strong
drink.
10 For יהוה has poured out on you the
spirit of deep sleep, and has closed your
eyes, the prophets. And He has covered
your heads, the seers.
11 And the entire vision is to you like the
words of a book that is sealed, which men
give to one who knows books, saying,
"Read this, please." And he said, "I am
unable, for it is sealed."
12 And the book is given to one who does
not know books, saying, "Read this,
please." And he said, "I have not known
books."
13 And יהוה says, "Because this people
has drawn near with its mouth, and with its
lips they have esteemed Me, and
it has kept its heart far from Me, and their
fear of Me has become a command of men
that is taught! [a]
14 "Therefore, see, I am again doing a
marvellous work among this people, a
marvellous work and a wonder. And the
wisdom of their wise men shall perish, and
the understanding of their clever men shall
be hidden."
15 Woe to those who seek deep to hide
their counsel far from יהוה, and their
works are in the dark; they say, "Who sees
us?" and, "Who knows us?"
16 How perverse of you! Should the potter
be reckoned as the clay? Should what is
made say of its Maker, "He did not make

29a Mt. 15:8-9, Mq. 7:6-7.

me"? And what is formed say of Him who
formed it, "He did not understand"?
17 Is it not yet a little while, and Leḇanon
shall be turned into garden land, and
garden land be reckoned as a forest?
18 And in that day the deaf shall hear the
words of the book, and the eyes of the
blind shall see out of gloom, and out of
darkness.
19 And the meek ones shall increase their
joy in יהוה, and the poor among men
rejoice in the Set-apart One of Yisra'ěl.
20 For the ruthless one is brought to
naught, the scorner is consumed, and all
who watch for evil shall be cut off,
21 those who make a man to sin in word,
and lay a snare for him who reproves in the
gate, and turn aside the righteous with
empty *reasoning*.
22 Therefore thus said יהוה, who ransomed Aḇraham, concerning the house
of Ya'aqoḇ, "Ya'aqoḇ is no longer put to
shame, no longer does his face grow pale.
23 "For when he sees his children, the
work of My hands, in his midst, they shall
set apart My Name, and set apart the Set-
apart One of Ya'aqoḇ, and fear the Elohim
of Yisra'ěl.
24 "And those who went astray in spirit
shall come to understanding, and the
grumblers accept instruction."

30 "Woe to the stubborn children,"
declares יהוה, "to make counsel,
but not from Me, and to devise plans, but
not of My Spirit, in order to add sin to sin;
2 who are setting out to go down to
Mitsrayim, and have not asked My mouth,
to be strengthened in the strength of
Pharaoh, and to seek refuge in the shadow
of Mitsrayim!
3 "And the strength of Pharaoh shall
become your shame, and the refuge in the
shadow of Mitsrayim your confusion.
4 "For his princes were at Tso'an, and his
messengers came to Ḥanes.
5 "They were all ashamed of a people
who do not profit them, not for help or
profit, but a shame and also a reproach."
6 The message concerning the beasts of
the South. Through a land of trouble and
distress, from which came the lioness and
lion, the adder and fiery flying serpent,
they convey their riches on the backs of
young donkeys, and their treasures on the
humps of camels, to an unprofitable people,
7 even Mitsrayim, whose help is vain and
empty. Therefore I have called her Rahaḇ-
Hěm-Sheḇeth.
8 And go, write it before them on a tablet,
and inscribe it on a scroll, that it is for a
latter day, a witness forever:
9 that this is a rebellious people, lying
children, children who refuse to hear the
Torah of יהוה,
10 who say to the seers, "Do not see," and
to the prophets, "Do not prophesy to us
what is right. Speak to us what is smooth,
prophesy deceits.
11 "Turn aside from the way, swerve from
the path, cause the Set-apart One of
Yisra'ěl to cease from before us."
12 Therefore thus said the Set-apart One
of Yisra'ěl, "Because you despise this
word, and trust in oppression and perverseness, and rely on them,
13 therefore this crookedness is to you like
a breach ready to fall, a bulge in a high
wall, whose breaking comes suddenly,
swiftly."
14 And He shall break it like the breaking
of the potter's vessel, which is broken in
pieces, without sparing, so that there is not
found among its fragments a sherd to take
fire from the hearth, or to take water from
the cistern.
15 For thus said the Master יהוה, the Set-
apart One of Yisra'ěl, "In returning and
rest you are saved, in stillness and trust is
your strength." But you would not,
16 and you said, "No, for we flee upon
horses," therefore you flee! And, "We ride
on swift horses," therefore those who pursue you are swift!
17 One thousand *flee* at the rebuke of one;
at the rebuke of five you shall flee until
you are left as a pole on top of a mountain
and as a sign on a hill.
18 And therefore יהוה shall wait, to show
you favour. And therefore He shall be
exalted, to have compassion on you. For

יהוה is an Elohim of right-ruling. Blessed
are all those who wait for Him.
19 For the people shall dwell in Tsiyon at
Yerushalayim, you shall weep no more. He
shall show much favour to you at the
sound of your cry; when He hears, He shall
answer you.
20 Though יהוה gave you bread of adversity and water of affliction, your Teacher [a]
shall no longer be hidden. But your eyes
shall see your Teacher, [b]
21 and your ears hear a word behind you,
saying, "This is the Way, walk in it,"
whenever you turn to the right, or whenever you turn to the left.
22 And you shall defile the covering of
your graven images of silver, and the
plating of your moulded images of gold.
You shall throw them away as a menstrual
cloth and say to them, "Be gone!"
23 And He shall give the rain for your seed
with which you sow the ground, and bread
of the increase of the earth. And it shall be
fat and rich, your cattle grazing in an
enlarged pasture in that day,
24 and the oxen and the young donkeys
that work the ground eat seasoned fodder
winnowed with shovel and fan.
25 And on every high mountain and on
every high hill there shall be rivers and
streams of waters, in the day of great
killing, when the towers fall.
26 And the light of the moon shall be as
the light of the sun, and the light of the sun
be sevenfold, as the light of seven days, in
the day that יהוה binds up the breach of
His people, and heals the wound of His
blows.
27 See, the Name of יהוה is coming from
afar, burning with His wrath, and heavy
smoke. His lips shall be filled with rage,
and His tongue be as a devouring fire;
28 and His breath shall be as an overflowing stream, which reaches up to the neck,
to sift [c] the nations with a sieve of falsehood, and a misleading bridle on the jaws
of the peoples.
29 Let the song be to you as in a night set
apart for a festival, and gladness of heart as
he who is going with a flute, to come into
the mountain of יהוה, to the Rock of
Yisra'ĕl.
30 And יהוה shall cause His excellent
voice to be heard, and show the coming
down of His arm, with raging wrath and
the flame of a consuming fire, with scattering, downpour and hailstones.
31 For through the voice of יהוה Ashshur
is broken down, with a rod He strikes.
32 And every passage of the ordained staff
which יהוה lays on him, shall be with tambourines and lyres, when He shall fight
with it, battling with a brandishing arm.
33 For Topheth was ordained of old, even
for the sovereign it has been prepared. He
has made it deep and large, its fire pit with
much wood; the breath of יהוה, as a stream
of burning sulphur, is burning in it!

31 Woe to those who go down to
Mitsrayim for help, and rely on
horses, who trust in chariots because they
are many, and in horsemen because they
are very strong, but who do not look to the
Set-apart One of Yisra'ĕl, nor seek יהוה!
2 And He also is wise, and has brought
evil, and has not turned aside His words.
And He shall rise up against the house of
evil-doers, and against the help of workers
of wickedness.
3 And the Mitsrites are men, and not Ěl.
And their horses are flesh, and not spirit.
And when יהוה stretches out His hand,
both he who helps shall stumble, and he
who is helped shall fall. And they shall all
fall, together.
4 For this is what יהוה has said to me,
"As a lion roars, and a young lion over his
prey, though a band of shepherds is called
out against him, he is not afraid of their
voice nor disturbed by their noise, so יהוה
of hosts shall come down to fight upon
Mount Tsiyon and upon its hill.
5 "Like hovering birds, so does יהוה of
hosts protect Yerushalayim – protecting
and delivering, passing over and rescuing."
6 Turn back to Him from whom the children of Yisra'ĕl have deeply fallen away.

30a Or *teachers*. *30b* Or *teachers*. See also Yo'ĕl 2:23. *30c* Amos 9:9.

7 For in that day, let each man reject his
idols of silver and his idols of gold, which
your own hands have made for yourselves,
as a sin.
8 "And Ashshur shall fall by a sword not
of man, and a sword not of mankind shall
devour him. But he shall flee from the
sword, and his young men shall become
slave labour,
9 and his strength pass away because of
fear, and his commanders shall be afraid of
the banner," declares יהוה, whose light is
in Tsiyon and whose furnace is in Yerushalayim.

32 See, a sovereign shall reign in
righteousness, and rulers rule in
right-ruling.
2 And each one shall be as a hiding place
from the wind, and a shelter from the
downpour, as rivers of water in a dry place,
as the shadow of a great rock in a weary
land.
3 And the eyes of those who see are not
dim, and the ears of those who hear listen.
4 And the heart of the rash understand
knowledge, and the tongue of the stam-
merers hurries to speak plainly.
5 A fool is no longer called noble, nor the
scoundrel said to be respectable;
6 for a fool speaks folly, and his heart
works wickedness: to practise filthiness,
and to speak against יהוה that which misleads, to starve the being of the hungry,
and to withhold the drink from the thirsty.
7 And the methods of the scoundrel are
evil – he has devised wicked plans to
destroy the poor with words of falsehood,
even when the needy pleads for right-
ruling.
8 But the generous one devises what is
generous, and by generous deeds he rises
up.
9 Rise up, you women who are at ease,
hear my voice; *rise up* you complacent
daughters, listen to my speech.
10 In little more than a year you shall be
troubled, you complacent women; for the
grape harvest shall fail, the ingathering
shall not come.
11 Tremble, you women who are at ease;
be troubled, you complacent ones; strip
yourselves, make yourselves bare, and gird
sackcloth on your waists.
12 Lament upon the breasts for the pleasant fields, for the fruit-bearing vine.
13 Weeds and thornbushes come up over
the ground of My people, indeed, over all
the houses of joy, the city of revelry;
14 for the palace is abandoned, the crowd-
ed city deserted. Hill and watchtower serve
as caves forever, a joy of wild donkeys, a
pasture of flocks;
15 until the Spirit is poured upon us from
on high, and the wilderness shall become
garden-land, and the garden-land be reckoned as a forest.
16 Then right-ruling shall dwell in the
wilderness, and righteousness remain in
the garden-land.
17 The work of righteousness shall be
peace, and the service of righteousness be
rest and safety forever.
18 And My people shall dwell in a home
of peace, and in safe dwellings, and in
undisturbed resting places,
19 even when hail shall fall, felling the
forest, and the city be brought low in
humiliation.
20 Blessed are you who sow beside all
waters, who send out the foot of the ox and
the donkey.

33 Woe to you ravager, while you
have not been ravaged, and you
treacherous, while they have not betrayed
you! When you have ceased ravaging, you
shall be ravaged. And when you stop
betraying, they shall betray you.
2 O יהוה, show us favour, for we have
waited for You. Be their arm every morning, our deliverance also in time of
distress.
3 At the noise of the rumbling the people
shall flee. When You lift Yourself up, the
nations shall be scattered.
4 And Your plunder shall be gathered like
the gathering of the caterpillar; as locusts
rush about, they rush upon them.
5 יהוה is exalted, for He dwells on high;
He has filled Tsiyon with right-ruling and
righteousness.

6 And He shall be the trustworthiness of your times, a wealth of deliverance, wisdom and knowledge. The fear of יהוה – that is His treasure.

7 See, their brave ones shall cry outside, the messengers of peace weep bitterly.

8 The highways shall be deserted, the wayfaring man shall have ceased. He has broken the covenant, he has despised the cities, he respected no man.

9 The earth shall mourn and languish, Leḇanon shall be ashamed. Sharon shall be withered like a desert, and Bashan and Karmel be shaking.

10 "Now I rise up," declares יהוה. "Now I am exalted, now I am lifted up.

11 "You conceive chaff, you bring forth stubble, your spirit devours you like fire.

12 "And peoples shall be like the burnings of lime, like thorns cut up they are burned in the fire.

13 "You who are afar off, hear what I shall do; and you who are near, know My might."

14 Sinners in Tsiyon shall be afraid; trembling shall grip the defiled ones, "Who of us shall dwell with the devouring fire? Who of us shall dwell with everlasting burnings?"

15 He who walks righteously and speaks what is straight, he who rejects the gain of oppressions, who keeps his hands from accepting bribes, who stops his ears from hearing of bloodshed, and shuts his eyes from seeing evil –

16 he shall inhabit the heights; strongholds of rocks be his refuge. His bread shall be given him, his water be steadfast.

17 Your eyes shall see the Sovereign in His comeliness, see a land that is far off.

18 Your heart ponders fear, "Where is the scribe? Where is he who weighs? Where is he who counts the towers?"

19 No longer shall you see a fierce people, a people of too deep a lip to hear, of a jabbering tongue no one understands.

20 See Tsiyon, the city of our appointed time; your eyes shall see Yerushalayim, an undisturbed home, a tent not taken down. Its stakes are never removed, nor any of its cords broken.

21 But there, great is יהוה for us; a place of broad rivers, streams, in which no boat with oars sails, nor big ships pass by –

22 for יהוה is our Judge, יהוה is our Inscriber, יהוה is our Sovereign, He saves us –

23 your ropes shall be slack, they do not strengthen their mast, they shall not spread the sail. Then the prey of great plunder shall be divided, the lame shall take the prey.

24 Neither shall the inhabitant say, "I am sick." The people who dwell in it is forgiven their crookedness!

34 Come near, you nations, to hear. And listen, you people! Let the earth hear, and all that is in it, the world and all its offspring.

2 For the displeasure of יהוה is against all the nations,[a] and His wrath against all their divisions. He shall put them under the ban, He shall give them over to the slaughter,

3 and their slain be thrown out, and their stench rise from their corpses. And mountains shall be melted with their blood.

4 And all the host of the heavens shall rot away. And the heavens shall be rolled up like a scroll, and all their host fade like a leaf fading on the vine, and like the fading one of a fig tree.

5 "For My sword shall be drenched in the heavens. Look, it comes down on Eḏom, and on the people of My curse, for judgment.

6 "The sword of יהוה shall be filled with blood, it shall be made overflowing with fatness, and with the blood of lambs and goats, with the fat of the kidneys of rams. For יהוה has a slaughtering in Botsrah, and a great slaughter in the land of Eḏom.

7 "And wild oxen shall come down with them, and young bulls with bulls. And their land shall be drenched with blood, and their dust made fat with fatness."

8 For it is the day of the vengeance of

34a See footnote Yirm. 30:11.

יהוה', the year of recompense for the cause
of Tsiyon.
9 And its streams shall be turned into tar,
and its dust into sulphur, and its land shall
become burning tar,
10 that is not quenched night or day, its
smoke going up forever. From generation
to generation it lies waste, no one passes
through it forever and ever,
11 so that the pelican and the porcupine
possess it, also the owl and the raven dwell
in it. And He shall stretch out over it the
line of formlessness and stones of emptiness.
12 Its caves, with no one in them, is called
a reign, but all its rulers have vanished.
13 And thorns shall come up in its palaces,
nettles and brambles in its strongholds.
And it shall be a home for jackals, a courtyard for ostriches.
14 And the wild beasts of the desert shall
also meet with the jackals, and the shaggy
goat call to its companion. The night creature shall also settle there, and shall find
for herself a place of rest.
15 The arrow snake shall nest there, and
lay eggs and hatch, and gather them under
her shadow. There too the vultures shall
gather, each with its mate.
16 Search from the book of יהוה', and
read: not one of these shall be missing, not
one shall be without a mate, for He has
commanded my mouth. And His Spirit
shall gather them.
17 And He shall cast the lot for them, and
His hand shall divide it among them with a
measuring line – they possess it forever,
from generation to generation they dwell
in it.

35 Let the wilderness and the dry
place be glad for them, and let the
desert rejoice, and blossom as the rose.
2 It blossoms much and rejoices, even
with joy and singing. The esteem of
Leḇanon shall be given to it, the excellence
of Karmel and Sharon. They shall see
the esteem of יהוה', the excellency of our
Elohim.
3 Strengthen the weak hands, and make
firm the weak knees.
4 Say to those with anxious heart, "Be
strong, do not fear! See, your Elohim
comes with vengeance, with the recompense of Elohim. He is coming to save
you."
5 Then the eyes of the blind shall be
opened, and the ears of the deaf be opened.
6 Then the lame shall leap like a deer,
and the tongue of the dumb sing, because
waters shall burst forth in the wilderness,
and streams in the desert.
7 And the parched ground shall become a
pool, and the thirsty land springs of water
– in the home for jackals, where each lay,
grass with reeds and rushes.
8 And there shall be a highway, and a
way, and it shall be called "The Way of
Set-apartness."[a] The unclean does not pass
over it, but it is for those who walk the
way, and no fools wander *on it.*
9 No lion is there, nor any ravenous beast
go up on it, it is not found there. But the
redeemed shall walk there.
10 And the ransomed of יהוה' shall return
and enter Tsiyon with singing, with everlasting joy on their heads. They shall
obtain joy and gladness, and sorrow and
sighing shall flee away.

36 And it came to be in the fourteenth
year of Sovereign Ḥizqiyahu that
Sanḥěriḇ sovereign of Ashshur came up
against all the walled cities of Yehuḏah
and took them.
2 And the sovereign of Ashshur sent the
Raḇshaqěh with a great army from Laḵish
to Sovereign Ḥizqiyahu at Yerushalayim.
And he stood by the channel of the upper
pool, on the highway to the Launderer's
Field.
3 And there came to him Elyaqim son of
Ḥilqiyahu, who was over the household,
and Sheḇnah the scribe, and Yo'aḥ son of
Asaph, the recorder.
4 The Raḇshaqěh then said to them,
"Please say to Ḥizqiyahu, 'Thus said the
great sovereign, the sovereign of Ashshur,

35a Teh. 77:13.

"What trust is this in which you trust?
5 "I say: You speak of having counsel and strength for battle, but they are vain words. Now in whom do you trust, that you have rebelled against me?
6 "Look! You are trusting in the staff of this broken reed, Mitsrayim, on which if a man leans, it shall go into his hand and pierce it. So is Pharaoh the sovereign of Mitsrayim to all who trust in him.
7 "But if you say to me, 'We trust in יהוה' our Elohim,' is it not He whose high places and whose slaughter-places Ḥizqiyahu has taken away, and has said to Yehuḏah and to Yerushalayim, 'Bow yourselves before this slaughter-place'?
8 "And now, I urge you, please give a pledge to my master the sovereign of Ashshur, and I give you two thousand horses, if you are able on your part to put riders on them!
9 "And how do you refuse one officer of the least of my master's servants, and put your trust in Mitsrayim for chariots and horsemen?
10 "And now, have I come up without יהוה' against this land to destroy it? יהוה' said to me, 'Go up against this land, and destroy it.' "
11 And Elyaqim, Sheḇnah, and Yo'aḥ said to the Raḇshaqĕh, "Please speak to your servants in Aramaic, for we understand it. And do not speak to us in the language of Yehuḏah in the hearing of the people who are on the wall."
12 But the Raḇshaqĕh said, "Has my master sent me to your master and to you to speak these words, and not to the men who sit on the wall, to eat their own dung and drink their own urine with you?"
13 And the Raḇshaqĕh stood and called out with a loud voice in the language of Yehuḏah, and said, "Hear the words of the great sovereign, the sovereign of Ashshur!
14 "Thus said the sovereign, 'Do not let Ḥizqiyahu deceive you, for he is unable to deliver you,
15 and do not let Ḥizqiyahu make you trust in יהוה', saying, "יהוה' shall certainly deliver us, this city is not given into the hand of the sovereign of Ashshur." '
16 "Do not listen to Ḥizqiyahu, for thus said the sovereign of Ashshur, 'Make peace with me by a present and come out to me. And let each of you eat from his own vine and each from his own fig tree, and each of you drink the waters of his own cistern,
17 until I come. Then I shall take you away to a land like your own land, a land of grain and new wine, a land of bread and vineyards.
18 'Beware lest Ḥizqiyahu mislead you, saying, "יהוה' shall deliver us." Has any one of the mighty ones of the nations delivered its land from the hand of the sovereign of Ashshur?
19 'Where are the mighty ones of Ḥamath and Arpaḏ? Where are the mighty ones of Sepharwayim? And when have they delivered Shomeron from my hand?
20 'Who among all the mighty ones of these lands have delivered their land from my hand, that יהוה' should deliver Yerushalayim from my hand?' "
21 But they were silent and answered him not a word, for the command of the sovereign was, "Do not answer him."
22 And Elyaqim son of Ḥilqiyahu, who was over the household, Sheḇnah the scribe, and Yo'aḥ son of Asaph, the recorder, came to Ḥizqiyahu with their garments torn, and they reported to him the words of the Raḇshaqĕh.

37 And it came to be, when Sovereign Ḥizqiyahu heard it, that he tore his clothes, and covered himself with sackcloth, and went into the House of יהוה',
2 and sent Elyaqim, who was over the household, and Sheḇnah the scribe, and the elders of the priests, covering themselves with sackcloth, to Yeshayahu the prophet, the son of Amots.
3 And they said to him, "Thus said Ḥizqiyahu, 'This day is a day of distress and rebuke and scorn, for the children have come to birth, but there is no strength to bring forth.
4 'It could be that יהוה' your Elohim does hear the words of the Raḇshaqĕh, whom his master the sovereign of Ashshur has

sent to reproach the living Elohim, and
shall rebuke the words which יהוה your
Elohim has heard. Therefore lift up your
prayer for the remnant that is left.' "
5 So the servants of Sovereign Ḥizqiyahu
came to Yeshayahu,
6 and Yeshayahu said to them, "Say this
to your master, 'Thus said יהוה, "Do not
be afraid of the words which you have
heard, with which the servants of the
sovereign of Ashshur have reviled Me.
7 "See, I am putting a spirit in him, and
he shall hear a report and return to his own
land. And I shall cause him to fall by the
sword in his own land." ' "
8 And the Raḇshaqěh returned and found
the sovereign of Ashshur fighting against
Liḇnah, for he had heard that he had left
Laḵish.
9 And he heard concerning Tirhaqah sovereign of Kush, "He has come out to fight
with you." And when he heard it, he sent
messengers to Ḥizqiyahu, saying,
10 "Speak to Ḥizqiyahu the sovereign of
Yehuḏah, saying, 'Do not let your Elohim
in whom you trust deceive you, saying,
"Yerushalayim is not given into the hand
of the sovereign of Ashshur."
11 'See, you have heard what the sovereigns of Ashshur have done to all lands by
putting them under the ban. And are you
going to be delivered?
12 'Have the mighty ones of the nations
delivered those whom my fathers have
destroyed, Gozan and Ḥaran and Retseph,
and the sons of Ěḏen who were in
Telassar?
13 'Where is the sovereign of Ḥamath, and
the sovereign of Arpaḏ, and the sovereign
of the city of Sepharwayim, Hěna, and
Iwwah?' "
14 And Ḥizqiyahu received the letter from
the hand of the messengers, and read it.
And Ḥizqiyahu went up to the House of
יהוה, and spread it before יהוה.
15 And Ḥizqiyahu prayed to יהוה, saying,
16 "O יהוה of hosts, Elohim of Yisra'ěl,
the One who dwells between the keruḇim,
You are Elohim, You alone, of all the
reigns of the earth. You have made the
heavens and earth.
17 "Incline Your ear, O יהוה, and hear.
Open Your eyes, O יהוה, and see. And
hear all the words of Sanḥěriḇ, who has
sent to reproach the living Elohim.
18 "Truly, יהוה, the sovereigns of Ashshur
have laid waste all the lands, and their
land,
19 and have put their mighty ones into the
fire, for they were not mighty ones, but the
work of men's hands, wood and stone.
And they destroyed them.
20 "And now, O יהוה our Elohim, save us
from his hand, so that all the reigns of the
earth know that You are יהוה, You alone."
21 Then Yeshayahu son of Amots sent to
Ḥizqiyahu, saying, "Thus said יהוה
Elohim of Yisra'ěl, 'Because you have
prayed to Me against Sanḥěriḇ sovereign
of Ashshur,
22 this is the word which יהוה has spoken
concerning him, "The maiden, the daughter of Tsiyon, has despised you, mocked
you; the daughter of Yerushalayim has
shaken her head behind you!
23 "Whom have you reproached and
reviled? And against whom have you
raised your voice, and lifted up your eyes
in pride? Against the Set-apart One of
Yisra'ěl!
24 "By the hand of your servants you have
reproached יהוה, and said, 'With my many
chariots I have come up to the height of the
mountains, to the limits of Leḇanon. And I
cut down its tall cedars and its choice
cypress trees. And I enter its farthest
height, its thickest forest.
25 'I have dug and drunk water, and with
the soles of my feet I have dried up all the
streams of defence.'
26 "Have you not heard long ago how I
made it, from days of old, that I formed it?
Now I have brought it about, that you
should be for crushing walled cities into
heaps of ruins.
27 "And their inhabitants were powerless,
they were overthrown and put to shame.
They were as the grass of the field and as
the green plant, as the grass on the house-
tops and as grain blighted before it is
grown.
28 "But I know your sitting down, and

your going out and your coming in, and
your rage against Me.
29 "Because your rage against Me and
your pride have come up to My ears, I
shall put My hook in your nose and My
bridle in your lips, and I shall turn you
back by the way which you came.
30 "And this shall be the sign for you: This
year you eat such as grows of itself, and
the second year what springs from that,
and in the third year sow and reap, plant
vineyards, and eat the fruit of them.
31 "And the remnant who have escaped of
the house of Yehuḏah shall again take root
downward, and be fruitful upward.
32 "For out of Yerushalayim comes forth
a remnant, and those who escape from
Mount Tsiyon – the ardour of יהוה of hosts
does this.
33 "Therefore thus said יהוה concerning
the sovereign of Ashshur, 'He does not
come into this city, nor does he shoot an
arrow there, nor does he come before it
with shield, nor does he build a siege
mound against it.
34 'By the way that he came, by the same
he turns back. And into this city he does
not come,' declares יהוה.
35 'And I shall defend this city, to save it
for My own sake and for the sake of My
servant Dawiḏ.' "
36 And a messenger of יהוה went out, and
struck in the camp of Ashshur one hundred
and eighty-five thousand. And they arose
early in the morning, and saw all of them,
dead bodies.
37 And Sanḥěriḇ the sovereign of Ashshur
broke camp and went away, and turned
back, and remained at Nineweh.
38 And it came to be, as he was bowing
himself in the house of Nisroḵ his mighty
one, that his sons Aḏrammeleḵ and
Shar'etser struck him with the sword, and
they escaped into the land of Ararat. And
his son Ěsarḥaddon reigned in his place.

38 In those days Ḥizqiyahu was sick
and near death. And Yeshayahu the
prophet, the son of Amots, came to him,
and said to him, "Thus said יהוה,
'Command your house, for you are going
to die and not live.' "
2 And Ḥizqiyahu turned his face toward
the wall, and prayed to יהוה,
3 and said, "I pray, O יהוה, please
remember how I have walked before You
in truth and with a perfect heart, and have
done what is good in Your eyes." And
Ḥizqiyahu wept bitterly.
4 And the word of יהוה came to Yeshayahu, saying,
5 "Go and say to Ḥizqiyahu, 'Thus said
יהוה, the Elohim of Dawiḏ your father, "I
have heard your prayer, I have seen your
tears. See, I am adding fifteen years to
your days.
6 "And out of the hand of the sovereign
of Ashshur I shall deliver you and this city,
and protect this city." '
7 "And this is the sign to you from יהוה,
that יהוה does this word which He has
spoken:
8 "See, I am bringing the shadow on the
sundial, which has gone down with the sun
on the sundial of Aḥaz, ten degrees backward." And the sun returned ten degrees
on the dial by which it had gone down.
9 This is the writing of Ḥizqiyahu sovereign of Yehuḏah, when he had been sick
and had recovered from his sickness:
10 I said, "Am I to go into the gates of
She'ol in the prime of my life? Shall I be
deprived of the rest of my years?"
11 I said, "I shall not see Yah – Yah in the
land of the living! I shall no longer look on
man with the inhabitants of the world!
12 "My dwelling is plucked up, taken
from me like a shepherd's tent. I have cut
off my life like a weaver; He cuts me off
from the loom. From day to night You
make an end of me.
13 "I soothed myself until morning. Like a
lion, so He shatters all my bones. From day
to night You make an end of me.
14 "Like a swallow or a thrush, so I chat-
tered; I moaned like a dove; my eyes look
weakly on high. O יהוה, I am oppressed,
undertake for me!
15 "What do I say? For He has spoken to
me, and He Himself has acted. Softly I go,
all my years, because of the bitterness of
my being.

16 "O יהוה, by these do *men* live, and my
spirit finds life in all of them. Restore me
and make me live.
17 "See, for peace I had what was bitter,
bitter. But You have lovingly delivered my
being from the pit of corruption, for You
have cast all my sins behind Your back.
18 "For She'ol does not thank You, nor
death praise You; those who go down to
the pit do not watch for Your truth.
19 "The living, the living – he is praising
You, as I do this day. A father makes
known Your truth to his children.
20 "יהוה, *come* to save me! And let us
sing my songs with stringed instruments
all the days of our life in the House of
יהוה."
21 For Yeshayahu had said, "Let them take
a cake of figs, and apply it on the boil, so
that he lives."
22 And Ḥizqiyahu asked, "What is the
sign that I go up to the House of יהוה?"

39 At that time Meroḏaḵ-Balaḏan son
of Balaḏan, sovereign of Baḇel,
sent letters and a present to Ḥizqiyahu, for
he heard that he had been sick and had
become strong.
2 And Ḥizqiyahu was pleased with them,
and showed them the house of his treasures, the silver and gold, the spices and
precious ointment, and all his armoury, and
all that was found among his treasures.
There was not an object in his house or in
all his rule that Ḥizqiyahu did not show
them.
3 And Yeshayahu the prophet went to
Sovereign Ḥizqiyahu, and said to him,
"What did these men say, and from where
did they come to you?" And Ḥizqiyahu
said, "They came to me from a distant
land, from Baḇel."
4 And he said, "What have they seen in
your house?" And Ḥizqiyahu said, "They
have seen all that is in my house; there is
not an object among my treasures that I did
not show them."
5 So Yeshayahu said to Ḥizqiyahu, "Hear
the word of יהוה of hosts:
6 'See, the days are coming when all that
is in your house, and what your fathers
have stored up until this day, shall be taken
away to Baḇel; not a matter shall be left,'
declares יהוה.
7 'And they shall take some of your sons
who are born to you, whom you bring
forth. And they shall be eunuchs in the
palace of the sovereign of Baḇel.' "
8 And Ḥizqiyahu said to Yeshayahu,
"The word of יהוה which you have spoken
is good!" And he said, "Because there is
peace and truth in my days."

40 "Comfort, comfort My people!"
says your Elohim.
2 "Speak to the heart of Yerushalayim,
and cry out to her, that her hard service is
completed, that her crookedness is pardoned, that she has received from the hand
of יהוה double for all her sins."
3 The voice of one crying in the wilderness, "Prepare the way of יהוה; make
straight in the desert a highway for our
Elohim.
4 "Let every valley be raised, and every
mountain and hill made low. And the steep
ground shall become level, and the rough
places smooth.
5 "And the esteem of יהוה shall be
revealed, and all flesh together shall see it.
For the mouth of יהוה has spoken."
6 The voice said, "Cry out!" and he said,
"What do I cry?" "All flesh is grass, and
all its loving-commitment is like the
flower of the field.
7 "Grass shall wither, the flower shall
fade, when the Spirit of יהוה has blown on
it! Truly the people is grass!
8 "Grass shall wither, the flower shall
fade, but the Word of our Elohim stands
forever." [a]
9 You who bring good news to Tsiyon,
get up into the high mountain. You who
bring good news to Yerushalayim, lift
up your voice with strength, lift it up,
be not afraid. Say to the cities of Yehuḏah,

40a Kěpha א 1:24-25.

"See your Elohim!"

10 See, the Master יהוה comes with strength, and His arm rules for Him. See, His reward is with Him, and His recompense before Him.

11 He feeds His flock like a shepherd, He gathers the lambs with His arm, and carries them in His bosom, gently leading those who are with young.

12 Who has measured the waters in the hollow of his hand, and measured the heavens with a span, and contained the dust of the earth in a measure, and weighed the mountains in scales and the hills in a balance?

13 Who has meted out the Spirit of יהוה, or as His counsellor taught Him?

14 With whom did He take counsel, and who instructed Him, and taught Him in the path of right-ruling? Who taught Him knowledge, and showed Him the way of understanding?

15 See, nations are as a drop in a bucket, and are reckoned as dust on the balance. See, He lifts up isles as fine dust.

16 And Leḇanon is not enough to burn, nor its beasts enough for an ascending offering.

17 All nations before Him are as a non-entity, and they are reckoned by Him as less than a speck, and emptiness.

18 And to whom would you liken Ěl? And what likeness would you compare to Him?

19 The workman moulds a graven image, and the goldsmith overspreads it with gold, and the silversmith casts silver chains.

20 He who is too poor for such an offering chooses a tree that does not rot. He seeks for himself a skilled craftsman to prepare a carved image that does not totter.

21 Did you not know? Have you not heard? Has it not been declared to you from the beginning? Have you not understood from the foundations of the earth?

22 It is He who sits above the circle of the earth, and its inhabitants are like grasshoppers, who stretches out the heavens like a curtain, and spreads them out like a tent to dwell in,

23 who brings princes to naught, shall make the rulers of the earth as emptiness.

24 Hardly have they been planted, hardly have they been sown, hardly has their stock taken root in the earth, when He shall blow on them and they wither, and a whirlwind take them away like stubble.

25 "And to whom then do you liken Me, or *to whom* am I compared?" says the Set-apart One.

26 Lift up your eyes on high and see. Who has created these? He is bringing out their host by number, He calls them all by name, by the greatness of ability and potent of power, a man is not lacking.

27 Why do you say, O Ya'aqoḇ, and speak, O Yisra'ěl, "My way is hidden from יהוה, and my rights are overlooked by my Elohim"?

28 Did you not know? Have you not heard? The everlasting Elohim, יהוה, the Creator of the ends of the earth, neither faints nor is weary. His understanding is unsearchable.

29 He gives power to the faint, and to those who have no might He increases strength.

30 Even youths shall faint and be weary, and young men stumble and fall,

31 but those who wait on יהוה renew their strength, they raise up the wing like eagles, they run and are not weary, they walk and do not faint.

41

"Be silent before Me, you coastlands, and let peoples renew their power! Let them come near, then let them speak. Let us come together for right-ruling.

2 "Who raised up the righteous one from the east, called him to His foot, gave the nations before him, and made sovereigns submit to him? He gave them as the dust to his sword, as driven stubble to his bow.

3 "He pursued them, passed over in safety, by a path that he had not gone with his feet.

4 "Who has performed and done it, calling the generations from the beginning? 'I, יהוה, am the first, and with the last I am He.' "

5 Coastlands see it and fear, the ends of the earth are afraid – they draw near and

come.
6 Everyone helps his neighbour, and says
to his brother, “Be strong!”
7 And the craftsman strengthens the
goldsmith. He who smooths with the hammer inspires him who strikes the anvil,
saying of the joining, “It is good.” And he
strengthens it with nails, so it does not totter.
8 “But you, Yisra’ĕl, are My servant,
Ya‘aqoḇ, whom I have chosen, the descendants of Aḇraham who loved Me,
9 whom I have strenghtened from the
ends of the earth, and called from its farthest parts, and said to You, ‘You are My
servant, I have chosen you and have not
rejected you.
10 ‘Do not fear, for I am with you. Do not
look around, for I am your Elohim. I shall
fortify you, I shall also help you, I shall
also uphold you with the right hand of My
righteousness.’
11 “See, all those who raged against you
are ashamed and blush, they are as non-
existent. And the men who strive with you
perish.
12 “You seek them but do not find them,
those who struggle with you. Those who
fight you are as non-existent, as naught.
13 “For I, יהוה your Elohim, am strengthening your right hand, saying to you, ‘Do
not fear, I shall help you.’
14 “Do not fear, you worm Ya‘aqoḇ, you
men of Yisra’ĕl! I shall help you,” declares
יהוה and your Redeemer, the Set-apart
One of Yisra’ĕl.
15 “See, I shall make you into a new
threshing sledge with sharp teeth, let you
thresh mountains and beat them small, and
make hills like chaff.
16 “You winnow them, the wind lifts them
up, and the whirlwind scatters them; but
you, you rejoice in יהוה, and boast in the
Set-apart One of Yisra’ĕl.
17 “When the poor and needy seek water,
and there is none, and their tongues have
failed for thirst, I, יהוה, do answer them; I,
the Elohim of Yisra’ĕl, do not forsake
them.
18 “I open rivers on bare hills, and fountains in the midst of valleys; I make a
wilderness become a pool of water, and a
dry land springs of water.
19 “I set in the wilderness cedar, acacia
and myrtle and oil tree; I place in the desert
cypress, pine and box tree together.
20 “So that they see and know, and consider and understand together, that the hand of
יהוה has done this, and the Set-apart One
of Yisra’ĕl has created it.
21 “Present your case,” says יהוה. “Let
your strong *ones* come near,” says the
Sovereign of Ya‘aqoḇ.
22 “Let them draw near and declare to us
what is going to take place; let them
declare the former *events*, what they were,
and we consider them, and know the latter
end of them; or announce to us what is
coming.
23 “Declare the *events* that are going to
come hereafter, and we know that you are
mighty ones; yes, do good or do evil, and
let us be amazed and see it together.
24 “See, you are of naught, and your work
a breath; he who chooses you is an abomination.
25 “I have stirred up one from the north,
and he comes; from the rising of the sun he
calls on My Name. And he comes against
princes as though mortar, as the potter
treads clay.
26 “Who has declared from the beginning,
and we know? and former times, and we
say, ‘He is righteous’? No, no one is
declaring; no, no one is proclaiming; no,
no one is hearing your words.
27 “He who is First *said* to Tsiyon, ‘See,
see them!’ And to Yerushalayim I give one
who brings good news.
28 “And I see that there is no man, and of
these, there is no counsellor, who, when I
ask of them, answers a word.
29 “See, all of them are useless, their
works are naught, their moulded images
are wind and confusion.

42 “See, My Servant whom I uphold,
My Chosen One My being has
delighted in! I have put My Spirit upon
Him; He brings forth right-ruling to the
nations.
2 “He does not cry out, nor lifts up *His*

voice, nor causes His voice to be heard in
the street.
3"A crushed reed He does not break, and
smoking flax He does not quench. He
brings forth right-ruling in accordance
with truth.
4"He does not become weak or crushed,
until He has established right-ruling in the
earth. And the coastlands wait for His
Torah."
5Thus said the Ěl, יהוה, who created the
heavens and stretched them out, who
spread forth the earth and that which
comes from it, who gives breath to the
people on it, and spirit to those who walk
on it:
6"I, יהוה, have called You in righteousness, and I strengthen[a] Your hand and
guard You, and give You for a covenant to
a people, for a light to the nations,
7to open blind eyes, to bring out prisoners from the prison, those who sit in darkness from the prison house.
8"I am יהוה, that is My Name, and My
esteem I do not give to another, nor My
praise to idols.
9"See, the former *predictions* have
come, and new ones I am declaring; before
they spring forth I let you hear them."
10Sing to יהוה a new song; His praise
from the ends of the earth, you who go
down to the sea, and all that is in it, you
coastlands and you inhabitants of them!
11Let the wilderness and its cities lift up
their voice, the villages where Qěḏar
dwells. Let the inhabitants of Sela sing, let
them shout from the top of the mountains.
12Let them give esteem to יהוה, and
declare His praise in the coastlands.
13יהוה goes forth like a mighty man. He
stirs up ardour like a fighter. He cries out,
yes, shout aloud. Over His enemies He
shows Himself mighty.
14"I have kept silent from of old, I have
been still and held Myself back. Like a
woman in labour I *now* cry out, I pant and
gasp at once.
15"I lay waste mountains and hills, and I
dry up all their plants. And I shall make
rivers become coastlands, and I dry up
pools.
16"And I shall lead the blind by a way
they have not known – in paths they have
not known I lead them. I make darkness
light before them, and crooked places
straight. These matters I shall do for them,
and I shall not forsake them.
17"Those who trust in idols, who say to
the moulded images, 'You are our mighty
ones,' shall be turned back, utterly
ashamed.
18"Hear, you deaf! And look, you blind,
and see.
19"Who is blind but My servant, or deaf
as My messenger whom I send? Who is
blind as he who is at peace, and blind as
servant of יהוה?
20"You see much, but do not guard; ears
are open, but do not hear."
21It has delighted יהוה, for the sake of
His righteousness, to make the Torah great
and esteemed.
22But this is a people robbed and plundered, all of them are snared in holes, and
they are hidden in prison houses. They
have become a prey, with no one to deliver
– for plunder, and no one to say, "Restore!"
23Who among you gives ear to this, pays
attention and hears for the time to come?
24Who gave Ya'aqoḇ for plunder, and
Yisra'ěl to the robbers? Was it not יהוה,
He against whom we sinned? For they
would not walk in His ways, and they did
not obey His Torah!
25So He has poured on him His burning
displeasure and the strength of battle, and
it set him on fire all around, yet he did not
understand. And it burned against him,
yet he did not take it to heart!

43

But now, thus said יהוה, your
Creator, O Ya'aqoḇ, and He who
formed you, O Yisra'ěl, "Do not fear, for I
have redeemed you. I have called you by
your name, you are Mine.
2"When you pass through the waters, I
am with you; and through rivers, they do
not overflow you. When you walk through

42a Commonly understood as "take hold of."

fire, you are not scorched, and a flame does not burn you.

3 "For I am יהוה your Elohim, the Set-apart One of Yisra'ěl, your Saviour; I gave Mitsrayim for your ransom, Kush and Seḇa in your place.

4 "Since you were precious in My eyes, you have been esteemed, and I have loved you. And I give men in your place, and peoples for your life.

5 "Do not fear, for I am with you. I shall bring your seed from the east, and gather you from the west.

6 "I shall say to the north, 'Give them up!' And to the south, 'Do not keep them back!' Bring My sons from afar, and My daughters from the ends of the earth –

7 all those who are called by My Name, whom I have created, formed, even made for My esteem."

8 He shall bring out a blind people who have eyes, and deaf ones who have ears.

9 All the nations shall be assembled, and the peoples be gathered. Who among them declares this, and show us former *events*? Let them give their witnesses, to be declared right; or let them hear and say, "It is truth."

10 "You are My witnesses," declares יהוה, "And My servant whom I have chosen, so that you know and believe Me, and understand that I am He. Before Me there was no Ěl formed, nor after Me there is none.

11 "I, I am יהוה, and besides Me there is no saviour.

12 "I, I have declared and saved, and made known, and there was no foreign mighty one among you. And you are My witnesses," declares יהוה, "that I am Ěl.

13 "Even from the day I am He, and no one delivers out of My hand. I work, and who turns it back?"

14 Thus said יהוה, your Redeemer, the Set-apart One of Yisra'ěl, "For your sake I shall send to Baḇel, and bring them all down as fugitives, even the Kasdim, who rejoice in their ships.

15 "I am יהוה, your Set-apart One, Creator of Yisra'ěl, your Sovereign."

16 Thus said יהוה, who makes a way in the sea and a path through the mighty waters,

17 who brings forth the chariot and horse, the army and the power (they lie down together, they do not rise, they have been extinguished, they have been quenched like a wick):

18 "Do not remember the former *events*, nor consider the *events* of old.

19 "See, I am doing what is new, let it now spring forth. Do you not know it? I am even making a way in the wilderness and rivers in the desert.

20 "The beast of the field esteems Me, the jackals and the ostriches, because I have given waters in the wilderness and rivers in the desert, to give drink to My people, My chosen,

21 this people I have formed for Myself, let them relate My praise.

22 "But you have not called on Me, O Ya'aqoḇ, for you have been weary of Me, O Yisra'ěl.

23 "You have not brought Me the sheep for your ascending offerings, nor have you esteemed Me with your slaughterings. I have not caused you to serve with grain offerings, nor wearied you with incense.

24 "You have not bought Me sweet cane with silver, nor have you satisfied Me with the fat of your slaughterings. You have only burdened Me with your sins, you have wearied Me with your crookednesses.

25 "I, I am He who blots out your transgressions for My own sake, and remember your sins no more.

26 "Remind Me, let us enter into judgment, together; relate, that you might be declared right.

27 "Your first father sinned, and your interpreters have transgressed against Me.

28 "So I have profaned the chief ones of the set-apart place, and I have delivered up Ya'aqoḇ to the curse, and Yisra'ěl to scorn.

44

"But now hear, O Ya'aqoḇ My servant, and Yisra'ěl whom I have chosen.

2 Thus said יהוה who made you and formed you from the womb, who helps you, 'Do not fear, O Yaʽaqoḇ My servant, and Yeshurun,[a] whom I have chosen.

3 'For I pour water on the thirsty, and floods on the dry ground. I pour My Spirit on your seed, and My blessing on your offspring,

4 and they shall spring up among the grass like willows by streams of water.'

5 "One says, 'I belong to יהוה'; another calls himself by the name of Yaʽaqoḇ; another writes with his hand, 'Unto יהוה,' and names himself by the name of Yisra'ĕl.

6 "Thus said יהוה, Sovereign of Yisra'ĕl, and his Redeemer, יהוה of hosts, 'I am the First and I am the Last, besides Me there is no Elohim.

7 'And who is like Me? Let him call and declare it, and lay it before Me, since I appointed the everlasting people. And the events that are coming and those that do come, let them declare these to them.

8 'Do not fear, nor be afraid. Have I not since made you hear, and declared it? You are My witnesses. Is there an Eloah besides Me? There is no other Rock, I know not one.' "

9 Those who make an idol, all of them are emptiness, and their delights do not profit. And they are their own witnesses; they neither see nor know, so that they are put to shame.

10 Who would form a mighty one or cast an idol that is of no value?

11 See, all his companions are ashamed, and the workmen, they are but men. Let them all be gathered together, let them stand up, let them fear, let them be put to shame, altogether.

12 The craftsman in iron with the tools works one in the coals, and fashions it with hammers, and works it with the strength of his arms. Even so, he shall be hungry, and has no strength; he drinks no water and is weary.

13 The carpenter stretches out his rule, he outlines it with chalk; he fashions it with a plane, and he outlines it with the compass, and makes it like the figure of a man, according to the comeliness of a man, to remain in the house.

14 He cuts down cedars for himself, and takes cypress and oak, which he raised among the trees of the forest. He has planted a pine, and the rain nourishes it.

15 And it shall be for a man to burn, for he takes some of it and warms himself. He also kindles it and shall bake bread. He also makes a mighty one and bows himself to it – has made it a carved image and falls down before it.

16 Half of it he shall burn in the fire; with this half he eats meat. He roasts a roast, and is satisfied. He also warms himself and says, "Aha, I am warm, I have seen the fire."

17 And the rest of it he makes into a mighty one, his carved image. He falls down before it and worships, prays to it and says, "Deliver me, for you are my mighty one."

18 They do not know nor understand, for He has smeared their eyes from seeing, and their hearts from understanding.

19 And no one recalls it to his heart, nor is there knowledge nor understanding to say, "I have burned half of it in the fire, and I have also baked bread on its coals; I have roasted meat and eaten it. And shall I make the rest of it an abomination? Should I fall down before a log of wood?"

20 Feeding on ashes, a deceived heart turns him aside, and he does not deliver his being, nor says, "Is there not a lie in my right hand?"

21 "Remember these *matters*, O Yaʽaqoḇ, and Yisra'ĕl, for you are My servant! I have formed you, you are My servant, O Yisra'ĕl, do not forget Me!

22 "I shall wipe out your transgressions like a cloud, and your sins like a mist. Return to Me, for I shall redeem you."

23 Sing, O heavens, for יהוה shall do it! Shout, O depths of the earth! Break forth into singing, O mountains, forest, and

44a A poetical title for Yisra'ĕl, meaning the *Straight One* or the *Upright One*. This poetical title is also found in Deḇ. 32:15, 33:5 & 33:26.

every tree in it! For יהוה shall redeem
Ya'aqoḇ, and make Himself clear in
Yisra'ĕl.
24 Thus said יהוה, your Redeemer, and He
who formed you from the womb, "I am
יהוה, doing all, stretching out the heavens
all alone, spreading out the earth, with
none beside Me,
25 frustrating the signs of the babblers,
and driving diviners mad, turning wise
men backward, and making their knowledge foolish,
26 confirming the word of His servant,
and completing the counsel of His messengers, who says of Yerushalayim, 'Be
inhabited,' and of the cities of Yehuḏah,
'They shall be built, and her ruins raised
up by Me,'
27 who is saying to the deep, 'Be dry, and
your rivers I dry up,'
28 who is saying of Koresh, 'He is My
shepherd, and he completes all My pleasure, even saying to Yerushalayim, "Let
her be built," and to the Hěḵal, "Let her
foundation be laid." '

45 "Thus said יהוה to His anointed, to
Koresh, whose right hand I have
strengthened, to subdue nations before him
and ungird the loins of sovereigns, to open
before him the double doors, so that gates
are not shut:
2 'I go before you and make the crooked
places straight; I shatter the gates of bronze
and cut down the bars of iron.
3 'And I shall give you the treasures of
darkness and hoarded wealth of secret
places, so that you know that I, יהוה, who
are calling you by your name, am the
Elohim of Yisra'ĕl.
4 'For the sake of Ya'aqoḇ My servant,
and of Yisra'ĕl My chosen, I also call you
by your name, I give you a title, though
you have not known Me.
5 'I am יהוה, and there is none else –
there is no Elohim besides Me. I gird you,
though you have not known Me,
6 so that they know from the rising of the
sun to its setting that there is none but Me.
I am יהוה, and there is none else,
7 forming light and creating darkness,
making peace and creating evil. I, יהוה, do
all these.'
8 "Rain down, O heavens, from above,
and let clouds pour down righteousness.
Let the earth open, let them bring forth
deliverance, and let righteousness spring
up together. I, יהוה, have created it.
9 "Woe to him who strives with his
Maker! (a potsherd with the potsherds of
the earth). Does clay say to him who forms
it, 'What are you making?' Or your handi-
work say, 'He has no hands'?
10 "Woe to him who says to his father,
'What are you bringing forth?' Or to the
woman, 'What are you labouring over?' "
11 Thus said יהוה, the Set-apart One of
Yisra'ĕl, and his Maker, "Do you ask Me
about My sons what is to come? And about
the work of My hands do you command
Me?
12 "I have made the earth, and created
man on it. I, My hands have stretched out
the heavens, and all their host I have commanded.
13 "I have stirred him up in righteousness,
and all his ways I make straight. He builds
My city and lets My exiles go, not for price
nor reward," declares יהוה of hosts.
14 Thus said יהוה, "The labour of Mitsrayim and merchandise of Kush and of the
Seḇaites, men of size, come over to you
and they are yours. They walk behind you,
they come over in chains, and they bow
down to you. They make supplication to
you, saying, 'Indeed, Ěl is in you, and
there is none else, no mighty one.' "
15 Truly You are Ěl, who hide Yourself, O
Elohim of Yisra'ĕl, Saviour!
16 They shall be put to shame, and even be
humiliated, all of them – the makers of
idols shall go away together in humiliation.
17 Yisra'ĕl shall be saved by יהוה with an
everlasting deliverance. You are not to be
ashamed nor hurt, forever and ever.
18 For thus said יהוה, Creator of the heavens, He is Elohim, Former of earth and its
Maker, He established it, He did not create
it to be empty, He formed it to be inhabited: "I am יהוה, and there is none else.
19 "I have not spoken in secret, in a dark

place of the earth. I have not said to the
seed of Ya'aqoḇ, 'Seek Me in vain.' I am
יהוה, speaking righteousness, declaring
matters that are straight.
20 "Gather yourselves and come; draw
near together, you who have escaped from
the nations. No knowledge have they who
are lifting up the wood of their carved
image, and pray to a mighty one that does
not save.
21 "Declare and bring near, let them even
take counsel together. Who has announced
this from of old? Who has declared it from
that time? Is it not I, יהוה? And there is no
mighty one besides Me, a righteous Ěl and
a Saviour, there is none besides Me.
22 "Turn to Me and be saved, all you ends
of the earth! For I am Ěl, and there is none
else.
23 "I have sworn by Myself, a word has
gone out of My mouth in righteousness,
and shall not return, so that to Me every
knee shall bow, every tongue swear.
24 "One shall say, 'Only in יהוה do I have
righteousness and strength' – he comes to
Him. And all those displeased with Him
shall be put to shame.
25 "In יהוה all the seed of Yisra'ěl shall be
declared right and boast."

46

Běl has bowed down, Neḇo is
stooping, their idols were on the
beasts and on the cattle. That which is carried is burdensome, a burden to the weary.
2 They have stooped, they have bowed
down together, they were unable to deliver
the burden, but they themselves went into
captivity.
3 "Listen to Me, O house of Ya'aqoḇ, and
all the remnant of the house of Yisra'ěl,
who are borne from the belly, who are carried from the womb:
4 even to your old age, I am He, and even
to grey hairs I carry! I have made and I
bear, and I carry and rescue.
5 "To whom do you liken Me, and compare Me and make Me similar, that we
should be alike?
6 "They pour gold out of the bag, and
weigh silver on the scale. They hire a goldsmith, and he makes it a mighty one. They
fall down, they also bow themselves.
7 "They bear it on the shoulder, they
carry it and set it in its place, and it stands
– from its place it does not move. Though
one cries out to it, it does not answer, nor
save him from his distress.
8 "Remember this, and show yourselves
men; turn it back, you transgressors.
9 "Remember the former *events* of old,
for I am Ěl, and there is no one else –
Elohim, and there is no one like Me,
10 declaring the end from the beginning,
and from of old that which has not *yet* been
done, saying, 'My counsel does stand, and
all My delight I do,'
11 calling a bird of prey from the east, the
man who executes My counsel, from a distant land. Indeed I have spoken it, I also
bring it to pass. I have planned it, I also do
it.
12 "Listen to Me, you stubborn-hearted,
who are far from righteousness:
13 "I shall bring My righteousness near, it
is not far off, and My deliverance, it is not
delayed. And I shall give deliverance in
Tsiyon, My esteem to Yisra'ěl.

47

"Come down and sit in the dust, O
maiden daughter of Baḇel. Sit on
the ground without a throne, O daughter of
the Kasdim! For no more do they call you
tender and delicate.
2 "Take the millstones and grind flour.
Remove your veil, lift up the skirt, uncover
the leg, pass through rivers.
3 "Let your nakedness be uncovered, let
your shame also be exposed. I take
vengeance, and meet no man."
4 Our Redeemer, יהוה of hosts is His
Name, the Set-apart One of Yisra'ěl.
5 "Sit silent, and go into darkness, O
daughter of Kasdim! For no more do they
call you Mistress of Reigns.
6 "I was wroth with My people, I have
profaned My inheritance and I gave them
into your hand. You showed them no compassion, you made your yoke very heavy
on the elderly.
7 "And you said, 'I am mistress forever,'
so that you did not take these *matters* to
heart, and did not remember the latter end

of them.
8 "And now, hear this, you who are given
to pleasures, who dwells complacently,
who says in your heart, 'I am, and there is
none but me. I do not sit as a widow, nor
do I know the loss of children.'
9 "Both of these come to you suddenly,
in one day: the loss of children, and widowhood. They shall come upon you in
completeness, because of your many
witchcrafts, for your numerous great
potent spells.
10 "And you have trusted in your evil, you
have said, 'No one sees me.' Your wisdom
and your knowledge have led you astray.
And you have said in your heart, 'I am, and
there is none but me.'
11 "But evil shall come upon you, you not
knowing from where it arises, and trouble
fall upon you, you being unable to put it
off, and ruin come upon you suddenly,
which you know not.
12 "Stand now with your potent spells and
your many witchcrafts, in which you have
laboured from your youth, if so be you are
able to profit, if so be you find strength.
13 "You are exhausted by your many
counsels; let the astrologers, the stargazers,
and those who prognosticate by the new
moons stand up and save you from what is
coming upon you.
14 "See, they shall be as stubble, fire shall
burn them, they do not deliver themselves
from the power of the flame, there is not a
coal to be warmed by, nor a fire to sit
before it!
15 "So they shall be to you with whom
you have laboured, your merchants from
your youth. They shall wander, each one
his own way, there is none to save you.

48

"Hear this, O house of Ya'aqoḇ,
who are called by the name of
Yisra'ěl, and have come from the waters of
Yehuḏah, who swear by the Name of יהוה,
and profess the Elohim of Yisra'ěl –
though not in truth or in righteousness –
2 for they call themselves after the set-
apart city, and lean on the Elohim of
Yisra'ěl – יהוה of hosts is His Name:
3 "I have declared the former *events* from
the beginning, and they went forth from
My mouth, and I made you hear them.
Suddenly I acted, and they came to be.
4 "Because I knew that you were hard,
and your neck was an iron sinew, and your
forehead bronze,
5 therefore I declared it to you long ago.
Before it came I made you hear, lest you
should say, 'My idol has done them, and
my carved image and my moulded image
commanded them.'
6 "You have heard, look at them all. And
do you not declare it? From now on I shall
make you hear new ones, even hidden
ones, which you have not known.
7 "Now they shall be created and not
long ago. And before this day you have not
heard them, lest you should say, 'Look, I
knew them.'
8 "No, you have not heard; no, you have
not known; no, from of old your ear has
not been open. Because I knew that you
are indeed treacherous, and are called 'a
transgressor from the womb.'
9 "For My Name's sake I postponed My
displeasure, and for My praise I held it
back from you, so as not to cut you off.
10 "See, I have refined you, but not as
silver; I have chosen you in the furnace of
affliction. [a]
11 "For My own sake, for My own sake, I
do it. For how is it profaned? And My
esteem I do not give to another.
12 "Listen to Me, O Ya'aqoḇ, and Yisra'ěl,
My called: I am He, I am the First, I am
also the Last.
13 "Also, My hand has laid the foundation
of the earth, and My right hand has
stretched out the heavens. I call to them, let
them stand together.
14 "All of you, gather yourselves, and
hear! Who among them has declared
these? יהוה has loved him. Let him do His
pleasure on Baḇel, and His arm be on the
Kasdim.
15 "I, I have spoken, I have also called
him, I have brought him, and he shall make

48a See also Deḇ. 8:2-16. Yesh. 48:10.

his way prosperous.
16 "Come near to Me, hear this: I have not
spoken in secret from the beginning; from
the time that it was, I was there. And now
the Master יהוה has sent Me, and His
Spirit."
17 Thus said יהוה, your Redeemer, the
Set-apart One of Yisra'ěl, "I am יהוה your
Elohim, teaching you what is best, leading
you by the way you should go.
18 "If only you had listened to My commands! Then your peace would have been
like a river, and your righteousness like the
waves of the sea.
19 "And your seed would have been like
the sand, and the offspring of your inward
parts like the grains of sand. His name
would not have been cut off nor destroyed
from before Me.
20 "Come out of Baḇel! Flee from the
Kasdim! Declare this with a voice of
singing, proclaim it, send it out to the end
of the earth! Say, 'יהוה has redeemed His
servant Ya'aqoḇ!' "
21 And they did not thirst when He led
them through the deserts; He caused
waters from a rock to flow for them; He
split the rock, and waters gushed out.
22 "There is no peace for the wrong," said
יהוה."

49

Listen to Me, O coastlands, and
hear, you peoples from afar! יהוה
has called Me from the womb, from My
mother's belly He has caused My Name to
be remembered.
2 And He made My mouth like a sharp
sword, in the shadow of His hand He hid
Me, and made Me a polished shaft. In His
quiver He hid Me."
3 And He said to Me, 'You are My servant, O Yisra'ěl, in whom I am adorned.'
4 And I said, 'I have laboured in vain, I
have spent my strength for emptiness, and
in vain. But my right-ruling is with יהוה,
and my work with my Elohim.' "
5 And now said יהוה – who formed Me
from the womb to be His Servant, to bring
Ya'aqoḇ back to Him, though Yisra'ěl is
not gathered to Him, yet I am esteemed in
the eyes of יהוה, and My Elohim has been
My strength –
6 and He says, "Shall it be a small *matter*
for You to be My Servant to raise up the
tribes of Ya'aqoḇ, and to bring back the
preserved ones of Yisra'ěl? And I shall
give You as a light to the nations, to be My
deliverance to the ends of the earth!"
7 Thus said יהוה, the Redeemer of
Yisra'ěl, their Set-apart One, to the
despised , to the loathed One of the nation,
to the Servant of rulers, "Sovereigns shall
see and arise, rulers also shall bow themselves, because of יהוה who is steadfast,
the Set-apart One of Yisra'ěl. And He has
chosen You!"
8 Thus said יהוה, "In a favourable time I
shall answer You, and in the day of deliverance I shall help You – and I guard You
and give You for a covenant of the people,
to restore the earth, to cause them to inherit the ruined inheritances,
9 to say to the prisoners, 'Go out,' to
those who are in darkness, 'Show yourselves.' Let them feed on the ways, and let
their pasture be on all bare hills.
10 "They shall not hunger nor thirst, neither heat or sun strike them, for He who
has compassion on them shall lead them,
even by fountains of water guide them.
11 "And I shall make all My mountains a
way, and My highways raised up.
12 "See, these come from far away, and
see, those from the north and the west, and
these from the land of Sinim."
13 Sing, O heavens, rejoice, O earth! And
break out in singing, O mountains! For
יהוה shall comfort His people and have
compassion on His afflicted ones.
14 But Tsiyon says, "יהוה has forsaken
me, and יהוה has forgotten me."
15 "Would a woman forget her nursing
child, and not have compassion on the son
of her womb? Though they forget, I never
forget you.
16 "See, I have inscribed you on the palms
of My hands; your walls are always before
Me.
17 "Your sons shall hurry, your destroyers
and those who laid you waste depart from
you.
18 "Lift up your eyes round about and see,

all of them gather together and come to
you. As I live," declares יהוה, "you shall
put on all of them as an ornament, and bind
them on you as a bride does.
19 "For your wastes, and your deserted
places, and the land of your destruction,
shall soon be too narrow for the inhabitants, while those who swallowed you up
are far away.
20 "The sons of your bereavement shall
yet say in your ears, 'The place is too narrow for me, make room for me to live.'
21 "And you shall say in your heart, 'Who
has brought forth these for me, since I am
bereaved and barren, an exile, and wandering to and fro? And who reared them? See,
I was left alone – from where did these
come?' "
22 Thus said the Master יהוה, "See, I lift
My hand up to the nations, and set up My
banner for the peoples; and they shall bring
your sons in their arms, and your daughters
carried on their shoulders;
23 "And sovereigns shall be your foster
fathers, and their sovereignesses your
nursing mothers. They bow down to you
with their faces to the earth, and lick up the
dust of your feet. And you shall know that
I am יהוה – those who wait for Me shall
not be ashamed."
24 Is prey taken from the mighty, and the
captives of the righteous delivered?
25 Yet thus said יהוה, "Even the captives
of the mighty are taken away, and the prey
of the ruthless is delivered; and I strive
with him who strives with you, and I save
your children.
26 "And I shall feed those who oppress
you with their own flesh, and let them
drink their own blood as sweet wine. All
flesh shall know that I, יהוה, am your
Saviour, and your Redeemer, the Mighty
One of Ya'aqoḇ."

50 Thus says יהוה, "Where is the certificate of your mother's divorce,
whom I have put away? Or which of My
creditors is it to whom I have sold you?
Look, you were sold for your crookednesses, and your mother was put away for your
transgressions.
2 "When I came, why was there no man?
When I called, why was there no one to
answer? Was My hand too short to ransom? Or have I no power to deliver? See,
by My rebuke I dry up the sea, I make the
rivers a wilderness; their fish stink for
there is not water, and die of thirst.
3 "I clothe the heavens with darkness,
and I make sackcloth their covering."
4 The Master יהוה has given Me the
tongue of taught ones, that I should know
to help the weary with a word. He wakes
Me morning by morning, he wakes My ear
to hear as taught ones.
5 The Master יהוה has opened My ear,
and I was not rebellious, nor did I turn
away.
6 I gave My back to those who struck
Me, and My cheeks to those who plucked
out the beard, I did not hide My face from
humiliation and spitting.
7 And the Master יהוה helps Me, therefore I shall not be humiliated. So I have set
My face like a flint, and I know that I am
not put to shame.
8 Near is He who declares Me right. Who
would contend with Me? Let us stand
together. Who is My adversary? Let him
come near Me.
9 See, the Master יהוה helps Me. Who
would declare Me wrong? See, all of them
wear out like a garment, a moth eats them.
10 Who among you is fearing יהוה, obeying the voice of His Servant, that has
walked in darkness and has no light? Let
him trust in the Name of יהוה and lean
upon his Elohim!
11 See, all you who light a fire, girding on
burning arrows: walk in the light of your
fire and in the burning arrows you have lit.
From My hand you shall have this: you
shall lie down in grief!

51 "Listen to Me, you who pursue
righteousness, seeking יהוה: Look
to the rock you were hewn from, and to the
hole of the pit you were dug from.
2 "Look to Aḇraham your father, and to
Sarah who bore you. For he was alone
when I called him, and I blessed him and
increased him.

3 "For יהוה shall comfort Tsiyon, He
shall comfort all her waste places. For He
makes her wilderness like Ěden, and her
desert like the garden of יהוה. Joy and
gladness are found in it, thanksgiving and
the voice of song.

4 "Listen to Me, My people, and give ear
to Me, O My nation, for the Torah goes
forth from Me, and My right-ruling I set as
a light to peoples.

5 "My righteousness is near, My deliverance shall go forth, and My arms judge
peoples. Coastlands wait upon Me, and for
My arm they wait expectantly.

6 "Lift up your eyes to the heavens, and
look on the earth beneath, for the heavens
shall vanish like smoke, and the earth wear
out like a garment, and those who dwell in
it die as gnats. But My deliverance is forever, and My righteousness is not broken.

7 "Listen to Me, you who know righteousness, a people in whose heart is My
Torah: do not fear the reproach of men, nor
be afraid of their revilings.

8 "For a moth eats them like a garment,
and a worm eats them like wool; but My
righteousness is forever, and My deliverance to all generations."

9 Awake, awake, put on strength, O arm
of יהוה! Awake as in days of old, everlasting generations. Was it not You who cut
Rahab̲ apart, and pierced the Crocodile?

10 Was it not You who dried up the sea,
the waters of the great deep, who made the
depths of the sea a way for the redeemed to
pass over?

11 And let the ransomed of יהוה return.
And they shall come to Tsiyon with
singing, with everlasting joy on their
heads. Let them attain joy and gladness;
sorrow and sighing shall flee away.

12 "I, I am He who comforts you. Who are
you that you should be afraid of man that
dies, and of the son of man who is made
like grass?

13 "And you have forgotten יהוה your
Maker who stretched out the heavens and
laid the foundations of the earth, and you
continually fear, all the day, because of the
rage of the oppressor, as he has prepared to
destroy. And where is the rage of the
oppressor?

14 "Bowed, he hastens to be loosened, that
he should not die in the pit, and that his
bread should not fail.

15 "But I am יהוה your Elohim, stirring up
the sea, and its waves roar. יהוה of hosts is
His Name.

16 "And I have put My Words in your
mouth, and with the shadow of My hand I
have covered you, to plant the heavens and
lay the foundations of the earth, and to say
to Tsiyon, 'You are My people.' "

17 Awake, awake yourself! Rise up, O
Yerushalayim, you who have drunk at the
hand of יהוה the cup of His wrath. You
have drunk the dregs of the cup of reeling,
and drained it out.

18 Of all the sons she bore, she has none to
guide her. And of all the sons she has
brought up, none is strengthening her
hand.

19 Both these are coming upon you – who
is sorry for you?: Ruin and destruction,
scarcity of food and sword. How shall I
comfort you?

20 Your sons have fainted, they lie at the
head of all the streets, like a gazelle in a
net. They are filled with the wrath of יהוה,
the rebuke of your Elohim.

21 Therefore please hear this, you afflicted
and drunk, but not with wine.

22 Thus said your Master, יהוה and your
Elohim, who pleads the cause of His people, "See, I shall take out of your hand the
cup of reeling, the dregs of the cup of My
wrath – never again shall you drink it.

23 "And I shall put it into the hand of
those who afflict you, who have said to
your being, 'Bow down, and we pass over
you.' And you made your back like the
ground, and as the street, to walk over."

52 Awake, awake! Put on your
strength, O Tsiyon, put on your
garments of splendour, O Yerushalayim,
the set-apart city! For no more do the
uncircumcised and the unclean come into
you.

2 Shake yourself from the dust, arise, and
sit down, O Yerushalayim. Loose yourself
from the bonds of your neck, O captive

daughter of Tsiyon!
3 For thus said יהוה, "You have been
sold for naught, and you are redeemed not
with silver."
4 For thus said the Master יהוה, "At first
My people went down into Mitsrayim to
sojourn there, and Ashshur oppressed them
without cause.
5 "And now, what have I here," declares
יהוה, "that My people are taken away for
naught? Those who rule over them make
them wail," declares יהוה, "and My Name
is despised [a] all day continually.
6 "Therefore My people shall know My
Name, in that day, for I am the One who is
speaking. See, it is I."
7 How pleasant upon the mountains are
the feet of him who brings good news, who
proclaims peace, who brings good news,
who proclaims deliverance, who says to
Tsiyon, "Your Elohim reigns!"
8 The voice of your watchmen! They
shall lift up their voices, together they
shout for joy, because eye to eye they see
the return of יהוה to Tsiyon.
9 Break forth into joy, sing together, you
waste places of Yerushalayim! For יהוה
shall comfort His people, He shall redeem
Yerushalayim.
10 יהוה shall lay bare His set-apart arm in
the eyes of all the nations. And all the ends
of the earth shall see the deliverance of our
Elohim.
11 Turn aside! Turn aside! Come out from
there, touch not the unclean. Come out of
her midst, be clean, you who bear the
vessels of יהוה.
12 For you shall not come out in haste, nor
go in flight. For יהוה is going before you,
and the Elohim of Yisra'ěl is your rear
guard.
13 See, My Servant shall work wisely, He
shall be exalted and lifted up and very
high.
14 As many were astonished at You – so
the disfigurement beyond any man's and
His form beyond the sons of men –
15 He shall likewise startle many nations.
Sovereigns shut their mouths at Him, for
what had not been recounted to them they
shall see, and what they had not heard they
shall understand.

53 Who has believed our report? And
to whom was the arm of יהוה
revealed?
2 For He grew up before Him as a tender
plant, and as a root out of dry ground. He
has no form or splendour that we should
look upon Him, nor appearance that we
should desire Him –
3 despised and rejected by men, a man of
pains and knowing sickness. And as one
from whom the face is hidden, being
despised, and we did not consider Him.
4 Truly, He has borne our sicknesses and
carried our pains. Yet we reckoned Him
smitten, stricken by Elohim, and afflicted.
5 But He was pierced for our transgressions, He was crushed for our crookednesses. The chastisement for our peace
was upon Him, and by His stripes we are
healed.
6 We all, like sheep, went astray, each
one of us has turned to his own way. And
יהוה has laid on Him the crookedness of
us all.
7 He was oppressed and He was afflicted,
but He did not open His mouth. He was led
as a lamb to the slaughter, and as a sheep
before its shearers is silent, but He did not
open His mouth.
8 He was taken from prison and from
judgment. And as for His generation, who
considered that He shall be cut off from the
land of the living? For the transgression of
My people He was stricken.
9 And He was appointed a burial-site
with the wrong, and with the rich at His
death, because He had done no violence,
nor was deceit in His mouth. [a]
10 But יהוה was pleased to crush Him, He
laid sickness on Him, that when He made
Himself an offering for guilt, He would see
a seed, He would prolong His days and the
pleasure of יהוה prosper in His hand.

52a See Teh. 74:10 & 18, Shem. 20:7 & Deḇ. 5:11. *53a* Kěpha א 2:22.

11 He would see the result of the suffering
of His life and be satisfied. Through His
knowledge My righteous Servant makes
many righteous, and He bears their
crookednesses.
12 Therefore I give Him a portion among
the great, and He divides the spoil with the
strong, because He poured out His being
unto death, and He was counted with the
transgressors, and He bore the sin of many,
and made intercession for the transgressors.

54 "Sing, O barren one, you who did
not bear! Break forth into singing,
and cry aloud, you who have not been in
labour! For the children of the deserted one
are more than the children of the married
woman," said יהוה.
2 "Enlarge the place of your tent, and let
them stretch out the curtains of your
dwellings, spare not. Lengthen your cords,
and strengthen your stakes.
3 "For you shall break forth to the right
and to the left, and your seed inherit the
nations, and make the deserted cities
inhabited.
4 "Do not fear, for you shall not be put to
shame, nor hurt, you shall not be humiliated. For the shame of your youth you shall
forget, and not remember the reproach of
your widowhood any more.
5 "For your Maker is your husband, יהוה
of hosts is His Name, and the Set-apart
One of Yisra'ěl is your Redeemer. He is
called the Elohim of all the earth.
6 "For יהוה has called you like a woman
forsaken and grieved in spirit, like a wife
of youth when you were refused," declares
your Elohim.
7 "For a little while I have forsaken you,
but with great compassion I shall gather
you.
8 "In an overflow of wrath I hid My face
from you for a moment, but with everlasting loving-commitment I shall have compassion on you," said יהוה, your
Redeemer.
9 "For this is the waters of Noaḥ to Me,
in that I have sworn that the waters of
Noaḥ would never again cover the earth,
so have I sworn not to be wroth with you,
nor to rebuke you.
10 "For though the mountains be removed
and the hills be shaken, My loving-commitment is not removed from you, nor is
My covenant of peace shaken," said יהוה,
who has compassion on you.
11 "O you afflicted one, tossed with storm,
and not comforted, see, I am setting your
stones in antimony, and shall lay your
foundations with sapphires,
12 and shall make your battlements of
rubies, your gates of crystal, and all your
walls of precious stones,
13 and all your children taught by יהוה,
and the peace of your children great.
14 "In righteousness you shall be established – far from oppression, for you shall
not fear, and *far* from ruin, for it does not
come near you.
15 "See, they shall indeed assemble, but
not because of Me. Whoever shall assemble against you falls for your sake!
16 "See, I Myself have created the blacksmith who blows the coals in the fire, who
brings forth an instrument for his work.
And I have created the waster to destroy.
17 "No weapon formed against you shall
prosper, and every tongue which rises
against you in judgment you shall prove
wrong. This is the inheritance of the servants of יהוה, and their righteousness from
Me," declares יהוה.

55 "Oh everyone who thirsts, come to
the waters. And you who have no
silver, come, buy and eat. Come, buy wine
and milk without silver and without price.
2 "Why do you weigh out silver for what
is not bread, and your labour for what does
not satisfy? Listen, listen to Me, and eat
what is good, and let your being delight
itself in fatness.
3 "Incline your ear, and come to Me.
Hear, so that your being lives. And let Me
make an everlasting covenant with you,
the trustworthy loving-commitments of
Dawiḏ.
4 "See, I have given Him as a witness to
the people, a Leader and a Commander for
the people.

5“See, a nation you do not know you
shall call, and a nation who does not know
you run to you, because of יהוה your
Elohim, and the Set-apart One of Yisra’ěl,
for He has adorned you.”
6Seek יהוה while He is to be found, call
on Him while He is near.
7Let the wrong forsake his way, and the
unrighteous man his thoughts. Let him
return to יהוה, who has compassion on
him, and to our Elohim, for He pardons
much.
8“For My thoughts are not your
thoughts, neither are your ways My ways,”
declares יהוה.
9“For as the heavens are higher than the
earth, so are My ways higher than your
ways, and My thoughts than your thoughts.
10“For as the rain comes down, and the
snow from the heavens, and do not return
there, but water the earth, and make it
bring forth and bud, and give seed to the
sower and bread to the eater,
11so is My Word that goes forth from My
mouth – it does not return to Me empty,
but shall do what I please, and shall certainly accomplish what I sent it for.
12“For with joy you go out, and with
peace you are brought in – the mountains
and the hills break forth into singing before
you, and all the trees of the field clap the
hands.
13“Instead of the thorn the cypress comes
up, and instead of the nettle the myrtle
comes up. And it shall be to יהוה for a
name, for an everlasting sign which is not
cut off.”

56 Thus said יהוה, “Guard right-ruling, and do righteousness, for near
is My deliverance to come, and My righteousness to be revealed.
2“Blessed is the man who does this, and
the son of man who becomes strong in it,
guarding the Sabbath lest he profane it,
and guarding his hand from doing any evil.
3“And let not the son of the foreigner
who has joined himself to יהוה speak, saying, ‘יהוה has certainly separated me from
His people,’ nor let the eunuch say, ‘Look I
am a dry tree.’ ”
4For thus said יהוה, “To the eunuchs
who guard My Sabbaths, and have chosen
what pleases Me, and are holding onto My
covenant:
5to them I shall give in My house and
within My walls a place and a name better
than that of sons and daughters – I give
them an everlasting name that is not cut
off.
6“Also the sons of the foreigner who
join themselves to יהוה, to serve Him, and
to love the Name of יהוה, to be His servants, all who guard the Sabbath, and not
profane it, and are holding onto My
covenant –
7them I shall bring to My set-apart
mountain, and let them rejoice in My
house of prayer. Their ascending offerings
and their slaughterings are accepted on My
slaughter-place, for My house is called a
house of prayer for all the peoples.”
8The Master יהוה, who gathers the
outcasts of Yisra’ěl, declares, “I gather still
others to him besides those who are
gathered to him.”
9All you beasts of the field, come to
devour, all you beasts in the forest.
10His watchmen are blind, all of them,
they have not known. All of them are
dumb dogs, unable to bark, dreaming,
lying down, loving to slumber.
11And the dogs have a strong appetite,
they never have enough. And they are
shepherds! They have not known understanding. All of them look to their own
way, every one for his own gain, from his
own end, *saying*,
12“Come, let me bring wine and fill ourselves with strong drink. And tomorrow
shall be as today, even much greater.”

57 The righteous one has perished,
and no one takes it to heart. And
committed men are taken away, while no
one understands that the righteous one is
taken away from the presence of evil,
2he enters into peace. They who walk in
integrity rest on their beds.
3“But come here, you sons of the sorcer-
ess, you offspring of the adulterer and the
whore!

4 Against whom are you sporting? Against whom do you make a wide mouth and stick out the tongue? Are you not children of transgression, offspring of falsehood,

5 being inflamed with mighty ones under every green tree, slaying the children in the valleys, under the clefts of the rocks?

6 "Among the smooth stones of the stream is your portion; they, they, are your lot! Also to them you have poured a drink offering, you have offered a grain offering. Am I comforted in these?

7 "On a high and lofty mountain you have set your bed. There, too, you went up to slaughter a slaughtering.

8 "Also behind the doors and their posts you have set up your remembrance. For you have departed from Me, and have gone up to them. You have made your bed wide and made a covenant with them. You have loved their bed, where you saw their hand.

9 "And you went to the sovereign with ointment, and increased your perfumes. And you sent your messengers far off, and lowered yourself even to She'ol.

10 "You have wearied yourselves with your many wanderings, yet you did not say, 'I give up!' You have found the life of your hand, therefore you were not grieved.

11 "And of whom have you been afraid, or feared, that you have lied and not remembered Me, nor taken it to your heart? Have I not been silent, even from of old, and you have not feared Me?

12 "Let Me declare your righteousness and your works, for they do not profit you.

13 "When you cry out, let your collection *of idols* deliver you. But the wind shall bear them all away, a breath take them. But he who takes refuge in Me shall inherit the land, and possess My set-apart mountain."

14 And one shall say, "Heap it up! Heap it up! Prepare the way, take the stumbling-block out of the way of My people."

15 For thus declares the high and exalted One who dwells forever, whose Name is set-apart, "I dwell in the high and set-apart place, with him who has a bruised and humble spirit, to revive the spirit of the humble, and to revive the heart of bruised ones.

16 "For I would not strive forever, nor am I wroth forever, for the spirit would grow faint before Me, even the beings I have made.

17 "For the crookedness of his unfair gain I was wroth and I struck him. I hid Myself and was wroth, and he went on backsliding in the way of his heart.

18 "I have seen his ways, but *now* I heal him, and I lead him, and restore comforts to him and to his mourners,

19 creating the fruit of the lips: peace, peace to him who is far off and to him who is near," said יהוה, "and I shall heal him."

20 But the wrong are like the troubled sea, for it is unable to rest, and its waters cast up mud and dirt.

21 "There is no peace," said my Elohim, "for the wrong."

58 "Cry aloud, do not spare. Lift up your voice like the shophar. Declare to My people their transgression, and the house of Ya'aqoḇ their sins.

2 "Yet they seek Me day by day, and delight to know My ways, as a nation that did righteousness, and did not forsake the right-ruling of their Elohim. They ask of Me rulings of righteousness, they delight in drawing near to Elohim.

3 *They say*, 'Why have we fasted, and You have not seen? Why have we afflicted our beings, and You took no note?' "Look, in the day of your fasting you find pleasure, and drive on all your labourers.

4 "Look, you fast for strife and contention, and to strike with the fist of wrongness. You do not fast as you do this day, to make your voice heard on high.

5 "Is it a fast that I have chosen, a day for a man to afflict his being? Is it to bow down his head like a bulrush, and to spread out sackcloth and ashes? Do you call this a fast, and an acceptable day to יהוה?

6 "Is this not the fast that I have chosen: to loosen the tight cords of wrongness, to undo the bands of the yoke, to exempt the oppressed, and to break off every yoke?

7 "Is it not to share your bread with the

hungry, and that you bring to your house
the poor who are cast out; when you see
the naked, and cover him, and not hide
yourself from your own flesh?
[8]"Then your light would break forth like
the morning, your healing spring forth
speedily. And your righteousness shall go
before you, the esteem of יהוה would be
your rear guard.
[9]"Then, when you call, יהוה would
answer; when you cry, He would say,
'Here I am.' "If you take away the yoke
from your midst, the pointing of the finger,
and the speaking of unrighteousness,
[10]if you extend your being to the hungry
and satisfy the afflicted being, then your
light shall dawn in the darkness, and your
darkness be as noon.
[11]"Then יהוה would guide you continually, and satisfy your being in drought, and
strengthen your bones. And you shall be
like a watered garden, and like a spring of
water, whose waters do not fail.
[12]"And those from among you shall build
the old waste places. You shall raise up
the foundations of many generations. And
you would be called the Repairer of the
Breach, the Restorer of Streets to Dwell In.
[13]"If you do turn back your foot from the
Sabbath, from doing your pleasure on My
set-apart day, and shall call the Sabbath
'a delight,' the set-apart *day* of יהוה
'esteemed,' and shall esteem it, not doing
your own ways, nor finding your own
pleasure, nor speaking your own words,
[14]then you shall delight yourself in יהוה.
And I shall cause you to ride on the heights
of the earth, and feed you with the inheritance of Ya'aqoḇ your father. For the
mouth of יהוה has spoken!"

59

Look, the hand of יהוה has not
become too short to save, nor His
ear too heavy to hear.
[2]But your crookednesses have separated
you from your Elohim. And your sins have
hidden His face from you, from hearing.
[3]For your hands have been defiled with
blood, and your fingers with crookedness;
your lips have spoken falsehood, your
tongue mutters unrighteousness.
[4]No one calls for righteousness, and no
one pleads for truth. They trust in emptiness and speak worthlessness; they conceive trouble and bring forth wickedness.
[5]They have hatched adders' eggs and
they weave the spider's web. Whoever eats
their eggs dies, and when one is broken an
adder is hatched.
[6]Their webs do not become garments,
nor do they cover themselves with their
works. Their works are works of wickedness, and a deed of violence is in their
hands.
[7]Their feet run to evil, and they hurry to
shed innocent blood. Their thoughts are
thoughts of wickedness, wasting and ruin
are in their highways.
[8]The way of peace they have not known,
and there is no right-ruling in their ways.
They have made crooked paths for themselves, whoever treads in them shall not
know peace.
[9]Therefore right-ruling has been far from
us, and righteousness does not reach us.
We look for light, but there is darkness; for
brightness, but we walk in thick darkness!
[10]We feel for the wall like the blind, and
we feel as without eyes. At noon we stumble as at twilight, in deserted places, like
the dead.
[11]All of us growl like bears, and moan
sadly like doves. We look for right-ruling,
but there is none; for deliverance, but it is
far from us.
[12]For our transgressions have increased
before You, and our sins witnessed against
us. For our transgressions are with us, and
as for our crookednesses, we know them:
[13]transgressing, and being untrue to יהוה,
and turning away from our Elohim, speaking oppression and apostasy, conceiving
and pondering words of falsehood from the
heart.
[14]And right-ruling is driven back, and
righteousness stands far off. For truth has
fallen in the street, and right is unable to
enter. [a]

59a Amos 5:7.

15 And the truth is lacking, and whoever
turns away from evil makes himself a prey.
And יהוה saw, and it displeased Him that
there was no right-ruling.
16 And He saw that there was no man, and
was astonished that there was no intercessor. So His own arm saved for Him, and
His righteousness upheld him.
17 And He put on righteousness as a
breastplate, and a helmet of deliverance on
His head. And He put on garments of
vengeance for clothing, and wrapped
Himself with ardour as a mantle.
18 According to their deeds, so He repays,
wrath to His adversaries, recompense to
His enemies. He repays recompense to the
coastlands.
19 And they shall fear the Name of יהוה
from the west, and His esteem from the rising of the sun, when distress comes like a
flood, the Spirit of יהוה drives at [b] it.
20 "And the Redeemer shall come to
Tsiyon, [c] and to those turning from transgression in Ya'aqob," declares יהוה.
21 "As for Me, this is My covenant with
them," said יהוה: "My Spirit that is upon
you, and My Words that I have put in your
mouth, shall not be withdrawn from your
mouth, nor from the mouth of your descendants, nor from the mouth of your descendants' descendants," said יהוה, "from this
time and forever."

60 "Arise, shine, for your light has
come! And the esteem of יהוה has
risen upon you.
2 "For look, darkness covers the earth,
and thick darkness the peoples. But יהוה
arises over you, and His esteem is seen
upon you.
3 "And the nations shall come to your
light, [a] and sovereigns to the brightness of
your rising.
4 "Lift up your eyes all around and see:
all of them have gathered, they have come
to you; your sons come from afar, and your
daughters are supported on the side.
5 "Then you shall see and be bright, and
your heart shall throb and swell, for the
wealth of the sea is turned to you, the riches of the nations come to you.
6 "A stream of camels cover your land,
the dromedaries of Midyan and Ěphah; all
those from Sheba come, bearing gold and
incense, and proclaiming the praises of
יהוה.
7 "All the flocks of Qědar are gathered to
you, the rams of Nebayoth serve you; they
come up for acceptance on My slaughter-
place, and I embellish My esteemed
House.
8 "Who are these who fly like a cloud,
and like doves to their windows?
9 "Because the coastlands wait for Me,
and the ships of Tarshish first, to bring
your sons from afar, their silver and their
gold with them, to the Name of יהוה your
Elohim, and to the Set-apart One of
Yisra'ěl, because He has adorned you.
10 "And the sons of foreigners shall build
your walls, and their sovereigns serve you.
For in My wrath I have stricken you, but in
My delight I shall have compassion on
you.
11 "And your gates shall be open continually, they are not shut day or night, to bring
to you the wealth of the nations, and their
sovereigns in procession.
12 "For the nation and the reign that do not
serve you shall perish, and those nations
shall be utterly laid waste.
13 "The esteem of Lebanon shall come to
you, cypress, pine, and the box tree together, to embellish the place of My set-apart
place. And I shall make the place of My
feet esteemed.
14 "And the sons of those who afflicted
you come bowing to you, and all those
who despised you shall bow themselves at
the soles of your feet. And they shall call
you: City of יהוה, Tsiyon of the Set-apart
One of Yisra'ěl.
15 "Instead of you being forsaken and
hated, so that no one passes through you, I
shall make you an everlasting excellence, a
joy of many generations.
16 "And you shall suck the milk of the
nations, and shall suckle the breast of sov-

59b Lit. "in" it. *59c* See footnote at 24:23. *60a* Yesh. 60:19,20, Ḥazon 21:23,24.

ereigns. And you shall know that I, יהוה,
your Saviour and your Redeemer, am the
Mighty *One* of Ya'aqoḇ.
17 "Instead of bronze I bring gold, and
instead of iron I bring silver, and bronze
instead of wood, and iron instead of stones.
And I shall make your officers peace, and
your magistrates righteousness.
18 "Violence shall no longer be heard in
your land, neither wasting nor ruin within
your borders. And you shall call your walls
Deliverance, and your gates Praise.
19 "No longer is the sun your light by day,
nor does the moon give light to you for
brightness, but יהוה shall be to you an
everlasting light, and your Elohim your
comeliness.
20 "No longer does your sun go down, nor
your moon withdraw itself, for יהוה shall
be your everlasting light, and the days of
your mourning shall be ended.
21 "And your people, all of them righteous, shall inherit the earth forever – a
branch of My planting, a work of My
hands, to be adorned.
22 "The little shall become a thousand,
and the small one a strong nation. [b] I, יהוה,
shall hasten it in its time."

61 The Spirit of the Master יהוה is
upon Me, because יהוה has anointed Me to bring good news to the meek. He
has sent Me to bind up the broken-hearted,
to proclaim release to the captives, and the
opening of the prison to those who are
bound,
2 to proclaim the acceptable year of יהוה,
and the day of vengeance of our Elohim, to
comfort all who mourn,
3 to appoint unto those who mourn in
Tsiyon: to give them embellishment for
ashes, the oil of joy for mourning, the garment of praise for the spirit of heaviness.
And they shall be called trees of righteousness, a planting of יהוה, to be adorned.
4 And they shall rebuild the old ruins,
raise up the former wastes. And they shall
restore the ruined cities, the wastes of
many generations.
5 And strangers shall stand and feed your
flocks, and the sons of the foreigner be
your ploughmen and your vinedressers.
6 But you shall be called, 'Priests of
יהוה,' 'Servants of our Elohim' shall be
said of you. You shall consume the
strength of the nations, and boast in their
esteem.
7 Instead of your shame and reproach,
they rejoice a second time in their portion.
Therefore they take possession a second
time in their land, everlasting joy is theirs.
8 "For I, יהוה, love right-ruling; I hate
robbery for ascending offering. And I shall
give their reward in truth, and make an
everlasting covenant with them.
9 "And their seed shall be known among
the nations, and their offspring in the midst
of the peoples. All who see them shall
acknowledge them, that they are the seed
יהוה has blessed."
10 I greatly rejoice in יהוה, my being
exults in my Elohim. For He has put garments of deliverance on me, He has covered me with the robe of righteousness, as
a bridegroom decks himself with ornaments, and as a bride adorns herself with
her jewels.
11 For as the earth brings forth its bud, as
the garden causes the seed to shoot up, so
the Master יהוה causes righteousness and
praise to shoot up before all the nations!

62 For Tsiyon's sake I am not silent,
and for Yerushalayim's sake I do
not rest, until her righteousness goes forth
as brightness, and her deliverance as a
lamp that burns.
2 And the nations shall see your righteousness, and all sovereigns your esteem.
And you shall be called by a new name,
which the mouth of יהוה designates.
3 And you shall be a crown of comeliness
in the hand of יהוה, and a royal head-dress
in the hand of your Elohim.
4 No longer are you called "Forsaken,"
and no longer is your land called
"Deserted." But you shall be called
"Ḥephtsiḇah," and your land "Married,"

60b See 41:14, Dan. 2:34-44.

for יהוה shall delight in you, and your
land be married.
5 For as a young man marries a maiden,
so shall your sons marry you. And as the
bridegroom rejoices over the bride, so
shall your Elohim rejoice over you.
6 I have set watchmen on your walls, O
Yerushalayim, all the day and all the night,
continually, who are not silent. You who
remember יהוה, give yourselves no rest,
7 and give Him no rest till He establishes
and till He makes Yerushalayim a praise in
the earth.
8 יהוה has sworn by His right hand and
by the arm of His strength, "No more do
I give your grain to be food for your
enemies, nor do sons of the foreigner drink
your new wine, for which you have
laboured;
9 but those gathering it shall eat it, and
praise יהוה. And those collecting it shall
drink it in My set-apart courts."
10 Pass through, pass through the gates!
Prepare the way for the people. Build up,
build up the highway! Remove the stones.
Lift up a banner for the peoples!
11 See, יהוה has proclaimed to the end of
the earth: "Say to the daughter of Tsiyon,
'See, your deliverance has come; see, His
reward is with Him, and His work before
Him.' "
12 And they shall be called, "The Set-
apart People, the Redeemed of יהוה." And
you shall be called, "Sought Out, a City
Not Forsaken."

63 Who is this coming from Eḏom,
with garments of glowing colours
from Botsrah, who is robed in splendour,
striding forward in the greatness of His
strength? "It is I who speak in righteousness, mighty to save."
2 Why is there red on Your raiment, and
Your garments like one who treads in the
winepress?
3 "I have trodden the winepress alone,
and from the peoples no one was with Me.
And I trod them down in My displeasure,
and I trampled them in My wrath. Their
blood is sprinkled upon My garments, and
I have defiled all My raiment.
4 "For a day of vengeance is in My heart,
and the year of My redeemed has come.
5 "And I looked, but there was none
helping, and I was astonished that there
was none upholding. So My own arm
saved for Me, and My wrath upheld Me.
6 "And I trod down peoples in My displeasure, and made them drunk in My
wrath, and brought down their strength to
earth."
7 Let me recount the loving-commitments of יהוה and the praises of יהוה,
according to all that יהוה has done for us,
and the great goodness toward the house of
Yisra'ěl, which He has done for them
according to His compassion, and according to His many loving-commitments.
8 And He said, "They are My people,
children who do not act falsely." And He
became their Saviour.
9 In all their distress He was distressed,
and the Messenger of His Presence saved
them. In His love and in His compassion
He redeemed them, and He lifted them up
and carried them all the days of old.
10 But they rebelled and grieved His Set-
apart Spirit, so He turned against them as
an enemy, and He fought against them.
11 Then He remembered the days of old,
Mosheh, His people, "Where is He who
brought them up out of the sea with the
shepherd of His flock? Where is He who
put His Set-apart Spirit within him,
12 who led them by the right hand of
Mosheh, with His comely arm, dividing
the water before them to make for Himself
an everlasting Name,
13 who led them through the deep? Like a
horse in the wilderness they did not stumble."
14 As a beast goes down into the valley,
and the Spirit of יהוה causes him to rest, so
You led Your people, to make Yourself a
comely Name.
15 Look down from the heavens, and see
from Your set-apart and comely dwelling.
Where are Your ardour and Your might,
the stirring of Your inward parts and Your
compassion toward me? Are they withheld?
16 For You are our Father, though Aḇra-

ham does not know us, and Yisra'ěl does
not recognise us. You, O יהוה, are our
Father, our Redeemer – Your Name is from
of old.
17 O יהוה, why do You make us stray
from Your ways, and harden our heart
from Your fear? Turn back, for the sake
of Your servants, the tribes of Your inheritance.
18 For a little while Your set-apart people
possessed it – our adversaries have trodden
down Your set-apart place.[a]
19 We have become like those over whom
You never ruled – Your Name is not called
on them!

64 Oh, that You would tear the heavens open, come down, that mountains shall shake before You –
2 as when fire burns twigs, as fire makes
water boil – to make Your Name known to
Your adversaries, so that nations tremble
before You.
3 When You did awesome *matters*, which
we did not expect, You came down, mountains did shake before You!
4 Since the beginning of the ages they
have not heard nor perceived by the ear,
nor has the eye seen any Elohim besides
You, who acts for those who wait for Him.
5 You shall meet him who rejoices and
does righteousness, who remembers You
in Your ways. See, You were wroth when
we sinned in them a long time. And should
we be saved?
6 And all of us have become as one
unclean, and all our righteousnesses are as
soiled rags. And all of us fade like a leaf,
and our crookednesses, like the wind, have
taken us away.
7 And there is no one who calls on Your
Name, who stirs himself up to be strengthened[a] in You; for You have hidden Your
face from us, and have consumed us
because of our crookednesses.
8 And now, O יהוה, You are our Father.
We are the clay, and You our potter. And
we are all the work of Your hand.
9 Do not be wroth, O יהוה, nor remember crookedness forever. See, please look,
all of us are Your people!
10 Your set-apart cities have become a
wilderness, Tsiyon has become a wilderness, Yerushalayim a waste.
11 Our set-apart and comely House, where
our fathers praised You, has been burned
up with fire. And all that we treasured has
become a ruin.
12 In view of all this, would You restrain
Yourself, O יהוה? Would You keep silent
and afflict us beyond measure?

65 "I have let Myself be inquired of,
not by those who asked; I was
found, not by those who sought Me. I said,
'Here I am, here I am,' to a nation not calling on My Name.
2 "I have held out My hands all day long
to a stubborn people, who walk in a way
that is not good, after their own thoughts;
3 the people who provoke Me continually
to My face, who slaughter in gardens, and
burn incense on slaughter-places of brick;
4 who sit among the burial-sites, and
spend the night in secret places, who eat
flesh of pigs,[a] and the broth of unclean
meat is in their pots,
5 who say, 'Keep to yourself, do not
come near me, for I am set-apart to you!'
These are smoke in My nostrils, a fire that
burns all day.
6 "See, it is written before Me: I am not
silent, but shall repay, and I shall repay
into their bosom,
7 your crookednesses and the crookednesses of your fathers together," said יהוה,
"who burned incense on the mountains and
reproached Me on the hills. And I shall
measure their former work into their
bosom."
8 Thus said יהוה, "As the new wine is
found in the cluster, and one shall say, 'Do
not destroy it, for there is blessing in it,'
so I do for My servants' sake, not to
destroy them all.
9 "And I shall bring forth a seed from

63a Teh. 74, Teh. 79, Yirm 51:51, Ěḵah 1:10, Dan. 8:13, Dan. 11:31, Mt. 24:15.
64a Commonly understood as "Take hold of." *65a* See 66:17.

Ya'aqob, and from Yehuḏah an heir of My mountains. And My chosen ones shall inherit it, and My servants dwell there.

10 “And Sharon shall be a fold of flocks, and the Valley of Aḵor a place for herds to lie down, for My people who have sought Me.

11 “But you are those who forsake יהוה, who forget My set-apart mountain, who prepare a table for Gad, and who fill a drink offering for Meni.

12 “And I shall allot you to the sword, and let you all bow down to the slaughter, because I called and you did not answer, I spoke and you did not hear, and you did evil before My eyes and chose that in which I did not delight.”

13 Therefore thus said the Master יהוה, “See, My servants eat, but you hunger; see, My servants drink, but you thirst; see, My servants rejoice, but you are put to shame;

14 see, My servants sing for joy of heart, but you cry for sorrow of heart, and wail for breaking of spirit.

15 “And you shall leave your name as a curse to My chosen, for the Master יהוה shall put you to death, and call His servants by another name,

16 so that he who blesses himself in the earth does bless himself in the Elohim of truth. And he who swears in the earth does swear by the Elohim of truth. Because the former distresses shall be forgotten, and because they shall be hidden from My eyes.

17 “For look, I am creating new heavens and a new earth, and the former shall not be remembered, nor come to heart.

18 “But be glad and rejoice forever in what I create; for look, I create Yerushalayim a rejoicing, and her people a joy.

19 “And I shall rejoice in Yerushalayim, and shall joy in My people, and let the voice of weeping no more be heard in her, nor the voice of crying.

20 “No more is an infant from there going to live but a few days, nor an old man who does not complete his days, for the youth dies one hundred years old, but the sinner being one hundred years old shall be lightly esteemed.

21 “And they shall build houses and inhabit them, and plant vineyards and eat their fruit.

22 “They shall not build and another inhabit; they shall not plant and another eat. For the days of My people are going to be as the days of a tree, and My chosen ones outlive the work of their hands.

23 “They shall not labour in vain, nor bring forth children for trouble. For they are the seed of the blessed of יהוה, and their offspring with them.

24 “And it shall be that before they call, I answer. And while they are still speaking, I hear.

25 “Wolf and lamb feed together, a lion eats straw as an ox, and dust is the snake's food. They shall do no evil, nor destroy in all My set-apart mountain,” said יהוה.

66 Thus said יהוה, “The heavens are My throne, and the earth is My footstool. Where is this house that you build for Me? And where is this place of My rest?

2 “And all these My hand has made, and all these that exist,” declares יהוה. “Yet to such a one I look: on him who is poor and bruised of spirit, and who trembles at My Word.

3 “*But* whoever slays the bull strikes a man; whoever slaughters the lamb breaks a dog's neck; whoever brings a grain offering – pig's blood; whoever burns incense blesses an idol. Indeed, they have chosen their own ways, and their being delights in their abominations.

4 “I shall also choose their punishments, and bring their fears on them. Because I called, but no one answered. I spoke and they did not hear, and they did evil before My eyes, and chose what was displeasing to Me.”

5 Hear the Word of יהוה, you who tremble at His Word, “Your brothers who hate you, who cast you out for My Name's sake, said, 'Let יהוה be esteemed, so that we see your joy.' But they are put to shame.”

6 “A roaring sound from the city, a voice from the Hěḵal, the voice of יהוה, repay-

ing His enemies!
7 "Before she laboured, she gave birth; before a pain came to her, she was delivered of a male child.
8 "Who has heard the like of this? Who has seen the like of these? Is a land brought forth in one day? Is a nation born at once? For as soon as Tsiyon laboured, she gave birth to her children.
9 "Shall I bring to birth, and not give delivery?" says יהוה. "Shall I who give delivery restrain birth?" said your Elohim.
10 "Rejoice with Yerushalayim, and be glad with her, all you who love her; rejoice greatly with her, all you who mourn for her;
11 so that you feed, and shall be satisfied with the breast of her comforts, so that you drink deeply, and shall delight yourselves in her overflowing esteem."
12 For thus said יהוה, "See, I am extending peace to her like a river, and the esteem of the nations like a flowing stream. And you shall feed; you shall be carried on the side, and be fondled on her knees.
13 "As one whom his mother comforts, so I comfort you. And in Yerushalayim you are comforted."
14 "And you shall see, and your heart shall rejoice, and your bones flourish as tender grass. And the hand of יהוה shall be known to His servants, and His displeasure to His enemies.
15 "For look, יהוה comes with fire and with His chariots, like a whirlwind, to render His displeasure with burning, and His rebuke with flames of fire.
16 "For by fire and by His sword יהוה shall judge all flesh, and the slain of יהוה shall be many –
17 those who set themselves apart and cleanse themselves at the gardens after 'One' in the midst, eating flesh of pigs [a] and the abomination and the mouse, are snatched away, together," declares יהוה.
18 "And I, because of their works and their imaginations, am coming to gather all nations and tongues. And they shall come and see My esteem.
19 "And I shall set a sign among them, and shall send some of those who escape to the nations – Tarshish and Pul and Luḏ, who draw the bow, and Tuḇal and Yawan, the coastlands afar off who have not heard My report nor seen My esteem. And they shall declare My esteem among the nations.
20 "And they shall bring all your brothers as an offering to יהוה out of all the nations, on horses and in chariots and in litters, on mules and on camels, to My set-apart mountain Yerushalayim," declares יהוה, "as the children of Yisra'ěl bring an offering in a clean vessel into the House of יהוה.
21 "And from them too I shall take for priests – for Lěwites," declares יהוה.
22 "For as the new heavens and the new earth that I make stand before Me," declares יהוה, "so your seed and your name shall stand.
23 "And it shall be that from New Moon to New Moon, and from Sabbath to Sabbath, [b] all flesh shall come to worship before Me," declares יהוה.
24 "And they shall go forth and look upon the corpses of the men who have transgressed against Me. [c] For their worm shall not die, and their fire not be quenched. And they shall be repulsive to all flesh!"

66a See 65:4. *66b* Possible meaning: *Every week on the Sabbath.*
66c See 24:6, 34:2-3, Teh. 110:6, Yirm. 25:33.

YIRMEYAHU

JEREMIAH

1 The words of Yirmeyahu the son of
Ḥilqiyahu, of the priests who were in
Anathoth in the land of Binyamin,
2 to whom the word of יהוה came in the
days of Yoshiyahu son of Amon, sovereign
of Yehuḏah, in the thirteenth year of his
reign.
3 And it came in the days of Yehoyaqim,
son of Yoshiyahu, sovereign of Yehuḏah,
until the end of the eleventh year of
Tsiḏqiyahu, son of Yoshiyahu, sovereign
of Yehuḏah, until the exile of
Yerushalayim in the fifth new *moon*.
4 Now the word of יהוה came to me, saying,
5 "Before I formed you in the belly I
knew you, and before you came out of the
womb I did set you apart – I appointed you
a prophet to nations."
6 And said I, "Ah, Master יהוה! See, I do
not know how to speak, for I am a youth."
7 And יהוה said to me, "Do not say, 'I am
a youth,' but go to all to whom I send you,
and speak whatever I command you.
8 "Do not fear their faces, for I am with
you to deliver you," declares יהוה.
9 Then יהוה put forth His hand and
touched my mouth, and יהוה said to me,
"See, I have put My words in your mouth.
10 "See, I have this day set you over the
nations and over the reigns, to root out and
to pull down, to destroy and to overthrow,
to build and to plant."
11 And the word of יהוה came to me, saying, "What do you see, Yirmeyahu?" And I
said, "I see a branch of an almond tree."
12 And יהוה said to me, "You have seen
well, for I am watching over My word to
do it."
13 And the word of יהוה came to me a
second time, saying, "What do you see?"
And I said, "I see a boiling pot, and it is
facing away from the north."
14 And יהוה said to me, "Out of the north
evil is set loose on all the inhabitants of the
land.
15 "For look, I am calling all the clans of
the reigns of the north," declares יהוה.
"And they shall come and each one set his
throne at the entrance of the gates of Yerushalayim, against all its walls all around,
and against all the cities of Yehuḏah.
16 "And I shall pronounce My judgments
against them concerning all their evil,
because they have forsaken Me, burned
incense to other mighty ones, and bowed
themselves to the works of their own
hands.
17 "Now, gird up your loins and arise, and
speak to them all that I command you. Do
not break down before their faces, lest I
break you before them.
18 "For look, I have made you this day a
walled city and an iron column, and bronze
walls against all the land, against the sovereigns of Yehuḏah, against her heads,
against her priests, and against the people
of the land.
19 "And they shall fight against you, but
not prevail against you. For I am with
you," declares יהוה, "to deliver you."

2 And the word of יהוה came to me,
saying,
2 "Go, and you shall cry in the hearing of
Yerushalayim, saying, 'Thus said יהוה,
"I remember you, the loving-commitment
of your youth, the love of your bridehood,
when you went after Me in the wilderness,
in a land that was not sown.
3 "Yisra'ěl was set-apart to יהוה, the
first-fruits of His increase. All who ate of it
became guilty – evil came upon them,"
declares יהוה.' "
4 Hear the word of יהוה, O house of
Ya'aqoḇ and all the clans of the house of
Yisra'ěl.
5 Thus said יהוה, "What unrighteousness
have your fathers found in Me, that they
have gone far from Me, and went after

worthlessness, and became worthless?
6"And did not they say, 'Where is יהוה',
who brought us up out of the land of
Mitsrayim, who led us through the wilderness, through a land of deserts and pits,
through a land of drought and the shadow
of death, a land that no one passed through
and where no one dwelt?'
7"Then I brought you into a garden land,
to eat its fruit and its goodness. But when
you entered, you defiled My land and
made My inheritance an abomination.
8"The priests did not say, 'Where is
יהוה?' And those who handle the Torah
did not know Me, and the shepherds [a]
transgressed against Me, and the prophets
prophesied by Baʽal, and walked after *matters* that did not profit.
9"Therefore I still contend with you,"
declares יהוה, "and with your children's
children I contend.
10"For, pass beyond the isles of Kittim
and see, and send to Qěḏar and observe
well, and see if there has been any like this.
11"Has a nation changed its mighty ones,
which are not mighty ones? But My people
have changed My esteem [b] for that which
does not profit.
12"Be amazed, O heavens, at this, and be
frightened, be utterly dried up," declares
יהוה.
13"For My people have done two evils:
they have forsaken Me, the fountain of
living waters, [c] to hew out for themselves
cisterns, cracked cisterns, which do not
hold water.
14"Is Yisra'ěl a servant? Was he born in
the house? Why is he given to plunder?
15"The young lions roared at him, they
growled, and made his land waste; his
cities have been burned, without inhabitant.
16"Even the sons of Noph and of
Taḥpanḥes have shaven the crown of your
head.
17"Have you not done this to yourself, by
forsaking יהוה your Elohim when He led
you in the way?
18"And now why take the way to
Mitsrayim, to drink the waters of Shiḥor?
Or why take the way to Ashshur, to drink
the waters of the River?
19"Your own evil instructs you, and your
backslidings reprove you. Know therefore
and see that it is evil and bitter that you
have forsaken יהוה your Elohim, and that
My fear is not in you," declares the Master
יהוה of hosts.
20"For of old I have broken your yoke
and torn off your chastisements. And you
said, 'I am not serving [d] *You*,' when on
every high hill and under every green tree
you lay down, a whore.
21"Yet I had planted you a choice vine, all
of it a true seed. How then have you turned
before Me into the degenerate plant of a
strange vine?
22"Although you wash yourself with lye,
and use much soap, yet your crookedness
is ingrained before Me," declares the
Master יהוה.
23"How do you say, 'I am not defiled, I
have not gone after the Baʽals'? See your
way in the valley, know what you have
done: a swift dromedary breaking loose in
her ways,
24a wild donkey used to the wilderness,
sniffing the wind in the desire of her being
– in her time of mating, who turns her
away? All those who seek her need not
weary themselves; in her month [e] they find
her. [f]
25"Keep your foot from being bare, and
your throat from thirst. But you said, 'It is
useless, because I love strangers, and after
them I go.'
26"As the thief is ashamed when he is
found out, so is the house of Yisra'ěl
ashamed – they and their sovereigns and
their heads, and their priests and their
prophets,
27saying to a tree, 'You are my father,'
and to a stone, 'You gave birth to me.' For
they have turned their back to Me, and not
their face. But in the time of their calamity
they say, 'Arise and save us.'

2a See 10:21, 12:10-11, 50:6-7. *2b* Symbolic name for His Ark. *2c* See 17:13. *2d* Heb. Or "transgressing".
2e Hebrew: Chodesh - New *Moon*. *2f* On heat.

28 "But where are your mighty ones that
you have made for yourselves? Let them
arise, *see* if they save you in the time of
your calamity. Because your mighty ones
have become as many as your cities, O
Yehuḏah.
29 "Why do you complain to Me? You all
have transgressed against Me," declares
יהוה.
30 "In vain have I stricken your children –
they received no instruction. Your sword
has devoured your prophets like a destroying lion.
31 "O generation, see the word of יהוה!
Have I been a wilderness to Yisra'ěl, Or
a land of darkness? Why do My people
say, 'We have broken loose; we come to
You no more'?
32 "Would a maiden forget her ornaments,
or a bride her headband? Yet My people
have forgotten Me, days without number.
33 "Why do you embellish your way to
seek love? Therefore you have even taught
the evil women your ways.
34 "Even on your skirts is found the blood
of the lives of the poor innocents. You did
not find them breaking in, but in spite of
all these,
35 you say, 'Because I am innocent, certainly His displeasure shall turn from me.'
See, I shall bring judgment on you,
because you say, 'I have not sinned.'
36 "Why do you go about so much to
change your way? Even of Mitsrayim you
are to be ashamed, as you were ashamed of
Ashshur.
37 "Even from this one you shall go forth,
with your hands on your head. For יהוה
has rejected those you trust, and you shall
not prosper by them.

3 *Elohim* said, "If a man puts away his
wife, and she goes from him and
becomes another man's, does he return to
her again? Would not that land be made
greatly unclean? But you have committed
whoring with many lovers. And would you
return to Me?" declares יהוה.
2 "Lift up your eyes to the bare heights
and see: where have you not lain with
men? Besides the ways you have sat for
them like an Araḇian in the wilderness.
And you made the land unclean with your
whorings and your evil.
3 "Therefore the showers have been
withheld, and there has been no latter rain.
You have had a whore's forehead, you
refuse to be ashamed.
4 "Shall you not from now on cry to Me,
'My father, You are the guide of my youth?
5 'Does one bear a grudge forever? Does
one keep it to the end?' See, you have spoken and done the evils that you could."
6 And יהוה said to me in the days of
Yoshiyahu the sovereign, "Have you seen
what backsliding Yisra'ěl has done? She
has gone up on every high mountain and
under every green tree, and there committed whoring.
7 "And after she had done all these, I said
'Return to Me.' But she did not return.
And her treacherous sister Yehuḏah saw it.
8 "And I saw that for all the causes for
which backsliding Yisra'ěl had committed
adultery, I had put her away and given her
a certificate of divorce; yet her treacherous
sister Yehuḏah did not fear, but went and
committed whoring too.
9 "And it came to be, through her frivo-
lous whoring, that she defiled the land and
committed adultery with stones and wood.
10 "And yet for all this her treacherous sister Yehuḏah has not turned to Me with all
her heart, but falsely," declares יהוה.
11 And יהוה said to me, "Backsliding
Yisra'ěl has shown herself more righteous
than treacherous Yehuḏah.
12 "Go and proclaim these words toward
the north, and say, 'Return, O backsliding
Yisra'ěl,' declares יהוה, 'I shall not look
on you in displeasure, for I am lovingly-
committed,' declares יהוה, 'and I do not
bear a grudge forever.
13 'Only, acknowledge your crookedness,
because you have transgressed against
יהוה your Elohim, and have scattered your
ways to strangers under every green tree,
and you have not obeyed My voice,'
declares יהוה.
14 "Return, O backsliding children,"
declares יהוה, "for I shall rule over you,
and shall take you, one from a city and two

from a clan,[a] and shall bring you to Tsiyon.
15 “And I shall give you shepherds
according to My heart, and they shall feed
you with knowledge and understanding.
16 “And it shall be, when you have
increased, and shall be fruitful in the land
in those days,” declares יהוה, “that they no
longer say, ‘The ark of the covenant of
יהוה.’ Neither would it come to heart, nor
would they remember it, nor would they
visit it, nor would it be made again.
17 “At that time Yerushalayim shall be
called the throne of יהוה, and all the
nations shall be gathered to it, to the Name
of יהוה, to Yerushalayim, and no longer
walk after the stubbornness of their evil
heart.
18 “In those days the house of Yehuḏah
shall go to the house of Yisra’ĕl, and they
shall come together out of the land of the
north to the land that I have given as an
inheritance to your fathers.
19 “But I said, ‘How would I put you
among the children and give you a pleasant
land, a splendid inheritance of the hosts of
nations?’ “And I said, ‘Call Me, “My
Father,” and do not turn away from Me.’
20 “But indeed as a wife betrays her husband, so have you betrayed Me, O house of
Yisra’ĕl,” declares יהוה.
21 A voice was heard on the bare heights,
weeping supplications of the children of
Yisra’ĕl, because they have perverted their
way, they have forgotten יהוה their
Elohim.
22 “Return, O backsliding children, I shall
make your backslidings cease.” “See, we
have come to You, for You are יהוה our
Elohim.
23 “Truly, delusion comes from the high
hills, the noisy throng *on* the mountains.
Truly, in יהוה our Elohim is the deliverance of Yisra’ĕl.
24 “For shame has devoured the labour of
our fathers from our youth, their flocks and
their herds, their sons and their daughters.
25 “We shall lie down in our shame, while
our reproach covers us. For we have
sinned against יהוה our Elohim, we and
our fathers, from our youth even to this
day, and have not obeyed the voice of
יהוה our Elohim.”

4

“If you do return, O Yisra’ĕl,”
declares יהוה, “return to Me. And if
you remove your abominations from My
presence, and cease straying,
2 and shall swear, ‘As יהוה lives,’ in
truth, in right-ruling, and in righteousness
– then nations shall bless themselves in
Him, and they shall boast in Him!”
3 For this is what יהוה said to the men of
Yehuḏah and Yerushalayim, “Break up
your tillable ground, and do not sow
among thorns.
4 “Circumcise yourselves unto יהוה, and
take away the foreskins of your hearts, you
men of Yehuḏah and inhabitants of Yerushalayim, lest My wrath come forth like
fire and burn, with none to quench it,
because of the evil of your deeds.”
5 Declare in Yehuḏah and let it be heard
in Yerushalayim, and say, “Blow a shophar
in the land. Cry aloud and say, ‘Gather
yourselves, and let us go into the walled
city.’
6 “Lift up the banner toward Tsiyon. Be
strong, do not stand still! For I am bringing
evil from the north, and great destruction.”
7 “A lion has come up from his bush, and
the destroyer of nations is on his way. He
has set out from his place to make your
land a ruin. Your cities are laid waste,
without inhabitant.
8 “For this, gird yourself with sackcloth,
lament and wail. For the burning displeasure of יהוה has not turned back from us.
9 “And in that day it shall be,” declares
יהוה, “that the heart of the sovereign shall
perish, and the heart of the heads. And the
priests shall be astonished, and the
prophets wonder.”
10 Then I said, “Ah, Master יהוה! Truly,
You have greatly deceived this people and
Yerushalayim, saying, ‘Peace is for you,’
whereas the sword reaches to the heart.”
11 At that time it shall be said to this people and to Yerushalayim, “A scorching

3a See Yesh. 27:12.

wind of the bare heights blows in the
wilderness toward the daughter of My people, not to fan or to cleanse.
12 "A wind too strong for this shall come
for Me. Now it is I who speak judgments
against them.
13 "See, he comes up like clouds, and his
chariots like a whirlwind. His horses shall
be swifter than eagles. Woe to us, for we
shall be ravaged!"
14 O Yerushalayim, wash your heart from
evil, and be saved. Till when would your
wicked thoughts remain within you?
15 For a voice is declaring from Dan, and
is proclaiming trouble from Mount
Ephrayim:
16 "Announce to the nations, look, proclaim against Yerushalayim, that besiegers
are coming from a distant land and raise
their voice against the cities of Yehuḏah.
17 "Like keepers of a field they are against
her all around, because she has rebelled
against Me," declares יהוה.
18 "Your ways and your deeds have
brought this upon you. This is your evil,
because it is bitter, because it has reached
into your heart."
19 O my inward parts, my inward parts!
I am in pain! O the walls of my heart! My
heart pounds in me, I am not silent. For
you have heard, O my being, a voice of a
shophar, a shout of battle!
20 Destruction upon destruction is cried,
for all the land is ravaged. Suddenly my
tents are ravaged – my curtains in a
moment.
21 How long shall I see a banner, and hear
a voice of a shophar?
22 "For My people are foolish, they have
not known Me. They are stupid children,
and they have no understanding. They are
wise to do evil, but to do good they have
no knowledge."
23 I looked at the earth, and saw it was
formless and empty. And the heavens, they
had no light.
24 I looked at the mountains, and saw they
shook, and all the hills were swaying.
25 I looked, and saw there was no man,
and all the birds of the heavens had fled.
26 I looked, and saw the garden land was a
wilderness, and all its cities were broken
down at the presence of יהוה, by His burning displeasure.
27 For thus said יהוה, "All the earth shall
be a ruin, but I shall not make a complete
end.
28 "On account of this, let the earth mourn
and the heavens above be dark, because I
have spoken, because I have purposed and
shall not relent, nor do I turn back from it."
29 All the city is fleeing from the noise of
the horsemen and bowmen. They shall go
into bushes and climb up on the rocks. All
the city is forsaken, and no one is dwelling
in it.
30 And when you are ravaged, what would
you do? Though you put on crimson,
though you adorn yourself with ornaments
of gold, though you enlarge your eyes with
paint, you beautify yourself in vain. Your
lovers despise you, they seek your life.
31 For I have heard a voice as of a woman
in labour, the distress as of her who brings
forth her first child, the voice of the daughter of Tsiyon! She bewails herself, she
spreads out her hands, saying, "Woe to me,
for my being faints because of killers!"

5 "Diligently search the streets of
Yerushalayim, and please look, and
know and seek in her open places if you
find a man, if there is anyone doing right-
ruling, seeking the truth, then I shall pardon her.
2 "Even when they say, 'As יהוה lives,'
they swear falsely, for certain."
3 O יהוה, are Your eyes not on truth? You
have stricken them, but they have not
grieved. You have consumed them, but
they have refused to receive instruction.
They made their faces stronger than rock,
they refused to turn back.
4 Then I said, "These are only the poor.
They have been foolish, for they have not
known the way of יהוה, the right-ruling of
their Elohim.
5 "Let me go to the great men and speak
to them, for they have known the way of
יהוה, the right-ruling of their Elohim." But
these have altogether broken the yoke and
torn off the bonds.

6 Therefore a lion from the forest shall
strike them, a wolf of the deserts ravage
them. A leopard is watching over their
cities, whoever comes out of them is torn
in pieces. For their transgressions have
been many, their backslidings have been
numerous.
7 "Why should I pardon you for this?
Your children have forsaken Me and sworn
by those that are not mighty ones. When I
had filled them up, they then committed
adultery and they thronged to the house of
a whore.
8 "They were like well-fed horses, every
one neighed after his neighbour's wife.
9 "Would I not punish them for this?"
declares יהוה. "And would I not revenge
Myself on such a nation as this?
10 "Go up on her walls and destroy, but do
not make a complete end. Take away her
branches, for they do not belong to יהוה.
11 "For the house of Yisra'ěl and the
house of Yehuḏah have utterly betrayed
Me," declares יהוה.
12 They have been untrue to יהוה, and
said, "It is not He. No evil comes upon us,
nor do we see sword or scarcity of food."
13 And the prophets have become wind,
and the Word is not in them. Thus shall be
done to them:
14 Therefore thus said יהוה Elohim of
hosts, "Because you speak this word, see, I
am making My words in your mouth fire,
and this people wood, and it shall devour
them.
15 "See, I am bringing a nation against
you from afar, O house of Yisra'ěl,"
declares יהוה. "It is an enduring nation, it
is an ancient nation, a nation whose language you do not know, nor do you understand what they say.
16 "Their quiver is like an open burial-
site, all of them are mighty men.
17 "And they shall eat up your harvest and
your bread, which your sons and daughters
should eat. They shall eat up your flocks
and your herds, they shall eat up your
vines and your fig trees. With the sword
they shall demolish your walled cities, in
which you are trusting.
18 "But even in those days," declares
יהוה, "I shall not make a complete end of
you.
19 "And it shall be, when they say, 'Why
does יהוה our Elohim do all this to us?'
then you shall answer them, 'As you have
forsaken Me and served foreign mighty
ones in your land, so you shall serve
foreigners in a land that is not yours.'
20 "Declare this in the house of Ya'aqoḇ
and proclaim it in Yehuḏah, saying,
21 'Hear this now, O foolish people without heart, who have eyes and see not, and
who have ears and hear not:
22 'Do you not fear Me?' declares יהוה.
'Do you not tremble at My presence, who
have placed the sand as the boundary of
the sea, by an everlasting law, and it does
not pass over it? Though its waves toss to
and fro, they are not able; though they roar,
they do not pass over it.
23 'But this people has a backsliding and
rebellious heart, they have turned aside
and gone away.
24 'And they do not say in their heart, "Let
us now fear יהוה our Elohim, who gives
rain, both the former and the latter, in its
season. He guards for us, the *required-by-*
law, weeks [a] of the harvest."
25 'Your crookednesses have turned these
away, and your sins have kept the good
from you.
26 'For among My people are found
wrong men who lie in wait as one who sets
snares. They have set up a trap, they catch
men.
27 'As a cage is filled with birds, so their
houses are filled with deceit. Therefore
they have become great and grown rich.
28 'They have become fat, they are sleek.
They also overlook the deeds of the wrong.
They did not rightly rule the cause of the
fatherless, so that they prosper. And the
right of the needy they did not rightly rule.
29 'Would I not punish them for this?'
declares יהוה. 'Would I not revenge
Myself on such a nation as this?'
30 "An astounding and horrible matter has

5a - Lit. Shaḇu'oth

come to be in the land:
31 The prophets have prophesied falsely,[b]
and the priests rule by their own hand, and
My people have loved it so.[c] And what are
you going to do at the end of it?

6

"O children of Binyamin, gather yourselves to flee out of the midst of
Yerushalayim! Blow a shophar in Teqowa,
and set up a signal-fire in Bĕyth
Hakkerem, for evil has been seen from the
north, and great destruction.
2 "I shall cut off the lovely and delicate
one, the daughter of Tsiyon.
3 "The shepherds with their flocks shall
come to her, they shall pitch their tents
against her all around. They shall pasture,
each one in his own place."
4 "Set apart battle against her. Arise, and
let us go up at noon. Woe to us, for the day
goes away, for the shadows of the evening
are lengthening.
5 "Arise, and let us go by night, and let us
destroy her palaces."
6 For thus said יהוה of hosts, "Cut down
her trees, and cast up a siege mound
against Yerushalayim. She is the city to be
punished, in whose midst there is only
oppression.
7 "As a well flows with water, so she
flows with her evil. Violence and destruction are heard in her. Before Me continually are suffering and smiting.
8 "Be instructed, O Yerushalayim, lest
My being be torn from you, lest I make
you a waste, a land not inhabited."
9 Thus said יהוה of hosts, "Let them
thoroughly glean as a vine the remnant of
Yisra'ĕl; pass your hand again over the
branches like a grape-gatherer."
10 To whom shall I speak and give warning, so that they hear? See, their ear is
uncircumcised, and they are unable to
listen. See, the word of יהוה is a reproach
to them, they do not delight in it.
11 Therefore I am filled with the wrath of
יהוה. I have become weary of containing
it. "Pour it out on the children outside, and
on the company of young men together, for
even husband and wife shall be taken, the
aged and the very old.
12 "And their houses shall be turned over
to others, fields and wives together. For I
shall stretch out My hand against the
inhabitants of the land," declares יהוה.
13 "For from the least of them even to the
greatest of them, they are all greedy for
gain. And from the prophet even to the
priest, all act falsely.
14 "And they heal the breach of My people slightly, saying, 'Peace, peace,' when
there is no peace.
15 Were they ashamed when they had
done abomination? No! They were not at
all ashamed, nor did they know how to
blush. Therefore they shall fall among
those who fall. They shall stumble at the
time I visit them," said יהוה.
16 Thus said יהוה, "Stand in the ways and
see, and ask for the old paths, where the
good way is, and walk in it; and find rest
for yourselves. But they said, 'We do not
walk *in it.*'
17 "And I raised up watchmen over you,
and said, 'Listen to a voice of a shophar!'
But they said, 'We do not listen.'
18 "Therefore hear, you nations, and
know, O congregation, what is upon them!
19 "Hear, O earth! See, I am bringing evil
upon this people, even the fruit of their
thoughts, because they have not listened to
My words, nor My Torah – and they rejected it.
20 "What need have I of frankincense
from Sheḇa, and sweet cane from a distant
land? Your ascending offerings are not
acceptable, and your slaughterings have
not been sweet to Me."
21 Therefore thus said יהוה, "See, I am
laying stumbling-blocks before this people. And the fathers and the sons together
shall stumble on them, the neighbour and
his friend shall perish."
22 Thus said יהוה, "See, a people shall
come from the land of the north, and a
great nation is stirred up from the farthest

5b See 27:14,15. *5c* Yesh. 30:10, Tim. ב 4:3.

parts of the earth,
23 they strengthen *their* bow and spear,
they are cruel and have no compassion,
their voice roars like the sea. And they ride
on horses, set in array as a man for battle
against you, O daughter of Tsiyon."
24 We have heard the report of it, our
hands grow weak. Distress has taken hold
of us, pain as of a woman in labour.
25 Do not go out into the field, nor walk
by the way. Because of the sword of the
enemy, fear is on every side.
26 O daughter of my people, gird on sackcloth, and roll about in ashes! Make
mourning as for an only son, most bitter
lamentation because suddenly the ravager
shall come upon us.
27 "I have made you a trier and a stronghold among My people, so that you know,
and shall try their way.
28 "All of them are rebels of rebels, walking as slanderers. They are bronze and
iron, all of them are corrupters.
29 "The bellows have burned, the lead has
been consumed by fire. The refiner has
refined in vain, for those who are evil have
not been separated.
30 "They shall call them rejected silver,
because יהוה has rejected them."

7 The word that came to Yirmeyahu
from יהוה, saying,
2 "Stand in the gate of the House of יהוה,
and you shall proclaim there this word, and
shall say, 'Hear the word of יהוה, all you
of Yehuḏah who enter in at these gates to
bow before יהוה!' "
3 Thus said יהוה of hosts, the Elohim of
Yisra'ěl, "Make your ways and your deeds
good, then I let you dwell in this place.
4 "Do not trust in these false words, saying, 'This is the Hěḵal of יהוה, the Hěḵal
of יהוה, the Hěḵal of יהוה!'
5 "For if you truly make your ways and
your deeds good, if you truly do right-
ruling between a man and his neighbour,
6 if you do not oppress the stranger, the
fatherless, and the widow, and do not shed
innocent blood in this place, or walk after
other mighty ones to your own evil,
7 then I shall let you dwell in this place,
in the land that I gave to your fathers forever and ever.
8 "See, you are trusting in false words,
which do not profit –
9 stealing, murdering, and committing
adultery, and swearing falsely, and burning
incense to Baʽal, and walking after other
mighty ones you have not known.
10 "And you came and stood before Me in
this house which is called by My Name,
and said, 'We have been delivered' – in
order to do all these abominations!
11 "Has this house, which is called by My
Name, become a den of robbers in your
eyes? Look, I, even I Myself have seen it,"
declares יהוה.
12 "But go now to My place at Shiloh,
where I set My Name at the first, and see
what I did to it because of the evil of My
people Yisra'ěl.
13 "And now, because you have done all
these works," declares יהוה, "and I spoke
to you, rising up early and speaking, but
you did not hear, and I called you, but you
did not answer,
14 "I shall also do to this house, which is
called by My Name, in which you trust,
and to this place which I gave to you and
your fathers, as I did to Shiloh.
15 "And I shall cast you out of My presence, as I have cast out all your brothers,
all the seed of Ephrayim.
16 "And you, do not pray for this people,
nor lift up a cry or prayer for them, nor
make intercession to Me, for I do not hear
you.
17 "Do you not see what they are doing in
the cities of Yehuḏah and in the streets of
Yerushalayim?
18 "The children are gathering wood, the
fathers are lighting the fire, and the women
are kneading their dough, to make cakes
for the sovereigness of the heavens, and to
pour out drink offerings to other mighty
ones, to provoke Me.
19 "Is it Me they are provoking?" declares
יהוה. "Is it not themselves – unto the
shame of their own faces?"
20 Therefore, thus said the Master יהוה,
"See, My displeasure and My wrath is
poured out on this place, on man and on

beast, and on the trees of the field and on
the fruit of the ground. And it shall burn
and not be quenched."
21 Thus said יהוה of hosts, the Elohim of
Yisra'ěl, "Add your ascending offerings to
your slaughterings and eat meat.
22 "For I did not speak to your fathers, or
command them in the day that I brought
them out of the land of Mitsrayim, about
matters of ascending offerings or slaughterings.
23 "But this word I did command them,
saying, 'Obey My voice,[a] and I shall be
your Elohim, and you be My people. And
walk in all the ways that I have commanded you, so that it be well with you.'
24 "But they did not obey or incline their
ear, but walked in the counsels, in the
stubbornness of their evil heart, and went
backward and not forward.
25 "From the day that your fathers came
out of the land of Mitsrayim until this day,
I have even sent to you all My servants the
prophets, daily rising up early and sending
them.
26 "But they did not obey Me or incline
their ear, but stiffened their neck. They did
evil, more than their fathers.
27 "And you shall speak all these words to
them, though they do not listen to you.
And you shall also call to them, though
they do not answer you.
28 "But you shall say to them, 'This is a
nation that did not obey the voice of יהוה
their Elohim, nor did they accept instruction. Truth has perished and has been cut
off from their mouth.
29 'Cut off your hair and throw it away,
and take up a lamentation on the bare
heights, for יהוה has rejected and forsaken
the generation of His wrath.'
30 "For the children of Yehuḏah have
done what is evil in My eyes," declares
יהוה. "They have set their abominations in
the house which is called by My Name, to
defile it.
31 "And they have built the high places of
Topheth, which is in the Valley of the Son
of Hinnom, to burn their sons and their
daughters in the fire, which I did not command, nor did it come into My heart.
32 "Therefore see, the days are coming,"
declares יהוה, "when it shall no longer be
called Topheth, or the Valley of the Son of
Hinnom, but the Valley of Slaughter, for
they shall bury in Topheth until no room is
left.
33 "And the corpses of this people shall be
food for the birds of the heavens and for
the beasts of the earth, with none to fright-
en them away.
34 "And in the cities of Yehuḏah and in
the streets of Yerushalayim I shall make to
cease the voice of rejoicing and the voice
of gladness, the voice of the bridegroom
and the voice of the bride. For the land
shall become a waste!

8 "At that time," declares יהוה, "they
shall bring the bones of the sovereigns
of Yehuḏah, and the bones of its heads, and
the bones of the priests, and the bones of
the prophets, and the bones of the inhabitants of Yerushalayim, out of their burial-
sites,
2 and shall spread them before the sun
and the moon and all the host of the heavens, which they have loved and which they
have served and after which they have
walked, which they have sought, and to
which they have bowed themselves. They
shall not be gathered nor buried, they shall
be for dung on the face of the earth.
3 "And death shall be preferred to life by
all the rest of those who remain of this evil
people, who remain in all the places where
I have driven them," declares יהוה of
hosts.
4 "And you shall say to them, 'Thus said
יהוה, "Would they fall, and not rise? Does
one turn away and not return?
5 "Why then has this people, Yerushalayim, turned away in a continual backsliding? They are strengthened in deceit, they
refuse to turn back.
6 "I have listened and heard – they do not
speak right. No man has repented of his
evil, saying, 'What have I done?' They all

7a See also Ber. 26:5, Shem. 19:5, Yn. 3:36, Rom. 6:16, Iḇ`rim 4:11, 5:9 and Ḥazon 22:14).

turned to their own course, like a horse
rushing into battle.
7 “Even a stork in the heavens knows her
appointed times. And a turtledove, and a
swallow, and a thrush guard the time of
their coming. But My people do not know
the right-ruling of יהוה.
8 “How do you say, ‘We are wise, and the
Torah of יהוה is with us’? But look, the
false pen of the scribe has worked falsehood.
9 “The wise shall be put to shame, they
shall be broken down and caught. See, they
have rejected the Word of יהוה, so what
wisdom do they have?
10 “Therefore I give their wives to others,
and their fields to possessing ones. For
from the least even to the greatest, they are
all greedy for gain. From the prophet to the
priest, all act falsely.
11 “And they heal the breach of the daughter of My people slightly, saying, ‘Peace,
peace!’ when there is no peace.
12 “Were they ashamed when they had
done abomination? No! They were not at
all ashamed, nor did they know how to
blush. So they shall fall among those who
fall. They shall stumble in the time of their
visitation,” said יהוה.
13 “I shall snatch them away,” declares
יהוה. “There are no grapes on the vine, nor
figs on the fig tree, and the leaf has faded.
And what I gave them shall pass away
from them.” ’ ”
14 Why are we sitting still? Gather yourselves, and let us go into the walled cities,
and let us be silent there. For יהוה our
Elohim has let us perish and given us poisoned water to drink, because we have
sinned against יהוה.
15 We looked for peace, but there was no
good; *and* for a time of healing, but see –
fear!
16 The snorting of his horses was heard
from Dan. All the land shook at the sound
of the neighing of his strong ones.
They came and devoured the land and all
that fills it, the city and those who dwell in
it.
17 “For look, I am sending among you serpents, adders, which have no enchanter,
and they shall bite you,” declares יהוה.
18 When in grief I would seek comfort;
my heart is sick within me.
19 Observe! The voice, the cry of the
daughter of my people from a distant land,
“Is יהוה not in Tsiyon? Is her Sovereign
not in her?” “Why have they provoked Me
with their carved images, and with foreign
worthlessnesses?”
20 “The harvest is past, the summer is
ended, and we have not been saved!”
21 For the breach of the daughter of my
people I have been broken. I have grown
sad; astonishment has taken hold of me.
22 Is there no balm in Gilʽaḏ, is there no
healer there? Why has the healing of the
daughter of my people not come?

9 Oh, that my head were waters, and my
eyes a fountain of tears, and I would
weep day and night for the slain of the
daughter of my people!
2 Oh, that I had in the wilderness a lodging place for wayfaring men, and I would
leave my people, and go from them! For
they are all adulterers, an assembly of
treacherous men.
3 “And they bend their tongue like a bow.
Falsehood, and not truth, prevails on the
earth. For they proceed from evil to evil,
and they have not known Me,” declares
יהוה.
4 “Let everyone beware of his neighbour
and not trust any brother. For every brother
catches by the heel, and every neighbour
walks with slanderers.
5 “And everyone deceives his neighbour,
and no one speaks the truth. They have
taught their tongue to speak falsehood, and
have wearied themselves to crook.
6 “You live in the midst of deceit;
through deceit they have refused to know
Me,” declares יהוה.
7 Therefore thus said יהוה of hosts, “See,
I shall refine them, and shall try them, for
what shall I do because of the daughter of
My people?
8 “Their tongue is a slaying arrow. It
speaks deceit – speaks peaceably to his
neighbour with his mouth, but in his heart
he sets his ambush.

9 "Would I not punish them for this?" declares יהוה. "Would I not revenge Myself on such a nation as this?"

10 "I shall take up a weeping and wailing for the mountains, and for the pastures of the wilderness a lamentation, because they have been burned up, without any passing over, nor has the voice of cattle been heard. Both the birds of the heavens and the beasts have fled, they have gone.

11 "And I shall make Yerushalayim a heap of ruins, a habitation for jackals; and the cities of Yehuḏah I shall make a waste, without an inhabitant."

12 Who is the wise man, that he understands this? And to whom has the mouth of יהוה spoken, that he declares it? Why has the land perished, has it been burned up like a wilderness, with none passing through?

13 And יהוה says, "Because they have forsaken My Torah which I set before them, and have not obeyed My voice, [a] nor walked according to it,

14 but they have walked according to the stubbornness of their own heart and after the Ba'als, which their fathers had taught them."

15 Therefore thus said יהוה of hosts, the Elohim of Yisra'ěl, "See, I am making this people eat wormwood, and I shall make them drink poisoned water.

16 "And I shall scatter them among the nations, whom neither they nor their fathers have known. And I shall send a sword after them until I have consumed them."

17 Thus said יהוה of hosts, "Discern! And call for the mourning women, that they come. And send for the wise women, that they come.

18 "And let them hasten and take up a wailing for us, and let our eyes run with tears and our eyelids gush with water.

19 "For a voice of wailing is heard from Tsiyon, 'How we are ravaged! We are greatly ashamed, because we have forsaken the land, because we have been thrown out of our dwellings.' "

20 But hear the word of יהוה, O women, and let your ear receive the word of His mouth. And teach your daughters wailing, and each one her neighbour a lamentation.

21 For death has come through our windows, has entered our palaces, cutting off the children from the streets, and the young men from the squares.

22 Speak, "Thus declares יהוה, 'The corpses of men shall fall as dung on the face of the field, like cuttings after the reaper, with none to gather them.' "

23 Thus said יהוה, "Let not the wise boast in his wisdom, let not the mighty boast in his might, nor let the rich boast in his riches,

24 but let him who boasts boast of this, that he understands and knows Me, that I am יהוה, doing loving-commitment, right-ruling, and righteousness in the earth. For in these I delight," declares יהוה.

25 "See, the days are coming," declares יהוה, "when I shall punish all circumcised with the uncircumcised –

26 "Mitsrayim, and Yehuḏah, and Eḏom, and the children of Ammon, and Mo'aḇ, and all those trimmed on the edges, who dwell in the wilderness. For all the nations are uncircumcised, and all the house of Yisra'ěl are uncircumcised in heart!"

10

Hear the word which יהוה speaks to you, O house of Yisra'ěl.

2 Thus said יהוה, "Do not learn the way of the nations, [a] and do not be awed by the signs of the heavens, for the nations are awed by them. [b]

3 "For the laws of these peoples are worthless, for one cuts a tree from the forest, work for the hands of a craftsman with a cutting tool.

4 "They beautify it with silver and gold, they strengthen it with nails and hammers so that it does not topple.

5 "They are like a rounded post, and they

9a See footnote at 7:23.
10a Way. 18:3, Deḇ. 12:30 & 18:9, Yeḥez. 11:12 & 20:32, Eph. 4:17, Kěpha א 4:3.
10b Deḇ. 4:19 & 17:3.

do not speak. They have to be carried, because they do not walk. Do not be afraid of them, for they do no evil, nor is it in them to do any good."

6 There is none like You, O יהוה. You are great, and great is Your Name in might.

7 Who would not fear You, O Sovereign of the nations? For this is Your due, for among all the wise men of the nations, and in all their reigns, there is none like You.

8 They are both brutish and foolish, an instruction of worthlessness is the tree.

9 Silver is beaten into plates; it is brought from Tarshish, and gold from Uphaz, the work of the craftsman and of the hands of the smith; draped in blue and purple; all of them are the work of skilled ones.

10 But יהוה is truly Elohim. He is the living Elohim and the everlasting Sovereign. At His wrath the earth shakes, and nations are unable to stand His displeasure.

11 Say to them this, "The elah [c] that did not make the heavens and the earth shall perish from the earth and from under these heavens."

12 He has made the earth by His power, He has established the world by His wisdom, and has stretched out the heavens by His understanding.

13 When He makes His voice heard, there is a roaring of waters in the heavens. And He makes vapours rise from the ends of the earth. The lightnings for rain He has made, and brings wind from His treasuries.

14 Everyone is brutish in knowledge; every smith is put to shame by his idol. For his moulded image is falsehood, and there is no spirit in them.

15 They are worthless, a work of mockery. In the time of their punishment they perish.

16 The Portion of Ya'aqoḇ is not like these, for He is the Maker of all, and Yisra'ěl is the tribe of His inheritance – יהוה of hosts is His Name.

17 Gather up your bundle from the ground, you who live under siege!

18 For thus said יהוה, "See, at this time I am hurling out the inhabitants of the land, and shall distress them, so that they feel it."

19 Woe to me for my breaking! My wound is grievous, but I say, "This is my sickness, and I bear it.

20 "My tent has been ravaged, and all my cords have been broken. My children have gone from me, and they are no more. There is no one to pitch my tent any more, or to set up my curtains.

21 For the shepherds have become brutish, and they have not sought יהוה. Therefore they did not understand, and all their flock scattered." [d]

22 See, it has come, the voice of a report, and a great shaking out of the land of the north, to make the cities of Yehuḏah a waste, a habitation of jackals.

23 O יהוה, I know the way of man is not in himself, it is not for man who walks to direct his own steps.

24 O יהוה, chastise me, but with right-ruling – not in Your displeasure, lest You bring me to naught.

25 Pour out Your wrath on the nations who do not know You, and on the tribes who do not call on Your Name. For they have eaten up Ya'aqoḇ, devoured him and consumed him, and laid waste his home. [e]

11

The word that came to Yirmeyahu from יהוה, saying,

2 "Hear the words of this covenant, and speak to the men of Yehuḏah and to the inhabitants of Yerushalayim.

3 "And you shall say to them, 'Thus said יהוה Elohim of Yisra'ěl, "Cursed is the man who does not obey the words of this covenant,

4 which I commanded your fathers in the day when I brought them out of the land of Mitsrayim, from the iron furnace, saying, 'Obey My voice, [m] and you shall do according to all that I command you, and you shall be My people, and I be your Elohim,'

5 in order to establish the oath which I have sworn to your fathers, to give them a

10c Elah - Aramaic for mighty one - See Explanatory notes under El, Eloah etc. *10d* See 2:8, 12:10-11, 50:6-7, Yeḥez. 34:1-23, Tim. ב 4:3-4, Kěpha ב 2:1-22. *10e* Teh. 79:6, Miḵ. 4:5. *11a* See footnote 7:23.

land flowing with milk and honey, as it is
this day." ' " And I answered and said,
"Amĕn, יהוה."
6 And יהוה said to me, "Proclaim all
these words in the cities of Yehuḏah and in
the streets of Yerushalayim, saying, 'Hear
the words of this covenant and do them.
7 'For I earnestly warned your fathers in
the day that I brought them up out of the
land of Mitsrayim, until this day, rising
early and warning, saying, "Obey My
voice."
8 'But they did not obey or incline their
ear, but everyone walked in the stubbornness of his evil heart. So I brought on them
all the words of this covenant, which I
commanded them to do, and they did not
do.' "
9 And יהוה said to me, "There is a conspiracy among the men of Yehuḏah and
among the inhabitants of Yerushalayim.
10 "They have turned back to the crookednesses of their forefathers who refused to
hear My words, and they have gone after
other mighty ones to serve them. The
house of Yisra'ĕl and the house of Yehuḏah have broken My covenant I made with
their fathers."
11 Therefore thus said יהוה, "See, I am
bringing evil on them which they are
unable to escape. Then they shall cry out to
Me, but I shall not listen to them.
12 "And the cities of Yehuḏah and the
inhabitants of Yerushalayim shall go and
cry out to the mighty ones to whom they
burn incense, but they shall bring no deliverance to them at all in the time of their
evil.
13 "For your mighty ones have become as
many as your cities, O Yehuḏah. And you
have set up as many slaughter-places to
shame as there are streets in Yerushalayim
– slaughter-places to burn incense to Baʽal.
14 "And you, do not pray for this people,
or lift up a cry or prayer for them, for I do
not hear them in the time that they cry out
to Me because of their evil.
15 "Why should My beloved be in My
house – she has done wickedness with
many. And does the set-apart flesh remove
your evil from you? Then you rejoice?
16 "יהוה has named you, 'Green Olive
Tree, Beautiful, of Goodly Fruit.' With the
noise of a great sound He has set it on fire,
and its branches shall be broken.
17 "And יהוה of hosts, who planted you,
has spoken evil against you for the evil of
the house of Yisra'ĕl and of the house of
Yehuḏah, which they have done against
themselves to provoke Me, by burning
incense to Baʽal."
18 And יהוה made it known to me, and I
know it. Then You showed me their deeds.
19 But I was like a gentle lamb brought to
the slaughter. And I did not know that they
had plotted against me, saying, "Let us
destroy the tree with its fruit, and let us cut
him off from the land of the living, and let
his name be remembered no more."
20 But, O יהוה of hosts, who judges righteously, who tries kidneys and heart, let me
see Your vengeance upon them, for unto
You I have revealed my cause.
21 "Therefore thus said יהוה concerning
the men of Anathoth who are seeking your
life, saying, 'Do not prophesy in the Name
of יהוה, lest you die by our hand' –
22 therefore thus said יהוה of hosts, 'See,
I am punishing them, the young men shall
die by the sword, their sons and their
daughters shall die by scarcity of food.
23 'And there shall be no remnant of them,
for I bring evil on the men of Anathoth –
the year of their punishment.' "

12

Righteous are You, O יהוה, when I
plead with You. Indeed, let me
speak with You about right-rulings. Why
has the way of the wrong prospered? All
the workers of treachery are at ease? [a]
2 You have planted them and they have
taken root, they grow and they bear fruit.
You are near in their mouth but far from
their kidneys.
3 But You have known me, O יהוה. You
see me, and You have tried my heart
toward You. Draw them away like sheep
for slaughter, and separate them for the day

12a See footnote Teh. 73:3.

of slaughter.
4 How long shall the land mourn, and the
plants of every field wither? The beasts
and birds are consumed, for the evil of
those who dwell there, because they said,
"He does not see our latter ending."
5 "If you have run with the footmen, and
they have wearied you, then how do you
contend with horses? And if in the land of
peace, you feel safe, then how do you manage in the Yardĕn jungle?
6 "For even your brothers, the house of
your father, even they have betrayed you,
even they have cried aloud after you. Do
not believe them, even though they speak
smooth words to you.
7 "I have forsaken My house, I have left
My inheritance, I have given the beloved
of My being into the hand of her enemies.
8 "My inheritance has become to Me like
a lion in the forest. It cries out against Me,
therefore I have hated it.
9 "My inheritance is to Me like a speckled bird of prey, the birds of prey all
around are against her. Go, gather all the
beasts of the field, bring them to devour!
10 "Many shepherds have destroyed My
vineyard, they have trodden My portion
under foot, they have made My pleasant
portion become a deserted wilderness. [b]
11 "They have laid it waste – a waste, it
mourns to Me. All the land is laid waste,
because no one takes it to heart.
12 "The ravagers have come on all the
bare heights in the wilderness, for the
sword of יהוה is devouring from one end
of the land to the other end of the land.
There is no peace to any flesh.
13 "They have sown wheat but reaped
thorns, they have exhausted themselves –
they do not profit. And they shall be
ashamed of your harvest because of the
burning displeasure of יהוה."
14 Thus said יהוה, "As for all My evil
neighbours who touch the inheritance
which I have caused My people Yisra'ĕl to
inherit; see, I am plucking them out of
their land, and I shall pluck out the house
of Yehuḏah from their midst.
15 "And it shall be, after My plucking
them out, I shall return, and have compassion on them and bring them back, everyone to his inheritance and everyone to his
land.
16 "And it shall be, if they learn well the
ways of My people, to swear by My Name,
'As יהוה lives,' as they taught My people
to swear by Ba'al, then they shall be established in the midst of My people.
17 "But if they do not obey, I shall pluck
up, pluck up and destroy that nation,"
declares יהוה.

13

Thus יהוה said to me, "Go and get
yourself a linen girdle, and put it
on your loins, but do not put it in water."
2 So I bought a girdle according to the
word of יהוה, and put it on my loins.
3 And the word of יהוה came to me the
second time, saying,
4 "Take the girdle that you have bought,
which is on your loins, and arise, go to the
Euphrates, and hide it there in a hole in the
rock."
5 And I went and hid it by the Euphrates,
as יהוה commanded me.
6 And it came to be after many days that
יהוה said to me, "Arise, go to the
Euphrates, and take from there the girdle
which I commanded you to hide there."
7 So I went to the Euphrates and dug, and
I took the girdle from the place where I had
hidden it. And there was the girdle, ruined.
It was completely useless.
8 "And the word of יהוה came to me,
saying,
9 "Thus said יהוה, 'Thus I ruin the pride
of Yehuḏah and the great pride of Yerushalayim.
10 'This evil people, who refuse to hear
My Words, who walk in the stubbornness
of their heart, and walk after other mighty
ones to serve them and to bow themselves
to them, is like this girdle which is completely useless.
11 'For as the girdle clings to the loins of a
man, so I have caused all the house of
Yisra'ĕl and all the house of Yehuḏah to

12b See footnote 10:21.

cling to Me,’ declares יהוה, ‘to become Mine – for a people, and for a name, and for a praise, and for an adorning. But they did not listen.’

12 “And you shall speak to them this word, ‘Thus said יהוה Elohim of Yisra’ĕl, “Every bottle is to be filled with wine.” ’ And when they say to you, ‘Do we not know that every bottle should be filled with wine?’

13 “Then say to them, ‘Thus said יהוה, “See, I am filling all the inhabitants of this land, and the sovereigns who sit on the throne of Dawiḏ, and the priests, and the prophets, and all the inhabitants of Yerushalayim with drunkenness!

14 “And I shall dash them one against another, both the fathers and the sons together,” declares יהוה. “I do not spare nor pardon nor have compassion, that I should not destroy them.” ’ ”

15 Listen and give ear, do not be proud, for יהוה has spoken.

16 Give esteem to יהוה your Elohim before He brings darkness, and before your feet stumble on the dark mountains, and while you are looking for light. He turns it into the shadow of death, makes it gross darkness.

17 And if you do not listen, my being shall weep in secret for your pride, and my eyes bitterly weep and run down with tears, because the flock of יהוה shall be taken captive.

18 Say to the sovereign and to the sovereigness mother, “Humble yourselves. Sit down, for your rule, the crown of your comeliness, has come down.”

19 The cities of the South shall be shut up, with no one to open them. Yehuḏah shall be taken into exile, all of it. She shall be taken into exile, completely.

20 Lift up your eyes and see those who come from the north. Where is the flock that was given to you, your fair sheep?

21 What would you say when He visits you? For you have taught them to be chiefs, to be head over you. Do not pangs seize you, like a woman in labour?

22 And when you say in your heart, “Why has this come upon me?” It is because of your great crookedness that your skirts have been uncovered, your heels made bare.

23 Does a Kushite change his skin and a leopard its spots? You who are taught to do evil are also unable to do good!

24 “So I shall scatter them like stubble that passes away by the wind of the wilderness.

25 “This is your lot, your measured portion from Me,” declares יהוה, “because you have forgotten Me, and trust in falsehood.

26 “I shall even draw your skirts over your face, and your shame shall be seen,

27 your adulteries and your neighings, the wickedness of your whoring! I have seen your abominations on the hills in the fields. Woe to you, O Yerushalayim! How long before you would be made clean?”

14 The word of יהוה that came to Yirmeyahu concerning the matter of droughts.

2 “Yehuḏah has mourned, and her gates have languished. They have mourned on the ground, and the cry of Yerushalayim has gone up.

3 “And their nobles have sent their little ones for water, they went to the cisterns and found no water, they returned with their vessels empty. They were put to shame, and blushed and covered their heads.

4 “Because the ground became cracked, for there has been no rain in the land. The ploughmen were put to shame, they covered their heads.

5 “Even the deer gave birth in the field, but left because there was no grass.

6 “And wild donkeys stood in the bare heights, they sniffed at the wind like jackals. Their eyes have failed because there was no grass.”

7 O יהוה, though our crookednesses witness against us, act, for Your Name’s sake. For our backslidings have been many, we have sinned against You.

8 O Expectation of Yisra’ĕl, its Saviour in time of distress, why should You be like a stranger in the land, or like a traveller who turns aside to lodge?

9 Why should You be as one who is
stunned, as a mighty man that is unable to
save? Yet You, O יהוה, are in our midst,
and Your Name has been called on us. Do
not leave us!
10 Thus said יהוה to this people, "So they
have loved to wander, they have not
restrained their feet. Therefore יהוה has
not accepted them. Now He does remember their crookedness and punish their
sins."
11 And יהוה said to me, "Do not pray for
this people for their good.
12 "When they fast, I do not hear their cry.
And when they offer ascending offering
and grain offering, I do not accept them.
Instead, I am consuming them by sword,
and by scarcity of food, and by pestilence."
13 But I said, "Ah, Master יהוה! See, the
prophets say to them, 'You are not to see a
sword, nor have scarcity of food, for I give
you true peace in this place.' "
14 Then יהוה said to me, "The prophets
prophesy falsehood [a] in My Name. I have
not sent them, nor commanded them, nor
spoken to them. They are prophesying to
you a false vision, worthless divination,
and the deceit of their own heart.
15 "Therefore thus said יהוה concerning
the prophets who prophesy in My Name,
whom I did not send, and who say, 'Sword
and scarcity of food shall not be in this
land.' 'By sword and scarcity of food
those prophets shall be consumed!
16 'And the people to whom they are
prophesying shall be thrown out in the
streets of Yerushalayim because of the
scarcity of food and the sword, with no one
to bury them – them nor their wives, their
sons nor their daughters. For I shall pour
their evil on them.'
17 "And you shall say this word to them,
'Let my eyes flow with tears night and day,
and let them not cease; for the maiden
daughter of my people has been crushed
with a mighty blow, with a very severe
wound.
18 'If I go out to the field, then see those
slain with the sword! And if I enter the
city, then see those sick from scarcity of
food! For both prophet and priest go about
in a land they do not know.' "
19 Have You completely rejected Yehuḏah? Has Your being loathed Tsiyon? Why
have You stricken us so that there is no
healing for us? We looked for peace, but
there was no good; and for the time of
healing, but see – fear!
20 O יהוה, we know our wrong and the
crookedness of our fathers, for we have
sinned against You.
21 Do not scorn us, for Your Name's sake.
Do not despise the throne of Your esteem.
Remember, do not break Your covenant
with us.
22 Are there among the worthless idols of
the nations any causing rain? And do the
heavens give showers? Are You not He, O
יהוה our Elohim? And we wait for You,
for You are the One who does all this.

15 And יהוה said to me, "Even if
Mosheh and Shemu'ěl were to
stand before Me, My being is not toward
this people. Send them away from My
presence, let them go.
2 "And it shall be, when they say to you,
'Where do we go?' then you shall say to
them, 'Thus said יהוה, "Those for death,
to death. And those for the sword, to the
sword. And those for scarcity of food, to
scarcity of food. And those for captivity,
to captivity." '
3 "And I shall appoint over them four
kinds," declares יהוה, "the sword to kill,
the dogs to drag, the birds of the heavens
and the beasts of the earth to devour and
destroy.
4 "And I shall make them for a horror to
all the reigns of the earth, on account of
Menashsheh son of Ḥizqiyahu, sovereign
of Yehuḏah, because of what he did in
Yerushalayim.
5 "For who has compassion on you, O
Yerushalayim? And who mourns for you?
And who turns aside to ask how you are
doing?
6 "You who have forsaken Me," declares

14a 23:11-36.

יהוה, "you have gone backward. Therefore
I shall stretch out My hand against you and
destroy you. I have been weary of relenting!
7 "And I shall winnow them with a winnowing fan in the gates of the land. I shall
bereave, I shall destroy My people. They
would not turn back from their ways.
8 "Their widows shall be more numerous
than the sand of the seas. I shall bring
against them, against the mother of the
young men, a ravager at noon. I shall cause
agitation and sudden alarm to fall on her,
suddenly.
9 "She who has borne seven shall pine
away. She shall breathe her last. Her sun
shall go down while it is yet day. She shall
be put to shame and be humiliated. And
their remnant I give up to the sword before
their enemies," declares יהוה.
10 Woe to me, my mother, that you have
borne me, a man of strife and a man of
contention to all the earth! I have neither
lent for interest, nor have men lent to me
for interest. All of them are reviling me.
11 יהוה said, "Did I not direct you for
your good? Did I not intercede for you in a
time of evil and in a time of distress
against the enemy?
12 "Does one break iron, iron or bronze
from the north?
13 "Your wealth and your treasures I give
as plunder, not for price, because of all
your sins, even in all your borders.
14 "And I shall cause them to pass over
with your enemies into a land which you
did not know, for a fire is kindled in My
displeasure, which burns upon you."
15 You Yourself know, O יהוה. Remember
me and visit me, and take vengeance for
me on these who persecute me. In Your
patience, do not take me away. Know that
for You I have suffered reproach.
16 Your words were found, and I ate them,
and Your word was to me the joy and
rejoicing of my heart. For Your Name is
called on me, O יהוה Elohim of hosts.
17 I have not sat in the company of the
mockers, nor do I exult. I have sat alone
because of Your hand, for You have filled
me with displeasure.
18 Why is my pain without end and my
wound incurable, which refuses to be
healed? Are You to me like a failing
stream, as waters not steadfast?
19 Therefore thus said יהוה, "If you turn
back, then I shall bring you back. Before
Me you shall stand. And if you take out the
precious from the worthless, you shall
become as My mouth. Let them return to
you, but do not return to them.
20 "And I shall make you to this people a
strong bronze wall. And they shall fight
against you, but not overcome you. For I
am with you to save you and deliver you,"
declares יהוה.
21 "And I shall deliver you from the hand
of evil-doers, and I shall ransom you from
the grip of the ruthless."

16 And the word of יהוה came to me,
saying,
2 "Do not take a wife, nor have sons or
daughters in this place."
3 For thus said יהוה concerning the sons
and daughters who are born in this place,
and concerning their mothers who bear
them and their fathers who bring them
forth in this land,
4 "They shall die of deaths from diseases,
they shall not be lamented nor be buried,
but be like dung on the face of the earth,
and be consumed by sword and by scarcity
of food. And their corpses shall be meat
for the birds of the heavens and for the
beasts of the earth."
5 For thus said יהוה, "Do not enter the
house of mourning, neither go to lament or
mourn for them, for I have withdrawn My
peace from this people," declares יהוה,
"even the loving-commitment and the
compassions.
6 "Both great and small shall die in this
land. They shall not be buried, and no one
shall lament for them, or cut themselves, or
make themselves bald for them.
7 "Neither shall they break bread in
mourning for them to comfort them for the
dead, nor give them the cup of comfort to
drink for their father or their mother.
8 "Do not enter the house of feasting to
sit with them, to eat and drink."

9For thus said יהוה of hosts, the Elohim
of Yisra'ěl, "See, before your eyes and in
your days, I am making the voice of rejoicing and the voice of gladness, the voice of
the bridegroom and the voice of the bride
to cease in this place.
10"And it shall be, when you declare to
this people all these words, and they shall
say to you, 'Why has יהוה pronounced all
this great evil against us? And what is our
crookedness, and what is our sin that we
have committed against יהוה our Elohim?'
11then you shall say to them, 'Because
your fathers have forsaken Me,' declares
יהוה, 'and have walked after other mighty
ones and served them and bowed themselves to them, and have forsaken Me, and
did not guard My Torah.
12'And you have done more evil than
your fathers, for look, each one walks
according to the stubbornness of his own
evil heart, without listening to Me.
13'So I shall throw you out of this land
into a land that you do not know, neither
you nor your fathers. And there you shall
serve other mighty ones day and night,
where I show you no favour.'
14"Therefore see, the days are coming,"
declares יהוה, "when it is no longer said,
'יהוה lives who brought up the children of
Yisra'ěl from the land of Mitsrayim,'
15but, 'יהוה lives who brought up the
children of Yisra'ěl from the land of the
north and from all the lands where He had
driven them.' For I shall bring them back
into their land I gave to their fathers.
16"See, I am sending for many fishermen," declares יהוה, "and they shall fish
them. And after that I shall send for many
hunters, and they shall hunt them from
every mountain and every hill, and out of
the holes of the rocks.
17"For My eyes are on all their ways;
they have not been hidden from My face,
nor has their crookedness been hidden
from My eyes.
18"And first I shall repay double for their
crookedness and their sin, because they
have defiled My land with the dead bodies
of their disgusting *matters*, and have filled
My inheritance with their abominations."
19O יהוה, my strength and my stronghold
and my refuge, in the day of distress the
nations shall come to You from the ends of
the earth and say, "Our fathers have inherited only falsehood, futility, and there is no
value in them." [a]
20Would a man make mighty ones for
himself, which are not mighty ones?
21"Therefore see, I am causing them to
know, this time I cause them to know My
hand and My might. And they shall know
that My Name is יהוה!"

17

"The sin of Yehuḏah is written
with a pen of iron, engraved with
the point of a diamond on the tablet of their
heart, and on the horns of your slaughter-
places,
2while their children remember their
slaughter-places and their Ashěrim by the
spreading trees on the high hills.
3"My mountain in the field, I give as
plunder your wealth, all your treasures,
your high places of sin, throughout all your
borders.
4"And you, even of yourself, shall let go
of your inheritance which I gave you. And
I shall make you serve your enemies in a
land which you have not known, for you
have kindled a fire in My displeasure
which burns forever."
5Thus said יהוה, "Cursed is the man
who trusts in man and makes flesh his arm,
and whose heart turns away from יהוה.
6"For he shall be like a shrub in the
desert, and not see when good comes, and
shall inhabit the parched places in the
wilderness, a salt land that is not inhabited.
7"Blessed is the man who trusts in יהוה,
and whose trust is יהוה.
8"For he shall be like a tree planted by
the waters, which spreads out its roots by
the river, and does not see when heat
comes. And his leaf shall be green, and in
the year of drought he is not anxious, nor

16a See also Teh. 147:19, Yesh. 2:3, Yesh. 60:2-3, Yn. 4:22, Rom. 2:20, Rom. 3:2 and Rom. 9:4.
17a 7:24, 16:12, 18:12, 23:17.

does he cease from yielding fruit.
9 “The heart is crooked [a] above all, and
desperately sick – who shall know it?
10 “I, יהוה, search the heart, I try the kidneys, and give every man according to his
ways, according to the fruit of his deeds.
11 “As a partridge that broods but does not
hatch, so is he who gets riches, but not by
right. It leaves him in the midst of his days,
and at his end he is a fool.”
12 An esteemed throne, exalted from the
beginning, is the place of our set-apart
place.
13 O יהוה, the expectation of Yisra'ĕl, all
who forsake You are put to shame. “Those
who depart from Me shall be written in the
earth, because they have forsaken יהוה, the
fountain of living waters.” [b]
14 Heal me, O יהוה, so that I am healed.
Save me, so that I am saved, for You are
my praise.
15 See, they say to me, “Where is the word
of יהוה? Let it come now!”
16 And I have not run away from being a
shepherd who follows You, nor have I
longed for the desperately sick day. You
Yourself have known, that which came out
of my lips was before You.
17 Do not be a ruin to me, You are my
shelter in the day of evil.
18 Let these who persecute me be put to
shame, but do not let me be put to shame.
Let them be broken, but do not let me be
broken. Bring on them the day of evil, and
destroy them with double destruction!
19 Thus יהוה said to me, “Go and stand in
the gate of the children of the people, by
which the sovereigns of Yehuḏah come in
and by which they go out, and in all the
gates of Yerushalayim.
20 “And you shall say to them, ‘Hear the
word of יהוה, you sovereigns of Yehuḏah,
and all Yehuḏah, and all the inhabitants of
Yerushalayim, who enter by these gates.
21 ‘Thus said יהוה, “Guard yourselves,
and bear no burden on the Sabbath day, nor
bring it in by the gates of Yerushalayim,
22 nor take a burden out of your houses on
the Sabbath day, nor do any work. And you
shall set apart the Sabbath day, as I commanded your fathers.
23 “But they did not obey, or incline their
ear, and they made their neck stiff not to
hear and not to receive instruction.
24 “And it shall be, if you diligently obey
Me,” declares יהוה, “to bring in no burden
through the gates of this city on the
Sabbath day, and set apart the Sabbath day,
to do no work in it,
25 then sovereigns and heads sitting on the
throne of Dawiḏ shall enter in through the
gates of this city, riding in chariots and on
horses, they and their heads – the men of
Yehuḏah and the inhabitants of Yerushalayim. And this city shall be inhabited
forever.
26 “And they shall come from the cities of
Yehuḏah and from the places around Yerushalayim, and from the land of Binyamin
and from the low country, from the mountains and from the South, bringing ascending offerings and slaughterings, grain
offerings and incense, bringing offerings
of praise to the House of יהוה.
27 “But if you do not obey Me to set apart
the Sabbath day, and not to bear a burden
when entering the gates of Yerushalayim
on the Sabbath day, then I shall kindle a
fire in its gates, and it shall consume the
palaces of Yerushalayim, and not be
quenched.” ’ ”

18

The word which came to
Yirmeyahu from יהוה, saying,
2 “Arise, and go down to the potter's
house, and there I let you hear My words.”
3 So I went down to the potter's house,
and saw him doing a piece of work on the
wheel.
4 And the vessel that he made of clay was
ruined in the hand of the potter, so he
remade it into another vessel, as it seemed
good to the potter to do.
5 Then the word of יהוה came to me,
saying,
6 “O house of Yisra'ĕl, am I not able to
do with you as this potter?” declares יהוה.
“Look, as the clay is in the hand of the pot-

17b See 2:13.

ter, so are you in My hand, O house of
Yisra'ěl!
7 “The moment I speak concerning a
nation and concerning a reign, to pluck up,
to pull down, and to destroy it,
8 and that nation shall turn from its evil
because I have spoken against it, then I
shall repent of the evil that I thought to do
to it.
9 “And the moment I speak concerning a
nation and concerning a reign, to build and
to plant it,
10 and it shall do evil in My eyes in not
obeying My voice, then I shall repent concerning the good with which I spoke of
doing to it.
11 “And now, speak to the men of
Yehuḏah and to the inhabitants of Yerushalayim, saying, ‘Thus said יהוה, “See, I
am forming evil and devising a plan
against you. Return now every one from
his evil way, and make your ways and your
deeds good.” ’ ”
12 But they shall say, “It is no use! For we
walk according to our own plans, and we
do each one the stubbornness of his evil
heart.” [a]
13 Therefore thus said יהוה, “Ask now
among the nations, who has heard the like
of this? The maiden of Yisra'ěl has done
what is most horrible.
14 “Does the snow of Leḇanon cease from
the rock of the field? Or the cool flowing
waters from afar dry up?
15 “But My people have forgotten Me,
they have burned incense to what is false,
and they have stumbled from their ways,
from the ancient paths, to walk in bypaths
and not on a highway,
16 to make their land become a ruin, a
hissing forever – everyone who passes by
it is appalled and shakes his head.
17 “I shall scatter them as with an east
wind before the enemy; I shall show them
the back and not the face in the day of their
calamity.”
18 Then they said, “Come and let us
devise plans against Yirmeyahu, for the
Torah shall not perish from the priest, nor
counsel from the wise, nor the word from
the prophet. Come and let us strike him
with the tongue, and let us not listen to any
of his words.”
19 Attend to me, O יהוה, and listen to the
voice of my adversaries!
20 Should good be repaid with evil? For
they have dug a pit for my life. Remember
that I stood before You to speak good for
them, and to turn away Your wrath from
them.
21 So give their children over to scarcity
of food, and hand them over to the power
of the sword. Let their wives become
widows and bereaved of their children.
Let their men be killed to death, their
young men be stricken by the sword in battle.
22 Let a cry be heard from their houses,
when You bring a raiding party suddenly
upon them. For they have dug a pit to take
me, and laid snares for my feet.
23 But You, O יהוה, You know all their
counsel against me, to slay me. Do not pardon their crookedness, nor blot out their
sin from Your presence, and let them be
overthrown before You. Deal with them in
the time of Your displeasure.

19

Thus said יהוה, “Go and get a potter's earthen jug, and take some of
the elders of the people and some of the
elders of the priests.
2 “Then you shall go out to the Valley of
the Son of Hinnom, which is by the entry
of the Potsherd Gate, and shall proclaim
there the words that I speak to you,
3 and shall say, ‘Hear the word of יהוה,
O sovereigns of Yehuḏah and inhabitants
of Yerushalayim. Thus said יהוה of hosts,
the Elohim of Yisra'ěl, “See, I am bringing
evil on this place, that makes the ears
tingle of all who hear it.
4 “Because they have forsaken Me and
have profaned this place, and have burned
incense in it to other mighty ones whom
neither they, their fathers, nor the sovereigns of Yehuḏah have known, and they
have filled this place with the blood of the

18a 7:24, 16:12, 17:9, 23:17.

innocents,
[5]and have built the high places of Ba'al,
to burn their sons with fire for ascending
offerings to Ba'al, which I did not command or speak, nor did it come into My
heart.
[6]"Therefore see, the days are coming,"
declares יהוה, "that this place shall no
more be called Topheth or the Valley of the
Son of Hinnom, but *rather* the Valley of
Slaughter.
[7]"And I shall pour out the counsel of
Yehuḏah and Yerushalayim in this place,
and I shall make them fall by the sword
before their enemies and by the hands of
those who seek their lives. And I shall give
their corpses as meat for the birds of the
heavens and for the beasts of the earth.
[8]"And I shall make this city a ruin, and a
hissing – everyone who passes by it is
appalled and hisses because of all its
plagues.
[9]"And I shall make them to eat the flesh
of their sons and the flesh of their daughters, and eat one another's flesh in the
siege and in the distress with which their
enemies and those who seek their lives
distress them." '
[10]"And you shall break the jug before the
eyes of the men who go with you,
[11]and shall say to them, 'Thus said יהוה
of hosts, "Even so I break this people and
this city, as one breaks a potter's vessel,
which one is unable to repair again. And
let them bury them in Topheth till there is
no place to bury.
[12]"This is what I shall do to this place,"
declares יהוה, "and to its inhabitants, so as
to make this city like Topheth.
[13]"And the houses of Yerushalayim and
the houses of the sovereigns of Yehuḏah
shall be as unclean as the place of Topheth,
because of all the houses on whose roofs
they have burned incense to all the host of
the heavens, and poured out drink offerings to other mighty ones." ' "
[14]And when Yirmeyahu returned from
Topheth, where יהוה had sent him to
prophesy, he stood in the courtyard of the
House of יהוה and said to all the people,
[15]"Thus said יהוה of hosts, the Elohim of
Yisra'ěl, 'See, I am bringing on this city
and on all her towns all the evil that I have
pronounced against it, because they have
stiffened their necks so as not to hear My
words.' "

20 And Pashhur son of Imměr, the
priest who was also chief governor
in the House of יהוה, heard that Yirmeyahu prophesied these words,
[2]And Pashhur struck Yirmeyahu the
prophet, and put him in the stocks that
were in the high gate of Binyamin, which
was by the House of יהוה.
[3]And it came to be on the next day that
Pashhur brought Yirmeyahu out of the
stocks, and Yirmeyahu said to him, "יהוה
has not called your name Pashhur, but
Maḡor-Missaḇiḇ.
[4]"For thus said יהוה, 'See, I am making
you a fear to yourself and to all your loved
ones. And they shall fall by the sword of
their enemies, while your eyes see it. And I
shall give all Yehuḏah into the hand of the
sovereign of Baḇel, and he shall exile them
to Baḇel and strike them with the sword.
[5]'And I shall give all the wealth of this
city and all its labour, and all its valuables,
and all the treasures of the sovereigns of
Yehuḏah, I give into the hand of their
enemies, who shall plunder them, seize
them, and shall bring them to Baḇel.
[6]'And you, Pashhur, and all who dwell
in your house, shall go into captivity, and
enter into Baḇel. And there you shall die,
and be buried there, you and all your loved
ones, to whom you have prophesied falsehood.' "
[7]O יהוה, You enticed me, and I was
enticed. You are stronger than I, and have
prevailed. I have been ridiculed all day
long, everyone mocks me.
[8]For when I speak, I cry out, proclaiming violence and ruin. Because the word of
יהוה was made to me a reproach and a
derision daily.
[9]Whenever I said, "Let me not mention
Him, nor speak in His Name again," it was
in my heart like a burning fire shut up in
my bones. And I became weary of holding
it back, and was helpless.

10 For I heard many mocking, "Fear on every side!" "Expose," they say, "yes, let us expose him!" All my friends watched for my stumbling, *saying*, "He might be lured away, so that we prevail against him, and take our revenge on him."

11 But יהוה is with me like a mighty, awesome one. Therefore my persecutors shall stumble, and not prevail. They shall be greatly ashamed, for they have not acted wisely – an everlasting reproach never to be forgotten.

12 But, O יהוה of hosts, trying the righteous, and seeing the kidneys and heart, let me see Your vengeance on them, for I have revealed my cause to You.

13 Sing to יהוה! Praise יהוה! For He has delivered the being of the poor from the hand of evil ones.

14 Cursed be the day in which I was born! Let the day not be blessed in which my mother bore me!

15 Let the man be cursed who brought news to my father, saying, "A male child has been born to you," making him very glad.

16 And let that man be like the cities which יהוה overthrew, and repented not. Let him hear the cry in the morning and the shouting at noon,

17 because I was not slain from the womb, so that my mother should have been my burial-site and her womb forever great.

18 Why did I come forth from the womb to see toil and sorrow, and spend my days in shame?

21 The word that came to Yirmeyahu from יהוה when Sovereign Tsiḏqiyahu sent to him Pashhur son of Malkiyah, and Tsephanyah the son of Ma‛asěyah, the priest, saying,

2 "Please inquire of יהוה on our behalf, for Neḇuḵaḏretstsar sovereign of Baḇel has *started* fighting against us. It might be that יהוה deals with us according to all His wondrous works, so that he withdraws from us."

3 But Yirmeyahu said to them, "Say this to Tsiḏqiyahu,

4 'Thus said יהוה Elohim of Yisra'ěl, "See, I am turning back the weapons of battle that are in your hands, with which you fight against the sovereign of Baḇel and the Kasdim who besiege you outside the wall. And I shall gather them inside this city.

5 "And I Myself shall fight against you with an outstretched hand, and with a strong arm, even in displeasure and rage and great wrath.

6 "And I shall strike the inhabitants of this city, both man and beast – let them die of a great pestilence.

7 "And afterward," declares יהוה, "I give Tsiḏqiyahu sovereign of Yehuḏah, his servants and the people, and such as are left in this city from the pestilence and the sword and the scarcity of food, into the hand of Neḇuḵaḏretstsar sovereign of Baḇel, into the hand of their enemies, and into the hand of those who seek their life. And he shall strike them with the edge of the sword. He shall not pardon them, nor spare nor have compassion." '

8 "You shall also say to this people, 'Thus said יהוה, "See, I set before you the way of life and the way of death.

9 "Whoever stays in this city dies by the sword, by scarcity of food, and by pestilence. But whoever goes out and shall go over to the Kasdim who besiege you, is going to live, and his life shall be as a prize to him.

10 "For I have set My face against this city for evil and not for good," declares יהוה. "It is given into the hand of the sovereign of Baḇel, and he shall burn it with fire." '

11 "And to the house of the sovereign of Yehuḏah, *say*, 'Hear the word of יהוה,

12 'O house of Dawiḏ! Thus said יהוה, "Render right-ruling in the morning, and deliver him who has been robbed out of the hand of the oppressor, lest My wrath go out like fire and burn, with no one to quench it, because of the evil of your deeds.

13 "See, I am against you, O inhabitant of the valley, rock of the plain," declares יהוה, "who are saying, 'Who would come down against us? And who would come into our dwellings?'

14 “And I shall punish you according to
the fruit of your deeds,” declares יהוה.
“And I shall kindle a fire in its forest, and
it shall consume all that is around her.” ’ ”

22 Thus said יהוה, “Go down to the
house of the sovereign of Yehuḏah.
And there you shall speak this word,
2 and shall say, ‘Hear the word of יהוה,
O sovereign of Yehuḏah, you who sit on
the throne of Dawiḏ, you and your servants
and your people who enter these gates!
3 ‘Thus said יהוה, “Do right-ruling and
righteousness, and deliver him who is
robbed out of the hand of the oppressor.
Do not maltreat nor do violence to the
stranger, the fatherless, or the widow, nor
shed innocent blood in this place.
4 “For if you certainly do this word, then
there shall enter in by the gates of this
house sovereigns sitting on the throne of
Dawiḏ, riding on horses and in chariots, he
and his servants and his people.
5 “But if you do not obey these words, I
swear by Myself,” declares יהוה, “that this
house shall become a ruin.” ’ ”
6 For thus said יהוה to the house of the
sovereign of Yehuḏah, “You are *like* Gilʽaḏ
to Me, the head of Leḇanon. But I shall
make you a wilderness, and cities which
are not inhabited.
7 “And I shall prepare destroyers against
you, each with his weapons. And they shall
cut down your choice cedars and throw
them into the fire.
8 “And many nations shall pass by this
city, and they shall say to one another,
‘Why has יהוה done so to this great city?’
9 “Then they shall say, ‘Because they
have forsaken the covenant of יהוה their
Elohim, and bowed themselves to other
mighty ones and served them.’ ”
10 Do not weep for the dead, nor mourn
for him. Weep bitterly for him who goes
away, for he shall never come back nor see
the land of his birth.
11 For thus said יהוה concerning Shallum
son of Yoshiyahu, sovereign of Yehuḏah,
who reigned instead of Yoshiyahu his
father, who went from this place, “He shall
never come back,
12 but he shall die in the place where they
have exiled him, and not see this land
again.
13 “Woe to him who builds his house
without righteousness and his rooms without right-ruling, who uses his neighbour’s
service without wages and does not give
him his wages,
14 who says, ‘I am going to build myself a
wide house with spacious rooms, and cut
out windows for it, panelling it with cedar
and painting it in red.’
15 “Do you reign because you enclose
yourself in cedar? Did not your father eat
and drink, and do right-ruling and righteousness? Then it was well with him.
16 “He defended the cause of the poor and
needy – then it was well. Was this not to
know Me?” declares יהוה.
17 “But your eyes and your heart are only
upon your own greedy gain, and on shedding innocent blood, and on oppression
and on doing violence.”
18 Therefore thus said יהוה concerning
Yehoyaqim son of Yoshiyahu, sovereign of
Yehuḏah, “Let them not lament for him:
‘Alas, my brother!’ or ‘Alas, my sister!’
Let them not lament for him: ‘Alas, master!’ or ‘Alas, his excellency!’
19 “He shall be buried – the burial-place
of a donkey – dragged and thrown outside
the gates of Yerushalayim.
20 “Go up to Leḇanon, and cry out, and lift
up your voice in Bashan. And cry from
Aḇarim, for all your lovers are destroyed.
21 “I have spoken to you in your ease, but
you said, ‘I do not listen.’ This has been
your way from your youth, for you did not
obey My voice.
22 “Let all your shepherds be devoured by
the wind, and your lovers go into captivity.
Then you shall be ashamed and humiliated
for all your evil.
23 “You who dwell in Leḇanon, being
nested in the cedars, how you shall groan
when pangs come upon you, like the pains
of a woman giving birth!
24 “As I live,” declares יהוה, “though
Konyahu son of Yehoyaqim, sovereign of
Yehuḏah, were the signet on My right
hand, I would still pull you off from there;

25 and I shall give you into the hand of
those who seek your life, and into the hand
of those whose face you fear, into the hand
of Neḇuḵaḏretstsar sovereign of Baḇel and
the hand of the Kasdim.
26 "And I shall hurl you out, and your
mother who bore you, into another land
where you were not born, and there you
shall die.
27 "But they shall not return to the land to
which their being yearns to return.
28 "Is this man Konyahu a despised broken pot, or an undesirable vessel? Why are
they hurled out, he and his descendants,
and cast into a land which they do not
know?
29 "O land, land, land! Hear the word of
יהוה!
30 "Thus said יהוה, 'Write this man down
as childless, a strong man who is not to
prosper in his days, for none of his descendants shall prosper, sitting on the throne of
Dawiḏ, or rule any more in Yehuḏah.' "

23

"Woe to the shepherds destroying
and scattering the sheep of My pasture!" [a] declares יהוה.
2 Therefore thus said יהוה Elohim of
Yisra'ěl against the shepherds who feed
My people, "You have scattered My flock,
driven them away, and have not tended
them. See, I am punishing you for the evil
of your deeds," declares יהוה.
3 "Therefore I shall gather the remnant of
My flock out of all the lands where I have
driven them, and shall bring them back to
their fold. And they shall bear and
increase.
4 "And I shall raise up shepherds over
them, and they shall feed them. [b] And they
shall fear no more, nor be discouraged, nor
shall they be lacking," declares יהוה.
5 "See, the days are coming," declares
יהוה, "when I shall raise for Dawiḏ a
Branch [c] of righteousness, and a Sovereign
shall reign and act wisely, and shall do
right-ruling and righteousness in the earth.
6 "In His days Yehuḏah shall be saved,
and Yisra'ěl dwell safely. And this is His
Name whereby He shall be called: 'יהוה
our Righteousness.'
7 "Therefore, see, the days are coming,"
declares יהוה, "when they shall say no
more, 'As יהוה lives who brought up the
children of Yisra'ěl out of the land of
Mitsrayim,'
8 but, 'As יהוה lives who brought up and
led the seed of the house of Yisra'ěl out of
the land of the north and from all the lands
where I had driven them.' And they shall
dwell on their own soil."
9 My heart within me is broken because
of the prophets; all my bones shake. I am
like a drunken man, and like a man overcome by wine, because of יהוה, and
because of His set-apart words.
10 For the land is filled with adulterers; for
the land mourns because of a curse. The
pastures of the wilderness are dried up.
And their course is evil, and their might
is not right.
11 "For both prophet and priest have
become defiled. Even in My house I have
found their evil," declares יהוה.
12 "Therefore their way is to them like
slippery ways in the dark. They are driven
on and they shall fall in them. For I bring
evil on them, the year of their punishment," declares יהוה.
13 "And I have seen folly in the prophets
of Shomeron: they prophesied by Ba'al
and led My people Yisra'ěl astray.
14 "And among the prophets of Yerushalayim I have seen a horrible matter:
committing adultery and walking in falsehood. And they strengthen the hands of
evil ones, so that no one turns back from
his evil. All of them are like Seḏom to Me,
and her inhabitants like Amorah.
15 "Therefore thus said יהוה of hosts concerning the prophets, 'See, I am making
them eat wormwood, and shall make them
drink poisoned water. For defilement has
gone out into all the land from the prophets
of Yerushalayim.' "
16 Thus said יהוה of hosts, "Do not listen
to the words of the prophets who prophesy
to you, they lead you astray. They speak a

23a 10:21, 50:5-6, Yeḥez. 34:1-23, Zeḵ. 10:2, Mt. 9:36. *23b* 3:14-17. *23c* Or *Sprout*.

vision of their own heart, not from the mouth of יהוה.

17 “They keep on saying to those who despise Me, ‘יהוה has said you shall have peace.’ And to all who walk according to the stubbornness of their own heart *they say*, ‘No evil comes upon you.’ ”

18 For who has stood in the counsel of יהוה, and has seen and heard His word? Who has listened to His word and obeyed it?

19 See, a storm of יהוה shall go forth in a rage, a whirling storm! It whirls on the head of the wrong.

20 The displeasure of יהוה shall not turn back until He has done and established the purposes of His heart. In the latter days you shall understand it perfectly.[d]

21 “I did not send these prophets, yet they ran. I have not spoken to them, yet they prophesied.[e]

22 “But if they had stood in My counsel, then they would have let My people hear My Words, and they would have turned them from their evil way and from the evil of their deeds.

23 “Am I an Elohim close by,” declares יהוה, “and not an Elohim afar off?

24 “If anyone is hidden in secret places, would I not see him?” declares יהוה. “Do I not fill the heavens and earth?” declares יהוה.

25 “I have heard what the prophets have said who prophesy falsehood in My Name, saying, ‘I have dreamed, I have dreamed!’

26 “Till when shall it be in the heart of the prophets? – the prophets of falsehood and prophets of the deceit of their own heart,

27 who try to make My people forget My Name by their dreams which everyone relates to his neighbour, as their fathers forgot My Name for Ba‘al.

28 “The prophet who has a dream, let him relate the dream, and he who has My Word, let him speak My Word in truth. What is the chaff to the wheat?” declares יהוה.

29 “Is not My Word like a fire?” declares יהוה, “and like a hammer that shatters a rock?

30 “Therefore see, I am against the prophets,” declares יהוה, “who steal My Words every one from his neighbour.

31 “See, I am against the prophets,” declares יהוה, “who use their tongues and say, ‘He declares.’

32 “See, I am against those who prophesy false dreams,” declares יהוה, “and relate them, and lead My people astray by their falsehoods and by their reckless boasting. But I Myself did not send them nor have I commanded them. And they do not profit this people at all,” declares יהוה.

33 “And when these people or the prophet or the priest ask you, saying, ‘What is the message of יהוה?’ then you shall say to them, ‘What message?’ I shall forsake you,” declares יהוה.

34 “As for the prophet and the priest and the people who say, ‘The message of יהוה,’ I shall punish that man and his house.

35 “This is what each one says to his neighbour, and each one to his brother, ‘What has יהוה answered?’ and, ‘What has יהוה spoken?’

36 “But the message of יהוה you no longer remember! For every man’s message is his own word, for you have changed[f] the Words of the living Elohim, יהוה of hosts, our Elohim!

37 “This is what you say to the prophet, ‘What has יהוה answered you?’ and, ‘What has יהוה spoken?’

38 “But since you say, ‘The message of יהוה!’ therefore thus said יהוה, ‘Because you say this word, “The message of יהוה!” and I have sent to you, saying, “Do not say, ‘The message of יהוה!’ ”

39 therefore see, I, I shall utterly forget you and cast you away from My presence, along with the city that I gave you and your fathers.

40 ‘And I shall put an everlasting reproach on you, and an everlasting shame that is not forgotten.’ ”

23d 30:24. *23e* 14:14-15, 23:32, 28:15, 29:9. *23f* Or *overthrown*. See Yesh. 24:5.

24

יהוה showed me, and look, there were two baskets of figs set before the Hěkal of יהוה, after Neḇuḵaḏrets-tsar sovereign of Baḇel had exiled Yeḵonyahu son of Yehoyaqim, sovereign of Yehuḏah, and the heads of Yehuḏah with the craftsmen and smiths, from Yerushalayim, and had brought them to Baḇel.

2 One basket had very good figs, like the figs that are first ripe. And the other basket had very spoilt figs which could not be eaten, they were so spoilt."

3 And יהוה said to me, "What do you see, Yirmeyahu?" And I said, "Figs, the good figs, very good. And the spoilt, very spoilt, which could not be eaten, they are so spoilt."

4 Again the word of יהוה came to me, saying,

5 "Thus said יהוה, the Elohim of Yisra'ěl, 'Like these good figs, so do I acknowledge the exiles of Yehuḏah, whom I have sent out of this place for their own good, into the land of the Kasdim.

6 'And I shall set My eyes on them for good, and shall bring them back to this land. And I shall build them and not pull them down, and shall plant them and not pluck them up.

7 'And I shall give them a heart to know Me, that I am יהוה. And they shall be My people and I shall be their Elohim, for they shall turn back to Me with all their heart.

8 'And as the spoilt figs that could not be eaten because they are so spoilt,' for thus said יהוה, 'so do I give up Tsiḏqiyahu, the sovereign of Yehuḏah, his heads, the rest of Yerushalayim who remain in this land, and those who dwell in the land of Mitsrayim.

9 'And I shall make them a horror to all the reigns of the earth, for evil, to be a reproach and a byword, a mockery and a curse, in all the places to which I drive them.

10 'And I shall send the sword, the scarcity of food, and the pestilence among them, till they are consumed from the land that I gave to them and their fathers.' "

25

The word that came to Yirmeyahu concerning all the people of Yehuḏah, in the fourth year of Yehoyaqim son of Yoshiyahu, the sovereign of Yehuḏah, which was the first year of Neḇuḵaḏretstsar sovereign of Baḇel,

2 which Yirmeyahu the prophet spoke to all the people of Yehuḏah and to all the inhabitants of Yerushalayim, saying,

3 "From the thirteenth year of Yoshiyahu son of Amon, sovereign of Yehuḏah, even to this day, this is the twenty-third year in which the word of יהוה has come to me. And I have spoken to you, rising early and speaking, but you have not listened.

4 "Moreover, יהוה has sent to you all His servants the prophets, rising early and sending them, but you have not listened nor inclined your ear to hear,

5 saying, 'Turn back now everyone from his evil way and from the evil of your deeds, and dwell on the soil which יהוה has given to you and your fathers forever and ever.

6 'And do not go after other mighty ones to serve them and to bow down to them. And do not provoke Me with the works of your hands, so that I do you no evil.'

7 "But you did not listen to Me," declares יהוה, "so as to provoke Me with the works of your hands, for your own evil.

8 "Therefore thus said יהוה of hosts, 'Because you did not obey My words,

9 see, I am sending and taking all the tribes of the north,' declares יהוה, 'and Neḇuḵaḏretstsar the sovereign of Baḇel, My servant, and shall bring them against this land and against its inhabitants, and against these nations all around, and shall put them under the ban, and make them an astonishment, and a hissing, and everlasting ruins.

10 'And I shall banish from them the voice of rejoicing and the voice of gladness, the voice of the bridegroom and the voice of the bride, the sound of the millstones and the light of the lamp.

11 'And all this land shall be a ruin and a waste, and these nations shall serve the sovereign of Baḇel seventy years.

12 'And it shall be, when seventy years are

completed, that I shall punish the sovereign of Baḇel and that nation, the land of
the Kasdim, for their crookedness,'
declares יהוה, 'and shall make it everlasting ruins.
13 'And I shall bring on that land all My
words which I have pronounced against it,
all that is written in this book, which
Yirmeyahu has prophesied concerning all
the nations.
14 'For they too shall be enslaved by many
nations and great sovereigns. And I shall
repay them according to their deeds and
according to the works of their hands.' "
15 For thus said יהוה Elohim of Yisra'ěl to
me, "Take this wine cup of wrath from My
hand, and make all the nations, to whom I
send you, drink it.
16 "And they shall drink, and shake, and
go mad because of the sword that I am
sending among them."
17 I then took the cup from the hand of
יהוה, and made all the nations drink, to
whom יהוה had sent me,
18 *namely* Yerushalayim and the cities of
Yehuḏah, and its sovereigns, its heads, to
make them a ruin, an object of astonishment, a hissing, and a curse, as it is this
day;
19 Pharaoh sovereign of Mitsrayim, and
his servants, and his heads, and all his people;
20 and all the mixed multitude, and all the
sovereigns of the land of Uts, and all the
sovereigns of the land of the Philistines –
even Ashqelon, and Azzah, and Eqron, and
the remnant of Ashdoḏ;
21 Eḏom, and Mo'aḇ, and the children of
Ammon;
22 and all the sovereigns of Tsor, and all
the sovereigns of Tsiḏon, and the sovereigns of the coastlands which are beyond
the sea;
23 Deḏan, and Těma, and Buz, and all
who are in the farthest corners;
24 and all the sovereigns of Araḇia and all
the sovereigns of the mixed multitude who
dwell in the wilderness;
25 and all the sovereigns of Zimri, and all
the sovereigns of Ěylam, and all the sovereigns of the Medes;
26 and all the sovereigns of the north, far
and near, one with another, and all the
reigns of the earth which are on the face of
the ground. Also the sovereign of Shěshaḵ
shall drink after them.
27 "And you shall say to them, 'Thus said
יהוה of hosts, the Elohim of Yisra'ěl,
"Drink, be drunk, and vomit! Fall and rise
no more, because of the sword which I
am sending among you." '
28 "And it shall be, when they refuse to
take the cup from your hand to drink, then
you shall say to them, 'Thus said יהוה of
hosts, "You shall drink!
29 "For look, I am beginning to bring evil
upon the city which is called by My Name,
and should you be entirely unpunished?
You are not going unpunished, for I am
calling for a sword on all the inhabitants of
the earth," declares יהוה of hosts.'
30 "And you shall prophesy against them
all these words, and say to them, 'יהוה
roars from on high, and utters His voice
from His set-apart dwelling place. He roars
mightily over His fold, a shout as those
who tread the grapes, against all the inhabitants of the earth.
31 "Tumult shall come to the ends of the
earth, for יהוה has a controversy with the
nations. He shall enter into judgment with
all flesh. The wrong He shall give to the
sword,' declares יהוה."
32 Thus said יהוה of hosts, "See, evil is
going forth from nation to nation, and a
great whirlwind is raised up from the farthest parts of the earth.
33 "And in that day the slain of יהוה shall
be from one end of the earth even to the
other end of the earth.[a] They shall not be
lamented, or gathered, or buried, for they
are dung on the face of the ground.
34 "Howl, you shepherds, and cry! And
roll yourselves *in the ashes*, you leaders of
the flock! For the days of your slaughter
and your scatterings are completed, and
you shall fall like a choice vessel.
35 "And a place of refuge shall perish

25a See footnote Yesh. 66:24.

from the shepherds, and escape from the
leaders of the flock.
36 "Hear the cry of the shepherds, and a
wailing of the leaders of the flock, for יהוה
is ravaging their pasture!
37 "And the pastures of peace shall be cut
down because of the burning displeasure
of יהוה.
38 "Like a lion He shall leave His hiding
place, for their land shall become a waste
because of the sword of oppressors, and
because of His burning displeasure."

26 In the beginning of the reign of
Yehoyaqim the son of Yoshiyahu,
the sovereign of Yehuḏah, this word came
from יהוה, saying,
2 "Thus said יהוה, 'Stand in the courtyard of the House of יהוה, and speak to all
the cities of Yehuḏah, which come to bow
themselves in the House of יהוה, all the
words that I command you to speak to
them. Do not diminish a word.
3 'If so be that they listen and each turn
from his evil way, then I shall repent of the
evil that I plan to do to them, because of
the evil of their deeds.'
4 "And you shall say to them, 'Thus said
יהוה, "If you do not listen to Me, to walk
in My Torah which I set before you,
5 to listen to the words of My servants
the prophets I am sending you, even rising
up early and sending them – though you
have not listened –
6 then I shall make this house like Shiloh,
and make this city a curse to all the nations
of the earth." ' "
7 And the priests and the prophets and all
the people heard Yirmeyahu speaking
these words in the House of יהוה.
8 And it came to be, when Yirmeyahu
had ended speaking all that יהוה had commanded him to speak to all the people, that
the priests and the prophets and all the
people seized him, saying, "You shall
certainly die!
9 "Why have you prophesied in the
Name of יהוה, saying, 'This house shall be
like Shiloh, and this city be dried up, without an inhabitant'?" And all the people
were gathered against Yirmeyahu in the
House of יהוה.
10 And the heads of Yehuḏah heard this,
and they came up from the sovereign's
house to the House of יהוה and sat down in
the entrance of the new gate of the House
of יהוה.
11 And the priests and the prophets spoke
to the heads and all the people, saying, "A
death sentence for this man! For he has
prophesied against this city, as you have
heard with your ears."
12 And Yirmeyahu spoke to all the heads
and all the people, saying, "יהוה sent me to
prophesy against this house and against
this city with all the words you heard.
13 "And now, make good your ways and
your deeds, and obey the voice of יהוה
your Elohim, then יהוה shall relent concerning the evil He has pronounced against
you.
14 "And I, look I am in your hand. Do
with me as seems good and right to you.
15 "But know for certain that if you put
me to death, you are bringing innocent
blood on yourselves, and on this city, and
on its inhabitants. For truly יהוה has sent
me to you to speak all these words in your
hearing."
16 Then the heads and all the people said
to the priests and the prophets, "No death
sentence for this man. For he has spoken to
us in the Name of יהוה our Elohim."
17 And some of the elders of the land rose
up and spoke to all the assembly of the
people, saying,
18 "Miḵayah of Moresheth prophesied in
the days of Ḥizqiyahu the sovereign of
Yehuḏah, and he spoke to all the people of
Yehuḏah, saying, 'Thus said יהוה of hosts,
"Tsiyon shall become a ploughed field, and
Yerushalayim be heaps, and the mountain
of the House like the bare hills of the
forest." '
19 "Did Ḥizqiyahu sovereign of Yehuḏah
and all Yehuḏah indeed put him to death?
Did he not fear יהוה and seek the favour of
יהוה? And the Master relented concerning
the evil which He had pronounced against
them. But we are doing great evil against
ourselves."
20 There was however a man who prophe-

sied in the Name of יהוה, Uriyahu the son
of Shemayahu of Qiryath Ye'arim, who
prophesied against this city and against
this land according to all the words of
Yirmeyahu.
21 And when Yehoyaqim the sovereign,
with all his mighty men and all the heads,
heard his words, the sovereign sought to
put him to death. But Uriyahu heard of it,
and was afraid and fled, and went to Mitsrayim.
22 Then Yehoyaqim the sovereign sent
men to Mitsrayim: Elnathan the son of
Aḵbor, and some men who went with him
to Mitsrayim.
23 And they brought Uriyahu from Mitsrayim and brought him to Yehoyaqim the
sovereign, who struck him with the sword
and threw his dead body into the burial-
sites of the common people.
24 However, the hand of Aḥiqam son of
Shaphan was with Yirmeyahu, so as not to
give him into the hand of the people to put
him to death.

27 In the beginning of the reign of
Yehoyaqim son of Yoshiyahu, the
sovereign of Yehuḏah, this word came to
Yirmeyah from יהוה, saying,
2 "This is what יהוה said to me, 'Make
for yourselves bands and yokes. Then you
shall put them on your neck,
3 and shall send them to the sovereign of
Eḏom, and the sovereign of Mo'aḇ, and the
sovereign of the Ammonites, and the
sovereign of Tsor, and the sovereign of
Tsiḏon, by the hand of the messengers who
come to Yerushalayim to Tsiḏqiyahu, the
sovereign of Yehuḏah.
4 'And you shall command them to say to
their masters, "Thus said יהוה of hosts, the
Elohim of Yisra'ěl, 'Say this to your masters,'
5 'I have made the earth, the man and the
beast that are on the face of the earth, by
My great power and by My outstretched
arm. And I shall give it to whom it seemed
right in My eyes.
6 'And now, I have given all these lands
into the hand of Neḇuḵaḏnetstsar the
sovereign of Baḇel, My servant. And the
beasts of the field I have also given him to
serve him.
7 'And all nations shall serve him and his
son and his son's son, until the time of his
land comes. And then many nations and
great sovereigns shall make him serve
them.
8 'And it shall be, the nation and reign
that do not serve Neḇuḵaḏnetstsar the sovereign of Baḇel, and the one that does not
put its neck under the yoke of the sovereign of Baḇel, that nation I shall punish,'
declares יהוה, 'with the sword, and the
scarcity of food, and the pestilence, until I
have consumed them by his hand.
9 'So do not listen to your prophets, or to
your diviners, or to your dreamers, or to
your observers of clouds, or your sorcerers, who speak to you, saying, "Do not
serve the sovereign of Baḇel."
10 'For they are prophesying falsehood to
you, to remove you far from your land.
And I shall drive you out, and you shall
perish.
11 'But the nations that bring their necks
under the yoke of the sovereign of Baḇel
and serve him, I shall leave in their own
land,' declares יהוה, 'and they shall till it
and dwell in it.' "
12 And I spoke to Tsiḏqiyah the sovereign
of Yehuḏah according to all these words,
saying, "Bring your necks under the yoke
of the sovereign of Baḇel, and serve him
and his people, and live!
13 "Why should you die, you and your
people, by the sword, by the scarcity of
food, and by the pestilence, as יהוה has
spoken against the nation that does not
serve the sovereign of Baḇel?
14 "Do not listen to the words of the
prophets who speak to you, saying, 'Do
not serve the sovereign of Baḇel,' for they
prophesy falsehood to you,
15 for I have not sent them," declares
יהוה, "yet they prophesy falsehood in My
Name, in order that I drive you out. Then
you shall perish, you and the prophets who
prophesy to you."
16 Then I spoke to the priests and to all
this people, saying, "Thus said יהוה, 'Do
not listen to the words of your prophets

who are prophesying to you, saying, "See,
the vessels of the House of יהוה are
brought back from Baḇel soon now,"
for they prophesy falsehood to you.
17 'Do not listen to them. Serve the sovereign of Baḇel, and live! Why should this
city become a ruin?
18 'But if they are prophets, and if the
word of יהוה is with them, let them now
make intercession to יהוה of hosts, that the
vessels which are left in the House of יהוה,
and in the house of the sovereign of
Yehuḏah, and at Yerushalayim, shall not
go to Baḇel.'
19 "For thus said יהוה of hosts concerning
the columns, and concerning the Sea, and
concerning the stands, and concerning the
remainder of the vessels which are left in
this city,
20 which Neḇuḵaḏnetstsar the sovereign
of Baḇel did not take, when he exiled
Yeḵonyah the son of Yehoyaqim, the sovereign of Yehuḏah, from Yerushalayim to
Baḇel, and all the nobles of Yehuḏah and
Yerushalayim –
21 thus said יהוה of hosts, the Elohim of
Yisra'ĕl, concerning the vessels that
remain in the House of יהוה, and in the
house of the sovereign of Yehuḏah and of
Yerushalayim:
22 'They shall be brought to Baḇel, and be
there until the day that I visit them,'
declares יהוה. 'Then I shall bring them
back and restore them to this place.' "

28

And it came to be in that year, at
the beginning of the reign of
Tsiḏqiyah sovereign of Yehuḏah, in the
fourth year and in the fifth new *moon*, that
Ḥananyah son of Azzur the prophet, who
was from Giḇʽon, spoke to me in the House
of יהוה in the presence of the priests and of
all the people, saying,
2 "Thus spoke יהוה of hosts, the Elohim
of Yisra'ĕl, saying, 'I have broken the yoke
of the sovereign of Baḇel.
3 'Within two years I am going to bring
back to this place all the vessels of the
House of יהוה, that Neḇuḵaḏnetstsar sovereign of Baḇel removed from this place
and took to Baḇel.
4 'And I am going to bring back to this
place Yeḵonyah son of Yehoyaqim, sovereign of Yehuḏah, with all the exiles of
Yehuḏah who went to Baḇel,' declares
יהוה, 'for I am going to break the yoke of
the sovereign of Baḇel.' "
5 Then the prophet Yirmeyah spoke to
the prophet Ḥananyah in the presence of
the priests and in the presence of all the
people who stood in the House of יהוה,
6 and the prophet Yirmeyah said, "Amĕn!
יהוה do so! יהוה establish your words
which you have prophesied, to bring back
the vessels of the House of יהוה and all the
exiles from Baḇel to this place!
7 "Only, hear now this word that I speak
in your hearing and in the hearing of all the
people:
8 "The prophets who have been before
me and before you of old prophesied
against many lands and great reigns, of
battle and of evil and of pestilence.
9 "The prophet who prophesies of peace
– when the word of the prophet comes to
pass, that prophet is known as one whom
יהוה has truly sent."
10 And Ḥananyah the prophet took the
yoke off the prophet Yirmeyah's neck and
broke it.
11 And Ḥananyah spoke in the presence of
all the people, saying, "Thus said יהוה, 'So
I shall break the yoke of Neḇuḵaḏnetstsar
sovereign of Baḇel from the neck of all
nations within two years.' " And the
prophet Yirmeyah went his way.
12 And the word of יהוה came to Yirmeyah, after Ḥananyah the prophet had broken the yoke from the neck of the prophet
Yirmeyah, saying,
13 "Go and speak to Ḥananyah, saying,
'Thus said יהוה, "You have broken the
yokes of wood, but you shall make yokes
of iron instead."
14 'For thus said יהוה of hosts, the Elohim
of Yisra'ĕl, "I have put a yoke of iron on
the neck of all these nations, to serve
Neḇuḵaḏnetstsar sovereign of Baḇel. And
they shall serve him. And I have also given
him the beasts of the field." ' "
15 And the prophet Yirmeyah said to
Ḥananyah the prophet, "Listen, please,

Ḥananyah, יהוה has not sent you, but you
have made this people trust in falsehood.
16 "Therefore thus said יהוה, 'See, I am
sending you away from the face of the
earth. This year you shall die, for you have
spoken apostasy against יהוה.' "
17 And Ḥananyah the prophet died the
same year, in the seventh new *moon*.

29 And these are the words of the letter which Yirmeyah the prophet
sent from Yerushalayim to the rest of the
elders of the exile, and to the priests, and to
the prophets and to all the people whom
Neḇuḵaḏnetstsar had exiled from
Yerushalayim to Baḇel –
2 after Yeḵonyah the sovereign, and the
sovereigness mother, and the eunuchs, and
the heads of Yehuḏah and Yerushalayim,
and the craftsmen, and the smiths had gone
into exile from Yerushalayim –
3 by the hand of El'asah son of Shaphan,
and Gemaryah the son of Ḥilqiyah, whom
Tsiḏqiyah sovereign of Yehuḏah sent to
Baḇel, to Neḇuḵaḏnetstsar the sovereign of
Baḇel, saying,
4 "Thus said יהוה of hosts, Elohim of
Yisra'ĕl, to all the exiles whom I exiled
from Yerushalayim to Baḇel,
5 'Build houses and dwell *in them*, plant
gardens and eat their fruit.
6 'Take wives and bring forth sons and
daughters. And take wives for your sons
and give your daughters to husbands, and
let them bear sons and daughters, and be
increased there, and not diminished.
7 'And seek the peace of the city where
I have exiled you, and pray to יהוה for it,
for in its peace you have peace.'
8 "For thus said יהוה of hosts, Elohim of
Yisra'ĕl, 'Let not your prophets and your
diviners who are in your midst deceive
you, neither listen to the dreams which you
are dreaming.
9 'For they are prophesying falsely to
you in My Name. I have not sent them,'
declares יהוה.
10 "For thus said יהוה, 'When seventy
years are completed, at Baḇel I shall visit
you and establish My good word toward
you, to bring you back to this place.
11 'For I know the plans I am planning for
you,' declares יהוה, 'plans of peace and
not of evil, to give you a future and an
expectancy.
12 'Then you shall call on Me, and shall
come and pray to Me, and I shall listen to
you.
13 'And you shall seek Me, and shall find
Me, when you search for Me with all your
heart. [a]
14 'And I shall be found by you,' declares
יהוה, 'and I shall turn back your captivity,
and shall gather you from all the nations
and from all the places where I have driven
you, declares יהוה. And I shall bring you
back to the place from which I have exiled
you.'
15 "Because you have said, 'יהוה has
raised up prophets for us in Baḇel' –
16 thus said יהוה concerning the sovereign
who sits on the throne of Dawiḏ, concerning all the people who dwell in this city,
and concerning your brothers who have
not gone out with you into exile,
17 thus said יהוה of hosts, 'See, I am
sending on them the sword, the scarcity of
food, and the pestilence. And I shall make
them like spoilt figs, so spoilt as to be
uneatable.
18 'And I shall pursue them with the
sword, with scarcity of food, and with
pestilence. And I shall make them a horror
among all the reigns of the earth, to be a
curse, and an astonishment, and a hissing,
and a reproach among all the nations
where I have driven them.
19 'For they did not heed My words,'
declares יהוה, 'which I sent to them by My
servants the prophets, rising up early and
sending them, yet you did not listen,'
declares יהוה.
20 "You, therefore, hear the word of יהוה,
all you exiles whom I have sent from
Yerushalayim to Baḇel.
21 "Thus said יהוה of hosts, the Elohim of
Yisra'ĕl, concerning Aḥaḇ son of Qolayah,
and Tsiḏqiyahu son of Ma'asĕyah, who are

29a Deḇ. 4:29, Yo'ĕl 2:12.

prophesying falsely to you in My Name,
'See, I am giving them into the hand of
Neḇuḵaḏretstsar sovereign of Baḇel, and
he shall strike them before your eyes.
22 'And because of them all the exiles of
Yehuḏah who are in Baḇel shall use a
curse, saying, "יהוה make you like
Tsiḏqiyahu and Aḥaḇ, whom the sovereign
of Baḇel roasted in the fire,"
23 because they have done wickedness in
Yisra'ěl, and committed adultery with their
neighbours' wives, and have spoken a
word in My Name falsely which I have not
commanded them. And I am He who
knows, and a witness,' declares יהוה.
24 "And speak to Shemayahu the Neḥelamite, saying,
25 "Thus speaks יהוה of hosts, the Elohim
of Yisra'ěl, saying, 'Because you have sent
letters in your name to all the people who
are at Yerushalayim, to Tsephanyah son of
Ma'aséyah the priest, and to all the priests,
saying,
26 "יהוה has made you priest instead of
Yehoyaḏa the priest, so that there are overseers in the House of יהוה over everyone
who is mad and makes himself a prophet,
that you should put him in the stocks and
in the iron collar.
27 "So why have you not reproved Yirmeyahu of Anathoth who makes himself a
prophet to you?
28 "For he has sent to us in Baḇel, saying,
'This *captivity* is long – build houses and
dwell *in them*, and plant gardens and eat
their fruit.' " ' "
29 And Tsephanyah the priest read this
letter in the hearing of Yirmeyahu the
prophet.
30 Then the word of יהוה came to Yirmeyahu, saying,
31 "Send to all those in exile, saying,
'Thus said יהוה concerning Shemayah the
Neḥelamite, "Because Shemayah has
prophesied to you, and I have not sent him,
and he has made you to trust on falsehood,"
32 therefore thus said יהוה, "See, I am
bringing punishment upon Shemayah the
Neḥelamite and his seed: he shall have no
one to dwell among this people, nor is he
to see the good that I am about to do for
My people," declares יהוה, "because he
has spoken apostasy against יהוה." ' "

30

The word that came to Yirmeyahu
from יהוה, saying,
2 "Thus spoke יהוה Elohim of Yisra'ěl,
saying, 'Write in a book for yourself all the
words that I have spoken to you.
3 'For look, the days are coming,'
declares יהוה, 'when I shall turn back the
captivity of My people Yisra'ěl and Yehuḏah,' declares יהוה, 'and I shall bring them
back to the land that I gave to their fathers,
and let them possess it.' "
4 And these are the words יהוה spoke
concerning Yisra'ěl and Yehuḏah.
5 "For this is what יהוה said, 'We have
heard a voice of trembling, of fear, and not
of peace.
6 'Ask now, and see if a man is giving
birth. Why do I see every man with his
hands on his loins like a woman in labour,
and all faces turned pale?
7 'Oh! For great is that day, there is none
like it. And it is the time of Ya'aqoḇ's distress, but he shall be saved out of it.
8 'And it shall be in that day,' declares
יהוה of hosts, 'that I break his yoke from
your neck, and tear off your bonds, and
foreigners no more enslave them.
9 'And they shall serve יהוה their Elohim
and Dawiḏ their sovereign, whom I raise
up for them.
10 'And you, do not fear, O Ya'aqoḇ My
servant,' declares יהוה, 'nor be discouraged, O Yisra'ěl. For look, I am saving you
from afar, and your seed from the land of
their captivity. And Ya'aqoḇ shall return,
and have rest and be at ease, with no one to
trouble him.
11 'For I am with you,' declares יהוה, 'to
save you. Though I make a complete end
of all nations [a] where I have scattered you,
yet I do not make a complete end of you.
But I shall reprove you in judgment, and
by no means leave you unpunished.'

30a See 46:28, Yesh. 34:2, Yesh. 45:17, Dan. 2:44, Amos 9:8, Ḥagg. 2:22.

12 "For thus said יהוה, 'Your breach is
incurable, your wound is grievous.
13 'No one pleads your cause, to bind up.
There are no healing medicines for you.
14 'All those loving you have forgotten
you, they do not seek you. For I struck you
as an enemy strikes, with cruel chastisement, because your crookedness is great,
your sins have increased.
15 'Why do you cry about your breach?
Your pain is incurable. Because of your
many crookednesses, because your sins
have increased, I have done this to you.
16 'However, all those who devour you
shall be devoured. And all your adversaries, every one of them, shall go into
captivity. And those who exploit you shall
be exploited, and all who prey upon you I
shall make a prey.
17 'For I restore health to you and heal
you of your wounds,' declares יהוה, 'for
they have called you an outcast saying,
"This is Tsiyon, no one is seeking her." '
18 "Thus said יהוה, 'See, I turn back the
captivity of Yaʽaqoḇ's tents, and have compassion on his dwelling places. And the
city shall be built upon its own mound, and
the palace stand on its right place.
19 'And out of them shall arise thanksgiving and the voice of those who are
laughing. And I shall increase them, and
they shall not diminish. And I shall esteem
them, and they shall not be small.
20 'And his children shall be as before,
and his congregation shall be established
before Me. And I shall punish all who
oppress them.
21 'And his Prince shall be from him, and
his Ruler shall come from among him.
And I shall bring him near, and he shall
approach Me, for who is this who pledged
his heart to approach Me?' declares יהוה.
22 'And you shall be My people, and I
shall be your Elohim.' "
23 See, the storm of יהוה shall go forth in
a rage, a whirling storm! It bursts upon the
head of the wrong.
24 The burning displeasure of יהוה shall
not turn back until He has done and established the purposes of His heart. In the
latter days you shall understand it. [b]

31 "At that time," declares יהוה, "I
shall be the Elohim of all the clans
of Yisra'ĕl, and they shall be My people."
2 Thus said יהוה, "A people escaped
from the sword found favour in the wilderness, Yisra'ĕl, when it went to find rest."
3 יהוה appeared to me from afar, *saying*,
"I have loved you with an everlasting love,
therefore I shall draw you with loving-
commitment.
4 "I am going to build you again. And
you shall be rebuilt, O maiden of Yisra'ĕl!
Again you shall take up your tambourines,
and go forth in the dances of those who
rejoice.
5 "Again you shall plant vines on the
mountains of Shomeron. The planters shall
plant and treat them as common.
6 "For there shall be a day when the
watchmen cry on Mount Ephrayim, 'Arise,
and let us go up to Tsiyon, to יהוה our
Elohim.' "
7 For thus said יהוה, "Sing with gladness
for Yaʽaqoḇ, and shout among the chief of
the nations. Cry out, give praise, and say,
'O יהוה, save Your people, the remnant of
Yisra'ĕl!'
8 "See, I am bringing them from the land
of the north, and shall gather them from
the ends of the earth, among them the blind
and the lame, those with child and those in
labour, together – a great assembly returning here.
9 "With weeping they shall come, and
with *their* prayers I bring them. I shall
make them walk by rivers of waters, in a
straight way in which they do not stumble.
For I shall be a Father to Yisra'ĕl, and
Ephrayim – he is My first-born.
10 "Hear the word of יהוה, O nations, and
declare it in the isles afar off, and say, 'He
who scattered Yisra'ĕl gathers him, and
shall guard him as a shepherd his flock.'
11 "For יהוה shall ransom Yaʽaqoḇ, and
redeem him from the hand of one stronger
than he.

30b See 23:20.

12 "And they shall come in and shall sing
on the height of Tsiyon, and stream to the
goodness of יהוה, for grain and for new
wine and for oil, and for the young of the
flock and the herd. And their being shall be
like a well-watered garden, and never languish again.
13 "Then shall a maiden rejoice in a
dance, and young men and old, together.
And I shall turn their mourning to joy, and
shall comfort them, and shall make them
rejoice from their sorrow,
14 and shall fill the being of the priests
with fatness. And My people shall be satisfied with My goodness," declares יהוה.
15 Thus said יהוה, "A voice was heard in
Ramah, wailing, bitter weeping, Raḥěl
weeping for her children, refusing to be
comforted for her children, because they
are no more."
16 Thus said יהוה, "Hold back your voice
from weeping, and your eyes from tears,
for there is a reward for your work,"
declares יהוה, "and they shall return from
the land of the enemy.
17 "And there is expectancy for your latter
end," declares יהוה, "and your children
shall return to their own country.
18 "I have clearly heard Ephrayim lamenting, 'You have chastised me, and I was
chastised, like an untrained calf. Turn me
back, and I shall turn back, for You are
יהוה my Elohim.
19 'For after my turning back, I repented.
And after I was instructed, I struck myself
on the thigh. I was ashamed, even humiliated, for I bore the reproach of my youth.'
20 "Is Ephrayim a precious son to Me, a
child of delights? For though I spoke
against him, I still remembered him. That
is why My affections were deeply moved
for him. I have great compassion for him,"
declares יהוה.
21 "Set up signposts, make landmarks; set
your heart toward the highway, the way in
which you went. Turn back, O maiden of
Yisra'ěl, turn back to these cities of yours!
22 "Till when would you turn here and
there, O backsliding daughter? For יהוה
has created what is new on earth: a woman
encompasses a man!"
23 Thus said יהוה of hosts, the Elohim of
Yisra'ěl, "Let them once again say this
word in the land of Yehuḏah and in its
cities, when I turn back their captivity,
'יהוה bless you, O home of righteousness,
mountain of set-apartness!'
24 "And in Yehuḏah and all its cities farmers and those who journey with flocks,
shall dwell together.
25 "For I shall fill the weary being, and I
shall replenish every grieved being."
26 At this I awoke and looked around, and
my sleep was sweet to me.
27 "See, the days are coming," declares
יהוה, "that I shall sow the house of
Yisra'ěl and the house of Yehuḏah with the
seed of man and the seed of beast.
28 "And it shall be, that as I have watched
over them to pluck up, and to break down,
and to throw down, and to destroy, and to
afflict, so I shall watch over them to build
and to plant," declares יהוה.
29 "In those days they shall no longer say,
'The fathers ate sour grapes, and the children's teeth are blunted.'
30 "But each one shall die for his own
crookedness – whoever eats sour grapes,
his teeth shall be blunted.
31 "See, the days are coming," declares
יהוה, "when I shall make a renewed
covenant with the house of Yisra'ěl and
with the house of Yehuḏah, [a]
32 not like the covenant I made with their
fathers in the day when I strengthened [b]
their hand to bring them out of the land of
Mitsrayim, My covenant which they
broke, though I was a husband to them,"
declares יהוה.
33 "For this is the covenant I shall make
with the house of Yisra'ěl after those days,
declares יהוה: I shall put My Torah in their
inward parts, and write it on their hearts.
And I shall be their Elohim, and they shall
be My people.
34 "And no longer shall they teach, each
one his neighbour, and each one his brother, saying, 'Know יהוה,' for they shall all

31a Iḇ'rim 8:8-12, 10:16-17. *31b* Commonly understood as "take hold of."

know Me, from the least of them to the
greatest of them," declares יהוה. "For I
shall forgive their crookedness, and
remember their sin no more."
35 Thus said יהוה, who gives the sun for a
light by day, and the laws of the moon and
the stars for a light by night, who stirs up
the sea, and its waves roar – יהוה of hosts
is His Name:
36 "If these laws vanish from before Me,"
declares יהוה, "then the seed of Yisra'ĕl
shall also cease from being a nation before
Me forever."
37 Thus said יהוה, "If the heavens above
could be measured, and the foundations of
the earth searched out beneath, I would
also cast off all the seed of Yisra'ĕl for all
that they have done," declares יהוה.
38 "See, the days are coming," declares
יהוה, "that the city shall be built for יהוה
from the Tower of Ḥanan'ĕl to the Corner
Gate.
39 "And the measuring line shall again
extend straight ahead to the hill Garĕḇ,
then it shall turn toward Go'ah.
40 "And all the valley of the dead bodies
and of the ashes, and all the fields as far as
the wadi Qiḏron, to the corner of the Horse
Gate toward the east, is to be set-apart to
יהוה. It shall not be plucked up or thrown
down any more forever."

32 The word that came to Yirmeyahu
from יהוה in the tenth year of
Tsiḏqiyahu sovereign of Yehuḏah, which
was the eighteenth year of Neḇuḵaḏretstsar.
2 Now at that time the army of the sovereign of Baḇel besieged Yerushalayim, and
Yirmeyahu the prophet was shut up in the
court of the guard, which was in the house
of the sovereign of Yehuḏah.
3 For Tsiḏqiyahu sovereign of Yehuḏah
had shut him up, saying, "Why are you
prophesying, saying, 'Thus said יהוה,
"See, I am giving this city into the hand of
the sovereign of Baḇel, and he shall take it,
4 and Tsiḏqiyahu sovereign of Yehuḏah
shall not escape from the hand of the
Kasdim, but certainly be given into the
hand of the sovereign of Baḇel, and shall
speak with him face to face, and see him
eye to eye,
5 and he shall lead Tsiḏqiyahu to Baḇel,
and be there until I visit him," declares
יהוה, "though you fight with the Kasdim,
you shall not prosper" '?"
6 And Yirmeyahu said, "The word of
יהוה came to me, saying,
7 'See, Ḥaname'ĕl son of Shallum your
uncle is coming to you, saying, "Buy my
field which is in Anathoth, for the right of
redemption is yours to buy it." '
8 "So Ḥaname'ĕl my uncle's son came to
me in the court of the guard according to
the word of יהוה, and said to me, 'Please
buy my field that is in Anathoth, which is
in the land of Binyamin, for the right of
inheritance is yours, and the redemption.
Buy it for yourself.' And I knew that this
was the word of יהוה.
9 "And I bought the field which was at
Anathoth from Ḥaname'ĕl, my uncle's
son, and weighed out to him the silver,
seventeen sheqels of silver.
10 "And I signed the deed and sealed it,
took witnesses, and weighed the silver in
the scales.
11 "Then I took the deed of purchase –
that which was sealed according to the
command and law, and that which was
open –
12 and I gave the deed of purchase to
Baruḵ son of Nĕriyah, son of Maḥsĕyah, in
the presence of Ḥaname'ĕl my uncle's son,
and in the presence of the witnesses who
signed the deed of purchase, before all the
Yehuḏim who sat in the court of the guard.
13 "And I commanded Baruḵ before their
eyes, saying,
14 'Thus said יהוה of hosts, the Elohim of
Yisra'ĕl, "Take these deeds, both this deed
of purchase which is sealed and this deed
which is open, and put them in an earthen
vessel, so that they remain many days."
15 'For thus said יהוה of hosts, the Elohim
of Yisra'ĕl, "Houses and fields and vineyards shall again be bought in this land." '
16 "And after I had given the deed of purchase to Baruḵ son of Nĕriyah, I prayed to
יהוה, saying,
17 'Ah, Master יהוה! See, You have made

the heavens and the earth by Your great
power and outstretched arm. There is no
matter too hard for You,
18 who show loving-commitment to thousands, and repay the crookedness of the
fathers into the bosom of their children
after them – the Great, the Mighty Ěl, יהוה
of hosts is His Name,
19 great in counsel and mighty in work,
for Your eyes are open to all the ways of
the sons of men, to give everyone according to his ways and according to the fruit
of his deeds.
20 'For You have set signs and wonders in
the land of Mitsrayim, to this day, and in
Yisra'ěl and among other men. And You
have made Yourself a Name, as it is this
day.
21 'And You have brought Your people
Yisra'ěl out of the land of Mitsrayim with
signs and wonders, with a strong hand and
an outstretched arm, and with great fearsome deeds.
22 'And You gave them this land, of which
You swore to their fathers to give them, a
land flowing with milk and honey.
23 'And they came in and possessed it, but
they did not obey Your voice nor did they
walk in Your Torah. They did not do all
that You commanded them to do, so You
brought all this evil upon them.
24 'See the siege mounds! They have
come to the city to take it. And the city has
been given into the hand of the Kasdim
who fight against it, because of the sword
and the scarcity of food and the pestilence.
And what You have spoken has come
about, and look, You see it!
25 'Yet You, O Master יהוה, have said to
me, "Buy the field for silver, and take witnesses"! although the city has been given
into the hand of the Kasdim.' "
26 Then the word of יהוה came to
Yirmeyahu, saying,
27 "See, I am יהוה, the Elohim of all flesh.
Is there any matter too hard for Me?"
28 Therefore thus said יהוה, "See, I am
giving this city into the hand of the
Kasdim, into the hand of Neḇuḵaḏretstsar
sovereign of Baḇel, and he shall take it.
29 "And the Kasdim who fight against this
city shall come and set fire to this city and
burn it, with the houses on whose roofs
they burned incense to Ba'al and poured
out drink offerings to other mighty ones, to
provoke Me.
30 "For the children of Yisra'ěl and the
children of Yehuḏah have done only evil
before Me, from their youth. For the children of Yisra'ěl have only provoked Me
with the work of their hands," declares
יהוה.
31 "For this city has been a cause for My
displeasure and My wrath from the day
that they built it, even to this day that I
should remove it from before My face,
32 because of all the evil of the children of
Yisra'ěl and the children of Yehuḏah,
which they have done to provoke Me –
they, their sovereigns, their heads, their
priests, their prophets, and the men of
Yehuḏah, and the inhabitants of Yerushalayim.
33 "And they have turned their back to
Me, and not their face – though I taught
them, rising up early and teaching them,
they did not listen to receive instruction.
34 "And they set their abominations in the
house which is called by My Name, to
defile it.
35 "And they built the high places of Ba'al
which are in the Valley of the Son of
Hinnom, to offer up their sons and their
daughters to Moleḵ, which I did not command them, nor did it come into My heart,
that they should do this abomination, to
make Yehuḏah sin.
36 "And now, thus said יהוה, the Elohim
of Yisra'ěl, concerning this city of which
you say, 'It shall be given into the hand of
the sovereign of Baḇel by the sword, and
by scarcity of food, and by pestilence':
37 'See, I am gathering them out of all the
lands where I have driven them in My displeasure, and in My wrath, and in great
rage. And I shall bring them back to this
place, and shall let them dwell in safety.
38 'And they shall be My people, and I
shall be their Elohim.
39 'And I shall give them one heart and
one way, to fear Me all the days, for the
good of them and of their children after

them.
40 'And I shall make an everlasting covenant with them, that I do not turn back from doing good to them. And I shall put My fear in their hearts so as not to turn aside from Me.
41 'And I shall rejoice over them to do good to them, and shall plant them in this land in truth, with all My heart and with all My being.'
42 "For thus said יהוה, 'As I have brought all this great evil on this people, so I am bringing on them all the good that I am speaking to them.
43 'And fields shall be bought in this land of which you are saying, "It is a wasteland, without man or beast. It has been given into the hand of the Kasdim."
44 'Fields shall be bought for silver, and deeds signed and sealed, and witnesses be called, in the land of Binyamin, and in the places around Yerushalayim, and in the cities of Yehuḏah, and in the cities of the mountains, and in the cities of the low country, and in the cities of the South. For I shall turn back their captivity,' declares יהוה."

33 And the word of יהוה came to Yirmeyahu a second time, while he was still shut up in the court of the guard, saying,
2 "Thus said יהוה who made it, יהוה who formed it to establish it, יהוה is His Name,
3 'Call unto Me, and I shall answer you, and show you great and inaccessible *matters*, which you have not known.'
4 "For thus said יהוה, the Elohim of Yisra'ěl, concerning the houses of this city and the houses of the sovereigns of Yehuḏah, which are thrown down against the siege mounds and the sword,
5 while coming to fight with the Kasdim, and to fill their places with the corpses of men whom I shall strike in My displeasure and My wrath, all for whose evil I have hidden My face from this city.
6 'See, I am bringing to it relief and healing. And I shall heal them and reveal to them the riches of peace and truth.
7 'And I shall turn back the captivity of Yehuḏah and the captivity of Yisra'ěl, and shall build them as at the first,
8 and shall cleanse them from all their crookedness that they have sinned against Me. And I shall pardon all their crookednesses that they have sinned and by which they have transgressed against Me.
9 'And it shall be to Me a name of joy, a praise, and a pride before all nations of the earth, who hear all the good I am doing to them, and they shall fear and tremble for all the goodness and all the peace I am doing to it.'
10 "Thus said יהוה, 'In this place of which you say, "It is dried up, without man and without beast," in the cities of Yehuḏah, in the streets of Yerushalayim that are deserted, without man and without inhabitant and without beast, there shall once again be heard
11 the voice of joy and the voice of gladness, the voice of the bridegroom and the voice of the bride, the voice of those who are saying, "Praise יהוה of hosts, for יהוה is good, for His loving-commitment is forever," of those who are bringing the offering of praise into the House of יהוה. For I shall turn back the captivity of the land, as at the first,' declares יהוה.
12 "Thus said יהוה of hosts, 'In this place which is dried up, without man and without beast, and in all its cities, there shall once again be a home of shepherds causing their flocks to lie down.
13 'In the cities of the mountains, in the cities of the low country, and in the cities of the South, and in the land of Binyamin, and in the places around Yerushalayim, and in the cities of Yehuḏah, the flocks once again pass under the hands of him who counts them,' declares יהוה.
14 'See, the days are coming,' declares יהוה, 'when I shall establish the good word which I have promised to the house of Yisra'ěl and to the house of Yehuḏah:
15 'In those days and at that time I cause a Branch of righteousness to spring forth for Dawiḏ. And He shall do right-ruling and righteousness in the earth.
16 'In those days Yehuḏah shall be saved, and Yerushalayim dwell in safety. And this

is that which shall be proclaimed to her:
'יהוה' our Righteousness.'
17"For thus said יהוה', 'For Dawiḏ there
is not to cease a man to sit on the throne of
the house of Yisra'ěl.
18'And for the priests, the Lěwites, there
is not to cease a man to offer ascending
offerings before Me, to kindle grain offerings, and to slaughter continually.' "
19And the word of יהוה' came to Yirmeyahu, saying,
20"Thus said יהוה', 'If you could break
My covenant with the day and My covenant with the night, so that there be not
day and night in their season,
21then My covenant could also be broken
with Dawiḏ My servant – so that he shall
not have a son to reign upon his throne –
and with the Lěwites, the priests, My attendants.
22'As the host of the heavens is not
counted, nor the sand of the sea measured,
so I increase the descendants of Dawiḏ My
servant and the Lěwites who attend upon
Me.' "
23And the word of יהוה' came to Yirmeyahu, saying,
24"Have you not observed what these
people have spoken, saying, 'The two
clans which יהוה' has chosen have been
rejected by Him'? So they have despised
My people, [a] no more to be a nation before
them.
25"Thus said יהוה', 'If My covenant is not
with day and night, and if I have not
appointed the laws of the heavens and
earth,
26then I would also reject the descendants
of Ya'aqoḇ and Dawiḏ My servant, so that
I should not take of his descendants to be
rulers over the descendants of Aḇraham,
Yitsḥaq, and Ya'aqoḇ. For I shall turn back
their captivity, and have compassion on
them.' "

34 The word which came to Yirmeyahu from יהוה', when Neḇuḵaḏnetstsar sovereign of Baḇel and all his
army, and all the reigns of the earth under
his rule, and all the people, fought against
Yerushalayim and all its cities, saying,
2"Thus said יהוה' the Elohim of Yisra'ěl,
'Go and speak to Tsiḏqiyahu sovereign of
Yehuḏah and say to him, "Thus said יהוה',
'See, I am giving this city into the hand of
the sovereign of Baḇel. And he shall burn
it with fire,
3and you shall not escape out of his
hand, but certainly be taken and given into
his hand. And your eyes shall see the eyes
of the sovereign of Baḇel, and his mouth
shall speak with your mouth, and you shall
go to Baḇel.' " '
4"But hear the word of יהוה', O Tsiḏqiyahu sovereign of Yehuḏah! Thus said
יהוה' concerning you, 'You shall not die by
the sword.
5'In peace you are to die, and as in the
burnings of spices for your fathers, the former sovereigns who were before you, so
they shall burn spices for you and lament
for you, saying, "Alas, master!" ' For I
have spoken the word," declares יהוה'.
6And Yirmeyahu the prophet spoke all
these words to Tsiḏqiyahu the sovereign of
Yehuḏah in Yerushalayim,
7while the sovereign of Baḇel's army
was fighting against Yerushalayim and all
the cities of Yehuḏah that were left, against
Laḵish and Azěqah. For only these walled
cities remained of the cities of Yehuḏah.
8The word which came to Yirmeyahu
from יהוה', after Sovereign Tsiḏqiyahu had
made a covenant with all the people who
were at Yerushalayim to proclaim release
to them:
9that everyone was to set free his male
and female slave, the Hebrew man and the
Hebrew woman, no one was to keep a
Yehuḏi, his brother, enslaved.
10And when all the heads and all the people who had come into the covenant heard
that each one was to set free his male and
female slaves, and not keep them enslaved
any longer, they obeyed and released them.
11But afterward they changed their minds
and made the male and female slaves
return, whom they had set free, and

33a Teh. 83:3-4, Yeḥez. 28:24-26, 36:2-6.

brought them into subjection as male and
female slaves.
12 Therefore the word of יהוה came to
Yirmeyahu from יהוה, saying,
13 "Thus said יהוה the Elohim of Yisra'ěl,
'I Myself made a covenant with your
fathers in the day that I brought them out
of the land of Mitsrayim, out of the house
of bondage, saying,
14 "At the end of seven years each one
should set free his Hebrew brother, who
has been sold to him. And when he has
served you six years, you shall let him go
free from you." But your fathers did not
obey Me nor incline their ear.
15 'And you recently turned and did what
was right in My eyes, each man proclaiming release to his neighbour. And you
made a covenant before Me in the house
which is called by My Name.
16 'But you turned back and profaned My
Name, and each one of you took back his
male and female slaves, whom he had set
free, at their pleasure, and brought them
into subjection, to be your male and female
slaves.'
17 "Therefore thus said יהוה, 'You have
not obeyed Me in proclaiming release,
each one to his brother and each one to his
neighbour. See, I am proclaiming release
to you,' declares יהוה, 'to the sword, to the
pestilence, and to the scarcity of food! And
I shall make you a horror to all reigns of
the earth.
18 'And I shall give the men who are
transgressing My covenant, who have not
established the words of the covenant
which they made before Me, when they cut
the calf in two and passed between the
parts of it:
19 the heads of Yehuḏah, and the heads of
Yerushalayim, the eunuchs, and the priests,
and all the people of the land who passed
between the parts of the calf.
20 'And I shall give them into the hand of
their enemies and into the hand of those
who seek their life. And their corpses shall
be for food to the birds of the heavens and
the beasts of the earth.
21 'And I shall give Tsiḏqiyahu sovereign
of Yehuḏah and his heads into the hand of
their enemies, and into the hand of those
who seek their life, and into the hand of the
sovereign of Baḇel's army that has withdrawn from you.
22 'See, I am commanding,' declares
יהוה, 'and shall bring them back to this
city, and they shall fight against it and take
it and burn it with fire. And I shall make
the cities of Yehuḏah a ruin without inhabitant.' "

35 The word which came to Yirmeyahu from יהוה in the days of
Yehoyaqim son of Yoshiyahu, sovereign of
Yehuḏah, saying,
2 "Go to the house of the Rěḵaḇites. And
you shall speak to them, and bring them
into the House of יהוה, into one of the
rooms, and give them wine to drink."
3 And I took Ya'azanyah the son of
Yirmeyahu, the son of Ḥaḇatstsinyah, and
his brothers and all his sons, and all the
house of the Rěḵaḇites,
4 and brought them into the House of
יהוה, into the room of the sons of Ḥanan
son of Yiḡdalyahu, a man of Elohim,
which was by the chamber of the heads,
above the room of Ma'asěyahu son of
Shallum, the keeper of the door.
5 And I set before the sons of the house
of the Rěḵaḇites bowls filled with wine,
and cups, and I said to them, "Drink wine."
6 But they said, "We do not drink wine,
because Yonaḏaḇ the son of Rěḵaḇ, our
father, commanded us, saying, 'You shall
not drink wine, neither you nor your sons,
forever.
7 'And do not build a house, neither sow
seed, nor plant a vineyard, nor have any of
these, but dwell in tents all your days, so
that you live many days on the face of the
land where you are sojourners.'
8 "So we obeyed the voice of Yonaḏaḇ
son of Rěḵaḇ, our father, in all that he
commanded us, to drink no wine all our
days, we, our wives, our sons, and our
daughters,
9 nor to build ourselves houses to dwell
in. And we have no vineyard, field or seed.
10 "But we dwell in tents, and have
obeyed and done according to all that

Yonaḏaḇ our father commanded us.
11 "And it came to be, whenNeḇuḵaḏretst-
sar sovereign of Baḇel came up into the
land, that we said, 'Come, let us go to
Yerushalayim for fear of the army of the
Kasdim and for fear of the army of the
Arameans.' So we dwell at Yerushalayim."
12 And the word of יהוה came to
Yirmeyahu, saying,
13 "Thus said יהוה of hosts, the Elohim of
Yisra'ěl, 'Go, and you shall say to the men
of Yehuḏah and to the inhabitants of
Yerushalayim, "Have you not received
instruction, to obey My words?" declares
יהוה.
14 "The words of Yonaḏaḇ son of Rěḵaḇ,
which he commanded his sons, not to
drink wine, are established, and they have
not drunk unto this day, for they have
obeyed their father's command. And as for
Me, I have spoken to you, rising early and
speaking, but you have not obeyed Me.
15 "And I sent to you all My servants the
prophets, rising up early and sending them,
saying, 'Turn, each one from his evil way,
and make good your deeds, and do not go
after other mighty ones to serve them, and
you shall dwell in the land which I have
given you and your fathers.' But you have
not inclined your ear, nor obeyed Me.
16 "The sons of Yonaḏaḇ son of Rěḵaḇ
have indeed carried out the command of
their father which he commanded them,
but this people has not obeyed Me." '
17 "Therefore thus said יהוה Elohim of
hosts, the Elohim of Yisra'ěl, 'See, I am
bringing on Yehuḏah and on all the inhabitants of Yerushalayim all the evil I have
pronounced against them, because I have
spoken to them but they did not listen, and
I have called to them but they did not
answer.' "
18 And Yirmeyahu said to the house of the
Rěḵaḇites, "Thus said יהוה of hosts, the
Elohim of Yisra'ěl, 'Because you have
obeyed the command of Yonaḏaḇ your
father, and guarded all his commands and
done according to all that he commanded
you,
19 therefore thus said יהוה of hosts, the
Elohim of Yisra'ěl, "Of Yonaḏaḇ son of
Rěḵaḇ there shall never cease to be a man
to stand before Me." ' "

36 And it came to be in the fourth
year of Yehoyaqim son of
Yoshiyahu, sovereign of Yehuḏah, that this
word came to Yirmeyahu from יהוה, saying,
2 "Take a scroll and write on it all the
words that I have spoken to you against
Yisra'ěl, and against Yehuḏah, and against
all the nations, from the day I spoke to you,
from the days of Yoshiyahu even to this
day.
3 "It could be that the house of Yehuḏah
hears of all the evil which I plan to bring
upon them, so that each one turns back
from his evil way, and I shall pardon their
crookedness and their sin."
4 And Yirmeyahu called Baruḵ son of
Něriyah. And Baruḵ wrote on a scroll from
the mouth of Yirmeyahu, all the words of
יהוה which He had spoken to him.
5 And Yirmeyahu commanded Baruḵ,
saying, "I am shut up, I am unable to enter
the House of יהוה.
6 "But you shall enter, and shall read
from the scroll which you have written
from my mouth, the words of יהוה, in the
hearing of the people in the House of יהוה
on the day of fasting. And also read them
in the hearing of all Yehuḏah who come
from their cities.
7 "It could be that they present their supplication before יהוה, and they turn back,
each one from his evil way. For great is the
displeasure and the wrath that יהוה has
spoken against this people."
8 And Baruḵ son of Něriyah did according to all that Yirmeyahu the prophet
commanded him, reading from the book
the words of יהוה in the House of יהוה.
9 And it came to be in the fifth year of
Yehoyaqim son of Yoshiyahu, sovereign of
Yehuḏah, in the ninth new *moon*, that they
called a fast before יהוה to all the people in
Yerushalayim, and to all the people who
came from the cities of Yehuḏah to
Yerushalayim.
10 And Baruḵ read from the book the
words of Yirmeyahu in the House of יהוה,

in the room of Gemaryahu son of Shaphan
the scribe, in the upper courtyard at the
entry of the New Gate of the House of
יהוה, in the hearing of all the people.
11 And Miḵayehu son of Gemaryahu, son
of Shaphan, heard all the words of יהוה
from the book,
12 And then he went down to the sovereign's house, into the scribe's room. And
there all the heads were sitting: Elishama
the scribe, and Delayahu son of Shemayahu, and Elnathan son of Aḵbor, and
Gemaryahu son of Shaphan, and Tsiḏqiyahu son of Ḥananyahu, and all the heads.
13 And Miḵayehu told them all the words
which he heard when Baruḵ read the book
in the hearing of the people.
14 Then all the heads sent Yehuḏi son of
Nethanyahu, son of Shelemyahu, son of
Kushi, to Baruḵ, saying, "Take in your
hand the scroll from which you have read
in the hearing of the people, and come." So
Baruḵ son of Nĕriyahu took the scroll in
his hand and came to them.
15 And they said to him, "Sit down,
please, and read it in our hearing." Then
Baruḵ read it in their hearing.
16 And it came to be, when they had heard
all the words, that they looked at each
other in fear, and said to Baruḵ, "We are
certainly going to report all these words to
the sovereign."
17 And they asked Baruḵ, saying, "Please
explain to us, how did you write all these
words? From his mouth?"
18 And Baruḵ answered them, "From his
mouth he spoke all these words to me, and
I wrote them with ink in the book."
19 Then the heads said to Baruḵ, "Go,
hide, you and Yirmeyahu, and let no one
know where you are."
20 And they went to the sovereign, into
the court. But they put the scroll in the
room of Elishama the scribe, and told all
the words in the hearing of the sovereign.
21 The sovereign therefore sent Yehuḏi to
bring the scroll, and he took it from the
room of Elishama the scribe. And Yehuḏi
read it in the hearing of the sovereign and
in the hearing of all the heads standing
beside the sovereign.
22 And the sovereign was sitting in the
winter house in the ninth new *moon*, with a
fire burning on the hearth before him.
23 Then it came to be, when Yehuḏi had
read three or four columns, that the sovereign cut it with the scribe's knife and threw
it into the fire that was on the hearth, until
the entire scroll was burned in the fire that
was on the hearth.
24 Yet the sovereign and all his servants
who heard all these words were not afraid,
nor did they tear their garments.
25 Moreover, Elnathan, and Delayahu, and
Gemaryahu pleaded with the sovereign not
to burn the scroll, but he did not listen to
them.
26 And the sovereign commanded Yeraḥme'ĕl son of the sovereign, and Serayahu
son of Azri'ĕl, and Shelemyahu son of
Aḇde'ĕl, to seize Baruḵ the scribe and
Yirmeyahu the prophet, but יהוה had hid
them.
27 And after the sovereign had burned the
scroll with the words which Baruḵ had
written from the mouth of Yirmeyahu, the
word of יהוה came to Yirmeyahu, saying,
28 "Take another scroll, and write on it all
the former words that were in the first
scroll which Yehoyaqim the sovereign of
Yehuḏah has burned,
29 and say to Yehoyaqim sovereign of
Yehuḏah, 'Thus said יהוה, "You have
burned this scroll, saying, 'Why have you
written in it that the sovereign of Baḇel is
certainly coming to destroy this land, and
cause man and beast to cease from here?' "
30 'Therefore thus said יהוה concerning
Yehoyaqim sovereign of Yehuḏah, "He
shall have no one to sit on the throne of
Dawiḏ, and his dead body is to be thrown
out, to the heat of the day and the frost of
the night.
31 "And I shall punish him, and his seed,
and his servants for their crookedness. And
I shall bring on them, and on the inhabitants of Yerushalayim, and on the men of
Yehuḏah all the evil I have spoken against
them. But they did not listen." ' "
32 So Yirmeyahu took another scroll and
gave it to Baruḵ the scribe, son of Nĕriyahu, who wrote on it from the mouth of

Yirmeyahu all the words of the book which Yehoyaqim sovereign of Yehuḏah had burned in the fire. And many similar words were added to them.

37 And Sovereign Tsiḏqiyahu son of Yoshiyahu reigned instead of Konyahu son of Yehoyaqim, whom Neḇukaḏretstsar sovereign of Baḇel set up to reign in the land of Yehuḏah.
2 But neither he nor his servants nor the people of the land had listened to the words of יהוה which He spoke by the prophet Yirmeyahu.
3 And Tsiḏqiyahu the sovereign sent Yehuḵal son of Shelemyah, and the priest, Tsephanyahu son of Ma'asěyah, to the prophet Yirmeyahu, saying, "Please pray to יהוה our Elohim for us."
4 Now Yirmeyahu was still coming and going among the people, for they had not yet put him in prison.
5 Meanwhile, Pharaoh's army had set out from Mitsrayim. And when the Kasdim who were besieging Yerushalayim heard news of them, they withdrew from Yerushalayim.
6 And the word of יהוה came to Yirmeyahu the prophet, saying,
7 "Thus said יהוה the Elohim of Yisra'ěl, 'Say this to the sovereign of Yehuḏah, who sent you to Me to inquire of Me, "See, Pharaoh's army which has come up to help you, shall turn back to Mitsrayim, to their own land.
8 "And the Kasdim shall return and fight against this city, and take it and burn it with fire." '
9 "Thus said יהוה, 'Do not deceive yourselves, saying, "The Kasdim shall go away from us," for they do not go.
10 'For though you had stricken the entire army of the Kasdim who are fighting against you, and there remained only wounded men among them, they would get up, each man in his tent, and burn the city with fire.' "
11 And it came to be, when the army of the Kasdim left the siege of Yerushalayim for fear of Pharaoh's army,
12 that Yirmeyahu went out of Yerushalayim to go into the land of Binyamin to receive his portion there in the midst of the people.
13 And it came to be, as he was in the gate of Binyamin, a master of the guard was there whose name was Yiriyah son of Shelemyah, son of Ḥananyah. And he seized Yirmeyahu the prophet, saying, "You are deserting to the Kasdim!"
14 But Yirmeyahu said, "It is a lie! I am not deserting to the Kasdim." But he did not listen to him, and Yiriyah seized Yirmeyahu and brought him to the heads.
15 And the heads were wroth with Yirmeyahu, and struck him and put him in prison in the house of Yehonathan the scribe. For they had made that for a prison.
16 When Yirmeyahu had entered into the dungeon and into the cells, then Yirmeyahu remained there many days.
17 And Tsiḏqiyahu the sovereign sent and took him out. And the sovereign asked him secretly in his house, and said, "Is there any word from יהוה?" And Yirmeyahu said, "There is." And he said, "You are given into the hand of the sovereign of Baḇel!"
18 And Yirmeyahu said to Tsiḏqiyahu the sovereign, "What have I sinned against you, and against your servants, and against this people, that you have put me into prison?
19 "Where are your prophets who prophesied to you, saying, 'The sovereign of Baḇel is not coming against you or against this land?'
20 "But now, please hear, O my master the sovereign. Please, let my petition be accepted before you, and do not make me return to the house of Yehonathan the scribe, lest I die there."
21 Tsiḏqiyahu the sovereign then commanded Yirmeyahu to be placed in the court of the guard, and that they should give him daily a piece of bread from the bakers' street, until all the bread in the city was gone. So Yirmeyahu remained in the court of the guard.

38 And Shephatyah son of Mattan, and Geḏalyahu son of Pashhur, and

Yuḵal son of Shelemyahu, and Pashḥur son
of Malkiyah heard the words which
Yirmeyahu had spoken to all the people,
saying,
2 "Thus said יהוה, 'He who remains in
this city shall die by the sword, by scarcity
of food, and by pestilence, but whoever
goes over to the Kasdim shall live. And his
life shall be as a prize to him, and he shall
live.'
3 "Thus said יהוה, 'This city is certainly
given into the hand of the sovereign of
Baḇel's army, and he shall take it.' "
4 Then the heads said to the sovereign,
"Please, let this man be put to death,
because he is weakening the hands of the
men of battle who are left in this city, and
the hands of all the people, by speaking
such words to them. For this man does not
seek the peace of this people, but the evil."
5 And Tsiḏqiyahu the sovereign said,
"Look, he is in your hand. For the sovereign is unable to do any matter against
you."
6 And they took Yirmeyahu and threw
him into the dungeon of Malkiyahu the
sovereign's son, which was in the court of
the guard, and they let Yirmeyahu down
with ropes. And in the dungeon there was
no water, but mud. So Yirmeyahu sank in
the mud.
7 And Eḇeḏ-Meleḵ the Kushite, one of
the eunuchs, who was in the sovereign's
house, heard that they had put Yirmeyahu
in the dungeon. And the sovereign was sitting at the Gate of Binyamin,
8 And Eḇeḏ-Meleḵ came from the sovereign's house and spoke to the sovereign,
saying,
9 "My master the sovereign, these men
have done evil in all that they have done to
Yirmeyahu the prophet, whom they have
thrown into the dungeon, and he is likely
to die from hunger in the place where he is,
for there is no more bread in the city."
10 And the sovereign commanded Eḇeḏ-
Meleḵ the Kushite, saying, "Take thirty
men from here with you, and lift Yirmeyahu the prophet out of the dungeon before
he dies."
11 So Eḇeḏ-Meleḵ took the men with him
and went into the house of the sovereign
under the treasury, and took old clothes
and old rags from there, and let them down
by ropes into the dungeon to Yirmeyahu.
12 And Eḇeḏ-Meleḵ the Kushite said to
Yirmeyahu, "Please put these old clothes
and rags under your armpits, under the
ropes." And Yirmeyahu did so,
13 and they pulled Yirmeyahu up with
ropes and lifted him out of the dungeon.
And Yirmeyahu remained in the court of
the guard.
14 Then Tsiḏqiyahu the sovereign sent and
had Yirmeyahu the prophet brought to him
at the third entrance of the House of יהוה.
And the sovereign said to Yirmeyahu, "I
am asking you a matter. Do not hide a matter from me."
15 And Yirmeyahu said to Tsiḏqiyahu, "If
I declare it to you, shall you not put me to
death? And if I give you advice, you shall
not listen to me."
16 But Tsiḏqiyahu the sovereign swore
secretly to Yirmeyahu, saying, "As יהוה
lives, who made us this life, I do not put
you to death, nor do I give you into the
hand of these men who seek your life."
17 And Yirmeyahu said to Tsiḏqiyahu,
"Thus said יהוה, the Elohim of hosts, the
Elohim of Yisra'ěl, 'If you do indeed surrender to the heads of the sovereign of
Baḇel, then your being shall live, and this
city not be burned with fire. And you and
your house shall live.
18 'But if you do not surrender to the
heads of the sovereign of Baḇel, then this
city shall be given into the hand of the
Kasdim, and they shall burn it with fire,
and you shall not escape from their hand.'
"
19 Then Tsiḏqiyahu the sovereign said to
Yirmeyahu, "I am afraid of the Yehuḏim
who have gone over to the Kasdim, lest
they give me into their hand, and they maltreat me."
20 But Yirmeyahu said, "They shall not
hand you over. Please, obey the voice of
יהוה which I speak to you, and let it be
well with you, and your life be spared.
21 "But if you refuse to surrender, this is
the word that יהוה has shown me:

22 ‘Then see, all the women who are left in the sovereign of Yehuḏah’s house shall be surrendered to the heads of the sovereign of Baḇel, and see, they are saying, “Your close friends have set upon you and prevailed against you; your feet have sunk in the mire; they have turned away again.”

23 ‘And they are going to surrender all your wives and children to the Kasdim, and you yourself shall not escape from their hand, but be taken by the hand of the sovereign of Baḇel, and this city shall be burned with fire.’ ”

24 Then Tsiḏqiyahu said to Yirmeyahu, “Let no one know of these words, and you shall not die.

25 “But if the heads hear that I have spoken with you, and they come to you and say to you, ‘Declare to us now what you have said to the sovereign, and also what the sovereign said to you. Do not hide it from us, and we do not put you to death,’

26 then you shall say to them, ‘I presented my petition before the sovereign, not to send me back to the house of Yonathan to die there.’ ”

27 And all the heads came to Yirmeyahu and asked him. And he informed them according to all these words that the sovereign had commanded. And they said no more to him, for the matter was not heard.

28 So Yirmeyahu remained in the court of the guard until the day that Yerushalayim was taken, and he was *there* when Yerushalayim was taken.

39

In the ninth year of Tsiḏqiyahu sovereign of Yehuḏah, in the tenth new *moon*, Neḇuḵaḏretstsar sovereign of Baḇel and all his army came against Yerushalayim, and besieged it.

2 In the eleventh year of Tsiḏqiyahu, in the fourth new *moon*, on the ninth day of the new *moon*, the city was broken into.

3 And all the heads of the sovereign of Baḇel came in and sat in the Middle Gate: Něrḡal-Shar’etser, Samgar-Neḇo, Sarseḵim, Raḇsaris, Něrḡal-Sarezer, Raḇmaḡ, and all the rest of the heads of the sovereign of Baḇel.

4 And it came to be, when Tsiḏqiyahu the sovereign of Yehuḏah and all the men of battle saw them, they fled and left the city by night, by way of the sovereign’s garden, by the gate between the two walls. And he went out toward the desert plain.

5 But the army of the Kasdim pursued them and overtook Tsiḏqiyahu in the desert plains of Yeriḥo. And they captured him, and brought him up to Neḇuḵaḏnetstsar sovereign of Baḇel, to Riḇlah in the land of Ḥamath, where he spoke judgment on him.

6 And the sovereign of Baḇel slew the sons of Tsiḏqiyahu before his eyes in Riḇlah. The sovereign of Baḇel also slew all the nobles of Yehuḏah.

7 And he put out the eyes of Tsiḏqiyahu, and bound him with bronze shackles to bring him to Baḇel.

8 And the Kasdim burned the house of the sovereign and the houses of the people with fire, and they broke down the walls of Yerushalayim.

9 And Neḇuzaraḏan, chief of the guard, exiled to Baḇel the remnant of the people who remained in the city and those who defected to him, with the rest of the people who were left.

10 But Neḇuzaraḏan, chief of the guard, left in the land of Yehuḏah the poor people, who had naught whatever, and gave them vineyards and fields on the same day.

11 And Neḇuḵaḏretstsar the sovereign of Baḇel gave a command concerning Yirmeyahu to Neḇuzaraḏan, chief of the guard, saying,

12 “Take him and look after him, and do no harm whatsoever to him, but do to him even as he shall speak to you.”

13 And Neḇuzaraḏan, chief of the guard, and Neḇushazban the Raḇsaris, Něrḡal-Shar’etser the Raḇmaḡ, and all the sovereign of Baḇel’s chief officers sent,

14 and had Yirmeyahu taken from the court of the guard, and gave him to Geḏalyahu son of Aḥiqam, son of Shaphan, to take him home. And he dwelt among the people.

15 And the word of יהוה had come to Yirmeyahu while he was shut up in the court of the guard, saying,

16 “Go, and you shall speak to Eḇeḏ-

Meleḵ the Kushite, saying, 'Thus said
יהוה of hosts, the Elohim of Yisra'ěl, "See,
I am bringing My words upon this city for
evil and not for good, and they shall be
before you in that day.
17 "And I shall deliver you in that day,"
declares יהוה, "so that you are not given
into the hand of the men of whom you are
afraid.
18 "For I shall rescue you, and you shall
not fall by the sword. But your life shall be
as a prize to you, for you have put your
trust in Me," declares יהוה.' "

40 The word that came to Yirmeyahu
from יהוה after Neḇuzaraḏan,
chief of the guard, had let him go from
Ramah, when he had taken him bound in
chains among all the exiles from
Yerushalayim and Yehuḏah, who were
being exiled to Baḇel.
2 And the chief of the guard took
Yirmeyahu and said to him, "יהוה your
Elohim has spoken this evil on this place.
3 "And יהוה has brought it on, and has
done, as He has said. Because you have
sinned against יהוה, and did not obey His
voice, therefore this matter has come upon
you.
4 "And now, see, I loosen you today from
the chains that were on your hand. If it
seems good to you to come with me to
Baḇel, come, and I shall look after you.
But if it seems wrong for you to come with
me to Baḇel, remain here. See, all the land
is before you, go wherever it seems good
and right for you to go."
5 And before he replied, *Neḇuzaraḏan
said*, "Or go back to Geḏalyah son of
Aḥiqam, son of Shaphan, whom the sovereign of Baḇel has made governor over the
cities of Yehuḏah, and dwell with him
among the people, or go wherever it seems
right for you to go." And the chief of the
guard gave him provisions and a gift and
let him go.
6 So Yirmeyahu went to Geḏalyah son of
Aḥiqam, to Mitspah, and dwelt with him
among the people who were left in the
land.
7 And all the commanders of the armies
who were in the fields, they and their men,
heard that the sovereign of Baḇel had made
Geḏalyahu son of Aḥiqam governor in the
land, and had put him in charge of the men,
and women, and children, and the poor of
the land who had not been exiled to Baḇel.
8 So they came to Geḏalyah at Mitspah –
Yishma'ěl the son of Nethanyahu, and
Yoḥanan and Yonathan the sons of Qarěaḥ,
and Serayah the son of Tanḥumeth, and the
sons of Ophai the Netophathite and Yezan-
yahu the son of a Ma'aḵathite, they and
their men.
9 And Geḏalyahu son of Aḥiqam, son of
Shaphan, swore to them and their men,
saying, "Do not be afraid of serving the
Kasdim. Dwell in the land and serve the
sovereign of Baḇel, and it shall be well
with you.
10 "And I, see, I am dwelling at Mitspah,
to serve the Kasdim who come to us. But
you, gather wine and summer fruit and oil,
and put them in your vessels, and dwell in
your cities which you have taken."
11 Also, when all the Yehuḏim who were
in Mo'aḇ, and among the Ammonites, and
in Eḏom, and who were in all the lands,
heard that the sovereign of Baḇel had left a
remnant of Yehuḏah, and that he had set
over them Geḏalyahu son of Aḥiqam, son
of Shaphan,
12 then all the Yehuḏim returned from all
the places where they had been driven, and
came to the land of Yehuḏah, to Geḏalyahu
at Mitspah, and gathered wine and summer
fruit in large quantities.
13 And Yoḥanan son of Qarěaḥ and all the
commanders of the army that were in the
fields came to Geḏalyahu at Mitspah,
14 and they said to him, "Do you certainly
know that Ba'alis sovereign of the
Ammonites has sent Yishma'ěl son of
Nethanyah to strike you – a being?" But
Geḏalyahu son of Aḥiqam would not
believe them.
15 Then Yoḥanan son of Qarěaḥ spoke
secretly to Geḏalyahu in Mitspah, saying,
"Please let me go and strike Yishma'ěl son
of Nethanyah, without anyone knowing it.
Why should he murder you, and so let
all the Yehuḏim who are gathered to you

be scattered, and the remnant in Yehuḏah
perish?"
16 But Geḏalyahu son of Aḥiqam said to
Yoḥanan son of Qarěaḥ, "Do not do this
matter, for what you are saying about
Yishma'ěl is not true."

41 And in the seventh new *moon* it
came to be that Yishma'ěl son of
Nethanyah, son of Elishama, of the royal
seed, and of the officers of the sovereign,
came with ten men to Geḏalyahu son of
Aḥiqam, at Mitspah. And while they ate
bread together there in Mitspah,
2 Yishma'ěl son of Nethanyah, and the
ten men who were with him, arose and
struck Geḏalyahu son of Aḥiqam, son of
Shaphan, with the sword, and killed him
whom the sovereign of Baḇel had made
governor over the land.
3 And Yishma'ěl struck all the Yehuḏim
who were with him, with Geḏalyahu at
Mitspah, and the Kasdim who were found
there, the men of battle.
4 And it came to be, on the second day
after he had killed Geḏalyahu, when no
one yet knew it,
5 that men came from Sheḵem, from
Shiloh, and from Shomeron, eighty men
with their beards shaved and their garments torn, having cut themselves, with
offerings and incense in their hand, to
bring them to the House of יהוה.
6 And Yishma'ěl son of Nethanyah went
out from Mitspah to meet them, weeping
as he walked along. And it came to be, as
he met them, that he said to them, "Come
to Geḏalyahu son of Aḥiqam!"
7 And it came to be, when they came
inside the city, that Yishma'ěl son of
Nethanyah slew them, *throwing* them into
a pit, he and the men who were with him.
8 But ten men were found among them
who said to Yishma'ěl, "Do not kill us, for
we have wheat, and barley, and oil, and
honey hidden in the field." So he held back
and did not kill them among their brothers.
9 And the pit into which Yishma'ěl had
thrown all the corpses of the men whom he
had struck, because of Geḏalyahu, was the
same one Asa the sovereign had made for
fear of Ba'asha sovereign of Yisra'ěl –
Yishma'ěl son of Nethanyahu had filled it
with the slain.
10 Then Yishma'ěl took captive all the rest
of the people who were in Mitspah, the
sovereign's daughters and all the people
who were left in Mitspah, whom Neḇuzaraḏan, chief of the guard, had entrusted
to Geḏalyahu son of Aḥiqam. And Yishma'ěl son of Nethanyahu took them captive and went to go over to the Ammonites.
11 But Yoḥanan son of Qarěaḥ and all the
commanders of the army that were with
him heard of all the evil that Yishma'ěl son
of Nethanyah had done,
12 so they took all the men and went to
fight with Yishma'ěl son of Nethanyah.
And they found him by the great pool that
is in Giḇ'on.
13 And it came to be, when all the people
who were with Yishma'ěl saw Yoḥanan
son of Qarěaḥ, and all the commanders of
the army who were with him, that they
were glad.
14 And all the people whom Yishma'ěl
had taken captive from Mitspah turned
around, and came back, and went to
Yoḥanan son of Qarěaḥ.
15 But Yishma'ěl the son of Nethanyah
escaped from Yoḥanan with eight men and
went to the Ammonites.
16 Then Yoḥanan son of Qarěaḥ, and all
the commanders of the army that were
with him, took from Mitspah all the rest of
the people whom he had recovered from
Yishma'ěl son of Nethanyah after he had
struck Geḏalyah son of Aḥiqam – the
mighty men of battle and the women and
the children and the eunuchs, whom he had
brought back from Giḇ'on.
17 And they set out and dwelt in the lodging place of Kimham, which is near Běyth
Leḥem, to go to enter Mitsrayim,
18 because of the Kasdim. For they were
afraid of them, because Yishma'ěl son of
Nethanyah had struck Geḏalyahu son of
Aḥiqam, whom the sovereign of Baḇel had
made governor in the land.

42 Then all the commanders of the
army, and Yoḥanan son of Qarěaḥ,

and Yezanyah son of Hoshayah, and all the
people, from the least to the greatest, came
near
2and said to Yirmeyahu the prophet,
"We beg you, let our petition be acceptable
to you, and pray for us to יהוה your
Elohim, for all this remnant, for we are few
left of many, as your eyes see us.
3"And let יהוה your Elohim show us the
way in which we should walk and the word
we should do."
4And Yirmeyahu the prophet said to
them, "I have heard. See, I am praying to
יהוה your Elohim according to your
words, and it shall be that I declare to you
all the word יהוה answers you. I withhold
not a word from you."
5And they said to Yirmeyahu, "Let יהוה
be a true and steadfast witness between us,
if we do not do according to all the word
which יהוה your Elohim sends us by you.
6"Whether good or evil, let us obey the
voice of יהוה our Elohim to whom we
send you, in order that it might be well
with us when we obey the voice of יהוה
our Elohim."
7And after ten days it came to be that the
word of יהוה came to Yirmeyahu.
8So he called Yoḥanan son of Qarěaḥ,
and all the commanders of the army which
were with him, and all the people from the
least even to the greatest,
9and said to them, "Thus said יהוה, the
Elohim of Yisra'ěl, to whom you sent me
to present your petition before Him,
10'If you would indeed stay in this land,
then I shall build you and not pull you
down, and I shall plant you and not pluck
you up. For I have relented of the evil I
have done to you.
11'Do not be afraid of the sovereign of
Baḇel, of whom you are afraid. Do not be
afraid of him,' declares יהוה, 'for I am
with you, to save you and deliver you from
his hand.
12'And I shall show you compassion, so
that he has compassion on you and let you
return to your own land.'
13"But if you say, 'We are not staying in
this land,' and so disobey the voice of יהוה
your Elohim,
14saying, 'No, but we are going to the
land of Mitsrayim so that we see no fighting, nor hear a voice of a shophar, nor
hunger for bread, and there we shall stay,'
15then hear the word of יהוה, O remnant
of Yehuḏah! Thus said יהוה of hosts, the
Elohim of Yisra'ěl, 'If you indeed set your
faces to enter Mitsrayim, and shall go to
sojourn there,
16then it shall be that the sword which
you feared overtakes you there in the land
of Mitsrayim, and the scarcity of food of
which you were afraid clings to you there
in Mitsrayim, and you die there.
17'And so it shall be with all the men who
set their faces to go to Mitsrayim to
sojourn there: they shall die by the sword,
by scarcity of food, and by pestilence, and
not one of them shall survive or escape
from the evil I am bringing upon them.'
18"For thus said יהוה of hosts, the
Elohim of Yisra'ěl, 'As My displeasure
and My wrath have been poured out on the
inhabitants of Yerushalayim, so shall My
wrath be poured out on you when you
enter Mitsrayim. And you shall be an oath,
and an astonishment, and a curse, and a
reproach, and you shall see this place no
more.'
19"יהוה has spoken about you, O remnant
of Yehuḏah, 'Do not go to Mitsrayim!'
Know for certain that I have warned you
this day.
20"For you deceived yourselves when
you sent me to יהוה your Elohim, saying,
'Pray for us to יהוה our Elohim, and
according to all that יהוה your Elohim
says, so declare to us and we shall do it.'
21"So I have declared it to you today, but
you have not obeyed the voice of יהוה
your Elohim in all which He has sent me to
you.
22"And now, know for certain that you
shall die by the sword, by scarcity of food,
and by pestilence in the place where you
have desired to go to sojourn."

43 And it came to be, when
Yirmeyahu had ended speaking all
these words to all the people – all the
words of יהוה their Elohim, for which

יהוה their Elohim had sent him to them –
2 that Azaryah son of Hoshayah, and
Yoḥanan son of Qarĕaḥ, and all the proud
men spoke, saying to Yirmeyahu, “You are
speaking a lie! יהוה our Elohim has not
sent you to say, ‘Do not go to Mitsrayim to
sojourn there.’
3 “For Baruḵ son of Nĕriyah is moving
you against us, to give us into the hand of
the Kasdim, to put us to death or exile us to
Baḇel.”
4 So Yoḥanan son of Qarĕaḥ, and all the
commanders of the army, and all the people disobeyed the voice of יהוה, to stay in
the land of Yehuḏah.
5 And Yoḥanan son of Qarĕaḥ and all the
commanders of the army took all the remnant of Yehuḏah who had returned to dwell
in the land of Yehuḏah, from all nations
where they had been driven –
6 the men, and the women, and the
children, and the sovereign’s daughters,
and every being whom Neḇuzaraḏan, chief
of the guard, had left with Geḏalyahu son
of Aḥiqam, son of Shaphan, and Yirmeyahu the prophet, and Baruḵ son of Nĕriyahu.
7 So they went to the land of Mitsrayim,
for they disobeyed the voice of יהוה. And
they went as far as Taḥpanḥes.
8 And the word of יהוה came to Yirmeyahu in Taḥpanḥes, saying,
9 “Take large stones in your hand, and
you shall hide them before the eyes of the
men of Yehuḏah, in the clay in the brick
courtyard which is at the entrance to
Pharaoh’s house in Taḥpanḥes.
10 “Then you shall say to them, ‘Thus said
יהוה of hosts, the Elohim of Yisra’ĕl, “See,
I am sending, and I shall bring Neḇuḵaḏretstsar the sovereign of Baḇel, My servant. And I shall set his throne above these
stones that I have hidden. And he shall
spread his canopy over them.
11 “And he shall come and strike the land
of Mitsrayim, *bringing* death to those
appointed for death, and captivity to those
for captivity, and the sword to those for the
sword.
12 “And he shall set fire to the houses of
the mighty ones of Mitsrayim. And he
shall burn them and take them captive.
And he shall cover himself with the land
of Mitsrayim, as a shepherd puts on his
garment, and he shall go out from there in
peace.
13 “And he shall break the stone pillars of
the House of the Sun which are in the land
of Mitsrayim, and he shall burn the houses
of the mighty ones of the Mitsrites with
fire.” ’ ”

44 The word that came to Yirmeyahu
concerning all the Yehuḏim who
were dwelling in the land of Mitsrayim –
who were dwelling at Miḡdol, and at
Taḥpanḥes, and at Noph, and in the land of
Pathros, saying,
2 “Thus said יהוה of hosts, the Elohim of
Yisra’ĕl, ‘You yourselves have seen all the
evil that I have brought on Yerushalayim
and on all the cities of Yehuḏah. And see,
this day they are a ruin, and no one dwells
in them,
3 because of their evil which they have
done to provoke Me, by going to burn
incense by serving other mighty ones
whom they did not know, they nor you nor
your fathers.
4 ‘And I sent to you all My servants the
prophets, rising early and sending them,
saying, “Please do not do this abominable
matter that I hate!”
5 ‘But they did not listen or incline their
ear, to turn from their evil, not to burn
incense to other mighty ones.
6 ‘So My wrath and My displeasure were
poured out and burned in the cities of
Yehuḏah and in the streets of Yerushalayim, and they became a ruin and a
wasteland, as it is this day.’
7 “And now, thus said יהוה, the Elohim
of hosts, the Elohim of Yisra’ĕl, ‘Why are
you doing this great evil against your lives,
to cut off from you man and woman, child
and infant, from the midst of Yehuḏah,
leaving none to remain,
8 by provoking Me with the works of
your hands, by burning incense to other
mighty ones in the land of Mitsrayim
where you have gone to dwell, to cut yourselves off and be a curse and a reproach

among all the nations of the earth?
9 'Have you forgotten the evils of your fathers, and the evils of the sovereigns of Yehuḏah, and the evils of their wives, and your own evils, and the evils of your wives, which they have done in the land of Yehuḏah and in the streets of Yerushalayim?
10 'To this day they have not been humbled, nor have they feared, nor have they walked in My Torah and in My laws that I set before you and your fathers.'
11 "Therefore thus said יהוה of hosts, the Elohim of Yisra'ěl, 'See, I am setting My face against you for evil and for cutting off all Yehuḏah.
12 'And I shall take the remnant of Yehuḏah who have set their faces to go into the land of Mitsrayim to sojourn there. And they shall all be consumed in the land of Mitsrayim – fall by the sword, consumed by scarcity of food. From the least to the greatest they shall die, by the sword and by scarcity of food. And they shall be an oath and an astonishment and a curse and a reproach!
13 'And I shall punish those dwelling in the land of Mitsrayim, as I have punished Yerushalayim, by the sword, by scarcity of food, and by pestilence.
14 'And none of the remnant of Yehuḏah who have gone into the land of Mitsrayim to sojourn there shall escape or survive, lest they return to the land of Yehuḏah, to which they are longing to return to dwell there. For they shall not return, except those who escape.' "
15 Then all the men who knew that their wives had burned incense to other mighty ones, and all the women who stood by, a great assembly, and all the people who dwelt in the land of Mitsrayim, in Pathros, answered Yirmeyahu, saying,
16 "We are not going to listen to you in the matter about which you spoke to us in the Name of יהוה!
17 "But we shall do whatever has gone out of our own mouth, to burn incense to the sovereigness of the heavens and pour out drink offerings to her, as we have done, we and our fathers, our sovereigns and our heads, in the cities of Yehuḏah and in the streets of Yerushalayim. And we had plenty of food, and were well-off, and saw no evil.
18 "But since we ceased burning incense to the sovereigness of the heavens and pouring out drink offerings to her, we have lacked all and have been consumed by the sword and by scarcity of food.
19 "And when we burned incense to the sovereigness of the heavens and poured out drink offerings to her, did we make cakes for her, to idolize her, and pour out drink offerings to her, without our husbands?"
20 Then Yirmeyahu spoke to all the people – to the men and to the women, and to all the people who had given him that answer, saying,
21 "As for the incense that you burned in the cities of Yehuḏah and in the streets of Yerushalayim, you and your fathers, your sovereigns and your heads, and the people of the land, did not יהוה remember them? And it came into His heart!
22 "And יהוה could no longer bear it, because of the evil of your deeds and because of the abominations which you did. Therefore your land is a ruin, an object of astonishment, a curse, and without an inhabitant, as it is this day.
23 "Because you have burned incense and because you have sinned against יהוה, and did not obey the voice of יהוה or walk in His Torah, in His laws or in His witnesses, therefore this evil did befall you, as at this day."
24 And Yirmeyahu said to all the people and to all the women, "Hear the word of יהוה, all Yehuḏah who are in the land of Mitsrayim!
25 "Thus spoke יהוה of hosts, the Elohim of Yisra'ěl, saying, 'You and your wives have spoken with your mouths, and have filled with your hands, saying, "We shall perform our vows that we have made, to burn incense to the sovereigness of the heavens and pour out drink offerings to her." Then confirm your vows and perform your vows!'
26 "Therefore hear the word of יהוה, all

Yehuḏah who are dwelling in the land of
Mitsrayim, 'See, I have sworn by My great
Name,' declares יהוה, 'My Name shall no
longer be called upon by the mouth of any
man of Yehuḏah in all the land of
Mitsrayim, saying, "As the Master יהוה
lives..."
27 'See, I am watching over them for evil
and not for good. And all the men of
Yehuḏah who are in the land of Mitsrayim
shall be consumed by the sword and by
scarcity of food, until they come to an end.
28 'And those who escape the sword, few
in number, shall return from the land of
Mitsrayim to the land of Yehuḏah. And all
the remnant of Yehuḏah, who came into
the land of Mitsrayim to sojourn there,
shall know whose word is established,
Mine or theirs.
29 'And this is the sign to you,' declares
יהוה, 'that I am punishing you in this
place, so that you know that My words are
certainly established against you for evil.'
30 "Thus said יהוה, 'See, I am giving
Pharaoh Ḥophra sovereign of Mitsrayim
into the hand of his enemies and into the
hand of those who seek his life, as I gave
Tsiḏqiyahu sovereign of Yehuḏah into the
hand of Neḇuḵaḏretstsar sovereign of
Baḇel, his enemy who sought his life.' "

45 The word that Yirmeyahu the
prophet spoke to Baruḵ son of
Nĕriyah, when he had written these words
in a book from the mouth of Yirmeyahu, in
the fourth year of Yehoyaqim son of
Yoshiyahu, sovereign of Yehuḏah, saying,
2 "Thus said יהוה, the Elohim of Yisra'ĕl, concerning you, Baruḵ:
3 'You have said, "Woe to me now! For
יהוה has added grief to my pain. I have
been wearied with my sighing, and I have
found no rest." '
4 "Say this to him, 'Thus said יהוה, "See,
what I have built I am breaking down, and
what I have planted I am plucking up, that
is, the entire land.
5 "And do you seek great matters for
yourself? Do not seek them, for look, I am
bringing evil on all flesh," declares יהוה.
"But I shall give your life to you as a prize
in all places, wherever you go." ' "

46 The word of יהוה which came to
Yirmeyahu the prophet concerning
the nations:
2 For Mitsrayim, concerning the army of
Pharaoh Neḵo, sovereign of Mitsrayim,
which was by the River Euphrates in
Karkemish, and which Neḇuḵaḏretstsar the
sovereign of Baḇel had stricken in the
fourth year of Yehoyaqim, son of Yoshiyahu, sovereign of Yehuḏah:
3 "Prepare the large and the small shield,
and draw near to battle!
4 "Harness the horses, and mount up, you
horsemen! Stand with helmets, polish the
spears, put on the armour!
5 "Why do I see them afraid, turned
back? And their fighters are beaten down.
And they have fled in haste, and did not
look back, for fear was all around,"
declares יהוה.
6 Do not let the swift flee away, nor the
mighty man escape. They shall stumble
and fall toward the north, by the River
Euphrates.
7 Who is this rising like a flood, whose
waters surge about like the rivers?
8 Mitsrayim rises like a flood, and its
waters surge about like the rivers. And he
says, 'Let me rise and cover the earth; let
me destroy the city and its inhabitants.'
9 Go up, O horses, and rage, O chariots!
And let the mighty men go forth – Kush
and Put who handle the shield, and Luḏ
who handle and bend the bow.
10 For this is the day of the Master יהוה of
hosts, a day of vengeance, to revenge
Himself on His adversaries. And the sword
shall devour, and be satisfied and made
drunk with their blood. For the Master
יהוה of hosts has a slaughtering in the land
of the north by the River Euphrates.
11 Go up to Gil'aḏ and take balm, O maid-
en, the daughter of Mitsrayim. In vain you
have used many remedies, there is no healing for you.
12 Nations have heard of your shame, and
your cry has filled the land. For the mighty
has stumbled against the mighty, they have
both fallen together.

13 The word which יהוה spoke to Yirme-
yahu the prophet, about the coming of Neḇuḵaḏretstsar sovereign of Baḇel, to strike the land of Mitsrayim:
14 "Declare in Mitsrayim, and let it be heard in Miḡdol. And let it be heard in Noph and in Taḥpanḥes. Say, 'Stand fast and be prepared, for a sword shall devour all around you.'
15 "Why were your strong ones swept away? They did not stand because יהוה drove them away.
16 "He made many stumble; indeed, they fell over each other, and said, 'Arise! Let us go back to our own people, and to the land of our birth, away from the oppressing sword.'
17 "There they cried, 'Pharaoh, sovereign of Mitsrayim, is but a noise. He has let the appointed time pass by!'
18 "As I live," declares the Sovereign, whose Name is יהוה of hosts, "For as Taḇor is among the mountains, and as Karmel by the sea, he shall come.
19 "O you daughter dwelling in Mitsrayim, prepare yourself to go into exile! For Noph shall become a waste and a ruin, and be burned, without inhabitant.
20 "Mitsrayim is like a very pretty heifer, but destruction comes, it comes from the north.
21 "Her hired ones too, in her midst, are like fattened calves, for they too shall turn, they shall flee away together. They shall not stand, for the day of their calamity has come upon them, the time of their punishment.
22 "Its sound moves along like a serpent, for they move on like an army and come against her with axes, like woodcutters.
23 "They shall cut down her forest," declares יהוה, "for it is not searched, because they are more numerous than locusts, and without number.
24 "The daughter of Mitsrayim shall be put to shame. She shall be given into the hand of the people of the north."
25 יהוה of hosts, the Elohim of Yisra'ěl, has said, "See, I am bringing punishment on Amon of No, and on Pharaoh, and on Mitsrayim, and on their mighty ones, and on their sovereigns, and on Pharaoh and on those trusting in him.
26 "And I shall give them into the hand of those who seek their lives, into the hand of Neḇuḵaḏretstsar sovereign of Baḇel and into the hand of his servants. And afterward it shall be inhabited as in the days of old," declares יהוה.
27 "But as for you, do not fear, O My servant Ya'aqoḇ, and do not be discouraged, O Yisra'ěl! For look, I am saving you from afar, and your descendants from the land of their captivity. And Ya'aqoḇ shall return, and shall have rest and be at ease, with no one disturbing.
28 "Do not fear, O Ya'aqoḇ My servant," declares יהוה, "for I am with you. Though I make a complete end of all the nations to which I have driven you, yet I do not make a complete end of you. [a] But I shall reprove you in right-ruling, and by no means leave you unpunished."

47 The word of יהוה that came to Yirmeyahu the prophet concerning the Philistines, before Pharaoh struck Azzah:
2 Thus said יהוה, "See, waters are rising out of the north, and shall be an overflowing flood. And they shall overflow the land and all that is in it, the city and those who dwell within. And men shall cry, and all the inhabitants of the land shall wail.
3 "At the noise of the stamping hooves of his strong horses, at the rushing of his chariots, at the rumbling of his wheels, the fathers shall not look to their children, because of weakness of hands,
4 because of the day that shall come to ravage all the Philistines, to cut off from Tsor and Tsiḏon every helper that survives. For יהוה is ravaging the Philistines, the remnant of the isle of Kaphtor.
5 "Baldness shall come upon Azzah, Ashqelon shall be cut off with the remnant of their valley. Till when would you cut yourself?

46a See footnote 30:11.

6 "O you sword of יהוה, how long till you rest? Put yourself up into your sheath, rest and be still!

7 "How shall it rest, when יהוה has given it a command? Against Ashqelon and against the seashore – there He has appointed it."

48 Concerning Mo'aḇ. This is what יהוה of hosts, the Elohim of Yisra'ěl said, "Woe to Neḇo! For it is ravaged, Qiryathayim is put to shame, captured. The high stronghold is put to shame and broken down.

2 "There is praise for Mo'aḇ no longer. In Ḥeshbon they have devised evil against her, 'Come and let us cut it off as a nation.' O Maḏměn, you are also cut off, a sword goes after you.

3 "Listen! An outcry from Ḥoronayim, ravaging and great destruction!

4 "Mo'aḇ shall be destroyed, her little ones shall cry out.

5 "For on the ascent to Luḥith they go up weeping bitterly. For in the descent of Ḥoronayim the enemies shall hear a cry of destruction.

6 "Flee, deliver your own lives! And be like a bush in the wilderness.

7 "For because you have trusted in your works and your treasures, you shall be captured. And Kemosh shall go forth into exile, his priests and his heads together.

8 "And a ravager shall come into every city, no one escapes. And the valley shall perish, and the plain be destroyed, as יהוה has spoken.

9 "Give wings to Mo'aḇ, for she has to flee away, and her cities become a ruin, with no one to dwell in them.

10 (Cursed is he who is slack in doing the work of יהוה, and cursed is he who withholds his sword from blood).

11 "Mo'aḇ has been at ease from his youth, and he has settled on his dregs, and has not been emptied from vessel to vessel, nor has he gone into exile. Therefore his flavour has stayed in him, and his fragrance is unchanged.

12 "Therefore see, the days are coming," declares יהוה, "when I shall send him tilters, who shall tilt him over and empty his vessels and break the bottles.

13 "And Mo'aḇ shall be ashamed because of Kemosh, as the house of Yisra'ěl was ashamed of Běyth Ěl, their refuge.

14 "How do you say, 'We are mighty and strong men for battle'?

15 "Mo'aḇ is ravaged and her cities have been entered. And her chosen young men have gone down to the slaughter," declares the Sovereign, whose Name is יהוה of hosts.

16 "The calamity of Mo'aḇ is near to come and his affliction hurries fast.

17 "Lament for him, all you who are around him. And all you who know his name, say, 'How the strong sceptre has been broken, the staff of splendour!'

18 "Come down from your esteem, and sit in thirst, O inhabitant, daughter of Diḇon. For the ravager of Mo'aḇ shall come against you, he shall destroy your strongholds.

19 "Stand by the way and watch, O inhabitant of Aro'ěr. Ask him who flees and her who escapes; say, 'What has been done?'

20 "Mo'aḇ has been put to shame, for it has been broken down. Howl and cry! Let it be heard in Arnon that Mo'aḇ is ravaged.

21 "And judgment has come on the plain country, on Ḥolon and on Yaḥtsah and on Mopha'ath,

22 and on Diḇon and Neḇo and on Běyth Diḇlathayim,

23 and on Qiryathayim and on Běyth Gamul and on Běyth Me'on,

24 and on Qeriyoth and on Botsrah, and on all the cities of the land of Mo'aḇ, far or near.

25 "The horn of Mo'aḇ has been cut off, and his arm has been broken," declares יהוה.

26 "Make him drunk, because he has made himself great against יהוה. Mo'aḇ shall splash in his vomit, and he shall also be in mockery.

27 "And was not Yisra'ěl a mockery to you? Was he found among thieves? For whenever you speak of him, you shake your head.

28 "O inhabitants of Mo'aḇ, leave the

cities and dwell in the rock, and be like the
dove making a nest in the sides of the
cave's mouth.
29"We have heard of the pride of Mo'aḇ
(he is very proud!), of his loftiness and
arrogance and pride, and of the haughti-
ness of his heart."
30"I know his wrath," declares יהוה, "and
his boastings are untrue, *and* his deeds are
false.
31"Therefore I wail for Mo'aḇ, and I cry
out for all Mo'aḇ. I mourn for the men of
Qir Ḥeres.
32"O vine of Siḇmah! I weep for you with
the weeping of Ya'zĕr. Your branches have
passed over the sea, they have come to the
sea of Ya'zĕr. The ravager has fallen on
your summer fruit and your grape harvest.
33"Joy and gladness have been taken
away from the orchard and from the land
of Mo'aḇ. And I have made wine to cease
from the winepresses. No one treads with
shouting – the shouting is no shouting!
34"From the outcry of Ḥeshbon unto
El'alĕh, unto Yahats, they shall raise their
voice, from Tso'ar to Ḥoronayim, like a
three-year-old heifer, for even the waters
of Nimrim are dried up.
35"And I shall make an end in Mo'aḇ to
him who offers in the high places and
burns incense to his mighty ones," declares
יהוה.
36"So My heart sounds for Mo'aḇ like
flutes, and My heart sounds for the men of
Qir Ḥeres like flutes. Therefore the wealth
they made shall be gone.
37"For every head is bald, and every
beard clipped – cuts on all the hands, and
sackcloth on the loins.
38"On all the house-tops of Mo'aḇ and in
its streets it is all lamentation, for I have
broken Mo'aḇ like a vessel in which no
one delights," declares יהוה.
39"How has she been broken down! They
shall wail! How has Mo'aḇ turned her back
with shame! So Mo'aḇ shall be a mockery
and a horror to all those about her."
40For thus said יהוה, "See, he soars like
an eagle, and shall spread his wings over
Mo'aḇ.
41"Qeriyoth shall be captured, and the
strongholds seized. And the heart of the
mighty men in Mo'aḇ on that day shall be
like the heart of a woman in labour.
42"And Mo'aḇ shall be destroyed as a
people, because he has made himself great
against יהוה.
43"Fear and the pit and the snare are upon
you, O inhabitant of Mo'aḇ," declares
יהוה.
44"He who flees from the fear falls into
the pit, and he who gets out of the pit is
caught in the snare. For I am bringing upon
Mo'aḇ the year of their punishment,"
declares יהוה.
45"Those who fled stood powerless under
the shadow of Ḥeshbon. But a fire shall
come out of Ḥeshbon, and a flame from
the midst of Siḥon, and consume the brow
of Mo'aḇ and the crown of the head of the
sons of uproar.
46"Woe to you, O Mo'aḇ! The people of
Kemosh have perished, for your sons have
been taken into exile, and your daughters
into exile.
47"But I shall turn back the captivity of
Mo'aḇ in the latter days," declares יהוה.
Thus far is the judgment of Mo'aḇ.

49 Concerning the Ammonites: Thus
said יהוה, "Has Yisra'ĕl no sons?
Has he no heir? Why has Malkam taken
possession of Gaḏ, and his people dwell in
its cities?
2"Therefore see, the days are coming,"
declares יהוה, "when I shall sound a battle
cry in Rabbah of the Ammonites. And it
shall be a heap, a wasteland, and her
villages shall be burned with fire. Then
Yisra'ĕl shall dispossess those who dispossessed him," declares יהוה.
3"Howl, O Ḥeshbon, for Ai is ravaged!
Cry, daughters of Rabbah, gird on sackcloth! Lament and diligently search by the
walls, for Malkam shall go into exile, with
his priests and his heads.
4"Why do you boast in the valleys, your
flowing valley, O backsliding daughter
who is trusting in her treasures, saying,
'Who would come against me?'
5"See, I am bringing fear upon you,
from all those around you," declares the

Master יהוה of hosts. "And you shall be
driven out, each one straight ahead, with
no one to bring home the wanderer.
6"And after this I turn back the captivity
of the children of Ammon," declares יהוה.
7Concerning Eḏom: Thus said יהוה of
hosts, "Is there no more wisdom in
Těman? Has counsel been lost to those
with understanding? Has their wisdom
vanished?
8"Flee, turn back, dwell in the depths, O
inhabitants of Deḏan! For I shall bring the
calamity of Ěsaw upon him, the time that I
shall punish him.
9"If grape-gatherers came to you, would
they not leave some gleaning grapes? Even
thieves by night would destroy *only* until
they had enough!
10"But as for Me, I shall make Ěsaw bare.
I shall uncover his hiding places, so that he
is unable to conceal himself. His seed is
ravaged, his brothers and his neighbours,
and he is no more.
11"Leave your fatherless children, let Me
keep them alive. And let your widows trust
in Me."
12For thus said יהוה, "See, those whose
judgment was not to drink of the cup have
certainly drunk. And are you the one to go
unpunished? You shall not go unpunished,
but certainly drink of it.
13"For I have sworn by Myself," declares
יהוה, "that Botsrah is to become a ruin, a
reproach, a waste, and a curse, and all its
cities become everlasting wastes."
14I have heard a report from יהוה, and an
envoy has been sent to the nations, "Gather
together, come against her, and rise up to
battle!
15"For look, I shall make you small
among nations, despised among men.
16"The dread for you, the pride of your
heart, has deceived you, O you who dwell
in the clefts of the rock, holding the height
of the hill! Though you make your nest as
high as the eagle, from there I bring you
down," declares the Master.
17"And Eḏom shall be a ruin, everyone
who passes by it is astonished and whistles
at all its plagues.
18"As in the overthrow of Seḏom and
Amorah and their neighbouring cities,"
declares יהוה, "No one shall dwell there,
nor would a son of man sojourn in it.
19"See, he comes up like a lion from the
Yarděn jungle against the home of the
strong. But in an instant I shall make him
run away from her. And who is the Chosen
One, to appoint over her? For who is like
Me? And who summons Me? And who is
that Shepherd who stands before Me?"
20Therefore hear the counsel of יהוה
which He has counselled concerning
Eḏom, and the purposes He has purposed
concerning the inhabitants of Těman: the
least of the flock shall drag them away! He
shall make their pasture a waste before
them!
21The earth shall be shaken at the noise of
their fall. There is an outcry! Its noise is
heard at the Sea of Reeds.
22See, like an eagle he flies up, and
spreads his wings over Botsrah. And the
heart of the mighty men of Eḏom in that
day shall be like the heart of a woman in
her pain.
23Concerning Dammeseq: "Ḥamath and
Arpaḏ have been put to shame, for they
have heard an evil report. They have been
melted in anxiety, like the sea, unable to
rest.
24"Dammeseq has become feeble, she
has turned to flee, and trembling has taken
hold of her. Distress and pain have seized
her like a woman in labour.
25"How is the city of praise deserted, the
city of My joy!
26"Therefore her young men fall in her
streets, and all the men of battle are cut off
in that day," declares יהוה of hosts.
27"And I shall kindle a fire in the wall of
Dammeseq, and it shall consume the
palaces of Ben-Haḏaḏ."
28To Qěḏar and to the reigns of Ḥatsor,
which Neḇuḵaḏretstsar sovereign of Baḇel
struck: Thus said יהוה, "Arise, go up to
Qěḏar, and ravage the men of the East!
29"Their tents and their flocks, their curtains and all their vessels shall be taken.
And they shall take away their camels for
themselves. And they shall cry out to them,
'Fear is on every side!'

30"Flee, go away! Dwell in the depths, O
inhabitants of Ḥatsor!" declares יהוה. "For
Neḇuḵaḏretstsar sovereign of Baḇel has
taken counsel against you, and has devised
a plan against you.
31"Arise, go up to the nation at ease that
dwells safely," declares יהוה. "It has no
gates or bars, they dwell alone.
32"And their camels shall become plunder, and their large herds booty. And I shall
scatter them to all winds, those who cut off
the corner, and bring their calamity from
all its sides," declares יהוה.
33"Ḥatsor shall be a habitation for jackals, a desert forever. No one dwells there,
nor does son of man sojourn in it."
34The word of יהוה that came to Yirmeyahu the prophet concerning Ěylam, in the
beginning of the reign of Tsiḏqiyah, the
sovereign of Yehuḏah, saying,
35"Thus said יהוה of hosts, 'See, I am
breaking the bow of Ěylam, the chief of
their might.
36'And I shall bring upon Ěylam the four
winds from the four quarters of the heavens, and scatter them toward all those
winds. And there shall be no nation where
the outcasts of Ěylam do not go.
37'And I shall break Ěylam before their
enemies and before those who seek their
life. And I shall bring evil upon them, my
burning displeasure,' declares יהוה. 'And I
shall send the sword after them until I have
consumed them.
38'And I shall set My throne in Ěylam,
and destroy from there the sovereign and
the heads,' declares יהוה.
39'And it shall be in the latter days that I
turn back the captivity of Ěylam,' declares
יהוה."

50

The word that יהוה spoke concerning Baḇel, concerning the land of
the Kasdim by Yirmeyahu the prophet.
2"Declare among the nations, and let it
be heard. And lift up a banner, let it be
heard, and do not conceal it. Say, 'Baḇel
shall be taken, Běl shall be put to shame,
Meroḏaḵ shall be broken, her images shall
be put to shame, her idols shall be broken.'
3For a nation shall come up against her
from the north, which shall make her land
waste, and none shall dwell in it. They
shall flee, they shall go, both man and
beast.
4"In those days and at that time,"
declares יהוה, "the children of Yisra'ěl
shall come, they and the children of
Yehuḏah together, weeping as they come,
and seek יהוה their Elohim.
5"They shall ask the way to Tsiyon, their
faces toward it, 'Come and let us join ourselves to יהוה, in an everlasting covenant,
never to be forgotten.'
6"My people have been wandering [a]
sheep. Their shepherds have led them
astray, turning them away on the mountains. They have gone from mountain to
hill, they have forgotten their resting place.
7"All who found them have devoured
them. And their adversaries have said, 'We
are not guilty, because they have sinned
against יהוה, the Home of righteousness,
and the Expectation of their fathers: יהוה.'
8"Flee from the midst of Baḇel, come
out [b] of the land of the Kasdim. And be as
rams before a flock.
9"For look, I am stirring up and bringing
up against Baḇel an assembly of great
nations from a land of the north, and they
shall array themselves against her. From
there she shall be captured – their arrows
are like those of a mighty skilled man, not
returning empty-handed.
10"And Chaldea shall become plunder, all
who plunder her shall satisfy themselves,"
declares יהוה.
11"Because you were glad, because you
rejoiced, you who plunder My inheritance,
because you have grown fat like a heifer
threshing grain, and you neigh like stal-
lions,
12your mother shall be greatly ashamed.
She who bore you shall be humiliated.
Look, the last of the nations, a wilderness,
a dry land and a desert.
13"Because of the wrath of יהוה she shall
not be inhabited, but she shall be deserted

50a Or *lost*, or *straying*, or *perishing*. *50b* Ḥazon 18:4.

– all of it. Everyone passing by Baḇel shall
be astonished and whistle at all her
plagues.
14 “Set yourselves in array against Baḇel
all around, all you who bend the bow.
Shoot at her, spare no arrows, for she has
sinned against יהוה.
15 “Shout against her all around. She has
given her hand, her foundations have fall-
en, her walls are thrown down, for it is the
vengeance of יהוה. Take vengeance on her.
As she has done, so do to her.
16 “Cut off the sower from Baḇel, and him
who handles the sickle at harvest time.
From before the sword of the oppressor
each one turns to his own people, and each
one flees to his own land.
17 “Yisra'ěl is a scattered sheep, the lions
have driven him away. First the sovereign
of Ashshur devoured him, and now, at last,
this Neḇuḵaḏretstsar sovereign of Baḇel
has broken his bones.”
18 Therefore thus said יהוה of hosts, the
Elohim of Yisra'ěl, “See, I am punishing
the sovereign of Baḇel and his land, as I
have punished the sovereign of Ashshur.
19 “And I shall bring back Yisra'ěl to his
pasture, and he shall feed on Karmel and
Bashan. And his being shall be satisfied on
Mount Ephrayim and Gil'aḏ.
20 “In those days and at that time,”
declares יהוה, “the crookedness of Yisra'ěl
shall be searched for, but there shall be
none; and the sin of Yehuḏah, but none
shall be found. For I shall pardon those
whom I leave as a remnant.
21 “Go up against the land of Merathayim,
against it, and against the inhabitants of
Peqoḏ. Slay and put them under the ban,”
declares יהוה, “and do according to all that
I have commanded you.
22 “There is a sound of battle in the land,
and of great destruction.
23 “How the hammer of all the earth has
been cut off and broken! How Baḇel has
become a ruin among the nations!
24 “I have laid a snare for you, and you
were captured, O Baḇel, and you yourself
did not know! You have been found and
also caught, because you strove against
יהוה.”
25 יהוה has opened His armoury, and has
brought out the weapons of His displeasure, for the Master Elohim of hosts has a
work to do in the land of the Kasdim.
26 Come against her from every quarter,
open her storehouses, pile her up as heaps
of ruins, and put her under the ban. Let her
have no remnant.
27 Slay all her bulls, let them go down to
the slaughter. Woe to them! For their day
has come, the time of their punishment.
28 Listen! They flee and escape from the
land of Baḇel, to declare in Tsiyon the
vengeance of יהוה our Elohim, the
vengeance of His Hěḵal.
29 “Summon archers against Baḇel. All
you who bend the bow, encamp against it
all around, let no one escape. Repay her
according to her work, do to her according
to all she has done. For she has been proud
against יהוה, against the Set-apart One of
Yisra'ěl.
30 “Therefore her young men shall fall in
the streets, and all her men of battle shall
perish in that day,” declares יהוה.
31 “See, I am against you, O proud one!”
declares the Master יהוה of hosts, “for
your day has come, the time for your punishment.
32 “And the proud one shall stumble, and
he shall fall, with no one to raise him up.
And I shall kindle a fire in his cities, and it
shall devour all around him.”
33 Thus said יהוה of hosts, “The children
of Yisra'ěl were oppressed, along with the
children of Yehuḏah. And all who took
them captive have held them fast, they
refused to let them go.
34 “Their Redeemer is strong, יהוה of
hosts is His Name. He shall strongly plead
their case, so as to give rest to the land, but
unrest to the inhabitants of Baḇel.
35 “A sword is upon the Kasdim,”
declares יהוה, “and it is upon the inhabitants of Baḇel, and upon her heads and
upon her wise men.
36 “A sword is upon the liars, and they
shall be fools. A sword is upon her mighty
men, and they shall be broken down.
37 “A sword is upon their horses, and
upon their chariots, and upon all the mixed

peoples who are in her midst, and they
shall become like women. A sword is upon
her treasures, and they shall be plundered.
38 "A sword is upon her waters, and they
shall be dried up. For it is a land of carved
images, and they boast about their idols.
39 "Therefore the wild desert beasts shall
dwell with the jackals, and the ostriches
dwell in it. And it shall never again be
inhabited, nor dwelt in, unto all generations.
40 "As Elohim overthrew Seḏom and
Amorah and their neighbouring cities,"
declares יהוה, "so no one would dwell
there, nor would son of man sojourn in it.
41 "See, a people shall come from the
north, and a great nation and many sovereigns stirred up from the ends of the earth.
42 "They strengthen *their* bow and spear,
they are cruel and they show no compassion. They sound like the roaring sea, and
ride on horses, set in array, like a man for
the battle, against you, O daughter of
Baḇel.
43 "The sovereign of Baḇel has heard the
report about them, and his hands became
weak. Distress has taken hold of him, pain
like that of a woman in labour.
44 "See, he comes up like a lion from
the Yarděn jungle, against the enduring
pasture. But in an instant I shall make them
run away from her. And who is the Chosen
One whom I appoint against her? For who
is like Me? Who summons Me? And who
is that Shepherd who stands before Me?"
45 Therefore hear the counsel of יהוה
which He has counselled concerning
Baḇel, and His purposes He has purposed
concerning the land of the Kasdim: the
least of the flock shall drag them away! He
shall make their pasture a waste before
them!
46 At the sound of Baḇel's capture the
earth shall be shaken, and the outcry shall
be heard among the nations.

51 Thus said יהוה, "See, I am stirring
up the spirit of a destroyer against
Baḇel, against those who dwell in Lěḇ –
My opponents.
2 And I shall send winnowers to Baḇel,
who shall winnow her and empty her land.
For they shall be against her all around, in
the day of evil.
3 "Let the archer draw his bow, and let
him stand ready in his armour. Do not
spare her young men, put all her army
under the ban.
4 "And the slain shall fall in the land of
the Kasdim, and the pierced-through in her
streets.
5 "For neither Yisra'ěl nor Yehuḏah is
widowed by his Elohim, יהוה of hosts,
though their land has been filled with sin
against the Set-apart One of Yisra'ěl."
6 Flee from the midst of Baḇel, [a] and let
each one save his life! Do not be cut off in
her crookedness, for this is the time of the
vengeance of יהוה, the recompense He is
repaying her.
7 Baḇel was a golden cup in the hand of
יהוה, making drunk all the earth. [b] The
nations drank her wine, that is why the
nations went mad!
8 Baḇel shall suddenly fall and be broken. Howl for her! Take balm for her pain
– if so be, she might be healed.
9 We would have healed Baḇel, but she is
not healed. Let us leave her and each go to
his own land, for her judgment reaches to
the heavens and is lifted up to the clouds.
10 יהוה has brought forth our righteousness. Come and let us relate in Tsiyon the
work of יהוה our Elohim.
11 Polish the arrows! Put on the shields!
יהוה has stirred up the spirit of the sovereigns of the Medes. For His plan is against
Baḇel to destroy it, because it is the
vengeance of יהוה, the vengeance for His
Hěḵal.
12 Lift up a banner on the walls of Baḇel,
strengthen the watch, station the watchmen, prepare the ambush. For יהוה has
both planned and done what He spoke concerning the inhabitants of Baḇel.
13 You who dwell upon many waters,
great in treasures, your end has come, the
measure of your greedy gain.

51a Ḥazon 18:4. *51b* Ḥazon 17:1-18.

14 יהוה of hosts has sworn by Himself, "I shall certainly fill you with men, as with locusts, and they shall lift up a shout against you."

15 He made the earth by His power, He established the world by His wisdom, and stretched out the heavens by His understanding.

16 When He gives forth His voice the waters in the heavens roar, and He makes vapours to ascend from the ends of the earth; He makes lightnings for the rain, and He brings the wind out of His treasuries.

17 All mankind has become too brutish to know, every smith has been put to shame by the carved image, for his moulded image is falsehood, and there is no breath in them.

18 They are worthless, a work of mockery. In the time of their punishment they perish.

19 The Portion of Yaʽaqoḇ is not like them, for He is the Maker of all, and Yisra'ěl is the tribe of His inheritance. יהוה of hosts is His Name.

20 "You are My battle-axe, weapons of battle, and with you I shall break nations in pieces, and with you I shall destroy reigns.

21 "And with you I shall break in pieces the horse and its rider, and with you I shall break in pieces the chariot and its rider.

22 "And with you I shall break in pieces man and woman, and with you I shall break in pieces old and young, and with you I shall break in pieces the young man and the maiden.

23 "And with you I shall break in pieces the shepherd and his flock, and with you I shall break in pieces the farmer and his yoke of oxen. And with you I shall break in pieces governors and rulers.

24 "And I shall repay Baḇel and all the inhabitants of Chaldea for all the evil they have done in Tsiyon before your eyes," declares יהוה.

25 "See, I am against you, O destroying mountain, who destroys all the earth," declares יהוה. "And I shall stretch out My hand against you. And I shall roll you down from the rocks, and make you a burnt mountain.

26 "And they shall not take from you a stone for a corner nor a stone for a foundation, but you shall be a waste forever," declares יהוה.

27 Lift up a banner in the land, blow a shophar among the nations! Prepare the nations against her, call the reigns together against her: Ararat, Minni, and Ashkenaz. Appoint a commander against her, bring up horses like hairy locusts.

28 Separate the nations against her, with the sovereigns of the Medes, its governors and all its rulers, all the land of his rule,

29 so that the land shakes and writhes in pain. For every plan of יהוה shall be established against Baḇel, to make the land of Baḇel a ruin, without inhabitant.

30 The mighty men of Baḇel have ceased to fight, they remained in their strongholds. Their might has failed, they became like women, they have burned her dwelling places. The bars of her gate have been broken.

31 One runner runs to meet another, and one reporter to meet another, to report to the sovereign of Baḇel that his city is taken on all sides,

32 and the fords have been captured, and they have burned the reeds with fire, and the soldiers are startled.

33 For thus said יהוה of hosts, the Elohim of Yisra'ěl, "The daughter of Baḇel is like a threshing-floor at the time it is trodden. Yet a little while and the time of her harvest shall come."

34 "Neḇuḵaḏretstsar the sovereign of Baḇel has devoured us, he has crushed us, he has made us an empty vessel, he has swallowed us up like a monster. He has filled his stomach with my delicacies, he has driven us away.

35 "Let the violence done to me and my flesh be upon Baḇel," says the inhabitant of Tsiyon. And, "Let my blood be upon the inhabitants of Chaldea," says Yerushalayim.

36 Therefore thus said יהוה, "See, I am pleading your case. And I shall take vengeance for you and dry up her sea and make her fountain dry.

37 "And Baḇel shall become a heap, a

habitation of jackals, an astonishment and
a hissing, without inhabitant.
38 "Together they roar like lions, they
shall growl like lions' cubs.
39 "In their heat I prepare their feasts. And
I shall make them drunk, so that they
rejoice, and sleep a neverending sleep and
not awake," declares יהוה.
40 "I shall bring them down like lambs to
the slaughter, like rams with male goats.
41 "Oh, how Shěshak has been captured,
the praise of all the earth been seized! How
Baḇel has become a ruin among the
nations!
42 "The sea has risen over Baḇel, she has
been covered with the roaring of its waves.
43 "Her cities have become a ruin, a dry
land and a desert, a land where no one
dwells, neither does son of man pass by it.
44 "And I shall punish Běl in Baḇel. And I
shall make him spew out what he has swallowed, and nations shall no longer stream
to him. Even the wall of Baḇel shall fall.
45 "Come out [c] of her midst, My people!
And let everyone deliver his being from
the burning displeasure of יהוה.
46 "And lest your heart grow faint, and
you fear the report heard in the land – for a
report shall come one year, and after that,
in another year a report shall come, and
violence in the land, ruler against ruler –
47 therefore see, the days are coming that I
shall bring punishment on the carved
images of Baḇel, and all her land shall be
put to shame, and all her slain fall in her
midst.
48 "And the heavens and the earth and all
that is in them shall shout for joy over
Baḇel, for the ravagers shall come to her
from the north," declares יהוה.
49 As Baḇel is to fall for the slain of
Yisra'ěl, so for Baḇel the slain of all the
earth shall fall.
50 You who have escaped the sword, go
away! Do not stand still! Remember יהוה
from afar, and let Yerushalayim come to
your heart.
51 We are ashamed because we have heard
reproach. Shame has covered our faces, for
strangers have come into the set-apart
places of the House of יהוה. [d]
52 "Therefore see, the days are coming,"
declares יהוה, "that I shall bring punishment on her carved images, while the
wounded groan throughout all her land.
53 "Though Baḇel should mount up to the
heavens, and though she should make the
height of her strength inaccessible, ravagers shall come to her from Me," declares
יהוה.
54 Listen! A cry from Baḇel, and great
destruction from the land of the Kasdim,
55 because יהוה is ravaging Baḇel, and
shall silence her loud voice. And her
waves shall roar like great waters, the
noise of their voice shall resound,
56 because the ravager shall come against
her, against Baḇel, and her mighty men
shall be captured. Every one of their bows
shall be broken, for יהוה is the Ěl of
recompense, He shall certainly repay.
57 "And I shall make her rulers drunk, and
her wise men, her governors, and her
deputies, and her mighty men. And they
shall sleep a lasting sleep, and not awake,"
declares the Sovereign, whose Name is
יהוה of hosts.
58 Thus said יהוה of hosts, "The broad
walls of Baḇel are completely demolished,
and her high gates are burned with fire,
and peoples labour in vain, and the nations
weary themselves for fire."
59 The word that Yirmeyahu the prophet
commanded Serayah son of Něriyah, son
of Maḥsěyah, when he went with Tsiḏqiyahu the sovereign of Yehuḏah to Baḇel in
the fourth year of his reign. And Serayah
was a quartermaster.
60 So Yirmeyahu wrote in a book all the
evil that would come upon Baḇel, all these
words which have been written concerning
Baḇel.
61 And Yirmeyahu said to Serayah,
"When you come to Baḇel and see it, and
read all these words,
62 then you shall say, 'O יהוה, You have
spoken concerning this place to cut it off,
so that none shall dwell in it, neither man

51c Ḥazon 18:4. *51d* Teh. 79:1-7, Ěḵah 1:10, Dan. 8:13, 11:31, Mt. 24:15.

nor beast, for it is a ruin forever.’
63 “And it shall be, when you have ended
reading this book, that you shall tie a stone
to it and throw it into the midst of the
Euphrates,
64 and shall say, ‘So does Baḇel sink and
not rise from the evil that I am bringing
upon her, and they shall weary themselves.’ ” Thus far are the words of
Yirmeyahu.

52 Tsiḏqiyahu was twenty-one years
old when he began to reign, and he
reigned eleven years in Yerushalayim. And
his mother’s name was Ḥamutal the
daughter of Yirmeyahu of Liḇnah.
2 And he did evil in the eyes of יהוה,
according to all that Yehoyaqim had done.
3 For through the displeasure of יהוה this
came to be against Yerushalayim and
Yehuḏah, until He had cast them out from
His presence. And Tsiḏqiyahu rebelled
against the sovereign of Baḇel.
4 And it came to be in the ninth year of
his reign, in the tenth new *moon*, on the
tenth of the new *moon*, that Neḇuḵaḏretstsar sovereign of Baḇel and all his army
came against Yerushalayim and encamped
against it. And they built a siege wall
against it all around.
5 And the city was under siege until the
eleventh year of Sovereign Tsiḏqiyahu.
6 On the ninth of the fourth new *moon*
the scarcity of food was so severe in the
city that there was no food for the people
of the land.
7 Then the city wall was breached, and
all the men of battle fled and went out of
the city at night by way of the gate
between the two walls, which was by the
sovereign’s garden, while the Kasdim
were near the city all around. And they
went by way of the desert plain.
8 But the army of the Kasdim pursued the
sovereign, and they overtook Tsiḏqiyahu
in the desert plains of Yeriḥo, and his
entire army was scattered from him.
9 Then they captured the sovereign and
brought him up to the sovereign of Baḇel
at Riḇlah in the land of Ḥamath, and he
pronounced judgments on him.
10 And the sovereign of Baḇel slew the
sons of Tsiḏqiyahu before his eyes, and he
also slew all the heads of Yehuḏah in
Riḇlah.
11 And he put out the eyes of Tsiḏqiyahu.
And the sovereign of Baḇel bound him in
bronze shackles, and took him to Baḇel,
and put him in prison till the day of his
death.
12 And on the tenth of the fifth new *moon*,
which was the nineteenth year of sovereign
Neḇuḵaḏretstsar sovereign of Baḇel,
Neḇuzaraḏan, chief of the guard, who
served the sovereign of Baḇel, came to
Yerushalayim,
13 and he burned the House of יהוה, and
the sovereign’s house, and all the houses
of Yerushalayim, and all the houses of the
great men, he burned with fire.
14 And all the army of the Kasdim who
were with the chief of the guard broke
down all the walls of Yerushalayim all
around.
15 And Neḇuzaraḏan, chief of the guard,
exiled some of the poor people, and the
rest of the people who were left in the city,
and the defectors who had gone over to the
sovereign of Baḇel, and the rest of the
craftsmen.
16 But Neḇuzaraḏan, chief of the guard,
left some of the poor of the land as vinedressers and farmers.
17 And the Kasdim broke the bronze
columns that were in the House of יהוה,
and the stands and the bronze Sea that
were in the House of יהוה, and brought all
their bronze to Baḇel.
18 They also took away the pots, and the
shovels, and the snuffers, and the bowls,
and the ladles, and all the bronze utensils
with which they served,
19 and the basins, and the fire holders,
and the bowls, and the pots, and the lampstands, and the ladles, and the cups, whatever was of solid gold and whatever was of
solid silver, the chief of the guard took.
20 The two columns, one Sea, the twelve
bronze bulls which were under it, and the
stands, which Sovereign Shelomoh had
made for the House of יהוה – the bronze of
all these vessels was beyond weighing.

[21] As for the columns, the height of one column was eighteen cubits, and its circumference was twelve cubits, and its thickness was four fingers, hollow.

[22] And a capital of bronze was on it. And the height of one capital was five cubits, with a network and pomegranates all around the capital, all of bronze. And the second column, with pomegranates was the same.

[23] And there were ninety-six pomegranates on the sides. All the pomegranates on the network were one hundred, all around.

[24] And the chief of the guard took Serayah the chief priest, and Tsephanyah the second priest, and the three doorkeepers.

[25] And from the city he took one eunuch who was in charge of the men of battle, and seven men who saw the sovereign's face, who were found in the city, and the scribe of the commander of the army who mustered the people of the land, and sixty men of the people of the land who were found in the city.

[26] And Neḇuzaraḏan, chief of the guard, took these and brought them to the sovereign of Baḇel at Riḇlah,

[27] and the sovereign of Baḇel struck them and put them to death at Riḇlah in the land of Ḥamath. Thus Yehuḏah was exiled from its own land.

[28] These are the people whom Neḇuḵaḏretstsar exiled: in the seventh year, three thousand and twenty-three Yehuḏim;

[29] in the eighteenth year of Neḇuḵaḏretstsar he exiled from Yerushalayim eight hundred and thirty-two beings;

[30] in the twenty-third year of Neḇuḵaḏretstsar, Neḇuzaraḏan, chief of the guard, exiled of the Yehuḏim seven hundred and forty-five beings. All the beings were four thousand six hundred.

[31] And it came to be in the thirty-seventh year of the exile of Yehoyaḵin sovereign of Yehuḏah, in the twelfth new *moon*, on the twenty-fifth of the new *moon*, that Ewil-Meroḏaḵ sovereign of Baḇel, in the first year of his reign, lifted up the head of Yehoyaḵin sovereign of Yehuḏah and brought him out of prison,

[32] and spoke kindly to him and set his throne above those of the sovereigns who were with him in Baḇel.

[33] So he changed his prison garments, and he ate bread continually before the sovereign all the days of his life.

[34] And as for his allowance, there was a continual allowance given him by the sovereign of Baḇel, a portion for each day until the day of his death, all the days of his life.

YEḤEZQĚL

EZEKIEL

1 And it came to be in the thirtieth year, in the fourth *month*, on the fifth of the new *moon*, as I was among the exiles by the River Keḇar, the heavens were opened and I saw visions of Elohim.

2 On the fifth of the new *moon*, in the fifth year of Sovereign Yehoyaḵin's exile,

3 the word of יהוה came expressly to Yeḥezqěl the priest, the son of Buzi, in the land of the Kasdim by the River Keḇar. And the hand of יהוה came upon him there.

4 And I looked and saw a whirlwind coming out of the north, a great cloud with fire flashing itself. And brightness was all around it, and out of its midst like glowing metal, out of the midst of the fire,

5 and out of the midst of it came what looked like four living creatures. And this was their appearance: they had the likeness of a man.

6 And each one had four faces, and each one had four wings.

7 And their feet were straight feet, and the soles of their feet were like the sole of a calves' foot. And they sparkled like the appearance of polished bronze,

8 and under their wings on their four sides were the hands of a man. And each of the four had faces and wings –

9 their wings touched one another. They did not turn when they went, but each one went straight forward.

10 And the likeness of their faces: the face of a man, and each of the four had the face of a lion on the right side, and each of the four had the face of an ox on the left side, and each of the four had the face of an eagle.

11 Such were their faces. Their wings were spread upward, two of each touched one another, and two covered their bodies.

12 And each one went straight forward, going wherever the spirit was to go, and they did not turn when they went.

13 And the likeness of the living creatures: their appearance was like burning coals of fire, and like the appearance of torches, moving back and forth among the living creatures. And the fire was bright, and out of the fire went lightning.

14 And the living creatures ran back and forth, like the appearance of a flash of lightning.

15 And I looked at the living creatures, and saw a wheel on the earth beside each living creature with its four faces.

16 The appearance of the wheels and their works was like the appearance of beryl, and all four had the same form. The appearance of their works was, as it were, a wheel in the middle of a wheel.

17 When they went, they went in any one of four directions, they did not turn aside when they went.

18 And their rims were high and awesome, and their rims were covered with eyes, all around the four of them.

19 And when the living creatures went, the wheels went beside them. And when the living creatures were lifted up from the earth, the wheels were lifted up.

20 Wherever the spirit was to go, they went, because there the spirit went. And the wheels were lifted together with them, for the spirit of the living creatures was in the wheels.

21 When those went, these went; when those stood, these stood. And when those were lifted up from the earth, the wheels were lifted up together with them, for the spirit of the living creatures was in the wheels.

22 And a likeness was over the heads of the living creatures, an expanse like the appearance of an awesome crystal, stretched out over their heads.

23 And under the expanse their wings were straight, one toward another. Each one had two which covered one side, and

each one had two which covered the other
side of the body.
24 And when they went, I heard the noise
of their wings, like the noise of many
waters, like the voice of the Almighty, a
tumult like the noise of an army. And when
they stood still, they let down their wings.
25 And a voice came from above the
expanse that was over their heads. When
they stood, they dropped their wings.
26 And above the expanse over their heads
was the likeness of a throne, in appearance
like a sapphire stone. And on the likeness
of the throne was a likeness as the appearance of a man high above it.
27 And from the appearance of His waist
and upward I saw what looked like glowing metal with the appearance of fire all
around within it. And from the appearance
of His waist and downward I saw what
looked like fire, and brightness all around.
28 As the appearance of a rainbow in a
cloud on a rainy day, so was the appearance of the brightness all around it. This
was the appearance of the likeness of the
esteem of יהוה. And when I saw it, I fell
on my face, and I heard a voice of One
speaking.

2 And He said to me, "Son of man,
stand on your feet, so that I speak to
you."
2 And the Spirit entered into me when He
spoke to me, and set me on my feet. And I
heard Him who was speaking to me.
3 And He said to me, "Son of man, I am
sending you to the children of Yisra'ĕl, to a
nation of rebels who have rebelled against
Me. They and their fathers have transgressed against Me, until this day.
4 "And the children are stiff of face and
hard of heart to whom I am sending you,
and you shall say to them, 'Thus said the
Master יהוה.'
5 "And they – whether they hear or
whether they refuse, for they are a rebellious house – shall know that a prophet has
been in their midst.
6 "And you, son of man, do not be afraid
of them, nor be afraid of their words,
though thistles and thorns are with you and
you dwell among scorpions. Do not be
afraid of their words or discouraged by
their looks, for they are a rebellious house.
7 "And you shall speak My words to
them, whether they hear or whether they
refuse, for they are rebellious.
8 "And you, son of man, hear what I
am speaking to you. Do not be rebellious
like that rebellious house, open your
mouth and eat what I am giving you."
9 And I looked and saw a hand stretched
out to me. And see, a scroll of a book was
in it,
10 and He spread it before me, and it was
written on the inside and on the outside.
And written on it were lamentations and
mourning and woe.

3 And He said to me, "Son of man, eat
what you find, eat this scroll, and go,
speak to the house of Yisra'ĕl."
2 And I opened my mouth, and He fed
me the scroll.
3 And He said to me, "Son of man, feed
your stomach, and fill your stomach with
this scroll that I am giving you." And I ate
it, and it was as sweet as honey in my
mouth. [a]
4 And He said to me, "Son of man, go to
the house of Yisra'ĕl, and you shall speak
to them with My words.
5 "For you are not sent to a people of
foreign speech and of difficult language,
but to the house of Yisra'ĕl,
6 not to many people of foreign speech
and of difficult language, whose words you
do not understand. If I had rather sent you
to them, they would have listened to you.
7 "But the house of Yisra'ĕl is going to
refuse to listen to you, for they refuse to
listen to Me. For all the house of Yisra'ĕl
are hard of head, and hard of heart.
8 "See, I shall make your face as hard as
their faces and your forehead as hard as
their foreheads.
9 "Like adamant stone, harder than flint,
I shall make your forehead. Do not be

3a Teh. 19:10, 119:103, Ḥazon 10:9-10.

afraid of them, nor be discouraged at their
looks, for they are a rebellious house."
10 And He said to me, "Son of man,
receive into your heart all My words that
I speak to you, and hear with your ears.
11 "And go! Come to the exiles, to the
children of your people, and speak to them
and say to them, 'Thus said the Master
יהוה,' whether they hear, or whether they
refuse."
12 And the Spirit lifted me up, and behind
me I heard the sound of a great rumbling
voice, "Blessed be the esteem of יהוה from
His place,"
13 and the sound of the wings of the living
creatures touching one another, and the
sound of the wheels beside them, and the
sound of a great rushing.
14 And the Spirit lifted me and took me
away, and I went in bitterness, in the heat
of my spirit, while the hand of יהוה was
strong upon me.
15 And I came to the exiles at Tĕl Aḇiḇ,
who were dwelling by the River Keḇar.
And I sat where they were sitting, and sat
there, stunned among them, seven days.
16 And it came to be at the end of seven
days that the word of יהוה came to me,
saying,
17 "Son of man, I have made you a watchman for the house of Yisra'ĕl. And you
shall hear a word from My mouth, and
shall warn them from Me.
18 "When I say to the wrong, [b] 'You shall
certainly die,' and you have not warned
him, nor spoken to warn the wrong from
his wrong way, to save his life, that same
wrong man shall die in his crookedness,
and his blood I require at your hand.
19 "But if you have warned the wrong and
he does not turn from his wrong, nor from
his wrong way, he shall die in his crookedness, and you have delivered your being.
20 "And when a righteous one turns from
his righteousness and shall do unrighteousness, when I have put a stumbling-block
before him, he shall die. Because you did
not warn him, he shall die in his sin, and
his righteousness which he has done is not
remembered, and his blood I require at
your hand.
21 "But if you have warned the righteous
one that the righteous should not sin, and
he did not sin, he shall certainly live
because he has been warned, and you have
delivered your being."
22 And the hand of יהוה came upon me
there, and He said to me, "Arise, go out
into the plain, so that I might speak to you
there."
23 So I got up and went out into the plain,
and see, the esteem of יהוה stood there,
like the esteem which I saw by the River
Keḇar, and I fell on my face.
24 And the Spirit entered me and set me
on my feet, and spoke with me and said to
me, "Go, shut yourself inside your house.
25 "And you, O son of man, see, they shall
put cords on you and bind you with them,
so that you do not go out in their midst.
26 "And I make your tongue stick to the
roof of your mouth, so that you shall be
dumb and not be a reprover to them, for
they are a rebellious house.
27 "But when I speak with you, I open
your mouth, and you shall say to them,
'Thus said the Master יהוה.' He who
hears, let him hear. And he who refuses, let
him refuse, for they are a rebellious house.

4 "And you, son of man, take a clay
tablet, and you shall lay it before you,
and shall inscribe on it a city, Yerushalayim,
2 and shall lay siege against it, and build
a siege wall against it, and heap up a
mound against it, and set camps against it,
and place battering rams against it all
around.
3 "Then take an iron plate, and set it as an
iron wall between you and the city. And
you shall set your face against it, and it
shall be besieged, and you shall lay siege
against it. It is a sign to the house of
Yisra'ĕl.
4 "And lie on your left side, and you shall
put the crookedness of the house of Yisra'ĕl on it. As many days as you lie on it,

3b This passage is almost the same as in 18:20-32 and 33:8-20.

you shall bear their crookedness.
5 "For I Myself have laid on you the
years of their crookedness, according to
the number of the days, three hundred and
ninety days. And you shall bear the
crookedness of the house of Yisra'ěl.
6 "And when you have completed them,
you shall lie again on your right side and
shall bear the crookedness of the house of
Yehuḏah forty days, a day for a year. I
have laid on you a day for a year.
7 "Then you shall set your face toward
the siege of Yerushalayim, with your arm
bared, and you shall prophesy against it.
8 "And see, I shall put cords on you so
that you do not turn from one side to
another untill you have completed the days
of your siege.
9 "And take wheat, and barley, and
beans, and lentils, and millet, and spelt.
And you shall put them into one vessel,
and make bread of them. You shall eat it,
as many days as you lie on your side, three
hundred and ninety days.
10 "And your food which you eat is by
weight, twenty sheqels a day, to be eaten
from time to time.
11 "And drink water by measure, one-
sixth of a hin, to be drunk from time to
time.
12 "And eat it as a barley cake. And bake
it, before their eyes, on human dung."
13 And יהוה said, "Even so the children of
Yisra'ěl shall eat their defiled bread among
the nations, to whom I drive them."
14 Then I said, "Ah, Master יהוה! See, I
have never defiled myself from my youth
till now. I have never eaten what died of
itself or was torn by beasts, nor has
unclean meat ever come into my mouth."
15 And He said to me, "See, I am giving
you the dung of cattle instead of human
dung, and you shall prepare your bread
over it."
16 And He said to me, "Son of man, see, I
am going to cut off the supply of bread in
Yerushalayim, and they shall eat bread by
weight and with fear, and drink water by
measure and with dread,
17 so that they lack bread and water, and
shall be appalled with one another, and be
consumed in their crookedness.

5 "And you, son of man, take a sharp
sword, take it as a barber's razor, and
you shall pass it over your head and your
beard. And you shall take scales to weigh
and divide the hair.
2 "Burn with fire one-third in the midst
of the city when the days of the siege are
completed. And you shall take one-third
and strike around it with the sword, and
scatter one-third in the wind. And I shall
draw out a sword after them.
3 "And you shall take a few *hairs* from
there and bind them in the edge of your
garment.
4 "And take again some of them, and
throw them into the midst of the fire, and
burn them in the fire. From it a fire shall
spread unto all the house of Yisra'ěl.
5 "Thus said the Master יהוה, 'This is
Yerushalayim which I have set in the midst
of the nations, with the *other* lands all
around her.
6 'But she rebelled against My right-
rulings, doing wrong, more than the
nations, and My laws more than the lands
all around her. For they have rejected My
right-rulings, and they have not walked in
My laws.'
7 "Therefore thus said the Master יהוה,
'Because you have rebelled more than the
nations all around you, and have not
walked in My laws, nor done My right-
rulings, nor even done according to the
right-rulings of the nations all around you,'
8 therefore thus said the Master יהוה,
'Look I Myself am against you and shall
execute judgments in your midst before the
eyes of the nations.
9 'And I shall do among you what I have
never done, and the like of which I never
do again, because of all your abominations.
10 'Therefore fathers are going to eat their
sons in your midst, and sons eat their
fathers. And I shall execute judgments
among you and scatter all your remnant to
all the winds.
11 'Therefore, as I live,' declares the
Master יהוה, 'because you have defiled

My set-apart place with all your disgusting
matters and with all your abominations,
therefore I also withdraw. And My eye
shall not pardon, nor shall I spare.
12 'One-third of you shall die of pestilence, and be consumed with scarcity of
food in your midst. And one-third shall fall
by the sword all around you. And I shall
scatter another third to all the winds, and
draw out a sword after them.
13 'And My displeasure shall be completed. And I shall bring My wrath to rest upon
them, and I shall be eased. And they shall
know that I, יהוה, have spoken it in My
ardour, when I have completed My wrath
upon them.
14 'And I shall make you a waste and a
reproach among the nations that are all
around you, before the eyes of all who pass
by.
15 'And it shall be a reproach, an object of
scorn, a warning, and an astonishment to
the nations that are all around you, when
I execute judgments among you in displeasure and in wrath and in heated chastisements. I, יהוה, have spoken.
16 'When I send against them the evil
arrows of scarcity of food which shall be
for their destruction, which I send to
destroy you, I shall increase the scarcity of
food upon you and cut off your supply of
bread.
17 'And I shall send against you scarcity
of food and evil beasts, and they shall
bereave you. And pestilence and blood
shall pass through you, while I bring the
sword against you. I, יהוה, have spoken.' "

6 And the word of יהוה came to me,
saying,
2 "Son of man, set your face toward the
mountains of Yisra'ěl, and prophesy
against them.
3 "And you shall say, 'O mountains of
Yisra'ěl, hear the word of the Master
יהוה!' Thus said the Master יהוה to the
mountains, to the hills, to the ravines, and
to the valleys, "Look, I Myself am bringing a sword against you, and I shall destroy
your high places.
4 "And your slaughter-places shall be
ruined, your sun-pillars shall be broken in
pieces. And I shall make your slain fall in
front of your idols,
5 and lay the corpses of the children of
Yisra'ěl in front of their idols, and scatter
your bones all around your slaughter-
places.
6 "In all your dwelling places the cities
shall be destroyed and the high places
deserted, so that your slaughter-places are
broken and bear their punishment. And
your idols shall be smashed and made to
cease, and your sun-pillars cut down, and
your works blotted out.
7 "And the slain shall fall in your midst,
and you shall know that I am יהוה.
8 "But I shall leave a remnant, in that
some of you shall escape the sword among
the nations, when you are scattered
throughout the lands.
9 "And those of you who escape shall
remember Me among the nations where
they have been taken captive, because I
have been broken by their adulterous heart
which has turned away from Me, and by
their eyes which whored after their idols.
And they shall loathe themselves for the
evils which they have done in all their
abominations.
10 "And they shall know that I am יהוה,
and not for naught have I spoken to do this
evil to them."
11 'Thus said the Master יהוה, "Strike
with your hand and stamp your feet, and
say, 'Alas, because of all the evil abominations of the house of Yisra'ěl who shall fall
by sword, by scarcity of food, and by pestilence!
12 'He who is far off shall die by pestilence, he who is near fall by the sword, and
he who is left over and is besieged die by
scarcity of food. And I shall complete My
wrath upon them.
13 'And you shall know that I am יהוה,
when their slain are among their idols all
around their slaughter-places, on every
high hill, on all the mountaintops, under
every green tree, and under every thick
oak, wherever they offered sweet incense
to all their idols.
14 'And I shall stretch out My hand

against them and make the land a wasteland, even more waste than the wilderness
toward Diḇlah, in all their dwelling places.
And they shall know that I am יהוה.’ ” ’ ”

7 And the word of יהוה came to me,
saying,
2 “And you, son of man, this is what the
Master יהוה said to the land of Yisra’ěl,
‘An end! The end has come upon the four
corners of the land.
3 ‘Now the end is upon you, and I shall
send My displeasure against you, and
judge you according to your ways, and
repay you for all your abominations.
4 ‘And My eye shall not pardon you, nor
would I spare, for I repay your ways while
your abominations are in your midst. And
you shall know that I am יהוה!’
5 “Thus said the Master יהוה, ‘A calamity, an only calamity, look, it has come!
6 ‘An end has come, the end has come! It
has awakened against you, look, it has
come!
7 ‘The turn has come to you, O inhabitants of the land. The time has come, a day
of uproar is near, and not of rejoicing in the
mountains.
8 ‘Soon I shall pour out My wrath, and
shall complete My displeasure upon you,
and judge you according to your ways, and
repay you for all your abominations.
9 ‘And My eye shall not pardon, nor
would I spare. I give you according to your
ways while your abominations are in your
midst. And you shall know that I am יהוה
who strikes.
10 ‘See, the day! See, it has come! The
turn has come, the rod has blossomed,
pride has budded.
11 ‘The violence has grown into a rod of
wrongdoing. There is none of them, and
none of its crowd, and none of their riches,
and none eminent among them.
12 ‘The time has come, *and* the day has
arrived. ‘Let not the buyer rejoice, nor the
seller mourn, for wrath is on all its crowd.
13 ‘For the seller shall not return to what
has been sold, though they are still alive.
For the vision is for all its crowd – it shall
not turn back. And in the crookedness of
his life a man shall not strengthen himself.
14 ‘They have blown the trumpet and all is
prepared, but no one goes to battle, for My
wrath is on all its crowd.
15 ‘The sword is outside, and the pestilence and the scarcity of food inside. He
who is in the field dies by the sword, and
he who is in a city, scarcity of food and
pestilence devour him,
16 while they who escape of them shall
escape and be on the mountains like doves
of the valleys, all of them mourning, each
for his crookedness.
17 ‘All hands go limp, and all knees
become as water.
18 ‘And they shall gird on sackcloth, and
be covered with trembling. And shame
shall be on every face, and baldness on all
their heads.
19 ‘They throw their silver into the streets,
and their gold becomes as filth. Their
silver and their gold is unable to deliver
them in the day of the wrath of יהוה.
They do not satisfy their appetite, nor fill
their stomachs, because it has been their
stumbling-block of crookedness.
20 ‘And the splendour of His ornaments,
He set it in excellency. But they made from
it the images of their abominations and
their disgusting *matters*. Therefore I shall
make it like filth to them.
21 ‘And I shall give it for a prey into the
hands of strangers, and to the wrong of the
earth for a spoil, and they shall profane it.
22 ‘And I shall turn My face from them.
And they shall profane My secret place,
for destroyers shall enter it and profane it.
23 ‘Make a chain, for the land has been
filled with crimes of blood, and the city
has been filled with violence.
24 ‘And I shall bring the evil ones of
the nations, and they shall possess their
houses. And I shall cause the pride of the
strong to cease, and their set-apart places
shall be profaned.
25 ‘Destruction shall come. And they shall
seek peace, but there is none.
26 ‘Calamity upon calamity shall come,
and report shall be upon report. And they
shall seek a vision from a prophet. But the
teaching has perished from the priest, and

counsel from the elders!
[27] 'Let the sovereign mourn, and let the
prince put on despair, and let the hands of
the common people tremble. And I shall
deal with them according to their way, and
judge them with their own right-rulings.
And they shall know that I am יהוה!' "

8

And it came to be in the sixth year, in
the sixth *month*, on the fifth of the
new *moon*, as I sat in my house with the
elders of Yehuḏah sitting before me, that
the hand of the Master יהוה fell upon me
there.
[2] And I looked and saw a likeness, like
the appearance of fire. From His waist
and downward the appearance was like
fire, and from His waist and upward the
appearance of brightness, like glowing
metal.
[3] And He stretched out the form of a
hand, and took me by a lock of my hair.
And the Spirit lifted me up between the
earth and the heavens, and brought me in
visions of Elohim to Yerushalayim, to the
door of the north gate of the inner court,
where the seat of the image of jealousy
was, which causes jealousy.
[4] And see, the esteem of the Elohim of
Yisra'ěl was there, like the vision that I
saw in the plain.
[5] And He said to me, "Son of man, please
lift your eyes toward the north." And I lifted my eyes northward, and north of the
slaughter-place gate I saw this image of
jealousy in the entrance.
[6] And He said to me, "Son of man, do
you see what they are doing, the great
abominations which the house of Yisra'ěl
are doing here, driving Me away from My
set-apart place? And you are to see still
greater abominations."
[7] Then He brought me to the door of the
court. And I looked and saw a hole in the
wall.
[8] And He said to me, "Son of man, please
dig into the wall." And when I dug into the
wall I saw a door.
[9] And He said to me, "Go in, and see the
evil abominations [a] which they are doing
there."
[10] And I went in and looked and saw all
kinds of creeping creatures, abominable
beasts, and all the idols of the house of
Yisra'ěl, carved all around on the walls.
[11] And facing them stood seventy men of
the elders of the house of Yisra'ěl, and in
their midst stood Ya'azanyahu son of
Shaphan. Each one had a censer in his
hand, and a thick cloud of incense went up.
[12] And He said to me, "Son of man, have
you seen what the elders of the house of
Yisra'ěl are doing in the dark, each one in
the room of his idols? For they say, 'יהוה
does not see us, יהוה has forsaken the
land.' "
[13] And He said to me, "You are to see still
greater abominations which they are
doing."
[14] And He brought me to the door of the
north gate of the House of יהוה, and I saw
women sitting there, weeping for Tammuz.
[15] Then He said to me, "Have you seen
this, O son of man? You are to see still
greater abominations than these."
[16] And He brought me into the inner court
of the House of יהוה. And there, at the
door of the Hěḵal of יהוה, between the
porch and the slaughter-place, were about
twenty-five men with their backs toward
the Hěḵal of יהוה and their faces toward
the east, and they were bowing themselves
eastward to the sun.
[17] And He said to me, "Have you seen, O
son of man? Is it a small matter to the
house of Yehuḏah to do the abominations
which they have done here? For they have
filled the land with violence, and turn back
to provoke Me. And see, they are putting
the branch to My nose.
[18] "Therefore I shall indeed deal in wrath.
My eye shall not pardon nor would I spare.
And they shall cry in My ears with a loud
voice, but I shall not hear them."

8a See also 6:4, Deḇ. 4:19, Deḇ. 17:3, Mel. ב 23:4-11, Diḇre ב 14:5, Iyoḇ 31:29, Yirm. 19:13, 44:17 and Ma. 7:42.

9 And He called out in my hearing with a loud voice, saying, "Let the punishers of the city draw near, each with his weapon of destruction in his hand."

2 And look, six men came from the direction of the upper gate, which faces north, each with his battle-axe in his hand. And one man in their midst was clothed with linen and had a writer's ink-horn at his side. And they came in and stood beside the bronze slaughter-place.

3 And the esteem of the Elohim of Yisra'ěl went up from the keruḇ, where it had been, to the threshold of the House. And He called to the man clothed with linen, who had the writer's ink-horn at his side,

4 and יהוה said to him, "Pass on into the midst of the city, into the midst of Yerushalayim, and you shall put a mark on the foreheads of the men who sigh and cry over all the abominations that are done within it."

5 And to the others He said in my hearing, "Pass on into the city after him and strike, do not let your eye pardon nor spare.

6 "Kill to destruction old, young men, maidens and children and women, but do not come near anyone upon whom is the mark, and begin at My set-apart place." So they began with the elders who were in front of the House.

7 And He said to them, "Defile the House, and fill the courts with the slain. Go out!" And they went out and struck in the city.

8 And as they were striking them it came to be that I alone was left. And I fell on my face and cried out, and said, "Ah, Master יהוה! Are You destroying all the remnant of Yisra'ěl in pouring out Your wrath on Yerushalayim?"

9 And He said to me, "The crookedness of the house of Yisra'ěl and Yehuḏah is exceedingly great, and the land is filled with bloodshed, and the city filled with that which is warped. For they say, 'יהוה has forsaken the land, and יהוה is not seeing!'

10 "But as for Me, My eye shall not pardon, nor would I spare, I shall recompense their deeds on their own head."

11 And see, the man clothed with linen, who had the ink-horn at his side, reported back and said, "I have done as You commanded me."

10 And I looked and saw in the expanse that was above the head of the keruḇim, like a sapphire stone, having the appearance of the likeness of a throne.

2 And He spoke to the man clothed with linen, and said, "Go in among the wheels, under the keruḇ, and fill your hands with coals of fire from among the keruḇim, and scatter over the city." And he went in before my eyes.

3 And the keruḇim were standing on the south side of the House when the man went in, and the cloud filled the inner court.

4 And the esteem of יהוה went up from the keruḇ, over the threshold of the House. And the House was filled with the cloud, and the court was filled with the brightness of the esteem of יהוה.

5 And the sound of the wings of the keruḇim was heard in the outer court, like the voice of Ěl Shaddai when He speaks.

6 And it came to be, when He commanded the man clothed in linen, saying, "Take fire from among the wheels, from among the keruḇim," that he went in and stood beside the wheel.

7 And the keruḇ stretched out his hand from among the keruḇim to the fire that was among the keruḇim, and took some, and put it into the hands of the man clothed with linen, who took it and went out.

8 And the form of a man's hand was seen under the wings of the keruḇim.

9 And I looked and saw four wheels beside the keruḇim, one wheel beside each keruḇ, and the wheels' appearance was like the colour of beryl stone.

10 As for their appearance, all four looked alike; as if a wheel in the middle of a wheel.

11 When they went, they went on their four sides; they did not turn aside when they went, but went in the direction the

head was facing. They did not turn aside
when they went.
12 And their entire bodies, and their backs,
and their hands, and their wings, and the
wheels that the four had, were covered
with eyes all around.
13 The wheels were called in my hearing,
"Wheel."
14 And each one had four faces: the first
face was the face of a keruḇ, and the
second face the face of a man, and the third
the face of a lion, and the fourth the face
of an eagle.
15 And the keruḇim were lifted up – it was
the living creature I saw by the River
Keḇar.
16 And when the keruḇim went the wheels
went beside them. And when the keruḇim
lifted their wings to mount up from the
earth, the same wheels also did not turn
from beside them.
17 When they stood still, the wheels stood
still, and when one was lifted up, the other
lifted itself up, for the spirit of the living
creature was in them.
18 And the esteem of יהוה went from the
threshold of the House and stood over the
keruḇim.
19 And the keruḇim lifted their wings and
rose from the earth before my eyes. When
they went out, the wheels were beside
them. And it stood at the door of the east
gate of the House of יהוה, and the esteem
of the Elohim of Yisra'ěl was above them.
20 It was the living creature I saw under
the Elohim of Yisra'ěl by the River Keḇar,
and I knew they were keruḇim.
21 Each one had four faces and each one
four wings, and the likeness of the hands
of a man was under their wings.
22 And the likeness of their faces was the
same as the faces which I had seen by the
River Keḇar, their appearances and themselves. Each one went straight forward.

11 And the Spirit lifted me up and
brought me to the east gate of the
House of יהוה, which faces east. And see,
at the door of the gate were twenty-five
men, among whom I saw Ya'azanyah son
of Azzur, and Pelatyahu son of Benayahu,
heads of the people.
2 And He said to me, "Son of man, these
are the men who plot wickedness and give
evil counsel in this city,
3 who are saying, 'It is not near, let us
build houses. This *city* is the cooking pot,
and we are the meat.'
4 "Therefore prophesy against them,
prophesy, O son of man!"
5 And the Spirit of יהוה fell upon me,
and said to me, "Speak! 'Thus said יהוה,
"Thus you have said, O house of Yisra'ěl.
For I know what comes up in your spirit.
6 "You have increased your slain in this
city, and filled its streets with the slain."
7 'Therefore thus said the Master יהוה,
"Your slain whom you have laid in its
midst, they are the meat, and this city is the
cooking pot. But I shall bring you out of
the midst of it.
8 "You have feared the sword, and I bring
a sword upon you," declares the Master
יהוה.
9 "And I shall bring you out of its midst,
and give you into the hands of strangers,
and execute judgments on you.
10 "By the sword you fall. At the border of
Yisra'ěl I judge you. And you shall know
that I am יהוה.
11 "This *city* is not your cooking pot, nor
are you the meat in its midst. At the border
of Yisra'ěl I judge you.
12 "And you shall know that I am יהוה,
for you have not walked in My laws nor
executed My right-rulings, but have done
according to the rulings of the nations[a]
which are all around you." ' "
13 And it came to be, while I was prophesying, that Pelatyahu son of Benayah
died. And I fell on my face and cried out
with a loud voice, and said, "Ah, Master
יהוה! Are You making an end of the remnant of Yisra'ěl?"
14 Then the word of יהוה came to me,
saying,
15 "Son of man, your brothers, your relatives, your kinsmen, and all the house of

11a See footnote at Yirm. 10:2.

Yisra'ĕl, all of it, are those about whom the inhabitants of Yerushalayim said, 'Keep far from יהוה, this land has been given to us as a possession.'
16 "Therefore say, 'Thus said the Master
יהוה, "Although I have sent them far off among the nations, and although I have scattered them among the lands, yet I was for them a set-apart place for a little while in the lands to which they came." '
17 "Therefore say, 'Thus said the Master
יהוה, "And I shall gather you from the peoples, and I shall assemble you from the lands where you have been scattered, and I shall give you the land of Yisra'ĕl." '
18 "And they shall go there, and shall take away all its disgusting *matters* and all its abominations from there.
19 "And I shall give them one heart, and put a new spirit within you. And I shall take the stony heart out of their flesh, and give them a heart of flesh,
20 so that they walk in My laws, and guard My right-rulings, and shall do them. And they shall be My people and I shall be their Elohim.
21 "But to those whose hearts walk after the heart of their disgusting *matters* and their abominations, I shall recompense their deeds on their own heads," declares the Master יהוה.
22 And the keruḇim lifted up their wings, with the wheels beside them, and the esteem of the Elohim of Yisra'ĕl was high above them.
23 And the esteem of יהוה went up from the midst of the city and stood upon the mountain, which is on the east side of the city.
24 And the Spirit lifted me up and brought me in a vision by the Spirit of Elohim into Kasdima, to those in exile. And the vision that I had seen went up from me.
25 And I spoke to those in exile of all the words of יהוה which He had shown me.

12 And the word of יהוה came to me, saying,
2 "Son of man, you are dwelling in the midst of a rebellious house. They have eyes to see but they have not seen, they have ears to hear but they have not heard, for they are a rebellious house.
3 "Therefore, son of man, prepare your baggage for exile, and go into exile by day before their eyes. And you shall go from your place into exile to another place before their eyes. It could be that they see, though they are a rebellious house.
4 "And you shall bring out your baggage for exile before their eyes by day, and at evening go before their eyes, like those who go into exile.
5 "Dig through the wall before their eyes, and you shall bring *them* out through it –
6 take them on your shoulders and bring them out at dark before their eyes. Cover your face, so that you do not see the land, for I have made you a sign to the house of Yisra'ĕl."
7 And so I did, as I was commanded. I brought out my baggage for exile by day, and at evening I dug through the wall with my hand. I brought them out at dark, and I took them on my shoulder before their eyes.
8 And in the morning the word of יהוה came to me, saying,
9 "Son of man, did not the house of Yisra'ĕl, the rebellious house, say to you, 'What are you doing?'
10 "Say to them, 'Thus said the Master
יהוה, "This message is to the prince in Yerushalayim and all the house of Yisra'ĕl who are in their midst." '
11 "Say, 'I am a sign to you. As I have done, so it is done to them – they are to go into exile, into captivity.'
12 "And the prince who is in their midst is to bear his baggage on his shoulder at dark and go out. They are to dig through the wall to bring them out through it. He is to cover his face, so that he does not see the land with his eyes.
13 "And I shall spread My net over him, and he shall be caught in My snare. And I shall bring him to Baḇel, the land of the Kasdim, but he shall not see it, and yet die there.
14 "And I shall scatter to every wind all who are around him to help him, and all his bands, and I shall draw out the sword

after them.
15 "And they shall know that I am יהוה,
when I scatter them among the nations.
And I shall disperse them throughout the
lands.
16 "But I shall let a few of their men
escape from the sword, from scarcity of
food, and from pestilence, so that they
recount all their abominations among the
nations wherever they go. And they shall
know that I am יהוה."
17 And the word of יהוה came to me,
saying,
18 "Son of man, eat your bread with trembling, and drink your water with fear and
with anxiety.
19 "And you shall say to the people of the
land, 'Thus said the Master יהוה to the
inhabitants of Yerushalayim and to the
land of Yisra'ěl, "Let them eat their bread
with anxiety, and drink their water with
astonishment, for her land is emptied of all
who are in it, because of the violence of all
those who dwell in it.
20 "And the cities that are inhabited
shall be laid waste, and the land shall
become a wasteland. And you shall know
that I am יהוה." ' "
21 And the word of יהוה came to me,
saying,
22 "Son of man, what is this proverb that
you people have about the land of Yisra'ěl,
which says, 'The days go by, and every
vision shall come to naught'?
23 "Therefore say to them, 'Thus said the
Master יהוה, "I shall make this proverb to
cease, so that they no longer use it as a
proverb in Yisra'ěl." But say to them, "The
days have drawn near, as well as the matter
of every vision.
24 "For no longer is there to be any false
vision or flattering divination within the
house of Yisra'ěl.
25 "For I am יהוה, I speak. And the word
which I speak is done. It is no longer
deferred. For in your days, O rebellious
house, when I speak the word I shall do it,"
declares the Master יהוה.' "
26 Again the word of יהוה came to me,
saying,
27 "Son of man, see, the house of Yisra'ěl
is saying, 'The vision that he is seeing is
for many days from now, and he is prophesying of times far off.'
28 "Therefore say to them, 'Thus said the
Master יהוה, "None of My words are
deferred any longer. When I speak a word
it is done," declares the Master יהוה.' "

13

And the word of יהוה came to me,
saying,
2 "Son of man, prophesy against the
prophets of Yisra'ěl who prophesy, and say
to those who prophesy out of their own
heart, 'Hear the word of יהוה!' "
3 Thus said the Master יהוה, "Woe to the
foolish prophets, who are following their
own spirit, without having had a vision!
4 "O Yisra'ěl, your prophets have been
like foxes among ruins.
5 "You have not gone up into the breaches, nor do you build a wall for the house of
Yisra'ěl to stand in battle on the day of
יהוה.
6 "Their visions are false and their
divinations a lie, saying, 'Thus declares
יהוה,' when יהוה has not sent them, yet
they expected the word to be confirmed!
7 "Have you not seen a false vision, and
have you not spoken a divination of lies?
You say, 'יהוה declares,' when I have not
spoken."
8 Therefore thus said the Master יהוה,
"Because you have spoken falsehood and
seen lies, therefore see, I am against you,"
declares the Master יהוה.
9 "My hand shall be against the prophets
who see falsehood and who divine lies.
They shall not be in the council of My people, nor be written in the record of the
house of Yisra'ěl, and they shall not enter
into the land of Yisra'ěl. And you shall
know that I am the Master יהוה.
10 "Because, yes because they have led
My people astray, saying, 'Peace!' when
there is no peace. And when one is building a wall, see, they are coating it with
whitewash!
11 "Say to those who coat it with whitewash: it shall fall! There shall be flooding
rain, and you, O great hailstones: fall! –
and a stormy wind breaks it down,

12 and see, the wall shall fall! Shall you
not be asked, 'Where is the coating with
which you coated it?' "
13 Therefore thus said the Master יהוה,
"I shall break down with a stormy wind
in My wrath, and a flooding rain in My
displeasure, and great hailstones in wrath,
to consume.
14 "And I shall throw down the wall you
have coated with whitewash, and bring it
down to the ground, and its foundation
shall be uncovered. And it shall fall, and
you shall be consumed in the midst of it.
And you shall know that I am יהוה.
15 "So I shall complete My wrath on the
wall and on those coating it with whitewash, and say to you, 'The wall is no
more, nor those whitewashing it –
16 the prophets of Yisra'ěl who are prophesying concerning Yerushalayim, and who
are seeing visions of peace for her when
there is no peace,' " declares the Master
יהוה.
17 "And you, son of man, set your face
against the daughters of your people, who
are prophesying out of their own heart, and
prophesy against them.
18 "And you shall say, 'This is what the
Master יהוה said, "Woe to the women
sewing cushions for all joints of the hand,
and to those making veils for the heads of
people of every size, to hunt beings! You
hunt the beings of My people, while you
keep alive your own beings!
19 "And you have profaned Me among
My people for handfuls of barley and for
pieces of bread, to put to death beings that
should not die, and to keep alive beings
who should not live, by your lying to
My people who listen to lies!"
20 'Therefore thus said the Master יהוה,
"See, I am against your cushions by which
you hunt the beings there like birds. And I
shall tear them from your arms, and shall
let the beings go, the beings you hunt like
birds.
21 "And I shall tear off your veils, and
shall deliver My people out of your hand,
and they shall no longer be as prey in your
hand. And you shall know that I am
יהוה." ' "
22 "Because with falsehood you have
made the heart of the righteous sad, whom
I have not made sad. And you have
strengthened the hands of the wrong, so
that he does not turn from his evil way, to
keep him alive.
23 "Therefore you shall no longer see false
visions, nor practise divination. And I shall
deliver My people out of your hand, and
you shall know that I am יהוה." ' "

14 And some of the elders of Yisra'ěl
came to me and sat before me.
2 And the word of יהוה came to me,
saying,
3 "Son of man, these men have set up
their idols in their hearts, and have put
the stumbling-block of their crookedness
before their face. Should I let them inquire
of Me at all?
4 "Therefore speak to them, and you
shall say to them, 'Thus said the Master
יהוה, "Everyone of the house of Yisra'ěl
who sets up his idols in his heart, and puts
the stumbling-block of his crookedness
before his face, and shall come to the
prophet – I יהוה shall answer him who
comes, according to his many idols,
5 in order to lay hold of the house of
Yisra'ěl by their heart, for they have
become estranged from Me by their idols,
all of them." '
6 "Therefore say to the house of Yisra'ěl,
'Thus said the Master יהוה, "Repent, and
turn back from your idols, and turn back
your faces from all your abominations.
7 "For anyone of the house of Yisra'ěl, or
of the strangers who sojourn in Yisra'ěl,
who separates himself from Me and sets up
his idols in his heart and puts the stumbling-block of his crookedness before his
face, and shall come to a prophet to inquire
of him concerning Me, I יהוה shall answer
him Myself.
8 "And I shall set My face against that
man and make him a sign and a proverb,
and I shall cut him off from the midst of
My people. And you shall know that I am
יהוה.
9 "And if the prophet is deceived, and
shall speak a word, I יהוה have deceived

that prophet, and shall stretch out My hand against him and destroy him from the midst of My people Yisra’ěl.

10 “And they shall bear their crookedness, the crookedness of the prophet is the same as the crookedness of the inquirer,

11 so that the house of Yisra’ěl no longer strays from Me, nor be made unclean any more with all their transgressions. And they shall be My people and I be their Elohim,” declares the Master יהוה.’ ”

12 And the word of יהוה came again to me, saying,

13 “Son of man, when a land sins against Me to commit a trespass, and I shall stretch out My hand against it, and cut off its supply of bread and send scarcity of food on it, and cut off man and beast from it,

14 even though these three men, Noaḥ, Dani’ěl, and Iyoḇ, were in it, they would deliver only themselves by their righteousness,” declares the Master יהוה.

15 “If I cause an evil beast to pass through the land, and it shall bereave it, and it shall be a wasteland, so that no man passes through because of the beasts,

16 even though these three men were in it, as I live,” declares the Master יהוה, “they would deliver neither sons nor daughters. They alone would be delivered, but the land be a wasteland.

17 “Or if I bring a sword on that land, and I shall say, ‘Sword, go through the land,’ and I shall cut off man and beast from it,

18 even though these three men were in its midst, as I live,” declares the Master יהוה, “they would deliver neither sons nor daughters, for they alone would be delivered.

19 “Or if I send a pestilence into that land, and I shall pour out My wrath on it in blood, to cut off from it man and beast,

20 even though Noaḥ, Dani’ěl, and Iyoḇ were in it, as I live,” declares the Master יהוה, “they would deliver neither son nor daughter. They would deliver their own lives by their righteousness.”

21 For thus said the Master יהוה, “How much more it shall be when I send My four evil judgments on Yerushalayim: the sword and scarcity of food and evil beasts and pestilence, to cut off man and beast from it?

22 “But see, there shall be left in it a remnant who are brought out, both sons and daughters. See, they are coming out to you, and you shall see their ways and their deeds, and shall be comforted concerning the evil which I have brought upon Yerushalayim – all that I have brought upon it.

23 “And they shall comfort you, when you see their ways and their deeds. And you shall know that it was not for naught that I have done whatever I did in it,” declares the Master יהוה.

15 Then the word of יהוה came to me, saying,

2 “Son of man, how is the vine tree better than any tree, the vine branch that has been among the trees of the forest?

3 “Is wood taken from it to be made into any work? Do they take a peg from it to hang any vessel on?

4 “See, into the fire it shall be given for fuel. Both ends of it the fire shall burn, and its middle shall be scorched. Is it fit for any work?

5 “See, when it was intact, it was not made for work, how much less when the fire has burned it and it is scorched shall it still be used for work?

6 “Therefore thus said the Master יהוה, ‘As the vine tree among the trees of the forest, which I have given to the fire for fuel, so I shall give up the inhabitants of Yerushalayim.

7 ‘And I shall set My face against them. They shall go out from fire, but fire consumes them. And you shall know that I am יהוה, when I set My face against them.

8 ‘And I shall make the land a wasteland, because they committed trespass,’ declares the Master יהוה.”

16 Again the word of יהוה came to me, saying,

2 “Son of man, make known to Yerushalayim her abominations,

3 and say, ‘Thus said the Master יהוה to Yerushalayim, “Your origin and your birth

are from the land of Kenaʽan. Your father
was an Amorite and your mother a Ḥittite.
4 "As for your birth, on the day you were born your navel cord was not cut, nor were you washed in water for cleansing, and you were not rubbed with salt at all, nor wrapped in cloth at all.
5 "No eye felt sorry for you, to do any of these for you, to have compassion on you. But you were thrown out into the open field, to the loathing of your life on the day you were born.
6 "Then I passed by you and saw you trampled down in your own blood, and I said to you in your blood, 'Live!' And I said to you in your blood, 'Live!'
7 "I have let you grow like a plant in the field. And you are grown and are great, and you come in the finest ornaments. – breasts were formed, your hair grew, and you were naked and bare.
8 "Again I passed by you and looked upon you and saw that your time was the time of *carnal*-love. And I spread My skirt over you and covered your nakedness. And I swore an oath to you and entered into a covenant with you, and you became Mine," declares the Master יהוה.
9 "And I washed you in water, and I washed off your blood, and I anointed you with oil.
10 "And I dressed you in embroidered work and gave you sandals of leather. And I wrapped you in fine linen and covered you with silk.
11 "And I adorned you with ornaments, and I put bracelets on your wrists, and a chain on your neck.
12 "And I put a ring on your nose, and earrings in your ears, and a crown of adorning on your head.
13 "Thus you were adorned with gold and silver, and your dress was of fine linen, and silk, and embroidered cloth. You ate fine flour, and honey, and oil. And you were exceedingly beautiful, and became fit for royalty.
14 "And your name went out among the nations because of your loveliness, for it was perfect, by My splendour which I had put on you," declares the Master יהוה.
15 "But you trusted in your own loveliness, and whored because of your name, and poured out your whorings on everyone passing by who would have it.
16 "And you took some of your garments and made multi-coloured high places for yourself, and whored on them – which should not have come about, nor shall it be.
17 "And you took your splendid adornments, of My gold and My silver that I gave you, and made for yourself images of a male and whored with them.
18 "And you took your embroidered garments and covered them, and you set My oil and My incense before them.
19 "And My food which I gave you, fine flour and oil and honey which I fed you, you set it before them as sweet incense – and so it was," declares the Master יהוה.
20 "And you took your sons and your daughters, whom you bore to Me, and these you slaughtered as food to them. Were your whorings a small matter,
21 that you have slain My children and gave them up to them by causing them to pass through *the fire*?
22 "And in all your abominations and whorings you did not remember the days of your youth, when you were naked and bare, trampled down in your blood.
23 "Then it came to be after all your evil – 'Woe, woe to you!' declares the Master יהוה –
24 that you also built an arched place for yourself, and made a high place in every street for yourself.
25 "You built your high places at the head of every way, and made your loveliness to be loathed. And you parted your feet to everyone who passed by, and increased your whorings.
26 "And you whored with the sons of Mitsrayim, your neighbours, great of flesh. And you increased your whorings to provoke Me.
27 "And see, I have stretched out My hand against you, and withdrew *what is* lawfully yours, and gave you up to the desire of those who hate you, the daughters of the Philistines, who are ashamed of your

wicked way.
28"And you whored with the sons of
Ashshur, without being satisfied. And
you whored with them and still were not
satisfied.
29"And you increased your whorings as
far as the land of traders, Kasdima, and
even then you were not satisfied.
30"How weak is your heart!" declares the
Master יהוה, "seeing you do all this, the
deeds of a shameless whore.
31"You built your arched place at the
head of every way, and built your high
place in every street. Yet you were unlike a
whore, you scorned a harlot-fee!
32"The wife who commits adultery who
takes strangers instead of her husband!
33"To all whores they give gifts, but you
gave gifts to all your lovers, and bribed
them to come to you from all around in
your whorings.
34"Thus you are different from other
women in your whorings, because no one
whores after you, and in you giving a harlot-fee,
while a harlot-fee was not given to
you. Thus you are different."
35'Therefore, O whore, hear the word of
יהוה!
36'Thus said the Master יהוה, "Because
your copper was poured out and your
nakedness uncovered in your whorings
with your lovers, and with the idols of your
abominations, and because of the blood of
your children which you gave to them,
37therefore, see, I am gathering all your
lovers with whom you took pleasure, all
those you loved, with all those you hated.
And I shall gather them from all around
against you and shall uncover your nakedness
to them, and they shall see all your
nakedness.
38"And I shall judge you with judgments
of adulteresses and shedders of blood. And
I shall bring on you the blood of wrath and
jealousy.
39"And I shall give you into their hand,
and they shall throw your arched place
down, and they shall break down your high
places. And they shall strip you of your
garments, and they shall take your splendid
adornments, and leave you naked and
bare.
40"And they shall bring up an assembly
against you, and they shall stone you with
stones and thrust you through with their
swords,
41and burn your houses with fire, and
execute judgments on you before the eyes
of many women. And I shall make you
stop whoring, and no longer give harlot-fees.
42"So I shall bring My wrath to rest upon
you, and My jealousy shall turn away from
you. And I shall be calm, and no longer be
vexed.
43"Because you did not remember the
days of your youth, but troubled Me with
all this, so see, I shall also bring your way
on your own head," declares the Master
יהוה. "And shall I not do this thought for
all your abominations?
44"See, all who use proverbs shall use
this proverb against you, 'Like mother, like
daughter!'
45"You are your mother's daughter, who
despises her husband and her children.
And you are the sister of your sisters, who
despised their husbands and their children.
Your mother was a Ḥittite and your father
an Amorite.
46"And your elder sister is Shomeron, she
and her daughters, who is dwelling to the
north of you. And your younger sister, who
is dwelling to the south of you, is Seḏom
and her daughters.
47"And have you not walked in their
ways and did according to their abominations?
But in all your ways you soon
became more corrupt than they.
48"As I live," declares the Master יהוה,
"neither your sister Seḏom nor her
daughters have done as you and your
daughters have done.
49"See, this was the crookedness of your
sister Seḏom: She and her daughter had
pride, sufficiency of bread, and unconcerned
ease. And she did not help the poor
and needy.
50"And they were haughty and did abomination
before Me, and I took them away
when I saw it.
51"And Shomeron did not commit half of

your sins, but you have increased your
abominations more than they, and by all
the abominations which you have done
you made your sisters seem righteous!
52 "You also, who pleaded for your sisters,
bear your own shame, because the sins
which you committed were more abominable than theirs. They are more righteous
than you. So be ashamed too, and bear
your own shame, because you have made
your sisters seem righteous.
53 "And I shall turn back their captivity,
the captivity of Seḏom and her daughters,
and the captivity of Shomeron and her
daughters, and the captivity of your captives with them,
54 so that you bear your shame, and shall
blush for all that you did when you comforted them,
55 "and your sisters, Seḏom and her
daughters, return to their former state, and
Shomeron and her daughters return to their
former state, and you and your daughters
return to your former state.
56 "Was not your sister Seḏom a byword
in your mouth in the days of your pride,
57 before your evil was exposed, as the
time of the reproach of the daughters of
Aram and all who were around her, and of
the daughters of the Philistines, who are
despising you everywhere?
58 "You shall bear your wickedness and
your abominations," declares יהוה.
59 'For thus said the Master יהוה, "I shall
deal with you as you have done, in that you
have despised the oath by breaking the
covenant.
60 "But I shall remember My covenant
with you in the days of your youth, and I
shall establish an everlasting covenant
with you.
61 "And you shall remember your ways
and be ashamed, when you receive your
older and your younger sisters. And I shall
give them to you for daughters, though not
by your own covenant.
62 "And I Myself shall establish My
covenant with you. And you shall know
that I am יהוה,
63 so that you remember. And you shall be
ashamed, and never open your mouth any
more because of your shame, when I pardon you for all you have done," declares
the Master יהוה.' "

17 And the word of יהוה came to me,
saying,
2 "Son of man, put forth a riddle, and
speak a parable to the house of Yisra'ěl.
3 "And you shall say, 'Thus said the
Master יהוה, "The great eagle with large
wings of long pinions, covered with feathers of various colours, came to Leḇanon
and took the top of the cedar.
4 "He plucked off the topmost of its
young twigs and brought it to a land of
traders. In a city of merchants he placed it.
5 "He also took some of the seed of the
land and planted it in a field for seed. He
took it by many waters, set it like a willow
tree.
6 "So it grew and became a low, spreading vine. Its branches turned toward him,
and its roots were under it. And it became
a vine, and brought forth branches, and
sent out shoots.
7 "And there was another great eagle
with large wings and many feathers. And
see, this vine bent its roots toward him, and
stretched its branches toward him, to water
it, away from the beds where it was planted.
8 "It was planted in a good field by many
waters, to bring forth branches, and to bear
fruit, to be a splendid vine." '
9 "Say, 'Thus said the Master יהוה, "Is
it going to thrive? Is he not going to pull up
its roots, and cut off its fruit, and let it
wither? All of its sprouting leaves wither,
without great power or many people, to
pluck it up by its roots.
10 "See, it is planted, is it going to thrive?
Would it not utterly wither when the east
wind touches it – wither in the beds where
it grows?" ' "
11 And the word of יהוה came to me,
saying,
12 "Please say to the rebellious house, 'Do
you not know what these mean?' Say,
'See, the sovereign of Baḇel went to
Yerushalayim and took its sovereign and
heads, and brought them with him to

Baḇel.
13 'And he took one of the royal seed, and
made a covenant with him, and put him
under oath. And he took away the mighty
of the land,
14 so that the reign would be brought low
and not lift itself up, but guard his covenant, that it might stand.
15 'But he rebelled against him by sending
his messengers to Mitsrayim, to give him
horses and many people. Shall he thrive?
Shall he escape who is doing these? And
shall he break a covenant and still escape?
16 'As I live,' declares the Master יהוה',
'in the place where the sovereign dwells
who set him up to reign, whose oath he
despised and whose covenant he broke,
with him in the midst of Baḇel he shall die!
17 'And Pharaoh with his great army and
great company is not going to help him in
battle, when they heap up a siege mound
and build a wall to cut off many beings.
18 'And he despised the oath by breaking
the covenant. And see, he has given his
hand and he has done all this, he is not
going to escape.' "
19 Therefore thus said the Master יהוה',
"As I live, My oath which he has despised,
and My covenant which he has broken,
shall I not put it on his own head?
20 "And I shall spread My net over him,
and he shall be taken in My snare. And I
shall bring him to Baḇel and enter into
judgment with him there for the trespass
which he committed against Me,
21 and all his fugitives with all his bands
fall by the sword, and those who are left be
scattered to every wind. And you shall
know that I, יהוה', have spoken."
22 Thus said the Master יהוה', "And I shall
take of the top of the highest cedar and set
it out. And I Myself shall pluck off a tender
one from the topmost of its young twigs,
and plant it on a high and lofty mountain.
23 "On the mountain height of Yisra'ěl I
plant it. And it shall bring forth branches,
and bear fruit, and become a big cedar.
And under it shall dwell birds of every
sort, in the shadow of its branches they
shall dwell.
24 "And all the trees of the field shall
know that I, יהוה', have brought down the
high tree and exalted the low tree, dried
up the green tree and made the dry tree
flourish. I, יהוה', have spoken and shall do
it."

18 And the word of יהוה' came to me,
saying,
2 "What do you mean when you use this
proverb concerning the land of Yisra'ěl,
saying, 'The fathers have eaten sour
grapes, and the children's teeth are blunted'?
3 "As I live," declares the Master יהוה',
"you shall no longer use this proverb
in Yisra'ěl.
4 "See, all beings are Mine, the being of
the father as well as the being of the son is
Mine. The being that is sinning shall die.
5 "But if a man is righteous and shall do
right-ruling and righteousness,
6 if he has not eaten on the mountains,
nor lifted up his eyes to the idols of the
house of Yisra'ěl, nor defiled his neighbour's wife, nor comes near a woman
during her uncleanness,
7 if he does not oppress anyone, does
return to the debtor his pledge, does not
commit robbery, does give his bread to the
hungry and covers the naked with a
garment,
8 if he does not lend on interest or take
increase, turns back his hand from unrighteousness, executes right-ruling in truth
between man and man,
9 if he walks in My laws, and he has
guarded My right-rulings in truth – he is
righteous, he shall certainly live!" declares
the Master יהוה'.
10 "But if he has brought forth a son who
is a robber or a shedder of blood, who does
any of these –
11 whereas he himself did not do any of
these – that also he has eaten on the mountains or defiled his neighbour's wife,
12 if he has oppressed the poor and needy,
has committed robbery, he does not return
a pledge, has lifted his eyes to the idols, or
did abomination,
13 if he has lent on interest or taken
increase – shall he live? He shall not live!

If he has done any of these abominations,
he shall certainly die, his blood is upon
him.
14 "But see, if he has brought forth a
son who sees all the sins which his father
has done, but he fears and does not do likewise,
15 has not eaten on the mountains, and has
not lifted his eyes to the idols of the house
of Yisra'ěl, has not defiled his neighbour's
wife,
16 has not oppressed anyone, nor withheld
a pledge, nor committed robbery, has given
his bread to the hungry and covered the
naked with a garment,
17 turns back his hand from *wronging* the
poor, and he has not taken interest or
increase, has executed My right-rulings
and walked in My laws – he shall not die
for the crookedness of his father, he shall
certainly live!
18 "His father, because he used oppression, robbed his brother, and did what is
not good among his people, see, he shall
die for his crookedness.
19 "And you said, 'Why should the son
not bear the crookedness of the father?'
But the son has done right-ruling and righteousness, he has guarded all My laws and
he does them, he shall certainly live.
20 "The being who sins shall die. The son
shall not bear the crookedness of the
father, nor the father bear the crookedness
of the son. The righteousness of the righteous is upon himself, and the wrongness
of the wrong is upon himself.
21 "But the wrong,[a] if he turns from all
his sins which he has done, and he shall
guard all My laws, and shall do right-
ruling and righteousness, he shall certainly
live, he shall not die.
22 "All the transgressions which he has
done shall not be remembered against him
– in his righteousness that he has done, he
shall live.
23 "Have I any pleasure in the death of the
wrong?" declares the Master יהוה. "Is it
not that he should turn from his ways, and
live?

24 "But when a righteous one turns away
from his righteousness and does unrighteousness, according to all the abominations that the wrong one has done, shall he
live? All his righteousness which he has
done shall not be remembered. For his
trespass which he has committed, and for
his sin which he has committed, for them
he shall die.
25 "And you said, 'The way of יהוה is not
right.' Hear now, O house of Yisra'ěl, is
My way not right? Is it not your ways that
are not right?
26 "When a righteous one turns away from
his righteousness, and does unrighteousness, and he dies in it, it is because of his
unrighteousness which he has done that he
dies.
27 "And when the wrong turns away from
the wrong which he has done, and he does
right-ruling and righteousness, he keeps
himself alive.
28 "Because he sees and turns away from
all the transgressions which he has done,
he shall certainly live, he shall not die.
29 "And the house of Yisra'ěl have said,
'The way of יהוה is not right.' Are My
ways not right, O house of Yisra'ěl? Is it
not your ways that are not right?
30 "Therefore I judge you, O house of
Yisra'ěl, every one according to his ways,"
declares the Master יהוה. "Repent, and
turn back from all your transgressions, and
let not crookedness be a stumbling-block
to you.
31 "Cast away from you all the transgressions, by which you have transgressed, and
make for yourselves a new heart and a new
spirit. For why should you die, O house of
Yisra'ěl?
32 "For I have no pleasure in the death of
one who dies," declares the Master יהוה.
"So turn back and live!"

19 "And take up a lamentation for the
leaders of Yisra'ěl,
2 and you shall say, 'What a lioness was
your mother among the lions! She lay
down among the lions, in the midst of the

18a Similar passages in 3:18-21, 33:8-20.

young lions she reared her cubs.
3 ‘And she brought up one of her cubs,
and he became a young lion. And he
learned to tear the prey, he devoured men.
4 ‘Then nations heard of him. He was
caught in their pit, and they brought him
with chains to the land of Mitsrayim.
5 ‘When she saw, as she waited, that her
expectancy was lost, she took another of
her cubs and made him a young lion.
6 ‘And he went about among the lions,
and became a young lion. And he learned
to tear the prey, he devoured men.
7 ‘And he knew their widows, and laid
waste their cities. And the land and all who
filled it was stunned by the noise of his
roaring.
8 ‘Then nations set against him from the
provinces on every side, and spread their
net over him, he was caught in their pit.
9 ‘And they put him in a cage in chains,
and brought him to the sovereign of Baḇel.
They brought him in nets, so his roar was
no longer heard on the mountains of
Yisra’ěl.
10 ‘Your mother was like a vine in your
vineyard, planted by the waters, a bearer of
fruit and branching, because of many
waters.
11 ‘And she had strong rods for sceptres of
rulers. And her stature was exalted among
the thick branches, and was seen in her
height with the mass of its branches.
12 ‘But she was uprooted in wrath, she
was cast down to the ground, and the east
wind dried her fruit. Her strong rods were
broken and withered, fire consumed them.
13 ‘And now she is planted in the wilderness, in a dry and thirsty land.
14 ‘And fire went out from a rod of her
branches. It devoured her fruit, so that she
has no strong rod, a sceptre to rule.’ ” This
is a lament, and it shall be a lament.

20 And it came to be in the seventh
year, in the fifth *month*, on the
tenth of the new *moon*, that certain of the
elders of Yisra’ěl came to inquire of יהוה,
and sat before me.
2 And the word of יהוה came to me,
saying,
3 “Son of man, speak to the elders of
Yisra’ěl, and say to them, ‘Thus said the
Master יהוה, “Have you come to inquire of
Me? As I live, I am not being inquired of
by you,” declares the Master יהוה.’
4 “Judge them, son of man, judge them!
Make known to them the abominations of
their fathers.
5 “And you shall say to them, ‘Thus said
the Master יהוה, “On the day when I chose
Yisra’ěl and lifted My hand in an oath to
the seed of the house of Ya‘aqoḇ, and made
Myself known to them in the land of
Mitsrayim, I lifted My hand in an oath to
them, saying, ‘I am יהוה your Elohim.’
6 “On that day I lifted My hand in an oath
to them, to bring them out of the land of
Mitsrayim into a land that I had searched
out for them, flowing with milk and honey,
the splendour of all lands.
7 “And I said to them, ‘Each one of you,
throw away the abominations which are
before his eyes, and do not defile yourselves with the idols of Mitsrayim! I am
יהוה your Elohim.’
8 “But they rebelled against Me, and
would not obey Me. All of them did not
throw away the abominations which were
before their eyes, nor did they forsake the
idols of Mitsrayim. So I resolved to pour
out My wrath on them to complete My
displeasure against them in the midst of the
land of Mitsrayim.
9 “But I acted for My Name’s sake, that
it should not be profaned before the eyes of
the nations among whom they were –
before whose eyes I had made Myself
known to them, to bring them out of the
land of Mitsrayim.
10 “So I took them out of the land of
Mitsrayim, and I brought them into the
wilderness.
11 “And I gave them My laws and showed
them My right-rulings, ‘which, if a man
does, he shall live by them.’
12 “And I also gave them My Sabbaths, to
be a sign [a] between them and Me, to know

20a See also Shem. 31:13-17.

that I am יהוה who sets them apart.
13 “But the house of Yisra’ĕl rebelled
against Me in the wilderness. They did not
walk in My laws, and they rejected My
right-rulings, which, if a man does, he
shall live by them. And they greatly profaned My Sabbaths. Then I said I would
pour out My wrath on them in the wilderness, to consume them.
14 “But I acted for My Name’s sake, not
to profane it before the nations, before
whose eyes I had brought them out.
15 “And I Myself also lifted My hand in
an oath to them in the wilderness, not to
bring them into the land which I had given
them, flowing with milk and honey, the
splendour of all lands,
16 because they rejected My right-rulings
and did not walk in My laws, and they profaned My Sabbaths. For their heart went
after their idols.
17 “And My eye pardoned them, from
destroying them. And I did not make an
end of them in the wilderness.
18 “And I said to their children in the
wilderness, ‘Do not walk in the laws of
your fathers, nor observe their rulings, nor
defile yourselves with their idols.
19 ‘I am יהוה your Elohim. Walk in My
laws, and guard My right-rulings, and do
them.
20 ‘And set apart My Sabbaths, and they
shall be a sign between Me and you, to
know that I am יהוה your Elohim.’
21 “But the children rebelled against Me.
They did not walk in My laws, and My
right-rulings they did not guard to do them,
which, if a man does, he shall live by them.
They profaned My Sabbaths, so I resolved
to pour out My wrath on them to complete
My displeasure against them in the wilderness.
22 “But I held back My hand and acted for
My Name’s sake, not to profane it before
the eyes of the nations, before whose eyes
I had brought them out.
23 “Also, I Myself lifted My hand in an
oath to those in the wilderness, to scatter
them among the nations and disperse them
throughout the lands,
24 because they had not done My right-
rulings, and they rejected My laws, and
they profaned My Sabbaths, and their eyes
were on their fathers’ idols.
25 “And I also gave them up to laws that
were not good, and right-rulings by which
they would not live. *b*
26 “And I defiled them by their own gifts,
as they passed all their first-born through
the fire, so that I might stun them, so that
they know that I am יהוה.” ’
27 “Therefore, son of man, speak to the
house of Yisra’ĕl, and you shall say to
them, ‘Thus said the Master יהוה, “In this
your fathers have further reviled Me,
by committing trespass against Me.
28 “When I brought them into the land for
which I had lifted My hand in an oath to
give them, and they saw all the high hills
and all the thick trees, they slaughtered
their slaughterings there and provoked Me
with their offerings there. And they sent up
their sweet fragrance there and poured out
their drink offerings there.
29 “And I said to them, ‘What is this high
place to which you go?’ So its name is
called High Place to this day.” ’
30 “Therefore say to the house of Yisra’ĕl,
‘Thus said the Master יהוה, “Are you
defiling yourselves in the way of your
fathers? And do you whore after their
abominations?
31 “For when you lift up your gifts and
make your sons pass through the fire, you
defile yourselves with all your idols, even
to this day. And shall I be inquired of by
you, O house of Yisra’ĕl? As I live,”
declares the Master יהוה, “I am not being
inquired of by you.
32 “And what comes up in your spirit shall
never be, when you say, ‘Let us be like the
nations, like the tribes in other lands, serving wood and stone.’
33 “As I live,” declares the Master יהוה,
“do not I, with a mighty hand, with an
outstretched arm, and with wrath poured
out, reign over you?
34 “And I shall bring you out from the

20b Teh. 81:12, Yesh. 30:28, Ma. 7:42, Rom. 1:24-28, Tas. ב 2:11.

peoples and gather you out of the lands where you are scattered, with a mighty hand, and with an outstretched arm, and with wrath poured out.
35 "And I shall bring you into the wilderness of the peoples, and shall enter into judgment with you face to face there.
36 "As I entered into judgment with your fathers in the wilderness of the land of Mitsrayim, so I shall enter into judgment with you," declares the Master יהוה.
37 "And I shall make you pass under the rod, and shall bring you into the bond of the covenant,
38 and purge the rebels from among you, and those who transgress against Me. From the land where they sojourn I bring them out, but they shall not come into the land of Yisra'ěl. And you shall know that I am יהוה.
39 "As for you, O house of Yisra'ěl," thus said the Master יהוה, "Go, serve each of you his idols, and afterwards, if you are not listening to Me. But do not profane My set-apart Name any more with your gifts and your idols.
40 "For on My set-apart mountain, on the mountain height of Yisra'ěl," declares the Master יהוה, "there all the house of Yisra'ěl, all of them in the land, shall serve Me. There I shall accept them, and there I shall require your offerings and the first-fruits of your offerings, together with all your set-apart gifts.
41 "As a sweet fragrance I shall accept you when I bring you out from the peoples. And I shall gather you out of the lands where you have been scattered. And I shall be set-apart in you before the nations.
42 "And you shall know that I am יהוה, when I bring you into the land of Yisra'ěl, into the land for which I lifted My hand in an oath to give to your fathers.
43 "And there you shall remember your ways and all your deeds with which you were defiled. And you shall loathe yourselves in your own sight because of all the evils that you did.
44 "And you shall know that I am יהוה, when I have dealt with you for My Name's sake, not according to your evil ways nor according to your corrupt deeds, O house of Yisra'ěl," declares the Master יהוה.' "
45 And the word of יהוה came to me, saying,
46 "Son of man, set your face toward the south, and drop *word* against the south and prophesy against the forest land, the South.
47 "And you shall say to the forest of the South, 'Hear the word of יהוה! Thus said the Master יהוה, "See, I am kindling a fire in you, and it shall devour every green tree and every dry tree in you – the blazing flame is not quenched. And it shall burn all faces from the south to the north.
48 "And all flesh shall see that I, יהוה, have kindled it, it is not quenched." ' "
49 And I said, "Ah, Master יהוה! They are saying of me, 'Is he not speaking parables?' "

21 And the word of יהוה came to me, saying,
2 "Son of man, set your face toward Yerushalayim, and drop *word* against the set-apart places, and prophesy against the land of Yisra'ěl.
3 "And you shall say to the land of Yisra'ěl, 'Thus said יהוה, "See, I am against you, and I shall draw My sword out of its sheath and cut off from you the righteous and the wrong.
4 "Because I shall cut off from you the righteous and the wrong, therefore My sword shall go out of its sheath against all flesh from south to north.
5 "And all flesh shall know that I, יהוה, have drawn My sword out of its sheath, not to turn back again." '
6 "And you, son of man, sigh with a breaking of loins, and sigh with bitterness before their eyes.
7 "And it shall be when they say to you, 'Why are you sighing?' that you shall say, 'Because of the report that is coming. And every heart shall melt, and all hands shall go limp, and every spirit become faint, and all knees be weak as water. See, it is coming, and it shall be,' declares the Master יהוה."
8 And the word of יהוה came to me, saying,

9 "Son of man, prophesy, and you shall say, 'Thus said יהוה! "Say, 'A sword, a sword is sharpened and also polished!

10 'It is sharpened to make a slaughter, it is polished to flash like lightning!' Or shall we rejoice? My son, you have despised the rod, every stick!

11 "And He has given it to be polished, to be taken by the hand. This sword is sharpened and polished, to be given into the hand of the killer.

12 "Cry and wail, son of man, for it shall be on My people, on all the leaders of Yisra'ěl. They shall be delivered to the sword together with My people, therefore strike your thigh.

13 "For it is a trier, and what if it even despises the rod? Shall it not be?" declares the Master יהוה.

14 "And you, son of man, prophesy, and strike your hands striking. And let the sword come down twice, thrice, the sword for the slain. It is the sword of the slain, the great one, which surrounds them.

15 "I have set the point of the sword against all their gates, to melt the heart and that the overthrown be many. Ah! It is made like lightning, keen for slaughter.

16 "Sharpen yourself on the right, set yourself on the left, wherever your edge is appointed!

17 "And I too, I shall strike My hands together and cause My wrath to rest. I, יהוה, have spoken."

18 And the word of יהוה came to me again, saying,

19 "And you, son of man, appoint for yourself two ways for the sword of the sovereign of Baḇel to go, both of them coming from one land. And place a signpost, put it at the head of the way to the city.

20 "Appoint a way for the sword to go to Rabbah of the Ammonites, and to Yehuḏah, into the walled Yerushalayim.

21 "For the sovereign of Baḇel shall stand at the parting of the way, at the fork of the two ways, to practise divination. He shall shake the arrows, he shall ask the household idols, he shall look at the liver.

22 "In his right hand shall be the divination for Yerushalayim: to set up battering rams, to call for murder, to lift the voice with shouting, to set battering rams against the gates, to heap up a siege mound, to build a wall.

23 "And it shall be to them as a false divination in the eyes of those who have sworn oaths to them. But he is bringing their crookedness to remembrance, so that they are taken.

24 "Therefore thus said the Master יהוה, 'Because you have made your crookedness to be remembered, in that your transgressions are uncovered, so that your sins are seen in all your deeds. Because you have been remembered, you are taken by hand.

25 'And to you, O profane, wrong one, leader of Yisra'ěl, whose day has come, in the time of the crookedness of the end,

26 thus said the Master יהוה, 'Remove the turban, and take off the crown! This shall not remain! Exalt the humble, and humble the exalted.

27 'Overthrown, overthrown, I make it overthrown! It shall be no longer, until He comes to whom it rightly belongs – and I shall give it!'

28 "And you, son of man, prophesy and say, 'Thus said the Master יהוה concerning the Ammonites and concerning their reproach.' And you shall say, 'A sword, a sword, drawn for slaughter, polished to the utmost like lightning –

29 while they see false visions for you, while they divine a lie to you – to put you on the necks of the profaned ones, the wrong ones whose day has come, in the time of the crookedness of the end.

30 'Return it to its sheath. In the place where you were created, in the land of your origin, I shall judge you.

31 'And I shall pour out My displeasure on you, blow against you with the fire of My wrath, and shall give you into the hands of beastly men, skilled to destroy.

32 'You are to be fuel for the fire, your blood to be in the midst of the land. You are not to be remembered, for I יהוה have spoken.' "

22 And the word of יהוה came to me,
saying,
2 "And now, son of man, judge, judge
the city of blood! And you shall show her
all her abominations!
3 "And you shall say, 'Thus said the
Master יהוה, "The city sheds blood in her
midst, that her time might come. And she
has made idols within herself to become
defiled.
4 "You have become guilty by the blood
which you have shed, and have defiled
yourself with the idols which you have
made. Thus you have brought your days
near, and have come to the end of your
years. Therefore I shall make you a
reproach to the nations, and a mockery to
all lands.
5 "Those near and those far from you
mock you – defiled is your name and great
the confusion!
6 "See the leaders of Yisra'ěl: each one
has used his arm to shed blood in you.
7 "They have despised father and mother
within you. They have oppressed the
stranger in your midst. They have wronged
the fatherless and the widow within you.
8 "You have despised that which is set-
apart to Me, and you have profaned My
Sabbaths.
9 "Slanderous men have been in you to
shed blood. And in you are those who eat
on the mountains. They have done wickedness in your midst.
10 "In you they have uncovered the nakedness of a father. In you they have humbled
women who are defiled during their uncleanness.
11 "And the one has done abomination
with his neighbour's wife. And another has
wickedly defiled his daughter-in-law. And
another within you has humbled his sister,
his father's daughter.
12 "In you they have taken a bribe to shed
blood. You have taken interest and
increase. You have cut off your neighbour
by extortion. And you have forgotten Me,"
declares the Master יהוה.
13 "And see, I shall strike My hand
because of your greedy gain which you
have made, and at the bloodshed which has
been in your midst.
14 "Would your heart stand, your hands be
strong, in the days when I deal with you? I,
יהוה, have spoken, and shall do it.
15 "And I shall scatter you among the
nations, and shall disperse you throughout
the lands, and shall consume your filthiness out of you.
16 "And you shall profane yourself before
the eyes of the nations. And you shall
know that I am יהוה." ' "
17 And the word of יהוה came to me, saying,
18 "Son of man, the house of Yisra'ěl has
become dross to Me. All of them are
bronze, and tin, and iron, and lead, in the
midst of a furnace – they have become the
dross of silver.
19 "Therefore thus said the Master יהוה,
'Because all of you have become dross,
therefore see, I am gathering you into the
midst of Yerushalayim.
20 'As they gather silver, and bronze, and
iron, and lead, and tin into the midst of a
furnace, to blow fire on it, to melt it, so I
gather you in My displeasure and in My
wrath. And I shall blow and melt you.
21 'And I shall gather you and blow on
you with the fire of My wrath, and you
shall be melted in its midst.
22 'As silver is melted in the midst of a
furnace, so are you melted in its midst.
And you shall know that I, יהוה, have
poured out My wrath on you.' "
23 And the word of יהוה came to me,
saying,
24 "Son of man, say to her, 'You are a land
that is not cleansed or rained upon in the
day of displeasure.'
25 "There is a conspiracy of her prophets
in her midst, like a roaring lion tearing the
prey. They have devoured life, they have
taken wealth and precious *matters*, they
have made many widows in her midst.
26 "Her priests have done violence to My
teaching [a] and they profane My set-apart
matters. They have not distinguished

22a Tseph. 3:4, Lq. 16:16.

between the set-apart and profane, nor have they made known *the difference* between the unclean and the clean. And they have hidden their eyes from My Sabbaths, and I am profaned in their midst.

27 “Her leaders in her midst are like wolves tearing the prey, to shed blood, to destroy lives, and to get greedy gain.

28 “And her prophets have coated them with whitewash, seeing a false vision, and divining a lie for them, saying, ‘Thus said the Master יהוה,’ when יהוה had not spoken.

29 “The people of the land have practised oppression, and committed robbery, and have wronged the poor and needy. And they oppressed the stranger without right-ruling.

30 “And I sought for a man among them who would make a wall, and stand in the breach before Me on behalf of the land, that I should not destroy it – but I did not find one!

31 “Therefore I have poured out My displeasure on them, I have consumed them with the fire of My wrath. And I have put their way on their own head,” declares the Master יהוה.

23 And the word of יהוה came to me, saying,

2 “Son of man, there were two women, daughters of one mother.

3 “And they whored in Mitsrayim, they whored in their youth. There their breasts were handled, and there their maiden nipples were squeezed.

4 “And their names were: Oholah the elder and Oholiḇah her sister. And they were Mine, and they bore sons and daughters. And their names: Shomeron is Oholah, and Yerushalayim is Oholiḇah.

5 “And Oholah whored while she was Mine. And she lusted for her lovers, the neighbouring Ashshurians,

6 dressed in purple, officers and rulers, all of them desirable young men, horsemen riding on horses.

7 “So she gave her whorings on them, all of them choice sons of Ashshur. And with all for whom she lusted, with all their idols, she defiled herself.

8 “And she did not forsake her whorings from Mitsrayim, for in her youth they had lain with her, and they squeezed her maiden nipples, and poured out their whorings on her.

9 “Therefore I have given her into the hand of her lovers, into the hand of the Ashshurians, for whom she lusted.

10 “They uncovered her nakedness, they took away her sons and daughters, and killed her with the sword. And she became a byword among women, and they executed judgments on her.

11 “And her sister Oholiḇah saw this, yet she became more corrupt in her lust than she, and in her whorings more corrupt than her sister’s whorings.

12 “She lusted for the sons of Ashshur, officers and rulers, the ones near, perfectly dressed, horsemen riding on horses, all of them desirable young men.

13 “And I saw that she was defiled, they both took the same way.

14 “But she increased her whorings, and she looked at men carved on the wall, images of Kasdim inscribed in red,

15 girded with belts around their loins, flowing turbans on their heads, all of them looking like officers, like the sons of Baḇel of Kasdim, the land of their birth.

16 “As soon as her eyes saw them, she lusted for them and sent messengers to them in Kasdima.

17 “And the sons of Baḇel came to her, into the bed of *carnal*-love, and they defiled her with their whorings. And she was defiled by them, and her being turned from them in disgust.

18 “And she uncovered her whorings and uncovered her nakedness. Then I turned My being from her in disgust, as My being had turned from her sister in disgust.

19 “And she increased her whorings, remembering the days of her youth, when she whored in the land of Mitsrayim.

20 “And she lusted after her lovers, whose flesh is like the flesh of donkeys, and whose emission is like the emission of horses.

21 "Thus you longed for the wickedness of your youth, when the Mitsrites squeezed your nipples because of the breasts of your youth.

22 "Therefore, Oholiḇah, thus said the Master יהוה, 'See, I am stirring up your lovers against you, from whom your being turned in disgust, and shall bring them against you from every side:

23 the children of Baḇel, and all the Kasdim, Peqoḏ, and Showa, and Qowa, all the sons of Ashshur with them, all of them desirable young men, governors and rulers, officers and men of name, all of them riding on horses.

24 'And they shall come against you with battle-axe, chariots, and vehicles, and with an assembly of peoples. They shall set against you armour, and shield, and helmet all around. And I shall commit the judgment to them, and they shall judge you according to their rulings.

25 'And I shall set My jealousy against you and they shall deal heatedly with you. They shall cut off your nose and your ears, while the rest of you fall by the sword. Your sons and your daughters they shall take away, while the rest of you shall be consumed by fire.

26 'And they shall strip you of your garments and shall take your pretty jewels.

27 'And I shall put an end to your wickedness and to your whorings from the land of Mitsrayim, so that you do not lift your eyes to them neither remember Mitsrayim any more.'

28 "For thus said the Master יהוה, 'See, I am giving you into the hand of those whom you hate, into the hand of those from whom your being turned in disgust.

29 'And they shall deal with you in hatred, and they shall take away all you have worked for, and they shall leave you naked and bare. And the nakedness of your whorings shall be uncovered, and the wickedness of your whorings.

30 'I do this to you because of your whoring after the nations, because you have been defiled by their idols.

31 'You have walked in the way of your sister, and I shall give her cup into your hand.'

32 "Thus said the Master יהוה, 'Drink of your sister's cup, the deep and wide one – you being laughed at and mocked at – for it holds much.

33 'Be filled with drunkenness and sorrow, the cup of astonishment and ruin, the cup of your sister Shomeron.

34 'And you shall drink it and shall drain it, and gnaw its shards, and tear at your own breasts. For I have spoken,' declares the Master יהוה.

35 "Therefore thus said the Master יהוה, 'Because you have forgotten Me and cast Me behind your back, therefore you shall bear your wickedness and your whorings.' "

36 And יהוה said to me, "Son of man, judge Oholah and Oholiḇah! And declare to them their abominations.

37 "For they have committed adultery, and blood is on their hands. And they have committed adultery with their idols, and even offered their sons whom they bore to Me, passing them through *the fire*, to devour.

38 "They also did this to Me: They have defiled My set-apart place on the same day, and they have profaned My Sabbaths.

39 "For when they had slain their children for their idols, on the same day they came into My set-apart place to profane it. And see, that is what they did in the midst of My House.

40 "And they even sent for men to come from afar, to whom a messenger was sent. And see, they came – for whom you washed yourself, painted your eyes, and adorned yourself with ornaments.

41 "And you sat on a splendid couch, with a table prepared before it, on which you had set My incense and My oil.

42 "And the sound of a crowd at ease was with her, and drunkards were brought from the wilderness with men of the commonest sort. And they put bracelets on their wrists and pretty crowns on their heads.

43 "Then I said concerning the one worn out in adulteries, 'Now let them commit her whorings, even hers!'

44 "And they went in to her, as men go in

to a woman who is a whore. Thus they
went in to Oholah and Oholiḇah, the
wicked women.
45 "But let righteous men judge them with
the judgment of adulteresses, and the judgment of women who shed blood, for they
are adulteresses, and blood is on their
hands.
46 "For thus said the Master יהוה, 'Bring
up an assembly against them, give them up
to maltreatment and plunder.
47 'And the assembly shall stone them
with stones and cut them with their
swords. They shall kill their sons and their
daughters, and burn their houses with fire.
48 'And I shall put an end to wickedness
in the land, and all the women shall be
instructed not to commit wickedness as
you have done.
49 'And they shall put your wickedness on
you, and you shall bear the sins of your
idols. And you shall know that I am the
Master יהוה.' "

24 And in the ninth year, in the tenth
new *moon*, on the tenth of the new
moon, the word of יהוה came to me,
saying,
2 "Son of man, write down the name of
the day, for on this same day the sovereign
of Baḇel has thrown himself against Yerushalayim.
3 "And speak a parable to the rebellious
house, and you shall say to them, 'Thus
said the Master יהוה, "Put on a pot, put it
on, and also pour water into it.
4 "Gather pieces of meat in it, every good
piece, the thigh and the shoulder, fill it
with choice bones.
5 "Take the choice of the flock, also pile
bones under it, cook it thoroughly, also let
the bones cook in it."
6 'Therefore thus said the Master יהוה,
"Woe to the city of blood, to the pot in
which there is rust, and whose rust has not
gone out of it! Bring it out piece by piece,
on which no lot has fallen.
7 "For her blood is in her midst. She has
set it on a shining rock. She did not pour it
on the ground, to cover it with dust.
8 "To stir up wrath and take vengeance, I
have set her blood on a shining rock, so
that it would not be covered."
9 'Therefore thus said the Master יהוה,
"Woe to the city of blood! Let Me also
make the pile great.
10 "Heap on the wood, kindle the fire,
cook the meat well, mixing in the spices,
and let the bones be burned up.
11 "And set it on the coals, empty, so that
it gets hot, and its bronze glows. And its
filthiness shall be melted in it, and its rust
be consumed.
12 "She has wearied herself with sorrows,
and her great rust has not gone from her.
Into the fire with her rust!
13 "In your filthiness is wickedness.
Because I have cleansed you, but you are
not clean. You shall not be cleansed of
your filthiness any more, till I have caused
My wrath to rest upon you.
14 "I, יהוה, have spoken. It shall come,
and I shall do it. I do not hold back, nor do
I pardon, nor do I relent. According to your
ways and according to your deeds they
shall judge you," declares the Master
יהוה.' "
15 And the word of יהוה came to me,
saying,
16 "Son of man, see, I am taking away
from you the desire of your eyes with one
stroke. But do not mourn, nor weep, nor let
your tears run down.
17 "Groan silently, make no mourning for
the dead. Bind your turban on your head,
and put your sandals on your feet. Do not
cover your upper lip, and do not eat man's
bread of sorrow."
18 And I spoke to the people in the morning, and in the evening my wife died. And
the next morning I did as I was commanded.
19 And the people said to me, "Would you
not explain to us what these matters you
are doing mean to us?"
20 And I said to them, "The word of יהוה
came to me, saying,
21 'Speak to the house of Yisra'ěl, "Thus
said the Master יהוה, 'See, I am profaning
My set-apart place – the pride of your
strength, the desire of your eyes, and the
delight of your being. And your sons and

daughters whom you left behind shall fall by the sword.

22 'And you shall do as I have done, do not cover your upper lip nor eat man's bread of sorrow,

23 and let your turbans remain on your heads and your sandals on your feet. Do not mourn, nor weep, but you shall pine away in your crookednesses and groan with one another.

24 'And Yeḥezqěl shall be a sign to you. Do according to all that he has done. When this comes, you shall know that I am the Master יהוה.' "

25 'And you, son of man, on the day when I take from them their stronghold, the joy of their adorning, the desire of their eyes, and the lifting up of their being, their sons and their daughters,

26 on that day one that has escaped shall come to you to let you hear it with your ears.

27 'On that day your mouth shall be opened to him who has escaped, and you shall speak and no longer be silent. And you shall be a sign to them. And they shall know that I am יהוה.' "

25

And the word of יהוה came to me, saying,

2 "Son of man, set your face against the Ammonites, and prophesy against them.

3 "And you shall say to the Ammonites, 'Hear the word of the Master יהוה! Thus said the Master יהוה, "Because you said, 'Aha!' against My set-apart place when it was profaned, and against the land of Yisra'ěl when it was ruined, and against the house of Yehuḏah when they went into exile,

4 therefore, see, I am giving you as a possession to the men of the East, and they shall set their encampments among you and make their dwellings among you – they shall eat your fruit, and they shall drink your milk.

5 "And I shall make Rabbah a pasture for camels and Ammon a resting place for flocks. And you shall know that I am יהוה."

6 'For this is what the Master יהוה said, "Because you clapped your hands, and you stamped your feet, and rejoiced with all the scorn of your being against the land of Yisra'ěl,

7 therefore see, I Myself shall stretch out My hand against you, and give you as plunder to the nations. And I shall cut you off from the peoples, and make you perish from the lands. I shall destroy you, and you shall know that I am יהוה."

8 'This is what the Master יהוה said, "Because Mo'aḇ and Sě'ir say, 'See, the house of Yehuḏah is like all the nations,'

9 therefore, see, I am opening the flank of Mo'aḇ on the side of the cities, on the side of his cities on its frontiers, the splendour of the land, Běyth Yeshimoth, Ba'al Me'on, and Qiryathayim,

10 and I shall give it, together with the Ammonites, as a possession to the men of the East, so that the Ammonites are no more remembered among the nations.

11 "Also on Mo'aḇ I execute judgments, and they shall know that I am יהוה."

12 'Thus said the Master יהוה, "Because of what Eḏom has done against the house of Yehuḏah by taking vengeance, so that they became very guilty, and they have taken vengeance on them,"

13 therefore thus said the Master יהוה, "I shall stretch out My hand against Eḏom, and I shall cut off man and beast from it and lay it waste – from Těman even to Deḏan they shall fall by the sword.

14 "And I shall lay My vengeance on Eḏom by the hand of My people Yisra'ěl. And they shall do in Eḏom according to My displeasure and according to My wrath. So they shall know My vengeance," declares the Master יהוה.

15 'Thus said the Master יהוה, "Because the Philistines have acted in vengeance, and took vengeance with scorn in *their* being, to destroy with lasting enmity,"

16 therefore thus said the Master יהוה, "See, I am stretching out My hand against the Philistines, and I shall cut off the Kerěthites and destroy the remnant of the seacoast,

17 and execute great vengeance on them with raging reproofs. And they shall know

that I am יהוה', when I lay My vengeance
upon them." ' "

26 And it came to be in the eleventh
year, on the first of the new *moon*,
the word of יהוה' came to me, saying,
2 "Son of man, because Tsor has spoken
against Yerushalayim, 'Aha! She, the gateway of the peoples, has been broken, she
has been turned over to me. Let me be
filled, she has been ruined.'
3 "Therefore thus said the Master יהוה',
'See, I am against you, O Tsor, and shall
cause many nations to come up against
you, as the sea causes its waves to come
up.
4 'And they shall destroy the walls of
Tsor, and they shall break down her towers. And I shall scrape her dust from her,
and shall make her like a shining rock.
5 'She shall be a place for spreading nets
in the midst of the sea, for I have spoken,'
declares the Master יהוה'. 'And she shall
become plunder for the nations,
6 while her daughter villages which are
in the fields are killed by the sword. And
they shall know that I am יהוה'.'
7 "For thus said the Master יהוה', 'See,
I am bringing against Tsor from the north
Neḇuḵaḏretstsar sovereign of Baḇel, a sovereign of sovereigns, with horses, and with
chariots, and with horsemen, even an
assembly, and many people.
8 'With the sword he shall kill your
daughters in the field. And he shall heap
up a siege mound against you, and shall
build a wall against you, and shall raise a
large shield against you,
9 and set the blow of his battering rams
against your walls, and break down your
towers with his weapons.
10 'From his many horses, their dust shall
cover you. From the noise of the horsemen, and vehicles, and chariots, your walls
shall shake as he enters your gates, as men
enter a city that is breached.
11 'With the hooves of his horses he tramples all your streets, he kills your people
by the sword, and the columns of your
strength shall fall to the ground.
12 'And they shall plunder your riches,
and they shall loot your merchandise. And
they shall break down your walls and
destroy your pleasant houses. And they
shall put your stones, and your timber, and
your dust in the midst of the water.
13 'And I shall cause the sound of your
songs to cease, and let the sound of your
lyres be heard no more.
14 'And I shall make you like a shining
rock, and let you be a place for spreading
nets, never to be rebuilt, for I יהוה' have
spoken,' declares the Master יהוה'.
15 "Thus said the Master יהוה' to Tsor,
'Would the coastlands not shake at the
sound of your fall, when the wounded cry,
when the killing occurs [a] in your midst?
16 'And all the princes of the sea shall
come down from their thrones, and they
shall lay aside their robes, and take off
their embroidered garments, and put on
trembling, and sit on the ground. And they
shall tremble continuously, and they shall
be astonished at you.
17 'And they shall take up a lamentation
for you, and say to you, "How you have
perished, O one inhabited by seafaring
men, the city well-praised, who was strong
at sea, she and her inhabitants, who put
their fear on all her inhabitants!
18 Now the coastlands tremble on the day
of your fall! And the coastlands by the sea
shall shudder at your going out." '
19 "For thus said the Master יהוה', 'When
I make you a ruined city, like cities no
longer inhabited, when I bring the deep
upon you, and great waters cover you,
20 then I shall bring you down with those
who go down into the pit, to the people of
old. And I shall make you dwell in the
lowest part of the earth, in wastes of old,
with those who go to the pit, so that you do
not return. But I shall establish splendour
in the land of the living.
21 'I make you a horror, and let you be no
more. And you are sought for, but never
found again,' declares the Master יהוה'."

26a Lit. - Is being killed.

27 The word of יהוה came again to
me, saying,
2 "Now, son of man, take up a lamentation for Tsor,
3 and you shall say to Tsor, 'You who
dwell at the entrance to the sea, merchant
of the peoples on many coastlands, thus
said the Master יהוה, "O Tsor, you yourself have said, 'I am perfect in loveliness.'
4 "Your borders are in the heart of the
seas. Your builders have perfected your
loveliness.
5 "They have made all your timbers of fir
trees from Senir. They took a cedar from
Leḇanon to make a mast for you.
6 "From the oaks of Bashan they made
your oars. They made your deck with ivory
from the coasts of Kittim.
7 "Of fine embroidered linen from Mitsrayim was your sail to serve you as banner.
Of blue and purple from the coasts of
Elishah was your covering.
8 "The inhabitants of Tsiḏon and Arwaḏ
were your seamen. Your wise men, O Tsor,
were in you, they were your sailors.
9 "The elders of Geḇal and its wise men
were in you repairing your seams. All the
ships of the sea and their seamen were in
you to trade your merchandise.
10 "Those from Persia, Luḏ, and Put were
in your army as men of battle. Shield and
helmet they hung up within you, they gave
splendour to you.
11 "The sons of Arwaḏ, and your army
were on your walls all around, and the
Gammaḏites were in your towers. They
hung their shields on your walls all around,
they perfected your loveliness.
12 "Tarshish was your merchant because
of your great wealth. They gave you silver,
iron, tin, and lead for your merchandise.
13 "Yawan, Tuḇal, and Meshek̲ were your
traders. They exchanged slaves and objects
of bronze for your merchandise.
14 "Those from the house of Toḡarmah
exchanged horses, and horsemen, and
mules for your merchandise.
15 "The men of Deḏan traded with you.
Many isles were your market, they brought
you ivory tusks and ebony as payment.
16 "Aram was your merchant because of
the multitude of your works. They gave
you emeralds, purple, and embroidery, and
fine linen, and corals, and rubies for your
wares.
17 "Yehuḏah and the land of Yisra'ěl were
your traders. For your merchandise they
exchanged wheat of Minnith, and early
figs, and honey, and oil, and balm.
18 "Dammeseq was your merchant
because of the multitude of your works,
because of your great wealth of goods,
with the wine of Ḥelbon and with white
wool.
19 "Weḏan and Yawan from Uzal paid for
your wares, they exchanged wrought iron,
cassia, and cane for your merchandise.
20 "Deḏan traded with you in saddlecloths
for riding.
21 "Araḇia, and all princes of Qěḏar, were
merchants for you. In lambs, and rams, and
goats they were your merchants.
22 "The traders of Sheḇa and Raʽmah were
your traders. They paid for your wares
with the choicest spices, and all kinds of
precious stones, and gold.
23 "Ḥaran, and Kanneh, and Ěḏen, traders
of Sheḇa, Ashshur, and Kilmaḏ traded with
you.
24 "They traded with you in perfect items,
in purple clothes, in embroidered garments, in chests of multi-coloured clothes,
in strong twined cords, among your
merchandise.
25 "The ships of Tarshish were the travellers of your merchandise. And you were
filled and richly laden in the heart of the
seas.
26 "Your seamen brought you into many
waters, but the east wind broke you in the
heart of the seas.
27 "Your wealth, and your wares, your
merchandise, your mariners and your
sailors, your repairers of seams, and your
dealers in merchandise, and all your fighting men who are in you, and the entire
company which is in your midst, shall go
down into the heart of the seas on the day
of your fall,
28 the coasts shaking at the sound of the
cry of your sailors.
29 "And all the oarsmen, the mariners, all

the sailors of the sea shall come down from
their ships. They shall stand on the shore,
30 and they shall raise their voice and cry
bitterly over you, and cast dust on their
heads, rolling themselves in ashes.
31 "And they shall shave themselves bald
because of you, and shall gird themselves
with sackcloth. And they shall weep for
you with bitterness of heart and bitter wailing.
32 "And in their wailing for you they shall
take up a lamentation. And they shall
lament for you, 'Who is cut off in the midst
of the sea like Tsor?
33 'When your wares went out by sea, you
have filled many peoples; with your great
wealth and your merchandise you have
made the sovereigns of the earth rich.
34 'In the time you are broken by the seas
in the depths of the waters, your merchandise and all your company shall fall in your
midst.
35 'All the inhabitants of the isles shall be
astonished at you, and their sovereigns
shall be greatly afraid, their faces shall be
troubled.
36 'The merchants among the peoples
shall whistle at you. You shall become a
horror, and be no more, forever.' " ' "

28 And the word of יהוה came to me,
saying,
2 "Son of man, say to the prince of Tsor,
'Thus said the Master יהוה, "Because your
heart is lifted up, and you say, 'I am Ěl,
I sit in the seat of Elohim, in the heart of
the seas,' whereas you are a man, and not
Ěl, though you set your heart as the heart
of Elohim!
3 "Look, are you wiser than Dani'ěl? Has
no secret been hidden from you?
4 "By your wisdom and your understanding you have made riches for yourself, and
gathered gold and silver into your treasuries.
5 "By your great wisdom, by your trade
you have increased your riches, and your
heart is lifted up because of your riches."
6 'Therefore thus said the Master יהוה,
"Because you have set your heart as the
heart of Elohim,
7 therefore see, I am bringing against you
strangers, the ruthless ones of the nations.
And they shall draw their swords against
the loveliness of your wisdom, and they
shall profane your splendour.
8 "Down into the pit they shall bring you,
and you shall die the death of the slain in
the heart of the seas.
9 "Would you still say before him who
slays you, 'I am Elohim', whereas you are
man, and not Ěl, in the hand of him who
kills you?
10 "The death of the uncircumcised you
shall die, by the hand of foreigners. For I
have spoken," declares the Master יהוה.' "
11 And the word of יהוה came to me,
saying,
12 "Son of man, take up a lamentation for
the sovereign of Tsor, and you shall say to
him, 'Thus said the Master יהוה, "You
were sealing up a pattern, complete in
wisdom and perfect in loveliness.
13 "You were in Ěḏen, the garden of
Elohim. Every precious stone was your
covering: the ruby, topaz, and diamond,
beryl, shoham, and jasper, sapphire,
turquoise, and emerald and gold. The
workmanship of your settings and mount-
ings was prepared for you on the day you
were created.
14 "You were the anointed keruḇ that
covered. And I placed you, you were on
the set-apart mountain of Elohim. You
walked up and down in the midst of stones
of fire.
15 "You were perfect in your ways from
the day you were created, until unrighteousness was found in you.
16 "By the greatness of your trade you
became filled with violence within, and
you sinned. So I thrust you from the mountain of Elohim, and I destroyed you, O
covering keruḇ, from the midst of the
stones of fire.
17 "Your heart was lifted up because of
your loveliness, you corrupted your wisdom for the sake of your splendour. I threw
you to the earth, I laid you before sovereigns, to look at you.
18 "You profaned your set-apart places by
your many crookednesses, by the unright-

eousness of your trading. Therefore I
brought forth fire from your midst. It has
devoured you, and I turned you to ashes
upon the earth before the eyes of all who
see you.
19 "All who knew you among the peoples
were astonished at you. Waste you shall
be, and cease to be, forever." ' "
20 And the word of יהוה came to me, saying,
21 "Son of man, set your face toward
Tsiḏon, and prophesy against her,
22 and you shall say, 'Thus said the
Master יהוה, "See, I am against you, O
Tsiḏon, and I shall be esteemed in your
midst. And they shall know that I am יהוה,
when I execute judgments in her. And I
shall be set-apart in her.
23 "And I shall send pestilence upon her,
and blood in her streets. And the slain shall
fall in her midst by the sword against her,
from all sides. And they shall know that I
am יהוה.
24 "And there shall no longer be a prick-
ing brier or a paining thorn for the house of
Yisra'ěl from among all who are around
them, who despise them. And they shall
know that I am the Master יהוה."
25 'Thus said the Master יהוה, "When
I have gathered the house of Yisra'ěl from
the peoples among whom they are scattered, I shall be set-apart in them before
the eyes of the nations. And they shall
dwell in their own land which I gave to My
servant Ya'aqoḇ.
26 "And they shall dwell safely, and build
houses, and plant vineyards, and dwell
safely, when I execute judgments on all
those around them who despise them. And
they shall know that I am יהוה their
Elohim." ' "

29 In the tenth year, in the tenth
month, on the twelfth of the new
moon, the word of יהוה came to me, saying,
2 "Son of man, set your face against
Pharaoh the sovereign of Mitsrayim, and
prophesy against him, and against Mitsrayim, all of it.
3 "Speak, and you shall say, 'Thus said
the Master יהוה, "See, I am against you, O
Pharaoh sovereign of Mitsrayim, O great
monster who lies in the midst of his rivers,
who has said, 'My River is my own, and I,
I have made it for myself.'
4 "And I shall put hooks in your jaws,
and I shall make the fish of your rivers
cling to your scales. And I shall bring you
up out of the midst of your rivers, and all
the fish in your rivers cling to your scales.
5 "And I shall leave you in the wilderness, you and all the fish of your rivers. On
the face of the field you shall fall, and you
shall not be picked up or gathered. I shall
give you as food to the beasts of the field
and to the birds of the heavens.
6 "And all the inhabitants of Mitsrayim
shall know that I am יהוה, because they
have been a staff of reed to the house of
Yisra'ěl.
7 "When they grasped you with the hand,
you broke and tore all their shoulders.
When they leaned on you, you broke and
made all their loins shake."
8 'Therefore thus said the Master יהוה,
"See, I am bringing a sword upon you and
shall cut off from you man and beast.
9 "And the land of Mitsrayim shall
become a desert and a waste. And they
shall know that I am יהוה, because he said,
'The River is mine, and I have made it.'
10 "Therefore see, I am against you and
against your rivers, and shall make the
land of Mitsrayim an utter waste and a
desert, from Miḡdol to Sewěněh, as far as
the border of Kush.
11 "No foot of man shall pass through it,
nor foot of beast pass through it, neither
shall it be inhabited for forty years.
12 "And I shall make the land of Mitsrayim a desert in the midst of the lands that
are waste. And among the cities that are
ruined, her cities shall be a waste forty
years. And I shall scatter the Mitsrites
among the nations, and I shall disperse
them throughout the lands."
13 'For thus said the Master יהוה, "At the
end of forty years I shall gather the
Mitsrites from the peoples among whom
they were scattered.
14 "And I shall turn back the captivity of

Mitsrayim and I shall bring them back to
the land of Pathros, to the land of their
birth, and there they shall be a lowly reign,
15 being the lowliest of reigns, and never
again exalt itself above the nations. And I
shall make them few so as not to rule over
the nations.
16 "And no longer is it to be the refuge of
the house of Yisra'ěl, bringing to remembrance their crookedness when they turned
to follow them. And they shall know that I
am the Master יהוה." ' "
17 And it came to be in the twenty-seventh
year, in the first *month*, on the first of the
new *moon*, that the word of יהוה came to
me, saying,
18 "Son of man, Neḇuḵaḏretstsar sovereign of Baḇel made his army to serve a
great service against Tsor, every head was
made bald and every shoulder worn bare.
But he and his army received no reward
from Tsor, for the service he served against
it.
19 "Therefore thus said the Master יהוה,
'See, I am giving the land of Mitsrayim to
Neḇuḵaḏretstsar sovereign of Baḇel. And
he shall take away her wealth, take her
spoil, and remove her pillage. And it shall
be a reward for his army.
20 'I have given him the land of Mitsrayim
as a reward for his labour, because they
worked for Me,' declares the Master יהוה.
21 'In that day I shall make the horn of the
house of Yisra'ěl to spring forth, while I
open your mouth to speak in their midst.
And they shall know that I am יהוה.' "

30 And the word of יהוה came to me,
saying,
2 "Son of man, prophesy and say, 'Thus
said the Master יהוה, "Howl, 'Woe to the
day!'
3 "For the day is near, even the day of
יהוה is near. It is a day of clouds, the time
of the nations.
4 "The sword shall come upon Mitsrayim, and great anguish shall be in Kush,
when the slain fall in Mitsrayim, and they
take away her wealth, and her foundations
are broken down.
5 "Kush, and Put, and Luḏ, all the mixed
people, and Kuḇ, and the sons of the land
of the covenant, shall fall with them by the
sword."
6 'Thus said יהוה, "Those who lean on
Mitsrayim shall fall, and the pride of her
power shall come down. From Miḡdol to
Sewěněh those within her shall fall by the
sword," declares the Master יהוה.
7 "They shall be ruined amidst the wasted lands, and her cities shall be in the
midst of the cities that are dried up.
8 "And they shall know that I am יהוה,
when I have set a fire in Mitsrayim and all
her helpers are crushed.
9 "On that day messengers shall go forth
before Me in ships to make the complacent
Kushites afraid, and great anguish shall
come upon them, as on the day of Mitsrayim – for look, it is coming!"
10 'Thus said the Master יהוה, "I shall
cause the crowd of Mitsrayim to cease, by
the hand of Neḇuḵaḏretstsar sovereign of
Baḇel.
11 "He and his people with him, the ruthless ones of the nations, are brought to
destroy the land. And they shall draw their
swords against Mitsrayim, and shall fill the
land with the slain.
12 "And I shall make the rivers dry, and I
shall sell the land into the hand of evil
ones. And I shall lay the land waste, and all
that is in it, by the hand of foreigners. I,
יהוה, have spoken."
13 'Thus said the Master יהוה, "And I
shall destroy the idols, and make an end of
the images in Noph, and there shall no
longer be a prince from the land of Mitsrayim, and I shall put fear in the land of
Mitsrayim.
14 "And I shall make Pathros a waste, and
I shall set fire to Tso'an, and I shall execute
judgments in No.
15 "And I shall pour out My wrath on Sin,
the stronghold of Mitsrayim. And I shall
cut off the crowd of No.
16 "And I shall set a fire in Mitsrayim, Sin
shall writhe in anguish, No is to be split
open, and Noph has adversaries daily.
17 "The young men of Awen and Pi
Ḇeseth shall fall by the sword, while these
cities go into captivity.

18"And in Teḥaphneḥes the day shall be
darkened, when I shatter the yokes of
Mitsrayim there. And the pride of her
strength shall cease in her, a cloud shall
cover her. And her daughters shall go into
captivity.
19"And I shall execute judgments on
Mitsrayim, and they shall know that I
am יהוה." ' "
20And it came to be in the eleventh year,
in the first *month*, on the seventh of the
new *moon*, that the word of יהוה came to
me, saying,
21"Son of man, I have broken the arm of
Pharaoh sovereign of Mitsrayim. And see,
it has not been bound up for healing, to put
a bandage to bind it, to make it strong to
hold a sword.
22"Therefore thus said the Master יהוה,
'See, I am against Pharaoh sovereign of
Mitsrayim, and shall break his arms, both
the strong one and the one that was broken,
and shall make the sword fall out of his
hand,
23and shall scatter the Mitsrites among
the nations, and disperse them throughout
the lands,
24and strengthen the arms of the sovereign of Baḇel. And I shall put My sword in
his hand. And I shall break Pharaoh's
arms, and he shall groan before him with
the groanings of the slain before him.
25'And I shall strengthen the arms of the
sovereign of Baḇel, but the arms of
Pharaoh shall fall. And they shall know
that I am יהוה, when I put My sword into
the hand of the sovereign of Baḇel and he
shall stretch it out against the land of
Mitsrayim.
26'And I shall scatter the Mitsrites among
the nations, and I shall disperse them
throughout the lands. And they shall know
that I am יהוה.' "

31

And it came to be in the eleventh
year, in the third *month*, on the first
of the new *moon*, that the word of יהוה
came to me, saying,
2"Son of man, say to Pharaoh sovereign
of Mitsrayim and to his crowd, 'To whom
are you to be compared in your greatness?
3'See, Ashshur was a cedar in Leḇanon,
beautiful branches and forest shade, and of
high stature. And its top was among the
thick foliage.
4'The waters made him great, the deep
gave it height with its rivers running
around its planting, and sent their channels
to all the trees of the field.
5'Therefore its height was lifted up
above all the trees of the field, and its
boughs were increased, and its branches
became long because of the many waters,
as it sent them out.
6'All the birds of the heavens made their
nests in its boughs, and under its branches
all the beasts of the field gave birth. And in
its shadow all great nations dwelt.
7'And it was beautiful in greatness and
in the length of its branches, for its roots
reached to many waters.
8'Cedars in the garden of Elohim did not
hide it, fir trees were not like its boughs,
and the chestnut trees were not like its
branches. No tree in the garden of Elohim
was as pretty as it.
9'I made it beautiful by its many branches, so that all the trees of Ěḏen which were
in the garden of Elohim were jealous of it.'
10"Therefore thus said the Master יהוה,
'Because you have increased in height, and
it set its top among the thick foliage, and
its heart was lifted up in its height,
11'I give it into the hand of the mighty
one of the nations, and he shall certainly
deal with it. I have driven it out for its
wrong.
12'And foreigners, the most ruthless of
the nations, shall cut it down and leave it.
Its branches shall fall on the mountains and
in all the valleys, its boughs lie broken by
all the rivers of the land. And all the
peoples of the earth shall come out from
under its shadow and leave it.
13'On its ruin shall dwell all the birds of
the heavens, and all the beasts of the field
shall be on its *fallen* branches,
14so that none of the trees by the waters
would exalt themselves because of their
height, nor set their tops among the thick
foliage, and that no tree which drinks
water would ever be high enough to reach

up to them. 'For all of them shall be given up to death, to the depths of the earth, among the children of men who go down to the pit.'

15 "Thus said the Master יהוה, 'In the day when it is brought down to She'ol I shall cause mourning. I shall cover the deep because of it and hold back its streams, and many waters shall be confined. And I shall make Leḇanon mourn for it, and all the trees of the field shall wither away because of it.

16 'I shall make the nations shake at the sound of its fall, when I bring it down to She'ol together with those who descend into the pit. And all the trees of Ěḏen, the choice and best of Leḇanon, all that drink water, shall be comforted in the depths of the earth.

17 'They too shall go down to She'ol with it, with those slain by the sword. And those who were its strength shall dwell in its shadows among the nations.

18 'To whom are you to be compared in esteem and greatness among the trees in Ěḏen? But you shall be brought down with the trees of Ěḏen to the depths of the earth, lie in the midst of the uncircumcised, with those slain by the sword. This is Pharaoh and all his crowd,' declares the Master יהוה."

32 And it came to be in the twelfth year, in the twelfth new *moon*, on the first of the new *moon*, that the word of יהוה came to me, saying,

2 "Son of man, take up a lamentation for Pharaoh sovereign of Mitsrayim, and you shall say to him, 'You were like a young lion among the nations, and you are like a monster in the seas, and you burst forth in your rivers, and trouble the waters with your feet, and muddy their rivers.'

3 "Thus said the Master יהוה, 'And I shall spread My net over you with an assembly of many peoples, and they shall bring you up in My net.

4 'And I shall leave you on the land, hurl you out on the open fields, and make all the birds of the heavens dwell on you. And with you I shall satisfy the beasts of all the earth.

5 'And I shall put your flesh on the mountains, and fill the valleys with your height,

6 and water the land with the flow of your blood unto the mountains, and let streams be filled with you.

7 'And when I extinguish you, I shall cover the heavens, and make its stars dark. I shall cover the sun with a cloud, and the moon shall not give her light.

8 'All the bright lights of the heavens I shall make dark over you, and I shall bring darkness upon your land,' declares the Master יהוה.

9 'And I shall trouble the hearts of many peoples, when I bring your destruction among the nations, into the lands which you have not known.

10 'And I shall make many peoples appalled at you, and their sovereigns shall be greatly afraid of you when I swing My sword before them. And they shall tremble continually, every man for his own life, in the day of your fall.'

11 "For thus said the Master יהוה, 'The sword of the sovereign of Baḇel shall come upon you.

12 'By the swords of the mighty men, all of them the ruthless ones of the nations, I shall make your host fall. And they shall ravage the arrogance of Mitsrayim, and all its host shall be destroyed.

13 'And I shall destroy all its beasts from beside its great waters, and let the foot of man trouble them no more, nor let the hooves of beasts trouble them.

14 'Then I shall make their waters clear, and make their rivers run like oil,' declares the Master יהוה.

15 'When I lay the land of Mitsrayim waste, and the land shall be stripped of all that once filled it, when I have stricken all who dwell in it, then they shall know that I am יהוה.

16 'This is the lamentation, and they shall lament her, the daughters of the nations lament her. Over Mitsrayim and over all her crowd they shall lament her,' declares the Master יהוה."

17 And it came to be in the twelfth year,

on the fifteenth of the new *moon*, that the word of יהוה came to me, saying,

18 "Son of man, wail over the crowd of Mitsrayim, and send them down to the depths of the earth, her and the daughters of the mighty nations, with those going down to the pit.

19 'Are you more pleasant than others? Go down, be placed with the uncircumcised.'

20 "In the midst of those slain by the sword they fall. She shall be given to the sword, drawing her and all her crowds.

21 "The mightiest among the mighty speak to him out of the midst of She'ol with those who help him, 'They have gone down, they lie with the uncircumcised, slain by the sword.'

22 "Ashshur is there, and all her assembly, with their burial-sites all around her, all of them slain, fallen by the sword,

23 whose burial-sites are set in the sides of the pit, and her assembly is all around her burial-place, all of them slain, fallen by the sword, because they instilled fear in the land of the living.

24 "There is Ěylam and all her crowd, around her burial-place, all of them slain, fallen by the sword, who have gone down uncircumcised to the lower parts of the earth, because they instilled fear in the land of the living. And they bear their shame with those going down to the pit.

25 "They have set her bed in the midst of the slain, with all her crowd, with her burial-sites all around it, all of them uncircumcised, slain by the sword, for the fear they instilled in the land of the living. So they bear their shame with those going down to the pit. In the midst of the slain they have been placed.

26 "There are Mesheḵ and Tuḇal and all her crowd, with all their burial-sites around it, all of them uncircumcised, slain by the sword, because they instilled fear in the land of the living.

27 "And they shall not lie with the mighty who are fallen of the uncircumcised, who have gone down to She'ol with their battle gear, and whose swords were laid under their heads. But their crookednesses are on their bones, because of the fear of the mighty in the land of the living.

28 "And you shall be broken in the midst of the uncircumcised, and lie with those slain by the sword.

29 "There is Eḏom, her sovereigns and all her princes, who shall be given up in their might, with those slain by the sword. With the uncircumcised they lie, and with those going down to the pit.

30 "There are the princes of the north, all of them, and all the Tsiḏonians, who have gone down with the slain, because of the fear they instilled. They are ashamed of their might. And they lie uncircumcised with those slain by the sword, and bear their shame with those going down to the pit.

31 "Pharaoh – Pharaoh and all his army – shall see them, and he shall be comforted for all his host that were slain by the sword," declares the Master יהוה.

32 "For I have put a fear of him in the land of the living, yet he shall be placed in the midst of the uncircumcised with those slain by the sword – Pharaoh and all his host," declares the Master יהוה.

33

And the word of יהוה came to me, saying,

2 "Son of man, speak to the children of your people, and you shall say to them, 'When I bring the sword upon a land, and the people of the land shall take a man from their borders and shall make him their watchman,

3 and he sees the sword coming upon the land, and shall blow with the shophar and shall warn the people,

4 then whoever shall hear the voice of the shofar and shall not take warning, if the sword comes and takes him away, his blood is on his own head.

5 'He heard the voice of the shophar, but he did not take warning, his blood is on himself. But he who takes warning shall deliver his being.

6 'But if the watchman sees the sword coming and shall not blow with the shophar, and the people shall not be warned, and the sword comes and takes any being from among them, he is taken

away in his crookedness, and his blood I
require at the watchman's hand.'
7 "And you, son of man, I have made you
a watchman for the house of Yisra'ěl. And
you shall hear a word from My mouth and
you shall warn them for Me.
8 "When I say to the wrong, 'O wrong
one, you shall certainly die!' and you have
not spoken to warn the wrong from his
way, that wrong one shall die in his
crookedness, and his blood I require at
your hand.
9 "But when you have warned[a] the
wrong to turn from his way, and he has not
turned from his way, he shall die in his
crookedness, but you have delivered your
being.
10 "And you, O son of man, say to the
house of Yisra'ěl, 'This is what you have
said, "If our transgressions and our sins lie
upon us, and we pine away in them, how
then shall we live?" '
11 "Say to them, 'As I live,' declares the
Master יהוה, 'I have no pleasure in the
death of the wrong, but that the wrong turn
from his way and live. Turn back, turn
back from your evil ways! For why should
you die, O house of Yisra'ěl?'
12 "And you, O son of man, say to the
children of your people, 'The righteousness of the righteous man shall not deliver
him in the day of his transgression. And as
for the wrongness of the wrong, he shall
not stumble because of it in the day that he
turns from his wrong. And the righteous
shall not be able to live because of his
righteousness in the day that he sins.'
13 "When I say to the righteous that he
shall live, and he has trusted in his righteousness, and shall do unrighteousness,
none of his righteousness shall be remembered, but because of his unrighteousness
that he has done, he shall die.
14 "Again, when I say to the wrong, 'You
shall certainly die,' if he turns from his sin
and does right and righteousness,
15 if the wrong restores the pledge, gives
back what he has stolen, and walks in the
laws of life without doing crookedness, he
shall certainly live; he shall not die.
16 "None of his sins which he has committed shall be remembered against him – he
has done right and righteousness; he shall
certainly live.
17 "And the children of your people have
said, 'The way of יהוה is not fair.' But it is
their way which is not fair!
18 "When the righteous turns from his
righteousness and does unrighteousness,
he shall die because of it.
19 "But when the wrong turns from his
wrongness and does right and righteousness, he shall live because of it.
20 "And you have said, 'The way of יהוה
is not fair.' O house of Yisra'ěl, I shall
judge every one of you according to his
own ways."
21 And it came to be in the twelfth year of
our exile, in the tenth *month*, on the fifth of
the new *moon*, that one who had escaped
from Yerushalayim came to me and said,
"The city has been stricken!"
22 And the hand of יהוה came upon me
the evening before the man came who had
escaped. And He had opened my mouth,
before he came to me in the morning. And
my mouth was opened. And I was no
longer silent.
23 Then the word of יהוה came to me,
saying,
24 "Son of man, they who inhabit those
ruins in the land of Yisra'ěl are saying,
'Aḇraham was only one, and he inherited
the land. But we are many, let the land be
given to us as a possession.'
25 "Therefore say to them, 'Thus said the
Master יהוה, "You eat meat with blood,
and you lift up your eyes toward your
idols, and shed blood. Should you then
possess the land?
26 "You depend on your sword, and you
commit abominations, and each of you
defiles his neighbour's wife. Should you
then possess the land?" '
27 "Say this to them, 'Thus said the
Master יהוה, "As I live, those who are in
the ruins shall fall by the sword, and the
one who is in the open field I shall give to

33a Similar messages in 3:18-21, 18:20-30.

the beasts to be devoured, and those who are in the strongholds and caves shall die of the pestilence.

28 “And I shall make the land a desert and a waste, the arrogance of her strength shall cease, and the mountains of Yisra’ěl shall be a waste, with none passing through.

29 “And they shall know that I am יהוה, when I have made the land a desert and a waste, because of all their abominations which they have done.” ’

30 “As for you, son of man, the children of your people are talking about you beside the walls and in the doors of the houses. And they speak to each other, each saying to his brother, ‘Please come and hear what the word is that comes from יהוה.’

31 “And they come to you as people do, and they sit before you as My people, and they hear your words, but they do not do them. For with their mouth they show much love – their hearts pursue their greedy gain.

32 “And see, you are to them as a very lovely song of one who has a beautiful voice and playing well on an instrument. And they hear your words, but they do not do them.

33 “And when it comes – see, it shall come – then they shall know that a prophet has been in their midst.”

34

And the word of יהוה came to me, saying,

2 “Son of man, prophesy against the shepherds of Yisra’ěl, prophesy and say to them, ‘Thus said the Master יהוה to the shepherds, “Woe to the shepherds [a] of Yisra’ěl who have been feeding themselves! Should not the shepherds feed the flock?

3 “You eat the fat and you put on the wool. You slaughter the fatlings – you do not feed the flock.

4 “You have not strengthened the weak, nor have you healed the sick, nor bound up the broken, nor brought back the straying, nor sought what was lost; but you have ruled them with might and harshness.

5 “And they were scattered because there was no shepherd. And they became food for all the beasts of the field when they were scattered.

6 “My sheep wandered through all the mountains, and on every high hill. And My sheep were scattered over all the face of the earth, and no one was seeking or searching for them.”

7 ‘Therefore, you shepherds, hear the word of יהוה:

8 “As I live,” declares the Master יהוה, “because My flock became a prey, and My flock became food for every beast of the field, from not having a shepherd, and My shepherds did not search for My flock, but the shepherds fed themselves and did not feed My flock,”

9 therefore, O shepherds, hear the word of יהוה!

10 ‘Thus said the Master יהוה, “See, I am against the shepherds, and shall require My flock at their hand, and shall make them cease feeding the sheep, and the shepherds shall feed themselves no more. And I shall deliver My flock from their mouths, and they shall no longer be food for them.”

11 ‘For thus said the Master יהוה, “See, I Myself shall search for My sheep and seek them out.

12 “As a shepherd seeks out his flock on the day he is among his scattered sheep, so I shall seek out My sheep and deliver them from all the places where they were scattered in a day of cloud and thick darkness.

13 “And I shall bring them out from the peoples and gather them from the lands, and shall bring them to their own land. And I shall feed them on the mountains of Yisra’ěl, in the valleys, and in all the dwellings of the land.

14 “In good pasture I shall feed them, and their fold shall be on the high mountains of Yisra’ěl. They shall lie there in a good fold and feed in rich pasture on the mountains of Yisra’ěl.

15 “I shall feed My flock and make them lie down,” declares the Master יהוה.

16 “I shall seek out the lost and bring back

34a See footnote at Yirm. 10:21.

the strayed. And I shall bind up the broken
and strengthen what was sick, but the fat
and the strong I shall destroy. I shall feed
them with right-ruling."
17 'And as for you, O My flock, thus said
the Master יהוה, "See, I am judging
between sheep and sheep, between rams
and goats.
18 "Is it not enough for you to have eaten
up the good pasture, and the rest of your
pasture you trample with your feet. Or that
you should drink of the clear waters, and
the rest you muddy with your feet?
19 "And as for My flock, they eat what
you have trampled with your feet, and they
drink what you have muddied with your
feet."
20 'Therefore thus said the Master יהוה to
them, "See, I Myself shall judge between
fat and lean sheep.
21 "Because you have pushed with flank
and shoulder, and thrust at all the weak
ones with your horns, and scattered them
abroad,
22 therefore I shall save My flock, and let
them no longer be a prey. And I shall judge
between sheep and sheep.
23 "And I shall raise up over them one
shepherd, My servant Dawiḏ, and he shall
feed them. He shall feed them and be their
shepherd.
24 "And I, יהוה, shall be their Elohim, and
My servant Dawiḏ a prince in their midst.
I, יהוה, have spoken.
25 "And I shall make a covenant of peace
with them, and make evil beasts cease
from the land. And they shall dwell safely
in the wilderness and sleep in the forest.
26 "And I shall make them and the places
all around My hill a blessing, and shall
cause showers to come down in their season – showers of blessing they are.
27 "And the trees of the field shall yield
their fruit and the earth yield her increase,
and they shall be safe in their land. And
they shall know that I am יהוה, when I
have broken the bars of their yoke. And I
shall deliver them from the hand of those
who enslaved them,
28 and they shall no longer be a prey for
the nations, and the beast of the earth shall
not devour them. And they shall dwell
safely, with no one to make them afraid.
29 "And I shall raise up for them a planting place of name, and they shall no longer
be consumed by hunger in the land, nor
bear the shame of the nations any more.
30 "And they shall know that I, יהוה their
Elohim, am with them, and that they, the
house of Yisra'ěl, are My people," declares
the Master יהוה.' "
31 "And you, My flock, the flock of My
pasture, are men, and I am your Elohim,"
declares the Master יהוה.' "

35

And the word of יהוה came to me,
saying,
2 "Son of man, set your face against
Mount Sě'ir and prophesy against it,
3 and you shall say to it, 'Thus said the
Master יהוה, "See, O Mount Sě'ir, I am
against you, and shall stretch out My hand
against you, and shall make you a ruin and
a waste.
4 "Your cities I destroy, and let you be a
ruin. And you shall know that I am יהוה.
5 "Because you have had a continuous
enmity, and handed the children of Yisra'ěl
over to the power of the sword at the time
of their calamity, at the time of the
crookedness of the end.
6 "Therefore, as I live," declares the
Master יהוה, "I shall appoint you for
blood, and let blood pursue you. Since you
did not hate blood, therefore blood shall
pursue you.
7 "And I shall make Mount Sě'ir a ruin
and a waste, and cut off from it the one
who leaves and the one who returns,
8 and shall fill its mountains with the
slain, those slain by the sword falling on
your hills and in your valleys and in all
your ravines.
9 "I shall make you an everlasting ruin,
and your cities uninhabited. And you shall
know that I am יהוה.
10 "Because you have said, 'These two
nations and these two lands are mine, and
we shall possess them,' although יהוה was
there,
11 therefore, as I live," declares the Master
יהוה, "I shall do according to your displea-

sure and according to your envy which you showed in your hatred against them. And I shall make Myself known among them when I judge you.

12 "And you shall know that I am יהוה. I have heard all your scorns which you have spoken against the mountains of Yisra'ěl, saying, 'They are laid waste, they were given to us for food.'

13 "And with your mouth you have boasted against Me and increased your words against Me – I Myself have heard."

14 'Thus said the Master יהוה, "As all the earth is rejoicing I shall make you a ruin.

15 "As you rejoiced because the inheritance of the house of Yisra'ěl was laid waste, so I do to you: be a ruin, O Mount Sě'ir, as well as all of Eḏom, all of it! And they shall know that I am יהוה." '

36

"And you, son of man, prophesy to the mountains of Yisra'ěl, and you shall say, 'O mountains of Yisra'ěl, hear the word of יהוה!

2 'Thus said the Master יהוה, "Because the enemy has said of you, 'Aha! The heights of old have become our possession,' " '

3 therefore prophesy, and you shall say, 'Thus said the Master יהוה, "Because they laid you waste and swallowed you up on every side, so that you became the possession of the rest of the nations, and you are taken up by the lips of talkers and slandered by the people,"

4 therefore, O mountains of Yisra'ěl, hear the word of the Master יהוה! Thus said the Master יהוה to the mountains, and to the hills, to the rivers, and to the valleys, and to the deserted ruins, and to the cities that have been forsaken, which became a prey and a mocking to the rest of the nations all around;

5 therefore thus said the Master יהוה, "Have I not spoken in My burning jealousy against the rest of the nations and against all Eḏom, who gave My land to themselves as a possession, with all joy of heart, with scorn in their being, to drive it out for a prey?" '

6 "Therefore prophesy concerning the land of Yisra'ěl, and you shall say to mountains, and to hills, to rivers, and to valleys, 'Thus said the Master יהוה, "See, I have spoken in My jealousy and My wrath, because you have borne the shame of the nations."

7 'Therefore thus said the Master יהוה, "I have lifted My hand in an oath that the nations that are around you shall bear their own shame.

8 "But you, O mountains of Yisra'ěl, put forth your branches and bear your fruit to My people Yisra'ěl, for they are about to come!

9 "For look, I am for you, and I shall turn to you, and you shall be tilled and sown.

10 "And I shall increase men upon you, all the house of Yisra'ěl, all of it. And the cities shall be inhabited and the ruins rebuilt.

11 "And I shall increase upon you man and beast, and they shall increase and bear young. And I shall make you inhabited as of old, and do better for you than at your beginnings. And you shall know that I am יהוה.

12 "And I shall let men, My people Yisra'ěl, walk upon you, and let them possess you, and you shall be their inheritance, and no longer let you add to their bereavement."

13 'Thus said the Master יהוה, "Because they say to you, 'You devour men and have bereaved your nation,'

14 therefore you shall no longer devour men, and no longer bereave your nation," declares the Master יהוה.

15 "And no longer shall I let you hear the insults of the nations. And the reproach of the peoples you shall bear no more, and no longer cause your nations to stumble," declares the Master יהוה.' "

16 And the word of יהוה came to me, saying,

17 "Son of man, when the house of Yisra'ěl dwelt in their own land, they defiled it by their own ways and deeds. To Me their way was like the uncleanness of a woman in her monthly period.

18 "So I poured out My wrath on them for the blood they had shed on the land, and

for their idols they defiled it.
19 "And I scattered them among the
nations, and they were dispersed throughout the lands. I have judged them according to their ways and their deeds.
20 "And when they came to the nations,
wherever they went, they profaned My set-
apart Name for it was said of them, 'These
are the people of יהוה', and yet they have
gone out of His land.'
21 "But I had compassion on My set-apart
Name, which the house of Yisra'ěl had
profaned among the nations wherever they
went.
22 "Therefore say to the house of Yisra'ěl,
'Thus said the Master יהוה', "I do not
do this for your sake, O house of Yisra'ěl,
but for My set-apart Name's sake, which
you have profaned among the nations
wherever you went.
23 "And I shall set apart My great Name,
which has been profaned among the
nations, which you have profaned in their
midst. And the nations shall know that I
am יהוה'," declares the Master יהוה', "when
I am set-apart in you before their eyes.
24 "And I shall take you from among the
nations, and I shall gather you out of all
lands, and I shall bring you into your own
land.
25 "And I shall sprinkle clean water on
you, and you shall be clean – from all your
filthiness and from all your idols I cleanse
you.
26 "And I shall give you a new heart and
put a new spirit within you. And I shall
take the heart of stone out of your flesh,
and I shall give you a heart of flesh,
27 and put My Spirit within you. [a] And I
shall cause you to walk in My laws and
guard My right-rulings and shall do them.
28 "And you shall dwell in the land that I
gave to your fathers. And you shall be My
people, and I shall be your Elohim.
29 "And I shall save you from all your
uncleannesses. And I shall call for the
grain and increase it, and I shall bring no
scarcity of food upon you.
30 "And I shall increase the fruit of your
trees and the increase of your fields, so that
you need never again bear the reproach of
scarcity of food among the nations.
31 "And you shall remember your evil
ways and your deeds that were not good.
And you shall loathe yourselves in your
own eyes, for your crookednesses and your
abominations.
32 "Not for your sake am I acting,"
declares the Master יהוה', "let it be known
to you. Be ashamed and blush for your
ways, O house of Yisra'ěl!"
33 'Thus said the Master יהוה', "On the
day that I cleanse you from all your
crookednesses, I shall cause the cities to be
inhabited, and the ruined places shall be
rebuilt,
34 and the land that was laid waste tilled
instead of being a ruin before the eyes of
all who pass by.
35 "And they shall say, 'This land that was
laid waste has become like the garden of
Ěḏen. And the wasted, the deserted, and
the destroyed cities are now walled and
inhabited.'
36 "Then the nations which are left all
around you shall know that I, יהוה', have
rebuilt the destroyed places and planted
what was laid waste. I, יהוה', have spoken
it, and I shall do it."
37 'Thus said the Master יהוה', "Once
again I shall let the house of Yisra'ěl
inquire of Me to do for them: I shall
increase their men like a flock.
38 "As a set-apart flock, as the flock at
Yerushalayim at her appointed times, so
shall the wasted cities be filled with flocks
of men. And they shall know that I am
יהוה'." ' "

37 The hand of יהוה' was upon me and
took me out by the Spirit of יהוה',
and set me down in the midst of the valley.
And it was filled with bones.
2 And He made me pass among them, all
around, and see, there were very many on
the surface of the valley, and see, they
were very dry.
3 And He said to me, "Son of man, would

36a See 11:19-20, 37:6-14, 39:29.

these bones live?" And I said, "O Master
יהוה, You know."
4 Again He said to me, "Prophesy to
these bones, and you shall say to them, 'O
dry bones, hear the word of יהוה!
5 'Thus said the Master יהוה to these
bones, "See, I am bringing into you a spirit, and you shall live.
6 "And I shall put sinews on you and
bring flesh upon you, and cover you with
skin and put a spirit in you, and you shall
live. And you shall know that I am
יהוה." ' "
7 And I prophesied as I was commanded.
And as I prophesied, there was a noise, and
there was a rattling. And the bones came
together, bone to bone.
8 And I looked and saw sinews and flesh
came upon them, and skin covered them,
but there was no spirit in them.
9 He then said to me, "Prophesy to the
spirit, prophesy, son of man, and you shall
say to the spirit, 'Thus said the Master
יהוה, "Come from the four winds, O spirit,
and breathe on these killed ones, so that
they live." ' "
10 And I prophesied as He commanded
me, and the spirit came into them, and they
lived, and stood upon their feet, a very
great army.
11 And He said to me, "Son of man, these
bones are all the house of Yisra'ěl. See,
they say, 'Our bones are dry, our expectancy has perished, and we ourselves have
been cut off!'
12 "Therefore prophesy, and you shall say
to them, 'Thus said the Master יהוה, "See,
O My people, I am opening your burial-
sites and shall bring you up from your burial-sites, and shall bring you into the land
of Yisra'ěl.
13 "And you shall know that I am יהוה,
when I open your burial-sites, My people,
and bring you up from your burial-sites.
14 "And I shall put My Spirit in you, and
you shall live, and I shall settle you in your
own land. And you shall know that I יהוה
have spoken, and I have done it," declares
יהוה.' "
15 And the word of יהוה came to me,
saying,
16 "And you, son of man, take a stick for
yourself and write on it, 'For Yehuḏah and
for the children of Yisra'ěl, his companions.' Then take another stick and write on
it, 'For Yosěph, the stick of Ephrayim, and
for all the house of Yisra'ěl, his companions.'
17 "Then bring them together for yourself
into one stick, and they shall become one
in your hand.
18 "And when the children of your people
speak to you, saying, 'Won't you show us
what you mean by these?'
19 say to them, 'Thus said the Master
יהוה, "See, I am taking the stick of
Yosěph, which is in the hand of Ephrayim,
and the tribes of Yisra'ěl, his companions.
And I shall give them unto him, with the
stick of Yehuḏah, and make them one
stick, and they shall be one in My hand." '
20 "And the sticks on which you write
shall be in your hand before their eyes.
21 "And speak to them, 'Thus said the
Master יהוה, "See, I am taking the children
of Yisra'ěl from among the nations,
wherever they have gone, and shall gather
them from all around, and I shall bring
them into their land.
22 "And I shall make them one nation in
the land, on the mountains of Yisra'ěl. And
one sovereign shall be sovereign over them
all, and let them no longer be two nations,
and let them no longer be divided into two
reigns.
23 "And they shall no longer defile themselves with their idols, nor with their disgusting *matters*, nor with any of their
transgressions. And I shall save them from
all their dwelling places in which they
have sinned, and I shall cleanse them. And
they shall be My people, and I be their
Elohim,
24 while Dawiḏ My servant is sovereign
over them. And they shall all have one
shepherd and walk in My right-rulings and
guard My laws, and shall do them.
25 "And they shall dwell in the land that I
have given to Ya'aqoḇ My servant, where
your fathers dwelt. And they shall dwell
in it, they and their children and their
children's children, forever, and My ser-

vant Dawiḏ be their prince forever.
26 "And I shall make a covenant of peace
with them – an everlasting covenant it is
with them. And I shall place them and
increase them, and shall place My set-apart
place in their midst, forever.
27 "And My Dwelling Place shall be over
them. And I shall be their Elohim, and they
shall be My people.
28 "And the nations shall know that I,
יהוה, am setting Yisra'ěl apart, when
My set-apart place is in their midst –
forever." ' "

38 And the word of יהוה came to me,
saying,
2 "Son of man, set your face against Goḡ,
of the land of Maḡoḡ, the prince of Rosh,
Mesheḵ, and Tuḇal, and prophesy against
him.
3 "And you shall say, 'Thus says the
Master יהוה, "See, I am against you, O
Goḡ, the prince of Rosh, Mesheḵ, and
Tuḇal.
4 "And I shall turn you around, and I
shall put hooks into your jaws, and shall
lead you out, with all your army, horses
and horsemen, clad perfectly, a great
assembly with armour and shields, all of
them handling swords.
5 "Persia, Kush, and Put are with them,
all of them with shield and helmet,
6 "Gomer and all its bands, the house of
Toḡarmah from the far north and all its
bands, many peoples with you.
7 "Be ready, prepare yourself, you and all
your assemblies that are assembled unto
you. And you shall be a guard for them.
8 "After many days you shall be called
up. In the latter years you shall come into
the land of those brought back from the
sword and gathered from many people on
the mountains of Yisra'ěl, which had been
a continual waste. But they were brought
out of the peoples, and all of them shall
dwell safely.
9 "And you shall go up, coming like a
storm, covering the land like a cloud, you
and all your bands and many peoples with
you."
10 'Thus said the Master יהוה, "And it
shall be in that day that words arise in your
heart, and you shall devise an evil plan:
11 "And you shall say, 'Let me go up
against a land of unwalled villages, let me
go to those at rest who dwell safely, all of
them dwelling without walls, and having
neither bars nor gates,'
12 to take plunder and to take booty, to
stretch out your hand against the waste
places that are again inhabited, and against
a people gathered from the peoples,
acquiring livestock and goods, who dwell
in the middle of the land.
13 "Sheḇa, and Deḏan, and the merchants
of Tarshish, and all their young lions shall
say to you, 'Have you come to take plunder? Have you gathered your army to take
booty, to bear away silver and gold, to take
away livestock and goods, to take great
plunder?' " '
14 "Therefore, son of man, prophesy, and
you shall say to Goḡ, 'Thus said the
Master יהוה, "In that day when My people
Yisra'ěl dwell safely, would you not
know?
15 "And you shall come from your place
out of the far north, you and many peoples
with you, all of them riding on horses, a
great assembly and a mighty army.
16 "And you shall come up against My
people Yisra'ěl like a cloud, to cover the
land – in the latter days it shall be. And I
shall bring you against My land, in order
that the nations know Me, when I am set
apart in you, O Goḡ, before their eyes."
17 'Thus said the Master יהוה, "Are you
the one I spoke of in former days by My
servants the prophets of Yisra'ěl, who
prophesied for years in those days, to bring
you against them?
18 "And it shall be on that day, on the day
when Goḡ comes against the land of
Yisra'ěl," declares the Master יהוה, "that
My wrath shall come up in My face.
19 "For in My jealousy and in the fire of
My wrath I have spoken, 'On that day
there shall be a great shaking in the land of
Yisra'ěl,
20 so that the fish of the sea, and the birds
of the heavens, and the beasts of the field,
and all creeping creatures that creep on the

earth, and all men who are on the face of
the earth shall shake at My presence. And
the mountains shall be thrown down, and
the steep places shall fall, and every wall
fall to the ground.'
21 "And I shall call for a sword against
Goḡ on all My mountains," declares the
Master יהוה, "the sword of each one being
against his brother.
22 "And I shall judge him with pestilence
and blood, and rain down flooding rain and
hailstones, fire and sulphur, on him and on
his bands and on the many peoples who are
with him.
23 "And I shall exalt Myself and set
Myself apart, and I shall be known in the
eyes of many nations. And they shall know
that I am יהוה." '

39 "And you, son of man, prophesy
against Goḡ, and you shall say,
'Thus said the Master יהוה, "See, I am
against you, O Goḡ, the prince of Rosh,
Meshek, and Tuḇal,
2 and shall turn you around and lead you
on, and bring you up from the uttermost
parts of the north, and bring you against
the mountains of Yisra'ěl,
3 and shall strike the bow out of your left
hand, and make the arrows fall from your
right hand.
4 "On the mountains of Yisra'ěl you shall
fall, you and all your bands and the peoples who are with you. To the birds of prey
of every sort and to the beasts of the field I
shall give you for food.
5 "On the face of the field you shall fall,
for I have spoken," declares the Master
יהוה.
6 "And I shall send fire upon Maḡoḡ and
on those who live undisturbed in the coastlands. And they shall know that I am יהוה.
7 "And I shall make My set-apart Name
known in the midst of My people Yisra'ěl,
and not let My set-apart Name be profaned
any more. And the nations shall know that
I am יהוה, the Set-apart One in Yisra'ěl.
8 "See, it shall come, and it shall be
done," declares the Master יהוה. "This is
the day of which I have spoken.
9 "And those who inhabit the cities of
Yisra'ěl shall go out and set on fire and
burn the weapons, both the shields and
armour, the bows and arrows, the clubs and
spears. And they shall make fires with
them for seven years,
10 and take no wood from the field nor cut
down any from the forests, for with the
weapons they make fire. And they shall
plunder those who plundered them, and
loot those who looted them," declares the
Master יהוה.
11 "And it shall be on that day that I give
Goḡ a place for a burial-site there in
Yisra'ěl, the valley of those passing by east
of the sea, and stopping those passing by,
because there they shall bury Goḡ and all
his crowd, and shall call it the Valley of
Hamon Goḡ.
12 "And the house of Yisra'ěl shall bury
them for seven new *moons*, in order to
cleanse the land.
13 "And all the people of the land shall
bury them, and it shall be for a name to
them on the day that I am esteemed,"
declares the Master יהוה.
14 "And they shall separate men who continually pass through the land, burying
those who were passing through, those left
on the surface of the ground, in order to
cleanse it. At the end of seven new *moons*
they shall search,
15 and those passing through shall pass
through the land, and when anyone sees a
man's bone, he shall set up a sign beside it,
till the buriers have buried it in the Valley
of Hamon Goḡ.
16 "And also a city named Hamonah shall
be there. So they shall cleanse the land." '
17 "And you, son of man, thus said the
Master יהוה, 'Speak to every sort of bird
and to every beast of the field, "Assemble
yourselves and come, gather from all
around to My slaughtering which I am
slaughtering for you, a great slaughtering
on the mountains of Yisra'ěl, and you shall
eat flesh and drink blood.
18 "Eat the flesh of the mighty, drink the
blood of the princes of the earth, of rams
and lambs, of goats and bulls, all of them
fatlings of Bashan.
19 "And you shall eat fat till you are filled,

and drink blood till you are drunk, at My slaughtering which I am slaughtering for you.

20 "And you shall be satisfied at My table with horses and riders, with mighty men and with all the men of battle," declares the Master יהוה.

21 "And I shall set My esteem among the nations. And all nations shall see My judgment which I have executed, and My hand which I have laid on them.

22 "And the house of Yisra'ěl shall know that I am יהוה their Elohim from that day onward.

23 "And the nations shall know that the house of Yisra'ěl went into exile for their crookedness, because they have trespassed against Me, so that I hid My face from them, and I gave them into the hand of their adversaries, and they all fell by the sword.

24 "According to their uncleanness and according to their transgressions I have dealt with them, and hidden My face from them." '

25 "Therefore thus said the Master יהוה, 'Now I am going to bring back the captives of Yaʽaqoḇ. And I shall have compassion on all the house of Yisra'ěl, and shall be jealous for My set-apart Name.

26 'And they shall have borne their shame, and all their trespass they committed against Me, when they dwell safely in their own land, with none to make them afraid,

27 when I have brought them back from the peoples and gathered them out of the lands of their enemies. And I shall be set apart in them before the eyes of many nations.

28 'And they shall know that I am יהוה their Elohim, who sent them into exile among the nations, and then gathered them back to their own land, and left none of them behind.

29 'And no longer do I hide My face from them, for I shall have poured out My Spirit on the house of Yisra'ěl,' declares the Master יהוה."

40 In the twenty-fifth year of our exile, at Rosh [a] haShanah, [b] on the tenth of the new *moon*, in the fourteenth year after the city was stricken, on that same day the hand of יהוה came upon me and He brought me there.

2 In visions of Elohim He brought me into the land of Yisra'ěl and set me on a very high mountain, and upon it toward the south was as the structure of a city.

3 So He brought me there, and look, a man whose appearance was like the appearance of bronze, and a line of flax and a measuring rod in his hand, and he stood in the gateway.

4 And the man said to me, "Son of man, see with your eyes and hear with your ears, and set your heart on all that I am showing you, for you were brought here in order to show them to you. Declare to the house of Yisra'ěl all that you are seeing."

5 And look: a wall all around the outside of the House, and in the man's hand a measuring rod six cubits long, each being a cubit and a handbreadth. And he measured the width of the wall structure, one rod, and the height one rod.

6 Then he came to the gate facing east. And he went up its stairs and measured the threshold of the gate, one rod wide, and the other threshold, one rod wide,

7 and the little room one rod long and one rod wide, and between the little rooms a space of five cubits. And the threshold of the gate inwards from the porch of the gate was one rod.

8 Then he measured the porch of the inside gate, one rod.

9 And he measured the porch of the gate, eight cubits, and its posts two cubits. And the porch of the gate was on the inside.

10 And the little rooms of the east gate three on one side and three on the other, all three of the same size. And posts were of the same size on this side and that side.

11 And he measured the width of the entrance of the gate, ten cubits, and the length of the gate thirteen cubits.

12 And the border in front of the little

40a - Head. *40b Of* the year.

rooms, one cubit on this side and one cubit
on that side. And the gate room was six
cubits on this side and six cubits on that
side.
13 And he measured the gate from the roof
of one little room to the roof of the other,
the width was twenty-five cubits, door to
door.
14 And he measured the posts, sixty cubits
high, even to the post of the courtyard all
around the gate.
15 And from the front of the entrance gate
to the front of the porch of the inner gate
was fifty cubits.
16 And there were narrowed window
frames in the little rooms and to their posts
at the inside of the gate all around, and for
the porches too. And there were windows
all around on the inside. And on each post
were palm trees.
17 And he brought me into the outer courtyard, and look, rooms and a pavement
made all around the courtyard, thirty
rooms on the pavement.
18 And the pavement was by the side of
the gates, equal to the length of the gates –
the lower pavement.
19 And he measured the width from the
front of the lower gate to the front of the
inner courtyard on the outside, one hundred cubits toward the east and the north.
20 And the gate of the outer courtyard
facing north he measured its length and its
width.
21 And its little rooms, three on this side
and three on that side, its posts and its
porches, had the same measurements as
the first gate, its length was fifty cubits and
its width twenty-five cubits.
22 And its windows and its porches, and
its palm trees, had the same measurements
as the gate facing east. And they went up
to it by seven steps, and its porch was in
front of it.
23 And the gate of the inner courtyard was
opposite the northern gate, and at the
eastern gate. And he measured from gate
to gate, one hundred cubits.
24 And he took me toward the south, and
look, a gate toward the south. And he measured its posts and porches according to
these measurements.
25 And windows were in it and in its
porches all around like those windows, its
length was fifty cubits and its width twenty-five cubits.
26 And seven steps led up to it, and its
porch was in front of them. And it had
palm trees on its posts, one on this side and
one on that side.
27 And the inner courtyard had a gate
toward the south. And he measured from
gate to gate toward the south, one hundred
cubits.
28 And he brought me to the inner courtyard through the south gate, and he measured the southern gate according to these
measurements.
29 And its little rooms, and its posts, and
its porches were according to these measurements. And windows were in it and in
its porches all around – fifty cubits long
and twenty-five cubits wide.
30 And there were porches all around,
twenty-five cubits long and five cubits
wide.
31 And its porches were toward the outer
courtyard, and palm trees were on its posts,
and eight steps led up to it.
32 And he brought me into the inner courtyard toward the east, and he measured the
gate according to these measurements.
33 And its little rooms, and its posts, and
its porches were according to these measurements. And windows were in it and in
its porches all around – fifty cubits long
and twenty-five cubits wide.
34 And its porches were toward the outer
courtyard, and palm trees were on its posts
on this side and on that side, and eight
steps led up to it.
35 And he brought me to the north gate,
and he measured it according to these
measurements,
36 its little rooms, its posts, and its porches. And it had windows all around, its
length was fifty cubits and its width twenty-five cubits.
37 And its posts were toward the outer
courtyard, and palm trees were on its posts
on this side and on that side, and eight
steps led up to it.

38 And there was a room with its entrance
by the posts of the gate, where they
washed the ascending offering.
39 And in the porch of the gate were two
tables on this side and two tables on that
side, on which to slay the ascending offering, and the sin offering, and the guilt
offering.
40 And on the outer side, as one went up
to the entrance of the north gate, were two
tables. And on the other side of the porch
of the gate were two tables.
41 Four tables were on this side and four
tables on that side, by the side of the gate,
eight tables on which they slew.
42 And there were four tables of hewn
stone for the ascending offering, one cubit
and a half long, one cubit and a half wide,
and one cubit high. On these they placed
the instruments with which they slew the
ascending offering and the slaughterings.
43 And the double hooks, a handbreadth
wide, were fastened all around. And on the
tables was the flesh of the offerings.
44 And on the outside of the inner gate
were the rooms for the singers in the inner
courtyard, one at the side of the north gate
and facing south, and the other at the side
of the south gate facing north.
45 And he said to me, "This room facing
south is for the priests who guard the duty
of the House.
46 "And the room facing north is for the
priests who guard the duty of the slaughter-place, they are the sons of Tsaḏoq, from
the sons of Lěwi, who come near יהוה to
serve Him."
47 And he measured the courtyard, one
hundred cubits long and one hundred
cubits wide, a square. And the slaughter-
place was in front of the House.
48 And he brought me to the porch of the
House and measured the doorposts of the
porch, five cubits on this side and five
cubits on that side. And the width of the
gate was three cubits on this side and three
cubits on that side.
49 The length of the porch was twenty
cubits, and the width eleven cubits. And by
the steps which led up to it there were
columns by the doorposts, one on this side
and one on that side.

41

1 And he brought me into the Hěḵal,
and he measured the doorposts, six
cubits wide on one side and six cubits wide
on the other side, the width of the Tent.
2 And the entrance was ten cubits wide,
and the side walls of the entrance were five
cubits on this side and five cubits on the
other side. And he measured its length,
forty cubits, and twenty cubits wide.
3 And he went inside and measured the
doorposts, two cubits, and the entrance six
cubits high, and the width of the entrance
seven cubits.
4 And he measured the length, twenty
cubits, and the width twenty cubits, to the
front of the Hěḵal. And he said to me,
"This is the Most Set-apart Place."
5 And he measured the wall of the
House, six cubits, and the width of each
side room all around the House was four
cubits on every side.
6 And the side rooms were on three *levels*, one above the other, thirty rooms on
each *level*, they rested on ledges which
were for the side rooms all around, to be
supported, but not fastened to the wall of
the House.
7 And there was a broadening and a
winding upwards for the side rooms, for
the winding around the House went up like
steps. And the width of the structure
increased as one went up from the lowest
level to the highest by way of the middle
one.
8 And I saw the height all around the
House: the foundation of the side rooms, a
rod's length of six cubits.
9 The thickness of the outer wall of the
side rooms was five cubits, and that which
was left between the side rooms of the
House
10 and the rooms was a width of twenty
cubits all around the House on every side.
11 And the door of the side room was
toward the open space, one door toward
the north and another toward the south.
And the width of the place of the open
space was five cubits all around.
12 And the building that was in front of

the separate place at the side toward the west was seventy cubits wide, and the wall of the building was five cubits thick all around, and its length ninety cubits.

13 Then he measured the House, one hundred cubits long. And the separate place with the building and its walls, were one hundred cubits long,

14 and the width of the front of the House, and of the separate place eastward, was one hundred cubits.

15 And he measured the length of the building to the front of the separate place behind it, and its galleries on the one side and on the other side, one hundred cubits, as well as the inner Hěḵal and the porches of the courtyard.

16 The doorposts and the narrowed window frames, and the galleries all around, their three *levels* opposite the threshold, were panelled with wood. From the ground to the windows, and the windows were covered,

17 from the space above the door, even to the inner house, as well as outside, and on every wall all around, inside and outside, by measure.

18 And it was made with kerubim and palm trees, and a palm tree between kerub and kerub. A kerub had two faces,

19 so that the face of a man was toward a palm tree on one side, and the face of a young lion toward a palm tree on the other side – made on all the House all around.

20 From the floor to the space above the door, and on the wall of the Hěḵal, kerubim and palm trees were carved.

21 The doorposts of the Hěḵal were square, and the front of the set-apart place, the appearance of one was like the appearance of the other.

22 The slaughter-place was of wood, three cubits high, and its length two cubits. And its corners, and its length, and its sides were of wood. And he said to me, "This is the table that is before יהוה."

23 And the Hěḵal and the set-apart place had two doors.

24 And each of the doors had two panels, two folding panels, two panels for one door and two panels for the other door.

25 And kerubim and palm trees were carved on the doors of the Hěḵal, like those carved on the walls. And thick wood was on the front of the porch outside.

26 And narrowed window frames and palm trees were on one side and on the other, on the sides of the porch, and on the side rooms of the House, and thick wood.

42 And he brought me out into the outer courtyard, the way toward the north. And he brought me into the room which was opposite the separate place, and which was opposite the building to the north.

2 Along the length which was one hundred cubits, was the north door, the width was fifty cubits.

3 Opposite the inner courtyard of twenty *cubits*, and opposite the pavement of the outer courtyard, gallery against gallery in three *levels*.

4 And before the rooms, toward the inside, was a walk ten cubits wide, a way of one cubit. And their doors were to the north.

5 And the upper rooms were shorter, because the galleries took away space from them more than from the lower and middle *levels* of the building.

6 For they were in three *levels* and had no columns like the columns of the courtyards, so the upper *level* was set back more than the lower and middle *levels* from the ground up.

7 As for the outer wall by the side of the rooms, toward the outer courtyard facing the rooms, its length was fifty cubits.

8 For the length of the rooms toward the outer courtyard was fifty cubits, and that facing the Hěḵal was one hundred cubits.

9 And below these rooms was the entrance on the east side, as one enters them from the outer courtyard.

10 In the thickness of the wall of the courtyard toward the east, opposite the separate place and opposite the building, were rooms.

11 And the way in front of them was like the appearance of the rooms which were toward the north, as long and as wide as

the others, and all their exits and entrances were according to plan.

12 And according to the doors of the rooms that were toward the south, there was a door in front of the way, the way in front of the wall toward the east, as one enters them.

13 And he said to me, "The north rooms and the south rooms, which are opposite the separate place, are the set-apart rooms where the priests who approach יהוה eat the most set-apart offerings. There they place the most set-apart *items*, and the grain offering, and the sin offering, and the guilt offering, for the place is set-apart.

14 "When the priests enter, they are not to go out of the set-apart room into the outer courtyard, but leave their garments in which they attend there, for they are set-apart, and shall put on other garments and shall draw near to that which is for the people."

15 And when he had ended measuring the inner House, he brought me out through the gate that faces east, and measured it all around.

16 He measured the east side with the measuring rod, five hundred rods by the measuring rod all around.

17 He measured the north side, five hundred rods by the measuring rod all around.

18 He measured the south side, five hundred rods by the measuring rod.

19 He turned round to the west side and measured five hundred rods by the measuring rod.

20 On the four sides he measured it. It had a wall all around, five hundred *cubits* long and five hundred wide, to separate the set-apart places from the common.

43

And he led me to the gate, the gate facing east.

2 And see, the esteem of the Elohim of Yisra'ěl came from the way of the east. And His voice was like the sound of many waters, and the earth shone from His esteem.

3 And it was like the appearance of the vision which I saw, like the vision which I saw when He came to destroy the city. And the visions were like the vision which I saw by the River Keḇar, and I fell on my face.

4 And the esteem of יהוה came into the House by way of the gate facing east.

5 And the Spirit took me up and brought me into the inner courtyard. And see, the esteem of יהוה filled the House.

6 And I heard someone speaking to me from the House, while a man stood beside me.

7 And He said to me, "Son of man, this is the place of My throne and the place of the soles of My feet, when I dwell in the midst of the children of Yisra'ěl forever, and the house of Yisra'ěl shall no longer defile My set-apart Name, they nor their sovereigns, by their whoring and by the corpses of their sovereigns on their high places.

8 "When they placed their threshold by My threshold, and their doorpost by My doorpost, with a wall between them and Me, they defiled My set-apart Name by the abominations which they have done. So I consumed them in My displeasure.

9 "Now let them put their whoring and the corpses of their sovereigns far away from Me, and I shall dwell in their midst forever.

10 "Son of man, explain the House to the house of Yisra'ěl, and when they are ashamed of their crookednesses, they shall measure the measurements.

11 "And since they shall be ashamed of all that they did, make known to them the design of the House and its structure, and its exits and its entrances, its entire design and all its laws, and all its forms and all its Torot. And write it down before their eyes, so that they observe its entire design and all its laws, and shall do them.

12 "This is the Torah of the House: Upon the mountaintop, all the boundary of it, all around, is most set-apart. See, this is the Torah of the House.

13 "And these are the measurements of the slaughter-place in cubits, that cubit being one cubit and a handbreadth, and the base one cubit high and one cubit wide, with a rim all around its edge of one span. And this is the upper part of the slaughter-place.

14 “And from the base on the ground
to the lower ledge, two cubits, and the
width of the ledge one cubit, and from the
smaller ledge to the larger ledge four
cubits, and the width of the ledge one
cubit.
15 “And the slaughter-place hearth is four
cubits high, and four horns extending
upward from the hearth.
16 “And the slaughter-place hearth is
twelve cubits long, and twelve wide,
square at its four corners.
17 “And the ledge is fourteen long and
fourteen wide on its four sides, with a rim
of half a cubit around it, and its base one
cubit all around, and its steps face east.”
18 And He said to me, “Son of man, thus
said the Master יהוה, ‘These are the laws
for the slaughter-place on the day when it
is made, for offering ascending offerings
on it, and for sprinkling blood on it.
19 ‘And you shall give a young bull for a
sin offering to the priests, the Lěwites, who
are of the seed of Tsaḏoq, who approach
unto Me,’ declares the Master יהוה.
20 ‘And you shall take some of its blood
and put it on the four horns of the slaughter-place, on the four corners of the ledge,
and on the rim around it, and shall cleanse
it and make atonement for it.
21 ‘And you shall take the bull of the sin
offering, and shall burn it in the appointed
place of the House, outside the set-apart
place.
22 ‘And on the second day you bring a
male goat, a perfect one, for a sin offering.
And they shall cleanse the slaughter-place,
as they cleansed it with the bull.
23 ‘When you have ended cleansing it,
bring a young bull, a perfect one, and a
ram from the flock, a perfect one.
24 ‘And you shall bring them before יהוה,
and the priests shall throw salt on them and
offer them up as an ascending offering to
יהוה.
25 ‘Prepare a goat for a sin offering daily
for seven days, and prepare a young bull
and a ram from the flock, perfect ones.
26 ‘For seven days they shall make atonement for the slaughter-place and cleanse it,
and ordain it.
27 ‘And when these days are completed it
shall be, on the eighth day and thereafter,
that the priests make your ascending offerings and your peace offerings on the
slaughter-place, and I shall accept you,’
declares the Master יהוה.”

44

And He brought me back to the
outer gate of the set-apart place
which faces east, and it was shut.
2 And יהוה said to me, “This gate is shut,
it is not opened, and no one enters it,
because יהוה Elohim of Yisra’ěl has
entered by it, and it shall be shut.
3 “The prince, as prince, he sits in it to
eat bread before יהוה, coming in by way of
the porch of the gate, and going out the
same way.”
4 And He brought me by way of the north
gate to the front of the House. And I
looked and saw the esteem of יהוה filled
the House of יהוה, and I fell on my face.
5 And יהוה said to me, “Son of man, set
your heart and see with your eyes and hear
with your ears, all that I say to you concerning all the laws of the House of יהוה
and all its Torot. And you shall set your
heart to the entrance of the house, with all
the exits of the set-apart place,
6 and shall say to the rebellious, to the
house of Yisra’ěl, ‘Thus said the Master
יהוה, “O house of Yisra’ěl, enough of all
these abominations of yours,
7 that you brought in sons of a foreigner,
uncircumcised in heart and uncircumcised
in flesh, to be in My set-apart place to profane it, My house! That you brought near
My food, the fat and the blood, and you
broke My covenant because of all your
abominations.
8 “And you did not guard the charge of
that which is set-apart to Me, but you have
set others to guard the charge of My set-
apart place for you.”
9 ‘Thus said the Master יהוה, “No son of
a foreigner, uncircumcised in heart or
uncircumcised in flesh, comes into My set-
apart place, even any son of a foreigner
who is among the children of Yisra’ěl.
10 “And the Lěwites who went far from
Me, when Yisra’ěl went astray, who

strayed away from Me after their idols,
they shall bear their crookedness.
11 "And they were attendants in My set-
apart place, as gatekeepers of the house
and attendants of the house, slaying the
ascending offering and the slaughtering for
the people, and standing before them to
attend to them.
12 "Because they attended to them before
their idols and became a stumbling-block
of crookedness to the house of Yisra'ěl,
therefore I have lifted My hand in an oath
against them," declares the Master יהוה,
"that they shall bear their crookedness,
13 and not come near Me to serve as My
priest, nor come near any of that which is
set-apart to Me, nor into the Most Set-apart
Place. And they shall bear their shame and
their abominations which they have done.
14 "Yet I shall make them those who
guard the duty of the House, for all its
work, and for all that has to be done in it.
15 "But the priests, the Lěwites, the sons
of Tsaḏoq, who guarded the duty of My
set-apart place when the children of
Yisra'ěl went astray from Me, they shall
draw near to Me to serve Me, and shall
stand before Me to bring to Me the fat and
the blood," declares the Master יהוה.
16 "They shall enter My set-apart place,
and they shall draw near to My table to
serve Me, and they shall guard My charge.
17 "And it shall be, when they enter the
gates of the inner courtyard, that they put
on linen garments, and no wool shall come
upon them while they attend within the
gates of the inner courtyard or within the
house.
18 "They shall have linen turbans on their
heads and linen trousers on their bodies,
they shall not gird themselves with sweat.
19 "And when they go out to the outer
courtyard, to the outer courtyard to the
people, they shall take off their garments in
which they have attended, and shall leave
them in the set-apart rooms, and shall put
on other garments. And they shall set apart
the people in their set-apart garments.
20 "And their heads they shall not shave,
nor shall they let their hair grow long –
they shall keep their hair well trimmed.
21 "And no priest is to drink wine when he
comes into the inner court.
22 "And they do not take as wife a widow
or a divorced woman, but take maidens of
the seed of the house of Yisra'ěl, or widows of priests.
23 "And they are to teach My people the
difference between the set-apart and the
profane, and make them know what is
unclean and clean.
24 "And they are to stand as judges in a
dispute, and judge it according to My
right-rulings. And they are to guard My
Torot and My laws in all My appointed
festivals, and set apart My Sabbaths.
25 "And they are not to defile themselves
by coming near a dead man. Only for a
father or mother, for a son or daughter, for
a brother or unmarried sister they defile
themselves.
26 "And after his cleansing, they count
seven days for him,
27 and on the day that he comes into the
inner court of the set-apart place to attend
in the set-apart place, he brings his sin
offering," declares the Master יהוה.
28 "And it shall be to them for an inheritance, I am their inheritance. And you give
them no possession in Yisra'ěl – I am their
possession.
29 "The grain offering, and the sin offering, and the guilt offering they are to eat,
and all that is dedicated in Yisra'ěl is
theirs.
30 "And the first of all the first-fruits of
all, and every contribution of all, of all
your contributions, belong to the priests.
And the first of your ground meal you give
to the priest, so that a blessing rests on
your house.
31 "The priests are not to eat any bird or
beast found dead or torn to pieces.

45 "And when you divide the land by
lot into inheritance, offer a contribution to יהוה, a set-apart portion of the
land, in length twenty-five thousand *cubits*
long, and in width ten thousand, this being
set-apart throughout its border all around.
2 "Of this a square plot is to be for the
set-apart place, five hundred by five

hundred, with fifty cubits around it for an
open space.
3 "And from this measure you are to
measure: twenty-five thousand *cubits* long
and ten thousand wide. And in it is to be
the set-apart place, the Most Set-apart
Place.
4 "This is to be a set-apart portion of the
land, belonging to the priests, the attendants of the set-apart place, who draw near
to serve יהוה. And it shall be a place for
their houses and set-apart ground for the
set-apart place.
5 "And twenty-five thousand *cubits* in
length and ten thousand in width is for the
Lěwites, the attendants of the House, for
them for a possession, twenty rooms.
6 "And give the city as possession: five
thousand *cubits* wide and twenty-five
thousand long, beside the contribution of
the set-apart portion – it belongs to all the
house of Yisra'ěl.
7 "And the prince is to have a portion on
one side and the other of the set-apart contribution and of the possession of the city.
And bordering on the set-apart contribution and the possession of the city, on the
west side westward and on the east side
eastward, and the length alongside one of
the portions, from the west border to the
east border.
8 "Of the land this is his possession in
Yisra'ěl, and My princes shall no longer
oppress My people. And they shall give
the land to the house of Yisra'ěl, according
to their tribes."
9 'Thus said the Master יהוה, "Enough,
you princes of Yisra'ěl! Put away violence
and plundering, and do right-ruling and
righteousness, and stop your evictions of
My people," declares the Master יהוה.
10 "Have right scales, and a right ěphah,
and a right bath.
11 "Let the ěphah and the bath be of the
same measure, so that the bath contains
one-tenth of a ḥomer, and the ěphah one-
tenth of a ḥomer. Let their measure be
according to the ḥomer.
12 "And the sheqel is twenty gěrahs. Your
mina is twenty sheqels, twenty-five
sheqels, fifteen sheqels.
13 "This is the contribution which you
present: you shall give one-sixth of an
ěphah from a ḥomer of wheat, and one-
sixth of an ěphah from a ḥomer of barley.
14 "And the law concerning oil, the bath
of oil, is one-tenth of a bath from a kor. A
kor is a ḥomer or ten baths, for ten baths
are a ḥomer.
15 "And one lamb from a flock, from two
hundred, from the watered pastures of
Yisra'ěl, for grain offerings, and for an
ascending offering, and for peace offerings, to make atonement for them,"
declares the Master יהוה.
16 "All the people of the land are to give
this contribution to the prince in Yisra'ěl.
17 "And on the prince are the ascending
offerings, and the grain offerings, and
drink offerings, at the festival, the new
moons, the sabbaths – in all the appointed
times of the house of Yisra'ěl. He is to prepare the sin offering, and the grain offering, and the ascending offering, and the
peace offerings to make atonement for the
house of Yisra'ěl."
18 'Thus said the Master יהוה, "In the first
month, on the first of the new *moon*, you
are to take a young bull, a perfect one, and
shall cleanse the set-apart place.
19 "And the priest shall take some of the
blood of the sin offering and put it on the
doorposts of the House, on the four corners
of the ledge of the slaughter-place, and on
the posts of the gate of the inner courtyard.
20 "And do the same on the seventh of the
new *moon* for anyone who makes a mistake or is foolish. And you shall make
atonement for the House.
21 "In the first *month*, on the fourteenth
day of the new *moon*, you have the Pěsaḥ,
a festival of seven days, unleavened bread
is eaten.
22 "And on that day the prince shall prepare for himself and for all the people of
the land a bull for a sin offering.
23 "And *during* the seven days of the festival he prepares an ascending offering to
יהוה, seven bulls and seven rams, perfect
ones, daily for seven days, and a male goat
daily for a sin offering.
24 "And he prepares a grain offering of

one ěphah for each bull and one ěphah for each ram, together with a hin of oil for each ěphah.

25 "In the seventh *month*, on the fifteenth day of the new *moon*, at the festival, he prepares like these seven days, as the sin offering, as the ascending offering, as the grain offering, and as the oil."

46 'Thus said the Master יהוה, "The gate of the inner courtyard facing east is shut the six days of work, but on the sabbath it is opened, and on the day of the new *moon* it is opened.

2 "And the prince shall enter by way of the porch of that gate from the outside, and he shall stand by the post. And the priests shall prepare his ascending offering and his peace offerings. And he shall bow himself at the threshold of the gate, and shall go out, but the gate is not shut until evening.

3 "And the people of the land shall also bow themselves at the entrance to this gate before יהוה, on the sabbaths and on the new *moons*.

4 "And the ascending offering which the prince brings to יהוה on the sabbath day is six lambs, perfect ones, and a ram, a perfect one.

5 "And the grain offering is one ěphah for a ram, and the grain offering for the lambs, a gift of his hand, and a hin of oil for an ěphah.

6 "And on the day of the new *moon*: a young bull, a perfect one, six lambs, and a ram, they should be perfect.

7 "And he prepares a grain offering of an ěphah for a bull, and an ěphah for a ram, and for the lambs as his hand attains, and a hin of oil for an ěphah.

8 "And when the prince enters, he comes in by way of the porch of that gate, and goes out the same way.

9 "And when the people of the land enter before יהוה at the appointed times, whoever shall enter by way of the north gate to bow himself, goes out by way of the south gate. And whoever enters by way of the south gate, goes out by way of the north gate, he shall not return by way of the gate through which he came, but goes out through the opposite one.

10 "And the prince is to be in their midst, entering when they enter, and going out when they go out.

11 "And in the festivals and in the appointed times the grain offering is an ěphah for a bull, and an ěphah for a ram, and for lambs the gift of his hand, and a hin of oil for an ěphah.

12 "And when the prince makes a spontaneous ascending offering or spontaneous peace offerings to יהוה, the gate facing east shall be opened for him. And he shall prepare his ascending offering and his peace offerings as he did on the Sabbath day. And he shall go out, and after he goes out the gate shall be shut.

13 "And make a daily ascending offering to יהוה of a lamb a year old, a perfect one, preparing it morning by morning.

14 "And prepare a grain offering with it morning by morning, a sixth of an ěphah, and a third of a hin of oil to moisten the fine flour, a grain offering to יהוה – continual everlasting laws.

15 "And prepare the lamb, and the grain offering, and the oil, morning by morning, a continual ascending offering."

16 'Thus said the Master יהוה, "When the prince gives a gift of some of his inheritance to any of his sons, it belongs to his sons, it is their possession by inheritance.

17 "And when he gives a gift of some of his inheritance to one of his servants, then it shall be his till the year of release, then it shall return to the prince. Only the inheritance of his sons is theirs.

18 "And the prince does not take any of the people's inheritance by evicting them from their possession. He is to give his sons their inheritance from his own possession, so that none of My people are separated from his possession." ' "

19 And he brought me through the entrance, which was at the side of the gate, into the set-apart rooms of the priests facing north. And look, there was a place at the extreme rear toward the west.

20 And he said to me, "This is the place where the priests cook the guilt offering

and the sin offering, where they bake the
grain offering, so as not to bring them out
into the outer courtyard to set the people
apart."
21 And he brought me out into the outer
courtyard and made me pass along to the
four corners of the courtyard. And look, in
every corner of the courtyard was another
courtyard.
22 In the four corners of the courtyard
were courtyards covered over, forty cubits
long and thirty wide, these four corners
having one measure,
23 and a row of building stones all around
in them, all around the four of them, and
places for fire were made under the rows,
all around.
24 And he said to me, "These are the
kitchens where the attendants of the House
cook the slaughterings of the people."

47 And he turned me back to the door
of the House. And look, water was
flowing from under the threshold of the
House toward the east, for the House faced
east, and the water was flowing from under
the right side of the House, from the south
of the slaughter-place.
2 And he led me out by way of the north
gate, and took me round on the outside to
the outer gate facing east. And look, water
trickling out on the right side.
3 As the man went out to the east with the
line in his hand, he measured one thousand
cubits, and he made me pass over into
water, water to the ankles.
4 And he measured one thousand and
made me pass over into water, water to the
knees. And he measured one thousand and
made me pass over, water to the loins.
5 And he measured one thousand, a
stream that I was unable to pass over, for
the water had risen, water to swim, a
stream that is not passed over.
6 And he said to me, "Son of man, have
you seen this?" And he led me and brought
me back to the bank of the stream.
7 When I returned, then look, along the
bank of the stream were very many trees
on one side and the other.
8 And he said to me, "These waters are
flowing toward the eastern country, and go
down into the Araḇah, and enter the sea,
being made to flow into the sea, and the
waters shall be healed.
9 "And it shall be that every swarming
creature, wherever the stream goes, shall
live. And there shall be very many fish, for
these waters shall go there, and they are
healed. And wherever the stream flows all
shall live.
10 "And it shall be that fishermen stand
along it, from Ěn Geḏi to Ěn Eğlayim,
being places for spreading their nets. Their
fish is to be of the same kind as the fish of
the Great Sea, very many.
11 "Its swamps and marshes shall not be
healed, they shall be given over to salt.
12 "And by the bank of the stream, on
both sides, grow all kinds of trees used for
food, whose leaves do not wither and fruit
do not fail. They bear fruit every new
moon, because their water flows from the
set-apart place. And their fruit shall be for
food, and their leaves for healing."
13 Thus said the Master יהוה, "This is the
border by which you inherit the land,
according to the twelve tribes of Yisra'ěl,
two portions for Yosěph.
14 "And you shall inherit it, each one the
same as his brother. For I lifted My hand in
an oath to give it to your fathers, and this
land shall fall to you as your inheritance.
15 "And this is the border of the land on
the north: from the Great Sea, the way of
Ḥethlon, as one goes to Tseḏaḏ,
16 "Ḥamath, Běrothah, Siḇrayim, which is
between the border of Dammeseq and the
border of Ḥamath, Ḥatsar Hattiḵon, which
is on the border of Ḥawran.
17 "And the border shall be from the Sea
to Ḥatsar Ěnan, the border of Dammeseq,
and on the north toward the north is the
border of Ḥamath. This is the north side.
18 "And the east side is from between
Ḥawran, and Dammeseq, and Gil'aḏ, and
the land of Yisra'ěl; the Yarděn, from the
border to the eastern side of the sea you are

47a Yesh. 14:1, Yesh. 56:6-8, Rom. 11:17-26, Eph. 2:19, Eph. 3:6, Ḥazon 21:12.

to measure. This is the east side.
19 “And the south side toward the South is
from Tamar to the waters of Meriḇah by
Qaḏěsh, along the Wadi to the Great Sea.
This is the south side toward the South.
20 “And the west side is the Great Sea,
from the border to the point opposite
Ḥamath. This is the west side.
21 “And you shall divide this land among
yourselves according to the tribes of Yisra'ěl.
22 “And it shall be that you divide it by lot
as an inheritance for yourselves, and for
the strangers who sojourn in your midst
and who bear children among you. And
they shall be to you as native-born among
the children of Yisra'ěl – with you they
have an inheritance in the midst of the
tribes of Yisra'ěl. [a]
23 “And it shall be that in whatever tribe
the stranger sojourns, there you give him
his inheritance,” declares the Master יהוה.

48 “And these are the names of the
tribes: From the north end along
the way to Ḥethlon at the entrance of
Ḥamath, to Ḥatsar Ěnan, the border of
Dammeseq northward by the side of
Ḥamath, from its east to its west side, Dan:
one.
2 “And by the border of Dan, from the
east side to the west, Ashěr: one.
3 “And by the border of Ashěr, from the
east side to the west, Naphtali: one.
4 “And by the border of Naphtali, from
the east side to the west, Menashsheh: one.
5 “And by the border of Menashsheh,
from the east side to the west, Ephrayim:
one.
6 “And by the border of Ephrayim, from
the east side to the west, Re'uḇěn: one.
7 “And by the border of Re'uḇěn, from
the east side to the west, Yehuḏah: one.
8 “And by the border of Yehuḏah, from
the east side to the west, is the contribution
which you offer up, twenty-five thousand
cubits in width, and in length the same as
one of the portions, from the east side to
the west, with the set-apart place in its
midst.
9 “The contribution that you offer up to
יהוה is twenty-five thousand *cubits* in
length and ten thousand in width.
10 “And of these is the set-apart contribution for the priests: on the north twenty-
five thousand *cubits*, and on the west ten
thousand in width, and on the east ten
thousand in width, and on the south twenty-five thousand in length. And the set-
apart place of יהוה shall be in its midst –
11 for the priests of the sons of Tsaḏoq,
who are set-apart, who did guard My
Charge, who did not go astray when the
children of Yisra'ěl went astray, as the
Lěwites went astray.
12 “So this contribution shall be to them,
from the contribution of the land, a most
set-apart place by the border of the
Lěwites.
13 “And alongside the border of the
priests, the Lěwites have twenty-five thousand *cubits* in length and ten thousand in
width, its entire length is twenty-five thousand and its width ten thousand.
14 “And they do not sell any of it, nor
exchange it, nor transfer this best part of
the land, for it is set-apart to יהוה.
15 “And the five thousand *cubits* in width
that is left, facing the twenty-five thousand, is for common use by the city, for
dwellings and open land. And the city shall
be in its midst.
16 “And these are its measurements: the
north side four thousand five hundred
cubits, and the south side four thousand
five hundred, and the east side four thousand five hundred, and the west side four
thousand five hundred.
17 “And the open land of the city shall be:
to the north two hundred and fifty *cubits*,
and to the south two hundred and fifty, and
to the east two hundred and fifty, and to the
west two hundred and fifty.
18 “And the rest of the length, alongside
the contribution of the set-apart portion, is
ten thousand *cubits* to the east and ten
thousand to the west. And it shall be alongside the contribution of the set-apart
portion, and its increase shall be food for
the workers of the city.
19 “And the workers of the city, from all
the tribes of Yisra'ěl, shall till it.

20 "The entire contribution is twenty-five thousand *cubits* by twenty-five thousand cubits, foursquare. You are to offer up the set-apart contribution with the possession of the city.
21 "And the rest is for the prince, on one side and on the other of the set-apart contribution and of the possession of the city, facing the twenty-five thousand *cubits* of the set-apart contribution as far as the eastern border, and westward facing the twenty-five thousand as far as the western border, alongside the portions of the prince. And the set-apart contribution, and the set-apart place of the House shall be in its midst.
22 "So the possession of the Lěwites and the possession of the city are in the midst of what belongs to the prince – between the border of Yehuḏah and the border of Binyamin, it belongs to the prince.
23 "As for the rest of the tribes, from the east side to the west side, Binyamin: one.
24 "And by the border of Binyamin, from the east side to the west side, Shimʽon: one.
25 "And by the border of Shimʽon, from the east side to the west side, Yissasḵar: one.
26 "And by the border of Yissasḵar, from the east side to the west side, Zeḇulun: one.
27 "And by the border of Zeḇulun, from the east side to the west side, Gaḏ: one.
28 "And by the border of Gaḏ, on the south side toward the South, the border shall be from Tamar to the waters of Meriḇah by Qaḏěsh, along the Wadi to the Great Sea.
29 "This is the land which you divide by lot as an inheritance among the tribes of Yisra'ěl, and these are their portions," declares the Master יהוה.
30 "And these are the exits of the city, the gates of the city according to the names of the tribes of Yisra'ěl: [a] On the north side, measuring four thousand five hundred *cubits*,
31 the three gates northward: one gate for Re'uḇěn, one gate for Yehuḏah, one gate for Lěwi.
32 "And on the east side, four thousand five hundred *cubits*, three gates: one gate for Yosěph, one gate for Binyamin, one gate for Dan.
33 "And on the south side, measuring four thousand five hundred *cubits*, three gates: one gate for Shimʽon, one gate for Yissasḵar, one gate for Zeḇulun.
34 "And on the west side, four thousand five hundred *cubits* with their three gates: one gate for Gaḏ, one gate for Ashěr, one gate for Naphtali.
35 "All around: eighteen thousand cubits. And the name of the city from that day is: יהוה is there!" [b]

48a See 47:22-23, Ḥazon 21:12. *48b* In Hebrew: יהוה Shammah. See also 43:7 & 9.

DANI'ĚL

1 In the third year of the reign of
Yehoyaqim, sovereign of Yehuḏah,
Neḇuḵaḏnetstsar, sovereign of Baḇel came
to Yerushalayim and besieged it.
2 And יהוה gave Yehoyaqim sovereign of
Yehuḏah into his hand, with some of the
utensils of the House of Elohim, which he
brought to the land of Shinʽar to the house
of his mighty one. And he brought the
utensils into the treasure house of his
mighty one.
3 And the sovereign said to Ashpenaz,
the chief of his eunuchs, to bring some of
the children of Yisra'ěl and some of the
sovereign's descendants and some of the
nobles,
4 young men in whom there was no blemish, but good-looking, having insight in all
wisdom, having knowledge and understanding learning, capable to stand in the
sovereign's palace, and to teach them the
writing and speech of the Kasdim.
5 And the sovereign appointed for them
a daily ration of the sovereign's food and
of the wine which he drank, and three years
of training for them, so that at the end
thereof they should stand before the sovereign.
6 Now among them were from the sons of
Yehuḏah: Dani'ěl, Ḥananyah, Misha'ěl,
and Azaryah.
7 And the chief of the eunuchs gave them
names. For he called Dani'ěl, Bělteshatstsar; and Ḥananyah, Shaḏraḵ; and
Misha'ěl, Měyshaḵ; and Azaryah, Aḇěḏ-
Neḡo.
8 But Dani'ěl laid it upon his heart
that he would not defile himself with the
portion of the sovereign's food, nor with
the wine which he drank. So he asked *permission* from the chief of the eunuchs not
to defile himself.
9 And Elohim granted Dani'ěl loving-
commitment and compassion from the
chief of the eunuchs,
10 but the chief of the eunuchs said to
Dani'ěl, "I fear my master the sovereign,
who has appointed your food and drink.
For why should he see your faces looking
worse than the young men who are your
age? Then you would make my head guilty
before the sovereign!"
11 And Dani'ěl said to the overseer whom
the chief of the eunuchs had set over
Dani'ěl, Ḥananyah, Misha'ěl, and Azaryah,
12 "Please try your servants for ten days,
and let them give us vegetables to eat and
water to drink.
13 "Then let our appearances be examined
before you, and the appearances of the
young men who eat the portion of the sovereign's food. And do with your servants as
you see fit."
14 And he listened to them in this matter,
and tried them ten days.
15 And at the end of ten days their appearances looked better and fatter in flesh than
all the young men who ate the portion of
the sovereign's food.
16 And it came to be that the overseer took
away their portion of food and the wine
they were to drink, and gave them vegetables.
17 As for these four young men, Elohim
gave them knowledge and skill in all learning and wisdom. And Dani'ěl had understanding in all visions and dreams.
18 And at the end of the days, when the
sovereign had said that they should be
brought in, the chief of the eunuchs
brought them in before Neḇuḵaḏnetstsar.
19 And the sovereign spoke with them,
and none among them all were found like
Dani'ěl, Ḥananyah, Misha'ěl, and Azaryah,
so they stood before the sovereign.
20 And in any word of wisdom and understanding about which the sovereign examined them, he found them ten times better
than all the magicians, the astrologers, who
were in all his reign.

21 And Dani’ěl continued until the first year of Sovereign Koresh.

2 And in the second year of the reign of Neḇuḵaḏnetstsar, Neḇuḵaḏnetstsar had dreams. And his spirit was so troubled that his sleep left him.

2 And the sovereign gave orders to call the magicians, and the astrologers, and the practisers of witchcraft, and the Kasdim to declare to the sovereign his dreams. So they came and stood before the sovereign.

3 And the sovereign said to them, “I have had a dream, and my spirit is troubled to know the dream.”

4 And the Kasdim spoke to the sovereign in Aramaic,[a] “O sovereign, live forever! Relate the dream to your servants, and we shall reveal the interpretation.”

5 The sovereign answered and said to the Kasdim, “My decision is firm: if you do not make known the dream and its interpretation to me, your limbs shall be taken from you, and your houses made dunghills.

6 “But if you reveal the dream and its interpretation, you shall receive gifts, and rewards, and great esteem from me. So reveal to me the dream and its interpretation.”

7 They answered again and said, “Let the sovereign relate to his servants the dream, and we shall reveal its interpretation.”

8 The sovereign answered and said, “I know for certain that you would gain time, because you see that my decision is firm:

9 “If you do not make known the dream to me, there is only one decree for you! For you have agreed to speak lying and corrupt words before me till the time has changed. So relate the dream to me, then I shall know that you shall reveal its interpretation for me.”

10 The Kasdim answered the sovereign, and said, “There is no one on earth who is able to reveal the matter of the sovereign. Because no sovereign, master, or ruler has ever asked a matter like this of any magician, or astrologer, or Kasdim.

11 “And the matter that the sovereign is asking is difficult, and there is no other who is able to reveal it to the sovereign except the elahin, whose dwelling is not with flesh.”

12 Because of this the sovereign was enraged and very wroth, and gave orders to destroy all the wise ones of Baḇel.

13 So the decree went out, and they began killing· the wise ones. And they sought Dani’ěl and his companions, to kill· them.

14 Then with counsel and wisdom Dani’ěl answered Aryoḵ, the chief of the sovereign’s guard, who had gone out to kill· the wise ones of Baḇel –

15 he answered and said to Aryoḵ the sovereign’s officer, “Why is the decree from the sovereign so urgent?” So Aryoḵ made the decision known to Dani’ěl.

16 And Dani’ěl went in and asked the sovereign to give him time, and he would show the sovereign the interpretation.

17 Then Dani’ěl went to his house, and made the decision known to Ḥananyah, Misha’ěl, and Azaryah, his companions,

18 to seek compassion from the Elah of the heavens concerning this secret, so that Dani’ěl and his companions should not perish with the rest of the wise ones of Baḇel.

19 Then the secret was revealed to Dani’ěl in a night vision, and Dani’ěl blessed the Elah of the heavens.

20 Dani’ěl responded and said, “Blessed be the Name of Elah forever and ever, for wisdom and might are His.

21 “And He changes the times and the seasons. He removes sovereigns and raises up sovereigns. He gives wisdom to the wise and knowledge to those who possess understanding.

22 “He reveals deep and secret matters. He knows what is in the darkness, and light dwells with Him.

23 “I thank You and praise You, O Elah of my fathers. You have given me wisdom and might, and have now made known to me what we asked of You, for You have made known to us the sovereign’s matter.”

24 So Dani’ěl went to Aryoḵ, whom the

2a The Aramaic text starts here, chapter 2 verse 4 and ends at chapter 7 verse 28.

sovereign had appointed to destroy the wise ones of Baḇel. He went and said this to him, "Do not destroy the wise ones of Baḇel. Bring me in before the sovereign, and I shall show the interpretation to the sovereign."

25 Then Aryoḵ brought Dani'ěl in a hurry before the sovereign, and said thus to him, "I have found a man among the sons of the exile of Yehuḏah, who does make known to the sovereign the interpretation."

26 The sovereign answered and said to Dani'ěl, whose name was Bělteshatstsar, "Are you able to make known to me the dream which I have seen, and its interpretation?"

27 Dani'ěl answered before the sovereign, and said, "The secret which the sovereign is asking – the wise ones, the astrologers, the magicians, and the diviners are unable to show it to the sovereign.

28 "But there is an Elah in the heavens who reveals secrets, and He has made known to Sovereign Neḇuḵaḏnetstsar what is to be in the latter days. Your dream, and the visions of your head upon your bed, were these:

29 "As for you, O sovereign, on your bed your thoughts came up: What is going to take place after this. And He who reveals secrets has made known to you what shall be *after this*.

30 "As for me, this secret has not been revealed to me because I have more wisdom than anyone living, but for our sakes who make known the interpretation to the sovereign, and that you should know the thoughts of your heart.

31 "You, O sovereign, were looking on, and saw a great image! This great image, and its brightness excellent, was standing before you, and its form was awesome.

32 "This image's head was of fine gold, its chest and arms of silver, its belly and thighs of bronze,

33 its legs of iron, its feet partly of iron and partly of clay.

34 "You were looking on, until a stone was cut out without hands, and it smote the image on its feet of iron and clay, and broke them in pieces.

35 "Then the iron, the clay, the bronze, the silver, and the gold were crushed together, and became like chaff from the summer threshing-floors. And the wind took them away so that no trace of them was found. And the stone that smote the image became a great mountain and filled all the earth.

36 "This is the dream, and its interpretation we declare before the sovereign.

37 "You, O sovereign, are a sovereign of sovereigns. For the Elah of the heavens has given you a reign, power, and strength, and preciousness,

38 and wherever the children of men dwell, or the beasts of the field and the birds of the heavens, He has given them into your hand, and has made you ruler over them all. You are the head of gold.

39 "And after you rises up another reign lower than yours, and another third reign of bronze that rules over all the earth.

40 "And the fourth reign is as strong as iron, because iron crushes and shatters all. So, like iron that breaks in pieces, it crushes and breaks all these.

41 "Yet, as you saw the feet and toes, partly of potter's clay and partly of iron, the reign is to be divided. But some of the strength of the iron is to be in it, because you saw the iron mixed with muddy clay.

42 "And as the toes of the feet were partly of iron and partly of clay, so the reign is partly strong and partly brittle.

43 "And as you saw iron mixed with muddy clay, they are mixing themselves with the seed of men, but they are not clinging to each other, even as iron does not mix with clay.

44 "And in the days of these sovereigns the Elah of the heavens shall set up a reign which shall never be destroyed, nor the reign pass on to other people – it crushes and puts to an end all these reigns, and it shall stand forever. [b]

45 "Because you saw that the stone was cut out of the mountain without hands, and that it crushed the iron, the bronze, the clay,

2b Dan. 7, Teh. 22:28, Yirm. 30:11, Yo'ěl 3:16, Oḇaḏ. 15-17, Ḥaḇ. 3:12-13, Tseph. 3:8, Ḥagg. 2:22, Ḥazon 11:15.

the silver, and the gold, the great Elah has made known to the sovereign what shall be after this. And the dream is true, and its interpretation is trustworthy."

46 Then Sovereign Neḇuḵaḏnetstsar fell on his face, and did obeisance before Dani'ěl, and gave orders to present to him an offering and incense.

47 The sovereign answered Dani'ěl, and said, "Truly your Elah is the Elah of elahin, the Master of sovereigns, and a revealer of secrets, since you were able to reveal this secret."

48 Then the sovereign made Dani'ěl great and gave him many great gifts, and made him ruler over all the province of Baḇel, and chief of the nobles, over all the wise ones of Baḇel.

49 And Dani'ěl asked of the sovereign, and he set Shaḏraḵ, Měyshaḵ, and Aḇěḏ-Neḡo over the work of the province of Baḇel, and Dani'ěl in the gate of the sovereign.

3 Neḇuḵaḏnetstsar the sovereign made an image of gold, whose height was sixty cubits and its width six cubits. He set it up in the plain of Dura, in the province of Baḇel.

2 And Sovereign Neḇuḵaḏnetstsar sent word to gather together the viceroys, the nobles, and the governors, the counsellors, the treasurers, the judges, the magistrates, and all the officials of the provinces, to come to the dedication of the image which Sovereign Neḇuḵaḏnetstsar had set up.

3 Then the viceroys, the nobles, and the governors, the counsellors, the treasurers, the judges, the magistrates, and all the officials of the provinces gathered together for the dedication of the image that Sovereign Neḇuḵaḏnetstsar had set up. And they stood before the image that Neḇuḵaḏnetstsar had set up.

4 Then a herald loudly proclaimed, "To you it is commanded, O peoples, nations, and languages,

5 that as soon as you hear the sound of the horn, the flute, the zither, the lyre, the harp, the pipes, and all kinds of instruments, you shall fall down and do obeisance to the gold image that Sovereign Neḇuḵaḏnetstsar has set up.

6 "And whoever does not fall down and do obeisance is immediately thrown into the midst of a burning furnace of fire."

7 So as soon as all the people heard the sound of the horn, the flute, the zither, the lyre, the harp, all kinds of instruments, all the people, nations, and languages fell down and did obeisance to the gold image that Sovereign Neḇuḵaḏnetstsar had set up.

8 Thereupon, at that time, certain Kasdim came forward and accused the Yehuḏim.

9 They spoke and said to Sovereign Neḇuḵaḏnetstsar, "O sovereign, live forever!

10 "You, O sovereign, have made a decree that everyone who hears the sound of the horn, the flute, the zither, the lyre, the harp, the pipes, and all kinds of instruments, shall fall down and do obeisance to the gold image,

11 and whoever does not fall down and do obeisance is thrown into the midst of a burning furnace of fire.

12 "There are certain Yehuḏim whom you have set over the work of the province of Baḇel: Shaḏraḵ, Měyshaḵ, and Aḇěḏ-Neḡo. These men, O sovereign, pay no heed to you. They do not serve your elahin, and they are not doing obeisance to the gold image which you have set up."

13 Then Neḇuḵaḏnetstsar, in rage and wrath, gave orders to bring Shaḏraḵ, Měyshaḵ, and Aḇěḏ-Neḡo. Then they brought these men before the sovereign.

14 Neḇuḵaḏnetstsar spoke and said to them, "Is it true, Shaḏraḵ, Měyshaḵ, and Aḇěḏ-Neḡo, that you do not serve my elahin, and you do not do obeisance to the gold image which I have set up?

15 "Now if you are ready when you hear the sound of the horn, the flute, the zither, the lyre, the harp, the pipes, and all kinds of instruments, and you fall down and do obeisance to the image which I have made, good! But if you do not do obeisance, you are immediately thrown into the midst of a burning furnace of fire. And who is the elah who does deliver you from my hands?"

16 Shaḏraḵ, Mĕyshaḵ, and Aḇĕḏ-Neḡo answered and said to the sovereign, “O Neḇuḵaḏnetstsar, we have no need to answer you in this matter.

17 “For if so, our Elah whom we serve is able to deliver us from the burning furnace of fire and from your hand, O sovereign – He does deliver!

18 “But if not, let it be known to you, O sovereign, that we do not serve your elahin, nor do we do obeisance to the gold image which you have set up.”

19 Then Neḇuḵaḏnetstsar was filled with wrath, and the expression on his face changed toward Shaḏraḵ, Mĕyshaḵ, and Aḇĕḏ-Neḡo. He responded and gave orders that they heat the furnace seven times more than it was usual to heat it.

20 And he commanded some of the strongest men of his army to bind Shaḏraḵ, Mĕyshaḵ, and Aḇĕḏ-Neḡo, and throw them into the burning furnace of fire.

21 So these men were bound in their coats, their trousers, and their turbans, and their other garments, and were thrown into the midst of the burning furnace of fire.

22 Thereupon, because the sovereign’s order was urgent, and the furnace exceedingly hot, the flame of the fire killed those men who took up Shaḏraḵ, Mĕyshaḵ, and Aḇĕḏ-Neḡo.

23 And these three men, Shaḏraḵ, Mĕyshaḵ, and Aḇĕḏ-Neḡo, fell down bound into the midst of the burning furnace of fire.

24 Then Sovereign Neḇuḵaḏnetstsar was amazed, and stood up in haste and spoke and said to his counsellors, “Did we not throw three men bound into the midst of the fire?” They answered and said to the sovereign, “Certainly, O sovereign.”

25 He answered and said, “Look! I see four men loose, walking in the midst of the fire. And they are not hurt, and the form of the fourth is like the Son of Elah.”

26 Then Neḇuḵaḏnetstsar went near the mouth of the burning furnace of fire. He spoke and said, “Shaḏraḵ, Mĕyshaḵ, and Aḇĕḏ-Neḡo, servants of the Most High Elah, come out, and come here.” Then Shaḏraḵ, Mĕyshaḵ, and Aḇĕḏ-Neḡo came from the midst of the fire.

27 And the viceroys, the nobles, and the governors, and the sovereign’s counsellors gathered together, seeing these men on whose bodies the fire had no power, and the hair of their head was not singed nor were their garments changed, nor did the smell of fire come on them.

28 Neḇuḵaḏnetstsar responded and said, “Blessed be the Elah of Shaḏraḵ, Mĕyshaḵ, and Aḇĕḏ-Neḡo, who sent His Messenger and delivered His servants who trusted in Him, and changed the sovereign’s order, and gave up their bodies, that they should not serve nor do obeisance to any elah except their own Elah!

29 “Therefore I make a decree that whoever of any people, nation, or language who speaks any wrong against the Elah of Shaḏraḵ, Mĕyshaḵ, and Aḇĕḏ-Neḡo, his limbs shall be taken, and his house made a dunghill, because there is no other Elah who is able to deliver like this.”

30 Then the sovereign promoted Shaḏraḵ, Mĕyshaḵ, and Aḇĕḏ-Neḡo in the province of Baḇel.

4 Neḇuḵaḏnetstsar the sovereign, to all peoples, nations and languages that dwell in all the earth: Peace be increased to you.

2 I thought it good to declare the signs and wonders which the Most High Elah has worked for me.

3 How great are His signs, and how mighty His wonders! His reign is an everlasting reign, and His rulership is from generation to generation.

4 I, Neḇuḵaḏnetstsar, was at rest in my house, and prospering in my palace.

5 I saw a dream and it frightened me, and the thoughts on my bed and the visions of my head alarmed me.

6 So I issued a decree to bring in all the wise ones of Baḇel before me, to make known to me the interpretation of the dream.

7 So the magicians, the astrologers, the Kasdim, and the diviners came in, and I related the dream to them, but its interpretation they did not make known to me.

8 And at last Dani'ěl, whose name is Bělteshatstsar, according to the name of my elah, came before me. In him is the Spirit of the Set-apart Elah. So I related the dream to him, saying,

9 "Bělteshatstsar, chief of the magicians, because I know that the Spirit of the Set-apart Elah is in you, and no secret is too difficult for you, explain to me the visions of my dream that I have seen, and its interpretation.

10 "Now the visions of my head on my bed were these: I looked, and saw a tree in the midst of the earth, and its height great.

11 "The tree became great and strong, and its height reached to the heavens, and it was visible to the ends of all the earth.

12 "Its leaves were lovely, and its fruit plenty, and in it was food for all. The beasts of the field found shade under it, and the birds of the heavens dwelt in its branches, and all flesh was fed from it.

13 "In the visions of my head on my bed, I looked and saw a Watcher, even a set-apart one, coming down from the heavens.

14 "He cried aloud and said this, 'Hew down the tree and cut off its branches, strip off its leaves and scatter its fruit. Let the beasts flee from under it, and the birds from its branches.

15 'But leave the stump of its roots in the earth, even with a band of iron and bronze, in the tender grass of the field. And let it be wet with the dew of the heavens, and let his portion be with the beasts on the grass of the earth.

16 'Let his heart be changed from man's, let him be given the heart of a beast, and seven times pass over him.

17 'This matter is by the decree of the watchers, and the command by the word of the set-apart ones, so that the living know that the Most High is ruler in the reign of men, and gives it to whomever He wishes, and sets over it the lowest of men.'

18 "This dream have I seen, I, Sovereign Neḇuḵaḏnetstsar. And you, Běltshatstsar, reveal its interpretation, since all the wise ones of my reign are unable to make known to me the interpretation. But you are able, for the Spirit of the Set-apart Elah is in you."

19 Then Dani'ěl, whose name was Běltshatstsar, was stunned for a short time, and his thoughts alarmed him. The sovereign responded and said, "Běltshatstsar, do not let the dream or its interpretation alarm you." Běltshatstsar answered and said, "My master, the dream is to those who hate you, and its interpretation to your enemies!

20 "The tree you saw, which became great and strong, whose height reached to the heavens and was visible to all the earth,

21 whose leaves were lovely and its fruit plenty, and in it was food for all, under which the beasts of the field dwelt, and on whose branches the birds of the heavens sat –

22 it is you, O sovereign, for you have become great and strong. And your greatness has grown, and has reached to the heavens and your rulership to the end of the earth.

23 "And as the sovereign saw a Watcher, even a set-apart one, coming down from the heavens, and he said, 'Hew down the tree and destroy it, but leave the stump of its roots in the earth, even with a band of iron and bronze in the tender grass of the field. And let it be wet with the dew of the heavens, and let his portion be with the beasts of the field, till seven times pass over him' –

24 this is the interpretation, O sovereign, and this is the decree of the Most High, which has come upon my master the sovereign:

25 "That you are going to be driven away from men, and your dwelling be with the beasts of the field, and you be given grass to eat like oxen, and you be wetted with the dew of the heavens, and seven times pass over you, till you know that the Most High is ruler in the reign of men, and that He gives it to whomever He wishes.

26 "And they that gave the command to leave the stump of its roots of the tree: your reign remains yours, from the time you come to know that the heavens are ruling.

27 "Therefore, O sovereign, let my counsel be acceptable to you, and break off your

sins by righteousness, and your crookednesses by showing favour to the poor –
your prosperity might be extended."
28 All this came upon Sovereign Neḇuḵaḏnetstsar.
29 At the end of the twelve months he was
walking about the palace of the reign of
Baḇel.
30 The sovereign spoke and said, "Is not
this great Baḇel, which I myself have built,
for the house of the reign, by the might of
my power and for the esteem of my
splendour?"
31 The word was still in the sovereign's
mouth, when a voice fell from the heavens,
"Sovereign Neḇuḵaḏnetstsar, to you it is
spoken: the reign has been taken away
from you,
32 and you are driven away from men, and
your dwelling is to be with the beasts of the
field. You are given grass to eat like oxen,
and seven seasons shall pass over you, until
you know that the Most High is ruler in the
reign of men, and He gives it to whomever
He wishes."
33 In that hour the word was executed on
Neḇuḵaḏnetstsar, and he was driven from
men and he ate grass like oxen, and his
body was wet with the dew of the heavens
till his hair had grown like eagles' *feathers*
and his nails like birds' *claws*.
34 And at the end of the days I,
Neḇuḵaḏnetstsar, lifted my eyes to the
heavens, and my understanding returned to
me. And I blessed the Most High and
praised and made Him great who lives forever, whose rule is an everlasting rule, and
His reign is from generation to generation.
35 And all the inhabitants of the earth are
of no account, and He does as He wishes
with the host of the heavens and among the
inhabitants of the earth. And there is none
to strike against His hand or say to Him,
"What have You done?"
36 At the same time my understanding
returned to me, and for the preciousness
of my reign, my esteem and splendour
were returning to me. And my counsellors
and nobles sought me out, and I was re-
established to my reign, and excellent
greatness was added to me.
37 Now I, Neḇuḵaḏnetstsar, am praising
and exalting and esteeming the Sovereign
of the heavens, for all His works are truth,
and His ways right. And those who walk in
pride He is able to humble.

5 Bělshatstsar the sovereign made a
great feast for a thousand of his great
men, and drank wine in the presence of the
thousand.
2 While tasting the wine, Bělshatstsar
gave orders to bring the gold and silver
vessels which his father Neḇuḵaḏnetstsar
had taken from the Hěḵal which had been
in Yerushalayim, that the sovereign and his
great men, his wives, and his concubines
could drink from them.
3 Then they brought the gold vessels that
had been taken from the Hěḵal of the
House of Elah which had been in
Yerushalayim. And the sovereign and his
great men, his wives, and his concubines
drank out of them.
4 They drank wine, and praised the elahin
of gold, and of silver, of bronze, of iron, of
wood and of stone.
5 At that moment the fingers of a man's
hand appeared and wrote opposite the
lampstand on the plaster of the wall of the
sovereign's palace. And the sovereign saw
the part of the hand that wrote.
6 Then the sovereign's colour changed,
and his thoughts alarmed him, so that the
joints of his hips were loosened and his
knees knocked against each other.
7 The sovereign called loudly to bring in
the astrologers, the Kasdim, and the diviners. The sovereign spoke and said to the
wise ones of Baḇel, "Whoever reads this
writing, and shows me its interpretation, is
robed in purple and has a chain of gold
around his neck, and shall be the third ruler
in the reign."
8 So all the sovereign's wise ones came,
but they were unable to read the writing, or
to make known its interpretation to the sovereign.
9 Then Sovereign Bělshatstsar was greatly alarmed, and his colour changed, and his
great men were puzzled.
10 The sovereigness, because of the words

of the sovereign and his great men, came to
the banquet hall. And the sovereigness
spoke and said, "O sovereign, live forever!
Do not let your thoughts alarm you, nor let
your colour change.
11 "There is a man in your reign in whom
is the Spirit of the Set-apart Elah. And in
the days of your father, light and understanding and wisdom, like the wisdom of
the elahin, were found in him. And
Sovereign Neḇuḵaḏnetstsar your father,
your father the sovereign, made him chief
of the magicians, astrologers, Kasdim, and
diviners,
12 because an excellent spirit, knowledge
and understanding, interpreting dreams,
and explaining riddles, and solving difficult problems were found in this Dani'ěl,
whom the sovereign named Bělteshatstsar.
Now let Dani'ěl be called, and let him
show the interpretation."
13 So Dani'ěl was brought in before the
sovereign. The sovereign spoke and said to
Dani'ěl, "Are you that Dani'ěl who is one
of the sons of the exile from Yehuḏah,
whom my father the sovereign brought
from Yehuḏah?
14 "I have heard of you, that the Spirit of
Elah is in you, and that light and understanding and excellent wisdom are found in
you.
15 "And the wise ones, the astrologers,
have been brought in before me, that they
should read this writing and make known
to me its interpretation, but they were
unable to show the interpretation of the
word.
16 "And I myself have heard of you, that
you are able to give interpretations and to
solve difficult problems. Now if you are
able to read the writing and make known
its interpretation to me, you are to be robed
in purple and have a chain of gold around
your neck, and shall be the third ruler in the
reign."
17 Then Dani'ěl answered and said before
the sovereign, "Let your gifts be for yourself, and give your rewards to another. Yet I
shall read the writing to the sovereign, and
make known the interpretation to him.
18 "O sovereign, the Most High Elah gave
Neḇuḵaḏnetstsar your father a reign and
greatness, and preciousness and esteem.
19 "And because of the greatness which
He gave him, all peoples, nations, and
languages trembled and feared before him.
Whomever he wished he killed, and
whomever he wished he kept alive, and
whomever he wished he raised up, and
whomever he wished he made low.
20 "But when his heart was lifted up, and
his spirit was so strong as to act proudly, he
was put down from his throne of reign, and
they took his preciousness from him.
21 "Then he was driven from the sons of
men, and his heart was made like the
beasts, and his dwelling was with the wild
donkeys. He was given grass to eat like
oxen, and his body was wet with the dew
of the heavens, till he knew that the Most
High Elah is ruler in the reign of men, and
He sets up over it whomever He wishes.
22 "And you his son, Bělshatstsar, have
not humbled your heart, although you
knew all this.
23 "And you have lifted yourself up
against the Master of the heavens. And
they brought before you the vessels of His
house, and you and your great men, your
wives and your concubines, have been
drinking wine from them. And you have
praised the elahin of silver, and of gold, of
bronze, of iron, of wood, and of stone,
which neither see nor hear nor know. But
the Elah who holds your breath in His hand
and owns all your ways, you have not
made great.
24 "Then the part of the hand was sent
from Him, and this writing was inscribed.
25 "And this is the writing that was
inscribed: MENĚ, MENĚ, TEQĚL,
UPHARSIN.
26 "This is the interpretation of each word:
MENĚ – Elah has numbered your reign,
and put an end to it.
27 "TEQĚL – You have been weighed on
the scales, and found lacking.
28 "PERES – Your reign has been divided,
and given to the Medes and Persians."
29 Then Bělshatstsar gave orders, and they
robed Dani'ěl in purple and put a chain of
gold around his neck, and they proclaimed

concerning him that he is the third ruler in
the reign.
30 In that night Bĕlshatstsar, sovereign of
the Kasdim, was killed.
31 And Dareyawesh the Mede took over
the reign, being about sixty-two years old.

6 It pleased Dareyawesh to appoint over
the reign one hundred and twenty
viceroys, to be over all the reign,
2 and over them three governors, of
whom Dani’ĕl was one, so that these
viceroys should give account to them, and
the sovereign suffer no loss.
3 Then this Dani’ĕl distinguished himself
above the governors and viceroys, because
an excellent spirit was in him. And the sovereign planned to appoint him over all the
reign.
4 Then the governors and viceroys sought
to find occasion against Dani’ĕl concerning
the reign. But they were unable to find
occasion or corruption, because he was
steadfast, and no negligence or corruption
was found in him.
5 Then these men said, “We shall not find
any occasion against this Dani’ĕl unless we
find it against him concerning the law of
his Elah.”
6 Then these governors and viceroys
tumultuously gathered before the sovereign, and said this to him, “Sovereign
Dareyawesh, live forever!
7 “All the governors of the reign, the
nobles and viceroys, the counsellors and
advisors, have consulted together to establish a royal decree and to make a strong
interdict, that whoever petitions any elah or
man for thirty days, except you, O sovereign, is thrown into the den
of lions.
8 “Now, O sovereign, establish the interdict and sign the writing, so that it is not to
be changed, according to the law of the
Medes and Persians, which does not pass
away.”
9 So Sovereign Dareyawesh signed the
written interdict.
10 And Dani’ĕl, when he knew that the
writing was signed, went home and in his
upper room with his windows open toward
Yerushalayim he knelt down on his knees
three times a day, and prayed and gave
thanks before his Elah, as he had done
before.
11 Then these men tumultuously gathered
and found Dani’ĕl praying and entreating
before his Elah.
12 Then they approached the sovereign,
and spoke concerning the sovereign’s
interdict, “Have you not signed a interdict
that every man who petitions any elah or
man within thirty days, except you, O sovereign, is thrown into the den of lions?”
The sovereign answered and said, “The
word is certain, according to the law of the
Medes and Persians, which does not pass
away.”
13 Then they answered and said before the
sovereign, “Dani’ĕl, who is one of the sons
of the exile from Yehuḏah, pays no heed to
you, O sovereign, nor for the interdict that
you have signed, but makes his petition
three times a day.”
14 Then the sovereign, when he heard
these words, was greatly displeased with
himself, and set his heart on Dani’ĕl to
deliver him. And he laboured till the going
down of the sun to deliver him.
15 Then these men tumultuously gathered
before the sovereign, and said to the sovereign, “Know, O sovereign, that it is the
law of the Medes and Persians that any
interdict or decree which the sovereign
establishes is not to be changed.”
16 Then the sovereign gave orders, and
they brought Dani’ĕl and threw him into
the den of lions. But the sovereign spoke
and said to Dani’ĕl, “Your Elah, whom you
serve continually, He Himself delivers
you.”
17 And a stone was brought and laid on the
mouth of the den, and the sovereign sealed
it with his own signet and with the signets
of his great men, that the situation concerning Dani’ĕl might not be changed.
18 And the sovereign went to his palace
and spent the night fasting. And no enter-
tainment was brought before him, and his
sleep fled from him.
19 Then the sovereign rose up very early in
the morning and hurried to the den of lions.

[20] And when he came to the den, he called
with a grieved voice to Dani'ěl. The sovereign spoke and said to Dani'ěl, "Dani'ěl,
servant of the living Elah, has your Elah,
whom you serve continually, been able to
deliver you from the lions?"
[21] Then Dani'ěl said to the sovereign, "O
sovereign, live forever!
[22] "My Elah has sent His messenger and
has shut the lions' mouths, and they did not
harm me, because I was found innocent
before Him. And also before you, O sovereign, I have done no harm."
[23] Then the sovereign was very glad and
gave orders that Dani'ěl be taken up out of
the den. And Dani'ěl was taken up out of
the den, and no harm was found on him,
because he trusted in his Elah.
[24] And the sovereign gave orders and they
brought those men who had accused
Dani'ěl, and they threw them, their
children, and their wives into the den of
lions. And the lions overpowered them,
and broke all their bones in pieces before
they reached the floor of the den.
[25] Then Sovereign Dareyawesh wrote to
all peoples, nations, and languages that
dwell in all the earth: "Peace be increased
to you.
[26] "From before me is made a decree that
throughout every rule of my reign men are
to tremble and fear before the Elah of
Dani'ěl, for He is the living Elah, and
steadfast forever. And His reign is one
which is not destroyed, and His rule is unto
the end.
[27] "He delivers and rescues, and He works
signs and wonders in the heavens and on
earth, for He has delivered Dani'ěl from
the power of the lions."
[28] And this Dani'ěl prospered in the reign
of Dareyawesh and in the reign of Koresh
the Persian.

7 In the first year of Bělshatstsar sovereign of Baḇel, Dani'ěl had a dream
and visions of his head on his bed. Then he
wrote down the dream, giving a summary
of the matters.
[2] Dani'ěl spoke and said, "I was looking
in my vision by night and saw the four
winds of the heavens stirring up the Great
Sea.
[3] "And four great beasts came up from
the sea, different from one another.
[4] "The first was like a lion, and had
eagle's wings. I was looking until its wings
were plucked off, and it was lifted up from
the earth and made to stand on two feet like
a man, and it was given a man's heart.
[5] "And see, another beast, a second, like
a bear. And it was raised up on one side,
and had three ribs in its mouth between its
teeth. And they said this to it, 'Arise,
devour much flesh!'
[6] "After this I looked and saw another,
like a leopard, which had on its back four
wings of a bird. The beast also had four
heads, and rule was given to it.
[7] "After this I looked in the night visions
and saw a fourth beast, fearsome and burly,
exceedingly strong. And it had great iron
teeth. It devoured and crushed, and trampled down the rest with its feet. And it was
different from all the beasts that were
before it, and it had ten horns.
[8] "I was thinking about the horns, then
saw another horn, a little one, coming up
among them, and three of the first horns
were plucked out by the roots before it.
And see, eyes like the eyes of a man were
in this horn, and a mouth speaking great
words.
[9] "I was looking until thrones were set
up, and the Ancient of Days was seated.
His garment was white as snow, and the
hair of His head was like clean wool, His
throne was flames of fire, its wheels burning fire.
[10] "A stream of fire was flowing and coming forth from His presence, and a thousand thousands served Him, and ten thousand times ten thousand stood before Him,
the Judge was seated, and the books were
opened.
[11] "I was looking. Then, because of the
sound of the great words which the horn
was speaking, I was looking until the beast
was kiiled', and its body destroyed and
given to the burning fire,

12 and the rest of the beasts had their rule
taken away. But a lengthening of life was
given to them, for a season and a time.
13 "I was looking in the night visions and
saw One like the Son of Enosh, [a] coming
with the clouds of the heavens! And He
came to the Ancient of Days, and they
brought Him near before Him.
14 "And to Him was given rulership and
preciousness and a reign, that all peoples,
nations, and languages should serve Him.
His rule is an everlasting rule which shall
not pass away, and His reign that which
shall not be destroyed.
15 "As for me, Dani'ĕl, my spirit was
pierced within my body, and the visions of
my head alarmed me.
16 "I drew near to one of those who stood
by, and asked him the certainty of all this.
And he spoke to me and made known to
me the interpretation of the matters:
17 'These great beasts, which are four, are
four sovereigns which rise up from the
earth.
18 'Then the set-apart ones of the Most
High shall receive the reign, and possess
the reign forever, even forever and ever.'
19 "Then I desired for certainty concerning
the fourth beast, which was different from
all the others, very fearsome, with its teeth
of iron and its nails of bronze, which
devoured, crushed, and trampled down the
rest with its feet,
20 and concerning the ten horns that were
on its head, and of the other *horn* that came
up, before which three fell – this horn
which had eyes and a mouth which spoke
great *words*, whose appearance was greater
than his fellows.
21 "I was looking, and this horn was fighting against the set-apart ones, and was prevailing against them,
22 until the Ancient of Days came, and
right-ruling was given to the set-apart ones
of the Most High, and the time came and
the set-apart ones took possession of the
reign.
23 "This is what he said, 'The fourth beast
is the fourth reign on earth, which is different from all other reigns, and it devours all
the earth, tramples it down and crushes it.
24 'And the ten horns are ten sovereigns
from this reign. They shall rise, and another shall rise after them, and it is different
from the first ones, and it humbles three
sovereigns,
25 and it speaks words against the Most
High, and it wears out the set-apart ones of
the Most High, and it intends to change
appointed times [b] and law, and they are
given into its hand for a time and times and
half a time.
26 'But the Judgment shall sit, and they
shall take away its rule, to cut off and to
destroy, until the end.
27 'And the reign, and the rulership, and
the greatness of the reigns under all the
heavens, shall be given to the people, the
set-apart ones of the Most High. His reign
is an everlasting reign, and all rulerships
shall serve and obey Him.'
28 "This is the end of the matter. As for
me, Dani'ĕl, my thoughts greatly alarmed
me, and my colour changed. And I kept the
matter in my heart." [c]

8 In the third year of the reign of
Bĕlshatstsar the sovereign, a vision
appeared to me, Dani'ĕl, after the one that
appeared to me the first time.
2 And I looked in the vision, and it came
to be while I was looking, that I was in the
citadel of Shushan, which is in the province
of Ĕylam. And I looked in the vision, and I
was by the River Ulai.
3 And I lifted my eyes and looked and
saw a ram standing beside the river, and it
had two horns, and the two horns were
high. And the one was higher than the
other, and the higher one came up last.
4 I saw the ram pushing westward, and
northward, and southward, so that no beast
could stand before him, and there was no
one to deliver from his hand, while he did
as he pleased and became great.
5 And I was observing and saw a male

7a *Son of Enosh* - This Aramaic term is similar to the Hebrew 'Ben Aḏam,' (Son of Aḏam) but not the exact equivalent of it. 7b This is another word for *festivals*. 7c The end of the Aramaic text.

goat came from the west, over the surface of all the earth, without touching the ground. And the goat had a conspicuous horn between his eyes.

6 And he came to the ram that had two horns, which I had seen standing beside the river, and ran at him in the rage of his power.

7 And I saw him come close to the ram, and he became embittered against him, and struck the ram, and broke his two horns. And there was no power in the ram to withstand him, but he threw him down to the ground and trampled on him. And there was no one to deliver the ram from his hand.

8 And the male goat became very great. But when he was strong, the large horn was broken, and in place of it four conspicuous ones came up toward the four winds of the heavens.

9 And from one of them came a little horn which became exceedingly great toward the south, and toward the east, and toward the Splendid *Land*.

10 And it became great, up to the host of the heavens. And it caused some of the host and some of the stars to fall to the earth, and trampled them down.

11 It even exalted itself as high as the Prince of the host. And it took that which is continual away from Him, and threw down the foundation of His set-apart place.

12 And because of transgression, an army was given over *to the horn* to oppose that which is continual. And it threw the truth down to the ground, [a] and it acted and prospered.

13 Then I heard a certain set-apart one speaking. And another set-apart one said to that certain one who was speaking, "Till when is the vision, concerning that which is continual, and the transgression that lays waste, to make both the set-apart place and the host to be trampled under foot?" [b]

14 And he said to me, "For two thousand three hundred nights, [c] then that which is set-apart shall be made right."

15 And it came to be, when I, Dani'ěl, had seen the vision, that I sought understanding, and see, before me stood one having the appearance of a mighty man.

16 And I heard a man's voice between *the banks of* Ulai, who called, and said, "Gaḇri'ěl, make this man understand the vision."

17 He then came near where I stood. And when he came I feared and I fell on my face, but he said to me, "Understand, son of man, for the vision is for the time of the end."

18 And, as he was speaking with me, I fell stunned upon my face to the ground, but he touched me, and made me stand up straight,

19 and said, "Look, I am making known to you what shall take place in the latter time of the wrath, for at the appointed time shall be the end.

20 "The ram which you saw, having two horns, are the sovereigns of Media and Persia.

21 "And the male goat is the sovereign of Greece, and the large horn between its eyes is the first sovereign.

22 "And that it was broken and four stood up in its place: are four rulerships arising out of that nation, but not in its power.

23 "And in the latter time of their rule, when the transgressors have filled up their measure, a sovereign, fierce of face and skilled at intrigues, shall stand up.

24 "And his power shall be mighty, but not by his own power, and he shall destroy incredibly, and shall prosper and thrive, and destroy mighty men, and the set-apart people.

25 "And through his skill he shall make deceit prosper in his hand, and hold himself to be great in his heart, and destroy many who are at ease, and even stand against the Prince of princes – yet without hand he shall be broken.

26 "And what was said in the vision of the evening and morning is truth. And hide the vision, for it is after many days."

27 And I, Dani'ěl, was stricken and became sick for days. Then I rose up and

8a Yesh. 59:14. *8b* See 11:31, Mt.24:15. *8c* Lit. evening-morning.

went about the sovereign's work. And I was amazed at the vision, but there was no understanding.

9 In the first year of Dareyawesh the son of Aḥashwĕrosh, of the seed of the Medes, who was set up as sovereign over the reign of the Kasdim –

2 in the first year of his reign I, Dani'ĕl, observed from the Scriptures the number of the years, according to the word of יהוה given to Yirmeyah the prophet, for the completion of the wastes of Yerushalayim would be seventy years.

3 So I set my face toward יהוה the Elohim to seek by prayer and supplications, with fasting, and sackcloth, and ashes.

4 And I prayed to יהוה my Elohim, and made confession, and said, "O יהוה, great and awesome Ĕl, guarding the covenant and the loving-commitment to those who love Him, and to those who guard His commands.

5 "We have sinned and did crookedness, and did wrong and rebelled, to turn aside from Your commands and from Your right-rulings.

6 "And we have not listened to Your servants the prophets, who spoke in Your Name to our sovereigns, our heads, and our fathers, and to all the people of the land.

7 "O יהוה, to You is the righteousness, and to us the shame of face, as it is this day – to the men of Yehuḏah, to the inhabitants of Yerushalayim and all Yisra'ĕl, those near and those far off in all the lands to which You have driven them, because of their trespass which they have trespassed against You.

8 "O Master, to us is the shame of face, to our sovereigns, to our heads, and to our fathers, because we have sinned against You.

9 "To יהוה our Elohim are the compassions and forgivenesses, for we have rebelled against Him.

10 "And we have not obeyed the voice of יהוה our Elohim, to walk in His Torot, which He set before us through His servants the prophets.

11 "And all Yisra'ĕl have transgressed Your Torah, and turned aside, so as not to obey Your voice. So the curse and the oath written in the Torah of Mosheh the servant of Elohim have been poured out on us, for we have sinned against Him.

12 "And He has confirmed His words, which He spoke against us and against our rulers who judged us, by bringing upon us great evil. For under all the heavens there has not been done like what was done to Yerushalayim.

13 "As it is written in the Torah of Mosheh, all this evil has come upon us, and we have not entreated the face of יהוה our Elohim, to turn back from our crookednesses, and to study Your truth.

14 "Hence יהוה has watched over the evil and has brought it upon us. For יהוה our Elohim is righteous in all the works which He has done, but we have not obeyed His voice.

15 "And now, O יהוה our Elohim, who brought Your people out of the land of Mitsrayim with a strong hand, and made Yourself a Name, as it is this day – we have sinned, we have done wrong!

16 "O יהוה, according to all Your righteousness, I pray, let Your displeasure and Your wrath be turned away from Your city Yerushalayim, Your set-apart mountain. For, because of our sins, and because of the crookednesses of our fathers, Yerushalayim and Your people have become a reproach to all those around us.

17 "And now, our Elohim, hear the prayer of Your servant, and his supplications, and for the sake of יהוה cause Your face to shine on Your set-apart place, which is laid waste.

18 "O my Elohim, incline Your ear and hear. Open Your eyes and see our wastes, and the city which is called by Your Name. For we do not present our supplications before You because of our righteous deeds, but because of Your great compassions.

19 "O יהוה, hear! O יהוה, forgive! O יהוה, listen and act! Do not delay for Your own sake, my Elohim, for Your city and Your people are called by Your Name."

20 And while I was speaking, and praying,

and confessing my sin and the sin of my
people Yisra'ěl, and presenting my supplication before יהוה my Elohim for the set-
apart mountain of my Elohim,
21 while I was still speaking in prayer, the
man Gaḇri'ěl, whom I had seen in the
vision at the beginning, came close to me,
in swift flight about the time of the evening
offering.
22 And he made me understand, and talked
with me, and said, "O Dani'ěl, I have now
come forth to make you wise concerning
understanding.
23 "At the beginning of your supplications
a word went out, and I have come to make
it known, for you are greatly appreciated.
So consider the word and understand the
vision:
24 "Seventy weeks are decreed for your
people and for your set-apart city, to put an
end to the transgression, and to seal up
sins, and to cover crookedness, and to
bring in everlasting righteousness, and to
seal up vision and prophet, and to anoint
the Most Set-apart.
25 "Know, then, and understand: from the
going forth of the command to restore and
build Yerushalayim until Messiah the
Prince is seven weeks and sixty-two weeks.
It shall be built again, with streets and a
trench, but in times of affliction.
26 "And after the sixty-two weeks Messiah
shall be cut off and have naught. And the
people of a coming prince shall destroy the
city and the set-apart place. And the end of
it is with a flood. And wastes are decreed,
and fighting until the end.
27 "And he shall confirm a covenant with
many for one week. And in the middle of
the week he shall put an end to slaughtering and meal offering. And on the wing of
abominations he shall lay waste, even until
the complete end and that which is decreed
is poured out on the one who lays waste." [a]

10 In the third year of Koresh sovereign of Persia a word was revealed
to Dani'ěl, whose name was called
Bělteshatstsar. And the word was true, and
the conflict great. And he understood the
word, and had understanding of the vision.
2 In those days I, Dani'ěl, was mourning
three weeks of days.
3 I did not eat desirable food, and meat
and wine did not come into my mouth,
and I did not anoint myself at all, till the
completion of three weeks of days.
4 And on the twenty-fourth day of the first
new *moon*, while I was by the side of the
great river, that is Ḥiddeqel,
5 then I lifted my eyes and looked and
saw a certain man dressed in linen, whose
loins were girded with gold of Uphaz!
6 And his body was like beryl, and his
face like the appearance of lightning, and
his eyes like torches of fire, and his arms
and feet like polished bronze in appearance,
and the sound of his words like the sound of
a crowd.
7 And I, Dani'ěl, alone saw the vision, for
the men who were with me did not see the
vision, but a great trembling fell upon them,
and they ran away to hide themselves.
8 So I was left alone when I saw this great
vision, and no strength remained in me, for
my comeliness was destroyed in me, and I
retained no strength.
9 But I heard the sound of his words. And
while I heard the sound of his words I was
stunned lying with my face to the ground.
10 And see, a hand touched me, and set me
trembling on my knees and on the palms of
my hands.
11 And he said to me, "O Dani'ěl, man
greatly appreciated, understand the words
that I speak to you, and stand upright, for I
have now been sent to you." And while
he was speaking this word to me, I stood
trembling.
12 And he said to me, "Do not fear,
Dani'ěl, for from the first day that you set
your heart to understand and to humble
yourself before your Elohim, your words
were heard, and I have come because of
your words.
13 "But the head of the rule of Persia withstood me twenty-one days. And see,
Miḵa'ěl, one of the chief heads, came to

9a Mt. 24:15.

help me, for I had been left alone there with the sovereigns of Persia.

14 "And I have come to make you understand what is to befall your people in the latter days. For the vision is yet for days to come."

15 And when he had spoken such words to me, I turned my face toward the ground and kept silent.

16 And see, one who looked like the sons of men touched my lips, and I opened my mouth and spoke and said to him who stood before me, "My master, because of the vision I have been seized with pains, and I have retained no strength.

17 "So how was this servant of my master able to speak with you, my master? As for me, no strength remains in me now, nor is any breath left in me."

18 And again the one who looked like a man touched me and strengthened me.

19 And he said, "Do not fear, O man greatly appreciated! Peace be to you, be strong now, be strong!" So when he spoke to me I was strengthened, and said, "Let my master speak, for you have strengthened me."

20 And he said, "Do you know why I have come to you? And now I return to fight with the head of Persia. And when I have left, see, the head of Greece shall come.

21 "But let me declare to you what is written in the Scripture of Truth, and there is not one strengthening [a] himself with me concerning these, except Miḵa'ěl your head.

11 "And in the first year of Dareyawesh the Mede, I myself stood up to support and protect him.

2 "And now I declare the truth to you: See, three more sovereigns are to arise in Persia, and the fourth is to become far richer than them all. And by his power, through his riches, he stirs up all against the rulership of Greece.

3 "And a mighty sovereign shall arise, and he shall rule with great authority, and do as he pleases.

4 "But when he has arisen, his rule shall be broken up and divided toward the four winds of the heavens, but not among his descendants nor according to his authority with which he ruled, because his rule shall be uprooted, even for others besides these.

5 "And a sovereign of the South shall become strong, and one of his princes; and he shall be strong over him and shall rule – his rule shall be a great rule.

6 "And at the end of years they shall join themselves together, and a daughter of the sovereign of the South shall come to the sovereign of the North to make an alliance. But she shall not retain the strength of her power, nor would he or his power stand. And she shall be given up, with those who brought her, and he who brought her forth, and he who supported her in those times.

7 "But from a branch of her roots one shall arise in his place, and he shall come into the defence and come into a stronghold of the sovereign of the North, and shall act against them, and shall prevail,

8 and also their mighty ones, with their princes and their precious utensils of silver and gold he shall seize and bring to Mitsrayim. And he shall stand more years than the sovereign of the North.

9 "Then he shall enter the reign of the sovereign of the South, but shall return to his own land.

10 "But his sons shall stir themselves up, and assemble a great army. And he shall certainly come and overflow and pass through, then return to his stronghold, and be stirred up.

11 "Then the sovereign of the South shall be enraged and go out to fight with him, with the sovereign of the North, who shall raise a large army. But the army shall be given into the hand of his enemy,

12 and he shall capture the army, his heart being exalted. And he shall cause tens of thousands to fall, but not prevail.

13 "And the sovereign of the North shall return and raise an army greater than the former, and certainly come at the end of some years with a great army and much supplies.

14 "And in those times many shall rise up against the sovereign of the South, while some violent ones among your people exalt themselves to establish the vision, but they

shall stumble.
15 "Then the sovereign of the North shall
come in and build a siege mound, and
capture a city of strongholds. And the arms
of the South shall not stand, nor his choice
people, for there is no strength to stand.
16 "So his opponent shall do as he pleases
– with no one standing against him – and
stand in the Splendid Land with destruction
in his hand.
17 "And he shall set his face to enter with
the strength of his entire rule, and make an
alliance with him. And he shall do so, and
give him the daughter of women to corrupt
her. But she shall not stand, neither be for
him.
18 "Then he shall turn his face to the coastlands and capture many. But a ruler shall
bring the reproach against them to an end.
And with the reproach removed, he shall
turn back on him.
19 "Then he shall turn his face toward the
strongholds of his own land, but shall stumble and fall, and not be found.
20 "And in his place one shall stand up
who imposes taxes on the adorned *city* of
the rule, but within a few days he is
destroyed, but not in wrath or in battle.
21 "And in his place shall arise a despised
one, to whom they shall not give the excellency of the rule. But he shall come in
peaceably, and seize the rule by flatteries.
22 "And the arms of the flood shall be
swept away from before him and be broken,
and also the prince of the covenant.
23 "And after they joined him, he shall
work deceit, and shall come up and become
strong with a small nation.
24 "He shall enter peaceably, even into
the richest places of the province, and do
what his fathers have not done, nor his forefathers: distribute among them plunder and
spoil and supplies, and devise his plots
against the strongholds, but only for a time.
25 "And he shall stir up his power and his
heart against the sovereign of the South
with a great army, and the sovereign of the
South shall be stirred up to battle with a
very great and mighty army, but not stand,
for they shall devise plots against him.
26 "And those who have been eating his
food shall destroy him, and his army be
swept away, and many fall down slain.
27 "And both these sovereigns' hearts are
to do evil, and speak lies at the same table,
but not prosper, for the end is still for an
appointed time.
28 "Then he shall return to his land with
much supplies, and his heart be against the
set-apart covenant. And he shall act, and
shall return to his land.
29 "At the appointed time he shall return
and go toward the south, but it shall not be
like the former or the latter.
30 "For ships from Kittim shall come
against him, and he shall lose heart, and
shall return in rage against the set-apart
covenant, and shall act, and shall return and
consider those who forsake the set-apart
covenant.
31 "And strong ones shall arise from him
and profane the set-apart place, the stronghold, and shall take away that which is continual, and set up the abomination that lays
waste. [a]
32 "And by flatteries he shall profane those
who do wrong against the covenant, but the
people who know their Elohim shall be
strong, and shall act.
33 "And those of the people who have
insight shall give understanding to many.
And they shall stumble by sword and flame,
by captivity and plundering, for days.
34 "And when they stumble, they shall be
helped, a little help, but many shall join
them, by flatteries.
35 "And some of those who have insight
shall stumble, to refine them, and to cleanse
them, and to make them white, until the
time of the end, for it is still for an appointed time.
36 "And the sovereign shall do as he pleases, and exalt himself and show himself to
be great above every mighty one, and speak
incredible matters against the Ěl of mighty
ones, and shall prosper until the wrath has
been accomplished – for what has been
decreed shall be done –

11a See 8:13, 9:27, Mt. 24:15.

37 and have no regard for the mighty ones of his fathers nor for the desire of women, nor have regard for any mighty one, but exalt himself above them all.

38 "But in his place he shall give esteem to a mighty one of strongholds. And to a mighty one which his fathers did not know he shall give esteem with gold and silver, with precious stones and costly gifts.

39 "And he shall act against the strongest strongholds with a foreign mighty one, which he shall acknowledge. He shall increase in esteem and cause them to rule over many, and divide the land for gain.

40 "At the time of the end the sovereign of the South shall push at him, and the sovereign of the North rush against him like a whirlwind, with chariots, and with horsemen, and with many ships. And he shall enter the lands, and shall overflow and pass over,

41 and shall enter the Splendid Land, and many shall stumble, but these escape from his hand: Eḏom, and Mo'aḇ, and the chief of the sons of Ammon.

42 "And he shall stretch out his hand against the lands, and the land of Mitsrayim shall not escape.

43 "And he shall rule over the treasures of gold and silver, and over all the riches of Mitsrayim, and Libyans and Kushites shall be at his steps.

44 "Then reports from the east and the north shall disturb him, and he shall go out with great wrath to destroy and put many under the ban,

45 and he shall pitch the tents of his palace between the seas and the splendid set-apart mountain, but shall come to his end with none to help him.

12 "Now at that time Miḵa'ěl shall stand up, the great head who is standing over the sons of your people. And there shall be a time of distress, such as never was since there was a nation, until that time. And at that time your people shall be delivered, every one who is found written in the book,

2 and many of those who sleep in the dust of the earth wake up, some to everlasting life, and some to reproaches, everlasting abhorrence.

3 "And those who have insight shall shine like the brightness of the expanse, and those who lead many to righteousness like the stars forever and ever.

4 "But you, Dani'ěl, hide the words, and seal the book until the time of the end. [a] Many shall diligently search and knowledge shall increase."

5 Then I, Dani'ěl, looked and saw two others standing, one on this bank of the river and the other on that bank.

6 And one said to the man dressed in linen, who was above the waters of the river, "How long until the end of these wonders?"

7 And I heard the man dressed in linen, who was above the waters of the river, and he held up his right hand and his left hand to the heavens, and swore by Him who lives forever, that it would be for an appointed time, appointed times, and half *a time*. And when they have ended scattering the power of the set-apart people, then all these shall be completed.

8 And I heard, but I did not understand, so I said, "My master, what is the latter end of these *matters*?"

9 And he said, "Go, Dani'ěl, for the words are hidden and sealed till the time of the end. [b]

10 "Many shall be cleansed and made white, and refined. But the wrong shall do wrong – and none of the wrong shall understand, but those who have insight shall understand.

11 "And from the time that which is continual is taken away, and the abomination that lays waste is set up, is one thousand two hundred and ninety days.

12 "Blessed is he who is waiting earnestly, and comes to the one thousand three hundred and thirty-five days.

13 "But you, go your way till the end. And rest, and arise to your lot at the end of the days."

12a See v. 9. *12b* See v. 4.

HOSHĔA

HOSEA

1 The word of יהוה that came to Hoshĕa son of Be'ĕri, in the days of Uzziyah, Yotham, Aḥaz, and Yeḥizqiyah, sovereigns of Yehuḏah, and in the days of Yaroḇʽam son of Yo'ash, sovereign of Yisra'ĕl.

2 The beginning of the word of יהוה with Hoshĕa. And יהוה said to Hoshĕa, "Go, take yourself a woman of whoring and children of whoring, for the land has utterly whored away from יהוה."

3 So he went and took Gomer, daughter of Diḇlayim, and she conceived and bore him a son.

4 And יהוה said to him, "Call his name Yizreʽĕl, for in a little while I shall revenge the bloodshed of Yizreʽĕl on the house of Yĕhu, and put an end to the reign of the house of Yisra'ĕl.

5 "And it shall be in that day that I shall break the bow of Yisra'ĕl in the Valley of Yizreʽĕl."

6 And she conceived again and bore a daughter. And He said to him, "Call her name Lo-Ruḥamah, for no longer do I have compassion on the house of Yisra'ĕl so as to forgive them at all.

7 "But I shall have compassion on the house of Yehuḏah and save them by יהוה their Elohim, and not save them by bow or by sword or battle, by horses or horsemen."

8 And she weaned Lo-Ruḥamah, and conceived and bore a son,

9 then He said, "Call his name Lo-Ammi, for you are not My people, and I am not for you.

10 "Yet the number of the children of Yisra'ĕl shall be as the sand of the sea, which is not measured nor counted. And it shall be in the place where it was said to them, 'You are not My people,' they shall be called, 'You are the sons of the living Ĕl.'

11 "And the children of Yehuḏah and the children of Yisra'ĕl shall be gathered together, and appoint for themselves one head, and shall come up out of the earth, for great is the day of Yizreʽĕl!

2 "Say to your brothers, 'O my people,' and to your sisters, 'O, compassioned one.'

2 "Strive with your mother, strive, for she is not My wife, nor am I her Husband! Let her put away her whorings from her face, and her adulteries from between her breasts,

3 lest I strip her naked, and shall set her up as on the day she was born, and shall make her like a wilderness, and shall set her like a dry land, and shall put her to death with thirst.

4 "And I shall not have compassion on her children, for they are the children of whorings.

5 "For their mother has whored, she who conceived them has acted shamelessly. For she said, 'I go after my lovers, who give me my bread and my water, my wool and my linen, my oil and my drink.'

6 "Therefore, see, I am hedging up your way with thorns, and I shall wall her in, so that she does not find her paths.

7 "And she shall pursue her lovers but not overtake them, and shall seek them but not find them. Then she shall say, 'Let me go and return to my first husband, for then it was better for me than now.'

8 "And she did not acknowledge that I gave her grain, and new wine, and oil, and increased her silver and gold which they prepared for Baʽal.

9 "Therefore I shall turn back and shall take my grain in its time and My new wine in its appointed time, and I shall take away My wool and My linen covering her nakedness.

10 "And now I shall uncover her shame before the eyes of her lovers, and no one shall deliver her from My hand.

11 "And I shall cause all her rejoicing, her festivals, her New Moons, and her

Sabbaths, even all her appointed times, to cease,

12 and lay waste her vines and her fig trees, of which she has said, 'these are my harlot-fees that my lovers have given me.' And I shall make them a forest, and the beasts of the field shall eat them.

13 "And I shall punish her for the days of the Baʽals to which she burned incense and adorned herself with her rings and jewelry, and went after her lovers, and forgot Me," declares יהוה.

14 "Therefore, see, I am alluring her, and shall lead her into the wilderness, and shall speak to her heart,

15 and give to her vineyards from there, and the Valley of Aḵor as a door of expectation. And there she shall respond as in the days of her youth, as in the day when she came up from the land of Mitsrayim.

16 "And it shall be, in that day," declares יהוה, "that you call Me 'My Husband,' and no longer call Me 'My Baʽal.'

17 "And I shall remove the names of the Baʽals from her mouth, and they shall no more be remembered by their name.

18 "And in that day I shall make a covenant for them with the beasts of the field, and with the birds of the heavens, and with the creeping creatures of the ground, when bow, and sword, and battle I break from the earth. And I shall make them lie down in safety.

19 "And I shall take you as a bride unto Me forever, and take you as a bride unto Me in righteousness, and in right-ruling, and loving-commitment and compassion.

20 "And I shall take you as a bride unto Me in trustworthiness, and you shall know יהוה.

21 "And it shall be in that day that I answer," declares יהוה, "that I answer the heavens, and they answer the earth,

22 and the earth answer the grain and the new wine and the oil, and they answer Yizreʽěl.

23 "And I shall sow her for Myself in the earth, and I shall have compassion on her who had not obtained compassion. And I shall say to those who were not My people, 'You are My people,' while they say, 'My Elohim!' "

3 Then יהוה said to me, "Go again, love a woman loved by a friend, and an adulteress, according to the love of יהוה for the children of Yisra'ěl, though they are turning to other mighty ones and love their raisin cakes."

2 So I bought her for myself for fifteen pieces of silver, and one and one-half ḥomers of barley.

3 And I said to her, "You are to remain with me many days, you are not to whore, nor become any man's, and so I shall also be towards you."

4 For many days the children of Yisra'ěl are to remain without sovereign and without prince, and without slaughtering, and without pillar, and without shoulder garment or house idols.

5 Afterward the children of Yisra'ěl shall return, and seek יהוה their Elohim, and Dawiḏ their sovereign, and fear יהוה and His goodness, in the latter days.

4 Hear the word of יהוה, you children of Yisra'ěl, for יהוה has a case against the inhabitants of the land: "For there is no truth or loving-commitment or knowledge of Elohim in the land.

2 "Swearing, and lying, and murdering, and stealing, and committing adultery have increased. And bloodshed follows bloodshed.

3 "Therefore the land mourns, and everyone living there languishes, with the beasts of the field and the birds of the heavens. And the fish of the sea are taken away.

4 "However, let no one strive or reprove another, for your people are like those striving with a priest.

5 "And you shall stumble in the day, and the prophet shall also stumble with you in the night. And I shall make your mother perish.

6 "My people have perished for lack of knowledge. Because you have rejected knowledge, I reject you from being priest for Me. Since you have forgotten the Torah of your Elohim, I also forget your children.

7 "As they were increased, so they sinned

against Me. My esteem they have changed into shame.

8 “They eat the sin of My people, and lift up their desire to their crookedness.

9 “And it shall be: like people, like priest. And I shall punish them for their ways, and reward them for their deeds.

10 “And they shall eat but not be satisfied, they shall whore but not increase, for they have stopped obeying יהוה.

11 “Whoring, and wine, and new wine enslave the heart.

12 “My people ask from their Wood, and their Staff declares to them. For a spirit of whorings has led them astray, and they went whoring from under their Elohim.

13 “They slaughter on the mountaintops, and burn incense on the hills, under oak and poplars and terebinth, because its shade is good. Therefore your daughters commit whoring, and your brides commit adultery.

14 “I would not punish your daughters when they commit whoring, nor your brides when they commit adultery, for *the men* themselves go aside with whores, and slaughter with cult prostitutes – a people that do not understand are thrust down!

15 “Though you are a whore, Yisra’ěl, let not Yehuḏah become guilty. Do not come up to Gilgal, nor go up to Běyth Awen, nor swear an oath, saying, ‘As יהוה lives!’

16 “For Yisra’ěl is stubborn, like a stubborn calf. Would יהוה now feed them like a lamb in a broad place?

17 “Ephrayim is joined to idols, let him alone.

18 “Their drink is sour, they have whored continually. Her rulers wildly loved shame.

19 “A wind has bound her up in its wings, and they are ashamed because of their slaughterings.

5 “Hear this, O priests! And listen, O house of Yisra’ěl! Give ear, O house of the sovereign! For the judgment is for you, for you have been a snare to Mitspah and a net spread on Taḇor.

2 “And revolters have gone deep in slaying, and I reprove them all.

3 “I have known Ephrayim, and Yisra’ěl has not been hidden from Me. For now, O Ephrayim, you have whored, Yisra’ěl is defiled.

4 “Their deeds do not allow them to turn back to their Elohim, for the spirit of whorings is among them, and they do not know יהוה.

5 “And the Excellency of Yisra’ěl shall witness to his face, and Yisra’ěl and Ephrayim stumble in their crookedness. Yehuḏah shall also stumble with them.

6 “With their flocks and herds they go to seek יהוה, but do not find Him – He has withdrawn from them.

7 “They have acted treacherously against יהוה, for they have brought forth strange children. Now a new moon shall devour them with their portions.

8 “Blow a shophar in Giḇʽah, the trumpet in Ramah! Shout, O Běyth Awen! Behind you, O Binyamin!

9 “Ephrayim is laid waste in the day of rebuke. Among the tribes of Yisra’ěl I shall make known what is certain.

10 “The chiefs of Yehuḏah shall be like those who remove a border – on them I pour out my wrath like water.

11 “Ephrayim is oppressed, crushed in judgment, because he walked after the command when it pleased him.

12 “So I am to Ephrayim like a moth, and to the house of Yehuḏah like rottenness.

13 “When Ephrayim saw his sickness, and Yehuḏah saw his wound, then Ephrayim went to Ashshur and sent to Sovereign Yarěḇ. But he is unable to heal you, or to remove the wound from you.

14 “For I am like a lion to Ephrayim, and like a young lion to the house of Yehuḏah. I Myself tear them and go, I take them away, and there is no one to deliver.

15 “I shall go, I shall return to My place, until they confess their guilt and seek My face, in their distress diligently search for Me, *and say*,

6 ‘Come, and let us turn back to יהוה. For He has torn but He does heal us, He has stricken but He binds us up.

2 ‘After two days He shall revive us, on the third day He shall raise us up, so that

we live before Him.

3 'So let us know, let us pursue to know יהוה. His going forth is as certain as the morning. And He comes to us like the rain, like the latter rain watering the earth.'

4 "Ephrayim, what would I do with you? Yehuḏah, what would I do with you? For your loving-commitment is like a morning cloud, and like the early dew it goes away.

5 "Therefore I have hewn *them* by the prophets, I have killed them by the words of My mouth. And my right-rulings break forth as the light.

6 "For I delight in loving-commitment and not slaughtering, and in the knowledge of Elohim more than ascending offerings.

7 "But like Aḏam they transgressed the covenant. There they acted treacherously against Me.

8 "Gil'aḏ is a city of workers of wickedness – tracked up with blood.

9 "And as bands of robbers lie in wait for a man, so the company of priests murder on the way to Sheḵem, for they have done wickedness.

10 "I have seen a horrible matter in the house of Yisra'ĕl: the whoring of Ephrayim is there, Yisra'ĕl is defiled.

11 "Also, a harvest is appointed for you, O Yehuḏah, when I turn back the captivity of My people.

7 "Whenever I would heal Yisra'ĕl, then the crookedness of Ephrayim is uncovered, and the evil deeds of Shomeron. For they have wrought falsehood, and a thief comes in, a band of robbers raids outside.

2 "And they do not say to their hearts that I remember all their evil. Now their own deeds have surrounded them, they have been before Me.

3 "With their evil they make a sovereign glad, and rulers with their lies.

4 "All of them are adulterers, as an oven heated by a baker, who ceases stirring the fire after kneading the dough, until it is leavened.

5 "In the day of our sovereign rulers became sick, inflamed with wine. He extended his hand with scoffers.

6 "For they have drawn near, their heart is like an oven. While they lie in wait all the night their baker sleeps. In the morning it burns like a flaming fire.

7 "All of them are as hot as an oven, and they consumed their rulers. All their sovereigns have fallen – not one among them calls on Me.

8 "Ephrayim mixes himself among the peoples, Ephrayim has become a cake unturned.

9 "Strangers have devoured his strength, but he does not know it. Grey hairs are also sprinkled on him, and he does not know it.

10 "And the Excellency of Yisra'ĕl did witness to his face, but they did not return to יהוה their Elohim, nor did they seek Him for all this.

11 "And Ephrayim has become a simple dove without heart, they have called on Mitsrayim, they have gone to Ashshur.

12 "When they go I spread My net over them, I bring them down like the birds of the heavens, I chastise them as their congregation has heard.

13 "Woe to them, for they have strayed from Me! Destruction to them, because they have transgressed against Me! And I Myself have ransomed them, yet they have spoken falsehoods against Me,

14 and did not cry out to Me with their heart when they wailed upon their beds. For grain and new wine they assemble themselves; they turn away from Me.

15 "And I instructed, I strengthened their arms, but they plot evil against Me.

16 "They return but not above. They have been like a slack bow. Their rulers fall by the sword for the cursings of their tongue. This is their scorn in the land of Mitsrayim.

8 "Put a shophar to your mouth, like an eagle against the House of יהוה, because they have transgressed My covenant, and they have rebelled against My Torah.

2 "They cry out to Me, 'My Elohim – we, Yisra'ĕl, know You!'

3 "Yisra'ĕl has rejected what is good, an enemy pursues him.

4 “They have made sovereigns, but not
from Me. They have made rulers, but I
have not known. From their silver and gold
they made idols for themselves, so that
they are cut off.
5 “O Shomeron, your calf has been cast
off! My wrath has burned against them.
How long shall they be incapable of innocence?
6 “For from Yisra’ěl is even this: a workman made it, and it is not Elohim! For the
calf of Shomeron is splinters!
7 “For they sow the wind, and reap the
whirlwind. The stalk has no bud, it yields
no grain. If it does yield, strangers swallow
it up.
8 “Yisra’ěl has been swallowed up. They
have now become among the nations as a
vessel in which is no pleasure.
9 “For they themselves have gone up to
Ashshur. A wild donkey alone by itself is
Ephrayim, they have hired lovers.
10 “Also, although they sold themselves
among the nations, this time I shall gather
them, when they have suffered for a while
from the burden of a sovereign, of rulers.
11 “Since Ephrayim has made many
slaughter-places for sin, they have been
slaughter-places for sinning to him.
12 “I have written for him numerous matters of My Torah – they were regarded as
strange.
13 “As for My slaughterings: they slaughter flesh and they eat. יהוה shall not accept
them. Now does He remember their
crookedness and punish their sins. Let
them return to Mitsrayim!
14 “For Yisra’ěl has forgotten his Maker,
and has built palaces. And Yehuḏah has
increased walled cities. But I shall send
fire upon his cities, and it shall devour his
strongholds.”

9 O Yisra’ěl, do not rejoice with exulta-
tion like the peoples, for you have
whored from your Elohim. You have loved
a harlot-fee at all threshing-floors.
2 Threshing floor and winepress shall not
feed them, and new wine shall fail in her.
3 They shall not dwell in the land of
יהוה, but Ephrayim shall return to
Mitsrayim, and eat unclean *food* in
Ashshur.
4 They do not pour wine *offerings* to
יהוה, nor are they pleasing to Him. Their
slaughterings are like bread of mourners to
them, all who eat it are defiled. For their
bread is for their beings, it does not come
into the House of יהוה.
5 What do you do for the Day of
Appointment, and in the day of the
Festival of יהוה?
6 For look, they shall go because of
destruction – Mitsrayim gathers them up,
Moph buries them, nettles possess their
valuables of silver, thorns are in their tents.
7 The days of punishment have come, the
days of retribution have come. Yisra’ěl
knows! The prophet is a fool, the ‘man of
the Spirit’ is mad, because of the greatness
of your crookedness, and great is the enmity.
8 Elohim’s watchman over you, Ephrayim, is the prophet, but a trapper’s snare is
in all his ways. Enmity is in the House of
his Elohim.
9 They have deeply corrupted themselves, as in the days of Giḇ‘ah. He
remembers their crookedness, He punishes
their sins.
10 “I found Yisra’ěl like grapes in the
wilderness. I saw your fathers as the first-
fruits on the fig tree in its beginning. They
themselves have gone to Ba‘al Pe‘or, and
separated themselves to shame, and
became as abominable as that which they
loved.
11 “Ephrayim is like a bird, their esteem
has flown away – no birth, and none with
child, and no conception!
12 “Though they bring up their children, I
shall make them childless, without man.
For it is woe to them when I turn away
from them!
13 “I have seen Ephrayim, like Tsor, planted in a pleasant place. But Ephrayim shall
bring out his children to the killer.”
14 Give them, O יהוה – give what? Give
them a miscarrying womb and dry breasts.
15 “All their evil is in Gilgal, for there I
have hated them. Because of the evil of
their deeds I drive them from My house,

no more do I love them. All their rulers are
rebels.
16 "Ephrayim has been stricken, their root
has dried up, they yield no fruit. Even if
they bear children, I shall put to death the
precious ones of their womb."
17 My Elohim rejects them, because they
have not obeyed Him, so that they become
wanderers among the nations! [a]

10 Yisra'ěl is a degenerate vine, he
brings forth fruit for himself. As
his fruit increased, he increased the slaughter-places. And the better his land, the better they made the pillars.
2 Their heart has been slippery, now they
are guilty. He breaks down their slaughter-
places, He destroys their pillars.
3 For now they say, "We have no sovereign, because we did not fear יהוה. What
would the sovereign do for us?"
4 They have spoken words, swearing
falsely in making a covenant. Therefore
judgment shall spring up like poisonous
weeds in the furrows of the field.
5 The inhabitants of Shomeron fear
because of the calf of Běyth Awen. For its
people shall mourn for it, as well as its
priests who used to rejoice over it, because
of its esteem that has departed from it.
6 It is also brought to Ashshur as a present for Sovereign Yarěḇ. Ephrayim does
receive shame, and Yisra'ěl is put to shame
through his counsel.
7 Shomeron is cut off, her sovereign is
like a twig on the surface of the water.
8 And the high places of Awen, the sin of
Yisra'ěl, shall be destroyed, thorn and thistle come up on their slaughter-places. And
they shall say to the mountains, "Cover
us!" and to the hills, "Fall on us!"
9 "O Yisra'ěl, you have sinned from the
days of Giḇ'ah. There they stood! The
battle in Giḇ'ah against the children of
perversity did not overtake them.
10 "When I desire, then I bind them. And
peoples shall be gathered against them
when I bind them for their double guilt.
11 "And Ephrayim is a trained heifer,
loving to thresh grain. But I Myself shall
pass over her comely neck – I put
Ephrayim to the yoke, Yehuḏah ploughs,
Ya'aqoḇ harrows for him."
12 Sow for yourselves righteousness, reap
according to loving-commitment, break up
your tillable ground, it is time to seek יהוה,
till He comes and rains [a] righteousness on
you.
13 You have ploughed wrongness, you
have reaped unrighteousness, you have
eaten the fruit of lying, because you trusted
in your own way, in your many mighty
men.
14 And uproar shall arise among your people, and all your strongholds shall be ravaged as Shalman ravaged Běyth Arběl in
the day of battle – a mother dashed in
pieces on her children.
15 Thus it shall be done to you, O Běyth
Ěl, because of the evil of your wickedness.
At dawn the sovereign of Yisra'ěl is completely cut off!

11 "When Yisra'ěl was a child, I loved
him, and out of Mitsrayim I called
My son.
2 "They called to them, so they went
from their face. They slaughtered to the
Ba'als, and burned incense to carved
images.
3 "And I taught Ephrayim to walk, taking
them by their arms, but they did not know
that I healed them.
4 "I drew them with ropes of man, with
cords of love, and I was to them as those
who take the yoke from their neck. And I
bent down, fed them.
5 "No, let him return to the land of
Mitsrayim, and let Ashshur be his sovereign, because they refused to repent!
6 "And the sword shall whirl in his cities,
and it shall demolish his gate bars, and
consume, because of their own counsels.
7 "My people are bent towards backsliding from Me. Though they call to *the One*
Above, none of them exalt *Him*.
8 "How could I give you up, Ephrayim?
How could I hand you over, Yisra'ěl? How

9a Refer Deḇ. 28:36.

could I make you like Aḏmah? How could
I set you like Tseḇoyim? My heart turns
within Me, all My compassion is kindled.
9 "I shall not let the heat of My wrath
burn, I shall not turn to destroy Ephrayim.
For I am Ěl, and not man, the Set-apart
One in your midst, and I shall not come in
enmity.
10 "Let them follow יהוה. Like a lion He
roars. When He roars, then sons shall tremble from the west.
11 "They shall tremble like a bird from
Mitsrayim, and like a dove from the land
of Ashshur. And I shall let them dwell in
their own houses," declares יהוה.
12 "Ephrayim has surrounded Me with
lying, and the house of Yisra'ěl with
deceit. But Yehuḏah is still wandering with
Ěl, and is true to the Set-apart One."

12 Ephrayim is feeding on wind, and
pursuing an east wind. All the day
he increases falsehood and ruin. And they
make a covenant with Ashshur, and oil is
sent to Mitsrayim.
2 And יהוה has a controversy with
Yehuḏah, to punish Ya'aqoḇ according to
his ways, to repay him according to his
deeds.
3 He took his brother by the heel in the
womb, and in his strength he strove with
Elohim.
4 He strove with the Messenger and overcame, [a] he wept and sought His favour. He
found Him in Běyth Ěl, and there He spoke
to us –
5 even יהוה Elohim of hosts, יהוה is His
remembrance.
6 Therefore, return to your Elohim.
Guard loving-commitment and right-ruling, and wait on your Elohim continually.
7 A merchant! In his hand are scales of
deceit, he loved to oppress.
8 And Ephrayim says, "Indeed, I have
become rich, I have found wealth for
myself. In all my labours they shall find in
me no crookedness that is sin."
9 "But I am יהוה your Elohim since the
land of Mitsrayim, again I shall make you
dwell in tents as in the days of the appointed time. [12b]
10 "And I have spoken to the prophets,
and have increased visions. And through
the prophets I gave parables."
11 Is Gil'aḏ wicked? Certainly, they have
been false! In Gilgal they have slaughtered
bulls. Also their slaughter-places are as
heaps on a ploughed field.
12 And when Ya'aqoḇ fled to the country
of Aram, Yisra'ěl served for a wife, and for
a wife he kept watch.
13 And by a prophet יהוה brought Yisra'ěl
out of Mitsrayim, and by a prophet he was
watched over.
14 Ephrayim has provoked most bitterly.
So his Master left his blood-guilt on him,
and repaid him for his reproach.

13 When Ephrayim spoke there was
trembling, he was lifted up in Yisra'ěl. But through Ba'al he became guilty,
and he died.
2 And now they sin more and more, and
make for themselves moulded images from
their silver, idols according to their skill,
all of them the work of craftsmen. They
say of them, "Let the men who slaughter
kiss the calves!"
3 Therefore they shall be like a morning
cloud, and like dew that goes away early,
like chaff blown off from a threshing-floor,
and like smoke from a window.
4 "But I am יהוה your Elohim since the
land of Mitsrayim, and an Elohim besides
Me you shall not know, for there is no
Saviour besides Me.
5 "I knew you in the wilderness, in the
land of drought.
6 "When they were fed they were satisfied. They were satisfied and their heart
was exalted, therefore they forgot Me.
7 "So I am become like a lion to them,
like a leopard I watch by the way,
8 like a bear robbed of her young I attack
them and rip open the enclosure of their
heart. And there I devour them like a lion,
a wild beast tear them apart.
9 "You have destroyed yourself, O

12a Ber. 32:28. *12b* Or *festival.*

Yisra'ěl, but your help is in Me.
10 "Where is your sovereign now to save
you in all your cities, and your rulers of
whom you said, 'Give me a sovereign and
rulers'?
11 "I gave you a sovereign in My displeasure, but I took *him* away in My wrath.
12 "The crookedness of Ephrayim is
bound up, his sin is hidden.
13 "Pains of a woman in labour shall come
upon him. He is not a wise son, for it is not
the time that he should delay at the breaking forth of children.
14 "From the power of She'ol I ransom
them, from death I redeem them. Where
is your plague, O Death? Where is your
destruction, O She'ol? Repentance is
hidden from My eyes.
15 "Though he bears fruit among his
brothers, an east wind comes, a wind from
יהוה comes up from the wilderness, and it
dries up his fountain, and his spring
becomes dry – it plunders a treasure of all
desirable objects.
16 "Shomeron is held guilty, for she has
rebelled against her Elohim – they fall by
the sword, their infants are dashed in
pieces, and their pregnant women ripped
open."

14 O Yisra'ěl, return to יהוה your
Elohim, for you have stumbled by
your crookedness.
2 Take words with you, and return to
יהוה. Say to Him, "Take away all crookedness, and accept what is good, and we render the bulls of our lips. [a]
3 "Ashshur does not save us. We do not
ride on horses, nor ever again do we say to
the work of our hands, 'Our mighty ones.'
For the fatherless finds compassion in
You."
4 "I shall heal their backsliding, I shall
love them spontaneously, for My displeasure has turned away from him.
5 "I shall be like the dew to Yisra'ěl. He
shall blossom like the lily, and strike out
his roots like Leḇanon.
6 "His branches shall spread, and his
splendour shall be like an olive tree, and
his fragrance like Leḇanon.
7 "Those who dwell under his shadow
shall return. They shall revive like grain,
and blossom like the vine, and become as
fragrant as the wine of Leḇanon.
8 "What more has Ephrayim to do with
idols? It is I who answer and look after
him. I am like a green cypress tree, your
fruit comes from Me."
9 Who is wise and understands these
words, discerning and knows them? For
the ways of יהוה are straight, and the righteous walk in them, but the transgressors
stumble in them.

14a Iḇ`rim 13:15 - bulls, referring to offerings.

YO'ĚL

JOEL

1 The word of יהוה that came to Yo'ěl
son of Pethu'ěl.
2 Hear this, you elders, and give ear, all
you inhabitants of the land! Has this *ever*
been in your days, or even in the days of
your fathers?
3 Relate it to your children, and your children to their children, and their children to
the generation after them.
4 What the gnawing locust left the
swarming locust has eaten, and what the
swarming locust left the crawling locust
has eaten, and what the crawling locust left
the consuming locust has eaten.
5 Wake up, you drunkards, and weep.
And wail, all you drinkers of wine, on
account of the new wine, for it has been cut
off from your mouth.
6 For a nation has come up against My
land, strong, and innumerable. Its teeth are
the teeth of a lion, and it has the fangs of a
lioness.
7 It has laid waste My vine and splintered
My fig tree. It has made it entirely bare and
cast it away, its branches became white.
8 Wail like a maiden girded with sackcloth for the husband of her youth.
9 The grain offering and the drink offering have been cut off from the House of
יהוה. The priests, servants of יהוה, have
mourned.
10 The field is ravaged, the ground has
mourned, for the grain is ruined, the new
wine has dried up, the oil fails.
11 The farmers are ashamed, the vinedressers wail over the wheat and over the
barley, for the harvest of the field is
destroyed.
12 The vine has dried up, and the fig tree
droops, pomegranate, also palm, and apple
tree, all the trees of the field are dried up,
because joy has dried up among the sons of
men.
13 Gird yourselves and lament, you
priests. Wail, you attendants of the slaughter-place. Come, lie all night in sackcloth,
you attendants of my Elohim. For the grain
offering and the drink offering are withheld
from the house of your Elohim.
14 Set apart a fast. Call an assembly,
gather the elders, all the inhabitants of the
land, into the House of יהוה your Elohim,
and cry out to יהוה.
15 Alas for the day! For the day of יהוה is
near, and it comes as destruction from the
Almighty.
16 Is not the food cut off before our eyes,
joy and gladness from the House of our
Elohim?
17 The seed has rotted under their clods,
storehouses are laid waste, granaries are
broken down, for the grain has withered.
18 How the beasts moan! The herds of
cattle are restless, because they have no
pasture. The flocks of sheep also perish.
19 I cry to You יהוה, for fire has consumed
the pastures of the wilderness, and a flame
has set on fire all the trees of the field.
20 Even the beasts of the field cry out to
You, for the water streams are dried up, and
fire has consumed the pastures of the
wilderness.

2 Blow a shophar in Tsiyon, and sound
an alarm in My set-apart mountain!
Let all the inhabitants of the earth tremble,
for the day of יהוה is coming, for it is near:
2 a day of darkness and gloom, a day of
clouds and thick darkness, like the morning
clouds spread over the mountains – a people many and strong, the like of whom has
never been, nor shall there ever be again
after them, to the years of many generations.
3 Ahead of them a fire has consumed, and
behind them a flame burns. Before them
the land is like the Garden of Ěḏen, and
behind them a desert waste. And from them
there is no escape.

4 Their appearance is like the appearance
of horses, and they run like steeds.
5 As the noise of chariots they leap over
mountaintops, as the noise of a flaming fire
consuming stubble, as a mighty people set
in battle array.
6 Before them peoples are in anguish, all
faces become flushed.
7 They run like mighty men, they climb
the wall like men of battle, every one goes
on his way, and they do not break ranks.
8 And they do not press one another,
every one goes in his path. They fall among
the weapons, but they do not stop.
9 They rush on the city, they run on the
wall. They climb into the houses, they enter
at the windows like a thief.
10 The earth shall tremble before them, the
heavens shall shake. Sun and moon shall be
darkened, and the stars withdraw their
brightness.
11 And יהוה shall give forth His voice
before His army, for His camp is very
great, for mighty is the doer of His word.
For the day of יהוה is great and very
awesome, and who does bear it?
12 "Yet even now," declares יהוה, "turn to
Me with all your heart, and with fasting,
and with weeping, and with mourning."
13 And tear your heart and not your
garments, and turn back to יהוה your
Elohim, for He shows favour and is compassionate, patient, and of great loving-
commitment, and He shall relent concerning the evil.
14 Who knows – He might turn and relent,
and leave a blessing behind Him, a grain
offering and a drink offering for יהוה your
Elohim?
15 Blow a shophar in Tsiyon, set apart a
fast, call an assembly.
16 Gather the people, set the assembly
apart, assemble the elders, gather the children and nursing babes. Let a bridegroom
come out from his room, and a bride from
her dressing room.
17 Let the priests, servants of יהוה, weep
between the porch and the slaughter-place.
And let them say, "Spare Your people, O
יהוה, and do not give Your inheritance to
reproach, for the nations to rule over them.
Why should they say among the peoples,
'Where is their Elohim?' "
18 And let יהוה be jealous for His land,
and spare His people.
19 And let יהוה answer and say to His people, "See, I am sending you the grain and
the new wine and the oil, and you shall be
satisfied by them. And no longer do I make
you a reproach among the nations.
20 "And the Northerner I shall remove far
from you, and drive him away into a dry
and deserted land, with his face toward the
eastern sea and his rear toward the western
sea. And his stench shall come up and his
smell rise, for he has done greatly."
21 Do not fear, O soil, be glad and rejoice,
for יהוה has done greatly!
22 Do not fear, you beasts of the field, for
the pastures of the wilderness shall spring
forth, and the tree shall bear its fruit, the fig
tree and the vine shall yield their strength.
23 And you children of Tsiyon, be glad and
rejoice in יהוה your Elohim, for He shall
give you the Teacher of Righteousness, and
cause the rain to come down for you, the
former rain and the latter rain, as before.
24 And the threshing-floors shall be filled
with grain, and the vats shall overflow with
new wine and oil.
25 "Then I shall repay you the years that
the swarming locust has eaten, the crawling
locust, and the consuming locust, and the
gnawing locust, My great army which I
sent among you.
26 "Then you shall eat – eat and be satisfied – and shall praise the Name of יהוה
your Elohim, who has done with you so
wondrously. And My people shall never be
put to shame.
27 "And you shall know that I am in the
midst of Yisra'ĕl,[a] and that I am יהוה your
Elohim and there is no one else. And My
people shall never be put to shame.
28 "And after this it shall be that I pour out
My Spirit on all flesh. And your sons and
your daughters shall prophesy, your old
men dream dreams, your young men see

2a See footnote Yesh. 24:23.

visions.

29 “And also on the male servants and on the female servants I shall pour out My Spirit in those days.

30 “And I shall give signs in the heavens and upon the earth: blood and fire and columns of smoke,

31 the sun is turned into darkness, and the moon into blood, before the coming of the great and awesome day of יהוה.

32 “And it shall be that everyone who calls on the Name of יהוה shall be delivered. [b] For on Mount Tsiyon and in Yerushalayim there shall be an escape [c] as יהוה has said, and among the survivors whom יהוה calls.

3

“For look, in those days and at that time, when I turn back the captivity of Yehuḏah and Yerushalayim,

2 then I shall gather all nations, and bring them down to the Valley of Yehoshaphat. And I shall enter into judgment with them there for My people, My inheritance Yisra’ěl, whom they have scattered among the nations, and they have divided up My land.

3 “And they have cast lots for My people, and have given a young man for a whore, and sold a girl for wine, and drank it.

4 “And also, what are you to Me, O Tsor and Tsiḏon, and all the coasts of Philistia? Are you repaying Me? And if you are repaying Me, I would swiftly and speedily return your reward on your own head.

5 “For you have taken My silver and My gold, and brought My treasures into your temples,

6 and the people of Yehuḏah and the people of Yerushalayim you have sold to the sons of Yawan, to remove them far from their borders.

7 “See, I am stirring them up out of the place to which you have sold them, and I shall return on your own head what you have done,

8 and shall sell your sons and your daughters into the hand of the people of Yehuḏah, and they shall sell them to the Sheḇaites, to a nation far off. For יהוה has spoken.”

9 Proclaim this among the nations, “Prepare for battle! Wake up the mighty men, let all the men of battle draw near, let them come up.

10 “Beat your ploughshares into swords and your pruning-hooks into spears, let the weak say, ‘I am strong.’ ”

11 Hasten and come, all you nations, and gather together all around. O יהוה, let Your mighty men come down here.

12 “Let the nations be aroused, and come up to the Valley of Yehoshaphat. For there I shall sit to judge all the nations on every side.

13 “Put in the sickle, for the harvest has grown ripe. Come, go down, for the winepress is filled, the vats overflow, for their evil is great.”

14 Crowds, crowds in the valley of decision! For the day of יהוה is near in the valley of decision.

15 Sun and moon shall become dark, and stars shall withdraw their brightness.

16 And יהוה shall roar from Tsiyon, and give forth His voice from Yerushalayim. And the heavens and earth shall shake, but יהוה shall be a refuge for His people, and a stronghold for the children of Yisra’ěl.

17 “Then you shall know that I am יהוה your Elohim, dwelling in Tsiyon, My set-apart mountain. [a] And Yerushalayim shall be set-apart, and foreigners shall not pass through her again.

18 “And it shall be in that day that the mountains drip with new wine, and the hills flow with milk. And all the streams of Yehuḏah shall be flooded with water, and a fountain flow from the House of יהוה and water the wadi Shittim.

19 “Mitsrayim shall become a ruin, and Eḏom a ruin, a wilderness, because of violence done to the people of Yehuḏah, whose innocent blood they shed in their land.

20 “But Yehuḏah shall dwell forever, and Yerushalayim to all generations.

21 “And I shall avenge their blood, which I have not avenged. And יהוה shall be dwelling in Tsiyon!”

2b Ma. 2:21, Rom. 10:13. *2c* Yesh. 4:2-3, Oḇaḏ. v. 17, Rev. 14:1. *3a* See v. 21, and footnote at Yesh. 24:23.

AMOS

1 The words of Amos, who was among
the herdsmen of Teqowa, which he saw
concerning Yisra'ěl in the days of Uzziyah
sovereign of Yehuḏah, and in the days of
Yaroḇʽam son of Yo'ash, sovereign of
Yisra'ěl, two years before the earthquake.
2 And he said, "יהוה roars from Tsiyon,
and gives forth His voice from Yerushalayim. And the pastures of the shepherds
shall mourn, and the top of Karmel shall
wither."
3 Thus said יהוה, "For three transgressions of Dammeseq, and for four, I do not
turn it back, because they threshed Gilʽaḏ
with threshing implements of iron.
4 "But I shall send fire upon the house of
Ḥaza'ěl, and it shall consume the palaces of
Ben-Haḏaḏ.
5 "And I shall break the bar of
Dammeseq, and cut off the inhabitant from
the Valley of Awen, and the one who holds
the sceptre from Běyth Ěḏen. And the
people of Aram shall go exiled to Qir," said
יהוה.
6 Thus said יהוה, "For three transgressions of Azzah, and for four, I do not turn it
back, because they took into exile an entire
exile, to surrender it to Eḏom.
7 "But I shall send fire upon the wall of
Azzah, and it shall consume its palaces.
8 "And I shall cut off the inhabitant from
Ashdoḏ, and the one who holds the sceptre
from Ashqelon. And I shall turn My hand
against Eqron, and the remnant of the
Philistines shall perish," said the Master
יהוה.
9 Thus said יהוה, "For three transgressions of Tsor, and for four, I do not turn it
back, because they surrendered an entire
exile to Eḏom, and did not remember the
brotherly covenant.
10 "But I shall send fire upon the wall of
Tsor, and it shall consume its palaces."
11 Thus said יהוה, "For three transgressions of Eḏom, and for four, I do not turn it
back, because he pursued his brother with
the sword, and cast off all compassion. And
his displeasure tore incessantly, and he kept
his wrath forever.
12 "But I shall send fire upon Těman, and it
shall consume the palaces of Botsrah."
13 Thus said יהוה, "For three transgressions of the children of Ammon, and for
four, I do not turn it back, because they
ripped open the pregnant women in Gilʽaḏ,
to enlarge their border.
14 "So I shall kindle a fire upon the wall of
Rabbah, and it shall consume its palaces,
with a shout in the day of battle, with a
storm in the day of the whirlwind.
15 "And their sovereign shall go into exile,
he and his heads together," said יהוה.

2 Thus said יהוה, "For three transgressions of Mo'aḇ, and for four, I do not
turn it back, because he burned the bones of
the sovereign of Eḏom to lime.
2 "But I shall send fire upon Mo'aḇ, and it
shall consume the palaces of Qeriyoth. And
Mo'aḇ shall die amid uproar, with a cry and
with a voice of a shophar.
3 "And I shall cut off the judge from its
midst, and kill all its heads with him," said
יהוה.
4 Thus said יהוה, "For three transgressions of Yehuḏah, and for four, I do not turn
it back, because they have rejected the
Torah of יהוה, and did not guard His laws.
And their lies after which their fathers
walked lead them astray.
5 "But I shall send fire upon Yehuḏah, and
it shall consume the palaces of Yerushalayim."
6 Thus said יהוה, "For three transgressions of Yisra'ěl, and for four, I do not turn
it back, because they sell the righteous for
silver, and the poor for a pair of sandals,
7 who crush the head of the poor ones in
the dust of the earth, and turn aside the way
of the meek. And a man and his father go in
to the same girl, to defile My set-apart
Name.

8 "And they lie down by every slaughter-
place on garments taken in pledge, and in
the house of their mighty one they drink the
wine of those who have been fined.
9 "Yet I destroyed the Amorite before
them, whose height was like the height of
the cedars. And he was as strong as the
oaks, yet I destroyed his fruit from above
and his roots from beneath.
10 "And I brought you up from the land of
Mitsrayim, and led you forty years through
the wilderness, to possess the land of the
Amorite.
11 "And I raised up some of your sons as
prophets, and some of your young men as
Nazirites. Not so? O you children of Yisra'ěl?" declares יהוה.
12 "But you made the Nazirites drink wine,
and commanded the prophets saying, 'Do
not prophesy!'
13 "See, I am weighed down by you, as a
wagon is weighed down when filled with
sheaves.
14 "And a place to flee shall perish from
the swift, and the strong not fortify his
power, and the mighty not save his life,
15 and he who handles the bow not stand,
and the swift of foot not save, nor he who
rides a horse save his life,
16 and the one potent of his heart among
the mighty flee naked, in that day," declares
יהוה.

3 Hear this word that יהוה has spoken
against you, O children of Yisra'ěl,
against the entire clan which I brought up
from the land of Mitsrayim, saying,
2 "You alone have I known of all the clans
of the earth, therefore I punish you for all
your crookednesses."
3 Would two walk together, without having met?
4 Does a lion roar in the forest, when he
has no prey? Does a young lion give forth
his voice out of his den unless he has
caught?
5 Does a bird fall into a snare on the earth,
where there is no trap for it? Does a snare
spring up from the earth, if it has not captured prey?
6 If a shophar is blown in a city, do the
people not tremble? If there is calamity in a
city, shall not יהוה have done it?
7 For the Master יהוה does no matter
unless He reveals His secret to His servants
the prophets.
8 A lion has roared! Who is not afraid?
The Master יהוה has spoken! Who would
not prophesy?
9 "Cry out at the palaces in Ashdoḏ, and at
the palaces in the land of Mitsrayim, and
say, 'Gather on the mountains of Shomeron,
and see the many unrests in her midst, and
the oppressed ones within her.
10 'But they do not know to do what is
right,' declares יהוה, 'these who store up
plunder and loot in their palaces.' "
11 Therefore thus said the Master יהוה,
"An enemy, even all around the land! And
he shall bring down your strength from you,
and your palaces shall be plundered."
12 Thus said יהוה, "As a shepherd rescues
from the mouth of a lion two legs or a piece
of an ear, so are the children of Yisra'ěl who
dwell in Shomeron to be rescued – in the
corner of a bed and on the edge of a couch!
13 "Hear and witness against the house of
Ya'aqoḇ," declares the Master יהוה, the
Elohim of hosts.
14 "For in the day I visit Yisra'ěl for their
transgressions, I shall also punish concerning the slaughter-places of Běyth Ěl. And
the horns of the slaughter-place shall be
broken, and they shall fall to the ground.
15 "And I shall strike the winter house
along with the summer house. And the
houses of ivory shall perish, and the great
houses shall be swept away," declares יהוה.

4 Hear this word, you cows of Bashan,
who are on the mountain of Shomeron,
who are oppressing the poor, who are crushing the needy, who are saying to their masters, "Bring wine, let us drink!"
2 The Master יהוה has sworn by His set-
apartness, "See, days are coming upon you
when He shall take you away with hooks,
and your descendants with fish-hooks,
3 and let you go out at the breaches, each
woman before her, and you shall be cast out
toward Harmon," declares יהוה.
4 "Come to Běyth Ěl and transgress, to

Gilgal, increase transgression. And bring
your slaughterings every morning, your
tithes every three days.
5 "And burn an offering of thanksgiving
with leaven, proclaim voluntary offerings,
loudly. For you have loved this, you
children of Yisra'ěl!" declares the Master
יהוה.
6 "And I also gave you cleanness of teeth
in all your cities, and lack of bread in all
your places. But you did not turn back to
Me," declares יהוה.
7 "And I also withheld rain from you,
three new *moons* before the harvest. Then I
would send rain on one city, and on another
city I would not send rain. One part was
rained upon, and where it did not rain the
part would dry up.
8 "Then two or three cities would wander
to another city to drink water, but they were
not satisfied. But you did not turn back to
Me," declares יהוה.
9 "I have stricken you with blight and with
mildew. The creeping locust devoured your
many gardens, and your vineyards, and
your fig trees, and your olive trees. But you
did not turn back to Me," declares יהוה.
10 "I have sent among you a plague in the
way of Mitsrayim. I have killed your young
men with a sword, along with your captured
horses. And I made the stench of your
camps come up into your nostrils. But you
did not turn back to Me," declares יהוה.
11 "I have overthrown some of you, as
Elohim overthrew Seḏom and Amorah, and
you were like a burning stick plucked from
the burning. But you did not turn back to
Me," declares יהוה.
12 "Therefore I am doing this to you, O
Yisra'ěl. And because I do this to you,
prepare to meet your Elohim, O Yisra'ěl!"
13 For look, He who forms mountains, and
creates the wind, and who declares to man
what His thought is, and makes the morning
darkness, and who treads the high places of
the earth, יהוה Elohim of hosts
is His Name.

5 Hear this word which I take up against
you, this lamentation, O house of
Yisra'ěl:
2 The maiden of Yisra'ěl has fallen, not to
rise again. She lies forsaken on her land,
with no one to lift her up.
3 For thus said the Master יהוה, "The city
that goes out by a thousand has a hundred
left, and that which goes out by a hundred
has ten left to the house of Yisra'ěl."
4 For thus said יהוה to the house of
Yisra'ěl, "Seek Me and live,
5 but do not seek Běyth Ěl, nor enter
Gilgal, nor pass over to Be'ěrsheḇa. For
Gilgal shall certainly go into exile, and
Běyth Ěl become a non-entity.
6 "Seek יהוה and live, lest He break out
like fire upon the house of Yosěph, and shall
consume it, with no one to quench it in
Běyth Ěl.
7 "O you who are turning right-ruling to
wormwood, and have cast down righteousness to the earth!"
8 He who made Kimah and Kesil, and
who turns the shadow of death into morning and darkened day into night, who is
calling for the waters of the sea and pours
them out on the face of the earth – יהוה is
His Name –
9 who is flashing forth destruction upon
the strong, so that destruction comes upon
the stronghold.
10 They hated the one who reproves in the
gate, and they despise the one who speaks
the truth.[a]
11 Therefore, because you trample on the
poor and take grain taxes from him – you
have built houses of hewn stone but you are
not going to dwell in them, you have planted pleasant vineyards but not drink wine
from them.
12 For I know your transgressions are many
and your sins are great, afflicting the righteous and accepting bribes, and turning aside
the poor at the gate.
13 Therefore the wise keep silent at that
time, for it is an evil time.
14 Seek good and not evil, so that you live.

5a Yesh. 59:15, Tim. ב 4:4.

And let יהוה Elohim of hosts be with you,
as you have spoken.
15 Hate evil and love good, and set up
right-ruling in the gate. It might be that יהוה
Elohim of hosts shows favour to the remnant of Yosĕph.
16 Therefore יהוה Elohim of hosts, יהוה,
said this, "There is wailing in all open
squares, and in all the streets they say,
'Alas! Alas!' and shall call the farmer to
mourning, and skilled lamenters to wailing.
17 "And in all vineyards there is wailing,
for I pass through your midst," said יהוה.
18 Woe to you who are longing for the day
of יהוה! What does the day of יהוה mean to
you? It is darkness, and not light,
19 as when a man flees from a lion, and a
bear shall meet him; or entered his house,
rested his hand on the wall, and a serpent
shall bite him.
20 Is not the day of יהוה darkness, and not
light? Is it not very dark, with no brightness
in it?
21 "I have hated, I have despised your
festivals, and I am not pleased with your
assemblies.
22 "Though you offer Me ascending offerings and your grain offerings, I do not
accept them, nor do I look on your fattened
peace offerings.
23 "Take away from Me the noise of your
songs, for I do not hear the sound of your
stringed instruments.
24 "And let right-ruling roll on like water,
and righteousness like a mighty stream.
25 "You brought Me slaughterings and
meal offerings in the wilderness for forty
years, O house of Yisra'ĕl,
26 but you took up Sikkuth your sovereign
and Kiyyun, your idols, your astral mighty
ones, [b] which you made for yourselves!
27 "Therefore I shall send you into exile
beyond Dammeseq," said יהוה Elohim of
hosts – His Name.

6 Woe to those at ease in Tsiyon, and
those trusting in Mount Shomeron, the
distinguished ones among the chief of the
nations, to whom the house of Yisra'ĕl
comes!
2 Pass over to Kalneh and see, and from
there go to Ḥamath the great. Then go down
to Gath of the Philistines. Are you better
than these reigns, or is their border greater
than your border?
3 You who are putting off the day of evil,
yet bring near the seat of violence,
4 who are lying on beds of ivory, and are
stretched out on your couches, and are
eating lambs from the flock and calves from
the midst of the stall,
5 who are singing to the sound of the harp,
having composed songs for themselves like
Dawiḏ,
6 who are drinking wine from bowls, and
anoint with the finest ointments, yet they
have not been pained over the breach of
Yosĕph!
7 Therefore they shall now go into exile,
with the first of the exiles, and the feasting
of the stretched-out ones shall cease!
8 The Master יהוה has sworn by Himself,
יהוה Elohim of hosts declares, "I am
loathing the pride of Ya'aqoḇ, and I have
hated his palaces. Therefore I shall deliver
up the city and all that is in it."
9 And it shall be, that if ten men remain in
one house, they shall die.
10 And if an uncle, or his undertaker, brings
the remains out of the house, he shall say to
one inside the house, "Is anyone with you?"
and he says, "No," then he shall say,
"Hush!" For we have not remembered the
Name of יהוה!
11 For look, יהוה is commanding, and He
shall strike the great house with breaches,
and the little house with clefts.
12 Do horses run on a rock? Does one
plough it with oxen? For you have turned
right-ruling into poison, and the fruit of
righteousness into wormwood,
13 you who are rejoicing over a matter of
naught, who say, "Have we not taken horns
for ourselves by our own strength?"
14 "For look, I am raising up a nation
against you, O house of Yisra'ĕl," declares
יהוה Elohim of hosts, "and they shall
oppress you from the entrance of Ḥamath to

5b Ma. 7:43.

the wadi Araḇah."

7 This is what the Master יהוה showed
me, and see, He was forming locust
swarms at the beginning of the late crop.
And see, it was the late crop after the mow-
ings of the sovereign.
2 And it came to be, when they had finished eating the grass of the land, that I said,
"O Master יהוה, forgive, I pray! How does
Ya'aqoḇ survive, for he is small?"
3 יהוה relented concerning this. "It shall
not be," said יהוה.
4 This is what the Master יהוה showed
me, and see, the Master יהוה was calling to
contend by fire, and it consumed the great
deep and did consume the portion,
5 and I said, "O Master יהוה, please stop!
How does Ya'aqoḇ survive, for he is
small?"
6 יהוה relented concerning this. "This
shall not be either," said the Master יהוה.
7 This is what He showed me, and see,
יהוה stood on a wall made with a plumb-
line, with a plumb-line in His hand,
8 and יהוה said to me, "Amos, what do
you see?" And I said, "A plumb-line." And
יהוה said, "See, I am setting a plumb-line in
the midst of My people Yisra'ěl, no longer
do I pardon them.
9 "And the high places of Yitsḥaq shall be
laid waste, and the set-apart places of
Yisra'ěl shall be destroyed. And I shall rise
with the sword against the house of
Yaroḇ'am."
10 Then Amatsyah the priest of Běyth Ěl
sent to Yaroḇ'am sovereign of Yisra'ěl, saying, "Amos has conspired against you in the
midst of the house of Yisra'ěl. The land is
not able to endure all his words,
11 for this is what Amos said, 'Yaroḇ'am
shall die by the sword, and Yisra'ěl
certainly be exiled from their own land.' "
12 And Amatsyah said to Amos, "Go, you
seer! Flee to the land of Yehuḏah, and eat
bread and prophesy there,
13 but do not prophesy any more at Běyth
Ěl, for it is the sovereign's set-apart place
and it is the house of the reign."
14 And Amos answered and said to
Amatsyah, "I am not a prophet, nor am I a
son of a prophet, for I am a herdsman and a
grower of sycamore figs.
15 "But יהוה took me from behind the
flock, and יהוה said to me, 'Go, prophesy to
My people Yisra'ěl.'
16 "And now, hear the word of יהוה. You
are saying, 'Do not prophesy against
Yisra'ěl, and do not drop *words* against the
house of Yitsḥaq.'
17 "Therefore thus said יהוה, 'Your wife
shall become a whore in the city, and your
sons and daughters fall by the sword, and
your land be divided by a *measuring* line,
and you die in a defiled land, and Yisra'ěl
shall certainly be exiled from its land.' "

8 This is what the Master יהוה showed
me, and see, a basket of summer fruit.
2 And He said, "Amos, what do you see?"
And I said, "A basket of summer fruit."
And יהוה said to me, "The end has come
upon my people Yisra'ěl, no longer do I
pardon them.
3 "And the songs of the Hěḵal shall be
wailing in that day," declares the Master
יהוה, "many dead bodies everywhere,
thrown into any place – hush!"
4 Hear this, you who are swallowing up
the needy, to do away with the poor of the
land,
5 saying, "When does the New Moon pass
so that we sell grain, and the Sabbath so that
we trade our wheat, to make the ěphah
small and the sheqel large, and to falsify the
scales by deceit,
6 to buy the poor for silver, and the needy
for a pair of sandals, and sell the chaff of the
wheat?"
7 יהוה has sworn by the Excellency of
Ya'aqoḇ, "I shall never forget any of their
works.
8 "Shall the land not tremble for this, and
everyone mourn who dwells in it? And all
of it shall swell like the River, heave and
subside like the River of Mitsrayim.
9 "And it shall be in that day," declares the
Master יהוה, "that I shall cause the sun to
go down at noon, and shall darken the earth
on a day of brightness,
10 and shall turn your festivals into mourning, and all your songs into lamentation, and

bring sackcloth on all loins, and baldness on
every head, and shall make it like mourning
for an only son, and its end like a day of bitterness.
11 "See, days are coming," declares the
Master יהוה, "that I shall send a hunger in
the land, not a hunger for bread, nor a thirst
for water, but for hearing the Words of יהוה.
12 "And they shall wander from sea to sea,
and from north to east – they shall diligently
search, seeking the Word of יהוה, but they
shall not find it. [a]
13 "In that day the beautiful maidens and
strong young men shall faint from thirst,
14 those swearing by the guilt of Shomeron, who say, 'As your mighty one lives, O
Dan!' and, 'As the way of Be'ĕrsheḇa
lives!' And they shall fall and never rise
again."

9 I saw יהוה standing by the slaughter-
place, and He said, "Strike the column
head, so that the thresholds shake, and break
them off by the head, all of them. And the
last of them I kill with the sword. Not one of
them fleeing gets away, and not one fugitive
of them escapes.
2 "If they dig into She'ol, from there my
hand does take them; and if they climb up to
the heavens, from there I bring them down.
3 "And if they hide themselves on top of
Karmel, from there I shall search, and take
them. And if they hide from before My eyes
at the bottom of the sea, from there I shall
command the serpent, and it shall bite them.
4 "And if they go into captivity before
their enemies, from there I shall command
the sword, and it shall kill them. And I shall
set My eyes on them for evil and not for
good."
5 And the Master יהוה of hosts is He who
touches the earth so that it melts, and all
who dwell in it mourn, and all of it come up
like the River, and subside like the River of
Mitsrayim –
6 who is building His upper room in the
heavens, and has founded His firmament on
the earth, who is calling for the waters of the
sea, and pours them out on the face of the
earth – יהוה is His Name.
7 "Are you not like the people of Kush to
Me, O children of Yisra'ĕl?" declares יהוה.
"Did I not bring up Yisra'ĕl from the land of
Mitsrayim, and the Philistines from
Kaphtor, and Aram from Qir?
8 "Look, the eyes of the Master יהוה are
on the sinful reign, [a] and I shall destroy it
from the face of the earth, except that, I do
not completely destroy the house of
Ya'aqoḇ," declares יהוה.
9 "For look, I am commanding, and I shall
sift [b] the house of Yisra'ĕl among all the
nations, as one sifts [b] with a sieve, yet not a
grain falls to the ground.
10 "All the sinners of My people are going
to die by the sword, those who are saying,
'Evil does not overtake us nor meet us.'
11 "In that day I shall raise up the Booth of
Dawiḏ which has fallen down. And I shall
repair its breaches and raise up its ruins.
And I shall build it as in the days of old,
12 so that they possess the remnant of
Eḏom, [c] and all the nations on whom My
Name is called," [d] declares יהוה who does
this.
13 "Look, the days are coming," declares
יהוה, "that the ploughman shall overtake
the reaper, and the treader of grapes him
who sows seed. And the mountains shall
drip new wine, and all the hills melt.
14 "And I shall turn back the captivity of
My people Yisra'ĕl. And they shall build
the waste cities and inhabit them. And they
shall plant vineyards and drink wine from
them, and shall make gardens and eat their
fruit.
15 "And I shall plant them on their own
soil, and not uproot them any more from
their own soil I have given them," said יהוה
your Elohim!

8a Yirm. 5:13, Hosh. 8:12, Yeḥez. 34:3-10.
9a Yesh. 34:2, Yirm. 30:11, Yirm. 46:28, Dan. 2:44, Tseph. 3:8, Ḥagg. 2:22, Lq. 4:5-6. *9b* Or *shake – shakes.*
9c The vowels which the Massoretes added later on makes this read *Eḏom*, but it was probably a mistake. It should be *Aḏam*, meaning *mankind.* *9d* Ma. 15:16-17.

OḆAḎYAH

OBADIAH

1 The vision of Oḇaḏyah: This is what
the Master יהוה said concerning
Eḏom. We have heard a report from יהוה,
and a messenger has been sent among the
nations, saying, "Arise, and let us rise up
against her for battle!"
2 "See, I have made you small among the
nations, you are greatly despised.
3 "The pride of your heart has deceived
you, you who dwell in the clefts of the rock,
whose dwelling is high, who say in your
heart, 'Who shall bring me down to the
ground?'
4 "Though you rise high as the eagle, and
though you set your nest among the stars,
from there I shall bring you down," declares
יהוה.
5 "If thieves came to you, if robbers by
night, how ruined you would have been!
Would they not steal till they had enough?
If grape-gatherers had come to you, would
they not leave gleanings?
6 "How Ěsaw shall be searched out! His
hidden treasures shall be sought out!
7 "All your allies shall send you forth to the
border, your friends shall deceive you and
overpower you. They make your bread a
snare under you, without you discerning it!
8 "In that day," declares יהוה, "I shall
destroy the wise men from Eḏom, and
discernment from the mountains of Ěsaw!
9 "And your mighty men shall be discouraged, O Těman, so that everyone from the
mountains of Ěsaw is cut off by killing.
10 "Because of your violence against your
brother Ya'aqoḇ, let shame cover you. And
you shall be cut off forever.
11 "In the day that you stood on the other
side, in the day that strangers took captive
his wealth, when foreigners entered his
gates and cast lots for Yerushalayim, you
also were like one of them!
12 "And you should not have looked on
your brother's day in the day of his
estrangement, nor rejoiced over the children of Yehuḏah in the day of their destruction, nor made your mouth great in the day
of distress,
13 nor have entered the gate of My people
in the day of their calamity, nor looked
down on their evil in the day of their
calamity, nor have seized their wealth in the
day of their calamity,
14 nor have stood at the parting of the way
to cut off his fugitives, nor handed over his
survivors in the day of distress.
15 "For the day of יהוה is near upon all the
nations. As you have done, it shall be done
to you, your reward shall come back on
your own head.
16 "For as you have drunk on my set-apart
mountain, so do all the nations drink continually. And they shall drink and shall
swallow, and they shall be as though they
had never been.
17 "But on Mount Tsiyon there shall be an
escape, [a] and they shall be set-apart. And
the house of Ya'aqoḇ shall possess their
possessions.
18 "And the house of Ya'aqoḇ shall be a
fire, and the house of Yosěph a flame, but the
house of Ěsaw for stubble. And they shall
burn among them and they shall consume
them, so that no survivor is left of the house
of Ěsaw." For יהוה has spoken.
19 And they shall possess the South with
the mountains of Ěsaw, and low country
with the Philistines. And they shall possess
the fields of Ephrayim and the fields of
Shomeron, and Binyamin with Gil'aḏ,
20 and the exiles of this host of the children
of Yisra'ěl *possess* that of the Kena'anites
as far as Tsarephath, and the exiles of
Yerushalayim who are in Sepharaḏ possess
the cities of the South.
21 And saviours shall come to Mount
Tsiyon to judge the mountains of Ěsaw.
And the reign shall belong to יהוה. [b]

1a Yesh. 4:2-3, Yo'ěl 2:32, Ḥazon 14:1.
1b Teh. 2:8, Teh. 22:28, Dan. 2:44, Dan. 7:13-14 & 27, Zeḵ. 14: 9, Ḥazon 11:15, 12:10.

YONAH

JONAH

1 And the word of יהוה came to Yonah
son of Amittai, saying,
2 “Arise, go to Ninewĕh, the great city,
and cry out against it, for their evils have
come up before Me.”
3 But Yonah rose up to flee to Tarshish
from the presence of יהוה, and went down
to Yapho, and found a ship going to
Tarshish. And he paid the fare, and went
down into it, to go with them to Tarshish
from the presence of יהוה.
4 And יהוה sent out a great wind on the
sea, and there was a great storm on the sea,
so that the ship was thought to be broken
up.
5 And the seamen were afraid, and each
one cried out to his mighty one, and threw
the cargo which was in the ship into the
sea, to lighten the load. But Yonah had
gone down into the lowest parts of the
ship, and he lay down, and was fast asleep.
6 And the captain came to him, and said
to him, “What do you mean, sleeper?
Arise, cry out to your Elohim, if so be that
Elohim shall think about us, so that we do
not perish.”
7 And they said to each other, “Come,
and let us cast lots, so that we know for
whose sake this evil has come upon us.”
So they cast lots, and the lot fell on Yonah.
8 So they said to him, “Please explain to
us! For whose sake is this evil upon us?
What is your occupation? And where do
you come from? What is your country?
And from what people are you?”
9 And he said to them, “I am a Hebrew.
And I am fearing יהוה, the Elohim of the
heavens, who made the sea and the dry
land.”
10 And the men were exceedingly afraid,
and said to him, “Why have you done
this?” For the men knew that he fled from
the presence of יהוה, for he had informed
them.
11 And they said to him, “What are we to
do to you to make the sea calm for us?”
For the sea was growing more stormy.
12 And he said to them, “Take me and
throw me into the sea, so that the sea
becomes calm for you. For I know that this
great storm is because of me.”
13 However, the men rowed hard to bring
the ship to land, but were unable, for the
sea continued to grow more stormy against
them.
14 And they cried out to יהוה and said,
“We pray, O יהוה, please, let us not perish
for this man’s life, and do not lay on us
innocent blood. For You, O יהוה, have
done as it pleased You.”
15 Then they took Yonah and threw him
into the sea, and the sea stopped raging.
16 And the men feared יהוה exceedingly,
and slaughtered a slaughtering to יהוה and
made vows.
17 But יהוה appointed a great fish to
swallow Yonah. And Yonah was in the
stomach of the fish three days and three
nights.

2 And Yonah prayed to יהוה his Elohim
from the stomach of the fish.
2 And he said, “I called to יהוה because
of my distress, and He answered me. From
the stomach of She’ol I cried, and You
heard my voice.
3 “For You threw me into the deep, into
the heart of the seas, and the floods
surrounded me. All Your breakers and
Your waves passed over me.
4 “So I said, ‘I have been driven away
from Your eyes. Would I ever look again
toward Your set-apart Hĕḵal?’
5 “Waters encompassed me, unto life, the
deep closed around me, weeds were
wrapped around my head.
6 “I went down to the base of the mountains, the earth with its bars were behind
me forever. But You brought up my life
from the pit, O יהוה, my Elohim.
7 “When my life fainted within me, I
remembered יהוה. And my prayer went up

to You, into Your set-apart Hěkal.
8 "Those observing false worthlessnesses
forsake their own loving-commitment.
9 "But I slaughter to You with the voice
of thanksgiving, I pay what I have vowed.
Deliverance is of יהוה."
10 Then יהוה spoke to the fish, and it
vomited Yonah on the dry land.

3 And the word of יהוה came to Yonah
the second time, saying,
2 "Arise, go to Nineweh, that great city,
and proclaim to it the message that I am
speaking to you."
3 And Yonah arose and went to Nineweh,
according to the word of יהוה. Now
Nineweh was a great city before Elohim,
of three day's journey.
4 And Yonah began to go in to the city on
the first day's walk. And he cried out and
said, "Yet forty days, and Nineweh shall be
overthrown!"
5 And the men of Nineweh believed in
Elohim, and proclaimed a fast, and put on
sackcloth, from the greatest to the least of
them.
6 And the word reached the sovereign of
Nineweh, so he arose from his throne and
took off his robe, and covered himself with
sackcloth and sat in ashes.
7 And he proclaimed and said throughout
Nineweh, "By decree of the sovereign and
his nobles: No man or beast, herd or flock,
shall taste whatever – let them not eat, let
them not even drink water.
8 "But let man and beast be covered with
sackcloth, and call mightily to Elohim.
And let each one turn from his evil way
and from the violence that is in his hands.
9 "Who knows whether Elohim does turn
and relent, and shall turn away from the
heat of His displeasure, so that we do not
perish?"
10 And Elohim saw their works, that they
turned from their evil way. And Elohim
relented from the evil which He had said
He would do to them, and He did not do it.

4 But it greatly displeased Yonah, and
he was grieved.
2 And he prayed to יהוה, and he said,
"Please, יהוה, was this not what I said
while I was in my own land? This is why I
went ahead and fled to Tarshish. For I
know that You are an Ěl showing favour,
and compassionate, patient and of great
loving-commitment, and relenting from
doing evil.
3 "And now, O יהוה, please take my life
from me, for it is better for me to die than
to live!"
4 And יהוה said, "Are you right to be displeased?"
5 Then Yonah went out of the city and sat
on the east side of the city, and made
himself a shelter there, and sat under it in
the shade, to see what would become of
the city.
6 And יהוה Elohim appointed a plant and
made it come up over Yonah, to be a shade
for his head to deliver him from his dis-
comfort. And Yonah greatly rejoiced over
the plant.
7 But as morning dawned the next day
Elohim appointed a worm which struck the
plant so that it withered.
8 And it came to be when the sun came
up, that Elohim appointed a scorching east
wind, and the sun struck on Yonah's head,
so that he grew faint, and asked for his life
to die, and said, "It is better for me to die
than to live."
9 And Elohim said to Yonah, "Have you
rightly become displeased over the plant?"
And he said, "I have rightly become displeased, even to death!"
10 And יהוה said, "You felt sorry for the
plant for which you have not laboured, nor
made it grow, which came up in a night
and perished in a night.
11 "And should I not pardon Nineweh,
that great city, in which are more than one
hundred and twenty thousand beings who
have not known their right hand from their
left, and much cattle?"

MIḴAH

MICAH

1 The word of יהוה that came to Miḵah
of Moresheth in the days of Yotham,
Aḥaz, Ḥizqiyah, sovereigns of Yehuḏah,
which he saw concerning Shomeron and
Yerushalayim.
2 Hear, all you peoples! Listen, O earth,
and all who are in it! And let the Master
יהוה be a witness against you – יהוה from
His set-apart Hěḵal.
3 For look, יהוה is coming out of His
place,[a] and He shall come down and shall
tread on the high places of the earth.
4 And the mountains shall melt under
Him,[b] and the valleys be cleft as wax
before the fire, as waters poured down a
steep place.
5 All this is for the transgression of
Ya'aqoḇ and for the sins of the house of
Yisra'ěl. What is the transgression of
Ya'aqoḇ? Is it not Shomeron? And what
are the high places of Yehuḏah? Are they
not Yerushalayim?
6 "And I shall make Shomeron a heap in
the field, places for planting a vineyard.
And I shall pour down her stones into the
valley, and uncover her foundations.
7 "And all her carved images shall be
beaten in pieces, and all her harlot-fees be
burned with the fire. And all her idols I
shall lay waste, for she gathered it from the
harlot-fee of a whore, and they shall return
to the harlot-fee of a whore."
8 Because of this I lament and howl. I go
stripped and naked. I make a lamentation
like jackals, and a mourning like ostriches.
9 For her wounds are incurable. For it has
come to Yehuḏah, it has come to the gate
of My people, to Yerushalayim.
10 Do not declare it in Gath, weep not at
all in Běyth Aphrah, roll yourself in the
dust.
11 Pass by in nakedness and shame, you
inhabitant of Shaphir. The inhabitant of
Tsa'anan has not gone out. The lamentation of Běyth Ětsel takes from you its
standing place.
12 Though the inhabitants of Maroth waited for good, yet evil came down from יהוה
to the gate of Yerushalayim.
13 O inhabitant of Laḵish, harness the
chariot to the horse – she was the
beginning of sin to the daughter of Tsiyon
– for the transgressions of Yisra'ěl were
found in you.
14 Therefore you shall give parting gifts to
Moresheth Gath, the houses of Aḵziḇ
becoming a deception to the sovereigns of
Yisra'ěl.
15 Again I shall bring a dispossessor to
you, O inhabitant of Marěshah. The esteem
of Yisra'ěl shall come to Aḏullam.
16 Make yourself bald and cut off your
hair for the children of your delight.
Enlarge your baldness like an eagle, for
they shall be exiled from you.

2 Woe to those plotting wickedness, and
working out evil upon their beds! In
the light of the morning they practise it,
because it is in the might of their hand.
2 And they coveted fields and seized
them, also houses, and took them away.
And they oppressed a man and his house, a
man and his inheritance.
3 Therefore thus said יהוה, "See, against
this clan I am planning evil, from which
you do not remove your necks, nor walk
proudly, for this is a time of evil.
4 "In that day one shall lift up a proverb
against you, and he shall lament with a
bitter lamentation, and shall say, 'We have
been utterly ravaged! He changes the
inheritance of my people. How He
removes it from me! He apportions our
fields to the backslider.' "

1a Yesh. 26:21. *1b* Teh. 97:5.

5 “Therefore you shall have no one in the
assembly of יהוה to divide the land by lot.
6 “You do not preach, they preach. They
do not preach to these, reproaches are not
turned back.
7 “Are you called ‘House of Ya‛aqoḇ’?
Has the Spirit of יהוה been limited? Are
these His doings? Do not My words do
good to the one walking uprightly?
8 “And lately My people have risen up as
an enemy. You strip off the robe with the
garment from those who trust you, as they
pass by – those returning from battle.
9 “You have driven the women of My
people from their pleasant houses. You
have taken away My splendour from their
children forever.
10 “Arise and go, for this is not your rest,
because uncleanness destroys, and the
destruction is grievous.
11 “If a man walking after wind and falsehood has lied: ‘I preach to you of wine and
of strong drink,’ he shall be the ‘preacher’
of this people!
12 “I shall certainly gather all of you, O
Ya‛aqoḇ, I shall bring together the remnant
of Yisra’ĕl, put them together like sheep of
the fold, like a flock in the midst of their
pasture, they being noisy because of men.
13 “The breach-maker shall go up before
them. They shall break out, and pass
through the gate, and go out by it, and their
sovereign pass before them, with יהוה at
their head!”

3 Then I said, “Hear now, O heads of
Ya‛aqoḇ, and you rulers of the house
of Yisra’ĕl: Should you not know right-
ruling,
2 you who are hating good and loving
evil, tearing away the skin from My
people, and the flesh from their bones,
3 and who have eaten the flesh of My
people, and stripped off their skin, and
have broken their bones, and have cut it up
as into a pot, like flesh in the cooking
pot?”
4 Therefore, when they cry to יהוה He
does not answer them, and hides His face
from them at that time, as they have made
their deeds evil.
5 Thus said יהוה concerning the prophets
who lead my people astray, who are biting
with their teeth and have called out,
“Peace!” They even set apart a battle
against him who does not give for their
mouths.
6 Therefore it shall be night to you
without vision, and darkness to you
without divination. The sun shall go down
on the prophets, and the day shall be dark
for them.
7 And the seers shall be ashamed, and the
diviners embarrassed. And they shall all
cover their lips, for there is no answer, O
Elohim.
8 But truly I am filled with power, with
the Spirit of יהוה, and with right-ruling
and with might, to declare to Ya‛aqoḇ his
transgression and to Yisra’ĕl his sin. [a]
9 Hear this, please, you heads of the
house of Ya‛aqoḇ and you rulers of the
house of Yisra’ĕl, who despise right-ruling
and distort all that is straight,
10 those building up Tsiyon with bloodshed and Yerushalayim with unrighteousness.
11 Her heads judge for a bribe, her priests
teach for pay, [b] and her prophets divine for
a price. Yet they lean on יהוה, and say, “Is
not יהוה in our midst? Evil does not come
upon us.”
12 Therefore, because of you, Tsiyon is
ploughed like a field, and Yerushalayim
becomes heaps, and the mountain of the
House like a wooded height.

4 And in the latter days it shall be that
the mountain of the House of יהוה is
established on the top of the mountains,
and shall be exalted above the hills. And
peoples shall flow to it.
2 And many nations shall come and say,
“Come, and let us go up to the mountain of
יהוה, to the House of the Elohim of
Ya‛aqoḇ, and let Him teach us His ways,
and let us walk in His paths. For out of
Tsiyon comes forth the Torah, and the

3a Diḇre ב 24:20, Yn. 16:8. *3b* Yn. 10:12.

word of יהוה from Yerushalayim." [a]
3 And He shall judge among many peoples, and reprove strong nations afar off.
They shall beat their swords into ploughshares, and their spears into pruning hooks
– nation shall not lift up sword against
nation, neither teach battle any more.
4 But each one shall sit under his vine
and under his fig tree, with no one to make
them afraid, for the mouth of יהוה of hosts
has spoken.
5 For all the peoples walk, each one in
the name of his mighty one, but we walk in
the Name of יהוה our Elohim forever and
ever. [b]
6 "In that day," declares יהוה, "I gather
the lame, and I bring together the outcast
and those whom I have afflicted.
7 "And I shall make the lame a remnant,
and the outcast a strong nation. And יהוה
shall reign over them in Mount Tsiyon, [c]
from now on and forever.
8 "And you, O tower of the flock, stronghold of the daughter of Tsiyon, it shall
come to you, the former rule shall come,
the reign of the daughter of Yerushalayim."
9 Now why do you cry aloud? Is there no
sovereign in you? Has your counsellor perished? For pain has gripped you like a
woman in labour.
10 Be in pain, and deliver, O daughter of
Tsiyon, like a woman in labour. For now
you are to leave the city, and you shall
dwell in the field. And you shall go to
Baḇel, there you shall be delivered, there
יהוה shall redeem you from the hand of
your enemies.
11 And now, many nations shall be
gathered against you, who are saying, "Let
her be defiled, and let our eyes look upon
Tsiyon!"
12 But they do not know the thoughts of
יהוה, nor do they understand His counsel.
For He has gathered them like sheaves to
the threshing-floor.
13 "Arise and thresh, O daughter of
Tsiyon, for I make your horn iron and your
hooves bronze. And you shall beat many
peoples into pieces, and I shall seclude
their gain to יהוה, and their wealth to the
Master of all the earth."

5

Now you are raided, O daughter of
raiders, a siege has been laid against
us. They strike the Judge of Yisra'ěl with a
rod on the cheek.
2 "But you, Běyth Leḥem Ephrathah, you
who are little among the clans of Yehuḏah,
out of you shall come forth to Me the One
to become Ruler in Yisra'ěl. And His com-
ings forth [a] are of old, from everlasting."
3 Therefore He shall give them up, until
the time that she who is in labour has given
birth, and the remnant of His brothers
return to the children of Yisra'ěl.
4 And He shall stand and shepherd [b] in
the strength of יהוה, in the excellency of
the Name of יהוה His Elohim. And they
shall dwell, for at that time He shall be
great, to the ends of the earth.
5 And this shall be peace. When Ashshur
comes into our land, and when he treads in
our palaces, we shall raise against him
seven shepherds and eight leaders of men.
6 And they shall shepherd the land of
Ashshur with the sword, and the land of
Nimroḏ at its entrances. And He shall
deliver us from Ashshur, when he comes
into our land and when he treads within
our borders.
7 And the remnant of Ya'aqoḇ shall be in
the midst of many peoples, as dew from
יהוה, as showers on the grass, which do
not wait for man nor delay for the sons of
men.
8 And the remnant of Ya'aqoḇ shall be
among the nations, in the midst of many
peoples, like a lion among the beasts of a
forest, like a young lion among flocks of
sheep, who, if he passes through, shall
both tread down and shall tear, and there is
no one to deliver.
9 Let your hand be lifted up against your
adversaries, and all your enemies be cut
off.
10 "And it shall be in that day," declares
יהוה, "that I shall cut off your horses out

4a Yesh. 2:3. 4b Zeḵ. 10:12. 4c See footnote Yesh. 24:23. 5a Or *His appearances*. 5b Yeḥez. 34:13-14.

of your midst, and I shall destroy your
chariots.
11 "And I shall cut off the cities of your
land, and I shall pull down all your strongholds.
12 "And I shall cut off witchcrafts out of
your hand, and let you have no magicians.
13 "And I shall cut off your carved
images, and your pillars from your midst,
so that you no longer bow down to the
work of your hands.
14 "And I shall pluck your Ashěrim out of
your midst, and I shall destroy your cities.
15 "And I shall take vengeance in wrath
and rage on the nations who did not obey."

6 Hear now what יהוה is saying, "Arise,
strive with the mountains, and let the
hills hear your voice.
2 "Hear, O you mountains, the controversy of יהוה, and you everlasting
foundations of the earth! For יהוה has a
controversy with His people and He shall
reprove Yisra'ěl.
3 "My people, what have I done to you?
And how have I wearied you? Answer Me,
4 for I brought you up from the land of
Mitsrayim, and I ransomed you from the
house of bondage. And I sent Mosheh,
Aharon, and Miryam before you.
5 "My people, remember, please, what
Balaq sovereign of Mo'aḇ counselled, and
what Bil'am son of Be'or answered him,
from Shittim to Gilgal, in order to know
the righteousness of יהוה."
6 With what shall I come before יהוה,
bow myself before the high Elohim? Shall
I come before Him with ascending offerings, with calves a year old?
7 Is יהוה pleased with thousands of rams
or ten thousand rivers of oil? Shall I give
my first-born for my transgression, the
fruit of my body for the sin of my being?
8 He has declared to you, O man, what is
good. And what does יהוה require of you
but to do right, and to love loving-
commitment, and to walk humbly with
your Elohim?
9 The voice of יהוה cries to the city – and
let sound wisdom see Your Name! "Hear
the Rod and Him who appointed it!
10 "Are there still treasures of wrongness
in the house of the wrong, and the short
measure that is an abomination?"
11 Would I be innocent with wrong scales,
and with a bag of false weights?
12 "For her rich men are filled with cruel
unrighteousness, and her inhabitants have
spoken falsehood, and their tongue is
deceit in their mouth.
13 "So I also, I shall strike you with a
grievous wound, to lay you waste because
of your sins:
14 "You shall eat but not be satisfied, and
your inside be empty. And you shall store
up but not save, and what you save I shall
give to the sword.
15 "You shall sow but not reap, you shall
tread the olives but not anoint yourselves
with oil, and make sweet wine but not
drink wine.
16 "For the laws of Omri are strictly
observed, and all the works of the house of
Aḥab, and you walk in their counsels.
Therefore I give you for a ruin, and your
inhabitants for a hissing, and let you bear
the reproach of My people."

7 Woe to me! For I am as gatherings of
summer fruit, as gleanings of the
grape harvest. There is no cluster to eat.
My being has desired the first-ripe fruit.
2 The lovingly-committed one has perished from the earth, and there is no one
straight among men. All of them lie in wait
for blood, everyone hunts his brother with
a net.
3 Both hands are on the evil, to do it well.
The prince asks for gifts, the judge seeks a
bribe, and the great man speaks the desire
of his being. And they weave it together.
4 The best of them is like a prickly plant,
the most straight is sharper than a thorn
hedge. The day of your watchman and
your punishment has come, now is their
confusion.
5 Trust no friend, rely on no companion,
guard the doors of your mouth from her
who lies in your bosom.
6 For son is despising father, daughter
rises up against her mother, daughter-in-
law against her mother-in-law, the enemies

of a man are the men of his own house.
[7]As for me, I look to יהוה, I wait for the
Elohim of my deliverance, my Elohim
does hear me.
[8]Do not rejoice over me, O my enemy.
When I have fallen I have risen, when I sit
in darkness יהוה is a light to me.
[9]I bear the displeasure of יהוה, for I
have sinned against Him, until He pleads
my case, and shall execute right-ruling for
me, *until* He brings me out into the light
and I look on His righteousness.
[10]And let my enemy see it, and let shame
cover her who said to me, "Where is יהוה
your Elohim?" Let my eyes look on her:
now she is trampled down like mud in the
streets.
[11]The day for building your walls! Let
the law go far and wide in that day –
[12]that day when they come to you from
Ashshur and the besieged cities of
Mitsrayim, and from the siege [a] to the
River, and from sea to sea, and mountain to
mountain.
[13]But the earth shall become a waste
because of those who dwell in it, and for
the fruit of their deeds.
[14]Shepherd Your people with Your rod,
the flock of Your inheritance, who dwell
alone in a forest, in the midst of Karmel.
Let them feed in Bashan and Gil'aḏ, as in
days of old.
[15]"As in the days when you came out of
the land of Mitsrayim, I shall let him see
wonders."
[16]Let the nations see and be ashamed of
all their might, let them put their hand over
their mouth, let their ears be deaf.
[17]Let them lick the dust like a serpent, let
them come trembling from their strongholds like snakes of the earth, let them be
afraid of יהוה our Elohim and fear because
of You.
[18]Who is an Ěl like You – taking away
crookedness and passing over the transgression of the remnant of His inheritance?
He shall not retain His wrath forever, for
He Himself delights in loving-
commitment.
[19]He shall turn back, He shall have compassion on us, He shall trample upon our
crookednesses! And You throw all our sins
into the depths of the sea!
[20]You give truth to Ya'aqoḇ, loving-commitment to Aḇraham, which You swore to
our fathers from the days of old!

7a "Siege" in this verse could be another name for Mitsrayim.

NAḤUM

NAHUM

1 The message concerning Nineweh.
The book of the vision of Naḥum the
Elqoshite.
2 יהוה is a jealous and revenging Ěl,
יהוה is a revenger and a possessor of
wrath. יהוה takes vengeance on His adversaries, and He watches for His enemies.
3 יהוה is patient and great in power, but
by no means leaves unpunished. יהוה has
His way in the whirlwind and in the storm,
and the clouds are the dust of His feet.
4 He is rebuking the sea and dries it up.
And all the floods He has made dry,
Bashan and Karmel are withering, and the
flower of Leḇanon is languishing.
5 Mountains have shaken before Him,
and the hills have melted. And the earth is
lifted up at His presence, and the world
and all who dwell in it.
6 Who does stand before His rage? And
who rises up in the heat of His displeasure?
His wrath is poured out like fire, and the
rocks have been broken by Him.
7 יהוה is good, as a stronghold in the day
of distress. And He knows those who take
refuge in Him.
8 But with an overwhelming flood He
makes a complete end of the place of
Nineweh, and darkness does pursue His
enemies.
9 What do you plot against יהוה? He
makes a complete end of it. Distress does
not rise up a second time.
10 Though they are as entangled thorns,
and as drunkards with their drink, they
shall be consumed like stubble thoroughly
dried.
11 From you came forth one who plots
evil against יהוה, a counsellor of Beliya'al.
12 Thus said יהוה, "Though they are
strong and many, even so, they shall be cut
off and pass away. Though I have afflicted
you, I afflict you no more.
13 "So now I break his yoke from you, and
tear off your shackles."
14 And יהוה has commanded concerning
you, "Your name shall no longer be sown.
From the house of your mighty ones I shall
cut off the carved image and the moulded
image. I shall appoint your burial-site, for
you have been of no account."
15 See, on the mountains the feet of him
who brings good news, who proclaims
peace! O Yehuḏah, celebrate your festivals, perform your vows. For Beliya'al
shall no more pass through you. He has
been cut off completely.

2 He who breaks in pieces has come up
before your face. Guard the ramparts!
Watch the way! Strengthen your loins!
Fortify your power very much.
2 For יהוה shall turn back the splendour
of Ya'aqoḇ like the splendour of Yisra'ěl,
for the emptiers have emptied them out
and ruined their vine branches.
3 The shields of his mighty men have
become red, the men of battle are in scarlet. The chariots are like flaming torches in
the day of his preparation, and the cypress-
es shall be shaken.
4 The chariots dash about in the streets,
they rush one another in the broad ways.
They look like flaming torches, they run
like lightning.
5 He remembers his noble ones, they
stumble in their walk, they hurry to her
walls, and the defence is prepared.
6 The river gates have been opened, and
the palace is melted.
7 And it is established: she shall be
exiled, she shall be led away. And her
female servants are moaning as with the
voice of doves, beating on their breasts.
8 And Nineweh of old was like a pool of
water, now they flee away. "Stop! Stop!"
they cry, but no one turns back.
9 Plunder the silver! Plunder the gold!
There is no limit to the treasure – a wealth
of all precious objects.
10 She is empty, even emptiness and
waste! And the heart has melted, and the

knees have knocked together, and much
pain is in all loins, and all their faces have
become flushed.
11 Where is the den of the lions, and the
feeding place of the young lions, where the
lion, the lioness and the lion's cub walked,
with no one to disturb them?
12 The lion tore in pieces enough for his
cubs, and strangled for his lionesses, and
filled his caves with prey, and his dens
with torn prey.
13 "See, I am against you," declares יהוה
of hosts, "and I shall burn your chariots in
smoke, and the sword devour your young
lions. And I shall cut off your prey from
the earth, and no longer is the voice of
your messengers heard."

3 Woe to the city of blood! All of it is a
lie, filled with plunder, the prey is not
lacking.
2 The sound of a whip and the sound of
rattling wheels, of galloping horses, of jolt-
ing chariots,
3 mounted horsemen with bright sword
and glittering spear, and many wounded,
and a mass of dead bodies, and no end of
corpses, they stumble over the corpses –
4 because of the many whorings of the
well-favoured whore, the mistress of
sorceries, who sells nations by her
whorings, and clans by her sorceries.
5 "See, I am against you," declares יהוה
of hosts, "and shall lift up your skirts over
your face, and shall show nations your
nakedness, and reigns your shame.
6 "And I shall cast abominations upon
you, and treat you as foolish, and make a
spectacle of you.
7 "And it shall be that all who see you
flee from you, and say, 'Ninewĕh is laid
waste! Who does mourn for her?' Where
do I seek comforters for you?"
8 Are you better than No Amon, who
dwelt by the Nile-streams, with waters
around her, whose rampart was like the
sea, whose wall was like the sea?
9 Kush and Mitsrayim were her strength,
even unlimited. Put and Luḇim were your
helpers.
10 Yet she was exiled, she went into
captivity. At the head of every street her
young children were dashed to pieces. Lots
were cast for her esteemed men, and all her
great men were bound in chains.
11 You too are to become drunk, you are
to go into hiding. You too are to seek
refuge from the enemy.
12 All your strongholds are fig trees with
ripened figs, when shaken they shall fall
into the mouth of the eater.
13 See, your people in your midst are
women! The gates of your land shall be
opened wide to your enemies. Fire shall
consume your gate bars.
14 Draw for yourself water for the siege!
Strengthen your defences! Go into the clay
and tread the mortar, lay hold of the brick
mould!
15 There a fire shall consume you, a sword
cut you off, eat you up like a locust. Make
yourself many like the locust, make yourself many like the swarming locust!
16 You have increased your merchants
more than the stars of the heavens. The
locust shall strip off and fly away.
17 Your officials are like the locusts, and
your marshals are like the great grasshoppers, which settle in the hedges on a cold
day – when the sun rises they flee away,
and the place where they are is unknown.
18 Your shepherds have slumbered, O sovereign of Ashshur, your nobles lie down to
rest. Your people are scattered on the
mountains, and no one gathers them.
19 Your injury has no healing, your wound
is grievous. All who hear news of you shall
clap their hands over you. For over whom
did your evil not pass continually?

ḤAḆAQQUQ

HABAKKUK

1 The message which the prophet
Ḥaḇaqquq saw.
2 O יהוה, till when shall I cry, and You
not hear? I cry to You, "Violence!" and
You do not save.
3 Why do You show me wickedness, and
cause me to see perversity? For ruin and
violence are before me. And there is strife,
and contention arises.
4 Therefore the Torah ceases, and right-
ruling never goes forth. For the wrong hem
in the righteous, so that right-ruling comes
out twisted.
5 "Look among the nations and see, and
be amazed, be amazed! For a work is being
wrought in your days which you would not
believe if it were told.
6 "See, I am raising up the Kasdim, a bitter and hasty nation, who is going through
the breadth of the earth, to possess
dwelling places that are not theirs.
7 "They are frightening and fearsome,
their right-ruling and their exaltation
proceed from themselves.
8 "Their horses shall be swifter than
leopards, and more fierce than evening
wolves. And their horsemen shall charge
ahead, and their horsemen come from afar.
They fly as the eagle, rushing to eat.
9 "All of them come for violence, the
direction of their faces is like the east
wind, and they gather captives like sand.
10 "And they scoff at sovereigns, and
princes are a laughing matter to them.
They laugh at every stronghold, for they
pile up earth and seize it.
11 "Then shall he pass on as a wind, and
transgress and be guilty, and ascribe this
power to his mighty one."
12 Are You not from everlasting, O יהוה
my Elohim, my Set-apart One? You do not
die! O יהוה, You have appointed them for
right-ruling, O Rock, You have established
them for reproof.
13 *You*, whose eyes are too clean to see
evil, You are not able to look on wrong.
Why do You look on those who act treacherously – keep silent when the wrong
devours one more righteous than he?
14 And would You make men like fish of
the sea, like creeping creatures that have
no ruler over them?
15 *The wicked foe* has pulled all of them
up with a hook, caught them in his net, and
gathers them in his dragnet. Therefore he
rejoices and exults.
16 Therefore he slaughters to his net, and
burns incense to his dragnet, for by them is
his portion fat and his food is rich.
17 Is he therefore to keep on emptying his
net, and killing nations without sparing?

2 I stand at my watch, and station
myself on the watch-tower, and wait
to see what He says to me, and what to
answer when I am reproved.
2 And יהוה answered me and said,
"Write the vision and inscribe it on tablets,
so that he who reads it runs.
3 "For the vision is yet for an appointed
time, and it speaks of the end, and does not
lie. If it lingers, wait for it, for it shall
certainly come, it shall not delay.
4 "See, he whose being is not upright in
him is puffed up. But the righteous one
lives by his steadfastness.
5 "And also, because wine betrays him, a
man is proud, and he does not stay at
home. Because he enlarges his appetite as
She'ol, and he is like death, and is not satisfied, and gathers to himself all nations
and heaps up for himself all peoples.
6 "Shall not all these lift up a proverb
against him, and a mocking riddle against
him, and say, 'Woe to him who increases
what is not his! Till when is he to load on
himself many pledges'?
7 "Do not your creditors rise up suddenly? And those who make you tremble wake
up and you be plunder for them?
8 "Because you have plundered many
nations, all the remnant of the people shall

plunder you, because of men's blood, and doing violence to the land, to the city, and to all who dwell in it.

9 "Woe to him who is getting evil gain for his house, in order to set his nest on high, to escape the clutches of evil!

10 "You have counselled shame for your house, to cut off many peoples, and your being is sinning.

11 "For a stone from the wall cries out, and a beam from the timbers answers it.

12 "Woe to him who builds a town by blood, and establishes a city by unrighteousness!

13 "See, it is not from יהוה of hosts that peoples labour only for fire, and nations weary themselves for naught,

14 for the earth shall be filled with the knowledge of the esteem of יהוה, as the waters cover the sea! [a]

15 "Woe to him who gives drink to his neighbour, pouring out your wineskin, and also making him drunk – in order to look on their nakedness!

16 "You shall be filled with shame instead of esteem. Drink, you too, and be exposed as uncircumcised! The cup of the right hand of יהוה shall come around to you, and great shame upon your esteem.

17 "For the violence done to Leḇanon is to overwhelm you – and the ravaging of beasts by which you made them afraid – because of men's blood and the violence to the land, to the city and of all who dwell in it.

18 "Of what use shall a carved image be? For its maker has carved it: a moulded image and teacher of falsehood! For the maker trusts what he has made: to make dumb idols!

19 "Woe to him who says to wood, 'Awake!' to silent stone, 'Arise!' Is it a teacher? See, it is overlaid with gold and silver, and there is no spirit at all inside it.

20 "But יהוה is in His set-apart Hěḵal. Let all the earth be silent before Him."

3 A prayer of Ḥaḇaqquq the prophet, on Shiḡionoth.

2 O יהוה, I have heard your report, I was afraid.
O יהוה, renew Your work in the midst of the years!
Make it known in the midst of the years.
In wrath remember compassion.
3 Eloah comes from Těman,
And the Set-apart One from Mount Paran. Selah.
His splendour shall cover the heavens,
And His praise shall fill the earth.
4 And the brightness is as the light,
He has rays from His hand,
And there His power is hidden.
5 Before Him goes pestilence,
And a burning flame goes forth at His feet.
6 He shall stand and measure the earth.
He shall look and shake the nations.
And the ancient mountains are shattered,
The age-old hills shall bow.
His ways are everlasting.
7 I saw the tents of Kushan under sorrow,
The curtains of the land of Miḏyan tremble.
8 Shall יהוה burn against the rivers?
Is Your displeasure against the rivers,
Is Your wrath against the sea,
That You ride on Your horses,
Your chariots of deliverance?
9 You uncover Your bow,
The oaths of the rod of the Word. Selah.
You cut through the earth with rivers.
10 The mountains shall see You, they tremble.
The storm of water shall pass over.
The deep shall give forth its voice,
It shall lift up its hands.
11 Sun, moon shall stand still in their places.
Like light Your arrows fly,
Like lightning is Your glittering spear.
12 You step through the earth in rage,
You thresh the nations in wrath.
13 You shall go forth to save Your people,

2a Yesh. 11:9.

To save Your Anointed.
You shall smite the Head from the house of the wrong,
By laying bare from foundation to neck. Selah.
14 You shall pierce with his own arrows
The head of his leaders.
They stormed along to scatter me,
Rejoicing as if to devour the poor in secret.
15 You shall tread the sea with Your horses,
The foaming of many waters.
16 I heard, and my body trembled,
My lips quivered at the sound,
Rottenness came into my bones.
And I trembled within myself,
That I might rest for the day of distress,
To come upon the people who would attack us.
17 Though the fig tree does not blossom,
And there is no fruit on the vine,
The yield of the olive has failed,
And the fields brought forth no food,
The flock has been cut off from the fold,
And there is no herd in the stalls,
18 Yet I exult in יהוה,
I rejoice in the Elohim of my deliverance.
19 יהוה the Master is my strength.
And He makes my feet like those of deer,
And makes me walk on my high places.
To the chief singer with my stringed instruments.

TSEPHANYAH

ZEPHANIAH

1 The word of יהוה which came to
Tsephanyah son of Kushi, son of
Geḏalyah, son of Amaryah, son of
Ḥizqiyah, in the days of Yoshiyahu son of
Amon, sovereign of Yehuḏah.
2 “I shall snatch away all from the face of
the earth,” declares יהוה –
3 “I snatch away man and beast, I snatch
away the birds of the heavens, and the fish
of the sea, and the stumbling-blocks, with
the wrong, when I shall cut off man from
the face of the earth,” declares יהוה.
4 “And I shall stretch out My hand
against Yehuḏah, and against all the
inhabitants of Yerushalayim, and cut off
every trace of Ba‘al from this place, the
names of the idolatrous priests, with the
priests,
5 and those bowing down to the host of
the heavens on the house-tops, and those
bowing themselves, swearing by יהוה and
swearing by Malkam;
6 and those who turn away from following יהוה, and who have not sought יהוה or
inquired of Him.”
7 Hush! in the presence of the Master
יהוה. For the day of יהוה is near, for יהוה
has prepared a slaughter, He has set apart
His invited ones.
8 “And it shall be, in the day of the
slaughter of יהוה, that I shall punish the
rulers and the sons of the sovereign, and all
such as are clad in foreign garments.
9 “And I shall punish on that day all who
leap over the threshold, who fill their masters’ houses with violence and deceit.
10 “And on that day there shall be,”
declares יהוה, “the sound of a cry from the
Fish Gate, and of a howling from the
Second Quarter, and of a great crashing
from the hills.
11 “Howl, you inhabitants of Maḵtěsh, for
all the merchant people shall be silenced,
all those weighing out silver shall be cut
off.
12 “And at that time it shall be, that I
search Yerushalayim with lamps and
punish the men who are settled on their
dregs, who say in their heart, ‘יהוה does no
good, nor does He evil.’
13 “And their wealth shall become plunder, and their houses laid waste. And they
shall build houses but not inhabit them,
and they shall plant vineyards but not drink
their wine.”
14 Near is the great day of יהוה, near and
hurrying greatly, the noise of the day of
יהוה. Let the mighty man then bitterly cry
out!
15 That day is a day of wrath, a day of
distress and trouble, a day of waste and
ruin, a day of darkness and gloominess, a
day of clouds and thick darkness,
16 a day of a shophar and sounding –
against the walled cities and against the
corner towers.
17 “And I shall bring distress on men, and
they shall walk like blind men – because
they have sinned against יהוה, and their
blood shall be poured out like dust and
their flesh like dung.”
18 Neither their silver nor their gold shall
be able to deliver them in the day of the
wrath of יהוה. And by the fire of His jealousy all the earth shall be consumed, for
He makes a sudden end of all those who
dwell in the earth.

2 Gather together, gather together, O
nation without shame,
2 before the law gives birth – the day
shall pass on like chaff – before the burning wrath of יהוה comes upon you, before
the day of wrath of יהוה comes upon you!
3 Seek יהוה, all you meek ones of the
earth, who have done His right-ruling.
Seek righteousness, seek meekness, if so
be that you are hidden in the day of wrath
of יהוה.

4 For Azzah is abandoned and Ashqelon laid waste, Ashdoḏ is driven out at noonday and Eqron is uprooted.

5 Woe to the inhabitants of the seacoast, the nation of the Kerĕthites! The word of יהוה is against you, O Kenaʻan, land of the Philistines, "And I shall destroy you, so that there is no inhabitant."

6 And the seacoast shall be pastures, shepherds' meadows and enclosures for flocks.

7 And the coast shall be for the remnant of the house of Yehuḏah. They shall feed their flocks on it, at evening they lie down in the houses of Ashqelon. For יהוה their Elohim shall visit them and turn back their captivity.

8 "I have heard the reproach of Mo'aḇ, and the revilings of the children of Ammon, with which they have reproached My people, and exalted themselves against their borders.

9 "Therefore, as I live," declares יהוה of hosts, the Elohim of Yisra'ĕl, "Mo'aḇ shall be like Seḏom, and the children of Ammon like Amorah – a possession for weeds and a pit of salt, and a waste forever, the remnant of My people plunder them, and the rest of My nation possess them."

10 This is what they get for their pride, because they have reproached and exalted themselves against the people of יהוה of hosts.

11 יהוה shall be awesome to them, for He shall make all the mighty ones of the earth to shrivel, while all the coastlands of the nations bow down to Him, each one from his place.

12 "You too, O Kushites, are to be slain by My sword."

13 And He shall stretch out His hand against the north, and destroy Ashshur, and make Ninewĕh a waste, as dry as a wilderness.

14 And droves shall lie down in her midst, every beast of the nation, both pelican and bittern lodge in the tops of her columns, a voice singing at the window, ruin be at the threshold, for the cedar work is exposed.

15 This is the exultant city that is dwelling in safety, that said in her heart, "I am it, and there is none but me." How has she become a waste, a place for beasts to lie down! Everyone who passes by her whistles and shakes his fist.

3

Woe to her who is rebellious and defiled, the oppressing city!

2 She did not obey the voice, she did not accept instruction, she did not trust in יהוה, she did not draw near to her Elohim.

3 Her rulers in her midst are roaring lions, her judges are evening wolves, they shall leave no bone until morning.

4 Her prophets are reckless, treacherous men. Her priests have profaned the set-apart place, they have done violence to the Torah. [a]

5 יהוה is righteous in her midst, He does no unrighteousness. Morning by morning He brings His right-ruling to light, it has not been lacking, yet the unrighteous one knows no shame.

6 "I have cut off nations, their corner towers are in ruins. I have made their streets deserted, with no one passing by. Their cities are destroyed, without man, without inhabitant.

7 "I have said, 'Only fear Me, accept instruction.' And her dwelling would not be cut off, all that I have appointed for her. But they rose up early, they corrupted all their deeds.

8 "Therefore wait for Me," declares יהוה, "until the day I rise up for plunder. For My judgment is to gather nations, to assemble reigns, to pour out on them My rage, all My burning wrath. For by the fire of My jealousy all the earth shall be consumed.

9 "For then I shall turn unto the peoples a clean lip, [b] so that they all call on the Name of יהוה, to serve Him with one shoulder.

10 "From beyond the rivers of Kush my worshippers, the daughter of My dispersed ones, shall bring My offering.

11 "In that day you shall not be put to shame for any of your deeds in which you have transgressed against Me, for then I

3a Yeḥez. 22:26, Lq. 16:16. *3b* Or *language*.

shall remove from your midst your proud
exulting ones, and you shall no more be
haughty in My set-apart mountain.
12 "But I shall leave in your midst an
oppressed and poor people, and they shall
trust in the Name of יהוה.
13 "The remnant of Yisra'ěl shall do no
unrighteousness and speak no falsehood, [c]
nor is a tongue of deceit found in their
mouth. For they shall feed their flocks and
lie down, with none to frighten them."
14 Shout for joy, O daughter of Tsiyon!
Shout, O Yisra'ěl! Be glad and rejoice
with all your heart, O daughter of Yerushalayim!
15 יהוה has turned aside your judgments.
He has faced your enemy. The Sovereign
of Yisra'ěl, יהוה, is in your midst. [d] No
longer need you fear evil.
16 In that day it shall be said to Yerushalayim, "Do not fear, Tsiyon, do not let
your hands be weak.
17 "יהוה your Elohim in your midst, is
mighty to save. He rejoices over you with
joy, He is silent in His love, He rejoices
over you with singing."
18 "I shall gather those who grieve about
the appointed time, who are among you, to
whom its reproach is a burden.
19 "See, I am dealing with all those afflicting you at that time. And I shall save the
lame, and gather those who were cast out.
And I shall give them for a praise and for a
name in all the earth where they were put
to shame.
20 "At that time I shall bring you in, even
at the time I gather you, for I shall give you
for a name, and for a praise, among all the
peoples of the earth, when I turn back your
captivity before your eyes," said יהוה.

3c See Ḥazon 14:5. *3d* See v. 17, and footnotes at Yesh. 12:6.

ḤAGGAI

HAGGAI

1 In the second year of Dareyawesh the
sovereign, in the sixth new *moon*, on
the first day of the new *moon*, the word of
יהוה came by Ḥaggai the prophet to
Zerubbaḇel son of She'alti'ěl, governor of
Yehuḏah, and to Yehoshua son of
Yehotsaḏaq, the high priest, saying,
2 "Thus spoke יהוה of hosts, saying,
'This people have said, "The time has not
come, the time the House of יהוה is to be
built." ' "
3 Then the word of יהוה came by Ḥaggai
the prophet, saying,
4 "Is it time for you yourselves to dwell
in your panelled houses, and this House be
in ruins?"
5 And now, thus said יהוה of hosts,
"Consider your ways!
6 "You have sown much, but brought in
little; eat, but do not have enough; drink,
but you are not filled with drink; clothe
yourselves, but no one is warm; and he
who earns wages, earns wages to put into a
bag with holes."
7 Thus said יהוה of hosts, "Consider
your ways!
8 Go up to the mountain, and you shall
bring wood and build the House. And I
will be pleased with it, and let Me be
esteemed," said יהוה.
9 "When you looked for much, then see,
it came to little. And when you brought it
home, I would blow on it. Why?" declares
יהוה of hosts. "Because of My House
which lies in ruins, while each of you runs
to his own house.
10 "Therefore the heavens above you have
withheld the dew, and the earth has withheld its fruit.
11 "And I called for a drought on the land,
and on the mountains, and on the grain,
and on the new wine, and on the oil, and on
whatever the ground brings forth, and on
man, and on livestock, and on all the
labour of the hands."
12 Then Zerubbaḇel son of She'alti'ěl, and
Yehoshua son of Yehotsaḏaq, the high
priest, with all the remnant of the people,
obeyed the voice of יהוה their Elohim, and
the words of Ḥaggai the prophet, as יהוה
their Elohim had sent him. And the people
feared the presence of יהוה.
13 And Ḥaggai, the messenger of יהוה,
spoke the message of יהוה to the people,
saying, "I am with you, declares יהוה."
14 And יהוה stirred up the spirit of
Zerubbaḇel son of She'alti'ěl, governor of
Yehuḏah, and the spirit of Yehoshua son of
Yehotsaḏaq, the high priest, and the spirit
of all the remnant of the people. And they
came and worked on the House of יהוה of
hosts, their Elohim,
15 on the twenty-fourth day of the sixth
new *moon*, in the second year of
Dareyawesh the sovereign.

2 In the seventh *month*, on the twenty-
first of the new *moon*, the word of
יהוה came by Ḥaggai the prophet, saying,
2 "Speak, please, to Zerubbaḇel son of
She'alti'ěl, governor of Yehuḏah, and to
Yehoshua son of Yehotsaḏaq, the high
priest, and to the remnant of the people,
saying,
3 'Who is there left among you who saw
this House in its former esteem? And how
do you see it now? Is it not in your eyes as
naught when compared to it?
4 'And now, be strong, Zerubbaḇel,'
declares יהוה. 'And be strong, Yehoshua,
son of Yehotsaḏaq, the high priest. And be
strong, all you people of the land,' declares
יהוה, 'and work. For I am with you,'
declares יהוה of hosts –
5 the Word that I covenanted with you
when you came out of Mitsrayim, and My
Spirit is remaining in your midst, do not
fear!'
6 "For thus said יהוה of hosts, 'Once
more, in a little while, and I am shaking the
heavens and earth, the sea and dry land.
7 'And I shall shake all the nations, and

they shall come to the Delight of all the nations, and I shall fill this House with esteem,' said יהוה of hosts.

8 'The silver is Mine, and the gold is Mine,' declares יהוה of hosts.

9 'Let the esteem of this latter House be greater than the former,' said יהוה of hosts. 'And in this place I give peace,' declares יהוה of hosts."

10 On the twenty-fourth of the ninth *month*, in the second year of Dareyawesh, the word of יהוה came unto Ḥaggai the prophet, saying,

11 "Thus said יהוה of hosts, 'Now, ask the priests concerning the Torah, saying,

12 "If one bears set-apart meat in the fold of his garment, and with the edge he touches bread or stew, or wine or oil, or any food, is it set-apart?" ' " And the priests answered and said, "No."

13 And Ḥaggai said, "If someone defiled by a dead body touches any of these, is it defiled?" And the priests answered and said, "It is defiled."

14 And Ḥaggai answered and said, " 'So is this people, and so is this nation before Me,' declares יהוה, 'and so is every work of their hands. And whatever they bring near there is defiled.

15 'But now, please consider, from this day onward: Before a stone was laid on a stone in the Hěḵal of יהוה,

16 since those days – one came to a heap of twenty ěphahs, and there were ten; one came to the winepress to draw out fifty baths from the press, and there were twenty –

17 'I struck you with blight and mildew and hail in all the labours of your hands, and there was none of you with Me,' declares יהוה.

18 'Consider now from this day forward, from the twenty-fourth day of the ninth *month*, from the day that the foundation of the Hěḵal of יהוה was laid, consider it:

19 'Is the seed yet in the storehouse? And until now the vine, and the fig tree, and the pomegranate, and the olive tree have not yielded fruit! From this day on I shall bless you!' "

20 And a second time the word of יהוה came to Ḥaggai on the twenty-fourth day of the new *moon*, saying,

21 "Speak to Zerubbaḇel, the governor of Yehuḏah, saying, 'I am shaking the heavens and earth.

22 'And I shall overturn the throne of reigns. And I shall destroy the might of the reigns of the nations, [b] and overturn the chariots and their riders. And the horses and their riders shall come down, each by the sword of his brother.

23 'In that day,' declares יהוה of hosts, 'I shall take you, Zerubbaḇel My servant, son of She'alti'ěl,' declares יהוה, 'and shall make you as a signet, for I have chosen you,' declares יהוה of hosts."

2b See footnote at Dan. 2:44.

ZEḴARYAH

ZECHARIAH

1 In the eighth new *moon* of the second year of Dareyawesh, the word of יהוה came to Zeḵaryah son of Bereḵyah, son of Iddo the prophet, saying,

2 "יהוה was very wroth with your fathers.

3 "And you shall say to them, 'Thus said יהוה of hosts, "Turn back to Me," declares יהוה of hosts, "and I shall turn back to you," declares יהוה of hosts.

4 "Do not be like your fathers, to whom the former prophets proclaimed, saying, 'Thus said יהוה of hosts, "Turn back now from your evil ways and your evil deeds." ' But they did not obey or give heed to Me," declares יהוה.

5 "Your fathers, where are they? And the prophets, do they live forever?

6 "But My words and My laws, which I commanded My servants the prophets, did they not overtake your fathers?" "Then they turned back and said, 'As יהוה of hosts planned to do to us, according to our ways and according to our deeds, so He has done with us.' " ' "

7 On the twenty-fourth day of the eleventh new *moon*, which is the new *moon* Sheḇat, in the second year of Dareyawesh, the word of יהוה came to Zeḵaryah son of Bereḵyahu, son of Iddo the prophet, saying,

8 "I looked at night and saw a man riding on a red horse, and he was standing among the myrtle trees in the shade. And behind him were horses: red, sorrel, and white."

9 And I said, "My master, what are these?" And the messenger who was speaking to me said to me, "Let me show you what they are."

10 And the man who stood among the myrtle trees answered and said, "They are the ones יהוה has sent to go throughout the earth."

11 And they answered the messenger of יהוה, who stood among the myrtle trees, and said, "We have gone throughout the earth, and see, all the earth is at peace and rest."

12 And the messenger of יהוה answered and said, "O יהוה of hosts, how long would You have no compassion on Yerushalayim and on the cities of Yehuḏah, against which You were enraged these seventy years?"

13 And יהוה answered the messenger who talked to me, good words, comforting words.

14 And the messenger who spoke with me said to me, "Proclaim, saying, 'Thus said יהוה of hosts, "I have been jealous for Yerushalayim and for Tsiyon with great jealousy.

15 "And I am very wroth with the nations who are at ease, for when I was a little wroth, they furthered the evil!"

16 'Therefore thus said יהוה, "I shall return to Yerushalayim with compassion. My house shall be built in it," declares יהוה of hosts, "and a surveyor's line be stretched out over Yerushalayim." '

17 "Again proclaim, saying, 'Thus said יהוה of hosts, "Again My cities shall overflow with goodness. And יהוה shall again comfort Tsiyon, and shall again choose [a] Yerushalayim." ' "

18 And I lifted up my eyes and looked, and saw four horns.

19 And I said to the messenger who was speaking to me, "What are these?" And he said to me, "These are the horns that have scattered Yehuḏah, Yisra'ěl, and Yerushalayim."

20 And יהוה showed me four craftsmen.

21 And I said, "What are these coming to do?" And he spoke saying, "These are the

1a See 2:12, and footnote at Yesh. 14:1.

horns that scattered Yehuḏah, so that no
one lifted up his head. But these come to
trouble them, to throw down the horns of
the nations that lifted up their horn against
the land of Yehuḏah to scatter it."

2 And I lifted up my eyes and looked,
and saw a man with a measuring line
in his hand.
2 And I said, "Where are you going?"
And he said to me, "To measure Yerushalayim, to see what is its width and what is
its length."
3 And see, the messenger who was
speaking to me was going out. And another messenger was coming out to meet him,
4 and he said to him, "Run, speak to this
young man, saying, 'Yerushalayim is to
remain unwalled, because of the many
men and livestock in it.
5 'For I Myself am to her,' declares יהוה,
'a wall of fire all around, and for esteem I
am in her midst.' "
6 "Oh, Oh! And flee from the land of the
north," declares יהוה, "for I have scattered
you like the four winds of the heavens,"
declares יהוה.
7 "Oh, Tsiyon! Escape, you who dwell
with the daughter of Baḇel."
8 For thus said יהוה of hosts (for the sake
of esteem He sent me to the nations which
plunder you): "For he who touches you
touches the apple of My eye. [a]
9 "For look, I am waving My hand
against them, and they shall become spoil
for their servants. And you shall know that
יהוה of hosts has sent Me.
10 "Sing and rejoice, O daughter of
Tsiyon! For look, I am coming, and shall
dwell in your midst [b]," declares יהוה.
11 "And many nations shall be joined to
יהוה in that day, [c] and they shall become
My people. And I shall dwell in your
midst. And you shall know that יהוה of
hosts has sent Me to you.
12 "And יהוה shall inherit Yehuḏah, His
portion in the Set-apart Land. And He shall
again choose Yerushalayim. [d]
13 "Hush, all flesh, before יהוה, for He
has roused Himself out of His set-apart
dwelling!"

3 And he showed me Yehoshua the high
priest standing before the messenger
of יהוה, and Satan standing at his right
hand to be an adversary to him.
2 And יהוה said to Satan, "יהוה rebuke
you, Satan! יהוה who has chosen Yerushalayim rebuke you! Is this not a brand
plucked from the fire?"
3 And Yehoshua was dressed in filthy
garments, and was standing before the
messenger.
4 And He answered and spoke to those
who stood before Him, saying, "Remove
the filthy garments from him." And to him
He said, "See, I have removed your guilt
from you, and shall put costly robes on
you."
5 And I said, "Let them put a clean
turban on his head." Then they put a clean
turban on his head, and they put garments
on him. And the messenger of יהוה stood
by.
6 And the messenger of יהוה witnessed
to Yehoshua, saying,
7 "Thus said יהוה of hosts, 'If you walk
in My ways, and if you guard My duty,
then you shall also rule My house, and also
guard My courts. And I shall give you
access among these standing here.
8 'Now listen, Yehoshua the high priest,
you and your companions who sit before
you, for they are men of symbol. For look,
I am bringing forth My Servant – the
Branch. [a]
9 'See the stone which I have put before
Yehoshua: on one stone are seven eyes.
See, I am engraving its inscription,'
declares יהוה of hosts, 'and I shall remove
the guilt of that land in one day.
10 'In that day,' declares יהוה of hosts,
'you shall invite one another, under the
vine and under the fig tree.' "

2a Deḇ. 32:10. *2b* See footnote at Yesh. 12:6.
2c Yesh. 14:1, Yesh. 56:6-8, Yesh. 60:3, Yeḥez. 47:22-23, Yn. 10:16, Ma. 15:14-17. *2d* See 1:17.
3a Or *Sprout*. See Yesh. 4:2, Yesh. 11:1, Yirm. 23:5, Yirm. 33:15, Zeḵ. 6:12.

4 And the messenger who was speaking to me came back and woke me up as a man is awakened from sleep.

2 And he said to me, "What do you see?" So I said, "I have looked, and see: a lampstand all of gold with a bowl on top of it, and on the stand seven lamps with seven spouts to the seven lamps.

3 "And two olive trees are by it, one at the right of the bowl and the other at its left."

4 Then I responded and spoke to the messenger who was speaking to me, saying, "What are these, my master?"

5 And the messenger who was speaking to me answered and said to me, "Do you not know what these are?" And I said, "No, my master."

6 And he answered and said to me, "This is the word of יהוה to Zerubbaḇel, 'Not by might nor by power, but by My Spirit,' said יהוה of hosts.

7 'Who are you, great mountain, before Zerubbaḇel? A plain! And he shall bring forth the capstone with shouts of "Favour, favour to it!" ' "

8 And the word of יהוה came to me, saying,

9 "The hands of Zerubbaḇel have laid the foundation of this House, and his hands shall complete it. And you shall know that יהוה of hosts has sent Me to you.

10 "For who has despised the day of small *beginnings*? They shall rejoice when they see the plumb-line in the hand of Zerubbaḇel. These seven are the eyes of יהוה, which diligently search throughout all the earth."

11 Then I responded and said to him, "What are these two olive trees, one at the right of the lampstand and the other at its left?"

12 And I responded a second time and said to him, "What are these two olive branches which empty golden *oil* from themselves by means of the two gold pipes?"

13 And he answered me and said, "Do you not know what these are?" And I said, "No, my master."

14 And he said, "These are the two anointed ones, who stand beside the Master [a] of all the earth."

5 And I lifted up my eyes again, and looked and saw a flying scroll.

2 And he said to me, "What do you see?" And I answered, "I see a flying scroll, twenty cubits long and ten cubits wide."

3 And he said to me, "This is the curse that goes forth over the face of all the earth: 'everyone who is stealing shall go unpunished,' on the one side, according to it, and, 'everyone who has sworn *falsely* shall go unpunished,' on the other side, according to it."

4 "I shall send it out," declares יהוה of hosts, "and it shall come into the house of the thief and the house of the one who shall swear falsely by My Name. And it shall remain in the midst of his house and shall consume it, both its timber and stones."

5 And the messenger who was speaking with me came out and said to me, "Lift up your eyes now, and see what this is that is going forth."

6 And I said, "What is it?" And he said, "It is an ĕphah-measure that is going forth." Again he said, "This is their appearance throughout the earth:

7 "And see, a lead cover lifted up, and this: a woman sitting inside the ĕphah-measure!"

8 And he said, "This is Wrongness!" And he threw her down into the ĕphah-measure, and threw the lead weight over its mouth.

9 And I lifted up my eyes, and looked and saw two women, coming with the wind in their wings. And they had wings like the wings of a stork, and they lifted up the ĕphah-measure between earth and the heavens.

10 Then I said to the messenger who was speaking to me, "Where are they taking the ĕphah-measure?"

11 And he said to me, "To build a house for it in the land of Shinʽar. And it shall be established and set there on its own base."

4a See vv. 3 & 11, also Mt. 17:3-4, Ḥazon 11:3-10.

6 And I lifted up my eyes again, and
looked and saw four chariots coming
from between two mountains, and the
mountains were mountains of bronze.
2 With the first chariot were red horses,
and with the second chariot black horses,
3 and with the third chariot white horses,
and with the fourth chariot strong speckled
horses.
4 So I responded and said to the messenger who was speaking to me, "What are
these, my master?"
5 And the messenger answered and said
to me, "These are four spirits of the
heavens, coming forth from presenting
themselves before the Master of all the
earth.
6 "The one with the black horses is going
out to the land of the north, and the white
ones have gone out after them, and the
speckled ones have gone out to the land of
the south."
7 And the strong ones went out, eager to
go, to walk to and fro in the earth. And He
said, "Go, walk to and fro in the earth." So
they walked to and fro in the earth.
8 And He called to me, and spoke to me,
saying, "See, those who go toward the land
of the north have given rest to My Spirit in
the land of the north."
9 And the word of יהוה came to me, saying,
10 "Receive the gift from the exiles, from
Ḥeldai, Toḇiyah, and Yeḏayah, who have
come from Baḇel. Then you shall go the
same day and enter the house of Yoshiyah
son of Tsephanyah.
11 "And you shall take the silver and gold,
make a crown, and set it on the head of
Yehoshua the son of Yehotsaḏaq, the high
priest,
12 and shall speak to him, saying, 'Thus
said יהוה of hosts, saying, "See, the Man
whose name is the Branch! [a] And from His
place He shall branch out, and He shall
build the Hěḵal of יהוה.
13 "It is He who is going to build the
Hěḵal of יהוה. It is He who is going to
bear the splendour. And He shall sit and
rule on His throne, and shall be a priest on
His throne, and the counsel of peace shall
be between Them both," '
14 while the crown is for a remembrance
in the Hěḵal of יהוה to Ḥělem, and to
Toḇiyah, and to Yeḏayah, and to Ḥěn son
of Tsephanyah.
15 "And those who are far away shall
come and build the Hěḵal of יהוה. And
you shall know that יהוה of hosts has sent
Me to you. And this shall be, if you diligently obey the voice of יהוה your
Elohim."

7 And in the fourth year of Sovereign
Dareyawesh it came to be that the
word of יהוה came to Zeḵaryah, on the
fourth of the ninth new *moon*, Kislěw.
2 Now Běyth Ěl had sent Shar'etser, with
Reḡem-Meleḵ and his men, to pray before
יהוה,
3 speaking to the priests who belonged to
the House of יהוה of hosts, and to the
prophets, saying, "Should I weep in the
fifth new *moon* and fast as I have done for
so many years?"
4 Then the word of יהוה of hosts came to
me, saying,
5 "Speak to all the people of the land, and
to the priests, saying, 'When you fasted
and lamented in the fifth and seventh
months all these seventy years, did you
truly fast for Me – for Me?
6 'And when you ate and when you
drank, was it not for those eating and for
those drinking?
7 'Are these not the words which יהוה
proclaimed through the former prophets
when Yerushalayim and the cities around it
were inhabited and in safety, and the South
and the low country were inhabited?' "
8 And the word of יהוה came to
Zeḵaryah, saying,
9 "Thus said יהוה of hosts, 'Execute true
right-ruling, show loving-commitment and
compassion everyone to his brother.
10 "Do not oppress the widow or the
fatherless, the stranger or the poor. And do
not plot evil in your hearts against one

6a See 3:8.

another.'
11 "But they refused to listen, and they
shrugged their shoulders, and stopped their
ears from hearing.
12 "And they made their hearts like flint
against hearing the Torah, and the words,
which יהוה of hosts had sent by His Spirit
through the former prophets. Therefore
great wrath came from יהוה of hosts.
13 "And it came to be: as He called and
they did not hear, so let them call, but I
shall not hear," said יהוה of hosts.
14 "And I scattered them with a storm
wind among all the nations which they had
not known. And the land was laid waste
behind them, no one passing through or
returning, for they made the pleasant land
a waste."

8 And the word of יהוה of hosts came,
saying,
2 "Thus said יהוה of hosts, 'I shall be
jealous for Tsiyon with great jealousy, with
great wrath I shall be jealous for her.'
3 "Thus said יהוה, 'I shall return to
Tsiyon, and I shall dwell in the midst of
Yerushalayim. [a] And Yerushalayim shall
be called: City of the Truth, and the
Mountain of יהוה of hosts, the Set-apart
Mountain.'
4 "Thus said יהוה of hosts, 'Again old
men and old women shall dwell in the
streets of Yerushalayim, each one with his
staff in his hand because of great age,
5 and the streets of the city shall be filled
with boys and girls playing in its streets.'
6 "Thus said יהוה of hosts, 'If it is
marvellous in the eyes of the remnant of
this people in these days, should it also be
marvellous in My eyes?' declares יהוה of
hosts.
7 "Thus said יהוה of hosts, 'See, I am
saving My people from the land of the sunrise and from the land of the sunset.
8 'And I shall bring them back, and they
shall dwell in the midst of Yerushalayim.
And they shall be My people, and I shall
be their Elohim, in truth and in righteousness.'
9 "Thus said יהוה of hosts, 'Let your
hands be strong, you who are listening in
these days to these words, from the mouth
of the prophets, of the day the foundation
was laid for the House of יהוה of hosts, the
Hěḵal that was to be rebuilt.
10 'For before these days there was not a
wage for a man, nor a hire for beast, and
there was no peace for him who went out
or came in, because of his enemies, and I
set all men one against another.
11 'But now I am not as in the former days
to the remnant of this people,' declares
יהוה of hosts.
12 'Because of the sowing of peace the
vine does give its fruit, the ground does
give her increase, and the heavens do give
their dew. And I shall cause the remnant of
this people to inherit all these.
13 'And it shall be, as you were a curse
among the nations, O house of Yehuḏah
and house of Yisra'ěl, so I shall save you,
and you shall be a blessing. Do not fear, let
your hands be strong.'
14 "For thus said יהוה of hosts, 'As I
purposed to do evil to you when your
fathers provoked Me,' declares יהוה of
hosts, 'and I did not relent,
15 so again in these days I have purposed
to do good to Yerushalayim and to the
house of Yehuḏah. Do not fear!
16 'These are the words you should do:
speak the truth to one another, judge with
truth and right-ruling for peace in your
gates.
17 'And do not plot evil in your heart
against another, and do not love a false
oath. For all these I hate,' declares יהוה."
18 And the word of יהוה of hosts came to
me, saying,
19 "Thus said יהוה of hosts, 'The fast of
the fourth, and the fast of the fifth, and the
fast of the seventh, and the fast of the tenth
months, are to be joy and gladness, and
pleasant appointed times for the house of
Yehuḏah – and they shall love the truth and
the peace.'
20 "Thus said יהוה of hosts, 'Peoples shall
yet come, inhabitants of many cities,

8a See footnote Yesh. 12:6.

21 and the inhabitants of the one go to another, saying, "Let us earnestly go and pray before יהוה, and seek יהוה of hosts. I myself am going."

22 'And many peoples and strong nations shall come to seek יהוה of hosts in Yerushalayim, and to pray before יהוה.'

23 "Thus said יהוה of hosts, 'In those days ten men from all languages of the nations take hold, yes, they shall take hold of the edge of the garment of a man, a Yehuḏi, saying, "Let us go with you, for we have heard that Elohim is with you." ' " [b]

9

The message of the word of יהוה against the land of Ḥaḏraḵ, and Dammeseq its resting place – when the eye of man and all the tribes of Yisra'ěl are on יהוה –

2 and Ḥamath also borders on it, Tsor and Tsiḏon, though they are very wise.

3 For Tsor built herself a tower, heaped up silver like the dust, and gold like the mud of the streets.

4 See, יהוה shall dispossess her, and He shall strike her power in the sea, and she shall be consumed by fire.

5 Ashqelon sees it and fears, Azzah too, writhing in anguish, and Eqron, for her expectation has dried up. And the sovereign shall perish from Azzah, and Ashqelon shall not be inhabited.

6 "And a mamzer [a] shall settle in Ashdoḏ. So I shall cut off the pride of the Philistines,

7 and shall take away his blood from his mouth, and the abominations from between his teeth. And he shall remain, even he, to our Elohim, and he shall be like a leader in Yehuḏah, and Eqron like a Yeḇusite.

8 And I shall encamp around My house, against an army, against him who passes by and him who returns, so that no oppressor passes through them again, for now I have seen with My eyes.

9 "Rejoice greatly, O daughter of Tsiyon! Shout, O daughter of Yerushalayim! See, your Sovereign is coming to you, He is righteous and endowed with deliverance, humble and riding on a donkey, a colt, the foal of a donkey. [b]

10 "And I shall cut off the chariot from Ephrayim and the horse from Yerushalayim. And the battle bow shall be cut off. And He shall speak peace to the nations, and His rule is from sea to sea, and from the River to the ends of the earth.

11 "Also you, because of the blood of your covenant, I shall send your prisoners out of the pit.

12 "Return to the stronghold, you prisoners of the expectation. Even today I declare that I return double to you.

13 "For I shall bend Yehuḏah for Me, I shall fill the bow with Ephrayim, and I shall stir up your sons, O Tsiyon, against your sons, O Greece, and I shall make you like the sword of a mighty man."

14 And יהוה shall appear for them, and His arrow go forth like lightning, and the Master יהוה sound with the shophar. And He shall go with whirlwinds from the south,

15 יהוה of hosts shall shield them. And they shall devour and trample on sling stones. And they shall drink, roar as if with wine, and they shall be filled like basins, like the corners of the slaughter-place.

16 And יהוה their Elohim shall save them in that day, as the flock of His people, for the stones of a diadem, sparkling over His land.

17 For what goodness is His, and what comeliness is His. Grain make the young men thrive, and new wine the maidens!

10

Ask יהוה for rain in the time of the latter rain, יהוה who makes storm clouds. And He gives them showers of rain, the plants in the field to everyone.

2 For the household idols spoke emptiness, the diviners saw falsehood, and relate dreams of deceit, they comfort in vain. Therefore they have wandered about like sheep. They are afflicted, for there is no shepherd. [a]

3 "My wrath burns against the shepherds,

8b Yn. 4:22. *9a* See Explan. Notes. *9b* Mt. 21:5, Yn. 12:15. *10a* Yeḥez. 34:5 & 8.

and I lay a charge against the leaders. For יהוה of hosts shall visit His flock, the house of Yehuḏah, and make them like His splendid horse in battle.

4 “From him comes the corner-stone, from him the tent peg, from him the battle bow, from him every ruler, together.

5 “And they shall be like mighty men, who trample down the mud of the streets in the battle. And they shall fight because יהוה is with them, and the riders on horses shall be put to shame.

6 “And I shall make the house of Yehuḏah mighty, and save the house of Yosěph. And I shall bring them back, because I have compassion on them. And they shall be as though I had not pushed them aside. For I am יהוה their Elohim, and I answer them.

7 “And Ephrayim shall be as a mighty man, and their heart shall rejoice as if with wine. And their children shall see and rejoice, their heart exulting in יהוה.

8 “I shall whistle for them and gather them, for I shall ransom them. And they shall increase as they once increased.

9 “Though I sow them among peoples, they shall remember Me in places far away. And they shall live, together with their children, and they shall return.

10 “And I shall bring them back from the land of Mitsrayim, and gather them from Ashshur, and bring them into the land of Gil‘aḏ and Leḇanon, until no more room is found for them.

11 “And He shall pass through the sea of distress, and strike the waves of the sea, and all the depths of the River shall dry up. And the pride of Ashshur shall be brought down, and the sceptre of Mitsrayim be taken away.

12 “And I shall make them mighty in יהוה, so that they walk up and down in His Name,” declares יהוה.

11 Open your doors, O Leḇanon, and let fire devour your cedars.

2 Howl, O cypress, for the cedar has fallen, because the mighty are ravaged. Howl, O oaks of Bashan, for the dense forest has come down.

3 Listen! The howling of shepherds, for their splendour is ravaged. Listen! The roaring of lions, for the pride of the Yarděn is ravaged.

4 Thus said יהוה my Elohim, “Feed the flock for slaughter,

5 whose owners kill them and feel no guilt, and their sellers say, ‘Blessed be יהוה, for I have become rich.’ And their own shepherds do not spare them.

6 “For I shall no longer spare the inhabitants of the land,” declares יהוה. “But see, I am delivering up mankind, each one into his neighbour’s hand and into the hand of his sovereign. And they shall crush the earth, but I do not deliver from their hand.”

7 So I shepherded the flock meant for slaughter, the truly poor of the flock. And I took for myself two staffs, the one I called Pleasantness, and the other I called Unity, and I shepherded the flock.

8 Then I sent off the three shepherds in one month, for my being despised them, and their being also loathed me.

9 So I said, “I am not shepherding you. Let the dying die, and the straying stray, and let those who are left eat each other’s flesh.”

10 And I took my staff, Pleasantness, and cut it in two, to break the covenant which I had made with all the peoples.

11 So it was broken on that day. And the poor of the flock, who were watching me, knew that it was the word of יהוה.

12 And I said to them, “If it is good in your eyes, give me my wages. And if not, refrain.” So they weighed out for my wages thirty pieces of silver.

13 And יהוה said to me, “Throw it to the potter,” the splendid price at which I was valued by them. And I took the thirty pieces of silver and threw them into the House of יהוה for the potter.

14 Then I cut in two my other staff, Unity, to break the brotherhood between Yehuḏah and Yisra’ěl.

15 And יהוה said to me, “Take again the implements of a foolish shepherd.

16 “For look, I am raising up a shepherd in the land who does not visit those straying, nor seek the young, nor heal those that are

broken, nor feed those that still stand. But he does eat the flesh of the fat and tear off their hooves.

17 "Woe to the worthless shepherd forsaking the flock! Let a sword be upon his arm and upon his right eye! His arm shall wither and his right eye shall be dimmed."

12 The message of the word of יהוה against Yisra'ěl. יהוה, stretching out the heavens, and laying the foundation of the earth, and forming the spirit of man within him, declares,

2 "See, I am making Yerushalayim a cup of reeling to all the people all around, and also against Yehuḏah it is in the siege against Yerushalayim.

3 "And in that day it shall be that I make Yerushalayim a very heavy stone for all peoples – all lifting it are severely injured. And all the nations of the earth shall be gathered against it.

4 "In that day," declares יהוה, "I strike every horse with bewilderment and its rider with madness. And on the house of Yehuḏah I open My eyes, but every horse of the peoples I strike with blindness.

5 "And the leaders of Yehuḏah shall say in their heart, 'The inhabitants of Yerushalayim are a strength to me, through יהוה of hosts, their Elohim.'

6 "In that day I make the leaders of Yehuḏah like a fire pot among trees, and like a torch of fire in the sheaves. And they shall consume all the peoples all around, on the right and on the left. And Yerushalayim shall dwell again in her own place, in Yerushalayim.

7 "And יהוה shall save the tents of Yehuḏah first, so that the comeliness of the house of Dawiḏ and the comeliness of the inhabitants of Yerushalayim would not become greater than that of Yehuḏah.

8 "In that day יהוה shall shield the inhabitants of Yerushalayim. And the feeble among them in that day shall be like Dawiḏ, and the house of Dawiḏ like Elohim, like the Messenger of יהוה before them!

9 "And it shall be in that day that I seek to destroy all the nations that come against Yerushalayim.

10 "And I shall pour on the house of Dawiḏ and on the inhabitants of Yerushalayim a spirit of favour and prayers. And they shall look on Me whom they pierced, and they shall mourn for Him as one mourns for his only son. And they shall be in bitterness over Him as a bitterness over the first-born.

11 "In that day the mourning in Yerushalayim is going to be great, like the mourning at Haḏaḏ Rimmon in the valley of Meḡiddo.

12 "And the land shall mourn, every clan by itself: the clan of the house of Dawiḏ by itself, and their women by themselves; the clan of the house of Nathan by itself, and their women by themselves;

13 the clan of the house of Lěwi by itself, and their women by themselves; the clan of Shim'i by itself, and their women by themselves;

14 all the rest of the clans, every clan by itself, and their women by themselves.

13 "In that day a fountain shall be opened for the house of Dawiḏ and for the inhabitants of Yerushalayim, for sin and for uncleanness.

2 "And it shall be in that day," declares יהוה of hosts, "that I cut off the names of the idols from the earth, [a] and they shall be remembered no more, and I shall also remove the prophets and the unclean spirit from the earth.

3 "And it shall be, when one prophesies again, then his father and mother who brought him forth shall say to him, 'You shall not to live, because you have spoken falsehood in the Name of יהוה.' And his father and mother who brought him forth shall pierce him through when he prophesies.

4 "And it shall be in that day that the prophets shall be ashamed, everyone of his vision when he prophesies, and not put a hairy robe on in order to deceive,

13a Shem. 23:13, Deḇ. 12:3, Yeh. 23:7, Hosh. 2:17, Tseph. 3:9.

5 but shall say, 'I am no prophet, I am a
farmer, for a man sold me as a slave in my
youth.'
6 "And one shall say to him, 'What are
these wounds in your hands?' And he shall
say, 'Because I was struck at home by
those who love me.'
7 "O sword, awake against My Shepherd,
against the Man who is My Companion,"
declares יהוה of hosts. "Strike the
Shepherd, and let the sheep be scattered.
But I shall turn My hand upon the little
ones.
8 And it shall be throughout all the soil,"
declares יהוה, "that two thirds therein are
cut off and die, and one third is left therein.
9 "And I shall bring the third into fire,
and refine them as silver is refined, and try
them as gold is tried. They shall call on My
Name, [b] and I shall answer them. I shall
say, 'This is My people,' while they say,
'יהוה is my Elohim.' "

14

See, a day shall come for יהוה, and
your spoil shall be divided in your
midst.
2 And I shall gather all the nations to battle against Yerushalayim. [a] And the city
shall be taken, the houses plundered, and
the women ravished. Half of the city shall
go into exile, but the remnant of the people
shall not be cut off from the city.
3 And יהוה shall go forth, and He shall
fight against those nations, as He fights in
the day of battle.
4 And in that day His feet shall stand
upon the Mount of Olives, which faces
Yerushalayim on the east. And the Mount
of Olives shall be split in two, from east to
west, a very great valley, and half of the
mountain shall move toward the north and
half of it toward the south.
5 And you shall flee to the valley of My
mountain – for the valley of the mountains
reaches to Atsal. And you shall flee as you
fled from the earthquake in the days of
Uzziyah sovereign of Yehuḏah. And יהוה
my Elohim shall come – all the set-apart
ones with You.
6 And in that day it shall be: there is no
light, it is dark.
7 And it shall be one day which is known
to יהוה, neither day nor night, but at
evening time there shall be light.
8 And in that day it shall be that living
waters flow from Yerushalayim, [b] half of
them toward the eastern sea and half of
them toward the western sea, in summer as
well as in winter.
9 And יהוה shall be Sovereign over all
the earth. [c] In that day there shall be one
יהוה, and His Name one.
10 All the land shall be changed into a
desert plain from Geḇa to Rimmon south
of Yerushalayim, and she shall be raised up
and inhabited in her place from
Binyamin's Gate to the place of the First
Gate and the Corner Gate, and from the
Tower of Ḥanan'ěl to the winepresses of
the sovereign.
11 And they shall dwell in her, and there
shall be no more utter destruction, [d] but
Yerushalayim shall be safely inhabited.
12 And this is the plague with which יהוה
plagues all the people who fought against
Yerushalayim: their flesh shall decay while
they stand on their feet, and their eyes
decay in their sockets, and their tongues
decay in their mouths.
13 And it shall be in that day that a great
confusion from יהוה is among them, and
everyone of them shall seize the hand of
his neighbour, and his hand rise up against
his neighbour's hand.
14 And Yehuḏah shall fight at Yerushalayim as well. And the wealth of all the
nations round about shall be gathered
together: gold, and silver, and garments in
great quantities.
15 So also is the plague on the horse and
the mule, on the camel and the donkey, and
on all the cattle that are in those camps – as
this plague.
16 And it shall be that all who are left from
all the nations which came up against
Yerushalayim, shall go up from year to

13b Tseph. 3:9. *14a* Yo'ěl 3:2, Tseph. 3:8, Ḥazon 16:14. *14b* Ḥazon 22:1-2.
14c See footnote Yesh. 24:23, also Dan. 2:44, Ḥazon 11:15. *14d* Mal. 4:6.

year to bow themselves to the Sovereign, יהוה of hosts, and to celebrate the Festival of Sukkot. [e]

17 And it shall be, that if anyone of the clans of the earth does not come up to Yerushalayim to bow himself to the Sovereign, יהוה of hosts, on them there is to be no rain.

18 And if the clan of Mitsrayim does not come up and enter in, then there is no *rain*. On them is the plague with which יהוה plagues the nations who do not come up to celebrate the Festival of Sukkot. [e]

19 This is the punishment of Mitsrayim and the punishment of all the nations that do not come up to celebrate the Festival of Sukkot. [e]

20 In that day "SET-APART TO יהוה" shall be engraved on the bells of the horses. And the pots in the House of יהוה shall be like the bowls before the slaughter-place.

21 And every pot in Yerushalayim and Yehuḏah shall be set-apart to יהוה of hosts. And all those who slaughter shall come and take them and cook in them. And there shall no longer be a merchant in the House of יהוה of hosts, in that day.

MAL’AḴI

MALACHI

1 The message of the word of יהוה to
Yisra’ĕl by Mal’aḵi.
2 “I have loved you,” said יהוה. “But you
asked, ‘In what way have You loved us?’
“Was not Ěsaw Ya‘aqoḇ’s brother?”
declares יהוה. “And I love Ya‘aqoḇ,
3 but I have hated Ěsaw, and have laid
waste his mountains and his inheritance for
the jackals of the wilderness.”
4 If Eḏom says, “We have been beaten
down, let us return and build the ruins,”
יהוה of hosts said thus: “Let them build,
but I tear down. And they shall be called
‘Border of Wrongness’, and the people
against whom יהוה is enraged forever.
5 And your eyes shall see, and you shall
say, ‘Great is יהוה beyond the border of
Yisra’ĕl!’
6 “A son esteems his father, and a servant
his master. And if I am the Father, where is
My esteem? And if I am a Master, where is
My fear? said יהוה of hosts to you priests
who despise My Name. But you asked, ‘In
what way have we despised Your Name?’
7 “You are presenting defiled food on My
slaughter-place. But you asked, ‘In what
way have we defiled You?’ Because you
say, ‘The table of יהוה is despicable.’
8 “And when you present the blind as a
slaughtering, is it not evil? And when you
present the lame and sick, is it not evil?
Bring it then to your governor! Would he
be pleased with you? Would he accept you
favourably?” said יהוה of hosts.
9 “And now, entreat the face of Ěl to
show favour to us. This has been done by
your hands. Would He show favour to
you?” said יהוה of hosts.
10 “Who among you who would shut the
doors, so that you would not kindle fire on
My slaughter-place for naught? I have no
pleasure in you,” said יהוה of hosts, “Nor
do I accept an offering from your hands.
11 “For from the rising of the sun, even to
its going down, My Name is great among
nations. And in every place incense is presented to My Name, and a clean offering.
For My Name is great among nations,”
said יהוה of hosts.
12 “But you are profaning Me, in that you
say, ‘The table of יהוה is defiled, and its
fruit, its food, is despicable.’
13 “And you said, ‘Oh, what weariness!’
and you sneered at it,” said יהוה of hosts.
“And you brought in plunder, and the
lame, and the sick – thus you have brought
in the offering! Should I accept this from
your hand?” said יהוה.
14 “But cursed be the deceiver who has a
male in his flock, and makes a vow, but is
slaughtering to יהוה what is blemished.
For I am a great Sovereign,” said יהוה of
hosts, “and My Name is feared among
nations.

2 “And now, O priests, this command is
for you.
2 “If you do not hear, and if you do not
take it to heart, to give esteem to My
Name,” said יהוה of hosts, “I shall send a
curse upon you, and I shall curse your
blessings. And indeed, I have cursed them,
because you do not take it to heart.
3 “See, I shall rebuke your seed, and scatter dung before your faces, the dung of
your festivals. And you shall be taken
away with it.
4 “And you shall know that I have sent
this command to you, as being My
covenant with Lĕwi,” said יהוה of hosts.
5 “My covenant with him was life and
peace, and I gave them to him, to fear. And
he feared Me, and stood in awe of My
Name.
6 “The Torah of truth [a] was in his mouth,

2a See footnote Neḥ. 9:13.

and unrighteousness was not found on his lips. He walked with Me in peace and straightness, and turned many away from crookedness.

7 "For the lips of a priest should guard knowledge, and they seek the Torah from his mouth, for he is the messenger of יהוה of hosts.

8 "But you, you have turned from the way, you have caused many to stumble in the Torah. You have corrupted the covenant of Lěwi," said יהוה of hosts.

9 "And I also, I shall make you despised and low before all the people, because you are not guarding My ways, and are showing partiality in the Torah."

10 Have we not all one Father? Did not one Ěl create us? Why do we act treacherously against one another, to profane the covenant of the fathers?

11 Yehuḏah has acted treacherously, and an abomination has been done in Yisra'ěl and in Yerushalayim, for Yehuḏah has profaned what is set-apart to יהוה – which He had loved – and has married the daughter of a foreign mighty one.

12 Let יהוה cut off from the tents of Ya'aqoḇ the man who does this – stirring up or answering, and bringing an offering to יהוה of hosts!

13 And this you have done a second time: you cover the slaughter-place of יהוה with tears, with weeping and crying, because He no longer regards the offering, nor receives it with pleasure from your hands.

14 And you said, "Why?" Because יהוה has been witness between you and the wife of your youth, against whom you have acted treacherously, though she is your companion and the wife of your covenant.

15 And did He not make one? And He had the remnant of the Spirit? And what is the one *alone*? He seeks a seed of Elohim. So you shall guard your spirit, and let none act treacherously against the wife of his youth.

16 "For I hate divorce," said יהוה Elohim of Yisra'ěl, "and the one who covers his garment with cruelty," said יהוה of hosts. "So you shall guard your spirit, and do not act treacherously."

17 You have wearied יהוה with your words, and you have said, "In what way have we wearied Him?" In that you say, "Everyone who does evil is good in the eyes of יהוה, and He is delighting in them," or, "Where is the Elohim of right-ruling?"

3

"See, I am sending My messenger, and he shall prepare the way before Me. Then suddenly the Master you are seeking comes to His Hěḵal, even the Messenger of the covenant, in whom you delight. See, He is coming," said יהוה of hosts.

2 "And who is able to bear the day of His coming, and who is able to stand when He appears? For He is like the fire of a refiner, and like the soap of a launderer.

3 "And He shall sit as a refiner and a cleanser of silver. And He shall cleanse the sons of Lěwi, and refine them as gold and silver, and they shall belong to יהוה, bringing near an offering in righteousness.

4 "Then shall the offering of Yehuḏah and Yerushalayim be pleasant to יהוה, as in the days of old, as in former years.

5 "And I shall draw near to you for right-ruling. And I shall be a swift witness against the practisers of witchcraft, and against adulterers, and against them that swear to falsehood, and against those who oppress the wage earner in his wages and widows and the fatherless, and those who turn away a sojourner and do not fear Me," said יהוה of hosts.

6 "For I am יהוה, I shall not change,[a] and you, O sons of Ya'aqoḇ, shall not come to an end.

7 "From the days of your fathers you have turned aside from My laws and did not guard them. Turn back to Me, and I shall turn back to you," said יהוה of hosts. "But you said, 'In what shall we turn back?'

8 "Would a man rob Elohim? Yet you are robbing Me! But you said, 'In what have we robbed You?' In the tithe and the

3a Ya'aqoḇ 1:17.

offering!
9"You have cursed Me with a curse, for
you are robbing Me, this nation, all of it!
10"Bring all the tithes into the storehouse,
and let there be food in My house. And
please prove Me in this," said יהוה of
hosts, "whether I do not open for you the
windows of the heavens, and shall pour out
for you boundless blessing!
11"And I shall rebuke the devourer for
you, so that it does not destroy the fruit of
your ground, nor does the vine fail to bear
fruit for you in the field," said יהוה of
hosts.
12"And all nations shall call you blessed,
for you shall be a land of delight," said
יהוה of hosts.
13"Your words have been strong against
Me," said יהוה, "but you have said, 'What
have we spoken against You?'
14"You have said, 'It is worthless to serve
Elohim. And what did we gain when we
guarded His Charge, and when we walked
as mourners before יהוה of hosts?
15'And now we are calling the proud
blessed – not only are the doers of wrongness built up, but they also try Elohim and
escape.' "
16Then shall those who fear יהוה speak
to one another, and יהוה listens and hears,
and a book of remembrance be written
before Him, of those who fear יהוה, and
those who think upon His Name.
17"And they shall be Mine," said יהוה of
hosts, "on the day that I prepare a treasured
possession. And I shall spare them as a
man spares his own son who serves him.
18"Then you shall again see the *difference* between the righteous and the wrong,
between one who serves Elohim and one
who does not serve Him.

4 "For look, the day shall come, burning
like a furnace, and all the proud, and
every wrongdoer shall be stubble. And the
day that shall come shall burn them up,"
said יהוה of hosts, "which leaves to them
neither root nor branch.
2"But to you who fear My Name the Sun
of Righteousness shall arise with healing
in His wings. And you shall go out and
leap for joy like calves from the stall.
3"And you shall trample the wrongdoers, for they shall be ashes under the soles
of your feet on the day that I do this," said
יהוה of hosts.
4"Remember the Torah of Mosheh, My
servant, which I commanded him in Ḥorěḇ
for all Yisra'ěl – laws and right-rulings.
5"See, I am sending you Ěliyah the
prophet before the coming of the great and
awesome day of יהוה.
6"And he shall turn the hearts of the
fathers to the children, and the hearts of the
children to their fathers, lest I come and
strike the earth with utter destruction." [a]

4b See also Zeḵ. 14:13.

TEHILLIM

PSALMS

1 Blessed is the man who shall not walk
in the counsel of the wrong,
And shall not stand in the path of
sinners,
And shall not sit in the seat of scoffers,
2 But his delight is in the Torah of יהוה,
And he meditates in His Torah day and
night.
3 For he shall be as a tree
Planted by the rivers of water,
That yields its fruit in its season,
And whose leaf does not wither,
And whatever he does prospers.
4 The wrong are not so,
But are like the chaff which the wind
blows away.
5 Therefore the wrong shall not rise in
the judgment,
Nor sinners in the congregation of the
righteous.
6 For יהוה knows the way of the
righteous,
But the way of the wrong comes to
naught.

2 Why do the nations rage, [a]
And the peoples meditate
emptiness?
2 The sovereigns of the earth take their
stand,
And the rulers take counsel together,
Against יהוה and against His Messiah,
and say,
3 "Let us tear apart Their bonds,
And throw away Their ropes from us."
4 He who is sitting in the heavens
laughs,
יהוה mocks at them.
5 Then He speaks to them in His wrath,
And troubles them in His rage, *saying*,
6 "But I, I have set My Sovereign on
Tsiyon,
My set-apart mountain."
7 "I inscribe for a law:
יהוה has said to Me, 'You are My Son,
Today I have brought You forth.
8 'Ask of Me, and I make the nations
Your inheritance,
And the ends of the earth
Your possession.
9 'Break them with a rod of iron,
Dash them to pieces like a potter's
vessel.' "
10 And now, be wise, O sovereigns;
Be instructed, you rulers of the earth.
11 Serve יהוה with fear,
And rejoice with trembling.
12 Kiss the Chosen, [b] lest He be enraged,
And you perish in the way,
For soon His wrath is to be kindled.
Blessed are all those taking refuge in
Him.

3 O יהוה, how my adversaries have
increased!
Many rising up against me.
2 Many are saying of me,
"There is no deliverance for him in
Elohim." Selah.
3 But You, O יהוה, are a shield for me,
My esteem, and the One lifting up my
head.
4 I cried to יהוה with my voice,
And He heard me from His set-apart
mountain. Selah.
5 I, I laid down and slept;
I awoke, for יהוה sustained me.
6 I am not afraid of ten thousands of
people
Who have set themselves against me
all around.
7 Arise, O יהוה;
Save me, O my Elohim!
Because You have stricken all my ene-

2a Quoted in Ma. 4:25-26. See also Dan. 2:44, Dan. 7:13-28, Ḥagg. 2:22, Zeḵ. 14:9 & Ḥazon 11:15.
2b Hebrew, Nashqu ḇar. Ḇar - Chosen in Hebrew but Son in Aramaic.

mies on the cheek;
You have broken the teeth of the wrong.
8 Deliverance belongs to יהוה.
Your blessing is on Your people. Selah.

4

Answer me when I call,
O Elohim of my righteousness!
You gave relief to me when I was in distress;
Show favour to me, and hear my prayer.
2 Till when, O you sons of men,
Would you turn my esteem to shame,
Would you love emptiness, seek falsehood? Selah.
3 But know that יהוה has separated a lovingly-committed one for Himself;
יהוה hears when I call to Him.
4 Tremble, and do not sin.
Speak within your heart on your bed, and be still. Selah.
5 Slaughter slaughterings of righteousness,
And trust in יהוה.
6 Many are saying, "Who would show us good?"
יהוה, lift up the light of Your face upon us.
7 You have put more gladness in my heart,
Than in the season that their grain and wine increased.
8 I lie down in peace altogether, and sleep;
For You alone, O יהוה, make me dwell in safety.

5

Give ear to my words, O יהוה,
Consider my meditation.
2 Attend to the voice of my cry,
My Sovereign and my Elohim,
For unto You I pray.
3 O יהוה, in the morning You hear my voice;
I present myself to You in the morning,
And I look up.
4 For You are not an Ěl taking delight in wrong,
Nor does evil dwell with You.
5 The boasters do not stand before Your eyes;
You hate all workers of wickedness.
6 You destroy those speaking falsehood;
יהוה loathes a man of blood and deceit.
7 But I, I enter Your house
In the greatness of Your loving-commitment;
I bow myself toward Your set-apart Hěḵal in Your fear.
8 O יהוה, lead me in Your righteousness because of those watching me;
Make Your way straight before my face.
9 For there is no stability in their mouth;
Their inward part is destruction;
Their throat is an open burial-site;
They flatter with their tongue.
10 Declare them guilty, O Elohim!
Let them fall by their own counsels;
Thrust them away for their many transgressions,
Because they have rebelled against You.
11 But let all who take refuge in You rejoice;
Let them ever shout for joy, because You shelter them;
And let those who love Your Name exult in You.
12 For You bless the righteous, O יהוה;
You surround him with favour as with a shield.

6

O יהוה, do not rebuke me in Your displeasure,
Nor discipline me in Your wrath.
2 Show favour to me, O יהוה, for I am fading away;
O יהוה, heal me, for my bones have been troubled.
3 And my being has been greatly troubled;
And You, O יהוה – till when?
4 Return, O יהוה, rescue my life!
Oh, save me for Your loving-commitment' sake!
5 For in death there is no remembrance of You;
Who gives You thanks in She'ol?
6 I have grown weary with my groaning;
Every night I flood my bed;

I drench my couch with my tears.
7 My eye has grown dim because of grief;
It grows old because of all my adversaries.
8 Depart from me, all you workers of wickedness;
For יהוה has heard the voice of my weeping.
9 יהוה has heard my pleading;
יהוה receives my prayer.
10 Let all my enemies be ashamed and greatly troubled;
They turn back suddenly, ashamed.

7 O יהוה my Elohim, in You I have taken refuge;
Save me from all my pursuers;
And deliver me,
2 Lest they tear at my throat like a lion,
Rending in pieces, with no one to deliver.
3 O יהוה my Elohim, if I have done this:
If there is unrighteousness in my hands,
4 If I have done evil to him who was at peace with me,
Or have plundered my enemy without cause,
5 Let the enemy pursue me and overtake my being,
And trample my life to the ground,
And lay my esteem in the dust. Selah.
6 Arise, O יהוה, in Your displeasure;
Lift Yourself up against the rage of my adversaries,
And awake for me!
You shall command judgment!
7 And let the congregation of the peoples gather about You;
And over them return on high.
8 יהוה judges the peoples;
Judge me, O יהוה, according to my righteousness,
And according to my integrity within me.
9 Please let the evil of the wrong be ended,
And establish the righteous;
For the righteous Elohim is a trier of hearts and kidneys.
10 My shield is upon Elohim,
Who saves the upright in heart.
11 Elohim is a righteous judge.
And Ěl is enraged every day,
12 If one does not repent!
He sharpens His sword,
He bends His bow and makes it ready,
13 And He has prepared for Himself instruments of death,
He makes His arrows hot for pursuers.
14 See, he who is bound with wickedness,
And has conceived trouble and brought forth falsehood,
15 He has made a pit and dug it out,
And falls into the ditch he made!
16 His trouble turns back upon his own head,
And his wrongdoing comes down on the top of his head.
17 I give thanks to יהוה according to His righteousness,
And praise the Name of יהוה Most High.

8 O יהוה, our Master, how excellent is Your Name in all the earth,
You who set Your splendour above the heavens!
2 Out of the mouth of babes and infants
You have founded strength,
Because of Your adversaries,
To put an end to enemy and avenger.
3 For I see Your heavens, the work of Your fingers,
The moon and the stars, which You have established.
4 What is man that You remember him?
And the son of man that You visit him?
5 Yet You have made him a little less than Elohim, [a]
And have crowned him with esteem and splendour.
6 You made him rule over the works of Your hands;
You have put all under his feet,
7 All sheep and oxen,
And also the beasts of the field,

8a Or - elohim.

8 The birds of the heavens,
And the fish of the sea,
Passing through the paths of the seas.
9 O יהוה, our Master,
How excellent is Your Name in all the earth!

9 **Aleph** I praise You, O יהוה, with all my heart;
I declare all Your wonders.
2 I rejoice and exult in You;
I sing praise to Your Name, O Most High.
3 **Bĕt** When my enemies turn back,
They stumble and perish before You.
4 For You executed my right and my cause,
You sat on the throne judging in righteousness.
5 **Gimel** You have rebuked the nations,
You have destroyed the wrong,
You have wiped out their name forever and ever.
6 **Hĕ** The enemy is no more – ruins everlasting!
And You have uprooted the cities;
Even their remembrance has perished.
7 But יהוה abides forever,
He is preparing His throne for judgment.
8 And He judges the world in righteousness,
He judges the peoples in straightness.
9 **Waw** And יהוה is a refuge for the crushed one,
A refuge in times of distress.
10 And those who know Your Name trust in You,
For You have not forsaken those who seek You, O יהוה.
11 **Zayin** Sing praises to יהוה, who dwells in Tsiyon!
Declare His deeds among the peoples.
12 For He remembers the seekers of bloodshed,
He does not forget the cry of the afflicted.
13 **Ḥet** Show favour to me, O יהוה!
See my affliction by those who hate me,
You who lift me up from the gates of death,
14 So that I declare all Your praise
In the gates of the daughter of Tsiyon.
I rejoice in Your deliverance.
15 **Tet** The nations have sunk down in the pit which they made;
In the net which they hid, their own foot is caught.
16 יהוה has made Himself known,
He has done right-ruling;
The wrong is snared in the work of his own hands.
Meditation. Selah.
17 **Yod** The wrong return to She'ol,
All the nations that forget Elohim.
18 **Kaph** For the needy is not always forgotten;
Neither the expectancy of the poor lost forever.
19 Arise, O יהוה,
Do not let man prevail;
Let the nations be judged before Your face.
20 Put them in fear, O יהוה,
Let the nations know they are *but* men. Selah.

10 **Lamed** Why do You stand afar off, O יהוה, hiding in times of dis tress?
2 In arrogance the wrongdoer hotly pursues the poor;
They are caught by the schemes which they devised.
3 For the wrongdoer boasted of his cravings;
And the greedy one cursed and despised יהוה.
4 In the pride of his face
The wrongdoer does not seek *Him*,
In all his thoughts there is no Elohim!
5 His ways are always prosperous!
Your right-rulings are on high, out of his sight!
He snorts at all his adversaries!
6 He has said in his heart,
"I shall not be moved;
From generation to generation, never be in evil!"
7 **Pĕ** His mouth is filled with cursing and deceit and oppression;

Under his tongue is trouble and
wickedness.
8 He sits in the hiding places of the
villages;
In the secret places he kills the innocent;
Ayin His eyes are on the lookout for
the helpless.
9 He lies in wait in a secret place,
as a lion in his den;
He lies in wait to catch the poor;
He catches the poor, drawing him into
his net.
10 And he crouches, he lies low,
And the helpless fall under his
strength.
11 He has said in his heart,
"Ěl has forgotten,
He has hidden His face,
He shall never see."
12 **Qoph** Arise, O יהוה! O Ěl, lift up Your
hand!
Do not forget the lowly ones.
13 Why do the wrong scorn Elohim?
He has said in his heart,
"It is not required."
14 **Rěsh** You have seen it, for You observe
trouble and grief,
To repay with Your hand.
The poor commits himself to You;
You are the helper of the fatherless.
15 **Shin** Break the arm of the wrong one
and the evil one;
Search out his wrongness that would
not be found out.
16 יהוה is Sovereign forever and ever;
The nations shall perish from His land.
17 **Taw** יהוה, You have heard the desire
of the lowly ones;
You prepare their heart;
You incline Your ear,
18 To defend the fatherless and the
downtrodden;
So that man who is of the earth no
longer oppresses!

11

In יהוה I have taken refuge;
Why do you say to me,
"Flee to your mountain like a bird"?
2 For look! The wrong bend a bow,
They set their arrow on the string,
To shoot in darkness at the upright in
heart.
3 When the foundations are destroyed,
What shall the righteous do?
4 יהוה is in His set-apart Hěḵal,
The throne of יהוה is in the heavens.
His eyes see, His eyelids examine the
sons of men.
5 יהוה tries the righteous,
But His being shall hate the wrong
And the one who loves violence.
6 Upon the wrong He rains snares,
Fire and sulphur and a scorching wind
Are the portion of their cup.
7 For יהוה is righteous,
He has loved righteousness;
The upright shall see His face.

12

Save, יהוה, for the lovingly-
committed one is no more!
For the trustworthy have ceased from
among the sons of men.
2 They speak falsehood with each other;
They speak *with* flattering lips,
a double heart.
3 יהוה does cut off all flattering lips,
A tongue that speaks swelling words,
4 Who have said, "With our tongue we
do mightily;
Our lips are our own;
Who is master over us?"
5 "Because of the oppression of the poor,
because of the sighing of the needy,
I now arise," says יהוה, "I set in safety
– he pants for it."
6 The Words of יהוה are clean Words,
Silver tried in a furnace of earth,
Refined seven times. [a]
7 You guard them, O יהוה,
You preserve them from this
generation forever.
8 The wrong walk around on every side,
When worthlessness is exalted among
the sons of men.

13

How long would You forget me,
O יהוה? Forever?

12a Teh. 18:30, Teh. 119:140, Mish. 30:4.

How long would You hide Your face from me?
2 How long would I take counsel in my being,
Grief in my heart day by day?
How long would my enemy be exalted over me?
3 Look! Answer me, O יהוה my Elohim;
Enlighten my eyes,
Lest I sleep in death;
4 Lest my enemy say, "I have prevailed against him,"
Lest my adversaries rejoice when I am moved.
5 But I have trusted in Your loving-commitment;
My heart rejoices in Your deliverance.
6 I sing to יהוה,
Because He has been good to me.

14 The fool has said in his heart, "There is no יהוה."
They have done corruptly,
They have done an abominable deed,
There is no one who does good.
2 יהוה looked down from the heavens on the sons of mankind,
To see if there is a wise one, seeking יהוה.
3 They have all turned aside,
They have together become filthy;
No one is doing good, not even one.
4 Have all the workers of wickedness no knowledge,
Who eat up my people as they eat bread,
And do not call on יהוה?
5 There they are in great fear,
For יהוה is with the generation of the righteous.
6 You would put to shame the counsel of the poor,
But יהוה is his refuge.
7 O that the deliverance of Yisra'ěl
Would be given out of Tsiyon!
When יהוה turns back the captivity of His people,
Let Ya'aqoḇ rejoice, let Yisra'ěl be glad.

15 יהוה, who does sojourn in Your Tent?
Who does dwell in Your set-apart mountain?
2 He who walks blamelessly,
And does righteousness,
And speaks the truth in his heart.
3 He has not slandered with his tongue,
He has not done evil to his neighbour,
Nor lifted up a reproach against his friend;
4 In whose eyes a reprobate one is despised,
But he esteems those who fear יהוה;
He who swears to his own hurt and does not change;
5 He has not put out his silver at interest,
And has not taken a bribe against the innocent.
He who does these is never moved.

16 Guard me, O Ěl, for I have taken refuge in You.
2 I have said to יהוה,
"You are יהוה,
I have no good beside You."
3 As for the set-apart ones who are on the earth,
They are the excellent ones, in whom is all my delight.
4 The sorrows of those who run after another one are increased;
I would not pour out their drink offerings of blood,
Nor take up their names on my lips.
5 יהוה is the portion of my inheritance and my cup;
You uphold my lot.
6 *Boundary* lines have fallen to me in pleasant places;
Indeed, a good inheritance is mine.
7 I bless יהוה who has given me counsel;
My kidneys also instruct me in the nights.
8 I have set יהוה always before me;
Because *He* is at my right hand I am not shaken.
9 Therefore my heart was glad, and my esteem rejoices;
My flesh also dwells in safety.
10 For You do not leave my being in

She'ol,
Neither let Your Lovingly-committed One see corruption.
11 You show me the path of life;
In Your presence is joy to satisfaction;
At Your right hand are pleasures forever.

17

Hear righteousness, יהוה,
Listen to my cry;
Give ear to my prayer,
From lips without deceit.
2 Let my right-ruling go out from Your presence;
Let Your eyes see what is straight.
3 You have examined my heart;
You have visited me in the night;
You have tried me –
You find I have not schemed;
My mouth would not transgress.
4 As for the deeds of men –
By the word of Your lips,
I have kept myself from the paths of the destroyer.
5 My steps have held fast to Your paths,
My feet have not slipped.
6 I have called upon You, for You answer me, O Ěl;
Incline Your ear to me, hear my speech.
7 Let Your loving-commitment be distinguished,
You who save by Your right hand those who take refuge
From those who rise up.
8 Guard me as the apple of Your eye.
Hide me under the shadow of Your wings,
9 From the face of the wrong who ravage me,
From my deadly enemies who surround me.
10 They are enclosed in their own fat,
They speak proudly with their mouths,
11 They have now surrounded us in our steps,
They set their eyes to cast *us* to the ground,
12 Like a lion who is eager to tear his prey,
And as a young lion crouching in cover.
13 Arise, O יהוה,
Confront him, cause him to bend;
Deliver my being from the wrong by Your sword,
14 From men by Your hand, O יהוה,
From men of the world whose portion is in *this* life,
And You fill their bellies with Your treasure,
They are satisfied with children,
And shall leave their riches to their babes.
15 As for me, let Me see Your face in righteousness;
I am satisfied *to see* Your appearance when I awake.

18

I love You, O יהוה,
My strength.
2 יהוה is my rock and my stronghold and my deliverer;
My Ěl is my rock, I take refuge in Him;
My shield and the horn of my deliverance, my high tower.
3 I call upon יהוה, the One to be praised,
And I am saved from my enemies.
4 The cords of death surrounded me,
And the floods of Beliyaʿal made me afraid.
5 The cords of She'ol were all around me;
The snares of death were before me.
6 In my distress I called upon יהוה,
And to my Elohim I cried;
He heard my voice from His Hěḵal,
And my cry went before Him, into His ears.
7 And the earth shook and trembled;
Even the foundations of the mountains were troubled
And they shook, because He was wroth.
8 Smoke went up from His nostrils,
And consuming fire from His mouth;
Coals were kindled by it.
9 And He bowed the heavens and came down,
And thick darkness was under His feet.
10 And He rode upon a keruḇ, and flew;

He flew upon the wings of the wind.
11 He made darkness His covering;
Around Him His booth,
Darkness of waters, thick clouds of the skies.
12 From the brightness before Him,
His thick clouds passed, hail and coals of fire.
13 And יהוה thundered in the heavens,
And the Most High sent forth His voice,
Hail and coals of fire.
14 And He sent out His arrows and scattered them,
And much lightning, and confused them.
15 And the channels of waters were seen,
And the foundations of the world were uncovered
At Your rebuke, O יהוה,
At the blast of the breath of Your nostrils.
16 He sent from above, He took me;
He drew me out of many waters.
17 He delivered me from my strong enemy,
And from those hating me,
For they were stronger than I.
18 They confronted me in the day of my calamity,
But יהוה was my support.
19 And He brought me out into a large place;
He delivered me for He delighted in me.
20 יהוה rewarded me according to my righteousness;
According to the cleanness of my hands He repaid me.
21 For I have guarded the ways of יהוה,
And have not acted wrongly against my Elohim.
22 For all His right-rulings are before me,
And I did not turn from His laws.
23 And I am perfect before Him,
And I guard myself from my crookedness.
24 And יהוה repays me according to my righteousness,
According to the cleanness of my hands before His eyes.
25 With the lovingly-committed You show Yourself lovingly-committed;
With the perfect one You show Yourself perfect;
26 With the clean You show Yourself clean;
And with the crooked You show Yourself twisted.
27 For You save the afflicted people,
But bring down those whose eyes are haughty.
28 For You Yourself light my lamp;
יהוה my Elohim makes my darkness light.
29 For with You I run against a band,
And with my Elohim I leap over a wall.
30 The Ěl – His way is perfect;
The Word of יהוה is proven; [a]
He is a shield to all who take refuge in Him.
31 For who is Eloah, besides יהוה?
And who is a rock, except our Elohim?
32 It is Ěl who girds me with strength,
And makes my way perfect,
33 Making my feet like the feet of deer,
And sets me on my high places,
34 Teaching my hands for battle,
So that my arms shall bend a bow of bronze.
35 And You give me the shield of Your deliverance;
And Your right hand supports me,
And Your lowliness makes me great.
36 You enlarge my step under me;
And my feet shall not slip.
37 I pursue my enemies and overtake them;
And do not turn back till they are destroyed.
38 I crush them, and they are unable to rise;
They fall under my feet.
39 And You gird me with strength for battle;
Cause my adversaries to bow under me.

18a Teh. 12:6, Teh. 119:140, Mish. 30:5.

40 And You have made my enemies turn
their backs,
As for those hating me, I cut them off.
41 They cry – but no one is there to save,
To יהוה – but He answers them not.
42 And I beat them as dust before the
wind;
I empty them out like dirt in the streets.
43 You deliver me from the strivings of
the people,
You set me at the head of the nations;
A people I have not known serve me.
44 As soon as they hear of me they obey
me;
The foreigners submit to me.
45 The foreigners fade away,
And come frightened from their strongholds.
46 יהוה lives! And blessed is my Rock!
And exalted is the Elohim of my
deliverance,
47 The Ěl who avenges me,
And He humbles the peoples under me;
48 My deliverer from my enemies.
You lift me up above those who rise
against me;
You deliver me from a man of
violence.
49 Therefore I give thanks to You,
O יהוה, among nations,
And I sing praise to Your Name,
50 Making great the deliverance of His
sovereign,
And showing loving-commitment to
His anointed,
To Dawiḏ and his seed, forever.

19

The heavens are proclaiming the
esteem of Ěl;
And the expanse is declaring the work
of His hand.
2 Day to day pours forth speech,
And night to night reveals knowledge.
3 There is no speech, and there are no
words,
Their voice is not heard.
4 Their line has gone out through all the
earth,
And their words to the end of the
world.
In them He set up a tent for the sun,
5 And it is like a bridegroom coming out
of his room,
It rejoices like a strong man to run the
path.
6 Its rising is from one end of the
heavens,
And its circuit to the other end;
And naught is hidden from its heat.
7 The Torah of יהוה is perfect,
bringing back the being;
The witness of יהוה is trustworthy,
making wise the simple;
8 The orders of יהוה are straight,
rejoicing the heart;
The command of יהוה is clear,
enlightening the eyes;
9 The fear of יהוה is clean, standing forever;
The right-rulings of יהוה are true,
They are righteous altogether,
10 More desirable than gold,
Than much fine gold;
And sweeter than honey and the
honeycomb.
11 Also, Your servant is warned by them,
In guarding them there is great reward.
12 Who discerns mistakes?
Declare me innocent from those that
are secret,
13 Also keep Your servant back from
presumptuous ones,
Do not let them rule over me.
Then shall I be perfect, and innocent of
great transgression.
14 Let the words of my mouth and the
meditation of my heart
Be pleasing before You,
O יהוה, my rock and my redeemer.

20

יהוה does answer you in the day
of distress!
The Name of the Elohim of Ya'aqoḇ
does set you on high!
2 He does send you help from the set-
apart place,
And does uphold you from Tsiyon!
3 He does remember all your offerings,
And does accept your ascending offering! Selah.
4 He does give you according to your
heart,

And fills all your plans!
5 We sing of Your deliverance,
And in the Name of our Elohim we set up a banner!
יהוה does fill all your requests!
6 Now I know that יהוה shall save His Anointed;
He answers him from His set-apart heavens
With the saving might of His right hand.
7 Some *trust* in chariots, and some in horses,
But we remember the Name of יהוה our Elohim.
8 They, they have bowed down and fallen;
But we have risen and are established.
9 Save, יהוה!
Let the Sovereign answer us in the day we call.

21

The sovereign rejoices in Your strength, O יהוה;
And how greatly he exults in Your deliverance!
2 You have given him the desire of his heart,
And You have not withheld the request of his lips. Selah.
3 For You put before him the blessings of goodness;
You set a crown of fine gold on his head.
4 He asked life from You, and You gave it to him –
Length of days forever and ever.
5 Through Your deliverance his esteem is great;
You have laid excellency and splendour on him.
6 For You have made him most blessed forever;
You have made him glad with the joy of Your presence.
7 For the sovereign is trusting in יהוה,
And through the loving-commitment of the Most High he is not moved.
8 Your hand reaches all Your enemies;
Your right hand reaches those who hate You.
9 You make them as a furnace of fire in the time of Your presence;
יהוה does swallow them up in His wrath,
And fire does consume them.
10 You destroy their fruit from the earth,
And their seed from among the sons of men.
11 For they held out evil against You;
They devised a plot; they do not prevail.
12 For You make them turn their back,
When You aim with Your bowstring toward their faces.
13 Be exalted, O יהוה, in Your strength!
We sing and we praise Your might.

22

My Ěl, My Ěl, why have You forsaken Me –
Far from saving Me, *far from* the words of My groaning?
2 O My Elohim, I call by day, but You do not answer;
And by night, but I find no rest.
3 Yet You are set-apart,
Enthroned on the praises of Yisra'ěl.
4 Our fathers trusted in You;
They trusted, and You delivered them.
5 They cried to You, and were delivered;
They trusted in You, and were not ashamed.
6 But I am a worm, and no man;
A reproach of men, and despised by the people.
7 All those who see Me mock Me;
They shoot out the lip, they shake the head, *saying*,
8 "He trusted in יהוה, let Him rescue Him;
Let Him deliver Him, seeing He has delighted in Him!"
9 For You are the One who took Me out of the womb;
Causing Me to trust *while* on My mother's breasts.
10 I was cast upon You from birth.
From My mother's belly You have been My Ěl.
11 Do not be far from Me,
For distress is near;
For there is none to help.

12 Many bulls have surrounded Me;
Strong ones of Bashan have encircled Me.
13 They have opened their mouths against Me,
As a raging and roaring lion.
14 I have been poured out like water,
And all My bones have been spread apart;
My heart has become like wax;
It has melted in the midst of My inward parts.
15 My strength is dried like a potsherd,
And My tongue is cleaving to My jaws;
And to the dust of death You are appointing Me.
16 For dogs have surrounded Me;
A crowd of evil ones have encircled Me,
Piercing My hands and My feet;
17 I count all My bones.
They look, they stare at Me.
18 They divide My garments among them,
And for My raiment they cast lots.
19 But You, O יהוה, do not be far off;
O My Strength, hasten to help Me!
20 Deliver My life from the sword,
My only *life* from the power of the dog.
21 Save Me from the mouth of the lion,
And from the horns of the wild beasts!
You have answered Me.
22 I make known Your Name to My brothers;
In the midst of the assembly I praise You.
23 You who fear יהוה, praise Him!
All you seed of Yaʽaqoḇ, esteem Him,
And fear Him, all you seed of Yisra'ĕl!
24 For He has not despised
Nor hated the affliction of the afflicted;
Nor has He hidden His face from Him;
But when He cried to Him, He heard.
25 From You is My praise in the great assembly;
I pay My vows before those who fear Him.
26 The meek ones do eat and are satisfied;
Let those who seek Him praise יהוה.
Let your heart live forever!
27 Let all the ends of the earth
Remember and turn to יהוה,
And all clans of the nations
Bow themselves before You.
28 For the reign belongs to יהוה,
And He is ruling over the nations.
29 All the fat ones of the earth
Shall eat and bow themselves;
All who go down to the dust bow before Him,
Even he who did not keep alive his own life.
30 A seed shall serve Him.
It is declared of יהוה to the *coming* generation.
31 They shall come and declare His righteousness
To a people *yet* to be born,
For He shall do it!

23

יהוה is my shepherd;
I do not lack.
2 He makes me to lie down in green pastures;
He leads me beside still waters.
3 He turns back [a] my being;
He leads me in paths of righteousness
For His Name's sake.
4 When I walk through the valley of the shadow of death,
I fear no evil.
For You are with me;
Your rod and Your staff, they comfort me.
5 You spread before me a table in the face of my enemies;
You have anointed my head with oil;
My cup runs over.
6 Only goodness and loving-commitment follow me
All the days of my life;
And I shall dwell in the House of יהוה,
To the length of days!

24

The earth belongs to יהוה,
And all that fills it –
The world and those who dwell in it.

23a Or *He converts*.

2 For He has founded it upon the seas,
And upon the waters He does establish it.
3 Who does go up into the mountain of יהוה?
And who does stand in His set-apart place?
4 He who has innocent hands and a clean heart,
Who did not bring his life to naught,
And did not swear deceivingly.
5 He receives a blessing from יהוה,
And righteousness from the Elohim of his deliverance.
6 This is the generation of those who seek Him;
Ya'aqoḇ, who seek Your face. Selah.
7 Lift up your heads, O you gates!
And be lifted up, you everlasting doors!
And let the Sovereign of esteem come in.
8 Who is this Sovereign of esteem?
יהוה strong and mighty,
יהוה mighty in battle.
9 Lift up your heads, O you gates!
Even lift up, you everlasting doors!
And let the Sovereign of esteem come in.
10 Who is this Sovereign of esteem?
יהוה of hosts,
He is the Sovereign of esteem! Selah.

25

Aleph To You, O יהוה,
I lift up my being.
2 **Bĕt** O my Elohim, in You I have put my trust;
Let me not be ashamed;
Let not my enemies exult over me.
3 **Gimel** Indeed, let no one who waits on You be ashamed;
Let those who are treacherous without cause be ashamed.
4 **Dalet** Show me Your ways, O יהוה;
Teach me Your paths.
5 **Hĕ** Lead me in Your truth (**Waw**) and teach me,
For You are the Elohim of my deliverance;
On You I wait all the day.
6 **Zayin** Remember, O יהוה, Your compassion and Your loving-commitments,
For they are from everlasting.
7 **Ḥet** Do not remember the sins of my youth, and my transgressions;
According to Your loving-commitment remember me,
For Your goodness' sake, O יהוה.
8 **Tet** Good and straight is יהוה;
Therefore He teaches sinners in the way.
9 **Yod** He guides the meek ones in right-ruling,
And He teaches the meek ones His way.
10 **Kaph** All the paths of יהוה are loving-commitment and truth,
To those who guard His covenant and His witnesses.
11 **Lamed** For Your Name's sake, O יהוה,
You shall pardon my crookedness, though it is great.
12 **Mem** Who, then, is the man that fears יהוה?
He teaches him in the way he should choose.
13 **Nun** His life dwells in good,
And his seed inherits the earth.
14 **Samek** The secret of יהוה is with those who fear Him,
And He makes His covenant known to them.
15 **Ayin** My eyes are ever toward יהוה,
For He brings my feet out of the net.
16 **Pĕ** Turn Your face to me, and show me favour,
For I am lonely and afflicted.
17 **Tsadi** The distresses of my heart have enlarged;
Oh, bring me out of my distresses!
18 **Rĕsh** Look on my affliction and my toil,
And forgive all my sins.
19 **Rĕsh** See how many my enemies have become;
And they hate me with a violent hatred.
20 **Shin** Oh, guard my life, and deliver me;
Let me not be ashamed, for I have taken refuge in You.
21 **Taw** Let integrity and straightness

guard me,
. or I have waited for You.
22 Redeem Yisra'ěl, O Elohim,
Out of all his distresses!

26

Rule me rightly, O יהוה,
For I have walked in my integrity.
And I have trusted in יהוה,
without wavering.
2 Examine me, O יהוה, and prove me;
Try my kidneys and my heart.
3 For Your loving-commitment is before
my eyes,
And I have walked in Your truth.
4 I have not sat with men of falsehood,
Nor do I enter with pretenders.
5 I have hated the assembly of evil-
doers,
And I do not sit with the wrong.
6 I wash my hands in innocence;
And I walk around Your slaughter-
place, O יהוה,
7 To raise a voice of thanksgiving,
And to declare all Your wonders.
8 יהוה, I have loved the abode of Your
house,
And the place where Your esteem
dwells.
9 Do not gather my being together with
sinners,
Nor my life with bloodthirsty men,
10 In whose hands is a plot,
And their right hand is filled with
bribes.
11 But as for me, I walk in my integrity;
Redeem me and show me favour.
12 My foot shall stand on a level place;
In the assemblies I bless יהוה.

27

יהוה is my light and my
deliverance;
Whom should I fear? יהוה is the
refuge of my life;
Whom should I dread?
2 When evil-doers come against me
To eat up my flesh,
My adversaries and my enemies,
They shall stumble and fall.
3 Though an army encamps against me,
My heart does not fear;
Though battle comes up against me,
Even then I would be trusting.
4 One *matter* I asked of יהוה – this I
seek:
To dwell in the House of יהוה
All the days of my life,
To see the pleasantness of יהוה,
And to inquire in His Hěkal.
5 For in the day of evil He hides me in
His booth;
In the covering of His Tent He hides
me;
On a rock He raises me up.
6 And now my head is lifted up above
my enemies all around me;
And I slaughter in His Tent with
slaughters of sounding;
I sing, yes, I sing praises to יהוה.
7 Hear, O יהוה, when I cry with my
voice!
And show me favour, and answer me.
8 To my heart You have said,
"Seek My face."
Your face, יהוה, I seek.
9 Do not hide Your face from me;
Do not turn Your servant away in
displeasure;
You have been my help;
Do not leave me nor forsake me,
O Elohim of my deliverance.
10 When my father and my mother have
forsaken me,
Then יהוה does take me in.
11 Teach me Your way, O יהוה,
And lead me in a smooth path, because
of my enemies.
12 Do not give me over
To the desire of my adversaries;
For false witnesses have risen against
me,
And they breathe out cruelty to me.
13 What if I had not believed
To see the goodness of יהוה
In the land of the living!
14 Wait on יהוה, be strong,
And let Him strengthen your heart!
Wait, I say, on יהוה!

28

I cry to You, O יהוה my Rock:
Do not be deaf to me!
For if You are silent to me,
I shall be like those who go down to

the pit.
2 Hear the voice of my prayers when I
cry to You,
When I lift up my hands
Toward Your Set-apart Speaking Place.
3 Do not draw me away with the wrong
And with the workers of wickedness,
Who speak peace to their neighbours,
But evil is in their hearts.
4 Give to them according to their deeds,
And according to the evil of their practices;
Give to them according to the work of
their hands;
Bring back to them what they deserve.
5 Because they do not heed the works of
יהוה,
Nor the works of His hands, He throws
them down,
And does not build them up.
6 Blessed be יהוה,
Because He has heard the voice of my
prayers!
7 יהוה is my strength, and my shield;
My heart has trusted in Him, and I
have been helped;
Therefore my heart exults,
And with my song I thank Him.
8 יהוה is the strength of His people,
And He is the stronghold of
deliverance of His anointed.
9 Save Your people, and bless Your
inheritance;
And be their Shepherd, and bear them
up forever.

29

Ascribe to יהוה, O you sons of the
mighty,
Ascribe to יהוה esteem and strength.
2 Ascribe to יהוה the esteem of His
Name;
Bow yourselves to יהוה in the
splendour of set-apartness.
3 The voice of יהוה is over the waters;
The Ěl of esteem thunders;
יהוה is over many waters.
4 The voice of יהוה is with power,
The voice of יהוה is with greatness.
5 The voice of יהוה is breaking the
cedars,
יהוה is breaking the cedars of Leḇanon
in pieces.
6 And He makes them skip like a calf,
Leḇanon and Siryon like a young wild
ox.
7 The voice of יהוה cuts through the
flames of fire.
8 The voice of יהוה shakes the wilderness;
יהוה shakes the Wilderness of Qaḏěsh.
9 The voice of יהוה makes the deer give
birth,
And strips the forests bare;
And in His Hěḵal everyone says,
"Esteem!"
10 יהוה sat enthroned at the Flood,
And יהוה sits as Sovereign forever.
11 יהוה gives strength to His people;
יהוה blesses His people with peace.

30

I exalt You, O יהוה, for You have
drawn me up,
And have not let my enemies rejoice
over me.
2 יהוה my Elohim, I have cried to You,
And You have healed me.
3 יהוה, You brought me up from She'ol;
You have kept me alive, from going
down into the pit.
4 Sing praise to יהוה,
You lovingly-committed ones of
His,
And give thanks at the remembrance of
His Set-apartness.
5 For His displeasure is for a moment,
His delight is for life;
Weeping might last for the night,
But joy comes in the morning.
6 As for me, I have said in my ease,
"Never would I be shaken!"
7 יהוה, in Your good pleasure
You have made my mountain
to stand strong;
You hid Your face, and I was troubled.
8 I cried out to You, O יהוה;
And to יהוה I prayed:
9 "What gain is there in my blood,
When I go down to the pit?
Would dust praise You?
Would it declare Your truth?
10 "Hear, O יהוה, and show me favour;
יהוה, be my helper!"

11 You have turned my mourning into
dancing for me;
You have torn off my sackcloth and
girded me with gladness,
12 So that esteem might praise You
and not be silent.
O יהוה my Elohim, I thank You
forever.

31 In You, O יהוה, I have taken
refuge;
Let me never be ashamed;
Deliver me in Your righteousness.
2 Incline Your ear to me,
Deliver me speedily;
Be a rock of refuge to me,
A house of defence to save me.
3 For You are my rock and my
stronghold;
For Your Name's sake lead me and
guide me.
4 Bring me out of the net which they
have hidden for me,
For You are my stronghold.
5 Into Your hand I commit my spirit;
You have redeemed me, O יהוה Ěl of
truth.
6 I have hated those who observe
lying vanities;
But I trust in יהוה.
7 I exult and rejoice in Your loving-
commitment,
For You have seen my affliction;
You have known the distresses of my
life,
8 And You have not shut me up into the
hand of the enemy.
You have set my feet in a large place.
9 Show me favour, O יהוה, for I am in
distress;
My eye, my being and my body have
become old with grief!
10 For my life is consumed in sorrow,
And my years in sighing;
My strength fails because of my
crookedness,
And my bones have become old.
11 I am a reproach among all my
adversaries,
But most of all among my neighbours,
And a dread to my friends;
Those who see me outside flee from
me.
12 I have been forgotten like someone
dead from the heart;
I have been like a missing vessel.
13 For I hear the evil report of many;
Fear is from all around;
When they take counsel together
against me,
They plot to take away my life.
14 But I, I have put my trust in You,
O יהוה;
I have said, "You are my Elohim."
15 My times are in Your hand;
Deliver me from the hand of my
enemies,
And from those who pursue me.
16 Make Your face shine upon Your
servant;
Save me in Your loving-commitment.
17 Do not let me be ashamed, O יהוה,
For I have called upon You;
Let the wrong be ashamed;
Let them be silenced in She'ol.
18 Let lips of falsehood be stilled,
Which speak recklessly against the
righteous,
With pride and scorn.
19 How great is Your goodness,
Which You have laid up for those
fearing You,
Which You have prepared for those
taking refuge in You
In the sight of the sons of men!
20 In the secrecy of Your presence
You shall hide them from the plots of
man;
You shelter them in a booth from the
strife of tongues.
21 Blessed be יהוה,
For He has made marvellous His
loving-commitment to me in a
strong city!
22 And I, I have said in my haste, "I am
cut off from before Your eyes,"
Yet You heard the voice of my prayers
When I cried out to You.
23 Love יהוה, all you His lovingly-
committed ones!
For יהוה guards the trustworthy ones,
And exceedingly repays the doer of

pride.
24 Be strong, and let Him fortify your
heart,
All you who are waiting for יהוה.

32

Blessed is he whose transgression
is forgiven,
Whose sin is covered.
2 Blessed is the man to whom יהוה
imputes no crookedness,
And in whose spirit there is no deceit.
3 When I kept silent, my bones became
old
Through my groaning all the day.
4 For day and night Your hand was
heavy upon me;
My sap was turned into the droughts of
summer. Selah.
5 I acknowledged my sin to You,
And my crookedness I did not hide.
I have said, "I confess my transgressions to יהוה,"
And You forgave the crookedness of
my sin. Selah.
6 Therefore, let every lovingly-committed one pray to You
While *You* might be found;
Even in a flood of great waters
They would not reach him.
7 You are my hiding place;
You preserve me from distress;
You surround me with songs of
deliverance. Selah.
8 "Let Me instruct you and teach you in
the way you should go;
Let Me counsel, My eye be on you.
9 Do not be like the horse, like the mule,
With no understanding, with bit and
bridle,
Else they do not come near you."
10 Many are the sorrows of the wrong;
But as for the one trusting in יהוה,
Loving-commitment surrounds him.
11 Be glad in יהוה and exult,
you righteous;
And shout for joy, all you upright in
heart!

33

Shout for joy in יהוה, you
righteous!
Praise is fitting for the straight!
2 Praise יהוה with the lyre;
Sing to Him with an instrument of ten
strings.
3 Sing to Him a new song;
Play sweetly with a shout of joy.
4 For the Word of יהוה is straight,
And all His works are in truth,
5 Loving righteousness and right-ruling;
The earth is filled with the loving-
commitment of יהוה.
6 By the Word of יהוה the heavens were
made,
And all their host by the Spirit of His
mouth,
7 Gathering the waters of the sea
together as a heap;
Laying up the deep in storehouses.
8 Let all the earth fear יהוה;
Let all the inhabitants of the world
stand in awe of Him.
9 For He spoke, and it came to be;
He commanded, and it stood fast.
10 יהוה brings the counsel of the nations
to naught;
He thwarts the plans of the peoples.
11 The counsel of יהוה stands forever,
The plans of His heart to all
generations.
12 Blessed is the nation whose Elohim is
יהוה,
The people whom He has chosen as
His own inheritance.
13 יהוה has looked from the heavens;
He has seen all the sons of men.
14 He looked from His dwelling place
On all the inhabitants of the earth –
15 He who fashions the hearts of them all,
He who understands all their works.
16 The sovereign is not saved by the
multitude of an army;
A mighty man is not delivered by great
strength.
17 A horse is a vain means of safety;
Neither does it rescue any by its great
power.
18 See, the eye of יהוה is on those
fearing Him,
On those waiting for His loving-
commitment,
19 To deliver their being from death,
And to keep them alive during scarcity

of food.
20 Our being has longed for יהוה;
Our help and our shield is He.
21 For our heart does rejoice in Him,
For we have put our trust in His set-apart Name.
22 Let Your loving-commitment, O יהוה, be upon us,
Even as we wait for You.

34 **Aleph** I bless יהוה at all times;
His praise is continually in my mouth.
2 **Bět** My being makes its boast in יהוה;
Let the humble hear and be glad.
3 **Gimel** Oh, make יהוה great with me,
And let us exalt His Name together.
4 **Dalet** I sought יהוה, and He answered me,
And delivered me from all my fears.
5 **Hě** They looked to Him and were lightened,
Waw And their faces were not ashamed.
6 **Zayin** This poor one cried out and יהוה heard him,
And saved him out of all his distresses.
7 **Ḥet** The messenger of יהוה encamps all around those who fear Him,
And rescues them.
8 **Tet** Oh, taste and see that יהוה is good;
Blessed is the man that takes refuge in Him!
9 **Yod** Fear יהוה, you His set-apart ones,
For there is no lack to them who fear Him!
10 **Kaph** Young lions have lacked and been
hungry;
But those who seek יהוה lack not any good *matter*.
11 **Lamed** Come, you children, listen to me;
Let me teach you the fear of יהוה.
12 **Mem** Who is the man who desires life,
Who loves many days, in order to see good?
13 **Nun** Keep your tongue from evil,
And your lips from speaking deceit.
14 **Samek** Turn away from evil and do good;
Seek peace, and pursue it.
15 **Ayin** The eyes of יהוה are on the righteous,
And His ears unto their cry.
16 **Pě** The face of יהוה is against evil-doers,
To cut off their remembrance from the earth.
17 **Tsadi** *The righteous* cried out, and יהוה heard,
And delivered them out of all their distresses.
18 **Qoph** יהוה is near to the broken-hearted,
And saves those whose spirit is crushed.
19 **Rěsh** Many are the evils of the righteous, [a]
But יהוה delivers him out of them all.
20 **Shin** He is guarding all his bones;
Not one of them is broken.
21 **Taw** Evil does slay the wrong,
And those who hate the righteous are guilty.
22 יהוה redeems the lives of His servants,
And none of those taking refuge in Him are guilty.

35 O יהוה, strive with those who strive with me;
Fight against those who fight against me.
2 Take hold of shield and armour,
And rise for my help.
3 And draw out spear and lance,
To meet those who pursue me.
Say to my life, "I am your deliverance."
4 Let those be ashamed and blush
Who seek my life;
Let those be turned back and abashed
Who plot evil to me.
5 Let them be as chaff before the wind,
With a messenger of יהוה driving on.
6 Let their way be dark and slippery,

34a Teh. 71:20, Tim. ב 3:11-12.

With a messenger of יהוה pursuing them.
7 For without cause they hid their net for me;
Without cause they dug *a pit* for my life.
8 Let ruin come upon him unawares,
And let his net that he hid catch himself;
Let him fall in it, into ruin.
9 But let my own being exult in יהוה;
Let it rejoice in His deliverance.
10 Let all my bones say, "יהוה, who is like You,
Delivering the poor from one stronger than he,
And the poor and the needy from him who robs him?"
11 Ruthless witnesses rise up;
They ask me that which I knew not.
12 They reward me evil for good, bereaving my life.
13 But I, when they were sick,
I put on sackcloth;
I humbled my being with fastings;
And my prayer would return to my own bosom.
14 I walked about as though he were my friend or brother;
I bowed down mourning, as one mourning for a mother.
15 But they rejoiced at my stumbling
And gathered together;
The smiters gathered against me,
And I did not know it;
They tore in pieces without ceasing,
16 With unclean ones, mockers at feasts,
Gnashing at me with their teeth.
17 יהוה, how long would You look on?
Rescue my being from their destructions,
My only *life* from the lions.
18 I give You thanks in the great assembly;
I praise You among a mighty people.
19 Let not my lying enemies rejoice over me;
Or those who hate me without cause wink their eyes.
20 For they do not speak peace,
But they devise words of deceit
Against the peaceable ones of the land.
21 And they open their mouth wide against me,
They said, "Aha, aha! Our eyes have seen it."
22 This You have seen, O יהוה;
Do not be silent.
O יהוה, do not be far from me.
23 Stir up Yourself and awake to my right-ruling –
To my cause, my Elohim and my Master.
24 Rule me rightly, O יהוה my Elohim,
According to Your righteousness;
And let them not rejoice over me.
25 Let them not say in their hearts,
"Aha, our desire!"
Let them not say, "We have swallowed him up."
26 Let those who are rejoicing at my evil
Be ashamed and abashed altogether;
Let those who are exalting themselves over me
Be clad in shame and humiliation.
27 Let those who delight in my righteous cause
Shout for joy and be glad,
And let them always say,
"Let יהוה be made great,
Who is desiring the peace of His servant."
28 And my tongue shall speak of
Your righteousness, Your praise,
All day long.

36

Transgression speaks to the wrong within his heart;
Fear of Elohim is not before his eyes.
2 For he flatters himself in his own eyes,
To find his crookedness to be hated.
3 The words of his mouth are wickedness and deceit;
He has ceased to be wise, to do good.
4 He plots wickedness on his bed;
He sets himself in a way that is not good;
He does not despise evil.
5 O יהוה, Your loving-commitment is in the heavens,
And Your trustworthiness reaches to the clouds.

6 Your righteousness is like the mighty mountains;
Your right-rulings are a great deep;
O יהוה, You save man and beast.
7 How precious is Your loving-commitment, O Elohim!
And the sons of men take refuge in the shadow of Your wings.
8 They are filled from the fatness of Your house,
And You give them drink from the river of Your pleasures.
9 For with You is the fountain of life;
In Your light we see light.
10 Draw out Your loving-commitment to those who know You,
And Your righteousness to the upright in heart.
11 Let not the foot of pride come against me,
And the hand of the wrong drive me away.
12 There the workers of wickedness have fallen;
They have been overthrown
And have been unable to rise.

37 **Aleph** Do not fret because of evil-doers, Do not be envious of the workers of unrighteousness.
2 For they soon wither like grass,
And fade like green plants.
3 **Bĕt** Trust in יהוה, and do good;
Dwell in the earth, and feed on steadfastness.
4 And delight yourself in יהוה,
And let Him give you the desires of your heart.
5 **Gimel** Commit your way to יהוה,
And trust in Him, and He does it.
6 And He shall bring forth your righteousness as the light,
And your right-ruling as midday.
7 **Dalet** Rest in יהוה, and wait patiently for Him;
Do not fret because of him who prospers in his way,
Because of the man doing wicked devices.
8 **Hĕ** Abstain from displeasure, and forsake wrath;
Do not fret, also to do evil.
9 For evil-doers are cut off;
But those who wait on יהוה,
They shall inherit the earth. [a]
10 **Waw** Yet a little while and the wrong is no more;
And you shall look on his place,
But it is not.
11 But the meek ones shall inherit the earth,
And delight themselves in plenty of peace.
12 **Zayin** The wrong plots against the righteous,
And gnashes his teeth at him.
13 יהוה laughs at him,
For He sees that his day is coming.
14 **Ḥet** The wrong have drawn the sword
And have bent their bow,
To cause the poor and needy to fall,
To slay those who walk straightly.
15 Their sword does enter into their own heart,
And their bows are broken.
16 **Tet** Better is the little of the righteous one,
Than the riches of many wrongdoers.
17 For the arms of the wrongdoers are broken,
But יהוה sustains the righteous.
18 **Yod** יהוה knows the days of the perfect,
And their inheritance is forever.
19 They are not ashamed in a time of evil,
And in the days of scarcity of food they are satisfied.
20 **Kaph** But the wrongdoers shall perish;
And the enemies of יהוה,
Like the splendour of the meadows they vanish,
Like smoke they vanish away.
21 **Lamed** The wrongdoer is borrowing and does not repay,
But the righteous one shows favour and gives.
22 For His blessed ones inherit the earth,
But those cursed by Him are cut off.

37a Also see vv. 11, 22, 29 & 34 and Mt. 5:5.

23 **Mem** The steps of a man are ordered
by יהוה,
And He delights in his way.
24 Though he falls, he is not cast down,
For יהוה is supporting his hand.
25 **Nun** I have been young, and now I am
old;
Yet I have not seen the righteous
forsaken,
Or his seed begging bread.
26 All day long he is showing favour and
lending;
And his seed is for a blessing.
27 **Samek** Turn away from evil, and do
good;
And dwell forever.
28 For יהוה loves right-ruling,
And does not forsake His lovingly-
committed ones;
They shall be guarded forever,
But the seed of the wrongdoers is cut
off.
29 The righteous shall inherit the earth,
And dwell in it forever.
30 **Pě** The mouth of the righteous speaks
wisdom,
And his tongue talks of right-ruling.
31 The Torah of his Elohim is in his
heart; [b]
His steps do not slide.
32 **Tsadi** The wrong one is watching for
the righteous,
And is seeking to slay him.
33 יהוה does not leave him in his hand,
Or let him be declared wrong when he
is judged.
34 **Qoph** Wait on יהוה and guard His
way,
And He shall exalt you to inherit the
earth –
When the wrongdoers are cut off, you
shall see it.
35 **Rěsh** I have seen the wrongdoer in
great power,
And spreading himself like a native
green tree.
36 Yet he passed away, and see, he was
not;
And I sought him, but he was not
found.
37 **Shin** Watch the perfect, and observe
the straight;
For the latter end of each is peace.
38 But the transgressors shall be destroyed
together;
The latter end of the wrong shall be cut
off.
39 **Taw** But the deliverance of the righteous is from יהוה,
Their strength in time of distress.
40 And יהוה does help them and deliver
them;
He delivers them from the wrongdoers
and saves them,
Because they took refuge in Him.

38 O יהוה, do not rebuke me in
Your wrath,
Nor chastise me in Your hot
displeasure!
2 For Your arrows have pierced me,
And Your hand comes down on me.
3 There is no soundness in my flesh
because of Your rage,
Nor peace in my bones
because of my sin.
4 For my crookednesses have passed
over my head;
Like a heavy burden, too heavy for me.
5 My wounds have become stinky,
festering
Because of my folly.
6 I have been bent down;
I have been bowed down very much;
All day long I have gone mourning.
7 For my loins have become filled with
burning,
And there is no soundness in my flesh.
8 I have become weak and greatly
crushed;
I howled from the groaning of my
heart.
9 יהוה, all my desire is before You;
And my sighing has not been hid from
You.
10 My heart is throbbing, my strength has
forsaken me;
And the light of my eyes also is not

37b Deḇ. 6:6, Teh. 40:8, Teh. 119:11, Yesh. 51:7.

with me.
11 My loved ones and my friends stand
back from my plague,
And my neighbours stand far away.
12 And those seeking my life lay a snare;
And those seeking my evil have
spoken of destruction,
And utter deceit all day long.
13 But I, as one deaf, do not hear;
And as a dumb one who does not open
his mouth.
14 I am like a man who does not hear,
And who has no rebukes in his mouth.
15 For on You, O יהוה, I have waited;
You do answer, O יהוה my Elohim.
16 For I said, "Otherwise they would
rejoice over me,
When my foot slips they would exalt
themselves over me."
17 For I am ready to fall,
And my pain is always with me.
18 For I confess my crookedness;
I am sorry over my sin.
19 But my enemies are alive;
They have become strong;
And those hating me falsely are many.
20 And those who repay evil for good,
They oppose me, because I follow
what is good.
21 Do not forsake me, O יהוה;
O my Elohim, be not far from me!
22 Hasten to help me, O יהוה,
my deliverance!

39

I have said,"Let me guard my ways
Against sinning with my tongue;
Let me guard my mouth with a muzzle,
While the wrongdoer is before me."
2 I became dumb, keeping still;
I was silent, from good;
And my pain was stirred.
3 My heart was hot within me;
While I was meditating, the fire
burned.
Then I spoke with my tongue:
4 "יהוה, let me know my end,
And the measure of my days, what it
is,
Let me know how short-lived I am.
5 "See, You have made my days as
handbreadths,
And my lifetime is as non-existence
before You;
Only, all men standing, are all breath.
Selah.
6 "As but a shadow each one walks;
They busy themselves, only in vain;
He heaps up *wealth*,
But knows not who gathers them.
7 "And now, יהוה, what do I wait for?
My expectancy is in You.
8 "Deliver me from all my transgres-
sions;
Do not make me the reproach of the
foolish.
9 "I was dumb, I did not open my mouth,
Because it was You who did it.
10 "Turn aside Your stroke from me;
I am overcome by the blow of Your
hand.
11 "When You chastise man for
crookedness with reproofs,
You consume what he loves, like a
moth;
All men are but a breath. Selah.
12 "Hear my prayer, O יהוה,
And give ear to my cry;
Do not be silent at my tears;
For I am a stranger with You,
A sojourner, as all my fathers were.
13 "Look away from me,
That I might brighten up,
Before I go away and am no more."

40

I waited, waited for יהוה;
And He inclined to me, and heard
my cry.
2 And He drew me
Out of the pit of destruction,
Out of the muddy clay,
And He set my feet upon a rock,
He is establishing my steps.
3 Then He put a new song in my mouth;
Praise to our Elohim;
Many do see it and fear,
And trust in יהוה.
4 Blessed is that man who has made
יהוה his trust,
And has not turned to the proud,
And those turning aside to falsehood.
5 O יהוה my Elohim, many are the
wonders

Which You have done, and Your
purposes toward us;
There is no one to compare with You;
I declare and speak:
They are too many to be numbered.
6 Slaughtering [a] and meal offering You
did not desire;
You have opened my ears;
Ascending offering and sin offering
You did not ask for.
7 Then I said, "See, I have come;
In the scroll of the Book it is pre-
scribed for me.
8 I have delighted to do Your pleasure,
O my Elohim,
And Your Torah is within my heart." [b]
9 I have proclaimed the good news of
righteousness,
In the great assembly;
See, I do not restrain my lips, O יהוה,
You know.
10 I did not conceal Your righteousness
within my heart;
I have declared Your trustworthiness
and Your deliverance;
I did not hide Your loving-commitment
and Your truth
From the great assembly.
11 Do not withhold Your compassion
from me, O יהוה;
Let Your loving-commitment and Your
truth always watch over me.
12 For evils without number have
surrounded me;
My crookednesses have overtaken me,
And I have been unable to see;
They became more than the hairs of
my head;
And my heart has failed me.
13 Be pleased, O יהוה, to deliver me;
O יהוה, hasten to help me!
14 Let those who seek to destroy my life
Be ashamed and abashed altogether;
Let those who are desiring my evil
Be driven back and put to shame.
15 Let those who say to me, "Aha, aha!"
Be appalled at their own shame.
16 Let all those who seek You
Rejoice and be glad in You;
Let those who love Your deliverance
always say,
"יהוה be exalted!"
17 But I am poor and needy;
Let יהוה think upon me.
You are my help and my deliverer;
O my Elohim, do not delay!

41

Blessed is he who considers the
poor;
יהוה does deliver him in a day of evil.
2 יהוה does guard him and keep him
alive;
He is blessed on the earth,
And You do not hand him over
To the desire of his enemies.
3 יהוה sustains him on his sickbed;
In his weakness on his bed You bring
a change.
4 As for me, I said,
"O יהוה, show me favour;
Heal me, for I have sinned against
You."
5 My enemies speak evil of me,
"When he dies his name shall perish."
6 And when one comes to visit,
he speaks falsely;
His heart gathers wickedness to itself;
He goes out, he speaks of it.
7 All who hate me whisper together
against me;
They plot evil to me, *saying*,
8 "A matter of Beliya'al is poured out
on him,
That when he lies down, he would not
rise again."
9 Even my own friend in whom I trusted,
who ate my bread,
Has lifted up his heel against me.
10 But You, יהוה, show me favour and
raise me up,
And let me repay them.
11 By this I know that You did delight
in me,
Because my enemy does not shout
for joy over me.
12 And I, You uphold me in my integrity,
And set me before Your face forever.
13 Blessed be יהוה Elohim of Yisra'ĕl

40a See Iḇ'rim 10:5,6. *40b* Teh. 37:31, Teh. 119:11, Yesh. 51:7, Iḇ'rim 10:7-9.

From everlasting to everlasting!
Amĕn and Amĕn.

42 As a deer longs for the water streams,
So my being longs for You, O Elohim.
2 My being thirsts for Elohim, for the living Ěl.
When shall I enter in to appear before Elohim?
3 My tears have been my food day and night,
While they say to me all day,
"Where is your Elohim?"
4 These I remember, and pour out my being within me.
For I used to pass along with the throng;
I went with them to the House of Elohim,
With the voice of joy and praise,
A multitude celebrating a festival!
5 Why are you depressed, O my being?
And *why* are you restless within me?
Wait for Elohim: for I shall yet thank Him,
For the deliverance of His face!
6 O my Elohim, my being is depressed within me;
Therefore I remember You from the land of the Yardĕn,
And from the heights of Ḥermon,
From Mount Mitsʽar.
7 Deep calls to deep at the sound of Your waterfalls;
All Your waves and breakers passed over me.
8 By day יהוה commands His loving-commitment,
And by night His song is with me;
A prayer to the Ěl of my life.
9 I say to Ěl my Rock, "Why have You forgotten me?
Why do I go mourning because of the oppression of the enemy?"
10 With murder in my bones,
My enemies have reproached me,
While they say to me all day long,
"Where is your Elohim?"
11 Why are you depressed, O my being?
And why are you restless within me?
Wait for Elohim: for I shall yet thank Him, the deliverance of my face,
And my Elohim.

43 Rule me rightly, O Elohim,
And plead my cause against a nation without loving-commitment.
Oh, deliver me from a man of deceit and unrighteousness!
2 For You are the Elohim of my strength.
Why have You rejected me?
Why do I go mourning because of the oppression of the enemy?
3 Send forth Your light and Your truth!
Let them lead me,
Let them bring me to Your set-apart mountain
And to Your dwelling places.
4 That I might come to the slaughter-place of Elohim,
To Ěl, the joy of my delight,
And praise You with the lyre,
O Elohim, my Elohim.
5 Why are you depressed, O my being?
And why are you restless within me?
Wait for Elohim: for I shall yet thank Him, the deliverance of my face,
And my Elohim.

44 O Elohim, we have heard with our ears,
Our fathers have related to us,
The work You did in their days,
In the days of old.
2 You drove out the nations with Your hand,
But them You planted.
You afflicted peoples, and sent them out.
3 For not by their own sword did they possess the land,
Neither did their own arm save them;
But it was Your right hand and Your arm,
And the light of Your face,
Because You delighted in them.
4 You Yourself are my Sovereign, O Elohim;
Command deliverances for Yaʽaqoḇ.
5 Through You we push our enemies;

Through Your Name we tread down those who rise up against us.
6 For I do not trust in my bow,
And my sword does not save me.
7 For You have saved us from our enemies,
And have put to shame those who hated us.
8 In Elohim we shall boast all day long,
And praise Your Name forever. Selah.
9 Yet You have rejected us and put us to shame,
And You do not go with our armies.
10 You make us turn back from the adversary,
And those who hate us have plundered us.
11 You do give us as sheep to be eaten,
And You have scattered us among the nations.
12 You sell Your people for no value,
And have set no high price on them.
13 You make us a reproach to our neighbours,
A scorn and a mockery to those round about us.
14 You make us a proverb among the nations,
A shaking of the head among the peoples.
15 My reproach is always before me,
And the shame of my face has covered me,
16 Because of the voice of the slanderer and blasphemer,
Because of the enemy and avenger.
17 All this has come upon us;
But we have not forgotten You,
Neither have we been false to Your covenant.
18 Our heart has not turned back,
Neither has our step swerved from Your way,
19 Yet You have crushed us in the place of jackals,
And covered us with the shadow of death.
20 If we have forgotten the Name of our Elohim,
Or stretched out our hands to a foreign mighty one,
21 Would Elohim not search this out?
For He knows the secrets of the heart.
22 But for Your sake we are killed all day long;
Reckoned as sheep for the slaughter.
23 Awake! Why do You sleep, O יהוה? Arise!
Do not reject us forever.
24 Why do You hide Your face,
Ignoring our affliction and our oppression?
25 For our being is bowed down to the dust;
Our body cleaves to the earth.
26 Arise, be our help,
And redeem us for Your loving-commitment' sake.

45

My heart is overflowing with a goodly word;
I address my works to the Sovereign;
My tongue is the pen of a speedy writer.
2 You are more handsome than the sons of men;
Favour has been poured upon Your lips;
Therefore Elohim has blessed You forever.
3 Gird Your sword upon *Your* thigh, O Mighty One,
Your excellency and Your splendour.
4 And ride prosperously in Your splendour,
On the matter of truth and humility, righteousness;
And let Your right hand lead You to awesome *matters* .
5 Your arrows are sharp
In the heart of the Sovereign's enemies –
Peoples fall under You.
6 Your throne, O Elohim, is forever and ever;
The sceptre of Your reign
Is a sceptre of straightness.
7 You have loved righteousness and

hated wrongness; [a]
Therefore Elohim, Your Elohim, has anointed You
With the oil of gladness more than Your companions.
8 All Your garments are myrrh and aloes, cassia;
Out of the palaces of ivory,
Stringed instruments have made You glad.
9 Daughters of sovereigns are among Your precious ones;
At Your right hand stands the sovereigness in gold from Ophir.
10 Listen, O daughter, and see,
And incline your ear,
And forget your own people and your father's house;
11 And let the Sovereign delight in your loveliness;
Because He is your Master – bow yourself to Him.
12 And the daughter of Tsor with a gift,
The rich among the people seek your favour.
13 The daughter of the Sovereign
Is all esteemed within *the palace*;
Her dress is embroidered with gold.
14 She is brought to the Sovereign in embroidered work;
Maidens, her companions following her,
Are brought to You.
15 They are brought with gladness and rejoicing;
They enter the Sovereign's palace.
16 Instead of Your fathers are Your sons,
Whom You appoint princes in all the earth.
17 I cause Your Name to be remembered in all generations;
Therefore the people praise You forever and ever.

46 Elohim is our refuge and strength,
A help in distress, soon found.
2 Therefore we do not fear,
Though the earth reels
And mountains topple into the heart of the seas.
3 Let its waters rage, foam;
Let mountains shake with its swelling. Selah.
4 A river whose streams
Make glad the city of Elohim,
The set-apart dwelling of the Most High.
5 Elohim is in her midst, she does not topple;
Elohim does help her when morning turns.
6 The nations shall rage,
Reigns shall topple;
He shall give forth His voice,
The earth melts.
7 יהוה of hosts is with us;
The Elohim of Ya'aqoḇ is our refuge. Selah.
8 Come, see the works of יהוה,
The ruins He has wrought on the earth,
9 Causing *all* fighting to cease,
Unto the end of the earth.
He breaks the bow and shatters the spear;
He burns the chariot with fire.
10 Be still, and know that I am Elohim;
I am exalted among nations,
I am exalted in the earth!
11 יהוה of hosts is with us;
The Elohim of Ya'aqoḇ is our refuge. Selah.

47 Oh, clap your hands, all you peoples!
Shout to Elohim with a voice of singing!
2 For יהוה Most High is awesome;
A great Sovereign over all the earth.
3 He subdues peoples under us,
And nations under our feet.
4 He chooses our inheritance for us,
The excellence of Ya'aqoḇ whom He loves. Selah.
5 Elohim shall go up with a shout,
יהוה with a voice of a shophar.
6 Sing praises to Elohim, sing praises!
Sing praises to our Sovereign, sing praises!

45a Quoted in Iḇ`rim 1:8-9 where the Greek text has *lawlessness* instead of *wrongness*.

7 For Elohim is Sovereign of all the
earth;
Sing praises with understanding.
8 Elohim shall reign over the nations;
Elohim shall sit on His set-apart
throne.
9 Nobles of peoples shall be gathered
together,
The people of the Elohim of Aḇraham.
For the shields of the earth belong to
Elohim;
He shall be greatly exalted.

48

Great is יהוה, and greatly to be
praised
In the city of our Elohim,
His set-apart mountain.
2 Beautiful on high,
The joy of all the earth,
Is Mount Tsiyon on the sides of the
north,
The city of the great Sovereign.
3 Elohim is in her citadels;
He is known as her refuge.
4 For look, the sovereigns met,
They passed by together.
5 They saw, so they marvelled;
They were alarmed, they hastened
away.
6 Trembling took hold of them there,
Pain, as of a woman in labour,
7 With an east wind You break the ships
of Tarshish.
8 As we have heard, so we have seen
In the city of יהוה of hosts,
In the city of our Elohim,
Elohim establishes her forever.
Selah.
9 We have thought, O Elohim, of Your
loving-commitment,
In the midst of Your Hěḵal.
10 According to Your Name, O Elohim,
So is Your praise to the ends of the
earth;
Your right hand is filled with
righteousness.
11 Let Mount Tsiyon rejoice,
Let the daughters of Yehuḏah exult,
Because of Your right-rulings.
12 Walk about Tsiyon,
And go all around her.
Count her towers;
13 Set your heart upon her rampart;
Go through her citadels;
So that you report it to the coming
generation.
14 For this Elohim is our Elohim,
Forever and ever;
He Himself leads us,
Even to death.

49

Hear this, all you peoples;
Give ear, all you inhabitants of
the world,
2 Both sons of mankind and sons of man,
Rich and poor together.
3 My mouth speaks wisdom,
And the meditation of my heart brings
understanding.
4 I incline my ear to a parable;
I expound my riddle on the lyre.
5 Why should I fear in the days of evil,
When the crookedness of my
supplanters surrounds me?
6 Those who are trusting in their riches
And who are boasting in their great
wealth?
7 A brother does not redeem anyone at
all,
Neither give to Elohim a ransom for
him;
8 For the redemption of their lives is
costly,
And it shall cease forever;
9 That he should still live forever,
And not see the pit.
10 For he sees wise men die,
The foolish and the ignorant
both perish,
And shall leave their wealth to others.
11 Their graves are their houses, forever;
Their dwelling places, to all
generations;
They call *their* lands after
their own names.
12 But man does not remain in esteem,
He is like the beasts that perish.
13 This way of theirs is folly to them,
Yet their followers are pleased with
their words. Selah.
14 Like sheep they shall be laid in the
grave;

Death shall shepherd them;
And the upright rule over them in the morning;
And their form is consumed in She'ol,
Far from their dwelling.
15 But Elohim does redeem my being
From the power of She'ol,
For He does receive me. Selah.
16 Do not be afraid when a man becomes rich,
When the wealth of his house increases;
17 For when he dies he takes none of it;
His wealth does not go down after him.
18 Though while he lived he blessed himself,
And though they praise you when you do well for yourself,
19 He has to go to the generation of his fathers;
They never see the light.
20 Man, who is rich,
Yet does not understand,
Shall be like the beasts,
They shall perish.

50 Ěl Elohim יהוה shall speak,
And He shall call the earth
From the rising of the sun to its going down.
2 From Tsiyon, the perfection of loveliness,
Elohim shall shine forth.
3 Our Elohim comes, and is not silent –
A fire consumes before Him,
And it shall be very stormy all around Him.
4 He calls to the heavens from above,
And to the earth, to rightly rule His people:
5 "Gather My lovingly-committed ones together to Me,
Those who have made a covenant with Me by slaughtering."
6 Then the heavens declared His righteousness,
For Elohim Himself is Judge. Selah.
7 "Hear, O My people, and I speak,
O Yisra'ěl, and I witness against you:
I am Elohim, your Elohim!
8 "I do not reprove you for your slaughterings,
And your ascending offerings are continually before Me.
9 "I do not take a bull from your house,
Nor goats out of your pens.
10 "For every beast of the forest is Mine,
The cattle on a thousand hills.
11 "I know all the birds of the mountains,
And all moving in My field are Mine.
12 "If I were hungry,
I would not speak to you;
For the world is Mine,
and all that fills it.
13 "Do I eat the flesh of bulls,
Or drink the blood of goats?
14 "Slaughter thanksgiving to Elohim,
And pay your vows to the Most High.
15 "And call upon Me in the day of distress –
Let Me rescue you,
and you esteem Me."
16 But to the wrong Elohim said,
"What right have you to recite My laws,
Or take My covenant in your mouth,
17 "While you hated instruction
And cast My Words behind you?
18 "When you saw a thief,
you were pleased with him,
And you take part with adulterers.
19 "You let your mouth loose to evil,
And your tongue frames deceit.
20 "You sit, speak against your brother;
You slander your own mother's son.
21 "You have done this, and I kept silent;
You have thought that I was altogether like you –
I rebuke you, and set it in order before your eyes.
22 "Understand this please, you who forget Eloah,
Lest I tear you in pieces,
With no one to deliver:
23 "Whoever slaughters praise esteems Me;
And to him who prepares a way,
I show the deliverance of Elohim."

51 Show me favour, O Elohim,
According to Your loving-commitment;

According to the greatness of
Your compassion,
Blot out my transgressions.
2 Wash me completely from my guilt,
And cleanse me from my sin.
3 For I know my transgressions,
And my sin is ever before me.
4 Against You, You alone, have I sinned,
And done evil in Your eyes;
That You might be proven right in
Your words;
Be clear when You judge.
5 See, I was brought forth in
crookedness,
And in sin my mother conceived me.
6 See, You have desired truth in the
inward parts,
And in the hidden part You make me
know wisdom.
7 Cleanse me with hyssop, and I am
clean;
Wash me, and I am whiter than snow.
8 Let me hear joy and gladness,
Let the bones You have crushed
rejoice.
9 Hide Your face from my sins,
And blot out all my crookednesses.
10 Create in me a clean heart, O Elohim,
And renew a steadfast spirit within me.
11 Do not cast me away from Your
presence,
And do not take Your Set-apart Spirit
from me.
12 Restore to me the joy of Your
deliverance,
And uphold me, Noble Spirit!
13 Let me teach transgressors Your ways,
So that sinners turn back to You.
14 Deliver me from blood-guilt,
O Elohim,
Elohim of my deliverance,
Let my tongue sing aloud of Your
righteousness.
15 O יהוה, open my lips,
And that my mouth declare Your
praise.
16 For You do not desire slaughtering,
or I would give it;
You do not delight in ascending offering.
17 The slaughterings of Elohim are a broken spirit,
A heart broken and crushed,
O Elohim,
These You do not despise.
18 Do good in Your good pleasure to
Tsiyon;
Build the walls of Yerushalayim.
19 Then You would delight in slaughter-
ings of righteousness,
In ascending offering and complete
ascending offering;
Then young bulls would be offered on
Your slaughter-place.

52 Why do you boast in evil, O
mighty man?
The loving-commitment of Ěl
is all day long!
2 Your tongue devises destruction,
Like a sharp razor, working deceit.
3 You loved evil more than good,
Lying more than speaking
righteousness. Selah.
4 You loved all devouring words,
O tongue of deceit.
5 Let Ěl also break you down forever,
Take you and pluck you out of your
tent.
And He shall uproot you
From the land of the living. Selah.
6 And let the righteous see and fear,
And laugh at him, *saying*,
7 "See the man who did not make
Elohim his strength,
But trusted in his many riches,
Being strong in his destruction."
8 But I am like a green olive tree
In the House of Elohim,
I have trusted in the loving-
commitment of Elohim
Forever and ever.
9 I thank You forever,
Because You have done it;
And in the presence of Your
lovingly-committed ones
I wait on Your Name, for it is good.

53 The fool has said in his heart,
"There is no Elohim."
They have done corruptly,
And they have done abominable

unrighteousness;
No one does good.
2 Elohim looked down from the heavens
on the children of men,
To see if there is a wise one, seeking
Elohim.
3 They have all turned aside;
They have together become filthy;
No one is doing good, not even one.
4 Have the workers of wickedness no
knowledge,
Who eat up my people as they eat
bread,
And do not call on Elohim?
5 There they are in great fear,
Where no fear was,
For Elohim shall scatter the bones
Of him who encamps against you.
You shall put them to shame,
For Elohim has rejected them.
6 O that the deliverance of Yisra'ěl
Would be given out of Tsiyon!
When Elohim turns back the captivity
of His people,
Let Ya'aqoḇ rejoice, let Yisra'ěl be
glad.

54 O Elohim, save me by Your Name,
And rightly rule me by Your
might.
2 Hear my prayer, O Elohim;
Give ear to the words of my mouth.
3 For strangers have risen up against me,
And cruel men have sought after my
life;
They have not set Elohim before them.
Selah.
4 See, Elohim is my helper;
יהוה is with those who sustain my life.
5 He repays evil to my enemies.
Cut them off in Your truth.
6 Voluntarily I slaughter to You;
I praise Your Name, O יהוה, for it is
good.
7 For He has delivered me out of all
distress;
And my eye has looked upon my
enemies.

55 Give ear to my prayer, O Elohim,
And do not hide Yourself from my
plea.
2 Give heed to me, and answer me;
I wander and moan in my complaint,
3 Because of the noise of the enemy,
Because of the outcry of the wrong;
For they bring down wickedness upon
me,
And in wrath they hate me.
4 My heart is pained within me,
And the frights of death have fallen
upon me.
5 Fear and trembling have come upon
me,
And shuddering covers me.
6 And I said, "Who would give me
wings like a dove!
I would fly away and be at rest.
7 "See, I would wander far off,
I would lodge in the wilderness. Selah.
8 "I would hasten my escape
From the raging wind and storm."
9 Confuse, O יהוה, divide their tongues,
For I saw violence and strife in the city.
10 Day and night they go around it on its
walls;
Wickedness and trouble are also in the
midst of it.
11 Covetings are in its midst;
Oppression and deceit do not vanish
from its streets.
12 It is not an enemy who reproaches
me –
That I could bear;
Nor one who hates me who is making
himself great against me –
Then I could hide from him.
13 But it was you, a man my equal,
My companion and my friend.
14 We took sweet counsel together,
We walked to the House of Elohim in
the throng.
15 Let death come upon them;
Let them go down into She'ol alive,
For evil is in their dwellings, in their
midst.
16 I, I call upon Elohim,
And יהוה saves me.
17 Evening and morning and at noon
I complain and moan,
And He hears my voice.
18 He has redeemed my life in peace

From the battle against me,
For there were many against me.
19 Ěl, even He who sits *enthroned* from of old,
Does hear and afflict them – Selah –
Those with whom there are no changes,
Those who do not fear Elohim.
20 He has put forth his hands against those
Who were at peace with him;
He has broken his covenant.
21 His mouth was smoother than curds,
Yet in his heart is fighting;
His words were softer than oil,
But they are drawn swords.
22 Cast your burden on יהוה,
And let Him sustain you;
He never allows the righteous to be shaken.
23 For You, O Elohim, do bring them down
To the pit of destruction;
Men of blood and deceit do not reach half their days;
But I, I trust in You.

56

Show me favour, O Elohim,
For man would swallow me up;
Fighting all day long, he oppresses me.
2 My enemies would swallow me up all day long,
For many are fighting against me, O *Most* High.
3 In the day I am afraid, I trust in You.
4 In Elohim, whose Word I praise,
In Elohim I have trusted;
I do not fear;
What could flesh do to me?
5 All day long they twist my words;
All their thoughts are against me for evil.
6 They stir up strife, they hide,
They watch my steps,
As they lie in wait for my life.
7 Because of wickedness, cast them out.
Put down the peoples in displeasure, O Elohim!
8 You have counted my wanderings;
You put my tears into Your bottle;
Are they not in Your book?
9 My enemies turn back in the day I call;
This I know, because Elohim is for me.
10 In Elohim, whose Word I praise,
In יהוה, whose Word I praise,
11 In Elohim I have trusted;
I do not fear;
What could man do to me?
12 On me, O Elohim, are Your vows;
I render praises to You,
13 For You have delivered my life from death,
My feet from stumbling,
That I might walk before Elohim,
In the light of the living!

57

Show me favour, O Elohim, show me favour!
For in You my being is taking refuge;
And in the shadow of Your wings I take refuge,
Until destruction passes by.
2 I cry out to the Most High Elohim,
To Ěl who is perfecting *all matters* for me.
3 He sends from the heavens and saves me;
He reproaches the one who would swallow me up. Selah.
Elohim sends forth His loving-commitment and His truth.
4 My being is in the midst of lions;
I lie *among* those who breathe fire,
Whose teeth are spears and arrows,
And their tongue is a sharp sword.
5 Be exalted, O Elohim, above the heavens;
Let Your esteem be above all the earth.
6 They have prepared a net for my footsteps;
My being was bowed down;
They have dug a pit before me;
They fell into the midst of it! Selah.
7 My heart is firm, O Elohim,
My heart is firm;
I sing and praise.
8 Awake, my esteem!
Awake, harp and lyre!
I awake the dawn.
9 I praise You among the peoples, O יהוה;
I sing to You among the nations.

[10] For Your loving-commitment is great
up to the heavens,
And Your truth unto the clouds.
[11] Be exalted above the heavens,
O Elohim;
Let Your esteem be above all the earth.

58 Would you indeed speak
righteousness, in silence?
Do you judge straightly,
you sons of men?
[2] No, in heart you work unrighteousness;
On earth you weigh out the violence of
your hands.
[3] The wrong have been estranged from
the womb;
These who speak lies go astray from
birth.
[4] Their poison is like the poison of a
snake;
Like a deaf cobra that stops its ear,
[5] So as not to hear the voice of
whisperers,
Or a skilled caster of spells.
[6] O Elohim, break their teeth in their
mouth!
Break out the fangs of the young lions,
O יהוה!
[7] Let them melt, let them vanish as
water;
Let Him aim His arrows that they be
cut down;
[8] Like a snail which melts away as it
moves,
Like a woman's stillbirth,
Let them not see the sun!
[9] Before your pots feel the thorns,
Whether green or ablaze,
He sweeps them away.
[10] The righteous rejoices when he has
seen the vengeance,
He washes his feet in the blood of the
wrong,
[11] And man says,
"Truly, the righteous are rewarded;
Truly, there is an Elohim judging in the
earth."

59 Deliver me from my enemies,
O my Elohim;
Set me on high from those who rise up
against me.
[2] Deliver me from the workers of
wickedness,
And save me from men of blood.
[3] For look, they have lain in wait for my
life;
Mighty men assemble against me,
For no transgression or sin of mine,
O יהוה,
[4] For no guilt *of mine*!
They run and prepare themselves.
Awake to help me, and see!
[5] And You, יהוה Elohim of hosts,
Elohim of Yisra'ěl,
Awake to punish all the nations;
Show no favour to any wicked traitors.
Selah.
[6] They return at evening,
They howl like a dog,
And go around the city.
[7] See, they belch out with their mouth,
Swords are in their lips,
For who is listening?
[8] But You, יהוה, laughs at them,
You mock all the nations.
[9] O my Strength, I wait for You;
For Elohim is my strong tower.
[10] My Elohim of loving-commitment,
Elohim does go before me.
He lets me look upon my enemies.
[11] Do not kill them, lest my people forget;
Scatter them by Your power,
And bring them down,
O יהוה our shield.
[12] The sin of their mouth is the words of
their lips,
And they are captured in their pride,
And for the cursing and lying they
utter.
[13] Bring *them* to an end in wrath,
Bring *them* to an end,
That they be no more;
And let them know
That Elohim is ruling in Ya'aqoḇ
To the ends of the earth. Selah.
[14] And at evening they return,
They howl like a dog,
And go around the city.
[15] They wander up and down for food,
And whine if they are not satisfied.
[16] And I, I sing of Your power;

And in the morning
I sing aloud of Your loving-
commitment;
For You have been my strong tower
And a refuge in the day of my distress.
17 O my Strength, to You I sing praises;
For Elohim is my strong tower,
My Elohim of loving-commitment.

60 O Elohim, You have rejected us;
You have broken us;
You have been displeased;
Turn back to us!
2 You have made the earth tremble;
You have broken it;
Heal its breaches, for it is shaken.
3 You have let Your people see hardship;
You have made us drink the wine of
trembling.
4 You have given a banner to those who
fear You,
That it might be lifted up
Because of the truth. Selah.
5 That those You love might be rescued,
Save with Your right hand and answer
me.
6 Elohim has spoken in His set-apart-
ness,
"I exult, I portion out Sheḵem
And measure out the Valley of
Sukkoth.
7 "Gil'aḏ is Mine and Menashsheh is
Mine,
And Ephrayim is the defence of My
head,
Yehuḏah is My inscriber. [a]
8 "Mo'aḇ is My wash-pot,
Over Eḏom I cast My shoe,
Shout loud, O Philistia,
because of Me."
9 Who would bring me to the strong
city?
Who shall lead me to Eḏom?
10 Have not You, O Elohim, rejected us?
And You do not go out, O Elohim,
With our armies!
11 Give us help from distress,
For the help of man is naught.
12 In Elohim we do mightily,
And He treads down our adversaries!

61 Hear my cry, O Elohim,
Listen to my prayer.
2 From the end of the earth I call unto
You,
When my heart is faint;
Lead me to the rock that is higher
than I.
3 For You have been my refuge,
A strong tower in the face of the
enemy.
4 Let me dwell in Your Tent forever,
Let me take refuge in the shelter of
Your wings. Selah.
5 For You, O Elohim, have heard my
vows;
You have given me the inheritance
Of those who fear Your Name.
6 You add days to the days of the
sovereign,
His years as many generations.
7 Let him dwell forever before Elohim.
Prepare loving-commitment and truth
to preserve him!
8 So I sing praise to Your Name forever,
When I pay my vows day by day.

62 My being finds rest in
Elohim alone;
From Him is my deliverance.
2 He alone is my rock and my
deliverance, my strong tower;
I am not greatly shaken.
3 How long would you shout at a man?
– Murder! – Like a leaning wall, a
tottering fence.
4 They plotted to topple him from his
high position;
They delight in lies;
They bless with their mouth,
But in their heart they curse. Selah.
5 My being, find rest in Elohim alone,
Because my expectation is from Him.
6 He alone is my rock and my
deliverance, my strong tower;
I am not shaken.
7 My deliverance and my esteem *depend*
on Elohim;

60a - See Ber. 49:10

The rock of my strength, my refuge is in Elohim.
8 Trust in Him at all times, you people;
Pour out your heart before Him;
Elohim is a refuge for us. Selah.
9 Sons of Aḏam are but a breath,
Sons of men are a lie;
If weighed in the scales,
They are altogether lighter than breath.
10 Do not trust in oppression.
And do not become vain in robbery;
If riches increase,
Do not set your heart on them.
11 Elohim has spoken once,
Twice I have heard this:
That strength belongs to Elohim.
12 And loving-commitment is Yours, O יהוה;
For You reward each one according to his work.

63

O Elohim, You are my Ěl;
I earnestly seek You;
My being has thirsted for You;
My flesh has longed for You
In a dry and thirsty land without water.
2 Therefore I have had a vision of You
In the set-apart place,
To see Your power and Your esteem.
3 Because Your loving-commitment is better than life,
My lips do praise You.
4 Therefore I bless You while I live;
In Your Name I lift up my hands.
5 My being is satisfied as with marrow and fat,
And my mouth praises You with singing lips.
6 When I remember You on my bed,
I meditate on You in the night watches.
7 For You have been my help,
And in the shadow of Your wings I sing.
8 My being has closely followed You;
Your right hand did uphold me.
9 But those who seek to destroy my life,
Go into the lower parts of the earth.
10 They are handed over
To the power of the sword;
They become a portion for jackals.
11 But let the sovereign rejoice in Elohim;
Let everyone who swears by Him exult;
For the mouth of those speaking lies are stopped.

64

Hear my voice, O Elohim, in my meditation;
Guard my life from the threats of the enemy.
2 Hide me from the secret plans of the evil-doers,
From the tumult of the workers of wickedness,
3 Who sharpen their tongue like a sword,
And aim their arrows, a bitter word,
4 To shoot in ambush at someone blameless,
They shoot at him suddenly and do not fear.
5 They arm themselves with an evil word;
They talk of hiding snares;
They have said, "Who sees them?"
6 They search out unrighteousnesses,
"We have perfected a well searched out plan."
For the inward part of man, and heart, are deep.
7 But Elohim does shoot at them with an arrow;
Their wounds shall be sudden.
8 And they cause one to stumble,
Their own tongue is against them;
All who see them flee away.
9 And all men fear,
And declare the work of Elohim.
And they shall wisely consider
What He has done.
10 The righteous rejoice in יהוה,
And shall take refuge in Him,
And all the upright in heart praise *Him*.

65

To You, stillness, praise, in Tsiyon, O Elohim;
And to You a vow is paid.
2 To You who hears all prayer, all flesh comes.
3 Crooked matters were mightier than I;
As for our transgressions, You do cover them.
4 Blessed is the one You choose,

And bring near to dwell in Your courts.
We are satisfied with the goodness of
Your house,
Your set-apart Hĕḵal.
5 By awesome deeds in righteousness
You answer us,
O Elohim of our deliverance,
The Trust of all the ends of the earth,
And the distant seas;
6 Who established the mountains by
His strength,
Being girded with might;
7 Who stills the roaring of the seas,
The roaring of their waves,
And the uproar of the peoples.
8 And they who dwell in the farthest
parts,
Are afraid of Your signs;
You make the outgoings of the
morning and evening rejoice.
9 You have visited the earth
and watered it,
You greatly enrich it;
The river of Elohim is filled with
water;
You provide their grain,
For so You have prepared it.
10 Its ridges have been filled,
Its furrows have been deepened,
You make it soft with showers,
You bless its growth.
11 You have crowned the year with Your
goodness,
And Your paths drip with fatness.
12 The pastures of the wilderness drip,
And the hills are girded with rejoicing.
13 The meadows are dressed in flocks,
And valleys are covered with grain;
They shout for joy and sing.

66 Shout with joy to Elohim,
All the earth!
2 Sing out the splendour of His Name;
Make His praise esteemed.
3 Say to Elohim, "How awesome are
Your works!
Through the greatness of Your power
Your enemies pretend obedience to
You.
4 "All the earth bow to You,
They sing praises to You,
They praise Your Name." Selah.
5 Come and see the works of Elohim,
Awesome acts toward the sons of men.
6 He has turned the sea into dry land,
They went through the river on foot.
There we rejoiced in Him,
7 Who rules by His power forever;
His eyes keeping watch on the nations;
Let the rebellious not exalt themselves.
Selah.
8 Bless our Elohim, you peoples!
And sound His praise abroad,
9 Who keeps us in life,
And does not allow our feet to be
moved.
10 For You, O Elohim, have proved us;
You have refined us as silver is refined.
11 You brought us into the net;
You laid affliction on our loins.
12 You have let men ride at our head;
We went through fire and through
water;
But You brought us out to plenty.
13 I enter Your house with ascending
offerings;
I complete my vows to You,
14 That which my lips have uttered
And my mouth spoke in my distress.
15 Ascending offerings of fatlings I offer
to You,
With the incense of rams;
I offer bulls with goats. Selah.
16 Come, hear, all you who fear Elohim,
And I relate what He has done for my
being.
17 I called to Him with my mouth,
And praise was in my tongue.
18 If I have seen wickedness in my heart,
יהוה would not hear.
19 Truly, Elohim has heard me;
He has given heed to the voice of my
prayer.
20 Blessed be Elohim,
Who has not turned away my prayer,
Nor His loving-commitment from me!

67 Elohim does favour us and bless us,
Cause His face to shine upon us.
Selah.
2 For Your way to be known on earth,
Your deliverance among all nations.

3 Let the peoples praise You, O Elohim,
Let all the peoples praise You.
4 Let the nations be glad and sing for joy!
For You judge the peoples uprightly,
And lead the nations on earth. Selah.
5 Let the peoples praise You, O Elohim;
Let all the peoples praise You.
6 The earth shall give her increase;
Elohim, our own Elohim, blesses us!
7 Elohim blesses us!
And all the ends of the earth fear Him!

68 Elohim arises,
His enemies are scattered.
And those who hate Him flee before Him!
2 As smoke is driven away,
You drive *them* away;
As wax melts before the fire,
The wrong perish before Elohim.
3 But the righteous are glad,
They exult before Elohim.
And they rejoice with gladness.
4 Sing to Elohim, sing praises to His Name.
Raise up a highway for Him
Who rides through the deserts,
By His Name Yah,
And exult before Him.
5 Father of the fatherless,
And Right-ruler of widows,
Is Elohim in His set-apart dwelling.
6 Elohim makes a home for the lonely;
He brings out into prosperity
Those who are bound with chains;
Only the rebellious shall dwell in a dry land.
7 O Elohim, when You went out before Your people,
When You stepped through the wilderness, Selah.
8 The earth shook and the heavens dropped before Elohim,
This Sinai, shook before Elohim, the Elohim of Yisra'ěl.
9 You, O Elohim, sent a shower of plenty,
You confirmed Your inheritance,
When it was weary.
10 Your flock dwelt in it;
You provided from Your goodness for the poor, O Elohim.
11 יהוה gave the word;
The women who proclaimed it was a great company:
12 "Sovereigns of armies flee in haste!
And she who remains at home divides the spoil."
13 If you lie down among the sheepfolds,
The wings of a dove are covered with silver,
And her feathers with yellow gold.
14 When the Almighty scattered sovereigns in it,
It did snow in Tsalmon.
15 A mountain of Elohim is the mountain of Bashan;
A mountain of peaks is the mountain of Bashan.
16 O mountain of peaks, why do you gaze in envy
At the mountain which Elohim desired to dwell in;
יהוה even dwells *there* forever.
17 The chariots of Elohim are twenty thousand,
Thousands of thousands;
יהוה came from Sinai
Into the Set-apart Place.
18 You have ascended on high,
You have led captivity captive,
You have received gifts among men,
And even the rebellious,
That Yah Elohim might dwell *there*.
19 Blessed be יהוה,
Day by day He bears our burden,
The Ěl of our deliverance! Selah.
20 Our Ěl is the Ěl of deliverance;
And to יהוה, the Master, belong escapes from death.
21 Indeed, Elohim smites the head of His enemies,
The hairy scalp of him who walks about in His guilt.
22 יהוה said, "I bring back from Bashan,
I bring back from the depths of the sea,
23 "So that you plunge your foot in blood;
That the tongues of your dogs
Have their portion from the enemies."
24 They have seen Your goings, O Elohim,

The goings of my Ěl, my Sovereign,
Into the set-apart place.
25 The singers went in front,
The players on instruments after them;
Among them were the young women [a]
playing tambourines.
26 Bless Elohim in the assemblies,
יהוה, from the fountain of Yisra'ěl.
27 There is Binyamin, the smallest, their
ruler,
The leaders of Yehuḏah, their
company,
The leader of Zeḇulun, the leader of
Naphtali.
28 Your Elohim has commanded your
strength, be strong!
O Elohim, this You have worked out
for us!
29 Because of Your Hěḵal at
Yerushalayim,
Sovereigns bring presents to You.
30 Rebuke the wild beasts of the reeds,
The herd of bulls, with the calves of
the peoples,
Each one humbling himself with pieces
of silver.
Scatter the peoples who delight in
conflicts!
31 Ambassadors come out of Mitsrayim;
Kush stretches out her hands to
Elohim.
32 Sing to Elohim, you reigns of the earth,
Praises to יהוה, Selah.
33 To Him who rides on the ancient
highest heavens!
See, He sends out His voice, a mighty
voice.
34 Ascribe strength to Elohim;
His excellence is over Yisra'ěl,
And His strength is in the clouds.
35 O Elohim, awesome from Your set-
apart places,
The Ěl of Yisra'ěl is He
Who gives strength and power to His
people.
Blessed be Elohim!

69 Save me, O Elohim!
For waters have come up to my
neck.
2 I have sunk in deep mud,
And there is no place to stand;
I have come into deep waters,
And the floods overflow me.
3 I am worn out from my crying;
My throat is dry;
My eyes grow dim
As I wait for my Elohim.
4 Those who hate me without a cause
Are more than the hairs of my head;
They are mighty who would destroy
me,
My lying enemies;
What I did not steal, I restored.
5 O Elohim, You Yourself know my
foolishness;
And my guilt has not been hidden from
You.
6 Let not those who wait for You,
O Master יהוה of hosts,
Be ashamed because of me;
Let not those who seek You
Be humbled because of me,
O Elohim of Yisra'ěl.
7 Because I have borne reproach
for Your sake;
Shame has covered my face.
8 I have become a stranger to my
brothers,
And a foreigner to my mother's
children;
9 Because ardour for Your house has
eaten me up,
And the reproaches of those who
reproach You have fallen on me.
10 And I wept in my being with fasting,
And it became my reproach.
11 And when I put on sackcloth,
I became a proverb to them.
12 They who sit in the gate talk about me,
And I am the song of the drunkards.
13 But as for me, my prayer is to You,
O יהוה,
At an acceptable time, O Elohim.
In the greatness of Your loving-
commitment,
Answer me in the truth of Your
deliverance.

68a See Explanatory notes: Maiden.

14 Rescue me out of the mire,
And let me not sink.
Let me be rescued from those who hate
me,
And out of the deep waters.
15 Let not a flood of waters overflow me,
Nor let the deep swallow me up,
Nor let the pit shut its mouth on me.
16 Answer me, O יהוה, for Your loving-
commitment is good.
According to the greatness of Your
compassion, turn to me.
17 And do not hide Your face from Your
servant,
For I am in distress;
Answer me speedily.
18 Draw near to my being, redeem it;
Ransom me because of my enemies.
19 You Yourself know my reproach,
And my shame and my confusion;
My adversaries are all before You.
20 Reproach has broken my heart and I
am sick;
I looked for sympathy, but there was
none;
And for comforters, but I found none.
21 And they gave me gall for my food,
And for my thirst they gave me vinegar
to drink.
22 Let their table before them become a
snare,
And a trap to those at ease.
23 Let their eyes be darkened, so as not to
see;
And make their loins shake
continually.
24 Pour out Your wrath upon them,
And let Your burning displeasure
overtake them.
25 Let their encampments be deserted;
Let no one dwell in their tents.
26 For they persecute him whom You
have stricken,
And talk about the pain of those You
have wounded.
27 Add crookedness to their crookedness,
And let them not enter into Your
righteousness.
28 Let them be blotted out of the book of
the living,
And not be written with the righteous.
29 But I am poor and in pain;
Let Your deliverance, O Elohim, set
me up on high.
30 I praise the Name of Elohim with a
song,
And I make Him great with
thanksgiving.
31 And this pleases יהוה more than an ox,
A bull with horns *and* hooves.
32 The humble shall see, they rejoice,
You who seek Elohim, and your hearts
live.
33 For יהוה hears the poor,
And He shall not despise His captives.
34 Let the heavens and earth praise Him,
The seas and all that moves in them.
35 For Elohim shall save Tsiyon
And build the cities of Yehuḏah.
And they shall dwell there
and possess it,
36 And the seed of His servants inherit it,
And those who love His Name
dwell in it. [a]

70 O Elohim, deliver me!
Hasten to my help, O יהוה!
2 Let those who seek my life
Be ashamed and abashed,
Let those who are desiring my evil
Be turned back and humiliated.
3 Let those who say, "Aha, aha!"
Be turned back because of their shame.
4 Let all those who seek You
Rejoice and be glad in You;
And let those who love Your
deliverance always say,
"Let Elohim be made great!"
5 But I am poor and needy;
Hasten to me, O Elohim!
You are my help and my deliverer;
O יהוה, do not delay.

71 In You, O יהוה, I have taken
refuge;
Let me never be ashamed.
2 In Your righteousness deliver and
rescue me;

69a Teh. 5:11, Teh. 119:132, Yesh. 56:6.

Incline Your ear to me, and save me.
3 Be to me a rock to dwell in,
To go into continually.
You have given the command to save me,
For You are my rock and my stronghold.
4 Rescue me, O my Elohim,
Out of the hand of the wrong,
Out of the hand of the unrighteous and cruel.
5 For You are my expectation,
Master יהוה, my Trust from my youth.
6 Upon You I have leaned from my birth;
You took me out of my mother's womb.
My praise is continually of You.
7 I have become as a wonder to many,
But You are my strong refuge.
8 My mouth is filled *with* Your praise,
Your splendour, all the day.
9 Do not cast me off in the time of old age,
When my strength fails, do not forsake me.
10 For my enemies have spoken against me.
And those who watch for my life
Have taken counsel together,
11 Saying, "Elohim has forsaken him;
Pursue and take him, for there is no one to deliver."
12 O Elohim, do not be far from me;
My Elohim, hasten to my help!
13 Let those who are adversaries of my life
Be ashamed, consumed,
Let those who seek my evil
Be covered with reproach and confusion.
14 But I continually wait,
And shall praise You more and more.
15 My mouth recounts Your righteousness
Your deliverance all the day,
Though I do not know *their* numbers.
16 I come in the might of the Master יהוה;
I make mention of Your righteousness, Yours alone.
17 Elohim, You have taught me from my youth;
And to this day I declare Your wonders.
18 And also when I am old and grey,
O Elohim, do not forsake me,
Until I declare Your strength to a generation,
Your might to all those who are to come.
19 For Your righteousness, O Elohim, is very high,
You who have done great *deeds*.
O Elohim, who is like You?
20 You who have shown me great and evil distresses,
Revive me again and bring me up again
From the depths of the earth.
21 You increase my greatness,
And comfort me on every side.
22 Also with the lyre I praise You
For Your trustworthiness, O my Elohim!
I sing to You with the lyre,
O Set-apart One of Yisra'ěl.
23 My lips shout for joy when I sing to You,
Even my being, which You have redeemed.
24 My tongue, too, utters Your righteousness all day long;
For those who have been seeking my evil
Have been put to shame,
Have become abashed.

72

O Elohim, give the sovereign Your right-rulings,
And Your righteousness to the Son of a sovereign.
2 Let Him rule Your people with righteousness,
And Your poor with right-ruling.
3 Let the mountains bring peace to the people,
And the hills, by righteousness.
4 Let Him rightly rule the poor of the people,
Save the children of the needy,
And crush the oppressor.
5 Let them fear You with the sun, *shining*
And before the moon, in all generations.

6 Let Him come down like rain upon the mown grass,
Like showers, watering the earth.
7 Let the righteous flourish in His days,
With plenty of peace,
Till the moon is no more.
8 And let Him rule from sea to sea,
And from the River to the ends of the earth.
9 Let those dwelling in the desert bow before Him,
And His enemies lick the dust.
10 Let the sovereigns of Tarshish and of the isles bring presents;
The sovereigns of Sheḇa and Seḇa offer gifts.
11 And let all sovereigns bow down before Him,
All nations serve Him.
12 For He delivers the needy when he cries,
And the poor, who has no helper.
13 He spares the poor and needy,
And He saves the lives of the needy.
14 He redeems their life from oppression and from violence;
And their blood is precious in His eyes.
15 And He shall live,
And the gold of Sheḇa be given to Him,
And prayer be made for Him continually;
Let Him be blessed all day long.
16 Let there be plenty of grain in the earth,
On the top of the mountains,
Let its fruit wave like Leḇanon,
And those of the city flourish like grass of the earth.
17 Let His Name be forever,
His Name continue before the sun;
And let them bless themselves in Him;
Let all nations call Him blessed.
18 Blessed be יהוה Elohim,
Elohim of Yisra'ěl,
He alone is doing wonders!
19 And blessed be His esteemed Name forever!
And let all the earth
Be filled with His esteem.
Aměn and Aměn.
20 The prayers of Dawiḏ the son of Yishai are ended.

73

Elohim is truly good to Yisra'ěl,
To those whose heart is clean.
2 But as for me, my feet had almost stumbled,
My steps had nearly slipped.
3 For I was envious of the boasters,
When I saw the peace of the wrong-doers. [a]
4 For death has no pangs for them,
And their strength is firm.
5 They are not in trouble as other men,
And they are not plagued like other men.
6 So pride is their necklace,
The garment of violence covers them.
7 Their eyes bulge from fatness;
Their heart overflows with imaginations.
8 They mock and speak in the evil of oppression;
They speak loftily.
9 They have set their mouth against the heavens,
And their tongue walks through the earth, *saying*:
10 "Therefore His people return here,
And waters of a filled *cup* are drained by them!"
11 And they have said, "How could Ěl know?
And is there knowledge in the Most High?"
12 See, these are the wrong,
And always at ease,
They have amassed wealth!
13 Indeed, in vain have I cleansed my heart,
And washed my hands in innocence.
14 For I am plagued all day long,
And my reproof is every morning.
15 If I had said, "Let me speak thus,"
See, I would have deceived
A generation of Your children.
16 Yet, when I tried to understand this,

73a See Iyoḇ 21:7, Yirm. 12:1-2, Teh. 73:17 and Teh. 92:6-7.

It was labour to my eyes –
17 Until I went into the set-apart place of Ěl;
Then I perceived their end.
18 Indeed, You set them in slippery places;
You make them fall to ruins.
19 How suddenly they are ruined!
Completely swept away through destructions.
20 יהוה, when You awake You despise their image,
As one does a dream after waking.
21 For my heart was in a ferment,
And I was pierced in my kidneys.
22 I was stupid and ignorant,
I was like a beast toward You.
23 Yet I am always with You,
You took hold of my right hand.
24 You lead me by Your counsel,
And afterward receive me unto esteem.
25 Whom do I have in the heavens?
And I have desired no one besides You on earth.
26 My flesh and my heart shall waste away,
But Elohim is the rock of my heart
And my portion forever.
27 For look, those who are far from You perish;
You shall cut off all those
Who go whoring away from You.
28 But as for me, it is good to be near Elohim.
I have made my refuge in the Master יהוה,
To declare all Your works.

74 O Elohim, why do You forever reject us?
Why does Your displeasure smoke
Against the sheep of Your pasture?
2 Remember Your congregation.
You did purchase of old,
The tribe of Your inheritance.
You did redeem,
This Mount Tsiyon where You have dwelt.
3 Lift up Your steps to the endless ruins;
The enemy has done all evil
in the set-apart place. [a]
4 Your adversaries have roared
In the midst of Your appointments;
They have set up their own signs as signs.
5 It seems as if one had lifted up
Axes among the thick trees.
6 And now all its carved work,
They have broken down with axe and hammer.
7 They have set fire to Your set-apart place,
They have profaned the dwelling place of Your Name to the ground.
8 They said in their hearts, "Let us suppress them altogether."
They burned all the Appointment *Places* of Ěl in the land.
9 We do not see our signs,
There is no longer a prophet,
Nor any among us who knows how long.
10 O Elohim, how long would the adversary reproach?
Would the enemy despise Your Name forever? [b]
11 Why do You hold back Your hand, even Your right hand?
From the midst of Your bosom – end it!
12 For Elohim is my Sovereign from of old,
Working deliverance in the midst of the earth.
13 You divided the sea by Your might;
You broke the heads of the sea serpents in the waters.
14 You broke the heads of Liwiathan in pieces,
You made him food for the people
Living in the wilderness.
15 You did cleave open the fountain and the flood,
You did dry up mighty rivers.
16 The day is Yours, the night is Yours too,
You have established the light and the sun.

74a See Teh. 79. *74b* See v. 18.

17 You have set all the borders of the earth,
You have made summer and winter.
18 Remember this: the enemy has reproached יהוה,
And a foolish people has despised Your Name.
19 Do not give the being of Your turtle-dove to the wild beast!
Do not forget the life of Your afflicted ones forever.
20 Look to the covenant,
For the dark places of the earth are filled
With haunts of violence.
21 Let not the crushed one return ashamed!
Let the poor and needy praise Your Name.
22 Arise, O Elohim, plead Your own cause,
Remember how the foolish man reproaches You daily.
23 Do not forget the voice of Your enemies,
The uproar of those rising up against You increases continually.

75

We shall give thanks to You,
O Elohim, we shall give thanks!
And Your Name is near!
Your wonders shall be declared!
2 "When I seize the appointed time,
It is I who judge in uprightness.
3 "The earth and all its inhabitants are melted;
It is I who set its columns firm. Selah.
4 "I said to the boasters, 'Do not boast,'
And to the wrong, 'Do not lift up the horn.
5 "Do not lift up your horn on high
(You speak with a stiff neck).' "
6 For exaltations are neither from the east,
Nor from the west nor from the wilderness.
7 But Elohim is the Judge – He puts down one,
And exalts another.
8 For a cup is in the hand of יהוה,
And the wine shall foam;
It is filled with a mixture,
And He pours it out.
All the wrong of the earth drink,
Draining it to the dregs.
9 But I, I declare forever,
I sing praises to the Elohim of Ya'aqob.
10 "And all the horns of the wrong I cut off;
The horns of the righteous are lifted up."

76

In Yehudah Elohim is known;
His Name is great in Yisra'ĕl.
2 And His booth is in Shalĕm, [a]
And His dwelling place in Tsiyon.
3 There He broke the arrows of the bow,
The shield and the sword and the battle-axe. Selah.
4 You are resplendent,
More excellent than mountains of prey.
5 The stout-hearted have been stripped;
They slept their sleep;
And none of the mighty men have found their hands.
6 At Your rebuke, O Elohim of Ya'aqob,
Both the rider and horse lay stunned.
7 You, You are to be feared;
And who would stand in Your presence
When You are displeased?
8 From heaven You shall cause judgment to be heard;
The earth shall fear, and shall be still,
9 When Elohim arises to right-ruling,
To save all the meek of the earth. Selah.
10 For the wrath of mankind praises You,
With the remainder of wrath You gird Yourself!
11 Make vows to יהוה your Elohim, and pay them.
Let all who are around Him bring presents
To the One to be feared.
12 He cuts off the spirit of leaders,
He is awesome to the sovereigns of the earth!

76a A previous name of Yerushalayim.

77 My voice is to Elohim, and I cry;
My voice is to Elohim, and He listened to me.
2 In the day of my distress I sought יהוה;
My hand was stretched out in the night
And it did not cease,
My being refused to be comforted.
3 I remembered Elohim, and groaned;
I complained, and my spirit grew faint. Selah.
4 You ceased the watches of my eyes,
I was too troubled to speak.
5 I have thought about the days of old,
The years long past.
6 I remember my song in the night,
I meditate within my heart,
And my spirit searches diligently.
7 Would יהוה reject forever,
And never again be pleased?
8 Has His loving-commitment ceased forever,
Has the promise failed for all generations?
9 Has Ěl forgotten to show favour?
Has He shut up His compassions in displeasure? Selah.
10 And I said, "This is my grief:
That the right hand of the
Most High has changed."
11 I remember the deeds of Yah,
For I remember Your wonders of old.
12 And I shall meditate on all Your work,
And talk of Your deeds.
13 Your way, O Elohim, is in Set-apartness; [a]
Who is a great Ěl like Elohim?
14 You are the Ěl who does wonders;
You have made known Your strength among the peoples.
15 By Your arm You have redeemed Your people,
The sons of Ya'aqoḇ and Yosěph. Selah.
16 The waters saw You, O Elohim;
The waters saw You, they were afraid;
The depths also trembled.
17 The clouds poured out water;
The heavens rumbled;
Also, Your arrows flashed back and forth.
18 The voice of Your thunder rolled along;
Lightnings lit up the world;
The earth trembled and shook.
19 Your way was in the sea,
And Your path in the great waters,
And Your footsteps were not known.
20 You did lead Your people like a flock
By the hand of Mosheh and Aharon.

78 My people, give ear to my Torah,
Incline your ears to the words of my mouth.
2 I open my mouth in a parable;
I utter riddles of old,
3 Which we have heard and known,
For our fathers have related *them* to us.
4 We do not hide *them* from their children,
Relating to the generation to come the praises of יהוה,
And His strength and His wonders which He has done.
5 For He raised a witness in Ya'aqoḇ,
And set a Torah in Yisra'ěl,
Which He commanded our fathers,
To teach them to their children;
6 That it might be known to a generation to come,
To children who would be born,
To rise up and relate *them* to their children,
7 And place their trust in Elohim,
And not forget the works of Ěl,
But watch over His commands,
8 And not be like their fathers,
A stubborn and rebellious generation,
A generation which did not prepare its heart,
Whose spirit was not steadfast to Ěl.
9 The children of Ephrayim, armed bowmen,
Turned back in the day of battle.
10 They did not guard the covenant of Elohim,
And they refused to walk in His Torah,
11 And they forgot His deeds

77a Yesh. 35:8.

And His wonders which He had shown
them.
12 He did wonders in the sight of their
fathers,
In the land of Mitsrayim, in the field
of Tsoʿan.
13 He split the sea and caused them to
pass through,
And He made the waters stand up like
a heap,
14 And led them with the cloud by day,
And all the night with a light of fire.
15 He split the rocks in the wilderness,
And made them drink, as from the
great depths,
16 And brought forth streams from
the rock,
And caused waters to come down
as rivers.
17 Yet they sinned still more
against Him
To rebel against the Most High
in the desert.
18 And they tried Ěl in their heart
By asking food according to their
desire.
19 And they spoke against Elohim.
They said, "Is Ěl able to set a table
in the wilderness?
20 "Look, He struck the rock,
So that the waters gushed out,
And the streams overflowed.
Is He able to give bread also?
Would He provide meat for His
people?"
21 Therefore יהוה heard, and He was
wroth;
So a fire was kindled against Yaʿaqoḇ,
And displeasure also came up against
Yisra'ěl,
22 Because they did not believe in
Elohim,
Neither did they trust in His
deliverance.
23 Yet He had commanded the clouds
above,
And opened the doors of the heavens,
24 And He rained down manna on them
to eat,
And He gave them the grain of the
heavens.
25 Men ate bread of the mighty;
He sent them provisions to satisfaction.
26 He made an east wind blow in the
heavens;
And by His power He brought in the
south wind.
27 And He rained meat on them like the
dust,
And winged birds like the sand of the
seas,
28 And let them fall in the midst of His
camp,
All around His Dwelling Place.
29 So they ate and were completely
satisfied,
For He brought them what they
desired.
30 They had not turned away from their
desire,
Their food was still in their mouths,
31 When the wrath of Elohim came
against them,
And He killed among their fat ones,
And He struck down the choice ones
of Yisra'ěl.
32 In spite of all this they still sinned,
And did not believe in His wonders.
33 So He ended their days in a breath,
And their years in trouble.
34 When He killed them, then they sought
Him,
And they returned and did earnestly
seek Ěl.
35 And they remembered that Elohim was
their rock,
And the Most High Ěl their redeemer.
36 But they flattered Him with their
mouth,
And they lied to Him with their tongue,
37 For their heart was not steadfast with
Him,
And they were not true to His
covenant.
38 But He, the Compassionate One,
Pardoned crookedness,
And did not destroy them.
And many a time He turned His
displeasure away,
And did not stir up all His wrath.
39 For He remembered that they were
but flesh,

A passing breath that does not return.
40 How often they rebelled against Him in the wilderness,
And grieved Him in the desert!
41 And again and again they tried Ěl,
And provoked the Set-apart One of Yisra'ěl.
42 They did not remember His hand,
The day when He redeemed them from the adversary,
43 How He worked His signs in Mitsrayim,
And His wonders in the field of Tsoʽan.
44 He turned their rivers into blood,
And they could not drink their streams.
45 He sent among them swarms of flies which devoured them,
And frogs which destroyed them,
46 And gave their crops to the caterpillar,
And their labour to the locust.
47 He destroyed their vines with hail,
And their sycamore trees with frost,
48 And gave their beasts over to the hail,
And their livestock to bolts of fire.
49 He sent on them the burning of His displeasure,
Wrath, and rage, and distress,
A deputation of messengers of evils.
50 He made a path for His displeasure;
He did not spare their being from death,
But gave their life over to the plague.
51 And He struck all the first-born in Mitsrayim,
The first-fruits of strength in the tents of Ḥam,
52 Then made His own people go forth like sheep,
And led them in the wilderness like a flock.
53 And He led them on safely,
And they did not fear,
But the sea covered their enemies.
54 And He brought them to the border of His set-apart place,
This mountain which His right hand had gained,
55 And drove out nations before them,
And allotted them a measured inheritance,
And made the tribes of Yisra'ěl dwell in their tents.
56 Yet they tried and rebelled
Against the Most High Elohim,
And did not guard His witnesses,
57 But they turned back
And acted treacherously like their fathers;
They twisted like a treacherous bow.
58 For they enraged Him with their high places,
And moved Him to jealousy with their carved images.
59 When Elohim heard this, He was wroth,
And greatly despised Yisra'ěl,
60 And He left the Dwelling Place of Shiloh,
The Tent which He had set up among men.
61 And He gave His strength into captivity,
And His comeliness into the hand of the adversary.
62 And He gave His people over to the sword,
And He was wroth with His inheritance.
63 His young men were consumed by fire,
And His maidens were not praised.
64 His priests fell by the sword,
And their widows could not weep.
65 Then יהוה awoke as one asleep,
As a mighty man who shouts because of wine.
66 And He struck His adversaries backward,
He put them to an everlasting reproach.
67 Then He rejected the tent of Yosěph,
And did not choose the tribe of Ephrayim,
68 But chose the tribe of Yehuḏah,
Mount Tsiyon, which He loved.
69 And He built His set-apart place like the heights,
Like the earth He founded it forever.
70 And He chose Dawiḏ His servant,
And took him from the sheepfolds;
71 He brought him in from tending the ewes,
To shepherd Yaʽaqoḇ His people,
And Yisra'ěl His inheritance.

72 And he shepherded them
According to the integrity of his heart,
And led them by the skill of his hands.

79

O Elohim, the nations [a] have come into Your inheritance;
They have defiled Your set-apart Hěḵal;
They turned Yerushalayim into ruins.
2 They have given the dead bodies of Your servants
As food for the birds of the heavens,
The flesh of Your lovingly-committed ones to the wild beast of the earth.
3 They have poured out their blood
Like water all around Yerushalayim,
With no one to bury *them*.
4 We have become a reproach to our neighbours,
A scorn and a mockery to those who are around us.
5 How long, O יהוה,
Would You be enraged forever?
Would Your jealousy burn like fire?
6 Pour out Your wrath on the nations
Who have not known You,
And on reigns that have not called on Your Name.
7 For they have devoured Yaʽaqoḇ,
And laid waste his pasture.
8 Do not remember against us
The crookednesses of the fathers!
Let Your compassion speedily meet us,
For we have been greatly weakened.
9 Help us, O Elohim of our deliverance,
For the sake of the esteem of Your Name.
And deliver us, and cover over our sins,
For Your Name's sake!
10 Why should the nations say,
"Where is their Elohim?"
Let the vengeance of the outpoured blood of Your servants
Be known among the nations,
Before our eyes.
11 Let the groaning of the prisoner come before You.
According to the greatness of Your arm
Preserve those appointed to death.
12 And repay to our neighbours sevenfold
Their reproach, into their bosom,
With which they have reproached You, O יהוה.
13 And we, Your people and the sheep of Your pasture,
We give thanks to You forever;
From generation to generation we show forth Your praise.

80

Give ear, O Shepherd of Yisra'ěl,
Who leads Yosěph like a flock;
Who dwells between the keruḇim, shine forth!
2 Before Ephrayim, Binyamin, and Menashsheh,
Stir up Your might,
And come and save us!
3 Cause us to turn back, O Elohim,
And cause Your face to shine,
That we might be saved!
4 O יהוה Elohim of hosts,
How long shall You be wroth
Against the prayer of Your people?
5 You have caused them to eat the bread of tears,
And have caused them to drink
With tears, a third time.
6 You have made us a strife to our neighbours,
And our enemies laugh among themselves.
7 Turn us back, O Elohim of hosts,
And cause Your face to shine,
That we might be saved!
8 You brought a vine out of Mitsrayim;
You drove out the nations, and planted it.
9 You cleared a place for it,
And caused it to take deep root,
And it filled the land.
10 Hills were covered with its shadow,
And the mighty cedars with its twigs.
11 She spread her branches to the Sea,
And her shoots to the River.
12 Why have You broken down her hedges,
So that every passer-by plucked her

79a See also vv. 6-7, Teh. 74:1-23, Yesh. 63:18, Yirm. 51:51, Ěḵah 1:10, Dan. 8:13, Dan. 11:31, Mt. 24:15.

fruit?
13 The boar out of the forest ravages it,
And the wild beast of the field devours it.
14 Return, we beg You, O Elohim of hosts;
Look down from heaven, and see,
And visit this vine,
15 And the stock which Your right hand has planted,
And the Son whom You made strong for Yourself.
16 It is burned with fire, it is cut down;
They perish at the rebuke of Your face.
17 Let Your hand be upon the One at Your right hand,
Upon the Son of Aḏam whom You made strong for Yourself,
18 And we shall not backslide from You.
Revive us, and let us call upon Your Name.
19 Turn us back, O יהוה Elohim of hosts,
And cause Your face to shine,
That we might be saved!

81 Shout for joy to Elohim our strength;
Raise a shout to the Elohim of Ya'aqoḇ.
2 Lift up a song and beat the tambourine,
The pleasant lyre and with the harp.
3 Blow a shophar in the New *Moon*,
in the covering for the day of our festival.
4 For this is a law [a] for Yisra'ěl,
And a right-ruling of the Elohim of Ya'aqoḇ.
5 He appointed it in Yehosěph for a witness,
When He went throughout the land of Mitsrayim;
I heard a language that I did not know.
6 *He says*, "I removed his shoulder from the burden;
His hands were freed from the baskets.
7 "You called in distress, and I rescued you;
I answered you in the covering of thunder;
I proved you at the waters of Meriḇah. Selah.
8 "Hear, O My people, and let Me warn you,
O Yisra'ěl, if you would listen to Me!
9 "Let there be no strange mighty one among you,
And do not bow down to a foreign mighty one.
10 "I am יהוה your Elohim,
Who brought you out of the land of Mitsrayim;
Open your mouth wide, and I fill it.
11 "But My people did not listen to My voice,
And Yisra'ěl would not submit to Me.
12 "So I gave them over to their own stubborn heart,
To walk in their own counsels.
13 "O, if My people had listened to Me,
Yisra'ěl would walk in My ways,
14 "I would subdue their enemies at once,
And turn My hand against their adversaries!
15 "Those who hate יהוה would cringe before Him;
And their time *of punishment* be forever.
16 "He would feed them with the finest of wheat;
And with honey from the rock I would satisfy you."

82 Elohim stands in the congregation of Ěl;
He judges in the midst of the elohim.
2 How long would you judge perversely,
And show partiality to the wrong? Selah.
3 Give right-ruling to the poor and fatherless,
Do right to the afflicted and needy.
4 Rescue the poor and needy;
Deliver them from the hand of the wrong.
5 They do not know, nor do they understand,
They walk about in darkness.
All the foundations of the earth are

81a Way. 23:24, Bem. 10:10, 29:1.

shaken.
6 I, I said, "You are elohim,
And all of you are sons of the Most High.
7 "But as men you die,
And fall as one of the heads."
8 Arise, O Elohim, judge the earth,
For You shall possess all the nations.

83 O Elohim, do not remain silent!
Do not be speechless,
And do not be still, O Ěl!
2 For look, Your enemies make an uproar,
And those hating You have lifted up their head.
3 They craftily plot against Your people,
And conspire against Your treasured ones.
4 They have said, "Come,
And let us wipe them out as a nation,
And let the name of Yisra'ěl be remembered no more."
5 For they have conspired together with one heart;
They have made a covenant against You –
6 The tents of Eḏom and the Yishma'ělites,
Mo'aḇ and the Haḡarites,
7 Geḇal, and Ammon, and Amalěq,
Philistia with the inhabitants of Tsor,
8 Ashshur also has joined with them,
They have helped the children of Lot. Selah.
9 Do to them as to Miḏyan,
As to Sisera,
As to Yaḇin at the wadi Qishon,
10 Who perished at Ěndor,
Who became as dung for the ground.
11 Make their nobles like Orěḇ and like Ze'ěḇ,
And all their princes like Zeḇaḥ and Tsalmunna,
12 Who have said, "Let us take possession of the pastures of Elohim
For ourselves."
13 O my Elohim, make them as whirling dust,
As stubble before the wind!
14 As a fire consumes a forest,
And as a flame sets mountains on fire,
15 So pursue them with Your whirlwind,
And frighten them with Your storm.
16 Fill their faces with shame,
And let them seek Your Name, [a] O יהוה.
17 Let them be ashamed and alarmed forever;
And let them become abashed and perish,
18 And let them know that You,
Whose Name is יהוה,
You alone are the Most High over all the earth.

84 How lovely are Your dwelling places,
O יהוה of hosts!
2 My being has longed, and even fainted,
For the courts of יהוה;
My heart and my flesh cry out for the living Ěl.
3 Even the sparrow has found a home,
And the swallow a nest for herself,
Where she has put her young ones –
Your slaughter-places, O יהוה of hosts,
My Sovereign and my Elohim.
4 Blessed are those who dwell in Your house,
They are ever praising You. Selah.
5 Blessed is the man whose strength is in You,
Your Highways are in their heart.
6 Passing through the valley of weeping,
They make it a fountain;
The Teacher also covers it with blessings.
7 They go from strength to strength,
Appearing before Elohim in Tsiyon.
8 O יהוה Elohim of hosts, hear my prayer;
Give ear, O Elohim of Ya'aqoḇ! Selah.
9 O Elohim, see our shield,
And look upon the face of Your anointed.
10 For a day in Your courts
Is better than a thousand *days*.

83a See also 44:21-22, 74:18, Yesh. 52:5, Yirm. 23:26-27.

I have chosen rather to be a doorkeeper
In the House of my Elohim,
Than to dwell in the tents of the wrong.
11 For יהוה Elohim is a sun and a shield;
יהוה gives favour and esteem;
He withholds no good *matter*
From those who walk blamelessly.
12 O יהוה of hosts,
Blessed is the man who trusts in You!

85 יהוה, You shall take pleasure in
Your land;
You shall turn back the captivity of
Ya'aqoḇ.
2 You shall take away the crookedness of
Your people;
You shall cover all their sin. Selah.
3 You shall withdraw all Your wrath;
You shall turn from Your fierce
displeasure.
4 Turn back to us, O Elohim of our
deliverance,
And cause Your vexation toward us
to cease.
5 Would You be enraged with us
forever?
Would You draw out Your displeasure
From generation to generation?
6 Would You not revive us again,
For Your people to rejoice in You?
7 Show us Your loving-commitment,
O יהוה,
And give us Your deliverance.
8 Let me hear what Ěl יהוה speaks,
For He speaks peace to His people
And to His lovingly-committed ones;
And let them not turn again to folly.
9 Truly, His deliverance is near to those
who fear Him,
For esteem to dwell in our land.
10 Loving-commitment and truth shall
meet,
Righteousness and peace shall kiss.
11 Truth sprouts forth from the earth,
And righteousness looks down from
heaven,
12 Indeed, יהוה gives what is good,
And our land yields its increase.
13 Righteousness goes before Him,
And prepares a way for His footsteps.

86 Incline Your ear, O יהוה,
Answer me, for I am poor and
needy.
2 Guard my being, for I am
lovingly-committed;
You are my Elohim;
Save Your servant who is trusting
in You!
3 Show favour to me, O יהוה,
For I cry to You all day long.
4 Bring joy to the being of Your servant,
For to You, O יהוה, I lift up my being.
5 For You, יהוה, are good, and ready to
forgive,
And great in loving-commitment to all
those who call upon You.
6 Give ear, O יהוה, to my prayer;
And listen to the voice of my
pleadings.
7 In the day of my distress I call upon
You,
For You answer me.
8 There is none like You among the
mighty ones, O יהוה;
And like Your works there are none.
9 Let all nations You have made
Come and bow themselves before You,
O יהוה,
And give esteem to Your Name.
10 For You are great, and are doing
wonders;
You are Elohim, You alone.
11 Teach me Your way, O יהוה;
Let me walk in Your truth;
Unite my heart to fear Your Name.
12 I praise You, O יהוה my Elohim,
with all my heart,
And I esteem Your Name forever.
13 For Your loving-commitment is great
toward me,
And You have delivered my being
From the depths of She'ol.
14 O Elohim, the proud have risen
against me,
And a band of dreaded men have
sought my life,
And have not set You before them.
15 But You, O יהוה,
Are a compassionate Ěl and showing
favour,
Patient and great in loving-commit-

ment and truth.
16 Turn to me, and show favour to me!
Give Your strength to Your servant,
And save the son of Your female servant.
17 Show me a sign for good,
And let those hating me see it and be ashamed,
For You, יהוה, have helped me and comforted me.

87 His foundation is
In the set-apart mountains.
2 יהוה loves the gates of Tsiyon
More than all the dwellings of Ya'aqoḇ.
3 Esteemed *matters* are spoken of you,
O city of Elohim: Selah.
4 "I mention Rahaḇ and Baḇel to those who know Me;
See, O Philistia and Tsor, with Kush,
'This and that one was born there.' "
5 And of Tsiyon it is said,
"Each one was born in her;
For the Most High Himself does establish her."
6 יהוה does write,
In the register of the peoples,
"This one was born there." Selah.
7 And the singers and the players on instruments –
All my fountains, are in you.

88 O יהוה, Elohim of my deliverance,
By day I have cried out,
In the night *also* before You,
2 Let my prayer come before You,
Incline Your ear to my cry.
3 For my being is filled with evils,
And my life draws near to She'ol.
4 I have been reckoned among those
Who go down to the pit;
I have become like a man
Who has no strength,
5 Released among the dead,
Like slain ones lying in the burial-site,
Whom You have remembered no more,
And who have been cut off from Your hand.
6 You have put me in the lowest pit,
In dark places, in the depths.
7 Your wrath has rested heavily upon me,
And You have afflicted me with all Your breakers. Selah.
8 You have put away my friends far from me;
You have made me an abomination to them;
I am shut in and do not go out;
9 My eye grows dim because of affliction.
יהוה, I have called upon You, all day long;
I have stretched out my hands to You.
10 Would You work wonders for the dead?
Would the dead rise to praise You? Selah.
11 Is Your loving-commitment declared in the burial-site?
Your trustworthiness in the place of destruction?
12 Are Your wonders known in the dark?
And Your righteousness in the land of no remembrance?
13 But I, unto You I have cried, O יהוה,
And in the morning my prayer comes before You.
14 יהוה, why do You reject me?
Why do You hide Your face from me?
15 I am afflicted and dying from childhood;
I have borne frightening *matters* from You;
I am in despair.
16 Your fierce wrath has gone over me;
Your onslaughts have cut me off.
17 They surrounded me like water all day long;
They close in upon me altogether.
18 You have put loved one and companion far from me,
Darkness is my close friend!

89 I sing of the loving-commitment of יהוה forever;
With my mouth I make known Your trustworthiness
To all generations.
2 For I said, "Loving-commitment is built up forever;
You establish Your trustworthiness in

the heavens."
3 *You said*, "I have made a covenant with My chosen,
I have sworn to My servant Dawiḏ:
4 'I establish your seed forever,
And shall build up your throne to all generations.' " Selah.
5 And the heavens praise Your wonders, O יהוה,
Your trustworthiness, too,
In the assembly of the set-apart ones.
6 For who in the heavens is comparable to יהוה?
Who among the sons of the mighty is like יהוה?
7 Ěl is greatly feared
In the company of the set-apart ones,
And awesome above all those around Him.
8 O יהוה Elohim of hosts,
Who is mighty like You, O Yah?
And Your trustworthiness is all around You.
9 You rule the swelling of the sea;
When its waves rise, You still them.
10 You have broken Rahaḇ in pieces, as one who is slain;
You have scattered Your enemies
With the arm of Your strength.
11 The heavens are Yours,
The earth also is Yours;
The world and all that fills it.
You have founded them.
12 North and south –
You have created them;
Taḇor and Ḥermon rejoice in Your Name.
13 You have a mighty arm,
Your hand is strong,
Your right hand exalted.
14 Righteousness and right-ruling
Are the foundation of Your throne;
Loving-commitment and truth go before Your face.
15 Blessed are the people
Who know the sounding!
They walk, O יהוה, in the light of Your face.
16 In Your Name they rejoice all day long,
And they are exalted in Your righteousness .
17 For You are the comeliness of their strength,
And by Your good pleasure our horn is exalted.
18 For יהוה is our shield,
And the Set-apart One of Yisra'ěl is our Sovereign.
19 Then You spoke in a vision to Your lovingly-committed one,
And You said, "I have given help to one who is mighty,
I have exalted one chosen from the people.
20 "I have found My servant Dawiḏ;
With My set-apart oil I anointed him,
21 "With whom My hand is established;
My arm also strengthens him.
22 "No enemy subjects him to tribute,
And no son of wickedness afflicts him.
23 "And I shall beat down
His adversaries before his face,
And plague those who hate him.
24 "But My trustworthiness
And My loving-commitment are with him,
And in My Name his horn is exalted.
25 "And I shall set his hand on the sea,
And his right hand on the rivers.
26 "He calls out to Me, 'You are my Father,
My Ěl, and the rock of my deliverance.'
27 "I also appoint him first-born,
Highest of the sovereigns of the earth.
28 "I guard My loving-commitment for him forever,
And My covenant is steadfast with him.
29 "And I shall establish his seed forever,
And his throne as the days of the heavens.
30 "If his sons forsake My Torah
And do not walk in My right-rulings,
31 "If they profane My laws
And do not guard My commands,
32 "Then I shall visit their transgression with the rod,
And their crookedness with flogging.
33 "But My loving-commitment I do not take away from him,

Nor be false to My trustworthiness.
34 "I shall not profane My covenant,
Neither would I change what has gone out from My lips.
35 "Once I have sworn by My set-apartness,
I do not lie to Dawiḏ:
36 "His seed shall be forever,
And his throne as the sun before Me;
37 "Like the moon, it is established forever,
And the witness in the heaven is steadfast." Selah.
38 Yet You have rejected and spurned,
You have been wroth with Your anointed.
39 You have disowned the covenant of Your servant,
You have defiled his diadem in the dust.
40 You have broken down all his hedges,
You have brought his strongholds to ruin.
41 All who pass by the way plunder him;
He is a reproach to his neighbours.
42 You have exalted the right hand of his adversaries,
You have made all his enemies rejoice.
43 Moreover You have turned back the edge of his sword,
And have not made him stand in battle.
44 You have brought an end to his splendour,
And have hurled his throne to the ground.
45 You have shortened the days of his youth,
You have covered him with shame. Selah.
46 How long, O יהוה, would You be hidden?
Would Your wrath burn like fire forever?
47 Please remember how short my time is;
Why should you have created all the sons of men for naught?
48 What man would live and not see death?
Who rescues his life from the power of She'ol? Selah.
49 יהוה, where are Your former loving-commitments,
Which You swore to Dawiḏ in Your trustworthiness?
50 יהוה, remember the reproach of Your servants,
That I have borne in my bosom –
Of all the many peoples,
51 With which Your enemies have reproached, O יהוה,
With which they have reproached the footsteps of Your anointed.
52 Blessed be יהוה forever!
Amĕn and Amĕn.

90 יהוה, You have been our refuge
In all generations.
2 Before the mountains were born,
Or You had brought forth the earth and the world,
Even from everlasting to everlasting
You are Ěl.
3 You turn man back to dust,
And say, "Return, O children of men."
4 For a thousand years in Your eyes
Are like yesterday that has past,
Or like a watch in the night.
5 You have swept them away,
They are as a sleep,
Like grass that springs up in the morning.
6 In the morning it flourishes and springs up,
At evening it is cut down and withered.
7 For we have been consumed by Your displeasure,
And by Your wrath we are alarmed.
8 You have set our crookednesses before You,
Our secret *sin* in the light of Your face.
9 For all our days have passed away in Your wrath,
We spend our years like a whisper.
10 The days of our lives are seventy years;
Or if due to strength, eighty years,
Yet the best of them is but toil and exertion;
For it is soon cut off, and we fly away.
11 Who knows the power of Your displeasure?
And your wrath, according to the fear of You?

[12] Teach us to number our days,
And let us bring the heart to wisdom.
[13] Return, O יהוה! How long?
And be sorry for Your servants.
[14] Satisfy us in the morning with Your loving-commitment,
And let us sing for joy all our days!
[15] Give us joy according to
The days You have afflicted us,
The years we have seen evil.
[16] Reveal Your work to Your servants,
And Your splendour to their children.
[17] And let the pleasantness
Of יהוה our Elohim be upon us,
And confirm the work of our hands for us;
O confirm the work of our hands!

91

He who dwells in the secret place of the Most High,
Who abides under the shadow of the Almighty,
[2] He is saying of יהוה, "My refuge and my stronghold,
My Elohim, in whom I trust!"
[3] For He delivers you from the snare of a trapper,
From the destructive pestilence.
[4] He covers you with His feathers,
And under His wings you take refuge;
His truth is a shield and armour.
[5] You are not afraid of the dread by night,
Of the arrow that flies by day,
[6] Of the pestilence that walks in darkness,
Of destruction that ravages at midday.
[7] A thousand fall at your side,
And ten thousand at your right hand;
But it does not come near you.
[8] Only with your eyes you look on,
And see the reward of the wrong ones.
[9] Because you have made יהוה –
My refuge, the Most High – your dwelling place,
[10] No evil befalls you,
And a plague does not come near your tent;
[11] For He commands His messengers concerning you,
To guard you in all your ways.
[12] They bear you up in their hands,
Lest you dash your foot against a stone.
[13] You tread upon lion and cobra,
Young lion and serpent you trample under foot.
[14] "Because he cleaves to Me in love,
Therefore I deliver him;
I set him on high,
Because he has known My Name.
[15] "When he calls on Me, I answer him;
I am with him in distress;
I deliver him and esteem him.
[16] "With long life I satisfy him,
And show him My deliverance."

92

It is good to give thanks to יהוה,
And to sing praises to Your Name, O Most High;
[2] To declare Your loving-commitment in the morning,
And Your trustworthiness each night,
[3] On ten strings, and on the harp,
To the sounding chords of the lyre.
[4] For You have made me rejoice with Your work, O יהוה,
I shout for joy at the works of Your hands.
[5] O יהוה, how great are Your works!
Your thoughts are very deep!
[6] A senseless man does not know,
And a fool does not understand this.
[7] When the wrong spring up like grass,
And all the workers of wickedness blossom,
It is for them to be destroyed forever.
[8] But You, יהוה, are on high forever.
[9] For look, Your enemies, O יהוה,
For look, Your enemies do perish;
All the workers of wickedness are scattered.
[10] But You lift up my horn like a wild ox;
I have been anointed with fresh oil.
[11] And my eye looks upon my enemies;
My ears hear the evil-doers
Who rise up against me.
[12] The righteous one flourishes like a palm tree,
He grows like a cedar in Leḇanon.
[13] Those who are planted in the House

of יהוה
Flourish in the courts of our Elohim.
14 They still bear fruit in old age;
They are fresh and green,
15 To declare that יהוה is straight,
My rock, and in Him is no unrighteousness.

93 יהוה shall reign,
He shall put on excellency;
יהוה shall put on strength;
He shall gird Himself.
Indeed, the world is established, immovable.
2 Your throne is established from of old;
You are from everlasting.
3 Rivers shall lift up, O יהוה,
Rivers shall lift up their voice;
Rivers lift up their breakers.
4 יהוה on high is mightier
Than the noise of many waters,
The mighty breakers of the sea.
5 Your witnesses have been very trustworthy.
Set-apartness befits Your house, O יהוה, forever.

94 O יהוה, Ěl of vengeance;
O Ěl of vengeance, shine forth!
2 Raise Yourself up, O Judge of the earth;
Render punishment to the proud.
3 יהוה, how long are the wrong,
How long are the wrong going to exult?
4 They pour forth *words*,
They speak arrogantly;
All the workers of wickedness boast in themselves.
5 They crush Your people, O יהוה,
And they afflict Your inheritance.
6 They kill the widow and the stranger,
And murder the fatherless.
7 Yet they say, "Yah does not see,
And the Elohim of Ya'aqoḇ pays no heed."
8 Take heed, you senseless among the people;
And you fools, when would you become wise?
9 He who planted the ear, does He not hear?
He who formed the eye, does He not see?
10 He who disciplines the nations,
Does He not reprove –
The One teaching man knowledge?
11 יהוה knows the thoughts of man,
That they are *but* a breath.
12 Blessed is the man You discipline, O Yah,
And instruct out of Your Torah,
13 To give him rest from the days of evil,
Until the pit is dug for the wrong.
14 For יהוה does not leave His people,
Nor does He forsake His inheritance.
15 For right-ruling returns *man* to righteousness,
And all the upright in heart follow it.
16 Who would rise up for me against evil-doers?
Who would stand up for me against workers of wickedness?
17 If יהוה had not been my help,
My being would soon have settled in silence.
18 When I said, "My foot has slipped,"
Your loving-commitment, O יהוה, supported me.
19 When anxiety was great within me,
Your comforts delighted my being.
20 Would a throne of destruction,
Which devises trouble by law,
Be joined with You?
21 They band together against the life of the righteous,
And declare innocent blood wrong.
22 But יהוה is my defence,
And my Elohim the rock of my refuge,
23 And brings back on them their own wickedness,
And cuts them off in their own wrong-doing;
יהוה our Elohim does cut them off.

95 Come, let us sing to יהוה!
Let us raise a shout to the Rock of our deliverance.
2 Let us come before His face with thanksgiving;
Let us raise a shout to Him in song.
3 For יהוה is a great Ěl,

And a great Sovereign above all
mighty ones.
4 In whose hand are the depths of the
earth;
The mountain peaks are His also.
5 His is the sea, for He made it;
And His hands formed the dry land.
6 Come, let us bow down and bend low,
Let us kneel before יהוה our Maker.
7 For He is our Elohim,
And we are the people of His pasture,
And the sheep of His hand.
Today, if you would hear His voice:
8 "Do not harden your hearts as in
Meriḇah,
And as in the day of Massah in the
wilderness,
9 "When your fathers tried Me,
Have proved Me, though they saw My
work.
10 "For forty years I was grieved with *that*
generation,
And said, 'They are a people who go
astray in their hearts,
And they do not know My ways.'
11 "As I swore in My wrath, 'If they enter
into My rest...' "

96

Sing to יהוה a new song,
Sing to יהוה, all the earth!
2 Sing to יהוה, bless His Name,
Proclaim His deliverance from day to
day.
3 Declare His esteem among the nations,
His wonders among all peoples.
4 For great is יהוה and greatly to be
praised,
He is to be feared above all mighty
ones.
5 For all the mighty ones of the peoples
are matters of naught,
But יהוה made the heavens.
6 Excellency and splendour are before
Him,
Strength and comeliness are in His
set-apart place.
7 Ascribe to יהוה, O clans of the
peoples,
Ascribe to יהוה esteem and strength.
8 Ascribe to יהוה the esteem of His
Name;
Bring an offering, and come into His
courts.
9 Bow yourselves to יהוה,
In the splendour of set-apartness!
Tremble before Him, all the earth.
10 Say among nations, "יהוה shall reign.
The world also is established,
immovable.
He judges the peoples in straightness."
11 Let the heavens rejoice, and let the
earth be glad;
Let the sea roar, and all that fills it;
12 Let the field exult, and all that is in it.
Let all the trees of the forest then shout
for joy,
13 At the presence of יהוה.
For He shall come,
For He shall come to judge the earth.
He judges the world in righteousness, [a]
And the peoples with His truth.

97

יהוה shall reign.
The earth rejoices.
Many isles are glad!
2 Clouds and darkness all around Him,
Righteousness and right-ruling are the
foundation of His throne.
3 Fire goes before Him,
And burns up His adversaries round
about.
4 His lightnings shall light the world,
The earth shall see and tremble.
5 The mountains shall melt like wax
before the face of יהוה,
Before the face of the Master of all
the earth.
6 The heavens shall declare His
righteousness,
And all the peoples shall see His
esteem.
7 All are put to shame who serve carved
images,
Those boasting of matters of naught.
Bow yourselves to Him,
all you mighty ones.
8 Tsiyon shall hear and be glad,
And the daughters of Yehuḏah rejoice

96a See also 98:9, Ma. 17:31, Ḥazon 19:11.

Because of Your right-rulings, O יהוה.
9 For You, יהוה, are the Most High over all the earth,
You shall be greatly exalted, over all mighty ones.
10 You who love יהוה, hate evil!
He guards the lives of His lovingly-committed ones,
He delivers them out of the hand of the wrong.
11 Light is sown for the righteous,
And gladness for the upright in heart.
12 Rejoice in יהוה, you righteous,
And give thanks at the remembrance of His Set-apartness.

98 Sing to יהוה a new song!
For He has done wonders;
His right hand and His set-apart arm
Have brought Him deliverance.
2 יהוה has made known His deliverance;
His righteousness He has openly shown
Before the eyes of the nations.
3 He has remembered His loving-commitment
And His trustworthiness to the house of Yisra'ěl;
All the ends of the earth have seen
The deliverance of our Elohim.
4 Raise a shout to יהוה, all the earth;
Break forth in song, rejoice, and sing praises.
5 Sing to יהוה with the lyre,
With the lyre and the voice of a song,
6 With trumpets and a voice of a shophar;
Raise a shout before יהוה, the Sovereign.
7 Let the sea roar, and all that fills it,
The world and those who dwell in it.
8 Let the rivers clap their hands,
Let the mountains sing together for joy before יהוה,
9 For He shall come to judge the earth.
He judges the world in righteousness,
And the people in straightness.

99 יהוה shall reign;
Peoples tremble!
He is enthroned on the keruḇim;
The earth shakes!
2 יהוה is great in Tsiyon,
And He is high above all the peoples.
3 They praise Your Name, great and awesome,
It is set-apart.
4 And the strength of the Sovereign
Shall love right-ruling;
You Yourself shall establish straightness;
You shall execute right-ruling
And righteousness in Ya'aqoḇ.
5 Exalt יהוה our Elohim,
And bow yourselves at His footstool,
He is set-apart.
6 Mosheh and Aharon were among His priests,
And Shemu'ěl was among those calling upon His Name.
They called upon יהוה, and He answered them.
7 He spoke to them in the column of cloud;
They guarded His witnesses
And the law He gave them.
8 You answered them, O יהוה our Elohim.
You were a forgiving Ěl to them,
Though You took vengeance on their deeds.
9 Exalt יהוה our Elohim,
And bow down towards His set-apart mountain;
For יהוה our Elohim is set-apart.

100 Raise a shout for יהוה,
All the earth!
2 Serve יהוה with gladness;
Come before His presence with singing.
3 Know that יהוה, He is Elohim;
He has made us, and we are His –
His people and the sheep of His pasture.
4 Enter into His gates with thanksgiving,
And into His courts with praise.
Give thanks to Him; bless His Name.
5 For יהוה is good;
His loving-commitment is everlasting,
And His truth, to all generations.

101 I sing of loving-commitment
and right-ruling;
To You, O יהוה, I sing praises.
2 I act wisely in a perfect way.
When do You come to me?
I walk in the midst of my house with a
perfect heart.
3 I set no matter of Beliya'al before my
eyes;
I hate the work of those who fall away;
It does not cleave to me.
4 A perverse heart turns away from me;
I do not know evil.
5 Him who secretly slanders his
neighbour I cut off;
I do not tolerate one
Who has a haughty look and a proud
heart.
6 My eyes are on the trustworthy of the
land,
To dwell with me;
He who walks in a perfect way,
He serves me.
7 He who practises deceit
Does not dwell in my house;
He who speaks lies
Does not stand in my presence.
8 Each morning I uproot all the wrong
of the land,
To cut off all the workers of
wickedness
From the city of יהוה.

102 O יהוה, hear my prayer,
And let my cry come to You.
2 Do not hide Your face from me
In the day of my distress;
Incline Your ear to me;
In the day I call, answer me speedily.
3 For my days are consumed like smoke,
And my bones are burned like a hearth.
4 My heart is stricken and withered like
grass,
For I have forgotten to eat my bread.
5 Because of the sound of my sighing
My bones have cleaved to my flesh.
6 I have been like a pelican of the
wilderness,
I have been like an owl of the desert.
7 I have watched, and I am
As a bird alone on the house-top.
8 My enemies reproached me all day
long,
Those who rave against me have sworn
against me.
9 For I have eaten ashes like bread,
And mixed my drink with tears,
10 Because of Your displeasure and Your
wrath;
For You have lifted me up
And thrown me down.
11 My days are like a shadow that
lengthens,
And I wither away like grass.
12 But You, O יהוה, shall be enthroned
forever,
And the remembrance of You be to all
generations.
13 You Yourself shall arise
And have compassion on Tsiyon,
For the time to favour her,
The appointed time, has come.
14 For Your servants have been pleased
with her stones,
And they favour her dust.
15 And the nations shall fear the Name of
יהוה,
And all the sovereigns of the earth
Your esteem,
16 For יהוה shall build up Tsiyon,
He shall appear in His esteem.
17 He shall turn unto the prayer of the
destitute,
And He shall not despise their prayer.
18 This is written for a generation to
come,
So that a people to be created [a] praise
Yah.
19 For He looked down
From the height of His set-apart place;
From heaven יהוה viewed the earth,
20 To hear the groaning of the prisoner,
To release those appointed to death,
21 To declare the Name of יהוה in Tsiyon,
And His praise in Yerushalayim,
22 When peoples gather together,
And reigns, to serve יהוה.
23 He has humbled my strength in the

102a Teh. 22:31.

way;
He has shortened my days.
24 I said, "O my Ěl,
Do not take me away in the midst of my days;
Your years are throughout all generations.
25 "You did found the earth of old,
And the heavens are the work of Your hands.
26 "They shall perish, but You remain;
And all of them grow old like a garment;
You change them like a coat,
And they are changed.
27 "But You are the same,
And Your years have no end.
28 "The sons of Your servants continue,
And their seed is established before You."

103

Bless יהוה, O my being,
And all that is within me,
Bless His set-apart Name!
2 Bless יהוה, O my being,
And do not forget all His dealings,
3 Who forgives all your crookednesses,
Who heals all your diseases,
4 Who redeems your life from destruction,
Who crowns you with loving-commitment and compassion,
5 Who satisfies your desire with the good,
Your youth is renewed like the eagle's.
6 יהוה is doing righteousness
And right-ruling for all the oppressed.
7 He made known His ways to Mosheh,
His acts to the children of Yisra'ěl.
8 יהוה is compassionate and showing favour,
Patient, and great in loving-commitment.
9 He does not always strive, nor maintain it forever.
10 He has not done to us according to our sins,
Nor rewarded us according to our crookednesses.
11 For as the heavens are high above the earth,
So great is His loving-commitment toward those who fear Him;
12 As far as east is from west,
So far has He removed our transgressions from us.
13 As a father has compassion for his children,
So יהוה has compassion for those who fear Him.
14 For He knows how we are made;
He remembers that we are dust.
15 A man's days are like grass;
As a flower of the field, so he flourishes.
16 For the wind blows over it, and it is no more,
And its place no longer remembers it.
17 But the loving-commitment of יהוה
Is from everlasting to everlasting
Upon those who fear Him,
And His righteousness to children's children,
18 To those who guard His covenant,
And to those who remember His orders to do them.
19 יהוה has established His throne in the heavens,
And His reign shall rule over all.
20 Bless יהוה, you His messengers,
Mighty in power, who do His Word,
Listening to the voice of His Word.
21 Bless יהוה, all you His hosts,
You His servants, who do His pleasure.
22 Bless יהוה, all His works,
In all places of His rule.
Bless יהוה, O my being!

104

Bless יהוה, O my being!
O יהוה my Elohim,
You have been very great:
You have put on excellency and splendour,
2 Covering Yourself with light as with a garment,
Stretching out the heavens like a curtain,
3 Who is laying the beams of His upper rooms in the waters,
Who is making thick clouds His chariot,
Who is walking on the wings of the

wind,
4 Making His messengers the winds,
His servants a flame of fire.
5 He established the earth on its foundations,
So that it would not totter forever,
6 You covered it with the deep as with a garment;
The waters stood above the mountains.
7 At Your rebuke they flee;
At the voice of Your thunder they hurry away.
8 They go up the mountains;
They go down the valleys,
To the place which You founded for them.
9 You did set a boundary, they do not pass over,
They do not return to cover the earth.
10 Who is sending the springs into the valleys,
They flow among the hills.
11 They give drink to every beast of the field;
Wild donkeys break their thirst.
12 The birds of the heavens dwell beside them;
They sing from between the branches.
13 Watering the hills from His upper rooms;
The earth is satisfied with the fruit of Your works.
14 Causing the grass to grow for the cattle,
And plants for the service of mankind,
To bring forth food from the earth,
15 And wine that makes glad the heart of man,
Oil to make the face shine,
And bread which sustains man's heart.
16 The trees of יהוה are satisfied,
The cedars of Leḇanon which He planted,
17 Where the birds do make nests;
The stork has her home in the fir trees.
18 The high hills are for wild goats;
Rocks a refuge for rock badgers.
19 He made the moon for appointed times;
The sun knows its going down.
20 You put darkness, and it is night,
In it all the beasts of the forest creep.
21 The young lions are roaring for prey,
And seeking their food from Ěl.
22 The sun arises – they withdraw
And lie down in their dens.
23 Man goes out to his work,
And to his labour, till evening.
24 O יהוה, how many have been Your works!
You have made all of them in wisdom.
The earth is filled with Your possessions.
25 There is the sea, great and wide,
In which are innumerable swarms,
Living creatures, small with great.
26 There do ships go;
That Liwiathan which You made, to play there.
27 All of them wait for You,
To give their food in due season.
28 You give to them, they gather in;
You open Your hand, they are satisfied with good.
29 You hide Your face, they are alarmed;
You take away their breath, they die and return to their dust;
30 You send forth Your Spirit, they are created;
And You renew the face of the earth.
31 The esteem of יהוה is forever,
יהוה rejoices in His works,
32 Who looks on the earth,
and it trembles;
He touches the mountains,
and they smoke.
33 I sing to יהוה as long as I live,
I sing praise to my Elohim while I exist.
34 My meditation on Him is sweet;
I rejoice in יהוה.
35 Let sinners be consumed from the earth,
And let the wrong be no more.
Bless יהוה, O my being!
Praise Yah!

105

Give thanks to יהוה!
Call upon His Name,
Make known His deeds
among the peoples.
2 Sing to Him, sing praise to Him;

Speak of all His wonders.
3 Make your boast in His set-apart Name;
Let the hearts rejoice of those seeking יהוה.
4 Seek יהוה and His strength;
Seek His face always.
5 Remember His wonders which He has done,
His miracles, and the right-rulings of His mouth,
6 O seed of Aḇraham His servant,
Children of Ya'aqoḇ, His chosen ones!
7 He is יהוה our Elohim;
His right-rulings are in all the earth.
8 He has remembered His covenant forever,
The Word He commanded, for a thousand generations,
9 *The covenant* He made with Aḇraham,
And His oath to Yitsḥaq,
10 And established it to Ya'aqoḇ for a law,
To Yisra'ěl – an everlasting covenant,
11 Saying, "To you I give the land of Kena'an,
The portion of your inheritance."
12 When they were few in number,
Few indeed, and sojourners in it,
13 And they went about from one nation to another,
From one reign to another people,
14 He allowed no one to oppress them,
And He reproved sovereigns for their sakes,
15 *Saying*, "Do not touch My anointed ones,
And do My prophets no evil."
16 And He called for a scarcity of food in the land;
He cut off all the supply of bread.
17 He sent ahead of them a man,
Yosěph, sold as a slave.
18 They afflicted his feet with shackles,
His neck was put in irons.
19 Until the time that His Word came,
The Word of יהוה tried him.
20 The sovereign sent and released him,
The ruler of the people let him loose.
21 He made him master of his house,
And ruler over all his possessions,
22 To bind his chiefs at his pleasure,
And to teach his elders wisdom.
23 Then Yisra'ěl came to Mitsrayim,
And Ya'aqoḇ sojourned in the land of Ḥam.
24 And He increased His people greatly,
And made them stronger than their enemies.
25 He turned their heart to hate His people,
To conspire against His servants.
26 He sent Mosheh His servant,
Aharon whom He had chosen.
27 They set among them the matters of His signs,
And wonders in the land of Ḥam.
28 He sent darkness, and made it dark;
And they did not rebel against His word.
29 He turned their waters into blood,
And killed their fish.
30 Their land teemed with frogs,
In the rooms of their sovereigns.
31 He spoke, and swarms of flies came,
Gnats in all their borders.
32 He gave them hail for rain,
A flaming fire in their land.
33 And He struck their vines and their fig trees,
And broke the trees of their borders.
34 He spoke, and locusts came,
And larvae, innumerable,
35 And they devoured all the plants in their land,
And they devoured the fruit of their ground.
36 Then He struck all the first-born in their land,
The first-fruit of all their strength,
37 And brought them out with silver and gold,
And among His tribes no one faltered.
38 Mitsrayim was glad when they left,
For the fear of them had fallen upon them.
39 He spread a cloud for a covering,
And fire to give light in the night.
40 They asked, and He brought quail,
And satisfied them with the bread of heaven.
41 He opened the rock, and water gushed out;

It ran in the dry places, a river.
42 For He remembered His set-apart word,
To Aḇraham His servant.
43 So He brought out His people with joy,
His chosen ones with singing.
44 And He gave to them the lands of the nations,
And they inherited the labour of peoples,
45 In order that they might guard His laws,
And watch over His Torot.[a] Praise Yah!

106

Praise Yah!
Oh, give thanks to יהוה,
For He is good!
For His loving-commitment is everlasting.
2 Who does relate the mighty acts of יהוה?
Or declare all His praise?
3 Blessed are those who guard right-ruling,
Who do righteousness at all times!
4 Remember me, O יהוה, in the acceptance of Your people;
Visit me with Your deliverance,
5 To see the good of Your chosen ones,
To rejoice in the gladness of Your nation,
To make my boast with Your inheritance.
6 We have sinned with our fathers,
We have acted perversely,
We have done wrong.
7 Our fathers in Mitsrayim did not understand Your wonders;
They did not remember Your many loving-commitments,
But rebelled by the sea, the Sea of Reeds.
8 But He saved them for His Name's sake,
To make known His might.
9 And He rebuked the Sea of Reeds, and it dried up;
And He led them through the depths,
Through a wilderness.
10 And He saved them from the hand of the hater,
And redeemed them from the hand of the enemy.
11 And waters covered their adversaries;
Not one of them was left.
12 Then they believed His words;
They sang His praise.
13 They soon forgot His works;
They did not wait for His counsel,
14 But greedily lusted in the wilderness,
And tried Ěl in the desert.
15 And He gave them their request,
But sent leanness within their being.
16 And they were jealous of Mosheh in the camp,
Of Aharon, the set-apart one of יהוה,
17 *Then* the earth opened up and swallowed Dathan,
And covered the company of Aḇiram.
18 And a fire burned in their company;
A flame consumed the wrong.
19 They made a calf in Ḥorěḇ,
And bowed down to a moulded image.
20 Thus they changed My esteem
Into the form of an ox that eats grass.
21 They forgot Ěl their Saviour,
The Doer of great *deeds* in Mitsrayim,
22 Of wonders in the land of Ḥam,
Of awesome *deeds* by the Sea of Reeds.
23 Then He said that He would destroy them,
Had not Mosheh His chosen one stood before Him in the breach,
To turn away His wrath from destroying *them*.
24 They then despised the pleasant land;
They did not believe His word,
25 And they grumbled in their tents,
They did not listen to the voice of יהוה.
26 So He lifted up His hand *in an oath* against them,
To make them fall in the wilderness,
27 And to make their seed fall among the nations,
And to scatter them in the lands.

105a Torot - plural of Torah - teaching

28 And they joined themselves to Ba'al Pe'or,
And ate slaughterings made to the dead.
29 Thus they provoked Him with their deeds,
And the plague broke out among them.
30 Then Pineḥas stood up and intervened,
And the plague was stopped.
31 And that was reckoned to him for righteousness
To all generations forever.
32 And they provoked wrath at the waters of Meriḇah,
And Mosheh suffered on account of them;
33 Because they embittered his spirit,
And he spoke rashly with his lips.
34 They did not destroy the peoples,
As יהוה had commanded them,
35 But mixed with the nations
And learned their works,
36 And served their idols,
And they became a snare to them.
37 And they slaughtered their sons
And their daughters to demons,
38 And they shed innocent blood,
The blood of their sons and daughters,
Whom they slaughtered to the idols of Kena'an;
And the land was defiled with blood.
39 So they became unclean by their own works,
And went whoring by their own deeds.
40 And the wrath of יהוה burned against His people,
And He loathed His own inheritance.
41 Then He gave them into the hand of the nations,
And those who hated them ruled over them.
42 And their enemies oppressed them,
And they were humbled under their hand.
43 Many times He delivered them;
But they rebelled in their plans,
So they were brought low for their crookedness.
44 But He would look on their distress,
When He heard their cry,
45 And remember His covenant for their sake,
And relent according to the greatness of His loving-commitment.
46 And He would let them find compassion,
Before all those holding them captive.
47 Save us, O יהוה our Elohim,
And gather us from among the nations,
To give thanks to Your set-apart Name,
To exult in Your praise.
48 Blessed be יהוה Elohim of Yisra'ěl
From everlasting to everlasting!
And all the people shall say, "Aměn!"
Praise Yah!

107 Give thanks to יהוה! For *He is* good,
For His loving-commitment is everlasting.
2 Let the redeemed of יהוה say *so*,
Whom He has redeemed from the hand of the adversary,
3 And gathered out of the lands,
From east and from west,
From north and from south.
4 They wandered in a wilderness, in a desert way;
They found no city to dwell in.
5 Hungry and thirsty,
Their being in them grew faint.
6 Then they cried out to יהוה in their distress,
He delivered them out of their troubles.
7 And He guided them by the right way,
To go to a city to settle.
8 Let them give thanks to יהוה for His loving-commitment,
And His wonders to the children of men!
9 For He has satisfied a longing being,
And has filled the hungry being with goodness.
10 Some sat in darkness and in the shadow of death,
Bound in affliction and irons,
11 Because they rebelled against the words of Ěl,
And despised the counsel of the Most High.
12 And He humbled their heart by toil;
They stumbled, and there was no one

to help.
13 And they cried out to יהוה in their
distress,
And He saved them out of their
troubles.
14 He brought them out of darkness and
the shadow of death,
And He broke their chains in pieces.
15 Let them give thanks to יהוה for His
loving-commitment,
And His wonders to the children of
men!
16 For He has broken the gates of bronze,
And He cut the bars of iron in two.
17 Fools, because of their transgression,
And because of their crookednesses,
were afflicted.
18 Their being loathed all food,
And they drew near to the gates of
death,
19 And cried out to יהוה in their distress,
He saved them out of their troubles.
20 He sent His word and healed them,
And delivered them from their
destructions.
21 Let them give thanks to יהוה for His
loving-commitment,
And His wonders to the children of
men!
22 And let them slaughter slaughterings of
thanksgiving,
And relate His works with rejoicing.
23 Those who go down to the sea in ships,
Doing work in many waters,
24 They see the works of יהוה,
And His wonders in the deep.
25 For He commands and raises the
stormy wind,
Which lifts up the waves of the sea.
26 They go up to the heavens,
They go down to the depths;
Their being is melted because of evil.
27 They celebrate and stagger like a
drunkard,
And all their wisdom is swallowed up.
28 Then they cry out to יהוה in their
distress,
And He brings them out of their
troubles.
29 He caused the storm to be still,
So that its waves were silent.
30 And they rejoice because they are
hushed;
And He leads them to the haven of
their delight.
31 Let them give thanks to יהוה for His
loving-commitment,
And His wonders to the children of
men!
32 And let them exalt Him in the
assembly of the people,
And praise Him in the
seat of the elders.
33 He makes rivers become a wilderness,
And the fountains of water become a
dry ground;
34 A land of fruit becomes a salty desert,
For the evil of those who dwell in it.
35 He makes a wilderness become a pool
of water,
And dry land become fountains of
waters.
36 And He causes the hungry to dwell
there,
And they build a city to settle in,
37 And they sow fields and plant
vineyards,
And they make fruits of increase.
38 And He blesses them,
And they increase greatly;
And He lets not their cattle diminish.
39 But when they are diminished and
brought low
Through oppression, evil and sorrow,
40 He pours scorn on nobles,
And causes them to wander in a
pathless waste;
41 But He raises the poor up from
affliction,
And makes *their* clans like a flock.
42 The straight ones see, and rejoice,
And all unrighteousness shuts its
mouth.
43 Who is wise? Then let him observe
these *matters*!
Let them understand the loving-
commitments of יהוה.

108 O Elohim, my heart is steadfast;
I sing and give praise – even
my esteem.
2 Awake, harp and lyre!

I awake the dawn.
3 I praise You, O יהוה, among peoples,
And I sing praises to You among the nations.
4 For Your loving-commitment is great above the heavens,
And Your truth reaches to the clouds.
5 Exalt Yourself above the heavens, O Elohim,
And Your esteem above all the earth;
6 In order that those You love
Might be delivered.
Save with Your right hand,
And answer me.
7 Elohim has spoken in His set-apartness,
"I exult, I portion out Sheḵem,
And I measure out the Valley of Sukkoth.
8 "Gil'aḏ is Mine, Menashsheh is Mine,
And Ephrayim is My chief defence,
Yehuḏah is My inscriber. [a]
9 "Mo'aḇ is My wash-pot,
Over Eḏom I cast My shoe,
Over Philistia I raise a shout."
10 Who would bring me into the strong city?
Who shall lead me to Eḏom?
11 Have You not rejected us, O Elohim?
And You do not go out with our armies, O Elohim!
12 Give us help from distress,
For the help of man is naught.
13 In Elohim we do mightily,
For it is He who treads down our adversaries.

109

Do not be silent,
O Elohim of my praise!
2 For the mouth of the wrong
And the mouth of the deceiver
Have opened against me;
They have spoken against me with a false tongue.
3 They have surrounded me with words of hatred,
And they attack me without a cause.
4 In return for my love they accuse me,
While I am *in* prayer.
5 And they repay me evil for good,
And hatred for my love.
6 Appoint over him one who is wrong,
And let an accuser stand at his right hand.
7 When he is judged, let him be found wrong,
And let his prayer become sin.
8 Let his days be few,
Let another take his office.
9 Let his children be fatherless,
And his wife a widow.
10 And let his children always wander and beg,
And seek *food* out of their ruins.
11 Let the creditor lay a snare for all that he has,
And let strangers plunder his labour.
12 Let him have no one to extend loving-commitment,
Nor any to show favour to his fatherless children.
13 Let his descendants be cut off,
Their name be blotted out in the next generation.
14 Let the crookedness of his fathers
Be remembered before יהוה,
And let not the sin of his mother be blotted out.
15 Let them always be before יהוה,
And let Him cut off their remembrance from the earth;
16 Because he did not remember to show loving-commitment,
But persecuted the poor and needy man;
And the broken-hearted, to put to death.
17 He also loved cursing, so let it come to him;
And he did not delight in blessing, so let it be far from him.
18 And he put cursing on as with his garment,
So let it enter his inward parts like water,
Into his bones and like oil.
19 Let it be to him like a cloak he wraps around him,

108a - See Ber. 49:10 & Teh. 60:7.

And as a girdle that he always girds on.
20 This is the reward of my accusers from
יהוה,
And to those speaking evil against my
being.
21 But You, O יהוה, Master,
Deal with me for Your Name's sake;
Because Your loving-commitment is
good, deliver me.
22 For I am poor and needy,
And my heart is pierced within me.
23 I have gone like a lengthening
shadow,
I have been driven away like a locust.
24 My knees are weak through fasting,
And my flesh grows lean from fatness.
25 And I, I have become a reproach to
them;
They see me, they shake their heads.
26 Help me, O יהוה my Elohim!
Save me according to Your loving-
commitment,
27 And let them know that this is Your
hand.
You, יהוה, You have done it!
28 Let them curse, but You bless.
They shall arise, but be ashamed,
And let Your servant rejoice.
29 Let my accusers put on shame,
And be wrapped in their own
confusion as in a cloak.
30 I greatly thank יהוה with my mouth,
And I praise Him in the midst of the
throng.
31 For He stands at the right hand of the
poor,
To save from those judging his being.

110

יהוה said to my Master,
"Sit at My right hand,
Until I make Your enemies a
footstool for Your feet."
2 יהוה sends Your mighty sceptre out of
Tsiyon.
Rule in the midst of Your enemies!
3 Your people volunteer in the day of
Your might,
In the splendours of set-apartness!
From the womb, from the morning,
You have the dew of Your youth!
4 יהוה has sworn and does not relent,
"You are a priest forever
According to the order of
Malkitseḏeq."
5 יהוה at Your right hand
Shall smite sovereigns in the day of
His wrath.
6 He judges among the nations,
He shall fill *the nations* with dead
bodies,
He shall crush the Head over the
mighty earth!
7 He drinks of the stream by the
wayside,
Therefore He does lift up the head!

111

Aleph Praise Yah! I thank יהוה
with all my heart,
Bět In the company of the straight,
and of the congregation.
2 **Gimel** Great are the works of יהוה,
Dalet Searched for by all who delight
in them.
3 **Hě** Splendour and greatness are His
work,
Waw And His righteousness stands
forever.
4 **Zayin** He has made His wonders to be
remembered;
Ḥet יהוה shows favour and is
compassionate.
5 **Tet** He has given food to those who
fear Him;
Yod He remembers His covenant forever.
6 **Kaph** He has shown His people the
power of His works,
Lamed To give to them the inheritance
of the nations.
7 **Mem** The works of His hands are truth
and right-ruling,
Nun All His orders are trustworthy,
8 **Samek** They are upheld forever and
ever,
Ayin Performed in truth and straightness.
9 **Pě** He sent redemption to His people,
Tsadi He has commanded His
covenant forever.
Qoph Set-apart and awesome is His
Name.
10 **Rěsh** The fear of יהוה is the beginning

of wisdom,
Shin All those doing them have a good understanding.
Taw His praise is standing forever.

112

Aleph Praise Yah!
Blessed is the man,
Who fears יהוה,
Bĕt Who has greatly delighted in His commands.
2 **Gimel** Mighty in the earth shall be his seed,
Dalet The generation of the straight ones shall be blessed.
3 **Hĕ** Wealth and riches are in his house,
Waw And his righteousness is standing forever.
4 **Zayin** Light has risen in the darkness to the straight ones,
Those showing favour,
Ḥet The compassionate,
And the righteous.
5 **Tet** Good is a man showing favour and lending,
Yod He sustains his matters in right-ruling.
6 **Kaph** For he is never shaken;
Lamed The righteous is remembered forever.
7 **Mem** He is not afraid of an evil report.
Nun His heart is steadfast, trusting in יהוה.
8 **Samek̲** His heart is upheld, he is not afraid,
Ayin While he looks on his adversaries.
9 **Pĕ** He scattered abroad,
He gave to the poor,
Tsadi His righteousness is standing forever.
Qoph His horn is exalted with esteem.
10 **Rĕsh** The wrong one sees it and shall be vexed;
Shin He gnashes his teeth and shall melt.
Taw The desire of the wrong ones does perish.

113

Praise Yah!
Praise, O servants of יהוה,
Praise the Name of יהוה!
2 Blessed be the Name of יהוה,
Now and forever!
3 From the rising of the sun to its going down,
The Name of יהוה is praised.
4 יהוה is high above all nations,
His esteem above the heavens.
5 Who is like יהוה our Elohim,
Who is enthroned on high?
6 He looks down on the heavens and in the earth;
7 He raises the poor out of the dust,
Lifts the needy from a dunghill,
8 To make him sit with the nobles,
With the nobles of His people,
9 Causing the barren *woman* to dwell in a house,
A rejoicing mother of children.
Praise Yah!

114

When Yisra'ĕl went out of Mitsrayim,
The house of Ya'aqob̲ from a people of strange language,
2 Yehud̲ah became His set-apart place,
And Yisra'ĕl His rule.
3 The sea saw it and fled;
The Yardĕn turned back.
4 The mountains skipped like rams,
The little hills like lambs.
5 Why was it, O sea, that you fled?
O Yardĕn, that you turned back?
6 O mountains, that you skipped like rams?
O little hills, like lambs?
7 Tremble, O earth,
from the face of the Master,
From the face of the Eloah of Ya'aqob̲,
8 Who turned the rock into a pool of water,
The flint into a fountain of water.

115

Not to us, O יהוה, not to us,
But to Your Name give esteem,
For Your loving-commitment,
For Your truth.
2 Why should the nations say,
"Where now is their Elohim?"
3 But our Elohim is in the heavens;
Whatever pleased Him, He has done.
4 Their idols are silver and gold,

The work of men's hands.
5 They have mouths, but they do not speak;
They have eyes, but they do not see;
6 They have ears, but they do not hear;
They have noses, but they do not smell;
7 They have hands, but they do not handle;
They have feet, but they do not walk;
They make no sound through their throat.
8 The ones who make them, shall become like them –
All who trust in them.
9 O Yisra'ěl, trust in יהוה;
He is their help and their shield.
10 O house of Aharon, trust in יהוה;
He is their help and their shield.
11 You who fear יהוה, trust in יהוה;
He is their help and their shield.
12 יהוה has remembered us;
He blesses us;
He blesses the house of Yisra'ěl;
He blesses the house of Aharon.
13 He blesses those who fear יהוה,
The small and the great.
14 יהוה gives you increase more and more,
You and your children.
15 You are blessed by יהוה,
Who made the heavens and earth.
16 The heavens are the heavens of יהוה;
But He has given the earth to the children of men.
17 The dead do not praise Yah,
Nor any going down to silence.
18 But we, we bless Yah
Now and forever.
Praise Yah!

116 I love יהוה, because He has heard my voice, my pleas.
2 Because He has inclined His ear to me,
And I shall call throughout my days.
3 The cords of death were around me,
And the pains of She'ol came upon me;
I found distress and sorrow.
4 Then I called upon the Name of יהוה,
"O יהוה, I pray to You, deliver my being!"
5 יהוה shows favour and is righteous;
And our Elohim is compassionate.
6 יהוה guards the simple;
I was brought low, but He saved me.
7 Return to your rest, O my being,
For יהוה has treated you well.
8 For You have delivered my being from death,
My eyes from tears,
My feet from falling.
9 I shall walk before יהוה in the land of the living.
10 I have believed, for I speak;
I have been greatly afflicted.
11 I said in my haste, "All men are liars."
12 What shall I return to יהוה?
All His bounties are upon me.
13 I lift up the cup of deliverance,
And call upon the Name of יהוה.
14 I pay my vows to יהוה
Now in the presence of all His people.
15 Precious in the eyes of יהוה
Is the death of His lovingly-committed ones.
16 O יהוה, I am truly Your servant,
I am Your servant, the son of Your female servant;
You have loosed my bonds.
17 I slaughter You a slaughtering of thanksgiving,
And call upon the Name of יהוה.
18 I pay my vows to יהוה
In the presence of all His people,
19 In the courts of the House of יהוה,
In your midst, O Yerushalayim.
Praise Yah!

117 Praise יהוה, all you nations!
Extol Him, all you peoples!
2 For His loving-commitment is mighty over us,
And the truth of יהוה is everlasting.
Praise Yah!

118 Oh, give thanks to יהוה, for He is good!
Because His loving-commitment is everlasting.
2 Let Yisra'ěl now say,
"His loving-commitment is everlasting."
3 Let the house of Aharon now say,

"His loving-commitment is
everlasting."
4 Let those who fear יהוה now say,
"His loving-commitment is
everlasting."
5 I called on Yah in distress;
Yah answered me in a broad place.
6 יהוה is on my side;
I do not fear what man does to me!
7 יהוה is for me among those helping
me;
Therefore I look on those hating me.
8 It is better to take refuge in יהוה
Than to trust in man.
9 It is better to take refuge in יהוה
Than to trust in princes.
10 All the nations surrounded me,
In the Name of יהוה I shall cut them
off.
11 They surrounded me,
Yes, they surrounded me;
In the Name of יהוה shall I cut them
off.
12 They surrounded me like bees;
They were extinguished like burning
thorns;
In the Name of יהוה I shall cut them
off.
13 Pushing, *the enemy* pushed me to fall,
But יהוה helped me.
14 Yah is my strength and song,
And He has become my deliverance. [a]
15 The voice of rejoicing and deliverance
Is in the tents of the righteous;
The right hand of יהוה is doing
mightily.
16 The right hand of יהוה is exalted,
The right hand of יהוה acts mightily.
17 Let me not die, but live,
And declare the works of Yah.
18 Yah has punished me severely,
But did not give me over to death.
19 Open to me the gates of righteousness;
I enter through them, I thank Yah.
20 This is the gate of יהוה,
The righteous enter through it.
21 I thank You,
For You have answered me,
And have become my deliverance.
22 The stone which the builders rejected
Has become the chief corner-stone. [b]
23 This was from יהוה,
It is marvellous in our eyes.
24 This is the day יהוה has made,
Let us rejoice and be glad in it.
25 I pray, O יהוה, please save *us* now; [c]
I pray, O יהוה, please send prosperity.
26 Blessed is He who is coming in the
Name of יהוה! [d]
We shall bless you from the
House of יהוה.
27 יהוה is Ěl, and He gave us light;
Bind the festival *offering*
With cords to the horns of the slaugh-
ter-place.
28 You are my Ěl, and I praise You;
You are my Elohim, I exalt You.
29 Give thanks to יהוה, for He is good!
For His loving-commitment is
everlasting.

119

Aleph Blessed are the perfect
in the way,
Who walk in the Torah of יהוה!
2 Blessed are those who observe His
witnesses,
Who seek Him with all the heart!
3 Yes, they shall do no
unrighteousness;
They shall walk in His ways.
4 You have commanded us
To guard Your orders diligently.
5 Oh, that my ways were established
To guard Your laws!
6 Then I would not be ashamed,
When I look into all Your commands.
7 I thank You with uprightness of heart,
When I learn the right-rulings of Your
righteousness.
8 I guard Your laws;
Oh, do not leave me entirely!
9 **Bět** How would a young man cleanse
his path?
To guard it according to Your word.
10 I have sought You with all my heart;
Let me not stray from Your commands!

118a See footnote at Shem. 15:2. *118b* See also Ma. 4:11. *118c* Hebrew: Hoshianah. *118d* Also see Mt. 21:9, Yoḥ. 12:13 and Deḇ. 18:18-20.

11 I have treasured up Your word in
my heart,
That I might not sin against You.
12 Blessed are You, O יהוה!
Teach me Your laws.
13 With my lips I have recounted
All the right-rulings of Your mouth.
14 I have rejoiced in the way of Your
witnesses,
As over all riches.
15 I meditate on Your orders,
And regard Your ways.
16 I delight [a] myself in Your laws;
I do not forget Your word.
17 **Gimel** Do good to Your servant,
Let me live and I guard Your word.
18 Open my eyes, that I might see
Wonders from Your Torah.
19 I am a sojourner in the earth;
Do not hide Your commands from me.
20 My being is crushed with longing
For Your right-rulings at all times.
21 You rebuked the proud, cursed ones,
Who are straying from Your
commands.
22 Remove from me reproach and scorn,
For I have observed Your witnesses.
23 Though princes sat, speaking against
me,
Your servant meditates on Your laws.
24 Your witnesses also are my delight,
My counsellors.
25 **Dalet** My being has been clinging to
the dust;
Revive me according to Your word.
26 I have recounted my ways and You
answered me;
Teach me Your laws.
27 Make me understand the way of
Your orders;
That I might meditate on
Your wonders.
28 My being has wept from grief;
Strengthen me according to
Your word.
29 Remove from me the way of falsehood,
And favour me with Your Torah.
30 I have chosen the way of truth;
Your right-rulings I have held level.

31 I have clung to Your witnesses;
O יהוה, do not put me to shame!
32 I run the way of Your commands,
For You enlarge my heart.
33 **Hĕ** Teach me, O יהוה, the way of
Your laws,
And I observe it to the end.
34 Make me understand, that I might
observe Your Torah,
And guard it with all my heart.
35 Make me walk in the path of
Your commands,
For I have delighted in it.
36 Incline my heart to Your witnesses,
And not to own gain.
37 Turn away my eyes from looking at
falsehood,
And revive me in Your way.
38 Establish Your word to Your servant,
Which leads to the fear of You.
39 Turn away my reproach which I dread,
For Your right-rulings are good.
40 See, I have longed for Your orders;
Revive me in Your righteousness.
41 **Waw** And let Your loving-commit-
ments come to me, O יהוה;
Your deliverance, according to
Your word,
42 So that I answer my reprover,
For I have trusted in Your word.
43 And do not take away from my mouth
The word of truth entirely,
For I have waited for
Your right-rulings;
44 That I might guard Your Torah
continually,
Forever and ever;
45 That I might walk in a broad place,
For I have sought Your orders;
46 That I might speak of Your witnesses
before sovereigns,
And not be ashamed;
47 That I might delight myse
Your commands,
Which I have loved;
48 That I might lift up my
Your commands,
Which I have loved;
While I meditate on Y

119a See also vv. 24, 35, 47, 70, 77, 92, 143, 174, Rom. 7:22.

49 **Zayin** Remember the word to Your servant,
On which You have caused me to wait.
50 This is my comfort in my affliction,
For Your word has given me life.
51 The proud have utterly scorned me,
I did not turn aside from Your Torah.
52 I remembered Your right-rulings of old, O יהוה,
And I comfort myself.
53 Rage has seized me because of the wrong
Who forsake Your Torah.
54 Your laws have been my songs
In the place of my sojournings.
55 I have remembered Your Name in the night, O יהוה,
And I guard Your Torah.
56 This has become mine,
Because I have observed Your orders.
57 **Ḥet** You are my portion, O יהוה;
I have promised to guard Your words.
58 I have sought Your face with all my heart;
Show me favour according to Your word.
59 I have thought upon my ways,
And turned my feet to Your witnesses.
60 I have hurried, and did not delay
To guard Your commands.
61 The cords of the wrong have surrounded me,
Your Torah I have not forgotten.
62 At midnight I rise to give thanks to You,
For Your righteous right-rulings.
63 I am a companion of all who fear You,
And of those guarding Your orders.
64 O יהוה, Your loving-commitment has filled the earth;
Teach me Your laws.
65 **Tet** You have done good to Your servant, O יהוה,
According to Your word.
66 Teach me good sense and knowledge,
For I have trusted in Your commands.
67 Before I was afflicted I myself was going astray,
But now I have guarded Your word.
68 You are good, and do good;
Teach me Your laws.
69 The proud have forged a lie against me,
With all *my* heart I observe Your orders.
70 Their heart has become like fat,
Without feeling;
I have delighted in Your Torah.
71 It was good for me that I was afflicted,
That I might learn Your laws.
72 The Torah of Your mouth is better to me
Than thousands of gold and silver pieces.
73 **Yod** Your hands have made me and formed me;
Make me understand, that I might learn Your commands.
74 Those who fear You see me and rejoice,
For I have waited for Your Word.
75 I know, O יהוה,
That Your right-rulings are righteous,
And in trustworthiness You have afflicted me.
76 Please let Your loving-commitment be for my comfort,
According to Your word to Your servant.
77 Let Your compassions come to me,
That I might live,
For Your Torah is my delight.
78 Let the proud be put to shame,
For with lies they perverted me;
But I study Your orders.
79 Let those who fear You turn to me,
And those who know Your witnesses.
80 Let my heart be perfect in Your laws,
So that I am not put to shame.
81 **Kaph** For Your deliverance my being has pined away,
For I have waited for Your word.
82 My eyes have pined away for Your word,
Saying, "When would it comfort me?"
83 For I have become like a wineskin in the smoke,
Your laws I have not forgotten.
84 How many are the days of Your servant?
When do You execute right-ruling

On those who persecute me?
85 The proud have dug pits for me,
Which is not according to
Your Torah.
86 All Your commands are trustworthy;
They have persecuted me with lies;
Help me!
87 They almost made an end of me on
earth,
But I, I did not forsake Your orders.
88 Revive me according to Your loving-
commitment,
That I might guard the witness of
Your mouth.
89 **Lamed** Forever, O יהוה, Your word
stands firm in the heavens.
90 Your trustworthiness is to all
generations;
You established the earth,
and it stands.
91 According to Your right-rulings
They have stood to this day,
For all are Your servants.
92 If Your Torah had not been my delight,
I would have perished in my affliction.
93 Let me never forget Your orders,
For by them You have given me life.
94 I am Yours, save me;
For I have sought Your orders.
95 The wrong have waited for me to
destroy me;
I understand Your witnesses.
96 I have seen an end of all perfection;
Your command is exceedingly broad.
97 **Mem** O how I love [b] Your Torah!
It is my study all day long.
98 Your commands make me wiser
than my enemies;
For it is ever before me.
99 I have more understanding
than all my teachers,
For Your witnesses are my study.
100 I understand more than the aged,
For I have observed Your orders.
101 I have restrained my feet from every
evil way,
That I might guard Your word.
102 I have not turned aside from
Your right-rulings,
For You Yourself have taught me.
103 How sweet to my taste has
Your word been,
More than honey to my mouth!
104 From Your orders I get understanding;
Therefore I have hated every false way.
105 **Nun** Your word is a lamp to my feet
And a light to my path.
106 I have sworn, and I confirm,
To guard Your righteous right-rulings.
107 I have been afflicted very much;
O יהוה, revive me according to
Your word.
108 Please accept the voluntary offerings
Of my mouth, O יהוה,
And teach me Your right-rulings.
109 My life is in my hand continually,
And Your Torah I have not forgotten.
110 The wrong have laid a snare for me,
But I have not strayed from
Your orders.
111 Your witnesses are my inheritance
forever,
For they are the joy of my heart.
112 I have inclined my heart to do
Your laws
Forever, to the end.
113 **Samek** I have hated doubting thoughts,
But I have loved Your Torah.
114 You are my hiding place
and my shield;
I have waited for Your word.
115 Turn away from me, you evil-doers,
For I observe the commands of my
Elohim!
116 Support me according to Your word,
That I might live;
And put me not to shame
Because of my expectation.
117 Sustain me, that I might be saved,
And always look to Your laws.
118 You have made light of all those
Who stray from Your laws,
For falsehood is their deceit.
119 You have made to cease
All the wrong of the earth, like dross;
Therefore I have loved Your witnesses.
120 My flesh has trembled for fear of You,
And I am in awe of Your right-rulings.

119b See also vv. 113, 119, 127, 163, 165, 167.

121 **Ayin** I have done right-ruling and
righteousness;
Leave me not to my oppressors.
122 Guarantee Your servant's well-being;
Let not the proud oppress me.
123 My eyes have pined away for
Your deliverance,
And for the word of
Your righteousness.
124 Do with Your servant according to
Your loving-commitment,
And teach me Your laws.
125 I am Your servant – make me
understand,
That I might know Your witnesses.
126 It is time for יהוה to act!
For they have broken Your Torah.
127 Therefore I have loved
Your commands
More than gold, even fine gold!
128 Therefore all *Your* orders I count as
right;
I have hated every false way.
129 **Pě** Your witnesses are wonders;
So my being observes them.
130 The opening up of Your words
gives light,
Giving understanding to the simple.
131 I have opened my mouth and panted,
For I have longed for Your commands.
132 Turn to me and show me favour,
According to Your right-ruling, toward
those who love Your Name.
133 Establish my footsteps by Your word,
And let no wickedness have rule
over me.
134 Redeem me from the oppression
of man,
That I might guard Your orders.
135 Make Your face shine upon Your
servant,
And teach me Your laws.
136 Streams of water have run down from
my eyes,
Because they did not guard
Your Torah.
137 **Tsadi** Righteous are You, O יהוה,
And Your right-rulings are straight.
138 You have commanded Your witnesses
In righteousness and truth,
exceedingly.
139 My ardour has consumed me,
For my adversaries have forgotten
Your words.
140 Your word is tried, exceedingly;
And Your servant has loved it.
141 I am small and despised;
I have not forgotten Your orders.
142 Your righteousness is righteousness
forever,
And Your Torah is truth.
143 Distress and anguish have found me;
Your commands are my delight.
144 The righteousness of Your witnesses
is forever;
Make me understand, that I might live.
145 **Qoph** I have called with all my heart;
Answer me, O יהוה!
I observe Your laws.
146 I have called upon You;
Save me, that I might guard
Your witnesses.
147 I rise before dawn, and cry for help;
I have waited for Your word.
148 My eyes have gone before the night
watches,
To study Your word.
149 Hear my voice according to
Your loving-commitment;
O יהוה, revive me according to
Your right-ruling.
150 Those who pursue mischief have
drawn near;
They have been far from
Your Torah.
151 You are near, O יהוה,
And all Your commands are truth.
152 Of old I have known Your witnesses,
That You have founded them forever.
153 **Rěsh** See my affliction and deliver me,
For I have not forgotten Your Torah.
154 Plead my cause and redeem me;
Revive me according to Your word.
155 Deliverance is far from the
wrong ones,
For they have not sought Your laws.
156 Your compassions are many, O יהוה;
Revive me according to
Your right-rulings.
157 My persecutors and adversaries
are many;
I have not turned aside from

Your witnesses.
158 I saw traitors and was grieved,
Because they did not guard Your word.
159 See how I have loved Your orders,
יהוה, revive me according to
Your loving-commitment.
160 The sum of Your word is truth,
And all Your righteous right-rulings
are forever.
161 **Shin** Rulers have persecuted me
without a cause,
But at Your word my heart
stood in awe.
162 I rejoice at Your word
As one who finds great treasure.
163 I have hated falsehood and loathe it,
Your Torah I have loved.
164 I have praised You seven times a day,
Because of Your righteous
right-rulings.
165 Great peace have those loving
Your Torah,
And for them there is no
stumbling-block.
166 יהוה, I have waited for
Your deliverance,
And I have done Your commands.
167 My being has guarded Your witnesses,
And I love them exceedingly.
168 I have guarded
Your orders and Your witnesses,
For all my ways are before You.
169 **Taw** My cry comes before You, O
יהוה;
Make me understand according to Your
word.
170 Let my prayer come before You;
Deliver me according to Your word.
171 My lips pour forth praise,
For You teach me Your laws.
172 My tongue sings of Your word,
For all Your commands are
righteousness.
173 Your hand is a help to me,
For I have chosen Your orders.
174 I have longed for Your deliverance,
O יהוה,
And Your Torah is my delight.
175 My being lives, and it praises You;
And Your right-rulings help me.
176 I have strayed like a lost sheep;
Seek Your servant,
For I have not forgotten
Your commands.

120

In my distress I cried to יהוה,
And He answered me.
2 יהוה, deliver my being from false lips,
From a treacherous tongue.
3 What would one give to you,
Or what would one do to you,
O treacherous tongue?
4 Sharp arrows of a mighty man,
With coals of the broom-wood!
5 Woe to me for I have sojourned in
Meshek̲,
I have dwelt among the tents of Qĕd̲ar!
6 My being has dwelt too long
With him who hates peace.
7 I am *for* peace;
But when I speak, they are for fighting.

121

I lift up my eyes to the hills;
Where does my help come
from?
2 My help comes from יהוה,
Maker of the heavens and earth.
3 He does not allow your foot to be
moved;
He who watches over you does not
slumber.
4 See, He who is guarding Yisra'ĕl
Neither slumbers nor sleeps.
5 יהוה is your guard;
יהוה is your shade at your right hand.
6 The sun does not strike you by day,
Nor the moon by night.
7 יהוה guards you from all evil;
He guards your being.
8 יהוה guards your going out and your
coming in
Now and forever.

122

I was glad when they said to
me, "Let us go into the House
of יהוה."
2 Our feet have been standing
Within your gates, O Yerushalayim!
3 Yerushalayim is built
As a city that is bound together,
4 Where the tribes have come up,
The tribes of Yah,

A witness to Yisra'ěl,
To give thanks to the Name of יהוה.
5 For there the thrones of right-ruling were set,
The thrones of the house of Dawiḏ.
6 Pray for the peace of Yerushalayim,
Let those who love You be at rest.
7 Peace be within your walls,
Rest in your citadels.
8 For the sake of my brothers and companions,
I say, "Peace be within you."
9 For the sake of the House of יהוה our Elohim
I seek your good.

123

I shall lift up my eyes
Unto You who dwell in the heavens.
2 See, as the eyes of servants
Are toward the hand of their masters,
As the eyes of a female servant
Are toward the hand of her mistress,
So are our eyes toward יהוה our Elohim,
Until He shows favour to us.
3 Show favour to us,
O יהוה, show favour to us!
For we are exceedingly filled with mockery.
4 Our being is exceedingly filled
With the scoffing of those who are at ease,
With the mockery of the proud.

124

"If it had not been יהוה who was on our side,"
Let Yisra'ěl now say;
2 "If it had not been יהוה who was on our side,
When men rose up against us,
3 "Then they would have swallowed us alive,
In their burning rage against us;
4 "Then the waters would have overwhelmed us,
The stream would have gone over our being;
5 "Then the proud waters
Would have gone over our being."
6 Blessed be יהוה,
Who did not give us as prey to their teeth.
7 Our being has escaped like a bird
From the snare of the trappers;
The snare was broken, and we have escaped.
8 Our help is in the Name of יהוה,
Maker of the heavens and earth.

125

Those who trust in יהוה
Are like Mount Tsiyon –
It is not shaken, it remains forever.
2 As the mountains surround Yerushalayim,
So יהוה surrounds His people,
Now and forever.
3 For the sceptre of wrongness shall not rest
On the land allotted to the righteous,
Lest the righteous stretch forth their hands to unrighteousness.
4 Do good, O יהוה, to those who are good,
And to those who are upright in their hearts.
5 But those who turn aside to their crooked ways,
יהוה shall lead them away
With the workers of wickedness.
Peace be upon Yisra'ěl!

126

When יהוה turns back the captivity of Tsiyon,
We shall be like dreamers.
2 Then our mouth shall be filled with laughter,
And our tongue with singing,
Then shall they say among the nations,
"יהוה has done great *deeds* for them."
3 יהוה shall do great *deeds* for us,
We shall be glad.
4 Turn back our captivity, O יהוה,
Like the streams in the South.
5 Those sowing in tears,
shall reap with songs of joy.
6 He who goes on and weeps,
Bearing seed for sowing,
Shall indeed come in with rejoicing,
Bearing his sheaves.

127 If יהוה does not build the house,
Its builders have laboured in vain.
If יהוה does not guard the city,
The watchman has stayed awake in vain.
2 In vain do you rise up early,
To sit up late, to eat the bread of toil;
So He gives His beloved sleep.
3 Look, children are an inheritance from יהוה,
The fruit of the womb is the reward.
4 As arrows in the hand of a mighty man,
So are the children of one's youth.
5 Blessed is the man
Who has filled his quiver with them.
They are not ashamed,
When they speak with their enemies in the gate.

128 Blessed are all who fear יהוה,
Who walk in His ways.
2 You shall eat the labour of your hands.
Be blessed, and let it be well with you.
3 Let your wife be
As a fruit-bearing vine within your house,
Your sons like olive plants all around your table.
4 Look, so shall the man be blessed
Who fears יהוה.
5 יהוה shall bless you out of Tsiyon,
And let you see the good of Yerushalayim
All the days of your life,
6 And let you see your children's children!
Peace be upon Yisra'ĕl!

129 "Often they have distressed me from my youth."
Let Yisra'ĕl now say,
2 "Often they have distressed me from my youth,
But they have not overcome me.
3 "The ploughers ploughed on my back,
They made their furrows long."
4 יהוה is righteous,
He has cut the cords of the wrong in two.
5 Let all those who hate Tsiyon
Be put to shame and turned back.
6 Let them be as the grass on the house-tops,
Which withers before it grows up,
7 That shall not fill the reaper's hand,
Nor the sheaves *fill* the binder's bosom.
8 And those who pass by shall not say,
"The blessing of יהוה be upon you;
We have blessed you in the Name of יהוה!"

130 Out of the depths I have cried to You, O יהוה.
2 O יהוה, hear my voice!
Let Your ears be attentive
To the voice of my prayers.
3 O Yah, if You should watch crookednesses,
O יהוה, who would stand?
4 But with You there is forgiveness,
That You might be feared.
5 I looked to יהוה,
My being has looked,
And for His word I have waited.
6 My being *looks* to יהוה
More than those watching for morning, watching for morning.
7 O Yisra'ĕl, wait for יהוה;
For with יהוה there is loving-commitment.
And with Him is much redemption,
8 For He shall redeem Yisra'ĕl
From all his crookednesses.

131 O יהוה, my heart has not been proud,
Nor have my eyes been haughty.
Neither have I concerned myself with great matters,
Nor with those too wondrous for me.
2 Have I not calmed, and kept my being silent,
Like one weaned by its mother?
My being is like one weaned.
3 O Yisra'ĕl, wait for יהוה,
Now and forever.

132 O יהוה, remember Dawiḏ,
All his afflictions;

2 How he swore to יהוה,
Vowed to the Mighty One of Ya'aqoḇ:
3 "Not to enter into my dwelling-house,
Not to get into my bed,
4 "Not to give sleep to my eyes,
Or slumber to my eyelids,
5 "Until I find a place for יהוה,
A dwelling place for the Mighty One
of Ya'aqoḇ."
6 See, we heard of it in Ephrathah;
We found it in the fields of the forest.
7 Let us go into His dwelling places;
Let us bow ourselves at His footstool.
8 Arise, O יהוה, to Your place of rest,
You and the ark of Your strength.
9 Let Your priests put on righteousness,
And Your lovingly-committed ones
shout for joy.
10 For the sake of Your servant Dawiḏ,
Do not turn away the face of Your
Anointed One.
11 יהוה has sworn in truth to Dawiḏ;
He does not turn from it,
"Of the fruit of your body I set upon
your throne.
12 "If your sons guard My covenant
And My witnesses that I teach them,
Their sons shall sit upon your throne
forever."
13 For יהוה has chosen Tsiyon,
He has desired it for His dwelling:
14 "This is My place of rest forever;
Here I dwell, for I have desired it.
15 "I greatly bless her provision,
I satisfy her poor with bread.
16 "And I put deliverance on her priests,
And her lovingly-committed ones sing
for joy.
17 "There I make the horn of Dawiḏ
grow;
I shall set up a lamp for My
Anointed One.
18 "I put shame on his enemies,
While on Him His diadem shall shine."

133 See how good and how pleasant it is for brothers to dwell
together in unity –
2 Like the precious oil on the head,
Running down on the beard,
The beard of Aharon,
Running down on the collar of his
robes –
3 Like the dew of Ḥermon,
That comes down on the mountains of
Tsiyon.
For there יהוה commanded the
blessing,
Life forever!

134 Come, bless יהוה,
All you servants of יהוה,
Who are standing in the House of
יהוה by night!
2 Lift up your hands in the set-apart
place,
And bless יהוה.
3 יהוה, Maker of the heavens and earth,
Does bless you from Tsiyon!

135 Praise Yah!
Praise the Name of יהוה;
Praise, you servants of יהוה,
2 Who are standing in the House of יהוה,
In the courts of the House of our
Elohim,
3 Praise Yah, for יהוה is good;
Sing praises to His Name, for it is
pleasant.
4 For Yah has chosen Ya'aqoḇ for
Himself,
Yisra'ěl for His treasured possession.
5 For I know that יהוה is great,
And our Master is above all mighty
ones.
6 יהוה has done whatever pleased Him,
In the heavens and in earth,
In the seas and in all the depths,
7 Causing vapours to go up
From the ends of the earth;
He made lightning for the rain,
Bringing forth wind from His
treasuries;
8 Who struck the first-born of
Mitsrayim,
From man to beast.
9 He sent signs and wonders
Into your midst, O Mitsrayim,
On Pharaoh and on all his servants;
10 Who struck many nations,
And killed mighty sovereigns,
11 Even Siḥon sovereign of the Amorites,

And Oḡ sovereign of Bashan,
And all the reigns of Kenaʽan.
12 And He gave their land as an inheritance,
An inheritance to Yisra'ěl His people.
13 O יהוה, Your Name is forever,
O יהוה, Your remembrance to all generations,
14 For יהוה rightly rules His people,
And has compassion on His servants.
15 The idols of the nations are silver and gold,
The work of men's hands.
16 They have mouths, but they do not speak;
They have eyes, but they do not see;
17 They have ears, but they do not hear;
Also there is no breath in their mouth.
18 Those making them become like them,
Everyone who is trusting in them.
19 Bless יהוה, O house of Yisra'ěl!
Bless יהוה, O house of Aharon!
20 Bless יהוה, O house of Lěwi!
You who fear יהוה, bless יהוה!
21 Blessed from Tsiyon, יהוה be,
Who dwells in Yerushalayim!
Praise Yah.

136

Give thanks to יהוה, for He is good!
For His loving-commitment is everlasting.
2 Give thanks to the Elohim of mighty ones!
For His loving-commitment is everlasting.
3 Give thanks to the Master of masters!
For His loving-commitment is everlasting:
4 To Him who alone does great wonders,
For His loving-commitment is everlasting;
5 To Him who by wisdom made the heavens,
For His loving-commitment is everlasting;
6 To Him who spread the earth on the waters,
For His loving-commitment is everlasting;
7 To Him who made great lights,
For His loving-commitment is everlasting;
8 The sun to rule by day,
For His loving-commitment is everlasting;
9 The moon and stars to rule by night,
For His loving-commitment is everlasting.
10 To Him who struck Mitsrayim in their first-born,
For His loving-commitment is everlasting;
11 And brought out Yisra'ěl from their midst,
For His loving-commitment is everlasting;
12 With a strong hand, and with an outstretched arm,
For His loving-commitment is everlasting;
13 To Him who split apart the Sea of Reeds,
For His loving-commitment is everlasting;
14 And made Yisra'ěl pass through the midst of it,
For His loving-commitment is everlasting;
15 But shook off Pharaoh and his army in the Sea of Reeds,
For His loving-commitment is everlasting;
16 To Him who led His people through the wilderness,
For His loving-commitment is everlasting;
17 To Him who struck great sovereigns,
For His loving-commitment is everlasting;
18 And killed mighty sovereigns,
For His loving-commitment is everlasting;
19 Even Siḥon sovereign of the Amorites,
For His loving-commitment is everlasting;
20 And Oḡ sovereign of Bashan,
For His loving-commitment is everlasting;
21 And gave their land as an inheritance,
For His loving-commitment is everlasting;

22 An inheritance to Yisra'ěl His servant,
For His loving-commitment is everlasting.
23 Who remembered us in our humiliation,
For His loving-commitment is everlasting;
24 And rescued us from our adversaries,
For His loving-commitment is everlasting;
25 Who gives food to all flesh,
For His loving-commitment is everlasting.
26 Give thanks to the Ěl of the heavens!
For His loving-commitment is everlasting.

137 By the rivers of Baḇel,
There we sat down and we wept
As we remembered Tsiyon.
2 We hung our lyres
Upon the willows in the midst of it.
3 For there our captors
Asked us for the words of a song,
And our plunderers for rejoicing, *saying*,
"Sing to us a song of Tsiyon!"
4 How could we sing the song of יהוה
On foreign soil?
5 If I forget you, O Yerushalayim,
Let my right hand forget.
6 Let my tongue cleave to my palate,
If I do not remember you,
If I do not exalt Yerushalayim
Above my chief joy.
7 Remember, O יהוה, against the sons of Eḏom
The day of Yerushalayim,
Who said, "Lay it bare, lay it bare,
To its foundation!"
8 O daughter of Baḇel, who are to be destroyed,
Blessed is he who repays you your deed,
What you did to us!
9 Blessed is he who shall take
And dash your little ones against the rock.

138 I give You thanks with all my heart;
Before the mighty ones
I sing praises to You.
2 I bow myself toward Your set-apart Hěḵal,
And give thanks to Your Name
For Your loving-commitment and for Your truth;
For You have made great Your Word, Your Name, above all.
3 On the day I called You did answer me,
You made me bold with strength in my being.
4 Let all the sovereigns of the earth
Give thanks to You, O יהוה,
When they shall hear the words of Your mouth.
5 And let them sing of the ways of יהוה,
For great is the esteem of יהוה.
6 Though יהוה is exalted,
He looks on the humble;
But the proud He perceives from a distance.
7 Though I walk in the midst of distress,
You revive me;
You stretch out Your hand
Against the wrath of my enemies,
And Your right hand saves me.
8 יהוה does perfect for me.
O יהוה, Your loving-commitment is everlasting.
Do not forsake the works of Your hands.

139 O יהוה, You have searched me
And know me.
2 You know my sitting down and my rising up;
You understand my thought from afar.
3 You sift my path and my lying down,
And know well all my ways.
4 For there is not a word on my tongue,
But see, O יהוה, You know it all!
5 You have closed me in, behind and before,
And laid Your hand upon me –
6 Knowledge too wondrous for me,
It is high, I am unable to *reach* it.
7 Where would I go from Your Spirit?
Or where would I flee from Your face?
8 If I go up into the heavens, You are there;

If I make my bed in She'ol, see,
You are there.
9 I take the wings of the morning,
I dwell in the uttermost parts of the sea,
10 There, too, Your hand would lead me,
And Your right hand hold me.
11 If I say, "Darkness shall cover me,"
Then night would be light to me;
12 Even darkness is not dark for You,
But night shines as the day –
As is darkness, so is light.
13 For You, You possessed my kidneys,
You have covered me in my mother's womb.
14 I give thanks to You,
For I am awesomely and wondrously made!
Wondrous are Your works,
And my being knows it well.
15 My bones were not concealed from You,
When I was shaped in a hidden place,
Knit together in the depths of the earth.
16 Your eyes saw my unformed body.
And in Your book all of them were written,
The days they were formed,
While none was among them.
17 And how precious are Your thoughts to me, O Ěl!
How great has been the sum of them!
18 If I should count them,
They would be more than the sand;
When I wake up, I am still with You.
19 Oh, that You would kill the wrong,
O Eloah!
Depart from me, therefore,
men of bloodshed!
20 They speak against You wickedly.
Bring Your enemies to naught!
21 O יהוה, do I not hate them,
who hate You?
And do I not loathe those who rise up against You?
22 With a complete hatred I hate them;
They have become my enemies.
23 Search me, O Ěl, and know my heart;
Try me, and know my thoughts;
24 And see if an idolatrous way is in me,
And lead me in the way everlasting.

140

Rescue me, O יהוה,
from men of evil;
Preserve me from men of violence,
2 Who have devised evils in their hearts;
They stir up conflicts all day long.
3 They sharpen their tongues like a snake;
The poison of cobras is under their lips. Selah.
4 Guard me, O יהוה, from the hands of the wrong;
Guard me from a man of violence,
Who have schemed to trip up my steps.
5 The proud have hidden a trap for me, and cords;
They have spread a net by the wayside;
They have set snares for me. Selah.
6 I said to יהוה, "You are my Ěl;
Hear the voice of my prayers, O יהוה.
7 "O Master יהוה, my saving strength,
You have screened my head in the day of battle.
8 "Do not grant the desires of the wrong, O יהוה;
Do not promote his scheme. Selah.
9 "Those who surround me lift up their head;
The trouble of their lips cover them;
10 "Let burning coals fall on them;
Let them be made to fall into the fire,
Into deep pits, let them not rise again.
11 "Let not a slanderer be established in the earth;
Let evil hunt the man of violence speedily."
12 I have known that יהוה maintains
The cause of the afflicted,
The right-ruling of the poor.
13 Only, let the righteous give thanks to Your Name,
Let the straight ones dwell in Your presence.

141

יהוה, I have cried out to You;
Hasten to me!
Give ear to my voice when
I cry out to You.
2 Let my prayer be prepared before You as incense,
The lifting up of my hands as the evening offering.

3 O יהוה, set a guard for my mouth;
Watch over the door of my lips.
4 Let not my heart be inclined to evil,
To practise deeds of wrongness
With men working wickedness,
And let me not eat of their delicacies.
5 Let the righteous one smite me
Or reprove me in loving-commitment –
It is oil on my head.
Let my head not refuse it.
My prayer is still against their evil deeds.
6 Their judges have been thrown down
By the sides of the rock,
But they have heard my words,
For they have been pleasant.
7 Our bones are scattered at the mouth of She'ol,
As when one ploughs and breaks up the earth.
8 But my eyes are upon You,
O Master יהוה.
In You I take refuge;
Do not pour out my life.
9 Guard me from the clutches
Of the trap they have laid for me,
And from the snares
Of the workers of wickedness.
10 Let the wrong fall into their own nets,
While I pass by.

142

I cry out to יהוה with my voice;
I pray to יהוה with my voice.
2 I pour out my complaint before Him;
I declare before Him my distress.
3 When my spirit grew faint within me,
Then You know my path.
In the way in which I walk
They have hidden a trap for me.
4 Look to the right hand and see,
And no one is concerned for me;
No refuge remains to me;
No one inquires after my being.
5 I cried out to You, O יהוה:
I said, "You are my refuge,
My portion in the land of the living.
6 "Listen to my cry,
For I am brought very low;
Deliver me from my persecutors,
For they are too strong for me.
7 "Bring my being out of prison,
To give thanks to Your Name.
Let the righteous gather around me,
Because You deal kindly with me."

143

Hear my prayer, O יהוה,
Give ear to my pleadings
In Your trustworthiness.
Answer me in Your righteousness.
2 And do not enter into right-ruling with Your servant,
For before You no one living is in the right.
3 For the enemy has pursued my being;
He has crushed my life to the ground;
He has made me dwell in dark places,
Like the dead of old.
4 Therefore my spirit grew faint within me,
My heart within me is stunned.
5 I remembered the days of old;
I meditated on all Your works;
I ponder on the work of Your hands.
6 I have spread out my hands to You;
My being is like a thirsty land for You. Selah.
7 Hasten, answer me, O יהוה;
My spirit fails! Do not hide Your face from me,
Lest I be like those going down into the pit.
8 Let me hear Your loving-commitment in the morning,
For in You I have put my trust;
Let me know the way in which I should walk,
For I have lifted up my being to You.
9 Deliver me from my enemies, O יהוה;
I take refuge in You.
10 Teach me to do Your good pleasure,
For You are my Elohim.
Let Your good Spirit lead me
In the land of straightness.
11 For the sake of Your Name,
O יהוה, revive me!
In Your righteousness,
Bring my being out of distress.
12 And in Your loving-commitment,
Cut off my enemies.
And destroy all the adversaries of my life,
For I am Your servant!

144 Blessed be יהוה my Rock,
Who is teaching my hands for fighting,
My fingers for battle;
2 My loving-commitment and my stronghold,
My tower and my deliverer,
My shield, and in whom I take refuge,
Who is subduing peoples under me.
3 יהוה, what is man, that You should know him?
Son of man, that You should think of him?
4 Man is like a breath,
His days like a passing shadow.
5 Incline Your heavens, O יהוה, and come down;
Touch the mountains that they smoke.
6 Send forth lightning and scatter them,
Send forth Your arrows and confuse them.
7 Send forth Your hand from above;
Rescue me and deliver me out of great waters,
From the hand of foreigners,
8 Whose mouth has spoken falsehood,
And whose right hand is a right hand of lies.
9 O Elohim, a new song I sing to You;
On a harp of ten strings I sing praises to You,
10 Who gives deliverance to sovereigns,
Who rescues Dawiḏ His servant
From the evil sword.
11 Rescue me and deliver me from the hand of foreigners,
Whose mouth has spoken falsehood,
And whose right hand is a right hand of lies;
12 Because our sons are like plants
Grown up in their youth;
Our daughters like hewn stones,
Polished, like a palace building;
13 Let our storehouses be filled,
Supplying all kinds;
Let our sheep bring forth thousands
And ten thousands in our fields;
14 Our cattle well-laden;
No breaking in, no going out;
And no crying in our streets.
15 Blessed are the people who have it so;
Blessed are the people
whose Elohim is יהוה!

145 I exalt You, my Elohim, O Sovereign;
And bless Your Name
forever and ever.
2 All day long I bless You,
And praise Your Name forever and ever.
3 Great is יהוה, and greatly to be praised;
And His greatness is unsearchable.
4 Generation after generation praise Your works,
And they declare Your mighty acts.
5 I declare the esteemed splendour of Your excellency,
And the matters of Your wondrous works.
6 And they speak of the might of Your awesome acts,
And I recount Your greatness.
7 They send forth the remembrance of Your great goodness,
And they sing of Your righteousness.
8 יהוה shows favour and is compassionate,
Patient and great in loving-commitment.
9 יהוה is good to all,
And He has compassion on all His works.
10 All Your works give thanks to You, O יהוה,
And Your lovingly-committed ones bless You.
11 They speak of the esteem of Your reign,
And talk of Your might,
12 To make known to the sons of men His mighty acts,
And the esteemed splendour of His reign.
13 Your reign is an everlasting reign,
And Your rule is throughout all generations.
14 יהוה is supporting all who are falling,
And raising up all who are bowed down.
15 The eyes of all look to You

expectantly,
And You are giving them their food in its season,
16 Opening Your hand and satisfying
The desire of all that live.
17 יהוה is righteous in all His ways,
And lovingly-committed in all His works.
18 יהוה is near to all who call upon Him,
To all who call upon Him in truth.
19 He does the desire of those who fear Him;
And He hears their cry and saves them.
20 יהוה preserves all those loving Him,
But all the wrong ones He destroys.
21 My mouth speaks the praise of יהוה,
And let all flesh bless
His set-apart Name,
Forever and ever.

146 Praise Yah!
Praise יהוה, O my being!
2 While I live I praise יהוה;
I sing praises to my Elohim while I exist.
3 Do not put your trust in princes,
In a son of man, in whom is no deliverance.
4 His spirit goes out, he returns to his earth;
In that day his plans perish.
5 Blessed is he who has the Ěl of Ya'aqoḇ for his help,
Whose expectancy is in יהוה his Elohim,
6 Maker of the heavens and earth,
The sea and all that is in them,
Who is guarding truth forever,
7 Doing right-ruling for the oppressed,
Giving bread to the hungry.
יהוה releases those who are bound,
8 יהוה opens *the eyes of* the blind,
יהוה raises those who are bowed down,
יהוה loves the righteous.
9 יהוה guards the strangers,
He lifts up the fatherless and widow,
But the way of the wrong ones
He turns upside down.
10 יהוה reigns forever, O Tsiyon,
Your Elohim to all generations.
Praise Yah!

147 Praise Yah!
For it is good to sing praises to our Elohim.
For it is pleasant – praise is fitting.
2 יהוה builds up Yerushalayim,
He gathers the outcasts of Yisra'ěl –
3 *He* heals the broken-hearted
And binds up their wounds.
4 *He* appoints the number of the stars,
He gives names to all of them.
5 Great is our Master and mighty in power,
There is no limit to His understanding.
6 יהוה lifts up the meek ones,
He throws the wrong ones down to the ground.
7 Respond to יהוה with thanksgiving;
Sing praises on a lyre to our Elohim,
8 Who covers the heavens with clouds,
Who prepares rain for the earth,
Who makes grass to sprout on the mountains,
9 Giving to the beast its food,
To the young ravens that cry.
10 He does not delight in the strength of the horse,
He takes no pleasure in the legs of a man.
11 יהוה takes pleasure in those who fear Him,
In those who wait for His loving-commitment.
12 Extol יהוה, O Yerushalayim!
Praise your Elohim, O Tsiyon!
13 For He has strengthened the bars of your gates,
He has blessed your children in your midst,
14 Who makes peace in your borders,
He satisfies you with the finest wheat;
15 Who sends out His command to the earth,
His word runs very speedily;
16 Who gives snow like wool,
He scatters the frost like ashes;
17 Throwing out His hail like pieces;
Who does stand before His cold?
18 He sends out His word and melts them,
He causes His wind to blow – the

waters flow;
19 Declaring His Word to Ya'aqoḇ,
His laws and His right-rulings to Yisra'ěl. [a]
20 He has not done so with any nation;
And they have not known *His* right-rulings! Praise Yah!

148

Praise Yah!
Praise יהוה from the heavens,
Praise Him in the heights!
2 Praise Him, all His messengers;
Praise Him, all His hosts!
3 Praise Him, sun and moon;
Praise Him, all you stars of light!
4 Praise Him, heavens of heavens,
And you waters above the heavens!
5 Let them praise the Name of יהוה,
For He commanded
and they were created.
6 And He established them
forever and ever,
He gave a law and they pass not beyond.
7 Praise יהוה from the earth,
You great sea creatures and all the depths,
8 Fire and hail, snow and clouds,
Stormy wind that does His word,
9 The mountains and all hills,
Fruit tree and all cedars,
10 Wild beasts and all cattle,
Creeping creatures and flying birds,
11 Sovereigns of the earth and all peoples,
Rulers and all judges of the earth,
12 Both young men and maidens,
Old men and children.
13 Let them praise the Name of יהוה,
For His Name alone is exalted,
His splendour is above the earth and heavens.
14 He also lifts up the horn of His people,
The praise of all His lovingly-committed ones;
Of the children of Yisra'ěl,
A people near to Him. Praise Yah!

149

Praise Yah!
Sing to יהוה a new song,
His praise in an assembly of lovingly-committed ones.
2 Let Yisra'ěl rejoice in their Maker;
Let the children of Tsiyon exult in their Sovereign.
3 Let them praise His Name in a dance;
Let them sing praises to Him with the tambourine and lyre.
4 For יהוה takes pleasure in His people;
He embellishes the meek ones with deliverance.
5 Let the lovingly-committed ones exult in esteem;
Let them sing aloud on their beds.
6 Let the exaltation of Ěl be in their mouth,
And a two-edged sword in their hand,
7 To execute vengeance on the nations,
Punishments on the peoples;
8 To bind their sovereigns with chains,
And their nobles with iron bands;
9 To execute on them the written right-ruling;
A splendour it is for all His lovingly-committed ones. Praise Yah!

150

Praise Yah!
Praise Ěl in His set-apart place;
Praise Him in His mighty expanse!
2 Praise Him for His mighty acts;
Praise Him according to His excellent greatness!
3 Praise Him with the blowing of a shophar;
Praise Him with the harp and lyre!
4 Praise Him with tambourine and dance;
Praise Him with stringed instruments and flutes!
5 Praise Him with sounding cymbals;
Praise Him with resounding cymbals!
6 Let all that have breath praise Yah.
Praise Yah!

147a See also Rom. 2:20, 3:2, and 9:4.

MISHLĚ

PROVERBS

1 The proverbs of Shelomoh son of
Dawiḏ, sovereign of Yisra'ěl:
2 For knowing wisdom and discipline,
For understanding the words of
understanding,
3 For receiving the discipline of wisdom,
Righteousness, right-ruling, and
straightness;
4 For giving insight to the simple,
Knowledge and discretion to the
young.
5 The wise one hears and increases
learning,
And the understanding one gets wise
counsel,
6 For understanding a proverb and a
figure,
The words of the wise and their
riddles.
7 The fear of יהוה is the beginning of
knowledge; [a]
Fools despise wisdom and discipline.
8 My son, heed the discipline of your
father,
And do not forsake the Torah of your
mother;
9 For they are a fair wreath on your head,
And chains about your neck.
10 My son, if sinners entice you,
do not give in.
11 If they say, "Come with us, let us lie in
wait for blood,
Let us ambush the innocent without
cause.
12 "Let us swallow them alive like She'ol,
And entirely, like those going down to
the pit.
13 "Let us find all precious goods,
Let us fill our houses with spoil.
14 "Cast in your lot among us,
Let us all have one purse,"
15 My son, do not walk in the way
with them,
Keep your foot from their path;
16 For their feet run to evil,
And they hurry to shed blood.
17 For in vain the net is spread
In the sight of any bird.
18 But they lie in wait for their own
blood,
They ambush their own lives.
19 Such are the ways of everyone greedy
for gain;
It takes away the life of its owners.
20 Wisdom calls aloud outside;
She raises her voice in the broad
places.
21 At the head of the noisy streets she
cries out,
At the openings of the gates,
In the city she speaks her words:
22 "How long, you simple ones,
Would you love simplicity,
And shall scoffers delight in their
scoffing,
And fools hate knowledge?
23 "Turn at my reproof.
See, I pour out my spirit on you,
I make my words known to you. [b]
24 "Because I called and you refused,
I have stretched out my hand and no
one inclined,
25 "And you spurned all my counsel,
And would not yield to my reproof,
26 "Let me also laugh at your calamity,
Mock when your dread comes,
27 "When your dread comes like a storm,
And your calamity comes like a
whirlwind,
When distress and anguish come upon
you.
28 "Let them then call on me,
but I answer not;
Let them seek me, but not find me.
29 "Because they hated knowledge
And did not choose the fear of יהוה,

1a See also 9:10, Teh. 111:10. *1b* See footnote, Teh. 33:6.

30 "They did not accept my counsel,
They despised all my reproof,
31 "Therefore let them eat the fruit of
their own way,
And be filled with their own counsels.
32 "For the turning away of the simple
kills them,
And the complacency of fools destroys
them.
33 "But whoever listens to me dwells
safely,
And is at ease from the dread of evil."

2 My son, if you accept my words,
And treasure up my commands with
you,
2 So that you make your ear attend to
wisdom,
Incline your heart to understanding;
3 For if you cry for discernment,
Lift up your voice for understanding,
4 If you seek her as silver,
And search for her as hidden treasures,
5 Then you would understand the
fear of יהוה,
And find the knowledge of Elohim.
6 For יהוה gives wisdom;
Out of His mouth *come* knowledge
and understanding.
7 And He treasures up stability for the
straight,
A shield to those walking blamelessly,
8 To watch over the paths of right-ruling,
And the way of His lovingly-commited
ones He guards.
9 Then you would understand
righteousness
And right-ruling, and straightness –
Every good path.
10 For wisdom would enter your heart,
And knowledge be pleasant to your
being,
11 Discretion would guard you;
Understanding would watch over you,
12 To deliver you from the evil way,
From the man who speaks perversities,
13 Those who leave the paths of
straightness
To walk in the ways of darkness;
14 Who rejoice to do evil;
They delight in the perversities of evil;
15 Whose paths are crooked,
And they are perverted in their ways;
16 To deliver you from the strange
woman,
From the foreigner who flatters with
her words,
17 Who forsakes the companion of her
youth,
And has forgotten the covenant of her
Elohim.
18 For her house has sunk down to death,
And her paths to the dead;
19 None going in to her does return,
Nor do they reach the paths of life –
20 So walk in the way of goodness,
And guard the paths of righteousness.
21 For the straight shall dwell in the earth,
And the perfect be left in it;
22 But the wrong shall be cut off from
the earth,
And the treacherous ones plucked
out of it.

3 My son, do not forget my Torah,
And let your heart watch over my
commands;
2 For length of days and long life
And peace they add to you.
3 Let not loving-commitment and truth
forsake you –
Bind them around your neck,
Write them on the tablet of your heart,
4 Thus finding favour and good insight
In the eyes of Elohim and man.
5 Trust in יהוה with all your heart,
And lean not on your own
understanding;
6 Know Him in all your ways,
And He makes all your paths straight.
7 Do not be wise in your own eyes; [a]
Fear יהוה and turn away from evil. [b]
8 It is healing to your navel,
And moistening to your bones.
9 Esteem יהוה with your goods,
And with the first-fruits of all your
increase;
10 Then your storehouses shall be filled

3a Yesh. 5:21. *3b* Iyoḇ 28:28.

with plenty,
And your vats overflow with new wine.
11 My son, do not despise the discipline of יהוה,
And do not loathe His reproof;
12 For whom יהוה loves He reproves,
As a father the son whom he delights in. [c]
13 Blessed is the man who has found wisdom,
And the man who gets understanding;
14 For the gain from it is better
Than gain from silver,
And its increase than fine gold.
15 She is more precious than rubies,
And all your delights are not comparable to her.
16 Length of days is in her right hand,
Riches and esteem in her left hand.
17 Her ways are pleasant ways,
And all her paths are peace.
18 She is a tree of life to those taking hold of her,
And blessed are all who retain her.
19 יהוה founded the earth by wisdom;
He established the heavens by understanding;
20 By His knowledge the depths were broken up,
And clouds drop down dew.
21 My son, let them not depart from your eyes;
Watch over sound wisdom and discretion;
22 Then they become life to your being
And an adorning to your neck.
23 Then you would walk safely in your way,
And your foot would not stumble.
24 When you lie down, you need not be afraid.
And you shall lie down and your sleep shall be sweet.
25 Do not be afraid of sudden dread,
Nor of the ruin of the wrong when it comes;
26 For יהוה is at your side,
And He shall guard your foot from being caught.
27 Do not withhold good from those who deserve it,
When it is in the power of your hand to do so.
28 Do not say to your neighbour,
"Go, and come back, and tomorrow I give it,"
When you have it with you.
29 Do not plan evil against your neighbour,
Seeing he dwells safely beside you.
30 Do not strive with a man without cause,
If he has done you no evil.
31 Do not envy a cruel man,
And choose none of his ways;
32 For the perverse one is an abomination to יהוה,
And His secret counsel is with the straight.
33 The curse of יהוה is on the house of the wrong,
But He blesses the home of the righteous.
34 He certainly scoffs the scoffers,
But gives favour to the humble.
35 The wise do inherit esteem,
But fools are bearing away shame!

4 Children, listen to the discipline of a father,
And give attention to know understanding;
2 For I gave you good instruction:
Do not forsake my Torah.
3 For I was my father's son,
Tender and the only one in the eyes of my mother,
4 Then he taught me and said to me,
"Let your heart hold fast my words;
Guard my commands, and live.
5 "Get wisdom! Get understanding!
Do not forget, and do not turn away
From the words of my mouth.
6 "Do not leave her, and let her guard you;
Love her, and let her watch over you.
7 "The beginning of wisdom is:

3c Verses 11-12 are quoted in Ib`rim 12:5-6.

Get wisdom!
And with all your getting,
get understanding.
8 "Exalt her, and let her uplift you;
She brings you esteem when you
embrace her.
9 "She gives your head a fair wreath,
She shields you with an adorning
crown."
10 Hear, my son, and accept my words,
And let the years of your life be many.
11 I have taught you in the way of
wisdom,
I have led you in straight paths.
12 When you walk your steps shall not be
hindered,
And if you run you shall not stumble.
13 Become strong in discipline, do not let
go;
Watch over her, for she is your life.
14 Do not enter the path of the wrong,
And do not walk in the way of
evil-doers.
15 Avoid it, do not pass by it;
Turn away from it and pass on.
16 For they do not sleep unless they have
done evil.
And their sleep is taken away unless
they make someone fall.
17 For they have eaten the bread of
wrongdoing,
And they drink the wine of violence.
18 But the path of the righteous is like the
light of dawn,
That shines ever brighter unto the
perfect day.
19 The way of the wrong is like darkness;
They do not know at what they
stumble.
20 My son, listen to my words;
Incline your ear to my sayings.
21 Let them not depart from your eyes;
Guard them in the midst of your heart;
22 For they are life to those who find
them,
And healing to all their flesh.
23 Watch over your heart with all
diligence,
For out of it are the sources of life.
24 Turn away from you a crooked mouth,
And put perverse lips far from you.
25 Let your eyes look forward,
And your eyelids look straight before
you.
26 Consider the path of your feet,
And all your ways are established.
27 Do not turn to the right or the left;
Turn your foot away from evil.

5 My son, listen to my wisdom;
Incline your ear to my understanding,
2 So as to watch over discretion,
And your lips guard knowledge.
3 For the lips of a strange woman drip
honey,
And her mouth is smoother than oil;
4 But in the end she is bitter as
wormwood,
Sharp as a two-edged sword.
5 Her feet go down to death,
Her steps lay hold of She'ol.
6 She does not consider the path of life;
Her ways are unstable – you do not
know it.
7 So now, listen to me, you children,
And do not turn away from the words
of my mouth.
8 Keep your way far from her,
And do not come near the door of her
house,
9 Lest you give your splendour to others,
And your years to one who is cruel;
10 Lest strangers be filled with your
strength,
And your labours go to the house of a
foreigner.
11 Then you shall howl in your latter end,
When your flesh and your body are
consumed,
12 And shall say,
"How I have hated discipline,
And my heart has despised reproof!
13 "And I have not heeded the voice of
my teachers,
And I have not inclined my ear to those
who instructed me!
14 "In a little while I was in all evil,
In the midst of an assembly
and a congregation."
15 Drink water from your own cistern,
And running water from your own
well.

16 Should your springs be scattered
abroad,
Rivers of water in the streets?
17 Let them be only your own,
And not for strangers with you.
18 Let your fountain be blessed,
And rejoice with the wife of your
youth –
19 A loving deer and a pleasant doe!
Let her nipples satisfy you at all times.
And be captivated by her love always.
20 For why should you, my son,
Be captivated by a strange woman,
And embrace the bosom of a
foreigner?
21 For the ways of man
Are before the eyes of יהוה,
And He considers all his paths.
22 The wrong one is entrapped
In his own crookednesses,
And he is caught in the cords of his sin.
23 He dies for lack of discipline,
And in the greatness of his folly
He goes astray.

6 My son, if you:
Have become guarantor for your
friend,
Have shaken hands in pledge for a
stranger,
2 Have been snared by the words of your
own mouth,
Have been caught by the words of your
mouth –
3 Do this at once, my son, and deliver
yourself,
For you have come into the hand of
your friend:
Go, humble yourself, and urge your
friend.
4 Give no sleep to your eyes,
Nor slumber to your eyelids.
5 Deliver yourself like a gazelle from *the
hunter's* hand,
And like a bird from the hand of the
trapper.
6 Go to the ant, you lazy one!
See her ways and be wise,
7 Which, having no commander,
overseer or ruler,
8 Provides her supplies in the summer,
Gathers her food in the harvest.
9 How long would you lie down,
O lazy one?
When do you arise from your sleep?
10 A little sleep, a little slumber,
A little folding of the hands to lie
down;
11 And your poverty shall come like a
prowler,
And your need as an armed man.
12 A man of Beliya'al, a wicked man,
Walks with a perverse mouth,
13 Winks with his eyes, shuffles his feet,
Points with his fingers;
14 Perverseness is in his heart,
Plotting evil at all times,
He sends out strife.
15 Therefore his calamity comes
suddenly;
Instantly he is broken,
And there is no healing.
16 These six *matters* יהוה hates,
And seven are an abomination to Him:
17 A proud look,
A lying tongue,
And hands shedding innocent blood,
18 A heart devising wicked schemes,
Feet quick to run to evil,
19 A false witness breathing out lies,
And one who causes strife among
brothers.
20 My son, watch over your father's
command,
And do not forsake the Torah of your
mother.
21 Bind them on your heart always;
Tie them around your neck.
22 When you are walking about, it leads
you;
When you lie down, it guards you.
And when you have woken up,
It talks to you.
23 For the command is a lamp,
And the Torah a light, [a]
And reproofs of discipline a way of
life,
24 To guard you against an evil woman,

6a Teh. 119:105.

From the flattering tongue of a strange woman.
25 Do not desire her prettiness in your heart,
Neither let her captivate you with her eyelids.
26 For because of a whore
One is brought to a crust of bread.
And an adulteress hunts a precious life.
27 Would a man take fire to his bosom,
And his garments not be burned?
28 Would a man walk on hot coals,
And his feet not be scorched?
29 So is he who goes in to his neighbour's wife;
None who touches her goes unpunished.
30 They do not despise a thief
If he steals to satisfy his appetite when he is starving.
31 Yet if he is caught he repays sevenfold;
He gives all the wealth of his house.
32 He who commits adultery with a woman lacks heart;
He who does it destroys his own life.
33 He finds smiting and shame,
And his reproach is not wiped away.
34 For jealousy enrages a man,
And he does not spare in the day of vengeance.
35 He does not regard any ransom,
Nor accept your bribe, however great!

7 My son, guard my words,
And treasure up my commands with you.
2 Guard my commands and live,
And my Torah as the apple of your eye.
3 Bind them on your fingers;
Write them on the tablet of your heart.
4 Say to wisdom, "You are my sister,"
And call understanding a close friend,
5 To guard you against the strange woman,
Against the foreigner who flatters with her words.
6 For at the window of my house
I looked through my lattice,
7 And I saw among the simple,
I perceived among the youths,
A young man lacking heart,
8 Passing through the street near her corner;
And he went the way to her house
9 In the twilight, in the evening,
In the black and dark night.
10 And look, a woman met him,
Dressed like a whore,
With a hidden heart.
11 She was boisterous and stubborn,
Her feet did not stay at her own house.
12 Now in the street,
Now in the square,
And at every corner she lurks.
13 And she took hold of him and kissed him;
She hardened her face and said to him:
14 "Slaughterings of peace *offerings* are with me;
Today I have paid my vows.
15 "Therefore I came out to meet you,
To earnestly seek your face, and I found you.
16 "I have spread my bed with coverings,
Coloured linens of Mitsrayim.
17 "I have sprinkled my bed with myrrh, aloes, and cinnamon.
18 "Come, let us take our fill of *carnal-*love until morning;
Let us delight ourselves with love.
19 "For my husband is not at home;
He has gone on a long journey;
20 "He took a bag of silver with him;
He comes home on the day of the covering."
21 With her many words she leads him astray,
With her smooth lips she seduces him.
22 He goes after her immediately,
Like an ox he goes to the slaughter,
And as in chains, a fool to the punishment,
23 Till an arrow strikes through his liver;
Like a bird rushing into a snare,
And did not know it would take his life.
24 And now, listen to me, you children;
Pay attention to the words of my mouth:
25 Do not let your heart turn aside to her ways,
Do not go astray in her paths.

26 For many are the wounded she has caused to fall,
And numerous all her killed ones.
27 Her house is the way to She'ol,
Going down to the rooms of death.

8 Does not wisdom call,
And understanding lift up her voice?
2 On the top of the heights along the way,
Between the paths she has taken her stand.
3 Beside the gates, leading to the city,
At the entrances, she shouts:
4 "O men, I call, to you,
And my voice is to the sons of men.
5 "You simple ones, understand insight,
And you fools, be of an understanding heart.
6 "Listen, for I speak noble words,
And the opening of my lips is about straightness;
7 "For my mouth speaks truth;
And wrongness is an abomination to my lips.
8 "All the words of my mouth are in righteousness,
None of them twisted or crooked,
9 "All of them plain to him who understands,
And straight to those who find knowledge.
10 "Accept my discipline, and not silver,
And knowledge rather than choice gold;
11 "For wisdom is better than rubies,
And all delights are not comparable to her.
12 "I, wisdom, have dwelt with insight,
And I find knowledge, foresight.
13 "The fear of יהוה is to hate evil.
I have hated pride and arrogance,
And the evil way,
And the perverse mouth.
14 "Counsel is mine, and sound wisdom;
I am understanding, mightiness is mine.
15 "By me sovereigns reign,
And rulers make righteous inscriptions.
16 "By me princes rule, and nobles,
All the judges of the earth.
17 "I love those who love me,
And those who earnestly seek me do find me.
18 "Riches and esteem are with me,
Enduring wealth and righteousness.
19 "My fruit is better than gold and fine gold,
And my increase than choice silver.
20 "I walk in the way of righteousness,
In the midst of the paths of right-ruling,
21 "To bestow substance on those who love me,
And to fill their treasuries.
22 "יהוה possessed me,
The beginning of His way,
As the first of His works of old.
23 "I was set up ages ago, at the first,
Before the earth ever was.
24 "When there were no depths I was brought forth,
When there were no springs heavy with water.
25 "Before mountains were sunk,
Before the hills, I was brought forth,
26 "Before He had made the earth and the fields,
Or the first dust of the world.
27 "When He prepared the heavens, I was there,
When He inscribed a circle on the face of the deep,
28 "When He set the clouds above,
When He made the fountains of the deep strong,
29 "When He gave to the sea its law,
So that the waters would not transgress His mouth,
When He inscribed the foundations of the earth,
30 "Then I was beside Him, a master workman,
And I was *His* delight, day by day
Rejoicing before Him all the time,
31 "Rejoicing in the world, His earth;
And my delights were with the sons of men.
32 "And now, listen to me, you children,
For blessed are they who guard my ways.
33 "Listen to discipline and become wise,

And do not refuse it.
34 "Blessed is the man who listens to me,
Watching daily at my gates,
Waiting at the posts of my doors.
35 "For whoever finds me shall find life,
And obtain favour from יהוה,
36 "But he who sins against me injures himself;
All who hate me love death!"

9 Wisdom has built her house,
She has hewn out its seven columns,
2 She has slaughtered her meat,
She has mixed her wine,
She has also prepared her table.
3 She has sent out her young women,
She cries out from the highest places of the city:
4 "Who is simple? Let him turn in here!"
As for him who lacks heart, she says to him,
5 "Come, eat of my bread and drink of the wine I have mixed."
6 Leave the simple ones and live,
And walk in the way of understanding.
7 He who reproves a scoffer gets shame for himself,
And he who rebukes a wrong one gets himself a blemish.
8 Do not reprove a scoffer, lest he hate you;
Reprove a wise one, and he loves you.
9 Give *instruction* to a wise one, and he is wiser still;
Teach a righteous one, and he increases in learning.
10 The fear of יהוה is the beginning of wisdom,
And the knowledge of the Set-apart One is understanding. [a]
11 For by me your days become many,
And years of life are added to you.
12 If you have become wise,
You have become wise for yourself,
And if you have scoffed,
You alone bear it.
13 A foolish woman is loud,
Simple, and without knowledge.
14 For she has seated herself
At the door of her house,
On a seat by the highest places of the city,
15 To call to those who pass by,
Who go straight on their way:
16 "Who is simple? Let him turn in here."
And as for him who lacks heart, she says to him,
17 "Stolen waters are sweet,
And bread *eaten* in secret is pleasant."
18 But he does not know that the dead are there,
Her guests are in the depths of She'ol.

10 Proverbs of Shelomoh:
A wise son makes a father rejoice,
But a foolish son is his mother's sorrow.
2 Treasures of wrongness are of no value,
But righteousness delivers from death.
3 יהוה does not let the being of the righteous go hungry,
But He thrusts away the desire of the wrong.
4 Poor is he who works with a lazy hand,
But the hand of the hard worker makes rich.
5 He who gathers in summer is a wise son,
He who sleeps in harvest is a son who causes shame.
6 Blessings are on the head of the righteous,
But violence covers the mouth of the wrong.
7 The remembrance of the righteous is blessed,
But the name of the wrong ones rot.
8 The wise in heart accepts commands, [a]
But one with foolish lips falls.
9 He who walks in integrity walks safely,
But he who perverts his ways becomes known.
10 He who winks with the eye causes sorrow,
And one with foolish lips falls.
11 The mouth of the righteous is a fountain of life,

9a See 1:7. *10a* Hosh. 14:9.

But violence covers the mouth of the wrong.
12 Hatred stirs up strife,
But love covers all transgressions.
13 Wisdom is found on the lips of him who has understanding,
But a rod is for the back of him who lacks heart.
14 The wise treasure up knowledge,
But the mouth of a fool is near ruin.
15 The rich man's wealth is his strong city;
The ruin of the poor is their poverty.
16 The wage of the righteous is for life,
The increase of the wrong is for sin.
17 He who heeds discipline is in the way of life,
But he who refuses reproof goes astray.
18 He who hides hatred has lying lips,
And he who sends out a slander is a fool.
19 When words are many,
Transgression is not absent,
But he who restrains his lips is wise.
20 The tongue of the righteous is choice silver;
The heart of the wrong is of little *value*.
21 The lips of the righteous shepherd many,
But fools die for lack of heart.
22 The blessing of יהוה makes one rich,
And He adds no pain with it.
23 To work out wicked schemes
Is like sport to a fool,
But wisdom is for a man of understanding.
24 What the wrong one fears comes upon him,
But the desire of the righteous is granted.
25 As the whirlwind passes by,
The wrong one is no more,
But the righteous *has* an everlasting foundation.
26 As vinegar to the teeth and smoke to the eyes,
So is the lazy one to those who send him.
27 The fear of יהוה prolongs days,
But the years of the wrong ones are shortened.
28 The righteous look forward to joy,
But the expectancy of the wrong ones perish.
29 The way of יהוה is a stronghold for the perfect,
But ruin to the workers of wickedness.
30 The righteous is never shaken,
While the wrong shall not dwell in the earth.
31 The mouth of the righteous brings forth wisdom,
But the tongue of perverseness is cut out.
32 The lips of the righteous know what is pleasing,
But the mouth of the wrong *speaks* perverseness.

11 A false scale is an abomination to יהוה,
But a perfect weight is His delight.
2 Pride comes, then comes shame;
But with the humble is wisdom.
3 The integrity of the straight ones guides them,
But the slipperiness of the treacherous destroys them.
4 Riches do not profit in the day of wrath,
But righteousness delivers from death.
5 The righteousness of the perfect
Makes his way straight,
But by his own wrongness the wrong one falls.
6 The righteousness of the straight ones delivers them,
But the treacherous are caught by greed.
7 When a wrong man dies, expectancy perishes,
And the ambition of the wicked shall be lost.
8 The righteous is delivered from distress,
And the wrong one takes his place.
9 The defiled one destroys his neighbour with his mouth,
But the righteous is delivered by knowledge.
10 When the righteous prosper, the city

rejoices.
And when the wrong perish, there is
shouting.
11 By the blessing of the straight the city
is exalted,
But by the mouth of the wrong it is
overthrown.
12 He who lacks heart despises his
neighbour,
But a man of understanding keeps
silence.
13 A slanderer is a revealer of secrets,
But one with a trustworthy spirit
conceals a matter.
14 Without guidance the people fall,
But in a great counsellor there is
safety.
15 He who is guarantor for a stranger
suffers harm,
But one who hates shaking hands in
pledge is safe.
16 A woman showing favour obtains
esteem,
But ruthless men obtain riches.
17 A lovingly-commited man is rewarding
his being,
But he who is cruel troubles his own
flesh.
18 The wrong one earns false wages,
But the one sowing righteousness,
a true reward.
19 Thus righteousness *leads* to life,
And one pursuing evil, to his own
death.
20 The perverse of heart are an
abomination to יהוה,
But the perfect in the Way are His
delight.
21 Hand to hand, the evil one does not
go unpunished,
But the seed of the righteous shall
escape.
22 Like a ring of gold in a pig's snout,
Is a beautiful woman who lacks good
sense.
23 The desire of the righteous is only
good,
The expectancy of the wrong is wrath.
24 There is one who scatters,
yet increases more.
And one who withholds more than is
right,
But it *comes* to poverty.
25 The generous being is enriched,
And he who waters is also watered
himself.
26 The people curse him who withholds
grain,
But blessing is on the head of him
who sells it.
27 He who earnestly seeks good,
Seeks what is pleasing;
But to him who seeks evil,
It comes to him.
28 He who trusts in his riches falls,
But the righteous flourish like a leaf.
29 He who troubles his own house
inherits wind,
And the fool is servant to the wise
of heart.
30 The fruit of the righteous is a tree
of life,
And he who is winning lives is wise.
31 See, the righteous in the earth shall be
rewarded,
How much more the wrong and the
sinner!

12 Whoever loves discipline loves
knowledge,
But he who hates reproof is stupid.
2 The good obtains favour from יהוה,
But the man of wicked devices He
declares wrong.
3 A man is not established by
wrongness,
But the root of the righteous shall not
be moved.
4 A capable wife is the crown of her
husband,
But one causing shame is like
rottenness in his bones.
5 The thoughts of the righteous are
right-ruling,
The counsels of the wrong are deceit.
6 The words of the wrong are,
"Lie in wait for blood,"
But the mouth of the straight delivers
them.
7 The wrong are overthrown,
And are no more,
But the house of the righteous stands.

8 A man is praised according to his
wisdom,
But the perverted of heart becomes
despised.
9 Better to be lightly esteemed and have
a servant,
Than the highly esteemed who lacks
bread.
10 The righteous regards the life of his
beast,
But the compassion of the wrong is
cruelty.
11 He who tills his land is satisfied
with bread,
But he who pursues vanities is lacking
heart.
12 The wrong shall covet the catch of
evil-doers,
But the root of the righteous yields
fruit.
13 In the transgression of the lips is an
evil snare,
But the righteous gets out of distress.
14 From the fruit of his mouth one is
filled with good,
And the work of a man's hands is
given back to him.
15 The way of a fool is right in his own
eyes,
But he who listens to advice is wise.
16 A fool's wrath is known at once,
But a clever one covers shame.
17 He who speaks truth declares
righteousness,
But a false witness, deceit.
18 Rash speaking is like piercings of a
sword,
But the tongue of the wise is healing.
19 The lip of truth is established forever,
But a lying tongue is but for a moment.
20 Deceit is in the heart of those who plot
evil,
But counsellors of peace have joy.
21 No harm befalls the righteous,
But the wrong shall be filled with evil.
22 Lying lips are an abomination to יהוה,
But those who deal truly are His
delight.
23 A clever man is concealing knowledge,
But the heart of fools proclaims folly.
24 The hand of the hard worker rules,
But the lazy is put to compulsory
labour.
25 Anxiety in the heart of man causes
depression,
But a good word makes him glad.
26 The righteous is a guide to his
neighbour,
But the way of the wrong leads them
astray.
27 The lazy one has no game to roast,
But the hard worker prizes his
possessions.
28 In the way of righteousness is life,
And in its pathway there is no death.

13 A wise son *accepts* his father's
discipline,
But a scoffer shall not listen to rebuke.
2 From the fruit of the mouth a man eats
the good,
But the desire of the treacherous is for
violence.
3 He who watches over his mouth guards
his being,
But he who opens wide his lips comes
to ruin.
4 The being of the lazy one craves,
but has not;
While the being of the hard workers
are enriched.
5 A righteous one hates a lying word,
But a wrong man is loathsome and
comes to shame.
6 Righteousness watches over him who
is perfect in the way,
But wrongness overthrows the sinner.
7 There is one who makes himself rich,
Yet *has* none at all.
And one who makes himself poor,
Yet has great riches.
8 The ransom of a man's life is his
riches,
But the poor does not hear rebuke.
9 The light of the righteous rejoices,
But the lamp of the wrong is put out.
10 By pride comes only strife,
But wisdom is with those who take
advice.
11 Wealth from vanity diminishes,
But he who gathers by hand increases.
12 Expectancy drawn out makes the heart

sick,
But a longing come true is a tree of life.
13 He who despises the Word is destroyed,
But he who fears the command is rewarded.
14 The Torah of the wise is a fountain of life,
Turning one away from the snares of death.
15 Good understanding gains favour,
But the way of the treacherous is hard.
16 Every one with insight acts with knowledge,
But a fool spreads folly.
17 A messenger that is wrong falls into evil,
But a trustworthy envoy is a healing.
18 Poverty and shame are for him
Who ignores discipline,
But he who heeds reproof is esteemed.
19 A desire accomplished is sweet to the being,
But to turn away from evil is an abomination to fools.
20 He who walks with the wise, shall be wise,
But the companion of fools suffers evil.
21 Evil pursues sinners,
But good is repaid to the righteous.
22 A good man leaves an inheritance to his children's children,
But the wealth of the sinner is stored up for the righteous.
23 Much food is in the tillable ground of the poor,
But lack of right-ruling sweeps it away.
24 He who spares his rod hates his son,
But he who loves him, seeks him with discipline.
25 The righteous eats to the satisfying of his being,
But the stomach of the wrong is lacking.

14 Every wise woman has built her house,
But the foolish breaks it down with her hands.
2 He who walks in his straightness fears יהוה,
But he whose ways are crooked despises Him.
3 In the mouth of a fool is a rod of pride,
But the lips of the wise guard them.
4 Where there are no oxen, the crib is clean;
But from the strength of an ox comes much increase.
5 A trustworthy witness does not lie,
But a false witness breathes out lies.
6 A scoffer shall seek wisdom but *find* none,
But knowledge is swift to him who has understanding.
7 Leave the presence of a foolish man,
For you shall not perceive the lips of knowledge.
8 The wisdom of the clever is to understand His way,
But the folly of fools is deceit.
9 Fools scoff at guilt,
But among the straight there is delight.
10 The heart knows its own bitterness,
And no stranger shares its joy.
11 The house of the wrong is destroyed,
But the tent of the straight flourishes.
12 There is a way which seems right to a man,
But its end is the way of death. [a]
13 Even in laughter the heart is in pain,
And the end of that joy is heaviness.
14 The backslider in heart is satisfied with his own ways,
But a good man *is satisfied* from his.
15 The simple believes every word,
But the clever one watches his step.
16 The wise fears and turns away from evil,
But a fool rushes on and is reckless.
17 He who is impatient acts foolishly,
And a man who plans wickedness is hated.
18 The simple shall inherit folly,
But the clever are crowned with knowledge.

14a 16:25.

[19]The evil ones shall bow before the
good,
And the wrong ones at the gates of the
righteous.
[20]The poor is hated even by his own
neighbour,
But the rich has many friends.
[21]He who despises his neighbour sins;
But he who shows favour to the poor,
O blessed is he.
[22]Do not those who plan evil go astray?
But loving-commitment and truth are
to those who plan good.
[23]In all labour there is profit,
But talk of the lips *leads* only to
poverty.
[24]The crown of the wise is their wealth,
The folly of fools is folly.
[25]A true witness saves lives,
But he who breathes out lies is a
betrayer.
[26]In the fear of יהוה is strong trust,
And His children have a place of
refuge.
[27]The fear of יהוה is a fountain of life,
To turn away from the snares of death.
[28]In a multitude of people
Is a sovereign's splendour,
But in the lack of people
Is the ruin of a prince.
[29]He who is patient has great
understanding,
But he who is short of spirit exalts
folly.
[30]A healthy heart is life to the body,
But envy is rottenness to the bones.
[31]He who oppresses the poor reproaches
his Maker,
But he who esteems Him shows favour
to the needy.
[32]By his own evildoing the wrong is
thrust down,
But the righteous has a refuge in his
death.
[33]Wisdom rests in the heart of him who
has understanding,
And *even* among fools it becomes
known.
[34]Righteousness exalts a nation;
And loving-commitment,
To the peoples is sin.
[35]The sovereign's delight is toward a
wise servant,
But his wrath is towards him who
causes shame.

15 A soft answer turns away wrath,
But a harsh word stirs up
displeasure.
[2]The tongue of the wise makes
knowledge good,
But the mouth of fools pours out
foolishness.
[3]The eyes of יהוה are in every place,
Watching the evil and the good.
[4]A healing tongue is a tree of life,
But perverseness in it crushes the
spirit.
[5]A fool despises his father's discipline,
But he who heeds reproof is clever.
[6]The household of the righteous is a
great treasure,
But in the income of the wrong is
trouble.
[7]The lips of the wise scatter knowledge,
But the heart of fools is not so.
[8]The slaughtering of the wrong ones
Is an abomination to יהוה,
But the prayer of the straight is His
delight.
[9]The way of the wrong one
Is an abomination to יהוה,
But He loves him who pursues
righteousness.
[10]Discipline is grievous to him who
forsakes the way;
He who hates reproof dies.
[11]She'ol and destruction are before יהוה,
How much more the hearts of the sons
of men.
[12]A scoffer does not love his reprover,
Nor does he go to the wise.
[13]A glad heart makes good a face,
But by sorrow of heart the spirit is
stricken.
[14]The heart of the understanding one
seeks knowledge,
But the mouth of fools feeds on folly.
[15]All the days of the afflicted are evil,
But gladness of heart is a continual
feast.
[16]Better is a little with the fear of יהוה,

Than great treasure with trouble.
17 Better is a meal of vegetables where love is,
Than a fatted calf with hatred.
18 A man of wrath stirs up strife,
But he who is patient appeases strife.
19 The way of a lazy one is like a hedge of thorns,
But the way of the straight is a highway.
20 A wise son makes a father glad,
But a foolish man despises his mother.
21 Folly is joy to one lacking heart,
But a man of understanding walks straight.
22 Without counsel, plans go wrong,
But by great counsellors they are established.
23 A man has joy by the answer of his mouth,
And how good is a word *spoken* in its season!
24 The path of life is upward for the wise,
To turn away from She'ol below.
25 יהוה tears down the house of the proud,
And He sets up the boundary of the widow.
26 Evil thoughts are an abomination to יהוה,
But pleasant words are clean.
27 He who is greedy for gain, troubles his own house,
But he who hates bribes lives.
28 The heart of the righteous ponders how to answer,
But the mouth of the wrong pours out evil.
29 יהוה is far from the wrong ones,
But He hears the prayer of the righteous. [a]
30 The light of the eyes rejoices the heart,
A good report gives marrow to the bones.
31 An ear that hears the reproof of life
Does dwell among the wise.
32 He who ignores discipline hates himself,
But he who listens to reproof gets understanding.
33 The fear of יהוה is the discipline of wisdom,
And before esteem is humility.

16 To man belongs the preparations of the heart,
But from יהוה is the answer of the tongue.
2 All the ways of a man are clean in his own eyes,
But יהוה weighs the spirits.
3 Commit your works to יהוה,
And your plans shall be established.
4 יהוה has made all for His purpose,
And also the wrong for the day of evil.
5 Everyone proud in heart is an abomination to יהוה;
Hand to hand: he goes not unpunished.
6 By loving-commitment and truth crookedness is pardoned.
And in the fear of יהוה one turns away from evil.
7 When a man's ways please יהוה,
He makes even his enemies to be at peace with him.
8 Better is a little with righteousness,
Than a large income without right-ruling.
9 A man's heart plans his way,
But יהוה establishes his steps.
10 An oath is on the lips of the sovereign,
In right-ruling his mouth trespasses not.
11 A right scale and balances are of יהוה;
All the weights in the bag are His work.
12 It is an abomination for sovereigns
To commit wrongness,
For a throne is established by righteousness.
13 Righteous lips are the delight of sovereigns,
And they love him who speaks what is straight.
14 The sovereign's wrath is a messenger of death,
But a wise man appeases it.
15 In the light of a sovereign's face is life,

15a 28:9.

And his delight is like a cloud of the latter rain.
16 How much better it is to get wisdom than gold!
And to get understanding is preferable to silver.
17 The highway of the straight
Is to turn away from evil;
He who guards his life watches over His way.
18 Before destruction *comes* pride,
And before a fall a haughty spirit!
19 Better to be lowly in spirit with the poor,
Than to divide the spoil with the proud.
20 He who acts wisely concerning the Word finds good,
And blessed is he who trusts in יהוה.
21 The wise-hearted is called discerning,
And sweetness of lips increases learning.
22 Understanding is a fountain of life to him who has it,
But the disciplining of fools is folly.
23 The heart of the wise gives discretion to his mouth,
And he increases learning to his lips.
24 Pleasant words are like a honeycomb,
Sweet to the being, and healing to the bones.
25 There is a way that seems right to a man,
But its end is the way of death. [a]
26 He who labours, labours for himself,
For his mouth drives him on.
27 A man of Beliyaʿal plots evil,
And on his lips it is like a burning fire.
28 A perverse man sends forth strife,
And a whisperer separates intimate friends.
29 A ruthless man entices his neighbour,
And leads him in a way that is not good,
30 Winking with his eye to plot perversity,
Moving his lips he shall bring about evil.
31 Grey hair is a crown of adorning,
It is found in the way of righteousness.
32 He who is patient is better than the mighty,
And he who rules over his spirit than he who takes a city.
33 The lot is cast into the lap,
But every decision by it is from יהוה.

17 Better is a dry piece of bread and rest with it,
Than a house filled with slaughters of strife.
2 A wise servant rules over a son who causes shame,
And shares an inheritance among the brothers.
3 A refining pot is for silver and a furnace for gold,
But יהוה tries the hearts.
4 An evil-doer gives heed to wicked lips;
A liar gives ear to a tongue of desire.
5 He who mocks the poor reproaches his Maker;
He who rejoices at calamity does not go unpunished.
6 Children's children are the crown of old men,
And the adornment of children is their fathers.
7 Excellent speech is not fitting for a fool,
Much less lying lips for a noble.
8 A bribe is a stone of favour in the eyes of its owner;
Wherever he turns, he prospers.
9 He who covers a transgression seeks love,
But he who repeats a matter separates intimate friends.
10 Reproof enters deeper into a wise man
Than a hundred strikes on a fool.
11 An evil one seeks only rebellion,
So a cruel messenger is sent against him.
12 Let a bereaved bear meet a man,
Rather than a fool in his folly.
13 Whoever rewards evil for good,
Evil does not leave his house.
14 The beginning of strife is like releasing water;

16a 14:12.

Therefore stop fighting before it breaks
out.
15 He who declares the wrong right,
And he who condemns the righteous,
Both of them are an abomination to
יהוה.
16 Why is this – a price in the hand
Of a fool to buy wisdom,
When there is no heart?
17 A friend loves at all times,
And a brother is born for adversity.
18 A man lacking heart shakes hands in a
pledge,
He becomes a guarantor for his friend.
19 He who loves transgression loves
strife,
He who exalts his door seeks
destruction.
20 He who has a crooked heart finds no
good,
And he who has a perverse tongue falls
into evil.
21 He who brings forth a fool has sorrow
for it,
And the father of a fool has no joy.
22 A rejoicing heart causes good healing,
But a stricken spirit dries the bones.
23 One who is wrong accepts a bribe
behind the back
To pervert the paths of right-ruling.
24 Wisdom is before the face of the
understanding one,
But the eyes of a fool are on the ends
of the earth.
25 A foolish son is a grief to his father,
And bitterness to her who bore him.
26 It is also not good to punish the
righteous one,
To strike noble ones for straightness.
27 He who has knowledge spares his
words,
And a man of understanding is cool of
spirit.
28 Even a fool keeping silence is regarded
as wise,
As understanding, when he closes
his lips.

18 The separatist seeks *his* own
desire;
He breaks out against all sound
wisdom.
2 A fool does not delight in
understanding,
But in uncovering his own heart.
3 When a wrong one comes, scorn
comes too.
And with shame *comes* reproach.
4 The words of a man's mouth are deep
waters;
The fountain of wisdom is a flowing
stream.
5 It is not good to show partiality to the
wrong,
Or to turn aside the righteous in
right-ruling.
6 A fool's lips enter into strife,
And his mouth calls for blows.
7 A fool's mouth is his ruin,
And his lips are the snare of his life.
8 The words of a slanderer are like
delicacies,
And they go down into the inner parts
of the heart.
9 Also, he who is slack in his work
Is a brother of a master destroyer.
10 The Name of יהוה is a strong tower;
The righteous run into it and are safe.
11 The rich man's wealth is his strong
city,
And like a high wall in his own
imagination.
12 Before destruction the heart of a man is
haughty,
And before esteem is humility.
13 He who answers a matter before he
hears it,
It is folly and shame to him.
14 The spirit of a man sustains him in
sickness,
But who does bear a broken spirit?
15 The heart of the understanding one
gets knowledge,
And the ear of the wise seeks
knowledge.
16 A man's gift makes room for him,
And brings him before great men.
17 The first to state his own case,
seems right,
Until another comes and
examines him.
18 The lot settles disputes,

And separates between the mighty.
19 A brother transgressed against is
a strong city,
And contentions are like the bars of
a citadel.
20 A man's stomach is satisfied
From the fruit of his mouth;
He is satisfied *with* the increase of his
lips.
21 Death and life are in the power of the
tongue,
And those loving it eat its fruit.
22 He who has found a wife has found
good,
And receives favour from יהוה.
23 The poor speaks beseechingly,
But the rich answers fiercely.
24 A man of *many* friends might come to
ruin,
But there is a Loving One
Who sticks closer than a brother!

19 Better is the poor walking in his
integrity
Than one of perverse lips,
who is a fool.
2 Also, desire without knowledge is not
good;
And he who hurries with his feet sins.
3 The foolishness of a man perverts his
way,
And his heart is wroth against יהוה.
4 Wealth adds many friends,
But the poor is separated from his
friend.
5 A false witness does not go unpunished,
And he who breaths out lies does not
escape.
6 Many entreat the favour of the noble.
And all are friends to him who gives
gifts.
7 All the brothers of the poor shall hate
him;
How much more shall his friends go
far from him!
He pursues promises – they are gone!.
8 He who gets heart loves his own life;
He who guards understanding finds
good.
9 A false witness does not go
unpunished,
And he who breathes out lies perishes.
10 Luxury is not fitting for a fool,
Much less for a servant to rule over
princes.
11 A man's discretion makes him patient,
And his adorning is to pass over a
transgression.
12 The sovereign's wrath is like the
roaring of a lion,
But his delight is like dew on the grass.
13 A foolish son is a calamity to his
father,
And the contentions of a wife are a
continual dripping.
14 Houses and riches are the inheritance
from fathers,
But an understanding wife is from
יהוה.
15 Laziness makes one fall into a deep
sleep,
And an idle being suffers hunger.
16 He who guards the command guards
his life,
He who despises His ways dies.
17 He who shows favour to the poor lends
to יהוה,
And He repays his deed.
18 Discipline your son because there is
expectation,
And do not set your being on his
destruction.
19 One of great wrath bears punishment;
For if you rescue *him*,
You only have to do it again.
20 Listen to counsel and accept discipline,
So that you are wise in your latter end.
21 Many are the plans in a man's heart,
But it is the counsel of יהוה that
stands.
22 What is desirable in a man is his
loving-commitment,
And a poor man is better than a liar.
23 The fear of יהוה *leads* to life,
And he remains satisfied,
He is not visited by evil.
24 A lazy one buries his hand in a dish,
And does not bring it back to his
mouth.
25 Strike a scoffer,
and the simple is made wise;

And reprove one who has
understanding,
And he discerns knowledge.
26 He who plunders a father,
Chases away his mother,
Is a son causing shame and bringing
reproach.
27 Cease, my son, to hear discipline,
And you shall stray from the words of
knowledge.
28 A witness of Beliya'al scorns
right-ruling,
And the mouth of the wrong ones
Devours wickedness.
29 Judgments are in store for scoffers,
And beatings for the backs of fools.

20 Wine is a scoffer, strong drink a
brawler,
And whoever is led astray by it is not
wise.
2 The dread of a sovereign is like the
roaring of a lion;
Whoever provokes him sins against
his own life.
3 For a man to cease from strife is
esteem,
But every fool bursts out.
4 The lazy one does not plough after
the autumn;
At harvest time he inquires – there is
none!
5 Counsel in the heart of man is like
deep water,
But a man of understanding draws it
up.
6 Most men proclaim each his own
loving-commitment,
But who finds a trustworthy man?
7 The righteous man walks in his
integrity;
His children are blessed after him.
8 A sovereign who sits on the throne of
judgment
Is scattering all evil with his eyes.
9 Who says, "I have cleansed my heart,
I am purged of my sin"?
10 Differing weights and differing
measures,
Both of them are an abomination
to יהוה.
11 Even a child is known by his deeds,
Whether his work is clear and right.
12 The hearing ear and the seeing eye,
יהוה has made both of them.
13 Do not love sleep,
lest you become poor;
Open your eyes,
be satisfied with bread.
14 "Evil! Evil!" cries the buyer;
But when he has gone his way, then he
boasts.
15 There is gold and a multitude of rubies,
But the lips of knowledge are a
precious vessel.
16 Take the garment of one who is
guarantor for a stranger,
And hold it as a pledge when it is for
foreigners.
17 Bread gained by deceit might be sweet
to a man,
But afterward his mouth is filled with
gravel.
18 By counsel plans are established;
And by wise guidance wage a battle.
19 He who goes about as a slanderer
reveals secrets;
Therefore do not associate with him
Who speaks smoothly with his lips.
20 Whoever curses his father or his
mother,
His lamp is put out in deep darkness.
21 An inheritance obtained with greed at
the beginning
Is not blessed at the end.
22 Do not say, "I repay evil."
Wait for יהוה, and He saves you.
23 Differing weights are an abomination
to יהוה,
And a false scale is not good.
24 The steps of a man are from יהוה;
What does a man know about his own
way?
25 It is a snare for a man to say rashly,
"It is set-apart,"
And only later to reconsider his vows.
26 A wise sovereign winnows out the
wrong,
And turns the wheel over them.
27 The spirit of a man is the lamp of יהוה,
Searching all his inmost parts.
28 Loving-commitment and truth watch

over the sovereign,
And he shall support his throne by loving-commitment.
29 The comeliness of young men is their strength,
And the splendour of old men is their grey hair.
30 The blows that wound cleanse away evil,
And strokes the inner parts of the heart.

21 The sovereign's heart is as channels of water
In the hand of יהוה;
He turns it wherever He wishes.
2 All a man's ways are right in his own eyes,
But יהוה weighs the hearts.
3 To do righteousness and right-ruling
Is more acceptable to יהוה than a slaughtering.
4 A haughty look, a proud heart,
The lamp of the wrong, are sin.
5 The plans of the hard worker *lead* only to plenty,
But all rash haste only to poverty.
6 Gaining treasures by a lying tongue
Is a fleeting vapour, heading for death.
7 The spoil of the wrong catches them,
Because they refused to do right-ruling.
8 The way of a guilty man is perverse;
But as for the innocent,
his work is right.
9 It is better to dwell in a corner of a roof,
Than in a house shared with a contentious woman.
10 The desire of the wrong is set upon evil;
His neighbour finds no favour in his eyes.
11 When the scoffer is punished,
the simple is made wise;
But when the wise is instructed, he receives knowledge.
12 The righteous one understands the house of the wrong;
He overthrows the wrong for their evil.
13 Whoever shuts his ears to the cry of the poor,
Let him also cry and not be heard.
14 A gift in secret subdues displeasure,
And a bribe in the bosom, strong wrath.
15 To do right-ruling is joy to the righteous,
But ruin to the workers of wickedness.
16 A man who strays from the way of understanding,
Rests in the assembly of the dead.
17 He who loves pleasure is a poor man;
He who loves wine and oil does not become rich.
18 The wrong is a ransom for the righteous,
And the treacherous for the straight.
19 It is better to dwell in the wilderness,
Than with a contentious and vexed woman.
20 Desirable treasure and oil,
Are in the dwelling of the wise,
But a foolish man swallows it up.
21 He who pursues righteousness and loving-commitment
Finds life, righteousness and esteem.
22 A wise one scales the city of the mighty,
And brings down the trusted stronghold.
23 Whoever guards his mouth and tongue
Guards his life from distresses.
24 Proud, haughty, "Scoffer" is his name;
He acts with arrogant pride.
25 The desire of the lazy man slays him,
For his hands refused to work.
26 He covets greedily all day long,
But the righteous gives and does not withhold.
27 The slaughtering of the wrong is an abomination;
How much more when he brings it with wickedness!
28 A false witness perishes,
But the man who obeys speaks forever.
29 A wrong man hardens his face,
But as for the straight, he establishes his way.
30 There is no wisdom or understanding
Or counsel against יהוה.
31 The horse is prepared for the day of battle,

But the deliverance is of יהוה.

22 A *good* name is preferable to great riches.
Favour is better than silver and gold.
2 The rich and the poor meet together –
יהוה is the Maker of them all.
3 A clever one foresees evil and hides himself,
But the simple go on and are punished.
4 The reward of humility is the fear of יהוה,
Riches, and esteem and life.
5 Thorns, snares are in the way of the perverse;
He who guards his life keeps far away from them.
6 Train up a child in the way he should go,
Even when he is old he turns not away from it.
7 The rich rules over the poor,
And the borrower is servant to the lender.
8 He who sows unrighteousness reaps trouble,
And the rod of his wrath perishes.
9 He who has a good eye is blessed,
For he gives of his bread to the poor.
10 Cast out the scoffer and strife goes out,
And contention and shame cease.
11 He who loves cleanness of heart,
Whose speech is pleasant,
A sovereign is his friend.
12 The eyes of יהוה shall watch over knowledge,
But He overthrows the words of the treacherous.
13 The lazy one says:
"There is a lion outside!"
"I am going to be murdered in the streets!"
14 The mouth of a strange woman is a deep pit;
The one denounced by יהוה falls in there.
15 Folly is bound up in the heart of a child;
The rod of discipline drives it far from him.
16 One oppresses the poor to increase his *wealth*,
Another gives to the rich, only to come to poverty.
17 Incline your ear and hear the words of the wise,
And apply your heart to my knowledge;
18 For they are pleasant
If you guard them within you;
Let all of them be ready on your lips.
19 That your trust might be in יהוה,
I caused you to know today, even you:
20 Have I not previously written to you
Of counsels and knowledge,
21 To cause you to know
The certainty of the words of truth,
To return words of truth to those who send to you?
22 Do not rob the poor because he is poor,
And oppress not the afflicted at the gate.
23 For יהוה pleads their cause,
And shall plunder those who plunder them.
24 Make no friendship with one given to wrath,
And do not go with a man of rage,
25 Lest you learn his ways,
And find yourself ensnared.
26 Do not be one of those who shakes hands in a pledge,
One of those who are guarantors for debts.
27 If you do not have the means to pay,
Why should he take away your bed from under you?
28 Do not move the ancient boundary
Which your fathers have set.
29 Do you see a man who is skilled in his work?
He does stand before sovereigns,
He does not stand before obscure ones.

23 When you sit down to eat with a ruler,
Look well what is before you;
2 And put a knife to your throat
If you are a man given to appetite.
3 Do not desire his delicacies,
For that food is deceptive.

4 Do not labour to be rich.
Cease from your own understanding!
5 Do you set your eyes on that which is not?
For riches certainly make themselves wings;
They fly away like an eagle to the heavens.
6 Do not eat the bread of *one having* an evil eye,
Nor desire his delicacies;
7 For as he reckons in his life, so is he.
"Eat and drink!" he says to you,
But his heart is not with you.
8 You vomit the piece you have eaten,
And lose your sweet words.
9 Do not speak in the ears of a fool,
For he treads on the wisdom of your words.
10 Do not move the ancient boundary,
And do not enter the fields of the fatherless;
11 For their Redeemer is strong;
He shall plead their cause against you.
12 Bring your heart to discipline,
And your ears to words of knowledge.
13 Do not withhold discipline from a child;
If you strike him with a rod, he does not die.
14 Strike him with a rod
And deliver his being from She'ol.
15 My son, if your heart shall be wise,
My heart rejoices, even I,
16 And my kidneys exult
When your lips speak what is straight.
17 Do not let your heart envy sinners,
But be in the fear of יהוה all day long;
18 For certain, there is a hereafter,
And let your expectancy not be cut off.
19 Hear, my son, and be wise,
And guide your heart in the way.
20 Be not among heavy drinkers of wine
Or with gluttonous eaters of meat;
21 For the drunkard and the glutton become poor,
And slumber puts rags on *a man*.
22 Listen to your father who brought you forth,
And do not despise your mother when she is old.
23 Buy the truth and do not sell it –
Wisdom and discipline and understanding.
24 The father of the righteous greatly rejoices,
And he who brings forth a wise one delights in him.
25 Let your father and your mother rejoice,
And let her who bore you exult.
26 My son, give me your heart,
And let your eyes watch my ways.
27 For a whore is a deep pit,
And a strange woman is a narrow well.
28 She too lies in wait as for a prey,
And increases the treacherous among men.
29 Who has woe?
Who has sorrow?
Who has contentions?
Who has complaints?
Who feels hurt without cause?
Who has redness of eyes?
30 Those staying long at the wine,
Those going in to search out mixed wine.
31 Do not look on the wine when it is red,
When it gives its colour in the cup,
As it flows smoothly;
32 In the end it bites like a snake,
And stings like an adder –
33 Your eyes look on strange women,
And your heart speaks perversities.
34 And you shall be as one
Lying down in the midst of the sea,
And as one lying at the top of the mast, saying,
35 "They struck me, I was not sick!
They beat me, I did not know!
When shall I wake up? Let me seek it again!"

24 Do not envy evil men,
Nor desire to be with them;
2 For their heart plots to ravage,
And their lips talk of trouble.
3 By wisdom a house is built,
And by understanding it is established;
4 And by knowledge the rooms are filled
With all precious and pleasant riches.
5 Mighty is the wise in strength,

And a man of knowledge strengthens
power;
6 For by wise guidance you wage your
own battle,
And delivery is by a great counsellor.
7 Wisdom is high for a fool;
He does not open his mouth in the
gate.
8 He who plots to do evil
Is called a master of evil plots.
9 The purpose of folly is sin,
And the scoffer is an abomination to
men.
10 If you falter in the day of distress,
Your strength is small!
11 Deliver those taken to death,
And hold back those stumbling to the
kill,
12 If you say, "See, we did not know
this,"
Would not He who weighs the hearts
discern it?
He who watches over your life,
Would He not know it?
And shall He not repay man according
to his work?
13 My son, eat honey, for it is good,
And the honeycomb, sweet to your
taste;
14 Know that wisdom is thus to your
being;
If you have found it, there is a future,
And your expectancy is not cut off.
15 Do not lie in wait, O wrong one,
Against the dwelling of the righteous;
Do not ravage his resting place;
16 For seven times a righteous man falls
and rises,
But the wrong one stumbles into evil.
17 Do not exult when your enemy falls,
And let not your heart rejoice when he
stumbles;
18 Lest יהוה see and it be evil in His eyes,
And He turn away His wrath from him.
19 Do not fret because of evil-doers,
And do not envy the wrong;
20 For there is no future for the evil-doer;
The lamp of the wrongdoers is put out.
21 My son, fear יהוה and the sovereign;
Do not mingle with those who change;
22 For their calamity arises suddenly,
And who knows the ruin of both of
them?
23 These also are for the wise:
It is not good to show partiality in
right-ruling.
24 He who says to the wrong,
"You are righteous" – peoples curse
him,
Nations despise him.
25 But those who rebuke *the wrong*,
It is pleasant, and a good blessing
comes on them.
26 He who gives a right answer kisses the
lips.
27 Prepare your outside work,
And make it fit for yourself in the
field;
Then you shall build your house.
28 Do not witness against your neighbour
without cause,
And do not deceive with your lips.
29 Do not say, "Let me do to him as he
did to me;
I repay each according to his work."
30 I passed by the field of the lazy,
And by the vineyard of the man
lacking heart;
31 And see, it was all overgrown with
thorns;
Its surface was covered with nettles;
And its stone wall was broken down.
32 When I saw it, I set my heart on it;
I looked and received discipline:
33 A little sleep, a little slumber,
A little folding of the hands to rest;
34 And your poverty shall come,
a prowler,
And your need like an armed man.

25

These too are proverbs of
Shelomoh which the men of
Ḥizqiyah sovereign of Yehuḏah
copied:
2 It is the esteem of Elohim to hide a
matter,
And the esteem of sovereigns to search
out a matter.
3 The heavens for height and the earth
for depth,
But the heart of sovereigns is
unsearchable.

4 Take away the dross from silver,
And a vessel comes forth for the refiner.
5 Take away the wrong from before the sovereign,
And his throne is established in righteousness.
6 Do not exalt yourself before a sovereign,
And do not stand in the place of great men;
7 For it is better for him to say to you, "Come up here,"
Than that you should be put lower
Before a noble whom your eyes have seen.
8 Do not go forth to strive in haste,
For what would you do in the end,
When your neighbour has put you to shame?
9 Plead your case with your neighbour himself,
And do not disclose the secret of another;
10 Lest he who hears it put you to shame,
And your evil report turn not back.
11 A word spoken at the right time
Is like apples of gold in settings of silver.
12 A ring of gold, and an ornament of fine gold,
Is a wise one's reproof to an ear that hears.
13 Like the cold of snow in time of harvest
Is a trustworthy messenger to those who send him,
For he refreshes the life of his masters.
14 He who boasts of his gifts falsely
Is like clouds and wind without rain.
15 Through patience a ruler is persuaded,
And a soft tongue shatters a bone.
16 Have you found honey?
Eat only as much as you need,
Lest you be satisfied with it and vomit.
17 Make your foot rare in your neighbour's house,
Lest he gets enough of you and hate you.
18 A man bearing false witness against his neighbour
Is like a club and a sword and a sharp arrow.
19 Trust in a treacherous man in time of distress
Is like a broken tooth or a foot out of joint.
20 One who takes away a garment in cold weather,
Is like vinegar on soda,
And a singer of songs on an evil heart.
21 If your enemy is hungry give him bread to eat,
And if he is thirsty give him water to drink,
22 For you are heaping coals of fire on his head,
And יהוה rewards you.
23 The north wind brings rain,
And a secret tongue an enraged face.
24 It is better to dwell in a corner of a roof,
Than in a house shared with a contentious woman.
25 *Like* cold water to a parched throat,
Is good news from a distant land.
26 A righteous man who gives way before the wrong,
Is like a muddied spring and a ruined fountain.
27 It is not good to eat much honey.
Is it esteem to seek one's own esteem?
28 A man who has no control over his spirit
Is like a broken-down city without a wall.

26 Like snow in summer,
and rain in harvest,
So esteem is not fitting for a fool.
2 As a bird wanders,
as a swallow flies about,
So a curse without cause does not come.
3 A whip for a horse, a bridle for a donkey,
And a rod for the fool's back.
4 Do not answer a fool according to his folly,
Lest you also become like him.
5 Answer a fool according to his folly,
Lest he become wise in his own eyes.

6 He who sends a message by the hand
of a fool
Cuts off feet, drinks damage.
7 The legs of the lame hang limp
So is a proverb in the mouth of fools.
8 Like one binding a stone in a sling,
So is he who gives esteem to a fool.
9 A thorn goes into the hand of a
drunkard
So is a proverb in the mouth of fools.
10 An archer who wounds anyone,
Is he who hires a fool or any passer-by.
11 As a dog returns to his own vomit,
So a fool repeats his folly.
12 Have you seen a man wise in his own
eyes?
There is more expectancy for a fool
than for him.
13 The lazy one says,
"There is a lion in the way!
A fierce lion is in the streets!"
14 *As* a door turns on its hinges,
So does the lazy one turn on his bed.
15 The lazy one buries his hand in a dish;
It tires him to bring it back to his
mouth.
16 The lazy one is wiser in his own eyes
Than seven rendering advice.
17 A passer-by meddling in a strife not his
own
Is like one who takes hold of a dog by
the ears.
18 Like a madman who throws sparks,
arrows, and death,
19 So is a man who deceived his
neighbour,
And says, "I was only joking!"
20 For lack of wood, the fire goes out.
And without a slanderer, strife ceases.
21 *As* charcoal is to burning coals, and
wood to fire,
So is a contentious man to kindle strife.
22 The words of a slanderer are as dainty
morsels,
Which go down into the inner parts of
the heart.
23 Burning lips with an evil heart
Are like earthenware covered with
silver dross.
24 He who hates, pretends with his lips,
And lays up deceit within him;
25 Though he speaks kindly,
do not believe him,
For there are seven abominations in his
heart.
26 Hatred is covered by deceit.
His evil is disclosed in the assembly.
27 Whoever digs a pit falls into it,
And whoever rolls a stone,
it turns back on him.
28 A lying tongue hates its bruised ones,
And a flattering mouth works ruin.

27 Do not boast of tomorrow,
For you do not know what a day
brings forth.
2 Let another man praise you,
And not your own mouth –
A stranger, and not your own lips.
3 A stone is heavy and sand is weighty,
But a fool's wrath is heavier than both.
4 Wrath is cruel and displeasure
overwhelming,
But who is able to stand before
jealousy?
5 Open reproof is better than hidden
love.
6 The wounds of a loved one are true,
But the kisses of an enemy are profuse.
7 One satisfied loathes the honeycomb,
But to a hungry one any bitter *food* is
sweet.
8 Like a bird that wanders from its nest,
So is a man who wanders from his
place.
9 Ointment and perfume gladden the
heart,
So one's counsel is sweet to his friend.
10 Do not forsake your own friend or your
father's friend,
And do not go into your brother's
house
In the day of your calamity –
Better is a neighbour nearby than a
brother far away.
11 My son, be wise, and gladden my
heart,
That I might have a word for him who
reproaches me.
12 A clever man foresees calamity, hides
himself;
The simple shall go on, they are

punished.
13 Take the garment of him who is guarantor for a stranger,
And for a strange woman pledge it.
14 He who greets his friend loudly early in the morning,
Shall have it reckoned to him as a curse.
15 Drops that never cease on a very rainy day
And a contentious woman are alike;
16 Whoever represses her represses the wind,
And his right hand encounters oil.
17 Iron is sharpened by iron,
And a man sharpens the face of his friend.
18 He who tends the fig tree eats its fruit;
And he who guards his master is esteemed.
19 As in water face *reflects* face,
So a man's heart *reflects* a man.
20 She'ol and destruction are not satisfied;
So the eyes of man are not satisfied.
21 A refining pot is for silver and a furnace for gold,
So a man *is tried* by his praise.
22 Even if you pound a fool in a mortar with a pestle
Along with crushed grain,
His folly shall not leave him.
23 Know well the state of your flocks;
Set your heart to your herds;
24 For riches are not forever,
Nor a diadem to all generations.
25 Grass vanishes, and new grass appears,
And the vegetation of the mountains are gathered in.
26 The lambs are for your garments,
And the goats for the price of a field;
27 And goats' milk enough for your food,
For the food of your household,
And sustenance for your girls.

28

The wrong shall flee though no one pursues,
But the righteous are as bold as a lion.
2 Because of transgression of a land,
Many are its rulers;
But by a man of understanding and knowledge,
Right is maintained.
3 A poor man who oppresses the poor
Is like a sweeping rain that leaves no food.
4 Those who forsake the Torah praise the wrong,
Those who guard the Torah strive with them.
5 Evil men do not understand right-ruling,
But those who seek יהוה understand all.
6 Better is the poor who walks in his integrity
Than one perverse in his ways, who is rich.
7 He who watches over the Torah is a discerning son,
But a companion of gluttons shames his father.
8 He who increases his possessions by interest and profit
Gathers it for him who shows favour to the poor.
9 He who turns away his ear from hearing the Torah,
Even his prayer is an abomination. [a]
10 He who causes the straight to go astray in an evil way,
Falls into his own pit;
But the perfect inherit the good.
11 A rich man is wise in his own eyes,
But the poor who has understanding searches him out.
12 When the righteous exult, there is great comeliness;
But when the wrong arise, a man is searched for.
13 He who hides his transgressions does not prosper,
But he who confesses and forsakes them finds compassion.
14 Blessed is the man who always fears *Elohim*,
But he who hardens his heart falls into

28a See also 15:29, Yesh. 59:1-2, Yn. 9:31, Yn. א 3:22.

evil.
15 A roaring lion and a charging bear
Is a wrongdoing ruler over poor people.
16 A leader who lacks understanding is a great oppressor,
But the hater of greed prolongs his days.
17 A man oppressed by blood-guilt flees into a pit;
Let no one help him.
18 He who walks blamelessly is saved,
But the perverted of ways falls at once.
19 He who tills his land is satisfied with bread,
But he who pursues vanities is filled with poverty.
20 A man of truth has many blessings,
But one in a hurry to be rich does not go unpunished.
21 To show partiality is not good,
Because for a piece of bread a man would transgress.
22 A man with an evil eye runs after wealth,
And does not know that poverty awaits him.
23 He who reproves a man finds more favour afterward
Than he who flatters with the tongue.
24 He who robs his father or his mother,
And says, "It is no transgression,"
He is a companion to a destroyer.
25 He who is greedy stirs up strife,
But he who trusts in יהוה prospers.
26 He who trusts in his own heart is a fool,
But he who walks wisely is delivered.
27 He who gives to the poor does not lack,
But he who hides his eyes does have many curses.
28 When the wrong rise up, men hide themselves;
But when they perish, the righteous increase.

29 One often reproved, hardening his neck,
Is suddenly broken, and there is no healing.
2 When the righteous increase, the people rejoice;
But when a wrong one rules, the people sigh.
3 He who loves wisdom gladdens his father,
But a companion of whores destroys wealth.
4 A sovereign establishes a land by right-ruling,
But one who receives bribes throws it down.
5 A man who flatters his neighbour
Spreads a net for his own feet.
6 An evil man is ensnared by transgression,
But the righteous sings and rejoices.
7 The righteous knows the plea of the poor,
The wrong does not understand *such* knowledge.
8 Scoffers ensnare a city,
But the wise turn away wrath.
9 When a wise man disputes with a foolish man,
Whether he rages or laughs, there is no peace.
10 Bloodthirsty men hate the perfect,
And seek the life of the straight.
11 A fool lets out all his breath,
But the wise keeping it back calms it down.
12 If a ruler listens to lying words,
All his servants become wrong.
13 The poor man and the oppressor have this in common:
יהוה gives light to the eyes of both.
14 The sovereign who rightly rules the poor with truth,
His throne is established forever.
15 A rod and reproof give wisdom,
But a child unrestrained brings shame to his mother.
16 When the wrong become many, transgression increases;
But the righteous look on their fall.
17 Discipline your son,
And he brings you rest and delight to your life.
18 Where there is no vision, the people are let loose,
But blessed is he who guards the

Torah.
19 A servant is not disciplined by words;
Though he understands, he does not respond.
20 Have you seen a man hasty in his words?
There is more expectancy for a fool than for him.
21 He who deals tenderly
With his servant from youth,
Has him as a son in the end.
22 A man of displeasure stirs up strife,
And a master of rage has many a transgression.
23 The pride of man brings him low,
But the humble in spirit obtains esteem.
24 He who shares with a thief hates his own life;
He hears an oath, but does not report.
25 The fear of man brings a snare,
But whoever trusts in יהוה is set on high.
26 Many seek the face of a ruler,
But right-ruling for man comes from יהוה.
27 An unrighteous man
Is an abomination to the righteous,
And he who is straight in the way
Is an abomination to the wrong.

30 The words of Aḡur son of Yaqeh, a message.
This man declared to Ithi'ěl,
to Ithi'ěl and Uḵal:
2 For I am more stupid than anyone,
And do not have the understanding of a man.
3 And I have not learned wisdom
That I should know the knowledge of the Set-apart One.
4 Who has gone up to the heavens and come down?
Who has gathered the wind in His fists?
Who has bound the waters in a garment?
Who established all the ends of the earth?
What is His Name,
And what is His Son's Name,
If you know it?
5 Every Word of Eloah is tried; [a]
He is a shield to those taking refuge in Him.
6 Do not add to His Words, [b]
Lest He reprove you,
and you be found a liar.
7 Two *matters* I have asked of You –
Deny them not to me before I die:
8 Remove falsehood and a lying word far from me;
Give me neither poverty nor riches;
Feed me my lawfull bread;
9 Lest I become satisfied and deny *You*,
And say, "Who is יהוה?"
And lest I be poor, and steal,
And seize the Name of my Elohim.
10 Do not slander a servant to his master,
Lest he curse you,
And you be found guilty.
11 There is a generation that curses its father,
And does not bless its mother –
12 There is a generation, clean in its own eyes,
But not washed from its own filth.
13 There is a generation;
Oh, how haughty are their eyes!
And their eyelids are lifted up.
14 There is a generation whose teeth are swords,
And whose jaw-teeth are knives,
To devour the poor from off the earth,
And the needy from *among* men.
15 The leech has two daughters:
"Give! Give!"
Three are not satisfied,
Four that never say, "Enough":
16 She'ol, and the barren womb,
Soil not satisfied with water,
And fire which never says, "Enough."
17 An eye that mocks his father,
And scorns to obey his mother –
Ravens of the wadi dig it out,
And young eagles eat it!
18 Three *matters* are too marvellous for me,

30a Teh. 12:6, Teh. 18:30. *30b* Deḇ. 4:2 & 12:32, Ḥazon 22:18-19.

And four which I do not understand:
19 The way of an eagle in the heavens,
The way of a snake on a rock,
The way of a ship in the heart of the sea,
And the way of a man with a young woman. [c]
20 This is the way of an adulterous woman:
She shall eat and wipe her mouth, and say,
"I have not done wickedness."
21 Under three *matters* the earth trembles,
And under four, it is unable to bear:
22 Under a servant when he reigns,
And a fool when he is satisfied with food,
23 Under a hated *woman* who marries,
And a female servant who supplants her mistress.
24 There are four *matters*
Which are little on the earth,
But they are exceedingly wise:
25 The ants are a people not strong,
Yet they prepare their food in the summer;
26 The rock badgers are a weak folk,
Yet they make their homes in the crags;
27 The locusts have no sovereign,
Yet they all go out in formation;
28 A spider takes hold with two hands,
And is in sovereigns' palaces.
29 There are three *matters*
That are going well,
And four are good in walking:
30 A lion, which is mighty among beasts
And does not turn away from facing all;
31 A greyhound, and a male goat,
And a sovereign whose army is with him.
32 If you have been foolish in lifting up yourself,
Or if you have plotted evil,
Put your hand on your mouth.
33 For as milk under pressure brings forth curds,
And as a nose under pressure brings forth blood,
So wrath under pressure brings forth strife.

31

The words of Sovereign Lemu'ĕl, a message which his mother taught him:
2 What, my chosen?
And what, chosen of my womb?
And what, chosen of my vows?
3 Do not give your strength to women,
Nor your ways to wiping away sovereigns.
4 Not for sovereigns, O Lemu'ĕl,
Not for sovereigns to drink wine,
Nor for princes to desire strong drink;
5 Lest they drink and forget *what is* inscribed,
And pervert the right of all the afflicted.
6 Give strong drink to him who is perishing,
And wine to those embittered in being.
7 Let him drink and forget his poverty,
And remember his trouble no more.
8 Open your mouth for the dumb,
In the cause of all the sons of the departed.
9 Open your mouth, judge righteously,
And plead the cause of the poor and needy.
10 Who does find a capable wife?
For she is worth far more than rubies.
11 The heart of her husband shall trust her,
And he has no lack of gain.
12 She shall do him good, and not evil,
All the days of her life.
13 She shall seek wool and flax,
And with delight she works with her hands.
14 She shall be as the ships of Tarshish,
She brings in her food from afar.
15 She also rises while it is still night,
And provides food for her household,
And what is law*full* for her girls.
16 She shall consider a field and buy it;
From her profits she shall plant a vineyard.
17 She shall gird herself with strength,

30c See Explanatory notes: Maiden

And strengthen her arms.
18 She shall taste when her gain is good;
Her lamp does not go out by night.
19 She shall stretch out her hands to the distaff,
And her hand shall hold the spindle.
20 She shall extend her hand to the poor,
And she shall reach out her hands to the needy.
21 She is not afraid of snow for her household,
For all her household is dressed in scarlet.
22 She shall make tapestry for herself;
She is dressed in fine linen and purple.
23 Her husband is known in the gates,
When he sits among the elders of the land.
24 She shall make fine linen and sell them,
And shall give girdles for the merchants.
25 Strength and splendour are her garments,
And she rejoices in time to come.
26 She shall open her mouth with wisdom,
And on her tongue is the Torah of loving-commitment.
27 She watches over the ways of her household,
And does not eat the bread of idleness.
28 Her children shall rise up and call her blessed;
Her husband *too*, and he praises her:
29 "Many daughters have done nobly,
But you have risen over them all."
30 Loveliness is deceptive
And prettiness is vain,
A woman who fears יהוה is to be praised.
31 Give her of the fruit of her hands,
And let her works praise her in the gates.

IYOḆ

JOB

1 There was a man in the land of Uts, whose name was Iyoḇ. And that man was perfect and straight, and one who feared Elohim and turned aside from evil.

2 And seven sons and three daughters were born to him.

3 And his possessions were seven thousand sheep, and three thousand camels, and five hundred yoke of oxen, and five hundred female donkeys, and a very large body of servants, so that this man was the greatest of all the people of the East.

4 And his sons went and had a feast in the house of each on his day, and sent and invited their three sisters to eat and to drink with them.

5 And it came to be, when the days of feasting had gone round, that Iyoḇ would send and set them apart, and he would rise early in the morning and offer ascending offerings – the number of them all – for Iyoḇ said, "It might be that my sons have sinned and cursed Elohim in their hearts." This Iyoḇ always did.

6 And the day came to be that the sons of Elohim came to present themselves before יהוה, and Satan also came among them.

7 And יהוה said to Satan, "From where do you come?" And Satan answered יהוה and said, "From diligently searching in the earth, and from walking up and down in it."

8 And יהוה said to Satan, "Have you considered My servant Iyoḇ, that there is none like him on the earth, a perfect and straight man, one who fears Elohim and turns aside from evil?"

9 And Satan answered יהוה and said, "Is Iyoḇ fearing Elohim for naught?

10 "Have You not made a hedge around him, and around his household, and around all that he has on every side? You have blessed the work of his hands, and his possessions have increased in the land.

11 But stretch out Your hand, please, and strike all that he has – if he would not curse You to Your face!"

12 And יהוה said to Satan, "See, all that he has is in your hand. Only do not lay a hand on himself." And Satan went out from the presence of יהוה.

13 And the day came to be when his sons and daughters were eating and drinking wine in the house of their brother, the first-born.

14 And a messenger came to Iyoḇ and said, "The oxen were ploughing and the donkeys feeding alongside them,

15 when Sheḇa fell upon them and took them away, and they struck the servants with the edge of the sword. And I alone have escaped to inform you!"

16 While he was still speaking, another also came and said, "The fire of Elohim fell from the heavens and burned up the sheep and the servants, and consumed them. And I alone have escaped to inform you!"

17 While he was still speaking, another also came and said, "The Kasdim formed three bands, and made a raid on the camels and took them away, and they struck the servants with the edge of the sword. And I alone have escaped to inform you!"

18 While he was still speaking, another also came and said, "Your sons and daughters were eating and drinking wine in the house of their brother, the first-born,

19 and see, a great wind came from the wilderness and struck the four corners of the house, and it fell on the young men, and they are dead. And I alone have escaped to inform you!"

20 Then Iyoḇ rose up and tore his robe, and shaved his head, and he fell to the ground and did obeisance.

21 And he said, "Naked I came from my mother's womb, and naked I return there. יהוה has given, and יהוה has taken away. Blessed be the Name of יהוה."

22 In all this Iyoḇ did not sin nor ascribe
wrong-doing unto Elohim.

2

Again the day came to be that the sons
of Elohim came to present themselves
before יהוה, and Satan also came among
them to present himself before יהוה.
2 And יהוה said to Satan, "From where
do you come?" And Satan answered יהוה
and said, "From diligently searching in the
earth, and from walking up and down in
it."
3 And יהוה said to Satan, "Have you
considered My servant Iyoḇ, that there is
none like him on the earth, a perfect and
straight man, one who fears Elohim and
turns aside from evil? And still he holds
fast to his integrity, although you incited
Me against him, to destroy him without
cause."
4 And Satan answered יהוה and said,
"Skin for skin, and all that a man has he
would give for his life!
5 "But stretch out Your hand, please, and
strike his bone and his flesh – if he would
not curse You to Your face!"
6 And יהוה said to Satan, "See, he is in
your hand, only spare his life."
7 And Satan went out from the presence
of יהוה, and struck Iyoḇ with loathsome
sores from the sole of his foot to the crown
of his head.
8 And he took a potsherd with which to
scrape himself while he sat in the midst of
the ashes.
9 And his wife said to him, "Do you still
hold fast to your integrity? Curse Elohim
and die!"
10 But he said to her, "You speak as one of
the foolish women speaks. Indeed, should
we accept *only* good from Elohim, and not
accept evil?" In all this Iyoḇ did not sin
with his lips.
11 And three of the friends of Iyoḇ heard
of all this evil that came on him, and each
one came from his own place – Eliphaz the
Tĕmanite, and Bildaḏ the Shuḥite, and
Tsophar the Na'amathite – and they met
together to come to sympathise with him
and to comfort him.
12 And they lifted up their eyes from a distance, and did not recognise him, and they
lifted their voices and wept. And each one
tore his robe and sprinkled dust on his head
toward the heavens.
13 Then they sat down with him on the
ground seven days and seven nights, and
no one spoke a word to him, for they saw
that the pain was very great.

3

After this Iyoḇ opened his mouth and
cursed the day of his birth.
2 And Iyoḇ spoke, and said,
3 "Let the day perish on which I was
born, and the night it was said, 'A male
child has been conceived.'
4 Let that day be darkness. Let not Eloah
from above seek for it, nor let light shine
upon it.
5 Let darkness and the shadow of death
buy it back, let a cloud dwell on it, let all
that blackens the day frighten it.
6 That night – let darkness seize it. Let it
not be included among the days of the
year, let it not come into the number of the
months.
7 Look, let that night be silent! Let no
singing come into it!
8 Let those curse it who curse the day,
who are ready to stir up Liwiathan.
9 Let the stars of its twilight be dark. Let
it wait for light, but have none. And let it
not see the eyelashes of the dawn.
10 For it did not shut up the doors of my
mother's womb, nor hide trouble from my
eyes.
11 Why did I not die from the womb,
come forth from the belly and expire?
12 Why were there knees to receive me?
Or breasts for me to suck?
13 For now I would have been lying in
peace. I would have slept – then I would
have been at rest,
14 with sovereigns and counsellors of the
earth, who built ruins for themselves,
15 or with rulers who had gold, who filled
their houses with silver,
16 or as a hidden untimely birth, as infants
who never saw light?
17 There the wrong cease raging, and
there the weary are at rest,
18 the prisoners rest together, they do not

hear the voice of the oppressor.
19 The small and great are there, and the
servant is free from his master.
20 Why does He give light to the sufferer,
and life to the bitter of being,
21 who are waiting for death, but it does
not come, and search for it more than
treasures;
22 who rejoice exceedingly, they are glad
when they find the burial-site?
23 Why does He give light to a man whose
way has been hidden, and whom Eloah has
hedged in?
24 For my sighing comes before I eat, and
my groanings pour out like water.
25 For that which I greatly feared has
come upon me, and that which I dreaded
has overtaken me.
26 I have not been at ease, nor have I been
undisturbed, nor been at rest, yet trouble
comes!"

4 And Eliphaz the Tĕmanite answered
and said,
2 "If one tries a word with you, would
you become impatient? But who is able to
withhold himself from speaking?
3 See, you have instructed many, and you
have made weak hands strong.
4 Your words have raised up him who
was stumbling, and you have strengthened
the weak knees.
5 But now it has come to you, and you
are impatient; it strikes you, and you are
troubled.
6 Is not your reverence your trust, the
integrity of ways your expectancy?
7 Remember, please: Who, being innocent, has ever perished? And where have
the straight ones ever been cut off?
8 According to what I have seen, those
who plough wickedness and sow suffering
reap the same.
9 Through the breath of Eloah they
perish, and through the Spirit of His nostrils they are consumed.
10 The roaring of the lion, and the voice of
the fierce lion, but the teeth of the young
lions shall be broken.
11 An old lion perishes for lack of prey,
and the cubs of the lioness are scattered.
12 And unto me a word was secretly
brought, and my ear received a little of it.
13 Amid thoughts from visions of the
night, when deep sleep falls on men,
14 fear came upon me, and trembling,
causing my bones to shake greatly.
15 Then a spirit passed before my face, the
hair on my body stood up.
16 It stood still, but I could not discern its
appearance. A form was before my eyes –
silence, then a voice I heard,
17 'Is mortal man more righteous than
Eloah? Is man more clean than his Maker?
18 'Look, He puts no trust in His servants,
and He charges His messengers with
straying.
19 'How much more those who dwell in
houses of clay, whose foundation is in the
dust, who are crushed like a moth?
20 'From morning till evening they are
beaten down, they perish forever, with no
one regarding.
21 'Are not the cords of their tents pulled
up? They die, without wisdom!'

5 "Call out, please, is there anyone to
answer you? And to which of the set-
apart ones would you turn?
2 For wrath kills the fool, and envy slays
the simple.
3 I myself have seen the fool taking root,
but suddenly his home was cursed.
4 His sons are far from safety, they are
crushed in the gate, with no one to deliver.
5 The hungry eat up his harvest, taking it
even from the thorns, and the snare snaps
up their wealth.
6 For evil does not come from the dust,
nor does trouble spring from the ground;
7 for man is born for trouble, and the
sparks fly upward.
8 But as for me, I would seek Ěl, and I
would submit my case to Elohim,
9 who is doing great and unsearchable
deeds, innumerable wonders,
10 who is giving rain on the earth's face,
and is sending waters on the field's face;
11 to set the lowly on high, and those who
mourn shall be lifted to safety,
12 thwarting the schemes of the crafty, so
that their hands do not work effectively;

13 catching the wise in their own craftiness, and the counsel of schemers are
swept away.
14 By day they encounter darkness, and at
noon they grope as in the night.
15 But He saves the needy from the sword
of their mouth, from the clutches of the
strong.
16 Thus the poor have expectancy, and unrighteousness shuts her mouth.
17 Look, blessed is the man whom Eloah
does reprove, so do not despise the discipline [a] of the Almighty.
18 For He bruises, but He binds up; He
smites, but His hands heal. [b]
19 In six distresses He delivers you, and in
seven no evil strikes you.
20 In scarcity of food He shall redeem you
from death, and in battle from the power of
the sword.
21 When the tongue scourges you are
shielded, and you have no fear when
destruction comes.
22 At destruction and at starvation you
laugh, and you have no fear of the beasts
of the earth.
23 For your covenant is with the stones of
the field, and the beasts of the field shall be
at peace with you.
24 And you shall know that your tent is in
peace, and shall visit your tent and not sin,
25 and shall know that your seed are
many, and your offspring like the grass of
the earth.
26 You shall come to the burial-site in ripe
old age, like the stacking of grain in its
season.
27 Look, this we have searched out, it is
so. Hear it, and know for yourself."

6 And Iyoḇ answered and said,
2 "Oh, that my grief were thoroughly
weighed, and my calamity be placed on the
scales!
3 For it would outweigh the sand of the
sea, therefore my words have been rash.
4 For the arrows of the Almighty are
within me, my spirit drinks in their poison,
the onslaughts of Eloah are arrayed against
me.
5 Does the wild donkey bray when it has
grass, or does the ox bellow over its
fodder?
6 Is tasteless food eaten without salt? Is
there any flavour in the juice of mallows?
7 I refuse to touch it, they are like food
when I am sick.
8 Oh that I might have my desire, that
Eloah would grant me what I long for!
9 That it would please Eloah to crush me,
loose His hand and cut me off!
10 Then I would still have comfort, and I
would rejoice in pain, though not spared,
for I have not hidden the words of the Set-
apart One.
11 What strength do I have, that I should
wait? And what is my end, that I should
prolong my life?
12 Is my strength the strength of stones? Is
my flesh of bronze?
13 Is my help not within me? And is
ability driven from me?
14 To him who is afflicted: loving-
commitment, even the one leaving the fear
of the Almighty.
15 My brothers are as undependable as a
wadi, as a bed on which streams once ran,
16 which are dark because of the ice, in
which the snow is hidden.
17 When it is warm, they cease to flow;
when it is hot, they vanish from their place.
18 The paths of their way turn aside, they
enter wastes and perish.
19 Passengers of Tēma looked expectantly, travellers of Sheḇa waited for them.
20 They were ashamed because they had
trusted, they came there and were disap-
pointed.
21 Indeed, you have now become the
same! You see *my* downfall and are afraid.
22 Did I ever say, 'Give to me'? or, 'Offer
a bribe for me from your wealth'?
23 or, 'Rescue me from the hand of the
enemy?' or, 'Redeem me from the hand of
oppressors'?
24 Teach me, and I shall be silent. And
show me where I have gone astray.
25 Words of uprightness are harsh! But

5a Mish. 3:12, Iḇ`rim 12:6-8. *5b* Yirm. 32:42, Ěḵah 3:31-32, Hosh. 6:1.

what does your reproving reprove?
26Do you reckon to reprove my words,
and the sayings of one in despair, which
are as wind?
27You would cast lots over the fatherless,
and make merchandise of your friend!
28But now, please look at me – whether I
would lie to your face.
29Relent, please, let there be no unrighteousness. Relent! My righteousness is still
in it.
30Is there unrighteousness on my tongue?
Does my taste not discern what is perverse?

7 "Does not man have to struggle on
earth? For his days are like the days of
a hired man.
2Like a servant who sighs for the shade,
and like a hireling longing for his wages,
3so am I allotted months of futility. And
nights of trouble have been appointed to
me.
4When I lie down, I say, 'When am I
going to rise, and the night be ended?' For
I have had my fill of tossing till dawn.
5My body is covered with worms and
dirt, my skin is cracked and it festers.
6My days are swifter than a weaver's
shuttle, and are spent without expectancy.
7Remember that my life is a breath! My
eye is never again to see good.
8The eye of him who sees me sees me no
longer. Your eyes are upon me, and I am no
more.
9The cloud fades and vanishes away, so
he who goes down to She'ol does not come
up.
10He returns no more to his house, nor
does his place know him any more.
11I also, I do not hold my mouth, I speak
in the distress of my spirit, I complain in
the bitterness of my being.
12Am I the sea, or a sea monster, that You
set a guard over me?
13When I say, 'My bed does comfort me,
my couch does ease my complaint,'
14then You frighten me with dreams and
make me afraid with visions,
15so that my being chooses strangling,
death rather than my bones.
16I have wasted away, I would not live
forever. Leave me alone, for my days are a
breath.
17What is man, that You should make
him great, that You should set Your heart
on him,
18that You should visit him every morning, trying him every moment?
19How long do You not look away from
me, nor leave me alone till I swallow my
saliva?
20Have I sinned? What have I done to
You, O Watcher of men? Why have You
set me as Your target, so that I am a burden
to You?
21And why do You not pardon my transgression, and take away my crookedness?
For now I lie down in the dust, and You
shall seek me, but I am not."

8 And Bildad̲ the Shuḥite answered and
said,
2"How long are you going to speak like
this, since the words of your mouth are a
strong wind?
3Does Ěl twist right-ruling? Or does the
Almighty twist what is right?
4If your sons have sinned against Him,
and He delivers them into the hand of their
transgression,
5if you diligently seek Ěl and plead with
the Almighty,
6if you were clear and straight, then
indeed He would awake for you, and shall
bless your righteous dwelling place.
7Though your beginning was small, yet
your latter end would greatly increase.
8Indeed, please ask the former generation, and prepare for the research of their
fathers,
9for we are but of yesterday, and know
not, because our days on earth are as a
shadow.
10Do they not teach you, speak to you,
and bring forth words from their heart?
11Does papyrus grow without a marsh, a
reed thrive without water?
12While it is yet green, not cut down, it
dries out before any plant.
13So are the paths of all who forget Ěl,
and the expectancy of a defiled one does

perish,
14 whose refuge is cut off, and whose trust
is a spider’s web.
15 He leans on his house, but it does not
stand. He holds it fast, but it does not last.
16 He is moist before the sun, and his
branches spread out in his garden.
17 His roots wrap around a heap, and look
for a place in the stones.
18 If he is destroyed from his place, then it
shall deny him: ‘I have not seen you.’
19 See, this is the joy of His way, and out
of the dust others grow.
20 See, Ěl does not cast away the perfect,
neither hold the hand of evil-doers.
21 While He fills your mouth with laughter, and your lips with rejoicing,
22 those hating you put on shame, and the
tent of the wrong is no more.”

9 And Iyoḇ answered and said,
2 “Truly I know it is so. But how is
man right with Elohim?
3 If one wished to dispute with Him, he
would not answer Him one time out of a
thousand.
4 Wise in heart and potent of power –
who has hardened himself against Him and
is at peace?
5 He who removes mountains, and they
do not know it, when He overturns them in
His displeasure;
6 who shakes the earth out of its place,
and its columns tremble;
7 who commands the sun, and it does not
rise; and He seals up the stars,
8 stretching out the heavens by Himself,
and treading upon the waves of the sea;
9 who made Ash, Kesil, and Kimah, and
the rooms of the south;
10 who performs great and unsearchable
deeds, and innumerable wonders.
11 Look, He goes by me, and I do not see;
and He moves past, but I do not discern
Him.
12 Look, He snatches away, who brings it
back? Who says to Him, ‘What are You
doing?’
13 Eloah does not turn back His displeasure, the helpers of pride stoop under
Him.
14 How much less would I answer Him,
choose my words with Him?
15 For though I were righteous, I would
not answer Him. I pray to Him for my
right-ruling.
16 Though I had called and He answered
me, I would not believe that He was listening to my voice.
17 For He crushes me with a storm, and
has multiplied my wounds for no cause.
18 He does not allow me to recover my
breath, but fills me with bitterness.
19 If *I speak* of power? Look, He is potent.
And if of right-ruling? Who sets me a
time?
20 If I am righteous? My mouth would
declare me wrong. Am I perfect? It would
declare me perverse.
21 Am I perfect? Do I not know my own
being? I despise my life!
22 It is all the same, therefore I say, ‘He
destroys the perfect and the wrong.’
23 If the scourge slays suddenly, He
laughs at the trial of the innocent.
24 Earth has been given into the hand of
the wrong. He covers the faces of its
judges. If it is not He, then who is it?
25 My days have become swifter than a
runner – they have fled, they have not seen
good.
26 They have passed by like swift ships,
like an eagle swooping on its prey.
27 If I say, ‘Let me forget my complaint,
let me put off my sad face, and let me
smile,’
28 I shall be afraid of all my sufferings. I
know that You do not hold me innocent.
29 If I am wrong, why should I labour in
vain?
30 If I washed myself with snow water,
and cleansed my hands with soap,
31 then You would plunge me into a ditch,
and my garments shall abhor me.
32 For *He is* not a man as I am that I
answer Him, and we come together into
right-ruling.
33 There is no mediator between us, to lay
his hand upon us both.
34 Let Him take His rod away from me,
and let His dread frighten me.
35 *Then* I would speak and not fear Him,

for I am not so within myself.

10 "My being has grown weary of
life. I let loose my complaint, I
speak in the bitterness of my being.
2 I say to Eloah, 'Do not declare me
wrong, show me why You strive with me.
3 Is it good to You that You should crush,
that You should despise the work of Your
hands, and shine on the counsel of the
wrong?
4 Do You have eyes of flesh? Do You see
as man sees?
5 Are Your days like the days of a mortal
man? Are Your years like the days of a
mighty man,
6 that You should seek for my crookedness and search out my sin?
7 For You know that I am not wrong, and
there is no one to deliver from Your hand.
8 Your hands have made me and shaped
me, together all around, yet You destroy
me.
9 Remember, please, that You have made
me like clay. And would You turn me into
dust again?
10 Did You not pour me out like milk, and
curdle me like cheese?
11 Skin and flesh you put on me, and
wove me with bones and sinews.
12 Life and loving-commitment You have
bestowed on me, and Your visitation has
preserved my spirit.
13 And these You have laid up in Your
heart, I know that this was with You:
14 If I sin, then You watch me, and let no
crookedness of mine go unpunished.
15 If I am wrong, woe to me! And if I am
righteous, I would not lift up my head –
filled with shame and seeing my grief!
16 If I lift it up high, you hunt me as a lion,
and again You would show Yourself marvellous against me.
17 You renew Your witnesses against me,
and increase Your vexation toward me;
changes and a host are with me.
18 So why have You brought me forth
from the womb? Oh, that I had perished
and no eye had seen me!
19 I should have been as though I had not
been – brought from the womb to the
burial-site.
20 Are not my days few? Then cease!
Leave me alone, so that I brighten up a
little,
21 Before I go, and not return, to the land
of darkness and the shadow of death,
22 a land as dark as darkness itself, as the
shadow of death, without any order, whose
light is as darkness."

11 And Tsophar the Naʽamathite
answered and said,
2 "Should a multitude of words go un-
answered? And should a man of lips be
declared right?
3 Should your babblings silence men?
And should you mock, and no one make
you ashamed?
4 Since you have said, 'My discourse is
flawless, and I have been clean in Your
eyes.'
5 But if only Eloah would speak, and
open His lips against you,
6 and show you the secrets of wisdom,
doubling your ability. Know then that
Eloah forgets *some* of your crookedness
for you.
7 Would you find out Eloah by searching,
or search out the end of the Almighty?
8 It is higher than the heavens – what
would you do? Deeper than She'ol – what
would you know?
9 Their measure is longer than the earth,
and broader than the sea.
10 If He passes through and shuts up, and
gathers, then who does reverse it?
11 For He knows false men. When He sees
wickedness does He not consider it?
12 But a senseless man takes heart when a
wild donkey's colt is born a man!
13 If you would prepare your heart, and
stretch out your hands toward Him;
14 if wickedness were in your hand, put it
far away and do not let perverseness dwell
in your tents;
15 then indeed you shall lift up your face
without spot; and you shall stand firm, and
not be afraid,
16 because you would forget sorrow, and
remember it as waters that have passed
away,

17 and your life would be brighter than noon. You would soar upward, you would be like the morning.

18 And you shall trust, because there is expectancy. And when you have searched you shall lie down in safety.

19 And you shall rest, and no one would make you afraid, and many shall seek your favour.

20 But the eyes of the wrong are consumed, and they shall not escape, and their expectancy is the breathing out of life!"

12

And Iyoḇ answered and said,
2 "Truly you are the people, and wisdom would die with you!

3 But I, like you, have a heart too; I am not less than you. And who does not know such as these?

4 I have become a laughing-stock to my friends – one who has called on Eloah and He answered him! A laughing-stock is the righteous, the perfect one!

5 A lamp is despised in the thought of one who is at ease – prepared for those whose feet slip.

6 The tents of robbers are at peace, and those who provoke Ěl are complacent, to him who brings Eloah into his hand!

7 But now ask the beasts, and they teach you; and the birds of the heavens, and they declare it to you;

8 or speak to the earth, and it teaches you; and the fish of the sea inform you.

9 Who among all these does not know that the hand of יהוה has done this,

10 in whose hand is the life of all that live, and the breath of all mankind?

11 Does the ear not try words? And the mouth taste food for itself?

12 With the aged is wisdom, and understanding with length of days.

13 With Him are wisdom and might, He has counsel and understanding.

14 Look, He breaks down, and it is not rebuilt. If He imprisons a man, there is no release.

15 Look, He withholds the waters, and they dry up. And He sends them out, and they overwhelm the earth.

16 With Him are strength and ability. The misled and the misleader are His.

17 He leads counsellors away stripped, and makes judges go mad.

18 He loosens the bonds of sovereigns, and binds a girdle on their loins;

19 who leads away priests as a spoil, and overthrows the mighty;

20 turning aside the lip of the trusted ones, and takes away the discernment of the elders;

21 pouring scorn on nobles, and loosens the girdle of the strong;

22 revealing deep *matters* out of darkness, and He brings the shadow of death to light;

23 making nations great, and He destroys them; spreading out the nations, and He leads them out.

24 turning aside the heart of the chiefs of the people of the earth, and He makes them wander in a pathless waste.

25 They grope in darkness, having no light, and He makes them stagger like a drunkard.

13

"Look, my eye has seen it all, my ear has heard and understood it.

2 What you know, I know too; I am not less than you.

3 But I would speak to the Almighty, and I delight to reason with Ěl.

4 But you smear with falsehood, worthless healers, all of you!

5 If you would only be silent, then it would be your wisdom!

6 Please hear my reasoning, and listen to the pleadings of my lips.

7 Would you speak perversely for Ěl, and speak deceit for Him?

8 Would you be partial towards Him? Would you plead for Ěl?

9 Would it be well when He searches you out? Or could you deceive Him as one deceives a man?

10 He would certainly reprove you if you secretly show partiality.

11 Should not His excellence make you afraid, and the dread of Him fall upon you?

12 Your weighty sayings are proverbs of ashes, your shields are shields of clay.

13 Be silent before me, and let me speak, and let whatever come upon me!

14 Why do I take my flesh in my teeth,
and put my life in my hands?
15 Though, He kills me – in Him I expect!
But I show my ways to be right before
Him.
16 He also is my deliverance, for a defiled
one does not come before Him.
17 Listen closely to my words, and with
your ears to what I say.
18 Look, please, I have prepared my case,
I know that I am in the right.
19 Who is he who would strive with me?
For then I would keep silent and die.
20 Only two *matters* do not do to me, then
I am not hidden from Your face:
21 Withdraw Your hand far from me, and
let not dread of You make me afraid.
22 Then call, and let me answer; or let me
speak, and You reply to me.
23 How many are my crookednesses and
sins? Let me know my transgression and
my sin.
24 Why do You hide Your face, and reckon me as Your enemy?
25 Would You frighten a leaf driven to and
fro? And would You pursue dry stubble?
26 For You write bitter *charges* against
me, and make me inherit the crookednesses of my youth,
27 and put my feet in the stocks, and look
closely to all my paths. You set a limit for
the soles of my feet.
28 And he, like that which is rotten, wastes
away, as a garment that is moth-eaten.

14 "Man born of woman is of few
days and turmoil-filled.
2 He comes forth like a flower and
withers. He flees like a shadow and does
not continue.
3 Yet on such a one You open Your eyes,
and bring me to right-ruling with Yourself!
4 Who brings the clean out of the unclean? No one!
5 Since his days are decided, the number
of his new *moons* is with You, You have
made his laws, and he does not pass over.
6 Look away from him and let him rest,
till like a hired man he enjoys his day.
7 For there is expectancy for a tree, if it is
cut down, that it does sprout again, and
that its tender branch does not cease.
8 Though its root grows old in the earth,
and its stump dies in the ground,
9 at the scent of water it buds and brings
forth foliage like a plant.
10 But man dies and is powerless, and
man expires, and where is he?
11 Water disappears from the sea, and a
river dries up and is parched,
12 and man shall lie down and not rise.
Till the heavens are no more, they awake
not, nor are aroused from their sleep.
13 If only You would hide me in She'ol,
conceal me until Your wrath turns away.
Set for me a law, and remember me!
14 If a man dies, would he live again? All
the days of my struggle I wait, till my
change comes.
15 You would call, and I would answer
You. You have yearned for the work of
Your hands.
16 For now You count my steps – do You
not watch over my sin?
17 My transgression is sealed up in a bag,
and You cover over my crookedness.
18 But a falling mountain crumbles away,
and a rock is moved from its place,
19 as water wears away stones, its out-
pouring washes away the soil of the earth –
so You have destroyed the expectancy of
man.
20 You overpower him, forever, and he is
gone – his face changes and You send him
away.
21 His sons come to esteem, and he does
not know it. And they are brought low, and
he does not perceive it.
22 He feels only the pain of his flesh, and
he mourns over himself."

15 And Eliphaz the Těmanite
answered and said,
2 "Would a wise man answer with vain
knowledge, or fill his belly with the east
wind?
3 Would he reason with useless talk, or
by speeches with which do not profit?
4 Indeed, you do away with reverence,
and withhold prayer before Ěl.
5 For your crookedness teaches your
mouth *what to say*, and you choose the

tongue of the crafty.

6 Not I, but your own mouth condemns you. And your own lips witness against you.

7 Were you the first one born? Or were you made before the hills?

8 Have you heard the secret counsel of Eloah? And do you limit wisdom to yourself?

9 What do you know that we do not know – understand, that is not within us?

10 Both the grey-haired and the aged are among us, much older than your father.

11 Are the comforts of Ěl not enough for you – and a word that deals gently with you?

12 What have you taken to heart? And why do your eyes flash?

13 That you should turn your spirit against Ěl, and let *such* words go out of your mouth?

14 What is man, that he should be clean? And one born of a woman, that he should be righteous?

15 Look, He puts no trust in His set-apart ones, and the heavens are not clean in His eyes,

16 how much less one who is loathsome and corrupt, drinking unrighteousness like water!

17 Let me show you – hear me – and this I have seen and declare,

18 which the wise declare, and have not hidden from their fathers,

19 to them alone the land was given, and no stranger passed over into their midst:

20 All the days of the wrong one he is paining himself, and few years have been stored up for the ruthless.

21 A frightening sound is in his ears; in peace a destroyer comes to him.

22 He believes not to return from darkness, and he is reserved for the sword.

23 He wanders about for food – where is it? He knows that a day of darkness is prepared for him.

24 Distress and pain frighten him – they overwhelm him, like a sovereign ready for the attack.

25 Because he has stretched out his hand against Ěl, and acts mightily against the Almighty.

26 He runs against Him defiantly, with thick-bossed shields.

27 For he has covered his face with his fatness, and he has put layers of fat on his loins.

28 But he dwells in ruined cities, in houses which no one lives in, which have been ready to become heaps.

29 He shall not be rich, and his wealth shall not rise, and his possessions shall not overspread the earth.

30 He does not turn away from darkness. The flame dries up his branches, and he turns aside by the breath of His mouth.

31 Let him not trust in falsehood, deceiving himself, for falsehood is his reward.

32 Before his day it is accomplished, and his branch shall not be green.

33 He shakes off his unripe grape like a vine, and throws off his blossom like an olive tree.

34 For the company of the defiled ones is barren, and fire consumes the tents of bribery.

35 They conceive trouble and bring forth wickedness, even their womb prepares deception."

16 And Iyoḇ answered and said,
2 "I have heard many *matters* like these; all of you are comforters of trouble!

3 Is there an end to words of wind? Or what provokes you that you answer?

4 I might also speak like you, if you were in my place. I might heap up words against you, and shake my head at you.

5 I might strengthen you with my mouth, and my moving lips might bring relief.

6 If I speak, my pain is not relieved; and if I refrain, does it leave me?

7 But now He has wearied me. You have stunned all my company.

8 And You have plucked me, and it is a witness. And my failure rises up against me, it bears witness to my face.

9 He has torn in His wrath, and He hates me. He has gnashed at me with His teeth; my adversary sharpens His eyes upon me.

10 They open wide their mouths at me, in scorn they have stricken my cheeks, they

mass themselves together against me.
11 Ěl has handed me over to the perverse,
and cast me into the hands of the wrong.
12 I was at ease, but He broke me. And He
took me by my neck and shattered me, and
He has set me up for His target.
13 His archers surround me, He splits my
kidneys in two and does not spare, He
pours out my bile on the ground.
14 He made a breach in me, breach upon
breach. He runs upon me like a mighty
man.
15 I sewed sackcloth over my skin, and
laid my horn in the dust.
16 My face is reddened from weeping, and
on my eyelids is the shadow of death;
17 though no violence was on my hand,
and my prayer sincere.
18 O earth, do not cover my blood, and let
my cry have no resting place!
19 See, even now my witness is in the
heavens, and my defender is on high.
20 My friends are they that scorn me; my
eyes pour out tears to Eloah.
21 O that one might plead for a man with
Eloah, as a man with his neighbour!
22 When a few years are past, then I shall
go the way of no return.

17 "My spirit has been broken, my
days have been extinguished, burial-sites are for me.
2 Truly, mockeries are with me, and my
eye rests on their insults!
3 Please lay down a pledge for me with
Yourself. Who would strike hands with
me?
4 For You have hidden their heart from
understanding, therefore You do not exalt
them.
5 He who denounces friends for a share,
even the eyes of his children shall fail.
6 But He has made me a byword of the
people, whereas in former times I was as a
drum.
7 And from sorrow my eye has grown
dim, and all my members are like shadows.
8 Upright ones are astonished at this, and
the innocent stirs himself up against the
defiled one.
9 And the righteous holds to his way, and
he who has clean hands becomes stronger
and stronger.
10 But please, come back again, all of you,
for I do not find a wise one among you.
11 My days have passed by, my plans have
been broken off – the desires of my heart.
12 They would turn night into day, *saying*
that light is near, in the presence of darkness!
13 If I wait – She'ol is my house, I shall
make my bed in darkness,
14 I shall say to corruption, 'You are my
father,' – to the worm, 'You are my mother
and my sister.'
15 Where then is my expectancy? As for
my expectancy, who would see it?
16 Would it sink down into She'ol? Would
we together go down into the dust?"

18 And Bildaḏ the Shuḥite answered
and said,
2 "When do you put an end to words?
Understand, and let us then talk.
3 Why should we be reckoned as beasts,
as stupid in your eyes?
4 You who tear yourself to pieces in displeasure – would the earth be forsaken for
your sake? Or the rock move from its
place?
5 Indeed, the light of the wrong goes out,
and the flame of his fire does not shine.
6 The light shall be dark in his tent, and
his lamp beside him is put out.
7 The steps of his strength are impeded,
and his own counsel overthrows him.
8 For he is sent into a net by his own feet,
and he walks on a pit-fall.
9 The net seizes his heel, a snare prevails
over him.
10 A noose is hidden on the ground for
him, and a trap for him in the path.
11 Alarms frighten him on all sides, and
chase him at his heels.
12 His strength is starved, and calamity is
ready at his side.
13 It devours parts of his skin, the first-
born of death devours his parts.
14 He is torn from the shelter of his tent,
and they parade him before the sovereign
of alarms.
15 In his tent dwells that which is none of

his; brimstone is scattered on his house.
[16]His roots below dry up, and his branch
is cut off above.
[17]Remembrance of him perishes from the
earth, and he has no name on the street.
[18]They thrust him from light into darkness, and chase him out of the world.
[19]He leaves no offspring or descendant
among his people, nor any survivor in his
dwellings.
[20]Those in the west are astonished at his
day, as those in the east are frightened.
[21]Indeed, such are the dwellings of the
perverse, and this is the place of him who
does not know Ěl."

19 And Iyoḇ answered and said,
[2]"How long would you grieve my
life, and crush me with words?
[3]These ten times you have insulted me,
shamelessly you attack me.
[4]Even if I have truly gone astray, my
straying remains with me.
[5]If indeed you would exalt yourselves
above me, and plead against me my
reproach,
[6]know then that Eloah has overthrown
me, and has surrounded me with His net.
[7]See, I cry, 'Violence!' but I am not
heard. I cry aloud, but there is no right-
ruling.
[8]He has fenced up my way, and I pass
not over. And He has placed darkness in
my paths.
[9]He has stripped me of my esteem, and
taken the crown from my head.
[10]He breaks me down on every side, and
I am gone; and uproots my expectancy like
a tree.
[11]And He kindled His wrath against me,
and He counts me as one of His enemies.
[12]His companies come together, and they
cast up their way against me, and encamp
all around my tent.
[13]He has removed my brothers far away
from me, and my friends are completely
estranged from me.
[14]My near ones have fallen away, and my
close friends have forgotten me.
[15]The guests in my house, and my female
servants, reckon me for a stranger – I am a
foreigner in their eyes.
[16]I have called my servant, but he gives
no answer – I have to beg him with my
mouth.
[17]My spirit is strange to my wife, and my
loving-commitment to the children of my
own body.
[18]Even young children have scorned me.
I rise, and they speak against me.
[19]All my intimate friends loathe me, and
those whom I love have turned against me.
[20]My bone clings to my skin and to my
flesh, and I have escaped by the skin of my
teeth.
[21]Show favour to me, show favour to me,
O you my friends, for the hand of Eloah
has struck me!
[22]Why do you persecute me like Ěl *does*,
and are not satisfied with my flesh?
[23]Oh, that my words were written down!
Oh, that they were inscribed in a book,
[24]engraved on a rock with an iron pen
and lead, forever!
[25]For I know that my Redeemer lives,
and as the Last shall rise over the dust;
[26]and after my skin has been struck off,
then in my flesh I shall see Eloah,
[27]whom I myself shall see on my side,
and not a stranger. My kidneys have failed
within me!
[28]If you say, 'Why do we persecute him?'
Seeing the root of the matter has been
found in me,
[29]fear the sword yourselves, for wrath
brings the punishment of the sword, so that
you know there is a judgment."

20 Then Tsophar the Naʽamathite
answered and said,
[2]"Truly, my thoughts make me respond,
even because of my haste within me.
[3]I have listened to the reproof which
insults me, and the spirit of my understanding makes me answer.
[4]You have known this of old, since man
was placed on earth,
[5]that the singing of the wrong is short-
lived, and the joy of the defiled one is but
for a moment?
[6]Although his pride mounts up to the
heavens, and his head does reach to the

clouds,
[7] he perishes forever like his own dung.
Those who have seen him say, 'Where is
he?'
[8] He flies away like a dream, and is not
found. And he is driven away like a vision
of the night.
[9] Eyes that saw him do so no more, nor
does his place see him any more.
[10] His sons seek the favour of the poor,
and his hands give back his wealth.
[11] His bones shall be filled with his youth,
but it lies down with him in the dust.
[12] Though evil is sweet in his mouth, he
hides it under his tongue,
[13] *though* he fondles it and does not
forsake it, but still keeps it in his mouth,
[14] his food is turned in his stomach, the
bitterness of cobras is in him.
[15] He has swallowed down riches, then
vomits them up – Ěl drives it out of his
stomach.
[16] He sucks the poison of cobras; the
tongue of the poisonous snake kills him.
[17] He looks not on streams, the rivers
flowing with honey and cream.
[18] He is giving back what he laboured for,
and does not eat it – like wealth from his
trade, but he does not enjoy.
[19] For he has oppressed, he has forsaken
the poor, he has seized a house which he
did not build.
[20] For he shall not know ease in his inner-
most, neither save what he desires.
[21] There is no left-over after he has eaten,
therefore his good does not last.
[22] With all his plenty he is in distress; the
hand of every labourer comes against him.
[23] It shall be, at the filling of his stomach,
that He casts on him His burning wrath,
and rains it down on him while he is
eating.
[24] He shall flee from the iron weapon, a
bronze bow pierce him through.
[25] It is drawn, and comes out of the body,
and the gleaming point comes out of his
gall. Fears come upon him.
[26] All darkness waits for his treasures. A
fire not blown consumes him, it destroys
what remains in his tent.
[27] The heavens reveal his crookedness,
and the earth rises up against him.
[28] The increase of his house departs,
flowing away in the day of His wrath.
[29] This is the portion from Elohim for a
wrong man, and the heritage Ěl has
decreed for him."

21

And Iyoḇ answered and said,
[2] "Listen closely to my word, and
let this be your comfort.
[3] Bear with me and let me speak, and
after I have spoken, keep mocking.
[4] As for me, is my complaint against
man? And why should I not be impatient?
[5] Look at me and be appalled, then put
your hand on your mouth.
[6] And when I consider it I am frightened,
and my body shudders.
[7] Why do the wrong live, become old,
and become mighty in power? [a]
[8] Their seed is established with them
before their face, and their offspring before
their eyes.
[9] Their houses are peace without fear,
neither is the rod of Eloah upon them.
[10] Their bull breeds and does not fail,
their cow calves without miscarriage.
[11] They send forth their little ones like a
flock, and their children dance.
[12] They sing to the tambourine and lyre,
and rejoice to the sound of the flute.
[13] They spend their days in goodness, and
in a moment go down to She'ol.
[14] And they say to Ěl, 'Turn aside from
us, for we have no desire to know Your
ways.
[15] Who is the Almighty, that we should
serve Him? And what profit do we have if
we pray to Him?'
[16] See, is their good not in their own
hand? (The counsel of the wrong has been
far from me).
[17] How often is the lamp of the wrong put
out, and does come upon them their
calamity, sorrows He allots in His displeasure?
[18] They are like straw before the wind,

21a Teh. 73: 3 & 17, Yirm. 12:1-2 and Teh. 73: 17.

and like chaff that a storm steals away.
19 *You say*, 'Eloah stores up one's wickedness for his children.' Let Him repay him,
so that he knows it.
20 Let his eyes see his destruction, and let
him drink of the wrath of the Almighty.
21 For what is his delight in his house after
him, when the number of his new *moons* is
cut off?
22 Does anyone teach Ěl knowledge, since
He judges those that are exalted?
23 One dies in his perfect strength, completely at ease and satisfied;
24 His pails are filled with milk, and his
bones are juicy with marrow.
25 Another one dies in the bitterness of his
being, and never eats with pleasure.
26 Together they lie down in the dust, and
worms cover them.
27 Look, I know your thoughts, and the
plots with which you would wrong me.
28 For you say, 'Where is the house of the
noble one? And where is the tent, the
dwelling place of the wrong ones?'
29 Have you not asked those passing by
the way? And do you not know their signs?
30 That the wicked is kept for the day of
calamity. They are brought to the day of
wrath.
31 Who declares his way to his face? And
who repays him for what he has done?
32 As for him, he is brought to the burial-
site, and a watch is kept over the heap.
33 The clods of the wadi shall be sweet to
him, and all men follow him, innumerable
are those before him.
34 How then do you comfort me in vain,
seeing that perverseness remains in your
answers?"

22 And Eliphaz the Těmanite answered and said,
2 "Would a strong man be of use to Ěl?
Even he who is wise be of use to Him?
3 Is it a delight to the Almighty that you
are righteous? Or gain, that you make your
ways perfect?
4 Is it because of your fear of Him that
He reproves you, or enters into right-ruling
with you?
5 Is not your evil great? And is there no
end to your crookednesses?
6 For you take pledges from your brother
for naught, and strip the naked of their
garments.
7 You do not give the weary water to
drink, and you have withheld bread from
the hungry.
8 But the man of strength, he has the
earth, and the highly respected man dwells
in it.
9 You have sent widows away empty, and
the arms of the fatherless are crushed.
10 Therefore snares are all around you,
and sudden fear alarms you,
11 or darkness, so that you do not see, and
a flood of water covers you.
12 Is not Eloah in the height of heaven?
And see the highest stars, how lofty they
are!
13 And you have said, 'What does Ěl
know? Would He judge through the dark
cloud?
14 'Clouds screen Him, so that He does
not see, and He moves about the circuit of
the heavens.'
15 Do you observe the old way which
wicked men have trod,
16 who were cut down before their time,
whose foundations were swept away by a
flood?
17 They said to Ěl, 'Turn aside from us!'
And what did the Almighty do to them?
18 Yet He filled their houses with the
good! (But the counsel of the wrong has
been far from me).
19 The righteous see it and are glad, and
the innocent mock at them *and say*,
20 'Truly, our adversaries are cut off, and
fire has consumed their excess.'
21 Be of service to Him, and be at peace;
thereby blessing shall come to you.
22 Please accept the Torah from His
mouth, and lay up His words in your heart.
23 If you return to the Almighty, you are
built up. If you remove unrighteousness far
from your tents,
24 and lay *your* gold in the dust, and *the
gold of* Ophir among the stones of the
wadis,
25 then the Almighty shall be your gold
and your silver, strength to you.

26 Then you shall certainly delight in the
Almighty, and lift up your face to Eloah,
27 make your prayer to Him. And He shall
hear you, and you shall pay your vows.
28 And whatever you decide on shall be
established for you, and light shine on your
ways.
29 For they have made low, and you say,
'Up!' And He saves the lowly of eyes.
30 Would He deliver one who is not innocent? So by the cleanness of your hands
you shall be delivered."

23 And Iyoḇ answered and said,
2 "Even today my complaint is bitter; my hand is heavy on account of my
groaning.
3 If only I knew where to find Him,
I would come to His dwelling-place!
4 I would present my case before Him,
and fill my mouth with proofs.
5 I would know the words which He
would answer me, and understand what He
would say to me.
6 Would He contend with me in great
power? No! But He would pay attention to
me.
7 There the upright might reason with
Him, and I would go safe forever from my
Judge.
8 See, I go forward, but He is not; and
backward, but I do not perceive Him;
9 to the left where He is working, but I do
not see; He turns to the right, but I do not
see.
10 For He knows the way that I take.
When He has tried me, I would come forth
as gold.
11 My foot has held fast to His steps. I
have guarded His way, and did not turn
aside.
12 I have not strayed from the command
of His lips. I have treasured the words of
His mouth more than my *own* law.
13 But He is One, and who does turn Him?
And He does whatever His being has
desired.
14 For He makes complete my law, and
many like these are with Him.
15 Therefore I am troubled at His presence; I consider, and I am afraid of Him.
16 For Ěl has made me faint-hearted, and
the Almighty has alarmed me;
17 because I was not cut off before darkness, and from my face He has covered the
thick darkness.

24 "Times are not hidden from the
Almighty, and why have not those
who know Him seen His days?
2 They remove landmarks; they rob and
feed on flocks;
3 they drive away the donkey of the
fatherless; they take the widow's ox as a
pledge;
4 they turn the needy out of the way; the
poor of the earth have hidden together.
5 See, as wild donkeys in the wilderness
they go about their tasks, eager seekers for
prey; the desert *gives* his bread, for the
children.
6 They reap his fodder in a field and they
glean the vineyard of the wrong.
7 They spend the night naked, without a
garment, and without covering in the cold.
8 They are wet with the showers of the
hills, and have embraced a rock for lack of
shelter.
9 They snatch away the fatherless from
the breast, and take a pledge from the poor;
10 naked, they shall go about without a
garment; and hungry, they shall take away
sheaves.
11 They press out oil within their walls;
winepresses they shall tread, yet suffer
thirst.
12 Men groan in the city, and the beings of
the wounded cry out, and Eloah does not
regard it as foolish.
13 They have become rebels against the
light; they have not known His ways nor
remained in His paths.
14 The murderer rises at daylight, he kills
the poor and needy, and in the night he is
as a thief.
15 And the eye of the adulterer watches
for dusk, saying, 'No eye sees me.' And he
puts a covering on the face.
16 In the dark he has broken into houses;
by day they shut themselves up; they have
not known light.
17 For all of them morning is the same as

the shadow of death, when he discerns the
extreme fears of the shadow of death.
18 He is swift on the face of the waters;
their portion is cursed in the earth; he does
not turn into the way of vineyards.
19 Drought and heat snatch away snow
waters – She'ol *those who* have sinned.
20 The womb forgets him, the worm feeds
sweetly on him; he is remembered no
more, and wickedness is broken like a tree;
21 treating evil the barren who does not
bear, and does no good for the widow.
22 But He draws the mighty away with
His power – He rises up, and no one is
certain of life.
23 He gives him safety, and he leans on it;
yet His eyes are on their ways.
24 They are lifted up for a little while, then
they are gone, then they shall be brought
low. Like all *else* they are gathered up, and
they are cut off like the heads of grain.
25 And if it is not so, who does prove me a
liar, and make my word worthless?"

25

And Bildaḏ the Shuḥite answered
and said,
2 "Rule and fear belong to Him, making
peace in His high places.
3 Is there any number to His armies? And
on whom does His light not rise?
4 So how could man be righteous before
Ěl? Or how could he be flawless who is
born of a woman?
5 See, even the moon does not shine, and
the stars have not been flawless in His
eyes,
6 how much less man, a maggot, and a
son of man, a worm?"

26

And Iyoḇ answered and said,
2 "How have you helped the powerless, saved an arm not strong?
3 How have you given counsel to the
unwise, or declared sound advice to many?
4 With whom have you spoken words?
And whose spirit came from you?
5 The dead wait – those under the waters
and those inhabiting them.
6 She'ol is naked before Him, and
destruction has no covering.
7 *He it was* who stretched out the north
over emptiness, hanging the earth upon
space,
8 binding up waters in His thick clouds,
and the cloud is not torn under them,
9 covering the surface of His throne,
spreading His cloud over it.
10 A law of encirclement on the face of
the waters – until the end of light with
darkness.
11 The columns of the heavens tremble,
and are stunned at His reproof.
12 By His power He has calmed the sea,
and by His understanding He struck down
Rahaḇ.
13 By His Spirit He adorned the heavens.
His hand whirled the fleeing serpent.
14 See, these are the fringes of His ways,
and how little a matter is heard of Him!
And who understands the thunder of His
power?"

27

And Iyoḇ again took up his discourse, and said,
2 "As Ěl lives, who has turned aside my
right-ruling, and the Almighty, who has
made my life bitter,
3 as long as my breath is in me, and the
spirit of Eloah in my nostrils,
4 my lips do not speak unrighteousness,
nor my tongue utter deceit.
5 Far be it from me that I grant that you
are right. Until I die I would not turn aside
my integrity from me.
6 My righteousness I hold fast, and I do
not let it go. My heart does not reproach
me as long as I live.
7 Let my enemy be like the wrongdoer,
and he who rises up against me like the
unrighteous.
8 For what is the expectancy of the
defiled one, when He does cut off, when
Eloah takes away his life?
9 Would Ěl hear his cry when distress
comes upon him?
10 Would he delight himself in the
Almighty – call on Eloah at all times?
11 Let me teach you by the hand of Ěl, that
which is with the Almighty I do not hide.
12 See, all of you have seen it. Why then
are you altogether vain?
13 This is the portion of a wrong man with

Ěl, and the inheritance of cruel ones, which
they receive from the Almighty:
14 If his children are increased, it is for the
sword; and his offspring shall not have
enough to eat.
15 Those who remain of him are buried in
death, and their widows do not weep.
16 Though he heaps up silver like dust,
and lays up garments like clay –
17 he lays up, but the righteous puts it on,
and the innocent divides the silver.
18 He built his house like a moth, like a
booth which a watchman made.
19 He lies down, a rich man, but he is not
gathered. When he opens his eyes, it is no
more!
20 Alarms overtake him like a flood; a
storm wind shall steal him away in the
night.
21 The east wind takes him away, and he
is gone; for it sweeps him from his place.
22 And it hurls itself against him and does
not spare; he swiftly flees from its power.
23 It claps its hands at him, and it hisses
him out of his place.

28 "Indeed, there is a mine for silver,
and a place where gold is refined.
2 Iron is taken from the earth, and copper
is smelted from ore.
3 An end to darkness he has set, and to
every limit he is searching, to rocks in
deepest darkness.
4 He opens a shaft far away from people;
they are forgotten by feet; they hang far
away from men; they swing to and fro.
5 Earth, out of which grows food, is
turned underneath as by fire;
6 its stones are the place of sapphires,
and it has dust of gold.
7 No bird of prey knows the path, nor has
the hawk's eye seen it.
8 The proud beasts have not trodden it,
nor has the fierce lion passed over it.
9 He puts his hand on the flint; he shall
overturn the mountains at the roots.
10 He cuts out channels in the rocks, and
his eye sees every precious *gem*.
11 He dams up the sources of the rivers;
and he brings to light what is hidden.
12 And wisdom – where is it found? And
where is the place of understanding? [d]
13 Man does not know its value, and it is
not found in the land of the living.
14 The deep has said, 'It is not in me,' and
the sea has said, 'It is not with me.'
15 Gold is not given for it, nor is silver
weighed out as its price.
16 It is not valued in the gold of Ophir, in
precious shoham or sapphire.
17 Gold or crystal are not to be compared
with it, nor is it exchanged for a vessel of
fine gold.
18 No mention is made of coral or crystal,
for the price of wisdom is above rubies.
19 The topaz of Kush is not to be compared with it, nor is it valued in clean gold.
20 And wisdom – from where does it
come? And where is the place of understanding?
21 It has been hidden from the eyes of all
living, and concealed from the birds of the
heavens.
22 Destruction and death have said, 'With
our ears we have heard a report of it.'
23 Elohim has understood its way, and He
has known its place.
24 For He looks to the ends of the earth,
sees under all the heavens,
25 making a weight for the wind, and measuring out the waters by measure.
26 When He made a law for the rain, and a
way for the lightning of thunder,
27 then He saw wisdom and declared it;
He prepared it and also searched it out.
28 And He said to man, 'See, the fear of
יהוה', that is wisdom, and to turn from evil
is understanding.' "

29 And Iyoḇ again took up his discourse, and said,
2 "Oh, that I were as in months past, as in
the days when Eloah protected me;
3 when His lamp shone on my head,
when I walked in the dark by His light;
4 as I was in the days of my autumn,
when the intimacy of Eloah was on my
tent;
5 when the Almighty was still with me,
when my children were around me;
6 when my steps were bathed with
cream, and the rock poured out rivers of oil

for me.
[7] When I went out to the gate by the city,
to take my seat in the open square,
[8] the young men saw me and hid, and the
aged rose up, they stood;
[9] rulers held back their words, and laid a
hand on their mouth;
[10] the voice of leaders was hushed, and
their tongue clung to the roof of their
mouth.
[11] For when the ear heard, it blessed me,
and when the eye saw, it gave witness of
me;
[12] because I rescued the poor who cried
out, and the fatherless who had no helper.
[13] The blessing of the perishing one
would come upon me, and I made the widow's heart sing for joy.
[14] I put on righteousness, and it robed me;
right-ruling was my cloak and turban.
[15] I was eyes to the blind, and I was feet to
the lame.
[16] I was a father to the poor, and I investi-
gated the case which I did not know.
[17] And I broke the jaws of the perverse,
and snatched the prey from his teeth.
[18] Then I thought I would die in my nest,
and increase my days as the sand,
[19] my root reaching out to the waters, and
dew lying all night on my branch,
[20] my esteem fresh within me, and my
bow renewed in my hand.
[21] To me they listened, and they waited,
and kept silence at my counsel.
[22] After my words they did not speak
again, and my speech settled on them.
[23] And they waited for me like the rain,
and they opened their mouth wide as for
the latter rain.
[24] I smiled at those who did not believe,
and the light of my face they did not dim.
[25] I chose the way for them, and sat as
chief, and I dwelt like a sovereign in the
army, like one who comforts mourners.

30 "But now they laugh at me, those
younger than I, whose fathers I
would have refused to put with my sheep
dogs.
[2] Of what use to me is the strength of
their hands, since their manhood power
has perished?
[3] They are dried up from lack and
hunger, they flee to a parched land,
formerly a waste and ruin.
[4] They pluck salt herbs by the bushes,
and broom tree roots for their food.
[5] They were driven out from among *men*,
they shouted at them as at a thief,
[6] to dwell in the gullies of wadis, holes of
the ground and clefts.
[7] Among the bushes they cry out, under
the nettles they huddled together –
[8] sons of fools, even sons without a
name, they have been whipped out of the
land.
[9] And now I have become their song, and
I am a byword to them.
[10] They have loathed me, they have kept
far from me, and did not refrain from
spitting in my face.
[11] Because He has loosed my bowstring
and afflicted me, they have thrown off
restraint in my presence.
[12] At my right hand a brood rises; they
pushed away my feet, and they raise up
against me their destructive ways.
[13] They have broken up my path, they
gain by my ruin; no one restrains them.
[14] They come as *through* a wide breach;
rushing on me under the ruins.
[15] Destructions are turned upon me; they
pursue my life as the wind, and my welfare
has passed like a cloud.
[16] And now my life pours itself out; days
of affliction seize me.
[17] My bones have been pierced in me at
night, and my gnawings never lie down.
[18] By great exertion is my garment
changed – it girds me as the collar of my
coat,
[19] throwing me into the mud, and I have
become like dust and ashes.
[20] I cry out to You, but You do not answer
me; I stand up, but You *only* look at me.
[21] You have become cruel to me; with the
power of Your hand You oppose me.
[22] You lift me up to the wind, making me
to ride it; and You melt me in a storm.
[23] For I have known that You bring me to
death, and to the house of appointment for
all living.

24 Yet does not one in a heap of ruins
stretch out his hand, or in calamity cry out
for help?
25 Did I not weep for him who was in
trouble? Was my being not grieved for the
poor?
26 When I looked for good, then evil came
to me. And when I waited for light, darkness came.
27 My inward parts boiled and did not
rest; days of affliction went before me.
28 I went about blackened, but not by the
sun; I stood up in the assembly, I cried for
help.
29 I became a brother of jackals, and a
companion of ostriches.
30 My skin became black upon me, and
my bones burned with heat.
31 So my lyre becomes mourning, and my
flute the sound of weeping.

31 “I have made a covenant with my
eyes. How then could I gaze at a
maiden?
2 For what is the portion of Eloah from
above, and the inheritance of the Almighty
from on high?
3 Is it not calamity to the perverse, and
strangeness to the workers of wickedness?
4 Does He not see my ways, and number
all my steps?
5 If I have walked with falsehood, or if
my foot has hurried to deceit,
6 let Him weigh me in a right scale, and
let Eloah know my integrity.
7 If my step does turn from the way, or
my heart has gone after my eyes, or if any
spot has clung to my hands,
8 let me sow, and another eat; and let my
harvest be rooted out.
9 If my heart has been enticed by a
woman, or if I have lurked at my neighbour’s door,
10 let my wife grind for another, and let
others bow down over her.
11 For that would be a wicked scheme,
and a punishable crookedness.
12 For that would be a fire that burns to
destruction, and take root among all my
increase.
13 If I have refused the plea of my male
servant or my female servant when they
complained against me,
14 then what should I do when Ěl rises up?
And when He punishes, what should I
answer Him?
15 Did not He who made me in the womb
make him? And did not One fashion us in
the womb?
16 If I have withheld the poor from pleasure, or caused the widow’s eyes to fail,
17 or eaten my piece of bread by myself,
and the fatherless did not eat of it –
18 but from my youth he grew up with me
as *with* a father, and from my mother’s
womb I guided her –
19 if I have seen anyone perish for lack of
garments, or a poor one without covering;
20 if his loins have not blessed me, and he
warmed himself with the fleece of my
sheep;
21 if I have raised my hand against the
fatherless, when I saw I had help in the
gate;
22 let my arm fall from my shoulder, and
my arm be broken from the bone.
23 For I am in dread of destruction from
Ěl, and from His excellence I could not
escape.
24 If I have put my trust in gold, or called
fine gold my refuge;
25 if I have rejoiced because my wealth
was great, and because my hand had
gained much;
26 if I have looked at the sun when it
shines, or the moon moving in brightness,
27 so that my heart has been secretly
enticed, and my mouth has kissed my
hand –
28 that too is a punishable crookedness,
for I would have denied Ěl above.
29 If I have rejoiced when he who hated
me was ruined, or lifted myself up when
evil found him –
30 also I have not allowed my mouth to sin
by asking for a curse on his life –
31 if the men of my tent did not say, ‘Who
is there that has not been satisfied with his
meat?’
32 The stranger did not have to spend the
night in the street, for I have opened my
doors to the way.

33 If I have covered my transgressions like
Aḏam, by hiding my crookedness in my
bosom,
34 then let me fear the great crowd, and
dread the scorn of clans, then I would be
silent, and go out of the door!
35 Who would give me a hearing? See, my
signature, let the Almighty answer me, and
let my accuser write a bill!
36 Would I not take it up on my shoulder,
bind it on me for a crown?
37 I would declare to Him the number of
my steps – I would approach Him like a
prince.
38 If my land cries out against me, or its
furrows weep together;
39 if I have eaten its fruit without payment, or caused its owners to die;
40 let thistles grow instead of wheat, and
useless weed instead of barley." The words
of Iyoḇ are ended.

32 Then these three men ceased to
answer Iyoḇ, because he was righteous in his own eyes.
2 And the wrath of Elihu, son of Baraḵ'ěl
the Buzite, of the clan of Ram, burned
against Iyoḇ. His wrath burned because he
declared himself right rather than Elohim.
3 And against his three friends his wrath
burned, because they had found no answer,
and pronounced Elohim wrong.
4 And because they were years older than
he, Elihu had waited to speak to Iyoḇ.
5 And when Elihu saw that there was no
answer in the mouth of these three men,
his wrath burned.
6 And Elihu, son of Baraḵ'ěl the Buzite,
responded and said, "I am young in years,
and you are aged. Therefore I was afraid to
let you know my opinion.
7 I said, 'Days should speak, and many
years should teach wisdom.'
8 But truly it is the spirit in man and the
breath of the Almighty that gives him
understanding.
9 The multitude are not wise, nor do the
aged understand right-ruling.
10 Therefore I have said, 'Listen to me, let
me also make my opinion known to you.'
11 Look, I waited for your words, I
listened to your reasonings, while you
searched out what to say.
12 And I paid close attention to you. But
look, not one of you proved Iyoḇ wrong,
nor answered his words.
13 Lest you say, 'We have found wisdom'
– it is Ěl that drives him away, not man.
14 Now he has not ordered words against
me, so I would not answer him with your
words.
15 They have broken down; they have not
answered again; words have departed from
them.
16 And I have waited, but they do not
speak, because they have stood still, they
answered no more.
17 Let me answer on my part, let me also
make my opinion known.
18 For I am filled with words; the spirit
within me presses me.
19 See, within me it is like wine not
opened; it shall burst like new wineskins.
20 Let me speak, so that I find relief; let
me open my lips and answer.
21 Please, let me not show partiality to
anyone, nor let me flatter any man.
22 For I do not know how to flatter, lest
my Maker should soon take me away!

33 "And yet, O Iyoḇ, please hear my
speech and listen to all my words.
2 See, please! I shall open my mouth, my
tongue shall speak in my mouth.
3 My words are from the uprightness of
my heart, my lips shall speak knowledge
clearly.
4 The Spirit of Ěl has made me, and the
breath of the Almighty gives me life.
5 If you are able, answer me, set yourself
in order before me, take your stand.
6 See, I am like you before Ěl, I too have
been formed out of clay.
7 See, no fear of me should alarm you,
nor should pressure by me be heavy on
you.
8 But you have spoken in my hearing,
and the sound of words I hear, *saying*,
9 'I am clear, without transgression; I am
innocent, and I have no crookedness.
10 See, He finds occasions against me, He
counts me as His enemy;

[11]He puts my feet in the stocks, He watches all my paths.'
[12]See, in this you have not been righteous. Let me answer you: Eloah is greater than man!
[13]Why have you complained against Him? Because He does not answer all His matters?
[14]For Ěl does speak once, or twice – *though* one does not notice it –
[15]in a dream, in a vision of the night, when deep sleep falls upon men, while slumbering on a bed,
[16]then He opens the ears of men, and seals their instruction,
[17]to turn man *from his* deed, and conceal pride from man.
[18]He keeps back his being from the pit, and his life from passing away by the sword.
[19]And he is reproved with pain on his bed, and with unceasing distress in his bones,
[20]so that his life loathes bread, and his being desirable food.
[21]His flesh wastes away, and his bones which were not seen stick out.
[22]And his being draws near the pit, and his life to the destroyers.
[23]If there is a messenger for him, a mediator, one among a thousand, to show man His straightness,
[24]then He shows favour to him, and says, 'Release him from going down to the pit, I have found an atonement.
[25]'Let his flesh become fresher than a child's, let him return to the days of his youth.'
[26]He prays to Eloah, and He accepts him. And he sees His face with joy, and He restores to man his righteousness.
[27]He sings to men and says, 'I have sinned, and I have perverted what was right, and it did not profit me.
[28]He has redeemed my being from going down to the pit, and my life sees the light.'
[29]See, Ěl does all these – twice, three times with a man,
[30]to bring back his being from the pit, to be enlightened with the light of the living.
[31]Pay attention, Iyoḇ, listen to me, keep silent, and let me speak.
[32]If there are words, answer me; speak, for I desire to declare you right.
[33]If not, listen to me, keep silent, and let me teach you wisdom."

34

Then Elihu responded and said,
[2]"Hear my words, you wise men; give ear to me, you who have knowledge.
[3]For the ear tries words as the palate tastes food.
[4]Let us choose what is right for us; let us know among us what is good.
[5]For Iyoḇ has said, 'I am righteous, but Ěl has taken away my right.
[6]Would I lie concerning my right? My wound is incurable – without transgression.'
[7]What man is like Iyoḇ, who drinks mocking like water,
[8]who goes in company with the workers of wickedness, and walks with men of wrongness?
[9]For he has said, 'It does not profit a man that he takes delight in Elohim.'
[10]Therefore, listen to me, you men of heart: far be it from Ěl to do wrong, and from the Almighty to commit unrighteousness.
[11]For He repays man's work to him, and makes man to find a reward according to his path.
[12]The truth is, Ěl does not do wrong, and the Almighty does not twist right-ruling.
[13]Who has assigned to Him the earth? And who has laid out all the world?
[14]If He sets His heart on him, should He gather to Himself his spirit and his breath,
[15]all flesh would expire together and man return to dust.
[16]If *you have* understanding, hear this! Give ear to the sound of my words:
[17]Should the one who hates right-ruling govern? Or would you declare a most righteous one wrong?
[18]Who shall say to a sovereign:
'Beliya'al,' to nobles: 'Wrong one'? –
[19]who is not partial to princes, nor regards the rich more than the poor? For they are all the work of His hands.
[20]In a moment they die, in the middle of

the night; the people are shaken and pass
away; and the mighty are taken away
without a hand.
21 For His eyes are on the ways of man,
and He sees all his steps.
22 There is no darkness nor shadow of
death where the workers of wickedness
hide themselves.
23 For He sets a man no stated time to
appear before Ěl in right-ruling.
24 He breaks in pieces the mighty, without
inquiry, and puts others in their place.
25 Truly, He knows their works, and He
shall overthrow in the night, and they are
crushed.
26 As wrong ones He slaps them in the
presence of onlookers,
27 because they turned from following
Him, and they regarded not all His ways,
28 so as to cause the cry of the poor to
come to Him; for He hears the cry of the
afflicted.
29 And when He is silent, who would then
condemn? And when He hides His face,
who then sees Him, whether it is against a
nation or a man alone?
30 So that a defiled one should not reign,
lest the people be ensnared.
31 For has anyone said to Ěl, ‘I have taken
away, I do not act corruptly.
32 ‘Teach me what I do not see. If I have
done unrighteousness, I shall not do so
again’?
33 Should He repay you because you have
refused? For you choose, and not I, therefore speak what you know.
34 Let men of heart say to me, and a wise
man who listens to me:
35 ‘Iyoḇ does not speak with knowledge,
and his words are without wisdom.’
36 Would that Iyoḇ be tried to the end,
since his answers are like those of wicked
men!
37 For he adds rebellion to his sin – he
claps *his hands* among us, and multiplies
his words against Ěl.”

35 And Elihu responded and said,
2 “Do you think this is right? Do
you say, ‘My righteousness is more than
that of Ěl’?
3 For you say, ‘Of what use is it to you?
What do I gain more than if I had sinned?’
4 Let me answer you and your friends
with you.
5 Look to the heavens, and see. And consider the clouds which are higher than you.
6 If you sin, what would you do against
Him? If your transgressions are increased,
what would you do to Him?
7 If you are righteous, what do you give
Him? Or what does He receive from your
hand?
8 Your wrong is for a man like yourself,
and your righteousness for a son of man.
9 Because of the multitude of oppressions they cry out; they cry out for help
because of the arm of the many.
10 And no one says, ‘Where is Eloah my
Maker, who gives songs in the night,
11 teaching us more than the beasts of the
earth, and makes us wiser than the birds of
the heavens?’
12 There they cry, but He answers not,
because of the pride of evil ones.
13 Only, it is false that Ěl does not hear,
and that the Almighty pays no attention to
it.
14 Although you say you do not see Him,
yet right-ruling is before Him, and you
wait for Him.
15 And now, is it for naught that His displeasure has come? Yet He has not taken
note of extreme arrogance,
16 so Iyoḇ opens his mouth in vain, he
increases words without knowledge.”

36 Then Elihu continued and said,
2 “Bear with me a little, and let me
show you there is still more to say for
Eloah.
3 I bring my knowledge from afar and
ascribe righteousness to my Maker.
4 For truly my words are not false; the
One perfect in knowledge is with you.
5 See, Ěl is mighty, but rejects no one –
mighty in power *and* heart.
6 He does not keep the wrongdoer alive,
but *He* gives right-ruling to the oppressed
ones.
7 He does not withdraw His eyes from
the righteous, and sovereigns on the

throne, and seats them forever, and they
are exalted.
8 And if they are bound in shackles,
caught in the cords of affliction,
9 then He reveals to them their work, and
their transgressions, that they behaved
proudly.
10 And He opens their ear for discipline,
and commands that they turn back from
wickedness.
11 If they obey and serve, they complete
their days in blessedness, and their years in
pleasantness.
12 But if they do not obey, they perish by
the sword, and die without knowledge.
13 But the defiled ones in heart become
enraged – let them not cry for help when
He binds them.
14 Their being dies in youth, and their life
among the male prostitutes.
15 He rescues the afflicted one in his
affliction, and opens their ears in oppression.
16 And He also would have brought you
out of distress, into a broad place where
there is no restraint. And what is set on
your table would be filled with rich food.
17 But you are filled with the judgment of
the wrong, judgment and right-ruling take
hold of you.
18 *Beware*, that rage does not entice you to
scoffing. And do not let a large bribe turn
you aside.
19 Would He value your riches? No, not
precious ore, nor all your strength!
20 Do not long for the night, when people
go up in their place.
21 Beware, do not turn to wickedness, for
you have chosen this rather than affliction.
22 See, Ěl is exalted by His power; who is
a Teacher like Him?
23 Who has appointed Him His way, or
who has said, 'You have worked unrighteousness'?
24 Remember to extol His work, of which
men have sung.
25 All men have seen it, man looks on it
from afar.
26 See, Ěl is great, beyond our understanding, and we do not know the number
of His years.
27 For He draws up drops of water, which
distil as rain from the mist,
28 which the clouds drop down – pour
down in showers on man.
29 Also, who understands the spreading of
clouds, the crashing from His booth?
30 See, He has spread his light upon it, and
He has covered the depths of the sea.
31 For by these He judges the peoples; He
gives plenty of food.
32 He has covered His hands with lightning, and commands it to strike.
33 Its noise declares concerning Him, also
the cattle, as to what is coming up.

37

"At this too my heart trembles, and
leaps from its place.
2 Listen, listen to the trembling of His
voice, and the sound that comes from His
mouth.
3 He lets it loose under all the heavens,
and His lightning to the ends of the earth.
4 After it a voice roars. He thunders with
the voice of His excellency, and He does
not hold them back when His voice is
heard.
5 Ěl thunders wondrously with His voice;
doing great deeds, which we do not understand.
6 For He says to the snow, 'Be on the
earth,' also to the gentle rain and the heavy
rain of His strength.
7 He seals up the hand of every man, for
all men to know His work.
8 Then the beast goes into its lair, and
they stay in their dens.
9 From the room of the south comes the
whirlwind, and cold from the scattering
winds of the north.
10 By the breath of Ěl ice is given, and the
expanse of water becomes solid.
11 He also loads the thick clouds with
moisture; He scatters His bright clouds.
12 And they swirl about, being turned by
His guidance, to do whatever He commands them on the face of the earthly
world.
13 He causes it to come, whether as a rod,
or for His land, or for loving-commitment.
14 Listen to this, O Iyoḇ, stand still and
consider the wonders of Ěl.

15 Do you know when Eloah placed them,
and caused the lightning of His cloud to
shine?
16 Do you know the balancing of the
clouds, the wonders of the One perfect in
knowledge?
17 Why are your garments hot, when the
earth is stilled from the south?
18 Did you, with Him, spread out the
clouds, strong as a hard mirror?
19 Teach us what we should say to Him;
we do not set in order because of darkness.
20 Should He be told that I would speak?
Would any man ask to be swallowed up?
21 And now, they shall not look on the
light that is bright behind the clouds, when
the wind has passed and cleared them.
22 From the golden north it comes – with
Eloah is awesome excellency.
23 The Almighty, we have not found Him
out, He is exalted in power and right-ruling
and great in righteousness – He does not
oppress.
24 Therefore men fear Him. He does not
regard any who are wise of heart."

38 Then יהוה answered Iyoḇ out of
the whirlwind, and said,
2 "Who is this who darkens counsel by
words without knowledge?
3 Now gird up your loins like a man, and
I ask you, and you answer Me.
4 Where were you when I laid the foundations of the earth? Declare, if you have
understanding.
5 Who set its measurements, if you
know? Or who stretched the line upon it?
6 Upon what were its foundations sunk?
Or who laid its corner-stone,
7 when the morning stars sang together,
and all the sons of Elohim shouted for joy?
8 Or *who* enclosed the sea with doors,
when it burst forth and came from the
womb;
9 when I made the clouds its garment,
and thick darkness its swaddling band;
10 and assigned for it My law, and set bars
and doors;
11 and said, 'This far you have come, but
no farther, and here your proud waves
stop?'
12 Have you ever commanded the morning, and caused the dawn to know its place,
13 to take hold of the ends of the earth,
and the wrong be shaken out of it?
14 It is changed like clay under a seal, and
they stand out like a garment.
15 And their light is withheld from the
wrong, and the arm lifted up is broken.
16 Have you come to the sources of the
sea? Or have you walked about in the
recesses of the deep?
17 Were the gates of death revealed to
you? Or have you seen the gates of the
shadow of death?
18 Have you understood the breadth of the
earth? Declare, if you know it all.
19 Where is the way to the dwelling of
light? And darkness, where is its place,
20 that you should take it to its boundary,
and know the paths to its home?
21 Do you know? For you would have
been born then, and the number of your
days been many!
22 Have you entered into the storehouses
of snow, or have you seen the storehouses
of hail,
23 which I have kept for the time of
distress, for the day of fighting and battle?
24 Where is the way that light is divided,
or the east wind scattered over the earth?
25 Who has cleft a channel for the overflowing water, or a way for the thunder-
claps,
26 to make rain fall on land where no one
is, a wilderness in which there is no man;
27 to satisfy the wild and waste places,
and to make the seeds of grass to sprout?
28 Does the rain have a father? Or who has
brought forth the drops of dew?
29 From whose belly comes the ice? And
who gave birth to the frost of the heavens?
30 The waters harden like stone, and the
surface of the deep is frozen.
31 Do you bind the bands of Kimah, or
loosen the cords of Kesil?
32 Do you bring out the constellations in
its season? Or do you lead the Bear with its
sons?
33 Do you know the laws of the heavens?
Or do you set their rule over the earth?
34 Do you lift up your voice to the clouds,

so that floods of water cover you?
35 Do you send out lightnings, and they go
and say to you, 'Here we are!'?
36 Who has put wisdom in the inward
parts? Or who has given understanding to
the heart?
37 Who has wisdom to count the clouds,
or to tip over the bottles of the heavens,
38 when the dust hardens in clumps, and
the clods cling together?
39 Do you hunt the prey for the lion, or
satisfy the appetite of the young lions,
40 when they crouch in dens, sit in the
cover of their hiding place?
41 Who provides food for the raven, when
its young ones cry to Ěl, *and* wander about
without food?

39 "Do you know the time when the
wild mountain goats bear young?
Or do you observe when the deer gives
birth?
2 Do you number the months they complete? Or do you know the time when they
bear young?
3 They bow down, they bring forth their
young, their labour pains are ended.
4 Their young ones are thriving, they
grow up in the field. They shall leave and
shall not return to them.
5 Who set the wild donkey free? Who
loosed the bonds of the wild donkey,
6 whose home I have made the desert,
and the salt land his dwelling?
7 He laughs at the commotion of the city;
he does not hear the shouts of the driver.
8 The range of the mountains is his
pasture, and he searches for all that is
green.
9 Would the wild ox be pleased to serve
you? Or spend the night by your feeding
trough?
10 If you bind the wild ox in the furrow
with ropes, would he plough the valleys
behind you?
11 Would you rely on his great strength?
Or would you leave your labour to him?
12 Would you trust him to bring home
your grain, and gather it to your threshing-
floor?
13 The wings of the ostrich flap joyously,
but they are not the pinions and plumage of
a stork! [a]
14 She leaves her eggs on the ground, and
warms them in the dust;
15 and she forgets that a foot might crush
them, or a wild beast tread on them.
16 She treats her young harshly, as if not
hers; her toil is in vain, without fear,
17 because Eloah has made her forget
wisdom, and did not endow her with
understanding.
18 When she lifts herself on high, she
laughs at the horse and its rider.
19 Have you given the horse strength?
Have you covered his neck with a mane?
20 Would you make him leap like a
locust? His splendid snorting is frightening.
21 He paws in the valley, and rejoices in
strength. He gallops into the clash of arms.
22 He laughs at fear, and is not frightened;
nor does he turn back from the sword.
23 The quiver rattles against him, the glittering spear and lance.
24 He eats up the ground with fierceness
and rage, and he does not stand still
because of a voice of a shophar.
25 At the blast of the shophar he says,
'Aha!' And from afar he smells the battle,
the thunder of commanders and shouting.
26 Does the hawk fly by your wisdom,
spreading its wings toward the south?
27 Does the eagle mount up at your
mouth, and make its nest on high?
28 It dwells on the rock, and lodges on the
crag of the rock and the stronghold.
29 From there it searches out the prey, its
eyes see it from afar.
30 And its young ones suck up blood. And
where the slain are, there it is!"

40 And יהוה answered Iyoḇ, and said,
2 "Should a reprover contend with
the Almighty? Let him who reproves
Eloah answer it."
3 And Iyoḇ answered יהוה and said,
4 "See, I am insignificant, what would I

39a - Hebrew: Ḥacidah.

answer You? I lay my hand over my
mouth.
5 Once I have spoken, but I have no
answer – and twice, but I say no more."
6 Then יהוה answered Iyoḇ out of the
whirlwind, and said,
7 "Now gird up your loins like a man;
I ask you, and you answer Me.
8 Would you also set aside My judgment? Would you pronounce Me wrong,
and you be declared righteous?
9 Or do you have an arm like Ěl? Or do
you thunder with a voice like His?
10 Deck yourself, please, with excellency
and grandeur, and put on esteem and splendour.
11 Scatter abroad the rage of your wrath,
and look on everyone who is proud and
bring him low.
12 Look on everyone who is proud,
humble him. And tread down the wrongdoers in their place.
13 Hide them in the dust together, bind
their faces in obscurity.
14 Then even I would confess to you that
your own right hand does save you.
15 See now, Behĕmoth, which I made
along with you – he eats grass like an ox.
16 See now, his strength is in his loins, and
his power is in his stomach muscles.
17 He bends his tail like a cedar; the
sinews of his thighs are knit together.
18 His bones are like tubes of bronze, his
ribs like bars of iron.
19 He is the beginning of the ways of Ěl.
His Maker brings near His sword.
20 For the mountains yield food for him,
and all the beasts of the field play there.
21 He lies under the slender trees, under
cover of reed and swamp.
22 The slender trees cover him with their
shade; the willows by the stream surround
him.
23 See, if a river rages, he is not alarmed;
he feels safe, even if the Yardĕn gushes
into his mouth,
24 Before his eyes, shall he be caught,
with snares? Or *his* nose pierced?

41 "Would you draw out Liwiathan
with a hook, or snare his tongue
with a line which you lower?
2 Would you put a cord through his nose,
or pierce his jaw with a hook?
3 Would he keep on pleading with you?
Would he speak softly to you?
4 Would he make a covenant with you to
be taken as a servant forever?
5 Would you play with him as with a
bird? Or leash him for your young girls?
6 Would *trading* partners bargain over
him? Would they divide him among the
merchants?
7 Fill his skin with harpoons? Or his head
with fishing spears?
8 Put your hand on him – think of the
struggle! Do not do it again!
9 See, any expectation of him is disap-
pointed – he is laid low even at the sight of
him!
10 No one is so foolhardy to wake him up.
Who then is able to stand against Me?
11 Who has given to Me first, that I should
repay him – under all the heavens that is
Mine?
12 I would not keep silent concerning his
limbs, or his mighty power, or his fair
frame.
13 Who shall take off the surface of his
skin? Who approaches him with a double
bridle?
14 Who shall open the doors of his face,
with his frightening teeth all around?
15 Rows of scales are *his* pride – closed
up, a binding seal.
16 One to the other they fit closely, not
even a breath enters between them.
17 They are joined one to another, they
stick together and are not separated.
18 His sneezings flash forth light, and his
eyes are like the eyelids of the morning.
19 Out of his mouth go firebrands – sparks
of fire shoot out.
20 Out of his nostrils comes smoke, like a
boiling pot or kettle.
21 His breath sets coals on fire, and a
flame goes out of his mouth.
22 Strength dwells in his neck, and fear
leaps before him.
23 The folds of his flesh cleave together.
They are firm on him, immovable.
24 His heart is as hard as stone, even as

hard as the lower millstone.

25 When he raises himself up, the mighty are afraid. Because of his crashings they are bewildered.

26 No sword that reaches him does prevail, *neither* spear, dart, or lance.

27 He reckons iron as straw, bronze as rotten wood.

28 The arrow does not make him flee, sling-stones become like stubble to him.

29 Clubs are reckoned as straw, he laughs at the rattle of a lance.

30 His undersides are like sharp potsherds. He sprawls on the mud like a threshing-sledge.

31 He makes the deep boil like a pot, he makes the sea like a pot of ointment.

32 He leaves a shining path behind him. One would think the deep to be grey-haired.

33 No one on earth is like him – one made without fear.

34 He sees all that is haughty. He is sovereign over all the sons of pride."

42

And Iyoḇ answered יהוה and said,

2 "You know that You are able to do all, and that no purpose is withheld from You.

3 Who is this that hides counsel without knowledge? Therefore I declared but I did not understand, *matters* too marvellous for me, which I did not know.

4 Listen, please, and let me speak. I ask You, then would You make it known to me?'

5 I have heard of You by the hearing of the ear, but now my eye sees You.

6 Therefore I despise *myself*, and repent in dust and ashes."

7 And it came to be, after יהוה had spoken these words to Iyoḇ, that יהוה said to Eliphaz the Tĕmanite, "My wrath has burned against you and your two friends, for you have not spoken of Me what is right, as did My servant Iyoḇ.

8 And now, take seven bulls and seven rams, and go to My servant Iyoḇ, and offer up an ascending offering for yourselves. And let My servant Iyoḇ pray for you – for I accept him – lest I punish you; because you have not spoken of Me what is right, as did My servant Iyoḇ."

9 So Eliphaz the Tĕmanite and Bildaḏ the Shuḥite, Tsophar the Naʽamathite went and did as יהוה commanded them. And יהוה accepted the face of Iyoḇ.

10 And יהוה turned the captivity of Iyoḇ when he prayed for his friends. And יהוה gave Iyoḇ twice as much as he had before.

11 And all his brothers, and all his sisters, and all those who had been his friends before, came to him and ate food with him in his house. And they sympathised with him and comforted him for all the evil that יהוה had brought upon him. And they each gave him a qesitah [a] and each one a ring of gold.

12 And יהוה blessed the latter days of Iyoḇ more than his beginning; for he had fourteen thousand sheep, and six thousand camels, and one thousand yoke of oxen, and one thousand female donkeys.

13 And he had seven sons and three daughters.

14 And he called the name of the first Yemimah, and the name of the second Qetsiʽah, and the name of the third Qeren-Happuḵ.

15 And in all the land were found no women so beautiful as the daughters of Iyoḇ. And their father gave them an inheritance among their brothers.

16 And after this Iyoḇ lived one hundred and forty years, and saw his children and grandchildren for four generations.

17 And Iyoḇ died, old and satisfied with days.

42a A monetary unit of uncertain value, perhaps in the form of a lamb.

SHIR haSHIRIM

SONG OF SONGS

1 The song of songs,
which is Shelomoh's.
2 Let him kiss me with the kisses of his mouth,
For your *carnal*-love are better than wine.
3 For fragrance your oils are good.
Your name is oil poured forth, [a]
Therefore the young women [b] love you.
4 Draw me! We run after you.
The sovereign has brought me into his inner rooms.
We exult and rejoice in you.
We praise your *carnal*-love more than wine.
Rightly do they love you.
5 I am dark, but lovely,
O daughters of Yerushalayim,
Like the tents of Qĕḏar,
Like the curtains of Shelomoh.
6 Do not look upon me,
because I am dark,
Because the sun has tanned me.
My mother's sons were displeased with me.
They made me the keeper of the vineyards,
My own vineyard I have not kept.
7 Make known to me,
O you whom my being loves,
Where you feed *your flock*,
Where you make it rest at noon.
For why should I be as one who is veiled
Beside the flocks of your companions?
8 If you do not know, O beautiful among women,
Go in the footsteps of the flock,
And feed your little goats beside the shepherds' dwellings.
9 I have compared you, my love,
To my filly among Pharaoh's chariots.
10 Your cheeks are pretty with ornaments,
Your neck with strings of beads.
11 Let us make you ornaments of gold
with studs of silver.
12 While the sovereign is at his table,
My nard shall give its fragrance.
13 My beloved is a bundle of myrrh to me,
Lying between my breasts.
14 My beloved is to me a cluster of henna blooms
In the vineyards of Ěn Geḏi.
15 See, you are beautiful, my love!
See, you are beautiful!
Your eyes are as doves.
16 See, you are handsome, my beloved!
Yes, pleasant! Also our bed is green.
17 The beams of our houses are cedar,
our rafters are of fir.

2 I am the rose of Sharon,
The lily of the valleys.
2 Like a lily among thorns,
So is my love among the daughters.
3 Like an apple tree among the trees of the forest,
So is my beloved among the sons.
I delighted in his shade and sat down,
And his fruit was sweet to my taste.
4 He brought me to the house of wine,
And his banner over me was love.
5 "Strengthen me with raisin cakes,
Refresh me with apples, for I am faint with love."
6 His left hand is under my head,
And his right hand embraces me.
7 I have put you under oath,
O daughters of Yerushalayim,
By the gazelles or by the does of the field,
Do not stir up nor awaken love until it pleases.
8 The voice of my beloved!
See, he is coming,
Leaping on the mountains, skipping on

1a See also Qoheleth 7:1. *1b* See Explanatory notes: Maiden.

the hills.
9 My beloved is like a gazelle or like a
young stag.
See, he is standing behind our wall,
Looking through the windows,
Peering through the lattice.
10 My beloved responded and said to me,
"Rise up, my love, my beautiful one,
and come away.
11 "For look, the winter is past,
the rain is over, gone.
12 "The flowers have appeared in the
earth;
The time of singing has come,
And the voice of the turtledove has
been heard in our land.
13 "The fig tree has ripened her figs,
And the vines with the tender grapes
have given a good fragrance.
Rise up, my love, my beautiful one,
and come away!
14 "O my dove, in the clefts of the rock,
In the covering of the cliff,
Let me see your appearance,
Let me hear your voice;
For your voice is sweet,
And your appearance is lovely."
15 Catch the foxes for us,
The little foxes that spoil the vines,
And our vines are all blossom.
16 My beloved is mine, and I am his.
He feeds *his flock* among the lilies.
17 Until the day breaks and
the shadows have fled,
Turn, my beloved,
And be like a gazelle or a young stag
On the mountains of Bether.

3 On my bed at night I sought the
beloved of my being;
I sought him, but I did not find him.
2 "Come, let me arise,
and go about the city,
In the streets and in the broad places
I seek the beloved of my being."
I sought him, but I did not find him.
3 The watchmen who go about the city
found me, to whom I said,
"Have you seen the beloved of my
being?"
4 Scarcely had I passed by them,
When I found the beloved of my being.
I held him and would not let him go,
Until I had brought him to the house
of my mother,
And into the room of her who
conceived me.
5 I have put you under oath,
O daughters of Yerushalayim,
By the gazelles or by the does of the
field,
Do not stir up nor awaken love until it
pleases.
6 Who is this coming out of the
wilderness
Like columns of smoke,
Perfumed with myrrh and frankincense,
From all the merchant's fragrant
powders?
7 See, it is Shelomoh's couch –
Sixty mighty men are around it,
Of the mighty men of Yisra'ěl,
8 All of them holding swords,
Skilled in battle,
Each one has his sword on his thigh
Because of fear in the night.
9 Sovereign Shelomoh made himself
A litter of the wood of Leḇanon;
10 He made its posts of silver,
Its support of gold, its seat of purple,
Within it was decked with love
By the daughters of Yerushalayim.
11 Go forth, O daughters of Tsiyon,
And see Sovereign Shelomoh with the
crown
With which his mother crowned him on
the day of his wedding,
And on the day of his gladness of heart.

4 See, you are beautiful, my love!
See, you are beautiful!
Your eyes are as doves
behind your veil.
Your hair is like a flock of goats,
Going down from Mount Gilʿaḏ.
2 Your teeth are like a flock of shorn
sheep
Which have come up from the
washing,
All of them bear twins, and not one
loses her young.
3 Your lips are like a cord of scarlet,

And your speech is lovely.
Your cheeks behind your veil are like a
piece of pomegranate.
4 Your neck is like the tower of Dawiḏ,
Built for an armoury,
On which hang a thousand shields,
All the armour of mighty men.
5 Your two breasts are like two fawns,
Twins of a gazelle,
pasturing among the lilies.
6 Until the day breaks and the shadows
have fled,
I shall go my way to the mountain of
myrrh,
And to the hill of frankincense.
7 You are all beautiful, my love,
and not a blemish is on you.
8 Come with me from Leḇanon,
My bride, with me from Leḇanon.
Look from the top of Amana,
From the top of Shenir and Ḥermon,
From the dens of lions,
From the mountains of the leopards.
9 You have put heart into me,
My sister, my bride;
You have put heart into me
With one *glance* of your eyes,
With one bead of your necklace.
10 How beautiful have been your
carnal-love,
My sister, my bride!
How much better than wine is your
carnal-love,
And the fragrance of your perfumes
than all spices!
11 Your lips, O my bride,
drip as the honeycomb;
Honey and milk are under your tongue.
And the fragrance of your garments
Is like the fragrance of Leḇanon.
12 A garden locked is my sister, my bride,
A fountain locked, a spring sealed up.
13 Your plants are an orchard of
pomegranates with pleasant fruits,
With henna, nard,
14 Nard and saffron,
Calamus and cinnamon,
With all trees of frankincense,
Myrrh and aloes,
With all the chief spices;
15 A garden spring,
A well of living waters,
And streams from Leḇanon.
16 Awake, O north wind, and come,
O south!
Blow upon my garden, let its spices
flow out.
Let my beloved come to his garden
And eat its pleasant fruits.

5 I have come to my garden,
My sister, my bride;
I have plucked my myrrh
with my spice;
I have eaten my honeycomb
with my honey;
I have drunk my wine
with my milk.
Eat, O friends!
Drink, and drink deeply,
O beloved ones!
2 I was sleeping,
But my heart was awake – the voice of
my beloved!
He knocks, "Open for me, my sister,
My love, my dove, my perfect one;
For my head is drenched with dew,
My locks with the drops of the night."
3 I have taken off my robe, should I put it
on?
I have washed my feet, should I dirty
them?
4 My beloved put his hand by the latch,
And my feelings were deeply moved
for him.
5 I rose to open for my beloved,
And my hands dripped with myrrh,
My fingers with flowing myrrh,
On the handles of the lock.
6 I opened for my beloved,
But my beloved had turned away,
had gone.
My being went out when he spoke.
I sought him, but I could not find him;
I called him,
but he gave me no answer.
7 The watchmen who went about the city
found me.
They struck me, they bruised me;
The keepers of the walls lifted my veil
from me.
8 I have put you under oath,

O daughters of Yerushalayim,
If you find my beloved,
That you inform him that I am faint
with love!
9 What kind of a beloved is your
beloved,
O beautiful among women?
What kind of a beloved is your
beloved,
That you have put us under oath?
10 My beloved is dazzling and ruddy,
Chief among ten thousand.
11 His head is refined gold;
His locks are wavy,
black as a raven.
12 His eyes are like doves by streams of
waters,
Washed with milk, and fitly set.
13 His cheeks are like a bed of spices,
Raised bed of scented plants.
His lips are lilies, dripping flowing
myrrh.
14 His hands are rods of gold set with
beryl.
His body is carved ivory, covered with
sapphires.
15 His legs are columns of marble
Founded on sockets of fine gold.
His appearance is like Leḇanon,
Choice as the cedars.
16 His mouth is most sweet,
And he is altogether lovely.
This is my beloved,
and this is my friend,
O daughters of Yerushalayim!

6 "Where has your beloved gone,
O beautiful among women?
Where has your beloved turned aside?
Let us seek him with you."
2 My beloved went down to his garden,
To the beds of spices,
To feed *his flock* in the gardens,
And to gather lilies.
3 I am my beloved's, and my beloved is
mine.
He feeds *his flock* among the lilies.
4 O my love, you are as beautiful as
Tirtsah,
Lovely as Yerushalayim,
Awesome as an army with banners!
5 Turn your eyes away from me,
Because they overcome me.
Your hair is like a flock of goats
That have hopped down from Gil'aḏ.
6 Your teeth are like a flock of sheep
That have come up from the washing;
All of them bear twins,
And not one among them has lost her
young.
7 Your cheeks behind your veil are like
a piece of pomegranate.
8 There are sixty sovereignesses and
eighty concubines,
And innumerable young women.
9 My dove, my perfect one,
Is the only one, the only one of her
mother,
The choice of the one who bore her.
The daughters saw, and called her
blessed,
Sovereignesses and concubines,
And they praised her.
10 Who is she who shines forth as the
morning,
Beautiful as the moon, clear as the sun,
Awesome as an army with banners?
11 I went down to the garden of nuts
To see the budding of the wadi,
To see whether the vine had budded
and the pomegranates had bloomed.
12 I did not know, my desire made me as
the chariots of my noble people.
13 Return, return, O Shulammith;
Return, return,
and let us look upon you!
Why should you look upon the
Shulammith,
As it were the dance of two armies?

7 How beautiful are your feet in
sandals, O daughter of a noble!
The curves of your thighs are like
ornaments,
The work of a craftsman's hands.
2 Your navel is a rounded bowl
Let it not lack mixed wine.
Your body is a heap of wheat,
Hedged about with lilies.
3 Your two breasts are like two fawns,
twins of a gazelle.
4 Your neck is like an ivory tower,

Your eyes pools in Ḥeshbon
By the gate of Bath Rabbim.
Your nose is like the tower of Leḇanon
looking to Dammeseq.
5 Your head upon you is like Mount
Karmel,
And the hair of your head like purple;
The sovereign is held captive by the
ringlets.
6 How beautiful and how pleasant you
are, O love, in delights!
7 This stature of yours compares to a
palm tree,
And your breasts to clusters.
8 I said, "Let me go up to the palm tree,
Let me take hold of its tips."
And please, let your breasts be like
clusters of the vine,
And the fragrance of your breath like
apples,
9 And your palate like the best wine,
Going down smoothly for my beloved,
Flowing gently, slumbering lips.
10 I am my beloved's, and his desire is
toward me.
11 Come, my beloved, let us go forth to
the field;
Let us stay in the villages.
12 Let us get up early to the vineyards;
Let us see whether the vine has budded,
The grape blossoms have opened,
The pomegranates have bloomed.
There I give you my *carnal*-loves.
13 The love-apples have given fragrance,
And at our gates are all pleasant *fruit*,
New and old, which I have laid up for
you, my beloved.

8 Who would make you a brother to me,
Who nursed at my mother's breasts!
Should I find you outside,
I would kiss you;
I would not be despised.
2 I would lead you,
I would bring you into the house of
my mother,
She who has taught me.
I would give you spiced wine to drink,
Of the juice of my pomegranate.
3 His left hand is under my head,
And his right hand embraces me.
4 I have put you under oath,
O daughters of Yerushalayim,
Do not stir up or awake love until
it pleases.
5 Who is this coming up from the wilder-
ness,
Leaning upon her beloved?
Under the apple tree I awakened you.
There your mother was in labour with
you;
There she was in labour,
gave birth to you.
6 Set me as a seal upon your heart,
As a seal upon your arm;
For love is as strong as death,
Jealousy as cruel as She'ol;
Its flames are flames of fire,
a flame of Yah!
7 Many waters are unable to extinguish
love,
And floods do not wash it away.
If one would give all the wealth of his
house for love,
It would be utterly scorned.
8 We have a little sister, and she has no
breasts.
What do we do for our sister in the day
when she is spoken for?
9 If she is a wall, we build upon her a
battlement of silver.
And if she is a door, we would enclose
her with boards of cedar.
10 I am a wall, and my breasts like towers;
So I became in his eyes as one who
found peace.
11 Shelomoh had a vineyard in Ba'al
Hamon;
He let out the vineyard to keepers;
Each one was to bring for its fruit a
thousand pieces of silver.
12 My own vineyard is before me.
O Shelomoh, a thousand belongs to
you,
And two hundred to those who keep
its fruit.
13 You who sit in the gardens,
The companions listen for your voice;
Let me hear it!
14 Hurry, my beloved,
And be like a gazelle or a young stag
On the mountains of spices.

RUTH

1 And it came to be, in the days when the rulers ruled, that there was a scarcity of food in the land. And a man from Běyth Leḥem, Yehuḏah, went to sojourn in the fields of Mo'aḇ, he and his wife and his two sons.

2 And the name of the man was Elimeleḵ, and the name of his wife was Na'omi, and the names of his two sons were Maḥlon and Kilyon – Ephrathites of Běyth Leḥem, Yehuḏah. And they went to the fields of Mo'aḇ and came to be there.

3 And Elimeleḵ, husband of Na'omi, died. And she was left with her two sons.

4 And they took wives of the women of Mo'aḇ, the name of the one was Orpah, and the name of the other Ruth. And they dwelt there about ten years.

5 And Maḥlon and Kilyon also died, both of them, so the woman was bereaved of her two sons and of her husband.

6 And she rose up, with her daughters-in-law, and returned from the fields of Mo'aḇ, for she had heard in the fields of Mo'aḇ that יהוה had visited His people in giving them bread.

7 And she left the place where she was, and her two daughters-in-law with her. And they went on the way to return to the land of Yehuḏah.

8 And Na'omi said to her two daughters-in-law, "Go, return each to her mother's house. יהוה show loving-commitment to you, as you have shown to the dead and to me.

9 "יהוה grant that you find rest, each in the house of her husband." Then she kissed them, and they lifted up their voices and wept.

10 And they said to her, "No, we shall go back with you to your people."

11 But Na'omi said, "Go back, my daughters, why go with me? Have I still sons in my womb, that they should become your husbands?

12 "Go back, my daughters, go your way, for I am too old to have a husband. If I should say I have expectancy, even if I should have a husband tonight and should also bear sons,

13 would you wait for them till they were grown? Would you shut yourselves up, not to have a husband? No, my daughters, for it is much more bitter for me than for you, because the hand of יהוה has gone out against me!"

14 And they lifted up their voices and wept again. And Orpah kissed her mother-in-law, but Ruth clung to her.

15 And she said, "Look, your sister-in-law has gone back to her people and to her mighty ones. Go back, follow your sister-in-law."

16 But Ruth said, "Do not urge me to leave you, or to go back from following after you. For wherever you go, I go; and wherever you stop over, I stop over. Your people is my people, and your Elohim is my Elohim. [a]

17 "Where you die, I die, and there I shall be buried. יהוה do so to me, and more also – for death itself parts you and me."

18 And when she saw that she was strengthening herself to go with her, she ceased to speak to her.

19 And both of them went until they came to Běyth Leḥem. And it came to be, when they had come to Běyth Leḥem, that all the city was moved because of them, and they said, "Is this Na'omi?"

20 And she said to them, "Do not call me Na'omi, call me Mara, for the Almighty has dealt very bitterly with me.

21 "I went out filled, and יהוה has brought me back empty. Why do you call me Na'omi, since יהוה has witnessed against me, and the Almighty has done evil to me?"

1a Ruth, great-grandmother of Dawiḏ.

22 Thus Na'omi returned, and Ruth the
Mo'aḇitess her daughter-in-law with her,
who returned from the fields of Mo'aḇ, and
they came to Běyth Leḥem at the beginning of barley harvest.

2

And Na'omi had a relative on her husband's side, a man of great wealth, of
the clan of Elimeleḵ, and his name was
Bo'az.
2 And Ruth, the Mo'aḇitess, said to
Na'omi, "Please let me go to the field, and
glean heads of grain after him in whose
eyes I find favour." So she said to her, "Go,
my daughter."
3 And she left, and went and gleaned in
the field after the reapers. As it turned out,
she came to the part of the field belonging
to Bo'az, the near relative of Elimeleḵ.
4 And see, Bo'az had come from Běyth
Leḥem, and said to the reapers, "יהוה be
with you!" And they answered him, "יהוה
bless you!"
5 And Bo'az said to his servant who was
appointed over the reapers, "Whose young
woman is this?"
6 So the servant who was appointed over
the reapers answered and said, "It is the
young Mo'aḇite woman who came back
with Na'omi from the fields of Mo'aḇ,
7 and she said, 'Please let me glean, and
gather among the sheaves behind the
reapers.' And she came and has remained
from morning until now – she sat a little in
the house."
8 And Bo'az said to Ruth, "You have
heard, have you not, my daughter? Do not
go to glean in another field, nor go from
here, but stay close to my young women.
9 "Let your eyes be on the field which
they reap, and you shall go after them.
Have I not commanded the young men not
to touch you? And when you are thirsty, go
to the vessels and drink from what the
young men have drawn."
10 And she fell on her face, bowed down
to the ground, and said to him, "Why have
I found favour in your eyes, that you
should take notice of me, seeing I am a
foreigner?"
11 And Bo'az answered and said to her, "I
have been told all that you have done for
your mother-in-law since the death of your
husband, and how you have left your
father and your mother and the land of
your birth, and have come to a people
whom you did not know before.
12 "יהוה repay your work, and your
reward is complete from יהוה Elohim of
Yisra'ěl, under whose wings you have
come to seek refuge."
13 And she said, "Let me find favour in
your eyes, my master, because you have
comforted me, and have spoken to the
heart of your female servant, though I am
not like one of your female servants."
14 And Bo'az said to her, "Come here at
mealtime. Then you shall eat of the bread
and dip your piece of bread in the vinegar."
And she sat beside the reapers, and he
passed roasted grain to her. And she ate
and was satisfied, and had left over.
15 And she rose up to glean, and Bo'az
commanded his young men, saying, "Let
her glean even among the sheaves, and do
not embarrass her.
16 "Rather, draw out from the bundles for
her, and leave it for her to glean, and do
not restrain her."
17 And she gleaned in the field until
evening, and beat out that which she had
gleaned, and it was about an ěphah of barley.
18 And she took it up and went into the
city, and her mother-in-law saw what she
had gleaned. And she brought out and gave
to her what she had left over after she was
satisfied.
19 Then her mother-in-law asked her,
"Where have you gleaned today? And
where did you work? Blessed be the one
who took notice of you." And she told her
mother-in-law with whom she had worked,
and said, "The name of the man I worked
today with is Bo'az."
20 And Na'omi said to her daughter-in-
law, "Blessed be he of יהוה, who has not
forsaken His loving-commitment to the
living and the dead!" And Na'omi said to
her, "The man is a relative of ours, one of
our redeemers."
21 And Ruth the Mo'aḇitess said, "He also

said to me, 'Stay close to my young people until they have completed all my harvest.' "

22 And Naʿomi said to Ruth her daughter-in-law, "It is good, my daughter, that you go out with his young women, and that they do not meet you in any other field."

23 And she stayed close by the young women of Boʿaz to glean, till the completion of barley harvest and wheat harvest, but she dwelt with her mother-in-law.

3 And Naʿomi her mother-in-law said to her, "My daughter, should I not seek rest for you, so that it is well with you?

2 "And now, is not Boʿaz, with whose young women you have been, our relative? See, he is winnowing barley tonight at the threshing-floor.

3 "And, you shall bathe and anoint yourself, and put your garments on and go down to the threshing-floor. Do not make yourself known to the man until he has finished eating and drinking.

4 "And it shall be, when he lies down, that you shall notice the place where he lies, and shall go in and uncover his feet, and lie down. And let him make known to you what you should do."

5 And she said to her, "All that you say to me, I do."

6 And she went down to the threshing-floor and did according to all that her mother-in-law commanded her.

7 And Boʿaz ate and drank, and his heart was glad, and he went to lie down at the end of the heap of grain. And she came softly and uncovered his feet, and lay down.

8 And it came to be at midnight that the man was startled, and turned himself, and saw a woman lying at his feet!

9 And he said, "Who are you?" And she answered, "I am Ruth, your female servant. Now you shall spread your covering over your female servant – for you are a redeemer."

10 And he said, "Blessed are you of יהוה, my daughter! For you have shown more loving-commitment at the end than at the beginning, not to go after young men, whether poor or rich.

11 "And now, my daughter, do not fear. All that you say I do for you, for all the people of my town know that you are a capable woman.

12 "And now, it is true that I am your redeemer. However, there is a redeemer nearer than I.

13 "Stop over tonight, and in the morning it shall be that if he does redeem you, good – let him do it. But if he is not pleased to redeem you, then I shall redeem you, as יהוה lives! Lie down until morning."

14 And she lay at his feet until morning, and she arose before one could recognise another. And he said, "Let it not be known that the woman came to the threshing-floor."

15 And he said, "Bring the shawl that is on you and hold it." So she held it and he measured six *measures* of barley, and laid it on her. And she went into the city.

16 And when she came to her mother-in-law, she said, "Is that you, my daughter?" And she explained to her all that the man had done for her.

17 And she said, "He gave me these six *measures* of barley, for he said to me, 'Do not go empty-handed to your mother-in-law.' "

18 And she said, "Wait, my daughter, until you know how the matter falls, for the man is not going to rest until he has completed the matter this day."

4 And Boʿaz went up to the gate and sat down there. And see, the redeemer of whom Boʿaz had spoken came by. And Boʿaz said, "Turn aside, So-and-so, sit down here." And he turned aside and sat down.

2 And he took ten men of the elders of the city, and said, "Sit down here." So they sat down.

3 He then said to the redeemer, "Naʿomi, who has come back from the fields of Moʼaḇ, sold the piece of land which belonged to our brother Elimeleḵ.

4 "And I thought that I should disclose it to you, saying, 'Buy it back in the presence of the inhabitants and the elders of my

people. If you do redeem it, redeem it. But
if you do not redeem it, inform me, so that
I know. For there is no one but you to
redeem it, and I am next after you.' " And
he said, "I redeem it."
5 And Boʿaz said, "On the day you buy
the field from the hand of Naʿomi, you
shall also acquire Ruth the Mo'aḇitess, the
wife of the dead, to raise up the name of
the dead on his inheritance."
6 And the redeemer said, "I am not able
to redeem it for myself, lest I ruin my own
inheritance. Redeem my right of redemption for yourself, for I am not able to
redeem it."
7 And this was formerly done in Yisra'ěl
concerning redeeming and exchanging, to
confirm every word: one man took off his
sandal and gave it to the other, and this was
a witness in Yisra'ěl.
8 So the redeemer said to Boʿaz, "Buy it
for yourself." Then he took off his sandal.
9 And Boʿaz said to the elders and to all
the people, "You are witnesses this day
that I have bought all that was Elimeleḵ's,
and all that was Kilyon's and Maḥlon's,
from the hand of Naʿomi.
10 "And also, Ruth the Mo'aḇitess, the
wife of Maḥlon, I have acquired as my
wife, to raise up the name of the dead on
his inheritance, so that the name of the
dead should not be cut off from among his
brothers and from the gate of his place.
You are witnesses today."
11 And all the people who were at the
gate, and the elders, said, "Witnesses! יהוה
make the woman who is coming to your
house as Raḥěl and as Lě'ah, the two who
built the house of Yisra'ěl. And prove your
worth in Ephrathah and proclaim the Name
in Běyth Leḥem.
12 "And let your house be like the house
of Perets, whom Tamar bore to Yehuḏah,
of the seed which יהוה does give you from
this young woman."
13 And Boʿaz took Ruth and she became
his wife. And he went in to her, and יהוה
granted her conception, and she bore a son.
14 And the women said to Naʿomi,
"Blessed be יהוה, who has not left you this
day without a redeemer. And let his Name
be proclaimed in Yisra'ěl!
15 "And he shall be to you a restorer of
life and a sustainer of your old age. For
your daughter-in-law, who loves you, who
is better to you than seven sons, has borne
him."
16 And Naʿomi took the child and laid him
on her bosom, and became a nurse to him.
17 And the women, her neighbours, gave
him a name, saying, "There is a son born to
Naʿomi." And they called his name Oḇěḏ.
He was the father of Yishai, the father of
Dawiḏ.
18 And this is the genealogy of Perets:
Perets brought forth Ḥetsron.
19 And Ḥetsron brought forth Ram, and
Ram brought forth Amminaḏaḇ.
20 And Amminaḏaḇ brought forth
Naḥshon, and Naḥshon brought forth
Salmon.
21 And Salmon brought forth Boʿaz, and
Boʿaz brought forth Oḇěḏ.
22 And Oḇěḏ brought forth Yishai, and
Yishai brought forth Dawiḏ.

ĔḴAH

LAMENTATIONS

1 How alone she sits,
The city once great with people!
Like a widow she has become,
One great among the nations!
A princess among provinces has
become a slave!
2 She weeps bitterly at night,
And her tears are upon her cheeks.
Among all her lovers there is no
comforter for her.
All her friends have betrayed her,
They have become her enemies.
3 Yehuḏah has gone into exile,
Because of affliction and because
of harsh labour.
She has dwelt among nations,
She has found no rest.
All her pursuers have overtaken her
Between narrow places.
4 The ways to Tsiyon mourn
For no one comes to the appointed
times. [a]
All her gates are deserted,
Her priests sigh, her maidens are
afflicted,
And she has bitterness.
5 Her adversaries have become chief,
Her enemies have become at ease.
For יהוה has afflicted her
Because of her many transgressions.
Her children have gone into captivity
before the enemy.
6 And all the splendour has departed
From the daughter of Tsiyon.
Her rulers have become like buck,
They have found no pasture,
And they go powerless before the
pursuer.
7 In the days of her affliction and
wandering,
Yerushalayim remembered all her
precious *matters*
She had in the days of old.
When her people fell into the hand
of the enemy,
With no one to help her,
The adversaries saw her,
They mocked at her destruction.
8 Yerushalayim has sinned greatly,
Therefore she has become defiled.
All who esteemed her despised her
Because they have seen her nakedness.
She herself has sighed and turned
away.
9 Her uncleanness is in her skirts.
She did not keep in mind her latter end,
And has gone down appallingly,
There was no one to comfort her.
"See, O יהוה, my affliction,
For the enemy has made himself
great!"
10 The adversary has spread his hand
Over all her precious *matters*;
Indeed, she has seen:
The nations have entered her set-apart
place,
Those whom You commanded not to
enter Your assembly.
11 All her people are sighing, seeking
bread.
They have given their precious *matters*
For food, to bring back life.
"See, O יהוה, and look,
For I have become despised."
12 "Is it naught to you,
All you who pass by?
Look and see if there is any pain
like my pain,
Which has been brought on me,
Which יהוה has inflicted on me
In the day of His burning displeasure.
13 "From above He has sent fire into
my bones,
And it overpowered them;
He has spread a net for my feet and
turned me back;

1a Or *festivals*.

He has laid me waste and faint all the day.
14 "The yoke of my transgressions
Has been bound by His hand,
Woven together and thrust upon my neck.
He has made my strength stumble,
יהוה has given me into hands
Which I am unable to withstand.
15 "יהוה has trodden down all my strong men in my midst,
He has called an appointed time
Against me to crush my young men.
יהוה has trodden down as in a winepress
The maiden daughter of Yehuḏah.
16 "This is why I weep.
My eye, my eye is running down with water,
Because the comforter,
Who could bring back my life,
Has been far from me.
My children are stunned,
For the enemy has prevailed."
17 Tsiyon spreads out her hands,
There is no comforter for her.
יהוה has commanded concerning Yaʿaqoḇ,
His neighbours are his adversaries.
Yerushalayim has become an uncleanness among them.
18 יהוה is righteous,
for I rebelled against His mouth.
Hear now, all peoples,
and see my pain.
My maidens and my young men have gone into captivity.
19 I called for my lovers, but they deceived me.
My priests and my elders breathed their last in the city,
While they sought food to bring back their life.
20 "See, O יהוה, that I am in distress.
My inward parts are boiling up,
My heart is overturned within me,
For I have been very rebellious.
From without the sword has bereaved,
At home it is like death.
21 "They have heard that I sighed,
With no one to comfort me.
All my enemies have heard of my calamity,
They have rejoiced that You have done it.
You shall bring on the day that You have announced,
So let them become like me.
22 "Let all their evil come before You,
And do to them as You have done to me
For all my transgressions.
For my sighs are many, and my heart is faint."

2 How יהוה in His displeasure
Has covered the daughter of Tsiyon with a cloud!
He has cast down from the heavens to the earth
The comeliness of Yisra'ěl,
And has not remembered His footstool in the day of His displeasure.
2 יהוה has swallowed up,
without compassion,
All the pastures of Yaʿaqoḇ.
In His wrath He has thrown down
The strongholds of the daughter of Yehuḏah.
He has brought them down to the ground.
He has profaned the reign and its rulers.
3 In the heat of displeasure
He has cut off every horn of Yisra'ěl.
He has withdrawn His right hand from before the enemy.
And He burns against Yaʿaqoḇ
Like a flaming fire, consuming all around.
4 He has bent His bow like an enemy.
He has set His right hand like an adversary.
And He kills all who delighted the eye.
In the tent of the daughter of Tsiyon,
He has poured out His wrath like fire.
5 יהוה has been like an enemy.
He has swallowed up Yisra'ěl,
He has swallowed up all her palaces,
He has destroyed her strongholds.
And He increases mourning and lamentation

In the daughter of Yehuḏah.
6 He has demolished His booth like a garden,
He has destroyed His place of meeting.
יהוה has made the appointed times [a] and Sabbaths
To be forgotten in Tsiyon,
And despises sovereign and priest
In His raging displeasure.
7 יהוה has cast off His slaughter-place,
He has rejected His set-apart place,
He has delivered the walls of her palaces
Into the hand of the enemy.
They have made a noise in the House of יהוה
As on the day of an appointed time.
8 יהוה has planned to destroy
The wall of the daughter of Tsiyon.
He has stretched out a line.
He has not turned back His hand from destroying.
And He has made the rampart and wall to lament;
Together they have languished.
9 Her gates have sunk into the ground.
He has destroyed and broken her bars.
Her sovereign and her rulers are among the nations.
The Torah is no more,
And her prophets have found no vision from יהוה.
10 The elders of the daughter of Tsiyon
Sit on the ground, are silent.
They have thrown dust on their heads,
They have girded themselves with sackcloth.
The maidens of Yerushalayim
Have let their heads hang to the ground.
11 My eyes are spent with tears,
My inward parts ferment,
My bile has been poured on the ground
Because of the destruction of the daughter of my people,
As children and the infants languish
In the streets of the city.
12 They say to their mothers,
"Where is grain and wine?"
As they languish like the wounded
In the streets of the city,
As their life is poured out in their mothers' bosom.
13 How shall I admonish you,
To what shall I compare you,
O daughter of Yerushalayim?
To what shall I liken you to comfort you,
O maiden daughter of Tsiyon?
For your breach is as great as the sea.
Who shall heal you?
14 Your prophets have seen
Falsehood and folly for you,
And have not shown you your crookedness,
To turn back your captivity.
But their visions for you
Are false and misleading messages.
15 All who pass by have clapped their hands at you.
They have whistled,
And they shake their heads
At the daughter of Yerushalayim,
"Is this the city that is called
'The perfection of loveliness,
The joy of all the earth'?"
16 All your enemies have opened
Their mouth against you;
They have whistled and they gnash their teeth.
They say, "We have swallowed her up!
This is certainly the day we waited for;
We have found it, we have seen it."
17 יהוה has done what He planned,
He has filled His word
Which He commanded in days of old.
He has torn down, without compassion,
And He has let your enemy rejoice over you.
He has exalted the horn of your adversaries.
18 Their heart cried out to יהוה,
"O wall of the daughter of Tsiyon,
Let tears run down like a river day and night.
Give yourself no numbness,
Let your eyes have no rest.

2a Or *festivals*.

19 "Arise, cry out in the night,
At the beginning of the watches,
Pour out your heart like water
Before the face of יהוה.
Lift your hands toward Him
For the life of your young children,
Who languish from hunger
At the head of every street.
20 "See, O יהוה, and look attentively
To whom have You done thus.
Should the women eat their offspring,
Infants of a hand breadth?
Should the priest and prophet be killed
In the set-apart place of יהוה?
21 "Young and old lie on the ground in the streets.
My maidens and my young men have fallen by the sword.
You have killed them in the day of Your displeasure,
You have slaughtered without compassion.
22 "Would You proclaim, as in a day of appointed time,
The fears that surround me?
And no one escaped or survived
In the day of the displeasure of יהוה.
Those whom I have nursed and brought up
My enemy has destroyed."

3 I am the man who has seen affliction
By the rod of His wrath.
2 He has led me and made me walk
In darkness and not light.
3 Indeed, He has turned back,
He has turned His hand against me all the day.
4 He has worn out my flesh and my skin,
He has broken my bones.
5 He has piled up against me,
And surrounded me with bitterness and hardship.
6 He has made me dwell in dark places
Like the dead of old.
7 He has hedged me in and I do not go out,
He has made my chain heavy.
8 Also, when I cry and shout,
He shuts out my prayer.
9 He has blocked my ways with hewn stone,
He has made my paths crooked.
10 He is to me like a bear lying in wait,
A lion in hiding.
11 He has turned aside my ways
And torn me in pieces,
He has laid me waste.
12 He has bent His bow
And set me up as a target for the arrow.
13 He made the arrows of His quiver pierce my kidneys.
14 I have been a mockery to all my people,
Their *mocking* song all the day.
15 He has filled me with bitterness,
He drenched me with wormwood.
16 And He has broken my teeth with gravel,
He has covered me with ashes.
17 And You have removed my being far from peace,
I have forgotten goodness.
18 And I said, "My strength and my expectancy
Have perished from יהוה."
19 Remember my affliction and my anguish,
The wormwood and the gall.
20 Your being indeed remembers
And bows down upon me.
21 This I recall to my mind, therefore I wait:
22 The loving-commitments of יהוה!
For we have not been consumed,
For His compassions have not ended.
23 They are new every morning,
Great is Your trustworthiness.
24 "יהוה is my Portion," says my being,
"Therefore I wait for Him!"
25 יהוה is good to those waiting for Him,
To the being who seeks Him.
26 It is good – both to wait and to be silent,
For the deliverance of יהוה.
27 It is good for a man to bear a yoke in his youth.
28 Let him sit alone and be silent,
Because He has laid it on him.
29 Let him put his mouth in the dust,
There might yet be expectancy.
30 Let him give his cheek

To the one who strikes him –
He is filled with reproach.
31 For יהוה does not cast off forever.
32 For though He afflicted,
Yet He shall show compassion
According to the greatness of His loving-commitments.
33 For He has not afflicted from His heart,
Nor does He grieve the children of men.
34 To crush under His feet
All the prisoners of the earth,
35 To turn aside the right-ruling of man
Before the face of the Most High,
36 Or wrong a man in his cause –
This יהוה does not approve.
37 Who was it that spoke,
And it came to be!
Has יהוה not commanded it?
38 Do not the evils and the good
Come out of the mouth of the Most High?
39 What? Should mankind complain,
A living man, because of his sins?
40 Let us search and examine our ways,
And turn back to יהוה.
41 Let us lift our hearts and hands
To Ěl in the heavens *and say*:
42 We, we have transgressed and rebelled.
You, You have not forgiven.
43 You have wrapped Yourself
With displeasure and pursued us.
You have killed,
You have not shown compassion.
44 You have wrapped Yourself
With a cloud, so that prayer does not pass through.
45 You make us as scum and refuse
In the midst of the peoples.
46 All our enemies have opened their mouth against us.
47 Fear and a snare have come upon us,
Shame and ruin.
48 Streams of water run down my eye
For the ruin of the daughter of my people.
49 My eye flows out and does not cease,
Without stopping,
50 Until יהוה looks down and sees from the heavens.
51 My eye pains my being
Because of all the daughters of my city.
52 My enemies hunted me down
Like a bird, without cause.
53 They have cut off my life in the pit,
And they threw stones at me.
54 Waters flowed over my head;
I said, "I am cut off!"
55 I called on Your Name,
O יהוה, from the lowest pit.
56 You have heard my voice,
Do not hide Your ear from my groaning,
From my outcry!
57 You drew near on the day I called on You;
You said, "Do not fear!"
58 O יהוה, You did plead the case for my being;
You have redeemed my life.
59 O יהוה, You have seen my oppression;
Judge my case.
60 You have seen all their vengeance,
All their plans against me.
61 You have heard their reproach,
O יהוה, all their plans against me,
62 The lips of those rising against me,
And their scheming against me all the day.
63 Look at their sitting down and their rising up;
I am their song.
64 Repay them, O יהוה,
According to the work of their hands.
65 Give them a veiled heart,
Your curse upon them!
66 Pursue and destroy them in displeasure,
From under the heavens of יהוה.

4 How dim the gold has become,
The fine gold changed!
The stones of the set-apart place
Are scattered at the head of every street.
2 The precious sons of Tsiyon
Who were weighed against fine gold,
How they have been reckoned as clay pots,
The work of the hands of the potter!
3 Even jackals have presented their breasts,

They have nursed their young.
The daughter of my people has become as cruel,
As ostriches in the wilderness.
4 The tongue of the infant has clung
To the roof of its mouth for thirst;
Children asked for bread,
No one breaks it for them.
5 Those who ate delicacies
Have been laid waste in the streets;
Those who were brought up in scarlet
Have embraced dunghills.
6 And the crookedness of the daughter of my people
Is greater than the punishment of the sin of Seḏom,
Which was overthrown in a moment,
And no hands were wrung over her!
7 Her Nazirites were brighter than snow
And whiter than milk;
More ruddy in body than rubies,
Their cut like sapphire.
8 Their appearance has become blacker than soot;
They have become unrecognised in the streets;
Their skin has shrivelled on their bones,
It has become dry, it has become as wood.
9 Better off were those pierced by the sword
Than those pierced by hunger;
For these pine away,
Pierced through for lack of the fruits of the field.
10 The hands of the compassionate women
Have boiled their own children;
They became food for them
In the destruction of the daughter of my people.
11 יהוה has completed His wrath,
He has poured out His burning displeasure.
And He kindled a fire in Tsiyon,
And it consumed her foundations.
12 The sovereigns of the earth did not believe,
Nor any of the inhabitants of the world,
That an adversary and enemy
Would enter the gates of Yerushalayim.
13 It was because of the sins of her prophets,
The crookednesses of her priests,
Who shed in her midst the blood of the righteous.
14 They staggered, blind, in the streets;
They have defiled themselves with blood,
So that no one was able to touch their garments.
15 They shouted at them,
"Away! Unclean! Away! Away! Touch not!"
When they fled and staggered,
They said, among the nations,
"They shall stay no longer."
16 The face of יהוה scattered them.
He no longer regards them.
They showed no respect for the priests
Nor favour to the elders.
17 While we exist, our eyes are consumed,
Watching vainly for our help.
In our watch-tower we watched for a nation
That could not save.
18 They have hunted our steps
From going in our streets.
Our end was near,
Our days were completed,
For our end had come.
19 Our pursuers were swifter
Than the eagles of the heavens.
They came hotly after us on the mountains
And lay in wait for us in the wilderness.
20 The breath of our nostrils, the anointed of יהוה,
Was caught in their pits,
In whose shadow we had thought
To live among the nations.
21 Rejoice and be glad, O daughter of Eḏom,
You who dwell in the land of Uz!
The cup is to pass over to you too,
So that you become drunk and make yourself naked.
22 Your crookedness has been completed,
O daughter of Tsiyon.

He no longer prolongs your exile.
He shall punish your crookedness,
O daughter of Eḏom,
He shall uncover your sins!

5 Remember, O יהוה,
what has come upon us.
Look, and see our reproach!
2 Our inheritance has been turned over to strangers,
And our houses to foreigners.
3 We have become orphans, fatherless,
Our mothers are like widows.
4 We had to pay for our drinking water,
And our wood comes at a price.
5 We have been pursued close onto our neck,
We have laboured and had no rest.
6 To Mitsrayim we have given a hand;
To Ashshur, to be satisfied with bread.
7 Our fathers sinned, they are no more.
We have borne their crookednesses.
8 Servants have ruled over us;
There is no one to deliver from their hand.
9 With our lives we bring in our bread,
Because of the sword of the wilderness.
10 Our skin has become as hot as an oven,
Because of the burning heat of scarcity of food.
11 They have humbled the women in Tsiyon,
The maidens in the cities of Yehuḏah.
12 Rulers were hung up by their hands,
And elders were not respected.
13 They have taken young men to grind,
And youths stumbled under *loads of* wood.
14 Elders have ceased from the gate,
Young men from their song.
15 The joy of our heart has ceased,
Our dancing has turned into mourning.
16 The crown has fallen from our head.
Woe to us, for we have sinned!
17 Because of this our heart has been sick,
Because of these our eyes have become dim,
18 Because of Mount Tsiyon which is laid waste;
Foxes have gone roaming in it.
19 You, O יהוה, remain forever,
Your throne from generation to generation.
20 Why do You forget us forever,
Forsake us for length of days?
21 Turn us back to You, O יהוה,
And let us turn back,
Renew our days as of old.
22 For have You completely rejected us?
You have been wroth with us, exceedingly!

QOHELETH

ECCLESIASTES – CONVENER

1 The words of Qoheleth,[a] son of Dawiḏ, sovereign in Yerushalayim.
2 "Futility! Futility!" says Qoheleth. "Futility, futility, all is futile!"
3 What does man gain from all his labour in which he toils under the sun?
4 A generation passes away, and a generation comes, but the earth stands forever.
5 The sun also rises, and the sun sets, and hurries back to the place where it arose.
6 Going to the south, and turning round to the north, turning, turning, and on its rounds the wind returns.
7 All the rivers run into the sea, yet the sea never overflows. To the place from which the rivers come, there they return again.
8 All matters are wearisome, no one is able to speak of it. The eye is not satisfied with seeing, nor the ear filled with hearing.
9 What has been is what shall be, what has been done is what shall be done, and there is no new *matter* under the sun.
10 Is there a matter of which it is said, "See, this is new"? It was here already, long ago.
11 There is no remembrance of former ones, nor is there any remembrance of those that are to come by those who come later on.
12 I, Qoheleth, was sovereign over Yisra'ěl in Yerushalayim.
13 And I set my heart to seek and search out by wisdom concerning all that has been done under the heavens; this evil task Elohim has given to the sons of man, to be humbled by it.
14 I have seen all the works that are done under the sun. And see, all was futile and feeding on wind.
15 The crooked could not be straightened, and what is lacking could not be counted.
16 So I spoke to my heart, saying, "See, I have attained greatness, and have gained more wisdom than all who were before me in Yerushalayim. And my heart has seen much wisdom and knowledge."
17 And I set my heart to know wisdom – and to know madness and folly. I know that this too is feeding on wind.
18 For in much wisdom is much grief, and he who increases knowledge increases suffering.

2 I said in my heart, "Come now, let me try you with rejoicing and find out what is good." But see, that too was futile.
2 I said of laughter, "It is madness," and of rejoicing, "What does it do?"
3 I searched in my heart how to stimulate my body with wine, while guiding my heart with wisdom, and how to lay hold on folly, until I could see what was good for the sons of men to do under the heavens all the days of their lives.
4 I made my works great, I built myself houses, I planted vineyards for myself.
5 I made gardens and parks for myself, and I planted all kinds of fruit trees in them.
6 I made pools of water for myself, to water from them a plantation of growing trees.
7 I bought male and female servants, and I came to have sons of the household. Also, I had greater possessions of herds and flocks than all who were before me in Yerushalayim.
8 I also gathered for myself silver and gold and the treasures of sovereigns and of the provinces. I provided male and female singers for myself, and the pleasures of men – a woman and women.
9 Thus I became great and increased

[a] This Hebrew word means Assembler or Convener, an appelative. The author could have been Shelomoh, or else some post-exilic writer.

more than all who were before me in Yerushalayim. Also my wisdom remained with me.

10 And all that my eyes desired I did not keep from them. I did not withhold my heart from any pleasure, for my heart rejoiced in all my labour. And this was my portion from all my labour.

11 But when I looked on all the works that my hands had done and on the labour in which I had toiled, see, all was futile and feeding on wind, and there was no gain under the sun.

12 And I turned myself to look at wisdom, and madness, and folly. For what would the man do who comes after the sovereign *except* what already has been done?

13 Then I saw that wisdom is better than folly, as light is better than darkness.

14 The wise one's eyes are in his head, but the fool walks in darkness. And I also knew that one event befalls them all.

15 And I said in my heart, "As the event of the fool, even so it befalls me, and why was I then more wise?" Then I said in my heart, "This also is futile."

16 For there is no more lasting remembrance of the wise than of the fool, since in the days to come all is forgotten. And how does a wise man die? With the fool!

17 And I hated life because the work that was done under the sun was evil on me, for all is futile and feeding on wind.

18 And I hated all my labour in which I had toiled under the sun, because I leave it to a man who would come after me.

19 And who knows whether he is wise or foolish? Yet he shall rule over all my labour in which I toiled and in which I have shown myself wise under the sun. That too is futile.

20 So I turned my heart and despaired of all the labour in which I had toiled under the sun.

21 For a man might labour with wisdom, knowledge, and skill; yet he leaves his heritage to a man who has not laboured for it. That too is futile and a great evil.

22 For what does a man get for all his labour and strain of his heart with which he has toiled under the sun?

23 For all his days are sufferings, and his work grievous; even in the night his heart takes no rest. That too is futile.

24 A man could do no better but to eat and drink, and enjoy himself in his labour! That too, I saw, was from the hand of Elohim.

25 For who eats or who finds enjoyment without Him?

26 For He gives wisdom and knowledge and joy to a man who is good in His eyes. But to the sinner He gives the task of gathering and collecting, to give *to him* who is good before Elohim. That too is futile and feeding on wind.

3 For every *matter* there is an appointed time, even a time for every pursuit under the heavens:

2 A time to be born, and a time to die; a time to plant, and a time to uproot;

3 a time to kill, and a time to heal; a time to break down, and a time to build up;

4 a time to weep, and a time to laugh; a time to mourn, and a time to dance;

5 a time to throw away stones, and a time to gather stones; a time to embrace, and a time to refrain from embracing;

6 a time to seek, and a time to lose; a time to keep, and a time to throw away;

7 a time to tear, and a time to sew; a time to be silent, and a time to speak;

8 a time to love, and a time to hate; a time for battle, and a time for peace.

9 What does the worker gain from his toil?

10 I have seen the task Elohim has given to the sons of men to be humbled by it.

11 He has made it all, beautiful in its time. Even the ages He has put in their hearts, except that no one finds out the work that Elohim does from beginning to end.

12 I know that there is no good for them but to rejoice, and to do good in their lives,

13 and also that every man should eat and drink and enjoy the good of all his labour, it is a gift of Elohim.

14 I know that whatever Elohim does is forever. There is no adding to it, and there is no taking from it. Elohim does it, that men should fear before Him.

15 Whatever is has already been, and what shall be has been before. But Elohim seeks out what has been pursued.

16 Then again I saw under the sun: In the place of right-ruling, wrongness was there. And in the place of righteousness, wrongness was there.

17 I said in my heart, "Elohim judges the righteous and the wrong, for there is a time for every matter and for every work."

18 I said in my heart, "Concerning the matter of the sons of men, Elohim selects them, so as to see that they themselves are beasts."

19 For the event of the sons of men is also the event of beasts – one event befalls them: as one dies, so dies the other. Indeed, they all have one breath – man has no advantage over beasts. For all is futile.

20 All are going to one place – all came from the dust, and all return to dust.

21 Who knows the spirit of the sons of men, which goes upward, and the spirit of the beast, which goes down to the earth?

22 So I saw that man could do no better but to rejoice in his own works, for that is his portion. For who would bring him to see what shall be after him?

4 Then I looked again at all the oppression that is done under the sun: And see! The tears of the oppressed, but they have no comforter; and power on the side of their oppressors, but they have no comforter.

2 Therefore I commended the dead who were already dead, more than the living who are still alive.

3 And better than both is he who has never existed, who has not seen the evil work that is done under the sun.

4 And I saw that all the toil and skill of the work bring envy between man and his neighbour. That too is futile and feeding on wind.

5 The fool folds his hands and consumes his own flesh.

6 Better is a hand filled with rest than both hands filled with toil and feeding on wind.

7 Then I looked again at futility under the sun:

8 There is one, without a second, who has neither son nor brother. And there is no end to all his labours. His eye also is not satisfied with riches. "And for whom am I toiling and depriving myself of good?" That too is futility, and an evil task.

9 Two are better than one, because they have a good reward for their labour.

10 For if they fall, one lifts his companion up. But woe to him who is alone when he falls, for he has no one to help him up.

11 Also, if two lie down together, they keep warm; but how does one keep warm *by himself?*

12 Although one might be overpowered, two withstand him. And a threefold cord is not readily broken.

13 A poor and wise youth is better than an old and foolish sovereign who no longer knows how to take warning.

14 For he comes out of prison to be sovereign, although in his reign he was born poor.

15 I have seen all the living who walk under the sun; they were with the second youth who stands in his place.

16 There was no end of all the people; all of whom he headed. But the ones who come afterward do not rejoice in him. For that too is futile and feeding on wind.

5 Guard your steps when you go to the House of Elohim. And draw near to listen rather than to give the slaughtering of fools, for they do not know that they do evil.

2 Do not be hasty with your mouth, and let not your heart hurry to bring forth a word before Elohim. For Elohim is in the heavens, and you on earth, therefore let your words be few.

3 For a dream comes through the greatness of the task, and a fool's voice is known by his many words.

4 When you make a vow to Elohim, do not delay to pay it, for *He takes* no pleasure in fools. Pay that which you have vowed.

5 It is better not to vow than to vow and not pay.

6 Do not allow your mouth to cause your
flesh to sin, nor say before the messenger
of Elohim that it was a mistake. Why
should Elohim be wroth at your voice and
destroy the work of your hands?
7 For in much dreaming and many words
there is futility. But fear Elohim.
8 If you see the oppression of the poor,
and denial of right-ruling and righteousness in a province, do not be astonished at
the matter. For a higher than the high is
guarding, and there are higher ones over
them.
9 And the increase of the land is for all.
The sovereign himself is served from the
field.
10 He who loves silver is not satisfied with
silver; nor he who loves wealth, *and*
increase. That too is futile.
11 With the increase of goods, there is an
increase of those consuming them. What
advantage then is there to their owners, but
to look on?
12 Sweet is the sleep of a labourer whether
he eats little or much, but the plenty of the
rich does not let him sleep.
13 There is a sickly evil I have seen under
the sun: riches kept for their owner, for his
evil.
14 But those riches perish through evil
use. And he brings forth a son, and there is
naught in his hand.
15 As he came naked from his mother's
womb, so he returns, to go as he came.
And from his labour which goes into his
hand he takes none whatsoever.
16 And this too is a grievous evil – exactly
as he came, so he goes. And what gain has
he since he toiled for the wind?
17 All his days he also eats in darkness,
and with much sorrow and sickness and
wrath.
18 See what I have seen: It is good and
beautiful for one to eat and drink, and to
enjoy the good of all his labour in which he
toils under the sun all the days of his life
which Elohim gives him, for it is his
portion.
19 Further, when Elohim has given any
man riches and wealth, and permitted him
to enjoy them, and to receive his portion
and rejoice in his labour, this is a gift of
Elohim.
20 Though it not be much, let him remember the days of his life, because Elohim
bears witness by the gladness of his heart.

6

There is an evil which I have seen
under the sun, and it is great among
men:
2 A man to whom Elohim has given
riches and wealth and esteem, so that his
being lacks none at all of what he desires,
but Elohim does not permit him to eat of it,
and a foreigner consumes it. This is futile,
and it is an evil disease.
3 If a man brings forth a hundred *children* and lives many years, so that the days
of his years are many, but his being is not
satisfied with goodness, or indeed he has
no burial-place, I say that a premature birth
is better than he,
4 for it comes in futility and goes away in
darkness, and in darkness its name is covered;
5 even the sun it has not seen – it has
more rest than that man.
6 And though he lives a thousand years
twice over, yet he shall not see goodness.
Do not all go to one place?
7 All the labour of man is for his mouth,
and yet the appetite is not satisfied.
8 For what advantage has the wise over
the fool? What *advantage* does the poor
have who knows how to walk before the
living?
9 What the eyes see is better than what
the desire goes after. That too is futile and
feeding on wind.
10 Whatever shall be, has already been
named, and it is known that he is son of
Adam. And he is unable to contend with
Him who is mightier than he.
11 The more words, the more futility –
what is to man the advantage?
12 For who knows what is good for man in
life, all the days of his futile life, which he
passes like a shadow? For who declares to
man what shall be after him, under the
sun?

7 A *good* name is better than precious
oil, and the day of death than the day
of one's birth.
2 It is better to go to the house of mourning than to go to the house of feasting, for
that is the end of all men. And the living
take it to heart.
3 Sorrow is better than laughter, for by
the sadness of the face the heart becomes
better.
4 The heart of the wise is in the house of
mourning, but the heart of fools is in the
house of rejoicing.
5 It is better to hear the rebuke of the
wise than for man to hear the song of fools.
6 For as the crackling of thorns under a
pot, so is the laughter of a fool. That too is
futile.
7 For oppression makes a wise one mad,
and a bribe destroys the heart.
8 The end of a matter is better than its
beginning. The patient in spirit is better
than the proud in spirit.
9 Do not be hasty in your spirit to be
vexed, for vexation rests in the bosom of
fools.
10 Do not say, "Why were the former days
better than these?" For it is not wise of you
to have asked about this.
11 Wisdom is good with an inheritance,
and an advantage to those who see the sun.
12 For wisdom protects as silver protects,
but the advantage of knowledge is that
wisdom gives life to those who have it.
13 See the work of Elohim: For who is
able to make straight what He has made
crooked?
14 Be glad in the day of prosperity, but in
the evil day take note that Elohim has also
appointed the one as well as the other, so
that man should not uncover whatever
shall be after him.
15 I have seen it all in my days of futility:
There is a righteous one perishing in his
righteousness, and there is a wrong one
living long in his evil.
16 Do not be overrighteous, neither be
overwise – why destroy yourself?
17 Do not be wrong overmuch, and do not
be a fool – why die before your time?
18 It is good that you should take hold of
this, and also not withhold your hand from
the other. For he who fears Elohim comes
forth with all of them.
19 Wisdom makes the wise strong, more
than ten rulers that are in the city.
20 For there is not a righteous man on
earth who does good and does not sin.
21 Also do not take to heart all the words
they speak, lest you hear your servant cursing you.
22 For you know in your heart that many
times you have cursed others.
23 All this I have proved by wisdom. I
said, "I am wise," but it was far from me.
24 That which is, is far off and exceedingly deep – who does find it?
25 I have turned round, even my heart, to
know and to search, and to seek out wisdom and a conclusion, to know the wrongness of folly, even of foolishness and
madness.
26 And I found more bitter than death, the
woman whose heart is snares and nets,
whose hands are shackles. He who pleases
Elohim escapes from her, but the sinner is
captured by her.
27 "See, this I have found," says Qoheleth,
"*Counting* one by one, to find a conclusion,
28 which my being still seeks but have not
found: I have found one man among a
thousand, but a woman among all these I
have not found.
29 Truly, this only I have found: that
Elohim made man straight, but they have
sought out many devices."

8 Who is like a wise one? And who
knows the meaning of a matter? A
man's wisdom makes his face shine, and
the hardness of his face is changed.
2 I *say*, "Guard the sovereign's command
because of the oath before Elohim.
3 Do not be in a hurry to go from his
presence. Do not take a stand in an evil
matter, for he does whatever he pleases."
4 Where the word of a sovereign is, there
is power. And who says to him, "What are
you doing?"
5 He who guards the command knows no
evil matter. And the heart of the wise

discerns both time and right-ruling,
6 Because for every matter there is a time
and right-ruling, though the trouble of man
is heavy upon him.
7 For he does not know what shall be; so
who declares to him when it shall be?
8 No one has power over the spirit to
retain the spirit, and no one has power in
the day of death. There is no discharge in
battle, and wrongness does not release
those who are given to it.
9 All this I have seen; I applied my heart
to every work that is done under the sun:
There is a time in which a man rules over a
man for his evil.
10 And so I saw the wrong ones buried,
and they came and went from the place of
set-apartness, and they were forgotten in
the city where they had so done. That too
is futile.
11 Because the sentence against an evil
deed is not executed speedily, therefore the
heart of the sons of men is filled in them to
do evil.
12 Although a sinner is doing evil a hundred times, and his *life* is prolonged, yet I
know that there is good to those who fear
Elohim, who fear before Him.
13 But it shall not be well with the wrong
one, nor would he prolong his days as a
shadow, because he does not fear before
Elohim.
14 There is a futility which has been done
on earth, that there are righteous ones who
get according to the deeds of the wrong.
And there are wrong ones who get according to the deeds of the righteous. I said that
this too is futile.
15 Therefore I praised enjoyment, because
there is no good to man except to eat, and
to drink, and to rejoice – and it remains
with him in his labour for the days of his
life which Elohim has given him under the
sun.
16 When I gave my heart to know wisdom
and to see the task which has been done on
earth, even though one sees no sleep day or
night,
17 then I saw all the work of Elohim, that
man is unable to find out the work that has
been done under the sun. For though a man
labours to seek, yet he does not find it. And
even though a wise one claims to know, he
is unable to find it.

9 For all this I took to heart, even to
search out all this: that the righteous
and the wise and their deeds are in the
hand of Elohim. No man knows whether
love or hatred awaits him.
2 It is the same for all: One event to the
righteous and to the wrong; to the good,
and to the clean, and to the unclean; and to
the one slaughtering and to the one not
slaughtering. As is the good one, so is the
sinner; the one swearing as the one fearing
an oath.
3 This is an evil in all that is done under
the sun: there is one event to all. Truly the
hearts of the sons of men are filled with
evil, and madness is in their hearts while
they live, and then – to the dead!
4 But for him who is joined to all the
living there is trust, for a living dog is
better than a dead lion.
5 For the living know that they shall die,
but the dead know naught, nor do they
have any more reward, for their remembrance is forgotten.
6 Also their love, and their hatred, and
their envy have now perished; and they no
longer have a share in all that is done under
the sun.
7 Go, eat your bread with joy, and drink
your wine with a glad heart; for Elohim
has already approved your works.
8 Let your garments be white at all times,
and let your head lack no oil.
9 See life with the wife whom you love
all the days of your futile life which He has
given you under the sun, all your days of
futility. For that is your share in life, and in
your toil which you have laboured under
the sun.
10 All that your hand finds to do, do it
with your might; for there is no work or
planning or knowledge or wisdom in
She'ol where you are going.
11 I again saw under the sun that the race
is not to the swift, nor the battle to the
mighty, nor even bread to the wise, nor
even riches to men of understanding, nor

even favour to men of knowledge – for time and chance meets with them all.

12 For even man does not know his time. Like fish taken in an evil net, and like birds caught in a snare, so the sons of men are snared in an evil time, when it comes down on them suddenly.

13 Also this I saw as wisdom under the sun, and it is great to me:

14 A little city, and few men in it, and a great sovereign came against it, and besieged it, and built huge siege-works against it.

15 And there was found in it a poor wise man, and by his wisdom he delivered the city, yet no one remembered that poor man.

16 And I said, "Wisdom is better than might. But the wisdom of the poor man is despised, and his words are not heard."

17 The words of the wise, spoken calmly, should be heard rather than the shout of a ruler of fools.

18 Wisdom is better than weapons of conflict, but one sinner destroys much good.

10 Dead flies make the perfumer's ointment stink, ferment; a little folly outweighs wisdom, esteem.

2 A wise man's heart is at his right hand, but a fool's heart at his left.

3 And also, when a fool walks along the way, his heart fails, and he shows everyone that he is a fool.

4 If the spirit of the ruler rises against you, do not leave your post, for calmness lays to rest great faults.

5 There is an evil I have seen under the sun, as a mistake coming from the ruler:

6 Folly is set in many high *positions*, while the rich sit in a humble place.

7 I have seen servants on horses – and rulers walking on the ground like servants.

8 He who digs a pit falls into it, and whoever breaks through a wall is bitten by a snake.

9 He who quarries stones is hurt by them. He who splits wood is endangered by it.

10 If an iron tool is blunt, and one does not sharpen the edge, then he needs more strength, and wisdom is advantageous to make right.

11 If the snake bites without enchantment, then 'the master of the tongue' is no better!

12 Words of a wise man's mouth show favour, but the lips of a fool swallow him up;

13 the beginning of the words of his mouth is foolishness, and the end of his talk is wicked madness.

14 And a fool increases words; a man knows not what shall come to be; and who declares to him what shall be after him?

15 The labour of fools wearies them, because not one knows how to go to the city!

16 Woe to you, O land, when your sovereign is a youth, and your rulers feast in the morning!

17 Blessed are you, O land, when your sovereign is the son of nobles, and your rulers feast in due season – for strength and not for drunkenness!

18 Because of laziness the framework tumbles, and through idleness of hands the house leaks.

19 A feast is made for laughter, and wine gladdens life; and the silver answers all.

20 Do not curse the sovereign, even in your thought; do not curse the rich, even in your bedroom; for a bird of the heavens conveys the voice, and a bird in flight makes the matter known.

11 Send out your bread on the face of the waters, for after many days you shall find it.

2 Give a portion to seven, and also to eight, for you do not know what evil might be on the earth.

3 If the clouds are filled with rain, they empty themselves upon the earth. And if a tree falls to the south or the north, in the place where the tree falls, there it is.

4 He who watches the wind does not sow, and he who looks at the clouds does not reap.

5 As you do not know what is the way of the wind, or how the bones grow in the womb of her who is with child, so you do not know the works of Elohim who makes all.

[6]Sow your seed in the morning, and until evening do not let your hand rest; since you do not know which prosper, this or that, or whether both alike are good.
[7]Sweet also is the light, and good for the eyes to see the sun;
[8]But if a man lives many years, let him rejoice in them all. But let him remember the days of darkness, for they are many. All that is coming is futility.
[9]Rejoice, O young man, in your youth, and let your heart gladden you in the days of your youth. And walk in the ways of your heart, and in the sight of your eyes, but know that for all these Elohim brings you into right-ruling.
[10]Therefore remove vexation from your heart, and put away evil from your flesh, for youth and dawn of life are futility.

12

Remember also your Creator in the days of your youth, before the evil days come, and the years draw near when you say, "I have no pleasure in them":
[2]Before the sun and the light, the moon and the stars, are darkened, and the clouds return after the rain;
[3]in the day when the guards of the house tremble, and the strong men shall bow down; when the grinders shall cease because they are few, and those that look through the windows shall become dim;
[4]and the doors shall be shut in the streets, and the sound of grinding is low; and one rises up at the sound of a bird, and all the daughters of song are bowed down;
[5]furthermore, they are afraid of what is high, and of low places in the way; and the almond tree blossoms, and the grasshopper becomes a burden, and desire perishes. For man is going to his everlasting home, and the mourners shall go about the streets.
[6]*Remember Him* before the silver cord is loosed, or the golden bowl is broken, or the jar shattered at the fountain, or the wheel broken at the well,
[7]and the dust returns to the earth as it was, and the spirit returns to Elohim who gave it.
[8]"Futility! Futility!" said the Qoheleth, "All is futile."
[9]And besides being wise, Qoheleth also taught the people knowledge, and he listened and sought out – set in order many proverbs.
[10]Qoheleth sought to find out words of delight, and words of truth, rightly written.
[11]The words of the wise are like goads, and as nails driven by the masters of collections – they were given by one Shepherd.
[12]And besides these, my son, be warned – the making of many books has no end, and much study is a wearying of the flesh.
[13]Let us hear the conclusion of the entire matter: Fear Elohim and guard His commands, for this *applies to* all mankind!
[14]For Elohim shall bring every work into right-ruling, including all that is hidden, whether good or whether evil.

ESTĚR

ESTHER

1 And it came to be in the days of
Aḥashwĕrosh – he is the
Aḥashwĕrosh who reigned from India to
Kush, a hundred and twenty-seven
provinces –
2 in those days, when Sovereign
Aḥashwĕrosh sat on the throne of his
reign, which was in the citadel of Shushan,
3 that in the third year of his reign he
made a feast for all his officials and
servants. The power of Persia and Media,
the nobles and the princes of the provinces
were before him,
4 when he showed the riches of his
esteemed reign and the splendour of his
excellent greatness for many days, a hundred and eighty days.
5 And when these days were completed,
the sovereign made a feast lasting seven
days for all the people who were present in
the citadel of Shushan, from great to small,
in the courtyard of the garden of the sovereign's palace.
6 White and blue tapestries were fastened
with cords of fine linen and purple on
silver rods and marble columns – the
couches were of gold and silver on a mosa-
ic pavement of porphyry, marble, mother-
of-pearl, and black marble.
7 And they served drinks in golden
vessels, the vessels being different from
one another, with much royal wine,
according to the hand of the sovereign.
8 And drinking was according to the law,
no one was compelled, for so the sovereign
had ordered all the officers of his house,
that they should do according to each one's
pleasure.
9 Sovereigness Vashti also made a feast
for the women in the royal palace which
Sovereign Aḥashwĕrosh owned.
10 On the seventh day, when the heart of
the sovereign was glad with wine, he
ordered Mehuman, Biztha, Ḥarḇona,
Biḡtha, and Aḇaḡtha, Zĕthar, and Karkas,
the seven eunuchs who were in attendance
in the presence of Sovereign
Aḥashwĕrosh,
11 to bring Sovereigness Vashti before the
sovereign, with her royal crown, in order
to show her loveliness to the people and
the officials, for she was lovely to look
upon.
12 But Sovereigness Vashti refused to
come at the sovereign's command brought
by his eunuchs. And the sovereign was
very wroth, and his rage burned within
him.
13 So the sovereign said to the wise men
who understood the times (for in this way
the sovereign's matter *came* before all who
knew law and right-ruling,
14 and who were close to him: Karshena,
Shĕthar, Aḏmatha, Tarshish, Meres,
Marsena, Memuḵan, the seven princes of
Persia and Media, who saw the sovereign's
face, who sat first in the reign):
15 "According to law, what is to be done
to Sovereigness Vashti, because she did
not perform the command of Sovereign
Aḥashwĕrosh, through the eunuchs?"
16 And Memuḵan answered before the
sovereign and the princes, "Sovereigness
Vashti has misbehaved not only toward the
sovereign, but also toward all the princes,
and all the people who are in all the
provinces of Sovereign Aḥashwĕrosh.
17 "For the matter of the sovereigness
shall go forth to all women, to make their
husbands despised in their eyes, when they
say, 'Sovereign Aḥashwĕrosh commanded
Sovereigness Vashti to be brought in
before him, but she did not come.'
18 "And this day the princesses of Persia
and Media shall say to all the sovereign's
officials that they have heard of the matter
of the sovereigness – with plenty of scorn
and wrath.
19 "If it pleases the sovereign, let a royal
decree go out from him, and let it be
recorded in the laws of the Persians and the
Medes, so that it does not pass away, that

Vashti shall come no more before
Sovereign Aḥashwĕrosh. And let the
sovereign give her royal position to
another who is better than she.
20 "And the sovereign's decree which he
makes shall be proclaimed throughout all
his rule, great as it is, and all the wives
give esteem to their husbands, both great
and small."
21 And the word was good in the eyes of
the sovereign and the princes, and the
sovereign did according to the word of
Memuḵan.
22 So he sent letters to all the sovereign's
provinces, to each province in its own
writing, and to every people in their own
language, that each man should be master
in his own house and speak in the language
of his people.

2 After these events, when the wrath of
Sovereign Aḥashwĕrosh had ceased,
he remembered Vashti, what she had done,
and what had been decreed against her.
2 Then the sovereign's servants who
attended him said, "Let lovely young
maidens be sought for the sovereign,
3 and let the sovereign appoint officers in
all the provinces of his reign, and let them
gather all the lovely young maidens to the
citadel of Shushan, into the women's quarters, under the hand of Hĕgai the
sovereign's eunuch, guardian of the
women, to give their preparations.
4 "And let the young woman who pleases
the sovereign be sovereigness instead of
Vashti." And the word pleased the sovereign, and he did so.
5 In the citadel of Shushan there was a
certain man, a Yehuḏi whose name was
Mordeḵai son of Ya'ir, son of Shimʿi, son
of Qish, a Binyamite,
6 who had been exiled from Yerushalayim with the captives who had been
exiled with Yeḵonyah sovereign of Yehuḏah, whom Neḇuḵaḏnetstsar the sovereign
of Baḇel had exiled.
7 And it came to be that he was raising
Haḏassah, that is Estĕr, his uncle's
daughter, for she had neither father nor
mother. The young woman was beautiful
and of good appearance. And when her
father and mother died, Mordeḵai took her
as his own daughter.
8 And it came to be, when the sovereign's command and decree were heard,
and when many young women were gathered at the citadel of Shushan, into the
hand of Hĕḡai, that Estĕr, too, was taken to
the sovereign's palace, into the hand of
Hĕḡai, guardian of the women.
9 And the young woman pleased him,
and she received loving-commitment from
him. So he hastened to give her preparations and her portions, and gave her seven
choice female servants from the sovereign's palace. And he moved her and her
female servants to the best *place* in the
house of the women.
10 Estĕr had not made known her people
or her relatives, for Mordeḵai had commanded her not to make it known.
11 And every day Mordeḵai walked about
in front of the courtyard of the women's
quarters, to learn of Estĕr's welfare and
what is done to her.
12 Now when the turn of each young
woman came to go in to Sovereign
Aḥashwĕrosh after she had completed
twelve new *moons* according to the regulations for the women – for the days of their
preparation were completed as follows: six
new *moons* with oil of myrrh, and six new
moons with perfumes and with the preparations of women –
13 thus prepared, the young woman went
to the sovereign, and whatever she asked
for was given to take with her from the
house of the women to the sovereign's
palace.
14 In the evening she went, and in the
morning she returned to the second house
of the women, into the hand of Shaʿashgaz,
the sovereign's eunuch, guardian of the
concubines. She would not come in to the
sovereign again unless the sovereign
delighted in her and called for her by
name.
15 And when the turn came for Estĕr, the
daughter of Aḇihayil the uncle of
Mordeḵai, who had taken her as his
daughter, to come in to the sovereign, she

sought no matter but what Hěḡai the sovereign's eunuch, guardian of the women, advised. And Estěr found favour in the eyes of all who saw her.

16 And Estěr was taken to Sovereign Aḥashwěrosh, into his royal palace, in the tenth new *moon,* which is the new *moon* of Těḇěth, in the seventh year of his reign.

17 And the sovereign loved Estěr more than all the women, and she found favour and loving-commitment in his eyes more than all the maidens. And he set the royal crown upon her head and made her sovereigness instead of Vashti.

18 And the sovereign made a great feast, the Feast of Estěr, for all his officials and servants. And he proclaimed a release in the provinces and gave gifts according to the means of a sovereign.

19 And when maidens were assembled a second time, Mordeḵai sat within the sovereign's gate.

20 Estěr had not made known her relatives and her people *yet,* as Mordeḵai commanded her, for Estěr obeyed the command of Mordeḵai as when she was being raised by him.

21 In those days, while Mordeḵai sat within the sovereign's gate, two of the sovereign's eunuchs, Biḡthan and Teresh, doorkeepers, were wroth and sought to lay hands on Sovereign Aḥashwěrosh.

22 And the matter became known to Mordeḵai, who informed Sovereigness Estěr, and Estěr spoke to the sovereign in Mordeḵai's name.

23 And when the matter was searched into, it was confirmed, and both were hanged on a wood*en structure*. And it was written in the book of the annals in the presence of the sovereign.

3 After these events Sovereign Aḥashwěrosh promoted Haman, son of Hammeḏatha the Aḡaḡite, and exalted him and seated him higher than all the princes with him.

2 And all the sovereign's servants who were in the sovereign's gate bowed and did obeisance to Haman, for so the sovereign had commanded concerning him. But Mordeḵai would not bow or do obeisance.

3 And the sovereign's servants who were in the sovereign's gate said to Mordeḵai, "Why do you disobey the sovereign's command?"

4 And it came to be, when they spoke to him daily and he would not listen to them, that they told Haman, to see whether the words of Mordeḵai would stand – for he had told them that he was a Yehuḏi.

5 And when Haman saw that Mordeḵai did not bow or do obeisance, Haman was filled with wrath.

6 But it was despicable in his eyes to lay hands on Mordeḵai alone, for they had informed him of the people of Mordeḵai. Therefore Haman sought to destroy all the Yehuḏim who were throughout all the reign of Aḥashwěrosh, the people of Mordeḵai.

7 In the first new *moon,* which is the new *moon* of Nisan, in the twelfth year of Sovereign Aḥashwěrosh, someone cast Pur – that is, the lot – before Haman from day to day, and from new *moon* to new *moon,* until it fell on the twelfth *month,* which is the new *moon* of Aḏar.

8 Haman then told Sovereign Aḥashwěrosh, "There is a certain people scattered and dispersed among the people in all the provinces of your reign, whose laws are different from all people, and they do not do the sovereign's laws. Therefore it is not in the sovereign's interest to let them remain.

9 "If it pleases the sovereign, let a decree be written to destroy them, and let me pay ten thousand talents of silver into the hands of those who do the work, to bring it into the sovereign's treasuries."

10 And the sovereign took his signet ring from his hand and gave it to Haman, son of Hammeḏatha the Aḡaḡite, the enemy of the Yehuḏim.

11 And the sovereign said to Haman, "The silver and the people are given to you, to do with them as seems good to you."

12 And the sovereign's scribes were called on the thirteenth day of the first new *moon,* and a decree was written according to all that Haman commanded – to the viceroys

of the sovereign, and to the governors who
were over each province, and to the officials of all people, to every province
according to its writing, and to every
people in their language. It was written in
the name of Sovereign Aḥashwěrosh, and
sealed with the sovereign's signet ring.
13 And the letters were sent by the runners
into all the sovereign's provinces, to cut
off, to kill, and to destroy all the Yehuḏim,
both young and old, little children and
women, in one day, on the thirteenth day of
the twelfth new *moon*, which is the new
moon of Aḏar, and to plunder their possessions.
14 A copy of the writing, to be made law
in every province, was published for all
people, to be ready for that day.
15 The runners went out, hastened by the
sovereign's command, and the decree was
given out in the citadel of Shushan. The
sovereign and Haman then sat down to
drink, but the city of Shushan was in confusion.

4 And Mordeḵai learned of all that had
been done, and Mordeḵai tore his
garments and put on sackcloth and ashes,
and went out into the midst of the city, and
cried out with a loud and bitter cry.
2 And he went up to the front of the
sovereign's gate, for no one might enter
the sovereign's gate wearing sackcloth.
3 And in every province where the sovereign's command and decree came, there
was great mourning among the Yehuḏim,
and fasting, and weeping, and wailing.
And many lay in sackcloth and ashes.
4 And Estěr's young women and eunuchs
came and told her, and the sovereigness
was deeply pained, and sent garments to
Mordeḵai to wear, and to take away his
sackcloth from him, but he refused.
5 And Estěr called Hathaḵ, one of the
sovereign's eunuchs whom he had
appointed to attend her, and she gave him a
command concerning Mordeḵai, to learn
what and why this was.
6 And Hathaḵ went out to Mordeḵai, to
an open space of the city, in front of the
sovereign's gate.
7 And Mordeḵai told him all that befell
him, and all about the silver that Haman
promised to pay into the sovereign's
treasuries to destroy the Yehuḏim.
8 And he gave him a copy of the written
decree to destroy them, which was given at
Shushan, to show it to Estěr and explain it
to her, and to command her to go in to the
sovereign to make supplication to him, and
plead before him for her people.
9 And Hathaḵ came and told Estěr the
words of Mordeḵai.
10 And Estěr spoke to Hathaḵ, and gave
him a command for Mordeḵai,
11 "All the sovereign's servants and the
people of the sovereign's provinces know
that any man or woman who goes into the
inner court to the sovereign, who has not
been called, he has but one law: to be put
to death, except the one to whom the
sovereign holds out the golden sceptre,
who then shall live. But I have not been
called to come in to the sovereign these
thirty days."
12 And they declared to Mordeḵai the
words of Estěr.
13 And Mordeḵai commanded them to
answer Estěr, "Do not think within yourself to escape in the sovereign's palace any
more than all the other Yehuḏim.
14 "For if you keep entirely silent at this
time, relief and deliverance shall arise for
the Yehuḏim from another place, while
you and your father's house perish. And
who knows whether you have come to the
reign for such a time as this?"
15 And Estěr commanded to reply to
Mordeḵai,
16 "Go, gather all the Yehuḏim who are
present in Shushan, and fast for me, and do
not eat or drink for three days, night or day.
I too, and my young women shall fast in
the same way, then I shall go to the sovereign, which is against the law. And if I
shall perish, I shall perish!"
17 Mordeḵai then went away and did
according to all that Estěr commanded
him.

5 And it came to be on the third day that
Estěr put on royal apparel and stood in

the inner court of the sovereign's palace, in front of the sovereign's house, while the sovereign sat on his royal throne in the royal house, opposite the entrance of the house.

2 And it came to be, when the sovereign saw Sovereigness Estĕr standing in the court, that she found favour in his eyes, and the sovereign held out to Estĕr the golden sceptre which was in his hand. And Estĕr went near and touched the top of the sceptre.

3 And the sovereign said to her, "What is it, Sovereigness Estĕr, and what is your request? Up to half my reign, and it is given to you!"

4 And Estĕr answered, "If it pleases the sovereign, let the sovereign and Haman come today to the feast which I have prepared for him."

5 And the sovereign said, "Get Haman at once, to do as Estĕr has said." Then the sovereign and Haman went to the feast which Estĕr had prepared.

6 And the sovereign said to Estĕr at the feast of wine, "What is your petition? And it is given you. And what is your request? Up to half my reign, and it is done!"

7 And Estĕr answered and said, "My petition and request is this:

8 "If I have found favour in the eyes of the sovereign, and if it pleases the sovereign to give my petition and perform my request, then let the sovereign and Haman come to the feast which I make for them, and tomorrow I shall do according to the word of the sovereign."

9 And Haman went out that day rejoicing and with a glad heart. But when Haman saw Mordeḵai in the sovereign's gate, and that he did not stand or tremble before him, he was filled with wrath against Mordeḵai.

10 But Haman held himself in, and came to his house, and he sent and called for his loved ones and Zeresh his wife.

11 And Haman recounted to them the esteem of his wealth, and his many sons, and all in which the sovereign had promoted him, and how he had exalted him above the officials and servants of the sovereign.

12 And Haman said, "Besides, Estĕr the sovereigness let no one but me come in with the sovereign to the feast which she prepared. And tomorrow too I am invited by her, along with the sovereign.

13 "But all this does not suit me, as long as I see Mordeḵai the Yehuḏi sitting at the sovereign's gate."

14 So his wife Zeresh and all his loved ones said to him, "Let a wood*en structure* be made, fifty cubits high, and in the morning speak to the sovereign that Mordeḵai be hanged on it. And go with the sovereign to the feast, rejoicing." And the word pleased Haman, and he had the wood*en structure* made.

6 On that night the sleep of the sovereign fled, and he commanded to bring the book of the records of the annals. And they were read before the sovereign.

2 And it was found written that Mordeḵai had told of Biḡthana and Teresh, two of the sovereign's eunuchs, the doorkeepers who had sought to lay hands on Sovereign Aḥashwĕrosh.

3 Then the sovereign said, "What has been done in value or in greatness to Mordeḵai for this?" And the sovereign's servants who attended him said, "Naught has been done for him."

4 And the sovereign said, "Who is in the court?" Now Haman had come into the outer court of the sovereign's palace to speak to the sovereign to hang Mordeḵai on the wood*en structure* that he had prepared for him.

5 And the sovereign's servants said to him, "Look, Haman is standing in the court." And the sovereign said, "Let him come in."

6 And when Haman came in, the sovereign asked him, "What is to be done for the man whom the sovereign delights to value?" Now Haman thought in his heart, "Whom would the sovereign delight to value more than me?"

7 And Haman answered the sovereign, "For the man whom the sovereign delights to value,

8 let a royal robe be brought which the

sovereign has worn, and a horse on which
the sovereign has ridden, one with a royal
crest placed on its head.
9 “And let this robe and horse be given
into the hand of one of the sovereign’s
most noble princes. Let them dress the
man whom the sovereign delights to value.
And make him ride on horseback through
the city square, and proclaim before him,
‘Thus it is done to the man whom the
sovereign delights to value!’ ”
10 And the sovereign said to Haman,
“Hurry, take the robe and the horse, as you
have spoken, and do so for Mordeḵai the
Yehuḏi who sits in the sovereign’s gate.
Let no word fail of all that you have spoken.”
11 And Haman took the robe and the
horse, and robed Mordeḵai and led him on
horseback through the city square, and
proclaimed before him, “Thus it is done to
the man the sovereign delights to value.”
12 Then Mordeḵai went back to the
sovereign’s gate. But Haman hurried to his
house, mourning and with covered head.
13 And when Haman related to his wife
Zeresh and all his loved ones all that had
befallen him, his wise men and his wife
Zeresh said to him, “If Mordeḵai, before
whom you have begun to fall, is from the
seed of the Yehuḏim, you are not going to
prevail against him but certainly fall before
him.”
14 While they were still speaking with
him, the sovereign’s eunuchs came, and
hurried to bring Haman to the feast which
Estĕr had prepared.

7 And the sovereign and Haman came
in, to drink with Sovereigness Estĕr.
2 And again on the second day, at the
feast of wine, the sovereign said to Estĕr,
“What is your petition, Sovereigness
Estĕr? And it is given to you. And what is
your request? Up to half my reign, and it is
done!”
3 And Sovereigness Estĕr answered and
said, “If I have found favour in your eyes,
O sovereign, and if it pleases the sovereign, let my life be given me at my petition, and my people at my request.
4 “For we have been sold, my people and
I, to be cut off, to be killed, and to be
destroyed. And if we had been sold as
male and female slaves, I would have kept
silent, although the adversary could not
make up for the sovereign’s loss.”
5 Then Sovereign Aḥashwĕrosh asked
Sovereigness Estĕr, “Who is he, and where
is he, whose heart is set to do so?”
6 And Estĕr said, “The adversary and
enemy is this evil Haman!” Then Haman
was afraid before the sovereign and
sovereigness.
7 And the sovereign, arising in his wrath
from the feast of wine, *went* into the palace
garden. And Haman remained before
Sovereigness Estĕr, pleading for his life,
for he saw that evil had been decided
against him by the sovereign.
8 And when the sovereign returned from
the palace garden to the place of the feast
of wine, Haman was falling on the couch
where Estĕr was. Then the sovereign said,
“Also to ravish the sovereigness while I
am in the house?” As the word left the sovereign’s mouth, they covered Haman’s
face.
9 And Ḥarḇonah, one of the eunuchs,
said to the sovereign, “Also, see the wood-
en structure, fifty cubits high, which
Haman made for Mordeḵai, who spoke
good on behalf of the sovereign, is standing at the house of Haman.” And the sovereign said, “Impale him on it!”
10 And they hanged Haman on the wood-
en structure that he had prepared for
Mordeḵai, and the sovereign’s wrath abat-
ed.

8 On that day Sovereign Aḥashwĕrosh
gave to Sovereigness Estĕr the house
of Haman, the adversary of the Yehuḏim.
And Mordeḵai came before the sovereign,
for Estĕr had explained what he was to her.
2 And the sovereign took off his signet
ring, which he had taken from Haman, and
gave it to Mordeḵai. And Estĕr appointed
Mordeḵai over the house of Haman.
3 And Estĕr spoke to the sovereign again,
and fell down at his feet and begged him
with tears to put an end to the evil of

Haman the Aḡaḡite, and his plot which he
had plotted against the Yehuḏim.
4 And the sovereign held out the golden
sceptre toward Estĕr. And Estĕr arose and
stood before the sovereign,
5 and said, “If it pleases the sovereign,
and if I have found favour in his sight and
the matter is right before the sovereign and
I am pleasing in his eyes, let it be written
to bring back the letters, the plot by
Haman, son of Hammeḏatha the Aḡaḡite,
which he wrote to destroy the Yehuḏim
who are in all the sovereign’s provinces.
6 “For how could I bear to see the evil
coming to my people? Or how could I bear
to see the destruction of my relatives?”
7 And Sovereign Aḥashwĕrosh said to
Sovereigness Estĕr and Mordeḵai the
Yehuḏi, “Look, I have given Estĕr the
house of Haman, and they have hanged
him on the wood*en structure* because he
laid his hand on the Yehuḏim.
8 “Now you write on behalf of the Yehuḏim, as it pleases you, in the sovereign’s
name, and seal it with the sovereign’s
signet ring. For a letter which is written in
the sovereign’s name and sealed with the
sovereign’s signet ring no one turns back.”
9 So the sovereign’s scribes were called
at that time, in the third new *moon*, which
is the new *moon* of Siwan, on the twenty-
third day. And it was written, according to
all that Mordeḵai commanded to the
Yehuḏim, and to the viceroys, and the
governors, and the princes of the provinces
from India to Kush, a hundred and twenty-
seven provinces, to every province in its
own writing, to every people in their own
language, and to the Yehuḏim in their own
writing, and in their own language.
10 And he wrote in the name of Sovereign
Aḥashwĕrosh, and sealed it with the
sovereign’s signet ring, and sent letters by
runners on horseback, riding on royal
horses bred from speedy mares:
11 That the sovereign has granted to the
Yehuḏim who were in every city to be
assembled and stand for their lives – to cut
off, to kill, and to destroy all the power of
the people or province that would distress
them, little children and women, and to
plunder their possessions,
12 on one day in all the provinces of
Sovereign Aḥashwĕrosh, on the thirteenth
day of the twelfth new *moon*, which is the
new *moon* of Aḏar.
13 The copy of the writing to be made law
in every province was announced to all the
peoples, so that the Yehuḏim would be
ready on that day to be avenged on their
enemies.
14 The runners, riding on royal horses,
went out, hastened and pressed on by the
sovereign’s command. And the decree was
given out in the citadel of Shushan.
15 And Mordeḵai went out from the
presence of the sovereign wearing royal
garments of blue and white, with a great
crown of gold and a garment of fine linen
and purple. And the city of Shushan
rejoiced and was glad.
16 For the Yehuḏim there was light and
gladness and joy and value.
17 And in every province and in every city
where the sovereign’s command and
decree came, the Yehuḏim had joy and
gladness, a feast and a good day. And
many of the people of the land were
becoming Yehuḏim, for the fear of the
Yehuḏim had fallen upon them.

9 And in the twelfth new *moon*, that is,
the new *moon* of Aḏar, on the thirteenth day, when the sovereign’s command
and his decree came to be done, on the day
that the enemies of the Yehuḏim had waited to overpower them, it turned around, so
that the Yehuḏim overpowered those who
hated them.
2 The Yehuḏim assembled in their cities,
throughout all the provinces of Sovereign
Aḥashwĕrosh to lay hands on those who
sought their evil. And no one stood against
them, because fear of them fell upon all
people.
3 And all the officials of the provinces,
and the viceroys, and the governors, and
all those doing the sovereign’s work,
helped the Yehuḏim, because the fear of
Mordeḵai fell upon them.
4 For Mordeḵai was great in the palace of
the sovereign, and his report spread into all

the provinces, for this man Mordeḵai became greater and greater.

5 And the Yehuḏim struck all their enemies with the stroke of the sword, with killing and destruction, and did what they pleased to those who hated them.

6 And in the citadel of Shushan the Yehuḏim killed and destroyed five hundred men.

7 And Parshandatha, and Dalphon, and Aspatha,

8 and Poratha, and Aḏalya, and Ariḏatha,

9 and Parmashta, and Arisai, and Ariḏai, and Wayezatha,

10 the ten sons of Haman son of Hammeḏatha, the enemy of the Yehuḏim, they killed. But they did not lay a hand on the plunder.

11 On that day the number of those who were killed in the citadel of Shushan came before the sovereign.

12 And the sovereign said to Sovereigness Estĕr, "The Yehuḏim have killed and destroyed five hundred men in the citadel of Shushan, and the ten sons of Haman. What have they done in the rest of the sovereign's provinces? And what is your petition? And it is given to you. And what is your further request? And it is done."

13 And Estĕr said, "If it pleases the sovereign, let it be given to the Yehuḏim who are in Shushan to do again tomorrow according to today's decree, and let Haman's ten sons be hanged on the wooden *structure*."

14 And the sovereign commanded this to be done. And the decree was given in Shushan, and they hanged Haman's ten sons.

15 And the Yehuḏim who were in Shushan also assembled on the fourteenth day of the new *moon* of Aḏar and they killed three hundred men at Shushan. But they did not lay a hand on the plunder.

16 And the rest of the Yehuḏim in the sovereign's provinces assembled and stood for their lives, and to get rest from their enemies, and to kill seventy-five thousand of their enemies. But they did not lay a hand on the plunder.

17 *That was* on the thirteenth day of the new *moon* of Aḏar, and on the fourteenth they rested in it and made it a day of feasting and gladness.

18 But the Yehuḏim who were at Shushan assembled on the thirteenth *day*, as well as on the fourteenth *day*. And on the fifteenth they rested in it, and made it a day of feasting and gladness.

19 Therefore the Yehuḏim of the villages who dwelt in the unwalled towns were making the fourteenth day of the new *moon* of Aḏar a good day of gladness and feasting, and for sending portions to one another.

20 And Mordeḵai wrote these matters and sent letters to all the Yehuḏim who were in all the provinces of Sovereign Aḥashwĕrosh, both near and far,

21 to establish among them, to perform [a] the fourteenth and fifteenth days of the new *moon* of Aḏar, yearly,

22 as the days on which the Yehuḏim had rest from their enemies, as the new *moon* which was turned from sorrow to joy for them, and from mourning to a good day, that they should make them days of feasting and joy, of sending portions to one another and gifts to the poor.

23 And the Yehuḏim undertook to do as they had begun, and as Mordeḵai had written to them,

24 because Haman, son of Hammeḏatha the Aḡaḡite, the adversary of all the Yehuḏim, had plotted against the Yehuḏim to destroy them, and had cast Pur – that is, the lot – to crush them and to destroy them.

25 But when she came before the sovereign, he commanded by letter that his evil plot which Haman had plotted against the Yehuḏim should return on his own head, and that he and his sons should be hanged on the wood*en structure*.

26 Therefore they called these days Purim, after the name Pur. Therefore, because of all the words of this letter, what they had seen concerning this matter, and what had come upon them,

27 the Yehuḏim established and imposed it
upon themselves and upon their seed and
all who should join them, that without fail
they should perform [a] these two days every
year, according to their writing and at their
appointed time,
28 and that these days should be remembered and performed [a] throughout every
generation, every clan, every province, and
every city, and that these days of Purim
should not fail from among the Yehuḏim,
and that the remembrance of them should
not cease from their seed.
29 And Sovereigness Estĕr, the daughter
of Aḇiḥayil, with Mordeḵai the Yehuḏi,
wrote with all authority to confirm this
second letter about Purim.
30 And Mordeḵai sent letters to all the
Yehuḏim, to the hundred and twenty-seven
provinces of the reign of Aḥashwĕrosh,
words of peace and truth,
31 to establish these days of Purim at their
appointed times, as Mordeḵai the Yehuḏi
and Sovereigness Estĕr had established for
them, and as they had established for
themselves and their seed concerning
matters of their fastings and lamenting.
32 And the decree of Estĕr established
these matters of Purim, and it was written
in the book.

10 And Sovereign Aḥashwĕrosh laid
compulsory labour on the land and
the islands of the sea.
2 And all the acts of his power and his
might, and the exact account of the greatness of Mordeḵai, with which the
sovereign made him great, are they not
written in the book of the annals of the
sovereigns of Media and Persia?
3 For Mordeḵai the Yehuḏi was second to
Sovereign Aḥashwĕrosh, and great among
the Yehuḏim and pleasing to his many
brothers, seeking the good of his people
and speaking peace to all his seed.

9a - To memorialise

EZRA

1 And in the first year of Koresh sovereign of Persia, that the word of יהוה
by the mouth of Yirmeyah might be
accomplished, יהוה stirred up the spirit of
Koresh sovereign of Persia, to proclaim
throughout all his reign, and also in
writing, saying,
2 “Thus said Koresh sovereign of Persia,
‘יהוה Elohim of the heavens has given me
all the reigns of the earth. And He has
commanded me to build Him a house in
Yerushalayim which is in Yehuḏah.
3 Who is among you of all His people?
His Elohim be with him! And let him go
up to Yerushalayim, which is in Yehuḏah,
and build the House of יהוה Elohim of
Yisra’ěl – He is Elohim – which is in Yerushalayim.
4 And whoever is left from all the places
where he sojourns, let the men of his place
help him with silver and gold, with goods
and livestock, besides the voluntary offerings for the House of Elohim which is in
Yerushalayim.’ ”
5 And the heads of the fathers’ *houses* of
Yehuḏah and Binyamin, and the priests
and the Lěwites, with all those whose
spirits Elohim had stirred, rose up to go up
and build the House of יהוה which is in
Yerushalayim.
6 And all those round about them
strengthened their hands with objects of
silver and gold, with goods and livestock,
and with valuables, besides all that was
voluntarily offered.
7 And Sovereign Koresh brought out the
utensils of the House of יהוה, which
Neḇuḵaḏnetstsar had taken from Yerushalayim and put in the house of his
mighty ones,
8 and Koresh sovereign of Persia brought
them out by the hand of Mithreḏath the
treasurer, and counted them out to
Shěshbatstsar the leader of Yehuḏah.
9 And this was their number: thirty gold
dishes, one thousand silver dishes, twenty-
nine knives,
10 thirty gold basins, next, four hundred
and ten silver basins, one thousand other
utensils.
11 All the utensils of gold and silver were
five thousand four hundred. Shěshbatstsar
took all of them with the exiles who were
brought from Baḇel to Yerushalayim.

2 And these are the sons of the province
who came back from the captivity of
the exiles, whom Neḇuḵaḏnetstsar the
sovereign of Baḇel had exiled to Baḇel,
and who returned to Yerushalayim and
Yehuḏah, each to his own city,
2 who came with Zerubbaḇel: Yěshua,
Neḥemyah, Serayah, Re‘ělayah, Mordeḵai,
Bilshan, Mispar, Biḡwai, Reḥum, Ba‘anah.
The number of the men of the people of
Yisra’ěl:
3 sons of Parosh, two thousand one hundred and seventy-two;
4 sons of Shephatyah, three hundred and
seventy-two;
5 sons of Araḥ, seven hundred and seventy-five;
6 sons of Paḥath-Mo’aḇ, of the sons of
Yěshua and Yo’aḇ, two thousand eight
hundred and twelve;
7 sons of Ěylam, one thousand two hundred and fifty-four;
8 sons of Zattu, nine hundred and forty-
five;
9 sons of Zakkai, seven hundred and
sixty;
10 sons of Bani, six hundred and forty-
two;
11 sons of Běḇai, six hundred and twenty-
three;
12 sons of Azgaḏ, one thousand two hundred and twenty-two;
13 sons of Aḏoniqam, six hundred and
sixty-six;
14 sons of Biḡwai, two thousand and fifty-
six;
15 sons of Aḏin, four hundred and fifty-

four;
[16] sons of Atěr of Ḥizqiyah, ninety-eight;
[17] sons of Bětsai, three hundred and twenty-three;
[18] sons of Yorah, one hundred and twelve;
[19] sons of Ḥashum, two hundred and
twenty-three;
[20] sons of Gibbar, ninety-five;
[21] sons of Běyth Leḥem, one hundred and
twenty-three;
[22] men of Netophah, fifty-six;
[23] men of Anathoth, one hundred and
twenty-eight;
[24] sons of Azmaweth, forty-two;
[25] sons of Qiryath Arim, Kephirah, and
Be'ěroth, seven hundred and forty-three;
[26] sons of Ramah and Geḇa, six hundred
and twenty-one;
[27] men of Miḵmas, one hundred and
twenty-two;
[28] men of Běyth Ěl and Ai, two hundred
and twenty-three;
[29] sons of Neḇo, fifty-two;
[30] sons of Mağbish, one hundred and
fifty-six;
[31] sons of the other Ěylam, one thousand
two hundred and fifty-four;
[32] sons of Ḥarim, three hundred and
twenty;
[33] sons of Loḏ, Ḥaḏiḏ, and Ono, seven
hundred and twenty-five;
[34] sons of Yeriḥo, three hundred and
forty-five;
[35] sons of Sena'ah, three thousand six
hundred and thirty.
[36] The priests: sons of Yeḏayah, of the
house of Yěshua, nine hundred and seventy-three;
[37] sons of Imměr, one thousand and fifty-
two;
[38] sons of Pashhur, one thousand two hundred and forty-seven;
[39] sons of Ḥarim, one thousand and
seventeen.
[40] The Lěwites: sons of Yěshua and
Qadmi'ěl, of the sons of Hoḏawyah,
seventy-four.
[41] The singers: sons of Asaph, one hundred and twenty-eight.
[42] Sons of the gatekeepers: sons of
Shallum, sons of Atěr, sons of Talmon,
sons of Aqquḇ, sons of Ḥatita, sons of
Shoḇai, one hundred and thirty-nine in all.
[43] The Nethinim: sons of Tsiḥa, sons of
Ḥasupha, sons of Tabba'oth,
[44] sons of Qěros, sons of Si'aha, sons of
Paḏon,
[45] sons of Leḇanah, sons of Ḥağaḇah, sons
of Aqquḇ,
[46] sons of Ḥağaḇ, sons of Shamlai, sons of
Ḥanan,
[47] sons of Gidděl, sons of Gaḥar, sons of
Re'ayah,
[48] sons of Retsin, sons of Neqoḏa, sons of
Gazzam,
[49] sons of Uzza, sons of Paseaḥ, sons of
Běsai,
[50] sons of Asnah, sons of Me'unim, sons
of Nephusim,
[51] sons of Baqbuq, sons of Ḥaqupha, sons
of Ḥarḥur,
[52] sons of Batsluth, sons of Meḥiḏa, sons
of Ḥarsha,
[53] sons of Barqos, sons of Sisera, sons of
Těmaḥ,
[54] sons of Netsiyaḥ, sons of Ḥatipha.
[55] Sons of Shelomoh's servants: sons of
Sotai, sons of Sophereth, sons of Peruḏa,
[56] sons of Ya'ala, sons of Darqon, sons of
Gidděl,
[57] sons of Shephatyah, sons of Ḥattil, sons
of Poḵereth of Tseḇayim, sons of Ami.
[58] All the Nethinim and the children of
Shelomoh's servants were three hundred
and ninety-two.
[59] And these were those who came up
from Těl Melaḥ, Těl Ḥarsha, Kerub,
Addan, Imměr; but they were unable to
show their father's house, and their seed,
whether they were of Yisra'ěl:
[60] sons of Delayah, sons of Toḇiyah, sons
of Neqoḏa, six hundred and fifty-two;
[61] and of the sons of the priests: sons of
Ḥaḇayah, sons of Qots, sons of Barzillai,
who took a wife of the daughters of
Barzillai the Gil'aḏite, and was called by
their name.
[62] These sought their register *among* those
who were counted by genealogy, but they
were not found, so they were *barred* from
the priesthood as defiled.
[63] And the governor said to them that they

should not eat of the most set-apart gifts
until there stood up a priest with the Urim
and Tummim.
64 The entire assembly was forty-two
thousand three hundred and sixty,
65 besides their male and female servants
– these were seven thousand three hundred
and thirty-seven. They also had two hundred men and women singers.
66 Their horses were seven hundred and
thirty-six, their mules two hundred and
forty-five,
67 their camels four hundred and thirty-
five, donkeys six thousand seven hundred
and twenty.
68 And some of the heads of the fathers'
houses, when they came to the House of
יהוה which is in Yerushalayim, offered
voluntarily for the House of Elohim, to
establish it in its place.
69 They gave according to their ability to
the treasury for the work sixty-one thousand gold drachmas, and five thousand
minas of silver, and one hundred priestly
garments.
70 And the priests and the Lěwites, and
some of the people, and the singers, and
the gatekeepers, and the Nethinim, dwelt
in their cities, and all Yisra'ěl in their
cities.

3 Now when the seventh new *moon*
came, and the children of Yisra'ěl
were in the cities, the people gathered as
one man to Yerushalayim.
2 And Yěshua son of Yotsaḏaq and his
brothers the priests, and Zerubbaḇel son of
She'alti'ěl and his brothers, arose and built
the slaughter-place of the Elohim of
Yisra'ěl, to offer ascending offerings on it,
as it is written in the Torah of Mosheh, the
man of Elohim.
3 So they set the slaughter-place on its
stands, being afraid of the peoples of the
lands. And they offered ascending offerings on it to יהוה, both the morning and
evening ascending offerings.
4 And they performed the Festival of
Sukkot,[a] as it is written, and the daily
ascending offerings by number, according
to the right-ruling for each day,
5 and afterward the continual ascending
offering, and those for new *moons* and for
all the appointed times of יהוה that were
set-apart, also for everyone who volunteered a voluntary offering to יהוה.
6 From the first day of the seventh new
moon they began to offer ascending offerings to יהוה. But the foundation of the
Hěḵal of יהוה had not been laid.
7 And they gave silver to the stonemasons and the carpenters, and food, and
drink, and oil to the people of Tsiḏon and
Tsor to bring cedar logs from Leḇanon to
the sea at Yapho, according to the permission which they had from Koresh
sovereign of Persia.
8 And in the second new *moon* of the second year of their coming to the House of
Elohim, to Yerushalayim, Zerubbaḇel son
of She'alti'ěl, and Yěshua son of Yotsaḏaq,
and the rest of their brothers the priests and
the Lěwites, and all those who had come
out of the captivity to Yerushalayim,
began, and they appointed the Lěwites
from twenty years old and above to oversee the work of the House of יהוה.
9 And Yěshua stood up, his sons and his
brothers, Qadmi'ěl with his sons, the sons
of Yehuḏah together, to oversee those
working on the House of Elohim: the sons
of Ḥěnaḏaḏ with their sons and their
brothers the Lěwites.
10 And when the builders laid the foundation of the Hěḵal of יהוה, they appointed
the priests in their robes, with trumpets,
and the Lěwites, the sons of Asaph, with
cymbals, to praise יהוה, after the order of
Dawiḏ sovereign of Yisra'ěl.
11 And they responded by praising and
giving thanks to יהוה, "For He is good, for
His loving-commitment towards Yisra'ěl
is forever." And all the people shouted
with a great shout, when they praised יהוה,
because the foundation of the House of
יהוה was laid.
12 And many of the priests and Lěwites
and heads of the fathers' *houses*, the old

3a - Booths.

men who had seen the first House, wept
with a loud voice when the foundation of
this House was laid before their eyes, and
many shouted aloud for joy,
13 and the people could not distinguish the
noise of the shout of joy from the noise of
the weeping of the people, for the people
shouted with a loud shout, and the sound
was heard far away.

4 And when the adversaries of Yehuḏah
and Binyamin heard that the sons of
the exile were building the Hěḵal of יהוה
Elohim of Yisra'ěl,
2 they came to Zerubbaḇel and the heads
of the fathers' *houses* and said to them,
"Let us build with you, for we seek your
Elohim as you do. And we have slaughtered to Him since the days of Ěsarḥaddon
sovereign of Ashshur, who brought us
here."
3 But Zerubbaḇel and Yěshua and the
rest of the heads of the fathers' *houses* of
Yisra'ěl said to them, "It is not for you and
for us to build a house for our Elohim, but
we alone build to יהוה Elohim of Yisra'ěl,
as Sovereign Koresh the sovereign of
Persia has commanded us."
4 And it came to be that the people of the
land were weakening the hands of the people of Yehuḏah and troubling them in their
building,
5 and hiring counsellors against them to
thwart their plans all the days of Koresh
sovereign of Persia, even until the reign of
Dareyawesh sovereign of Persia.
6 And in the reign of Aḥashwěrosh, in
the beginning of his reign, they wrote an
accusation against the inhabitants of
Yehuḏah and Yerushalayim.
7 And in the days of Artaḥshashta,
Bishlam, Mithreḏath, Taḇe'ěl, and the rest
of their companions wrote to Artaḥshashta
sovereign of Persia. And the letter was
written in Aramaic, and translated *from*
Aramaic.
8 Reḥum the governor and Shimshai the
scribe wrote a letter against Yerushalayim
to Sovereign Artaḥshashta, thus:
9 Reḥum the governor, and Shimshai the
scribe, and the rest of their companions –
the judges, and the emissaries, the consuls,
the officials, the people of Ereḵ and of
Baḇel and of Shushan, the Dehawites, the
Ěylamites,
10 and the rest of the nations whom the
great and noble Osnapper took into exile
and settled in the cities of Shomeron and
the rest beyond the River. And now,
11 this is a copy of the letter that they sent
him, to Sovereign Artaḥshashta from your
servants the men beyond the River. And
now,
12 let it be known to the sovereign that the
Yehuḏim who came up from you have
come to us at Yerushalayim, and are building the rebellious and evil city, and are
completing its walls and repairing the
foundations.
13 Now let it now be known to the
sovereign that, if this city is built and the
walls completed, they are not going to pay
tax, excise, or toll, and cause the revenue
of the sovereign to suffer loss.
14 Now, because we have eaten salt from
the palace, it was not fitting for us to see
the sovereign's shame. Therefore we have
sent and informed the sovereign,
15 so that search be made in the book of
the records of your fathers, and you find in
the book of the records, and know, that this
city is a rebellious city, and causing loss to
sovereigns and provinces. And revolt was
stirred up in it since days of old, for which
cause this city was destroyed.
16 We inform the sovereign that if this city
is rebuilt and its walls are completed, then
you have no portion beyond the River.
17 The sovereign sent a message: To
Reḥum the governor, and Shimshai the
scribe, to the rest of their companions who
dwell in Shomeron, and the rest beyond
the River: Peace! And now,
18 the letter you sent to us has been plainly
read before me.
19 And I made the decree, and a search
has been made, and it was found that this
city in days of old has lifted up itself
against sovereigns, and that rebellion and
revolt have been made in it.
20 And mighty sovereigns have been over
Yerushalayim, who have ruled over all

beyond the River. And tax, excise, and toll
were paid to them.
21 Now, make a decree to make these men
cease, and that this city be not built until
the command is given by me.
22 And beware of negligence to do this.
Why should damage increase to the hurt of
the sovereigns?
23 Now when the copy of the letter of
Sovereign Artaḥshashta was read before
Reḥum, and Shimshai the scribe, and their
companions, they went up in a hurry to
Yerushalayim against the Yehuḏim, and
made them cease by might and power.
24 Then the work of the House of Elah
which is at Yerushalayim ceased, and it
ceased until the second year of the reign of
Dareyawesh sovereign of Persia.

5 Then the prophets, Ḥaggai the prophet
and Zeḵaryah son of Iddo, prophesied
to the Yehuḏim who were in Yehuḏah and
Yerushalayim, in the Name of the Elah of
Yisra'ěl upon them.
2 Then Zerubbaḇel son of She'alti'ěl and
Yěshua son of Yotsaḏaq rose up and began
to build the House of Elah which is in
Yerushalayim. And the prophets of Elah
were with them, helping them.
3 At that time Tattenai the governor
beyond the River and Shethar-Bozenai and
their companions came to them and said
this to them, "Who has made you a decree
to build this House and to complete this
wall?"
4 Then we told them what the names
were of the men who were building this
building.
5 And the eye of their Elah was upon the
elders of the Yehuḏim, so that they could
not make them cease until the matter went
to Dareyawesh. And then they sent back a
letter concerning this.
6 This is a copy of the letter that Tattenai,
governor beyond the River, had sent, and
Shethar-Bozenai, and his companions the
officials beyond the River, to Dareyawesh
the sovereign.
7 They sent a letter to him, and this was
written in it: To Dareyawesh the sovereign:
All peace.
8 Let it be known to the sovereign that
we went into the province of Yehuḏah, to
the House of the great Elah, which is being
built with heavy stones, and timber is
being laid in the walls. And this work goes
on speedily and is blessed in their hands.
9 Then we asked those elders, saying this
to them, "Who made you a decree to build
this House and to complete these walls?"
10 And we also asked them their names, in
order to inform you, so we could write the
names of the men at their head.
11 And this is the answer they gave us,
saying, "We are the servants of the Elah of
heaven and earth, and we are rebuilding
the House that was built many years ago,
which a great sovereign of Yisra'ěl built
and completed.
12 "But because our fathers provoked the
Elah of heaven, He gave them into the
hand of Neḇuḵaḏnetstsar sovereign of
Baḇel, the Kasdaia, who destroyed this
House and exiled the people to Baḇel.
13 "But in the first year of Koresh sovereign of Baḇel, Koresh the sovereign made
a decree to build this House of Elah.
14 "And also, the gold and silver utensils
of the House of Elah, which Neḇuḵaḏnetstsar had taken from the Hěḵal that was
in Yerushalayim and brought to the hěḵal
of Baḇel, those Sovereign Koresh took
from the hěḵal of Baḇel and they were
given to one named Shěshbatstsar, whom
he had made governor,
15 and said to him, 'Take these utensils,
go, deposit them in the Hěḵal in
Yerushalayim, and let the House of Elah be
built on its place.'
16 "Then the same Shěshbatstsar came,
laid the foundation of the House of Elah
which is in Yerushalayim, and since that
time even until now it has been in building,
and it is not completed."
17 And now, if it seems good to the sovereign, let a search be made in the sovereign's treasure-house, which is there in
Baḇel, whether it is so that a decree was
made by Sovereign Koresh to build this
House of Elah at Yerushalayim, and let the
sovereign send us his decision concerning
this.

6 Then Dareyawesh the sovereign made
a decree, and a search was made in the
house of the books wherein also the
treasures of Baḇel were kept.
2 And at Aḥmetha, in the palace which is
in the province of Media, a scroll was
found, and this was written in it:
3 In the first year of Sovereign Koresh,
Sovereign Koresh made a decree concerning the House of Elah at Yerushalayim,
"Let the house be built in the place where
they brought offerings, and its foundations
strongly laid, its height sixty cubits, its
width sixty cubits,
4 three rows of heavy stones and one row
of new timber. Let the expenses be paid
from the sovereign's house.
5 "And let the gold and silver utensils of
the House of Elah, which Neḇuḵaḏnetstsar
took from the Hěḵal which is in
Yerushalayim and brought to Baḇel, be
returned and go to the Hěḵal which is in
Yerushalayim, to its place, and deposit
them in the House of Elah,"
6 Now, Tattenai, governor beyond the
River, and Shethar-Bozenai, and your
companions the officials beyond the River,
stay away from there.
7 Leave the work of this House of Elah
alone. Let the governor of the Yehuḏim
and the elders of the Yehuḏim build this
House of Elah on its place.
8 And I make a decree as to what you
should do for the elders of these Yehuḏim,
for the building of this House of Elah: Let
the exact expense be paid to these men
from the sovereign's resources, out of the
taxes beyond the River, so that they are not
stopped.
9 And whatever they need – both young
bulls and rams, and lambs for the ascending offerings of the Elah of heaven, wheat,
salt, wine, and oil, according to the request
of the priests who are in Yerushalayim – let
it be given them day by day without fail,
10 so that they bring pleasing offerings to
the Elah of heaven, and pray for the life of
the sovereign and his sons.
11 And I make a decree that whoever
changes this word, let a timber be pulled
from his house, and let him be impaled,
hanged on it. And let his house be made a
dunghill because of this.
12 And Elah, who has caused His Name to
dwell there does overthrow any sovereign
or people who put their hand to change, to
destroy this House of Elah which is in
Yerushalayim! I Dareyawesh make the
decree – let it be done promptly.
13 Then Tattenai, governor beyond the
River, Shethar-Bozenai, and their companions promptly did according to what
Dareyawesh the sovereign had sent.
14 And the elders of the Yehuḏim were
building, and they were blessed through
the prophesying of Ḥaggai the prophet and
Zeḵaryah son of Iddo. And they built and
finished it, according to the decree of the
Elah of Yisra'ěl, and according to the
decree of Koresh, and Dareyawesh, and
Artaḥshashta sovereign of Persia.
15 And this House was completed on the
third day of the month of Aḏar, which was
in the sixth year of the reign of Sovereign
Dareyawesh.
16 Then the children of Yisra'ěl, the
priests and the Lěwites and the rest of the
sons of the exile, did the dedication of this
House of Elah with joy,
17 and offered at the dedication of this
House of Elah one hundred bulls, two hundred rams, four hundred lambs, and as a
sin offering for all Yisra'ěl twelve male
goats, according to the number of the
tribes of Yisra'ěl.
18 And they appointed the priests to their
divisions and the Lěwites to their
divisions, over the service of Elah in Yerushalayim, as it is written in the Book of
Mosheh.
19 And the sons of the exile performed the
Pěsaḥ on the fourteenth *day* of the first
new *moon*,
20 for the priests and the Lěwites had
cleansed themselves – all of them were
clean. And they slew the Pěsaḥ for all the
sons of the exile, and for their brothers the
priests, and for themselves.
21 And the children of Yisra'ěl who had
returned from the exile ate together with
all who had separated themselves from the
uncleanness of the nations of the land in

order to seek יהוה Elohim of Yisra'ĕl.

22 And they performed the Festival of Matzot[a] seven days with joy, for יהוה caused them to rejoice, and turned the heart of the sovereign of Ashshur toward them, to strengthen their hands in the work of the House of Elohim, the Elohim of Yisra'ĕl.

7 And after these events, in the reign of Artaḥshashta sovereign of Persia, Ezra son of Serayah, son of Azaryah, son of Ḥilqiyah,

2 son of Shallum, son of Tsaḏoq, son of Aḥituḇ,

3 son of Amaryah, son of Azaryah, son of Merayoth,

4 son of Zeraḥyah, son of Uzzi, son of Buqqi,

5 son of Aḇishua, son of Phineḥas, son of El'azar, son of Aharon the chief priest –

6 this Ezra came up from Baḇel. And he was a scribe, skilled in the Torah of Mosheh, which יהוה Elohim of Yisra'ĕl had given. And the sovereign gave him all he asked, according to the hand of יהוה his Elohim upon him.

7 And some of the children of Yisra'ĕl, and the priests, and the Lĕwites, and the singers, and the gatekeepers, and the Nethinim came up to Yerushalayim in the seventh year of Sovereign Artaḥshashta.

8 And he came to Yerushalayim in the fifth new *moon*, which was in the seventh year of the sovereign.

9 For on the first *day* of the first new *moon* he began to go up from Baḇel, and on the first day of the fifth new *moon* he came to Yerushalayim, according to the good hand of his Elohim upon him.

10 For Ezra had prepared his heart to seek the Torah of יהוה, and to do it, and to teach laws and right-rulings in Yisra'ĕl.

11 And this is the copy of the letter that Sovereign Artaḥshashta gave Ezra the priest, the scribe, a scribe in the words of the commands of יהוה, and of His laws to Yisra'ĕl:

12 Artaḥshashta, sovereign of sovereigns, to Ezra the priest, a perfect scribe of the law of the Elah of heaven. And now,

13 I make a decree that all those of the people of Yisra'ĕl and the priests and Lĕwites in my reign, who volunteer to go up to Yerushalayim, go with you.

14 Since you are being sent by the sovereign and his seven counsellors to inquire about Yehuḏah and Yerushalayim, with regard to the law of your Elah which is in your hand;

15 and to bring the silver and gold which the sovereign and his counsellors have voluntarily given to the Elah of Yisra'ĕl, whose dwelling is in Yerushalayim,

16 and all the silver and gold that you find in all the province of Baḇel, along with the gift of the people and the priests, voluntarily given for the House of their Elah in Yerushalayim,

17 therefore, with this silver promptly buy bulls, rams, lambs, with their grain offerings and their drink offerings, and offer them on the slaughter-place of the House of your Elah in Yerushalayim.

18 And whatever seems good to you and your brothers to do with the rest of the silver and the gold, do it according to the desire of your Elah.

19 And the utensils that are given to you for the service of the House of your Elah, put back before the Elah of Yerushalayim.

20 And the rest of the needs for the House of your Elah, which falls to you to give, give from the sovereign's treasure-house.

21 And I, I Artaḥshashta the sovereign, do make a decree to all the treasurers who are beyond the River, that whatever Ezra the priest, the scribe of the law of the Elah of heaven, does ask of you, let it be done promptly,

22 up to one hundred talents of silver, and up to one hundred kors of wheat, and up to one hundred baths of wine, and up to one hundred baths of oil, and salt without reckoning.

23 Whatever is commanded by the Elah of heaven, let it be diligently done for the House of the Elah of heaven. For why

6a - Unleavened Bread.

should there be wrath against the reign of
the sovereign and his sons?
24 We further inform you that there is no
authority to impose tax, excise, or toll on
any of the priests and Lĕwites, singers,
gatekeepers, Nethinim, and servants of this
House of Elah.
25 And you, Ezra, according to the wisdom of your Elah that is in your hand,
appoint magistrates and judges to judge all
the people who are beyond the River, all
such as know the laws of your Elah. And
teach those who do not know them.
26 And whoever does not do the law of
your Elah and the law of the sovereign, let
judgment be promptly executed on him,
whether it be death, or banishment, or con-
fiscation of goods, or imprisonment.
27 Blessed be יהוה Elohim of our fathers,
who has put this in the sovereign's heart,
to embellish the House of יהוה which is in
Yerushalayim,
28 and has extended loving-commitment
to me before the sovereign and his counsellors, and before all the sovereign's
mighty princes. So I was strengthened, as
the hand of יהוה my Elohim was upon me.
And I gathered heads from Yisra'ĕl to go
up with me.

8 These are the heads of their fathers'
houses, and this is the genealogy of
those who went up with me from Baḇel, in
the reign of Sovereign Artaḥshashta:
2 of the sons of Phineḥas, Gĕreshom; of
the sons of Ithamar, Dani'ĕl; of the sons of
Dawiḏ, Ḥattush;
3 of the sons of Sheḵanyah, of the sons of
Parosh, Zeḵaryah, and registered with him
were one hundred and fifty males;
4 of the sons of Paḥath-Mo'aḇ, Elyeho-
ʽĕynai son of Zeraḥyah, and with him two
hundred males;
5 of the sons of Sheḵanyah, the son of
Yaḥazi'ĕl, and with him three hundred
males;
6 and of the sons of Aḏin, Eḇeḏ son of
Yehonathan, and with him fifty males;
7 and of the sons of Ĕylam, Yeshayah son
of Athalyah, and with him seventy males;
8 and of the sons of Shephatyah, Zeḇaḏyah son of Miḵa'ĕl, and with him eighty
males;
9 of the sons of Yo'aḇ, Oḇaḏyah son of
Yeḥi'ĕl, and with him two hundred and
eighteen males;
10 and of the sons of Shelomith, the son of
Yosiphyah, and with him one hundred and
sixty males;
11 and of the sons of Bĕḇai, Zeḵaryah son
of Bĕḇai, and with him twenty-eight males;
12 and of the sons of Azgaḏ, Yoḥanan son
of Haqqatan, and with him one hundred
and ten males;
13 and of the last sons of Aḏoniqam,
whose names are these; Eliphelet, Yeʽi'ĕl,
and Shemayah, and with them sixty males;
14 and of the sons of Biḡwai, Uthai and
Zabbuḏ, and with them seventy males.
15 And I assembled them at the river that
flows to Ahawa, and we camped there
three days. And I looked among the people
and the priests, and did not find any of the
sons of Lĕwi there.
16 Then I sent for Eliʽezer, for Ari'ĕl, for
Shemayah, and for Elnathan, and for
Yariḇ, and for Elnathan, and for Nathan,
and for Zeḵaryah, and for Meshullam,
leaders – also for Yoyariḇ and Elnathan,
men of understanding.
17 And I gave them a command for Iddo
the chief man at the place Kasiphya, and
put in their mouth words to speak to Iddo
and his brothers the Nethinim at the place
Kasiphya, to bring us servants for the
House of our Elohim.
18 Then, by the good hand of our Elohim
upon us, they brought us a man of understanding, of the sons of Maḥli son of Lĕwi,
son of Yisra'ĕl, and Shĕrĕḇyah, with his
sons and brothers, eighteen;
19 and Ḥashaḇyah, and with him Yeshayah of the sons of Merari, his brothers and
their sons, twenty;
20 and of the Nethinim, whom Dawiḏ and
the leaders had appointed for the service of
the Lĕwites, two hundred and twenty
Nethinim, all of them designated by name.
21 I then proclaimed a fast there, at the
river of Ahawa, to humble ourselves
before our Elohim, to seek from Him the
right way for us and our little ones and all

our possessions,
22 for I was ashamed to ask of the sovereign a group of soldiers and horsemen to
help us against the enemy on the way,
because we had spoken to the sovereign,
saying, "The hand of our Elohim is upon
all those for good who seek Him, but His
power and His wrath are against all those
who forsake Him."
23 So we fasted and prayed to our Elohim
for this, and He answered our prayer.
24 And I separated twelve of the leaders of
the priests: Shĕrĕḇyah, Ḥashaḇyah, and ten
of their brothers with them;
25 and weighed out to them the silver, and
the gold, and the utensils, the contribution
for the House of our Elohim which the
sovereign and his counsellors and his
heads, and all Yisra'ĕl who were there, had
presented.
26 Thus I weighed into their hand six hundred and fifty talents of silver, and silver
objects of one hundred talents, one hundred talents of gold,
27 and twenty gold basins of a thousand
drachmas, and two utensils of fine polished bronze, precious as gold.
28 And I said to them, "You are set-apart
to יהוה, and the objects are set-apart. And
the silver and the gold are a voluntary
offering to יהוה Elohim of your fathers.
29 "Watch and guard them until you weigh
them before the leaders of the priests and
the Lĕwites and heads of the fathers' *houses* of Yisra'ĕl in Yerushalayim, in the
rooms of the House of יהוה."
30 So the priests and the Lĕwites took the
weight of the silver and the gold and the
utensils, to bring them to Yerushalayim to
the House of our Elohim.
31 Then we set out from the Ahawa River
on the twelfth of the first new *moon*, to go
to Yerushalayim. And the hand of our
Elohim was upon us, and He delivered us
from the hand of the enemy and from
ambush along the way.
32 And when we came to Yerushalayim,
we dwelt there three days.
33 And on the fourth day the silver and the
gold and the utensils were weighed in the
House of our Elohim by the hand of
Merĕmoth son of Uriyah the priest, and
with him was El'azar son of Phineḥas. And
with them were the Lĕwites, Yozaḇaḏ son
of Yĕshua and No'aḏyah son of Binnui,
34 with the number and weight of all. And
all the weight was written down at that
time.
35 The sons of the exile, who had come
from the captivity, brought ascending
offerings to the Elohim of Yisra'ĕl: twelve
bulls for all Yisra'ĕl, ninety-six rams, seventy-seven lambs, and twelve male goats
as a sin offering – all as a ascending offering to יהוה.
36 And they gave the sovereign's orders to
the sovereign's viceroys and the governors
beyond the River. And they lifted up the
people and the House of Elohim.

9 And when these *matters* had been
done, the leaders came to me, saying,
"The people of Yisra'ĕl and the priests and
the Lĕwites have not separated themselves
from the peoples of the lands, as to their
abominations, *those* of the Kena'anites, the
Ḥittites, the Perizzites, the Yeḇusites, the
Ammonites, the Mo'aḇites, the Mitsrites,
and the Amorites,
2 for they have taken some of their
daughters as wives for themselves and
their sons, so that the set-apart seed is
intermingled with the peoples of those
lands. And the hand of the leaders and
rulers has been foremost in this trespass."
3 And when I heard this word, I tore my
garment and my robe, and plucked out
some of the hair of my head and beard, and
sat down astonished.
4 Then all those who trembled at the
words of the Elohim of Yisra'ĕl gathered
to me, because of the trespass of the exiles,
and I sat astonished until the evening
offering.
5 And at the evening offering I rose from
my affliction. And having torn my garment
and my robe, I fell on my knees and spread
out my hands to יהוה my Elohim,
6 and said, "O my Elohim, I am too
ashamed and wounded to lift up my face to
You, my Elohim, for our crookednesses
have risen higher than our heads, and our

guilt has grown up to the heavens.
7 "Since the days of our fathers to this
day we have been very guilty, and for our
crookednesses we, our sovereigns, and our
priests have been given into the hand of the
sovereigns of the lands, to the sword, to
captivity, and to plunder, and to shame of
faces, as it is this day.
8 "But now, for a short while, favour has
been shown from יהוה our Elohim, to
leave us a remnant to escape, and to give
us a peg in His set-apart place, that our
Elohim might enlighten our eyes and give
us a little reviving in our bondage.
9 "For we were slaves, but in our
bondage our Elohim did not forsake us,
and extended loving-commitment to us in
the presence of the sovereigns of Persia, to
revive us, to raise up the House of our
Elohim, to restore its ruins, and to give us a
wall in Yehuḏah and Yerushalayim.
10 "And now, O our Elohim, what do we
say after this? For we have forsaken Your
commands,
11 which You have commanded by Your
servants the prophets, saying, 'The land
which you are going in to possess is a land
unclean through the uncleanness of the
peoples of the lands, by their abominations
with which they have filled it, from one
end to another, by their uncleanness.
12 'And now, do not give your daughters
as wives for their sons, nor take their
daughters to your sons. And do not seek
their peace or wealth ever, so that you are
strong, and shall eat the good of the land,
and leave it as an inheritance to your
children forever.'
13 "And after all that has come upon us for
our evil deeds and for our great guilt, since
You our Elohim have held back the rod
upon our crookednesses, and have given us
such deliverance as this,
14 should we turn back, to break Your
commands, and join in marriage with the
people of these abominations? Would You
not be enraged with us until You had
consumed us, so that there would be no
remnant or survivor?
15 "O יהוה Elohim of Yisra'ěl, You are
righteous, for we are left as a remnant, as it
is this day. See, we are before You, in our
guilt, for there is no one to stand before
You concerning this!"

10

And while Ezra was praying, and
while he was confessing, weeping,
and bowing down before the House of
Elohim, a very large assembly – men and
women and children – gathered unto him
from Yisra'ěl, for the people wept very
bitterly.
2 And Sheḵanyah son of Yeḥi'ěl, one of
the sons of Olam, spoke up and said to
Ezra, "We have trespassed against our
Elohim, and have taken foreign women
from the peoples of the land. And now
there is expectancy in Yisra'ěl concerning
this.
3 "Now then, let us make a covenant with
our Elohim to put away all these wives and
those who have been born to them, according to the counsel of יהוה and of those who
tremble at the command of our Elohim.
And let it be done according to the Torah.
4 "Arise, for the matter is upon you, but
we are with you. Be strong and act."
5 And Ezra rose, and made the leaders of
the priests, the Lěwites, and all Yisra'ěl, to
swear to do according to this word. And
they swore.
6 Then Ezra rose up from before the
House of Elohim, and went into the room
of Yehoḥanan son of Elyashiḇ. And he
went there – he ate no bread and drank no
water for he mourned because of the
trespass of the exiles.
7 And they passed a call throughout
Yehuḏah and Yerushalayim to all the sons
of the exile, to gather at Yerushalayim,
8 and that whoever would not come
within three days, according to the counsel
of the leaders and elders, all his goods
would be put under a ban, and himself
separated from the assembly of the exiles.
9 Then all the men of Yehuḏah and
Binyamin gathered at Yerushalayim within
three days. It was the ninth new *moon*, on
the twentieth of the new *moon*. And all the
people sat in the open space of the House
of Elohim, trembling because of the matter
and because of showers of rain.

10And Ezra the priest stood up and said to
them, "You, you have trespassed and have
taken foreign women, adding to the guilt
of Yisra'ĕl.
11"And now, make confession to יהוה
Elohim of your fathers, and do His desire,
and separate yourselves from the peoples
of the land, and from the foreign women."
12And all the assembly answered and said
with a loud voice, "Right! It is upon us to
do according to your word.
13"But the people are many, and it is the
season of showers of rain, and we are not
able to stand outside. And the work not of
one or two days, for we have greatly
transgressed in this matter.
14"Please, let the leaders of all the assembly stand. And let all those in our cities
who have taken foreign women come at
appointed times, together with the elders
and judges of their cities, until the burning
wrath of our Elohim is turned away from
us in this matter."
15Only Yonathan son of Asah'ĕl and
Yaḥzeyah son of Tiqwah opposed this, and
Meshullam and Shabbethai the Lĕwite
gave them support.
16Then the sons of the exile did so. And
Ezra the priest, with certain heads of the
fathers' *houses*, were separated by the
fathers' *houses*, each of them by name.
And they sat down on the first day of the
tenth new *moon* to examine the matter.
17And they finished with all the men who
had taken foreign women by the first day
of the first new *moon*.
18And among the sons of the priests who
had taken foreign women were found of
the sons of Yĕshua son of Yotsaḏaq, and
his brothers: Ma'asĕyah, and Eli'ezer, and
Yariḇ, and Geḏalyah.
19And they gave their hand *in pledge* to
put away their wives. And being guilty,
they presented a ram of the flock for their
guilt.
20And of the sons of Immĕr: Ḥanani and
Zeḇaḏyah;
21and of the sons of Ḥarim: Ma'asĕyah,
and Ĕliyah, and Shemayah, and Yeḥi'ĕl,
and Uzziyah;
22and of the sons of Pashhur: Elyo'ĕynai,
Ma'asĕyah, Yishma'ĕl, Nethanĕ'l, Yozaḇaḏ, and El'asah.
23And of the Lĕwites: Yozaḇaḏ, Shim'i,
Qĕlayah – he is Qelita – Pethaḥyah, Yehuḏah, and Eli'ezer.
24And of the singers: Elyashiḇ. And of
the gatekeepers: Shallum, and Telem, and
Uri.
25And of Yisra'ĕl of the sons of Parosh:
Ramyah, and Yizziyah, and Malkiyah, and
Miyamin, and El'azar, and Malkiyah, and
Benayah;
26and of the sons of Ĕylam: Mattanyah,
Zeḵaryah, and Yeḥi'ĕl, and Aḇdi, and
Yerĕmoth, and Ĕliyah;
27and of the sons of Zattu: Elyo'ĕynai,
Elyashiḇ, Mattanyah, and Yerĕmoth, and
Zaḇaḏ, and Aziza;
28and of the sons of Bĕḇai: Yehoḥanan,
Ḥananyah, Zabbai, and Athlai;
29and of the sons of Bani: Meshullam,
Malluḵ, and Aḏayah, Yashuḇ, and She'al,
Ramoth;
30and of the sons of Paḥath-Mo'aḇ:
Aḏna, and Kelal, Benayah, Ma'asĕyah,
Mattanyah, Betsal'ĕl, and Binnui, and
Menashsheh;
31and of the sons of Ḥarim: Eli'ezer,
Yishshiyah, Malkiyah, Shemayah,
Shim'on,
32Binyamin, Malluḵ, and Shemaryah;
33of the sons of Ḥashum: Mattenai,
Mattattah, Zaḇaḏ, Eliphelet, Yerĕmai,
Menashsheh, and Shim'i;
34of the sons of Bani: Ma'aḏai, Amram,
and U'ĕl,
35Benayah, Bĕḏeyah, Keluhu,
36Wanyah, Merĕmoth, Elyashiḇ,
37Mattanyah, Mattenai, and Ya'asu,
38and Bani, and Binnui, Shim'i,
39and Shelemyah, and Nathan, and
Aḏayah,
40Maḵnaḏeḇai, Shashai, Sharai,
41Azar'ĕl, and Shelemyahu, Shemaryah,
42Shallum, Amaryah, and Yosĕph;
43of the sons of Neḇo: Ye'i'ĕl,
Mattithyah, Zaḇaḏ, Zeḇina, Yaddu, and
Yo'ĕl, Benayah.
44All these had taken foreign women, and
some of them had women who had borne
children.

NEḤEMYAH

NEHEMIAH

1 The words of Neḥemyah son of
Ḥakalyah. And it came to be in the
new *moon* of Kislěw, in the twentieth year,
as I was in the citadel of Shushan,
2 that Ḥanani, one of my brothers, came
with men from Yehuḏah. And I asked them
concerning the Yehuḏim who had escaped,
who had survived the captivity, and concerning Yerushalayim.
3 And they said to me, "The remnant
who are left of the captivity in the province
are there in great evil and reproach. And
the wall of Yerushalayim is broken down,
and its gates are burned with fire."
4 And it came to be, when I heard these
words, that I sat down and wept, and
mourned for many days. And I was fasting
and praying before the Elohim of the
heavens,
5 and I said, "I pray, יהוה Elohim of the
heavens, O great and awesome Ěl, guarding the covenant and loving-commitment
with those who love You, and with those
guarding Your commands,
6 please let Your ear be attentive and
Your eyes open, to hear the prayer of Your
servant which I am praying before You
now, day and night, for the children of
Yisra'ěl Your servants, and confess the sins
of the children of Yisra'ěl which we have
sinned against You. Both my father's
house and I have sinned.
7 "We have acted very corruptly against
You, and have not guarded the commands,
nor the laws, nor the right-rulings which
You commanded Your servant Mosheh.
8 "Please remember the word that You
commanded Your servant Mosheh, saying,
'If you trespass, I shall scatter you among
the peoples,
9 but if you shall turn back to Me, and
guard My commands and do them, though
you were cast out to the end of the
heavens, I shall gather them from there,
and bring them to the place which I have
chosen, to make My Name dwell there.'
10 "And they are Your servants and Your
people, whom You have ransomed by Your
great power, and by Your strong hand.
11 "O יהוה, I pray, please let Your ear be
attentive to the prayer of Your servant, and
to the prayer of Your servants who delight
to fear Your Name. And let Your servant
prosper this day, I pray, and grant him
compassion in the presence of this man."
For I was cupbearer to the sovereign.

2 And it came to be in the new *moon* of
Nisan, in the twentieth year of Artaḥshashta the sovereign, when wine was
before him, that I took the wine and gave it
to the sovereign. And I had never been sad
in his presence.
2 And the sovereign said to me, "Why is
your face sad, since you are not sick? This
is none else but sorrow of heart." Then I
was very much afraid,
3 and said to the sovereign, "Let the
sovereign live forever! Why should my
face not be sad, when the city, the place of
my fathers' burial-sites, lies waste, and its
gates are burned with fire?"
4 And the sovereign said to me, "What
are you asking for?" Then I prayed to the
Elohim of the heavens,
5 and said to the sovereign, "If it seems
good to the sovereign, and if your servant
is pleasing before you, I ask that you send
me to Yehuḏah, to the city of my fathers'
burial-sites, so that I build it."
6 And the sovereign, with the sovereigness sitting beside him, said to me,
"How long would your journey take? And
when do you return?" So it seemed good
before the sovereign to send me. And I set
him a time.
7 And I said to the sovereign, "If it seems
good to the sovereign, let letters be given
to me for the governors beyond the River,
that they should let me to pass through till I

come to Yehuḏah,

8 and a letter to Asaph the keeper of the sovereign's forest, that he should give me timber to make beams for the gates of the palace that belongs to the House, and for the city wall, and for the house I would enter." And the sovereign gave them to me according to the good hand of my Elohim upon me.

9 Then I came to the governors beyond the River, and gave to them the letters of the sovereign. Now the sovereign had sent commanders of the army and horsemen with me.

10 And Sanballat the Ḥoronite and Toḇiyah the Ammonite official heard of it, and to them it was evil, a great evil that a man had come to seek good for the children of Yisra'ěl.

11 Then I came to Yerushalayim and was there three days.

12 And I rose up in the night, I and a few men with me, but informed no one what my Elohim had put in my heart to do at Yerushalayim, nor was there any beast with me, except the beast on which I rode.

13 And I went out by night through the Valley Gate to the Jackals' Fountain and the Dung Gate, and examined the walls of Yerushalayim which were broken down and its gates which were burned with fire.

14 And I went on to the Fountain Gate and to the Sovereign's Pool, but there was no room for the beast that was under me to pass.

15 And I went up in the night by the wadi, and examined the wall, and turned back, and entered by the Valley Gate, and returned.

16 And the deputy rulers did not know where I had gone nor what I had done. Nor had I yet informed the Yehuḏim, or the priests, or the nobles, or the deputy rulers, or the others who did the work.

17 Then I said to them, "You see the evil which we are in, how Yerushalayim lies waste, and its gates are burned with fire. Come and let us build the wall of Yerushalayim, and let us no longer be a reproach."

18 And I informed them of the hand of my Elohim which had been good upon me, and also of the sovereign's words he had spoken to me. And they said, "Let us rise up and we shall build." So they made their hands strong for good.

19 But when Sanballat the Ḥoronite heard, and Toḇiyah the servant, the Ammonite, and Geshem the Araḇ, they mocked us and despised us, and said, "What is this you are doing? Are you rebelling against the sovereign?"

20 And I answered them, and said to them, "The Elohim of the heavens, He shall bless us and let us, His servants, rise and build, but you have no portion or right or remembrance in Yerushalayim."

3

And Elyashiḇ the high priest rose up with his brothers the priests and built the Sheep Gate. They set it apart and set up its doors, even as far as the Tower of Ḥanan'ěl they set it apart, as far as the Tower of Ḥanane'ěl.

2 And at his hand the men of Yeriḥo built. And at his hand Zakkur son of Imri built.

3 And the sons of Hassena'ah built the Fish Gate, who laid its beams and set up its doors, its bolts and bars.

4 And at their hand Merěmoth son of Uriyah, son of Qots, strengthened. And at their hand Meshullam son of Bereḵyah, son of Meshěyzaḇ'ěl, strengthened. And at their hand Tsaḏoq son of Baʽana strengthened.

5 And at their hand the Teqowites strengthened, but their nobles did not put their shoulders to the work of their Master.

6 And Yehoyaḏa son of Paseaḥ and Meshullam son of Besoḏeyah strengthened the Old Gate. They laid its beams and set up its doors, and its bolts and its bars.

7 And at their hand Melatyah the Giḇʽonite, and Yaḏon the Měronothite, the men of Giḇʽon and Mitspah, strengthened the official seat of the governor beyond the River.

8 At his hand Uzzi'ěl son of Ḥarhayah, one of the goldsmiths, strengthened. And at his hand Ḥananyah, one of the perfumers, strengthened. And they

restored Yerushalayim as far as the Broad Wall.

9 And at their hand Rephayah son of Ḥur, ruler of half the district of Yerushalayim, strengthened.

10 And at their hand Yeḏayah son of Ḥarumaph strengthened, even opposite his house. And at his hand Ḥattush son of Ḥashaḇneyah strengthened.

11 Malkiyah son of Ḥarim and Ḥashshuḇ son of Paḥath-Mo'aḇ strengthened another section, and the Tower of the Ovens.

12 And at his hand Shallum son of Halloḥěsh ruler of half the district of Yerushalayim strengthened, he and his daughters.

13 Ḥanun and the people of Zanowaḥ strengthened the Valley Gate. They built it, and set up its doors, its bolts and bars – and a thousand cubits of the wall as far as the Dung Gate.

14 And the Dung Gate was strengthened by Malkiyah son of Rěḵaḇ, ruler of the district of Běyth Hakkerem. He built it and set up its doors, its bolts and bars.

15 And the Fountain Gate was strengthened by Shallun son of Kol-Ḥozeh, ruler of the district of Mitspah. He built it and covered it, and set up its doors, its bolts and bars – also the wall of the Pool of Shelaḥ by the Sovereign's Garden, as far as the stairs going down from the City of Dawiḏ.

16 After him Neḥemyah son of Azbuq, ruler of half the district of Běyth Tsur, strengthened as far as opposite the burial-sites of Dawiḏ, and to the man-made pool, and as far as the house of the mighty men.

17 After him the Lěwites, Reḥum son of Bani, strengthened. At his hand strengthened Ḥashaḇyah, ruler of half the district of Qe'ilah, for his district.

18 After him their brothers, Bawwai son of Ḥěnaḏaḏ, ruler of the other half of the district of Qe'ilah, strengthened.

19 And at his hand Ězer son of Yěshua, the ruler of Mitspah, strengthened another section before the going up to the armoury at the corner.

20 After him Baruḵ son of Zabbai eagerly strengthened the other section, from the buttress to the door of the house of Elyashiḇ the high priest.

21 After him Merěmoth son of Uriyah, son of Qots, strengthened another section, from the door of the house of Elyashiḇ to the end of the house of Elyashiḇ.

22 And after him the priests, the men of the neighbourhood, strengthened.

23 After him Binyamin and Ḥashshuḇ strengthened opposite their house. After them Azaryah son of Ma'aśěyah, son of Ananyah, strengthened near his house.

24 After him Binnui son of Ḥěnaḏaḏ strengthened another section, from the house of Azaryah to the angle, even as far as the corner.

25 Palal son of Uzai *strengthened* opposite the corner, and on the tower which projects from the sovereign's upper house that was by the courtyard of the prison. After him Peḏayah son of Parosh.

26 Now the Nethinim dwelt in Ophel as far as opposite the Water Gate toward the east, and on the projecting tower.

27 After him the Teqowites strengthened another section, opposite the great projecting tower, and as far as the wall of Ophel.

28 Beyond the Horse Gate the priests strengthened, each opposite his own house.

29 After them Tsaḏoq son of Imměr strengthened opposite his own house. After him Shemayah son of Sheḵanyah, keeper of the East Gate, strengthened.

30 After him Ḥananyah son of Shelemyah, and Ḥanun, the sixth son of Tsalaph, strengthened another section. After him Meshullam son of Bereḵyah strengthened opposite his room.

31 After him Malkiyah, one of the goldsmiths, strengthened as far as the house of the Nethinim and of the merchants, opposite the Miphqaḏ Gate, and as far as the going up of the corner.

32 And between the going up of the corner to the Sheep Gate, the goldsmiths and the merchants strengthened.

4 And it came to be, when Sanballat heard that we were rebuilding the wall, that he was wroth and highly offended, and mocked the Yehuḏim.

2 And he spoke before his brothers and

the army of Shomeron, and said, "What are these feeble Yehuḏim doing? Are they going to restore, slaughter, complete it in a day? Are they going to bring to life the stones from the heaps of rubbish which are burned?"

3 And Toḇiyah the Ammonite was beside him, and he said, "Whatever they build, if a fox should climb on it, he shall break down their stone wall."

4 "Hear, O our Elohim, for we have become despised. And turn back their reproach on their own heads, and give them as a prey in a land of captivity!

5 "And do not cover over their crookedness, and do not let their sin be blotted out from before You, for they have provoked You before the builders."

6 So we built the wall, and the entire wall was joined together up to the half of it, for the people had a heart to work.

7 And it came to be, when Sanballat and Toḇiyah, and the Araḇs, and the Ammonites, and the Ashdoḏites heard that the walls of Yerushalayim were being repaired and the broken places began to be filled, that they became very wroth,

8 and all of them conspired together to come to fight against Yerushalayim and to do harm to it.

9 But we prayed to our Elohim, and set a watch against them day and night, because of them.

10 And Yehuḏah said, "The strength of the burden bearers is weakening, and there is so much rubbish that we are unable to build the wall."

11 And our adversaries said, "Let them not know or see it until we come into their midst and shall kill them, and cause the work to cease."

12 And it came to be, when the Yehuḏim who dwelt near them came, that they said to us ten times, "From whatever place you turn, *they are* against us."

13 So I set *men* behind the lower parts of the wall, at the openings – I set the people according to their clans, with their swords, their spears, and their bows.

14 And I looked, and rose up and said to the nobles, and to the deputy rulers, and to the rest of the people, "Do not be afraid of them. Remember the great and awesome, יהוה, and fight for your brothers, your sons and your daughters, your wives and your houses."

15 And it came to be, when our enemies heard that it was known to us, and that Elohim had brought their counsel to naught, that all of us returned to the wall, everyone to his work.

16 And it came to be, from that time on, that half of my servants were working in the work, while the other half were holding the spears, the shields, and the bows, and the breastplates. And the rulers were behind all the house of Yehuḏah,

17 who were building on the wall, and those bearing burdens, those loading, working with one hand in the work, and with the other holding a weapon.

18 As for the builders, each one had his sword girded at his side as he built. And the one who sounded with the shophar was beside me.

19 And I said to the nobles, and to the deputy rulers, and to the rest of the people, "The work is great and large, and we are separated far from one another on the wall.

20 "In whatever place you hear the voice of the shophar, join us there. Our Elohim fights for us."

21 So we laboured in the work, and half of them held the spears from the break of day until the stars appeared.

22 At that time I also said to the people, "Let each man and his servant spend the night in Yerushalayim, and they shall be our guard by night, and for the work by day."

23 So neither I, nor my brothers, nor my servants, nor the men of the guard who followed me, none of us took off our garments, each one his weapon *even* at the water.

5 And there was a great outcry of the people and their wives against their brothers, the Yehuḏim.

2 And there were some who were saying, "We, our sons, and our daughters are many. Let us get grain for them, and eat,

and live."
[3] And there were some who were saying,
"We have mortgaged our lands and vineyards and houses. Let us buy grain because
of the scarcity of food."
[4] And there were those who were saying,
"We have borrowed silver for the
sovereign's tax on our lands and vineyards.
[5] "And now our flesh is like the flesh of
our brothers, our children like their
children. And see, we are subjecting our
sons and our daughters to be slaves, and
some of our daughters have *already* been
subjected, and there is no power in our
hands, for other men have our lands and
vineyards."
[6] And it was very displeasing to me when
I heard their outcry and these words.
[7] And my heart ruled over me, and I
strove with the nobles and with the deputy
rulers, and said to them, "You are exacting
interest, each one from his brother." And I
called a great assembly against them,
[8] and said to them, "According to our
ability we have redeemed our brothers, the
Yehuḏim, who were sold to the nations.
And you even sell your brothers! Or
should they be sold to us?" And they were
silent and found not a word *to say*.
[9] I also said, "What you are doing is not
good. Should you not walk in the fear of
our Elohim because of the reproach of the
nations, our enemies?
[10] "And also, I, my brothers and my
servants, am lending them silver and grain.
Please, let us leave off this interest!
[11] "Please, give back to them, even today,
their lands, their vineyards, their olive-
trees, and their houses, also the hundredth
part of the silver and of the grain, and of
the new wine, and of the oil, that you have
taken from them."
[12] And they said, "Let us give it back, and
ask no more from them, we do as you say."
Then I called the priests, and made them
swear to do according to this word.
[13] I also shook out the fold of my garment
and said, "Let Elohim in this way shake
out each man from his house, and from his
property, who does not do this word, even
to be thus shaken out and emptied." And
all the assembly said, "Aměn!" and praised
יהוה. And the people did according to this
word.
[14] Also, from the day I was commanded
to be their governor in the land of
Yehuḏah, from the twentieth year until the
thirty-second year of Sovereign
Artaḥshashta, twelve years, neither I nor
my brothers ate the governor's food.
[15] But the former governors who were
before me laid burdens on the people, and
took from them bread and wine, besides
forty sheqels of silver. Their servants also
oppressed the people, but I did not do so,
because of the fear of Elohim.
[16] And I also *worked* strongly in the work
on this wall. We did not buy any land. And
all my servants were gathered there for the
work.
[17] And at my table were one hundred and
fifty of the Yehuḏim and deputy rulers,
besides those who came to us from the
nations around us.
[18] And that which was prepared for me
daily was one ox and six choice sheep, and
birds were prepared for me, and once
every ten days plenty of all kinds of wine.
And in spite of this I did not seek the
governor's food, because the bondage was
heavy on this people.
[19] O my Elohim, remember me for the
good – all that I have done for this people.

6 And it came to be when Sanballat, and
Toḇiyah, and Geshem the Araḇ, and
the rest of our enemies heard that I had
rebuilt the wall, and that there were no
breaks left in it – though at that time I had
not set up the doors in the gates –
[2] that Sanballat and Geshem sent to me,
saying, "Come, let us meet together in the
villages in the plain of Ono." But they
were planning to do evil to me.
[3] So I sent messengers to them, saying, "I
am doing a great work, and I am unable to
come down. Why should the work cease
while I leave it and come down to you?"
[4] However, they sent me the same word
four times, and I answered them the same
word.

5Then Sanballat sent his servant to me
with an open letter in his hand, the same
word, the fifth time.
6In it was written: Among the nations it
has been heard, and Gashmu is saying, that
you and the Yehuḏim are planning to rebel,
therefore you are rebuilding the wall, and
you are to be their sovereign – according to
these words.
7And you have also appointed prophets
to proclaim concerning you at Yerushalayim, saying, 'A sovereign is in
Yehuḏah!' And now these words are heard
by the sovereign. Therefore come now, and
let us take counsel together.
8Then I sent to him, saying, "There are
no such matters done as you are saying,
but you are inventing them in your own
heart."
9For all of them were making us afraid,
saying, "Let their hands slacken for the
work, and it not be done." But now, make
my hands strong.
10And when I came to the house of
Shemayah son of Delayah, son of
Mehĕtaḇ'ĕl, who was restrained, he said,
"Let us meet together in the House of
Elohim, inside the Hĕḵal, and let us close
the doors of the Hĕḵal, for they are coming
to kill you – by night they are coming to
kill you."
11 And I said, "Should a man like me flee?
And who is there like me who would go
into the Hĕḵal to save his life? I do not go
in!"
12And see, I perceived that Elohim had
not sent him, but that he spoke this
prophecy against me because Toḇiyah and
Sanballat had hired him –
13because he was a hireling – that I
should be afraid, and do so, and shall sin,
and so they could give me an evil name, to
reproach me.
14My Elohim, remember Toḇiyah and
Sanballat, according to these works of
theirs, and the prophetess No'aḏyah and
the rest of the prophets who would have
made me afraid.
15And the wall was completed on the
twenty-fifth of *the month* of Elul, in fifty-
two days.
16And it came to be, when all our
enemies heard, and all the nations around
us saw, that they fell greatly in their own
eyes, and knew that this work was done by
our Elohim.
17In those days the nobles of Yehuḏah
also sent many letters to Toḇiyah, while
those of Toḇiyah came to them.
18For many in Yehuḏah were sworn to
him, because he was the son-in-law of
Sheḵanyah son of Araḥ, and his son
Yehoḥanan had married the daughter of
Meshullam son of Bereḵyah.
19They were also speaking about his
good deeds before me, and reported my
words to him. Toḇiyah sent letters to
frighten me.

7 And it came to be, when the wall was
rebuilt, that I set up the doors, and the
gatekeepers, and the singers, and the
Lĕwites were appointed.
2And I put my brother Ḥanani in command of Yerushalayim, and Ḥananyah the
head of the palace, for he was a trustworthy man and feared Elohim more than
many.
3And I said to them, "Let not the gates
of Yerushalayim be opened until the sun is
hot. And while they are standing by, let
them shut the doors and bolt them. And
appoint guards from among the inhabitants
of Yerushalayim, each at his post, and each
in front of his own house."
4And the city was wide on both sides
and great, but the people in it were few,
and the houses were not rebuilt.
5And my Elohim put it into my heart to
gather the nobles, and the deputy rulers,
and the people, in order to be registered by
genealogy. And I found a register of the
genealogy of those who had come up at the
beginning, and I found written in it:
6These are the sons of the province who
came back from the captivity of the exiles
whom Neḇuḵaḏnetstsar the sovereign of
Baḇel had exiled, and who returned to
Yerushalayim and Yehuḏah, each to his
city,
7who came with Zerubbaḇel, Yĕshua,
Neḥemyah, Azaryah, Ra'amyah,

Naḥamani, Mordeḵai, Bilshan, Mispereth,
Biḡwai, Neḥum, Ba'anah. The number of
the men of the people of Yisra'ĕl:
8 sons of Parosh, two thousand one hundred and seventy-two;
9 sons of Shephatyah, three hundred and
seventy-two;
10 sons of Araḥ, six hundred and fifty-
two;
11 sons of Paḥath-Mo'aḇ, of the sons of
Yĕshua and Yo'aḇ, two thousand eight
hundred and eighteen;
12 sons of Ĕylam, one thousand two hundred and fifty-four;
13 sons of Zattu, eight hundred and forty-
five;
14 sons of Zakkai, seven hundred and
sixty;
15 sons of Binnui, six hundred and forty-
eight;
16 sons of Bĕḇai, six hundred and twenty-
eight;
17 sons of Azgaḏ, two thousand three hundred and twenty-two;
18 sons of Aḏoniqam, six hundred and
sixty-seven;
19 sons of Biḡwai, two thousand and
sixty-seven;
20 sons of Aḏin, six hundred and fifty-
five;
21 sons of Atĕr of Ḥizqiyah, ninety-eight;
22 sons of Ḥashum, three hundred and
twenty-eight;
23 sons of Bĕtsai, three hundred and
twenty-four;
24 sons of Ḥariph, one hundred and
twelve;
25 sons of Giḇ'on, ninety-five;
26 men of Bĕyth Leḥem and Netophah,
one hundred and eighty-eight;
27 men of Anathoth, one hundred and
twenty-eight;
28 men of Bĕyth Azmaweth, forty-two;
29 men of Qiryath Ye'arim, Kephirah, and
Be'ĕroth, seven hundred and forty-three;
30 men of Ramah and Geḇa, six hundred
and twenty-one;
31 men of Miḵmas, one hundred and
twenty-two;
32 men of Bĕyth Ĕl and Ai, one hundred
and twenty-three;
33 men of the other Neḇo, fifty-two;
34 sons of the other Ĕylam, one thousand
two hundred and fifty-four;
35 sons of Ḥarim, three hundred and twenty;
36 sons of Yeriḥo, three hundred and
forty-five;
37 sons of Loḏ, Ḥaḏiḏ, and Ono, seven
hundred and twenty-one;
38 sons of Sena'ah, three thousand nine
hundred and thirty.
39 The priests: sons of Yeḏayah, of the
house of Yĕshua, nine hundred and
seventy-three;
40 sons of Immĕr, one thousand and fifty-
two;
41 sons of Pashḥur, one thousand two hundred and forty-seven;
42 sons of Ḥarim, one thousand and
seventeen.
43 The Lĕwites: sons of Yĕshua, of
Qaḏmi'ĕl, of the sons of Hoḏewah,
seventy-four.
44 The singers: sons of Asaph, one hundred and forty-eight.
45 The gatekeepers: sons of Shallum, sons
of Atĕr, sons of Talmon, sons of Aqquḇ,
sons of Ḥatita, sons of Shoḇai, one hundred and thirty-eight.
46 The Nethinim: sons of Tsiḥa, sons of
Ḥasupha, sons of Tabba'oth,
47 sons of Qĕyros, sons of Si'a, sons of
Paḏon,
48 sons of Leḇanah, sons of Ḥaḡaḇa, sons
of Salmai,
49 sons of Ḥanan, sons of Giddĕl, sons of
Gaḥar,
50 sons of Re'ayah, sons of Retsin, sons of
Neqoḏa,
51 sons of Gazzam, sons of Uzza, sons of
Pasĕaḥ,
52 sons of Bĕsai, sons of Me'unim, sons of
Nephishesim,
53 sons of Baqbuq, sons of Ḥaqupha, sons
of Ḥarḥur,
54 sons of Batslith, sons of Meḥiḏa, sons
of Ḥarsha,
55 sons of Barqos, sons of Sisera, sons of
Temaḥ,
56 sons of Netsiyaḥ, and sons of Ḥatipha.
57 The sons of Shelomoh's servants: sons

of Sotai, sons of Sophereth, sons of Periḏa,
58 sons of Ya'ala, sons of Darqon, sons of
Giddĕl,
59 sons of Shephatyah, sons of Ḥattil, sons
of Poḵereth of Tseḇayim, sons of Amon.
60 All the Nethinim, and the sons of
Shelomoh's servants, were three hundred
and ninety-two.
61 And these were the ones who came up
from Tĕl Melaḥ, Tĕl Ḥarsha, Keruḇ,
Addon, and Immĕr, but they were unable
to show their father's house, and their
seed, whether they were of Yisra'ĕl:
62 sons of Delayah, sons of Toḇiyah, sons
of Neqoḏa, six hundred and forty-two.
63 And of the priests: sons of Ḥaḇayah,
sons of Qots, sons of Barzillai, who took a
wife of the daughters of Barzillai the
Gil'aḏite, and was called by their name.
64 These sought their register *among* those
who were counted by genealogy, but it was
not found, so they were *barred* from the
priesthood as defiled.
65 And the governor said to them that they
should not eat of the most set-apart gifts
until a priest stood up with the Urim and
Tummim.
66 All the assembly together was forty-
two thousand three hundred and sixty,
67 besides their male and female servants,
these were seven thousand three hundred
and thirty-seven. And they had two
hundred and forty-five men and women
singers.
68 Their horses were seven hundred and
thirty-six, their mules two hundred and
forty-five,
69 camels four hundred and thirty-five,
donkeys six thousand seven hundred and
twenty.
70 And some of the heads of the fathers'
houses contributed to the work. The governor gave to the treasury one thousand gold
drachmas, fifty basins, and five hundred
and thirty priestly garments.
71 Some of the heads of the fathers'
houses gave to the treasury of the work
twenty thousand gold drachmas, and two
thousand two hundred silver minas.
72 And the rest of the people gave twenty
thousand gold drachmas, two thousand
silver minas, and sixty-seven priestly
garments.
73 So the priests, and the Lĕwites, and the
gatekeepers, and the singers, and some of
the people, and the Nethinim, and all
Yisra'ĕl dwelt in their cities.

8 And when the seventh new *moon*
came, the children of Yisra'ĕl were in
their cities. And all the people gathered
together as one man in the open space that
was in front of the Water Gate. And they
spoke to Ezra the scribe to bring the Book
of the Torah of Mosheh, which יהוה had
commanded Yisra'ĕl.
2 And Ezra the priest brought the Torah
before the assembly of both men and
women and all who could hear with understanding, on the first day of the seventh
new *moon*.
3 And he read from it in the open space in
front of the Water Gate from morning until
midday, before the men and women and
those who could understand. And the ears
of all the people *listened* to the Book of the
Torah.
4 And Ezra the scribe stood on a platform
of wood which they had made for the purpose. And beside him on his right stood
Mattithyah, and Shema, and Anayah, and
Uriyah, and Ḥilqiyah, and Ma'asĕyah. And
on his left *stood* Peḏayah, and Misha'ĕl,
and Malkiyah, and Ḥashum, and Ḥashbad-
danah, Zeḵaryah, Meshullam.
5 And Ezra opened the book in the sight
of all the people, for he was above all the
people. And when he opened it, all the
people stood up.
6 And Ezra blessed יהוה, the great
Elohim. Then all the people answered,
"Amĕn, Amĕn!" while lifting up their
hands. And they bowed their heads and
worshipped יהוה with faces to the ground.
7 And Yĕshua, and Bani, and Shĕrĕḇyah,
Yamin, Aqquḇ, Shabbethai, Hoḏiyah,
Ma'asĕyah, Qelita, Azaryah, Yozaḇaḏ,
Ḥanan, Pelayah, and the Lĕwites, caused
the people to understand the Torah while
the people were in their place.
8 And they read in the Book of the Torah
of Elohim, translating to give the sense,

and caused *them* to understand the reading.
[9]And Neḥemyah, who was the governor,
and Ezra the priest, the scribe, and the
Lěwites who taught the people said to all
the people, "This day is set-apart to יהוה
your Elohim. Do not mourn or weep." For
all the people wept when they heard the
words of the Torah.
[10]Then he said to them, "Go, eat the fat,
drink the sweet, and send portions to those
for whom none is prepared. For this day is
set-apart to our יהוה. Do not be sad, for the
joy of יהוה is your strength."
[11]And the Lěwites were silencing all the
people, saying, "Hush, for the day is set-
apart, do not be sad."
[12]And all the people went to eat and to
drink, and to send portions and make a
great rejoicing, because they understood
the words that were made known to them.
[13]And on the second day the heads of the
fathers' *houses* of all the people, with the
priests and Lěwites, were gathered to Ezra
the scribe, in order to study the words of
the Torah.
[14]And they found written in the Torah,
which יהוה had commanded by Mosheh,
that the children of Yisra'ěl should dwell
in booths in the festival of the seventh new
moon,
[15]and that they should announce and
proclaim in all their cities and in Yerushalayim, saying, "Go out to the mountain,
and bring olive branches, branches of oil
trees, and myrtle branches, and palm
branches, and branches of leafy trees, to
make booths, as it is written."
[16]So the people went out and brought
them and made themselves booths, each
one on the roof of his house, and in their
courtyards and in the courtyards of the
House of Elohim, and in the open space of
the Water Gate and in the open space of the
Gate of Ephrayim.
[17]And the entire assembly of those who
had come back from the captivity made
booths and sat under the booths, for since
the days of Yeshua son of Nun until that
day the children of Yisra'ěl had not done
so. And there was very great rejoicing.
[18]And day by day, from the first day until
the last day, he read from the Book of the
Torah of Elohim. And they performed the
festival seven days. And on the eighth day
there was an assembly, according to the
right-ruling.

9 And on the twenty-fourth day of this
new *moon* the children of Yisra'ěl
were assembled with fasting, and in sackcloth, and with earth on them.
[2]And the descendants of Yisra'ěl separated themselves from all foreigners, and
stood and confessed their sins, and the
crookednesses of their fathers,
[3]and they stood up in their place and
read from the Book of the Torah of יהוה
their Elohim a fourth part of the day, and a
fourth part they were confessing and worshipping יהוה their Elohim.
[4]Then Yěshua and Bani, Qaḏmi'ěl,
Sheḇanyah, Bunni, Shěrěḇyah, Bani,
Kenani stood on the stairs of the Lěwites
and cried out with a loud voice to יהוה
their Elohim.
[5]Then the Lěwites, Yěshua and
Qaḏmi'ěl, Bani, Ḥashaḇneyah, Shěrěḇyah,
Hoḏiyah, Sheḇanyah, Pethaḥyah, said,
"Rise, bless יהוה your Elohim forever and
ever! And let them bless Your esteemed
Name, which is exalted above all blessing
and praise!
[6]"You are יהוה, You alone. You have
made the heavens, the heavens of the
heavens, with all their host, the earth and
all that are on it, the seas and all that are in
them, and You give life to them all. And
the host of the heavens are bowing
themselves to You.
[7]"You are יהוה, the Elohim who chose
Aḇram, and brought him out of Ur of the
Chaldees, and gave him the name of
Aḇraham,
[8]and found his heart trustworthy before
You, and made a covenant with him to give
the land of the Kena'anites, the Ḥittites, the
Amorites, and the Perizzites, and the
Yeḇusites, and the Girgashites – to give it
to his seed. And You have established Your
words, for You are righteous,
[9]and saw the affliction of our fathers in
Mitsrayim, and heard their cry by the Sea

of Reeds,
[10]and gave signs and wonders against
Pharaoh, and against all his servants, and
against all the people of his land. For You
knew that they acted proudly against them.
And You made a Name for Yourself, as it
is this day.
[11]"And You split the sea before them, and
they passed over into the midst of the sea
on the dry land. And their pursuers You
threw into the deep as a stone into the
mighty waters.
[12]"And You led them by day with a
cloudy column, and by night with a column of fire, to give them light in the way
they were to go.
[13]"And You came down on Mount Sinai,
and spoke with them from the heavens,
and gave them straight right-rulings and
Torah of truth, [a] good laws and commands.
[14]"And You made known to them Your
set-apart Sabbath, and You commanded
them commands and laws and Torot, [b] by
the hand of Mosheh Your servant.
[15]"And You gave them bread from the
heavens for their hunger, and brought them
water out of the rock for their thirst, and
said to them to go in to possess the land
which You had sworn to give them.
[16]"But they and our fathers acted
proudly, and hardened their necks, and did
not obey Your commands.
[17]"And they refused to obey, and they
remembered not Your wonders that You
did among them, and hardened their necks,
and in their rebellion they appointed a
leader to return to their bondage. But You
are a forgiving Eloah, showing favour, and
compassionate, patient, and of great loving-commitment, and did not forsake
them.
[18]"Even when they made a moulded calf
for themselves, and said, 'This is your
mighty one that brought you up out of
Mitsrayim,' and worked great blasphemies,
[19]yet You, in Your great compassion did
not forsake them in the wilderness. The
column of the cloud did not turn away
from them by day to lead them on the way,
nor the column of fire by night to give
them light in the way they were to go.
[20]"You also gave Your good Spirit to
instruct [c] them, and did not withhold Your
manna from their mouth, and gave them
water for their thirst.
[21]"And for forty years You sustained
them in the wilderness – they lacked not.
Their garments did not wear out and their
feet did not swell.
[22]"And You gave them reigns and
peoples, and apportioned them their lot. So
they took possession of the land of Siḥon,
and the land of the sovereign of Ḥeshbon,
and the land of Oḡ sovereign of Bashan.
[23]"And You increased their children as
the stars of the heavens, and brought them
into the land which You had said to their
fathers to go in and possess.
[24]"So the sons went in and possessed the
land, and You humbled before them the
people of the land, the Kenaʿanites, and
gave them into their hands, with their
sovereigns and the people of the land, to
do with them as they desired.
[25]"And they captured walled cities and a
rich land, and possessed houses filled with
all good, cisterns already dug, vineyards,
and olive-trees, and fruit trees, in plenty.
So they ate and were satisfied and grew
fat, and delighted themselves in Your great
goodness.
[26]"But they became disobedient and
rebelled against You, and cast Your Torah
behind their backs. And they kill Your
prophets who had warned them, to bring
them back to Yourself. And they worked
great blasphemies.
[27]"Therefore You gave them into the
hand of their enemies, who distressed
them. And in the time of their distress,
when they cried to You, You heard from
the heavens. And according to Your great
compassion You gave them saviours who
saved them from the hand of their enemies.
[28]"But after they had rest, they turned

9a Traditionally rendered *laws of truth*, of which we also read in Mal. 2:6, while it is rendered in Rom. 2:20 as *the truth in the law*. *9b* Torot - plural of Torah - teaching. *9c* Mishle 1:23, Yeḥez. 36:27, Zeḵ. 7:12.

back to do evil before You. Then You left
them in the hand of their enemies, so that
they ruled over them. But when they
turned back and cried out to You, You
heard from the heavens, and delivered
them according to Your compassion, many
times,
29 and warned them, to bring them back to
Your Torah. But they acted proudly, and
did not obey Your commands, and sinned
against Your right-rulings, 'which if a man
does, he shall live [d] by them.' And they
gave the rebellious shoulder and hardened
their necks, and would not hear.
30 "And You had patience with them for
many years, and did warn them by Your
Spirit, by the hand of Your prophets, yet
they would not give ear. Therefore You
gave them into the hand of the peoples of
the lands.
31 "But in Your great compassion You did
not make an end of them nor forsake them,
for You are an Ěl of favour and compassion.
32 "And now, our Elohim, the great, the
mighty, and awesome Ěl, guarding the
covenant and the loving-commitment, let
not all the trouble that has come upon us,
our sovereigns and our heads, our priests
and our prophets, our fathers and on all
Your people, from the days of the sovereigns of Ashshur until this day, seem little
before You.
33 "And in all that has come upon us You
are righteous, for You have done truth, but
we have done wrong.
34 "And our sovereigns, our rulers, our
priests, and our fathers, have not done
Your Torah, nor heeded Your commands
and Your witnesses, with which You witnessed against them.
35 "For they have not served You in their
reign, or in Your great goodness that You
gave them, or in the large and rich land
which You set before them – neither turned
back from their evil deeds.
36 "See, we are servants today! And the
land that You gave to our fathers, to eat its
fruit and the good of it, see, we are
servants in it!
37 "And its rich yield goes to the
sovereigns You have set over us, because
of our sins. And they rule over our bodies
and our livestock at their pleasure, and we
are in great distress.
38 "And because of all this, we are making
a trustworthy pledge, and write it. And our
rulers, our Lěwites, our priests set their
seal on it."

10 And those who set their seal were:
Neḥemyah the governor, son of
Ḥaḵalyah, and Tsiḏqiyah,
2 Serayah, Azaryah, Yirmeyah,
3 Pashhur, Amaryah, Malkiyah,
4 Ḥattush, Sheḇanyah, Malluḵ,
5 Ḥarim, Merěmoth, Oḇaḏyah,
6 Dani'ěl, Ginnethon, Baruḵ,
7 Meshullam, Aḇiyah, Miyamin,
8 Ma'azyah, Bilgai, and Shemayah.
These were the priests.
9 And the Lěwites: both Yěshua son of
Atsanyah, Binnui of the sons of Ḥěnaḏaḏ,
Qaḏmi'ěl.
10 And their brothers: Sheḇanyah, Hoḏiyah, Qelita, Pelayah, Ḥanan,
11 Miḵa, Reḥoḇ, Ḥashaḇyah,
12 Zakkur, Shěrěḇyah, Sheḇanyah,
13 Hoḏiyah, Bani, and Beninu.
14 The leaders of the people: Parosh,
Paḥath-Mo'aḇ, Ěylam, Zattu, Bani,
15 Bunni, Azgaḏ, Běḇai,
16 Aḏoniyah, Biḡwai, Aḏin,
17 Atěr, Ḥizqiyah, Azzur,
18 Hoḏiyah, Ḥashum, Bětsai,
19 Ḥariph, Anathoth, Něḇai,
20 Maḡpi'ash, Meshullam, Ḥězir,
21 Meshěyzaḇ'ěl, Tsaḏoq, Yaddua,
22 Pelatyah, Ḥanan, Anayah,
23 Hoshěa, Ḥananyah, Ḥashshuḇ,
24 Halloḥěsh, Pilḥa, Shoḇěq,
25 Reḥum, Ḥashaḇnah, Ma'asěyah,
26 Aḥiyah, Ḥanan, Anan,
27 Malluḵ, Ḥarim, Ba'anah.
28 And the rest of the people, the priests,
the Lěwites, the gatekeepers, the singers,
the Nethinim, and all those who had
separated themselves from the peoples of

9d Way. 18:5, Mt. 19:17, Lq. 10:28 & Yn. 12:50.

the lands unto the Torah of Elohim, their
wives, their sons, and their daughters, all
who had knowledge and understanding,
29 were strengthening their brothers, their
nobles, and were entering into a curse and
into an oath to walk in the Torah of
Elohim, which was given by Mosheh the
servant of Elohim, and to guard and do all
the commands of יהוה our Master, and His
right-rulings and His laws,
30 and that we would not give our
daughters as wives to the peoples of the
land, nor take their daughters for our sons,
31 and that if the peoples of the land bring
wares or any grain to sell on the Sabbath
day, we would not buy it from them on the
Sabbath, or on a set-apart day, and we
would forego the seventh year and the
interest of every hand.
32 And we imposed commands on ourselves, to give from ourselves yearly one-
third of a sheqel for the service of the
House of our Elohim:
33 for the showbread, and for the continual grain offering, and for the continual
ascending offering of the Sabbaths, of the
New Moons, for the appointed times, and
for the set-apart offerings, and for the sin
offerings to make atonement for Yisra'ěl,
and all the work of the House of our
Elohim.
34 And we cast lots among the priests, and
the Lěwites, and the people, for bringing
the wood offering into the House of our
Elohim, according to our fathers' houses,
at the appointed times year by year, to burn
on the slaughter-place of יהוה our Elohim
as it is written in the Torah,
35 and to bring the first-fruits of our soil
and the first-fruits of all fruit of all trees,
year by year, to the House of יהוה,
36 also to bring the first-born of our sons
and our livestock, as it is written in the
Torah, and the firstlings of our herds and
our flocks, to the House of our Elohim, to
the priests attending in the House of our
Elohim.
37 And that we should bring the first-fruits
of our dough, and our contributions, and
the fruit from all kinds of trees, of new
wine and of oil, to the priests, to the storerooms of the House of our Elohim; and the
tithes of our land to the Lěwites, for the
Lěwites should receive the tithes in all our
rural towns.
38 And the priest, son of Aharon, shall be
with the Lěwites when the Lěwites receive
tithes, and the Lěwites bring up a tenth of
the tithes to the House of our Elohim, to
the rooms of the storehouse.
39 For the children of Yisra'ěl and the
children of Lěwi bring the offering of the
grain, of the new wine and the oil, to the
storerooms where the vessels of the set-
apart place are, where the priests who
attend and the gatekeepers and the singers
are, and we should not neglect the House
of our Elohim.

11 Now the rulers of the people dwelt
at Yerushalayim, and the rest of the
people cast lots to bring one out of ten to
dwell in Yerushalayim, the set-apart city,
and nine-tenths were to dwell in other
cities.
2 And the people blessed all the men who
volunteered to dwell at Yerushalayim.
3 And these are the heads of the province
who dwelt in Yerushalayim, but in the
cities of Yehuḏah everyone dwelt in his
own possession in their cities – Yisra'ěl,
the priests, and the Lěwites, and the
Nethinim, and the sons of Shelomoh's servants.
4 And in Yerushalayim dwelt certain of
the children of Yehuḏah and of the children of Binyamin. Of the children of
Yehuḏah: Athayah son of Uzziyah, son of
Zeḵaryah, son of Amaryah, son of
Shephatyah, son of Mahalal'ěl, of the
children of Perets;
5 and Ma'aséyah son of Baruḵ, son of
Kol-Ḥozeh, son of Ḥazayah, son of
Aḏayah, son of Yoyariḇ, son of Zeḵaryah,
son of Shiloni.
6 All the sons of Perets who dwelt at
Yerushalayim were four hundred and
sixty-eight brave men.
7 And these are the sons of Binyamin:
Sallu son of Meshullam, son of Yow'ěḏ,
son of Peḏayah, son of Qolayah, son of
Ma'aséyah, son of Ithi'ěl, son of Yeshayah;

8 and after him Gabbai, Sallai, nine hundred and twenty-eight.
9 And Yo'ĕl son of Zikri was their
overseer, and Yehuḏah son of Senuah was
second over the city.
10 Of the priests: Yeḏayah son of Yoyariḇ,
Yaḵin,
11 Serayah son of Ḥilqiyah, son of
Meshullam, son of Tsaḏoq, son of
Merayoth, son of Aḥituḇ, was the leader of
the House of Elohim.
12 And their brothers who did the work of
the House were eight hundred and twenty-
two; and Aḏayah son of Yeroḥam, son of
Pelalyah, son of Amtsi, son of Zeḵaryah,
son of Pashhur, son of Malkiyah,
13 and his brothers, heads of the fathers'
houses, were two hundred and forty-two;
and Amashai son of Azar'ĕl, son of Aḥzai,
son of Meshillĕmoth, son of Immĕr,
14 and their brothers, mighty brave ones,
were one hundred and twenty-eight. And
their overseer was Zaḇdi'ĕl, son of the
great ones.
15 Also of the Lĕwites: Shemayah son of
Ḥashshuḇ, son of Azriqam, son of
Ḥashaḇyah, son of Bunni;
16 and Shabbethai and Yozaḇaḏ, of the
heads of the Lĕwites, over the outside
work of the House of Elohim;
17 and Mattanyah son of Miḵa, son of
Zaḇdi, son of Asaph, who was the leader
who began the thanksgiving with prayer,
and Baqbuqyah the second among his
brothers, and Aḇda son of Shammua, son
of Galal, son of Yeḏuthun.
18 All the Lĕwites in the set-apart city
were two hundred and eighty-four.
19 And the gatekeepers, Aqquḇ, Talmon,
and their brothers keeping guard at the
gates, were one hundred and seventy-two.
20 And the rest of Yisra'ĕl, of the priests,
Lĕwites, were in all the cities of Yehuḏah,
each one in his inheritance.
21 But the Nethinim dwelt in Ophel. And
Tsiḥa and Gishpa were over the Nethinim.
22 And the overseer of the Lĕwites at
Yerushalayim was Uzzi son of Bani, son of
Ḥashaḇyah, son of Mattanyah, son of
Miḵa. Of the sons of Asaph, the singers
were over the work of the House of
Elohim,
23 for the sovereign's command was upon
them – and support for the singers, a matter day by day.
24 And Pethaḥyah son of Meshĕyzaḇ'ĕl,
of the children of Zeraḥ son of Yehuḏah,
was the sovereign's deputy in all matters
concerning the people.
25 And at the villages with their fields,
some of the children of Yehuḏah dwelt in
Qiryath Arba and its villages, and in Diḇon
and its villages, and in Yeqaḇtse'ĕl and its
villages,
26 and in Yĕshua, and in Molaḏah, and in
Bĕyth Pelet,
27 and in Ḥatsar Shu'al, and in Be'ĕrsheḇa
and its villages,
28 and in Tsiqlaḡ, and in Meḵonah and its
villages,
29 and in Ĕn Rimmon, and in Tsorah, and
in Yarmuth,
30 Zanowaḥ, Aḏullam, and their villages;
in Laḵish and its fields; in Azĕqah and its
villages. So they dwelt from Be'ĕrsheḇa to
the Valley of Hinnom.
31 And the children of Binyamin: from
Geḇa, Miḵmash, and Ayyah, and Bĕyth Ĕl,
and their villages;
32 Anathoth, Noḇ, Ananyah;
33 Ḥatsor, Ramah, Gittayim;
34 Ḥaḏiḏ, Tseḇo'im, Neḇallat;
35 Loḏ, and Ono, and the Valley of
Craftsmen.
36 And of the Lĕwites, the divisions of
Yehuḏah were for Binyamin.

12 And these were the priests and the
Lĕwites who came up with
Zerubbaḇel son of She'alti'ĕl, and Yĕshua:
Serayah, Yirmeyah, Ezra,
2 Amaryah, Malluḵ, Ḥattush,
3 Sheḵanyah, Reḥum, Merĕmoth,
4 Iddo, Ginnethoi, Aḇiyah,
5 Miyamin, Ma'aḏyah, Bilgah,
6 Shemayah, and Yoyariḇ, Yeḏayah,
7 Sallu, Amoq, Ḥilqiyah, and Yeḏayah.
These were the heads of the priests and
their brothers in the days of Yĕshua.
8 And the Lĕwites: Yĕshua, Binnui,
Qaḏmi'ĕl, Shĕrĕḇyah, Yehuḏah, Mattanyah
over the thanksgiving, he and his brothers.

9 And Baqbuqyah and Unni, their brothers, were opposite them for guard duties.
10 And Yĕshua brought forth Yoyaqim,
and Yoyaqim brought forth Elyashiḇ, and
Elyashiḇ brought forth Yoyaḏa,
11 and Yoyaḏa brought forth Yonathan,
and Yonathan brought forth Yaddua.
12 And in the days of Yoyaqim, the
priests, the heads of the fathers' *houses*
were: of Serayah, Merayah; of Yirmeyah,
Ḥananyah;
13 of Ezra, Meshullam; of Amaryah,
Yehoḥanan;
14 of Meliḵu, Yonathan; of Sheḇanyah,
Yosĕph;
15 of Ḥarim, Aḏna; of Merayoth, Ḥelqai;
16 of Iddo, Zeḵaryah; of Ginnethon,
Meshullam;
17 of Aḇiyah, Ziḵri, *son* of Minyamin; of
Mo'aḏyah, Piltai;
18 of Bilgah, Shammua; of Shemayah,
Yehonathan;
19 of Yoyariḇ, Mattenai; of Yeḏayah,
Uzzi;
20 of Sallai, Qallai; of Amoq, Ĕḇer;
21 of Ḥilqiyah, Ḥashaḇyah. And of
Yeḏayah, Nethanĕ'l.
22 The Lĕwites and priests in the days of
Elyashiḇ, Yoyaḏa, Yoḥanan, and Yaddua,
were recorded heads of their fathers'
houses, also the priests in the reign of
Dareyawesh the Persian.
23 The sons of Lĕwi, the heads of the
fathers' *houses* until the days of Yoḥanan
son of Elyashiḇ, were written in the book
of the annals.
24 And the heads of the Lĕwites were
Ḥashaḇyah, Shĕrĕḇyah, and Yĕshua son of
Qaḏmi'ĕl, with their brothers opposite
them, to praise, to give thanks, watch
opposite watch, according to the command
of Dawiḏ the man of Elohim.
25 Mattanyah, and Baqbuqyah, Oḇaḏyah,
Meshullam, Talmon, Aqquḇ were gatekeepers guarding at the storerooms of the
gates.
26 These were in the days of Yoyaqim son
of Yĕshua, son of Yotsaḏaq, and in the
days of Neḥemyah the governor, and of
Ezra the priest, the scribe.
27 And at the dedication of the wall of
Yerushalayim they sought out the Lĕwites
in all their places, to bring them to
Yerushalayim to perform the dedication
with gladness, and with thanksgivings, and
with singing, cymbals, harps and lyres.
28 And the sons of the singers gathered
together from the countryside around
Yerushalayim, from the villages of the
Netophathites,
29 and from the house of Gilgal, and from
the fields of Geḇa and Azmaweth – for the
singers had built themselves villages all
around Yerushalayim.
30 And the priests and Lĕwites cleansed
themselves, and they cleansed the people,
and the gates, and the wall.
31 And I brought the rulers of Yehuḏah up
on the wall, and appointed two large
thanksgiving choirs, to go to the right on
the wall toward the Dung Gate,
32 and after them went Hoshayah and half
of the rulers of Yehuḏah,
33 then Azaryah, Ezra, and Meshullam,
34 Yehuḏah, and Binyamin, and Shemayah, and Yirmeyah,
35 and of the sons of the priests with trumpets: Zeḵaryah son of Yonathan, son of
Shemayah, son of Mattanyah, son of
Miḵayah, son of Zakkur, son of Asaph,
36 and his brothers Shemayah and Azar'ĕl,
Milalai, Gilalai, Ma'ai, Nethanĕ'l, and
Yehuḏah, Ḥanani with instruments of
songs of Dawiḏ the man of Elohim, with
Ezra the scribe before them.
37 And at the Fountain Gate and straight
ahead of them, they went up the stairs of
the City of Dawiḏ, on the stairway of the
wall, beyond the house of Dawiḏ, as far as
the Water Gate eastward.
38 And the other thanksgiving choir went
over against them, and I behind them with
half of the people on the wall, going past
the Tower of the Ovens as far as the Broad
Wall,
39 and above the Gate of Ephrayim, and
above the Old Gate, and above the Fish
Gate, and the Tower of Ḥanan'ĕl, and the
Tower of the Hundred, as far as the Sheep
Gate. And they stood still at the Gate of the
Prison.
40 Then the two thanksgiving choirs took

their stand in the House of Elohim, and I
and half of the deputy rulers with me,
41 and the priests, Elyaqim, Ma'asěyah,
Minyamin, Miḵayah, Elyo'ěynai, Zeḵaryah, and Ḥananyah, with trumpets,
42 and Ma'asěyah, and Shemayah, and
El'azar, and Uzzi, and Yehoḥanan, and
Malkiyah, and Ěylam, and Ězer. And the
singers sang aloud, with Yizraḥyah in
charge.
43 And on that day they slaughtered great
slaughterings and rejoiced, for Elohim had
made them rejoice with great joy. And the
women and the children also rejoiced, so
that the joy of Yerushalayim was heard far
away.
44 And on that day some were appointed
over the rooms for the stores, for the contributions, for the first-fruits, and for tithes,
to gather into them from the fields of the
cities the portions required by the Torah
for the priests and for the Lěwites. For
Yehuḏah rejoiced over the priests and the
Lěwites who stood up.
45 Both the singers and the gatekeepers
guarded the charge of their Elohim and the
charge of the cleansing, according to the
command of Dawiḏ and Shelomoh his son.
46 For in the days of Dawiḏ and Asaph of
old there were chiefs of the singers, and
songs of praise and thanksgiving to
Elohim.
47 And in the days of Zerubbaḇel and in
the days of Neḥemyah all Yisra'ěl gave the
portions for the singers and the gatekeepers, a portion for each day. And they set
apart what was for the Lěwites, and the
Lěwites set apart what was for the children
of Aharon.

13 On that day was read from the
Book of Mosheh in the hearing of
the people, and in it was found written that
an Ammonite and Mo'aḇite should not
come into the assembly of Elohim forever,
2 because they had not met the children
of Yisra'ěl with bread and water, and hired
Bil'am against them to curse them,
although our Elohim turned the curse into
a blessing.
3 And it came to be, when they had heard
the Torah, that they separated all the mixed
multitude from Yisra'ěl.
4 And before this, Elyashiḇ the priest,
having authority over the storerooms of the
House of our Elohim, was a relative of
Toḇiyah,
5 and he had prepared for him a large
room, where previously they had stored
the grain offerings, the frankincense, and
the utensils, and the tithes of grain, the new
wine and the oil, which were commanded
to be given to the Lěwites and the singers
and the gatekeepers, and the contributions
for the priests.
6 But in all this I was not in Yerushalayim, for in the thirty-second year of
Artaḥshashta sovereign of Baḇel I came to
the sovereign. And after some days I asked
leave from the sovereign *to return*,
7 and I came to Yerushalayim and
learned of the evil which Elyashiḇ had
done for Toḇiyah, in preparing a room for
him in the courts of the House of Elohim.
8 And it was very displeasing to me.
Therefore I threw all the household goods
of Toḇiyah out of the room,
9 and I commanded them to cleanse the
rooms. And I put back into them the utensils of the House of Elohim, with the grain
offering and the frankincense.
10 And I learned that the portions for the
Lěwites had not been given them, for each
of the Lěwites and the singers who did the
work had gone back to his field.
11 Then I contended with the deputy
rulers, and said, "Why is the House of
Elohim forsaken?" And I gathered them
together and set them in their place.
12 And all Yehuḏah brought the tithe of
the grain and the new wine and the oil to
the storehouse.
13 And I appointed as treasurers over the
storehouse Shelemyah the priest and
Tsaḏoq the scribe, and Peḏayah of the
Lěwites. And at their hand was Ḥanan son
of Zakkur, son of Mattanyah. For they
were reckoned trustworthy, and it was on
them to distribute to their brothers.
14 Remember me, O my Elohim, concerning this, and do not wipe out my loving-
commitments that I have done for the

House of my Elohim, and for its charges!

15 In those days I saw in Yehuḏah those treading wine presses on the Sabbath, and bringing in sheaves, and loading donkeys with wine, grapes, and figs, and all kinds of burdens, which they brought into Yerushalayim on the Sabbath day. So I warned *them* on the day they sold food.

16 And men of Tsor dwelt there, bringing in fish and all kinds of goods, and sold them on the Sabbath to the children of Yehuḏah, and in Yerushalayim.

17 Then I contended with the nobles of Yehuḏah, and said to them, "What evil matter is this that you are doing, profaning the Sabbath day?

18 "Did not your fathers do the same so that our Elohim brought all this evil on us and on this city? Yet you bring added wrath on Yisra'ěl by profaning the Sabbath."

19 And it came to be, when the gates of Yerushalayim were shaded before the Sabbath, that I commanded the doors to be shut, and commanded that they should not be opened till after the Sabbath. And I stationed some of my servants at the gates, so that no burdens would be brought in on the Sabbath day.

20 And the merchants and sellers of all kinds of wares spent the night outside Yerushalayim once or twice,

21 and I warned them, and said to them, "Why do you spend the night around the wall? If you do so again, I lay hands on you!" From that time on they came no more on the Sabbath.

22 And I commanded the Lěwites that they should cleanse themselves, and they should come, guarding the gates, to set apart the Sabbath day. Remember me, O my Elohim, concerning this also, and pardon me according to the greatness of Your loving-commitment!

23 In those days I also saw Yehuḏim who had married women of Ashdoḏ, Ammon, Mo'aḇ.

24 And half of their children spoke the language of Ashdoḏ, and could not speak the language of Yehuḏah, but spoke according to the language of one or the other people.

25 Then I contended with them and cursed them, and struck some of them and pulled out their hair, and made them swear by Elohim, saying, "You do not give your daughters as wives to their sons, nor take their daughters for your sons or yourselves.

26 "Did not Shelomoh sovereign of Yisra'ěl sin because of them? Among the many nations there was no sovereign like him, who was beloved of his Elohim, and Elohim made him sovereign over all Yisra'ěl. Even him foreign women caused to sin.

27 "Should we then hear of your doing all this great evil, trespassing against our Elohim by marrying foreign wives?"

28 And one of the sons of Yoyaḏa, son of Elyashiḇ the high priest, was a son-in-law of Sanballat the Ḥoronite. And I drove him from me.

29 Remember them, O my Elohim, because they have defiled the priesthood and the covenant of the priesthood, and of the Lěwites.

30 Thus I cleansed them from all that is foreign. And I appointed duties to the priests and the Lěwites, each in his task,

31 and for the wood offering and the firstfruits at appointed times. Remember me, O my Elohim, for good!

DIḆRE haYAMIM ALEPH

1 CHRONICLES (1 ANNALS)

1 Aḏam, Shěth, Enosh,
[2] Qěnan, Mahalal'ěl, Yereḏ,
[3] Ḥanoḵ, Methushelaḥ, Lemeḵ,
[4] Noaḥ, Shěm, Ḥam, and Yepheth.
[5] The sons of Yepheth: Gomer, and
Maḡoḡ, and Maḏai, and Yawan, and Tuḇal,
and Mesheḵ, and Tiras.
[6] And the sons of Gomer: Ashkenaz, and
Diphath [a], and Toḡarmah.
[7] And the sons of Yawan: Elishah and
Tarshishah, Kittim and Roḏanim.
[8] The sons of Ḥam: Kush and Mitsrayim,
Put and Kenaʽan.
[9] And the sons of Kush: Seḇa, and
Ḥawilah, and Saḇta, and Raʽmah, and
Saḇteḵa. And the sons of Raʽmah: Sheḇa
and Deḏan.
[10] And Kush brought forth Nimroḏ; he
began to be a mighty one on the earth.
[11] And Mitsrayim brought forth the
Luḏim, and the Anamim, and the Lehaḇim,
and the Naphtuḥim,
[12] and the Pathrusim, and the Kasluḥim
from whom came the Philistines, and the
Kaphtorim.
[13] And Kenaʽan brought forth Tsiḏon, his
first-born, and Ḥěth,
[14] and the Yeḇusite, and the Amorite, and
the Girgashite,
[15] and the Ḥiwwite, and the Arqite, and
the Sinite,
[16] and the Arwaḏite, and the Tsemarite,
and the Ḥamathite.
[17] The sons of Shěm: Ěylam, and Asshur,
and Arpaḵshaḏ, and Luḏ, and Aram, and
Uts, Ḥul, and Gether, and Mesheḵ.
[18] And Arpaḵshaḏ brought forth Shelaḥ,
and Shelaḥ brought forth Ěḇer.
[19] To Ěḇer were born two sons: the name
of one was Peleḡ, for in his days the earth
was divided, and his brother's name was
Yoqtan.
[20] And Yoqtan brought forth Almoḏaḏ,
and Sheleph, and Ḥatsarmaweth, and
Yeraḥ,
[21] and Haḏoram, and Uzal, and Diqlah,
[22] and Ěyḇal, and Aḇima'ěl, and Sheḇa,
[23] and Ophir, and Ḥawilah, and Yoḇaḇ.
All these were the sons of Yoqtan.
[24] Shěm, Arpaḵshaḏ, Shělah,
[25] Ěḇer, Peleḡ, Reʽu,
[26] Seruḡ, Naḥor, Teraḥ,
[27] and Aḇram, that is Aḇraham.
[28] The sons of Aḇraham: Yitsḥaq and
Yishmaʽěl.
[29] These are their genealogies: The first-
born of Yishmaʽěl was Neḇayoth, and
Qěḏar, and Aḏbe'ěl, and Miḇsam,
[30] Mishma, and Dumah, and Massa,
Haḏaḏ, and Těma,
[31] Yetur, Naphish, and Qěḏemah. These
were the sons of Yishmaʽěl.
[32] And the sons born to Qeturah,
Aḇraham's concubine: Zimran, and
Yoqshan, and Meḏan, and Miḏyan, and
Yishbaq, and Shuwaḥ. The sons of
Yoqshan: Sheḇa and Deḏan.
[33] And the sons of Miḏyan: Ěphah, and
Ěpher, and Ḥanoḵ, and Aḇiḏa, and
Eldaʽah. All these were the children of
Qeturah.
[34] And Aḇraham brought forth Yitsḥaq.
The sons of Yitsḥaq: Ěsaw and Yisra'ěl.
[35] The sons of Ěsaw: Eliphaz, Reʽu'ěl,
and Yeʽush, and Yaʽlam, and Qoraḥ.
[36] And the sons of Eliphaz: Těman, and
Omar, Tsephi, and Gatam, and Qenaz, and
Timna, and Amalěq.
[37] The sons of Reʽu'ěl: Naḥath, Zeraḥ,
Shammah, and Mizzah.
[38] And the sons of Sěʽir: Lotan, and
Shoḇal, and Tsiḇʽon, and Anah, and
Dishon, and Ětser, and Dishan.
[39] And the sons of Lotan: Ḥori and

1a - or Riphath - See Ber. 10:3. Also see Explanatory Note - Thigh.

Homam; Lotan's sister was Timna.
40 The sons of Shoḇal: Alyan, and
Manaḥath, and Ěyḇal, Shephi, and Onam.
The sons of Tsiḇʽon: Ayah and Anah.
41 The son of Anah was Dishon. The sons
of Dishon: Ḥamran, and Eshban, and
Yithran, and Keran.
42 The sons of Ětser: Bilhan, and
Zaʽawan, and Yaʽaqan. The sons of Dishan:
Uts and Aran.
43 And these were the sovereigns who
reigned in the land of Eḏom before any
sovereign reigned over the children of
Yisra'ěl: Bela son of Beʽor, and the name
of his city was Dinhaḇah.
44 And when Bela died, Yoḇaḇ son of
Zeraḥ of Botsrah reigned in his place.
45 And Yoḇaḇ died, and Ḥusham of the
land of the Těmanites reigned in his place.
46 And when Ḥusham died, Haḏaḏ son of
Beḏaḏ, who struck Miḏyan in the field of
Mo'aḇ, reigned in his place. The name of
his city was Awith.
47 And Haḏaḏ died, and Samlah of
Masrěqah reigned in his place.
48 And Samlah died, and Sha'ul of
Reḥoḇoth-by-the-River reigned in his
place.
49 And Sha'ul died, and Baʽal-Ḥanan son
of Aḵbor reigned in his place.
50 And Baʽal-Ḥanan died, and Haḏaḏ
reigned in his place. And the name of his
city was Pai. And his wife's name was
Mehětab'ěl the daughter of Matrěḏ, the
daughter of Měyzahaḇ.
51 And Haḏaḏ died. And the chiefs of
Eḏom were Chief Timnah, Chief Alyah,
Chief Yethěth,
52 Chief Oholiḇamah, Chief Ělah, Chief
Pinon,
53 Chief Qenaz, Chief Těman, Chief
Miḇtsar,
54 Chief Maḡdi'ěl, and Chief Iram. These
were the chiefs of Eḏom.

2 These were the sons of Yisra'ěl:
Re'uḇěn, Shimʽon, Lěwi and
Yehuḏah, Yissasḵar and Zeḇulun,
2 Dan, Yosěph and Binyamin, Naphtali,
Gaḏ and Ashěr.
3 The sons of Yehuḏah: Ěr, and Onan,
and Shělah, the three born to him by the
daughter of Shuwa, the Kenaʽanitess. And
Ěr, the first-born of Yehuḏah, was evil in
the eyes of יהוה, and He slew him.
4 And Tamar, his daughter-in-law, bore
him Perets and Zeraḥ. All the sons of
Yehuḏah were five.
5 The sons of Perets: Ḥetsron and Ḥamul.
6 And the sons of Zeraḥ: Zimri, and
Ěythan, and Hěman, and Kalkol, and Dara,
five of them in all.
7 And the son of Karmi was Aḵar, the
troubler of Yisra'ěl, who trespassed in that
which was under the ban.
8 And the son of Ěythan was Azaryah.
9 And the sons of Ḥetsron who were
born to him: Yeraḥme'ěl, and Ram, and
Keluḇai.
10 Ram brought forth Amminaḏaḇ, and
Amminaḏaḇ brought forth Naḥshon, leader
of the children of Yehuḏah;
11 Naḥshon brought forth Salma, and
Salma brought forth Boʽaz;
12 Boʽaz brought forth Oḇěḏ, and Oḇěḏ
brought forth Yishai;
13 Yishai brought forth Eliyaḇ his first-
born, and Aḇinaḏaḇ the second, and
Shimʽa the third,
14 Nethaně'l the fourth, Raddai the fifth,
15 Otsem the sixth, Dawiḏ the seventh.
16 And their sisters: Tseruyah and
Aḇiḡayil. And the sons of Tseruyah:
Aḇishai, and Yo'aḇ, and Asah'ěl, three.
17 And Aḇiḡayil bore Amasa. And the
father of Amasa was Yether the Yish-
maʽělite.
18 And Kalěḇ son of Ḥetsron brought
forth children by Azuḇah, his wife, and by
Yeriyoth. Now these were her sons:
Yěsher, and Shoḇaḇ, and Ardon.
19 And Azuḇah died, and Kalěḇ took
Ephrath as his wife, who bore him Ḥur.
20 And Ḥur brought forth Uri, and Uri
brought forth Betsal'ěl.
21 And afterward Ḥetsron went in to the
daughter of Maḵir the father of Gilʽaḏ,
whom he took when he was sixty years
old. And she bore him Seḡuḇ.
22 And Seḡuḇ brought forth Ya'ir, who
had twenty-three cities in the land of
Gilʽaḏ.

23 And he took from them Geshur and Aram, with the towns of Ya'ir, with Qenath and its towns, sixty towns. All these *belonged to* the sons of Maḵir the father of Gil'aḏ.

24 And after the death of Ḥetsron in Kalěḇ Ephrathah, Ḥetsron's wife Aḇiyah bore him Ashḥur the father of Teqowa.

25 And the sons of Yeraḥme'ěl the first-born of Ḥetsron were: Ram the first-born, and Bunah, and Oren, and Otsem, and Aḥiyah.

26 And Yeraḥme'ěl had another wife, whose name was Atarah; she was the mother of Onam.

27 And the sons of Ram, the first-born of Yeraḥme'ěl, were Ma'ats, and Yamin, and Ěqer.

28 And the sons of Onam were Shammai and Yaḏa. And the sons of Shammai: Naḏaḇ and Aḇishur.

29 And the name of the wife of Aḇishur was Aḇiḥayil, and she bore him Aḥban and Moliḏ.

30 And the sons of Naḏaḇ: Seleḏ and Appayim, and Seleḏ died without children.

31 And the son of Appayim was Yishi, and the son of Yishi was Shěshan, and the son of Shěshan was Aḥlai.

32 And the sons of Yaḏa, the brother of Shammai: Yether and Yonathan, and Yether died without children.

33 And the sons of Yonathan: Peleth and Zaza. These were the sons of Yeraḥme'ěl.

34 And Shěshan had no sons, only daughters. And Shěshan had a Mitsrian servant whose name was Yarḥa.

35 And Shěshan gave his daughter to Yarḥa his servant as wife, and she bore him Attai.

36 And Attai brought forth Nathan, and Nathan brought forth Zaḇaḏ,

37 and Zaḇaḏ brought forth Ephlal, and Ephlal brought forth Oḇěḏ,

38 and Oḇěḏ brought forth Yěhu, and Yěhu brought forth Azaryah,

39 and Azaryah brought forth Ḥelets, and Ḥelets brought forth El'asah,

40 and El'asah brought forth Sismai, and Sismai brought forth Shallum,

41 and Shallum brought forth Yeqamyah, and Yeqamyah brought forth Elishama.

42 And the sons of Kalěḇ the brother of Yeraḥme'ěl: Měysha his first-born, who was the father of Ziph, and the sons of Marěshah the father of Ḥeḇron.

43 And the sons of Ḥeḇron: Qoraḥ, and Tappuwaḥ, and Reqem, and Shema.

44 And Shema brought forth Raḥam the father of Yorqe'am, and Reqem brought forth Shammai.

45 And the son of Shammai was Ma'on, and Ma'on was the father of Běyth Tsur.

46 And Ěphah, Kalěḇ's concubine, bore Ḥaran, and Motsa, and Gazěz. And Ḥaran brought forth Gazěz.

47 And the sons of Yahdai: Reḡem, and Yotham, and Gěyshan, and Pelet, and Ěphah, and Sha'aph.

48 Ma'aḵah, Kalěḇ's concubine, bore Sheḇer and Tirḥanah.

49 And she bore Sha'aph the father of Maḏmannah, Shewa the father of Maḵběna and the father of Giḇ'a. And the daughter of Kalěḇ was Aḵsah.

50 These were the descendants of Kalěḇ: The sons of Ḥur, the first-born of Ephrathah: Shoḇal the father of Qiryath Ye'arim,

51 Salma the father of Běyth Leḥem, Ḥarěph the father of Běyth Gaḏer.

52 And Shoḇal the father of Qiryath Ye'arim had descendants: Haro'eh, half of the Menuḥothites.

53 And the clans of Qiryath Ye'arim: the Yithrites, and the Puthites, and the Shumathites, and the Mishraites. From these came the Tsor'athites and the Eshta'olites.

54 The sons of Salma: Běyth Leḥem, the Netophathites, Atroth Běyth Yo'aḇ, and half of the Menaḥtites, and the Tsor'ites.

55 And the clans of the scribes who dwelt at Yaḇěts: the Tirathites, the Shim'athites, the Suḵathites. These were the Qěynites who came from Ḥammath, the father of the house of Rěḵaḇ.

3 And these were the sons of Dawiḏ who were born to him in Ḥeḇron: The first-born was Amnon, by Aḥino'am the Yizre'ělitess; the second, Dani'ěl, by

Aḇiḡayil the Karmelitess;
2 the third, Aḇshalom son of Ma‘aḵah,
the daughter of Talmai, sovereign of
Geshur; the fourth, Aḏoniyah son of Ḥaggith;
3 the fifth, Shephatyah, by Aḇital; the
sixth, Yithre‘am, by his wife Eḡlah.
4 Six were born to him in Ḥeḇron. And
he reigned there seven years and six new
moons, and in Yerushalayim he reigned
thirty-three years.
5 And these were born to him in
Yerushalayim: Shim‘a, and Shoḇaḇ, and
Nathan, and Shelomoh – four by Bathshua
the daughter of Ammi’ěl.
6 Yiḇḥar also, and Elishama, and Eliphelet,
7 and Noḡah, and Nepheḡ, and Yaphiya,
8 and Elishama, and Elyaḏa, and
Eliphelet, nine,
9 all the sons of Dawiḏ, besides the sons
of the concubines, and Tamar their sister.
10 And Shelomoh’s son was Reḥaḇ‘am,
Aḇiyah his son, Asa his son, Yehoshaphat
his son,
11 Yoram his son, Aḥazyahu his son,
Yo’ash his son,
12 Amatsyahu his son, Azaryah his son,
Yotham his son,
13 Aḥaz his son, Ḥizqiyahu his son,
Menashsheh his son,
14 Amon his son, Yoshiyahu his son.
15 And the sons of Yoshiyahu: Yoḥanan
the first-born, the second Yehoyaqim, the
third Tsiḏqiyahu, the fourth Shallum.
16 And the sons of Yehoyaqim: Yeḵonyah
his son and Tsiḏqiyah his son.
17 And the sons of Yeḵonyah the captive:
She’alti’ěl his son,
18 and Malkiram, and Peḏayah, and
Shenatstsar, Yeqamyah, Hoshama, and
Neḏaḇyah.
19 And the sons of Peḏayah: Zerubbaḇel
and Shim‘i. The sons of Zerubbaḇel:
Meshullam, and Ḥananyah, and Shelomith
their sister,
20 and Ḥashuḇah, and Ohel, and Bereḵyah, and Ḥasaḏyah, Yushaḇ-Ḥeseḏ, five.
21 And the sons of Ḥananyah: Pelatyah
and Yeshayah, the sons of Rephayah, the
sons of Arnan, the sons of Oḇaḏyah, the
sons of Sheḵanyah.
22 And the son of Sheḵanyah: Shemayah.
The sons of Shemayah: Ḥattush, and
Yiḡ’al, and Bariyaḥ, and Ne‘aryah, and
Shaphat, six.
23 And the sons of Ne‘aryah: Elyo‘ěynai,
and Ḥizqiyah, and Azriqam, three.
24 And the sons of Elyo‘ěynai: Hoḏawyah,
and Elyashiḇ, and Pelayah, and Aqquḇ,
and Yoḥanan, and Delayah, and Anani,
seven.

4 The sons of Yehuḏah: Perets, Ḥetsron,
and Karmi, and Ḥur, and Shoḇal.
2 And Re’ayah son of Shoḇal brought
forth Yaḥath, and Yaḥath brought forth
Aḥumai and Lahaḏ. These were the clans
of the Tsor‘athites.
3 And these were of the father of Ěytam:
Yizre‘ěl, and Yishma, and Yiḏbash. And
the name of their sister was Hatselelponi;
4 and Penu’ěl was the father of Geḏor,
and Ězer was the father of Ḥushah. These
were the sons of Ḥur, the first-born of
Ephrathah the father of Běyth Leḥem.
5 And Ashḥur the father of Teqowa had
two wives, Ḥelah and Na‘arah.
6 And Na‘arah bore him Ahuzzam, and
Ḥěpher, and Těmeni, and Ha’aḥashtari.
These were the sons of Na‘arah.
7 And the sons of Ḥelah: Tsereth, and
Tsoḥar, and Ethnan;
8 and Qots brought forth Anuḇ, and
Tsoḇěḇah, and the clans of Aḥarḥěl son of
Harum.
9 And Yaḇěts was more esteemed than
his brothers, and his mother called his
name Yaḇěts, saying, “Because I bore him
in pain.”
10 And Yaḇěts called on the Elohim of
Yisra’ěl saying, “Oh, that You would bless
me indeed, and enlarge my border, and that
Your hand would be with me, and that You
would keep me from evil, not to be my
pain!” And Elohim gave him what he
asked.
11 And Keluḇ the brother of Shuḥah
brought forth Meḥir, who was the father of
Eshton.
12 And Eshton brought forth Běyth-
Rapha, and Paseaḥ, and Teḥinnah the

father of Ir-Naḥash. These were the men of
Rěḵah.
13 And the sons of Qenaz: Othni'ěl and
Serayah. And sons of Othni'ěl: Ḥathath,
14 and Meʽonothai, who brought forth
Ophrah. And Serayah brought forth Yo'aḇ
the father of Gě-Ḥarashim, for they were
craftsmen.
15 And the sons of Kaleḇ the son of
Yephunneh: Iru, Ělah, and Naʽam. And the
son of Ělah was Qenaz.
16 And the sons of Yehallel'ěl: Ziph, and
Ziphah, Tireya, and Asar'ěl.
17 And the sons of Ezrah: Yether, and
Mereḏ, and Ěpher, and Yalon. And she
bore Miryam, and Shammai, and Yishbaḥ
the father of Eshtemoa.
18 And his wife Yehuḏiyah bore Yereḏ the
father of Geḏor, and Ḥeḇer the father of
Soḵo, and Yequthi'ěl the father of
Zanowaḥ. And these were the sons of
Bithyah the daughter of Pharaoh, whom
Mereḏ took.
19 And the sons of Hoḏiyah's wife, the
sister of Naḥam, were the fathers of
Qeʽilah the Garmite and of Eshtemoa the
Maʽaḵathite.
20 And the sons of Shimon: Amnon, and
Rinnah, Ben-Ḥanan, and Tulon. And the
sons of Yishi: Zoḥěth and Ben-Zoḥěth.
21 The sons of Shělah the son of Yehuḏah:
Ěr the father of Lěḵah, and Laʽdah the
father of Marěshah, and the clans of the
house of the linen workers of the house of
Ashběa;
22 and Yoqim, and the men of Kozěḇa,
and Yo'ash, and Saraph who ruled in
Mo'aḇ, and Yashuḇi-Leḥem. But the
records were ancient.
23 These were the potters and those who
dwell at Netaʽim and Geḏěrah; there they
dwelt with the sovereign for his work.
24 The sons of Shimʽon: Nemu'ěl, and
Yamin, Yariḇ, Zeraḥ, Sha'ul,
25 Shallum his son, Miḇsam his son,
Mishma his son.
26 And the sons of Mishma: Ḥammu'ěl
his son, Zakkur his son, Shimʽi his son.
27 And Shimʽi had sixteen sons and six
daughters, but his brothers did not have
many children, nor did any of their clans
increase as much as the children of
Yehuḏah.
28 And they dwelt at Be'ěrsheḇa, and
Molaḏah, and Ḥatsar Shuʽal,
29 and at Bilhah, and at Etsem, and at
Tolaḏ,
30 and at Bethu'ěl, and at Ḥormah, and at
Tsiqlaḡ,
31 and at Běyth Markaḇoth, and at Ḥatsar
Susim, and at Běyth Birʽi, and at
Shaʽarayim. These were their cities until
the reign of Dawiḏ.
32 And their villages were Ěytam, and
Ayin, and Rimmon, and Toḵen, and Ashan,
five cities,
33 and all the villages that were around
these cities as far as Baʽal. These were
their dwelling places, and they kept their
genealogy.
34 And Meshoḇaḇ, and Yamlěḵ, and
Yoshah son of Amatsyah;
35 and Yo'ěl, and Yěhu son of Yoshiḇyah,
son of Serayah, son of Asi'ěl;
36 and Elyoʽěynai, and Yaʽaqoḇah, and
Yeshoḥayah, and Asayah, and Aḏi'ěl, and
Yesimi'ěl, and Benayah;
37 and Ziza son of Shiphi, son of Allon,
son of Yeḏayah, son of Shimri, son of
Shemayah.
38 These mentioned by name were leaders
in their clans, and their father's house
increased greatly.
39 And they went to the entrance of
Geḏor, as far as the east side of the valley,
to look for pasture for their flocks,
40 and they found rich, good pasture,
and the land was broad, undisturbed and
safe, for some Ḥamites had dwelt there
formerly.
41 And these written by name came in the
days of Ḥizqiyahu sovereign of Yehuḏah,
and struck their tents, and the homes that
were found there, and put them under the
ban, as it is to this day, and dwelt in their
place, because there was pasture for their
flocks there.
42 And some of them, five hundred men
of the sons of Shimʽon, went to Mount
Sěʽir, having as their chiefs Pelatyah, and
Neʽaryah, and Rephayah, and Uzzi'ěl, the
sons of Yishi.

43 And they struck the rest of the Amalěqites who had escaped, and dwelt there to this day.

5 As for the sons of Re'uḇěn the first-born of Yisra'ěl – he was the first-born, but because he profaned his father's bed, his birthright was given to the sons of Yosěph, son of Yisra'ěl, so that the genealogy is not listed according to the birthright,

2 for Yehuḏah prevailed over his brothers, and from him came a ruler, although the birthright was Yosěph's –

3 the sons of Re'uḇěn the first-born of Yisra'ěl: Ḥanoḵ and Pallu, Ḥetsron and Karmi.

4 The sons of Yo'ěl: Shemayah his son, Goḡ his son, Shimʿi his son,

5 Miḵah his son, Re'ayah his son, Baʿal his son,

6 and Be'ěrah his son, whom Tiglath-Pileser sovereign of Ashshur took into exile. He was leader of the Re'uḇěnites.

7 And his brothers by their clans, when the genealogy of their generations was registered: the chief, Yeʿi'ěl, and Zeḵaryahu,

8 and Bela son of Azaz, son of Shema, son of Yo'ěl, who dwelt in Aroʿěr, as far as Neḇo and Baʿal Meʿon.

9 And he dwelt eastward as far as the entrance of the wilderness from the River Euphrates, because their livestock had increased in the land of Gilʿaḏ.

10 And in the days of Sha'ul they fought against the Haḡrites, who fell by their hand. And they dwelt in their tents over all the eastern part of Gilʿaḏ.

11 And the children of Gaḏ dwelt next to them in the land of Bashan as far as Salḵah:

12 Yo'ěl was the chief, Shapham the next, then Yaʿanai and Shaphat in Bashan;

13 and their brothers of their father's house: Miḵa'ěl, and Meshullam, and Sheḇa, and Yorai, and Yakan, and Ziya, and Ěḇer, seven.

14 These were the children of Aḇiḥayil son of Ḥuri, son of Yarowaḥ, son of Gilʿaḏ, son of Miḵa'ěl, son of Yeshishai, son of Yaḥdo, son of Buz;

15 Aḥi son of Aḇdi'ěl, son of Guni, was chief of their father's house.

16 And they dwelt in Gilʿaḏ, in Bashan and in its villages, and in all the open lands of Sharon within their borders.

17 All these were registered by genealogies in the days of Yotham sovereign of Yehuḏah, and in the days of Yaroḇʿam sovereign of Yisra'ěl.

18 The sons of Re'uḇěn, and the Gaḏites, and half the tribe of Menashsheh had forty-four thousand seven hundred and sixty brave men, men able to bear shield and sword, to shoot with the bow, and skilled in battle, going out to the army.

19 And they fought against the Haḡrites, and Yetur, and Naphish, and Noḏaḇ.

20 And they were helped against them, and the Haḡrites were given into their hand, and all who were with them. For they cried out to Elohim in the battle, and He answered their prayer, because they put their trust in Him.

21 And they took away their livestock: fifty thousand of their camels, and two hundred and fifty thousand of their sheep, and two thousand of their donkeys, also one hundred thousand of their men,

22 for many fell dead, because the battle was of Elohim. And they dwelt in their place until the exile.

23 And the children of the half-tribe of Menashsheh dwelt in the land. They increased from Bashan to Baʿal Ḥermon, that is, to Senir, or Mount Ḥermon.

24 And these were the heads of their fathers' houses: Ěpher, and Yishi, and Eli'ěl, and Azri'ěl, and Yirmeyah, Hoḏawyah, and Yaḥdi'ěl – mighty brave men, men of name, and heads of their fathers' houses.

25 But they trespassed against the Elohim of their fathers, and whored after the mighty ones of the peoples of the land, whom Elohim had destroyed before them.

26 So the Elohim of Yisra'ěl stirred up the spirit of Pul sovereign of Ashshur, even the spirit of Tiglath-Pileser sovereign of Ashshur. And he took the Re'uḇěnites, and the Gaḏites, and the half-tribe of Menashsheh into exile, and brought them to Ḥalaḥ, and Ḥaḇor, and Hara, and the

river of Gozan, unto this day.

6 The sons of Lĕwi: Gĕreshom, Qehath, and Merari.

2 And the sons of Qehath: Amram, Yitshar, and Ḥeḇron, and Uzzi'ĕl.

3 And the children of Amram: Aharon, and Mosheh, and Miryam. And the sons of Aharon: Naḏaḇ and Aḇihu, El'azar and Ithamar.

4 El'azar brought forth Pineḥas, Pineḥas brought forth Aḇishua;

5 and Aḇishua brought forth Buqqi, and Buqqi brought forth Uzzi;

6 and Uzzi brought forth Zeraḥyah, and Zeraḥyah brought forth Merayoth;

7 Merayoth brought forth Amaryah, and Amaryah brought forth Aḥituḇ;

8 and Aḥituḇ brought forth Tsaḏoq, and Tsaḏoq brought forth Aḥima'ats;

9 and Aḥima'ats brought forth Azaryah, and Azaryah brought forth Yoḥanan;

10 and Yoḥanan brought forth Azaryah – it was he who served as priest in the House that Shelomoh built in Yerushalayim;

11 and Azaryah brought forth Amaryah, and Amaryah brought forth Aḥituḇ;

12 and Aḥituḇ brought forth Tsaḏoq, and Tsaḏoq brought forth Shallum;

13 and Shallum brought forth Ḥilqiyah, and Ḥilqiyah brought forth Azaryah;

14 and Azaryah brought forth Serayah, and Serayah brought forth Yehotsaḏaq.

15 And Yehotsaḏaq went away when יהוה sent Yehuḏah and Yerushalayim into exile by the hand of Neḇuḵaḏnetstsar.

16 The sons of Lĕwi: Gĕreshom, Qehath, and Merari.

17 And these are the names of the sons of Gĕreshom: Liḇni and Shim'i.

18 And the sons of Qehath: Amram, and Yitshar, and Ḥeḇron, and Uzzi'ĕl.

19 The sons of Merari: Maḥli and Mushi. And these are the clans of the Lĕwites according to their fathers:

20 Of Gĕreshom were Liḇni his son, Yaḥath his son, Zimmah his son,

21 Yo'aḥ his son, Iddo his son, Zeraḥ his son, Ye'atherai his son.

22 The sons of Qehath: Amminaḏaḇ his son, Qoraḥ his son, Assir his son,

23 Elqanah his son, Eḇyasaph his son, Assir his son,

24 Taḥath his son, Uri'ĕl his son, Uzziyah his son, and Sha'ul his son.

25 And the sons of Elqanah: Amasai and Aḥimoth.

26 Elqanah – the sons of Elqanah: Tsophai his son, and Naḥath his son,

27 Eliyaḇ his son, Yeroḥam his son, Elqanah his son.

28 And the sons of Shemu'ĕl: *Yo'ĕl* the first-born, and Aḇiyah the second.

29 The sons of Merari: Maḥli, Liḇni his son, Shim'i his son, Uzzah his son,

30 Shim'a his son, Ḥaggiyah his son, and Asayah his son.

31 And these are the men whom Dawiḏ appointed over the service of song in the House of יהוה, after the ark came to rest.

32 And they were rendering service in song before the dwelling place of the Tent of Appointment, until Shelomoh had built the House of יהוה in Yerushalayim, and they performed their duties according to their ruling.

33 And these are the ones who stood with their sons: Of the sons of the Qehathites were Hĕman the singer, son of Yo'ĕl, son of Shemu'ĕl,

34 son of Elqanah, son of Yeroḥam, son of Eli'ĕl, son of Towaḥ,

35 son of Tsuph, son of Elqanah, son of Maḥath, son of Amasai,

36 son of Elqanah, son of Yo'ĕl, son of Azaryah, son of Tsephanyah,

37 son of Taḥath, son of Assir, son of Eḇyasaph, son of Qoraḥ,

38 son of Yitshar, son of Qehath, son of Lĕwi, son of Yisra'ĕl.

39 And his brother Asaph, who stood at his right hand, was Asaph son of Bereḵyahu, son of Shim'a,

40 son of Miḵa'ĕl, son of Ba'asĕyah, son of Malkiyah,

41 son of Ethni, son of Zeraḥ, son of Aḏayah,

42 son of Ĕythan, son of Zimmah, son of Shim'i,

43 son of Yaḥath, son of Gĕreshom, son of Lĕwi.

44 And their brothers, the sons of Merari,

on the left hand, were Ěythan son of Qishi, son of Aḇdi, son of Malluḵ,
45 son of Ḥashaḇyah, son of Amatsyah, son of Ḥilqiyah,
46 son of Amtsi, son of Bani, son of Shemer,
47 son of Maḥli, son of Mushi, son of Merari, son of Lěwi.
48 And their brothers, the Lěwites, were appointed to every kind of service of the Dwelling Place of the House of Elohim.
49 But Aharon and his sons offered on the slaughter-place of ascending offering and on the slaughter-place of incense, for all the work of the Most Set-apart Place, and to make atonement for Yisra'ěl, according to all that Mosheh the servant of Elohim had commanded.
50 And these are the sons of Aharon: El'azar his son, Pineḥas his son, Aḇishua his son,
51 Buqqi his son, Uzzi his son, Zeraḥyah his son,
52 Merayoth his son, Amaryah his son, Aḥituḇ his son,
53 Tsaḏoq his son, Aḥima'ats his son.
54 And these were their dwelling places throughout their settlements within their borders, of the sons of Aharon, of the clan of the Qehathites, for the lot was theirs.
55 And they gave them Ḥeḇron in the land of Yehuḏah, with its surrounding open lands.
56 But the fields of the city and its villages they gave to Kalěḇ son of Yephunneh.
57 And to the sons of Aharon they gave the cities of refuge: Ḥeḇron, and Liḇnah with its open lands, and Yattir, and Eshtemoa with its open lands,
58 and Ḥilěn with its open lands, Deḇir with its open lands,
59 and Ashan with its open lands, and Běyth Shemesh with its open lands.
60 And from the tribe of Binyamin: Geḇa with its open lands, and Alemeth with its open lands, and Anathoth with its open lands. All their cities among their clans were thirteen.
61 And to the rest of the clan of the tribe of the Qehathites by lot ten cities from half the tribe of Menashsheh.
62 And to the sons of Gěreshom, throughout their clans, thirteen cities from the tribe of Yissasḵar, and from the tribe of Ashěr, and from the tribe of Naphtali, and from the tribe of Menashsheh in Bashan.
63 To the sons of Merari, throughout their clans, by lot twelve cities from the tribe of Re'uḇěn, and from the tribe of Gaḏ, and from the tribe of Zeḇulun.
64 So the children of Yisra'ěl gave cities with their open lands to the Lěwites.
65 And they gave by lot from the tribe of the children of Yehuḏah, and from the tribe of the children of Shim'on, and from the tribe of the children of Binyamin these cities which are mentioned by name.
66 And some of the clans of the sons of Qehath had cities of their borders from the tribe of Ephrayim.
67 And they gave them the cities of refuge: Sheḵem with its open lands, in the mountains of Ephrayim, and Gezer with its open lands,
68 and Yoqme'am with its open lands, and Běyth Ḥoron with its open lands,
69 and Ayalon with its open lands, and Gath Rimmon with its open lands.
70 And from the half-tribe of Menashsheh: Aněr with its open lands, and Bil'am with its open lands, for the rest of the clan of the sons of Qehath.
71 From the clan of the half-tribe of Menashsheh the sons of Gěreshom: Golan in Bashan with its open lands and Ashtaroth with its open lands.
72 And from the tribe of Yissasḵar: Qeḏesh with its open lands, Daḇerath with its open lands,
73 Ramoth with its open lands, and Aněm with its open lands.
74 And from the tribe of Ashěr: Mashal with its open lands, and Aḇdon with its open lands,
75 and Ḥuqoq with its open lands, and Reḥoḇ with its open lands.
76 And from the tribe of Naphtali: Qeḏesh in Galil with its open lands, and Ḥammon with its open lands, and Qiryathayim with its open lands.
77 From the tribe of Zeḇulun the rest of the children of Merari: Rimmon with its

open lands and Taḇor with its open lands.
78 And from beyond the Yarděn of Yeriḥo,
on the east side of the Yarděn, from the
tribe of Re'uḇěn: Betser in the wilderness
with its open lands, and Yahtsah with its
open lands,
79 Qeḏěmoth with its open lands, and
Měpha'ath with its open lands.
80 And from the tribe of Gaḏ: Ramoth in
Gil'aḏ with its open lands, and Maḥanayim
with its open lands,
81 and Ḥeshbon with its open lands, and
Ya'zěr with its open lands.

7 And the sons of Yissasḵar: Tola, and
Pu'ah, Yashuḇ, and Shimron, four.
2 And the sons of Tola: Uzzi, and
Rephayah, and Yeri'ěl, and Yaḥmai, and
Yiḇsam, and Shemu'ěl, heads of their
father's house. Of Tola there were great
men of might in their generations; their
number in the days of Dawiḏ was twenty-
two thousand six hundred.
3 And the son of Uzzi: Yizraḥyah, and
the sons of Yizraḥyah: Miḵa'ěl, and
Oḇaḏyah, and Yo'ěl, Yishshiyah. All five
of them were heads.
4 And with them, by their generations,
according to their fathers' houses, were
thirty-six thousand, bands of the army for
battle, for they had many wives and sons.
5 And their brothers among all the clans
of Yissasḵar were mighty brave men, listed
by their genealogies, eighty-seven thousand in all.
6 Of Binyamin: Bela, and Beḵer, and
Yeḏiya'ěl, three.
7 And the sons of Bela: Etsbon, and Uzzi,
and Uzzi'ěl, and Yerimoth, and Iri, five –
heads of their fathers' houses, and they
were listed by their genealogies, twenty-
two thousand and thirty-four mighty brave
men.
8 And the sons of Beḵer: Zemirah, and
Yo'ash, and Eli'ezer, and Elyo'ěynai, and
Omri, and Yerimoth, and Aḇiyah, and
Anathoth, and Alemeth. All these were the
sons of Beḵer,
9 with their genealogy according to their
generations, heads of their fathers' houses,
twenty thousand two hundred mighty
brave men.
10 And the son of Yeḏiya'ěl: Bilhan, and
the sons of Bilhan: Ye'ush, and Binyamin,
and Ěhuḏ, and Kena'anah, and Zěthan, and
Tarshish, and Aḥishaḥar.
11 All these sons of Yeḏiya'ěl were heads
of their fathers' houses, seventeen thousand two hundred mighty brave men going
out to the army for battle.
12 And Shuppim and Ḥuppim were the
sons of Ir, and Ḥushim was the son of
Aḥěr.
13 The sons of Naphtali: Yaḥtsi'ěl, and
Guni, and Yětser, and Shallum, sons of
Bilhah.
14 The sons of Menashsheh: his Aramean
concubine bore him Maḵir the father of
Gil'aḏ, the father of Asri'ěl.
15 And Maḵir took wives for Ḥuppim and
Shuppim; and the name of one was
Ma'aḵah, and the name of the second
was Tselophḥaḏ. And Tselophḥaḏ had
daughters.
16 But Ma'aḵah the wife of Maḵir bore a
son, and she called his name Peresh. And
the name of his brother was Sheresh, and
his sons were Ulam and Raqem.
17 And the son of Ulam: Beḏan. These
were the sons of Gil'aḏ, son of Maḵir, son
of Menashsheh.
18 And his sister Hammoleḵeth bore
Ishhod, and Aḇi'ezer, and Maḥlah.
19 And the sons of Shemiḏa: Aḥyan, and
Sheḵem, and Liqḥi, and Aniyam.
20 And the sons of Ephrayim: Shuthelaḥ,
and Bereḏ his son, and Taḥath his son, and
Elaḏah his son, and Taḥath his son,
21 and Zaḇaḏ his son, and Shuthelaḥ his
son, and Ezer and El'aḏ. But the men
of Gath who were born in that land killed
them because they came down to take their
livestock.
22 And Ephrayim their father mourned
many days, and his brothers came to comfort him.
23 And when he went in to his wife, she
conceived and bore a son. And he called
his name Beri'ah, because evil had come
upon his house.
24 And his daughter was She'erah, who
built Lower and Upper Běyth Ḥoron and

Uzzen She'erah.
25 And Rephaḥ was his son, as well as Resheph, and Telaḥ his son, and Taḥan his son,
26 La'dan his son, Ammihuḏ his son, Elishama his son,
27 Nun his son, Yehoshua his son.
28 And their possessions and dwelling places were Běyth Ěl and its towns: to the east Na'aran, and to the west Gezer and its towns, and Sheḵem and its towns, as far as Ayyah and its towns.
29 And by the borders of the children of Menashsheh were Běyth She'an and its towns, Ta'anaḵ and its towns, Meḡiddo and its towns, Dor and its towns. In these dwelt the children of Yosěph, son of Yisra'ěl.
30 The sons of Ashěr: Yimnah, and Yishwah, and Yishwi, and Beri'ah, and their sister Seraḥ.
31 And the sons of Beri'ah: Ḥeḇer and Malki'ěl, who was the father of Birzoth.
32 And Ḥeḇer brought forth Yaphlět, and Shoměr, and Ḥotham, and their sister Shuwa.
33 And the sons of Yaphlět: Pasaḵ, and Bimhal, and Ashwath. These were the children of Yaphlět.
34 And the sons of Shemer: Aḥi, and Rohagah, Yeḥubbah, and Aram.
35 And the sons of his brother Ḥělem: Tsophaḥ, and Yimna, and Shelesh, and Amal.
36 The sons of Tsophaḥ: Suwah, and Ḥarnepher, and Shu'al, and Běri, and Yimrah,
37 Betser, and Hoḏ, and Shamma, and Shilshah, and Yithran, and Be'ěra.
38 And the sons of Yether: Yephunneh, and Pispah, and Ara.
39 And the sons of Ulla: Araḥ, and Ḥanni'ěl, and Ritsya.
40 All these were the children of Ashěr, heads of their fathers' houses, chosen ones, mighty brave men, chief leaders. And when they registered by genealogy for the army, for battle, their number was twenty-six thousand.

8 And Binyamin brought forth Bela his first-born, Ashběl the second, Aḥraḥ the third,
2 Noḥah the fourth, and Rapha the fifth.
3 And the sons of Bela: Addar, and Gěra, and Aḇihuḏ,
4 and Aḇishua, and Na'aman, and Aḥowaḥ,
5 and Gěra, and Shephuphan, and Ḥuram.
6 And these are the sons of Ěḥuḏ. They were the heads of the fathers' houses of the inhabitants of Geḇa, and they were exiled to Manaḥath.
7 And Na'aman, and Aḥiyah, and Gěra – he exiled them. And Ěḥuḏ brought forth Uzza and Aḥihuḏ.
8 And Shaḥarayim brought forth children in the field of Mo'aḇ, after he had sent away Ḥushim and Ba'ara his wives.
9 And by Ḥoḏesh his wife he brought forth Yoḇaḇ, and Tsiḇya, and Měysha, and Malkam,
10 and Ye'uts, and Shoḇyah, and Mirmah. These were his sons, heads of their fathers' houses.
11 And by Ḥushim he brought forth Aḇituḇ and Elpa'al.
12 And the sons of Elpa'al: Ěḇer, and Mish'am, and Shemer, who built Ono and Loḏ with its towns;
13 and Beri'ah and Shema, who were heads of their fathers' houses of the inhabitants of Ayalon, who drove out the inhabitants of Gath.
14 and Aḥyo, Shashaq, and Yerěmoth,
15 and Zeḇaḏyah, and Araḏ, and Ěḏer,
16 and Miḵa'ěl, and Yispah, and Yoḥa were the sons of Beri'ah.
17 And Zeḇaḏyah, and Meshullam, and Ḥizqi, and Ḥeḇer,
18 and Yishmerai, and Yizli'ah, and Yoḇaḇ were the sons of Elpa'al.
19 And Yaqim, and Ziḵri, and Zaḇdi,
20 and Eli'ěynai, and Tsillethai, and Eli'ěl,
21 and Aḏayah, and Berayah, and Shimrath were the sons of Shim'i.
22 And Yishpan, and Ěḇer, and Eli'ěl,
23 and Aḇdon, and Ziḵri, and Ḥanan,
24 and Ḥananyah, and Ěylam, and Antothiyah,

25 and Yiphdeyah, and Penu'ĕl were the sons of Shashaq.

26 And Shamsherai, and Sheḥaryah, and Athalyah,

27 and Yaʽareshyah, and Ĕliyah, and Ziḵri were the sons of Yeroḥam.

28 These were heads of the fathers' houses by their generations, heads. These dwelt in Yerushalayim.

29 And the father of Giḇʽon, whose wife's name was Maʽaḵah, dwelt at Giḇʽon.

30 And his first-born son was Aḇdon, then Tsur, and Qish, and Baʽal, and Naḏaḇ,

31 and Geḏor, and Aḥyo, and Zeḵer,

32 and Miqloth, who brought forth Shimʽah. And they also dwelt alongside their relatives in Yerushalayim, with their brothers.

33 And Nĕr brought forth Qish, and Qish brought forth Sha'ul, and Sha'ul brought forth Yehonathan, and Malkishua, and Aḇinaḏaḇ, and Esh-Baʽal.

34 And the son of Yehonathan was Meriḇ-Baʽal, and Meriḇ-Baʽal brought forth Miḵah.

35 And the sons of Miḵah: Pithon, and Meleḵ, and Ta'arĕa, and Aḥaz.

36 And Aḥaz brought forth Yehoʽaddah, and Yehoʽaddah brought forth Alemeth, and Azmaweth, and Zimri. And Zimri brought forth Motsa.

37 And Motsa brought forth Binʽa, Raphah his son, Elʽasah his son, Atsĕl his son.

38 And Atsĕl had six sons whose names were these: Azriqam, Boḵeru, and Yishmaʽĕl, and Sheʽaryah, and Oḇaḏyah, and Ḥanan. All these were the sons of Atsĕl.

39 And the sons of Ĕsheq his brother: Ulam his first-born, Yeʽush the second, and Eliphelet the third.

40 And the sons of Ulam were mighty brave men, archers, and had many sons and grandsons, one hundred and fifty. These were all sons of Binyamin.

9 And all Yisra'ĕl registered themselves by genealogy. And see, they were written in the book of the sovereigns of Yisra'ĕl. And Yehuḏah was exiled to Baḇel for their trespass.

2 And the first inhabitants who were in their possessions in their cities of Yisra'ĕl, were the priests, the Lĕwites, and the Nethinim.

3 And in Yerushalayim dwelt some of the children of Yehuḏah, and some of the children of Binyamin, and some of the children of Ephrayim and Menashsheh:

4 Uthai son of Ammihuḏ, son of Omri, son of Imri, son of Bani, of the sons of Perets, the son of Yehuḏah.

5 And of the Shilonites: Asayah the first-born and his sons.

6 And of the sons of Zeraḥ: Yeʽu'ĕl, and their brothers, six hundred and ninety.

7 And of the sons of Binyamin: Sallu son of Meshullam, son of Hoḏawyah, son of Hasenu'ah;

8 and Yiḇneyah son of Yeroḥam; and Ĕlah son of Uzzi, son of Miḵri; and Meshullam son of Shephatyah, son of Reʽu'ĕl, son of Yiḇniyah;

9 and their brothers, according to their generations, nine hundred and fifty-six. All these men were heads of a father's house in their fathers' houses.

10 And of the priests: Yeḏayah, and Yehoyariḇ, and Yaḵin;

11 and Azaryah son of Ḥilqiyah, son of Meshullam, son of Tsaḏoq, son of Merayoth, son of Aḥituḇ, the officer over the House of Elohim;

12 and Aḏayah son of Yeroḥam, son of Pashḥur, son of Malkiyah; and Maʽasai son of Aḏi'ĕl, son of Yaḥzĕrah, son of Meshullam, son of Meshillĕmith, son of Immĕr;

13 and their brothers, heads of their fathers' houses, one thousand seven hundred and sixty, able men for the work of the service of the House of Elohim.

14 And of the Lĕwites: Shemayah son of Ḥashshuḇ, son of Azriqam, son of Ḥashaḇyah, of the sons of Merari;

15 and Baqbaqqar, Ḥeresh, and Galal, and Mattanyah son of Miḵa, son of Ziḵri, son of Asaph;

16 and Oḇaḏyah son of Shemayah, son of Galal, son of Yeḏuthun; and Bereḵyah son of Asa, son of Elqanah, who dwelt in the villages of the Netophathites.

17 And the gatekeepers: Shallum, and
Aqqub̲, and Talmon, and Aḥiman, and
their brothers – Shallum the chief.
18 And up till then they were gatekeepers
for the camps of the children of Lĕwi at the
Sovereign's Gate on the east.
19 And Shallum son of Qorĕ, son of
Eb̲yasaph, son of Qoraḥ, and his brothers,
from his father's house, the Qorḥites, were
over the work of the service, guards of the
thresholds of the Tent. And their fathers
had been guards of the entrance to the
camp of יהוה.
20 And Pineḥas son of El'azar was leader
over them in time past. יהוה was with him.
21 Zek̲aryah son of Meshelemyah was
gatekeeper at the entrance of the Tent of
Appointment.
22 All those chosen as gatekeepers at the
thresholds were two hundred and twelve.
They were registered by genealogy, in their
villages. Dawiḏ and Shemu'ĕl the seer had
appointed them to their office of trust.
23 So they and their sons were over the
gates of the House of יהוה, the House of
the Tent, by watches.
24 The gatekeepers were on the four sides:
the east, west, north, and south.
25 And their brothers in their villages had
to come with them from time to time for
seven days.
26 For the four chief gatekeepers were in
an office of trust. They were Lĕwites, and
they were over the rooms and treasuries of
the House of Elohim.
27 And they spent the night all around the
House of Elohim because they had the
duty, and they were to open it morning by
morning.
28 And some of them were over the vessels of service, for they brought them in
and took them out by count.
29 And some of them were appointed over
the vessels, even over all the vessels of the
set-apart place, and over the fine flour and
the wine and the oil and the incense and
the spices.
30 And some of the sons of the priests
blended the compound of spices.
31 And Mattithyah of the Lĕwites, the
first-born of Shallum the Qorḥite, was
entrusted with the making of the flat cakes.
32 And some of their brothers of the sons
of the Qehathites were over the showbread, to prepare every Sabbath.
33 And these were the singers, heads of
the fathers' houses of the Lĕwites, in the
rooms, and were exempted from other
duties, for they were employed in that
work day and night.
34 These heads of the fathers' houses of
the Lĕwites were heads throughout their
generations. They dwelt at Yerushalayim.
35 And Ye'i'ĕl the father of Gib̲'on, whose
wife's name was Ma'ak̲ah, dwelt at
Gib̲'on.
36 And his first-born son was Ab̲don, then
Tsur, and Qish, and Ba'al, and Nĕr, and
Naḏab̲,
37 and Geḏor, and Aḥyo, and Zek̲aryah,
and Miqloth.
38 And Miqloth brought forth Shim'am.
And they too dwelt alongside their relatives in Yerushalayim, with their brothers.
39 And Nĕr brought forth Qish, and Qish
brought forth Sha'ul, and Sha'ul brought
forth Yehonathan, and Malkishua, and
Ab̲inaḏab̲, and Esh-Ba'al.
40 And the son of Yehonathan was Merib̲-
Ba'al, and Merib̲-Ba'al brought forth
Mik̲ah.
41 And the sons of Mik̲ah: Pithon, and
Melek̲, and Taḥrĕa,
42 and Aḥaz, who brought forth Yarah;
and Yarah brought forth Alemeth, and
Azmaweth, and Zimri. And Zimri brought
forth Motsa;
43 and Motsa brought forth Bin'a, and
Rephayah was his son, El'asah his son,
Atsĕl his son.
44 And Atsĕl had six sons whose names
were these: Azriqam, Bok̲eru, and
Yishma'ĕl, and She'aryah, and Ob̲aḏyah,
and Ḥanan. These were the sons of Atsĕl.

10 And the Philistines fought against
Yisra'ĕl. And the men of Yisra'ĕl
fled from before the Philistines, and fell
slain on Mount Gilboa.
2 And the Philistines pursued Sha'ul and
his sons, and the Philistines struck Yonathan, and Ab̲inaḏab̲, and Malkishua, sons

of Sha'ul.
3 And the battle was heavy on Sha'ul.
And the archers hit him, and he was
wounded by the archers.
4 And Sha'ul said to his armour-bearer,
"Draw your sword, and thrust me through
with it, lest these uncircumcised ones
come and abuse me." But his armour-bearer would not, for he was much afraid, so
Sha'ul took a sword and fell on it.
5 And when his armour-bearer saw that
Sha'ul was dead, he also fell on his sword
and died.
6 Thus Sha'ul and his three sons died,
and all his house – they died together.
7 And when all the men of Yisra'ěl who
were in the valley saw that they had fled
and that Sha'ul and his sons were dead,
they forsook their cities and fled, and the
Philistines came and dwelt in them.
8 And the next day it came to be, when
the Philistines came to strip the slain, that
they found Sha'ul and his sons fallen on
Mount Gilboa.
9 And they stripped him and took his
head and his armour, and sent word
throughout the land of the Philistines to
proclaim the news among their idols and
among the people,
10 and put his armour in the house of their
mighty ones, and fastened his head in the
house of Daḡon.
11 And all Yaḇěsh Gil'aḏ heard of all that
the Philistines had done to Sha'ul,
12 and all the brave men arose and took
the body of Sha'ul and the bodies of his
sons. And they brought them to Yaḇěsh,
and buried their bones under the tamarisk
tree at Yaḇěsh, and fasted seven days.
13 Thus Sha'ul died for his trespass which
he had trespassed against יהוה, because he
did not guard the Word of יהוה, and also
for asking a medium for to make inquiry,
14 and did not inquire of יהוה. So He put
him to death, and turned the reign over to
Dawiḏ son of Yishai.

11

And all Yisra'ěl came together to
Dawiḏ at Ḥeḇron, saying, "See, we
are your bone and your flesh.
2 "Also, in time past, even when Sha'ul
was sovereign, you were the one who led
Yisra'ěl out and brought them in. And
יהוה your Elohim said to you, 'Shepherd
My people Yisra'ěl, and be ruler over My
people Yisra'ěl.' "
3 So all the elders of Yisra'ěl came to the
sovereign at Ḥeḇron, and Dawiḏ made a
covenant with them at Ḥeḇron before יהוה.
And they anointed Dawiḏ sovereign over
Yisra'ěl, according to the word of יהוה by
Shemu'ěl.
4 And Dawiḏ and all Yisra'ěl went to
Yerushalayim, which is Yeḇus, where the
Yeḇusites were, the inhabitants of the land.
5 And the inhabitants of Yeḇus said to
Dawiḏ, "You do not come in here." But
Dawiḏ captured the stronghold of Tsiyon,
the City of Dawiḏ.
6 And Dawiḏ said, "Whoever strikes the
Yeḇusites first becomes chief and commander." And Yo'aḇ son of Tseruyah went
up first, and became chief.
7 And Dawiḏ dwelt in the stronghold, so
they called it the City of Dawiḏ.
8 And he built the city around it, from
Millo round about, and Yo'aḇ revived the
rest of the city.
9 And Dawiḏ went on and became great,
and יהוה of hosts was with him.
10 And these were the heads of the mighty
men whom Dawiḏ had, who strengthened
themselves with him in his reign, with all
Yisra'ěl, to set him up to reign over
Yisra'ěl, according to the word of יהוה.
11 And this is the number of the mighty
men whom Dawiḏ had: Yashoḇ'am son of
a Ḥaḵmonite, chief of the thirty. He had
lifted up his spear against three hundred,
slain at one time.
12 And after him was El'azar son of Doḏo,
the Aḥoḥite, who was one of the three
mighty men.
13 He was with Dawiḏ at Pasdammim,
and the Philistines were gathered there for
battle, and a portion of the field was filled
with barley, and the people had fled before
the Philistines.
14 But they took their stand in the midst of
that field, and delivered it, and struck the
Philistines. Thus יהוה saved them by a
great deliverance.

15 And three of the thirty chiefs went
down to the rock to Dawiḏ, into the cave of
Aḏullam, while the army of the Philistines
encamped in the Valley of Repha'im.
16 And Dawiḏ was then in the stronghold,
and the watch-post of the Philistines was
then in Běyth Leḥem.
17 And Dawiḏ longed and said, "Oh, that
someone would give me a drink of water
from the well of Běyth Leḥem, which is by
the gate!"
18 And the three broke through the camp
of the Philistines, and drew water from the
well of Běyth Leḥem that was by the gate,
and took it and brought it to Dawiḏ. But
Dawiḏ would not drink it, but poured it out
to יהוה.
19 And he said, "Far be it from me, O my
Elohim, that I should do this! Should I
drink the blood of these men who have
risked their lives? For at the risk of their
lives they brought it." And he would not
drink it. This is what the three mighty men
did.
20 And Aḇishai the brother of Yo'aḇ was
chief of another three. And he had lifted up
his spear against three hundred men, who
were slain, and won a name among the
three.
21 Of the three he was more esteemed than
the other two men, so he became their
head. However he did not come to the first
three.
22 Benayah was the son of Yehoyaḏa, the
son of a brave man from Qaḇtse'ěl, who
had done many deeds. He struck two lion-
like Mo'aḇites. He also went down and
struck a lion in the midst of a pit on a
snowy day.
23 And he struck a Mitsrian, a man of
great height, five cubits tall. And in the
Mitsrian's hand was a spear like a
weaver's beam, and he went down to him
with a staff and wrenched the spear out of
the Mitsrian's hand, and killed him with
his own spear.
24 This is what Benayahu son of Yehoyaḏa did, and won a name among the three
mighty men.
25 See, he was more esteemed than the
thirty, but he did not come to the first three.
And Dawiḏ set him over his court.
26 And the mighty men of the armies were
Asah'ěl the brother of Yo'aḇ, Elḥanan son
of Doḏo of Běyth Leḥem,
27 Shammoth the Harorite, Ḥělets the
Pelonite,
28 Ira son of Iqqěsh the Teqowite,
Aḇi'ezer the Anathothite,
29 Sibbeḵai the Ḥushathite, Ilai the
Aḥoḥite,
30 Maharai the Netophathite, Ḥěleḏ son of
Ba'anah the Netophathite,
31 Ithai son of Riḇai of Giḇ'ah, of the
children of Binyamin, Benayah the
Pirathonite,
32 Ḥurai of the wadis of Ga'ash, Aḇi'ěl the
Arbathite,
33 Azmaweth the Baḥarumite, Elyaḥba
the Sha'albonite,
34 the sons of Hashěm the Gizonite,
Yonathan son of Shaḡě the Hararite,
35 Aḥyam son of Saḵar the Hararite,
Eliphal son of Ur,
36 Ḥěpher the Mekěrathite, Aḥiyah the
Pelonite,
37 Ḥetsro the Karmelite, Na'arai son of
Ezbai,
38 Yo'ěl the brother of Nathan, Miḇḥar
son of Haḡri,
39 Tseleq the Ammonite, Naḥarai the
Běrothite (the armour-bearer of Yo'aḇ son
of Tseruyah),
40 Ira the Yithrite, Garěḇ the Yithrite,
41 Uriyah the Ḥittite, Zaḇaḏ son of Aḥlai,
42 Aḏina son of Shiza the Re'uḇěnite, the
head of the Re'uḇěnites, and thirty with
him,
43 Ḥanan son of Ma'aḵah, and Yoshaphat
the Mithnite,
44 Uzziya the Ashterathite, Shama and
Ye'i'ěl the sons of Ḥotham the Aro'ěrite,
45 Yeḏiya'ěl son of Shimri, and Yoḥa his
brother, the Titsite,
46 Eli'ěl the Maḥawite, and Yeriḇai and
Yoshawyah the sons of Elna'am, Yithmah
the Mo'aḇite,
47 Eli'ěl, and Oḇěḏ, and Ya'asi'ěl of
Metsoḇayah.

12 Now these are they who came to
Dawiḏ at Tsiqlaḡ while he was still

in hiding from Sha'ul son of Qish. And
they were among the mighty men, helping
the battle,
2 armed with bows, using both the right
hand and the left, with stones, and with
arrows, with bows, of the brothers of
Sha'ul, of Binyamin.
3 The chief was Aḥi'ezer and Yo'ash, the
sons of Shema'ah the Giḇ'athite; and
Yezaw'ĕl and Pelet, the sons of Azmaweth;
and Beraḵah, and Yĕhu the Anathothite;
4 and Yishmayah the Giḇ'onite, a mighty
man among the thirty, and over the thirty;
and Yirmeyah, and Yaḥazi'ĕl, and
Yoḥanan, and Yozaḇaḏ the Geḏĕrathite;
5 Eluzai, and Yerimoth, and Be'alyah,
and Shemaryahu, and Shephatyahu the
Ḥaruphite;
6 Elqanah, and Yishshiyahu, and Azar'ĕl,
and Yow'ezer, and Yashoḇ'am the
Qorḥites;
7 and Yo'ĕlah and Zeḇaḏyah, the sons of
Yeroḥam of Geḏor.
8 And some Gaḏites separated themselves to Dawiḏ at the stronghold in the
wilderness, mighty brave men, men trained
for battle, who could handle shield and
spear, whose faces were like the faces of
lions, and were as swift as gazelles on the
mountains:
9 Ĕzer the chief, Oḇaḏyah the second,
Eliyaḇ the third,
10 Mishmannah the fourth, Yirmeyah the
fifth,
11 Attai the sixth, Eli'ĕl the seventh,
12 Yoḥanan the eighth, Elzaḇaḏ the ninth,
13 Yirmeyahu the tenth, Maḵbannai the
eleventh.
14 These were from the sons of Gaḏ,
chiefs of the army. The least was over a
hundred, and the greatest was over a thousand.
15 These were the ones who passed over
the Yardĕn in the first new *moon*, when it
was overflowing all its banks, and put to
flight all those in the valleys, to the east
and to the west.
16 And some of the children of Binyamin
and Yehuḏah came to Dawiḏ at the stronghold.
17 And Dawiḏ went out to face them, and
answered and said to them, "If you have
come peaceably to me to help me, my
heart shall be united with you; but if to
betray me to my enemies – there is no
violence in my hands – let the Elohim of
our fathers see and reprove."
18 Then the Spirit came upon Amasai,
chief of the officers, "Yours, O Dawiḏ!
And with you, O son of Yishai! Peace,
peace to you, and peace to your helpers!
For your Elohim shall help you." And
Dawiḏ received them, and put them among
the chiefs of the raiding band.
19 And some from Menashsheh went over
to Dawiḏ when he was going with the
Philistines to battle against Sha'ul. But
they did not help them, for the princes of
the Philistines took advice and sent him
away, saying, "He might go over to his
master Sha'ul with our heads!"
20 When he went to Tsiqlaḡ, those of
Menashsheh who went over to him were
Aḏnah, and Yozaḇaḏ, and Yeḏiya'ĕl, and
Miḵa'ĕl, and Yozaḇaḏ, and Elihu, and
Tsillethai, chiefs of the thousands who
were from Menashsheh.
21 And they helped Dawiḏ against the
raiding bands, for they were all mighty
brave men, and they were commanders in
the army.
22 For at that time they came to Dawiḏ
day by day to help him, until it was a great
army, like an army of Elohim.
23 And these were the numbers of the
chiefs of those that were armed for battle,
and came to Dawiḏ at Ḥeḇron to turn over
the reign of Sha'ul to him, according to the
word of יהוה:
24 Of the children of Yehuḏah bearing
shield and spear, six thousand eight hundred armed for battle;
25 of the children of Shim'on, mighty
brave men for the army, seven thousand
one hundred;
26 of the children of Lĕwi four thousand
six hundred;
27 and Yehoyaḏa, the leader of the
Aharonites, and with him three thousand
seven hundred;
28 and Tsaḏoq, a young man, a mighty
brave man, and from his father's house

twenty-two commanders;
29 and the children of Binyamin, relatives
of Sha'ul, three thousand – until then the
greatest part of them guarded the charge of
the house of Sha'ul;
30 and the children of Ephrayim twenty
thousand eight hundred, mighty brave
ones, men of name throughout their
father's house;
31 and the half-tribe of Menashsheh eighteen thousand, who were designated by
name to come and set up Dawiḏ to reign;
32 and the children of Yissasḵar who had
understanding of the times, to know what
Yisra'ěl should do, their chiefs were two
hundred. And all their brothers *acted* at
their mouth;
33 of Zeḇulun there were fifty thousand
going out to the army, arranging battle with
all weapons of battle, giving support with
undivided heart;
34 and of Naphtali one thousand commanders, and with them thirty-seven thousand
with shield and spear;
35 and of the Danites, arranging battle,
twenty-eight thousand six hundred;
36 and of Ashěr, going out to the army,
arranging battle, forty thousand;
37 and of the Re'uḇěnites and the Gaḏites
and the half-tribe of Menashsheh, from
beyond the Yarděn, one hundred and twenty thousand armed for battle with every
kind of weapon of battle.
38 All these men of battle, keeping rank,
came to Ḥeḇron with a perfect heart, to set
up Dawiḏ to reign over all Yisra'ěl. And
all the rest of Yisra'ěl were of one heart to
set up Dawiḏ to reign.
39 And they were there with Dawiḏ three
days, eating and drinking, for their brothers had prepared for them.
40 And also those who were near to them,
from as far away as Yissasḵar and Zeḇulun
and Naphtali, were bringing food on
donkeys and camels, on mules and cattle –
food of flour and cakes of figs and cakes of
raisins, wine and oil and cattle and sheep
in great quantities, for there was joy in
Yisra'ěl.

13 And Dawiḏ consulted with the
commanders of thousands and
hundreds, and with every leader.
2 And Dawiḏ said to all the assembly of
Yisra'ěl, "If it seems good to you, and if it
is of יהוה our Elohim, let us send out to
our brothers everywhere who are left in all
the land of Yisra'ěl, and with them to the
priests and Lěwites who are in their cities
of their open lands, and let them be
gathered to us;
3 and let us bring the ark of our Elohim
back to us, for we sought Him not since the
days of Sha'ul."
4 And all the assembly agreed to do so,
for the matter was right in the eyes of all
the people.
5 So Dawiḏ assembled all Yisra'ěl, from
Shiḥor in Mitsrayim to as far as the
entrance of Ḥamath, to bring the ark of
Elohim from Qiryath Ye'arim.
6 And Dawiḏ and all Yisra'ěl went up to
Ba'alah, to Qiryath Ye'arim of Yehuḏah, to
bring up from there the ark of Elohim,
יהוה, who dwells between the keruḇim,
where the Name is called on.
7 And they placed the ark of Elohim on a
new wagon from the house of Aḇinaḏaḇ,
and Uzza and Aḥyo were leading the
wagon.
8 And Dawiḏ and all Yisra'ěl were
playing before Elohim with all their might,
and with songs, and with lyres, and with
harps, and with tambourines, and with
cymbals, and with trumpets.
9 And when they came to the threshing-
floor of Kiḏon, Uzza put out his hand to
hold the ark, for the oxen stumbled.
10 Then the wrath of יהוה burned against
Uzza, and He struck him because he put
his hand to the ark. And he died there
before Elohim.
11 And Dawiḏ was displeased because
יהוה had broken out against Uzza, therefore that place is called Perets Uzza, until
this day.
12 And Dawiḏ was afraid of Elohim that
day, saying, "How shall I bring the ark of
Elohim to me?"
13 So Dawiḏ did not take the ark with him
into the City of Dawiḏ, but took it aside

into the house of Oḇěḏ-Eḏom the Gittite.
14 And the ark of Elohim remained with
the household of Oḇěḏ-Eḏom in his house
three new *moons*. And יהוה blessed the
house of Oḇěḏ-Eḏom and all that he had.

14 And Ḥiram sovereign of Tsor sent
messengers to Dawiḏ, and cedar
trees, with stonemasons and carpenters, to
build him a house.
2 And Dawiḏ knew that יהוה had established him as sovereign over Yisra'ěl, for
his reign was highly exalted for the sake of
His people Yisra'ěl.
3 And Dawiḏ took more wives in
Yerushalayim, and Dawiḏ brought forth
more sons and daughters.
4 And these are the names of his children
whom he had in Yerushalayim: Shammua
and Shoḇaḇ, Nathan and Shelomoh,
5 and Yiḇḥar, and Elishua, and Elpelet,
6 and Noḡah, and Nepheḡ, and Yaphiya,
7 and Elishama, and Be'elyaḏa, and
Eliphelet.
8 And when the Philistines heard that
Dawiḏ had been anointed sovereign over
all Yisra'ěl, all the Philistines went up to
seek Dawiḏ. And Dawiḏ heard and went
out against them.
9 And the Philistines came and made a
raid on the Valley of Repha'im.
10 And Dawiḏ inquired of Elohim, saying,
"Do I go up against the Philistines? And
shall You give them into my hand?" And
יהוה said to him, "Go up, and I shall give
them into your hand."
11 And they went up to Ba'al Peratsim,
and Dawiḏ struck them there. Then Dawiḏ
said, "Elohim has broken through my
enemies by my hand like a breakthrough of
water." So they called the name of that
place Ba'al Peratsim.
12 And they left their mighty ones there,
so Dawiḏ commanded, and they were
burned with fire.
13 And the Philistines once again made a
raid on the valley.
14 And Dawiḏ again inquired of Elohim,
and Elohim said to him, "Do not go up
after them. Go around them, and come
upon them in front of the mulberry trees.
15 "And it shall be, when you hear a sound
of stepping in the tops of the mulberry
trees, then go out to battle, for Elohim shall
go out before you to strike the camp of the
Philistines."
16 And Dawiḏ did as Elohim commanded
him, and they struck the army of the
Philistines from Giḇ'on as far as Gezer.
17 And the name of Dawiḏ went out into
all lands, and יהוה put the dread of him
upon all nations.

15 And he built houses for himself in
the City of Dawiḏ. And he prepared a place for the ark of Elohim, and
pitched a tent for it.
2 Then Dawiḏ said, "No one is to lift the
ark of Elohim but the Lěwites, for יהוה has
chosen them to lift the ark of Elohim and
to serve Him forever."
3 And Dawiḏ assembled all Yisra'ěl at
Yerushalayim, to bring up the ark of יהוה
to its place, which he had prepared for it.
4 And Dawiḏ gathered the children of
Aharon and the Lěwites;
5 of the sons of Qehath: Uri'ěl the chief,
and one hundred and twenty of his
brothers;
6 of the sons of Merari: Asayah the chief,
and two hundred and twenty of his
brothers;
7 of the sons of Gěreshom: Yo'ěl the
chief, and one hundred and thirty of his
brothers;
8 of the sons of Elitsaphan: Shemayah
the chief, and two hundred of his brothers;
9 of the sons of Ḥeḇron: Eli'ěl the chief,
and eighty of his brothers;
10 of the sons of Uzzi'ěl: Amminaḏaḇ the
chief, and one hundred and twelve of his
brothers.
11 And Dawiḏ called for Tsaḏoq and
Eḇyathar the priests, and for the Lěwites,
for Uri'ěl, Asayah, and Yo'ěl, Shemayah,
and Eli'ěl, and Amminaḏaḇ,
12 and said to them, "You are the heads of
the fathers' *houses* of the Lěwites. Set
yourselves apart, you and your brothers,
then you shall bring up the ark of יהוה
Elohim of Yisra'ěl to the place I have prepared for it.

13 "Because you did not do it the first
time, יהוה our Elohim broke out against
us, because we did not ask Him about the
right-ruling."
14 So the priests and the Lěwites set themselves apart, to bring up the ark of יהוה
Elohim of Yisra'ěl.
15 And the children of the Lěwites bore
the ark of Elohim on their shoulders, by its
poles, as Mosheh had commanded according to the word of יהוה.
16 And Dawiḏ spoke to the leaders of the
Lěwites to appoint their brothers the
singers with instruments of song, harps,
and lyres, and cymbals, to lift up the voice
with joy.
17 And the Lěwites appointed Hěman son
of Yo'ěl, and of his brothers, Asaph son of
Bereḵyahu; and of their brothers, the sons
of Merari, Ěythan son of Qushayahu;
18 and with them their brothers of the second rank: Zeḵaryahu, Běn, and Ya'azi'ěl,
and Shemiramoth, and Yeḥi'ěl, and Unni,
Eliyaḇ, and Benayahu, and Ma'asěyahu,
and Mattithyahu, and Elipheleěhu, and
Miqněyahu, and Oḇěḏ-Eḏom, and Ye'i'ěl,
the gatekeepers;
19 and the singers Hěman, Asaph, and
Ěythan, were to sound the cymbals of
bronze;
20 and Zeḵaryah, and Azi'ěl, and Shemiramoth, and Yeḥi'ěl, and Unni, and Eliyaḇ,
and Ma'asěyahu, and Benayahu, with
harps according to Alamoth;
21 and Mattithyahu, and Elipheleěhu, and
Miqněyahu, and Oḇěḏ-Eḏom, and Ye'i'ěl,
and Azazyahu, to lead with lyres on the
Sheminith;
22 and Kenanyahu, leader of the Lěwites,
in the song, because he was skilled;
23 and Bereḵyah and Elqanah were doorkeepers for the ark;
24 and Sheḇanyahu, and Yoshaphat, and
Nethaně'l, and Amasai, and Zeḵaryahu,
and Benayahu, and Eli'ezer, the priests,
were to blow the trumpets before the ark of
Elohim. And Oḇěḏ-Eḏom and Yeḥiyah,
were doorkeepers for the ark.
25 And it was Dawiḏ and the elders of
Yisra'ěl, and the commanders over thousands, who went to bring up the ark of the
covenant of יהוה from the house of Oḇěḏ-
Eḏom with joy.
26 And it came to be, when Elohim helped
the Lěwites who bore the ark of the
covenant of יהוה, that they slaughtered
seven bulls and seven rams.
27 And Dawiḏ was dressed in a robe of
fine linen, as were all the Lěwites who
bore the ark, the singers, and Kenanyah the
leader of the service with the singers. And
Dawiḏ wore a linen shoulder garment.
28 So all Yisra'ěl brought up the ark of the
covenant of יהוה with shouting and with a
voice of a shophar, with trumpets and with
cymbals, sounding with harps and lyres.
29 And it came to be, as the ark of the
covenant of יהוה came to the City of
Dawiḏ, that Miḵal the daughter of Sha'ul,
looking through a window, saw Sovereign
Dawiḏ dancing and playing. And she
despised him in her heart.

16 And they brought the ark of
Elohim, and set it in the midst of
the Tent that Dawiḏ had pitched for it. And
they brought ascending offerings and
peace offerings before Elohim.
2 And when Dawiḏ had made an end of
offering the ascending offerings and the
peace offerings, he blessed the people in
the Name of יהוה,
3 and gave a portion to everyone of
Yisra'ěl, both man and woman, to everyone a loaf of bread, a measure, and a cake
of raisins.
4 And he appointed some of the Lěwites
to serve before the ark of יהוה, to bring to
remembrance, and to thank, and to praise
יהוה Elohim of Yisra'ěl:
5 Asaph the chief, and his second
Zeḵaryah, Ye'i'ěl, and Shemiramoth, and
Yeḥi'ěl, and Mattithyah, and Eliyaḇ, and
Benayahu, and Oḇěḏ-Eḏom, and Ye'i'ěl,
with harps and lyres, but Asaph was
sounding with cymbals;
6 and Benayahu and Yaḥazi'ěl the priests
continually blew the trumpets before the
ark of the covenant of Elohim.
7 And on that day Dawiḏ first gave
thanks to יהוה by the hand of Asaph and
his brothers:

[8] Give thanks to יהוה, call upon His Name,
Make known His deeds among the peoples!
[9] Sing to Him, sing praise to Him,
Speak of all His wonders!
[10] Boast in His set-apart Name,
Let the hearts of those seeking יהוה rejoice!
[11] Seek יהוה and His strength,
Seek His face continually!
[12] Remember His wonders which He has done,
His signs and the right-rulings of His mouth,
[13] O seed of Yisra'ěl, His servant;
O children of Ya'aqoḇ, His chosen ones!
[14] He is יהוה our Elohim,
His right-rulings are in all the earth.
[15] Remember His covenant forever,
The Word He commanded for a thousand generations,
[16] Which He made with Aḇraham,
And His oath to Yitsḥaq,
[17] And He established it to Ya'aqoḇ for a law,
To Yisra'ěl as an everlasting covenant,
[18] Saying, "To you I give the land of Kena'an,
The portion of your inheritance,"
[19] When you were but few in number,
Few indeed, and sojourners in it.
[20] And they went up and down,
From one nation to another,
And from one reign to another people.
[21] He allowed no one to oppress them,
And He reproved sovereigns for their sakes, *saying*:
[22] "Do not touch My anointed ones,
And do My prophets no evil."
[23] Sing to יהוה, all the earth;
Proclaim His deliverance from day to day.
[24] Declare His esteem among the nations,
His wonders among all peoples.
[25] For great is יהוה and greatly to be praised;
And He is to be feared above all mighty ones.
[26] For all the mighty ones of the peoples are matters of naught, [a]
But יהוה made the heavens.
[27] Excellency and splendour are before Him,
Strength and gladness are in His place.
[28] Ascribe to יהוה, O clans of the peoples,
Ascribe to יהוה esteem and strength.
[29] Ascribe to יהוה the esteem of His Name;
Bring an offering, and come before Him;
Bow yourself to יהוה
In the splendour of set-apartness!
[30] Tremble before Him, all the earth.
The world also is firmly established, immovable.
[31] Let the heavens rejoice, and let the earth be glad;
And let them say among the nations,
"יהוה shall reign."
[32] Let the sea roar, and all that fills it;
Let the field rejoice, and all that is in it.
[33] Let the trees of the forest then sing before יהוה,
For He shall come to judge the earth.
[34] Give thanks to יהוה, for He is good,
For His loving-commitment is everlasting!
[35] And say, "Save us, O Elohim of our deliverance;
And gather us together,
And deliver us from the nations,
To give thanks to Your set-apart Name,
And boast in Your praise."
[36] Blessed be יהוה Elohim of Yisra'ěl
From everlasting to everlasting!
And all the people said, "Aměn!" and praised יהוה.

[37] So he left Asaph and his brothers there
before the ark of the covenant of יהוה to
perform regular service before the ark, as
each day required;
[38] also, Oḇěḏ-Eḏom with his sixty-eight
brothers, including Oḇěḏ-Eḏom son of
Yeḏuthun, and Ḥosah, to be gatekeepers;
[39] and Tsaḏoq the priest and his brothers

16a See Teh. 96:5.

the priests, before the Dwelling Place of
יהוה at the high place that was at Giḇʻon,
40 to offer ascending offerings to יהוה on
the slaughter-place of ascending offering
regularly morning and evening, and to do
according to all that is written in the Torah
of יהוה which He commanded Yisra'ěl;
41 and with them Hěman and Yeḏuthun
and the rest who were chosen, who were
designated by name, to give thanks to
יהוה, because His loving-commitment is
everlasting;
42 and with them Hěman and Yeḏuthun, to
sound aloud with trumpets and cymbals
and instruments for the songs of Elohim,
and the sons of Yeḏuthun for the gate.
43 And all the people went, each one to his
house, and Dawiḏ returned to bless his
house.

17 And it came to be, when Dawiḏ
was dwelling in his house, that
Dawiḏ said to Nathan the prophet, "See, I
am dwelling in a house of cedar, but the
ark of the covenant of יהוה is under curtains."
2 And Nathan said to Dawiḏ, "Do all that
is in your heart, for Elohim is with you."
3 And it came to be that night that the
word of Elohim came to Nathan, saying,
4 "Go, and you shall say to My servant
Dawiḏ, 'Thus said יהוה, "You do not build
Me a house to dwell in.
5 "For I have not dwelt in a house since
the time that I brought up Yisra'ěl, even to
this day, but have gone from tent to tent,
and from *one* Dwelling Place *to another*.
6 "Wherever I have moved about with all
Yisra'ěl, have I ever spoken a word to any
of the rulers of Yisra'ěl, whom I commanded to shepherd My people, saying,
'Why have you not built Me a house of
cedar?' " '
7 "And now, say this to My servant
Dawiḏ, 'Thus said יהוה of hosts, "I took
you from the sheepfold, from following
the sheep, to be ruler over My people
Yisra'ěl.
8 "And I have been with you wherever
you have gone, and have cut off all your
enemies from before you, and have made
you a name like the name of the great men
who are on the earth.
9 "And I shall prepare a place for My
people Yisra'ěl and plant them, and they
shall dwell in a place of their own and
move no more, nor shall the sons of
wickedness oppress them any more, as
at the first,
10 since the time that I commanded rulers
to be over My people Yisra'ěl, and I have
humbled all your enemies. And I declared
to you that יהוה does build you a house.
11 "And it shall be, when your days are
filled to go to be with your fathers, that I
shall raise up your seed after you, who is
of your sons. And I shall establish his
reign.
12 "He does build Me a house, and I shall
establish his throne forever.
13 "I am to be his Father, and he is to be
My son. And My loving-commitment I do
not turn away from him, as I took it from
him who was before you.
14 "And I shall establish him in My house
and in My reign forever, and let his throne
be established forever." ' "
15 According to all these words and
according to all this vision, so did Nathan
speak to Dawiḏ.
16 And Sovereign Dawiḏ came in and sat
before יהוה, and said, "Who am I, O יהוה
Elohim? And what is my house, that You
have brought me this far?
17 "And this was a small matter in Your
eyes, O Elohim, but You have spoken of
Your servant's house for a great while to
come, and have looked upon me as though
I were an exalted man , O יהוה Elohim.
18 "What more could Dawiḏ add to You
for the esteem of Your servant? For You
know Your servant.
19 "O יהוה, for Your servant's sake, and
according to Your own heart, You have
done all this greatness, in making known
all these great matters.
20 "O יהוה, there is none like You, nor is
there any Elohim besides You, according
to all that we have heard with our ears.
21 "And who is like Your people Yisra'ěl,
the one nation on the earth whom Elohim
went to redeem for Himself as a people; to

make for Yourself a great and awesome
Name, by driving out nations from before
Your people whom You redeemed from
Mitsrayim?
22 "For You appointed Your people
Yisra'ěl to be Your own people forever.
And You, יהוה, have become their Elohim.
23 "And now, O יהוה, the word which
You have spoken concerning Your servant
and concerning his house, let it stand fast
forever, and do as You have said.
24 "So let it stand fast, and Your Name be
great forever, saying, 'יהוה of hosts,
Elohim of Yisra'ěl, is Elohim to Yisra'ěl.
And let the house of Your servant Dawiḏ
be established before You.'
25 "For You, O my Elohim, have revealed
to Your servant to build a house for him.
Therefore Your servant has found *courage*
to pray before You.
26 "And now, יהוה, You are Elohim, and
have promised this goodness to Your servant.
27 "And now, You have been pleased to
bless the house of Your servant to be
before You forever. For You have blessed
it, O יהוה, and it is blessed forever."

18

And after this it came to be that
Dawiḏ struck the Philistines, and
humbled them, and took Gath and its
towns from the hand of the Philistines.
2 And he struck the Mo'aḇites, and the
Mo'aḇites became Dawiḏ's servants, and
brought presents.
3 And Dawiḏ struck Haḏaḏezer sovereign of Tsoḇah as far as Ḥamath, as he
went to establish his power by the River
Euphrates.
4 And Dawiḏ took from him one thousand chariots, and seven thousand horsemen, and twenty thousand foot soldiers.
And Dawiḏ also hamstrung all the chariot
horses, but left of them for one hundred
chariots.
5 And when Aram of Darmeseq came to
help Haḏaḏezer sovereign of Tsoḇah,
Dawiḏ struck twenty-two thousand of
Aram,
6 and Dawiḏ stationed *men* in Aram of
Darmeseq, and the Arameans became
Dawiḏ's servants, and brought presents.
And יהוה saved Dawiḏ wherever he went.
7 And Dawiḏ took the shields of gold
that were on the servants of Haḏaḏezer,
and brought them to Yerushalayim.
8 And from Tiḇḥath and from Kun, cities
of Haḏaḏezer, Dawiḏ brought a large
amount of bronze, with which Shelomoh
made the bronze Sea, and the columns, and
the vessels of bronze.
9 And when To'u sovereign of Ḥamath
heard that Dawiḏ had stricken all the army
of Haḏaḏezer sovereign of Tsoḇah,
10 he sent Haḏoram his son to Sovereign
Dawiḏ, to ask peace of him and bless him,
because he had fought against Haḏaḏezer
and struck him – because Haḏaḏezer had
been fighting against To'u – with all kinds
of objects of gold, and silver, and bronze.
11 Sovereign Dawiḏ also set these apart to
יהוה, along with the silver and gold that he
had brought from all these nations, from
Eḏom, and from Mo'aḇ, and from the
children of Ammon, and from the
Philistines, and from Amalěq.
12 And Aḇishai son of Tseruyah struck
eighteen thousand Eḏomites in the Valley
of Salt,
13 and he put watch-posts in Eḏom, and
all the Eḏomites became Dawiḏ's servants.
And יהוה saved Dawiḏ wherever he went.
14 So Dawiḏ reigned over all Yisra'ěl, and
he was doing right-ruling and righteousness to all his people.
15 And Yo'aḇ son of Tseruyah was over
the army, and Yehoshaphat son of Aḥiluḏ
was recorder,
16 and Tsaḏoq son of Aḥituḇ and
Aḇimeleḵ son of Eḇyathar were the priests,
and Shawsha was the scribe,
17 and Benayahu son of Yehoyaḏa was
over the Kerěthites and the Pelěthites. And
the sons of Dawiḏ were chiefs at the sovereign's side.

19

And after this it came to be that
Naḥash the sovereign of the children of Ammon died, and his son reigned
in his place.
2 And Dawiḏ said, "Let me show loving-commitment to Ḥanun son of Naḥash,

because his father showed loving-commitment to me." So Dawiḏ sent messengers to
comfort him concerning his father. And the
servants of Dawiḏ came to Ḥanun in the
land of the children of Ammon to comfort
him.
3 And the chiefs of the children of
Ammon said to Ḥanun, "Is Dawiḏ esteeming your father, in your eyes, because he
has sent comforters to you? Have his
servants not come to you to search and to
overthrow and to spy out the land?"
4 So Ḥanun took Dawiḏ's servants, and
shaved them, and cut off their garments in
the middle, at their buttocks, and sent them
away.
5 And when *some* went and informed
Dawiḏ about the men, he sent to meet
them, because the men were greatly
ashamed. And the sovereign said, "Remain
at Yeriḥo until your beards have grown,
then return."
6 And when the children of Ammon saw
that they had made themselves a stench to
Dawiḏ, Ḥanun and the children of Ammon
sent a thousand talents of silver to hire
chariots and horsemen from Aram-
Naharayim, and from Aram-Maʿaḵah, and
from Tsoḇah.
7 So they hired for themselves thirty-two
thousand chariots, with the sovereign of
Maʿaḵah and his people, who came and
encamped before Měyḏeḇa. And the children of Ammon had gathered from their
cities, and came to battle.
8 And when Dawiḏ heard, he sent Yo'aḇ
and the entire army of the mighty men,
9 and the children of Ammon came out
and put themselves in battle array before
the gate of the city, and the sovereigns who
had come were by themselves in the field.
10 And when Yo'aḇ saw that the battle had
been set against him before and behind, he
chose some of the choice ones of Yisra'ěl,
and put them in battle array to meet Aram.
11 And the rest of the people he put under
the command of Aḇishai his brother, and
they set themselves in battle array to meet
the children of Ammon.
12 And he said, "If Aram is too strong for
me, then you shall help me; but if the
children of Ammon are too strong for you,
then I shall help you.
13 "Be strong, and let us show strength for
our people and for the cities of our Elohim,
and let יהוה do what is good in His eyes."
14 And Yo'aḇ drew near, and the people
with him, to battle against Aram, and they
fled before him.
15 And when the children of Ammon saw
that the Arameans were fleeing, they also
fled before Aḇishai his brother, and went
into the city. And Yo'aḇ came to Yerushalayim.
16 And when Aram saw that they had been
smitten before Yisra'ěl, they sent messengers and brought the Arameans who were
beyond the River, and Shophaḵ the
commander of Haḏaḏezer's army went
before them.
17 And it was reported to Dawiḏ, and he
gathered all Yisra'ěl, and passed over the
Yarděn and came upon them, and set up in
battle array against them. And Dawiḏ set
up in battle array against Aram, and they
fought with him.
18 And Aram fled before Yisra'ěl, and
Dawiḏ killed seven thousand charioteers
and forty thousand foot soldiers of the
Arameans, and smote Shophaḵ the
commander of the army.
19 And the servants of Haḏaḏezer saw that
they were smitten by Yisra'ěl, and they
made peace with Dawiḏ and became his
servants. And the Arameans would not
help the children of Ammon any more.

20 And it came to be at the turn of the
year, at the time sovereigns go out
to battle, that Yo'aḇ led out the power of
the army and destroyed the land of the
children of Ammon, and came and
besieged Rabbah. But Dawiḏ remained at
Yerushalayim. And Yo'aḇ struck Rabbah
and overthrew it.
2 And Dawiḏ took their sovereign's
crown from his head, and found it weighed
a talent of gold, and there were precious
stones in it. And it was set on Dawiḏ's
head. And he also brought out the spoil of
the city, a very great amount.
3 And he brought out the people who

were in it, and put them to work with saws, and with iron picks, and with axes. And thus Dawiḏ did to all the cities of the children of Ammon. Then Dawiḏ and all the people returned to Yerushalayim.

4 And afterward it came to be that fighting broke out at Gezer with the Philistines. Then Sibbeḵai the Ḥushathite struck Sippai of the sons of the giant, and they were humbled.

5 And there was fighting again with the Philistines, and Elḥanan son of Ya'ir struck Laḥmi the brother of Golyath the Gittite, the shaft of whose spear was like a weaver's beam.

6 And there was fighting again at Gath, where there was a man of great size, with twenty-four fingers and toes, six and six. And he too was born to the giant.

7 And he reproached Yisra'ĕl, and Yehonathan son of Shimʽa, Dawiḏ's brother, struck him.

8 These were born to the giant in Gath, and they fell by the hand of Dawiḏ and by the hand of his servants.

21 And Satan stood up against Yisra'ĕl, and moved Dawiḏ to number Yisra'ĕl.

2 And Dawiḏ said to Yo'aḇ and to the rulers of the people, "Go, number Yisra'ĕl from Be'ĕrsheḇa to Dan, and bring the number of them to me so that I know it."

3 And Yo'aḇ answered, "יהוה does add to His people a hundred times more than they are. But, my master the sovereign, are they not all my master's servants? Why does my master seek to do this? Why should he be a cause of guilt in Yisra'ĕl?"

4 But the sovereign's word was strong against Yo'aḇ. And Yo'aḇ left and went throughout all Yisra'ĕl and came to Yerushalayim.

5 And Yo'aḇ gave the sum of the number of the people to Dawiḏ. And all Yisra'ĕl had one million one hundred thousand men who drew the sword, and Yehuḏah had four hundred and seventy thousand men who drew the sword.

6 But he did not number Lĕwi and Binyamin among them, for the sovereign's word was loathsome to Yo'aḇ.

7 And it was evil in the eyes of Elohim, concerning this matter, and He struck Yisra'ĕl.

8 Then Dawiḏ said to Elohim, "I have sinned greatly, because I have done this matter. But now, I pray, take away the crookedness of Your servant, for I have done very foolishly."

9 And יהוה spoke to Gaḏ, Dawiḏ's seer, saying,

10 "Go, and you shall speak to Dawiḏ, saying, 'Thus said יהוה, "I hold three *options* before you – choose one of them for yourself, and I do it to you." ' "

11 So Gaḏ came to Dawiḏ and said to him, "Thus said יהוה, 'Choose for yourself

12 either three years of scarcity of food, or three new *moons* to be defeated by your foes with the sword of your enemies overtaking you, or else for three days the sword of יהוה, even the plague in the land, with the messenger of יהוה destroying throughout all the borders of Yisra'ĕl.' And now consider what answer I am to return to Him who sent me."

13 And Dawiḏ said to Gaḏ, "I am in great trouble. Please let me fall into the hand of יהוה, for His compassion is very great, but do not let me fall into the hand of man."

14 And יהוה sent a plague upon Yisra'ĕl, and seventy thousand men of Yisra'ĕl fell.

15 And Elohim sent a messenger to Yerushalayim to destroy it. And as he was destroying, יהוה saw, and relented about the evil, and said to the messenger who was destroying, "Enough! Now stop your hand." And the messenger of יהוה was standing by the threshing-floor of Ornan the Yeḇusite.

16 And Dawiḏ lifted his eyes and saw the messenger of יהוה standing between earth and the heavens, having in his hand a drawn sword stretched out over Yerushalayim. And Dawiḏ and the elders, wrapped in sackcloth, fell on their faces.

17 And Dawiḏ said to Elohim, "Was it not I who commanded the people to be numbered? I am the one who has sinned and done evil indeed. But these, the sheep, what have they done? Let Your hand, I

pray, O יהוה my Elohim, be against me
and my father's house, but not against
Your people, to be plagued."
18 And the messenger of יהוה commanded Gad to say to Dawid that Dawid should
go up to raise a slaughter-place to יהוה on
the threshing-floor of Ornan the Yebusite.
19 So Dawid went up at the word of Gad,
which he had spoken in the Name of יהוה.
20 And Ornan turned and saw the messenger. And his four sons with him hid themselves, and Ornan was threshing wheat.
21 And Dawid came to Ornan, and Ornan
looked and saw Dawid, and he went out
from the threshing-floor, and bowed down
to Dawid with his face to the ground.
22 And Dawid said to Ornan, "Give me
the site of the threshing-floor, so that I
build a slaughter-place to יהוה on it. Give
it to me at the complete price, so that the
plague is restrained from the people."
23 And Ornan said to Dawid, "Take it for
yourself, and let my master the sovereign
do what is good in his eyes. See, I shall
give you the cattle for ascending offerings,
the threshing implements for wood, and
the wheat for the grain offering. I give it
all."
24 And Sovereign Dawid said to Ornan,
"No, but I shall certainly buy it at the complete price, for I do not take what is yours
for יהוה, nor offer an ascending offering
without cost."
25 And Dawid gave Ornan six hundred
sheqels of gold by weight for the place.
26 And Dawid built there a slaughter-place to יהוה, and offered ascending offerings and peace offerings, and called on
יהוה. And He answered him from the
heavens by fire on the slaughter-place of
ascending offering.
27 Then יהוה commanded the messenger,
and he returned his sword to its sheath.
28 At that time, when Dawid saw that
יהוה had answered him on the threshing-floor of Ornan the Yebusite, he slaughtered
there,
29 for the Dwelling Place of יהוה and the
slaughter-place of the ascending offering,
which Mosheh had made in the wilderness,
were at that time at the high place in
Gib'on.
30 But Dawid was unable to go before it to
inquire of Elohim, for he was afraid of the
sword of the messenger of יהוה.

22

Dawid then said, "This is the
House of יהוה Elohim, and this is
the slaughter-place of ascending offering
for Yisra'ěl."
2 And Dawid commanded to gather the
foreigners who were in the land of
Yisra'ěl. And he appointed stonemasons to
cut hewn stones to build the House of
Elohim.
3 And Dawid prepared large quantities of
iron for the nails of the doors of the gates
and for the clamps, and more bronze than
could be weighed,
4 and cedar trees beyond number, for the
Tsidonians and those from Tsor brought
much cedar wood to Dawid.
5 And Dawid said, "Shelomoh my son is
young and tender, and the house that is to
be built for יהוה is to be exceedingly great,
for a splendid Name, to all the lands.
Please, let me make preparation for it." So
Dawid made extensive preparations before
his death.
6 He also called for his son Shelomoh,
and commanded him to build a house for
יהוה Elohim of Yisra'ěl.
7 And Dawid said to Shelomoh, "My
son, as for me, it has been in my heart to
build a house to the Name of יהוה my
Elohim,
8 but the word of יהוה came to me,
saying, 'You have shed much blood and
have fought great battles. You do not build
a house for My Name, because you have
shed much blood on the earth in My presence.
9 'See, a son is to be born to you, who is
a man of rest. And I shall give him rest
from all his enemies all around, for
Shelomoh is his name, and peace and rest I
give to Yisra'ěl in his days.
10 'He does build a house for My Name,
and he is to be My son, and I am to be his
Father. And I shall establish the throne of
his reign over Yisra'ěl forever.'
11 "Now, my son, יהוה be with you, then

you shall prosper and build the House of
יהוה your Elohim, as He has said to you.
12 "Only, let יהוה give you wisdom and
understanding, and command you concerning Yisra'ĕl, so that you guard the Torah of
יהוה your Elohim,
13 then you shall prosper, if you guard to
do the laws and right-rulings with which
יהוה commanded Mosheh concerning
Yisra'ĕl. Be strong and brave, do not fear
nor be discouraged.
14 "See, in my affliction I have prepared
for the House of יהוה one hundred thousand talents of gold and one million talents
of silver, and bronze and iron beyond measure, for it is plenty. And I have prepared
timber and stone, and you shall add to
them.
15 "And with you there are many workmen: hewers and workers of stone and
timber, and all types of skilled men for
every kind of work.
16 "Of gold and silver and bronze and iron
there is no limit. Rise up and do, and יהוה
is with you."
17 And Dawiḏ commanded all the rulers
of Yisra'ĕl to help Shelomoh his son,
saying,
18 "Is not יהוה your Elohim with you?
And has He not given you rest all around?
For He has given the inhabitants of the
land into my hand, and the land has been
subdued before יהוה and before His people.
19 "Now, give your heart and your being
to seek יהוה your Elohim. And rise up and
build the set-apart place of יהוה Elohim, to
bring the ark of the covenant of יהוה and
the set-apart vessels of Elohim into the
house that is to be built for the Name
of יהוה."

23 And Dawiḏ was old and satisfied
with days, and he made his son
Shelomoh to reign over Yisra'ĕl,
2 and he gathered all the rulers of
Yisra'ĕl, with the priests and the Lĕwites.
3 And the Lĕwites were numbered from
the age of thirty years and above. And their
number, head by head, was thirty-eight
thousand males.
4 Of these, twenty-four thousand were to
oversee the work of the House of יהוה, and
six thousand were officers and judges,
5 and four thousand were gatekeepers,
and four thousand to give praise to יהוה,
"which I made for giving praise."
6 And Dawiḏ divided them into divisions, of the sons of Lĕwi: of Gĕrshon,
Qehath, and Merari.
7 Of the Gĕrshonites: La'dan and Shim'i.
8 The sons of La'dan: Yeḥi'ĕl the head,
then Zĕtham and Yo'ĕl, three.
9 The sons of Shim'i: Shelomith, and
Ḥazi'ĕl, and Haran, three. These were the
heads of the fathers' houses of La'dan.
10 And the sons of Shim'i: Yaḥath, Zina,
and Ye'ush, and Beri'ah. These were the
four sons of Shim'i.
11 And Yaḥath was the head and Zizah the
second. But Ye'ush and Beri'ah did not
have many sons, so they were reckoned as
one father's house.
12 The sons of Qehath: Amram, Yitshar,
Ḥeḇron, and Uzzi'ĕl, four.
13 The sons of Amram: Aharon and
Mosheh. And Aharon was set apart, he and
his sons forever, that he should set apart
the most set-apart, to burn incense before
יהוה, to serve Him, and to give the blessing in His Name forever.
14 Now Mosheh, the man of Elohim, his
sons were named after the tribe of Lĕwi.
15 The sons of Mosheh: Gĕreshom and
Eli'ezer.
16 The sons of Gĕreshom: Sheḇu'ĕl was
the head.
17 And the sons of Eli'ezer: Reḥaḇyah was
the head. And Eli'ezer had no other sons,
but the sons of Reḥaḇyah were very many.
18 The sons of Yitshar: Shelomith was the
head.
19 The sons of Ḥeḇron: Yeriyahu was the
head, Amaryah the second, Yaḥazi'ĕl the
third, and Yeqam'am the fourth.
20 The sons of Uzzi'ĕl: Miḵah was the
head and Yishshiyah the second.
21 The sons of Merari: Maḥli and Mushi.
The sons of Maḥli: El'azar and Qish.
22 And El'azar died, and had no sons, but
only daughters. And their brothers, the
sons of Qish, took them.

23 The sons of Mushi: Maḥli, Ěḏer, and
Yerěmoth, three.
24 These were the sons of Lěwi by their
fathers' houses, the heads of the fathers'
houses as they were counted head by head
by the number of their names, who did the
work for the service of the House of יהוה,
from the age of twenty years and above.
25 For Dawiḏ said, "יהוה Elohim of
Yisra'ěl has given rest to His people, and
He dwells in Yerushalayim forever,"
26 and also of the Lěwites, "They shall no
longer bear the Dwelling Place, or any of
the vessels for its service."
27 For by the last words of Dawiḏ the
Lěwites were numbered from twenty years
old and above,
28 because their duty was to help the sons
of Aharon in the service of the House of
יהוה, in the courtyards and in the rooms, in
the cleansing of all that was set-apart, and
the work of the service of the House of
Elohim,
29 both with the showbread and the fine
flour for the grain offering, and with the
unleavened cakes and what is baked on the
griddle, and with what is mixed and with
all kinds of measures and sizes;
30 and to stand every morning to thank
and praise יהוה, and so at evening;
31 and for all the ascending offerings to
יהוה on the sabbaths and on the new
moons and on the appointed times, by
number according to the right-ruling upon
them, continually before יהוה;
32 and that they should guard the duty of
the Tent of Appointment, the duty of the
set-apart place, and the duty of the sons of
Aharon their brothers in the service of the
House of יהוה.

24 And the divisions of the sons of
Aharon: The sons of Aharon were
Naḏaḇ and Aḇihu, El'azar and Ithamar.
2 But Naḏaḇ and Aḇihu died before their
father, and had no children, so El'azar and
Ithamar served as priests.
3 And Dawiḏ, with Tsaḏoq of the sons of
El'azar, and Aḥimeleḵ of the sons of
Ithamar, divided them according to their
offices in their service.
4 And there were more leaders found of
the sons of El'azar than of the sons of
Ithamar. So they divided the sons of
El'azar into sixteen heads of their fathers'
houses, and the sons of Ithamar into eight
heads of their fathers' houses.
5 And they were divided by lot, one
group as another, for there were officials of
the set-apart place and officials of Elohim,
from the sons of El'azar and from the sons
of Ithamar.
6 And the scribe, Shemayah son of
Nethaně'l, one of the Lěwites, wrote them
down before the sovereign, and the rulers,
and Tsaḏoq the priest, and Aḥimeleḵ son
of Eḇyathar, and the heads of the fathers'
houses of the priests and Lěwites, one
father's house taken for El'azar and one for
Ithamar.
7 And the first lot came forth to
Yehoyariḇ, the second to Yeḏayah,
8 the third to Ḥarim, the fourth to
Se'orim,
9 the fifth to Malkiyah, the sixth to
Miyamin,
10 the seventh to Haqqots, the eighth to
Aḇiyah,
11 the ninth to Yěshua, the tenth to
Sheḵanyahu,
12 the eleventh to Elyashiḇ, the twelfth to
Yaqim,
13 the thirteenth to Ḥuppah, the fourteenth
to Yesheḇ'aḇ,
14 the fifteenth to Bilgah, the sixteenth to
Imměr,
15 the seventeenth to Ḥězir, the eighteenth
to Happitstsěts,
16 the nineteenth to Pethaḥyah, the twentieth to Yeḥezqěl,
17 the twenty-first to Yaḵin, the twenty-
second to Gamul,
18 the twenty-third to Delayahu, the twenty-fourth to Ma'azyahu.
19 These were their offices in their service
for coming into the House of יהוה according to their right-ruling by the hand of
Aharon their father, as יהוה Elohim of
Yisra'ěl had commanded him.
20 And the rest of the sons of Lěwi: of the
sons of Amram, Shuḇa'ěl; of the sons of
Shuḇa'ěl, Yeḥdeyahu.

21 Concerning Reḥaḇyahu, of the sons of
Reḥaḇyahu, the head was Yishshiyah.
22 Of the Yitsharites, Shelomoth; of the
sons of Shelomoth, Yaḥath.
23 Of the sons *of Ḥeḇron*, Yeriyahu *was
the head*, Amaryahu the second, Yaḥazi'ěl
the third, and Yeqam'am the fourth.
24 Of the sons of Uzzi'ěl, Miḵah; of the
sons of Miḵah, Shamir.
25 The brother of Miḵah, Yishshiyah; of
the sons of Yishshiyah, Zeḵaryahu.
26 The sons of Merari: Maḥli and Mushi;
the son of Ya'aziyahu, Beno.
27 The sons of Merari by Ya'aziyahu:
Beno, and Shoham, and Zakkur, and Iḇri.
28 Of Maḥli: El'azar, who had no sons.
29 Of Qish: the son of Qish, Yeraḥme'ěl.
30 And the sons of Mushi: Maḥli, Ěḏer,
and Yerimoth. These were the sons of the
Lěwites according to their fathers' houses.
31 These also cast lots, they too, as their
brothers the sons of Aharon, in the
presence of Sovereign Dawiḏ, and Tsaḏoq,
and Aḥimeleḵ, and the heads of the
fathers' houses of the priests and Lěwites –
the head of the fathers, as well as his
younger brothers.

25 And Dawiḏ and the commanders
of the army separated for the service some of the sons of Asaph, and of
Hěman, and of Yeḏuthun, who should
prophesy with lyres, with harps, and with
cymbals. And the number of the workmen
according to their service was:
2 Of the sons of Asaph: Zakkur, and
Yosěph, and Nethanyah, and Ashar'ělah,
the sons of Asaph at the hands of Asaph,
who prophesied at the hands of the sovereign.
3 Of Yeḏuthun, the sons of Yeḏuthun:
Geḏalyahu, and Tseri, and Yeshayahu,
Ḥashaḇyahu, and Mattithyahu, six, under
the hands of their father Yeḏuthun, who
prophesied with a lyre to give thanks and
to praise יהוה.
4 Of Hěman, the sons of Hěman:
Buqqiyahu, Mattanyahu, Uzzi'ěl, Sheḇu'ěl, and Yerimoth, Ḥananyah, Ḥanani,
Eliyathah, Giddalti, and Romamti-Ezer,
Yoshbeqashah, Mallothi, Hothir, Maḥaziyoth.
5 All these were the sons of Hěman the
sovereign's seer in the words of Elohim, to
exalt his horn. For Elohim gave Hěman
fourteen sons and three daughters.
6 All these were at the hands of their
father for song in the House of יהוה, with
cymbals, harps and lyres, for the service of
the House of Elohim: Asaph, Yeḏuthun,
and Hěman, at the hands of the sovereign.
7 And the number of them, with their
brothers who were taught in the songs of
יהוה, all who were skilled, was two hundred and eighty-eight.
8 And they cast lots for their duty, the
small as well as the great, the teacher with
the student.
9 And the first lot for Asaph came forth
for Yosěph; Geḏalyahu the second, he, and
his brothers and sons, twelve;
10 the third Zakkur, his sons and his brothers, twelve;
11 the fourth Yitsri, his sons and his brothers, twelve;
12 the fifth Nethanyahu, his sons and his
brothers, twelve;
13 the sixth Buqqiyahu, his sons and his
brothers, twelve;
14 the seventh Yesar'ělah, his sons and his
brothers, twelve;
15 the eighth Yeshayahu, his sons and his
brothers, twelve;
16 the ninth Mattanyahu, his sons and his
brothers, twelve;
17 the tenth Shim'i, his sons and his brothers, twelve;
18 the eleventh Azar'ěl, his sons and his
brothers, twelve;
19 the twelfth Ḥashaḇyah, his sons and his
brothers, twelve;
20 the thirteenth Shuḇa'ěl, his sons and his
brothers, twelve;
21 the fourteenth Mattithyahu, his sons
and his brothers, twelve;
22 the fifteenth Yerěmoth, his sons and his
brothers, twelve;
23 the sixteenth Ḥananyahu, his sons and
his brothers, twelve;
24 the seventeenth Yoshbeqashah, his sons
and his brothers, twelve;
25 the eighteenth Ḥanani, his sons and his

brothers, twelve;
26 the nineteenth Mallothi, his sons and his brothers, twelve;
27 the twentieth Eliyathah, his sons and his brothers, twelve;
28 the twenty-first Hothir, his sons and his brothers, twelve;
29 the twenty-second Giddalti, his sons and his brothers, twelve;
30 the twenty-third Maḥaziyoth, his sons and his brothers, twelve;
31 the twenty-fourth Romamti-Ezer, his sons and his brothers, twelve.

26 For the divisions of the gatekeepers: Of the Qorḥites, Meshelemyahu son of Qorĕ, of the sons of Asaph.
2 And the sons of Meshelemyahu: Zeḵaryahu the first-born, Yeḏiya'ĕl the second, Zeḇaḏyahu the third, Yathni'ĕl the fourth,
3 Ěylam the fifth, Yehoḥanan the sixth, Elyo'ĕynai the seventh.
4 And the sons of Oḇĕḏ-Eḏom: Shemayah the first-born, Yehozaḇaḏ the second, Yo'aḥ the third, Saḵar the fourth, Nethanĕ'l the fifth,
5 Ammi'ĕl the sixth, Yissasḵar the seventh, Pe'ullethai the eighth, for Elohim blessed him.
6 Also to Shemayah his son were sons born who ruled their fathers' houses, because they were able mighty men.
7 The sons of Shemayah: Othni, and Repha'ĕl, and Oḇĕḏ, Elzaḇaḏ, whose brothers Elihu and Semaḵyahu were able men.
8 All these were of the sons of Oḇĕḏ-Eḏom, they and their sons and their brothers, able men with strength for the work: sixty-two of Oḇĕḏ-Eḏom.
9 And Meshelemyahu had sons and brothers, eighteen able men.
10 Also Ḥosah, of the children of Merari, had sons: Shimri the head (although he was not the first-born, his father made him the head),
11 Ḥilqiyahu the second, Teḇalyahu the third, Zeḵaryahu the fourth. All the sons and brothers of Ḥosah were thirteen.
12 These divisions of the gatekeepers, among the chief men, had duties like their brothers, to serve in the House of יהוה.
13 And they cast lots for each gate, the small as well as the great, according to their father's house.
14 And the lot to the east fell to Shelemyahu. Then they cast lots for his son Zeḵaryahu, a wise counsellor, and his lot came out to the north;
15 to Oḇĕḏ-Eḏom to the south, and to his sons the storehouse;
16 to Shuppim and Ḥosah to the west, with the Shalleḵeth Gate on the ascending highway; guard corresponding with guard.
17 On the east were six Lĕwites, on the north four each day, on the south four each day, and for the storehouse two by two.
18 As for the Parbar on the west, there were four on the highway and two at the Parbar.
19 These were the divisions of the gatekeepers among the sons of Qoraḥ and among the sons of Merari.
20 And of the Lĕwites, Aḥiyah was over the treasuries of the House of Elohim and over the treasuries of the set-apart *gifts*.
21 The sons of La'dan, the sons of the Gĕrshonites of La'dan, heads of their fathers' houses, of La'dan the Gĕrshonite: Yeḥi'ĕli.
22 The sons of Yeḥi'ĕli, Zĕtham and Yo'ĕl his brother, were over the treasuries of the House of יהוה.
23 Of the Amramites, the Yitsharites, the Ḥeḇronites, and the Uzzi'ĕlites,
24 even Sheḇu'ĕl son of Gĕreshom, son of Mosheh, was overseer of the treasuries.
25 And his brothers by Eli'ezer were Reḥaḇyahu his son, and Yeshayahu his son, and Yoram his son, and Ziḵri his son, and Shelomoth his son.
26 This Shelomoth and his brothers were over all the treasuries of the set-apart *gifts* which Sovereign Dawiḏ and the heads of fathers' houses, the commanders over thousands and hundreds, and the commanders of the army, had set apart.
27 Some of the booty won in battles they set apart to maintain the House of יהוה.
28 And all that Shemu'ĕl the seer, and

Sha'ul son of Qish, and Aḇněr son of Něr,
and Yo'aḇ son of Tseruyah had set apart,
all who were setting apart, were under the
hand of Shelomith and his brothers.
29 Of the Yitsharites, Kenanyahu and his
sons were for the outward duties as officials and judges over Yisra'ěl.
30 Of the Ḥeḇronites, Ḥashaḇyahu and his
brothers, one thousand seven hundred able
men, had the oversight of Yisra'ěl beyond
the Yarděn westward, for all the work of
יהוה, and in the service of the sovereign.
31 Of the Ḥeḇronites, Yeriyah was head of
the Ḥeḇronites according to his genealogy
of the fathers. In the fortieth year of the
reign of Dawiḏ they were sought, and there
were found among them able men at Ya'zěr
of Gil'aḏ.
32 And his brothers were two thousand
seven hundred able men, heads of fathers'
houses, whom Sovereign Dawiḏ made
officials over the Re'uḇěnites, and the
Gaḏites, and the half-tribe of Menashsheh,
in all matters of Elohim and matters of the
sovereign.

27 And the children of Yisra'ěl,
according to their number, the
heads of fathers' *houses*, and the commanders of thousands and hundreds and their
officers, served the sovereign in all matters
of the divisions which came in and went
out new *moon* by new *moon* throughout all
the new *moons* of the year, each division
having twenty-four thousand.
2 Over the first division for the first new
moon was Yashoḇ'am son of Zaḇdi'ěl, and
in his division were twenty-four thousand;
3 of the sons of Perets, and the chief of
all the commanders of the army for the
first new *moon*.
4 And over the division of the second
new *moon* was Doḏai an Aḥoḥite, and of
his division Miqloth also was the leader,
and in his division were twenty-four thousand.
5 The third commander of the army for
the third new *moon* was Benayahu, son of
Yehoyaḏa the priest, who was chief, and in
his division were twenty-four thousand.
6 This was the Benayahu who was
mighty among the thirty, and was over the
thirty, and in his division was Ammizaḇaḏ
his son.
7 The fourth for the fourth new *moon* was
Asah'ěl the brother of Yo'aḇ, and
Zeḇaḏyah his son after him, and in his
division were twenty-four thousand.
8 The fifth for the fifth new *moon* was
Shamhuth the Yizraḥite, and in his division
were twenty-four thousand.
9 The sixth for the sixth new *moon* was
Ira son of Iqqěsh the Teqowite, and in his
division were twenty-four thousand.
10 The seventh for the seventh new *moon*
was Ḥělets the Pelonite, of the children of
Ephrayim, and in his division were twenty-
four thousand.
11 The eighth for the eighth new *moon*
was Sibbeḵai the Ḥushathite, of the
Zarḥites, and in his division were twenty-
four thousand.
12 The ninth for the ninth new *moon* was
Aḇi'ezer the Anathothite, of the
Binyamites, and in his division were twenty-four thousand.
13 The tenth for the tenth new *moon* was
Maharai the Netophathite, of the Zarḥites,
and in his division were twenty-four thousand.
14 The eleventh for the eleventh new
moon was Benayah the Pirathonite, of the
children of Ephrayim, and in his division
were twenty-four thousand.
15 The twelfth for the twelfth new *moon*
was Ḥeldai the Netophathite, of Othni'ěl,
and in his division were twenty-four thousand.
16 And over the tribes of Yisra'ěl: the
chief officer over Re'uḇěn: Eli'ezer son of
Ziḵri; over Shim'on: Shephatyahu son of
Ma'aḵah;
17 Lěwi: Ḥashaḇyah son of Qemu'ěl; over
Aharon: Tsaḏoq;
18 Yehuḏah: Elihu, one of Dawiḏ's
brothers; Yissasḵar: Omri son of Miḵa'ěl;
19 Zeḇulun: Yishmayahu son of Oḇaḏyahu; Naphtali: Yerimoth son of Azri'ěl;
20 the children of Ephrayim: Hoshěa son
of Azazyahu; the half-tribe of Menashsheh: Yo'ěl son of Peḏayahu;
21 the half-tribe of Menashsheh in Gil'aḏ:

Iddo son of Zekaryahu; Binyamin: Ya'asi'ěl son of Aḇněr;
22 Dan: Azar'ěl son of Yeroḥam. These were the rulers of the tribes of Yisra'ěl.
23 But Dawiḏ did not take the number of those twenty years old and under, because יהוה had said He would increase Yisra'ěl like the stars of the heavens.
24 Yo'aḇ son of Tseruyah began a census, but he did not finish, for wrath came upon Yisra'ěl because of this census; nor was the number recorded in the account of the annals of Sovereign Dawiḏ.
25 And Azmaweth son of Aḏi'ěl was over the sovereign's treasuries. And Yehonathan son of Uzziyahu was over the storehouses in the field, in the cities, and in the villages, and in the watchtowers.
26 And Ezri son of Keluḇ was over those who did the work of the field for tilling the ground.
27 And Shim'i the Ramathite was over the vineyards, and Zaḇdi the Shiphmite was over the increase of the vineyards for the wine cellars.
28 And Ba'al-Ḥanan the Geḏěrite was over the olive trees and the sycamore trees that were in the low country, and Yo'ash was over the oil-stores.
29 And Shitrai the Sharonite was over the herds that fed in Sharon, and Shaphat son of Aḏlai was over the herds that were in the valleys.
30 And Oḇil the Yishma'ělite was over the camels, and Yeḥdeyahu the Měronothite was over the donkeys,
31 and Yaziz the Haḡrite was over the flocks. All of these were heads over the property of Sovereign Dawiḏ.
32 Also Yehonathan, Dawiḏ's uncle, was a counsellor, a wise man and a scribe. And Yeḥi'ěl son of Ḥakmoni was with the sovereign's sons.
33 And Aḥithophel was the sovereign's counsellor, and Ḥushai the Arkite was the sovereign's companion.
34 And after Aḥithophel was Yehoyaḏa son of Benayahu, then Eḇyathar. And the chief of the sovereign's army was Yo'aḇ.

28 And Dawiḏ assembled at Yerushalayim all the rulers of Yisra'ěl: the rulers of the tribes and the commanders of the divisions who served the sovereign, the commanders over thousands and commanders over hundreds, and the heads over all the property and possessions of the sovereign and of his sons, with the officials, the mighty men, and all the mighty brave men.
2 Then Sovereign Dawiḏ rose to his feet and said, "Hear me, my brothers and my people: I had it in my heart to build a house of rest for the ark of the covenant of יהוה, and for the footstool of our Elohim, and had made preparations to build it.
3 "But Elohim said to me, 'You do not build a house for My Name, because you have been a man of battle and have shed blood.'
4 "Yet יהוה Elohim of Yisra'ěl chose me above all the house of my father to be sovereign over Yisra'ěl forever, for He has chosen Yehuḏah to be the ruler. And of the house of Yehuḏah, the house of my father, and among the sons of my father, He was pleased with me to make me reign over all Yisra'ěl.
5 "And of all my sons – for יהוה has given me many sons – He has chosen my son Shelomoh to sit on the throne of the reign of יהוה over Yisra'ěl,
6 and said to me, 'Shelomoh your son is the one to build My house and My courtyards, for I have chosen him to be My son, and I Myself am a Father to him.
7 'And I shall establish his reign forever, if he is strong to do My commands and My right-rulings, as it is this day.'
8 "And now, before the eyes of all Yisra'ěl, the assembly of יהוה, and in the hearing of our Elohim, guard and seek all the commands of יהוה your Elohim, so that you possess this good land, and leave it as an inheritance for your children after you forever.
9 "As for you, my son Shelomoh, know the Elohim of your father, and serve Him with a perfect heart and with a pleasing life, for יהוה searches all hearts and understands all the intent of the thoughts. If you

do seek Him, He is found by you; but if you forsake Him, He rejects you forever.

10 "See, now, for יהוה has chosen you to build a house for the set-apart place. Be strong, and do it."

11 And Dawiḏ gave his son Shelomoh the plans for the porch, and its houses, and its treasuries, and its upper rooms, and its inner rooms, and the place of atonement;

12 and the plans for all that he had by the Spirit, of the courtyards of the House of יהוה, and of all the rooms all around, and of the treasuries of the House of Elohim, and of the treasuries for the set-apart *gifts*;

13 and for the divisions of the priests and the Lĕwites, and for all the work of the service of the House of יהוה, and for all the vessels of service in the House of יהוה;

14 even gold by weight for *utensils* of gold, for all utensils used in every kind of service; for silver for all utensils of silver by weight, for all utensils used in every kind of service;

15 and by weight for the lampstands of gold, and their lamps of gold, by weight for each lampstand and its lamps; and for the lampstands of silver by weight, for the lampstand and its lamps, according to the use of each lampstand;

16 and by weight gold for the tables of the showbread, for each table, and silver for the tables of silver;

17 and clean gold for the forks, and the basins, and the jars of clean gold, and the golden bowls, by weight for every bowl; and for the silver bowls, silver by weight for every bowl;

18 and refined gold by weight for the slaughter-place of incense, and for the pattern of the chariot of the gold keruḇim, spreading out their wings and covering over the ark of the covenant of יהוה.

19 "יהוה made me understand all this in writing, by His hand upon me, all the works of these plans."

20 And Dawiḏ said to his son Shelomoh, "Be strong and courageous, and do it. Do not fear nor be afraid, for יהוה Elohim, my Elohim, is with you. He shall not leave you nor forsake you, until you have completed all the work for the service of the House of יהוה.

21 "And see, the divisions of the priests and the Lĕwites for all the service of the House of Elohim, and every volunteer of any skill is with you in all work, for every kind of service. And the rulers and all the people are entirely at your command."

29 And Dawiḏ the sovereign said to all the assembly, "My son Shelomoh, the one whom Elohim has chosen, is young and tender. And the work is great, because the palace is not for man but for יהוה Elohim.

2 "And with all my power I have prepared for the House of my Elohim: the gold for the gold, and the silver for the silver, and the bronze for the bronze, the iron for the iron, and the wood for the wood, shoham stones, and settings, and fair stones of various colours, and all kinds of precious stones, and marble slabs – in large quantities.

3 "And also, because I delighted in the House of my Elohim, I have treasure of gold and silver; I give for the House of my Elohim even more than all that I have prepared for the Set-apart House:

4 three thousand talents of gold, of the gold of Ophir, and seven thousand talents of refined silver, to overlay the walls of the houses;

5 the gold for the gold and the silver for the silver, and for all kinds of work to be done by the hands of craftsmen. Who then is moved to fill his hand today for יהוה?"

6 And the leaders of the fathers' *houses*, and the leaders of the tribes of Yisra'ĕl, and the commanders of thousands and of hundreds, with the heads over the sovereign's work, volunteered

7 and gave for the work of the House of Elohim five thousand talents and ten thousand darics of gold, and ten thousand talents of silver, and eighteen thousand talents of bronze, and one hundred thousand talents of iron.

8 And those with whom were found precious *stones* gave them to the treasury of the House of יהוה, into the hand of Yeḥi'ĕl the Gĕrshonite.

9 And the people rejoiced, for they had given voluntarily, because with a perfect heart they had given voluntarily to יהוה. And Dawiḏ the sovereign also rejoiced greatly.

10 And Dawiḏ blessed יהוה before all the assembly. And Dawiḏ said, “Blessed are You, יהוה Elohim of Yisra’ěl, our Father, forever and ever.

11 “Yours, O יהוה, is the greatness, the power and the comeliness, the pre-eminence and the excellency, because of all that is in the heavens and in the earth. Yours is the reign, O יהוה, and You are exalted as head above all.

12 “And the riches and the esteem come from Your presence, and You rule over all. And in Your hand is power and might, and in Your hand to make great and to give strength to all.

13 “And now, our Elohim, we thank You and praise Your comely Name.

14 “But who am I, and who are my people, that we should be able to give so voluntarily as this? For all comes from You, and we have given to You out of Your hand.

15 “For we are sojourners and pilgrims before You, as were all our fathers; our days on earth are as a shadow, and without permanence.

16 “O יהוה our Elohim, all this store that we have prepared to build You a house for Your set-apart Name is from Your hand, and all is of You.

17 “And I know, my Elohim, that You are trying the heart and desire uprightness. As for me, in the uprightness of my heart I have voluntarily given all these. And now with joy I have seen Your people, who are present here to give voluntarily to You.

18 “O יהוה Elohim of Aḇraham, Yitsḥaq, and Yisra’ěl, our fathers, guard this forever in the intent of the thoughts of the heart of Your people, and prepare their heart toward You.

19 “And give my son Shelomoh a perfect heart to guard Your commands and Your witnesses and Your laws, to do all, and to build the palace for which I have prepared.”

20 And Dawiḏ said to all the assembly, “Now bless יהוה your Elohim.” And all the assembly blessed יהוה Elohim of their fathers, and bowed their heads and did obeisance to יהוה and the sovereign.

21 And they slaughtered slaughterings to יהוה and offered ascending offerings to יהוה on the next day: a thousand bulls, a thousand rams, a thousand lambs, with their drink offerings, and slaughterings in large numbers for all Yisra’ěl.

22 And they ate and drank before יהוה with great joy on that day. And they set up Shelomoh son of Dawiḏ to reign the second time, and anointed him before יהוה to be leader, and Tsaḏoq to be priest.

23 And Shelomoh sat on the throne of יהוה as sovereign instead of Dawiḏ his father, and prospered; and all Yisra’ěl obeyed him.

24 And all the rulers and the mighty men, and also all the sons of Sovereign Dawiḏ, submitted themselves to Shelomoh the sovereign.

25 And יהוה exalted Shelomoh exceedingly in the eyes of all Yisra’ěl, and put upon him such royal splendour as had not been on any sovereign before him in Yisra’ěl.

26 Thus Dawiḏ son of Yishai reigned over all Yisra’ěl.

27 And the days that he reigned over Yisra’ěl was forty years. He reigned seven years in Ḥeḇron, and he reigned thirty-three years in Yerushalayim.

28 And he died in a good old age, satisfied with days, riches and esteem. And Shelomoh his son reigned in his place.

29 And the acts of Sovereign Dawiḏ, first and last, see, they are written in the book of Shemu’ěl the seer, in the book of Nathan the prophet, and in the book of Gaḏ the seer,

30 with all his reign and his might, and the times that passed over him, and over Yisra’ěl, and over all the reigns of the lands.

DIḆRE haYAMIM BĚT

2 CHRONICLES (2 ANNALS)

1 And Shelomoh son of Dawiḏ strengthened himself over his reign, and יהוה his Elohim was with him and made him exceedingly great.

2 And Shelomoh spoke to all Yisra'ěl, to the commanders of the thousands and of the hundreds, to the judges, and to every leader in all Yisra'ěl, the heads of the fathers' *houses*.

3 And Shelomoh, and all the assembly with him, went to the high place that was at Giḇ'on, for Elohim's Tent of Meeting was there, which Mosheh the servant of יהוה had made in the wilderness.

4 However, Dawiḏ had brought up the ark of Elohim from Qiryath Ye'arim to the place Dawiḏ had prepared for it, for he had pitched a tent for it in Yerushalayim.

5 And the bronze slaughter-place that Betsal'ěl son of Uri son of Ḥur had made, he put before the Dwelling Place of יהוה. And Shelomoh and the assembly sought it.

6 And Shelomoh went up there to the bronze slaughter-place before יהוה, which was at the Tent of Appointment, and offered a thousand ascending offerings on it.

7 That night Elohim appeared to Shelomoh, and said to him, "Ask what should I give you!"

8 And Shelomoh said to Elohim, "You have shown great loving-commitment to Dawiḏ my father, and have made me sovereign in his place.

9 "Now, יהוה Elohim, let Your promise to Dawiḏ my father stand fast, for You have set me up to reign over a people as numerous as the dust of the earth.

10 "Now give me wisdom and knowledge, so that I go out and come in before this people. For who *is able to* rightly rule this great people of Yours?"

11 And Elohim said to Shelomoh, "Because this was in your heart, and you have not asked riches or wealth or esteem or the life of your enemies, nor have you asked long life, but have asked wisdom and knowledge for yourself, so as to rightly rule My people over whom I have set you up to reign,

12 wisdom and knowledge are given to you. And riches and wealth and esteem I *also* give you, such as none of the sovereigns have had who have been before you, nor any after you have."

13 And Shelomoh went to Yerushalayim from the high place that was at Giḇ'on, from before the Tent of Appointment, and reigned over Yisra'ěl.

14 And Shelomoh gathered chariots and horsemen, and he had one thousand four hundred chariots and twelve thousand horsemen, whom he stationed in the chariot cities and with the sovereign in Yerushalayim.

15 And the sovereign made silver and gold to be as stones in Yerushalayim, and he made cedars to be as plenty as the sycamores which are in the low country.

16 And Shelomoh had horses imported from Mitsrayim and from Quě – the sovereign's merchants bought them in Quě at a price.

17 And they came up and brought from Mitsrayim a chariot for six hundred pieces of silver, and a horse for one hundred and fifty. And so, for all the sovereigns of the Ḥittites and the sovereigns of Aram, they brought them out by their hand.

2 And Shelomoh gave word to build a House for the Name of יהוה, and a house for his reign.

2 Then Shelomoh enrolled seventy thousand men to bear burdens, eighty thousand hewing *stone* in the mountains, and three thousand six hundred to oversee them.

3 And Shelomoh sent to Ḥuram sovereign of Tsor, saying, "As you did for my father Dawiḏ, and sent him cedars to build

himself a house to dwell in –
4 see, I am building a House for the
Name of יהוה my Elohim, to set it apart to
Him, to burn before Him sweet incense,
and for the continual showbread, and for
the ascending offerings morning and
evening, on the sabbaths, and on the new
moons, and on the appointed times of יהוה
our Elohim. This is for Yisra'ěl forever.
5 "And the House which I build is great,
for our Elohim is greater than all mighty
ones.
6 "But who is able to build Him a House,
since the heavens and the heavens of the
heavens are unable to contain Him? Who
am I then, that I should build Him a House,
except to offer before Him?
7 "And now, send me at once a man who
knows to work in gold, and in silver, and in
bronze, and in iron, and in purple and crimson and blue, and knowing to engrave with
the skilled men who are with me in
Yehuḏah and Yerushalayim, whom Dawiḏ
my father has prepared.
8 "And send me cedar, cypress and algum
logs from Leḇanon, for I know that your
servants know to cut timber in Leḇanon.
And see, my servants are with your servants,
9 even to prepare plenty of timber for me,
for the House that I am building is great
and marvellous.
10 "And see, I have given servants to you,
the hewers who cut timber, twenty thousand kors of ground wheat, and twenty
thousand kors of barley, and twenty thousand baths of wine, and twenty thousand
baths of oil."
11 Then Ḥuram the sovereign of Tsor
answered in writing, which he sent to
Shelomoh, "Because יהוה loves His people, He has made you sovereign over
them."
12 And Ḥuram said, "Blessed be יהוה
Elohim of Yisra'ěl, who made the heavens
and earth, for He has given Sovereign
Dawiḏ a wise son, knowing wisdom and
understanding, to build a House for יהוה
and a house for his reign!
13 "And now I have sent a skilled man
having understanding, Ḥuram-aḇi,
14 the son of a woman of the daughters of
Dan, and his father was a man of Tsor, who
knows to work in gold, and in silver, in
bronze, in iron, in stone, and in wood, purple and blue, and in fine linen, and in crimson, and to make any engraving and to
accomplish any plan that is given to him,
with your skilled men and with the skilled
men of my master Dawiḏ your father.
15 "And now, the wheat and the barley, the
oil and the wine which my master has
spoken of, let him send to his servants.
16 "And let us cut wood from Leḇanon, as
much as you need, and bring it to you in
rafts by sea to Yapho, and you take it up to
Yerushalayim."
17 And Shelomoh numbered all the men,
the strangers who were in the land of
Yisra'ěl, according to the census in which
Dawiḏ his father had numbered them, and
they were found to be one hundred and
fifty-three thousand six hundred.
18 And he made seventy thousand of them
to bear burdens, and eighty thousand
hewers *of stone* in the mountain, and three
thousand six hundred overseers to make
the people work.

3 And Shelomoh began to build the
House of יהוה at Yerushalayim on
Mount Moriyah, where He appeared to his
father Dawiḏ, at the place that Dawiḏ had
prepared on the threshing-floor of Ornan
the Yeḇusite.
2 And he began to build on the second
day of the second new *moon* in the fourth
year of his reign.
3 And these are the foundations which
Shelomoh laid for building the House of
Elohim: The length by cubits according to
the former measure were sixty cubits, and
the width twenty cubits.
4 And the porch that was in front was
twenty cubits long according to the breadth
of the house, and the height was one
hundred and twenty. And he overlaid the
inside with clean gold.
5 And the great house he panelled with
cypress which he overlaid with fine gold,
and he carved palm trees and chainwork on
it.

[6]And he covered the house with precious
stones for comeliness, and the gold was
gold from Parwayim.
[7]And he overlaid the house, the beams,
the doorposts, and its walls, and its doors
with gold, and carved keruḇim on the
walls.
[8]And he made the House of the Most
Set-apart. Its length was according to the
width of the house, twenty cubits, and its
width twenty cubits. And he overlaid it
with fine gold, six hundred talents.
[9]And the weight of the nails was fifty
sheqels of gold. And he overlaid the upper
rooms with gold.
[10]In the Most Set-apart House he made
two keruḇim of sculptured work, and
overlaid them with gold.
[11]And the wings of the keruḇim: their
total length was twenty cubits, one wing
was five cubits, touching the wall of the
room, and the other wing was five cubits,
touching the wing of the other keruḇ,
[12]and the wing of the other keruḇ was
five cubits, touching the wall of the room,
and the other wing also was five cubits,
touching the wing of the other keruḇ.
[13]The wings of these keruḇim spread out
twenty cubits, and they stood on their feet,
and they faced inward.
[14]And he made the veil of blue and
purple and crimson and fine linen, and
worked keruḇim on it.
[15]And at the front of the House he made
two columns thirty-five cubits high, and
the capital that was on the top of each of
them was five cubits.
[16]And he made wreaths of chainwork, as
in the Speaking Place, and put them on top
of the columns. And he made one hundred
pomegranates, and put them on the wreaths
of chainwork.
[17]And he set up the columns before the
Hěḵal, one on the right and the other on the
left, and called the name of the one on the
right Yaḵin, and the name of the one on the
left Boʽaz.

4 And he made a slaughter-place of
bronze, twenty cubits long, and twenty cubits wide, and ten cubits high.
[2]And he made the Sea of cast *metal*, ten
cubits from one rim to the other, round all
about. And its height was five cubits, and a
line of thirty cubits measured around it.
[3]And figures like oxen were under it, all
around it, ten to a cubit, all the way around
the Sea. Two rows of oxen were cast when
it was cast.
[4]It stood on twelve oxen, three facing
north, and three facing west, and three
facing south, and three facing east. And the
Sea was set upon them, and all their back
parts were inward.
[5]And it was a handbreadth thick, and its
rim was shaped like the rim of a cup, like a
lily blossom. It held three thousand baths.
[6]And he made ten basins, and put five on
the right side and five on the left, to wash
in them. In them they rinsed off what pertains to the ascending offering, but the Sea
was for the priests to wash in.
[7]And he made ten lampstands of gold
according to their ruling, and set them in
the Hěḵal, five on the right side and five on
the left.
[8]And he made ten tables, and placed
them in the Hěḵal, five on the right side
and five on the left. And he made one hundred bowls of gold.
[9]And he made the courtyard of the
priests, and the great court and doors for
the court. And he overlaid these doors with
bronze.
[10]And he placed the Sea on the right side,
eastward over against the south.
[11]And Ḥuram made the pots and the
shovels and the bowls. So Ḥuram completed doing the work that he was to do for
Sovereign Shelomoh for the House of
Elohim:
[12]the two columns and the bowl-shaped
capitals that were on top of the two
columns, and the two networks to cover
the two bowl-shaped capitals which were
on top of the columns;
[13]and four hundred pomegranates for the
two networks, two rows of pomegranates
for each network, to cover the two bowl-
shaped capitals that were on the columns.
[14]And he made stands and the basins on
the stands,

15 one Sea and twelve oxen under it;
16 and the pots, and the shovels, and the
forks. And all their vessels Ḥuram his
master craftsman made of polished bronze
for Sovereign Shelomoh for the House of
יהוה.
17 On the plain of Yarděn the sovereign
had them cast in clay moulds, between
Sukkoth and Tserěḏathah.
18 And Shelomoh made so large a number
of all these vessels that the weight of the
bronze was not searched out.
19 And Shelomoh had all the furnishings
made for the House of Elohim, and the
slaughter-place of gold and the tables on
which was the showbread,
20 and the lampstands with their lamps of
refined gold, to burn according to right-ruling in front of the Speaking Place,
21 and the blossoms and the lamps and the
snuffers of gold, of perfect gold,
22 and the snuffers, and the bowls, and the
ladles, and the fire holders of refined gold.
And the entrance to the House, its inner
doors to the Most Set-apart Place, and the
doors of the Hěḵal of the House, were of
gold.

5 And all the work that Shelomoh had
done for the House of יהוה was completed. And Shelomoh brought in the set-
apart items of his father Dawiḏ: the silver
and the gold and all the utensils. And he
put them in the treasuries of the House of
Elohim.
2 And Shelomoh assembled the elders of
Yisra'ěl and all the heads of the tribes, the
chief fathers of the children of Yisra'ěl, in
Yerushalayim, to bring up the ark of the
covenant of יהוה from the City of Dawiḏ,
which is Tsiyon.
3 And all the men of Yisra'ěl assembled
to the sovereign at the festival, which was
in the seventh new *moon*.
4 And all the elders of Yisra'ěl came, and
the Lěwites took up the ark,
5 and they brought up the ark, the Tent of
Appointment, and all the set-apart utensils
that were in the Tent. The Lěwite priests
brought them up.
6 And Sovereign Shelomoh, and all the
congregation of Yisra'ěl who were assembled to him before the ark, were slaughtering so many sheep and cattle that could not
be counted or numbered.
7 And the priests brought in the ark of the
covenant of יהוה to its place, into the
Speaking Place of the House, to the Most
Set-apart Place, under the wings of the
keruḇim.
8 For the keruḇim spread their wings over
the place of the ark, and the keruḇim covered over the ark and its poles.
9 And the poles were so long that the
ends of the poles of the ark were seen from
the set-apart place, in front of the Speaking
Place, but they were not seen from outside.
And they are there to this day.
10 There was naught in the ark but the two
tablets which Mosheh put there at Ḥorěḇ,
when יהוה made a covenant with the
children of Yisra'ěl, when they came out of
Mitsrayim.
11 And it came to be when the priests
came out of the Most Set-apart Place – for
all the priests who were present had set
themselves apart, there was none to watch
by division –
12 and the Lěwite singers, all those of
Asaph and Hěman and Yeḏuthun, with
their sons and their brothers, stood at the
east end of the slaughter-place, dressed in
white linen, having cymbals and harps and
lyres, and with them one hundred and
twenty priests sounding with trumpets.
13 Then it came to be, as the trumpeters
and singers were as one, to make one
sound to be heard in praising and thanking
יהוה, and when they lifted up their voice
with the trumpets, and with cymbals, and
with instruments of song, and giving praise
to יהוה, "For He is good, for His loving-
commitment is everlasting," that the house,
the House of יהוה, was filled with a cloud,
14 and the priests were unable to stand and
perform the service because of the cloud,
for the esteem of יהוה filled the House of
Elohim.

6 Then Shelomoh said, "יהוה has said
He would dwell in the dark cloud.
2 "But I have built You an exalted house,

and a place for You to dwell in forever."

3 And the sovereign turned around and blessed all the assembly of Yisra'ěl, while all the assembly of Yisra'ěl stood.

4 And he said, "Blessed be יהוה Elohim of Yisra'ěl, who has filled with His hands what He spoke with His mouth to my father Dawiḏ, saying,

5 'From the day that I brought My people out of the land of Mitsrayim, I have chosen no city from any tribe of Yisra'ěl in which to build a house for My Name to be there, nor did I choose any man to be a leader over My people Yisra'ěl.

6 'But I have chosen Yerushalayim, for My Name to be there. And I have chosen Dawiḏ to be over My people Yisra'ěl.'

7 "And it was in the heart of my father Dawiḏ to build a House for the Name of יהוה Elohim of Yisra'ěl.

8 "But יהוה said to my father Dawiḏ, 'Because it was in your heart to build a House for My Name, you did well in that it was in your heart.

9 'But you do not build the house, for your son who comes forth from your loins, he does build the House for My Name.'

10 "Now יהוה has established His word which He spoke, and I have been raised up instead of my father Dawiḏ, and sit on the throne of Yisra'ěl, as יהוה promised. And I have built the House for the Name of יהוה Elohim of Yisra'ěl.

11 "And there I have placed the ark, in which is the covenant of יהוה which He made with the children of Yisra'ěl."

12 And he stood before the slaughter-place of יהוה in front of all the assembly of Yisra'ěl, and spread out his hands –

13 for Shelomoh had made a bronze platform five cubits long, and five cubits broad, and three cubits high, and had put it in the midst of the court. And he stood on it, and knelt down on his knees before all the assembly of Yisra'ěl, and spread out his hands toward the heavens –

14 and said, "יהוה Elohim of Yisra'ěl, there is no Elohim in the heavens or on earth like You, guarding the covenant and loving-commitment with Your servants who walk before You with all their heart,

15 who has guarded what You promised Your servant Dawiḏ my father. Indeed, You have both spoken with Your mouth and have filled it with Your hand, as it is this day.

16 "And now, יהוה Elohim of Yisra'ěl, guard what You promised Your servant Dawiḏ my father, saying, 'There is not to cease a man of yours before Me, sitting on the throne of Yisra'ěl – only, if your sons guard their way, to walk in My Torah as you have walked before Me.'

17 "And now, O יהוה Elohim of Yisra'ěl, let Your word come true which You have spoken to Your servant Dawiḏ.

18 "For is it true: Elohim dwells with men on the earth! See, the heavens and the heavens of the heavens are unable to contain You, how much less this House which I have built!

19 "Yet, shall You turn to the prayer of Your servant and his supplication, O יהוה my Elohim, to listen to the cry and to the prayer which Your servant is praying before You?

20 "For Your eyes to be open toward this House day and night, toward the place You have said to put Your Name there, to listen to the prayer which Your servant prays toward this place.

21 "And shall You give heed to the supplications of Your servant and of Your people Yisra'ěl, when they pray toward this place, and hear from Your dwelling place, in the heavens, and shall hear and forgive?

22 "If anyone sins against his neighbour, and he has lifted up an oath on him, to cause him to swear, and comes and swears before Your slaughter-place in this House,

23 then hear in the heavens, and act, and rightly rule Your servants, repaying the wrong by bringing his way on his own head, and declare right the righteous by giving him according to his righteousness.

24 "And if Your people Yisra'ěl are smitten before an enemy because they have sinned against You, and they shall turn back and confess Your Name, and pray and make supplication before You in this House,

25 then hear in the heavens and forgive the

sin of Your people Yisra'ĕl, and bring them
back to the land which You gave to them
and their fathers.
26 "When the heavens are shut up and
there is no rain because they have sinned
against You, and they shall pray toward
this place and confess Your Name, and turn
from their sin because You afflict them,
27 then hear in the heavens, and forgive
the sin of Your servants, Your people
Yisra'ĕl – for You teach them the good way
in which they should walk – and shall send
rain on Your land which You have given to
Your people as an inheritance.
28 "When there is scarcity of food in the
land; when there is pestilence or blight or
mildew, locusts or grasshoppers; when
their enemies distress them in the land of
their cities; any plague or any sickness;
29 whatever prayer, whatever supplication
is made by anyone, or by all Your people
Yisra'ĕl, when each one knows his own
plague and his own grief, and spreads out
his hands to this house,
30 then hear from the heavens Your
dwelling place, and forgive, and give to
everyone according to all his ways, whose
heart You know – for You alone know the
hearts of the sons of men –
31 so that they fear You, to walk in Your
ways as long as they live in the land which
You gave to our fathers.
32 "Also, concerning a foreigner, who is
not of Your people Yisra'ĕl, but who
comes from a far land for the sake of Your
great Name and Your strong hand and Your
outstretched arm, when they come and
pray in this House,
33 then hear from the heavens Your
dwelling place, and do according to all
which the foreigner calls to You for, so that
all the people of the earth know Your
Name and fear You, as do Your people
Yisra'ĕl, and to know that this House
which I have built is called by Your Name.
34 "When Your people go out to battle
against their enemies, in the way that You
send them, and they shall pray to You
toward this city which You have chosen
and toward the House which I have built
for Your Name,
35 then shall You hear from the heavens
their prayer and their supplication, and
maintain their cause?
36 "When they sin against You – for there
is no one who does not sin – and You
become enraged with them and give them
to the enemy, and they take them captive to
a land far or near,
37 and they shall turn back unto their
heart, in the land where they have been
taken captive, and shall turn, and make
supplication to You in the land of their captivity, saying, 'We have sinned, we have
acted crookedly, and have done wrong,'
38 and when they return to You with all
their heart and with all their being in the
land of their captivity, where they have
taken them captive, and they shall pray
toward their land which You gave to their
fathers, and the city which You have
chosen, and toward the House which I
have built for Your Name,
39 then shall You hear from the heavens,
Your dwelling place, their prayer and their
supplications, and maintain their cause,
and forgive Your people who have sinned
against You?
40 "Now, my Elohim, I pray, let Your eyes
be open and let Your ears be attentive to
the prayer of this place.
41 "And now, arise, O יהוה Elohim, to
Your resting place, You and the ark of Your
strength. Let Your priests, O יהוה Elohim,
be robed with deliverance, and let Your
lovingly-commited ones rejoice in
goodness.
42 "O יהוה Elohim, do not turn away the
face of Your anointed; remember the loving-commitment of Your servant Dawiḏ."

7 And when Shelomoh had ended
praying, fire came down from the
heavens and consumed the ascending
offering and the slaughterings. And the
esteem of יהוה filled the House.
2 And the priests were unable to enter the
House of יהוה, because the esteem of יהוה
had filled the House of יהוה.
3 And all the children of Yisra'ĕl saw
how the fire came down, and the esteem of
יהוה on the House, and they bowed their

faces to the ground on the pavement, and
did obeisance and gave thanks to יהוה,
saying, "For He is good, for His loving-
commitment is everlasting."
4 And the sovereign and all the people
slaughtered slaughterings before יהוה.
5 And Sovereign Shelomoh slaughtered a
slaughtering of twenty-two thousand bulls
and one hundred and twenty thousand
sheep. Thus the sovereign and all the people dedicated the House of Elohim.
6 And the priests were standing over their
duties, and the Lěwites with instruments of
the song to יהוה, which Sovereign Dawiḏ
had made to give thanks to יהוה, saying,
"For His loving-commitment is everlasting," whenever Dawiḏ praised by their
hand. And the priests were blowing trumpets before them, and all Yisra'ěl were
standing.
7 And Shelomoh set apart the middle of
the courtyard that was in front of the House
of יהוה, for there he made ascending offerings and the fat of the peace offerings,
because the bronze slaughter-place which
Shelomoh had made was not able to contain the ascending offerings and the grain
offerings and the fat.
8 And Shelomoh at that time observed
the Festival seven days, and all Yisra'ěl
with him, a very great assembly from the
entrance of Ḥamath to the wadi of
Mitsrayim.
9 And on the eighth day they held an
assembly, for they performed the dedication of the slaughter-place seven days, and
the festival seven days.
10 And on the twenty-third day of the
seventh new *moon* he sent the people away
to their tents, rejoicing and glad of heart
for the goodness that יהוה had done for
Dawiḏ, and for Shelomoh, and for His
people Yisra'ěl.
11 Thus Shelomoh finished the House of
יהוה and the sovereign's house. And all
that came into the heart of Shelomoh to do
in the House of יהוה and in his own house,
he prosperously executed.
12 And יהוה appeared to Shelomoh by
night, and said to him, "I have heard your
prayer, and have chosen this place for
Myself as a house of slaughtering.
13 "If I shut up the heavens and there is no
rain, or if I command the locusts to devour
the land, or if I send pestilence among My
people,
14 and My people upon whom My Name
is called, shall humble themselves, and
pray and seek My face, and turn from their
evil ways, then I shall hear from the heavens, and forgive their sin and heal their
land.
15 "Now, My eyes are open and My ears
attentive to the prayer of this place.
16 "And now, I have chosen and set this
house apart for My Name to be there forever. And My eyes and My heart shall always
be there.
17 "And you, if you walk before Me as
your father Dawiḏ walked, and do according to all that I have commanded you,
and if you guard My laws and My right-
rulings,
18 then I shall establish the throne of your
reign, as I covenanted with Dawiḏ your
father, saying, 'There is not to cease
a man of yours as ruler in Yisra'ěl.'
19 "But if you turn away and forsake My
laws and My commands which I have set
before you, and shall go and serve other
mighty ones, and bow yourself to them,
20 then I shall pluck them from My land,
which I have given them, and this house
which I have set apart for My Name I shall
cast out of My sight and make it to be a
proverb and a mockery among all peoples.
21 "And this house, which has been exalted, everyone who passes by it is shall be
astonished and say, 'Why has יהוה done
thus to this land and this house?'
22 "Then they shall say, 'Because they forsook יהוה Elohim of their fathers, who
brought them out of the land of Mitsrayim,
and embraced other mighty ones, and
bowed themselves to them and served
them, therefore He has brought all this evil
on them.' "

8 And it came to be at the end of twenty
years, that Shelomoh had built the
House of יהוה, and his own house.
2 As to the cities which Ḥuram had given

to Shelomoh, Shelomoh had built them,
and he settled the children of Yisra'ěl
there.
3 And Shelomoh went to Ḥamath Tsoḇah
and took hold of it.
4 And he built Taḏmor in the wilderness,
and all the storage cities which he built in
Ḥamath.
5 And he built Upper Běyth Ḥoron and
Lower Běyth Ḥoron, cities of defence, with
walls, gates, and bars,
6 also Ba'alath and all the storage cities
that Shelomoh had, and all the chariot
cities and the cities of the cavalry, and all
that Shelomoh desired to build in Yerushalayim, and in Leḇanon, and in all the
land of his rule.
7 All the people who were left of the Ḥittites, and the Amorites, and the Perizzites,
and the Ḥiwwites, and the Yeḇusites, who
were not of Yisra'ěl –
8 their descendants who were left in the
land after them, whom the children of
Yisra'ěl did not destroy – from these
Shelomoh raised compulsory labour, as it
is to this day.
9 And Shelomoh did not make slaves of
the children of Yisra'ěl for his work, but
they were men of battle, and chiefs of his
officers, and commanders of his chariots,
and his cavalry.
10 And these were the chiefs of the officials of Sovereign Shelomoh: two hundred
and fifty, who ruled over the people.
11 And Shelomoh brought the daughter of
Pharaoh up from the City of Dawiḏ to the
house he had built for her, for he said, "My
wife does not dwell in the house of Dawiḏ
sovereign of Yisra'ěl, for *the place* where
the ark of יהוה has come, is set-apart."
12 Then Shelomoh offered ascending
offerings to יהוה on the slaughter-place of
יהוה which he had built before the porch,
13 even as the duty of every day required,
offering according to the command of
Mosheh, for the sabbaths, and for the new
moons, and for the appointed times three
times a year: the Festival of Matzot,[a] and
the Festival of Shaḇu'ot,[b] and the Festival
of Sukkot.[c]
14 And according to the ruling of Dawiḏ
his father, he appointed the divisions of the
priests for their service, the Lěwites for
their duties, to praise and serve before the
priests, as the duty of each day required,
and the gatekeepers by their divisions at
each gate, for so was the command of
Dawiḏ the man of Elohim.
15 And they did not turn aside from the
command of the sovereign to the priests
and Lěwites concerning any matter or
concerning the treasuries.
16 And all the work of Shelomoh was
prepared from the day of the foundation of
the House of יהוה until it was completed.
And the House of יהוה was perfected.
17 Then Shelomoh went to Etsyon Geḇer
and Ěyloth on the seacoast, in the land of
Eḏom.
18 And Ḥuram sent him ships by the hand
of his servants, and servants who knew the
sea. And they went with the servants of
Shelomoh to Ophir, and took four hundred
and fifty talents of gold from there, and
brought it to Sovereign Shelomoh.

9 And the sovereigness of Sheḇa heard
of the report of Shelomoh, and came
to Yerushalayim to try Shelomoh with hard
questions, with a very great company, and
camels bearing spices, and much gold,
and precious stones. And she came to
Shelomoh, and she spoke with him about
all that was in her heart.
2 And Shelomoh answered all her questions. And there was no matter hidden for
Shelomoh which he did not make known to
her.
3 And the sovereigness of Sheḇa saw the
wisdom of Shelomoh, and the house that
he had built,
4 and the food on his table, and the seating of his servants, and the service of his
waiters and their attire, and his cupbearers
and their attire, and his ascending offerings
that he offered up in the House of יהוה,
and there was no more spirit in her.
5 Then she said to the sovereign, "True

8a - Unleavened Bread. *8b* - Weeks. *8c* - Booths.

was the word I heard in my own land about
your words and your wisdom.
6 “But I did not believe their words until I
came and saw with my own eyes. And see,
I have not been told the half of the greatness of your wisdom! You exceed the
report which I heard.
7 “Blessed are your men and blessed are
these your servants, who stand continually
before you and hear your wisdom!
8 “Blessed be יהוה your Elohim, who
delighted in you, to put you on His throne
to be sovereign for יהוה your Elohim!
Because your Elohim has loved Yisra’ěl, to
establish them forever, therefore He made
you sovereign over them, to do right-ruling
and righteousness.”
9 And she gave the sovereign one hundred and twenty talents of gold, and very
many spices, and precious stones. And
there has not been any spices such as those
the sovereigness of Sheḇa gave to
Sovereign Shelomoh.
10 And also, the servants of Ḥuram and
the servants of Shelomoh, who brought
gold from Ophir, brought algum wood and
precious stones.
11 And the sovereign made stairs of the
algum wood for the House of יהוה and for
the sovereign’s house, also lyres and harps
for singers. And there was never seen the
like of them before in the land of Yehuḏah.
12 And Sovereign Shelomoh gave to the
sovereigness of Sheḇa all she desired,
whatever she asked, besides that which she
had brought to the sovereign. And she
turned and went to her own land, she and
her servants.
13 And the weight of gold that came to
Shelomoh yearly was six hundred and
sixty-six talents of gold,
14 besides that which the merchants and
traders brought. And all the sovereigns of
Araḇia and governors of the land were
bringing gold and silver to Shelomoh.
15 And Sovereign Shelomoh made two
hundred large shields of beaten gold – six
hundred pieces of beaten gold went into
each shield,
16 and three hundred shields of beaten
gold – three hundred pieces of gold went
into each shield. And the sovereign put
them in the House of the Forest of
Leḇanon.
17 And the sovereign made a great throne
of ivory, and overlaid it with clean gold,
18 and six steps *led* to the throne, with a
footstool of gold, which were fastened to
the throne; and there were armrests on
either side of the place of the seat, and two
lions stood beside the armrests.
19 And twelve lions were standing there,
one on each side of the six steps. The like
of it was not in any reign.
20 And all the drinking vessels of
Sovereign Shelomoh were of gold, and all
the vessels of the House of the Forest of
Leḇanon were of refined gold – silver was
reckoned of little value in the days of
Shelomoh.
21 For the sovereign’s ships went to
Tarshish with the servants of Ḥuram. Once
in three years the ships of Tarshish came,
bringing gold, and silver, ivory, apes, and
baboons.
22 And Sovereign Shelomoh became
greater than all the sovereigns of the earth
in riches and wisdom.
23 And all the sovereigns of the earth
sought the presence of Shelomoh to hear
his wisdom, which Elohim had put in his
heart.
24 And each man brought his present:
objects of silver, and objects of gold, and
garments, and armour, and spices, horses
and mules, the matter of a year by year.
25 And Shelomoh had four thousand stalls
for horses and chariots, and twelve thousand horsemen whom he stationed in the
chariot cities and with the sovereign at
Yerushalayim.
26 And he ruled over all the sovereigns
from the River to the land of the
Philistines, as far as the border of Mitsrayim.
27 And the sovereign made silver in
Yerushalayim as the stones, and he made
cedar trees as plenty as the sycamores
which are in the low country.
28 And they were bringing horses to
Shelomoh from Mitsrayim and from all
lands.

29 And the rest of the acts of Shelomoh, first and last, are they not written in the book of Nathan the prophet, and in the prophecy of Aḥiyah the Shilonite, and in the visions of Iddo the seer concerning Yaroḇʽam son of Neḇat?

30 And Shelomoh reigned in Yerushalayim over all Yisra'ěl forty years.

31 So Shelomoh slept with his fathers, and was buried in the City of Dawiḏ his father. And Reḥaḇʽam his son reigned in his place.

10 And Reḥaḇʽam went to Sheḵem, for all Yisra'ěl had gone to Sheḵem to set him up to reign.

2 And it came to be, when Yaroḇʽam son of Neḇat heard it – he was in Mitsrayim where he had fled from the presence of Shelomoh the sovereign – that Yaroḇʽam returned from Mitsrayim.

3 So they sent for him and called him. And Yaroḇʽam and all Yisra'ěl came and spoke to Reḥaḇʽam, saying,

4 "Your father made our yoke hard, and now, lighten the hard service of your father and his heavy yoke which he put on us, then we shall serve you."

5 And he said to them, "Come back to me after three days." And the people went.

6 Then Sovereign Reḥaḇʽam consulted the elders who stood before his father Shelomoh while he still lived, saying, "What do you advise me to answer these people?"

7 And they spoke to him, saying, "If you are good to these people, and shall please them, and speak good words to them, they shall be your servants all the days."

8 But he ignored the advice the elders gave him, and consulted the young men who had grown up with him, who stood before him.

9 And he said to them, "What advice do you give? How should we answer this people who have spoken to me, saying, 'Lighten the yoke which your father put on us'?"

10 And the young men who had grown up with him spoke to him, saying, "Say this to the people who have spoken to you, saying, 'Your father made our yoke heavy, but you make it lighter on us.' Say this to them, 'My little finger is thicker than my father's waist!

11 'And now, my father put a heavy yoke on you, but I, I add to your yoke; my father chastised you with whips, but I with scourges!' "

12 So Yaroḇʽam and all the people came to Reḥaḇʽam on the third day, as the sovereign commanded, saying, "Come back to me the third day."

13 And the sovereign answered them harshly. Thus Sovereign Reḥaḇʽam ignored the advice of the elders,

14 and spoke to them according to the advice of the young men, saying, "My father made your yoke heavy, but I, I add to it; my father chastised you with whips, but I with scourges!"

15 So the sovereign did not listen to the people, for the turn *of events* was from Elohim, in order for יהוה to establish His word, which He had spoken by the hand of Aḥiyahu the Shilonite to Yaroḇʽam son of Neḇat.

16 And when all Yisra'ěl saw that the sovereign did not listen to them, the people answered the sovereign, saying, "What portion have we in Dawiḏ? And we have no inheritance in the son of Yishai. Every man to your mighty ones, O Yisra'ěl! Now see to your own house, O Dawiḏ!" So all Yisra'ěl went to their tents.

17 But as for the children of Yisra'ěl who dwelt in the cities of Yehuḏah, Reḥaḇʽam reigned over them.

18 Then Sovereign Reḥaḇʽam sent Haḏoram, who was over the compulsory labour, and the children of Yisra'ěl stoned him with stones, and he died. And Sovereign Reḥaḇʽam hastily mounted his chariot to flee to Yerushalayim.

19 Thus Yisra'ěl revolted against the house of Dawiḏ to this day.

11 And when Reḥaḇʽam came to Yerushalayim, he assembled from the house of Yehuḏah and Binyamin one hundred and eighty thousand chosen brave men to fight against Yisra'ěl, to bring back the reign to Reḥaḇʽam.

2 But the word of יהוה came to Shemayahu the man of Elohim, saying,
3 "Speak to Reḥaḇ'am son of Shelomoh,
sovereign of Yehuḏah, and to all Yisra'ěl in
Yehuḏah and Binyamin, saying,
4 'Thus said יהוה, "Do not go up or fight
against your brothers! Let every man
return to his house, for this matter is from
Me." ' " So they obeyed the words of יהוה,
and turned back from going against
Yaroḇ'am.
5 And Reḥaḇ'am dwelt in Yerushalayim,
and built cities for a defence in Yehuḏah.
6 And he built Běyth Leḥem, and Ěytam,
and Teqowa,
7 and Běyth Tsur, and Soḵo, and
Aḏullam,
8 and Gath, and Marěshah, and Ziph,
9 and Aḏorayim, and Laḵish, and
Azěqah,
10 and Tsor'ah, and Ayalon, and Ḥeḇron,
which are in Yehuḏah and Binyamin, cities
of defence.
11 And he strengthened the strongholds,
and put commanders in them, and stores of
food, and oil, and wine,
12 and shields and spears in every city, and
made them very strong. Thus Yehuḏah and
Binyamin were his.
13 And from all their borders the priests
and the Lěwites who were in all Yisra'ěl
took their stand with him.
14 For the Lěwites left their open lands
and their possessions and came to Yehuḏah
and Yerushalayim, for Yaroḇ'am and his
sons had rejected them from serving as
priests unto יהוה,
15 as he appointed for himself priests for
the high places, and for goats, and the calf
idols which he had made.
16 And after the Lěwites left, those from
all the tribes of Yisra'ěl, such as set their
heart to seek יהוה Elohim of Yisra'ěl,
came to Yerushalayim to slaughter to יהוה
Elohim of their fathers.
17 And they strengthened the reign of
Yehuḏah, and made Reḥaḇ'am son of
Shelomoh strong for three years, for they
walked in the way of Dawiḏ and Shelomoh
for three years.
18 And Reḥaḇ'am took for himself as wife
Maḥalath the daughter of Yerimoth son of
Dawiḏ, and of Aḇiḥayil the daughter of
Eliyaḇ son of Yishai.
19 And she bore him sons: Ye'ush, and
Shemaryah, and Zaham.
20 And after her he took Ma'aḵah the
granddaughter of Aḇshalom. And she bore
him Aḇiyah, and Attai, and Ziza, and
Shelomith.
21 And Reḥaḇ'am loved Ma'aḵah the
granddaughter of Aḇshalom more than all
his wives and his concubines. For he had
taken eighteen wives and sixty concubines,
and brought forth twenty-eight sons and
sixty daughters.
22 And Reḥaḇ'am appointed Aḇiyah son
of Ma'aḵah as chief, to be leader among
his brothers, in order to make him reign.
23 And he had understanding, and dispersed some of his sons throughout all the
lands of Yehuḏah and Binyamin, to all the
cities of defence, and gave them ample
provision. And he sought many wives *for
them*.

12

And it came to be, when Reḥaḇ'am
had established the reign and had
strengthened himself, that he forsook the
Torah of יהוה, and all Yisra'ěl with him.
2 And it came to be, in the fifth year
of Sovereign Reḥaḇ'am, that Shishaq
sovereign of Mitsrayim came up against
Yerushalayim – because they had trespassed against יהוה –
3 with twelve hundred chariots, and sixty
thousand horsemen, and innumerable people who came with him out of Mitsrayim:
the Luḇim, the Sukkites and the Kushites.
4 And he took the cities of defence of
Yehuḏah and came to Yerushalayim.
5 And Shemayah the prophet came to
Reḥaḇ'am and the rulers of Yehuḏah, who
had been gathered in Yerushalayim
because of Shishaq, and said to them,
"Thus said יהוה, 'You have forsaken Me,
and therefore I also have left you in the
hand of Shishaq.' "
6 Then the rulers of Yisra'ěl and the sovereign humbled themselves, and they said,
"יהוה is righteous."
7 And when יהוה saw that they humbled

themselves, the word of יהוה came to
Shemayah, saying, "They have humbled
themselves. I do not destroy them, but I
shall give to them some deliverance, and
not pour out My wrath on Yerushalayim by
the hand of Shishaq,
8 but they are to become his servants, so
that they know My service and the service
of the reigns of the lands."
9 And Shishaq sovereign of Mitsrayim
came up against Yerushalayim, and took
away the treasures of the House of יהוה
and the treasures of the sovereign's house.
He took all, he also took the gold shields
which Shelomoh had made.
10 And Sovereign Reḥaḇʽam made bronze
shields to replace them and committed
them into the hands of the chiefs of the
guard, who guarded the entrance of the
sovereign's house.
11 And it came to be, whenever the sovereign went into the House of יהוה, the
guard would go and bring them out, then
they would take them back into the guardroom.
12 And when he humbled himself, the
wrath of יהוה turned from him, so as not to
destroy him completely. And matters also
went well in Yehuḏah.
13 So Sovereign Reḥaḇʽam strengthened
himself in Yerushalayim and reigned. For
Reḥaḇʽam was forty-one years old when he
became sovereign, and he reigned seventeen years in Yerushalayim, the city which
יהוה had chosen out of all the tribes
of Yisra'ěl, to put His Name there. And
his mother's name was Naʽamah, the
Ammonitess.
14 And he did evil, because he did not
prepare his heart to seek יהוה.
15 And the acts of Reḥaḇʽam, the first and
the last, are they not written in the book of
Shemayah the prophet, and of Iddo the seer
concerning genealogies? And there was
fighting between Reḥaḇʽam and Yaroḇʽam
all the days.
16 So Reḥaḇʽam slept with his fathers, and
was buried in the City of Dawiḏ. And
Aḇiyah his son reigned in his place.

13 In the eighteenth year of Sovereign
Yaroḇʽam, Aḇiyah began to reign
over Yehuḏah.
2 He reigned three years in Yerushalayim. And his mother's name was Miḵayahu the daughter of Uri'ěl of Giḇʽah. And
there was fighting between Aḇiyah and
Yaroḇʽam.
3 And Aḇiyah joined battle with an army
of mighty men of battle, four hundred
thousand choice men. And Yaroḇʽam drew
up in battle formation against him with
eight hundred thousand choice men,
mighty brave men.
4 And Aḇiyah stood on Mount Tsemarayim, which is in the mountains of
Ephrayim, and said, "Hear me, Yaroḇʽam
and all Yisra'ěl:
5 "Do you not know that יהוה Elohim of
Yisra'ěl has given the reign over Yisra'ěl
to Dawiḏ forever, to him and his sons, by a
covenant of salt?
6 "Yet Yaroḇʽam son of Neḇat, the servant of Shelomoh son of Dawiḏ, rose up
and rebelled against his master.
7 "And vain men gathered to him, sons of
Beliyaʽal, and strengthened themselves
against Reḥaḇʽam son of Shelomoh, when
Reḥaḇʽam was young and tender of heart
and could not be strong against them.
8 "And now you think to be strong
against the reign of יהוה, which is in the
hand of the sons of Dawiḏ. And you are a
large crowd, and with you are the gold
calves which Yaroḇʽam made for you as
mighty ones.
9 "Have you not thrown out the priests of
יהוה, the sons of Aharon, and the Lěwites,
and made for yourselves priests, like the
peoples of the lands, so that whoever
comes to ordain himself with a young bull
and seven rams then becomes a priest of
what are not mighty ones?
10 "But as for us, יהוה is our Elohim, and
we have not forsaken Him, and priests are
serving יהוה, the sons of Aharon and the
Lěwites, in the work,
11 and are burning to יהוה every morning
and every evening ascending offerings and
sweet incense, and the showbread is *set* on
the clean table, and the lampstand of gold

with its lamps to burn every evening, for
we are guarding the Charge of יהוה our
Elohim. But you have forsaken Him.
12 "And see, with us as Head is Elohim
Himself, and His priests with sounding
trumpets to sound the alarm against you. O
children of Yisra'ěl, do not fight against
יהוה Elohim of your fathers, for you are
not going to prosper!"
13 But Yaroḇ'am sent round an ambush to
go behind them, so they were in front of
Yehuḏah, and the ambush was behind
them.
14 And Yehuḏah turned and saw the battle
was both in front and behind them. Then
they cried out to יהוה, and the priests
sounded the trumpets.
15 And the men of Yehuḏah gave a shout.
And it came to be, as the men of Yehuḏah
shouted, that Elohim smote Yaroḇ'am and
all Yisra'ěl before Aḇiyah and Yehuḏah.
16 And the children of Yisra'ěl fled before
Yehuḏah, and Elohim gave them into their
hand.
17 And Aḇiyah and his people struck them
with a great slaughter, and five hundred
thousand choice men of Yisra'ěl fell slain.
18 And the children of Yisra'ěl were humbled at that time, while the children of
Yehuḏah prevailed, because they relied on
יהוה Elohim of their fathers.
19 And Aḇiyah pursued Yaroḇ'am and
captured cities from him: Běyth Ěl with its
villages, and Yeshanah with its villages,
and Ephron with its villages.
20 And Yaroḇ'am did not regain power
again in the days of Aḇiyahu. And יהוה
smote him, and he died.
21 But Aḇiyah became strong, and took
fourteen wives, and brought forth twenty-
two sons and sixteen daughters.
22 And the rest of the acts of Aḇiyah, and
his ways, and his words are written in the
commentary of the prophet Iddo.

14 So Aḇiyah slept with his fathers,
and they buried him in the City of
Dawiḏ. And Asa his son reigned in his
place. In his days the land rested ten years.
2 And Asa did what was good and what
was right in the eyes of יהוה his Elohim,
3 and removed the slaughter-places of the
stranger, and the high places, and broke
down the pillars and cut down the
Ashěrim,
4 and commanded Yehuḏah to seek יהוה
Elohim of their fathers, and to do the Torah
and the command.
5 And he removed the high places and the
sun-pillars from all the cities of Yehuḏah,
and the reign rested under him.
6 And he built cities of defence in
Yehuḏah, since the land had rest and he
had no fighting in those years, because
יהוה had given him rest.
7 And he said to Yehuḏah, "Let us build
these cities and make walls around them,
and towers, gates, and bars, while the land
is yet before us, because we have sought
יהוה our Elohim. We have sought, and He
has given us rest all around." So they built
and prospered.
8 And Asa had an army of three hundred
thousand men from Yehuḏah bearing
shields and spears, and from Binyamin two
hundred and eighty thousand men bearing
shields and drew bows. All of them were
mighty brave men.
9 And Zeraḥ the Kushite came out
against them with an army of a million
men and three hundred chariots, and he
came to Marěshah.
10 And Asa went out against him, and they
set battle in array in the Valley of
Tsephathah at Marěshah.
11 And Asa called to יהוה his Elohim, and
said, "יהוה, there is no one but You to help
between the mighty and the powerless.
Help us, O יהוה our Elohim, for we rest on
You, and in Your Name we go against this
crowd. O יהוה, You are our Elohim, do not
let man prevail against You!"
12 So יהוה smote the Kushites before Asa
and Yehuḏah, and the Kushites fled.
13 And Asa and the people who were with
him pursued them to Gerar. And the
Kushites fell, until none was left alive for
them, for they were broken before יהוה
and His army. And they took very much
spoil,
14 and struck all the cities around Gerar,
for the fear of יהוה came upon them. And

they plundered all the cities, for there was exceedingly much spoil in them.

15 And they also struck the camps of the herdsmen, and captured many sheep and camels, and returned to Yerushalayim.

15 And the Spirit of Elohim came upon Azaryahu son of Oḏěḏ.

2 And he went out to face Asa, and said to him, "Hear me, Asa, and all Yehuḏah and Binyamin. יהוה is with you while you are with Him. And if you seek Him, He is found by you, but if you forsake Him, He forsakes you.

3 "And for many days Yisra'ěl has been without the true Elohim, and without a Torah priest, and without Torah.

4 "But in their distress they turned to יהוה Elohim of Yisra'ěl, and they sought Him, and He was found by them.

5 "And in those days there was no peace to the one who went out, nor to the one who came in, for great disturbances were on all the inhabitants of the lands,

6 and they were beaten down, nation by nation, and city by city, for Elohim troubled them with every distress.

7 "But you, be strong and do not let your hands be feeble, for there is a reward for your work!"

8 And when Asa heard these words and the prophecy of Oḏěḏ the prophet, he strengthened himself, and removed the abominations from all the land of Yehuḏah and Binyamin and from the cities which he had taken in the mountains of Ephrayim, and restored the slaughter-place of יהוה that was before the porch of יהוה,

9 and gathered all Yehuḏah and Binyamin, and those who sojourned with them from Ephrayim, and Menashsheh, and Shim'on, for they came over to him in great numbers from Yisra'ěl when they saw that יהוה his Elohim was with him.

10 And they gathered together at Yerushalayim in the third new *moon*, in the fifteenth year of the reign of Asa,

11 and slaughtered to יהוה on that day seven hundred bulls and seven thousand sheep from the spoil which they had brought.

12 And they entered into a covenant to seek יהוה Elohim of their fathers with all their heart and with all their being;

13 and whoever would not seek יהוה Elohim of Yisra'ěl would be put to death, from small to great, from man to woman.

14 And they swore to יהוה with a loud voice, with shouting and with trumpets and with shopharot.

15 And all Yehuḏah rejoiced concerning the oath, for they had sworn with all their heart and sought Him with all their being. And He was found by them, and יהוה gave them rest all around.

16 And he also removed Ma'aḵah, the mother of Asa the sovereign, from being sovereigness mother, because she had made an abominable image of Ashěrah. And Asa cut down her abominable image, and crushed it, and burned it by the wadi Qiḏron.

17 Yet the high places were not removed from Yisra'ěl. However, the heart of Asa was perfect all his days.

18 And he brought into the House of Elohim the set-apart items of his father and his own set-apart items: silver and gold and utensils.

19 And there was no more fighting until the thirty-fifth year of the reign of Asa.

16 In the thirty-sixth year of the reign of Asa, Ba'asha the sovereign of Yisra'ěl came up against Yehuḏah and built Ramah, to prevent anyone going out or coming in to Asa, sovereign of Yehuḏah.

2 And Asa brought silver and gold from the treasuries of the House of יהוה and of the sovereign's house, and sent to Ben-Haḏaḏ sovereign of Aram, who dwelt in Darmeseq, saying,

3 "Let there be a covenant between you and me, as there was between my father and your father. See, I have sent you silver and gold. Come, break your covenant with Ba'asha sovereign of Yisra'ěl, so that he withdraws from me."

4 And Ben-Haḏaḏ listened to Sovereign Asa and sent the commanders of his armies against the cities of Yisra'ěl, and they struck Iyon, and Dan, and Aḇěl Mayim,

and all the storage cities of Naphtali.

5 And it came to be, when Ba'asha heard it, that he stopped building Ramah and ceased his work.

6 Then Asa the sovereign brought all Yehuḏah, and they took away the stones and timber of Ramah, which Ba'asha had used for building. And with them he built Geḇa and Mitspah.

7 And at that time Ḥanani the seer came to Asa sovereign of Yehuḏah, and said to him, "Because you have relied on the sovereign of Aram, and have not relied on יהוה your Elohim, therefore the army of the sovereign of Aram has escaped from your hand.

8 "Were the Kushites and the Luḇim not a mighty army with very many chariots and horsemen? And because you relied on יהוה, He gave them into your hand.

9 "For the eyes of יהוה diligently search throughout all the earth, to show Himself *to be* strong on behalf of those whose heart is perfect to Him. You have acted foolishly in this, so from now on you shall have battles."

10 And Asa was wroth with the seer, and put him in prison, for *he was* enraged at him because of this. And Asa oppressed some of the people at that time.

11 And look, the acts of Asa, the first and the last, see, they are written in the book of the sovereigns of Yehuḏah and Yisra'ěl.

12 And in the thirty-ninth year of his reign, Asa became diseased in his feet, and his disease was severe. Yet even in his disease he did not seek יהוה, but the physicians.

13 So Asa slept with his fathers, and died in the forty-first year of his reign.

14 And they buried him in his burial-site, which he had made for himself in the City of Dawiḏ. And they laid him in the bed which was filled with spices and various kinds of ointments mixed by the perfumer's skill. And they made a very great burning for him.

17 And Yehoshaphat his son reigned in his place, and strengthened himself against Yisra'ěl,

2 and placed an army in all the walled cities of Yehuḏah, and set watch-posts in the land of Yehuḏah and in the cities of Ephrayim which Asa his father had taken.

3 And יהוה was with Yehoshaphat, for he walked in the former ways of his father Dawiḏ, and did not seek the Ba'als,

4 but sought the Elohim of his father, and walked in His commands and not according to the deeds of Yisra'ěl.

5 So יהוה established the reign in his hand. And all Yehuḏah gave presents to Yehoshaphat, and he had great riches and esteem.

6 And his heart was exalted in the ways of יהוה, and he again removed the high places and the Ashěrim from Yehuḏah.

7 And in the third year of his reign he sent his leaders, Ben-Ḥayil, and Oḇaḏyah, and Zeḵaryah, and Nethaně'l, and Miḵayahu, to teach in the cities of Yehuḏah.

8 And with them he sent Lěwites: Shemayahu, and Nethanyahu, and Zeḇaḏyahu, and Asah'ěl, and Shemiramoth, and Yehonathan, and Aḏoniyahu, and Toḇiyahu, and Toḇaḏoniyah, the Lěwites, and with them Elishama and Yehoram, the priests.

9 And they taught in Yehuḏah, and with them was the Book of the Torah of יהוה. And they went around into all the cities of Yehuḏah and taught the people.

10 And the fear of יהוה fell on all the reigns of the lands that were around Yehuḏah, and they did not fight against Yehoshaphat.

11 And some of the Philistines brought Yehoshaphat gifts and a load of silver. And the Araḇians brought him flocks, seven thousand seven hundred rams and seven thousand seven hundred male goats.

12 And Yehoshaphat became increasingly great, and he built palaces and storage cities in Yehuḏah.

13 And he had much work in the cities of Yehuḏah. And the men of battle, mighty brave men, were in Yerushalayim.

14 And these were their numbers, according to their fathers' houses: Of Yehuḏah, the commanders of thousands: Aḏnah the commander, and with him three hundred thousand mighty brave men;

15 and next to him was Yehoḥanan the
commander, and with him two hundred
and eighty thousand;
16 and next to him was Amasyah son of
Ziḵri, who volunteered himself to יהוה,
and with him two hundred thousand
mighty brave men.
17 And of Binyamin: Elyaḏa, a mighty
brave one, and with him two hundred thousand men armed with bow and shield;
18 and next to him was Yehozaḇaḏ, and
with him one hundred and eighty thousand
prepared for battle.
19 These were the ones serving the sovereign, besides those whom the sovereign
put in the walled cities throughout all
Yehuḏah.

18 And Yehoshaphat had great riches
and esteem, and allied himself with
Aḥaḇ by marriage.
2 And some years later he went down to
visit Aḥaḇ in Shomeron. And Aḥaḇ slaughtered many sheep and cattle for him and
the people with him, and incited him to go
up with him to Ramoth Gil'ad.
3 And Aḥaḇ sovereign of Yisra'ěl said to
Yehoshaphat sovereign of Yehuḏah, "Do
you go with me against Ramoth Gil'ad?"
And he answered him, "I am as you are,
and my people as your people, even with
you in battle."
4 And Yehoshaphat said to the sovereign
of Yisra'ěl, "Please inquire for the word of
יהוה today."
5 And the sovereign of Yisra'ěl gathered
the prophets together, four hundred men,
and said to them, "Do we go against
Ramoth Gil'ad to battle, or do I refrain?"
And they said, "Go up, for Elohim does
give it into the sovereign's hand."
6 But Yehoshaphat said, "Is there not still
a prophet of יהוה here, so that we inquire
of him?"
7 And the sovereign of Yisra'ěl said to
Yehoshaphat, "There is still one man to
inquire of יהוה from him; but I hate him,
because he never prophesies good
concerning me, but always evil. He is
Miḵayehu, the son of Yimla." And
Yehoshaphat said, "Let not the sovereign
say so!"
8 So the sovereign of Yisra'ěl called one
of his officers and said, "Bring Miḵahu son
of Yimla at once!"
9 And the sovereign of Yisra'ěl and
Yehoshaphat the sovereign of Yehuḏah,
dressed in their robes, sat each on his
throne. And they sat at a threshing-floor at
the entrance of the gate of Shomeron. And
all the prophets were prophesying before
them.
10 And Tsiḏqiyahu son of Kena'anah had
made horns of iron for himself, and said,
"Thus said יהוה, 'With these you push the
Arameans until they are destroyed.' "
11 And all the prophets were prophesying
so, saying, "Go up to Ramoth Gil'ad and
prosper, and יהוה shall give it into the hand
of the sovereign."
12 And the messenger who had gone to
call Miḵayehu spoke to him, saying, "See,
the words of the prophets with one mouth
are good towards the sovereign. So please
let your word be like the word of one of
them, and you shall speak good."
13 And Miḵayehu said, "As יהוה lives,
whatever my Elohim says, that I speak."
14 And he came to the sovereign. And the
sovereign said to him, "Miḵah, do we go
against Ramoth Gil'ad to battle, or do I
refrain?" And he said, "Go and prosper,
and they are given into your hand!"
15 And the sovereign said to him, "How
many times have I made you swear that
you do not speak to me, except the truth, in
the Name of יהוה?"
16 So he said, "I saw all Yisra'ěl scattered
on the mountains, as sheep that have no
shepherd. And יהוה said, 'These have no
master. Let each return to his house in
peace.' "
17 And the sovereign of Yisra'ěl said to
Yehoshaphat, "Did I not say to you that he
would not prophesy good concerning me,
but evil?"
18 Then he said, "Therefore hear the word
of יהוה: I saw יהוה sitting on His throne,
and all the host of the heavens standing on
His right and on His left.
19 "And יהוה said, 'Who shall entice
Aḥaḇ sovereign of Yisra'ěl to go up and

fall at Ramoth Gil'ad?' And one said this, and another said that.

20 "And a spirit came forward and stood before יהוה, and said, 'Let me entice him.' יהוה said to him, 'In what way?'

21 "And he said, 'I shall go out and be a spirit of falsehood in the mouth of all his prophets.' And He said, 'Entice him, and also prevail. Go out and do so.'

22 "And now, see, יהוה has put a spirit of falsehood [a] in the mouth of these prophets of yours, and יהוה has spoken evil concerning you."

23 And Tsidqiyahu son of Kena'anah came near and struck Mikayehu on the cheek, and said, "Which way did the spirit of יהוה pass over from me to speak to you?"

24 And Mikayehu said, "Look, you shall see on that day when you go into an inner room to hide!"

25 Then the sovereign of Yisra'ěl said, "Take Mikayehu, and return him to Amon the governor of the city and to Yo'ash the sovereign's son,

26 and say, 'Thus said the sovereign, "Put this one in prison, and feed him with bread of affliction and water of affliction until I return in peace." ' "

27 And Mikayehu said, "If you return at all in peace, יהוה has not spoken by me." And he said, "Hear, all you people!"

28 Then the sovereign of Yisra'ěl and Yehoshaphat the sovereign of Yehudah went up to Ramoth Gil'ad.

29 And the sovereign of Yisra'ěl said to Yehoshaphat, "Let me disguise myself and go into battle, but you put on your robes." And the sovereign of Yisra'ěl disguised himself, and they went into battle.

30 And the sovereign of Aram had commanded the commanders of the chariots who were with him, saying, "Fight with no one small or great, but only with the sovereign of Yisra'ěl."

31 And it came to be, when the commanders of the chariots saw Yehoshaphat, that they said, "It is the sovereign of Yisra'ěl!" So they turned around to fight against him, and Yehoshaphat cried out, and יהוה helped him, and Elohim moved them to turn away from him.

32 And it came to be, when the commanders of the chariots saw that it was not the sovereign of Yisra'ěl, that they turned back from pursuing him.

33 And a man drew a bow in his simplicity, and struck the sovereign of Yisra'ěl between the joints of his armour. And he said to the driver of his chariot, "Turn around and take me out of the battle, for I am wounded."

34 But the battle increased that day, and the sovereign of Yisra'ěl was propped up in his chariot facing the Arameans until evening, and he died at the time of the going down of the sun.

19 And Yehoshaphat the sovereign of Yehudah returned to his house in peace in Yerushalayim.

2 And Yěhu son of Ḥanani the seer went out to face him, and said to Sovereign Yehoshaphat, "Do you help the wrong and love those who hate יהוה? Therefore the wrath of יהוה is upon you.

3 "But good matters are found in you, in that you have removed the Ashěroth from the land, and have prepared your heart to seek Elohim."

4 So Yehoshaphat dwelt in Yerushalayim, and he went out again among the people from Be'ěrsheba to the hill country of Ephrayim, and brought them back to יהוה Elohim of their fathers.

5 And he appointed judges in the land in all the walled cities of Yehudah, city by city,

6 and said to the judges, "Watch what you are doing, for you do not judge for man, but for יהוה who is with you in the matter of right-ruling.

7 "And now, let the fear of יהוה be upon you. Guard and do it, for there is no unrighteousness with יהוה our Elohim, nor partiality, nor taking of bribes."

8 And in Yerushalayim Yehoshaphat also

18a Tas. ב 2:11.

appointed some of the Lěwites and priests, and some of the chief fathers of Yisra'ěl, for the right-ruling of יהוה and for dispute. Then they returned to Yerushalayim.

9 And he commanded them, saying, "Do this in the fear of יהוה, trustworthily and with a perfect heart:

10 "When any dispute comes to you from your brothers who dwell in their cities, between blood and blood, between Torah and command, laws and right-rulings, then you shall warn them, lest they trespass against יהוה and wrath come upon you and your brothers. Do this, and you shall not be guilty.

11 "And look, Amaryahu the chief priest is over you in all matters of יהוה. And Zeḇaḏyahu son of Yishma'ěl, the ruler of the house of Yehuḏah, for all the matters of the sovereign, and the Lěwites are officials before you. Be strong and do, and יהוה is with the good."

20 And after this it came to be that the children of Mo'aḇ and the children of Ammon came in, and with them some of the peoples, against Yehoshaphat to battle.

2 And they came and spoke to Yehoshaphat, saying, "A great army is coming against you from beyond the sea, from Aram. And see, they are in Ḥatsatson Tamar," which is Ěn Geḏi.

3 And Yehoshaphat was afraid, and set his face to seek יהוה, and proclaimed a fast throughout all Yehuḏah.

4 And Yehuḏah gathered to inquire of יהוה, even from all the cities of Yehuḏah they came to seek יהוה.

5 And Yehoshaphat stood in the assembly of Yehuḏah and Yerushalayim, in the House of יהוה, in front of the new courtyard,

6 and said, "O יהוה Elohim of our fathers, are You not Elohim in the heavens, and do You not rule over all the reigns of the nations, and in Your hand is there not power and might, so that no one is able to stand against You?

7 "Are You not our Elohim? You have driven out the inhabitants of this land before Your people Yisra'ěl, and gave it to the seed of Aḇraham who loves You forever.

8 "And they dwell in it, and have built You a set-apart place in it for Your Name, saying,

9 'If evil does come upon us, such as the sword, judgment, or pestilence, or scarcity of food, we shall stand before this House and in Your presence – for Your Name is in this House – and cry out to You in our distress, and You do hear and save.'

10 "And now, see, the children of Ammon and Mo'aḇ, and Mount Sě'ir, whom You would not let Yisra'ěl invade when they came out of the land of Mitsrayim, for they turned from them and did not destroy them,

11 and see, they are repaying us by coming in to drive us out of Your possession which You have given us to inherit.

12 "O our Elohim, would You not judge them? For we are powerless against this great army that is coming against us. And we do not know what to do, but our eyes are upon You."

13 And all Yehuḏah, with their little ones, their wives, and their children, stood before יהוה.

14 And the Spirit of יהוה came upon Yaḥazi'ěl son of Zeḵaryahu, son of Benayah, son of Ye'i'ěl, son of Mattanyah, a Lěwite of the sons of Asaph, in the midst of the assembly,

15 and he said, "Listen, all Yehuḏah, and you inhabitants of Yerushalayim, and Sovereign Yehoshaphat! Thus said יהוה to you, 'Do not fear, nor be afraid of the face of this great army, for the battle is not yours, but Elohim's.

16 'Go down against them tomorrow. See, they are coming up by the ascent of Tsits, and you shall find them at the end of the wadi before the Wilderness of Yeru'ěl.

17 'It is not for you to fight in this. Position yourselves, stand still and see the deliverance of יהוה with you, O Yehuḏah and Yerushalayim!' Do not be afraid nor fear, go out against them tomorrow, for יהוה is with you."

18 And Yehoshaphat bowed his head with his face to the ground, and all Yehuḏah and

the inhabitants of Yerushalayim fell down
before יהוה, to bow themselves before
יהוה.
19 And the Lĕwites, of the children of the
Qehathites and of the children of the
Qorḥites stood up to praise יהוה Elohim of
Yisra'ĕl with exceedingly loud voice.
20 And they rose early in the morning and
went out into the Wilderness of Teqowa.
And as they went out, Yehoshaphat stood
and said, "Hear me, O Yehuḏah and you
inhabitants of Yerushalayim: Trust in יהוה
your Elohim and be steadfast, trust His
prophets and prosper."
21 And after consulting with the people,
he appointed those who should sing to
יהוה, and who should praise the splendour
of set-apartness, as they went out before
the army and were saying, "Give thanks to
יהוה, for His loving-commitment is everlasting."
22 And when they began singing and
praising, יהוה set ambushes against the
children of Ammon, Mo'aḇ, and Mount
Sĕ'ir, who had come against Yehuḏah, and
they were smitten.
23 Then the children of Ammon and
Mo'aḇ stood up against the inhabitants of
Mount Sĕ'ir to destroy and annihilate them.
And when they had made an end of the
inhabitants of Sĕ'ir, they helped to destroy
one another.
24 And when Yehuḏah came at the lookout
in the wilderness, they looked toward the
army and saw their dead bodies, lying on
the ground, and none had escaped.
25 And Yehoshaphat and his people came
to take away their spoil, and they found
among them a great amount of valuables
on the dead bodies, and precious jewelry,
which they stripped off for themselves,
more than they could take away. And they
were three days plundering the spoil, for it
was much.
26 And on the fourth day they assembled
in the Valley of Beraḵah, for there they
blessed יהוה. Therefore the name of that
place was called The Valley of Beraḵah to
this day.
27 Then they returned, every man of
Yehuḏah and Yerushalayim, with Yehoshaphat in front of them, to go back to
Yerushalayim with joy, for יהוה had made
them rejoice over their enemies.
28 And they came to Yerushalayim, with
harps and lyres and trumpets, to the House
of יהוה.
29 And the fear of Elohim was on all the
reigns of the lands when they heard that
יהוה had fought against the enemies of
Yisra'ĕl.
30 Then the reign of Yehoshaphat was at
peace, for his Elohim gave him rest on all
sides.
31 Thus Yehoshaphat reigned over Yehuḏah – thirty-five years old when he began
to reign, and he reigned twenty-five years
in Yerushalayim. And his mother's name
was Azuḇah the daughter of Shilḥi.
32 And he walked in the way of his father
Asa and did not turn aside from it, doing
what was right in the eyes of יהוה.
33 Only, the high places were not taken
away, for as yet the people had not prepared their hearts for the Elohim of their
fathers.
34 And the rest of the acts of Yehoshaphat,
the first and the last, see, they are written in
the book of Yĕhu son of Ḥanani, which is
mentioned in the book of the sovereigns of
Yisra'ĕl.
35 And after this Yehoshaphat sovereign
of Yehuḏah joined himself with Aḥazyah
sovereign of Yisra'ĕl. He did wrong in
doing so.
36 And he joined himself with him to
make ships to go to Tarshish, and they
made the ships in Etsyon Geḇer.
37 Then Eli'ezer son of Doḏawahu of
Marĕshah prophesied against Yehoshaphat,
saying, "Because you have joined yourself
with Aḥazyahu, יהוה shall break up your
work." And the ships were wrecked, so
that they were unable to go to Tarshish.

21 And Yehoshaphat slept with his
fathers, and was buried with his
fathers in the City of Dawiḏ. And Yehoram
his son reigned in his place.
2 And he had brothers, the sons of
Yehoshaphat: Azaryahu, and Yeḥi'ĕl, and
Zeḵaryahu, and Azaryahu, and Miḵa'ĕl,

and Shephatyahu. All these were sons of
Yehoshaphat sovereign of Yisra'ěl.
3 And their father gave them many gifts
of silver and gold and precious items, with
walled cities in Yehuḏah, but he had given
the reign to Yehoram because he was the
first-born.
4 And when Yehoram had risen up over
the reign of his father and strengthened
himself, he killed all his brothers with the
sword, and also others of the heads of
Yisra'ěl.
5 Yehoram was thirty-two years old when
he began to reign, and he reigned eight
years in Yerushalayim.
6 And he walked in the way of the sovereigns of Yisra'ěl, as the house of Aḥaḇ had
done, for he had the daughter of Aḥaḇ as a
wife. And he did evil in the eyes of יהוה.
7 However, יהוה would not destroy the
house of Dawiḏ, because of the covenant
He had made with Dawiḏ, and since He
had promised to give a lamp to him and to
his sons, all the days.
8 In his days the Eḏomites revolted from
under the hand of Yehuḏah, and appointed
a sovereign over themselves.
9 Then Yehoram went out with his officers, and all his chariots with him. And it
came to be that he rose by night and struck
the Eḏomites who had surrounded him and
the commanders of the chariots.
10 Thus the Eḏomites revolted from under
the hand of Yehuḏah to this day. Then
Liḇnah revolted from under his hand,
because he had forsaken יהוה Elohim of
his fathers.
11 He had also made high places in the
mountains of Yehuḏah, and caused the
inhabitants of Yerushalayim to commit
whoring, and led Yehuḏah astray.
12 And a letter came to him from Ěliyahu
the prophet, saying, Thus said יהוה Elohim
of your father Dawiḏ, "Because you have
not walked in the ways of Yehoshaphat
your father, or in the ways of Asa sovereign of Yehuḏah,
13 but have walked in the way of the
sovereigns of Yisra'ěl, and have made
Yehuḏah and the inhabitants of Yerushalayim to commit whoring like the whorings of the house of Aḥaḇ, and also have
killed your brothers, those of your father's
household, who were better than yourself,
14 see, יהוה is going to strike with a great
blow among your people, your children,
your wives, and all your possessions,
15 and you, with many sicknesses, with
disease of your intestines, until your
intestines come out because of the sickness, day by day."
16 And יהוה stirred up the spirit of the
Philistines against Yehoram, and of the
Araḇians who were near the Kushites.
17 And they came up into Yehuḏah and
broke into it, and captured all the possessions that were found in the sovereign's
house, and also his sons and his wives, so
that there was not a son left to him except
Yeho'aḥaz, the youngest of his sons.
18 And after all this יהוה plagued him in
his intestines with a disease for which there
was no healing.
19 And it came to be in the course of time,
at the end of two years, that his intestines
came out because of his sickness, and he
died in great pain. And his people made no
burning for him, like the burning for his
fathers.
20 He was thirty-two years old when he
began to reign, and he reigned eight years
in Yerushalayim, to no one's regret, and
passed away. And they buried him in the
City of Dawiḏ, but not in the burial-sites of
the sovereigns.

22 And the inhabitants of Yerushalayim set up Aḥazyahu his
youngest son to reign in his place, for the
raiding band that came with the Araḇians
into the camp had killed all the older sons.
So Aḥazyahu son of Yehoram, sovereign
of Yehuḏah, reigned.
2 Aḥazyahu was forty-two years old
when he began to reign, and he reigned in
Yerushalayim one year. And his mother's
name was Athalyahu the granddaughter of
Omri.
3 He too walked in the ways of the house
of Aḥaḇ, for his mother counselled him to
do wrong.
4 And he did evil in the eyes of יהוה,

like the house of Aḥaḇ, for they were his
counsellors after the death of his father, to
his destruction.
5 He also walked in their counsel, and
went with Yehoram son of Aḥaḇ sovereign
of Yisra'ěl to fight against Ḥaza'ěl sovereign of Aram at Ramoth Gil'ad. And the
Arameans struck Yoram,
6 and he returned to Yizre'ěl to recover
from the strikings with which they struck
him at Ramah, when he fought against
Ḥaza'ěl sovereign of Aram. And Azaryahu
son of Yehoram, sovereign of Yehuḏah,
went down to see Yehoram son of Aḥaḇ in
Yizre'ěl, for he was sick.
7 But from Elohim came the downfall of
Aḥazyahu, through his coming to Yoram.
For when he came he went out with
Yehoram against Yěhu son of Nimshi,
whom יהוה had anointed to cut off the
house of Aḥaḇ.
8 And it came to be, when Yěhu was executing judgment on the house of Aḥaḇ, that
he found the rulers of Yehuḏah and the
sons of Aḥazyahu's brothers who served
Aḥazyahu, and killed them.
9 So he searched for Aḥazyahu, and they
caught him while he was hiding in
Shomeron, and brought him to Yěhu, and
put him to death, then buried him, for they
said, "He is the son of Yehoshaphat, who
sought יהוה with all his heart." And there
was none in the house of Aḥazyahu strong
enough to reign.
10 And when Athalyahu the mother of
Aḥazyahu saw that her son was dead, she
rose up and destroyed all the offspring of
the reign of the house of Yehuḏah.
11 But Yehoshaḇ'ath, the daughter of the
sovereign, took Yo'ash son of Aḥazyahu,
and stole him away from among the sovereign's sons who were slain, and put him
and his nurse in a bedroom. So Yehoshaḇ'ath, the daughter of Sovereign Yehoram, the wife of Yehoyaḏa the priest,
because she was the sister of Aḥazyahu,
hid him from Athalyahu so that she could
not put him to death.
12 And he was hidden with them in the
House of Elohim for six years, while
Athalyah was reigning over the land.

23 And in the seventh year Yehoyaḏa
strengthened himself, and made
a covenant with the commanders of
hundreds: Azaryah son of Yeroḥam, and
Yishma'ěl son of Yehoḥanan, and Azaryahu son of Oḇěḏ, and Ma'asěyahu son of
Aḏayahu, and Elishaphat son of Ziḵri.
2 And they went about through Yehuḏah
and gathered the Lěwites from all the cities
of Yehuḏah, and the chiefs of the fathers of
Yisra'ěl, and they came to Yerushalayim.
3 And all the assembly made a covenant
with the sovereign in the House of Elohim.
And he said to them, "See, the son of the
sovereign is to reign, as יהוה has said of
the sons of Dawiḏ.
4 "This is what you do: One-third of you
entering on the Sabbath, of the priests and
the Lěwites, gatekeepers of the thresholds;
5 and one-third are at the sovereign's
house, and one-third at the Gate of the
Foundation, while all the people are in the
courtyards of the House of יהוה.
6 "And let no one come into the House of
יהוה except the priests and those of the
Lěwites who serve – they go in, for they
are set-apart. But all the people are to
guard the Charge of יהוה.
7 "And the Lěwites shall surround the
sovereign on all sides, every man with his
weapons in his hand. And whoever comes
into the house, let him be put to death. And
be with the sovereign when he comes in
and when he goes out."
8 And the Lěwites and all Yehuḏah did
according to all that Yehoyaḏa the priest
commanded. And each man took his men
who were to come in on the Sabbath, with
those going out on the Sabbath, for
Yehoyaḏa the priest did not dismiss the
divisions.
9 And Yehoyaḏa the priest gave to the
commanders of hundreds the spears and
the large and small shields which had been
Sovereign Dawiḏ's, that were in the House
of Elohim.
10 And he set all the people, every man
with his weapon in his hand, from the right
side of the House to the left side of the
House, along by the slaughter-place and by
the House, all around the sovereign.

11 And they brought out the son of the sovereign and put on him the diadem and the Witness, and set him up to reign. Then Yehoyaḏa and his sons anointed him, and said, "Let the sovereign live!"

12 And Athalyahu heard the noise of the people running and praising the sovereign, and she came to the people in the House of יהוה,

13 and looked and saw the sovereign standing by his column at the entrance. And the chiefs and the trumpeters were beside the sovereign, and all the people of the land rejoicing and blowing trumpets, also the singers with instruments of song, and those who led in praise. Then Athalyahu tore her garments and said, "Treason! Treason!"

14 And Yehoyaḏa the priest brought out the commanders of hundreds who were set over the army, and said to them, "Take her outside the ranks, and slay with the sword whoever follows her." For the priest said, "Do not kill her in the House of יהוה."

15 So they laid hands on her, and she went by way of the entrance of the Horse Gate into the sovereign's house, and they put her to death there.

16 Yehoyaḏa then made a covenant – between himself and the people and the sovereign – to be the people of יהוה.

17 And all the people went to the house of Baʽal, and broke it down. They completely broke up its slaughter-places and images, and killed Mattan the priest of Baʽal before the slaughter-places.

18 And Yehoyaḏa put the offices of the House of יהוה into the hand of the priests, the Lĕwites, whom Dawiḏ had assigned in the House of יהוה, to offer the ascending offerings of יהוה, as it is written in the Torah of Mosheh, with rejoicing and with singing, by the hands of Dawiḏ.

19 And he set the gatekeepers at the gates of the House of יהוה, so that no one who was in any way unclean should enter.

20 And he took the commanders of hundreds, and the nobles, and the governors of the people, and all the people of the land, and brought the sovereign down from the House of יהוה. And they went through the Upper Gate to the sovereign's house, and set the sovereign on the throne of the reign.

21 And all the people of the land rejoiced. And the city had rest, for they had slain Athalyahu with the sword.

24

Yo'ash was seven years old when he began to reign, and he reigned forty years in Yerushalayim. And the name of his mother was Tsiḇyah of Be'ĕrsheḇa.

2 And Yo'ash did what was right in the eyes of יהוה all the days of Yehoyaḏa the priest.

3 And Yehoyaḏa took for him two wives, and he brought forth sons and daughters.

4 And after this it came to be that Yo'ash set his heart on restoring the House of יהוה.

5 And he gathered the priests and the Lĕwites, and said to them, "Go out to the cities of Yehuḏah, and gather from all Yisra'ĕl silver to repair the House of your Elohim from year to year, and see that you hurry the matter." But the Lĕwites did not hurry it.

6 And the sovereign called Yehoyaḏa the chief, and said to him, "Why have you not required the Lĕwites to bring in from Yehuḏah and from Yerushalayim the levy of Mosheh the servant of יהוה and of the assembly of Yisra'ĕl, for the Tent of the Witness?"

7 For the sons of Athalyahu, that wrong woman, had broken into the House of Elohim, and had also prepared all the set-apart *vessels* of the House of יהוה to the Baʽals.

8 So the sovereign commanded and they made a chest, and set it outside at the gate of the House of יהוה,

9 and made it known in Yehuḏah and in Yerushalayim to bring to יהוה the levy that Mosheh the servant of Elohim had imposed on Yisra'ĕl in the wilderness.

10 And all the rulers and all the people rejoiced, and they brought in and put them into the chest to completion.

11 And it came to be, at that time, when the chest was brought to the sovereign's official by the hand of the Lĕwites, and when they saw that there was much silver,

that the sovereign's scribe and the high priest's officer came and emptied the chest, and took it and returned it to its place. So they did day by day, and gathered a large amount of silver.

12 And the sovereign and Yehoyaḏa gave it to those who did the work of the service of the House of יהוה. And they hired stonemasons and carpenters to restore the House of יהוה, and also those who worked in iron and bronze to repair the House of יהוה.

13 And the workmen laboured, and the work of restoration progressed in their hands, and they established the House of Elohim to its proper form and strengthened it.

14 And when they had finished, they brought the rest of the silver before the sovereign and Yehoyaḏa, and they made utensils from it for the House of יהוה, utensils for serving and offering, ladles and vessels of gold and silver. And they offered ascending offerings in the House of יהוה continually all the days of Yehoyaḏa.

15 And Yehoyaḏa was old and satisfied with days, and died, one hundred and thirty years old when he died.

16 And they buried him in the City of Dawiḏ among the sovereigns, for he had done good in Yisra'ěl, both toward Elohim and His house.

17 And after the death of Yehoyaḏa the rulers of Yehuḏah came and bowed themselves to the sovereign. And the sovereign listened to them,

18 and they forsook the House of יהוה Elohim of their fathers, and served the Ashěrim and the idols. And wrath came upon Yehuḏah and Yerushalayim because of their trespass.

19 And He sent prophets to them, to bring them back to יהוה. And they witnessed against them, but they did not listen.

20 Then the Spirit of Elohim came upon Zeḵaryah son of Yehoyaḏa the priest, who stood above the people, and said to them, "Thus said Elohim, 'Why are you transgressing the commands of יהוה, [a] and do not prosper? Because you have forsaken יהוה, He has forsaken you.' "

21 And they conspired against him, and at the command of the sovereign they stoned him with stones in the courtyard of the House of יהוה.

22 Thus Yo'ash the sovereign did not remember the loving-commitment which Yehoyaḏa his father had done to him, and killed his son. And as he died, he said, "יהוה does see, and repay!"

23 And it came to be, at the turn of the year, that the army of Aram came up against him. And they came into Yehuḏah and Yerushalayim, and destroyed all the rulers of the people from among the people, and sent all their spoil to the sovereign of Darmeseq.

24 For the army of Aram came with few men, but יהוה gave a very great army into their hand, because they had forsaken יהוה Elohim of their fathers. So they executed judgment against Yo'ash.

25 And when they had withdrawn from him – for they left him very sick – his own servants conspired against him because of the blood of the sons of Yehoyaḏa the priest, and killed him on his bed, and he died. And they buried him in the City of Dawiḏ, but they did not bury him in the burial-sites of the sovereigns.

26 And these are the ones who conspired against him: Zaḇaḏ the son of Shimʽath the Ammonitess, and Yehozaḇaḏ the son of Shimrith the Mo'aḇitess.

27 As to his sons, and the many words about him, and the rebuilding of the House of Elohim, see, they are written in the commentary of the book of the sovereigns. And Amatsyahu his son reigned in his place.

25

Amatsyahu was twenty-five years old when he began to reign, and he reigned twenty-nine years in Yerushalayim. And the name of his mother was Yehoaddan of Yerushalayim.

2 And he did what was right in the eyes of יהוה, but not with a perfect heart.

3 And it came to be, upon his strong *con-*

24a Miḵ. 3:8, Yn. 16:8.

trol of the reign, that he killed his servants
who had struck his father the sovereign.
4 But he did not put their children to
death, but did as it is written in the Torah in
the Book of Mosheh, where יהוה commanded, saying, "Fathers are not put to
death for their children, and children are
not put to death for their fathers, but each
one has to die for his own sin."
5 And Amatsyahu gathered Yehuḏah and
set over them commanders of thousands
and commanders of hundreds, according to
the fathers' houses, for all Yehuḏah and
Binyamin. And he registered them from
twenty years old and above, and found
them to be three hundred thousand choice
men going out to the army, handling spear
and shield.
6 And he hired one hundred thousand
mighty brave ones from Yisra'ěl for one
hundred talents of silver.
7 But a man of Elohim came to him, saying, "O sovereign, do not let the army of
Yisra'ěl go with you, for יהוה is not with
Yisra'ěl, with all the children of Ephrayim.
8 "But if you are going, do it! Be strong
in battle, *else* Elohim would make you fall
before the enemy, for Elohim has power to
help and to overthrow."
9 And Amatsyahu said to the man of
Elohim, "But what do we do about the
hundred talents which I have given to the
army of Yisra'ěl?" And the man of Elohim
answered, "יהוה has more to give you than
this."
10 So Amatsyahu dismissed the army that
had come to him from Ephrayim, to go
back home. And they were greatly enraged
against Yehuḏah, and they returned home
in a rage.
11 And Amatsyahu strengthened himself,
and led his people, and went to the Valley
of Salt and struck ten thousand of the sons
of Sěʽir.
12 And the sons of Yehuḏah took captive
another ten thousand alive, and they
brought them to the top of the rock, and
threw them down from the top of the rock,
and all of them were dashed to pieces.
13 And the soldiers of the army which
Amatsyahu had sent back from going with
him to battle, they raided the cities of
Yehuḏah from Shomeron to Běyth Ḥoron,
and struck three thousand in them, and
took much spoil.
14 And it came to be, after Amatsyahu
came from striking the Eḏomites, that he
brought the mighty ones of the people of
Sěʽir, and set them up to be his mighty
ones, and bowed down before them and
burned incense to them.
15 Therefore the displeasure of יהוה
burned against Amatsyahu, and He sent
him a prophet who said to him, "Why have
you sought the mighty ones of the people,
which did not deliver their own people
from your hand?"
16 And it came to be, as he talked with
him, that the sovereign said to him, "Have
we appointed you counsellor to the
sovereign? Stop! Why should they strike
you?" Then the prophet stopped and said,
"I know that Elohim has counselled to
destroy you, because you have done this
and have not listened to my counsel."
17 And Amatsyahu sovereign of Yehuḏah
took counsel and sent to Yo'ash son of
Yeho'aḥaz, son of Yěhu, sovereign of
Yisra'ěl, saying, "Come, let us look each
other in the face!"
18 And Yo'ash sovereign of Yisra'ěl sent
to Amatsyahu sovereign of Yehuḏah, saying, "The thistle that was in Leḇanon sent
to the cedar that was in Leḇanon, saying,
'Give your daughter to my son as wife.'
And a wild beast that was in Leḇanon
passed by and trampled the thistle.
19 "You have said, 'See, I have stricken
Eḏom,' and your heart has lifted you up to
boast. Now stay at home, why should you
stir up yourself to evil, that you should fall
– you and Yehuḏah with you?"
20 But Amatsyahu did not listen, for it
came from Elohim, in order to give them
into the hand of their enemies, because
they had sought the mighty ones of Eḏom.
21 So Yo'ash sovereign of Yisra'ěl went
out. And he and Amatsyahu sovereign of
Yehuḏah faced one another at Běyth
Shemesh, which belongs to Yehuḏah.
22 And Yehuḏah was smitten before
Yisra'ěl, and they each fled to his tent.

23 And Yo'ash the sovereign of Yisra'ĕl caught Amatsyahu sovereign of Yehuḏah, son of Yo'ash, son of Yeho'aḥaz, at Bĕyth Shemesh, and brought him to Yerushalayim, and broke down the wall of Yerushalayim from the Gate of Ephrayim to the Corner Gate, four hundred cubits,

24 and *took* all the gold and the silver, and all the utensils that were found in the House of Elohim with Oḇĕḏ-Eḏom, and the treasures of the sovereign's house, and hostages, and returned to Shomeron.

25 And Amatsyahu son of Yo'ash, sovereign of Yehuḏah, lived fifteen years after the death of Yo'ash son of Yeho'aḥaz, sovereign of Yisra'ĕl.

26 And the rest of the acts of Amatsyahu, from the first to the last, see, are they not written in the book of the sovereigns of Yehuḏah and Yisra'ĕl?

27 And from the time that Amatsyahu turned away from following יהוה, they made a conspiracy against him in Yerushalayim, and he fled to Laḵish. And they sent after him to Laḵish and killed him there,

28 and they brought him on horses and buried him with his fathers in the City of Yehuḏah.

26 And all the people of Yehuḏah took Uzziyahu, who was sixteen years old, and set him up to reign instead of his father Amatsyahu.

2 He built Ĕyloth and restored it to Yehuḏah, after the sovereign slept with his fathers.

3 Uzziyahu was sixteen years old when he began to reign, and he reigned fifty-two years in Yerushalayim. And his mother's name was Yeḵolyah of Yerushalayim.

4 And he did what was right in the eyes of יהוה, according to all that his father Amatsyahu did.

5 And he sought Elohim in the days of Zeḵaryahu, who had understanding in the visions of Elohim. And while he sought יהוה, Elohim made him prosper.

6 And he went out and fought against the Philistines, and broke down the wall of Gath, and the wall of Yaḇneh, and the wall of Ashdoḏ, and built cities around Ashdoḏ and among the Philistines.

7 And Elohim helped him against the Philistines, and against the Araḇians who lived in Gur Ba'al, and the Me'unites.

8 And the Ammonites gave gifts to Uzziyahu. And his name spread as far as the entrance of Mitsrayim, for he strengthened himself greatly.

9 And Uzziyahu built towers in Yerushalayim at the Corner Gate, and at the Valley Gate, and at the corner buttress, and strengthened them.

10 And he built towers in the wilderness, and dug many wells, for he had much livestock, both in the low country and in the plain, farmers and vinedressers in the mountains and in Karmel, for he loved the soil.

11 And Uzziyah had an army of fighting men who went out to battle by divisions, according to the number on their roll as prepared by Ye'i'ĕl the scribe and Ma'asĕyahu the officer, under the hand of Ḥananyahu, one of the sovereign's commanders.

12 The total number of the clan chiefs of the mighty brave ones was two thousand six hundred.

13 And under their hand was an army of three hundred and seven thousand five hundred that fought with mighty power, to help the sovereign against the enemy.

14 And Uzziyahu prepared for them, for the entire army, shields, and spears, and helmets, and body armour, and bows, and sling stones.

15 And he made machines in Yerushalayim, devised by skilled men, to be on the towers and the corners, to shoot arrows and large stones. And his name spread far and wide, for he was marvellously helped till he became strong.

16 But when he became strong his heart was lifted up, to his destruction, for he trespassed against יהוה his Elohim by entering the Hĕḵal of יהוה to burn incense on the slaughter-place of incense.

17 And Azaryahu the priest went in after him, and with him were eighty priests of יהוה, who were brave men.

18 And they stood up against Sovereign
Uzziyahu, and said to him, “It is not for
you, Uzziyahu, to burn incense to יהוה, but
for the priests, the sons of Aharon, who are
set-apart to burn incense. Get out of the
set-apart place, for you have trespassed,
and there is no esteem to you from יהוה
Elohim.”
19 And Uzziyahu was wroth. And he had a
censer in his hand to burn incense. And
while he was wroth with the priests,
leprosy broke out on his forehead, before
the priests in the House of יהוה, beside the
incense slaughter-place.
20 And Azaryahu the chief priest and all
the priests looked at him, and saw that he
was leprous on his forehead. And they hurried him from there. And he also hurried to
get out, because יהוה had struck him.
21 And Sovereign Uzziyahu was a leper
until the day of his death, and dwelt in a
separate house, because he was a leper, for
he was cut off from the House of יהוה.
And Yotham his son was over the sovereign’s house, ruling the people of the land.
22 And the rest of the acts of Uzziyahu,
from the first to the last, the prophet
Yeshayahu the son of Amots wrote.
23 So Uzziyahu slept with his fathers, and
they buried him with his fathers in the field
of the burial-place which belonged to the
sovereigns, for they said, “He is a leper.”
And Yotham his son reigned in his place.

27 Yotham was twenty-five years old
when he began to reign, and he
reigned sixteen years in Yerushalayim.
And his mother’s name was Yerushah the
daughter of Tsaḏoq.
2 And he did what was right in the eyes
of יהוה, according to all that his father
Uzziyahu had done. Only, he did not come
into the Hěḵal of יהוה. And the people
continued to act corruptly.
3 He built the Upper Gate of the House of
יהוה, and he built much on the wall of
Ophel.
4 And he built cities in the hill country of
Yehuḏah, and in the forests he built palaces
and towers.
5 And he fought with the sovereign of
the Ammonites and *had* strong *victory* over
them. And the children of Ammon gave
him in that year one hundred talents of silver, and ten thousand kors of wheat, and
ten thousand of barley. This is what the
children of Ammon paid him, also in the
second and third years.
6 And Yotham strengthened himself, for
he prepared his ways before יהוה his
Elohim.
7 And the rest of the acts of Yotham, and
all his battles and his ways, see, they are
written in the book of the sovereigns of
Yisra’ěl and Yehuḏah.
8 He was twenty-five years old when he
began to reign, and he reigned sixteen
years in Yerushalayim.
9 So Yotham slept with his fathers, and
they buried him in the City of Dawiḏ. And
his son Aḥaz reigned in his place.

28 Aḥaz was twenty years old when
he began to reign, and he reigned
sixteen years in Yerushalayim. And he did
not do what was right in the eyes of יהוה,
as his father Dawiḏ had done,
2 and walked in the ways of the sovereigns of Yisra’ěl, and made moulded
images for the Baʿals.
3 And he himself burned incense in the
Valley of the Son of Hinnom, and burned
his children in the fire, according to the
abominations of the nations whom יהוה
dispossessed from before the children of
Yisra’ěl,
4 and slaughtered and burned incense on
the high places, and on the hills, and under
every green tree.
5 Therefore יהוה his Elohim gave him
into the hand of the sovereign of Aram,
and they struck him, and took many of
them away as captives, and brought them
to Darmeseq. And he was also given into
the hand of the sovereign of Yisra’ěl, who
struck him with a great slaughter.
6 And Peqaḥ son of Remalyahu killed
one hundred and twenty thousand in
Yehuḏah in one day, all brave men,
because they had forsaken יהוה Elohim of
their fathers.
7 And Ziḵri, a mighty man of Ephrayim,

killed Maʽasěyahu son of the sovereign, and Azriqam the officer over the house, and Elqanah who was second to the sovereign.
8 And the children of Yisra'ěl took captive from their brothers two hundred thousand women, sons and daughters. And they also seized from them much spoil, and they brought the spoil to Shomeron.
9 But a prophet of יהוה was there, whose name was Oḏěḏ. And he went out before the army that came to Shomeron, and said to them, "See, because יהוה Elohim of your fathers was displeased with Yehuḏah, He has given them into your hand, and you have killed them in a rage that reaches up to the heavens.
10 "And now you are planning to make the children of Yehuḏah and Yerushalayim your male and female slaves, but are you not also guilty before יהוה your Elohim?
11 "Now therefore, listen to me, and return the captives whom you have taken captive from your brothers, for the heat of the wrath of יהוה is upon you."
12 And some of the heads of the children of Ephrayim: Azaryahu son of Yehoḥanan, Bereḵyahu son of Meshillěmoth, and Yeḥizqiyahu son of Shallum, and Amasa son of Ḥaḏlai, stood up against those who came from the army,
13 and said to them, "Do not bring the captives here, to bring on us guilt before יהוה. Are you planning to add to our sins and to our guilt? For our guilt is great, and burning is the wrath on Yisra'ěl."
14 And the armed men left the captives and the spoil before the leaders and all the assembly.
15 And the men who were designated by name rose up and took the captives, and from the spoil they put on all the naked among them, dressed them and gave them sandals, and gave them food and drink, and anointed them, and let all the weak ones ride on donkeys, and brought them to their brothers at Yeriḥo, the city of palm trees, then returned to Shomeron.
16 At that time Sovereign Aḥaz sent to the sovereigns of Ashshur to help him.
17 For the Eḏomites had come again, and struck Yehuḏah, and took away captives.
18 And the Philistines invaded the cities of the low country and of the South of Yehuḏah, and captured Běyth Shemesh, and Ayalon, and Geḏěroth, and Soḵo with its villages, and Timnah with its villages, and Gimzo with its villages, and dwelt there.
19 For יהוה had brought Yehuḏah low because of Aḥaz sovereign of Yisra'ěl, for he brought about a lack of restraint in Yehuḏah and trespassed against יהוה.
20 And Tiglath-Pileser the sovereign of Ashshur came against him and distressed him, and did not strengthen him,
21 though Aḥaz had taken some of the treasures from the House of יהוה, from the house of the sovereign, and from the leaders, and he gave it to the sovereign of Ashshur, but he did not help him.
22 And in the time of his distress Sovereign Aḥaz trespassed even more against יהוה – this Sovereign Aḥaz –
23 and he slaughtered to the mighty ones of Darmeseq, those striking him, saying, "Because the mighty ones of the sovereigns of Aram help them, I slaughter to them and they help me." But they were to cause him and all Yisra'ěl to stumble.
24 And Aḥaz gathered the utensils of the House of Elohim, and cut in pieces the utensils of the House of Elohim, and shut the doors of the House of יהוה, and made for himself slaughter-places in every corner of Yerushalayim.
25 And in every city, even the cities of Yehuḏah, he made high places to burn incense to other mighty ones, and provoked יהוה Elohim of his fathers.
26 And the rest of his acts and all his ways, from first to last, see, they are written in the book of the sovereigns of Yehuḏah and Yisra'ěl.
27 So Aḥaz slept with his fathers, and they buried him in the city, in Yerushalayim, but they did not bring him into the burial-sites of the sovereigns of Yisra'ěl. And Ḥizqiyahu his son reigned in his place.

29 Ḥizqiyahu began to reign when he was twenty-five years old, and he

reigned twenty-nine years in Yerushalayim. And his mother's name was Aḇiyah the daughter of Zeḵaryahu.
2 And he did what was right in the eyes of יהוה, according to all that his father Dawiḏ did.
3 In the first year of his reign, in the first new *moon*, he opened the doors of the House of יהוה and repaired them,
4 and brought in the priests and the Lěwites, and gathered them in the open place to the east.
5 And he said to them, "Listen to me, O Lěwites! Now set yourselves apart, set apart the House of יהוה Elohim of your fathers, and remove the uncleanness from the set-apart place.
6 "For our fathers have trespassed and have done evil in the eyes of יהוה our Elohim, and have forsaken Him, and have turned their faces away from the Dwelling Place of יהוה, and have given their backs.
7 "And they have shut the doors of the porch, and put out the lamps, and they have not burned incense or offered ascending offerings in the set-apart place to the Elohim of Yisra'ěl.
8 "Therefore the wrath of יהוה fell upon Yehuḏah and Yerushalayim, and He has given them up for a trembling, for an astonishment, and for a hissing, as you see with your eyes.
9 "And see, because of this our fathers have fallen by the sword. And our sons, and our daughters, and our wives are in captivity for this.
10 "Now it is in my heart to make a covenant with יהוה Elohim of Yisra'ěl, so that the heat of His wrath turns away from us.
11 "My sons, do not be slack, for יהוה has chosen you to stand before Him, to serve Him, and to be attendants for Him and burn incense."
12 And the Lěwites rose up: Maḥath son of Amasai and Yo'ěl son of Azaryahu, of the sons of the Qehathites; and of the sons of Merari, Qish son of Aḇdi and Azaryahu son of Yehallel'ěl; and of the Gěreshonites, Yo'aḥ son of Zimmah and Ěḏen son of Yo'aḥ;
13 and of the sons of Elitsaphan, Shimri and Ye'i'ěl; and of the sons of Asaph, Zeḵaryahu and Mattanyahu;
14 and of the sons of Hěman, Yeḥi'ěl and Shim'i; and of the sons of Yeḏuthun, Shemayah and Uzzi'ěl.
15 And they gathered their brothers, and set themselves apart, and went according to the command of the sovereign, at the words of יהוה, to cleanse the House of יהוה.
16 And the priests came into the inner part of the House of יהוה to cleanse it, and brought out all the uncleanness they found in the Hěḵal of יהוה to the courtyard of the House of יהוה. Then the Lěwites received it to take it outside to the wadi Qiḏron.
17 And they began to set apart on the first day of the first new *moon*, and on the eighth day of the new *moon* they came to the porch of יהוה. And they set apart the House of יהוה in eight days, and on the sixteenth day of the first new *moon* they had finished.
18 Then they came in to Sovereign Ḥizqiyahu and said, "We have cleansed all the House of יהוה, and the slaughter-place of ascending offerings with all its utensils, and the table of the showbread with all its utensils.
19 "And all the utensils which Sovereign Aḥaz in his reign had pushed aside, when he trespassed, we have prepared and set apart. And see, they are before the slaughter-place of יהוה."
20 And Sovereign Ḥizqiyahu rose up early, and gathered the heads of the city, and went up to the House of יהוה.
21 And they brought seven bulls, and seven rams, and seven lambs, and seven male goats for a sin offering for the reign, for the set-apart place, and for Yehuḏah. And he said to the priests, the sons of Aharon, to offer them on the slaughter-place of יהוה.
22 So they slew the bulls, and the priests received the blood and sprinkled it on the slaughter-place. And they slew the rams and sprinkled the blood on the slaughter-place. And they slew the lambs and sprinkled the blood on the slaughter-place.

23 And they brought out the male goats of
the sin offering before the sovereign and
the assembly, and they laid their hands on
them,
24 and the priests slew them, and with
their blood made a sin offering on the
slaughter-place, to make an atonement for
all Yisra'ěl, for the sovereign said that the
ascending offering and the sin offering is
for all Yisra'ěl.
25 And he appointed the Lěwites in the
House of יהוה with cymbals, with harps,
and with lyres, according to the command
of Dawiḏ, and of Gaḏ, seer of the sovereign, and of Nathan the prophet, for the
command was by the hand of יהוה, by the
hand of His prophets.
26 And the Lěwites stood with the instruments of Dawiḏ, and the priests with the
trumpets.
27 And Ḥizqiyahu gave the order to offer
the ascending offering on the slaughter-
place. And when the ascending offering
began, the singing unto יהוה began, with
the trumpets and with the instruments of
Dawiḏ sovereign of Yisra'ěl.
28 And all the assembly were bowing, and
the singers singing, and the trumpeters
blowing – all this until the ascending offering was completed.
29 And at the completion of the offering,
the sovereign and all who were present
with him bowed and worshipped.
30 And Sovereign Ḥizqiyahu and the
rulers ordered the Lěwites to sing praise to
יהוה with the words of Dawiḏ and of
Asaph the seer. And they sang praises with
gladness, and they bowed their heads and
worshipped.
31 And Ḥizqiyahu responded and said,
"Now that you have ordained yourselves to
יהוה, come near, and bring slaughterings
and thank offerings into the House of
יהוה." And the assembly brought in
slaughterings and thank offerings, and all
those whose hearts were so moved brought
ascending offerings.
32 And the number of the ascending offerings which the assembly brought was seventy bulls, one hundred rams, two hundred
lambs – all these for an ascending offering
to יהוה.
33 And the set-apart gifts were six hundred
bulls and three thousand sheep.
34 Only, the priests were too few, and were
unable to skin all the ascending offerings,
so their brothers the Lěwites helped them
until the work was completed and until the
other priests had set themselves apart, for
the Lěwites were more upright of heart to
set themselves apart, than the priests.
35 And there were also many ascending
offerings, with the fat of the peace offerings and with the drink offerings for every
ascending offering. Thus the service of the
House of יהוה was re-established.
36 And Ḥizqiyahu and all the people
rejoiced that Elohim had prepared the
people, because the matter came about so
suddenly.

30 And Ḥizqiyahu sent to all Yisra'ěl
and Yehuḏah, and he also wrote
letters to Ephrayim and Menashsheh, to
come to the House of יהוה at
Yerushalayim, to perform the Pěsaḥ to
יהוה Elohim of Yisra'ěl.
2 But the sovereign and his leaders and
all the assembly in Yerushalayim had taken
counsel to perform the Pěsaḥ in the second
new *moon*.
3 For they were unable to perform it at its
time, because not enough priests had set
themselves apart, and the people had not
gathered at Yerushalayim.
4 And the matter was right in the eyes of
the sovereign and in the eyes of all the
assembly.
5 And they settled the matter, to send a
call to all Yisra'ěl, from Be'ěrsheḇa to
Dan, to come to perform a Pěsaḥ to יהוה
Elohim of Yisra'ěl at Yerushalayim, since
they had not done it for a long time, as it is
written.
6 And the runners went to all Yisra'ěl and
Yehuḏah with the letters from the sovereign and his leaders, and spoke according
to the command of the sovereign,
"Children of Yisra'ěl, turn back to יהוה
Elohim of Aḇraham, Yitsḥaq, and Yisra'ěl,
so that He returns to the remnant of you
who have escaped from the hand of the

sovereigns of Ashshur.

7 "And do not be like your fathers and like your brothers, who trespassed against יהוה Elohim of their fathers, so that He gave them up to ruin, as you see.

8 "Now do not stiffen your neck, like your fathers, stretch forth the hand to יהוה, and come to His set-apart place, which He has set apart forever, and serve יהוה your Elohim, so that His burning wrath turns away from you.

9 "For if you turn back to יהוה, your brothers and your children shall be shown compassion by their captors, even to return to this land. For יהוה your Elohim shows favour and compassion, and does not turn His face from you if you turn back to Him."

10 And the runners passed from city to city throughout the land of Ephrayim and Menashsheh, as far as Zeḇulun. But they were laughing at them and mocking them.

11 Some from Ashěr and Menashsheh and from Zeḇulun, however, humbled themselves and came to Yerushalayim.

12 Also the hand of Elohim was on Yehuḏah to give them one heart to do the command of the sovereign and the rulers, at the word of יהוה.

13 And many people, a very great assembly, gathered at Yerushalayim to perform the Festival of Matzot [a] in the second new *moon*.

14 And they rose up and removed the slaughter-places that were in Yerushalayim, and they removed all the incense slaughter-places and threw them into the wadi Qiḏron.

15 Then they slew the Pěsaḥ [b] on the fourteenth day of the second new *moon*. And the priests and the Lěwites were ashamed, and set themselves apart, and brought the ascending offerings to the House of יהוה.

16 And they stood in their place according to their right-ruling. According to the Torah of Mosheh, the man of Elohim, the priests sprinkled the blood from the hand of the Lěwites.

17 For many in the assembly had not set themselves apart. Therefore the Lěwites were over the slaughter of the Pěsaḥim [c] for everyone who was not clean, to set them apart to יהוה.

18 For many of the people, many from Ephrayim and Menashsheh, Yissasḵar and Zeḇulun, had not been cleansed, yet they ate the Pěsaḥ contrary to what was written. But Ḥizqiyahu prayed for them, saying, "יהוה who is good, provide atonement for everyone

19 who has prepared his heart to seek Elohim, יהוה Elohim of his fathers, though he is not cleansed according to the cleansing of the set-apart place."

20 And יהוה listened to Ḥizqiyahu and healed the people.

21 And the children of Yisra'ěl who were in Yerushalayim performed the Festival of Matzot [a] seven days with great joy. And the Lěwites and the priests praised יהוה day by day, with instruments of praise before יהוה.

22 And Ḥizqiyahu spoke to the heart of all the Lěwites, those having good understanding concerning יהוה. So they ate during the appointed time, seven days, slaughtering slaughterings of peace *offerings* and making confession to יהוה Elohim of their fathers.

23 And all the assembly took counsel to perform another seven days, and they performed it another seven days with joy.

24 For Ḥizqiyahu sovereign of Yehuḏah presented to the assembly a thousand bulls and seven thousand sheep, and the rulers presented to the assembly a thousand bulls and ten thousand sheep. And a great number of priests set themselves apart.

25 And all the assembly of Yehuḏah rejoiced, and the priests and Lěwites, and all the assembly who had come from Yisra'ěl, and the sojourners who came from the land of Yisra'ěl, and those who dwelt in Yehuḏah.

26 And there came to be great joy in Yerushalayim, for since the days of Shelomoh son of Dawiḏ, the sovereign of Yisra'ěl, the like of this had not been in

30a - Unleavened Bread. *30b* - Passover. *30c* Pěsaḥim - Plural of Pěsaḥ. See Explanatory notes - Passover.

Yerushalayim.

27 And the priests, the Lĕwites, rose and blessed the people, and their voice was heard. And their prayer came up to His set-apart dwelling place, to heaven.

31

And at the completion of all this, all Yisra'ĕl who were present went out to the cities of Yehuḏah and broke down the pillars, and cut down the Ashĕrim, and tore down the high places and the slaughter-places, from all Yehuḏah, and Binyamin, and in Ephrayim and Menashsheh, even to completion. Then all the children of Yisra'ĕl returned to their own cities, each to his possession.

2 And Ḥizqiyahu appointed the divisions of the priests and of the Lĕwites according to their divisions, each according to his service of the priests and Lĕwites for ascending offerings and peace offerings, to serve and to give thanks, and to praise in the gates of the camp of יהוה.

3 And the sovereign portioned of his possessions for the ascending offerings, for the morning and evening ascending offerings, and the ascending offerings for the sabbaths and for the new *moons* and for the appointed times, as it is written in the Torah of יהוה.

4 And he said to the people, those who dwelt in Yerushalayim, to give the portion for the priests and the Lĕwites, so that they are strengthened in the Torah of יהוה.

5 And as the word spread, the children of Yisra'ĕl brought large quantities of the first-fruits of grain and wine, and oil and honey, and of all the increase of the field. And they brought in the tithe of all, a large amount.

6 And the children of Yisra'ĕl and Yehuḏah, those who dwelt in the cities of Yehuḏah, brought the tithe of cattle and sheep. Even the tithe of set-apart gifts which were set apart to יהוה their Elohim were brought in, and they gave heaps, heaps.

7 In the third new *moon* they began to pile up the heaps, and they finished in the seventh new *moon*.

8 And Ḥizqiyahu and the leaders came and saw the heaps, and they blessed יהוה and His people Yisra'ĕl.

9 And Ḥizqiyahu asked the priests and the Lĕwites about the heaps.

10 And Azaryahu the chief priest, from the house of Tsaḏoq, answered him and said, "Since they began to bring the offerings into the House of יהוה, we have had enough to eat and have plenty left, for יהוה has blessed His people. And this great amount is left over."

11 And Ḥizqiyahu ordered them to prepare rooms in the House of יהוה, and they prepared them.

12 Then they brought in the contribution, and the tithes, and the set-apart gifts, trustworthily. And Konanyahu the Lĕwite was leader over them, and Shimʿi his brother was the next.

13 And Yeḥi'ĕl, and Azazyahu, and Naḥath, and Asah'ĕl, and Yerimoth, and Yozaḇaḏ, and Eli'ĕl, and Yismaḵyahu, and Maḥath, and Benayahu were overseers under the hand of Konanyahu and Shimʿi his brother, by order of Ḥizqiyahu the sovereign and Azaryahu the ruler of the House of Elohim.

14 And Qorĕ son of Yimnah the Lĕwite, the keeper of the East Gate, was over the voluntary offerings to Elohim, to distribute the offerings of יהוה and the most set-apart gifts.

15 And under his hand were Ěḏen, and Minyamin, and Yĕshua, and Shemayahu, Amaryahu, and Sheḵanyahu, in the cities of the priests, to distribute trustworthily to their brothers by divisions, to the great as well as the small.

16 Besides those males from three years old and up who were written in the genealogy, they distributed to everyone who entered the House of יהוה his daily portion for the work of his service, by his division,

17 and to the priests who were written in the genealogy according to their father's house, and to the Lĕwites from twenty years old upward, by their duties in their divisions,

18 and to all listed in the genealogy, their little ones and their wives, their sons and daughters, all the company of them. For in

their trustworthiness they set themselves
apart in set-apartness.
19 And for the sons of Aharon the priests,
who were in the fields of the open land of
their cities, in each and every city, there
were men who were called by name to distribute portions to all the males among the
priests and to all who were listed by
genealogies among the Lěwites.
20 And Ḥizqiyahu did this in all Yehuḏah,
and he did what was good and what was
right and what was true before יהוה his
Elohim.
21 And in every work that he began in the
service of the House of Elohim, in the
Torah and in the command, to seek his
Elohim, with all his heart, he did and prospered.

32 After these matters and this trustworthiness, Sanḥěriḇ sovereign of
Ashshur came. And he entered Yehuḏah
and encamped against the cities of defence,
and said to break them open to himself.
2 And Ḥizqiyahu saw that Sanḥěriḇ had
come, and his face set to fight against
Yerushalayim,
3 and he took counsel with his rulers and
mighty men to stop the water from the
springs which were outside the city. And
they helped him.
4 And many people were gathered, and
they stopped all the springs and the stream
that ran through the land, saying, "Why
should the sovereigns of Ashshur come
and find much water?"
5 And he strengthened himself, and built
up all the wall that was broken, and raised
it up to the towers, and outside of it another
wall, and strengthened Millo, the City of
Dawiḏ, and made large numbers of
weapons and shields.
6 And he appointed battle officers over
the people, and gathered them to him in the
open space at the city gate, and spoke to
their heart, saying,
7 "Be strong and courageous, do not be
afraid nor be cast down before the sovereign of Ashshur, nor before all the army
that is with him. For with us there are more
than with him.
8 "With him is an arm of flesh, but with
us is יהוה our Elohim, to help us and to
fight our battles." And the people leaned
on the words of Ḥizqiyahu sovereign of
Yehuḏah.
9 After this Sanḥěriḇ the sovereign of
Ashshur sent his servants to Yerushalayim
– but he himself, and all his power with
him against Laḵish – to Ḥizqiyahu sovereign of Yehuḏah, and to all Yehuḏah who
were in Yerushalayim, saying,
10 "Thus said Sanḥěriḇ the sovereign of
Ashshur, 'On what are you trusting, that
you remain in Yerushalayim under siege?
11 'Is Ḥizqiyahu not persuading you to
give yourselves over to die by scarcity of
food and by thirst, saying, "יהוה our
Elohim shall deliver us from the hand of
the sovereign of Ashshur"?
12 'Has not Ḥizqiyahu himself taken away
His high places and His slaughter-places,
and ordered Yehuḏah and Yerushalayim,
saying, "Bow yourselves before one
slaughter-place and burn incense on it"?
13 'Do you not know what I and my
fathers have done to all the peoples of
other lands? Were the mighty ones of the
nations of those lands in any way able to
deliver their lands out of my hand?
14 'Who was there among all the mighty
ones of those nations that my fathers put
under the ban that could deliver his people
from my hand, that your Elohim should be
able to deliver you from my hand?
15 'And now, do not let Ḥizqiyahu deceive
you or persuade you like this, and do not
believe him; for no mighty one of any
nation or reign was able to deliver his people from my hand or the hand of my fathers
– much less your Elohim, to deliver you
from my hand!' "
16 And his servants spoke even more
against יהוה Elohim and against His servant Ḥizqiyahu.
17 And he wrote letters to reproach יהוה
Elohim of Yisra'ěl, and to speak against
Him, saying, "As the mighty ones of the
nations of other lands have not delivered
their people from my hand, so the Elohim
of Ḥizqiyahu shall not deliver His people
from my hand."

[18]Then they called out with a loud voice
in the language of Yehuḏah to the people
of Yerushalayim who were on the wall, to
frighten them and to trouble them, in order
to capture the city.
[19]And they spoke against the Elohim of
Yerushalayim, as against the mighty ones
of the people of the earth, the work of
men's hands.
[20]And Sovereign Ḥizqiyahu and the
prophet Yeshayahu, son of Amots, prayed
about this, and cried out to the heavens.
[21]And יהוה sent a messenger who cut
down every mighty brave one, both the
leader and the commander in the camp of
the sovereign of Ashshur, and he returned
shamefaced to his own land, and went into
the house of his mighty one, and there
some of his own offspring caused him to
fall by the sword.
[22]Thus יהוה saved Ḥizqiyahu and the
inhabitants of Yerushalayim from the hand
of Sanḥěriḇ the sovereign of Ashshur, and
from the hand of all others, and guided
them on every side.
[23]And many brought gifts to יהוה at
Yerushalayim, and presents to Ḥizqiyahu
sovereign of Yehuḏah, and he was exalted
in the eyes of all nations thereafter.
[24]In those days Ḥizqiyahu was sick and
near death, and he prayed to יהוה. And He
spoke to him and appointed a sign for him.
[25]However, Ḥizqiyahu did not repay
according to the good done to him, for his
heart was lifted up, therefore wrath came
upon him and upon Yehuḏah and
Yerushalayim.
[26]Then Ḥizqiyahu humbled himself for
the pride of his heart, he and the inhabitants of Yerushalayim, so that the wrath of
יהוה did not come upon them in the days
of Ḥizqiyahu.
[27]And Ḥizqiyahu had much riches and
esteem. And he made himself treasuries for
silver, and for gold, and for precious
stones, and for spices, and for shields, and
for all desirable utensils;
[28]and storehouses for the harvest of grain,
and wine, and oil, and stalls for all kinds of
livestock, and folds for flocks.
[29]And he made cities for himself, and
possessions of great numbers of flocks and
herds, for Elohim gave him much property.
[30]And Ḥizqiyahu himself had stopped the
upper outlet of the waters of Giḥon, and
directed them to the west side of the City
of Dawiḏ. And Ḥizqiyahu prospered in all
his work.
[31]However with the envoys of the princes
of Baḇel, whom they sent to ask him about
the wonder that was done in the land,
Elohim left him, in order to try him, to
know all that was in his heart.
[32]And the rest of the acts of Ḥizqiyahu,
and his loving-commitment, see, they
arewritten in the vision of Yeshayahu the
prophet, son of Amots, in the book of the
sovereigns of Yehuḏah and Yisra'ěl.
[33]So Ḥizqiyahu slept with his fathers, and
they buried him in the upper burial-sites of
the sons of Dawiḏ. And all Yehuḏah and
the inhabitants of Yerushalayim esteemed
him at his death. And Menashsheh his son
reigned in his place.

33 Menashsheh was twelve years old
when he began to reign, and he
reigned fifty-five years in Yerushalayim.
[2]But he did evil in the eyes of יהוה,
according to the abominations of the
nations whom יהוה dispossessed from
before the children of Yisra'ěl.
[3]For again he rebuilt the high places
which Ḥizqiyahu his father had broken
down, and raised up slaughter-places for
the Ba'als, and made Ashěrim, and bowed
himself to all the host of the heavens and
served them.
[4]And he built slaughter-places in the
House of יהוה, of which יהוה had said, "In
Yerushalayim is My Name, forever."
[5]And he built slaughter-places for all the
host of the heavens in the two courtyards
of the House of יהוה.
[6]And he made his sons pass through the
fire in the Valley of the Son of Hinnom,
and practised magic, and used divination
and witchcraft, and consulted mediums
and spiritists. He did much evil in the eyes
of יהוה, to provoke Him.
[7]And he placed a carved image of the
idol which he had made, in the House of

Elohim, of which Elohim had said to Dawiḏ and to Shelomoh his son, “In this house and in Yerushalayim, which I have chosen out of all the tribes of Yisra’ěl, I put My Name forever,

8 and no more shall I remove the foot of Yisra’ěl from the soil which I have appointed for your fathers – only if they guard to do all that I have commanded them, according to all the Torah and the laws and the right-rulings by the hand of Mosheh.”

9 Thus Menashsheh led Yehuḏah and the inhabitants of Yerushalayim astray, to do more evil than the nations whom יהוה had destroyed before the children of Yisra’ěl.

10 And יהוה spoke to Menashsheh and to his people, but they did not listen.

11 Therefore יהוה brought upon them the commanders of the army of the sovereign of Ashshur, who captured Menashsheh with hooks, bound him with bronze shackles, and made him go to Baḇel.

12 And when he was in distress, he sought the face of יהוה his Elohim, and humbled himself greatly before the Elohim of his fathers,

13 and prayed to Him. And He was moved by his entreaty and heard his supplication, and brought him back to Yerushalayim into his reign. And Menashsheh knew that יהוה was Elohim.

14 And after this he built a wall outside the City of Dawiḏ on the west of Giḥon, in the wadi, and as far as the entrance of the Fish Gate, and it went round Ophel, and he made it exceedingly high. And he put army commanders in all the walled cities of Yehuḏah.

15 And he removed the foreign mighty ones and the idol from the House of יהוה, and all the slaughter-places that he had built in the mount of the House of יהוה and in Yerushalayim, and he threw them out of the city.

16 And he built the slaughter-place of יהוה, and slaughtered slaughterings of peace *offerings* and thank offerings on it, and ordered Yehuḏah to serve יהוה Elohim of Yisra’ěl.

17 But the people were still slaughtering on the high places, though only to יהוה their Elohim.

18 And the rest of the acts of Menashsheh, his prayer to his Elohim, and the words of the seers who spoke to him in the Name of יהוה Elohim of Yisra’ěl, see, they are written in the book of the sovereigns of Yisra’ěl.

19 And his prayer, and his entreaty, and all his sin, and his trespass, and the places where he built high places and set up the Asherim and the carved images, before he was humbled, see, they are written among the words of the seers.

20 So Menashsheh slept with his fathers, and they buried him in his own house. And his son Amon reigned in his place.

21 Amon was twenty-two years old when he began to reign, and he reigned two years in Yerushalayim.

22 But he did evil in the eyes of יהוה, as his father Menashsheh had done. And Amon slaughtered to all the carved images which his father Menashsheh had made, and served them.

23 And he did not humble himself before יהוה, as his father Menashsheh had humbled himself, for Amon trespassed more and more.

24 And his servants conspired against him, and killed him in his own house.

25 But the people of the land struck all those who had conspired against Sovereign Amon, and the people of the land set up his son Yoshiyahu to reign in his place.

34

Yoshiyahu was eight years old when he began to reign, and he reigned thirty-one years in Yerushalayim.

2 And he did what was right in the eyes of יהוה, and walked in the ways of his father Dawiḏ, and did not turn aside, right or left.

3 And in the eighth year of his reign, while he was still young, he began to seek the Elohim of his father Dawiḏ. And in the twelfth year he began to cleanse Yehuḏah and Yerushalayim from the high places, and the Asherim, and the carved images, and the moulded images.

4 And they broke down the slaughter-

places of the Baʿals in his presence, and the sun-pillars which were above them he cut down. And the Ashěrim, and the carved images, and the moulded images he smashed, and ground them up and strewed it on the surface of the burial-sites of those who had slaughtered to them.
5 And he burned the bones of the priests on their slaughter-places, and cleansed Yehuḏah and Yerushalayim,
6 and in the cities of Menashsheh, and Ephrayim, and Shimʿon, as far as Naphtali, in their ruins all around.
7 And he broke down the slaughter-places and the Ashěrim, and ground the carved images into dust, and cut down all the sun-pillars throughout all the land of Yisra'ěl, and returned to Yerushalayim.
8 And in the eighteenth year of his reign, when he had cleansed the land and the House, he sent Shaphan son of Atsalyahu, and Maʿasěyahu the head of the city, and Yo'aḥ son of Yo'aḥaz the recorder, to repair the House of יהוה his Elohim.
9 And they went to Ḥilqiyahu the high priest, and they gave the silver that was brought into the House of Elohim, which the Lěwites who kept the doors had gathered from the hand of Menashsheh and Ephrayim, and from all the remnant of Yisra'ěl, and from all Yehuḏah and Binyamin, and which they had brought back to Yerushalayim,
10 and they gave it in the hand of the workmen, those appointed over the House of יהוה. And they gave it to the workmen who worked in the House of יהוה, to repair and strengthen the house.
11 And they gave it to the craftsmen and to the builders, to buy hewn stone and timber for couplings and for beams for the houses which the sovereigns of Yehuḏah had destroyed.
12 And the men did the work trustworthily. And over them were appointed Yaḥath and Oḇaḏyahu the Lěwites, of the sons of Merari, and Zeḵaryah and Meshullam, of the sons of the Qehathites, to oversee; and of the Lěwites, all of whom were skilled in instruments of song,
13 and over the burden bearers, and overseers of all who did work in any kind of service. And of the Lěwites were scribes, and officers, and gatekeepers.
14 And when they brought out the silver that was brought into the House of יהוה, Ḥilqiyahu the priest found the Book of the Torah of יהוה given by Mosheh.
15 Then Ḥilqiyahu responded and said to Shaphan the scribe, "I have found the Book of the Torah in the House of יהוה." And Ḥilqiyahu gave the book to Shaphan.
16 And Shaphan brought the book to the sovereign, and brought the sovereign word, saying, "All that has been given into the hand of your servants, they are doing.
17 "And they have poured out the silver that was found in the House of יהוה, and have given it into the hand of those appointed and the workmen."
18 And Shaphan the scribe informed the sovereign, saying, "Ḥilqiyahu the priest has given me a book." And Shaphan read it before the sovereign.
19 And it came to be, when the sovereign heard the words of the Torah, that he tore his garments.
20 And the sovereign commanded Ḥilqiyahu, Aḥiqam son of Shaphan, and Aḇdon son of Miḵah, and Shaphan the scribe, and Asayah a servant of the sovereign, saying,
21 "Go, inquire of יהוה for me, and for him who is left in Yisra'ěl and in Yehuḏah, concerning the words of the book that is found. For great is the wrath of יהוה that is poured out on us, because our fathers have not guarded the Word of יהוה, to do according to all that is written in this book."
22 Then Ḥilqiyahu and those of the sovereign went to Ḥuldah the prophetess, the wife of Shallum son of Toqhath, son of Ḥasrah, keeper of the wardrobe, who was dwelling in Yerushalayim in the Second Quarter. And they spoke to her about this.
23 And she said to them, "Thus said יהוה Elohim of Yisra'ěl, 'Say to the man who sent you to Me,
24 "Thus said יהוה, 'See, I am bringing evil on this place and on its inhabitants, all the curses that are written in the book which they have read before the sovereign

of Yehuḏah,

25 because they have forsaken Me and burned incense to other mighty ones, to provoke Me with all the works of their hands. Therefore My wrath is poured out on this place, and is not quenched.' " '

26 "And to the sovereign of Yehuḏah, who sent you to inquire of יהוה, say this to him, 'Thus said יהוה Elohim of Yisra'ěl, whose words you have heard,

27 "Because your heart was tender, and you humbled yourself before Elohim when you heard His words against this place and against its inhabitants, and you humbled yourself before Me, and you tore your garments and wept before Me, I also have heard," declares יהוה.

28 "See, I am gathering you to your fathers, and you shall be gathered to your burial-site in peace, so that your eyes would not see all the evil that I am bringing on this place and its inhabitants." ' " So they brought back word to the sovereign.

29 And the sovereign sent and gathered all the elders of Yehuḏah and Yerushalayim.

30 And the sovereign went up to the House of יהוה with all the men of Yehuḏah and the inhabitants of Yerushalayim, and the priests and the Lěwites, and all the people, both great and small. And he read in their hearing all the words of the Book of the Covenant which had been found in the House of יהוה.

31 And the sovereign stood in his place and made a covenant before יהוה, to follow יהוה and to guard His commands and His witnesses and His laws, with all his heart and all his being, to do the words of the covenant that were written in this book.

32 And he made stand all who were present in Yerushalayim and Binyamin. And the inhabitants of Yerushalayim did according to the covenant of Elohim, the Elohim of their fathers.

33 And Yoshiyahu removed all the abominations from all the lands that belonged to the children of Yisra'ěl, and made all who were present in Yisra'ěl diligently serve יהוה their Elohim. All his days they did not turn away from following יהוה Elohim of their fathers.

35 And Yoshiyahu performed a Pěsaḥ to יהוה in Yerushalayim, and they slew the Pěsaḥ on the fourteenth day of the first new *moon*.

2 And he set the priests in their duties and strengthened them for the service of the House of יהוה,

3 and said to the Lěwites who were teaching all Yisra'ěl, who were set-apart to יהוה, "Put the set-apart ark in the house which Shelomoh son of Dawiḏ, sovereign of Yisra'ěl, built. It is no longer to be a burden on your shoulders. Now serve יהוה your Elohim and His people Yisra'ěl,

4 and prepare by the fathers' houses, according to your divisions, by the writing of Dawiḏ sovereign of Yisra'ěl and by the writing of Shelomoh his son.

5 "And stand in the set-apart place by the divisions of the fathers' houses of your brothers the lay people, and the portion of the father's house of the Lěwites.

6 "And slay the Pěsaḥ, and set yourselves apart, and prepare for your brothers, to do according to the word of יהוה by the hand of Mosheh."

7 And Yoshiyahu gave the lay people lambs and young goats from the flock, all for Pěsaḥim for everyone present, to the number of thirty thousand, and three thousand cattle – these were from the sovereign's possessions.

8 And his leaders contributed a voluntary offering to the people, to the priests, and to the Lěwites. Ḥilqiyah, and Zeḵaryahu, and Yeḥi'ěl, leaders of the House of Elohim, gave to the priests for the Pěsaḥim two thousand six hundred, and three hundred cattle;

9 and Konanyahu, his brothers Shemayahu and Nethaně'l, and Ḥashaḇyahu and Ye'i'ěl and Yozaḇaḏ, chiefs of the Lěwites, gave to the Lěwites for Pěsaḥim five thousand, and five hundred cattle.

10 And the service was prepared, and the priests stood in their places, and the Lěwites in their divisions, according to the command of the sovereign,

11 and they slew the Pěsaḥ. And the

priests sprinkled out of their hands, while the Lĕwites were skinning.
[12]And they removed the ascending offerings, to give them to the divisions of the fathers' houses of the lay people, to bring to יהוה, as it is written in the Book of Mosheh, and the same with the cattle.
[13]So they roasted the Pĕsaḥ with fire according to the right-ruling, and they boiled the set-apart offerings in pots, and in cauldrons, and in bowls, and brought them speedily to all the lay people.
[14]And afterward they prepared for themselves and for the priests, because the priests, the sons of Aharon, were offering ascending offerings and fat until night. So the Lĕwites prepared for themselves and for the priests, the sons of Aharon.
[15]And the singers, the sons of Asaph, were in their places, according to the command of Dawiḏ, and Asaph, and Hĕman, and Yeḏuthun the seer of the sovereign. And the gatekeepers at each gate did not have to leave their position, because their brothers the Lĕwites prepared for them.
[16]And all the service of יהוה was prepared that day, to perform the Pĕsaḥ and to offer ascending offerings on the slaughter-place of יהוה, according to the command of Sovereign Yoshiyahu.
[17]And the children of Yisra'ĕl who were present performed the Pĕsaḥ at that time, and the Festival of Matzot for seven days.
[18]There had not been a Pĕsaḥ performed in Yisra'ĕl like it since the days of Shemu'ĕl the prophet. And none of the sovereigns of Yisra'ĕl had performed such a Pĕsaḥ as Yoshiyahu performed, with the priests and the Lĕwites, and all Yehuḏah and Yisra'ĕl who were present, and the inhabitants of Yerushalayim.
[19]In the eighteenth year of the reign of Yoshiyahu this Pĕsaḥ was performed.
[20]After all this, when Yoshiyahu had prepared the House, Neḵo sovereign of Mitsrayim came up to fight against Karkemish by the Euphrates. And Yoshiyahu went out against him.
[21]And he sent messengers to him, saying, "What have I to do with you, sovereign of Yehuḏah? I am not coming against you this day, but against the house with which I am fighting, for Elohim commanded me to make haste. Leave Elohim alone, who is with me, lest He destroy you."
[22]However, Yoshiyahu would not turn his face from him, but disguised himself to fight against him, and did not listen to the words of Neḵo from the mouth of Elohim, and came to fight in the Valley of Meḡiddo.
[23]And the archers shot at Sovereign Yoshiyahu. And the sovereign said to his servants, "Take me away, for I am severely wounded."
[24]And his servants took him out of that chariot and put him in the second chariot that he had, and they brought him to Yerushalayim. And he died, and was buried in one of the burial-sites of his fathers. And all Yehuḏah and Yerushalayim were mourning for Yoshiyahu.
[25]And Yirmeyahu lamented for Yoshiyahu. And to this day all the singing men and the singing women speak of Yoshiyahu in their lamentations, and made it a law in Yisra'ĕl. And see, they are written in the Laments.
[26]And the rest of the acts of Yoshiyahu and his loving-commitment, according to what was written in the Torah of יהוה,
[27]and his acts from the first to the last, see, they are written in the book of the sovereigns of Yisra'ĕl and Yehuḏah.

36

And the people of the land took Yeho'aḥaz son of Yoshiyahu, and set him up to reign in his father's place in Yerushalayim.
[2]Yeho'aḥaz was twenty-three years old when he began to reign, and he reigned three new *moons* in Yerushalayim.
[3]And the sovereign of Mitsrayim turned him aside in Yerushalayim, and imposed on the land a levy of one hundred talents of silver and a talent of gold.
[4]And the sovereign of Mitsrayim made his brother Elyaqim sovereign over Yehuḏah and Yerushalayim, and changed his name to Yehoyaqim. And Neḵo took Yeho'aḥaz his brother and brought him to

Mitsrayim.
[5] Yehoyaqim was twenty-five years old when he began to reign, and he reigned eleven years in Yerushalayim. And he did evil in the eyes of יהוה his Elohim.
[6] Neḇuḵaḏnetstsar sovereign of Baḇel came up against him, and bound him in bronze shackles to take him away to Baḇel.
[7] And Neḇuḵaḏnetstsar brought some of the utensils from the House of יהוה to Baḇel, and put them in his hěḵal at Baḇel.
[8] And the rest of the acts of Yehoyaqim, the abominations which he did, and what was found against him, see, they are written in the book of the sovereigns of Yisra'ěl and Yehuḏah. Then Yehoyaḵin his son reigned in his place.
[9] Yehoyaḵin was eight years old when he began to reign, and he reigned in Yerushalayim three new *moons* [a] and ten days. And he did evil in the eyes of יהוה.
[10] And at the turn of the year Sovereign Neḇuḵaḏnetstsar sent and brought him to Baḇel, with the valuable utensils from the House of יהוה, and made Tsiḏqiyahu, Yehoyaqim's brother, sovereign over Yehuḏah and Yerushalayim.
[11] Tsiḏqiyahu was twenty-one years old when he began to reign, and he reigned eleven years in Yerushalayim.
[12] And he did evil in the eyes of יהוה his Elohim. He did not humble himself before Yirmeyahu the prophet, who spoke from the mouth of יהוה.
[13] And he also rebelled against Sovereign Neḇuḵaḏnetstsar, who had made him swear by Elohim, but he stiffened his neck and hardened his heart against turning to יהוה Elohim of Yisra'ěl.
[14] Also, all the heads of the priests and the people trespassed more and more, according to all the abominations of the nations, and they defiled the House of יהוה which He had set apart in Yerushalayim.
[15] And יהוה Elohim of their fathers sent to them, by His messengers, rising up early and sending them, for He had compassion on His people and on His dwelling place.
[16] But they were mocking the messengers of Elohim and despising His words and scoffing at His prophets, until the wrath of יהוה arose against His people, until there was no healing.
[17] Therefore He brought against them the sovereign of the Kasdim, and he killed their young men with the sword in the House of their set-apart place, and had no compassion on young man or maiden, on the aged or the weak – He gave all into his hand.
[18] And all the utensils from the House of Elohim, great and small, and the treasures of the House of יהוה, and the treasures of the sovereign and of his leaders, all these he brought to Baḇel.
[19] And they burned the House of Elohim, and broke down the wall of Yerushalayim, and burned all its palaces with fire, and destroyed all its valuable utensils.
[20] And those who escaped from the sword he exiled to Baḇel, where they became servants to him and his sons until the reign of the reign of Persia,
[21] in order to fill the word of יהוה by the mouth of Yirmeyahu, until the land had enjoyed her Sabbaths. As long as she lay waste she kept Sabbath, until seventy years were completed.
[22] And in the first year of Koresh sovereign of Persia, in order to accomplish the word of יהוה by the mouth of Yirmeyahu, יהוה stirred up the spirit of Koresh sovereign of Persia, so that he called out in all his reign, and also put it in writing, saying,
[23] "Thus said Koresh sovereign of Persia, 'יהוה Elohim of the heavens has given me all the reigns of the earth. And He has commanded me to build Him a house in Yerushalayim, which is in Yehuḏah. Whoever is among you of all His people, יהוה his Elohim be with him, and let him go up!' "

36a - Months.

THE

SECOND WRITINGS

Also called
Netzarim Writings, Messianic Writings, New Covenant,
haBrit haḤadasha or New Testament

MATTITHYAHU

MATTHEW

1 The book of the genealogy of יהושע Messiah, Son of Dawiḏ, Son of Aḇraham:

2 Aḇraham brought forth Yitsḥaq, and Yitsḥaq brought forth Yaʽaqoḇ, and Yaʽaqoḇ brought forth Yehuḏah and his brothers.

3 And Yehuḏah brought forth Perets and Zeraḥ by Tamar, and Perets brought forth Ḥetsron, and Ḥetsron brought forth Ram.

4 And Ram brought forth Amminaḏaḇ, and Amminaḏaḇ brought forth Naḥshon, and Naḥshon brought forth Salmon.

5 And Salmon brought forth Boʽaz by Raḥaḇ, and Boʽaz brought forth Oḇěḏ by Ruth, and Oḇěḏ brought forth Yishai.

6 And Yishai brought forth Dawiḏ the sovereign, and Dawiḏ the sovereign brought forth Shelomoh by Uriyah's wife.

7 And Shelomoh brought forth Reḥaḇʽam, [a] and Reḥaḇʽam brought forth Aḇiyah, and Aḇiyah brought forth Asa.

8 And Asa brought forth Yehoshaphat, and Yehoshaphat brought forth Yoram, and Yoram brought forth Uzziyah.

9 And Uzziyah brought forth Yotham, and Yotham brought forth Aḥaz, and Aḥaz brought forth Ḥizqiyahu.

10 And Ḥizqiyahu brought forth Menashsheh, and Menashsheh brought forth Amon, and Amon brought forth Yoshiyahu.

11 And Yoshiyahu brought forth Yeḵonyah and his brothers at the time of the exile to Baḇel.

12 And after the exile to Baḇel, Yeḵonyah brought forth She'alti'ěl, and She'alti'ěl brought forth Zerubbaḇel.

13 And Zerubbaḇel brought forth Aḇihuḏ, and Aḇihuḏ brought forth [Aḇner and Aḇner brought forth] [b] Elyaqim, and Elyaqim brought forth Azor.

14 And Azor brought forth Tsaḏoq, and Tsaḏoq brought forth Aqim, and Aqim brought forth Elihuḏ.

15 And Elihuḏ brought forth Elʽazar, and Elʽazar brought forth Mattan, and Mattan brought forth Yaʽaqoḇ.

16 And Yaʽaqoḇ brought forth Yosěph the husband of Miryam, of whom was born יהושע who is called Messiah.

17 So all the generations from Aḇraham to Dawiḏ were fourteen generations, and from Dawiḏ until the exile to Baḇel were fourteen generations, and from the exile to Baḇel until the Messiah were fourteen generations.

18 But the birth of יהושע Messiah was as follows: After His mother Miryam was engaged to Yosěph, before they came together, she was found to be pregnant from the Set-apart Spirit.

19 And Yosěph her husband, being righteous, and not wishing to make a show of her, had in mind to put her away secretly.

20 But while he thought about this, see, a messenger of יהוה appeared to him in a dream, saying, "Yosěph, son of Dawiḏ, do not be afraid to take Miryam as your wife, for that which is in her was brought forth from the Set-apart Spirit.

21 "And she shall give birth to a Son, and you shall call His Name יהושע for He shall save [c] His people from their sins."

22 And all this came to be in order to fill what was spoken by יהוה through the prophet, saying,

23 **"See, an 'almah' [d] shall conceive, and she shall give birth to a Son, and they shall call His Name Immanu'ěl,"** Yesh. 7:14 which translated, means, "Ěl with us."

24 And Yosěph, awaking from his sleep,

1a His mother was an Ammorite - Mel.א 14:21,31. *1b* [Aḇner and Aḇner brought forth] appears in the Du Tillit Hebrew text. *1c* This is the meaning of the Hebrew of His Name. *1d* According to the Shem Toḇ Hebrew text & Yesh. 7:14. Virgin / young woman. See also Explanatory note "Maiden".

did as the messenger of יהוה commanded him and took his wife,

25 but knew her not until she gave birth to her Son, the first-born. And he called His Name יהושע.

2 And יהושע having been born in Běyth Leḥem of Yehuḏah in the days of Herodes the sovereign, see, Magi from the east came to Yerushalayim,

2 saying, "Where is He who has been born Sovereign of the Yehuḏim? For we saw His star in the East and have come to do reverence to Him."

3 And Herodes the sovereign, having heard, was troubled, and all Yerushalayim with him.

4 And having gathered all the chief priests and scribes of the people together, he asked them where the Messiah was to be born.

5 And they said to him, "In Běyth Leḥem of Yehuḏah, for thus it has been written by the prophet,

6 **'But you, Běyth Leḥem, in the land of Yehuḏah, you are by no means least among the rulers of Yehuḏah, for out of you shall come a Ruler who shall shepherd My people Yisra'ěl.'** " Miḵ. 5:2

7 Then Herodes, having called the Magi secretly, learned exactly from them what time the star appeared.

8 And having sent them to Běyth Leḥem, he said, "Go and search diligently for the Child, and when you have found Him, bring back word to me, so that I too might go and do reverence to Him."

9 And having heard the sovereign, they went. And see, the star which they had seen in the East went before them, until it came and stood over where the Child was.

10 And seeing the star, they rejoiced with exceedingly great joy.

11 And coming into the house, they saw the Child with Miryam His mother, and fell down and did reverence to Him, and opening their treasures, they presented to Him gifts of gold, and frankincense, and myrrh.

12 And having been warned in a dream that they should not return to Herodes, they departed for their own country by another way.

13 And when they had left, see, a messenger of יהוה appeared to Yosěph in a dream, saying, "Arise, take the Child and His mother, and flee to Mitsrayim, and remain there until I bring you word, for Herodes is about to seek the Child to destroy Him."

14 And rising up, he took the Child and His mother by night and departed for Mitsrayim,

15 and remained there until the death of Herodes, to fill what was spoken by יהוה through the prophet, saying, **"Out of Mitsrayim I have called My Son."** Shem. 4:22-23, Hosh. 11:1, Ḥazon 21:7.

16 Then Herodes, having seen that he was fooled by the Magi, was greatly enraged, and he sent forth and slew all the male children in Běyth Leḥem and in all its borders, from two years old and under, according to the time which he had exactly learnt from the Magi.

17 Then was filled what was spoken by Yirmeyahu the prophet, saying,

18 **"A voice was heard in Ramah, wailing and weeping, and great mourning – Raḥěl weeping for her children, refusing to be comforted, because they were no more."** Yirm. 31:15

19 And Herodes having died, see, a messenger of יהוה appeared in a dream to Yosěph in Mitsrayim,

20 saying, "Arise, *and* take the Child and His mother, and go into the land of Yisra'ěl, for those seeking the life of the Child are dead."

21 And rising up, he took the Child and His mother, and came into the land of Yisra'ěl.

22 But hearing that Archelaos was reigning over Yehuḏah instead of his father Herodes, he was afraid to go there. And having been warned in a dream, he departed to the parts of Galil,

23 and came and dwelt in a city called Natsareth – thus to fill what was spoken [a]

2a *Spoken* (not written) by the prophets (plural).

by the prophets, "He shall be called a Natsarene."

3 And in those days Yoḥanan the Immerser came proclaiming in the wilderness of Yehuḏah,

2 and saying, "Repent, for the reign of the heavens has come near!"

3 For this is he who was spoken of by the prophet Yeshayahu, saying, **"A voice of one crying in the wilderness, 'Prepare the way of יהוה, make His paths straight.' "** Yesh. 40:3

4 And Yoḥanan had a garment of camel's hair, and a leather girdle around his waist. And his food was locusts and wild honey.

5 Then Yerushalayim, and all Yehuḏah, and all the country around the Yardĕn went out to him,

6 and they were immersed by him in the Yardĕn, confessing their sins.

7 And seeing many of the Pharisees and Sadducees coming to his immersion, he said to them, "Brood of adders! Who has warned you to flee from the coming wrath?

8 "Bear, therefore, fruits worthy of repentance,

9 and do not think to say to yourselves, 'We have Aḇraham as father.' [a] For I say to you that Elohim is able to raise up children [b] to Aḇraham from these stones. [b]

10 "And the axe is already laid to the root of the trees. Every tree, then, which does not bear good fruit is cut down and thrown into the fire.

11 "I indeed immerse you in water unto repentance, but He who is coming after me is mightier than I, whose sandals I am not worthy to bear. He shall immerse you in the Set-apart Spirit and fire.

12 "His winnowing fork is in His hand, and He shall thoroughly cleanse His threshing-floor, and gather His wheat into the storehouse, but the chaff He shall burn with unquenchable fire."

13 Then יהושע came from Galil to Yoḥanan at the Yardĕn to be immersed by him.

14 But Yoḥanan was hindering Him, saying, "I need to be immersed by You, and You come to me?"

15 But יהושע answering, said to him, "Permit it now, for thus it is fitting for us to fill all righteousness." Then he permitted Him.

16 And having been immersed, יהושע went up immediately from the water, and see, the heavens were opened, and He saw the Spirit of Elohim descending like a dove and coming upon Him,

17 and see, a voice out of the heavens, saying, "This is My Son, the Beloved, in whom I delight."

4 Then יהושע was led up by the Spirit into the wilderness to be tried by the devil.

2 And after having fasted forty days and forty nights, He was hungry.

3 And the trier came and said to Him, "If You are the Son of Elohim, command that these stones become bread."

4 But He answering, said, "It has been written, **'Man shall not live by bread alone, but by every word that comes from the mouth of יהוה.' "** Deḇ. 8:3

5 Then the devil took Him up into the set-apart city, set Him on the edge of the Set-apart Place,

6 and said to Him, "If You are the Son of Elohim, throw Yourself down. For it has been written, **'He shall command His messengers concerning you,'** Teh. 91:11 and, **'In their hands they shall bear you up, so that you do not dash your foot against a stone.' "** Teh. 91:12

7 יהושע said to him, "It has also been written, **'You shall not try יהוה your Elohim.' "** Deḇ. 6:16

8 Again, the devil took Him up on a very high mountain, and showed Him all the reigns of the world, and their esteem,

9 and said to Him, "All these I shall give You if You fall down and worship me."

10 Then יהושע said to him, "Go, Satan! For it has been written, **'You shall worship יהוה your Elohim, and Him alone**

3a See Yn. 8:33-44, Rom. 9:8 and Rom. 2:26-29. *3b* The only difference in Hebrew between children and stones is the first letter of the word. Children-banim. Stones-aḇanim.

you shall serve.' " Deḇ. 6:13

11 Then the devil left Him, and see, messengers came and attended Him.

12 And יהושע, having heard that Yoḥanan had been put in prison, withdrew into Galil.

13 And leaving Natsareth, He came and dwelt in Kephar Naḥum, which is by the sea, in the borders of Zeḇulun and Naphtali,

14 to fill what was spoken by Yeshayahu the prophet, saying,

15 **"Land of Zeḇulun and land of Naphtali, the way of the sea, beyond the Yardĕn, Galil of the nations –**

16 **the people who sat in darkness saw a great light, and upon those who sat in the land and shadow of death, light arose to them."** Yesh. 9:1-2

17 From that time יהושע began to proclaim and to say, "Repent, for the reign of the heavens has drawn near."

18 And יהושע, walking by the Sea of Galil, saw two brothers, Shim'on called Kĕpha, and Andri his brother, casting a net into the sea, for they were fishermen.

19 And He said to them, "Follow Me, and I shall make you fishers of men."

20 And immediately they left their nets and followed Him.

21 And going on from there, He saw two other brothers, Ya'aqoḇ *the son* of Zaḇdai, and Yoḥanan his brother, in the boat with Zaḇdai their father, mending their nets. And He called them,

22 and immediately they left the boat and their father, and followed Him.

23 And יהושע went about all Galil, teaching in their congregations, and proclaiming the Good News of the reign, and healing every disease and every bodily weakness among the people.

24 And news about Him went out into all Suria. And they brought to Him all who were sick, afflicted with various diseases and pains, and those who were demon-possessed, and epileptics, and paralytics. And He healed them.

25 And large crowds – from Galil, and Dekapolis, and Yerushalayim, and Yehuḏah, and beyond the Yardĕn – followed Him.

5

But when He saw the crowds, He went up on a mountain. And when He was seated His taught ones came to Him.

2 And having opened His mouth, He was teaching them, saying,

3 "Blessed are the poor in spirit, because theirs is the reign of the heavens.

4 "Blessed are those who mourn, because they shall be comforted.

5 **"Blessed are the meek, because they shall inherit the earth.** Teh. 37:11 [a]

6 "Blessed are those who hunger and thirst for righteousness, [b] because they shall be filled.

7 "Blessed are the compassionate, because they shall obtain compassion.

8 "Blessed are the clean in heart, [c] because they shall see Elohim.

9 "Blessed are the peacemakers, because they shall be called sons of Elohim.

10 "Blessed are those persecuted for righteousness' sake, [d] because theirs is the reign of the heavens.

11 "Blessed are you when they reproach and persecute you, and falsely say every wicked word against you, for My sake.

12 "Rejoice and be glad, because your reward in the heavens is great. For in this way they persecuted the prophets who were before you.

13 "You are the salt of the earth, but if the salt becomes tasteless, how shall it be seasoned? For it is no longer of any use but to be thrown out and to be trodden down by men.

14 "You are the light of the world. It is impossible for a city to be hidden on a mountain.

15 "Nor do they light a lamp and put it under a basket, but on a lampstand, and it shines to all those in the house.

16 "Let your light so shine before men, so that they see your good works and praise

5a Teh. 37:9, 11, 22, 29, 34. *5b* Yesh. 55:1-2, Mt. 4:4, Yn. 6:48-51. *5c* Teh. 24:3-4. *5d* Kĕpha א 3:14.

your Father who is in the heavens.

17 "Do not think that I came to destroy the Torah or the Prophets. [e] I did not come to destroy but to complete.

18 "For truly, I say to you, till the heaven and the earth pass away, one yod or one tittle shall by no means pass from the Torah till all be done. [f]

19 "Whoever, then, breaks one of the least of these commands, and teaches men so, shall be called least in the reign of the heavens; but whoever does and teaches them, he shall be called great in the reign of the heavens.

20 "For I say to you, that unless your righteousness exceeds that of the scribes and Pharisees, [g] you shall by no means enter into the reign of the heavens.

21 "You heard that it was said to those of old, **'You shall not murder,'** Shem. 20:13, Deḇ. 5:17 and whoever murders shall be liable to judgment.

22 "But I say to you that whoever is wroth with his brother without a cause shall be liable to judgment. And whoever says to his brother, 'Raka!' shall be liable to the Sanhedrin. But whoever says, 'You fool!' shall be liable to fire of GĕHinnom.

23 "If, then, you bring your gift to the slaughter-place, and there remember that your brother holds whatever against you,

24 leave your gift there before the slaughter-place, and go, first make peace with your brother, and then come and offer your gift.

25 "Be well-minded with your opponent, promptly, while you are on the way with him, lest your opponent deliver you to the judge, and the judge to the officer, and you be thrown into prison.

26 "Truly, I say to you, you shall by no means get out of there till you have paid the last penny.

27 "You heard that it was said to those of old, **'You shall not commit adultery.'** Shem. 20:14, Deḇ. 5:18

28 "But I say to you that everyone looking at a woman to lust for her has already committed adultery with her in his heart.

29 "And if your right eye causes you to stumble, pluck it out and throw it away from you. For it is better for you that one of your members perish, than for your entire body to be thrown into GĕHinnom.

30 "And if your right hand causes you to stumble, cut it off and throw it away from you. For it is better for you that one of your members perish, than for your entire body to be thrown into GĕHinnom.

31 "And it has been said, **'Whoever puts away his wife, let him give her a certificate of divorce.'** Deḇ. 24:1

32 "But I say to you that whoever puts away his wife, except for the matter of whoring, [h] makes her commit adultery. And whoever marries a woman who has been put away commits adultery.

33 "Again, you heard that it was said to those of old, **'You shall not swear falsely, but shall perform your oaths to יהוה.'** Way. 19:12, Bem. 30:2, Deḇ. 23:21

34 "But I say to you, do not swear [vainly] [i] at all, neither by **the heaven**, because it is Elohim's **throne**;

35 nor by **the earth**, for it is His **footstool**; Yesh. 66:1 nor by Yerushalayim, for it is **the city of the great Sovereign**; Teh. 48:2

36 nor swear by your head, because you are not able to make one hair white or black.

37 "But let your word 'Yes' be 'Yes,' and your 'No' be 'No.' And what goes beyond these is from the wicked one.

38 "You heard that it was said, **'An eye for an eye and a tooth for a tooth,'** Shem. 21:24 [j]

39 but I say to you, do not resist the wicked. But whoever slaps you on your right cheek, turn the other to him also.

40 "And he who wishes to sue you and take away your inner garment, let him have your outer garment as well.

41 "And whoever compels you to go one

5e The Law and the Prophets is a term used for the pre-Messianic Scriptures. *5f* Lq. 16:17. *5g* See also Mt. 23:28, Mt. 15:3-9, Mk. 7:7-13, Yn. 7:19, Ma. 7:53, Rom. 2:23-27, Gal. 6:13. *5h* See also Mt. 19:9 and Deḇ. 24:1. *5i* Shem Toḇ texts include 'vainly'= Hebrew: Shaw'. *5j* This was the principle for the judges to follow, while יהושע speaks in the next verse of our personal conduct.

mile, go with him two.
42 “Give to him who asks of you, and
from him who wishes to borrow from you,
do not turn away.
43 “You heard that it was said, **‘You shall**
love your neighbour Way. 19:18 and hate
your enemy.’ [k]
44 “But I say to you, love your enemies,
bless those cursing you, do good to those
hating you, and pray for those insulting
you and persecuting you,
45 so that you become sons of your Father
in the heavens. Because He makes His sun
rise on the wicked and on the good, and
sends rain on the righteous and on the
unrighteous. [l]
46 “For if you love those loving you, what
reward have you? Are the tax collectors
not doing the same too?
47 “And if you greet your brothers only,
what do you do more *than others*? Are the
tax collectors not doing so too?
48 “Therefore, be perfect, [m] as your Father
in the heavens is perfect.

6 “Beware of doing your kind deeds
before men, in order to be seen by
them. Otherwise you have no reward from
your Father in the heavens.
2 “Thus, when you do a kind deed, do not
sound a trumpet before you as the hypocrites do, in the congregations and in the
streets, to be praised by men. Truly, I say
to you, they have their reward.
3 “But when you do a kind deed, do not
let your left hand know what your right
hand is doing,
4 so that your kind deed shall be in
secret. And your Father who sees in secret
shall Himself reward you openly.
5 “And when you pray, you shall not be
like the hypocrites. For they love to pray
standing in the congregations and on the
corners of the streets, to be seen by men.
Truly, I say to you, they have their reward.
6 “But you, when you pray, go into your
room, and having shut your door, pray to
your Father who is in the secret place. And
your Father who sees in secret shall reward
you openly.
7 “And when praying, do not keep on
babbling like the nations. For they think
that they shall be heard for their many
words.
8 “Therefore do not be like them, for
your Father knows what you need before
you ask Him.
9 “This, then, is the way you should pray:
‘Our Father who is in the heavens, let Your
Name be set-apart,
10 let Your reign come, let Your desire be
done on earth as it is in heaven.
11 ‘Give us today our daily bread.
12 ‘And forgive us our debts, as we forgive our debtors.
13 ‘And do not lead us into trial, [a] but
deliver us from the wicked one – because
Yours is the reign and the power and the
esteem, forever. Amĕn.’
14 “For if you forgive men their trespasses, your heavenly Father shall also forgive
you.
15 “But if you do not forgive men
their trespasses, neither shall your Father
forgive your trespasses.
16 “And when you fast, do not be sad-
faced like the hypocrites. For they disfig-
ure their faces so that they appear to be
fasting to men. Truly, I say to you, they
have their reward.
17 “But you, when you fast, anoint your
head and wash your face,
18 so that you do not appear to men to be
fasting, but to your Father who is in the
secret place. And your Father who sees in
secret shall reward you openly.
19 “Do not lay up for yourselves treasures
on earth, where moth and rust destroy and
where thieves break in and steal,
20 but lay up for yourselves treasures in
heaven, where neither moth nor rust
destroys and where thieves do not break in
and steal.
21 “For where your treasure is, there your
heart shall be also.
22 “The lamp of the body is the eye. If

5k Hate your enemy was “said,” not “written.” *5l* Lq. 6:35, Ma. 14:16-17. *5m* Ber. 17:1, Teh. 119:1, Yn. א 2:5, Iḇ`rim 6:1. *6a* See 26:41.

therefore your eye is good, all your body shall be enlightened.

23 “But if your eye is evil, [b] all your body shall be darkened. If, then, the light that is within you is darkness, how great is that darkness!

24 “No one is able to serve two masters, for either he shall hate the one and love the other, or else he shall cleave to the one and despise the other. You are not able to serve Elohim and mammon. [c]

25 “Because of this I say to you, do not worry about your life, what you shall eat or drink, or about your body, what you shall put on. Is not life more than the food and the body more than the clothing?

26 “Look at the birds of the heaven, for they neither sow nor reap nor gather into storehouses, yet your heavenly Father does feed them. Are you not worth more than they?

27 “And which of you by worrying is able to add one cubit to his life's span?

28 “So why do you worry about clothing? Note well the lilies of the field, how they grow. They neither toil nor spin,

29 and I say to you that even Shelomoh in all his esteem was not dressed like one of these.

30 “But if Elohim so clothes the grass of the field, which exists today, and tomorrow is thrown into the furnace, how much more you, O you of little belief?

31 “Do not worry then, saying, 'What shall we eat?' or 'What shall we drink?' or 'What shall we wear?'

32 “For all these the nations seek for. And your heavenly Father knows that you need all these.

33 “But seek first the reign of Elohim, and His righteousness, and all these shall be added to you.

34 “Do not, then, worry about tomorrow, for tomorrow shall have its own worries. Each day has enough evil of itself.

7 “Do not judge, lest you be judged.
2 “For with what judgment you judge, you shall be judged. And with the same measure you use, it shall be measured to you.

3 “And why do you look at the splinter in your brother's eye, but do not notice the plank in your own eye?

4 “Or how is it that you say to your brother, 'Let me remove the splinter out of your eye,' and see, a plank is in your own eye?

5 “Hypocrite! First remove the plank from your own eye, and then you shall see clearly to remove the splinter out of your brother's eye.

6 “Do not give what is set-apart to the dogs, nor throw your pearls before the pigs, lest they trample them under their feet, and turn and tear you in pieces.

7 “Ask and it shall be given to you, seek and you shall find, knock and it shall be opened to you.

8 “For everyone who asks receives, and he who seeks finds, and to him who knocks it shall be opened.

9 “Or is there a man among you who, if his son asks for bread, shall give him a stone?

10 “Or if he asks for a fish, shall he give him a snake?

11 “If you then, being wicked, know how to give good gifts to your children, how much more shall your Father who is in the heavens give what is good to those who ask Him!

12 “Therefore, whatever you wish men to do to you, do also to them, for this is the Torah and the Prophets.

13 “Enter in through the narrow gate! Because the gate is wide – and the way is broad – that leads to destruction, and there are many who enter in through it.

14 “Because the gate is narrow and the way is hard pressed [a] which leads to life, and there are few who find it.

15 “But beware of the false prophets, [b] who come to you in sheep's clothing, but inwardly they are savage wolves.

16 “By their fruits you shall know them. Are grapes gathered from thornbushes or

6b This is a Hebrew idiom – *a good eye* means to be generous, while *an evil eye* means to be stingy. *6c* Personification of wealth. *7a* Or *the way is afflicted.* *7b* See also v. 23.

figs from thistles?
[17]"So every good tree yields good fruit,
but a rotten tree yields wicked fruit.
[18]"A good tree is unable to yield wicked
fruit, and a rotten tree to yield good fruit.
[19]"Every tree that does not bear good
fruit is cut down and thrown into the fire.
[20]"So then, by their fruits you shall know
them –
[21]"Not everyone who says to Me,
'Master, Master,' shall enter into the reign
of the heavens, but he who is doing the
desire of My Father in the heavens.
[22]"Many shall say to Me in that day,
'Master, Master, have we not prophesied in
Your Name, and cast out demons in Your
Name, and done many mighty works in
Your Name?'
[23]"And then I shall declare to them, 'I
never knew you, **depart from Me, you
who work lawlessness**!' Teh. 6:8 [c]
[24]"Therefore everyone who hears these
words of Mine, and does them, shall be
like a wise man who built his house on the
rock,
[25]and the rain came down, and the floods
came, and the winds blew and beat on that
house, and it did not fall, for it was founded on the rock.
[26]"And everyone who hears these words
of Mine, and does not do them, [d] shall be
like a foolish man who built his house on
the sand,
[27]and the rain came down, and the floods
came, and the winds blew, and they beat on
that house, and it fell, and great was its
fall."
[28]And it came to be, when יהושע had
ended these words, that the people were
astonished at His teaching,
[29]for He was teaching them as one possessing authority, and not as the scribes.

8 And when He came down from the
mountain, large crowds followed
Him.
[2]And see, a leper came, and bowed
before Him, saying, "Master, if You desire,
You are able to make me clean."
[3]And stretching out His hand יהושע
touched him, saying, "I desire it. Be
cleansed!" And immediately his leprosy
was cleansed.
[4]And יהושע said to him, "See, mention
it to no one. But go your way, show yourself to the priest, and offer the gift that
Mosheh commanded, as a witness to
them."
[5]And when יהושע had entered Kephar
Naḥum, a captain came to Him, appealing
to Him,
[6]saying, "Master, my servant is lying in
the house paralysed, grievously tortured."
[7]And יהושע said to him, "I shall come
and heal him."
[8]And the captain answering, said,
"Master, I am not worthy that You should
come under my roof. But only say a word,
and my servant shall be healed.
[9]"For I too am a man under authority,
having soldiers under me. And I say to this
one, 'Go,' and he goes, and to another,
'Come,' and he comes, and to my servant,
'Do this,' and he does it."
[10]And when יהושע heard, He marvelled,
and said to those who followed, "Truly, I
say to you, not even in Yisra'ěl have I
found such great belief!
[11]"And I say to you that many shall come
from east and west, and sit down with
Aḇraham, and Yitsḥaq, and Ya'aqoḇ in the
reign of the heavens,
[12]but the sons of the reign shall be cast
out into outer darkness – there shall be
weeping and gnashing of teeth."
[13]And יהושע said to the captain, "Go,
and as you have believed, so let it be done
for you." And his servant was healed that
hour.
[14]And when יהושע had come into the
house of Kěpha, He saw his wife's mother
lying sick with inflammation.
[15]And He touched her hand, and the
inflammation left her. And she arose and
served them.
[16]And when evening had come, they
brought to Him many who were demon-
possessed. And He cast out the spirits with

7c See v. 15, and also Mt. 13:41-42. *7d* See Yn. 3:36.

a word, and healed all who were sick,
17 that it might be filled what was spoken
by Yeshayahu the prophet, saying, **"He
Himself took our weaknesses and bore
our sicknesses."** Yesh. 53:4
18 And when יהושע saw large crowds
about Him, He gave a command to go off
to the other side.
19 And a certain scribe, having come near,
said to Him, "Teacher, I shall follow You
wherever You go."
20 And יהושע said to him, "The foxes
have holes and the birds of the heaven
nests, but the Son of Aḏam has nowhere to
lay His head."
21 And another of His taught ones said to
Him, "Master, first let me go and bury my
father."
22 But יהושע said to him, "Follow Me,
and leave the dead to bury their own
dead."
23 And when He entered into a boat, His
taught ones followed Him.
24 And see, a great gale arose on the sea,
so that the boat was covered by the waves.
But He was sleeping.
25 And His taught ones came to Him and
woke Him up, saying, "Master, save us!
We are perishing!"
26 And He said to them, "Why are you
afraid, O you of little belief?" Then,
having risen, He rebuked the winds and the
sea. And there was a great calm.
27 And the men marvelled, saying, "What
is this, that even the winds and the sea
obey Him?"
28 And when He came to the other side, to
the country of the Girgashites, two demon-
possessed ones met Him, coming out of
the tombs, very fierce, so that no one was
able to pass that way.
29 And see, they cried out, saying, "What
have we to do with You, יהושע, Son of
Elohim? Have You come here to torture us,
before the appointed time?"
30 And at a distance from them there was
a herd of many pigs feeding,
31 and the demons begged Him, saying,
"If You cast us out, send us into the herd
of pigs."
32 And He said to them, "Go." And they,
coming out, went into the herd of pigs.
And see, the entire herd of pigs rushed
down the steep place into the sea, and died
in the water.
33 And the herdsmen fled, and went away
into the city and reported all this, and
about those possessed by demons.
34 And see, all the city came out to meet
יהושע. And when they saw Him, they
begged Him to leave their borders.

9 And entering into a boat, He passed
over, and came to His own city.
2 And see, they were bringing to Him a
paralytic lying on a bed. And יהושע,
seeing their belief, said to the paralytic,
"Take courage, son, your sins have been
forgiven."
3 And see, some of the scribes said to
themselves, "This One blasphemes!"
4 And יהושע, knowing their thoughts,
said, "Why do you think wicked *thoughts*
in your hearts?
5 "For which is easier, to say, 'Your sins
have been forgiven,' or to say, 'Arise and
walk'?
6 "But in order for you to know that the
Son of Aḏam possesses authority on earth
to forgive sins..." He then said to the paralytic, "Rise, take up your bed, and go to
your house."
7 And he rose and went to his house.
8 And when the crowds saw it, they marvelled and praised Elohim who had given
such authority to men.
9 And as יהושע passed on from there, He
saw a man called Mattithyahu sitting at the
tax office. And He said to him, "Follow
Me." And he rose and followed Him.
10 And it came to be, as יהושע sat at the
table in the house, that see, many tax collectors and sinners came and sat down with
Him and His taught ones.
11 And when the Pharisees saw it, they
said to His taught ones, "Why does your
Teacher eat with tax collectors and
sinners?"
12 And יהושע hearing this, said to them,
"Those who are strong have no need of a
physician, but those who are sick.
13 "But go and learn what this means, **'I**

desire compassion and not offering.' Hosh. 6:6 For I did not come to call the righteous to repentance, but sinners."

14 Then the taught ones of Yoḥanan came to Him, saying, "Why do we and the Pharisees fast often, but Your taught ones do not fast?"

15 And יהושע said to them, "Are the friends of the bridegroom able to mourn as long as the bridegroom is with them? But the days shall come when the bridegroom is taken away from them, and then they shall fast.

16 "And no one puts a piece of unshrunk cloth on an old garment, for the patch pulls away from the garment, and the tear is made worse.

17 "Neither do they put new wine into old wineskins, or else the wineskins burst, and the wine is spilled, and the wineskins are ruined. But they put new wine into fresh wineskins, and both are preserved."

18 While He was saying all this to them, see, a ruler came and bowed down to Him, saying, "My daughter is dead by now, but come and lay Your hand on her and she shall live."

19 And יהושע rose and followed him, His taught ones too.

20 And see, a woman who had a flow of blood for twelve years came from behind and touched the tzitzit [a] of His garment.

21 For she said to herself, "If I only touch His garment, I shall be healed."

22 But יהושע turned, and when He saw her He said, "Take courage, daughter, your belief has healed you." And the woman was healed from that hour.

23 And when יהושע came into the ruler's house, and saw the flute players and the crowd making a noise,

24 He said to them, "Go back, for the girl is not dead, but sleeping." And they laughed at Him.

25 But when the crowd was put outside, He went in and took her by the hand, and the girl arose.

26 And this report went out into all that land.

27 And as יהושע passed on from there, two blind men followed Him, crying out and saying, "Son of Dawiḏ, have compassion on us!"

28 And when He came into the house, the blind men came to Him. And יהושע said to them, "Do you believe that I am able to do this?" They said to Him, "Yes, Master."

29 Then He touched their eyes, saying, "According to your belief let it be to you."

30 And their eyes were opened. And יהושע strictly ordered them, saying, "See, let no one know."

31 But when they went out, they made Him known in all that land.

32 And as they were going out, see, they brought to Him a man, dumb and demon-possessed.

33 And when the demon was cast out, the dumb one spoke. And the crowds marvelled, saying, "It was never seen like this in Yisra'ěl!"

34 But the Pharisees said, "He casts out demons by the ruler of the demons."

35 And יהושע went about all the cities and villages, teaching in their congregations, and proclaiming the Good News of the reign, and healing every disease and every bodily weakness among the people.

36 And having seen the crowds, He was moved with compassion for them, because they were weary and scattered, as sheep having no shepherd.

37 Then He said to His taught ones, "The harvest truly is great, but the workers are few.

38 "Pray then that the Master of the harvest would send out workers to His harvest."

10 And having called His twelve taught ones near, He gave them authority over unclean spirits, to cast them out, and to heal every disease and every bodily weakness.

2 And these are the names of the twelve emissaries: first, Shimʿon, who is called Kěpha, and Andri his brother; Yaʿaqoḇ the

9a See "Tzitzit" - Explanatory notes and Bem. 15:37-41, Deḇ. 22:12.

son of Zaḇdai, and Yoḥanan his brother;
3 Philip and Bartholomi; T'oma and
Mattithyahu the tax collector; Ya'aqoḇ the
son of Alphai, and Laḇai whose last name
was Taddai;
4 Shim'on the Kena'anite, and Yehuḏah
from Qerioth, who did also deliver Him
up.
5 יהושע sent these twelve out, having
commanded them, saying, "Do not go into
the way of the nations, and do not enter a
city of the Shomeronim,
6 but rather go to the lost sheep of the
house of Yisra'ěl.
7 "And as you go, proclaim, saying, 'The
reign of the heavens has drawn near.'
8 "Heal the sick, cleanse the lepers, raise
the dead, cast out demons. You have
received without paying, give without
being paid.
9 "Do not acquire gold or silver or copper
for your *money*-belts,
10 or a bag for the journey, or two undergarments, or sandals, or staffs, for the
worker is worthy of his food.
11 "And into whatever city or village you
enter, ask who is worthy in it, and stay
there until you leave.
12 "And as you enter into a house, greet it.
13 "And if the house is worthy, let your
peace come upon it. But if it is not worthy,
let your peace return to you.
14 "And whoever does not receive you nor
hear your words, when you leave that
house or city, shake off the dust from your
feet.
15 "Truly, I say to you, it shall be more
bearable for the land of Seḏom and
Amorah in the day of judgment than for
that city!
16 "See, I send you out as sheep in the
midst of wolves. Therefore be wise [a] as
serpents and innocent as doves.
17 "But beware of men, for they shall
deliver you up to sanhedrins and flog you
in their congregations.
18 "And you shall be brought before
governors and sovereigns for My sake, as
a witness to them and to the nations.
19 "But when they deliver you up, do not
worry about how or what you should
speak. For it shall be given to you in that
hour what you shall speak,
20 for it is not you who speak, but the
Spirit of your Father speaking in you.
21 "And brother shall deliver up brother to
death, and a father his child. And **children
shall rise up against parents** Mik 7:6 and
shall put them to death.
22 "And you shall be hated by all for My
Name's sake. But he who shall have
endured to the end shall be saved. [b]
23 "And when they persecute you in this
city, flee to another. For truly, I say to you,
you shall by no means have gone through
the cities of Yisra'ěl before the Son of
Aḏam comes.
24 "A taught one is not above his teacher,
nor a servant above his master.
25 "It is enough for the taught one to
become like his teacher, and a servant like
his master. If they have called the master
of the house Be'elzebul, how much more
those of his household!
26 "Therefore do not fear them. For whatever is covered shall be revealed, and
whatever is hidden shall be made known.
27 "What I say to you in the dark, speak in
the light. And what you hear in the ear,
proclaim on the house-tops.
28 "And do not fear those who kill the
body but are unable to kill the being. But
rather fear Him who is able to destroy both
being and body in GěHinnom.
29 "Are not two sparrows sold for a copper coin? And not one of them falls to the
ground without your Father.
30 "And even the hairs of your head are all
numbered.
31 "So do not fear, you are worth more
than many sparrows.
32 "Everyone, therefore, who shall confess Me before men, him I shall also
confess before My Father who is in the
heavens.
33 "But whoever shall deny Me before
men, him I shall also deny before My
Father who is in the heavens.

10a Or cautious, crafty, shrewd. *10b* See 24:13.

34 “Do not think that I have come to bring
peace on earth. I did not come to bring
peace but a sword, [c]
35 for I have come to bring division, **a
man against his father, a daughter
against her mother, and a daughter-in-
law against her mother-in-law –**
36 and **a man’s enemies are those of his
own household.** Mik. 7:6 [d]
37 “He who loves father or mother more
than Me is not worthy of Me, and he who
loves son or daughter more than Me is not
worthy of Me. [e]
38 “And he who does not take up his stake
and follow after Me is not worthy of Me.
39 “He who has found his life shall lose it,
and he that has lost his life for My sake
shall find it.
40 “He who receives you receives Me, and
he who receives Me receives Him who
sent Me.
41 “He who receives a prophet in the name
of a prophet shall receive a prophet’s
reward. And he who receives a righteous
one in the name of a righteous one shall
receive a righteous one’s reward.
42 “And whoever gives one of these little
ones a cup of cold *water* only in the name
of a taught one, truly, I say to you, he shall
by no means lose his reward.”

11

And it came to be, when יהושע
ended instructing His twelve taught
ones, that He set out from there to teach
and to proclaim in their cities.
2 And when Yoḥanan had heard in the
prison of the works of Messiah, he sent
two of his taught ones
3 and said to Him, “Are You the Coming
One, or do we look for another?”
4 And יהושע answering, said to them,
“Go, report to Yoḥanan what you hear and
see:
5 “**Blind receive sight** and **lame walk**,
lepers are cleansed and **deaf hear**, Yesh. 35:5-6
dead are raised up and **poor are brought
the Good News**. Yesh.61:1
6 “And blessed is he who does not stumble in Me.”
7 And as these were going, יהושע began
to say to the crowds concerning Yoḥanan,
“What did you go out into the wilderness
to see? A reed shaken by the wind?
8 “But what did you go out to see? A man
dressed in soft garments? Look, those
wearing soft *garments* are in the houses of
sovereigns.
9 “But what did you go out to see? A
prophet? Yes, I say to you, and more than a
prophet.
10 “For this is he of whom it was written,
**‘See, I send My messenger before Your
face, who shall prepare Your way before
You.’** Mal. 3:1
11 “Truly, I say to you, among those born
of women there has not risen one greater
than Yoḥanan the Immerser, yet the least
one in the reign of the heavens is greater
than he.
12 “And from the days of Yoḥanan the
Immerser till now the reign of the heavens
is violated, and the violent seize it. [a]
13 “For all the prophets and the Torah
prophesied till Yoḥanan.
14 “And if you wish to accept it, he is
Ěliyahu who was about to come.
15 “He who has ears to hear, let him hear!
16 “And to what shall I compare this
generation? It is like children sitting in the
market-places and calling to their companions,
17 and saying, ‘We played the flute for
you, and you did not dance; we lamented
to you, and you did not beat the breast.’
18 “For Yoḥanan came neither eating nor
drinking, and they say, ‘He has a demon.’
19 “The Son of Aḏam came eating and
drinking, and they say, ‘See, a man, a glutton and a winedrinker, a friend of tax
collectors and sinners!’ And wisdom was
declared right by her works.”
20 Then He began to reproach the cities in
which most of His miracles had been done,
because they did not repent:
21 “Woe to you, Korazin! Woe to you,
Běyth Tsaiḏa! Because if the miracles

10c In Lq. 12:51 the word “division” is used, while “sword” has the same meaning here. *10d* Lq. 12:53, Miḵ. 7:6. *10e* See 19:29, Lq. 14:26. *11a* See Lq. 16:16-17 which explains it more clearly.

which were done in you had been done in Tsor and Tsiḏon, they would have repented long ago in sackcloth and ashes.

22 "But I say to you, it shall be more bearable for Tsor and Tsiḏon in the day of judgment than for you.

23 "And you, Kephar Naḥum, who were **exalted to the heaven, shall be brought down to She'ol**! [b] Yesh. 14:13,15 Because if the miracles which were done in you had been done in Seḏom, it would have remained until this day.

24 "But I say to you that it shall be more bearable for the land of Seḏom in the day of judgment than for you."

25 At that time יהושע responding, said, "I thank You, Father, Master of the heavens and earth, because You have hidden these *matters* from clever and learned ones and have revealed them to babes. [c]

26 "Yes, Father, because so it was well-pleasing in Your sight.

27 "All have been handed over to Me by My Father, and no one knows the Son except the Father. Nor does anyone know the Father except the Son, and he to whom the Son wishes to reveal Him.

28 "Come to Me, all you who labour and are burdened, and I shall give you rest.

29 "Take My yoke upon you and learn from Me, for I am meek and humble in heart, and you shall find rest for your beings. [d]

30 "For My yoke is gentle and My burden is light."

12

At that time יהושע went through the grain fields on the Sabbath. And His taught ones were hungry, and began to pluck heads of grain, to eat.

2 And when the Pharisees saw it, they said to Him, "Look, Your taught ones are doing what is not right to do on the Sabbath!"

3 But He said to them, "Have you not read what Dawiḏ did when he was hungry, he and those who were with him:

4 how he went into the House of Elohim and ate the showbread which was not right for him to eat, nor for those who were with him, but only for the priests?

5 "Or did you not read in the Torah that on the Sabbath the priests in the Set-apart Place profane the Sabbath, and are blameless?

6 "But I say to you that in this place there is One greater than the Set-apart Place.

7 "And if you had known what this means, **'I desire compassion and not offering,'** Hosh. 6:6 you would not have condemned the blameless.

8 "For the Son of Aḏam is Master of the Sabbath." [a]

9 And having left there, He went into their congregation.

10 And see, there was a man having a withered hand. And they asked Him, saying, "Is it right to heal on the Sabbath?" – so as to accuse Him.

11 And He said to them, "What man is there among you who has one sheep, and if it falls into a pit on the Sabbath, shall not take hold of it and lift it out?

12 "How much more worth is a man than a sheep! So it is right to do good on the Sabbath."

13 Then He said to the man, "Stretch out your hand." And he stretched it out, and it was restored, as healthy as the other.

14 But the Pharisees went out and took counsel against Him, so as to destroy Him.

15 But יהושע, knowing it, withdrew from there. And large crowds followed Him, and He healed them all,

16 and warned them not to make Him known,

17 in order that what was spoken by Yeshayahu the prophet, might be filled, saying,

18 **"See, My Servant whom I have chosen, My Beloved in whom My being did delight. I shall put My Spirit upon Him, and He shall declare right-ruling to the nations.**

19 **"He shall not strive nor cry out, nor shall anyone hear His voice in the streets.**

20 **"A crushed reed He shall not break,**

11b See Explanatory notes - She'ol. *11c* Lq. 10:21 *11d* Yirm. 6:16. *12a* See also Ber. 2:2-3.

and smoking flax He shall not quench, till He brings forth right-ruling forever.
21 **"And the nations shall trust in His Name."** Yesh. 42:1-4 *b*
22 Then they brought to Him one who was demon-possessed, blind and dumb. And He healed him, so that the blind and dumb man both spoke and saw.
23 And all the crowds were amazed and said, "Is this the Son of Dawiḏ?"
24 But when the Pharisees heard it they said, "This one does not cast out demons except by Beʽelzebul, the ruler of the demons."
25 And יהושע knew their thoughts, and said to them, "Every reign divided against itself is laid waste, and every city or house divided against itself shall not stand.
26 "And if Satan casts out Satan, he is divided against himself. How then does his reign stand?
27 "And if I, by Beʽelzebul, do cast out demons, by whom do your sons cast them out? Because of this they shall be your judges.
28 "But if I cast out demons by the Spirit of Elohim, then the reign of Elohim has come upon you.
29 "Or how is one able to enter a strong man's house and plunder his goods, unless he first binds the strong man? And then he shall plunder his house.
30 "He who is not with Me is against Me, and he who does not gather with Me scatters abroad.
31 "Because of this I say to you, all sin and blasphemy shall be forgiven men, but the blasphemy against the Spirit shall not be forgiven men.
32 "And whoever speaks a word against the Son of Aḏam, it shall be forgiven him, but whoever speaks against the Set-apart Spirit, it shall not be forgiven him, either in this age or in the age to come.
33 "Either make the tree good and its fruit good, or else make the tree rotten and its fruit rotten, for a tree is known by its fruit.
34 "Brood of adders! How are you able to speak what is good – being wicked? For the mouth speaks from the overflow of the heart.
35 "The good man brings forth what is good from the good treasures of his heart, and the wicked man brings forth what is wicked from the wicked treasure.
36 "And I say to you that for every idle word men speak, they shall give an account of it in the day of judgment.
37 "For by your words you shall be declared righteous, and by your words you shall be declared unrighteous."
38 Then some of the scribes and Pharisees answered, saying, "Teacher, we wish to see a sign from You."
39 But He answering, said to them, "A wicked and adulterous generation seeks after a sign, and no sign shall be given to it except the sign of the prophet Yonah.
40 "For as **Yonah was three days and three nights in the stomach of the great fish,** Yonah 1:17 so shall the Son of Aḏam be three days and three nights in the heart of the earth.
41 "Men of Nineweh shall stand up in the judgment with this generation and condemn it, because they repented at the preaching of Yonah, and look, a greater than Yonah is here.
42 "The sovereigness of the South shall rise up in the judgment with this generation and shall condemn it, for she came from the ends of the earth to hear the wisdom of Shelomoh, and look, a greater than Shelomoh is here.
43 "Now when the unclean spirit goes out of a man, he goes through dry places, seeking rest, and finds none.
44 "Then it says, 'I shall return to my house from which I came.' And when it comes, it finds it empty, swept, and decorated.
45 "Then it goes and takes with it seven other spirits more wicked than itself, and they enter and dwell there. And the last of that man is worse than the first. So shall it also be with this wicked generation."

12b This is according to the Shem-Toḇ Hebrew text. However, this passage is a quote from Yesh. 42:1-3 where it reads *right-ruling unto truth*.

46 And while He was still talking to the crowds, see, His mother and brothers stood outside, seeking to speak with Him.

47 And one said to Him, "See, Your mother and Your brothers are standing outside, seeking to speak with You."

48 But He answering, said to the one who spoke to Him, "Who is My mother and who are My brothers?"

49 And having stretched out His hand toward His taught ones, He said, "See My mother and My brothers!

50 "For whoever does the desire of My Father who is in the heavens is My brother and sister and mother." [c]

13 And on that day יהושע went out of the house and sat by the sea.

2 And large crowds were gathered together to Him, so that He went into a boat and sat down. And all the crowd stood on the beach.

3 And He spoke to them much in parables, saying, "See, the sower went out to sow.

4 "And as he sowed, some indeed fell by the wayside, and the birds came and devoured them.

5 "And others fell on rocky places, where they did not have much soil, and immediately they sprang up, because they had no depth of soil.

6 "But when the sun was up they were scorched, and because they had no root they withered.

7 "And others fell among thorns, and the thorns came up and choked them.

8 "And others fell on good soil and yielded a crop, some a hundredfold, some sixty, some thirty.

9 "He who has ears to hear, let him hear!"

10 And the taught ones came and said to Him, "Why do You speak to them in parables?"

11 And He answering, said to them, "Because it has been given to you to know the secrets of the reign of the heavens, [a] but to them it has not been given. [b]

12 "For whoever possesses, to him more shall be given, and he shall have overflowingly; but whoever does not possess, even what he possesses shall be taken away from him. [c]

13 "Because of this I speak to them in parables, because seeing they do not see, and hearing they do not hear, nor do they understand.

14 "And in them the prophecy of Yeshayahu is completely filled, which says, **'Hearing you shall hear and by no means understand, and seeing you shall see and by no means perceive,**

15 **for the heart of this people has become thickened, and their ears are hard of hearing, and their eyes they have closed, lest they should see with their eyes and hear with their ears, lest they should understand with their heart, and turn back, and I heal them.'** Yesh. 6:9-10

16 "And blessed are your eyes because they see, and your ears because they hear,

17 for truly I say to you, that many prophets and righteous ones longed to see what you see, and did not see it, and to hear what you hear, and did not hear it.

18 "You, then, hear the parable of the sower:

19 "When anyone hears the word of the reign, and does not understand it, then the wicked one comes and snatches away what was sown in his heart. This is that sown by the wayside.

20 "And that sown on rocky places, this is he who hears the word and immediately receives it with joy,

21 yet he has no root in himself, but is short-lived, and when pressure or persecution arises because of the word, immediately he stumbles.

22 "And that sown among the thorns is he who hears the word, and the worry of this age and the deceit of riches choke the word, and it becomes fruitless. [d]

12c See Lq. 8:21 where the wording differs slightly. *13a* Mattithyahu uses the word "heaven(s)" as an euphemism for the Name or designation of the Father, while Mq. 4:11 and Lq. 8:10 use the Father's Name/designation. *13b* See also Mq. 4:33-34. *13c* Compare footnote at Lq. 8:18. *13d* Lq. 21:34, Tim. ב 3:4.

[23]"And that sown on the good soil is he who hears the word and understands it, who indeed bears fruit and yields – some a hundredfold, some sixty, some thirty."

[24]Another parable He put before them, saying, "The reign of the heavens has become like a man who sowed good seed in his field,

[25]but while men slept, his enemy came and sowed darnel [e] among the wheat and went away.

[26]"And when the blade sprouted and bore fruit, then the darnel also appeared.

[27]"And the servants of the master of the house came and said to him, 'Master, did you not sow good seed in your field? From where then does it have the darnel?'

[28]"And he said to them, 'A man, an enemy did this.' And the servants said to him, 'Do you wish then, that we go and gather them up?'

[29]"But he said, 'No, lest while you gather up the darnel you also uproot the wheat with them.

[30]'Let both grow together until the harvest, and at the time of harvest I shall say to the reapers, "First gather the darnel and bind them in bundles to burn them, but gather the wheat into my granary." ' "

[31]Another parable He put before them, saying, "The reign of the heavens is like a mustard seed, which a man took and sowed in his field,

[32]which indeed is less than all the seeds, but when it is grown it is greater than the plants and becomes a tree, so that **the birds of the heaven come and dwell in its branches."** Teh. 104:12, Yeḥ. 17:23; 31:6, Dan. 4:12

[33]Another parable He spoke to them, "The reign of the heavens is like leaven, which a woman took and hid in three measures of meal until all was leavened."

[34]יהושע said all this to the crowds in parables, and He did not speak to them without a parable,

[35]so that what was spoken by the prophet might be filled, saying, **"I shall open My mouth in parables, I shall pour forth what has been hidden from the foundation of the world."** Teh. 78:2

[36]Then, having sent the crowds away, יהושע went into the house. And His taught ones came to Him, saying, "Explain to us the parable of the darnel of the field."

[37]And He answering, said to them, "He who is sowing the good seed is the Son of Aḏam,

[38]and the field is the world. And the good seed, these are the sons of the reign, but the darnel are the sons of the wicked one,

[39]and the enemy who sowed them is the devil. And the harvest is the end of the age, and the reapers are the messengers.

[40]"As the darnel, then, is gathered and burned in the fire, so it shall be at the end of this age.

[41]"The Son of Aḏam shall send out His messengers, and they shall gather out of His reign **all the stumbling-blocks,** [f] **and those doing lawlessness,** Tseph. 1:3 [g]

[42]and shall throw them into the furnace of fire – there shall be wailing and gnashing of teeth.

[43]**"Then the righteous** [h] **shall shine forth as the sun** Dan. 12:3 in the reign of their Father. He who has ears to hear, let him hear!

[44]"Again, the reign of the heavens is like treasure hidden in a field, which a man having found it, hid, and for joy over it he goes and sells all that he has and buys that field.

[45]"Again, the reign of the heavens is like a man, a merchant, seeking fine pearls,

[46]who, when he had found one pearl of great price, went and sold all that he had and bought it.

[47]"Again, the reign of the heavens is like a dragnet that was thrown into the sea and gathered some of every kind,

[48]which, when it was filled, they drew to shore. And they sat down and gathered the good into containers, but threw the rotten away.

[49]"Thus shall it be at the end of the age: the messengers shall come forth, and sepa-

13e Darnel looks like wheat but is poisonous to man and beast. *13f* Or *all the causes of sinning/offence.* *13g* The Darnel of v.25. *13h* Teh. 37:29, Teh. 72:7, Teh. 75:10, Teh. 118:19-20, Teh. 146:8, Mal. 3:18, Ḥazon 22:11.

rate the wicked out of the midst of the
righteous,
50 and shall throw them into the furnace of
fire – there shall be wailing and gnashing
of teeth."
51 יהושע said to them, "Have you understood all this?" They said to Him, "Yes,
Master."
52 And He said to them, "Therefore every
scholar taught in the reign of the heavens is
like a householder who brings out of his
treasure *matters*, renewed and old."
53 And it came to be, when יהושע had
ended these parables, that He left there.
54 And when He had come to His own
country, He taught them in their congregation, so that they were astonished and said,
"Where did this One get this wisdom and
miracles?
55 "Is this not the son of the carpenter? Is
not His mother called Miryam? And His
brothers Ya'aqoḇ and Yosěph and Shim'on
and Yehuḏah?
56 "And His sisters, are they not all with
us? Where then did this One get all this?"
57 And they stumbled at Him. But יהושע
said to them, "A prophet is not unappreciated except in his own country and in his
own house."
58 And He did not do many miracles there
because of their unbelief.

14 At that time Herodes the district
ruler heard the report about יהושע,
2 and said to his servants, "This is
Yoḥanan the Immerser. He has risen from
the dead, and that is why these mighty
powers are at work in him."
3 For Herodes had arrested Yoḥanan,
bound him and put him in prison because
of Herodias, his brother Philip's wife,
4 for Yoḥanan had said to him, "It is not
right for you to have her."
5 And wishing to kill him, he feared the
crowd, because they held him as a prophet.
6 But as Herodes' birthday was being
held, the daughter of Herodias danced
before them and pleased Herodes,
7 so he promised with an oath to give her
whatever she asked.
8 And she, being urged on by her mother,
said, "Give me here the head of Yoḥanan
the Immerser on a dish."
9 And the sovereign was sad, but because
of the oaths and the guests he commanded
it to be given,
10 and sent and beheaded Yoḥanan in
prison.
11 And his head was brought on a dish and
given to the girl, and she brought it to her
mother.
12 And his taught ones came and took
away the body and buried it, and went and
reported to יהושע.
13 Now when יהושע heard it, He withdrew from there by boat to a deserted
place, by Himself. And when the crowds
heard it, they followed Him on foot from
the cities.
14 And when יהושע came out, He saw a
large crowd and was moved with compassion for them, and healed their sick.
15 And when evening came, His taught
ones came to Him, saying, "This is a
deserted place, and the hour is already late.
Dismiss the crowds, so that they might go
into the villages and buy food for themselves."
16 But יהושע said to them, "They do
not need to go away, give them to eat yourselves."
17 And they said to Him, "We have here
only five loaves and two fish."
18 And He said, "Bring them here to Me."
19 And commanding the crowds to sit
down on the grass, and taking the five
loaves and the two fish, and looking up to
the heaven, He blessed and broke and gave
the loaves to the taught ones. And the
taught ones gave to the crowds,
20 and all ate and were satisfied. And they
picked up the pieces left over – twelve baskets, filled.
21 And those who ate were about five
thousand men, besides women and children.
22 And immediately יהושע made His
taught ones enter into the boat and go
before Him to the other side, while He dismissed the crowds.
23 And having dismissed the crowds, He
went up to the mountain by Himself to

pray. And when evening had come, He was
alone there.
24 But the boat was now in the middle of
the sea, agitated by the waves, for the wind
was against it.
25 And in the fourth watch of the night
יהושע went to them, walking on the sea.
26 And when the taught ones saw Him
walking on the sea, they were troubled,
saying, "It is a phantom!" And from fear
they cried.
27 But immediately יהושע spoke to them,
saying, "Take courage, it is I, do not be
afraid."
28 And Kěpha answered Him and said,
"Master, if it is You, command me to come
to You on the water."
29 And He said, "Come." And when
Kěpha had come down out of the boat, he
walked on the water to go to יהושע.
30 But when he saw that the wind was
strong, he was afraid. And beginning to
sink, he cried out, saying, "Master, save
me!"
31 And immediately יהושע stretched out
His hand and took hold of him, and said to
him, "O you of little belief, why did you
doubt?"
32 And when they came into the boat, the
wind ceased.
33 And those in the boat came and did
bow to Him, saying, "Truly You are the
Son of Elohim."
34 And having passed over, they came to
the land of Gennĕsar.
35 And when the men of that place recognised Him, they sent out into all that surrounding country, and brought to Him all
who were sick,
36 and begged Him to let them only touch
the tzitzit [a] of His garment. And as many
as touched it were completely healed.

15

Then there came to יהושע scribes
and Pharisees from Yerushalayim,
saying,
2 "Why do Your taught ones transgress
the tradition of the elders? For they do not
wash their hands when they eat bread."
3 But He answering, said to them, "Why
do you also transgress the command of
Elohim [a] because of your tradition?
4 "For Elohim has commanded, saying,
'Respect your father and your mother,'
Shem. 20:12, Deḇ. 5:16 and, **'He who curses**
father or mother, let him be put to
death.' Shem. 21:17, Way. 20:9
5 "But you say, 'Whoever says to his
father or mother, "Whatever profit you
might have received from me has been
dedicated,"
6 is certainly released from respecting his
father or mother.' So you have nullified the
command of Elohim by your tradition.
7 "Hypocrites! Yeshayahu rightly prophesied about you, saying,
8 **'This people draw near to Me with**
their mouth, and respect Me with their
lips, but their heart is far from Me.
9 **'But in vain do they worship Me,**
teaching as teachings the commands of
men.' " Yesh. 29:13 [b]
10 And calling the crowd near, He said to
them, "Hear and understand:
11 "Not that which goes into the mouth
defiles the man, but that which comes out
of the mouth, this defiles the man."
12 Then His taught ones came and said to
Him, "Do You know that the Pharisees
stumbled when they heard this word?"
13 But He answering, said, "Every plant
which My heavenly Father has not planted
shall be uprooted.
14 "Leave them alone. They are blind
leaders of the blind. And if the blind leads
the blind, both shall fall into a ditch."
15 And Kěpha answering, said to Him,
"Explain this parable to us."
16 And יהושע said, "Are you also still
without understanding?
17 "Do you not understand that whatever
enters into the mouth goes into the stomach, and is cast out in the sewer?
18 "But what comes out of the mouth
comes from the heart, and these defile the
man.
19 "For out of the heart come forth wicked
reasonings, murders, adulteries, whorings,

14a See Explanatory notes - Tzitzit. *15a* See footnote 5:20. *15b* Mq. 7:7, Mel. ב 17:19.

thefts, false witnessings, slanders.
20 "These defile the man, but to eat with
unwashed hands [c] does not defile the
man."
21 And יהושע went out from there and
withdrew to the parts of Tsor and Tsiḏon.
22 And see, a woman of Kena'an came
from those borders and cried out to Him,
saying, "Have compassion on me, O
Master, Son of Dawiḏ! My daughter is
badly demon-possessed."
23 But He did not answer her a word. And
His taught ones came and asked Him, saying, "Send her away, because she cries
after us."
24 And He answering, said, "I was not
sent except to the lost sheep of the house of
Yisra'ĕl." [d]
25 But she came and was bowing to Him,
saying, "Master, help me!"
26 And He answering, said, "It is not good
to take the children's bread and throw it to
the little dogs."
27 But she said, "Yes Master, for even the
little dogs eat the crumbs which fall from
their masters' table."
28 And יהושע answering, said to her, "O
woman, your belief is great! Let it be to
you as you desire." And her daughter was
healed from that hour.
29 And moving from there, יהושע came
toward the Sea of Galil, and going up on
the mountain, He was sitting there.
30 And large crowds came to Him, having
with them those who were lame, blind,
dumb, crippled, and many others. And
they laid them down at the feet of יהושע,
and He healed them,
31 so that the crowd marvelled when they
saw the dumb speaking, the crippled well,
the lame walking, and the blind seeing.
And they praised the Elohim of Yisra'ĕl.
32 And יהושע, having called His taught
ones near, said, "I have compassion on the
crowd, because they have now continued
with Me three days and do not have whatever to eat. And I do not wish to send them
away hungry, lest they faint on the way."
33 And His taught ones said to Him,
"Where are we to get enough bread in the
desert to satisfy such a large crowd?"
34 And יהושע said to them, "How many
loaves do you have?" And they said,
"Seven, and a few little fish."
35 And He commanded the crowd to sit
down on the ground,
36 and taking the seven loaves and the
fish, giving thanks, He broke them and
gave to His taught ones, and the taught
ones to the crowd.
37 And all ate and were satisfied, and they
picked up what was left over of the broken
pieces – seven large baskets, filled.
38 And those who ate were four thousand
men, besides women and children.
39 And dismissing the crowd, He went
into the boat, and came to the borders of
Maḡdala.

16 And the Pharisees and Sadducees
came, and trying Him asked that
He would show them a sign from heaven.
2 And He answering, said to them,
"When it is evening you say, 'Fair weather,
for the heaven is red,'
3 and in the morning, 'Stormy weather
today, for the heaven is red and overcast.'
You know how to discern the face of the
heaven, but you are unable to *discern* the
signs of the times!
4 "A wicked and adulterous generation
seeks after a sign, and no sign shall be
given to it except the sign of the prophet
Yonah." And He left them and went away.
5 And His taught ones came to the other
side, and had forgotten to take bread.
6 And יהושע said to them, "Mind! And
beware of the leaven of the Pharisees and
the Sadducees."
7 And they reasoned among themselves,
saying, "Because we brought no bread!"
8 But יהושע, aware of this, said to them,
"O you of little belief, why do you reason
among yourselves because you brought no
bread?
9 "Do you still not understand, neither

15c This refers to the mistaken belief that demons entered the person eating bread with "unwashed hands". *15d* See footnote 10:6.

remember the five loaves of the five thousand and how many baskets you picked
up?
10 "Or the seven loaves of the four thousand and how many large baskets you
picked up?
11 "How is it that you do not understand
that I did not speak to you concerning
bread, *but* to beware of the leaven of the
Pharisees and Sadducees?"
12 Then they understood that He did not
say to beware of the leaven of bread, but of
the teaching of the Pharisees and the
Sadducees.
13 Now when יהושע came into the parts
of Caesarea Philippi, He asked His taught
ones, saying, "Who do men say the Son of
Aḏam is?"
14 And they said, "Some *say* Yoḥanan the
Immerser, and others Ěliyahu, and others
Yirmeyahu or one of the prophets."
15 He said to them, "And you, who do you
say I am?"
16 And Shim'on Kěpha answering, said,
"You are the Messiah, the Son of the living
Elohim." [a]
17 And יהושע answering, said to him,
"Blessed are you, Shim'on Bar-Yonah, for
flesh and blood has not revealed this to
you, but My Father in the heavens.
18 "And I also say to you that you are
Kěpha, and on this rock I shall build My
assembly, and the gates of She'ol [b] shall
not overcome it.
19 "And I shall give you the keys of the
reign of the heavens, and whatever you
bind on earth shall be having been bound
in the heavens, and whatever you loosen
on earth shall be having been loosened in
the heavens." [c]
20 Then He warned His taught ones that
they should say to no one that He is יהושע
the Messiah.
21 From that time יהושע began to show to
His taught ones that it was necessary for
Him to go to Yerushalayim, and to suffer
much from the elders and chief priests and
scribes, and be killed, and to be raised
again the third day.
22 And Kěpha took Him aside and began
to rebuke Him, saying, "Be kind to
Yourself, Master, this shall not be to You!"
23 But He turned and said to Kěpha, "Get
behind Me, Satan! You are a stumbling-
block to Me, for your thoughts are not
those of Elohim, but those of men."
24 Then יהושע said to His taught ones, "If
anyone wishes to come after Me, let him
deny himself, and take up his stake, and
follow Me.
25 "For whoever wishes to save his life
shall lose it, and whoever loses his life for
My sake shall find it.
26 "For what is a man profited if he gains
all the world, and loses his own life? Or
what shall a man give in exchange for his
life?
27 "For the Son of Aḏam is going to come
in the esteem of His Father with His messengers, and then He shall **reward each
according to his works.** Teh. 62:12, Mish. 24:12 [d]
28 "Truly, I say to you, there are some
standing here who shall not taste death at
all until they see the Son of Aḏam coming
in His reign:" [e]

17
And after six days יהושע took
Kěpha, and Ya'aqoḇ, and Yoḥanan
his brother, and brought them up on a high
mountain by themselves,
2 and He was transformed before them,
and His face shone like the sun, and His
garments became as white as the light.
3 And see, Mosheh and Ěliyahu appeared
to them, talking with Him.
4 And Kěpha answering, said to יהושע,
"Master, it is good for us to be here. If You
wish, let us make here three booths: one
for You, one for Mosheh, and one for
Ěliyahu." [a]
5 While he was still speaking, see, a
bright cloud overshadowed them. And see,

16a This is repeated in eight more places. *16b* Shem Toḇ reads: GěHinnom, i.e. 'valley of weeping'. *16c Binding and loosening* is a Hebrew idiom for *exercising authority* (to prohibit and permit). *16d* See also 21:44, Yn. 5:29, Rom. 2:6, Cor. ב 5:10, Eph. 2:10, Titos 2:7 & 14, Ya'aqoḇ 2:14-24, Ḥazon 22:12. *16e* See 17:2-5. *17a* See footnote Mq 9:4.

a voice came out of the cloud, saying, "This is My Son, the Beloved, in whom I did delight. Hear Him!"

6 And when the taught ones heard, they fell on their faces and were much afraid.

7 But יהושע came near and touched them and said, "Rise, and do not be afraid."

8 And having lifted up their eyes, they saw no one but יהושע only.

9 And as they were coming down from the mountain, יהושע commanded them, saying, "Do not mention the vision to anyone until the Son of Aḏam is raised from the dead."

10 And His taught ones asked Him, saying, "Why then do the scribes say that Ěliyahu has to come first?"

11 And יהושע answering, said to them, "Ěliyahu is indeed coming first, and shall restore all. [b]

12 "But I say to you that Ěliyahu has already come, and they did not recognise him but did to him whatever they wished. In this way the Son of Aḏam is also about to suffer by them."

13 Then the taught ones understood that He had spoken to them about Yoḥanan the Immerser.

14 And when they came to the crowd, a man came up to Him, kneeling down to Him and saying,

15 "Master, have compassion on my son, for he is an epileptic and suffers badly, for he often falls into the fire and often into the water.

16 "And I brought him to Your taught ones, but they were unable to heal him."

17 And יהושע answering, said, "O generation, unbelieving and perverted, how long shall I be with you? How long shall I put up with you? Bring him here to Me."

18 And יהושע rebuked the demon, and he came out of him. And the child was healed from that hour.

19 Then the taught ones came to יהושע by Himself and said, "Why were we unable to cast him out?"

20 And יהושע said to them, "Because of your unbelief, for truly, I say to you, if you have belief as a mustard seed, you shall say to this mountain, 'Move from here to there,' and it shall move. And no matter shall be impossible for you.

21 "But this kind does not go out except through prayer and fasting."

22 And while they were staying in Galil, יהושע said to them, "The Son of Aḏam is about to be delivered up into the hands of men,

23 and they shall kill Him, and the third day He shall be raised up." And they were deeply grieved.

24 And when they came into Kephar Naḥum, those who received the tax came to Kěpha and said, "Does your Teacher not pay the tax?"

25 He said, "Yes." And when he came into the house, יהושע spoke to him first, saying, "What do you think, Shimʽon? From whom do the sovereigns of the earth take toll or tax, from their own sons or from the strangers?"

26 Kěpha *then* said to Him, "From the strangers." יהושע said to him, "Then the sons are exempt.

27 "But, lest we cause them to stumble, go to the sea, cast in a hook, and take the fish that comes up first. And when you have opened its mouth, you shall find a stater. [c] Take that and give it to them for Me and you."

18

At that time the taught ones came to יהושע, saying, "Who, then, is greatest in the reign of the heavens?"

2 And יהושע called a little child to Him, set him in their midst,

3 and said, "Truly, I say to you, unless you turn and become as little children, you shall by no means enter into the reign of the heavens.

4 "Whoever then humbles himself as this little child is the greatest in the reign of the heavens.

5 "And whoever receives one little child like this in My Name receives Me.

6 "But whoever causes one of these little

17b See Mq. 9:12, and Ma. 3:21 in particular. *17c* A coin.

ones who believe in Me to stumble, it is better for him that a millstone be hung around his neck, and that he be drowned in the depth of the sea.

7 “Woe to the world because of stumbling-blocks! For it is necessary that stumbling-blocks come, but woe to that man by whom the stumbling-block comes!

8 “And if your hand or foot causes you to stumble, cut it off and throw it away from you. It is better for you to enter into life lame or crippled, rather than having two hands or two feet, to be thrown into the everlasting fire.

9 “And if your eye causes you to stumble, pluck it out and throw it away from you. It is better for you to enter into life with one eye, rather than having two eyes, to be thrown into the fire of GĕHinnom.

10 “See that you do not despise one of these little ones, for I say to you that in the heavens their messengers always see the face of My Father who is in the heavens.

11 “For the Son of Aḏam has come to save what was lost.

12 “What do you think? If a man has a hundred sheep, and one of them goes astray, would he not leave the ninety-nine on the mountains, going to seek the one that is straying?

13 “And if he should find it, truly, I say to you, he rejoices more over that sheep than over the ninety-nine that did not go astray.

14 “Thus it is not the desire of your Father who is in the heavens that one of these little ones should be lost.

15 “And if your brother sins against you, go and convict him, between you and him alone. If he hears you, you have gained your brother.

16 “But if he does not hear, take with you one or two more, that **‘by the mouth of two or three witnesses every word might be established.’** Deḇ. 19:15 [a]

17 “And if he refuses to hear them, say it to the assembly. And if he refuses even to hear the assembly, let him be to you like the nations and a tax collector.

18 “Truly, I say to you, whatever you bind on earth shall be having been bound in heaven, and whatever you loosen on earth shall be having been loosened in heaven. [b]

19 “Again I say to you that if two of you agree on earth concerning any matter that they ask, it shall be done for them by My Father in the heavens.

20 “For where two or three are gathered together in My Name, there I am in their midst.”

21 Then Kĕpha came to Him and said, “Master, how often shall my brother sin against me, and I forgive him? Up to seven times?”

22 יהושע said to him, “I do not say to you, up to seven times, but up to seventy times seven.

23 “Because of this the reign of the heavens is like a certain man, a sovereign who wished to settle accounts with his servants.

24 “And when he had begun to settle, one was brought to him who owed him ten thousand talents,

25 but as he was unable to pay, his master commanded that he be sold, with his wife and children and all that he had, and payment to be made.

26 “Then the servant fell down before him, saying, ‘Master, have patience with me, and I shall pay you all.’

27 “And the master of that servant was moved with compassion, released him, and forgave him the debt.

28 “And that servant went out and found one of his fellow servants who owed him a hundred denarii [c]. And he laid hands on him and took him by the throat, saying, ‘Pay me what you owe!’

29 “Then his fellow servant fell down at his feet and begged him, saying, ‘Have patience with me, and I shall pay you all.’

30 “But he would not, and went and threw him into prison till he should pay the debt.

31 “And when his fellow servants saw what had been done, they were deeply grieved, and came and reported to their master all that had taken place.

32 “Then his master called him and said to him, ‘Wicked servant! I forgave you all

18a Yoh. 8:17, Cor. א 13:1, Tim. ב 5:19, Iḇ`rim 10:28. *18b* See footnote 16:19. *18c* A Roman monetary unit.

that debt seeing you begged me.
33 'Should you not also have had compassion on your fellow servant, as I also had
compassion on you?'
34 "And his master was wroth, and delivered him to the torturers until he should
pay all that was due to him.
35 "So also My heavenly Father shall do
to you if each of you, from his heart, does
not forgive his brother his trespasses."

19 And it came to be, when יהושע
had ended these words, that He left
Galil and came to the borders of Yehuḏah
beyond the Yarděn.
2 And large crowds followed Him, and
He healed them there.
3 And the Pharisees came to Him, trying
Him, and saying to Him, "Is it right for a
man to put away his wife for every reason?"
4 And He answering, said to them, "Did
you not read that He who made them at the
beginning **made them male and female**,
Ber. 1:27; 5:2
5 and said, **'For this cause a man shall
leave his father and mother and cleave
to his wife, and the two shall become one
flesh'**? Ber. 2:24
6 "So that they are no longer two, but one
flesh. Therefore, what Elohim has joined
together, let man not separate."
7 They said to Him, "Why then did
Mosheh command to **give a certificate of
divorce**, Deḇ. 24:1,3 and to put her away?"
8 He said to them, "Because of the hardness of your hearts, Mosheh allowed you
to put away your wives, but from the
beginning it was not so.
9 "And I say to you, whoever puts away
his wife, except on the ground of whoring,
and marries another, commits adultery.
And whoever marries her who has been
put away commits adultery." [a]
10 His taught ones said to Him, "If such is
the case of the man with his wife, it is good
not to marry."
11 And He said to them, "Not all receive
this word, but only those to whom it has
been given,
12 for there are eunuchs who were so born
from their mother's womb, and there are
eunuchs who were made eunuchs by men,
and there are eunuchs who have made
themselves eunuchs for the sake of the
reign of the heavens. He who is able to
receive it, let him receive it."
13 Then young children were brought to
Him to lay His hands on them and pray,
and the taught ones rebuked them.
14 But יהושע said, "Allow the young children and do not stop them from coming to
Me, for of such is the reign of the heavens."
15 And having laid hands on them He
went from there.
16 And see, one came and said to Him,
"Good Teacher, what good shall I do to
have everlasting life?"
17 And He said to him, "Why do you call
Me good? No one is good except One –
Elohim. But if you wish to enter into life,
guard the commands." [b]
18 He said to Him, "Which?" And יהושע
said, " **'You shall not murder,' 'You shall
not commit adultery,' 'You shall not
steal,' 'You shall not bear false witness,'**
Shem. 20:13-16, Deḇ. 5:17-20
19 **'Respect your father and your mother,'** Shem. 20:12, Deḇ. 5:16 and **'You shall love
your neighbour as yourself.'** " Way. 19:18
20 The young man said to Him, "All these
I have watched over from my youth, what
do I still lack?"
21 יהושע said to him, "If you wish to be
perfect, go, [c] sell what you have and give
to the poor, and you shall have [d] treasure in
heaven. And come, follow Me."
22 And when the young man heard the
word, he went away sad, because he had
many possessions.
23 And יהושע said to His taught ones,
"Truly, I say to you that it is hard for a rich
man to enter into the reign of the heavens.
24 "And again I say to you, it is easier for
a camel [e] to go through the eye of a needle

19a See footnote 5:32. *19b* See also Lq. 10:28, Yn. 12:50, Ḥazon 22:14. *19c* Lq 12:33; 16:9, Ma. 2:45; 4:34. *19d* Mt. 6:20. *19e* Aramaic "gamla",which is camel or rope.

than for a rich man to enter into the reign of Elohim."

25 And when His taught ones heard it, they were very astonished, saying, "Who then is able to be saved?"

26 And looking intently יהושע said to them, "With men this is impossible, but with Elohim all is possible."

27 Then Kěpha answering, said to Him, "See, we have left all and followed You. What then shall we have?"

28 And יהושע said to them, "Truly I say to you, when the Son of Aḏam sits on the throne of His esteem, you who have followed Me in the rebirth, shall also sit on twelve thrones, judging the twelve tribes of Yisra'ěl.

29 "And everyone who has left houses or brothers or sisters or father or mother or wife or children or lands, for My Name's sake, shall receive a hundredfold, and shall inherit everlasting life.

30 "But many who are first shall be last, and the last first.

20

"For the reign of the heavens is like a man, a householder who went out early in the morning to hire workers for his vineyard.

2 "And when he had agreed with the workers for a denarius [a] a day, he sent them into his vineyard.

3 "And he went out about the third hour and saw others standing idle in the marketplace,

4 and said to them, 'You too go into the vineyard, and whatever is right I shall give you.' And they went.

5 "Having gone out again about the sixth and the ninth hour, he did likewise.

6 "And about the eleventh hour, having gone out, he found others standing idle, and said to them, 'Why do you stand here idle all day?'

7 "They said to him, 'Because no one hired us.' He said to them, 'You too go into the vineyard, and whatever is right you shall receive.'

8 "And when evening came, the master of the vineyard said to his manager, 'Call the workers and pay them their wages, beginning with the last to the first.'

9 "And when those came who were hired about the eleventh hour, they each received a denarius [a].

10 "And when the first came, they thought they would receive more. But they too received each a silver piece.

11 "And when they received it, they grumbled against the householder,

12 saying, 'These last have worked *only* one hour, and you made them equal to us who have borne the burden and the heat of the day.'

13 "But he answering, said to one of them, 'Friend, I do you no wrong. Did you not agree with me for a denarius? [a]

14 'Take yours and go. But I wish to give to this last man as also to you.

15 'Is it not right for me to do what I wish with my own? Or is your eye evil because I am good?'

16 "Thus the last shall be first, and the first last. For many are called, but few chosen." [b]

17 And יהושע, going up to Yerushalayim, took the twelve taught ones aside on the way and said to them,

18 "See, we are going up to Yerushalayim, and the Son of Aḏam shall be delivered up to the chief priests and to the scribes. And they shall condemn Him to death,

19 and deliver Him to the nations to mock and to flog and to impale. And the third day He shall be raised."

20 Then the mother of the sons of Zaḇdai came to Him with her sons, bowing down and making a request of Him.

21 And He said to her, "What do you wish?" She said to Him, "Command that these two sons of mine might sit, one on Your right hand and the other on the left, in Your reign."

22 But יהושע answering, said, "You do not know what you ask. Are you able to drink the cup that I am about to drink, and to be immersed with the immersion that I am immersed with?" They said to Him,

20a Roman monetary unit. *20b* See 22:14.

"We are able."

23 And He said to them, "You shall indeed drink My cup, and you shall be immersed with the immersion that I am immersed with. [c] But to sit on My right hand and on My left is not Mine to give, but it is for those for whom it has been prepared by My Father."

24 And when the ten heard it, they were displeased at the two brothers.

25 But יהושע called them near and said, "You know that the rulers of the nations are masters over them, and those who are great exercise authority over them.

26 "But it shall not be so among you, but whoever wishes to become great among you, let him be your servant.

27 "And whoever wishes to be first among you, let him be your servant,

28 even as the Son of Aḏam did not come to be served, but to serve, [d] and to give His life as a ransom for many."

29 And as they were leaving Yeriḥo, a large crowd followed Him.

30 And see, two blind men sitting by the way, having heard that יהושע was passing by, cried out, saying, "Have compassion on us, O Master, Son of Dawiḏ!"

31 And the crowd rebuked them that they should be silent, but they cried out all the more, saying, "Have compassion on us, O Master, Son of Dawiḏ!"

32 And יהושע stopped and called them, and said, "What do you wish Me to do for you?"

33 They said to Him, "Master, that our eyes be opened."

34 And having been moved with compassion, יהושע touched their eyes. And immediately their eyes received sight, and they followed Him.

21

And when they came near to Yerushalayim, and came to Bĕyth Phaḡi, at the Mount of Olives, then יהושע sent two taught ones,

2 saying to them, "Go into the village opposite you, and straightaway you shall find a donkey tied, and a colt with her, loosen *them*, and bring them to Me.

3 "And if anyone says whatever to you, you shall say, 'The Master needs them,' and immediately he shall send them."

4 And all this took place that it might be filled what was spoken by the prophet, saying,

5 **"Say to the daughter of Tsiyon, 'See, your Sovereign is coming to you, meek, and sitting on a donkey, even a colt, the foal of a donkey.' "** Zeḵ. 9:9

6 And the taught ones went, and having done as יהושע ordered them,

7 they brought the donkey and the colt, and laid their garments on them, and He sat on them.

8 And most of the crowd spread their garments on the way, while others cut down branches from the trees and spread them on the way.

9 And the crowds who went before and those who followed cried out, saying, "**Hoshia-na** to the Son of Dawiḏ! **Blessed is He who is coming in the Name of** יהוה! **Hoshia-na** in the highest!" Teh. 118:26

10 And as He entered into Yerushalayim, all the city was stirred, saying, "Who is this?"

11 And the crowds said, "This is יהושע, the prophet from Natsareth of Galil."

12 And יהושע went into the Set-apart Place of Elohim and drove out all those buying and selling in the Set-apart Place, and overturned the tables of the money-changers and the seats of those who sold doves.

13 And He said to them, "It has been written, **'My House shall be called a house of prayer,'** Yesh. 56:7 but you have made it a **'den of robbers.'** " Yirm. 7:11

14 And blind and lame ones came to Him in the Set-apart Place, and He healed them.

15 But when the chief priests and scribes saw the wonders which He did, and the children crying out in the Set-apart Place and saying, "**Hoshia-na** Teh. 118:26 to the Son of Dawiḏ!" they were greatly displeased,

16 and said to Him, "Do You hear what these say?" And יהושע said to them, "Yes,

20c See also Mq. 10:39, Lq. 12:50. *20d* Mq. 10:45, Yesh. 49:1-7.

have you never read, **'Out of the mouth of**
babes and nurslings You have perfected
praise'?" Teh. 8:2
17 And having left them He went out of
the city to Běyth Anyah, and spent the
night there.
18 And returning to the city early in the
morning, He became hungry.
19 And seeing a single fig tree by the way,
He came to it and found naught on it but
leaves, and said to it, "Let no fruit grow on
you ever again." And immediately the fig
tree withered.
20 And the taught ones, seeing it, marvelled, saying, "How did the fig tree wither
so soon?"
21 And יהושע answering, said to them,
"Truly, I say to you, if you have belief and
do not doubt, you shall not only do what
was done to the fig tree, but even if you
say to this mountain, 'Be removed and be
thrown into the sea,' it shall be done.
22 "And whatever you ask in prayer,
believing, you shall receive."
23 And when He had come into the Set-
apart Place, the chief priests and the elders
of the people came to Him as He was
teaching, and said, "By what authority are
You doing these? And who gave You this
authority?"
24 And יהושע answering, said to them, "I
shall ask you one question too, which if
you answer Me, I also shall say to you by
what authority I do these:
25 "The immersion of Yoḥanan, where did
it come from? From heaven or from men?"
So they reasoned among themselves, saying, "If we say, 'From heaven,' He shall
say to us, 'Then why did you not believe
him?'
26 "But if we say, 'From men,' we fear the
crowd, for all hold Yoḥanan as a prophet."
27 And they answered יהושע and said,
"We do not know." And He said to them,
"Neither do I say to you by what authority
I do these.
28 "But what do you think? A man had
two sons, and he came to the first and said,
'Son, go, work today in my vineyard.'
29 "And he answering, said, 'I do not wish
to,' but afterwards he repented and went.
30 "And having come to the second, he
said similarly. And he answering, said, 'I
go, master,' but he did not go.
31 "Which of the two did the desire of the
father?" They said to Him, "The first."
יהושע said to them, "Truly, I say to you
that tax collectors and whores are entering
into the reign of Elohim before you,
32 for Yoḥanan came to you in the way of
righteousness, and you did not believe
him, but tax collectors and whores
believed him. And when you saw it, you
did not repent afterwards, to believe him.
33 "Hear another parable: There was a
certain man, a householder who **planted a**
vineyard and placed a hedge around it,
and dug a winepress in it and built a
watchtower. Yesh. 5:1,2 And he leased it to
farmers and went abroad.
34 "And when the season of the fruits
drew near, he sent his servants to the farmers, to receive its fruit.
35 "And the farmers took his servants
and beat one, and they killed one, and they
stoned another.
36 "Again he sent other servants, more
than the first, and they did likewise to
them.
37 "And at last he sent his son to them,
saying, 'They shall respect my son.'
38 "But when the farmers saw the son,
they said among themselves, 'This is the
heir. Come, let us kill him, and let us possess his inheritance.'
39 "And they took him, and threw him out
of the vineyard, and killed him.
40 "Therefore, when the master of the
vineyard comes, what shall he do to those
farmers?"
41 They said to Him, "Evil ones! He shall
bring them to evil destruction, and lease
the vineyard to other farmers who shall
give to him the fruits in their seasons."
42 יהושע said to them, "Did you never
read in the Scriptures, **'The stone which**
the builders rejected has become the
chief corner-stone. This was from יהוה',
and it is marvellous in our eyes'?
Teh. 118:22-23
43 "Because of this I say to you: the reign
of Elohim shall be taken from you and

given to a nation bringing forth the fruits of it.

44 "And he who falls on this stone shall be broken, [a] but on whomever it falls, he shall be pulverised."

45 And the chief priests and Pharisees, having heard His parables, knew that He was speaking of them.

46 And seeking to lay hands on Him, they feared the crowds, seeing they held Him to be a prophet.

22

And יהושע responded and spoke to them again by parables and said,

2 "The reign of the heavens is like a man, a sovereign, who made a wedding feast for his son,

3 and sent out his servants to call those who were invited to the wedding feast. But they would not come.

4 "Again he sent out other servants, saying, 'Say to those who are invited, "See, I have prepared my dinner. My oxen and fattened cattle are slaughtered, and all is ready. Come to the wedding feast." '

5 "But they disregarded it and went their way – this one to his field, that one to his trade.

6 "And the rest, having seized his servants, insulted and killed them.

7 "But when the sovereign heard, he was wroth, and sent out his soldiers, destroyed those murderers, and set their city on fire.

8 "Then he said to his servants, 'The wedding feast, indeed, is ready, but those who were invited were not worthy.

9 'Therefore go into the street corners, and as many as you find, invite to the wedding feast.'

10 "And those servants went out into the street corners and gathered all whom they found, both wicked and good. And the wedding hall was filled with guests.

11 "And when the sovereign came in to view the guests, he saw there a man who had not put on a wedding garment,

12 and he said to him, 'Friend, how did you come in here not having a wedding garment?' And he was speechless.

13 "Then the sovereign said to the servants, 'Bind him hand and foot, take him away, and throw him out into the outer darkness – there shall be weeping and gnashing of teeth.'

14 "For many are called, but few are chosen." [a]

15 Then the Pharisees went and plotted how to trap Him in His words.

16 And they sent to Him their taught ones with the Herodians, saying, "Teacher, we know that You are true, and teach the way of Elohim in truth, and it does not concern You about anyone, for You are not partial to any man.

17 "Then say to us, what do You think? Is it right to pay taxes to Caesar, or not?"

18 But knowing their wickedness, יהושע said, "Why do you try Me, you hypocrites?

19 "Show Me the coin of the tax." And they brought Him a denarius. [b]

20 And He said to them, "Whose likeness and inscription is this?"

21 They said to Him, "Caesar's." And He said to them, "Then give to Caesar what is Caesar's, and to Elohim what is Elohim's."

22 And having heard, they marvelled, and left Him and went away.

23 On that day Sadducees, who say there is no resurrection, came to Him and asked Him,

24 saying, "Teacher, Mosheh said that if **anyone should die, having no children, his brother shall marry his wife and raise offspring for his brother.** Deb. 25:5

25 "And there were with us seven brothers, and the first died after he had married, and having no children, left his wife to his brother.

26 "In the same way the second also, and the third, unto the seventh.

27 "And last of all the woman died too.

28 "At the resurrection, then, whose wife of the seven shall she be – for all had her?"

29 And יהושע answering, said to them, "You go astray, not knowing the Scriptures [c] nor the power of Elohim.

30 "For in the resurrection they do not marry, nor are they given in marriage, but

21a Rom. 8:10 & 13, Qol. 3:5. *22a* See 20:16. *22b* Roman monetary unit. *22c* Mq. 12:24.

are as messengers of Elohim in heaven.
31 "And concerning the resurrection of the
dead, have you not read what was spoken
to you by Elohim, saying,
32 **'I am the Elohim of Aḇraham, and
the Elohim of Yitsḥaq, and the Elohim
of Ya'aqoḇ'**? Shem. 3:6 Elohim is not the
Elohim of the dead, but of the living."
33 And when the crowds heard, they were
astonished at His teaching.
34 But the Pharisees, having heard that He
had silenced the Sadducees, were gathered
together,
35 and one of them, one learned in the
Torah, did question, trying Him, and saying,
36 "Teacher, which is the great command
in the Torah?"
37 And יהושע said to him, " **'You shall
love יהוה your Elohim with all your
heart, and with all your being, and with
all your mind.'** Deḇ. 6:5
38 "This is the first and great command.
39 "And the second is like it, **'You shall
love your neighbour as yourself.'** Way. 19:18
40 "On these two commands hang all the
Torah and the Prophets."
41 And when the Pharisees were gathered
together, יהושע asked them,
42 saying, "What do you think concerning
the Messiah? Whose Son is He?" They
said to Him, "*The Son* of Dawiḏ."
43 He said to them, "Then how does
Dawiḏ in the Spirit call Him 'Master,' saying,
44 **'יהוה said to my Master, "Sit at My
right hand, until I make Your enemies a
footstool of Your feet" '**? Teh. 110:1
45 "If then Dawiḏ calls Him 'Master,' how
is He his Son?"
46 And no one was able to answer Him a
word, and from that day on no one was
bold *enough* to ask Him any more questions.

23 Then יהושע spoke to the crowds
and to His taught ones,
2 saying, "The scribes and the Pharisees
sit on the seat of Mosheh.
3 "Therefore, whatever they [a] say to you
to guard, guard and do. But do not do
according to their works, for they say, and
do not do.
4 "For they bind heavy burdens, hard to
bear, and lay them on men's shoulders, but
with their finger they do not wish to move
them.
5 "And they do all their works to be seen
by men, and they make their t'fillen [b] wide
and lengthen the tzitzit [c] of their garments,
6 and they love the best place at feasts,
and the best seats in the congregations,
7 and the greetings in the market-places,
and to be called by men, 'Rabbi, Rabbi.' [d]
8 "But you, do not be called 'Rabbi,' for
One is your Teacher, the Messiah, and you
are all brothers.
9 "And do not call *anyone* on earth your
father, for One is your Father, He who is in
the heavens.
10 "Neither be called leaders, for One is
your Leader, the Messiah.
11 "But the greatest among you shall be
your servant.
12 "And whoever exalts himself shall be
humbled, and whoever humbles himself
shall be exalted.
13 "But woe to you, scribes and Pharisees,
hypocrites! Because you shut up the reign
of the heavens before men, for you do not
go in, nor do you allow those who are
entering to go in.
14 "Woe to you, scribes and Pharisees,
hypocrites! Because you eat up widows'
houses, and for a show make long prayers.
Because of this you shall receive greater
judgment.
15 "Woe to you, scribes and Pharisees,
hypocrites! Because you go about the land
and the sea to win one convert, and when
he is won, you make him a son of
GěHinnom twofold more than yourselves.
16 "Woe to you, blind guides, who say,
'Whoever swears by the Dwelling Place,

23a Four of eleven available Shem Toḇ texts read "he says", referring to Mosheh, instead of "they say", referring to the Pharisees. *23b* See Explanatory notes - T'fillen. *23c* See Explanatory notes - "Tzitzit" and Bem. 15:37-41, Deḇ. 22:12. *23d* Rabbi - A Semitic term literaly meaning "My Great One."

it does not matter, but whoever swears by the gold of the Dwelling Place, is bound by oath.'

17 "Fools and blind! For which is greater, the gold or the Dwelling Place that sets the gold apart?

18 "And, 'Whoever swears by the slaughter-place, it does not matter, but whoever swears by the gift that is on it, is bound by oath.'

19 "Fools and blind! For which is greater, the gift or the slaughter-place that sets the gift apart?

20 "He, then, who swears by the slaughter-place, swears by it and by all that is upon it.

21 "And he who swears by the Dwelling Place, swears by it and by Him who is dwelling in it.

22 "And he who swears by the heaven, swears by the throne of Elohim and by Him who is sitting upon it.

23 "Woe to you, scribes and Pharisees, hypocrites! Because you tithe the mint and the anise and the cumin, and have neglected the weightier *matters* of the Torah: the right-ruling and the compassion and the belief. [d] These need to have been done, without neglecting the others.

24 "Blind guides – straining out a gnat and swallowing a camel!

25 "Woe to you, scribes and Pharisees, hypocrites! Because you clean the outside of the cup and dish, but inside they are filled with plunder and unrighteousness.

26 "Blind Pharisee, first clean the inside of the cup and dish, so that the outside of them becomes clean too.

27 "Woe to you, scribes and Pharisees, hypocrites! Because you are like whitewashed tombs which outwardly indeed look well, but inside are filled with dead men's bones and all uncleanness.

28 "So you too outwardly indeed appear righteous to men, but inside you are filled with hypocrisy and lawlessness. [e]

29 "Woe to you, scribes and Pharisees, hypocrites! Because you build the tombs of the prophets and decorate the monuments of the righteous,

30 and say, 'If we had lived in the days of our fathers, we would not have taken part with them in the blood of the prophets.'

31 "Thus you bear witness against yourselves that you are sons of those who did murder the prophets –

32 and you fill up the measure of your fathers!

33 "Serpents, brood of adders! How would you escape the judgment of GěHinnom?

34 "Because of this, see, I send you prophets, and wise men, and scholars *of Scripture.* [f] Some of them you shall kill and impale, and some of them you shall flog in your congregations and persecute from city to city,

35 so that on you should come all the righteous blood shed on the earth, from the blood of righteous Heḇel to the blood of Zeḵaryah, son of Bereḵyah, whom you murdered between the Dwelling Place and the slaughter-place.

36 "Truly, I say to you, all this shall come upon this generation. [g]

37 "Yerushalayim, Yerushalayim, killing the prophets and stoning those who are sent to her! How often I wished to gather your children together, the way a hen gathers her chickens under her wings, but you would not!

38 "**See! Your house is left to you laid waste,** Yirm. 22:5

39 for I say to you, from now on you shall by no means see Me, until you say, **'Blessed is He who is coming in the Name of יהוה!'** " Teh. 118:26

24

And going out, יהושע went away from the Set-apart Place, and His taught ones came near to point out to Him the buildings of the Set-apart Place.

2 And יהושע said to them, "Do you not see all these? Truly, I say to you, not one stone shall be left here upon another, at all, which shall not be thrown down."

3 And as He sat on the Mount of Olives, the taught ones came to Him separately, saying, "Say to us, when shall this be, and

23d The wording in Lq. 11:42 is somewhat different. *23e* See footnote 5:20. *23f* See 13:52. *23g* Or 'race'.

what is the sign of Your coming, and of the end of the age?"

4 And יהושע answering, said to them, "Take heed that no one leads you astray.

5 "For many shall come in My Name, saying, 'I am the Messiah,' and they shall lead many astray.

6 "And you shall begin to hear of fightings and reports of fightings. See that you are not troubled, for these have to take place, but the end is not yet.

7 "For nation shall rise against nation, and reign against reign. And there shall be scarcities of food, and deadly diseases, and earthquakes in places.

8 "And all these are the beginning of birth pains.

9 "Then they shall deliver you up to affliction and kill you, and you shall be hated by all nations for My Name's sake.

10 "And then many shall stumble, and they shall deliver up one another, and shall hate one another.

11 "And many false prophets shall rise up and lead many astray.

12 "And because of the increase in lawlessness, the love of many shall become cold.

13 "But he who shall have endured to the end shall be saved. [a]

14 "And this Good News of the reign shall be proclaimed in all the world as a witness to all the nations, and then the end shall come.

15 "So when you see the **'abomination that lays waste,'** Dan. 11:31 [b] spoken of by Dani'ĕl the prophet, set up in the set-apart place" – he who reads, let him understand –

16 "then let those who are in Yehuḏah flee to the mountains.

17 "Let him who is on the house-top not come down to take whatever out of his house.

18 "And let him who is in the field not turn back to get his garments.

19 "And woe to those who are pregnant and to those who are nursing children in those days!

20 "And pray that your flight does not take place in winter or on the Sabbath.

21 "For then there shall be great distress, [c] such as has not been since the beginning of the world until this time, no, nor ever shall be.

22 "And if those days were not shortened, no flesh would be saved, but for the sake of the chosen ones those days shall be shortened.

23 "If anyone then says to you, 'Look, here is the Messiah!' or 'There!' do not believe.

24 "For false messiahs and false prophets shall arise, and they shall show great signs and wonders, so as to lead astray, if possible, even the chosen ones.

25 "See, I have forewarned you.

26 "So if they say to you, 'Look, He is in the desert!' do not go out; or 'Look, He is in the inner rooms!' do not believe.

27 "For as the lightning comes from the east and shines to the west, so also shall the coming of the Son of Aḏam be.

28 "For wherever the dead body is, there the vultures [d] shall be gathered together.

29 "And immediately after the distress [e] of those days **the sun shall be darkened**, and **the moon shall not give its light**, and **the stars shall fall from the heaven,** Yesh. 13:10; 24:23, Yeḥ. 32:7,8, Yo'ĕl 2:10,31; 3:15 [f] and **the powers of the heavens shall be shaken.** Ḥag. 2:6,21 [g]

30 "And then the sign of the Son of Aḏam shall appear in the heaven, and then **all the tribes of the earth shall mourn,** Zeḵ. 12:10,14 and they shall see the **Son of Aḏam coming on the clouds** Dan. 7:13 of the heaven with power and much esteem. [h]

31 "And He shall send His messengers with **a great sound of a trumpet,** Yesh. 27:13 and they shall gather together His chosen ones from **the four winds,** Dan. 7:2 **from one end of the heavens to the other.** Deḇ. 4:32

32 "And learn this parable from the fig tree: When its branch has already become tender and puts forth leaves, you know that

24a See 10:22. *24b* See also Dan. 9:27 and *Abomination that lays waste* in Explanatory Notes. *24c* Or *great pressure*, or *great affliction*. *24d* Lq. 17:37. *24e* Or *pressure*. *24f* Also see Amos 5:20; 8:9. *24g* Also see Yesh. 34:4. *24h* Also see Dan. 12:14.

the summer is near.
33 "So you also, when you see all these, know that He is near, at the doors.
34 "Truly, I say to you, this generation shall by no means pass away until all this takes place.
35 "The heaven and the earth shall pass away, but My words shall by no means pass away.
36 "But concerning that day and the hour no one knows, not even the messengers of the heavens, but My Father only. [i]
37 "And as the days of Noaḥ, so also shall the coming of the Son of Aḏam be.
38 "For as they were in the days before the flood, eating and drinking, marrying and giving in marriage, until the day that **Noaḥ entered into the ark**, Ber. 7:7
39 and they did not know until the flood came and took them all away, so also shall the coming of the Son of Aḏam be.
40 "Then two [j] shall be in the field, the one is taken and the one is left.
41 "Two women [j] shall be grinding at the mill, one is taken and one is left.
42 "Watch therefore, for you do not know what hour your Master is coming.
43 "And know this, that if the master of the house had known what hour the thief would come, he would have watched and not allowed his house to be broken into.
44 "Because of this, be ready too, for the Son of Aḏam is coming at an hour when you do not expect Him.
45 "Who then is a trustworthy and wise servant, whom his master set over his household, to give them food in season?
46 "Blessed is that servant whom his master, having come, shall find so doing.
47 "Truly, I say to you that he shall set him over all his possessions.
48 "But if that evil servant says in his heart, 'My master is delaying his coming,'
49 and begins to beat his fellow servants, and to eat and drink with the drunkards,
50 the master of that servant shall come on a day when he does not expect it, and at an hour he does not know,
51 and shall cut him in two and appoint him his portion with the hypocrites – there shall be weeping and gnashing of teeth.

25 "Then the reign of the heavens shall be compared to ten maidens who took their lamps and went out to meet the bridegroom.
2 "And five of them were wise, and five foolish.
3 "Those who were foolish, having taken their lamps, took no oil with them,
4 but the wise took oil in their containers with their lamps.
5 "Now while the bridegroom took time, they all slumbered and slept.
6 "And at midnight a cry was heard, 'See, the bridegroom is coming, go out to meet him!'
7 "Then all those maidens rose up and trimmed their lamps.
8 "And the foolish said to the wise, 'Give us of your oil, because our lamps are going out.'
9 "But the wise answered, saying, 'No, indeed, there would not be enough for us and you. Instead, go to those who sell, and buy for yourselves.'
10 "And while they went to buy, the bridegroom came, and those who were ready went in with him to the wedding feast, and the door was shut.
11 "And later the other maidens also came, saying, 'Master, Master, open up for us!'
12 "But he answering, said, 'Truly, I say to you, I do not know you.'
13 "Watch therefore, because you do not know the day nor the hour in which the Son of Aḏam is coming,
14 for it is like a man going from home, who called his own servants and delivered his possessions to them.
15 "And to one he gave five talents, and to another two, and to another one, to each according to his own ability, and went from home.
16 "And he who had received the five talents went and worked with them, and made another five talents.

24i Mq. 13:32. *24j* A masculine plural can refer to either gender; feminine plural refers to females only.

[17]"In the same way, he with the two also, he gained two more.
[18]"But he who had received the one went away and dug in the ground, and hid the silver of his master.
[19]"And after a long time the master of those servants came and settled accounts with them.
[20]"And he who had received five talents came and brought five other talents, saying, 'Master, you delivered to me five talents. See, I have gained five more talents besides them.'
[21]"And his master said to him, 'Well done, good and trustworthy servant. You were trustworthy over a little, I shall set you over much. Enter into the joy of your master.'
[22]"Then he who had received two talents came and said, 'Master, you delivered to me two talents. See, I have gained two more talents besides them.'
[23]"His master said to him, 'Well done, good and trustworthy servant. You were trustworthy over a little, I shall set you over much. Enter into the joy of your master.'
[24]"And the one who had received the one talent also came and said, 'Master, I knew you to be a hard man, reaping where you have not sown, and gathering where you have not scattered seed,
[25]and being afraid, I went and hid your talent in the ground. See, you have what is yours.'
[26]"And his master answering, said to him, 'You wicked and lazy servant, you knew that I reap where I have not sown, and gather where I have not scattered seed.
[27]'Then you should have put my silver with the bankers, and at my coming I would have received back my own with interest.
[28]'Therefore take away the talent from him, and give it to him who possesses ten talents.
[29]'For to everyone who possesses, more shall be given, and he shall have overflowingly; but from him who does not possess, even what he possesses shall be taken away. [a]
[30]'And throw the worthless servant out into the outer darkness – there shall be weeping and gnashing of teeth.'
[31]"And when the Son of Aḏam comes in His esteem, and all the set-apart messengers with Him, then He shall sit on the throne of His esteem.
[32]"And all the nations shall be gathered before Him, and He shall separate them one from another, as a shepherd separates his sheep from the goats.
[33]"And He shall set the sheep on His right hand, but the goats on the left.
[34]"Then the Sovereign shall say to those on His right hand, 'Come, you blessed of My Father, inherit the reign prepared for you from the foundation of the world –
[35]for I was hungry and you gave Me food, I was thirsty and you gave Me drink, I was a stranger and you took Me in,
[36]was naked and you clothed Me, I was sick and you visited Me, I was in prison and you came to Me.'
[37]"Then the righteous shall answer Him, saying, 'Master, when did we see You hungry and we fed *You*, or thirsty and gave *You* to drink?
[38]'And when did we see You a stranger and took *You* in, or naked and clothed *You*?
[39]'And when did we see You sick, or in prison, and we came to You?'
[40]"And the Sovereign shall answer and say to them, 'Truly, I say to you, in so far as you did it to one of the least of these My brothers, you did it to Me.'
[41]"He shall then also say to those on the left hand, 'Go away from Me, accursed ones, into the everlasting fire prepared for the devil and his messengers –
[42]for I was hungry and you gave Me no food, I was thirsty and you gave Me no drink,
[43]'I was a stranger and you did not take Me in, was naked and you did not clothe Me, sick and in prison and you did not visit Me.'
[44]"Then they also shall answer Him, say-

25a See footnote Lq. 8:18.

ing, 'Master, when did we see You hungry
or thirsty or a stranger or naked or sick or
in prison, and did not serve You?'
45 "Then He shall answer them, saying,
'Truly, I say to you, in so far as you did
not do it to one of the least of these, you
did not do it to Me.'
46 "And these shall go away into everlasting punishment, but the righteous into
everlasting life."

26 And it came to be, when יהושע
ended all these words, He said to
His taught ones,
2 "You know that after two days the
Pěsaḥ takes place, and the Son of Aḏam is
to be delivered up to be impaled."
3 Then the chief priests, and the scribes,
and the elders of the people came together
at the court of the high priest, who was
called Qayapha,
4 and plotted to seize יהושע by trickery
and kill *Him*.
5 But they said, "Not at the festival lest
there be an uproar among the people."
6 And when יהושע was in Běyth Anyah
at the house of Shim'on the leper,
7 a woman came to Him, having an
alabaster flask of costly perfume, and she
poured it on His head as He sat at the table.
8 And when His taught ones saw it, they
were much displeased saying, "To what
purpose is this waste?
9 "For this perfume could have been sold
for much and given to the poor."
10 However, when יהושע noticed it, He
said to them, "Why do you trouble the
woman? For she has done a good work
toward Me.
11 "For you always have the poor with
you, but Me you do not have always.
12 "For in pouring this perfume on My
body, she did it for My burial.
13 "Truly, I say to you, wherever this
Good News is proclaimed in all the world,
what this woman has done shall be spoken
of also, to her remembrance."
14 Then one of the twelve, called Yehuḏah
from Qerioth, went to the chief priests,
15 and said, "What would you give me to
deliver Him to you?" And **they counted
out to him thirty pieces of silver.** Zek. 11:12
16 And from then on he was seeking an
occasion to deliver Him up.
17 And on the first *day* of Unleavened
Bread the taught ones came to יהושע,
saying to Him, "Where do You wish us to
prepare for You to eat the Pěsaḥ?"
18 And He said, "Go into the city to a certain man, and say to him, 'The Teacher
says, "My time is near. I am to perform
the Pěsaḥ at your house with My taught
ones." ' "
19 And the taught ones did as יהושע had
ordered them, and prepared the Pěsaḥ.
20 And when evening came, He sat down
with the twelve.
21 And while they were eating, He said,
"Truly, I say to you, one of you shall deliver Me up."
22 And they were deeply grieved, and
began to say to Him, each of them,
"Master, is it I?"
23 And He answering, said, "He who has
dipped his hand with Me in the dish, he
shall deliver Me up.
24 "Indeed, the Son of Aḏam goes as it has
been written concerning Him, but woe to
that man by whom the Son of Aḏam is
delivered up! It would have been good for
that man if he had not been born."
25 And Yehuḏah – he who delivered Him
up – answering, said, "Rabbi, is it I?" He
said to him, "You have said it."
26 And as they were eating, יהושע took
bread, and having blessed, broke and gave
it to the taught ones and said, "Take, eat,
this is My body."
27 And taking the cup, and giving thanks,
He gave it to them, saying, "Drink from it,
all of you.
28 "For this is My blood, that of the
renewed covenant, which is shed for many
for the forgiveness of sins.
29 "But I say to you, I shall certainly not
drink of this fruit of the vine from now on
till that day when I drink it anew with you
in the reign of My Father."

30 And having sung a song, they went out
to the Mount of Olives.
31 Then יהושע said to them, "All of you
shall stumble in Me this night, for it has
been written, **'I shall strike the Shepherd,
and the sheep of the flock shall be scattered.'** Zek. 13:7 *a*
32 "But after I have been raised, I shall go
before you into Galil."
33 And Kěpha answering, said to Him,
"Even if all stumble in You, I shall never
stumble."
34 יהושע said to him, "Truly, I say to you
that this night, before the cock crows, you
shall deny Me three times."
35 Kěpha said to Him, "Even if I have to
die with You, I shall not deny You!" All
the taught ones said the same too.
36 Then יהושע came with them to a place
called Gethsemane, and said to the taught
ones, "Sit here while I go over there and
pray."
37 And He took with Him Kěpha and the
two sons of Zaḇdai, and He began to be
grieved and deeply distressed.
38 Then He said to them, "My being is
exceedingly grieved, even to death. Stay
here and watch with Me."
39 And going forward a little, He fell on
His face, and prayed, saying, "O My
Father, if it is possible, let this cup pass
from Me. Yet not as I desire, but as You
desire."
40 And He came to the taught ones and
found them asleep, and said to Kěpha, "So,
were you not able to watch with Me one
hour?
41 "Watch and pray, lest you enter into
trial. The spirit indeed is eager, but the
flesh is weak."
42 Again He went away, a second time,
and prayed, saying, "O My Father, if it is
impossible for this to pass unless I drink it,
let Your desire be done."
43 And He came and found them asleep
again, for their eyes were heavy.
44 And He left them, went away again,
and prayed the third time, saying the same
words.
45 Then He came to His taught ones and
said to them, "Still sleeping and taking
rest? See, the hour has come near, and the
Son of Aḏam is delivered up into the hands
of sinners.
46 "Rise, let us go. See, he who delivers
Me up has come near."
47 And while He was still speaking, see,
Yehuḏah, one of the twelve, with a large
crowd with swords and clubs, came from
the chief priests and elders of the people.
48 And he who was delivering Him up
gave them a sign, saying, "Whomever I
kiss, it is He, seize Him."
49 And going straight up to יהושע he said,
"Greetings, Rabbi!" and kissed Him.
50 And יהושע said to him, "Friend, why
have you come?" Then they came and laid
hands on יהושע and seized Him.
51 And look, one of those with יהושע
put out his hand and drew his sword, and
striking the servant of the high priest he cut
off his ear.
52 Then יהושע said to him, "Return your
sword to its place, for all who take the
sword shall die by the sword.
53 "Or do you think that I am not able to
pray to My Father now, and He shall provide Me with more than twelve legions of
messengers?
54 "How then would the Scriptures be
filled that it has to be this way?"
55 In that hour יהושע said to the crowds,
"Have you come out, as against a robber,
with swords and clubs to arrest Me? Daily
I sat with you, teaching in the Set-apart
Place, and you did not seize Me.
56 "But all this came to be, so that the
Scriptures of the prophets might be filled."
Then all the taught ones left Him and fled.
57 And those who had seized יהושע led
Him away to Qayapha the high priest,
where the scribes and the elders were
gathered together.
58 But Kěpha followed Him at a distance
to the courtyard of the high priest, and he
went in and sat with the servants to see the
end.
59 And the chief priests, and the elders,

26a Also see Mq. 14:27, Yn. 16:32.

and all the council were seeking false
witness against יהושע to put Him to death,
60 but found none. Although many false
witnesses came forward, they found none.
But at last two false witnesses came forward,
61 and said, "This one said, 'I am able to
destroy the Dwelling Place of Elohim and
to build it in three days.' "
62 And the high priest stood up and said to
Him, "Have You no answer to make? What
do these witness against You?"
63 But יהושע remained silent. So the high
priest said to Him, "I put You to oath, by
the living Elohim that You say to us if You
are the Messiah, the Son of Elohim."
64 יהושע said to him, "You have said it.
Besides I say to you, from now you shall
see **the Son of Aḏam sitting at the right
hand of the Power,** Teh. 110:1 and **coming on
the clouds of the heaven."** Dan. 7:13
65 Then the high priest tore his garments,
saying, "He has blasphemed! Why do we
need any more witnesses? See, now you
have heard His blasphemy!
66 "What do you think?" And they
answering, said, "He is liable to death."
67 Then they spat in His face and beat
Him, and others slapped Him,
68 saying, "Prophesy to us, Messiah! Who
is the one who struck You?"
69 And Kěpha sat outside in the courtyard,
and a servant girl came to him, saying,
"And you were with יהושע of Galil."
70 But he denied it before them all, saying,
"I do not know what you say."
71 And as he was going out into the porch,
another girl saw him and said to those
there, "And this one was with יהושע of
Natsareth."
72 But again he denied with an oath, "I do
not know the Man!"
73 And after a while those who stood by
came to him and said to Kěpha, "Truly you
are one of them too, for even your speech
gives you away."
74 Then he began to curse and to swear,
saying, "I do not know the Man!" And
immediately a cock crowed.
75 And Kěpha remembered the word of
יהושע who had said to him, "Before a
cock crows, you shall deny Me three
times." And going out, he wept bitterly.

27 And morning having come, all the
chief priests and elders of the people took counsel against יהושע, so as to
put Him to death.
2 And having bound Him, they led Him
away and delivered Him to Pontius Pilate
the governor.
3 Then Yehuḏah – he who delivered Him
up – having seen that He had been
condemned, repented, returned the thirty
pieces of silver to the chief priests and to
the elders,
4 saying, "I have sinned in delivering up
innocent blood." And they said, "What is
that to us? You see to it!"
5 And throwing down the pieces of silver
in the Dwelling Place he left, and went and
hanged himself.
6 And the chief priests took the silver
pieces and said, "It is not right to put them
into the treasury, seeing they are the price
of blood."
7 So they took counsel and bought with
them the potter's field, for the burial of
strangers.
8 Therefore that field has been called the
Field of Blood, until today.
9 Then was filled what was spoken by
Yirmeyahu the prophet, saying, **"And they
took the thirty pieces of silver, the price
of Him who was pierced, on whom they
of the children of Yisra'ěl set a price,**
**10 and gave them for the potter's field,
as יהוה had ordered me."** Zeḵ. 11:12-13
11 And יהושע stood before the governor,
and the governor asked Him, saying, "Are
You the Sovereign of the Yehuḏim?" And
יהושע said to him, "You say it."
12 And as He was accused by the chief
priests and the elders, He answered not.
13 Then Pilate said to Him, "Do You not
hear how much they witness against You?"
14 And He did not answer him, not one
word, so that the governor wondered
much.
15 And at the festival the governor used to
release to the crowd one prisoner whom
they wished.

16 And they had then a well-known prisoner called Barabba.
17 So when they were assembled, Pilate
said to them, "Whom do you wish I release
to you? Barabba, or יהושע who is called
Messiah?"
18 For he knew that because of envy they
had delivered Him up.
19 And as he was sitting on the judgment
seat, his wife sent to him, saying, "Have
none at all to do with that righteous Man,
for I have suffered much today in a dream
because of Him."
20 But the chief priests and elders persuaded the crowds that they should ask for
Barabba and to destroy יהושע.
21 And the governor answering, said to
them, "Which of the two do you wish I
release to you?" They said, "Barabba!"
22 Pilate said to them, "What then shall I
do with יהושע who is called Messiah?"
They all said to him, "Let Him be
impaled!"
23 And the governor said, "Indeed, what
evil has He done?" And they were crying
out all the more, saying, "Let Him be
impaled!"
24 And when Pilate saw that he was getting nowhere, but rather an uproar was
starting, he took water and washed his
hands before the crowd, saying, "I am
innocent of the blood of this Righteous
One. You shall see to it."
25 And all the people answering, said,
"His blood be on us and on our children."
26 Then he released Barabba to them, but
having יהושע whipped, he delivered Him
over to be impaled.
27 Then the soldiers of the governor took
יהושע into the court and gathered the
entire company *of soldiers* around Him.
28 And having stripped Him, they put a
scarlet robe on Him.
29 And plaiting a crown of thorns, they
put it on His head, and a reed in His right
hand. And they kneeled down before Him
and mocked Him, saying, "Greetings,
Sovereign of the Yehuḏim!"
30 And spitting on Him they took the reed
and struck Him on the head.
31 And when they had mocked Him, they
took the robe off Him, then put His own
garments on Him, and led Him away to be
impaled.
32 And as they were going out, they found
a man of Cyrene, Shim'on by name – they
compelled him to bear His stake.
33 And when they came to a place called
Golgotha, that is to say, Place of a Skull,
34 they gave Him wine mixed with bile to
drink. And after tasting, He would not
drink it.
35 And having impaled Him, they divided
His garments, casting lots, that it might be
filled what was spoken by the prophet,
**"They divided My garments among
them, and for My clothing they cast
lots."** Teh. 22:18
36 And sitting down, they guarded Him
there.
37 And they put up over His head the written charge against Him: THIS IS יהושע,
THE SOVEREIGN OF THE YEHUḎIM.
38 Then two robbers were impaled with
Him, one on the right and another on the
left.
39 And those passing by were blaspheming Him, **shaking their heads**, Teh. 22:7
40 and saying, "You who destroy the
Dwelling Place and build it in three days,
save Yourself! If You are the Son of
Elohim, come down from the stake."
41 And likewise the chief priests, with the
scribes and elders, mocking, said,
42 "He saved others – He is unable to save
Himself. If He is the Sovereign of Yisra'ěl,
let Him now come down from the stake,
and we shall believe Him.
43 **"He trusted in Elohim, let Him rescue Him now if He desires Him,** Teh. 22:8
for He said, 'I am the Son of Elohim.' "
44 And also the robbers who were impaled
with Him reviled Him, *saying* the same.
45 And from the sixth hour there was
darkness over all the land, until the ninth
hour.
46 And about the ninth hour יהושע cried
out with a loud voice, saying, **"Ěli, Ěli,
lemah sheḇaqtani?"** that is, **"My Ěl, My
Ěl, why have You forsaken Me?"** Teh. 22:1
47 Some of those standing there, having
heard, said, "This One calls Ěliyahu!"

48 And immediately one of them ran and took a sponge, and filled it with **sour wine** and put it on a reed, and gave it to Him **to drink**. Teh. 69:21

49 But the rest said, "Leave it, let us see if Ěliyahu comes to save Him."

50 And יהושע cried out again with a loud voice, and gave up His spirit.

51 And see, the veil of the Dwelling Place was torn in two from top to bottom, and the earth was shaken, and the rocks were split,

52 and the tombs were opened, and many bodies of the set-apart ones who had fallen asleep were raised,

53 and coming out of the tombs after His resurrection, they went into the set-apart city and appeared to many.

54 And when the captain and those with him, who were guarding יהושע, saw the earthquake and all that took place, they feared exceedingly, saying, "Truly this was the Son of Elohim!"

55 And many women who followed יהושע from Galil, attending Him, were there, watching from a distance,

56 among whom were Miryam from Mağdala, and Miryam the mother of Ya'aqoḇ and Yosěph, and the mother of Zaḇdai's sons.

57 And when evening came, there came a rich man from Ramathayim, named Yosěph, who himself had also become a taught one of יהושע.

58 He went to Pilate and asked for the body of יהושע. Then Pilate commanded the body to be given.

59 And having taken the body, Yosěph wrapped it in clean linen,

60 and laid it in his new tomb which he had hewn out of the rock. And he rolled a large stone against the door of the tomb, and went away.

61 And Miryam from Mağdala was there, and the other Miryam, sitting opposite the tomb.

62 On the next day, which was after the preparation, the chief priests and Pharisees gathered together to Pilate,

63 saying, "Master, we remember, while He was still alive, how that deceiver said, 'After three days I am raised.'

64 "Command, then, that the tomb be safeguarded until the third day, lest His taught ones come by night and steal Him away, and should say to the people, 'He was raised from the dead.' And the last deception shall be worse than the first."

65 So Pilate said to them, "You have a watch, go, safeguard it as you know how."

66 And they went and safeguarded the tomb, sealing the stone and setting the watch.

28

But late in the sabbath, [a] as it was dawning into *day* one of *the* week, [b] Miryam from Mağdala and the other Miryam came to see the tomb.

2 And see, there was a great earthquake, for a messenger of יהוה came down out of heaven, and came and rolled back the stone from the door, and sat on it.

3 And his appearance was like lightning, and his garments as white as snow.

4 And the guards trembled for fear of him, and became like dead men.

5 And the messenger responding, said to the women, "Do not be afraid, for I know that you seek יהושע who was impaled.

6 "He is not here, for He was raised, as He said. Come, see the place where the Master lay.

7 "And go quickly, say to His taught ones that He was raised from the dead, and see, He is going before you to Galil. There you shall see Him. See, I have told you."

8 And they left the tomb quickly, with fear and great joy, and ran to report to His taught ones.

9 And as they were going to report to His taught ones, see, יהושע met them, saying, "Greetings!" And they came and held Him by the feet and did bow to Him.

10 Then יהושע said to them, "Do not be

28a Gk. Sabbaths *28b* Gk. one of *the* sabbaths. See also Mq. 16:2, Lq. 24:1, Yn. 20:1 and Cor. א 16:2. See Explanatory Notes - First Day of the Week.

afraid. Go, report to My brothers, to go to
Galil, and they shall see Me there."
11 And while they were going, see, some
of the watch having gone into the city,
reported to the chief priests all that took
place.
12 And when they came together with the
elders and taken counsel, they gave
enough silver to the soldiers,
13 saying, "Say that His taught ones came
at night and stole Him away while we
slept.
14 "And if this should be reported to the
governor, we shall win him over and keep
you out of trouble."
15 And having taken the silver they did as
they were instructed. And this account was
widely spread among the Yehuḏim, to this
day.
16 And the eleven taught ones went away
into Galil, to the mountain which יהושע
had appointed for them.
17 And when they saw Him, they bowed
to Him, but some doubted.
18 And יהושע came up and spoke to
them, saying, "All authority has been
given to Me in heaven and on earth.
19 "Therefore, go and make taught ones of
all the nations, immersing them in the
Name [c] of the Father and of the Son and of
the Set-apart Spirit, [d]
20 teaching them to guard all that I have
commanded you. And see, I am with you
always, until the end of the age." Aměn.

28c Note: The singular. *28d* Not found in the Hebrew Shem Toḇ text, "...and make taught ones of all the nations, immersing them in the Name of the Father and of the Son and of the Set-apart Spirit."

MARQOS

MARK

1 The beginning of the Good News of
יהושע Messiah, the Son of Elohim.
2 As it has been written in the Prophets,
**“See, I send My messenger before Your
face, who shall prepare Your way before
You,** Mal. 3:1
3 **a voice of one crying in the wilderness, ‘Prepare the way of יהוה, make His
paths straight.’ ”** Yesh. 40:3
4 Yoḥanan came immersing in the
wilderness and proclaiming an immersion
of repentance for the forgiveness of sins.
5 And all the country of Yehuḏah, and
those of Yerushalayim, went out to him
and were all immersed by him in the
Yarděn River, confessing their sins.
6 And Yoḥanan was clothed with camel’s
hair and a leather girdle around his waist,
and eating locusts and wild honey.
7 And he proclaimed, saying, “After me
comes One who is mightier than I, whose
sandal strap I am not worthy to stoop down
and loosen.
8 “I indeed did immerse you in water, but
He shall immerse you in the Set-apart
Spirit.”
9 And it came to be in those days that
יהושע came from Natsareth of Galil, and
was immersed by Yoḥanan in the Yarděn.
10 And immediately, coming up from the
water, He saw the heavens being torn open
and the Spirit coming down on Him like a
dove.
11 And a voice came out of the heavens,
“You are My Son, the Beloved, in whom I
did delight.”
12 And immediately the Spirit drove Him
into the wilderness.
13 And He was there in the wilderness
forty days, tried by Satan, and was with the
wild beasts. And the messengers attended
Him.
14 And after Yoḥanan was delivered up,
יהושע came to Galil, proclaiming the
Good News of the reign of Elohim,
15 and saying, “The time has been filled,
and the reign of Elohim has come near.
Repent, and believe in the Good News.”
16 And walking by the Sea of Galil, He
saw Shim‘on, and Andri his brother, casting a net into the sea, for they were fishers.
17 And יהושע said to them, “Come,
follow Me, and I shall make you become
fishers of men.”
18 And immediately they left their nets
and followed Him.
19 And having gone on a little from there,
He saw Ya‘aqoḇ the *son* of Zaḇdai, and
Yoḥanan his brother, and they were in the
boat mending their nets.
20 And immediately He called them, and
leaving their father Zaḇdai in the boat with
the hired servants, they went after Him.
21 And they went into Kephar Naḥum,
and immediately on the Sabbath He went
into the congregation and taught.
22 And they were astonished at His teaching, for He was teaching them as possessing authority, and not as the scribes.
23 And there was a man in their congregation with an unclean spirit, and he cried
out,
24 saying, “Ha! What have we to do with
You, יהושע of Natsareth? Did You come
to destroy us? I know who You are: the
Set-apart One of Elohim!”
25 And יהושע rebuked him, saying, “Be
silenced, and come out of him!”
26 And throwing him into convulsions, the
unclean spirit called out with a loud voice,
and came out of him.
27 And they were all so amazed, as to reason among themselves, saying, “What is
this, a fresh teaching? With authority He
commands even the unclean spirits, and
they obey Him!”
28 And news about Him immediately
spread into all the country around Galil.
29 And coming out of the congregation,
they went straight to the house of Shim‘on
and Andri, with Ya‘aqoḇ and Yoḥanan.
30 And the mother-in-law of Shim‘on lay

sick with inflammation, and immediately
they spoke to Him about her.
31 And having come, He took her by the
hand and lifted her up, and immediately
the inflammation left her, and she served
them.
32 And when evening came, when the
sun had set, they brought to Him all who
were sick and those who were demon-
possessed.
33 And the entire city had gathered at the
door.
34 And He healed many who were sick
with various diseases, and cast out many
demons, and was not allowing the demons
to speak, because they knew Him.
35 And having risen very early in the
morning, while still dark, He went out, and
went away to a lonely place, and there He
prayed.
36 And Shim'on and those who were with
Him searched for Him,
37 and when they found Him, they said to
Him, "All are seeking You."
38 And He said to them, "Let us go into
the neighbouring towns, so that I proclaim
there also, because for this I have come
forth."
39 And He was proclaiming in their congregations, in all Galil, and casting out
demons.
40 And a leper came to Him, calling upon
Him, kneeling down to Him and saying to
Him, "If You desire, You are able to make
me clean."
41 And יהושע, moved with compassion,
stretched out His hand and touched him,
and said to him, "I desire it. Be cleansed."
42 And immediately the leprosy left him,
and he was cleansed.
43 And having strictly warned him, He
immediately sent him away,
44 and said to him, "See, say none at all to
anyone, but go show yourself to the priest,
and offer for your cleansing what Mosheh
ordered, as a witness to them."
45 But he went out and began to publish it
so much, and to spread the word, that
יהושע was no longer able to openly enter
the city, but was outside in lonely places.
Yet they came to Him from all directions.

2 And some days later He again entered
into Kephar Naḥum, and it was heard
that He was in the house.
2 And so many gathered together, that
there was no more room, not even at the
door. And He spoke the Word to them.
3 And they came to Him, bringing a paralytic, carried by four.
4 And not being able to come near Him
because of the crowd, they uncovered the
roof where He was. And when they had
broken through, they let down the bed on
which the paralytic was lying.
5 And when יהושע saw their belief, He
said to the paralytic, "Son, your sins are
forgiven you."
6 Now some of the scribes were sitting
there, and reasoning in their hearts,
7 "Why does this One talk like this? He is
blaspheming! Who is able to forgive sins
but Elohim alone?"
8 And immediately יהושע, knowing in
His spirit that they were reasoning that
way within themselves, said to them,
"Why do you reason about all this in your
hearts?
9 "Which is easier, to say to the paralytic,
'Your sins are forgiven,' or to say, 'Rise,
take up your bed and walk'?
10 "But in order for you to know that the
Son of Aḏam possesses authority on earth
to forgive sins..." He said to the paralytic,
11 "I say to you, rise, take up your bed,
and go to your house."
12 And he rose straightaway, and took up
the bed, and went out before all, so that all
were amazed and praised Elohim, saying,
"We have never seen the like of it!"
13 And He went out again by the sea, and
all the crowd was coming to Him, and He
taught them.
14 And passing by, He saw Lěwi the *son*
of Alphai sitting at the tax office, and said
to him, "Follow Me." And having risen he
followed Him.
15 And it came to be, as He sat at the table
at his house, that many tax collectors and
sinners also sat with יהושע and His taught
ones, for there were many, and they followed Him.
16 And when the scribes and Pharisees

saw Him eating with the tax collectors and
sinners, they said to His taught ones, "Why
does He eat and drink with tax collectors
and sinners?"
17 And hearing this, יהושע said to them,
"Those who are strong have no need of a
physician, but those who are sick. I did not
come to call the righteous to repentance,
but sinners."
18 And the taught ones of Yoḥanan and of
the Pharisees were fasting. And they came
and said to Him, "Why do the taught ones
of Yoḥanan and of the Pharisees fast, but
Your taught ones do not fast?"
19 And יהושע said to them, "Are the
friends of the bridegroom able to fast while
the bridegroom is with them? As long as
they have the bridegroom with them they
are not able to fast.
20 "But the days shall come when the
bridegroom shall be taken away from
them, and then they shall fast in those
days.
21 "And no one sews a piece of unshrunk
cloth on an old garment, otherwise the
renewed piece pulls away from the old,
and the tear is made worse.
22 "And no one puts new wine into old
wineskins, otherwise the new wine bursts
the wineskins, and the wine runs out, and
the wineskins are ruined. But new wine is
to be put into fresh wineskins."
23 And it came to be that He went through
the grainfields on the Sabbath. And as they
went His taught ones began to pluck heads
of grain,
24 and the Pharisees said to Him, "Look,
why do they do what is not right on the
Sabbath?"
25 And He said to them, "Have you never
read what Dawiḏ did when he had need
and was hungry, he and those with him?
26 "How he went into the House of
Elohim, while Eḇyathar was high priest,
and ate the showbread, which is not right
to eat, except for the priests, and he gave it
also to those who were with him?"
27 And He said to them, "The Sabbath
was made for man, and not man for the
Sabbath.
28 "So the Son of Aḏam is also Master of
the Sabbath." [a]

3 And He went into the congregation
again, and a man who had a withered
hand was there.
2 And they were watching Him, whether
He would heal him on the Sabbath, so as to
accuse Him.
3 And He said to the man who had the
withered hand, "Get up to the middle."
4 And He said to them, "Is it right to do
good on the Sabbath, or to do evil, to save
life or to kill?" But they remained silent.
5 And having looked around on them
with displeasure, being grieved at the hardness of their hearts, He said to the man,
"Stretch out your hand." And he stretched
it out, and his hand was restored as healthy
as the other.
6 And the Pharisees went out and immediately plotted with the Herodians against
Him, how to destroy Him.
7 But יהושע withdrew with His taught
ones to the sea. And a great crowd from
Galil followed Him, and from Yehuḏah.
8 Even from Yerushalayim, and from
Eḏom and beyond the Yardĕn, and those
around Tsor and Tsiḏon, a large crowd
came to Him when they heard how much
He was doing.
9 And He spoke to His taught ones, that a
small boat should be kept ready for Him
because of the crowd, lest they should
press upon Him.
10 For He healed many, so that as many as
had afflictions fell upon Him to touch Him.
11 And the unclean spirits, whenever they
saw Him, fell down before Him and cried
out, saying, "You are the Son of Elohim."
12 But He warned them many times that
they should not make Him known.
13 And He went up on the mountain and
called to Him whom He wished, and they
came to Him.
14 And He appointed twelve to be with
Him, and to be sent out to proclaim,
15 and to possess authority to heal sick-

2a See also Ber. 2:2-3.

nesses and to cast out demons.
16 And He appointed the twelve: Shimʿon,
to whom He added the name Kĕpha;
17 and Yaʿaqoḇ the *son* of Zaḇdai, and
Yoḥanan the brother of Yaʿaqoḇ, to whom
He added the name Beni-Reḡes, that is,
"Sons of Thunder,"
18 and Andri, and Philip, and Bartholomi,
and Mattithyahu, and T'oma, and Yaʿaqoḇ
son of Alphai, and Taddai, and Shimʿon the
Kenaʿanite;
19 and Yehuḏah from Qerioth, who did
also deliver Him up. And they went into
a house,
20 and again the crowd came together, so
that they were unable even to eat bread.
21 And when His relatives heard about
this, they went out to seize Him, for they
said, "He is out of His mind."
22 And the scribes who came down from
Yerushalayim said, "He has Beʿelzebul,"
and, "He casts out demons by the ruler of
the demons."
23 And calling them near He said to them
in parables, "How is Satan able to cast out
Satan?
24 "And if a reign is divided against itself,
that reign is unable to stand.
25 "And if a house is divided against
itself, that house is unable to stand.
26 "And if Satan has risen up against himself, and is divided, he is unable to stand,
but has an end.
27 "No one is able to enter a strong man's
house and plunder his goods, unless he
first binds the strong man, and then he
shall plunder his house.
28 "Truly, I say to you, all the sins shall be
forgiven the sons of men, and whatever
blasphemies they speak,
29 but he who blasphemes against the Set-
apart Spirit has no forgiveness forever, but
is subject to everlasting judgment,"
30 because they said, "He has an unclean
spirit."
31 And His brothers and His mother came,
and standing outside they sent to Him,
calling Him.
32 And a crowd was sitting around Him.
And they said to Him, "See, Your mother
and Your brothers are outside seeking
You."
33 But He answered them, saying, "Who
is My mother, or My brothers?"
34 And looking about on those sitting
round Him, He said, "See My mother and
My brothers!
35 "For whoever does the desire of Elohim
is My brother and My sister and mother." [a]

4 And He began to teach again by the
sea, and a large crowd was gathered to
Him, so that He entered into a boat, to sit
in the sea. And all the crowd was on the
land facing the sea.
2 And He taught them much in parables,
and said to them in His teaching:
3 "Listen! See, a sower went out to sow. [a]
4 "And it came to be, as he sowed, some
fell by the wayside, and the birds of the
heaven came and devoured it.
5 "And other fell on rocky places, where
it had not much soil. And immediately it
sprang up because it had no depth of soil.
6 "But when the sun was up it was
scorched, and because it had no root it
withered away.
7 "And other fell among thorns. And the
thorns grew up and choked it, and it yielded no crop.
8 "And other fell on good soil and yielded a crop that came up, grew and yielded a
crop, some thirtyfold, and some sixty, and
some a hundred."
9 And He said to them, "He who has ears
to hear, let him hear!"
10 And when He was alone, those about
Him, with the twelve, asked Him about the
parable.
11 And He said to them, "To you it has
been given to know the secret of the reign
of Elohim, but to those who are outside, all
are done in parables,
12 so that **'seeing they see but do not
perceive, and hearing they hear but do
not understand, lest they should turn
and their sins be forgiven them.'** "
Yesh. 6:9-10 [b]

3a Mt. 12:50, Lq. 8:21. *4a* See Mt. 13 with its footnotes. *4b* See footnote Mt. 13:15.

13 And He said to them, "Do you not
understand this parable? How then shall
you understand all the parables?
14 "The sower sows the word.
15 "These, then, are the ones by the wayside where the word is sown. And when
they hear, Satan comes immediately and
takes away the word that was sown in their
hearts.
16 "And likewise these are the ones sown
on rocky places, who, when they hear the
word, immediately receive it with joy,
17 and they have no root in themselves,
but are short-lived. Then when pressure or
persecution arises because of the word,
immediately they stumble.
18 "And others are those sown among
thorns, these are they who hear the word,
19 and the worries of this age, and the
deceit of riches, and the desires for other
matters, entering in, choke the word, and it
becomes fruitless.
20 "And those sown on good soil, are
those who hear the word, and accept it, and
bear fruit, some thirtyfold, and some sixty,
and some a hundred."
21 And He said to them, "Would a lamp be
brought to be put under a basket or under a
bed? Is it not to be put on a lampstand?
22 "For whatever is hidden shall be revealed, and whatever has been kept secret,
shall come to light. [c]
23 "If anyone has ears to hear, let him
hear."
24 And He said to them, "Take heed what
you hear. With the same measure you use,
it shall be measured to you, and more shall
be added to you who hear.
25 "For whoever possesses, to him more
shall be given; but whoever does not possess, even what he possesses shall be taken
away from him." [d]
26 And He said, "The reign of Elohim is
as when a man scatters seed on the ground,
27 then sleeps by night and rises by day,
while the seed sprouts and grows, he himself does not know how.
28 "For the soil yields crops by itself: first
the blade, then the head, after that the completed grain in the head.
29 "And when the crop is ready, immediately he puts in the sickle, because the
harvest has come."
30 And He said, "To what shall we compare the reign of Elohim? Or with what
parable shall we present it?
31 "Like a mustard seed, which, when it is
sown on the ground, is smaller than all the
seeds on earth,
32 and when it is sown, it grows up and
becomes greater than all plants, and forms
large branches, so that the birds of the
heaven are able to nest under its shade."
33 And with many such parables He was
speaking to them the word as they were
able to hear,
34 and He was not speaking to them without parables. And when they were alone,
He explained all to His taught ones.
35 And on the same day, when evening
had come, He said to them, "Let us pass
over to the other side."
36 And having left the crowd, they took
Him along in the boat, as He was. And
other little boats were also with Him.
37 And there came a great windstorm, and
the waves beat into the boat, so that it was
already being filled.
38 And He was in the stern, asleep on a
cushion. And they woke Him up and said
to Him, "Teacher, is it no concern to You
that we perish?"
39 And having been awakened He rebuked
the wind, and said to the sea, "Peace, be
still!" And the wind ceased and there was a
great calm.
40 And He said to them, "Why are you so
afraid? Have you not yet belief?"
41 And they feared exceedingly, and asked
each other, "Who then is this, that even the
wind and the sea obey Him!"

5

And they came to the other side of the
sea, to the country of the Gaḏarenes.
2 And when He came out of the boat,
immediately there met Him out of the
tombs a man with an unclean spirit,
3 who had his dwelling among the tombs.

4c See footnote Lq. 8:17. *4d* See footnote Lq. 8:18.

And no one was able to bind him, not even
with chains,
4 because he had often been bound with
shackles and chains but the chains had
been pulled apart by him, and the shackles
broken in pieces, and no one was able to
tame him.
5 And continually, night and day, he was
in the mountains and in the tombs, crying
out and cutting himself with stones.
6 And seeing יהושע from a distance, he
ran and bowed down to Him,
7 and having called out with a loud voice,
said, "What have I to do with You, יהושע,
Son of the Most High Ěl? Swear to Elohim
not to torture me."
8 For He had said to him, "Come out of
the man, unclean spirit!"
9 And He was asking him, "What is your
name?" And he answered, saying, "My
name is Legion, because we are many."
10 And he begged Him very much that He
would not send them out of the country.
11 Now a great herd of pigs was there,
feeding near the mountains.
12 And all the demons begged Him, saying, "Send us to the pigs, so that we enter
into them."
13 And He gave them permission. And the
unclean spirits came out and entered into
the pigs – they were about two thousand –
and the herd rushed down the steep place
into the sea, and drowned in the sea.
14 And those who fed the pigs fled, and
reported it in the city and in the country.
And they went out to see what had taken
place.
15 So they came to יהושע, and saw the
demon-possessed one, him who had the
legion, sitting, and dressed, and in his right
mind. And they were afraid.
16 And those who saw it related to them
what was done to the demon-possessed
one, and about the pigs.
17 And they began to plead with Him to
leave their borders.
18 And as He was entering into the boat,
he who had been demon-possessed begged
Him that he might be with Him.
19 And יהושע did not allow him, but said
to him, "Go home to your friends, and
report to them what the Master has done
for you, and how He had compassion on
you."
20 And he left and began to proclaim in
Dekapolis all that יהושע had done for him,
and all marvelled.
21 And when יהושע had passed over
again by boat to the other side, a large
crowd assembled to Him, and He was by
the sea.
22 And see, one of the rulers of the congregation came, Ya'ir by name. And when
he saw Him, he fell at His feet,
23 and begged Him strongly, saying, "My
little daughter lies at the point of death.
Come, lay Your hands on her to heal her,
and she shall live."
24 And He went with him. And a large
crowd was following Him, and they were
thronging Him.
25 And a certain woman had a flow of
blood for twelve years,
26 and had suffered much from many
physicians, and spent all that she had and
was no better, but rather became worse.
27 Having heard about יהושע, she came
behind Him in the crowd and touched His
garment,
28 for she said, "If I only touch His garments, I shall be made well."
29 And immediately the fountain of her
blood was dried up, and she felt in her
body that she was healed of the affliction.
30 And immediately יהושע, knowing in
Himself that power had gone out of Him,
turned around in the crowd and said, "Who
touched My garments?"
31 And His taught ones said to Him, "You
see the crowd is thronging You, and You
say, 'Who touched Me?' "
32 And He was looking around to see her
who did this.
33 And the woman, fearing and trembling,
knowing what was done to her, came and
fell down before Him and spoke to Him all
the truth.
34 And He said to her, "Daughter, your
belief has healed you. Go in peace, and be
relieved from your affliction."
35 As He was speaking, they came from
the ruler of the congregation's *house*, say-

ing *to him*, "Your daughter is dead. Why trouble the Teacher any further?"
36 But having heard the word that was spoken, יהושע said to the ruler of the congregation, "Do not be afraid – only believe."
37 And He allowed no one to follow Him except Kěpha, and Ya'aqoḇ, and Yoḥanan the brother of Ya'aqoḇ.
38 So they came to the house of the ruler of the congregation, and saw a commotion, and much weeping and lamenting.
39 And coming in He said to them, "Why make this commotion and weep? The child has not died, but is sleeping."
40 And they were laughing at Him. And when He had put them all out, He took the father and the mother of the child, and those who were with Him, and went in where the child was lying.
41 And taking the child by the hand He said to her, "Talitha, qumi," which is translated, "Little girl, I say to you, arise."
42 And immediately the girl rose up and was walking, for she was twelve years old. And they were completely astonished.
43 But He ordered them many times that no one should know it, and said that she should be given *food* to eat.

6 And He went away from there and came to His own country, and His taught ones followed Him.
2 And Sabbath having come, He began to teach in the congregation. And many who heard *Him* were astonished, saying, "Where did He get all this? And what wisdom is this which is given to Him, that such miracles are done through His hands?
3 "Is this not the carpenter, the Son of Miryam, and brother of Ya'aqoḇ, and Yosěph, and Yehuḏah, and Shim'on? And are not His sisters here with us?" And they stumbled in Him.
4 And יהושע said to them, "A prophet is not unappreciated except in his own country, and among his own relatives, and in his own house."
5 And He was unable to do any miracle there, except that He laid His hands on a few sick ones and healed them.
6 And He marvelled because of their unbelief. And He was going around among the villages, teaching.
7 And He called the twelve near, and began to send them out two by two, and gave them authority over unclean spirits.
8 And He instructed them to take none at all for the journey except a staff – no bag, no bread, no copper in their money belts,
9 but to wear sandals, and not to wear two undergarments.
10 And He said to them, "Wherever you enter into a house, stay there until you leave that place.
11 "And any place that does not receive you or listen to you, when you leave there, shake off the dust under your feet as a witness against them. Truly, I say to you, it shall be more bearable for Seḏom and Amorah in the day of judgment than for that city!"
12 And they went out and proclaimed that *men* should repent.
13 And they were casting out many demons, and they were anointing with oil many who were sick, and they were healing them.
14 And Sovereign Herodes heard, for His Name had become well-known. And he said, "Yoḥanan the Immerser has been raised from the dead, and because of this these powers are at work in him."
15 Others said, "He is Ěliyahu." And others said, "He is a prophet – like one of the prophets."
16 But when Herodes heard, he said, "This one is Yoḥanan whom I beheaded, he has been raised from the dead!"
17 For Herodes himself had sent and seized Yoḥanan, and bound him in prison because of Herodias, his brother Philip's wife, because he had married her,
18 for Yoḥanan had said to Herodes, "It is not right for you to have your brother's wife."
19 So Herodias held a grudge against him and wished to kill him, but was unable,
20 for Herodes feared Yoḥanan, knowing that he was a righteous and set-apart man, and he protected him. And when he heard him, he was much perplexed, yet heard

him gladly.

21 And a suitable day came when Herodes on his birthday gave a feast for his great men, and the high officers, and the chief men of Galil.

22 And when the daughter of Herodias herself came in and danced, and pleased Herodes and those who sat with him, the sovereign said to the girl, "Ask me whatever you wish, and I shall give it to you."

23 And he swore to her, "Whatever you ask me, I shall give you, up to half of my reign."

24 And she went out and said to her mother, "What shall I ask?" And she said, "The head of Yoḥanan the Immerser!"

25 And coming in immediately with haste to the sovereign she asked, saying, "I wish that you give me at once the head of Yoḥanan the Immerser on a dish."

26 And the sovereign, becoming deeply grieved, because of the oaths, and because of those who sat with him, did not wish to refuse her.

27 And the sovereign straightaway sent an executioner and commanded his head to be brought. And he went and beheaded him in prison,

28 and brought his head on a dish, and gave it to the girl. And the girl gave it to her mother.

29 And when his taught ones heard of it, they came and took away his dead body and laid it in a tomb.

30 And the emissaries gathered to יהושע and reported to Him all, both what they had done and what they had taught.

31 And He said to them, "Come aside by yourselves to a lonely place and rest a little" – for there were many coming and going, and they did not even have time to eat.

32 And they went away to a lonely place in the boat by themselves.

33 But they saw them going, and many recognised Him and ran there on foot from all the cities, and came before them and came together to Him.

34 And having gone out, יהושע saw a large crowd and was moved with compassion for them because they were like sheep not having a shepherd. And He began to teach them many *matters*.

35 And as the hour grew late, His taught ones came to Him and said, "This is a lonely place, and now the hour is late.

36 "Send them away, so that they go into the surrounding country and villages and buy themselves bread, since they have no *food* to eat."

37 But He answering, said to them, "You give them to eat." And they said to Him, "Should we go and buy two hundred denarii [a] worth of bread and give them to eat?"

38 Then He said to them, "How many loaves do you have? Go and see." And when they found out they said, "Five, and two fishes."

39 And He ordered them to make them all sit down in groups on the green grass.

40 And they sat down in groups, in hundreds and in fifties.

41 And taking the five loaves and the two fishes, looking up to the heaven, He blessed and broke the loaves, and gave them to His taught ones to set before them. And the two fishes He divided among them all.

42 And all ate and were satisfied.

43 And they picked up twelve baskets, filled with pieces, also from the fishes.

44 Now those who ate the loaves were about five thousand men.

45 And immediately He made His taught ones enter into the boat, and to go before Him to the other side, to Běyth Tsaiḏa, while He was dismissing the crowd.

46 And having sent them away, He went away to the mountain to pray.

47 And when evening came, the boat was in the middle of the sea. And He was alone on the land.

48 And seeing them straining at rowing – for the wind was against them – at about the fourth watch of the night, He came to them walking on the sea, and *He* wished to

6a - Roman monetary unit.

pass them by.
49 And when they saw Him walking on
the sea, they thought it was a phantom, and
cried out,
50 for they all saw Him and were troubled.
And immediately He spoke to them and
said to them, "Take courage, it is I. Do not
be afraid."
51 And He went up to them, into the boat,
and the wind ceased. And they were
exceedingly amazed in themselves, and
marvelled.
52 For they did not understand about the
loaves, because their heart was hardened.
53 And having passed over, they came to
the land of Gennĕsar and drew to shore.
54 And when they came out of the boat,
He was immediately recognised,
55 and all that neighbourhood ran about,
and began to carry about on beds those
who were sick to wherever they heard He
was.
56 And wherever He went, into villages,
or cities, or the country, they were laying
the sick in the market-places, and begged
Him to let them touch if only the tzitzit [b] of
His garment. And as many as touched Him
were healed.

7 And the Pharisees and some of the
scribes assembled to Him, having
come from Yerushalayim.
2 And seeing some of His taught ones eat
bread with defiled, that is, with unwashed
hands, they found fault.
3 For the Pharisees, and all the Yehuḏim,
do not eat unless they wash their hands
thoroughly, holding fast the tradition of the
elders,
4 and *coming* from the market-place,
they do not eat unless they wash. And
there are many other *traditions* which they
have received and hold fast – the washing
of cups and utensils and copper vessels and
couches.
5 Then the Pharisees and scribes asked
Him, "Why do Your taught ones not walk
according to the tradition of the elders, but
eat bread with unwashed hands?"
6 And He answering, said to them,
"Well did Yeshayahu prophesy concerning
you hypocrites, as it has been written,
**'This people respect Me with their lips,
but their heart is far from Me.**
7 **And in vain do they worship Me,
teaching as teachings the commands of
men.'** Yesh. 29:13 *a*
8 "Forsaking the command of Elohim,
you hold fast the tradition of men."
9 And He said to them, "Well do you set
aside the command of Elohim, in order to
guard your tradition.
10 "For Mosheh said, **'Respect your
father and your mother,'** Shem. 20:12, Deḇ. 5:16
and, **'He who curses father or mother, let
him be put to death.'** Shem. 21:17, Way. 20:9
11 "But you say, 'If a man says to his
father or mother, "Whatever profit you
might have received from me, is Qorban
(that is, a gift),"'
12 you no longer let him do any *matter* at
all for his father or his mother,
13 nullifying the Word of Elohim through
your tradition which you have handed
down. And many such *traditions* you do."
14 And calling the crowd to Him, He said
to them, "Hear Me, everyone, and understand:
15 "There is no matter that enters a man
from outside which is able to defile him,
but it is what comes out of him that defiles
the man.
16 "If anyone has ears to hear, let him
hear!"
17 And when He went from the crowd into
a house, His taught ones asked Him concerning the parable.
18 And He said to them, "Are you also
without understanding? Do you not perceive that whatever enters a man from
outside is unable to defile him,
19 because it does not enter his heart but
his stomach, and is eliminated, thus purg-
ing all the foods?" *b*

6b See Explanatory notes - "Tzitzit" and Bem. 15:37-41; Deḇ. 22:12. *7a* Also see Mel. ב 17:19, and Mt. 15:3-9.
7b See footnote Mt. 15:20.

20 And He said, "What comes out of a man, that defiles a man.

21 "For from within, out of the heart of men, proceed evil reasonings, adulteries, whorings, murders,

22 thefts, greedy desires, wickednesses, deceit, indecency, an evil eye, blasphemy, pride, foolishness.

23 "All these wicked *matters* come from within and defile a man."

24 And rising up from there He went to the borders of Tsor and Tsiḏon. And entering into a house He wished no one to know it, but it was impossible to be hidden.

25 For a woman whose young daughter had an unclean spirit heard about Him, and she came and fell at His feet.

26 Now the woman was a Greek, a Syro-Phoenician by birth, and she kept asking Him to cast the demon out of her daughter.

27 And יהושע said to her, "Let the children be satisfied first, for it is not good to take the children's bread and throw it to the little dogs." [c]

28 But she answering, said to Him, "Yes, Master, for even the little dogs under the table eat from the children's crumbs."

29 And He said to her, "Because of this word go, the demon has gone out of your daughter."

30 And having come into her house, she found the demon gone out, and her daughter lying on the bed.

31 And again, going out from the borders of Tsor and Tsiḏon, He came to the Sea of Galil, through the midst of the borders of Dekapolis.

32 And they brought to Him one who was deaf and spoke with difficulty, and they begged Him to lay His hand upon him.

33 And taking him away from the crowd, He put His fingers in his ears, and having spit, He touched his tongue.

34 And looking up to the heaven, He sighed, and said to him, "Ephphatha," that is, "Be opened."

35 And immediately his ears were opened, and the binding of his tongue was loosed, and he was speaking plainly.

36 And He ordered them, that they should say it to no one, but the more He ordered them, the more they published it.

37 And they were immeasurably astonished, saying, "He has done all well. He makes even the deaf to hear and the dumb to speak."

8 In those days, the crowd being very great and not having any to eat, יהושע called His taught ones near and said to them,

2 "I have compassion on the crowd, for they have now been with Me three days and do not have *food* to eat.

3 "And if I dismiss them unfed to their home, they shall faint on the way, for some of them have come from far."

4 And His taught ones answered Him, "How shall anyone be able to feed these people with bread here in the desert?"

5 And He asked them, "How many loaves do you have?" And they said, "Seven."

6 And He commanded the crowd to sit down on the ground. And taking the seven loaves, giving thanks, He broke them and gave them to His taught ones to set before them. And they set them before the crowd.

7 And they had a few small fishes. And having blessed, He said to set them also before them.

8 And they ate and were satisfied, and they picked up seven large baskets of broken pieces.

9 And those eating were about four thousand, and He dismissed them.

10 And immediately entering into the boat with His taught ones, He came to the parts of Dalmanutha.

11 And the Pharisees came out and began to dispute with Him, seeking from Him a sign from heaven, trying Him.

12 And sighing deeply in His spirit He said, "Why does this generation seek a sign? Truly, I say to you, no sign shall be given to this generation."

13 And leaving them, again entering into the boat, He went away to the other side.

7c Also see Mt. 15:27.

14 And they had forgotten to take bread,
and they did not have more than one loaf
with them in the boat.
15 And He was warning them, saying,
"Mind! Beware of the leaven of the
Pharisees and of the leaven of Herodes."
16 And they were reasoning with one
another, saying, "Because we have no
bread."
17 And יהושע, being aware of it, said to
them, "Why do you reason because you
have no bread? Do you not yet perceive
nor understand? Is your heart still hardened?
18 "**Having eyes, do you not see? And
having ears, do you not hear**? [Yeḥ. 12:2] And
do you not remember?
19 "When I broke the five loaves for the
five thousand, how many baskets filled
with broken pieces did you pick up?" They
said to Him, "Twelve."
20 "And when I broke the seven for the
four thousand, how many large baskets
filled with broken pieces did you pick up?"
And they said, "Seven."
21 And He said to them, "How do you not
understand?"
22 And He came to Bĕyth Tsaiḏa, and they
brought a blind man to Him, and begged
Him to touch him.
23 And taking the blind man by the hand
He led him out of the village. And having
spit on his eyes, laying hands on him, He
asked him, "Do you see at all?"
24 And he looked up and said, "I see men
like trees, walking."
25 Then He placed His hands on his eyes
again and made him look up. And he was
restored, and saw all clearly.
26 And He sent him away to his home,
saying, "Do not go into the village."
27 And יהושע and His taught ones went
out to the villages of Caesarea Philippi.
And on the way He asked His taught ones,
saying to them, "Who do men say I am?"
28 And they said to Him, "Yoḥanan the
Immerser, and others, Ĕliyahu, but others,
one of the prophets."
29 And He asked them, "And you, who do
you say I am?" And Kĕpha answering, said
to Him, "You are the Messiah."
30 And He warned them that they should
speak to no one about Him.
31 And He began to teach them that the
Son of Aḏam has to suffer much, and be
rejected by the elders and chief priests and
scribes, and be killed, and after three days
to rise again.
32 And He was speaking about this openly. Then Kĕpha, taking Him aside, began to
rebuke Him.
33 And turning around and seeing His
taught ones, He rebuked Kĕpha, saying,
"Get behind Me, Satan! For your thoughts
are not those of Elohim, but those of men."
34 And calling near the crowd with His
taught ones, He said to them, "Whoever
desires to come after Me, let him deny
himself, and take up his stake, and follow
Me.
35 "For whoever desires to save his life
shall lose it, but whoever loses his life for
the sake of Me and the Good News, he
shall save it.
36 "For what shall it profit a man if he
gains all the world, and loses his own life?
37 "Or what shall a man give in exchange
for his life?
38 "For whoever is ashamed of Me and
My words in this adulterous and sinning
generation, of him the Son of Aḏam also
shall be ashamed when He comes in the
esteem of His Father with the set-apart
messengers."

9

And He said to them, "Truly, I say to
you that there are some standing here
who shall not taste of death at all until they
see the reign of Elohim having come in
power:"
2 And after six days יהושע took Kĕpha,
and Yaʽaqoḇ, and Yoḥanan, and led them
up on a high mountain alone by themselves. And He was transformed before
them.
3 And His garments became glittering,
exceedingly white, like snow, such as no
launderer on earth is able to whiten.

[4] And there appeared to them Ěliyahu with Mosheh, [a] and they were talking with יהושע.

[5] And Kěpha responding, said to יהושע, "Rabbi, it is good for us to be here. And let us make three booths, one for You, and one for Mosheh, and one for Ěliyahu,"

[6] because he did not know what to say, for they were exceedingly afraid.

[7] And there came a cloud overshadowing them, and a voice came out of the cloud, saying, "This is My Son, the Beloved. Hear Him!"

[8] And suddenly, looking around, they no longer saw anyone with them, but only יהושע.

[9] And as they were coming down from the mountain, He ordered them not to relate to anyone what they saw, till the Son of Aḏam had risen from the dead.

[10] And they kept this matter to themselves, debating what the rising from the dead meant.

[11] And they asked Him, saying, "Why do the scribes say that Ěliyahu has to come first?"

[12] And He said to them, "Ěliyahu indeed, having come first, restores all *matters*. [b] And how has it been written concerning the Son of Aḏam, that He is to suffer much and be despised?

[13] "But I say to you that even Ěliyahu has come, and they did to him whatever they wished, as it has been written of him."

[14] And coming to the taught ones, He saw a large crowd around them, and scribes disputing with them.

[15] And immediately, when all the crowd saw Him, they were greatly astonished, and running near, greeted Him.

[16] And He asked the scribes, "What are you disputing with them?"

[17] And one of the crowd answering, said, "Teacher, I brought You my son, who has a dumb spirit.

[18] "And wherever he seizes him, he throws him down, and he foams *at the mouth*, and gnashes his teeth, and he wastes away. And I spoke to Your taught ones, that they should cast him out, but they were not able."

[19] And He answered him and said, "O unbelieving generation, how long shall I be with you? How long shall I put up with you? Bring him to Me."

[20] So they brought him to Him. And when he saw Him, immediately the spirit threw him into convulsions. And falling on the ground, he rolled about, foaming *at the mouth*.

[21] And He asked his father, "How long has he been like this?" And he said, "From childhood,

[22] and often he has thrown him both into the fire and into the water to destroy him. But if it is at all possible for You, have compassion on us and help us."

[23] And יהושע said to him, "If you are able to believe, all is possible to him who believes."

[24] And immediately the father of the child cried out and said with tears, "I believe Master, help my unbelief!"

[25] And when יהושע saw that a crowd came running together, He rebuked the unclean spirit, saying to him, "You deaf and dumb spirit, I order you, come out of him, and never again enter into him!"

[26] And crying out, and convulsing him much, it came out of him. And he became as one dead, so that many said that he was dead.

[27] But יהושע, taking him by the hand, lifted him up, and he arose.

[28] And when He came into a house, His taught ones asked Him separately, "Why were we unable to cast him out?"

[29] And He said to them, "It is impossible for this kind to come out except through prayer and fasting."

[30] And going from there they passed through Galil. And He did not wish anyone to know,

[31] for He was teaching His taught ones and said to them, "The Son of Aḏam is being delivered into the hands of men, and they shall kill Him. And having been killed, He shall rise the third day."

9a See Mt. 17:2-9, Lq. 9:28-35, Lq. 16:31, Yn. 5:47, Mal. 4:4-5. *9b* See Mt. 17:11, and Ma.3:21.

32 But they did not understand the word,
and they were afraid to ask Him.
33 And they came to Kephar Naḥum, and
having come in the house He asked them,
"What was it you disputed among yourselves on the way?"
34 And they were silent, for on the way
they had disputed with one another who
was the greatest.
35 And sitting down, He called the twelve
and said to them, "If anyone wishes to be
first, he shall be last of all and servant of
all."
36 And He took a little child and set him in
their midst, and taking him in His arms, He
said to them,
37 "Whoever receives one of such little
children in My Name receives Me. And
whoever receives Me, receives not Me, but
the One who sent Me."
38 And Yoḥanan said to Him, "Teacher,
we saw someone, who does not follow us,
casting out demons in Your Name, and we
forbade him because he does not follow
us."
39 And יהושע said, "Do not forbid him,
for no one who works a miracle in My
Name is able to readily speak evil of Me.
40 "For he who is not against us is for us.
41 "For whoever gives you a cup of water
to drink in My Name, because you are of
Messiah, truly, I say to you, he shall by no
means lose his reward.
42 "And whoever causes one of these little
ones who believe in Me to stumble, [c] it is
better for him if a millstone were hung
around his neck, and he were thrown into
the sea.
43 "And if your hand makes you stumble,
cut it off. It is better for you to enter into
life crippled, than having two hands, to go
into GĕHinnom, into the unquenchable
fire,
44 where 'their worm does not die and the
fire is not quenched.' [d]
45 "And if your foot makes you stumble,
cut it off. It is better for you to enter into
life crippled, than having two feet, to be
thrown into GĕHinnom, into the unquenchable fire,
46 where 'their worm does not die and the
fire is not quenched.' [d]
47 "And if your eye makes you stumble,
pluck it out. It is better for you to enter into
the reign of Elohim with one eye, than
having two eyes, to be thrown into the fire
of GĕHinnom,
48 where **'their worm does not die and
the fire is not quenched.'** Yesh. 66:24
49 "For everyone shall be seasoned with
fire, and every offering shall be seasoned
with salt.
50 "Salt is good, but if the salt becomes
tasteless, how shall you season it? Have
salt in yourselves, and be at peace among
one another."

10 And rising up from there He came
into the borders of Yehuḏah by
the other side of the Yardĕn. And crowds
gathered to Him again, and as He usually
did, He was teaching them again.
2 And Pharisees came and asked Him,
"Is it right for a man to put away his wife?"
– trying Him.
3 And He answering, said to them, "What
did Mosheh command you?"
4 And they said, "Mosheh allowed a man
to **write a certificate of divorce,** Deḇ. 24:1,3
and to put *her* away."
5 And יהושע said to them, "Because of
the hardness of your heart he wrote you
this command.
6 "However, from the beginning of the
creation, Elohim **'made them male and
female.'** Ber. 1:27; 5:2
7 **'For this cause a man shall leave his
father and mother and cleave to his
wife,**
8 **and the two shall become one flesh,'**
Ber. 2:24 so that they are no longer two, but
one flesh.
9 "Therefore what Elohim has joined
together, let man not separate."
10 And in the house His taught ones asked
Him about this again.
11 And He said to them, "Whoever puts
away his wife and marries another com-

9c Or to sin. *9d* Verses 44 & 46 are omitted from some ancient manuscripts.

mits adultery against her.
12 "And if a woman puts away her husband and marries another, she commits
adultery." [a]
13 And they were bringing little children
for Him to touch them, but the taught ones
were rebuking those who were bringing
them.
14 And when יהושע saw it, He was much
displeased and said to them, "Let the little
children come to Me, and do not forbid
them, for of such is the reign of Elohim.
15 "Truly, I say to you, whoever does not
receive the reign of Elohim as a little child,
shall certainly not enter into it."
16 And taking them up in His arms, laying
His hands on them, He blessed them.
17 And as He was setting out on the way,
one came running, and knelt before Him,
and asked Him, "Good Teacher, what shall
I do to inherit everlasting life?"
18 And יהושע said to him, "Why do you
call Me good? No one is good except One
– Elohim.
19 "You know the commands, **'Do not
commit adultery,' 'Do not murder,'
'Do not steal,' 'Do not bear false witness,' 'Do not rob,' 'Respect your
father and your mother.'** " Shem. 20:12-16,
Deḇ. 5:16-20
20 And he answering, said to Him,
"Teacher, all these I have watched over
from my youth."
21 And יהושע, looking at him, loved him,
and said to him, "One *matter* you lack: Go,
sell all you possess and give to the poor,
and you shall have treasure in heaven. And
come, follow Me, taking up the stake."
22 But he, being sad at this word, went
away grieved, for he had many possessions.
23 And יהושע, looking around, said to His
taught ones, "How hard it is for those who
have money to enter into the reign of
Elohim!"
24 And the taught ones were astonished at
His words. And יהושע responding, said to
them again, "Children, how hard it is for
those who trust in riches to enter into the
reign of Elohim!
25 "It is easier for a camel [b] to enter
through the eye of a needle than for a rich
man to enter into the reign of Elohim."
26 And they were immeasurably astonished, saying among themselves, "Who
then is able to be saved?"
27 And looking at them, יהושע said,
"With men it is impossible, but not with
Elohim, for with Elohim all is possible."
28 And Kěpha began to say to Him, "See,
we have left all and we have followed
You."
29 יהושע said, "Truly, I say to you, there
is no one who has left house or brothers
or sisters or father or mother or wife or
children or lands, for the sake of Me and
the Good News,
30 who shall not receive a hundredfold
now in this time, houses and brothers and
sisters and mothers and children and lands,
with persecutions, and in the age to come,
everlasting life.
31 "But many who are first shall be last,
and the last first."
32 And they were on the way, going up to
Yerushalayim, and יהושע was going
before them. And they were astonished,
and those who followed were afraid. And
again He took the twelve aside and began
to say to them what was about to befall
Him:
33 "See, we are going up to Yerushalayim,
and the Son of Aḏam shall be delivered to
the chief priests and to the scribes, and
they shall condemn Him to death and shall
deliver Him to the nations,
34 and they shall mock Him, and flog
Him, and spit on Him, and kill Him. And
the third day He shall rise again."
35 And Ya'aqoḇ and Yoḥanan, the sons of
Zaḇdai, came up to Him, saying, "Teacher,
we wish that You would do for us whatever
we ask."
36 And He said to them, "What do you
wish Me to do for you?"
37 And they said to Him, "Grant us to be
seated in Your esteem, one on Your right
hand and the other on Your left."

10a See footnote Mt. 5:32. *10b* Aramaic "gamla", which is camel or rope.

38 But יהושע said to them, "You do not
know what you ask. Are you able to drink
the cup that I drink, and be immersed with
the immersion that I am immersed with?"
39 And they said to Him, "We are able."
And יהושע said to them, "You shall
indeed drink the cup that I drink, and with
the immersion I am immersed with you
shall be immersed, [c]
40 but to sit on My right hand and on My
left is not Mine to give, but it is for those
for whom it has been prepared."
41 And when the ten heard it, they began
to be sorely displeased with Ya'aqoḇ and
Yoḥanan.
42 And יהושע, calling them near, said to
them, "You know that those who think to
rule the nations are masters over them, and
their great ones exercise authority over
them.
43 "But it is not so among you, but whoever wishes to become great among you
shall be your servant.
44 "And whoever wishes to be first among
you, shall be servant of all.
45 "For even the Son of Aḏam did not
come to be served, but to serve, and to give
His life a ransom for many."
46 And they came to Yeriḥo. And as He
was leaving Yeriḥo with His taught ones
and a large crowd, blind Bartimai, the son
of Timai, was sitting by the way begging.
47 And when he heard that it was יהושע
of Natsareth, he began to cry out and to
say, "יהושע, Son of Dawiḏ, have compassion on me!"
48 And many were reprimanding him to
be silent, but he cried out all the more,
"Son of Dawiḏ, have compassion on me!"
49 And יהושע stopped and said, "Call
him." And they called the blind man, saying to him, "Take courage, arise, He is calling you."
50 And he, throwing aside his garment,
rose and came to יהושע.
51 And יהושע responding, said to him,
"What do you desire I do for you?" And
the blind man said to Him, "Rabboni, that I
receive my sight."
52 And יהושע said to him, "Go, your
belief has healed you." And immediately
he saw again and followed יהושע on the
way.

11

And when they came near Yerushalayim, to Běyth Phaği and
Běyth Anyah, at the Mount of Olives, He
sent out two of His taught ones,
2 and said to them, "Go into the village
opposite you, and immediately entering
into it, you shall find a colt tied, on which
no one has sat. Loosen it and bring it.
3 "And if anyone says to you, 'Why are
you doing this?' say, 'The Master needs it
and shall send it back straightaway.' "
4 So they went away, and found the colt
tied by the door outside on the street, and
they loosened it.
5 And some of those standing there said
to them, "What are you doing, loosening
the colt?"
6 And they said to them, as יהושע had
said. So they let them go.
7 And they brought the colt to יהושע and
threw their garments on it, and He sat on it.
8 And many spread their garments on the
way, and others were cutting down branches from the trees and were spreading them
on the way.
9 And those going before and those
following cried out, saying, **"Hoshia-na!
'Blessed is He who is coming in the
Name of יהוה!'** [Teh. 118:25-26]
10 Blessed is the coming reign of our
father Dawiḏ – in the Name of יהוה!
Hoshia-na [Teh. 118:25] in the highest!"
11 And יהושע went into Yerushalayim
and into the Set-apart Place. And having
looked around on all, He went out to Běyth
Anyah with the twelve, as the hour was
already late.
12 And on the next day, when they had
come out from Běyth Anyah, He was hungry.
13 And seeing at a distance a fig tree
having leaves, He went to see whether He
would find any *fruit* on it. And when He
came to it, He found none but leaves, for it

10c See also Mt. 20:23.

was not the season for figs.
[14]And יהושע, responding, said to it, "Let no one eat fruit from you ever again." And His taught ones heard it.
[15]And they came to Yerushalayim. יהושע, entering into the Set-apart Place, began to drive out those who bought and sold in the Set-apart Place, and overturned the tables of the money-changers and the seats of those selling doves.
[16]And He did not allow anyone to carry a vessel through the Set-apart Place.
[17]And He was teaching, saying to them, "Has it not been written, **'My House shall be called a house of prayer for all nations'**? Yesh. 56:7 But you have made it a **'den of robbers.'** " Yirm. 7:11
[18]And the scribes and the chief priests heard it and they were seeking how to destroy Him, for they feared Him, because all the crowd was astonished at His teaching.
[19]And when evening came, He went out of the city.
[20]And in the morning, passing by, they saw the fig tree dried up from the roots.
[21]Then Kěpha, remembering, said to Him, "Rabbi, look! The fig tree which You cursed has withered."
[22]And יהושע answering, said to them, "Have belief in Elohim.
[23]"For truly, I say to you, whoever says to this mountain, 'Be removed and be thrown into the sea,' and does not doubt in his heart, but believes that what he says, shall be done, he shall have whatever he says.
[24]"Because of this I say to you, whatever you ask when you pray, believe that you receive them, and you shall have them.
[25]"And whenever you stand praying, if you hold whatever against anyone, forgive, so that your Father in the heavens shall also forgive you your trespasses.
[26]"But if you do not forgive, neither shall your Father in the heavens forgive your trespasses."
[27]And they came again to Yerushalayim. And as He was walking in the Set-apart Place, the chief priests, and the scribes, and the elders came to Him,
[28]and they said to Him, "By what authority are You doing these? And who gave You this authority to do these?"
[29]And יהושע answering, said to them, "I shall ask you one question, and answer Me, and I shall say to you by what authority I do these:
[30]"The immersion of Yoḥanan – was it from heaven or from men? Answer Me."
[31]And they reasoned among themselves, saying, "If we say, 'From heaven,' He shall say, 'Then why did you not believe him?'
[32]"But if we say, 'From men' " – they feared the people, for all held that Yoḥanan was a prophet indeed.
[33]And answering they said to יהושע, "We do not know." And יהושע answering, said to them, "Neither do I say to you by what authority I do these."

12

And He began to speak to them in parables, **"A man planted a vineyard and put a hedge around it, and dug a vat for the winepress and built a watchtower,** Teh. 80:8, Yesh. 5:1,2 and let it out to farmers and went away.
[2]"And at *harvest* time he sent a servant to the farmers, to receive some of the fruit of the vineyard from the farmers.
[3]"And they seized him and beat *him* and sent *him* away empty-handed.
[4]"And again he sent them another servant, and throwing stones at him, they wounded *him* in the head, and sent him away, having insulted *him*.
[5]"And again he sent another, and they killed him; and many others, beating some and killing some.
[6]"He had one more son, his beloved. He sent him last of all, saying, 'They shall respect my son.'
[7]"But those farmers said among themselves, 'This is the heir. Come, let us kill him, and the inheritance shall be ours.'
[8]"So they took him and killed *him* and threw *him* out of the vineyard.
[9]"What then shall the owner of the vineyard do? He shall come and destroy the farmers, and give the vineyard to others.
[10]"Have you not read this Scripture, **'The stone which the builders rejected has become the chief corner-stone.** Teh. 118:22

[11] **'This was from יהוה, and it is marvellous in our eyes'?"** Teh. 118:23
[12] And they were seeking to seize Him, but feared the crowd, for they knew He had spoken the parable against them. And leaving Him, they went away.
[13] And they sent to Him some of the Pharisees and the Herodians, to catch Him in a word.
[14] And when they came, they said to Him, "Teacher, we know that You are true, and it does not concern You about anyone, for You are not partial to any, but teach the way of Elohim in truth. Is it right to pay taxes to Caesar, or not?
[15] "Should we pay, or should we not pay?" And He, knowing their hypocrisy, said to them, "Why do you try Me? Bring Me a denarius [a] to look at."
[16] And they brought it, and He said to them, "Whose likeness and inscription is this?" And they said to Him, "Caesar's."
[17] So יהושע said to them, "Give to Caesar what is Caesar's, and to Elohim what is Elohim's." And they marvelled at Him.
[18] And Sadducees, who say there is no resurrection, came to Him. And they asked Him, saying,
[19] "Teacher, Mosheh wrote to us that **if a brother of anyone dies, and leaves his wife behind, and leaves no children, his brother should take his wife and raise up offspring for his brother.** Deḇ. 25:5-6
[20] "There were seven brothers, and the first took a wife, and died, leaving no offspring.
[21] "And the second took her, and he died, leaving behind no offspring. And the third likewise.
[22] "And the seven left no offspring. Last of all the woman died too.
[23] "In the resurrection then, when they rise, whose wife shall she be? For seven had her as wife."
[24] And יהושע answering, said to them, "Is this not why you go astray, because you do not know the Scriptures [b] nor the power of Elohim?
[25] "For when they rise from the dead, they neither marry nor are given in marriage, but are as messengers in the heavens.
[26] "And concerning the dead, that they rise – have you not read in the book of Mosheh, at the bush, how Elohim spoke to him, saying, **'I am the Elohim of Aḇraham, and the Elohim of Yitsḥaq, and the Elohim of Ya'aqoḇ'**? Shem. 3:6
[27] "He is not the Elohim of the dead, but Elohim of the living. You, then, go greatly astray."
[28] And one of the scribes coming near, hearing them reasoning together, knowing that He had answered them well, asked Him, "Which is the first command of all?"
[29] And יהושע answered him, "The first of all the commands is, **'Hear, O Yisra'ěl, יהוה our Elohim, יהוה is one.** Deḇ. 6:4
[30] **'And you shall love יהוה your Elohim with all your heart, and with all your being, and with all your mind, and with all your strength.'** Deḇ. 6:5 This is the first command.
[31] "And the second, like it, is this, **'You shall love your neighbour as yourself.'** Way. 19:18 There is no other command greater than these."
[32] And the scribe said to Him, "Well said, Teacher. You have spoken the truth, **for there is one Elohim, and there is no other besides Him.** Deḇ. 4:35
[33] **"And to love Him with all the heart, and with all the understanding, and with all the being,** Deḇ. 6:5 **and with all the strength,** and to love one's neighbour as oneself, is more than all the ascending offerings and offerings."
[34] And when יהושע saw that he answered wisely, He said to him, "You are not far from the reign of Elohim." And after that no one was bold *enough* to question Him.
[35] And יהושע responding, said, while teaching in the Set-apart Place, "How is it that the scribes say that the Messiah is the Son of Dawiḏ?
[36] "Dawiḏ himself said by the Set-apart Spirit, **'יהוה said to my Master, "Sit at My right hand, until I make Your enemies a footstool of Your feet." '** Teh. 110:1

12a Roman monetary unit. *12b* Mt. 22:29.

37 "Dawiḏ himself calls Him 'Master.' In
what way then is He his Son?" And the
large crowd heard Him gladly.
38 And in His teaching He was saying to
them, "Beware of the scribes, who like to
walk around in long robes, and *like* greetings in the market-places,
39 and the best seats in the congregations,
and the best places at feasts,
40 who are devouring widows' houses,
and for a show make long prayers. These
shall receive greater judgment."
41 And sitting opposite the treasury He
saw how the people put copper into the
treasury. And many rich ones put in much.
42 And a poor widow came and threw in
two small copper coins, which amount to a
cent.
43 And calling near His taught ones He
said to them, "Truly, I say to you that this
poor widow has put in more than all those
putting into the treasury,
44 for they all put in out of their excess,
but she out of her poverty put in all that she
had, her entire livelihood."

13 And as He went out of the Set-
apart Place, one of His taught ones
said to Him, "Teacher, see what stones!
And what buildings!"
2 And יהושע answering, said to him,
"Do you see these great buildings? Not one
stone shall be left upon another at all,
which shall not be thrown down." [a]
3 And as He sat on the Mount of Olives
opposite the Set-apart Place, Kěpha, and
Ya'aqoḇ, and Yoḥanan, and Andri asked
Him separately,
4 "Say to us, when shall these *events* be?
And what shall be the sign when all this is
going to be accomplished?"
5 And יהושע began to say to them, "Take
heed that no one leads you astray,
6 for many shall come in My Name, saying, 'I am He,' and they shall lead many
astray.
7 "And when you hear of fightings and
reports of fightings, do not be troubled – it
has to take place, but the end is not yet.
8 "For nation shall rise against nation,
and reign against reign. And there shall be
earthquakes in various places, and there
shall be scarcities of food, and disturbances. These are the beginnings of birth-
pains.
9 "But take heed to yourselves, for they
shall deliver you up to councils and to congregations. You shall be beaten, and you
shall be brought before rulers and sovereigns for My sake, for a witness to them.
10 "And the Good News has to be proclaimed first to all the nations.
11 "And when they lead you away and
deliver you up, do not worry beforehand
what you are to say. But whatever is given
you in that hour, speak that, for it is not
you who are speaking, but the Set-apart
Spirit.
12 "And brother shall deliver up brother to
death, and a father his child. And children
shall rise up against parents and shall put
them to death.
13 "And you shall be hated by all because
of My Name. But he who shall have
endured to the end, he shall be saved. [b]
14 "And when you see the 'abomination
that lays waste,' [c] spoken of by Dani'ěl the
prophet, set up where it should not be" – he
who reads, let him understand – "then let
those who are in Yehuḏah flee to the
mountains.
15 "And he who is on the house-top, let
him not go down into the house, nor come
in to take whatever out of his house.
16 "And he who is in the field, let him not
go back to get his cloak.
17 "And woe to those who are pregnant
and to those nursing children in those days!
18 "And pray that your flight does not take
place in winter.
19 "For in those days there shall be distress, such as has not been from the beginning of creation which Elohim created
until this time, nor ever shall be.
20 "And if the Master had not shortened
those days, no flesh would have been

13a Mt. 24. *13b* Mt. 10:22, Mt. 24:13. *13c* See *Abomination that lays waste* in Explanatory Notes.

saved; but because of the chosen ones,
whom He chose, He shortened the days.
21 "And if anyone then says to you,
'Look, here is the Messiah!' or, 'Look,
there!' do not believe it.
22 "For false messiahs and false prophets
shall rise and show signs and wonders to
lead astray, if possible, even the chosen
ones.
23 "And you, take heed. See, I have forewarned you of it all.
24 "But in those days, after that distress,
**the sun shall be darkened, and the moon
shall not give its light,**
25 **and the stars of heaven shall fall,** Yesh.
13:10 and **the powers in the heavens shall
be shaken.** Yesh. 34:4 [d]
26 "And then they shall see the **Son of
Aḏam coming in the clouds** Dan. 7:13 with
much power and esteem.
27 "And then He shall send His messengers, and **assemble His chosen ones** from
the **four winds**, from the farthest part of
earth to the **farthest part of heaven**.
Deḇ. 30:4, Zeḵ. 2:6
28 "And learn this parable from the fig
tree: When its branch has already become
tender, and puts forth leaves, you know
that the summer is near.
29 "So you also, when you see these taking place, know that it is near, at the door.
30 "Truly, I say to you, this generation
shall by no means pass away till all this
takes place.
31 "The heaven and the earth shall pass
away, but My words shall by no means
pass away.
32 "But concerning that day and the hour
no one knows, not even the messengers in
heaven, nor the Son, but only the Father.
33 "Take heed, watch and pray, for you do
not know when the time is –
34 as a man going abroad, having left his
house and given authority to his servants,
and to each his work, and commanded the
doorkeeper to watch.
35 "Watch therefore, for you do not know
when the master of the house is coming –
in the evening or at midnight, or at the
crowing of the cock, or in the morning,
36 lest, coming suddenly, he should find
you sleeping.
37 "And what I say to you, I say to all:
Watch!"

14 Now the Pěsaḥ [a] and the *Festival of*
Matzot [b] was after two days. And
the chief priests and the scribes were seeking how to take Him through treachery and
put Him to death.
2 And they said, "Not at the festival, lest
there shall be an uproar of the people."
3 And while He was in Běyth Anyah in
the house of Shim'on the leper, and sitting
at the table, a woman came having an
alabaster flask of perfume, genuine nard,
very costly. And breaking the flask she
poured it on His head.
4 But there were some who were much
displeased among themselves, and said,
"Why was this perfume wasted?
5 "For it could have been sold for more
than three hundred denarii and given to the
poor." And they were scolding her.
6 But יהושע said, "Leave her alone. Why
do you trouble her? She has done a good
work for Me.
7 "For you have the poor with you
always, and you are able do good to them,
whenever you wish. But you do not always
have Me.
8 "What she had, she used. She took it
beforehand to anoint My body for the
burial.
9 "Truly, I say to you, wherever this
Good News is proclaimed in all the world,
what this woman did shall also be spoken
of, to her remembrance."
10 And Yehuḏah from Qerioth, one of the
twelve, went to the chief priests to deliver
Him up to them.
11 And when they heard it, they were glad,
and promised to give him silver. And
he was seeking how to deliver Him up,
conveniently.
12 And on the first day of Unleavened
Bread, when they were slaughtering the
Pěsaḥ [a] lamb, His taught ones said to Him,

13d Also see Yeḥ. 32:7, Yo'el 2:10,31; 3:15, Ḥag. 2:6,21 *14a* - Passover. *14b* - Unleavened Bread.

"Where do You wish us to go and prepare, for You to eat the Pěsaḥ?"
13 And He sent out two of His taught ones and said to them, "Go into the city, and there a man bearing a jar of water shall meet you, follow him.
14 "And wherever he enters, say to the master of the house, 'The Teacher says, "Where is the guest room in which I am to eat the Pěsaḥ with My taught ones?" '
15 "And he shall show you a large upper room, furnished, ready. Prepare for us there."
16 And His taught ones went out and came into the city, and found it as He said to them, and they prepared the Pěsaḥ.
17 And evening having come, He came with the twelve.
18 And as they sat and ate, יהושע said, "Truly, I say to you, one of you who is eating with Me shall deliver Me up."
19 And they began to be grieved, and to say to Him one by one, "Is it I?" And another, "Is it I?"
20 And He answering, said to them, "It is one of the twelve, he who is dipping with Me in the dish.
21 "The Son of Aḏam is indeed going, as it has been written of Him, but woe to that man by whom the Son of Aḏam is delivered up! It would have been good for that man if he had not been born."
22 And as they were eating, יהושע took bread, having blessed, broke it, gave it to them and said, "Take, eat, this is My body."
23 And taking the cup, giving thanks, He gave it to them, and they all drank from it.
24 And He said to them, "This is My blood, that of the renewed covenant, which is shed for many.
25 "Truly, I say to you, I shall certainly no more drink of the fruit of the vine till that day when I drink it anew in the reign of Elohim."
26 And having sung a song, they went out to the Mount of Olives.
27 And יהושע said to them, "All of you shall stumble in Me this night, for it has been written, **'I shall strike the shepherd, and the sheep shall be scattered.'** Zek. 13:7
28 "But after I am raised, I shall go before you to Galil."
29 And Kěpha said to Him, "Even if all shall stumble, yet not I."
30 And יהושע said to him, "Truly, I say to you that today, this night, before the cock shall crow twice, you shall deny Me three times."
31 But he spoke more strongly, "If I have to die with You, I shall not deny You!" And they all said the same.
32 And they came to a place called Gethsemane. And He said to His taught ones, "Sit here while I pray."
33 And He took with Him Kěpha, and Ya'aqoḇ, and Yoḥanan, and He began to be greatly amazed, and to be deeply distressed.
34 And He said to them, "My being is exceedingly grieved, even to death. Stay here and watch."
35 And He went on a little, and fell on the ground, and was praying that if it were possible, the hour might pass from Him.
36 And He said, "Abba, Father, all is possible for You. Make this cup pass from Me. Yet not what I desire, but what You *desire*."
37 And He came and found them sleeping, and said to Kěpha, "Shim'on, are you sleeping? You were not able to watch one hour!
38 "Watch and pray, lest you enter into trial. The spirit indeed is eager, but the flesh is weak."
39 And again He went away and prayed, and spoke the same words.
40 And having returned, He found them asleep again, for their eyes were heavy. And they did not know what to answer Him.
41 And He came the third time and said to them, "Are you still sleeping and resting? It is enough! The hour has come. See, the Son of Aḏam is being delivered up into the hands of the sinners.
42 "Rise up, let us go. See, he who is delivering Me up has drawn near."
43 And immediately, while He was still speaking, Yehuḏah, one of the twelve, with a large crowd with swords and clubs, came

from the chief priests and the scribes and
the elders.
44 And the one who was delivering Him
up had given them a signal, saying,
"Whomever I kiss, it is He – seize Him and
lead Him away safely."
45 And coming, going straight up to Him,
he said to Him, "Rabbi, Rabbi!" and kissed
Him.
46 And they laid their hands on Him and
seized Him.
47 And one of those standing by drew his
sword and struck the servant of the high
priest, and cut off his ear.
48 And יהושע answering, said to them,
"Have you come out as against a robber,
with swords and clubs, to take Me?
49 "Daily I was with you in the Set-apart
Place teaching, and you did not seize Me.
But let the Scriptures be filled."
50 And they all left Him and fled.
51 And a certain young man was following Him, having a linen cloth thrown
around *his* naked *body*. And when they
seized him,
52 he left the linen cloth and fled from
them naked.
53 And they led יהושע away to the high
priest. And all the chief priests, and the
elders, and the scribes came together to
Him.
54 And Kěpha followed Him at a distance,
even into the courtyard of the high priest.
And he was sitting with the officers and
warming himself at the fire.
55 And the chief priests and all the council
were seeking witness against יהושע to put
Him to death, and they were finding none.
56 For many bore false witness against
Him, but their evidences did not agree.
57 And some rose up and bore false witness against Him, saying,
58 "We heard Him saying, 'I shall destroy
this Dwelling Place that is made with
hands, and within three days I shall build
another made without hands.' "
59 And not even then did their witness
agree.
60 Then the high priest stood up in the
centre and asked יהושע, saying, "Have
You no answer to make? What do these
witness against You?"
61 But He remained silent and gave no
answer. Again the high priest asked Him,
saying to Him, "Are You the Messiah, the
Son of the Blessed?"
62 And יהושע said, "I am, and you shall
see the **Son of Aḏam sitting at the right
hand of the Power**, Teh. 110:1 and **coming
with the clouds of the heaven**." Dan. 7:13
63 And tearing his garments, the high
priest said, "What further need do we have
of witnesses?
64 "You have heard the blasphemy! What
do you think?" And they all condemned
Him to be liable to death.
65 And some began to spit on Him, and to
blindfold Him, and to beat Him, and to say
to Him, "Prophesy!" And the officers
struck Him with the palms of their hands.
66 And as Kěpha was below in the courtyard, one of the servant girls of the high
priest came,
67 and seeing Kěpha warming himself, she
looked at him and said, "And you were
with יהושע of Natsareth."
68 But he denied it, saying, "I do not know
nor understand what you are saying." And
he went out onto the porch, and a cock
crowed.
69 And the servant girl saw him again, and
began to say to those who stood by, "This
is one of them."
70 And again he was denying it. And after
a little while those who stood by again said
to Kěpha, "Truly you are one of them, for
you are a Galilean too, and your speech is
alike."
71 And he began to curse and swear, "I do
not know this Man of whom you speak!"
72 And a second time the cock crowed.
And Kěpha remembered the word that
יהושע had said to him, "Before the cock
crows twice, you shall deny Me three
times." And thinking on it, he wept.

15 And immediately, in the morning,
the chief priests had a council
meeting with the elders and scribes and all
the council. Having bound יהושע, they led
Him away, and delivered Him to Pilate.
2 And Pilate asked Him, "Are You the

Sovereign of the Yehuḏim?" And He
answering, said to him, "You say it."
3 And the chief priests accused Him of
much, but He made no answer.
4 And Pilate again asked Him, saying,
"Have You no answer? See how much they
witness against You!"
5 But יהושע still gave no answer, so that
Pilate marvelled.
6 And at a festival he released to them
one prisoner, whomever they were asking.
7 And there was one called Barabba,
chained with his fellow rebels, who had
committed murder in the uprising.
8 And the crowd, crying aloud, began to
ask, as he had always done for them.
9 But Pilate answered them, saying, "Do
you wish me to release for you the
Sovereign of the Yehuḏim?"
10 For he knew that the chief priests had
handed Him over because of envy.
11 And the chief priests stirred up the
crowd, that he should rather release
Barabba to them.
12 And Pilate answered and again said to
them, "What then do you wish me to do *to*
Him whom you call the Sovereign of the
Yehuḏim?"
13 And again they cried out, "Impale
Him!"
14 And Pilate said to them, "Why, what
evil has He done?" And they vehemently
cried out, "Impale Him!"
15 And Pilate, wishing to satisfy the
crowd, released Barabba to them, and having whipped *Him*, he delivered יהושע over
to be impaled.
16 And the soldiers led Him away into the
court, which is the palace, and they called
together the entire company *of soldiers*,
17 and decked Him with purple. And they
plaited a crown of thorns, put it on Him,
18 and they began to call out to Him,
"Greetings, Sovereign of the Yehuḏim!"
19 And they kept beating Him on the head
with a reed and were spitting on Him. And
bending the knee, they were bowing down
to Him.
20 And when they had mocked Him, they
took the purple off Him, and put His own
garments on Him, and led Him out to
impale Him.
21 And they compelled a passer-by,
Shim'on, a Cyrenian, coming from a field,
the father of Alexander and Rufus, to bear
His stake.
22 And they brought Him to the place Golgotha, which is translated, Place of a Skull.
23 And they were giving Him wine mixed
with myrrh to drink, but He did not take it.
24 And when they impaled Him, **they**
divided His garments, casting lots for
them, Teh. 22:18 what each one should take.
25 And it was the third hour, and they
impaled Him.
26 And the inscription of His accusation
was written above: THE SOVEREIGN OF
THE YEHUḎIM.
27 And with Him they impaled two robbers, one on His right and the other on His
left.
28 And the Scripture was filled which
says, **"And He was reckoned with the**
lawless." Yesh. 53:12
29 And those passing by were blaspheming Him, **shaking their heads** Teh. 22:7 and
saying, "Ah! You who destroy the
Dwelling Place and build it in three days,
30 save Yourself, and come down from the
stake!"
31 And likewise the chief priests and the
scribes, mocking to one another said, "He
saved others, He is unable to save Himself.
32 "The Messiah? The Sovereign of
Yisra'ěl? Come down now from the stake,
so that we see and believe." And those
who were impaled with Him were
reproaching Him.
33 And when the sixth hour came, darkness came over all the land until the ninth
hour.
34 And at the ninth hour יהושע cried out
with a loud voice, saying, "**Ěli, Ěli, lamah**
sheḇaqtani?" [a] which is translated, "**My**
Ěl, My Ěl, why have You forsaken Me?"
Teh. 22:1
35 And some of those standing by, when
they heard it, said, "See, He is calling for

15a - In Hebrew - "Eli, Eli lamah azaḇtani" - as per Teh.22:1

Ěliyahu!"
36 And someone ran and filled a sponge
with **sour wine**, and put it on a reed, and
offered it to Him **to drink**, [Teh. 69:21] saying,
"Leave Him, let us see if Ěliyahu does
come to take Him down."
37 And יהושע cried out with a loud voice,
and breathed His last.
38 And the veil of the Dwelling Place was
torn in two from top to bottom.
39 And when the captain, who was standing opposite Him, saw that He cried out
like this and breathed His last, he said,
"Truly this Man was the Son of Elohim!"
40 And there were also women watching
from a distance, among whom was also
Miryam from Maḡdala, and Miryam the
mother of Yaʽaqoḇ the Less and of Yosěph,
and Shelomah,
41 who also followed Him and attended
Him when He was in Galil, and many
other women who came up with Him to
Yerushalayim.
42 And when evening had come, because
it was the Preparation Day, that is, the day
before the Sabbath,
43 Yosěph of Ramathayim, a prominent
council member, who was himself waiting
for the reign of Elohim, came, boldly went
in to Pilate and asked for the body of
יהושע.
44 But Pilate wondered whether He was
already dead, so summoning the captain,
he asked him if He was already dead.
45 And when he learned *this* from the
captain, he gave the body to Yosěph.
46 And he, having bought fine linen, took
Him down, and wrapped Him in the linen.
And he laid Him in a tomb which had been
hewn out of the rock, and rolled a stone
against the entrance of the tomb.
47 And Miryam from Maḡdala, and
Miryam the *mother* of Yosěph, saw where
He was laid.

16 And when the Sabbath was past,
Miryam from Maḡdala, and
Miryam the *mother* of Yaʽaqoḇ, and
Shelomah bought spices, to go and anoint
Him.
2 And very early on *day* one of *the* week
[a], they came to the tomb when the sun had
risen.
3 And they said among themselves,
"Who shall roll away the stone from the
entrance of the tomb for us?"
4 And looking up, they saw that the stone
had been rolled away, for it was extremely
large.
5 And having entered into the tomb, they
saw a young man sitting on the right, wearing a white robe, and they were greatly
astonished.
6 And he said to them, "Do not be much
astonished. You seek יהושע of Natsareth,
who was impaled. He was raised – He is
not here! See the place where they laid
Him.
7 "And go, say to His taught ones, and
Kěpha, that He is going before you into
Galil. You shall see Him there as He said
to you."
8 And they went out and fled from the
tomb, and were trembling and bewildered.
And they spoke to no one, for they were
afraid.
9 And having risen early on the first *day*
of *the* week [b] He appeared first to Miryam
from Maḡdala, from whom He had cast out
seven demons. [c]
10 She went and reported to those who had
been with Him, mourning and weeping.
11 And when they heard that He was alive
and had been seen by her, they did not
believe.
12 And after this He appeared in another
form to two of them as they walked and
went into a field.
13 And they went and reported it to the
rest, but they did not believe them either.
14 Later He appeared to the eleven as they
sat at the table. And He reproached their
unbelief and hardness of heart, because
they did not believe those who had seen
Him after He was raised.
15 And He said to them, "Go into all the

16a Gk. one of *the* sabbaths. See footnote - Mt. 28:1 and Explanatory Notes - "First day of the week".
16b Gk. first of a sabbath. *16c* Some manuscripts omit vv. 9-20; Textus Receptus includes them.

world and proclaim the Good News to
every creature.
16 "He who has believed and has been
immersed, shall be saved, but he who has
not believed shall be condemned.
17 "And these signs shall accompany the
ones who believe: In My Name they shall
cast out demons, they shall speak with
renewed tongues,
18 they shall take up snakes, and if they
drink any deadly *drink* it shall by no means
hurt them, they shall lay hands on the sick
and they shall get well."
19 Then indeed, after the Master had spoken to them, He was received up into the
heaven, and **sat down at the right hand of
Elohim.** Teh. 110:1
20 And they went out and proclaimed it
everywhere, while the Master worked with
them, and confirmed the word through the
accompanying signs. Amĕn.

LUQAS

LUKE

1 Since many have indeed taken in hand to set in order an account of the matters completely confirmed among us,

2 as those who from the beginning were eyewitnesses and servants of the word delivered them to us,

3 it seemed good to me as well, having followed up all these matters exactly from the beginning, to write to you an orderly account, most excellent Theophilos,

4 that you might know the certainty of the words which you were taught.

5 There was in the days of Herodes, the sovereign of Yehuḏah, a certain priest named Zeḵaryah, of the division of Aḇiyah. And his wife was of the daughters of Aharon, and her name was Elisheḇa.

6 And they were both righteous before Elohim, blamelessly walking in all the commands and righteousnesses of יהוה.

7 And they had no child, because Elisheḇa was barren, and both were advanced in years.

8 And it came to be, that while he was serving as priest before Elohim in the order of his division,

9 according to the institute of the priesthood, he was chosen by lot to burn incense when he went into the Dwelling Place of יהוה.

10 And the entire crowd of people was praying outside at the hour of incense.

11 And a messenger of יהוה appeared to him, standing on the right side of the slaughter-place of incense.

12 And when Zeḵaryah saw *him*, he was troubled, and fear fell upon him.

13 But the messenger said to him, "Do not be afraid, Zeḵaryah, for your prayer is heard. And your wife Elisheḇa shall bear you a son, and you shall call his name Yoḥanan.

14 "And you shall have joy and gladness, and many shall rejoice at his birth.

15 "For he shall be great before יהוה, and shall drink no wine and strong drink at all. And he shall be filled with the Set-apart Spirit, even from his mother's womb.

16 "And he shall turn many of the children of Yisra'ěl to יהוה their Elohim.

17 "And he shall go before Him in the spirit and power of Ěliyahu, **'to turn the hearts of the fathers to the children,'** Mal. 4:6 and the disobedient to the insight of the righteous, to make ready a people prepared for יהוה."

18 And Zeḵaryah said to the messenger, "By what shall I know this? For I am old, and my wife advanced in years."

19 And the messenger answering, said to him, "I am Gaḇri'ěl, who stands in the presence of Elohim, and was sent to speak to you and announce to you this good news.

20 "But see, you shall be silent and unable to speak until the day this takes place, because you did not believe my words which shall be filled in their appointed time."

21 And the people waited for Zeḵaryah, and marvelled at his delay in the Dwelling Place.

22 And when he came out, he was unable to speak to them. And they recognised that he had seen a vision in the Dwelling Place, for he was beckoning to them and remained dumb.

23 And it came to be, as soon as the days of his service were completed, he went away to his house.

24 And after those days his wife Elisheḇa conceived. And she hid herself five months, saying,

25 "יהוה has done this for me, in the days when He looked upon me, to take away my reproach among men."

26 And in the sixth month the messenger Gaḇri'ěl was sent by Elohim to a city of Galil named Natsareth,

27 to a maiden engaged to a man whose name was Yosěph, of the house of Dawiḏ. And the maiden's name was Miryam.

28 And the messenger, coming to her, said, "Greetings, favoured one, the Master is with you. Blessed are you among women!"

29 But she was greatly disturbed at his word, and wondered what kind of greeting this was.

30 And the messenger said to her, "Do not be afraid, Miryam, for you have found favour with Elohim.

31 "And see, you shall conceive in your womb, and shall give birth to a Son, and call His Name יהושע. [a]

32 "He shall be great, and shall be called the Son of the Most High. And יהוה Elohim shall give Him the throne of His father Dawiḏ.

33 "And He shall reign over the house of Ya'aqoḇ forever, and there shall be no end to His reign." [b]

34 And Miryam said to the messenger, "How shall this be, since I do not know a man?"

35 And the messenger answering, said to her, "The Set-apart Spirit shall come upon you, and the power of the Most High shall overshadow you. And for that reason the Set-apart One born of you shall be called: Son of Elohim.

36 "And see, Elisheḇa your relative, she has also conceived a son in her old age. And this is now the sixth month to her who was called barren,

37 because with Elohim no matter shall be impossible."

38 And Miryam said, "See the female servant of יהוה! Let it be to me according to your word." And the messenger went away from her.

39 And Miryam arose in those days and went into the hill country with haste, to a city of Yehuḏah,

40 and entered into the house of Zeḵaryah and greeted Elisheḇa.

41 And it came to be, when Elisheḇa heard the greeting of Miryam, that the baby leaped in her womb. And Elisheḇa was filled with the Set-apart Spirit,

42 and called out with a loud voice and said, "Blessed are you among women, and blessed is the fruit of your womb!

43 "And who am I, that the mother of my Master should come to me?

44 "For look, when the sound of your greeting came to my ears, the baby in my womb leaped for joy.

45 "Blessed is she who believed, for that which יהוה has said to her shall be accomplished!"

46 And Miryam said, "My being makes יהוה great,

47 and my spirit has rejoiced in Elohim my Saviour.

48 "Because He looked on the humiliation of His female servant. For look, from now on all generations shall call me blessed. [c]

49 "For He who is mighty has done wonders for me, and set-apart is His Name. [d]

50 **"And His compassion is from generation to generation, to those who fear Him.** Teh. 103:17

51 "He did mightily with His arm; He scattered the proud in the thought of their hearts.

52 "He brought down rulers from their thrones, and exalted the lowly.

53 **"He has filled the hungry with good** *items*, Teh. 107:9 and the rich He has sent away empty.

54 "He sustained Yisra'ěl, His servant, in remembrance of His compassion,

55 as He spoke to our fathers, to Aḇraham and to his seed, forever."

56 And Miryam stayed with her about three months, and returned to her home.

57 And the time was filled for Elisheḇa to give birth, and she bore a son.

58 And her neighbours and relatives heard how יהוה had shown great compassion to her, and they rejoiced with her.

59 And it came to be, on the eighth day, that they came to circumcise the child. And they were calling him by the name of his father, Zeḵaryah.

60 And his mother answering, said, "Not

1a See Mt. 1:21. *1b* See Teh. 2, Teh. 89:14-34, Yesh. 9:7, Yesh. 16:5, Yirm. 23:3-6, Yirm. 30:9, Yeḥez. 37:24, Dan. 2:44, Dan. 7:18-27, Miḵ. 5:2-4, Ma. 1:6-7, Ḥazon 11:15. *1c* Also see Shem. א 1:11, 2:1.
1d Also see Teh. 111:9.

so, but he shall be called Yoḥanan."
61 And they said to her, "There is no one
among your relatives who is called by this
name."
62 Then they motioned to his father, what
he would like him to be called.
63 And having asked for a writing tablet,
he wrote, saying, "Yoḥanan is his name."
And they all marvelled.
64 And at once his mouth was opened and
his tongue loosed, and he was speaking,
praising Elohim.
65 And fear came on all those dwelling
around them, and all these matters were
spoken of in all the hill country of Yehuḏah.
66 And all who heard them kept them in
their hearts, saying, "What then shall this
child be?" And the hand of יהוה was with
him.
67 And Zeḵaryah, his father, was filled
with the Set-apart Spirit, and prophesied,
saying,
68 **"Blessed be יהוה Elohim of Yisra'ěl,**
Teh. 41:13 *e* for He did look upon and worked
redemption for His people,
69 and has raised up a horn of deliverance
for us in the house of His servant Dawiḏ,
70 as He spoke by the mouth of His set-
apart prophets, from of old –
71 deliverance **from our enemies and
from the hand of all those hating us,**
Teh. 106:10
72 to show compassion toward our fathers
and to remember His set-apart covenant,
73 an oath which He swore to our father
Aḇraham:
74 to give to us, being delivered from the
hand of our enemies, to serve Him without
fear,
75 in set-apartness and righteousness
before Him all the days of our life.
76 "And you, child, shall be called prophet
of the Most High, for you shall **go before
the face of יהוה to prepare His ways,**
Mal. 3:1 *f*
77 to give knowledge of deliverance to His
people, by the forgiveness of their sins,
78 through the tender compassion of our
Elohim, with which the daybreak from on
high has looked upon us,
79 **to give light to those who sit in darkness and the shadow of death,** Yesh. 9:1 to
guide our feet into the way of peace."
80 And the child grew and became strong
in spirit, and was in the deserts until the
day of showing himself openly to Yisra'ěl.

2 And it came to be in those days that a
decree went out from Caesar
Augustus for all the world to be registered.
2 This took place as a first registration
while Quirinius was governing Suria.
3 And all were going to be registered,
each one to his own city.
4 And Yosěph also went up from Galil,
out of the city of Natsareth to Yehuḏah, to
the city of Dawiḏ, which is called Běyth
Leḥem, because he was of the house and
lineage of Dawiḏ,
5 to be registered with Miryam, who was
engaged to him – being pregnant.
6 And it came to be, that while they were
there, the days were filled for her to give
birth.
7 And she gave birth to her first-born
Son, and wrapped Him up, and laid Him
down in a feeding trough, because there
was no room for them in a lodging place.
8 And in the same country there were
shepherds living out in the fields, keeping
watch over their flock by night.
9 And look, a messenger of יהוה stood
before them, and the esteem of יהוה shone
around them, and they were greatly afraid.
10 And the messenger said to them, "Do
not be afraid, for look, I bring you good
news of great joy which shall be to all
people.
11 "Because there was born to you today
in the city of Dawiḏ a Saviour, who is
Messiah, the Master.
12 "And this is the sign to you: You shall
find a baby wrapped up, lying in a feeding
trough."
13 And suddenly there was with the
messenger a crowd of the heavenly host
praising Elohim and saying,

1e Also see Teh. 72:18; 106:48. *1f* Yesh. 40:3, Yn. 1:23

14“Esteem to Elohim in the highest, and
on earth peace among men with whom He
is pleased!”
15And it came to be, when the messengers had gone away from them into the
heaven, that the shepherds said to each
other, “Indeed, let us go to Běyth Leḥem
and see this matter that has taken place,
which the Master has made known to us.”
16And they came in haste and found
Miryam and Yosěph, and the baby lying
in a feeding trough.
17And having seen, they made known the
matter which was spoken to them concerning the child.
18And all those who heard marvelled at
what the shepherds said to them.
19But Miryam kept all these matters, considering them in her heart.
20And the shepherds returned, boasting
and praising Elohim for all they had heard
and seen, as it was spoken to them.
21And when eight days were completed
for Him to be circumcised, His Name was
called יהושע, the Name given by the
messenger before He was conceived in
the womb.
22And when the days of her cleansing
according to the Torah of Mosheh were
completed, they brought Him to
Yerushalayim to present Him to יהוה –
23as it has been written in the Torah of
יהוה, **“Every male who opens the womb
shall be called set-apart to יהוה”** –
Shem. 13:2, 12, 15
24and to give an offering according to
what is said in the Torah of יהוה, **“A pair
of turtledoves or two young pigeons.”**
Way. 5:11; 12:8
25And see, there was a man in Yerushalayim whose name was Shim‘on, and
this man was righteous and dedicated,
looking for the comforting of Yisra’ěl. And
the Set-apart Spirit was upon him.
26And it had been revealed to him by the
Set-apart Spirit that he would not see death
before he sees the Messiah of יהוה.
27And he came in the Spirit into the Set-
apart Place. And as the parents brought in
the Child יהושע, to do for Him according
to the usual practice of the Torah,
28then he took Him up in his arms and
blessed Elohim and said,
29“Now let Your servant go in peace, O
Master, according to Your word,
30for my eyes have seen Your deliverance,
31which You have prepared before the
face of all the peoples,
32**a light for the unveiling of the
nations,** Yesh. 42:6; 49:6 and the esteem of Your
people Yisra’ěl.”
33And Yosěph and His mother were marvelling at what was said about Him.
34And Shim‘on blessed them, and said to
Miryam His mother, “See, this One is set
for a fall and rising of many in Yisra’ěl,
and for a sign spoken against –
35and a sword shall pierce through your
own being also – so as to reveal the
thoughts of many hearts.”
36And there was Ḥannah, a prophetess, a
daughter of Penu’ěl, of the tribe of Ashěr.
She was advanced in years, and had lived
with a husband seven years from her maidenhood,
37and she was a widow of about eighty-
four years, who did not leave the Set-apart
Place, but served Elohim with fastings and
prayers night and day.
38And she, coming in at that moment,
gave thanks to יהוה, and spoke of Him to
all who were waiting for redemption in
Yerushalayim.
39And when they had accomplished all
matters according to the Torah of יהוה,
they returned to Galil, to their city
Natsareth.
40And the Child grew and became strong
in spirit, being filled with wisdom. And the
favour of Elohim was upon Him.
41And His parents went to Yerushalayim
every year at the Festival of the Pěsaḥ.
42And when He was twelve years old,
they went up to Yerushalayim according to
the practice of the festival.
43When they had accomplished the days,
as they returned, the Child יהושע stayed
behind in Yerushalayim. And His parents
did not know it,
44but thinking He was in the company,
they went a day’s journey, and were seek-

ing Him among the relatives and friends.
45 And not having found Him, they
returned to Yerushalayim, seeking Him.
46 And it came to be, after three days, that
they found Him in the Set-apart Place,
sitting in the midst of the teachers, both listening to them and asking them questions.
47 And all who heard Him were astonished at His understanding and answers.
48 And having seen Him, they were
amazed. And His mother said to Him,
"Son, why have You done this to us? See,
Your father and I have been anxiously
seeking You."
49 And He said to them, "Why were you
seeking Me? Did you not know that I had
to be in the *matters* of My Father?"
50 But they did not understand the word
which He spoke to them.
51 And He went down with them and
came to Natsareth, and was subject to
them, but His mother kept all these matters
in her heart.
52 And יהושע increased in wisdom and
stature, and in favour with Elohim and
men.

3 And in the fifteenth year of the reign
of Tiberius Caesar, when Pontius
Pilate was governor of Yehuḏah, and
Herodes district ruler of Galil, and his
brother Philip district ruler of Yetur and the
country of Trachonitis, and Lusanias district ruler of Aḇilene,
2 Ḥanan and Qayapha being high priests,
the word of Elohim came to Yoḥanan the
son of Zeḵaryah in the wilderness.
3 And he went into all the neighbourhood
of the Yarděn, proclaiming an immersion
of repentance for the forgiveness of sins,
4 as it has been written in the book of the
words of Yeshayahu the prophet, saying,
"A voice of one crying in the wilderness,
'Prepare the way of יהוה', make His
paths straight.
5 **'Every valley shall be filled and every**
mountain and hill shall be made low,
and the crooked shall become straight,
and the rough become smooth ways,
6 **and all flesh shall see the deliverance**
of Elohim.' " Yesh. 40:3-5 *a*
7 He said therefore to the crowds that
came out to be immersed by him, "Brood
of adders, who warned you to flee from the
wrath to come?
8 "Therefore bear fruit worthy of repentance, and do not begin to say to yourselves, 'We have Aḇraham as our father.'
For I say to you that Elohim is able to raise
up children to Aḇraham from these stones.
9 "And even now the axe is laid to the
root of the trees. Therefore every tree that
does not bear good fruit is cut down and
thrown into the fire."
10 And the crowds asked him, saying,
"What, then, shall we do?"
11 And answering He said to them, "Let
him who has two undergarments share
with him who has none, and let him who
has food do likewise."
12 And tax collectors also came to be
immersed, and said to him, "Teacher, what
shall we do?"
13 And he said to them, "Collect no more
than what is appointed for you."
14 And soldiers also asked him, saying,
"And what shall we do?" And he said to
them, "Do not intimidate anyone or accuse
falsely, and be satisfied with your pay."
15 But as the people were in expectation,
and all were reasoning in their hearts about
Yoḥanan, whether he was the Messiah or
not,
16 Yoḥanan answered, saying to them all,
"I indeed immerse you in water, but One
mightier than I is coming, whose sandal
straps I am not worthy to loosen. He shall
immerse you in the Set-apart Spirit and
fire.
17 "His winnowing fork is in His hand,
and He shall thoroughly cleanse His
threshing-floor, and gather the wheat into
His storehouse, but the chaff He shall burn
with unquenchable fire."
18 And urging with many other *words*, he
brought the Good News to the people.
19 And Herodes the district ruler, being
convicted by him concerning Herodias his

3a Also see Yn. 1:23

brother Philip's wife, and for all the
wicked deeds which Herodes did,
20 added this also to them all – he locked
up Yoḥanan in prison.
21 And it came to be, when all the people
were immersed, יהושע also being
immersed, and praying, the heaven was
opened,
22 and the Set-apart Spirit descended in
bodily form like a dove upon Him, and a
voice came from heaven saying, "You are
My Son, the Beloved, in You I did
delight."
23 And when יהושע Himself began, He
was about thirty years of age, being, as
reckoned by law, son of Yosěph, of Ěli,
24 of Mattithyahu, of Lěwi, of Meleḵi, of
Yanah, of Yosěph,
25 of Mattithyahu, of Amots, of Naḥum,
of Ḥesli, of Noḡah,
26 of Maʽath, of Mattithyahu, of Shimʽi, of
Yosěph, of Yehuḏah,
27 of Yoḥanan, of Rephayah, of
Zerubbaḇel, of She'alti'ěl, of Neri,
28 of Meleḵi, of Addi, of Qosam, of
Elmoḏam, of Ěr,
29 of Yehoshua, of Eliʽezer, of Yorim, of
Mattithyahu, of Lěwi,
30 of Shimʽon, of Yehuḏah, of Yosěph, of
Yonam, of Elyaqim,
31 of Melea, of Menna, of Mattattah, of
Nathan, of Dawiḏ,
32 of Yishai, of Oḇěḏ, of Boʽaz, of
Salmon, of Naḥshon,
33 of Amminaḏaḇ, of Ram, of Ḥetsron, of
Perets, of Yehuḏah,
34 of Yaʽaqoḇ, of Yitsḥaq, of Aḇraham, of
Teraḥ, of Naḥor,
35 of Seruḡ, of Reʽu, of Peleḡ, of Ěḇer, of
Shělaḥ,
36 of Qěynan, of Arpaḵshaḏ, of Shěm, of
Noaḥ, of Lemeḵ,
37 of Methushelaḥ, of Ḥanoḵ, of Yereḏ, of
Mahalalěl, of Qěynan,
38 of Enosh, of Shěth, of Aḏam, of
Elohim.

4 And יהושע, being filled with the Set-
apart Spirit, returned from the Yarděn
and was led by the Spirit into the wilderness,
2 being tried for forty days by the devil.
And in those days He did not eat at all, and
afterward, when they had ended, He was
hungry.
3 And the devil said to Him, "If You are
the Son of Elohim, command this stone to
become bread."
4 But יהושע answered him, saying, "It
has been written, **'Man shall not live by
bread alone, but by every word of
Elohim.'** " Deḇ. 8:3 [a]
5 And the devil, taking Him up on a high
mountain, showed Him all the reigns of the
world in a moment of time.
6 And the devil said to Him, "All this
authority I shall give You, and their
esteem, for it has been delivered to me, [b]
and I give it to whomever I wish.
7 "If, then, You worship before me, all
shall be Yours."
8 And יהושע answering him, said, "Get
behind Me, Satan! For it has been written,
**'You shall worship יהוה your Elohim,
and Him only you shall serve.'** " Deḇ. 6:13
9 And he brought Him to Yerushalayim,
set Him on the edge of the Set-apart Place,
and said to Him, "If You are the Son of
Elohim, throw Yourself down from here,
10 for it has been written, **'He shall command His messengers concerning You,
to guard over You,'** Teh. 91:11
11 and, **'In their hands they shall bear
You up, lest You dash Your foot against
a stone.'** " Teh. 91:12
12 And יהושע answering, said to him, "It
has been said, **'You shall not try יהוה
your Elohim.'** " Deḇ. 6:16
13 And when the devil had ended every
trial, he went away from Him until a
convenient time.
14 And יהושע returned in the power of the
Spirit to Galil, and news of Him went out
through all the surrounding country.
15 And He was teaching in their congrega-

4a Mt. 4:4. *4b* See Cor. ב 4:4, Yn. 12:31, Yn. 14:30, Yn. 16:11, Yn. א 5:19.

tions, being praised by all.
16 And He came to Natsareth, where He
had been brought up. And according to His
practice, He went into the congregation on
the Sabbath day, and stood up to read.
17 And the scroll of the prophet Yeshayahu was handed to Him. And having
unrolled the scroll, He found the place
where it was written:
18 "The Spirit of יהוה is upon Me, [c]
**because He has anointed Me to bring the
Good News to the poor. He has sent Me
to heal the broken-hearted, to proclaim
release to the captives and recovery of
sight to the blind, to send away crushed
ones with a release,**
**19 to proclaim the acceptable year of
יהוה."** Yesh. 61:1-2 [d]
20 And having rolled up the scroll, He
gave it back to the attendant and sat down.
And the eyes of all in the congregation
were fixed upon Him.
21 And He began to say to them, "Today
this Scripture has been filled in your
hearing."
22 And all were bearing witness to Him,
and marvelled at the pleasant words that
came out of His mouth. And they said, "Is
this not the son of Yosĕph?"
23 And He said to them, "No doubt, you
shall say this proverb to Me, 'Physician,
heal yourself! Whatever we have heard
being done in Kephar Naḥum, do also here
in Your country.' "
24 And He said, "Truly, I say to you, no
prophet is accepted in his own country.
25 "But truly I say to you, many widows
were in Yisra'ĕl in the days of Ĕliyahu,
when the heaven was shut up for three
years and six months, and there was a great
scarcity of food in all the land,
26 and Ĕliyahu was sent to none of them,
but to Tsarephath of Tsiḏon, to a woman, a
widow.
27 "And many lepers were in Yisra'ĕl in
the time of Elisha the prophet, and none of
them was cleansed except Na'aman the
Aramean."
28 And all those in the congregation, when
they heard this, were filled with wrath.
29 And rising up they drove Him out of
the city, and brought Him to the brow of
the hill on which their city was built, in
order to throw Him down.
30 But He, passing through the midst of
them, went away.
31 And He came down to Kephar Naḥum,
a city of Galil, and was teaching them on
the Sabbaths.
32 And they were astonished at His teaching, for His word was with authority.
33 And in the congregation was a man
having a spirit of an unclean demon. And
he cried out with a loud voice,
34 saying, "Ha! What have we to do with
You, יהושע of Natsareth? Did You come
to destroy us? I know You, who You are,
the Set-apart One of Elohim!"
35 And יהושע rebuked him, saying, "Be
silenced, and come out of him!" And when
the demon had thrown him in their midst,
it came out of him without hurting him.
36 And astonishment came on all, and
they spoke to each other, saying, "What is
this word, that with authority and power
He commands the unclean spirits, and they
come out?"
37 And the report about Him went out into
every place of the neighbourhood.
38 And rising up from the congregation
He went into the house of Shim'on. But the
mother-in-law of Shim'on was sick with a
severe inflammation, and they asked Him
concerning her.
39 And standing over her He rebuked the
inflammation, and it left her, and instantly
rising up she served them.
40 And when the sun was setting, all
who had any who were sick with various
diseases brought them to Him. And He laid
His hands on each one of them and healed
them.
41 And also demons were coming out of
many, crying out and saying, "You are the
Messiah, the Son of Elohim!" And rebuking them, He did not allow them to speak,
for they knew that He was the Messiah.
42 And when day came, He went out and

4c See Yesh. 61:1-3. *4d* Also see Yesh. 58:6

proceeded to a lonely place, but the crowds
were seeking Him and came to Him, and
tried to keep Him from leaving them.
43 And He said to them, "To the other
cities I also have to bring the Good News:
the reign of Elohim, because for this I have
been sent."
44 And He was proclaiming in the congregations of Galil.

5 And it came to be, while the crowd
was pressing upon Him to hear the
word of Elohim, that He stood by the Lake
of Gennĕsar,
2 and He saw two boats standing by the
lake, but the fishermen had gone from
them and were washing their nets.
3 And entering into one of the boats,
which belonged to Shimʽon, He asked him
to pull away a little from the land. And He
sat down and was teaching the crowds
from the boat.
4 And when He ceased speaking, He said
to Shimʽon, "Pull out into the deep and let
down your nets for a catch."
5 And Shimʽon answering, said to Him,
"Master, we have toiled all night and
caught none, but at Your word I shall let
down the net."
6 And when they did so, they caught a
great number of fish, and their net was
breaking,
7 and they motioned to their partners in
the other boat to come and help them. And
they came and filled both the boats, so that
they were sinking.
8 And when Shimʽon Kĕpha saw it, he
fell down at the knees of יהושע, saying,
"Depart from me, for I am a man, a sinner,
O Master!"
9 For astonishment had seized him and
all those with him, at the catch of fish
which they took,
10 so too were Yaʽaqoḇ and Yoḥanan, the
sons of Zaḇdai, who were partners with
Shimʽon. Then יהושע said to Shimʽon,
"Do not fear, from now on you shall catch
men."
11 And having brought the boats to land,
they left all and followed Him.
12 And it came to be when He was in a
certain city, that see, a man covered with
leprosy saw יהושע. And he fell on his face
and begged Him, saying, "Master, if You
desire, You are able to cleanse me."
13 And He stretched out His hand and
touched him, saying, "I desire it. Be
cleansed." And immediately the leprosy
left him.
14 And He ordered him to say it to no one,
"**But go and show yourself to the priest**,
Way. 13:49; 14:2 and make an offering for your
cleansing, as a witness to them, as Mosheh
commanded."
15 And the news about Him was spreading
even more. And large crowds were coming
together to hear, and to be healed by Him
of their sicknesses.
16 But He was *often* withdrawing Himself
to lonely places and praying.
17 And on a certain day it came to be, as
He was teaching, that there were Pharisees
and teachers of the Torah sitting by, who
had come out of every village of Galil,
Yehuḏah, and Yerushalayim. And the
power of יהוה was *there* to heal them.
18 And see, men brought on a bed a man
who was paralysed. And they were seeking
to bring him in and lay him before Him.
19 But having found no way to bring him
in because of the crowd, they went up on
the house-top and let him down with his
bed through the tiles into the midst before
יהושע.
20 And having seen their belief, He said to
him, "Man, your sins are forgiven you."
21 And the scribes and the Pharisees
began to reason, saying, "Who is this who
speaks blasphemies? Who is able to forgive sins except Elohim alone?"
22 And יהושע, knowing their thoughts,
answering, said to them, "Why are you
reasoning in your hearts?
23 "Which is easier, to say, 'Your sins are
forgiven you,' or to say, 'Rise up and
walk'?
24 "But in order for you to know that the
Son of Aḏam possesses authority on earth
to forgive sins..." He said to the man who
was paralysed, "I say to you, rise, take up
your bed, and go to your house."
25 And at once, having risen up before

them, he took up what he had been lying on, and went away to his house, praising Elohim.

26 And astonishment seized them all, and they praised Elohim and were filled with fear, saying, "We have seen extra-ordinary *feats* today!"

27 And after this He went out and saw a tax collector named Lěwi, sitting at the tax office, and said to him, "Follow Me."

28 And he, having left all, rose up and followed Him.

29 And Lěwi made a great feast for Him in his house. And there were a great number of tax collectors and others who sat down with them.

30 And the Pharisees and their scribes grumbled against His taught ones, saying, "Why do You eat and drink with tax collectors and sinners?"

31 And יהושע answering, said to them, "Those who are well do not need a physician, but those who are sick.

32 "I have not come to call the righteous, but sinners, to repentance."

33 And they said to Him, "Why do the taught ones of Yoḥanan fast often and make prayers, and likewise those of the Pharisees, but Yours eat and drink?"

34 And He said to them, "Are you able to make the friends of the bridegroom fast while the bridegroom is with them?

35 "But days shall come when the bridegroom is taken away from them, then they shall fast in those days."

36 And He also spoke a parable to them, "No one puts a piece from a fresh garment on an old one, otherwise the fresh one makes a tear, and also the piece that was taken out of the fresh one does not match the old.

37 "And no one puts new wine into old wineskins, otherwise the new wine shall burst the wineskins and run out, and the wineskins shall be ruined.

38 "But new wine is put into fresh wineskins, and both are preserved.

39 "And no one, having drunk old wine, immediately desires new *wine*, for he says, 'The old is better.' "

6 And it came to be on a Sabbath [a] that He went through grainfields, and His taught ones were plucking the heads of grain and were eating, rubbing *them* with the hands.

2 And some of the Pharisees said to them, "Why are you doing what is not right to do on the Sabbath?"

3 And יהושע answering them, said, "Have you not read what Dawiḏ did when he was hungry, he and those who were with him,

4 how he went into the House of Elohim, took and ate the showbread, and also gave some to those with him, which is not right for any but the priests to eat?"

5 And He said to them, "The Son of Aḏam is Master of the Sabbath." [b]

6 And it also came to be on another Sabbath, that He entered into the congregation and taught, and there was a man whose right hand was withered.

7 And the scribes and Pharisees were watching Him closely, whether He would heal on the Sabbath, for them to find an accusation against Him.

8 And He knew their thoughts, and said to the man who had the withered hand, "Rise and stand in the midst." And he rose up and stood.

9 Then יהושע said to them, "I ask you, is it right to do good on the Sabbath, or to do evil, to save life or to destroy it?"

10 And looking around at them all, He said to the man, "Stretch out your hand." And he did so, and his hand was restored sound as the other.

11 But they were filled with folly, and were speaking with one another what they should do to יהושע.

12 And in those days it came to be that He went out to the mountain to pray, and was spending the night in prayer to Elohim.

13 And when it became day, He called near His taught ones and chose from them twelve, whom He also named emissaries:

14 Shim'on whom He also named Kěpha,

6a Some manuscripts read: On the second Sabbath after the first. *6b* Mt.12:8.

and his brother Andri, Ya'aqoḇ and Yoḥanan, Philip and Bartholomi,
15 Mattithyahu and T'oma, Ya'aqoḇ the
son of Alphai and Shim'on, the one called
the Ardent One,
16 Yehuḏah *the son* of Ya'aqoḇ and Yehuḏah from Qerioth who also became the
betrayer.
17 And coming down with them He stood
on a level place with a crowd of His taught
ones and a great number of people from all
Yehuḏah and Yerushalayim, and from the
coast country of Tsor and Tsiḏon, who
came to hear Him, and to be healed of their
diseases,
18 and those who were troubled with
unclean spirits – and they were healed.
19 And all the crowd were seeking to
touch Him, for power went out from Him,
and healing them all.
20 And He, lifting up His eyes toward His
taught ones, said, "Blessed are the poor, [c]
because yours is the reign of Elohim.
21 "Blessed are you who hunger now,
because you shall be satisfied. Blessed are
you who weep now, because you shall
laugh.
22 "Blessed are you when men shall hate
you, and when they shall cut you off, and
shall reproach you, and cast out your name
as wicked, for the sake of the Son of
Aḏam.
23 "Rejoice in that day and leap for joy,
for look, your reward is great in the heav-
en, for that is how their fathers treated the
prophets.
24 "But woe to you who are rich, because
you are receiving your comfort.
25 "Woe to you who have been filled,
because you shall hunger. Woe to you who
are laughing now, because you shall mourn
and weep.
26 "Woe to you when all men speak well
of you, for thus their fathers did to the false
prophets.
27 "But I say to you who are hearing:
Love your enemies, do good to those
hating you.
28 "Bless those cursing you, and pray for
those insulting you.
29 "And to him who hits you on the one
cheek, offer the other also. And from him
who takes away your outer garment, do not
withhold the inner garment either.
30 "And give to everyone who asks of
you. And from him who takes away what
is yours do not ask it back.
31 "And as you wish men should do to
you, you also do to them in the same way.
32 "And if you love those loving you,
what favour have you? For sinners, too,
love those loving them.
33 "And if you do good to those doing
good to you, what favour have you? For
even sinners do the same.
34 "And if you lend *to those* from whom
you expect to receive back, what favour
have you? For even sinners lend to sinners
to receive as much back.
35 "Rather, love your enemies, and do
good, and lend, expecting none in return.
And your reward shall be great, and you
shall be sons of the Most High. Because
He is kind to the thankless and wicked
ones. [d]
36 "Therefore be compassionate, as your
Father also is compassionate.
37 "And do not judge, and you shall not
be judged at all. Condemn not, and you
shall not be condemned at all. Forgive, and
you shall be forgiven.
38 "Give, and it shall be given to you. A
good measure, pressed down and shaken
together and running over shall be put into
your lap. For with the same measure with
which you measure, it shall be measured
back to you."
39 And He spoke a parable to them, "Is a
blind able to lead a blind? Shall they not
both fall into a pit?
40 "A taught one is not above his teacher,
but everyone perfected shall be like his
teacher.
41 "And why do you see the splinter in
your brother's eye, but are not aware of the
plank in your own eye?
42 "Or how are you able to say to your
brother, 'Brother, let me take out the splin-

6c Yesh. 11:4, Ya'aqoḇ 2:5. *6d* Mt. 5:45, Ma. 14:16-17.

ter that is in your eye,' not seeing the plank in your own eye? Hypocrite, first take the plank out of your own eye, and then you shall see clearly to take out the splinter that is in your brother's eye.

43 "For a good tree does not yield rotten fruit, nor does a rotten tree yield good fruit.

44 "For each tree is known by its own fruit. For they do not gather figs from thorns, nor do they gather grapes from a bramble bush.

45 "The good man brings forth what is good out of the good treasure of his heart, and the wicked man brings forth what is wicked out of the wicked treasure of his heart. For out of the overflow of the heart his mouth speaks.

46 "But why do you call Me 'Master, Master,' and do not do what I say? [e]

47 "Everyone who is coming to Me, and is hearing My words and is doing them, I shall show you whom he is like:

48 "He is like a man building a house, who dug deep and laid a foundation on the rock. And when a flood came, the stream burst against that house, but was unable to shake it, for it was founded on the rock.

49 "But the one hearing and not doing, is like a man who built a house on the earth without a foundation, against which the stream burst, and immediately it fell. And the ruin of that house was great."

7 And when He completed all His words in the hearing of the people, He went into Kephar Naḥum.

2 And a certain captain's servant, who was valuable to him, was sick and about to die.

3 And hearing about יהושע, he sent elders of the Yehuḏim to Him, asking Him to come and heal his servant.

4 And when they came to יהושע, they begged Him earnestly, saying, "He is worthy for You to grant this to him,

5 for he loves our nation, and has built the congregation for us."

6 So יהושע went with them. However, He was not far from the house when the captain sent friends to Him, saying to Him, "Master, do not trouble Yourself, for I am not worthy that You should come under my roof.

7 "For this reason I did not even think myself worthy to come to You. But say a word, and my servant shall be healed.

8 "For I too am a man appointed under authority, having soldiers under me. And I say to one, 'Go,' and he goes, and to another, 'Come,' and he comes, and to my servant, 'Do this,' and he does it."

9 And when יהושע heard this, He marvelled at him, and turned around and said to the crowd that followed Him, "I say to you, not even in Yisra'ěl have I found such great belief!"

10 And those who were sent, returning to the house, found the servant who had been sick in good health.

11 And it came to be the next day, that He went into a city called Na'im. And many of His taught ones went with Him, and a large crowd.

12 And see, as He came near the gate of the city a dead man was being carried out, the only son of his mother, and she was a widow. And a large crowd from the city was with her.

13 And when the Master saw her, He had compassion on her and said to her, "Do not weep."

14 And coming near He touched the bier, and those bearing it stood still. And He said, "Young man, I say to you, arise."

15 And he who was dead sat up and began to speak, and He gave him to his mother.

16 And fear seized all, and they praised Elohim, saying, "A great prophet has been raised up among us," and, "Elohim has visited His people."

17 And this news about Him went out in all Yehuḏah and all the neighbourhood.

18 And the taught ones of Yoḥanan reported to him about all this.

19 And Yoḥanan, calling two of his taught ones near, sent to יהושע, saying, "Are You the Coming One, or should we look for another?"

6e See vv. 47-49, Mt. 7:24-28, Lq. 8:21, Yn. 3:36, Ya'aqoḇ 2:17-24.

20 And coming to Him, the men said, "Yoḥanan the Immerser has sent us to You, saying, 'Are You the Coming One, or should we look for another?' "

21 And in the same hour He healed many of diseases, and afflictions, and wicked spirits. And He gave sight to many blind ones.

22 And יהושע answering, said to them, "Go, report to Yoḥanan what you have seen and heard: **blind receive sight, lame do walk**, lepers are cleansed, **deaf do hear**, Yesh. 35:5, 6 dead are raised, **the Good News is brought to the poor.** Yesh. 61:1

23 "And blessed is he who shall not stumble in Me."

24 And when the messengers of Yoḥanan had left, He began to speak to the crowds concerning Yoḥanan, "What did you go out into the wilderness to see? A reed shaken by the wind?

25 "But what did you go out to see? A man dressed in soft garments? Look, those who are splendidly dressed and living in luxury are in the houses of sovereigns.

26 "But what did you go out to see? A prophet? Yes, I say to you, and more than a prophet.

27 "This is he concerning whom it has been written, **'See, I send My messenger before Your face, who shall prepare Your way before You.'** Mal. 3:1

28 "For I say to you, among those born of women there is not a greater prophet than Yoḥanan the Immerser, but he who is least in the reign of Elohim is greater than he."

29 And all the people, even the tax collectors, when they heard, declared Elohim righteous, having been immersed with the immersion of Yoḥanan.

30 But the Pharisees and those learned in the Torah rejected the counsel of Elohim for themselves, not having been immersed by him.

31 And the Master said, "To what then shall I compare the men of this generation, and what are they like?

32 "They are like children sitting in the market-place and calling to each other, saying, 'We played the flute for you and you did not dance, we lamented for you and you did not weep.'

33 "For Yoḥanan the Immerser came neither eating bread nor drinking wine, and you say, 'He has a demon.'

34 "The Son of Aḏam has come eating and drinking, and you say, 'Look, a man, a glutton and a winedrinker, a friend of tax collectors and sinners!'

35 "And wisdom is declared right by all her children."

36 And one of the Pharisees asked Him to eat with him. And He went into the Pharisee's house, and sat down to eat.

37 And see, a woman in the city who was a sinner, when she knew that יהושע sat at the table in the Pharisee's house, brought an alabaster flask of perfume.

38 And standing behind, at His feet, weeping, she began to wet His feet with her tears, and wiping them with the hair of her head, and was kissing His feet and anointing them with the perfume.

39 And when the Pharisee who had invited Him saw this, he spoke to himself, saying, "This One, if He were a prophet, would know who and what kind of woman this is who is touching Him, for she is a sinner."

40 And יהושע answering, said to him, "Shim'on, I have somewhat to say to you." And he said, "Teacher, say it."

41 "A certain creditor had two debtors. The one owed five hundred denarii [a], and the other fifty.

42 "And when they were unable to repay, he forgave them both. Which of them, then, shall love him more?"

43 And Shim'on answering, said, "I suppose the one whom he forgave more." And He said to him, "You have rightly judged."

44 And turning to the woman He said to Shim'on, "Do you see this woman? I came into your house – you gave Me no water for My feet, but she has wetted My feet with her tears and wiped them with the hair of her head.

45 "You gave Me no kiss, but she has not ceased to kiss My feet since the time I

7a - Roman monetary unit.

came in.
46 "You did not anoint My head with oil,
but she anointed My feet with perfume.
47 "Therefore I say to you, her many sins
have been forgiven, because she loved
much. But to whom little is forgiven, he
loves little."
48 And He said to her, "Your sins have
been forgiven."
49 And those who were sitting at the table
with Him began to say among themselves,
"Who is this who even forgives sins?"
50 And He said to the woman, "Your
belief has saved you. Go in peace."

8 And it came to be, afterward, that He
went through every city and village,
proclaiming and bringing the Good News
of the reign of Elohim, and the twelve
were with Him,
2 and certain women who were healed of
wicked spirits and sicknesses: Miryam,
called 'from Mağdala,' out of whom had
come seven demons,
3 and Yoḥanah the wife of Kuza, manager of Herodes, and Shoshannah, and many
others who provided for Him from their
resources.
4 And when a large crowd had gathered,
and those who were coming to Him from
every city, He spoke by a parable:
5 "A sower went out to sow his seed.
And as he sowed, some indeed fell by the
wayside. And it was trodden down, and the
birds of the heaven devoured it.
6 "And other fell on rock, and when it
grew up, it withered because it had no
moisture.
7 "And other fell among thorns, and the
thorns grew up with it and choked it.
8 "And other fell on the good soil, and
grew up, and yielded a crop a hundredfold." Having said this He cried, "He who
has ears to hear, let him hear!"
9 And His taught ones were asking Him,
saying, "What does this parable mean?"
10 And He said, "To you it has been given
to know the secrets of the reign of Elohim,
but to the rest in parables, that **'Seeing
they do not see, and hearing they do not
understand.'** Yesh. 6:9
11 "And this is the parable: The seed is the
word of Elohim. [a]
12 "And those by the wayside are the ones
who hear, then the devil comes and takes
away the word from their hearts, lest
having believed, they should be saved.
13 "And those on the rock are those who,
when they hear, receive the word with joy.
And these have no root, who believe for a
while and in time of trial fall away.
14 "And that which fell among thorns are
those who, when they have heard, go out
and are choked with worries, and riches,
and pleasures of life, and bring no fruit to
perfection.
15 "And that on the good soil are those
who, having heard the word with a noble
and good heart, retain it, and bear fruit
with endurance.
16 "And no one having lit a lamp, covers
it with a vessel or puts it under a bed, but
he puts it on a lampstand, so that those
coming in see the light.
17 "For whatever is hidden shall be
revealed, and whatever is secret shall be
known and come to light.
18 "Therefore take heed how you hear. For
whoever possesses, to him *more* shall be
given; and whoever does not possess, even
what he thinks he possesses shall be taken
from him."
19 And His mother and brothers came to
Him, and were unable to get to Him
because of the crowd.
20 And it was reported to Him, saying,
"Your mother and Your brothers are standing outside, wishing to see You."
21 And He answering, said to them, "My
mother and My brothers are those who are
hearing the Word of Elohim and doing
it." [b]
22 And on a certain day it came to be, that
He entered into a boat with His taught
ones, and He said to them, "Let us go over
to the other side of the lake." And they set
out.
23 And as they were sailing He fell asleep.

8a Mt. 13 and Mq. 4. *8b* Mt. 12:50, Mq. 3:35.

And a windstorm came down on the lake,
and they were filling up, and were in danger.
24 And they came to Him and woke Him
up, saying, "Master, Master, we are perishing!" And He awoke and rebuked the wind
and the raging of the water. And they
ceased, and there came a calm.
25 And He said to them, "Where is your
belief?" And they were afraid, and
marvelled, saying to one another, "Who
then is this, that He even commands the
winds and water, and they obey Him?"
26 And they sailed to the country of the
Gaḏarenes, which is opposite Galil.
27 And as He went out onto the land, He
was met by a certain man, from the city,
who had demons for a long time. And he
wore no garments, and he was not living
in a house but in the tombs.
28 And when he saw יהושע, he cried out,
fell down before Him, and with a loud
voice said, "What have I to do with You,
יהושע, Son of the Most High Elohim? I
beg You, do not torture me!"
29 For He had commanded the unclean
spirit to come out of the man. For it had
seized him many times, and he was bound
with chains and shackles, being guarded.
And breaking the bonds, he was driven by
the demon into the lonely places.
30 And יהושע asked him, saying, "What
is your name?" And he said, "Legion,"
because many demons had entered into
him.
31 And they were begging Him that He
would not command them to go out into
the bottomless pit.
32 And a herd of many pigs was feeding
there on the mountain. And they begged
Him to allow them to go into them. And
He allowed them.
33 And the demons, having gone out of
the man, entered into the pigs, and the herd
rushed down the steep place into the lake
and drowned.
34 And when those feeding them saw what
had taken place, they fled and reported it in
the city and in the country.
35 So they came out to see what had taken
place, and came to יהושע, and found the
man from whom the demons had gone out,
sitting at the feet of יהושע, dressed, and in
his right mind. And they were afraid.
36 And those who had seen it reported to
them how he who had been possessed by
demons was healed.
37 And all the crowd of the neighbourhood of the Gaḏarenes asked Him to leave
them, for they were seized with great fear.
And He entered into the boat and returned.
38 And the man from whom the demons
had gone out was begging Him to be with
Him. But יהושע sent him away, saying,
39 "Go back to your house, and relate
what Elohim has done for you." And he
went away proclaiming through all the city
what יהושע did for him.
40 And it came to be, when יהושע
returned, that the crowd gladly received
Him, for they were all looking for Him.
41 And see, there came a man whose name
was Ya'ir, and he was a ruler of the congregation. And falling down at the feet of
יהושע he was calling upon Him to come to
his house,
42 because he had an only daughter about
twelve years of age, and she was dying.
And as He went, the crowds thronged upon
Him.
43 And a woman, having a flow of blood
for twelve years, who, having spent all her
livelihood on physicians, was unable to be
healed by any,
44 came from behind and touched the
tzitzit of His garment. And immediately
her flow of blood stopped.
45 And יהושע said, "Who touched Me?"
And when all denied it, Kěpha and those
with him said, "Master, the crowds throng
You and press upon You, and You say,
'Who touched Me?' "
46 But יהושע said, "Somebody did touch
Me, for I knew power went out from Me."
47 And the woman, seeing that she was
not hidden, came trembling, and falling
down before Him she declared to Him in
the presence of all the people why she had
touched Him and how she was healed
immediately.
48 And He said to her, "Take courage,
daughter, your belief has healed you. Go in

peace."

49 While He was still speaking, someone came from the ruler of the congregation's *house*, saying to him, "Your daughter is dead. Do not trouble the Teacher any further."

50 And יהושע, having heard, answered him, saying, "Do not be afraid, only believe, and she shall be healed."

51 And coming into the house, He allowed no one to go in except Kěpha, and Ya'aqoḇ, and Yoḥanan, and the girl's father and mother.

52 And they were all weeping and mourning for her, and He said, "Do not weep, she is not dead, but sleeps."

53 And they were laughing at Him, knowing that she was dead.

54 But taking her by the hand He called, saying, "Child, arise."

55 And her spirit returned, and she rose up immediately. And He directed that she be given *food* to eat.

56 And her parents were astonished, but He ordered them to say to no one what had taken place.

9 And having called His twelve taught ones together, He gave them power and authority over all demons, and to heal diseases.

2 And He sent them to proclaim the reign of Elohim and to heal the sick.

3 And He said to them, "Take no *matter* at all for the journey, neither staffs nor bag nor bread nor silver – neither have two undergarments.

4 "And whatever house you enter, stay there, and go out from there.

5 "And as for those who do not receive you, when you go out of that city, shake off the dust from your feet as a witness against them."

6 And going out they went through the villages, bringing the Good News and healing everywhere.

7 And Herodes the district ruler heard of all that was done by Him, and was perplexed, because it was said by some that Yoḥanan had been raised from the dead,

8 and by some that Ěliyahu had appeared, and by others that one of the old prophets has risen up.

9 And Herodes said, "Yoḥanan I have beheaded, but who is this of whom I hear such *reports*?" And he was seeking to see Him.

10 And the emissaries, when they had returned, related to Him all that they had done. And He took them and they withdrew by themselves to a city called Běyth Tsaiḏa.

11 And when the crowds knew it, they followed Him. And having received them, He was speaking to them about the reign of Elohim, and healed those who had need of healing.

12 And as the day began to decline, the twelve came and said to Him, "Send the crowd away, that going into the surrounding villages and country, they might lodge and get food, because here we are in a lonely place."

13 But He said to them, "You give them to eat." And they said, "We have no more than five loaves and two fishes, unless we go and buy food for all these people."

14 For there were about five thousand men. And He said to His taught ones, "Make them sit down in groups of fifty."

15 And they did so, and made them all sit down.

16 And taking the five loaves and the two fishes, having looked up to the heaven, He blessed and broke them, and gave them to the taught ones to set before the crowd.

17 So they all ate and were satisfied, and twelve baskets of the broken pieces were picked up by them.

18 And it came to be, as He was alone praying, the taught ones were with Him, and He asked them, saying, "Who do the crowds say that I am?"

19 And they answering, said, "Yoḥanan the Immerser, but others Ěliyahu, and others say that one of the old prophets has risen up."

20 And He said to them, "And you, who do you say I am?" And Kěpha answering, said, "The Messiah of Elohim."

21 And strictly warning them, He commanded them to say this to no one,

22 saying, "The Son of Aḏam has to suffer
much, and to be rejected by the elders and
chief priests and scribes, and to be killed,
and to be raised the third day."
23 And He said to them all, "If anyone
wishes to come after Me, let him deny
himself, and take up his stake daily, and
follow Me.
24 "For whoever wishes to save his life
shall lose it, but whoever loses his life for
My sake shall save it.
25 "For what is a man profited if he gains
all the world, and is himself destroyed or
lost?
26 "For whoever is ashamed of Me and
My words, of him the Son of Aḏam shall
be ashamed when He comes in His esteem,
and in His Father's, and of the set-apart
messengers.
27 "But truly I say to you, there are some
standing here who shall not taste death at
all till they see the reign of Elohim:"
28 And it came to be, about eight days
after these words, taking with Him Kěpha
and Yoḥanan and Yaʽaqoḇ, He went up to
the mountain to pray.
29 And it came to be, as He prayed, the
appearance of His face changed, and His
garment dazzling white.
30 And see, two men were talking with
Him, who were Mosheh and Ěliyahu, [a]
31 who having appeared in esteem, spoke
of His death which He was about to complete at Yerushalayim.
32 But Kěpha and those with him were
heavy with sleep. And having awakened,
they saw His esteem and the two men
standing with Him.
33 And it came to be, as they were parting
from Him, Kěpha said to יהושע, "Master,
it is good for us to be here. And let us
make three booths: one for You, and one
for Mosheh, and one for Ěliyahu," not
knowing what he said.
34 And as he was saying this, a cloud
came and overshadowed them. And they
were afraid as they entered the cloud.
35 And a voice came out of the cloud, saying, "This is My Son, the Beloved. Hear
Him!"
36 And when the voice had spoken, יהושע
was found alone. And they were silent, and
reported to no one in those days any of
what they had seen.
37 And it came to be on the next day,
when they came down from the mountain,
that a large crowd met Him.
38 And see, a man from the crowd cried
out, saying, "Teacher, I beg You, look at
my son, for he is my only child.
39 "And see, a spirit seizes him, and he
suddenly cries out, and it convulses him,
with foaming, and scarcely leaves him,
bruising him.
40 "And I begged Your taught ones to cast
it out, but they were unable."
41 And יהושע answering, said, "O generation, unbelieving and perverse, how long
shall I be with you and put up with you?
Bring your son here."
42 And as he was still coming, the demon
threw him down in convulsions. And
יהושע rebuked the unclean spirit, and
healed the child, and gave him back to his
father.
43 And they were all amazed at the greatness of Elohim. And while all were
marvelling at all that יהושע did, He said
to His taught ones,
44 "Lay up in your ears these words, for
the Son of Aḏam is about to be delivered
into the hands of men."
45 But they did not understand this saying,
and it was veiled from them so that they
did not perceive it. And they were afraid to
ask Him about this saying.
46 And a reasoning arose among them,
who might be the greater of them.
47 And יהושע, having seen the reasoning
of their heart, took a little child and placed
him by His side,
48 and said to them, "Whoever receives
this little child in My Name receives Me.
And whoever receives Me receives Him
who sent Me. For he who is least among
you all, he shall be great."
49 And Yoḥanan answering, said, "Master,
we saw someone casting out demons in

9a Mq. 9:4.

Your Name, and we forbade him because he does not follow with us."

50 But יהושע said to him, "Do not forbid him, for he who is not against us is for us."

51 And it came to be, when the days of His taking up were being completed, even He set His face to go to Yerushalayim,

52 and He sent messengers ahead of Him. And they went and entered into a village of the Shomeronim, to prepare for Him.

53 And they did not receive Him, because His face was set for the journey to Yerushalayim.

54 And His taught ones, Ya'aqoḇ and Yoḥanan, seeing it said, "Master, do You wish us to command fire to come down from the heaven and destroy them, as also Ěliyahu did?" [b]

55 But having turned, He rebuked them and said, "You do not know of what spirit you are,

56 for the Son of Aḏam did not come to destroy men's lives but to save them." And they went on to another village.

57 And it came to be, as they journeyed on the way, that someone said to Him, "Master, I shall follow You wherever You go."

58 And יהושע said to him, "The foxes have holes and the birds of the heaven nests, but the Son of Aḏam has nowhere to lay His head."

59 And He said to another, "Follow Me," but he said, "Master, let me first go and bury my father."

60 And יהושע said to him, "Let the dead bury their own dead, but you go and announce the reign of Elohim."

61 And another also said, "Master, I shall follow You, but let me first say good-bye to those in my house."

62 But יהושע said to him, "No one, having put his hand to the plough, and looking back, is fit for the reign of Elohim." [c]

10 And after this the Master appointed seventy others, and sent them two by two ahead of Him into every city and place where He Himself was about to go.

2 Then He said to them, "The harvest indeed is great, but the workers are few, therefore pray the Master of the harvest to send out workers into His harvest.

3 "Go! See, I send you out as lambs into the midst of wolves.

4 "Do not take a purse, nor a bag, nor sandals. And greet no one along the way.

5 "And whatever house you enter, first say, 'Peace to this house.'

6 "And if indeed a son of peace is there, your peace shall rest on it; and if not, it shall return to you.

7 "And stay in the same house, eating and drinking whatever with them, for the labourer is worthy of his wages. Do not move from house to house.

8 "And into whatever city you enter, and they receive you, eat whatever is placed before you,

9 and heal the sick there, and say to them, 'The reign of Elohim has come near to you.'

10 "And into whatever city you enter, and they do not receive you, go out into its streets and say,

11 'Even the dust of your city which clings to us, we wipe off against you, but know this, that the reign of Elohim has come near to you.'

12 "And I say to you that it shall be more bearable for Seḏom in that Day, than for that city.

13 "Woe to you, Korazin! Woe to you, Běyth Tsaiḏa! For if the miracles which were done in you had been done in Tsor and Tsiḏon, they would have repented long ago, sitting in sackcloth and ashes.

14 "But it shall be more bearable for Tsor and Tsiḏon at the judgment than for you.

15 "And you, Kephar Naḥum, who are **exalted to the heaven, shall be brought down to She'ol.** Yesh. 14:13,15 [a]

16 "He who hears you hears Me, he who rejects you rejects Me, and he who rejects Me rejects Him who sent Me."

17 And the seventy returned with joy, saying, "Master, even the demons are subject to us in Your Name."

9b Mel. ב 1:9-16 *9c* Lq. 14:26, 33, Yn. 12:24-26. *10a* See Explanatory notes - She'ol.

18 And He said to them, "I saw Satan falling out of the heaven as lightning.

19 "See, I give you the authority to trample on serpents and scorpions, and over all the power of the enemy, and none at all shall hurt you.

20 "But do not rejoice in this, that the spirits are subject to you, but rather rejoice because your names have been written in the heavens."

21 In that hour יהושע exulted in the Spirit and said, "I praise You, Father, Master of the heaven and of the earth, that You have hidden these *matters* from clever and learned ones, and did reveal them to babes. Yes, Father, because thus it was well-pleasing in Your sight.

22 "All has been delivered to Me by My Father, and no one knows who the Son is, except the Father, and who the Father is, except the Son, and he to whom the Son wishes to reveal *Him*."

23 And turning to His taught ones He said, separately, "Blessed are the eyes that see what you see,

24 for I say to you that many prophets and sovereigns have wished to see what you see, and have not seen it, and to hear what you hear, and have not heard it."

25 And see, a certain one learned in the Torah stood up, trying Him, and saying, "Teacher, what shall I do to inherit everlasting life?"

26 And He said to him, "What has been written in the Torah? How do you read it?"

27 And he answering, said, " **'You shall love יהוה your Elohim with all your heart, and with all your being, and with all your strength, and with all your mind,'** Deb. 6:5 and **'your neighbour as yourself.'** " Way. 19:18

28 And He said to him, "You have answered rightly. **Do this and you shall live.**" Way. 18:5 [b]

29 But he, wishing to declare himself righteous, said to יהושע, "And who is my neighbour?"

30 And replying, יהושע said, "A certain man was going down from Yerushalayim to Yeriḥo, and fell among robbers, who, both stripping and beating him, went away, leaving him half dead.

31 "And by a coincidence a certain priest was going down that way. And when he saw him, he passed by on the other side.

32 "And likewise a Lĕwite also, when he came to the place, and seeing, passed by on the other side.

33 "But a certain Shomeroni,[c] journeying, came upon him. And when he saw him, he had compassion on him,

34 and he went to him and bandaged his wounds, pouring on oil and wine. And having placed him on his own beast, he brought him to an inn, and looked after him.

35 "And going out on the next day, he took out two denarii, gave them to the innkeeper, and said to him, 'Look after him, and whatever more you spend I shall repay you when I return.'

36 "Who, then, of these three, do you think, was neighbour to him who fell among the robbers?"

37 And he said, "He who showed compassion on him." Then יהושע said to him, "Go and do likewise."

38 And it came to be as they went that He entered into a certain village. And a certain woman named Martha received Him into her house.

39 And she had a sister called Miryam, who also sat at the feet of יהושע and heard His word.

40 But Martha was distracted with much serving, and coming up she said, "Master, are You not concerned that my sister has left me to serve alone? Speak to her then, to help me."

41 And יהושע answering, said to her, "Martha, Martha, you are worried and troubled about many *matters*,

42 but one only is necessary, and Miryam has chosen the good portion, which shall not be taken away from her."

11 And it came to be while He was praying in a certain place, as He

10b See also Mt. 19:17; Yn. 12:50 & Ḥazon 22:14. *10c* See 17:18.

ceased, one of His taught ones said to Him,
"Master, teach us to pray, as Yoḥanan also
taught his taught ones."
2 And He said to them, "When you pray,
say: Our Father in the heavens, let Your
Name be set-apart, let Your reign come, let
Your desire be done on earth as it is in
heaven.
3 "Give us day by day our daily bread.
4 "And forgive us our sins, for we also
forgive everyone who is indebted to us.
And do not lead us into trial, but rescue us
from the wicked one."
5 And He said to them, "Which of you
shall have a friend, and go to him at midnight and say to him, 'Friend, lend me
three loaves,
6 since a friend of mine has come to me
on his journey, and I do not have *food* to
set before him,'
7 then the one inside answering, says,
'Do not trouble me, the door is already
locked, and my children with me are in
bed. I am unable to get up and give to
you'?
8 "I say to you, if he does not get up and
give to him because he is his friend, he
shall get up and give him as many as he
needs because of his persistence.
9 "And I say to you: ask and it shall be
given to you, seek and you shall find,
knock and it shall be opened to you.
10 "For everyone asking receives, and he
who is seeking finds, and to him who is
knocking it shall be opened.
11 "And what father among you whose
son asks for bread shall give him a stone,
or if he asks for a fish shall give him a
snake instead of a fish,
12 or if he asks for an egg shall give him a
scorpion?
13 "If you then, being wicked, know how
to give good gifts to your children, how
much more shall your Father from heaven
give the Set-apart Spirit to those asking
Him!"
14 And He was casting out a demon, and it
was dumb. And it came to be, when the
demon had gone out, that the dumb spoke.
And the crowds marvelled.
15 But some of them said, "He casts out
demons by Beʿelzebul, the ruler of the
demons,"
16 and others, trying *Him*, were seeking
from Him a sign from heaven.
17 And He, knowing their thoughts, said
to them, "Every reign divided against itself
is laid waste, and a house *divided* against a
house falls.
18 "So if Satan also is divided against
himself, how shall his reign stand?
Because you say I cast out demons by
Beʿelzebul.
19 "Now if I cast out demons by
Beʿelzebul, by whom do your sons cast
them out? Because of this they shall be
your judges.
20 "But if I cast out demons by the finger
of Elohim, [a] then the reign of Elohim has
come upon you.
21 "When a strong man, having been well
armed, watches over his own court, his
possessions are in peace.
22 "But when a stronger than he comes
upon him and overcomes him, he takes
from him all his armour in which he trusted, and divides his booty.
23 "He who is not with Me is against Me,
and he who does not gather with Me scatters.
24 "When the unclean spirit goes out of a
man, he goes through dry places, seeking
rest. And finding none, he says, 'I shall
return to my house from which I came.'
25 "And when he comes, he finds it swept
and decorated,
26 then he goes and takes with him seven
other spirits more wicked than himself,
and they enter and dwell there. And the
last *state* of that man becomes worse than
the first."
27 And it came to be, as He was saying
this, a certain woman from the crowd
raised her voice and said to Him, "Blessed
is the womb that bore You, and the breasts
which You sucked!"
28 But He said, "Blessed rather are those
hearing the Word of Elohim and watching

11a See Shem. 31:18.

over it!" [b]
29 And while the crowds were thronging,
He began to say, "This generation is
wicked. It seeks a sign, and no sign shall
be given to it except the sign of Yonah the
prophet.
30 "For as Yonah became a sign to the
Ninewites, so also the Son of Aḏam shall
be to this generation.
31 "The sovereigness of the South shall
rise up in the judgment with the men of
this generation and shall condemn them,
for she came from the ends of the earth to
hear the wisdom of Shelomoh, and look, a
greater than Shelomoh is here.
32 "The men of Nineweh shall rise up in
the judgment with this generation and condemn it, for they repented at the preaching
of Yonah, and look, a greater than Yonah is
here.
33 "And no one, when he has lit a lamp,
puts it in a hidden place or under a basket,
but on a lampstand, that those who come in
shall see the light.
34 "The lamp of the body is the eye.
Therefore, when your eye is good, all your
body also is enlightened. But when your
eye is evil, [c] your body also is darkened.
35 "See to it therefore that the light which
is in you is not darkness.
36 "If then all your body is enlightened,
having no part dark, all shall be enlightened, as when the bright shining of a lamp
gives you light."
37 And as He spoke, a certain Pharisee
asked Him to dine with him, so He went in
and sat down to eat.
38 And when the Pharisee saw it, he marvelled that He did not first wash before
dinner.
39 And the Master said to him, "Now you
Pharisees make the outside of the cup and
dish clean, but your inward part is filled
with greed and wickedness.
40 "Mindless ones! Did not He who made
the outside make the inside also?
41 "But give in kindness of that which is
within, and see, all are clean to you.
42 "But woe to you Pharisees, because
you tithe the mint and the rue and every
plant, and pass by the right-ruling and the
love of Elohim. These you should have
done, without leaving the others undone.
43 "Woe to you Pharisees, because you
love the best seats in the congregations and
the greetings in the market-places.
44 "Woe to you, scribes and Pharisees,
hypocrites, because you are like the unseen
tombs, and the men walking over them do
not know."
45 And one of those learned in the Torah,
answering, said to Him, "Teacher, when
You say this You insult us too."
46 And He said, "Woe to you also, you
learned in the Torah, because you load men
with burdens hard to bear, and you yourselves do not touch the burdens with one of
your fingers.
47 "Woe to you, because you build the
tombs of the prophets, and your fathers
killed them.
48 "So you bear witness that you approve
of the works of your fathers, because they
indeed killed them, and you build their
tombs.
49 "And because of this the wisdom of
Elohim said, 'I shall send them prophets
and emissaries, and some of them they
shall kill and persecute,'
50 so that the blood of all the prophets
which was shed from the foundation of the
world shall be required of this generation,
51 from the blood of Heḇel to the blood of
Zeḵaryah who perished between the
slaughter-place and the Dwelling Place.
Yes, I say to you, it shall be required of this
generation.
52 "Woe to you learned in the Torah,
because you took away the key of knowledge. You did not enter in yourselves, and
those who were entering in you hindered."
53 And as He was saying this to them, the
scribes and the Pharisees began to oppose
Him fiercely, and to draw Him out on
many subjects,
54 watching Him, and seeking to catch

11b See 8:21. *11c* This is Hebrew idiom – *a good eye* means to be generous, while *an evil eye* means to be stingy. Also see Mish. 22:9, 23:6 & 28:22.

Him in whatever He says, so as to accuse Him.

12

Meanwhile, when an innumerable crowd of people had gathered together, so that they trampled one another, He began to say to His taught ones, first, “Beware of the leaven of the Pharisees, which is hypocrisy.

2 “And whatever is concealed shall be revealed, and whatever is hidden shall be known.

3 “So, whatever you have said in the dark shall be heard in the light, and what you have spoken in the ear in inner rooms shall be proclaimed on the house-tops.

4 “But I say to you, My friends, do not be afraid of those who kill the body, and after that are unable to do any more.

5 “But I shall show you whom you should fear: Fear the One who, after killing, possesses authority to cast into GĕHinnom. Yes, I say to you, fear Him!

6 “Are not five sparrows sold for two copper coins? And not one of them is forgotten before Elohim.

7 “But even the hairs of your head have all been numbered. Do not fear, you are worth more than many sparrows.

8 “And I say to you, everyone who confesses Me before men, the Son of Aḏam shall also confess him before the messengers of Elohim.

9 “But he that has denied Me before men shall be denied before the messengers of Elohim.

10 “And everyone who shall speak a word against the Son of Aḏam, it shall be forgiven him, but to him who has blasphemed against the Set-apart Spirit, it shall not be forgiven.

11 “And when they bring you to the congregations and rulers and authorities, do not worry about how or what you should answer, or what you should say,

12 for the Set-apart Spirit shall teach you in that very hour what you should say.”

13 And someone from the crowd said to Him, “Teacher, speak to my brother, to divide the inheritance with me.”

14 But He said to him, “Man, who made Me a judge or divider over you?”

15 And He said to them, “Mind, and beware of greed, because one’s life does not consist in the excess of his possessions.”

16 He then spoke a parable to them, saying, “The land of a certain rich man yielded well.

17 “And he was reasoning within himself, saying, ‘What shall I do, because I have no room to store my crops?’

18 “And he said, ‘I am going to do this: pull down my storehouses and build greater, and store all my crops and my goods there,

19 then say to myself, “Life, you have many goods laid up for many years, take your ease, eat, drink, rejoice.” ’

20 “But Elohim said to him, ‘You mindless one! This night your life shall be demanded from you. And who shall own what you have prepared?’

21 “So is he who is storing up treasure for himself, and is not rich toward Elohim.”

22 And He said to His taught ones, “For this reason I say to you, do not worry about your life, what you shall eat; nor about the body, what you shall put on.

23 “The life is more than the food, and the body is more than the clothing.

24 “Look at the ravens, for they neither sow nor reap, which have neither storehouse nor granary, and Elohim feeds them. How much more valuable are you than the birds?

25 “And which of you by worrying is able to add one cubit to his life’s span?

26 “If then you are unable to do the least, why do you worry about the rest?

27 “Look at the lilies, how they grow. They neither toil nor spin, and I say to you, even Shelomoh in all his esteem was not dressed like one of these.

28 “And if Elohim so clothes the grass, which today exists in the field and tomorrow is thrown into the furnace, how much more you, O you of little belief?

29 “And do not seek what you shall eat or what you shall drink, and do not keep worrying.

30 “For the nations of the world seek all

these, and your Father knows that you
need these.
31 "But seek the reign of Elohim, and all
these shall be added to you.
32 "Do not fear, little flock, because your
Father did delight to give you the reign.
33 "Sell your possessions and give in
kindness. Make yourselves purses which
do not grow old, a treasure in the heavens
that does not fail, where no thief does
come near nor moth destroys.
34 "For where your treasure is, there your
heart shall be also.
35 "Let your loins be girded and your
lamps burning,
36 and be like men waiting for their master, when he shall return from the wedding,
that when he comes and knocks they open
to him immediately.
37 "Blessed are those servants whom the
master, when he comes, shall find watching. Truly, I say to you that he shall gird
himself and make them sit down to eat,
and shall come and serve them.
38 "And if he comes in the second watch,
or in the third watch, and find them so,
blessed are those servants.
39 "And know this, that if the master of
the house had known what hour the thief
comes, he would have watched and not
allowed his house to be broken into.
40 "And you, then, be ready, for the Son of
Aḏam is coming at an hour you do not
expect."
41 And Kěpha said to Him, "Master, do
You speak this parable to us, or also to
all?"
42 And the Master said, "Who then is the
trustworthy and wise manager, whom his
master shall appoint over his household, to
give the portion of food in due season?
43 "Blessed is that servant whom his master shall find so doing when he comes.
44 "Truly, I say to you that he shall
appoint him over all his possessions.
45 "But if that servant says in his heart,
'My master is delaying his coming,' and
begins to beat the male servants and
female servants, and to eat and drink and
be drunk,
46 the master of that servant shall come on
a day when he does not expect him, and at
an hour that he does not know, and shall
cut him in two and appoint his portion with
the unbelievers.
47 "And that servant who knew his master's desire, and did not prepare, nor did
according to his desire, shall be beaten
with many *stripes*.
48 "But he who did not know, yet did what
deserved flogging, shall be beaten with
few. And everyone to whom much is
given, from him much shall be demanded.
And to whom much has been entrusted,
from him much more shall be asked.
49 "I came to send fire on the earth, and
how I wish it were already kindled!
50 "But I have an immersion to be
immersed with, and how distressed I am
until it is accomplished!
51 "Do you think that I came to give peace
on earth? I say to you, no, but rather division.
52 "For from now on five in one house
shall be divided, three against two, and two
against three –
53 father shall be divided against son, and
son against father, mother against daughter, and **daughter against mother**, mother-in-law against her daughter-in-law, and
**daughter-in-law against her mother-in-
law.**" Miḵ. 7:6
54 And He also said to the crowds, "When
you see a cloud rising out of the west,
immediately you say, 'A storm is coming,'
and so it is.
55 "And when you see the south wind
blow, you say, 'There shall be hot weather,' and it is.
56 "Hypocrites! You know to discern the
face of the heaven and of the earth, but
how is it you do not discern this time?
57 "And why, also, do you not judge for
yourselves what is right?
58 "For, as you go with your opponent to a
ruler, try hard along the way to settle with
him, lest he drag you to the judge, and the
judge deliver you to the officer, and the
officer throw you into prison.
59 "I say to you, you shall certainly not
leave there until you have paid even the
last mite."

13 And some were present at that
time, reporting to Him about the
Galileans whose blood Pilate had mixed
with their offerings.
2 And יהושע answering, said to them,
"Do you think that these Galileans were
worse sinners than all *other* Galileans,
because they have suffered like this?
3 "I say to you, no! But unless you repent
you shall all perish in the same way.
4 "Or those eighteen on whom the tower
in Shiloaḥ fell and killed them, do you
think that they were greater offenders than
all other men who dwelt in Yerushalayim?
5 "I say to you, no! But unless you repent
you shall all perish in the same way."
6 And He spoke this parable, "A certain
man had a fig tree planted in his vineyard,
and he came seeking fruit on it and found
none.
7 "And he said to the gardener, 'Look,
for three years I have come seeking
fruit on this fig tree and find none. Cut it
down, why does it even make the ground
useless?'
8 "And he answering, said to him,
'Master, leave it this year too, until I dig
around it and throw manure.
9 'And if indeed it bears fruit, *good*. But
if not so, you shall cut it down.' "
10 And He was teaching in one of the congregations on the Sabbath,
11 and see, there was a woman having a
weakening spirit for eighteen years, and
was bent over and was unable to straighten
up at all.
12 And יהושע, seeing her, called her near
and said to her, "Woman, you are loosened
from your weakness."
13 And He laid His hands on her, and
immediately she was straightened up, and
praised Elohim.
14 But the ruler of the congregation,
responding, much displeased that יהושע
had healed on the Sabbath, said to the
crowd, "There are six days on which men
should work, so come and be healed on
them, and not on the Sabbath day."
15 Then the Master answered him and
said, "Hypocrite! Does not each one of you
on the Sabbath loosen his ox or his donkey
from the stall, and lead it away to water it?
16 "And this one, being a daughter of
Aḇraham, whom Satan has bound, look,
for eighteen years, should she not be loosened from this bond on the Sabbath?"
17 And when He said this, all His opponents were put to shame. And all the crowd
rejoiced for all the splendid *works* being
done by Him.
18 Therefore He said, "What is the reign
of Elohim like? And to what shall I compare it?
19 "It is like a mustard seed, which a man
took and threw into his garden. And it
grew and became a large tree, and the birds
of the heavens nested in its branches."
20 And again He said, "To what shall I
compare the reign of Elohim?
21 "It is like leaven, which a woman took
and hid in three measures of flour until it
was all leavened."
22 And He was going through the cities
and villages, teaching, and journeying
toward Yerushalayim,
23 and someone said to Him, "Master, are
there few who are being saved?" And He
said to them,
24 "Strive to enter through the narrow
gate, because many, I say to you, shall seek
to enter in and shall not be able.
25 "When once the Master of the house
has risen up and shut the door, and you
begin to stand outside and knock at the
door, saying, 'Master, Master, open for us,'
and He shall answer and say to you, 'I do
not know you, where you are from,'
26 then you shall begin to say, 'We ate and
drank in Your presence, and You taught in
our streets.'
27 "But He shall say, 'I say to you I do not
know you, where you are from. **Depart
from Me, all you workers of unrighteousness**.' Teh. 6:8
28 "There shall be weeping and gnashing
of teeth, when you see Aḇraham and
Yitsḥaq and Yaʽaqoḇ [a] and all the prophets
in the reign of Elohim, and yourselves

13a Mt. 16:28-17:3.

thrown outside.
29“And they shall come from the east and
the west, and from the north and the south,
and sit down in the reign of Elohim.
30“And see, there are last who shall be
first, and there are first who shall be last.”
31On the same day there came certain
Pharisees, saying to Him, “Get out and go
from here, for Herodes wishes to kill You.”
32And He said to them, “Go, say to that
fox, ‘See, I cast out demons and perform
healings today and tomorrow, and the third
day I shall be perfected.’
33“But I have to journey today, and
tomorrow, and the day following, because
it is not fitting for a prophet to perish
outside of Yerushalayim.
34“Yerushalayim, Yerushalayim, killing
the prophets and stoning those who are
sent to her! How often I wished to gather
your children together, the way a hen *gathers* her chickens under her wings, but you
would not!
35“See, your House is left to you laid
waste. And truly I say to you, you shall by
no means see Me until *the time* comes
when you say, **‘Blessed is He who is coming in the Name of יהוה!’** ” Teh. 118:26 *b*

14 And it came to be, as He went into
the house of one of the rulers of the
Pharisees to eat bread on the Sabbath, that
they were watching Him closely.
2And see, there was a certain man before
Him suffering from dropsy.
3And יהושע responding, spoke to those
learned in the Torah and the Pharisees, saying, “Is it right to heal on the Sabbath?”
4But they were silent. So taking hold of
him He healed him, and let him go.
5And to them He said, “Which of you,
having a donkey or an ox that has fallen
into a pit, shall not immediately pull him
out on the Sabbath day?”
6And they were unable to answer Him
regarding these *matters*.
7And He spoke a parable to those who
were invited, when He noted how they
chose the best places, saying to them:
8“When you are invited by anyone to a
wedding feast, do not sit down in the best
place, lest one more distinguished than you
be invited by him,
9and he who invited you and him come
and say to you, ‘Give this one place,’ and
then you begin with shame to take the last
place.
10“Rather, when you are invited, go and
sit down in the last place, so that when he
who invited you comes he shall say to you,
‘Friend, come up higher.’ Then you shall
have esteem in the presence of those who
sit at the table with you.
11“For everyone who is exalting himself
shall be humbled, and he who is humbling
himself shall be exalted.”
12And He also said to him who invited
Him, “When you give a dinner or a supper,
do not ask your friends, nor your brothers,
nor your relatives, nor your rich neighbours, lest they also invite you back, and
you be repaid.
13“But when you give a feast, invite poor
ones, crippled ones, lame ones, blind ones,
14and you shall be blessed, because they
do not have to repay you. For you shall be
repaid at the resurrection of the righteous.”
15And when one of those who sat at the
table with Him heard this, he said to Him,
“Blessed is he who eats bread in the reign
of Elohim!”
16But He said to him, “A certain man
gave a great supper and invited many,
17and he sent his servant at supper time to
say to those who were invited, ‘Come, for
all is now ready.’
18“But one by one they all began making
excuses. The first said to him, ‘I have
bought a field, and I need to go and see it. I
ask you to have me excused.’
19“And another said, ‘I have bought five
yoke of oxen, and I am going to try them
out. I ask you to have me excused.’
20“And another said, ‘I have married a
wife, and because of this I am unable to
come.’
21“And that servant came and reported
this to his master. Then the master of the

13b See Mt. 23:39.

house, being wroth, said to his servant,
'Hurry out into the streets and lanes of
the city, and bring in here the poor, and
crippled, and lame, and blind.'
22 "And the servant said, 'Master, it is
done as you commanded, and still there is
room.'
23 "And the master said to the servant,
'Go out into the street corners and hedges,
and compel them to come in, so that my
house is filled.
24 'For I say to you that none of those men
who were invited shall taste my supper.' "
25 And large crowds were going with
Him, and turning, He said to them,
26 "If anyone comes to Me and does not
hate [a] his father and mother, and wife, and
children, and brothers, and sisters, and his
own life too, he is unable to be My taught
one.
27 "And whoever does not bear his stake
and come after Me is unable to be My
taught one.
28 "For who of you, wishing to build a
tower, does not sit down first and count the
cost, whether he has *enough* to complete
it?
29 "Otherwise, when he has laid the foundation, and is unable to finish it, all who
see it begin to mock him,
30 saying, 'This man began to build and
was unable to finish.'
31 "Or what sovereign, going to fight
against another sovereign, does not sit
down first and take counsel whether he is
able with ten thousand to meet him who
comes against him with twenty thousand?
32 "And if not, while the other is still far
away, he sends a delegation and asks conditions of peace.
33 "So, then, everyone of you who does
not give up all that he has, is unable to be
My taught one. [b]
34 "The salt is good, but if the salt
becomes tasteless, with what shall it be
seasoned?
35 "It is not fit for land, nor for manure,
they throw it out. He who has ears to hear,
let him hear!"

15 Now all the tax collectors and the
sinners were coming to Him to
hear Him.
2 And the Pharisees and scribes grumbled, saying, "This One receives sinners
and eats with them."
3 And He spoke this parable to them,
saying,
4 "What man among you, having a hundred sheep, and having lost one of them,
does not leave the ninety-nine in the
wilderness and go after the one which is
lost until he finds it?
5 "And having found it, he lays it on his
shoulders, rejoicing.
6 "And having come home, he calls
together his friends and neighbours, saying
to them, 'Rejoice with me, for I have found
my sheep which was lost!'
7 "I say to you that in the same way there
shall be more joy in the heaven over one
sinner repenting, than over ninety-nine
righteous ones who need no repentance.
8 "Or what woman, having ten silver
coins, if she loses one coin, does not light
a lamp and sweep the house, and seek
diligently till she finds it?
9 "And having found it, she calls friends
and neighbours together, saying, 'Rejoice
with me, for I have found the coin which I
lost!'
10 "I say to you, in the same way there is
joy in the presence of the messengers of
Elohim over one sinner repenting."
11 And He said, "A certain man had two
sons,
12 and the younger of them said to his
father, 'Father, give me the portion of
goods falling *to me*.' And he divided his
livelihood between them.
13 "And not many days after, the younger
son, having gathered all together, went
away to a distant country, and there wasted
his goods with loose [a] living.
14 "And when he had spent all, there arose
a severe scarcity of food throughout that
land, and he began to be in need.
15 "And he went and joined himself to one
of the citizens of that country, and he sent

14a To *love less*. *14b* See 9:62, Yn. 12:24-26, Pilip. 3:7, Iḇ`rim 11:26. *15a* Or *unbridled*.

him to his fields to feed pigs.
16 “And he was longing to fill his stomach
with the pods which the pigs were eating,
and no one gave to him.
17 “But having come to himself, he said,
‘How many of my father’s hired servants
have bread enough and to spare, and I am
perishing with hunger!
18 ‘Having risen, I shall go to my father
and say to him, “Father, I have sinned
against the heaven, and before you,
19 and I am no longer worthy to be called
your son. Make me like one of your hired
servants.” ’
20 “And having risen, he went to his
father. And while he was still a long way
off, his father saw him and was moved
with compassion, and ran and fell on his
neck and kissed him.
21 “And the son said to him, ‘Father, I
have sinned against the heaven, and before
you, and I am no longer worthy to be
called your son.’
22 “But the father said to his servants,
‘Bring out the best robe and put it on him,
and put a ring on his hand and sandals on
his feet.
23 ‘And bring the fattened calf here and
slaughter it, and let us eat and rejoice,
24 because this son of mine was dead and
is alive again, and he was lost and is
found.’ And they began to rejoice.
25 “And his older son was in the field, and
when he came and approached the house,
he heard music and dancing.
26 “And having called one of the servants
he asked what this meant.
27 “And he said to him, ‘Your brother has
come, and your father has slaughtered the
fattened calf because he received him back
in health.’
28 “And he was wroth and would not go
in. So his father came out and pleaded with
him.
29 “And answering, he said to his father,
‘See, these many years I have been serving
you, and I have never transgressed a command of yours, but to me you have never
given a young goat, so I could rejoice with
my friends.
30 ‘But when this son of yours came, who
has devoured your livelihood with whores,
you slaughtered the fattened calf for him.’
31 “Then he said to him, ‘Son, you are
always with me, and all I have is yours.
32 ‘And we had to rejoice and be glad, for
your brother was dead and is alive, and
was lost and is found.’ ”

16 And He also said to His taught
ones, “There was a certain rich
man who had a manager and he was
accused to him as wasting his possessions.
2 “So having called him he said to him,
‘What is this I hear about you? Give an
account of your management, for you are
no longer able to be manager.’
3 “And the manager said within himself,
‘What shall I do? For my master is taking
the managership away from me. I am
unable to dig, I am ashamed to beg.
4 ‘I know what I shall do, that, when I am
removed from the managership, they
might receive me into their houses.’
5 “And calling every one of his master’s
debtors to him, he said to the first, ‘How
much do you owe my master?’
6 “And he said, ‘A hundred measures of
oil.’ And he said to him, ‘Take your bill,
and sit down quickly and write fifty.’
7 “Then to another he said, ‘And how
much do you owe?’ And he said, ‘A hundred measures of wheat.’ And he said to
him, ‘Take your bill, and write eighty.’
8 “And the master praised the unrighteous manager because he had acted
shrewdly, because the sons of this age are
more shrewd in their generation than the
sons of light.
9 “And I say to you, make friends for
yourselves by unrighteous mammon, [a] that
when you fail, they shall receive you into
everlasting dwellings.
10 “He who is trustworthy in what is least,
is trustworthy also in much. And he who is
unrighteous in what is least is unrighteous
also in much.
11 “If, therefore, you have not been trust-

16a Deity of wealth.

worthy in the unrighteous mammon, who
shall entrust to you the true?
12 "And if you have not been trustworthy
in what is another man's, who shall give
you what is your own?
13 "No servant is able to serve two masters, for either he shall hate the one and
love the other, or else he shall cling to the
one and despise the other. You are not able
to serve Elohim and mammon."
14 And the Pharisees, who loved silver,
also heard all this, and were sneering at
Him,
15 so He said to them, "You are those who
declare yourselves righteous before men,
but Elohim knows your hearts, because
what is highly thought of among men is an
abomination in the sight of Elohim.
16 "The Torah and the prophets are until
Yoḥanan. Since then the reign of Elohim is
being announced, and everyone is doing
violence [b] upon it.
17 "And it is easier for the heaven and the
earth to pass away than for one tittle of the
Torah to fall. [c]
18 "Everyone putting away his wife and
marrying another commits adultery. And
everyone marrying her who is put away
from her husband commits adultery. [d]
19 "But there was a certain rich man who
used to dress in purple and fine linen and
lived luxuriously every day.
20 "And there was a certain beggar named
Elʿazar, being covered with sores, who was
placed at his gate,
21 and longing to be fed with the crumbs
which fell from the rich man's table.
Indeed, even the dogs came and licked his
sores.
22 "And it came to be that the beggar died,
and was carried by the messengers to the
bosom of Aḇraham. And the rich man also
died and was buried.
23 "And while suffering tortures in She'ol,
having lifted up his eyes, he saw Aḇraham
far away, and Elʿazar in his bosom.
24 "And crying out he said, 'Father Aḇraham, have compassion on me, and send
Elʿazar to dip the tip of his finger in water
and cool my tongue, for I am suffering in
this flame.'
25 "But Aḇraham said, 'Son, remember
that in your life you received your good,
and likewise Elʿazar the evil, but now he is
comforted and you are suffering.
26 'And besides all this, between us and
you a great chasm has been set, so that
those who wish to pass from here to you
are unable, nor do those from there pass
to us.'
27 "And he said, 'Then I beg you, father,
that you would send him to my father's
house,
28 for I have five brothers, let him warn
them, lest they also come to this place of
torture.'
29 "Aḇraham said to him, 'They have
Mosheh and the prophets, let them hear
them.'
30 "And he said, 'No, father Aḇraham, but
if someone from the dead goes to them,
they shall repent.'
31 "But he said to him, 'If they do not hear
Mosheh and the prophets, [e] neither would
they be persuaded even if one should rise
from the dead.' "

17

And He said to the taught ones, "It
is inevitable that stumbling-blocks
should come, but woe to him through
whom they come!
2 "It would be better for him if a millstone is put around his neck, and he were
thrown into the sea, than that he should
cause one of these little ones to stumble.
3 "Take heed to yourselves. If your brother sins against you, rebuke him, and if he
repents, forgive him.
4 "And if he sins against you seven times
in a day, and seven times in a day comes
back to you, saying, 'I repent,' you shall
forgive him."
5 And the emissaries said to the Master,
"Give us more belief."
6 And the Master said, "If you have
belief as a mustard seed, you would say to

16b See Yeḥez. 22:26, Tseph. 3:4. *16c* See *Law* in Explanatory Notes. *16d* See footnote Mt. 5:32.
16e See 9:33, Mal. 4:4-5.

this mulberry tree, ‘Be pulled up by the
roots and be planted in the sea,’ and it
would obey you.
7 “But who of you, having a servant
ploughing or shepherding, would say to
him when he has come in from the field,
‘Come immediately and sit down to eat’?
8 “But would he not rather say to him,
‘Prepare somewhat for my supper, and gird
yourself and serve me while I eat and
drink, and afterward you shall eat and
drink’?
9 “Would he thank that servant because
he did what he was commanded? I think
not.
10 “So also you, when you have done all
that you were commanded, say, ‘We are
unworthy servants, we have done what
was our duty to do.’ ”
11 And it came to be, as He went to
Yerushalayim, that He passed through the
midst of Shomeron and Galil.
12 And as He was entering into a certain
village, He was met by ten leprous men,
who stood at a distance.
13 And they lifted up their voices, saying,
“יהושע, Master, have compassion on us!”
14 And having seen *them*, He said to them,
“Go, show yourselves to the priests.” And
it came to be, that as they were going, they
were cleansed.
15 And one of them, when he saw that he
was healed, returned, praising Elohim with
a loud voice,
16 and he fell down upon his face at His
feet, giving thanks to Him. And he was a
Shomeroni.
17 And יהושע answering, said, “Were
there not ten cleansed? But where are the
nine?
18 “Was no one found to return to give
praise to Elohim, except this foreigner?” [a]
19 And He said to him, “Rise, go your
way. Your belief has made you well.”
20 And having been asked by the
Pharisees when the reign of Elohim would
come, He answered them and said, “The
reign of Elohim does not come with intent
watching,
21 nor shall they say, ‘Look here!’ or
‘Look there!’ For look, the reign of Elohim
is in your midst!”
22 And He said to the taught ones, “Days
shall come when you shall long to see one
of the days of the Son of Aḏam, but you
shall not see it.
23 “And they shall say to you, ‘Look
here!’ or ‘Look there!’ Do not go after
them, nor follow.
24 “For as the lightning that flashes out of
one part under heaven shines to the other
part under heaven, so also the Son of
Aḏam shall be in His day.
25 “But first He has to suffer much and be
rejected by this generation.
26 “And as it came to be in the days of
Noaḥ, so also shall it be in the days of the
Son of Aḏam:
27 “They were eating, they were drinking,
they were marrying, they were given in
marriage, until the day that Noaḥ went into
the ark, and the flood came and destroyed
them all.
28 “And likewise, as it came to be in the
days of Lot: They were eating, they were
drinking, they were buying, they were selling, they were planting, they were building,
29 but on the day Lot went out of Seḏom it
rained fire and sulphur from heaven and
destroyed all.
30 “It shall be the same in the day the Son
of Aḏam is revealed.
31 “In that day, he who shall be on the
house-top, and his goods in the house, let
him not come down to take them away.
And likewise the one who is in the field,
let him not turn back.
32 “Remember the wife of Lot.
33 “Whoever seeks to save his life shall
lose it, and whoever loses his life shall preserve it.
34 “I say to you, in that night there shall be
two in one bed, the one shall be taken and
the other shall be left.
35 “Two *women* shall be grinding together, the one shall be taken and the other
shall be left.

17a The Greek word referring to this Shomeroni is *allogenes*, which means “of another race.”

36 "Two [b] shall be in the field, the one
shall be taken and the other shall be left."
37 And they answering, said to Him,
"Where, Master?" And He said to them,
"Where the body is, there also the
vultures [c] shall be gathered together."

18

And He spoke a parable to them,
that they should always pray and
not lose heart,
2 saying, "In a certain city there was a
certain judge, not fearing Elohim nor
regarding man.
3 "And a widow was in that city, and she
came to him, saying, 'Do right to me on
my adversary.'
4 "And he would not for a while, but
afterward he said within himself, 'Even if I
do not fear Elohim nor regard man,
5 yet because this widow troubles me I
shall do right to her, lest by her continual
coming she wears me out.' "
6 And the Master said, "Hear what the
unrighteous judge said.
7 "And shall Elohim not do right by all
means to His own chosen ones who are
crying out day and night to Him, and being
patient over them?
8 "I say to you that He shall do right to
them speedily. But when the Son of Aḏam
comes, shall He find the belief on the
earth?"
9 And He also spoke this parable to some
who relied on themselves that they were
righteous, and looking down on others:
10 "Two men went up to the Set-apart
Place to pray – the one a Pharisee and the
other a tax collector.
11 "The Pharisee stood and began to pray
with himself this way, 'Elohim, I thank
You that I am not like the rest of men,
swindlers, unrighteous, adulterers, or even
as this tax collector.
12 'I fast twice a week, I give tithes of all
that I possess.'
13 "But the tax collector standing at a distance would not even raise his eyes to the
heaven, but was beating his breast, saying,
'Elohim, show favour unto me, a sinner!'
14 "I say to you, this man went down
to his house declared right, rather than the
other. For everyone who is exalting himself shall be humbled, and he who is humbling himself shall be exalted."
15 And they also brought infants to Him to
touch them, but His taught ones seeing it,
rebuked them.
16 But יהושע called them to Him and
said, "Let the little children come to Me,
and do not forbid them, for of such is the
reign of Elohim.
17 "Truly, I say to you, whoever does not
receive the reign of Elohim as a little child,
shall certainly not enter into it."
18 And a certain ruler asked Him, saying,
"Good Teacher, what shall I do to inherit
everlasting life?"
19 So יהושע said to him, "Why do you
call Me good? No one is good except One
– Elohim.
20 "You know the commands, **'Do not
commit adultery,' 'Do not murder,'
'Do not steal,' 'Do not bear false witness,' 'Respect your father and your
mother.'** " Shem. 20:12-16, Deḇ. 5:16-20
21 And he said, "All these I have watched
over from my youth."
22 And hearing this, יהושע said to him,
"Yet one you lack: Sell all that you have
and distribute to the poor, and you shall
have treasure in heaven. And come, follow
Me."
23 But when he heard this, he became
intensely sad, for he was extremely rich.
24 And when יהושע saw that he became
intensely sad, He said, "How hard it is for
those who have money to enter into the
reign of Elohim!
25 "For it is easier for a camel to enter
through a needle's eye than for a rich man
to enter into the reign of Elohim."
26 And those who heard it said, "And who
is able to be saved?"
27 And He said, "What is impossible with
men is possible with Elohim."
28 And Kěpha said, "See, we have left all
and followed You."
29 And He said to them, "Truly, I say to

17b Mt. 24:40. Some manuscripts do not contain this verse, 17:36. *17c* See Mt. 24:28.

you, there is no one who has left house or
parents or brothers or wife or children, for
the sake of the reign of Elohim,
30 who shall not receive many times more
in this present time, and in the age to come
everlasting life." [a]
31 And taking the twelve aside, He said to
them, "See, we are going up to Yerushalayim, and all that have been written by the
prophets about the Son of Aḏam shall be
accomplished.
32 "For He shall be delivered up to the
nations and shall be mocked and insulted
and spat upon,
33 and having flogged Him they shall kill
Him. And on the third day He shall rise
again."
34 But they understood none of this, and
this word was hidden from them, and they
did not know what was being said.
35 And it came to be, that as He was coming near Yeriḥo, that a certain blind man
was sitting by the way begging.
36 And hearing a crowd passing by, he
asked what it meant.
37 And they reported to him that יהושע of
Natsareth was passing by.
38 And he cried out, saying, "יהושע, Son
of Dawiḏ, have compassion on me!"
39 And those going before were rebuking
him that he should be silent, but he was
crying out much more, "Son of Dawiḏ,
have compassion on me!"
40 And יהושע stopped and commanded
him to be brought to Him. And when he
had come near, He asked him,
41 saying, "What do you wish Me to do
for you?" And he said, "Master, to receive
my sight."
42 And יהושע said to him, "Receive your
sight! Your belief has saved you."
43 And immediately he received his sight,
and was following Him, praising Elohim.
And all the people, seeing it, gave praise to
Elohim.

19

And having entered, He was passing through Yeriḥo.
2 And see, a man called Zakkai! And he
was a chief tax collector, and he was rich,
3 and he was seeking to see who יהושע
was, but was unable because of the crowd,
for he was small in stature.
4 And having run ahead, he climbed up
into a sycamore tree to see Him, because
He was about to pass by.
5 And as יהושע came to the place, He
looked up and saw him, and said to him,
"Zakkai, hurry and come down, for I have
to stay at your house today."
6 And he hurried and came down, and
received Him, rejoicing.
7 And seeing it, they all grumbled, saying, "He has gone in to stay with a man
who is a sinner."
8 But Zakkai stood up and said to the
Master, "Look, Master, I give half of my
possessions to the poor. And if I have
taken whatever from anyone by false accusation, I repay fourfold."
9 And יהושע said to him, "Today deliverance has come to this house – since he
also is a son of Aḇraham.
10 "For the Son of Aḏam has come to seek
and to save what was lost."
11 And as they were hearing this, He
spoke another parable, because He was
near Yerushalayim and they thought the
reign of Elohim was about to be manifested straightaway.
12 He therefore said, "A certain nobleman
went to a distant country to receive for
himself a reign and to return.
13 "And calling ten of his servants, he
gave them ten minas, and said to them,
'Trade until I come.'
14 "But his subjects were hating him, and
sent a delegation after him, to say, 'We do
not wish this one to reign over us.'
15 "And it came to be, when he came
back, having received the reign, that he
sent for these servants to whom he had
given the silver, in order to know what
each had gained by trading.
16 "And the first came, saying, 'Master,
your mina has earned ten minas.'
17 "And he said to him, 'Well done, good
servant. Because you were trustworthy in a

18a See Mt. 6:33, Mt. 19:29, Mq. 10:29.

small *matter*, have authority over ten cities.’

18 “And the second came, saying, ‘Master, your mina has earned five minas.’

19 “And he said to him also, ‘And you – be over five cities.’

20 “And another came, saying, ‘Master, here is your mina, which I kept laid up in a handkerchief.

21 ‘For I was afraid of you, because you are a hard man. You take up what you did not lay down, and reap what you did not sow.’

22 “And he said to him, ‘Out of your own mouth I shall judge you, you wicked servant. You knew that I was a hard man, taking up what I did not lay down and reaping what I did not sow.

23 ‘Why did you not put the silver in the bank, that when I come I could have collected it with interest?’

24 “Then he said to those who stood by, ‘Take the mina from him, and give it to him who possesses ten minas.’

25 “But they said to him, ‘Master, he *already* possesses ten minas.’

26 ‘For I say to you, that to everyone who possesses shall be given; and from him who does not possess, even what he possesses shall be taken away from him.

27 ‘But those enemies of mine who did not wish me to reign over them, bring them here and slay them before me.’ ”

28 And having said this, He went on ahead, going up to Yerushalayim.

29 And it came to be, when He came near to Bĕyth Phaği and Bĕyth Anyah, at the mountain of Olives, that He sent two of His taught ones,

30 saying, “Go into the village opposite you, in which, as you enter, you shall find a colt tied, on which no one has ever sat. Loosen it and bring it here.

31 “And if anyone asks you, ‘Why do you loosen it?’ thus you shall say to him, ‘Because the Master has need of it.’ ”

32 And those who were sent went away and found it as He had said to them.

33 And as they were loosing the colt, the owners of it said to them, “Why do you loosen the colt?”

34 And they said, “The Master needs it.”

35 So they brought it to יהושע. And throwing their garments on the colt, they set יהושע on it.

36 And as He went, they were spreading their garments on the way.

37 And as He was coming near, already at the descent of the Mount of Olives, the entire crowd of the taught ones began rejoicing, to praise Elohim with a loud voice for all the miracles they had seen,

38 saying, “ **‘Blessed is** the Sovereign **who is coming in the Name of יהוה!** Teh. 118:26 *a* Peace in heaven and esteem in the highest!”

39 And some of the Pharisees from the crowd said to Him, “Teacher, rebuke Your taught ones.”

40 But He answering, said to them, “I say to you that if these shall be silent, the stones would cry out.”

41 And as He came near, He saw the city and wept over it,

42 saying, “If you only knew even today, the *matters* for your peace! But now they are hidden from your eyes.

43 “Because days shall come upon you when your enemies shall build a rampart around you, and surround you and press you on all sides,

44 and dash you to the ground, and your children within you. And they shall not leave in you one stone upon another, because you did not know the time of your visitation.”

45 And having entered into the Set-apart Place, He began to drive out those selling and buying in it,

46 saying to them, “It has been written, **‘My House is a house of prayer,’** Yesh. 56:7 but you have made it a **‘den of robbers.’** ” Yirm. 7:11

47 And He was teaching daily in the Set-apart Place. But the chief priests and the scribes and the leaders of the people were seeking to destroy Him,

48 but they did not find what they might

19a Mt. 23:39.

do, for all the people were hanging upon
Him, listening.

20 And it came to be, on one of those
days, as He was teaching the people in the Set-apart Place and bringing the
Good News, that the chief priests and the
scribes, together with the elders, came up
2 and spoke to Him, saying, "Say to us,
by what authority are You doing these? Or
who is he who gave You this authority?"
3 And He answering, said to them, "I
shall ask you one question too, and answer
Me:
4 "The immersion of Yoḥanan – was it
from heaven or from men?"
5 And they debated among themselves,
saying, "If we say, 'From heaven,' He shall
say, 'Then why did you not believe him?'
6 "But if we say, 'From men,' all the people shall stone us, for they are persuaded
that Yoḥanan was a prophet."
7 And they answered that they did not
know from where it was.
8 And יהושע said to them, "Neither do I
say to you by what authority I do these."
9 And He began to speak this parable to
the people, "A certain man planted a vineyard, and leased it to farmers, and went
away for a long time.
10 "And at *harvest* time he sent a servant
to the farmers, to give him some of the
fruit of the vineyard. But the farmers beat
him and sent him away empty-handed.
11 "And again he sent another servant.
And they beat him too and maltreated him,
and sent him away empty-handed.
12 "And again he sent a third. And they
wounded him too and cast him out.
13 "And the owner of the vineyard said,
'What shall I do? I shall send my son, the
beloved. They might respect him when
they see him.'
14 "But when the farmers saw him, they
reasoned among themselves, saying, 'This
is the heir. Come, let us kill him, so that the
inheritance becomes ours.'
15 "And they cast him out of the vineyard
and killed him. What, then, shall the owner
of the vineyard do to them?
16 "He shall come and destroy those farmers and give the vineyard to others." And
having heard, they said, "Let it not be!"
17 But He looked at them and said, "What
then is this that has been written, **'The
stone which the builders rejected has
become the chief corner-stone'**? Teh. 118:22
18 "Everyone who falls on that stone shall
be broken, but on whomever it falls, he
shall be pulverised."
19 And the chief priests and the scribes
sought to lay hands on Him in the same
hour, but they feared the people, for they
knew that He had spoken this parable
against them.
20 And keeping a close watch *on Him*,
they sent spies who pretended to be righteous, to catch Him in a word, in order to
deliver Him to the rule and to the authority
of the governor.
21 So they asked Him, saying, "Teacher,
we know that You say and teach rightly,
and You are not partial to any, but teach the
way of Elohim truly,
22 "Is it right for us to pay taxes to Caesar
or not?"
23 But perceiving their craftiness, He said
to them, "Why do you try Me?
24 "Show Me a denarius. Whose likeness
and inscription does it have?" And they
answering, said, "Caesar's."
25 And He said to them, "Then give to
Caesar what is Caesar's, and to Elohim
what is Elohim's."
26 And they were unable to catch Him in a
saying in the presence of the people, and
marvelling at His answer, they were silent.
27 And some of the Sadducees, who deny
that there is a resurrection, came to Him
and asked Him,
28 saying, "Teacher, Mosheh wrote to us
that **if a man's brother dies, having a
wife, and he dies childless, his brother
should take his wife and raise up offspring for his brother.** Deb. 25:5
29 "Now, there were seven brothers, and
the first took a wife, and died childless.
30 "And the second took her as wife, and
he died childless.
31 "And the third took her, and in the same
way the seven also. And they left no children, and died.

[32]"And last of all the woman died too.
[33]"At the resurrection, then, whose wife
does she become? For the seven had her as
wife."
[34]And יהושע answering, said to them,
"The sons of this age marry and are given
in marriage,
[35]but those who are counted worthy of
attaining that age, and the resurrection
from the dead, neither marry, nor are they
given in marriage,
[36]for neither is it possible for them to die
any more, because they are like messengers and are sons of Elohim, being sons of
the resurrection.
[37]"But that the dead are raised, even
Mosheh showed at the bush when he called
יהוה **'the Elohim of Aḇraham, and the
Elohim of Yitsḥaq, and the Elohim of
Ya'aqoḇ.'** Shem. 3:6
[38]"Now He is not the Elohim of the dead,
but of the living, for all live to Him."
[39]And some of the scribes answering,
said, "Teacher, You have spoken well."
[40]And they were not bold *enough* to
question Him any more.
[41]And He said to them, "How do they say
that the Messiah is the Son of Dawiḏ?
[42]"For Dawiḏ himself said in the Book of
Tehillim, **'יהוה' said to my Master, "sit at
My right hand,**
[43]**until I make Your enemies a footstool
of Your feet." '** Teh. 110:1
[44]"Dawiḏ then calls Him 'Master,' how is
He then his Son?"
[45]And in the hearing of all the people, He
said to His taught ones,
[46]"Beware of the scribes, who like to
walk in long robes, and love greetings in
the market-places, and the best seats in the
congregations, and the best places at
feasts,
[47]who devour widows' houses, and for
a show make long prayers. They shall
receive greater judgment."

21
And looking up He saw the rich
putting their gifts into the treasury,
[2]and He saw a certain poor widow
putting in two mites.
[3]And He said, "Truly I say to you that
this poor widow has put in more than all.
[4]"For all these out of their excess have
put in offerings for Elohim, but she out of
her poverty has put in all that she had to
live on."
[5]And as some were speaking about the
Set-apart Place, that it was adorned with
goodly stones and gifts, He said,
[6]"These that you see – the days are coming in which not one stone shall be left
upon another that shall not be thrown
down."
[7]And they asked Him, saying, "Teacher,
but when shall this be? And what is the
sign when this is about to take place?"
[8]And He said, "See that you are not led
astray, for many shall come in My Name,
saying, 'I am,' and, 'The time is near.'
Then do not go after them.
[9]"But when you hear of fightings and
unrests, do not be alarmed, for these have
to take place first, but the end is not immediately."
[10]Then He said to them, "Nation [a] shall
rise against nation, and reign against reign.
[11]"And there shall be great earthquakes
in various places, and scarcities of food
and deadly diseases. And there shall be
horrors, and great signs from heaven.
[12]"But before all this, they shall lay
their hands on you and persecute you,
delivering you up to the congregations and
prisons, being brought before sovereigns
and rulers for My Name's sake.
[13]"And it shall turn out to you for a
witness.
[14]"Therefore, resolve in your hearts not
to premeditate on what to answer.
[15]"For I shall give you a mouth and
wisdom which all your adversaries shall
not be able to refute or resist.
[16]"And you shall also be betrayed by parents and brothers and relatives and friends.
And some of you shall be put to death.
[17]"And you shall be hated by all because
of My Name.
[18]"But not a hair of your head shall be

21a The Greek word for nation is *ethnos* which could also mean "ethnic group."

lost at all.
19 "Possess your lives by your endurance!
20 "And when you see Yerushalayim
surrounded by armies, then know that its
laying waste is near.
21 "Then let those in Yehuḏah flee to the
mountains, and let those who are in the
midst of her go out, and let not those who
are in the fields enter her.
22 "Because these are days of vengeance,
to fill all that have been written.
23 "And woe to those who are pregnant
and to those who are nursing children in
those days! For there shall be great distress
in the earth and wrath upon this people.
24 "And they shall fall by the edge of the
sword, and be led away captive into all
nations. And Yerushalayim shall be trampled underfoot by the nations [b] until the
times of the nations are filled.
25 "And there shall be signs in the sun,
and moon, and stars, and on the earth
anxiety of nations, in bewilderment at the
roaring of the sea, and agitation,
26 men fainting from fear and the expectation of what is coming on the earth, for **the
powers of the heavens shall be shaken.**
Ḥag. 2:6,21
27 "And then they shall see **the Son of
Aḏam coming in a cloud** Dan. 7:13 with
power and much esteem.
28 "And when these *matters* begin to take
place, look up and lift up your heads,
because your redemption draws near."
29 And He spoke a parable to them, "Look
at the fig tree, and all the trees.
30 "When they have already budded,
observing it, you shall know for yourselves
that summer is now near.
31 "So you also, when you see these *matters* take place, know that the reign of
Elohim is near.
32 "Truly, I say to you, this generation
shall by no means pass away till all shall
have taken place.
33 "The heaven and the earth shall pass
away, but My words shall by no means
pass away.
34 "And take heed to yourselves, lest your
hearts be weighed down by gluttony, and
drunkenness, and worries of this life, and
that day come on you suddenly.
35 "For it shall come as a snare on all
those dwelling on the face of all the earth.
36 "Watch then at all times, and pray that
you be counted worthy to escape all this
about to take place, and to stand before the
Son of Aḏam."
37 And He was teaching in the Set-apart
Place by day, but at night He went out and
stayed on the mountain of Olives,
38 and early in the morning all the people
came to Him in the Set-apart Place to hear
Him.

22 And the Festival of Matzot [a] drew
near, which is called Pěsaḥ. [b]
2 And the chief priests and the scribes
were seeking how to kill Him, for they
feared the people.
3 And Satan entered into Yehuḏah, who
was called *man* from Qerioth, who was
numbered among the twelve.
4 And he went and spoke with the chief
priests and captains, how he might deliver
Him up to them.
5 And they were glad, and agreed to give
him silver.
6 And he promised, and was seeking an
occasion to deliver Him up to them, away
from the crowd.
7 And the Day of Unleavened Bread
came when the Pěsaḥ [b] had to be slaughtered.
8 And He sent Kěpha and Yoḥanan,
saying, "Go and prepare the Pěsaḥ for us to
eat."
9 And they said to Him, "Where do You
wish us to prepare?"
10 And He said to them, "See, as you enter
into the city, a man shall meet you carrying
a jar of water. Follow him into the house
he enters.
11 "And you shall say to the master of the
house, 'The Teacher says to you, "Where
is the guest room where I might eat the
Pěsaḥ with My taught ones?" '
12 "And he shall show you a large, fur-

21b See Ber. 48:19, Teh. 79:1, Rom. 11:25. *22a* - Unleavened Bread. *22b* - Passover.

nished upper room. Prepare it there."
13 And going they found it as He had said
to them, and they prepared the Pěsaḥ.
14 And when the hour had come, He sat
down, and the twelve emissaries with Him.
15 And He said to them, "With desire I
have desired to eat this Pěsaḥ with you
before My suffering,
16 for I say to you, I shall certainly not eat
of it again until it is filled in the reign of
Elohim."
17 And taking the cup, giving thanks, He
said, "Take this and divide it among yourselves,
18 for I say to you, I shall certainly not
drink of the fruit of the vine until the reign
of Elohim comes."
19 And taking bread, giving thanks, He
broke it and gave it to them, saying, "This
is My body which is given for you, do this
in remembrance of Me."
20 Likewise the cup also, after supper,
saying, "This cup is the renewed covenant
in My blood which is shed for you.
21 "But see, the hand of him delivering
Me up is with Me on the table.
22 "For indeed the Son of Aḏam goes as it
has been decreed, but woe to that man by
whom He is delivered up!"
23 And they began to ask among themselves, which of them it could be who was
about to do this.
24 And there also took place a dispute
among them, as to which of them seemed
to be greater.
25 And He said to them, "The sovereigns
of the nations rule over them, and those
who control them are called 'workers of
good.'
26 "But not so with you, but let him who is
greatest among you be as the youngest,
and the leader as one who serves.
27 "For who is greater, the one who sits at
the table, or the one who serves? Is it not
the one who sits at the table? But I am in
your midst as the One who serves.
28 "But you are those who have remained
with Me in My trials.
29 "And I covenant for you, as My Father
covenanted for Me, a reign,
30 to eat and drink at My table, in My
reign, and to sit on thrones, judging the
twelve tribes of Yisra'ěl."
31 And the Master said, "Shim'on,
Shim'on! See, Satan has asked for you to
sift *you* as wheat.
32 "But I have prayed for you, that your
belief should not fail. And when you have
turned, strengthen your brothers."
33 And he said to Him, "Master, I am prepared to go with You, both to prison and to
death."
34 And He said, "I say to you, Kěpha, the
cock shall not crow at all today until you
have denied three times that you know
Me."
35 And He said to them, "When I sent you
without purse and bag and sandals, did you
lack any?" And they said, "None at all."
36 And He said to them, "But now, let him
who has a purse take it, likewise also a
bag. And let him who has no sword sell his
garment and buy one.
37 "For I say to you that what has been
written has yet to be accomplished in Me,
**'And He was reckoned with lawless
ones.'** Yesh. 53:12 For that which refers to Me
has an end too."
38 And they said, "Master, look, here are
two swords." But He said to them, "That is
enough!"
39 And coming out, He went to the Mount
of Olives, according to usage, and His
taught ones also followed Him.
40 And coming to the place, He said to
them, "Pray that you do not enter into
trial."
41 And He withdrew from them about a
stone's throw, and falling on His knees He
was praying,
42 saying, "Father, if it be Your counsel,
remove this cup from Me. Yet not My
desire, but let Yours be done."
43 And there appeared a messenger from
heaven to Him, strengthening Him.
44 And being in agony, He was praying
more earnestly. And His sweat became like
great drops of blood falling down to the
ground.
45 And rising up from prayer, and coming
to His taught ones, He found them sleeping
from grief.

46 And He said to them, "Why do you sleep? Rise and pray, lest you enter into trial."

47 And while He was still speaking, see: a crowd! And he who was called Yehuḏah, one of the twelve, was going before them and came near to יהושע to kiss Him.

48 And יהושע said to him, "Yehuḏah, do you deliver up the Son of Aḏam with a kiss?"

49 And those around Him, seeing what was about to take place, said to Him, "Master, shall we strike with the sword?"

50 And one of them struck the servant of the high priest and cut off his right ear.

51 But יהושע answering, said, "Allow it this far." And touching his ear He healed him.

52 And יהושע said to those who had come against Him, the chief priests and captains of the Set-apart Place and the elders, "Have you come out as against a robber, with swords and clubs?

53 "While I was with you daily in the Set-apart Place, you did not lay hands on Me. But this is your hour and the authority of darkness."

54 And having seized Him, they led Him and brought Him to the house of the high priest. And Kěpha was following at a distance.

55 And when they had lit a fire in the midst of the courtyard, and sat down together, Kěpha sat among them.

56 And a certain servant girl, seeing him as he sat by the fire, looked intently at him and said, "And this one was with Him."

57 But he denied Him, saying, "Woman, I do not know Him."

58 And after a little while another saw him and said, "You are one of them too." But Kěpha said, "Man, I am not!"

59 And about an hour later, another insisted, saying, "Truly, this one was with Him too, for he is a Galilean too."

60 But Kěpha said, "Man, I do not know what you are saying!" And immediately, while he was still speaking, a cock crowed.

61 And the Master turned and looked at Kěpha, and Kěpha remembered the word of the Master, how He had said to him, "Before a cock crows, you shall deny Me three times."

62 And Kěpha went out and wept bitterly.

63 And the men who were holding יהושע were mocking Him, beating *Him*.

64 And having blindfolded Him, they were striking Him on the face and were asking Him, saying, "Prophesy! Who is it that struck You?"

65 And they said to Him much more, blaspheming.

66 And when it became day, the elders of the people, both chief priests and scribes, came together and they led Him into their council, saying,

67 "If You are the Messiah, say it to us." And He said to them, "If I say to you, you would not believe it at all,

68 and if I asked you, you would not answer Me at all.

69 "From now on the Son of Aḏam shall **sit on the right hand of the power of** Teh. 110:1 Elohim."

70 And they all said, "Are You then the Son of Elohim?" And He said to them, "You say that I am."

71 And they said, "Why do we need further witness? For we heard it ourselves from His mouth."

23

And the entire assembly of them, having risen up, led Him to Pilate,

2 and began to accuse Him, saying, "We found this one perverting the nation, and forbidding to pay taxes to Caesar, saying that He Himself is Messiah, a Sovereign."

3 And Pilate asked Him, saying, "Are You the Sovereign of the Yehuḏim?" And answering him He said, "You say it."

4 And Pilate said to the chief priests and the crowd, "I find no guilt in this Man."

5 But they were insisting, saying, "He stirs up the people, teaching through all Yehuḏah, beginning from Galil unto this place."

6 And when Pilate heard of Galil, he asked if the Man were a Galilean.

7 And when he learned that He was under the authority of Herodes, he sent Him to Herodes, who was also in Yerushalayim in those days.

8 And seeing יהושע, Herodes rejoiced greatly, for a long time he had wished to see Him, because he had heard much about Him, and was anticipating to see some miracle done by Him,

9 and was questioning Him with many words, but He gave him no answer.

10 And the chief priests and the scribes stood, accusing Him intensely.

11 And Herodes, with his soldiers, made light of Him and mocked Him, dressing Him in a splendid robe, and sent Him back to Pilate.

12 And on that day Pilate and Herodes became friends with each other, for before that they had been at enmity with each other.

13 And Pilate, having called together the chief priests and the rulers and the people,

14 said to them, "You brought this Man to me, as one who turns away the people. And look, I have examined Him in your presence and have found no guilt in this Man regarding the charges which you make against Him,

15 and neither did Herodes, for I sent you back to him. And look, He has done none at all deserving death.

16 "Having disciplined Him, then, I shall release *Him*" –

17 for he had to release one to them at the festival.

18 And they cried out, all together, saying, "Away with this One, and release to us Barabba"

19 (who had been thrown into prison for a certain uprising made in the city, and for murder).

20 Wishing to release יהושע, then, Pilate appealed to them again.

21 But they were calling out, saying, "Impale! Impale Him!"

22 And he said to them the third time, "Why, what evil has He done? I have found no reason for death in Him. Having disciplined Him then, I shall release *Him*."

23 But with loud voices they insisted, asking for Him to be impaled. And the voices of these men and of the chief priests were prevailing.

24 And Pilate pronounced sentence that what they asked should be done.

25 And he released the one they asked for, who for uprising and murder had been thrown into prison, but he handed יהושע over to their wishes.

26 And as they led Him away, they laid hold of a certain man, Shim'on a Cyrenian, who was coming from the field, and they put the stake on him, to bear it behind יהושע.

27 And a great number of the people were following Him, and women who also were mourning and lamenting Him.

28 But יהושע, turning to them, said, "Daughters of Yerushalayim, do not weep for Me, but weep for yourselves and for your children.

29 "For look, days are coming in which they shall say, 'Blessed are the barren, and wombs that never bore, and the breasts which never nursed!'

30 "Then they shall begin **'to say to the mountains, "Fall on us!" and to the hills, "Cover us!" '** Yesh. 2:19, 20; Hosh. 10:8 [a]

31 "Because if they do this to the green tree, what is going to be done to the dry *tree*?"

32 And two others also, evil-doers, were led with Him to be put to death.

33 And when they had come to the place called Golgotha, they impaled Him there, and the evil-doers, one on the right and the other on the left.

34 And יהושע said, "Father, forgive them, for they do not know what they do." **And they divided His garments and cast lots.** Teh. 22:18

35 And the people were standing, looking on, and the rulers also were sneering with them, saying, "He saved others, let Him save Himself if He is the Messiah, the chosen of Elohim."

36 And the soldiers were mocking Him too, coming and offering Him sour wine,

37 and saying, "If You are the Sovereign of the Yehuḏim, save Yourself."

38 And there was also an inscription

23a Also see Ḥazon 6:16.

written over Him in letters of Greek, and
Roman, and Hebrew: THIS IS THE
SOVEREIGN OF THE YEHUḎIM.
39 And one of the evil-doers who were
hanged, was speaking evil of Him, saying,
"If You are the Messiah, save Yourself and
us."
40 But the other, responding, rebuked him,
saying, "Do you not even fear Elohim,
since you are under the same judgment?
41 "And we, indeed, rightly so, for we
receive the due reward of our deeds, but
this One has done no wrong."
42 And he said to יהושע, "Master,
remember me when You come into Your
reign."
43 And יהושע said to him, "Truly, I say to
you today, you shall be with Me in paradise." [b]
44 And it was now about the sixth hour,
and darkness came over all the land, until
the ninth hour.
45 And the sun was darkened, and the veil
of the Dwelling Place was torn in two.
46 And crying out with a loud voice,
יהושע said, "Father, **into Your hands I
commit My spirit.**" Teh. 31:5 And having
said this, He breathed His last.
47 And the captain, seeing what took
place, praised Elohim, saying, "Truly, this
Man was righteous!"
48 And when all the crowds who had gathered to that sight saw what took place, they
beat their breasts and went away.
49 And all those who knew Him, and the
women who followed Him from Galil,
stood at a distance, watching this.
50 And see, a man named Yosěph, a council member, a good and righteous man –
51 he was not agreeing with their counsel
and deed – from Ramathayim, a city of the
Yehuḏim, who himself was also waiting
for the reign of Elohim,
52 he, going to Pilate, asked for the body
of יהושע.
53 And taking it down, he wrapped it in
linen, and laid it in a tomb hewn out of the
rock, where no one was yet laid.
54 And it was Preparation day, and the
Sabbath was approaching.
55 And the women who had come with
Him from Galil followed after, and saw the
tomb and how His body was laid.
56 And having returned, they prepared
spices and perfumes. And they rested on
the Sabbath according to the command.

24

But on *day* one of the week [a], at
early dawn, they came to the tomb,
bringing the spices which they had prepared,
2 and they found the stone rolled away
from the tomb.
3 And having entered, they did not find
the body of the Master יהושע.
4 And it came to be, as they were perplexed about this, that see, two men stood
by them in glittering garments.
5 And becoming frightened and bowing
their faces to the earth, these said to them,
"Why do you seek the living among the
dead?
6 "He is not here, but has been raised up!
Remember how He spoke to you when He
was still in Galil,
7 saying, 'The Son of Aḏam has to be
delivered into the hands of sinners, and be
impaled, and the third day rise again.' "
8 And they remembered His words.
9 And having returned from the tomb
they reported all this to the eleven and to
all the rest.
10 And it was Miryam from Maḡdala, and
Yoḥanah, and Miryam *the mother* of
Ya'aqoḇ, and the rest with them, who told
this to the emissaries.
11 And their words appeared to them to be
nonsense, and they did not believe them.
12 But Kěpha arose and ran to the tomb.
And stooping down, he saw the linen
wrappings lying by themselves. And he
went away home, marvelling at what took
place.
13 And see, two of them were going that
same day to a village called Amma'us,
which was sixty stadia [b] from Yerushalayim.
14 And they were talking to each other of

23b Lit. garden. *24a* Lit. Sabbath. *24b* Roman Monetory unit.

all this which had taken place.
15 And it came to be, as they were talking
and reasoning, that יהושע Himself drew
near and went with them.
16 But their eyes were restrained, so that
they did not know Him.
17 And He said to them, "What are these
words you are exchanging with each other
as you are walking – and you are sad?"
18 And the one whose name was Qleophas
answering, said to Him, "Are You the lone
visitor in Yerushalayim who does not
know what took place in it these days?"
19 And He said to them, "What?" And
they said to Him, "Concerning יהושע of
Natsareth, who was a Prophet mighty in
deed and word before Elohim and all the
people,
20 and how the chief priests and our rulers
delivered Him to be condemned to death,
and impaled Him.
21 "We, however, were expecting that it
was He who was going to redeem Yisra'ěl.
But besides all this, today is the third day
since these *matters* took place.
22 "But certain women of ours, who
arrived at the tomb early, also astonished
us,
23 when they did not find His body, they
came saying that they had also seen a
vision of messengers who said He was
alive.
24 "And some of those with us went to the
tomb and found it, as also the women had
said, but they did not see Him."
25 And He said to them, "O thoughtless
ones, and slow of heart to believe in all
that the prophets have spoken!
26 "Was it not necessary for the Messiah
to suffer these and to enter into His
esteem?"
27 And beginning at Mosheh and all the
Prophets, He was explaining to them in all
the Scriptures the *matters* concerning
Himself.
28 And they approached the village where
they were going, and He seemed to be
going on.
29 But they urged Him strongly, saying,
"Stay with us, for it is toward evening, and
the day has declined." And He went in to
stay with them.
30 And it came to be, when He sat at the
table with them, having taken the bread,
He blessed, and having broken, He was
giving it to them.
31 And their eyes were opened and they
recognised Him. And He disappeared from
their sight.
32 And they said to each other, "Was not
our heart burning within us as He was
speaking to us on the way, and as He was
opening the Scriptures to us?"
33 And rising up that same hour they
returned to Yerushalayim, and found the
eleven and those who were with them
gathered together,
34 saying, "The Master was truly raised,
and has appeared to Shimʽon!"
35 And they related what *took place* on the
way, and how He was recognised by them
in the breaking of the bread.
36 And as they were saying this, יהושע
Himself stood in the midst of them, and
said to them, "Peace to you."
37 And being startled and frightened, they
thought they had seen a spirit.
38 And He said to them, "Why are you
troubled? And why do doubts arise in your
hearts?
39 "See My hands and My feet, that it is I
Myself. Handle Me and see, for a spirit
does not have flesh and bones as you see I
have."
40 And saying this, He showed them His
hands and His feet.
41 And while they were still not believing
for joy, and marvelling, He said to them,
"Have you any food here?"
42 And they gave Him a piece of a broiled
fish and some honeycomb.
43 And taking it He ate in their presence.
44 And He said to them, "These are the
words which I spoke to you while I was
still with you, that all have to be filled that
were written in the Torah of Mosheh and
the Prophets and the Tehillim concerning
Me."
45 Then He opened their minds to understand the Scriptures,
46 and said to them, "Thus it has been
written, and so it was necessary for the

Messiah to suffer and to rise again from
the dead the third day,
47 and that repentance and forgiveness of
sins should be proclaimed in His Name to
all nations, beginning at Yerushalayim.
48 "And you are witnesses of these *matters*.
49 "And see, I am sending the Promise of
My Father upon you, but you are to remain
in the city of Yerushalayim until you are
clothed with power from on high." [c]

50 And He led them out as far as Běyth
Anyah, and lifting up His hands He
blessed them.
51 And it came to be, while He was
blessing them, that He was parted from
them and was taken up into the heaven.
52 And they, having bowed down to Him,
returned to Yerushalayim with great joy,
53 and were continually in the Set-apart
Place praising and blessing Elohim. Aměn.

24c Ma. 1:4-8.

YOḤANAN

JOHN

1 In the beginning was the Word, and the Word was with Elohim, and the Word was Elohim.

2 He was in the beginning with Elohim.

3 All came to be through Him, [a] and without Him not even one came to be that came to be.

4 In Him was life, and the life was the light of men.

5 And the light shines in the darkness, and the darkness has not overcome it.

6 There was a man sent from Elohim, whose name was Yoḥanan.

7 This one came for a witness, to bear witness of the Light, that all might believe through him.

8 He was not that Light, but that he might bear witness of that Light.

9 He was the true Light, which enlightens every man, coming into the world.

10 He was in the world, and the world came to be through Him, and the world did not know Him.

11 He came to His own, and His own did not receive Him.

12 But as many as received Him, to them He gave the authority to become children of Elohim, to those believing in His Name,

13 who were born, not of blood nor of the desire of flesh nor of the desire of man, but of Elohim.

14 And the Word became flesh and pitched His tent among us, and we saw His esteem, esteem as of an only brought-forth of a father, complete in favour and truth.

15 Yoḥanan bore witness of Him and cried out, saying, "This was He of whom I said, 'He who comes after me has become before me, because He was before me.' "

16 And out of His completeness we all did receive, and favour upon favour,

17 for the Torah was given through Mosheh – the favour and the truth came through יהושע Messiah.

18 No one has ever seen Elohim. [b] The only brought-forth Son, who is in the bosom of the Father, He did declare.

19 Now this was the witness of Yoḥanan when the Yehuḏim sent from Yerushalayim priests and Lěwites to ask him, "Who are you?"

20 And he confessed, and did not deny, but confessed, "I am not the Messiah."

21 And they asked him, "What then, are you Ěliyahu?" So he said, "I am not." "Are you the Prophet?" And he answered, "No."

22 Therefore they said to him, "Who are you, so that we give an answer to those who sent us? What do you say about yourself?"

23 He said, "I am a **voice of one crying in the wilderness, 'Make straight the way of יהוה,'** Yesh. 40:3 as the prophet Yeshayahu said."

24 And those sent were of the Pharisees,

25 and they asked him, saying, "Why then do you immerse if you are not the Messiah, nor Ěliyahu, nor the Prophet?"

26 Yoḥanan answered them, saying, "I immerse in water, but in your midst stands One whom you do not know,

27 the One coming after me, who has become before me, whose sandal strap I am not worthy to loosen."

28 This took place in Běyth Anyah beyond the Yarděn, where Yoḥanan was immersing.

29 On the next day Yoḥanan saw יהושע coming toward him, and said, "See, the Lamb of Elohim who takes away the sin of the world! [c]

30 "This is He of whom I said, 'After me

1a Eph. 3:9, Qol. 1:16, Iḇ`rim 1:2, Iḇ`rim 11:3, Kěpha ב 3:5, Teh. 33:6. *1b* 5:37, 6:46, Yn. א 4:12. *1c* Mt. 1:21, Titos 2:14, Yn. א 3:5 & 8.

comes a Man who has become before me, for He was before me.’ [d]

31 “And I did not know Him, but that He might be revealed to Yisra’ĕl, therefore I came immersing in water.”

32 And Yoḥanan bore witness, saying, “I have seen the Spirit coming down from heaven like a dove and remain on Him.

33 “And I did not know Him, but He who sent me to immerse in water said to me, ‘Upon whom you see the Spirit coming down and remaining on Him, this is He who immerses in the Set-apart Spirit.’

34 “And I have seen and have witnessed that this is the Son of Elohim.”

35 Again the following day, Yoḥanan was standing with two of his taught ones,

36 and looking at יהושע walking, he said, “See the Lamb of Elohim!”

37 And the two taught ones heard him speaking, and they followed יהושע.

38 And יהושע turning, and seeing them following, said to them, “What do you seek?” And they said to Him, “Rabbi” (which means Teacher), “where are You staying?”

39 He said to them, “Come and see.” They went and saw where He was staying, and remained with Him that day. Now it was about the tenth hour.

40 Andri, the brother of Shim‘on Kĕpha, was one of the two who heard from Yoḥanan, and followed Him.

41 First he found his own brother Shim‘on, and said to him, “We have found the Messiah” (which means the Anointed).

42 And he brought him to יהושע. And looking at him, יהושע said, “You are Shim‘on the son of Yonah, you shall be called Kĕpha” (which means a Stone).

43 On the following day יהושע wished to go to Galil, and He found Philip and said to him, “Follow Me.”

44 And Philip was from Bĕyth Tsaiḏa, the city of Andri and Kĕpha.

45 Philip found Nethanĕ’l and said to him, “We have found Him whom Mosheh wrote of in the Torah, and the prophets: יהושע of Natsareth – the son of Yosĕph.”

46 And Nethanĕ’l said to him, “Is it possible for any good *matter* to come out of Natsareth?” Philip said to him, “Come and see.”

47 יהושע saw Nethanĕ’l coming toward Him, and said of him, “See, truly a Yisra’ĕli, in whom is no deceit!”

48 Nethanĕ’l said to Him, “From where do You know me?” יהושע answered and said to him, “Before Philip called you, when you were under the fig tree, I saw you.”

49 Nethanĕ’l answered and said to Him, “Rabbi, You are the Son of Elohim! You are the Sovereign of Yisra’ĕl!”

50 יהושע answered and said to him, “Because I said to you, ‘I saw you under the fig tree,’ do you believe? Greater than that you shall see.”

51 And He said to him, “Truly, truly, I say to you, from now on you shall see the heaven opened, and the messengers of Elohim ascending and descending upon the Son of Aḏam.” [e]

2 And on the third day there was a wedding in Qanah of Galil, and the mother of יהושע was there.

2 And both יהושע and His taught ones were invited to the wedding.

3 And when they were short of wine, the mother of יהושע said to Him, “They have no wine.”

4 יהושע said to her, “Woman, what is that to Me and to you? My hour has not yet come.”

5 His mother said to the servants, “Do whatever He says to you.”

6 And there were six stone water-jugs standing there, according to the mode of cleansing of the Yehuḏim, each holding two or three measures.

7 יהושע said to them, “Fill the water-jugs with water.” And they filled them up to the brim.

8 And He said to them, “Now draw out and take it to the master of the feast.” So they took it.

9 But when the master of the feast had tasted the water that had become wine, and

1d See v. 15. *1e* Ber. 28:12

did not know where it came from – though
the servants who had drawn the water
knew – the master of the feast called the
bridegroom,
10 and said to him, "Every man at the
beginning sets out the good wine, and
when they have drunk, then that which is
poorer. You have kept the good wine until
now."
11 This, the beginning of the signs, יהושע
did in Qanah of Galil, and manifested His
esteem. And His taught ones believed in
Him.
12 After this He went down to Kephar
Naḥum, He and His mother, and His brothers, and His taught ones. And there they
stayed not many days.
13 And the Pěsaḥ of the Yehuḏim was
near, and יהושע went up to Yerushalayim.
14 And He found in the Set-apart Place
those selling oxen and sheep and doves,
and the moneychangers sitting.
15 And having made a whip of cords, He
drove them all out of the Set-apart Place,
with the sheep and the oxen, and poured
out the moneychangers' coins and overturned the tables.
16 And He said to those selling doves,
"Take these away! Do not make the house
of My Father a house of merchandise!"
17 And His taught ones remembered that it
was written, **"The ardour for Your house
has eaten Me up."** Teh. 69:9
18 And the Yehuḏim answered and said to
Him, "What sign do You show to us, since
You are doing these?"
19 יהושע answered and said to them,
"Destroy this Dwelling Place, and in three
days I shall raise it."
20 Then the Yehuḏim said, "It took forty-
six years to build this Dwelling Place, and
You are going to raise it in three days?"
21 But He spoke about the Dwelling Place
of His body.
22 So, when He was raised from the dead,
His taught ones remembered that He said
this to them. And they believed the
Scripture and the word which יהושע had
said.
23 And when He was in Yerushalayim at
the Pěsaḥ, at the festival, many believed in
His Name when they saw the signs which
He was doing.
24 But יהושע was not entrusting Himself
to them, because He knew all men,
25 and had no need that anyone should
witness of man, for He knew what was in
man.

3 And there was a man of the Pharisees,
Naḵdimon was his name, a ruler of the
Yehuḏim.
2 This one came to יהושע by night and
said to Him, "Rabbi, we know that You are
a teacher come from Elohim, for no one is
able to do these signs You do if Elohim is
not with him."
3 יהושע answered and said to him,
"Truly, truly, I say to you, unless one is
born from above, he is unable to see [a] the
reign of Elohim."
4 Naḵdimon said to Him, "How is a man
able to be born when he is old? Is he able to
enter into his mother's womb a second
time and be born?"
5 יהושע answered, "Truly, truly, I say to
you, unless one is born of water and the
Spirit, he is unable to enter into the reign of
Elohim.
6 "That which has been born of the flesh
is flesh, and that which has been born of
the Spirit is spirit.
7 "Do not marvel that I said to you, 'You
have to be born from above.'
8 "The wind [b] blows where it wishes, and
you hear the sound of it, but do not know
where it comes from and where it goes. So
is everyone who has been born of the
Spirit."
9 Naḵdimon answered and said to Him,
"How is it possible for this to take place?"
10 יהושע answered and said to him, "Are
you the teacher of Yisra'ěl, and do not
know this?
11 "Truly, truly, I say to you, We speak
what We know and witness what We have
seen, and you do not receive Our witness.
12 "If you do not believe when I spoke to

3a Or *perceive*. *3b* Wind and Spirit has the same underlying Hebrew and Greek words.

you about earthly *matters*, how are you
going to believe when I speak to you about
the heavenly *matters*?
13 "And no one has gone up into the heav-
en except He who came down from the
heaven – the Son of Aḏam.
14 "And as Mosheh lifted up the serpent in
the wilderness, even so the Son of Aḏam
has to be lifted up,
15 so that whoever is believing in Him
should not perish but possess everlasting
life.
16 "For Elohim so loved the world that
He gave His only brought-forth Son, so
that everyone who believes in Him should
not perish but possess everlasting life.
17 "For Elohim did not send His Son into
the world to judge the world, but that the
world through Him might be saved.
18 "He who believes in Him is not judged,
but he who does not believe is judged
already, because he has not believed in the
Name of the only brought-forth Son of
Elohim.
19 "And this is the judgment, that the light
has come into the world, and men loved the
darkness rather than the light, for their
works were wicked.
20 "For everyone who is practising evil
matters hates the light and does not come
to the light, lest his works should be
exposed.
21 "But the one doing the truth comes to
the light, so that his works are clearly seen,
that they have been wrought in Elohim."
22 After this, יהושע and His taught ones
came into the land of Yehuḏah, and He
remained there with them, and was immersing.
23 And Yoḥanan was also immersing in
Ayin near Salim, because there was plenty
of water there. And they were coming and
were being immersed,
24 for Yoḥanan had not yet been put into
prison.
25 Then a dispute arose between some of
Yoḥanan's taught ones and the Yehuḏim
about cleansing,
26 and they came to Yoḥanan and said to
him, "Rabbi, He who was with you beyond
the Yardĕn, to whom you have witnessed,
see, He is immersing, and all are coming to
Him!"
27 Yoḥanan answered and said, "No man
is able to receive any *matter* unless it is
given to him from the heaven.
28 "You yourselves are witnesses for me
that I said, 'I am not the Messiah but I am
sent ahead of Him.'
29 "He that has the bride is the bridegroom, but the friend of the bridegroom,
who stands and hears him, rejoices greatly
because of the voice of the bridegroom.
So this joy of mine is complete.
30 "It is right for Him to increase, but me
to decrease.
31 "He who comes from above is over all,
he who is from the earth is of the earth and
speaks of the earth. He who comes from
the heaven is over all.
32 "And what He has seen and heard, that
He witnesses. And no one receives His witness.
33 "He who receives His witness has set
his seal that Elohim is true.
34 "For He whom Elohim has sent speaks
the Words of Elohim, for Elohim does not
give the Spirit by measure.
35 "The Father loves the Son, and has
given all into His hand.
36 "He who believes in the Son possesses
everlasting life, but he who does not obey
the Son shall not see life, but the wrath of
Elohim remains on him."

4 So when the Master knew that the
Pharisees had heard that יהושע made
and immersed more taught ones than
Yoḥanan –
2 although יהושע Himself did not
immerse, but His taught ones –
3 He left Yehuḏah and went away again
to Galil.
4 And He had to pass through Shomeron.
5 So He came to a city of Shomeron,
called Sheḵem, near the piece of land
Ya'aqoḇ gave to his son Yosĕph.
6 And Ya'aqoḇ's fountain was there. So
יהושע, being wearied from the journey,
was sitting thus at the fountain. It was
about the sixth hour.
7 A woman of Shomeron came to draw

water. יהושע said to her, "Give Me to
drink."
8 For His taught ones had gone off into
the city to buy food.
9 The woman of Shomeron therefore said
to Him, "How is it that You, being a
Yehudi, ask a drink from me, a woman of
Shomeron?" For Yehudim do not associate
with Shomeronim.
10 יהושע answered and said to her, "If you
knew the gift of Elohim, and who it is who
says to you, 'Give Me to drink,' you would
have asked Him, and He would have given
you living water." [a]
11 The woman said to Him, "Master, You
have no vessel, and the well is deep. From
where, then, do You have living water?
12 "Are You greater than our father
Ya'aqob, who gave us the well, and drank
from it himself, and his sons, and his
cattle?"
13 יהושע answered and said to her,
"Everyone drinking of this water shall
thirst again,
14 but whoever drinks of the water I give
him shall certainly never thirst. And the
water that I give him shall become in him a
fountain of water springing up into everlasting life."
15 The woman said to Him, "Master, give
me this water, so that I do not thirst, nor
come here to draw."
16 יהושע said to her, "Go, call your husband, and come here."
17 The woman answered and said, "I have
no husband." יהושע said to her, "You have
well said, 'I have no husband,'
18 for you have had five husbands, and the
one whom you now have is not your husband. What you have said is true."
19 The woman said to Him, "Master, I see
that You are a prophet.
20 "Our fathers worshipped on this mountain, but you *people* say that in Yerushalayim is the place where one needs to
worship."
21 יהושע said to her, "Woman, believe
Me, the hour is coming when you shall neither on this mountain, nor in Yerushalayim,
worship the Father.
22 "You worship what you do not know.
We worship what we know, because the
deliverance is of the Yehuḏim. [b]
23 "But the hour is coming, and now is,
when the true worshippers shall worship
the Father in spirit and truth, for the Father
also does seek such to worship Him.
24 "Elohim is Spirit, and those who worship Him need to worship in spirit and
truth."
25 The woman said to Him, "I know that
Messiah is coming, the One who is called
Anointed. When that One comes, He shall
announce to us all."
26 יהושע said to her, "I who am speaking
to you am He."
27 And upon this His taught ones came,
and they were marvelling that He was
speaking with a woman, however, no one
said, "What do You seek?" or, "Why do
You speak with her?"
28 The woman then left her water-jug, and
went away to the city, and said to the men,
29 "Come, see a Man who told me all that
I have done. Is this not the Messiah?"
30 They went out of the city and were
coming to Him.
31 But in the meantime His taught ones
were asking Him, saying, "Rabbi, eat."
32 And He said to them, "I have food to
eat of which you do not know."
33 Then the taught ones said to each other,
"Did anyone bring Him *food* to eat?"
34 יהושע said to them, "My food is to do
the desire of Him who sent Me, and to
accomplish His work.
35 "Do you not say, 'There are still four
months, and the harvest comes'? See, I say
to you, lift up your eyes and see the fields,
for they are white for harvest – already!
36 "He who is reaping receives a reward,
and gathers fruit for everlasting life, so that
both he who is sowing and he who is reaping rejoice together.
37 "For in this the word is true, 'One sows
and another reaps.'

4a Yirm. 2:13, Yirm. 17:13, Zeḵ. 14:8, Yn. 7:37-39. *4b* Teh. 147:19, Yesh. 2:3, Yesh. 14:1, Yesh. 56:6-8, Yeḥez. 47:22-23, Zeḵ. 2:10-11, Zeḵ. 8:23, Rom. 2:20, Rom. 3:2, Rom. 9:4, Ḥazon 21:12 & 24.

38 “I sent you to reap that for which you
have not laboured. Others have laboured,
and you have entered into their labours.”
39 And many of the Shomeronim of that
city believed in Him because of the word
of the woman who witnessed, “He told me
all that I have done.”
40 Therefore when the Shomeronim came
to Him, they were asking Him to stay with
them, and He stayed there two days.
41 And many more believed because of
His word.
42 And they said to the woman, “We no
longer believe because of what you said,
for we ourselves have heard, and we know
that this is truly the Messiah, the Saviour of
the world.”
43 And after the two days He left there and
went to Galil.
44 For יהושע Himself witnessed that a
prophet is without appreciation in his own
country.
45 Therefore when He came to Galil, the
Galileans received Him, having seen all
that He had done in Yerushalayim at the
festival, for they also went to the festival.
46 Then יהושע came again to Qanah of
Galil where He had made the water wine.
And there was a certain nobleman whose
son was sick at Kephar Naḥum.
47 When he heard that יהושע had come
from Yehuḏah into Galil, he went to Him
and was asking Him to come down and
heal his son, for he was about to die.
48 יהושע then said to him, “If you *people*
do not see signs and wonders, you do not
believe at all.”
49 The nobleman said to Him, “Master,
come down before my child dies!”
50 יהושע said to him, “Go, your son
lives.” And the man believed the word that
יהושע spoke to him, and went.
51 And while he was going down, his
servants met him and reported, saying,
“Your son lives!”
52 He then asked from them the hour in
which he became better, and they said to
him, “Yesterday at the seventh hour the
inflammation left him.”
53 Then the father knew that it was at the
same hour in which יהושע said to him,
“Your son lives.” And he himself believed,
and all his household.
54 Again this was the second sign יהושע
did, when He had come from Yehuḏah into
Galil.

5 After this there was a festival of the
Yehuḏim, and יהושע went up to Yerushalayim.
2 And in Yerushalayim at the Sheep *Gate*
there is a pool, which is called in Hebrew,
Bĕyth Zatha, having five porches.
3 In these were lying a great number
of those who were sick, blind, crippled,
paralysed, waiting for the stirring of the
water.
4 For a messenger was going down at a
certain time into the pool and was stirring
the water. Whoever stepped in first, then,
after the stirring of the water, became well
of whatever disease he had.
5 And a certain man was there who had a
sickness thirty-eight years.
6 When יהושע saw him lying there, and
knowing that he already had been a long
time, He said to him, “Do you wish to
become well?”
7 The sick man answered Him, “Master, I
have no man to put me into the pool when
the water is stirred, but while I am coming,
another steps down before me.”
8 יהושע said to him, “Rise, take up your
bed and walk.”
9 And immediately the man became well,
and he took up his bed and was walking.
Now it was Sabbath on that day.
10 The Yehuḏim therefore said to him who
had been healed, “It is the Sabbath, it is not
right for you to take up the bed.”
11 He answered them, “He who made me
well said to me, ‘Take up your bed and
walk.’ ”
12 Therefore they asked him, “Who is the
Man who said to you, ‘Take up your bed
and walk’?”
13 But the one who was healed did not
know who it was, for יהושע had moved
away, a crowd being in that place.
14 Afterward יהושע found him in the Set-
apart Place, and said to him, “See, you
have been made well. Sin no more, so that

no worse *matter* befalls you." [a]

15 The man went away, and told the Yehuḏim that it was יהושע who made him well.

16 And because of this the Yehuḏim persecuted יהושע, and were seeking to kill Him, because He was doing these *healings* on the Sabbath.

17 But יהושע answered them, "My Father works until now, and I work."

18 Because of this, then, the Yehuḏim were seeking all the more to kill Him, 'because not only was He breaking the Sabbath, but He also called Elohim His own Father, making Himself equal with Elohim.'

19 Therefore יהושע responded and said to them, "Truly, truly, I say to you, the Son is able to do none at all by Himself, but only that which He sees the Father doing, because whatever He does, the Son also likewise does.

20 "For the Father loves the Son, and shows Him all that He Himself does. And greater works than these He is going to show Him, in order that you marvel.

21 "For as the Father raises the dead and makes alive, even so the Son makes alive whom He wishes.

22 "For the Father judges no one, but has given all the judgment to the Son,

23 that all should value the Son even as they value the Father. He who does not value the Son does not value the Father who sent Him.

24 "Truly, truly, I say to you, he who hears My word and believes in Him who sent Me possesses everlasting life, and does not come into judgment, but has passed from death into life.

25 "Truly, truly, I say to you, the hour is coming, and now is, when the dead shall hear the voice of the Son of Elohim. And those having heard shall live.

26 "For as the Father possesses life in Himself, so He gave also to the Son to possess life in Himself,

27 and He has given Him authority also to do judgment, because He is the Son of Aḏam.

28 "Do not marvel at this, because the hour is coming in which all those in the tombs shall hear His voice,

29 and shall come forth – those who have done good, to the resurrection of life, and those who have practised evil *matters*, to a resurrection of judgment.

30 "Of Myself I am unable to do any *matter*. As I hear, I judge, and My judgment is righteous, because I do not seek My own desire, but the desire of the Father who sent Me.

31 "If I bear witness of Myself, My witness is not true.

32 "There is another who bears witness of Me, and I know that the witness which He witnesses of Me is true.

33 "You have sent to Yoḥanan, and he bore witness to the truth.

34 "But I do not receive witness from man, but I say this in order that you might be saved.

35 "He was the burning and shining lamp, and for a while you wished to rejoice in his light.

36 "But I have a greater witness than that of Yoḥanan, for the works that the Father gave Me to accomplish, the works that I do, bear witness of Me, that the Father has sent Me.

37 "And the Father who sent Me, He bore witness of Me. You have neither heard His voice at any time, nor seen His form. [b]

38 "And you do not have His Word staying in you, because you do not believe Him whom He sent.

39 "You search the Scriptures, because you think you possess everlasting life in them. And these are the ones that bear witness of Me.

40 "But you do not desire to come to Me in order to possess life.

41 "I do not receive esteem from men,

42 but I know you, that you do not have the love of Elohim in you.

43 "I have come in My Father's Name and you do not receive Me, if another comes in his own name, him you would receive.

5a See also 8:11. *5b* See 1:18.

44 “How are you able to believe, when you
are receiving esteem from one another, and
the esteem that is from the only Elohim
you do not seek?
45 “Do not think that I shall accuse you to
the Father. There is one who accuses you:
Mosheh, in whom you have set your
expectation.
46 “For if you believed Mosheh, you
would have believed Me, since he wrote
about Me.
47 “But if you do not believe his
writings,[c] how shall you believe My
words?”

6 After this יהושע went away to the
other side of the Sea of Galil, that is
Lake Kinnereth.
2 And a large crowd was following Him,
because they saw His signs which He did
on those who were sick.
3 And יהושע went up on a mountain, and
there He sat down with His taught ones.
4 And the Pěsaḥ was near, the festival of
the Yehuḏim.
5 Then יהושע, lifting up His eyes and
seeing a large crowd coming toward Him,
said to Philip, “Where shall we buy bread
for them to eat?”
6 And this He said, trying him, for He
Himself knew what He would do.
7 Philip answered Him, “Two hundred
denarii[a] worth of bread is not sufficient for
them, for every one of them to receive a little.”
8 One of His taught ones, Andri, the
brother of Shim‛on Kěpha, said to Him,
9 “Here is a boy who has five barley
loaves and two fishes, but what are these
for so many?”
10 And יהושע said, “Make the people sit
down.” Now there was much grass in the
place, and the men, numbering about five
thousand, sat down.
11 And יהושע took the loaves, and having
given thanks He distributed them to the
taught ones, and the taught ones to those
sitting down. And the same with the fish,
as much as they wished.
12 And when they were filled, He said
to His taught ones, “Gather the broken
pieces that are left over, so that none gets
wasted.”
13 So they gathered them and filled twelve
baskets with broken pieces of the five
barley loaves which were left over by those
who had eaten.
14 Then the men, having seen the sign that
יהושע did, said, “This is truly the Prophet
who is coming to the world.”
15 Then יהושע, knowing that they were
about to come and seize Him, that they
might make Him sovereign, withdrew
again to the mountain, alone by Himself.
16 And when evening came, His taught
ones went down to the sea,
17 and entering into the boat, they were
going over the sea toward Kephar Naḥum.
And it had already become dark, and
יהושע had not yet come to them.
18 And the sea was rising because a great
wind was blowing.
19 When they had rowed about twenty-
five or thirty stadia[b], they saw יהושע
walking on the sea and coming near the
boat, and they were afraid.
20 And He said to them, “It is I, do not be
afraid.”
21 They wished therefore to take Him into
the boat, and at once the boat was at the
land where they were going.
22 On the next day, the crowd that was
standing on the other side of the sea saw
that there was no other boat there except
that one into which His taught ones had
entered, and that יהושע had not entered the
boat with His taught ones, but His taught
ones went away alone –
23 but other boats came from Kinnereth,
near the place where they ate bread after
the Master had given thanks –
24 therefore when the crowd saw that
יהושע was not there, nor His taught ones,
they themselves also entered into the boats
and came to Kephar Naḥum, seeking
יהושע.
25 And having found Him on the other
side of the sea, they asked Him, “Rabbi,

5c Lq. 16:31. *6a* Roman monetary unit. *6b* Approx. 5 to 6 kilometres or 3 to 4 miles.

when did You come here?"

26 יהושע answered them and said, "Truly, truly, I say to you, you seek Me, not because you saw signs, but because you ate of the loaves and were satisfied.

27 "Do not labour for the food that is perishing, but for the food that is remaining to everlasting life, which the Son of Aḏam shall give you, [c] for the Father, Elohim, has set His seal on Him."

28 So they said to Him, "What should we do to work the works of Elohim?"

29 יהושע answered and said to them, "This is the work of Elohim, that you believe in Him whom He sent."

30 So they said to Him, "What sign then would You do, so that we see and believe You? What would You do?

31 "Our fathers ate the manna in the wilderness, as it has been written, **'He gave them bread out of the heaven to eat.'** " Teh. 78:24; 105:40, Neḥ. 9:15

32 Therefore יהושע said to them, "Truly, truly, I say to you, Mosheh did not give you the bread out of the heaven, but My Father gives you the true bread out of the heaven.

33 "For the bread of Elohim is He who comes down out of the heaven and gives life to the world."

34 So they said to Him, "Master, give us this bread always."

35 And יהושע said to them, "I am the bread of life. He who comes to Me shall not get hungry at all, and he who believes in Me shall not get thirsty at all.

36 "But I said to you that you have seen Me, and still do not believe.

37 "All that the Father gives Me shall come to Me, and the one who comes to Me I shall by no means cast out.

38 "Because I have come down out of the heaven, not to do My own desire, but the desire of Him who sent Me.

39 "This is the desire of the Father who sent Me, that all He has given Me I should not lose of it, but should raise it in the last day.

40 "And this is the desire of Him who sent Me, that everyone who sees the Son and believes in Him should possess everlasting life. And I shall raise him up in the last day."

41 Therefore the Yehuḏim were grumbling against Him, because He said, "I am the bread which came down out of the heaven."

42 And they said, "Is not this יהושע, the son of Yosĕph, whose father and mother we know? How is it then that He says, 'I have come down out of the heaven'?"

43 Then יהושע answered and said to them, "Do not grumble with one another.

44 "No one is able to come to Me unless the Father who sent Me draws him. And I shall raise him up in the last day.

45 "It has been written in the prophets, **'And they shall all be taught by יהוה.'** Yesh. 54:13, Yirm. 31:34 Everyone, then, who has heard from the Father, and learned, comes to Me.

46 "Not that anyone has seen the Father, except He who is from Elohim – He has seen the Father.

47 "Truly, truly, I say to you, he who believes in Me possesses everlasting life.

48 "I am the bread of life.

49 "Your fathers ate the manna in the wilderness and they died.

50 "This is the bread which comes down out of the heaven, so that anyone might eat of it, and not die.

51 "I am the living bread which came down out of the heaven. If anyone eats of this bread, he shall live forever. And indeed, the bread that I shall give is My flesh, which I shall give for the life of the world."

52 The Yehuḏim, therefore, were striving with one another, saying, "How is this One able to give us *His* flesh to eat?"

53 יהושע therefore said to them, "Truly, truly, I say to you, unless you eat the flesh of the Son of Aḏam and drink His blood, you possess no life in yourselves.

54 "He who eats My flesh and drinks My blood possesses everlasting life, and I shall raise him up in the last day.

55 "For My flesh is truly food, and My

6c See vv. 35, 48, 51, 58, and Mt. 4:4.

blood is truly drink.
56 "He who eats My flesh and drinks My
blood stays in Me, and I in him.
57 "As the living Father sent Me, and I live
because of the Father, so he who feeds on
Me shall live because of Me.
58 "This is the bread which came down
out of the heaven, not as your fathers ate
the manna and died. He who eats this bread
shall live forever."
59 He said this in a congregation, teaching
in Kephar Naḥum.
60 Therefore many of His taught ones
having heard, said, "This word is hard,
who is able to hear it?"
61 But יהושע knowing within Himself
that His taught ones were grumbling about
this, said to them, "Does this make you
stumble?
62 "What if you see the Son of Aḏam
going up where He was before?
63 "It is the Spirit that gives life, the flesh
does not profit at all. The words that I
speak to you are Spirit and are life. [d]
64 "But there are some of you who do not
believe." For יהושע knew from the beginning who they were who did not believe,
and who would deliver Him up.
65 And He said, "Because of this I have
said to you that no one is able to come to
Me unless it has been given to him by My
Father."
66 From then on many of His taught ones
withdrew and were not walking with Him
any more.
67 יהושע therefore said to the twelve, "Do
you also wish to go away?"
68 Then Shimʽon Kěpha answered Him,
"Master, to whom shall we go? You
possess words of everlasting life.
69 "And we have believed, and we know
that You are the Messiah, the Son of the
living Elohim."
70 יהושע answered them, "Have I not
chosen you, the twelve, and one of you is a
devil?"
71 He was now speaking of Yehuḏah from
Qerioth, *the son* of Shimʽon, for he, one of
the twelve, was about to deliver Him up.

7 And after this יהושע was walking in
Galil, for He did not wish to walk in
Yehuḏah, because the Yehuḏim were seeking to kill Him.
2 And the festival of the Yehuḏim was
near, the Festival of Sukkot. [a]
3 So His brothers said to Him, 'Get away
from here and go into Yehuḏah, so that
Your taught ones also see the works that
You are doing.
4 "For no one acts in secret while he himself seeks to be known openly. If You do
these *works*, show Yourself to the world."
5 For even His brothers did not believe in
Him.
6 יהושע therefore said to them, "My time
has not yet come, but your time is always
ready.
7 "It is impossible for the world to hate
you, but it hates Me because I bear witness
of it, that its works are wicked.
8 "You go up to this festival. I am not yet
going up to this festival, for My time has
not yet been filled."
9 And having said this to them, He stayed
in Galil.
10 But when His brothers had gone up to
the festival, then He also went up, not
openly, but as it were in secret.
11 The Yehuḏim, therefore, were seeking
Him at the festival, and said, "Where is
He?"
12 And there was much grumbling about
Him among the crowd. Some were saying,
"He is good," but others were saying, "No,
but He is leading the crowd astray."
13 However, no one spoke openly of Him
for fear of the Yehuḏim.
14 And about the middle of the festival
יהושע went up into the Set-apart Place,
and He was teaching.
15 And the Yehuḏim were marvelling, saying, "How does this Man know letters, not
having learned?"
16 יהושע answered them and said, "My
teaching is not Mine, but His who sent

6d See v. 68, and Qor. א 15:45. *7a* - Booths.

Me. [b]
17 “If anyone desires to do His desire, he
shall know concerning the teaching,
whether it is from Elohim, or *whether* I
speak from Myself.
18 “He who speaks from himself is seeking his own esteem, but He who seeks the
esteem of the One who sent Him is true,
and no unrighteousness is in Him.
19 “Did not Mosheh give you the Torah?
Yet not one of you does the Torah! [c] Why
do you seek to kill Me?”
20 The crowd answered and said, “You
have a demon, who seeks to kill You?”
21 יהושע answered and said to them,
“I did one work, and you all marvel.
22 “Because of this Mosheh has given you
the circumcision – though it is not from
Mosheh, but from the fathers – and you circumcise a man on the Sabbath.
23 “If a man receives circumcision on the
Sabbath, so that the Torah of Mosheh
should not be broken, are you wroth with
Me because I made a man entirely well on
the Sabbath?
24 “Do not judge according to appearance,
but judge with righteous judgment.”
25 Therefore some of them from Yerushalayim said, “Is this not He whom they are
seeking to kill?
26 “And see! He speaks boldly, and they
say none at all to Him. Could it be that the
rulers truly know that this is truly the
Messiah?
27 “But we know where this One is from.
And when the Messiah comes, no one
knows where He is from.”
28 יהושע therefore cried out in the Set-
apart Place, teaching and saying, “You both
know Me, and you know where I am from.
And I have not come of Myself, but He
who sent Me is true, whom you do not
know.
29 “But I know Him, because I am from
Him, and He sent Me.”
30 So they were seeking to seize Him, but
no one laid a hand on Him, because His
hour had not yet come.
31 And many of the crowd believed in
Him, and said, “When the Messiah comes,
shall He do more signs than these which
this One did?”
32 The Pharisees heard the crowd mutter-
ing these *matters* concerning Him, and the
Pharisees and the chief priests sent officers
to seize Him.
33 Therefore יהושע said to them, “Yet a
little while I am with you, then I go to Him
who sent Me.
34 “You shall seek Me and you shall not
find *Me*, and where I am you are unable to
come.”
35 The Yehuḏim, therefore, said to themselves, “Where is He about to go that we
shall not find Him? Is He about to go to the
Dispersion among the Greeks, and to teach
the Greeks?
36 “What is this word which He said, ‘You
shall seek Me and you shall not find *Me*,
and where I am you are unable to come’?”
37 And on the last day, the great *day* of the
festival, יהושע stood and cried out, saying,
“If anyone thirsts, let him come to Me, and
let him who believes in Me drink.
38 “As the Scripture said, out of His inner-
most shall flow rivers of living water.” [d]
39 And this He said concerning the Spirit,
which those believing in Him were about
to receive, for the Set-apart Spirit was not
yet *given*, [e] because יהושע was not yet
esteemed.
40 Many from the crowd, when they heard
the word, then said, “This truly is the
Prophet.”
41 Others said, “This is the Messiah,” but
others said, “Does the Messiah then come
out of Galil?
42 “Did not the Scripture say that the
Messiah comes from the seed of Dawiḏ [f]
and from the village of Běyth Leḥem, [g]
where Dawiḏ was?”
43 So a division came about among the

7b יהושע says this in seven places in the Book of Yn: 3:34, 7:16, 8:28, 8:40, 12:49, 14:24, 17:8. See also Deḇ. 18:15-20. *7c* See footnote Mt. 5:20. *7d* Yesh. 44:3, Yirm 2:13, Yirm. 17:13, Zeḵ. 14:8, Teh. 36:8,9, Mish. 14:27, Yn. 4:10, Yn. 6:63, Qor. א 10:4, Ḥazon 7:17, Ḥazon 21:6, Ḥazon 22:1 & 17. *7e* Yeḥez. 36:26-27, Yo’ěl 2:28-32, Ma. 1:4-8, Ma. 2:4 & 33, Ma. 10:44-47, Ma. 11:15-16, Eph. 5:18. *7f* Shem. ב 7:12, Teh. 89:4. *7g* Miḵ. 5:2.

people because of Him.
44 And some of them wished to take Him,
but no one laid hands on Him.
45 The officers therefore came to the chief
priests and Pharisees. And they said to
them, "Why did you not bring Him?"
46 The officers answered, "Never has any
man spoken like this Man!"
47 The Pharisees, therefore, answered
them, "Have you also been led astray?
48 "Has anyone of the rulers or of the
Pharisees believed in Him?
49 "But this crowd that does not know the
Torah is accursed."
50 Naḵdimon – he who came to יהושע by
night, being one of them – said to them,
51 "Does our Torah judge the man unless it
hears first from him and knows what he is
doing?"
52 They answered and said to him, "Are
you also from Galil? Search and see that no
prophet has arisen out of Galil."
53 And each one went to his own house.

8

And יהושע went to the Mount of
Olives.
2 And at dawn He came again into the
Set-apart Place, and all the people were
coming to Him. And having sat down, He
was teaching them.
3 And the scribes and Pharisees brought
to Him a woman caught in adultery. And
having set her in the midst,
4 they said to Him, "Teacher, this woman
was caught in the act of adultery.
5 "And in the Torah Mosheh commanded
us that such should be stoned. What then
do You say?"
6 And this they said, trying Him, so that
they might accuse Him. But יהושע, bending down, wrote on the ground with the
finger, as though He did not hear.
7 But as they kept on questioning Him,
He straightened up and said to them, "He
who is without sin among you, let him be
the first to throw a stone at her."
8 And bending down again, He wrote on
the ground.
9 And when they heard it, being reproved
by *their* conscience, went out one by one,
beginning from the older ones until the
last. And יהושע was left alone, and the
woman standing in the middle.
10 And יהושע, straightening up and seeing no one but the woman, said to her,
"Woman, where are those accusers of
yours? Did no one condemn you?"
11 And she said, "No one, Master." And
יהושע said to her, "Neither do I condemn
you. Go and sin no more." [a]
12 Therefore יהושע spoke to them again,
saying, "I am the light of the world. He
who follows Me shall by no means walk in
darkness, but possess the light of life." [b]
13 The Pharisees, therefore, said to Him,
"You bear witness about Yourself, Your
witness is not true."
14 יהושע answered and said to them,
"Even if I witness concerning Myself, My
witness is true, for I know where I came
from and where I am going. But you do not
know from where I come, or where I go.
15 "You judge according to the flesh,
I judge no one.
16 "But even if I do judge, My judgment
is true, because I am not alone *in it*, but I
and the Father who sent Me.
17 "And in your Torah also, it has been
written that the witness of two men is true.
18 "I am One who witnesses concerning
Myself, and the Father who sent Me witnesses concerning Me."
19 Therefore they said to Him, "Where is
Your Father?" יהושע answered, "You
know neither Me nor My Father. If you
knew Me, you would have known My
Father also."
20 These words יהושע spoke in the treasury, teaching in the Set-apart Place. And
no one laid hands on Him, because His
hour had not yet come.
21 Therefore יהושע said to them again, "I
am going away, and you shall seek Me, and
you shall die in your sin. Where I go you
are unable to come."
22 Then the Yehuḏim said, "Shall He kill

8a See also Yn. 5:14, Rom. 6:16-20, Qor. א 15:34, Kěpha א 2:24, Kěpha א 4:1-2, Yn. א 3:4-10, Yn. א 5:18. *8b* See also 11:9-10. Ch. 7:53- 8:11 does not appear in the Aramaic Peshitta or Aramaic Old Syriac texts.

Himself, because He says, 'Where I go you
are unable to come'?"
23 And He said to them, "You are from
below, I am from above. You are of this
world, I am not of this world.
24 "Therefore I said to you that you shall
die in your sins. For if you do not believe
that I am He, you shall die in your sins."
25 Then they said to Him, "Who are You?"
And יהושע said to them, "Altogether that
which I even say to you!
26 "I have much to say and to judge concerning you. But He who sent Me is true,
and what I heard from Him, these *Words* I
speak to the world."
27 They did not know that He spoke to
them of the Father.
28 So יהושע said to them, "When you lift
up the Son of Aḏam, then you shall know
that I am He, and that I do none at all of
Myself, but as My Father taught Me, these
words I speak.
29 "And He who sent Me is with Me. The
Father has not left Me alone, for I always
do what pleases Him."
30 As He was speaking these words, many
believed in Him.
31 So יהושע said to those Yehuḏim who
believed Him, "If you stay in My Word,
you are truly My taught ones,
32 and you shall know the truth, and the
truth shall make you free."
33 They answered Him, "We are the seed
of Aḇraham, and have been servants to no
one at any time. How do you say, 'You
shall become free'?"
34 יהושע answered them, "Truly, truly, I
say to you, everyone doing sin is a servant
of sin.
35 "And the servant does not stay in the
house forever – a son stays forever.
36 "If, then, the Son makes you free, you
shall be free indeed.
37 "I know that you are the seed of Aḇraham, but you seek to kill Me, because My
Word has no place in you.
38 "I speak what I have seen with My
Father, and you do what you have heard
from your father."
39 They answered and said to Him,
"Aḇraham is our father [c]." יהושע said to
them, "If you were Aḇraham's children,
you would do the works of Aḇraham.
40 "But now you seek to kill Me, a Man
who has spoken to you the truth which I
heard from Elohim. Aḇraham did not do
this.
41 "You do the works of your father."
Then they said to Him, "We were not born
of whoring, we have one Father: Elohim."
42 יהושע said to them, "If Elohim were
your Father, you would love Me, for I
came forth from Elohim, and am here. For
I have not come of Myself, but He sent Me.
43 "Why do you not know what I say?
Because you are unable to hear My Word.
44 "You are of *your* father the devil, and
the desires of your father you wish to do.
He was a murderer from the beginning, and
has not stood in the truth, because there is
no truth in him. When he speaks the lie, he
speaks of his own, for he is a liar and the
father of it.
45 "And because I speak the truth, you do
not believe Me.
46 "Who of you proves Me wrong concerning sin? And if I speak the truth, why
do you not believe Me?
47 "He who is of Elohim hears the Words
of Elohim, therefore you do not hear
because you are not of Elohim."
48 The Yehuḏim answered and said to
Him, "Do we not say well that You are a
Shomeroni and have a demon?"
49 יהושע answered, "I do not have a
demon, but I value My Father, and you do
not value Me.
50 "And I do not seek My own esteem,
there is One who is seeking and is judging.
51 "Truly, truly, I say to you, if anyone
guards My Word he shall never see death at
all."
52 The Yehuḏim said to Him, "Now we
know that You have a demon! Aḇraham
died, and the prophets. And You say, 'If
anyone guards My Word he shall never
taste death at all.'
53 "Are You greater than our father

8c See footnote Mt. 3:9, Rom. 9:8.

Aḇraham, who died? And the prophets
died. Whom do You make Yourself?"
54 יהושע answered, "If I esteem Myself,
My esteem is none at all. It is My Father
who esteems Me, of whom you say that He
is your Elohim.
55 "And you have not known Him, but I
know Him. And if I say, 'I do not know
Him,' I shall be like you, a liar. But I do
know Him and I guard His Word. [d]
56 "Your father Aḇraham was glad that he
should see My day, and he saw it and did
rejoice."
57 The Yehuḏim, therefore, said to Him,
"You are not yet fifty years old, and have
You seen Aḇraham?"
58 יהושע said to them, "Truly, truly, I say
to you, before Aḇraham came to be, I
am." [e]
59 Therefore they picked up stones to
throw at Him, but יהושע was hidden and
went out of the Set-apart Place, going
through the midst of them, and so passed
by.

9 And passing by, He saw a man, blind
from birth.
2 And His taught ones asked Him, saying, "Rabbi, who sinned, this man or his
parents, that he should be born blind?"
3 יהושע answered, "Neither this man nor
his parents sinned, but that the works of
Elohim might be made manifest in him.
4 "It is necessary for Me to work the
works of Him who sent Me while it is day
– night is coming, when no one is able to
work.
5 "While I am in the world, I am the light
of the world."
6 Having said this, He spat on the ground
and made clay with the saliva, and applied
the clay to the eyes of the blind man.
7 And He said to him, "Go, wash in the
pool of Shiloaḥ" (which means Sent). So
he went and washed, and came seeing.
8 Therefore the neighbours and those
who saw him before, that he was blind,
said, "Is not this he who was sitting and
begging?"
9 Others said, "This is he." Others *said*,
"He is like him." He said, "I am."
10 So they said to him, "How were your
eyes opened?"
11 He answered and said, "A Man called
יהושע made clay and applied it to my eyes
and said to me, 'Go to the pool of Shiloaḥ
and wash.' And I went and washed, and I
received sight."
12 And they said to him, "Where is He?"
He said, "I do not know."
13 They brought to the Pharisees the one
who was once blind.
14 Now it was a Sabbath when יהושע
made the clay and opened his eyes.
15 Therefore the Pharisees also asked him
again how he had received his sight. He
said to them, "He put clay on my eyes, and
I washed, and I see."
16 Therefore some of the Pharisees said,
"This Man is not from Elohim, because He
does not guard the Sabbath." Others said,
"How is a man who is a sinner able to do
such miracles?" And there was a division
among them.
17 So they said to the blind one again,
"What do you say about Him because He
opened your eyes?" And he said, "He is a
prophet."
18 However, the Yehuḏim did not believe
concerning him, that he had been blind and
received his sight, till they called the
parents of him who had received his sight.
19 And they asked them, saying, "Is this
your son, who you say was born blind?
How then does he now see?"
20 His parents answered them and said,
"We know that this is our son, and that he
was born blind,
21 but how he now sees we do not know,
or who opened his eyes we do not know.
He is of age, ask him, he shall speak concerning himself."
22 His parents said this because they were
afraid of the Yehuḏim, for the Yehuḏim
had already agreed that if anyone confessed that He was Messiah, he should be put
out of the congregation.
23 Because of this his parents said, "He is

8d See also 15:10. *8e* See also 1:1, 6:62, 17:5, Iḇ`rim 11:26.

of age, ask him."
[24]So for the second time they called the
man who was blind, and said to him, "Give
esteem to Elohim, we know that this Man
is a sinner."
[25]Then he answered and said, "Whether
He is a sinner, I do not know. I only know
that I was blind, now I see."
[26]And they asked him once more, "What
did He do to you? How did He open your
eyes?"
[27]He answered them, "I have told you
already, and you did not hear. Why do you
wish to hear it again? Do you wish to
become His taught ones too?"
[28]Then they abused him and said, "You
are His taught one, but we are taught ones
of Mosheh.
[29]"We know that Elohim has spoken to
Mosheh, but this One, we do not know
where He is from."
[30]The man answered and said to them,
"Why, this is a wonder! You do not know
where He is from, yet He opened my eyes!
[31]"And we know that Elohim does not
hear sinners. But if anyone fears Elohim
and does His desire, He hears him. [a]
[32]"From of old it has never been heard
that anyone opened the eyes of one who
was born blind.
[33]"If this One were not from Elohim, He
could have done none at all."
[34]They answered and said to him, "You
were completely born in sins – and are you
teaching us?" And they cast him out.
[35]יהושע heard that they had cast him out,
and when He had found him, He said to
him, "Do you believe in the Son of
Elohim?"
[36]He answered and said, "Who is He,
Master, that I might believe in Him?"
[37]And יהושע said to him, "You have both
seen Him and He who speaks with you is
He."
[38]And he said, "Master, I believe," and
bowed before Him.
[39]And יהושע said, "For judgment I have
come into this world, that those not seeing
might see, and those seeing might become
blind."
[40]And those of the Pharisees who were
with Him heard these words, and said to
Him, "Are we blind, too?"
[41]יהושע said to them, "If you were blind,
you would have no sin, but now you say,
'We see,' therefore your sin remains.

10 "Truly, truly, I say to you, he who
does not enter through the door
into the sheepfold, but climbs up by another way, that one is a thief and a robber.
[2]"But he who enters through the door is
the shepherd of the sheep.
[3]"The doorkeeper opens for him, and the
sheep hear his voice. And he calls his own
sheep by name and leads them out.
[4]"And when he has brought out his own
sheep, he goes before them. And the sheep
follow him, because they know his voice.
[5]"And they shall by no means follow a
stranger, but shall flee from him, because
they do not know the voice of strangers."
[6]יהושע used this figure of speech, but
they did not know what He had been saying to them.
[7]יהושע therefore said to them again,
"Truly, truly, I say to you, I am the door of
the sheep.
[8]"All who came before Me are thieves
and robbers, but the sheep did not hear
them.
[9]"I am the door. Whoever enters through
Me, he shall be saved, and shall go in and
shall go out and find pasture.
[10]"The thief does not come except to
steal, and to slaughter, and to destroy. I
have come that they might possess life, and
that they might possess it beyond measure.
[11]"I am the good shepherd. The good
shepherd lays down His life for the sheep.
[12]"But the hireling, and not being a shepherd, one who does not own the sheep, sees
the wolf coming and leaves the sheep and
flees. And the wolf snatches the sheep and
scatters them.
[13]"Now the hireling flees because he is a
hireling and is not concerned about the
sheep.

9a See footnote Mish. 28:9.

14 "I am the good shepherd. [a] And I know
Mine, and Mine know Me,
15 even as the Father knows Me, and I
know the Father. And I lay down My life
for the sheep.
16 "And other sheep I have which are not
of this fold – I have to bring them as well,
and they shall hear My voice, and there
shall be one flock, one shepherd. [b]
17 "Because of this the Father loves Me,
because I lay down My life, in order to
receive it again.
18 "No one takes it from Me, but I lay it
down of Myself. I have authority to lay it
down, and I have authority to receive it
again. This command I have received from
My Father."
19 Again there came a division among the
Yehuḏim because of these words,
20 and many of them said, "He has a
demon and is mad, why do you listen to
Him?"
21 Others said, "These are not the words of
one possessed by a demon. Is a demon able
to open the eyes of the blind?"
22 At that time the Ḥanukkah [c] came to be
in Yerushalayim, and it was winter.
23 And יהושע was walking in the Set-
apart Place, in the porch of Shelomoh.
24 So the Yehuḏim surrounded Him and
said to Him, "How long do You keep us in
suspense? If You are the Messiah, say to us
plainly."
25 יהושע answered them, "I have told
you, and you do not believe. The works
that I do in My Father's Name, they bear
witness concerning Me.
26 "But you do not believe, because you
are not of My sheep, as I said to you.
27 "My sheep hear My voice, and I know
them, and they follow Me. [d]
28 "And I give them everlasting life, and
they shall by no means ever perish, and no
one shall snatch them out of My hand.
29 "My Father, who has given them to Me,
is greater than all. And no one is able to
snatch them out of My Father's hand.
30 "I and My Father are one." [e]
31 Again the Yehuḏim picked up stones to
stone Him.
32 יהושע answered them, "Many good
works I have shown you from My Father.
Because of which of these works do you
stone Me?"
33 The Yehuḏim answered Him, saying,
"We do not stone You for a good work, but
for blasphemy, and because You, being a
Man, make Yourself Elohim."
34 יהושע answered them, "Is it not written
in your own Torah, 'I said, **"You are elohim"** '? Teh. 82:6
35 "If He called them elohim, to whom the
word of Elohim came – and it is impossible
for the Scripture to be broken –
36 do you say of Him whom the Father set
apart and sent into the world, 'You are
blaspheming,' because I said, 'I am the Son
of Elohim'?
37 "If I do not do the works of My Father,
do not believe Me;
38 but if I do, though you do not believe
Me, believe the works, so that you know
and believe that the Father is in Me, and I
in Him."
39 Therefore they were seeking again to
seize Him, but He went forth out of their
hand,
40 and went once more to the other side of
the Yarděn to the place where Yoḥanan was
immersing at first, and there He stayed.
41 And many came to Him and said,
"Yoḥanan indeed did no sign, [f] yet all that
Yoḥanan said about this Man was true."
42 And many believed in Him there.

11 And a certain one was sick, El'azar
from Běyth Anyah, the village of
Miryam and her sister Martha.
2 (Now it was Miryam who anointed the
Master with perfume and wiped His feet
with her hair, whose brother El'azar was
sick).

10a Yeḥ. 34 (all) esp. vv. 11,12, Iḇ`rim 13:20, Kěpha א 2:25, Kěpha א 5:4. *10b* 11:52, Eph. 2:13-19, Yesh. 56:8, Yeḥez. 34:23, Yeḥez. 37:24. *10c* Feast of Dedication, during which candles are lit every evening to commemorate Maccabean victory over Greeks in 165 BCE. - *10d* See also Ḥazon 14:4-5. *10e* One- Hebrew: Eḥaḏ. See also 17:11, 17:21-23. Also Deḇ. 6:4. *10f* Or *miracle*.

3 Therefore the sisters sent to Him, saying, “Master, see, he whom You love is sick.”

4 But when יהושע heard, He said, “This sickness is not unto death, but for the esteem of Elohim, so that the Son of Elohim might be esteemed by it.”

5 Now יהושע loved Martha and her sister and El‘azar .

6 Therefore, when He heard that he was sick, then indeed He stayed at the place where He was, two more days.

7 Then after this He said to the taught ones, “Let us go back to Yehuḏah.”

8 The taught ones said to Him, “Rabbi, the Yehuḏim were but now seeking to stone You, and are You going back there?”

9 יהושע answered, “Are there not twelve hours in the day? If anyone walks in the day, he does not stumble, because he sees the light of this world.

10 “But if anyone walks in the night, he stumbles, because the light is not in him.”

11 He said this, and after that He said to them, “Our friend El‘azar has fallen asleep, but I am going there, to wake him up.”

12 Therefore the taught ones said to Him, “Master, if he has fallen asleep he shall recover.”

13 But יהושע had spoken about his death, whereas they thought that He spoke of taking rest in sleep.

14 So then יהושע said to them plainly, “El‘azar has died.

15 “And for your sake I am glad I was not there, in order for you to believe. But let us go to him.”

16 T’oma, who is called the Twin, then said to his fellow taught ones, “Let us also go, so that we die with Him.”

17 Therefore, when יהושע arrived, He found that he had already been four days in the tomb.

18 Now Bĕyth Anyah was near Yerushalayim, about fifteen stadia [a] away.

19 And many of the Yehuḏim had come to Martha and Miryam, to comfort them concerning their brother.

20 Martha, then, when she heard that יהושע was coming, met Him, but Miryam was sitting in the house.

21 Martha, then, said to יהושע, “Master, if You had been here, my brother would not have died.

22 “But even now I know that whatever You might ask of Elohim, Elohim shall give You.”

23 יהושע said to her, “Your brother shall rise again.”

24 Martha said to Him, “I know that he shall rise again in the resurrection at the last day.”

25 יהושע said to her, “I am the resurrection and the life. He who believes in Me, though he dies, he shall live.

26 “And everyone that is living and believing in Me shall never die at all. Do you believe this?”

27 She said to Him, “Yes, Master, I believe that You are the Messiah, the Son of Elohim, who is coming into the world.”

28 And having said this she went away and called her sister Miryam secretly, saying, “The Teacher is here and calls you.”

29 When she heard, she rose up quickly and came to Him.

30 And יהושע had not yet come into the village, but was in the place where Martha met Him.

31 Therefore the Yehuḏim who were with her in the house, and were comforting her, when they saw that Miryam rose up quickly and went out, followed her, saying, “She is going to the tomb to weep there.”

32 Miryam, therefore, when she came where יהושע was, and saw Him, she fell down at His feet, saying to Him, “Master, if You had been here, my brother would not have died.”

33 יהושע, therefore, when He saw her weeping, and the Yehuḏim who came with her weeping, He groaned in the spirit and was troubled,

34 and said, “Where have you laid him?” They said to Him, “Master, come and see.”

35 יהושע wept.

36 The Yehuḏim therefore said, “See how He loved him!”

11a About 3 kilometres or 2 miles.

37 And some of them said, "Was this One, who opened the eyes of the blind, not also able to prevent this one from dying?"

38 יהושע, therefore, again groaning in Himself, came to the tomb. Now it was a cave, and a stone lay against it.

39 יהושע said, "Take away the stone." Martha, the sister of him who had died, said to Him, "Master, already he smells, for it is four days."

40 יהושע said to her, "Did I not say to you that if you believe, you shall see the esteem of Elohim?"

41 So they took away the stone where the dead man was laid. And יהושע lifted up His eyes and said, "Father, I thank You that You have heard Me.

42 "And I know that You always hear Me, but because of the crowd standing by I said this, in order that they believe that You sent Me."

43 And when He had said this, He cried with a loud voice, "El'azar, come out!"

44 And he who died came out bound feet and hands with wrappings, and his face was wrapped with a cloth. יהושע said to them, "Loosen him, and let him go."

45 Therefore many of the Yehuḏim who had come to Miryam, and had seen what יהושע did, believed in Him.

46 But some of them went away to the Pharisees and told them what יהושע did.

47 So the chief priests and the Pharisees gathered a council and said, "What shall we do? Because this Man does many signs.

48 "If we let Him alone like this, they all shall believe in Him, and the Romans shall come and take away from us both our place and nation."

49 And one of them, Qayapha, being high priest that year, said to them, "You know naught,

50 neither do you consider that it is better for us that one man die for the people than that the entire nation should perish."

51 But he did not say this from himself, but being high priest that year he prophesied that יהושע was about to die for the nation,

52 and not for the nation only, but to gather together into one the children of Elohim who were scattered abroad.

53 So from that day on they plotted to kill Him.

54 יהושע therefore no longer went openly among the Yehuḏim, but went from there into the country near the wilderness, to a city called Ephrayim, and remained there with His taught ones.

55 Now the Pěsaḥ of the Yehuḏim was near, and many went from the country up to Yerushalayim before the Pěsaḥ, to set themselves apart.

56 And so they were seeking יהושע, and spoke among one another, standing in the Set-apart Place, "What do you think? Is He not coming to the festival at all?"

57 And both the chief priests and the Pharisees had given a command, that if anyone knew where He was, he should disclose it, in order for them to seize Him.

12 Accordingly יהושע, six days before the Pěsaḥ, came to Běyth Anyah, where El'azar was, who had died, whom He raised from the dead.

2 So they made Him a supper there, and Martha served, while El'azar was one of those who sat at the table with Him.

3 Then Miryam took a pound of costly perfume of nard, anointed the feet of יהושע, and wiped His feet with her hair. And the house was filled with the fragrance of the perfume.

4 Then one of His taught ones, Yehuḏah from Qerioth, *son* of Shim'on, who was about to deliver Him up, said,

5 "Why was this perfume not sold for three hundred denarii and given to the poor?"

6 And he said this, not because he was concerned about the poor, but because he was a thief, and had the bag, and he used to take what was put in it.

7 יהושע then said, "Let her alone, she has kept this for the day of My burial.

8 "For the poor you have with you always, but Me you do not have always."

9 Then a great crowd of the Yehuḏim learned that He was there. And they came, not on account of יהושע only, but also to see El'azar, whom He had raised from the

dead.
[10]And the chief priests resolved to kill
El'azar as well,
[11]because on account of him many of the
Yehuḏim went away and believed in
יהושע.
[12]On the next day a great crowd who had
come to the festival, when they heard that
יהושע was coming to Yerushalayim,
[13]took the branches of palm trees and
went out to meet Him, and were crying out,
"Hoshia-na! Teh. 118:25 **Blessed is He who is
coming in the Name of יהוה,** Teh. 118:26 *a*
the Sovereign of Yisra'ěl!"
[14]And יהושע, having found a young
donkey, sat on it, as it has been written:
[15]**"Do not fear, daughter of Tsiyon, see,
your Sovereign is coming, sitting on the
colt of a donkey."** Zek. 9:9
[16]At first His taught ones did not understand this. But when יהושע was esteemed,
then they remembered that this was written
about Him and that they had done this to
Him.
[17]Therefore the crowd, who were with
Him when He called El'azar out of his
tomb and raised him from the dead, were
bearing witness.
[18]On account of this the crowd also met
Him, because they heard that He had done
this sign.
[19]The Pharisees then said among themselves, "You see how you are getting
nowhere at all. Look, the world has gone
after Him!"
[20]And there were certain Greeks among
those coming up to worship at the festival.
[21]These then came to Philip, who was
from Běyth Tsaiḏa of Galil, and were asking him, saying, "Master, we wish to see
יהושע."
[22]Philip came and told Andri, and in turn
Andri and Philip told יהושע.
[23]And יהושע answered them, saying,
"The hour has come for the Son of Aḏam
to be esteemed.
[24]"Truly, truly, I say to you, unless a grain
of wheat falls into the ground and dies, it
remains alone. But if it dies, it bears much
fruit.
[25]"He who loves his life shall lose it, and
he who hates his life in this world shall preserve it for everlasting life.
[26]"If anyone serves Me, let him follow
Me. And where I am, there My servant also
shall be. If anyone serves Me, the Father
shall value him.
[27]"Now I Myself am troubled, and what
shall I say? 'Father, save Me from this
hour'? But for this reason I came to this
hour.
[28]"Father, esteem Your Name." Then a
voice came from the heaven, "I have both
esteemed it and shall esteem it again."
[29]So the crowd who stood by and heard it
were saying there had been thunder. Others
said, "A messenger has spoken to Him."
[30]יהושע answered and said, "This voice
did not come because of Me, but for your
sake.
[31]"Now is the judgment of this world,
now the ruler of this world *b* shall be cast
out.
[32]"And I, if I am lifted up from the earth,
shall draw all *men* unto Myself."
[33]This He said, signifying by what death
He was about to die.
[34]The crowd answered Him, "We have
heard out of the Torah that the Messiah
remains forever. And how do You say, 'The
Son of Aḏam has to be lifted up'? Who is
this Son of Aḏam?"
[35]יהושע, therefore, said to them, "Yet a
little while the light is with you. Walk
while you have the light, lest darkness
overtake you. And he who walks in darkness does not know where he is going.
[36]"While you have the light, believe in
the light, so that you become sons of light."
These *words* יהושע spoke, and went off
and was hidden from them.
[37]But though He had done so many signs
before them, they did not believe in Him,
[38]that the word of Yeshayahu the prophet
might be filled, which he spoke, **"יהוה,
who has believed our report? And to
whom has the arm of יהוה been
revealed?"** Yesh. 53:1

12a See Mt. 23:39 & Teh. 118:26. *12b* See Lq. 4:6.

39 Because of this they were unable to believe, because again Yeshayahu said:

40 **"He has blinded their eyes and hardened their heart, so that they should not see with their eyes and understand with their heart, and turn, and I should heal them."** Yesh. 6:10 [c]

41 Yeshayahu said this when he saw His esteem and spoke of Him.

42 Still, even among the rulers many did believe in Him, but because of the Pharisees they did not confess *Him*, lest they should be put out of the congregation,

43 for they loved the praise of men more than the praise of Elohim.

44 Then יהושע cried out and said, "He who believes in Me, believes not in Me but in Him who sent Me.

45 "And he who sees Me sees Him who sent Me.

46 "I have come as a light into the world, so that no one who believes in Me should stay in darkness.

47 "And if anyone hears My Words but does not watch over them, I do not judge him. For I did not come to judge the world but to save the world.

48 "He who rejects Me, and does not receive My Words, has one who judges him: the Word that I have spoken shall judge him in the last day. [d]

49 "Because I spoke not from Myself, but the Father who sent Me has given Me a command, [e] what I should say and what I should speak.

50 "And I know that His command is everlasting life. [f] Therefore, whatever I speak, as the Father has said to Me, so I speak."

13 And before the Festival of the Pěsaḥ, יהושע knowing that His hour had come that He should move out of this world unto the Father, having loved His own who were in the world, He loved them to the end.

2 And supper taking place, the devil having already put it into the heart of Yehuḏah from Qerioth, *son* of Shim'on, to deliver Him up,

3 יהושע, knowing that the Father had given all into His hands, and that He had come from Elohim and was going to Elohim,

4 rose from supper and laid aside His garments, and having taken a towel, He girded Himself.

5 After that He put water into a basin and began to wash the feet of the taught ones, and to wipe them with the towel with which He was girded.

6 And so He came to Shim'on Kěpha, and he said to Him, "Master, do You wash my feet?"

7 יהושע answered and said to him, "You do not know what I am doing now, but you shall know after this."

8 Kěpha said to Him, "By no means shall You wash my feet, ever!" יהושע answered him, "If I do not wash you, you have no part with Me."

9 Shim'on Kěpha said to Him, "Master, not my feet only, but also my hands and my head!"

10 יהושע said to him, "He who has had a bath does not need to wash, except his feet, but is clean altogether. And you are clean, but not all of you."

11 For He knew who would deliver Him up, so He said, "You are not all clean."

12 So when He had washed their feet and taken His garments, and sat down again, He said to them, "Do you know what I have done to you?

13 "You call me Teacher and Master, and you say well, for I am.

14 "Then if I, Master and Teacher, have washed your feet, you also ought to wash one another's feet.

15 "For I gave you an example, that you should do as I have done to you.

16 "Truly, truly, I say to you, a servant is not greater than his master, nor is an emissary greater than he who sent him.

17 "If you know these *teachings*, blessed are you if you do them.

18 "I do not speak concerning all of you. I know whom I have chosen, but that the Scripture might be filled, **'He who eats**

12c See Mt. 13:15. *12d* See also 3:18,19; 7:16. *12e* See 7:16. *12f* See Mt. 19:17; Yn. 3:36.

bread with Me has lifted up his heel
against Me.’ Teh. 41:9
19 “Now I say to you, before it takes place,
that when it does take place, you shall
believe that I am.
20 “Truly, truly, I say to you, he who
receives whomever I send, receives Me.
And he who receives Me, receives Him
who sent Me.”
21 When יהושע had said this He was troubled in spirit, and witnessed and said,
“Truly, truly, I say to you, one of you shall
deliver Me up.”
22 The taught ones looked at one another,
doubting of whom He spoke.
23 And one of His taught ones, whom
יהושע loved, was reclining on the bosom
of יהושע.
24 Shim‘on Kěpha then motioned to him to
ask who it was of whom He spoke.
25 And leaning back on the breast of
יהושע he said to Him, “Master, who is it?”
26 יהושע answered, “It is he to whom I
shall give a piece of bread when I have
dipped it.” And having dipped the bread,
He gave it to Yehuḏah from Qerioth, *son* of
Shim‘on.
27 And after the piece of bread, Satan
entered into him. יהושע, therefore, said to
him, “What you do, do quickly.”
28 But no one at the table knew why He
said this to him,
29 for some were supposing, because
Yehuḏah had the bag, that יהושע was saying to him, “Buy what we need for the festival,” or that he should give somewhat to
the poor.
30 So, having received the piece of bread,
he then went out straightaway, and it was
night.
31 When, therefore, he went out, יהושע
said, “Now the Son of Aḏam has been
esteemed, and Elohim has been esteemed
in Him.
32 “If Elohim has been esteemed in Him,
Elohim shall also esteem Him in Himself,
and straightaway esteem Him.
33 “Little children, yet a little while I am
with you. You shall seek Me, and as I said
to the Yehuḏim, ‘Where I am going, you
are unable to come,’ I now also say to you.
34 “A renewed command I give to you,
that you love one another, as I have loved
you, that you also love one another.
35 “By this shall all know that you are My
taught ones, if you have love for one another.”
36 Shim‘on Kěpha said to Him, “Master,
where are You going?” יהושע answered
him, “Where I am going you are unable to
follow Me now, but afterwards you shall
follow Me.”
37 Kěpha said to Him, “Master, why am I
unable to follow You now? I shall lay
down my life for You.”
38 יהושע answered him, “Shall you lay
down your life for Me? Truly, truly, I say to
you, the cock shall not crow at all until you
have denied Me three times.

14 “Let not your heart be troubled.
Believe in Elohim, believe also in
Me.
2 “In My Father’s house are many staying places. And if not, I would have told
you. I go to prepare a place for you.
3 “And if I go and prepare a place for
you, I shall come again and receive you to
Myself, that where I am, you might be too.
4 “And where I go you know, and the
way you know.”
5 T’oma said to Him, “Master, we do not
know where You are going, and how are
we able to know the way?”
6 יהושע said to him, “I am the Way, and
the Truth, and the Life. No one comes to
the Father except through Me.
7 “If you had known Me, you would have
known My Father too. From now on you
know Him, and have seen.”
8 Philip said to Him, “Master, show us
the Father, and it is enough for us.”
9 יהושע said to him, “Have I been with
you so long, and you have not known Me,
Philip? He who has seen Me has seen the
Father, and how do you say, ‘Show us the
Father’?
10 “Do you not believe that I am in the
Father, and the Father is in Me? The words
that I speak to you I do not speak from
Myself. But the Father who stays in Me
does His works.

11 "Believe Me that I am in the Father and
the Father in Me, otherwise believe Me
because of the works themselves.
12 "Truly, truly, I say to you, he who
believes in Me, the works that I do he shall
do also. And greater *works* than these he
shall do, because I go to My Father.
13 "And whatever you ask in My Name,
that I shall do, in order that the Father
might be esteemed in the Son.
14 "If you ask whatever in My Name, I
shall do it.
15 "If you love Me, you shall guard My
commands. [a]
16 "And I shall ask the Father, and He
shall give you another Helper, to stay with
you forever –
17 the Spirit of the Truth, whom the world
is unable to receive, because it does not see
Him or know Him. But you know Him, for
He stays with you and shall be in you.
18 "I shall not leave you orphans – I am
coming to you.
19 "Yet a little while, and the world no
longer sees Me, but you shall see Me,
because I live, and you shall live.
20 "In that day you shall know that I am in
My Father, and you in Me, and I in you.
21 "He who possesses My commands and
guards them, it is he who loves Me. And he
who loves Me shall be loved by My Father,
and I shall love him and manifest Myself to
him."
22 Yehuḏah – not the one from Qerioth –
said to Him, "Master, what has come about
that You are about to manifest Yourself to
us, and not to the world?"
23 יהושע answered him, "If anyone loves
Me, he shall guard My Word. And My
Father shall love him, and We shall come
to him and make Our stay with him.
24 "He who does not love Me does not
guard My Words. And the Word which you
hear is not Mine but of the Father Who sent
Me.
25 "These *Words* I have spoken to you
while still with you.
26 "But the Helper, the Set-apart Spirit,
whom the Father shall send in My Name,
He shall teach you all, and remind you of
all that I said to you.
27 "Peace I leave with you – My peace I
give to you. I do not give to you as the
world gives. Do not let your heart be
troubled, neither let it be afraid.
28 "You heard that I said to you, 'I am
going away and I am coming to you.' If
you did love Me, you would have rejoiced
that I said, 'I am going to the Father,' for
My Father is greater than I.
29 "And now I have told you before it
takes place, that when it does take place,
you shall believe.
30 "I shall no longer talk much with you,
for the ruler of this world [b] is coming, and
he possesses none at all in Me,
31 but, in order for the world to know that
I love the Father, and that as the Father
commanded Me, so I am doing. Rise up, let
us go from here.

15 "I am the true vine, and My Father
is the gardener.
2 "Every branch in Me that bears no fruit
He takes away. And every branch that
bears fruit He prunes, so that it bears more
fruit.
3 "You are already clean because of the
Word which I have spoken to you.
4 "Stay in Me, and I *stay* in you. As the
branch is unable to bear fruit of itself,
unless it stays in the vine, so neither you,
unless you stay in Me.
5 "I am the vine, you are the branches. He
who stays in Me, and I in him, he bears
much fruit. Because without Me you are
able to do naught!
6 "If anyone does not stay in Me, he is
thrown away as a branch and dries up. And
they gather them and throw them into the
fire, and they are burned.
7 "If you stay in Me, and My Words stay
in you, you shall ask whatever you wish,
and it shall be done for you.
8 "In this My Father is esteemed, that you
bear much fruit, and you shall be My

14a See also vv. 21 & 23; Shem. 20:6; Yn. א 5:2-3 and Yn. ב v. 6. *14b* See footnote Lq. 4:6.

taught ones.

9 "As the Father has loved Me, I have also loved you. Stay in My love.

10 "If you guard My commands, you shall stay in My love, [a] even as I have guarded My Father's commands and stay in His love.

11 "These *words* I have spoken to you, so that My joy might be in you, and that your joy might be complete.

12 "This is My command, that you love one another, as I have loved you. [b]

13 "No one has greater love than this: that one should lay down his life for his friends.

14 "You are My friends if you do whatever I command you.

15 "No longer do I call you servants, for a servant does not know what his master is doing. But I have called you friends, for all *teachings* which I heard from My Father I have made known to you.

16 "You did not choose Me, but I chose you and appointed you that you should go and bear fruit, and that your fruit should remain, so that whatever you ask the Father in My Name He might give you.

17 "These *words* I command you, so that you love one another. [c]

18 "If the world hates you, you know that it hated Me before *it hated* you.

19 "If you were of the world, the world would love its own. But because you are not of the world, but I chose you out of the world, for that reason the world hates you.

20 "Remember the word that I said to you, 'A servant is not greater than his master.' If they persecuted Me, they shall persecute you too. If they have guarded My Word, they would guard yours too.

21 "But all this they shall do to you because of My Name, because they do not know Him who sent Me.

22 "If I had not come and spoken to them, they would have no sin, but now they have no excuse for their sin.

23 "He who hates Me hates My Father as well.

24 "If I did not do among them the works which no one else did, they would have no sin. But now they have both seen and have hated both Me and My Father,

25 but... that the word might be filled which was written in their Torah, **'They hated Me without a cause.'** Teh. 35:19, 69:4

26 "And when the Helper comes, whom I shall send to you from the Father, the Spirit of the Truth, who comes from the Father, He shall bear witness of Me,

27 but you also bear witness, because you have been with Me from the beginning.

16 "These *words* I have spoken to you, so that you do not stumble.

2 "They shall put you out of the congregations, but an hour is coming when everyone who kills you shall think he is rendering service to Elohim.

3 "And this they shall do to you because they did not know the Father, nor Me.

4 "But I have said these *words* to you, so that when the hour comes you remember that I told them to you. And these *words* I did not say to you at the beginning, for I was with you.

5 "But now I go away to Him who sent Me, and not one of you asks Me, 'Where are You going?'

6 "But because I have said these *words* to you, grief has filled your heart.

7 "But I say the truth to you. It is better for you that I go away, for if I do not go away, the Helper shall not come to you at all, but if I go, I shall send Him to you.

8 "And having come, He shall convict [a] the world concerning sin, [b] and concerning righteousness, and concerning judgment –

9 concerning sin because they do not believe in Me,

10 concerning righteousness because I go to My Father and you see Me no more,

11 concerning judgment because th of this world [c] is judged.

12 "I still have many *words* to s

15a See 14:15. *15b* See 13:34 and 15:17. *15c* See 13:34, and 15:12. *16a* Or *confute* or *prove wrong*
16b Diḇre. ב 24:20, Neḥ. 9:30, Yeḥez. 36:27, Miḵ. 3:8, Ma. 28:25-27. *16c* See Lq. 4:6.

but you are not able to bear them now.
13 "But when He comes, the Spirit of the
Truth, He shall guide you into all the truth.
For He shall not speak from Himself, but
whatever He hears He shall speak, and He
shall announce to you what is to come.
14 "He shall esteem Me, for He shall take
of what is Mine and announce it to you.
15 "All that the Father has is Mine. That is
why I said that He takes from what is Mine
and announces it to you.
16 "A little while, and you do not see Me,
and again a little while, and you shall see
Me."
17 Therefore some of His taught ones said
to one another, "What is this that He says
to us, 'A little while, and you do not see
Me, and again a little while, and you shall
see Me,' and, 'because I am going to the
Father'?"
18 So they said, "What is this that He says,
'A little while'? We do not know what He
is saying."
19 יהושע, therefore, knew that they were
wishing to ask Him, and He said to them,
"Are you asking one another about what I
said, 'A little while, and you do not see
Me, and again a little while, and you shall
see Me'?
20 "Truly, truly, I say to you that you shall
weep and lament, but the world shall
rejoice. And you shall be grieved, but your
grief shall become joy.
21 "The woman has grief when she is in
labour, because her hour has come, but as
soon as she has given birth to the child, she
no longer remembers the affliction, for joy
that a man was born into the world.
22 "And you, therefore, have grief now,
but I shall see you again and your heart
shall rejoice, and no one takes your joy
away from you.
23 "And in that day you shall ask Me none
at all. Truly, truly, I say to you, whatever
you ask the Father in My Name He shall
give you.
24 "Until now you have asked naught in
My Name. Ask, and you shall receive, in
order that your joy might be complete.
25 "These *words* I have spoken to you in
figures of speech, but an hour is coming
when I shall no longer speak to you in
figures of speech, but I shall declare the
Father plainly to you.
26 "In that day you shall ask in My Name,
and I do not say to you that I shall pray the
Father on your behalf,
27 for the Father Himself does love you,
because you have loved Me, and have
believed that I came forth from Elohim.
28 "I came forth from the Father and have
come into the world. Again, I leave the
world and go to the Father."
29 His taught ones said to Him, "See, now
You are speaking plainly, and not using
figure of speech!
30 "Now we know that You know all, and
have no need that anyone should question
You. By this we believe that You came
forth from Elohim."
31 יהושע answered them, "Do you now
believe?
32 "See, an hour is coming, and has now
come, that you are scattered, each to his
own, and leave Me alone. Yet I am not
alone, because the Father is with Me.
33 "These *words* I have spoken to you, that
in Me you might have peace. In the world
you have pressure, but take courage, I have
overcome the world."

17 יהושע said these *words*, and lifted
up His eyes to the heaven, and
said, "Father, the hour has come. Esteem
Your Son, so that Your Son also might
esteem You,
2 as You have given Him authority over
all flesh, that He should give everlasting
life to all whom You have given Him.
3 "And this is everlasting life, that they
should know You, the only true Elohim,
and יהושע Messiah whom You have sent.
4 "I have esteemed You on the earth, having accomplished the work You have given
Me that I should do.
5 "And now, esteem Me with Yourself,
Father, with the esteem which I had with
You before the world was.

6 "I have revealed Your Name to the men
whom You gave Me out of the world. They
were Yours, and You gave them to Me, and
they have guarded Your Word. [a]
7 "Now they have come to know that all
You gave to Me, is from You.
8 "Because the Words which You gave to
Me, I have given to them. And they have
received them, and have truly known that I
came forth from You, and they believed
that You sent Me.
9 "I pray for them. I do not pray for the
world but for those whom You have given
Me, for they are Yours.
10 "And all Mine are Yours, and Yours are
Mine, and I have been esteemed in them.
11 "And I am no more in the world, but
these are in the world, and I come to You.
Set-apart Father, guard them in Your Name
which You have given Me, so that they
might be one, [b] as We are.
12 "When I was with them in the world, I
was guarding them in Your Name which
You have given Me, and I watched over
them, and not one of them perished except
the son of destruction, that the Scripture
might be filled.
13 "And now I come to You. And I speak
these *words* in the world, so that they have
My joy completed in them.
14 "I have given them Your Word, and the
world hated them because they are not of
the world, as I am not of the world.
15 "I do not pray that You should take
them out of the world, but that You keep
them from the wicked *one*.
16 "They are not of the world, as I am not
of the world.
17 "Set them apart in Your truth – Your
Word is truth. [c]
18 "As You sent Me into the world, I also
sent them into the world.
19 "And for them I set Myself apart, so
that they too might be set apart in truth.
20 "And I do not pray for these alone, but
also for those believing in Me through their
word,
21 so that they all might be one, as You,
Father, are in Me, and I in You, so that they
too might be one in Us, so that the world
might believe that You have sent Me.
22 "And the esteem which You gave Me I
have given them, so that they might be one
as We are one,
23 "I in them, and You in Me, so that they
might be perfected into one, so that the
world knows that You have sent Me, and
have loved them as You have loved Me.
24 "Father, I desire that those whom You
have given Me, might be with Me where I
am, so that they see My esteem which You
have given Me, because You loved Me
before the foundation of the world.
25 "O righteous Father, indeed the world
did not know You, but I knew You, and
these knew that You sent Me.
26 "And I have made Your Name known
to them, [d] and shall make it known, so that
the love with which You loved Me might
be in them, and I in them."

18 Having said these *words*, יהושע
went out with His taught ones
beyond the Qiḏron torrent, where there was
a garden, into which He and His taught
ones entered.
2 And Yehuḏah, who delivered Him up,
also knew the place, because יהושע often
met there with His taught ones.
3 Yehuḏah, then, having received the
company *of soldiers*, and officers from the
chief priests and Pharisees, came there
with lanterns, and torches, and weapons.
4 יהושע, then, knowing all that would
come upon Him, went forward and said to
them, "Whom do you seek?"
5 They answered Him, "יהושע of
Natsareth." יהושע said to them, "I am."
And Yehuḏah, who delivered Him up, was
also standing with them.
6 When, therefore, He said to them, "I
am," they drew back and fell to the ground.
7 Once more He asked them, "Whom do
you seek?" And they said, "יהושע of
Natsareth."
8 יהושע answered, "I said to you that I

17a Also see Teh. 138:2. *17b* Also see 10:30. *17c* Teh. 119:142, 151, 160. *17d* See also v. 6, as well as Teh. 22:22, Iḇ`rim 2:12.

am. If, then, you seek Me, allow these to
go,”
9 in order that the word might be filled
which He spoke, “Of those whom You
have given Me, I have lost none.”
10 Then Shim‘on Kěpha, having a sword,
drew it and struck the high priest’s servant,
and cut off his right ear. And the servant’s
name was Meleḵ.
11 Then יהושע said to Kěpha, “Put your
sword into the sheath. Shall I not drink the
cup which My Father has given Me?”
12 Then the company *of soldiers* and the
commander and the officers of the
Yehuḏim seized יהושע and bound Him,
13 and they led Him away to Ḥanan first,
for he was the father-in-law of Qayapha
who was high priest that year.
14 Now Qayapha was the one who gave
counsel to the Yehuḏim that it was better
that one man should die for the people.
15 And Shim‘on Kěpha followed יהושע,
with another taught one, and that taught
one was known to the high priest, and went
with יהושע into the courtyard of the high
priest.
16 But Kěpha was standing outside at the
door. So the other taught one, who was
known to the high priest, went out and
spoke to her who kept the door, and
brought Kěpha in.
17 Then the servant girl who kept the door
said to Kěpha, “Are you also one of this
Man’s taught ones?” He said, “I am not.”
18 And the servants and officers who had
made a fire of coals stood there, because it
was cold, and they warmed themselves.
And Kěpha was standing with them and
warming himself.
19 Then the high priest asked יהושע about
His taught ones and His teaching.
20 יהושע answered him, “I spoke openly
to the world. I always taught in the congregation and in the Set-apart Place, where the
Yehuḏim always meet, and I spoke no
word in secret.
21 “Why do you ask Me? Ask those who
have heard Me what I said to them. See,
they know what I said.”
22 And when He had said this, one of the
officers who stood by slapped יהושע in the
face, saying, “Do You answer the high
priest this way?”
23 יהושע answered him, “If I have spoken
evilly, bear witness of the evil, but if well,
why do you strike Me?”
24 Then Ḥanan sent Him bound to the high
priest, Qayapha.
25 And Shim‘on Kěpha was standing and
warming himself. Then they said to him,
“Are you also one of His taught ones?” He
denied it and said, “I am not!”
26 One of the servants of the high priest, a
relative of the one whose ear Kěpha cut off,
said, “Did I not see you in the garden with
Him?”
27 Then Kěpha again denied it, and immediately a cock crowed.
28 Then they led יהושע from Qayapha to
the palace, and it was early. And they
themselves did not go into the palace, lest
they should be defiled, but that they might
eat the Pěsaḥ.
29 Pilate, therefore, came out to them and
said, “What accusation do you bring
against this Man?”
30 They answered and said to him, “If He
were not an evil-doer, we would not have
delivered Him up to you.”
31 Then Pilate said to them, “You take
Him and judge Him according to your
law.” The Yehuḏim said to him, “It is not
right for us to put anyone to death,”
32 in order that the word of יהושע might
be filled which He spoke, signifying by
what death He was about to die.
33 Then Pilate went back into the palace,
and called יהושע, and said to Him, “Are
You the Sovereign of the Yehuḏim?”
34 יהושע answered him, “Do you say this
from yourself, or did others talk to you
about Me?”
35 Pilate answered, “Am I a Yehuḏi? Your
own nation and the chief priests have delivered You to me. What did You do?”
36 יהושע answered, “My reign is not of
this world. If My reign were of this world,
My servants would fight, so that I should
not be delivered to the Yehuḏim. But now
My reign is not from here.”
37 Then Pilate said to Him, “You are a
sovereign, then?” יהושע answered, “You

say it, because I am a sovereign. For this I
was born, and for this I have come into the
world, that I should bear witness to the
truth. Everyone who is of the truth hears
My voice."
38 Pilate said to Him, "What is truth?"
And when he had said this, he went out
again to the Yehuḏim, and said to them, "I
find no guilt in Him.
39 "But you have a habit that I shall
release someone to you at the Pěsaḥ. Do
you wish, then, that I release to you the
Sovereign of the Yehuḏim?"
40 Then they all shouted again, saying,
"Not this One, but Barabba!" And Barabba
was a robber.

19 Then, therefore, Pilate took יהושע
and flogged *Him*.
2 And the soldiers plaited a crown of
thorns and placed it on His head, and they
put a purple robe on Him,
3 and came to Him and said, "Greetings,
Sovereign of the Yehuḏim!" And they
slapped Him in the face.
4 And Pilate went outside again, and said
to them, "See, I am bringing Him out to
you, to let you know that I find no guilt in
Him."
5 Then יהושע came outside, wearing the
crown of thorns and the purple robe. And
Pilate said to them, "See the Man!"
6 So when the chief priests and officers
saw Him, they shouted, saying, "Impale!
Impale!" Pilate said to them, "You take
Him and impale Him, for I find no guilt in
Him."
7 The Yehuḏim answered him, "We have
a law, and according to our law He ought to
die, for He has made Himself the Son of
Elohim."
8 So when Pilate heard this word, he was
more afraid,
9 and went back into the palace, and
asked יהושע, "Where are You from?" But
יהושע gave him no answer.
10 Then Pilate said to Him, "Do You not
speak to me? Do You not know that I possess authority to impale You, and I possess
authority to release You?"
11 יהושע answered, "You would possess
no authority against Me if it were not given
you from above. Because of this, he who
delivered Me to you has greater sin."
12 From then on Pilate was seeking to
release Him, but the Yehuḏim shouted,
saying, "If you release this One, you are
not Caesar's friend. Everyone who makes
himself a sovereign, does speak against
Caesar."
13 Therefore, when Pilate heard these
words, he brought יהושע out and sat down
in the judgment seat in a place that is called
Pavement, but in Hebrew, Gabbatha.
14 And it was the Preparation *Day* of
the Pěsaḥ *week*, and about the sixth hour.
And he said to the Yehuḏim, "See your
Sovereign!"
15 But they shouted, "Away, away, impale
Him!" Pilate said to them, "Shall I impale
your Sovereign?" The chief priests
answered, "We have no sovereign except
Caesar!"
16 At that time, then, he delivered Him to
them to be impaled. And they took יהושע
and led *Him* away.
17 And bearing His stake, He went out to
the so-called Place of a Skull, which is
called in Hebrew, Golgotha,
18 where they impaled Him, and two others with Him, one on this side and one on
that side, and יהושע in the middle.
19 And Pilate wrote a title too, and put it
on the stake, and it was written: יהושע OF
NATSARETH, THE SOVEREIGN OF
THE YEHUḎIM.
20 Many of the Yehuḏim therefore read
this title, for the place where יהושע was
impaled was near the city, and it was written in Hebrew, in Greek, in Roman.
21 So the chief priests of the Yehuḏim said
to Pilate, "Do not write, 'The Sovereign of
the Yehuḏim,' but, 'He said, "I am the
Sovereign of the Yehuḏim." ' "
22 Pilate answered, "What I have written, I
have written."
23 Then the soldiers, when they had
impaled יהושע, took His outer garments
and made four parts, to each soldier a part,
and the inner garment. But the inner
garment was without seam, woven from
the top in one piece.

24 So they said to each other, "Let us not
tear it, but cast lots for it – whose it shall
be," in order that the Scripture might be
filled which says, **"They divided My garments among them, and for My clothing
they cast lots."** Teh. 22:18 The soldiers therefore indeed did this.
25 And by the stake of יהושע stood His
mother, and His mother's sister, Miryam
the wife of Qlophah, and Miryam from
Maḡdala.
26 Then יהושע, seeing His mother and the
taught one whom He loved standing by, He
said to His mother, "Woman, see your
son!"
27 Then to the taught one He said, "See,
your mother!" And from that hour that
taught one took her to his own *home*.
28 After this, יהושע, knowing that all had
been accomplished, in order that the Scripture might be accomplished, said, "I
thirst!"
29 A bowl of sour wine stood there, and
they filled a sponge with sour wine, put it
on hyssop, and held it to His mouth.
30 So when יהושע took the sour wine He
said, "It has been accomplished!" And
bowing His head, He gave up His spirit.
31 Therefore, since it was the Preparation
Day, that the bodies should not remain on
the stake on the Sabbath – for that Sabbath
was a high one – the Yehuḏim asked Pilate
to have their legs broken, and that *they* be
taken away.
32 Therefore the soldiers came and broke
the legs of the first, and of the other who
was impaled with Him,
33 but when they came to יהושע and saw
that He was already dead, they did not
break His legs.
34 But one of the soldiers pierced His side
with a spear, and instantly blood and water
came out.
35 And he who has seen has witnessed,
and his witness is true. And he knows that
he is speaking the truth, in order that you
might believe.
36 For this took place in order for the
Scripture to be filled: **"Not one of His
bones shall be broken."** Teh. 34:20 [a]
37 And again another Scripture says,
**"They shall look on Him whom they
pierced."** Zeḵ. 12:10
38 And after this, Yosĕph of Ramathayim,
being a taught one of יהושע, but secretly,
for fear of the Yehuḏim, asked Pilate that
he might take the body of יהושע, and
Pilate gave permission. Therefore he came
and took the body of יהושע.
39 And Naḵdimon, who at first came to
יהושע by night, also came, bringing a mixture of myrrh and aloes, about a hundred
pounds.
40 Then they took the body of יהושע, and
bound it in linen wrappings with the spices,
as was the habit of the Yehuḏim for burial.
41 And at the place where He was impaled
there was a garden, and in the garden a
fresh tomb in which no one had yet been
laid.
42 There, then, because of the Preparation
Day of the Yehuḏim, they laid יהושע,
because the tomb was near.

20

And on *day* one of the week [a]
Miryam from Maḡdala came early
to the tomb, while it was still dark, [b] and
saw that the stone had been removed from
the tomb.
2 So she ran and came to Shim'on Kĕpha,
and to the other taught one whom יהושע
loved, and said to them, "They have taken
the Master out of the tomb, and we do not
know where they laid Him."
3 Then Kĕpha and the other taught one
went out, and they were going to the tomb,
4 and the two were running together, but
the other taught one outran Kĕpha and
came to the tomb first.
5 And stooping down he saw the linen
wrappings lying, but he did not go in.
6 Then Shim'on Kĕpha came, following
him, and went into the tomb. And he saw
the linen wrappings lying,
7 and the cloth which had been on His
head, not lying with the linen wrappings,

19a Also see Shem. 12:46, Bem. 9:12. *20a* Gk. one of the sabbaths - See Explanatory notes - First day of the week. *20b* Gk. dimness or obscurity.

but folded up in a place by itself.
8 So, then, the other taught one, who
came to the tomb first, also went in. And he
saw and believed.
9 For they did not yet know the Scripture,
that He has to rise again from the dead.
10 Therefore the taught ones went away
again, by themselves.
11 But Miryam was standing outside by
the tomb weeping. Then as she wept, she
stooped down to the tomb,
12 and saw two messengers in white sitting, one at the head and the other at the
feet, where the body of יהושע had been
laid.
13 And they said to her, "Woman, why do
you weep?" She said to them, "Because
they took away my Master, and I do not
know where they laid Him."
14 And having said this, she turned around
and saw יהושע standing, but she did not
know that it was יהושע.
15 יהושע said to her, "Woman, why do
you weep? Whom do you seek?" Thinking
He was the gardener, she said to Him,
"Master, if You have carried Him away,
say to me where You put Him, and I shall
take Him away."
16 יהושע said to her, "Miryam!" She
turned and said to Him, "Rabboni!" (which
means Teacher).
17 יהושע said to her, "Do not hold on to
Me, for I have not yet ascended to My
Father. But go to My brothers and say to
them, 'I am ascending to My Father and
your Father, and to My Elohim and your
Elohim.' "
18 Miryam from Maḡdala came announcing to the taught ones that she had seen the
Master, and that He had told her this.
19 When therefore it was evening on that
day, *day* one of the week [c], and when the
doors were shut where the taught ones met,
for fear of the Yehuḏim, יהושע came and
stood in the midst, and said to them, "Peace
to you."
20 And having said this, He showed them
His hands and His side. The taught ones
therefore rejoiced when they saw the
Master.
21 Then יהושע said to them again, "Peace
to you! As the Father has sent Me, I also
send you."
22 And having said this, He breathed on
them, and said to them, "Receive the Set-
apart Spirit.
23 "If you forgive the sins of any, they are
forgiven them; if you retain the sins of any,
they have been retained."
24 But T'oma, called the Twin, one of the
twelve, was not with them when יהושע
came,
25 so the other taught ones said to him,
"We have seen the Master." But he said to
them, "Unless I see in His hands the mark
of the nails, and put my finger into the
imprint of the nails, and put my hand into
His side, I shall by no means believe."
26 And after eight days His taught ones
were again inside, and T'oma with them.
יהושע came, the doors having been shut,
and He stood in the midst, and said, "Peace
to you!"
27 Then He said to T'oma, "Bring your
finger here, and see My hands. And bring
your hand and put it into My side – and do
not be unbelieving, but believing."
28 And T'oma answered and said to Him,
"My Master and my Elohim!"
29 יהושע said to him, "T'oma, because
you have seen Me, you have believed.
Blessed are those who have not seen and
have believed."
30 There were indeed many other signs
that יהושע did in the presence of His
taught ones, which are not written in this
book,
31 but these have been written so that you
believe that יהושע is the Messiah, the Son
of Elohim, and that, believing, you might
possess life in His Name.

21 After this יהושע manifested Himself again to the taught ones at the
Sea of Kinnereth, and He manifested this
way:
2 Shim'on Kěpha, and T'oma called the
Twin, and Nethaně'l of Qanah in Galil, the

20c Gk. one of the sabbaths - See Explanatory notes - First day of the week.

sons of Zaḇdai, and two others of His
taught ones were together.
3 Shimʿon Kěpha said to them, "I am
going to fish." They said to him, "We are
also coming with you." They went out and
immediately entered into the boat. And that
night they caught none at all.
4 But when it became early morning,
יהושע stood on the beach. However, the
taught ones did not know that it was
יהושע.
5 Then יהושע said to them, "Children,
have you any food?" They answered Him,
"No."
6 And He said to them, "Throw the net on
the right side of the boat, and you shall
find." So they threw, and they were no
longer able to draw it in because of the
large number of fish.
7 That taught one whom יהושע loved
then said to Kěpha, "It is the Master!" Then
Shimʿon Kěpha, hearing that it was the
Master, put on his outer garment – for he
was stripped – and plunged into the sea.
8 And the other taught ones came in the
little boat – for they were not far from land,
but about two hundred cubits – dragging
the net with fish.
9 So when they had come to land, they
saw a fire of coals there, and fish laid on it,
and bread.
10 יהושע said to them, "Bring some of the
fish which you have now caught."
11 Shimʿon Kěpha went up and dragged
the net to land, filled with one hundred and
fifty-three big fishes. And though there
were so many, the net was not broken.
12 יהושע said to them, "Come, have
breakfast." And not one of the taught ones
had the courage to ask Him, "Who are
You?," knowing that it was the Master.
13 יהושע came and took the bread and
gave it to them, and the same with the fish.
14 This was now the third time יהושע was
manifested to His taught ones after He was
raised from the dead.
15 When, therefore, they had eaten breakfast, יהושע said to Shimʿon Kěpha,
"Shimʿon, *son* of Yonah, do you love Me
more than these?" He said to Him, "Yes,
Master, You know that I love You." He said
to him, "Feed My lambs."
16 He said to him again, the second time,
"Shimʿon, *son* of Yonah, do you love Me?"
He said to Him, "Yes, Master, You know
that I love You." He said to him, "Shepherd
My sheep."
17 He said to him the third time, "Shimʿon,
son of Yonah, do you love Me?" Kěpha
was sad because He said to him the third
time, "Do you love Me?" And he said to
Him, "Master, You know all, You know
that I love You." יהושע said to him, "Feed
My sheep.
18 "Truly, truly, I say to you, when you
were younger you girded yourself and
walked where you wished, but when you
are old you shall stretch out your hands,
and another shall gird you and bring you
where *you* do not wish."
19 Now this He said, signifying by what
death he would esteem Elohim. And having said this, He said to him, "Follow Me."
20 And Kěpha, turning around, saw the
taught one whom יהושע loved following,
who also had leaned on His breast at the
supper, and said, "Master, who is the one
who is delivering You up?"
21 Seeing him, Kěpha said to יהושע, "But
Master, what about this one?"
22 יהושע said to him, "If I wish him to
remain till I come, what is that to you? You
follow Me."
23 Therefore this word went out among
the brothers that this taught one would not
die. However, יהושע did not say to him
that he would not die, but, "If I desire him
to remain until I come, what is it to you?"
24 This is the taught one who bears witness about these *matters*, and wrote these
matters. And we know that his witness is
true.
25 Now there is much else that יהושע did.
If every one of them were written down, I
think that the world itself would not contain the written books. Aměn.

MAʿASEI

ACTS

1 The first account I made, O Theophilos,[a] of all that יהושע began both to do and to teach,

2 until the day when He was taken up, after giving instructions through the Set-apart Spirit to the emissaries whom He had chosen,

3 to whom He also presented Himself alive after His suffering by many infallible proofs, being seen by them for forty days, speaking concerning the reign of Elohim.

4 And meeting with them, He commanded them not to leave Yerushalayim, but to wait for the Promise of the Father,[b] "which you have heard from Me –

5 because Yoḥanan truly immersed in water, but you shall be immersed in the Set-apart Spirit not many days from now."

6 So when they had come together, they asked Him, saying, "Master, would You at this time restore the reign to Yisra'ěl?"[c]

7 And He said to them, "It is not for you to know times or seasons which the Father has put in His own authority.

8 "But you shall receive power when the Set-apart Spirit has come upon you, and you shall be My witnesses in Yerushalayim, and in all Yehuḏah and Shomeron, and to the end of the earth."

9 And having said this, while they were looking on, He was taken up, and a cloud hid Him from their sight.

10 And as they were gazing into the heaven as He went up, see, two men stood by them dressed in white,

11 who also said, "Men of Galil, why do you stand looking up into the heaven? This same יהושע, who was taken up from you into the heaven, shall come in the same way[d] as you saw Him go into the heaven."

12 Then they went back to Yerushalayim from the Mount of Olives, which is near Yerushalayim, a Sabbath day's journey.

13 And when they came in, they went up into the upper room where they were staying: both Kěpha and Yaʿaqoḇ and Yoḥanan and Andri, Philip and T'oma, Bartholomi and Mattithyahu, Yaʿaqoḇ *the son* of Alphai and Shimʿon the Zealot, and Yehuḏah *the son* of Yaʿaqoḇ.

14 All these were continuing with one mind in prayer and supplication, with the women and Miryam the mother of יהושע, and with His brothers.

15 And in those days Kěpha, standing up in the midst of the taught ones – and there was a gathering of about a hundred and twenty – said,

16 "Men and brothers, this Scripture had to be filled which the Set-apart Spirit spoke before by the mouth of Dawiḏ concerning Yehuḏah, who became a guide to those who seized יהושע,

17 because he was numbered with us and did receive his share in this service."

18 (This one, therefore, purchased a field with the wages of unrighteousness, and falling forward, he burst open in the middle and all his intestines gushed out.

19 And it became known to all those dwelling in Yerushalayim, so that in their own language that field was called, Ḥaqal Dema, that is, Field of Blood).

20 "For it has been written in the Book of Tehillim, **'Let his dwelling lie waste, and let no one live in it,'** Teh. 69:25 and, **'Let another take his office.'** Teh. 109:8

21 "It is therefore necessary that of the men who have been with us all the time that the Master יהושע went in and out among us,

22 beginning from the immersion of Yoḥanan to that day when He was taken up from us, that one of these should become a witness with us of His resurrection."

23 And they put forward two: Yosěph

1a Compare Lq. 1:1-3. It appears that Luqas was the author of both accounts. *1b* Lq. 24:49, Yn. 14:16 & 26.
1c Also see Lq. 1:33. *1d* See Zeḵ. 14:4. Note: these men were standing on the Mount of Olives (v. 12).

called Barsabba, who was also called
Justus, and Mattithyahu.
24 And praying they said, "You, יהוה',
who know the hearts of all, show which
one of these two You have chosen
25 to receive the share in this service and
office of the emissary from which Yehuḏah
by transgression fell, to go to his own
place."
26 And they cast their lots, and the lot fell
on Mattithyahu. And he was numbered
with the eleven emissaries.

2 And when the Day of the Festival of
Shaḇu'ot[a] had come, they were all
with one mind in one place.
2 And suddenly there came a sound from
the heaven, as of a rushing mighty wind,
and it filled all the house where they were
sitting.
3 And there appeared to them divided
tongues, as of fire, and settled on each one
of them.
4 And they were all filled with the Set-
apart Spirit and began to speak with other
tongues, as the Spirit gave them to speak.
5 Now in Yerushalayim there were dwelling Yehuḏim, dedicated men from every
nation under the heaven.
6 And when this sound came to be, the
crowd came together, and were confused,
because everyone heard them speak in his
own language.
7 And they were all amazed and marvelled, saying to each other, "Look, are not
all these who speak Galileans?
8 "And how do we hear, each one in our
own language in which we were born?
9 "Parthians and Medes and Ěylamites,
and those dwelling in Aram Naharayim,
both Yehuḏah and Kappadokia, Pontos and
Asia,
10 both Phrygia and Pamphulia, Mitsrayim and the parts of Libya around
Cyrene, visitors from Rome, both Yehuḏim and converts,
11 "Cretans and Araḇs, we hear them
speaking in our own tongues the great
deeds of Elohim."
12 And they were all amazed, and were
puzzled, saying to each other, "What does
this mean?"
13 And others mocking said, "They have
been filled with sweet wine."
14 But Kěpha, standing up with the
eleven, lifted up his voice and said to them,
"Men of Yehuḏah and all those dwelling in
Yerushalayim, let this be known to you,
and listen closely to my words.
15 "For these men are not drunk, as you
imagine, since it is only the third hour of
the day.
16 "But this is what was spoken by the
prophet Yo'ěl:
17 **'And it shall be in the last days, says
Elohim, that I shall pour out of My
Spirit on all flesh. And your sons and
your daughters shall prophesy, and your
young men shall see visions, and your
old men shall dream dreams,**
18 **and also on My male servants and
on My female servants I shall pour out
My Spirit in those days, and they shall
prophesy.**
19 **'And I shall show wonders in the
heaven above and signs in the earth
beneath: blood and fire and vapour of
smoke.**
20 **'The sun shall be turned into darkness, and the moon into blood, before
the coming of the great and splendid day
of יהוה'.**
21 **'And it shall be that everyone who
calls on the Name of יהוה' shall be
saved.'** Yo'ěl 2:28-32 *b*
22 "Men of Yisra'ěl, hear these words:
יהושע' of Natsareth, a Man from Elohim,
having been pointed out to you by mighty
works, and wonders, and signs which
Elohim did through Him in your midst,
as you yourselves also know,
23 this One, given up by the set purpose
and foreknowledge of Elohim, you have
impaled and put to death through the hands
of lawless men –
24 "Him Elohim raised up, having loosed
the pangs of death, because it was impossible that He could be held in its grip.

2a - Weeks. *2b* - Rom. 10:13.

25 "For Dawiḏ says concerning Him, **'I
saw יהוה before me continually, because
He is at my right hand, in order that I
should not be shaken.**
26 **'For this reason my heart rejoiced,
and my tongue was glad, and now my
flesh shall also rest in expectation,**
27 **because You shall not leave my being
in She'ol, nor shall You give Your Kind
One to see corruption.**
28 **'You have made known to me the
ways of life, You shall fill me with joy in
Your presence.'** Teh. 16:8-11
29 "Men and brothers, let me speak boldly
to you of the ancestor Dawiḏ, that he died
and was buried, [c] and his tomb is with us
to this day.
30 "Being a prophet, then, and knowing
that Elohim had sworn with an oath to him:
of the fruit of his loins, according to the
flesh, to raise up the Messiah to sit on his
throne,
31 foreseeing this he spoke concerning the
resurrection of the Messiah, that His being
was neither left in She'ol, nor did His flesh
see corruption.
32 "Elohim has raised up this יהושע, of
which we are all witnesses.
33 "Therefore, having been exalted to the
right hand of Elohim, and having received
from the Father the promise of the Set-
apart Spirit, He poured out this which you
now see and hear.
34 "For Dawiḏ did not ascend into the
heavens, but he himself said, **'יהוה said to
my Master, "Sit at My right hand,**
35 **until I make Your enemies a footstool
for Your feet." '** Teh. 110:1
36 "Therefore let all the house of Yisra'ěl
know for certain that Elohim has made this
יהושע, whom you impaled, both Master
and Messiah."
37 And having heard this, they were
pierced to the heart, and said to Kěpha and
the rest of the emissaries, "Men, brothers,
what shall we do?"
38 And Kěpha said to them, "Repent, and
let each one of you be immersed in the
Name of יהושע Messiah for the forgiveness of sins. [d] And you shall receive the
gift of the Set-apart Spirit.
39 "For the promise is to you and to your
children, and to all who are far off, as
many as יהוה our Elohim shall call."
40 And with many other words he earnestly witnessed and urged them, saying, "Be
saved from this crooked generation." [e]
41 Then those, indeed, who gladly
received his word, were immersed. And on
that day about three thousand beings were
added to them.
42 And they were continuing steadfastly in
the teaching of the emissaries, and in the
fellowship, and in the breaking of bread,
and in the prayers.
43 And fear came upon every being, and
many wonders and signs were being done
through the emissaries.
44 And all those who believed were
together, and had all in common,
45 and sold their possessions and property,
and divided them among all, as anyone
might have need.
46 And day by day, continuing with one
mind in the Set-apart Place, and breaking
bread from house to house, they ate their
food with gladness and simplicity of heart,
47 praising Elohim and having favour with
all the people. And the Master added to the
assembly those who were being saved, day
by day.

3

And Kěpha and Yoḥanan were going
up to the Set-apart Place at the hour of
prayer, the ninth hour.
2 And a certain man, lame from his birth,
was carried, whom they laid daily at the
gate of the Set-apart Place which is called
Yaphah,[a] to ask alms from those entering
into the Set-apart Place,
3 who, seeing Kěpha and Yoḥanan about
to go into the Set-apart Place, asked for
alms.
4 And Kěpha, with Yoḥanan, looking
steadfastly at him, said, "Look at us."
5 And he gave heed to them, expecting to
receive whatever from them.
6 But Kěpha said, "I do not have silver

2c See v. 34. *2d* Also see 2:40, 3:19, 3:26. *2e* Yirm. 51:6, Pilip. 2:15, Ḥazon 18:4. *3a* Beautiful or Lovely.

and gold, but what I do possess, this I give
you: In the Name of יהושע Messiah of
Natsareth, rise up and walk."
7 And taking him by the right hand he
lifted him up, and immediately his feet and
ankle bones were made firm.
8 And leaping up, he stood and walked,
and went in with them into the Set-apart
Place, walking and leaping and praising
Elohim.
9 And all the people saw him walking
and praising Elohim.
10 And they recognised him, that it was he
who sat begging alms at the Lovely Gate
of the Set-apart Place. And they were filled
with wonder and amazement at what befell
him.
11 And as the lame man who was healed
was clinging to Kěpha and Yoḥanan, all
the people ran together to them in the
porch which is called Shelomoh's, greatly
amazed.
12 And seeing it, Kěpha responded to the
people, "Men of Yisra'ěl, why do you marvel at this? Or why look so intently at us,
as though by our own power or reverence
we have made him walk?
13 "**The Elohim of Aḇraham, and of
Yitsḥaq, and of Ya'aqoḇ, the Elohim of
our fathers**, Shem. 3:6,13,15 esteemed His
Servant יהושע, whom you delivered up
and denied in the presence of Pilate, when
he had decided to release Him.
14 "But you denied the Set-apart and
Righteous One, and asked that a man, a
murderer, be granted you.
15 "But you killed the Prince [b] of life,
whom Elohim raised from the dead, of
which we are witnesses.
16 "And by the belief in His Name, this
one whom you see and know, His Name
made strong, and the belief which comes
through Him has given him this perfect
healing before all of you.
17 "And now, brothers, I know that you
did it in ignorance, as your rulers did too.
18 "But this is how Elohim has filled what
He had announced beforehand through the
mouth of all the prophets, that His Messiah
was to suffer.
19 "Repent therefore and turn back, for
the blotting out of your sins, in order that
times of refreshing might come from the
presence of the Master,
20 and that He sends יהושע Messiah, pre-
appointed for you,
21 whom heaven needs to receive until the
times of restoration of all *matters*, of
which Elohim spoke through the mouth of
all His set-apart prophets since of old.
22 "For Mosheh truly said to the fathers,
**'יהוה' your Elohim shall raise up for you
a Prophet like me from your brothers.
Him you shall hear according to all *matters*, whatever He says to you.**
23 **'And it shall be that every being who
does not hear that Prophet shall be
utterly destroyed from among the people.'** Deḇ. 18:15-19
24 "And likewise, all the prophets who
have spoken, from Shemu'ěl and those following, have also announced these days.
25 "You are sons of the prophets, and of
the covenant which Elohim made with our
fathers, saying to Aḇraham, **'And in your
seed all the nations of the earth shall be
blessed.'** Ber. 12:3, 22:18, 26:4
26 "To you first, Elohim, having raised up
His Servant יהושע, sent Him to bless you,
in turning away each one of you from your
wicked ways." [c]

4

And as they were speaking to the
people, the priests and the captain of
the Set-apart Place, and the Sadducees,
came upon them,
2 being annoyed because they taught the
people and announced the resurrection
from the dead in יהושע.
3 And they arrested them, and put them
in jail until the next day, for it was already
evening.
4 But many of those who had heard the
word believed, and the number of the men
became about five thousand.
5 And it came to be, on the next day, that
their rulers and elders and scribes assembled in Yerushalayim,

3b 5:31. *3c* Also see 2:38.

6 as well as Ḥanan the high priest, and Qayapha, and Yoḥanan, and Alexander, and as many as were of high priestly descent.

7 And having placed them in the middle, they asked, "By what power or in what Name did you do this?"

8 Then Kěpha, filled with the Set-apart Spirit, said to them, "Rulers of the people and elders of Yisra'ěl:

9 "If today we are called to account for a good deed towards a sick man, by whom he has been healed,

10 let it be known to all of you, and to all the people of Yisra'ěl, that in the Name of יהושע Messiah of Natsareth, whom you impaled, whom Elohim raised from the dead, by Him this one stands before you, healthy.

11 "This is **'the stone which was rejected by you builders, which has become the chief cornerstone.'** Teh. 118:22

12 "And there is no deliverance in anyone else, for there is no other Name under the heaven given among men by which we need to be saved."

13 And seeing the boldness of Kěpha and Yoḥanan, and perceiving that they were unlearned and ordinary men, they marvelled. And they recognised that they had been with יהושע.

14 And seeing the man who had been healed standing with them, they could not contradict it.

15 But when they had commanded them to go aside out of the council, they consulted with one another,

16 saying, "What shall we do to these men? For, indeed, that an outstanding miracle has been done through them is apparent to all those dwelling in Yerushalayim, and we are unable to deny it.

17 "But in order that it spreads no further among the people, let us strongly threaten them, to speak no more to anyone in this Name."

18 And they called them and commanded them not to speak at all nor to teach in the Name of יהושע.

19 But Kěpha and Yoḥanan answering them, said, "Whether it is right in the sight of Elohim to listen to you more than to Elohim, [a] you judge.

20 "For it is impossible for us not to speak of what we saw and heard."

21 And having threatened them further, they released them, finding no way of punishing them, because of the people, because they were all praising Elohim for what had been done.

22 For the man was over forty years old on whom this miracle of healing had been done.

23 And having been released, they went to their own *people* and reported all that the chief priests and elders said to them.

24 And having heard that, they lifted up their voice to Elohim with one mind and said, "יהוה, You are Elohim, who **made the heaven and the earth and the sea, and all that is in them,** Teh. 146:6 *b*

25 who by the mouth of Your servant Dawiḏ have said, **'Why did the nations rage, and the people plot in vain?**

26 **'The sovereigns of the earth stood up, and the rulers were gathered together against יהוה and against His Messiah.'** Teh. 2:1-2

27 "For truly, in this city there were gathered together against Your set-apart Servant יהושע, whom You anointed, both Herodes and Pontius Pilate, with the nations and the people of Yisra'ěl

28 to do whatever Your hand and Your purpose decided before to be done.

29 "And now, יהוה, look on their threats, and give to Your servants all boldness to speak Your word,

30 by stretching out Your hand for healing, and signs, and wonders to take place through the Name of Your set-apart Servant יהושע."

31 And when they had prayed, the place where they came together was shaken. And they were all filled with the Set-apart Spirit, and they spoke the word of Elohim with boldness.

32 And the group of those who believed

4a See 5:29. *4b* Also see Shem. 20:11.

were of one heart and one being. And no
one claimed that any of his possessions
was his own, but they had all in common.
33 And with great power the emissaries
gave witness to the resurrection of the
Master יהושע, and great favour was upon
them all.
34 For there was not anyone needy among
them, for all who were possessors of lands
or houses sold them, and brought the
prices of what was sold,
35 and laid them at the feet of the emissaries, and they distributed to each as anyone had need.
36 And Yosěph, who was also called
Barnaḇa by the emissaries (which means
Son of Encouragement), a Lěwite, a native
of Cyprus,
37 having land, sold it, and brought the
money and laid it at the feet of the emissaries.

5 But a certain man named Ḥananyah,
with Shappirah his wife, sold a possession.
2 And he kept back from the price, his
wife also being aware of it, and brought a
certain part and laid it at the feet of the
emissaries.
3 But Kěpha said, "Ḥananyah, why has
Satan filled your heart to lie to the Set-
apart Spirit and keep back from the price
of the land for yourself?
4 "While it remained, did it not remain
your own? And after it was sold, was it not
in your authority? Why have you conceived this deed in your heart? You have
not lied to men but to Elohim."
5 Then Ḥananyah, hearing these words,
fell down and breathed his last. And great
fear came upon all those who heard of this.
6 But the young men arose and wrapped
him up, carried him out and buried him.
7 And it came to be, about three hours
later, that his wife came in, not knowing
what had taken place.
8 And Kěpha responded to her, "Say to
me whether you sold the land for so
much?" And she said, "Yes, for so much."
9 So Kěpha said to her, "Why have you
agreed to try the Spirit of יהוה? Look, the
feet of those who have buried your husband are at the door, and they shall carry
you out."
10 And immediately she fell down at his
feet and breathed her last. And the young
men came in and found her dead, and
carrying her out, they buried her beside her
husband.
11 And great fear came upon all the
assembly and upon all who heard of this.
12 And through the hands of the emissaries many signs and wonders were done
among the people. And they were all with
one mind in Shelomoh's Porch.
13 But of the rest no one had the courage
to join them, however, the people made
much of them.
14 And more believers were added to the
Master, large numbers of both men and
women,
15 so that they brought the sick out into
the streets and laid them on beds and
couches, that at least the shadow of Kěpha,
passing by, might fall on some of them.
16 A large number also gathered from the
surrounding cities to Yerushalayim, bringing sick ones and those who were troubled
by unclean spirits, and they were all
healed.
17 But the high priest rose up, and all
those with him, which is the sect of the
Sadducees, and they were filled with
jealousy,
18 and seized the emissaries and put them
in the public jail.
19 But a messenger of יהוה opened the
prison doors at night and brought them out,
and said,
20 "Go and stand in the Set-apart Place
and speak to the people all the words of
this life."
21 Now when they heard, they went into
the Set-apart Place early in the morning,
and were teaching. But the high priest and
those with him came and called the council
together, with all the elders of the children
of Yisra'ěl, and sent to the prison for them
to be brought.
22 But having come, the officers did not
find them in the prison, and they went back
and reported it,

23 saying, "We found the prison shut in all
safety, and the watches standing outside
before the doors. But having opened them,
we found no one inside!"
24 And as the high priest and the captain
of the Set-apart Place and the chief priests
heard these words, they were puzzled and
wondered what this might be.
25 But one came and reported to them,
saying, "Look, the men whom you put in
prison are standing in the Set-apart Place
and teaching the people!"
26 Then the captain went with the officers
and brought them, not with force, for they
feared the people, lest they should be
stoned.
27 And having brought them, they set
them before the council and the high priest
asked them,
28 saying, "Did we not strictly command
you not to teach in this Name? And look,
you have filled Yerushalayim with your
teaching, and intend to bring the blood of
this Man upon us!"
29 And Kěpha and the other emissaries
answering, said, "We have to obey Elohim
rather than men. [a]
30 "**The Elohim of our fathers** Shem. 3:15
raised up יהושע whom you laid hands on,
hanging *Him* on a timber. Deḇ. 21:22-23
31 "Him, a Prince [b] and a Saviour, Elohim
has exalted **to His right hand**, Teh. 110:1 to
give repentance to Yisra'ěl and forgiveness
of sins.
32 "And we are His witnesses to these
matters, and so also is the Set-apart Spirit
whom Elohim has given to those who obey
Him." [c]
33 And those hearing were cut *to the
heart*, and took counsel to kill them.
34 But a certain one in the council stood
up, a Pharisee named Gamli'ěl, a teacher
of the Torah, respected by all the people,
and ordered them to put the emissaries outside for a little while,
35 and said to them, "Men of Yisra'ěl, take
heed to yourselves what you intend to do
to these men.
36 "For before these days Toḏah rose up,
claiming to be somebody. A number of
men, about four hundred, did join him. He
was slain, and all who obeyed him were
dispersed, and came to naught.
37 "After him, Yehuḏah of Galil rose up in
the days of the census, and drew away
many people after him. He also perished,
and all who obeyed him were scattered.
38 "And now I say to you, stay away from
these men and leave them alone, because if
this plan or this work is of men, it shall be
overthrown,
39 but if it is of Elohim, you are unable to
overthrow it, lest you even be found to
fight against Elohim."
40 And they heeded his advice, and having
called for the emissaries, beating them,
they commanded that they should not
speak in the Name of יהושע, and let them
go.
41 Then indeed they went rejoicing from
the presence of the council, because they
were counted worthy to suffer shame for
His Name.
42 And daily in the Set-apart Place, and in
every house, they did not cease teaching
and bringing the Good News: יהושע the
Messiah!

6 And in those days, when the taught
ones were increasing, there arose a
grumbling against the Hebrews by the
Hellenists, because their widows were
overlooked in the daily serving.
2 So the twelve summoned the group of
the taught ones and said, "It is not pleasing
for us to leave the Word of Elohim and
serve tables.
3 "Therefore, brothers, seek out from
among you seven men who are known to
be filled with the Set-apart Spirit and wisdom, whom we shall appoint for this duty,
4 but we shall give ourselves continually
to prayer and to serving the Word."
5 And the word pleased the entire group.
And they chose Stephanos, a man filled
with belief and the Set-apart Spirit, and
Philip, and Prochoros, and Nikanor, and
Timon, and Parmenas, and Nikolaos, a

5a See 4:19. *5b* 3:15. *5c* See also Yn. א 3:24.

convert from Antioch,
6 whom they set before the emissaries.
And when they had prayed, they laid hands
on them.
7 And the Word of Elohim spread, and
the number of the taught ones increased
greatly in Yerushalayim, and a great many
of the priests were obedient to the belief.
8 And Stephanos, filled with belief and
power, did great wonders and signs among
the people.
9 But some of those of the so-called
Congregation of the Freedmen (Cyrenians,
Alexandrians, and those from Kilikia and
Asia), rose up, disputing with Stephanos,
10 but they were unable to resist the wisdom and the Spirit by which he spoke.
11 Then they instigated men to say, "We
have heard him speak blasphemous words
against Mosheh and Elohim."
12 And they stirred up the people, and the
elders, and the scribes, so they came upon
him, seized him, and brought him to the
council.
13 And they set up false witnesses who
said, "This man does not cease to speak
blasphemous words against this set-apart
place and the Torah,
14 for we have heard him saying that this
יהושע of Natsareth shall overthrow this
place and change the institutes which
Mosheh delivered unto us."
15 And all who sat in the council, looking
steadily at him, saw his face was like the
face of a *heavenly* messenger.

7 And the high priest said, "Is this so?"
2 And he replied, "Men, brothers and
fathers, listen: The Elohim of esteem
appeared to our father Aḇraham when he
was in Aram Naharayim, before he dwelt
in Ḥaran,
3 **and said to him, 'Come out of your
land and from your relatives, and come
here, into a land that I shall show you.'**
Ber. 12:1
4 "Then he came out of the land of the
Kasdim and dwelt in Ḥaran. And from
there, after the death of his father, He
removed him to this land in which you
now dwell.
5 "And He gave him no inheritance in it,
not a foot of it. Deḇ. 2:5 But He promised to
**give it to him for a possession, and to his
seed after him,** Ber. 12:7, 17:8 [a] when as yet he
had no child.
6 "And Elohim spoke in this way: that
**his seed would be sojourning in a for-
eign land, and that they would be
enslaved and mistreated four hundred
years.** Ber. 15:13
7 **'And the nation to whom they shall
be enslaved, I shall judge,'** Ber. 15:13 said
Elohim, **'and after that they shall come
out and serve Me in this place.'** Ber. 15:14,
Shem. 3:12
8 "And He gave him the covenant of
circumcision. And so he brought forth
Yitsḥaq and circumcised him on the eighth
day. And Yitsḥaq *brought forth* Ya'aqoḇ,
and Ya'aqoḇ *brought forth* the twelve
ancestors.
9 "And the ancestors, **becoming jealous,
sold Yosěph into Mitsrayim**. But **Elohim
was with him,** Ber. 37:11,28; 39:2,21
10 and delivered him out of all his afflictions, and **gave him favour** Ber. 39:21 and
wisdom **before Pharaoh, sovereign of
Mitsrayim. And he appointed him
governor over Mitsrayim and all his
house.** Ber. 41:37-46
11 **"Then a scarcity of food and great
distress came over all the land of Mitsrayim and Kena'an,** Ber. 41:54; 42:5 and our
fathers found no food.
12 "But **Ya'aqoḇ heard that there was
grain in Mitsrayim,** Ber. 42:2 and he sent out
our fathers the first time,
13 and at the second time Yosěph was
made known to his brothers, and Yosěph's
race became known to the Pharaoh.
14 "And Yosěph sent and called his father
Ya'aqoḇ and all his relatives to him, seventy-five people.
15 "And **Ya'aqoḇ went down to Mitsrayim, and died, he and our fathers,**
Ber. 46:5; 49:33, Shem. 1:6
16 and they were brought over to Sheḵem

7a Also see Ber. 13:15; 15:4,7,18-21; 24:7; 48:4

and laid in the tomb that Aḇraham bought
for a price of silver from the sons of
Ḥamor, *the father* of Sheḵem.
17 "But as the time of the promise drew
near which Elohim had sworn to Aḇraham,
the people increased and multiplied in
Mitsrayim
18 until **another sovereign arose who did
not know Yosěph**. Shem. 1:8
19 "Having dealt treacherously with our
race, this one mistreated our fathers, making them expose their babies, so that they
should not live.
20 "At that time Mosheh was born, and he
was well-pleasing to Elohim. And he was
reared three months in the house of his
father.
21 "But when he was exposed, the daughter of Pharaoh took him up and reared him
as her own son.
22 "And Mosheh was instructed in all the
wisdom of the Mitsrites, and was mighty
in words and works.
23 "And when he was forty years old, it
came into his heart to visit his brothers, the
children of Yisra'ěl.
24 "And seeing one of them being
wronged, he defended and revenged him
who was oppressed, smiting the Mitsrian.
25 "And he thought that his brothers
would have understood that Elohim would
give deliverance to them by his hand, but
they did not understand.
26 "And the next day he appeared to two
of them as they were fighting, and urged
them to peace, saying, 'Men, you are
brothers, why do you wrong one another?'
27 "But he who was wronging his neighbour pushed him away, saying, **'Who
made you a ruler and a judge over us?**
28 **'Do you wish to kill me as you killed
the Mitsrian yesterday?'** Shem. 2:14
29 "And at this saying, **Mosheh fled and
became a sojourner in the land of
Miḏyan**, Shem. 2:15 where he fathered two
sons.
30 "And after forty years were completed,
a **Messenger of יהוה' appeared to him in
a flame of fire in a bush**, Shem. 3:2 in the
wilderness of Mount Sinai.
31 "And Mosheh, seeing it, marvelled at
the sight, and coming near to look, the
voice of יהוה' came to him,
32 saying, **'I am the Elohim of your
fathers, the Elohim of Aḇraham and the
Elohim of Yitsḥaq and the Elohim of
Ya'aqoḇ.' And Mosheh trembled and
did not have the courage to look.**
33 **'But יהוה' said to him, "Take your
sandals off your feet, for the place where
you stand is set-apart ground.**
34 **"I have certainly seen the evil treatment of my people who are in
Mitsrayim, and I have heard their
groaning and have come down to deliver
them. And now come, let Me send you to
Mitsrayim." '** Shem. 3:6-10
35 "This Mosheh whom they had refused,
saying, **'Who made you a ruler and a
judge?'** Shem. 2:14 – this one Elohim sent to
be a ruler and a deliverer by the hand of the
Messenger who appeared to him in the
bush.
36 "This one led them out, after he had
done wonders and signs in the land of
Mitsrayim, and in the Red Sea, and in the
wilderness forty years.
37 "This is the Mosheh who said to the
children of Yisra'ěl, **'יהוה' your Elohim
shall raise up for you a Prophet like me
from your brothers. Him you shall
hear.'** Deḇ. 18:15
38 "This is he who was in the assembly in
the wilderness with the Messenger who
spoke to him on Mount Sinai, and with our
fathers, who received the living Words to
give to us,
39 unto whom our fathers would not
become obedient, but thrust away, and in
their hearts they turned back to Mitsrayim,
40 saying to Aharon, **'Make us mighty
ones to go before us, for this Mosheh
who led us out of the land of Mitsrayim,
we do not know what has become of
him.'** Shem. 32:1, 23
41 "And they made a calf in those days,
and brought an offering to the idol, and
were rejoicing in the works of their own
hands.
42 "So Elohim turned and gave them up to
worship the host of the heaven, [b] as it has

been written in the book of the Prophets, **'Did you bring slaughtered beasts and offerings unto Me during forty years in the wilderness, O house of Yisra'ěl?**

43 **'And you took up the tent of Moleḵ, and the star of your mighty one Kiyyun, images which you made to bow before them. Therefore I shall remove you beyond Baḇel.'** Amos 5:25-27

44 "The Tent of Witness was with our fathers in the wilderness, as He appointed, instructing Mosheh to make it according to the pattern that he had seen,

45 which our fathers, having received it in turn, also brought with Yehoshua into the land possessed by the nations, whom Elohim drove out before the face of our fathers until the days of Dawiḏ,

46 who found favour before Elohim and asked to find a dwelling for the Elohim of Yaʽaqoḇ,

47 but Shelomoh built Him a house.

48 "However, the Most High does not dwell in dwellings made with hands,[c] as the prophet says:

49 **'The heaven is My throne, and earth is My footstool. What house shall you build for Me? says יהוה, or what is the place of My rest?**

50 **'Has My hand not made all these?'** Yesh. 66:1,2

51 **"You stiff-necked** Shem. 32:9; 33:3,5 **and uncircumcised in heart and ears!** Way. 26:41, Yirm. 6:10 You always resist the Set-apart Spirit, as your fathers did, you also do.

52 "Which of the prophets did your fathers not persecute? And they killed those who before announced the coming of the Righteous One, of whom you now have become the betrayers and murderers,

53 who received the Torah as it was ordained by messengers, but did not watch over[d] it."

54 And hearing this they were cut to the hearts and gnashed the teeth at him.

55 But he, being filled with the Set-apart Spirit, looked steadily into the heaven and saw the esteem of Elohim, and יהושע **standing at the right hand of Elohim,**

56 and he said, "Look! I see the heavens opened and the Son of Aḏam **standing at the right hand of Elohim**!" Teh. 110:1

57 And crying out with a loud voice, they stopped their ears, and rushed upon him with one mind,

58 and threw him out of the city and stoned him. And the witnesses laid down their garments at the feet of a young man named Sha'ul.

59 And they were stoning Stephanos as he was calling and saying, "Master יהושע, receive my spirit."

60 And kneeling down he cried out with a loud voice, "Master, do not hold this sin against them." And having said this, he fell asleep.

8 And Sha'ul was giving approval to his death. And on that day there was a great persecution against the assembly which was at Yerushalayim, and they were all scattered throughout the countries of Yehuḏah and Shomeron, except the emissaries.

2 And dedicated men buried Stephanos, and made great lamentation over him.

3 But Sha'ul was ravaging the assembly, entering every house, and dragging off men and women, putting them in prison.

4 Then those who had been scattered went everywhere bringing the Good News: the Word!

5 And going down to the city of Shomeron Philip proclaimed Messiah to them.

6 And the crowds with one mind heeded what Philip said, hearing and seeing the miracles which he did.

7 For unclean spirits came out of many who were possessed, crying with a loud voice, and many who were paralysed and lame were healed.

8 And there came to be great joy in that city.

9 Now there was a certain man called Shimʽon, who formerly was practising magic in the city and astonishing the people of Shomeron, claiming to be someone great,

7b (Previous page) Deḇ. 4:19; 17:3; Mel.ב 23:5. 7c See also 17:24. 7d See Mt. 5:20.

10 to whom they all were giving heed,
from the least to the greatest, saying, "This
one is the power of Elohim, which is
great."
11 And they were giving heed to him
because for a long time he had amazed
them with his magic.
12 And when they believed Philip as he
brought the Good News about the reign of
Elohim and the Name of יהושע Messiah,
both men and women were immersed.
13 And Shimʻon himself also believed.
And when he was immersed he continued
with Philip, and was amazed, seeing the
miracles and signs which took place.
14 And when the emissaries who were at
Yerushalayim heard that Shomeron had
received the Word of Elohim, they sent
Kěpha and Yoḥanan to them,
15 who, when they had come down,
prayed for them to receive the Set-apart
Spirit,
16 for He had not yet fallen on any of
them, but they had only been immersed in
the Name of the Master יהושע.
17 Then they laid hands on them, and they
received the Set-apart Spirit.
18 And Shimʻon, seeing that through the
laying on of the hands of the emissaries the
Set-apart Spirit was given, he offered them
money,
19 saying, "Give me this authority too, so
that anyone I lay hands on shall receive the
Set-apart Spirit."
20 But Kěpha said to him, "Let your silver
perish with you, because you thought to
buy the gift of Elohim through money!
21 "You have neither part nor lot in this
matter, for your heart is not right before
Elohim.
22 "Repent therefore of this evil of yours,
and plead with Elohim to forgive you the
intention of your heart.
23 "For I see that you are poisoned by
bitterness and bound by unrighteousness."
24 But Shimʻon answering, said, "Plead
with the Master for me, so that none of
what you had said shall come upon me."
25 Then after they had earnestly witnessed
and spoken the Word of יהוה, they
returned to Yerushalayim, bringing the
Good News in many villages of the
Shomeronim.
26 But a messenger of יהוה spoke to
Philip, saying, "Arise and go toward the
south along the way which goes down
from Yerushalayim to Azzah." This is
desert.
27 And he arose and went, and saw, a man
of Kush, a eunuch of great authority under
Kandake the sovereigness of the Kushites,
who was in charge of all her treasury, and
had come to Yerushalayim to worship,
28 and was returning. And sitting in his
chariot, he was reading the prophet Yeshayahu.
29 And the Spirit said to Philip, "Go near
and join him in that chariot."
30 And running up, Philip heard him reading the prophet Yeshayahu, and said, "Do
you know what you are reading?"
31 And he said, "How am I able, unless
someone guides me?" And he called Philip
near, to come up and sit with him.
32 And the passage of the Scripture which
he was reading was this, **"He was led as a
sheep to slaughter, and like a lamb silent
before its shearer, so He opened not His
mouth.**
33 **"In His humiliation He was deprived
of right-ruling. And who shall declare
His generation? Because His life was
taken from the earth."** Yesh. 53:7-8
34 And the eunuch, answering Philip, said,
"I ask you, about whom does the prophet
say this, about himself or about some
other?"
35 And Philip opening his mouth, and
beginning at this Scripture, brought to him
the Good News: יהושע!
36 And as they were going on the way,
they came to some water. And the eunuch
said, "Look, water! What hinders me from
being immersed?"
37 And Philip said, "If you believe with all
your heart, it is permitted." And he
answering, said, "I believe the Son of
Elohim [a] to be יהושע the Messiah."

8a See Mt. 16:16 - Some manuscripts omit verse 8:37.

38 And he commanded the chariot to stand still. And both Philip and the eunuch went down into the water, and he immersed him.

39 And when they came up out of the water, the Spirit of יהוה caught Philip away, and the eunuch saw him no more, for he went his way, rejoicing.

40 Philip, however, was found at Ashdoḏ. And passing through, he brought the Good News in all the cities until he came to Caesarea.

9 But Sha'ul, still breathing threats and murder against the taught ones of the Master, having come to the high priest,

2 asked from him letters to the congregations of Dammeseq, so that if he found any who were of the Way, whether men or women, to bring them bound to Yerushalayim.

3 And it came to be, that as he journeyed, he came near Dammeseq, and suddenly a light flashed around him from the heaven.

4 And he fell to the ground, and heard a voice saying to him, "Sha'ul, Sha'ul, why do you persecute Me?"

5 And he said, "Who are You, Master?" And the Master said, "I am יהושע, whom you persecute. It is hard for you to kick against the prods."

6 Both trembling, and being astonished, he said, "Master, what do You wish me to do?" And the Master *said* to him, "Arise and go into the city, and you shall be told what you have to do."

7 And the men journeying with him stood speechless, hearing indeed the voice but seeing no one.

8 And Sha'ul arose from the ground, but when his eyes were opened he saw no one. And leading him by the hand they brought him into Dammeseq.

9 And he was three days without sight, and did not eat nor drink.

10 And there was at Dammeseq a certain taught one, by name Ḥananyah. [a] And the Master said unto him in a vision, "Ḥananyah!" And he said, "Here I am, Master."

11 And the Master *said* to him, "Arise and go to the street called Straight, and seek in the house of Yehuḏah for one called Sha'ul of Tarsos, for look, he is praying,

12 and has seen in a vision a man named Ḥananyah coming in and laying his hand on him, so as to see again."

13 And Ḥananyah answered, "Master, I have heard from many about this man, how many evils he did to Your set-apart ones in Yerushalayim,

14 and here he has authority from the chief priests to bind all those calling on Your Name."

15 But the Master said to him, "Go, for he is a chosen vessel of Mine to bear My Name before nations, sovereigns, and the children of Yisra'ěl.

16 "For I shall show him how much he has to suffer for My Name."

17 And Ḥananyah went away and went into the house. And laying his hands on him he said, "Brother Sha'ul, the Master יהושע, who appeared to you on the way as you came, has sent me, so that you might see again and be filled with the Set-apart Spirit."

18 And immediately there fell from his eyes, as it were scales, and he received his sight. And rising up, he was immersed.

19 And having received food, he was strengthened. And Sha'ul was with the taught ones at Dammeseq some days.

20 And immediately he proclaimed the Messiah in the congregations, that He is the Son of Elohim.

21 And all who heard were amazed, and said, "Is this not he who destroyed those calling on this Name in Yerushalayim, and has come here for this, to take them bound to the chief priests?"

22 But Sha'ul kept increasing in strength, and was confounding the Yehuḏim who dwelt in Dammeseq, proving that this is the Messiah.

23 And after many days had elapsed, the Yehuḏim plotted to kill him.

24 But their plot became known to Sha'ul. And they were watching the gates day and

9a See 22:12.

night, to kill him.
25 But taking him by night, the taught
ones let him down through the wall, lower-
ing him in a basket.
26 And having arrived at Yerushalayim,
Sha'ul tried to join the taught ones, but
they were all afraid of him, not believing
that he was a taught one.
27 But Barnaḇa took him and brought him
to the emissaries, and told them how he
had seen the Master on the way, and that
He had spoken to him, and how he was
speaking boldly at Dammeseq in the Name
of יהושע.
28 And he was with them at Yerushalayim,
coming in and going out,
29 and speaking boldly in the Name of the
Master יהושע and disputed with the
Hellenists, but they undertook to kill him.
30 And when the brothers learned of this,
they brought him down to Caesarea and
sent him out to Tarsos.
31 Then indeed the assemblies throughout
all Yehuḏah, and Galil, and Shomeron had
peace and were built up, and walking in
the fear of יהוה and in the encouragement
of the Set-apart Spirit, they were being
increased.
32 And it came to be, as Kěpha was passing through all *places*, that he also came
down to the set-apart ones who were
dwelling at Lod.
33 And there he found a certain man
named Aeneas, who had been bedridden
for eight years, being paralytic.
34 And Kěpha said to him, "Aeneas,
יהושע the Messiah heals you! Rise up and
make your bed." And immediately he rose
up.
35 And all those dwelling at Lod and
Sharon saw him and did turn to the Master.
36 And in Yapho there was a certain taught
one named Taḇitha, which means Dorkas.
This woman was filled with good works
and kind deeds which she did.
37 And it came to be in those days that she
became sick and died. And having washed
her, they laid her in an upper room.
38 And Lod being near to Yapho, and the
taught ones having heard that Kěpha was
there, they sent two men to him, urging
him not to delay in coming to them.
39 And having risen up, Kěpha went with
them. And when he arrived, they brought
him to the upper room. And all the widows
stood beside him weeping, showing the
inner garments and outer garments which
Dorkas had made while she was with
them.
40 But Kěpha sent them all out, and knelt
down and prayed. And turning to the body
he said, "Taḇitha, arise." And she opened
her eyes, and seeing Kěpha, she sat up.
41 And giving her his hand, he lifted her
up. And calling the set-apart ones and widows, he presented her alive.
42 And it became known throughout all
Yapho, and many believed on the Master.
43 And it came to be that he stayed for
many days in Yapho with Shim'on, a
leather-tanner.

10 Now there was a certain man in
Caesarea called Cornelius, a captain of what was called the Italian
Regiment,
2 dedicated, and fearing Elohim with all
his household, doing many kind deeds to
the people, and praying to Elohim always.
3 He clearly saw in a vision, about the
ninth hour of the day, a messenger of
Elohim coming to him, and saying to him,
"Cornelius!"
4 And looking intently at him, and
becoming afraid, he said, "What is it, master?" And he said to him, "Your prayers
and your kind deeds have come up for a
remembrance before Elohim.
5 "And now send men to Yapho, and
send for Shim'on who is also called Kěpha.
6 "He is staying with Shim'on, a leather-
tanner, whose house is by the sea."
7 And when the messenger who spoke to
him went away, Cornelius called two of his
household servants, and a dedicated soldier from among those who waited on him
continually.
8 And having explained to them all, he
sent them to Yapho.
9 And on the next day, as they were on
their way and approaching the city, Kěpha
went up on the house-top to pray, about the

sixth hour.
10 And he became hungry and wished to
eat. But while they were preparing, he fell
into a trance,
11 and he saw the heaven opened and a
certain vessel like a great sheet bound at
the four corners, descending to him and let
down to the earth,
12 in which were all kinds of four-footed
beasts of the earth, and wild beasts, and
creeping *creatures*, and the birds of the
heaven.
13 And a voice came to him, "Rise up,
Kěpha, slay and eat."
14 But Kěpha said, "Not at all, Master!
Because I have never eaten whatever is
common or unclean."
15 And a voice *came* to him again the second time, "What Elohim has cleansed you
do not consider common."
16 And this took place three times, and the
vessel was taken back to the heaven.
17 And while Kěpha was doubting within
himself about what the vision might mean,
look, the men who had been sent from
Cornelius, having asked for the house of
Shimʽon, stood at the gate,
18 and calling out, they enquired whether
Shimʽon, also known as Kěpha, was staying there.
19 And as Kěpha was thinking about the
vision, the Spirit said to him, "See, three
men seek you.
20 "But rise up, go down and go with
them, not doubting at all, for I have sent
them."
21 So Kěpha went down to the men who
had been sent to him from Cornelius, and
said, "Look, I am the one you seek. Why
have you come?"
22 And they said, "Cornelius the captain, a
righteous man and one who fears Elohim
and well spoken of by the entire nation of
the Yehuḏim, was instructed by a set-apart
messenger to send for you to his house,
and to hear words from you."
23 So inviting them in, he housed them.
And on the next day Kěpha went away
with them, and some brothers from Yapho
went with him.
24 And the following day they entered into
Caesarea. And Cornelius was waiting for
them, having called together his relatives
and close friends.
25 And it came to be, that when Kěpha
entered, Cornelius met him and fell down
at his feet and bowed before him.
26 But Kěpha raised him up, saying,
"Stand up, I myself am also a man."
27 And talking with him, he went in and
found many who had come together.
28 And he said to them, "You know that a
Yehuḏi man is not allowed [a] to associate
with, or go to one of another race. But
Elohim has shown me that I should not call
any man [b] common or unclean.
29 "That is why I came without hesitation
when I was sent for. So I ask, why have
you sent for me?"
30 And Cornelius said, "Four days ago I
was fasting until this hour. And at the ninth
hour I prayed in my house, and see, a man
stood before me in shining garments,
31 and said, 'Cornelius, your prayer has
been heard, and your kind deeds were
remembered before Elohim.
32 'Now send to Yapho and call Shimʽon
here, who is also called Kěpha. He is
staying in the house of Shimʽon, a leather-
tanner, by the sea. When he comes, he
shall speak to you.'
33 "So I sent to you immediately, and you
have done well to come. And now, we are
all present before Elohim, to hear all that
you have been commanded by Elohim."
34 And opening his mouth, Kěpha said,
"Truly I see that Elohim shows no
partiality,
35 but in every nation, he who fears Him
and works righteousness is accepted by
Him.
36 "He sent the word to the children of
Yisra'ěl, bringing the Good News: peace
through יהושע Messiah! He is Master of
all.
37 "You know what word came to be
throughout all Yehuḏah, beginning from
Galil after the immersion which Yoḥanan

10a This was a man-made law. See Mt. 15:3,9, Mq. 7:7-8, Qol. 2:14, 20 & 22. *10b* Not animal - See also v. 35.

proclaimed:
38 how Elohim did anoint יהושע of
Natsareth with the Set-apart Spirit and
with power, who went about doing good
and healing all who were oppressed by the
devil, for Elohim was with Him.
39 “And we are witnesses of all He did,
both in the country of the Yehuḏim and
in Yerushalayim, whom they even killed
by hanging on a timber. Deb. 21:22,23
40 “Elohim raised up this One on the third
day, and let Him be seen,
41 not to all the people, but to witnesses,
those having been chosen before by
Elohim – to us who ate and drank with
Him after He arose from the dead.
42 “And He commanded us to proclaim to
the people, and to witness that it is He who
was appointed by Elohim to be Judge of
the living and the dead. [c]
43 “To this One all the prophets bear witness, that through His Name, everyone
believing in Him does receive forgiveness
of sins.”
44 While Kěpha was still speaking these
words, the Set-apart Spirit fell upon all
those hearing the word.
45 And those of the circumcision who
believed were astonished, as many as came
with Kěpha, because the gift of the Set-
apart Spirit had been poured out on the
nations also,
46 for they were hearing them speaking
with tongues and extolling Elohim. Then
Kěpha answered,
47 “Is anyone able to forbid water, that
these should not be immersed who have
received the Set-apart Spirit – even as also
we?”
48 And he commanded them to be
immersed in the Name of יהושע Messiah.
Then they asked him to remain a few days.

11 And the emissaries and brothers
who were in Yehuḏah heard that
the nations also received the word of
Elohim.
2 And when Kěpha went up to Yerushalayim, those of the circumcision were
contending with him,
3 saying, “You went in to uncircumcised
men and ate with them!”
4 But Kěpha began and set it forth in
order, saying:
5 “I was in the city of Yapho praying.
And in a trance I saw a vision, a certain
vessel descending like a great sheet, let
down from the heaven by four corners, and
it came to me.
6 “Having looked into it, I perceived and
I saw four-footed beasts of the earth, and
wild beasts, and creeping *creatures*, and
the birds of heaven.
7 “And I heard a voice saying to me,
‘Rise up, Kěpha, slay and eat.’
8 “But I said, ‘Not at all, Master!
Because whatever is common or unclean
has never entered into my mouth.’
9 “And the voice answered me again
from the heaven, ‘What Elohim has
cleansed you do not consider common.’
10 “And this took place three times, and
all were drawn up again into the heaven.
11 “And see, immediately three men stood
before the house where I was, having been
sent to me from Caesarea.
12 “And the Spirit said to me to go with
them, not doubting at all. And these six
brothers also went with me, and we went
into the man’s house.
13 “And he told us how he had seen a messenger standing in his house, who said to
him, ‘Send men to Yapho, and call for
Shimʽon who is also called Kěpha,
14 who shall speak to you words, by
which you shall be saved, you and all your
house.’
15 “And as I began to speak, the Set-apart
Spirit fell upon them, as upon us at the
beginning.
16 “And I remembered the word of the
Master, how He said, ‘Yoḥanan indeed
immersed in water, but you shall be
immersed in the Set-apart Spirit.’
17 “So if Elohim gave them the same gift
as He gave us when we believed on the
Master יהושע Messiah, how was I able to
withstand Elohim?”

10c See 17:31, Yn. 5:29, Teh. 96:13, Teh. 98:9, Ḥazon 19:11.

18 And having heard this, they were silent, and praised Elohim, saying, "Then Elohim has indeed also given to the nations repentance to life." [a]

19 Then, indeed, they who were scattered because of the pressure that arose over Stephanos passed through to Phoenicia, and Cyprus, and Antioch, speaking the word to no one except the Yehuḏim only.

20 But some of them were men from Cyprus and Cyrene, who, when they had come to Antioch, spoke to the Hellenists, bringing the Good News: the Master יהושע!

21 And the hand of the Master was with them, and a great number having believed turned to the Master.

22 And word of it came to the ears of the assembly in Yerushalayim, and they sent out Barnaḇa to go as far as Antioch,

23 who, having come, and seeing the favour of Elohim, was glad, and encouraged them all with purpose of heart to cleave to the Master.

24 Because he was a good man, and filled with the Set-apart Spirit and with belief. And large numbers were added to the Master.

25 Then Barnaḇa went to Tarsos to seek Sha'ul,

26 and having found him, he brought him to Antioch. And it came to be that for an entire year they came together in the assembly and taught large numbers. And the taught ones were called 'Messianics' first in Antioch.

27 And in those days prophets came from Yerushalayim to Antioch.

28 And one of them, named Ḥaḡaḇ, stood up and indicated by the Spirit that there was going to be a great scarcity of food over all the world – which also took place under Claudius Caesar.

29 So the taught ones, each according to his ability, decided to send relief to the brothers dwelling in Yehuḏah.

30 This they also did, and sent it to the elders by the hands of Barnaḇa and Sha'ul.

12 And about that time Herodes the sovereign put forth his hands to do evil to some from the assembly.

2 And he killed Ya'aqoḇ the brother of Yoḥanan with the sword.

3 And seeing that it was pleasing to the Yehuḏim, he proceeded further to arrest Kěpha as well – and they were the Days of Unleavened Bread.

4 So when he had seized him, he put him in prison, and delivered him to four squads of soldiers to watch over him, intending to bring him before the people after Pěsaḥ.

5 So Kěpha was indeed kept in prison, but prayer was earnestly made to Elohim on his behalf by the assembly.

6 And when Herodes was about to bring him out, that night Kěpha was sleeping, bound with two chains between two soldiers. And the guards before the door were keeping the prison.

7 And see, a messenger of יהוה stood by, and a light shone in the building. And smiting the side of Kěpha he raised him up, saying, "Get up quickly!" And his chains fell off his hands.

8 And the messenger said to him, "Gird yourself and bind on your sandals," and he did so. And he said to him, "Put on your garment and follow me."

9 And coming out he followed him, and knew not that what was done by the messenger was true, but thought he was seeing a vision.

10 And when they had passed the first and the second guard posts, they came to the iron gate that leads to the city, which opened to them by itself. And they went out and went down one street, and the messenger instantly withdrew from him.

11 And when Kěpha had come to himself, he said, "Now I truly know that יהוה has sent His messenger, and delivered me from the hand of Herodes and *from* all the Yehuḏi people were anticipating."

12 And having realised this, he went to the house of Miryam, the mother of Yoḥanan who was also called Marqos, where many had gathered to pray.

11a See 10:35.

13 And when Kěpha knocked at the door
of the gate, a girl named Rhode came to
answer.
14 And when she recognised Kěpha's
voice, she did not open the gate because of
her joy, but ran in and reported that Kěpha
stood before the gate.
15 And they said to her, "You are mad!"
But she kept insisting that it was so, and
they said, "It is his messenger."
16 And Kěpha continued knocking, and
having opened they saw him and were
amazed.
17 And motioning to them with his hand to
be silent, he told them how the Master
brought him out of the prison. And he said,
"Report this to Yaʽaqoḇ and to the brothers." And he left and went to another place.
18 Now when day came, there was no
small stir among the soldiers about what
had become of Kěpha.
19 And when Herodes had searched for
him and did not find him, he examined the
guards and ordered them to be led away.
And he went down from Yehuḏah to
Caesarea, and stayed there.
20 Now Herodes had been highly displeased with the people of Tsor and
Tsiḏon, but with one mind they came to
him, and having made Blastos the sovereign's eunuch their friend, they were
asking for peace, because their country
was supplied with food by the sovereign's
country.
21 And on an appointed day Herodes,
having put on his royal clothes, sat on his
throne and gave an address to them.
22 And the people kept shouting, "The
voice of a mighty one and not of a man!"
23 And instantly a messenger of יהוה
smote him, because he did not give the
esteem to Elohim. And becoming worm-
eaten, he died.
24 And the word of Elohim went on growing and spreading.
25 And Barnaḇa and Sha'ul returned from
Yerushalayim, having completed the service, and having taken with them Yoḥanan
who was also called Marqos.

13

And in the assembly that was at
Antioch there were certain
prophets and teachers: both Barnaḇa and
Shimʽon who was called Niger, and Lucius
of Cyrene, and Manaḥěm who had been
brought up with Herodes the district ruler,
and Sha'ul.
2 And as they were doing service to the
Master and fasted, the Set-apart Spirit said,
"Separate unto Me Barnaḇa and Sha'ul for
the work to which I have called them."
3 Then having fasted and prayed, and
having laid hands on them, they sent them
away.
4 So they, having been sent out by the
Set-apart Spirit, went down to Seleukeia,
and from there they sailed to Cyprus.
5 And having come into Salamis, they
proclaimed the word of Elohim in the
congregations of the Yehuḏim. And they
also had Yoḥanan as an attendant.
6 And having passed through all the
island to Paphos, they found a certain
magician, a false prophet, a Yehuḏi whose
name was Bar-Yehoshua,
7 who was with the proconsul, Sergius
Paulus, a man of understanding. This man,
having called for Barnaḇa and Sha'ul,
earnestly sought to hear the word of
Elohim.
8 But Elumas the magician – for so his
name is translated – withstood them, seeking to turn the proconsul away from the
belief.
9 Then Sha'ul, who also *is* Paul [a] – filled
with the Set-apart Spirit, looked intently at
him,
10 and said, "O son of the devil, filled with
all deceit and all recklessness, you enemy
of all righteousness, shall you not cease
perverting the straight ways of יהוה?
11 "And now, see, the hand of יהוה is
upon you, and you shall be blind, not seeing the sun for a time." And instantly a
dark mist fell on him, and he went around
seeking someone to lead him by the hand.
12 And having seen what took place, the
proconsul believed, being astonished at the
teaching of the Master.

13a - See Explanatory Notes - Paul.

13 And having put out from Paphos, Sha'ul and those with him came to Perge in Pamphulia. And Yoḥanan, having left them, returned to Yerushalayim.

14 But passing through from Perge, they came to Antioch in Pisidia, and went into the congregation on the Sabbath day and sat down.

15 And after the reading of the Torah and the Prophets, the rulers of the congregation sent to them, saying, "Men, brothers, if you have any word of encouragement for the people, speak."

16 And Sha'ul, standing up and motioning with his hand said, "Men, Yisra'ělis, and those fearing Elohim, listen:

17 "The Elohim of this people Yisra'ěl did choose our fathers, and exalted the people in their sojourning in the land of Mitsrayim, and with a high arm He brought them out of it.

18 "Now for a time of about forty years He sustained them in the wilderness.

19 "And having destroyed seven nations in the land of Kena'an, He gave their land to them as an inheritance.

20 "And after that He gave judges for about four hundred and fifty years, until Shemu'ěl the prophet.

21 "But then they asked for a sovereign, and Elohim gave them Sha'ul the son of Qish, a man of the tribe of Binyamin, for forty years.

22 "And having removed him, He raised up for them Dawiḏ as sovereign, to whom also He gave witness and said, 'I have found Dawiḏ the son of Yishai, a man after My own heart, who shall do all My desires.'

23 "From this one's seed, according to the promise, Elohim raised up for Yisra'ěl a Saviour, יהושע,

24 after Yoḥanan had first proclaimed the immersion of repentance to all the people of Yisra'ěl, before His coming.

25 "And as Yoḥanan was completing his mission, he said, 'Who do you suppose I am? I am not He. But see, there comes One after me, the sandals of whose feet I am not worthy to loose.'

26 "Men, brothers, sons of the race of Aḇraham, and those among you fearing Elohim, to you the word of this deliverance has been sent,

27 for those dwelling in Yerushalayim, and their rulers, because they did not know Him, nor even the voices of the Prophets which are read every Sabbath, have filled them in having judged Him.

28 "And having found not one cause for death, they asked Pilate that He should be put to death.

29 "And when they had accomplished all that was written concerning Him, taking Him down from the timber, they laid Him in a tomb.

30 "But Elohim raised Him from the dead,

31 and He was seen for many days by those who came up with Him from Galil to Yerushalayim, who are His witnesses to the people.

32 "And we bring you the Good News, the promise made to the fathers,

33 that Elohim has filled this for us, their children, having raised up יהושע, as it has also been written in the second Tehillah, **'You are My Son, today I have brought You forth.'** Teh. 2:7

34 "And that He raised Him out of the dead, no more to return to corruption, He has said thus, **'I shall give you the trustworthy kindnesses of Dawiḏ.'** Yesh. 55:3

35 "For this reason He also says in another Tehillah, **'You shall not give Your Kind One to see corruption.'** Teh. 16:10

36 "For Dawiḏ, indeed, having served his own generation by the counsel of Elohim, fell asleep, was buried with his fathers, and saw corruption,

37 but He whom Elohim raised up saw no corruption.

38 "Let it therefore be known to you, brothers, that through this One forgiveness of sins is proclaimed to you,

39 and by Him everyone who believes is declared right from all *sins* from which you were not able to be declared right by the Torah of Mosheh.

40 "Watch then that what was said in the prophets does not come upon you:

41 **"See, you despisers, marvel and per-**

ish, for I work a work in your days, a
work which you would in no way believe
if someone were to declare it to you.' "
Ḥab. 1:5
42 And when the Yehuḏim went out of the
congregation, the nations begged to have
these words spoken to them the next
Sabbath.
43 And when *the meeting of* the congregation had broken up, many of the Yehuḏim
and of the worshipping converts followed
Sha'ul and Barnaḇa, who, speaking to
them, were urging them to continue in the
favour of Elohim.
44 And on the next Sabbath almost all the
city came together to hear the Word of
Elohim.
45 But when the Yehuḏim saw the crowds,
they were filled with jealousy. And contradicting and speaking evil, they opposed
what Sha'ul was saying.
46 But speaking boldly, Sha'ul and
Barnaḇa said, "It was necessary that the
word of Elohim should be spoken to you
first, but since you thrust it away, and
judge yourselves unworthy of everlasting
life, see, we turn to the nations.
47 "For so the Master has commanded us,
'I have set you to be a light to the
nations, that you should be for deliver-
ance to the ends of the earth.' " Yesh. 49:6
48 And when the nations heard this, they
were glad and praised the Word of יהוה.
And as many as had been appointed to
everlasting life believed.
49 And the Word of יהוה was being spread
throughout the entire country.
50 But the Yehuḏim stirred up the worshipping and noble women and the chief
men of the city, and raised up persecution
against Sha'ul and Barnaḇa, and threw
them out of their borders.
51 And shaking off the dust from their feet
against them, they came to Ikonion.
52 And the taught ones were filled with
joy and the Set-apart Spirit.

14 And it came to be in Ikonion that
they went together into the congregation of the Yehuḏim, and spoke in such a
way that a great number of both Yehuḏim
and Greeks believed.
2 But the Yehuḏim who would not obey
stirred up the nations and evilly influenced
their beings against the brothers.
3 So they remained a long time, speaking
boldly in the Master, who was bearing
witness to the word of His favour, giving
signs and wonders to be done by their
hands.
4 And the crowd of the city was divided,
and some sided with the Yehuḏim, and
some with the emissaries.
5 But when a move took place by both
the nations and Yehuḏim, with their rulers,
to mistreat and stone them,
6 they became aware of it and fled to
Lustra and Derbe, cities of Lukaonia, and
the country round about.
7 And they were bringing the Good News
there.
8 And in Lustra there was sitting a certain
man, disabled in his feet, a cripple from his
mother's womb, who had never walked.
9 This one heard Sha'ul speaking, who,
looking intently at him and seeing that he
had belief to be healed,
10 said with a loud voice, "Stand upright
on your feet!" And he sprang up and began
to walk.
11 And when the crowds saw what Sha'ul
had done, they lifted up their voices, saying in Lukaonian, "The mighty ones have
become like men and come down to us!"
12 And they called Barnaḇa Zeus, and
Sha'ul Hermes, since he was the chief
speaker.
13 And the priest of Zeus, being in front of
their city, brought oxen and wreaths to the
gates, and wished to offer with the crowds.
14 And when the emissaries Barnaḇa and
Sha'ul heard this, they tore their garments
and ran in among the crowd, crying out
15 and saying, "Men, why are you doing
this? We also are men with the same nature
as you, bringing to you the Good News: to
turn from these worthless matters to the
living Elohim, **who made the heaven, and**
the earth, and the sea, and all that is in
them, Shem. 20:11, Teh. 146:6
16 who in past generations allowed all the
nations to walk in their own ways, [a]

17 though, indeed, He did not leave
Himself without witness, doing good –
giving us rain from heaven and fruit-
bearing seasons, filling our hearts with
food and gladness."[b]
18 Even with these words they still had
difficulty in stopping the crowds from
offering to them.
19 But Yehuḏim arrived from Antioch and
Ikonion, and having won over the crowds,
they stoned Sha'ul, dragged him out of the
city, thinking he was dead.
20 But while the taught ones gathered
around him, he rose up and went into the
city. And on the next day he went away
with Barnaḇa to Derbe.
21 And having brought the Good News to
that city, and having made many taught
ones, they returned to Lustra, and Ikonion,
and Antioch,
22 strengthening the beings of the taught
ones, encouraging them to continue in the
belief, and that through many pressures we
have to enter the reign of Elohim.
23 And having appointed elders in every
assembly, having prayed with fasting, they
committed them to the Master in whom
they had believed.
24 And having passed through Pisidia,
they came to Pamphulia.
25 And having spoken the word in Perge,
they went down to Attaleia,
26 and from there they sailed to Antioch,
where they had been committed to the
favour of Elohim for the work which they
had completed.
27 And having arrived, and having gathered together the assembly, they related all
that Elohim had done with them, and that
He had opened the door of belief to the
nations.
28 And they remained there a long time
with the taught ones.

15

And certain men came down from
Yehuḏah and were teaching the
brothers, "Unless you are circumcised,
according to the practice of Mosheh, you
are unable to be saved."
2 So when Sha'ul and Barnaḇa had no
small dissension and dispute with them,
they arranged for Sha'ul and Barnaḇa and
certain others of them to go up to Yerushalayim, to the emissaries and elders, about
this question.
3 So, being sent on their way by the
assembly, they passed through Phoenicia
and Shomeron, relating the conversion of
the nations. And they were causing great
joy to all the brothers.
4 And having arrived in Yerushalayim,
they were received by the assembly and
the emissaries and the elders. And they
reported all that Elohim had done with
them.
5 And some of the believers who belonged to the sect of the Pharisees, rose up,
saying, "It is necessary to circumcise them,
and to command them to keep the Torah of
Mosheh."
6 And the emissaries and elders came
together to look into this matter.
7 And when there had been much dispute, Kĕpha rose up and said to them,
"Men, brothers, you know that a good
while ago Elohim chose among us, that by
my mouth the nations should hear the word
of the Good News and believe.
8 "And Elohim, who knows the heart,
bore witness to them, by giving them the
Set-apart Spirit, as also to us,
9 and made no distinction between us and
them, cleansing their hearts by belief.
10 "Now then, why do you try Elohim by
putting a yoke on the neck of the taught
ones which neither our fathers nor we were
able to bear?
11 "But through the favour of the Master
יהושע Messiah we trust to be saved, in the
same way as they."
12 And all the crowd was silent and were
listening to Barnaḇa and Sha'ul declaring
how many miracles and wonders Elohim
did among the nations, through them.
13 And after they were silent, Ya'aqoḇ
answered, saying, "Men, brothers, listen to
me:
14 "Shim'on has declared how Elohim

14a (previous page) 17:30. *14b* See Mt. 5:45.

first visited the nations to take out of them
a people for His Name.
15 "And the words of the prophets agree
with this, as it has been written:
16 **'After this I shall return and rebuild
the Booth of Dawiḏ which has fallen
down. And I shall rebuild its ruins, and I
shall set it up,**
17 **so that the remnant of mankind shall
seek יהוה, even all the nations on whom
My Name has been called, says יהוה who
is doing all this,'**
18 **who has made this known from of
old.** Amos 9:11-12
19 "Therefore I judge that we should not
trouble those from among the nations who
are turning to Elohim,
20 but that we write to them to abstain
from the defilements of idols, [a] and from
whoring, [b] and from what is strangled, [c]
and from blood. [d]
21 "For from ancient generations Mosheh
has, in every city, those proclaiming him –
being read in the congregations every
Sabbath."
22 Then it seemed good to the emissaries
and elders, with all the assembly, to send
chosen men from among them to Antioch
with Sha'ul and Barnaḇa: Yehuḏah being
called Barsabba, and Silas, leading men
among the brothers,
23 having written by their hand this: The
emissaries and the elders and the brothers,
To the brothers who are of the nations in
Antioch, and Suria, and Kilikia: Greetings.
24 Since we have heard that some who
went out from us have troubled you with
words, unsettling your lives, to whom we
gave no command –
25 it seemed good to us, having become of
one mind, to send chosen men to you with
our beloved Barnaḇa and Sha'ul,
26 men who have given up their lives for
the Name of our Master יהושע Messiah.
27 We have therefore sent Yehuḏah and
Silas, who are also confirming this by
word of mouth.
28 For it seemed good to the Set-apart
Spirit, and to us, to lay upon you no greater
burden than these necessities:
29 that you abstain from what is offered to
idols, and blood, and what is strangled, and
whoring. [e] If you keep yourselves from
these, you shall do well. Be strong!
30 They, therefore, being sent off, went to
Antioch. And having gathered the crowd
together, they delivered the letter.
31 And having read it, they rejoiced over
its encouragement.
32 And Yehuḏah and Silas, being themselves also prophets, encouraged the brothers with many words and strengthened
them.
33 And having spent some time, they were
sent back in peace from the brothers to the
emissaries.
34 But it seemed good to Silas to remain.
35 And Sha'ul and Barnaḇa continued in
Antioch, teaching and bringing, with many
others also, the Good News: the Word of
יהוה!
36 And after some days Sha'ul said to
Barnaḇa, "Let us now go back and visit our
brothers in every city where we proclaimed the Word of יהוה, and see how
they are."
37 And Barnaḇa purposed to take with
them Yoḥanan called Marqos.
38 But Sha'ul thought it not fit to take with
them the one who withdrew from them in
Pamphulia, and had not gone with them to
the work.
39 A sharp feeling therefore came to be, so
that they parted from one another. And so
Barnaḇa took Marqos and sailed to Cyprus.
40 And Sha'ul chose Silas and went off,
being committed by the brothers to the
favour of Elohim.
41 And he went through Suria and Kilikia,
strengthening the assemblies.

15a Shem. 22:20; Way. 17:7; Deḇ. 32:17,21; Cor. א 10:14, 20, 21. *15b* Bem. 25:1-3; Way. 17:7. *15c* Ber. 9:4; Yeḥ. 33:25 (Strangled - One way of eating meat with blood) Ma. 21:25. *15d* Way. 3:17 & 17:10-12,26; Deḇ. 12:23, 24. *15e* See v. 20.

16

And he came to Derbe and Lustra. And see, a certain taught one was there, named Timotiyos, the son of a certain Yehuḏi woman who believed – but his father was Greek –

2 who was well spoken of by the brothers who were at Lustra and Ikonion.

3 Sha'ul wished to have this one go with him. And he took him and circumcised him because of the Yehuḏim who were in those places, for they all knew that his father was Greek.

4 And as they went through the cities, they delivered to them the regulations to keep, which were decided by the emissaries and elders at Yerushalayim.

5 Then, indeed, the assemblies were strengthened in the belief, and increased in number every day.

6 And having passed through Phrygia and the Galatian country, they were forbidden by the Set-apart Spirit to speak the word in Asia.

7 When they came to Musia, they tried to go into Bithunia, but the Spirit did not allow them.

8 And having passed by Musia, they came down to Troas.

9 And in the night a vision appeared to Sha'ul: A man of Makedonia was standing, begging him and saying, "Come over to Makedonia and help us."

10 And when he saw the vision, immediately we sought to go to Makedonia, concluding that the Master had called us to bring the Good News to them.

11 Therefore, sailing from Troas, we ran a straight course to Samothrake, and the next day came to Neapolis,

12 and from there to Philippi, which is the principal city of that part of Makedonia, a colony. And we were staying in that city for some days.

13 And on the Sabbath day we went outside the city by a river, where there used to be prayer. And having sat down we were speaking to the women who met there.

14 And a certain woman named Ludia, [a] a seller of purple from the city of Thyatira, worshipping Elohim, was hearing, whose heart the Master did open to pay attention to what Sha'ul said.

15 And when she was immersed, and her household, she begged us, saying, "If you have judged me to be believing in the Master, come to my house and stay." And she urged us.

16 And it came to be, as we went to prayer, that a certain slave girl possessed with a spirit of Puthon, did meet us, who brought her masters much profit by foretelling.

17 Having followed Sha'ul and us, she cried out, saying, "These men are the servants of the Most High Elohim, who proclaim to us the way of deliverance."

18 And she was doing this for many days. But Sha'ul, greatly annoyed, turned and said to the spirit, "I command you in the Name of יהושע Messiah to come out of her." And it came out that same hour.

19 But when her masters saw that their anticipation of money-making was gone, they seized Sha'ul and Silas and dragged them into the market-place to the rulers.

20 And having brought them to the captains, they said, "These men, being Yehuḏim, greatly disturb our city,

21 and they proclaim practices which are not right for us to receive nor to do, being Romans."

22 And the crowd rose up together against them. And the captains tore off their garments and commanded them to be beaten with rods.

23 And having laid many blows upon them, they threw them into prison, commanding the jailer to keep them safely,

24 who, having received such a command, put them into the inner prison and fastened their feet in the stocks.

25 And at midnight Sha'ul and Silas were praying and singing songs to Elohim, and the prisoners were listening to them.

26 And suddenly a great earthquake took place, so that the foundations of the prison were shaken, and immediately all the doors were opened and all the chains came

16a Most probably a gentile by birth, converted to יהושע.

loose.
27 And the jailer, awaking from sleep and
seeing the prison doors open, thinking the
prisoners had fled, drew his sword and was
about to kill himself.
28 But Sha'ul called with a loud voice,
saying, "Do no harm to yourself, for we
are all here."
29 And asking for a light, he ran in, and
fell down trembling before Sha'ul and
Silas.
30 And having led them outside he said,
"Masters, what do I have to do to be
saved?"
31 And they said, "Believe on the Master
יהושע Messiah, and you shall be saved,
you and your household."
32 And they spoke the Word of יהוה to
him and to all who were in his house.
33 And taking them in that hour of the
night, he washed their wounds, and immediately he was immersed, he and all that
were his.
34 And having brought them into his
house, he set food before them. And he
rejoiced with all his household, having
believed in Elohim.
35 And when day came, the authorities
sent the officers, saying, "Let these men
go."
36 And the jailer reported these words to
Sha'ul, saying, "The captains have sent to
let you go. Now then, come out and go in
peace."
37 But Sha'ul said to them, "They have
beaten us publicly, uncondemned, being
Romans. They have thrown us into prison,
and now, do they throw us out secretly? No
indeed! Let them come themselves and
bring us out."
38 And the officers reported these words
to the authorities, and they were afraid
when they heard that they were Romans.
39 And having come, they pleaded with
them and brought them out, and asked
them to leave the city.
40 So coming out of the prison they went
to Ludia, and seeing the brothers, they
encouraged them, and went forth.

17 And having passed through
Amphipolis and Apollonia, they
came to Thessalonike, where there was a
congregation of the Yehuḏim.
2 And according to his practice, Sha'ul
went in unto them, and for three Sabbaths
was reasoning with them from the
Scriptures,
3 explaining and pointing out that the
Messiah had to suffer and rise again from
the dead, and *saying*, "This is the Messiah,
יהושע, whom I proclaim to you."
4 And some of them did believe, and a
large number of the worshipping Greeks,
and not a few of the leading women, joined
Sha'ul and Silas.
5 But the Yehuḏim who did not believe,
having become envious, took some of the
wicked men from the market-place, and
gathering a mob, set all the city in an
uproar and came upon the house of Jason,
and were seeking to bring them out to the
people.
6 But not finding them, they dragged
Jason and some of the brothers to the city
rulers, crying out, "They who have turned
the world upside down have come here
too,
7 whom Jason has received. And all of
them are acting contrary to the dogmas of
Caesar, saying there is another sovereign,
יהושע."
8 And they troubled the crowd and the
city rulers when they heard this.
9 And when they had received a pledge
from Jason and the rest, they let them go.
10 And the brothers immediately sent
Sha'ul and Silas away by night to Beroia,
who, having come, went into the congregation of the Yehuḏim.
11 Now these were more noble than those
in Thessalonike, who received the word
with great eagerness, and searched the
Scriptures daily, if these *words* were so.
12 Then many of them truly believed, and
also not a few of the Greeks, decent
women as well as men.
13 And when the Yehuḏim from Thessalonike came to know that the word of
Elohim was proclaimed by Sha'ul at
Beroia, they came there also and stirred up

the crowds.
14 And then immediately the brothers sent
Sha'ul away, to go to the sea, but both
Silas and Timotiyos stayed there.
15 And those who arranged for Sha'ul
brought him to Athens. And receiving a
command for Silas and Timotiyos to join
him as soon as possible, they departed.
16 But while Sha'ul was waiting for them
at Athens, his spirit was stirred up within
him when he saw that the city was utterly
idolatrous.
17 Therefore, indeed, he was reasoning in
the congregation with the Yehuḏim and
with the worshippers, and in the market-
place daily with those who met there.
18 And some of the Epicurean and Stoic
philosophers encountered him. And some
were saying, "What does this babbler wish
to say?" Others said, "He seems to be a
proclaimer of strange mighty ones" –
because to them he brought the Good
News: 'יהושע' and the resurrection!
19 So they laid hold of him and brought
him to the Areopagus, saying, "Are we
able to know what this fresh teaching is of
which you speak?
20 "For you are bringing some strange
matters to our ears. We wish, then, to know
what these mean."
21 For all the Athenians and the strangers
living there spent their leisure time in
doing naught but to speak or to hear what
is fresh.
22 And having stood in the midst of the
Areopagus Sha'ul said, "Men of Athens, I
see that you are very religious in every
matter.
23 "For passing through and observing the
objects of your worship, I even found a
slaughter-place with this inscription: TO
THE UNKNOWN MIGHTY ONE. Not
knowing then whom you worship, I make
Him known to you:
24 "'יהוה', who made the world and all that
is in it, this One being Master of heaven
and earth, does not dwell in dwellings
made with hands. [a]
25 "Nor is He served with men's hands –
as if needing any – Himself giving to all
life, and breath, and all *else*.
26 "And He has made from one blood
every nation of men to dwell on all the face
of the earth, having ordained beforehand
the times and the boundaries of their
dwelling,
27 to seek the Master, if at least they
would reach out for Him and find Him,
though He is not far from each one of us.
28 "For in Him we live and move and are,
as also some of your own poets have said,
'For we are also His offspring.'
29 "Now then, since we are the offspring
of Elohim, we should not think that the
Elohim is like gold or silver or stone, an
image made by the skill and thought of
man.
30 "Truly, then, having overlooked these
times of ignorance, Elohim now commands all men everywhere to repent,
31 because He has set a day on which He
is going to judge the world in righteousness by a Man whom He has appointed, [b]
having given proof of this to all by raising
Him from the dead."
32 And hearing of the resurrection of the
dead, some indeed mocked, while others
said, "We shall hear you again concerning
this."
33 And so Sha'ul went out from among
them.
34 But some men joined him and believed,
among them Dionusios the Areopagite,
and a woman named Damaris, and others
with them.

18 And after this Sha'ul left Athens
and went to Corinth.
2 And he found a certain Yehuḏi named
Aqulas, born in Pontos, who had recently
come from Italy with his wife Priscilla –
because Claudius had commanded all the
Yehuḏim to leave Rome – and he came to
them.
3 And because he was of the same trade,
he stayed with them and was working, for
they were tentmakers by trade.
4 And he was reasoning in the congrega-

17a See 7:48. *17b* See 10:42.

tion every Sabbath, and won over both Yehuḏim and Greeks.

5 And when Silas and Timotiyos came down from Makedonia, Sha'ul was pressed by the Spirit, and earnestly witnessed to the Yehuḏim that יהושע is the Messiah.

6 However, when they resisted and blasphemed, he shook his garments and said to them, "Your blood is upon your head, I am clean. From now on I shall go to the nations."

7 And having left there he came to the house of a certain man named Justus, who worshipped Elohim, whose house was next to the congregation.

8 And Crispus, the ruler of the congregation, did believe in the Master with all his household. And many of the Corinthians, hearing, believed and were immersed.

9 And the Master spoke to Sha'ul in the night by a vision, "Do not be afraid, but speak, and do not be silent,

10 because I am with you, and no one shall attack you to do you evil, because I have much people in this city."

11 And he remained a year and six months, teaching the Word of יהוה among them.

12 And when Gallion was proconsul of Achaia, the Yehuḏim with one mind rose up against Sha'ul and brought him to the judgment seat,

13 saying, "This one does seduce men to worship Elohim contrary to the Torah."

14 And as Sha'ul was about to open his mouth, Gallion said to the Yehuḏim, "If it were a matter of wrongdoing or wicked recklessness, O Yehuḏim, there would be reason why I should bear with you.

15 "But if it is a question of words and names and a law which is among you, see to it yourselves, for I do not wish to be a judge of these *matters*."

16 And he drove them away from the judgment seat.

17 And all the Greeks took Sosthenes, the ruler of the congregation, and beat him before the judgment seat. But Gallion showed no concern whatever.

18 And Sha'ul, having stayed several days more, having taken leave of the brothers, was sailing for Suria, and Priscilla and Aqulas were with him, having shaved his hair at Kenḥrea, for he had taken a vow.

19 And he came to Ephesos, and left them there, but he himself went into the congregation and reasoned with the Yehuḏim.

20 And when they asked him to stay a longer time with them, he declined,

21 but took leave of them, saying, "I have to keep this coming festival in Yerushalayim by all means, but I shall come back to you, Elohim desiring so." And he sailed from Ephesos.

22 And having come to Caesarea, going up and greeting the assembly, he went down to Antioch.

23 And having spent some time there, he went forth, passing through the country of Galatia and on through Phrygia, strengthening all the taught ones.

24 And a certain Yehuḏi named Apollos, born at Alexandria, a learned man and mighty in the Scriptures, came to Ephesos.

25 This one had been instructed in the way of the Master. And being fervent in spirit, he was speaking and teaching the *matters* about the Master exactly, though he knew only the immersion of Yoḥanan.

26 And he began to speak boldly in the congregation. And when Aqulas and Priscilla heard him, they took him aside and explained to him the way of Elohim more exactly.

27 And when he intended to pass through to Achaia, the brothers, having encouraged him, wrote to the taught ones to receive him, who, having arrived, greatly helped those who believed through favour,

28 for with power he refuted the Yehuḏim publicly, showing from the Scriptures that יהושע is the Messiah.

19 And it came to be, while Apollos was at Corinth, that Sha'ul, having passed through the upper parts, came to Ephesos. And having found some taught ones,

2 he said to them, "Did you receive the Set-apart Spirit when you believed?" And they said to him, "No, we have not even

heard that there is a Set-apart Spirit."
3 And he said to them, "Into what then
were you immersed?" And they said, "Into
Yoḥanan's immersion."
4 And Sha'ul said, "Yoḥanan indeed
immersed with an immersion of repentance, saying to the people that they should
believe in the One who is coming after
him, that is, in Messiah יהושע."
5 And when they heard this, they were
immersed into the Name of the Master
יהושע.
6 And when Sha'ul had laid hands on
them, the Set-apart Spirit came upon them,
and they were speaking in tongues and
prophesying.
7 And all the men were about twelve.
8 And having gone into the congregation
he spoke boldly for three months, reasoning and persuading concerning the reign of
Elohim.
9 But when some were hardened and did
not believe, speaking evil of the Way
before the crowd, he withdrew from them
and separated the taught ones, reasoning
daily in the school of Turannos.
10 And this took place for two years, so
that all who dwelt in Asia heard the word
of the Master יהושע, both Yehuḏim and
Greeks.
11 And Elohim worked unusual miracles
through the hands of Sha'ul,
12 so that even handkerchiefs or aprons
were brought from his body to the sick,
and the diseases left them and the wicked
spirits went out of them.
13 But certain roving Yehuḏi exorcists
took it upon themselves to call the Name
of the Master יהושע over those who had
wicked spirits, saying, "We exorcise you
by יהושע whom Sha'ul proclaims."
14 And there were seven sons of a certain
Skeua, a Yehuḏi chief priest, who were
doing this.
15 And the wicked spirit answering, said,
"יהושע I know, and Sha'ul I know, but
who are you?"
16 And the man in whom the wicked spirit
was leaped on them, overpowered them,
and prevailed against them, so that they
fled out of that house naked and wounded.
17 And this became known to all, both
Yehuḏim and Greeks dwelling in Ephesos.
And fear fell on them all, and the Name of
the Master יהושע was made great.
18 And many who had believed came confessing and declaring their deeds.
19 And many of those who had practised
magic brought their books together, burning them before all. And they reckoned up
the value of them, and found it to be fifty
thousand pieces of silver.
20 So the word of the Master was growing
mightily and prevailing.
21 Now when these *matters* had been
completed, Sha'ul purposed in the Spirit,
when he had passed through Makedonia
and Achaia, to go to Yerushalayim, saying,
"After I have been there, I have to see
Rome too."
22 And having sent into Makedonia two of
those assisting him, Timotiyos and Ěrastos, he himself remained in Asia for a time.
23 And about that time there came to be a
great commotion about the Way.
24 For a certain man named Demetrios, a
silversmith, who made silver shrines of
Artemis, provided no little business to the
craftsmen,
25 who, having called them together, with
the workers of similar *trade*, said, "Men,
you know that our wealth is from this business.
26 "And you see and hear that not only at
Ephesos, but throughout almost all Asia,
this Sha'ul has persuaded and turned away
a large number, saying that they are not
mighty ones which are made with hands.
27 "And not only is this trade of ours in
danger of coming to rejection, but also that
the temple of the great female mighty one
Artemis whom all Asia and the world worship, shall be regarded as worthless and
her greatness diminished."
28 And having heard this, they were filled
with rage and cried out, saying, "Great is
Artemis of the Ephesians!"
29 And the entire city was filled with
confusion, and they rushed with one mind
into the theatre, having seized Gaios and
Aristarchos, Makedonians, Sha'ul's fellow
travellers.

30 And Sha'ul, intending to go in among
the mob, the taught ones did not allow him.
31 And some of the officials of Asia,
being his friends, sent to him begging him
not to risk himself into the theatre.
32 Then others indeed shouted this and
others that, for the assembly was confused,
and most of them did not know why they
had come together.
33 And some of the crowd instructed
Alexander – the Yehuḏim putting him forward. And Alexander motioned with his
hand, and wished to make his defence to
the people.
34 But having recognised that he was a
Yehuḏi, all with one voice cried out for
about two hours, "Great is Artemis of the
Ephesians!"
35 And the city clerk, having calmed the
crowd, said, "Men of Ephesos, what man
is there who does not know that the city of
the Ephesians is the guardian of the temple
of the great female mighty one Artemis,
and of that which fell down from Zeus?
36 "Therefore, if these *matters* are undeni-
able, you need to be calm, and do not act
rashly.
37 "For you have brought these men here
who are neither temple-robbers nor speaking evil of your female mighty one.
38 "If truly then Demetrios and his fellow
craftsmen have a case against anyone, the
courts are open and there are proconsuls.
Let them accuse one another.
39 "And if you have any further complaint, it shall be settled in the regular
assembly.
40 "For we are in danger of being accused
of riot concerning today, there being no
reason which we could give to account for
this disorderly gathering."
41 And having said this, he dismissed the
assembly.

20 After the uproar had ceased, Sha'ul
called the taught ones to him, and
having embraced them, went away to go to
Makedonia.
2 And having gone through those parts,
and having encouraged them with many
words, he came to Greece,
3 where he spent three months. When he
was about to sail to Suria, he decided to
return through Makedonia, as a plot was
made against him by the Yehuḏim.
4 And he was accompanied by Sopater of
Beroia, and Aristarchos and Sekundos of
the Thessalonians, and Gaios of Derbe,
and Timotiyos, and Tuchikos and
Trophimos of Asia.
5 And these, going ahead, waited for us
at Troas.
6 And we sailed away from Philippi after
the Days of Unleavened Bread, and came
to them at Troas in five days, where we
stayed seven days.
7 And on *day* one of the week[a], the
taught ones having gathered together to
break bread, Sha'ul, intending to depart the
next day, was reasoning with them and was
extending the word till midnight.
8 And there were many lamps in the
upper room where they were assembled.
9 And a certain young man, by name
Eutuchos, was sitting in a window, being
overpowered by a deep sleep. As Sha'ul
kept on reasoning, he was overcome by
sleep and fell down from the third story,
and was picked up dead.
10 And Sha'ul, having gone down, fell on
him, and embracing him said, "Do not be
upset, for his life is in him."
11 Then going up again, and having
broken bread and eaten, he talked a long
while, even till daybreak, and so went
forth.
12 And they brought the young man in
alive, and were encouraged, not a little.
13 And we, going ahead to the ship, sailed
to Assos, intending to take Sha'ul on board
there, for so he had arranged, intending
himself to go on foot.
14 And when he met us at Assos, we took
him on board and came to Mitulene.
15 And from there we sailed, and the next
day came opposite Chios. And the next
day we arrived at Samos and remained at
Trogullion. And the following day we

20a Gk. Sabbaths.

came to Miletos.
16 For Sha'ul had decided to sail past
Ephesos, so that he might lose no time in
Asia, for he was hurrying to be at
Yerushalayim, if possible, on the Day of
the Festival of Shaḇu'ot. [b]
17 And from Miletos he sent to Ephesos
and called for the elders of the assembly.
18 And when they had come to him, he
said to them, "You know, from the first day
that I came to Asia, how I was with you all
the time,
19 serving the Master with all humility,
with many tears and trials which befell me
by the plotting of the Yehuḏim,
20 as I kept back no *matter* that was profitable, but proclaimed it to you, and taught
you publicly and from house to house,
21 witnessing to Yehuḏim, and also to
Greeks: repentance toward Elohim and
belief in our Master יהושע Messiah.
22 "And now see, I go bound in the spirit
to Yerushalayim, not knowing what is
going to meet me there,
23 except that the Set-apart Spirit witnesses in every city, saying that chains and
pressures await me.
24 "But I do not count my life of any value
to me, so that I might accomplish my mission with joy, and the service which I
received from the Master יהושע, to bear
witness to the Good News of the favour of
Elohim.
25 "And now see, I know that you all,
among whom I went about proclaiming the
reign of Elohim, shall see my face no
more.
26 "Therefore I witness to you this day
that I am clear from the blood of all.
27 "For I kept not back from declaring to
you all the counsel of Elohim.
28 "Therefore take heed to yourselves and
to all the flock, among which the Set-apart
Spirit has made you overseers, to shepherd
the assembly of Elohim which He has
purchased with His own blood.
29 "For I know this, that after my departure savage wolves [c] shall come in among
you, not sparing the flock.
30 "Also from among yourselves men
shall arise, speaking distorted *teachings*, to
draw away the taught ones after themselves.
31 "Therefore watch, remembering that
for three years, night and day, I did not
cease to warn each one with tears.
32 "And now, brothers, I commit you to
Elohim and to the word of His favour,
which is able to build you up and give you
an inheritance among all those having been
set apart.
33 "I have coveted no one's silver or gold
or garments.
34 "And you yourselves know that these
hands supplied my needs, and for those
who were with me.
35 "All this I did show you, by labouring
like this, that you ought to help the weak.
And remember the words of the Master
יהושע, that He said, 'It is more blessed to
give than to receive.' "
36 And having said this, he knelt down
and prayed with them all.
37 And there was much weeping among
them all, and falling on Sha'ul's neck, they
kissed him,
38 distressed most of all because of the
word which he had said, that they would
see his face no more. And they went with
him to the ship.

21 And it came to be, when we had
torn ourselves away from them,
and had set sail, we ran a straight course
and came to Cos, and the next day to
Rhodes, and from there to Patara.
2 And having found a ship passing over
to Phoenicia, we went aboard and set sail.
3 And having sighted Cyprus, and having
passed it on the left, we sailed to Suria, and
landed at Tsor, for the ship was to unload
her cargo there.
4 And having found taught ones, we
remained there seven days. And they told

20b Counted from the day on which the sheaf of the first-fruits is waved during the Festival of Matzot (Unleavened Bread) - See Way. 23:10-21. (The morrow after the Sabbath.) See also Ma. 2:1. *20c* Mt. 7:15-23; 10:16, Lq. 10:3, Yn. 10:12; Ma. 20:29.

Sha'ul through the Spirit not to go up to Yerushalayim.
5 And when it came to be that our days there were ended, we left and went on, all of them accompanying us, with wives and children, till we were out of the city. And kneeling down on the beach, we prayed.
6 And having embraced one another, we boarded the ship, and they returned to their homes.
7 And when we had completed our voyage from Tsor, we came to Ptolemais. And having greeted the brothers we stayed with them one day.
8 And on the next day we left and came to Caesarea, and went into the house of Philip the evangelist, who was one of the seven, and stayed with him.
9 Now this one had four maiden daughters who prophesied.
10 And as we were staying many days, a certain prophet named Ḥaḡaḇ came down from Yehuḏah,
11 and having come to us, he took the girdle of Sha'ul, bound his own hands and feet, and said, "Thus says the Set-apart Spirit, 'Thus shall the Yehuḏim at Yerushalayim bind the man who owns this girdle, and deliver him into the hands of the nations.' "
12 And when we heard this, both we and those from that place begged him not to go up to Yerushalayim.
13 And Sha'ul answered, "What do you mean by weeping and breaking my heart? For I am ready not only to be bound, but also to die at Yerushalayim for the Name of the Master יהושע."
14 And as he could not be persuaded, we ceased, saying, "Let the desire of the Master be done."
15 And after those days, having made ready, we went up to Yerushalayim.
16 And also some of the taught ones from Caesarea went with us and brought with them one, Mnason of Cyprus, an early taught one, with whom we were to lodge.
17 And when we had arrived in Yerushalayim, the brothers received us gladly.
18 And on the following day Sha'ul went in with us to Yaʽaqoḇ, and all the elders came.
19 And having greeted them, he was relating one by one what Elohim had done among the nations through his service.
20 And when they heard it, they praised the Master. And they said to him, "You see, brother, how many thousands of Yehuḏim there are who have believed, and all are ardent for the Torah,
21 "But they have been informed about you that you teach all the Yehuḏim who are among the nations to forsake Mosheh, saying not to circumcise the children nor to walk according to the practices.
22 "What then is it? They shall certainly hear that you have come.
23 "So do this, what we say to you: We have four men who have taken a vow.
24 "Take them and be cleansed with them, and pay their expenses so that they shave their heads. And all shall know that what they have been informed about you is not so, but that you yourself also walk orderly, keeping the Torah.
25 "But concerning the nations who believe, we have written and decided that they should keep themselves from what is offered to idols, and blood, and what is strangled, and whoring." [a]
26 Then Sha'ul took the men on the next day, and having been cleansed with them, went into the Set-apart Place to announce the completion of the days of separation – until the offering should be presented for each one of them.
27 And when the seven days were almost ended, the Yehuḏim from Asia, seeing him in the Set-apart Place, were stirring up all the crowd, and they laid hands on him,
28 crying out, "Men of Yisra'ěl, help! This is the man who is teaching all men everywhere against the people, and the Torah, and this place. And besides, he also brought Greeks into the Set-apart Place and has profaned this Set-apart Place."
29 Because they had previously seen Trophimos the Ephesian with him in the

21a See 15:20.

city, whom they thought that Sha'ul had
brought into the Set-apart Place.
30 And the entire city was moved, and the
people rushed together, seized Sha'ul, and
dragged him out of the Set-apart Place.
And immediately the doors were shut.
31 And while they were seeking to kill
him, a report came to the commander of
the company *of soldiers* that all Yerushalayim was in confusion.
32 At once he took soldiers and captains,
and ran down to them. And they, having
seen the commander and the soldiers, stopped beating Sha'ul.
33 Then the commander came near and
took him, and commanded him to be
bound with two chains, and was asking
who he was and what he had done.
34 And in the crowd some were shouting
this and others that. And not being able to
ascertain the truth because of the uproar,
he commanded him to be taken into the
barracks.
35 And when he came to the stairs, he had
to be carried by the soldiers because of the
violence of the crowd.
36 For a large number of the people followed after, crying out, "Away with him!"
37 And as Sha'ul was about to be led into
the barracks, he said to the commander,
"Am I allowed to say somewhat to you?"
And he said, "Do you know Greek?
38 "Are you not the Mitsrian who some
time ago stirred up a revolt and led the four
thousand assassins out into the wilderness?"
39 But Sha'ul replied, "I am a Yehuḏi
from Tarsos, in Kilikia, a citizen of no
mean city. And I beg you, allow me to
speak to the people."
40 And having given him permission,
Sha'ul, standing on the stairs motioned
with his hand to the people. And when
there was a great silence, he spoke in the
Hebrew language, [b] saying,

22

"Men, brothers, and fathers, hear
my defence before you now."
2 And when they heard that he spoke to
them in the Hebrew language, [a] they kept
greater silence. And he said:
3 "I am indeed a Yehuḏi, having been
born in Tarsos of Kilikia, but brought up in
this city at the feet of Gamli'ěl, having
been instructed according to the exactness
of the Torah of our fathers, being ardent for
Elohim, as you all are today,
4 who persecuted this Way to the death,
binding and delivering up into prisons both
men and women,
5 as also the high priest bears me witness,
and all the eldership, from whom I also
received letters to the brothers, and went to
Dammeseq to bring in chains even those
who were there to Yerushalayim to be punished.
6 "And it came to be, as I was journeying
and coming near Dammeseq, about noon,
suddenly a great light shone around me out
of the heaven,
7 and I fell to the ground and heard a
voice saying to me, 'Sha'ul, Sha'ul, why
do you persecute Me?'
8 "And I answered, 'Who are You,
Master?' And He said to me, 'I am יהושע
of Natsareth, whom you persecute.'
9 "And those who were with me indeed
saw the light and were afraid, but they did
not hear His voice speaking to me.
10 "And I said, 'What shall I do, Master?'
And the Master said to me, 'Rise up, go
into Dammeseq, and there you shall be
told all that you have been appointed to
do.'
11 "And as I could not see because of the
esteem of that light, being led by the hand
of those who were with me, I came into
Dammeseq.
12 "And a certain Ḥananyah, [b] a dedicated
man according to the Torah, being well
spoken of by all the Yehuḏim dwelling
there,
13 came to me, and stood by and said to
me, 'Brother Sha'ul, look up.' And at that
same hour I looked up at him.
14 "And he said, **'The Elohim of our
fathers** [Shem. 3:15] has appointed you to know
His desire, and to see the Righteous One,

21b See 26:14. *22a* See 21:40, 26:14. *22b* See 9:10 & 17.

and to hear the voice from His mouth.
15 'Because you shall be His witness to all
men of what you have seen and heard.
16 'And now, why do you delay? Rise up,
be immersed, and wash away your sins,
calling on the Name of יהוה.'
17 "And it came to be, when I returned to
Yerushalayim, and while I was praying in
the Set-apart Place, I came to be in a
trance,
18 and I saw Him saying to me, 'Hurry
and get out of Yerushalayim, speedily,
because they shall not accept your witness
concerning Me.'
19 "And I said, 'Master, they know that in
every congregation I was imprisoning and
beating those who believe on You.
20 'And when the blood of Your witness
Stephanos was shed, I also was standing
by giving my approval to his death, and
keeping the garments of those who were
killing him.'
21 "And He said to me, 'Go, because
I shall send you far from here to the
nations.' "
22 And they were listening to him until
this word, and then they lifted up their
voice, saying, "Away with such a one from
the earth, for it is not fit that he should
live!"
23 As they were shouting and tearing their
garments, and throwing dust into the air,
24 the commander ordered him to be
brought into the barracks, and said that he
should be examined by flogging, in order
to find out why they were shouting so
against him.
25 And as they were stretching him out
with straps, Sha'ul said to the captain who
was standing by, "Is it permitted for you to
whip a man who is a Roman, and uncondemned?"
26 And when the captain heard, he went
and reported to the commander, saying,
"Watch what you are about to do, for this
man is a Roman."
27 And having come, the commander said
to him, "Say to me, are you a Roman?"
And he said, "Yes."
28 And the commander answered, "With a
large sum I obtained this citizenship." And
Sha'ul said, "But I was even born so."
29 Then at once those who were about to
examine him withdrew from him. And the
commander was also afraid after he found
out that he was a Roman, and because he
had bound him.
30 And on the next day, intending to know
for certain why he was accused by the
Yehuḏim, he released him, and commanded the chief priests and all their council to
come, and brought Sha'ul down and set
him before them.

23 And Sha'ul, looking intently at the
council, said, "Men, brothers, I
have lived in all good conscience before
Elohim until this day."
2 And the high priest Ḥananyah commanded those who stood by him to strike
him on the mouth.
3 Then Sha'ul said to him, "Elohim is
going to strike you, whitewashed wall!
And do you sit judging me according to the
Torah, and do you command me to be
struck contrary to the Torah?"
4 And those who stood by said, "Do you
revile the high priest of Elohim?"
5 And Sha'ul said, "I did not know,
brothers, that he was the high priest, for it
has been written, **'You shall not speak
evil of the ruler of your people.'** "
Shem. 22:28
6 Now Sha'ul, perceiving that one part
were Sadducees and the other Pharisees,
cried out in the council, "Men, brothers, I
am a Pharisee, the son of a Pharisee, I am
being judged concerning the expectation
and resurrection of the dead!"
7 And when he had said this, there came
a dissension between the Pharisees and the
Sadducees. And the crowd was divided.
8 For the Sadducees say that there is no
resurrection, nor messenger nor spirit, but
the Pharisees confess both.
9 And there was a great uproar. And certain of the scribes of the party of Pharisees
were earnestly contending, saying, "We
find no evil in this man. And if a spirit or a
messenger has spoken to him, let us not
fight against Elohim."
10 And a great dissension having come,

the commander, fearing lest Sha'ul would be pulled to pieces by them, commanded the body of soldiers to go down and seize him from their midst, and bring him into the barracks.

11 And on the following night the Master stood by him and said, "Take courage, Sha'ul, for as you have witnessed for Me in Yerushalayim, so you have to bear witness at Rome too."

12 And when it became day, some of the Yehuḏim made a conspiracy and bound themselves under an oath, saying that they would neither eat nor drink until they had killed Sha'ul.

13 And those making this conspiracy were more than forty,

14 who, having come to the chief priests and elders, said, "We have bound ourselves under a great oath not to eat at all until we have killed Sha'ul.

15 "Now, then, you, with the council, inform the commander to have him brought down to you tomorrow, as intending to examine more exactly all about him. And we are ready to kill him before he comes near."

16 And when Sha'ul's sister's son heard of their ambush, he went and entered into the barracks and reported to Sha'ul.

17 And Sha'ul, having called one of the captains to him, said, "Take this young man to the commander, for he has somewhat to report to him."

18 He indeed then took him and led him to the commander and said, "The prisoner Sha'ul called me to him and asked me to bring this young man to you, having somewhat to say to you."

19 And the commander, having taken him by the hand, went aside by themselves and asked, "What is it that you have to report to me?"

20 And he said, "The Yehuḏim have agreed to ask that you bring Sha'ul down to the council tomorrow, as intending to inquire more exactly about him.

21 "Therefore, do not let them persuade you, for more than forty of them lie in wait for him, men who have bound themselves by an oath neither to eat nor to drink until they have killed him. And now they are ready, waiting for the promise from you."

22 Then the commander dismissed the young man, having commanded him, "Inform no one that you reported this to me."

23 And having called near a certain two captains, he said, "Get two hundred soldiers ready to go to Caesarea, and seventy horsemen, and two hundred spearmen, after the third hour of the night,

24 and provide beasts, on which to place Sha'ul, and bring him safely to Felix the governor,"

25 having written a letter in this form:

26 Claudius Lysias, to the most excellent governor Felix: Greetings.

27 This man, having been seized by the Yehuḏim, and being about to be killed by them, I rescued, having come with the body of soldiers, having learned that he was a Roman.

28 And, desiring to know the reason they accused him, I brought him before their council.

29 I found out that he was accused concerning questions of their Torah, but there was no charge against him deserving death or chains.

30 And when I was informed that there was to be a plot against the man by the Yehuḏim, I sent him immediately to you, having also commanded his accusers to state before you the charges against him. Be strong!

31 So the soldiers, as they were commanded, took Sha'ul and brought him by night to Antipatris.

32 And on the next day they left the horsemen to go on with him, and returned to the barracks,

33 who, having come to Caesarea, and delivered the letter to the governor, they also presented Sha'ul to him.

34 And the governor, having read it, and having asked of what province he was, and being informed that he was from Kilikia,

35 said, "I shall hear you when your accusers arrive also." And he commanded him to be kept in Herodes' palace.

24 And after five days the high priest
Ḥananyah came down, with the
elders, and a certain speaker – Tertullus.
And they brought charges against Sha'ul
before the governor.
2 And when he was called upon,
Tertullus began to accuse him, saying,
"Having obtained great peace through you,
and reforms being brought to this nation by
your forethought,
3 we accept it always and in all places,
most excellent Felix, with all thanks.
4 "But in order not to hinder you any
further, I beg you to hear us briefly in your
gentleness.
5 "For having found this man a plague,
who stirs up dissension among all the
Yehuḏim throughout the world, and a ring-
leader of the sect of the Natsarenes,
6 who also tried to profane the Set-apart
Place, and whom we seized, and wished to
judge him according to our law,
7 but the commander Lysias came along
and with much violence took him out of
our hands,
8 commanding his accusers to come to
you. And by examining him yourself you
shall be able to know all these *matters* of
which we accuse him."
9 And the Yehuḏim also agreed, maintaining that these *matters* were so.
10 And when the governor had motioned
him to speak, Sha'ul answered, "Knowing
that for many years you have been a judge
of this nation, I gladly defend myself,
11 seeing you are able to know that it is
not more than twelve days since I went up
to Yerushalayim to worship.
12 "And they neither found me in the
Set-apart Place disputing with anyone nor
stirring up the crowd, either in the congregations or in the city.
13 "Nor are they able to prove the charges
of which they now accuse me.
14 "And this I confess to you, that according to the Way which they call a sect, so I
worship the **Elohim of my fathers**,
Shem. 3:15 believing all that has been written
in the Torah and in the Prophets,
15 having an expectation in Elohim, which
they themselves also wait for, that there is
to be a resurrection of the dead, both of the
righteous and the unrighteous.
16 "And in this I exercise myself to have a
clear conscience toward Elohim and men
always.
17 "And after many years I came to bring
kind deeds to my nation and offerings,
18 at which time certain Yehuḏim from
Asia found me cleansed in the Set-apart
Place, neither with a crowd nor with
disturbance,
19 who ought to be present before you to
bring charges if they have any *matter*
against me.
20 "Or else let these themselves say if they
found any wrongdoing in me while I stood
before the council,
21 other than for this one declaration
which I cried out, standing among them,
'Concerning the resurrection of the dead I
am being judged by you today.' "
22 And having heard this, having known
more exactly about the Way, Felix put
them off, saying, "When Lysias the commander comes down, I shall decide your
case."
23 And he ordered the captain to keep
Sha'ul and to have ease, and not to forbid
any of his friends to attend to him.
24 And after some days, when Felix came
with his wife Drusilla, who was a female
Yehuḏi, he sent for Sha'ul and heard him
concerning the belief in Messiah.
25 And as he reasoned about righteousness, and self-control, and the judgment to
come, Felix became frightened and said,
"For the present, go. And when I find time
I shall send for you."
26 At the same time too he was anticipating that money would be given him by
Sha'ul, that he might release him.
Therefore he sent for him more often and
conversed with him.
27 But after two years had passed Porcius
Festus succeeded Felix. And wishing to do
the Yehuḏim a favour, Felix left Sha'ul
bound.

25 Festus therefore, having come to
the province, three days later went
up from Caesarea to Yerushalayim.

2 And the high priest and the chief men
of the Yehuḏim informed him against
Sha'ul, and they begged him,
3 asking a favour against him, that he
would send him to Yerushalayim – making
a plot along the way to kill him.
4 Then, indeed, Festus answered that
Sha'ul should be kept at Caesarea, and that
he himself was about to set out shortly.
5 "Therefore," he said, "let those who
have authority among you go down with
me and accuse this man, to see if there is
any fault in him."
6 And having spent more than ten days
among them, he went down to Caesarea.
And on the next day, sitting on the judgment seat, he commanded Sha'ul to be
brought.
7 And when he had come, the Yehuḏim
who had come down from Yerushalayim
stood about, bringing many and heavy
charges against Sha'ul, which they were
unable to prove,
8 while Sha'ul said in his own defence,
"Neither against the Torah of the Yehuḏim,
nor against the Set-apart Place, nor against
Caesar did I commit any sin."
9 But Festus, wishing to do the Yehuḏim
a favour, answering Sha'ul, said, "Do you
wish to go up to Yerushalayim and be
judged before me there concerning these
matters?"
10 And Sha'ul said, "I am standing at
Caesar's judgment seat, where I should be
judged. To the Yehuḏim I have done no
wrong, as you know well enough.
11 "For if indeed I do wrong, or have committed whatever deserving death, I do not
refuse to die. But if there is none at all in
these *matters* of which these men accuse
me, no one is able to give me up to them. I
appeal to Caesar."
12 Then Festus, having talked with the
council, answered, "You have appealed to
Caesar? To Caesar you shall go!"
13 And certain days having passed,
Sovereign Agrippa and Bernike came to
Caesarea to greet Festus.
14 And when they had spent many days
there, Festus laid Sha'ul's case before the
sovereign, saying, "There is a man here
whom Felix left as a prisoner,
15 about whom the chief priests and the
elders of the Yehuḏim informed me, when
I was in Yerushalayim, asking for a judgment against him.
16 "To them I answered, 'It is not the
Roman practice to give up any man to
destruction before the accused meets the
accusers face to face, and has a chance to
answer for himself concerning the charge
against him.'
17 "They, therefore, having come together,
without any delay, I sat on the judgment
seat the next day and commanded the man
to be brought in.
18 "When the accusers stood up, they
brought no charge against him such as I
expected,
19 but had some questions against him
about their own worship and about a certain יהושע, who had died, whom Sha'ul
was claiming to be alive.
20 "And being uncertain how to investi-
gate these matters, I asked whether he
wished to go to Yerushalayim and there be
judged concerning these matters.
21 "But when Sha'ul appealed to be kept
for the decision of Augustus, I ordered him
to be kept until I send him to Caesar."
22 And Agrippa said to Festus, "I was
wishing also to hear the man myself." And
he said, "Tomorrow, you shall hear him."
23 Therefore, on the next day, Agrippa and
Bernike having come with great show, and
having entered the place of hearing with
the commanders and the eminent men of
the city, Sha'ul was brought in at the order
of Festus.
24 And Festus said, "Sovereign Agrippa
and all the men present here with us, you
see this one about whom all the community of the Yehuḏim pleaded with me, both at
Yerushalayim and here, shouting that he
ought not to be living any longer.
25 "But I, having found that he had committed none at all deserving death, and that
he himself had appealed to Augustus, I
decided to send him.
26 "I have no definite *matter* to write to
my master concerning him. Therefore I
have brought him out before you, and most

of all before you, Sovereign Agrippa, so
that after the examination has taken place I
might have somewhat to write.
27 “For it seems to me unreasonable to
send a prisoner and not to signify the
charges against him.”

26 And Agrippa said to Sha’ul, “You
are allowed to speak for yourself.”
Then Sha’ul stretched out his hand and
made his defence:
2 “I think myself blessed, Sovereign
Agrippa, because today I shall make my
defence before you concerning all of
which I am accused by the Yehuḏim,
3 you being most of all an expert, knowing of all practices and questions which
have to do with the Yehuḏim. So, please
hear me patiently.
4 “Truly, then, all the Yehuḏim know my
way of life from youth, which I led from
the beginning among my own nation at
Yerushalayim,
5 since they have known me from the
first, if they wish to witness, that I lived as
a Pharisee according to the strictest sect of
our observance.
6 “And now I stand and am judged for
the expectation of the promise made by
Elohim to our fathers,
7 to which our twelve tribes, earnestly
serving Elohim night and day, expect to
attain. Concerning this expectation, O
Sovereign Agrippa, I am accused by the
Yehuḏim.
8 “Why is it considered ‘unbelievable’
among you if Elohim raises the dead?
9 “Therefore, indeed, I thought within
myself that I ought to do much against the
Name of יהושע of Natsareth,
10 which also I did in Yerushalayim, and I
shut up many of the set-apart ones in
prison, having received authority from the
chief priests. And when they were put to
death, I gave my vote against them.
11 “And punishing them often in all the
congregations, I compelled them to blaspheme. And being exceedingly enraged
against them, I persecuted them even to
foreign cities.
12 “While thus engaged, as I was journeying to Dammeseq with authority and commission from the chief priests,
13 at midday along the highway, O
sovereign, I saw a light from heaven,
brighter than the sun, shining around me
and those who journeyed with me.
14 “And when we had all fallen to the
ground, I heard a voice speaking to me,
and saying in the Hebrew language, [a]
‘Sha’ul, Sha’ul, why do you persecute Me?
It is hard for you to kick against the prods.’
15 “And I said, ‘Who are You, Master?’
And He said, ‘I am יהושע’, whom you
persecute.
16 ‘But rise up, and stand on your feet, for
I have appeared to you for this purpose, to
appoint you a servant and a witness both of
what you saw and of those which I shall
reveal to you,
17 delivering you from the people, and the
nations, to whom I now send you,
18 to open their eyes, to turn them from
darkness to light, [b] and the authority of
Satan to Elohim, in order for them to
receive forgiveness of sins and an inheritance among those who are set-apart by
belief in Me.’
19 “Therefore, Sovereign Agrippa, I was
not disobedient to the heavenly vision,
20 but declared first to those in Dammeseq
and in Yerushalayim, and in all the country
of Yehuḏah, and to the nations, that they
should repent, and turn to Elohim, and do
works worthy of repentance. [c]
21 “That is why the Yehuḏim seized me in
the Set-apart Place and tried to kill me.
22 “Therefore, having obtained help from
Elohim, to this day I stand, witnessing both
to small and great, saying nil else than
what the prophets and Mosheh said would
come –
23 that the Messiah would suffer, would
be the first to rise from the dead, He would
proclaim light to the people and to the
nations.”
24 And while saying this in his defence,
Festus said with a loud voice, “Sha’ul, you

26a See 21:40, 22:2. *26b* Yesh. 42:6-7, Yesh. 60:2-3, Ḥazon 21:24. *26c* See footnote Mt. 16:27.

are mad! Much learning is turning you to
madness!"
25 But Sha'ul said, "I am not mad, most
excellent Festus, but I speak words of truth
and sense.
26 "For the sovereign, before whom I also
speak boldly, knows these *matters*. For I
am persuaded that none of these are hidden
from him, for this has not been done in a
corner.
27 "Sovereign Agrippa, do you believe the
prophets? I know that you do believe."
28 And Agrippa said to Sha'ul, "With a little you might persuade me to become a
Messianite!"
29 And Sha'ul said, "Much or little, I pray
to Elohim that not only you, but also all
who hear me today, might become such as
I also am, except for these chains."
30 And having said this, the sovereign
stood up, as well as the governor and
Bernike and those sitting with them,
31 and having withdrawn, they spoke to
each other, saying, "This man is doing
none at all deserving death or chains."
32 And Agrippa said to Festus, "This man
could have been released if he had not
appealed to Caesar."

27 And when it was decided that we
should sail to Italy, they delivered
Sha'ul and some other prisoners to one
named Julius, a captain of the Augustan
regiment.
2 And having embarked in a ship from
Adramyttium, about to sail along the
coasts of Asia, did set sail. Aristarchos, a
Makedonian of Thessalonike, was with us.
3 And on the next day we landed at
Tsiḏon. And Julius treated Sha'ul kindly
and allowed him to go to his friends to
receive attention.
4 And from there we put out to sea and
sailed close to Cyprus, because the winds
were against us.
5 And having sailed over the sea along
Kilikia and Pamphulia, we came to Mura,
of Lukia.
6 And there the captain, having found an
Alexandrian ship sailing to Italy, did put us
on board.
7 And having sailed slowly many days,
and arriving with difficulty off Knidos, the
wind not allowing us to proceed, we sailed
close to Crete, off Salmone.
8 And passing it with difficulty, we came
to a place called Fair Havens, near the city
of Lasea.
9 And much time having passed, and the
sailing now being dangerous, because the
Fast was already over, Sha'ul advised
them,
10 saying, "Men, I see that this voyage is
going to end with damage and great loss,
not only of the cargo and ship, but also our
lives."
11 But the captain was persuaded by the
pilot and the owner of the ship, rather than
what Sha'ul said.
12 And because the harbour was unsuit-
able to winter in, the greater part advised
to set sail from there too, if somehow they
were able to reach Phoenix, a harbour of
Crete facing southwest and northwest, to
pass the winter.
13 And a south wind blowing softly, thinking they had obtained their purpose, having lifted *anchor*, they sailed along Crete,
close *inshore*.
14 And not long after, a stormy head wind
rushed down from it, called Northeaster.
15 And when the ship was caught *in it*, and
unable to head against the wind, we let her
go and were driven.
16 And having run under a small island
called Klauda, we were hardly able to control the small boat.
17 And having hoisted it, they used helps
to undergird the ship. And fearing lest they
should run aground on Surtis, they lowered
the tackle and so were driven.
18 And because we were exceedingly
storm-tossed, the next day they began to
throw overboard.
19 And on the third day we threw out the
ship's tackle with our own hands.
20 When, now, neither sun nor stars
appeared for many days, and no small
storm beat on us, all expectancy that we
would be saved was taken away.
21 And when there had been a long absti-
nence from food, then Sha'ul, standing in

the midst of them, said, “Truly, men, you
should have listened to me not to have
sailed from Crete and sustained this damage and loss.
22 “And now I urge you to take courage,
for there shall be no loss of life among
you, but only of the ship.
23 “For tonight a messenger of the Elohim
to whom I belong and whom I serve, stood
by me,
24 saying, ‘Do not be afraid, Sha’ul, you
have to be brought before Caesar. And
look, Elohim has favourably given you all
those who sail with you.’
25 “Therefore take courage, men, for I
believe Elohim that it shall be according to
the way it was spoken to me.
26 “However, we need to run aground on
some island.”
27 And when the fourteenth night came, as
we were driven up and down in the
Adriatic Sea, about midnight the sailors
suspected that they were drawing near
some land.
28 So, taking soundings, they found it to
be twenty fathoms. And a little farther on
they took soundings again and found it to
be fifteen fathoms.
29 And, fearing lest we should run
aground on the rocks, they dropped four
anchors from the stern, and were praying
for day to come.
30 But when the sailors were seeking to
escape from the ship, when they had let
down the boat into the sea, under pretence
of going to cast out anchors from the prow,
31 Sha’ul said to the captain and the
soldiers, “If these do not remain in the
ship, it is impossible for you to be saved.”
32 Then the soldiers did cut the ropes of
the boat and let it fall off.
33 And when day was about to come,
Sha’ul urged them all to take food, saying,
“Today is the fourteenth day you have continued without food, and eaten none at all.
34 “So I urge you to take food, for this
concerns your safety, since not a hair shall
fall from the head of any of you.”
35 And having said this, he took bread and
gave thanks to Elohim in the presence of
them all. And when he had broken it he
began to eat.
36 And they were all encouraged, and also
took food themselves.
37 And all of us were two hundred and
seventy-six beings in the ship.
38 And being satisfied with food, they
were lightening the ship, throwing out the
wheat into the sea.
39 And when day came, they did not
recognise the land, but they noted a certain
bay with a beach, onto which they planned
to run the ship if possible.
40 And having cast off the anchors, they
left them in the sea, meanwhile untying the
rudder ropes. And they hoisted the foresail
to the wind and made for the beach.
41 But coming upon a place where two
seas met, they grounded the ship, and the
prow stuck fast and remained immovable,
but the stern was broken by the pounding
of the surf.
42 And the soldiers intended to kill the
prisoners, lest any of them should swim
away and escape.
43 But the captain, intending to save
Sha’ul, kept them from their intention, and
commanded those able to swim to jump
first and get to land,
44 and the rest, some indeed on boards,
and some on *items* of the ship. And so
it came to be that all reached the land in
safety.

28 And having come to safety, they
then learned that the island was
called Melite.
2 And the foreigners showed us extraordinary kindness, for they kindled a fire and
received us all, because of the rain that was
falling and because of the cold.
3 But Sha’ul, having gathered a bundle of
sticks, and having laid them on the fire, an
adder came out because of the heat, and
fastened itself on his hand.
4 And when the foreigners saw the creature hanging from his hand, they said to
each other, “This man is certainly a murderer, whom, though saved from the sea,
still right-ruling does not allow to live.”
5 Then, indeed, he shook off the creature
into the fire and suffered no evil.

6 And expecting that he would swell up
or suddenly fall down dead, they waited
for a long time and saw no harm come to
him, changing their minds they said that he
was a mighty one.
7 And in the neighbourhood of that place
there were lands of the chief of the island,
whose name was Poplius, who received us
and housed us in a friendly way for three
days.
8 And it came to be that the father of
Poplius lay sick with inflammation and
dysentery. Sha'ul went in to him, and having prayed he laid his hands on him and
healed him.
9 And when this took place, the rest of
those on the island who had diseases also
came and were healed,
10 who also respected us in many ways.
And when we were setting sail, they provided *us* with our needs.
11 And after three months we set sail in an
Alexandrian ship which had wintered at
the island, and whose figurehead was
"Dioscuri." [a]
12 And having landed at Syracuse, we
stayed three days,
13 from which place we went round and
arrived at Rhegium. And after one day the
south wind blew, and the second day we
came to Puteoli,
14 where we found brothers, and were
invited to stay with them seven days. And
so we went toward Rome.
15 And when the brothers there heard
about us, they came to meet us as far as
Forum of Appius and Three Taverns.
When Sha'ul saw them, he thanked
Elohim and took courage.
16 And when we came to Rome, the captain delivered the prisoners to the captain
of the guard, but Sha'ul was allowed to
stay by himself with the soldier guarding
him.
17 And it came to be after three days that
Sha'ul called the leaders of the Yehuḏim
together. And when they had come together, he said to them, "Men, brothers, though
I have done none at all against our people
or the practices of our fathers, I was delivered as a prisoner from Yerushalayim into
the hands of the Romans,
18 who, when they had examined me,
intended to let me go, because there was
no cause for putting me to death.
19 "But the Yehuḏim spoke against it, and
I was compelled to appeal to Caesar, not
that I had any accusation against my
nation.
20 "This therefore is the reason I called for
you, to see you and speak with you. It is
because of the expectation of Yisra'ěl that
I am bound with this chain."
21 And they said to him, "We neither
received letters from Yehuḏah concerning
you, nor have any of the brothers who
came reported or spoken whatever wicked
about you.
22 "And we think it right to hear from you
what you think, for indeed, concerning this
sect, we know that it is spoken against
everywhere."
23 And having appointed him a day, many
came to him where he was staying, to
whom he was explaining, earnestly witnessing about the reign of Elohim, and persuading them concerning יהושע from both
the Torah of Mosheh and the Prophets,
from morning until evening.
24 And some indeed were persuaded by
what was said, but some believed not.
25 And disagreeing with one another, they
began to leave, after Sha'ul had spoken
one word, "The Set-apart Spirit rightly
spoke through Yeshayahu the prophet to
our fathers,
26 saying, **'Go to this people and say,**
"Hearing you shall hear but by no
means understand, and seeing you shall
see but by no means perceive,
27 **for the heart of this people has**
become thickened, and with their ears
they heard heavily, and they have closed
their eyes, lest they should see with their
eyes and hear with their ears, and
understand with their heart, and turn

28a Which means: Twin Brothers, who were *Sons of Zeus*, named *Castor and Pollux*. They were tutelary deities of sailers.

back, and I should heal them." ' Yesh. 6:9-10
28 "Therefore let it be known to you that
the deliverance of Elohim has been sent
to the nations, and they shall hear!"
29 And when he had said these words,
the Yehuḏim went away and had a great
dispute among themselves.
30 And Sha'ul stayed two entire years in
his own rented house, and was receiving
all who came to him,
31 proclaiming the reign of Elohim and
teaching about the Master יהושע Messiah
with all boldness, unhindered.

ROMIYIM

ROMANS

1 Sha'ul, a servant of יהושע Messiah, a called emissary, separated to the Good News of Elohim,

2 which He promised before through His prophets in the Set-apart Scriptures,

3 concerning His Son, who came of the seed of Dawiḏ according to the flesh,

4 who was designated Son of Elohim with power, according to the Set-apart Spirit, by the resurrection from the dead: יהושע Messiah, the Master of us,

5 through whom we have received favour and office of the emissary for belief-obedience among all the nations on behalf of His Name,

6 among whom you also are the called ones of יהושע Messiah.

7 To all who are in Rome, beloved of Elohim, called, set-apart ones: Favour to you and peace from Elohim our Father and the Master יהושע Messiah.

8 First, I truly thank my Elohim through יהושע Messiah for you all, that your belief is spoken of in all the world.

9 For Elohim is my witness, whom I serve with my spirit in the Good News of His Son, how unceasingly I make mention of you,

10 always asking in my prayers, if at all possible, I shall be blessed by the desire of Elohim, to come to you.

11 For I long to see you, so as to impart some spiritual gift to you, for you to be established,

12 and that is, to be encouraged together among you, each by the other's belief – both yours and mine.

13 And I do not wish you to be unaware, brothers, that I often purposed to come to you, but was hindered until now, in order to have some fruit among you, as also among the other nations.

14 I am a debtor both to Greeks and to foreigners, both to wise and to foolish.

15 That is why I am so eager to bring the Good News also to you who are in Rome.

16 For I am not ashamed of the Good News of Messiah, for it is the power of Elohim for deliverance to everyone who believes, to the Yehuḏi first and also to the Greek.

17 For in it the righteousness of Elohim is revealed from belief to belief, as it has been written, **"But the righteous shall live by belief."** Ḥab. 2:4

18 For the wrath of Elohim is revealed from heaven against all wickedness and unrighteousness of men, who suppress the truth in unrighteousness,

19 because that which is known of Elohim is manifest among them, for Elohim has manifested it to them.

20 For since the creation of the world His invisible *qualities* have been clearly seen, being understood from what has been made, both His everlasting power and Mightiness, for them to be without excuse,

21 because, although they knew Elohim, they did not esteem Him as Elohim, nor gave thanks, but became vain in their reasonings, and their undiscerning heart was darkened.

22 Claiming to be wise, they became fools,

23 and changed the esteem of the incorruptible Elohim into the likeness of an image of corruptible man, and of birds and of four-footed beasts and of reptiles.

24 Therefore Elohim gave them up to uncleanness in the lust of their hearts, to disrespect their bodies among themselves,

25 who changed the truth of Elohim into the falsehood, and worshipped and served what was created rather than the Creator, who is blessed forever. Aměn.

26 Because of this Elohim gave them over to degrading passions. For even their women exchanged natural relations for what is against nature,

27 and likewise, the men also, having left natural relations with woman, burned in their lust for one another, men with men

committing indecency, and receiving back
the reward which was due for their straying.
28 And even as they did not think it worth-
while to possess the knowledge of Elohim,
Elohim gave them over to a worthless
mind, to do what is improper,
29 having been filled with all unrighteousness, whoring, wickedness, greed, evil;
filled with envy, murder, fighting, deceit,
evil habits; whisperers,
30 slanderers, haters of Elohim, insolent,
proud, boasters, devisers of evils, disobedient to parents,
31 without discernment, covenant breakers, unloving, unforgiving, ruthless;
32 who, though they know the righteousness of Elohim, that those who practise
such deserve death, not only do the same
but also approve of those who practise
them.

2 Therefore, O man, you are without
excuse, everyone who judges, for in
which you judge another you condemn
yourself, since you who judge practise the
same *wrongs*.
2 And we know that the judgment of
Elohim is according to truth against those
who practise such *wrongs*.
3 And do you think, O man, you who
judge those practising such *wrongs*, and
doing the same, that you shall escape the
judgment of Elohim?
4 Or do you despise the riches of His
kindness, and tolerance, and patience, [a] not
knowing that the kindness of Elohim leads
you to repentance?
5 But according to your hardness and
your unrepentant heart you are treasuring
up for yourself wrath in the day of wrath
and revelation of the righteous judgment of
Elohim,
6 who **"shall render to each one
according to his works"**: Teh. 62:12 [b]
7 everlasting life to those who by persistence in good work seek for esteem, and
respect, and incorruptibility;
8 but wrath and displeasure to those who
are self-seeking and do not obey the truth,
but obey unrighteousness;
9 affliction and distress on every human
being working what is evil, of the Yehuḏi
first, and also of the Greek;
10 but esteem, respect, and peace to everyone working what is good, to the Yehuḏi
first and also to the Greek.
11 For there is no partiality with Elohim.
12 For as many as sinned without Torah
shall also perish without Torah, and as
many as sinned in the Torah shall be
judged by the Torah.
13 For not the hearers of the Torah are
righteous in the sight of Elohim, but the
doers of the Torah [c] shall be declared right.
14 For when nations, who do not have the
Torah, by nature do what is in the Torah,
although not having the Torah, they are a
torah to themselves,
15 who show the work of the Torah written in their hearts, their conscience also
bearing witness, and between themselves
their thoughts accusing or even excusing,
16 in the day when Elohim shall judge the
secrets of men through יהושע Messiah,
according to my Good News.
17 See, you are called a Yehuḏi, and rest
on the Torah, and make your boast in
Elohim,
18 and know the desire *of Elohim*, and
approve what is superior, being instructed
out of the Torah,
19 and are trusting that you yourself are a
guide to the blind, a light to those who are
in darkness,
20 an instructor of foolish ones, a teacher
of babes, having the form of knowledge
and of the truth in the Torah. [d]
21 You, then, who teach another, do you
not teach yourself? You who proclaim that
a man **should not steal**, Shem. 20:15 [e] do you
steal?
22 You who say, **"Do not commit adultery,"** Shem. 20:14 [f] do you commit adultery?

2a Kěpha ב 3:9. *2b* See footnote Mt. 16:27. *2c* Mt. 7:21-27, Yaʽaqoḇ 2:14-24. *2d* Teh. 147:19, Rom. 3:2, Rom. 9:4. 2e Deḇ. 5:18. *2f* Deḇ. 5:19.

You who abominate idols, do you rob temples?
23 You who make your boast in the Torah,
through the transgression of the Torah do
you disrespect Elohim?
24 For **"The Name of Elohim is blasphemed among the nations because of
you,"** Yesh. 52:5 as it has been written.
25 For circumcision indeed profits if you
practise the Torah, but if you are a transgressor of the Torah, your circumcision has
become uncircumcision.
26 So, if an uncircumcised one watches
over the righteousnesses of the Torah, shall
not his uncircumcision be reckoned as
circumcision?
27 And the uncircumcised by nature, who
perfects the Torah, shall judge you who
notwithstanding letter and circumcision
are a transgressor of the Torah!
28 For he is not a Yehuḏi who is *so* outwardly, neither is circumcision that which
is outward in the flesh.
29 But a Yehuḏi is he who is *so* inwardly,
and circumcision is that of the heart,[g] in
Spirit, not literally, whose praise is not
from men but from Elohim.

3 What then is the advantage of the
Yehuḏi, or what is the value of the circumcision?
2 Much in every way! Because firstly
indeed, that they were entrusted with the
Words of Elohim.[a]
3 For what if some did not believe? Shall
their unbelief nullify the trustworthiness of
Elohim?
4 Let it not be! But let Elohim be true,
and every man a liar, as it has been written,
**"That You should be declared right in
Your words, and prevail in Your judging."** Teh. 51:4
5 But if our unrighteousness establishes
the righteousness of Elohim, what shall we
say? Is Elohim unrighteous who is inflict-
ing wrath? I speak as a man.
6 Let it not be! Otherwise how shall
Elohim judge the world?
7 For if the truth of Elohim has increased
through my lie, to His esteem, why am I
also still judged as a sinner?
8 And *why* not *say*, "Let us do evil so that
the good might come"? – as we are wrongly accused and as some claim that we say.
Their judgment is in the right.
9 What then? Are we better *than they*?
Not at all, for we have previously accused
both Yehuḏim and Greeks that they are all
under sin.
10 As it has been written, **"There is none
righteous, no, not one!**
11 **"There is no one who is understanding, there is none who is seeking Elohim.**
12 **"They all have turned aside, they
have together become worthless. There
is none who does good, no, not one."**
Teh. 14:1-3, 53:1-4
13 **"Their throat is an open tomb, with
their tongues they have deceived,"** Teh. 5:9
**"The poison of adders is under their
lips,"** Teh. 140:3
14 **"Whose mouth is filled with cursing
and bitterness."** Teh. 10:7
15 **"Their feet are swift to shed blood,**
Mish. 1:16
16 **ruin and wretchedness are in their
ways,**
17 **and the way of peace they have not
known."** Yesh. 59:7
18 **"There is no fear of Elohim before
their eyes."** Teh. 36:1
19 And we know that whatever the Torah
says, it says to those who are in the Torah,
so that every mouth might be stopped, and
all the world come under judgment before
Elohim.
20 Therefore by works of Torah **no flesh
shall be declared right before Him,**
Teh. 143:2 for by the Torah is the knowledge
of sin.[b]
21 But now, apart from the Torah, a righteousness of Elohim has been revealed,
being witnessed by the Torah and the
Prophets,
22 and the righteousness of Elohim is
through belief in יהושע Messiah to all

2g Cor. א 7:19, Shem. 19:5, Deḇ. 10:12-16, Deḇ. 30:6-8. *3a* See 2:20. *3b* Shem. 20:20, Rom. 4:15, Rom. 7:7.

and on all who believe. For there is no
difference,
23 for all have sinned and fall short of the
esteem of Elohim,
24 being declared right, without paying,
by His favour through the redemption
which is in Messiah יהושע,
25 whom Elohim set forth as an atonement, through belief in His blood, to
demonstrate His righteousness, because in
His tolerance Elohim had passed over the
sins that had taken place before,
26 to demonstrate at the present time His
righteousness, that He is righteous and
declares righteous the one who has belief
in יהושע.
27 Where, then, is the boasting? It is shut
out. By what torah? Of works? No, but by
the torah of belief.
28 For we reckon that a man is declared
right by belief without works of Torah.
29 Or *is He* the Elohim of the Yehuḏim
only, and not also of the nations? Yes,
of the nations also,
30 since it is one Elohim who shall declare
right the circumcised by belief and the
uncircumcised through belief.
31 Do we then nullify the Torah through
the belief? Let it not be! On the contrary,
we establish the Torah. [c]

4 What, then, shall we say Aḇraham our
father, to have found, according to the
flesh?
2 For if Aḇraham was declared right by
works, he has *ground for* boasting, but not
before Elohim.
3 For what does the Scripture say?
**"Aḇraham believed Elohim, and it was
reckoned to him for righteousness."**
Ber. 15:6 [a]
4 And to him who is working, the reward
is not reckoned as a favour but as a debt.
5 And to him who is not working
but believes on Him who is declaring
right the wicked, his belief is reckoned for
righteousness,
6 even as Dawiḏ also says of the blessedness of the man to whom Elohim reckons
righteousness without works:
7 **"Blessed are those whose lawlessnesses are forgiven, and whose sins are
covered,**
8 **blessed is the man to whom יהוה
shall by no means reckon sin."** Teh. 32:1,2
9 Is this blessing then upon the circumcised *only*, or also upon the uncircumcised? For we affirm: **Belief was reckoned
unto Aḇraham for righteousness.** Ber. 15:6
10 How then was it reckoned? Being in
circumcision, or in uncircumcision? Not in
circumcision, but in uncircumcision.
11 And he received the sign of circumcision, a seal of the righteousness of the
belief *while* in uncircumcision, for him to
be a father of all those believing through
uncircumcision, for righteousness to be
reckoned to them also,
12 and the father of circumcision to those
who not only are of the circumcision, but
who also walk in the steps of the belief
which our father Aḇraham had in uncircumcision.
13 For the promise that he should be the
heir of the world, was not to Aḇraham or to
his seed through the Torah, but through a
righteousness of belief.
14 For if those who are of the Torah are
heirs, belief has been made useless, and the
promise has been nullified,
15 for the Torah works out wrath, for
where there is no Torah there is no transgression.
16 On account of this it is of belief, that it
be according to favour, for the promise to
be made certain to all the seed, not only to
those who are of the Torah, but also to
those who are of the belief of Aḇraham,
who is father of us all –
17 as it has been written, **"I have made
you a father of many nations"** Ber. 17:5 – in
the presence of Him whom he believed,
even Elohim, who gives life to the dead
and calls that which does not exist as existing,
18 who against *all* expectation did believe,
in expectation, so that he should become
father of many nations, according to what

3c See 7:12. 4a See also Gal. 3:6.

was said, **"So shall your seed be."** Ber. 15:5

19 And not having grown weak in belief, he did not consider his own body, already dead, being about a hundred years old, and the deadness of Sarah's womb,

20 he did not hesitate about the promise of Elohim through unbelief, but was strengthened in belief, giving esteem to Elohim,

21 and being completely persuaded that what He had promised He was also able to do.

22 Therefore also **"it was reckoned to him for righteousness."** Ber. 15:6

23 And not because of him alone was it written that **it was reckoned to him,** Ber. 15:6

24 but also because of us, to whom it shall be reckoned, to us who believe in Him who raised up יהושע our Master from the dead,

25 who was delivered up because of our trespasses, and was raised for us to be declared right.

5

Therefore, having been declared right by belief, we have peace with Elohim through our Master יהושע Messiah,

2 through whom also we have access by belief into this favour in which we stand, and we exult in the expectation of the esteem of Elohim.

3 And not only this, but we also exult in pressures, knowing that pressure works endurance;

4 and endurance, approvedness; and approvedness, expectation.

5 And expectation does not disappoint, because the love of Elohim has been poured out in our hearts by the Set-apart Spirit which was given to us.

6 For when we were still weak, Messiah in due time died for the wicked.

7 For one shall hardly die for a righteous one, though possibly for a good one someone would even have the courage to die.

8 But Elohim proves His own love for us, in that while we were still sinners, Messiah died for us.

9 Much more then, having now been declared right by His blood, we shall be saved from wrath through Him.

10 For if, being enemies, we were restored to favour with Elohim through the death of His Son, much more, having been restored to favour, we shall be saved by His life.

11 And not only this, but we also exult in Elohim through our Master יהושע Messiah, through whom we have now received the restoration to favour.

12 For this reason, even as through one man sin did enter into the world, and death through sin, and thus death spread to all men, because all sinned –

13 for until the Torah, sin was in the world, but sin is not reckoned when there is no Torah.

14 But death reigned from Aḏam until Mosheh, even over those who had not sinned according to the likeness of the transgression of Aḏam, who is a type of Him who was to come.

15 But the favourable gift is not like the trespass. For if by the one man's trespass many died, much more the favour of Elohim, and the gift in favour of the one Man, יהושע Messiah, overflowed to many.

16 And the favourable gift is not as by one having sinned. For indeed the judgment was of one to condemnation, but the favourable gift is of many trespasses unto righteousness.

17 For if by the trespass of the one, death did reign through the one, much more those who receive the overflowing favour and the gift of righteousness shall reign in life through the One, יהושע Messiah.

18 So then, as through one trespass there resulted condemnation to all men, so also through one righteous act there resulted righteous-declaring of life to all men.

19 For as through the disobedience of one man many were made sinners, so also through the obedience of the One many shall be made righteous.

20 And the Torah came in beside, so that the trespass would increase. But where sin increased, favour increased still more,

21 so that as sin did reign in death, even so favour might reign through righteousness to everlasting life through יהושע Messiah our Master.

6 What, then, shall we say? Shall we
continue in sin, to let favour increase?
2 Let it not be! How shall we who died to
sin [a] still live in it?
3 Or do you not know that as many of us
as were immersed into Messiah יהושע
were immersed into His death?
4 We were therefore buried with Him
through immersion into death, that as
Messiah was raised from the dead by the
esteem of the Father, so also we should
walk in newness of life.
5 For if we have come to be grown
together in the likeness of His death, we
shall be also of the resurrection,
6 knowing this, that our old man was
impaled with Him, so that the body of sin
might be rendered powerless, to serve sin
no longer.
7 For he who has died has been made
right from sin.
8 And if we died with Messiah, we
believe that we shall also live with Him,
9 knowing that Messiah, having been
raised from the dead, dies no more – death
no longer rules over Him.
10 For in that He died, He died to sin once
for all; but in that He lives, He lives to
Elohim.
11 So you also, reckon yourselves to be
dead indeed to sin, but alive to Elohim in
Messiah יהושע our Master.
12 Therefore do not let sin reign in your
mortal body, to obey it in its desires,
13 neither present your members as instruments of unrighteousness to sin, but present yourselves to Elohim as being alive
from the dead, and your members as
instruments of righteousness to Elohim.
14 For sin shall not rule over you, [b] for you
are not under the law but under favour.
15 What then? Shall we sin because we are
not under Torah but under favour? Let it
not be!
16 Do you not know that to whom you
present yourselves servants for obedience,
you are servants of the one whom you
obey, whether of sin to death, or of obedience to righteousness?
17 But thanks to Elohim that you were servants of sin, yet you obeyed from the heart
that form of teaching to which you were
entrusted.
18 And having been set free from sin, you
became servants of righteousness.
19 I speak as a man, because of the weakness of your flesh. For even as you did
present your members as servants of
uncleanness, and of lawlessness resulting
in lawlessness, so now present your members as servants of righteousness resulting
in set-apartness.
20 For when you were servants of sin, you
were free from righteousness.
21 What fruit, therefore, were you having
then, over which you are now ashamed?
For the end thereof is death.
22 But now, having been set free from sin,
and having become servants of Elohim,
you have your fruit resulting in set-apartness, and the end, everlasting life.
23 For the wages of sin is death, [c] but the
favourable gift of Elohim is everlasting life
in Messiah יהושע our Master.

7 Or do you not know, brothers – for I
speak to those knowing the Torah –
that the Torah rules over a man as long as
he lives?
2 For the married woman has been bound
by Torah to the living husband, but if the
husband dies, she is released from the
Torah *concerning* her husband.
3 So then, while her husband lives, she
shall be called an adulteress if she becomes
another man's. But if her husband dies, she
is free from that *part of the* Torah, so that
she is not an adulteress, having become
another man's.
4 So my brothers, you also were put to
death to the Torah through the body of
Messiah, for you to become another's, the
One who was raised from the dead, that we
should bear fruit to Elohim.
5 For when we were in the flesh, the
passions of sins, through the Torah, were

6a See Rom. 8:13, Qol. 3:3, Kěpha א 2:24. *6b* Ber. 4:7. *6c* See 8:13.

working in our members to bear fruit to
death.
6 But now we have been released from
the Torah, having died to what we were
held by, so that we should serve in newness of Spirit and not in oldness of letter.
7 What, then, shall we say? Is the Torah
sin? Let it not be! However, I did not know
sin except through the Torah. For also the
covetousness I knew not if the Torah had
not said, **"You shall not covet."** Shem. 20:17,
Deḇ. 5:21
8 But sin, having taken the occasion
through the command, did work in me all
sorts of covetousness. For apart from
Torah sin is dead.
9 And I was alive apart from the Torah
once, but when the command came, the sin
revived, and I died.
10 And the command which was to result
in life, this I found to result in death.
11 For sin, having taken the occasion
through the command, deceived me, and
through it killed *me*.
12 So that the Torah truly is set-apart, and
the command set-apart, and righteous, and
good.
13 Therefore, has that which is good
become death to me? Let it not be! But the
sin, that sin might be manifest, was working death in me through what is good, so
that sin through the command might
become an exceedingly great Sinner.
14 For we know that the Torah is Spiritual,
but I am fleshly, sold under sin.
15 For what I work, I know not. For what I
wish, that I do not practise, but what I hate,
that I do.
16 But if I do what I do not wish, I agree
with the Torah that it is good.
17 And now, it is no longer I that work it,
but the sin dwelling in me.
18 For I know that in me, that is in my
flesh, dwells no good. For to wish is
present with me, but to work the good I do
not find.
19 For the good that I wish to do, I do not
do; but the evil I do not wish to do, this I
practise.
20 And if I do that which I do not wish, it
is no longer I who work it, but the sin
dwelling in me.
21 I find therefore this law, that when I
wish to do the good, that the evil is present
with me.
22 For I delight in the Torah of Elohim [a]
according to the inward man,
23 but I see another torah in my members,
battling against the torah of my mind, and
bringing me into captivity to the torah of
sin which is in my members.
24 Wretched man that I am! Who shall
deliver me from this body of death?
25 Thanks to Elohim, through יהושע
Messiah our Master! So then, with the
mind I myself truly serve the Torah of
Elohim, but with the flesh the torah of sin.

8 There is, then, now no condemnation
to those who are in Messiah יהושע,
who do not walk according to the flesh, but
according to the Spirit.
2 For the torah of the Spirit of the life in
Messiah יהושע has set me free from the
torah of sin and of death.
3 For the Torah being powerless, in that
it was weak through the flesh, Elohim,
having sent His own Son in the likeness of
flesh of sin, and concerning sin, condemned sin in the flesh,
4 so that the righteousness of the Torah
should be completed in us who do not walk
according to the flesh but according to the
Spirit.
5 For those who live according to the
flesh set their minds on the *matters* of the
flesh, but those *who live* according to the
Spirit, the *matters* of the Spirit.
6 For the mind of the flesh is death, but
the mind of the Spirit is life and peace.
7 Because the mind of the flesh is enmity
towards Elohim, for it does not subject
itself to the Torah of Elohim, neither
indeed is it able,
8 and those who are in the flesh are
unable to please Elohim.
9 But you are not in the flesh but in the
Spirit, if indeed the Spirit of Elohim dwells

7a See Teh. 119:16.

in you. And if anyone does not have the Spirit of Messiah, this one is not His.
10 And if Messiah is in you, the body is truly dead on account of sin, but the Spirit is life on account of righteousness.
11 And if the Spirit of Him who raised יהושע from the dead dwells in you, He who raised Messiah from the dead shall also give life to your mortal bodies through His Spirit dwelling in you.
12 So then, brothers, we are not debtors to the flesh, to live according to the flesh.
13 For if you live according to the flesh, you are going to die; but if by the Spirit you put to death the deeds of the body, you shall live.
14 For as many as are led by the Spirit of Elohim, these are sons of Elohim.
15 For you did not receive the spirit of bondage again to fear, but you received the Spirit of adoption by whom we cry out, "Abba, Father."
16 The Spirit Himself bears witness with our spirit that we are children of Elohim,
17 and if children, also heirs – truly heirs of Elohim, and co-heirs with Messiah, if indeed we suffer with Him, in order that we also be exalted together.
18 For I reckon that the sufferings of this present time are not worth comparing with the esteem that is to be revealed in us.
19 For the intense longing [a] of the creation eagerly waits for the revealing of the sons of Elohim.
20 For the creation was subjected to futility, not from choice, but because of Him who subjected it, in anticipation,
21 that the creation itself also shall be delivered from the bondage to corruption into the esteemed freedom of the children of Elohim.
22 For we know that all the creation groans together, and suffers the pains of childbirth together until now.
23 And not only so, but even we ourselves who have the first-fruits of the Spirit, we ourselves also groan within ourselves, eagerly waiting for the adoption, the redemption of our body.
24 For in this expectation we were saved, but expectation that is seen is not expectation, for when anyone sees, does he expect it?
25 And if we expect what we do not see, we eagerly wait for it with endurance.
26 And in the same way the Spirit does help in our weaknesses. For we do not know what we should pray, but the Spirit Himself pleads our case for us with groanings unutterable.
27 And He who searches the hearts knows what the mind of the Spirit is, because He makes intercession for the set-apart ones according to Elohim.
28 And we know that all *matters* work together for good to those who love Elohim, to those who are called according to *His* purpose.
29 Because those whom He knew beforehand, He also ordained beforehand *to be* conformed to the likeness of His Son, for Him to be the first-born among many brothers.
30 And whom He ordained beforehand, these He also called, and whom He called, these He also declared right. And whom He declared right, these He also esteemed.
31 What then shall we say to this? If Elohim is for us, who is against us?
32 Truly, He who did not spare His own Son, but delivered Him up on behalf of us all – how shall He not, along with Him, freely give us all else?
33 Who shall bring any charge against Elohim's chosen ones? It is Elohim who is declaring right.
34 Who is he who is condemning? It is Messiah who died, and furthermore is also raised up, who is also at the right hand of Elohim, who also makes intercession for us.
35 Who shall separate us from the love of the Messiah? Shall pressure, or distress, or persecution, or scarcity of food, or nakedness, or danger, or sword?
36 As it has been written, **"For Your sake we are killed all day long, we are reckoned as sheep of slaughter."** Teh. 44:22

8a Lit. *anxiously looking with outstretched head.*

37 But in all this we are more than overcomers through Him who loved us.

38 For I am persuaded that neither death nor life, nor messengers nor principalities nor powers, neither the present nor the future,

39 nor height nor depth, nor any other creature, shall be able to separate us from the love of Elohim which is in Messiah יהושע our Master.

9 I speak the truth in Messiah, I do not lie, my conscience also bearing me witness in the Set-apart Spirit,

2 that I have great sadness and continual grief in my heart.

3 For I myself could have wished to be banished from Messiah for the sake of my brothers, my relatives according to the flesh,

4 who are *the children of* Yisra'ěl, to whom is the adoption, and the esteem, and the covenants, and the giving of the Torah, and the worship, and the promises,

5 whose are the fathers, and from whom is the Messiah according to the flesh, who is over all, Elohim-blessed forever. Aměn.

6 However, it is not as though the word of Elohim has failed. For they are not all Yisra'ěl who are of Yisra'ěl, [a]

7 neither are they all children because they are the seed of Aḇraham, but, **"In Yitsḥaq your seed shall be called."** Ber. 21:12

8 That is, those who are the children of the flesh, these are not the children of Elohim, but the children of the promise are reckoned as the seed.

9 For this is the word of promise, **"At this time I shall come and Sarah shall have a son."** Ber. 18:10

10 And not only so, but Riḇqah having conceived by one, our father Yitsḥaq.

11 Yet, before they were born or had done any good or evil – in order that the purpose of Elohim, according to choice, might stand, not of works but of Him who calls –

12 it was said to her, **"The greater shall serve the lesser,"** Ber. 25:23

13 as it has been written, **"Ya'aqoḇ I have loved, but Ěsaw I have hated."** Mal. 1:2-3

14 What, then, shall we say? Is there unrighteousness with Elohim? Let it not be!

15 For He says to Mosheh, **"I shall favour whomever I favour, and I shall have compassion on whomever I have compassion."** Shem. 33:19

16 So, then, it is not of him who is wishing, nor of him who is running, but of Elohim who shows favour.

17 For the Scripture says to Pharaoh, **"For this same purpose I have raised you up, to show My power in you, and that My Name be declared in all the earth."** Shem. 9:16

18 So, then, He favours whom He wishes, and He hardens whom He wishes.

19 Then you shall say to me, "Why does He still find fault? For who has resisted His counsel?"

20 But who are you, O man, to talk back to Elohim? **Shall that which is formed say to him who formed it, "Why have you made me like this?"** Yesh. 29:16; 45:9

21 Does not the potter have authority over the clay, from the same lump to make one vessel for value and another not for value?

22 And if Elohim, desiring to show wrath, and to make His power known, with much patience tolerated the vessels of wrath prepared for destruction,

23 and that He might make known the riches of His esteem on vessels of compassion, which He had prepared beforehand for esteem,

24 even whom He called, not only us of the Yehuḏim, but also of the nations?

25 As He says in Hoshěa too, **"I shall call them My people, who were not My people, and her beloved, who was not beloved."** Hosh. 2:23

26 **"And it shall be in the place where it was said to them, 'You are not My people,' there they shall be called sons of the living Elohim."** Hosh. 1:10

27 And Yeshayahu cries out on behalf of Yisra'ěl, **"Though the number of the**

9a A play on words. See Explanatory Note on "Overcomers."

children of Yisra'ěl be as the sand of the
sea, the remnant shall be saved. Yesh. 10:22,
Ber. 22:17, Hosh. 1:10
28 **For He is bringing a matter to an**
end, and is cutting it short in righteous-
ness, because יהוה shall cut short a mat-
ter on the earth." Yesh. 10:23
29 And as Yeshayahu said before, **"If יהוה**
of hosts had not left us a seed, we would
have become like Sedom, and we would
have been made like Amorah." Yesh. 1:9,
Deb. 29:23 *b*
30 What shall we say then? That nations
not following after righteousness, have
obtained righteousness, even the righteousness of belief,
31 but Yisra'ěl following after the Torah
of righteousness, has not arrived at the
Torah of righteousness.
32 Why? Because *it was* not of belief, but
as by works of Torah. For they stumbled at
the **Stone of stumbling.** Yesh. 8:14
33 As it has been written, **"See, I lay in**
Tsiyon a Stone of stumbling and a Rock
that makes for falling, and everyone
who is believing on Him shall not be put
to shame." Yesh. 8:14, 28:16

10

Truly brothers, my heart's desire
and prayer to Elohim for Yisra'ěl is
for deliverance.
2 For I bear them witness that they have
an ardour for Elohim, but not according to
knowledge.
3 For not knowing the righteousness of
Elohim, and seeking to establish their own
righteousness, they did not subject themselves to *a* the righteousness of Elohim.
4 For Messiah is the goal *b* of the 'Torah
unto righteousness' to everyone who
believes.
5 For Mosheh writes about the righteousness which is of the Torah, **"The man who**
does these shall live by them." Way. 18:5
6 But the righteousness of belief speaks
in this way, **"Do not say in your heart,**
'Who shall ascend into the heavens?' "
Deb. 30:12 – that is, to bring Messiah down;
or,
7 " 'Who shall descend into the abyss?' "
– that is, to bring Messiah up from the
dead.
8 But what does it say? **"The word is**
near you, in your mouth and in your
heart" Deb. 30:14 – that is, the word of belief
which we are proclaiming:
9 That if you confess with your mouth
the Master יהושע and believe in your heart
that Elohim has raised Him from the dead,
you shall be saved.
10 For with the heart one believes unto
righteousness, and one confesses with the
mouth, and so is saved.
11 Because the Scripture says, **"Whoever**
puts his trust in Him shall not be put to
shame." Yesh. 28:16
12 Because there is no distinction between
Yehudi and Greek, for the same Master of
all is rich to all those calling upon Him.
13 For **"everyone who calls on the Name**
of יהוה shall be saved." Yo'el 2:32 *c*
14 How then shall they call on Him in
whom they have not believed? And how
shall they believe in Him of whom they
have not heard? And how shall they hear
without one proclaiming?
15 And how shall they proclaim if they are
not sent? As it has been written, **"How**
pleasant are the feet of those who bring
the Good News of peace, who bring the
Good News of the good!" Yesh. 52:7
16 However, not all obeyed the Good
News. For Yeshayahu says, **"יהוה, who**
has believed our report?" Yesh. 53:1
17 So then belief comes by hearing, and
hearing by the word of Elohim.
18 But I ask, Did they not hear? Yes
indeed, **"Their voice went out to all the**
earth, and their words to the ends of the
world." Teh. 19:4
19 But I ask, Did Yisra'ěl not know?
First Mosheh says, **"I shall provoke you**
to jealousy by those who are not a
nation, I shall enrage you by an unwise
nation." Deb. 32:21
20 And Yeshayahu boldly says, **"I was**

9b See Yirm. 49:18; 50:40, Amos 4:11 *10a* Or *did not obey*. *10b* Or end purpose; not termination.
10c Ma. 2:21

**found by those not seeking Me, I was
made manifest to those not asking for
Me."** Yesh. 65:1
21 And to Yisra'ěl He says, **"All day long
I have stretched out My hands to a disobedient and back-talking people."**
Yesh. 65:2

11 I say then, has Elohim rejected His
people? Let it not be! For I also am
of Yisra'ěl, of the seed of Aḇraham, of the
tribe of Binyamin.
2 **Elohim has not rejected His people**
Teh. 94:14 whom He knew beforehand. Or do
you not know what the Scripture says of
Ěliyahu, how he pleads with Elohim
against Yisra'ěl, saying,
3 **"יהוה', they have killed Your
prophets and overthrown Your slaughter-places, and I alone am left, and they
seek my life"**? Mel. א 19:10, 14
4 But what does the answer *of Elohim* say
to him? **"I have left for Myself seven
thousand men who have not bowed the
knee to Ba'al."** Mel. א 19:18
5 So therefore also, at this present time a
remnant according to the choice of favour
has come to be.
6 And if by favour, it is no longer of
works, otherwise favour is no longer
favour. And if it is of works, it is no longer
favour, otherwise work is no longer work.
7 What then? Yisra'ěl has not obtained
what it seeks, but the chosen did obtain it,
and the rest were hardened.
8 As it has been written, **"יהוה' has given
them a spirit of deep sleep, eyes not to
see and ears not to hear, unto this day."**
Deḇ. 29:4, Yesh. 29:10
9 Dawiḏ also says, **"Let their table
become for a snare, and for a trap, and
for a stumbling-block and a recompense
to them,**
10 **let their eyes be darkened, not to see,
and bow down their back always."**
Teh. 69:22, 23
11 I say then, have they stumbled that they
should fall? Let it not be! But by their fall
deliverance has come to the nations, to
provoke them to jealousy. Deḇ. 32:21
12 And if their fall is riches for the world,
and their failure riches for the nations, how
much more their completeness!
13 For I speak to you, the nations, inasmuch as I am an emissary to the nations,
I esteem my service,
14 if somehow I might **provoke to jealousy** Deḇ. 32:21 *those who are* my flesh and
save some of them.
15 For if their casting away is the restoration to favour of the world, what is their
acceptance but life from the dead?
16 Now if the first-fruit is set-apart, the
lump is also. And if the root is set-apart, so
are the branches.
17 And if some of the branches were broken off, and you, being a wild olive tree,
have been grafted in among them, and
came to share the root and fatness of the
olive tree,
18 do not boast against the branches. And
if you boast, *remember*: you do not bear
the root, but the root *bears* you!
19 You shall say then, "The branches were
broken off that I might be grafted in."
20 Good! By unbelief they were broken
off, and you stand by belief. Do not be
arrogant, but fear.
21 For if Elohim did not spare the natural
branches, He might not spare you either.
22 See then the kindness and sharpness of
Elohim: on those who fell sharpness, but
toward you kindness, if you continue in
His kindness, otherwise you also shall be
cut off.
23 And they also, if they do not continue
in unbelief, shall be grafted in, for Elohim
is able to graft them in again.
24 For if you were cut out of the olive tree
which is wild by nature, and were grafted
contrary to nature into a good olive tree,
how much more shall these who are the
natural *branches*, be grafted into their own
olive tree?
25 For I do not wish you to be ignorant of
this secret, brothers, lest you should be
wise in your own estimation, that hardening in part has come over Yisra'ěl, until the

11a Ber. 48:19.

completeness of the nations [a] has come in.

26 And so all Yisra'ěl shall be saved, as it has been written, **"The Deliverer shall come out of Tsiyon, and He shall turn away wickedness from Ya'aqoḇ,**

27 **and this is My covenant with them, when I take away their sins."** Yesh. 59:20-21

28 Truly, as regards the Good News *they are* enemies for your sake, but concerning the choice *they are* beloved for the sake of the fathers.

29 For the gifts and the calling of Elohim are not to be repented of.

30 For as you also at one time disobeyed Elohim, but now have obtained compassion through their disobedience,

31 so also these have now disobeyed, that through the compassion shown you they also might obtain compassion.

32 For Elohim has shut them all up to disobedience, in order to have compassion on all.

33 Oh, the depth of riches, and wisdom and knowledge of Elohim! How unsearchable His judgments and untraceable His ways!

34 "For **who has known the mind of יהוה? Or who has become His counsellor?"** Yesh. 40:13

35 "Or **who first gave to Him, and it shall be given back to him**?" Iyoḇ. 35:7; 41:11

36 Because of Him, and through Him, and to Him, are all, to whom be esteem forever. Aměn.

12

I call upon you, therefore, brothers, through the compassion of Elohim, to present your bodies a living offering – set-apart, well-pleasing to Elohim – your reasonable worship.

2 And do not be conformed to this world, but be transformed by the renewing of your mind, so that you prove what is that good and well-pleasing and perfect desire of Elohim.

3 For I say, through the favour which has been given to me, to everyone who is among you, not to think *of himself* more highly than he should think, but to think soberly, as Elohim has given to each a measure of belief.

4 For as we have many members in one body, but all members do not have the same function,

5 so we, the many, are one body in Messiah, and members each one of one another.

6 Now having different gifts, according to the favour which was given to us, *let us use them accordingly*: if prophecy, according to the proportion of belief;

7 if serving, in the serving; or he who is teaching, in the teaching;

8 or he who encourages, in the encouragement; or he who is sharing, in sincerity; he who is leading, in diligence; he who shows compassion, joyously.

9 Let love be without hypocrisy. Shrink from what is wicked, cling to what is good.

10 In brotherly love, tenderly loving towards one another, in appreciation, giving preference to each other;

11 not idle in duty, ardent in spirit, serving the Master;

12 rejoicing in the expectancy, enduring under pressure, continuing steadfastly in prayer;

13 imparting to the needs of the set-apart ones, pursuing kindness towards strangers.

14 Bless those who persecute you – bless and do not curse.

15 Rejoice with those who rejoice, and weep with those who weep.

16 Be of the same mind toward one another. Do not be proud in mind, but go along with the lowly. Do not be wise in your own estimation.

17 Repay no one evil for evil. Respect what is right in the sight of all men.

18 If possible, on your part, be at peace with all men.

19 Beloved, do not revenge yourselves, but give place to the wrath, for it has been written, **"Vengeance is Mine, I shall repay,"** says יהוה. Deḇ. 32:35

20 **"Instead, if your enemy hungers, feed him; if he thirsts, give him a drink, for in so doing you shall heap coals of fire on his head."** Mish. 25:21-22

21 Do not be overcome by evil, but overcome evil with good.

13

Let every being be in subjection to the governing authorities. For there is no authority except from Elohim, and the authorities that exist are appointed by Elohim.

2 So he who opposes the authority withstands the institution of Elohim, and those who withstand shall bring judgment on themselves.

3 For those ruling are an object of fear, not to good works, but to evil. Do you wish to be not afraid of the authority? Do the good, and you shall have praise from it,

4 for it is a servant of Elohim to you for good. But if you do evil, be afraid, for it does not bear the sword in vain. For it is a servant of Elohim, a revenger to execute wrath on him who practises evil.

5 Therefore, it is necessary to be subject, not only because of wrath but also because of the conscience.

6 For because of this you also pay taxes, for they are servants of Elohim attending continually to these duties.

7 Render therefore to all what is due to them: tax to whom tax *is due*, toll to whom toll, fear to whom fear, respect to whom respect.

8 Owe no one any *matter* except to love one another, for he who loves another has filled the Torah.

9 For this, **"You shall not commit adultery," "You shall not murder," "You shall not steal," "You shall not bear false witness," "You shall not covet,"** Shem. 20:13-17, Deḇ. 5:17-21 and if there is any other command, it is summed up in this word, **"You shall love your neighbour as yourself."** Way. 19:18

10 Love does no evil to a neighbour. Therefore, love is completion of the Torah.

11 And *do* this, knowing the time, that it is already the hour for us to wake up from sleep, for now our deliverance is nearer than when we did believe.

12 The night is far advanced, the day has come near. So let us put off the works of darkness, and let us put on the armour of light.

13 Let us walk becomingly, as in the day, not in wild parties and drunkenness, not in living together and indecencies, not in fighting and envy,

14 but put on the Master יהושע Messiah, and make no provision for the lusts of the flesh.

14

And receive him who is weak in the belief, not criticising *his* thoughts.

2 One indeed believes to eat all *food*, but he who is weak eats only vegetables.

3 He that eats, let him not despise him who does not eat, and he that does not eat, let him not judge him who eats, for Elohim received him.

4 Who are you that judges another's servant? To his own master he stands or falls. But he shall be made to stand, for Elohim is able to make him stand.

5 One indeed judges one day above another, another judges every day *alike*. Let each one be completely persuaded in his own mind.

6 He who minds the day, minds it to יהוה. And he who does not mind the day, to יהוה he does not mind it. He who eats, eats to יהוה, for he gives Elohim thanks. And he who does not eat, to יהוה he does not eat, and gives Elohim thanks.

7 For not one of us lives to himself, and not one dies to himself.

8 For both, if we live, we live unto the Master, and if we die, we die unto the Master. Therefore, whether we live or die, we are the Master's.

9 For unto this Messiah died and rose and lived again, to rule over both the dead and the living.

10 But why do you judge your brother? Or why do you despise your brother? For we shall all stand before the judgment seat of Messiah.

11 For it has been written, **"As I live, says יהוה, every knee shall bow to Me, and every tongue shall confess to Elohim."** Yesh. 45:23

12 Each one of us, therefore, shall give account of himself to Elohim.

13 Therefore let us not judge one another any longer, but rather judge this, not to put an obstacle or a stumbling-block in our

brother's way.

14 I know and am persuaded in the Master יהושע that none at all is common of itself. But to him who regards whatever to be common, to him it is common.

15 And if your brother is grieved because of your food, you are no longer walking in love. Do not by your food ruin the one for whom Messiah died.

16 Do not then allow your good to be spoken of as evil.

17 For the reign of Elohim is not eating and drinking, but righteousness and peace and joy in the Set-apart Spirit.

18 For he who is serving Messiah in these *matters* is well-pleasing to Elohim and approved by men.

19 So, then, let us pursue the *matters* of peace and the *matters* for building up one another.

20 Do not destroy the work of Elohim for the sake of food. All indeed are clean, but evil to that man who eats so as to cause stumbling.

21 It is good not to eat meat or drink wine, nor *to do whatever* by which your brother stumbles.

22 Do you have belief? Have it to yourself before Elohim. Blessed is he who does not condemn himself in what he approves.

23 But he who doubts, if he eats, is condemned, because it is not of belief, and all that is not of belief is sin.

15

But we who are strong ought to bear with the failings of the weak, and not to please ourselves.

2 Let each one of us please his neighbour for his good, to build him up.

3 For even the Messiah did not please Himself, but, as it has been written, **"The reproaches of those who reproached You fell upon Me."** Teh. 69:9

4 For whatever was written before was written for our instruction, [a] that through endurance and encouragement of the Scriptures we might have the expectation.

5 And the Elohim of endurance and encouragement give you to be of the same mind toward one another, according to Messiah יהושע,

6 that with one mind and one mouth, you might praise the Elohim and Father of our Master יהושע Messiah.

7 So accept one another, as Messiah also did accept us, to the esteem of Elohim.

8 And I say that יהושע Messiah has become a servant of the circumcised for the truth of Elohim, to confirm the promises made to the fathers,

9 and for the nations to praise Elohim for His compassion, as it has been written, **"Because of this I shall confess to You among the nations, and I shall sing to Your Name."** Shem. ב 22:50, Teh. 18:49

10 And again it says, **"Rejoice, O nations, with His people!"** Deb. 32:43

11 And again, **"Praise יהוה, all you nations! Praise Him, all you peoples!"** Teh. 117:1

12 And again, Yeshayahu says, **"There shall be a root of Yishai, and He who shall rise to reign over the nations, on Him the nations shall set their expectation."** Yesh. 11:10

13 And the Elohim of expectation fill you with all joy and peace in believing, that you overflow with expectation by the power of the Set-apart Spirit.

14 Now I myself am persuaded concerning you, my brothers, that you too are filled with goodness, complete in all knowledge, able also to admonish one another.

15 But I have written more boldly to you, in part, as reminding you, because of the favour given to me by Elohim,

16 to be a servant of יהושע Messiah to the nations, with the priestly duty of bringing the Good News of Elohim, so that the offering of the nations becomes acceptable, set apart by the Set-apart Spirit.

17 Therefore I have cause for boasting in Messiah יהושע in the *matters* pertaining to Elohim.

18 For I shall not presume to speak of any *matter* except what Messiah has worked

15a Qor. א 10:11, Tim. ב 3:16-17.

out through me, in word and deed, to make
the nations obedient,
19 in power of signs and wonders, in
power of the Spirit of Elohim, so that from
Yerushalayim and round about to Illurikon
I have completed the preaching of the
Good News of Messiah.
20 And so I was ambitious to bring the
Good News where Messiah had not been
named, lest I should build on another
man's foundation,
21 but as it has been written, **"To whom it
was not announced concerning Him,
they shall see, and those that have not
heard shall understand."** Yesh. 52:15
22 This is why I was often hindered from
coming to you.
23 But now, no longer having a place in
these parts, and having a longing to come
to you for many years,
24 I shall come to you when I go to Spain.
For I expect to see you on my journey, and
to be helped on my way there by you,
if first I be somewhat filled with your
company.
25 But now I am going to Yerushalayim to
serve the set-apart ones.
26 For it pleased those from Makedonia
and Achaia to make some contribution for
the poor among the set-apart ones who are
in Yerushalayim.
27 For they were pleased, and they are
their debtors. For if the nations have
shared in their spiritual matters, their duty
is also to serve them in material matters.
28 Having completed this, then, and having put my seal on this fruit of theirs, I
shall return through you to Spain.
29 And I know that when I come to you, I
shall come in the completeness of the
blessing of the Good News of Messiah.
30 But I urge you, brothers, through our
Master יהושע Messiah, and through the
love of the Spirit, to strive together with
me in prayers for me, unto Elohim,
31 that I might be delivered from those in
Yehuḏah who do not believe, and that my
service for Yerushalayim be well received
by the set-apart ones,
32 that I might come to you with joy,
through the desire of Elohim, and be
refreshed together with you.
33 And the Elohim of peace be with you
all. Amĕn.

16 And I commend to you Phoebe our
sister, who is a servant of the
assembly in Kenḥrea,
2 that you receive her in יהוה, worthy of
the set-apart ones, and assist her in whatever matter she has need of you. For she
has been a great help to many, including
me.
3 Greet Priscilla and Aqulas, my fellow
workers in Messiah יהושע,
4 who risked their own necks for my life,
to whom not only I give thanks, but also all
the assemblies of the nations,
5 and the assembly that is in their house.
Greet my beloved Epainetos, who is the
first-fruits of Achaia to Messiah.
6 Greet Miryam, who worked very hard
for us.
7 Greet Andronikos and Junias, my relatives and my fellow prisoners, who are
eminent among the emissaries, who also
were in Messiah before me.
8 Greet Amplias, my beloved in יהוה.
9 Greet Urbanus, our fellow worker in
Messiah, and Stachus, my beloved.
10 Greet Apelles, the approved in
Messiah. Greet those who are of
Aristobulos.
11 Greet Herodion, my relative. Greet
those who are of Narcissus who are in
יהוה.
12 Greet Truphaina and Truphosa, who
work in יהוה. Greet the beloved Persis,
who worked very hard in יהוה.
13 Greet Rufus, chosen in יהוה and his
mother and mine.
14 Greet Asugritos, Phlegon, Hermas,
Patrobas, Hermes, and the brothers who
are with them.
15 Greet Philologos and Julia, Nereus and
his sister, and Olumpas, and all the set-
apart ones who are with them.
16 Greet one another with a set-apart kiss.
The assemblies of Messiah greet you.
17 Now I call upon you, brothers, watch
out for those who cause divisions and
stumbling, contrary to the teaching which

you learned, and turn away from them.
18 For such ones do not serve our Master
יהושע Messiah, but their own stomach,
and by smooth words and flattering speech
they deceive the hearts of the innocent.
19 Your obedience, indeed, is reported to
all. Therefore I rejoice concerning you, but
I wish you to be wise indeed as to the
good, and simple toward the evil.
20 And the Elohim of peace shall crush
Satan under your feet shortly. The favour
of our Master יהושע Messiah be with you.
Amĕn.
21 Timothy, my fellow worker, and
Lucius, and Jason, and Sosipater, my relatives, greet you.
22 I, Tertius, who wrote this letter, greet
you in יהוה.
23 Gaios, the host of all the assembly and
me, greets you. Ĕrastos, the treasurer of the
city, greets you, and Quartus, a brother.
24 The favour of our Master יהושע
Messiah be with you all. Amĕn.
25 And to Him who is able to establish
you according to my Good News and the
preaching of יהושע Messiah, according to
the revelation of the secret which was kept
silent since times of old,
26 but now has been made manifest, and
by the prophetic Scriptures has been made
known to all nations, according to the
command of the everlasting Elohim, for
belief-obedience.
27 To Elohim, wise alone, be the esteem,
through יהושע Messiah forever. Amĕn.

QORINTIYIM ALEPH

1 CORINTHIANS

1 Sha'ul, a called emissary of יהושע
Messiah by the desire of Elohim, and
brother Sosthenes,
2 to the assembly of Elohim which is at
Corinth, to those who are set-apart in
Messiah יהושע, called set-apart ones, with
all those calling on the Name of יהושע
Messiah our Master in every place, theirs
and ours:
3 Favour to you and peace from Elohim
our Father and the Master יהושע Messiah.
4 I thank my Elohim always concerning
you for the favour of Elohim which was
given to you by Messiah יהושע,
5 that in Him you were enriched in all –
in every word and all knowledge –
6 as the witness of Messiah was confirmed in you,
7 so that you are not lacking in any gift,
eagerly waiting for the revelation of our
Master יהושע Messiah,
8 who shall also confirm you to the end,
unreprovable in the day of our Master
יהושע Messiah.
9 Elohim is trustworthy, by whom you
were called into the fellowship of His Son,
יהושע Messiah our Master.
10 And I appeal to you, brothers, by the
Name of our Master יהושע Messiah, that
you all agree, and that there be no divisions among you, but that you be knit
together in the same mind and in the same
opinion.
11 For I have been informed concerning
you, my brothers, by those of *the house of*
Chloe, that there are strifes among you.
12 What I mean is this, that each one of
you says, "I am of Sha'ul," or "I am of
Apollos," or "I am of Kěpha," or "I am of
Messiah."
13 Has the Messiah been divided? Was
Sha'ul impaled for you? Or were you
immersed in the name of Sha'ul?
14 I thank Elohim that I immersed not one
of you except Crispus and Gaios,
15 that no one should say that I immersed
into my own name.
16 Now I did also immerse the household
of Stephanas. For the rest, I do not know
whether I immersed anyone else.
17 For Messiah did not send me to
immerse, but to bring the Good News, not
with wisdom of words, that the stake of
Messiah should not be nullified.
18 For the word of the stake is indeed foolishness to those who are perishing, but to
us who are being saved it is the power of
Elohim.
19 For it has been written, **"I shall
destroy the wisdom of the wise, and set
aside the learning of the learned
ones."** Yesh. 29:14 *a*
20 Where is the wise? Where is the scholar? Where is the debater of this age? Has
not Elohim made foolish the wisdom of
this world?
21 For since, in the wisdom of Elohim, the
world through wisdom did not know
Elohim, it pleased Elohim through the
foolishness of preaching to save those who
believe.
22 And since Yehuḏim ask a sign, and
Greeks seek wisdom,
23 yet we proclaim Messiah impaled, to
the Yehuḏim a stumbling-block and to the
Greeks foolishness,
24 but to those who are called – both
Yehuḏim and Greeks – Messiah the power
of Elohim and the wisdom of Elohim.
25 For the foolishness of Elohim is wiser
than men, and the weakness of Elohim is
stronger than men.
26 For look at your calling, brothers, that
there were not many wise according to the
flesh, not many mighty, not many noble.
27 But Elohim has chosen the foolish *matters* of the world to put to shame the wise,
and Elohim has chosen the weak of the

1a See Mt. 11:25, Rom. 1:22.

world to put to shame the strong.
28 And Elohim has chosen the low-born of the world and the despised, and the ones that are not, that He might bring to naught the ones that are,
29 so that no flesh should boast in His presence.
30 And of Him you are in Messiah יהושע, who became for us wisdom from Elohim, righteousness also, and set-apartness and redemption,
31 that, as it has been written, **"He who boasts, let him boast in יהוה."** Yirm. 9:23, 24

2 And, when I came to you, brothers, I did not come with excellence of speech or wisdom, proclaiming to you the witness of Elohim.
2 For I resolved not to know any *matter* among you except יהושע Messiah and Him impaled.
3 And I was with you in weakness, and in fear, and in much trembling.
4 And my word and my preaching were not with persuasive words of man's wisdom, but in demonstration of the Spirit and of power,
5 in order that your belief should not be in the wisdom of men but in the power of Elohim.
6 Yet we speak wisdom among those who are perfect, and not the wisdom of this age, nor of the rulers of this age that are being brought to naught.
7 But we speak the wisdom of Elohim, which was hidden in a secret, and which Elohim ordained before the ages for our esteem,
8 which no one of the rulers of this age knew, for if they had known, they would not have impaled the Master of esteem.
9 But as it has been written, **"Eye has not seen, and ear has not heard, nor have entered into the heart of man what Elohim has prepared for those who love Him."** Yesh. 64:4
10 But Elohim has revealed them to us through His Spirit. For the Spirit searches all *matters*, even the depths of Elohim.
11 For who among men knows the *thoughts* of a man except the spirit of the man that is in him? So also, the *thoughts* of Elohim no one has known, except the Spirit of Elohim.
12 And we have received, not the spirit of the world, but the Spirit that is from Elohim, in order to know what Elohim has favourably given us,
13 which we also speak, not in words which man's wisdom teaches but which the Set-apart Spirit teaches, comparing spiritual *matters* with spiritual *matters*.
14 But the natural man does not receive the *matters* of the Spirit of Elohim, for they are foolishness to him, and he is unable to know them, because they are spiritually discerned.
15 But he who is spiritual discerns indeed all *matters*, but he himself is discerned by no one.
16 For **"Who has known the mind of יהוה? Who shall instruct Him?"** Yesh. 40:13 But we have the mind of Messiah.

3 And I, brothers, was not able to speak to you as to spiritual ones but as to fleshly, as to babes in Messiah.
2 I fed you with milk and not with solid food, for until now you were not able to receive it, and even now you are still not able,
3 for you are still fleshly. For since there is envy, and strife, and divisions among you, are you not fleshly and walking according to man?
4 For when one says, "I am of Sha'ul," and another, "I am of Apollos," are you not fleshly?
5 What then is Apollos, and what is Sha'ul, but servants through whom you believed, as the Master assigned to each?
6 I planted, Apollos watered, but Elohim was giving growth.
7 So neither he who plants nor he who waters is any at all, but Elohim who gives the increase.
8 And he who plants and he who waters are one, and each one shall receive his own reward according to his own labour.
9 For we are fellow workers of Elohim, you are the field of Elohim, the building of Elohim.

10 According to the favour of Elohim
which was given to me, as a wise master
builder I have laid the foundation, and
another builds on it. But each one should
look how he builds on it.
11 For no one is able to lay any other foundation except that which is laid, which is
יהושע Messiah.
12 And if anyone builds on this foundation
with gold, silver, precious stones, wood,
hay, straw,
13 each one's work shall be revealed, for
the day shall show it up, because it is
revealed by fire. And the fire shall prove
the work of each one, what sort it is.
14 If anyone's work remains, which he has
built on, he shall receive a reward.
15 If anyone's work is burned, he shall
suffer loss, but he himself shall be saved,
but so as through fire.
16 Do you not know that you are a
Dwelling Place of Elohim and that the
Spirit of Elohim dwells in you?
17 If anyone destroys the Dwelling Place
of Elohim, Elohim shall destroy him. For
the Dwelling Place of Elohim is set-apart,
which you are.
18 Let no one deceive himself. If anyone
among you seems to be wise in this age, let
him become foolish, so that he might
become wise.
19 For the wisdom of this world is foolishness with Elohim. For it has been written,
"He catches the wise in their craftiness,"
Iyoḇ 5:13
20 and again, **"יהוה knows the thoughts
of the wise, that they are worthless."**
Teh. 94:11
21 So then, let no one boast in men, for all
belongs to you,
22 whether Sha'ul or Apollos or Kěpha, or
the world, or life, or death, or the present
or the future – all belongs to you.
23 And you belong to Messiah, and
Messiah belongs to Elohim.

4 Let a man regard us as servants of
Messiah and trustees of the secrets of
Elohim.
2 For the rest, it is sought in trustees, that
those should be found trustworthy.
3 But with me it is a small matter that I
should be judged by you or by a man's
court. But not even myself I judge.
4 For I am not conscious of any *matter*
against myself, yet I am not declared right
by this, but He who judges me is יהוה.
5 So do not judge any at all before the
time, until the Master comes, who shall
bring to light what is hidden in darkness
and reveal the thoughts of the hearts. And
then each one's praise shall come from
Elohim.
6 And these *matters*, brothers, I have
applied in a figure to myself and Apollos
for your sakes, so that in us you might
learn not to think beyond what is written,
so that none of you be puffed up on behalf
of one against the other.
7 For who makes you to differ? And what
do you have that you did not receive? And
if you did indeed receive it, why do you
boast as if you had not received it?
8 You are already satisfied! You are
already enriched! You have reigned as sovereigns, apart from us! And I wish, indeed,
you did reign, that we also might reign
with you!
9 For I think that Elohim has exhibited
us, the emissaries, last, as appointed to
death, because we became a spectacle to
the world, both to messengers and to men.
10 We are fools for the sake of Messiah,
but you are wise in Messiah! We are weak,
but you are strong! You are in esteem, but
we are not appreciated!
11 Until the present hour we both hunger
and thirst, and we are scantily clad, and
beaten, and homeless,
12 and labour, working with our own
hands. Being cursed, we bless; being
persecuted, we suffer;
13 being insulted, we help. We have been
made as the filth of the world – dirt wiped
off by all until now.
14 I do not write this to shame you, but to
warn you as my beloved children.
15 For if you should have ten thousand
instructors in Messiah, yet not many
fathers, for in Messiah יהושע I have
brought you forth through the Good News.
16 Therefore I appeal to you, to become

imitators of me.
17 For this reason I have sent Timotiyos to
you, who is my beloved and trustworthy
son in the Master, who shall remind you of
my ways in Messiah, as I teach everywhere in every assembly.
18 Now some are puffed up, as though I
were not coming to you.
19 But I shall come to you shortly, if the
Master desires, and I shall know, not the
word of those who are puffed up, but the
power.
20 For the reign of Elohim is not in
speech, but in power.
21 What do you wish? Shall I come to you
with a rod, or in love and a spirit of meekness?

5 It is commonly reported that there is
whoring among you, and such whoring as is not even named among the
nations, so as one to have his father's wife!
2 And you have been puffed up, and did
not rather mourn, so that he who has done
this deed, be removed from among you!
3 For I indeed, as absent in body but
present in spirit, have already judged the
one who did this, as though I were present.
4 In the Name of our Master יהושע
Messiah, when you are gathered together,
and my spirit, with the power of our
Master יהושע Messiah,
5 deliver such a one to Satan for destruction of the flesh, in order that his spirit be
saved in the day of the Master יהושע.
6 Your boasting is not good. Do you not
know that a little leaven leavens the entire
lump?
7 Therefore cleanse out the old leaven, so
that you are a new lump, as you are
unleavened. For also Messiah our Pěsaḥ
was slaughtered for us.
8 So then let us celebrate the festival, not
with old leaven, nor with the leaven of evil
and wickedness, but with the unleavened
bread of sincerity and truth.
9 I wrote to you in my letter not to keep
company with those who whore.
10 And I certainly did not mean with those
of this world who whore, or with the
greedy of gain, or swindlers, or idolaters,
since then you would need to go out of the
world.
11 But now I have written to you not to
keep company with anyone called 'a brother,' if he is one who whores, or greedy of
gain, or an idolater, or a reviler, or a drunkard, or a swindler – not even to eat with
such a one.
12 For what have I to do with judging outsiders? Do you not judge those who are
inside?
13 But Elohim judges those who are outside. And **put away the wicked one from
among you**! Deḇ. 13:5 *a*

6 Should any of you, holding a matter
against another, go to be judged
before the unrighteous, and not before the
set-apart ones?
2 Do you not know that the set-apart ones
shall judge the world? And if the world is
judged by you, are you unworthy to judge
the smallest matters?
3 Do you not know that we shall judge
messengers? How much more, matters of
this life?
4 If then you truly have judgments of this
life, do you appoint them as judges who
are least esteemed by the assembly?
5 I say this to your shame. Is it so, that
there is not a wise one among you, not
even one, who shall be able to judge
between his brothers?
6 But brother against brother goes to be
judged and that before unbelievers!
7 Already, then, there is a failure with
you, that you have lawsuits among you.
Why not rather be wronged? Why not
rather be cheated?
8 But you yourselves do wrong and
cheat, and that to your brothers!
9 Do you not know that the unrighteous
shall not inherit the reign of Elohim? Do
not be deceived. Neither those who whore,
nor idolaters, nor adulterers, nor effemi-
nate, nor homosexuals,
10 nor thieves, nor greedy of gain, nor

5a See Deḇ. 17:7, 12; 19:19; 21:21; 22:21

drunkards, nor revilers, nor swindlers shall inherit the reign of Elohim. [a]

11 And such were some of you. But you were washed, but you were set apart, but you were declared right in the Name of the Master יהושע and by the Spirit of our Elohim.

12 All is permitted me, but not all do profit. All is permitted me, but I shall not be under authority of any.

13 Foods for the stomach and the stomach for foods – but Elohim shall destroy both it and them. And the body is not for whoring but for the Master, and the Master for the body.

14 And Elohim, who raised up the Master, shall also raise us up through His power.

15 Do you not know that your bodies are members of Messiah? Shall I then take the members of Messiah and make them members of a whore? Let it not be!

16 Or do you not know that he who is joined to a whore is one body? For He says, **"The two shall become one flesh."** Ber. 2:24

17 And he who is joined to the Master is one spirit.

18 Flee whoring. Every sin that a man does is outside the body, but he who commits whoring sins against his own body.

19 Or do you not know that your body is the Dwelling Place of the Set-apart Spirit who is in you, which you have from Elohim, and you are not your own?

20 For you were bought with a price, therefore esteem Elohim in your body and in your spirit, [b] which are of Elohim.

7

And concerning the *matters* you wrote to me: It is good for a man not to touch a woman.

2 But because of whoring, let each one have his own wife, and let each woman have her own husband.

3 Let the husband render to his wife what is her due, and likewise also the wife to her husband.

4 The wife does not have authority over her own body, but the husband does. And likewise the husband does not have authority over his own body, but the wife does.

5 Do not deprive one another except with agreement for a time, to give yourselves to fasting and prayer. And come together again so that Satan does not try you because of your lack of self-control.

6 And I say this as a concession, not as a command.

7 For I wish that all men were even as I myself. But each one has his own gift from Elohim, one in this way and another in that.

8 And I say to the unmarried and to the widows: It is good for them if they remain even as I am,

9 but if they do not have self-control, let them marry, for it is better to marry than to burn.

10 And to the married I command, not I, but the Master: A wife should not separate from a husband.

11 But if she is indeed separated, let her remain unmarried or be restored to favour with her husband, and let a husband not send away a wife.

12 And to the rest I say, not the Master: If any brother has an unbelieving wife, and she thinks well to live with him, let him not send her away.

13 And a woman who has an unbelieving husband, and he thinks well to live with her, let her not send him away.

14 For the unbelieving husband has been set-apart in the wife, and the unbelieving wife has been set-apart in the husband. Otherwise your children would be unclean, but now they are set-apart.

15 And, if the unbelieving one separates, let him separate himself. A brother or a sister has not been enslaved in such matters. But Elohim has called us to peace.

16 For how do you know, O wife, whether you shall save your husband? Or how do you know, O husband, whether you shall save your wife?

17 Only, as Elohim has distributed to each

6a See Gal. 5:19-21, Eph. 5:3-5. *6b* See 7:23, Kěpha א 1:18-19.

one, as the Master has called each one, so
let him walk. And so I order in all the
assemblies.
18 Was anyone called while circumcised?
Let him not become uncircumcised. Was
anyone called while uncircumcised? Let
him not be circumcised.
19 The circumcision is naught, and the
uncircumcision is naught, but the guarding
of the commands of Elohim *does matter*! [a]
20 Let each one remain in the same calling
in which he was called.
21 Were you called while a slave? It matters not to you, but if you are able to
become free too, rather use it.
22 For he who is called in the Master
while a slave is the Master's freed man.
Likewise he who is called while free is a
slave of Messiah. [b]
23 You were bought with a price, do not
become slaves of men.
24 Brothers, let each one remain with
Elohim in that calling in which he was
called.
25 And concerning maidens: I have no
command from the Master, but I give
judgment as one whom the Master in His
compassion has made trustworthy.
26 I think then that this is good because of
the present necessity, that it is good for a
man to remain as he is.
27 Are you bound to a wife? Do not seek
to be loosed. Are you loosed from a wife?
Do not seek a wife.
28 But even if you should marry, you have
not sinned. And if a maiden should marry,
she has not sinned. But such shall have
pressure in the flesh, but I would spare
you.
29 And this I say, brothers, the time is
short, so that from now on even those who
have wives should be as though they had
none,
30 and those who weep as though they did
not weep, and those who rejoice as though
they did not rejoice, and those who buy as
though they did not possess,
31 and those who use this world as not
misusing it. For the scene of this world is
passing away.
32 And I wish you to be without concern.
He who is unmarried is concerned about
the *matters* of the Master – how to please
the Master.
33 But he who is married is concerned
about the *matters* of the world – how to
please his wife.
34 There is a difference between a wife
and a maiden. The unmarried woman is
concerned about the *matters* of the Master,
that she might be set-apart both in body
and in spirit. But she who is married is
concerned about the *matters* of the world –
how to please her husband.
35 And this I say for your own good, not
to put a restraint on you, but for what is
proper, and to attend to the Master without
distraction.
36 And if anyone thinks he is behaving
improperly toward his maiden, if she is
past the flower of her youth, and so it
should be, let him do what he desires, he
does not sin – let them marry.
37 But he who stands steadfast in his
heart, having no necessity, and has authority over his own desire, and has so decided
in his heart to guard his own maiden, does
well.
38 So then he who gives her in marriage
does well, but he who does not give her in
marriage does better.
39 A wife is bound by Torah as long as her
husband lives, and if her husband dies, she
is free to be married to whom she desires,
only in the Master.
40 But she is better off if she remains as
she is, according to my opinion. And I
think I also have the Spirit of Elohim.

8

And concerning *food* offered to idols:
We know that we all have knowledge.
Knowledge puffs up, but love builds up.
2 If anyone thinks that he knows somewhat, he does not yet know as he should
know.
3 But if anyone loves Elohim, this one is
known by Him.
4 So then, concerning the eating of *food*

7a See Rom. 2:26-29. 7b Eph. 6:6, Kěpha א 2:16.

offered to idols, we know that an idol is no
matter at all in the world, and that there is
no other Elohim but one.
5 For even if there are so-called mighty
ones, whether in heaven or on earth – as
there are many mighty ones and many
masters –
6 for us there is one Elohim, [a] the Father,
from whom all came and for whom we
live, and one Master יהושע Messiah,
through whom all came and through whom
we *live*.
7 However, not all have this knowledge.
But some, being aware of the idol, until
now eat it as having been offered to an
idol, so their conscience, being weak, is
defiled.
8 But food does not commend us to
Elohim, for we are none the better if we
eat, nor any worse for not eating.
9 But look to it, lest somehow this right
of yours becomes a stumbling-block to
those who are weak.
10 For if anyone sees you who have
knowledge eating in an idol's place, shall
not his conscience, if he is weak, be built
up to eat *food* offered to idols?
11 So this weak brother, for whom
Messiah died, shall perish through your
knowledge!
12 Now sinning in this way against the
brothers, and wounding their weak conscience, you sin against Messiah.
13 Therefore, if food makes my brother
stumble, I am never again going to eat
meat, lest I make my brother stumble.

9 Am I not an emissary? Am I not free?
Have I not seen יהושע Messiah our
Master? Are you not my work in the
Master?
2 If to others I am not an emissary, I
certainly am to you. For you are the seal of
my office of the emissary in the Master.
3 My defence to those who examine me
is this:
4 Do we not have a right to eat and drink?
5 Do we not have a right to take along a
sister – a wife – as do also the other emissaries, and the brothers of the Master, and
Kěpha?
6 Or do only Barnaḇa and I have no right
to refrain from working?
7 Who serves as a soldier at his own
expense? Who plants a vineyard and does
not eat of its fruit? Or who shepherds a
flock and does not feed on the milk of the
flock?
8 Do I say this as a man? Or does not the
Torah say the same too?
9 For it has been written in the Torah of
Mosheh, **"You shall not muzzle an ox
while it treads out the grain."** Deḇ. 25:4 Is it
about oxen Elohim is concerned?
10 Or does He say it because of us all? For
this was written because of us, that he who
ploughs should plough in expectation, and
the thresher in expectation of sharing.
11 If we have sown spiritual *seed* among
you, is it too much if we reap material
goods from you?
12 If others share authority over you,
should not rather we? But we have not
used this authority, but we put up with all,
lest we hinder the Good News of Messiah.
13 Do you not know that those serving the
Set-apart Place eat from the Set-apart
Place, and those attending at the slaughter-
place have their share of the offerings of
the slaughter-place?
14 So also the Master instituted that those
announcing the Good News should live
from the Good News.
15 But I have used none of these, nor have
I written this that it should be done so to
me. For it would be better for me to die
than that anyone should make my boasting
empty.
16 For if I bring the Good News, it is no
boasting for me, for necessity is laid on
me, and it is woe to me if I do not bring the
Good News!
17 For if I do this voluntarily I have a
reward, but if not voluntarily, I am entrusted with a management.
18 What then is my reward? That in bringing the Good News, I should offer the
Good News of Messiah without cost, so as

8a Eph. 4:6, Tim. א 2:5, Mq. 12:32,34.

not to abuse my authority in the Good
News.
19 For though I am free from all, I made
myself a servant to all, in order to win
more,
20 and to the Yehuḏim I became as a
Yehuḏi, that I might win Yehuḏim; to those
who are under Torah, as under Torah, so as
to win those who are under Torah;
21 to those without Torah, as without
Torah – not being without Torah toward
Elohim, but under Torah of Messiah – so
as to win those who are without Torah.
22 To the weak I became as weak, so as to
win the weak. To all *men* I have become
all, so as to save some, by all means.
23 And I do this because of the Good
News, so as to become a fellow-partaker
with it.
24 Do you not know that those who run in
a race indeed all run, but one receives the
prize? Run in such a way as to obtain it.
25 And everyone who competes controls
himself in every way. Now they do it to
receive a corruptible crown, but we for an
incorruptible crown.
26 Therefore I run accordingly, not with
uncertainty. Thus I fight, not as one who
beats the air.
27 But I treat my body severely and
make it my slave, lest having proclaimed
to others, I myself might be rejected.

10 For I do not wish you to be ignorant, brothers, that all our fathers
were under the cloud, and all passed
through the sea,
2 and all were immersed into Mosheh in
the cloud and in the sea,
3 and all ate the same spiritual food,
4 and all drank the same spiritual drink.
For they drank of that spiritual Rock that
followed, and the Rock was Messiah.
5 However, with most of them Elohim
was not well pleased, for they were laid
low in the wilderness.
6 And these became examples for us, so
that we should not lust after evil, as those
indeed lusted.
7 And do not become idolaters as some
of them, as it has been written, **"The people sat down to eat and to drink, and
stood up to play."** Shem. 32:6
8 Neither should we commit whoring, as
some of them did, and in one day twenty-
three thousand fell,
9 neither let us try Messiah, as some of
them also tried, and were destroyed by
serpents,
10 neither grumble, as some of them also
grumbled, and were destroyed by the
destroyer.
11 And all these came upon them as
examples, and they were written as a warning to us, on whom the ends of the ages
have come,
12 so that he who thinks he stands, let him
take heed lest he fall.
13 No trial has overtaken you except such
as is common to man, and Elohim is trustworthy, who shall not allow you to be tried
beyond what you are able, but with the
trial shall also make the way of escape,
enabling you to bear it.
14 Therefore, my beloved ones, flee from
idolatry.
15 I speak as to wise men, judge for yourselves what I say.
16 The cup of blessing which we bless, is
it not a sharing in the blood of Messiah?
The bread that we break, is it not a sharing
in the body of Messiah?
17 Because there is one bread, we, who are
many, are one body, for we all partake of
the one bread.
18 Look at Yisra'ěl after the flesh: Are not
those who eat of the slaughterings sharers
in the slaughter-place?
19 What then do I say? That an idol is of
any *value*? Or that which is slaughtered to
idols is of any *value*?
20 No, but what the nations slaughter they
slaughter to demons [a] and not to Elohim,
and I do not wish you to become sharers
with demons.
21 You are not able to drink the cup of the
Master and the cup of demons, you are not
able to partake of the table of the Master

10a See Way. 17:7, Deḇ. 32:17

and of the table of demons.
22 Do we provoke the Master to jealousy?
Are we stronger than He?
23 All is permitted me, but not all do profit. All is permitted me, but not all build up.
24 Let no one seek his own, but each one
that of the other.
25 You eat whatever is sold in the meat
market, asking no questions because of
conscience,
26 for **"The earth belongs to יהוה, and
all that fills it."** Teh. 24:1; 50:12
27 And if any of the unbelievers invite
you, and you wish to go, you eat whatever
is set before you, asking no question on
account of the conscience.
28 And if anyone says to you, "This was
slaughtered to idols," do not eat it because
of the one pointing it out to you, and on
account of the conscience, for "The earth
belongs to יהוה, and all that fills it."
29 Now I say conscience, not your own,
but that of the other. For why is my freedom judged by another's conscience?
30 But if I partake with thanks, why am I
evil spoken of for what I give thanks?
31 Therefore, whether you eat or drink, or
whatever you do, do all to the esteem of
Elohim.
32 Cause no stumbling, either to the
Yehuḏim or to the Greeks or to the assembly of Elohim,
33 as I also please all *men* in all *matters*,
not seeking my own advantage, but that of
the many, that they might be saved.

11 Become imitators of me, as I also
am of Messiah.
2 And I praise you, brothers, that you
remember me in every way and keep the
traditions as I delivered them to you.
3 And I wish you to know that the head
of every man is the Messiah, [a] and the head
of woman is the man, [b] and the head of
Messiah is Elohim. [c]
4 Every man praying or prophesying,
having his head covered, brings shame to
his Head.
5 And every woman praying or prophesying with her head uncovered brings
shame to her head, for that is one and the
same as if her head were shaved.
6 For if a woman is not covered, let her
also be shorn. But if it is a shame for a
woman to be shorn or shaved, let her be
covered. [d]
7 For a man indeed should not cover his
head, since he is the likeness and esteem of
Elohim, but woman is the esteem of man.
8 For man is not from woman, but
woman from man.
9 For man also was not created for the
woman, but woman for the man.
10 Because of this the woman ought to
have authority [e] on her head, because of the
messengers.
11 However, man is not independent of
woman, nor woman independent of man,
in the Master.
12 For as the woman was from the man,
even so the man also is through the
woman. But all are from Elohim.
13 Judge for yourselves: is it proper for a
woman to pray to Elohim with her head
uncovered?
14 Does not nature itself teach you that if a
man indeed has long hair, it is a disrespect
to him?
15 And if a woman has long hair, it is an
esteem to her, because the long hair has
been given to her over against a veil.
16 If, however, anyone seems to be contentious, we do not have such a habit, nor
do the assemblies of Elohim.
17 And in declaring this I do not praise
you, since you come together not for the
better but for the worse.
18 For in the first place, I hear that when
you come together as an assembly, there
are divisions among you, and to some
extent I believe it.
19 For there have to be factions even
among you, so that the approved ones
might be revealed among you.

11a Eph. 1:22; 4:15; 5:23. *11b* Ber. 3:16. *11c* Cor. א 3:23, Yn. 14:28. *11d* Bem. 5:18. *11e* Some say "*a symbol of* authority."

[20]So when you come together in one
place, it is not to eat the Master's supper.
[21]For, when you eat, each one takes his
own supper first, and one is hungry and
another is drunk.
[22]Have you not houses to eat and drink
in? Or do you despise the assembly of
Elohim and shame those who have not?
What shall I say to you? Shall I praise you
in this? I do not praise!
[23]For I received from the Master that
which I also delivered to you: that the
Master יהושע in the night in which He
was delivered up took bread,
[24]and having given thanks, He broke it
and said, "Take, eat, this is My body which
is broken for you; do this in remembrance
of Me."
[25]In the same way also the cup, after
supper, saying, "This cup is the renewed
covenant in My blood. As often as you
drink it, do this in remembrance of Me."
[26]For as often as you eat this bread and
drink this cup, you proclaim the death of
the Master until He comes.
[27]So that whoever should eat this bread
or drink this cup of the Master unworthily
shall be guilty of the body and blood of the
Master.
[28]But let a man examine himself, and so
let him eat of that bread and drink of that
cup.
[29]For the one who is eating and drinking
unworthily, eats and drinks judgment to
himself, not discerning the body of the
Master.
[30]Because of this many are weak and sick
among you, and many sleep.
[31]For if we were to examine ourselves,
we would not be judged.
[32]But when we are judged, we are disciplined by the Master, that we should not be
condemned with the world.
[33]So then, my brothers, when you come
together to eat, wait for one another.
[34]And if anyone is hungry, let him eat
at home, lest you come together for
judgment. And the rest I shall set in order
w

12
bro
ignorant.
[2]You know tha
away to the dumb id
be led.
[3]Therefore I make know
one speaking by the Spirit of
יהושע is a curse, and no one is a
that יהושע is Master except by th
apart Spirit.
[4]And there are different kinds of gifts,
but the same Spirit.
[5]There are different kinds of services,
but the same Master.
[6]And there are different kinds of work-
ings, but it is the same Elohim who is
working all in all.
[7]And to each one is given the manifestation of the Spirit for profiting,
[8]for to one is given a word of wisdom
through the Spirit, and to another a word of
knowledge according to the same Spirit,
[9]and to another belief by the same Spirit,
and to another gifts of healing by the same
Spirit,
[10]and to another operations of powers,
and to another prophecy, and to another
discerning of spirits, and to another kinds
of tongues, and to another interpretation of
tongues.
[11]But one and the same Spirit works all
these, distributing to each one individually
as He intends.
[12]For as the body is one and has many
members, but all the members of that one
body, being many, are one body, so also is
the Messiah.
[13]For indeed by one Spirit we were all
immersed into one body, whether Yehuḏim
or Greeks, whether slaves or free, and we
were all made to drink into one Spirit.
[14]For indeed the body is not one member
but many.
[15]If the foot says, "Because I am not a
hand, I do not belong to the body," does it

12a See also Eph. 2:11, Eph. 4:17, Kěpha א 4:3, Tas. א 4:5.

ı the
body w... ...aker are
necessary.
23 And to those of the body which we
think to be less respected, these we present
greater respect. And our unseemly *members* have greater seemliness,
24 whereas our seemly *members* have
no need. But Elohim blended together the
body, having given greater respect to that
member which lacks it,
25 that there should be no division in the
body, but that the members should have the
same concern one for another.
26 And if one member suffers, all the
members suffer with it; or if one member
is esteemed, all the members rejoice with
it.
27 And you are a body of Messiah, and
members individually.
28 And Elohim has appointed these in the
assembly: firstly emissaries, secondly
prophets, thirdly teachers, after that miracles, then gifts of healings, helps, ministra-
tions, kinds of tongues.
29 Are all emissaries? Are all prophets?
Are all teachers? Are all workers of miracles?
30 Do all have gifts of healings? Do all
speak with tongues? Do all interpret?
31 But earnestly seek the better gifts. And
yet I show you a more excellent way.

I speak with the tongues of men
d of messengers, but do not have
ve become as sounding brass or a
cymbal.
if I have prophecy, and know all
and all knowledge, and if I have all
so as to remove mountains, but do
e love, I am none at all.
d if I give out all my possessions to
he poor, and if I give my body to be
d, but do not have love, I am not
ted at all.
ove is patient, is kind, love does not
y, love does not boast, is not puffed up,
does not behave indecently, does not
ek its own, is not provoked, reckons not
the evil,
6 does not rejoice over the unrighteousness, but rejoices in the truth,
7 it covers all, believes all, expects all,
endures all.
8 Love never fails. And whether *there be*
prophecies, they shall be inactive; or
tongues, they shall cease; or knowledge, it
shall be inactive.
9 For we know in part and we prophesy
in part.
10 But when that which is perfect has
come, then that which is in part shall be
inactive.
11 When I was a child, I spoke as a child, I
thought as a child, I reasoned as a child.
But when I became a man, I did away with
childish matters.
12 For now we see in a mirror, dimly, but
then face to face. Now I know in part, but
then I shall know, as I also have been
known.
13 And now belief, expectation, and love
remain – these three. But the greatest of
these is love.

14 Pursue love, and earnestly seek the
spiritual gifts, but rather that you
prophesy.
2 For he who is speaking in a tongue does
not speak to men but to Elohim, for no one
understands, but in the Spirit he speaks
secrets.
3 But he who is prophesying speaks
upbuilding and encouragement and com-

fort to men.
4 He who is speaking in a tongue builds
up himself, but he who is prophesying
builds up the assembly.
5 Now I wish you all spoke with tongues,
but rather that you might prophesy, for he
who is prophesying is greater than he who
is speaking with tongues, unless he interprets, so that the assembly might receive
upbuilding.
6 But now, brothers, if I come to you
speaking with tongues, what shall I profit
you unless I speak to you, either by revelation, or by knowledge, or by prophesying,
or by teaching?
7 Nevertheless, lifeless *instruments* making a sound, whether flute or harp, if they
do not make a distinction in the sound,
how shall it be known what is played on
the flute or on the harp?
8 For indeed, if the trumpet makes an
indistinct sound, who shall prepare himself
for battle?
9 So also you, if you do not give speech
by the tongue that is clear, how shall it be
known what is spoken? For you shall be
speaking into the air.
10 There are, undoubtedly, so many kinds
of sounds in the world, and none of them is
without *distinct* sound.
11 If then I do not know the power of the
voice, I shall be a foreigner to him who
speaks, and he who speaks be a foreigner
to me.
12 So also you, since you are ardent for
spiritual gifts, seek to excel in the upbuilding of the assembly.
13 Therefore, he who is speaking in a
tongue, let him pray that he might interpret.
14 For if I am praying in a tongue, my
spirit is praying, but my understanding is
without fruit.
15 What then is it? I shall pray with the
spirit, and I shall also pray with the understanding. I shall sing with the spirit, and I
shall also sing with the understanding.
16 Otherwise, if you bless with the spirit,
how shall he who fills up the place of the
unlearned say "Aměn" at your giving of
thanks, since he does not know what you
say?
17 For you truly give thanks well, but the
other is not built up.
18 I thank my Elohim I speak with tongues
more than you all,
19 but in an assembly I wish to speak five
words with my understanding that I might
instruct others also, than ten thousand
words in a tongue.
20 Brothers, do not be children in *your*
thinking, but in evil be babes, and in *your*
thinking be perfect.
21 In the Torah it has been written, **"With
men of other tongues and other lips I
shall speak to this people. And even so,
they shall not hear Me, says יהוה."**
Yesh. 28:11
22 So then tongues are for a sign, not to
those who believe but to unbelievers, and
prophesying is not for unbelievers but for
those who believe.
23 If then all the assembly comes together
in one place, and all speak with tongues,
and there come in those who are unlearned
or unbelievers, shall they not say that you
are mad?
24 But if all prophesy, and an unbeliever
or an unlearned one comes in, he is
reproved by all, he is discerned by all.
25 And so the secrets of his heart are
revealed. And so, falling down on his face,
he shall worship Elohim, declaring that
Elohim is truly among you.
26 What then is it, brothers? Whenever
you come together, each one has a psalm,
has a teaching, has a tongue, has a revelation, has an interpretation. Let all be done
for upbuilding.
27 If anyone speaks in a tongue, let there
be two or at the most three, each in turn,
and let one interpret.
28 And if there is no interpreter, let him be
silent in an assembly, and let him speak to
himself and to Elohim.
29 And let two or three prophets speak,
and let the others discern.
30 And if there should be a revelation to
another who sits by, let the first be silent.
31 For you are all able to prophesy one by
one, so that all learn and all be encouraged.
32 And the spirits of the prophets are

subject to the prophets.
33 For Elohim is not *Elohim* of disorder
but of peace, as in all the assemblies of the
set-apart ones.
34 Let your women be silent in the assemblies, for they are not allowed to speak, but
let them subject themselves, as the Torah
also says. [a]
35 And if they wish to learn whatever, let
them ask their own husbands at home, for
it is improper for women to speak in an
assembly.
36 Or did the word of Elohim go out from
you? Or did it reach only to you?
37 If anyone thinks himself to be a prophet
or spiritual, let him acknowledge what I
write to you, that they are a command of
the Master.
38 And if anyone is ignorant, let him be
ignorant.
39 So, then, brothers, earnestly seek to
prophesy, and do not forbid speaking in
tongues.
40 Let all be done decently and in order.

15 But brothers, I make known to you
the Good News, which I brought as
Good News to you, which you also did
receive, and in which you stand,
2 through which also you are being
saved, if you hold fast that word I brought
as Good News to you. Otherwise, you have
believed in vain.
3 For I delivered to you at the first that
which I also received: that Messiah died
for our sins according to the Scriptures,
4 and that He was buried, and that He
was raised the third day, according to the
Scriptures,
5 and that He was seen by Kěpha, then by
the twelve.
6 After that He was seen by over five
hundred brothers at one time, of whom the
greater part remain till now, but some have
fallen asleep.
7 After that He was seen by Yaʽaqoḇ,
then by all the emissaries.
8 And last of all He was seen by me also,
as if to one born prematurely.
9 For I am the least of the emissaries,
who am not worthy to be called an emissary, because I persecuted the assembly of
Elohim.
10 But by the favour of Elohim I am what
I am, and His favour toward me was not in
vain, but I laboured much more than they
all, yet not I, but the favour of Elohim with
me.
11 Whether, then, it was I or they, so we
proclaimed and so you believed.
12 And if Messiah is proclaimed that He
has been raised from the dead, how do
some among you say that there is no resurrection of the dead?
13 And if there is no resurrection of the
dead, then Messiah has not been raised.
14 And if Messiah has not been raised,
then our proclaiming is empty, and your
belief also empty,
15 and we are also found false witnesses
of Elohim, because we have witnessed of
Elohim that He raised up Messiah, whom
He did not raise up, if then the dead are not
raised.
16 For if the dead are not raised, then neither Messiah has been raised.
17 And if Messiah has not been raised,
your belief is to no purpose, you are still in
your sins!
18 Then also those who have fallen asleep
in Messiah have perished.
19 If in this life only we have expectation
in Messiah, we are of all men the most
wretched.
20 But now Messiah has been raised from
the dead, and has become the first-fruit of
those having fallen asleep.
21 For since death is through a man, resurrection of the dead is also through a Man.
22 For as all die in Aḏam, so also all shall
be made alive in Messiah.
23 And each in his own order: Messiah the
first-fruits, then those who are of Messiah
at His coming,
24 then the end, when He delivers up the
reign to Elohim the Father, when He has
brought to naught all rule and all authority
and power.

14a Ber. 3:16

25 For He has to reign until He has put all enemies under His feet.

26 The last enemy to be brought to naught is death.

27 For **"He has put all under His feet."** Teh. 8:6 But when He says "all are put under Him," it is clear that He who put all under Him is excepted.

28 And when all are made subject to Him, then the Son Himself shall also be subject to Him who put all under Him, in order that Elohim be all in all.

29 Otherwise, what shall they do who are immersed for the dead, if the dead are not raised at all? Why indeed are they immersed for the dead?

30 And why do we stand in danger every hour?

31 I affirm, by the boasting in you which I have in Messiah יהושע our Master, I die day by day.

32 If, as men do, I have fought with beasts at Ephesos, of what good is it to me? If the dead are not raised, **"Let us eat and drink, for tomorrow we die."** Yesh. 22:13; 56:12

33 Do not be led astray, "Evil company corrupts good habits."

34 Wake up to soberness, righteously, and do not sin, for some do not have the knowledge of Elohim. I speak this to your shame.

35 But someone might say, "How are the dead raised up? And with what body do they come?"

36 Senseless one! What you sow is not made alive unless it dies.

37 And as to what you sow: you do not sow the body which is to be, but a bare grain, it might be wheat or some other grain.

38 But Elohim gives it a body as He wishes, and to each seed a body of its own.

39 All flesh is not the same flesh, but there is one flesh of men, and another flesh of beasts, and another of fishes, and another of birds.

40 And *there are* heavenly bodies and earthly bodies, but the esteem of the heavenly is truly one, and the esteem of the earthly is another,

41 one esteem of the sun, and another esteem of the moon, and another esteem of the stars – for star differs from star in esteem.

42 So also is the resurrection of the dead: it is sown in corruption, it is raised in incorruption;

43 it is sown in disrespect, it is raised in esteem; it is sown in weakness, it is raised in power;

44 it is sown a natural body, it is raised a spiritual body; there is a natural body, and there is a spiritual body.

45 And so it has been written, "The first man Aḏam **became a living being**," Ber. 2:7 the last Aḏam a life-giving Spirit.

46 The spiritual, however, was not first, but the natural, and afterward the spiritual.

47 The first man was of the earth, earthy; the second Man is the Master from heaven.

48 As is the earthy, so also are those who are earthy; and as is the heavenly, so also are those who are heavenly.

49 And as we have borne the likeness of the earthy, we shall also bear the likeness of the heavenly.

50 And this I say, brothers, that flesh and blood is unable to inherit the reign of Elohim, neither does corruption inherit incorruption.

51 See, I speak a secret to you: We shall not all sleep, but we shall all be changed,

52 in a moment, in the twinkling of an eye, at the last trumpet. For the trumpet shall sound, and the dead shall be raised incorruptible, and we shall be changed.

53 For this corruptible has to put on incorruption, and this mortal to put on immortality.

54 And when this corruptible has put on incorruption, and this mortal has put on immortality, then shall come to be the word that has been written, **"Death is swallowed up in overcoming."** Yesh. 28:5

55 **"O Death, where is your sting? O grave, where is your overcoming?"** Hosh. 13:14

56 And the sting of death is the sin, and the power of the sin is the Torah.

57 But thanks to Elohim who gives us the overcoming through our Master יהושע

Messiah.

58 Therefore, my beloved brothers, be steadfast, immovable, always excelling in the work of the Master, knowing that your labour is not in vain in the Master.

16

And concerning the collections for the set-apart ones, you are to do as I gave orders to the assemblies of Galatia:

2 Every *day* one of *the* week [a] let each one of you set aside, storing up whatever he is prospered, so that there are no collections when I come.

3 And when I come, whomever you approve by your letters, I shall send to bear your gift to Yerushalayim.

4 And if it is fitting for me to go, they shall go with me.

5 And I shall come to you when I pass through Makedonia, for I am passing through Makedonia.

6 And possibly I shall stay with you, or even spend the winter, so that you send me forward, wherever I go.

7 For I do not wish to see you now on the way, but I expect to stay a while with you, if the Master permits.

8 And I shall remain in Ephesos until the Festival of Shaḇu‘ot. [b]

9 For a great and effective door has opened to me, and many are opposing.

10 And if Timotiyos comes, see that he is with you without fear, for he does the work of the Master, even as I.

11 Therefore let no one despise him. And send him forward in peace, so that he comes to me, for I am waiting for him with the brothers.

12 And concerning our brother Apollos, I strongly urged him to come to you with the brothers, but he had no desire at all to come at this time; however, he shall come when it is convenient.

13 Watch, stand fast in the belief, be men, be strong.

14 Let all that you do be done in love.

15 And I urge you, brothers, you know the household of Stephanas, that it is the first-fruit of Achaia, and that they have assigned themselves for service to the set-apart ones,

16 that you also be subject to such, and to everyone who works and labours with us.

17 And I rejoice about the coming of Stephanas, and Fortunatos, and Achaikos, for what was lacking on your part they supplied.

18 For they refreshed my spirit and yours, therefore give recognition to such ones.

19 The assemblies of Asia greet you. Aqulas and Priscilla greet you heartily in the Master, with the assembly that is in their house.

20 All the brothers greet you. Greet one another with a set-apart kiss.

21 The greeting with my own hand – Sha’ul.

22 If anyone does not love the Master יהושע Messiah, let him be a curse. Maranatha!

23 The favour of our Master יהושע Messiah be with you.

24 My love be with you all in Messiah יהושע. Amĕn.

16a Gk. one of *the* sabbath (singular). *16b* - Weeks.

QORINTIYIM BĚT

2 CORINTHIANS

1 Sha'ul, an emissary of יהושע
Messiah, by the desire of Elohim, and
Timotiyos the brother, to the assembly of
Elohim that is at Corinth, with all the set-
apart ones who are in all Achaia:
2 Favour to you and peace from Elohim
our Father and the Master יהושע Messiah.
3 Blessed be the Elohim and Father of
our Master יהושע Messiah, the Father of
compassion and Elohim of all comfort,
4 who is comforting us in all our pressure, enabling us to comfort those who are
in every pressure, through the comfort
with which we ourselves are comforted by
Elohim.
5 Because, as the sufferings of Messiah
overflow in us, so our comfort also overflows through Messiah.
6 And if we suffer pressure, it is for your
comfort and deliverance, being worked out
in enduring the same sufferings which we
also suffer. If we are comforted, it is for
your comfort and deliverance.
7 And our expectation for you is steadfast, because we know that as you are sharing in the sufferings – so also in the comfort.
8 For we do not wish you to be ignorant,
brothers, of our pressure which came to us
in Asia, that we were weighed down,
exceedingly, [a] beyond ability, so that we
despaired even of life.
9 Indeed, we had the sentence of death in
ourselves, that we should not trust in ourselves but in Elohim who raises the dead,
10 who rescued us from so great a death,
and does rescue, in whom we trust that He
shall still rescue us,
11 you also helping together in prayer for
us, that thanks shall be given by many on
our behalf for the favour bestowed upon us
through many.
12 For our boasting is this: the witness of
our conscience that we behaved ourselves
in the world in simplicity and sincerity of
Elohim, not in fleshly wisdom but in the
favour of Elohim, and much more toward
you.
13 For we are not writing any other *matters* to you than what you read or understand. Now I trust you shall understand,
even to the end,
14 as also you have understood us in part,
that we are your boast as you also are ours,
in the day of the Master יהושע.
15 And relying on this I intended to come
to you before, that you might twice receive
a favour,
16 and to pass your way into Makedonia,
and again from Makedonia come to you,
and to be sent by you on my way to
Yehuḏah.
17 Since I intended this, did I do it lightly?
Or what I plan, do I plan according to the
flesh, that with me there should be Yes,
Yes, and No, No?
18 But Elohim is trustworthy, that our
word to you was not Yes and No.
19 For the Son of Elohim, יהושע Messiah,
who was proclaimed among you by us – by
me, Silas, and Timotiyos – was not Yes
and No, but in Him was Yes.
20 For as many promises as are of Elohim,
in Him they are Yes, and in Him Amĕn, to
the esteem of Elohim through us.
21 But He who establishes us with you in
Messiah and has anointed us is Elohim,
22 who also sealed us, and gave the Spirit
in our hearts as a pledge.
23 And I call Elohim as witness against
my being, that to spare you I came no more
to Corinth.
24 Not that we rule over your belief, but
we are fellow workers for your joy, for you
stand by belief.

2 And I decided this within myself, not
to come to you again in sadness.

1a See 4:8-9 & 17.

2 For if I make you sad, then who is he who makes me glad but the one who is made sad by me?

3 And I wrote to you as I did, so that having come, I might not have sadness over those from whom I should have joy, trusting in you all that my joy is that of you all.

4 For out of much pressure and distress of heart I wrote to you, with many tears, not that you should be sad, but that you might know the love which I so richly have for you.

5 But if anyone has caused sadness, he has not made me sad, but in some degree you all – not to be too harsh.

6 For such a one this punishment, by the many, is sufficient,

7 so that, on the contrary, you should rather forgive and comfort, lest somehow such a one be swallowed up with too much sadness.

8 So I appeal to you to confirm your love to him.

9 Besides, I wrote for this purpose also, that I might know the proof of you, if you are obedient in all *matters*.

10 And whom you forgive any *matter*, I do also. For indeed, if I have forgiven any *matter*, I have forgiven that one for your sakes in the sight of Messiah,

11 lest Satan should take advantage of us, for we are not ignorant of his thoughts.

12 And when I came to Troas for the Good News of Messiah, and a door was opened to me by the Master,

13 I had no rest in my spirit, because I did not find Titos my brother. But taking my leave of them, I went on to Makedonia.

14 But thanks be to Elohim who always leads us on, to overcome in Messiah, and manifests through us the fragrance of His knowledge in every place.

15 Because we are to Elohim the fragrance of Messiah among those who are being saved and among those who are perishing.

16 To the one we are the smell of death to death, and to the other the fragrance of life to life. And who is competent for these?

17 For we are not, as so many, adulterating the Word of Elohim *for gain* – but as of sincerity, but as from Elohim, in the sight of Elohim, we speak in Messiah.

3 Are we to begin to recommend ourselves again? Or do we need, as some, letters of recommendation to you, or from you?

2 You are our letter, having been written in our hearts, known and read by all men,

3 making it obvious that you are a letter of Messiah, served by us, written not with ink but by the Spirit of the living Elohim, not on tablets of stone but on fleshly tablets of the heart.

4 And such trust we have toward Elohim, through the Messiah.

5 Not that we are competent in ourselves to reckon any *matter* as from ourselves, but our competence is from Elohim,

6 who also made us competent as servants of a renewed covenant, not of the letter but of the Spirit, for the letter kills but the Spirit gives life.

7 But if the administering of death in letters, engraved on stones, was esteemed, so that the children of Yisra'ěl were unable to look steadily at the face of Mosheh because of the esteem of his face, which was passing away,

8 how much more esteemed shall the administering of the Spirit not be?

9 For if the administering of condemnation had esteem, the administering of righteousness exceeds much more in esteem.

10 For indeed what was made esteemed had no esteem in this respect, in view of the esteem that excels.

11 For if that which is passing away was esteemed, much more that which remains in esteem.

12 Having then such expectation, we use much boldness of speech,

13 and not like Mosheh, who put a veil over his face[a] so that the children of Yisra'ěl should not look steadily at the end of what was passing away.

14 But their minds were hardened, for to this day, when the old covenant is being

3a See Shem. 34:33-35.

read, that same veil remains, not lifted,
because in Messiah it is taken away.
15 But to this day, when Mosheh is being
read, a veil lies on their heart.
16 **And when one turns to the Master,**
the veil is taken away. Shem. 34:34
17 Now יהוה is the Spirit, and where the
Spirit of יהוה is, there is freedom.
18 And we all, as with unveiled face we
see as in a mirror the esteem of יהוה, are
being transformed into the same likeness
from esteem to esteem, as from יהוה, the
Spirit. [b]

4 Therefore, having this service, even as
we received compassion, we do not
lose heart,
2 but have renounced the secret *ways*
of shame, not walking in craftiness nor
falsifying the Word of Elohim, but by the
manifestation of the truth recommending
ourselves to every human conscience, in
the sight of Elohim.
3 And indeed, if our Good News has
been veiled, it has been veiled in those
who are perishing,
4 in whom the mighty one of this age [a]
has blinded the minds of the unbelieving,
so that the enlightening of the Good News
of the esteem of Messiah, who is the likeness of Elohim, does not shine on them.
5 For we do not proclaim ourselves, but
Messiah יהושע the Master, and ourselves
your servants for the sake of יהושע.
6 For Elohim, who said, "Let light shine
out of darkness," is the One who has shone
in our hearts for the enlightening of the
knowledge of the esteem of Elohim in the
face of יהושע Messiah.
7 And we have this treasure in earthen
vessels, so that the excellence of the power
might be of Elohim, and not of us –
8 being hard pressed on every side, [b] but
not crushed; being perplexed, but not in
despair;
9 being persecuted, but not forsaken;
being thrown down, but not destroyed;
10 always bearing about in the body the
dying of the Master יהושע, that the life of
יהושע might also be manifested in our
body.
11 For we, the living, are always delivered
to death for the sake of יהושע, that the life
of יהושע might also be manifested in our
mortal flesh,
12 so that death indeed is working in us,
but the life in you.
13 But having the same spirit of belief,
according to what has been written,
"I believed, therefore I spoke," Teh. 116:10
we also believe, therefore we also speak,
14 knowing that He who raised up the
Master יהושע shall also raise us up
through יהושע, and shall present *us* with
you.
15 For all this is for your sake, so that
favour, having spread through the many,
would cause thanksgiving to overflow,
unto the esteem of Elohim.
16 Therefore we do not lose heart, but
even if our outward man is perishing, the
inward man is being renewed day by day.
17 For this slight momentary pressure is
working for us a far more exceeding and
everlasting weight of esteem.
18 We are not looking on what is seen, but
on what is not seen. For what is seen passes away, but what is not seen is everlasting. [c]

5 For we know that if the tent of our
earthly house is destroyed, we have a
building from Elohim, a house not made
with hands, everlasting in the heavens.
2 For indeed in this we groan, longing to
put on our dwelling which is from heaven,
3 so that, having put it on, we shall not be
found naked.
4 For indeed, we who are in this tent
groan, being burdened, not because we
wish to put it off, but to put on *the other*,
so that what is to die might be swallowed
up by life.
5 Now He who has prepared us for this
same purpose is Elohim, who has given us
the Spirit as a pledge of what is to come.

3b See also verses 17 and 18. *4a* See Lq. 4:6. *4b* See 1:8. *4c* See 5:7, and Rom. 8:24, Iḇ`rim 11:1 & 13.

6 Therefore, being always of good
courage, and knowing that while we are at
home in the body we are absent from the
Master –
7 for we walk by belief, not by sight [a] –
8 we are of good courage, and are well
pleased rather to be absent from the body
and to be present with the Master.
9 So we also make it our aim to be well-
pleasing to Him, whether being at home, or
being away from home.
10 For we all have to appear before the
judgment seat of Messiah, in order for
each one to receive according to what he
has done in the body, whether good or
evil. [b]
11 Knowing, therefore, the fear of יהוה,
we persuade men, but we have been made
manifest to Elohim, and I also trust in your
consciences to have been manifested.
12 For we do not again commend ourselves to you, but give you an occasion to
boast on our behalf, in order that you have
an answer for those who take pride in
appearance and not in heart.
13 For whether we are beside ourselves, it
was for Elohim, or whether we are of
sound mind, it is for you.
14 For the love of Messiah compels us,
having judged this: that if One died for all,
then all died;
15 and He died for all, that those who live
should no longer live for themselves, [c] but
for Him who died for them, and was
raised.
16 So from now onwards we know no one
according to the flesh. And if we have
known Messiah according to the flesh, yet
now we no longer know *Him thus*.
17 Therefore, if anyone is in Messiah, *he
is* a renewed creature – the old *matters*
have passed away, see, all *matters* have
become renewed! [d]
18 And all *matters* are from Elohim, who
has restored us to favour with Himself
through יהושע Messiah, and has given us
the service of restoration to favour,
19 that is, that Elohim was in Messiah
restoring the world to favour unto Himself,
not reckoning their trespasses to them, and
has committed to us the word of restoration to favour.
20 Therefore we are envoys on behalf of
Messiah, as though Elohim were pleading
through us. We beg, on behalf of Messiah:
Be restored to favour with Elohim.
21 For He made Him who knew no sin to
be sin for us, so that in Him we might
become the righteousness of Elohim.

6 And working together, we also call
upon you not to receive the favour of
Elohim in vain –
2 For He says, **“In an acceptable time I
have heard you, and in a day of deliverance I have helped you.”** See, now is the
well-accepted time, see, now is a **day of
deliverance** – Yesh. 49:8
3 giving no cause of stumbling in whatever, so that the service is not blamed.
4 Rather, we commend ourselves as servants of Elohim in every way: in much
endurance, in pressures, in hardships, in
distresses,
5 in stripes, in imprisonments, in disturbances, in toils, in watchings, in fastings,
6 in cleanness, in knowledge, in patience,
in kindness, in the Set-apart Spirit, in love
unfeigned,
7 in the word of truth, in the power of
Elohim, through the weapons of righteousness, on the right and on the left,
8 through esteem and disrespect, through
evil report and good report; *regarded* as
deceivers, and yet true;
9 as unknown, and yet well-known; as
dying, and see, we live; as disciplined, and
yet not killed;
10 as sad, yet always rejoicing; as poor,
yet enriching many; as having none, and
yet possessing all.
11 Our mouth has spoken openly to you, O
Corinthians, our heart is wide open.
12 You are not restrained by us, but you

5a See 4:18, and Qor. א 2:14. *5b* See Mt. 16:27, Yn. 5:29. *5c* Rom 14:7-8, Gal. 2:20.
5d Rom. 6:2-22, Gal. 2:20, Eph. 4:22-24, Qol. 3:10, Yn. א 3:9-10.

are restrained by your own affections.
13 But for the same reward – I speak as to
children – open wide *your hearts* too.
14 Do not become unevenly yoked with
unbelievers. For what partnership have
righteousness and lawlessness? And what
fellowship has light with darkness?
15 And what agreement has Messiah with
Beliya'al? Or what part does a believer
have with an unbeliever?
16 And what union has the Dwelling Place
of Elohim with idols? For you are a
Dwelling Place of the living Elohim, as
Elohim has said, **"I shall dwell in them
and walk among them, and I shall be
their Elohim, and they shall be My people."** Way. 26:12 [a]
17 Therefore, **"Come out from among
them and be separate, says יהוה, and do
not touch what is unclean, and I shall
receive you.** Yesh. 52:11
18 **"And I shall be a Father to you, and
you shall be sons and daughters to Me,
says יהוה the Almighty."** Yesh. 43:6, Hosh. 1:10

7 Having, then, these promises,
beloved, let us cleanse ourselves from
all defilement of the flesh and spirit,
perfecting set-apartness in the fear of
Elohim. [a]
2 Make room for us, we wronged no one,
we corrupted no one, we exploited no one.
3 I do not say this to condemn, for I
previously said that you are in our hearts,
to die together and to live together.
4 Great is my boldness of speech toward
you, great is my boasting on your behalf.
I have been filled with encouragement,
I overflow with joy in all our pressure.
5 For, indeed, when we came into
Makedonia, our flesh had no rest, but we
were hard pressed on every side – conflicts
without, fears within.
6 But Elohim, who encourages the down-
cast, encouraged us by the coming of
Titos,
7 and not only by his coming, but also by
the encouragement with which he was
encouraged over you, when he reported to
us your longing, your mourning, your
ardour for me, so that I greatly rejoiced.
8 For even if I made you sad with my
letter, I do not regret it, though I did regret
it. For I perceive that the same letter made
you sad, even if for an hour.
9 I now rejoice, not that you were made
sad, but that you were saddened into
repenting. For you were made sad according to Elohim, so that you suffered no loss
from us.
10 For sadness according to Elohim works
repentance to deliverance, not to be regret-
ted, but the sadness of the world works
death.
11 For see how you have been saddened
according to Elohim – how much it
worked out in you eagerness; indeed,
clearing of yourselves; indeed, displeasure;
indeed, fear; indeed, longing; indeed,
ardour; indeed, righting of wrong! In every
way you proved yourselves to be clear in
the matter.
12 So although I wrote to you, it was not
for the sake of him who had done the
wrong, nor for the sake of him who suffered wrong, but for the sake of revealing
our diligence for you, before Elohim.
13 For this reason we have been encouraged in your encouragement. And we
rejoiced exceedingly more for the joy of
Titos, because his spirit has been refreshed
by all of you.
14 Because if I have boasted somewhat
about you to him, I am not ashamed. But as
we spoke to you in all truth, even so our
boasting to Titos was found true.
15 And his tender feelings are greater for
you as he remembers the obedience of all
of you, as you received him with fear and
trembling.
16 I rejoice that in every way I am of good
courage by reason of you.

8 Now brothers, we make known to you
the favour of Elohim which has been
given in the assemblies of Makedonia:

6a See also Shem. 29:45, Way. 26:12, Yirm. 31:1, Yeḥ. 37:27.
7a See also Ber. 12:1, Shem. 19:5-6, and Ḥazon 18:4.

2 that in much trial of pressure the overflowing of their joy and their deep poverty
overflowed into the riches of their generosity.
3 Because I bear witness that according
to their ability, and beyond their ability,
they gave voluntarily,
4 begging us with much urgency for the
favour of taking part in this service to the
set-apart ones.
5 And, not as we had expected, they gave
themselves first to the Master, and then to
us by the desire of Elohim,
6 that we should urge Titos, that as he
had begun, so he would also complete this
kind gift in you as well.
7 But as you excel in every way – in
belief, and speech, and knowledge, and all
diligence, and in your love for us – that
you should excel in this kind gift as well.
8 I speak not by command, but I am
proving the genuineness of your love by
the eagerness of others.
9 For you know the favour of our Master
יהושע Messiah, that being rich, He
became poor for your sake, so that you
might become rich through His poverty.
10 And in this I give an opinion: It is to
your advantage not only to be doing what
you began and were desiring to do a year
ago,
11 and now also complete the work, that
as *there was* a readiness in desiring it, so
there also should be a completion out of
what you have.
12 For if the readiness is present, it is well
received according to what one has, not
according to what he does not have –
13 not, however, that others should be
eased and you hard pressed,
14 but by fair sharing, that now at this time
your plenty for their need, so that their
plenty might also be for your need – that
there might be fair sharing.
15 As it has been written, **"He who** *gath-*
ered **much did not have too much, and**
he who *gathered* **little had not less."**
Shem. 16:18
16 But thanks be to Elohim who puts the
same eagerness for you into the heart of
Titos.
17 Because he received the appeal, indeed,
but being more eager, he went to you of his
own accord.
18 And we sent with him the brother
whose praise is in the Good News through
all the assemblies,
19 and not only so, but who was also chosen by the assemblies to travel with us with
this gift that is administered by us to the
esteem of the Master Himself, and your
ready mind,
20 avoiding this: that anyone should blame
us in this generous gift which is administered by us.
21 For we provide what is right, not only
in the sight of יהוה, but also in the sight
of men. Mish. 3:4
22 And we sent with them our brother
whom we have often proved eager in many
ways, but now much more eager, because
of the great reliance which we have in you.
23 As for Titos, he is my partner and
fellow worker for you. As for our brothers,
they are messengers of the assemblies,
the esteem of Messiah.
24 Therefore show to them the proof of
your love and of our boasting on your
behalf, and in the presence of the assemblies.

9 Indeed, concerning the service to the
set-apart ones, it is unnecessary for
me to write to you;
2 for I know your eagerness, about which
I boast of you to the Makedonians, that
Achaia was ready a year ago. And your
ardour has stirred up most of them.
3 But I sent the brothers, lest our boasting
on behalf of you should be made empty in
this part, in order that, as I said, you were
ready,
4 lest if some Makedonians come with
me and find you not ready, we – not to
speak of you – should be put to shame
because of our belief.
5 So I thought it necessary to appeal to
the brothers to come to you in advance,
and arrange your promised blessing
beforehand – this to be ready as a blessing
and not as greediness.
6 And this: He who sows sparingly shall

also reap sparingly, and he who sows on
blessing shall also reap on blessing.
7 Let each one *give* as he purposes in his
heart, not of grief or of necessity, for
Elohim loves a joyous giver.
8 And Elohim is able to make all favour
overflow toward you, that you, always
having all you need in every way, have
plenty for every good work.
9 As it has been written, **"He scattered
abroad, He gave to the poor, His righteousness remains forever."** Teh. 112:9
10 And He who supplies seed to the sower,
and bread for food, shall supply and
increase the seed you have sown and
increase the fruit of your righteousness,
11 being enriched in every way for all
simplicity, which works out thanksgiving
to Elohim through us.
12 Because the rendering of this service
not only supplies the needs of the set-apart
ones, but also is overflowing through
many thanksgivings to Elohim.
13 Through the proof of this service, they
esteem Elohim on the submission of your
confession to the Good News of Messiah,
and generosity in sharing with them and all
men,
14 and by their prayer for you, who long
for you because of the exceeding favour of
Elohim in you.
15 Thanks also to Elohim for His unspeakable gift!

10 And I, Sha'ul, myself appeal to
you, through the meekness and
gentleness of Messiah – I who am indeed
lowly when face to face with you, but bold
toward you when absent!
2 But I pray, that when I am present, I
might not be bold with that bravery by
which I think to be bold against some who
reckon us as if we walked according to the
flesh.
3 For though we walk in the flesh, we do
not fight according to the flesh.
4 For the weapons we fight with are
not fleshly but mighty in Elohim for overthrowing strongholds,
5 overthrowing reasonings and every
high matter that exalts itself against the
knowledge of Elohim, taking captive every
thought to make it obedient to the Messiah,
6 and being ready to punish all disobedience, when your obedience is complete. [a]
7 Take a look at what you are facing. If
anyone seems to trust in himself that he is
of Messiah, let him reckon again for himself, that as he is of Messiah, so also are
we.
8 For even if I should boast somewhat
more about our authority, which the Master
gave us for building up, and not for overthrowing you, I shall not be put to shame,
9 lest I seem to frighten you away by
letters.
10 Because they say, "His letters are truly
weighty and strong, but his bodily presence is weak, and his speech amounts to
naught."
11 Let such a one take this into account,
that what we are in word by letters when
absent, such *we are* also in deed when we
are present.
12 For we do not presume to count ourselves or compare ourselves with those
who commend themselves. But they,
measuring themselves by themselves, and
comparing themselves among themselves,
are not wise.
13 But we shall not boast beyond measure,
but within the measure of the limits
Elohim assigned unto us, to reach even to
you.
14 For we are not overextending ourselves, as if we did not reach to you, for we
also came to you with the Good News of
the Messiah,
15 not boasting beyond measure in the
labours of others, but having an expectation, that as your belief grows, we shall be
greatly enlarged by you, according to our
limits,
16 to bring the Good News in the parts
beyond you – not to boast in another's
limits in what has been accomplished.
17 But **"He who boasts, let him boast in
יהוה."** Yirm. 9:24

10a See also Yn. 3:36.

18 For not he who commends himself is approved, but he whom the Master commends.

11

I wish that you would bear with me in a little folly. But indeed, you are bearing with me.

2 For I am jealous for you with a jealousy according to Elohim. For I gave you in marriage to one husband, to present you as an innocent maiden to Messiah.

3 But I am afraid, lest, as the serpent deceived Ḥawwah by his trickery, so your minds should be corrupted from the simplicity that is in Messiah.

4 For, indeed, if he who is coming proclaims another יהושע, [a] whom we have not proclaimed, or if you receive a different spirit which you have not received, or a different Good News which you have not accepted, you put up with it well enough!

5 For I reckon that I am not inferior to the most eminent emissaries.

6 But even if I am unskilled in word, [b] yet not in knowledge; but, in every way we have been manifested among you in all *matters*.

7 Or did I commit sin in humbling myself in order to exalt you, because I brought good news, the Good News of Elohim to you without being paid?

8 Other assemblies I robbed, by receiving wages *from them* to serve you.

9 And when I was present with you, and in need, I was not a burden to anyone, for what was lacking to me the brothers who came from Makedonia supplied. And in every way I kept myself – and shall keep – from being a burden to you.

10 It is a truth of Messiah in me, that this boasting in me shall not be stopped in the districts of Achaia.

11 Why? Is it that I do not love you? Elohim knows!

12 And I shall go on doing as I do, in order to cut off the occasion from those desiring an occasion, so that in that which they boast, they might be found also as we are.

13 For such are false emissaries, deceptive workers, masquerading as emissaries of Messiah.

14 And no wonder! For Satan himself masquerades as a messenger of light!

15 It is not surprising, then, if his servants also masquerade as servants of righteousness, [c] whose end shall be according to their works! [d]

16 Again I say, let no one think me to be a fool. And if otherwise, at least receive me as a fool, for me to also boast a little.

17 What I speak, I speak not according to the Master, but as in foolishness, in this boldness of boasting.

18 Since many boast according to the flesh, I too shall boast.

19 For you, being wise, put up with fools gladly!

20 For you put up with it if anyone enslaves you, if anyone devours you, if anyone takes from you, if anyone exalts himself, if one hits you in the face.

21 To *my* shame, I say that we were too weak for that! But in whatever anyone is bold – I say it in foolishness – I am bold also.

22 Are they Hebrews? So am I. Are they of Yisra'ěl? So am I. Are they the seed of Aḇraham? So am I.

23 Are they servants of Messiah? – I speak as beside myself – I am more, in labours much more, in stripes above measure, in prisons more frequently, in deaths many times.

24 Five times I received from the Yehuḏim forty stripes less one. [e]

25 Three times I was beaten with rods, once I was stoned, three times I was shipwrecked, a night and a day I have been in the deep,

26 in many travels, in dangers of waters, in dangers of robbers, in dangers from my own race, in dangers from the nations, in dangers in the city, in dangers in the desert, in dangers in the sea, in dangers among

11a Mt. 24:5 & 23-24, Yn. 5:43. *11b* Or *speech.* *11c* See Mt. 7:15-23, Kěpha ב 2:1-22. *11d* See Mt. 13:41-42. *11e* See Deḇ. 25:3.

false brothers;
27 in toil and hardship, in watchings often,
in hunger and thirst, in fastings often, in
cold and nakedness,
28 besides the *matters* from outside, what
comes upon me daily: the anxiety for all
the assemblies.
29 Who is weak, and I am not weak? Who
is made to stumble, and I do not burn
inwardly?
30 If I have to boast, I shall boast of matters that show up my weakness.
31 The Elohim and Father of our Master
יהושע Messiah, who is blessed forever,
knows that I am not lying.
32 In Dammeseq the governor, under
Aretas the sovereign, was guarding the city
of the Dammasqiyim, wishing to seize me,
33 but through a window I was let down in
a basket by the wall, and escaped from his
hands.

12 To boast, indeed, is useless for me,
for I shall go on to visions and revelations of יהוה.
2 I know a man in Messiah who fourteen
years ago – whether in the body I do not
know, or whether out of the body I do not
know, Elohim knows – such a one was
caught up to the third heaven.
3 And I know such a man – whether in
the body or out of the body I do not know,
Elohim knows –
4 that he was caught up into paradise [a]
and heard unspeakable words, which it is
not right for a man to speak.
5 Of such a one I shall boast, but of
myself I shall not boast, except in my
weaknesses.
6 For if I shall wish to boast, I shall not
be a fool, for I shall speak the truth. But I
refrain, lest anyone should think more of
me than what he sees in me, or hears of
me.
7 And to keep me from exalting myself
because of the exceeding greatness of the
revelations, a thorn in the flesh was given
to me, a messenger of Satan to hit me, to
keep me from exalting myself.
8 Concerning this I pleaded with the
Master three times to take it away from
me.
9 And He said to me, "My favour is sufficient for you, for My power is perfected in
weakness." Most gladly, then, I shall rather
boast in my weaknesses, so that the power
of Messiah rests on me.
10 Therefore I take pleasure in weaknesses, in insults, in needs, in persecutions, in
distresses, for the sake of Messiah. For
when I am weak, then I am strong.
11 I have become a fool – you have compelled me. For I should have been commended by you, for in no respect was I
behind the most eminent emissaries,
though I am a nobody.
12 Indeed, the signs of an emissary were
wrought among you with all endurance, in
signs and wonders and powers.
13 For what is there in which you were
inferior to other assemblies, except that I
myself was not a burden to you? Forgive
me this wrong!
14 See, I am ready to come to you for the
third time. And I shall not be a burden
to you, for I do not seek yours, but you.
For the children should not lay up for the
parents, but the parents for the children.
15 And I shall most gladly spend and be
spent for your lives. If I love you more and
more, am I to be loved less?
16 But be it so, I did not burden you. But
being crafty, did I catch you with guile?
17 Did I take advantage of you by any of
those whom I sent to you?
18 I urged Titos, and sent our brother with
him. Did Titos take advantage of you? Did
we not walk in the same spirit – not in the
same steps?
19 Again, do you think that we defend
ourselves to you? We speak before Elohim
in Messiah. But all this, beloved, is for
your upbuilding.
20 For I fear lest, when I come, I do not
find you such as I wish, and I be found by
you such as you do not wish – lest there
be strife, jealousies, outbursts of wrath,
selfish ambitions, slander, gossip, puffings

12a Lit. garden.

up, unrests,
21 and lest, when I come again, my
Elohim should humble me among you, and
I shall mourn for many who have sinned
before and have not repented of the
uncleanness, and whoring, and indecency
which they have practised.

13 This is the third time I am coming
to you. **"By the mouth of two or
three witnesses every word shall be
established."** Deb. 19:15
2 I have previously said, and I say
beforehand, as being present the second
time, and now being absent I write to those
who have sinned before, and to all the rest,
that if I come again I shall not spare,
3 since you are seeking for proof of
Messiah speaking in me, who is not weak
toward you, but mighty in you.
4 For though He was impaled in weakness, yet He lives by the power of Elohim.
For we also are weak in Him, but we shall
live with Him by the power of Elohim
toward you.
5 Examine yourselves whether you are in
the belief – prove yourselves. Or do you
not know yourselves, that יהושע Messiah
is in [a] you, unless you are disapproved.
6 And I trust that you shall know that we
are not disapproved.
7 And we pray to Elohim that you do no
evil at all – not that we should appear
approved, but that you should do what is
right, even though we should appear unap-
proved.
8 For we have no power at all against the
truth, but for the truth.
9 For we rejoice when we are weak and
you are strong. And this also we pray for:
your perfection. [b]
10 For this reason I write this in my
absence, so that, being present I should not
use sharpness, according to the authority
which the Master has given me for
upbuilding and not for overthrowing.
11 For the rest, brothers, rejoice. Be made
perfect, [c] be encouraged, be of one mind,
live in peace. And the Elohim of love and
peace shall be with you.
12 Greet one another with a set-apart kiss.
13 All the set-apart ones greet you.
14 The favour of the Master יהושע
Messiah, and the love of Elohim, and the
fellowship of the Set-apart Spirit be with
all of you. Amĕn.

13a Rom. 8:10, Gal. 2:20, Eph. 3:17, Qol. 1:27, Yn. א 4:4. *13b* Mt. 5:48. *13c* See v. 9, Mt. 5:48.

GALATIYIM

GALATIANS

1 Sha'ul, an emissary – not from men, nor by a man, but by יהושע Messiah and Elohim the Father who raised Him from the dead –

2 and all the brothers who are with me, to the assemblies of Galatia:

3 Favour to you and peace from Elohim the Father and our Master יהושע Messiah,

4 who gave Himself for our sins, to deliver us out of this present wicked age, according to the desire of our Elohim and Father,

5 to whom be the praise forever and ever. Amĕn.

6 I marvel that you are so readily turning away from Him who called you in the favour of Messiah, to a different 'Good News,' [a]

7 which is not another, only there are some who are troubling you and wishing to pervert the Good News of Messiah.

8 However, even if we, or a messenger out of heaven, bring a 'Good News' to you beside what we announced to you, let him be accursed.

9 As we have said before, and now I say again, if anyone brings a 'Good News' to you beside what you have received, let him be accursed.

10 For do I now persuade men, or Elohim? Or do I seek to please men? For if I still pleased men, I should not be a servant of Messiah.

11 And I make known to you, brothers, that the Good News announced by me is not according to man.

12 For I did not receive it from man, nor was I taught it, but through a revelation of יהושע Messiah.

13 For you have heard of my former behaviour in Yehuḏaism, how intensely I persecuted the assembly of Elohim, and ravaged it.

14 And I progressed in Yehuḏaism beyond many of my age in my race, being more exceedingly ardent for the traditions of my fathers.

15 But when it pleased Elohim, who separated me from my mother's womb and called me by His favour,

16 to reveal His Son in me, that I might bring Him, the Good News, to the nations, I did not immediately consult with flesh and blood,

17 neither did I go up to Yerushalayim, to those who were emissaries before me. But I went to Araḇia, and returned again to Dammeseq.

18 Then after three years I went up to Yerushalayim to learn from Kĕpha, and remained with him for fifteen days.

19 And I saw no other of the emissaries except Ya'aqoḇ, the brother of the Master.

20 And what I write to you, see, before Elohim, I do not lie.

21 Then I went into the districts of Suria and of Kilikia.

22 And I was *still* not known by sight to the assemblies of Yehuḏah which were in Messiah,

23 but they were hearing only that, "The one who once persecuted us now brings as Good News the belief which he once ravaged."

24 So they were esteeming Elohim in me.

2 Then after fourteen years I again went up to Yerushalayim, with Barnaḇa, taking Titos along too.

2 And I went up by revelation, and laid before them that Good News which I proclaim among the nations, but separately to those who were esteemed, lest somehow I run, or had run, in vain.

3 But not even Titos who was with me, though a Greek, was compelled to be cir-

1a Qor. ב 11:4.

cumcised.

4 But as for the false brothers, sneakingly brought in, who sneaked in to spy out our freedom which we have in Messiah יהושע in order to enslave us,

5 to these we did not yield in subjection, not even for an hour, so that the truth of the Good News remains with you.

6 But from those who were esteemed to be whatever – what they were, it makes no difference to me, Elohim shows no partiality – for those who were esteemed contributed naught to me.

7 But on the contrary, when they saw that the Good News to the uncircumcised had been entrusted to me, even as Kěpha to the circumcised –

8 for He who worked in Kěpha to make him an emissary to the circumcised also worked in me for the nations.

9 So when Ya'aqoḇ, Kěpha, and Yoḥanan, who seemed to be supports, came to know the favour that had been given to me, they gave me and Barnaḇa the right hand of fellowship, in order that we *go* to the nations and they to the circumcised,

10 only that we might remember the poor, which I myself was eager to do.

11 And when Kěpha had come to Antioch, I withstood him to his face, because he was at fault.

12 For before some came from Ya'aqoḇ, he was eating with the nations, but when they came, he began to withdraw and separate himself, in fear of those of the circumcision.

13 And the rest of the Yehuḏim joined him in hypocrisy, so that even Barnaḇa was led away by their hypocrisy.

14 But when I saw that they are not walking straight according to the truth of the Good News, I said to Kěpha before them all, "If you, being a Yehuḏi, live as the nations and not as the Yehuḏim, why do you compel nations to live as Yehuḏim?

15 "We, Yehuḏim by nature, and not of the nations, sinners,

16 knowing that a man is not declared right by works of Torah, but through belief in יהושע Messiah, even we have believed in Messiah יהושע, in order to be declared right by belief in Messiah and not by works of Torah, because by works of Torah no flesh shall be declared right.

17 "And if, while seeking to be declared right by Messiah, we ourselves also are found sinners, is Messiah then a servant of sin? Let it not be!

18 "For if I rebuild what I *once* overthrew, I establish myself a transgressor.

19 "For through Torah I died to Torah [a], in order to live to Elohim.

20 "I have been impaled with Messiah, and I no longer live, but Messiah lives in me. [b] And that which I now live in the flesh I live by belief in the Son of Elohim, who loved me and gave Himself for me.

21 "I do not set aside the favour of Elohim, for if righteousness is through Torah, then Messiah died for naught."

3 O senseless Galatians! Who has put you under a spell, not to obey the truth – before whose eyes יהושע Messiah was clearly portrayed among you as impaled?

2 This only I wish to learn from you: Did you receive the Spirit by works of Torah, or by the hearing of belief?

3 Are you so senseless? Having begun in the Spirit, do you now end in the flesh?

4 Have you suffered so much in vain – if indeed in vain?

5 Is He, then, who is supplying the Spirit to you and working miracles among you, doing it by works of Torah, or by hearing of belief?

6 Even so Aḇraham **"did believe Elohim, and it was reckoned unto him as righteousness."** Ber. 15:6

7 Know, then, that those who are of belief are sons of Aḇraham.

8 And the Scripture, having foreseen that Elohim would declare right the nations by belief, announced the Good News to Aḇraham beforehand, saying, **"All the nations shall be blessed in you,"** Ber. 12:3 [a]

2a See Rom. 7. *2b* Rom. 8:10, Qor. ב 6:16, 13:5, Eph. 3:17, Qol. 1:27, Yn. א 4:4. *3a* Ber. 18:18.

9 so that those who are of belief are blessed with Aḇraham, the believer.

10 For as many as are of works of Torah are under the curse, for it has been written, **"Cursed is everyone who does not continue in all that has been written in the Book of the Torah, to do them."** Deḇ. 27:26

11 And that no one is declared right by Torah before Elohim is clear, for **"The righteous shall live by belief."** Ḥab. 2:4

12 And the Torah is not of belief, but **"The man who does them shall live by them."** Way. 18:5

13 Messiah redeemed us from the curse of the Torah, having become a curse for us – for it has been written, **"Cursed is everyone who hangs upon a tree."** – Deḇ. 21:23

14 in order that the blessing of Aḇraham might come upon the nations in Messiah יהושע, to receive the promise of the Spirit through belief.

15 Brothers, as a man I say it: a covenant, even though it is man's, yet if it is confirmed, no one sets it aside, or adds to it.

16 But the promises were spoken to Aḇraham, and to his Seed. He does not say, "And to seeds," as of many, but as of one, **"And to your Seed,"** Ber. 12:7*b* who is Messiah.

17 Now this I say, Torah, that came four hundred and thirty years later, does not annul a covenant previously confirmed by Elohim in Messiah, so as to do away with the promise.

18 For if the inheritance is by Torah, it is no longer by promise, but Elohim gave it to Aḇraham through a promise.

19 Why, then, the Torah? It was added because of transgressions, until the Seed should come to whom the promise was made. And it was ordained through messengers in the hand of a mediator.

20 The Mediator, however, is not of one, but Elohim is one.

21 Is the Torah then against the promises of Elohim? Let it not be! For if a torah had been given that was able to make alive, truly righteousness would have been by Torah.

22 But the Scripture has shut up all *mankind* under sin, that the promise by belief in יהושע Messiah might be given to those who believe.

23 But before belief came, we were being guarded under Torah, having been shut up for the belief being about to be revealed.

24 Therefore the Torah became our trainer unto Messiah, in order to be declared right by belief.

25 And after belief has come, we are no longer under a trainer.

26 For you are all sons of Elohim through belief in Messiah יהושע.

27 For as many of you as were immersed into Messiah have put on Messiah.

28 There is not Yehuḏi nor Greek, there is not slave nor free, there is not male and female, for you are all one in Messiah יהושע.

29 And if you are of Messiah, then you are seed of Aḇraham, and heirs according to promise.

4 And I say, for as long as the heir is a child, he is no different from a slave, though he is master of all,

2 but is under guardians and trustees till the time prearranged by the father.

3 So we also, when we were children, were under the elementary matters of the world, being enslaved.

4 But when the completion of the time came, Elohim sent forth His Son, born of a woman, born under Torah,

5 to redeem those who were under Torah, in order to receive the adoption as sons.

6 And because you are sons, Elohim has sent forth the Spirit of His Son into your hearts, crying, "Abba, Father!"

7 So you are no longer a slave but a son, and if a son, also an heir of Elohim through Messiah.

8 But then, indeed, not knowing Elohim, you served those which by nature are not mighty ones.

9 But now after you have known Elohim, or rather are known by Elohim, how do you turn again to the weak and poor

3b Also see Ber. 17:7, 22:18, 24:7. *4a* See v.3, Qol. 2:8 & 20.

elementary matters, [a] to which you wish to
be enslaved again?
10 You closely observe days and months
and seasons and years.
11 I fear for you, lest by any means I have
laboured for you in vain.
12 Brothers, I beg you to become as I am,
because I am as you are. You did not wrong
me at all.
13 But you know that through weakness of
the flesh I brought the Good News to you
before.
14 And my trial which was in my flesh you
did not despise or reject, but you received
me as a messenger of Elohim, as Messiah
יהושע.
15 What then was your blessedness? For I
bear you witness, that if possible, you
would have plucked out your own eyes and
given them to me.
16 So then, have I become your enemy,
speaking truth to you?
17 They are ardent towards you, for no
good, but they wish to shut you out, that
you might be ardent towards them.
18 And it is good always to be ardent
in what is good, and not only when I am
present with you.
19 My little children, for whom I am again
in birth pains until Messiah is formed in
you,
20 even now I wish to be present with you
now and to change my voice, for I have
doubts about you.
21 Say to me, you who wish to be under
Torah, do you not hear the Torah?
22 For it has been written that Aḇraham
had two sons, one by a female servant, the
other by a free woman.
23 But he who was of the female servant
was born according to the flesh, and he of
the free woman through promise.
24 This is allegorical, for these are the two
covenants: one indeed from Mount Sinai
which brings forth slavery, which is Haḡar,
25 for this Haḡar is Mount Sinai in Araḇia,
and corresponds to Yerushalayim which
now is, and is in slavery with her children.
26 But the Yerushalayim above is free,
which is the mother of us all.
27 For it has been written, **"Rejoice, O
barren, you who do not bear! Break
forth and shout, you who do not have
birth pains! For the deserted one has
many more children than she who has a
husband."** Yesh. 54:1
28 And we, brothers, as Yitsḥaq was, are
children of promise.
29 But, as he who was born according to
the flesh then persecuted him *born* according to the Spirit, so also now.
30 But what does the Scripture say? **"Cast
out the female servant and her son, for
the son of the female servant shall by no
means be heir with the son of the free
woman."** Ber. 21:10
31 Therefore, brothers, we are not children
of the female servant but of the free
woman.

5

In the freedom with which Messiah
has made us free, stand firm, then,
and do not again be held with a yoke of
slavery.
2 See, I, Sha'ul, say to you that if you
become circumcised, Messiah shall be of
no use to you.
3 And I witness again to every man being
circumcised that he is a debtor to do the
entire Torah.
4 You who are declared right by Torah
have severed yourselves from Messiah, you
have fallen from favour.
5 For we, in Spirit, by belief, eagerly wait
for the expectation of righteousness.
6 For in Messiah יהושע neither circumcision nor uncircumcision has any strength,
but belief working through love.
7 You were running well, who held you
back from obeying the truth?
8 That persuasion does not come from
Him who calls you.
9 A little leaven leavens all the lump.
10 I trust in you, in the Master, that you
shall have no other mind. And he who is
troubling you shall bear his judgment, whoever he is.
11 And I, brothers, if I still proclaim
circumcision, why am I still persecuted?
Then the stumbling-block of the stake has
been set aside.
12 O that those who disturb you would

even cut themselves off!
[13] For you, brothers, have been called to freedom, only do not use freedom as an occasion for the flesh, but through love serve one another.
[14] For the entire Torah is completed in one word, in this, **"You shall love your neighbour as yourself."** Way. 19:18
[15] And if you bite and devour one another, beware lest you be consumed by one another!
[16] And I say: Walk in the Spirit, and you shall not accomplish the lust of the flesh.
[17] For the flesh lusts against the Spirit, and the Spirit against the flesh. And these are opposed to each other, so that you do not do what you desire to do.
[18] But if you are led by the Spirit, you are not under Torah.
[19] And the works of the flesh are well-known, which are *these*: adultery [a], whoring, uncleanness, indecency,
[20] idolatry, drug sorcery, hatred, quarrels, jealousies, fits of rage, selfish ambitions, dissensions, factions,
[21] envy, murders, drunkenness, wild parties, and the like – of which I forewarn you, even as I also said before, that those who practise such as these shall not inherit the reign of Elohim. [b]
[22] But the fruit of the Spirit is love, joy, peace, patience, kindness, goodness, trustworthiness,
[23] gentleness, self-control. Against such there is no Torah.
[24] And those who are of Messiah have impaled the flesh with its passions and the desires.
[25] If we live in the Spirit, let us also walk in the Spirit.
[26] Let us not become conceited, provoking one another, envying one another.

6 Brothers, if a man is overtaken in some trespass, you the spiritual ones, set such a one straight in a spirit of meekness, looking at yourself lest you be tried too.
[2] Bear one another's burdens, and so complete the Torah of Messiah.
[3] For if anyone thinks himself to be somebody, when he is not, he deceives himself.
[4] But let each one examine his own work, and then he shall have boasting in himself alone, and not in another.
[5] For each one shall bear his own burden.
[6] And let him who is instructed in the Word share in all that is good, with him who is instructing.
[7] Do not be led astray: Elohim is not mocked, for whatever a man sows, that he shall also reap.
[8] Because he who sows to his own flesh shall reap corruption from the flesh, but he who sows to the Spirit shall reap everlasting life from the Spirit.
[9] And let us not lose heart in doing good, for in due season we shall reap if we do not grow weary.
[10] So then, as we have occasion, let us do good to all, especially to those who are of the household of the belief.
[11] See with what big letters I have written to you with my own hand!
[12] As many as wish to make a good show in the flesh, these compel you to be circumcised, only so that they should not be persecuted for the stake of Messiah.
[13] For those who are circumcised do not even watch over the Torah, but they wish to have you circumcised so that they might boast in your flesh.
[14] And for me, let it not be that I should boast except in the stake of our Master יהושע Messiah, through whom the world has been impaled to me, and I to the world.
[15] For in Messiah יהושע neither circumcision nor uncircumcision has any strength, but a renewed creature. [a]
[16] And as many as walk according to this rule, peace and compassion be upon them, and upon the Yisra'ěl of Elohim.

[5a] Some manuscripts omit *adultery*. [5b] See Qor. א 6:10. [6a] See Qor. א 7:19, Rom. 2:26-29, and Qor. ב 5:17.

17 From now on let no one trouble me, for I bear in my body the scars of the Master יהושע.

18 The favour of our Master יהושע Messiah be with your spirit, brothers. Aměn.

EPH`SIYIM

EPHESIANS

1 Sha'ul, an emissary of יהושע Messiah
by the desire of Elohim, to the set-
apart ones who are in Ephesos, and true to
Messiah יהושע:
2 Favour to you and peace from Elohim
our Father and the Master יהושע Messiah.
3 Blessed be the Elohim and Father of
our Master יהושע Messiah, who has
blessed us with every spiritual blessing in
the heavenlies in Messiah,
4 even as He chose us in Him before the
foundation of the world, that we should be
set-apart and blameless before Him, in
love, [a]
5 having previously ordained us to adoption as sons through יהושע Messiah to
Himself, according to the good pleasure of
His desire,
6 to the praise of the esteem of His favour
with which He favoured us in the Beloved,
7 in whom we have redemption through
His blood, the forgiveness of trespasses,
according to the riches of His favour,
8 which He has lavished on us in all
wisdom and insight,
9 having made known to us the secret of
His desire, according to His good pleasure
which He purposed in Him,
10 to administer at the completion of time,
to gather together in one all in Messiah,
both which are in the heavens and which
are on earth, in Him,
11 in whom also we did obtain an inheritance, being previously ordained according
to the purpose of Him working all *matters*
according to the counsel of His desire,
12 for us to be the praise of His esteem –
those having first trusted in Messiah,
13 in whom you also, having heard the
word of the truth, the Good News of your
deliverance, in whom also, having
believed, you were sealed with the Set-
apart Spirit of promise,
14 who is the pledge of our inheritance,
until the redemption of the purchased possession, to the praise of His esteem.
15 For this reason I too, having heard of
your belief in the Master יהושע and your
love for all the set-apart ones,
16 do not cease giving thanks for you,
making mention of you in my prayers,
17 that the Elohim of our Master יהושע
Messiah, the Father of esteem, would give
you a spirit of wisdom and revelation in
the knowledge of Him,
18 the eyes of your understanding [b] being
enlightened, so that you know what is the
expectation of His calling, and what are
the riches of the esteem of His inheritance
in the set-apart ones,
19 and what is the exceeding greatness of
His power toward us who are believing,
according to the working of His mighty
strength,
20 which He wrought in the Messiah when
He raised Him from the dead and seated
Him at His right hand in the heavenlies,
21 far above all rule and authority and
power and mastery, and every name that is
named, not only in this age but also in that
which is to come.
22 **And He put all under His feet,** Teh. 8:6
and gave Him to be head over all, to the
assembly,
23 which is His body, the completeness of
Him who fills all in all.

2 And you were dead in trespasses and
sins, [a]
2 in which you once walked according to
the course of this world, according to the
ruler of the authority of the air, of the spirit
that is now working in the sons of disobedience, [b]

1a See also Tas. ב 2:13. *1b* Lq. 24:45. *2a* See also v.5, as well as Mt. 8:22, Rom. 8:6, Qol. 2:13, Tim. א 5:6, Yn. א 3:14, Ḥazon 3:1. *2b* Eph. 5:6, Qol. 3:6.

3 among whom also we all once lived in
the lusts of our flesh, doing the desires of
the flesh and of the mind, and were by
nature children of wrath, as also the rest.
4 But Elohim, who is rich in compassion,
because of His great love with which He
loved us,
5 even when we were dead in trespasses,
made us alive together with Messiah – by
favour you have been saved –
6 and raised us up together, and made us
sit together in the heavenlies in Messiah
יהושע,
7 in order to show in the coming ages the
exceeding riches of His favour in kindness
toward us in Messiah יהושע.
8 For by favour you have been saved,
through belief, and that not of yourselves,
it is the gift of Elohim,
9 it is not by works, so that no one should
boast.
10 For we are His workmanship, created
in Messiah יהושע unto good works, which
Elohim prepared beforehand that we
should walk in them.
11 Therefore remember that you, once
nations [c] in the flesh, who are called 'the
uncircumcision' by what is called 'the circumcision' made in the flesh by hands,
12 that at that time you were without
Messiah, excluded from the citizenship of
Yisra'ěl and strangers from the covenants
of promise, having no expectation and
without Elohim in the world.
13 But now in Messiah יהושע you who
once were far off have been brought near
by the blood of the Messiah.
14 For He is our peace, who has made
both one, and having broken down the
partition of the barrier,
15 having abolished in His flesh the
enmity [d] – the torah of the commands in
dogma – so as to create in Himself one
renewed man from the two, thus making
peace,
16 and to completely restore to favour
both of them unto Elohim in one body
through the stake, having destroyed the
enmity by it.
17 And having come, He **brought as
Good News peace to you who were far
off, and peace to those near**. Yesh. 57:19
18 Because through Him we both have
access to the Father by one Spirit.
19 So then you are no longer strangers and
foreigners, but fellow citizens of the set-
apart ones and members of the household
of Elohim, [e]
20 having been built upon the foundation
of the emissaries and prophets, יהושע
Messiah Himself being chief corner-stone,
21 in whom all the building, being joined
together, grows into a set-apart Dwelling
Place in יהוה,
22 in whom you also are being built
together into a dwelling of Elohim in the
Spirit.

3 Because of this I, Sha'ul, *am* the prisoner of יהושע Messiah on behalf of
you nations –
2 if indeed you have heard of the administration of the favour of Elohim that was
given to me for you,
3 that by revelation was made known to
me the secret, as I wrote before briefly.
4 In reading this, then, you are able to
understand my insight into the secret of
Messiah,
5 which was not made known to the sons
of men in other generations, as it has now
been revealed by the Spirit to His set-apart
emissaries and prophets:
6 The nations to be co-heirs, united in the
same body, and partakers together [a] in the
promise in Messiah through the Good
News,
7 of which I became a servant according
to the gift of the favour of Elohim given to
me, according to the working of His
power.
8 To me, the very least of all the set-apart
ones, this favour was given, to bring the
Good News of the unsearchable riches of

2c See Qor. א 12:2. *2d* Also see Qol. 2:14, 20; Ma. 11:1-3. *2e* See Rom. 11:17-24, Yesh. 14:1. *3a* See Rom. 11:17-24, Yesh. 14:1.

Messiah among the nations,

9 and to make all see how this secret is administered, which for ages past has been hidden in Elohim who created all through יהושע Messiah, [b]

10 so that now, through the assembly, the many-sided wisdom of Elohim might be known to the principalities and authorities in the heavenlies,

11 according to the everlasting purpose which He made in Messiah יהושע our Master,

12 in whom we have boldness and access, with reliance, through belief in Him.

13 I pray therefore, that you do not lose heart at my pressures on your behalf, which is your esteem.

14 For this reason I bow my knees to the Father of our Master יהושע Messiah,

15 from whom all fatherhood [c] in the heavens and earth is named,

16 in order that He might give you, according to the riches of His esteem by power, to be strengthened in the inner man, through His Spirit,

17 that the Messiah might dwell in your hearts [d] through belief – having become rooted and grounded in love,

18 in order that you might be strengthened to firmly grasp, with all the set-apart ones, what is the width and length and depth and height,

19 to know the love of Messiah which surpasses knowledge, in order that you might be filled to all the completeness of Elohim.

20 And to Him who is able to do exceedingly above what we ask or think, according to the power that is working in us,

21 to Him be esteem in the assembly by Messiah יהושע unto all generations, for ever and ever. Amĕn.

4

I call upon you therefore, I the prisoner of the Master, to walk worthily of the calling with which you were called,

2 with all humility and meekness, with patience, bearing with one another in love,

3 being eager to guard the unity of the Spirit in the bond of peace –

4 one body and one Spirit, as you also were called in one expectation of your calling,

5 one Master, one belief, one immersion,

6 one Elohim and Father of all, who is above all, [a] and through all, and in you all.

7 But to each one of us favour was given according to the measure of the gift of Messiah.

8 That is why it says, **"When He went up on high, He led captivity captive, and gave gifts to men."** Teh. 68:18

9 But what does "He went up" mean, except that He also first went down into the lower parts of the earth?

10 He who went down is also the One who went up far above all the heavens, to fill all.

11 And He Himself gave some as emissaries, and some as prophets, and some as evangelists, and some as shepherds and teachers

12 for the perfecting of the set-apart ones, to the work of service to a building up of the body of the Messiah,

13 until we all come to the unity of the belief and of the knowledge of the Son of Elohim, to a perfect man, to the measure of the stature of the completeness of Messiah,

14 so that we should no longer be children, tossed and borne about by every wind of teaching, by the trickery of men, in cleverness, unto the craftiness of leading astray, [b]

15 but, maintaining the truth in love, we grow up in all respects into Him who is the head, Messiah,

16 from whom the entire body, joined and knit together by what every joint supplies, according to the working by which each part does its share, causes growth of the body for the building up of itself in love.

17 So this I say, and witness in the Master, that you should no longer walk as the nations walk, [c] in the futility of their mind,

18 having been darkened in their under-

3b See Yn. 1:3. *3c* Or *lineage*, or *paternal descent*. *3d* See Gal. 2:20. *4a* See Mq. 12:32,34, Cor. א 8:6, Tim. א 2:5, Mq. 12:29-34. *4b* See 5:6, also Qor. ב 10:5, Qor. ב 11:3-14, Gal. 1:6-9, Tim. ב 3:1-8, Tim. ב 4:2-4, Kĕpha ב 2:2-22, Yehuḏ. vv. 10-19. *4c* See Qor. א 12:2, and Yirm. 10:2.

standing, having been estranged from the
life of Elohim, because of the ignorance
that is in them, because of the hardness of
their heart,
19 who, having become callous, have
given themselves up to indecency, to work
all uncleanness with greediness.
20 But you have not so learned Messiah,
21 if indeed you have heard Him and were
taught by Him, as truth is in יהושע:
22 that you put off – with regard to your
former behaviour – the old man, being corrupted according to the desires of the
deceit,
23 and to be renewed in the spirit of your
mind,
24 and that you put on the renewed man [d]
which was created according to Elohim, in
righteousness and set-apartness of the
truth.
25 Therefore, having put off the false,
**speak truth, each one with his neigh-
bour,** Zek. 8:16 for we are members of one
another.
26 **"Be wroth, but do not sin."** Teh. 4:4 Do
not let the sun go down on your rage, [e]
27 nor give place to the devil.
28 Let him who stole steal no more, but
rather let him labour, working with his
hands what is good, so that he has *somewhat* to share with those in need.
29 Let no corrupt word come out of your
mouth, but only such as is good for the use
of building up, so as to impart what is
pleasant to the hearers.
30 And do not grieve the Set-apart Spirit
of Elohim, by whom you were sealed for
the day of redemption.
31 Let all bitterness, and wrath, and displeasure, and uproar, and slander be put
away from you, along with all evil.
32 And be kind towards one another,
tenderhearted, forgiving one another, as
Elohim also forgave you in Messiah.

5 Become, then, imitators of Elohim as
beloved children.
2 And walk in love, as Messiah also has
loved us, and gave Himself for us, a gift
and an offering to Elohim for a sweet-
smelling fragrance.
3 But whoring and all uncleanness, or
greed of gain, let it not even be named
among you, as is proper among set-apart
ones –
4 neither filthiness, nor foolish talking,
nor coarse jesting, which are not fitting,
but rather thanksgiving.
5 For this you know, that no one who
whores, nor unclean one, nor one greedy of
gain, who is an idolater, has any inheritance in the reign of Messiah and Elohim.
6 Let no one deceive you with empty
words, [a] for because of these the wrath of
Elohim comes upon the sons of disobedience.
7 Therefore do not become partakers
with them.
8 For you were once darkness, [b] but now
you are light in the Master. Walk as children of light –
9 for the fruit of the Spirit [c] is in all
goodness, and righteousness, and truth –
10 proving what is well-pleasing to the
Master.
11 And have no fellowship with the fruitless works of darkness, but rather convict [d]
them.
12 For it is a shame even to speak of what
is done by them in secret.
13 But all *matters* being convicted [d] are
manifested by the light, for whatever is
manifested is light.
14 That is why He says, **"Wake up, you
who sleep,** Yesh. 26:19 and arise from the
dead, and Messiah shall shine on you."
15 See then that you walk exactly, not as
unwise, but as wise,
16 redeeming the time, because the days
are wicked.
17 So then do not be foolish, but understand what the desire of יהוה is.
18 And do not be drunk with wine, in
which is loose behaviour, but be filled with
the Spirit,
19 speaking to each other in psalms and

4d See Rom. 8:1. *4e* Deḇ. 24:15 *5a* See 4:14. *5b* See 2:2, 4:18, Qol. 3:7.
5c See Pilip. 1:11. *5d* See Yn. 16:8.

songs of praise and spiritual songs, singing and striking the strings in your heart to the Master,

20 giving thanks always for all to Elohim the Father, in the Name of our Master יהושע Messiah,

21 subjecting yourselves to each other in the fear [e] of Elohim.

22 Wives, subject yourselves to your own husbands, as to the Master.

23 Because the husband is head of the wife, as also the Messiah is head of the assembly, and He is Saviour of the body.

24 But as the assembly is subject to Messiah, so also let the wives be to their own husbands in every respect.

25 Husbands, love your wives, as Messiah also did love the assembly and gave Himself for it,

26 in order to set it apart and cleanse it with the washing of water by the Word, [f]

27 in order to present it to Himself a splendid assembly, not having spot or wrinkle or any of this sort, but that it might be set-apart and blameless.

28 In this way husbands ought to love their own wives as their own bodies. He who loves his wife loves himself.

29 For no one ever hated his own flesh, but feeds and cherishes it, as also the Master does the assembly.

30 Because we are members of His body, of His flesh and of His bones.

31 **"For this cause a man shall leave his father and mother and be joined to his wife, and the two shall become one flesh."** Ber. 2:24

32 This secret is great, but I speak concerning Messiah and the assembly.

33 However, you too, everyone, let each one love his own wife as himself, and let the wife see that she fears her husband.

6

Children, obey your parents in the Master, for this is right.

2 **"Respect your father and mother,"** which is the first command with promise,

3 **in order that it might be well with you, and you might live long on the earth."** Shem. 20:12, Deb. 5:16

4 And you, fathers, do not provoke your children, but bring them up in the instruction and admonition of the Master.

5 Servants, obey your masters according to the flesh, with fear and trembling, in sincerity of heart, as to Messiah;

6 not with eye-service as men-pleasers, but as servants of Messiah, doing the desire of Elohim from the inner self, [a]

7 rendering service with pleasure, as to the Master, and not to men,

8 knowing that whatever good anyone does, he shall receive the same from the Master, whether he is slave or free.

9 And, masters, do the same to them, refrain from threatening, knowing that your own Master also is in the heavens, and there is no partiality with Him.

10 For the rest, my brothers, be strong in the Master and in the mightiness of His strength.

11 Put on the complete armour of Elohim, for you to have power to stand against the schemes of the devil.

12 Because we do not wrestle against flesh and blood, but against principalities, against authorities, against the world-rulers of the darkness of this age, against spiritual *matters* of wickedness in the heavenlies.

13 Because of this, take up the complete armour of Elohim, so that you have power to withstand in the wicked day, and having done all, to stand.

14 Stand, then, **having girded your waist with truth,** Yesh. 11:5 and having **put on the breastplate of righteousness,** Yesh. 59:17

15 and having fitted your **feet with the preparation of the Good News of peace;** Yesh. 52:7

16 above all, having taken up the shield of belief with which you shall have power to quench all the burning arrows of the wicked one.

17 Take also the **helmet of deliverance,** Yesh. 59:17 and the sword of the Spirit, which is the Word of Elohim,

18 praying at all times, with all prayer and supplication in the Spirit, watching in all

5e See Shem. 20:20. *5f* Ḥazon 19:8-9. *6a* Rom. 6:16-23.

perseverance and supplication for all the
set-apart ones;
[19] also for me, that a word might be given
to me in the opening of my mouth, to be
bold in making known the secret of the
Good News,
[20] for which I am an envoy in chains, that
in it I might speak boldly, as I should
speak.
[21] Now, in order that you also might know
about me, how I am doing, Tuchikos, a
beloved brother and trustworthy servant in
the Master, shall make all *matters* known
to you,
[22] whom I did send to you for this same
purpose, so that you know about us, and
might encourage your hearts.
[23] Peace to the brothers, and love, with
belief, from Elohim the Father and the
Master יהושע Messiah.
[24] Favour be with all those who love our
Master יהושע Messiah, undecayingly!
Amĕn.

PILIPIYIM

PHILLIPPIANS

1 Sha'ul and Timotiyos, servants of
יהושע Messiah, to all the set-apart
ones in Messiah יהושע who are in
Philippi, with the overseers and attendants:
2 Favour to you and peace from Elohim
our Father and the Master יהושע Messiah.
3 I thank my Elohim in all my remembrance of you.
4 In all my prayers for all of you, I
always pray with joy,
5 for your fellowship in the Good News
from the first day until now,
6 being persuaded of this, that He
who has begun a good work in you shall
perfect [a] it until the day of יהושע Messiah.
7 It is right for me to think this of you all,
because I have you in my heart, all of you
being sharers of the favour with me, both
in my chains and in the defence and confirmation of the Good News.
8 For Elohim is my witness, how I long
for you all with the affection of יהושע
Messiah.
9 And this I pray, that your love might
extend more and more in knowledge and
all discernment,
10 for you to examine the *matters* that
differ, in order to be sincere, and not stumbling, until the day of Messiah,
11 being filled with the fruit of righteousness, [b] through יהושע Messiah, to the
esteem and praise of Elohim.
12 And I wish you to know, brothers, that
what has befallen me has turned out for the
advancement of the Good News,
13 so that it has become known to all the
palace guard, and to all the rest, that my
chains are in Messiah;
14 and most of the brothers, trusting in the
Master because of my chains, are much
more bold to fearlessly speak the word.
15 Some indeed proclaim Messiah even
from envy and strife, but some also out of
pleasure –
16 the former announce Messiah from
selfish ambition, not sincerely, thinking to
add distress to my chains,
17 but the latter out of love, knowing that I
am appointed for the defence of the Good
News.
18 What then? Only that in every way,
whether in pretence or in truth, Messiah is
announced. And in this I rejoice, in fact, I
shall rejoice.
19 For I know that this shall turn out for
my deliverance [c] through your prayer and
the supply of the Spirit of יהושע Messiah,
20 according to my intense longing and
anticipation that I shall not be ashamed at
all, but that with all boldness, as always, so
now also Messiah shall be made great in
my body, whether by life or by death.
21 For to me, to live is Messiah, and to die
is gain.
22 And if to live in the flesh is to me a
fruit of work, then what shall I choose? I
do not know.
23 For I am pressed down by the two, having a desire to depart and be with Messiah,
which is much better,
24 but to remain in the flesh is more necessary for your sake.
25 And being persuaded of this, I know
that I shall stay and continue with you all,
for your progress and joy of belief,
26 so that your boasting might overflow in
יהושע Messiah on account of me, through
my coming to you again.
27 Only, behave yourselves worthily of
the Good News of Messiah, in order that
whether I come and see you or am absent, I
hear about you, that you stand fast in one
spirit, with one being, striving together for
the belief of the Good News,

1a See Mt. 5:48. *1b* Mt. 3:8-10, Rom. 6:22, Rom. 14:17, Qor. ב 9:10, Eph. 5:9, Gal. 5:22, Qol. 1:10, Iḇ`rim 12:11, Ya'aqoḇ 3:18. *1c* Iyoḇ 13:16

28 without being frightened in any way by
those who oppose, which to them truly is a
proof of destruction, but to you of deliverance, and that from Elohim.
29 Because to you it has been given as a
favour, on behalf of Messiah, not only to
believe in Him, but also to suffer for His
sake,
30 having the same struggle which you
saw in me, and now hear to be in me.

2 If, then, there is any encouragement in
Messiah, if any comfort of love, if any
fellowship of Spirit, if any affection and
compassion,
2 make my joy complete by being of the
same mind, having the same love, one in
being and of purpose,
3 doing none at all through selfishness or
self-conceit, but in humility consider others better than yourselves.
4 Each one should look out not only for
his own interests, but also for the interests
of others.
5 For, let this mind be in you which was
also in Messiah יהושע,
6 who, being in the form of Elohim, did
not regard equality with Elohim a matter to
be grasped,
7 but emptied Himself, taking the form of
a servant, and came to be in the likeness of
men.
8 And having been found in fashion as a
man, He humbled Himself and became
obedient unto death, death even of a stake.
9 Elohim, therefore, has highly exalted
Him and given Him the Name [a] which is
above every name,
10 that at the Name of יהושע **every knee
should bow**, of those in heaven, and of
those on earth, and of those under the
earth,
11 **and every tongue should confess**
Yesh. 45:23 that יהושע Messiah is Master, to
the esteem of Elohim the Father.
12 So that, my beloved, as you always
obeyed – not only in my presence, but now
much rather in my absence – work out
your own deliverance with **fear and trembling**, Teh. 2:11
13 for it is Elohim who is working in you
both to desire and to work for *His* good
pleasure.
14 Do all *matters* without grumblings and
disputings,
15 in order that you be blameless and
faultless, children of Elohim without blemish in the midst of a **crooked and perverse
generation**, Deb. 32:5 among whom you
shine as lights in the world,
16 holding on to the Word of life, for a
boast to me in the day of Messiah, that I
have not run in vain or laboured in vain.
17 In fact, even if I am being poured out as
a drink offering on the offering and service
of your belief, I am glad and rejoice with
you all.
18 So you too should be glad and rejoice
with me.
19 But I trust in the Master יהושע to send
Timotiyos to you shortly, so that I too am
encouraged by news from you.
20 For I have no one *else* of the same
mind, who takes a genuine interest in your
welfare.
21 For all seek their own *interests*, not
those of Messiah יהושע.
22 But you know he has proven himself,
that as a son with his father he served with
me for the Good News.
23 So I expect to send him as soon as I see
how it goes with me,
24 and I trust in the Master that I myself
shall also come shortly.
25 But I thought it necessary to send
to you Epaphroditos, my brother, fellow
worker, and fellow soldier, and your emissary and servant to my need,
26 since he was longing for you all, and
being troubled because you had heard that
he was sick.
27 For indeed he was sick, near to death,
but Elohim had compassion on him, and
not only on him but on me as well, lest I
should have sadness upon sadness.
28 Therefore I sent him more eagerly, so
that on seeing him again you might rejoice,
and I be less sad.
29 Receive him therefore in the Master
with all joy, and hold such as he in esteem,
30 because for the work of Messiah he was
near death, risking his life, to fill up what

was lacking in your service toward me.

3 For the rest, my brothers, rejoice in יהוה. To write the same *matters* to you is truly no trouble to me, and for you it is safe.

2 Look out for dogs, look out for the evil workers, look out for the mutilation!

3 For we are the circumcision, who are serving Elohim in the Spirit, and boasting in Messiah יהושע, and do not trust in the flesh,

4 though I too might have trust in the flesh. If anyone else thinks to trust in the flesh, I more –

5 circumcised the eighth day, of the race of Yisra'ěl, of the tribe of Binyamin, a Hebrew of Hebrews, according to Torah a Pharisee,

6 according to ardour, persecuting the assembly; according to righteousness that is in the law, having become blameless.

7 But what might have been a gain to me, I have counted as loss, because of Messiah.

8 What is more, I even count all to be loss because of the excellence of the knowledge of Messiah יהושע my Master, for whom I have suffered the loss of all, and count them as refuse, in order to gain Messiah,

9 and be found in Him, not having my own righteousness, which is of the law, but that which is through belief in Messiah, the righteousness which is from Elohim on the basis of belief,

10 to know Him, and the power of His resurrection, and the fellowship of His sufferings, being conformed to His death,

11 if somehow I might attain to the resurrection from the dead.

12 Not that I have already received, or already been perfected, but I press on, to lay hold of that for which Messiah יהושע has also laid hold of me.

13 Brothers, I do not count myself to have laid hold of it yet, but only this: forgetting what is behind and reaching out for what lies ahead,

14 I press on toward the goal for the prize of the high calling of Elohim in Messiah יהושע.

15 As many, then, as are perfect, should have this mind. And if you think differently in any respect, Elohim shall also reveal this to you.

16 But to what we have *already* attained – walk by the same rule, be of the same mind.

17 Become joint imitators of me, brothers, and look at those who so walk, as you have us for a pattern.

18 For many – of whom I have often told you, and now say to you even weeping – walk *as* enemies of the stake of Messiah.

19 Their end is destruction, their mighty one is their stomach, and their esteem is in their shame – they mind the earthly.

20 For our citizenship is in the heavens, from which we also eagerly wait for the Saviour, the Master יהושע Messiah,

21 who shall change our lowly body, to be conformed to His esteemed body, according to the working by which He is able even to bring all under His control.

4 So then, my brothers, beloved and longed-for, my joy and crown, stand firm in the Master, beloved.

2 I appeal to Euodia and I appeal to Suntuche to be of the same mind in the Master.

3 And I also ask you, true companion, help these women who laboured with me in the Good News, with Qlemes also, and the rest of my fellow workers, whose names are in the Book of Life.

4 Rejoice in יהוה always, again I say, rejoice!

5 Let your gentleness be known to all men. The Master is near.

6 Do not worry at all, but in every *matter*, by prayer and petition, with thanksgiving, let your requests be made known to Elohim.

7 And the peace of Elohim, which surpasses all understanding, shall guard your hearts and minds through Messiah יהושע.

8 For the rest, brothers, whatever is true, whatever is noble, whatever is righteous, whatever is clean, whatever is lovely, whatever is of good report, if there is any uprightness and if there is any praise –

think on these.
9 And what you have learned and
received and heard and saw in me, practise
these, and the Elohim of peace shall be
with you.
10 And I rejoiced in יהוה greatly that now
at last your concern for me has revived
again – though you were concerned, but
had no chance.
11 Not that I speak concerning need, for I
have learned to be content in whatever
state I am.
12 I know what it is to be humbled, and I
know what it is to have in excess. In any
and every *situation* I have learned both to
be filled, and to be hungry, both to have in
excess, and to be in need.
13 I have strength to do all, through
Messiah [a] who empowers me.
14 Yet you did well in sharing in my
pressure.
15 And you know too, Philippians, that in
the beginning of the Good News, when I
went out from Makedonia, no assembly
shared with me concerning giving and
receiving, except you only,
16 because, even in Thessalonike you sent
to my need, once and twice.
17 Not that I seek the gift, but I seek the
fruit that is multiplying to your account.
18 Indeed I have all and more than
enough. I have been filled, having received
from Epaphroditos what you sent, **a sweet-
smelling fragrance**, [Shem. 29:18] [b] an acceptable offering, well-pleasing to Elohim.
19 And my Elohim shall fill all your need
according to His riches in esteem by
Messiah יהושע.
20 And to our Elohim and Father be
esteem forever and ever. Amĕn.
21 Greet every set-apart one in Messiah
יהושע. The brothers with me greet you.
22 All the set-apart ones greet you, but
most of all those of Caesar's household.
23 The favour of our Master יהושע
Messiah be with you all. Amĕn.

4a Yn. 15:5, Qor. ב 3:5-6, Qor. ב 12:9, Eph. 3:20, Pilip. 2:13, Iḇ`rim 13:20-21, Yn. א 4:4.
4b Qor. ב 2:14, 15, Eph. 5:2

QOLASIM

COLOSSIANS

1 Sha'ul, an emissary of יהושע Messiah by the desire of Elohim, and Timotiyos our brother,

2 to the set-apart ones in Colosse, and true brothers in Messiah: Favour to you and peace from Elohim our Father and the Master יהושע Messiah.

3 We give thanks to the Elohim and Father of our Master יהושע Messiah, praying always for you,

4 having heard of your belief in Messiah יהושע and of your love for all the set-apart ones,

5 because of the expectation that is laid up for you in the heavens, of which you heard before in the word of the truth of the Good News,

6 which has come to you, as also in all the world it is bearing fruit and growing, as also among you, since the day you heard and knew the favour of Elohim in truth,

7 as you also learned from Epaphras, our beloved fellow servant, who is a true servant of Messiah on your behalf,

8 who also declared to us your love in the Spirit.

9 That is also why we, from the day we heard, have not ceased praying for you, and asking that you be filled with the knowledge of His desire in all wisdom and spiritual understanding,

10 to walk worthily of the Master, pleasing all, bearing fruit in every good work and increasing in the knowledge of Elohim,

11 being empowered with all power, according to the might of His esteem, for all endurance and patience with joy,

12 giving thanks to the Father who has made us fit to share in the inheritance of the set-apart ones in the light,

13 who has delivered us from the authority of darkness [a] and transferred us into the reign of the Son of His love,

14 in whom we have redemption through His blood, the forgiveness of sins,

15 who is the likeness of the invisible Elohim, the first-born of all creation. [b]

16 Because in Him were created all that are in the heavens and that are on earth, visible and invisible, whether thrones or rulerships or principalities or authorities – all have been created through Him and for Him. [c]

17 And He is before all, and in Him all hold together.

18 And He is the Head of the body, the assembly, who is the beginning, the first-born from the dead, that He might become the One who is first in all.

19 Because in Him all the completeness was well pleased to dwell,

20 and through Him to completely restore to favour all unto Himself, whether on earth or in the heavens, having made peace through the blood of His stake.

21 And you, who once were estranged and enemies in the mind by wicked works, but now He has completely restored to favour

22 in the body of His flesh through death, to present you set-apart, and blameless, and unreprovable before Him,

23 if indeed you continue in the belief, founded and steadfast, and are not moved away from the expectation of the Good News which you heard, which was proclaimed to every creature under the heaven, of which I, Sha'ul, became a servant,

24 who now rejoice in my sufferings for you, and fill up in my flesh what is lacking in Messiah's afflictions, for the sake of His Body, which is the assembly,

25 of which I became a servant according to the administration of Elohim which was given to me for you, to fill the word of Elohim,

26 the secret which has been hidden from ages and from generations, but now has been revealed to His set-apart ones,

1a Lq. 11:35, Yn. 8:12, Yn. 12:46-50, Ma. 26:18, Eph. 5:8. *1b* Iḇ`rim 1:6, Ḥazon 3:14. *1c* Yn. 1:3.

27 to whom Elohim desired to make
known what are the riches of the esteem of
this secret among the nations: which is
Messiah in you, the expectancy of esteem,
28 whom we announce, warning every
man and teaching every man in all wisdom, in order to present every man perfect
in Messiah יהושע,
29 for which I also labour, striving according to the working of Him who works in
me in power.

2 For I wish you to know what a great
struggle I have for you and those in
Laodikeia, and for as many as have not
seen my face in the flesh,
2 in order that their hearts might be
encouraged, being knit together in love,
and to all riches of the entire confirmation
of understanding, to a true knowledge of
the secret of Elohim, and of the Father, and
of the Messiah,
3 in whom are hidden all the treasures of
wisdom and knowledge. [a]
4 And this I say, so that no one deceives
you with enticing words.
5 For though I am absent in the flesh, yet
I am with you in spirit, rejoicing to see
your good order and the steadfastness of
your belief in Messiah.
6 Therefore, as you accepted Messiah
יהושע the Master, walk in Him,
7 having been rooted and built up in Him,
and established in the belief, as you were
taught, overflowing in it with thanksgiving.
8 See to it that no one makes a prey of
you through philosophy and empty deceit,
according to the tradition of men, according to the elementary matters of the
world, [b] and not according to Messiah.
9 Because in Him dwells all the completeness of Elohim-ness bodily,
10 and you have been made complete in
Him, who is the Head of all principality
and authority.
11 In Him you were also circumcised with
a circumcision not made with hands, in the
putting off of the body of the sins of the
flesh, by the circumcision of Messiah,
12 having been buried with Him in immersion, in which you also were raised with
Him through the belief in the working of
Elohim, who raised Him from the dead.
13 And you, being dead in your trespasses [c] and the uncircumcision of your
flesh, He has made alive together with
Him, having forgiven you all trespasses,
14 having blotted out that which was written by hand against us – by the dogmas [d] –
which stood against us. And He has taken
it out of the way, having nailed it to the
stake.
15 Having stripped the principalities and
the authorities, He made a public display
of them, having prevailed over them in it.
16 Let no one therefore judge you in
eating or in drinking, or in respect of a
festival or a new moon or Sabbaths –
17 which are a shadow of what is to come
– but the Body of the Messiah. [e]
18 Let no one deprive you of the prize, one
who takes delight in false humility and
worship of messengers, taking his stand on
what he has not seen, puffed up by his
fleshly mind,
19 and not holding fast to the Head, from
whom all the Body – nourished and knit
together by joints and ligaments – grows
with the growth of Elohim.
20 If, then, you died with Messiah from
the elementary matters [f] of the world, why,
as though living in the world, do you subject yourselves to dogmas: [d]
21 "Do not touch, do not taste, do not
handle" –
22 which are all to perish with use –
according to the **commands and teachings of men**? Yesh. 29:13 [g]
23 These indeed have an appearance of
wisdom in self-imposed worship, humiliation and harsh treatment of the body – of
no value at all, *only* for satisfaction of the
flesh.

2a Yesh. 11:2, Qol. 2:9. *2b* See v. 20, and Gal. 4:3 & 9. *2c* Eph. 2:1. *2d* Dogmas - also see v. 20 and Eph. 2:15 .
2e The Body of Messiah is to give ruling on all matters, not the outsiders! See also Mt. 18:15-20. *2f* See v. 8, and Gal. 4:3 & 9. *2g* See also Mt. 15:8-9, Mq. 7:6-7.

3 If, then, you were raised with
Messiah, seek the *matters* which are
above, where Messiah is, **seated at the
right hand of Elohim**. Teh. 110:1
2 Mind the *matters* above, not those on
the earth.
3 For you have died, and your life has
been hidden with Messiah in Elohim.
4 When the Messiah, who is our life, is
manifested, then you also shall be manifested with Him in esteem.
5 Therefore put to death your members
which are on the earth: whoring, uncleanness, passion, evil desire and greed of gain,
which is idolatry.
6 Because of these the wrath of Elohim is
coming upon the sons of disobedience, [a]
7 in which you also once walked when
you lived in them.
8 But now, also put off all these: displeasure, wrath, evil, blasphemy, filthy talk
from your mouth.
9 Do not lie to each other, since you have
put off the old man [b] with his practices,
10 and have put on the new one who is
renewed in knowledge according to the
likeness of Him who created him,
11 where there is not Greek and Yehuḏi,
circumcised and uncircumcised, foreigner,
Scythian, slave, free, but Messiah is all,
and in all.
12 Therefore, as chosen ones of Elohim,
set-apart and beloved, put on compassion,
kindness, humbleness of mind, meekness,
patience,
13 bearing with one another, and forgiving
each other if anyone has a complaint
against another, indeed, as Messiah forgave you so also should you.
14 But above all these *put on* love, which
is a bond of the perfection.
15 And let the peace of Elohim rule in
your hearts, to which indeed you were
called in one Body, and be filled with
thanks.
16 Let the Word of Messiah [c] dwell in you
richly, teaching and admonishing one
another in all wisdom, singing with pleasure in your hearts to the Master in psalms
and songs of praise and spiritual songs.
17 And whatever you do in word or deed,
do all in the Name of the Master יהושע,
giving thanks to Elohim the Father through
Him.
18 Wives, subject yourselves to your own
husbands, as is proper in the Master.
19 Husbands, love your wives and do not
be bitter toward them.
20 Children, obey your parents in all, for
this is well-pleasing to the Master.
21 Fathers, do not provoke your children,
lest they become discouraged.
22 Servants, obey your masters according
to the flesh in all respects, not with eye-
service, as men-pleasers, but in sincerity of
heart, fearing Elohim.
23 And whatever you do, do it heartily, as
to the Master and not to men,
24 knowing that from the Master you shall
receive the reward of the inheritance. It is
the Master, Messiah, you serve.
25 But he who does wrong shall be repaid
for the wrong which he has done, and there
is no partiality.

4 Masters, give your servants what is
righteous and fair, knowing that you
also have a Master in the heavens.
2 Continue in prayer, watching therein,
with thanksgiving,
3 praying at the same time also for us,
that Elohim would open to us a door for
the word, to speak the secret of Messiah,
for which I am also in chains,
4 so that I make it clear, as I should
speak.
5 Walk in wisdom toward those who are
outside, redeeming the time.
6 Let your word always be with favour,
seasoned with salt, so that you know how
you ought to answer each one.
7 Tuchikos, who is a beloved brother, a
true servant, and a fellow servant in the
Master, shall give you all the news about
me.
8 I am sending him to you for this purpose, to know your circumstances and to
encourage your hearts,

3a Eph. 2:2, Eph. 5:6. *3b* Rom. 6:6, Eph. 4:22. *3c* See Yn. 12:48, Deḇ. 18:19, Ḥazon 19:13.

9 with Onesimos, a true and beloved
brother, who is one of you. They shall let
you know all the news here.
10 Aristarchos my fellow prisoner greets
you, with Marqos the relative of Barnaḇa
about whom you received instructions: if
he comes to you, welcome him,
11 also Yeshua who is called Justus. These
are my only fellow workers for the reign of
Elohim who are of the circumcision, who
were to me a comfort.
12 Epaphras, who is one of you, a servant
of Messiah, greets you, always wrestling
for you in prayers, so that you stand
perfect [a] and complete in all the desire of
Elohim.
13 For I bear him witness that he has a
deep concern for you, and for those who
are in Laodikeia and those in Hierapolis.
14 Luke the beloved physician and Demas
greet you.
15 Greet the brothers in Laodikeia, and
Numpha and the assembly that is in his
house.
16 And when this letter is read among you,
see that it is read also in the assembly of
the Laodikeians, and that you likewise
read the letter from Laodikeia.
17 And say to Archippos, "See to the
service which you have received in the
Master, so that you complete it."
18 This greeting is in my own hand –
Sha'ul. Remember my chains. Favour be
with you. Amĕn.

4a Mt. 5:48.

TAS`LONIQIM ALEPH

1 THESSALONIANS

1 Sha'ul, and Silas, and Timotiyos, to
the assembly of the Thessalonians in
Elohim the Father and the Master יהושע
Messiah: Favour to you and peace from
Elohim our Father and the Master יהושע
Messiah.
2 We give thanks to Elohim always for
you all, making mention of you in our
prayers,
3 remembering without ceasing your
work of the belief, and the labour of love,
and the endurance of the expectation in our
Master יהושע Messiah in the presence of
our Elohim and Father,
4 knowing, brothers beloved by Elohim,
that you were chosen.
5 Because our Good News did not come
to you in word only, but also in power, and
in the Set-apart Spirit and in entire confirmation, as you know what kind of men we
were among you for your sake.
6 And you became imitators of us and of
the Master, having received the word in
much pressure, with joy of the Set-apart
Spirit,
7 so that you became an example to all
who believe in Makedonia and Achaia.
8 For from you the word of the Master
has sounded forth, not only in Makedonia
and Achaia, but also in every place your
belief toward Elohim has gone out, so that
it is unnecessary for us to say whatever.
9 For they themselves report what kind of
reception we had with you, and how you
turned to Elohim from idols, to serve the
living and true Elohim,
10 and to wait for His Son from the heavens, whom He raised from the dead,
יהושע, who is delivering us from the
wrath to come.

2 For you yourselves know, brothers,
that our coming to you was not in
vain.
2 But having suffered before and having
been mistreated at Philippi, as you know,
we were bold in our Elohim to speak to
you the Good News of Elohim in much
struggle.
3 For the appeal we make does not come
from delusion, nor from uncleanness, nor
from deceit.
4 But as we have been approved by
Elohim to be entrusted with the Good
News, so we speak, not as pleasing men,
but Elohim who proves our hearts.
5 For we never came with a word of
flattery, as you know, nor with a cloak for
greed – Elohim is witness –
6 nor were we looking for praise from
men, not from you nor from others, though
we could have been a burden to you, as
emissaries of Messiah.
7 But we were gentle in your midst, like a
nursing mother warmly loving her own
children.
8 So, having a tender affection for you,
we were well pleased to share with you not
only the Good News of Elohim, but also
our own lives, because you have become
beloved to us.
9 For you remember, brothers, our toil
and hardship, for labouring night and day,
in order not to burden any of you, we proclaimed to you the Good News of Elohim.
10 You are witnesses, Elohim also, how
set-apart and righteously and blamelessly
we behaved ourselves among you who
believe,
11 even as you know how each one of you,
as a father to his children, encouraging and
comforting and bearing witness to you,
12 that you would walk worthily of
Elohim who is calling you into His own
reign and esteem.
13 And because of this we thank Elohim
without ceasing, that when you received
the Word of Elohim which you heard from

us, you welcomed it not as the word of men, but as it is truly, the Word of Elohim, which also works in you who believe. [a]

14 For you, brothers, became imitators of the assemblies of Elohim which are in Yehuḏah in Messiah יהושע, because you also suffered the same *treatment* from your own countrymen as they also from the Yehuḏim,

15 who killed both the Master יהושע and their own prophets, and have persecuted us, and who displease Elohim and are hostile to all men,

16 forbidding us to speak to the nations that they might be saved, so as to fill up their sins always. But the wrath has come upon them to the utmost.

17 But we, brothers, having been taken away from you for a short while – in presence, not in heart – were much more eagerly trying to see your face, with much longing.

18 We would therefore have come to you, I indeed, Sha'ul, more than once, but Satan hindered us.

19 For what is our expectation, or joy, or crown of boasting? Is it not even you, before our Master יהושע Messiah at His coming?

20 For you are our esteem and joy.

3 So, when we could no longer stand it, we thought it good to be left in Athens alone,

2 and sent Timotiyos, our brother and servant of Elohim, and our fellow worker in the Good News of Messiah, to establish you and encourage you concerning your belief,

3 that no one should be unsettled by these pressures, for you yourselves know that we are appointed to this.

4 For indeed, we did inform you beforehand, when we were with you, that we would suffer pressure, and so it came to be, as you know.

5 Because of this, when I could no longer stand it, I sent to find out about your belief, lest the trying one might have tried you, and our labour should be in vain.

6 But now that Timotiyos has come to us from you, and having brought us good news of your belief and love, and that you always have good remembrance of us, longing to see us, as we also *to see* you,

7 therefore, brothers, in all our pressure and distress we were encouraged concerning you by your belief.

8 Because we now live, if you stand fast in the Master.

9 For what thanks are we able to return to Elohim for you, for all the joy with which we rejoice for your sake in the presence of our Elohim,

10 night and day praying exceedingly, to see your face and make complete what is lacking in your belief?

11 And our Elohim and Father Himself, and our Master יהושע Messiah, direct our way to you!

12 And the Master make you increase and overflow in love to each other and to all, as we also do to you,

13 to establish your hearts blameless in set-apartness before our Elohim and Father at the coming of our Master יהושע Messiah with all His set-apart ones!

4 For the rest then, brothers, we beg you and call upon you in the Master יהושע, that as you received from us how you should walk and to please Elohim, you should excel still more,

2 for you know what commands we gave you through the Master יהושע.

3 For this is the desire of Elohim: your set-apartness! – that you should abstain from whoring,

4 that each one of you should know how to possess his own vessel in set-apartness and respect,

5 not in passion of lust, like the nations who do not know Elohim,

6 not to overstep and take advantage of his brother in this matter, because the Master is the revenger of all such, as we indeed said to you before and earnestly warned.

2a Iḇ`rim 13:21.

7 For Elohim did not call us to uncleanness, but in set-apartness.

8 Therefore he who rejects this does not reject man, but Elohim, who also gives us His Set-apart Spirit.

9 And it is not necessary to write to you about brotherly love, for you yourselves are taught by Elohim to love one another,

10 for, in fact, you do so toward all the brothers who are in all Makedonia. But we call upon you, brothers, that you do so more and more,

11 and to make it your ambition to live peaceably, and to attend to your own, and to work with your own hands, as we commanded you,

12 so that you behave decently toward those who are outside, and not be in any need.

13 Now, brothers, we do not wish you to be ignorant concerning those who have fallen asleep, lest you be sad as others who have no expectation.

14 For if we believe that יהושע died and rose again, so also Elohim shall bring with Him those who sleep [a] in יהושע.

15 For this we say to you by the word of the Master, that we, the living who are left over at the coming of the Master shall in no way go before those who are asleep.

16 Because the Master Himself shall come down from heaven with a shout, with the voice of a chief messenger, and with the trumpet of Elohim, and the dead in Messiah shall rise first.

17 Then we, the living who are left over, shall be caught away together with them in the clouds to meet the Master in the air – and so we shall always be with the Master.

18 So, then, encourage one another with these words.

5 Now, brothers, as to the times and the seasons, you do not need to be written to.

2 For you yourselves know very well that the day of יהוה comes as a thief in the night.

3 For when they say, "Peace and safety!" then suddenly destruction comes upon them, as labour pains upon a pregnant woman, and they shall not escape.

4 But you, brothers, are not in darkness, so that this Day should overtake you as a thief.

5 For you are all sons of light and sons of the day. We are not of the night nor of darkness.

6 So, then, we should not sleep, as others do, but we should watch and be sober.

7 For those who sleep, sleep at night, and those who get drunk are drunk at night.

8 But we who are of the day should be sober, putting on the **breastplate** of belief and love, and as **a helmet the expectation of deliverance**. Yesh. 59:17

9 Because Elohim did not appoint us to wrath, but to obtain deliverance through our Master יהושע Messiah,

10 who died for us, so that we, whether awake or asleep, should live together with Him.

11 Therefore encourage one another, and build up one another, as indeed you do.

12 But brothers, we beg you to know those who labour among you, and are over you in the Master and admonish you,

13 and to hold them in the highest regard in love because of their work. Be at peace among yourselves.

14 And we appeal to you, brothers, warn those who are disorderly, encourage the faint-hearted, uphold the weak, be patient with all.

15 See that no one renders evil for evil to anyone, but always pursue what is good both for yourselves and for all.

16 Rejoice always,

17 pray without ceasing,

18 in all *circumstances* give thanks, for this is the desire of Elohim in Messiah יהושע for you.

19 Do not quench the Spirit.

20 Do not despise prophecies,

21 prove them all. Hold fast what is good.

22 Keep back from every form of wickedness.

23 And the Elohim of peace Himself set

4a A euphemism for death.

you completely apart, and your entire
spirit, and being, and body - be preserved
blameless at the coming of our Master
יהושע Messiah!
24 He who calls you is trustworthy, who
also shall do it.
25 Brothers, pray for us.
26 Greet all the brothers with a set-apart
kiss.
27 I charge you by the Master that this
letter be read to all the set-apart brothers.
28 The favour of our Master יהושע
Messiah be with you. Aměn.

TAS`LONIQIM BĚT

2 THESSALONIANS

1 Sha'ul, and Silas, and Timotiyos, to
the assembly of the Thessalonians in
Elohim our Father and the Master יהושע
Messiah:
2 Favour to you and peace from Elohim
our Father and the Master יהושע Messiah.
3 We ought to give thanks to Elohim
always for you, brothers, as it is proper,
because your belief grows exceedingly,
and the love every one of you has for each
other is increasing,
4 so that we ourselves boast of you
among the assemblies of Elohim for your
endurance and belief in all your persecutions and afflictions which you are bearing,
5 clear evidence of the righteous judgment of Elohim, in order for you to be
counted worthy of the reign of Elohim, for
which you also suffer,
6 since Elohim shall rightly repay with
affliction those who afflict you,
7 and to give you who are afflicted rest
with us when the Master יהושע is revealed
from heaven with His mighty messengers,
8 in flaming fire taking vengeance on
those who do not know Elohim, and on
those who do not obey the Good News of
our Master יהושע Messiah,
9 who shall be punished with everlasting
destruction from the presence of the
Master and from the esteem of His
strength,
10 when He comes to be esteemed in His
set-apart ones and to be admired among all
those who believe in that Day, because our
witness to you was believed.
11 To this end we always pray for you that
our Elohim would count you worthy of this
calling, and complete all the good pleasure
of goodness, and the work of belief with
power,
12 so that the Name of our Master יהושע
Messiah is esteemed in you, and you in
Him, according to the favour of our
Elohim and the Master יהושע Messiah.

2 As to the coming of our Master יהושע
Messiah and our gathering together to
Him, we ask you, brothers,
2 not to become easily unsettled in mind
or troubled, either by spirit or by word or
by letter, as if from us, as if the day of יהוה
has come.
3 Let no one deceive you in any way,
because the falling away is to come first,
and the man of lawlessness [a] is to be
revealed, the son of destruction,
4 who opposes and exalts himself above
all that is called Elohim or that is worshipped, so that he sits as Elohim in the
Dwelling Place of Elohim, showing himself that he is Elohim.
5 Do you not remember that I told you
this while I was still with you?
6 And now you know what restrains, for
him to be revealed in his time.
7 For the secret of lawlessness is already
at work – only until he who now restrains
comes out of the midst.
8 And then the lawless one shall be
revealed, whom the Master **shall consume**
with the Spirit of His mouth Yesh. 11:4 and
bring to naught with the manifestation of
His coming.
9 The coming of the *lawless one* is
according to the working of Satan, with all
power and signs and wonders of falsehood,
10 and with all deceit of unrighteousness
in those perishing, because they did not
receive the love of the truth, in order for
them to be saved.
11 And for this reason Elohim sends them
a working of delusion, for them to believe
the falsehood, [b]
12 in order that all should be judged who
did not believe the truth, but have delighted in the unrighteousness.
13 But we ought to give thanks to Elohim

2a See Dan. 11:36-39. *2b* See also Yn. 9:39, Yn. 12:40, Ma. 7:42, Rom. 1:24-28.

always for you, brothers, beloved by the
Master, because Elohim from the beginning chose you to be saved – in set-apartness of Spirit, and belief in the truth [c] –
14 unto which He called you by our Good
News, for the obtaining of the esteem of
our Master יהושע Messiah.
15 So, then, brothers, stand fast and hold
the traditions which you were taught,
whether by word or by our letter.
16 And our Master יהושע Messiah Himself, and our Elohim and Father, who has
loved us and given us everlasting encouragement and good expectation, through
favour,
17 encourage your hearts and establish
you in every good word and work.

3 For the rest, brothers, pray for us, so
that the Word of יהוה spreads rapidly
and be praised, as also with you,
2 and that we might be delivered from
unreasonable and wicked men, for not all
have belief.
3 But the Master is trustworthy, who
shall establish you and guard you from the
wicked one.
4 And we trust in the Master as to you,
both that you do and shall do what we
command you.
5 And the Master direct your hearts into
the love of Elohim and into the endurance
for Messiah.
6 But we command you, brothers, in the
Name of our Master יהושע Messiah, that
you withdraw from every brother who
walks disorderly and not according to the
tradition which you received from us.
7 For you yourselves know how you
ought to imitate us, for we were not disorderly among you,
8 nor did we eat anyone's bread without
paying for it, but worked with labour and
toil night and day, in order not to burden
any of you,
9 not because we do not have authority,
but to make ourselves an example, for you
to imitate us.
10 For even when we were with you, we
commanded you this: If anyone does not
wish to work, neither let him eat.
11 For we hear of some among you walking disorderly, not working at all, but are
busybodies.
12 But we command and urge such,
through our Master יהושע Messiah, to settle down, work and eat their own bread.
13 And you, brothers, do not grow weary
in doing good.
14 And if anyone does not obey our word
in this letter, note that one, and do not keep
company with him, so that he is put to
shame.
15 However, do not regard him as an
enemy, but admonish him as a brother.
16 And the Master of peace Himself give
you peace always in every way. The
Master be with you all.
17 The greeting of Sha'ul with my own
hand, which is a sign in every letter, thus I
write.
18 The favour of our Master יהושע
Messiah be with you all. Amĕn.

2c See Eph. 1:4.

TIMOTIYOS ALEPH

1 TIMOTHY

1 Sha'ul, an emissary of יהושע Messiah, according to a command of Elohim our Saviour, and of the Master יהושע Messiah, our expectation,

2 to Timotiyos, a genuine child in the belief: Favour, compassion, peace from Elohim our Father and יהושע Messiah our Master.

3 As I appealed to you when I went into Makedonia, to remain in Ephesos, in order to command some not to teach differently,

4 nor to pay attention to fables and endless genealogies, which cause disputes rather than an administration of Elohim which is in belief.

5 Now the goal of this command is love from a clean heart, from a good conscience and a sincere belief,

6 which some, having missed *the goal*, turned aside to senseless talk,

7 wishing to be teachers of Torah, understanding neither what they say nor concerning what they strongly affirm.

8 And we know that the Torah is good if one uses it legitimately,

9 knowing this: that Torah is not laid down for a righteous being, but for the lawless and unruly, for the wicked and for sinners, for the wrong-doers and profane, for those who kill their fathers or mothers, for murderers,

10 for those who whore, for sodomites, for kidnappers, for liars, for perjurers, and for whatever else that is contrary to sound teaching,

11 according to the esteemed Good News of the blessed Elohim which was entrusted to me.

12 And I thank Messiah יהושע our Master who empowered me, because He counted me trustworthy, putting me into service,

13 me, although I was formerly a blasphemer, and a persecutor, and an insulter. But compassion was shown me because being ignorant I did it in unbelief.

14 And the favour of our Master was exceedingly increased, with belief and love which are in Messiah יהושע.

15 Trustworthy is the word and worthy of all acceptance, that Messiah יהושע came into the world to save sinners, of whom I am foremost.

16 But because of this I received compassion, so that in me first, יהושע Messiah might display all patience, as an example to those who are going to believe on Him for everlasting life.

17 Now to the Sovereign of the ages, incorruptible, invisible, to Elohim who alone is wise, be respect and esteem forever and ever. Amĕn.

18 This charge I entrust to you, son Timotiyos, according to the prophecies previously made concerning you, that by them you might wage the good campaign,

19 having belief and a good conscience, which some have thrust aside and suffered shipwreck concerning their belief.

20 Among these are Humenaios and Alexander, whom I delivered to Satan, in order to be taught not to blaspheme.

2 First of all, then, I urge that petitions, prayers, intercessions, and thanksgiving be made for all men,

2 for sovereigns and all those who are in authority, in order that we lead a calm and peaceable life in all reverence and seriousness.

3 For this is good and acceptable before Elohim our Saviour,

4 who desires all men to be saved and to come to the knowledge of the truth.

5 For there is one Elohim, [a] and one Mediator between Elohim and men, the Man Messiah יהושע,

2a Qor. א 8:6, Eph. 4:6, Mq. 12:29-34.

6 who gave Himself a ransom for all, to
be witnessed in its own seasons,
7 for which I was appointed a proclaimer
and an emissary – I am speaking the truth
in Messiah and not lying – a teacher of the
nations in belief and truth.
8 So I resolve that the men pray everywhere, lifting up hands that are set-apart,
without wrath and disputing.
9 Likewise, that the women dress
themselves becomingly, with decency and
sensibleness, not with braided hair or gold
or pearls or costly garments,
10 but with good works, [b] which is becoming for women undertaking worship of
Elohim.
11 Let a woman learn in silence, in all
subjection.
12 But I do not permit a woman to teach
or to have authority over a man, rather,
to be in silence.
13 Because Aḏam was formed first, then
Ḥawwah.
14 And Aḏam was not deceived, but the
woman, having been deceived, fell into
transgression.
15 But she shall be saved in childbearing if
they continue in belief, and love, and set-
apartness, with sensibleness.

3 Trustworthy is the word: If a man
longs for the position of an overseer,
he desires a good work.
2 An overseer, then, should be blameless,
the husband of one wife, sober, sensible,
orderly, kind to strangers, able to teach,
3 not given to wine, no brawler, but gentle, not quarrelsome, no lover of silver, [a]
4 one who rules his own house well,
having his children in subjection with all
reverence,
5 for if a man does not know how to rule
his own house, how shall he look after the
assembly of Elohim?
6 Not a new convert, lest he become
puffed up with pride and fall into the judgment of the devil.
7 And he should even have a good witness from those who are outside, lest he
fall into reproach and the snare of the
devil.
8 Likewise attendants are to be reverent,
not double-tongued, not given to much
wine, not greedy for filthy gain,
9 holding to the secret of the belief with a
clean conscience.
10 And let these also be proved first, then
let them serve, if they are unreprovable.
11 Wives in the same way: reverent, not
false accusers, sober, trustworthy in every
way.
12 Let attendants be the husbands of *only*
one wife, ruling children and their own
houses well.
13 For those who have served well as
attendants gain good standing for themselves, and much boldness in the belief
that is in Messiah יהושע.
14 I am writing you this, expecting to
come to you shortly,
15 but if I delay, that you might know how
you should behave in the House of Elohim,
which is the assembly of the living Elohim
– a *strong* support and foundation of the
truth.
16 And, beyond all question, the secret of
reverence is great – who was revealed in
the flesh, declared right in Spirit, was seen
by messengers, was proclaimed among
nations, was believed on in the world, was
taken up in esteem.

4 But the Spirit distinctly says that in
latter times some shall fall away from
the belief, paying attention to misleading
spirits, and teachings of demons,
2 speaking lies in hypocrisy, having been
branded on their own conscience,
3 forbidding to marry, *saying* to abstain
from foods which Elohim created to be
received with thanksgiving by those who
believe and know the truth.
4 Because every creature of Elohim is
good, and none is to be rejected if it is
received with thanksgiving,
5 for it is set apart by the Word of
Elohim [a] and prayer. [b]
6 If you present these *matters* to the

2b Mt. 16:27. *3a* Implying money. *4a* Way. 11 & Deḇ. 14. *4b* Qor. א 10:31.

brothers, you shall be a good servant of
יהושע Messiah, being nourished in the
words of belief and of the good teaching
which you have followed closely.
7 But refuse profane and old wives'
fables, and exercise yourself rather to
reverence.
8 For bodily exercise is profitable for a
little, but reverence is profitable for all,
having promise of the present life, and of
that which is to come.
9 Trustworthy is the word, and worthy of
all acceptance.
10 It is for this that we labour and struggle,
because we trust in the living Elohim, who
is the Saviour of all men, particularly of
those who believe.
11 Command and teach these *matters*.
12 Let no one look down on your youth,
but be an example to the believers in word,
in behaviour, in love, in spirit, in belief, in
cleanliness.
13 Until I come, give attention to reading
of Scripture, to encouragement, to teaching.
14 Do not neglect the gift that is in you,
which was given to you by prophecy with
the laying on of the hands of the elder-
hood.
15 Practise these *matters*, be in them, so
that your progress might be plain to all.
16 Pay attention to yourself and to the
teaching. Continue in them, for in doing
this you shall save both yourself and those
who hear you.

5 Do not rebuke an older man, but
appeal to him as a father, younger
ones as brothers,
2 elderly women as mothers, younger
ones as sisters, in all cleanliness.
3 Respect widows who are truly widows.
4 But if any widow has children or grandchildren, let them first learn to treat their
own house reverently, and to repay their
parents. For this is good and acceptable
before Elohim.
5 And she who is truly a widow, and left
alone, trusts in Elohim and continues in
petitions and prayers night and day.
6 But she who is living in luxury is dead
while she lives.
7 And command these *matters*, in order
for them to be blameless.
8 And if anyone does not provide for his
own, and especially for those of his household, he has denied the belief and is worse
than an unbeliever.
9 Do not enrol a widow unless she is over
sixty years of age, having been the wife
of one man,
10 well reported for good works, if she has
brought up children, if she has lodged
strangers, if she has washed the feet of the
set-apart ones, if she has assisted the
afflicted, if she has closely followed every
good work.
11 But refuse the younger widows, for
when they become headstrong against the
Messiah, they desire to marry,
12 having guilt because they set aside their
first belief.
13 Moreover, they learn to be idle, going
about from house to house, and not only
idle but also gossips and busybodies,
speaking what is improper.
14 So I resolve that the younger widows
marry, bear children, manage the house,
giving no occasion to the adversary for
reviling.
15 For already some have turned aside
after Satan.
16 If any believing man or woman has
widows, let such assist them, and do not let
the assembly be burdened, in order to
assist those who are truly widows.
17 Let the elders who rule well be counted
worthy of double respect, especially those
who labour in the word and teaching.
18 For the Scripture says, **"You shall not
muzzle an ox while it treads out the
grain,"** Deḇ. 25:4 and, **"The labourer is worthy of his wages."** Way. 19:13
19 Do not receive an accusation against an
elder except **from two or three witnesses**.
Deḇ. 17:6; 19:15
20 Reprove those who are sinning, in the
presence of all, so that the rest also might
fear.
21 I earnestly witness before Elohim and
the Master יהושע Messiah, and the chosen
messengers, that you watch over these

matters without prejudice, doing none at all with partiality.

22 Do not lay hands on anyone hastily, nor share in sins of others. Keep yourself clean.

23 No longer drink only water, but use a little wine for your stomach's sake and your frequent ailments.

24 The sins of some men are obvious, leading on to judgment, but those of some men follow later.

25 In the same way, the good works are obvious, while it is impossible to conceal those that are otherwise.

6 Let those who are servants under a yoke regard their own masters worthy of all respect, lest the Name of Elohim and His teaching be blasphemed.

2 And those who have believing masters, let them not disregard them because they are brothers, but rather serve them because they are believing and beloved ones, those receiving of the good service in return. Teach and urge these *matters*.

3 If anyone teaches differently and does not agree to the sound words, those of our Master יהושע Messiah, and to the teaching which is according to reverence,

4 he is puffed up, understanding none at all, but is sick about questionings and verbal battles from which come envy, strife, slander, wicked suspicions,

5 worthless disputes of men of corrupt minds and deprived of the truth, who think that reverence is a means of gain – withdraw from such.

6 But reverence with contentment is great gain.

7 For we brought naught into the world, and it is impossible to take any out.

8 When we have food and covering, we shall be satisfied with these.

9 But those wishing to be rich fall into trial and a snare, and into many foolish and injurious lusts which plunge men in ruin and destruction.

10 For the love of silver [a] is a root of all kinds of evil, for which some, by longing for it, have strayed from the belief, and pierced themselves through with many pains.

11 But you, O man of Elohim, flee from all this, and pursue righteousness, reverence, belief, love, endurance, meekness.

12 Fight the good fight of the belief, lay hold on everlasting life, to which you were also called and have confessed the good confession before many witnesses.

13 In the sight of Elohim who gives life to all, and of Messiah יהושע who witnessed the good confession before Pontius Pilate, I charge you:

14 that you guard the command [b] spotlessly, blamelessly, until the appearing of our Master יהושע Messiah,

15 which in His own seasons He shall reveal – the blessed and only Ruler, the Sovereign of sovereigns and Master of masters,

16 who alone has immortality, dwelling in unapproachable light, whom no one has seen or is able to see, to whom be respect and everlasting might. Aměn.

17 Charge those who are rich in this present age not to be high-minded, nor to trust in the uncertainty of riches, but in the living Elohim, who gives us richly all for enjoyment,

18 to do good, to be rich in good works, [c] to be generous, ready to share,

19 storing up for themselves a good foundation for the time to come, so that they lay hold on everlasting life.

20 O Timotiyos! Watch over that which has been entrusted to you, turning aside from the profane and empty babblings and contradictions of the falsely called 'knowledge,'

21 which some, having professed it, have missed *the goal* concerning the belief. Favour be with you. Aměn.

6a Implying money. *6b* Command (singular) often means commands, e.g. Deḇ. 17:20, Teh. 19:8. *6c* See Mt. 16:27.

TIMOTIYOS BĚT

2 TIMOTHY

1 Sha'ul, an emissary of יהושע Messiah
by the desire of Elohim, according to
the promise of life which is in Messiah
יהושע,
2 to Timotiyos, my beloved son: Favour,
compassion, peace from Elohim the
Father, and Messiah יהושע our Master.
3 I thank Elohim, whom I serve with a
clear conscience, as my forefathers did, as
I unceasingly remember you in my prayers
night and day,
4 longing to see you, as I remember your
tears, so that I might be filled with joy.
5 For I recollect the sincere belief which
is in you, which dwelt first in your grandmother Lois and your mother Eunike, and I
am persuaded is in you too.
6 For this reason I remind you to stir up
the gift of Elohim which is in you through
the laying on of my hands.
7 For Elohim has not given us a spirit of
cowardice, but of power and of love and of
self-control.
8 So do not be ashamed of the witness of
our Master, nor of me His prisoner, but
suffer hardship with me for the Good
News according to the power of Elohim,
9 who has saved us and called us with a
set-apart calling, not according to our
works, but according to His own purpose
and favour which was given to us in
Messiah יהושע before times of old,
10 but now revealed by the appearing of
our Saviour יהושע Messiah, who indeed
abolished death and brought life and incorruptibility to light through the Good News,
11 for which I was appointed a proclaimer,
and an emissary, and a teacher of the
nations.
12 For this reason I also suffer these *matters*, but I am not ashamed, for I know
whom I have believed and am persuaded
that He is able to watch over that which I
have entrusted to Him until that Day.
13 Hold the pattern of sound words which
you have heard from me, in belief and love
which are in Messiah יהושע.
14 Watch over the good deposit that was
entrusted to you, by the Set-apart Spirit
dwelling in us.
15 You know this, that all those in Asia
have turned away from me, among whom
are Phugellos and Hermogenes.
16 The Master grant compassion unto the
household of Onesiphoros, for he often
refreshed me, and was not ashamed of my
chain,
17 but when he was in Rome, he eagerly
searched for me and found me.
18 The Master grant to him to find compassion from the Master in that Day. And
you know very well how many ways he
attended to me at Ephesos.

2 You then, my son, be strong in the
favour that is in Messiah יהושע.
2 And what you have heard from me
among many witnesses, entrust these to
trustworthy men who shall be competent to
teach others as well.
3 Suffer hardship with *us* as a good soldier of יהושע Messiah.
4 No one serving as a soldier gets
involved in the affairs of this life, in order
to please *only* him who enlisted him as a
soldier.
5 And if anyone competes in a game, he
is not crowned unless he competes according to the rules.
6 The hard-working farmer ought to be
first to receive his share of the crops.
7 Think over what I say, for the Master
shall give you understanding into all this.
8 Remember that יהושע Messiah, of the
seed of Dawiḏ, was raised from the dead
according to my Good News,
9 for which I suffer hardship, as a crimi-
nal, unto chains, but the Word of Elohim is
not chained.
10 So I endure through it all for the sake
of the chosen, so that they too obtain deliverance which is in Messiah יהושע with

everlasting esteem.
11 Trustworthy is the word: For if we died
with Him, we shall also live with Him.
12 If we endure, we shall also reign with
Him. If we deny *Him*, He also shall deny
us.
13 If we are not trustworthy, He remains
trustworthy, it is impossible for Him to
deny Himself.
14 Remind them of this, earnestly witnessing before the Master, not to wage verbal
battles – which is useless – to the overthrowing of the hearers.
15 Do your utmost to present yourself
approved to Elohim, a worker who does
not need to be ashamed, rightly handling
the Word of Truth.
16 But keep away from profane, empty
babblings, for they go on to more wickedness,
17 and their word shall eat its way like
gangrene. Humenaios and Philetos are of
this sort,
18 who have missed *the goal* concerning
the truth, saying that the resurrection has
already taken place, and overthrow the
belief of some.
19 However, the solid foundation of
Elohim stands firm, having this seal, "**יהוה**
knows those who are His," Bem. 16:5 and, let
everyone who names the Name of Messiah
turn away from unrighteous-ness.
20 But in a large house there are not only
vessels of gold and silver, but also of wood
and clay, some unto value and some unto
no value.
21 If, then, anyone cleanses himself from
these *matters*, he shall be a vessel unto
value, having been set apart, of good use to
the Master, having been prepared for every
good work.
22 And flee from the lusts of youth, but
pursue righteousness, belief, love, peace
with those calling on the Master out of a
clean heart.
23 But refuse foolish and stupid questions,
knowing that they breed quarrels.
24 And a servant of the Master should not
quarrel but be gentle towards all, able to
teach, patient when wronged,
25 in meekness instructing those who are
in opposition, lest somehow Elohim gives
them repentance unto a thorough knowledge of the truth,
26 and they come to their senses, out of
the snare of the devil, having been taken
captive by him to do his desire.

3 But know this, that in the last days
hard times shall come.
2 For men shall be lovers of self, lovers
of silver,[a] boasters, proud, blasphemers,
disobedient to parents, thankless, wrongdoers,
3 unloving, unforgiving, slanderers, without self-control, fierce, haters of good,
4 betrayers, reckless, puffed up, lovers of
pleasure rather than lovers of Elohim,
5 having a form of reverence but denying
its power. [b] And turn away from these!
6 For among them are those who creep
into households and captivate silly women
loaded down with sins, led away by
various lusts,
7 always learning and never able to come
to the knowledge of the truth.
8 And as Yoḥane and Mamrě opposed
Mosheh, so do these also oppose the truth
– men of corrupt minds, found worthless
concerning the belief;
9 but they shall not go on further, for
their folly shall be obvious to all, as also
that of those men became.
10 But you did closely follow my teaching, the way of life, the purpose, the belief,
the patience, the love, the endurance,
11 the persecutions, the sufferings, which
came to me at Antioch, at Ikonion, *and* at
Lustra – what persecutions I bore. Yet out
of them all the Master delivered me.
12 And indeed, all those wishing to live
reverently in Messiah יהושע, shall be
persecuted. [c]
13 But evil men and impostors shall go on
to the worse, [d] leading astray and being led
astray.

3a Implying money. *3b* See v. 13, and also Yesh. 24:5-6, Mt. 24:12, Rom. 1:30-31, Tas. ב 2:3-11. *3c* Mt. 5:10. *3d* Mt. 24:12, Ḥazon 22:11.

14 But you, stay in what you have learned
and trusted, having known from whom you
have learned,
15 and that from a babe you have known
the Set-apart Scriptures, which are able to
make you wise for deliverance through
belief in Messiah יהושע.
16 All Scripture is breathed out by Elohim
and profitable for teaching, for reproof, for
setting straight, for instruction in righteousness,
17 that the man of Elohim might be fitted,
equipped for every good work.

4 In the sight of Elohim and the Master
יהושע Messiah, who shall judge the
living and the dead at His appearing and
His reign, I earnestly charge you:
2 Proclaim the Word! Be urgent in season, out of season. Convict, [a] warn, appeal,
with all patience and teaching.
3 For there shall be a time when they
shall not bear sound teaching, but according to their own desires, they shall heap up
for themselves teachers tickling the ear, [b]
4 and they shall indeed turn their ears
away from the truth, and be turned aside to
myths.
5 But you be sober in all *matters*, suffer
hardships, do the work of an evangelist,
accomplish your service completely.
6 For I am already being poured out, and
the time of my departure has arrived.
7 I have fought the good fight, I have
finished the race, I have guarded the belief.
8 For the rest, there is laid up for me the
crown of righteousness, which the Master,
the righteous Judge, shall give to me on
that Day, and not to me only but also to all
those loving His appearing.
9 Do your best to come to me soon,
10 for Demas, having loved this present
world, has deserted me and went to
Thessalonike, Crescens to Galatia, Titos to
Dalmatia.
11 Luqas alone is with me. Take Marqos
and bring him with you, for he is of good
use to me for service.
12 And Tuchikos I have sent to Ephesos.
13 Bring the cloak that I left with Karpos
at Troas when you come, and the books,
especially the parchments.
14 Alexander the coppersmith did many
evils to me. The Master shall **repay him
according to his works**. Teh. 28:4; 62:12
15 You, too, beware of him, for he
strongly opposed our words.
16 At my first defence no one stood with
me, but all forsook me. Let it not be held
against them.
17 But the Master stood with me and did
strengthen me, so that through me the
preaching might be completely accomplished, and that all the nations should
hear. And I was **rescued out of the lion's
mouth**. Teh. 22:21
18 And the Master shall rescue me from
every wicked work and save me for His
heavenly reign. To Him be esteem forever
and ever. Aměn!
19 Greet Prisca and Aqulas, and the house
of Onesiphoros.
20 Ěrastos stayed in Corinth, but I left
Trophimos sick in Miletos.
21 Do your best to come before winter.
Eubulos greets you, and Pudes, and Linos,
and Klaudia, and all the brothers.
22 The Master יהושע Messiah be with
your spirit. Favour be with you. Aměn.

4a Or: *confute*, or *prove them wrong*. *4b* Yesh. 30:10, Yirm. 5:31, Rom. 16:18.

TITOS

TITUS

1

Sha'ul, a servant of Elohim and an emissary of יהושע Messiah, according to the belief of Elohim's chosen ones and knowledge of the truth according to reverence,

2 in expectation of everlasting life which Elohim, who does not lie, promised before times of old,

3 but in its own times has manifested His word through preaching, with which I was entrusted according to the command of Elohim our Saviour,

4 to Titos, a genuine child according to our common belief: Favour, compassion, peace from Elohim the Father and the Master יהושע Messiah our Saviour.

5 The reason I left you in Crete was that you should straighten out what was left undone, and appoint elders in every city as I commanded you:

6 if anyone is unreprovable, the husband of one wife, having believing children not accused of loose behaviour, or unruly.

7 For an overseer has to be unreprovable, as a managing one of Elohim, not self-pleasing, not wroth, not given to wine, no brawler, not greedy for filthy gain,

8 but kind to strangers, a lover of what is good, sensible, righteous, set-apart, self-controlled,

9 clinging to the trustworthy word, according to the teaching, in order to be able both to encourage by sound teaching, and to convict [a] those who oppose it.

10 For there are many unruly men, senseless talkers and deceivers, especially those of the circumcision,

11 whose mouths have to be stopped, who upset entire households, teaching what they should not *teach*, for the sake of filthy gain.

12 One of them, a prophet of their own, said, "Cretans are always liars, evil beasts, lazy gluttons."

13 This witness is true. Therefore rebuke them sharply, in order for them to be sound in the belief,

14 not paying attention to Yehuḏi fables, and commands of men who turn from the truth.

15 Indeed, all *matters* are clean to the clean, but to those who are defiled and unbelieving no *matter* is clean, but both their mind and conscience are defiled.

16 They profess to know Elohim, but in works they deny Him, being abominable, and disobedient, and unfit for any good work. [b]

2

But you, speak what is fitting for sound teaching:

2 the older men are to be sober, serious, sensible, sound in belief, in love, in endurance,

3 the older women likewise are to be set-apart in behaviour, not slanderers, not given to much wine, teachers of what is good,

4 in order for them to train the young women to love their husbands, to love their children,

5 to be sensible, blameless, workers at home, good, subject to their own husbands, in order that the word of Elohim is not evil spoken of.

6 Likewise urge the young men to be sensible.

7 Show yourself *to them* an example of good works [a] in all *matters*. In teaching *show* uncorruptness, seriousness,

8 soundness of speech beyond reproach, in order that the opponent is put to shame, having no evil *word* to say about you.

9 Servants should be subject to their own masters, to be well-pleasing in every way, not back-talking,

10 not stealing, but showing all good trustworthiness, so that they adorn the teaching

1a Rather: *confute*, or *prove wrong*. *1b* Mt. 7:21-23, Kěpha ב 2:1-22, Yn. א 2:4, Yehuḏ. v. 4. *2a* Mt. 16:27.

of Elohim our Saviour in every way.
11 For the saving Gift of Elohim has
appeared to all men,
12 instructing us to renounce wickedness
and worldly lusts, and to live sensibly,
righteously, and reverently in the present
age,
13 looking for the blessed expectation and
esteemed appearance of the great Elohim
and our Saviour יהושע Messiah,
14 who gave Himself for us, to redeem us
from all lawlessness [b] and to cleanse for
Himself a people, *His* own possession,
ardent for good works. [c]
15 Speak these *matters*, urge, and
convict [d] with all authority. Let no one
despise you.

3 Remind them to be subject to rulers
and authorities, to obey, to be ready
for every good work,
2 not to slander anyone, not to be quarrelsome, to be gentle, showing all meekness
to all men.
3 For we ourselves were also once foolish, disobedient, led astray, serving various
lusts and pleasures, living in evil and envy,
being hated and hating one another.
4 But when the kindness and the love of
Elohim our Saviour toward man appeared,
5 He saved us, not by works of righteousness which we have done but according to
His compassion, through the washing of
rebirth, and renewal by the Set-apart Spirit,
6 which He poured out on us richly
through יהושע Messiah our Saviour,
7 that having been declared right by His
favour we should become heirs according
to the expectation of everlasting life.
8 Trustworthy is the word, and in this
regard I wish you to strongly affirm, that
those who have believed in Elohim should
keep their minds on maintaining good
works. This is good and profitable to men.
9 But keep away from foolish questions,
and genealogies, and strife and quarrels
about the Torah, for they are unprofitable
and useless.
10 Reject a divisive man after the first and
second warning,
11 knowing that such a one has been
perverted, and sins, being self-condemned.
12 When I shall send Artemas to you, or
Tuchikos, do your best to come to me at
Nikopolis, for I have decided to spend the
winter there.
13 Do your best to send Zenas the lawyer
and Apollos on their journey, so that they
lack none at all.
14 And our *brothers* should also learn to
maintain good works, to meet urgent
needs, so that they shall not be without
fruit.
15 All those with me greet you. Greet
those who love us in the belief. Favour be
with you all. Aměn.

2b See also Yn. א 3:4, Mt. 1:21, Ma. 3:19 & 26, Ma. 26:18, Rom. 6:1-22, Eph. 2:1-10, Yn. א 3:8, Titos 3:5.
2c Mt. 16:27. *2d* Or *confute*.

PILEYMON

PHILEMON

1 Sha'ul, a prisoner of Messiah יהושע,
and Timotiyos the brother, to
Pileymon our beloved one and fellow
worker,
2 and Apphia our sister, and Archippos
our fellow soldier, and the assembly at
your house:
3 Favour to you and peace from Elohim
our Father and the Master יהושע Messiah.
4 I always thank my Elohim when I mention you in my prayers,
5 hearing of your love and the belief
which you have toward the Master יהושע
and toward all the set-apart ones,
6 so that the sharing of your belief might
become working in the knowledge of all
the good which is in you toward Messiah
יהושע.
7 For we have much joy and encouragement in your love, because the tender
affections of the set-apart ones have been
refreshed by you, brother.
8 Therefore, although I have much boldness in Messiah to command you what is
fitting,
9 because of love, I rather appeal – being
such a one as Sha'ul, the aged, and now
also a prisoner of יהושע Messiah –
10 I appeal to you for my child Onesimos,
whom I brought forth while in my chains,
11 who formerly was of no use to you, but
now is of good use to you and to me,
12 whom I sent back to you, and receive
him, that is, my own tender affections,
13 whom I wished to keep with me, that
on your behalf he might serve me in my
chains for the Good News.
14 But without your opinion I wished to
do none at all, so that your good deed
should not be by way of necessity, but
voluntary.
15 For he parted *from you* for a while,
possibly because of this, so that you might
have him back forever,
16 no longer as a slave but more than a
slave, as a beloved brother, especially to
me, and how much more to you, both in
the flesh and in the Master.
17 So, if you regard me as your partner,
receive him as you would me.
18 But if he has wronged you or owes you
whatever, put that on my account.
19 I, Sha'ul, wrote with my own hand. I
shall repay – not to mention to you that
you indeed owe yourself to me also.
20 Yes, brother, let me derive pleasure
from you in the Master, refresh my tender
affections in the Master.
21 Trusting in your obedience, I wrote to
you, knowing that you shall do even more
than I say.
22 And at the same time also prepare a
place for me to stay, for I trust that through
your prayers I shall be given to you.
23 Epaphras, fellow prisoner of me in
Messiah יהושע, greets you,
24 *and* Marqos, Aristarchos, Demas,
Luqas, my fellow workers.
25 The favour of our Master יהושע
Messiah be with your spirit. Aměn.

IḆ`RIM

HEBREWS

1 Elohim, having of old spoken in many
portions and many ways to the fathers
by the prophets,
2 has in these last days spoken to us by
the Son, whom He has appointed heir of
all, through whom also He made the
ages, [a]
3 who being the brightness of the esteem
and the exact representation of His substance, and sustaining all by the word of
His power, having made a cleansing of our
sins through Himself, **sat down at the
right hand** Teh. 110:1 of the Greatness on
high,
4 having become so much better than the
messengers, as He has inherited a more
excellent Name than them.
5 For to which of the messengers did He
ever say, **"You are My Son, today I have
brought You forth"**? Teh. 2:7 And again, **"I
shall be to Him a Father, and He shall be
to Me a Son"**? Shem. ב 7:14 [b]
6 And when He again brings the first-
born into the world, He says, **"Let all the
messengers of Elohim do reverence to
Him."** Teh. 97:7
7 And of the messengers indeed He says,
**"... who is making His messengers spirits
and His servants a flame of fire."** Teh. 104:4
8 But to the Son *He says*, **"Your throne,
O Elohim, is forever and ever, a sceptre
of straightness is the sceptre of Your
reign.**
9 **"You have loved righteousness and
hated lawlessness. Because of this,
Elohim, Your Elohim, has anointed You
with the oil of gladness more than Your
companions."** Teh. 45:6-7
10 And, **"You, Master, did found the
earth in the beginning, and the heavens
are the work of Your hands.**
11 **"They shall perish, but You remain.
And they shall all grow old like a garment,**
12 **and like a mantle You shall fold them
up, and they shall be changed. But You
are the same, and Your years shall not
fail."** Teh. 102:25-27
13 And to which of the messengers did He
ever say, **"Sit at My right hand, until I
make Your enemies a footstool for Your
feet"**? Teh. 110:1
14 Are they not all serving spirits sent out
to attend those who are about to inherit
deliverance?

2 Because of this we have to pay more
attention to what we have heard, lest
we drift away.
2 For if the word spoken through messengers proved to be firm, and every transgression and disobedience received a right
reward,
3 how shall we escape if we neglect so
great a deliverance, which first began to be
spoken by the Master, and was confirmed
to us by those that heard,
4 Elohim also bearing witness both with
signs and wonders, with various miracles,
and gifts of the Set-apart Spirit, distributed
according to His own desire?
5 For it is not to messengers that He has
subjected the world to come, concerning
which we speak.
6 But somewhere one has witnessed, saying, **"What is man that You remember
him, or the son of man that You look
after him?**
7 **"You have made him a little lower
than Elohim.** [a] **You have crowned him
with esteem and respect, and set him
over the works of Your hands.**
8 **"You have put all in subjection under
his feet."** Teh. 8:4-6 For in that He put all in

1a See Yn. 1:3. *1b* See also Diḇre ב 17:13. *2a* According to the Greek text - messengers; however, this verse is quoted from Teh. 8:5.

subjection under him, He left none that is
not subjected to him. But now we do not
yet see all subjected to him.
9 But we do see Him who was made for a
little while lower than the messengers,
יהושע, because of the suffering of death
crowned with esteem and respect, that by
the favour of Elohim He should taste death
for everyone.
10 For it was fitting for Him, because of
whom all are and through whom all are, in
bringing many sons to esteem, to make the
Prince of their deliverance perfect through
sufferings.
11 For both He who sets apart and those
who are being set apart are all of One, for
which reason He is not ashamed to call
them brothers,
12 saying, **"I shall announce Your Name
to My brothers,** [b] **in the midst of the
congregation I shall sing praise to You."**
Teh. 22:22
13 And again, **"I shall put My trust in
Him."** Yesh. 8:17 And again, **"See, I and the
children whom Elohim gave Me."** Yesh. 8:18
14 Therefore, since the children share in
flesh and blood, He Himself similarly
shared in the same, so that by means of His
death He might destroy him having the
power of death, that is, the devil,
15 and deliver those who throughout life
were held in slavery by fear of death.
16 For, doubtless, He does not take hold of
messengers, but He does take hold of the
seed of Aḇraham. [c]
17 So in every way He had to be made like
His brothers, in order to become a compassionate and trustworthy High Priest in matters related to Elohim, to make atonement
for the sins of the people.
18 For in what He had suffered, Himself
being tried, He is able to help those who
are tried.

3 Therefore, set-apart brothers, partakers of the heavenly calling, closely
consider the Emissary and High Priest of
our confession, Messiah יהושע,
2 who was trustworthy to Him who
appointed Him, as also Mosheh in all His
house. [a]
3 For this One has been deemed worthy
of more esteem than Mosheh, as much as
He who built the house enjoys more
respect than the house.
4 For every house is built by someone,
but He who built all is Elohim.
5 And Mosheh indeed was trustworthy in
all His house as a servant, for a witness of
what would be spoken *later*,
6 but Messiah as a Son over His own
house, whose house we are if we hold
fast the boldness and the boasting of the
expectation firm to the end.
7 Therefore, as the Set-apart Spirit says,
"Today, if you hear His voice,
8 **do not harden your hearts as in the
rebellion, in the day of trial in the
wilderness,**
9 **where your fathers tried Me, proved
Me, and saw My works forty years.**
10 **"Therefore I was grieved with that
generation, and said, 'They always go
astray in their heart, and they have not
known My ways.'**
11 **"As I swore in My wrath, 'If they
shall enter into My rest ...' "** Teh. 95:7-11
12 Look out, brothers, lest there be in any
of you a wicked heart of unbelief in falling
away from the living Elohim,
13 but encourage one another daily, while
it is called "Today," lest any of you be
hardened by the deceivableness of sin.
14 For we have become partakers of
Messiah if we hold fast the beginning of
our trust firm to the end,
15 while it is said, **"Today, if you hear
His voice, do not harden your hearts as
in the rebellion."** Teh. 95:7-8
16 For who, having heard, rebelled? Was it
not all who came out of Mitsrayim, led by
Mosheh?
17 And with whom was He grieved forty
years? Was it not with those who sinned,
whose corpses fell in the wilderness?
18 And to whom did He swear that they
would not enter into His rest, but to those
who did not obey?

2b See also Teh. 45:17, Yn. 17:6 & 26. *2c* See Yesh. 41:8-9. *3a* See Bem. 12:7.

19 So we see that they were unable to enter in because of unbelief.

4 Therefore, since a promise remains of entering into His rest, let us fear lest any of you seem to have come short of it.

2 For indeed the Good News was brought to us as well as to them, but the word which they heard did not profit them, not having been mixed with belief in those who heard it.

3 For we who have believed do enter into that rest, as He has said, **"As I swore in My wrath, if they shall enter into My rest..."** Teh. 95:11 And yet His works have come into being from the foundation of the world.

4 For somewhere He has said thus about the seventh day, **"And Elohim rested on the seventh day from all His works,"** Ber. 2:2

5 and in this again, **"If they shall enter into My rest..."** Teh. 95:11

6 Since then it remains for some to enter into it, and those who formerly received the Good News did not enter in because of disobedience,

7 He again defines a certain day, **"Today,"** saying through Dawiḏ so much later, as it has been said, **"Today, if you hear His voice, do not harden your hearts."** Teh. 95:7-8

8 For if Yehoshua had given them rest, He would not have spoken of another day after that.

9 So there remains a Sabbath-keeping [a] for the people of Elohim.

10 For the one, having entered into His rest, has himself also rested from his works, as Elohim *rested* from His own.

11 Let us therefore do our utmost to enter into that rest, lest anyone fall after the same example of disobedience.

12 For the Word of Elohim is living, and working, and sharper than any two-edged sword, cutting through even to the dividing of being and spirit, and of joints and marrow, and able to judge the thoughts and intentions of the heart.

13 And there is no creature hidden from His sight, but all are naked and laid bare before the eyes of Him with whom is our account.

14 Therefore, since we have a great High Priest who has passed through the heavens, יהושע the Son of Elohim, let us hold fast our confession.

15 For we do not have a High Priest unable to sympathize with our weaknesses, but One who was tried in all respects as we are, apart from sin.

16 Therefore, let us come boldly to the throne of favour, in order to receive compassion, and find favour for timely help.

5 For every priest taken from among men is appointed on behalf of men in matters relating to Elohim, to offer both gifts and offerings for sins,

2 being able to have a measure of feeling for those not knowing and being led astray, since he himself is also surrounded by weakness.

3 And on account of this he has to offer for sins – as for the people, so also for himself.

4 And no one obtains this esteem for himself, but he who is called by Elohim, even as Aharon also was.

5 So also the Messiah did not extol Himself to become High Priest, but it was He who said to Him, **"You are My Son, today I have brought You forth."** Teh. 2:7 [a]

6 As He also says in another place, **"You are a priest forever according to the order of Malkitseḏeq,"** Teh. 110:4

7 who, in the days of His flesh, when He had offered up prayers and petitions with strong crying and tears to Him who was able to save Him from death, and was heard because of His reverent fear,

8 though being a Son, He learned obedience by what He suffered.

9 And having been perfected, He became the Causer of everlasting deliverance to all those obeying Him, [b]

4a The Greek word is sabattismos, which means Sabbath-keeping. *5a* See 1:5 & Teḥ. 2:7. *5b* Yn. 3:36, Yn. 14:15, Yn. 14:23, Yn. 15:10, Ma. 3:22-23.

10 having been designated by Elohim a High Priest "according to the order of Malkitseḏeq,"

11 concerning whom we have much to say, and hard to explain, since you have become dull of hearing.

12 For indeed, although by this time you ought to be teachers, you need someone to teach you again the first elements of the Words of Elohim. And you have become such as need milk and not solid food.

13 For everyone partaking of milk is inexperienced in the word of righteousness, for he is a babe.

14 But solid food is for the mature whose senses have been trained by practice to discern both good and evil.

6

Therefore, having left the word of the beginning of the Messiah, let us go on to perfection, [a] not laying again the foundation of repentance from dead works, and of belief toward Elohim,

2 of the teaching of immersions, and of laying on of hands, and of resurrection of the dead, and of everlasting judgment.

3 And this we shall do, if Elohim indeed permits.

4 For it is impossible for those who were once enlightened, and have tasted the heavenly gift, and have become partakers of the Set-apart Spirit,

5 and have tasted the good Word of Elohim and the powers of the age to come,

6 and fall away, to renew them again to repentance – having impaled for themselves the Son of Elohim again, and put Him to open shame. [b]

7 For ground that is drinking the rain often falling on it, and is bearing plants fit for those by whom it is tilled, receives blessing from Elohim,

8 but if it **brings forth thorns and thistles,** Ber. 3:18 it is rejected and near to being cursed, and ends up by being burned.

9 But although we speak in this way, beloved, we are persuaded, concerning you, of better matters which possess deliverance.

10 For Elohim is not unrighteous to forget your work and labour of love which you have shown toward His Name, in that you have attended to the set-apart ones, and *still* attend.

11 And we desire that each one of you show the same eagerness, to the entire confirmation of expectation until the end,

12 in order that you do not become sluggish, but imitate those who through belief and patience inherit the promises.

13 For Elohim, having promised Aḇraham, since He could swear by no one greater, swore by Himself, [c]

14 saying, **"Truly, blessing I shall bless you, and increasing I shall increase you."** Ber. 22:18

15 And so, after being patient, he obtained the promise.

16 For men do indeed swear by the one greater, and an oath for confirmation is for them an end of all dispute.

17 In this way Elohim, resolving to show even more clearly to the heirs of promise the unchangeableness of His purpose, confirmed it by an oath,

18 so that by two unchangeable matters in which it is impossible for Elohim to lie, we might have strong encouragement, we who have fled for refuge to lay hold of the expectation set before us,

19 which we have as an anchor of the life, both safe and firm, and entering into that within the veil,

20 where יהושע has entered as a forerunner for us, having become **High Priest forever according to the order of Malkitseḏeq.** Teh. 110:4

7

For this Malkitseḏeq, sovereign of Shalĕm, priest of the Most High Elohim, who met Aḇraham returning from the slaughter of the sovereigns and blessed him, [a]

2 to whom also Aḇraham gave a tenth part of all, *his name* being translated, indeed, first, 'sovereign of righteousness,' and then also sovereign of Shalĕm, that is, 'sovereign of peace,'

6a Mt. 5:48. *6b* Iḇ`rim 10:26-31. *6c* Ber. 22:16. *7a* See Ber. 14:17-20.

3 without father, without mother, without
genealogy, having neither beginning of
days nor end of life, but having been made
like the Son of Elohim, remains a priest for
all time.
4 Now see how great this one was, to
whom even the ancestor Aḇraham gave a
tenth of the choicest booty.
5 And truly, those who are of the sons of
Lěwi, who receive the priesthood, have a
command to receive tithes from the people
according to the Torah, that is, from their
brothers, though they have come from the
loins of Aḇraham,
6 however, the one whose genealogy is
not derived from them received tithes from
Aḇraham, and blessed the one who held
the promises.
7 And it is beyond all dispute that the
lesser is blessed by the better.
8 And here it is men who die that receive
tithes, but there it is someone of whom it is
witnessed that he lives.
9 And one might say that through Aḇraham even Lěwi, who received tithes, gave
tithes,
10 for he was still in the loins of his father
when Malkitseḏeq met him.
11 Truly, then, if perfection were through
the Lěwitical priesthood – for under it the
people were given the Torah – why was
there still need for another priest to arise
according to the order of Malkitseḏeq, and
not be called according to the order of
Aharon?
12 For the priesthood being changed, [b] of
necessity there takes place a change of law
also.
13 For He of whom this is said belongs to
another tribe, from which no one had
attended at the slaughter-place. [c]
14 For it is perfectly clear that our Master
arose from Yehuḏah, a tribe about which
Mosheh never spoke of concerning priesthood,
15 and this is clearer still, if another priest
arises in the likeness of Malkitseḏeq,
16 who has become, not according to the
torah of fleshly command, but according to
the power of an endless life,
17 for He does witness, **"You are a priest
forever according to the order of Malkitseḏeq."** Teh. 110:4
18 For there is indeed a setting aside of the
former command [d] because of its weakness
and unprofitableness,
19 for the Torah [e] perfected naught, but the
bringing in of a better expectation, through
which we draw near to Elohim.
20 And it was not without an oath!
21 For they indeed became priests without
an oath, but He *became Priest* with an oath
by Him who said to Him, "יהוה has sworn
and shall not regret, **'You are a priest
forever according to the order of Malkitseḏeq.'** " Teh. 110:4
22 By as much as this יהושע has become a
guarantor of a better covenant.
23 And indeed, those that became priests
were many, because they were prevented
by death from continuing,
24 but He, because He remains forever,
has an unchangeable priesthood.
25 Therefore He is also able to save completely those who draw near to Elohim
through Him, ever living to make intercession for them.
26 For it was fitting that we should have
such a High Priest – kind, innocent, undefiled, having been separated from sinners,
and exalted above the heavens,
27 who does not need, as those high
priests, to offer up slaughter *offerings* day
by day, first for His own sins and then for
those of the people, for this He did once
for all when He offered up Himself.
28 For the Torah appoints as high priests
men who have weakness, but the word of
the oath which came after the Torah,
appoints the Son having been perfected
forever.

8 Now the summary of what we are saying is: We have such a High Priest,
who is seated at the right hand of the
throne of the Greatness in the heavens,

7b From Malkitseḏeq to Aharon. *7c* See "Altar" in the Explanatory Notes. *7d* Or former *Lěwitical* command.
7e *Lěwitical* Torah.

2 and who serves in the set-apart place and of the true Tent, which יהוה set up, and not man.

3 For every high priest is appointed to offer both gifts and slaughters. So it was also necessary for this One to have somewhat to offer.

4 For if indeed He were on earth, He would not be a priest, since there are priests who offer the gifts according to the Torah,

5 who serve a copy and shadow of the heavenly, as Mosheh was warned when he was about to make the Tent. For He said, **"See that you make all according to the pattern shown you on the mountain."** Shem. 25:40

6 But now He has obtained a more excellent service, inasmuch as He is also Mediator [a] of a better covenant, which was constituted on better promises.

7 For if that first *covenant* had been faultless, then no place would have been sought for a second.

8 **For finding fault with them, He says, "See, the days are coming," says יהוה, "when I shall conclude with the house of Yisra'ěl and with the house of Yehuḏah a renewed covenant,**

9 **not according to the covenant that I made with their fathers in the day when I took them by the hand to lead them out of the land of Mitsrayim, because they did not continue in My covenant, and I disregarded them," says יהוה.**

10 **"Because this is the covenant that I shall make with the house of Yisra'ěl after those days, says יהוה, giving My laws in their mind, and I shall write them on their hearts, and I shall be their Elohim, and they shall be My people.**

11 **"And they shall by no means teach each one his neighbour, and each one his brother, saying, 'Know יהוה,' because they all shall know Me, from the least of them to the greatest of them.**

12 **"Because I shall forgive their unrighteousness, and their sins and their lawlessnesses I shall no longer remember."** Yirm. 31:31-34 [b]

13 By saying, 'renewed,' He has made the first old. Now what becomes old and growing aged is near disappearing.

9 Now the first *covenant* indeed had regulations of worship and the earthly set-apart place.

2 For a Tent was prepared: the first part, in which was the lampstand, and the table, and the showbread, which is called the Set-apart Place.

3 And after the second veil, the part of the Tent which is called Most Set-apart,

4 to which belonged the golden censer, and the ark of the covenant overlaid on all sides with gold, in which were the golden pot that held the manna, and the rod of Aharon that budded, and the tablets of the covenant,

5 and above it the keruḇim of esteem were overshadowing the place of atonement – about which we do not now speak in detail.

6 And these having been prepared like this, the priests always went into the first part of the Tent, accomplishing the services.

7 But into the second part the high priest went alone once a year, not without blood, which he offered for himself and for sins of ignorance of the people, [a]

8 the Set-apart Spirit signifying this, that the way into the Most Set-apart Place was not yet made manifest while the first Tent has a standing,

9 which was a parable for the present time in which both gifts and slaughters are offered which are unable to perfect the one serving, as to his conscience,

10 only as to foods and drinks, and different washings, and fleshly regulations imposed until a time of setting *matters* straight.

11 But Messiah, having become a High Priest of the coming good *matters*, through the greater and more perfect Tent not made

8a Messiah is called the Mediator of the New (Renewed) Covenant in Hebrews, in three places: 8:6, 9:15, 12:24.
8b See also Iḇ`rim 10:16-17. *9a* Bem. 15:15-28.

with hands, that is, not of this creation,
12 entered into the Most Set-apart Place
once for all, not with the blood of goats
and calves, but with His own blood, having
obtained everlasting redemption.
13 For if the blood of bulls and goats and
the ashes of a heifer, sprinkling the defiled,
sets apart for the cleansing of the flesh,
14 how much more shall the blood of the
Messiah, who through the everlasting
Spirit offered Himself unblemished to
Elohim, cleanse your conscience from
dead works to serve the living Elohim?
15 And because of this He is the Mediator
of a renewed covenant, so that, death
having taken place for redemption of the
transgressions under the first covenant,
those who are called might receive the
promise of the everlasting inheritance.
16 For where a covenant is, it is necessary
for the death of the covenanted one to be
established.
17 For a covenant over those dead is firm,
since it is never valid while the covenanted
one is living.
18 Therefore not even the first *covenant*
was instituted without blood.
19 For when, according to Torah, every
command had been spoken by Mosheh to
all the people, he took the blood of calves
and goats, with water, and scarlet wool,
and hyssop, and sprinkled both the book
itself and all the people,
20 saying, **"This is the blood of the covenant which Elohim commanded you."**
Shem. 24:8
21 And in the same way he sprinkled with
blood both the Tent and all the vessels of
the service.
22 And, according to the Torah, almost all
is cleansed with blood, and without shedding of blood there is no forgiveness.
23 It was necessary, then, that the copies
of the heavenly ones should be cleansed
with these, but the heavenly ones themselves with better slaughter *offerings* than
these.
24 For Messiah has not entered into a Set-
apart Place made by hand – figures of the
true – but into the heaven itself, now to
appear in the presence of Elohim on our
behalf,
25 not that He should offer Himself often,
as the high priest enters into the Set-apart
Place year by year with blood not his own.
26 For if so, He would have had to suffer
often, since the foundation of the world.
But now He has appeared once for all at
the end of the ages to put away sin by the
offering of Himself.
27 And as it awaits men to die once, and
after this the judgment,
28 so also the Messiah, having been
offered once to **bear the sins of many,**
Yesh. 53:12 shall appear a second time, apart
from sin, to those waiting for Him, unto
deliverance.

10 For the Torah, having a shadow of
the good *matters* to come, and not
the image itself of the matters, was never
able to make perfect those who draw near
with the same slaughter *offerings* which
they offer continually year by year.
2 Otherwise, would they not have ceased
to be offered? Because those who served,
once cleansed, would have had no more
consciousness of sins.
3 But in those *offerings* is a reminder of
sins year by year.
4 For it is impossible for blood of bulls
and goats to take away sins.
5 Therefore, coming into the world, He
says, **"Slaughtering and meal offering
You did not desire, but a body You have
prepared for Me.**
6 **"In ascending offerings and *offerings*
for sin You did not delight.**
7 **"Then I said, 'See, I come – in the
roll of the book it has been written concerning Me – to do Your desire, O
Elohim.' "** Teh. 40:6-8
8 Saying above, **"Slaughter and meal
offering, and ascending offerings, and
offerings for sin You did not desire, nor
delighted in,"** Teh. 40:6 which are offered
according to the Torah,
9 then He said, **"See, I come to do Your
desire, O Elohim."** Teh. 40:8 He takes away
the first to establish the second.
10 By that desire we have been set apart
through the offering of the body of יהושע
Messiah once for all.

11 And indeed every priest stands day by
day doing service, and repeatedly offering
the same slaughter *offerings* which are
never able to take away sins.
12 But He, having offered one slaughter
offering for sins for all time, sat down at
the right hand of Elohim,
13 waiting from that time onward **until
His enemies are made a footstool for His
feet**. Teh. 110:1
14 For by one offering He has perfected
for all time those who are being set apart.
15 And the Set-apart Spirit also witnesses
to us, for after having said before,
16 **"This is the covenant that I shall
make with them after those days, says
יהוה, giving My laws into their hearts,
and in their minds I shall write
them,"** Yirm. 31:33 *a*
17 and, **"Their sins and their lawlessnesses I shall remember no more."**
Yirm. 31:34
18 Now where there is forgiveness of
these, there is no longer a slaughter *offering* for sin.
19 So, brothers, having boldness to enter
into the Set-apart Place by the blood of
יהושע,
20 by a new and living way which He
instituted for us, through the veil, that is,
His flesh,
21 and *having* a High Priest over the
House of Elohim,
22 let us draw near with a true heart in
completeness of belief, having our hearts
sprinkled from a wicked conscience and
our bodies washed with clean water. *b*
23 Let us hold fast the confession of our
expectation without yielding, for He who
promised is trustworthy.
24 And let us be concerned for one another
in order to stir up love and good works, *c*
25 not forsaking the assembling of ourselves together, as is the habit of some, but
encouraging, and so much more as you see
the day coming near.
26 For if we sin purposely after we have
received the knowledge of the truth, there
no longer remains a slaughter *offering* for
sins, *d*
27 but some fearsome anticipation of judgment, and **a fierce fire which is about to
consume the opponents**. Yesh. 26:11
28 Anyone who has disregarded the Torah
of Mosheh dies without compassion on the
witness of two or three witnesses.
29 How much worse punishment do you
think shall he deserve who has trampled
the Son of Elohim underfoot, counted the
blood of the covenant by which he was set
apart as common, and insulted the Spirit of
favour?
30 For we know Him who has said,
**"Vengeance is Mine, I shall repay, says
יהוה."** And again, **"יהוה shall judge His
people."** Deḇ. 32:35-36
31 It is fearsome to fall into the hands of
the living Elohim.
32 But remember the former days, when,
after you were enlightened, you endured a
great struggle with sufferings.
33 On the one hand you were exposed to
reproaches and pressures, and on the other
hand you became sharers with those who
were so treated,
34 for you sympathised with me in my
chains, and you accepted with joy the
seizure of your possessions, knowing that
you have a better and a lasting possession
for yourselves in the heavens.
35 Do not, then, lose your boldness, which
has great reward.
36 For you have need of endurance, so that
when you have done the desire of Elohim,
you receive the promise:
37 **"For yet a little while – He who is
coming shall come and shall not delay."**
38 **"But the righteous shall live by
belief, but if anyone draws back, my
being has no pleasure in him."** Haḇ. 2:3-4
39 But we are not of those who draw back
to destruction, but of belief to the preserva-
tion of life.

11 And belief is the substance of what
is expected, the proof of what is

10a See also Iḇ`rim 8:8-12. *10b* Yeḥ. 36:25. *10c* Mt. 16:27. *10d* See also 6:6. This type of sinning is in contrast with sinning ignorantly – Iḇ`rim 9:7, Bem. 15:15-28.

not seen.

2 For by this the elders obtained witness.

3 By belief, we understand that the ages were prepared by the word of Elohim, so that what is seen was not made of what is visible.

4 By belief, Heḇel offered to Elohim a greater slaughter *offering* than Qayin, through which he obtained witness that he was righteous, Elohim witnessing of his gifts. And through it, having died, he still speaks.

5 By belief, Ḥanoḵ was translated so as not to see death, **"and was not found because Elohim had translated him."** Ber. 5:24 For before his translation he obtained witness, that he pleased Elohim.

6 But without belief it is impossible to please Him, for he who comes to Elohim has to believe that He is, and that He is a rewarder of those who earnestly seek Him.

7 By belief, Noaḥ, having been warned of what was yet unseen, having feared, prepared an ark to save his house, through which he condemned the world and became heir of the righteousness which is according to belief.

8 By belief, Aḇraham obeyed when he was called to go out to the place which he was about to receive as an inheritance. And he went out, not knowing where he was going.

9 By belief, he sojourned in the land of promise as a stranger, dwelling in tents with Yitsḥaq and Ya'aqoḇ, the heirs with him of the same promise,

10 for he was looking for the city having foundations, whose builder and maker is Elohim.

11 By belief also, Sarah herself was enabled to conceive seed, and she bore a child when she was past the normal age, because she deemed Him trustworthy who had promised.

12 And so from one, and him as good as dead, were born **as numerous as the stars of the heaven, as countless as the sand which is by the seashore.** Ber. 15:5; 22:17

13 In belief all these died, not having received the promises, [a] but seeing them from a distance, welcomed and embraced them, and confessed that they were aliens and strangers on the earth.

14 For those who speak this way make it clear that they seek a fatherland.

15 And yet, if they had indeed kept remembering that *place* from which they had come out, they would have had the chance to return.

16 But now they long for a better *place*, that is, a heavenly. Therefore Elohim is not ashamed to be called their Elohim, for He has prepared a city for them.

17 By belief, Aḇraham, when he was tried, offered up Yitsḥaq, and he who had received the promises offered up his only brought-forth son,

18 of whom it was said, **"In Yitsḥaq your seed shall be called,"** Ber. 21:12

19 reckoning that Elohim was able to raise, even from the dead, from which he received him back, as a type.

20 By belief, Yitsḥaq blessed Ya'aqoḇ and Ěsaw concerning that which was to come.

21 By belief, Ya'aqoḇ, when he was dying, blessed each of the sons of Yosěph, and did reverence on the top of his staff.

22 By belief, Yosěph, when he was dying, made mention of the outgoing of the children of Yisra'ěl, and gave orders concerning his bones.

23 By belief, Mosheh, having been born, was hidden three months by his parents, because they saw he was a comely child, [b] and were not afraid of the sovereign's command.

24 By belief, Mosheh, having become great, refused to be called the son of the daughter of Pharaoh,

25 choosing rather to be afflicted with the people of Elohim than to enjoy the pleasures of sin for a time,

26 deeming the reproach of Messiah greater riches than the treasures in Mitsrayim, for he was looking to the reward.

27 By belief, he left Mitsrayim, not fearing the wrath of the sovereign, for he was

11a See v. 39. *11b* Shem. 2:2

steadfast, as seeing Him who is invisible.

28 By belief, he performed the Pěsaḥ and the sprinkling of blood, lest he who destroyed the first-born should touch them.

29 By belief, they passed through the Red Sea as by dry land, and when the Mitsrites tried it, they were drowned.

30 By belief, the walls of Yeriḥo fell, having been surrounded for seven days.

31 By belief, Raḥaḇ the whore did not perish with those who did not believe, having received the spies with peace.

32 And what more shall I say? For the time would fail me to relate of Gid'on and Baraq and Shimshon and Yiphtaḥ, also of Dawiḏ and Shemu'ěl and the prophets,

33 who through belief, overcame reigns, worked righteousness, obtained promises, stopped the mouths of lions,

34 quenched the power of fire, escaped the edge of the sword, out of weakness were made strong, became mighty in battle, put foreign armies to flight.

35 Women received *back* their dead by resurrection. And others were tortured, not accepting release, to obtain a better resurrection.

36 And others had trial of mockings and floggings and more, of chains and imprisonment.

37 They were stoned, they were tried, they were sawn in two, they were slain with the sword. They went about in sheepskins, in goatskins, being in need, afflicted, mistreated,

38 of whom the world was not worthy – wandering in deserts and mountains and caves and holes of the earth.

39 And having obtained witness through the belief, all these did not receive the promise, [c]

40 Elohim having provided what is better for us, that they should not be made perfect apart from us.

12

We too, then, having so great a cloud of witnesses all around us, let us lay aside every weight and the sin which so easily entangles us, and let us run with endurance the race set before us,

2 looking to the Prince and Perfecter of our belief, יהושע, who for the joy that was set before Him endured the stake, having despised the shame, and sat down at the right hand of the throne of Elohim.

3 For consider Him who endured such opposition from sinners against Himself, lest you become weary and faint in your lives.

4 You have not yet resisted unto blood, striving against sin.

5 And you have forgotten the appeal which speaks to you as to sons, **"My son, do not despise the discipline of יהוה, nor faint when you are reproved by Him,**

6 **for whom יהוה loves, He disciplines, and flogs every son whom He receives."** Mish. 3:11-12

7 If you endure discipline, Elohim is treating you as sons. For what son is there whom a father does not discipline?

8 But if you are without discipline, of which all have become sharers, then you are illegitimate and not sons.

9 Moreover, we indeed had fathers of our flesh disciplining us, and we paid them respect. Shall we not much rather be subject to the Father of spirits, and live?

10 For they indeed disciplined us for a few days as seemed best to them, but He does it for our profit, so that we might share His apartness.

11 And indeed, no discipline seems pleasant at the time, but grievous, but afterward it yields the peaceable fruit of righteousness to those who have been trained by it. [a]

12 So, **strengthen the hands which hang down and the weak knees**, Yesh. 35:3

13 and make straight paths for your feet, lest the lame be turned aside, but instead, to be healed.

14 Pursue peace with all, and *pursue* apartness without which no one shall see the Master.

15 See to it that no one falls short of the favour of Elohim, that no root of bitterness springing up causes trouble, by which many become defiled,

11c See v. 13. *12a* See also Deḇ. 8:2.

16 lest there be anyone who whores, or profane one, like Ěsaw, who for a single meal sold his birthright. [b]

17 For you know that afterward, when he wished to inherit the blessing, he was rejected, for he found no place for repentance, though he sought it with tears.

18 For you have not drawn near to a mountain touched and scorched with fire, and to blackness, and darkness and storm,

19 and a sound of a trumpet, and a voice of words, so that those who heard it begged that no further Word should be spoken to them, [c]

20 for they could not bear what was commanded, **"If even a beast touches the mountain, it shall be stoned or shot through with an arrow."** Shem. 19:12

21 And so fearsome was the sight that Mosheh said, **"I exceedingly fear and tremble."** Deḇ. 9:19

22 But you have drawn near to Mount Tsiyon and to the city of the living Elohim, to the heavenly Yerushalayim, to myriads of messengers,

23 to the entire gathering and assembly of the first-born having been enrolled in heaven, and to Elohim the Judge of all, and to the spirits of righteous men made perfect,

24 and to יהושע the Mediator [d] of a new covenant, and to the blood of sprinkling which speaks better than *the blood* of Heḇel.

25 Take heed not to refuse the One speaking. For if those did not escape who refused the warning on earth, much less we who turn away from Him from heaven,

26 whose voice shook the earth then, but now He has promised, saying, **"Yet once more I shake not only the earth, but also the heaven."** Ḥag. 2:6

27 And this, **"Yet once more,"** makes clear the removal of what is shaken – as having been made – so that the unshaken *matters* might remain.

28 Therefore, receiving an unshakeable reign, let us hold the favour, through which we serve Elohim pleasingly with reverence and awe,

29 for indeed, our **Elohim is a consuming fire.** Deḇ. 4:24

13

Let the brotherly love continue.

2 Do not forget to receive strangers, for by so doing some have unwittingly entertained messengers.

3 Remember the prisoners as if chained with them, and those being mistreated, since you yourselves also are in the body.

4 Let marriage be respected by all, and the bed be undefiled. But Elohim shall judge those who whore, and adulterers.

5 *Let your* way of life be without the love of silver,[a] and be satisfied with what you have. For He Himself has said, **"I shall never leave you nor forsake you,"** Deḇ. 31:6

6 so that we boldly say, **"יהוה is my helper, I shall not fear what man shall do to me."** Teh. 118:6

7 Remember those leading you, who spoke the Word of Elohim to you. Consider the outcome of their behaviour and imitate their belief.

8 יהושע Messiah is the same yesterday, and today, and forever.

9 Do not be borne about by various and strange teachings. [b] For it is good for the heart to be established by favour, not with foods which have not profited those who have been occupied with them.

10 We have a slaughter-place from which those serving the Tent have no authority to eat.

11 For the bodies of those beasts whose blood is brought into the Set-apart Place by the high priest for sin, are burned outside the camp.

12 And so יהושע also suffered outside the gate, to set apart the people with His own blood.

13 Let us, then, go to Him outside the camp, bearing His reproach.

14 For we have no lasting city here, but we seek the one coming.

15 Through Him then, let us continually

12b Ber. 25:32-33. *12c* See Shem. 20:19. *12d* See 8:6. *13a* Implying money. *13b* Eph. 4:14.

offer up a slaughter *offering* of praise to
Elohim, that is, the fruit [c] of our lips, giving thanks to His Name.
16 And do not forget to do good and to
share, for with such slaughter *offerings*
Elohim is well pleased.
17 Obey those leading you, and be subject
to them, for they watch for your lives, as
having to give account. Let them do so
with joy and not groaning, for that would
be of no advantage to you.
18 Pray for us, for we trust that we have a
good conscience, desiring to behave well
in every way.
19 But I particularly encourage you to do
this, that I might be restored to you the
sooner.
20 And the Elohim of peace who brought
up our Master יהושע from the dead, that
great Shepherd of the sheep, through the
blood of the everlasting covenant,
21 make you perfect [d] in every good work
to do His desire, working in you [e] what is
pleasing in His sight, through יהושע
Messiah, to whom be esteem forever and
ever. Amĕn.
22 And I call upon you, brothers, bear with
the word of encouragement for I have written to you in few words.
23 Know that brother Timotiyos has been
released, with whom I shall see you if he
comes shortly.
24 Greet all those leading you, and all the
set-apart ones. Those from Italy greet you.
25 Favour be with you all. Amĕn.

13c Or "bulls of our lips" – See Hosh. 14:2. *13d* Mt. 5:48. *13e* See Gal. 2:20, Pilip. 2:13.

YA`AQOḆ

JAMES

1 Yaʿaqoḇ, a servant of Elohim and of
the Master יהושע Messiah, to the
twelve tribes who are in the dispersion:
Greetings.
2 My brothers, count it all joy when you
fall into various trials,
3 knowing that the proving of your belief
works endurance.
4 And let endurance have a perfect work,
so that you be perfect and complete, lacking in naught.
5 If any of you lacks wisdom, let him ask
of Elohim, who gives to all generously and
without reproach, and it shall be given to
him.
6 But he should ask in belief, not doubting, for he who doubts is like a wave of the
sea driven and tossed by the wind.
7 For that man should not think that he
shall receive whatever from the Master –
8 he is a double-minded man, unstable in
all his ways.
9 And let the lowly brother boast in his
exaltation,
10 but the rich in his humiliation, because
as a flower of the field he shall pass away.
11 For the sun rose with burning heat, and
withered the grass, and its flower fell, and
its pretty appearance perished. So also the
rich man shall fade away in his ways.
12 Blessed is the man who does endure
trial, for when he has been proved, he shall
receive the crown of life which the Master
has promised to those who love Him.
13 Let no one say when he is enticed,
"I am enticed by Elohim," for Elohim is
not enticed by evil *matters*, and He entices
no one.
14 But each one is enticed when he is
drawn away by his own desires and
trapped.
15 Then, when desire has conceived, it
gives birth to sin. And sin, when it has
been accomplished, brings forth death.
16 Do not go astray, my beloved brothers.
17 Every good gift and every perfect gift is
from above, coming down from the Father
of lights, with whom there is no change,
nor shadow of turning. [a]
18 Having purposed it, He brought us
forth by the Word of truth, for us to be a
kind of first-fruits of His creatures.
19 So then, my beloved brothers, let every
man be swift to hear, slow to speak, slow
to wrath,
20 for the wrath of man does not work the
righteousness of Elohim.
21 Therefore put away all filthiness and
overflow of evil, and receive with meekness the implanted Word, [b] which is able to
save your lives.
22 And become doers of the Word, and not
hearers only, [c] deceiving yourselves.
23 Because if anyone is a hearer of the
Word and not a doer, he is like a man who
looks at his natural face in a mirror,
24 for he looks at himself, and goes away,
and immediately forgets what he was like.
25 But he that looked into the perfect
Torah, that of freedom, [d] and continues in
it, not becoming a hearer that forgets, but a
doer of work, this one shall be blessed in
his doing *of the Torah*.
26 If anyone among you thinks he is religious, and does not bridle his tongue but
deceives his own heart, this one's religion
is worthless.
27 Clean and undefiled religion before the
Elohim and Father is this: to visit orphans
and widows in their affliction, *and* to keep
oneself unstained from the world.

2 My brothers, do not hold the belief of
our Master יהושע Messiah, the

1a See Mal. 3:6. *1b* See Mt. 13:4-23. *1c* See Mt. 7:24-27, Lq. 6:46-49, Lq. 8:21, Rom. 2:13, Iḇ`rim 4:11, Ḥazon 22:14. *1d* See 2:12.

Master of esteem, with partiality.
2 For if there should come into your
meeting place a man with gold rings, in a
splendid robe, and there should also come
in a poor one dressed in rags,
3 and you pay attention to the one wearing the splendid robe and say to him, "You
sit here in a good place," and say to the
poor one, "You stand there," or, "Sit here
by my feet,"
4 have you not discriminated among
yourselves, and become judges with
wicked thoughts?
5 Listen, my beloved brothers: Has
Elohim not chosen the poor of this world,
rich in belief and heirs of the reign which
He promised to those who love Him?
6 But you have shown disrespect towards
the poor man. Do not the rich oppress you
and drag you into the courts?
7 Do they not blaspheme that good Name
by which you are called?
8 If you truly accomplish the sovereign
law according to the Scripture, **"You shall
love your neighbour as yourself,"** Way. 19:18
you do well,
9 but if you show partiality, you commit
sin, being found guilty by the Torah as
transgressors.
10 For whoever shall guard all the Torah,
and yet stumble in one point, he is guilty of
all.
11 For He who said, **"Do not commit
adultery,"** Shem. 20:14 also said, **"Do not
murder."** Shem. 20:13 Now if you do not commit adultery, but you do murder, you have
become a transgressor of Torah.
12 So speak and so do as those who are to
be judged by a Torah of freedom. [a]
13 For the judgment is without compassion to the one who has shown no compassion. And compassion boasts over
judgment.
14 My brothers, what use is it for anyone
to say he has belief but does not have
works? This belief is unable to save him.
15 And if a brother or sister is naked and
in need of daily food,
16 but one of you says to them, "Go in
peace, be warmed and be filled," but you
do not give them the bodily needs, what
use is it?
17 So also belief, if it does not have works,
is in itself dead.
18 But someone might say, "You have
belief, and I have works." Show me your
belief without your works, and I shall
show you my belief by my works.
19 You believe that **Elohim is one.** Deḇ. 6:4
You do well. The demons also believe –
and shudder!
20 But do you wish to know, O foolish
man, that the belief without the works is
dead?
21 Was not Aḇraham our father declared
right by works when he offered Yitsḥaq his
son on the slaughter-place?
22 Do you see that the belief was working
with his works, and by the works the belief
was perfected?
23 And the Scripture was filled which
says, **"Aḇraham believed Elohim, and it
was reckoned to him for righteousness."**
Ber. 15:6 And He called him, **"he who loves
Elohim."** Yesh. 41:8, 2 Diḇ. 20:7
24 You see, then, that a man is declared
right by works, and not by belief alone.
25 In the same way, was not Raḥaḇ the
whore also declared right by works when
she received the messengers and sent them
out another way?
26 For as the body without the spirit is
dead, so also the belief is dead without the
works.

3 Not many of you should become
teachers, my brothers, knowing that
we shall receive greater judgment.
2 For we all stumble in many *matters*. If
anyone does not stumble in word, he is a
perfect man, able also to bridle the entire
body.
3 Look, we put bits in the mouths of
horses, for them to obey us, and we turn
their body.
4 Look at the ships too: although they are
so big and are driven by strong winds, they
are turned by a very small rudder wherever

2a See 1:25, and Yn. 8:32-36.

the pilot intends.

5 So too the tongue is a little member, yet boasts greatly. See how a little fire kindles a great forest!

6 And the tongue is a fire, the world of unrighteousness. Among our members the tongue is set, the one defiling the entire body, and setting on fire the wheel of life, and it is set on fire by GĕHinnom.

7 For every kind of beast and bird, of reptile and creature of the sea, is tamed and has been tamed by mankind.

8 But no man is able to tame the tongue. It is unruly, evil, filled with deadly poison.

9 With it we bless our Elohim and Father, and with it we curse men, who have been made **in the likeness of Elohim**. Ber. 1:26, 27

10 Out of the same mouth proceed blessing and cursing. My brothers, this should not be so.

11 Does the fountain send forth the sweet and the bitter from the same opening?

12 My brothers, is a fig tree able to bear olives, or a grapevine figs? So neither is a fountain *able* to make salt and sweet water.

13 Who is wise and understanding among you? Let him show by his good behaviour his works in meekness of wisdom.

14 But if you have bitter jealousy and self-seeking in your hearts, do not boast against and lie against the truth.

15 This is not the wisdom coming down from above, but it is earthly, unspiritual, demonic.

16 For where jealousy and self-seeking are, there is confusion and every foul deed.

17 But the wisdom from above is first clean, then peaceable, gentle, ready to obey, filled with compassion and good fruits, without partiality and without hypocrisy.

18 And the fruit of righteousness [a] is sown in peace by those who make peace.

4

Where do fightings and strivings come from among you? Do they not come from your pleasures that battle in your members?

2 You desire, and do not have. You murder, and are jealous, and are unable to obtain. You strive and fight, and you do not possess, because you do not ask.

3 You ask and do not receive, because you ask evilly, in order to spend it on your pleasures.

4 Adulterers and adulteresses! Do you not know that friendship with the world is enmity with Elohim? [a] Whoever therefore intends to be a friend of the world makes himself an enemy of Elohim.

5 Or do you think that the Scripture speaks to no purpose? Does the Spirit which dwells in us intensely crave unto envy?

6 But He gives greater favour. Because of this He says, **"Elohim resists the proud, but gives favour to the humble."** Mish. 3:34

7 So then subject yourselves to Elohim. Resist the devil [b] and he shall flee from you.

8 Draw near to Elohim and He shall draw near to you. Cleanse hands, sinners. And cleanse the hearts, you double-minded!

9 Lament and mourn and weep! Let your laughter be turned to mourning and your joy to dejection.

10 Humble yourselves in the sight of the Master, and He shall lift you up.

11 Brothers, do not speak against one another. He that speaks against a brother and judges his brother, speaks against Torah and judges Torah. And if you judge Torah, you are not a doer of Torah but a judge.

12 There is one Lawgiver and Judge, who is able to save and to destroy. Who are you to judge another?

13 Come now, you who say, "Today or tomorrow, let us go to such and such a city, spend a year there, and trade, and make a profit,"

14 when you do not know of tomorrow. For what is your life? For it is a vapour that appears for a little, and then disappears –

15 instead of your saying, "If the Master desires, we shall live and do this or that."

16 But now you boast in your proud speeches. All such boasting is wicked.

3a See Pilip. 1:11. *4a* Mt. 13:22, Lq. 4:5-6, Lq. 14:33, Rom. 12:2, Yn. א 2:15-17. *4b* Or adversary.

17 To him, then, who knows to do good and does not do it, to him it is sin.

5

Come now, rich ones, weep, crying aloud over the hardships coming upon you!

2 Your riches have rotted, and your garments have become moth-eaten.

3 Your gold and silver have become rusty, and their rust shall be a witness against you and shall eat your flesh like fire. You have laid up treasure in the last days.

4 See, the wages of the workmen who mowed your fields, which you kept back, cry out. And the cries of the reapers have reached the ears of יהוה of hosts. [a]

5 You have lived on the earth in pleasure and luxury, you have fattened your hearts, as in a day of slaughter.

6 You have condemned, you have murdered the righteous – he does not resist you.

7 So, brothers, be patient until the coming of the Master. See, the farmer waits for the precious fruit of the earth, waiting patiently for it until it receives the early and latter rain.

8 You too, be patient. Establish your hearts, for the coming of the Master has drawn near.

9 Do not grumble against each other, brothers, lest you be judged. See, the Judge is standing at the door!

10 My brothers, as an example of suffering and patience, take the prophets, who spoke in the Name of יהוה.

11 See, we call those blessed who endure. You have heard of the endurance of Iyoḇ and saw the purpose of יהוה, that He is very sympathetic and compassionate.

12 But above all, my brothers, do not swear, either by the heaven or by the earth or with any other oath. But let your Yes be Yes, and your No, No, lest you fall into judgment.

13 Is any of you suffering evil? Let him pray. Is anyone in good spirits? Let him sing psalms.

14 Is anyone among you sick? Let him call for the elders of the assembly, and let them pray over him, having anointed him with oil in the Name of the Master.

15 And the prayer of the belief shall save the sick, and the Master shall raise him up. And if he has committed sins, he shall be forgiven.

16 Confess your trespasses to one another, and pray for one another, so that you are healed. The earnest prayer of a righteous one accomplishes much.

17 Ěliyahu was a man with feelings like us, and he prayed earnestly that it would not rain. And it did not rain on the land for three years and six months.

18 And he prayed again, and the heaven gave rain, and the land brought forth its fruit.

19 Brothers, if anyone among you goes astray from the truth, and someone turns him back,

20 let him know that he who turns a sinner from the straying of his way shall save a life from death and **cover a great number of sins**. Mish. 10:12

5a Yirm. 22:13.

KĚPHA ALEPH

1 PETER

1 Kěpha, an emissary of יהושע Messiah, to the chosen, strangers of the dispersion in Pontos, Galatia, Kappadokia, Asia, and Bithunia,

2 *chosen* according to the foreknowledge of Elohim the Father, set apart by the Spirit unto obedience [a] and sprinkling of the blood of יהושע Messiah: Favour and peace be increased to you.

3 Blessed be the Elohim and Father of our Master יהושע Messiah, who according to His great compassion has caused us to be born again to a living expectation through the resurrection of יהושע Messiah from the dead,

4 to an inheritance incorruptible and undefiled and unfading, having been kept in the heavens for you,

5 who are protected by the power of Elohim through belief, for a deliverance ready to be revealed in the last time,

6 in which you exult, even though for a little while, if need be, you have been grieved by manifold trials,

7 in order that the proving of your belief – much more precious than gold that perishes, and proven by fire – might be found to result in praise and respect and esteem at the revelation of יהושע Messiah,

8 whom having not seen, you love; in whom you exult with unspeakable and esteemed joy, yet not seeing, but believing,

9 obtaining the goal of your belief: a deliverance of lives.

10 Concerning this deliverance the prophets have sought out and searched out, prophesying concerning the favour for you,

11 searching to know what, or what sort of time, the Spirit which was in them was pointing out concerning Messiah, when it was bearing witness beforehand the sufferings of Messiah, and the esteems that would follow,

12 to whom it was revealed that they were serving, not themselves, but you, in these *matters* which now have been announced to you through those who brought the Good News to you by the Set-apart Spirit sent from heaven – into which messengers long to look into.

13 Therefore, having girded up the loins of your mind, being sober, set your expectation perfectly upon the favour that is to be brought to you at the revelation of יהושע Messiah,

14 as obedient children, not conforming yourselves to the former lusts in your ignorance,

15 instead, as the One who called you is set-apart, so you also should become set-apart in all behaviour,

16 because it has been written, **"Be set-apart, for I am set-apart."** Way. 11:44, 19:2

17 And if you call on the Father, who without partiality judges according to each one's work, pass the time of your sojourning in fear,

18 knowing that you were redeemed from your futile behaviour inherited from your fathers, not with what is corruptible, silver or gold,

19 but with the precious blood of Messiah, as of a lamb unblemished and spotless,

20 foreknown, indeed, before the foundation of the world, but manifested in these last times for your sakes,

21 who through Him believe in Elohim who raised Him from the dead and gave Him esteem, so that your belief and expectation are in Elohim.

22 Now that you have cleansed your lives in obeying the truth through the Spirit to unfeigned brotherly love, love one another fervently with a clean heart,

1a Obedience is also stressed in vv. 14 & 22.

23 having been born again – not of corruptible seed, but incorruptible – through the living Word of Elohim, which remains forever,

24 because **"All flesh is as grass, and all the esteem of man as the flower of the grass. The grass withers, and its flower falls away,**

25 **but the Word of Elohim remains forever."** Yesh. 40:6-8 And this is the Word, announced as Good News to you.

2

Having put aside, then, all evil, and all deceit, and hypocrisies, and envyings, and all evil words,

2 as newborn babes, desire the unadulterated milk of the Word, in order that you grow by it,

3 if indeed you have tasted that the Master is good.

4 Drawing near to Him, a living Stone – rejected indeed by men, but chosen by Elohim and precious –

5 you also, as living stones, are being built up, a spiritual house, a set-apart priesthood, to offer up spiritual slaughter *offerings* acceptable to Elohim through יהושע Messiah.

6 Because it is contained in the Scripture, **"See, I lay in Tsiyon a chief corner-stone, chosen, precious, and he who believes on Him shall by no means be put to shame."** Yesh. 28:16

7 This preciousness, then, is for you who believe; but to those who are disobedient, **"The stone which the builders rejected has become the chief corner-stone,"** Teh. 118:22.

8 and **"A stone of stumbling and a rock that makes for falling,"** Yesh. 8:14 who stumble because they are disobedient [a] to the Word, to which they also were appointed.

9 But you are **a chosen race,** Deḇ. 10:15 [b] **a royal priesthood,** Yesh. 61:6 [c] **a set-apart nation,** Shem. 19:6 [d] **a people for a possession,** Yesh. 43:21 [e] that you should proclaim the praises of Him who called you out of darkness into His marvellous light,

10 who once were **not a people**, but now **the people of Elohim**; who had **not obtained compassion**, but now **obtained compassion.** Hosh. 1:9,10; 2:23 [f]

11 Beloved ones, I appeal to you as sojourners and pilgrims, to abstain from fleshly lusts which battle against the being,

12 having your behaviour among the nations good so that when they speak against you as evil-doers, let them, by observing your good works, [g] esteem Elohim in a day of visitation.

13 Be subject to every institution of man because of the Master, whether to the sovereign as supreme,

14 or to governors, as to those who are sent by him for the punishment of doers of evil, and a praise for those who do good.

15 Because such is the desire of Elohim, that by doing good you should put to silence the ignorance of foolish men,

16 as free, yet not using your freedom as a cloak for evil, but as servants of Elohim.

17 Respect all, love the brotherhood, fear Elohim, respect the sovereign.

18 Servants, be subject to your masters with all fear, not only to the good and gentle, but also to the crooked ones.

19 For this is favour, if because of conscience toward Elohim anyone bears up under grief, suffering unrighteously.

20 For what credit is there in enduring a beating when you sin? But if you suffer for doing good and you endure, this *finds* favour with Elohim.

21 For to this you were called, because Messiah also suffered for us, [h] leaving us [h] an example, that you should follow His steps, [i]

22 **"who committed no sin,** [j] **nor was deceit found in His mouth,"** Yesh. 53:9

23 who, being reviled, did not revile in return; suffering, did not threaten, but committed *Himself* to Him who judges righteously;

2a See Yn. 3:36, Iḇ`rim 3:18. *2b* Also see Yesh. 43:20. *2c* Also see Yesh. 66:21. *2d* Also see Deḇ. 7:6. *2e* Also see Shem. 19:5, Titos 2:14. *2f* Also see Yesh. 65:1, Hosh. 1:9, Yesh. 63:16; 64:8, Rom. 9:25,26. *2g* Mt. 5:16. *2h* *NA* reads "you". *2i* Qor. א 11:1, Yn. א 2:6. *2j* Yn 8:55, Yn. 15:10, Qor. ב 5:21, Yn. א 3:5.

24 who Himself **bore our sins** Yesh. 53:4 in His body on the timber, so that we, having died to sins, might live unto righteousness [k] – **by whose stripes you were healed**. Yesh. 53:5

25 For you were **like sheep going astray**, Yesh. 53:6 but have now returned to the Shepherd and Overseer of your beings.

3 In the same way, wives, be subject to your own husbands, so that if any are disobedient to the Word, they, without a word, might be won by the behaviour of their wives,

2 having seen your blameless behaviour in fear.

3 Your adornment should not be outward – arranging the hair, wearing gold, or putting on dresses –

4 but the hidden man of the heart, with the incorruptible ornament of a meek and peaceable spirit, which is of great value before Elohim.

5 For in this way, in former times, the set-apart women who trusted in Elohim also adorned themselves, being subject to their own husbands,

6 as Sarah obeyed Aḇraham, calling him master, of whom you became children, doing good, and not frightened by any fear.

7 In the same way, husbands, live understandingly together, giving respect to the wife, as to the weaker vessel, and as being heirs together of the favour of life, so that your prayers are not hindered.

8 To sum up, let all of you be like-minded, sympathetic, loving as brothers, tenderhearted, humble-minded,

9 not returning evil for evil or reviling for reviling, but on the contrary blessing, knowing that you were called to this, in order to inherit a blessing.

10 For **"He who wishes to love life and see good days, let him keep his tongue from evil, and his lips from speaking deceit,**

11 **let him turn away from evil and do good, let him seek peace and pursue it.**

12 **"Because the eyes of יהוה are on the righteous, and his ears are open to their prayers, but the face of יהוה is against those who do evil."** Teh. 34:12-16

13 And who is the one doing evil to you, if you become imitators of the good?

14 But even if you suffer for righteousness' sake, you are blessed. [a] **"And do not fear their threats, neither be troubled."** Yesh. 8:12

15 But set apart יהוה Elohim in your hearts, and always be ready to give an answer to everyone asking you a reason concerning the expectation that is in you, with meekness and fear,

16 having a good conscience, so that when they speak against you as doers of evil, those who falsely accuse your good behaviour in Messiah, shall be ashamed.

17 For it is better, if it is the desire of Elohim, to suffer for doing good than for doing evil.

18 Because even Messiah once suffered for sins, the righteous for the unrighteous, to bring you to Elohim, [b] having been put to death indeed in flesh but made alive in the Spirit,

19 in which also He went and proclaimed unto the spirits in prison,

20 who were disobedient at one time when the patience of Elohim waited in the days of Noaḥ, while the ark was being prepared, in which a few, that is, eight beings, were saved through water,

21 which figure now also saves us: immersion – not a putting away of the filth of the flesh, but the answer of a good conscience toward Elohim – through the resurrection of יהושע Messiah,

22 who, having gone into heaven, **is at the right hand of Elohim**, Teh. 110:1 messengers and authorities and powers having been subjected to Him.

4 Therefore, since Messiah suffered in the flesh, arm yourselves also with the same mind, because he who has suffered in the flesh has ceased from sin, [a]

2 so that he no longer lives the rest of his time in the flesh for the lusts of men, but

2k Rom. 6:2, Kěpha א 4:1-2. *3a* Mt. 5:10. *3b* Rom. 5:18. *4a* Rom. 6:2-22, Kěpha א 2:25.

according to the desire of Elohim.
3 For we *have spent* enough of our past
lifetime in doing the desire of the nations,
having walked in indecencies, lusts, drunkenness, orgies, wild parties, and abominable idolatries,
4 in which they are surprised that you do
not run with them in the same flood of
loose behaviour, blaspheming,
5 who shall give an account to Him who
is ready to judge the living and the dead.
6 For this reason the Good News was
also brought to those who are dead, so that,
whereas they are judged according to men
in the flesh, they might live according to
Elohim in the spirit.
7 But the end of all has drawn near.
Therefore be sober-minded, and be attentive in the prayers.
8 And above all have fervent love for
one another, because **love covers a great
number of sins.** Mish. 10:12
9 Welcome one another without grumbling.
10 As each one has received a gift, serve
one another, as good trustees of the manifold favour of Elohim.
11 If anyone speaks, *let it be* as the Words
of Elohim. If anyone serves, *let it be* as
with the strength which Elohim provides,
so that Elohim might be praised in it all
through יהושע Messiah, to whom belong
the esteem and the rule forever and ever.
Amĕn.
12 Beloved ones, do not be surprised at the
fiery trial that is coming upon you, to try
you, as though some unusual matter has
befallen you,
13 but as you share Messiah's sufferings, [b]
rejoice, in order that you might rejoice
exultingly at the revelation of His esteem.
14 If you are reproached for the Name of
Messiah, *you are* blessed, because the
Spirit of esteem and of Elohim rests upon
you. On their part He is blasphemed, but
on your part He is praised.
15 For do not let any of you suffer as a
murderer, or thief, or doer of evil, or as a
meddler.
16 But if *one suffers* being Messianic, let
him not be ashamed, but let him esteem
Elohim in this matter.
17 Because it is time for judgment to begin
from the House of Elohim. And if firstly
from us, what is the end of those who do
not obey the Good News of Elohim?
18 **And if the righteous one is scarcely
saved, where shall the wicked and the
sinner appear?** Mish. 11:31
19 So then, those who suffer according to
the desire of Elohim should commit their
lives to a trustworthy Creator, in doing
good.

5 Therefore, as a fellow elder and a witness of the sufferings of Messiah, and
also a sharer of the esteem that is to be
revealed, I appeal to the elders among you:
2 Shepherd the flock of Elohim which is
among you, serving as overseers, not by
compulsion but voluntarily, not out of
greed for filthy gain, but eagerly,
3 neither as being masters over those
entrusted to you, but being examples to the
flock.
4 And when the Chief Shepherd [a]
appears, you shall receive the never-fading
crown of esteem.
5 In the same way, you younger ones, be
subject to elders. And gird yourselves with
humility toward one another, for **"Elohim
resists the proud, but gives favour to the
humble."** Mish. 3:34
6 Humble yourselves, then, under the
mighty hand of Elohim, so that He exalts
you in due time,
7 casting all your worry upon Him, for
He is concerned about you.
8 Be sober, watch, because your adversary the devil walks about like a roaring
lion, seeking someone to devour.
9 Resist him, firm in the belief, knowing
that the same hardships are experienced by
your brotherhood in the world.
10 And the Elohim of all favour, who
called you to His everlasting esteem by
Messiah יהושע, after you have suffered a
while, Himself perfect, establish, strength-
en, and settle you.
11 To Him be the esteem and the might
forever and ever. Amĕn.
12 Through Silas the trustworthy brother,

as I reckon, I have written to you briefly,
encouraging and witnessing that this is the
true favour of Elohim. In this stand fast.
13 She who is in Baḇel, chosen together
with you, greets you, also my son, Marqos.
14 Greet one another with a kiss of love.
Peace to all of you who are in Messiah
יהושע. Amĕn.

KĔPHA BĔT

2 PETER

1 Shim'on Kĕpha, a servant and emissary of יהושע Messiah, to those who
have obtained a belief as precious as ours
by the righteousness of our Elohim and
Saviour יהושע Messiah:
2 Favour and peace be increased to you
in the knowledge of Elohim and of יהושע
our Master,
3 as His Mighty-like power has given to
us all we need for life and reverence,
through the knowledge of Him who called
us to esteem and uprightness.
4 Through these there have been given
to us exceedingly great and precious
promises, so that through these you might
be partakers of the Mighty-like nature,
having escaped from the corruption in the
world, caused by lust.
5 And for this reason do your utmost to
add to your belief uprightness, to uprightness knowledge,
6 to knowledge self-control, to self-
control endurance, to endurance reverence,
7 to reverence brotherly affection, and to
brotherly affection love.
8 For if these are in you and increase,
they cause you to be neither inactive nor
without fruit in the knowledge of our
Master יהושע Messiah.
9 For he in whom these are not present is
blind, being shortsighted, and has forgotten that he has been cleansed from his old
sins.
10 For this reason, brothers, all the more
do your utmost to make firm your calling
and choosing [a], for if you are doing these
matters you shall never stumble at all,
11 for in this way an entrance into the
everlasting reign of our Master and
Saviour יהושע Messiah shall be richly
supplied to you.
12 And so I intend to remind you of these
matters again and again, though you know
them and have been established in the
present truth.
13 But I think it is right, as long as I am in
this tent, to stir you up by a reminder,
14 knowing that the putting off of my tent
is soon, even as our Master יהושע
Messiah made clear to me.
15 And I shall do my utmost also, to see to
it that you always have a reminder of these
matters after my departure.
16 For we did not follow cleverly devised
stories when we made known to you the
power and coming of our Master יהושע
Messiah, but were eye-witnesses of His
superbness.
17 For when He received respect and
esteem from Elohim the Father, such a
voice came to Him from the Excellent
Esteem, "This is My Son, the Beloved in
whom I did delight."
18 And we heard this voice which came
from heaven when we were with Him on
the set-apart mountain.
19 And we have the prophetic word made
more certain, which you do well to heed as
a light that shines in a dark place, until the
day dawns and the morning star rises in
your hearts,
20 knowing this first, that no prophecy
of Scripture came to be of one's own interpretation,
21 for prophecy never came by the desire
of man, but men of Elohim spoke, being
moved by the Set-apart Spirit.

2 But there also came to be false
prophets [a] among the people, as also
among you there shall be false teachers,
who shall secretly bring in destructive
heresies, and deny the Master who bought
them, bringing swift destruction on themselves.
2 And many shall follow their destructive

1a Mt. 20:16, Mt. 22:14, Ḥazon 17:14. *2a* See also v. 7-8, 21 & Mt. 7:15-23.

ways, because of whom the way of truth
shall be evil spoken of,
3 and in greed, with fabricated words,
they shall use you for gain. From of old
their judgment does not linger, and their
destruction does not slumber.
4 For if Elohim did not spare the messengers who sinned, but sent them to
Tartaros,[b] and delivered them into chains
of darkness, to be kept for judgment,
5 and did not spare the world of old, but
preserved Noaḥ, a proclaimer of righteousness, and seven others, bringing in the
flood on the world of the wicked,
6 and having reduced to ashes the cities
of Seḏom and Amorah condemned them to
destruction – having made them an example to those who afterward would live
wickedly,
7 and rescued righteous Lot, who was
oppressed with the indecent behaviour of
the lawless [c]
8 (for day after day that righteous man,
dwelling among them, tortured his righteous being by seeing and hearing their
lawless works),
9 *then* יהוה knows how to rescue the reverent ones from trial and to keep the
unrighteous unto the day of judgment, to
be punished,
10 and most of all those walking after the
flesh in filthy lust and despising authority
– bold, headstrong, speaking evil of
esteemed ones,
11 whereas messengers who are greater in
strength and power do not bring a slanderous accusation against them before the
Master.
12 But these, like natural unreasoning
beasts, having been born to be caught and
destroyed, blaspheme that which they do
not know, shall be destroyed in their
destruction,
13 being about to receive the wages of
unrighteousness, deeming indulgence in
the day of pleasure, spots and blemishes,
revelling in their own deceptions while
they feast with you,
14 having eyes filled with an adulteress,
and unable to cease from sin, enticing
unstable beings, having a heart trained in
greed, children of a curse,
15 having left the right way they went
astray, having followed the way of Bilʿam
the son of Beʿor, who loved the wages of
unrighteousness, [d]
16 but he was rebuked for his transgression: a dumb donkey speaking with the
voice of a man restrained the madness of
the prophet.
17 These are fountains without water,
clouds driven by a storm, to whom the
blackest darkness is kept forever.
18 For speaking arrogant nonsense, they
entice – through the lusts of the flesh,
through indecencies – the ones who have
indeed escaped from those living in
delusion,
19 promising them freedom, though themselves being slaves of corruption – for one
is a slave to whatever overcomes him.
20 For if, after they have escaped the
defilements of the world through the
knowledge of the Master and Saviour
יהושע Messiah, they are again entangled
in them and overcome, the latter end is
worse for them than the first.
21 For it would have been better for them
not to have known the way of righteousness, than having known it, to turn from
the set-apart command [e] delivered unto
them.
22 For them the proverb has proved true,
"A dog returns to his own vomit," Mish.
26:11 and, "A washed sow *returns* to her
rolling in the mud."

3 This is now, beloved ones, the second
letter I write to you, in which I stir up
your sincere mind, to remember
2 the words previously spoken by the
set-apart prophets, and of the command of
the Master and Saviour, *spoken* by your
emissaries,

2b Possibly from Hebrew: Taḥti - See Explanatory notes - She'ol. *2c* The Greek word here, and in 3:17, is *athesmos* (not the usual one, *anomos*) but it also means "lawless." *2d* vv. 11-15; compare with Yeh. 7-11.
2e The singular "command" often means "commands" – see Tim. א 6:14, Deḇ. 17:20, Teh. 19:8.

3 knowing this first: that mockers shall come in the last days with mocking, walking according to their own lusts,

4 and saying, "Where is the promise of His coming? For since the fathers fell asleep, all continues as from the beginning of creation."

5 For they choose to have this hidden from them: that the heavens were of old, and the earth standing out of water and in the water, by the Word of Elohim, [a]

6 through which the world at that time was destroyed, being flooded with water.

7 And the present heavens and the earth are treasured up by the same Word, being kept for fire, to a day of judgment and destruction of wicked men.

8 But, beloved ones, let not this one *matter* be hidden from you: that with יהוה one day is as a thousand years, and **a thousand years as one day**. Teh. 90:4

9 יהוה is not slow in regard to the promise, as some count slowness, but is patient toward us, not wishing that any should perish but that all should come to repentance. [b]

10 But the day of יהוה shall come as a thief in the night, in which the heavens shall pass away with a great noise, and the elements shall melt with intense heat, and the earth and the works that are in it shall be burned up.

11 Seeing all these are to be destroyed in this way, what kind of people ought you to be in set-apart behaviour and reverence,

12 looking for and hastening the coming of the day of Elohim, through which the heavens shall be destroyed, being set on fire, and the elements melt with intense heat!

13 But according to His promise we wait for a **renewed heavens and a renewed earth** Yesh. 65:17; 66:22 in which righteousness dwells.

14 So then, beloved ones, looking forward to this, do your utmost to be found by Him in peace, spotless and blameless,

15 and reckon the patience of our Master as deliverance, as also our beloved brother Sha'ul wrote to you, according to the wisdom given to him,

16 as also in all *his* letters, speaking in them concerning these *matters*, in which some are hard to understand, [c] which those who are untaught and unstable twist to their own destruction, as they do also the other Scriptures.

17 You, then, beloved ones, being forewarned, watch, lest you also fall from your own steadfastness, being led away with the delusion of the lawless,

18 but grow in the favour and knowledge of our Master and Saviour יהושע Messiah. To Him be the esteem both now and to a day that abides. Amĕn.

3a Iḇ`rim 11:3. *3b* Tim. א 2:4. *3c* See Qor. ב 11:6.

YOḤANAN ALEPH

1 JOHN

1 What was from the beginning, what
we have heard, what we have seen
with our eyes, what we have looked upon,
and our hands have handled, concerning
the Word of life:
2 And the life was manifested, and we
have seen, and bear witness, and announce
to you that everlasting life which was with
the Father and was manifested to us.
3 We announce to you what we have seen
and heard, so that you too might have fellowship with us. And truly our fellowship
is with the Father and with His Son יהושע
Messiah.
4 And we write this to you in order that
your joy might be complete.
5 And this is the message which we have
heard from Him and announce to you, that
Elohim is light and in Him is no darkness
at all.
6 If we say that we have fellowship with
Him, and walk in darkness, we lie and are
not doing the truth.
7 But if we walk in the light as He is in
the light, we have fellowship with one
another, and the blood of יהושע Messiah
His Son cleanses us from all sin.
8 If we say that we have no sin, we are
misleading ourselves, and the truth is not
in us.
9 If we confess our sins, He is trustworthy and righteous to forgive us the sins and
cleanse us from all unrighteousness.
10 If we say that we have not sinned, we
make Him a liar, and His Word is not in us.

2 My little children, I write this to you,
so that you do not sin. And if anyone
sins, we have an Intercessor with the
Father, יהושע Messiah, a righteous One.
2 And He Himself is an atoning offering
for our sins, and not for ours only but also
for all the world.
3 And by this we know that we know
Him, if we guard His commands. [a]
4 The one who says, "I know Him," and
does not guard His commands, is a liar,
and the truth is not in him.
5 But whoever guards His Word, truly the
love of Elohim has been perfected [b] in
him. By this we know that we are in Him. [c]
6 The one who says he stays in Him
ought himself also to walk, even as He
walked.
7 Beloved, I write no fresh command to
you, but an old command which you have
had from the beginning. The old command
is the Word which you heard from the
beginning. [d]
8 Again I write you a fresh command,
which is true in Him and in you, because
the darkness is passing away, and the true
light now shines.
9 The one who says he is in the light, and
hates his brother, is in the darkness until
now.
10 The one who loves his brother stays in
the light, and there is no stumbling-block
in him.
11 But the one who hates his brother is in
the darkness and walks in the darkness,
and does not know where he is going,
because the darkness has blinded his eyes.
12 I write to you, little children, because
your sins have been forgiven on account of
His Name.
13 I write to you, fathers, because you
have known Him from the beginning. I
write to you, young men, because you have
overcome the wicked one. I write to you,
little children, because you have known
the Father.
14 I wrote to you, fathers, because you
have known Him from the beginning. I
wrote to you, young men, because you are

2a See 3:6. *2b* Ber. 17:1, Teh. 119:1, Mt. 5:48. *2c* See 3:24. *2d* See v. 24.

strong, and the Word of Elohim stays in
you, and you have overcome the wicked
one.
15 Do not love the world nor that which is
in the world. If anyone loves the world, the
love of the Father is not in him. [e]
16 Because all that is in the world – the
lust of the flesh, the lust of the eyes, and
the pride of life – is not of the Father but is
of the world.
17 And the world passes away, and the lust
of it, but the one doing the desire of
Elohim remains forever.
18 Little children, it is the last hour. And
as you have heard that the anti-messiah is
coming, even now many anti-messiahs
have come. This is how we know that it is
the last hour.
19 They went out from us, but they were
not of us, for if they had been of us, they
would have stayed with us – but in order
that it might be made manifest that none of
them were of us.
20 And you have an anointing from the
Set-apart One, and you know all.
21 I did not write to you because you do
not know the truth, but because you know
it, and because no falsehood is of the truth.
22 Who is the liar, except the one denying
that יהושע is the Messiah? This is the anti-
messiah, the one denying the Father and
the Son.
23 No one denying the Son has the Father.
The one confessing the Son has the Father
as well.
24 As for you, let that stay in you which
you heard from the beginning. If what you
heard from the beginning stays in you, you
also shall stay in the Son and in the Father.
25 And this is the promise that He has
promised us: everlasting life.
26 I have written this to you concerning
those who lead you astray.
27 But the anointing which you have
received from Him stays in you, and you
have no need that anyone should teach
you. But as the same anointing does teach
you concerning all, and is true, and is no
falsehood, and even as it has taught you,
you stay in Him.
28 And now, little children, stay in Him,
so that when He appears, we might have
boldness and not be ashamed before Him
at His coming.
29 If you know that He is righteous, you
know that everyone doing righteousness
has been born of Him. [f]

3 See what love the Father has given us,
that we should be called children of
Elohim! For this reason the world does not
know us, because it did not know Him.
2 Beloved ones, now we are children of
Elohim. And it has not yet been revealed
what we shall be, but we know that when
He is revealed, we shall be like Him, for
we shall see Him as He is.
3 And everyone having this expectation
in Him cleanses himself, as He is clean.
4 Everyone doing sin also does lawlessness, and sin is lawlessness.
5 And you know that He was manifested
to take away our sins, and in Him there is
no sin.
6 Everyone staying in Him does not sin.
Everyone sinning has neither seen Him nor
known Him. [a]
7 Little children, let no one lead you
astray. The one doing righteousness is
righteous, even as He is righteous. [b]
8 The one doing sin is of the devil,
because the devil has sinned from the
beginning. For this purpose the Son of
Elohim was manifested: to destroy the
works of the devil. [c]
9 Everyone having been born of Elohim
does not sin, because His seed stays in
him, and he is powerless to sin, because he
has been born of Elohim.
10 In this the children of Elohim and the
children of the devil are manifest: Everyone not doing righteousness is not of
Elohim, [d] neither the one not loving his
brother.
11 Because this is the message that you
heard from the beginning, that we should

2e Ya'aqoḇ 4:4. *2f* See 3:7-10, 5:4, 5:18. *3a* See 2:4 & 3 Yn. v. 11. *3b* See 2:29. *3c* See Titos 2:14.
3d See Yn. ג v. 11.

love one another,
12 not as Qayin who was of the wicked
one and killed his brother. And why did he
kill him? Because his works were wicked
but those of his brother were righteous.
13 Do not marvel, my brothers, if the
world hates you. [e]
14 We know that we have passed out of
death into life, because we love the brothers. The one not loving his brother stays in
death.
15 Everyone hating his brother is a murderer, and you know that no murderer has
everlasting life staying in him.
16 By this we have known love, because
He laid down His life for us. And we ought
to lay down *our* lives for the brothers.
17 But whoever has this world's goods,
and sees his brother in need, and shuts up
his tender affections from him, how does
the love of Elohim stay in him?
18 My little children, let us not love in
word or in tongue, but in deed and in truth.
19 And by this we know that we are of the
truth, and shall set our hearts at rest before
Him,
20 that if our heart condemns us, Elohim is
greater than our heart, and knows all.
21 Beloved ones, if our heart does not condemn us, we have boldness toward
Elohim.
22 And whatever we ask we receive from
Him, because we guard His commands and
do what is pleasing in His sight. [f]
23 And this is His command, that we
should believe in the Name of His Son
יהושע Messiah and love one another, as
He gave us command.
24 And the one guarding His commands
stays in Him, and He in him. And by this
we know that He stays in us, by the Spirit
which He gave us. [g]

4 Beloved ones, do not believe every
spirit, but prove the spirits, whether
they are of Elohim, because many false
prophets have gone out into the world.
2 By this you know the Spirit of Elohim:
Every spirit that confesses that יהושע
Messiah has come in the flesh is of
Elohim,
3 and every spirit that does not confess
that יהושע Messiah has come in the flesh
is not of Elohim. And this is the *spirit* of
the anti-messiah which you heard is coming, and now is already in the world.
4 You are of Elohim, little children, and
have overcome them, because He who is in
you is greater than he who is in the world.
5 They are of the world, therefore they
speak as of the world, and the world hears
them.
6 We are of Elohim – the one knowing
Elohim hears us. He who is not of Elohim
does not hear us. By this we know the
Spirit of the Truth and the spirit of the
delusion.
7 Beloved ones, let us love one another,
because love is of Elohim, and everyone
who loves has been born of Elohim, and
knows Elohim.
8 The one who does not love does not
know Elohim, for Elohim is love.
9 By this the love of Elohim was manifested in us, that Elohim has sent His only
brought-forth Son into the world, in order
that we might live through Him.
10 In this is love, not that we loved
Elohim, but that He loved us and sent His
Son to be an atoning offering for our sins.
11 Beloved ones, if Elohim so loved us,
we also ought to love one another.
12 No one has seen Elohim at any time. If
we love one another, Elohim does stay in
us, and His love has been perfected in us.
13 By this we know that we stay in Him,
and He in us, because He has given us of
His Spirit.
14 And we have seen and bear witness that
the Father has sent the Son, Saviour of the
world.
15 Whoever confesses that יהושע is the
Son of Elohim, Elohim stays in him, and
he in Elohim.
16 And we have known and believed the
love that Elohim has for us. Elohim is love,

3e See Yn. 15:18-19, Yn. 17:14. *3f* Mish. 28:9, Yn. 9:31, Ya'aqoḇ 5:16.
3g Yn. 14:23-24, Ma. 5:32, Rom. 8:7-11, Yn. א 2:5, Yn. א 4:13.

and he who stays in love stays in Elohim, and Elohim in him.

17 By this love has been perfected with us, in order that we might have boldness in the day of judgment, because as He is so are we in this world.

18 There is no fear in love, but perfect love casts out fear, because fear holds punishment, and he who fears has not been made perfect in love.

19 We love Him because He first loved us.

20 If someone says, "I love Elohim," and hates his brother, he is a liar. For the one not loving his brother whom he has seen, how is he able to love Elohim whom he has not seen?

21 And we have this command from Him, that the one loving Elohim should love his brother too.

5

Everyone who believes that יהושע is the Messiah has been born of Elohim, and everyone who loves the One bringing forth also loves the one having been born of Him.

2 By this we know that we love the children of Elohim, when we love Elohim and guard His commands.

3 For this is the love for Elohim, that we guard His commands, [a] and His commands are not heavy,

4 because everyone having been born of Elohim overcomes the world. And this is the overcoming that has overcome the world: our belief.

5 Who is the one who overcomes the world but he who believes that יהושע is the Son of Elohim?

6 This is the One that came by water and blood: יהושע Messiah, not only by water, but by water and blood. And it is the Spirit who bears witness, because the Spirit is the Truth.

7 Because there are three who bear witness:

8 the Spirit, and the water, and the blood. And the three are in agreement.

9 If we receive the witness of men, the witness of Elohim is greater, because this is the witness of Elohim which He has witnessed concerning His Son.

10 The one who believes in the Son of Elohim has the witness in himself, the one who does not believe Elohim has made Him a liar, because he has not believed the witness that Elohim has given concerning His Son.

11 And this is the witness: that Elohim has given us everlasting life, and this life is in His Son.

12 He who possesses the Son possesses life, he who does not possess the Son of Elohim does not possess life.

13 I have written this to you who believe in the Name of the Son of Elohim, so that you know that you possess everlasting life, and so that you believe in the Name of the Son of Elohim.

14 And this is the boldness that we have in Him, that if we ask whatever according to His desire, He hears us.

15 And if we know that He hears us, whatever we ask, we know that we have the petitions that we have asked of Him.

16 If anyone sees his brother sinning a sin, not unto death, he shall ask, and He shall give him life for those not sinning unto death. There is a sin unto death. I do not say that he should pray about that.

17 All unrighteousness is sin, and there is a sin not unto death.

18 We know that everyone having been born of Elohim does not sin, [b] but the one having been born of Elohim guards himself, and the wicked one does not touch him. [c]

19 We know that we are of Elohim, and all the world lies in the wicked one.

20 And we know that the Son of Elohim has come and has given us an understanding, so that we might know the true One. And we are in the true One, in His Son יהושע Messiah. This is the true Elohim and everlasting life.

21 Little children, keep yourselves from idols. [d] Amĕn.

5a See 5:2, Yn. ב v. 6, and Yn. 14:15. *5b* See 3:6-9. *5c* See 4:4. *5d* See Qor. א 10:14.

YOḤANAN BĔT

2 JOHN

1 The elder, to a chosen Kuria and her
children, whom I love in truth, and not
only I, but also all those who have known
the truth,
2 because of the truth which stays in us
and shall be with us forever:
3 Favour, compassion, peace be with you
from Elohim the Father, and from the
Master יהושע Messiah, the Son of the
Father, in truth and love.
4 I rejoiced greatly because I found some
of your children walking in truth, as we
received a command from the Father.
5 And now I ask you, Kuria, not as
though I wrote a fresh command to you,
but that which we have had from the
beginning: that we love one another.
6 And this is the love, that we walk
according to His commands. [a] This is the
command, that as you have heard from the
beginning, you should walk in it.
7 Because many who are leading astray
went out into the world who do not confess יהושע Messiah as coming in the
flesh. This one is he who is leading astray
and the anti-messiah.
8 See to yourselves, that we do not lose
what we worked for, but that we might
receive a complete reward.
9 Everyone who is transgressing and not
staying in the teaching of Messiah does not
possess Elohim. [b] The one who stays in the
teaching of Messiah possesses both the
Father and the Son. [c]
10 If anyone comes to you and does not
bring this teaching, do not receive him into
your house nor greet him,
11 for he who greets him shares in his
wicked works.
12 Having much to write to you, I did not
wish to do so with paper and ink, but I
expect to come to you and speak face to
face, so that our joy might be complete.
13 The children of your chosen sister greet
you. Amĕn.

1a See Yn. א 5:3, and Yn. 14:15. *1b* Tim. א 6:3. *1c* See Yn. א 1:3, Yn. א 2:22, Yn. א 5:20.

YOḤANAN GIMEL

3 JOHN

1 The elder, to the beloved Gaios,
whom I love in truth:
2 Beloved ones, I pray for you to do well
in every way, and be in health, as your life
is doing well.
3 For I rejoiced greatly when brothers
came and witnessed of the truth in you, as
you walk in the truth.
4 I have no greater joy than to hear of my
children walking in truth.
5 Beloved ones, you are acting trustworthily in whatever you do for the brothers and for strangers,
6 who have borne witness of your love
before the assembly. If you send them
forward worthily of Elohim, you shall do
well,
7 because they went out for the sake of
the Name, receiving naught from the
nations.
8 Therefore we ought to receive such, so
that we become fellow workers for the
truth.
9 I wrote to the assembly, but Diotrephes,
who loves to be the first among them, does
not receive us.
10 So if I come, I shall call to mind his
works which he does, babbling against us
with wicked words. And not satisfied
with that, he himself does not receive the
brothers, and forbids those who wish to,
putting them out of the assembly.
11 Beloved ones, do not imitate the evil,
but the good. The one who is doing good is
of Elohim, but he who is doing evil has not
seen Elohim. [a]
12 Demetrios has a good witness from all,
and from the truth itself. And we also bear
witness, and you know that our witness is
true.
13 I had much to write, but I do not wish
to write to you with pen and ink,
14 but I expect to see you shortly, and we
shall speak face to face. Peace to you. The
friends greet you. Greet the friends by
name.

1a See Yn. א 3:6-10.

YEHUḎAH

JUDE

1 Yehuḏah, a servant of יהושע Messiah,
and brother of Ya'aqoḇ, to those who
are called, set-apart by Elohim the Father,
and preserved in יהושע Messiah:
2 Compassion, and peace, and love be
increased to you.
3 Beloved ones, making all haste to write
to you concerning our common deliverance, I felt the necessity to write to you
urging you to earnestly contend for the
belief which was once for all delivered to
the set-apart ones.
4 For certain men have slipped in, whose
judgment was written about long ago,
wicked ones [a] perverting the favour of our
Elohim for indecency, and denying the
only Master יהוה and our Master יהושע
Messiah.
5 But I intend to remind you, though you
once knew this, that יהוה, having saved a
people out of the land of Mitsrayim, afterward destroyed those who did not believe.
6 And the messengers who did not keep
their own principality, but left their own
dwelling, He has kept in everlasting shackles under darkness for the judgment of the
great day.
7 Even as Seḏom and Amorah and the
cities around them in a similar way to
these, having given themselves over to
whoring and gone after strange flesh, are
set forth as an example, undergoing judi-
cial punishment of everlasting fire.
8 In the same way, indeed, these dreamers defile the flesh, and reject authority,
and speak evil of esteemed ones.
9 But Miḵa'ĕl the chief messenger, in
contending with the devil, when he disputed about the body of Mosheh, presumed
not to bring against him a blasphemous
accusation, but said, **"יהוה rebuke you!"**
Zeḵ. 3:2
10 But these blaspheme that which they
do not know. And that which they know
naturally, like unreasoning beasts, in these
they corrupt themselves.
11 Woe to them! Because they have gone
in the way of Qayin, and gave themselves
to the delusion of Bil'am for a reward, and
perished in the rebellion of Qoraḥ. [b]
12 These are rocky reefs in your love
feasts, feasting with you, feeding themselves without fear, waterless clouds borne
about by the winds, late autumn trees without fruit, twice dead, pulled up by the
roots,
13 wild waves of the sea foaming up their
own shame, straying stars for whom blackness of darkness is kept forever.
14 And Ḥanoḵ, the seventh from Adam,
also prophesied of these, saying, "See,
יהוה comes with His myriads of set-apart
ones,
15 to execute judgment on all, to punish
all who are wicked among them concerning all their wicked works which they have
committed in a wicked way, and concerning all the harsh *words* which wicked
sinners have spoken against Him."
16 These are grumblers, complainers, who
walk according to their own lusts, and their
mouth speaks proudly, admiring faces *of
others* for the sake of gain.
17 But you, beloved ones, remember the
words spoken before by the emissaries of
our Master יהושע Messiah,
18 because they told you that there would
be mockers in the last time who would
walk according to their own wicked lusts.
19 These are the ones who cause divisions,
not having the Spirit.
20 But you, beloved ones, building yourselves up on your most set-apart belief,
praying in the Set-apart Spirit,

1a See also Mt. 13 and Tas. ב 2. *1b* vv. 7-11; compare with Keph. ב 2:6-15.

21 keep yourselves in the love of Elohim,
looking for the compassion of our Master
יהושע Messiah unto everlasting life.
22 And show compassion toward some
who are doubting,
23 but others save with fear, snatching
them out of the fire, hating, even the garment defiled by the flesh. [c]
24 And to Him who is able to keep you
from stumbling, and to present you blameless before the presence of His esteem with
exceeding joy,
25 to the only wise Elohim, our Saviour,
be esteem and greatness and might and
authority, both now and forever. Amĕn.

1c See also Rom. 8:5-10 and Gal. 5:19-21.

ḤAZON

REVELATION

1 Revelation of יהושע Messiah, which Elohim gave Him to show His servants what has to take place with speed. And He signified it by sending His messenger to His servant Yoḥanan,

2 who bore witness to the Word of Elohim, and the witness of יהושע Messiah – to all he saw.

3 Blessed is he who reads and those who hear the words of this prophecy, and guard what is written in it, for the time is near.

4 Yoḥanan, to the seven assemblies that are in Asia: Favour to you and peace from Him who is and who was and who is coming, and from the seven Spirits that are before His throne,

5 and from יהושע Messiah, the trustworthy witness, the first-born from the dead, and the ruler of the sovereigns of the earth. To Him who loved us and washed us from our sins in His own blood,

6 and has made us sovereigns and priests to His Elohim and Father, to Him be esteem and rule forever and ever. Amĕn.

7 **See, He is coming with the clouds,** Dan. 7:13 **and every eye shall see Him, even they who pierced Him. And all the tribes of the earth shall mourn because of Him.** Zeḵ. 12:10 Yes, Amĕn.

8 "I am the 'Aleph' and the 'Taw', Beginning and End," says יהוה "who is and who was and who is to come, the Almighty."

9 I, Yoḥanan, both your brother and co-sharer in pressure, and in the reign and endurance of יהושע Messiah, came to be on the island that is called Patmos for the Word of Elohim and for the witness of יהושע Messiah.

10 I came to be in the Spirit on the Day of יהוה, [a] and I heard behind me a loud voice, as of a trumpet,

11 saying, "I am the 'Aleph' and the 'Taw', the First and the Last," and, "Write in a book what you see and send it to the seven assemblies of Asia – to Ephesos, and to Smurna, and to Pergamos, and to Thyatira, and to Sardis, and to Philadelphia, and to Laodikeia."

12 And I turned to see the voice which spoke with me. And having turned, I saw **seven golden lampstands,** Zeḵ. 4:2

13 and in the midst of the seven lampstands **One like the Son of Aḏam,** Dan. 7:13 **dressed in a robe** down to the feet and **girded about the chest with a golden band.** Dan. 10:5

14 And His head and hair were white as white wool, as snow, and **His eyes as a flame of fire,**

15 **and His feet like burnished brass,** Dan. 10:6 as if refined in a furnace, **and His voice as the sound of many waters.** Yeḥ. 1:24; 43:2

16 And in His right hand He held seven stars, and out of His mouth went a sharp two-edged sword, [b] and His face was as the sun shining in its strength.

17 And when I saw Him, I fell at His feet as dead, and He placed His right hand on me, saying, "Do not be afraid, **I am the First and the Last,** Yesh. 44:6; 48:12

18 and the living One. And I became dead, and see, I am living forever and ever. Amĕn. And I possess the keys of She'ol [c] and of Death.

19 "Write therefore what you have seen, both what is now and what shall take place after these:

20 "The secret of the seven stars which you saw in My right hand, and the seven golden lampstands: The seven stars are messengers of the seven assemblies, and the seven lampstands which you saw are seven assemblies.

1a See also Yesh. 13:6,9; Yeḥ. 13:5; Yo'ĕl 1:15, 2:1,11,31, 3:14; Amos 5:16-20; Oḇaḏ.1:15; Tseph. 1:7,14; Mal. 4:5; Ma. 2:20; Tas. א. 5:2; Tas. ב 2:2; Keph. ב 3:10. *1b* See 2:16, Yesh.49:2, Iḇ`rim 4:12. *1c* See Explanatory notes - She'ol.

2 "To the messenger of the assembly of
Ephesos write, 'He who is holding
the seven stars in His right hand, who is
walking in the midst of the seven golden
lampstands, says this:
2 "I know your works, and your labour,
and your endurance, and that you are not
able to bear evil ones, and have tried those
who say they are emissaries and are not,
and have found them false;
3 and you have been bearing up and have
endurance, and have laboured for My
Name's sake and have not become weary.
4 "But I hold this against you, that you
have left your first love.
5 "So remember from where you have
fallen, and repent and do the first works, or
else I shall come to you speedily and
remove your lampstand from its place,
unless you repent.
6 "Yet this you have, that you hate the
works of the Nikolaites, which I also hate.
7 "He who has an ear, let him hear what
the Spirit says to the assemblies. To him
who overcomes [a] I shall give to eat from
the **tree of life**, which is **in the midst of**
the paradise [b] of Elohim." ' Ber. 2:9; 3:22,24 [c]
8 "And to the messenger of the assembly
in Smurna write, 'This says the **First and**
the Last, Yesh. 44:6; 48:12 who became dead,
and came to life:
9 "I know your works, and pressure,
and poverty – yet you are rich – and the
blasphemy of those who say they are
Yehuḏim and are not, but are a congregation of Satan.
10 "Do not be afraid of what you are about
to suffer. See, the devil is about to throw
some of you into prison, in order to try
you, and you shall have pressure ten days.
Be trustworthy until death, and I shall give
you the crown of life.
11 "He who has an ear, let him hear what
the Spirit says to the assemblies. He who
overcomes shall by no means be harmed
by the second death." ' [d]
12 "And to the messenger of the assembly
in Pergamos write, 'He who has the sharp
two-edged sword, says this:
13 "I know your works, and where you
dwell, where the throne of Satan is. And
you hold fast to My Name, and did not
deny the belief in Me, even in the days in
which Antipas was My trustworthy witness, who was killed near you, where
Satan dwells.
14 "But I hold a few *matters* against you,
because you have there those who adhere
to the teaching of Bilʿam, who taught
Balaq to put a stumbling-block before the
children of Yisra'ěl, to eat *food* offered to
idols, and to commit whoring.
15 "So you also have those who adhere to
the teaching of the Nikolaites, which
teaching I hate.
16 "Repent, or else I shall come to you
speedily and fight against them with the
sword of My mouth.
17 "He who has an ear, let him hear what
the Spirit says to the assemblies. To him
who overcomes I shall give some of the
hidden manna to eat. And I shall give him
a white stone, and on the stone a renewed
Name written which no one knows except
him who receives it." '
18 "And to the messenger of the assembly
in Thyatira write, 'This says the Son of
Elohim, who has **eyes like a flame of fire**,
and **His feet like burnished brass**: Dan. 10:5-6
19 "I know your works, and love, and service, and belief, and your endurance. And
as for your works, the last are more than
the first.
20 "But I hold against you that you allow
that woman Izeḇel, who calls herself a
prophetess, to teach and lead My servants
astray to commit whoring and to eat *food*
offered to idols.
21 "And I gave her time to repent of her
whoring, and she did not repent.
22 "See, I am throwing her into a sickbed,
and those who commit adultery with her
into great affliction, unless they repent of
their works.
23 "And I shall slay her children with

2a This word (and its noun) is used 17 times in the Book of Revelation. The name Yisra'ěl means to *overcome with Ěl.* *2b* Lit. garden. *2c* See 22:2 & 14. *2d* See 20:6.

death. And all the assemblies shall know
that I am the One searching the kidneys
and hearts. And I shall give to each one of
you according to your works.
24 "And to you I say, and to the rest in
Thyatira, as many as do not possess this
teaching, and who have not known the
depths of Satan, as they call them, I am not
putting on you another burden.
25 "But hold fast what you have until I
come.
26 "And he who overcomes, and guards
My works until the end, **to him I shall
give authority over the nations,** Teh. 2:8
27 and he shall shepherd them **with a rod
of iron, as the potter's vessels shall be
broken to pieces,** Teh. 2:9 as I also have
received from My Father.
28 "And I shall give him the morning star.
29 "He who has an ear, let him hear what
the Spirit says to the assemblies." '

3 "And to the messenger of the assembly in Sardis write, 'He who has the
seven Spirits of Elohim and the seven
stars, says this, "I know your works, that
you have a name that you are alive, but
you are dead.
2 "Wake up, and strengthen what remains
and is about to die, for I have not found
your works complete before Elohim.
3 "Remember, then, how you have
received, and heard. And watch and
repent. If, then, you do not wake up, I shall
come upon you as a thief, and you shall not
know at all what hour I come upon you.
4 "Nevertheless, you have a few names
in Sardis who have not defiled their garments. And they shall walk with Me in
white, because they are worthy.
5 "He who overcomes shall be dressed in
white robes, and I shall by no means blot
out his name from the Book of Life, but I
shall confess his name before My Father
and before His messengers.
6 "He who has an ear, let him hear what
the Spirit says to the assemblies." '
7 "And to the messenger of the assembly
in Philadelphia write, 'He who is set-apart,
He who is true, He who has **the key of
Dawiḏ, He who opens and no one shuts,
and shuts and no one opens,** Yesh. 22:22 says
this:
8 "I know your works – see, I have set
before you an open door, and no one is
able to shut it – that you have little power,
yet have guarded My Word, and have not
denied My Name.
9 "See, I am giving up those of the congregation of Satan, who say they are
Yehuḏim and are not, but lie. See, I am
making them come and worship before
your feet, and to know that I have loved
you.
10 "Because you have guarded My Word
of endurance, I also shall guard you from
the hour of trial which shall come upon all
the world, to try those who dwell on the
earth.
11 "See, I am coming speedily! Hold what
you have that no one take your crown.
12 "He who overcomes, I shall make him
a supporting post in the Dwelling Place of
My Elohim, and he shall by no means go
out. And I shall write on him the Name of
My Elohim and the name of the city of My
Elohim, the renewed Yerushalayim, which
comes down out of the heaven from My
Elohim, and My renewed Name.
13 "He who has an ear, let him hear what
the Spirit says to the assemblies." '
14 "And to the messenger of the assembly
in Laodikeia write, 'The Amĕn, the
Trustworthy and True Witness, the Beginning of the creation of Elohim, [a] says this:
15 "I know your works, that you are neither cold nor hot. I would that you were
cold or hot.
16 "So, because you are lukewarm, and
neither cold nor hot, I am going to vomit
you out of My mouth.
17 "Because you say, **'Rich I am, and I
am made rich,** Hosh. 12:8 and need none at
all,' and do not know that you are
wretched, and pitiable, and poor, and blind,
and naked.
18 "I advise you to buy from Me gold
refined in the fire, [b] so that you become

3a Qol. 1:15, Iḇ`rim 1:6. *3b* Teh. 19:10, Teh. 119:72 & 127, Mish. 30:5.

rich; and white garments, so that you
become dressed, so that the shame of your
nakedness might not be shown; and anoint
your eyes with ointment, so that you see.
19 “As many as I love, I reprove and discipline. So be ardent and repent.
20 “See, I stand at the door and knock. If
anyone hears My voice and opens the door,
I shall come in to him and dine with him,
and he with Me.
21 “To him who overcomes I shall give to
sit with Me on My throne, as I also overcame and sat down with My Father on His
throne.
22 “He who has an ear, let him hear what
the Spirit says to the assemblies.” ’ ”

4 After this I looked and saw a door
having been opened in the heaven.
And the first voice which I heard was like
a trumpet speaking with me, saying,
“Come up here and I shall show you what
has to take place after this.”
2 And immediately I came to be in the
Spirit and saw a throne set in the heaven,
and One sat on the throne.
3 And He who sat there was like a jasper
and a ruby stone in appearance. And there
was a rainbow around the throne, like an
emerald in appearance.
4 And around the throne were twenty-
four thrones, and on the thrones I saw
twenty-four elders sitting, dressed in white
robes. And they had crowns of gold on
their heads.
5 And out of the throne came lightnings,
and thunders, and voices. And seven lamps
of fire were burning before the throne,
which are the seven Spirits of Elohim.
6 And before the throne there was a sea
of glass, like crystal. And in the midst of
the throne, and around the throne, were
four living creatures, covered with eyes in
front and in back.
7 And the first living creature was like a
lion, and the second living creature like a
calf, and the third living creature had a
face like a **man**, and the fourth living creature was like a flying **eagle**. Yeḥez. 1:10
8 And the four living creatures, **each
having six wings**, Yesh. 6:2 were covered
with eyes around and within. And they do
not cease, day or night, saying, **“Set-apart,
set-apart, set-apart, יהוה Ěl Shaddai**,
Yesh. 6:3 who was, and who is, and who is
coming!”
9 And when the living creatures give
esteem and respect and thanks to Him who
sits on the throne, who lives forever and
ever,
10 the twenty-four elders fall down before
Him who sits on the throne and bow before
Him who lives forever and ever, and they
cast their crowns before the throne, saying,
11 “You are worthy, O יהוה, to receive
esteem and respect and power, Diḇre א 29:11
for You have created all, and because of
Your desire they are, and were created.”

5 And I saw in the right hand of Him
who sat on the throne **a scroll written
inside and on the back**, Yeḥez. 2:10 having
been sealed with seven seals.
2 And I saw a strong messenger proclaiming with a loud voice, “Who is
worthy to open the scroll and to loosen its
seals?”
3 And no one in the heaven or on the
earth or under the earth was able to open
the scroll, or to look at it.
4 And I wept much, because no one was
found worthy to open and read the scroll,
or to look at it.
5 And one of the elders said to me, “Do
not weep. See, the Lion of the tribe of
Yehuḏah, [a] the Root of Dawiḏ, [b] overcame
to open the scroll and to loosen its seven
seals.”
6 And I looked and saw in the midst of
the throne and of the four living creatures,
and in the midst of the elders a Lamb
standing, as having been slain, having
seven horns and seven eyes, which are the
seven Spirits of Elohim sent out into all the
earth.
7 And He came and took the scroll out of
the right hand of Him sitting on the throne.
8 And when He took the scroll, the four

5a Ber. 49:9-10, Iḇ`rim 7:14. *5b* Yesh. 11:1 & 10.

living creatures and the twenty-four elders
fell down before the Lamb, each holding a
harp, and golden bowls filled with incense,
which are the prayers of the set-apart ones.
9 And they sang a renewed song, saying,
"You are worthy to take the scroll, and to
open its seals, because You were slain, and
have redeemed us to Elohim by Your blood
out of every tribe and tongue and people
and nation, [c]
10 and made us sovereigns and priests to
our Elohim, and we shall reign upon the
earth." [d]
11 And I looked, and I heard the voice of
many messengers around the throne, and
the living creatures, and the elders. And
the number of them was myriads of myriads, and thousands of thousands,
12 saying with a loud voice, "Worthy is
the Lamb having been slain to receive
power and riches and wisdom, and
strength and respect and esteem and blessing!"
13 And every creature which is in the
heaven and on the earth and under the
earth and such as are in the sea, and all that
are in them, I heard saying, "To Him sitting on the throne, and to the Lamb, be the
blessing and the respect and the esteem
and the might, forever and ever!"
14 And the four living creatures said,
"Amĕn!" And the twenty-four elders fell
down and bowed before Him who lives
forever and ever.

6 And I saw when the Lamb opened one
of the seals, and I heard one of the
four living creatures saying, like a sound
of thunder, "Come and see."
2 And I looked and saw a white horse [a],
and he who sat on it holding a bow. And a
crown was given to him, and he went out
overcoming and to overcome.
3 And when He opened the second seal, I
heard the second living creature saying,
"Come and see."
4 And another horse, fiery red, [b] went
out. And it was given to the one who sat on
it to take peace from the earth, and that
they should slay one another. And a great
sword was given to him.
5 And when He opened the third seal, I
heard the third living creature say, "Come
and see." And I looked and saw a black
horse, [c] and he who sat on it holding a pair
of scales in his hand. [d]
6 And I heard a voice in the midst of the
four living creatures saying, "A measure of
wheat for a denarius, [e] and three measures
of barley for a denarius. [e] And do not harm
the oil and the wine."
7 And when He opened the fourth seal, I
heard the voice of the fourth living creature saying, "Come and see."
8 And I looked and saw a pale horse. [f]
And he who sat on it had the name Death, [g]
and She'ol [g] followed with him. And
authority was given to them over a fourth
of the earth, to kill with sword, and with
hunger, and with death, and by the beasts
of the earth. [h]
9 And when He opened the fifth seal, I
saw under the slaughter-place the beings of
those having been slain for the Word of
Elohim and for the witness which they
held,
10 and they cried with a loud voice, saying, "How long, O Master, set-apart and
true, until You judge and avenge our blood
on those who dwell on the earth?"
11 And there was given to each one a
white robe, and they were told that they
should rest a little while longer, until both
the number of their fellow servants and
their brothers, who would be killed as they
were, was completed.
12 And I looked when He opened the sixth
seal and saw a great earthquake came to
be. And the sun became black as sackcloth
of hair, and the moon became as blood.
13 And the stars of the heaven fell to the
earth, as a fig tree drops its unripe figs,
being shaken by a strong wind.
14 And heaven departed like a scroll being
rolled up, and every mountain and island
was moved out of its place.

5c This fact is given in 6 other texts in the Book of Revelation. *5d* Dan. 7:18-27. *6a* Zeḵ. 6:3.
6b Zeḵ. 1:8; 6:2. *6c* Zeḵ. 6:2. *6d* Yeḥ. 4:16. *6e* Roman monetary unit - a day's wage. *6f* Zeḵ. 6:3. *6g* Hosh. 13:14.
6h Zeḵ. 5:12, 17; 14:13-19.

15 And the sovereigns of the earth, and the
great ones, and the rich ones, and the commanders, and the mighty, and every slave
and every free one, hid themselves in the
caves and in the rocks of the mountains,
16 and **said to the mountains and rocks,**
"Fall on us and hide us Hosh. 10:8 from the
face of Him sitting on the throne and from
the wrath of the Lamb,
17 because the great day of His wrath has
come, and who is able to stand?"

7 And after this I saw four messengers
standing at the four corners of the
earth, holding the four winds of the earth,
that the wind should not blow on the earth,
nor on the sea, nor on any tree.
2 And I saw another messenger coming
up from the rising of the sun, holding the
seal of the living Elohim. And he cried
with a loud voice to the four messengers to
whom it was given to harm the earth and
the sea,
3 saying, "Do not harm the earth, nor
the sea, nor the trees until we have sealed
the servants of our Elohim upon their foreheads." [a]
4 And I heard the number of those who
were sealed, one hundred and forty-four
thousand, sealed out of all the tribes of the
children of Yisra'ěl:
5 of the tribe of Yehuḏah twelve thousand were sealed, of the tribe of Re'uḇěn
twelve thousand were sealed, of the tribe
of Gaḏ twelve thousand were sealed,
6 of the tribe of Ashěr twelve thousand
were sealed, of the tribe of Naphtali twelve
thousand were sealed, of the tribe of
Menashsheh twelve thousand were sealed,
7 of the tribe of Shimʿon twelve thousand
were sealed, of the tribe of Lěwi twelve
thousand were sealed, of the tribe of
Yissasḵar twelve thousand were sealed,
8 of the tribe of Zeḇulun twelve thousand
were sealed, of the tribe of Yosěph twelve
thousand were sealed, of the tribe of
Binyamin twelve thousand were sealed.
9 After this I looked and saw a great
crowd which no one was able to count, out
of all nations and tribes and peoples and
tongues, standing before the throne and
before the Lamb, dressed in white robes,
and palm branches in their hands,
10 and crying out with a loud voice, saying, "Deliverance belongs to our Elohim
who sits on the throne, and to the Lamb!"
11 And all the messengers stood around
the throne and the elders and the four
living creatures, and fell on their faces
before the throne and worshipped Elohim,
12 saying, "Aměn! The blessing, and the
esteem, and the wisdom, and the thanksgiving, and the respect, and the power, and
the might, to our Elohim forever and ever.
Aměn."
13 And one of the elders responded, saying to me, "Who are these dressed in white
robes, and where did they come from?"
14 And I said to him, "Master, you know."
And he said to me, "These are those coming out of the great distress, having washed
their robes and made them white in the
blood of the Lamb.
15 "Because of this they are before the
throne of Elohim, and serve Him day and
night in His Dwelling Place. And He who
sits on the throne shall spread *His* Tent
over them.
16 **"They shall hunger no more, neither**
thirst any more, neither shall the sun
strike them, nor any heat, Yesh. 49:10
17 because the Lamb who is in the midst
of the throne **shall shepherd them** Yeḥ. 34:23
and lead them to **fountains of waters of**
life. Yirm. 2:13; 17:13 And Elohim **shall wipe**
away every tear from their eyes." Yesh. 25:8

8 And when He opened the seventh
seal, there came to be silence in the
heaven for about half an hour.
2 And I saw the seven messengers who
stand before Elohim, and to them were
given seven trumpets.
3 And another messenger came and stood
at the slaughter-place, holding a golden
censer, and much incense was given to
him, that he should offer it with the prayers
of all the set-apart ones upon the golden

7a See 9:4, 14:1, 22:4.

slaughter-place which was before the throne.
4 And the smoke of the incense, with the prayers of the set-apart ones, went up before Elohim from the hand of the messenger.
5 And the messenger took the censer, and filled it with fire from the slaughter-place, and threw it to the earth. And there were noises, and thunders, and lightnings, and an earthquake.
6 And the seven messengers who held the seven trumpets prepared themselves to sound.
7 And the first messenger sounded, and there came to be hail and fire mixed with blood, and they were thrown to the earth. And a third of the trees were burned up, and all green grass was burned up.
8 And the second messenger sounded, and *what looked* like a great mountain burning with fire was thrown into the sea, and a third of the sea became blood,
9 and a third of the living creatures in the sea died, and a third of the ships were destroyed.
10 And the third messenger sounded, and a great star fell from the heaven, burning like a torch, and it fell on a third of the rivers and on the fountains of water,
11 and the name of the star is called Wormwood. And a third of the waters became wormwood, and many men died from the waters, because they were made bitter.
12 And the fourth messenger sounded, and a third of the sun was struck, and a third of the moon, and a third of the stars, so that a third of them were darkened. And a third of the day did not shine, and likewise the night. [a]
13 And I looked, and I heard an eagle flying in mid-heaven, crying with a loud voice, "Woe, woe, woe to those dwelling upon the earth, because of the remaining blasts of the trumpet of the three messengers who are about to sound!"

9 And the fifth messenger sounded, and I saw a star from the heaven which had fallen to the earth. And the key to the pit of the deep was given to him.
2 And he opened the pit of the deep, and smoke went up out of the pit like the smoke of a great furnace. And the sun was darkened, also the air, because of the smoke of the pit.
3 And out of the smoke locusts came upon the earth, and authority was given to them as the scorpions of the earth possess authority.
4 And it was said to them that they shall not harm the grass of the earth, or any green *matter*, or any tree, but only those men who do not have the seal of Elohim upon their foreheads.
5 And it was given to them that they should not kill them, but to torture them for five months. And their torture was like the torture of a scorpion when it stings a man.
6 And in those days men shall seek death and shall not find it. And they shall long to die, but death shall flee from them.
7 And the locusts looked like horses prepared for battle, and on their heads were crowns like gold, and their faces were like the faces of men.
8 And they had hair like women's hair, and their teeth were like lions' teeth.
9 And they had breastplates like breastplates of iron, and the sound of their wings was like the sound of chariots of many horses running into battle.
10 And they have tails like scorpions, and stings. And in their tails is their authority to harm men five months.
11 And they have over them a sovereign, the messenger of the pit of the deep, whose name in Hebrew is Abaddon, but in Greek he has the name Apolluon.
12 The first woe is past. See, two woes are still coming after this.
13 And the sixth messenger sounded, and I heard a voice from the four horns of the golden slaughter-place which is before Elohim,

8a Verse 12 - compare with Shem. 10:21; Yesh. 50:3; Yirm. 4:23-29; Zeḵ. 13:8; Yo'ĕl 2:10, 31, 3:15.

14 saying to the sixth messenger who had
the trumpet, "Release the four messengers,
those having been bound at the great river
Euphrates."
15 And the four messengers, those having
been prepared for the hour and day and
month and year, were released to kill a
third of mankind.
16 And the number of the armies of the
horsemen was two hundred million, and I
heard the number of them.
17 And this is how I saw the horses in the
vision and those who sat on them, having
breastplates of fiery red, and hyacinth blue,
and sulphur yellow. And the heads of the
horses were like the heads of lions, and out
of their mouths came fire, and smoke, and
sulphur.
18 A third of mankind was killed by these
three *plagues*, by the fire and the smoke
and the sulphur which came out of their
mouths.
19 For the authority of the horses is in
their mouth and in their tails, for their tails
are like serpents, having heads. And with
them they do harm.
20 And the rest of mankind, who were not
killed by these plagues, did not repent of
the **works of their hands**, that they should
not worship the demons, and **idols of gold,
and of silver, and of brass, and of stone,
and of wood, which are neither able to
see, nor to hear, nor to walk.** Teh. 115:4-7;
135:15-17, Dan. 5:23
21 And they did not repent of their murders, nor of their drug sorceries, nor of
their whoring, nor of their thefts.

10

And I saw another strong messenger coming down from the heaven,
robed in a cloud, and a rainbow on his
head, and his face was like the sun, and his
feet like columns of fire,
2 and having in his hand a little book
opened. And he placed his right foot on the
sea and his left foot on the land,
3 and cried with a loud voice, as when a
lion roars. And when he cried out, seven
thunders spoke their sounds.
4 And when the seven thunders spoke
their sounds, I was about to write, but I
heard a voice from the heaven saying to
me, "Seal up what the seven thunders
spoke, and do not write them."
5 And the messenger whom I saw standing on the sea and on the land **lifted up his
right hand to the heaven,** Ber. 14:22, Deḇ. 32:40,
6 and swore by **Him who lives forever
and ever,** Dan. 12:7 **who created the heaven
and what is in it, the earth and what is in
it, and the sea and what is in it,** Neḥ. 9:6 [a]
that there shall be no further delay,
7 but in the days of the sounding of the
seventh messenger, when he is about to
sound, the secret of Elohim shall also be
ended, as He declared to His servants the
prophets.
8 And the voice which I heard out of the
heaven spoke to me again and said, "Go,
take the little book which is opened in the
hand of the messenger standing on the sea
and on the earth."
9 And I went to the messenger and said to
him, "Give me the little book." And he
said to me, "Take and eat it, [b] and it shall
make your stomach bitter, but it shall be as
sweet as honey in your mouth."
10 And I took the little book out of the
messenger's hand and ate it, and **it was as
sweet as honey in my mouth,** Yeḥ. 3:3 but
when I had eaten it, my stomach was made
bitter.
11 And he said to me, "You have to prophesy again concerning many peoples and
nations and tongues and sovereigns."

11

And a reed like a measuring rod
was given to me, and the messenger stood, saying, "Rise and measure the
Dwelling Place of Elohim, and the slaughter-place, and those worshipping in it.
2 "But cast out the court which is outside
the Dwelling Place, and do not measure it,
for it has been given to the nations, and
they shall trample the set-apart city under
foot for forty-two months.

10a Also see Shem. 20:11, Teh. 146:6, Ḥazon 4:11. *10b* Yeḥez. chs. 2 & 3. This is a Hebraism which means *to receive knowledge.*

3 "And I shall give unto my two witnesses, and they shall prophesy one thousand
two hundred and sixty days, clad in sackcloth."
4 These are the **two olive trees** [Zeḵ. 4:3] and
the two lampstands that are standing
before the Elohim of the earth.
5 And if anyone wishes to harm them,
fire comes out from their mouth and consumes their enemies. And if anyone wishes
to harm them, he has to be killed in that
way.
6 These possess authority to shut the
heaven, so that no rain falls in the days of
their prophecy. And they possess authority
over waters to turn them to blood, and to
smite the earth with all plagues, as often as
they wish.
7 And when they have ended their
witness, the beast coming up out of the
pit of the deep shall fight against them, and
overcome them, and kill them,
8 and their dead bodies *lie* in the street of
the great city which spiritually is called
Seḏom and Mitsrayim, where also our
Master was impaled,
9 and some of the peoples and tribes and
tongues and nations see their dead bodies
for three and a half days, and not allow
their dead bodies to be placed into tombs,
10 and those dwelling on the earth rejoice
over them and exult. And they shall send
gifts to each other, because these two
prophets tortured those dwelling on the
earth.
11 And after the three and a half days a
spirit of life from Elohim entered into
them, and they stood upon their feet, and
great fear fell on those who saw them.
12 And they heard a loud voice from the
heaven saying to them, "Come up here."
And they went up into the heaven in a
cloud, and their enemies saw them.
13 And in that hour there came to be a
great earthquake, and a tenth of the city
fell. And in the earthquake seven thousand
men were killed, and the rest became
afraid and gave esteem to the Elohim of
the heaven.
14 The second woe is past, and see, the
third woe is coming speedily.
15 And the seventh messenger sounded,
and there came to be loud voices in the
heaven, saying, "The reign of this world
has become *the reign* of our Master, and of
His Messiah, and He shall reign forever
and ever!" [a]
16 And the twenty-four elders sitting
before Elohim on their thrones fell on their
faces and worshipped Elohim,
17 saying, "We give You thanks, O יהוה
Ěl Shaddai, the One who is and who was
and who is coming, because You have
taken Your great power and reigned.
18 "And the **nations were enraged**, [Teh. 2:1]
and Your wrath has come, and the time of
the dead to be judged, and to give the
reward to Your servants the prophets and
to the set-apart ones, and to those who fear
Your Name, small and great, and to destroy
those who destroy the earth."
19 And the Dwelling Place of Elohim was
opened in the heaven, and the ark of His
covenant was seen in His Dwelling Place.
And there came to be lightnings, and
voices, and thunders, and an earthquake,
and great hail.

12

And a great sign was seen in the
heaven: a woman clad with the
sun, with the moon under her feet, and on
her head a crown of twelve stars.
2 And being pregnant, she cried out in
labour and in pain to give birth. [a]
3 And another sign was seen in the heav-
en: and see, a great, fiery red dragon
having seven heads and ten horns, and
seven crowns on his heads.
4 And his tail draws a third of the stars of
the heaven and throws them to the earth.
And the dragon stood before the woman
who was about to give birth, to devour her
child as soon as it was born.
5 And she bore a male child [a] who was to
shepherd all nations **with a rod of iron**.
[Teh. 2:9] And her child was caught away to

11a See 12:10, Teh. 2:8, Teh. 22:28, Dan. 2:44, Dan. 7:13-14, Oḇaḏ. 15-21, Ḥagg. 2:22, Zeḵ. 14:9. *12a* See also Yesh. 26:17, 66:7; Miḵ. 4:9,10.

Elohim and to His throne.
6 And the woman fled into the wilderness, where she has a place prepared by
Elohim, to be nourished there one thousand two hundred and sixty days.
7 And there came to be fighting in the
heaven: Mika'ĕl and his messengers
fought against the dragon. And the dragon
and his messengers fought,
8 but they were not strong enough, nor
was a place found for them in the heaven
any longer.
9 And the great dragon was thrown out,
that serpent of old, called the Devil and
Satan, who leads all the world astray. He
was thrown to the earth, and his messengers were thrown out with him.
10 And I heard a loud voice saying in the
heaven, "Now have come the deliverance
and the power and the reign of our
Elohim [b] and the authority of His Messiah,
for the accuser of our brothers, who
accused them before our Elohim day and
night, has been thrown down.
11 "And they overcame him because of
the Blood of the Lamb, and because of the
Word of their witness, and they did not
love their lives to the death.
12 "Because of this rejoice, O heavens,
and you who dwell in them! Woe to the
earth and the sea, because the devil has
come down to you, having great wrath,
knowing that he has little time."
13 And when the dragon saw that he had
been thrown to the earth, he persecuted the
woman who gave birth to the male child.
14 And the woman was given two wings
of a great eagle, to fly into the wilderness
to her place, where she is nourished **for a
time and times and half a time,** Dan. 7:25;
12:7 from the presence of the serpent.
15 And out of his mouth the serpent
spewed water like a river after the woman,
to cause her to be swept away by the river.
16 And the earth helped the woman, and
the earth opened its mouth and swallowed
up the river which the dragon had spewed
out of his mouth.
17 And the dragon was enraged with the
woman, and he went to fight with the remnant of her seed, those guarding the commands of Elohim and possessing the witness of יהושע Messiah.

13 And I stood on the sand of the sea.
And I saw a beast coming up out of
the sea, having seven heads and ten horns,
and on his horns ten crowns, and on his
heads names of blasphemy.
2 And the beast I saw was like a leopard,
and his feet were like the feet of a bear, and
his mouth like the mouth of a lion. And the
dragon gave him his power, and his throne,
and great authority.
3 And I saw one of his heads, as having
been slain to death, and his deadly wound
was healed. And all the earth marvelled
after the beast.
4 And they worshipped the dragon who
gave authority to the beast. And they worshipped the beast, saying, "Who is like the
beast? Who is able to fight with him?"
5 And he was given a mouth speaking
great *matters* and blasphemies, and he was
given authority to do so forty-two months.
6 And he opened his mouth in blasphemies against Elohim, to blaspheme His
Name, and His Tent, and those dwelling in
the heaven.
7 And it was given to him to fight with
the set-apart ones and to overcome them.
And authority was given to him over every
tribe and tongue and nation.
8 And all those dwelling on the earth,
whose names have not been written in
the Book of Life of the slain Lamb, from
the foundation of the world shall worship
him.
9 If anyone has an ear, let him hear.
10 **He who brings into captivity shall go
into captivity, he who kills with the
sword has to be killed with the sword.**
Yirm. 15:2; 43:11 [a] Here is the endurance and the
belief of the set-apart ones.
11 And I saw another beast coming up out
of the earth, and he had two horns like a
lamb and spoke like a dragon.
12 And he exercises all the authority of the

12b See 11:15. *13a* See also Ber. 9:6. Compare Chapter 13 with Dan. 7.

first beast in his presence, and causes the
earth and those who dwell in it to worship
the first beast, whose deadly wound was
healed.
13 And he does great signs, so that he even
makes fire come down from the heaven on
the earth before men.
14 And he leads astray those dwelling on
the earth because of those signs which he
was given to do before the beast, saying to
those dwelling on the earth to make an
image to the beast who was wounded by
the sword, yet lived.
15 And there was given to him to give
spirit to the image of the beast, that the
image of the beast should both speak and
cause to be killed as many as would not
worship the image of the beast.
16 And he causes all, both small and great,
and rich and poor, and free and slave, to be
given a mark upon their right hand or upon
their foreheads,
17 and that no one should be able to buy or
sell except he that has the mark or the
name of the beast, or the number of his
name.
18 Here is the wisdom! He who has understanding,
let him calculate the number of
the beast, for it is the number of a man, and
his number *is* six hundred *and* sixty six. [b]

14

And I looked and saw a Lamb
standing on Mount Tsiyon, and
with Him one hundred and forty-four thousand,
having His Father's Name [a] written
upon their foreheads.
2 And I heard a voice out of the heaven,
like the voice of many waters, and like the
voice of loud thunder, and I heard the
sound of harpists playing their harps.
3 And they sang a renewed song before
the throne, and before the four living creatures,
and the elders. And no one was able
to learn that song except the hundred and
forty-four thousand who were redeemed
from the earth.
4 They are those who were not defiled
with women, for they are maidens. They
are those following the Lamb wherever He
leads *them* on. They were redeemed from
among men, being first-fruits to Elohim
and to the Lamb.
5 And in their mouth was found no falsehood,
for they are blameless before the
throne of Elohim.
6 And I saw another messenger flying in
mid-heaven, holding the everlasting Good
News to announce to those dwelling on the
earth, even to every nation and tribe and
tongue and people,
7 saying with a loud voice, "Fear Elohim
and give esteem to Him, because the hour
of His judgment has come. And worship
Him who made the heaven and the earth,
and sea, and fountains of water."
8 And another messenger followed,
saying, "**Babel is fallen, is fallen,** Yesh. 21:9 [b]
that great city, because she has made all
nations drink of the wine of the wrath of
her whoring."
9 And a third messenger followed them,
saying with a loud voice, "If anyone worships
the beast and his image, and receives
his mark upon his forehead or upon his
hand,
10 he also shall drink of the wine of the
wrath of Elohim, which is poured out undiluted
into the cup of His wrath. And he
shall be tortured with fire and sulphur
before the set-apart messengers and before
the Lamb.
11 "And the smoke of their torture goes up
forever and ever. And they have no rest
day or night, those worshipping the beast
and his image, also if anyone receives the
mark of his name."
12 Here is the endurance of the set-apart
ones, [c] here are those guarding the commands
of Elohim and the belief of יהושע.
13 And I heard a voice out of the heaven
saying to me, "Write, 'Blessed are the dead
who die in the Master from now on.' "
"Yes," says the Spirit, "in order that they
rest from their labours, and their works follow
with them."
14 And I looked and saw a white cloud,

13b Some ancient manuscripts have *616* instead of *666*. *14a* Some texts read: *having His Name and His Father's Name.* *14b* Also see Yirm. 51:8. *14c* See also 12:17.

and sitting on the cloud was **One like the**
Son of Adam, Dan. 7:13 having on His head a
golden crown, and in His hand a sharp
sickle.
15 And another messenger came out of the
Dwelling Place, crying with a loud voice
to the One sitting on the cloud, "Send Your
sickle and reap, because the hour has come
for You to reap, because the harvest of the
earth is ripe."
16 And the One sitting on the cloud thrust
in His sickle on the earth, and the earth
was reaped.
17 And another messenger came out of the
Dwelling Place which is in the heaven, and
he too held a sharp sickle.
18 And another messenger came out from
the slaughter-place, having authority over
the fire, and he cried with a loud cry to him
having the sharp sickle, saying, "Send your
sharp sickle and gather the clusters of the
vine of the earth, because her grapes are
ripe."
19 And the messenger thrust his sickle into
the earth and gathered the vine of the earth,
and threw it into the great winepress of the
wrath of Elohim.
20 And the winepress was trodden outside
the city, and blood came out of the winepress, up to the bridles of the horses, for
about one thousand six hundred stadia [d].

15 And I saw another sign in the
heaven, great and marvellous:
seven messengers having the seven last
plagues, [a] for the wrath of Elohim was
ended in them.
2 And I saw like a sea of glass mixed
with fire, and those overcoming the beast
and his image and his mark and the number of his name, standing on the sea of
glass, holding harps of Elohim.
3 And they sing the song of Mosheh the
servant of Elohim, and the song of the
Lamb, saying, "Great and marvellous are
Your works, יהוה Ěl Shaddai! Righteous
and true are Your ways, O Sovereign of the
set-apart ones!
4 "Who shall not fear You, O יהוה, and
esteem Your Name? Because You alone
are kind. Because all nations shall come
and worship before You, for Your righteousnesses have been made manifest." [b]
5 And after this I looked and saw the
Dwelling Place of the Tent of Witness in
the heaven was opened.
6 And out of the Dwelling Place came the
seven messengers having the seven
plagues, dressed in clean bright linen, and
having their chests girded with golden
bands.
7 And one of the four living creatures
gave to the seven messengers seven golden
bowls filled with the wrath of Elohim who
lives forever and ever.
8 And the Dwelling Place was filled with
smoke from the esteem of Elohim and
from His power, and no one was able to
enter the Dwelling Place until the seven
plagues of the seven messengers were
ended.

16 And I heard a loud voice from the
Dwelling Place saying to the seven
messengers, "Go and pour out the bowls of
the wrath of Elohim on the earth."
2 And the first went and poured out his
bowl upon the earth, and an evil and
wicked sore came upon the men, those
having the mark of the beast and those
worshipping his image.
3 And the second messenger poured out
his bowl on the sea, and it became blood,
as of a dead one, and every living creature
in the sea died.
4 And the third messenger poured out his
bowl on the rivers and fountains of water,
and they became blood.
5 And I heard the messenger of the
waters saying, "You are righteous, O יהוה,
the One who is and who was and who shall
be, because You have judged these.
6 "Because they have shed the blood of
set-apart ones and prophets, and You have
given them blood to drink. For they
deserve it."
7 And I heard another out of the slaughter-place saying, "Yes, יהוה Ěl Shaddai,

14d Approx. 296 kilometres or 184 miles. *15a* See 21:9. *15b* See Yirm. 10:6,7; Teh. 86:9.

true and righteous are Your judgments.”

8 And the fourth messenger poured out his bowl on the sun, and it was given to him to burn men with fire.

9 And men were burned with great heat, and they blasphemed the Name of Elohim who possesses authority over these plagues. And they did not repent, to give Him esteem.

10 And the fifth messenger poured out his bowl on the throne of the beast, and his reign became darkened. And they gnawed their tongues from pain.

11 And they blasphemed the Elohim of the heaven for their pains and their sores, and did not repent of their works.

12 And the sixth messenger poured out his bowl on the great river Euphrates, and its water was dried up, in order to prepare the way of the sovereigns from the east.

13 And I saw *coming* out of the mouth of the dragon, and out of the mouth of the beast, and out of the mouth of the false prophet, three unclean spirits, as frogs,

14 for they are spirits of demons, doing signs, which go out to the sovereigns of the entire world, to gather them to the battle of that great day of יהוה the Almighty.

15 “See, I am coming as a thief. Blessed is he who is staying awake and guarding his garments, lest he walk naked and they see his shame.”

16 And they gathered them together to the place called in Hebrew, Har Meḡiddo.

17 And the seventh messenger poured out his bowl into the air, and a loud voice came out of the Dwelling Place of the heaven, from the throne, saying, “It is done!”

18 And there came to be noises and thunders and lightnings. And there came to be a great earthquake, such a mighty and great earthquake as had not came to be since men were on the earth.

19 And the great city became divided into three parts, and the cities of the nations fell. And great Baḇel was remembered before Elohim, to give her the cup of the wine of the fierceness of His wrath.

20 And every island fled away, and the mountains were not found.

21 And great hail from the heaven fell upon men, every hailstone about the weight of a talent. And men blasphemed Elohim for the plague of the hail, because that plague was exceedingly great.

17 And one of the seven messengers who had the seven bowls came and spoke with me, saying to me, “Come, I shall show you the judgment of the great whore sitting on many waters, [a]

2 with whom the sovereigns of the earth committed whoring, and the inhabitants of the earth were made drunk with the wine of her whoring.” [b]

3 And he carried me away in the Spirit into the wilderness. And I saw a woman sitting on a scarlet beast covered with names of blasphemy, having seven heads and ten horns.

4 And the woman was dressed in purple and scarlet, and adorned with gold and precious stones and pearls, holding in her hand a golden cup filled with abominations and the filthiness of her whoring, [b]

5 and upon her forehead a name written, a secret: BAḆEL THE GREAT, THE MOTHER OF THE WHORES AND OF THE ABOMINATIONS OF THE EARTH.

6 And I saw the woman, drunk with the blood of the set-apart ones, and with the blood of the witnesses of יהושע. And having seen her, I marvelled – greatly marvelled!

7 And the messenger said to me, “Why did you marvel? Let me explain to you the secret of the woman and of the beast she rides, which has the seven heads and the ten horns.

8 “The beast that you saw was, and is not, and is about to come up out of the pit of the deep and goes to destruction. And those dwelling on the earth, whose names are not written in the Book of Life from the foundation of the world, [c] shall marvel when they see the beast that was, and is not, and yet is.

9 “Here is the mind having wisdom: The

17a See v. 15. *17b* Yirm. 51:7. *17c* Dan. 12:1.

seven heads are seven mountains on which
the woman sits.
10 "And there are seven sovereigns: five
have fallen, and one is, and the other has
not yet come. And when he comes, he has
to remain a little while.
11 "And the beast that was, and is not, is
himself also the eighth, and is of the seven,
and goes to destruction.
12 "And the ten horns which you saw are
ten sovereigns who have not yet received a
reign, but receive authority as sovereigns
with the beast for one hour.
13 "They have one mind, and they shall
give their power and authority to the beast.
14 "They shall fight with the Lamb, and
the Lamb shall overcome them, for He is
Master of masters Deḇ.10:17 and Sovereign
of sovereigns. And those with Him are
called, and chosen, and trustworthy."
15 And he said to me, "The waters which
you saw, where the whore sits, are peoples,
and crowds, and nations, and tongues.
16 "And the ten horns which you saw on
the beast, these shall hate the whore, and
lay her waste and naked, and eat her flesh
and burn her with fire.
17 "For Elohim did give it into their hearts
to do His mind, to be of one mind, and to
give their reign to the beast, until the
words of Elohim shall be accomplished.
18 "And the woman whom you saw is that
great city having sovereignty over the sovereigns of the earth."

18 And after this I saw another messenger coming down from the
heaven, having great authority, and the
earth was lightened from his esteem.
2 And he cried with a mighty voice, saying, "**Baḇel** the great **is fallen, is fallen**,
Yesh. 21:9 and has become a dwelling place of
demons, a haunt for every unclean spirit,
and a haunt for every unclean and hated
bird,
3 because all the nations have drunk of
the wine of the wrath of her whoring, and
the sovereigns of the earth have committed
whoring with her, and the merchants of the
earth have become rich through the power
of her riotous living."
4 And I heard another voice from the
heaven saying, "Come out of her, my people, lest you share in her sins, and lest you
receive of her plagues. [a]
5 "Because her sins have piled up to
reach the heaven, and Elohim has remembered her unrighteousnesses.
6 "Render to her as she indeed did render,
and repay her double according to her
works. In the cup which she has mixed,
mix for her double.
7 "As much as she esteemed herself and
lived riotously, so much torture and grief
give to her, because in her heart she says, 'I
sit as sovereigness, and I am not a widow,
and I do not see mourning at all.'
8 "Because of this her plagues shall come
in one day: death and mourning and scarcity of food. And she shall be burned up with
fire, because יהוה Elohim who judges her
is mighty.
9 "And the sovereigns of the earth who
committed whoring and lived riotously
with her shall weep and mourn over her,
when they see the smoke of her burning,
10 standing at a distance for fear of her
torture, saying, 'Woe! Woe, the great city
Baḇel, the mighty city, because your judgment has come in one hour!'
11 "And the merchants of the earth weep
and mourn over her, because no one buys
their merchandise any more –
12 merchandise of gold and silver, and
precious stone and pearls, and fine linen
and purple, and silk and scarlet, and all
citron wood, and every object of ivory, and
every object of most precious wood and
bronze and iron and marble,
13 and cinnamon and incense, and fragrant
oil and frankincense, and wine and oil, and
fine flour and wheat, and cattle and sheep,
and horses and carriages, and bodies and
lives of men.
14 "And the fruit that your being longed
for has gone from you. And all your riches
and splendour are lost to you, and you
shall find them no more, not at all.

18a Yirm. 51:6, 9, 45. Also see Yirm. 50:8, 13, 28.

15 "The merchants of these, those who
became rich by her, shall stand at a
distance for fear of her torture, weeping
and mourning,
16 and saying, 'Woe! Woe, the great city
that was dressed in fine linen and purple
and scarlet, and adorned with gold and
precious stones and pearls!
17 'For in one hour such great riches was
laid waste.' And every shipmaster, and
every passenger, and sailors, and as many
as work the sea *for their living*, stood at a
distance,
18 and cried out when they saw the smoke
of her burning, saying, 'What is like this
great city?'
19 "And they threw dust on their heads
and cried out, weeping and mourning, and
saying, 'Woe! Woe, the great city, in which
all who had ships on the sea became rich
by her wealth! For in one hour she was laid
waste.'
20 "Rejoice over her, O heaven, and you
set-apart emissaries and prophets, for
Elohim has completely avenged you on
her!"
21 And one mighty messenger picked up a
stone like a great millstone and threw it
into the sea, saying, "With such a rush the
great city Baḇel shall be thrown down, and
shall not be found any more at all.
22 "And the sound of harpists, and musi-
cians, and flautists, and trumpeters shall
not be heard in you any more at all. And no
craftsman of any trade shall be found in
you any more at all. And the sound of a
millstone shall not be heard in you any
more at all.
23 "And the light of a lamp shall not shine
in you any more at all. And the voice of
bridegroom and bride shall not be heard in
you any more at all. For your merchants
were the great ones of the earth, for by
your drug sorcery all the nations were led
astray.
24 "And in her was found the blood of
prophets and set-apart ones, and of all who
were slain on the earth."

19 And after this I heard a loud voice
of a great crowd in the heaven,
saying, "Halleluyah! Deliverance and
esteem and respect and power to יהוה our
Elohim!
2 "**Because true and righteous are His
judgments**, Teh. 19:9 because He has judged
the great whore who corrupted the earth
with her whoring. And **He has avenged on
her the blood of His servants shed by
her**." Deb.32:43
3 And a second time they said,
"Halleluyah! And her smoke rises up forever and ever!"
4 And the twenty-four elders and the four
living creatures fell down and worshipped
Elohim who sat on the throne, saying,
"Aměn! Halleluyah!"
5 And a voice came from the throne,
saying, "Praise our Elohim, all you His
servants and **those who fear Him, both
small and great!**" Teh. 115:13
6 And I heard as the voice of a great
crowd, as the sound of many waters and as
the sound of mighty thunders, saying,
"Halleluyah, for יהוה Ěl Shaddai reigns!
7 "Let us be glad and rejoice and give
Him praise, for the marriage of the Lamb
has come, and His wife prepared herself."
8 And to her it was given to be dressed in
fine linen, clean and bright, for the fine
linen is the righteousnesses of the set-apart
ones.
9 And he said to me, "Write, 'Blessed are
those who have been called to the marriage
supper of the Lamb!' " And he said to me,
"These are the true words of Elohim."
10 And I fell at his feet to worship him,
but he said to me, "See, do not *do it*! I am
your fellow servant, and of your brothers
who possess the witness of יהושע.
Worship Elohim! For the witness of יהושע
is the spirit of prophecy."
11 And I saw the heaven opened, and there
was a white horse. And He who sat on him
was called Trustworthy and True, and in
righteousness He judges and fights. [a]
12 And His eyes were as a flame of fire,
and on His head were many crowns, hav-

19a See Ma. 10:42.

ing a Name that had been written, which no one had perceived except Himself[b] –

13 and having been dressed in a robe dipped in blood – and His Name is called: The Word of יהוה. [c]

14 And the armies in the heaven, dressed in fine linen, white and clean, followed Him on white horses.

15 And out of His mouth goes a sharp sword, that with it He should smite the nations. **And He shall shepherd them with a rod of iron.** Teh. 2:9 And He treads the winepress of the fierceness and wrath of Ěl Shaddai.

16 And on His robe and on His thigh [d] He has a name written: SOVEREIGN OF SOVEREIGNS AND MASTER OF MASTERS.

17 And I saw one messenger standing in the sun, and he cried with a loud voice, saying to all the birds that fly in mid-heaven, "Come and gather together for the supper of the great Elohim,

18 to eat the flesh of sovereigns, and the flesh of commanders, and the flesh of strong ones, and the flesh of horses and of those who sit on them, and the flesh of all people, free and slave, both small and great."

19 And I saw the beast, and the sovereigns of the earth, and their armies, gathered together to fight Him who sat on the horse and His army.

20 And the beast was seized, and with him the false prophet who worked signs in his presence, by which he led astray those who received the mark of the beast and those who worshipped his image. The two were thrown alive into the lake of fire burning with sulphur.

21 And the rest were killed with the sword which came from the mouth of Him who sat on the horse, and all the birds were filled with their flesh.

20

And I saw a messenger coming down from the heaven, having the key to the pit of the deep and a great chain in his hand.

2 And he seized the dragon, the serpent of old, who is the Devil and Satan, and bound him for a thousand years,

3 and he threw him into the pit of the deep, and shut him up, and set a seal on him, so that he should lead the nations no more astray until the thousand years were ended. And after that he has to be released for a little while.

4 And I saw thrones – and they sat on them, and judgment was given to them – and the lives of those who had been beheaded because of the witness they bore to יהושע and because of the Word of Elohim, and who did not worship the beast, nor his image, and did not receive his mark upon their foreheads or upon their hands. And they lived and reigned with Messiah for a thousand years

5 (and the rest of the dead did not come to life until the thousand years were ended) – this is the first resurrection.

6 Blessed and set-apart is the one having part in the first resurrection. The second death possesses no authority over these, but they shall be priests of Elohim and of Messiah, and shall reign with Him a thousand years.

7 And when the thousand years have ended, Satan shall be released from his prison,

8 and he shall go out to lead the nations astray which are in the four corners of the earth, **Goḡ and Maḡoḡ**, Yeḥez. 38:2 to gather them together for battle, whose number is as the sand of the sea.

9 And they came up over the breadth of the earth and surrounded the camp of the set-apart ones and the beloved city. And fire came down from Elohim out of the heaven and consumed them.

10 And the devil, who led them astray, was thrown into the lake of fire and sulphur where the beast and the false prophet are. And they shall be tortured day and night forever and ever.

11 And I saw a great white throne and Him who was sitting on it, from whose face the earth and the heaven fled away, and no

19b See 2:17. *19c* Yn. 1:1 & 14. *19d* "thigh", but possibly flag. See *Thigh* in the Explanatory Notes.

place was found for them.
[12]And I saw the dead, small and great,
standing before the throne, and books were
opened. And another book was opened,
which is *the Book* of Life. And the dead
were judged from what was written in the
books, according to their works.
[13]And the sea gave up the dead who were
in it, and Death and She'ol gave up the
dead who were in them. And they were
judged, each one according to his works.
[14]And Death and She'ol were thrown into
the lake of fire. This is the second death. [a]
[15]And if anyone was not found written in
the Book of Life, he was thrown into the
lake of fire.

21

And I saw a **renewed heaven and a renewed earth,** Yesh. 65:17 [a] for the
former heaven and the former earth had
passed away, and the sea is no more.
[2]And I, Yoḥanan, saw the set-apart city,
renewed Yerushalayim, coming down out
of the heaven from Elohim, prepared as a
bride adorned for her husband.
[3]And I heard a loud voice from the heav-
en saying, "See, the Booth of Elohim is
with men, and **He shall dwell with them,
and they shall be His people, and
Elohim Himself shall be with them and
be their Elohim.** Way. 26:11-12 [b]
[4]"And Elohim shall wipe away every
tear from their eyes, and there shall be no
more death, nor mourning, nor crying. And
there shall be no more pain, for the former
matters have passed away."
[5]And He who was sitting on the throne
said, "See, I make all *matters* new." And
He said to me, "Write, for these words are
true and trustworthy."
[6]And He said to me, "It is done! I am the
'Aleph' and the 'Taw', the Beginning and
the End. To the one who thirsts I shall give
of the fountain of the water of life without
payment.
[7]"The one who overcomes shall inherit
all this, and I shall be his Elohim and he
shall be My son.
[8]"But as for the cowardly, and untrust-
worthy, and abominable, and murderers,
and those who whore, and drug sorcerers,
and idolaters, and all the false, their part is
in the lake which burns with fire and sulphur, which is the second death."
[9]And one of the seven messengers who
held the seven bowls filled with the seven
last plagues came to me and spoke with
me, saying, "Come, I shall show you the
bride, the Lamb's wife."
[10]And he carried me away in the Spirit to
a great and high mountain, and showed me
the great city, the set-apart Yerushalayim,
descending out of the heaven from Elohim,
[11]having the esteem of Elohim, and her
light was like a most precious stone, like a
jasper stone, clear as crystal,
[12]and having a great and high wall, having twelve gates, and at the gates twelve
messengers, and names written on them,
which are *those* of the twelve tribes of the
children of Yisra'ěl: [c]
[13]three gates on the east, three gates on
the north, three gates on the south, and
three gates on the west.
[14]And the wall of the city had twelve
foundations, and on them were the names
of the twelve emissaries of the Lamb.
[15]And he who spoke with me had a gold-
en measuring rod, to measure the city, and
its gates, and its wall.
[16]And the city lies four-cornered, and
its length is as great as its breadth. And
he measured the city with the rod: twelve
thousand stadia [d] – the length, and the
breadth, and height of it are equal.
[17]And he measured its wall: hundred and
fourty-four foreams, [e] according to the
measure of a man, that is, of a messenger.
[18]And the structure of its wall was jasper.
And the city was clean gold, like clear
glass.
[19]And the foundations of the wall of the
city were adorned with all kinds of precious stones: the first foundation jasper,

20a See 2:11, 20:6, 21:8. *21a* Also see Yesh. 66:22. *21b* Also see Yesh. 7:14; 8:8,10; Yirm. 31:33; Yeḥ. 37:27; Diḇre. ב 6:18. *21c* See Yeḥez. 47:22-23, Yeḥez. 48:31-34. *21d* Approx. 2216 kilometres or 1377 miles.
21e Approx. 66 metres or 216 feet.

the second sapphire, the third agate, the
fourth emerald,
20 the fifth sardonyx, the sixth ruby, the
seventh chrysolite, the eighth beryl, the
ninth topaz, the tenth chrysoprase, the
eleventh jacinth, and the twelfth amethyst.
21 And the twelve gates were twelve
pearls – each one of the gates was a single
pearl. And the street of the city was clean
gold, like transparent glass.
22 And I saw no Dwelling Place in it, for
יהוה Ěl Shaddai is its Dwelling Place, and
the Lamb.
23 And the city had no need of the sun, nor
of the moon, to shine in it, for the esteem
of Elohim lightened it, and the Lamb is its
lamp.
24 And the nations, of those who are
saved, shall walk in its light,[f] and the sovereigns of the earth bring their esteem into
it.
25 And its gates shall not be shut at all by
day, for night shall not be there.
26 And they shall bring the esteem and the
appreciation of the nations into it.
27 And there shall by no means enter into
it whatever is unclean, neither anyone
doing abomination and falsehood,[g] but
only those **who are written in the** Lamb's
Book of Life. Dan. 12:1

22

And he showed me a river of water
of life, clear as crystal, coming
from the throne of Elohim and of the
Lamb.
2 In the middle of its street, and on either
side of the river, was the tree of life, which
bore twelve fruits, each tree yielding its
fruit every month. And the leaves of the
tree were for the healing of the nations.
3 And no longer shall there be any curse,
and the throne of Elohim and of the Lamb
shall be in it, and His servants shall serve
Him.
4 And they shall see His face, and His
Name *shall be* upon their foreheads.
5 And night shall be no more, and they
shall have no need of a lamp or the light of
the sun, because יהוה Elohim shall give
them light. And they shall reign forever
and ever.
6 And he said to me, "These words are
trustworthy and true. And יהוה Elohim of
the set-apart prophets has sent His messenger to show His servants what has to take
place with speed.
7 "See, I am coming speedily! Blessed is
he who guards the words of the prophecy
of this book."
8 And I, Yoḥanan, saw and heard these
matters. And when I heard and saw, I fell
down to worship before the feet of the
messenger who showed me these *matters*.
9 And he said to me, "See, do not! For I
am your fellow servant, and of your brothers the prophets, and of those who are
guarding the words of this book. Worship
Elohim."
10 And he said to me, "Do not **seal the
words of the prophecy of this book**, Dan.
12:4 because the time is near.
11 "He who does wrong, let him do more
wrong; he who is filthy, let him be more
filthy; he who is righteous, let him be more
righteous; he who is set-apart, let him be
more set-apart.
12 "And see, I am coming speedily, and
My reward is with Me, to give to each
according to his work.[a]
13 "I am the 'Aleph' and the 'Taw', the
Beginning and the End, the First and the
Last.
14 "Blessed are those doing[b] His commands,[c] so that the authority shall be
theirs unto the tree of life, and to enter
through the gates into the city.
15 "But outside are the dogs and those
who enchant with drugs, and those who
whore, and the murderers, and the idolaters, and all who love and do falsehood.[d]
16 "I, יהושע, have sent My messenger to
witness to you these *matters* in the assem-

21f See Yesh. 60:3. *21g* See 22:15, and Tas. ב 2:11. *22a* See Mt. 16:27, Yn. 5:29. *22b* See Mt. 19:17.
22c Long before the books were compiled to form "The New Testament," Ḥazon 22:14 was quoted, as it is here given, by Tertullian (CE 208), and by Cyprian (CE 251) – see the well-known *Antenicene Fathers*.
22d See 21:27, and also Tas. ב 2:11.

blies. I am the Root and the Offspring of Dawiḏ, [e] the Bright and Morning Star."
17 And the Spirit and the bride say, "Come!" And he who hears, let him say, "Come!" And he who thirsts, come! And he who desires it, take the water of life without paying!
18 For I witness to everyone hearing the words of the prophecy of this book: If anyone adds to them, Elohim shall add to him the plagues that are written in this book,
19 and if anyone takes away from the words of the book of this prophecy, Elohim shall take away his part from the Book [f] of Life, and out of the set-apart city, which are written in this Book.
20 He that bears witness of these *matters* says, "Yes, I am coming speedily." Amĕn. Yes, come, Master יהושע!
21 The favour of our Master יהושע Messiah be with the set-apart ones. Amĕn.

22e Yesh. 11:1 & 10, Ḥazon 5:5. *22f* Some manuscripts read 'tree of life'.

EXPLANATORY NOTES

The following notes are supplementary to what has already been explained in the Preface, and in the footnotes at the bottom of the pages of the main text:

Abomination That Lays Waste: We find this term in Dan. 9:27, Dan. 11:31 and Dan. 12:11. Who is the "Abomination that lays waste"? In 1 Macc. 1:54-57 and 2 Macc. 6:2 (during the time of Antiochus Epiphanes) it is referred to Zeus, or *Ba'al Shamen* as the Syriac version of 2 Macc. 6:2 renders it – the great sky-deity or sun-deity. Messiah, in Mt. 24:15,16 says: "So when you see the **'abomination that lays waste,'** spoken of by Dani'ěl the prophet, set up in the set-apart place" – he who reads, let him understand – "then let those who are in Yehuḏah flee to the mountains."

Afflict Your Beings: One way of afflicting your being is to fast. See Yesh 58:3, Teh. 35:13, Ezra 8:21, Dan. 10:1-2,12, Ma. 27:9 (probably referring to Yom Kippur).

Alleged Sabbath-breaking by Messiah: In *Dictionary of New Testament Theology* (Editor: Colin Brown), vol. 3, p. 410, after the author had critically examined all the alleged Sabbath-breaking texts, he says in conclusion, "We may conclude then, that though Jesus broke through rabbinic traditions about the sabbath, there was no annulling of the observance of the day." In the Mishnah, *Shabbath* 7, 2, we find a list of 39 additional laws on Sabbath-keeping which the Pharisees added, thereby making a burden of the Sabbath. In fact, the addition of these extra laws is against Scripture (Deḇ. 4:2 etc.). יהושע was indeed opposing the Pharisees who had made the Word of Elohim of no effect with their burdensome oral tradition. They had sought to make the observance of the Sabbath much more rigorous than יהוה had ever commanded. *The New Bible Dictionary*, 1st Edition, p. 1111, explicitly refutes the allegation that the Messiah broke the Sabbath, and referring to what Messiah and His taught ones did, says as follows, "It was not wrong to eat on the sabbath, even if the food must be obtained by plucking corn from the ears. Nor was it wrong to do good on the sabbath day." Furthermore, if יהושע was guilty of sabbath-breaking, it would have been used against Him at His trial.

Altar: Hebrew: *Mizḇeaḥ*; literally "Place of Slaughter" (from *zaḇaḥ*, 'he slaughtered'.) The Law of Mosheh allowed altars to be made from earth or unhewn stone (Shem. 20:24, 25). Altars were built for slaughtering of offerings (Ber. 8:20; Shem. 20:24), burning of incense (Shem. 37), or as memorials (Ber. 12:7, 13:18, 26:25, 35:1; Shem. 17:15).

Altar for Burnt Offering - Bronze Altar (Shem. 27, 30).

Altar for Incense - Golden Altar (Shem. 37).

Anti-Messiah: There are many Anti-Messiahs (Yn. א 2:18), and many theories have been presented throughout the centuries. If we study the Greek word *anti* we discover that it more frequently means "in place of" or "instead of" in the Messianic Writings than its other meaning of "against." Is this what the Messiah meant when He spoke of "another" one, in Yn. 5:43? Is it the same "another" one Sha'ul spoke about in Qor. ב 11:4? Whoever or whatever the anti-Messiahs are, they are all used by Satan, for he is behind them all. He even masquerades as a messenger of light. (Qor. ב 11:14).

Ba'al: The word Ba'al means lord or owner. Ba'al was the Phoenician or Kena'anite deity. This word, it seems, gradually became a proper name. A similar Semitic word derives from the Aryan root *Bhal*, which means "to shine," according to some. According to W. H. Roscher's well-known lexicon of mythology, *Ba'al (Bel, Belos)* was the ancestral and national deity of the Semites, and says that *Ba'al* was the founder of Baḇel (Babylon), according to secular history. He is identified with Zeus, Jupiter, Ammon, Asshur, Assur, Kronos, and Bel-Marduk. Morris Jastrow, Max Müller, and W. H. Roscher all three agree: *Ba'al* is the Babylonian sun-deity.

Beast: The Hebrew words translated as beast are *b'hemah,* plural *b'hemoth*. In some translations the Hebrew word *ḥai* (life) is often also rendered as beast or animal.

Believe, Belief: In the Greek of the Messianic Writings we find the word *pisteuo*. In classical Greek the word means "trust," and this is confirmed by the Greek of the Septuagint which uniformly translates the Hebrew *aman* by the word *pisteuo*. You might ask: Why not then translate *pisteuo* by "trust"? However, many other words also bore the meaning of trust, so in this case we opted to use the word "belief/believe." So, when reading *The Scriptures*, bear in mind that it means much more than uncommitted believing. It means to trust, to rely on, and even to prove your belief by obedience. It has been said, "He who believes shall obey, for by his obedience he proves that he believes."

Beliya'al: Often found as a compound expression, "Sons of Beliya'al" in the Scriptures. It is derived from two Hebrew words meaning "not" and "be of use," thus meaning "worthlessness." It could have been a proper name, originally. In Qor. ב 6:15 it is used as a synonym for Satan.

Between the Evenings: Hebrew, *bein arbayim*, an expression which according to the Pharisees means: between the decline of the sun immediately after midday and sunset, that is approximately 3 pm. in the afternoon - but according to the Sadducees means between sunset and dark, i.e. twilight.

Birth Pains: See *Great Distress*.

Bondage: To "be in bondage to," or to "be a slave of," or to "be a servant of," are three different ways of translating the same Hebrew word and its Greek equivalent. The decision to use any one of these three terms has always rested with the translator. The reader of *The Scriptures* might change them to suit himself. The bondage that we should beware of, and be set free from, is of course "bondage to sin" – as we read in Yn. 8:34 and Rom. 6:6-23.

Chaldeans: Hebrew - *Kasdim.*
Aramaic (Dan. 2:4-7:28; Ezra 5:12 - the various forms are rendered as:
Kasdaia - singular (Ezra 5:12)
Kasdaians - plural

Choose, Choice: The main word used in the Hebrew is the verb *baḥar*, which means to try, or by implication, to choose. One authority says it means "to choose after testing." As a nation, Yisra'ěl was, and still is, the chosen nation. Further, their Sovereign, יהושע, is the Chosen Servant. Elohim chooses His chosen ones for a certain task, for a High Calling, to comply with His conditions He laid down for them, namely to be "His treasured possession." We find it in the following texts: Shem. 19:5-6, Deḇ. 7:6-7, Deḇ. 10:15, Deḇ. 14:2, Deḇ. 26:18, Teh. 135:4, Yesh. 41:8, Yesh. 44:1-2. However, we find it even more clearly given to us in the Messianic Writings, namely in Eph. 1:4 (also confirmed in Tas. ב 2:13), which says that He has chosen us in Messiah "to be set-apart and blameless." Because of this High Calling we understand why "many are called, but few are chosen" (Mt. 20:16, Mt. 22:14). That is why there are few who find it (Mt. 7:14, confirmed also in Lq. 13:23-30). Yisra'ěl was "chosen in the furnace of affliction" (Yesh. 48:10), and it is no different for the Messianic believer (Mt. 7:14).

Commands (Commandments): The term "Ten Commandments, Ten Commands" is not found in Scripture at all. It is "Ten Words." The word "command(s)" and the word "word(s)" are often used as synonyms in Scripture, and often used interchangeably. See *Law* below.

Covenant: The Hebrew word *berith* means covenant, agreement or contract. This Hebrew word *berith* has been represented in Greek copies of the Messianic Writings as *diatheke.* A word which can carry the meaning of covenant or testament. Clearly the word *diatheke* was meant to carry the Hebraic meaning of covenant rather than testament. Dr. Bullinger in *The Companion Bible*, Appx. 95, wrote, "The word 'Testament,' as a translation of the Greek word *diatheke* (which means 'covenant'), has been nothing less than a great calamity; for, by its use, truth has been effectively veiled all through the centuries; causing a wrong turning to be taken ... errors of tradition have usurped the place of important truth. The word 'Testament' as a name for a collection of books is unknown to Scripture. It comes to us through the Latin Vulgate."

Darnel: In Mt. 13, Mq. 4, and Lq. 8 we read of the parable of the Sower (יהושע) sowing the wheat, and then (as we read in Mt. 13) comes the devil sowing the darnel (tares), which then grows among the wheat. It is generally agreed that the Greek *zizania* denotes "bearded darnel." This is a noxious plant, practically indistinguishable from wheat until the ear has developed. Messiah Himself reveals unto us in Mt. 13:41 that this darnel is sown by the devil, and shoots up among the true believers, right in the midst of the Messianic reign. This lawlessness of the darnel is manifested in people co-existing with the true believers in the Messiah's reign. At the end of this age the Messiah is going to send out His messengers to gather all these stumbling-blocks, as well as all "those doing lawlessness," and throw them into the furnace of fire.

Day of יהוה This expression appears some 30 times in the Scriptures, and this particular day is also referred to by means of equivalent phrases, about 300 times. It speaks of the visitation, the punishment, when יהוה actively intervenes to punish sin, especially at the end of the Age.

Deceit, Deception: The opposite of truth is "lie" or "falsehood," but so is "deceit" and "deception." Satan, the devil, is the father of all lies (Yn. 8:44). He is also the great deceiver (Ḥazon 12:9), deceiving the whole world. He started his work of deceiving in the garden of Ěḏen, and he has been doing it ever since, even coming as a messenger of light, and through his ministers who present themselves as ministers of righteousness (Qor. ב 11:13-15). In Mt. 24, speaking about the days prior to His return, יהושע warns us no less than four times against the deception (or leading astray) during the last days (vv. 4, 5, 11, 24). Sha'ul reveals this to us as well in Tas. ב 2, and explicitly warns us about "lawlessness" taking over in the Worship. This lawlessness is associated with "deceit", "falsehood" and "delusion" (Tas. ב 2:9-11).

Deʽu'ěl; Reʽu'ěl: In Hebrew the letter 'daleth' is very similar to the letter 'resh'; sometimes resulting in a mis-spelling and therefore this person is called both Deʽu'ěl and Reʽu'ěl. While the LXX and Syriac have Reʽu'ěl in Bem. 2:14 and elsewhere, the Samaritan, Vulgate, and Arabic have Deʽu'ěl instead. See also Bem. 7:42 & 10:20.

El, Eloah, Elohim, Elahin, Elyon:

El: Mighty One, Strength.

Elim: Plural of El.

Eloah: Singular form of Elohim, has same meaning as El.

Elohim: Plural of Eloah, Rulers, Messengers.

Elyon, El Elyon: The Most High El.

Hebrew	*Aramaic*
Eloah	Elah
Elyon	Illaya
Elohim	Elahin

Other languages: Ugaritic: "Il", plural: "Ilm", "Ilhm"; Phoenician: "l", plural: "lm."

The word *"El"* is a very ancient Semitic term. Among Semitic languages it is one of the most used terms for greatness, strength or deity. In Hebrew religious usage it does not denote a proper name but is used as a title. Used for the Creator's superiority over all other as a generic term in Dani'ěl 11:36 *"...the El of elahin..."*

El, Eloah, Elohim is used to refer to the Creator, but also applied to rulers, messengers and persons. (Referring to Mosheh in Shemoth 4:16, *"And it shall be that he shall be a mouth for you, and you shall be an elohim for him.")* Also Teh. 82:1.

Elyon is translated as Most High. Used in Tehillim 7:17 *"And praise the Name of יהוה (Elyon) Most High."*

The term *"Eli"* (my El) used by Messiah in the Messianic Writings in Marqos 15:34 "Eli, Eli lamah sheḇaqtani."

Emendations by the Sopherim: The 134 passages where the Sopherim (scribes) altered the Name יהוה to Adonai have been restored in *The Scriptures*, which are:

Berĕshith 18:3,27,30,31,32; 19:18; 20:4
Shemoth 4:10,13; 5:22; 15:17; 34:9(2)
Bemiḏbar 14:17
Yeshoshua 7:8
Shophetim 6:15; 13:8
Melaḵim א 3:10,15; 22:6
Melaḵim ב 7:6; 19:23
Yeshayahu 3:17,18; 4:4; 6:1,8,11; 7:14,20; 8:7; 9:8,17: 10:12; 11:11; 21:6,8,16; 28:2; 29:13; 30:20; 37:24; 38:14,16; 49:14
Yeḥezqĕl 18:25,29; 21:9; 33:17,20
Amos 5:16; 7:7,8; 9:1
Zeḵaryah 9:4
Miḵah 1:2
Mal'aḵi 1:12,14
Tehillim 2:4; 16:2; 22:30; 30:8; 35:17,22,23; 37:13; 38:9,15,22; 39:7; 40:17; 44:23; 51:15; 54:4; 55:9; 57:9; 59:11; 62:12; 66:18; 68:11,17,19,22,26,32; 73:20; 77:2,7; 78:65; 79:12; 86:3,4,5,8,9,12,15; 89:49,50; 90:1,17; 110:5; 130:2,3,6
Dani'ĕl 1:2; 9:3,4,7,9,15,16,17,19(3)
Ĕḵah 1:14,15(2); 2:1,2,5,7,18,19,20; 3:31,36,37,58
Ezra 10:3
Neḥemyah 1:11; 4:14
Iyoḇ 28:28

The additional passages where the Sopherim substituted the Name יהוה with Elohim are:
Tehillim 14:1,2,5; 53:1,2,4,5,6.

The 18 passages where the Sopherim "corrected" the text with good intentions to "revere" the Name of יהוה are:
Berĕshith 18:22
Bemiḏbar 11:15; 12:12
Shemu'el א 3:13
Shemu'el ב 16:12; 20:1
Melaḵim א 12:16
Diḇre haYamim ב 10:16
Iyoḇ 7:20; 32:3;
Tehillim 106:20
Yirmeyahu 2:11
Ĕḵah 3:20
Yeḥezqĕl 8:17
Hoshĕa 4:7
Ḥaḇaqquq 1:12
Zeḵaryah 2:8
Mal'aḵi 1:13

Eunuch: Careful consideration of the context of the passage must be given to understand the meaning of the word. The term eunuch can have a number of meanings:
- Official
- Someone who was castrated
- A childless / barren person

The meaning of the Hebrew word seems to be derived from an Assyrian term: 'He who is head (to the king)' (New Bible Dictionary, Jensen (ZA 7, 1892, 174A.1) and Zimmern (ZDMG 53, 1899, 116 A2). The Akkadian title ša rĕši (šarri) *"the one of the (king's) head."*

Another meaning of the word - a castrated person seems to come from the practice in eastern countries of utilising castrated men in high positions. Eunuchs were also employed in the Middle East and in China as guards and servants in harems and women's quarters.

First Day of the week: The underlying Greek text is "*mia ton sabbaton*", which when literally translated means "one of the sabbath/s", but is traditionally rendered as "first day of the week." The term "first day of the week" is literally translated as "*proté hemera tis hebdomata*" in Greek, but nowhere appears as such in the N.T. There is a strong argument that "*mia ton sabbaton"* should be rendered according to Semitic idiom as "day one of the week". See Mt. 28:1, Lq. 24:1, Yn. 20:1, Qor. א 16:2.

Gad: Apart from Gad, the son of Ya'aqoḇ, there was another "Gad." The astrologers of Baḇel called Jupiter (Zeus) by the name "Gad." He was also well known among the Canaanites (the Kena'anites) where his name was often coupled with Ba'al, Ba'al Gad, which according to the Massoretic vowel pointing in the Book of Yehoshua is pronounced: Ba'al Gahd. (Yeh. 11:17; 12:7; 13:5). This same name is discovered in the ancient Germanic languages as *Gott, Goda, Gode, God, Gud, Gade*. Gad (where the 'a' rimes with the the letter 'u' in "mud" is used as a proper name in Yesh. 65:11 as reference to the deity of fortune. And searching further back into its Indo-Germanic (Indo-European) roots, we find that it traces back to the word *GHODH*, which means "union," even "sexual union." No wonder this meaning is still evident in the Dutch and German *gade*.

Gentiles: In Hebrew, and in Greek, the word literally means "nations." Yisra'ěl is a nation, but is not numbered among the nations. (Bem. 23:9). It is for this reason that Yisra'ěl is rather referred to as a people whereas the word nation/s are used for those outside of covenant with יהוה. In Scripture the word nations has the meaning of non-Yisra'ělis or non-Yehuḏim, in most cases. In a few instances it means "many, or all nations, including Yisra'ěl." The true believer is repeatedly admonished not to learn the way of the gentiles (Way. 18:3, Deḇ. 12:30, Deḇ. 18:9, Yirm. 10:2, Yeḥez. 11:12, Yeḥez. 18:9, Miḵ. 4:5). And those who were gentiles before they came to conversion are admonished to "no longer walk as the gentiles walk" (Qor. א 12:2, Eph. 4:17, Kěpha א 4:3). Therefore, those who were gentiles, but came to belief, who are grafted in among Yisra'ěl (Rom. 11:17-24), simply have to unlearn their old gentile ways, and "come to the light" of Tsiyon (Yesh. 60:3), and "walk in the light" of the Renewed Yerushalayim (Ḥazon 21:24). They shall serve יהוה, they shall love the Name of יהוה, they shall no longer defile the Sabbath, and they shall hold fast the covenant of יהוה (Yesh. 56:6). They shall come to the House of the Elohim of Ya'aqoḇ, to Tsiyon, to Yerushalayim, and be taught the ways of Elohim, the Torah, the Word of יהוה (Yesh. 2:2-3, Miḵ. 4:2). What is the future of this unrepentant gentile world in which we live, who are outside the covenant of יהוה? None at all. Read this in Yesh. 34:2, Yirm. 25:26-33, Yirm. 30:11, Yirm. 46:28, Dan. 2:44, Dan. 7:27, Amos 9:8, Oḇaḏ. vv. 15-21, Ḥagg. 2:22, Ḥazon 11:15. Only Yisra'ěl, living true to Torah, shall be saved (Yesh. 45:17).

God: See *Gad*.

Great Distress: This was also prophesied in Deḇ. 4:30 and Dan. 12:1. Messiah prophesied that prior to His return, there shall be a time of Great Distress, or Great Pressure. He said so in Mt. 24:21 & 29, Mq. 13:24, and in Ḥazon 7:14. Some see this time also as the time of "birth pains," which is often found in the same passage. We read of this time of "birth pains" in Teh. 22:31, Teh. 102:18, Yesh. 66:7-9, Miḵ. 4:6-10, Miḵ. 5:3, Mt. 24:8, Ḥazon 12:5.

Heart: In Scripture this word is used figuratively in most instances, being one of the richest terms for the totality of man's inner nature. Whereas to the Greek (and also to the English speaker) heart refers to the emotions - to the Hebrew it refers rather to the centre of man's thoughts. We read in Yirm. 17:9 that "The heart is crooked above all, and very sick (or, desperately wicked)." Further, our Messiah teaches us that the heart is the source from which come all forms of sin (Mt. 15:19, Mq. 7:21-22). Those who still live according to the flesh have uncircumcised hearts, they have callous hearts, hardened hearts, hearts of stone. Those who do not yield "all their heart" unto Elohim, through His Son, are those who keep their hearts far away from Him (Yesh. 29:13, Mt. 15:8, Mq. 7:6). But those who have surrendered "all their heart," those whose "hearts are steadfast with Him," are living a life of overcoming, for they "are true to His covenant" (Teh. 78:37), their "eyes watch My ways" (Mish. 23:26), they no longer live according to the "teachings" which are but the "commands of men" (Yesh. 29:13, Mt. 15:8, Mq. 7:6). When the people of Yisra'ěl live up to their calling as Yisra'ěl (overcomers), their hearts are circumcised, (Deḇ. 30) they keep the Torah (law) as proof of their love towards Elohim (Rom. 2:26-29, Yn. א 5:2-3, Yn. ב v. 6). Elohim demands "all your heart" (Deḇ. 4:29-30; 6:4-9, Yirm. 29:13, Yo'ěl 2:12, Mt. 22:37, Mq. 12:29-30).

Jesus: Consider *Iesous*, rendered as "Jesus" in English versions up to now. For example the authoritative *Greek-English Lexicon* of Liddell & Scott, under *Iaso*: the Greek goddess of healing reveals that the name *Iaso* is *Ieso* in the Ionic dialect of the Greeks, *Iesous* being the contracted genitive form. In David Kravitz, *Dictionary of Greek and Roman Mythology*, we found a similar form, namely *Iasus*. There were four different Greek deities with the name of *Iasus*, one of them being the Son of Rhea. Further, it is well known that *Ies* is the abbreviated form of the name *Iesous*, and Dr.

Bullinger, in *The Apocalypse*, p. 396, says *Ies* was part of the name of Bacchus. Also see *Come out of her, My people*, by C.J. Koster.

The original KJV translators consistently translated the Greek term *Iesous* as Jesus even when referring to Joshua (Yehoshua) son of Nun in Heb. 4:8, thereby recognising that the same term should be used throughout. Modern translators have opted in Iḇ`rim 4:8 to render *Iesous* as Joshua (Yehoshua) thus recognising that the Greek term was a place holder for the original Hebrew Name, but have inconsistently not rendered *Iesous* as Joshua (Yehoshua) throughout the rest of the Messianic Writings (NT).

Kush: Usually taken as Ethiopia, the territory south of Mitsrayim (Egypt), including what is today known as Sudan. Some think that it could have been the Accadian *Kas*.

Law: a. In the Tanaḵ (pre-Messianic Scriptures):

(1) We have rendered *Torah* as "*Torah*," rather than translating it by an English word, thereby retaining the force and flavour of the original, as it appears in its various contexts. While the closest English word is the traditional "law" (and that is the rendering given in the Greek text of the Messianic Writings, from the Greek word *nomos*), the word *Torah* is far wider in meaning. It derives from the word *yarah* which carries the meanings "to cast," "to lay foundations," "to sprinkle," "to water," "to send out the hand," "to show," "to indicate," "to teach," "to instruct" (Gesenius). The word *Torah* is used in reference to precepts, commands, statutes, judgments, rules, whether in the singular or in groups. Understandably then, it carries the additional meanings of "body of law," "body of instruction," etc., and is used to refer also to the entire content of the *Ḥumash*, the first five books of the Tanaḵ (see Preface). Indeed, when context indicates that the "law of יהוה" is being referred to, the primary reference is to the *Ḥumash*.

Secondary references include for example the national law given on Mt. Sinai (Shem. 20-23) and its restatement on the plains of Moaḇ (Deḇ. 29:1,21.)

(2) We have rendered *ḥoq* and its feminine form *ḥuqqah* in most places as "law" instead of the traditional "statutes and "ordinances."

(3) We have rendered *mishpat* as "judgment" or as "right-ruling," and its verb *shaphat* as "judge" or "rightly rule."

(4) Expressions such as "command," "law," "teaching," "Torah," "word," etc. are often used in an inclusive way, whether in the singular or in the plural.

(5) Much of the Torah involves commands, laws, right-rulings, statutes, etc., which relate to a properly constituted society, such as that which prevailed under Mosheh or under the sovereigns of Yisra'ěl. As such, laws which clearly apply within a civil or national context are not to be misapplied by individuals living in a society that is not totally subject to the Torah as its constitution and legal code. Thus for example, you may not decide to stone someone to death for desecrating the sabbath. The decision would have to be made by a judge within the framework of such a Torah-based nation. Clearly then, although these laws are still applicable, since the context in which they are to be applied is lacking at present, they can only be applied when such a Torah-true nation comes into existence (for example, when Messiah returns to set up his Reign).

b. Law - In the Messianic Writings:

The word "law" (Torah) occurs throughout the Messianic Writings, usually in reference to the Torah, in whole or in part. In this respect, our comments above (Law - In the Tanaḵ) should be considered as a background to the correct understanding of the usage of those who wrote the Messianic Writings (New Testament).

However, a number of other points should also be borne in mind, viz.:

(1) Firstly, the text underlying all translations made today is Greek, not Hebrew, although the original Semitic structures and thought-patterns underlying the Greek text are frequently still discernible in the Greek text. This means that Greek words like *nomos* (law / Torah) may also represent expressions or ideas other than Torah from time to time in the Messianic

Writings. Thus, in Romiyim 7, 8 the word "law" sometimes refers to the "Torah", the Law of יהוה, the first five books of the Tanak̲ (Old Testament), as in Romiyim 7:14,16,22; Romiyim 8:3,4,7, but other times it refers to something else such as a body of rules or a fixed system or pattern of behaviour, as in Romiyim 7:21,23; 8:2. Both usages appear together in Romiyim 7:25, where the "law" of sin (torah of sin), i.e. the "fixed behaviour pattern" of sin (sin is "Law-breaking"- Yoḥanan א 3:4) is contrasted with the "Torah" of Elohim. The expression "the law of sin and death" (torah of sin and death) in Romiyim 8:2 is not a reference to the Torah as such, but to the system of sin and death in those who are walking in the flesh and not in the Spirit (Romiyim 8:1,2,6,7).

(2) There are times when *nomos* (law / Torah) is used to refer to a portion of the Torah such as that which applies to the Lĕwitical Priesthood, or to the Set-apart Place (K.J.V. "Sanctuary"), and a failure or refusal to see this could lead to the erroneous conclusion that the Torah / Law given at Sinai has been annulled, abolished, done away, or at least been changed, when in fact this is not the case at all. (Mattithyahu / Matthew 5:17-20). An example of this is in Ib̲`rim / Hebrews 7:12. The King James Version puts it this way: *"For the priesthood being changed, there is made of necessity a change also of the law."*

Since the "change" referred to is in reference to the "scaling down" from the heavenly original to the earthly shadow-copy (see Ib̲`rim / Hebrews 8:1,2,5), from a system in which the High Priest is eternal to one in which the human high priest keeps dying and having to be replaced by another, it would be wrong to see this verse as a proof-text for the position that the Torah / Law given through Mosheh has been changed. A careful look at the context makes abundantly clear the fact that the order of Malkitsed̲eq preceded that of Lĕwi, even as the heavenly Set-apart Place preceded that of the earthly one. The fact that יהושע began his High Priestly duties in the heavenly Set-apart Place after his death on Golgotha does not mean that the heavenly system only came into being at that time. The point made in Ib̲`rim / Hebrews 7:12 is that the present earthly / shadow-copy / "scale model" cannot produce perfection. Perfection requires nothing less than the ministry of "such a Kohĕn ha Gadol (High Priest), who is seated at the right hand of the throne of the Greatness in the heavens, and who serves in the set-apart place and of the true Tent, which יהוה set up, and not man" (8:1,2).

Lord: Substituting the Name of יהוה with "LORD" or "Lord," as has been done in most translations, is against all Scripture:

(1) It is a transgression of the Third Command(ment) which prohibits us from bringing His Name to naught, or falsifying it.

(2) It is a transgression of the command in Deb̲. 4:2, "Do not add to the Word which I command you, and do not take away from it." This is repeated in Deb̲. 12:32, Mish. 30:6, Ḥazon 22:18-19.

(3) יהוה reproves the prophets in Yirm. 23:36, "You have changed the Words of the living Elohim..."

(4) "Lord" is not an innocent title. We trace it back to the Roman house-deity, and further back to the name of an Etruscan sovereign, *Larth*, not forgetting that in those days the sovereigns were deities. So this is a transgression of the clear command of Shem. 23:13.

Maiden: In *The Scriptures* the Hebrew word 'almah' is translated as 'young woman' and 'bethulah' as 'maiden'. Similarly the Greek word 'parthenos' is translated as 'maiden' with the exception of Mt. 1:23 (a quotation from Yesh. 7:14, also confirmed in the Shem Tob̲ text of Mattithyahu). None of the Hebrew and Greek words can be translated exclusively as 'virgin' or 'non-virgin'. Here follows a complete list of the occurances.

Almah - Ber. 24:43; Shem. 2:8; Yesh. 7:14; Teh. 68:25; Mish. 30:19; Shir. 1:3, 6:8.

Bethulah - Ber. 24:16; Shem. 22:16,17; Way. 21:3,14; Deb̲. 22:19,23,28; 32:35; Shoph. 19:24; 21:12; Shem. ב 13:2,18; Mel. א 1:2; Mel. ב 19:21; Yesh. 23:4,12; 37:22; 47:1; 62:5; Yirm. 2:32; 14:17; 18:13; 31:4,13,21; 46:11; 51:22; Yeḥ. 9:6;

44:22; Yoĕl 1:8; Amos 5:2; 8:13; Zeḵ. 9:17; Teh. 45:14; 78:63; 148:12; Estĕr 2:2,3,17,19; Iyoḇ 31:1; Eḵah 1:4,15,18; 2:10,13,21; 5:11; Diḇre. ב 36:17.
Parthenos - Mt. 1:23; 25:1,7,11; Lq. 1:27; Ma. 21:9; Qor. א 7:25,28,34,36,37; Qor. ב 11:2; Ḥazon 14:4.
Parthenoia (maiden-hood) - Lq. 2:36.

Mamzer: This word occurs twice in Scripture, Deḇ. 23:2 & Zeḵ. 9:6. Some sources refer to this as someone born of a union between a man and woman of invalid marriage, such as between brother and sister, or other forms of incest. Others refer to this as a woman bearing a child from a man other than her husband. Yet other sources say that the meaning of the word is uncertain.

Mitsrayim: Egypt.

Naḥash: A proper name, meaning shining or shining one. Often translated as serpent. Also see 'Serpent.'

Name: The Hebrew word is *shĕm* (English : name), which is a label of identification. Flowing from this are the derived usages of *shĕm* as a reference to authority, fame, etc.

Overcome, Overcomers: Ya'aqoḇ's name was changed to Yisra'ĕl because Ya'aqoḇ "overcame (prevailed) with Ĕl." Ber. 32:28 & 35:10. Also see Yisra'ĕl.

Passover: The Hebrew word is *Pĕsaḥ*. As a verb, meaning to jump, skip or pass over. As a noun, referring primarily to the animal-victim that was slaughtered, but secondarily to the period of time connected with the slaughter of the victim. In Ma. 12:4 the KJV erroneously refers to this as easter, however the underlying word is the same word used throughout the rest of the Messianic Writings for Passover.

Paul: Who changed the name of Sha'ul to Paul (Paulus)? We find no evidence in Scripture as to why, when, and by whom this change of his name was instigated. All we could find was this: The ancient Romans had a national hero named Paulus. Was this change from "Sha'ul" to "Paulus" done in order to appease the Roman people? See Ma. 26:14, also in other translations where Messiah called him Sha'ul (Saul). There is of course the possibility that Paulus was used to represent the Hebrew name *Pallu* (Ber. 46:9; Shem. 6:14; Bem. 26:5,8; Diḇre. א 5:3.) meaning *separated* and that this was used by the believers in reference to his being especially set apart. To avoid taking sides we have used the form "Sha'ul" as per Messiah in Ma. 26:14.

Post-exilic Apostasy: Some (estimated to be 25%) of Yehuḏah and of the other tribes returned from exile in Baḇel and Assyria. After their return we find that apostasy had set in, or else started. Some proofs of this apostasy are:

(1) Babylonian month names were adopted which were clearly associated with Babylonian mythology: *Nisan, Siwan* etc., and we find them in the post-exilic books of Ezra, Neḥemyah, Estĕr, Zeḵaryah. In post-Scriptural times we find that they even adopted the name of the Babylonian sun-deity, *Tammuz*, by which to name one of their months.

(2) Estĕr's original name was Haḏassah (myrtle). The name Estĕr derives from *Ishtar* (the Babylonian female deity), or else from the Persian *stara* (star).

(3) The Name of יהוה began to be suppressed. At least by the 3rd century BCE the Name came to be avoided, and *Aḏonai* substituted in its place. Later on they substituted *HaShem* for the Name, according to the custom of the Samaritans. In the Talmud we find instructions that the Name was "to be hidden," and in another place we read, "to be kept secret," and again, "disguising it." They did exactly as was prophesied in Yirm. 23:26-27 (see also under *Lord*, above).

(4) Possibly for the same reason Yeho-, the abbreviated form of the Name of יהוה, became eliminated from the name of the successor to Mosheh, Yehoshua, who now became known as Yeshua (see Neḥ. 8:17). Deleting the Yeho- from Yehoshua's name, was probably the reason our Messiah became known as Yeshua in the Hebrew Shem-Toḇ text of Mattithyahu.

(5) This apostasy became worse and worse, and by the time יהושע began His ministry He repeatedly reproved the Pharisees (and others) for their lawlessness (Mt. 23:28, Yn. 7:19), and for keep-

ing their own man-made commands, whilst rejecting the commands of יהוה (Mt. 15:3-9, Mq. 7:7-13).

Prophets: A prophet is a spokesman for a deity. In times past "prophets" were often regarded as possesing a mystical or supernatural gift. Scripture defines יהוה true prophets as defined in Deḇ. 13:1-4 & 18:18-20. The prophets were persecuted (Ma. 7:52), and many of them were killed. Messiah said that false prophets were well spoken of (Lq. 6:26), and He reveals to us that the false prophets are those who work lawlessness (Mt. 7:15-23).

Renewed: Two Greek words, *neos* and *kainos*, have been rendered as "new" in almost all translations. The latter's meaning differs from the former, and is derived from the verb *kainoo*, which means "to make new." The Hebrew equivalent of this verb is *ḥadash*, which means "to renew." For this reason we have rendered *kainos* as "fresh" or as "renewed."

Reʽu'ěl: See Deʽu'ěl.

Righteousness: In Deḇ. 6:25 we read that righteousness requires of us "to guard to do all these commands before יהוה Elohim, as He commanded us." In Teh. 119:172 the Psalmist says, "For all Your commands are righteousness." In Yesh. 51:7 we read, "Listen to Me, you who know righteousness, you people in whose heart is My Torah (law)." This is explained in Yoḥ. א 3:4-10, "Everyone doing sin also does lawlessness, and sin is lawlessness. And you know that He was manifested to take away our sins, and in Him there is no sin. Everyone staying in Him does not sin. Everyone sinning has neither seen Him nor known Him. Little children, let no one lead you astray. The one doing righteousness is righteous, even as He is righteous. The one doing sin is of the devil, because the devil has sinned from the beginning. For this purpose the Son of Elohim was manifested: to destroy the works of the devil. Everyone having been born of Elohim does not sin, because His seed stays in him, and he is powerless to sin, because he has been born of Elohim. In this the children of Elohim and the children of the devil are manifest: Everyone not doing righteousness is not of Elohim, neither the one not loving his brother."

Right-ruling, Rightly rule: This noun and verb might at first appear to be unconventional, or rather unknown in the English language. They render the Hebrew noun *mishpat* and its verb *shaphat* often more precisely than the well-known "judgment" and "judge." Traditionally they have been rendered as "justice" and "justify" in some instances. We have avoided these latter two words because they derive from the name of a gentile deity.

Sabbath (Seventh Day of the Week): This day was blessed and set apart by Elohim at creation (Ber. 2:2-3). Later on it was instituted as the sign of the everlasting covenant between Elohim and His people, a sign that He sets them apart, an everlasting sign (Shem. 31:13-17, Yeḥez. 20:12-20). Sabbath-keeping is one of the Ten Words of the Covenant, standing forever, settled forever in heaven, founded forever (Teh. 89:34, Teh. 111:8-9, Teh. 119:89). We would like to point out the following:

(1) יהושע kept the Sabbath (Lq. 4:16, Yn. 15:10), and the women who were taught by Him still kept it at the time of Messiah's burial (Lq. 23:56).

(2) Sha'ul kept it (Ma. 13:14, Ma. 13:42-44, Ma. 17:2, Ma. 18:4 & 11).

(3) Ludia and the women kept it (Ma. 16:13).

(4) In Heb. 4:9 we are again reminded of the necessity of keeping the Sabbath.

(5) Finally: At the end of the age (Yesh. 66), we read in verse 23 that the Sabbath shall still be kept.

For further reading see *From Sabbath to Sunday* by Samuele Bacchiocchi and *Come out of her My people*, by C.J. Koster.

Serpent: **Hebrew**: Naḥash: Serpent, snake, image of a serpent, mythological fleeing serpent. King of the Ammonites during the time of king Shaul. Father of Aḇigail, the mother of Amasa. Commander of Aḇshalom's army.

Laḥash: Serpent-charming.

Neḥushtan: "A thing of brass": brazen serpent made by Mosheh in the wilderness that was worshipped in the time of king Ḥezekiah of Yehuḏah before he destroyed it.

Ir-naḥash: City of a serpent. Also a Yehuḏi.
Zoḥeleth: Boundary stone near Yerushalayim where Adoniyah slew sheep and oxen.
Muppim: a Binyamite, one of the 14 descendants of Raḥel.
Pethen: Snake, venomous serpent, cobra, adder, or viper.
Tsepha / Tsiphoni: Poisonous serpent, viper snake or Shephuphan or Shupham, serpent, son of Bela and grandson of Binyamin.
Shephiphon: Horned snake, adder.
Saraph: fiery serpent, poisonous serpent, seraph, seraphim majestic beings with 6 wings, human hands or voices in attendance upon Elohim.
Tannin / Tannim: dragon, serpent, sea monster, sea or river monster, serpent, venomous snake
Greek: Aspis: Asp, small and most venomous serpent.
Drakon: Dragon, Great serpent, Satan.
Ophis: Snake, serpent.

Set-apart Place: This could have been rendered or alternately read as "that which is set-apart," in most places. This would then give it an abstract meaning, e.g. in Teh. 74:3, Dan. 8:13, Dan. 11:31, Mt. 24:15.

She'ol: Place of the dead.

Shomeron: Samaria.

Sin: See Righteousness.

Slaughter, slaughters, slaughterings: The Hebrew word is *"za'ḇaḥ"* or *"ze'ḇaḥ"* which means to slaughter an animal, usually an offering. This word is sometimes translated as offer, offering or offerings. See also Altar.

Son of Aḏam: We used this term, rather than "Son of Man," as a designation for our Messiah, because "Man" comes from the German *Mann (Mannus)*, which was the great ancestor, progenitor, the ancestral deity of the Germanic race. The designation "Ben Aḏam" for our Messiah, is found in the Hebrew text of Teh. 80:17, as well as in the Hebrew of the Shem-Toḇ text of Mattithyahu, and in Delitzsch's Hebrew New Testament. The Aramaic equivalent term "Bar Enosh" is used in Daniel 7:13.

Tartaros: Kepha ב 2:4. A Greek term. Possibly from the Hebrew Taḥti, "the lower parts"; most probably of She'ol. Also see Deḇ. 32:22; Teh. 88:6.

Terms traditionally used to substitute the Name יהוה: Shemoth 20:7 "You do not bring the Name of יהוה your Elohim to naught, for יהוה does not leave the one unpunished who brings His Name to naught."

In the extreme and mistaken attempt to observe the Third Commandment, the Sopherim altered 134 passages from יהוה to "Adonai" to prevent the pronunciation of the Name.

For the same reason the Massoretes did not give the vocalisation for יהוה, but used instead the vowel signs for the alternative title "Adonai" and "Elohim." In many translations, this practice continues with the Name being substituted (in capitals) with "The LORD", "Die HERE", "God," "Pan Bog," "Modimo," "Utixo" and many other substitutes.

For these same reasons orthodox Jews today when reading the Scriptures do not vocalise the Name יהוה, instead pronouncing as a substitute terms such as "haShem" (the Name), "Adonai" (Master) etc.

In the Greek Manuscripts of the Messianic Writings we find the same practice where the Name is substituted by titles such as "Powers" or "Heavens" in order to abstain from using the proper Name.

Testament: See *Covenant*, above.

T`fillen: "And they do all their works to be seen by men, and they make their t'fillin wide ..." Mattityahu 23:5

In Deḇarim 6:4-9 (known as "the Shema") we read: "You ...shall bind them as a sign on your hand, and they shall be as frontlets between your eyes" (verse 8); similar words being found in Shemoth 13:9 and Deḇarim 11:18. While some have interpreted this symbolically, others have taken it literally, and so made containers which could be bound on hand and head containing portions of the Scripture text.

The prevailing Pharisee tradition at the time of יהושע, and also among Orthodox Rabbinic Judaism today, is to take the passages literally. This they do by inserting parchments containing these passages into two small leather boxes, one for the head and one for the the right arm (- left-handed people use the left arm). These are bound onto head and arm by leather straps. The box for the head has four sections, containing Shemoth 13:1-10; 13:11-16; Deḇarim 6:4-9; 11:13-21, respectively, whereas the same passages are found in the box for the arm without such divisions.

Torah refers to that bound on the hand by the term: *'ot*, meaning 'sign', and that for the head (between the eyes) by the term: *totafot* - usually rendered as 'frontlets' or 'bands'.

Torah does not specify the material to be used, how to attach the 'sign' and 'frontlet' , or to which hand it pertains.

In Mattityahu 23: 5, יהושע refers to the differing widths that were current, certain hypocritical 'rabbis' attempting to display their superior spirituality by having their sets somewhat wider than others. Thus, if meant to be interpreted literally, there is much potential variation in how they could look. On the other hand, none of these details matter if it is to be interpreted symbolically, since the real issue would only be the Torah-true attitude within, based on the love expressed in the Shema. The Rabbinic tradition has been to refer to both hand and headset together by the term: *t`fillin*, plural of the word *t`fillah* which means prayer or intercession. They call the handset *t`fillah shel yad* and the headset *t`fillah shel – rosh*, and they "put on t`fillin" during their daily customary prayer times.

So widespread is the usage of the term *t`fillin* that in the standard edition of the Ketuḇim Bĕt (known also as the Ketuḇim Netzarim, haBrit haḤadasha, and the New Testament) translated by the renowned Professor Franz Delitzsch, the term *t`fillin* is used rather than the terms *'ot* and *totafot*. See his rendering of Mattityahu 23:5 (Aramaic form: Mattai used in his translation).

Many traditional Christian 'New Testaments' use the word 'phylacteries', reflecting the Greek text of this passage, which uses the term: *phulakteria*, a word which appears to refer to a charm or amulet. This may have been their use by individuals or sectarians from time to time, but in all fairness it must be stated that the concept of charm or amulet is not integral to Orthodox Rabbinic Judaism. Of course it must be noted that such concepts are also entirely alien to the Torah itself, where the point of *'ot* and *totafot* is to focus our attention on יהוה himself as our Mighty One, Sustainer, and Shield.

Torah: Plural Torot - Hebrew for teachings or law. In general the Torah refers to the first five books of Scripture, but could also speak of others teachings of principles in the Messianic Writings, especially in the writings of Sha'ul. See also **Law**.

Thigh: Here we have a strong indication of Revelation originally being written in Hebrew. If this word was written in Hebrew, it would have been *regel*. It's possible though, that the copiers of Revelation could have overlooked the small extension on the *dalet* (ד), which would have made it a *resh* (ר). If the word was *degel,* it would have meant "banner", which makes much more sense than "thigh", because in the latter case two rules are broken:

(1) In Way. 19:28 we are forbidden to make tattoos on our bodies.

(2) A person whose thigh was exposed was considered naked. See Mq. 14:51, Shem. 28:42, Way. 16:4. When Revelation was copied it would have been easy to see the Hebrew "d" (ד) as an "r" (ר), if the former was not carefully written down. As the Hebrew script developed, the *dalet* and the *resh*, especially from around 700 BCE and onwards looked almost identical. It is also contrary to His dress in Ḥazon 1:13. It also seems that Messiah, when He appeared to His followers, spoke Hebrew, even though they could understand Greek very well (Ma. 26:14).

Similarly, compare Ber. 10:3 with Diḇre. א 1:6 - Riphath & Diphath.

Turn of the Year: Hebrew, "Tequphah". This is known to us as the time of year when day and night is of equal length. It is not the end of the year. (e.g. Shem. 34:22).

Tzitzit: Found in both the Torah and Messianic Writings. The tzitzit is worn as a remembrance of the Torah. Bem. 15:37-41; Deḇ. 22:12. יהושע also wore the tzitzit as found in the Messianic Writings. Mt. 9:20; 14:36.

Wadi: We have used this English word which is of Arabic origin, to translate the Hebrew *naḥal*. It is the only English word that aptly describes a wide river bed that only flows in times of rain, and occasionally very strongly, as a flood. This is to be distinguished from the word for river, which is *nahar* in Hebrew and *nehar* in Aramaic.

Works of Torah: Greek, *Ergon Nomou.* Hebrew, *Ma'ase Ha-Torah.* This term is used 9 times in 7 passages in the Messianic Wrtings in Rom. 3:20,28; 9:32, Gal. 2:16; 3:2,5,10. This may be interpreted in three ways.

(1) Referring to Torah obedience as a means toward being declared righteous, as apposed to Torah obedience as a result of being declared righteous.

(2) As a reference to a Dead Sea Scroll document called *Miqsat Ma'ase Ha-Torah* (MMT), variously translated as "Some of the Precepts of the Torah" (Strugnell and Qimron) or "Legal rulings of Torah" (Lawrence Schiffman), which refer to precepts of the Qumran community apparently for the purpose of right-standing before the Almighty. For further reference see the magazine Biblical Archaeology Review, Nov-Dec. 1994, Article, Paul, Works of the Law and MMT, pp.52 ff.

(3) A combination of (1) and (2).

Whichever of these views are taken, "Works of Torah" are shown to be in contrast to the teaching of Scripture as a whole, which declare that righteousness comes by belief and not by works.

Yehuḏah, Yehuḏi, Yehuḏim:

A. Yehuḏi; an individual belonging to Yehuḏah. Yehuḏim; the plural of Yehuḏi.

B. 1. Yehuḏah: The name of one of the sons of Ya'aqoḇ. The name Yehuḏah means: "Let יהוה be praised," or as Keil & Delitzsch's Commentary puts it: "The one for whom יהוה is praised." Ber. 29:35 says, "And she conceived again and bore a son, and said, "Now I praise יהוה." So she called his name Yehuḏah." Ya'aqoḇ's name was changed to Yisra'ěl. Thus Yehuḏah was a son of Yisra'ěl.

2. The sons of Yisra'ěl developed first into family clans, and then tribes, the tribes of Yisra'ěl. After the tribes of Yisra'ěl were led out of Mitsrayim by Mosheh they became the nation of Yisra'ěl. On entering the promised land each tribe (apart from Lěwi) was allocated a land area, and thus we have the land of Yehuḏah belonging to the Yehuḏim (individuals of the tribe of Yehuḏah).

3. When the twelve tribes were divided into two reigns the ten tribed reign was known as the reign or house of Yisra'ěl. It was also known as the house of Ephrayim after its chief tribe. The second reign or house (consisting of the two tribes Yehuḏah and Binyamin) was known as the reign or house of Yehuḏah.

4. It is therefore important to determine by context when reading the Scriptures the particular usage of the words Yehuḏah, Yehuḏi and Yehuḏim.

5. These terms contain the Name of יהוה, or rather, the first letters of it, (the so-called *Tri-grammaton*) the abbreviated form of His Name. The Massoretes vowel-pointed this name to read "Yehuḏah." In old Assyrian texts we find that they called them *Iaudaia* (probably pronounced: Ya-u-da-ia). So, which one is right – "Yehuḏah" or "Yahuḏah"?

Yisra'ěl: The name given to Ya'aqoḇ when he strove or overcame with Ěl. It literally means, He who rules with Ěl. See (Ber. 32:28). The sons if Yisra'ěl developed into the tribes of Yisra'ěl, ultimately becoming the twelve tribe nation of Yisra'ěl. Later the reign of Yisra'ěl divided into two reigns, one called the reign of Yehuḏah and one called the reign of Yisra'ěl. See explanatory note: Yehuḏah.

Yoḇel: The primary meaning of the word appears to be that of a ram's horn - See Shem. 19:13,16. The term is also used in Way. 25:8-16 for the proclamation of the Fiftieth Year (Jubilee) by the sounding of the Shophar on Yom haKippurim (Day of Atonement / Coverings).

WEIGHTS & MEASURES

The units for weights and measures used in Scripture (original languages) are difficult for people of today to understand or to visualize. In the tables below we have taken every precaution to convert the original units of weights and measures into our modern equivalents. Take note that units of weights and measures varied between countries and between time frames (eras). Units of weights and measures will be listed in two categories; (1) In the Tanaḵ (Pre-Messianic Scriptures, commonly referred to as the Old Testament) and, (2) Messianic Writings (commonly referred to as the New Testament.) Hebrew or Greek terms are shown below the translated terms.

Distance / Lenghts: The Scriptural standard measurement for length was the cubit, which was the length of an adult man's fore-arm, from the elbow to tip of the middle finger.

Dry measures: The homer or kor was the maximum weight that a donkey could carry. The standard for smaller measures was the ĕphah.

Liquid measures: The liquid measure 'bath' came from the word used in Hebrew for 'daughter' and may refer to the capacity of water that a young woman used to carry in a jar.

Weights: The terms used for weights (sheqels, minas and talents) were used to express amounts of money by weight.

Distance / Length - Tanaḵ / Pre-Messianic Writings:

Unit	**Equal to**	**Imperial** (Approx.)	**Metric** (Approx.)	**Examples**
Finger *Etzḇa (Heb)*		0.72"	18.5mm	Yirm. 52:21
Handbreadth *Tophaḥ (Heb)*	4 fingers	2.9"	74mm	Shem. 25:24 Shem. 37:11 Yeḥ. 40:5,42
Span *Zereth (Heb)*	3 handbreadths	8.75"	222mm	Shem. 28:16 Shem. 39:9 Yeḥ. 43:13
Cubit *Ammah (Heb)*	6 handbreadths	17.5"	445mm	Ber. 6:15 Shem. 25:10 Zeḵ. 5:2
'Extended' Cubit	7 handbreadths	20.4"	518mm	Yeḥ. 40:5 Yeḥ. 43:13
Reed *Qaneh (Heb)*	Six cubits	8.75-10 f t	2.7-3.1m	Yeḥ. 40:5 Yeḥ. 42:16
Day's journey				
Individual		30 miles	48 km	Mel. א 19:4
Group		10 miles	16 km	Shem. 3:18

Distance / Length - Messianic Writings:

Unit	**Equal to**	**Imperial** (Approx.)	**Metric** (Approx.)	**Examples**
Cubit *Pechus (Gk)*		17-19"	430-480mm	Mt. 6:27 Ḥaz. 21:17
Fathom *Orguia (Gk)*	4 cubits	6 ft	1.83m	Ma. 27:28
Reed	6 cubits	9 ft	2.74m	Ḥazon 11:1
Stadion *Stadia (Gk)*	400 cubits	600 ft	183m	Lq. 24:13 Yoḥ. 6:19 Ḥaz. 21:16
Mile *Milion (Gk)* *Latin origin*	3200 cubits 1000 paces	4858 ft	1.48km	Mt. 5:41
Sabbath Day's Journey	2000 cubits	3000 ft	914 m	Ma. 1:12

Weight - Tanaḵ / Pre-Messianic Writings:

Unit	**Equal to**	**Imperial** (Approx.)	**Metric** (Approx.)	**Examples**
Gerah *Gerah (Heb)*	1/20th shekel	0.02 oz	0.57 g	Yeḥ.45:12
Beka *Beqa (Heb)*	10 gerahs	0.20 oz	5.7 g	Shem. 38:26
Pim *Pim (Heb)*	1 1/3 bekas	0.27 oz	7.6 g	Shem. א 13:21
Shekel *Sheqel (Heb)*	20 gerahs 2 bekas	0.40 oz	11.4 g	Shem. 30:23 Shoph. 17:2 Yeḥ.45:12
Mina *Maneh (Heb)*	50 shekels	1.26 lb	572 g	Ezea 2:69 Neḥ.7:70
Talent *Kikar (Heb)*	3000 shekels	75.6 lb	34.3 kg	Shem. 38:24 Mel.א 9:14 Ezra 8:26

Weight - Messianic Writings:

Unit	Equal to	Imperial (Approx.)	Metric (Approx.)	Examples
Pounds *Litra (Gk)*		12 oz	340 g	Yoḥ. 19:39
Talent *Talanton (Gk)*		57-80 lb	26-36 kg	Mt. 25:15 Ḥaz. 16:21

Dry Measures - Tanak̲ / Pre-Messianic Writings:

Unit	Equal to	Imperial (Approx.)	Metric (Approx.)	Examples
qab *qab (Heb)*	1/6 seah 1/18 ĕphah	1.3 quarts	1.2 litres	Mel. ב 6:25
omer *omer (Heb)*	1/10 ĕphah	2.3 quarts	2.2 litres	Shem. 16:16 16:32,36
measure *seah (Heb.)* *	2 hins	8 quarts	7.3 litres	Mel. ב 7:1 7:16,18
ĕphah *ĕphah (Heb)*	3 seahs	24 quarts	22 litres	Shem. 16:36 29:40; Way. 5:11
lethek̲	1/2 ḥomer	3.12 bushels	110 litres	Hos. 3:2
kor *kor (Heb)*	10 ĕphahs ḥomer	6.25 bushels	220 litres	Yeḥ.45:14
ḥomer *ḥomer (Heb)*	kor 10 ĕphahs	6.25 bushels	220 litres	Way. 27:16 Yesh. 5:10, 45:11

* The *seah* was also used as a land measurement of 50 cubits long by 50 cubits wide.

Dry Measures - Messianic Writings:

basket *modius (Gk)*		0.5 bushels	7.4 litres	Mt. 5:15 Mq. 4:21

Also called: Grain measure, clay pot or bushel in some translations. In many instances the measures of the Tanak̲ are also used in the Messianic Writings.

Liquid Measures - Tanak̲ / Pre-Messianic Writings:

Unit	Equal to	Imperial (Approx.)	Metric (Approx.)	Examples
log *log (Heb)*	1/12 hin 1/72 bath	0.63 pints	0.35 litres	Way. 14:10; 14:12, 23
hin *hin (Heb)*	1/6 bath 12 logs	1 gallon	3.6 litres	Shem. 29:40; 30:24; Way. 19:36;
bath *bath (Heb)*	1/10 homer 6 hins 1 ĕphah	5.8 gallons	22 litres	Yesh. 5:10; Yeḥ.45:10,11
ḥomer *ḥomer (Heb)*	10 baths	58 gallons	220 litres	Yeḥ.45:11-14

Liquid Measures - Messianic Writings:

Unit	Equal to	Imperial (Approx.)	Metric (Approx.)	Examples
measure *metretes (Gk)*		10-30 gallons	38-115 litres	Yoḥ. 2:6

In many instances the measures of the Tanak̲ are also used in the Messianic Writings.

Monetary Measures - Tanak̲ / Pre-Messianic Scriptures:

In the Tanak̲ these measures overlap with weight measures, where measuring units were often used both for weight and money. It is difficult to express these in modern monetary units due to the fluctuation of monetary units.

Unit	Imperial Weight Equivalent	Metric Weight Equivalent	Other
Dram (daric)			The earliest coined money Yisraĕl used, equal to 130 grains weight.
Shekel (light) *Silver or Gold*	0.201 oz		
Shekel (heavy) *Silver or Gold*	0.403 oz		15 light shekels

Unit	Imperial Weight Equivalent	Metric Weight Equivalent	Other
Mina (lights) *Silver or Gold*	0.63 lb		50 light shekels
Mina (heavy) *Silver or Gold*	1.26 lb		50 heavy shekels
Talent (light) *Silver or Gold*	37.8 lb		60 light shekels
Talent (heavy) *Silver or Gold*	75.6 lb		60 heavy shekels
Qesitah			A unit of money of uncertain value, perhaps in the form of a lamb. Ber. 33:19, Yeh. 24:32, Iyoḇ 42:11

Monetary Measures - Messianic Writings:

Unit	Roman Equivalent	Greek Equivalent	Other
Mite *lepton*	1/2 quadran	1/2 fathing	
Fathering *(Quadrans; assaurius)*	2 mites	2 leptons	
Penny *(denarion)*	1 denarius	1 drachma	daily wage of a labourer
Didrachma	2 denarii	2 drachmas	
Stater *(tetradrachma)*	4 denarii	4 drachmas	A piece of silver
25 drachmas (Greek)	1 aureus		
Mina *pound*	100 denarii	100 drachmas	
Talent		240 aurei	

Study Notes:

ILLUSTRATIONS

he illustrations are mere artistic images to assist the reader in visualising the intended image and are ot drawn to scale or intended to be an accurate graphic representation of Scripture.

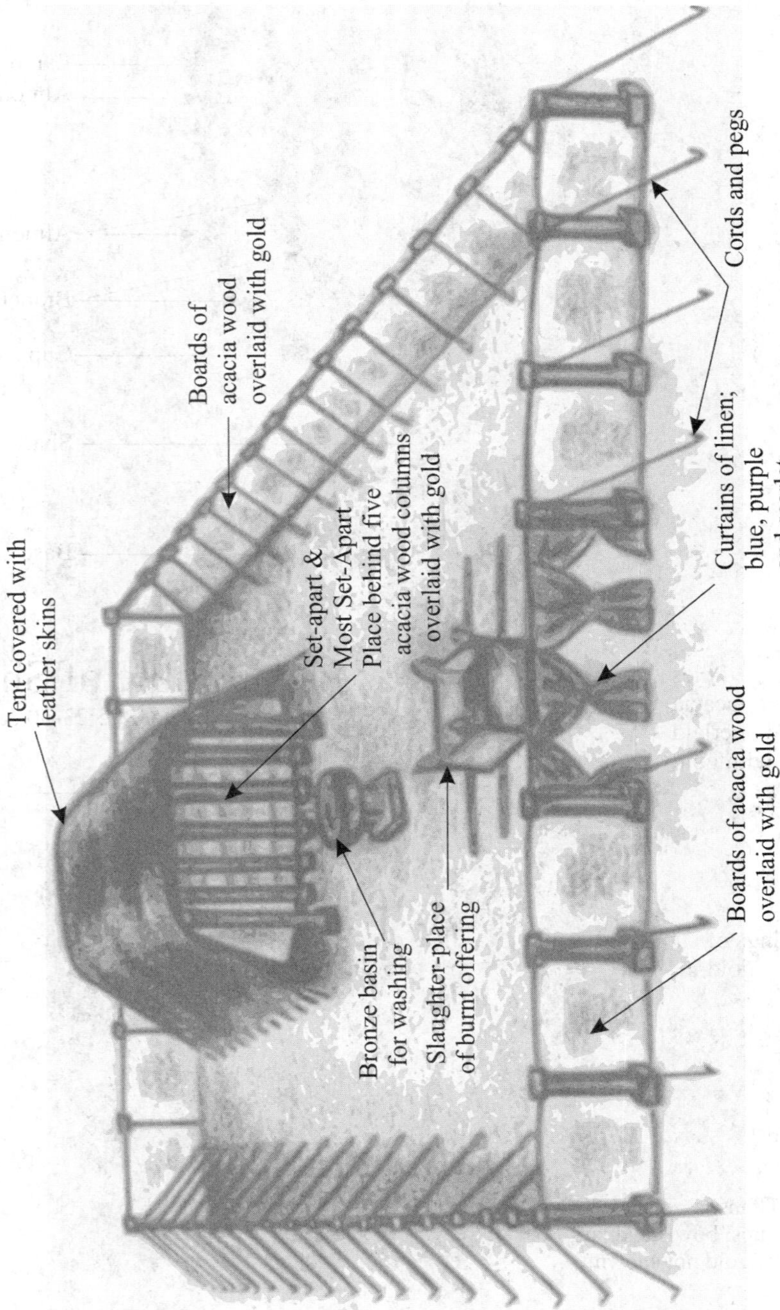

The Dwelling Place
Shemoth 26 & 36

Menorah / Lampstand of Gold

Shemoth 25:31-37 & 37:17-24

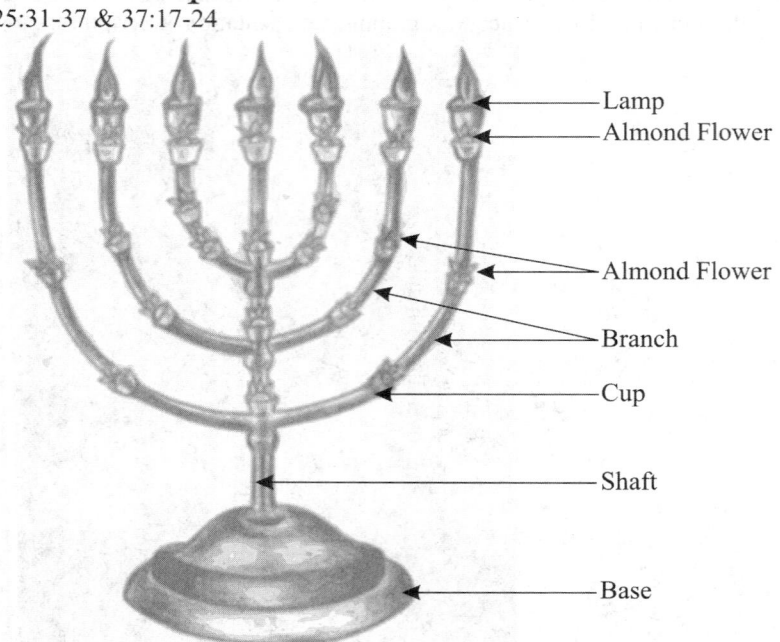

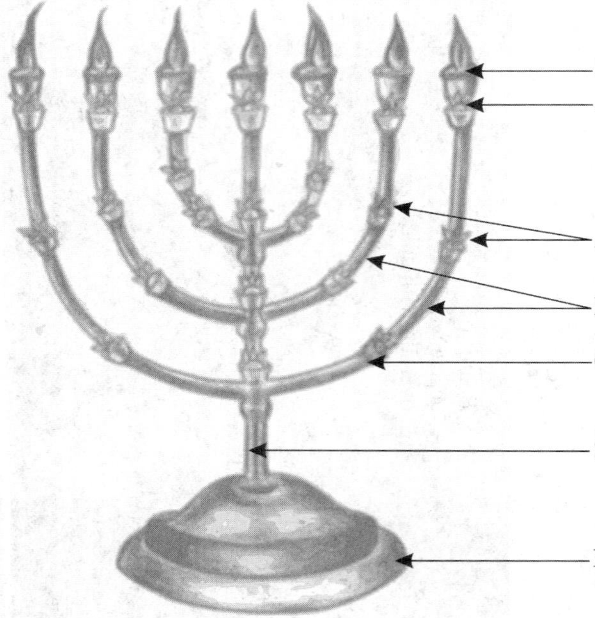

Table of Showbread

Shemoth 25:23-30 & 37:10-16

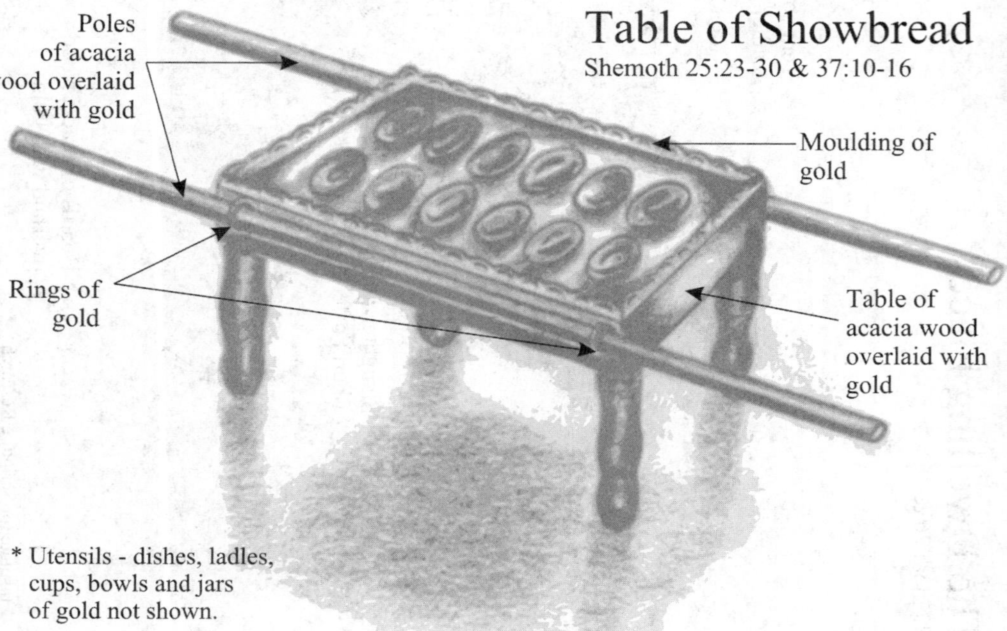

* Utensils - dishes, ladles, cups, bowls and jars of gold not shown.

Slaughter-place of Incense

Shemoth 30:1-5 & 37:25-28

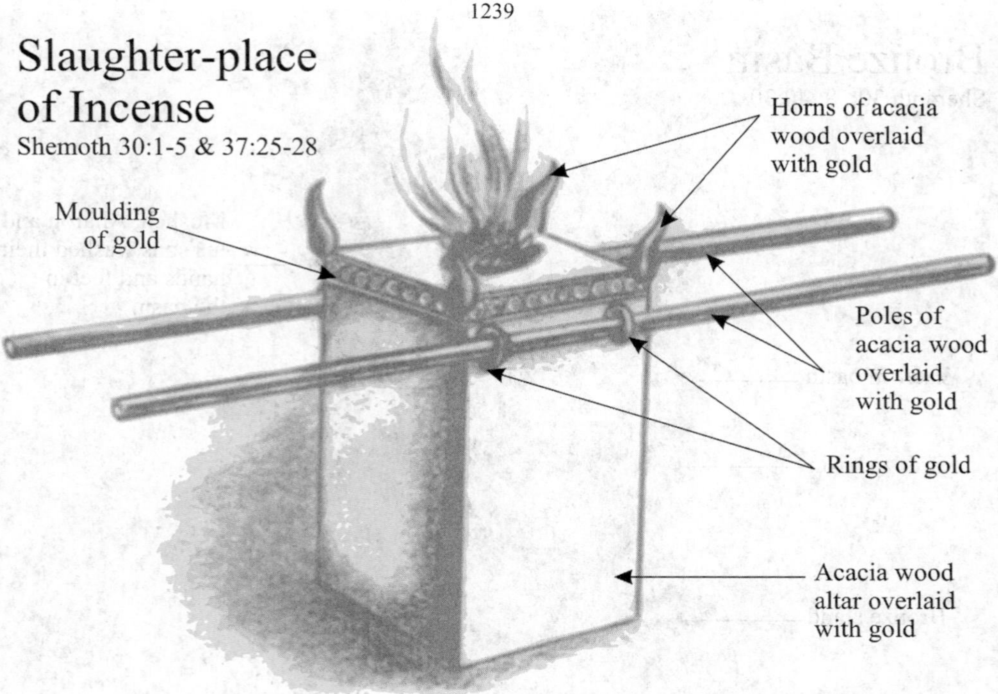

Slaughter-place of Burnt Offering

Shemoth 27:1-8 & 38:1-8

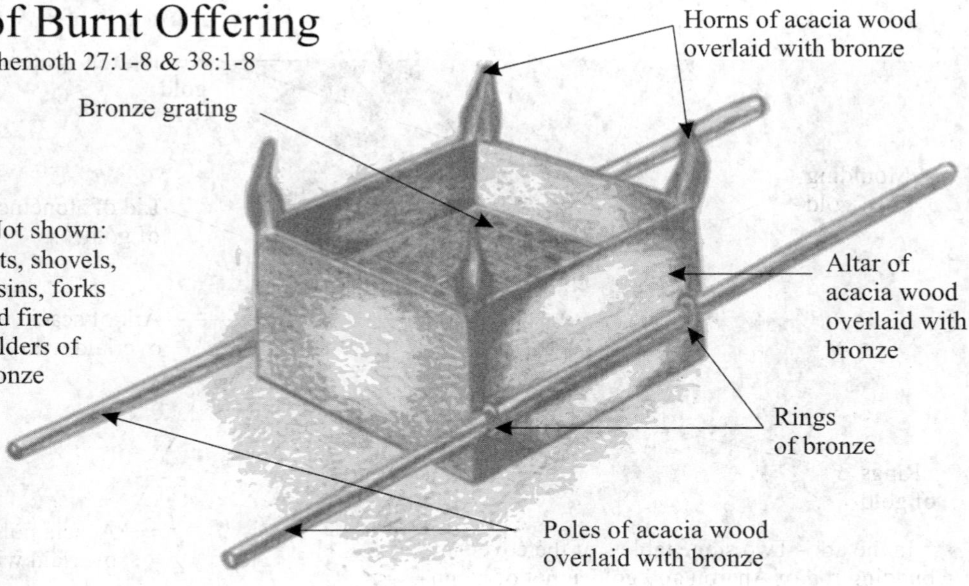

*Not shown: Pots, shovels, basins, forks and fire holders of bronze

Bronze Basin
Shemoth 30:18; 40:30

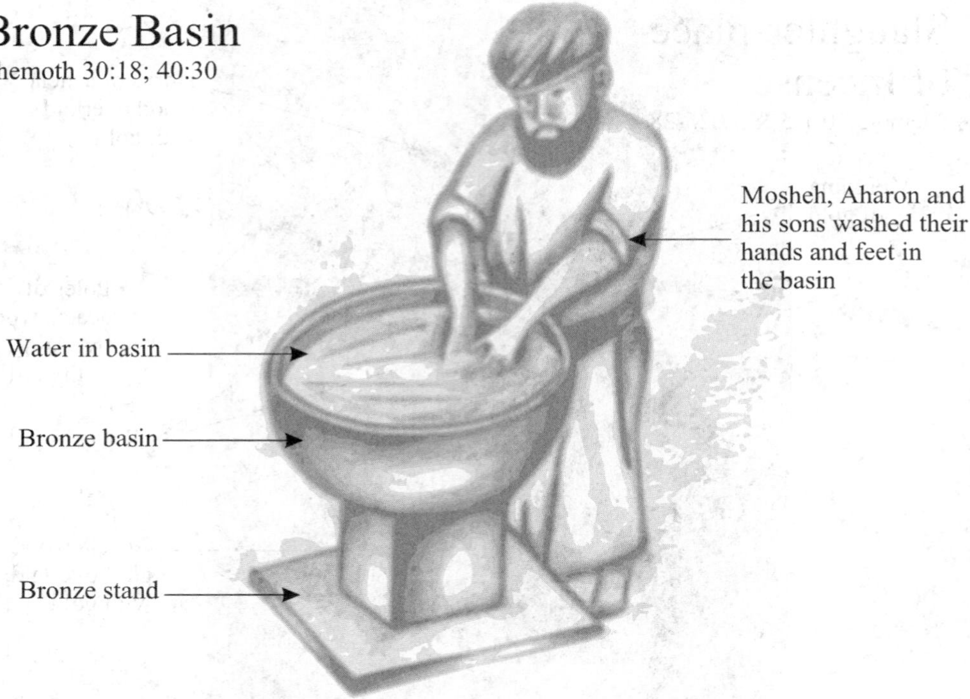

Ark of the Witness
Shemoth 25:10-22; 37:1-15

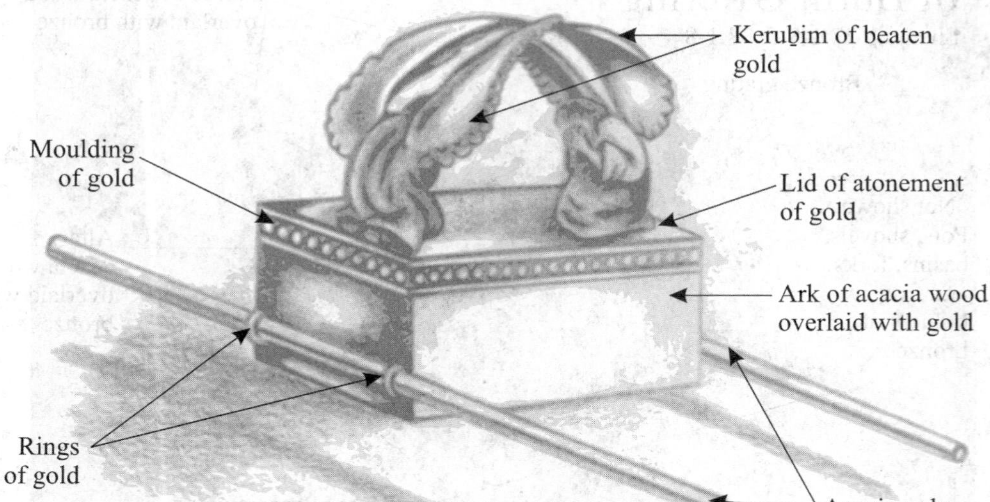

* In the ark - Two stone tablets of the covenant, budding rod of Aharon and golden pot of manna.

Garments of the High Priest

Shemoth 28 & 39:1-31

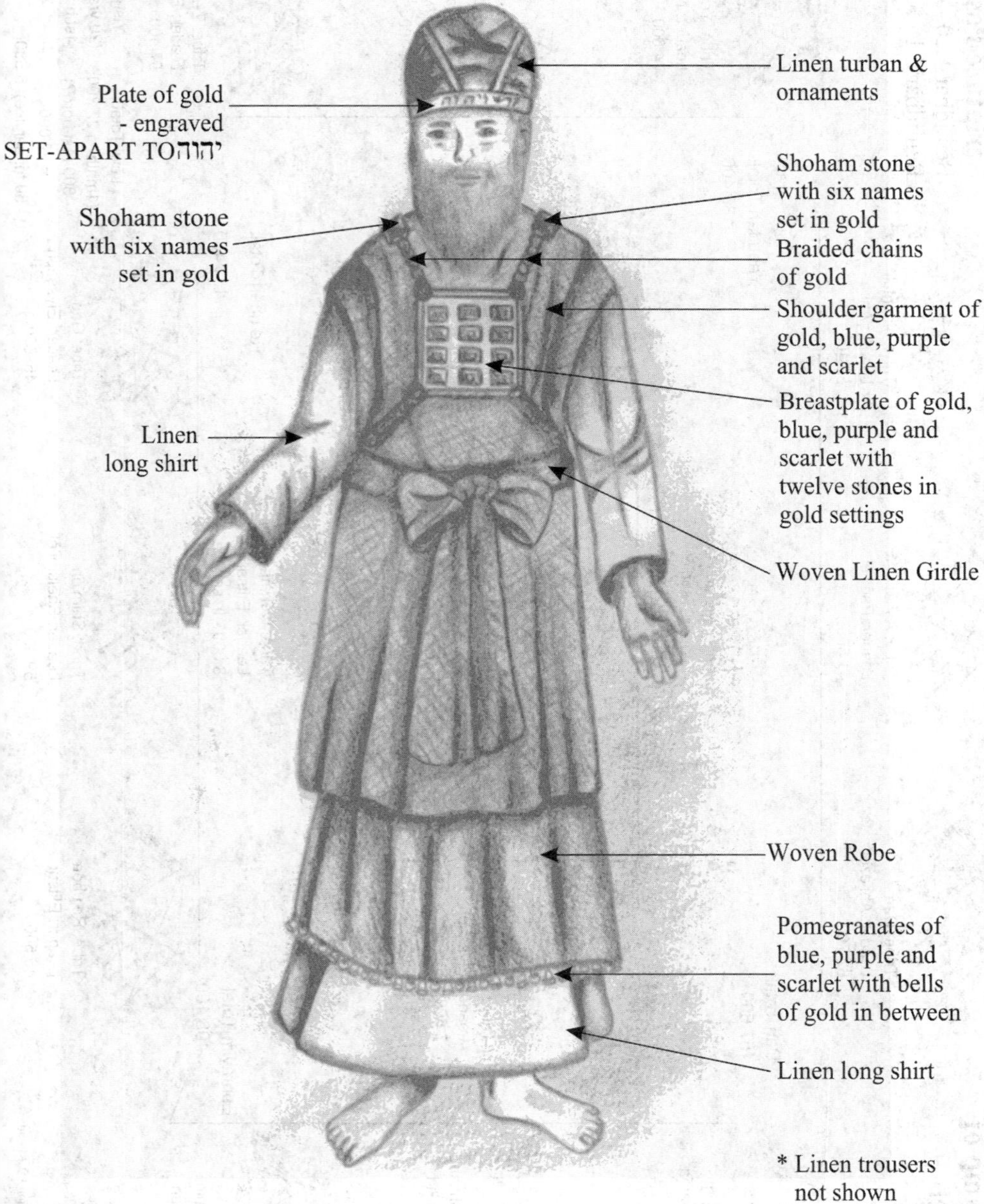
Linen turban & ornaments
Plate of gold - engraved SET-APART TOיהוה
Shoham stone with six names set in gold
Shoham stone with six names set in gold
Braided chains of gold
Shoulder garment of gold, blue, purple and scarlet
Breastplate of gold, blue, purple and scarlet with twelve stones in gold settings
Linen long shirt
Woven Linen Girdle
Woven Robe
Pomegranates of blue, purple and scarlet with bells of gold in between
Linen long shirt
* Linen trousers not shown

The Camp of Yisra'ěl

Scripture Pasages:
Bemiḏbar 1:20 - 46
Bemiḏbar 2:1 - 32

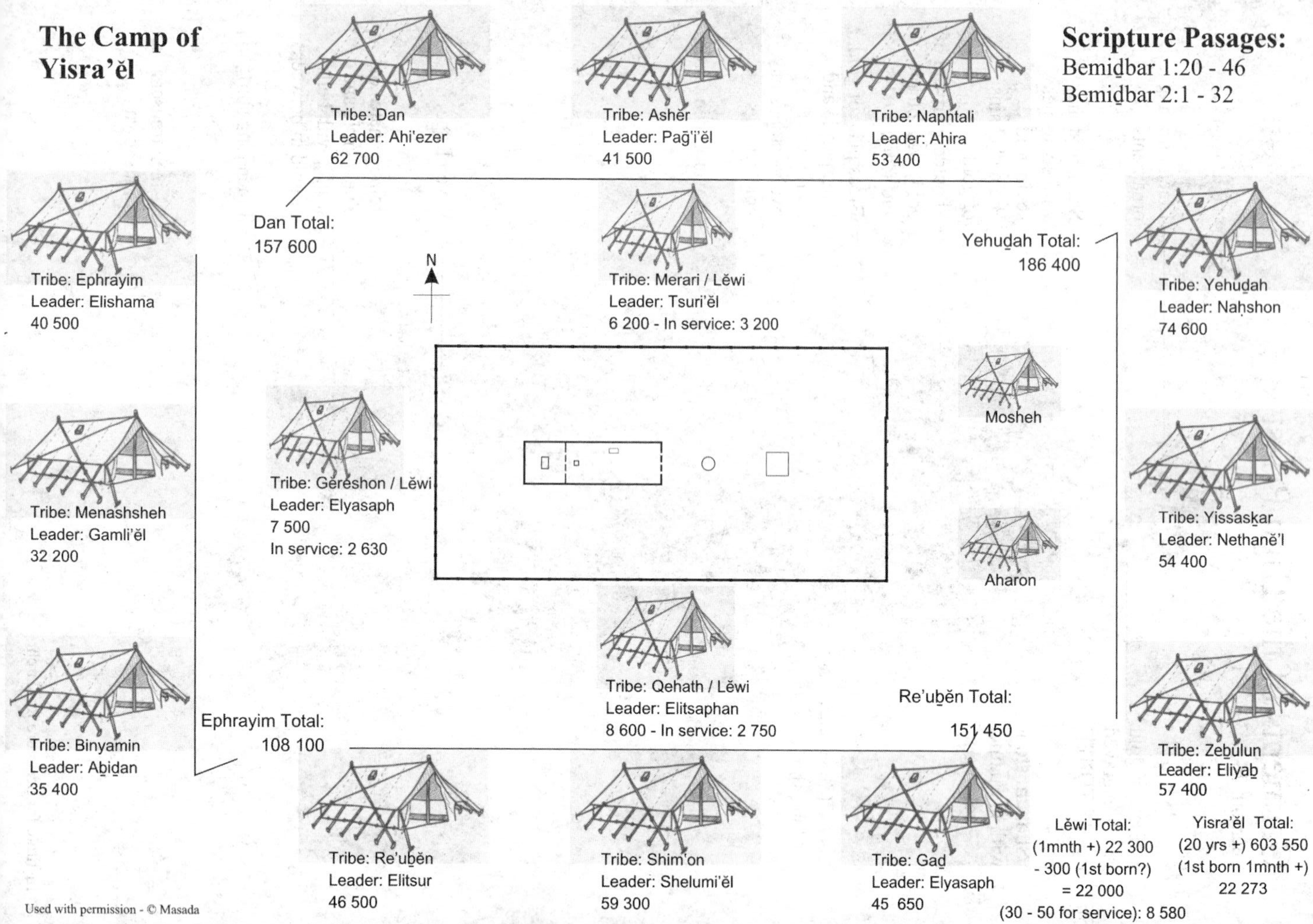

Lěwi Total:
(1mnth +) 22 300
- 300 (1st born?)
= 22 000
(30 - 50 for service): 8 580

Yisra'ěl Total:
(20 yrs +) 603 550
(1st born 1mnth +)
22 273

Although all possible care has been taken to ensure a precise representation of the timelines, we cannot guarantee that all are accurate, as interpretation of events vary.

Timeline - Flood

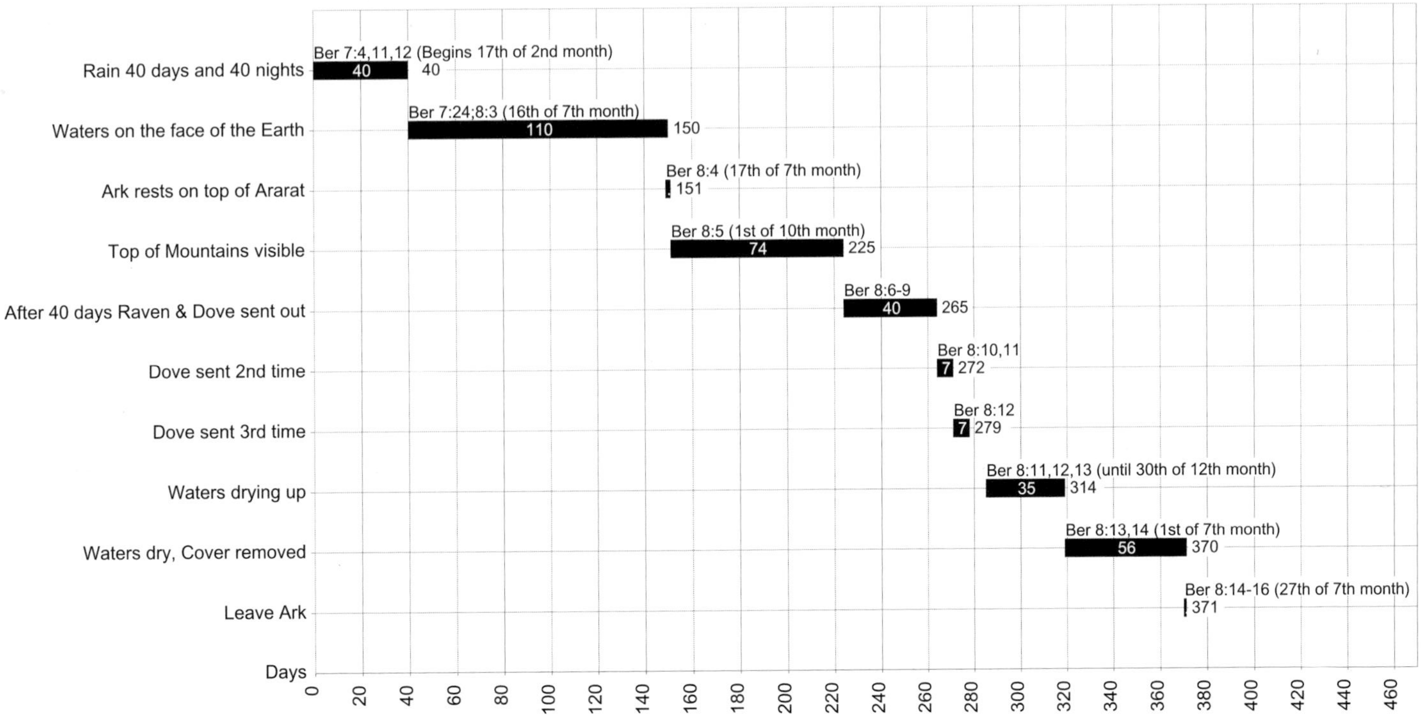

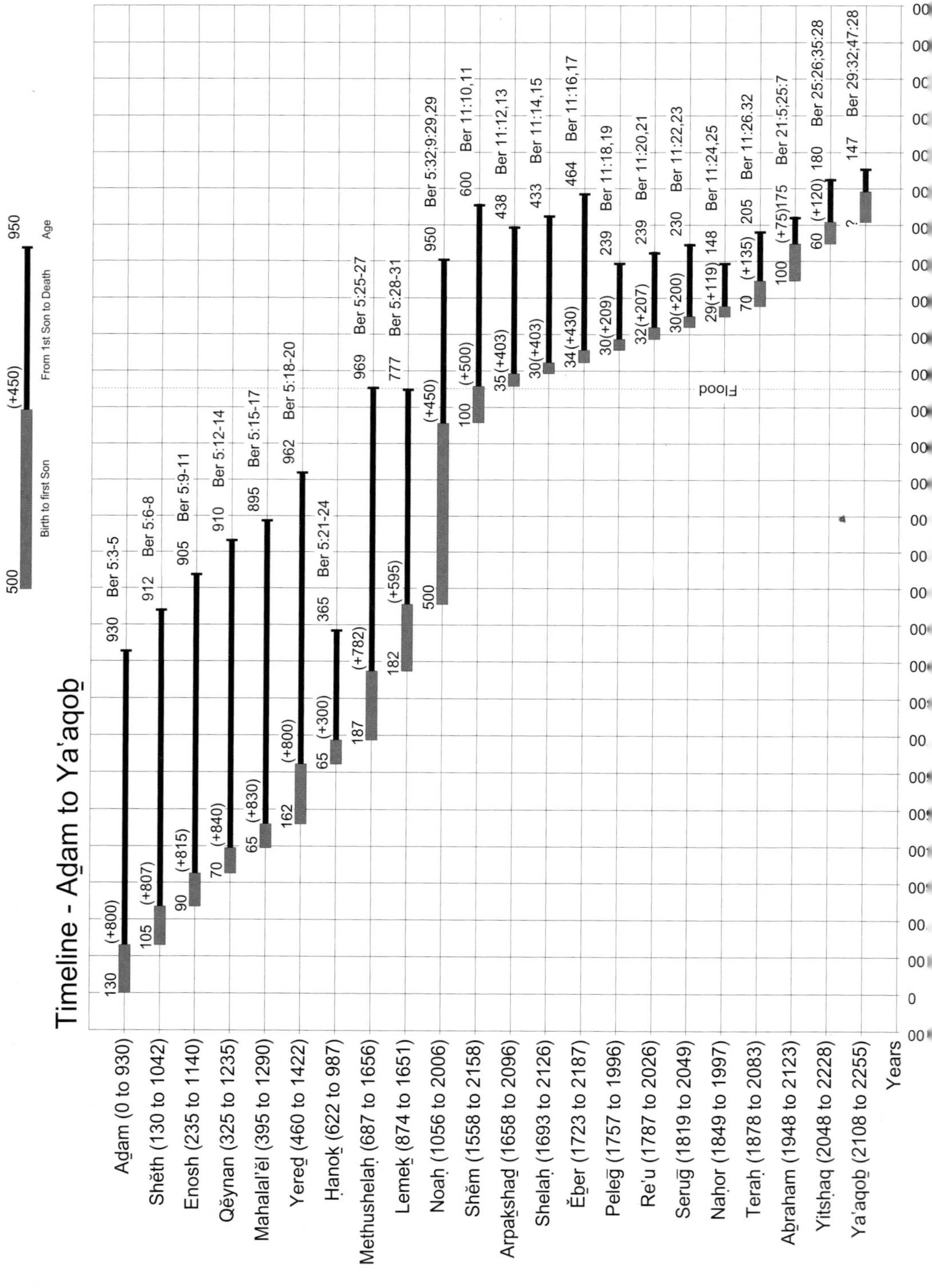
Timeline - Aḏam to Ya'aqoḇ
500
(+450)
950
Birth to first Son
From 1st Son to Death
Age
Aḏam (0 to 930)
Shěth (130 to 1042)
Enosh (235 to 1140)
Qěynan (325 to 1235)
Mahalal'ěl (395 to 1290)
Yereḏ (460 to 1422)
Ḥanoḵ (622 to 987)
Methushelaḥ (687 to 1656)
Lemeḵ (874 to 1651)
Noaḥ (1056 to 2006)
Shěm (1558 to 2158)
Arpaḵshaḏ (1658 to 2096)
Shelaḥ (1693 to 2126)
Ěḇer (1723 to 2187)
Peleḡ (1757 to 1996)
Re'u (1787 to 2026)
Seruḡ (1819 to 2049)
Naḥor (1849 to 1997)
Teraḥ (1878 to 2083)
Aḇraham (1948 to 2123)
Yitsḥaq (2048 to 2228)
Ya'aqoḇ (2108 to 2255)
Years
Flood
130 (+800) 930 Ber 5:3-5
105 (+807) 912 Ber 5:6-8
90 (+815) 905 Ber 5:9-11
70 (+840) 910 Ber 5:12-14
65 (+830) 895 Ber 5:15-17
162 (+800) 962 Ber 5:18-20
65 (+300) 365 Ber 5:21-24
187 (+782) 969 Ber 5:25-27
182 (+595) 777 Ber 5:28-31
500 (+450) 950 Ber 5:32;9:29,29
100 (+500) 600 Ber 11:10,11
35(+403) 438 Ber 11:12,13
30(+403) 433 Ber 11:14,15
34(+430) 464 Ber 11:16,17
30(+209) 239 Ber 11:18,19
32(+207) 239 Ber 11:20,21
30(+200) 230 Ber 11:22,23
29(+119) 148 Ber 11:24,25
70 (+135) 205 Ber 11:26.32
100 (+75)175 Ber 21:5;25:7
60 (+120) 180 Ber 25:26;35:28
? 147 Ber 29:32;47:28

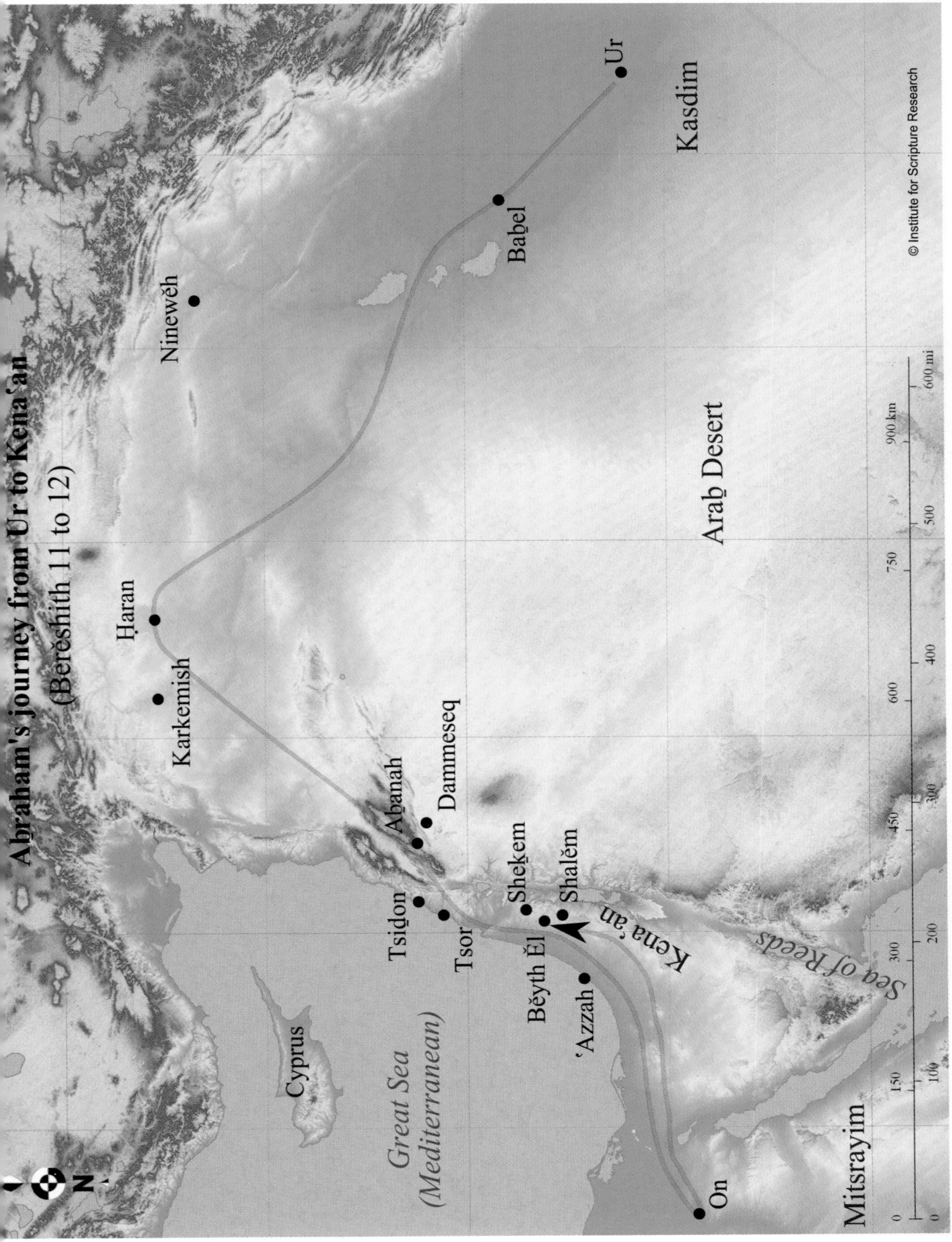
Aḇraham's journey from Ur to Kena'an
(Berĕshith 11 to 12)
N
Ur
Kasdim
Baḇel
Nineweh
Ḥaran
Karkemish
Arab Desert
Dammeseq
Aḇanah
Tsidon
Tsor
Sheḵem
Shalĕm
Bĕyth Ěl
'Azzah
Kena'an
Sea of Reeds
Cyprus
Great Sea
(Mediterranean)
Mitsrayim
On
0
150
300
450
600
750
900 km
0
100
200
300
400
500
600 mi
© Institute for Scripture Research

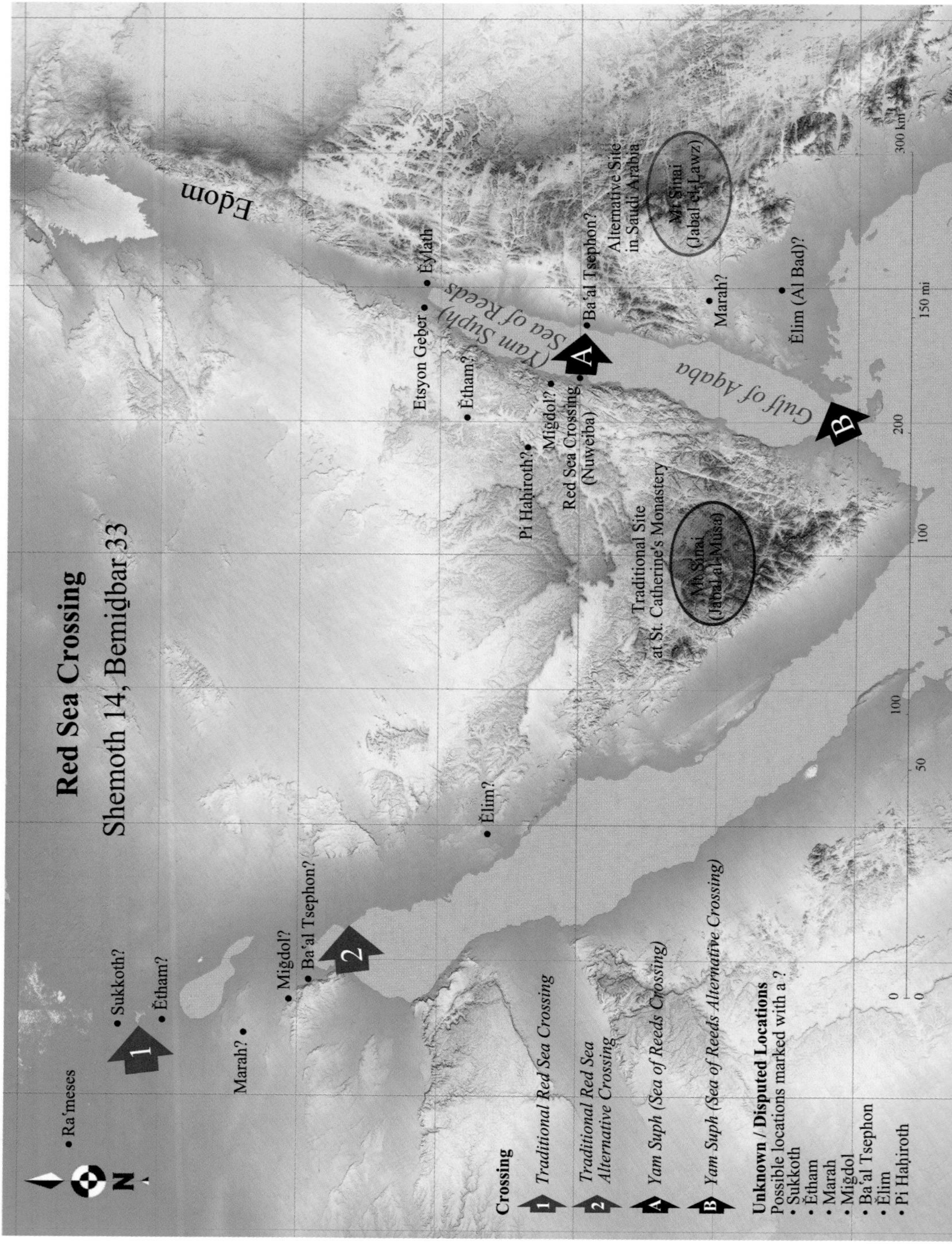
Red Sea Crossing
Shemoth 14, Bemidḇar 33
N
Crossing
1 Traditional Red Sea Crossing
2 Traditional Red Sea Alternative Crossing
A Yam Suph (Sea of Reeds Crossing)
B Yam Suph (Sea of Reeds Alternative Crossing)
Unknown / Disputed Locations
Possible locations marked with a ?
• Sukkoth
• Ěṫham
• Marah
• Miḡdol
• Ba'al Tsephon
• Ělim
• Pi Haḥiroth
• Ra'meses
• Sukkoth?
• Ěṫham?
Marah?
• Miḡdol?
• Ba'al Tsephon?
• Ělim?
Pi Haḥiroth?
Miḡdol?
Ěṫham?
Etsyon Geḇer
Ěylath
Red Sea Crossing (Nuweiba)
Ba'al Tsephon?
(Yam Suph) Sea of Reeds
Gulf of Aqaba
Ěḏom
Traditional Site at St. Catherine's Monastery
Mt Sinai (Jabal al-Musa)
Alternative Site in Saudi Arabia
Mt Sinai (Jabal el-Lawz)
Marah?
Ělim (Al Bad)?
0 50 100 150 mi
0 100 200 300 km

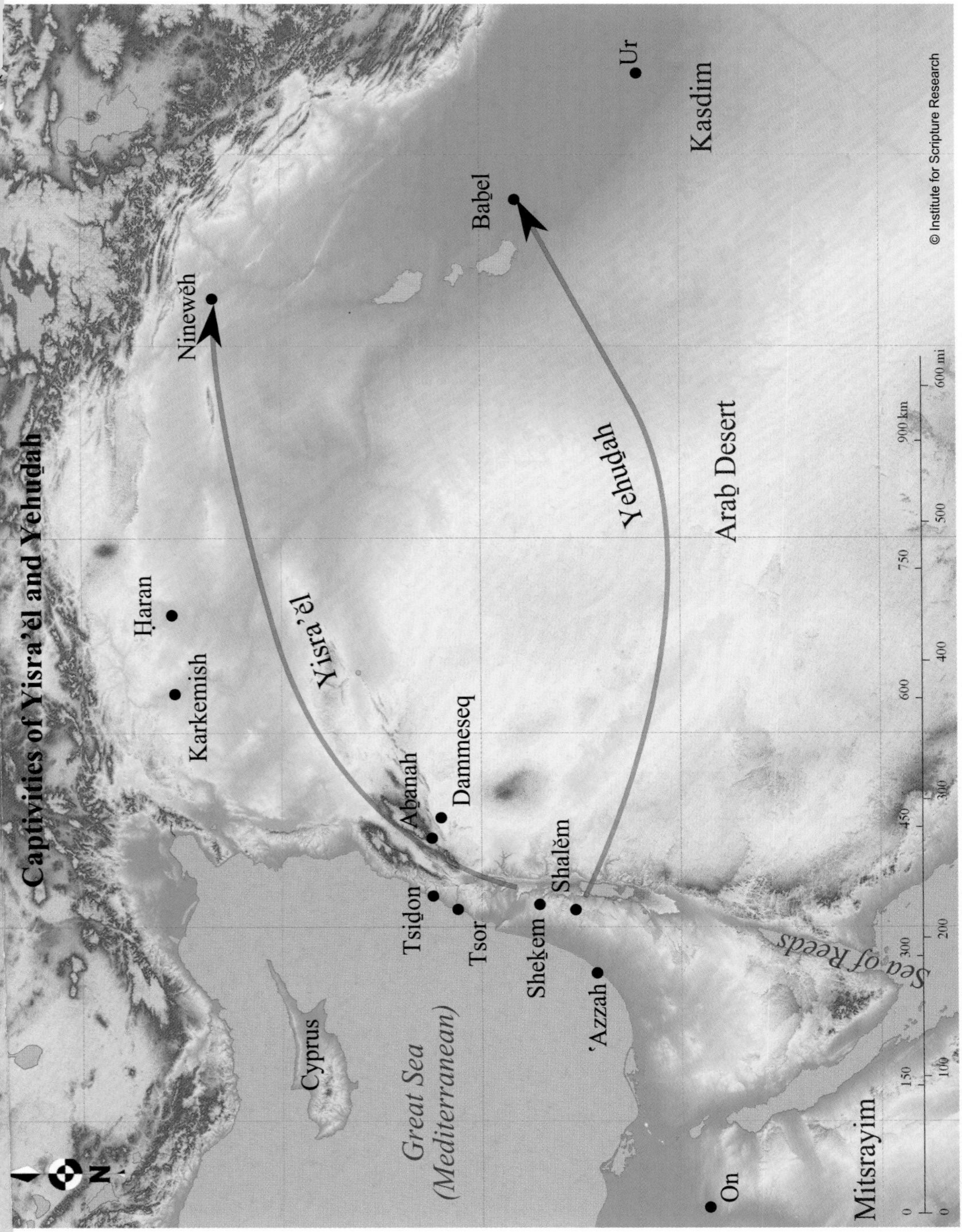
Captivities of Yisra'ĕl and Yehuḏah
N
Ḥaran
Karkemish
Nineweh
Babel
Ur
Kasdim
Dammeseq
Abanah
Tsiḏon
Tsor
Shekem
Shalĕm
'Azzah
Yisra'ĕl
Yehuḏah
Arab Desert
Cyprus
Great Sea
(Mediterranean)
Sea of Reeds
Mitsrayim
On
0 150 300 450 600 750 900 km
0 100 200 300 400 500 600 mi
© Institute for Scripture Research

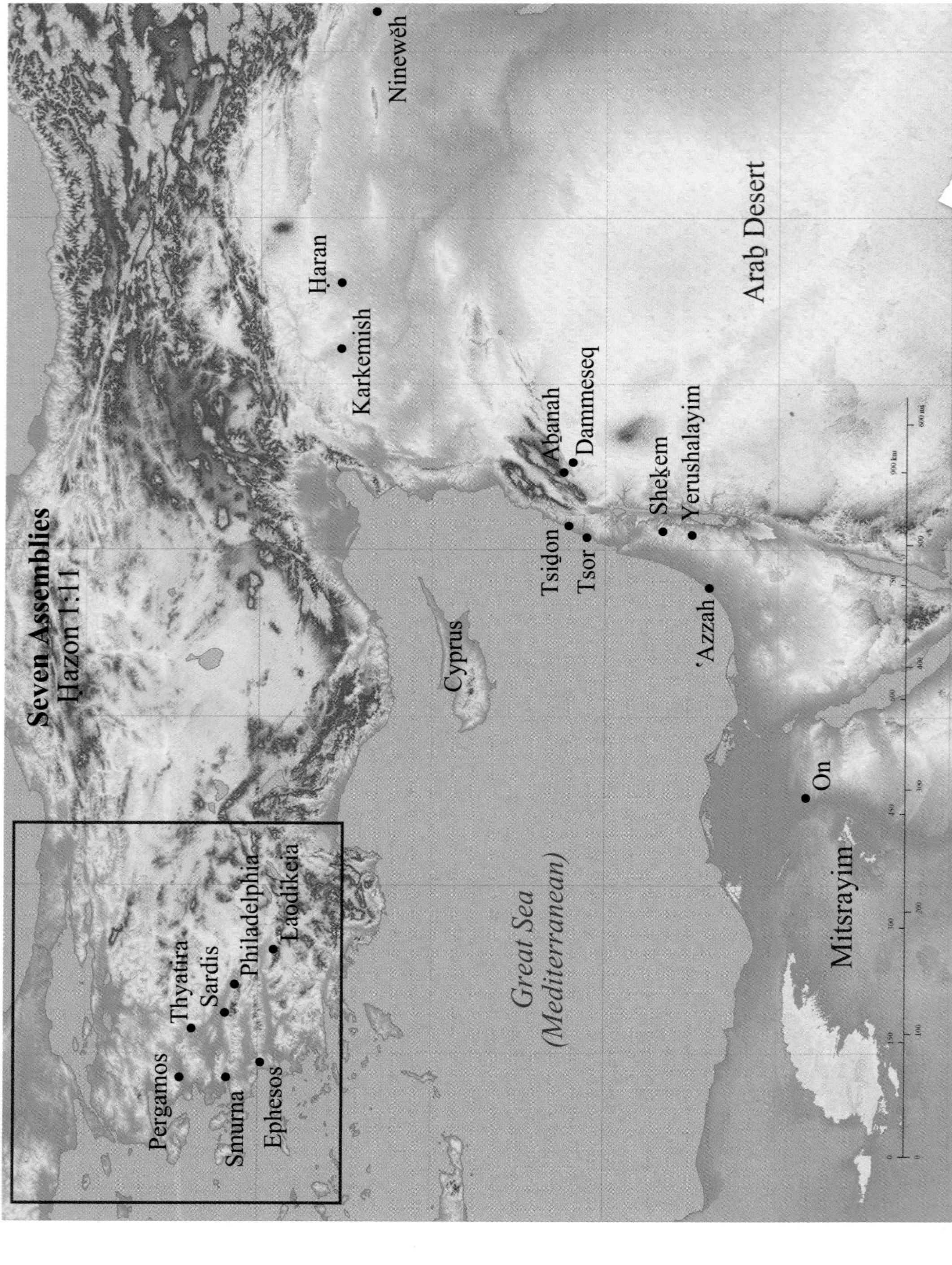
Seven Assemblies
Ḥazon 1:11
Pergamos
Thyatira
Sardis
Smurna
Ephesos
Philadelphia
Laodikeia
Great Sea
(Mediterranean)
Cyprus
Tsiḏon
Tsor
ʻAzzah
Sheḵem
Yerushalayim
Aḇanah
Dammeseq
Karkemish
Ḥaran
Ninewĕh
Araḇ Desert
Mitsrayim
On

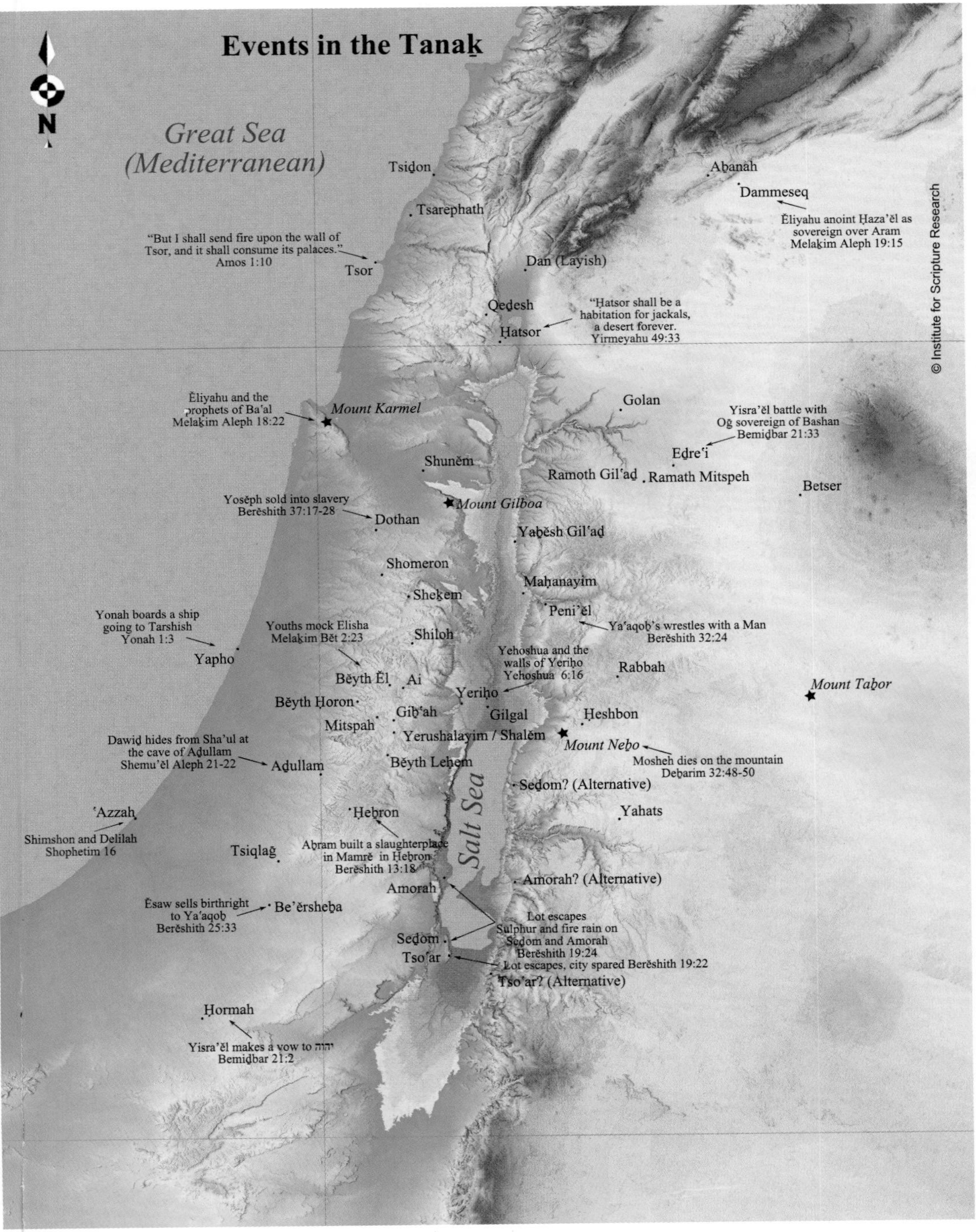
Events in the Tanaḵ
N
Great Sea (Mediterranean)
Tsiḏon
Tsarephath
Aḇanah
Dammeseq
Ěliyahu anoint Ḥaza'ěl as sovereign over Aram Melaḵim Aleph 19:15
"But I shall send fire upon the wall of Tsor, and it shall consume its palaces." Amos 1:10
Tsor
Dan (Layish)
Qeḏesh
Ḥatsor
"Ḥatsor shall be a habitation for jackals, a desert forever. Yirmeyahu 49:33
© Institute for Scripture Research
Ěliyahu and the prophets of Ba'al Melaḵim Aleph 18:22
Mount Karmel
Golan
Yisra'ěl battle with Oḡ sovereign of Bashan Bemiḏbar 21:33
Eḏre'i
Shuněm
Ramoth Gil'aḏ
Ramath Mitspeh
Betser
Yosěph sold into slavery Berěshith 37:17-28
Mount Gilboa
Dothan
Yaḇěsh Gil'aḏ
Shomeron
Maḥanayim
Sheḵem
Peni'ěl
Yonah boards a ship going to Tarshish Yonah 1:3
Youths mock Elisha Melaḵim Bět 2:23
Shiloh
Ya'aqoḇ's wrestles with a Man Berěshith 32:24
Yapho
Yehoshua and the walls of Yeriḥo Yehoshua 6:16
Rabbah
Běyth Ěl
Ai
Yeriḥo
Mount Taḇor
Běyth Ḥoron
Giḇ'ah
Gilgal
Ḥeshbon
Mitspah
Yerushalayim / Shalěm
Mount Neḇo
Dawiḏ hides from Sha'ul at the cave of Aḏullam Shemu'ěl Aleph 21-22
Aḏullam
Běyth Leḥem
Mosheh dies on the mountain Deḇarim 32:48-50
Seḏom? (Alternative)
Salt Sea
'Azzah
Ḥeḇron
Yahats
Shimshon and Delilah Shophetim 16
Tsiqlaḡ
Aḇram built a slaughterplace in Mamrě in Ḥeḇron Berěshith 13:18
Amorah
Amorah? (Alternative)
Ěsaw sells birthright to Ya'aqoḇ Berěshith 25:33
Be'ěrsheḇa
Lot escapes Sulphur and fire rain on Seḏom and Amorah Berěshith 19:24
Seḏom
Tso'ar
Lot escapes, city spared Berěshith 19:22
Tso'ar? (Alternative)
Ḥormah
Yisra'ěl makes a vow to יהוה Bemiḏbar 21:2

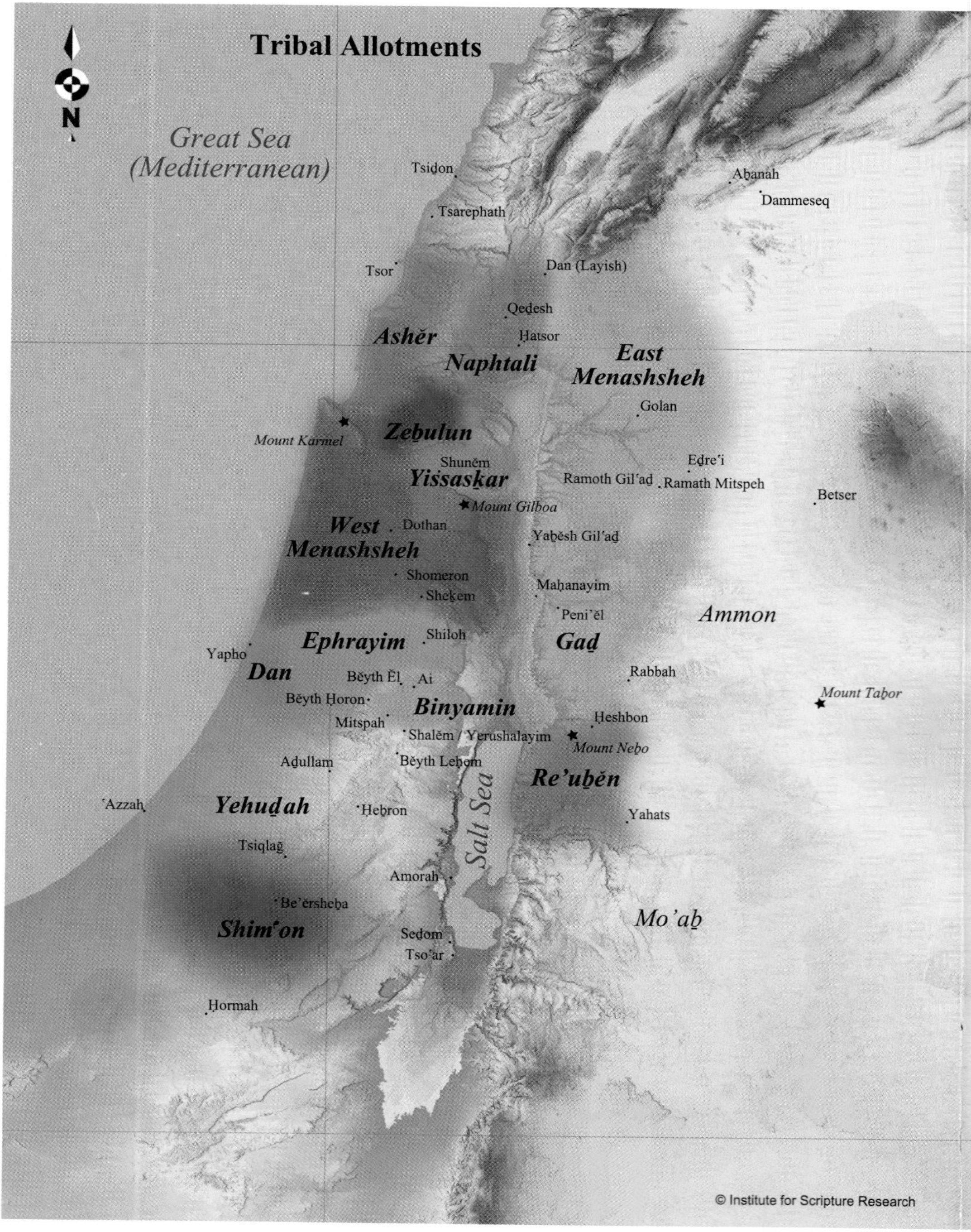
Tribal Allotments
N
Great Sea
(Mediterranean)
Tsidon
Tsarephath
Abanah
Dammeseq
Tsor
Dan (Layish)
Qedesh
Ashĕr
Hatsor
Naphtali
East
Menashsheh
Golan
Mount Karmel
Zebulun
Shunĕm
Yissaskar
Edre'i
Ramoth Gil'ad
Ramath Mitspeh
Betser
Mount Gilboa
West
Menashsheh
Dothan
Yabĕsh Gil'ad
Shomeron
Shekem
Mahanayim
Peni'ĕl
Ammon
Shiloh
Ephrayim
Gad
Yapho
Dan
Bĕyth Ĕl
Ai
Rabbah
Bĕyth Horon
Binyamin
Mount Tabor
Mitspah
Heshbon
Shalĕm / Yerushalayim
Mount Nebo
Adullam
Bĕyth Lehem
Re'ubĕn
'Azzah
Yehudah
Hebron
Salt Sea
Yahats
Tsiqlag
Amorah
Be'ĕrsheba
Mo'ab
Shim'on
Sedom
Tso'ar
Hormah